11. Format for Bank Reconciliation:

Cash balance according to bank statement			$xxx
Add: Additions by company not on bank			
statement		$xx	
Bank errors		xx	xx
			$xxx
Deduct: Deductions by company not on bank			
statement		$xx	
Bank errors		xx	xx
Adjusted balance..			$xxx
Cash balance according to company's records			$xxx
Add: Additions by bank not recorded by company ..		$xx	
Company errors		xx	xx
			$xxx
Deduct: Deductions by bank not recorded			
by company..		$xx	
Company errors		xx	xx
Adjusted balance..			$xxx

12. Inventory Costing Methods:

1. First-in, First-out (FIFO)
2. Last-in, First-out (LIFO)
3. Average Cost

13. Interest Computations:

$$\text{Interest} = \text{Face Amount (or Principal)} \times \text{Rate} \times \text{Time}$$

14. Methods of Determining Annual Depreciation:

STRAIGHT-LINE: $\dfrac{\text{Cost} - \text{Estimated Residual Value}}{\text{Estimated Life}}$

DOUBLE-DECLINING-BALANCE: Rate* × Book Value at Beginning of Period

*Rate is commonly twice the straight-line rate (1/Estimated Life).

15. Adjustments to Net Income (Loss) Using the Indirect Method

	Increase (Decrease)
Net income (loss)	$ XXX
Adjustments to reconcile net income to net cash flow from operating activities:	
Depreciation of fixed assets	XXX
Amortization of intangible assets	XXX
Losses on disposal of assets	XXX
Gains on disposal of assets	(XXX)
Changes in current operating assets and liabilities:	
Increases in noncash current operating assets	(XXX)
Decreases in noncash current operating assets	XXX
Increases in current operating liabilities	XXX
Decreases in current operating liabilities	(XXX)
Net cash flow from operating activities	$ XXX
	or
	$(XXX)

16. Contribution Margin Ratio $= \dfrac{\text{Sales} - \text{Variable Costs}}{\text{Sales}}$

17. Break-Even Sales (U

18. Sales (Units) $= \dfrac{\text{Fixed Costs} + \text{Target Profit}}{\text{Unit Contribution Margin}}$

19. Margin of Safety $= \dfrac{\text{Sales} - \text{Sales at Break-Even Point}}{\text{Sales}}$

20. Operating Leverage $= \dfrac{\text{Contribution Margin}}{\text{Income from Operations}}$

21. Variances

$\begin{aligned}\text{Direct Materials} \\ \text{Price Variance}\end{aligned} = \left(\begin{array}{l}\text{Actual Price} - \\ \text{Standard Price}\end{array}\right) \times \text{Actual Quantity}$

$\begin{aligned}\text{Direct Materials} \\ \text{Quantity Variance}\end{aligned} = \left(\begin{array}{l}\text{Actual Quantity} - \\ \text{Standard Quantity}\end{array}\right) \times \begin{array}{l}\text{Standard} \\ \text{Price}\end{array}$

$\begin{aligned}\text{Direct Labor} \\ \text{Rate Variance}\end{aligned} = \left(\begin{array}{l}\text{Actual Rate per Hour} - \\ \text{Standard Rate per Hour}\end{array}\right) \times \text{Actual Hours}$

$\begin{aligned}\text{Direct Labor} \\ \text{Time Variance}\end{aligned} = \left(\begin{array}{l}\text{Actual Direct Labor Hours} - \\ \text{Standard Direct Labor Hours}\end{array}\right) \times \begin{array}{l}\text{Standard Rate} \\ \text{per Hour}\end{array}$

$\begin{aligned}\text{Variable Factory} \\ \text{Overhead Controllable} \\ \text{Variance}\end{aligned} = \begin{array}{c}\text{Actual Variable} \\ \text{Factory} \\ \text{Overhead}\end{array} - \begin{array}{c}\text{Budgeted Variable} \\ \text{Factory Overhead}\end{array}$

$\begin{aligned}\text{Fixed Factory} \\ \text{Overhead} \\ \text{Volume} \\ \text{Variance}\end{aligned} = \left(\begin{array}{c}\text{Standard Hours} \\ \text{for 100\% of} \\ \text{Normal} \\ \text{Capacity}\end{array} - \begin{array}{c}\text{Standard} \\ \text{Hours for} \\ \text{Actual Units} \\ \text{Produced}\end{array}\right) \times \begin{array}{c}\text{Fixed Factory} \\ \text{Overhead} \\ \text{Rate}\end{array}$

22. Rate of Return on Investment (ROI) $= \dfrac{\text{Income from Operations}}{\text{Invested Assets}}$

Alternative ROI Computation:

$$\text{ROI} = \dfrac{\text{Income from Operations}}{\text{Sales}} \times \dfrac{\text{Sales}}{\text{Invested Assets}}$$

23. Capital Investment Analysis Methods:

1. Methods That Ignore Present Values:
   A. Average Rate of Return Method
   B. Cash Payback Method
2. Methods That Use Present Values:
   A. Net Present Value Method
   B. Internal Rate of Return Method

24. Average Rate of Return $= \dfrac{\text{Estimated Average Annual Income}}{\text{Average Investment}}$

25. Present Value Index $= \dfrac{\text{Total Present Value of Net Cash Flow}}{\text{Amount to Be Invested}}$

26. Present Value Factor for an Annuity of $1 $= \dfrac{\text{Amount to Be Invested}}{\text{Equal Annual Net Cash Flows}}$

Reeve Warren Duchac

ACCOUNTING

USING EXCEL FOR SUCCESS

Reeve Warren Duchac

ACCOUNTING
USING EXCEL FOR SUCCESS

James M. Reeve

Professor Emeritus of Accounting
University of Tennessee, Knoxville

Carl S. Warren

Professor Emeritus of Accounting
University of Georgia, Athens

Jonathan E. Duchac

Professor of Accounting
Wake Forest University

SOUTH-WESTERN
CENGAGE Learning™

Australia · Brazil · Canada · Mexico · Singapore · Spain · United Kingdom · United States

SOUTH-WESTERN
CENGAGE Learning™

Accounting Using Excel for Success
Reeve Warren Duchac

VP/Editorial Director: Jack W. Calhoun

Editor in Chief: Rob Dewey

Executive Editor: Sharon Oblinger

Developmental Editor: Tracy Newman

Editorial Assistant: Julie Warwick

Senior Marketing Manager: Kristen Hurd

Senior Marketing Communications Manager: Libby Shipp

Marketing Coordinator: Heather Moon

Senior Media Editor: Amir Nasiri

Senior Content Project Manager: Cliff Kallemeyn

Senior Art Director: Stacy Shirley

Senior Frontlist Buyer: Doug Wilke

Production: LEAP Publishing Services, Inc.

Composition: Cadmus Communications

Internal Design: Mike Stratton/Patti Hudepohl/Beckmeyer Design

Cover Design: Beckmeyer Design

Cover Image: Getty Images

For product information and technology assistance, contact us at
Cengage Learning Academic Resource Center, 1-800-423-0563

Library of Congress Control Number: 2009943509

Student Edition
ISBN 13: 978-0-324-59656-4
ISBN 10: 0-324-59656-1

Instructor Edition
ISBN 13: 978-0-538-47249-4
ISBN 10: 0-538-47249-9

South-Western Cengage Learning
5191 Natorp Boulevard
Mason, OH 45040
USA

Cengage Learning products are represented in Canada by Nelson Education, Ltd.

For your course and learning solutions, visit
www.cengage.com
Purchase any of our products at your local college store or at our preferred online store **www.ichapters.com**

Printed in the United States of America
1 2 3 4 5 6 7 13 12 11 10

James M. Reeve

Dr. James M. Reeve is Professor Emeritus of Accounting and Information Management at the University of Tennessee. Professor Reeve taught on the accounting faculty for 25 years, after graduating with his Ph.D. from Oklahoma State University. His teaching effort focused on undergraduate accounting principles and graduate education in the Master of Accountancy and Senior Executive MBA programs. Beyond this, Professor Reeve is also very active in the Supply Chain Certification program, which is a major executive education and research effort of the College. His research interests are varied and include work in managerial accounting, supply chain management, lean manufacturing, and information management. He has published over 40 articles in academic and professional journals, including the *Journal of Cost Management, Journal of Management Accounting Research, Accounting Review, Management Accounting Quarterly, Supply Chain Management Review*, and *Accounting Horizons*. He has consulted or provided training around the world for a wide variety of organizations, including Boeing, Procter and Gamble, Norfolk Southern, Hershey Foods, Coca-Cola, and Sony. When not writing books, Professor Reeve plays golf and is involved in faith-based activities.

Carl S. Warren

Dr. Carl S. Warren is Professor Emeritus of Accounting at the University of Georgia, Athens. Dr. Warren has taught classes at the University of Georgia, University of Iowa, Michigan State University, and University of Chicago. Professor Warren focused his teaching efforts on principles of accounting and auditing. He received his Ph.D. from Michigan State University and his B.B.A. and M.A. from the University of Iowa. During his career, Dr. Warren published numerous articles in professional journals, including *The Accounting Review, Journal of Accounting Research, Journal of Accountancy, The CPA Journal*, and *Auditing: A Journal of Practice & Theory*. Dr. Warren has served on numerous committees of the American Accounting Association, the American Institute of Certified Public Accountants, and the Institute of Internal Auditors. He has also consulted with numerous companies and public accounting firms. Warren's outside interests include playing handball, golfing, skiing, backpacking, and fly-fishing.

Jonathan Duchac

Dr. Jonathan Duchac is the Merrill Lynch and Co. Professor of Accounting and Director of the Program in Enterprise Risk Management at Wake Forest University. He earned his Ph.D. in accounting from the University of Georgia and currently teaches introductory and advanced courses in financial accounting. Dr. Duchac has received a number of awards during his career, including the Wake Forest University Outstanding Graduate Professor Award, the T.B. Rose award for Instructional Innovation, and the University of Georgia Outstanding Teaching Assistant Award. In addition to his teaching responsibilities, Dr. Duchac has served as Accounting Advisor to Merrill Lynch Equity Research, where he worked with research analysts in reviewing and evaluating the financial reporting practices of public companies. He has testified before the U.S. House of Representatives, the Financial Accounting Standards Board, and the Securities and Exchange Commission; and has worked with a number of major public companies on financial reporting and accounting policy issues. In addition to his professional interests, Dr. Duchac is the Treasurer of The Special Children's School of Winston-Salem; a private, nonprofit developmental day school serving children with special needs. Dr. Duchac is an avid long-distance runner, mountain biker, and snow skier. His recent events include the Grandfather Mountain Marathon, the Black Mountain Marathon, the Shut-In Ridge Trail run, and NO MAAM (Nocturnal Overnight Mountain Bike Assault on Mount Mitchell).

Accounting Using Excel for Success is an adaptation of *Accounting*, 23e. For nearly 80 years, *Accounting* has been used effectively to teach generations of businessmen and women. The text has been used by millions of business students. Over the years, the Warren series of accounting titles have provided the only exposure to accounting principles that students will ever receive. As the most successful business textbook of all time, it continues to introduce students to accounting through a variety of time-tested ways.

The original author of *Accounting*, James McKinsey, could not have imagined the success and influence this text has enjoyed, or that his original vision would continue to lead the market into the twenty-first century. With the increased development of software applications, this edition introduces students to a new learning approach that combines accounting concepts with spreadsheet mastery. As the current authors, we appreciate the responsibility of protecting and enhancing this vision, while continuing to refine it to meet the changing needs of students and instructors. Always in touch with a tradition of excellence but never satisfied with yesterday's success, this edition enthusiastically embraces a changing environment and continues to proudly lead the way. We sincerely thank our many colleagues who have helped to make it happen.

Carl S. Warren

Jonathan Duchac

"The teaching of accounting is no longer designed to train professional accountants only. With the growing complexity of business and the constantly increasing difficulty of the problems of management, it has become essential that everyone who aspires to a position of responsibility should have a knowledge of the fundamental principles of accounting."

— James O. McKinsey, Author, first edition, 1929

Unique Excel Success Learning System:

6 Formulas + 4 Steps = Excel Success

In developing this learning system, instructors expressed:

- Excel is the most important software students will use in business.
- Employers want graduates to know Excel.
- Many instructors *do not* use Excel because they believe they do not have the time to teach it in class.
- Many instructors *do* use Excel to learn and reinforce accounting concepts.

With the increased development of software applications, this textbook introduces students to a new learning approach. *Accounting Using Excel for Success* **effectively uses Excel to teach accounting in an easy way.**

The Power of Six Simple Formulas

By learning just six simple Excel formulas, students can solve most accounting problems, from posting a basic journal entry to calculating the internal rate of return. Here are the six basic formulas that are covered in the text:

1. =SUM
2. =MIN
3. =VLOOKUP (one time)
4. =IF (one time)
5. =IRR (one time) and =PV (one time)
6. $A$5 (absolute and relative references)

Four Easy Steps

The innovative four-step system encourages students to:

1. Read the accounting concept and illustration.
2. Follow the same concept using the Excel Success Example.
3. Practice using the "Try It" Tutorial.
4. Apply knowledge by completing the Excel Success Activity.

Here is a depiction of the four steps in the Excel Success Learning System:

Step 1

Step 1 is to Read and Learn the Accounting Concept. You can introduce the concept in lecture and your students will read the concept or illustration in the textbook. This example is Valuation at Lower of Cost or Market.

Valuation at Lower of Cost or Market

Dell Inc. recorded over $39.3 million of charges (expenses) in writing down its inventory of notebook computers. The remaining inventories of computers were then sold at significantly reduced prices.

If the cost of replacing inventory is lower than its recorded purchase cost, the **lower-of-cost-or-market (LCM) method** is used to value the inventory. *Market*, as used in *lower of cost or market*, is the cost to replace the inventory. The market value is based on normal quantities that would be purchased from suppliers.

The lower-of-cost-or-market method can be applied in one of three ways. The cost, market price, and any declines could be determined for the following:

1. Each item in the inventory.
2. Each major class or category of inventory.
3. Total inventory as a whole.

The amount of any price decline is included in the cost of merchandise sold. This, in turn, reduces gross profit and net income in the period in which the price declines occur. This matching of price declines to the period in which they occur is the primary advantage of using the lower-of-cost-or-market method.

To illustrate, assume the following data for 400 identical units of Item A in inventory on December 31, 2010:

Unit purchased cost	$10.25
Replacement cost on December 31, 2010	9.50

Since Item A could be replaced at $9.50 a unit, $9.50 is used under the lower-of-cost-or-market method.

Exhibit 8 illustrates applying the lower-of-cost-or-market method to each inventory item (A, B, C, and D). As applied on an item-by-item basis, the total lower-of-cost-or-market is $15,070, which is a market decline of $450 ($15,520 − $15,070). This market decline of $450 is included in the cost of merchandise sold.

In Exhibit 8, Items A, B, C, and D could be viewed as a class of inventory items. If the lower-of-cost-or-market method is applied to the class, the inventory would be valued at $15,472, which is a market decline of $48 ($15,520 − $15,472). Likewise, if Items A, B, C, and D make up the total inventory, the lower-of-cost-or-market method as applied to the total inventory would be the same amount, $15,472.

Step 2

Step 2 of Excel Success is to Reinforce the Accounting Concept Using the Excel Example:

- The Illustration is recreated using Excel.
- The *formulas* are displayed, not just the *solutions*.
- Students use easy steps to understand how to create a basic Excel formula.

excel success

The lower of cost or market inventory schedule from Exhibit 8 can be developed on a spreadsheet as follows:

	A	B	C	D	E a.	F b.	G c.
1							
2						Total	
3	Item	Inventory Quantity	Unit Cost Price	Unit Market Price	Cost	Market	Lower of C or M
4	A	400	$ 10.25	$ 9.50	=B4*C4	=B4*D4	=MIN(E4:F4)
5	B	120	22.50	24.10	=B5*C5	=B5*D5	=MIN(E5:F5)
6	C	600	8.00	7.75	=B6*C6	=B6*D6	=MIN(E6:F6)
7	D	280	14.00	14.75	=B7*C7	=B7*D7	=MIN(E7:F7)
8	Total				=SUM(E4:E7)	=SUM(F4:F7)	=SUM(G4:G7)
9							

d.

e.   f.

Develop the formulas by the following steps:

a.   Enter in cell E4 the formula for the total cost, =B4*C4.
b.   Enter in cell F4 the formula for the total market, =B4*D4.
c.   Enter in cell G4 a =MIN function to calculate the lower of cost or market, as follows:

=MIN(E4:F4)

This function will return the minimum value within the range of cells from E4 to F4.

d.   Copy E4:G4 to E5:G7.
e.   Enter in E8 a formula to sum the column, =SUM(E4:E7)
f.   Copy E8 to F8:G8

Copy cells by using the fill handle in the corner of the cell to be copied and dragging to the target cells.

 try it   Go to the hands-on *Excel Tutor* for this example!

Step 3

Step 3 is the Try It Tutorial. This is a hands-on tutorial that walks the student through the in-chapter example. Students actively participate in the learning process using the Try It Tutorial to use Excel to complete accounting problems. The Try It Tutorials are available to students 24/7. It's just that easy! Students receive an access code automatically with a new copy of the textbook that provides them access to the Try It Tutorials. The Tutorials are also built into CengageNOW, our premier online homework solution.

	A	B	C	D	E	F	G	H	I
						Total			
2	Item	Inventory Quantity	Unit Cost Price	Unit Market Price	Cost	Market	Lower of C or M		
3	A	400 $	10.25 $	9.50	4,100.00	3,800.00	=MIN(		
4	B	120	22.50	24.10					
5	C	600	8.00	7.75					
6	D	280	14.00	14.75					
7	Total								

Begin in cell **G3** (where the calculation result will display).

Start the formula with an equal sign (=) then type **MIN** and an open parenthesis (.

☞ **Note:** Remember that there are NEVER any spaces in an Excel formula.

Click in cell **E3**.

Step 4

Step 4 is the Excel Success End-of-Chapter Problem. At this point, students have learned the accounting concept, reinforced it in Excel, and learned how to create a simple Excel formula with the Try It Tutorial. Now it's time for them to complete their homework.

Excel Success Special Activities

SA 7-1
Lower of cost or market

excel
SUCCESS

All-Tech, Inc., has five inventory items with the following quantities, unit costs, and unit market values:

	A	B	C	D
1			Unit	Unit
2		Inventory	Cost	Market
3	Item	Quantity	Price	Price
4	A	250	$ 4.50	$ 4.20
5	B	340	9.20	8.90
6	C	90	12.90	13.50
7	D	125	18.90	21.80
8	E	440	11.30	11.40
9	Total			
10				

a. Open the spreadsheet file name *SA7-1*.
b. Complete the spreadsheet by determining the lower of cost or market valuation for inventory.
c. When you have completed the inventory table, perform a "save as," replacing the entire file name with the following:

   SA7-1_[your first name initial]_[your last name]

Here is what the problem looks like:

	A	B	C	D	E	F	G
1			All-Tech, Inc.				
2						Total	
3	Item	Inventory Quantity	Unit Cost Price	Unit Market Price	Cost	Market	Lower of C or M
4	A	250	$ 4.50	$ 4.20			
5	B	340	9.20	8.90			
6	C	90	12.90	13.50			
7	D	125	18.90	21.80			
8	E	440	11.30	11.40			
9	Total						
10							
11							
12	a. Enter in cell E4 the formula for the total cost.						
13	b. Enter in cell F4 the formula for the total market.						
14	c. Enter in cell G4 a formula to calculate the lower of cost or market.						
15	d. Copy these cells to the remaining items.						
16	e. Total the cost, market, and lower of cost or market columns.						
17							

This problem asks students to open up an Excel file and solve. At any time, students can refer to the Excel Success example within the chapter to help them successfully complete the problem.

Solution Files in Excel for Instructors

To help grade your students' homework, we have provided you with the solution file:

	A	B	C	D	E	F	G
1				All-Tech, Inc.			
2						Total	
3	Item	Inventory Quantity	Unit Cost Price	Unit Market Price	Cost	Market	Lower of C or M
4	A	250	$ 4.50	$ 4.20	$ 1,125	$ 1,050	$ 1,050
5	B	340	9.20	8.90	3,128	3,026	3,026
6	C	90	12.90	13.50	1,161	1,215	1,161
7	D	125	18.90	21.80	2,363	2,725	2,363
8	E	440	11.30	11.40	4,972	5,016	4,972
9	Total				$ 12,749	$ 13,032	$ 12,572
10							
11							
12	a. Enter in cell E4 the formula for the total cost.						
13	b. Enter in cell F4 the formula for the total market.						
14	c. Enter in cell G4 a formula to calculate the lower of cost or market.						
15	d. Copy these cells to the remaining items.						
16	e. Total the cost, market, and lower of cost or market columns.						
17							

Press Ctrl+~ to see the formulas!

If you want to see which of the basic six formulas was used, you can!

The Power of Using Six Basic Formulas

By just learning six simple Excel formulas, students can solve most accounting problems, from posting a basic journal entry to calculating the internal rate of return. Here are the types of accounting problems that students can solve using six basic Excel formulas:

- Make basic journal entries
- Post to ledger accounts
- Create an adjusted trial balance
- Generate financial statements
- Do inventory valuation
- Calculate straight-line depreciation
- Conduct horizontal and vertical analyses
- Calculate job order costing
- Calculate internal rate of return

Benefits of Accounting Using Excel for Success

- Students retain the accounting concepts better, because they practice in four ways: through reading the accounting concept, seeing the Excel Success example, doing the Try It Tutorial, and doing the homework.
- Students are more engaged in the course because they have many opportunities to practice. Learning the real-world skills of Excel helps motivate them.
- Students build basic Excel proficiency with the Excel Success system, which prepares them for the business world and later courses in accounting.

- After the course, students have an Excel "portfolio" to share with employers. They can show all of the spreadsheets from their homework to demonstrate mastery.
- Because this text offers so many opportunities for students to practice using Excel in accounting, instructors do not have to use valuable class time to teach Excel.
- Accounting Using Excel for Success is an adaptation of a market-leading principles text, guaranteeing a premier teaching and learning experience!

Hallmark Features of the *Accounting* Series

Textbooks continue to play an invaluable role in the teaching and learning environment. We reached out to accounting teachers in an effort to create the most effective textbook presentation. We extended our discussions by reaching out to students directly in order to learn what they value in a textbook. Here is a preview of our key features based on student input:

NEW! Guiding Principles System

Students can easily locate the information they need to master course concepts with the new "Guiding Principles System (GPS)." At the beginning of every chapter, this innovative system plots a course through the chapter content by displaying the chapter objectives, major topics, and related Example Exercises. The GPS reference to the chapter "At a Glance" summary completes the system.

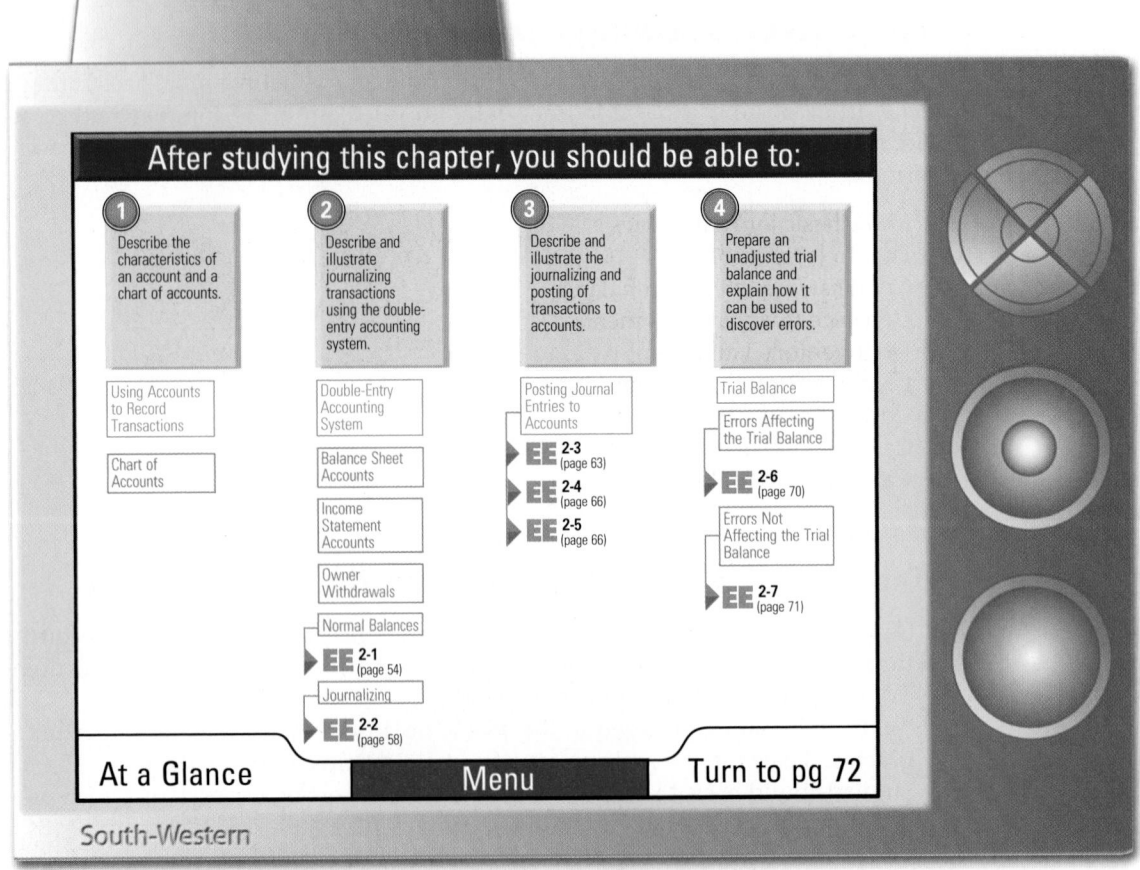

Leading by Example

NEW! Written for Today's Students

Designed for today's students, this edition uses an innovative, high-impact writing style that emphasizes topics in a concise and clearly written manner. Direct sentences, concise paragraphs, numbered lists, and step-by-step calculations provide students with an easy-to-follow structure for learning accounting. This is achieved without sacrificing content or rigor.

NEW! Mornin' Joe Financial Statements

Beginning after Chapter 6, "Accounting for Merchandising Businesses," and continuing through Chapter 15, "Investments and Fair Value Accounting," each chapter contains an excerpt from the full financial statements for Mornin' Joe, a coffee company. This example shows students the big picture of accounting by providing a consistent reference point for users who want to see an entire set of financial statements and the way each chapter topic fits within them. The financial statements were crafted by the authors to be consistent with the presentation in each chapter.

Investments Chapter

This chapter contains a conceptual discussion of fair value accounting and its increasing role in defining today's modern accounting methods.

Modern User-Friendly Design

Based on students' testimonials of what they find most useful, this streamlined presentation includes a wealth of helpful resources without the clutter. The use of spreadsheets reflects the changing environment of business. Visual learners will appreciate the generous number of exhibits and illustrations used to convey concepts and procedures.

Exhibit 4

Statement of Owner's Equity for Merchandising Business

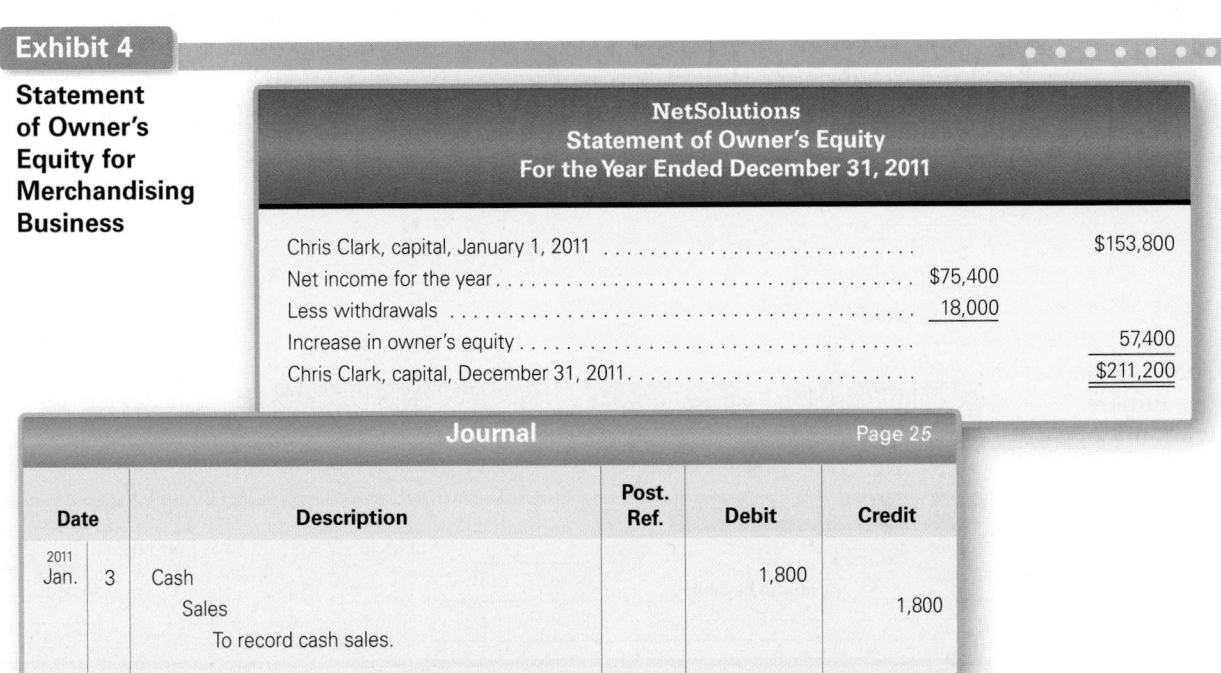

NetSolutions
Statement of Owner's Equity
For the Year Ended December 31, 2011

Chris Clark, capital, January 1, 2011		$153,800
Net income for the year	$75,400	
Less withdrawals	18,000	
Increase in owner's equity		57,400
Chris Clark, capital, December 31, 2011		$211,200

Journal — Page 25

Date		Description	Post. Ref.	Debit	Credit
2011 Jan.	3	Cash		1,800	
		Sales			1,800
		To record cash sales.			

Accounting Using Excel for Success, is unparalleled in pedagogical innovation. Our constant dialogue with accounting faculty continues to affect how we refine and improve the text to meet the needs of today's students. Our goal is to provide a logical framework and pedagogical system that caters to how students of today study and learn.

Clear Objectives and Key Learning Outcomes

To help guide students, the authors provide clear chapter objectives and important learning outcomes. All aspects of the chapter materials relate back to these key points and outcomes, which keeps students focused on the most important topics and concepts in order to succeed in the course.

1 Describe the nature of a business, the role of accounting, and ethics in business.

EX 6-1
Determining gross profit
obj. 1

During the current year, merchandise is sold for $795,000. The cost of the merchandise sold is $477,000.

a. What is the amount of the gross profit?
b. Compute the gross profit percentage (gross profit divided by sales).
c. ▬▬▶ Will the income statement necessarily report a net income? Explain.

Example Exercises

Example Exercises were developed to reinforce concepts and procedures in a bold, new way. Like a teacher in the classroom, students follow the authors' example to see how to complete accounting applications as they are presented in the text. This feature also provides a list of Practice Exercises that parallel the Example Exercises so students get the practice they need. In addition, the Practice Exercises also include references to the chapter Example Exercises so that students can easily cross-reference when completing homework.

See the example of the application being presented.

Follow along as the authors work through the Example Exercise.

Example Exercise 2-2   Journal Entry for Asset Purchase   **2**

Prepare a journal entry for the purchase of a truck on June 3 for $42,500, paying $8,500 cash and the remainder on account.

Follow My Example 2-2

June 3	Truck	42,500	
	Cash		8,500
	Accounts Payable		34,000

▶ For Practice: PE 2-2A, PE 2-2B

Try these corresponding end-of-chapter exercises for practice!

"At a Glance" Chapter Summary

The "At a Glance" summary grid ties everything together and helps students stay on track. First, the Key Points recap the chapter content for each chapter objective. Second, the related Key Learning Outcomes list all of the expected student performance capabilities that come from completing each objective. In case students need further practice on a specific outcome, the last two columns reference related Example Exercises and their corresponding Practice Exercises. In addition, the "At a Glance" grid guides struggling students from the assignable Practice Exercises to the resources in the chapter that will help them complete their homework. Through this intuitive grid, all of the chapter pedagogy links together in one cleanly integrated summary.

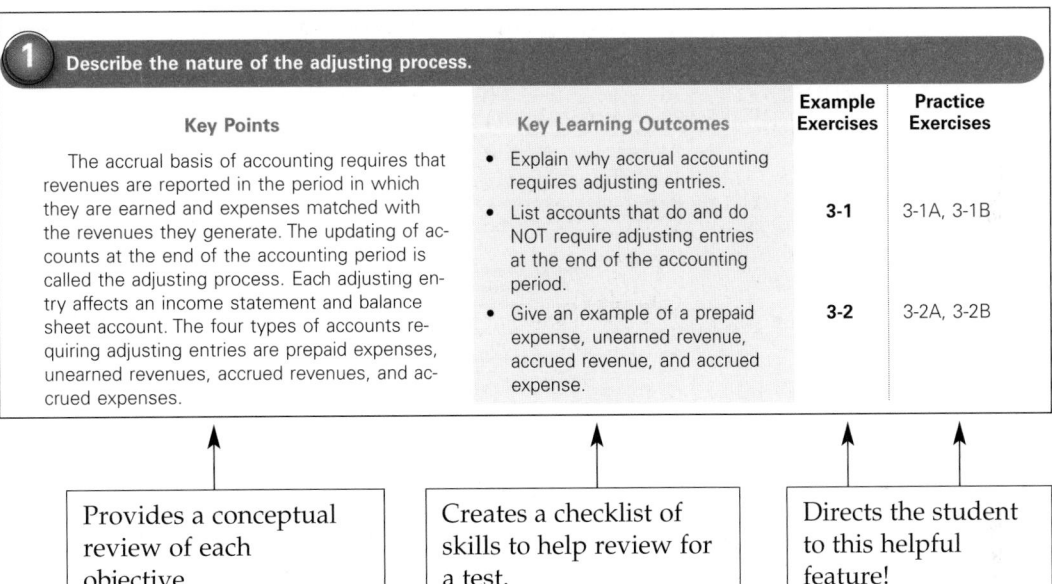

1 Describe the nature of the adjusting process.

Key Points	Key Learning Outcomes	Example Exercises	Practice Exercises
The accrual basis of accounting requires that revenues are reported in the period in which they are earned and expenses matched with the revenues they generate. The updating of accounts at the end of the accounting period is called the adjusting process. Each adjusting entry affects an income statement and balance sheet account. The four types of accounts requiring adjusting entries are prepaid expenses, unearned revenues, accrued revenues, and accrued expenses.	• Explain why accrual accounting requires adjusting entries. • List accounts that do and do NOT require adjusting entries at the end of the accounting period.	3-1	3-1A, 3-1B
	• Give an example of a prepaid expense, unearned revenue, accrued revenue, and accrued expense.	3-2	3-2A, 3-2B

Provides a conceptual review of each objective.

Creates a checklist of skills to help review for a test.

Directs the student to this helpful feature!

Real-World Chapter Openers

These openers continue to relate the accounting and business concepts in the chapter to students' lives. Examples of real companies provide invaluable insight into real practice. Several of the openers created especially for this edition focus on interesting companies such as Apple; Dollar Tree; Hasbro; and News Corporation (Fox), the parent company of the hit television shows *American Idol* and *The Simpsons*.

Financial Analysis and Interpretation

The "Financial Analysis and Interpretation" section at the end of each accounting chapter introduces relevant key ratios used throughout the textbook. Students connect with the business environment as they learn how stakeholders interpret financial reports. This section covers basic analysis tools that students will use again in Chapter 17, "Financial Statement Analysis." Furthermore, students get to test their proficiency with these tools through special activities and exercises at the end of each chapter. To ensure a consistent presentation, a unique icon is used for both the section and related end-of-chapter materials.

Financial Analysis and Interpretation

Comparing each item in a current statement with a total amount within that same statement is useful in analyzing relationships within a financial statement. *Vertical analysis* is the term used to describe such comparisons.

In vertical analysis of a balance sheet, each asset item is stated as a percent of the total assets. Each liability and owner's equity item is stated as a percent of the total liabilities and owner's equity. In vertical analysis of an income statement, each item is stated as a percent of revenues or fees earned.

Vertical analysis may be prepared for several periods to analyze changes in relationships over time. Vertical analysis of two years of income statements for J. Holmes, Attorney-at-Law, is shown below.

The preceding vertical analysis indicates both favorable and unfavorable trends affecting the income statement of J. Holmes, Attorney-at-Law. The increase in wages expense of 2% (32% − 30%) is an unfavorable trend, as is the increase in utilities expense of 0.7% (6.7% − 6.0%). A favorable trend is the decrease in supplies expense of 0.6% (2.0% − 1.4%). Rent expense and miscellaneous expense as a percent of fees earned were constant. The net result of these trends was that net income decreased as a percent of fees earned from 52.8% to 50.7%.

The analysis of the various percentages shown for J. Holmes, Attorney-at-Law, can be enhanced by comparisons with industry averages. Such averages are published by trade associations and financial information services. Any major differences between industry averages should be investigated.

J. Holmes, Attorney-at-Law
Income Statements
For the Years Ended December 31, 2010 and 2009

	2010		2009	
	Amount	Percent	Amount	Percent
Fees earned	$187,500	100.0%	$150,000	100.0%
Operating expenses:				
Wages expense	$ 60,000	32.0%	$ 45,000	30.0%*
Rent expense	15,000	8.0%	12,000	8.0%
Utilities expense	12,500	6.7%	9,000	6.0%
Supplies expense	2,700	1.4%	3,000	2.0%
Miscellaneous expense	2,300	1.2%	1,800	1.2%
Total operating expenses	$ 92,500	49.3%	$ 70,800	47.2%
Net income	$ 95,000	50.7%	$ 79,200	52.8%

*$45,000 ÷ $150,000

Business Connection and Comprehensive Real-World Notes

Students get a close-up look at how accounting operates in the marketplace through a variety of items in the margins and in the "Business Connection" boxed features.

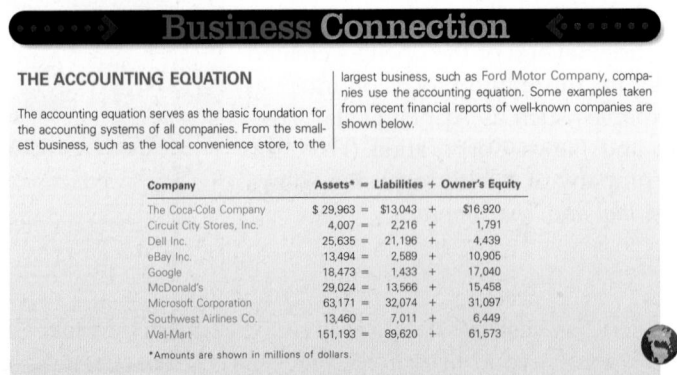

Business Connection

THE ACCOUNTING EQUATION

The accounting equation serves as the basic foundation for the accounting systems of all companies. From the smallest business, such as the local convenience store, to the largest business, such as Ford Motor Company, companies use the accounting equation. Some examples taken from recent financial reports of well-known companies are shown below.

Company	Assets*	=	Liabilities	+	Owner's Equity
The Coca-Cola Company	$ 29,963	=	$13,043	+	$16,920
Circuit City Stores, Inc.	4,007	=	2,216	+	1,791
Dell Inc.	25,635	=	21,196	+	4,439
eBay Inc.	13,494	=	2,589	+	10,905
Google	18,473	=	1,433	+	17,040
McDonald's	29,024	=	13,566	+	15,458
Microsoft Corporation	63,171	=	32,074	+	31,097
Southwest Airlines Co.	13,460	=	7,011	+	6,449
Wal-Mart	151,193	=	89,620	+	61,573

*Amounts are shown in millions of dollars.

In addition, a variety of end-of-chapter exercises and problems employ real-world data to give students a feel for the material that accountants see daily. No matter where they are found, elements that use material from real companies are indicated with a unique icon for a consistent presentation.

Integrity, Objectivity, and Ethics in Business

In each chapter, these cases help students develop their ethical compass. Often coupled with related end-of-chapter activities, these cases can be discussed in class or students can consider the cases as they read the chapter. Both the section and related end-of-chapter materials are indicated with a unique icon for a consistent presentation.

Integrity, Objectivity, and Ethics in Business

ACCOUNTING REFORM

The financial accounting and reporting failures of Enron, WorldCom, Tyco, Xerox, and others shocked the investing public. The disclosure that some of the nation's largest and best-known corporations had overstated profits and misled investors raised the question: Where were the CPAs?

In response, Congress passed the Investor Protection, Auditor Reform, and Transparency Act of 2002, called the Sarbanes-Oxley Act. The Act establishes a Public Company Accounting Oversight Board to regulate the portion of the accounting profession that has public companies as clients. In addition, the Act prohibits auditors (CPAs) from providing certain types of nonaudit services, such as investment banking or legal services, to their clients, prohibits employment of auditors by clients for one year after they last audited the client, and increases penalties for the reporting of misleading financial statements.

Continuing Case Study

@netsolutions   Students follow a fictitious company, NetSolutions, throughout Chapters 1–6, which demonstrates a variety of transactions. The continuity of using the same company facilitates student learning especially for Chapters 1–4, which cover the accounting cycle. Also, using the same company allows students to follow the transition of the company from a service business in Chapters 1–4 to a merchandising business in Chapters 5 and 6.

Summaries

Within each chapter, these synopses draw special attention to important points and help clarify difficult concepts.

Self-Examination Questions

Five multiple-choice questions, with answers at the end of the chapter, help students review and retain chapter concepts.

Illustrative Problem and Solution

A solved problem models one or more of the chapter's assignment problems so that students can apply the modeled procedures to end-of-chapter materials.

Market-Leading End-of-Chapter Material

Students need to practice accounting so that they can understand and use it. To give students the greatest possible advantage in the real world, *Accounting Using Excel for Success* goes beyond presenting theory and procedure with comprehensive, time-tested, end-of-chapter material.

South-Western, a division of Cengage Learning, offers a vast array of online solutions to suit your course needs. Choose the product that best meets your classroom needs and course goals. Please check with your Cengage representative for more details or for ordering information.

CengageNOW

CengageNOW for Reeve/Warren/Duchac *Accounting Using Excel for Success* is a powerful and fully integrated online teaching and learning system that provides you with flexibility and control. This complete digital solution offers a comprehensive set of digital tools to power your course. CengageNOW offers the following:

- Homework, including algorithmic variations
- Integrated E-book
- Personalized study plans, which include a variety of multimedia assets (from exercise demonstrations to video to iPod content) for students as they master the chapter materials
- Assessment options that include the full test bank, including algorithmic variations
- Reporting capability based on AACSB, AICPA, and IMA competencies and standards
- Course management tools, including grade book
- WebCT and blackboard integration

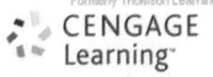

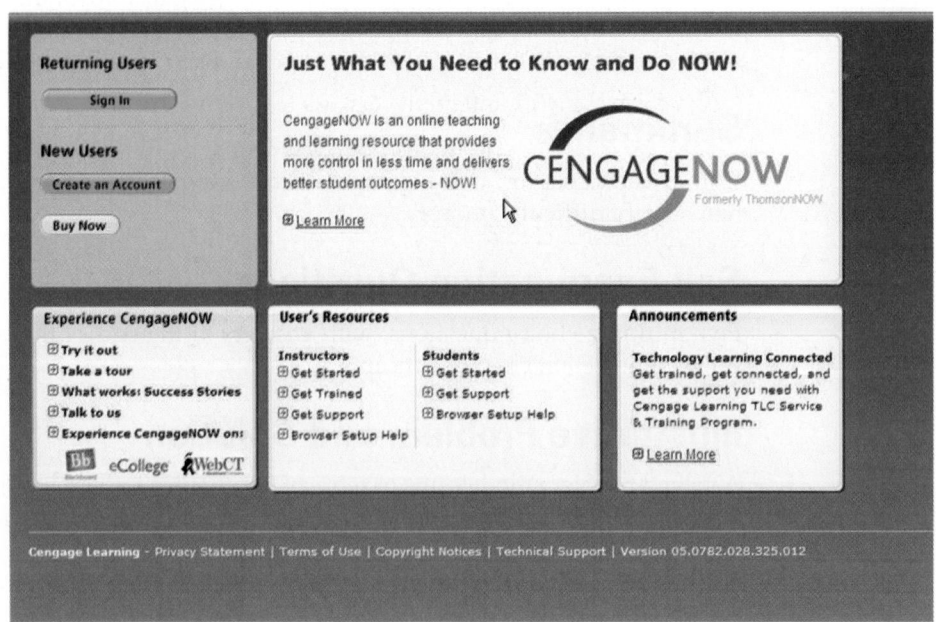

Aplia™

Aplia™ is an online interactive homework solution that improves learning by increasing student effort and engagement. Founded by Professor Paul Romer to enhance his own courses, Aplia provides auto-graded homework with detailed, immediate feedback on every question, and innovative teaching materials. Our easy-to-use system has

been used by more than 850,000 students at over 850 institutions. Aplia's accounting solution ensures that students stay on top of their coursework with regularly scheduled homework assignments. Interactive tools and content further increase engagement and understanding. The Aplia assignments match the language, style, and structure of your textbook, allowing your students to apply what they learn in the text directly to their homework.

WebTUTOR™ WebTutor™!

Webtutor may be packaged with Reeve/Warren/Duchac Accounting Using Excel for Success or purchased as a standalone item. Jumpstart your course with customizable, rich, text-specific content within your Course Management System.

- **Jumpstart**—Simply load a WebTutor cartridge into your Course Management System.
- **Customizable**—Easily blend, add, edit, reorganize, or delete content.
- **Content**—Rich, text-specific content, media assets, quizzing, test bank, weblinks, discussion topics, interactive games and exercises, and more.

Visit www.cengage.com/tlc for more information.

When it comes to supporting instructors, South-Western is unsurpassed. *Accounting Using Excel for Sucess* continues the tradition with powerful print and digital ancillaries aimed at facilitating greater course successes.

Instructor *Excel Success* Solution Files   Available online, these are Excel files (raw data populated) that follow the Excel Success example shown within the chapter. These files allow the student to download a file, practice creating Excel formulas, and reinforce the accounting concept. Additionally, these files are then saved by the student as a portfolio of activities completed during the course.

Instructor Excel® Templates   These templates provide the solutions for the problems and exercises that have Enhanced Excel® templates for students. Through these files, instructors can see the solutions in the same format as the students. All problems with accompanying templates are marked in the book with an icon and are listed in the information grid in the solutions manual. These templates are available for download on www.cengage.com/accounting/reeve or on the IRCD.

Instructor's Manual   The Instructors Manual will be on IRCD only.

Solutions Manual   The Solutions Manual contains answers to all exercises, problems, and activities that appear in the text. As always, the solutions are author-written and verified multiple times for numerical accuracy and consistency with the core text. Solutions transparencies are also available. The Solutions Manual will be on the IRCD only.

Test Bank   For each chapter, the Test Bank includes True/False questions, Multiple-Choice questions, and Problems, each marked with a difficulty level, and a tie-in to standard course outcomes. 2,800 test bank questions with variations of the Example Exercises offer multiple assignment options. In addition, the bank provides a grid for each chapter that compiles the correlation of each question to the individual chapter's objectives, as well as a ranking of difficulty based on a clearly described categorization. Through this helpful grid, making a test that is comprehensive and well-balanced is easy!

ExamView® Pro Testing Software   This intuitive software allows you to easily customize exams, practice tests, and tutorials and deliver them over a network, on the Internet, or in printed form. In addition, ExamView comes with searching capabilities that make sorting the wealth of questions from the printed test bank easy. The software and files are found on the IRCD.

PowerPoint®   Each presentation, which is included on the IRCD and on the product support site, enhances lectures and simplifies class preparation. Each chapter contains objectives followed by a thorough outline of the chapter that easily provide an entire lecture model. Also, exhibits from the chapter, such as the new Example Exercises, have been recreated as colorful PowerPoint slides to create a powerful, customizable tool.

Instructor's Resource CD-ROM   This convenient resource includes the PowerPoint® Presentations, Instructor's Manual, Solutions Manual, Test Bank, ExamView®, An Instructor's Guide to Online Resources, and Excel Application Solutions. Lively demonstrations of support technology are also included. All the basic material an instructor would need is available in one place on this IRCD.

Students come to accounting with a variety of learning needs. *Accounting Using Excel for Success* offers a broad range of supplements in both printed form and easy-to-use technology.

Try It Tutorials These tutorials are designed to walk you through in-chapter *Excel Success* examples. They require key strokes to complete the overall spreadsheet creation, ending with a display of the formulas created to solve the in-chapter example.

End-of-Chapter Special Activities These Excel spreadsheets will contain pre-populated raw data, ready for you to create various Excel formulas to solve many accounting problems. Additionally, once downloaded and completed, these files can comprise a *portfolio* of accounting problems, solved with the use of Excel.

Study Guide This author-written guide provides students Quiz and Test Hints, Matching questions, Fill-in-the-Blank questions (Parts A & B), Multiple-Choice questions, True/False questions, Exercises, and Problems for each chapter. Designed to assist students in comprehending the concepts and principles in the text, solutions for all of these items are available in the guide for quick reference.

Working Papers for Exercises and Problems The traditional working papers include problem-specific forms for preparing solutions for Exercises, A & B Problems, the Continuing Problem, and the Comprehensive Problems from the textbook. These forms, with preprinted headings, provide a structure for the problems, which helps students get started and saves them time. Additional blank forms are included.

Blank Working Papers These Working Papers are available for completing exercises and problems either from the text or prepared by the instructor. They have no preprinted headings. A guide at the front of the Working Papers tells students which form they will need for each problem.

 Enhanced Excel® Templates These templates are provided for selected long or complicated end-of-chapter exercises and problems and provide assistance to the student as they set up and work the problem. Certain cells are coded to display a red asterisk when an incorrect answer is entered, which helps students stay on track. Selected problems that can be solved using these templates are designated by an icon.

 Klooster & Allen General Ledger Software Prepared by Dale Klooster and Warren Allen, this best-selling, educational, general ledger package introduces students to the world of computerized accounting through a more intuitive, user-friendly system than the commercial software they'll use in the future. In addition, students have access to general ledger files with information based on problems from the textbook and practice sets. The program is enhanced with a problem checker that enables students to determine if their entries are correct and emulates commercial general ledger packages more closely than other educational packages. Problems that can be used with Klooster/Allen are highlighted by an icon. A free Network Version is available to schools whose students purchase Klooster/Allen GL.

Product Support Web Site www.cengage.com/accounting/reeve. This site provides students with a wealth of introductory accounting resources, including quizzing and supplement downloads and access to the Enhanced Excel® Templates.

Acknowledgments

The Excel Success learning system is a direct result of countless conversations we have had with accounting faculty and students over the past several years. These experiences and suggestions have helped us conceive this overall learning concept.

We would like to specially acknowledge and thank Craig Pence, who provided assistance in both the development of the end-of-chapter materials and the associated tutorials. Our Developmental Editor, Tracy Newman, brought invaluable vision, direction, and improvements that ensured the successful development of this title. And, lastly, we want to thank the many faculty and students for their perspectives and feedback.

Your comments and suggestions as you use this text are sincerely appreciated.

Jim Reeve, Carl Warren, and Jon Duchac

Donna T. Ascenzi
Bryant and Stratton College–Syracuse

Lisa Cooley Banks
Mott Community College

David H. Bland
Cape Fear Community College

Anna Marie Boulware
St. Charles Community College

Steven L. Ernest
Baton Rouge Community College

Christopher Gilbert
East Los Angeles College

Marina R. Grau
Accounting Program Chair, Houston Community College

Tabitha Hosty
Bradford School

Christine Jonick
Gainesville State College

Shirly A. Kleiner
Johnson County Community College

Jim Meir
Cleveland State Community College

Mary Ellen Morris
University of Massachusetts
Northern Essex Community College

Eric M. Primuth
Cuyahoga Community College

Rachel Pernia
Essex County College

Sherry Robertson
Tri-County Community College

Janice A. Stoudemire
Midlands Technical College

Melanie Torborg
Globe University/Minnesota School of Business/Utah Career College

Patricia Walczak
Lansing Community College

Shunda Ware
Atlanta Technical College

Wanda Y. Wong
Chabot College

Bucks County Community College
Instructors: Lori Grady, Judy Toland

Bernadette Allen Matarazzo
Vikas Patel
Erica Olsen
Eric Goldner
Shelly Rushbrook
Eamon Coleman
Tracy Bunsick

Baltimore City Community College
Instructors: Jeff Hillard, John Wiley

Sulaimon Adeyemi
Udeya Diour
Dwain White
Debra Witherspoon
Jacqueline Tuggle
Mabono Soumahoo

Des Moines Area Community College

Instructors: Shea Mears, Patty Holmes

Zach Schmidt
Angie Lee
Tim Hoffman
Richard Palmer
Sharon Beattie
Joseph J. Johnson
Armina Kahrimanovic
Ryan Wisnousky
Lindsay Tripp
Tiffany Shuey
Jenny Leonard
Susann Shaffner
Cori Shanahan
Nicholas Wallace
Kyle Melohn
Wendy Doolittle
LaRue Brannan
Nicholas Christopher Yaeger
Jason Aitchison

Kean University
Instructor: Gary Schader

Margherita Marjotta
Hugo Prado
Marta Domanska
Nicole Foy
Andrea Colbert
Khatija Bibi

Houston Community College
Instructor: Linda Flowers

Yildirim Kocoglu
Ana Zelaya
Seungkyu Kim
Mohammad Arsallan Bakali
Vanessa K. Rangel
Cher Lay
Sherika Gibson
Ulsi Ramos
Muhammad Shaikha
Hong Yang

Pamela Ruiz
Yvonne Ngo

Lansing Community College
Instructor: Patricia Walczak

Ana Topor
John Barrett
Brandon Smithwick
Bradley L. Moore
Cassandra DeVos
Elizabeth C. Escalera
Clara Powers
Lance Spencer
Jennifer Jones
Aristoteles Paiva Lopes

Oakland Community College
Instructor: Deborah Niemer

Paul Boker
Tracie M. Leitner
Thetnia Lynette Cobb
Vera Kolaj
Olivia Burke
Thomas J. Zuchowski
Ryan Shead
Austen Michaels
Michaele Jones
Bradlee J. VanAlstine
Tim Doherty
Vanya Jelezarova
Nilda Dervishaj
Maja Lulgjuraj
Pierce Radtke

Butler Community College
Instructors: Jennifer Brewer, Janice Akao

Sarah Kirkwood
Kimberly Brothers
Christine Brown
Chelsey Perkins
Thomas Mackay
Tucker Stewart
Austin Birkholtz

Santa Monica College
Instructors: Greg Brookins, Terri Bernstein, and Pat Halliday

Julieta Loreto
Noah Johnson
Matthew Nyby
Anitha Guna Wijaya
Jovani Rodriguez
Michelle Sharma
Marisol Granele
Prashila Sharma
Karlie Bryant
Wing San Kwong
Anthony Mitchell

Metropolitan Community College
Instructor: Idalene Williams

Suquett Saunders
Danette Cook
Ewokem Akohachere
Ivina Washington
Queen Esther Tucker
Jamie Rusch
Daisuke Motomura
Comlanri S. Zannou
Melissa Brunious
Marc Anderson
Keith Costello
Robyn Adler
Kelly Fitzgerald

Volunteer State Community College
Instructor: Brent Trentham

Kris Anderson
Jasmine Cox
Wendy Nabors
Patrick Farmer
Justin Gill
Kathryn Gambrell
Dana Mihalko
Kavitha Sudheendra
April Jeffries

BRIEF CONTENTS

CHAPTER	**1**	Introduction to Accounting and Business	1
CHAPTER	**2**	Analyzing Transactions	45
CHAPTER	**3**	The Adjusting Process	97
CHAPTER	**4**	Completing the Accounting Cycle	143
CHAPTER	**5**	Accounting Systems	204
CHAPTER	**6**	Accounting for Merchandising Businesses	252
CHAPTER	**7**	Inventories	311
CHAPTER	**8**	Sarbanes-Oxley, Internal Control, and Cash	351
CHAPTER	**9**	Receivables	393
CHAPTER	**10**	Fixed Assets and Intangible Assets	437
CHAPTER	**11**	Current Liabilities and Payroll	482
CHAPTER	**12**	Accounting for Partnerships and Limited Liability Companies	531
CHAPTER	**13**	Corporations: Organization, Stock Transactions, and Dividends	573
CHAPTER	**14**	Long-Term Liabilities: Bonds and Notes	612
CHAPTER	**15**	Investments and Fair Value Accounting	651
		Financial Statements for Mornin' Joe	700
CHAPTER	**16**	Statement of Cash Flows	704
CHAPTER	**17**	Financial Statement Analysis	757
CHAPTER	**18**	Managerial Accounting Concepts and Principles	812
CHAPTER	**19**	Job Order Costing	846
CHAPTER	**20**	Process Cost Systems	886
CHAPTER	**21**	Cost Behavior and Cost-Volume-Profit Analysis	936
CHAPTER	**22**	Budgeting	986
CHAPTER	**23**	Performance Evaluation Using Variances from Standard Costs	1032
CHAPTER	**24**	Performance Evaluation for Decentralized Operations	1075
CHAPTER	**25**	Differential Analysis and Product Pricing	1118
CHAPTER	**26**	Capital Investment Analysis	1163
APPENDIX	**A**	Interest Tables	A-2
APPENDIX	**B**	Reversing Entries	B-1
APPENDIX	**C**	End-of-Period Spreadsheet (Work Sheet) for a Merchandising Business	C-1
APPENDIX	**D**	Accounting for Deferred Income Taxes	D-1
APPENDIX	**E**	Nike, Inc., Annual Report	E-1
		Glossary	G-1
		Subject Index	I-1
		Company Index	I-18

Table of Contents

CHAPTER **1** Introduction to Accounting and Business 1

Nature of Business and Accounting 2
Types of Businesses 2
The Role of Accounting in Business 3
Role of Ethics in Accounting and Business 4
Opportunities for Accountants 6

Generally Accepted Accounting Principles 7
Business Entity Concept 7
The Cost Concept 8

The Accounting Equation 9

Business Transactions and the Accounting Equation 10

Financial Statements 14
Income Statement 15
Statement of Owner's Equity 16
Balance Sheet 16
Statement of Cash Flows 18
Interrelationships Among Financial Statements 20

Financial Analysis and Interpretation 20

CHAPTER **2** Analyzing Transactions 45

Using Accounts to Record Transactions 46
Chart of Accounts 48

Double-Entry Accounting System 49
Balance Sheet Accounts 49
Income Statement Accounts 49
Owner Withdrawals 50
Normal Balances 50
excel *success* Journalizing 50

excel *success* Posting Journal Entries to Accounts 55

excel *success* Trial Balance 63
Errors Affecting the Trial Balance 66
Errors Not Affecting the Trial Balance 67

Financial Analysis and Interpretation 69

CHAPTER **3** The Adjusting Process 97

Nature of the Adjusting Process 98
The Adjusting Process 99
Types of Accounts Requiring Adjustment 100

excel *success* Recording Adjusting Entries 102
Prepaid Expenses 103
Unearned Revenues 105

Accrued Revenues 106
Accrued Expenses 107
Depreciation Expense 109

Summary of Adjustment Process 111

excel *success* Adjusted Trial Balance 117

Financial Analysis and Interpretation 120

CHAPTER **4** Completing the Accounting Cycle 143

Flow of Accounting Information 144

excel *success* Financial Statements 146
Income Statement 146
Statement of Owner's Equity 148
Balance Sheet 149

Closing Entries 150
Journalizing and Posting Closing Entries 151
Post-Closing Trial Balance 153

Accounting Cycle 153

Illustration of the Accounting Cycle 156
Step 1. Analyzing and Recording Transactions in the Journal 158
Step 2. Posting Transactions to the Ledger 158
Step 3. Preparing an Unadjusted Trial Balance 160
Step 4. Assembling and Analyzing Adjustment Data 160
Step 5. Preparing an Optional End-of-Period Spreadsheet (Work Sheet) 160
Step 6. Journalizing and Posting Adjusting Entries 162
Step 7. Preparing an Adjusted Trial Balance 162
Step 8. Preparing the Financial Statements 163
Step 9. Journalizing and Posting Closing Entries 163
Step 10. Preparing a Post-Closing Trial Balance 165

Fiscal Year 166

Financial Analysis and Interpretation 172

Appendix: End-of-Period Spreadsheet (Work Sheet) 172
Step 1. Enter the Title 172A
Step 2. Enter the Unadjusted Trial Balance 172A
Step 3. Enter the Adjustments 172A
Step 4. Enter the Adjusted Trial Balance 172C
Step 5. Extend the Accounts to the Income Statement and Balance Sheet Columns 172C
Step 6. Total the Income Statement and Balance Sheet Columns, Compute the Net Income or Net Loss, and Complete the Spreadsheet 172C

Comprehensive Problem 1 199

CHAPTER **5** Accounting Systems.....................204

Basic Accounting Systems 205

Manual Accounting System 206
    Subsidiary Ledgers 206
    Special Journals 207
    Revenue Journal 208
    Cash Receipts Journal 211
    Accounts Receivable Control Account and Subsidiary
      Ledger 213
    Purchases Journal 214
    Cash Payments Journal 217
    Accounts Payable Control Account and Subsidiary
      Ledger 219

Adapting Manual Accounting Systems 220
    Additional Subsidiary Ledgers 220
    Modified Special Journals 220

Computerized Accounting Systems 221

E-Commerce 224

Financial Analysis and Interpretation 226

CHAPTER **6** Accounting for Merchandising
      Businesses 252

Nature of Merchandising Businesses 253

Financial Statements for a Merchandising Business 254
    Multiple-Step Income Statement 254
    Single-Step Income Statement 258
    Statement of Owner's Equity 258
    Balance Sheet 259

Merchandising Transactions 259
    Chart of Accounts for a Merchandising Business 259
    Sales Transactions 260
    Purchase Transactions 266
    Freight, Sales Taxes, and Trade Discounts 269
    Dual Nature of Merchandise Transactions 272

The Adjusting and Closing Process 274
    Adjusting Entry for Inventory Shrinkage 274
    Closing Entries 275

Financial Analysis and Interpretation 276

Appendix: Accounting Systems for Merchandisers 277
    Manual Accounting System 277
    Computerized Accounting Systems 279

Appendix: The Periodic Inventory system 280
    Cost of Merchandise Sold Using the Periodic Inventory
      System 280
    Chart of Accounts Under the Periodic Inventory
      System 281
    Recording Merchandise Transactions Under the Periodic
      Inventory System 282
    Adjusting Process Under the Periodic Inventory System 282
    Financial Statements Under the Periodic Inventory System 283
    Closing Entries Under the Periodic Inventory System 283

Comprehensive Problem 2 307

CHAPTER **7** Inventories 311

Control of Inventory 312
    Safeguarding inventory 312
    Reporting Inventory 313

Inventory Cost flow Assumptions 313

Inventory Costing Methods Under a Perpetual
    Inventory system 316
    First-In, First-Out Method 316
    Last-In, First-Out Method 318
    Average Cost Method 319
    Computerized Perpetual Inventory Systems 319

Inventory Costing Methods Under a Periodic Inventory
    System 320
    First-In, First-Out Method 320
    Last-In, First-Out Method 321
    Average Cost Method 322

Comparing Inventory Costing Methods 323

Reporting Merchandise Inventory in the Financial
    Statements 324
    Valuation at Lower of Cost or Market 325
    Valuation at Net Realizable Value 326
    Merchandise Inventory on the Balance Sheet 327
    Effect of Inventory Errors on the Financial Statement 327

Financial Analysis and Interpretation, 330

Appendix: Estimating Inventory Cost 331
    Retail Method of Inventory Costing 331
    Gross Profit Method of Inventory Costing 332

CHAPTER **8** Sarbanes-Oxley, Internal Control,
      and Cash 351

Sarbanes-Oxley Act of 2002 352

Internal Control 354
    Objectives of Internal Control 354
    Elements of Internal Control 354
    Control Environment 355
    Risk Assessment 356
    Control Procedures 356
    Monitoring 358
    Information and Communication 359
    Limitations of Internal Control 359

Cash Controls Over Receipts and Payments 359
    Control of Cash Receipts 360
    Control of Cash Payments 362

Bank Accounts 363
    Bank Statement 363
    Using the Bank Statement as a Control Over Cash 365

Bank Reconciliation 366

Special-Purpose Cash Funds 370

Financial Statement Reporting of Cash 371

Financial Analysis and Interpretation 372

Business Connection: Microsoft Corporation 373

CHAPTER **9** Receivables.....................................393

Classification of Receivables 394
    Accounts Receivable 394
    Notes Receivable 394
    Other Receivables 395

Uncollectible Receivables 395

Direct Write-Off Method for Uncollectible
    Accounts 396

Allowance Method for Uncollectible Accounts 397
    Write-Offs to the Allowance Account 397
    Estimating Uncollectibles 399

Comparing Direct Write-Off and Allowance
    Methods 405

Notes Receivable 406
    Characteristics of Notes Receivable 406
    Accounting for Notes Receivable 408

Reporting Receivables on the Balance Sheet 410

Financial Analysis and Interpretation 411

Appendix: Discounting Notes Receivable 412

CHAPTER **10** Fixed Assets and Intangible
    Assets 437

Nature of Fixed Assets 438
    Classifying Costs 439
    The Cost of Fixed Assets 440
    Capital and Revenue Expenditures 441
    Leasing Fixed Assets 442

Accounting for Depreciation 443
    Factors in Computing Depreciation Expense 444
    Straight-Line Method 445
    Units-of-Production Method 446
    Double-Declining Balance Method 447
    Comparing Depreciation Methods 448
    Depreciation for Federal Income Tax 450
    Revising Depreciation Estimates 450

Disposal of Fixed Assets 452
    Discarding Fixed Assets 452
    Selling Fixed Assets 453

Natural Resources 454

Intangible Assets 455
    Patents 455
    Copyrights and Trademarks 456
    Goodwill 456

Financial Reporting for Fixed Assets and Intangible
    Assets 458

Financial Analysis and interpretation 459

Appendix: Sum-of-the-Years-Digits Depreciation 459

Appendix: Exchanging Similar Fixed Assets 460
    Gain on Exchange 461
    Loss on Exchange 461

CHAPTER **11** Current Liabilities and Payroll.......482

Current Liabilities 483
    Accounts Payable 483
    Current Portion of Long-Term Debt 484
    Short-Term Notes Payable 484

Payroll and Payroll Taxes 487
    Liability for Employee Earnings 487
    Deductions from Employee Earnings 487
    Computing Employee Net Pay 490
    Liability for Employer's Payroll Taxes 492

Accounting Systems for Payroll and Payroll Taxes 493
    Payroll Register 494
    Employee's Earnings Record 497
    Payroll Checks 497
    Payroll System Diagram 498
    Internal Controls Payroll Systems 499

Employees' Fringe Benefits 501
    Vacation Pay 501
    Pensions 502
    Postretirement Benefits Other than Pensions 503
    Current Liabilities on the Balance Sheet 504

Contingent Liabilities 504
    Probable and Estimable 504
    Probable and Not Estimable 505
    Reasonably Possible 505
    Remote 505

Financial Analysis and Interpretation 507

Comprehensive Problem 3 526

CHAPTER **12** Accounting for Partnerships and
    Limited Liability Companies............531

Proprietorships, Partnerships, and Limited Liability
    Companies 532
    Proprietorships 532
    Partnerships 533
    Limited Liability Companies 534
    Comparing Proprietorships, Partnerships, and Limited
        Liability Companies 534

Forming and Dividing Income of a Partnership 534
    Forming a Partnership 535
    Dividing Income 536

Partner Admission and Withdrawal 540
    Admitting a Partner 540
    Withdrawal of a Partner 544
    Death of a Partner 545

Liquidating Partnerships 545
    Gain on Realization 546
    Loss on Realization 547
    Loss on Realization—Capital Deficiency 549
    Errors in Liquidation 552

Statement of Partnership Equity 552

Financial Analysis and Interpretation 553

CHAPTER **13** Corporations: Organization, Stock Transactions, and Dividends 573

Nature of a Corporation 574
Characteristics of a Corporation 574
Forming a Corporation 576

Stockholders' Equity 577

Paid-In Capital from Issuing Stock 577
Characteristics of Stock 578
Classes of Stock 578
Issuing Stock 579
Premium on Stock 581
No-Par Stock 582

Accounting for Dividends 583
Cash Dividends 583
Stock Dividends 585

Treasury Stock Transactions 586

Reporting Stockholders' Equity 587
Stockholders' Equity in the Balance Sheet 588
Reporting Retained Earnings 589
Statement of Stockholders' Equity 591
Reporting Stockholders' Equity for Mornin' Joe 591

Stock Splits 592

Financial Analysis and Interpretation 593

CHAPTER **14** Long-Term Liabilities: Bonds and Notes 612

Financing Corporations 613

Nature of Bonds Payable 616
Bond Characteristics and Terminology 616
Proceeds from Issuing Bonds 616

Accounting for Bonds Payable 617
Bonds Issued at Face Amount 617
Bonds Issued at a Discount 618
Amortizing a Bond Discount 619
Bonds Issued at a Premium 620
Amortizing a Bond Premium 621
Bond Redemption 622

Installment Notes 623
Issuing an Installment Note 623
Annual Payments 624

Reporting Long-Term Liabilities 626

Financial Analysis and Interpretation 627

Appendix: Present Value Concept and Pricing Bonds Payable 627
Present Value Concepts 628
Pricing Bonds 630

Appendix: Effective Interest Rate Method of Amortization 632
Amortization of Discount by the Interest Method 632
Amortization of Premium by the Interest Method 633

CHAPTER **15** Investments and Fair Value Accounting 651

Why Companies Invest 652
Investing Cash in Current Operations 652
Investing Cash in Temporary Investments 653
Investing Cash in Long-Term Investments 653

Accounting for Debt Investments 654
Purchase of Bonds 654
Interest Revenue 654
Sale of Bonds 655

Accounting for Equity Investments 656
Less Than 20% Ownership 656
Between 20%–50% Ownership 658
More Than 50% Ownership 660

Valuing and Reporting Investments 661
Trading Securities 661
Held-to-Maturity Securities 664
Available-for-Sale Securities 665
Summary 668

Fair Value Accounting 670
Trend to Fair Value Accounting 670
Effect of Fair Value Accounting on the Financial Statements 671
Future of Fair Value Accounting 671

Financial Analysis and Interpretation 672

Appendix: Accounting for Held-to-Maturity Investments 672
Purchase of Bonds 672
Amortization of Premium or Discount 673
Receipt of Maturity Value of Bond 674

Appendix: Comprehensive Income 675

Comprehensive Problem 4 697

Financial Statements for Mornin' Joe 700

CHAPTER **16** Statement of Cash Flows 704

Reporting Cash Flows 705
Cash Flows from Operating Activities 706
Cash Flows from Investing Activities 708
Cash Flows from Financing Activities 708
Noncash Investing and Financing Activities 708
No Cash Flow per Share 708

Statement of Cash Flows—The Indirect Method 709
Retained Earnings 709
Adjustments to Net Income 711
Dividends 716
Common Stock 717
Bonds Payable 718
Building 718
Land 719
Preparing the Statement of Cash Flows 719

Statement of Cash Flows—The Direct Method 720
Cash Received from Customers 721
Cash Payments for Merchandise 722

Cash Payments for Operating Expenses 723
Gain on Sale of Land 723
Interest Expense 723
Cash Payments for Income Taxes 724
Reporting Cash Flows from Operating Activities—Direct
    Method 724

Financial Analysis and Interpretation 725

Appendix: Spreadsheet (Work Sheet) for Statement of
    Cash Flows—The Indirect Method 726
Analyzing Accounts 726
Retained Earnings 726
Other Accounts 728
Preparing the Statement of Cash Flows 728

CHAPTER **17** Financial Statement Analysis 757

Basic Analytical Methods 758
Horizontal Analysis 759
Vertical Analysis 761
Common-Sized Statements 762
Other Analytical Measures 765

Solvency Analysis 765
Current Position Analysis 765
Accounts Receivable Analysis 768
Inventory Analysis 769
Ratio of Fixed Assets to Long-Term Liabilities 771
Ratio of Liabilities to Stockholders' Equity 771
Number of Times Interest Charges Earned 772

Profitability Analysis 773
Ratio of Net Sales to Assets 773
Rate Earned on Total Assets 774
Rate Earned on Stockholders' Equity 775
Rate Earned on Common Stockholders' Equity 776
Earning Per Share on Common Stock 777
Price-Earnings Ratio 778
Dividends Per Share 779
Dividend Yield 779
Summary of Analytical Measures 780

Corporate Annual Reports 780
Management Discussion and Analysis 780
Report on Internal Control 782
Report on Fairness of Financial Statements 782

Appendix: Unusual Items on the Income Statement 784
Unusual Items Affecting the Current Period's Income
    Statement 785
Unusual Items Affecting the Prior Period's Income
    Statement 786

Nike, Inc., Problem 808

CHAPTER **18** Managerial Accounting Concepts
                    and Principles 812

Managerial Accounting 813
Differences Between Managerial and Financial
    Accounting 814

The Management Accountant in the Organization 815
Managerial Accounting in the Management Process 816

Manufacturing Operations: Costs and Terminology 818
Direct and Indirect Cost 819
Manufacturing Cost 820

Financial Statements for a Manufacturing Business 824
Balance Sheet for a Manufacturing Business 824
Income Statement for a Manufacturing Company 825

Uses of Managerial Accounting 827

CHAPTER **19** Job Order Costing 846

Cost Accounting System Overview 847

Job Order Cost Systems for Manufacturing Businesses 848
Materials 849
Factory Labor 851
Factory Overhead Cost 853
Work in Process 858
Finished Goods 859
Sales and Cost of Goods Sold 860
Period Costs 860
Summary of Cost Flows for Legend Guitars 860

Job Order Costing for Decision Making 862

Job Order Cost Systems for Professional Service
    Businesses 863

CHAPTER **20** Process Cost Systems 886

Process Cost Systems 887
Comparing Job Order and Process Cost Systems 888
Cost Flows for a Process Manufacturer 890

Cost of Production Report 893
Step 1: Determine the Units to Be Assigned Costs 893
Step 2: Compute Equivalent Units of Production 895
Step 3: Determine the Cost per Equivalent Unit 898
Step 4: Allocate Costs to Units Transferred Out and Partially
    Completed Units 900
Preparing the Cost of Production Report 902

Journal Entries for a Process Cost System 904

Using the Cost of Production Report for Decision
    Making 906
Frozen Delight 906
Holland Beverage Company 907
Yield 908

Just-in-Time Processing 909

Appendix: Average Cost Method 912
Determining Costs Using the Average Cost Method 912
The Cost of Production Report 914

CHAPTER **21** Cost Behavior and Cost-Volume-
                    Profit Analysis................................936

Cost Behavior 937
Variable Costs 938
Fixed Costs 939

Mixed Costs 939
Summary of Cost Behavior Concepts 943

Cost-Volume-Profit Relationships 943
Contribution Margin 944
Contribution Margin Ratio 944
excel success Unit Contribution Margin 945

Mathematical Approach to Cost-Volume-Profit
Analysis 947
Break-Even Point 947
Target Profit 950

Graphic Approach to Cost-Volume-Profit Analysis 952
Cost-Volume-Profit (Break-Even) Chart 952
Profit-Volume Chart 954
Use of Computers in Cost-Volume-Profit Analysis 955
Assumptions of Cost-Volume-Profit Analysis 955

Special Cost-Volume-Profit Relationships 956
Sales Mix Considerations 957
Operating Leverage 958
Margin of Safety 960

Appendix: Variable Costing 961

CHAPTER 22 Budgeting 986
Nature and Objectives of Budgeting 987
Objectives of Budgeting 988
Human Behavior and Budgeting 988

Budgeting Systems 990
Static Budget 991
Flexile Budget 991
Computerized Budgeting Systems 993

Master Budget 993

Income Statement Budgets 995
excel success Sales Budget 995
excel success Production Budget 995
excel success Direct Materials Purchases Budget 997
excel success Direct Labor Cost Budget 998
excel success Factory Overhead Cost Budget 999
excel success Cost of Goods Sold Budget 1000
Selling and Administrative Expenses Budget 1002
Budgeted Income Statement 1002

Balance Sheet Budgets 1002
Cash Budget 1003
Capital Expenditures Budget 1006
Budgeted Balance Sheet 1007

CHAPTER 23 Performance Evaluation
Using Variances from Standard
Costs 1032
Standards 1033
Setting Standards 1034
Types of Standards 1034
Reviewing and Revising Standards 1035
Criticisms of Standard Costs 1035

Budgetary Performance Evaluation 1035
Budget Performance Report 1036
Manufacturing Cost Variances 1037

Direct Materials and Direct Labor Variances 1038
Direct Materials Variances 1038
excel success Direct Labor Variances 1041

Factory Overhead Variances 1043
excel success The Factory Overhead Flexile Budget 1043
excel success Variable Factory Overhead Controllable Variance 1044
excel success Fixed Factory Overhead Volume Variance 1046
Reporting Factory Overhead Variances 1047
Factory Overhead Account 1048

Recording and Reporting Variances from
Standards 1050

Nonfinancial Performance Measures 1053

Comprehensive Problem 5 1071

CHAPTER 24 Performance Evaluation for
Decentralized Operations.............1075
Centralized and Decentralized Operations 1076
Advantages of Decentralization 1077
Disadvantages of Decentralization 1077
Responsibility Accounting 1077

Responsibility Accounting for Cost Centers 1078

Responsibility Accounting for Profit Centers 1080
excel success Service Department Charges 1080
Profit Center Reporting 1084

Responsibility Accounting for Investment Centers 1085
Rate of Return on Investment 1086
Residual Income 1089
The Balanced Scorecard 1090

Transfer Pricing 1092
Market Price Approach 1093
Negotiated Price Approach 1093
Cost Price Approach 1096

CHAPTER 25 Differential Analysis and Product
Pricing 1118
Differential Analysis 1119
Lease or Sell 1121
Discontinue a Segment or Product 1122
Make or Buy 1124
Replace Equipment 1126
Process or Sell 1127
Accept Business at a Special Price 1128

Setting Normal Product Selling Prices 1130
Total Cost Concept 1130
Product Cost Concept 1133
Variable Cost Concept 1134
Choosing a Cost-Plus Approach Cost Concept 1136
Activity-Based Costing 1137
Target Costing 1137

Production Bottlenecks, Pricing, and Profits 1138
    Production Bottlenecks and Profits 1138
    Production Bottlenecks and Pricing 1139
Appendix: Activity-Based Costing 1140

CHAPTER **26** Capital Investment Analysis.........1163
Nature of Capital Investment analysis 1164
Methods Not Using Present Values 1165
    Average Rate of Return Method 1165
    Cash Payback Method 1166
Methods Using Present Values 1168
    Present Value Concepts 1168
    Net Present Value Method 1171
    Internal Rate of Return Method 1174
Factors that Complicate Capital Investment Analysis 1177
    Income Tax 1177
    Unequal Proposal Lives 1177
    Lease versus Capital Investment 1179
    Uncertainty 1179
    Changes in Price Levels 1179
    Qualitative Considerations 1180
Capital Rationing 1180

APPENDIX **A** Interest Tables A-2

APPENDIX **B** Reversing Entries............................B-1

APPENDIX **C** End-of-Period Spreadsheet
(Work Sheet) for a Merchandising
Business C-1

APPENDIX **D** Accounting for Deferred Income
Taxes...D-1
    Temporary Differences D-1
    Reporting Deferred Taxes D-3
    Permanent Differences D-3

APPENDIX **E** Nike, Inc., Annual Report................E-1
Glossary G-1
Subject Index I-1
Company Index I-18

excel
success
excel
success

Introduction to Accounting and Business

© AP Photo/Paul Sakuma

G O O G L E™

When two teams pair up for a game of football, there is often a lot of noise. The band plays, the fans cheer, and fireworks light up the scoreboard. Obviously, the fans are committed and care about the outcome of the game. Just like fans at a football game, the owners of a business want their business to "win" against their competitors in the marketplace. While having our football team win can be a source of pride, winning in the marketplace goes beyond pride and has many tangible benefits. Companies that are winners are better able to serve customers, to provide good jobs for employees, and to make more money for the owners.

One such successful company is Google, one of the most visible companies on the Internet. Many of us cannot visit the Web without first stopping at Google to power your search. As one writer said, "Google is the closest thing the Web has

to an ultimate answer machine." And yet, Google is a free tool—no one asks for your credit card when you use any of Google's search tools. So, do you think Google has been a successful company? Does it make money? How would you know? Accounting helps to answer these questions. Google's accounting information tells us that Google is a very successful company that makes a lot of money, but not from you and me. Google makes its money from advertisers.

In this textbook, we will introduce you to accounting, the language of business. In this chapter, we begin by discussing what a business is, how it operates, and the role that accounting plays.

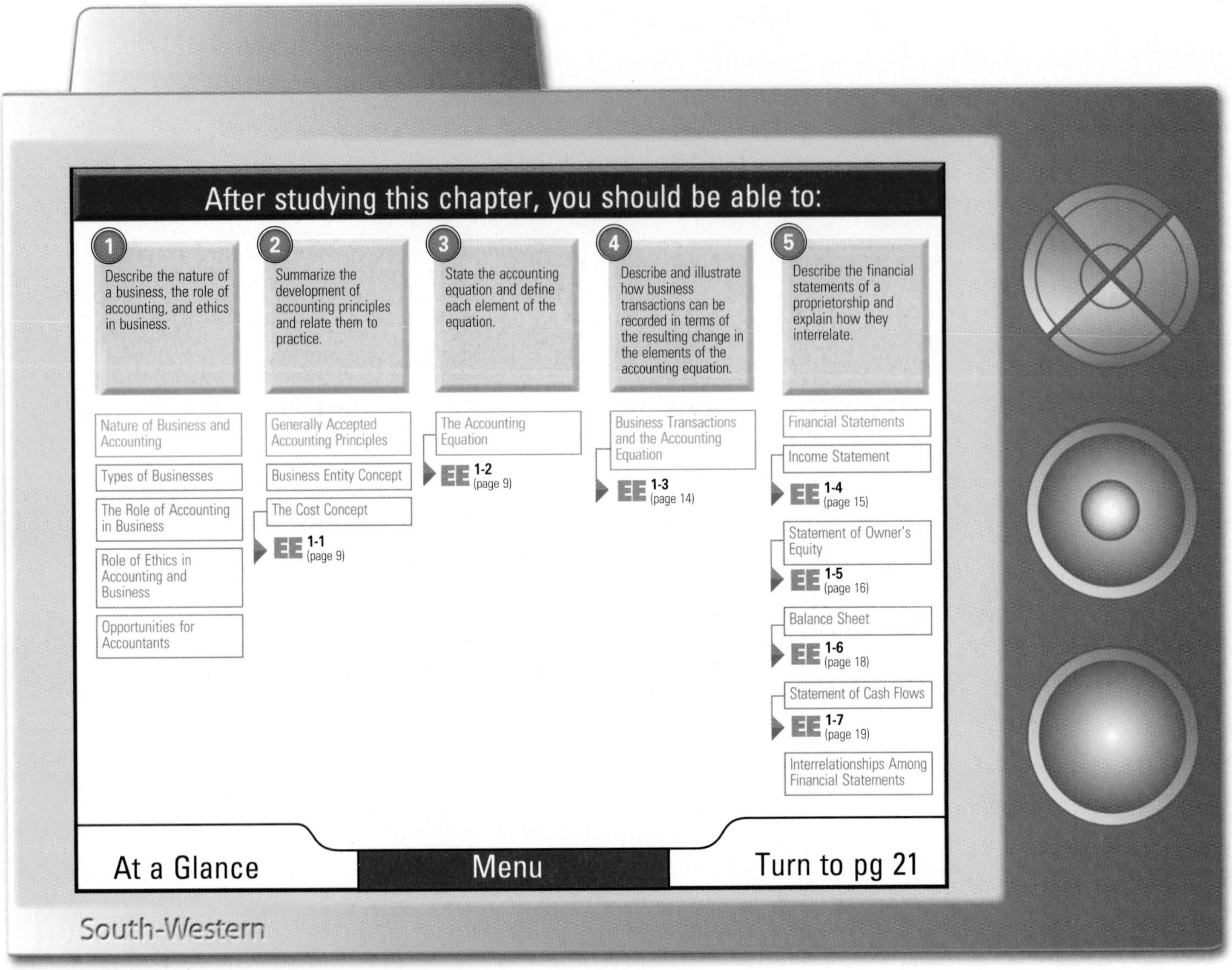

After studying this chapter, you should be able to:

1 Describe the nature of a business, the role of accounting, and ethics in business.

2 Summarize the development of accounting principles and relate them to practice.

3 State the accounting equation and define each element of the equation.

4 Describe and illustrate how business transactions can be recorded in terms of the resulting change in the elements of the accounting equation.

5 Describe the financial statements of a proprietorship and explain how they interrelate.

Nature of Business and Accounting

Types of Businesses

The Role of Accounting in Business

Role of Ethics in Accounting and Business

Opportunities for Accountants

Generally Accepted Accounting Principles

Business Entity Concept

The Cost Concept

EE 1-1 (page 9)

The Accounting Equation

EE 1-2 (page 9)

Business Transactions and the Accounting Equation

EE 1-3 (page 14)

Financial Statements

Income Statement

EE 1-4 (page 15)

Statement of Owner's Equity

EE 1-5 (page 16)

Balance Sheet

EE 1-6 (page 18)

Statement of Cash Flows

EE 1-7 (page 19)

Interrelationships Among Financial Statements

At a Glance   Menu   Turn to pg 21

South-Western

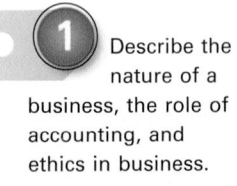

1 Describe the nature of a business, the role of accounting, and ethics in business.

Nature of Business and Accounting

A **business**[1] is an organization in which basic resources (inputs), such as materials and labor, are assembled and processed to provide goods or services (outputs) to customers. Businesses come in all sizes, from a local coffee house to Starbucks, which sells over $9 billion of coffee and related products each year.

The objective of most businesses is to earn a profit. **Profit** is the difference between the amounts received from customers for goods or services and the amounts paid for the inputs used to provide the goods or services. In this text, we focus on businesses operating to earn a profit. However many of the same concepts and principles also apply to not-for-profit organizations such as hospitals, churches, and government agencies.

Types of Businesses

Three types of businesses operated for profit include service, merchandising, and manufacturing businesses.

1 A complete glossary of terms appears at the end of the text.

Roughly eight out of every ten workers in the United States are service providers.

Each type of business and some examples are described below.

Service businesses provide services rather than products to customers.

Delta Air Lines (transportation services)
The Walt Disney Company (entertainment services)

Merchandising businesses sell products they purchase from other businesses to customers.

Wal-Mart (general merchandise)
Amazon.com (Internet books, music, videos)

Manufacturing businesses change basic inputs into products that are sold to customers.

General Motors Corporation (cars, trucks, vans)
Dell Inc. (personal computers)

The Role of Accounting in Business

What is the role of accounting in business? The simplest answer is that accounting provides information for managers to use in operating the business. In addition, accounting provides information to other users in assessing the economic performance and condition of the business.

Thus, **accounting** can be defined as an information system that provides reports to users about the economic activities and condition of a business. You may think of accounting as the "language of business." This is because accounting is the means by which businesses' financial information is communicated to users.

The process by which accounting provides information to users is as follows:

1. Identify users.
2. Assess users' information needs.
3. Design the accounting information system to meet users' needs.
4. Record economic data about business activities and events.
5. Prepare accounting reports for users.

As illustrated in Exhibit 1, users of accounting information can be divided into two groups: internal users and external users.

Exhibit 1

Users of Accounting Information

Providing Accounting Information to Users

1 Identify users
Internal users: Managers, employees
Users
External users: Customers, creditors, investors, government

2 Assess users' information needs

5 Prepare accounting reports for users
REPORT TO USERS

3 Design the accounting information system to meet users' needs

ACCOUNTING INFORMATION SYSTEM

4 Record economic data about business activities and events

Internal users of accounting information include managers and employees. These users are directly involved in managing and operating the business. The area of accounting that provides internal users with information is called **managerial accounting** or **management accounting**. The objective of managerial accounting is to provide relevant and timely information for managers' and employees' decision-making needs. Often times, such information is sensitive and is not distributed outside the business. Examples of sensitive information might include information about customers, prices, and plans to expand the business. Managerial accountants employed by a business are employed in **private accounting**.

External users of accounting information include customers, creditors, and the government. These users are not directly involved in managing and operating the business. The area of accounting that provides external users with information is called **financial accounting**. The objective of financial accounting is to provide relevant and timely information for the decision-making needs of users outside of the business. For example, financial reports on the operations and condition of the business are useful for banks and other creditors in deciding whether to lend money to the business. **General-purpose financial statements** are one type of financial accounting report that is distributed to external users. The term *general-purpose* refers to the wide range of decision-making needs that these reports are designed to serve. Later in this chapter, we describe and illustrate general-purpose financial statements.

Role of Ethics in Accounting and Business

The objective of accounting is to provide relevant, timely information for user decision making. Accountants must behave in an ethical manner so that the information they provide will be trustworthy and, thus, useful for decision making. Managers and employees must also behave in an ethical manner in managing and operating a business. Otherwise, no one will be willing to invest in or loan money to the business.

Ethics are moral principles that guide the conduct of individuals. Unfortunately, business managers and accountants sometimes behave in an unethical manner. A number of managers of the companies listed in Exhibit 2 engaged in accounting or business fraud. These ethical violations led to fines, firings, and lawsuits. In some cases, managers were criminally prosecuted, convicted, and sent to prison.

What went wrong for the managers and companies listed in Exhibit 2? The answer normally involved one or both of the following two factors:

Failure of Individual Character. An ethical manager and accountant is honest and fair. However, managers and accountants often face pressures from supervisors to meet company and investor expectations. In many of the cases in Exhibit 2, managers and accountants justified small ethical violations to avoid such pressures. However, these small violations became big violations as the company's financial problems became worse.

Culture of Greed and Ethical Indifference. By their behavior and attitude, senior managers set the company culture. In most of the companies listed in Exhibit 2, the senior managers created a culture of greed and indifference to the truth.

Integrity, Objectivity, and Ethics in Business

DOING THE RIGHT THING

Time Magazine named three women as "Persons of the Year 2002." Each of these not-so-ordinary women had the courage, determination, and integrity to do the right thing. Each risked her personal career to expose shortcomings in her organization. Sherron Watkins, an Enron vice president, wrote a letter to Enron's chairman, Kenneth Lay, warning him of improper accounting that eventually led to Enron's collapse. Cynthia Cooper, an internal accountant, informed WorldCom's Board of Directors of phony accounting that allowed WorldCom to cover up over $3 billion in losses and forced WorldCom into bankruptcy. Coleen Rowley, an FBI staff attorney, wrote a memo to FBI Director Robert Mueller, exposing how the Bureau brushed off her pleas to investigate Zacarias Moussaoui, who was indicted as a co-conspirator in the September 11 terrorist attacks.

Exhibit 2

Accounting and Business Fraud in the 2000s

Company	Nature of Accounting or Business Fraud	Result
Adelphia Communications	Rigas family treated the company assets as their own.	Bankruptcy. Rigas family members found guilty of fraud and lost their investment in the company.
American International Group, Inc. (AIG)	Used sham accounting transactions to inflate performance.	CEO resigned. Executives criminally convicted. AIG paid $126 million in fines.
America Online, Inc. and PurchasePro	Artificially inflated their financial results.	Civil charges filed against senior executives of both companies. $500 million fine.
Computer Associates International, Inc.	Fraudulently inflated its financial results.	CEO and senior executives indicted. Five executives pled guilty. $225 million fine.
Enron	Fraudulently inflated its financial results.	Bankrupcty. Senior executives criminally convicted. Over $60 billion in stock market losses.
Fannie Mae	Improperly shifted financial performance between periods.	CEO and CFO fired. Company made a $9 billion correction to previously reported earnings.
HealthSouth	Overstated performance by $4 billion in false entries.	Senior executives criminally convicted.
Qwest Communications International, Inc.	Improperly recognized $3 billion in false receipts.	CEO and six other executives criminally convicted of "massive financial fraud." $250 million SEC fine.
Tyco International, Ltd.	Failed to disclose secret loans to executives that were subsequently forgiven.	CEO forced to resign and subjected to frozen asset order and criminally convicted.
WorldCom	Misstated financial results by nearly $9 billion.	Bankruptcy. Criminal conviction of CEO and CFO. Over $100 billion in stock market losses. Directors forced to pay $18 million.
Xerox Corporation	Recognized $3 billion in revenue prior to when it should have been.	$10 million fine to SEC. Six executives forced to pay $22 million.

Exhibit 3

Guideline for Ethical Conduct

1. Identify an ethical decision by using your personal ethical standards of honesty and fairness.
2. Identify the consequences of the decision and its effect on others.
3. Consider your obligations and responsibilities to those that will be affected by your decision.
4. Make a decision that is ethical and fair to those affected by it.

As a result of the accounting and business frauds shown in Exhibit 2, Congress passed new laws to monitor the behavior of accounting and business. For example, the Sarbanes-Oxley Act of 2002 (SOX) was enacted. SOX established a new oversight body for the accounting profession called the Public Company Accounting Oversight Board (PCAOB). In addition, SOX established standards for independence, corporate responsibility, and disclosure.

How does one behave ethically when faced with financial or other types of pressure? A guideline for behaving ethically is shown in Exhibit 3.[2]

Opportunities for Accountants

Numerous career opportunities are available for students majoring in accounting. Currently, the demand for accountants exceeds the number of new graduates entering the job market. This is partly due to the increased regulation of business caused by the accounting and business frauds shown in Exhibit 2. Also, more and more businesses have come to recognize the importance and value of accounting information.

As we indicated earlier, accountants employed by a business are said to be employed in private accounting. Private accountants have a variety of possible career options within a company. Some of these career options are shown in Exhibit 4 along with their starting salaries. Accountants who provide audit services, called auditors, verify the accuracy of financial records, accounts, and systems. As shown in Exhibit 4, several private accounting careers have certification options.

Exhibit 4

Accounting Career Paths and Salaries

Accounting Career Track	Description	Career Options	Annual Starting Salaries[1]	Certification
Private Accounting	Accountants employed by companies, government, and not-for-profit entities.	Bookkeeper	$34,875	
		Payroll clerk	$33,500	Certified Payroll Professional (CPP)
		General accountant	$40,750	
		Budget analyst	$42,875	
		Cost accountant	$42,125	Certified Management Accountant (CMA)
		Internal auditor	$46,375	Certified Internal Auditor (CIA)
		Information technology auditor	$54,625	Certified Information Systems Auditor (CISA)
Public Accounting	Accountants employed individually or within a public accounting firm in tax or audit services.	Local firms	$43,625	Certified Public Accountant (CPA)
		National firms	$52,500	Certified Public Accountant (CPA)

Source: Robert Half 2008 Salary Guide (Finance and Accounting), Robert Half International, Inc.
[1]Median salaries of a reported range. Private accounting salaries are reported for large companies. Salaries may vary by region.

---

2 Many companies have ethical standards of conduct for managers and employees. In addition, the Institute of Management Accountants and the American Institute of Certified Public Accountants have professional codes of conduct.

Accountants and their staff who provide services on a fee basis are said to be employed in **public accounting**. In public accounting, an accountant may practice as an individual or as a member of a public accounting firm. Public accountants who have met a state's education, experience, and examination requirements may become **Certified Public Accountants (CPAs)**. CPAs generally perform general accounting, audit, or tax services. As can be seen in Exhibit 4, CPAs have slightly better starting salaries than private accountants. Career statistics indicate, however, that these salary differences tend to disappear over time.

Because all functions within a business use accounting information, experience in private or public accounting provides a solid foundation for a career. Many positions in industry and in government agencies are held by individuals with accounting backgrounds.

2 Summarize the development of accounting principles and relate them to practice.

Generally Accepted Accounting Principles

If a company's management could record and report financial data as it saw fit, comparisons among companies would be difficult, if not impossible. Thus, financial accountants follow **generally accepted accounting principles (GAAP)** in preparing reports. These reports allow investors and other users to compare one company to another.

Accounting principles and concepts develop from research, accepted accounting practices, and pronouncements of regulators. Within the United States, the **Financial Accounting Standards Board (FASB)** has the primary responsibility for developing accounting principles. The FASB publishes *Statements of Financial Accounting Standards* as well as *Interpretations* of these Standards. In addition, the **Securities and Exchange Commission (SEC),** an agency of the U.S. government, has authority over the accounting and financial disclosures for companies whose shares of ownership (stock) are traded and sold to the public. The SEC normally accepts the accounting principles set forth by the FASB. However, the SEC may issue *Staff Accounting Bulletins* on accounting matters that may not have been addressed by the FASB.

Many countries outside the United States use generally accepted accounting principles adopted by the **International Accounting Standards Board (IASB)**. The IASB issues *International Financial Reporting Standards (IFRSs)*. Significant differences currently exist between FASB and IASB accounting principles. However, the FASB and IASB are working together to reduce and eliminate these differences into a single set of accounting principles. Such a set of worldwide accounting principles would help facilitate investment and business in an increasingly global economy.

In this chapter and text, we emphasize accounting principles and concepts. It is by this emphasis on the "why" as well as the "how" that you will gain an understanding of accounting.

Business Entity Concept

The **business entity concept** limits the economic data in an accounting system to data related directly to the activities of the business. In other words, the business is viewed as an entity separate from its owners, creditors, or other businesses. For example, the accountant for a business with one owner would record the activities of the business only and would not record the personal activities, property, or debts of the owner.

A business entity may take the form of a proprietorship, partnership, corporation, or limited liability company (LLC). Each of these forms and their major characteristics are listed on the following chart.

Form of Business Entity	Characteristics
Proprietorship is owned by one individual.	• 70% of business entities in the United States. • Easy and cheap to organize. • Resources are limited to those of the owner. • Used by small businesses.
Partnership is owned by two or more individuals.	• 10% of business organizations in the United States (combined with limited liability companies). • Combines the skills and resources of more than one person.
Corporation is organized under state or federal statutes as a separate legal taxable entity.	• Generates 90% of business revenues. • 20% of the business organizations in the United States. • Ownership is divided into shares called stock. • Can obtain large amounts of resources by issuing stock. • Used by large businesses.
Limited liability company (LLC) combines the attributes of a partnership and a corporation.	• 10% of business organizations in the United States (combined with partnerships). • Often used as an alternative to a partnership. • Has tax and legal liability advantages for owners.

The three types of businesses we discussed earlier—service, merchandising, and manufacturing—may be organized as proprietorships, partnerships, corporations, or limited liability companies. Because of the large amount of resources required to operate a manufacturing business, most manufacturing businesses such as Ford Motor Company are corporations. Most large retailers such as Wal-Mart and Home Depot are also corporations.

The Cost Concept

Under the **cost concept**, amounts are initially recorded in the accounting records at their cost or purchase price. To illustrate, assume that Aaron Publishers purchased the following building on February 20, 2008:

Price listed by seller on January 1, 2008	$160,000
Aaron Publishers' initial offer to buy on January 31, 2008	140,000
Purchase price on February 20, 2008	150,000
Estimated selling price on December 31, 2010	220,000
Assessed value for property taxes, December 31, 2010	190,000

Under the cost concept, Aaron Publishers records the purchase of the building on February 20, 2008, at the purchase price of $150,000. The other amounts listed above have no effect on the accounting records.

The fact that the building has a higher estimated selling price on December 31, 2010, indicates that the building has increased in value. However, to use the $220,000 in the accounting records would be to record an illusory or unrealized profit. If Aaron Publishers sells the building on January 9, 2011, for $220,000, a profit of $70,000 is then realized and recorded. The new owner would record $220,000 as its cost of the building.

The cost concept also involves the objectivity and unit of measure concepts. The **objectivity concept** requires that the amounts recorded in the accounting records be based on objective evidence. In exchanges between a buyer and a seller, both try to get the best price. Only the final agreed-upon amount is objective enough to be recorded in the accounting records. If amounts in the accounting records were constantly being revised upward or downward based on offers, appraisals, and opinions, accounting reports could become unstable and unreliable.

The **unit of measure concept** requires that economic data be recorded in dollars. Money is a common unit of measurement for reporting financial data and reports.

Example Exercise 1-1   Cost Concept

On August 25, Gallatin Repair Service extended an offer of $125,000 for land that had been priced for sale at $150,000. On September 3, Gallatin Repair Service accepted the seller's counteroffer of $137,000. On October 20, the land was assessed at a value of $98,000 for property tax purposes. On December 4, Gallatin Repair Service was offered $160,000 for the land by a national retail chain. At what value should the land be recorded in Gallatin Repair Service's records?

Follow My Example 1-1

$137,000. Under the cost concept, the land should be recorded at the cost to Gallatin Repair Service.

For Practice: PE 1-1A, PE 1-1B

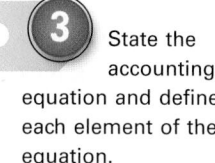

3 State the accounting equation and define each element of the equation.

The Accounting Equation

The resources owned by a business are its **assets**. Examples of assets include cash, land, buildings, and equipment. The rights or claims to the assets are divided into two types: (1) the rights of creditors and (2) the rights of owners. The rights of creditors are the debts of the business and are called **liabilities**. The rights of the owners are called **owner's equity**. The following equation shows the relationship among assets, liabilities, and owner's equity:

Assets = Liabilities + Owner's Equity

Example Exercise 1-2   Accounting Equation

John Joos is the owner and operator of You're A Star, a motivational consulting business. At the end of its accounting period, December 31, 2009, You're A Star has assets of $800,000 and liabilities of $350,000. Using the accounting equation, determine the following amounts:

a. Owner's equity, as of December 31, 2009.
b. Owner's equity, as of December 31, 2010, assuming that assets increased by $130,000 and liabilities decreased by $25,000 during 2010.

Follow My Example 1-2

a.   Assets = Liabilities + Owner's Equity
     $800,000 = $350,000 + Owner's Equity
   Owner's Equity = $450,000

b. First, determine the change in Owner's Equity during 2010 as follows:

     Assets = Liabilities + Owner's Equity
   $130,000 = −$25,000 + Owner's Equity
   Owner's Equity = $155,000

Next, add the change in Owner's Equity on December 31, 2009, to arrive at Owner's Equity on December 31, 2010, as shown below.

Owner's Equity on December 31, 2010 = $605,000 = $450,000 + $155,000

For Practice: PE 1-2A, PE 1-2B

This equation is called the **accounting equation**. Liabilities usually are shown before owner's equity in the accounting equation because creditors have first rights to the assets.

Given any two amounts, the accounting equation may be solved for the third unknown amount. To illustrate, if the assets owned by a business amount to $100,000 and the liabilities amount to $30,000, the owner's equity is equal to $70,000, as shown below.

Assets − Liabilities = Owner's Equity
$100,000 − $30,000 = $70,000

4   Describe and illustrate how business transactions can be recorded in terms of the resulting change in the elements of the accounting equation.

Business Transactions and the Accounting Equation

Paying a monthly telephone bill of $168 affects a business's financial condition because it now has less cash on hand. Such an economic event or condition that directly changes an entity's financial condition or its results of operations is a **business transaction**. For example, purchasing land for $50,000 is a business transaction. In contrast, a change in a business's credit rating does not directly affect cash or any other asset, liability, or owner's equity amount.

All business transactions can be stated in terms of changes in the elements of the accounting equation. We illustrate how business transactions affect the accounting equation by using some typical transactions. As a basis for illustration, we use a business organized by Chris Clark.

Assume that on November 1, 2009, Chris Clark begins a business that will be known as NetSolutions. The first phase of Chris's business plan is to operate NetSolutions as a service business assisting individuals and small businesses in developing Web pages and installing computer software. Chris expects this initial phase of the business to last

> All business transactions can be stated in terms of changes in the elements of the accounting equation.

one to two years. During this period, Chris plans on gathering information on the software and hardware needs of customers. During the second phase of the business plan, Chris plans to expand NetSolutions into a personalized retailer of software and hardware for individuals and small businesses.

Each transaction during NetSolutions' first month of operations is described in the following paragraphs. The effect of each transaction on the accounting equation is then shown.

Transaction A

> Nov. 1, 2009   Chris Clark deposits $25,000 in a bank account in the name of NetSolutions.

This transaction increases the asset cash (on the left side of the equation) by $25,000. To balance the equation, the owner's equity (on the right side of the equation) increases by the same amount. The equity of the owner is identified using the owner's name and "Capital," such as "Chris Clark, Capital."

The effect of this transaction on NetSolutions' accounting equation is shown below.

	Assets	=	Owner's Equity
	Cash	=	Chris Clark, Capital
a.	25,000		25,000

Since Chris Clark is the sole owner, NetSolutions is a proprietorship. Also, the accounting equation shown above is only for the business, NetSolutions. Under the business entity concept, Chris Clark's personal assets, such as a home or personal bank account, and personal liabilities are excluded from the equation.

Transaction B

> Nov. 5, 2009   NetSolutions paid $20,000 for the purchase of land as a future building site.

The land is located in a business park with access to transportation facilities. Chris Clark plans to rent office space and equipment during the first phase of the business plan. During the second phase, Chris plans to build an office and a warehouse on the land.

The purchase of the land changes the makeup of the assets, but it does not change the total assets. The items in the equation prior to this transaction and the effect of the transaction are shown below. The new amounts are called *balances*.

	Assets		=	Owner's Equity
	Cash +	Land	=	Chris Clark, Capital
Bal.	25,000			25,000
b.	−20,000	+20,000		
Bal.	5,000	20,000		25,000

Transaction C

> Nov. 10, 2009   NetSolutions purchased supplies for $1,350 and agreed to pay the supplier in the near future.

You have probably used a credit card to buy clothing or other merchandise. In this type of transaction, you received clothing for a promise to pay your credit card bill in the future. That is, you received an asset and incurred a liability to pay a future bill. NetSolutions entered into a similar transaction by purchasing supplies for $1,350 and agreeing to pay the supplier in the near future. This type of transaction is called a purchase *on account* and is often described as follows: *Purchased supplies on account, $1,350.*

The liability created by a purchase on account is called an **account payable**. Items such as supplies that will be used in the business in the future are called **prepaid expenses**, which are assets. Thus, the effect of this transaction is to increase assets (Supplies) and liabilities (Accounts Payable) by $1,350, as follows:

Other examples of common prepaid expenses include insurance and rent. Businesses often report these assets together as a single item, prepaid expenses.

	Assets			=	Liabilities + Owner's Equity	
					Accounts +	Chris Clark,
	Cash +	Supplies +	Land	=	Payable	Capital
Bal.	5,000		20,000			25,000
c.		+1,350			+1,350	
Bal.	5,000	1,350	20,000		1,350	25,000

Transaction D

> Nov. 18, 2009   NetSolutions received cash of $7,500 for providing services to customers.

You may have earned money by painting houses or mowing lawns. If so, you received money for rendering services to a customer. Likewise, a business earns money by selling goods or services to its customers. This amount is called **revenue**.

During its first month of operations, NetSolutions received cash of $7,500 for providing services to customers. The receipt of cash increases NetSolutions' assets and also increases Chris Clark's equity in the business. The revenues of $7,500 are recorded in a Fees Earned column to the right of Chris Clark, Capital. The effect of this transaction is to increase Cash and Fees Earned by $7,500, as shown below.

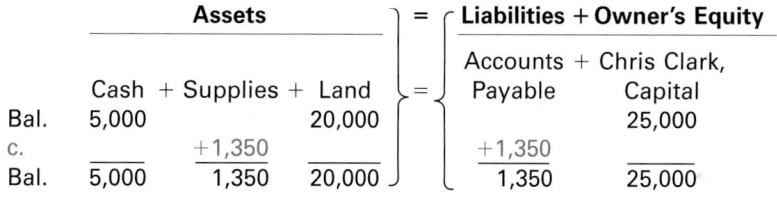

	Assets			=	Liabilities +	Owner's Equity	
					Accounts	Chris Clark,	Fees
	Cash +	Supplies +	Land	=	Payable +	Capital	+ Earned
Bal.	5,000	1,350	20,000		1,350	25,000	
d.	+7,500						+7,500
Bal.	12,500	1,350	20,000		1,350	25,000	7,500

Different terms are used for the various types of revenues. As illustrated above, revenue from providing services is recorded as **fees earned**. Revenue from the sale of merchandise is recorded as **sales**. Other examples of revenue include rent, which is recorded as **rent revenue**, and interest, which is recorded as **interest revenue**.

Instead of receiving cash at the time services are provided or goods are sold, a business may accept payment at a later date. Such revenues are described as *fees earned on account* or *sales on account*. For example, if NetSolutions had provided services on account instead of for cash, transaction (d) would have been described as follows: *Fees earned on account, $7,500.*

In such cases, the firm has an **account receivable**, which is a claim against the customer. An account receivable is an asset, and the revenue is earned and recorded as if cash had been received. When customers pay their accounts, Cash increases and Accounts Receivable decreases.

Transaction E

> Nov. 30, 2009 NetSolutions paid the following expenses during the month: wages, $2,125; rent, $800; utilities, $450; and miscellaneous, $275.

During the month, NetSolutions spent cash or used up other assets in earning revenue. Assets used in this process of earning revenue are called **expenses**. Expenses include supplies used and payments for employee wages, utilities, and other services.

NetSolutions paid the following expenses during the month: wages, $2,125; rent, $800; utilities, $450; and miscellaneous, $275. Miscellaneous expenses include small amounts paid for such items as postage, coffee, and newspapers. The effect of expenses is the opposite of revenues in that expenses reduce assets and owner's equity. Like fees earned, the expenses are recorded in columns to the right of Chris Clark, Capital. However, since expenses reduce owner's equity, the expenses are entered as negative amounts. The effect of this transaction is shown below.

	Assets		=	Liabilities +			Owner's Equity				
				Accounts	Chris Clark,	Fees	Wages	Rent	Utilities	Misc.
Cash +	Supplies +	Land	=	Payable +	Capital	+ Earned	− Exp.	− Exp.	− Exp.	− Exp.
Bal. 12,500	1,350	20,000		1,350	25,000	7,500				
e. −3,650							−2,125	−800	−450	−275
Bal. 8,850	1,350	20,000		1,350	25,000	7,500	−2,125	−800	−450	−275

Businesses usually record each revenue and expense transaction as it occurs. However, to simplify, we have summarized NetSolutions' revenues and expenses for the month in transactions (d) and (e).

Transaction F

> Nov. 30, 2009 NetSolutions paid creditors on account, $950.

When you pay your monthly credit card bill, you decrease the cash in your checking account and decrease the amount you owe to the credit card company. Likewise, when NetSolutions pays $950 to creditors during the month, it reduces assets and liabilities, as shown below.

	Assets		=	Liabilities +			Owner's Equity				
				Accounts	Chris Clark,	Fees	Wages	Rent	Utilities	Misc.
Cash +	Supplies +	Land	=	Payable +	Capital	+ Earned	− Exp.	− Exp.	− Exp.	− Exp.
Bal. 8,850	1,350	20,000		1,350	25,000	7,500	−2,125	−800	−450	−275
f. −950				−950						
Bal. 7,900	1,350	20,000		400	25,000	7,500	−2,125	−800	−450	−275

Paying an amount on account is different from paying an expense. The paying of an expense reduces owner's equity, as illustrated in transaction (e). Paying an amount on account reduces the amount owed on a liability.

Transaction G

> **Nov. 30, 2009**   Chris Clark determined that the cost of supplies on hand at the end of the month was $550.

The cost of the supplies on hand (not yet used) at the end of the month is $550. Thus, $800 ($1,350 − $550) of supplies must have been used during the month. This decrease in supplies is recorded as an expense, as shown below.

	Assets			=	Liabilities +			Owner's Equity					
	Cash +	Supplies +	Land	=	Accounts Payable +	Chris Clark, Capital	+ Fees Earned	− Wages Exp.	− Rent Exp.	− Supplies Exp.	− Utilities Exp.	− Misc. Exp.	
Bal.	7,900	1,350	20,000		400	25,000	7,500	−2,125	−800		−450	−275	
g.		−800								−800			
Bal.	7,900	550	20,000		400	25,000	7,500	−2,125	−800	−800	−450	−275	

Transaction H

> **Nov. 30, 2009**   Chris Clark withdrew $2,000 from NetSolutions for personal use.

At the end of the month, Chris Clark withdrew $2,000 in cash from the business for personal use. This transaction is the opposite of an investment in the business by the owner. Withdrawals by the owner should not be confused with expenses. Withdrawals *do not* represent assets or services used in the process of earning revenues. Instead, withdrawals are a distribution of capital to the owner. Owner withdrawals are identified by the owner's name and *Drawing*. For example, Chris Clark's withdrawal is identified as Chris Clark, Drawing. Like expenses, withdrawals are recorded in a column to the right of Chris Clark, Capital. The effect of the $2,000 withdrawal is shown as follows:

	Assets			=	Liabilities +			Owner's Equity					
	Cash +	Supp. +	Land	=	Accounts Payable +	Chris Clark, Capital	− Chris Clark, Drawing	+ Fees Earned	− Wages Exp.	− Rent Exp.	− Supplies Exp.	− Utilities Exp.	− Misc. Exp.
Bal.	7,900	550	20,000		400	25,000		7,500	−2,125	−800	−800	−450	−275
h.	−2,000						−2,000						
Bal.	5,900	550	20,000		400	25,000	−2,000	7,500	−2,125	−800	−800	−450	−275

Summary   The transactions of NetSolutions are summarized below. Each transaction is identified by letter, and the balance of each item is shown after every transaction.

	Assets			=	Liabilities +			Owner's Equity					
	Cash +	Supp. +	Land	=	Accounts Payable +	Chris Clark, Capital	− Chris Clark, Drawing	+ Fees Earned	− Wages Exp.	− Rent Exp.	− Supplies Exp.	− Utilities Exp.	− Misc. Exp.
a.	+25,000					+25,000							
b.	−20,000		+20,000										
Bal.	5,000		20,000			25,000							
c.		+1,350			+1,350								
Bal.	5,000	+1,350	20,000		+1,350	25,000							
d.	+7,500							+7,500					
Bal.	12,500	1,350	20,000		1,350	25,000		7,500					
e.	−3,650								−2,125	−800		−450	−275
Bal.	8,850	1,350	20,000		1,350	25,000		7,500	−2,125	−800		−450	−275
f.	−950				−950								
Bal.	7,900	1,350	20,000		400	25,000		7,500	−2,125	−800		−450	−275
g.		−800									−800		
Bal.	7,900	550	20,000		400	25,000		7,500	−2,125	−800	−800	−450	−275
h.	−2,000						−2,000						
Bal.	5,900	550	20,000		400	25,000	−2,000	7,500	−2,125	−800	−800	−450	−275

You should note the following in the preceding summary:

1. The effect of every transaction is *an increase or a decrease in one or more of the accounting equation elements.*
2. The two sides of the accounting equation are *always equal.*
3. The owner's equity is *increased by amounts invested by the owner* and is *decreased by withdrawals by the owner.* In addition, the owner's equity is *increased by revenues* and is *decreased by expenses.*

The effects of these four types of transactions on owner's equity are illustrated in Exhibit 5.

Exhibit 5

Effects of Transactions on Owner's Equity

Increased by
- Owner's investments
- Revenues

Decreased by
- Owner's withdrawals
- Expenses

Example Exercise 1-3   Transactions   4

Salvo Delivery Service is owned and operated by Joel Salvo. The following selected transactions were completed by Salvo Delivery Service during February:

1. Received cash from owner as additional investment, $35,000.
2. Paid creditors on account, $1,800.
3. Billed customers for delivery services on account, $11,250.
4. Received cash from customers on account, $6,740.
5. Paid cash to owner for personal use, $1,000.

Indicate the effect of each transaction on the accounting equation elements (Assets, Liabilities, Owner's Equity, Drawing, Revenue, and Expense) by listing the numbers identifying the transactions, (1) through (5). Also, indicate the specific item within the accounting equation element that is affected. To illustrate, the answer to (1) is shown below.

(1) Asset (Cash) increases by $35,000; Owner's Equity (Joel Salvo, Capital) increases by $35,000.

Follow My Example 1-3

(2) Asset (Cash) decreases by $1,800; Liability (Accounts Payable) decreases by $1,800.
(3) Asset (Accounts Receivable) increases by $11,250; Revenue (Delivery Service Fees) increases by $11,250.
(4) Asset (Cash) increases by $6,740; Asset (Accounts Receivable) decreases by $6,740.
(5) Asset (Cash) decreases by $1,000; Drawing (Joel Salvo, Drawing) increases by $1,000.

For Practice: PE 1-3A, PE 1-3B

 Describe the financial statements of a proprietorship and explain how they interrelate.

Financial Statements

After transactions have been recorded and summarized, reports are prepared for users. The accounting reports providing this information are called **financial statements**. The primary financial statements of a proprietorship are the income statement, the statement of owner's equity, the balance sheet, and the statement of cash flows. The order that the financial statements are prepared and the nature of each statement is described as follows.

Order Prepared	Financial Statement	Description of Statement
1.	**Income statement**	A summary of the revenue and expenses *for a specific period of time*, such as a month or a year.
2.	**Statement of owner's equity**	A summary of the changes in the owner's equity that have occurred *during a specific period of time*, such as a month or a year.
3.	**Balance sheet**	A list of the assets, liabilities, and owner's equity *as of a specific date*, usually at the close of the last day of a month or a year.
4.	**Statement of cash flows**	A summary of the cash receipts and cash payments for a *specific period of time*, such as a month or a year.

⊜netsolutions   The four financial statements and their interrelationships are illustrated in Exhibit 6, on page 17. The data for the statements are taken from the summary of transactions of NetSolutions on page 13.

All financial statements are identified by the name of the business, the title of the statement, and the *date* or *period of time*. The data presented in the income statement, the statement of owner's equity, and the statement of cash flows are for a period of time. The data presented in the balance sheet are for a specific date.

Income Statement

The income statement reports the revenues and expenses for a period of time, based on the **matching concept**. This concept is applied by *matching* the expenses with the revenue generated during a period by those expenses. The excess of the revenue over the expenses is called **net income** or **net profit**. If the expenses exceed the revenue, the excess is a **net loss**.

When you buy something at a store, you may *match* the cash register total with the amount you paid the cashier and with the amount of change, if any, you received.

The revenue and expenses for NetSolutions were shown in the equation as separate increases and decreases in each item. Net income for a period increases the owner's equity (capital) for the period. A net loss decreases the owner's equity (capital) for the period.

Example Exercise 1-4   Income Statement   ••••••••▶ 5

The assets and liabilities of Chickadee Travel Service at April 30, 2010, the end of the current year, and its revenue and expenses for the year are listed below. The capital of the owner, Adam Cellini, was $80,000 at May 1, 2009, the beginning of the current year.

Accounts payable	$ 12,200	Miscellaneous expense	$ 12,950
Accounts receivable	31,350	Office expense	63,000
Cash	53,050	Supplies	3,350
Fees earned	263,200	Wages expense	131,700
Land	80,000		

Prepare an income statement for the current year ended April 30, 2010.

Follow My Example 1-4

Chickadee Travel Service
Income Statement
For the Year Ended April 30, 2010

Fees earned		$263,200
Expenses:		
Wages expense.	$131,700	
Office expense	63,000	
Miscellaneous expense	12,950	
Total expenses.		207,650
Net income.		$ 55,550

For Practice: PE 1-4A, PE 1-4B

The revenue, expenses, and the net income of $3,050 for NetSolutions are reported in the income statement in Exhibit 6, on page 17. The order in which the expenses are listed in the income statement varies among businesses. Most businesses list expenses in order of size, beginning with the larger items. Miscellaneous expense is usually shown as the last item, regardless of the amount.

Statement of Owner's Equity

The statement of owner's equity reports the changes in the owner's equity for a period of time. It is prepared *after* the income statement because the net income or net loss for the period must be reported in this statement. Similarly, it is prepared *before* the balance sheet, since the amount of owner's equity at the end of the period must be reported on the balance sheet. Because of this, the statement of owner's equity is often viewed as the connecting link between the income statement and balance sheet.

Three types of transactions affected owner's equity for NetSolutions during November: (1) the original investment of $25,000, (2) the revenue and expenses that resulted in net income of $3,050 for the month, and (3) a withdrawal of $2,000 by the owner. This information is summarized in the statement of owner's equity in Exhibit 6.

Example Exercise 1-5 Statement of Owner's Equity ●●●●●●●▸ 5

Using the data for Chickadee Travel Service shown in Example Exercise 1-4, prepare a statement of owner's equity for the current year ended April 30, 2010. Adam Cellini invested an additional $50,000 in the business during the year and withdrew cash of $30,000 for personal use.

Follow My Example 1-5

Chickadee Travel Service
Statement of Owner's Equity
For the Year Ended April 30, 2010

Adam Cellini, capital, May 1, 2009		$ 80,000
Additional investment by owner during year	$ 50,000	
Net income for the year	55,550	
	$105,550	
Less withdrawals	30,000	
Increase in owner's equity		75,550
Adam Cellini, capital, April 30, 2010		$155,550

For Practice: PE 1-5A, PE 1-5B

Bank loan officers use a business's financial statements in deciding whether to grant a loan to the business. Once the loan is granted, the borrower may be required to maintain a certain level of assets in excess of liabilities. The business's financial statements are used to monitor this level.

Balance Sheet

The balance sheet in Exhibit 6 reports the amounts of NetSolutions' assets, liabilities, and owner's equity as of November 30, 2009. The asset and liability amounts are taken from the last line of the summary of transactions on page 13. Chris Clark, Capital as of November 30, 2009, is taken from the statement of owner's equity. The form of balance sheet shown in Exhibit 6 is called the **account form**. This is because it resembles the basic format of the accounting equation, with assets on the left side and the liabilities and owner's equity sections on the right side.[3]

The assets section of the balance sheet presents assets in the order that they will be converted into cash or used in operations. Cash is presented first, followed by receivables, supplies, prepaid insurance, and other assets. The assets of a more permanent nature are shown next, such as land, buildings, and equipment.

---

3 We illustrate an alternative form of balance sheet, called the *report form*, in Chapter 6. It presents the liabilities and owner's equity sections below the assets section.

Exhibit 6

Financial Statements for NetSolutions

NetSolutions
Income Statement
For the Month Ended November 30, 2009

Fees earned		$7,500
Expenses:		
Wages expense	$2,125	
Rent expense.	800	
Supplies expense	800	
Utilities expense.	450	
Miscellaneous expense	275	
Total expense		4,450
Net income		$3,050

NetSolutions
Statement of Owner's Equity
For the Month Ended November 30, 2009

Chris Clark, capital, November 1, 2009.		$ 0
Investment on November 1, 2009	$25,000	
Net income for November	3,050	
	$28,050	
Less withdrawals.	2,000	
Increase in owner's equity		26,050
Chris Clark, capital, November 30, 2009.		$26,050

NetSolutions
Balance Sheet
November 30, 2009

Assets		Liabilities	
Cash	$ 5,900	Accounts payable	$ 400
Supplies	550	**Owner's Equity**	
Land	20,000	Chris Clark, capital	26,050
Total assets	$26,450	Total liabilities and owner's equity . .	$26,450

NetSolutions
Statement of Cash Flows
For the Month Ended November 30, 2009

Cash flows from operating activities:		
Cash received from customers	$ 7,500	
Deduct cash payments for expenses and payments		
to creditors	4,600	
Net cash flow from operating activities.		$ 2,900
Cash flows from investing activities:		
Cash payments for purchase of land.		(20,000)
Cash flows from financing activities:		
Cash received as owner's investment.	$ 25,000	
Deduct cash withdrawal by owner	2,000	
Net cash flow from financing activities.		23,000
Net cash flow and November 30, 2009, cash balance		$ 5,900

In the liabilities section of the balance sheet in Exhibit 6, accounts payable is the only liability. When there are two or more liabilities, each should be listed and the total amount of liabilities presented as follows:

Liabilities		
Accounts payable	$12,900	
Wages payable	2,570	
Total liabilities		$15,470

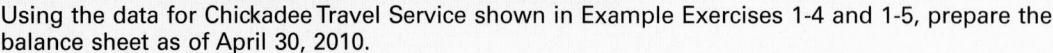

Example Exercise 1-6   Balance Sheet

Using the data for Chickadee Travel Service shown in Example Exercises 1-4 and 1-5, prepare the balance sheet as of April 30, 2010.

Follow My Example 1-6

Chickadee Travel Service
Balance Sheet
April 30, 2010

Assets		Liabilities	
Cash	$ 53,050	Accounts payable	$ 12,200
Accounts receivable	31,350		
Supplies	3,350	**Owner's Equity**	
Land	80,000	Adam Cellini, capital	155,550
Total assets	$167,750	Total liabilities and owner's equity	$167,750

For Practice: PE 1-6A, PE 1-6B

Statement of Cash Flows

The statement of cash flows consists of three sections, as shown in Exhibit 6: (1) operating activities, (2) investing activities, and (3) financing activities. Each of these sections is briefly described below.

Cash Flows from Operating Activities This section reports a summary of cash receipts and cash payments from operations. The net cash flow from operating activities normally differs from the amount of net income for the period. In Exhibit 6, NetSolutions reported net cash flows from operating activities of $2,900 and net income of $3,050. This difference occurs because revenues and expenses may not be recorded at the same time that cash is received from customers or paid to creditors.

Cash Flows from Investing Activities This section reports the cash transactions for the acquisition and sale of relatively permanent assets. Exhibit 6 reports that NetSolutions paid $20,000 for the purchase of land during November.

Cash Flows from Financing Activities This section reports the cash transactions related to cash investments by the owner, borrowings, and withdrawals by the owner. Exhibit 6 shows that Chris Clark invested $25,000 in the business and withdrew $2,000 during November.

Preparing the statement of cash flows requires that each of the November cash transactions for NetSolutions be classified as operating, investing, or financing activities. Using the summary of transactions shown on page 13, the November cash transactions for NetSolutions are classified as follows:

Transaction	Amount	Cash Flow Activity
a.	$25,000	Financing (Investment by Chris Clark)
b.	−20,000	Investing (Purchase of land)
d.	7,500	Operating (Fees earned)
e.	−3,650	Operating (Payment of expenses)
f.	−950	Operating (Payment of account payable)
h.	−2,000	Financing (Withdrawal by Chris Clark)

Transactions (c) and (g) are not listed here because they did not involve a cash receipt or payment. In addition, the payment of accounts payable in transaction (f) is classified as an operating activity since the account payable arose from the purchase of supplies, which are used in operations. Using the preceding classifications of November cash transactions, the statement of cash flows is prepared as shown in Exhibit 6.[4]

The ending cash balance shown on the statement of cash flows is also reported on the balance sheet as of the end of the period. To illustrate, the ending cash of $5,900 reported on the November statement of cash flows in Exhibit 6 is also reported as the amount of cash on hand in the November 30, 2009, balance sheet.

Since November is NetSolutions' first period of operations, the net cash flow for November and the November 30, 2009, cash balance are the same amount, $5,900, as shown in Exhibit 6. In later periods, NetSolutions will report in its statement of cash flows a beginning cash balance, an increase or a decrease in cash for the period, and an ending cash balance. For example, assume that for December NetSolutions has a decrease in cash of $3,835. The last three lines of NetSolutions' statement of cash flows for December would be as follows:

Decrease in cash	$3,835
Cash as of December 1, 2009	5,900
Cash as of December 31, 2009	$2,065

Example Exercise 1-7   Statement of Cash Flows 5

A summary of cash flows for Chickadee Travel Service for the year ended April 30, 2010, is shown below.

Cash receipts:	
Cash received from customers........................	$251,000
Cash received from additional investment of owner.........	50,000
Cash payments:	
Cash paid for expenses	210,000
Cash paid for land	80,000
Cash paid to owner for personal use	30,000

The cash balance as of May 1, 2009, was $72,050. Prepare a statement of cash flows for Chickadee Travel Service for the year ended April 30, 2010.

Follow My Example 1-7

Chickadee Travel Service
Statement of Cash Flows
For the Year Ended April 30, 2010

Cash flows from operating activities:		
Cash received from customers.......................	$251,000	
Deduct cash payments for expenses	210,000	
Net cash flows from operating activities..............		$ 41,000
Cash flows from investing activities:		
Cash payments for purchase of land		(80,000)
Cash flows from financing activities:		
Cash received from owner as investment..............	$ 50,000	
Deduct cash withdrawals by owner	30,000	
Net cash flows from financing activities..............		20,000
Net decrease in cash during year		$ (19,000)
Cash as of May 1, 2009............................		72,050
Cash as of April 30, 2010..........................		$ 53,050

For Practice: PE 1-7A, PE 1-7B

4 This method of preparing the statement of cash flows is called the "direct method." This method and the indirect method are discussed further in Chapter 16.

Interrelationships Among Financial Statements

Financial statements are prepared in the order of the income statement, statement of owner's equity, balance sheet, and statement of cash flows. This order is important because the financial statements are interrelated. These interrelationships for NetSolutions are shown in Exhibit 6 and are described below.[5]

Financial Statements	Interrelationship	NetSolutions Example (Exhibit 6)
Income Statement *and* Statement of Owner's Equity	Net income or net loss reported on the income statement is also reported on the statement of owner's equity as either an addition (net income) to or deduction (net loss) from the beginning owner's equity and any additional investments by the owner during the period.	NetSolutions' net income of $3,050 for November is added to Chris Clark's investment of $25,000 in the statement of owner's equity.
Statement of Owner's Equity *and* Balance Sheet	Owner's capital at the end of the period reported on the statement of owner's equity is also reported on the balance sheet as owner's capital.	Chris Clark, Capital of $26,050 as of November 30, 2009, on the statement of owner's equity also appears on the November 30, 2009, balance sheet as Chris Clark, Capital.
Balance Sheet *and* Statement of Cash Flows	The cash reported on the balance sheet is also reported as the end-of-period cash on the statement of cash flows.	Cash of $5,900 reported on the balance sheet as of November 30, 2009, is also reported on the November statement of cash flows as the end-of-period cash.

The preceding interrelationships are important in analyzing financial statements and the impact of transactions on a business. In addition, these interrelationships serve as a check on whether the financial statements are prepared correctly. For example, if the ending cash on the statement of cash flows doesn't agree with the balance sheet cash, then an error has occurred.

Financial Analysis and Interpretation

Financial statements are useful to bankers, creditors, owners, and other users in analyzing and interpreting the financial performance and condition of a business. Throughout this text, we discuss various tools that are often used to analyze and interpret the financial performance and condition of a business. The first such tool we introduce is useful in analyzing the ability of a business to pay its creditors.

The relationship between liabilities and owner's equity, expressed as a ratio, is computed as follows:

$$\text{Ratio of Liabilities to Owner's Equity} = \frac{\text{Total Liabilities}}{\text{Total Owner's Equity (or Total Stockholders' Equity)}}$$

To illustrate, NetSolutions' ratio of liabilities to owner's equity at the end of November is 0.015, as calculated at the top of the next column.

$$\text{Ratio of Liabilities to Owner's Equity} = \frac{\$400}{\$26,050} = 0.015$$

Corporations refer to total owner's equity as total stockholders' equity. Thus, you should substitute total stockholders' equity for total owner's equity when computing this ratio for a corporation.

The rights of creditors to a business's assets take precedence over the rights of the owners or stockholders. Thus, the lower the ratio of liabilities to owner's equity, the better able the business is to withstand poor business conditions and pay its obligations to creditors.

5 Depending on the method of preparing the cash flows from operating activities section of the statement of cash flows, net income (or net loss) may also appear on the statement of cash flows. This interrelationship or method of preparing the statement of cash flows, called the "indirect method," is described and illustrated in Chapter 16.

1 Describe the nature of a business, the role of accounting, and ethics in business.

Key Points	Key Learning Outcomes	Example Exercises	Practice Exercises
A business provides goods or services (outputs) to customers with the objective of earning a profit. Three types of businesses include service, merchandising, and manufacturing businesses. Accounting, called the "language of business," is an information system that provides reports to users about the economic activities and condition of a business. Ethics are moral principles that guide the conduct of individuals. Good ethical conduct depends on individual character and firm culture. Accountants are engaged in private accounting or public accounting.	• Distinguish among service, merchandising, and manufacturing businesses. • Describe the role of accounting in business and explain why accounting is called the "language of business." • Define ethics and list the two factors affecting ethical conduct. • Describe what private and public accounting means.		

2 Summarize the development of accounting principles and relate them to practice.

Key Points	Key Learning Outcomes	Example Exercises	Practice Exercises
Generally accepted accounting principles (GAAP) are used in preparing financial statements so that users can compare one company to another. Accounting principles and concepts develop from research, practice, and pronouncements of authoritative bodies such as the Financial Accounting Standards Board (FASB), Securities and Exchange Commission (SEC), and the International Accounting Standards Board (IASB). The business entity concept views the business as an entity separate from its owners, creditors, or other businesses. Businesses may be organized as proprietorships, partnerships, corporations, and limited liability companies. The cost concept requires that properties and services bought by a business be recorded in terms of actual cost. The objectivity concept requires that the accounting records and reports be based on objective evidence. The unit of measure concept requires that economic data be recorded in dollars.	• Explain what is meant by generally accepted accounting principles. • Describe how generally accepted accounting principles are developed. • Describe and give an example of what is meant by the business entity concept. • Describe the characteristics of a proprietorship, partnership, corporation, and limited liability company. • Describe and give an example of what is meant by the cost concept. • Describe and give an example of what is meant by the objectivity concept. • Describe and give an example of what is meant by the unit of measure concept.	1-1	1-1A, 1-1B

3 State the accounting equation and define each element of the equation.

Key Points	Key Learning Outcomes	Example Exercises	Practice Exercises
The resources owned by a business and the rights or claims to these resources may be stated in the form of an equation, as follows: Assets = Liabilities + Owner's Equity	• State the accounting equation. • Define assets, liabilities, and owner's equity. • Given two elements of the accounting equation, solve for the third element.	1-2	1-2A, 1-2B

4 Describe and illustrate how business transactions can be recorded in terms of the resulting change in the elements of the accounting equation.

Key Points	Key Learning Outcomes	Example Exercises	Practice Exercises
All business transactions can be stated in terms of the change in one or more of the three elements of the accounting equation.	• Define a business transaction. • Using the accounting equation as a framework, record transactions.	**1-3**	1-3A, 1-3B

5 Describe the financial statements of a proprietorship and explain how they interrelate.

Key Points	Key Learning Outcomes	Example Exercises	Practice Exercises
The primary financial statements of a proprietorship are the income statement, the statement of owner's equity, the balance sheet, and the statement of cash flows. The income statement reports a period's net income or net loss, which is also reported on the statement of owner's equity. The ending owner's capital reported on the statement of owner's equity is also reported on the balance sheet. The ending cash balance is reported on the balance sheet and the statement of cash flows.	• List and describe the financial statements of a proprietorship. • Prepare an income statement. • Prepare a statement of owner's equity. • Prepare a balance sheet. • Prepare a statement of cash flows. • Explain how the financial statements of a proprietorship are interrelated.	**1-4** **1-5** **1-6** **1-7**	1-4A, 1-4B 1-5A, 1-5B 1-6A, 1-6B 1-7A, 1-7B

Key Terms

account form (16)
account payable (11)
account receivable (12)
accounting (3)
accounting equation (9)
assets (9)
balance sheet (15)
business (2)
business entity concept (7)
business transaction (10)
Certified Public Accountant (CPA) (7)
corporation (8)
cost concept (8)
ethics (4)
expenses (12)
fees earned (11)
financial accounting (4)

Financial Accounting Standards Board (FASB) (7)
financial statements (14)
general-purpose financial statements (4)
generally accepted accounting principles (GAAP) (7)
income statement (15)
interest revenue (11)
International Accounting Standards Board (IASB) (7)
liabilities (9)
limited liability company (LLC) (8)
management (or managerial) accounting (4)
manufacturing business (3)
matching concept (15)
merchandising business (3)
net income (or net profit) (15)

net loss (15)
objectivity concept (8)
owner's equity (9)
partnership (8)
prepaid expenses (11)
private accounting (4)
profit (2)
proprietorship (8)
public accounting (7)
rent revenue (11)
revenue (11)
sales (11)
Securities and Exchange Commission (SEC) (7)
service business (3)
statement of cash flows (15)
statement of owner's equity (15)
unit of measure concept (8)

Illustrative Problem

Cecil Jameson, Attorney-at-Law, is a proprietorship owned and operated by Cecil Jameson. On July 1, 2009, Cecil Jameson, Attorney-at-Law, has the following assets and liabilities: cash, $1,000; accounts receivable, $3,200; supplies, $850; land, $10,000; accounts payable, $1,530. Office space and office equipment are currently being rented, pending the construction of an office complex on land purchased last year. Business transactions during July are summarized as follows:

a. Received cash from clients for services, $3,928.
b. Paid creditors on account, $1,055.
c. Received cash from Cecil Jameson as an additional investment, $3,700.
d. Paid office rent for the month, $1,200.
e. Charged clients for legal services on account, $2,025.
f. Purchased supplies on account, $245.
g. Received cash from clients on account, $3,000.
h. Received invoice for paralegal services from Legal Aid Inc. for July (to be paid on August 10), $1,635.
i. Paid the following: wages expense, $850; answering service expense, $250; utilities expense, $325; and miscellaneous expense, $75.
j. Determined that the cost of supplies on hand was $980; therefore, the cost of supplies used during the month was $115.
k. Jameson withdrew $1,000 in cash from the business for personal use.

Instructions

1. Determine the amount of owner's equity (Cecil Jameson's capital) as of July 1, 2009.
2. State the assets, liabilities, and owner's equity as of July 1 in equation form similar to that shown in this chapter. In tabular form below the equation, indicate the increases and decreases resulting from each transaction and the new balances after each transaction.
3. Prepare an income statement for July, a statement of owner's equity for July, and a balance sheet as of July 31, 2009.
4. (Optional). Prepare a statement of cash flows for July.

Solution

1.

$$\text{Assets} - \text{Liabilities} = \text{Owner's Equity (Cecil Jameson, capital)}$$

$$(\$1,000 + \$3,200 + \$850 + \$10,000) - \$1,530 = \text{Owner's Equity (Cecil Jameson, capital)}$$

$$\$15,050 - \$1,530 = \text{Owner's Equity (Cecil Jameson, capital)}$$

$$\$13,520 = \text{Owner's Equity (Cecil Jameson, capital)}$$

2.

	Assets			=	Liabilities +		Owner's Equity								
	Cash +	Accts. Rec. +	Supp. +	Land =	Accts. Pay. +	Cecil Jameson, Capital −	Cecil Jameson, Drawing +	Fees Earned −	Paralegal Exp. −	Wages Exp. −	Rent Exp. −	Utilities Exp. −	Answering Service Exp. −	Supp. Exp. −	Misc. Exp.
Bal.	1,000	3,200	850	10,000	1,530	13,520									
a.	+3,928							3,928							
Bal.	4,928	3,200	850	10,000	1,530	13,520		3,928							
b.	−1,055				−1,055										
Bal.	3,873	3,200	850	10,000	475	13,520		3,928							
c.	+3,700					+ 3,700									
Bal.	7,573	3,200	850	10,000	475	17,220		3,928							
d.	−1,200										−1,200				
Bal.	6,373	3,200	850	10,000	475	17,220		3,928			−1,200				
e.		+2,025						+2,025							
Bal.	6,373	5,225	850	10,000	475	17,220		5,953			−1,200				
f.			+ 245		+ 245										
Bal.	6,373	5,225	1,095	10,000	720	17,220		5,953			−1,200				
g.	+3,000	−3,000													
Bal.	9,373	2,225	1,095	10,000	720	17,220		5,953			−1,200				
h.					+1,635				−1,635						
Bal.	9,373	2,225	1,095	10,000	2,355	17,220		5,953	−1,635		−1,200				
i.	−1,500									−850		−325	−250		−75
Bal.	7,873	2,225	1,095	10,000	2,355	17,220		5,953	−1,635	−850	−1,200	−325	−250		−75
j.			− 115											−115	
Bal.	7,873	2,225	980	10,000	2,355	17,220		5,953	−1,635	−850	−1,200	−325	−250	−115	−75
k.	−1,000						−1,000								
Bal.	6,873	2,225	980	10,000	2,355	17,220	−1,000	5,953	−1,635	−850	−1,200	−325	−250	−115	−75

3.

Cecil Jameson, Attorney-at-Law
Income Statement
For the Month Ended July 31, 2009

Fees earned		$5,953
Expenses:		
Paralegal expense.	$1,635	
Rent expense.	1,200	
Wages expense	850	
Utilities expense.	325	
Answering service expense	250	
Supplies expense	115	
Miscellaneous expense	75	
Total expenses		4,450
Net income		$1,503

Cecil Jameson, Attorney-at-Law
Statement of Owner's Equity
For the Month Ended July 31, 2009

Cecil Jameson, capital, July 1, 2009.		$13,520
Additional investment by owner.	$3,700	
Net income for the month.	1,503	
	$5,203	
Less withdrawals	1,000	
Increase in owner's equity.		4,203
Cecil Jameson, capital, July 31, 2009.		$17,723

(continued)

Cecil Jameson, Attorney-at-Law
Balance Sheet
July 31, 2009

Assets		Liabilities	
Cash	$ 6,873	Accounts payable.	$ 2,355
Accounts receivable	2,225	**Owner's Equity**	
Supplies	980	Cecil Jameson, capital	17,723
Land	10,000	Total liabilities and	
Total assets	$20,078	owner's equity	$20,078

4. Optional.

Cecil Jameson, Attorney-at-Law
Statement of Cash Flows
For the Month Ended July 31, 2009

Cash flows from operating activities:		
Cash received from customers.	$6,928*	
Deduct cash payments for operating expenses	3,755**	
Net cash flows from operating activities		$3,173
Cash flows from investing activities		—
Cash flows from financing activities:		
Cash received from owner as investment	$3,700	
Deduct cash withdrawals by owner	1,000	
Net cash flows from financing activities		2,700
Net increase in cash during year		$5,873
Cash as of July 1, 2009		1,000
Cash as of July 31, 2009.		$6,873

   *$6,928 = $3,928 + $3,000
   **$3,755 = $1,055 + $1,200 + $1,500

Self-Examination Questions (Answers at End of Chapter)

1. A profit-making business operating as a separate legal entity and in which ownership is divided into shares of stock is known as a:
   A. proprietorship.   C. partnership.
   B. service business.   D. corporation.

2. The resources owned by a business are called:
   A. assets.   C. the accounting equation.
   B. liabilities.   D. owner's equity.

3. A listing of a business entity's assets, liabilities, and owner's equity as of a specific date is a(n):
   A. balance sheet.
   B. income statement.
   C. statement of owner's equity.
   D. statement of cash flows.

4. If total assets increased $20,000 during a period and total liabilities increased $12,000 during the same period, the amount and direction (increase or decrease) of the change in owner's equity for that period is a(n):
   A. $32,000 increase.   C. $8,000 increase.
   B. $32,000 decrease.   D. $8,000 decrease.

5. If revenue was $45,000, expenses were $37,500, and the owner's withdrawals were $10,000, the amount of net income or net loss would be:
   A. $45,000 net income.   C. $37,500 net loss.
   B. $7,500 net income.   D. $2,500 net loss.

Eye Openers

1. What is the objective of most businesses?
2. What is the difference between a manufacturing business and a service business? Is a restaurant a manufacturing business, a service business, or both?

3. Name some users of accounting information.
4. What is the role of accounting in business?
5. Why are most large companies like Microsoft, PepsiCo, Caterpillar, and AutoZone organized as corporations?
6. Barry Bergan is the owner of Elephant Delivery Service. Recently, Barry paid interest of $3,000 on a personal loan of $40,000 that he used to begin the business. Should Elephant Delivery Service record the interest payment? Explain.
7. On April 2, Gremlin Repair Service extended an offer of $100,000 for land that had been priced for sale at $125,000. On May 10, Gremlin Repair Service accepted the seller's counteroffer of $115,000. Describe how Gremlin Repair Service should record the land.
8. a. Land with an assessed value of $300,000 for property tax purposes is acquired by a business for $475,000. Ten years later, the plot of land has an assessed value of $500,000 and the business receives an offer of $900,000 for it. Should the monetary amount assigned to the land in the business records now be increased?
   b. Assuming that the land acquired in (a) was sold for $900,000, how would the various elements of the accounting equation be affected?
9. Describe the difference between an account receivable and an account payable.
10. A business had revenues of $600,000 and operating expenses of $715,000. Did the business (a) incur a net loss or (b) realize net income?
11. A business had revenues of $687,500 and operating expenses of $492,400. Did the business (a) incur a net loss or (b) realize net income?
12. What particular item of financial or operating data appears on both the income statement and the statement of owner's equity? What item appears on both the balance sheet and the statement of owner's equity? What item appears on both the balance sheet and the statement of cash flows?

Practice Exercises

PE 1-1A
Cost concept
obj. 2
EE 1-1   p. 9

On February 7, Snap Repair Service extended an offer of $75,000 for land that had been priced for sale at $85,000. On February 21, Snap Repair Service accepted the seller's counteroffer of $81,000. On April 30, the land was assessed at a value of $125,000 for property tax purposes. On August 30, Snap Repair Service was offered $130,000 for the land by a national retail chain. At what value should the land be recorded in Snap Repair Service's records?

PE 1-1B
Cost concept
obj. 2
EE 1-1   p. 9

On November 23, Terrier Repair Service extended an offer of $40,000 for land that had been priced for sale at $48,500. On December 2, Terrier Repair Service accepted the seller's counteroffer of $44,000. On December 27, the land was assessed at a value of $50,000 for property tax purposes. On April 1, Terrier Repair Service was offered $75,000 for the land by a national retail chain. At what value should the land be recorded in Terrier Repair Service's records?

PE 1-2A
Accounting equation
obj. 3
EE 1-2   p. 9

Paul Eberly is the owner and operator of You're Great, a motivational consulting business. At the end of its accounting period, December 31, 2009, You're Great has assets of $475,000 and liabilities of $115,000. Using the accounting equation, determine the following amounts:
a. Owner's equity, as of December 31, 2009.
b. Owner's equity, as of December 31, 2010, assuming that assets increased by $90,000 and liabilities increased by $28,000 during 2010.

PE 1-2B
Accounting equation
obj. 3
EE 1-2   p. 9

Lynn Doyle is the owner and operator of Star LLC, a motivational consulting business. At the end of its accounting period, December 31, 2009, Star has assets of $750,000 and liabilities of $293,000. Using the accounting equation, determine the following amounts:

a. Owner's equity, as of December 31, 2009.
b. Owner's equity, as of December 31, 2010, assuming that assets increased by $75,000 and liabilities decreased by $30,000 during 2010.

PE 1-3A
Transactions
obj. 4
EE 1-3   p. 14

Zany Delivery Service is owned and operated by Joey Bryant. The following selected transactions were completed by Zany Delivery Service during February:

1. Received cash from owner as additional investment, $15,000.
2. Paid advertising expense, $900.
3. Purchased supplies on account, $600.
4. Billed customers for delivery services on account, $9,000.
5. Received cash from customers on account, $5,500.

Indicate the effect of each transaction on the accounting equation elements (Assets, Liabilities, Owner's Equity, Drawing, Revenue, and Expense) by listing the numbers identifying the transactions, (1) through (5). Also, indicate the specific item within the accounting equation element that is affected. To illustrate, the answer to (1) is shown below.

(1) Asset (Cash) increases by $15,000; Owner's Equity (Joey Bryant, Capital) increases by $15,000.

PE 1-3B
Transactions
obj. 4
EE 1-3   p. 14

Yukon Delivery Service is owned and operated by Betty Pasha. The following selected transactions were completed by Yukon Delivery Service during June:

1. Received cash from owner as additional investment, $10,000.
2. Paid creditors on account, $1,500.
3. Billed customers for delivery services on account, $11,500.
4. Received cash from customers on account, $2,700.
5. Paid cash to owner for personal use, $2,000.

Indicate the effect of each transaction on the accounting equation elements (Assets, Liabilities, Owner's Equity, Drawing, Revenue, and Expense) by listing the numbers identifying the transactions, (1) through (5). Also, indicate the specific item within the accounting equation element that is affected. To illustrate, the answer to (1) is shown below.

(1) Asset (Cash) increases by $10,000; Owner's Equity (Betty Pasha, Capital) increases by $10,000.

PE 1-4A
Income statement
obj. 5
EE 1-4   p. 15

The assets and liabilities of Impeccable Travel Service at November 30, 2010, the end of the current year, and its revenue and expenses for the year are listed below. The capital of the owner, Charly Maves, was $380,000 at December 1, 2009, the beginning of the current year.

Accounts payable	$ 42,000	Miscellaneous expense	$ 12,700
Accounts receivable	75,500	Office expense	313,300
Cash	45,400	Supplies	5,100
Fees earned	754,000	Wages expense	450,000
Land	290,000		

Prepare an income statement for the current year ended November 30, 2010.

PE 1-4B
Income statement
obj. 5
EE 1-4   p. 15

The assets and liabilities of Express Travel Service at June 30, 2010, the end of the current year, and its revenue and expenses for the year are listed at the top of the following page. The capital of the owner, Janis Paisley, was $125,000 at July 1, 2009, the beginning of the current year.

Accounts payable	$ 12,000	Miscellaneous expense	$ 8,000
Accounts receivable	32,000	Office expense	111,000
Cash	78,000	Supplies	6,000
Fees earned	475,000	Wages expense	239,000
Land	150,000		

Prepare an income statement for the current year ended June 30, 2010.

PE 1-5A
Statement of owner's equity
obj. 5
EE 1-5 p. 16

Using the data for Impeccable Travel Service shown in Practice Exercise 1-4A, prepare a statement of owner's equity for the current year ended November 30, 2010. Charly Maves invested an additional $36,000 in the business during the year and withdrew cash of $20,000 for personal use.

PE 1-5B
Statement of owner's equity
obj. 5
EE 1-5 p. 16

Using the data for Express Travel Service shown in Practice Exercise 1-4B, prepare a statement of owner's equity for the current year ended June 30, 2010. Janis Paisley invested an additional $30,000 in the business during the year and withdrew cash of $18,000 for personal use.

PE 1-6A
Balance sheet
obj. 5
EE 1-6 p. 18

Using the data for Impeccable Travel Service shown in Practice Exercises 1-4A and 1-5A, prepare the balance sheet as of November 30, 2010.

PE 1-6B
Balance sheet
obj. 5
EE 1-6 p. 18

Using the data for Express Travel Service shown in Practice Exercises 1-4B and 1-5B, prepare the balance sheet as of June 30, 2010.

PE 1-7A
Statement of cash flows
obj. 5
EE 1-7 p. 19

A summary of cash flows for Impeccable Travel Service for the year ended November 30, 2010, is shown below.

Cash receipts:
Cash received from customers $700,000
Cash received from additional investment of owner   36,000
Cash payments:
Cash paid for operating expenses   730,000
Cash paid for land   54,000
Cash paid to owner for personal use   20,000

The cash balance as of December 1, 2009, was $113,400.
Prepare a statement of cash flows for Impeccable Travel Service for the year ended November 30, 2010.

PE 1-7B
Statement of cash flows
obj. 5
EE 1-7 p. 19

A summary of cash flows for Express Travel Service for the year ended June 30, 2010, is shown below.

Cash receipts:
Cash received from customers $460,000
Cash received from additional investment of owner   30,000
Cash payments:
Cash paid for operating expenses   355,000
Cash paid for land   104,000
Cash paid to owner for personal use   18,000

The cash balance as of July 1, 2009, was $65,000.
Prepare a statement of cash flows for Express Travel Service for the year ended June 30, 2010.

Exercises

EX 1-1
Types of businesses

obj. 1

Indicate whether each of the following companies is primarily a service, merchandise, or manufacturing business. If you are unfamiliar with the company, use the Internet to locate the company's home page or use the finance Web site of Yahoo.

1. H&R Block
2. eBay Inc.
3. Wal-Mart Stores, Inc.
4. Ford Motor Company
5. Citigroup
6. Boeing
7. SunTrust
8. Alcoa Inc.
9. Procter & Gamble
10. FedEx
11. Gap Inc.
12. Hilton Hospitality, Inc.
13. CVS
14. Caterpillar
15. The Dow Chemical Company

EX 1-2
Professional ethics

obj. 1

A fertilizer manufacturing company wants to relocate to Collier County. A 13-year-old report from a fired researcher at the company says the company's product is releasing toxic by products. The company has suppressed that report. A second report commissioned by the company shows there is no problem with the fertilizer.

➡ Should the company's chief executive officer reveal the context of the unfavorable report in discussions with Collier County representatives? Discuss.

EX 1-3
Business entity concept

obj. 2

Chalet Sports sells hunting and fishing equipment and provides guided hunting and fishing trips. Chalet Sports is owned and operated by Cliff Owen, a well-known sports enthusiast and hunter. Cliff's wife, Judy, owns and operates Joliet Boutique, a women's clothing store. Cliff and Judy have established a trust fund to finance their children's college education. The trust fund is maintained by City Bank in the name of the children, John and Morgan.

For each of the following transactions, identify which of the entities listed should record the transaction in its records.

Entities

C	Chalet Sports
B	City Bank Trust Fund
J	Joliet Boutique
X	None of the above

1. Cliff paid a local doctor for his annual physical, which was required by the workmen's compensation insurance policy carried by Chalet Sports.
2. Cliff received a cash advance from customers for a guided hunting trip.
3. Judy paid her dues to the YWCA.
4. Cliff paid a breeder's fee for an English springer spaniel to be used as a hunting guide dog.
5. Judy deposited a $5,000 personal check in the trust fund at City Bank.
6. Cliff paid for an advertisement in a hunters' magazine.
7. Judy authorized the trust fund to purchase mutual fund shares.
8. Judy donated several dresses from inventory for a local charity auction for the benefit of a women's abuse shelter.
9. Cliff paid for dinner and a movie to celebrate their fifteenth wedding anniversary.
10. Judy purchased two dozen spring dresses from a Seattle designer for a special spring sale.

EX 1-4
Accounting equation

obj. 3

✔ Coca-Cola,
$16,920

The total assets and total liabilities of Coca-Cola and PepsiCo are shown below.

	Coca-Cola (in millions)	PepsiCo (in millions)
Assets	$29,963	$29,930
Liabilities	13,043	14,483

Determine the owners' equity of each company.

EX 1-5
Accounting equation

obj. 3

✔ eBay, $10,905

The total assets and total liabilities of eBay and Google are shown below.

	eBay (in millions)	Google (in millions)
Assets	$13,494	$18,473
Liabilities	2,589	1,433

Determine the owners' equity of each company.

EX 1-6
Accounting equation

obj. 3

✔ a. 1,030,000

Determine the missing amount for each of the following:

	Assets	=	Liabilities	+	Owner's Equity
a.	?	=	$250,000	+	$780,000
b.	$125,000	=	?	+	39,500
c.	60,000	=	7,500	+	?

EX 1-7
Accounting equation

objs. 3, 4

✔ b. $568,000

Donna Ahern is the owner and operator of Omega, a motivational consulting business. At the end of its accounting period, December 31, 2009, Omega has assets of $760,000 and liabilities of $240,000. Using the accounting equation and considering each case independently, determine the following amounts:

a. Donna Ahern, capital, as of December 31, 2009.
b. Donna Ahern, capital, as of December 31, 2010, assuming that assets increased by $120,000 and liabilities increased by $72,000 during 2010.
c. Donna Ahern, capital, as of December 31, 2010, assuming that assets decreased by $60,000 and liabilities increased by $21,600 during 2010.
d. Donna Ahern, capital, as of December 31, 2010, assuming that assets increased by $100,000 and liabilities decreased by $38,400 during 2010.
e. Net income (or net loss) during 2010, assuming that as of December 31, 2010, assets were $960,000, liabilities were $156,000, and there were no additional investments or withdrawals.

EX 1-8
Asset, liability, owner's equity items

obj. 3

Indicate whether each of the following is identified with (1) an asset, (2) a liability, or (3) owner's equity:

a. accounts payable
b. cash
c. fees earned
d. land
e. supplies
f. wages expense

EX 1-9
Effect of transactions on accounting equation

obj. 4

Describe how the following business transactions affect the three elements of the accounting equation.

a. Invested cash in business.
b. Received cash for services performed.

c. Paid for utilities used in the business.
d. Purchased supplies for cash.
e. Purchased supplies on account.

EX 1-10
Effect of transactions on accounting equation
obj. **4**

✔ a. (1) increase $140,000

a. A vacant lot acquired for $150,000 is sold for $290,000 in cash. What is the effect of the sale on the total amount of the seller's (1) assets, (2) liabilities, and (3) owner's equity?
b. Assume that the seller owes $80,000 on a loan for the land. After receiving the $290,000 cash in (a), the seller pays the $80,000 owed. What is the effect of the payment on the total amount of the seller's (1) assets, (2) liabilities, and (3) owner's equity?

EX 1-11
Effect of transactions on owner's equity
obj. **4**

Indicate whether each of the following types of transactions will either (a) increase owner's equity or (b) decrease owner's equity:

1. expenses
2. revenues
3. owner's investments
4. owner's withdrawals

EX 1-12
Transactions
obj. **4**

The following selected transactions were completed by Lindbergh Delivery Service during October:

1. Received cash from owner as additional investment, $75,000.
2. Paid rent for October, $4,200.
3. Paid advertising expense, $4,000.
4. Received cash for providing delivery services, $39,750.
5. Purchased supplies for cash, $2,500.
6. Billed customers for delivery services on account, $81,200.
7. Paid creditors on account, $9,280.
8. Received cash from customers on account, $25,600.
9. Determined that the cost of supplies on hand was $900; therefore, $1,600 of supplies had been used during the month.
10. Paid cash to owner for personal use, $3,000.

Indicate the effect of each transaction on the accounting equation by listing the numbers identifying the transactions, (1) through (10), in a column, and inserting at the right of each number the appropriate letter from the following list:

a. Increase in an asset, decrease in another asset.
b. Increase in an asset, increase in a liability.
c. Increase in an asset, increase in owner's equity.
d. Decrease in an asset, decrease in a liability.
e. Decrease in an asset, decrease in owner's equity.

EX 1-13
Nature of transactions
obj. **4**

✔ d. $6,000

Murray Kiser operates his own catering service. Summary financial data for February are presented in equation form as follows. Each line designated by a number indicates the effect of a transaction on the equation. Each increase and decrease in owner's equity, except transaction (5), affects net income.

	Assets			=	Liabilities +		Owner's Equity			
	Cash +	Supplies +	Land	=	Accounts Payable +	Murray Kiser, Capital −	Murray Kiser, Drawing +	Fees Earned −	Expenses
Bal.	30,000	4,000	75,000		8,000	101,000			
1.	+35,000							35,000	
2.	−15,000		+15,000						
3.	−26,000								−26,000
4.		+1,500			+1,500				
5.	−2,000						−2,000		
6.	−7,200				−7,200				
7.		−3,000							−3,000
Bal.	14,800	2,500	90,000		2,300	101,000	−2,000	35,000	−29,000

a. Describe each transaction.
b. What is the amount of net decrease in cash during the month?
c. What is the amount of net increase in owner's equity during the month?
d. What is the amount of the net income for the month?
e. How much of the net income for the month was retained in the business?

EX 1-14
Net income and owner's withdrawals
obj. 5

The income statement of a proprietorship for the month of December indicates a net income of $75,000. During the same period, the owner withdrew $100,000 in cash from the business for personal use.

Would it be correct to say that the business incurred a net loss of $25,000 during the month? Discuss.

EX 1-15
Net income and owner's equity for four businesses
obj. 5

✔ Saturn: Net income, $108,000

Four different proprietorships, Jupiter, Mercury, Saturn, and Venus, show the same balance sheet data at the beginning and end of a year. These data, exclusive of the amount of owner's equity, are summarized as follows:

	Total Assets	Total Liabilities
Beginning of the year	$ 810,000	$324,000
End of the year	1,296,000	540,000

On the basis of the above data and the following additional information for the year, determine the net income (or loss) of each company for the year. (*Hint:* First determine the amount of increase or decrease in owner's equity during the year.)

Jupiter: The owner had made no additional investments in the business and had made no withdrawals from the business.

Mercury: The owner had made no additional investments in the business but had withdrawn $72,000.

Saturn: The owner had made an additional investment of $162,000 but had made no withdrawals.

Venus: The owner had made an additional investment of $162,000 and had withdrawn $72,000.

EX 1-16
Balance sheet items
obj. 5

From the following list of selected items taken from the records of Hoosier Appliance Service as of a specific date, identify those that would appear on the balance sheet:

1. Accounts Payable
2. Cash
3. Fees Earned
4. Land
5. Sarah Neil, Capital
6. Supplies
7. Supplies Expense
8. Utilities Expense
9. Wages Expense
10. Wages Payable

EX 1-17
Income statement
items

obj. 5

Based on the data presented in Exercise 1-16, identify those items that would appear on the income statement.

EX 1-18
Statement of
owner's equity

obj. 5

✔ Hedi Fry, capital,
April 30, 2010:
$799,100

Financial information related to Teflon Company, a proprietorship, for the month ended April 30, 2010, is as follows:

Net income for April	$ 93,780
Hedi Fry's withdrawals during April	10,000
Hedi Fry, capital, April 1, 2010	715,320

Prepare a statement of owner's equity for the month ended April 30, 2010.

EX 1-19
Income statement

obj. 5

✔ Net income:
$116,600

Relax Services was organized on May 1, 2010. A summary of the revenue and expense transactions for May follows:

Fees earned	$363,200
Wages expense	187,000
Rent expense	36,000
Supplies expense	11,500
Miscellaneous expense	12,100

Prepare an income statement for the month ended May 31.

EX 1-20
Missing amounts
from balance sheet
and income statement
data

obj. 5

✔ (a) $46,890

One item is omitted in each of the following summaries of balance sheet and income statement data for the following four different proprietorships:

	Earth	Mars	Neptune	Pluto
Beginning of the year:				
Assets	$216,000	$250,000	$100,000	(d)
Liabilities	129,600	130,000	76,000	$120,000
End of the year:				
Assets	268,200	350,000	90,000	248,000
Liabilities	117,000	110,000	80,000	136,000
During the year:				
Additional investment in the business	(a)	50,000	10,000	40,000
Withdrawals from the business	14,400	16,000	(c)	60,000
Revenue	71,190	(b)	115,000	112,000
Expenses	38,880	64,000	122,500	128,000

Determine the missing amounts, identifying them by letter. (*Hint:* First determine the amount of increase or decrease in owner's equity during the year.)

EX 1-21
Balance sheets, net
income

obj. 5

✔ b. $136,275

Financial information related to the proprietorship of Plexiglass Interiors for October and November 2010 is as follows:

	October 31, 2010	November 30, 2010
Accounts payable	$ 46,200	$ 49,800
Accounts receivable	102,000	117,375
Claudia Symonds, capital	?	?
Cash	180,000	306,000
Supplies	9,000	7,500

a. Prepare balance sheets for Plexiglass Interiors as of October 31 and as of November 30, 2010.
b. Determine the amount of net income for November, assuming that the owner made no additional investments or withdrawals during the month.
c. Determine the amount of net income for November, assuming that the owner made no additional investments but withdrew $37,500 during the month.

EX 1-22

Financial statements

obj. 5

Each of the following items is shown in the financial statements of ExxonMobil Corporation. Identify the financial statement (balance sheet or income statement) in which each item would appear.

a. Accounts payable
b. Cash equivalents
c. Crude oil inventory
d. Equipment
e. Exploration expenses
f. Income taxes payable
g. Investments
h. Long-term debt

i. Marketable securities
j. Notes and loans payable
k. Notes receivable
l. Operating expenses
m. Prepaid taxes
n. Sales
o. Selling expenses

EX 1-23

Statement of cash flows

obj. 5

Indicate whether each of the following activities would be reported on the statement of cash flows as (a) an operating activity, (b) an investing activity, or (c) a financing activity:

1. Cash received as owner's investment
2. Cash paid for land
3. Cash received from fees earned
4. Cash paid for expenses

EX 1-24

Statement of cash flows

obj. 5

A summary of cash flows for Pickerel Consulting Group for the year ended March 31, 2010, is shown below.

Cash receipts:	
Cash received from customers	$239,100
Cash received from additional investment of owner	50,000
Cash payments:	
Cash paid for operating expenses	162,900
Cash paid for land	75,000
Cash paid to owner for personal use	10,000

The cash balance as of April 1, 2009, was $30,800.

Prepare a statement of cash flows for Pickerel Consulting Group for the year ended March 31, 2010.

EX 1-25

Financial statements

obj. 5

✔ Correct amount of total assets is $176,400

Driftwood Realty, organized July 1, 2010, is owned and operated by Steffy Owen. How many errors can you find in the following statements for Driftwood Realty, prepared after its second month of operations?

Driftwood Realty
Income Statement
August 31, 2010

Sales commissions		$467,100
Expenses:		
Office salaries expense	$291,600	
Rent expense	99,000	
Automobile expense	22,500	
Miscellaneous expense	7,200	
Supplies expense	2,700	
Total expenses		423,000
Net income		$134,100

Steffy Owen
Statement of Owner's Equity
August 31, 2009

Steffy Owen, capital, August 1, 2010.	$ 93,600
Less withdrawals during August	18,000
	$ 75,600
Additional investment during August	22,500
	$ 98,100
Net income for the month.	134,100
Steffy Owen, capital, August 31, 2010	$232,200

Balance Sheet
For the Month Ended August 31, 2010

Assets		Liabilities	
Cash.	$29,700	Accounts receivable.	$128,700
Accounts payable.	34,200	Supplies	18,000
		Owner's Equity	
		Steffy Owen, capital	232,200
Total assets.	$63,900	Total liabilities and owner's equity	$378,900

EX 1-26

Ratio of liabilities to stockholders' equity

The Home Depot, Inc., is the world's largest home improvement retailer and one of the largest retailers in the United States based on net sales volume. The Home Depot operates over 2,000 Home Depot® stores that sell a wide assortment of building materials and home improvement and lawn and garden products. The Home Depot also operates over 30 EXPO Design Center stores that offer interior design products, such as kitchen and bathroom cabinetry, tiles, flooring, and lighting fixtures, and installation services.

The Home Depot reported the following balance sheet data (in millions):

	Jan. 28, 2007	Jan. 29, 2006
Total assets	$52,263	$44,405
Total stockholders' equity	25,030	26,909

a. Determine the total liabilities as of January 28, 2007, and January 29, 2006.
b. Determine the ratio of liabilities to stockholders' equity for 2007 and 2006. Round to two decimal places.
c. What conclusions regarding the margin of protection to the creditors can you draw from (b)?

EX 1-27

Ratio of liabilities to stockholders' equity

Lowe's, a major competitor of The Home Depot in the home improvement business, operates over 1,300 stores. For the years ending February 2, 2007, and February 3, 2006, Lowe's reported the following balance sheet data (in millions):

	2007	2006
Total assets	$27,767	$24,639
Total liabilities	12,042	10,343

a. Determine the total stockholders' equity as of February 2, 2007, and February 3, 2006.
b. Determine the ratio of liabilities to stockholders' equity for 2007 and 2006. Round to two decimal places.
c. What conclusions regarding the margin of protection to the creditors can you draw from (b)?
d. Using the balance sheet data for The Home Depot in Exercise 1-26, how does the ratio of liabilities to stockholders' equity of Lowe's compare to that of The Home Depot?

Problems Series A

PR 1-1A
Transactions

obj. 4

✔ Cash bal. at end
of July: $50,450

Jean Howard established an insurance agency on July 1 of the current year and completed the following transactions during July:

a. Opened a business bank account with a deposit of $50,000 from personal funds.
b. Purchased supplies on account, $1,600.
c. Paid creditors on account, $500.
d. Received cash from fees earned on insurance commissions, $9,250.
e. Paid rent on office and equipment for the month, $2,500.
f. Paid automobile expenses for month, $900, and miscellaneous expenses, $300.
g. Paid office salaries, $1,900.
h. Determined that the cost of supplies on hand was $550; therefore, the cost of supplies used was $1,050.
i. Billed insurance companies for sales commissions earned, $11,150.
j. Withdrew cash for personal use, $2,700.

Instructions

1. Indicate the effect of each transaction and the balances after each transaction, using the following tabular headings:

Assets			=	Liabilities	+			Owner's Equity					
Cash +	Accounts Receivable +	Supplies	=	Accounts Payable	+	Jean Howard, Capital	− Jean Howard, Drawing	+ Fees Earned	− Rent Expense	− Salaries Expense	− Supplies Expense	− Auto Expense	− Misc. Expense

2. ➤ Briefly explain why the owner's investment and revenues increased owner's equity, while withdrawals and expenses decreased owner's equity.

PR 1-2A
Financial statements

obj. 5

✔ 1. Net income:
$208,860

The amounts of the assets and liabilities of Heavenly Travel Service at April 30, 2010, the end of the current year, and its revenue and expenses for the year are listed below. The capital of Jennifer Burch, owner, was $45,540 at May 1, 2009, the beginning of the current year, and the owner withdrew $25,000 during the current year.

Accounts payable	$ 14,600	Supplies	$ 6,800
Accounts receivable	78,000	Supplies expense	13,200
Cash	159,200	Taxes expense	10,250
Fees earned	600,000	Utilities expense	49,150
Miscellaneous expense	5,000	Wages expense	232,640
Rent expense	80,900		

Instructions

1. Prepare an income statement for the current year ended April 30, 2010.
2. Prepare a statement of owner's equity for the current year ended April 30, 2010.
3. Prepare a balance sheet as of April 30, 2010.

PR 1-3A
Financial statements

obj. 5

✔ 1. Net income:
$22,975

Doug Van Buren established Ohm Computer Services on July 1, 2010. The effect of each transaction and the balances after each transaction for July are shown at the top of the following page.

Instructions

1. Prepare an income statement for the month ended July 31, 2010.
2. Prepare a statement of owner's equity for the month ended July 31, 2010.
3. Prepare a balance sheet as of July 31, 2010.
4. (Optional). Prepare a statement of cash flows for the month ending July 31, 2010.

	Cash	+ Receivable	+ Supplies	= Payable	+ Doug Van Buren, Capital	− Doug Van Buren, Drawing	+ Fees Earned	− Salaries Expense	− Rent Expense	− Auto Expense	− Supplies Expense	− Misc. Expense
	Assets			**= Liabilities +**	**Owner's Equity**							
a.	+30,000				+30,000							
b.			+2,600	+2,600								
Bal.	30,000		2,600	2,600	30,000							
c.	+29,500						+29,500					
Bal.	59,500		2,600	2,600	30,000		29,500					
d.	−8,000								−8,000			
Bal.	51,500		2,600	2,600	30,000		29,500		−8,000			
e.	−1,250			−1,250								
Bal.	50,250		2,600	1,350	30,000		29,500		−8,000			
f.		+20,750					+20,750					
Bal.	50,250	20,750	2,600	1,350	30,000		50,250		−8,000			
g.	−5,750									−3,875		−1,875
Bal.	44,500	20,750	2,600	1,350	30,000		50,250		−8,000	−3,875		−1,875
h.	−12,000							−12,000				
Bal.	32,500	20,750	2,600	1,350	30,000		50,250	−12,000	−8,000	−3,875		−1,875
i.			−1,525								−1,525	
Bal.	32,500	20,750	1,075	1,350	30,000		50,250	−12,000	−8,000	−3,875	−1,525	−1,875
j.	−7,500					−7,500						
Bal.	25,000	20,750	1,075	1,350	30,000	−7,500	50,250	−12,000	−8,000	−3,875	−1,525	−1,875

PR 1-4A
Transactions; financial statements
objs. 4, 5

✔ 2. Net income: $14,450

On April 1, 2010, Ryan Barnes established Coyote Realty. Ryan completed the following transactions during the month of April:

a. Opened a business bank account with a deposit of $25,000 from personal funds.
b. Paid rent on office and equipment for the month, $3,200.
c. Paid automobile expenses (including rental charge) for month, $1,200, and miscellaneous expenses, $800.
d. Purchased supplies (pens, file folders, and copy paper) on account, $900.
e. Earned sales commissions, receiving cash, $24,000.
f. Paid creditor on account, $400.
g. Paid office salaries, $3,600.
h. Withdrew cash for personal use, $3,000.
i. Determined that the cost of supplies on hand was $150; therefore, the cost of supplies used was $750.

Instructions
1. Indicate the effect of each transaction and the balances after each transaction, using the following tabular headings:

	Cash	+ Supplies	= Accounts Payable	+ Ryan Barnes, Capital	− Ryan Barnes, Drawing	+ Sales Commissions	− Office Salaries Expense	− Rent Expense	− Auto Expense	− Supplies Expense	− Misc. Expense
	Assets		**= Liabilities +**	**Owner's Equity**							

2. Prepare an income statement for April, a statement of owner's equity for April, and a balance sheet as of April 30.

PR 1-5A
Transactions; financial statements
objs. 4, 5

✔ 3. Net income: $13,950

Colfax Dry Cleaners is owned and operated by Maria Acosta. A building and equipment are currently being rented, pending expansion to new facilities. The actual work of dry cleaning is done by another company at wholesale rates. The assets and the liabilities of the business on November 1, 2010, are as follows: Cash, $34,200; Accounts Receivable, $40,000; Supplies, $5,000; Land, $50,000; Accounts Payable, $16,400. Business transactions during November are summarized as follows:

a. Maria Acosta invested additional cash in the business with a deposit of $35,000 in the business bank account.

b. Purchased land for use as a parking lot, paying cash of $30,000.

c. Paid rent for the month, $4,500.

d. Charged customers for dry cleaning revenue on account, $18,250.

e. Paid creditors on account, $9,000.

f. Purchased supplies on account, $2,800.

g. Received cash from cash customers for dry cleaning revenue, $31,750.

h. Received cash from customers on account, $27,800.

i. Received monthly invoice for dry cleaning expense for November (to be paid on December 10), $14,800.

j. Paid the following: wages expense, $8,200; truck expense, $1,875; utilities expense, $1,575; miscellaneous expense, $850.

k. Determined that the cost of supplies on hand was $3,550; therefore, the cost of supplies used during the month was $4,250.

l. Withdrew $10,000 for personal use.

Instructions

1. Determine the amount of Maria Acosta's capital as of November 1.

2. State the assets, liabilities, and owner's equity as of November 1 in equation form similar to that shown in this chapter. In tabular form below the equation, indicate increases and decreases resulting from each transaction and the new balances after each transaction.

3. Prepare an income statement for November, a statement of owner's equity for November, and a balance sheet as of November 30.

4. (Optional) Prepare a statement of cash flows for November.

PR 1-6A
Missing amounts from financial statements

obj. 5

✔ i. $515,610

The financial statements at the end of Four Corners Realty's first month of operations are shown below and on the next page.

Four Corners Realty
Income Statement
For the Month Ended July 31, 2010

Fees earned		$239,700
Expenses:		
Wages expense	$ (a)	
Rent expense	24,480	
Supplies expense	20,400	
Utilities expense	13,770	
Miscellaneous expense	8,415	
Total expenses		121,890
Net income		(b)

Four Corners Realty
Statement of Owner's Equity
For the Month Ended July 31, 2010

Jeremy Parks, capital, July 1, 2010		$ (c)
Investment on July 1, 2010.	$ (d)	
Net income for July	(e)	
	(f)	
Less withdrawals	(g)	
Increase in owner's equity		(h)
Jeremy Parks, capital, July 31, 2010.		(i)

Four Corners Realty
Balance Sheet
July 31, 2010

Assets		Liabilities	
Cash	$150,450	Accounts payable.	$12,240
Supplies	10,200	**Owner's Equity**	
Land	(j)	Jeremy Parks, capital	(l)
Total assets	(k)	Total liabilities and owner's equity . . .	(m)

Four Corners Realty
Statement of Cash Flows
For the Month Ended July 31, 2010

Cash flows from operating activities:		
Cash received from customers	$ (n)	
Deduct cash payments for expenses and payments to creditors	119,850	
Net cash flow from operating activities		$ (o)
Cash flows from investing activities:		
Cash payments for acquisition of land		(367,200)
Cash flows from financing activities:		
Cash received as owner's investment	$ 459,000	
Deduct cash withdrawal by owner.	61,200	
Net cash flow from financing activities		(p)
Net cash flow and July 31, 2010, cash balance		(q)

Instructions

By analyzing the interrelationships among the four financial statements, determine the proper amounts for (a) through (q).

Problems Series B

PR 1-1B
Transactions

obj. 4

✔ Cash bal. at end of November: $28,100

On November 1 of the current year, Rhea Quade established a business to manage rental property. She completed the following transactions during November:

a. Opened a business bank account with a deposit of $30,000 from personal funds.
b. Purchased supplies (pens, file folders, and copy paper) on account, $1,750.
c. Received cash from fees earned for managing rental property, $3,600.
d. Paid rent on office and equipment for the month, $1,300.
e. Paid creditors on account, $500.
f. Billed customers for fees earned for managing rental property, $4,800.
g. Paid automobile expenses (including rental charges) for month, $500, and miscellaneous expenses, $200.
h. Paid office salaries, $1,000.
i. Determined that the cost of supplies on hand was $800; therefore, the cost of supplies used was $950.
j. Withdrew cash for personal use, $2,000.

Instructions

1. Indicate the effect of each transaction and the balances after each transaction, using the following tabular headings:

Assets			= Liabilities +		Owner's Equity						
Cash +	Accounts Receivable +	Supplies =	Accounts Payable +	Rhea Quade, Capital −	Rhea Quade, Drawing +	Fees Earned −	Rent Expense −	Salaries Expense −	Supplies Expense −	Auto Expense −	Misc. Expense

2. ▬▬▶ Briefly explain why the owner's investment and revenues increased owner's equity, while withdrawals and expenses decreased owner's equity.

PR 1-2B
Financial statements

obj. 5

Following are the amounts of the assets and liabilities of St. Kitts Travel Agency at December 31, 2010, the end of the current year, and its revenue and expenses for the year. The capital of Robin Egan, owner, was $45,000 on January 1, 2010, the beginning of the current year. During the current year, Robin withdrew $7,500.

✔ 1. Net income: $68,750

Accounts payable	$ 6,250	Rent expense	$12,500
Accounts receivable	21,150	Supplies	1,350
Cash	90,000	Supplies expense	1,400
Fees earned	125,000	Utilities expense	9,100
Miscellaneous expense	750	Wages expense	32,500

Instructions

1. Prepare an income statement for the current year ended December 31, 2010.
2. Prepare a statement of owner's equity for the current year ended December 31, 2010.
3. Prepare a balance sheet as of December 31, 2010.

PR 1-3B
Financial statements
obj. 5

✔ 1. Net income: $8,800

Ashley Rhymer established Fair Play Financial Services on January 1, 2010. Fair Play Financial Services offers financial planning advice to its clients. The effect of each transaction and the balances after each transaction for January are shown below.

Instructions

1. Prepare an income statement for the month ended January 31, 2010.
2. Prepare a statement of owner's equity for the month ended January 31, 2010.
3. Prepare a balance sheet as of January 31, 2010.
4. (Optional). Prepare a statement of cash flows for the month ending January 31, 2010.

	Cash	+ Accounts Receivable	+ Supplies	= Accounts Payable	+ Ashley Rhymer, Capital	− Ashley Rhymer, Drawing	+ Fees Earned	− Salaries Expense	− Rent Expense	− Auto Expense	− Supplies Expense	− Misc. Expense
a.	+15,000				+15,000							
b.			+2,180	+2,180								
Bal.	15,000		2,180	2,180	15,000							
c.	− 600			−600								
Bal.	14,400		2,180	1,580	15,000							
d.	+28,000						+28,000					
Bal.	42,400		2,180	1,580	15,000		28,000					
e.	− 7,500								−7,500			
Bal.	34,900		2,180	1,580	15,000		28,000		−7,500			
f.	− 5,700									−4,500		−1,200
Bal.	29,200		2,180	1,580	15,000		28,000		−7,500	−4,500		−1,200
g.	−16,000							−16,000				
Bal.	13,200		2,180	1,580	15,000		28,000	−16,000	−7,500	−4,500		−1,200
h.			−1,500								−1,500	
Bal.	13,200		680	1,580	15,000		28,000	−16,000	−7,500	−4,500	−1,500	−1,200
i.		+11,500					+11,500					
Bal.	13,200	11,500	680	1,580	15,000		39,500	−16,000	−7,500	−4,500	−1,500	−1,200
j.	− 5,000					−5,000						
Bal.	8,200	11,500	680	1,580	15,000	−5,000	39,500	−16,000	−7,500	−4,500	−1,500	−1,200

PR 1-4B
Transactions;
financial statements
objs. 4, 5

✔ 2. Net income: $9,200

On August 1, 2010, Tanja Zier established Royal Realty. Tanja completed the following transactions during the month of August:

a. Opened a business bank account with a deposit of $20,000 from personal funds.
b. Purchased supplies (pens, file folders, paper, etc.) on account, $2,650.
c. Paid creditor on account, $1,600.
d. Earned sales commissions, receiving cash, $28,750.
e. Paid rent on office and equipment for the month, $4,200.
f. Withdrew cash for personal use, $5,000.
g. Paid automobile expenses (including rental charge) for month, $2,500, and miscellaneous expenses, $1,200.

h. Paid office salaries, $10,000.

i. Determined that the cost of supplies on hand was $1,000; therefore, the cost of supplies used was $1,650.

Instructions

1. Indicate the effect of each transaction and the balances after each transaction, using the following tabular headings:

Assets		= Liabilities +			Owner's Equity						
						Office					
		Accounts	Tanja Zier,	Tanja Zier,	Sales	Salaries	Rent	Auto	Supplies	Misc.
Cash	+ Supplies =	Payable	+ Capital	− Drawing	+ Commissions	+ Expense	− Expense	− Expense	− Expense	− Expense

2. Prepare an income statement for August, a statement of owner's equity for August, and a balance sheet as of August 31.

PR 1-5B
Transactions;
financial statements

objs. **4, 5**

✔ 3. Net income: $22,050

Swan Dry Cleaners is owned and operated by Peyton Keyes. A building and equipment are currently being rented, pending expansion to new facilities. The actual work of dry cleaning is done by another company at wholesale rates. The assets and the liabilities of the business on July 1, 2010, are as follows: Cash, $17,000; Accounts Receivable, $31,000; Supplies, $3,200; Land, $36,000; Accounts Payable, $10,400. Business transactions during July are summarized as follows:

a. Peyton Keyes invested additional cash in the business with a deposit of $25,000 in the business bank account.

b. Paid $24,000 for the purchase of land as a future building site.

c. Received cash from cash customers for dry cleaning revenue, $19,500.

d. Paid rent for the month, $3,000.

e. Purchased supplies on account, $1,550.

f. Paid creditors on account, $5,100.

g. Charged customers for dry cleaning revenue on account, $24,750.

h. Received monthly invoice for dry cleaning expense for July (to be paid on August 10), $8,200.

i. Paid the following: wages expense, $5,100; truck expense, $1,200; utilities expense, $800; miscellaneous expense, $950.

j. Received cash from customers on account, $26,750.

k. Determined that the cost of supplies on hand was $1,800; therefore, the cost of supplies used during the month was $2,950.

l. Withdrew $18,000 cash for personal use.

Instructions

1. Determine the amount of Peyton Keyes' capital as of July 1 of the current year.

2. State the assets, liabilities, and owner's equity as of July 1 in equation form similar to that shown in this chapter. In tabular form below the equation, indicate increases and decreases resulting from each transaction and the new balances after each transaction.

3. Prepare an income statement for July, a statement of owner's equity for July, and a balance sheet as of July 31.

4. (Optional). Prepare a statement of cash flows for July.

PR 1-6B
Missing amounts
from financial
statements

obj. **5**

The financial statements at the end of Palo Duro Realty's first month of operations are shown at the top of the next page.

✔ k. $180,000

Palo Duro Realty
Income Statement
For the Month Ended November 30, 2010

Fees earned..................................		$ (a)
Expenses:		
Wages expense	$51,000	
Rent expense	19,200	
Supplies expense	(b)	
Utilities expense....................................	10,800	
Miscellaneous expense	6,600	
Total expenses		105,600
Net income		$ 74,400

Palo Duro Realty
Statement of Owner's Equity
For the Month Ended November 30, 2010

Laura Biddle, capital, November 1, 2010.......................		$ (c)
Investment on November 1, 2010	$240,000	
Net income for November............................	(d)	
	(e)	
Less withdrawals	36,000	
Increase in owner's equity...............................		(f)
Laura Biddle, capital, November 30, 2010.....................		(g)

Palo Duro Realty
Balance Sheet
November 30, 2010

Assets		Liabilities	
Cash	$ 26,700	Accounts payable	$ 9,600
Supplies	21,300	**Owner's Equity**	
Land....................	240,000	Laura Biddle, capital	(i)
Total assets..............	(h)	Total liabilities and owner's equity ...	(j)

Palo Duro Realty
Statement of Cash Flows
For the Month Ended November 30, 2010

Cash flows from operating activities:		
Cash received from customers.....................	$ (k)	
Deduct cash payments for expenses and payments to creditors	117,300	
Net cash flow from operating activities......................		$ (l)
Cash flows from investing activities:		
Cash payments for acquisition of land....................		(m)
Cash flows from financing activities:		
Cash received as owner's investment...................	(n)	
Deduct cash withdrawal by owner	(o)	
Net cash flow from financing activities		(p)
Net cash flow and November 30, 2010, cash balance		(q)

Instructions

By analyzing the interrelationships among the four financial statements, determine the proper amounts for (a) through (q).

Continuing Problem

✔ 2. Net income: $1,480

Lee Chang enjoys listening to all types of music and owns countless CDs. Over the years, Lee has gained a local reputation for knowledge of music from classical to rap and the ability to put together sets of recordings that appeal to all ages.

During the last several months, Lee served as a guest disc jockey on a local radio station. In addition, Lee has entertained at several friends' parties as the host deejay.

On June 1, 2010, Lee established a proprietorship known as Music Depot. Using an extensive collection of music CDs, Lee will serve as a disc jockey on a fee basis for weddings, college parties, and other events. During June, Lee entered into the following transactions:

June 1. Deposited $8,000 in a checking account in the name of Music Depot.
2. Received $2,400 from a local radio station for serving as the guest disc jockey for June.
2. Agreed to share office space with a local real estate agency, Upstairs Realty. Music Depot will pay one-fourth of the rent. In addition, Music Depot agreed to pay a portion of the salary of the receptionist and to pay one-fourth of the utilities. Paid $750 for the rent of the office.
4. Purchased supplies (blank CDs, poster board, extension cords, etc.) from City Office Supply Co. for $350. Agreed to pay $100 within 10 days and the remainder by July 5, 2010.
6. Paid $600 to a local radio station to advertise the services of Music Depot twice daily for two weeks.
8. Paid $500 to a local electronics store for renting digital recording equipment.
12. Paid $250 (music expense) to Cool Music for the use of its current music demos to make various music sets.
13. Paid City Office Supply Co. $100 on account.
16. Received $400 from a dentist for providing two music sets for the dentist to play for her patients.
22. Served as disc jockey for a wedding party. The father of the bride agreed to pay $1,350 the 1st of July.
25. Received $500 from a friend for serving as the disc jockey for a cancer charity ball hosted by the local hospital.
29. Paid $240 (music expense) to Galaxy Music for the use of its library of music demos.
30. Received $1,000 for serving as disc jockey for a local club's monthly dance.
30. Paid Upstairs Realty $400 for Music Depot's share of the receptionist's salary for June.
30. Paid Upstairs Realty $300 for Music Depot's share of the utilities for June.
30. Determined that the cost of supplies on hand is $170. Therefore, the cost of supplies used during the month was $180.
30. Paid for miscellaneous expenses, $150.
30. Paid $800 royalties (music expense) to National Music Clearing for use of various artists' music during the month.
30. Withdrew $200 of cash from Music Depot for personal use.

Instructions
1. Indicate the effect of each transaction and the balances after each transaction, using the following tabular headings:

Assets			= Liabilities +			Owner's Equity									
Cash +	Accounts Receivable +	Supplies =	Accounts Payable +	Lee Chang, Capital −	Lee Chang, Drawing +	Fees Earned −	Music Expense −	Office Rent Expense −	Equipment Rent Expense −	Advertising Expense −	Wages Expense −	Utilities Expense −	Supplies Expense −	Misc. Expense	

2. Prepare an income statement for Music Depot for the month ended June 30, 2010.
3. Prepare a statement of owner's equity for Music Depot for the month ended June 30, 2010.
4. Prepare a balance sheet for Music Depot as of June 30, 2010.

Special Activities

You can access the special activities online at **www.cengage.com/accounting/reeve**.

Answers to Self-Examination Questions

1. **D**   A corporation, organized in accordance with state or federal statutes, is a separate legal entity in which ownership is divided into shares of stock (answer D). A proprietorship (answer A) is an unincorporated business owned by one individual. A service business (answer B) provides services to its customers. It can be organized as a proprietorship, partnership, corporation, or limited liability company. A partnership (answer C) is an unincorporated business owned by two or more individuals.

2. **A**   The resources owned by a business are called assets (answer A). The debts of the business are called liabilities (answer B), and the equity of the owners is called owner's equity (answer D). The relationship between assets, liabilities, and owner's equity is expressed as the accounting equation (answer C).

3. **A**   The balance sheet is a listing of the assets, liabilities, and owner's equity of a business at a specific date (answer A). The income statement (answer B) is a summary of the revenue and expenses of a business for a specific period of time. The statement of owner's equity (answer C) summarizes the changes in owner's equity for a proprietorship or partnership during a specific period of time. The statement of cash flows (answer D) summarizes the cash receipts and cash payments for a specific period of time.

4. **C**   The accounting equation is:

Assets = Liabilities + Owner's Equity

Therefore, if assets increased by $20,000 and liabilities increased by $12,000, owner's equity must have increased by $8,000 (answer C), as indicated in the following computation:

Assets	=	Liabilities	+	Owner's Equity
+$20,000	=	+$12,000	+	Owner's Equity
+$20,000 − $12,000	=			Owner's Equity
+$8,000	=			Owner's Equity

5. **B**   Net income is the excess of revenue over expenses, or $7,500 (answer B). If expenses exceed revenue, the difference is a net loss. Withdrawals by the owner are the opposite of the owner's investing in the business and do not affect the amount of net income or net loss.

Analyzing Transactions

© AP Photo/Paul Sakuma

A P P L E ,   I N C.™

Everyday it seems like we get an incredible amount of incoming e-mail messages; you get them from your friends, relatives, subscribed e-mail lists, and even spammers! But how do you organize all of these messages? You might create folders to sort messages by sender, topic, or project. Perhaps you use keyword search utilities. You might even use filters/rules to automatically delete spam or send messages from your best friend to a special folder. In any case, you are organizing information so that it is simple to retrieve and allows you to understand, respond, or refer to the messages.

In the same way that you organize your e-mail, companies develop an organized method for processing, recording, and summarizing financial transactions. For example, Apple, Inc., has a huge volume of financial transactions, resulting from sales of its innovative computers, digital media (like iPod music and video players), and iPhone mobile phones. When Apple sells an iPhone online or at The Apple Store, a customer has the option of paying with credit card, a debit or check card, an Apple gift card, a financing arrangement, or cash (using a cashier's check, a money order, or a wire transfer). In order to analyze only the information related to Apple's cash transactions, the company must record or summarize all these similar sales using a single category or "cash" account. This is comparable to how you summarize cash in the check register of your checkbook. Similarly, Apple will record credit card payments for iPhones and sales from financing arrangements in different accounts (records).

While Chapter 1 uses the accounting equation (Assets = Liabilities + Owner's Equity) to analyze and record financial transactions, this chapter presents more practical and efficient recording methods that most companies use. In addition, this chapter discusses possible accounting errors that may occur, along with methods to detect and correct them.

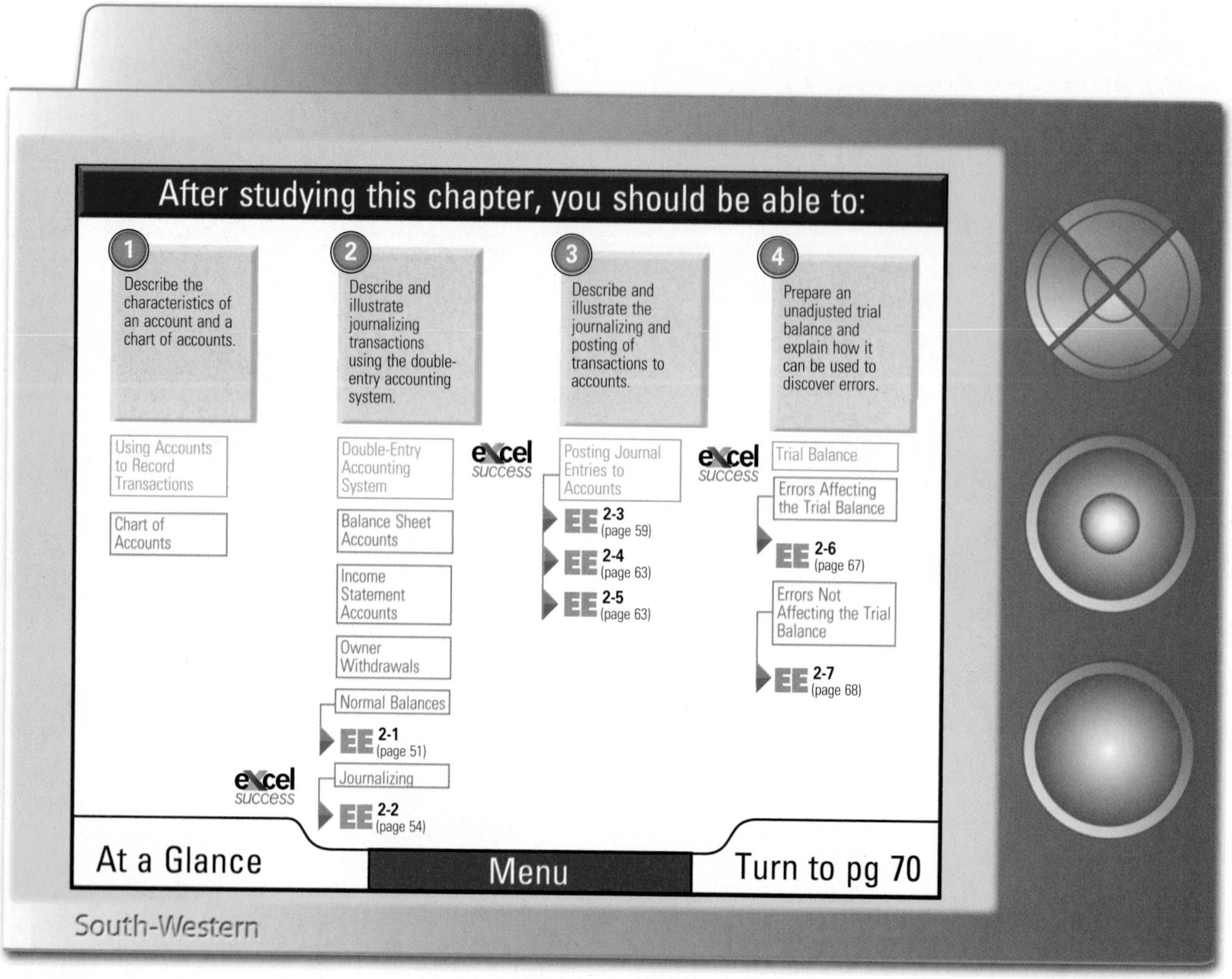

After studying this chapter, you should be able to:

1 Describe the characteristics of an account and a chart of accounts.

2 Describe and illustrate journalizing transactions using the double-entry accounting system.

3 Describe and illustrate the journalizing and posting of transactions to accounts.

4 Prepare an unadjusted trial balance and explain how it can be used to discover errors.

Using Accounts to Record Transactions	Double-Entry Accounting System	e**x**cel *success*	Posting Journal Entries to Accounts	e**x**cel *success*	Trial Balance
Chart of Accounts	Balance Sheet Accounts			Errors Affecting the Trial Balance

Double-Entry Accounting System

Balance Sheet Accounts

Income Statement Accounts

Owner Withdrawals

Normal Balances

EE 2-1 (page 51)

e**x**cel *success*

Journalizing

EE 2-2 (page 54)

Posting Journal Entries to Accounts

EE 2-3 (page 59)

EE 2-4 (page 63)

EE 2-5 (page 63)

e**x**cel *success*

Trial Balance

Errors Affecting the Trial Balance

EE 2-6 (page 67)

Errors Not Affecting the Trial Balance

EE 2-7 (page 68)

At a Glance   **Menu**   **Turn to pg 70**

South-Western

---

1 Describe the characteristics of an account and a chart of accounts.

Using Accounts to Record Transactions

In Chapter 1, we recorded the November transactions for NetSolutions using the accounting equation format shown in Exhibit 1. However, this format is not efficient or practical for companies that have to record thousands or millions of transactions daily. As a result, accounting systems are designed to show the increases and decreases in each accounting equation element as a separate record. This record is called an **account**.

To illustrate, the Cash column of Exhibit 1 records the increases and decreases in cash. Likewise, the other columns in Exhibit 1 record the increases and decreases in the other accounting equation elements. Each of these columns can be organized into a separate account.

An account, in its simplest form, has three parts.

1. A title, which is the name of the accounting equation element recorded in the account.
2. A space for recording increases in the amount of the element.
3. A space for recording decreases in the amount of the element.

The account form presented below is called a **T account** because it resembles the letter T. The left side of the account is called the *debit* side, and the right side is called the *credit* side.[1]

Title	
Left side	Right side
debit	*credit*

1 The terms *debit* and *credit* are derived from the Latin *debere* and *credere*.

Exhibit 1

NetSolutions November Transactions

	Assets			= Liabilities +		Owner's Equity							
	Cash +	Supp. +	Land =	Accounts Payable +	Chris Clark, Capital −	Chris Clark, Drawing +	Fees Earned −	Wages Exp. −	Rent Exp. −	Supplies Exp. −	Utilities Exp. −	Misc. Exp.
a.	+25,000				+25,000							
b.	−20,000		+20,000									
Bal.	5,000		20,000		25,000							
c.		+1,350		+1,350								
Bal.	5,000	1,350	20,000	1,350	25,000							
d.	+ 7,500						+7,500					
Bal.	12,500	1,350	20,000	1,350	25,000		7,500					
e.	− 3,650							−2,125	−800		−450	−275
Bal.	8,850	1,350	20,000	1,350	25,000		7,500	−2,125	−800		−450	−275
f.	− 950			− 950								
Bal.	7,900	1,350	20,000	400	25,000		7,500	−2,125	−800		−450	−275
g.		− 800								−800		
Bal.	7,900	550	20,000	400	25,000		7,500	−2,125	−800	−800	−450	−275
h.	−2,000					−2,000						
Bal.	5,900	550	20,000	400	25,000	−2,000	7,500	−2,125	−800	−800	−450	−275

The amounts shown in the Cash column of Exhibit 1 would be recorded in a cash account as follows:

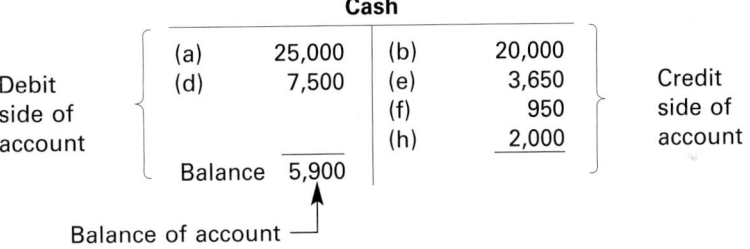

		Cash			
Debit side of account	(a) (d)	25,000 7,500	(b) (e) (f) (h)	20,000 3,650 950 2,000	Credit side of account
	Balance	5,900			

Balance of account ⤴

Many times when accountants analyze complex transactions, they use T accounts to simplify the thought process. In the same way, you will find T accounts a useful device in this and later accounting courses.

Recording transactions in accounts must follow certain rules. For example, increases in assets are recorded on the **debit** (left side) of an account. Likewise, decreases in assets are recorded on the **credit** (right side) of an account. The excess of the debits of an asset account over its credits is the **balance of the account**.

To illustrate, the receipt (increase in Cash) of $25,000 in transaction (a) is entered on the debit (left) side of the cash account shown above. The letter or date of the transaction is also entered into the account. This is done so if any questions later arise related to the entry, the entry can be traced back to the underlying transaction data. In contrast, the payment (decrease in Cash) of $20,000 to purchase land in transaction (b) is entered on the credit (right) side of the account. The balance of the cash account of $5,900 is the excess of the debits over the credits as shown below.

Debits ($25,000 + $7,500) $32,500
Less credits ($20,000 + $3,650 + $950 + $2,000)   26,600
Balance of Cash as of November 30, 2009 . . . . $ 5,900

The balance of the cash account is inserted in the account, in the Debit column. In this way, the balance is identified as a debit balance.[2] This balance represents NetSolutions' cash on hand as of November 30, 2009. This balance of $5,900 is reported on the November 30, 2009, balance sheet for NetSolutions as shown in Exhibit 6 of Chapter 1.

---

2 The totals of the debit and credit columns may be shown separately in an account. When this is done, these amounts should be identified in some way so that they are not mistaken for entries or the ending balance of the account.

In an actual accounting system, a more formal account form replaces the T account. Later in this chapter, we illustrate a four-column account. The T account, however, is a simple way to illustrate the effects of transactions on accounts and financial statements. For this reason, T accounts are often used in business to explain transactions.

Each of the columns in Exhibit 1 can be converted into an account form in a similar manner as was done for the Cash column of Exhibit 1. However, as we mentioned earlier, recording increases and decreases in accounts must follow certain rules. We discuss these rules after we describe and illustrate the chart of accounts.

Chart of Accounts

A group of accounts for a business entity is called a **ledger**. A list of the accounts in the ledger is called a **chart of accounts**. The accounts are normally listed in the order in which they appear in the financial statements. The balance sheet accounts are listed first, in the order of assets, liabilities, and owner's equity. The income statement accounts are then listed in the order of revenues and expenses. Each of these major account groups is described next.

Assets are resources owned by the business entity. These resources can be physical items, such as cash and supplies, or intangibles that have value. Examples of intangible assets include patent rights, copyrights, and trademarks. Examples of other assets include accounts receivable, prepaid expenses (such as insurance), buildings, equipment, and land.

Liabilities are debts owed to outsiders (creditors). Liabilities are often identified on the balance sheet by titles that include the word *payable*. Examples of liabilities include accounts payable, notes payable, and wages payable. Cash received before services are delivered creates a liability to perform the services. These future service commitments are called *unearned revenues*. Examples of unearned revenues are magazine subscriptions received by a publisher and tuition received by a college at the beginning of a term.

Owner's equity is the owner's right to the assets of the business after all liabilities have been paid. For a proprietorship, the owner's equity is represented by the balance of the owner's **capital account**. A **drawing** account represents the amount of withdrawals made by the owner.

Revenues are increases in owner's equity as a result of selling services or products to customers. Examples of revenues include fees earned, fares earned, commissions revenue, and rent revenue.

Expenses result from using up assets or consuming services in the process of generating revenues. Examples of expenses include wages expense, rent expense, utilities expense, supplies expense, and miscellaneous expense.

A chart of accounts should meet the needs of a company's managers and other users of its financial statements. The accounts within the chart of accounts are numbered for use as references. A numbering system is normally used, so that new accounts can be added without affecting other account numbers.

Exhibit 2 is NetSolutions' chart of accounts that we will use in this chapter. Additional accounts will be introduced in later chapters. In Exhibit 2, each account number has two digits. The first digit indicates the major account group of the ledger in which the account is located. Accounts beginning with 1 represent assets; 2, liabilities; 3, owner's equity; 4, revenue; and 5, expenses. The second digit indicates the location of the account within its group.

You should note that each of the columns in Exhibit 1 has been assigned an account number in the chart of accounts shown in Exhibit 2. In addition, we have added accounts for Accounts Receivable, Prepaid Insurance, Office Equipment, and Unearned Rent. These accounts will be used in recording NetSolutions' December transactions.

Procter & Gamble's account numbers have over 30 digits to reflect P&G's many different operations and regions.

Exhibit 2

Chart of
Accounts for
NetSolutions

Balance Sheet Accounts	Income Statement Accounts
1. Assets	4. Revenue
11 Cash	41 Fees Earned
12 Accounts Receivable	5. Expenses
14 Supplies	51 Wages Expense
15 Prepaid Insurance	52 Rent Expense
17 Land	54 Utilities Expense
18 Office Equipment	55 Supplies Expense
2. Liabilities	59 Miscellaneous Expense
21 Accounts Payable	
23 Unearned Rent	
3. Owner's Equity	
31 Chris Clark, Capital	
32 Chris Clark, Drawing	

2 Describe and illustrate journalizing transactions using the double-entry accounting system.

Double-Entry Accounting System

All businesses use what is called the **double-entry accounting system**. This system is based on the accounting equation and requires that every business transaction be recorded in at least two accounts. In addition, it requires that the total debits recorded for each transaction equal the total credits recorded. The double-entry accounting system also has specific **rules of debit and credit** for recording transactions in the accounts.

Balance Sheet Accounts

The double-entry accounting system is based on the accounting equation and specific rules for recording debits and credits. The debit and credit rules for balance sheet accounts are as follows:

Balance Sheet Accounts

ASSETS Asset Accounts			LIABILITIES Liability Accounts			OWNER'S EQUITY Owner's Equity Accounts	
Debit for increases (+)	Credit for decreases (−)	=	Debit for decreases (−)	Credit for increases (+)	+	Debit for decreases (−)	Credit for increases (+)

Income Statement Accounts

The debit and credit rules for income statement accounts are based on their relationship with owner's equity. As shown above, owner's equity accounts are increased by credits. Since revenues increase owner's equity, revenue accounts are increased by credits and decreased by debits. Since owner's equity accounts are decreased by debits, expense accounts are increased by debits and decreased by credits. Thus, the rules of debit and credit for revenue and expense accounts are as follows:

Income Statement Accounts

Revenue Accounts		Expense Accounts	
Debit for decreases (−)	Credit for increases (+)	Debit for increases (+)	Credit for decreases (−)

Owner Withdrawals

The debit and credit rules for recording owner withdrawals are based on the effect of owner withdrawals on owner's equity. Since owner's withdrawals decrease owner's equity, the owner's drawing account is increased by debits. Likewise, the owner's drawing account is decreased by credits. Thus, the rules of debit and credit for the owner's drawing account are as follows:

Drawing Account	
Debit for increases (+)	Credit for decreases (−)

Normal Balances

The sum of the increases in an account is usually equal to or greater than the sum of the decreases in the account. Thus, the **normal balance of an account** is either a debit or credit depending on whether increases in the account are recorded as debits or credits. For example, since asset accounts are increased with debits, asset accounts normally have debit balances. Likewise, liability accounts normally have credit balances.

The rules of debit and credit and the normal balances of the various types of accounts are summarized in Exhibit 3. Debits and credits are sometimes abbreviated as Dr. for debit and Cr. for credit.

Exhibit 3

Rules of Debit and Credit, Normal Balances of Accounts

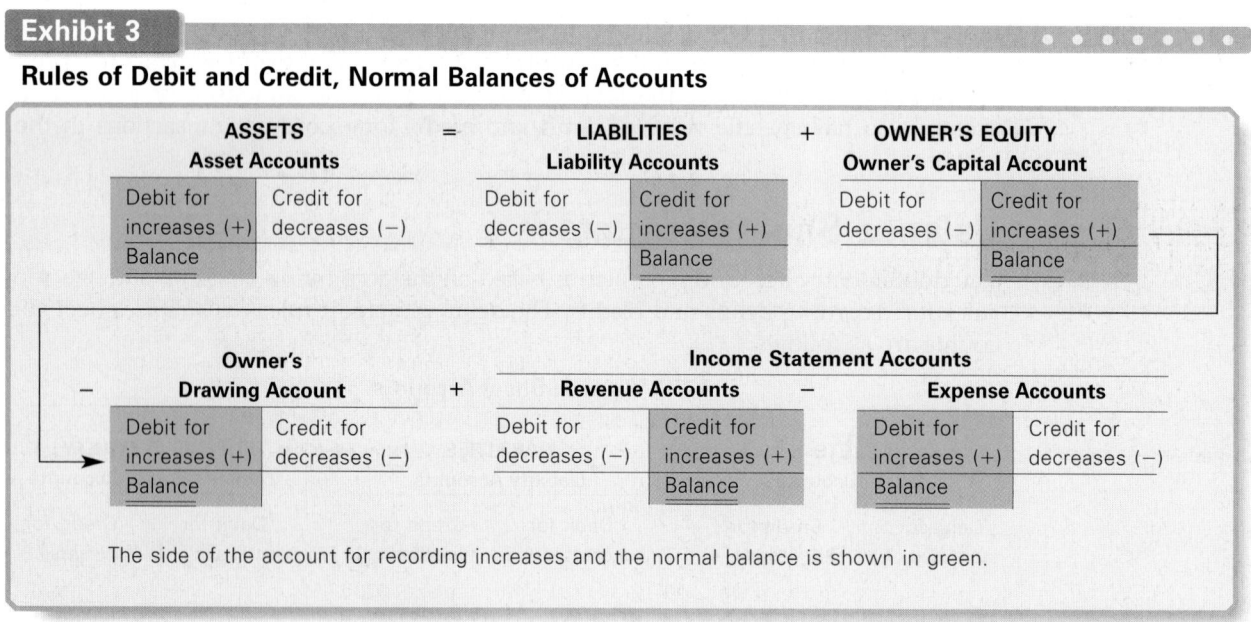

The side of the account for recording increases and the normal balance is shown in green.

When an account normally having a debit balance has a credit balance, or vice versa, an error may have occurred or an unusual situation may exist. For example, a credit balance in the office equipment account could result only from an error. This is because a business cannot have more decreases than increases of office equipment. On the other hand, a debit balance in an accounts payable account could result from an overpayment.

A journal can be thought of as being similar to an individual's diary of significant day-to-day life events.

Journalizing

Using the rules of debit and credit, transactions are initially entered in a record called a **journal**. In this way, the journal serves as a record of when transactions occurred and were recorded. To illustrate, we use the November transactions of NetSolutions from Chapter 1.

 Excel can be used to input a journal entry as follows:

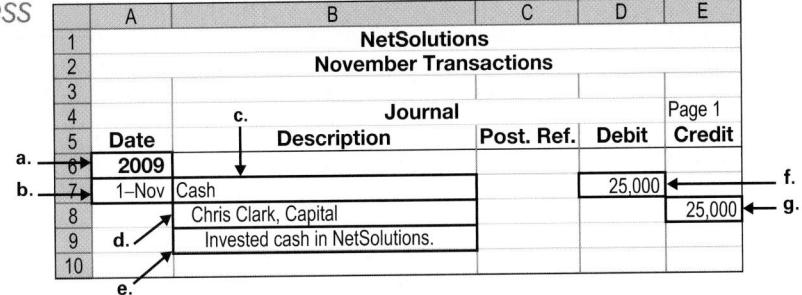

	A	B	C	D	E
1		NetSolutions			
2		November Transactions			
3					
4		c.	Journal		Page 1
5	Date	Description	Post. Ref.	Debit	Credit
6	2009				
7	1–Nov	Cash		25,000	
8		Chris Clark, Capital			25,000
9		Invested cash in NetSolutions.			
10					

a. → (cell A6)
b. → (cell A7)
d. (cell B8)
e. (cell B9)
f. ← (cell D7)
g. ← (cell E8)

a.   In cell A6, the journal year is entered (type 2009).
b.   The month and day is then entered for each transaction. In cell A7, type "11-1".
c.   The account to be **debited** is entered in cell B7 (type "Cash").
d.   The account to be **credited** is entered and indented in cell B8 (type "Chris Clark, Capital").
     Use the Excel indent format button to make indention.
e.   A description of the transaction is entered and indented, twice, in cell B9 (type "Invested
     cash in NetSolutions").
f.   The amount of the **debit** is entered in cell D7 (type 25000). Use the Excel comma format
     to insert commas.
g.   The amount of the **credit** is entered in cell E8 (type 25000).

tryit   Go to the hands-on *Excel Tutor* for this example!

Example Exercise 2-1 Rules of Debit and Credit and Normal Balances ····> ②

State for each account whether it is likely to have (a) debit entries only, (b) credit entries only, or (c) both debit and credit entries. Also, indicate its normal balance.

1. Amber Saunders, Drawing
2. Accounts Payable
3. Cash

4. Fees Earned
5. Supplies
6. Utilities Expense

Follow My Example 2-1

1. Debit entries only; normal debit balance
2. Debit and credit entries; normal credit balance
3. Debit and credit entries; normal debit balance

4. Credit entries only; normal credit balance
5. Debit and credit entries; normal debit balance
6. Debit entries only; normal debit balance

·····

For Practice: PE 2-1A, PE 2-1B

Chris Clark's first transaction (a) on November 1 was to deposit $25,000 in a bank account in the name of NetSolutions. The effect of this transaction on the balance sheet is to increase assets (Cash) and owner's equity (Chris Clark, Capital) by $25,000. This transaction is recorded in the journal using the following steps:

Step 1.   The date of the transaction is entered in the Date column.
Step 2.   The title of the account to be debited is recorded at the left-hand margin under the Description column, and the amount to be debited is entered in the Debit column.
Step 3.   The title of the account to be credited is listed below and to the right of the debited account title, and the amount to be credited is entered in the Credit column.
Step 4.   A brief description may be entered below the credited account.
Step 5.   The Post. Ref. (Posting Reference) column is left blank when the journal entry is initially recorded. We will use this column later in this chapter when we transfer the journal entry amounts to the accounts in the ledger.

Using the preceding steps, transaction (a) is recorded in the journal as follows:

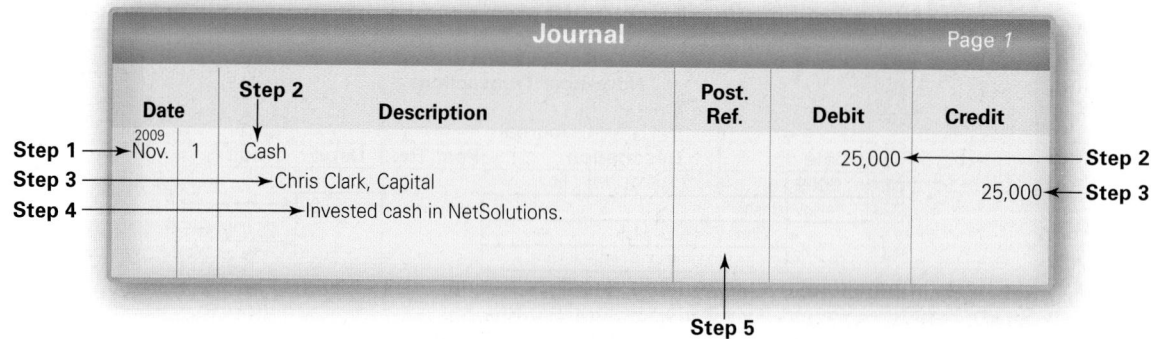

The process of recording a transaction in the journal is called **journalizing**. The entry in the journal is called a **journal entry**.

The following is a useful method for analyzing and journalizing transactions:

1. Carefully read the description of the transaction to determine whether an asset, a liability, an owner's equity, a revenue, an expense, or a drawing account is affected.
2. For each account affected by the transaction, determine whether the account increases or decreases.
3. Determine whether each increase or decrease should be recorded as a debit or a credit, following the rules of debit and credit shown in Exhibit 3.
4. Record the transaction using a journal entry.

The remaining transactions of NetSolutions for November are analyzed and journalized next.

Transaction B

> Nov. 5 NetSolutions paid $20,000 for the purchase of land as a future building site.

Analysis This transaction increases one asset account and decreases another. It is recorded in the journal as a $20,000 increase (debit) to Land and a $20,000 decrease (credit) to Cash.

Journal Entry

5	Land		20,000	
	Cash			20,000
	Purchased land for building site.			

Transaction C

> Nov. 10 NetSolutions purchased supplies on account for $1,350.

Analysis This transaction increases an asset account and increases a liability account. It is recorded in the journal as a $1,350 increase (debit) to Supplies and a $1,350 increase (credit) to Accounts Payable.

Journal Entry

10	Supplies		1,350	
	Accounts Payable			1,350
	Purchased supplies on account.			

Transaction D

Nov. 18   NetSolutions received cash of $7,500 from customers for services provided.

Analysis This transaction increases an asset account and increases a revenue account. It is recorded in the journal as a $7,500 increase (debit) to Cash and a $7,500 increase (credit) to Fees Earned.

Journal Entry

18	Cash	7,500	
	Fees Earned		7,500
	Received fees from customers.		

Transaction E

Nov. 30   NetSolutions incurred the following expenses: wages, $2,125; rent, $800; utilities, $450; and miscellaneous, $275.

Analysis This transaction increases various expense accounts and decreases an asset (Cash) account. You should note that regardless of the number of accounts, *the sum of the debits is always equal to the sum of the credits in a journal entry*. It is recorded in the journal as an increase (debit) to Wages Expense, $2,125; Rent Expense, $800; Utilities Expense, $450; Miscellaneous Expense, $275; and a decrease (credit) to Cash, $3,650.

Journal Entry

30	Wages Expense	2,125	
	Rent Expense	800	
	Utilities Expense	450	
	Miscellaneous Expense	275	
	Cash		3,650
	Paid expenses.		

Transaction F

Nov. 30   NetSolutions paid creditors on account, $950.

Analysis This transaction decreases a liability account and decreases an asset account. It is recorded in the journal as a $950 decrease (debit) to Accounts Payable and a $950 decrease (credit) to Cash.

Journal Entry

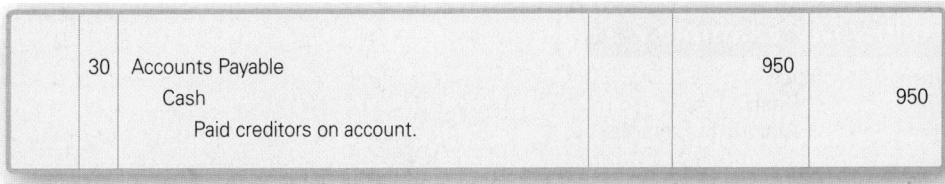

30	Accounts Payable	950	
	Cash		950
	Paid creditors on account.		

Integrity, Objectivity, and Ethics in Business

WILL JOURNALIZING PREVENT FRAUD?

While journalizing transactions reduces the possibility of fraud, it by no means eliminates it. For example, embez-zlement can be hidden within the double-entry book-keeping system by creating fictitious suppliers to whom checks are issued.

Transaction G

> Nov. 30 Chris Clark determined that the cost of supplies on hand at November 30 was $550.

Analysis NetSolutions purchased $1,350 of supplies on November 10. Thus, $800 ($1,350 − $550) of supplies must have been used during November. This transaction is recorded in the journal as an $800 increase (debit) to Supplies Expense and an $800 decrease (credit) to Supplies.

Journal Entry

30	Supplies Expense		800	
	Supplies			800
	Supplies used during November.			

Transaction H

> Nov. 30 Chris Clark withdrew $2,000 from NetSolutions for personal use.

Analysis This transaction decreases assets and owner's equity. This transaction is recorded in the journal as a $2,000 increase (debit) to Chris Clark, Drawing and a $2,000 decrease (credit) to Cash.

Journal Entry

		Journal			Page 2
Date		**Description**	**Post. Ref.**	**Debit**	**Credit**
2009 Nov.	30	Chris Clark, Drawing		2,000	
		Cash			2,000
		Chris Clark withdrew cash for personal use.			

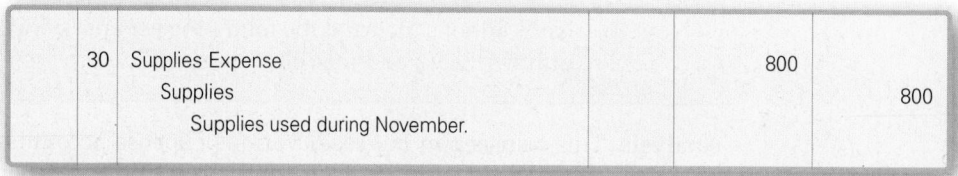

Example Exercise 2-2 Journal Entry for Asset Purchase

Prepare a journal entry for the purchase of a truck on June 3 for $42,500, paying $8,500 cash and the remainder on account.

Follow My Example 2-2

June 3	Truck	42,500	
	Cash		8,500
	Accounts Payable		34,000

For Practice: PE 2-2A, PE 2-2B

3   Describe and illustrate the journalizing and posting of transactions to accounts.

Posting Journal Entries to Accounts

As illustrated, a transaction is first recorded in a journal. Periodically, the journal entries are transferred to the accounts in the ledger. The process of transferring the debits and credits from the journal entries to the accounts is called **posting**.

We use the December transactions of NetSolutions to illustrate posting from the journal to the ledger. By using the December transactions, we also provide an additional review of analyzing and journalizing transactions.

Transaction

> Dec. 1   NetSolutions paid a premium of $2,400 for an insurance policy for liability, theft, and fire. The policy covers a one-year period.

Analysis Advance payments of expenses such as insurance are prepaid expenses. Prepaid expenses are assets. For NetSolutions, the asset purchased is insurance protection for 12 months. This transaction is recorded as a $2,400 increase (debit) to Prepaid Insurance and a $2,400 decrease (credit) to Cash.

Journal Entry

Dec.	1	Prepaid Insurance	15	2,400	
		Cash	11		2,400
		Paid premium on one-year policy.			

The posting of the preceding December 1 transaction is shown in Exhibit 4. You will notice that the T account form is not used. In practice, the T account is usually replaced with a standard account form similar to that shown in Exhibit 4.

Exhibit 4

Diagram of the Recording and Posting of a Debit and a Credit

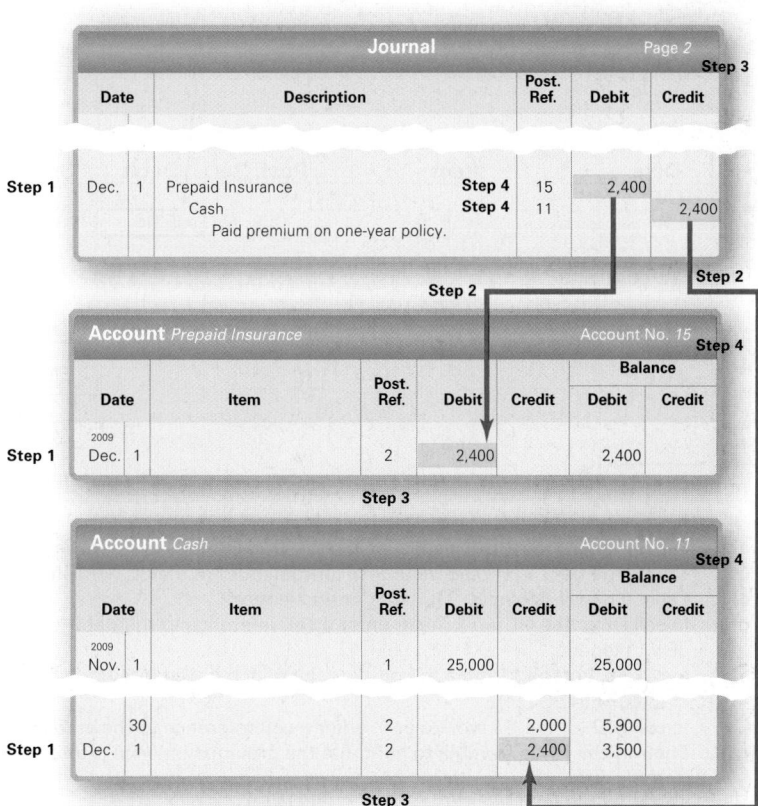

The debits and credits for each journal entry are posted to the accounts in the order they occur in the journal. To illustrate, the debit portion of the December 1 journal entry is posted to the prepaid account in Exhibit 4 using these four steps:

Step 1.   The date (Dec. 1) of the journal entry is entered in the Date column of Prepaid Insurance.

Step 2.   The amount (2,400) is entered into the Debit column of Prepaid Insurance.

Step 3.   The journal page number (2) is entered in the Posting Reference (Post. Ref.) column of Prepaid Insurance.

Step 4.   The account number (15) is entered in the Posting Reference (Post. Ref.) column in the journal.

As shown in Exhibit 4, the credit portion of the December 1 journal entry is posted to the cash account in a similar manner.

The remaining December transactions for NetSolutions are analyzed and journalized in the following paragraphs. These transactions are posted to the ledger in Exhibit 5 on pages 64–65. To simplify, some of the December transactions are stated in summary form. For example, cash received for services is normally recorded on a daily basis. However, only summary totals are recorded at the middle and end of the month for NetSolutions.

excel success

The general ledger can be created in the <u>same</u> workbook on a separate worksheet. The general ledger (*GL*) worksheet references cells from the journal worksheet (*JE*) in order to post the journal entries into the ledger accounts.

	A	B	C	D	E
1		**Journal**			Page 2
2	**Date**	**Description**	**Post. Ref.**	**Debit**	**Credit**
3	**2009**				
4	1–Dec	Prepaid Insurance	15	2,400	
5		Cash	11		2,400
6		Paid premium on one-year policy.			
7					
8					
9					

a. → (JE tab)   b.   d.

	A	B	C	D	E	F	G
1							
2	**Account**	*Prepaid Insurance*				**Account No.**	*15*
3						**Balance**	
4	**Date**	**Item**	**Post. Ref.**	**Debit**	**Credit**	**Debit**	**Credit**
5	**2009**						
6	=JE!A4		2	=JE!D4	e. →	=F5+D6-E6	
7							
8	**Account**	*Cash*				**Account No.**	*11*
9						**Balance**	
10	**Date**	**Item**	**Post. Ref.**	**Debit**	**Credit**	**Debit**	**Credit**
11	**2009**						
12	=JE!A4		2		=JE!E5	g. →	=G11+E12-D12
13							
14							
15							

c. → (GL tab)   f.

Always precede a cell reference or formula with an = sign.

Build a formula by clicking on a referenced cell.

a.   Label a worksheet JE. This will be used as the spreadsheet journal.
b.   Create the Dec. 1 *prepaid insurance* journal entry in the JE worksheet.
c.   Label a new worksheet "GL" for general ledger.
d.   In cell D6 of the GL worksheet, enter a cell reference to the **debit** of Prepaid insurance from the JE worksheet.
e.   In cell F6, enter a formula to compute the new balance (previous balance plus debits minus credits, =F5+D6-E6.)
f.   In cell E12 (of the GL worksheet), enter a cell reference to the **credit** to Cash from the JE worksheet.
g.   Enter in cell F14 a formula to compute the previous balance plus credits minus debits, =G11+E12-D12.

try it   Go to the hands-on *Excel Tutor* for this example!

Transaction

> Dec. 1   NetSolutions paid rent for December, $800. The company from which NetSolutions is renting its store space now requires the payment of rent on the first of each month, rather than at the end of the month.

Analysis The advance payment of rent is an asset, much like the advance payment of the insurance premium in the preceding transaction. However, unlike the insurance premium, this prepaid rent will expire in one month. When an asset that is purchased will be used up in a short period of time, such as a month, it is normal to debit an expense account initially. This avoids having to transfer the balance from an asset account (Prepaid Rent) to an expense account (Rent Expense) at the end of the month. Thus, this transaction is recorded as an $800 increase (debit) to Rent Expense and an $800 decrease (credit) to Cash.

Journal Entry

1	Rent Expense	52	800	
	Cash	11		800
	Paid rent for December.			

Transaction

> Dec. 1   NetSolutions received an offer from a local retailer to rent the land purchased on November 5. The retailer plans to use the land as a parking lot for its employees and customers. NetSolutions agreed to rent the land to the retailer for three months, with the rent payable in advance. NetSolutions received $360 for three months' rent beginning December 1.

Analysis By agreeing to rent the land and accepting the $360, NetSolutions has incurred an obligation (liability) to the retailer. This obligation is to make the land available for use for three months and not to interfere with its use. The liability created by receiving the cash in advance of providing the service is called **unearned revenue**. As time passes, the unearned rent liability will decrease and will become revenue. Thus, this transaction is recorded as a $360 increase (debit) to Cash and a $360 increase (credit) to Unearned Rent.

Journal Entry

Magazines that receive subscriptions in advance must record the receipts as unearned revenues. Likewise, airlines that receive ticket payments in advance must record the receipts as unearned revenues until the passengers use the tickets.

1	Cash	11	360	
	Unearned Rent	23		360
	Received advance payment for			
	three months' rent on land.			

Transaction

> Dec. 4   NetSolutions purchased office equipment on account from Executive Supply Co. for $1,800.

Analysis The asset (Office Equipment) and liability accounts (Accounts Payable) increase. This transaction is recorded as a $1,800 increase (debit) to Office Equipment and a $1,800 increase (credit) to Accounts Payable.

Journal Entry

4	Office Equipment	18	1,800	
	Accounts Payable	21		1,800
	Purchased office equipment			
	on account.			

Transaction

> Dec. 6   NetSolutions paid $180 for a newspaper advertisement.

Analysis An expense increases and an asset (Cash) decreases. Expense items that are expected to be minor in amount are normally included as part of the miscellaneous expense. This transaction is recorded as a $180 increase (debit) to Miscellaneous Expense and a $180 decrease (credit) to Cash.

Journal Entry

6	Miscellaneous Expense	59	180	
	Cash	11		180
	Paid for newspaper ad.			

Transaction

> Dec. 11   NetSolutions paid creditors $400.

Analysis A liability (Accounts Payable) and an asset (Cash) decrease. This transaction is recorded as a $400 decrease (debit) to Accounts Payable and a $400 decrease (credit) to Cash.

Journal Entry

In computerized accounting systems, some transactions may be automatically authorized and recorded when certain events occur. For example, the wages of employees may be paid automatically at the end of each pay period.

11	Accounts Payable	21	400	
	Cash	11		400
	Paid creditors on account.			

Transaction

> Dec. 13   NetSolutions paid a receptionist and a part-time assistant $950 for two weeks' wages.

Analysis This transaction is similar to the December 6 transaction, where an expense account is increased and Cash is decreased. This transaction is recorded as a $950 increase (debit) to Wages Expense and a $950 decrease (credit) to Cash.

Journal Entry

				Journal				Page *3*
Date			**Description**		**Post. Ref.**	**Debit**	**Credit**
2009 Dec.	13	Wages Expense			51	950	
		Cash			11		950
		Paid two weeks' wages.					

Transaction

Dec. 16   NetSolutions received $3,100 from fees earned for the first half of December.

Analysis An asset account (Cash) and a revenue account (Fees Earned) increase. This transaction is recorded as a $3,100 increase (debit) to Cash and a $3,100 increase (credit) to Fees Earned.

Journal Entry

16	Cash		11	3,100	
	Fees Earned		41		3,100
	Received fees from customers.				

Transaction

Dec. 16   Fees earned on account totaled $1,750 for the first half of December.

Analysis When a business agrees that a customer may pay for services provided at a later date, an **account receivable** is created. An account receivable is a claim against the customer. An account receivable is an asset, and the revenue is earned even though no cash has been received. Thus, this transaction is recorded as a $1,750 increase (debit) to Accounts Receivable and a $1,750 increase (credit) to Fees Earned.

Journal Entry

16	Accounts Receivable		12	1,750	
	Fees Earned		41		1,750
	Recorded fees earned on account.				

Example Exercise 2-3   Journal Entry for Fees Earned   3

Prepare a journal entry on August 7 for the fees earned on account, $115,000.

Follow My Example 2-3

Aug. 7	Accounts Receivable	115,000
	Fees Earned	115,000

For Practice: PE 2-3A, PE 2-3B

Transaction

Dec. 20   NetSolutions paid $900 to Executive Supply Co. on the $1,800 debt owed from the December 4 transaction.

Analysis This is similar to the transaction of December 11. This transaction is recorded as a $900 decrease (debit) to Accounts Payable and a $900 decrease (credit) to Cash.

Journal Entry

20	Accounts Payable	21	900	
	Cash	11		900
	Paid part of amount owed to			
	Executive Supply Co.			

Transaction

Dec. 21   NetSolutions received $650 from customers in payment of their accounts.

Analysis When customers pay amounts owed for services they have previously received, one asset increases and another asset decreases. This transaction is recorded as a $650 increase (debit) to Cash and a $650 decrease (credit) to Accounts Receivable.

Journal Entry

21	Cash	11	650	
	Accounts Receivable	12		650
	Received cash from customers			
	on account.			

Transaction

Dec. 23   NetSolutions paid $1,450 for supplies.

Analysis One asset account (Supplies) increases and another asset account (Cash) decreases. This transaction is recorded as a $1,450 increase (debit) to Supplies and a $1,450 decrease (credit) to Cash.

Journal Entry

23	Supplies	14	1,450	
	Cash	11		1,450
	Purchased supplies.			

Transaction

> Dec. 27   NetSolutions paid the receptionist and the part-time assistant $1,200 for two weeks' wages.

Analysis This is similar to the transaction of December 13. This transaction is recorded as a $1,200 increase (debit) to Wages Expense and a $1,200 decrease (credit) to Cash.

Journal Entry

27	Wages Expense	51	1,200	
	Cash	11		1,200
	Paid two weeks' wages.			

Transaction

> Dec. 31   NetSolutions paid its $310 telephone bill for the month.

Analysis This is similar to the transaction of December 6. This transaction is recorded as a $310 increase (debit) to Utilities Expense and a $310 decrease (credit) to Cash.

Journal Entry

31	Utilities Expense	54	310	
	Cash	11		310
	Paid telephone bill.			

Transaction

> Dec. 31   NetSolutions paid its $225 electric bill for the month.

Analysis This is similar to the preceding transaction. This transaction is recorded as a $225 increase (debit) to Utilities Expense and a $225 decrease (credit) to Cash.

Journal Entry

Journal				Page 4
Date	**Description**	**Post. Ref.**	**Debit**	**Credit**
2009 Dec. 31	Utilities Expense	54	225	
	Cash	11		225
	Paid electric bill.			

Transaction

> Dec. 31   NetSolutions received $2,870 from fees earned for the second half of December.

Analysis This is similar to the transaction of December 16. This transaction is recorded as a $2,870 increase (debit) to Cash and a $2,870 increase (credit) to Fees Earned.

Journal Entry

31	Cash	11	2,870	
	Fees Earned	41		2,870
	Received fees from customers.			

Transaction

> Dec. 31   Fees earned on account totaled $1,120 for the second half of December.

Analysis This is similar to the transaction of December 16. This transaction is recorded as a $1,120 increase (debit) to Accounts Receivable and a $1,120 increase (credit) to Fees Earned.

Journal Entry

31	Accounts Receivable	12	1,120	
	Fees Earned	41		1,120
	Recorded fees earned on account.			

Transaction

> Dec. 31   Chris Clark withdrew $2,000 for personal use.

Analysis This transaction decreases owner's equity and assets. This transaction is recorded as a $2,000 increase (debit) to Chris Clark, Drawing and a $2,000 decrease (credit) to Cash.

Journal Entry

31	Chris Clark, Drawing	32	2,000	
	Cash	11		2,000
	Chris Clark withdrew cash for personal use.			

Example Exercise 2-4   Journal Entry for Owner's Withdrawal   ••••••••> 3

Prepare a journal entry on December 29 for the payment of $12,000 to the owner of Smartstaff Consulting Services, Dominique Walsh, for personal use.

Follow My Example 2-4

Dec. 29	Dominique Walsh, Drawing	12,000	
	Cash		12,000

For Practice: PE 2-4A, PE 2-4B

Exhibit 5, on pages 64–65, shows the ledger for NetSolutions after the transactions for both November and December have been posted.

Example Exercise 2-5   Missing Amount from an Account   ••••••••> 3

On March 1, the cash account balance was $22,350. During March, cash receipts totaled $241,880 and the March 31 balance was $19,125. Determine the cash payments made during March.

Follow My Example 2-5

Using the following T account, solve for the amount of cash payments (indicated by ? below).

Cash			
Mar. 1 Bal.	22,350	?	Cash payments
Cash receipts	241,880		
Mar. 31 Bal.	19,125		

$19,125 = $22,350 + $241,880 − Cash payments
Cash payments = $22,350 + $241,880 − $19,125 = $245,105

For Practice: PE 2-5A, PE 2-5B

4 Prepare an unadjusted trial balance and explain how it can be used to discover errors.

Trial Balance

Errors may occur in posting debits and credits from the journal to the ledger. One way to detect such errors is by preparing a **trial balance**. Double-entry accounting requires that debits must always equal credits. The trial balance verifies this equality. The steps in preparing a trial balance are as follows:

Step 1: List the name of the company, the title of the trial balance, and the date the trial balance is prepared.

Step 2: List the accounts from the ledger and enter their debit or credit balance in the Debit or Credit column of the trial balance.

Step 3: Total the Debit and Credit columns of the trial balance.

Step 4: Verify that the total of the Debit column equals the total of the Credit column.

The trial balance for NetSolutions as of December 31, 2009, is shown in Exhibit 6. The account balances in Exhibit 6 are taken from the ledger shown in Exhibit 5. Before a trial balance is prepared, each account balance in the ledger must be determined. When the standard account form is used as in Exhibit 5, the balance of each account appears in the balance column on the same line as the last posting to the account.

Exhibit 5

Ledger NetSolutions

Ledger

Account *Cash*   Account No. 11

Date	Item	Post. Ref.	Debit	Credit	Balance Debit	Balance Credit
2009						
Nov. 1		1	25,000		25,000	
5		1		20,000	5,000	
18		1	7,500		12,500	
30		1		3,650	8,850	
30		1		950	7,900	
30		2		2,000	5,900	
Dec. 1		2		2,400	3,500	
1		2		800	2,700	
1		2	360		3,060	
6		2		180	2,880	
11		2		400	2,480	
13		3		950	1,530	
16		3	3,100		4,630	
20		3		900	3,730	
21		3	650		4,380	
23		3		1,450	2,930	
27		3		1,200	1,730	
31		3		310	1,420	
31		4		225	1,195	
31		4	2,870		4,065	
31		4		2,000	2,065	

Account *Accounts Receivable*   Account No. 12

Date	Item	Post. Ref.	Debit	Credit	Balance Debit	Balance Credit
2009						
Dec. 16		3	1,750		1,750	
21		3		650	1,100	
31		4	1,120		2,220	

Account *Supplies*   Account No. 14

Date	Item	Post. Ref.	Debit	Credit	Balance Debit	Balance Credit
2009						
Nov. 10		1	1,350		1,350	
30		1		800	550	
Dec. 23		3	1,450		2,000	

Account *Prepaid Insurance*   Account No. 15

Date	Item	Post. Ref.	Debit	Credit	Balance Debit	Balance Credit
2009						
Dec. 1		2	2,400		2,400	

Account *Land*   Account No. 17

Date	Item	Post. Ref.	Debit	Credit	Balance Debit	Balance Credit
2009						
Nov. 5		1	20,000		20,000	

Account *Office Equipment*   Account No. 18

Date	Item	Post. Ref.	Debit	Credit	Balance Debit	Balance Credit
2009						
Dec. 4		2	1,800		1,800	

Account *Accounts Payable*   Account No. 21

Date	Item	Post. Ref.	Debit	Credit	Balance Debit	Balance Credit
2009						
Nov. 10		1		1,350		1,350
30		1	950			400
Dec. 4		2		1,800		2,200
11		2	400			1,800
20		3	900			900

Account *Unearned Rent*   Account No. 23

Date	Item	Post. Ref.	Debit	Credit	Balance Debit	Balance Credit
2009						
Dec. 1		2		360		360

Account *Chris Clark, Capital*   Account No. 31

Date	Item	Post. Ref.	Debit	Credit	Balance Debit	Balance Credit
2009						
Nov. 1		1		25,000		25,000

Account *Chris Clark, Drawing*   Account No. 32

Date	Item	Post. Ref.	Debit	Credit	Balance Debit	Balance Credit
2009						
Nov. 30		2	2,000		2,000	
Dec. 31		4	2,000		4,000	

Account *Fees Earned*   Account No. 41

Date	Item	Post. Ref.	Debit	Credit	Balance Debit	Balance Credit
2009						
Nov. 18		1		7,500		7,500
Dec. 16		3		3,100		10,600
16		3		1,750		12,350
31		4		2,870		15,220
31		4		1,120		16,340

Account *Wages Expense*   Account No. 51

Date	Item	Post. Ref.	Debit	Credit	Balance Debit	Balance Credit
2009						
Nov. 30		1	2,125		2,125	
Dec. 13		3	950		3,075	
27		3	1,200		4,275	

(continued)

Exhibit 5

Account	Rent Expense					Account No. 52	
		Post.			Balance		
Date	Item	Ref.	Debit	Credit	Debit	Credit	
2009							
Nov. 30		1	800		800		
Dec. 1		2	800		1,600		

Account	Supplies Expense					Account No. 55	
		Post.			Balance		
Date	Item	Ref.	Debit	Credit	Debit	Credit	
2009							
Nov. 30		1	800		800		

Account	Utilities Expense					Account No. 54	
		Post.			Balance		
Date	Item	Ref.	Debit	Credit	Debit	Credit	
2009							
Nov. 30		1	450		450		
Dec. 31		3	310		760		
31		4	225		985		

Account	Miscellaneous Expense					Account No. 59	
		Post.			Balance		
Date	Item	Ref.	Debit	Credit	Debit	Credit	
2009							
Nov. 30		1	275		275		
Dec. 6		2	180		455		

The trial balance shown in Exhibit 6 is titled an **unadjusted trial balance**. This is to distinguish it from other trial balances that we will be preparing in later chapters. These other trial balances include an adjusted trial balance and a post-closing trial balance.[3]

Exhibit 6

Trial Balance

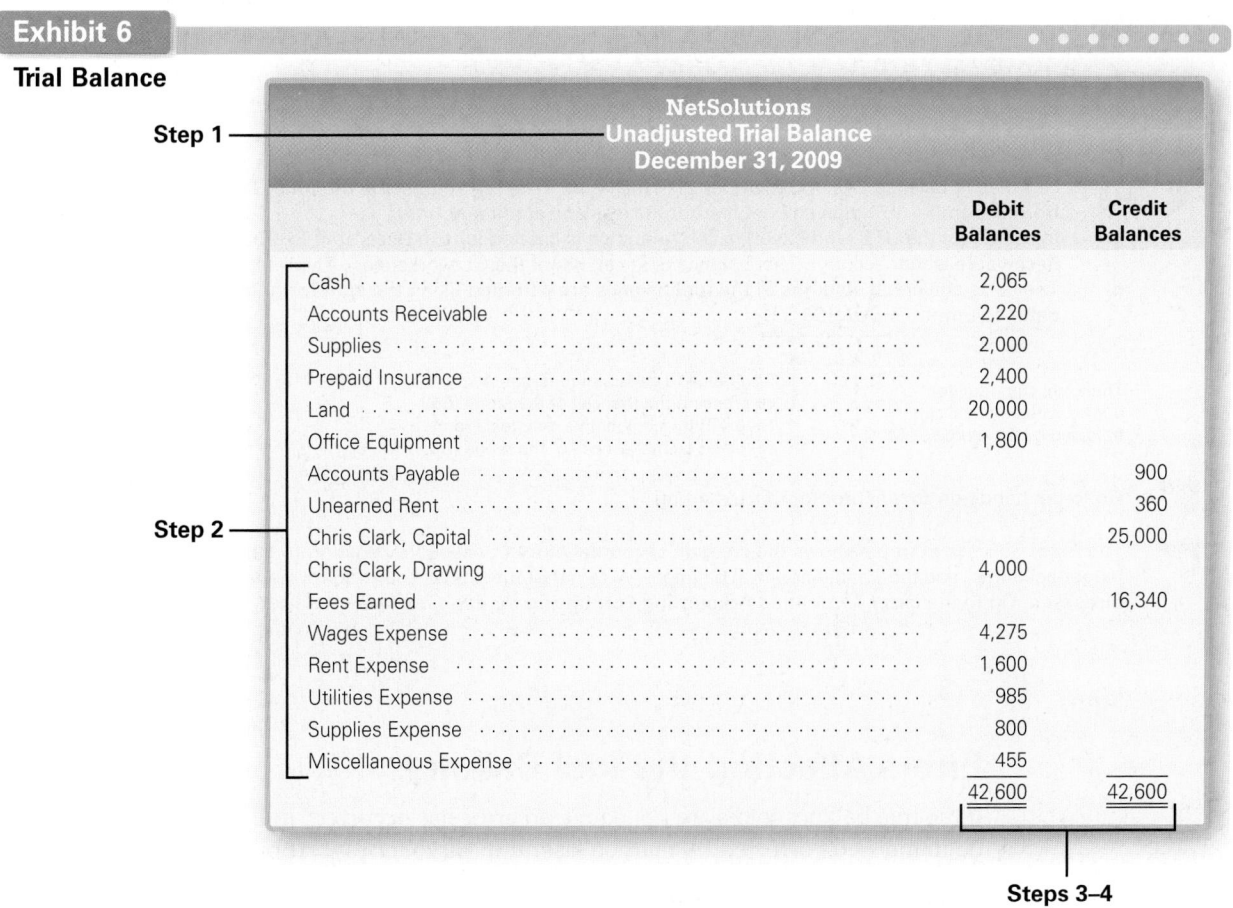

NetSolutions
Unadjusted Trial Balance
December 31, 2009

	Debit Balances	Credit Balances
Cash	2,065	
Accounts Receivable	2,220	
Supplies	2,000	
Prepaid Insurance	2,400	
Land	20,000	
Office Equipment	1,800	
Accounts Payable		900
Unearned Rent		360
Chris Clark, Capital		25,000
Chris Clark, Drawing	4,000	
Fees Earned		16,340
Wages Expense	4,275	
Rent Expense	1,600	
Utilities Expense	985	
Supplies Expense	800	
Miscellaneous Expense	455	
	42,600	42,600

Step 1 / Step 2 / Steps 3–4

3 The adjusted trial balance is discussed in Chapter 3, and the post-closing trial balance is discussed in Chapter 4.

The unadjusted trial balance can be created on a spreadsheet. The unadjusted trial balance references the ledger account balances. To illustrate, the relationship between the Accounts Receivable account and unadjusted trial balance is as follows:

	A	B	C	D	E	F	G
1							
2	**Account**	*Accounts Receivable*				**Account No.**	*15*
3						**Balance**	
4	**Date**	**Item**	**Post. Ref.**	**Debit**	**Credit**	**Debit**	**Credit**
5	2009						
6	16-Dec		3	1,750		=F5+D6-E6	
7	21-Dec		3		650	=F6+D7-E7	} b.
8	31-Dec		4	1,120		=F7+D8-E8	
9							

	A	B	C	D
1		NetSolutions		
2		Unadjusted Trial Balance		
3		31-Dec-09		
4		Debit	Credit	
5		Balances	Balances	
6	Cash	2,065		
7	Accounts Receivable	=GL!F8		c.
20	Supplies Expense	2,000		
21	Miscellaneous Expense	455		
22		=SUM(B6:B21)	=SUM(C6:C21)	d.
23				
24				
25				
26				
27				
28				
29				
30				

a. ⟶

‖ ◀ ▶ ‖ \ JE / GL / **UTB** /   ◀

a.   Label the third worksheet "UTB" for unadjusted trial balance.

b.   Previously, a formula that computes the account balance was created. This formula is copied down to create a cumulative balance. As of December 21st, the value in cell F7 represents the total. This total computes the total from December 16th plus any debit amounts less any credit amounts.

c.   In cell B7 (of the UTB worksheet), a cell reference is created for the December 31st balance in the Accounts Receivable ledger account. This balance is in cell F8 (of the GL worksheet). The reference is =GL!F8.

d.   The debit and credit columns of the trial balance are summed using the sum formula. The sum formula for the **debit** column is   =SUM(B6:B21)

The Excel sum function, begins with an equal sign "=" followed by the word "SUM"

The range to be summed is created by referencing the first cell of the range (B6) followed by a colon (this denotes a range) followed by the last cell of the range (B21).

 Go to the hands-on *Excel Tutor* for this example!

 The Excel Success example shows the creation of journal entry transactions, posting to general ledger accounts, and the unadjusted trial balance. Within that tutorial, accounting formatting is discussed. Go to the *Excel Tutor* titled **Accounting Formatting** for additional information!

Errors Affecting the Trial Balance

If the trial balance totals are not equal, an error has occurred. In this case, the error must be found and corrected. A method useful in discovering errors is as follows:

1. If the difference between the Debit and Credit column totals is 10, 100, or 1,000, an error in addition may have occurred. In this case, re-add the trial balance column totals. If the error still exists, recompute the account balances.

2. If the difference between the Debit and Credit column totals can be evenly divisible by 2, the error may be due to the entering of a debit balance as a credit balance, or vice versa. In this case, review the trial balance for account balances of one-half the difference that may have been entered in the wrong column. For example, if the Debit column total is $20,640 and the Credit column total is $20,236, the difference of $404 ($20,640 − $20,236) may be due to a credit account balance of $202 that was entered as a debit account balance.

3. If the difference between the Debit and Credit column totals is evenly divisible by 9, trace the account balances back to the ledger to see if an account balance was incorrectly copied from the ledger. Two common types of copying errors are transpositions and slides. A **transposition** occurs when the order of the digits is copied incorrectly, such as writing $542 as $452 or $524. In a **slide**, the entire number is copied incorrectly one or more spaces to the right or the left, such as writing $542.00 as $54.20 or $5,420.00. In both cases, the resulting error will be evenly divisible by 9.

4. If the difference between the Debit and Credit column totals is not evenly divisible by 2 or 9, review the ledger to see if an account balance in the amount of the error has been omitted from the trial balance. If the error is not discovered, review the journal postings to see if a posting of a debit or credit may have been omitted.

5. If an error is not discovered by the preceding steps, the accounting process must be retraced, beginning with the last journal entry.

The trial balance does not provide complete proof of the accuracy of the ledger. It indicates only that the debits and the credits are equal. This proof is of value, however, because errors often affect the equality of debits and credits.

Example Exercise 2-6   Trial Balance Errors   4

For each of the following errors, considered individually, indicate whether the error would cause the trial balance totals to be unequal. If the error would cause the trial balance totals to be unequal, indicate whether the debit or credit total is higher and by how much.

a. Payment of a cash withdrawal of $5,600 was journalized and posted as a debit of $6,500 to Salary Expense and a credit of $6,500 to Cash.

b. A fee of $2,850 earned from a client was debited to Accounts Receivable for $2,580 and credited to Fees Earned for $2,850.

c. A payment of $3,500 to a creditor was posted as a debit of $3,500 to Accounts Payable and a debit of $3,500 to Cash.

Follow My Example 2-6

a. The totals are equal since both the debit and credit entries were journalized and posted for $6,500..

b. The totals are unequal. The credit total is higher by $270 ($2,850 − $2,580).

c. The totals are unequal. The debit total is higher by $7,000 ($3,500 + $3,500).

For Practice: PE 2-6A, PE 2-6B

Errors Not Affecting the Trial Balance

An error may occur that does not cause the trial balance totals to be unequal. Such an error may be discovered when preparing the trial balance or may be indicated by an unusual account balance. For example, a credit balance in the supplies account indicates an error has occurred. This is because a business cannot have "negative" supplies.

When such errors are discovered, they should be corrected. If the error has already been journalized and posted to the ledger, a **correcting journal entry** is normally prepared.

To illustrate, assume that on May 5 a $12,500 purchase of office equipment on account was incorrectly journalized and posted as a debit to Supplies and a credit to Accounts Payable for $12,500. This posting of the incorrect entry is shown in the following T accounts:

Incorrect:

Supplies		Accounts Payable	
12,500			12,500

Before making a correcting journal entry, it is best to determine the debit(s) and credit(s) that should have been recorded. These are shown in the following T accounts:

Correct:

Office Equipment		Accounts Payable	
12,500			12,500

Comparing the two sets of T accounts shows that the incorrect debit to Supplies may be corrected by debiting Office Equipment for $12,500 and crediting Supplies for $12,500. The following correcting journal entry is then journalized and posted:

Entry to Correct Error:

May	31	Office Equipment	18	12,500	
		Supplies	14		12,500
		To correct erroneous debit			
		to Supplies on May 5. See invoice			
		from Bell Office Equipment Co.			

Example Exercise 2-7   Correcting Entries 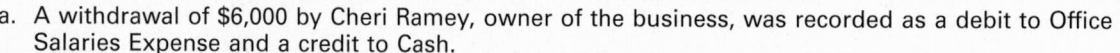 4

The following errors took place in journalizing and posting transactions:

a. A withdrawal of $6,000 by Cheri Ramey, owner of the business, was recorded as a debit to Office Salaries Expense and a credit to Cash.

b. Utilities Expense of $4,500 paid for the current month was recorded as a debit to Miscellaneous Expense and a credit to Accounts Payable.

Journalize the entries to correct the errors. Omit explanations.

Follow My Example 2-7

a.	Cheri Ramey, Drawing	. . . .	6,000	
	Office Salaries Expense	. . . .		6,000
b.	Accounts Payable	. . . .	4,500	
	Miscellaneous Expense	. . . .		4,500
	Utilities Expense	. . . .	4,500	
	Cash	. . . .		4,500

Note: The first entry in (b) reverses the incorrect entry, and the second entry records the correct entry. These two entries could also be combined into one entry; however, preparing two entries will make it easier for someone later to tunderstand what had happened and why the entries were necessary.

For Practice: PE 2-7A, PE 2-7B

Financial Analysis and Interpretation

A single item appearing in a financial statement is often useful in interpreting the financial results of a business. However, comparing this item in a current statement with the same item in prior statements often makes the financial information more useful. **Horizontal analysis** is the term used to describe such comparisons.

In horizontal analysis, the amount of each item on the current financial statements is compared with the same item on one or more earlier statements. The increase or decrease in the *amount* of the item is computed, together with the *percent* of increase or decrease. When two statements are being compared, the earlier statement is used as the base for computing the amount and the percent of change.

To illustrate, the horizontal analysis of two income statements for J. Holmes, Attorney-at-Law, is shown. The horizontal analysis indicates both favorable and unfavorable trends affecting the income statement of J. Holmes, Attorney-at-Law. The increase in fees earned is a favorable trend, as is the decrease in supplies expense. Unfavorable trends include the increase in wages expense, utilities expense, and miscellaneous expense. These expenses increased the same as or faster than the increase in revenues, with total operating expenses increasing by 30.6%. Overall, net income increased by $15,800, or 19.9%, a favorable trend.

The significance of the various increases and decreases in the revenue and expense items should be investigated to see if operations could be further improved. For example, the increase in utilities expense of 38.9% was the result of renting additional office space for use by a part-time law student in performing paralegal services. This explains the increase in rent expense of 25% and the increase in wages expense of 33.3%. The increase in revenues of 25% reflects the fees generated by the new paralegal.

The preceding example illustrates how horizontal analysis can be useful in interpreting and analyzing financial statements. Horizontal analyses similar to that shown can also be performed for the balance sheet, the statement of owner's equity, and the statement of cash flows.

J. Holmes, Attorney-at-Law
Income Statement
For the Years Ended December 31, 2010 and 2009

	2010	2009	Increase (Decrease) Amount	Increase (Decrease) Percent
Fees earned	$187,500	$150,000	$37,500	25.0%*
Operating expenses:				
Wages expense	$ 60,000	$ 45,000	$15,000	33.3
Rent expense	15,000	12,000	3,000	25.0
Utilities expense	12,500	9,000	3,500	38.9
Supplies expense	2,700	3,000	(300)	(10.0)
Miscellaneous expense	2,300	1,800	500	27.8
Total operating expenses	$ 92,500	$ 70,800	$21,700	30.6
Net income	$ 95,000	$ 79,200	$15,800	19.9

*$37,500 ÷ $150,000

1 Describe the characteristics of an account and a chart of accounts.

Key Points	Key Learning Outcomes	Example Exercises	Practice Exercises
The record used for recording individual transactions is an account. A group of accounts is called a ledger. The simplest form of an account, a T account, has three parts: (1) a title, which is the name of the item recorded in the account; (2) a left side, called the debit side; and (3) a right side, called the credit side. Amounts entered on the left side of an account, regardless of the account title, are called debits to the account. Amounts entered on the right side of an account are called credits. Periodically, the debits in an account are added, the credits in the account are added, and the balance of the account is determined. The system of accounts that make up a ledger is called a chart of accounts.	• Record transactions in T accounts. • Determine the balance of a T account. • Prepare a chart of accounts for a proprietorship.		

2 Describe and illustrate journalizing transactions using the double-entry accounting system.

Key Points	Key Learning Outcomes	Example Exercises	Practice Exercises
The double-entry accounting system is designed so that the sum of the debits always equals the sum of the credits for each journal entry. Transactions are initially entered in a record called a journal. The rules of debit and credit for recording increases or decreases in asset, liability, owner's equity, revenue, expense, and drawing accounts are shown in Exhibit 3. Each transaction is recorded so that the sum of the debits is always equal to the sum of the credits. The normal balance of an account is indicated by the side of the account (debit or credit) that receives the increases.	• Indicate the normal balance of an account. • Journalize transactions using the rules of debit and credit.	2-1 2-2	2-1A, 2-1B 2-2A, 2-2B

3 Describe and illustrate the journalizing and posting of transactions to accounts.

Key Points	Key Learning Outcomes	Example Exercises	Practice Exercises
Transactions are journalized and posted to the ledger using the rules of debit and credit. The debits and credits for each journal entry are posted to the accounts in the order in which they occur in the journal. In posting to the standard account, (1) the date is entered, and (2) the amount of the entry is entered. For future reference, (3) the journal page number is inserted in the Posting Reference column of the account, and (4) the account number is inserted in the Posting Reference column of the journal.	• Journalize transactions using the rules of debit and credit. • Determine whether an account has only debit entries, only credit entries, or both. • Determine the normal balance of an account. • Determine the missing amount from an account given its balance. • Post journal entries to a standard account. • Post journal entries to a T account.	2-3 2-4 2-5	2-3A, 2-3B 2-4A, 2-4B 2-5A, 2-5B

Prepare an unadjusted trial balance and explain how it can be used to discover errors.

		Example Exercises	Practice Exercises
Key Points	**Key Learning Outcomes**		

A trial balance is prepared by listing the accounts from the ledger and their balances. The totals of the Debit column and Credit column of the trial balance must be equal. If the two totals are not equal, an error has occurred. Errors may occur even though the trial balance totals are equal. Such errors may require a correcting journal entry.

- Prepare an unadjusted trial balance.
- Discover errors that cause unequal totals in the trial balance. **2-6** 2-6A, 2-6B
- Prepare correcting journal entries for various errors. **2-7** 2-7A, 2-7B

Key Terms

account (46)
account receivable (59)
assets (48)
balance of the account (47)
capital account (48)
chart of accounts (48)
correcting journal entry (68)
credit (47)
debit (47)
double-entry accounting
  system (49)

drawing (48)
expenses (48)
horizontal analysis (69)
journal (50)
journal entry (51)
journalizing (51)
ledger (48)
liabilities (48)
normal balance of an
  account (50)
owner's equity (48)

posting (55)
revenues (48)
rules of debit and credit (49)
slide (67)
T account (46)
transposition (67)
trial balance (63)
unadjusted trial balance (65)
unearned revenue (57)

Illustrative Problem

J. F. Outz, M.D., has been practicing as a cardiologist for three years. During April 2009, Outz completed the following transactions in her practice of cardiology:

Apr. 1. Paid office rent for April, $800.
  3. Purchased equipment on account, $2,100.
  5. Received cash on account from patients, $3,150.
  8. Purchased X-ray film and other supplies on account, $245.
  9. One of the items of equipment purchased on April 3 was defective. It was returned with the permission of the supplier, who agreed to reduce the account for the amount charged for the item, $325.
  12. Paid cash to creditors on account, $1,250.
  17. Paid cash for renewal of a six-month property insurance policy, $370.
  20. Discovered that the balances of the cash account and the accounts payable account as of April 1 were overstated by $200. A payment of that amount to a creditor in March had not been recorded. Journalize the $200 payment as of April 20.

Apr. 24.   Paid cash for laboratory analysis, $545.
27.   Paid cash from business bank account for personal and family expenses, $1,250.
30.   Recorded the cash received in payment of services (on a cash basis) to patients during April, $1,720.
30.   Paid salaries of receptionist and nurses, $1,725.
30.   Paid various utility expenses, $360.
30.   Recorded fees charged to patients on account for services performed in April, $5,145.
30.   Paid miscellaneous expenses, $132.

Outz's account titles, numbers, and balances as of April 1 (all normal balances) are listed as follows: Cash, 11, $4,123; Accounts Receivable, 12, $6,725; Supplies, 13, $290; Prepaid Insurance, 14, $465; Equipment, 18, $19,745; Accounts Payable, 22, $765; J. F. Outz, Capital, 31, $30,583; J. F. Outz, Drawing, 32; Professional Fees, 41; Salary Expense, 51; Rent Expense, 53; Laboratory Expense, 55; Utilities Expense, 56; Miscellaneous Expense, 59.

Instructions

1. Open a ledger of standard four-column accounts for Dr. Outz as of April 1. Enter the balances in the appropriate balance columns and place a check mark (✔) in the Posting Reference column. (*Hint:* Verify the equality of the debit and credit balances in the ledger before proceeding with the next instruction.)
2. Journalize each transaction in a two-column journal.
3. Post the journal to the ledger, extending the month-end balances to the appropriate balance columns after each posting.
4. Prepare an unadjusted trial balance as of April 30.

Solution 1., 2., and 3.

Journal					Page *27*

Date	Description	Post. Ref.	Debit	Credit
2009 Apr. 1	Rent Expense	53	800	
	Cash	11		800
	Paid office rent for April.			
3	Equipment	18	2,100	
	Accounts Payable	22		2,100
	Purchased equipment on account.			
5	Cash	11	3,150	
	Accounts Receivable	12		3,150
	Received cash on account.			
8	Supplies	13	245	
	Accounts Payable	22		245
	Purchased supplies.			
9	Accounts Payable	22	325	
	Equipment	18		325
	Returned defective equipment.			
12	Accounts Payable	22	1,250	
	Cash	11		1,250
	Paid creditors on account.			
17	Prepaid Insurance	14	370	
	Cash	11		370
	Renewed six-month property policy.			
20	Accounts Payable	22	200	
	Cash	11		200
	Recorded March payment to creditor.			

Journal					Page *28*

Date	Description	Post. Ref.	Debit	Credit
2009 Apr. 24	Laboratory Expense	55	545	
	Cash	11		545
	Paid for laboratory analysis.			
27	J. F. Outz, Drawing	32	1,250	
	Cash	11		1,250
	J. F. Outz withdrew cash for personal use.			
30	Cash	11	1,720	
	Professional Fees	41		1,720
	Received fees from patients.			
30	Salary Expense	51	1,725	
	Cash	11		1,725
	Paid salaries.			
30	Utilities Expense	56	360	
	Cash	11		360
	Paid utilities.			
30	Accounts Receivable	12	5,145	
	Professional Fees	41		5,145
	Recorded fees earned on account.			
30	Miscellaneous Expense	59	132	
	Cash	11		132
	Paid expenses.			

Account *Cash* Account No. *11*

Date	Item	Post. Ref.	Debit	Credit	Balance Debit	Balance Credit
2009 Apr. 1	Balance	✓			4,123	
1		27		800	3,323	
5		27	3,150		6,473	
12		27		1,250	5,223	
17		27		370	4,853	
20		27		200	4,653	
24		28		545	4,108	
27		28		1,250	2,858	
30		28	1,720		4,578	
30		28		1,725	2,853	
30		28		360	2,493	
30		28		132	2,361	

Account *Accounts Receivable* Account No. *12*

Date	Item	Post. Ref.	Debit	Credit	Balance Debit	Balance Credit
2009 Apr. 1	Balance	✓			6,725	
5		27		3,150	3,575	
30		28	5,145		8,720	

Account *Supplies* Account No. *13*

Date	Item	Post. Ref.	Debit	Credit	Balance Debit	Balance Credit
2009 Apr. 1	Balance	✓			290	
8		27	245		535	

Account *Prepaid Insurance*   Account No. *14*

Date	Item	Post. Ref.	Debit	Credit	Balance Debit	Balance Credit
2009 Apr. 1	Balance	✓			465	
17		27	370		835	

Account *Equipment*   Account No. *18*

Date	Item	Post. Ref.	Debit	Credit	Balance Debit	Balance Credit
2009 Apr. 1	Balance	✓			19,745	
3		27	2,100		21,845	
9		27		325	21,520	

Account *Accounts Payable*   Account No. *22*

Date	Item	Post. Ref.	Debit	Credit	Balance Debit	Balance Credit
2009 Apr. 1	Balance	✓				7,65
3		27		2,100		2,865
8		27		245		3,110
9		27	325			2,785
12		27	1,250			1,535
20		27	200			1,335

Account *J. F. Outz, Capital*   Account No. *31*

Date	Item	Post. Ref.	Debit	Credit	Balance Debit	Balance Credit
2009 Apr. 1	Balance	✓				30,583

Account *J. F. Outz, Drawing*   Account No. *32*

Date	Item	Post. Ref.	Debit	Credit	Balance Debit	Balance Credit
2009 Apr. 27		28	1,250		1,250	

Account *Professional Fees*   Account No. *41*

Date	Item	Post. Ref.	Debit	Credit	Balance Debit	Balance Credit
2009 Apr. 30		28		1,720		1,720
30		28		5,145		6,865

Account *Salary Expense*   Account No. *51*

Date	Item	Post. Ref.	Debit	Credit	Balance Debit	Balance Credit
2009 Apr. 30		28	1,725		1,725	

Account *Rent Expense*   Account No. *53*

Date	Item	Post. Ref.	Debit	Credit	Balance Debit	Balance Credit
2009 Apr. 1		27	800		800	

Account *Laboratory Expense*   Account No. *55*

Date	Item	Post. Ref.	Debit	Credit	Balance Debit	Balance Credit
2009 Apr. 24		28	545		545	

Account *Utilities Expense*   Account No. *56*

Date	Item	Post. Ref.	Debit	Credit	Balance Debit	Balance Credit
2009 Apr. 30		28	360		360	

Account *Miscellaneous Expense*   Account No. *59*

Date	Item	Post. Ref.	Debit	Credit	Balance Debit	Balance Credit
2009 Apr. 30		28	132		132	

4.

J. F. Outz, M.D. Unadjusted Trial Balance April 30, 2009	Debit Balances	Credit Balances
Cash	2,361	
Accounts Receivable	8,720	
Supplies	535	
Prepaid Insurance	835	
Equipment	21,520	
Accounts Payable		1,335
J. F. Outz, Capital		30,583
J. F. Outz, Drawing	1,250	
Professional Fees		6,865
Salary Expense	1,725	
Rent Expense	800	
Laboratory Expense	545	
Utilities Expense	360	
Miscellaneous Expense	132	
	38,783	38,783

Self-Examination Questions (Answers at End of Chapter)

1. A debit may signify a(n):
   A. increase in an asset account.
   B. decrease in an asset account.
   C. increase in a liability account.
   D. increase in the owner's capital account.

2. The type of account with a normal credit balance is:
   A. an asset.   C. a revenue.
   B. drawing.   D. an expense.

3. A debit balance in which of the following accounts would indicate a likely error?
   A. Accounts Receivable
   B. Cash
   C. Fees Earned
   D. Miscellaneous Expense

4. The receipt of cash from customers in payment of their accounts would be recorded by:
   A. a debit to Cash and a credit to Accounts Receivable.
   B. a debit to Accounts Receivable and a credit to Cash.
   C. a debit to Cash and a credit to Accounts Payable.
   D. a debit to Accounts Payable and a credit to Cash.

5. The form listing the titles and balances of the accounts in the ledger on a given date is the:
   A. income statement.
   B. balance sheet.
   C. statement of owner's equity.
   D. trial balance.

Eye Openers

1. What is the difference between an account and a ledger?
2. Do the terms *debit* and *credit* signify increase or decrease, or can they signify either? Explain.

3. Explain why the rules of debit and credit are the same for liability accounts and owner's equity accounts.
4. What is the effect (increase or decrease) of a debit to an expense account (a) in terms of owner's equity and (b) in terms of expense?
5. What is the effect (increase or decrease) of a credit to a revenue account (a) in terms of owner's equity and (b) in terms of revenue?
6. Carr Company adheres to a policy of depositing all cash receipts in a bank account and making all payments by check. The cash account as of March 31 has a credit balance of $1,250, and there is no undeposited cash on hand. (a) Assuming no errors occurred during journalizing or posting, what caused this unusual balance? (b) Is the $1,250 credit balance in the cash account an asset, a liability, owner's equity, a revenue, or an expense?
7. Longfellow Company performed services in July for a specific customer, for a fee of $8,380. Payment was received the following August. (a) Was the revenue earned in July or August? (b) What accounts should be debited and credited in (1) July and (2) August?
8. What proof is provided by a trial balance?
9. If the two totals of a trial balance are equal, does it mean that there are no errors in the accounting records? Explain.
10. Assume that a trial balance is prepared with an account balance of $18,500 listed as $1,850 and an account balance of $3,680 listed as $3,860. Identify the transposition and the slide.
11. Assume that when a purchase of supplies of $2,650 for cash was recorded, both the debit and the credit were journalized and posted as $2,560. (a) Would this error cause the trial balance to be out of balance? (b) Would the trial balance be out of balance if the $2,650 entry had been journalized correctly but the credit to Cash had been posted as $2,560?
12. Assume that JRQ Consulting erroneously recorded the payment of $10,000 of owner withdrawals as a debit to Salary Expense. (a) How would this error affect the equality of the trial balance? (b) How would this error affect the income statement, statement of owner's equity, and balance sheet?
13. Assume that Beebe Realty Co. borrowed $120,000 from City Bank and Trust. In recording the transaction, Beebe erroneously recorded the receipt as a debit to Cash, $120,000, and a credit to Fees Earned, $120,000. (a) How would this error affect the equality of the trial balance? (b) How would this error affect the income statement, statement of owner's equity, and balance sheet?
14. In journalizing and posting the entry to record the purchase of supplies for cash, the accounts payable account was credited in error. What is the preferred procedure to correct this error?
15. Checking accounts are the most common form of deposits for banks. Assume that Yellowstone Storage has a checking account at Livingston Savings Bank. What type of account (asset, liability, owner's equity, revenue, expense, drawing) does the account balance of $12,100 represent from the viewpoint of (a) Yellowstone Storage and (b) Livingston Savings Bank?

Practice Exercises

PE 2-1A
Rules of debit and credit and normal balances

obj. 2

EE 2-1   p. 51

State for each account whether it is likely to have (a) debit entries only, (b) credit entries only, or (c) both debit and credit entries. Also, indicate its normal balance.

1. Accounts Payable
2. Cash
3. Dorothy Holt, Drawing
4. Miscellaneous Expense
5. Prepaid Insurance
6. Rent Revenue

PE 2-1B
Rules of debit and credit and normal balances

obj. 2

EE 2-1   p. 51

State for each account whether it is likely to have (a) debit entries only, (b) credit entries only, or (c) both debit and credit entries. Also, indicate its normal balance.

1. Accounts Receivable
2. Commissions Earned
3. Notes Payable
4. Susan Wilks, Capital
5. Unearned Rent
6. Wages Expense

PE 2-2A
Journal entry for asset purchase

obj. 2

EE 2-2   p. 54

Prepare a journal entry for the purchase of office supplies on October 14 for $9,000, paying $1,800 cash and the remainder on account.

PE 2-2B
Journal entry for asset purchase

obj. 2

EE 2-2   p. 54

Prepare a journal entry for the purchase of office equipment on February 3 for $18,250, paying $3,650 cash and the remainder on account.

PE 2-3A
Journal entry for fees earned

obj. 3

EE 2-3   p. 59

Prepare a journal entry on April 2 for cash received for services rendered, $3,600.

PE 2-3B
Journal entry for fees earned

obj. 3

EE 2-3   p. 59

Prepare a journal entry on November 29 for fees earned on account, $11,375.

PE 2-4A
Journal entry for owner's withdrawal

obj. 3

EE 2-4   p. 63

Prepare a journal entry on January 19 for the withdrawal of $8,500 by Carla Hammond for personal use.

PE 2-4B
Journal entry for owner's withdrawal

obj. 3

EE 2-4   p. 63

Prepare a journal entry on December 23 for the withdrawal of $6,000 by Matt Nehls for personal use.

PE 2-5A
Missing amount
from an account

obj. 3

EE 2-5   p. 63

On July 1, the supplies account balance was $1,950. During July, supplies of $6,750 were purchased, and $1,851 of supplies were on hand as of July 31. Determine supplies expense for July.

PE 2-5B
Missing amount
from an account

obj. 3

EE 2-5   p. 63

On October 1, the cash account balance was $23,600. During October, cash payments totaled $315,700, and the October 31 balance was $36,900. Determine the cash receipts during October.

PE 2-6A
Trial balance errors

obj. 4

EE 2-6   p. 67

For each of the following errors, considered individually, indicate whether the error would cause the trial balance totals to be unequal. If the error would cause the trial balance totals to be unequal, indicate whether the debit or credit total is higher and by how much.

a. The payment of cash for the purchase of office equipment of $8,000 was debited to Land for $8,000 and credited to Cash for $8,000.
b. The payment of $6,750 on account was debited to Accounts Payable for $675 and credited to Cash for $6,750.
c. The receipt of cash on account of $4,150 was recorded as a debit to Cash for $4,510 and a credit to Accounts Receivable for $4,150.

PE 2-6B
Trial balance errors

obj. 4

EE 2-6   p. 67

For each of the following errors, considered individually, indicate whether the error would cause the trial balance totals to be unequal. If the error would cause the trial balance totals to be unequal, indicate whether the debit or credit total is higher and by how much.

a. The payment of an insurance premium of $3,600 for a two-year policy was debited to Prepaid Insurance for $3,600 and credited to Cash for $6,300.
b. A payment of $725 on account was debited to Accounts Payable for $752 and credited to Cash for $752.
c. A purchase of supplies of $900 was debited to Supplies for $900 and debited to Accounts Payable for $900.

PE 2-7A
Correcting entries

obj. 4

EE 2-7   p. 68

The following errors took place in journalizing and posting transactions:
a. The receipt of $6,480 for services rendered was recorded as a debit to Accounts Receivable and a credit to Fees Earned.
b. The purchase of supplies of $1,960 on account was recorded as a debit to Office Equipment and a credit to Supplies.

Journalize the entries to correct the errors. Omit explanations.

PE 2-7B
Correcting entries

obj. 4

EE 2-7   p. 68

The following errors took place in journalizing and posting transactions:
a. Advertising expense of $950 paid for the current month was recorded as a debit to Miscellaneous Expense and a credit to Advertising Expense.
b. The payment of $1,500 from a customer on account was recorded as a debit to Cash and a credit to Accounts Payable.

Journalize the entries to correct the errors. Omit explanations.

Exercises

EX 2-1
Chart of accounts
obj. 1

The following accounts appeared in recent financial statements of Continental Airlines:

Accounts Payable   Flight Equipment
Air Traffic Liability   Landing Fees
Aircraft Fuel Expense   Passenger Revenue
Cargo and Mail Revenue   Purchase Deposits for Flight Equipment
Commissions   Spare Parts and Supplies

Identify each account as either a balance sheet account or an income statement account. For each balance sheet account, identify it as an asset, a liability, or owner's equity. For each income statement account, identify it as a revenue or an expense.

EX 2-2
Chart of accounts
obj. 1

Humvee Interiors is owned and operated by Tony Newbaurer, an interior decorator. In the ledger of Humvee Interiors, the first digit of the account number indicates its major account classification (1—assets, 2—liabilities, 3—owner's equity, 4—revenues, 5—expenses). The second digit of the account number indicates the specific account within each of the preceding major account classifications.

Match each account number with its most likely account in the list below. The account numbers are 11, 12, 13, 21, 31, 32, 41, 51, 52, and 53.

Accounts Payable   Miscellaneous Expense
Accounts Receivable   Supplies Expense
Cash   Tony Newbaurer, Capital
Fees Earned   Tony Newbaurer, Drawing
Land   Wages Expense

EX 2-3
Chart of accounts
obj. 1

Monet School is a newly organized business that teaches people how to inspire and influence others. The list of accounts to be opened in the general ledger is as follows:

Accounts Payable   Miscellaneous Expense
Accounts Receivable   Prepaid Insurance
Cash   Rent Expense
Equipment   Supplies
Fees Earned   Supplies Expense
Jamie Bjork, Capital   Unearned Rent
Jamie Bjork, Drawing   Wages Expense

List the accounts in the order in which they should appear in the ledger of Monet School and assign account numbers. Each account number is to have two digits: the first digit is to indicate the major classification (1 for assets, etc.), and the second digit is to identify the specific account within each major classification (11 for Cash, etc.).

EX 2-4
Identifying transactions
objs. 1, 2

Cycle Tours Co. is a travel agency. The nine transactions recorded by Cycle Tours during February 2010, its first month of operations, are indicated in the following T accounts:

Cash		Equipment		Anita Rayle, Drawing	
(1) 25,000	(2) 1,750	(3) 18,000		(9) 2,500	
(7) 10,000	(3) 3,600				
	(4) 2,700				
	(6) 7,500				
	(9) 2,500				

Accounts Receivable		Accounts Payable		Service Revenue	
(5) 13,500	(7) 10,000	(6) 7,500	(3) 14,400		(5) 13,500

Supplies		Anita Rayle, Capital		Operating Expenses	
(2) 1,750	(8) 1,050		(1) 25,000	(4) 2,700	
				(8) 1,050	

Indicate for each debit and each credit: (a) whether an asset, liability, owner's equity, drawing, revenue, or expense account was affected and (b) whether the account was increased (+) or decreased (−). Present your answers in the following form, with transaction (1) given as an example:

Transaction	Account Debited		Account Credited	
	Type	Effect	Type	Effect
(1)	asset	+	owner's equity	+

EX 2-5
Journal entries

objs. 1,2

Based upon the T accounts in Exercise 2-4, prepare the nine journal entries from which the postings were made. Journal entry explanations may be omitted.

EX 2-6
Trial balance

obj. 4

Based upon the data presented in Exercise 2-4, prepare an unadjusted trial balance, listing the accounts in their proper order.

✔ Total Debit column:
$45,400

EX 2-7
Normal entries for accounts

obj. 2

During the month, Genesis Labs Co. has a substantial number of transactions affecting each of the following accounts. State for each account whether it is likely to have (a) debit entries only, (b) credit entries only, or (c) both debit and credit entries.

1. Accounts Payable
2. Accounts Receivable
3. Cash
4. Fees Earned

5. Insurance Expense
6. Meg Abdel, Drawing
7. Supplies Expense

EX 2-8
Normal balances of accounts

objs. 1, 2

Identify each of the following accounts of Sesame Services Co. as asset, liability, owner's equity, revenue, or expense, and state in each case whether the normal balance is a debit or a credit.

a. Accounts Payable
b. Accounts Receivable
c. Billy Eldrod, Capital
d. Billy Eldrod, Drawing
e. Cash

f. Fees Earned
g. Office Equipment
h. Rent Expense
i. Supplies
j. Wages Expense

EX 2-9
Rules of debit and credit

objs. 1, 2

The following table summarizes the rules of debit and credit. For each of the items (a) through (l), indicate whether the proper answer is a debit or a credit.

	Increase	Decrease	Normal Balance
Balance sheet accounts:			
Asset	Debit	(a)	(b)
Liability	Credit	(c)	(d)
Owner's equity:			
Capital	(e)	Debit	(f)
Drawing	(g)	(h)	Debit
Income statement accounts:			
Revenue	(i)	(j)	(k)
Expense	(l)	Credit	Debit

EX 2-10
Capital account balance

objs. 1, 2

As of January 1, Oh Kwon, Capital, had a credit balance of $37,100. During the year, withdrawals totaled $1,000, and the business incurred a net loss of $52,300.

a. Calculate the balance of Oh Kwon, Capital, as of the end of the year.

b. Assuming that there have been no recording errors, will the balance sheet prepared at December 31 balance? Explain.

EX 2-11
Cash account
balance

objs. 1, 2, 3

During the month, Racoon Co. received $319,750 in cash and paid out $269,900 in cash.

a. Do the data indicate that Racoon Co. earned $49,850 during the month? Explain.
b. If the balance of the cash account is $72,350 at the end of the month, what was the cash balance at the beginning of the month?

EX 2-12
Account balances

objs. 1, 2, 3

✔ c. $284,175

a. During July, $90,300 was paid to creditors on account, and purchases on account were $115,150. Assuming the July 31 balance of Accounts Payable was $39,000, determine the account balance on July 1.
b. On May 1, the accounts receivable account balance was $36,200. During May, $315,000 was collected from customers on account. Assuming the May 31 balance was $41,600, determine the fees billed to customers on account during May.
c. On April 1, the cash account balance was $18,275. During April, cash receipts totaled $279,100 and the April 30 balance was $13,200. Determine the cash payments made during April.

EX 2-13
Transactions

obj. 2

Derby Co. has the following accounts in its ledger: Cash; Accounts Receivable; Supplies; Office Equipment; Accounts Payable; Terri Burell, Capital; Terri Burell, Drawing; Fees Earned; Rent Expense; Advertising Expense; Utilities Expense; Miscellaneous Expense.

Journalize the following selected transactions for March 2009 in a two-column journal. Journal entry explanations may be omitted.

Mar. 1. Paid rent for the month, $3,000.
       2. Paid advertising expense, $1,800.
       5. Paid cash for supplies, $900.
       6. Purchased office equipment on account, $12,300.
      10. Received cash from customers on account, $4,100.
      15. Paid creditor on account, $1,200.
      27. Paid cash for repairs to office equipment, $500.
      30. Paid telephone bill for the month, $180.
      31. Fees earned and billed to customers for the month, $26,800.
      31. Paid electricity bill for the month, $315.
      31. Withdrew cash for personal use, $2,000.

EX 2-14
Journalizing and
posting

objs. 2, 3

On August 7, 2010, Mainsail Co. purchased $2,190 of supplies on account. In Mainsail Co.'s chart of accounts, the supplies account is No. 15, and the accounts payable account is No. 21.

a. Journalize the August 7, 2010, transaction on page 19 of Mainsail Co.'s two-column journal. Include an explanation of the entry.
b. Prepare a four-column account for Supplies. Enter a debit balance of $1,050 as of August 1, 2010. Place a check mark (✔) in the Posting Reference column.
c. Prepare a four-column account for Accounts Payable. Enter a credit balance of $15,600 as of August 1, 2010. Place a check mark (✔) in the Posting Reference column.
d. Post the August 7, 2010, transaction to the accounts.

EX 2-15
Transactions and
T accounts

objs. 2, 3

The following selected transactions were completed during February of the current year:

1. Billed customers for fees earned, $41,730.
2. Purchased supplies on account, $1,800.
3. Received cash from customers on account, $39,150.
4. Paid creditors on account, $1,100.

a. Journalize the above transactions in a two-column journal, using the appropriate number to identify the transactions. Journal entry explanations may be omitted.

b. Post the entries prepared in (a) to the following T accounts: Cash, Supplies, Accounts Receivable, Accounts Payable, Fees Earned. To the left of each amount posted in the accounts, place the appropriate number to identify the transactions.

EX 2-16

Trial balance

obj. 4

✔ Total of Credit column: $696,350

The accounts in the ledger of Aznar Co. as of October 31, 2010, are listed in alphabetical order as follows. All accounts have normal balances. The balance of the cash account has been intentionally omitted.

Accounts Payable	$ 28,000	Notes Payable	$ 60,000
Accounts Receivable	56,250	Prepaid Insurance	4,500
Cash	?	Rent Expense	90,000
Ellen Kubota, Capital	129,850	Supplies	3,150
Ellen Kubota, Drawing	30,000	Supplies Expense	11,850
Fees Earned	465,000	Unearned Rent	13,500
Insurance Expense	9,000	Utilities Expense	62,250
Land	127,500	Wages Expense	262,500
Miscellaneous Expense	13,350		

Prepare an unadjusted trial balance, listing the accounts in their proper order and inserting the missing figure for cash.

EX 2-17

Effect of errors on trial balance

obj. 4

Indicate which of the following errors, each considered individually, would cause the trial balance totals to be unequal:

a. A payment of $2,150 to a creditor was posted as a debit of $2,150 to Accounts Payable and a debit of $2,150 to Cash.

b. A fee of $4,600 earned and due from a client was not debited to Accounts Receivable or credited to a revenue account, because the cash had not been received.

c. A receipt of $3,100 from an account receivable was journalized and posted as a debit of $3,100 to Cash and a credit of $3,100 to Fees Earned.

d. A payment of $10,000 for equipment purchased was posted as a debit of $1,000 to Equipment and a credit of $1,000 to Cash.

e. Payment of a cash withdrawal of $15,000 was journalized and posted as a debit of $5,000 to Salary Expense and a credit of $15,000 to Cash.

EX 2-18

Errors in trial balance

obj. 4

✔ Total of Credit column: $181,600

The following preliminary unadjusted trial balance of Nevada-For-You Co., a sports ticket agency, does not balance:

Nevada-For-You Co.
Unadjusted Trial Balance
December 31, 2010

	Debit Balances	Credit Balances
Cash	47,350	
Accounts Receivable	22,100	
Prepaid Insurance		8,000
Equipment	7,500	
Accounts Payable		12,980
Unearned Rent		2,900
Tammy Gazboda, Capital	82,420	
Tammy Gazboda, Drawing	10,000	
Service Revenue		83,750
Wages Expense		42,000
Advertising Expense	7,200	
Miscellaneous Expense		1,425
	176,570	151,055

When the ledger and other records are reviewed, you discover the following: (1) the debits and credits in the cash account total $47,350 and $33,975, respectively; (2) a billing of $2,500 to a customer on account was not posted to the accounts receivable account;

(3) a payment of $1,800 made to a creditor on account was not posted to the accounts payable account; (4) the balance of the unearned rent account is $4,250; (5) the correct balance of the equipment account is $75,000; and (6) each account has a normal balance. Prepare a corrected unadjusted trial balance.

EX 2-19
Effect of errors
on trial balance

obj. 4

The following errors occurred in posting from a two-column journal:

1. A credit of $6,150 to Accounts Payable was not posted.
2. A debit of $1,500 to Cash was posted to Miscellaneous Expense.
3. A credit of $270 to Cash was posted as $720.
4. A debit of $4,520 to Wages Expense was posted as $4,250.
5. An entry debiting Accounts Receivable and crediting Fees Earned for $11,000 was not posted.
6. A debit of $900 to Accounts Payable was posted as a credit.
7. A debit of $1,150 to Supplies was posted twice.

Considering each case individually (i.e., assuming that no other errors had occurred), indicate: (a) by "yes" or "no" whether the trial balance would be out of balance; (b) if answer to (a) is "yes," the amount by which the trial balance totals would differ; and (c) whether the Debit or Credit column of the trial balance would have the larger total. Answers should be presented in the following form, with error (1) given as an example:

Error	(a) Out of Balance	(b) Difference	(c) Larger Total
1.	yes	$6,150	debit

EX 2-20
Errors in trial balance

obj. 4

✔ Total of Credit
column: $1,500,000

Identify the errors in the following trial balance. All accounts have normal balances.

Burgoo Co.
Unadjusted Trial Balance
For the Month Ending March 31, 2010

	Debit Balances	Credit Balances
Cash	90,000	
Accounts Receivable		196,800
Prepaid Insurance	43,200	
Equipment	600,000	
Accounts Payable	22,200	
Salaries Payable		15,000
Estelle Chatman, Capital		518,400
Estelle Chatman, Drawing		72,000
Service Revenue		944,400
Salary Expense	393,720	
Advertising Expense		86,400
Miscellaneous Expense	17,880	
	1,833,000	1,833,000

EX 2-21
Entries to correct
errors

obj. 4

The following errors took place in journalizing and posting transactions:

a. Rent of $6,000 paid for the current month was recorded as a debit to Rent Expense and a credit to Prepaid Rent.
b. A withdrawal of $18,000 by Juanita Jacobsen, owner of the business, was recorded as a debit to Wages Expense and a credit to Cash.

Journalize the entries to correct the errors. Omit explanations.

EX 2-22
Entries to correct
errors

obj. 4

The following errors took place in journalizing and posting transactions:

a. Cash of $3,750 received on account was recorded as a debit to Fees Earned and a credit to Cash.

b. A $1,500 purchase of supplies for cash was recorded as a debit to Supplies Expense and a credit to Accounts Payable.

Journalize the entries to correct the errors. Omit explanations.

EX 2-23
Horizontal analysis
of income statement

The following data (in millions) is taken from the financial statements of Williams-Sonoma for years ending 2007 and 2006:

	2007	2006
Net sales (revenues)	$3,728	$3,539
Total operating expenses	3,400	3,194

a. For Williams-Sonoma, comparing 2007 with 2006, determine the amount of change in millions and the percent of change for:
   1. Net sales (revenues)
   2. Total operating expenses
b. ⟶ What conclusions can you draw from your analysis of the net sales and the total operating expenses?

EX 2-24
Horizontal analysis
of income statement

The following data were adapted from the financial statements of Kmart Corporation, prior to its filing for bankruptcy:

	In millions	
For years ending January 31	2000	1999
Sales	$ 37,028	$ 35,925
Cost of sales (expense)	(29,658)	(28,111)
Selling, general, and administrative expenses	(7,415)	(6,514)
Operating income (loss)	$ (45)	$ 1,300

a. Prepare a horizontal analysis for the income statement showing the amount and percent of change in each of the following:
   1. Sales
   2. Cost of sales
   3. Selling, general, and administative expenses
   4. Operating income (loss)
b. Comment on the results of your horizontal analysis in part (a).

Problems Series A

PR 2-1A
Entries into T accounts
and trial balance

objs. 1, 2, 3, 4

✔ 3. Total of Debit
column: $62,700

Travis Fortney, an architect, opened an office on April 1, 2010. During the month, he completed the following transactions connected with his professional practice:

a. Transferred cash from a personal bank account to an account to be used for the business, $30,000.
b. Purchased used automobile for $19,500, paying $4,500 cash and giving a note payable for the remainder.
c. Paid April rent for office and workroom, $3,000.
d. Paid cash for supplies, $1,450.
e. Purchased office and computer equipment on account, $6,000.
f. Paid cash for annual insurance policies on automobile and equipment, $2,000.
g. Received cash from a client for plans delivered, $7,500.
h. Paid cash to creditors on account, $1,750.
i. Paid cash for miscellaneous expenses, $500.
j. Received invoice for blueprint service, due in May, $1,000.
k. Recorded fee earned on plans delivered, payment to be received in May, $5,200.

l. Paid salary of assistant, $1,600.

m. Paid cash for miscellaneous expenses, $325.

n. Paid installment due on note payable, $250.

o. Paid gas, oil, and repairs on automobile for April, $400.

Instructions

1. Record the above transactions directly in the following T accounts, without journalizing: Cash; Accounts Receivable; Supplies; Prepaid Insurance; Automobiles; Equipment; Notes Payable; Accounts Payable; Travis Fortney, Capital; Professional Fees; Rent Expense; Salary Expense; Blueprint Expense; Automobile Expense; Miscellaneous Expense. To the left of each amount entered in the accounts, place the appropriate letter to identify the transaction.

2. Determine account balances of the T accounts. Accounts containing a single entry only (such as Prepaid Insurance) do not need a balance.

3. Prepare an unadjusted trial balance for Travis Fortney, Architect, as of April 30, 2010.

PR 2-2A

Journal entries and trial balance

objs. 1, 2, 3, 4

✔ 4. c. $2,725

On October 1, 2010, Cody Doerr established Banyan Realty, which completed the following transactions during the month:

a. Cody Doerr transferred cash from a personal bank account to an account to be used for the business, $17,500.

b. Purchased supplies on account, $1,000.

c. Earned sales commissions, receiving cash, $12,250.

d. Paid rent on office and equipment for the month, $3,800.

e. Paid creditor on account, $600.

f. Withdrew cash for personal use, $3,000.

g. Paid automobile expenses (including rental charge) for month, $1,500, and miscellaneous expenses, $400.

h. Paid office salaries, $3,100.

i. Determined that the cost of supplies used was $725.

Instructions

1. Journalize entries for transactions (a) through (i), using the following account titles: Cash; Supplies; Accounts Payable; Cody Doerr, Capital; Cody Doerr, Drawing; Sales Commissions; Rent Expense; Office Salaries Expense; Automobile Expense; Supplies Expense; Miscellaneous Expense. Journal entry explanations may be omitted.

2. Prepare T accounts, using the account titles in (1). Post the journal entries to these accounts, placing the appropriate letter to the left of each amount to identify the transactions. Determine the account balances, after all posting is complete. Accounts containing only a single entry do not need a balance.

3. Prepare an unadjusted trial balance as of October 31, 2010.

4. Determine the following:

a. Amount of total revenue recorded in the ledger.

b. Amount of total expenses recorded in the ledger.

c. Amount of net income for October.

PR 2-3A

Journal entries and trial balance

objs. 1, 2, 3, 4

✔ 3. Total of Credit column: $53,400

On July 1, 2010, Jessie Halverson established an interior decorating business, Photogenic Designs. During the month, Jessie Halverson completed the following transactions related to the business:

July 1. Jessie transferred cash from a personal bank account to an account to be used for the business, $18,000.

4. Paid rent for period of July 4 to end of month, $1,750.

10. Purchased a truck for $15,000, paying $1,000 cash and giving a note payable for the remainder.

July 13. Purchased equipment on account, $7,000.
   14. Purchased supplies for cash, $1,200.
   15. Paid annual premiums on property and casualty insurance, $2,700.
   15. Received cash for job completed, $7,500.
   21. Paid creditor a portion of the amount owed for equipment purchased on July 13, $2,500.
   24. Recorded jobs completed on account and sent invoices to customers, $8,600.
   26. Received an invoice for truck expenses, to be paid in August, $800.
   27. Paid utilities expense, $900.
   27. Paid miscellaneous expenses, $315.
   29. Received cash from customers on account, $3,600.
   30. Paid wages of employees, $2,400.
   31. Withdrew cash for personal use, $2,000.

Instructions

1. Journalize each transaction in a two-column journal, referring to the following chart of accounts in selecting the accounts to be debited and credited. (Do not insert the account numbers in the journal at this time.) Journal entry explanations may be omitted.

11	Cash	31	Jessie Halverson, Capital
12	Accounts Receivable	32	Jessie Halverson, Drawing
13	Supplies	41	Fees Earned
14	Prepaid Insurance	51	Wages Expense
16	Equipment	53	Rent Expense
18	Truck	54	Utilities Expense
21	Notes Payable	55	Truck Expense
22	Accounts Payable	59	Miscellaneous Expense

2. Post the journal to a ledger of four-column accounts, inserting appropriate posting references as each item is posted. Extend the balances to the appropriate balance columns after each transaction is posted.
3. Prepare an unadjusted trial balance for Photogenic Designs as of July 31, 2010.

PR 2-4A
Journal entries and trial balance

objs. 1, 2, 3, 4

✔ 4. Total of Debit column: $560,750

Dodge City Realty acts as an agent in buying, selling, renting, and managing real estate. The unadjusted trial balance on July 31, 2010, is shown below.

Dodge City Realty
Unadjusted Trial Balance
July 31, 2010

		Debit Balances	Credit Balances
11	Cash	33,920	
12	Accounts Receivable	57,200	
13	Prepaid Insurance	7,200	
14	Office Supplies	1,600	
16	Land	—	
21	Accounts Payable		9,920
22	Unearned Rent		—
23	Notes Payable		—
31	Drew Harris, Capital		50,480
32	Drew Harris, Drawing	25,600	
41	Fees Earned		352,000
51	Salary and Commission Expense	224,000	
52	Rent Expense	28,000	
53	Advertising Expense	22,880	
54	Automobile Expense	10,240	
59	Miscellaneous Expense	1,760	
		412,400	412,400

The following business transactions were completed by Dodge City Realty during August 2010:

Aug. 1. Purchased office supplies on account, $2,100.
2. Paid rent on office for month, $4,000.
3. Received cash from clients on account, $44,600.
5. Paid annual insurance premiums, $5,700.
9. Returned a portion of the office supplies purchased on August 1, receiving full credit for their cost, $400.
17. Paid advertising expense, $5,500.
23. Paid creditors on account, $4,950.
29. Paid miscellaneous expenses, $500.
30. Paid automobile expense (including rental charges for an automobile), $1,500.
31. Discovered an error in computing a commission; received cash from the salesperson for the overpayment, $1,000.
31. Paid salaries and commissions for the month, $27,800.
31. Recorded revenue earned and billed to clients during the month, $83,000.
31. Purchased land for a future building site for $75,000, paying $10,000 in cash and giving a note payable for the remainder.
31. Withdrew cash for personal use, $5,000.
31. Rented land purchased on August 31 to a local university for use as a parking lot during football season (September, October, and November); received advance payment of $3,600.

Instructions

1. Record the August 1 balance of each account in the appropriate balance column of a four-column account, write *Balance* in the item section, and place a check mark (✔) in the Posting Reference column.
2. Journalize the transactions for August in a two-column journal. Journal entry explanations may be omitted.
3. Post to the ledger, extending the account balance to the appropriate balance column after each posting.
4. Prepare an unadjusted trial balance of the ledger as of August 31, 2010.

PR 2-5A
Errors in trial balance

obj. **4**

✔ 7. Total of Credit column: $43,338.10

If the working papers correlating with this textbook are not used, omit Problem 2-5A.

The following records of Hallmark Electronic Repair are presented in the working papers:

- Journal containing entries for the period May 1–31.
- Ledger to which the May entries have been posted.
- Preliminary trial balance as of May 31, which does not balance.

Locate the errors, supply the information requested, and prepare a corrected trial balance according to the following instructions. The balances recorded in the accounts as of May 1 and the entries in the journal are correctly stated. If it is necessary to correct any posted amounts in the ledger, a line should be drawn through the erroneous figure and the correct amount inserted above. Corrections or notations may be inserted on the preliminary trial balance in any manner desired. It is not necessary to complete all of the instructions if equal trial balance totals can be obtained earlier. However, the requirements of instructions (6) and (7) should be completed in any event.

Instructions

1. Verify the totals of the preliminary trial balance, inserting the correct amounts in the schedule provided in the working papers.

2. Compute the difference between the trial balance totals.
3. Compare the listings in the trial balance with the balances appearing in the ledger, and list the errors in the space provided in the working papers.
4. Verify the accuracy of the balance of each account in the ledger, and list the errors in the space provided in the working papers.
5. Trace the postings in the ledger back to the journal, using small check marks to identify items traced. Correct any amounts in the ledger that may be necessitated by errors in posting, and list the errors in the space provided in the working papers.
6. Journalize as of May 31 the payment of $120 for gas and electricity. The bill had been paid on May 31 but was inadvertently omitted from the journal. Post to the ledger. (Revise any amounts necessitated by posting this entry.)
7. Prepare a new unadjusted trial balance.

PR 2-6A
Corrected trial balance

obj. 4

✔ 1. Total of Debit column: $475,000

Yin & Yang Video has the following unadjusted trial balance as of January 31, 2010:

Yin & Yang Video
Unadjusted Trial Balance
January 31, 2010

	Debit Balances	Credit Balances
Cash	19,000	
Accounts Receivable	34,100	
Supplies	4,464	
Prepaid Insurance	4,800	
Equipment	108,000	
Notes Payable		45,000
Accounts Payable		9,650
Chea Wynn, Capital		69,400
Chea Wynn, Drawing	23,500	
Fees Earned		356,000
Wages Expense	204,000	
Rent Expense	41,700	
Advertising Expense	19,800	
Gas, Electricity, and Water Expense	11,340	
	470,704	480,050

The debit and credit totals are not equal as a result of the following errors:

a. The balance of cash was overstated by $10,000.
b. A cash receipt of $6,100 was posted as a debit to Cash of $1,600.
c. A debit of $3,500 to Accounts Receivable was not posted.
d. A return of $415 of defective supplies was erroneously posted as a $451 credit to Supplies.
e. An insurance policy acquired at a cost of $800 was posted as a credit to Prepaid Insurance.
f. The balance of Notes Payable was overstated by $9,000.
g. A credit of $1,450 in Accounts Payable was overlooked when the balance of the account was determined.
h. A debit of $2,500 for a withdrawal by the owner was posted as a debit to Chea Wynn, Capital.
i. The balance of $18,900 in Advertising Expense was entered as $19,800 in the trial balance.
j. Miscellaneous Expense, with a balance of $3,060, was omitted from the trial balance.

Instructions

1. Prepare a corrected unadjusted trial balance as of January 31 of the current year.
2. ➤ Does the fact that the unadjusted trial balance in (1) is balanced mean that there are no errors in the accounts? Explain.

Problems Series B

PR 2-1B
Entries into T accounts and trial balance

objs. 1, 2, 3, 4

✔ 3. Total of Debit column: $49,625

Brandy Corbin, an architect, opened an office on July 1, 2010. During the month, she completed the following transactions connected with her professional practice:

a. Transferred cash from a personal bank account to an account to be used for the business, $20,000.
b. Paid July rent for office and workroom, $2,500.
c. Purchased used automobile for $22,300, paying $5,000 cash and giving a note payable for the remainder.
d. Purchased office and computer equipment on account, $7,000.
e. Paid cash for supplies, $1,200.
f. Paid cash for annual insurance policies, $2,400.
g. Received cash from client for plans delivered, $4,175.
h. Paid cash for miscellaneous expenses, $240.
i. Paid cash to creditors on account, $2,500.
j. Paid installment due on note payable, $300.
k. Received invoice for blueprint service, due in August, $800.
l. Recorded fee earned on plans delivered, payment to be received in August, $3,150.
m. Paid salary of assistant, $1,500.
n. Paid gas, oil, and repairs on automobile for July, $410.

Instructions

1. Record the above transactions directly in the following T accounts, without journalizing: Cash; Accounts Receivable; Supplies; Prepaid Insurance; Automobiles; Equipment; Notes Payable; Accounts Payable; Brandy Corbin, Capital; Professional Fees; Rent Expense; Salary Expense; Automobile Expense; Blueprint Expense; Miscellaneous Expense. To the left of the amount entered in the accounts, place the appropriate letter to identify the transaction.
2. Determine account balances of the T accounts. Accounts containing a single entry only (such as Prepaid Insurance) do not need a balance.
3. Prepare an unadjusted trial balance for Brandy Corbin, Architect, as of July 31, 2010.

PR 2-2B
Journal entries and trial balance

objs. 1, 2, 3, 4

✔ 4. c. $11,025

On August 1, 2010, Cheryl Newsome established Titus Realty, which completed the following transactions during the month:

a. Cheryl Newsome transferred cash from a personal bank account to an account to be used for the business, $25,000.
b. Paid rent on office and equipment for the month, $2,750.
c. Purchased supplies on account, $950.
d. Paid creditor on account, $400.
e. Earned sales commissions, receiving cash, $18,100.
f. Paid automobile expenses (including rental charge) for month, $1,000, and miscellaneous expenses, $600.
g. Paid office salaries, $2,150.
h. Determined that the cost of supplies used was $575.
i. Withdrew cash for personal use, $2,000.

Instructions

1. Journalize entries for transactions (a) through (i), using the following account titles: Cash; Supplies; Accounts Payable; Cheryl Newsome, Capital; Cheryl Newsome, Drawing; Sales Commissions; Office Salaries Expense; Rent Expense;

Automobile Expense; Supplies Expense; Miscellaneous Expense. Explanations may be omitted.

2. Prepare T accounts, using the account titles in (1). Post the journal entries to these accounts, placing the appropriate letter to the left of each amount to identify the transactions. Determine the account balances, after all posting is complete. Accounts containing only a single entry do not need a balance.

3. Prepare an unadjusted trial balance as of August 31, 2010.

4. Determine the following:
   a. Amount of total revenue recorded in the ledger.
   b. Amount of total expenses recorded in the ledger.
   c. Amount of net income for August.

PR 2-3B
Journal entries and trial balance

objs. 1, 2, 3, 4

✔ 3. Total of Credit column: $57,000

On April 1, 2010, Jose Guadalupe established an interior decorating business, Lodge Designs. During the month, Jose completed the following transactions related to the business:

Apr. 1. Jose transferred cash from a personal bank account to an account to be used for the business, $15,000.
2. Paid rent for period of April 2 to end of month, $2,350.
6. Purchased office equipment on account, $10,000.
8. Purchased a used truck for $21,000, paying $2,000 cash and giving a note payable for the remainder.
10. Purchased supplies for cash, $1,200.
12. Received cash for job completed, $8,500.
15. Paid annual premiums on property and casualty insurance, $1,800.
23. Recorded jobs completed on account and sent invoices to customers, $6,000.
24. Received an invoice for truck expenses, to be paid in April, $1,000.
29. Paid utilities expense, $1,100.
29. Paid miscellaneous expenses, $500.
30. Received cash from customers on account, $3,500.
30. Paid wages of employees, $3,000.
30. Paid creditor a portion of the amount owed for equipment purchased on April 6, $2,500.
30. Withdrew cash for personal use, $1,750.

Instructions

1. Journalize each transaction in a two-column journal, referring to the following chart of accounts in selecting the accounts to be debited and credited. (Do not insert the account numbers in the journal at this time.) Explanations may be omitted.

11	Cash	31	Jose Guadalupe, Capital
12	Accounts Receivable	32	Jose Guadalupe, Drawing
13	Supplies	41	Fees Earned
14	Prepaid Insurance	51	Wages Expense
16	Equipment	53	Rent Expense
18	Truck	54	Utilities Expense
21	Notes Payable	55	Truck Expense
22	Accounts Payable	59	Miscellaneous Expense

2. Post the journal to a ledger of four-column accounts, inserting appropriate posting references as each item is posted. Extend the balances to the appropriate balance columns after each transaction is posted.

3. Prepare an unadjusted trial balance for Lodge Designs as of April 30, 2010.

PR 2-4B
Journal entries and
trial balance

objs. 1, 2, 3, 4

✔ 4. Total of Debit
column: $264,640

Ampere Realty acts as an agent in buying, selling, renting, and managing real estate. The unadjusted trial balance on October 31, 2010, is shown below.

Ampere Realty
Unadjusted Trial Balance
October 31, 2010

		Debit Balances	Credit Balances
11	Cash	13,150	
12	Accounts Receivable	33,750	
13	Prepaid Insurance	1,500	
14	Office Supplies	900	
16	Land	—	
21	Accounts Payable		6,510
22	Unearned Rent		—
23	Notes Payable		—
31	Maya Garmin, Capital		16,490
32	Maya Garmin, Drawing	1,000	
41	Fees Earned		130,000
51	Salary and Commission Expense	74,100	
52	Rent Expense	15,000	
53	Advertising Expense	8,900	
54	Automobile Expense	2,750	
59	Miscellaneous Expense	1,950	
		153,000	153,000

The following business transactions were completed by Ampere Realty during November 2010:

Nov. 1. Paid rent on office for month, $3,000.
2. Purchased office supplies on account, $1,000.
5. Paid annual insurance premiums, $2,400.
10. Received cash from clients on account, $25,000.
15. Purchased land for a future building site for $90,000, paying $10,000 in cash and giving a note payable for the remainder.
17. Paid creditors on account, $2,910.
20. Returned a portion of the office supplies purchased on November 2, receiving full credit for their cost, $200.
23. Paid advertising expense, $1,250.
27. Discovered an error in computing a commission; received cash from the salesperson for the overpayment, $400.
28. Paid automobile expense (including rental charges for an automobile), $900.
29. Paid miscellaneous expenses, $450.
30. Recorded revenue earned and billed to clients during the month, $31,750.
30. Paid salaries and commissions for the month, $13,500.
30. Withdrew cash for personal use, $1,000.
30. Rented land purchased on November 15 to local merchants association for use as a parking lot in December and January, during a street rebuilding program; received advance payment of $2,000.

Instructions
1. Record the November 1, 2010, balance of each account in the appropriate balance column of a four-column account, write *Balance* in the item section, and place a check mark (✔) in the Posting Reference column.
2. Journalize the transactions for November in a two-column journal. Journal entry explanations may be omitted.
3. Post to the ledger, extending the account balance to the appropriate balance column after each posting.
4. Prepare an unadjusted trial balance of the ledger as of November 30, 2010.

PR 2-5B
Errors in trial balance

obj. 4

✔ 7. Total of Debit column: $43,338.10

If the working papers correlating with this textbook are not used, omit Problem 2-5B.

The following records of Hallmark Electronic Repair are presented in the working papers:

- Journal containing entries for the period May 1–31.
- Ledger to which the May entries have been posted.
- Preliminary trial balance as of May 31, which does not balance.

Locate the errors, supply the information requested, and prepare a corrected trial balance according to the following instructions. The balances recorded in the accounts as of May 1 and the entries in the journal are correctly stated. If it is necessary to correct any posted amounts in the ledger, a line should be drawn through the erroneous figure and the correct amount inserted above. Corrections or notations may be inserted on the preliminary trial balance in any manner desired. It is not necessary to complete all of the instructions if equal trial balance totals can be obtained earlier. However, the requirements of instructions (6) and (7) should be completed in any event.

Instructions

1. Verify the totals of the preliminary trial balance, inserting the correct amounts in the schedule provided in the working papers.
2. Compute the difference between the trial balance totals.
3. Compare the listings in the trial balance with the balances appearing in the ledger, and list the errors in the space provided in the working papers.
4. Verify the accuracy of the balance of each account in the ledger, and list the errors in the space provided in the working papers.
5. Trace the postings in the ledger back to the journal, using small check marks to identify items traced. Correct any amounts in the ledger that may be necessitated by errors in posting, and list the errors in the space provided in the working papers.
6. Journalize as of May 31 the payment of $175 for advertising expense. The bill had been paid on May 31 but was inadvertently omitted from the journal. Post to the ledger. (Revise any amounts necessitated by posting this entry.)
7. Prepare a new unadjusted trial balance.

PR 2-6B
Corrected trial balance

obj. 4

✔ 1. Total of Debit column: $350,000

Damascus Carpet has the following unadjusted trial balance as of August 31, 2010.

Damascus Carpet
Unadjusted Trial Balance
August 31, 2010

	Debit Balances	Credit Balances
Cash	8,650	
Accounts Receivable	21,760	
Supplies	4,195	
Prepaid Insurance	1,550	
Equipment	98,000	
Notes Payable		45,675
Accounts Payable		13,825
Isaiah Betts, Capital		67,200
Isaiah Betts, Drawing	25,375	
Fees Earned		214,725
Wages Expense	122,500	
Rent Expense	29,050	
Advertising Expense	1,260	
Miscellaneous Expense	2,540	
	314,880	341,425

The debit and credit totals are not equal as a result of the following errors:

a. The balance of cash was understated by $5,250.
b. A cash receipt of $3,600 was posted as a debit to Cash of $6,300.
c. A debit of $2,250 to Accounts Receivable was not posted.

d. A return of $350 of defective supplies was erroneously posted as a $530 credit to Supplies.

e. An insurance policy acquired at a cost of $300 was posted as a credit to Prepaid Insurance.

f. The balance of Notes Payable was understated by $13,125.

g. A credit of $1,575 in Accounts Payable was overlooked when determining the balance of the account.

h. A debit of $6,125 for a withdrawal by the owner was posted as a credit to Isaiah Betts, Capital.

i. The balance of $12,600 in Advertising Expense was entered as $1,260 in the trial balance.

j. Gas, Electricity, and Water Expense, with a balance of $12,075 was omitted from the trial balance.

Instructions

1. Prepare a corrected unadjusted trial balance as of August 31, 2010.

2. ➡ Does the fact that the unadjusted trial balance in (1) is balanced mean that there are no errors in the accounts? Explain.

Continuing Problem

● ● ● ●

The transactions completed by Music Depot during June 2010 were described at the end of Chapter 1. The following transactions were completed during July, the second month of the business's operations:

July 1. Lee Chang made an additional investment in Music Depot by depositing $2,500 in Music Depot's checking account.

1. Instead of continuing to share office space with a local real estate agency, Lee decided to rent office space near a local music store. Paid rent for July, $2,000.

1. Paid a premium of $2,700 for a comprehensive insurance policy covering liability, theft, and fire. The policy covers a one-year period.

✔ 4. Total of Debit column: $38,680

2. Received $1,350 on account.

3. On behalf of Music Depot, Lee signed a contract with a local radio station, WHBD, to provide guest spots for the next three months. The contract requires Music Depot to provide a guest disc jockey for 80 hours per month for a monthly fee of $3,600. Any additional hours beyond 80 will be billed to WHBD at $40 per hour. In accordance with the contract, Lee received $7,200 from WHBD as an advance payment for the first two months.

3. Paid $250 on account.

4. Paid an attorney $500 for reviewing the July 3rd contract with WHBD. (Record as Miscellaneous Expense.)

5. Purchased office equipment on account from One-Stop Office Mart, $5,000.

8. Paid for a newspaper advertisement, $200.

11. Received $800 for serving as a disc jockey for a party.

13. Paid $600 to a local audio electronics store for rental of digital recording equipment.

14. Paid wages of $1,000 to receptionist and part-time assistant.

16. Received $1,750 for serving as a disc jockey for a wedding reception.

18. Purchased supplies on account, $680.

21. Paid $420 to Upload Music for use of its current music demos in making various music sets.

22. Paid $800 to a local radio station to advertise the services of Music Depot twice daily for the remainder of July.

23. Served as disc jockey for a party for $2,500. Received $750, with the remainder due August 4, 2010.

July 27. Paid electric bill, $560.
    28. Paid wages of $1,000 to receptionist and part-time assistant.
    29. Paid miscellaneous expenses, $150.
    30. Served as a disc jockey for a charity ball for $1,800. Received $400, with the remainder due on August 9, 2010.
    31. Received $2,800 for serving as a disc jockey for a party.
    31. Paid $1,100 royalties (music expense) to National Music Clearing for use of various artists' music during July.
    31. Withdrew $1,500 cash from Music Depot for personal use.

Music Depot's chart of accounts and the balance of accounts as of July 1, 2010 (all normal balances), are as follows:

11	Cash	$ 8,010	41	Fees Earned	$5,650
12	Accounts Receivable	1,350	50	Wages Expense	400
14	Supplies	170	51	Office Rent Expense	750
15	Prepaid Insurance	—	52	Equipment Rent Expense	500
17	Office Equipment	—	53	Utilities Expense	300
21	Accounts Payable	250	54	Music Expense	1,290
23	Unearned Revenue	—	55	Advertising Expense	600
31	Lee Chang, Capital	8,000	56	Supplies Expense	180
32	Lee Chang, Drawing	200	59	Miscellaneous Expense	150

Instructions

1. Enter the July 1, 2010, account balances in the appropriate balance column of a four-column account. Write *Balance* in the Item column, and place a check mark (✔) in the Posting Reference column. (*Hint:* Verify the equality of the debit and credit balances in the ledger before proceeding with the next instruction.)
2. Analyze and journalize each transaction in a two-column journal, omitting journal entry explanations.
3. Post the journal to the ledger, extending the account balance to the appropriate balance column after each posting.
4. Prepare an unadjusted trial balance as of July 31, 2010.

Special Activities

You can access the special activities online at **www.cengage.com/accounting/reeve**.

Excel Success Special Activities

SA 2-1

ImagePress—Journalize transactions

a. Open the Excel file *SA2-1,2,3*. Label the Sheet1 tab *JE*. On the worksheet page, journalize the following selected April 2011 transactions for ImagePress Printing. Omit posting references and journal entry explanations.

Apr. 1. Paid advertising expense, $460. [This has been entered for you.]
    2. Paid rent for the month, $2,500.
    6. Purchased office equipment on account, $9,450.
    9. Paid cash for supplies, $300.
    13. Paid creditor on account, $340.
    16. Received cash from customers on account, $1,080.
    20. Fees earned and billed to customers, $9,570.
    30. Paid salaries to employees, $1,900.
    30. Paid electricity bill for the month, $440.
    30. Ted Wright withdrew cash for personal use, $2,400.

b. When you have completed the journal transactions, perform a "save as," replacing the entire file name with the following:

SA2-1,2,3_[your first name initial]_[your last name]

SA 2-2

ImagePress—Post
transactions

a. Open your *SA2-1,2,3_[your first name initial]_[your last name]* file. Label Sheet2 as *GL* (for general ledger). Post the journal entries for ImagePress Printing from *SA2-1* to the appropriate accounts in the ledger, worksheet *GL*.

Insert the appropriate posting references as each item is posted. Extend the balances using spreadsheet formulas to the appropriate balance columns after each transaction is posted.

Using the following chart of accounts, placing the beginning balance in the first row of each account in the appropriate balance column.

ImagePress Printing
Unadjusted Trial Balance
March 31, 2011

Accounts		Debit Balances	Credit Balances
11	Cash	15,500	
12	Accounts Receivable	7,300	
13	Supplies	2,000	
14	Office Equipment	12,400	
21	Accounts Payable		1,300
31	Ted Wright, Capital		23,800
32	Ted Wright, Drawing	3,500	
41	Fees Earned		25,600
51	Advertising Expense	200	
52	Rent Expense	5,000	
53	Salaries Expense	3,600	
54	Utilities Expense	1,200	
		50,700	50,700

b. Save your file using the *same file name.*

SA 2-3

ImagePress—
Prepare a trial
balance

a. Open your *SA2-1,2,3_[your first name initial]_[your last name]* file. Label Sheet3 as *UTB* (for Unadjusted Trial Balance). Within this worksheet, use cell references to prepare an unadjusted trial balance for the April 30 balances of ImagePress Printing, from the ledger accounts of *SA2-2*.

b. Save your file using the *same file name.*

SA 2-4

Journalize
transactions

a. Open the Excel file *SA2-4,5,6*. Label Sheet1 *JE*. Journalize the following selected September 2011 transactions for Artscape in this worksheet. Omit posting references and journal entry explanations.

Sept. 1. Paid rent for the month, $1,150.
    3. Paid advertising expense, $670.
    8. Paid cash for supplies, $230.
    11. Purchased office equipment on account, $5,200.
    15. Paid creditor on account, $920.
    19. Fees earned and billed to customers, $7,200.
    25. Received cash from customers on account, $2,380.
    30. Paid telephone bill for the month, $240.
    30. Paid wages to employees, $1,450.
    30. Niki Yamura withdrew cash for personal use, $1,100.

b. When you have completed the journal transactions, perform a "save as," replacing the entire file name with the following:

SA2-4,5,6_[your first name initial]_[your last name]

SA 2-5

Post transactions

a. Open your *SA2-4,5,6_[your first name initial]_[your last name]* file. Label Sheet2, *GL*. Post the journal entries for Artscape from *SA2-4* to the appropriate accounts in the general ledger, worksheet *GL*.

Insert the appropriate posting references as each item is posted. Extend the balances using spreadsheet formulas to the appropriate balance columns after each transaction is posted.

Use the following chart of accounts, placing the beginning balance in the first row of each account in the appropriate balance column.

Artscape
Trial Balance
August 31, 2011

Accounts	Debit Balances	Credit Balances
11 Cash	12,700	
12 Accounts Receivable	9,100	
13 Supplies	1,500	
14 Office Equipment	11,900	
21 Accounts Payable		2,700
31 Niki Yamura, Capital		21,400
32 Niki Yamura, Drawing	3,100	
41 Fees Earned		23,100
51 Advertising Expense	300	
52 Rent Expense	4,200	
53 Utilities Expense	3,500	
54 Wages Expense	900	
	47,200	47,200

b. Save your file using the *same file name*.

SA 2-6

Prepare a trial balance

a. Open your *SA2-4,5,6_[your first name initial]_[your last name]* file. Label Sheet3, *UTB*. Use this worksheet to prepare an unadjusted trial balance for the September 30 balances of Artscape, from the ledger accounts of *SA2-5*.

b. Save your file using the *same file name*.

Answers to Self-Examination Questions

1. **A** A debit may signify an increase in an asset account (answer A) or a decrease in a liability or owner's capital account. A credit may signify a decrease in an asset account (answer B) or an increase in a liability or owner's capital account (answers C and D).

2. **C** Liability, capital, and revenue (answer C) accounts have normal credit balances. Asset (answer A), drawing (answer B), and expense (answer D) accounts have normal debit balances.

3. **C** Accounts Receivable (answer A), Cash (answer B), and Miscellaneous Expense (answer D) would all normally have debit balances. Fees Earned should normally have a credit balance. Hence, a debit balance in Fees Earned (answer C) would indicate a likely error in the recording process.

4. **A** The receipt of cash from customers on account increases the asset Cash and decreases the

asset Accounts Receivable, as indicated by answer A. Answer B has the debit and credit reversed, and answers C and D involve transactions with creditors (accounts payable) and not customers (accounts receivable).

5. **D** The trial balance (answer D) is a listing of the balances and the titles of the accounts in the ledger on a given date, so that the equality of the debits and credits in the ledger can be verified. The income statement (answer A) is a summary of revenue and expenses for a period of time. The balance sheet (answer B) is a presentation of the assets, liabilities, and owner's equity on a given date. The statement of owner's equity (answer C) is a summary of the changes in owner's equity for a period of time.

CHAPTER 3

The Adjusting Process

MARVEL ENTERTAINMENT, INC.

Do you subscribe to any magazines? Most of us subscribe to one or more magazines such as *Cosmopolitan*, *Sports Illustrated*, *Golf Digest*, *Newsweek*, or *Rolling Stone*. Magazines usually require you to prepay the yearly subscription price before you receive any issues. When should the magazine company record revenue from the subscriptions?

As we discussed in Chapter 2, sometimes revenues are earned and expenses are incurred at the point cash is received or paid. For transactions such as magazine subscriptions, the revenue is earned when the magazine is delivered, not when the cash is received. Most companies are required to account for revenues and expenses when the benefit is substantially provided or consumed, which may not be when cash is received or paid.

One company that records revenue from subscriptions is Marvel Entertainment, Inc. Marvel began in 1939 as a comic book publishing company, establishing such popular comic book characters as Spider-Man®, X-Men®, Fantastic Four®, and the Avengers®. From these humble beginnings, Marvel has grown into a full-line, multi-billion-dollar entertainment company. Marvel not only publishes comic books, but it has also added feature films, such as the *Spider-Man* movies, video games, and toys to its product offerings.

Most companies, like Marvel Entertainment, are required to update their accounting records for items such as revenues earned from magazine subscriptions before preparing their financial statements. In this chapter, we describe and illustrate this updating process.

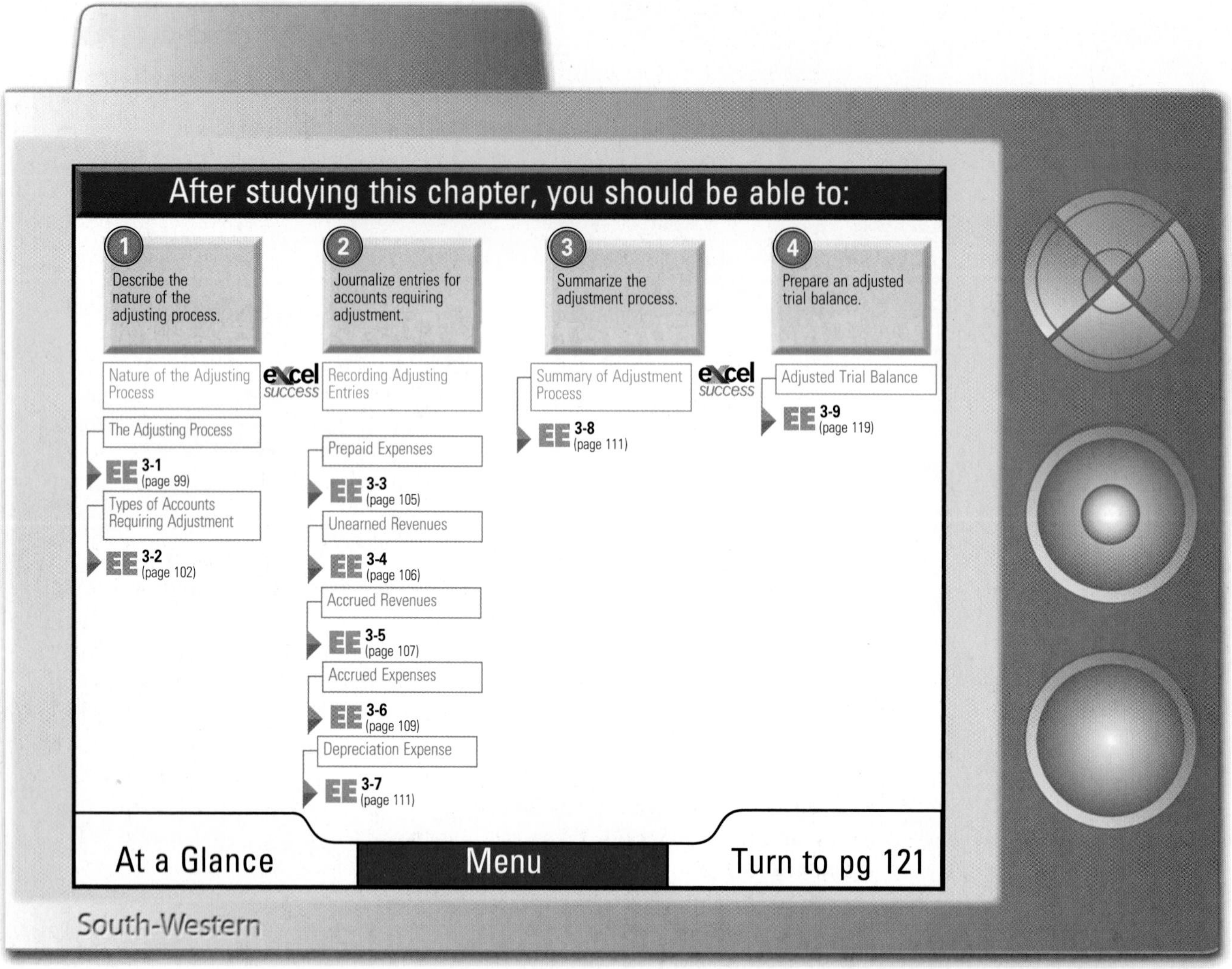

After studying this chapter, you should be able to:

1 Describe the nature of the adjusting process.

2 Journalize entries for accounts requiring adjustment.

3 Summarize the adjustment process.

4 Prepare an adjusted trial balance.

Nature of the Adjusting Process	**excel** *success* Recording Adjusting Entries	Summary of Adjustment Process	**excel** *success* Adjusted Trial Balance

The Adjusting Process

EE 3-1 (page 99)

Types of Accounts Requiring Adjustment

EE 3-2 (page 102)

Prepaid Expenses

EE 3-3 (page 105)

Unearned Revenues

EE 3-4 (page 106)

Accrued Revenues

EE 3-5 (page 107)

Accrued Expenses

EE 3-6 (page 109)

Depreciation Expense

EE 3-7 (page 111)

Summary of Adjustment Process

EE 3-8 (page 111)

Adjusted Trial Balance

EE 3-9 (page 119)

At a Glance   Menu   Turn to pg 121

South-Western

1 Describe the nature of the adjusting process.

Nature of the Adjusting Process

When preparing financial statements, the economic life of the business is divided into time periods. This **accounting period concept** requires that revenues and expenses be reported in the proper period. To determine the proper period, accountants use generally accepted accounting principles (GAAP). The use of the accrual basis of accounting is required by GAAP.

Under the **accrual basis of accounting**, revenues are reported in the income statement in the period in which they are earned. For example, revenue is reported when the services are provided to customers. Cash may or may not be received from customers during this period. The accounting concept supporting this reporting of revenues is called the **revenue recognition concept**.

Under the accrual basis, expenses are reported in the same period as the revenues to which they relate. For example, utility expenses incurred in December are reported as an expense and matched against December's revenues even though the utility bill may not be paid until January. The accounting concept supporting reporting revenues and related expenses in the same period is called the **matching concept**, or **matching principle**. By matching revenues and expenses, net income or loss for the period is properly reported on the income statement.

Although GAAP requires the accrual basis of accounting, some businesses use the **cash basis of accounting**. Under the cash basis of accounting, revenues and expenses are

American Airlines uses the accrual basis of accounting. Revenues are recognized when passengers take flights, not when the passenger makes the reservation or pays for the ticket.

reported in the income statement in the period in which cash is received or paid. For example, fees are recorded when cash is received from clients; likewise, wages are recorded when cash is paid to employees. The net income (or net loss) is the difference between the cash receipts (revenues) and the cash payments (expenses).

Small service businesses may use the cash basis, because they have few receivables and payables. For example, attorneys, physicians, and real estate agents often use the cash basis. For them, the cash basis provides financial statements similar to those of the accrual basis. For most large businesses, however, the cash basis will not provide accurate financial statements for user needs. For this reason, we use the accrual basis in this text.

The Adjusting Process

At the end of the accounting period, many of the account balances in the ledger can be reported in the financial statements without change. For example, the balances of the cash and land accounts are normally the amount reported on the balance sheet.

Under the accrual basis, however, some accounts in the ledger require updating.[1] This updating is required for the following reasons:

1. Some expenses are not recorded daily. For example, the daily use of supplies would require many entries with small amounts. Also, managers usually do not need to know the amount of supplies on hand on a day-to-day basis.
2. Some revenues and expenses are incurred as time passes rather than as separate transactions. For example, rent received in advance (unearned rent) expires and becomes revenue with the passage of time. Likewise, prepaid insurance expires and becomes an expense with the passage of time.
3. Some revenues and expenses may be unrecorded. For example, a company may have provided services to customers that it has not billed or recorded at the end of the accounting period. Likewise, a company may not pay its employees until the next accounting period even though the employees have earned their wages in the current period.

The analysis and updating of accounts at the end of the period before the financial statements are prepared is called the **adjusting process**. The journal entries that bring the accounts up to date at the end of the accounting period are called **adjusting entries**. All adjusting entries affect at least one income statement account and one balance sheet account. Thus, an adjusting entry will *always* involve a revenue or an expense account *and* an asset or a liability account.

Example Exercise 3-1 Accounts Requiring Adjustment

Indicate with a Yes or No whether or not each of the following accounts normally requires an adjusting entry.

a. Cash
b. Prepaid Rent
c. Wages Expense
d. Office Equipment
e. Accounts Receivable
f. Unearned Rent

Follow My Example 3-1

a. No
b. Yes
c. Yes
d. No
e. Yes
f. Yes

For Practice: PE 3-1A, PE 3-1B

[1] Under the cash basis of accounting, accounts do not require adjusting. This is because transactions are recorded only when cash is received or paid. Thus, the matching concept is not used under the cash basis.

Types of Accounts Requiring Adjustment

Four basic types of accounts require adjusting entries, as shown below.

1. Prepaid expenses
2. Unearned revenues
3. Accrued revenues
4. Accrued expenses

Prepaid expenses are the advance payment of *future* expenses and are recorded as assets when cash is paid. Prepaid expenses become expenses over time or during normal operations. To illustrate, the following transaction of NetSolutions from Chapter 2 is used.

The tuition you pay at the beginning of each term is an example of a prepaid expense to you, as a student.

> Dec. 1   NetSolutions paid $2,400 as a premium on a one-year insurance policy.

On December 1, the cash payment of $2,400 was recorded as a debit to Prepaid Insurance and credit to Cash for $2,400. At the end of December, only $200 ($2,400 divided by 12 months) of the insurance premium is expired and has become an expense. The remaining $2,200 of prepaid insurance will become an expense in future months. Thus, the $200 is insurance expense of December and should be recorded with an adjusting entry.

Other examples of prepaid expenses include supplies, prepaid advertising, and prepaid interest.

Unearned revenues are the advance receipt of *future* revenues and are recorded as liabilities when cash is received. Unearned revenues become earned revenues over time or during normal operations. To illustrate, we use the following December 1 transaction of NetSolutions.

> Dec. 1   NetSolutions received $360 from a local retailer to rent land for three months.

On December 1, the cash receipt of $360 was recorded as a debit to Cash and a credit to Unearned Rent for $360. At the end of December, $120 ($360 divided by 3 months) of the unearned rent has been earned. The remaining $240 will become rent revenue in future months. Thus, the $120 is rent revenue of December and should be recorded with an adjusting entry.

Other examples of unearned revenues include tuition received in advance by a school, an annual retainer fee received by an attorney, premiums received in advance by an insurance company, and magazine subscriptions received in advance by a publisher.

Exhibit 1 illustrates the nature of prepaid expenses and unearned revenues.

Exhibit 1

Type of Adjustments: Prepaid Expenses and Unearned Revenues

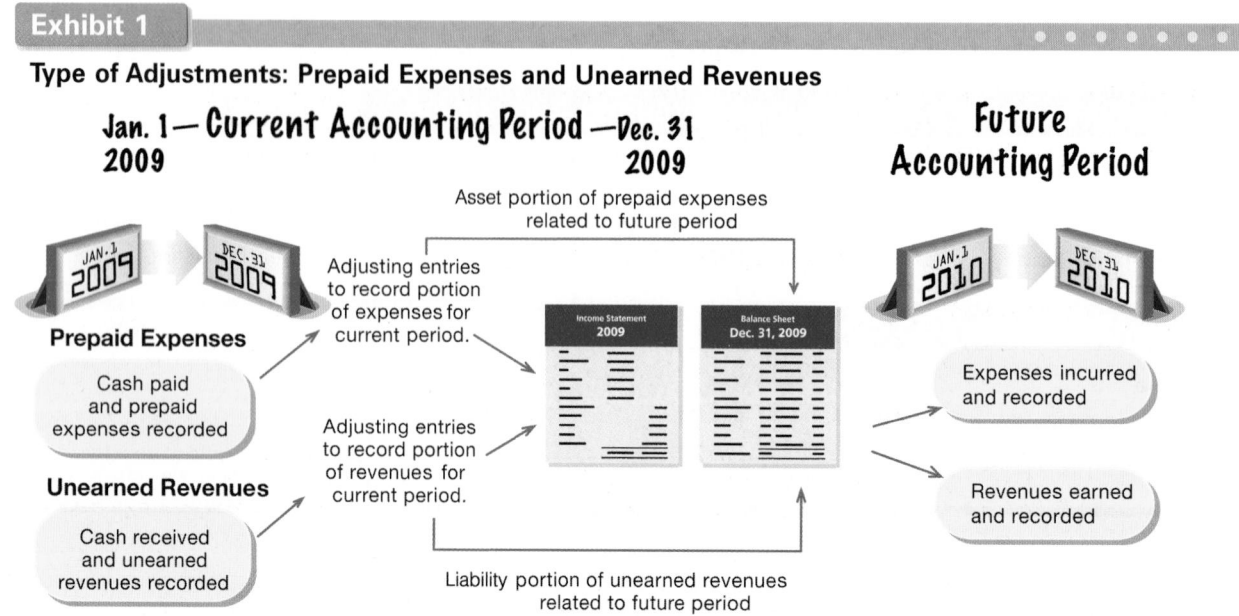

@netsolutions

Accrued revenues are unrecorded revenues that have been earned and for which cash has yet to be received. Fees for services that an attorney or a doctor has provided but not yet billed are accrued revenues. To illustrate, we use the following example involving NetSolutions and one of its customers.

> Dec. 15   NetSolutions signed an agreement with Dankner Co. on December 15 under which NetSolutions will bill Dankner Co. on the fifteenth of each month for services rendered at the rate of $20 per hour.

From December 16–31, NetSolutions provided 25 hours of service to Dankner Co. Although the revenue of $500 (25 hours × $20) has been earned, it will not be billed until January 15. Likewise, cash of $500 will not be received until Dankner pays its bill. Thus, the $500 of accrued revenue and the $500 of fees earned should be recorded with an adjusting entry on December 31.

Other examples of accrued revenues include accrued interest on notes receivable and accrued rent on property rented to others.

Accrued expenses are unrecorded expenses that have been incurred and for which cash has yet to be paid. Wages owed to employees at the end of a period but not yet paid is an accrued expense. To illustrate, the following example involving NetSolutions and its employees is used:

> Dec. 31   NetSolutions owes its employees wages of $250 for Monday and Tuesday, December 30 and 31.

NetSolutions paid wages of $950 on December 13 and $1,200 on December 27, 2009. These payments covered the biweekly pay periods that ended on those days. As of December 31, 2009, NetSolutions owes its employees wages of $250 for Monday and Tuesday, December 30 and 31. The wages of $250 will be paid on January 10, 2010, however, they are an expense of December. Thus, $250 of accrued wages should be recorded with an adjusting entry on December 31.

Other examples of accrued expenses include accrued interest on notes payable and accrued taxes.

As discussed above, accrued revenues are earned revenues that are unrecorded. The cash receipts for accrued revenues are normally received in the next accounting period. Accrued expenses are expenses that have been incurred, but are unrecorded. The cash payments for accrued expenses are normally paid in the next accounting period. Exhibit 2 illustrates the nature of accrued revenues and accrued expenses.

Exhibit 2

Type of Adjustments: Accrued Revenues and Expenses

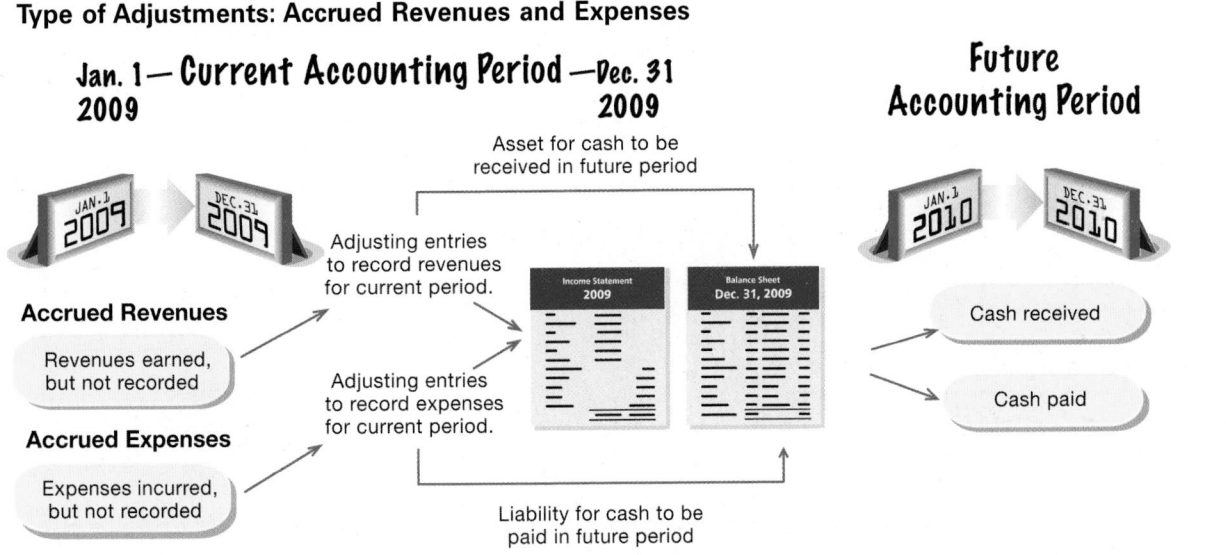

Prepaid expenses and unearned revenues are sometimes referred to as *deferrals*. This is because the recording of the related expense or revenue is deferred to a future period. Accrued revenues and accrued expenses are sometimes referred to as *accruals*. This is because the related revenue or expense should be recorded or accrued in the current period.

Example Exercise 3-2 Type of Adjustment •••••••⟩ **1**

Classify the following items as (1) prepaid expense, (2) unearned revenue, (3) accrued expense, or (4) accrued revenue.

a. Wages owed but not yet paid.

b. Supplies on hand.

c. Fees received but not yet earned.

d. Fees earned but not yet received.

Follow My Example 3-2

a. Accrued expense

b. Prepaid expense

c. Unearned revenue

d. Accrued revenue

For Practice: PE 3-2A, PE 3-2B

---

2 Journalize entries for accounts requiring adjustment.

Recording Adjusting Entries

To illustrate adjusting entries, we use the December 31, 2009, unadjusted trial balance of NetSolutions shown in Exhibit 3. An expanded chart of accounts for NetSolutions is shown in Exhibit 4. The additional accounts used in this chapter are shown in color. The rules of debit and credit shown in Exhibit 3 of Chapter 2 are used to record the adjusting entries.

Exhibit 3

Unadjusted Trial Balance for NetSolutions

@netsolutions

	NetSolutions Unadjusted Trial Balance December 31, 2009		
		Debit Balances	Credit Balances
Cash		2,065	
Accounts Receivable		2,220	
Supplies		2,000	
Prepaid Insurance		2,400	
Land		20,000	
Office Equipment		1,800	
Accounts Payable			900
Unearned Rent			360
Chris Clark, Capital			25,000
Chris Clark, Drawing		4,000	
Fees Earned			16,340
Wages Expense		4,275	
Rent Expense		1,600	
Utilities Expense		985	
Supplies Expense		800	
Miscellaneous Expense		455	
		42,600	42,600

Exhibit 4

Expanded Chart of Accounts for NetSolutions

Balance Sheet Accounts	Income Statement Accounts

1. Assets

11	Cash
12	Accounts Receivable
14	Supplies
15	Prepaid Insurance
17	Land
18	Office Equipment
19	Accumulated Depreciation—Office Equipment

2. Liabilities

21	Accounts Payable
22	Wages Payable
23	Unearned Rent

3. Owner's Equity

| 31 | Chris Clark, Capital |
| 32 | Chris Clark, Drawing |

4. Revenue

| 41 | Fees Earned |
| 42 | Rent Revenue |

5. Expenses

51	Wages Expense
52	Rent Expense
53	Depreciation Expense
54	Utilities Expense
55	Supplies Expense
56	Insurance Expense
59	Miscellaneous Expense

Prepaid Expenses

The balance in NetSolutions' supplies account on December 31 is $2,000. Some of these supplies (CDs, paper, envelopes, etc.) were used during December, and some are still on hand (not used). If either amount is known, the other can be determined. It is normally easier to determine the cost of the supplies on hand at the end of the month than to record daily supplies used. Assuming that on December 31 the amount of supplies on hand is $760, the amount to be transferred from the asset account to the expense account is $1,240, computed as follows:

Supplies available during December (balance of account)	$2,000
Supplies on hand, December 31	760
Supplies used (amount of adjustment)	$1,240

At the end of December, the supplies expense account should be increased (debited) for $1,240, and the supplies account should be decreased (credited) for $1,240 to record the supplies used during December. The adjusting journal entry and T accounts for Supplies and Supplies Expense are as follows:

			Journal			Page 5

Date		Description	Post. Ref.	Debit	Credit
2009					
Dec.	31	Supplies Expense	55	1,240	
		Supplies	14		1,240
		Supplies used ($2,000 − $760).			

Supplies				**Supplies Expense**	
Bal.	2,000	Dec. 31	1,240	Bal.	800
Adj. Bal.	760			Dec. 31	1,240
				Adj. Bal.	2,040

The adjusting entry is shown in color in the T accounts to separate it from other transactions. After the adjusting entry is recorded and posted, the supplies account has a debit balance of $760. This balance is an asset that will become an expense in a future period.

The debit balance of $2,400 in NetSolutions' prepaid insurance account represents a December 1 prepayment of insurance for 12 months. At the end of December, the insurance expense account should be increased (debited), and the prepaid insurance account should be decreased (credited) by $200, the insurance for one month. The adjusting journal entry and T accounts for Prepaid Insurance and Insurance Expense are as follows:

31	Insurance Expense	56	200	
	Prepaid Insurance	15		200
	Insurance expired ($2,400/12).			

Prepaid Insurance			**Insurance Expense**	
Bal.	2,400	Dec. 31	200	Dec. 31	200
Adj. Bal.	2,200				

After the adjusting entry is recorded and posted, the prepaid insurance account has a debit balance of $2,200. This balance is an asset that will become an expense in future periods. The insurance expense account has a debit balance of $200, which is an expense of the current period.

What is the effect of omitting adjusting entries? If the preceding adjustments for supplies ($1,240) and insurance ($200) are not recorded, the financial statements prepared as of December 31 will be misstated. On the income statement, Supplies Expense and Insurance Expense will be understated by a total of $1,440 ($1,240 + $200), and net income will be overstated by $1,440. On the balance sheet, Supplies and Prepaid Insurance will be overstated by a total of $1,440. Since net income increases owner's equity, Chris Clark, Capital will also be overstated by $1,440 on the balance sheet. The effects of omitting these adjusting entries on the income statement and balance sheet are as follows:

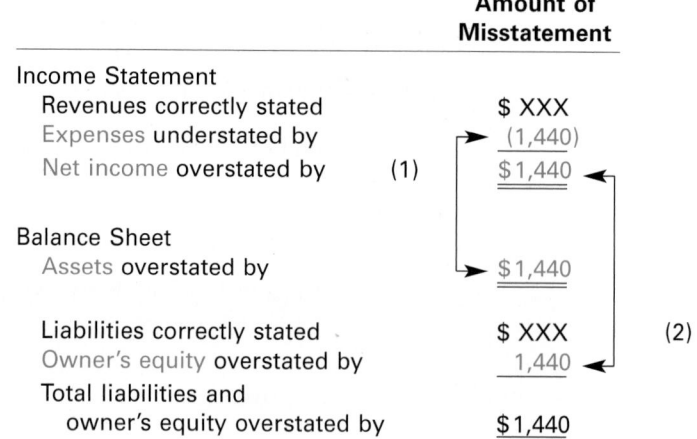

		Amount of Misstatement	
Income Statement			
Revenues correctly stated		$ XXX	
Expenses understated by		(1,440)	
Net income overstated by	(1)	$1,440	
Balance Sheet			
Assets overstated by		$1,440	
Liabilities correctly stated		$ XXX	(2)
Owner's equity overstated by		1,440	
Total liabilities and			
owner's equity overstated by		$1,440	

Arrow (1) indicates the effect of the understated expenses on assets. Arrow (2) indicates the effect of the overstated net income on owner's equity.

Integrity, Objectivity, and Ethics in Business

FREE ISSUE

Office supplies are often available to employees on a "free issue" basis. This means that employees do not have to "sign" for the release of office supplies but merely obtain the necessary supplies from a local storage area as needed. Just because supplies are easily available, however, doesn't mean they can be taken for personal use. There are many instances where employees have been terminated for taking supplies home for personal use.

Payments for prepaid expenses are sometimes made at the beginning of the period in which they will be *entirely used or consumed*. To illustrate, we use the following December 1 transaction of NetSolutions:

> Dec. 1   NetSolutions paid rent of $800 for the month.

On December 1, the rent payment of $800 represents Prepaid Rent. However, the Prepaid Rent expires daily, and at the end of December there will be no asset left. In such cases, the payment of $800 is recorded as Rent Expense rather than as Prepaid Rent. In this way, no adjusting entry is needed at the end of the period.[2]

Example Exercise 3-3   Adjustment for Prepaid Expense   ●●●●●●●● ❷

The prepaid insurance account had a beginning balance of $6,400 and was debited for $3,600 of premiums paid during the year. Journalize the adjusting entry required at the end of the year assuming the amount of unexpired insurance related to future periods is $3,250.

Follow My Example 3-3

```
Insurance Expense ...................................... 6,750
    Prepaid Insurance ..................................        6,750
        Insurance expired ($6,400 + $3,600 − $3,250).
```

For Practice: PE 3-3A, PE 3-3B

Unearned Revenues

The December 31 unadjusted trial balance of NetSolutions indicates a balance in the unearned rent account of $360. This balance represents the receipt of three months rent on December 1 for December, January, and February. At the end of December, one month's rent has been earned. Thus, the unearned rent account should be decreased (debited) by $120, and the rent revenue account should be increased (credited) by $120. The $120 represents the rental revenue for one month ($360/3). The adjusting journal entry and T accounts are shown below.

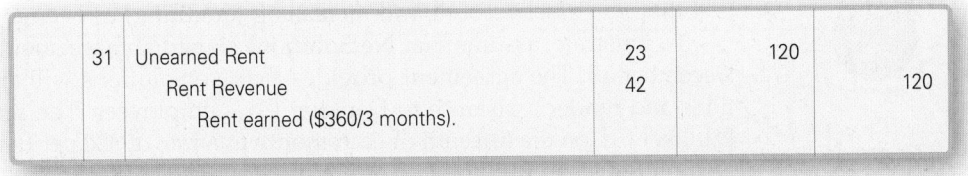

	31	Unearned Rent	23	120	
		Rent Revenue	42		120
		Rent earned ($360/3 months).			

Unearned Rent					Rent Revenue		
Dec. 31	120	Bal.	360			Dec. 31	120
		Adj. Bal.	240				

After the adjusting entry is recorded and posted, the unearned rent account has a credit balance of $240. This balance is a liability that will become revenue in a future period. Rent Revenue has a balance of $120, which is revenue of the current period.[3]

If the preceding adjustment of unearned rent and rent revenue is not recorded, the financial statements prepared on December 31 will be misstated. On the income statement, Rent Revenue and the net income will be understated by $120. On the balance sheet, Unearned Rent will be overstated by $120, and Chris Clark, Capital will be understated by $120. The effects of omitting this adjusting entry are shown at the top of the next page.

---

2 An alternative treatment of recording the cost of supplies, rent, and other prepayments of expenses is discussed in an appendix that can be downloaded from the book's companion Web site (www.cengage.com/accounting/reeve).

3 An alternative treatment of recording revenues received in advance of their being earned is discussed in an appendix that can be downloaded from the book's companion Web site (www.cengage.com/accounting/reeve).

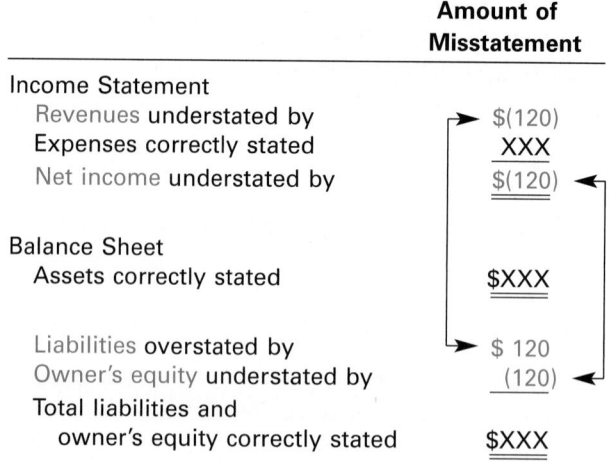

	Amount of Misstatement
Income Statement	
Revenues understated by	$(120)
Expenses correctly stated	XXX
Net income understated by	$(120)
Balance Sheet	
Assets correctly stated	$XXX
Liabilities overstated by	$ 120
Owner's equity understated by	(120)
Total liabilities and owner's equity correctly stated	$XXX

Example Exercise 3-4 Adjustment for Unearned Revenue

The balance in the unearned fees account, before adjustment at the end of the year, is $44,900. Journalize the adjusting entry required if the amount of unearned fees at the end of the year is $22,300.

Follow My Example 3-4

Unearned Fees	22,600	
Fees Earned		22,600
Fees earned ($44,900 − $22,300).		

For Practice: PE 3-4A, PE 3-4B

Accrued Revenues

During an accounting period, some revenues are recorded only when cash is received. Thus, at the end of an accounting period, there may be revenue that has been earned *but has not been recorded*. In such cases, the revenue should be recorded by increasing (debiting) an asset account and increasing (crediting) a revenue account.

To illustrate, assume that NetSolutions signed an agreement with Dankner Co. on December 15. The agreement provides that NetSolutions will answer computer questions and render assistance to Dankner Co.'s employees. The services will be billed to Dankner Co. on the fifteenth of each month at a rate of $20 per hour. As of December 31, NetSolutions had provided 25 hours of assistance to Dankner Co. The revenue of $500 (25 hours × $20) will be billed on January 15. However, NetSolutions earned the revenue in December.

The claim against the customer for payment of the $500 is an account receivable (*an asset*). Thus, the accounts receivable account should be increased (debited) by $500 and the fees earned account should be increased (credited) by $500. The adjusting journal entry and T accounts are shown below.

31	Accounts Receivable	12	500	
	Fees Earned	41		500
	Accrued fees (25 hrs. × $20).			

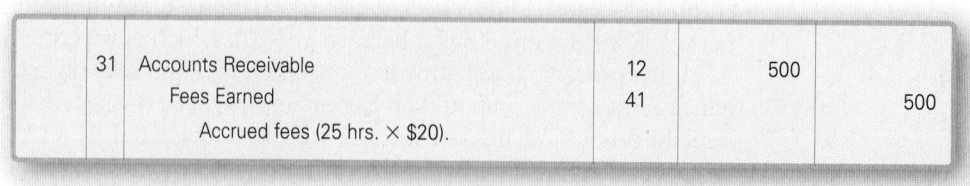

Accounts Receivable			Fees Earned	
Bal.	2,220		Bal.	16,340
Dec. 31	500		Dec. 31	500
Adj. Bal.	2,720		Adj. Bal.	16,840

If the adjustment for the accrued revenue ($500) is not recorded, Fees Earned and the net income will be understated by $500 on the income statement. On the balance sheet, Accounts Receivable and Chris Clark, Capital will be understated by $500. The effects of omitting this adjusting entry are shown below.

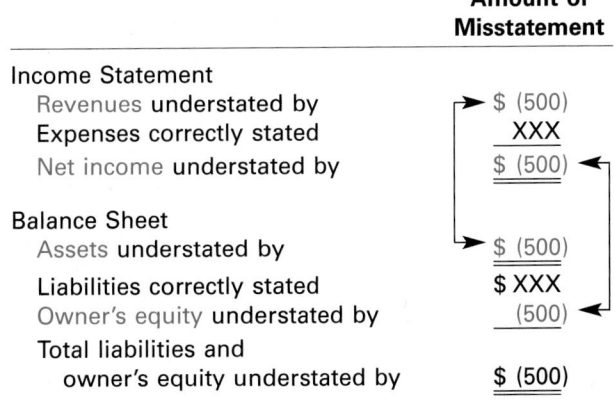

	Amount of Misstatement
Income Statement	
Revenues understated by	$ (500)
Expenses correctly stated	XXX
Net income understated by	$ (500)
Balance Sheet	
Assets understated by	$ (500)
Liabilities correctly stated	$ XXX
Owner's equity understated by	(500)
Total liabilities and owner's equity understated by	$ (500)

Example Exercise 3-5   Adjustment for Accrued Revenues   • • • • • • • •➤ ②

At the end of the current year, $13,680 of fees have been earned but have not been billed to clients. Journalize the adjusting entry to record the accrued fees.

Follow My Example 3-5

Accounts Receivable 13,680
    Fees Earned 13,680
        Accrued fees.

For Practice: PE 3-5A, PE 3-5B

Accrued Expenses

Some types of services used in earning revenues are paid for *after* the service has been performed. For example, wages expense is used hour by hour, but is paid only daily, weekly, biweekly, or monthly. At the end of the accounting period, the amount of such *accrued* but unpaid items is an expense and a liability.

For example, if the last day of the employees' pay period is not the last day of the accounting period, an accrued expense (wages expense) and the related liability (wages payable) must be recorded by an adjusting entry. This adjusting entry is necessary so that expenses are properly matched to the period in which they were incurred in earning revenue.

To illustrate, NetSolutions pays its employees biweekly. During December, NetSolutions paid wages of $950 on December 13 and $1,200 on December 27. These payments covered pay periods ending on those days as shown in Exhibit 5. As of December 31, NetSolutions owes $250 of wages to employees for Monday and Tuesday, December 30 and 31. Thus, the wages expense account should be increased (debited) by $250 and the wages payable account should be increased (credited) by $250. The adjusting journal entry and T accounts are shown below.

31	Wages Expense	51	250	
	Wages Payable	22		250
	Accrued wages.			

Wages Expense				Wages Payable	
Bal.	4,275			Dec. 31	250
Dec. 31	250				
Adj. Bal.	4,525				

After the adjusting entry is recorded and posted, the debit balance of the wages expense account is $4,525. This balance of $4,525 is the wages expense for two months, November and December. The credit balance of $250 in Wages Payable is the liability for wages owed on December 31.

As shown in Exhibit 5, NetSolutions paid wages of $1,275 on January 10. This payment includes the $250 of accrued wages recorded on December 31. Thus, on January 10, the wages payable account should be decreased (debited) by $250. Also, the wages expense account should be increased (debited) by $1,025 ($1,275 − $250), which is the wages expense for January 1–10. Finally, the cash account is decreased (credited) by $1,275. The journal entry for the payment of wages on January 10 is shown below.[4]

Jan.	10	Wages Expense	51	1,025	
		Wages Payable	22	250	
		Cash	11		1,275

What would be the effect on the financial statements if the adjustment for wages ($250) is not recorded? On the income statement, Wages Expense will be understated by $250, and the net income will be overstated by $250. On the balance sheet, Wages

Exhibit 5

Accrued Wages

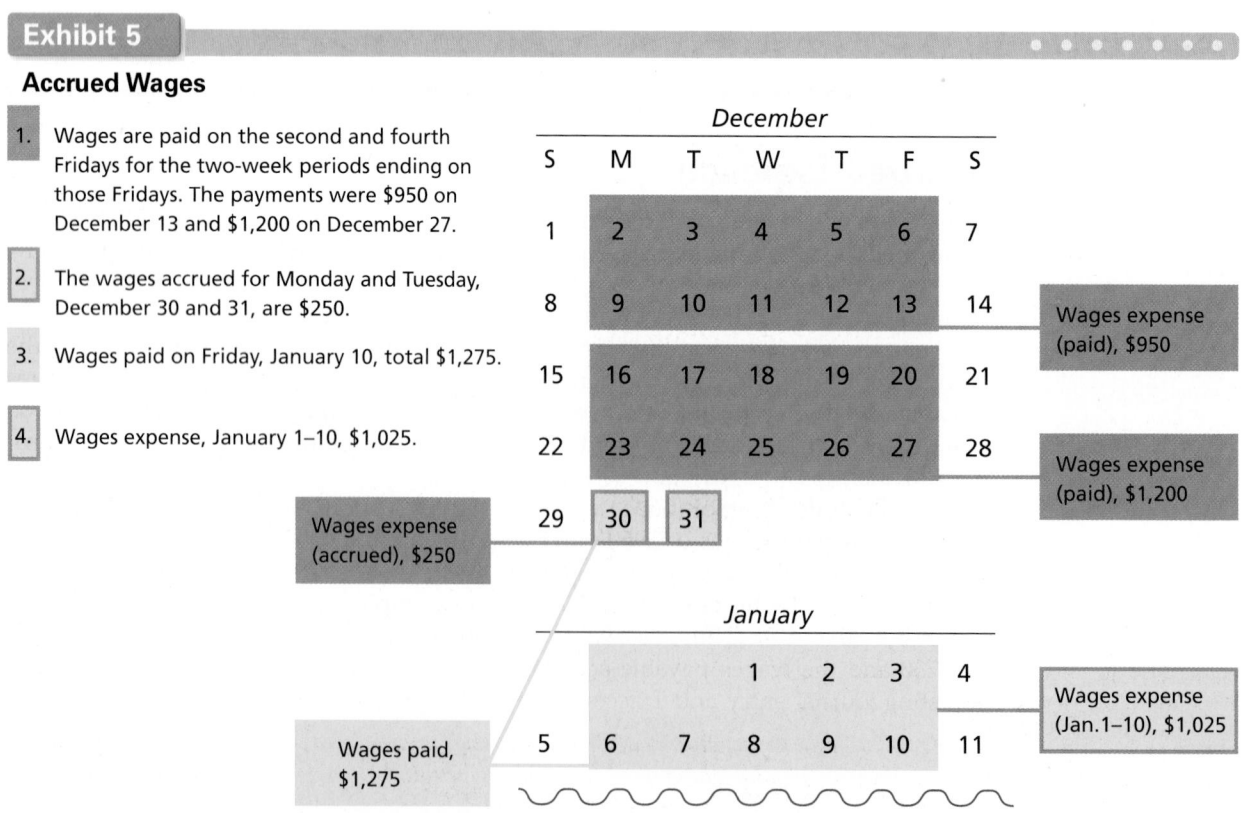

1. Wages are paid on the second and fourth Fridays for the two-week periods ending on those Fridays. The payments were $950 on December 13 and $1,200 on December 27.

2. The wages accrued for Monday and Tuesday, December 30 and 31, are $250.

3. Wages paid on Friday, January 10, total $1,275.

4. Wages expense, January 1–10, $1,025.

Payable will be understated by $250, and Chris Clark, Capital will be overstated by $250. The effects of omitting this adjusting entry are shown as follows:

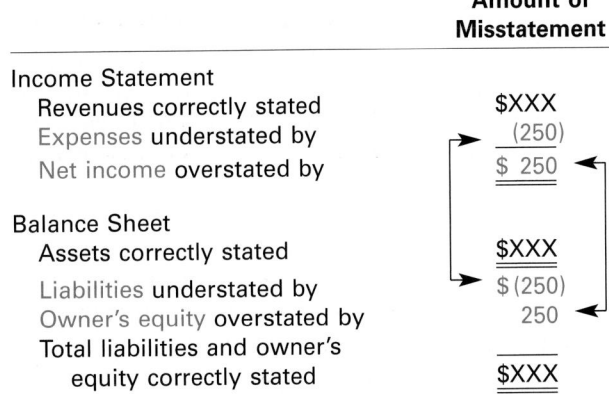

	Amount of Misstatement
Income Statement	
Revenues correctly stated	$XXX
Expenses understated by	(250)
Net income overstated by	$ 250
Balance Sheet	
Assets correctly stated	$XXX
Liabilities understated by	$ (250)
Owner's equity overstated by	250
Total liabilities and owner's equity correctly stated	$XXX

Example Exercise 3-6   Adjustment for Accrued Expense · · · · · · · · › 2

Sanregret Realty Co. pays weekly salaries of $12,500 on Friday for a five-day week ending on that day. Journalize the necessary adjusting entry at the end of the accounting period, assuming that the period ends on Thursday.

Follow My Example 3-6

Salaries Expense	10,000	
Salaries Payable		10,000
Accrued salaries [($12,500/5 days) × 4 days].		

For Practice: PE 3-6A, PE 3-6B

Depreciation Expense

Fixed assets, or **plant assets**, are physical resources that are owned and used by a business and are permanent or have a long life. Examples of fixed assets include land, buildings, and equipment. In a sense, fixed assets are a type of *long-term* prepaid expense. Because of their unique nature and long life, they are discussed separately from other prepaid expenses, such as supplies and prepaid insurance.

Fixed assets such as office equipment are used to generate revenue much like supplies are used to generate revenue. Unlike supplies, however, there is no visible reduction in the quantity of the equipment. Instead, as time passes, the equipment loses its ability to provide useful services. This decrease in usefulness is called **depreciation**.

All fixed assets, except land, lose their usefulness and, thus, are said to **depreciate**. As a fixed asset depreciates while being used to generate revenue, a portion of its cost should be recorded as an expense. This periodic expense is called **depreciation expense**.

The adjusting entry to record depreciation expense is similar to the adjusting entry for supplies used. The depreciation expense account is increased (debited) for the amount of depreciation. However, the fixed asset account is not decreased (credited). This is because both the original cost of a fixed asset and the depreciation recorded since its purchase are normally reported on the balance sheet. Instead, an account entitled **Accumulated Depreciation** is increased (credited).

Accumulated depreciation accounts are called **contra accounts**, or **contra asset accounts**. This is because accumulated depreciation accounts are deducted from their related fixed asset accounts on the balance sheet. The normal balance of a contra account is opposite to the account from which it is deducted. Since the normal balance of a fixed asset account is a debit, the normal balance of an accumulated depreciation account is a credit.

Lowe's Companies, Inc., reported land, buildings, and store equipment at a cost of over $18 billion and accumulated depreciation of over $4.1 billion.

The normal titles for fixed asset accounts and their related contra asset accounts are as follows:

Fixed Asset Account	Contra Asset Account
Land	None—Land is not depreciated.
Buildings	Accumulated Depreciation—Buildings
Store Equipment	Accumulated Depreciation—Store Equipment
Office Equipment	Accumulated Depreciation—Office Equipment

The December 31, 2009, unadjusted trial balance of NetSolutions (Exhibit 3) indicates that NetSolutions owns two fixed assets: land and office equipment. Land does not depreciate; however, an adjusting entry should be recorded for the depreciation of the office equipment for December. We assume that the office equipment has depreciated $50 during December.[5] Thus, the depreciation expense account should be increased (debited) by $50 and the accumulated depreciation—office equipment account should be increased (credited) by $50. The adjusting journal entry and T accounts are shown below.

31	Depreciation Expense	53	50	
	Accumulated Depreciation—Office Equip.	19		50
	Depreciation on office equipment.			

Office Equipment		Accumulated Depr.—Office Equip.	
Bal. 1,800			Dec. 31 50

Depreciation Expense	
Dec. 31 50	

After the adjusting journal entry is recorded and posted, the office equipment account still has a debit balance of $1,800. This is the original cost of the office equipment that was purchased on December 4. The accumulated depreciation—office equipment account has a credit balance of $50. The difference between these two balances of $1,750 ($1,800 − $50) is the cost of the office equipment that has not yet been depreciated. This amount of $1,750 is called the **book value of the asset** (or **net book value**).

The office equipment and its related accumulated depreciation are reported on the December 31, 2009 balance sheet as follows:

Office equipment	$1,800	
Less accumulated depreciation	50	$1,750

The market value of a fixed asset usually differs from its book value. This is because depreciation is an *allocation* method, not a *valuation* method. That is, depreciation allocates the cost of a fixed asset to expense over its estimated life. Depreciation does not measure changes in market values, which vary from year to year. Thus, on December 31, 2009, the market value of NetSolutions' office equipment could be more or less than $1,750.

If the adjustment for depreciation ($50) is not recorded, Depreciation Expense on the income statement will be understated by $50, and the net income will be overstated by $50. On the balance sheet, the book value of Office Equipment and Chris Clark, Capital will be overstated by $50. The effects of omitting the adjustment for depreciation are shown at the top of the next page.

5 We describe and illustrate methods of computing depreciation expense in Chapter 10.

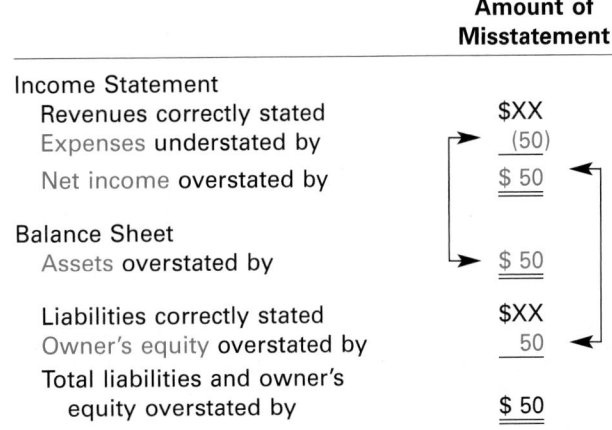

	Amount of Misstatement
Income Statement	
Revenues correctly stated	$XX
Expenses understated by	(50)
Net income overstated by	$ 50
Balance Sheet	
Assets overstated by	$ 50
Liabilities correctly stated	$XX
Owner's equity overstated by	50
Total liabilities and owner's equity overstated by	$ 50

Example Exercise 3-7 Adjustment for Depreciation   • • • • • • • • ➤ 2

The estimated amount of depreciation on equipment for the current year is $4,250. Journalize the adjusting entry to record the depreciation.

Follow My Example 3-7

Depreciation Expense	4,250	
Accumulated Depreciation—Equipment		4,250
Depreciation on equipment.		

For Practice: PE 3-7A, PE 3-7B

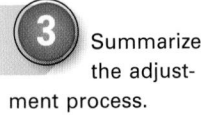

3 Summarize the adjustment process.

@netsolutions

Summary of Adjustment Process

We have described and illustrated the basic types of adjusting entries. A summary of these basic adjustments is shown in Exhibit 6 on pages 112–113.

The adjusting entries for NetSolutions are shown in Exhibit 7 on page 114. The adjusting entries are dated as of the last day of the period. However, because collecting the adjustment data requires time, the entries are usually recorded at a later date. An explanation is included with each adjusting entry.

NetSolutions' adjusting entries have been posted to the ledger shown in Exhibit 8 on pages 115–116. The adjustments are shown in color in Exhibit 8 to distinguish them from other transactions.

Example Exercise 3-8 Effect of Omitting Adjustments   • • • • • • • • ➤ 3

For the year ending December 31, 2010, Mann Medical Co. mistakenly omitted adjusting entries for (1) $8,600 of unearned revenue that was earned, (2) earned revenue that was not billed of $12,500, and (3) accrued wages of $2,900. Indicate the combined effect of the errors on (a) revenues, (b) expenses, and (c) net income for the year ended December 31, 2010.

Follow My Example 3-8

a. Revenues were understated by $21,100 ($8,600 + $12,500).

b. Expenses were understated by $2,900.

c. Net income was understated by $18,200 ($8,600 + $12,500 − $2,900).

For Practice: PE 3-8A, PE 3-8B

Exhibit 6

Summary of Adjustments

PREPAID EXPENSES

Examples	Reason for Adjustment	Adjusting Entry		Examples from NetSolutions	Financial Statement Impact if Adjusting Entry Is Omitted
		Dr.	Cr.		

Supplies, Prepaid Insurance	Prepaid expenses (assets) have been used or consumed in the business operations.	Expense	Asset	Supplies Expense 1,240 Supplies 1,240
				
				Insurance Expense 200 Prepaid Insurance 200
					Income Statement:
					  Revenues No effect
					  Expenses Understated
					  Net income Overstated
					Balance Sheet:
					  Assets Overstated
					  Liabilities No effect
					  Owner's Equity Overstated
					    (Capital)

UNEARNED REVENUES

Examples	Reason for Adjustment	Adjusting Entry		Examples from NetSolutions	Financial Statement Impact if Adjusting Entry Is Omitted
		Dr.	Cr.		

Unearned rent, magazine subscriptions received in advance, fees received in advance of services	Cash received before the services have been provided is recorded as a liability. Some services have been provided to customer before the end of the accounting period.	Liability	Revenue	Unearned Rent 120 Rent Revenue 120	Income Statement:
					  Revenues Understated
					  Expenses No effect
					  Net income Understated
					Balance Sheet:
					  Assets No effect
					  Liabilities Overstated
					  Owner's Equity Understated
					    (Capital)

ACCRUED REVENUES

Examples	Reason for Adjustment	Adjusting Entry		Examples from NetSolutions	Financial Statement Impact if Adjusting Entry Is Omitted
		Dr.	Cr.		

Services performed but not billed, interest to be received	Services have been provided to the customer, but have not been billed or recorded. Interest has been earned, but has not been received or recorded.	Asset	Revenue	Accounts Receivable 500 Fees Earned 500	Income Statement:
					  Revenues Understated
					  Expenses No effect
					  Net income Understated
					Balance Sheet:
					  Assets Understated
					  Liabilities No effect
					  Owner's Equity Understated
					    (Capital)

ACCRUED EXPENSES

Examples	Reason for Adjustment	Adjusting Entry	Examples from NetSolutions	Financial Statement Impact if Adjusting Entry Is Omitted
Wages or salaries incurred but not paid, interest incurred but not paid	Expenses have been incurred, but have not been paid or recorded.	Expense Dr. Liability Cr.	Wages Expense 250 Wages Payable 250	Income Statement: Revenues No effect Expenses Understated Net income Overstated Balance Sheet: Assets No effect Liabilities Understated Owner's Equity Overstated (Capital)

DEPRECIATION

Examples	Reason for Adjustment	Adjusting Entry	Examples from NetSolutions	Financial Statement Impact if Adjusting Entry Is Omitted

Depreciation of equipment and buildings	Fixed assets depreciate as they are used or consumed in the business operations.	Expense Dr.
		 Contra Asset Cr.
			Depreciation Expense—
			 Office Equipment 50
			 Accumulated Depr.—
			   Office Equipment 50
				Income Statement:
				 Revenues No effect
				 Expenses Understated
				 Net income Overstated
				 Balance Sheet:
				 Assets Overstated
				 Liabilities No effect
				 Owner's Equity Overstated
				   (Capital)

Exhibit 7

Adjusting Entries— NetSolutions

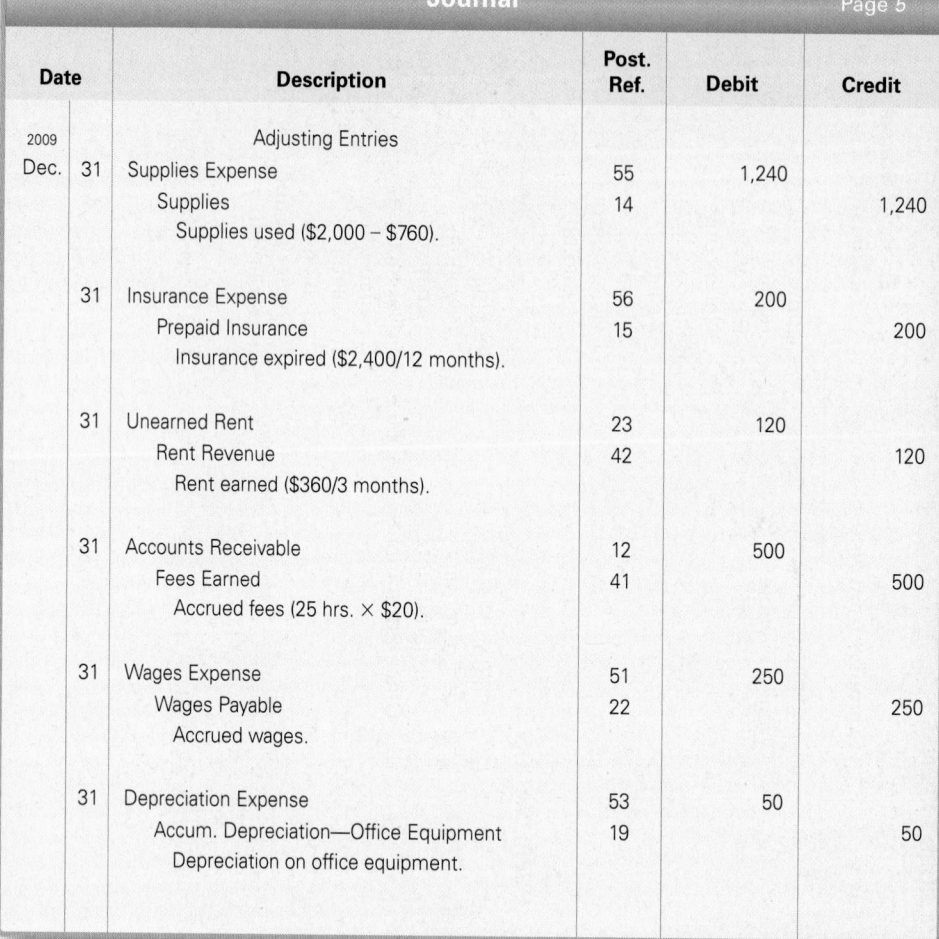

Date		Description	Post. Ref.	Debit	Credit
2009		Adjusting Entries			
Dec.	31	Supplies Expense	55	1,240	
		Supplies	14		1,240
		Supplies used ($2,000 – $760).			
	31	Insurance Expense	56	200	
		Prepaid Insurance	15		200
		Insurance expired ($2,400/12 months).			
	31	Unearned Rent	23	120	
		Rent Revenue	42		120
		Rent earned ($360/3 months).			
	31	Accounts Receivable	12	500	
		Fees Earned	41		500
		Accrued fees (25 hrs. × $20).			
	31	Wages Expense	51	250	
		Wages Payable	22		250
		Accrued wages.			
	31	Depreciation Expense	53	50	
		Accum. Depreciation—Office Equipment	19		50
		Depreciation on office equipment.			

Journal Page 5

One way for an accountant to check whether all adjustments have been made is to compare the current period's adjustments with those of the prior period.

Exhibit 8

Ledger with Adjusting Entries—NetSolutions

Account Cash — Account No. 11

Date	Item	Post. Ref.	Debit	Credit	Balance Debit	Balance Credit
2009						
Nov. 1		1	25,000		25,000	
5		1		20,000	5,000	
18		1	7,500		12,500	
30		1		3,650	8,850	
30		1		950	7,900	
30		2		2,000	5,900	
Dec. 1		2		2,400	3,500	
1		2		800	2,700	
1		2	360		3,060	
6		2		180	2,880	
11		2		400	2,480	
13		3		950	1,530	
16		3	3,100		4,630	
20		3		900	3,730	
21		3	650		4,380	
23		3		1,450	2,930	
27		3		1,200	1,730	
31		3		310	1,420	
31		4		225	1,195	
31		4	2,870		4,065	
31		4		2,000	2,065	

Account Accounts Receivable — Account No. 12

Date	Item	Post. Ref.	Debit	Credit	Balance Debit	Balance Credit
2009						
Dec. 16		3	1,750		1,750	
21		3		650	1,100	
31		4	1,120		2,220	
31	Adjusting	5	500		2,720	

Account Supplies — Account No. 14

Date	Item	Post. Ref.	Debit	Credit	Balance Debit	Balance Credit
2009						
Nov. 10		1	1,350		1,350	
30		1		800	550	
Dec. 23		3	1,450		2,000	
31	Adjusting	5		1,240	760	

Account Prepaid Insurance — Account No. 15

Date	Item	Post. Ref.	Debit	Credit	Balance Debit	Balance Credit
2009						
Dec. 1		2	2,400		2,400	
31	Adjusting	5		200	2,200	

Account Land — Account No. 17

Date	Item	Post. Ref.	Debit	Credit	Balance Debit	Balance Credit
2009						
Nov. 5		1	20,000		20,000	

Account Office Equipment — Account No. 18

Date	Item	Post. Ref.	Debit	Credit	Balance Debit	Balance Credit
2009						
Dec. 4		2	1,800		1,800	

Account Acc. Depr.—Office Equip. — Account No. 19

Date	Item	Post. Ref.	Debit	Credit	Balance Debit	Balance Credit
2009						
Dec. 31	Adjusting	5		50		50

Account Accounts Payable — Account No. 21

Date	Item	Post. Ref.	Debit	Credit	Balance Debit	Balance Credit
2009						
Nov. 10		1		1,350		1,350
30		1	950			400
Dec. 4		2		1,800		2,200
11		2	400			1,800
20		3	900			900

Account Wages Payable — Account No. 22

Date	Item	Post. Ref.	Debit	Credit	Balance Debit	Balance Credit
2009						
Dec. 31	Adjusting	5		250		250

Account Unearned Rent — Account No. 23

Date	Item	Post. Ref.	Debit	Credit	Balance Debit	Balance Credit
2009						
Dec. 1		2		360		360
31	Adjusting	5	120			240

Account Chris Clark, Capital — Account No. 31

Date	Item	Post. Ref.	Debit	Credit	Balance Debit	Balance Credit
2009						
Nov. 1		1		25,000		25,000

(continued)

Exhibit 8

Ledger with Adjusting Entries—NetSolutions *(concluded)*

Account Chris Clark, Drawing — Account No. 32

Date	Item	Post. Ref.	Debit	Credit	Balance Debit	Balance Credit
2009						
Nov. 30		2	2,000		2,000	
Dec. 31		4	2,000		4,000	

Account Fees Earned — Account No. 41

Date	Item	Post. Ref.	Debit	Credit	Balance Debit	Balance Credit
2009						
Nov. 18		1		7,500		7,500
Dec. 16		3		3,100		10,600
16		3		1,750		12,350
31		4		2,870		15,220
31		4		1,120		16,340
31	Adjusting	5		500		16,840

Account Rent Revenue — Account No. 42

Date	Item	Post. Ref.	Debit	Credit	Balance Debit	Balance Credit
2009						
Dec. 31	Adjusting	5		120		120

Account Wages Expense — Account No. 51

Date	Item	Post. Ref.	Debit	Credit	Balance Debit	Balance Credit
2009						
Nov. 30		1	2,125		2,125	
Dec. 13		3	950		3,075	
27		3	1,200		4,275	
31	Adjusting	5	250		4,525	

Account Rent Expense — Account No. 52

Date	Item	Post. Ref.	Debit	Credit	Balance Debit	Balance Credit
2009						
Nov. 30		1	800		800	
Dec. 1		2	800		1,600	

Account Depreciation Expense — Account No. 53

Date	Item	Post. Ref.	Debit	Credit	Balance Debit	Balance Credit
2009						
Dec. 31	Adjusting	5	50		50	

Account Utilities Expense — Account No. 54

Date	Item	Post. Ref.	Debit	Credit	Balance Debit	Balance Credit
2009						
Nov. 30		1	450		450	
Dec. 31		3	310		760	
31		4	225		985	

Account Supplies Expense — Account No. 55

Date	Item	Post. Ref.	Debit	Credit	Balance Debit	Balance Credit
2009						
Nov. 30		1	800		800	
Dec. 31	Adjusting	5	1,240		2,040	

Account Insurance Expense — Account No. 56

Date	Item	Post. Ref.	Debit	Credit	Balance Debit	Balance Credit
2009						
Dec. 31	Adjusting	5	200		200	

Account Miscellaneous Expense — Account No. 59

Date	Item	Post. Ref.	Debit	Credit	Balance Debit	Balance Credit
2009						
Nov. 30		1	275		275	
Dec. 6		2	180		455	

Exhibit 9

Adjusted Trial Balance

NetSolutions
Adjusted Trial Balance
December 31, 2009

	Debit Balances	Credit Balances
Cash	2,065	
Accounts Receivable	2,720	
Supplies	760	
Prepaid Insurance	2,200	
Land	20,000	
Office Equipment	1,800	
Accumulated Depreciation—Office Equipment		50
Accounts Payable		900
Wages Payable		250
Unearned Rent		240
Chris Clark, Capital		25,000
Chris Clark, Drawing	4,000	
Fees Earned		16,840
Rent Revenue		120
Wages Expense	4,525	
Rent Expense	1,600	
Depreciation Expense	50	
Utilities Expense	985	
Supplies Expense	2,040	
Insurance Expense	200	
Miscellaneous Expense	455	
	43,400	43,400

4 Prepare an adjusted trial balance.

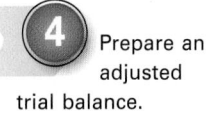

Adjusted Trial Balance

After the adjusting entries have been posted, an **adjusted trial balance** is prepared. The adjusted trial balance verifies the equality of the total debit and credit balances before the financial statements are prepared. If the adjusted trial balance does not balance, an error has occurred. However, as we discussed in Chapter 2, errors may occur even though the adjusted trial balance totals agree. For example, if an adjusting entry were omitted, the adjusted trial balance totals would still agree.

Exhibit 9 shows the adjusted trial balance for NetSolutions as of December 31, 2009. In Chapter 4, we discuss how financial statements, including a classified balance sheet, can be prepared from an adjusted trial balance.

A spreadsheet can be used to prepare adjusting entries, post adjustments to ledger accounts, and prepare an adjusted trial balance. This is illustrated for a single adjusting entry, NetSolutions' December 31 adjustment for supplies used.

a.   Posting adjusting entry to ledger.

	A	B	C	D	E
113					
114		**Journal**			Page 5
115	**Date**	**Description**	**Post. Ref.**	**Debit**	**Credit**
116	2009				
117	31-Dec	Supplies Expense	55	1,240	
118		Supplies	14		1,240
119		Supplies used ($2,000 – $760)			
120					

⏮ ◀ ▶ ⏭ **JE**   GL   UTB   ATB

— a.
b.
c.

	A	B	C	D	E	F	G
174	**Account**	*Supplies Expense*				**Account No.**	55
175						**Balance**	
176	**Date**	**Item**	**Post. Ref.**	**Debit**	**Credit**	**Debit**	**Credit**
177	2009						
178	30-Nov		1	800		800	
179	31-Dec	Adjusting	5	=JE!D117		=F178+D179-E179	← d.

⏮ ◀ ▶ ⏭ JE   **GL**   UTB   ATB

	A	B	C	D	E	F	G
38							
39	**Account**	*Supplies*				**Account No.**	14
40						**Balance**	
41	**Date**	**Item**	**Post. Ref.**	**Debit**	**Credit**	**Debit**	**Credit**
42	2009						
43	10-Nov		1	1,350		1,350	
44	30-Nov		1		800	550	
45	23-Dec		3	1,450		2,000	
46	31-Dec	Adjusting	5		=JE!E118	=F45+D46-E46	← e.

⏮ ◀ ▶ ⏭ JE   **GL**   UTB   ATB

b.   Enter into cell D179 (Ledger worksheet) the cell reference for the debit to *Supplies Expense* (Journal worksheet), =JE!D117

c.   Enter into cell E46 (Ledger worksheet) the cell reference for the debit to *Supplies Expense* (Journal worksheet), =JE!E118

d.   Copy (Ledger worksheet) the formula for the cumulative balance from cell F178 to F179. (The formula is =F178+D179-E179)

e.   Copy (Ledger worksheet) the formula for the cumulative balance from cell F45 to F46. (The formula is =F45+D46-E46)

Prepare the adjusted trial balance by referencing the cell addresses from the ledger:

	A	B	C
1	**NetSolutions**		
2	**Adjusted Trial Balance**		
3	**December 31, 2009**		
4		Debit	Credit
5		Balances	Balances
6	Cash	2.065	
7	Accounts Receivable	2,720	
8	Supplies	=GL!F46 ← g.	
9	Prepaid Insurance	2,200	
10	Land	20,000	
11	Office Equipment	1,800	
12	Accumulated Depreciation		50
13	Accounts Payable		900
14	Wages Payable		250
15	Unearned Rent		240
16	Chris Clark, Capital		25,000
17	Chris Clark, Drawing	4,000	
18	Fees Earned		16,840
19	Rent Revenue		120
20	Wages Expense	4,525	
21	Rent Expense	1,600	
22	Depreciation Expense	50	
23	Utilities Expense	985	
24	Supplies Expense	=GL!F179 ← g.	
25	Insurance Expense	200	
26	Miscellaneous Expense	455	
27		=SUM(B6:B26)	=SUM(B6:B26) } h.
28			
29			

f.

   JE   GL   UTB **ATB**

f.   Insert a new worksheet and label "ATB" for adjusted trial balance.
g.   Enter into the appropriate cell the adjusted ledger account balance cell references from the Ledger worksheet. (*Supplies,* =GL!F46; *Supplies Expense,* =GL!F179)
h.   Enter the formulas for the =SUM of the debit and credit balances for the adjusted trial balance.

tr*it*   Go to the hands-on *Excel Tutor* for this example!

Example Exercise 3-9   Effect of Errors on Adjusted Trial Balance   **4**

For each of the following errors, considered individually, indicate whether the error would cause the adjusted trial balance totals to be unequal. If the error would cause the adjusted trial balance totals to be unequal, indicate whether the debit or credit total is higher and by how much.

a. The adjustment for accrued fees of $5,340 was journalized as a debit to Accounts Payable for $5,340 and a credit to Fees Earned of $5,340.

b. The adjustment for depreciation of $3,260 was journalized as a debit to Depreciation Expense for $3,620 and a credit to Accumulated Depreciation for $3,260.

Follow My Example 3-9

a. The totals are equal even though the debit should have been to Accounts Receivable instead of Accounts Payable.

b. The totals are unequal. The debit total is higher by $360 ($3,620 − $3,260).

For Practice: PE 3-9A, PE 3-9B

Financial Analysis and Interpretation

Comparing each item in a current statement with a total amount within that same statement is useful in analyzing relationships within a financial statement. *Vertical analysis* is the term used to describe such comparisons.

In vertical analysis of a balance sheet, each asset item is stated as a percent of the total assets. Each liability and owner's equity item is stated as a percent of the total liabilities and owner's equity. In vertical analysis of an income statement, each item is stated as a percent of revenues or fees earned.

Vertical analysis may be prepared for several periods to analyze changes in relationships over time. Vertical analysis of two years of income statements for J. Holmes, Attorney-at-Law, is shown below.

The preceding vertical analysis indicates both favorable and unfavorable trends affecting the income statement of J. Holmes, Attorney-at-Law. The increase in wages expense of 2% (32% − 30%) is an unfavorable trend, as is the increase in utilities expense of 0.7% (6.7% − 6.0%). A favorable trend is the decrease in supplies expense of 0.6% (2.0% − 1.4%). Rent expense and miscellaneous expense as a percent of fees earned were constant. The net result of these trends was that net income decreased as a percent of fees earned from 52.8% to 50.7%.

The analysis of the various percentages shown for J. Holmes, Attorney-at-Law, can be enhanced by comparisons with industry averages. Such averages are published by trade associations and financial information services. Any major differences between industry averages should be investigated.

J. Holmes, Attorney-at-Law
Income Statements
For the Years Ended December 31, 2010, and 2009

	2010		2009	
	Amount	Percent	Amount	Percent
Fees earned	$187,500	100.0%	$150,000	100.0%
Operating expenses:				
Wages expense	$ 60,000	32.0%	$ 45,000	30.0%*
Rent expense	15,000	8.0%	12,000	8.0%
Utilities expense	12,500	6.7%	9,000	6.0%
Supplies expense	2,700	1.4%	3,000	2.0%
Miscellaneous expense	2,300	1.2%	1,800	1.2%
Total operating expenses	$ 92,500	49.3%	$ 70,800	47.2%
Net income	$ 95,000	50.7%	$ 79,200	52.8%

*$45,000 ÷ $150,000

1 Describe the nature of the adjusting process.

Key Points	Key Learning Outcomes	Example Exercises	Practice Exercises
The accrual basis of accounting requires that revenues are reported in the period in which they are earned and expenses matched with the revenues they generate. The updating of accounts at the end of the accounting period is called the adjusting process. Each adjusting entry affects an income statement and balance sheet account. The four types of accounts requiring adjusting entries are prepaid expenses, unearned revenues, accrued revenues, and accrued expenses.	• Explain why accrual accounting requires adjusting entries.		
	• List accounts that do and do NOT require adjusting entries at the end of the accounting period.	3-1	3-1A, 3-1B
	• Give an example of a prepaid expense, unearned revenue, accrued revenue, and accrued expense.	3-2	3-2A, 3-2B

2 Journalize entries for accounts requiring adjustment.

Key Points	Key Learning Outcomes	Example Exercises	Practice Exercises
Adjusting entries illustrated in this chapter include prepaid expenses, unearned revenues, accrued revenues, and accrued expenses. In addition, the adjusting entry necessary to record depreciation on fixed assets was illustrated.	• Prepare an adjusting entry for a prepaid expense.	3-3	3-3A, 3-3B
	• Prepare an adjusting entry for an unearned revenue.	3-4	3-4A, 3-4B
	• Prepare an adjusting entry for an accrued revenue.	3-5	3-5A, 3-5B
	• Prepare an adjusting entry for an accrued expense.	3-6	3-6A, 3-6B
	• Prepare an adjusting entry for depreciation expense.	3-7	3-7A, 3-7B

3 Summarize the adjustment process.

Key Points	Key Learning Outcomes	Example Exercises	Practice Exercises
A summary of adjustments, including the type of adjustment, reason for the adjustment, the adjusting entry, and the effect of omitting an adjustment on the financial statements, is shown in Exhibit 6.	• Determine the effect on the income statement and balance sheet of omitting an adjusting entry for prepaid expense, unearned revenue, accrued revenue, accrued expense, and depreciation.	3-8	3-8A, 3-8B

4 Prepare an adjusted trial balance.

Key Points	Key Learning Outcomes	Example Exercises	Practice Exercises
After all the adjusting entries have been posted, the equality of the total debit balances and total credit balances is verified by an adjusted trial balance.	• Prepare an adjusted trial balance.		
	• Determine the effect of errors on the equality of the adjusted trial balance.	3-9	3-9A, 3-9B

Key Terms

accounting period concept (98)
accrual basis of accounting (98)
accrued expenses (101)
accrued revenues (101)
accumulated depreciation (109)
adjusted trial balance (117)
adjusting entries (99)

adjusting process (99)
book value of the asset (or net book value) (110)
cash basis of accounting (98)
contra account (or contra asset account) (109)
depreciate (109)
depreciation (109)

depreciation expense (109)
fixed assets (or plant assets) (109)
matching concept (or matching principle) (98)
prepaid expenses (100)
revenue recognition concept (98)
unearned revenues (100)

Illustrative Problem

Three years ago, T. Roderick organized Harbor Realty. At July 31, 2010, the end of the current year, the unadjusted trial balance of Harbor Realty appears as shown below.

Harbor Realty
Unadjusted Trial Balance
July 31, 2010

	Debit Balances	Credit Balances
Cash	3,425	
Accounts Receivable	7,000	
Supplies	1,270	
Prepaid Insurance	620	
Office Equipment	51,650	
Accumulated Depreciation—Office Equipment		9,700
Accounts Payable		925
Wages Payable		0
Unearned Fees		1,250
T. Roderick, Capital		29,000
T. Roderick, Drawing	5,200	
Fees Earned		59,125
Wages Expense	22,415	
Depreciation Expense	0	
Rent Expense	4,200	
Utilities Expense	2,715	
Supplies Expense	0	
Insurance Expense	0	
Miscellaneous Expense	1,505	
	100,000	100,000

The data needed to determine year-end adjustments are as follows:

a. Supplies on hand at July 31, 2010, $380.
b. Insurance premiums expired during the year, $315.
c. Depreciation of equipment during the year, $4,950.
d. Wages accrued but not paid at July 31, 2010, $440.
e. Accrued fees earned but not recorded at July 31, 2010, $1,000.
f. Unearned fees on July 31, 2010, $750.

Instructions

1. Prepare the necessary adjusting journal entries. Include journal entry explanations.
2. Determine the balance of the accounts affected by the adjusting entries, and prepare an adjusted trial balance.

Solution

1.

	Journal			
Date	**Description**	**Post. Ref.**	**Debit**	**Credit**
2010 July 31	Supplies Expense		890	
	Supplies			890
	Supplies used ($1,270 – $380).			
31	Insurance Expense		315	
	Prepaid Insurance			315
	Insurance expired.			
31	Depreciation Expense		4,950	
	Accumulated Depreciation—Office Equipment			4,950
	Depreciation expense.			
31	Wages Expense		440	
	Wages Payable			440
	Accrued wages.			
31	Accounts Receivable		1,000	
	Fees Earned			1,000
	Accrued fees.			
31	Unearned Fees		500	
	Fees Earned			500
	Fees earned ($1,250 – $750).			

2.

Harbor Realty Adjusted Trial Balance July 31, 2010	Debit Balances	Credit Balances
Cash	3,425	
Accounts Receivable	8,000	
Supplies	380	
Prepaid Insurance	305	
Office Equipment	51,650	
Accumulated Depreciation—Office Equipment		14,650
Accounts Payable		925
Wages Payable		440
Unearned Fees		750
T. Roderick, Capital		29,000
T. Roderick, Drawing	5,200	
Fees Earned		60,625
Wages Expense	22,855	
Depreciation Expense	4,950	
Rent Expense	4,200	
Utilities Expense	2,715	
Supplies Expense	890	
Insurance Expense	315	
Miscellaneous Expense	1,505	
	106,390	106,390

Self-Examination Questions (Answers at End of Chapter)

1. Which of the following items represents a deferral?
   A. Prepaid insurance   C. Fees earned
   B. Wages payable   D. Accumulated
                              depreciation

2. If the supplies account, before adjustment on May 31, indicated a balance of $2,250, and supplies on hand at May 31 totaled $950, the adjusting entry would be:
   A. debit Supplies, $950; credit Supplies Expense, $950.
   B. debit Supplies, $1,300; credit Supplies Expense, $1,300.
   C. debit Supplies Expense, $950; credit Supplies, $950.
   D. debit Supplies Expense, $1,300; credit Supplies, $1,300.

3. The balance in the unearned rent account for Jones Co. as of December 31 is $1,200. If Jones Co. failed to record the adjusting entry for $600 of rent earned during December, the effect on the balance sheet and income statement for December would be:
   A. assets understated $600; net income overstated $600.

B. liabilities understated $600; net income understated $600.
C. liabilities overstated $600; net income understated $600.
D. liabilities overstated $600; net income overstated $600.

4. If the estimated amount of depreciation on equipment for a period is $2,000, the adjusting entry to record depreciation would be:
   A. debit Depreciation Expense, $2,000; credit Equipment, $2,000.
   B. debit Equipment, $2,000; credit Depreciation Expense, $2,000.
   C. debit Depreciation Expense, $2,000; credit Accumulated Depreciation, $2,000.
   D. debit Accumulated Depreciation, $2,000; credit Depreciation Expense, $2,000.

5. If the equipment account has a balance of $22,500 and its accumulated depreciation account has a balance of $14,000, the book value of the equipment would be:
   A. $36,500.   C. $14,000.
   B. $22,500.   D. $8,500.

Eye Openers

1. How are revenues and expenses reported on the income statement under (a) the cash basis of accounting and (b) the accrual basis of accounting?
2. Fees for services provided are billed to a customer during 2009. The customer remits the amount owed in 2010. During which year would the revenues be reported on the income statement under (a) the cash basis? (b) the accrual basis?
3. Employees performed services in 2009, but the wages were not paid until 2010. During which year would the wages expense be reported on the income statement under (a) the cash basis? (b) the accrual basis?
4. Is the matching concept related to (a) the cash basis of accounting or (b) the accrual basis of accounting?
5. Is the cash balance on the unadjusted trial balance the amount that should normally be reported on the balance sheet? Explain.
6. Is the supplies balance on the unadjusted trial balance the amount that should normally be reported on the balance sheet? Explain.
7. Why are adjusting entries needed at the end of an accounting period?
8. What is the difference between *adjusting entries* and *correcting entries*?
9. Identify the four different categories of adjusting entries frequently required at the end of an accounting period.
10. If the effect of the debit portion of an adjusting entry is to increase the balance of an asset account, which of the following statements describes the effect of the credit portion of the entry?
    a. Increases the balance of a liability account.
    b. Increases the balance of a revenue account.
    c. Increases the balance of an expense account.
11. If the effect of the credit portion of an adjusting entry is to increase the balance of a liability account, which of the following statements describes the effect of the debit portion of the entry?
    a. Increases the balance of an expense account.
    b. Increases the balance of a revenue account.
    c. Increases the balance of an asset account.
12. Does every adjusting entry have an effect on determining the amount of net income for a period? Explain.
13. What is the nature of the balance in the prepaid insurance account at the end of the accounting period (a) before adjustment? (b) after adjustment?
14. On July 1 of the current year, a business paid the July rent on the building that it occupies. (a) Do the rights acquired at July 1 represent an asset or an expense? (b) What is the justification for debiting Rent Expense at the time of payment?
15. (a) Explain the purpose of the two accounts: Depreciation Expense and Accumulated Depreciation. (b) What is the normal balance of each account? (c) Is it customary for the balances of the two accounts to be equal in amount? (d) In what financial statements, if any, will each account appear?

Practice Exercises

PE 3-1A
Accounts requiring
adjustment

obj. 1

EE 3-1   p. 99

Indicate with a Yes or No whether or not each of the following accounts normally requires an adjusting entry.
a. Building   c. Interest Payable   e. Nath Luken, Capital
b. Cash   d. Miscellaneous Expense   f. Prepaid Insurance

PE 3-1B
Accounts requiring
adjustment

obj. 1

EE 3-1   p. 99

Indicate with a Yes or No whether or not each of the following accounts normally requires an adjusting entry.
a. Accumulated Depreciation c. Land   e. Supplies
b. Klaire Reid, Drawing   d. Salaries Payable   f. Unearned Rent

---

PE 3-2A
Type of adjustment

obj. 1

EE 3-2   p. 102

Classify the following items as (1) prepaid expense, (2) unearned revenue, (3) accrued revenue, or (4) accrued expense.
a. Cash received for use of land next month   c. Rent expense owed but not yet paid
b. Fees earned but not received   d. Supplies on hand

PE 3-2B
Type of adjustment

obj. 1

EE 3-2   p. 102

Classify the following items as (1) prepaid expense, (2) unearned revenue, (3) accrued revenue, or (4) accrued expense.
a. Cash received for services not yet   c. Rent revenue earned but not
    rendered   received
b. Insurance paid   d. Salaries owed but not yet paid

PE 3-3A
Adjustment for
prepaid expense

obj. 2

EE 3-3   p. 105

The prepaid insurance account had a beginning balance of $6,000 and was debited for $7,200 of premiums paid during the year. Journalize the adjusting entry required at the end of the year assuming the amount of unexpired insurance related to future periods is $4,200.

PE 3-3B
Adjustment for
prepaid expense

obj. 2

EE 3-3   p. 105

The supplies account had a beginning balance of $1,815 and was debited for $3,790 for supplies purchased during the year. Journalize the adjusting entry required at the end of the year assuming the amount of supplies on hand is $1,675.

PE 3-4A
Adjustment for
unearned revenue

obj. 2

EE 3-4   p. 106

On October 1, 2009, Nautilus Co. received $15,300 for the rent of land for 12 months. Journalize the adjusting entry required for unearned rent on December 31, 2009.

PE 3-4B
Adjustment for
unearned revenue

obj. 2

EE 3-4   p. 106

The balance in the unearned fees account, before adjustment at the end of the year, is $31,850. Journalize the adjusting entry required assuming the amount of unearned fees at the end of the year is $6,195.

PE 3-5A
Adjustment for
accrued revenues

obj. 2

EE 3-5   p. 107

At the end of the current year, $12,400 of fees have been earned but have not been billed to clients. Journalize the adjusting entry to record the accrued fees.

PE 3-5B
Adjustment for
accrued revenues

obj. 2

EE 3-5   p. 107

At the end of the current year, $9,134 of fees have been earned but have not been billed to clients. Journalize the adjusting entry to record the accrued fees.

PE 3-6A
Adjustment for
accrued expense

obj. 2

EE 3-6   p. 109

Haifa Realty Co. pays weekly salaries of $29,100 on Monday for a six-day workweek ending the preceding Saturday. Journalize the necessary adjusting entry at the end of the accounting period assuming that the period ends on Thursday.

PE 3-6B
Adjustment for
accrued expense

obj. 2

EE 3-6   p. 109

Colossal Realty Co. pays weekly salaries of $19,375 on Friday for a five-day workweek ending on that day. Journalize the necessary adjusting entry at the end of the accounting period assuming that the period ends on Tuesday.

PE 3-7A
Adjustment for
depreciation

obj. 2

EE 3-7   p. 111

The estimated amount of depreciation on equipment for the current year is $5,500. Journalize the adjusting entry to record the depreciation.

PE 3-7B
Adjustment for
depreciation

obj. 2

EE 3-7   p. 111

The estimated amount of depreciation on equipment for the current year is $3,200. Journalize the adjusting entry to record the depreciation.

PE 3-8A
Effect of omitting
adjustments

obj. 3

EE 3-8   p. 111

For the year ending November 30, 2010, Towson Medical Services Co. mistakenly omitted adjusting entries for (1) $1,430 of supplies that were used, (2) unearned revenue of $11,150 that was earned, and (3) insurance of $6,000 that expired. Indicate the combined effect of the errors on (a) revenues, (b) expenses, and (c) net income for the year ended November 30, 2010.

PE 3-8B
Effect of omitting
adjustments

obj. 3

EE 3-8   p. 111

For the year ending February 28, 2009, Samaritan Medical Co. mistakenly omitted adjusting entries for (1) depreciation of $4,100, (2) fees earned that were not billed of $15,300, and (3) accrued wages of $3,750. Indicate the combined effect of the errors on (a) revenues, (b) expenses, and (c) net income for the year ended February 28, 2009.

PE 3-9A
Effect of errors on
adjusted trial balance

obj. 4

EE 3-9   p. 119

For each of the following errors, considered individually, indicate whether the error would cause the adjusted trial balance totals to be unequal. If the error would cause the adjusted trial balance totals to be unequal, indicate whether the debit or credit total is higher and by how much.

a. The adjustment for accrued wages of $4,150 was journalized as a debit to Wages Expense for $4,150 and a credit to Accounts Payable for $4,150.

b. The entry for $1,290 of supplies used during the period was journalized as a debit to Supplies Expense of $1,290 and a credit to Supplies of $1,920.

PE 3-9B
Effect of errors on
adjusted trial balance

obj. 4

EE 3-9   p. 119

For each of the following errors, considered individually, indicate whether the error would cause the adjusted trial balance totals to be unequal. If the error would cause the adjusted trial balance totals to be unequal, indicate whether the debit or credit total is higher and by how much.

a. The adjustment of $8,175 for accrued fees earned was journalized as a debit to Accounts Receivable for $8,175 and a credit to Fees Earned for $8,157.

b. The adjustment of depreciation of $2,700 was omitted from the end-of-period adjusting entries.

Exercises

EX 3-1
Classifying types of adjustments
obj. 1

Classify the following items as (a) prepaid expense, (b) unearned revenue, (c) accrued revenue, or (d) accrued expense.

1. A two-year premium paid on a fire insurance policy.
2. Fees earned but not yet received.
3. Fees received but not yet earned.
4. Salary owed but not yet paid.
5. Subscriptions received in advance by a magazine publisher.
6. Supplies on hand.
7. Taxes owed but payable in the following period.
8. Utilities owed but not yet paid.

EX 3-2
Classifying adjusting entries
obj. 1

The following accounts were taken from the unadjusted trial balance of Washington Co., a congressional lobbying firm. Indicate whether or not each account would normally require an adjusting entry. If the account normally requires an adjusting entry, use the following notation to indicate the type of adjustment:

AE—Accrued Expense
AR—Accrued Revenue
PE—Prepaid Expense
UR—Unearned Revenue

To illustrate, the answer for the first account is shown below.

Account	Answer
Accounts Receivable	Normally requires adjustment (AR).
Cash	
Interest Payable	
Interest Receivable	
Joyce Carns, Capital	
Land	
Office Equipment	
Prepaid Rent	
Supplies	
Unearned Fees	
Wages Expense	

EX 3-3
Adjusting entry for supplies
obj. 2

The balance in the supplies account, before adjustment at the end of the year, is $1,736. Journalize the adjusting entry required if the amount of supplies on hand at the end of the year is $813.

EX 3-4
Determining supplies purchased
obj. 2

The supplies and supplies expense accounts at December 31, after adjusting entries have been posted at the end of the first year of operations, are shown in the following T accounts:

Supplies		Supplies Expense	
Bal. 675		Bal. 2,718	

Determine the amount of supplies purchased during the year.

EX 3-5
Effect of omitting adjusting entry
objs. 2, 3

At March 31, the end of the first month of operations, the usual adjusting entry transferring prepaid insurance expired to an expense account is omitted. Which items will be incorrectly stated, because of the error, on (a) the income statement for March and (b) the balance sheet as of March 31? Also indicate whether the items in error will be overstated or understated.

EX 3-6
Adjusting entries for prepaid insurance
obj. 2

The balance in the prepaid insurance account, before adjustment at the end of the year, is $11,500. Journalize the adjusting entry required under each of the following *alternatives* for determining the amount of the adjustment: (a) the amount of insurance expired during the year is $8,750; (b) the amount of unexpired insurance applicable to future periods is $2,750.

EX 3-7
Adjusting entries for prepaid insurance
obj. 2

The prepaid insurance account had a balance of $5,400 at the beginning of the year. The account was debited for $6,000 for premiums on policies purchased during the year. Journalize the adjusting entry required at the end of the year for each of the following situations: (a) the amount of unexpired insurance applicable to future periods is $1,000; (b) the amount of insurance expired during the year is $10,400.

EX 3-8
Adjusting entries for unearned fees
obj. 2

✔ Amount of entry: $21,175

The balance in the unearned fees account, before adjustment at the end of the year, is $38,375. Journalize the adjusting entry required if the amount of unearned fees at the end of the year is $17,200.

EX 3-9
Effect of omitting adjusting entry
objs. 2, 3

At the end of February, the first month of the business year, the usual adjusting entry transferring rent earned to a revenue account from the unearned rent account was omitted. Indicate which items will be incorrectly stated, because of the error, on (a) the income statement for February and (b) the balance sheet as of February 28. Also indicate whether the items in error will be overstated or understated.

EX 3-10
Adjusting entry for accrued fees
obj. 2

At the end of the current year, $8,140 of fees have been earned but have not been billed to clients.

a. Journalize the adjusting entry to record the accrued fees.
b. If the cash basis rather than the accrual basis had been used, would an adjusting entry have been necessary? Explain.

EX 3-11
Adjusting entries for unearned and accrued fees
obj. 2

The balance in the unearned fees account, before adjustment at the end of the year, is $112,790. Of these fees, $69,735 have been earned. In addition, $13,200 of fees have been earned but have not been billed. Journalize the adjusting entries (a) to adjust the unearned fees account and (b) to record the accrued fees.

EX 3-12
Effect of omitting adjusting entry
objs. 2, 3

The adjusting entry for accrued fees was omitted at March 31, the end of the current year. Indicate which items will be in error, because of the omission, on (a) the income statement for the current year and (b) the balance sheet as of March 31. Also indicate whether the items in error will be overstated or understated.

EX 3-13
Adjusting entries for accrued salaries
obj. 2

✔ a. Amount of entry: $2,220

Canyon Realty Co. pays weekly salaries of $3,700 on Friday for a five-day workweek ending on that day. Journalize the necessary adjusting entry at the end of the accounting period assuming that the period ends (a) on Wednesday and (b) on Thursday.

EX 3-14
Determining wages paid
obj. 2

The wages payable and wages expense accounts at October 31, after adjusting entries have been posted at the end of the first month of operations, are shown in the following T accounts:

Wages Payable			Wages Expense		
	Bal.	3,175	Bal.	93,800	

Determine the amount of wages paid during the month.

EX 3-15
Effect of omitting adjusting entry
objs. 2, 3

Accrued salaries of $4,950 owed to employees for December 30 and 31 are not considered in preparing the financial statements for the year ended December 31. Indicate which items will be erroneously stated, because of the error, on (a) the income statement for the year and (b) the balance sheet as of December 31. Also indicate whether the items in error will be overstated or understated.

EX 3-16
Effect of omitting adjusting entry
objs. 2, 3

Assume that the error in Exercise 3-15 was not corrected and that the $4,950 of accrued salaries was included in the first salary payment in January. Indicate which items will be erroneously stated, because of failure to correct the initial error, on (a) the income statement for the month of January and (b) the balance sheet as of January 31.

EX 3-17
Adjusting entries for prepaid and accrued taxes
obj. 2

✔ b. $24,750

Northwest Financial Services was organized on April 1 of the current year. On April 2, Northwest prepaid $4,500 to the city for taxes (license fees) for the *next* 12 months and debited the prepaid taxes account. Northwest is also required to pay in January an annual tax (on property) for the *previous* calendar year. The estimated amount of the property tax for the current year (April 1 to December 31) is $21,375.

a. Journalize the two adjusting entries required to bring the accounts affected by the two taxes up to date as of December 31, the end of the current year.
b. What is the amount of tax expense for the current year?

EX 3-18
Adjustment for depreciation
obj. 2

The estimated amount of depreciation on equipment for the current year is $1,840. Journalize the adjusting entry to record the depreciation.

EX 3-19
Determining fixed asset's book value
obj. 2

The balance in the equipment account is $925,700, and the balance in the accumulated depreciation—equipment account is $311,100.

a. What is the book value of the equipment?
b. Does the balance in the accumulated depreciation account mean that the equipment's loss of value is $311,100? Explain.

EX 3-20
Book value of fixed assets
obj. 2

In a recent balance sheet, Microsoft Corporation reported *Property, Plant, and Equipment* of $7,223 million and *Accumulated Depreciation* of $4,179 million.

a. What was the book value of the fixed assets?
b. Would the book value of Microsoft Corporation's fixed assets normally approximate their fair market values?

EX 3-21
Effects of errors on
financial statements

objs. 2, 3

For a recent period, the balance sheet for Circuit City Stores, Inc., reported accrued expenses of $464,511,000. For the same period, Circuit City reported income before income taxes of $151,112,000. Assume that the accrued expenses apply to the current period and were not recorded at the end of the current period. What would have been the income (loss) before income taxes?

EX 3-22
Effects of errors on
financial statements

objs. 2, 3

For a recent year, the balance sheet for The Campbell Soup Company includes accrued expenses of $1,022,000,000. The income before taxes for The Campbell Soup Company for the year was $1,001,000,000.

a. Assume the accruals apply to the current year and were not recorded at the end of the year. By how much would income before taxes have been misstated?
b. What is the percentage of the misstatement in (a) to the reported income of $1,001,000,000? Round to one decimal place.

EX 3-23
Effects of errors on
financial statements

objs. 2, 3

✔ 1. a. Revenue
understated,
$21,950

The accountant for Mystic Medical Co., a medical services consulting firm, mistakenly omitted adjusting entries for (a) unearned revenue earned during the year ($21,950) and (b) accrued wages ($6,100). Indicate the effect of each error, considered individually, on the income statement for the current year ended July 31. Also indicate the effect of each error on the July 31 balance sheet. Set up a table similar to the following, and record your answers by inserting the dollar amount in the appropriate spaces. Insert a zero if the error does not affect the item.

	Error (a)		Error (b)	
	Over-stated	Under-stated	Over-stated	Under-stated
1. Revenue for the year would be	$ ___	$ ___	$ ___	$ ___
2. Expenses for the year would be	$ ___	$ ___	$ ___	$ ___
3. Net income for the year would be	$ ___	$ ___	$ ___	$ ___
4. Assets at July 31 would be	$ ___	$ ___	$ ___	$ ___
5. Liabilities at July 31 would be	$ ___	$ ___	$ ___	$ ___
6. Owner's equity at July 31 would be	$ ___	$ ___	$ ___	$ ___

EX 3-24
Effects of errors on
financial statements

objs. 2, 3

If the net income for the current year had been $424,300 in Exercise 3-23, what would have been the correct net income if the proper adjusting entries had been made?

EX 3-25
Adjusting entries for
depreciation; effect of
error

objs. 2, 3

On December 31, a business estimates depreciation on equipment used during the first year of operations to be $12,200.

a. Journalize the adjusting entry required as of December 31.
b. If the adjusting entry in (a) were omitted, which items would be erroneously stated on (1) the income statement for the year and (2) the balance sheet as of December 31?

EX 3-26
Adjusting entries from trial balances

obj. 4

The unadjusted and adjusted trial balances for Glockenspiel Services Co. on March 31, 2010, are shown below.

Glockenspiel Services Co.
Trial Balance
March 31, 2010

	Unadjusted		Adjusted	
	Debit Balances	Credit Balances	Debit Balances	Credit Balances
Cash	16		16	
Accounts Receivable	38		42	
Supplies	12		9	
Prepaid Insurance	20		12	
Land	26		26	
Equipment	40		40	
Accumulated Depreciation—Equipment		8		13
Accounts Payable		26		26
Wages Payable		0		1
Page Birch, Capital		92		92
Page Birch, Drawing	8		8	
Fees Earned		74		78
Wages Expense	24		25	
Rent Expense	8		8	
Insurance Expense	0		8	
Utilities Expense	4		4	
Depreciation Expense	0		5	
Supplies Expense	0		3	
Miscellaneous Expense	4		4	
	200	200	210	210

Journalize the five entries that adjusted the accounts at March 31, 2010. None of the accounts were affected by more than one adjusting entry.

EX 3-27
Adjusting entries from trial balances

obj. 4

✔ Corrected trial balance totals, $621,900

The accountant for Rooster Laundry prepared the following unadjusted and adjusted trial balances. Assume that all balances in the unadjusted trial balance and the amounts of the adjustments are correct. Identify the errors in the accountant's adjusting entries.

Rooster Laundry
Trial Balance
January 31, 2010

	Unadjusted		Adjusted	
	Debit Balances	Credit Balances	Debit Balances	Credit Balances
Cash	15,000		15,000	
Accounts Receivable	36,500		44,000	
Laundry Supplies	7,500		11,000	
Prepaid Insurance*	10,400		2,800	
Laundry Equipment	280,000		268,000	
Accumulated Depreciation		96,000		96,000
Accounts Payable		19,200		19,200
Wages Payable				2,400
Carlos Martinez, Capital		120,600		120,600
Carlos Martinez, Drawing	57,550		57,550	
Laundry Revenue		364,200		364,200
Wages Expense	98,400		98,400	
Rent Expense	51,150		51,150	
Utilities Expense	37,000		37,000	
Depreciation Expense			12,000	
Laundry Supplies Expense			3,500	
Insurance Expense			1,600	
Miscellaneous Expense	6,500		6,500	
	600,000	600,000	608,500	602,400

*$7,600 of insurance expired during the year.

EX 3-28
Vertical analysis of income statement

The following data (in millions) is taken from the financial statements of Williams-Sonoma for the years ending 2007 and 2006:

	2007	2006
Net sales (revenues)	$3,728	$3,539
Net income	209	215

a. Determine the amount of change (in millions) and percent of change in net income for 2007.
b. Determine the percentage relationship between net income and net sales (net income divided by net sales) for 2007 and 2008.
c. What conclusions can you draw from your analysis?

EX 3-29
Vertical analysis of income statement

The following income statement data (in thousands) for Dell Inc. and Gateway, Inc., were taken from their recent annual reports:

	Dell	Gateway
Net sales	$35,404,000	$ 4,171,325
Cost of goods sold (expense)	(29,055,000)	(3,605,120)
Operating expenses	(3,505,000)	(1,077,447)
Operating income (loss)	$ 2,844,000	$ (511,242)

a. Prepare a vertical analysis of the income statement for Dell.
b. Prepare a vertical analysis of the income statement for Gateway.
c. Based on (a) and (b), how does Dell compare to Gateway?

Problems Series A

PR 3-1A
Adjusting entries
obj. 2

On August 31, 2010, the following data were accumulated to assist the accountant in preparing the adjusting entries for Cobalt Realty:

a. Fees accrued but unbilled at August 31 are $9,560.
b. The supplies account balance on August 31 is $3,150. The supplies on hand at August 31 are $900.
c. Wages accrued but not paid at August 31 are $1,200.
d. The unearned rent account balance at August 31 is $9,375, representing the receipt of an advance payment on August 1 of three months' rent from tenants.
e. Depreciation of office equipment is $1,600.

Instructions

1. Journalize the adjusting entries required at August 31, 2010.
2. Briefly explain the difference between adjusting entries and entries that would be made to correct errors.

PR 3-2A
Adjusting entries
obj. 2

Selected account balances before adjustment for Oval Realty at April 30, 2010, the end of the current year, are shown at the top of the next page.

	Debits	Credits
Accounts Receivable	$ 65,000	
Accumulated Depreciation		$ 10,000
Depreciation Expense	—	
Equipment	100,000	
Fees Earned		379,500
Prepaid Rent	8,200	
Rent Expense	—	
Supplies	1,950	
Supplies Expense	—	
Unearned Fees		9,000
Wages Expense	128,000	
Wages Payable		—

Data needed for year-end adjustments are as follows:

a. Supplies on hand at April 30, $600.
b. Depreciation of equipment during year, $1,000.
c. Rent expired during year, $6,000.
d. Wages accrued but not paid at April 30, $1,900.
e. Unearned fees at April 30, $3,750.
f. Unbilled fees at April 30, $4,500.

Instructions

Journalize the six adjusting entries required at April 30, based on the data presented.

PR 3-3A
Adjusting entries

obj. 2

Wind River Outfitters Co., an outfitter store for fishing treks, prepared the following unadjusted trial balance at the end of its first year of operations:

Wind River Outfitters Co.
Unadjusted Trial Balance
February 28, 2010

	Debit Balances	Credit Balances
Cash	13,200	
Accounts Receivable	43,800	
Supplies	3,600	
Equipment	81,000	
Accounts Payable		6,100
Unearned Fees		9,600
Fran Fielding, Capital		111,400
Fran Fielding, Drawing	5,000	
Fees Earned		147,900
Wages Expense	76,400	
Rent Expense	27,500	
Utilities Expense	21,000	
Miscellaneous Expense	3,500	
	275,000	275,000

For preparing the adjusting entries, the following data were assembled:

a. Supplies on hand on February 28 were $750.
b. Fees earned but unbilled on February 28 were $2,900.
c. Depreciation of equipment was estimated to be $5,400 for the year.
d. Unpaid wages accrued on February 28 were $800.
e. The balance in unearned fees represented the February 1 receipt in advance for services to be provided. Only $1,600 of the services was provided between February 1 and February 28.

Instructions

Journalize the adjusting entries necessary on February 28.

PR 3-4A
Adjusting entries
objs. 2, 3, 4

Billy Board Company specializes in the maintenance and repair of signs, such as billboards. On March 31, 2010, the accountant for Billy Board Company prepared the following trial balances:

Billy Board Company
Trial Balance
March 31, 2010

	Unadjusted		Adjusted	
	Debit Balances	Credit Balances	Debit Balances	Credit Balances
Cash	4,750		4,750	
Accounts Receivable	17,400		17,400	
Supplies	6,200		1,850	
Prepaid Insurance	9,000		3,600	
Land	50,000		50,000	
Buildings	120,000		120,000	
Accumulated Depreciation—Buildings		51,500		58,100
Trucks	75,000		75,000	
Accumulated Depreciation—Trucks		12,000		14,300
Accounts Payable		6,920		7,520
Salaries Payable		—		1,180
Unearned Service Fees		10,500		5,100
William Elkins, Capital		156,400		156,400
William Elkins, Drawing	7,500		7,500	
Service Fees Earned		162,680		168,080
Salary Expense	80,000		81,180	
Depreciation Expense—Trucks	—		2,300	
Rent Expense	11,900		11,900	
Supplies Expense	—		4,350	
Utilities Expense	6,200		6,800	
Depreciation Expense—Buildings			6,600	
Taxes Expense	2,900		2,900	
Insurance Expense	—		5,400	
Miscellaneous Expense	9,150		9,150	
	400,000	400,000	410,680	410,680

Instructions

Journalize the seven entries that adjusted the accounts at March 31. None of the accounts were affected by more than one adjusting entry.

PR 3-5A
Adjusting entries and adjusted trial balances
objs. 2, 3, 4

✔ 2. Total of Debit column: $333,050

Jacksonville Financial Services Co., which specializes in appliance repair services, is owned and operated by Cindy Latty. Jacksonville Financial Services Co.'s accounting clerk prepared the unadjusted trial balance at December 31, 2010, shown below.

Jacksonville Financial Services Co.
Unadjusted Trial Balance
December 31, 2010

	Debit Balances	Credit Balances
Cash	10,200	
Accounts Receivable	34,750	
Prepaid Insurance	6,000	
Supplies	1,725	
Land	50,000	
Building	80,750	
Accumulated Depreciation—Building		37,850
Equipment	45,000	
Accumulated Depreciation—Equipment		17,650
Accounts Payable		3,750
Unearned Rent		3,600
Cindy Latty, Capital		103,550
Cindy Latty, Drawing	8,000	
Fees Earned		158,600
Salaries and Wages Expense	56,850	
Utilities Expense	14,100	
Advertising Expense	7,500	
Repairs Expense	6,100	
Miscellaneous Expense	4,025	
	325,000	325,000

The data needed to determine year-end adjustments are as follows:

a. Depreciation of building for the year, $2,100.
b. Depreciation of equipment for the year, $3,000.
c. Accrued salaries and wages at December 31, $800.
d. Unexpired insurance at December 31, $1,500.
e. Fees earned but unbilled on December 31, $2,150.
f. Supplies on hand at December 31, $600.
g. Rent unearned at December 31, $1,500.

Instructions

1. Journalize the adjusting entries. Add additional accounts as needed.
2. Determine the balances of the accounts affected by the adjusting entries and prepare an adjusted trial balance.

PR 3-6A
Adjusting entries and errors

obj. 3

✔ 2. Corrected Net Income: $135,375

At the end of July, the first month of operations, the following selected data were taken from the financial statements of Monita Forche, an attorney:

Net income for July	$135,800
Total assets at July 31	750,000
Total liabilities at July 31	250,000
Total owner's equity at July 31	500,000

In preparing the financial statements, adjustments for the following data were overlooked:

a. Unbilled fees earned at July 31, $6,700.
b. Depreciation of equipment for July, $3,000.
c. Accrued wages at July 31, $2,150.
d. Supplies used during July, $1,975.

Instructions

1. Journalize the entries to record the omitted adjustments.
2. Determine the correct amount of net income for July and the total assets, liabilities, and owner's equity at July 31. In addition to indicating the corrected amounts, indicate the effect of each omitted adjustment by setting up and completing a columnar table similar to the following. Adjustment (a) is presented as an example.

	Net Income	Total Assets	= Total Liabilities	+ Total Owner's Equity
Reported amounts	$135,800	$750,000	$250,000	$500,000
Corrections:				
Adjustment (a)	+ 6,700	+ 6,700	0	+ 6,700
Adjustment (b)				
Adjustment (c)				
Adjustment (d)				
Corrected amounts				

Problems Series B

PR 3-1B
Adjusting entries

obj. 2

On March 31, 2010, the following data were accumulated to assist the accountant in preparing the adjusting entries for Hackney Realty:

a. The supplies account balance on March 31 is $2,315. The supplies on hand on March 31 are $990.
b. The unearned rent account balance on March 31 is $7,950, representing the receipt of an advance payment on March 1 of three months' rent from tenants.
c. Wages accrued but not paid at March 31 are $800.

d. Fees accrued but unbilled at March 31 are $7,100.
e. Depreciation of office equipment is $700.

Instructions

1. Journalize the adjusting entries required at March 31, 2010.
2. Briefly explain the difference between adjusting entries and entries that would be made to correct errors.

PR 3-2B
Adjusting entries
obj. 2

Selected account balances before adjustment for Perfect Realty at October 31, 2010, the end of the current year, are as follows:

	Debits	Credits
Accounts Receivable	$ 40,000	
Equipment	100,000	
Accumulated Depreciation		$ 12,000
Prepaid Rent	9,000	
Supplies	1,800	
Wages Payable	—	
Unearned Fees		6,000
Fees Earned		215,000
Wages Expense	75,000	
Rent Expense	—	
Depreciation Expense	—	
Supplies Expense	—	

Data needed for year-end adjustments are as follows:

a. Unbilled fees at October 31, $2,900.
b. Supplies on hand at October 31, $400.
c. Rent expired, $6,000.
d. Depreciation of equipment during year, $3,000.
e. Unearned fees at October 31, $800.
f. Wages accrued but not paid at October 31, $1,400.

Instructions

Journalize the six adjusting entries required at October 31, based on the data presented.

PR 3-3B
Adjusting entries
obj. 2

Chinook Company, an electronics repair store, prepared the unadjusted trial balance shown below at the end of its first year of operations.

Chinook Company
Unadjusted Trial Balance
November 30, 2010

	Debit Balances	Credit Balances
Cash	6,900	
Accounts Receivable	45,000	
Supplies	10,800	
Equipment	227,400	
Accounts Payable		10,500
Unearned Fees		12,000
Neal Salmon, Capital		156,000
Neal Salmon, Drawing	9,000	
Fees Earned		271,500
Wages Expense	63,000	
Rent Expense	48,000	
Utilities Expense	34,500	
Miscellaneous Expense	5,400	
	450,000	450,000

For preparing the adjusting entries, the following data were assembled:

a. Fees earned but unbilled on November 30 were $1,300.
b. Supplies on hand on November 30 were $3,100.
c. Depreciation of equipment was estimated to be $3,500 for the year.
d. The balance in unearned fees represented the November 1 receipt in advance for services to be provided. Only $4,000 of the services was provided between November 1 and November 30.
e. Unpaid wages accrued on November 30 were $900.

Instructions

Journalize the adjusting entries necessary on November 30, 2010.

PR 3-4B
Adjusting entries
objs. 2, 3, 4

Luxor Company specializes in the repair of music equipment and is owned and operated by Amy Busby. On November 30, 2010, the end of the current year, the accountant for Luxor Company prepared the following trial balances:

Luxor Company
Trial Balance
November 30, 2010

	Unadjusted		Adjusted	
	Debit Balances	Credit Balances	Debit Balances	Credit Balances
Cash	38,250		38,250	
Accounts Receivable	109,500		109,500	
Supplies	11,250		2,700	
Prepaid Insurance	14,250		4,500	
Equipment	360,450		360,450	
Accumulated Depreciation—Equipment		94,500		102,000
Automobiles	109,500		109,500	
Accumulated Depreciation—Automobiles		54,750		61,200
Accounts Payable		24,930		26,400
Salaries Payable		—		6,000
Unearned Service Fees		18,000		8,700
Amy Busby, Capital		394,020		394,020
Amy Busby, Drawing	75,000		75,000	
Service Fees Earned		733,800		743,100
Salary Expense	516,900		522,900	
Rent Expense	54,000		54,000	
Supplies Expense	—		8,550	
Depreciation Expense—Equipment	—		7,500	
Depreciation Expense—Automobiles	—		6,450	
Utilities Expense	12,900		14,370	
Taxes Expense	8,175		8,175	
Insurance Expense	—		9,750	
Miscellaneous Expense	9,825		9,825	
	1,320,000	1,320,000	1,341,420	1,341,420

Instructions

Journalize the seven entries that adjusted the accounts at November 30. None of the accounts were affected by more than one adjusting entry.

PR 3-5B
Adjusting entries and adjusted trial balances
objs. 2, 3, 4

✔ 2. Total of Debit column: $822,180

Misfire Company is a small editorial services company owned and operated by Pedro Borman. On August 31, 2010, the end of the current year, Misfire Company's accounting clerk prepared the unadjusted trial balance shown on the next page.

The data needed to determine year-end adjustments are as follows:

a. Unexpired insurance at August 31, $1,800.
b. Supplies on hand at August 31, $750.
c. Depreciation of building for the year, $2,000.
d. Depreciation of equipment for the year, $5,000.
e. Rent unearned at August 31, $2,850.

f. Accrued salaries and wages at August 31, $2,800.
g. Fees earned but unbilled on August 31, $12,380.

Misfire Company
Unadjusted Trial Balance
August 31, 2010

	Debit Balances	Credit Balances
Cash	7,500	
Accounts Receivable	38,400	
Prepaid Insurance	7,200	
Supplies	1,980	
Land	112,500	
Building	200,250	
Accumulated Depreciation—Building		137,550
Equipment	135,300	
Accumulated Depreciation—Equipment		97,950
Accounts Payable		12,150
Unearned Rent		6,750
Pedro Borman, Capital		221,000
Pedro Borman, Drawing	15,000	
Fees Earned		324,600
Salaries and Wages Expense	193,370	
Utilities Expense	42,375	
Advertising Expense	22,800	
Repairs Expense	17,250	
Miscellaneous Expense	6,075	
	800,000	800,000

Instructions

1. Journalize the adjusting entries. Add additional accounts as needed.
2. Determine the balances of the accounts affected by the adjusting entries, and prepare an adjusted trial balance.

PR 3-6B
Adjusting entries and errors

obj. 3

✔ 2. Corrected Net Income: $136,850

At the end of April, the first month of operations, the following selected data were taken from the financial statements of Beth Cato, an attorney:

Net income for April	$125,750
Total assets at April 30	500,000
Total liabilities at April 30	180,000
Total owner's equity at April 30	320,000

In preparing the financial statements, adjustments for the following data were overlooked:

a. Supplies used during April, $3,100.
b. Unbilled fees earned at April 30, $18,750.
c. Depreciation of equipment for April, $2,700.
d. Accrued wages at April 30, $1,850.

Instructions

1. Journalize the entries to record the omitted adjustments.
2. Determine the correct amount of net income for April and the total assets, liabilities, and owner's equity at April 30. In addition to indicating the corrected amounts, indicate the effect of each omitted adjustment by setting up and completing a columnar table similar to the following. Adjustment (a) is presented as an example.

	Net Income	Total Assets	=	Total Liabilities	+	Total Owner's Equity
Reported amounts	$125,750	$500,000		$180,000		$320,000
Corrections:						
Adjustment (a)	−3,100	−3,100		0		−3,100
Adjustment (b)						
Adjustment (c)						
Adjustment (d)						
Corrected amounts						

Continuing Problem

✔ 3. Total of Debit column: $40,460

The unadjusted trial balance that you prepared for Music Depot at the end of Chapter 2 should appear as follows:

Music Depot
Unadjusted Trial Balance
July 31, 2010

	Debit Balances	Credit Balances
Cash	12,780	
Accounts Receivable	3,150	
Supplies	850	
Prepaid Insurance	2,700	
Office Equipment	5,000	
Accounts Payable		5,680
Unearned Revenue		7,200
Lee Chang, Capital		10,500
Lee Chang, Drawing	1,700	
Fees Earned		15,300
Wages Expense	2,400	
Office Rent Expense	2,750	
Equipment Rent Expense	1,100	
Utilities Expense	860	
Music Expense	2,810	
Advertising Expense	1,600	
Supplies Expense	180	
Miscellaneous Expense	800	
	38,680	38,680

The data needed to determine adjustments for the two-month period ending July 31, 2010, are as follows:

a. During July, Music Depot provided guest disc jockeys for WHBD for a total of 120 hours. For information on the amount of the accrued revenue to be billed to WHBD, see the contract described in the July 3, 2010, transaction at the end of Chapter 2.
b. Supplies on hand at July 31, $175.
c. The balance of the prepaid insurance account relates to the July 1, 2010, transaction at the end of Chapter 2.
d. Depreciation of the office equipment is $60.
e. The balance of the unearned revenue account relates to the contract between Music Depot and WHBD, described in the July 3, 2010, transaction at the end of Chapter 2.
f. Accrued wages as of July 31, 2010, were $120.

Instructions

1. Prepare adjusting journal entries. You will need the following additional accounts:

   18 Accumulated Depreciation—Office Equipment
   22 Wages Payable
   57 Insurance Expense
   58 Depreciation Expense

2. Post the adjusting entries, inserting balances in the accounts affected.
3. Prepare an adjusted trial balance.

Special Activities

You can access the special activities online at **www.cengage.com/accounting/reeve**.

Excel Success Special Activities

SA 3-1

Adjusting entries

Holly Company purchased a two-year insurance policy on January 2, 2010, for $1,800.

a. Open the Excel file *SA3-1.*

b. Journalize in a spreadsheet the adjusting entry to record insurance expired for the year on December 31, 2010. Label the worksheet J5 to journalize the adjusting entry.

c. Post the adjusting entry to the four-column general ledger accounts in the separate worksheet.

	A	B	C	D	E	F	G
1							
2	Account	*Prepaid Insurance*				*Account No.*	*18*
3						**Balance**	
4	**Date**	**Item**	**Post. Ref.**	**Debit**	**Credit**	**Debit**	**Credit**
5	Jan 2		5	1,800		1,800	
6	Dec. 31	Adjustment	5				
7							
8							
9	Account	*Insurance Expense*				Account No.	56
10						**Balance**	
11	**Date**	**Item**	**Post. Ref.**	**Debit**	**Credit**	**Debit**	**Credit**
12	Dec. 31	Adjustment	5				
13							
14							
15							
16							

|◄ ◄ ► ►|\ J5 \GL/\ **Sheet3** / ◄

d. When you have completed the journal entry and posted to the general ledger, perform a "save as," replacing the entire file name with the following:

SA3-1_[your first name initial]_[your last name]

SA 3-2

Adjusting entries

The accrued wages for Darrin Company at October 31, 2011, are $14,300.

a. Open the Excel file *SA3-2.*

b. Journalize in a spreadsheet the adjusting entry for accrued wages on October 31, 2011. Use a separate worksheet, J5, to journalize the adjusting entry.

c. Post the adjusting entry to the four-column general ledger accounts in the separate worksheet, *GL.*

	A	B	C	D	E	F	G
1							
2	Account	*Wages Payable*				*Account No.*	*34*
3						**Balance**	
4	**Date**	**Item**	**Post. Ref.**	**Debit**	**Credit**	**Debit**	**Credit**
5	Oct. 31	Adjustment	5				
6							
7							
8	Account	*Wages Expense*				Account No.	52
9						**Balance**	
10	**Date**	**Item**	**Post. Ref.**	**Debit**	**Credit**	**Debit**	**Credit**
11	Oct. 15			13,800		13,800	
12	Oct. 31	Adjustment	5				
13							
14							
15							
16							

|◄ ◄ ► ►|\ J5 \GL/\ **Sheet3** / ◄

d. When you have completed the journal entry and posted to the general ledger, perform a "save as," replacing the entire file name with the following:

SA3-2_[your first name initial]_[your last name]

SA 3-3

**ImagePress—
Adjusting entries**

success

Open the previously saved file, *SA2-1,2,3_[your first name initial]_[your last name].* (Note: This is the file saved in Chapter 2.)

ImagePress Printing (from *SA2-1,2,3*) prepared the following unadjusted trial balance for the end of ImagePress's first year of operations.

The following adjustments were assembled:

- Supplies on hand on April 30 were $600.
- Fees earned but unbilled on April 30 were $1,380.
- Depreciation of office equipment was estimated to be $4,250.
- Utility expenses accrued on April 30 were $900.

a. Journalize in the journal worksheet developed from SA2-1 for ImagePress Printing the necessary adjusting entries on April 30.

b. Post adjustments to the worksheet ledger accounts developed in SA2-2 for ImagePress Printing. Add accounts to the ledger for those adjustments requiring new accounts.

c. Prepare in a separate worksheet in the ImagePress Printing file the adjusted trial balance (labeled ATB).

d. When you have completed the adjustments, postings, and adjusted trial balance, perform a "save as," replacing the entire file name with the following:

SA3-3_[your first name initial]_[your last name]

Answers to Self-Examination Questions

1. **A**   A deferral is the delay in recording an expense already paid, such as prepaid insurance (answer A). Wages payable (answer B) is considered an accrued expense or accrued liability. Fees earned (answer C) is a revenue item. Accumulated depreciation (answer D) is a contra account to a fixed asset.

2. **D**   The balance in the supplies account, before adjustment, represents the amount of supplies available. From this amount ($2,250) is subtracted the amount of supplies on hand ($950) to determine the supplies used ($1,300). Since increases in expense accounts are recorded by debits and decreases in asset accounts are recorded by credits, answer D is the correct entry.

3. **C**   The failure to record the adjusting entry debiting Unearned Rent, $600, and crediting Rent Revenue, $600, would have the effect of overstating liabilities by $600 and understating net income by $600 (answer C).

4. **C**   Since increases in expense accounts (such as depreciation expense) are recorded by debits and it is customary to record the decreases in usefulness of fixed assets as credits to accumulated depreciation accounts, answer C is the correct entry.

5. **D**   The book value of a fixed asset is the difference between the balance in the asset account and the balance in the related accumulated depreciation account, or $22,500 − $14,000, as indicated by answer D ($8,500).

CHAPTER 4

Completing the Accounting Cycle

ELECTRONIC ARTS INC.

Most of us have had to file a personal tax return. At the beginning of the year, you estimate your upcoming income and decide whether you need to increase your payroll tax withholdings or perhaps pay estimated taxes. During the year, you earn income and enter into tax-related transactions, such as making charitable contributions. At the end of the year, your employer sends you a tax withholding information form (W-2) form, and you collect the tax records needed for completing your yearly tax forms. As the next year begins, you start the cycle all over again.

Businesses also go through a cycle of activities. For example, Electronic Arts Inc., the world's largest developer and marketer of electronic game software, begins its cycle by developing new or revised game titles, such as Madden NFL Football®, Need for Speed®, Tiger Woods PGA Tour®, The Sims®, and The Lord of the Rings®. These games are marketed and sold throughout the year. During the year, operating transactions of the business are recorded. For Electronic Arts, such transactions include the salaries for game developers, advertising expenditures, costs for producing and packaging games, and game revenues. At the

end of the year, financial statements are prepared that summarize the operating activities for the year. Electronic Arts publishes these statements on its Web site at **http://investor.ea.com**. Finally, before the start of the next year, the accounts are readied for recording the operations of the next year.

As we saw in Chapter 1, the initial cycle for NetSolutions began with Chris Clark's investment in the business on November 1, 2009. The cycle continued with recording NetSolutions' transactions for November and December, as we discussed and illustrated in Chapters 1 and 2. In Chapter 3, the cycle continued when the adjusting entries for the two months ending December 31, 2009, were recorded. In this chapter, we complete the cycle for NetSolutions by preparing financial statements and getting the accounts ready for recording transactions of the next period.

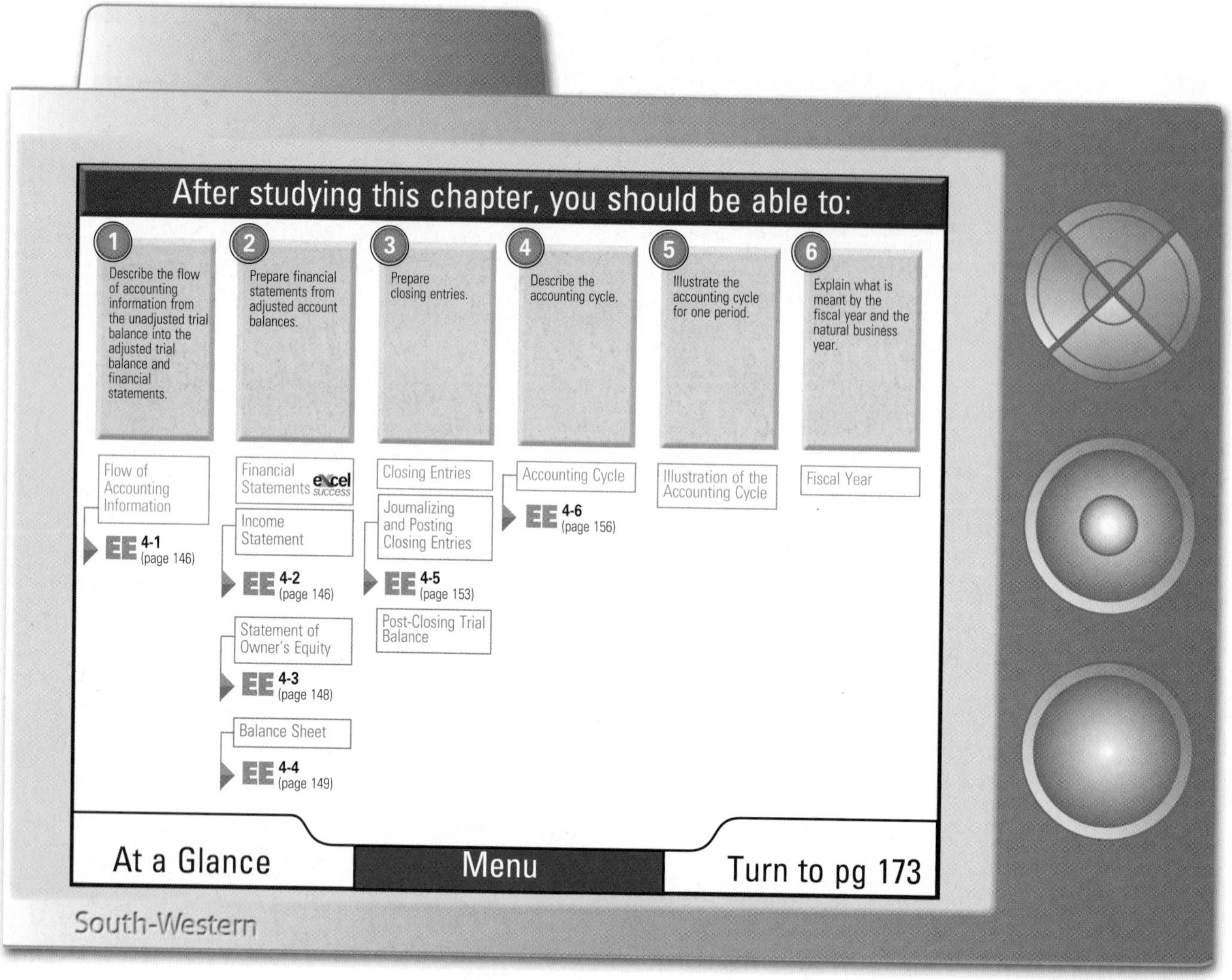

After studying this chapter, you should be able to:

1 Describe the flow of accounting information from the unadjusted trial balance into the adjusted trial balance and financial statements.

2 Prepare financial statements from adjusted account balances.

3 Prepare closing entries.

4 Describe the accounting cycle.

5 Illustrate the accounting cycle for one period.

6 Explain what is meant by the fiscal year and the natural business year.

Flow of Accounting Information

EE 4-1 (page 146)

Financial Statements   e**x**cel SUCCESS

Income Statement

EE 4-2 (page 146)

Statement of Owner's Equity

EE 4-3 (page 148)

Balance Sheet

EE 4-4 (page 149)

Closing Entries

Journalizing and Posting Closing Entries

EE 4-5 (page 153)

Post-Closing Trial Balance

Accounting Cycle

EE 4-6 (page 156)

Illustration of the Accounting Cycle

Fiscal Year

| At a Glance | Menu | Turn to pg 173 |

South-Western

Flow of Accounting Information

1 Describe the flow of accounting information from the unadjusted trial balance into the adjusted trial balance and financial statements.

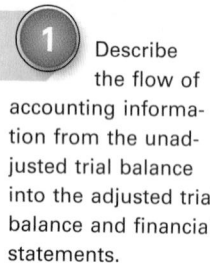

@netsolutions

Many companies use Microsoft's Excel® software to prepare end-of-period spreadsheets (work sheets).

The end-of-period process by which accounts are adjusted and the financial statements are prepared is one of the most important in accounting. Using our illustration of NetSolutions from Chapters 1–3, this process is summarized in spreadsheet form in Exhibit 1.

Exhibit 1 begins with the unadjusted trial balance as of the end of the period. The unadjusted trial balance verifies that the total of the debit balances equals the total of the credit balances. If the trial balance totals are unequal, an error has occurred. Any error must be found and corrected before the end-of-period process can continue.

The adjustments for NetSolutions from Chapter 3 are shown in the Adjustments columns of Exhibit 1. Cross-referencing (by letters) the debit and credit of each adjustment is useful in reviewing the impact of the adjustments on the unadjusted account balances. The adjustments are normally entered in the order in which the data are assembled. If the titles of the accounts to be adjusted do not appear in the unadjusted trial balance, the accounts are inserted in their proper order in the Account Title column. The total of the Adjustments columns verifies that the debits equals the credits for the adjustment data and adjusting entries. The total of the Debit column must equal the total of the Credit column.

The adjustment data are added to or subtracted from the amounts in the Unadjusted Trial Balance columns to arrive at the Adjusted Trial Balance columns. In this way, the Adjusted Trial Balance columns of Exhibit 1 illustrate the impact of the adjusting entries on the unadjusted accounts. The totals of the Adjusted Trial Balance columns verify the equality of the totals of the debit and credit balances after adjustment.

Exhibit 1 also illustrates the flow of accounts from the adjusted trial balance into the financial statements as follows:

1. The revenue and expense accounts are extended to (flow into) the Income Statement columns.

2. At the bottom of the Income Statement columns, the net income or net loss for the period is the difference between the total Credit column (revenues) and the total Debit column (expenses). If the Income Statement Credit column total (revenues) is greater than the Income Statement Debit column total (expenses), the difference is the net income. If the Income Statement Debit column total is greater than the Income Statement Credit column total, the difference is a net loss. Exhibit 1 shows that NetSolutions had net income of $7,105 for the period.

3. The assets, liabilities, owner's capital, and drawing accounts are extended (flow into) to the Balance Sheet columns.

4. At the bottom of the Balance Sheet column, the net income or net loss for the period is the difference between the total Debit column and the total Credit column. Since net income increases owner's capital, NetSolutions' net income of $7,105 is shown in the Balance Sheet Credit column.

To summarize, Exhibit 1 illustrates the end-of-period process by which accounts are adjusted. In addition, Exhibit 1 illustrates how the adjusted accounts flow into the financial statements. The financial statements for NetSolutions can be prepared directly from Exhibit 1.

The spreadsheet in Exhibit 1 is not a required part of the accounting process. However, many accountants prepare such a spreadsheet, often called a work sheet, in

Exhibit 1

End-of-Period Spreadsheet (Work Sheet)

NetSolutions
End-of-Period Spreadsheet (Work Sheet)
For the Two Months Ended December 31, 2009

	A	B	C	D	E	F	G	H	I	J	K
	Account Title	Unadjusted Trial Balance Dr.	Cr.	Adjustments Dr.	Cr.	Adjusted Trial Balance Dr.	Cr.	Income Statement Dr.	Cr.	Balance Sheet Dr.	Cr.
8	Cash	2,065				2,065				2,065	
9	Accounts Receivable	2,220		(d) 500		2,720				2,720	
10	Supplies	2,000			(a) 1,240	760				760	
11	Prepaid Insurance	2,400			(b) 200	2,200				2,200	
12	Land	20,000				20,000				20,000	
13	Office Equipment	1,800				1,800				1,800	
14	Accumulated Depreciation				(f) 50		50				50
15	Accounts Payable		900				900				900
16	Wages Payable				(e) 250		250				250
17	Unearned Rent		360	(c) 120			240				240
18	Chris Clark, Capital		25,000				25,000				25,000
19	Chris Clark, Drawing	4,000				4,000				4,000	
20	Fees Earned		16,340		(d) 500		16,840		16,840		
21	Rent Revenue				(c) 120		120		120		
22	Wages Expense	4,275		(e) 250		4,525		4,525			
23	Rent Expense	1,600				1,600		1,600			
24	Depreciation Expense			(f) 50		50		50			
25	Utilities Expense	985				985		985			
26	Supplies Expense	800		(a) 1,240		2,040		2,040			
27	Insurance Expense			(b) 200		200		200			
28	Miscellaneous Expense	455				455		455			
29		42,600	42,600	2,360	2,360	43,400	43,400	9,855	16,960	33,545	26,440
30	Net income							7,105			7,105
31								16,960	16,960	33,545	33,545

manual or electronic form, as part of their normal end-of-period process. The primary advantage in doing so is that it allows managers and accountants to see the impact of the adjustments on the financial statements. This is especially useful for adjustments that depend on estimates. We discuss such estimates and their impact on the financial statements in later chapters.[1]

Example Exercise 4-1 Flow of Accounts into Financial Statements

The balances for the accounts listed below appear in the Adjusted Trial Balance columns of the end-of-period spreadsheet (work sheet). Indicate whether each balance should be extended to (a) an Income Statement column or (b) a Balance Sheet column.

1. Amber Bablock, Drawing
2. Utilities Expense
3. Accumulated Depreciation—Equipment
4. Unearned Rent
5. Fees Earned
6. Accounts Payable
7. Rent Revenue
8. Supplies

Follow My Example 4-1

1. Balance Sheet column
2. Income Statement column
3. Balance Sheet column
4. Balance Sheet column
5. Income Statement column
6. Balance Sheet column
7. Income Statement column
8. Balance Sheet column

....

For Practice: PE 4-1A, PE 4-1B

Prepare financial statements from adjusted account balances.

Financial Statements

Using Exhibit 1, the financial statements for NetSolutions can be prepared. The income statement, the statement of owner's equity, and the balance sheet are shown in Exhibit 2.

Income Statement

@netsolutions

The income statement is prepared directly from the Income Statement or Adjusted Trial Balance columns of Exhibit 1 beginning with fees earned of $16,840. The expenses in the income statement in Exhibit 2 are listed in order of size, beginning with the larger items. Miscellaneous expense is the last item, regardless of its amount.

Example Exercise 4-2 Determining Net Income from End-of-Period Spreadsheet

In the Balance Sheet columns of the end-of-period spreadsheet (work sheet) for Dimple Consulting Co. for the current year, the Debit column total is $678,450, and the Credit column total is $599,750 before the amount for net income or net loss has been included. In preparing the income statement from the end-of-period spreadsheet (work sheet), what is the amount of net income or net loss?

Follow My Example 4-2

A net income of $78,700 ($678,450 − $599,750) would be reported. When the Debit column of the Balance Sheet columns is more than the Credit column, net income is reported. If the Credit column exceeds the Debit column, a net loss is reported.

....

For Practice: PE 4-2A, PE 4-2B

---

1 The appendix to this chapter describes and illustrates how to prepare the end-of-period spreadsheet (work sheet) shown in Exhibit 1.

Exhibit 2

Financial Statements Prepared from Work Sheet

NetSolutions
Income Statement
For the Two Months Ended December 31, 2009

Fees earned		$16,840	
Rent revenue		120	
Total revenues			$16,960
Expenses:			
Wages expense		$4,525	
Supplies expense		2,040	
Rent expense		1,600	
Utilities expense		985	
Insurance expense		200	
Depreciation expense		50	
Miscellaneous expense		455	
Total expenses			9,855
Net income			$ 7,105

NetSolutions
Statement of Owner's Equity
For the Two Months Ended December 31, 2009

Chris Clark, capital, November 1, 2009			$ 0
Investment on November 1, 2009		$25,000	
Net income for November and December		7,105	
		$32,105	
Less withdrawals		4,000	
Increase in owner's equity			28,105
Chris Clark, capital, December 31, 2009			$28,105

NetSolutions
Balance Sheet
December 31, 2009

Assets

Current assets:		
Cash	$ 2,065	
Accounts receivable	2,720	
Supplies	760	
Prepaid insurance	2,200	
Total current assets		$ 7,745
Property, plant, and equipment:		
Land	$20,000	
Office equipment	$1,800	
Less accum. depreciation	50	1,750
Total property, plant, and equipment		21,750
Total assets		$29,495

Liabilities

Current liabilities:		
Accounts payable	$900	
Wages payable	250	
Unearned rent	240	
Total liabilities		$ 1,390

Owner's Equity

Chris Clark, capital		28,105
Total liabilities and owner's equity		$29,495

Integrity, Objectivity, and Ethics in Business

THE ROUND TRIP

A common type of fraud involves artificially inflating revenue. One fraudulent method of inflating revenue is called "round tripping." Under this scheme, a selling company (S) "lends" money to a customer company (C). The money is then used by C to purchase a product from S. Thus, S sells product to C and is paid with the money just loaned to C! This looks like a sale in the accounting records, but in reality, S is shipping free product. The fraud is exposed when it is determined that there was no intent to repay the original loan.

Statement of Owner's Equity

The first item presented on the statement of owner's equity is the balance of the owner's capital account at the beginning of the period. The amount listed as owner's capital in the spreadsheet, however, is not always the account balance at the beginning of the period. The owner may have invested additional assets in the business during the period. Thus, for the beginning balance and any additional investments, it is necessary to refer to the owner's capital account in the ledger. These amounts, along with the net income (or net loss) and the drawing account balance, are used to determine the ending owner's capital account balance.

The basic form of the statement of owner's equity is shown in Exhibit 2. For NetSolutions, the amount of drawings by the owner was less than the net income. If the owner's withdrawals had exceeded the net income, the order of the net income and the withdrawals would have been reversed. The difference between the two items would then be deducted from the beginning capital account balance. Other factors, such as additional investments or a net loss, also require some change in the form, as shown below.

Allan Johnson, capital, January 1, 2009	$39,000	
Additional investment during the year	6,000	
Total		$45,000
Net loss for the year	$ 5,600	
Withdrawals	9,500	
Decrease in owner's equity		15,100
Allan Johnson, capital, December 31, 2009		$29,900

Example Exercise 4-3 Statement of Owner's Equity •••••••▷ 2

Zack Gaddis owns and operates Gaddis Employment Services. On January 1, 2009, Zack Gaddis, Capital had a balance of $186,000. During the year, Zack invested an additional $40,000 and withdrew $25,000. For the year ended December 31, 2009, Gaddis Employment Services reported a net income of $18,750. Prepare a statement of owner's equity for the year ended December 31, 2009.

Follow My Example 4-3

GADDIS EMPLOYMENT SERVICES
STATEMENT OF OWNER'S EQUITY
For the Year Ended December 31, 2009

Zack Gaddis, capital, January 1, 2009	$186,000	
Additional investment during 2009	40,000	
Total		$226,000
Withdrawals	$ 25,000	
Less net income	18,750	
Decrease in owner's equity		6,250
Zack Gaddis, capital, December 31, 2009 ...		$219,750

For Practice: PE 4-3A, PE 4-3B

Balance Sheet

The balance sheet is prepared directly from the Balance Sheet or Adjusted Trial Balance columns of Exhibit 1 beginning with Cash of $2,065.

The balance sheet in Exhibit 2 shows subsections for assets and liabilities. Such a balance sheet is a *classified balance sheet*. We describe these subsections next.

Assets Assets are commonly divided into two sections on the balance sheet: (1) current assets and (2) property, plant, and equipment.

Current Assets Cash and other assets that are expected to be converted to cash or sold or used up usually within one year or less, through the normal operations of the business, are called **current assets.** In addition to cash, the current assets may include notes receivable, accounts receivable, supplies, and other prepaid expenses.

Notes receivable are amounts that customers owe. They are written promises to pay the amount of the note and interest. Accounts receivable are also amounts customers owe, but they are less formal than notes. Accounts receivable normally result from providing services or selling merchandise on account. Notes receivable and accounts receivable are current assets because they are usually converted to cash within one year or less.

Property, Plant, and Equipment The property, plant, and equipment section may also be described as **fixed assets** or **plant assets**. These assets include equipment, machinery, buildings, and land. With the exception of land, as we discussed in Chapter 3, fixed assets depreciate over a period of time. The cost, accumulated depreciation, and book value of each major type of fixed asset are normally reported on the balance sheet or in the notes to the financial statements.

Liabilities Liabilities are the amounts the business owes to creditors. Liabilities are commonly divided into two sections on the balance sheet: (1) current liabilities and (2) long-term liabilities.

Current Liabilities Liabilities that will be due within a short time (usually one year or less) and that are to be paid out of current assets are called **current liabilities.** The most common liabilities in this group are notes payable and accounts payable. Other current liabilities may include Wages Payable, Interest Payable, Taxes Payable, and Unearned Fees.

Long-Term Liabilities Liabilities that will not be due for a long time (usually more than one year) are called **long-term liabilities.** If NetSolutions had long-term liabilities, they would be reported below the current liabilities. As long-term liabilities come due and are to be paid within one year, they are reported as current liabilities. If they are to be renewed rather than paid, they would continue to be reported as long term. When an asset is pledged as security for a liability, the obligation may be called a *mortgage note payable* or a *mortgage payable*.

Owner's Equity The owner's right to the assets of the business is presented on the balance sheet below the liabilities section. The owner's equity is added to the total liabilities, and this total must be equal to the total assets.

Example Exercise 4-4   Classified Balance Sheet   2

The following accounts appear in an adjusted trial balance of Hindsight Consulting. Indicate whether each account would be reported in the (a) current asset; (b) property, plant, and equipment; (c) current liability; (d) long-term liability; or (e) owner's equity section of the December 31, 2009, balance sheet of Hindsight Consulting.

1. Jason Corbin, Capital
2. Notes Receivable (due in 6 months)
3. Notes Payable (due in 2011)
4. Land
5. Cash
6. Unearned Rent (3 months)
7. Accumulated Depreciation—Equipment
8. Accounts Payable

(continued)

Follow My Example 4-4

1. Owner's equity
2. Current asset
3. Long-term liability
4. Property, plant, and equipment

5. Current asset
6. Current liability
7. Property, plant, and equipment
8. Current liability

For Practice: PE 4-4A, PE 4-4B

3 Prepare closing entries.

@netsolutions

Closing Entries

As discussed in Chapter 3, the adjusting entries are recorded in the journal at the end of the accounting period. For NetSolutions, the adjusting entries are shown in Exhibit 7 of Chapter 3.

After the adjusting entries are posted to NetSolutions' ledger, shown in Exhibit 6 (on pages 154–155), the ledger agrees with the data reported on the financial statements.

The balances of the accounts reported on the balance sheet are carried forward from year to year. Because they are relatively permanent, these accounts are called **permanent accounts** or **real accounts**. For example, Cash, Accounts Receivable, Equipment, Accumulated Depreciation, Accounts Payable, and Owner's Capital are all permanent accounts.

The balances of the accounts reported on the income statement are not carried forward from year to year. Also, the balance of the owner's drawing account, which is reported on the statement of owner's equity, is not carried forward. Because these accounts report amounts for only one period, they are called **temporary accounts** or **nominal accounts**. Temporary accounts are not carried forward because they relate only to one period. For example, the Fees Earned of $16,840 and Wages Expense of $4,525 for NetSolutions shown in Exhibit 2 are for the two months ending December 31, 2009, and should not be carried forward to 2010.

At the beginning of the next period, temporary accounts should have zero balances. To achieve this, temporary account balances are transferred to permanent accounts at the end of the accounting period. The entries that transfer these balances are called **closing entries**. The transfer process is called the **closing process** and is sometimes referred to as **closing the books**.

The closing process involves the following four steps:

1. Revenue account balances are transferred to an account called Income Summary.
2. Expense account balances are transferred to an account called Income Summary.
3. The balance of Income Summary (net income or net loss) is transferred to the owner's capital account.
4. The balance of the owner's drawing account is transferred to the owner's capital account.

Exhibit 3 diagrams the closing process.

Income Summary is a temporary account that is only used during the closing process. At the beginning of the closing process, Income Summary has no balance. During the closing process, Income Summary will be debited and credited for various amounts. At the end of the closing process, Income Summary will again have no balance. Because Income Summary has the effect of clearing the revenue and expense accounts of their balances, it is sometimes called a **clearing account**. Other titles used for this account include Revenue and Expense Summary, Profit and Loss Summary, and Income and Expense Summary.

The four closing entries required in the closing process are as follows:

1. Debit each revenue account for its balance and credit Income Summary for the total revenue.

Exhibit 3

The Closing Process

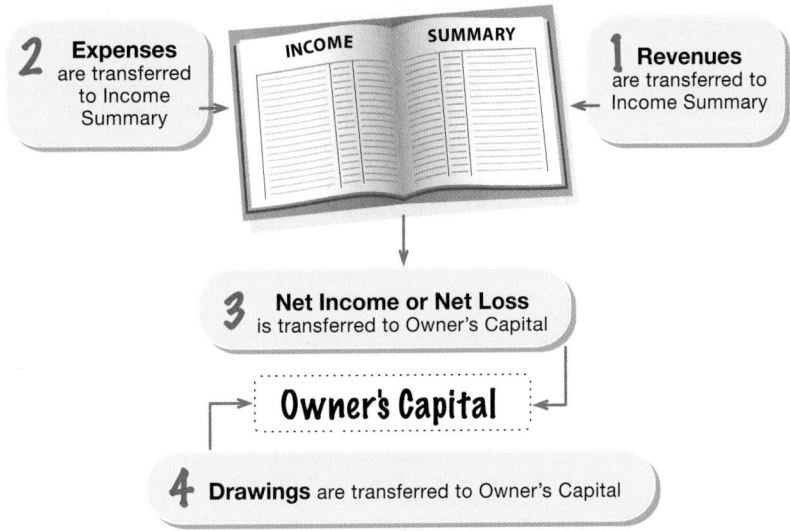

2 **Expenses** are transferred to Income Summary

INCOME SUMMARY

1 **Revenues** are transferred to Income Summary

3 **Net Income or Net Loss** is transferred to Owner's Capital

Owner's Capital

4 **Drawings** are transferred to Owner's Capital

2. Credit each expense account for its balance and debit Income Summary for the total expenses.
3. Debit Income Summary for its balance and credit the owner's capital account.
4. Debit the owner's capital account for the balance of the drawing account and credit the drawing account.

In the case of a net loss, Income Summary will have a debit balance after the first two closing entries. In this case, credit Income Summary for the amount of its balance and debit the owner's capital account for the amount of the net loss.

Closing entries are recorded in the journal and are dated as of the last day of the accounting period. In the journal, closing entries are recorded immediately following the adjusting entries. The caption, *Closing Entries*, is often inserted above the closing entries to separate them from the adjusting entries.

It is possible to close the temporary revenue and expense accounts without using a clearing account such as Income Summary. In this case, the balances of the revenue and expense accounts are closed directly to the owner's capital account. This process may be used in a computerized accounting system. In a manual system, the use of an income summary account aids in detecting and correcting errors.

Journalizing and Posting Closing Entries

A flowchart of the four closing entries for NetSolutions is shown in Exhibit 4. The balances in the accounts are those shown in the Adjusted Trial Balance columns of the end-of-period spreadsheet shown in Exhibit 1.

The closing entries for NetSolutions are shown in Exhibit 5. The account titles and balances for the these entries may be obtained from the end-of-period spreadsheet, the adjusted trial balance, the income statement, the statement of owner's equity, or the ledger.

The closing entries are posted to NetSolutions ledger as shown in Exhibit 6 (pages 154–155). Income Summary has been added to NetSolutions' ledger in Exhibit 6 as account number 33. After the closing entries are posted, NetSolutions' ledger has the following characteristics:

1. The balance of Chris Clark, Capital of $28,105 agrees with the amount reported on the statement of owner's equity and the balance sheet.
2. The revenue, expense, and drawing accounts will have zero balances.

Exhibit 4

Flowchart of Closing Entries for NetSolutions

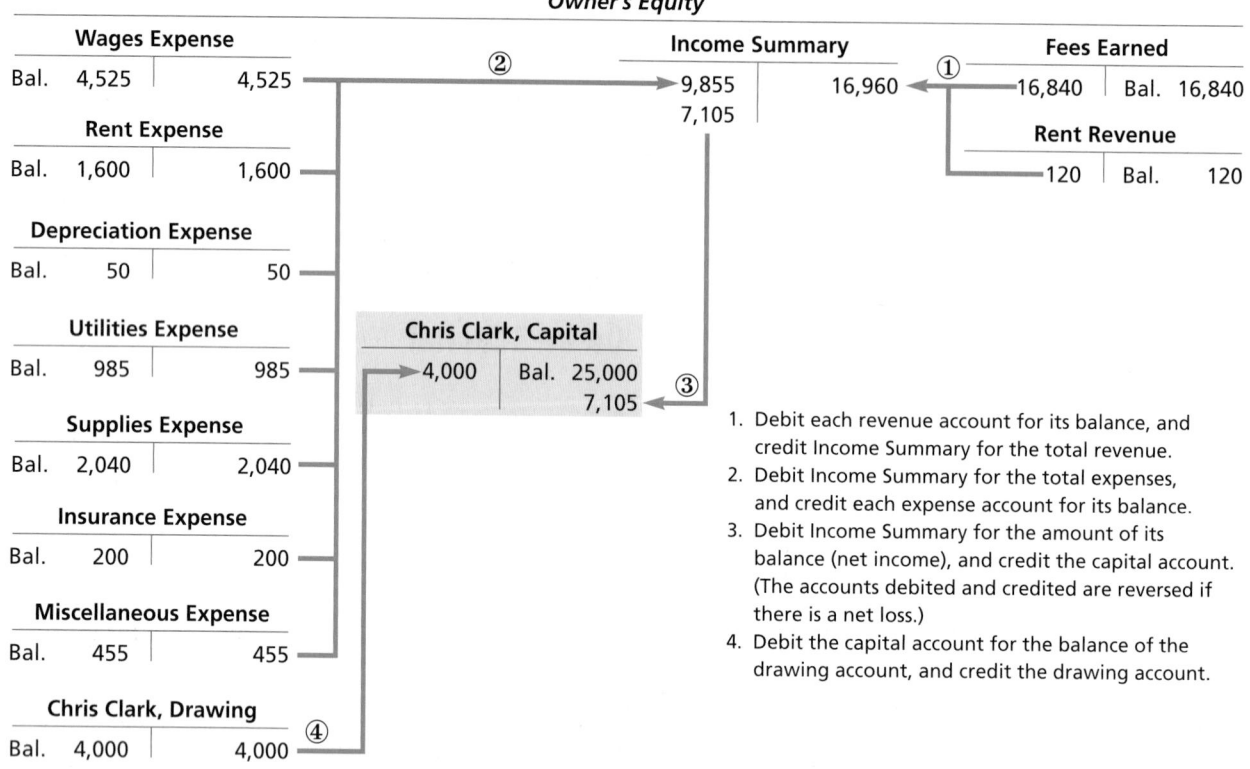

Owner's Equity

Wages Expense				Income Summary			Fees Earned	
Bal.	4,525	4,525	②	9,855	16,960	①	16,840	Bal. 16,840

Rent Expense						Rent Revenue	
Bal.	1,600	1,600		7,105		120	Bal. 120

Depreciation Expense		
Bal.	50	50

Utilities Expense			Chris Clark, Capital		
Bal.	985	985	4,000	Bal. 25,000	③
				7,105	

Supplies Expense		
Bal.	2,040	2,040

Insurance Expense		
Bal.	200	200

Miscellaneous Expense		
Bal.	455	455

Chris Clark, Drawing		
Bal.	4,000	4,000 ④

1. Debit each revenue account for its balance, and credit Income Summary for the total revenue.
2. Debit Income Summary for the total expenses, and credit each expense account for its balance.
3. Debit Income Summary for the amount of its balance (net income), and credit the capital account. (The accounts debited and credited are reversed if there is a net loss.)
4. Debit the capital account for the balance of the drawing account, and credit the drawing account.

Exhibit 5

Closing Entries for NetSolutions

Journal
Page 6

Date		Description	Post. Ref.	Debit	Credit
2009		Closing Entries			
Dec.	31	Fees Earned	41	16,840	
		Rent Revenue	42	120	
		Income Summary	33		16,960
	31	Income Summary	33	9,855	
		Wages Expense	51		4,525
		Rent Expense	52		1,600
		Depreciation Expense	53		50
		Utilities Expense	54		985
		Supplies Expense	55		2,040
		Insurance Expense	56		200
		Miscellaneous Expense	59		455
	31	Income Summary	33	7,105	
		Chris Clark, Capital	31		7,105
	31	Chris Clark, Capital	31	4,000	
		Chris Clark, Drawing	32		4,000

Example Exercise 4-5   Closing Entries

•••••••• ▷ ③

After the accounts have been adjusted at July 31, the end of the fiscal year, the following balances are taken from the ledger of Cabriolet Services Co.:

Terry Lambert, Capital	$615,850
Terry Lambert, Drawing	25,000
Fees Earned	380,450
Wages Expense	250,000
Rent Expense	65,000
Supplies Expense	18,250
Miscellaneous Expense	6,200

Journalize the four entries required to close the accounts.

Follow My Example 4-5

July	31	Fees Earned	380,450	
		Income Summary		380,450
	31	Income Summary	339,450	
		Wages Expense		250,000
		Rent Expense		65,000
		Supplies Expense		18,250
		Miscellaneous Expense		6,200
	31	Income Summary	41,000	
		Terry Lambert, Capital		41,000
	31	Terry Lambert, Capital	25,000	
		Terry Lambert, Drawing		25,000

For Practice: PE 4-5A, PE 4-5B

As shown in Exhibit 6, the closing entries are normally identified in the ledger as "Closing." In addition, a line is often inserted in both balance columns after a closing entry is posted. This separates next period's revenue, expense, and withdrawal transactions from those of the current period. Next period's transactions will be posted directly below the closing entry.

Post-Closing Trial Balance

A post-closing trial balance is prepared after the closing entries have been posted. The purpose of the post-closing (after closing) trial balance is to verify that the ledger is in balance at the beginning of the next period. The accounts and amounts should agree exactly with the accounts and amounts listed on the balance sheet at the end of the period. The post-closing trial balance for NetSolutions is shown in Exhibit 7 on page 156.

④ Describe the accounting cycle.

Accounting Cycle

The accounting process that begins with analyzing and journalizing transactions and ends with the post-closing trial balance is called the **accounting cycle**. The steps in the accounting cycle are as follows:

1. Transactions are analyzed and recorded in the journal.
2. Transactions are posted to the ledger.
3. An unadjusted trial balance is prepared.
4. Adjustment data are assembled and analyzed.
5. An optional end-of-period spreadsheet (work sheet) is prepared.
6. Adjusting entries are journalized and posted to the ledger.

Exhibit 6

Ledger for NetSolutions

Ledger

Account Cash — Account No. 11

Date	Item	Post. Ref.	Debit	Credit	Balance Debit	Balance Credit
2009						
Nov. 1		1	25,000		25,000	
5		1		20,000	5,000	
18		1	7,500		12,500	
30		1		3,650	8,850	
30		1		950	7,900	
30		2		2,000	5,900	
Dec. 1		2		2,400	3,500	
1		2		800	2,700	
1		2	360		3,060	
6		2		180	2,880	
11		2		400	2,480	
13		3		950	1,530	
16		3	3,100		4,630	
20		3		900	3,730	
21		3	650		4,380	
23		3		1,450	2,930	
27		3		1,200	1,730	
31		3		310	1,420	
31		4		225	1,195	
31		4	2,870		4,065	
31		4		2,000	2,065	

Account Accounts Receivable — Account No. 12

Date	Item	Post. Ref.	Debit	Credit	Balance Debit	Balance Credit
2009						
Dec. 16		3	1,750		1,750	
21		3		650	1,100	
31		4	1,120		2,220	
31	Adjusting	5	500		2,720	

Account Supplies — Account No. 14

Date	Item	Post. Ref.	Debit	Credit	Balance Debit	Balance Credit
2009						
Nov. 10		1	1,350		1,350	
30		1		800	550	
23		3	1,450		2,000	
Dec. 31	Adjusting	5		1,240	760	

Account Prepaid Insurance — Account No. 15

Date	Item	Post. Ref.	Debit	Credit	Balance Debit	Balance Credit
2009						
Dec. 1		2	2,400		2,400	
31	Adjusting	5		200	2,200	

Account Land — Account No. 17

Date	Item	Post. Ref.	Debit	Credit	Balance Debit	Balance Credit
2009						
Nov. 5		1	20,000		20,000	

Account Office Equipment — Account No. 18

Date	Item	Post. Ref.	Debit	Credit	Balance Debit	Balance Credit
2009						
Dec. 4		2	1,800		1,800	

Account Accumulated Depreciation — Account No. 19

Date	Item	Post. Ref.	Debit	Credit	Balance Debit	Balance Credit
2009						
Dec. 31	Adjusting	5		50		50

Account Accounts Payable — Account No. 21

Date	Item	Post. Ref.	Debit	Credit	Balance Debit	Balance Credit
2009						
Nov. 10		1		1,350		1,350
30		1	950			400
Dec. 4		2		1,800		2,200
11		2	400			1,800
20		3	900			900

Account Wages Payable — Account No. 22

Date	Item	Post. Ref.	Debit	Credit	Balance Debit	Balance Credit
2009						
Dec. 31	Adjusting	5		250		250

Account Unearned Rent — Account No. 23

Date	Item	Post. Ref.	Debit	Credit	Balance Debit	Balance Credit
2009						
Dec. 1		2		360		360
31	Adjusting	5	120			240

Account Chris Clark, Capital — Account No. 31

Date	Item	Post. Ref.	Debit	Credit	Balance Debit	Balance Credit
2009						
Nov. 1		1		25,000		25,000
Dec. 31	Closing	6		7,105		32,105
31	Closing	6	4,000			28,105

Account Chris Clark, Drawing — Account No. 32

Date	Item	Post. Ref.	Debit	Credit	Balance Debit	Balance Credit
2009						
Nov. 30		2	2,000		2,000	
Dec. 31		4	2,000		4,000	
31	Closing	6		4,000	—	—

Exhibit 6
(continued)

Account *Income Summary*   Account No. 33

Date	Item	Post. Ref.	Debit	Credit	Balance Debit	Balance Credit
2009						
Dec. 31	Closing	6		16,960		16,960
31	Closing	6	9,855			7,105
31	Closing	6	7,105		—	—

Account *Fees Earned*   Account No. 41

Date	Item	Post. Ref.	Debit	Credit	Balance Debit	Balance Credit
2009						
Nov. 18		1		7,500		7,500
Dec. 16		3		3,100		10,600
16		3		1,750		12,350
31		4		2,870		15,220
31		4		1,120		16,340
31	Adjusting	5		500		16,840
31	Closing	6	16,840		—	—

Account *Rent Revenue*   Account No. 42

Date	Item	Post. Ref.	Debit	Credit	Balance Debit	Balance Credit
2009						
Dec. 31	Adjusting	5		120		120
31	Closing	6	120		—	—

Account *Wages Expense*   Account No. 51

Date	Item	Post. Ref.	Debit	Credit	Balance Debit	Balance Credit
2009						
Nov. 30		1	2,125		2,125	
Dec. 13		3	950		3,075	
27		3	1,200		4,275	
31	Adjusting	5	250		4,525	
31	Closing	6		4,525	—	—

Account *Rent Expense*   Account No. 52

Date	Item	Post. Ref.	Debit	Credit	Balance Debit	Balance Credit
2009						
Nov. 30		1	800		800	
Dec. 1		2	800		1,600	
31	Closing	6		1,600	—	—

Account *Depreciation Expense*   Account No. 53

Date	Item	Post. Ref.	Debit	Credit	Balance Debit	Balance Credit
2009						
Dec. 31	Adjusting	5	50		50	
31	Closing	6		50	—	—

Account *Utilities Expense*   Account No. 54

Date	Item	Post. Ref.	Debit	Credit	Balance Debit	Balance Credit
2009						
Nov. 30		1	450		450	
Dec. 31		3	310		760	
31		4	225		985	
31	Closing	6		985	—	—

Account *Supplies Expense*   Account No. 55

Date	Item	Post. Ref.	Debit	Credit	Balance Debit	Balance Credit
2009						
Nov. 30		1	800		800	
Dec. 31	Adjusting	5	1,240		2,040	
31	Closing	6		2,040	—	—

Account *Insurance Expense*   Account No. 56

Date	Item	Post. Ref.	Debit	Credit	Balance Debit	Balance Credit
2009						
Dec. 31	Adjusting	5	200		200	
31	Closing	6		200	—	—

Account *Miscellaneous Expense*   Account No. 59

Date	Item	Post. Ref.	Debit	Credit	Balance Debit	Balance Credit
2009						
Nov. 30		1	275		275	
Dec. 6		2	180		455	
31	Closing	6		455	—	—

7. An adjusted trial balance is prepared.
8. Financial statements are prepared.
9. Closing entries are journalized and posted to the ledger.
10. A post-closing trial balance is prepared.[2]

2 Some accountants include the journalizing and posting of "reversing entries" as the last step in the accounting cycle. Because reversing entries are not required, we describe and illustrate them in Appendix B at the end of the book.

Exhibit 7

Post-Closing Trial Balance

NetSolutions
Post-Closing Trial Balance
December 31, 2009

	Debit Balances	Credit Balances
Cash	2,065	
Accounts Receivable	2,720	
Supplies	760	
Prepaid Insurance	2,200	
Land	20,000	
Office Equipment	1,800	
Accumulated Depreciation		50
Accounts Payable		900
Wages Payable		250
Unearned Rent		240
Chris Clark, Capital		28,105
	29,545	29,545

Exhibit 8 illustrates the accounting cycle in graphic form. It also illustrates how the accounting cycle begins with the source documents for a transaction and flows through the accounting system and into the financial statements.

Example Exercise 4-6 Accounting Cycle  4

From the following list of steps in the accounting cycle, identify what two steps are missing.

a. Transactions are analyzed and recorded in the journal.
b. Transactions are posted to the ledger.
c. Adjustment data are assembled and analyzed.
d. An optional end-of-period spreadsheet (work sheet) is prepared.
e. Adjusting entries are journalized and posted to the ledger.
f. Financial statements are prepared.
g. Closing entries are journalized and posted to the ledger.
h. A post-closing trial balance is prepared.

The following two steps are missing: (1) the preparation of an unadjusted trial balance and (2) the preparation of the adjusted trial balance. The unadjusted trial balance should be prepared after step (b). The adjusted trial balance should be prepared after step (e).

For Practice: PE 4-6A, PE 4-6B

---

5 Illustrate the accounting cycle for one period.

Illustration of the Accounting Cycle

In this section, we will illustate the complete accounting cycle for one period. We assume that for several years Kelly Pitney has operated a part-time consulting business from her home. As of April 1, 2010, Kelly decided to move to rented quarters and to operate the business on a full-time basis. The business will be known as Kelly Consulting. During April, Kelly Consulting entered into the following transactions:

Apr. 1. The following assets were received from Kelly Pitney: cash, $13,100; accounts receivable, $3,000; supplies, $1,400; and office equipment, $12,500. There were no liabilities received.

Exhibit 8

Accounting Cycle

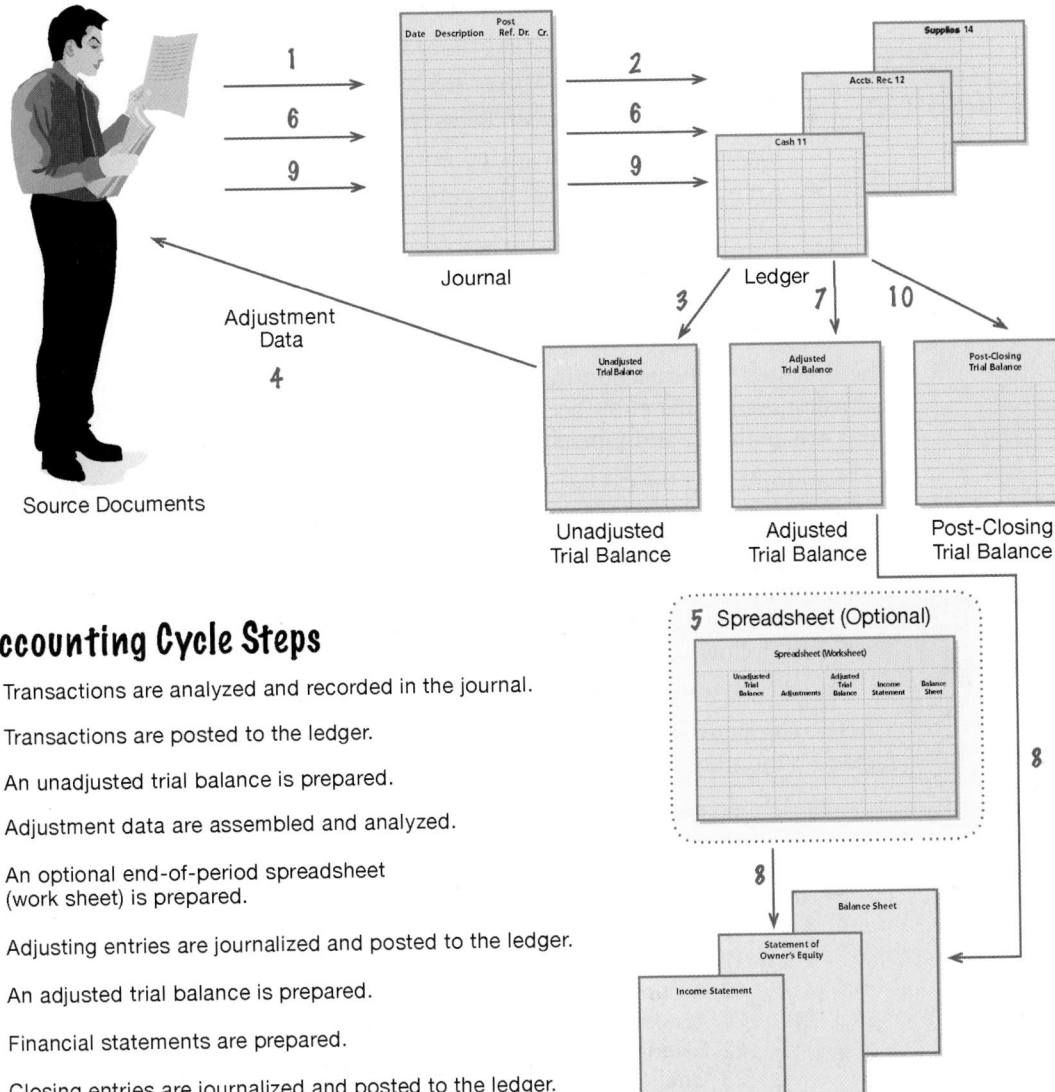

Accounting Cycle Steps

1 Transactions are analyzed and recorded in the journal.

2 Transactions are posted to the ledger.

3 An unadjusted trial balance is prepared.

4 Adjustment data are assembled and analyzed.

5 An optional end-of-period spreadsheet (work sheet) is prepared.

6 Adjusting entries are journalized and posted to the ledger.

7 An adjusted trial balance is prepared.

8 Financial statements are prepared.

9 Closing entries are journalized and posted to the ledger.

10 A post-closing trial balance is prepared.

Apr. 1. Paid three months' rent on a lease rental contract, $4,800.

2. Paid the premiums on property and casualty insurance policies, $1,800.

4. Received cash from clients as an advance payment for services to be provided and recorded it as unearned fees, $5,000.

5. Purchased additional office equipment on account from Office Station Co., $2,000.

6. Received cash from clients on account, $1,800.

10. Paid cash for a newspaper advertisement, $120.

12. Paid Office Station Co. for part of the debt incurred on April 5, $1,200.

12. Recorded services provided on account for the period April 1–12, $4,200.

14. Paid part-time receptionist for two weeks' salary, $750.

17. Recorded cash from cash clients for fees earned during the period April 1–16, $6,250.

18. Paid cash for supplies, $800.

Apr. 20. Recorded services provided on account for the period April 13–20, $2,100.
  24. Recorded cash from cash clients for fees earned for the period April 17–24, $3,850.
  26. Received cash from clients on account, $5,600.
  27. Paid part-time receptionist for two weeks' salary, $750.
  29. Paid telephone bill for April, $130.
  30. Paid electricity bill for April, $200.
  30. Recorded cash from cash clients for fees earned for the period April 25–30, $3,050.
  30. Recorded services provided on account for the remainder of April, $1,500.
  30. Kelly withdrew $6,000 for personal use.

Step 1. Analyzing and Recording Transactions in the Journal

The first step in the accounting cycle is to analyze and record transactions in the journal using the double-entry accounting system. As we illustrated in Chapter 2, transactions are analyzed and journalized using the following steps:

1. Carefully read the description of the transaction to determine whether an asset, liability, owner's equity, revenue, expense, or drawing account is affected.
2. For each account affected by the transaction, determine whether the account increases or decreases.
3. Determine whether each increase or decrease should be recorded as a debit or a credit, following the rules of debit and credit shown in Exhibit 3 of Chapter 2.
4. Record the transaction using a journal entry.

The company's chart of accounts is useful in determining which accounts are affected by the transaction. The chart of accounts for Kelly Consulting is as follows:

11 Cash	31 Kelly Pitney, Capital
12 Accounts Receivable	32 Kelly Pitney, Drawing
14 Supplies	33 Income Summary
15 Prepaid Rent	41 Fees Earned
16 Prepaid Insurance	51 Salary Expense
18 Office Equipment	52 Rent Expense
19 Accumulated Depreciation	53 Supplies Expense
21 Accounts Payable	54 Depreciation Expense
22 Salaries Payable	55 Insurance Expense
23 Unearned Fees	59 Miscellaneous Expense

After analyzing each of Kelly Consulting's transactions for April, the journal entries are recorded as shown in Exhibit 9.

Step 2. Posting Transactions to the Ledger

Periodically, the transactions recorded in the journal are posted to the accounts in the ledger. The debits and credits for each journal entry are posted to the accounts in the order in which they occur in the journal. As we illustrated in Chapters 2 and 3, journal entries are posted to the accounts using the following four steps:

1. The date is entered in the Date column of the account.
2. The amount is entered into the Debit or Credit column of the account.
3. The journal page number is entered in the Posting Reference column.
4. The account number is entered in the Posting Reference (Post. Ref.) column in the journal.

The journal entries for Kelly Consulting have been posted to the ledger shown in Exhibit 17 on pages 167–168.

Exhibit 9

Journal Entries for April, Kelly Consulting

		Journal			**Page 1**
Date		**Description**	**Post. Ref.**	**Debit**	**Credit**
2010 Apr.	1	Cash	11	13,100	
		Accounts Receivable	12	3,000	
		Supplies	14	1,400	
		Office Equipment	18	12,500	
		Kelly Pitney, Capital	31		30,000
	1	Prepaid Rent	15	4,800	
		Cash	11		4,800
	2	Prepaid Insurance	16	1,800	
		Cash	11		1,800
	4	Cash	11	5,000	
		Unearned Fees	23		5,000
	5	Office Equipment	18	2,000	
		Accounts Payable	21		2,000
	6	Cash	11	1,800	
		Accounts Receivable	12		1,800
	10	Miscellaneous Expense	59	120	
		Cash	11		120
	12	Accounts Payable	21	1,200	
		Cash	11		1,200
	12	Accounts Receivable	12	4,200	
		Fees Earned	41		4,200
	14	Salary Expense	51	750	
		Cash	11		750
	17	Cash	11	6,250	
		Fees Earned	41		6,250
	18	Supplies	14	800	
		Cash	11		800
	20	Accounts Receivable	12	2,100	
		Fees Earned	41		2,100
	24	Cash	11	3,850	
		Fees Earned	41		3,850
	26	Cash	11	5,600	
		Accounts Receivable	12		5,600
	27	Salary Expense	51	750	
		Cash	11		750
	29	Miscellaneous Expense	59	130	
		Cash	11		130

(continued)

Exhibit 9

Journal Entries for April, Kelly Consulting (*continued*)

	Journal				Page *2*
Date	**Description**	**Post. Ref.**	**Debit**	**Credit**
2010				
Apr. 30	Miscellaneous Expense	59	200	
	Cash	11		200
30	Cash	11	3,050	
	Fees Earned	41		3,050
30	Accounts Receivable	12	1,500	
	Fees Earned	41		1,500
30	Kelly Pitney, Drawing	32	6,000	
	Cash	11		6,000

Step 3. Preparing an Unadjusted Trial Balance

An unadjusted trial balance is prepared to determine whether any errors have been made in posting the debits and credits to the ledger. The unadjusted trial balance does not provide complete proof of the accuracy of the ledger. It indicates only that the debits and the credits are equal. This proof is of value, however, because errors often affect the equality of debits and credits. If the two totals of a trial balance are not equal, an error has occurred that must be discovered and corrected.

The unadjusted trial balance for Kelly Consulting is shown in Exhibit 10. The unadjusted account balances shown in Exhibit 10 were taken from Kelly Consulting's ledger shown in Exhibit 17, on pages 167–168, before any adjusting entries were recorded.

Step 4. Assembling and Analyzing Adjustment Data

Before the financial statements can be prepared, the accounts must be updated. The four types of accounts that normally require adjustment include prepaid expenses, unearned revenue, accrued revenue, and accrued expenses. In addition, depreciation expense must be recorded for fixed assets other than land. The following data have been assembled on April 30, 2010, for analysis of possible adjustments for Kelly Consulting:

   a.   Insurance expired during April is $300.
   b.   Supplies on hand on April 30 are $1,350.
   c.   Depreciation of office equipment for April is $330.
   d.   Accrued receptionist salary on April 30 is $120.
   e.   Rent expired during April is $1,600.
   f.   Unearned fees on April 30 are $2,500.

Step 5. Preparing an Optional End-of-Period Spreadsheet (Work Sheet)

Although an end-of-period spreadsheet (work sheet) is not required, it is useful in showing the flow of accounting information from the unadjusted trial balance to the adjusted trial balance and financial statements. In addition, an end-of-period spreadsheet is useful in analyzing the impact of proposed adjustments on the financial statements. The end-of-period spreadsheet for Kelly Consulting is shown in Exhibit 11.

Exhibit 10

Unadjusted Trial Balance, Kelly Consulting

Kelly Consulting
Unadjusted Trial Balance
April 30, 2010

	Debit Balances	Credit Balances
Cash	22,100	
Accounts Receivable	3,400	
Supplies	2,200	
Prepaid Rent	4,800	
Prepaid Insurance	1,800	
Office Equipment	14,500	
Accumulated Depreciation		0
Accounts Payable		800
Salaries Payable		0
Unearned Fees		5,000
Kelly Pitney, Capital		30,000
Kelly Pitney, Drawing	6,000	
Fees Earned		20,950
Salary Expense	1,500	
Rent Expense	0	
Supplies Expense	0	
Depreciation Expense	0	
Insurance Expense	0	
Miscellaneous Expense	450	
	56,750	56,750

Exhibit 11

End-of-Period Spreadsheet (Work Sheet)

Kelly Consulting
End-of-Period Spreadsheet (Work Sheet)
For the Month Ended April 30, 2010

	A	B	C	D	E	F	G	H	I	J	K
		Unadjusted Trial Balance		Adjustments		Adjusted Trial Balance		Income Statement		Balance Sheet	
6	Account Title	Dr.	Cr.	Dr.	Cr.	Dr.	Cr.	Dr.	Cr.	Dr.	Cr.
7											
8	Cash	22,100				22,100				22,100	
9	Accounts Receivable	3,400				3,400				3,400	
10	Supplies	2,200			(b) 850	1,350				1,350	
11	Prepaid Rent	4,800			(e) 1,600	3,200				3,200	
12	Prepaid Insurance	1,800			(a) 300	1,500				1,500	
13	Office Equipment	14,500				14,500				14,500	
14	Accum. Depreciation				(c) 330		330				330
15	Accounts Payable		800				800				800
16	Salaries Payable				(d) 120		120				120
17	Unearned Fees		5,000	(f) 2,500			2,500				2,500
18	Kelly Pitney, Capital		30,000				30,000				30,000
19	Kelly Pitney, Drawing	6,000				6,000				6,000	
20	Fees Earned		20,950		(f) 2,500		23,450		23,450		
21	Salary Expense	1,500		(d) 120		1,620		1,620			
22	Rent Expense			(e) 1,600		1,600		1,600			
23	Supplies Expense			(b) 850		850		850			
24	Depreciation Expense			(c) 330		330		330			
25	Insurance Expense			(a) 300		300		300			
26	Miscellaneous Expense	450				450		450			
27		56,750	56,750	5,700	5,700	57,200	57,200	5,150	23,450	52,050	33,750
28	Net income							18,300			18,300
29								23,450	23,450	52,050	52,050

Step 6. Journalizing and Posting Adjusting Entries

Based on the adjustment data shown in step 4, adjusting entries for Kelly Consulting are prepared as shown in Exhibit 12. Each adjusting entry affects at least one income statement account and one balance sheet account. Explanations for each adjustment including any computations are normally included with each adjusting entry.

Each of the adjusting entries shown in Exhibit 12 is posted to Kelly Consulting's ledger shown in Exhibit 17 on pages 167–168. The adjusting entries are identified in the ledger as "Adjusting."

Exhibit 12

Adjusting Entries, Kelly Consulting

		Journal			Page 3
Date			Post. Ref.	Debit	Credit
2010 Apr.	30	Adjusting Entries			
		Insurance Expense	55	300	
		Prepaid Insurance	16		300
		Expired Insurance.			
	30	Supplies Expense	53	850	
		Supplies	14		850
		Supplies used ($2,200 – $1,350).			
	30	Depreciation Expense	54	330	
		Accumulated Depreciation	19		330
		Depreciation of office equipment.			
	30	Salary Expense	51	120	
		Salaries Payable	22		120
		Accrued salary.			
	30	Rent Expense	52	1,600	
		Prepaid Rent	15		1,600
		Rent expired during April.			
	30	Unearned Fees	23	2,500	
		Fees Earned	41		2,500
		Fees earned ($5,000 – $2,500).			

Step 7. Preparing an Adjusted Trial Balance

After the adjustments have been journalized and posted, an adjusted trial balance is prepared to verify the equality of the total of the debit and credit balances. This is the last step before preparing the financial statements. If the adjusted trial balance does not balance, an error has occurred and must be found and corrected. The adjusted trial balance for Kelly Consulting as of April 30, 2010, is shown in Exhibit 13.

Exhibit 13

Adjusted Trial Balance, Kelly Consulting

Kelly Consulting Adjusted Trial Balance April 30, 2010	Debit Balances	Credit Balances
Cash	22,100	
Accounts Receivable	3,400	
Supplies	1,350	
Prepaid Rent	3,200	
Prepaid Insurance	1,500	
Office Equipment	14,500	
Accumulated Depreciation		330
Accounts Payable		800
Salaries Payable		120
Unearned Fees		2,500
Kelly Pitney, Capital		30,000
Kelly Pitney, Drawing	6,000	
Fees Earned		23,450
Salary Expense	1,620	
Rent Expense	1,600	
Supplies Expense	850	
Depreciation Expense	330	
Insurance Expense	300	
Miscellaneous Expense	450	
	57,200	57,200

Step 8. Preparing the Financial Statements

The most important outcome of the accounting cycle is the financial statements. The income statement is prepared first, followed by the statement of owner's equity and then the balance sheet. The statements can be prepared directly from the adjusted trial balance, the end-of-period spreadsheet, or the ledger. The net income or net loss shown on the income statement is reported on the statement of owner's equity, along with any additional investments by the owner and any withdrawals. The ending owner's capital is reported on the balance sheet and is added with total liabilities to equal total assets.

The financial statements for Kelly Consulting are shown in Exhibit 14. Kelly Consulting earned net income of $18,300 for April. As of April 30, 2010, Kelly Consulting has total assets of $45,720, total liabilities of $3,420, and total owner's equity of $42,300.

Step 9. Journalizing and Posting Closing Entries

As described earlier in this chapter, four closing entries are required at the end of an accounting period. These four closing entries are as follows:

1. Debit each revenue account for its balance and credit Income Summary for the total revenue.
2. Credit each expense account for its balance and debit Income Summary for the total expenses.
3. Debit Income Summary for its balance and credit the owner's capital account.
4. Debit the owner's capital account for the balance of the drawing account and credit the drawing account.

Exhibit 14

Financial Statements, Kelly Consulting

Kelly Consulting
Income Statement
For the Month Ended April 30, 2010

Fees earned		$23,450
Expenses:		
Salary expense	$1,620	
Rent expense	1,600	
Supplies expense	850	
Depreciation expense	330	
Insurance expense	300	
Miscellaneous expense	450	
Total expenses		5,150
Net income		$18,300

Kelly Consulting
Statement of Owner's Equity
For the Month Ended April 30, 2010

Kelly Pitney, capital, April 1, 2010		$ 0
Investment during the month	$30,000	
Net income for the month	18,300	
	$48,300	
Less withdrawals	6,000	
Increase in owner's equity		42,300
Kelly Pitney, capital, April 30, 2010		$42,300

Kelly Consulting
Balance Sheet
April 30, 2010

Assets			Liabilities		
Current assets:			Current liabilities:		
Cash	$22,100		Accounts payable	$ 800	
Accounts receivable	3,400		Salaries payable	120	
Supplies	1,350		Unearned fees	2,500	
Prepaid rent	3,200		Total liabilities		$ 3,420
Prepaid insurance	1,500				
Total current assets		$31,550			
Property, plant, and equipment:					
Office equipment	$14,500				
Less accumulated depreciation	330			Owner's Equity	
Total property, plant,			Kelly Pitney, capital		42,300
and equipment		14,170	Total liabilities and		
Total assets		$45,720	owner's equity		$45,720

The four closing entries for Kelly Consulting are shown in Exhibit 15. The closing entries are posted to Kelly Consulting's ledger as shown in Exhibit 17 (pages 167–168). After the closing entries are posted, Kelly Consulting's ledger has the following characteristics:

1. The balance of Kelly Pitney, Capital of $42,300 agrees with the amount reported on the statement of owner's equity and the balance sheet.
2. The revenue, expense, and drawing account will have zero balances.

The closing entries are normally identified in the ledger as "Closing." In addition, a line is often inserted in both balance columns after a closing entry is posted. This separates next period's revenue, expense, and withdrawal transactions from those of the current period.

Exhibit 15

Closing Entries, Kelly Consulting

	Journal				Page 4
Date	Description	Post. Ref.	Debit		Credit
	Closing Entries				
2010 Apr. 30	Fees Earned	41	23,450		
	Income Summary	33			23,450
30	Income Summary	33	5,150		
	Salary Expense	51			1,620
	Rent Expense	52			1,600
	Supplies Expense	53			850
	Depreciation Expense	54			330
	Insurance Expense	55			300
	Miscellaneous Expense	59			450
30	Income Summary	33	18,300		
	Kelly Pitney, Capital	31			18,300
30	Kelly Pitney, Capital	31	6,000		
	Kelly Pitney, Drawing	32			6,000

Step 10. Preparing a Post-Closing Trial Balance

A post-closing trial balance is prepared after the closing entries have been posted. The purpose of the post-closing trial balance is to verify that the ledger is in balance at the beginning of the next period. The accounts and amounts in the post-closing trial balance should agree exactly with the accounts and amounts listed on the balance sheet at the end of the period.

The post-closing trial balance for Kelly Consulting is shown in Exhibit 16. The balances shown in the post-closing trial balance are taken from the ending balances in the ledger shown in Exhibit 17 (pages 167–168). These balances agree with the amounts shown on Kelly Consulting's balance sheet in Exhibit 14.

Exhibit 16

Post-Closing Trial Balance, Kelly Consulting

Kelly Consulting
Post-Closing Trial Balance
April 30, 2010

	Debit Balances	Credit Balances
Cash	22,100	
Accounts Receivable	3,400	
Supplies	1,350	
Prepaid Rent	3,200	
Prepaid Insurance	1,500	
Office Equipment	14,500	
Accumulated Depreciation		330
Accounts Payable		800
Salaries Payable		120
Unearned Fees		2,500
Kelly Pitney, Capital		42,300
	46,050	46,050

6 Explain what is meant by the fiscal year and the natural business year.

Fiscal Year

The annual accounting period adopted by a business is known as its **fiscal year**. Fiscal years begin with the first day of the month selected and end on the last day of the following twelfth month. The period most commonly used is the calendar year. Other periods are not unusual, especially for businesses organized as corporations. For example, a corporation may adopt a fiscal year that ends when business activities have reached the lowest point in its annual operating cycle. Such a fiscal year is called the **natural business year**. At the low point in its operating cycle, a business has more time to analyze the results of operations and to prepare financial statements.

Because companies with fiscal years often have highly seasonal operations, investors and others should be careful in interpreting partial-year reports for such companies. That is, you should expect the results of operations for these companies to vary significantly throughout the fiscal year.

The financial history of a business may be shown by a series of balance sheets and income statements for several fiscal years. If the life of a business is expressed by a line moving from left to right, the series of balance sheets and income statements may be graphed as follows:

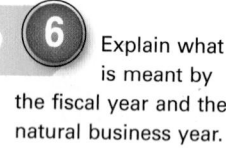

Percentage of Companies with Fiscal Years Ending in:			
January	5%	July	2%
February	1	August	2
March	3	September	7
April	2	October	3
May	3	November	2
June	7	December	63

Source: *Accounting Trends & Techniques*, 61st edition, 2007 (New York: American Institute of Certified Public Accountants).

Financial History of a Business

Income Statement for the year ended Dec. 31, 2008 → Dec. 31 2008

Income Statement for the year ended Dec. 31, 2009 → Dec. 31 2009

Income Statement for the year ended Dec. 31, 2010 → Dec. 31 2010

Balance Sheet Dec. 31, 2008

Balance Sheet Dec. 31, 2009

Balance Sheet Dec. 31, 2010

Exhibit 17

Ledger, Kelly Consulting

Ledger

Account *Cash* Account No. *11*

Date	Item	Post. Ref.	Debit	Credit	Balance Debit	Balance Credit
2010 Apr. 1		1	13,100		13,100	
1		1		4,800	8,300	
2		1		1,800	6,500	
4		1	5,000		11,500	
6		1	1,800		13,300	
10		1		120	13,180	
12		1		1,200	11,980	
14		1		750	11,230	
17		1	6,250		17,480	
18		1		800	16,680	
24		1	3,850		20,530	
26		1	5,600		26,130	
27		1		750	25,380	
29		1		130	25,250	
30		2		200	25,050	
30		2	3,050		28,100	
30		2		6,000	22,100	

Account *Accounts Receivable* Account No. *12*

Date	Item	Post. Ref.	Debit	Credit	Balance Debit	Balance Credit
2010 Apr. 1		1	3,000		3,000	
6		1		1,800	1,200	
12		1	4,200		5,400	
20		1	2,100		7,500	
26		1		5,600	1,900	
30		2	1,500		3,400	

Account *Supplies* Account No. *14*

Date	Item	Post. Ref.	Debit	Credit	Balance Debit	Balance Credit
2010 Apr. 1		1	1,400		1,400	
18		1	800		2,200	
30	Adjusting	3		850	1,350	

Account *Prepaid Rent* Account No. *15*

Date	Item	Post. Ref.	Debit	Credit	Balance Debit	Balance Credit
2010 Apr. 1		1	4,800		4,800	
30	Adjusting	3		1,600	3,200	

Account *Prepaid Insurance* Account No. *16*

Date	Item	Post. Ref.	Debit	Credit	Balance Debit	Balance Credit
2010 Apr. 2		1	1,800		1,800	
30	Adjusting	3		300	1,500	

Account *Office Equipment* Account No. *18*

Date	Item	Post. Ref.	Debit	Credit	Balance Debit	Balance Credit
2010 Apr. 1		1	12,500		12,500	
5		1	2,000		14,500	

Account *Accumulated Depreciation* Account No. *19*

Date	Item	Post. Ref.	Debit	Credit	Balance Debit	Balance Credit
2010 Apr. 30	Adjusting	3		330		330

Account *Accounts Payable* Account No. *21*

Date	Item	Post. Ref.	Debit	Credit	Balance Debit	Balance Credit
2010 Apr. 5		1		2,000		2,000
12		1	1,200			800

Account *Salaries Payable* Account No. *22*

Date	Item	Post. Ref.	Debit	Credit	Balance Debit	Balance Credit
2010 Apr. 30	Adjusting	3		120		120

Account *Unearned Fees* Account No. *23*

Date	Item	Post. Ref.	Debit	Credit	Balance Debit	Balance Credit
2010 Apr. 4		1		5,000		5,000
30	Adjusting	3	2,500			2,500

Account *Kelly Pitney, Capital* Account No. *31*

Date	Item	Post. Ref.	Debit	Credit	Balance Debit	Balance Credit
2010 Apr. 1		1		30,000		30,000
30	Closing	4		18,300		48,300
30	Closing	4	6,000			42,300

(continued)

Exhibit 17

Ledger, Kelly Consulting *(concluded)*

Account *Kelly Pitney, Drawing*   Account No. *32*

Date	Item	Post. Ref.	Debit	Credit	Balance Debit	Balance Credit
2010						
Apr. 30		2	6,000		6,000	
30	Closing	4		6,000	—	—

Account *Income Summary*   Account No. *33*

Date	Item	Post. Ref.	Debit	Credit	Balance Debit	Balance Credit
2010						
Apr. 30	Closing	4		23,450		23,450
30	Closing	4	5,150			18,300
30	Closing	4	18,300		—	—

Account *Fees Earned*   Account No. *41*

Date	Item	Post. Ref.	Debit	Credit	Balance Debit	Balance Credit
2010						
Apr. 12		1		4,200		4,200
17		1		6,250		10,450
20		1		2,100		12,550
24		1		3,850		16,400
30		2		3,050		19,450
30		2		1,500		20,950
30	Adjusting	3		2,500		23,450
30	Closing	4	23,450		—	—

Account *Salary Expense*   Account No. *51*

Date	Item	Post. Ref.	Debit	Credit	Balance Debit	Balance Credit
2010						
Apr. 14		1	750		750	
27		1	750		1,500	
30	Adjusting	3	120		1,620	
30	Closing	4		1,620	—	—

Account *Rent Expense*   Account No. *52*

Date	Item	Post. Ref.	Debit	Credit	Balance Debit	Balance Credit
2010						
Apr. 30	Adjusting	3	1,600		1,600	
30	Closing	4		1,600	—	—

Account *Supplies Expense*   Account No. *53*

Date	Item	Post. Ref.	Debit	Credit	Balance Debit	Balance Credit
2010						
Apr. 30	Adjusting	3	850		850	
30	Closing	4		850	—	—

Account *Depreciation Expense*   Account No. *54*

Date	Item	Post. Ref.	Debit	Credit	Balance Debit	Balance Credit
2010						
Apr. 30	Adjusting	3	330		330	
30	Closing	4		330	—	—

Account *Insurance Expense*   Account No. *55*

Date	Item	Post. Ref.	Debit	Credit	Balance Debit	Balance Credit
2010						
Apr. 30	Adjusting	3	300		300	
30	Closing	4		300	—	—

Account *Miscellaneous Expense*   Account No. *59*

Date	Item	Post. Ref.	Debit	Credit	Balance Debit	Balance Credit
2010						
Apr. 10		1	120		120	
29		1	130		250	
30		2	200		450	
30	Closing	4		450	—	—

The financial statements can be developed on a spreadsheet using the cell references from the adjusted trial balance. The adjusted trial balance for NetSolutions is prepared in a worksheet from Chapter 3, labeled ATB, as follows:

	A	B	C
1		NetSolutions	
2		Adjusted Trial Balance	
3		December 31, 2009	
4		Debit	Credit
5		Balances	Balances
6	Cash	2.065	
7	Accounts Receivable	2,720	
8	Supplies	760	
9	Prepaid Insurance	2,200	
10	Land	20,000	
11	Office Equipment	1,800	
12	Accumulated Depreciation		50
13	Accounts Payable		900
14	Wages Payable		250
15	Unearned Rent		240
16	Chris Clark, Capital		25,000
17	Chris Clark, Drawing	4,000	
18	Fees Earned		16,840
19	Rent Revenue		120
20	Wages Expense	4,525	
21	Rent Expense	1,600	
22	Depreciation Expense	50	
23	Utilities Expense	985	
24	Supplies Expense	2,040	
25	Insurance Expense	200	
26	Miscellaneous Expense	455	
27		43,400	43,400
28			

The financial statements are prepared in a separate worksheet labeled FS. Each financial statement could have its own separate worksheet; however, we'll combine the financial statements on to one worksheet in this text.

	A	B	C	D
1		NetSolutions		
2		Income Statement		
3		For the Two Months Ended December 31, 2009		
4				
5	Fees earned	a. →	=ATB!C18	
6	Rent revenue		=ATB!C19	
7	Total revenues			=C5+C6
8	Expenses:			
9	Wages expense		=ATB!B20	
10	Supplies expense		=ATB!B24	
11	Rent expense		=ATB!B21	
12	Utilities expense		=ATB!B23	
13	Insurance expense		=ATB!B25	
14	Depreciation expense		=ATB!B22	
15	Miscellaneous expense		=ATB!B26	
16	Total expenses			=SUM(C9:C15)
17	Net income			=D7–D16
18				

a. The *income statement* is prepared by referencing the appropriate adjusted trial balance cell locations.

For example, insert in cell B5 the adjusted trial balance cell reference for Fees Earned, =ATB!C18. The reference =ATB!C18 tells the spreadsheet software to insert into cell B5 the contents of cell C18 in worksheet ATB. The expenses can be done in the same way. The appropriate arithmetic spreadsheet formulas are entered to calculate the total expenses and net income.

b. The statement of owner's equity is prepared by referencing the ATB for beginning balances; referencing net income from the income statement; and, making the appropriate arithmetic formulas to determine the ending balance of Chris Clark, Capital as follows:

	A	B	C	D
1		NetSolutions		
2		Income Statement		
3		For the Two Months Ended December 31, 2009		
4				
5	Fees earned		=ATB!C18	
6	Rent revenue		=ATB!C19	
7	Total revenues			=C5+C6
8	Expenses:			
9	Wages expense		=ATB!B20	
10	Supplies expense		=ATB!B24	
11	Rent expense		=ATB!B21	
12	Utilities expense		=ATB!B23	
13	Insurance expense		=ATB!B25	
14	Depreciation expense		=ATB!B22	
15	Miscellaneous expense		=ATB!B26	
16	Total expenses			=SUM(C9:C15)
17	Net income			=D7–D16
18				
19				
20		NetSolutions		
21		Statement of Owner's Equity		
22		For the Two Months Ended December 31, 2009		
23				
24	Chris Clark, Capital, November 1, 2009			=ATB!C16
25	Net income			=D17
26				=SUM(D24:D25)
27	Less withdrawals			=ATB!C17
28	Chris Clark, Capital, December 31, 2009			=D26–D27
29				

b. Net income cell reference

c. The balance sheet is prepared by referencing the adjusted trial balance for all account balances except for the ending balance of the owner's capital account. The owner's capital account in cell G44 references the ending balance of the Statement of Owner's Equity, =D28. Appropriate spreadsheet formulas are then entered for subtotals and totals, as follows:

	A	B	C	D	E	F	G
19							
20		NetSolutions					
21		Statement of Owner's Equity					
22		For the Two Months Ended December 31, 2009					
23							
24	Chris Clark, Capital, November 1, 2009			=ATB!C16			
25	Net income			=D17			Ending balance from the *Statement of Owner's Equity.*
26				=SUM(D24:D25)			
27	Less withdrawals			=ATB!C17			
28	Chris Clark, Capital, December 31, 2009			=D26–D27			
29							
29							
30							
31				NetSolutions			
32				Balance Sheet			
33				December 31, 2009			
34	**Assets**					**Liabilities**	
35	Current assets:					Current liabilities:	
36	Cash		=ATB!B6			Accounts payable	=ATB!C13
37	Accounts receivable		=ATB!B7			Wages payable	=ATB!C14
38	Supplies		=ATB!B8			Unearned rent	=ATB!C15
39	Prepaid insurance		=ATB!B9			Total liabilities	=SUM(G36:G38)
40	Total current assets			=SUM(D36:C39)			
41	Property, plant, and equipment:						
42	Land		=ATB!B10				
43	Office equipment	=ATB!B11				**Owner's Equity**	
44	Less accum. depreciation	=ATB!C12	=B43-B44			Chris Clark, Capital	=D28
45	Total prop., plant, and equip.			=SUM(C42:C44)		Total liabilities and	
46	Total assets			=D40+D45		owner's equity	=G39+G44
47							

c.

	A	B	C	D	E	F	G
1	NetSolutions						
2	Income Statement						
3	For the Two Months Ended December 31, 2009						
4							
5	Fees earned		$ 16,840				
6	Rent revenue		120				
7	Total revenues			$16,960			
8	Expenses:						
9	Wages expense		$ 4,525				
10	Supplies expense		2,040				
11	Rent expense		1,600				
12	Utilities expense		985				
13	Insurance expense		200				
14	Depreciation expense		50				
15	Miscellaneous expense		455				
16	Total expenses			9,855			
17	Net income			$ 7,105			
18							
19							
20	NetSolutions						
21	Statement of Owner's Equity						
22	For the Two Months Ended December 31, 2009						
23							
24	Chris Clark, Capital, November 1, 2009			$ 25,000			
25	Net income			7,105			
26				$ 32,105			
27	Less withdrawals			4,000			
28	Chris Clark, Capital, December 31, 2009			$ 28,105			
29							
30							
31	NetSolutions						
32	Balance Sheet						
33	December 31, 2009						
34	Assets					Liabilities	
35	Current assets:		$ 2,065			Current liabilities:	
36	Cash		2,720			Accounts payable	$ 900
37	Accounts receivable		760			Wages payable	250
38	Supplies		2,200			Unearned rent	240
39	Prepaid insurance			$ 7,745		Total liabilities	$ 1,390
40	Total current assets						
41	Property, plant, and equipment:						
42	Land		$ 20,000				
43	Office equipment	$ 1,800				Owner's Equity	
44	Less accum. depreciation	50	1,750			Chris Clark, Capital	$ 28,105
45	Total prop., plant, and equip.			21,750		Total liabilities and	
46	Total assets			$ 29,495		owner's equity	$ 29,495

The financial statements should be formatted with currency format for leading numbers, single underline for totals; and double underlines for final summations.

See TryIt tutorial titled *Accounting Formatting* for more information!

trit Go to the hands-on *Excel Tutor* for this example!

After the net income or net loss is entered on the spreadsheet, the Income Statement and Balance Sheet columns are totaled. The totals of the two Income Statement columns must now be equal. The totals of the two Balance Sheet columns must also be equal.

Financial Analysis and Interpretation

The ability of a business to pay its debts is called *solvency*. Two financial measures for evaluating a business's short-term solvency are working capital and the current ratio. *Working capital* is the excess of the current assets of a business over its current liabilities, as shown below.

Working Capital = Current Assets − Current Liabilities

An excess of the current assets over the current liabilities implies that the business is able to pay its current liabilities. If the current liabilities are greater than the current assets, the business may not be able to pay its debts and continue in business.

To illustrate, NetSolutions' working capital at the end of 2009 is $675, as computed below. This amount of working capital implies that NetSolutions can pay its current liabilities.

Working Capital = Current Assets − Current Liabilities
Working Capital = $2,065 − $1,390
Working Capital = $675

The *current ratio* is another means of expressing the relationship between current assets and current liabilities.

The current ratio is computed by dividing current assets by current liabilities, as shown below.

Current Ratio = Current Assets/Current Liabilities

To illustrate, the current ratio for NetSolutions at the end of 2009 is 1.5, computed as follows:

Current Ratio = Current Assets/Current Liabilities
Current Ratio = $2,065/$1,390 = 1.5

The current ratio is useful in making comparisons across companies and with industry averages. To illustrate, assume that as of December 31, 2009, the working capital of a company that competes with NetSolutions is much greater than $675, but its current ratio is only 0.7. Considering these facts alone, NetSolutions is in a more favorable position to obtain short-term credit, even though the competing company has a greater amount of working capital.

f·a·i

A P P E N D I X 1

End-of-Period Spreadsheet (Work Sheet)

Accountants often use working papers for analyzing and summarizing data. Such working papers are not a formal part of the accounting records. This is in contrast to the chart of accounts, the journal, and the ledger, which are essential parts of an accounting system. Working papers are usually prepared by using a computer spreadsheet program such as Microsoft's Excel.™

@netsolutions

The end-of-period spreadsheet (work sheet) shown in Exhibit 1 is a working paper used to summarize adjusting entries and the account balances for the financial statements. In companies with few accounts and adjustments, an end-of-period spreadsheet may not be necessary. For example, the financial statements for NetSolutions can be prepared directly from the Adjusted Trial Balance columns in Exhibit 1. However, many companies use an end-of-period spreadsheet as an aid to analyzing adjustment data and preparing the financial statements.

Exhibits 18 through 22 on page 172B illustrate the step-by-step process of how to prepare an end-of-period spreadsheet. As a basis for this illustration, we use NetSolutions.

Step 1. Enter the Title

The spreadsheet is started by entering the following data:

1. Name of the business: *NetSolutions*
2. Type of working paper: *End-of-Period Spreadsheet*
3. The period of time: *For the Two Months Ended December 31, 2009*

Exhibit 18 shows the preceding data entered for NetSolutions.

Step 2. Enter the Unadjusted Trial Balance

Enter the unadjusted trial balance on the spreadsheet. The spreadsheet in Exhibit 18 shows the unadjusted trial balance for NetSolutions at December 31, 2009.

Step 3. Enter the Adjustments

The adjustments for NetSolutions from Chapter 3 are entered in the Adjustments columns, as shown in Exhibit 19. Cross-referencing (by letters) the debit and credit of each adjustment is useful in reviewing the spreadsheet. It is also helpful for identifying the adjusting entries that need to be recorded in the journal. This cross-referencing process is sometimes referred to as *keying* the adjustments.

The adjustments are normally entered in the order in which the data are assembled. If the titles of the accounts to be adjusted do not appear in the unadjusted trial balance, the accounts are inserted in their proper order in the Account Title column.

The adjusting entries for NetSolutions that are entered in the Adjustments columns are as follows:

(a) **Supplies**. The Supplies account has a debit balance of $2,000. The cost of the supplies on hand at the end of the period is $760. The supplies expense for December is the difference between the two amounts, or $1,240 ($2,000 − $760). The adjustment is entered as (1) $1,240 in the Adjustments Debit column on the same line as Supplies Expense and (2) $1,240 in the Adjustments Credit column on the same line as Supplies.

(b) **Prepaid Insurance**. The Prepaid Insurance account has a debit balance of $2,400. This balance represents the prepayment of insurance for 12 months beginning December 1. Thus, the insurance expense for December is $200 ($2,400 ÷ 12). The adjustment is entered as (1) $200 in the Adjustments Debit column on the same line as Insurance Expense and (2) $200 in the Adjustments Credit column on the same line as Prepaid Insurance.

Turn Exhibit 19

(c) **Unearned Rent**. The Unearned Rent account had a credit balance of $360. This balance represents the receipt of three months' rent, beginning with December. Thus, the rent revenue for December is $120 ($360 ÷ 3). The adjustment is entered as (1) $120 in the Adjustments Debit column on the same line as Unearned Rent and (2) $120 in the Adjustments Credit column on the same line as Rent Revenue.

(d) **Accrued Fees**. Fees accrued at the end of December but not recorded total $500. This amount is an increase in an asset and an increase in revenue. The adjustment is entered as (1) $500 in the Adjustments Debit column on the same line as Accounts Receivable and (2) $500 in the Adjustments Credit column on the same line as Fees Earned.

(e) **Wages**. Wages accrued but not paid at the end of December total $250. This amount is an increase in expenses and an increase in liabilities. The adjustment is entered as (1) $250 in the Adjustments Debit column on the same line as Wages Expense and (2) $250 in the Adjustments Credit column on the same line as Wages Payable.

(f) **Depreciation**. Depreciation of the office equipment is $50 for December. The adjustment is entered as (1) $50 in the Adjustments Debit column on the same line as Depreciation Expense and (2) $50 in the Adjustments Credit column on the same line as Accumulated Depreciation.

After the adjustments have been entered, the Adjustments columns are totaled to verify the equality of the debits and credits. The total of the Debit column must equal the total of the Credit column.

Exhibit 18

Spreadsheet (Work Sheet) with Unadjusted Trial Balance Entered

	A	B	C	D	E	F	G	H	I	J	K
1					NetSolutions						
2					End-of-Period Spreadsheet (Work Sheet)						
3					For the Two Months Ended December 31, 2009						
4		Unadjusted				Adjusted					
5		Trial Balance		Adjustments		Trial Balance		Income Statement		Balance Sheet	
6	Account Title	Dr.	Cr.	Dr.	Cr.	Dr.	Cr.	Dr.	Cr.	Dr.	Cr.
7											
8	Cash	2,065									
9	Accounts Receivable	2,220									
10	Supplies	2,000									
11	Prepaid Insurance	2,400									
12	Land	20,000									
13	Office Equipment	1,800									
14	Accumulated Depreciation										
15	Accounts Payable		900								
16	Wages Payable										
17	Unearned Rent		360								
18	Chris Clark, Capital		25,000								
19	Chris Clark, Drawing	4,000									
20	Fees Earned		16,340								
21	Rent Revenue										
22	Wages Expense	4,275									
23	Rent Expense	1,600									
24	Depreciation Expense										
25	Utilities Expense	985									
26	Supplies Expense	800									
27	Insurance Expense										
28	Miscellaneous Expense	455									
29		42,600	42,600								
30											
31											
32											

The spreadsheet (work sheet) is used for summarizing the effects of adjusting entries. It also aids in preparing financial statements.

Step 4. Enter the Adjusted Trial Balance

Turn Exhibit 20

The adjusted trial balance is entered by combining the adjustments with the unadjusted balances for each account. The adjusted amounts are then extended to the Adjusted Trial Balance columns, as shown in Exhibit 20.

To illustrate, the cash amount of $2,065 is extended to the Adjusted Trial Balance Debit column since no adjustments affected Cash. Accounts Receivable has an initial balance of $2,220 and a debit adjustment of $500. Thus, $2,720 ($2,220 + $500) is entered in the Adjusted Trial Balance Debit column for Accounts Receivable. The same process continues until all account balances are extended to the Adjusted Trial Balance columns.

After the accounts and adjustments have been extended, the Adjusted Trial Balance columns are totaled to verify the equality of debits and credits. The total of the Debit column must equal the total of the Credit column.

Step 5. Extend the Accounts to the Income Statement and Balance Sheet Columns

Turn Exhibit 21

The adjusted trial balance amounts are extended to the Income Statement and Balance Sheet columns. The amounts for revenues and expenses are extended to the Income Statement column. The amounts for assets, liabilities, owner's capital, and drawing are extended to the Balance Sheet columns.[3]

The first account listed in the Adjusted Trial Balance columns is Cash with a debit balance of $2,065. Cash is an asset, is listed on the balance sheet, and has a debit balance. Therefore, $2,065 is extended to the Balance Sheet Debit column. The Fees Earned balance of $16,840 is extended to the Income Statement Credit column. The same process continues until all account balances have been extended to the proper columns, as shown in Exhibit 21.

Step 6. Total the Income Statement and Balance Sheet Columns, Compute the Net Income or Net Loss, and Complete the Spreadsheet

Turn Exhibit 22

After the account balances are extended to the Income Statement and Balance Sheet columns, each of the columns is totaled. The difference between the two Income Statement column totals is the amount of the net income or the net loss for the period. This difference (net income or net loss) will also be the difference between the two Balance Sheet column totals.

If the Income Statement Credit column total (total revenue) is greater than the Income Statement Debit column total (total expenses), the difference is the net income. If the Income Statement Debit column total is greater than the Income Statement Credit column total, the difference is a net loss.

As shown in Exhibit 22, the total of the Income Statement Credit column is $16,960, and the total of the Income Statement Debit column is $9,855. Thus, the net income for NetSolutions is $7,105 as shown below.

Total of Income Statement Credit column (revenues)	$16,960
Total of Income Statement Debit column (expenses)	9,855
Net income (excess of revenues over expenses)	$ 7,105

The amount of the net income, $7,105, is entered in the Income Statement Debit column and the Balance Sheet Credit column. *Net income* is also entered in the Account Title column. Entering the net income of $7,105 in the Balance Sheet Credit column has the effect of transferring the net balance of the revenue and expense accounts to the owner's capital account.

If there was a net loss instead of net income, the amount of the net loss would be entered in the Income Statement Credit column and the Balance Sheet Debit column. *Net loss* would also be entered in the Account Title column.

3 The balances of the owner's capital and drawing accounts are extended to the Balance Sheet columns because the spreadsheet does not have separate Statement of Owner's Equity columns.

excel *success*

A spreadsheet can be used to prepare the income statement, the statement of owner's equity, and the balance sheet from the adjusted trial balance, as shown in the Excel Success section. The Excel Success sections from Chapters 2, 3, and 4 can be combined to perform steps 1–8 (excluding 5) of the accounting cycle, as diagramed in Exhibit 8 as follows:

Chapter 2:

1. Analyze and prepare journal entries in the spreadsheet.
2. Post transactions to spreadsheet ledger accounts.
3. Prepare in a spreadsheet an unadjusted trial balance from ledger balances.

Chapter 3:

4. Assemble and analyze adjustment data.
6. Journalize and post adjusting entries to the spreadsheet ledger accounts.
7. Prepare in a spreadsheet the adjusted trial balance from the adjusted ledger balances.

Chapter 4:

8. Prepare financial statements from the adjusted trial balance.

Thus, the spreadsheet can be used as an alternative to the manual accounting system. An accounting system on a spreadsheet has the advantage of minimizing mathematical errors and simplifying changes and corrections.

A spreadsheet can also be used as a multi-column worksheet summarizing the flow of adjustments to the final statements, as shown in Exhibit 2. The Exhibit 2 spreadsheet is not part of the formal accounting system, but can be used as an optional step within the accounting cycle, as shown in step five of Exhibit 8.

In the next chapter we will introduce accounting system approaches that are used with more complex businesses.

1 Describe the flow of accounting information from the unadjusted trial balance into the adjusted trial balance and financial statements.

Key Points	Key Learning Outcomes	Example Exercises	Practice Exercises
Exhibit 1 illustrates the end-of-period process by which accounts are adjusted and how the adjusted accounts flow into the financial statements.	• Using an end-of-period spreadsheet (work sheet), describe how the unadjusted trial balance accounts are affected by adjustments and how the adjusted trial balance accounts flow into the income statement and balance sheet.	4-1	4-1A, 4-1B

2 Prepare financial statements from adjusted account balances.

Key Points	Key Learning Outcomes	Example Exercises	Practice Exercises
Using the end-of-period spreadsheet (work sheet) shown in Exhibit 1, the income statement and balance sheet for NetSolutions can be prepared. The statement of owner's equity is prepared by referring to transactions that have been posted to owner's capital accounts in the ledger. A classified balance sheet has sections for current assets; property, plant, and equipment; current liabilities; long-term liabilities; and owner's equity.	• Describe how the net income or net loss from the period can be determined from an end-of-period spreadsheet (work sheet).		
	• Prepare an income statement, statement of owner's equity, and a balance sheet.	4-2 4-3	4-2A, 4-2B 4-3A, 4-3B
	• Indicate how accounts would be reported in a classified balance sheet.	4-4	4-4A, 4-4B

3 Prepare closing entries.

Key Points	Key Learning Outcomes	Example Exercises	Practice Exercises
Four entries are required in closing the temporary accounts. The first entry closes the revenue accounts to Income Summary. The second entry closes the expense accounts to Income Summary. The third entry closes the balance of Income Summary (net income or net loss) to the owner's capital account. The fourth entry closes the drawing account to the owner's capital account.	• Prepare the closing entry for revenues.	4-5	4-5A, 4-5B
	• Prepare the closing entry for expenses.	4-5	4-5A, 4-5B
After the closing entries have been posted to the ledger, the balance in the capital account agrees with the amount reported on the statement of owner's equity and balance sheet. In addition, the revenue, expense, and drawing accounts will have zero balances.	• Prepare the closing entry for transferring the balance of Income Summary to the owner's capital account.	4-5	4-5A, 4-5B
	• Prepare the closing entry for the owner's drawing account.	4-5	4-5A, 4-5B

(continued)

4 Describe the accounting cycle.

Key Points	Key Learning Outcomes	Example Exercises	Practice Exercises
The 10 basic steps of the accounting cycle are as follows: 1. Transactions are analyzed and recorded in the journal. 2. Transactions are posted to the ledger. 3. An unadjusted trial balance is prepared. 4. Adjustment data are assembled and analyzed. 5. An optional end-of-period spreadsheet (work sheet) is prepared. 6. Adjusting entries are journalized and posted to the ledger. 7. An adjusted trial balance is prepared. 8. Financial statements are prepared. 9. Closing entries are journalized and posted to the ledger. 10. A post-closing trial balance is prepared.	• List the 10 steps of the accounting cycle. • Determine whether any steps are out of order in a listing of accounting cycle steps. • Determine whether there are any missing steps in a listing of accounting cycle steps.	**4-6**	4-6A, 4-6B

5 Illustrate the accounting cycle for one period.

Key Points	Key Learning Outcomes	Example Exercises	Practice Exercises
The complete accounting cycle for Kelly Consulting for the month of April is described and illustrated on pages 156–168.	• Complete the accounting cycle for a period from beginning to end.		

6 Explain what is meant by the fiscal year and the natural business year.

Key Points	Key Learning Outcomes	Example Exercises	Practice Exercises
The annual accounting period adopted by a business is its fiscal year. A company's fiscal year that ends when business activities have reached the lowest point in its annual operating cycle is called the natural business year.	• Explain why companies use a fiscal year that is different from the calendar year.		

Key Terms

accounting cycle (153)
clearing account (150)
closing entries (150)
closing process (150)
closing the books (150)
current assets (149)

current liabilities (149)
fiscal year (166)
fixed (plant) assets (149)
Income Summary (150)
long-term liabilities (149)
natural business year (166)

notes receivable (149)
real (permanent)
  accounts (150)
temporary (nominal)
  accounts (150)

Illustrative Problem

Three years ago, T. Roderick organized Harbor Realty. At July 31, 2010, the end of the current fiscal year, the following end-of-period spreadsheet (work sheet) was prepared:

	A	B	C	D	E	F	G	H	I	J	K
1				Harbor Realty							
2				End-of-Period Spreadsheet (Work Sheet)							
3				For the Year Ended July 31, 2010							
4		Unadjusted				Adjusted					
5		Trial Balance		Adjustments		Trial Balance		Income Statement		Balance Sheet	
6	Account Title	Dr.	Cr.	Dr.	Cr.	Dr.	Cr.	Dr.	Cr.	Dr.	Cr.
7	Cash	3,425				3,425				3,425	
8	Accounts Receivable	7,000		(e) 1,000		8,000				8,000	
9	Supplies	1,270			(a) 890	380				380	
10	Prepaid Insurance	620			(b) 315	305				305	
11	Office Equipment	51,650				51,650				51,650	
12	Accum. Depreciation		9,700		(c) 4,950		14,650				14,650
13	Accounts Payable		925				925				925
14	Unearned Fees		1,250	(f) 500			750				750
15	Wages Payable				(d) 440		440				440
16	T. Roderick, Capital		29,000				29,000				29,000
17	T. Roderick, Drawing	5,200				5,200				5,200	
18	Fees Earned		59,125		(e) 1,000		60,625		60,625		
19					(f) 500						
20	Wages Expense	22,415		(d) 440		22,855		22,855			
21	Depreciation Expense			(c) 4,950		4,950		4,950			
22	Rent Expense	4,200				4,200		4,200			
23	Utilities Expense	2,715				2,715		2,715			
24	Supplies Expense			(a) 890		890		890			
25	Insurance Expense			(b) 315		315		315			
26	Miscellaneous Expense	1,505				1,505		1,505			
27		100,000	100,000	8,095	8,095	106,390	106,390	37,430	60,625	68,960	45,765
28	Net income							23,195			23,195
29								60,625	60,625	68,960	68,960
30											

Instructions

1. Prepare an income statement, a statement of owner's equity (no additional investments were made during the year), and a balance sheet.
2. On the basis of the data in the end-of-period spreadsheet (work sheet), journalize the closing entries.

Solution

1.

Harbor Realty
Income Statement
For the Year Ended July 31, 2010

Fees earned		$60,625
Expenses:		
Wages expense	$22,855	
Depreciation expense	4,950	
Rent expense	4,200	
Utilities expense	2,715	
Supplies expense	890	
Insurance expense	315	
Miscellaneous expense	1,505	
Total expenses		37,430
Net income		$23,195

Harbor Realty
Statement of Owner's Equity
For the Year Ended July 31, 2010

T. Roderick, capital, August 1, 2009		$29,000
Net income for the year	$23,195	
Less withdrawals	5,200	
Increase in owner's equity		17,995
T. Roderick, capital, July 31, 2010		$46,995

Harbor Realty
Balance Sheet
July 31, 2010

Assets			Liabilities		
Current assets:			Current liabilities:		
Cash	$ 3,425		Accounts payable	$ 925	
Accounts receivable	8,000		Unearned fees	750	
Supplies	380		Wages payable	440	
Prepaid insurance	305		Total liabilities		$ 2,115
Total current assets		$12,110			
Property, plant, and equipment:					
Office equipment	$51,650				
Less accumulated depreciation	14,650		**Owner's Equity**		
Total property, plant,			T. Roderick, capital		46,995
and equipment		37,000	Total liabilities and		
Total assets		$49,110	owner's equity		$49,110

2.

Journal					Page
Date		**Description**	**Post. Ref.**	**Debit**	**Credit**
		Closing Entries			
2010 July	31	Fees Earned		60,625	
		Income Summary			60,625
	31	Income Summary		37,430	
		Wages Expense			22,855
		Depreciation Expense			4,950
		Rent Expense			4,200
		Utilities Expense			2,715
		Supplies Expense			890
		Insurance Expense			315
		Miscellaneous Expense			1,505
	31	Income Summary		23,195	
		T. Roderick, Capital			23,195
	31	T. Roderick, Capital		5,200	
		T. Roderick, Drawing			5,200

Self-Examination Questions

1. Which of the following accounts in the Adjusted Trial Balance columns of the end-of-period spreadsheet (work sheet) would be extended to the Balance Sheet columns?
   A. Utilities Expense C. M. E. Jones, Drawing
   B. Rent Revenue   D. Miscellaneous Expense

2. Which of the following accounts would be classified as a current asset on the balance sheet?
   A. Office Equipment
   B. Land
   C. Accumulated Depreciation
   D. Accounts Receivable

3. Which of the following entries closes the owner's drawing account at the end of the period?
   A. Debit the drawing account, credit the income summary account.
   B. Debit the owner's capital account, credit the drawing account.

C. Debit the income summary account, credit the drawing account.
D. Debit the drawing account, credit the owner's capital account.

4. Which of the following accounts would not be closed to the income summary account at the end of a period?
   A. Fees Earned
   B. Wages Expense
   C. Rent Expense
   D. Accumulated Depreciation

5. Which of the following accounts would not be included in a post-closing trial balance?
   A. Cash
   B. Fees Earned
   C. Accumulated Depreciation
   D. J. C. Smith, Capital

Eye Openers

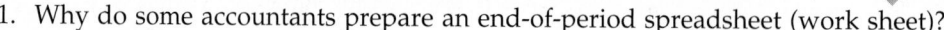

1. Why do some accountants prepare an end-of-period spreadsheet (work sheet)?
2. Is the end-of-period spreadsheet (work sheet) a substitute for the financial statements? Discuss.
3. In the Income Statement columns of the end-of-period spreadsheet (work sheet) for Steward Consulting Co. for the current year, the Debit column total is $675,450 and the Credit column total is $915,800 before the amount for net income or net loss has been included. In preparing the income statement from the end-of-period spreadsheet (work sheet), what is the amount of net income or net loss?
4. Describe the nature of the assets that compose the following sections of a balance sheet: (a) current assets, (b) property, plant, and equipment.
5. What is the difference between a current liability and a long-term liability?
6. What types of accounts are referred to as temporary accounts?
7. Why are closing entries required at the end of an accounting period?
8. What is the difference between adjusting entries and closing entries?
9. Describe the four entries that close the temporary accounts.
10. What is the purpose of the post-closing trial balance?
11. (a) What is the most important output of the accounting cycle? (b) Do all companies have an accounting cycle? Explain.
12. What is the natural business year?
13. Why might a department store select a fiscal year ending January 31, rather than a fiscal year ending December 31?
14. The fiscal years for several well-known companies are as follows:

Company	Fiscal Year Ending	Company	Fiscal Year Ending
Kmart	January 30	Toys "R" Us, Inc.	February 3
JCPenney	January 26	Federated Department Stores, Inc.	February 3
Target Corp.	January 28	The Limited, Inc.	February 2

What general characteristic shared by these companies explains why they do not have fiscal years ending December 31?

Practice Exercises

PE 4-1A
Flow of accounts into financial statements
obj. 1

EE 4-1   p. 146

The balances for the accounts listed below appear in the Adjusted Trial Balance columns of the end-of-period spreadsheet (work sheet). Indicate whether each balance should be extended to (a) an Income Statement column or (b) a Balance Sheet column.

1. Accumulated Depreciation—Equipment
2. Cash
3. Commissions Earned
4. Insurance Expense

5. Prepaid Rent
6. Supplies
7. Svend Tisdale, Drawing
8. Wages Expense

PE 4-1B
Flow of accounts into financial statements
obj. 1

EE 4-1   p. 146

The balances for the accounts listed below appear in the Adjusted Trial Balance columns of the end-of-period spreadsheet (work sheet). Indicate whether each balance should be extended to (a) an Income Statement column or (b) a Balance Sheet column.

1. Accounts Payable
2. Depreciation Expense—Equipment
3. Josh Neville, Capital
4. Office Equipment

5. Rent Revenue
6. Supplies Expense
7. Unearned Service Revenue
8. Wages Payable

PE 4-2A
Determining net
income from the
end-of-period spread-
sheet (work sheet)

obj. 2

EE 4-2 p. 146

In the Income Statement columns of the end-of-period spreadsheet (work sheet) for El Dorado Consulting Co. for the current year, the Debit column total is $186,200 and the Credit column total is $233,400 before the amount for net income or net loss has been included. In preparing the income statement from the end-of-period spreadsheet (work sheet), what is the amount of net income or net loss?

PE 4-2B
Determining net
income from the
end-of-period spread-
sheet (work sheet)

obj. 2

EE 4-2 p. 146

In the Balance Sheet columns of the end-of-period spreadsheet (work sheet) for Lancaster Consulting Co. for the current year, the Debit column total is $375,000 and the Credit column total is $505,200 before the amount for net income or net loss has been included. In preparing the income statement from the end-of-period spreadsheet (work sheet), what is the amount of net income or net loss?

PE 4-3A
Statement of owner's
equity

obj. 2

EE 4-3 p. 148

Meg Ostermiller owns and operates 4U Delivery Services. On January 1, 2009, Meg Ostermiller, Capital had a balance of $900,500. During the year, Meg made no additional investments and withdrew $60,000. For the year ended December 31, 2009, 4U Delivery Services reported a net loss of $24,900. Prepare a statement of owner's equity for the year ended December 31, 2009.

PE 4-3B
Statement of owner's
equity

obj. 2

EE 4-3 p. 148

Rod Zoot owns and operates Steuben Advertising Services. On January 1, 2009, Rod Zoot, Capital had a balance of $475,000. During the year, Rod invested an additional $75,000 and withdrew $30,000. For the year ended December 31, 2009, Steuben Advertising Services reported a net income of $110,000. Prepare a statement of owner's equity for the year ended December 31, 2009.

PE 4-4A
Classified balance
sheet

obj. 2

EE 4-4 p. 149

The following accounts appear in an adjusted trial balance of Gondola Consulting. Indicate whether each account would be reported in the (a) current asset; (b) property, plant, and equipment; (c) current liability; (d) long-term liability; or (e) owner's equity section of the December 31, 2009, balance sheet of Gondola Consulting.

1. Accounts Payable
2. Accounts Receivable
3. Accumulated Depreciation—Equipment
4. Cash

5. Holly Webb, Capital
6. Note Payable (due in 2016)
7. Supplies
8. Wages Payable

PE 4-4B
Classified balance
sheet

obj. 2

EE 4-4 p. 149

The following accounts appear in an adjusted trial balance of Resolve Consulting. Indicate whether each account would be reported in the (a) current asset; (b) property, plant, and equipment; (c) current liability; (d) long-term liability; or (e) owner's equity section of the December 31, 2009, balance sheet of Resolve Consulting.

1. Building
2. Clem Barnes, Capital
3. Mortgage Payable (due in 2015)
4. Prepaid Rent

5. Salaries Payable
6. Supplies
7. Taxes Payable
8. Unearned Service Fees

PE 4-5A
Closing entries
obj. 3

EE 4-5 p. 153

After the account have been adjusted at November 30, the end of the fiscal year, the following balances were taken from the ledger of Pond Landscaping Co.:

Brett Maxim, Capital	$978,500
Brett Maxim, Drawing	50,000
Fees Earned	779,000
Wages Expense	389,000
Rent Expense	60,000
Supplies Expense	7,200
Miscellaneous Expense	11,400

Journalize the four entries required to close the accounts.

PE 4-5B
Closing entries
obj. 3

EE 4-5 p. 153

After the accounts have been adjusted at July 31, the end of the fiscal year, the following balances were taken from the ledger of Rabbit Delivery Services Co.:

Sherry Kerney, Capital	$730,000
Sherry Kerney, Drawing	20,000
Fees Earned	515,000
Wages Expense	480,000
Rent Expense	75,000
Supplies Expense	12,100
Miscellaneous Expense	4,000

Journalize the four entries required to close the accounts.

PE 4-6A
Accounting cycle
obj. 4

EE 4-6 p. 156

From the following list of steps in the accounting cycle, identify what two steps are missing.

a. Transactions are analyzed and recorded in the journal.
b. Transactions are posted to the ledger.
c. An unadjusted trial balance is prepared.
d. An optional end-of-period spreadsheet (work sheet) is prepared.
e. Adjusting entries are journalized and posted to the ledger.
f. An adjusted trial balance is prepared.
g. Financial statements are prepared.
h. A post-closing trial balance is prepared.

PE 4-6B
Accounting cycle
obj. 4

EE 4-6 p. 156

From the following list of steps in the accounting cycle, identify what two steps are missing.

a. Transactions are analyzed and recorded in the journal.
b. An unadjusted trial balance is prepared.
c. Adjustment data are assembled and analyzed.
d. An optional end-of-period spreadsheet (work sheet) is prepared.
e. Adjusting entries are journalized and posted to the ledger.
f. An adjusted trial balance is prepared.
g. Closing entries are journalized and posted to the ledger.
h. A post-closing trial balance is prepared.

Exercises

EX 4-1
Extending account balances in an end-of-period spreadsheet (work sheet)

objs. 1, 2

The balances for the accounts listed below appear in the Adjusted Trial Balance columns of the end-of-period spreadsheet (work sheet). Indicate whether each balance should be extended to (a) an Income Statement column or (b) a Balance Sheet column.

1. Accounts Payable
2. Accounts Receivable
3. Cash
4. Dean Pinkerton, Drawing
5. Fees Earned
6. Supplies
7. Unearned Rent
8. Utilities Expense
9. Wages Expense
10. Wages Payable

EX 4-2
Classifying accounts

objs. 1, 2

Balances for each of the following accounts appear in an adjusted trial balance. Identify each as (a) asset, (b) liability, (c) revenue, or (d) expense.

1. Accounts Payable
2. Equipment
3. Fees Earned
4. Insurance Expense
5. Prepaid Advertising
6. Prepaid Insurance
7. Rent Revenue
8. Salary Expense
9. Salary Payable
10. Supplies
11. Supplies Expense
12. Unearned Rent

EX 4-3
Financial statements from the end-of-period spreadsheet (work sheet)

objs. 1, 2

Alpine Consulting is a consulting firm owned and operated by Scott Young. The end-of-period spreadsheet (work sheet) shown below was prepared for the year ended March 31, 2010.

	A	B	C	D	E	F	G	H	I	J	K
1		Alpine Consulting									
2		End-of-Period Spreadsheet (Work Sheet)									
3		For the Year Ended March 31, 2010									
4		Unadjusted				Adjusted					
5		Trial Balance		Adjustments		Trial Balance		Income Statement		Balance Sheet	
6	Account Title	Dr.	Cr.	Dr.	Cr.	Dr.	Cr.	Dr.	Cr.	Dr.	Cr.
7											
8	Cash	9,500				9,500				9,500	
9	Accounts Receivable	22,500				22,500				22,500	
10	Supplies	2,400			(a) 1,850	550				550	
11	Office Equipment	18,500				18,500				18,500	
12	Accumulated Depreciation		2,500		(b) 1,200		3,700				3,700
13	Accounts Payable		6,100				6,100				6,100
14	Salaries Payable				(c) 200		200				200
15	Scott Young, Capital		22,600				22,600				22,600
16	Scott Young, Drawing	3,000				3,000				3,000	
17	Fees Earned		43,800				43,800		43,800		
18	Salary Expense	17,250		(c) 200		17,450		17,450			
19	Supplies Expense			(a) 1,850		1,850		1,850			
20	Depreciation Expense			(b) 1,200		1,200		1,200			
21	Miscellaneous Expense	1,850				1,850		1,850			
22		75,000	75,000	3,250	3,250	76,400	76,400	22,350	43,800	54,050	32,600
23	Net income							21,450			21,450
24								43,800	43,800	54,050	54,050
25											

Based on the preceding spreadsheet, prepare an income statement, statement of owner's equity, and balance sheet for Alpine Consulting.

EX 4-4

Financial statements from the end-of-period spreadsheet (work sheet)

objs. 1, 2

Aardvark Consulting is a consulting firm owned and operated by Jan Sullivan. The following end-of-period spreadsheet (work sheet) was prepared for the year ended November 30, 2010.

	A	B	C	D	E	F	G	H	I	J	K
1					Aardvark Consulting						
2					End-of-Period Spreadsheet (Work Sheet)						
3					For the Year Ended November 30, 2010						
4		Unadjusted				Adjusted					
5		Trial Balance		Adjustments		Trial Balance		Income Statement		Balance Sheet	
6	Account Title	Dr.	Cr.	Dr.	Cr.	Dr.	Cr.	Dr.	Cr.	Dr.	Cr.
7											
8	Cash	7,500				7,500				7,500	
9	Accounts Receivable	18,500				18,500				18,500	
10	Supplies	3,000			(a) 2,250	750				750	
11	Office Equipment	30,500				30,500				30,500	
12	Accumulated Depreciation		4,500		(b) 900		5,400				5,400
13	Accounts Payable		3,300				3,300				3,300
14	Salaries Payable				(c) 400		400				400
15	Jan Sullivan, Capital		27,200				27,200				27,200
16	Jan Sullivan, Drawing	2,000				2,000				2,000	
17	Fees Earned		60,000				60,000		60,000		
18	Salary Expense	32,000		(c) 400		32,400		32,400			
19	Supplies Expense			(a) 2,250		2,250		2,250			
20	Depreciation Expense			(b) 900		900		900			
21	Miscellaneous Expense	1,500				1,500		1,500			
22		95,000	95,000	3,550	3,550	96,300	96,300	37,050	60,000	59,250	36,300
23	Net income							22,950			22,950
24								60,000	60,000	59,250	59,250
25											

Based on the preceding spreadsheet, prepare an income statement, statement of owner's equity, and balance sheet for Aardvark Consulting.

EX 4-5

Income statement

obj. 2

✔ Net income, $112,000

The following account balances were taken from the adjusted trial balance for 3 Rivers Messenger Service, a delivery service firm, for the current fiscal year ended September 30, 2010:

Depreciation Expense	$ 8,000	Rent Expense	$ 60,500
Fees Earned	425,000	Salaries Expense	213,800
Insurance Expense	1,500	Supplies Expense	2,750
Miscellaneous Expense	3,250	Utilities Expense	23,200

Prepare an income statement.

EX 4-6

Income statement; net loss

obj. 2

✔ Net loss, $44,275

The following revenue and expense account balances were taken from the ledger of Infinet Services Co. after the accounts had been adjusted on January 31, 2010, the end of the current fiscal year:

Depreciation Expense	$12,200	Service Revenue	$233,900
Insurance Expense	6,000	Supplies Expense	2,875
Miscellaneous Expense	4,750	Utilities Expense	18,750
Rent Expense	49,300	Wages Expense	184,300

Prepare an income statement.

EX 4-7

Income statement

obj. 2

FedEx Corporation had the following revenue and expense account balances (in millions) at its fiscal year-end of May 31, 2007:

Depreciation	$ 845	Purchased Transportation	$ 1,097
Fuel	2,946	Rentals and Landing Fees	1,598
Maintenance and Repairs	1,440	Revenues	22,527
Other Expense (Income) Net	4,566	Salaries and Employee Benefits	8,051
Provision for Income Taxes	733		

Internet Project

✔ a. Net income:
$1,251

a. Prepare an income statement.

b. ━━━━▶ Compare your income statement with the related income statement that is available at the FedEx Corporation Web site, which is linked to the text's Web site at **www.cengage.com/accounting/reeve**. What similarities and differences do you see?

EX 4-8
Statement of owner's equity
obj. 2

✔ Terry Collins, capital, Mar. 31, 2010: $899,900

Jackrabbit Systems Co. offers its services to residents in the Santa Cruz area. Selected accounts from the ledger of Jackrabbit Systems Co. for the current fiscal year ended March 31, 2010, are as follows:

Terry Collins, Capital			
Mar. 31	32,000	Apr. 1 (2009)	611,900
		Mar. 31	320,000

Terry Collins, Drawing			
June 30	8,000	Mar. 31	32,000
Sept. 30	8,000		
Dec. 31	8,000		
Mar. 31	8,000		

Income Summary			
Mar. 31	600,000	Mar. 31	920,000
31	320,000		

Prepare a statement of owner's equity for the year.

EX 4-9
Statement of owner's equity; net loss
obj. 2

✔ Margarita Castillo, capital, June 30, 2010: $201,300

Selected accounts from the ledger of Picasso Sports for the current fiscal year ended June 30, 2010, are as follows:

Margarita Castillo, Capital			
June 30	32,300	July 1 (2009)	237,600
30	4,000		

Margarita Castillo, Drawing			
Sept. 30	1,000	June 30	4,000
Dec. 31	1,000		
May 31	1,000		
June 30	1,000		

Income Summary			
June 30	511,900	June 30	479,600
		30	32,300

Prepare a statement of owner's equity for the year.

EX 4-10
Classifying assets
obj. 2

Identify each of the following as (a) a current asset or (b) property, plant, and equipment:

1. Accounts receivable
2. Building
3. Cash
4. Equipment
5. Prepaid rent
6. Supplies

EX 4-11
Balance sheet classification
obj. 2

At the balance sheet date, a business owes a mortgage note payable of $360,000, the terms of which provide for monthly payments of $2,000.

━━━━▶ Explain how the liability should be classified on the balance sheet.

EX 4-12
Balance sheet
obj. 2

✔ Total assets: $187,500

Optimum Weight Co. offers personal weight reduction consulting services to individuals. After all the accounts have been closed on June 30, 2010, the end of the current fiscal year, the balances of selected accounts from the ledger of Optimum Weight Co. are as follows:

Accounts Payable	$ 8,625	Land	$100,000
Accounts Receivable	20,780	Prepaid Insurance	4,800
Accumulated Depreciation—Equipment	25,975	Prepaid Rent	3,000
Carlos Kiser, Capital	173,000	Salaries Payable	3,375
Cash	?	Supplies	520
Equipment	75,000	Unearned Fees	2,500

Prepare a classified balance sheet that includes the correct balance for Cash.

EX 4-13
Balance sheet

obj. 2

✔ Corrected balance sheet, total assets: $540,000

List the errors you find in the following balance sheet. Prepare a corrected balance sheet.

Cabana Services Co.
Balance Sheet
For the Year Ended August 31, 2010

Assets			Liabilities		
Current assets:			Current liabilities:		
Cash	$ 15,840		Accounts receivable	$ 41,250	
Accounts payable	20,370		Accum. depr.—building	260,100	
Supplies	4,950		Accum. depr.—equipment	55,440	
Prepaid insurance	14,400		Net income	75,000	
Land	180,000		Total liabilities		$431,790
Total current assets		$235,560			
Property, plant,					
and equipment:			**Owner's Equity**		
Building	$470,100		Wages payable	$ 4,020	
Equipment	129,000		Hector Delgado, capital	515,610	
Total property, plant,			Total owner's equity		519,630
and equipment		715,860	Total liabilities and		
Total assets		$951,420	owner's equity		$951,420

EX 4-14
Identifying accounts to be closed

obj. 3

From the following list, identify the accounts that should be closed to Income Summary at the end of the fiscal year:

a. Accounts Receivable
b. Accumulated Depreciation—Equipment
c. Depreciation Expense—Equipment
d. Equipment
e. Erin Dowley, Capital
f. Erin Dowley, Drawing

g. Fees Earned
h. Land
i. Supplies
j. Supplies Expense
k. Wages Expense
l. Wages Payable

EX 4-15
Closing entries

obj. 3

Prior to its closing, Income Summary had total debits of $432,200 and total credits of $572,600.

➤ Briefly explain the purpose served by the income summary account and the nature of the entries that resulted in the $432,200 and the $572,600.

EX 4-16
Closing entries with net income

obj. 3

After all revenue and expense accounts have been closed at the end of the fiscal year, Income Summary has a debit of $193,400 and a credit of $258,600. At the same date, Laurie Engan, Capital has a credit balance of $300,000, and Laurie Engan, Drawing has a balance of $25,000. (a) Journalize the entries required to complete the closing of the accounts. (b) Determine the amount of Laurie Engan, Capital at the end of the period.

EX 4-17
Closing entries with net loss

obj. 3

Marina Services Co. offers its services to individuals desiring to improve their personal images. After the accounts have been adjusted at July 31, the end of the fiscal year, the following balances were taken from the ledger of Marina Services Co.

John O'Neil, Capital	$480,000	Rent Expense	$45,000
John O'Neil, Drawing	30,000	Supplies Expense	11,200
Fees Earned	215,000	Miscellaneous Expense	5,100
Wages Expense	190,000		

Journalize the four entries required to close the accounts.

EX 4-18
Identifying
permanent accounts

obj. 3

Which of the following accounts will usually appear in the post-closing trial balance?

a. Accounts Payable
b. Accumulated Depreciation
c. Bo Erath, Capital
d. Bo Erath, Drawing
e. Cash
f. Depreciation Expense

g. Fees Earned
h. Office Equipment
i. Salaries Expense
j. Salaries Payable
k. Supplies

EX 4-19
Post-closing trial
balance

obj. 3

✔ Correct column
totals, $175,000

An accountant prepared the following post-closing trial balance:

La Jolla Billiards Co.
Post-Closing Trial Balance
October 31, 2010

	Debit Balances	Credit Balances
Cash	13,200	
Accounts Receivable	29,350	
Supplies		1,850
Equipment		130,600
Accumulated Depreciation—Equipment	43,500	
Accounts Payable	15,800	
Salaries Payable		1,500
Unearned Rent	6,000	
Trisha Valentino, Capital	108,200	
	216,050	133,950

Prepare a corrected post-closing trial balance. Assume that all accounts have normal balances and that the amounts shown are correct.

EX 4-20
Steps in the
accounting cycle

obj. 4

Rearrange the following steps in the accounting cycle in proper sequence:

a. An unadjusted trial balance is prepared.
b. Transactions are posted to the ledger.
c. Transactions are analyzed and recorded in the journal.
d. An optional end-of-period spreadsheet (work sheet) is prepared.
e. An adjusted trial balance is prepared.
f. Financial statements are prepared.
g. A post-closing trial balance is prepared.
h. Adjustment data are asssembled and analyzed.
i. Closing entries are journalized and posted to the ledger.
j. Adjusting entries are journalized and posted to the ledger.

EX 4-21
Appendix: Steps in
completing an end-
of-period spreadsheet
(work sheet)

The steps performed in completing an end-of-period spreadsheet (work sheet) are listed below in random order.

a. Add the Debit and Credit columns of the Unadjusted Trial Balance columns of the spreadsheet (work sheet) to verify that the totals are equal.
b. Add the Debit and Credit columns of the Balance Sheet and Income Statement columns of the spreadsheet (work sheet) to verify that the totals are equal.
c. Add or deduct adjusting entry data to trial balance amounts, and extend amounts to the Adjusted Trial Balance columns.
d. Add the Debit and Credit columns of the Adjustments columns of the spreadsheet (work sheet) to verify that the totals are equal.

e. Add the Debit and Credit columns of the Balance Sheet and Income Statement columns of the spreadsheet (work sheet) to determine the amount of net income or net loss for the period.

f. Add the Debit and Credit columns of the Adjusted Trial Balance columns of the spreadsheet (work sheet) to verify that the totals are equal.

g. Enter the adjusting entries into the spreadsheet (work sheet), based on the adjustment data.

h. Enter the amount of net income or net loss for the period in the proper Income Statement column and Balance Sheet column.

i. Enter the unadjusted account balances from the general ledger into the Unadjusted Trial Balance columns of the spreadsheet (work sheet).

j. Extend the adjusted trial balance amounts to the Income Statement columns and the Balance Sheet columns.

Indicate the order in which the preceding steps would be performed in preparing and completing a spreadsheet (work sheet).

EX 4-22
Appendix:
Adjustment data on an end-of-period spreadsheet (work sheet)

✔ Total debits of Adjustments column: $16

Homeland Security Services Co. offers security services to business clients. The trial balance for Homeland Security Services Co. has been prepared on the end-of-period spreadsheet (work sheet) for the year ended October 31, 2010, shown below.

Homeland Security Services Co.
End-of-Period Spreadsheet (Work Sheet)
For the Year Ended October 31, 2010

	Unadjusted Trial Balance		Adjustments		Adjusted Trial Balance	
Account Title	Dr.	Cr.	Dr.	Cr.	Dr.	Cr.
Cash	6					
Accounts Receivable	40					
Supplies	4					
Prepaid Insurance	6					
Land	50					
Equipment	20					
Accum. Depr.—Equipment		2				
Accounts Payable		18				
Wages Payable		0				
Gloria Millard, Capital		85				
Gloria Millard, Drawing	4					
Fees Earned		45				
Wages Expense	10					
Rent Expense	6					
Insurance Expense	0					
Utilities Expense	3					
Depreciation Expense	0					
Supplies Expense	0					
Miscellaneous Expense	1					
	150	150				

The data for year-end adjustments are as follows:

a. Fees earned, but not yet billed, $4.
b. Supplies on hand, $1.
c. Insurance premiums expired, $5.
d. Depreciation expense, $2.
e. Wages accrued, but not paid, $2.

Enter the adjustment data, and place the balances in the Adjusted Trial Balance columns.

EX 4-23
Appendix:
Completing an end-
of-period spreadsheet
(work sheet)

✔ Net income: $17

Homeland Security Services Co. offers security services to business clients. Complete the following end-of-period spreadsheet (work sheet) for Homeland Security Services Co.

Homeland Security Services Co.
End-of-Period Spreadsheet (Work Sheet)
For the Year Ended October 31, 2010

Account Title	Adjusted Trial Balance		Income Statement		Balance Sheet	
	Dr.	Cr.	Dr.	Cr.	Dr.	Cr.
Cash	6					
Accounts Receivable	44					
Supplies	1					
Prepaid Insurance	1					
Land	50					
Equipment	20					
Accum. Depr.—Equipment		4				
Accounts Payable		18				
Wages Payable		2				
Gloria Millard, Capital		85				
Gloria Millard, Drawing	4					
Fees Earned		49				
Wages Expense	12					
Rent Expense	6					
Insurance Expense	5					
Utilities Expense	3					
Supplies Expense	3					
Depreciation Expense	2					
Miscellaneous Expense	1					
	158	158				
Net income (loss)						

EX 4-24
Appendix: Financial
statements from an
end-of-period spread-
sheet (work sheet)

✔ Gloria Millard,
capital, October 31,
2010: $98

Based on the data in Exercise 4-23, prepare an income statement, statement of owner's equity, and balance sheet for Homeland Security Services Co.

EX 4-25
Appendix: Adjusting
entries from an end-
of-period spreadsheet
(work sheet)

Based on the data in Exercise 4-22, prepare the adjusting entries for Homeland Security Services Co.

EX 4-26
Appendix: Closing
entries from an end-
of-period spreadsheet
(work sheet)

Based on the data in Exercise 4-23, prepare the closing entries for Homeland Security Services Co.

EX 4-27
Working capital and current ratio

The following data (in thousands) were taken from recent financial statements of Under Armour, Inc.:

	December 31	
	2007	**2006**
Current assets	$322,245	$244,952
Current liabilities	95,699	71,563

a. Compute the working capital and the current ratio as of December 31, 2007, and 2006. Round to two decimal places.
b. What conclusions concerning the company's ability to meet its financial obligations can you draw from part (a)?

EX 4-28
Working capital and current ratio

The following data (in thousands) were taken from recent financial statements of Starbucks Corporation:

	Sept. 30, 2007	**Oct. 1, 2006**
Current assets	$1,696,487	$1,529,788
Current liabilities	2,155,566	1,935,620

a. Compute the working capital and the current ratio as of September 30, 2007, and October 1, 2006. Round to two decimal places.
b. What conclusions concerning the company's ability to meet its financial obligations can you draw from part (a)?

Problems Series A

PR 4-1A
Financial statements and closing entries

objs. 1, 2, 3

✔ 1. Net loss: $14,150

Prison Watch Company offers legal consulting advice to prison inmates. Prison Watch Company prepared the end-of-period spreadsheet (work sheet) at the top of the following page at June 30, 2010, the end of the current fiscal year.

Instructions

1. Prepare an income statement for the year ended June 30.
2. Prepare a statement of owner's equity for the year ended June 30. No additional investments were made during the year.
3. Prepare a balance sheet as of June 30.
4. On the basis of the end-of-period spreadsheet (work sheet), journalize the closing entries.
5. Prepare a post-closing trial balance.

	A	B	C	D	E	F	G	H	I	J	K
1				Prison Watch Company							
2				End-of-Period Spreadsheet (Work Sheet)							
3				For the Year Ended June 30, 2010							
4		Unadjusted				Adjusted					
5		Trial Balance		Adjustments		Trial Balance		Income Statement		Balance Sheet	
6	**Account Title**	Dr.	Cr.	Dr.	Cr.	Dr.	Cr.	Dr.	Cr.	Dr.	Cr.
7											
8	Cash	5,100				5,100				5,100	
9	Accounts Receivable	12,750		(a) 1,200		13,950				13,950	
10	Prepaid Insurance	3,600			(b) 900	2,700				2,700	
11	Supplies	2,025			(c) 1,525	500				500	
12	Land	80,000				80,000				80,000	
13	Building	200,000				200,000				200,000	
14	Acc. Depr.—Building		90,000		(d) 2,500		92,500				92,500
15	Equipment	140,000				140,000				140,000	
16	Acc. Depr.—Equipment		54,450		(e) 6,000		60,450				60,450
17	Accounts Payable		9,750				9,750				9,750
18	Sal. & Wages Payable				(f) 1,900		1,900				1,900
19	Unearned Rent		4,500	(g) 4,000			500				500
20	Cassandra Jaffee, Capital		311,300				311,300				311,300
21	Cassandra Jaffee, Drawing	20,000				20,000				20,000	
22	Fees Revenue		280,000		(a) 1,200		281,200		281,200		
23	Rent Revenue				(g) 4,000		4,000		4,000		
24	Salaries & Wages Expense	145,100		(f) 1,900		147,000		147,000			
25	Advertising Expense	86,800				86,800		86,800			
26	Utilities Expense	30,000				30,000		30,000			
27	Travel Expense	18,750				18,750		18,750			
28	Depr. Exp.—Equipment			(e) 6,000		6,000		6,000			
29	Depr. Exp.—Building			(d) 2,500		2,500		2,500			
30	Supplies Expense			(c) 1,525		1,525		1,525			
31	Insurance Expense			(b) 900		900		900			
32	Misc. Expense	5,875				5,875		5,875			
33		750,000	750,000	18,025	18,025	761,600	761,600	299,350	285,200	462,250	476,400
34	Net loss								14,150	14,150	
35								299,350	299,350	476,400	476,400
36											

PR 4-2A
Financial statements and closing entries

objs. 2, 3

✔ 1. Jane Maines, capital, March 31: $467,000

The Hometown Services Company is a financial planning services firm owned and operated by Jane Maines. As of March 31, 2010, the end of the current fiscal year, the accountant for The Hometown Services Company prepared an end-of-period spreadsheet (work sheet), part of which is shown at the top of the next page.

Instructions

1. Prepare an income statement, a statement of owner's equity (no additional investments were made during the year), and a balance sheet.
2. Journalize the entries that were required to close the accounts at March 31.
3. If the balance of Jane Maines, Capital increased $35,000 after the closing entries were posted, and the withdrawals remained the same, what was the amount of net income or net loss?

	A	H	I	J	K
		The Hometown Services Company			
1					
2		**End-of-Period Spreadsheet (Work Sheet)**			
3		**For the Year Ended March 31, 2010**			
4		**Income Statement**		**Balance Sheet**	
5		**Dr.**	**Cr.**	**Dr.**	**Cr.**
6	Cash			12,950	
7	Accounts Receivable			28,150	
8	Supplies			4,400	
9	Prepaid Insurance			9,500	
10	Land			100,000	
11	Buildings			360,000	
12	Accumulated Depreciation—Buildings				117,200
13	Equipment			260,000	
14	Accumulated Depreciation—Equipment				152,700
15	Accounts Payable				33,300
16	Salaries Payable				3,300
17	Unearned Rent				1,500
18	Jane Maines, Capital				427,600
19	Jane Maines, Drawing			25,000	
20	Service Fees		475,000		
21	Rent Revenue		5,000		
22	Salary Expense	340,600			
23	Depreciation Expense—Equipment	18,500			
24	Rent Expense	15,500			
25	Supplies Expense	10,950			
26	Utilities Expense	9,900			
27	Depreciation Expense—Buildings	6,600			
28	Repairs Expense	5,450			
29	Insurance Expense	3,000			
30	Miscellaneous Expense	5,100			
31		415,600	480,000	800,000	735,600
32	Net income	64,400			64,400
33		480,000	480,000	800,000	800,000
34					

PR 4-3A

T accounts, adjusting entries, financial statements, and closing entries; optional end-of-period spreadsheet (work sheet)

objs. **2, 3**

✔ 2. Net income: $36,700

The unadjusted trial balance of Surf Suds Laundry at October 31, 2010, the end of the current fiscal year, is shown below.

Surf Suds Laundry
Unadjusted Trial Balance
October 31, 2010

	Debit Balances	Credit Balances
Cash	4,350	
Laundry Supplies	11,250	
Prepaid Insurance	7,200	
Laundry Equipment	163,500	
Accumulated Depreciation		61,500
Accounts Payable		9,300
Hilda Dinero, Capital		56,700
Hilda Dinero, Drawing	3,000	
Laundry Revenue		247,500
Wages Expense	107,250	
Rent Expense	54,000	
Utilities Expense	20,400	
Miscellaneous Expense	4,050	
	375,000	375,000

The data needed to determine year-end adjustments are as follows:

a. Wages accrued but not paid at October 31 are $1,250.

b. Depreciation of equipment during the year is $9,500.

c. Laundry supplies on hand at October 31 are $2,900.
d. Insurance premiums expired during the year are $6,000.

Instructions

1. For each account listed in the unadjusted trial balance, enter the balance in a T account. Identify the balance as "Oct. 31 Bal." In addition, add T accounts for Wages Payable, Depreciation Expense, Laundry Supplies Expense, Insurance Expense, and Income Summary.
2. **Optional:** Enter the unadjusted trial balance on an end-of-period spreadsheet (work sheet) and complete the spreadsheet. Add the accounts listed in Part (1) as needed.
3. Journalize and post the adjusting entries. Identify the adjustments by "Adj." and the new balances as "Adj. Bal."
4. Prepare an adjusted trial balance.
5. Prepare an income statement, a statement of owner's equity (no additional investments were made during the year), and a balance sheet.
6. Journalize and post the closing entries. Identify the closing entries by "Clos."
7. Prepare a post-closing trial balance.

PR 4-4A

Ledger accounts, adjusting entries, financial statements, and closing entries; optional end-of-period spreadsheet (work sheet)

objs. 2, 3

✔ 4. Net income: $22,645

If the working papers correlating with this textbook are not used, omit Problem 4-4A.

The ledger and trial balance of Mechanical Services Co. as of July 31, 2010, the end of the first month of its current fiscal year, are presented in the working papers.

Data needed to determine the necessary adjusting entries are as follows:

a. Service revenue accrued at July 31 is $3,000.
b. Supplies on hand at July 31 are $1,475.
c. Insurance premiums expired during July are $1,200.
d. Depreciation of the building during July is $1,300.
e. Depreciation of equipment during July is $1,250.
f. Unearned rent at July 31 is $1,700.
g. Wages accrued but not paid at July 31 are $500.

Instructions

1. **Optional:** Complete the end-of-period spreadsheet (work sheet) using the adjustment data shown above.
2. Journalize and post the adjusting entries, inserting balances in the accounts affected.
3. Prepare an adjusted trial balance.
4. Prepare an income statement, a statement of owner's equity, and a balance sheet.
5. Journalize and post the closing entries. Indicate closed accounts by inserting a line in both Balance columns opposite the closing entry. Insert the new balance of the capital account.
6. Prepare a post-closing trial balance.

PR 4-5A

Ledger accounts, adjusting entries, financial statements, and closing entries; optional end-of-period spreadsheet (work sheet)

objs. 2, 3

The unadjusted trial balance of Loose Leaf Co. at December 31, 2010, the end of the current year, is shown at the top of the next page. The data needed to determine year-end adjustments are as follows:

a. Supplies on hand at December 31 are $1,500.
b. Insurance premiums expired during the year are $2,500.
c. Depreciation of equipment during the year is $4,700.
d. Depreciation of trucks during the year is $3,100.
e. Wages accrued but not paid at December 31 are $750.

✔ 5. Net income:
$43,425

Loose Leaf Co.
Unadjusted Trial Balance
December 31, 2010

		Debit Balances	Credit Balances
11	Cash	1,825	
13	Supplies	4,820	
14	Prepaid Insurance	7,500	
16	Equipment	70,200	
17	Accumulated Depreciation—Equipment		12,050
18	Trucks	50,000	
19	Accumulated Depreciation—Trucks		27,100
21	Accounts Payable		12,015
31	Reed Barmack, Capital		27,885
32	Reed Barmack, Drawing	2,500	
41	Service Revenue		120,950
51	Wages Expense	48,010	
53	Rent Expense	7,600	
55	Truck Expense	5,350	
59	Miscellaneous Expense	2,195	
		200,000	200,000

Instructions

1. For each account listed in the unadjusted trial balance, enter the balance in the appropriate Balance column of a four-column account and place a check mark (✔) in the Posting Reference column.
2. **Optional:** Enter the unadjusted trial balance on an end-of-period spreadsheet (work sheet) and complete the spreadsheet. Add the accounts listed in part (3) as needed.
3. Journalize and post the adjusting entries, inserting balances in the accounts affected. The following additional accounts from Loose Leaf's chart of accounts should be used: Wages Payable, 22; Supplies Expense, 52; Depreciation Expense—Equipment, 54; Depreciation Expense—Trucks, 56; Insurance Expense, 57.
4. Prepare an adjusted trial balance.
5. Prepare an income statement, a statement of owner's equity (no additional investments were made during the year), and a balance sheet.
6. Journalize and post the closing entries. (Income Summary is account #33 in the chart of accounts.) Indicate closed accounts by inserting a line in both Balance columns opposite the closing entry.
7. Prepare a post-closing trial balance.

PR 4-6A
Complete accounting cycle

objs. 4, 5, 6

✔ 8. Net income:
$16,455

For the past several years, Emily Page has operated a part-time consulting business from her home. As of June 1, 2010, Emily decided to move to rented quarters and to operate the business, which was to be known as Bottom Line Consulting, on a full-time basis. Bottom Line Consulting entered into the following transactions during June:

June 1. The following assets were received from Emily Page: cash, $20,000; accounts receivable, $4,500; supplies, $2,000; and office equipment, $11,500. There were no liabilities received.
1. Paid three months' rent on a lease rental contract, $6,000.
2. Paid the premiums on property and casualty insurance policies, $2,400.
4. Received cash from clients as an advance payment for services to be provided and recorded it as unearned fees, $2,700.
5. Purchased additional office equipment on account from Office Depot Co., $3,500.
6. Received cash from clients on account, $3,000.
10. Paid cash for a newspaper advertisement, $200.
12. Paid Office Depot Co. for part of the debt incurred on June 5, $750.

June 12. Recorded services provided on account for the period June 1–12, $5,100.
14. Paid part-time receptionist for two weeks' salary, $1,100.
17. Recorded cash from cash clients for fees earned during the period June 1–16, $6,500.
18. Paid cash for supplies, $750.
20. Recorded services provided on account for the period June 13–20, $3,100.
24. Recorded cash from cash clients for fees earned for the period June 17–24, $5,150.
26. Received cash from clients on account, $6,900.
27. Paid part-time receptionist for two weeks' salary, $1,100.
29. Paid telephone bill for June, $150.
30. Paid electricity bill for June, $400.
30. Recorded cash from cash clients for fees earned for the period June 25–30, $2,500.
30. Recorded services provided on account for the remainder of June, $1,000.
30. Emily withdrew $5,000 for personal use.

Instructions

1. Journalize each transaction in a two-column journal, referring to the following chart of accounts in selecting the accounts to be debited and credited. (Do not insert the account numbers in the journal at this time.)

11	Cash	31	Emily Page, Capital
12	Accounts Receivable	32	Emily Page, Drawing
14	Supplies	41	Fees Earned
15	Prepaid Rent	51	Salary Expense
16	Prepaid Insurance	52	Rent Expense
18	Office Equipment	53	Supplies Expense
19	Accumulated Depreciation	54	Depreciation Expense
21	Accounts Payable	55	Insurance Expense
22	Salaries Payable	59	Miscellaneous Expense
23	Unearned Fees		

2. Post the journal to a ledger of four-column accounts.
3. Prepare an unadjusted trial balance.
4. At the end of June, the following adjustment data were assembled. Analyze and use these data to complete parts (5) and (6).
   a. Insurance expired during June is $200.
   b. Supplies on hand on June 30 are $650.
   c. Depreciation of office equipment for June is $250.
   d. Accrued receptionist salary on June 30 is $220.
   e. Rent expired during June is $2,000.
   f. Unearned fees on June 30 are $1,875.
5. **Optional:** Enter the unadjusted trial balance on an end-of-period spreadsheet (work sheet) and complete the spreadsheet.
6. Journalize and post the adjusting entries.
7. Prepare an adjusted trial balance.
8. Prepare an income statement, a statement of owner's equity, and a balance sheet.
9. Prepare and post the closing entries. (Income Summary is account #33 in the chart of accounts.) Indicate closed accounts by inserting a line in both the Balance columns opposite the closing entry.
10. Prepare a post-closing trial balance.

Problems Series B

PR 4-1B
Financial statements and closing entries
objs. 1, 2, 3

Lightworks Company maintains and repairs warning lights, such as those found on radio towers and lighthouses. Lightworks Company prepared the end-of-period spreadsheet (work sheet) shown below at July 31, 2010, the end of the current fiscal year:

	A	B	C	D	E	F	G	H	I	J	K
1						Lightworks Company					
2						End-of-Period Spreadsheet (Work Sheet)					
3						For the Year Ended July 31, 2010					
4		Unadjusted				Adjusted					
5		Trial Balance		Adjustments		Trial Balance		Income Statement		Balance Sheet	
6	Account Title	Dr.	Cr.	Dr.	Cr.	Dr.	Cr.	Dr.	Cr.	Dr.	Cr.
7											
8	Cash	5,800				5,800				5,800	
9	Accounts Receivable	18,900		(a) 3,300		22,200				22,200	
10	Prepaid Insurance	4,200			(b) 3,000	1,200				1,200	
11	Supplies	2,730			(c) 1,900	830				830	
12	Land	98,000				98,000				98,000	
13	Building	200,000				200,000				200,000	
14	Acc. Depr.—Building		100,300		(d) 1,400		101,700				101,700
15	Equipment	101,000				101,000				101,000	
16	Acc. Depr.—Equipment		85,100		(e) 3,200		88,300				88,300
17	Accounts Payable		5,700				5,700				5,700
18	Salaries & Wages Payable				(f) 1,800		1,800				1,800
19	Unearned Rent		2,100	(g) 1,000			1,100				1,100
20	Marisa Crider, Capital		103,100				103,100				103,100
21	Marisa Crider, Drawing	10,000				10,000				10,000	
22	Fees Revenue		303,700		(a) 3,300		307,000		307,000		
23	Rent Revenue				(g) 1,000		1,000		1,000		
24	Salaries & Wages Expense	113,100		(f) 1,800		114,900		114,900			
25	Advertising Expense	21,700				21,700		21,700			
26	Utilities Expense	11,400				11,400		11,400			
27	Repairs Expense	8,850				8,850		8,850			
28	Depr. Exp.—Equipment			(e) 3,200		3,200		3,200			
29	Insurance Expense			(b) 3,000		3,000		3,000			
30	Supplies Expense			(c) 1,900		1,900		1,900			
31	Depr. Exp.—Building			(d) 1,400		1,400		1,400			
32	Misc. Expense	4,320				4,320		4,320			
33		600,000	600,000	15,600	15,600	609,700	609,700	170,670	308,000	439,030	301,700
34	Net income							137,330			137,330
35								308,000	308,000	439,030	439,030
36											

✔ 1. Net income:
$137,330

Instructions

1. Prepare an income statement for the year ended July 31.
2. Prepare a statement of owner's equity for the year ended July 31. No additional investments were made during the year.
3. Prepare a balance sheet as of July 31.
4. Based on the end-of-period spreadsheet (work sheet), journalize the closing entries.
5. Prepare a post-closing trial balance.

PR 4-2B
Financial statements and closing entries

objs. 2, 3

✔ 1. Curtis Graves, capital, November 30: $176,300

Suspicions Company is an investigative services firm that is owned and operated by Curtis Graves. On November 30, 2010, the end of the current fiscal year, the accountant for Suspicions Company prepared an end-of-period spreadsheet (work sheet), a part of which is shown below.

	A	H	I	J	K
1	Suspicions Company				
2	End-of-Period Spreadsheet (Work Sheet)				
3	For the Year Ended November 30, 2010				
		Income Statement		Balance Sheet	
4		Dr.	Cr.	Dr.	Cr.
5	Cash			11,500	
6	Accounts Receivable			47,200	
7	Supplies			3,500	
8	Prepaid Insurance			4,800	
9	Equipment			175,000	
10	Accumulated Depreciation—Equipment				55,200
11	Accounts Payable				6,000
12	Salaries Payable				1,500
13	Unearned Rent				3,000
14	Curtis Graves, Capital				172,800
15	Curtis Graves, Drawing			30,000	
16	Service Fees		480,000		
17	Rent Revenue		20,000		
18	Salary Expense	375,000			
19	Rent Expense	62,500			
20	Supplies Expense	9,000			
21	Depreciation Expense—Equipment	5,000			
22	Utilities Expense	4,400			
23	Repairs Expense	3,200			
24	Insurance Expense	2,800			
25	Miscellaneous Expense	4,600			
26		466,500	500,000	272,000	238,500
27	Net income	33,500			33,500
28		500,000	500,000	272,000	272,000
29					

Instructions
1. Prepare an income statement, statement of owner's equity (no additional investments were made during the year), and a balance sheet.
2. Journalize the entries that were required to close the accounts at November 30.
3. If Curtis Graves, Capital decreased $40,000 after the closing entries were posted, and the withdrawals remained the same, what was the amount of net income or net loss?

PR 4-3B
T accounts, adjusting entries, financial statements, and closing entries; optional end-of-period spreadsheet (work sheet)

objs. 2, 3

✔ 2. Net income: $35,900

The unadjusted trial balance of Ocean Breeze Laundromat at April 30, 2010, the end of the current fiscal year, is shown below.

Ocean Breeze Laundromat
Unadjusted Trial Balance
April 30, 2010

	Debit Balances	Credit Balances
Cash	11,000	
Laundry Supplies	18,900	
Prepaid Insurance	8,600	
Laundry Equipment	284,000	
Accumulated Depreciation		150,400
Accounts Payable		9,800
Deanna Beaven, Capital		107,600
Deanna Beaven, Drawing	8,400	
Laundry Revenue		232,200
Wages Expense	104,000	
Rent Expense	39,300	
Utilities Expense	20,400	
Miscellaneous Expense	5,400	
	500,000	500,000

The data needed to determine year-end adjustments are as follows:

a. Laundry supplies on hand at April 30 are $4,000.
b. Insurance premiums expired during the year are $5,200.
c. Depreciation of equipment during the year is $6,000.
d. Wages accrued but not paid at April 30 are $1,100.

Instructions

1. For each account listed in the unadjusted trial balance, enter the balance in a T account. Identify the balance as "April 30 Bal." In addition, add T accounts for Wages Payable, Depreciation Expense, Laundry Supplies Expense, Insurance Expense, and Income Summary.
2. **Optional:** Enter the unadjusted trial balance on an end-of-period spreadsheet (work sheet) and complete the spreadsheet. Add the accounts listed in part (1) as needed.
3. Journalize and post the adjusting entries. Identify the adjustments by "Adj." and the new balances as "Adj. Bal."
4. Prepare an adjusted trial balance.
5. Prepare an income statement, a statement of owner's equity (no additional investments were made during the year), and a balance sheet.
6. Journalize and post the closing entries. Identify the closing entries by "Clos."
7. Prepare a post-closing trial balance.

PR 4-4B
Ledger accounts, adjusting entries, financial statements, and closing entries; optional end-of-period spreadsheet (work sheet)

obj. 2, 3

✔ 4. Net income: $22,820

If the working papers correlating with this textbook are not used, omit Problem 4-4B.

The ledger and trial balance of Handy Man Services Co. as of July 31, 2010, the end of the first month of its current fiscal year, are presented in the working papers.

Data needed to determine the necessary adjusting entries are as follows:

a. Service revenue accrued at July 31 is $2,200.
b. Supplies on hand at July 31 are $1,450.
c. Insurance premiums expired during July are $800.
d. Depreciation of the building during July is $1,000.
e. Depreciation of equipment during July is $750.
f. Unearned rent at July 31 is $1,800.
g. Wages accrued at July 31 are $600.

Instructions

1. **Optional:** Complete the end-of-period spreadsheet (work sheet) using the adjustment data shown above.
2. Journalize and post the adjusting entries, inserting balances in the accounts affected.
3. Prepare an adjusted trial balance.
4. Prepare an income statement, a statement of owner's equity, and a balance sheet.
5. Journalize and post the closing entries. Indicate closed accounts by inserting a line in both Balance columns opposite the closing entry. Insert the new balance of the capital account.
6. Prepare a post-closing trial balance.

PR 4-5B
Ledger accounts,
adjusting entries,
financial statements,
and closing entries;
optional spreadsheet
(work sheet)

objs. 2, 3

✔ 5. Net income:
$35,635

The unadjusted trial balance of Fix-It Co. at February 28, 2010, the end of the current year, is shown below.

Fix-It Co.
Unadjusted Trial Balance
February 28, 2010

	Debit Balances	Credit Balances
11 Cash	3,950	
13 Supplies	15,295	
14 Prepaid Insurance	2,735	
16 Equipment	100,650	
17 Accumulated Depreciation—Equipment		21,209
18 Trucks	36,300	
19 Accumulated Depreciation—Trucks		7,400
21 Accounts Payable		4,015
31 Tomas Guerrero, Capital		72,426
32 Tomas Guerrero, Drawing	5,000	
41 Service Revenue		119,950
51 Wages Expense	39,925	
53 Rent Expense	10,600	
55 Truck Expense	7,350	
59 Miscellaneous Expense	3,195	
	225,000	225,000

The data needed to determine year-end adjustments are as follows:

a. Supplies on hand at February 28 are $4,000.
b. Insurance premiums expired during year are $2,000.
c. Depreciation of equipment during year is $6,000.
d. Depreciation of trucks during year is $3,500.
e. Wages accrued but not paid at February 28 are $450.

Instructions

1. For each account listed in the trial balance, enter the balance in the appropriate Balance column of a four-column account and place a check mark (✔) in the Posting Reference column.
2. **Optional:** Enter the unadjusted trial balance on an end-of-period spreadsheet (work sheet) and complete the spreadsheet. Add the accounts listed in part (3) as needed.
3. Journalize and post the adjusting entries, inserting balances in the accounts affected. The following additional accounts from Fix-It's chart of accounts should be used: Wages Payable, 22; Supplies Expense, 52; Depreciation Expense—Equipment, 54; Depreciation Expense—Trucks, 56; Insurance Expense, 57.
4. Prepare an adjusted trial balance.
5. Prepare an income statement, a statement of owner's equity (no additional investments were made during the year), and a balance sheet.
6. Journalize and post the closing entries. (Income Summary is account #33 in the chart of accounts.) Indicate closed accounts by inserting a line in both Balance columns opposite the closing entry.
7. Prepare a post-closing trial balance.

PR 4-6B
Complete accounting
cycle

objs. 4, 5, 6

For the past several years, Kareem Ismail has operated a part-time consulting business from his home. As of October 1, 2010, Kareem decided to move to rented quarters and to operate the business, which was to be known as Iron Mountain Consulting, on a full-time basis. Iron Mountain Consulting entered into the following transactions during October:

Oct.   1.   The following assets were received from Kareem Ismail: cash, $18,000 accounts receivable, $5,000 supplies, $1,500; and office equipment, $10,750. There were no liabilities received.

✔ 8. Net income: $26,100

Oct. 1. Paid three months' rent on a lease rental contract, $4,800.
2. Paid the premiums on property and casualty insurance policies, $2,700.
4. Received cash from clients as an advance payment for services to be provided and recorded it as unearned fees, $3,150.
5. Purchased additional office equipment on account from Office Station Co., $1,250.
6. Received cash from clients on account, $2,000.
10. Paid cash for a newspaper advertisement, $325.
12. Paid Office Station Co. for part of the debt incurred on October 5, $750.
12. Recorded services provided on account for the period October 1–12, $5,750.
14. Paid part-time receptionist for two weeks' salary, $900.
17. Recorded cash from cash clients for fees earned during the period October 1–17, $9,250.
18. Paid cash for supplies, $600.
20. Recorded services provided on account for the period October 13–20, $4,100.
24. Recorded cash from cash clients for fees earned for the period October 17–24, $4,850.
26. Received cash from clients on account, $3,450.
27. Paid part-time receptionist for two weeks' salary, $900.
29. Paid telephone bill for October, $250.
31. Paid electricity bill for October, $300.
31. Recorded cash from cash clients for fees earned for the period October 25–31, $3,975.
31. Recorded services provided on account for the remainder of October, $2,500.
31. Kareem withdrew $7,500 for personal use.

Instructions

1. Journalize each transaction in a two-column journal, referring to the following chart of accounts in selecting the accounts to be debited and credited. (Do not insert the account numbers in the journal at this time.)

11	Cash	31	Kareem Ismail, Capital
12	Accounts Receivable	32	Kareem Ismail, Drawing
14	Supplies	41	Fees Earned
15	Prepaid Rent	51	Salary Expense
16	Prepaid Insurance	52	Rent Expense
18	Office Equipment	53	Supplies Expense
19	Accumulated Depreciation	54	Depreciation Expense
21	Accounts Payable	55	Insurance Expense
22	Salaries Payable	59	Miscellaneous Expense
23	Unearned Fees		

2. Post the journal to a ledger of four-column accounts.
3. Prepare an unadjusted trial balance.
4. At the end of October, the following adjustment data were assembled. Analyze and use these data to complete parts (5) and (6).
   a. Insurance expired during October is $225.
   b. Supplies on hand on October 31 are $875.
   c. Depreciation of office equipment for October is $400.
   d. Accrued receptionist salary on October 31 is $200.
   e. Rent expired during October is $1,600.
   f. Unearned fees on October 31 are $1,150.
5. **Optional:** Enter the unadjusted trial balance on an end-of-period spreadsheet (work sheet) and complete the spreadsheet.
6. Journalize and post the adjusting entries.
7. Prepare an adjusted trial balance.
8. Prepare an income statement, a statement of owner's equity, and a balance sheet.
9. Prepare and post the closing entries. (Income Summary is account #33 in the chart of accounts.) Indicate closed accounts by inserting a line in both the Balance columns opposite the closing entry.
10. Prepare a post-closing trial balance.

Continuing Problem

✔ 2. Net income: $6,920

The unadjusted trial balance of Music Depot as of July 31, 2010, along with the adjustment data for the two months ended July 31, 2010, are shown in Chapter 3.

Based on the adjustment data, the adjusted trial balance shown below was prepared.

Music Depot
Adjusted Trial Balance
July 31, 2010

	Debit Balances	Credit Balances
Cash	12,780	
Accounts Receivable	4,750	
Supplies	175	
Prepaid Insurance	2,475	
Office Equipment	5,000	
Accumulated Depreciation—Office Equipment		60
Accounts Payable		5,680
Wages Payable		120
Unearned Revenue		3,600
Lee Chang, Capital		10,500
Lee Chang, Drawing	1,700	
Fees Earned		20,500
Wages Expense	2,520	
Office Rent Expense	2,750	
Equipment Rent Expense	1,100	
Utilities Expense	860	
Music Expense	2,810	
Advertising Expense	1,600	
Supplies Expense	855	
Insurance Expense	225	
Depreciation Expense	60	
Miscellaneous Expense	800	
	40,460	40,460

Instructions

1. **Optional**. Using the data from Chapter 3, prepare an end-of-period spreadsheet (work sheet).
2. Prepare an income statement, a statement of owner's equity, and a balance sheet. (*Note:* Lee Chang made investments in Music Depot on June 1 and July 1, 2010.)
3. Journalize and post the closing entries. The income summary account is #33 in the ledger of Music Depot. Indicate closed accounts by inserting a line in both Balance columns opposite the closing entry.
4. Prepare a post-closing trial balance.

Comprehensive Problem 1

✔ 8. Net income, $27,665

Kelly Pitney began her consulting business, Kelly Consulting, on April 1, 2010. The accounting cycle for Kelly Consulting for April, including financial statements, was illustrated on pages 156–168. During May, Kelly Consulting entered into the following transactions:

May 3.   Received cash from clients as an advance payment for services to be provided and recorded it as unearned fees, $2,500.
　　 5.   Received cash from clients on account, $1,750.
　　 9.   Paid cash for a newspaper advertisement, $300.
　　 13.   Paid Office Station Co. for part of the debt incurred on April 5, $400.

May 15. Recorded services provided on account for the period May 1–15, $6,100.
    16. Paid part-time receptionist for two weeks' salary including the amount owed on April 30, $750.
    17. Recorded cash from cash clients for fees earned during the period May 1–16, $8,200.
    20. Purchased supplies on account, $400.
    21. Recorded services provided on account for the period May 16–20, $3,900.
    25. Recorded cash from cash clients for fees earned for the period May 17–23, $5,100.
    27. Received cash from clients on account, $9,500.
    28. Paid part-time receptionist for two weeks' salary, $750.
    30. Paid telephone bill for May, $120.
    31. Paid electricity bill for May, $290.
    31. Recorded cash from cash clients for fees earned for the period May 26–31, $3,875.
    31. Recorded services provided on account for the remainder of May, $3,200.
    31. Kelly withdrew $8,000 for personal use.

Instructions

1. The chart of accounts for Kelly Consulting is shown on page 158, and the post-closing trial balance as of April 30, 2010, is shown on page 166. For each account in the post-closing trial balance, enter the balance in the appropriate Balance column of a four-column account. Date the balances May 1, 2010, and place a check mark (✔) in the Posting Reference column. Journalize each of the May transactions in a two-column journal using Kelly Consulting's chart of accounts. (Do not insert the account numbers in the journal at this time.)
2. Post the journal to a ledger of four-column accounts.
3. Prepare an unadjusted trial balance.
4. At the end of May, the following adjustment data were assembled. Analyze and use these data to complete parts (5) and (6).
   a. Insurance expired during May is $300.
   b. Supplies on hand on May 31 are $600.
   c. Depreciation of office equipment for May is $330.
   d. Accrued receptionist salary on May 31 is $240.
   e. Rent expired during May is $1,600.
   f. Unearned fees on May 31 are $2,000.
5. **Optional:** Enter the unadjusted trial balance on an end-of-period spreadsheet (work sheet) and complete the spreadsheet.
6. Journalize and post the adjusting entries.
7. Prepare an adjusted trial balance.
8. Prepare an income statement, a statement of owner's equity, and a balance sheet.
9. Prepare and post the closing entries. (Income Summary is account #33 in the chart of accounts.) Indicate closed accounts by inserting a line in both the Balance columns opposite the closing entry.
10. Prepare a post-closing trial balance.

Special Activities

You can access the special activities online at **www.cengage.com/accounting/reeve**.

Excel Success Special Activities

SA 4-1
Financial statements

excel
success

The end-of-month adjusted trial balance for Impact Tools was as follows:

	A	B	C
1		**Impact Tools**	
2		**Adjusted Trial Balance**	
3		**August 31, 2011**	
4			
5		**Debit**	**Credit**
6		**Balance**	**Balance**
7	Cash	12,400	
8	Accounts Receivable	2,450	
9	Supplies	980	
10	Prepaid Rent	3,600	
11	Equipment	12,800	
12	Accumulated Depreciation		3,260
13	Accounts Payable		1,050
14	Salaries Payable		490
15	Oliver Reddy, Capital		22,570
16	Oliver Reddy, Drawing	7,500	
17	Fees Earned		21,300
18	Salary Expense	5,270	
19	Rent Expense	1,200	
20	Supplies Expense	1,140	
21	Depreciation Expense	820	
22	Miscellaneous Expense	510	
23		48,670	48,670
24			

a. Open the Excel file *SA4-1*.
b. On the worksheet labeled FS, complete the income statement, statement of owner's equity, and balance sheet from the adjusted trial balance.
c. When you have completed the financial statements, perform a "save as," replacing the entire file name with the following:

SA4-1_[your first name initial]_[your last name]

SA 4-2
Financial statements

The end-of-month adjusted trial balance for Fauna and Flowers was as follows:

	A	B	C
1	**Fauna and Flowers**		
2	**Adjusted Trial Balance**		
3	**August 31, 2011**		
4			
5		**Debit**	**Credit**
6		**Balance**	**Balance**
7	Cash	12,700	
8	Accounts Receivable	3,650	
9	Supplies	1,230	
10	Equipment	9,410	
11	Accumulated Depreciation		1,250
12	Accounts Payable		1,460
13	Salaries Payable		940
14	Unearned Revenue		560
15	Dawn Preston, Capital		21,820
16	Dawn Preston, Drawing	5,230	
17	Fees Earned		16,530
18	Salary Expense	6,790	
19	Rent Expense	1,800	
20	Supplies Expense	940	
21	Depreciation Expense	580	
22	Miscellaneous Expense	230	
23		42,560	42,560
24			

a. Open the Excel file *SA4-2*.

b. On the worksheet labeled FS, complete the income statement, statement of owner's equity and balance sheet from the adjusted trial balance.

c. When you have completed the creating the financial statements, perform a "save as," replacing the entire file name with the following:

   SA4-2_[your first name initial]_[your last name]

SA 4-3
ImagePress—
Financial Statements

ImagePress Printing's adjusted trial balance from SA3-3 is as follows:

	A	B	C
1	**ImagePress Printing**		
2	**Adjusted Trial Balance**		
3	**April 30, 2011**		
4		**Debit**	**Credit**
5		**Balances**	**Balances**
6	Cash	8,240	
7	Accounts Receivable	17,170	
8	Supplies	600	
9	Office Equipment	21,850	
10	Accumulated Depreciation		4,250
11	Accounts Payable		11,310
12	Ted Wright, Capital		23,800
13	Ted Wright, Drawing	5,900	
14	Fees Earned		36,550
15	Advertising Expense	660	
16	Rent Expense	7,500	
17	Salaries Expense	5,500	
18	Utilities Expense	2,540	
19	Depreciation Expense	4,250	
20	Supplies Expense	1,700	
21		75,910	75,910
22			

a. Open the Excel file *SA4-3*.

b. On the worksheet labeled FS, prepare the income statement, statement of owner's equity, and balance sheet from the adjusted trial balance.

c. When you have completed the creating the financial statements, perform a "save as," replacing the entire file name with the following:

SA4-3_[your first name initial]_[your last name]

Answers to Self-Examination Questions

1. **C** The drawing account, M. E. Jones, Drawing (answer C), would be extended to the Balance Sheet columns of the work sheet. Utilities Expense (answer A), Rent Revenue (answer B), and Miscellaneous Expense (answer D) would all be extended to the Income Statement columns of the work sheet.

2. **D** Cash or other assets that are expected to be converted to cash or sold or used up within one year or less, through the normal operations of the business, are classified as current assets on the balance sheet. Accounts Receivable (answer D) is a current asset, since it will normally be converted to cash within one year. Office Equipment (answer A), Land (answer B), and Accumulated Depreciation (answer C) are all reported in the property, plant, and equipment section of the balance sheet.

3. **B** The entry to close the owner's drawing account is to debit the owner's capital account and credit the drawing account (answer B).

4. **D** Since all revenue and expense accounts are closed at the end of the period, Fees Earned (answer A), Wages Expense (answer B), and Rent Expense (answer C) would all be closed to Income Summary. Accumulated Depreciation (answer D) is a contra asset account that is not closed.

5. **B** Since the post-closing trial balance includes only balance sheet accounts (all of the revenue, expense, and drawing accounts are closed), Cash (answer A), Accumulated Depreciation (answer C), and J. C. Smith, Capital (answer D) would appear on the post-closing trial balance. Fees Earned (answer B) is a temporary account that is closed prior to preparing the post-closing trial balance.

Accounting Systems

INTUIT INC.

Whether you realize it or not, you likely interact with accounting systems. For example, your checkbook register is a type of accounting system. When you make a deposit, you record an addition to your cash; when you write a check, you record a reduction in your cash. Such a simple accounting system works well for a person with just a few transactions per month. However, over time, you may find that your financial affairs will become more complex and involve many different types of transactions, including investments and loan payments. At this point, a simple checkbook register may not be sufficient for managing your financial affairs. Personal financial planning software, such as Intuit's Quicken®, can be useful when your financial affairs reach this level of complexity.

What happens if you decide to begin a small business? Now the transactions occurring every month have expanded and involve customers, vendors, and employees. As a result, the accounting system will need to grow with this complex-

ity. Thus, many small businesses will use small-business accounting software, such as Intuit's QuickBooks®, as their first accounting system. As a business grows, more sophisticated accounting systems will be needed. Companies such as SAP, Oracle, NetSuite Inc., and Sage Software, Inc. offer accounting system solutions for businesses that become larger with more complex accounting needs.

Accounting systems used by large and small businesses employ the basic principles of the accounting cycle discussed in the previous chapters. However, these accounting systems include features that sim-plify the recording and summary process. In this chapter, we will discuss these simplifying procedures as they apply to both manual and computerized systems.

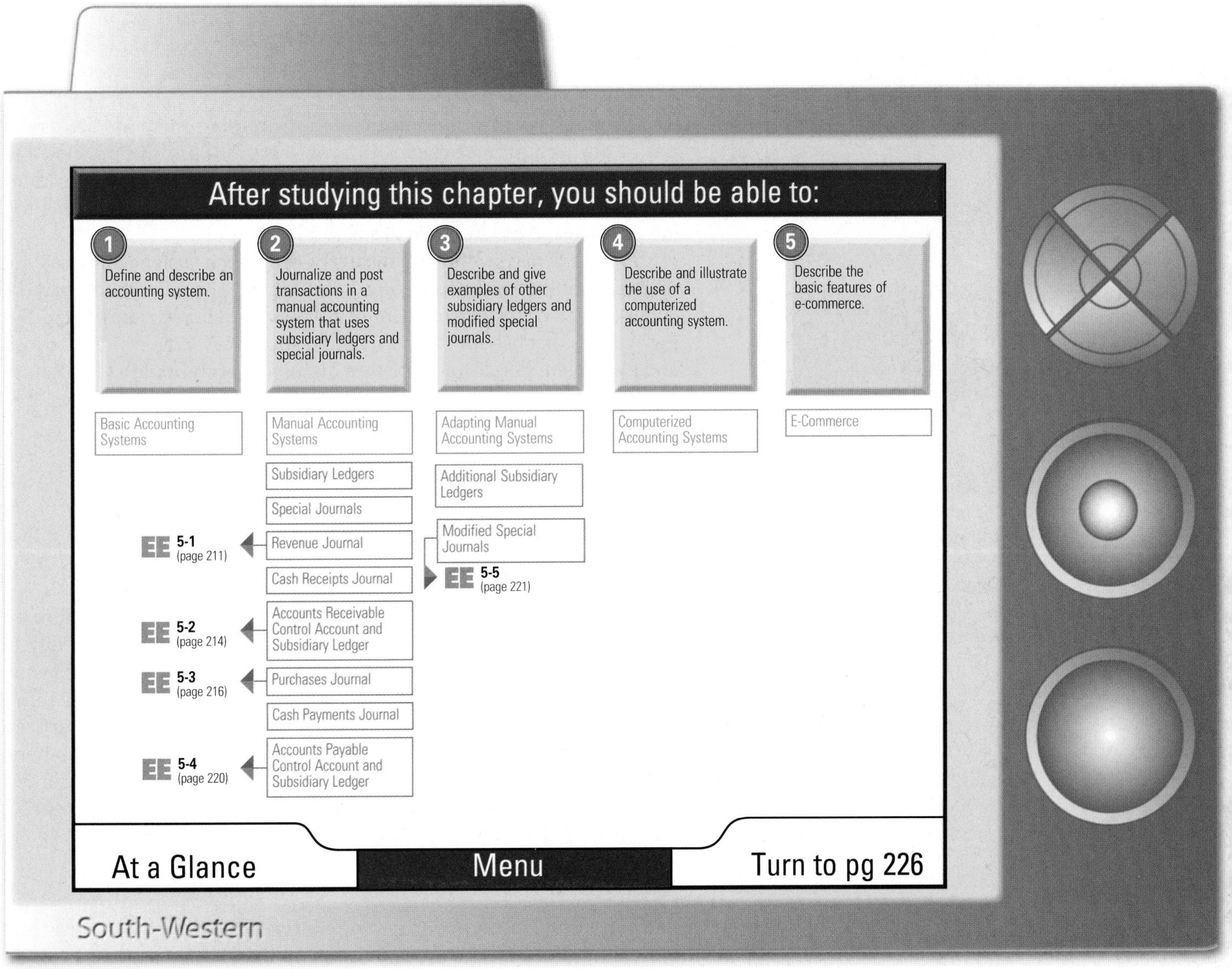

After studying this chapter, you should be able to:

1 Define and describe an accounting system.

2 Journalize and post transactions in a manual accounting system that uses subsidiary ledgers and special journals.

3 Describe and give examples of other subsidiary ledgers and modified special journals.

4 Describe and illustrate the use of a computerized accounting system.

5 Describe the basic features of e-commerce.

Basic Accounting Systems

Manual Accounting Systems

Subsidiary Ledgers

Special Journals

EE 5-1 (page 211) ← Revenue Journal

Cash Receipts Journal

EE 5-2 (page 214) ← Accounts Receivable Control Account and Subsidiary Ledger

EE 5-3 (page 216) ← Purchases Journal

Cash Payments Journal

EE 5-4 (page 220) ← Accounts Payable Control Account and Subsidiary Ledger

Adapting Manual Accounting Systems

Additional Subsidiary Ledgers

Modified Special Journals ▶ **EE** 5-5 (page 221)

Computerized Accounting Systems

E-Commerce

At a Glance   Menu   Turn to pg 226

South-Western

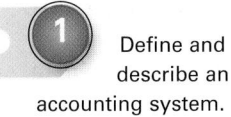

1 Define and describe an accounting system.

Basic Accounting Systems

In Chapters 1–4, an accounting system for NetSolutions was described and illustrated. An **accounting system** is the methods and procedures for collecting, classifying, summarizing, and reporting a business's financial and operating information. Most accounting systems, however, are more complex than NetSolutions'. For example, Southwest Airlines' accounting system not only records basic transaction data, but also records data on such items as ticket reservations, credit card collections, frequent-flier mileage, and aircraft maintenance.

As a business grows and changes, its accounting system also changes in a three-step process. This three-step process is as follows:

Step 1. *Analyze* user information needs.

Step 2. *Design* the system to meet the user needs.

Step 3. *Implement* the system.

For NetSolutions, our analysis determined that Chris Clark needed financial statements for the new business. We designed the system, using a basic manual system that included a chart of accounts, a two-column journal, and a general ledger. Finally, we implemented the system to record transactions and prepare financial statements.

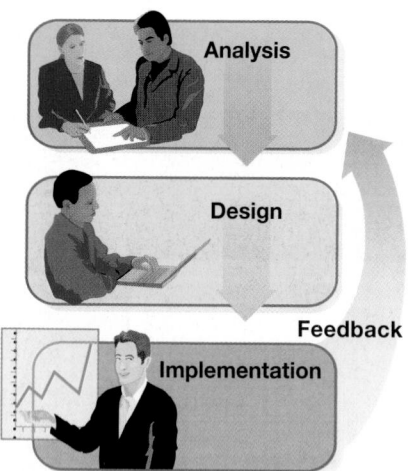

Once a system has been implemented, *feedback*, or input, from users is used to analyze and improve the system. For example, in later chapters NetSolutions expands its chart of accounts to record more complex transactions.

Internal controls and information processing methods are essential in an accounting system. **Internal controls** are the policies and procedures that protect assets from misuse, ensure that business information is accurate, and ensure that laws and regulations are being followed. Internal controls are discussed in Chapter 8.

Processing methods are the means by which the system collects, summarizes, and reports accounting information. These methods may be either *manual* or *computerized*. In the following sections, manual accounting systems that use special journals and subsidiary ledgers are described and illustrated. This is followed by a discussion of computerized accounting systems.

 Journalize and post transactions in a manual accounting system that uses subsidiary ledgers and special journals.

Manual Accounting Systems

Accounting systems are manual or computerized. Understanding a manual accounting system is useful in identifying relationships between accounting data and reports. Also, most computerized systems use principles from manual systems.

In prior chapters, the transactions for NetSolutions were manually recorded in an all-purpose (two-column) journal. The journal entries were then posted individually to the accounts in the ledger. Such a system is simple to use and easy to understand when there are a small number of transactions. However, when a business has a large number of *similar* transactions, using an all-purpose journal is inefficient and impractical. For example, in a given day, a company might earn fees on account from 20 customers. Recording each fee earned by debiting Accounts Receivable and crediting Fees Earned would be inefficient. Also, a record of the amount each customer owes must be kept. In such cases, subsidiary ledgers and special journals are useful.

Subsidiary Ledgers

An accounting system should be designed to provide information on the amounts due from various customers (accounts receivable) and amounts owed to various creditors (accounts payable). A separate account for each customer and creditor could be added to the ledger. However, as the number of customers and creditors increases, the ledger would become awkward.

A large number of individual accounts with a common characteristic can be grouped together in a separate ledger called a **subsidiary ledger**. The primary ledger, which contains all of the balance sheet and income statement accounts, is then called the **general ledger**. Each subsidiary ledger is represented in the general ledger by a summarizing account, called a **controlling account**. The sum of the balances of the accounts in a subsidiary ledger must equal the balance of the related controlling account. Thus, a subsidiary ledger is a secondary ledger that supports a controlling account in the general ledger.

Two of the most common subsidiary ledgers are as follows:

1. Accounts receivable subsidiary ledger
2. Accounts payable subsidiary ledger

The **accounts receivable subsidiary ledger**, or *customers ledger*, lists the individual customer accounts in alphabetical order. The controlling account in the general ledger that summarizes the debits and credits to the individual customer accounts is Accounts Receivable.

The **accounts payable subsidiary ledger**, *or creditors ledger*, lists individual creditor accounts in alphabetical order. The related controlling account in the general ledger is Accounts Payable.

The relationship between the general ledger and the accounts receivable and accounts payable subsidiary ledgers is illustrated in Exhibit 1.

Exhibit 1

General Ledger and Subsidiary Ledgers

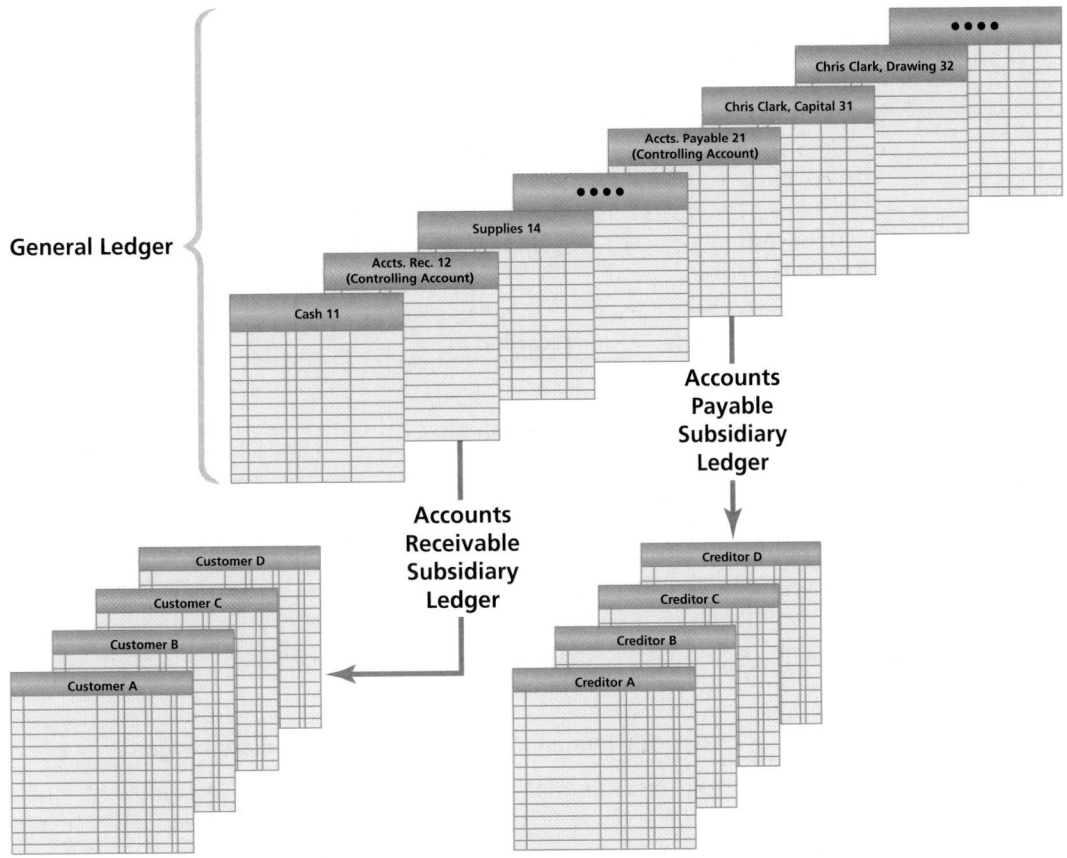

Special Journals

One method of processing data more efficiently in a manual accounting system is to expand the all-purpose two-column journal to a multicolumn journal. Each column in a multicolumn journal is used only for recording transactions that affect a certain account.

For example, a special column could be used only for recording debits to the cash account. Likewise, another special column could be used only for recording credits to the cash account. The addition of the two special columns would eliminate the writing of *Cash* in the journal for every receipt and every payment of cash. Also, there would be no need to post each individual debit and credit to the cash account. Instead, the *Cash Dr.* and *Cash Cr.* columns could be totaled periodically and only the totals posted. In a similar way, special columns could be added for recording credits to Fees Earned, debits and credits to Accounts Receivable and Accounts Payable, and for other entries that are repeated.

An all-purpose multicolumn journal may be adequate for a small business that has many transactions of a similar nature. However, a journal that has many columns for recording many different types of transactions is impractical for larger businesses.

The next logical extension of the accounting system is to replace the single multi-column journal with several **special journals**. Each special journal is designed to be used for recording a single kind of transaction that occurs frequently. For example, since most businesses have many transactions in which cash is paid out, they will likely use a special journal for recording cash payments. Likewise, they will use another special journal for recording cash receipts. Special journals are a method of summarizing transactions, which is a basic feature of any accounting system.

The format and number of special journals that a business uses depends on the nature of the business. A business that gives credit might use a special journal designed for recording only revenue from services provided on credit. In contrast, a business that does not give credit would have no need for such a journal.

The transactions that occur most often in a small service business and the special journals in which they are recorded are as follows:

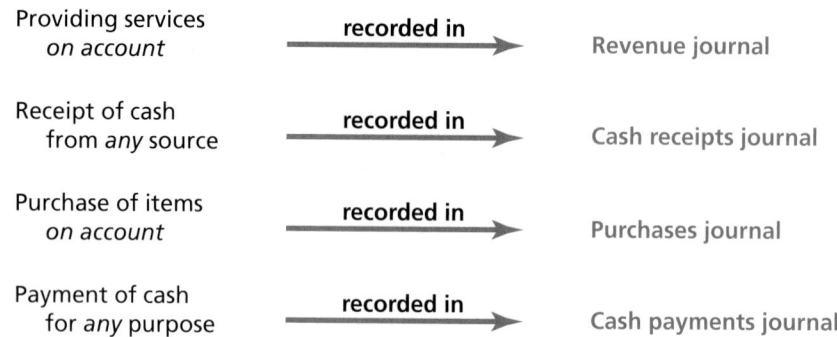

Providing services *on account*	recorded in →	Revenue journal
Receipt of cash from *any* source	recorded in →	Cash receipts journal
Purchase of items *on account*	recorded in →	Purchases journal
Payment of cash for *any* purpose	recorded in →	Cash payments journal

The all-purpose two-column journal, called the **general journal** or simply the *journal,* can be used for entries that do not fit into any of the special journals. For example, adjusting and closing entries are recorded in the general journal.

@netsolutions

Next, the following types of transactions, special journals, and subsidiary ledgers are described and illustrated for NetSolutions:

Transaction	Special Journal	Subsidiary Ledger
Fees earned on account	Revenue journal	Accounts receivable subsidiary ledger
Cash receipts	Cash receipts journal	Accounts receivable subsidiary ledger
Purchases on account	Purchases journal	Accounts payable subsidiary ledger
Cash payments	Cash payments journal	Accounts payable subsidiary ledger

As shown above, transactions that are recorded in the revenue and cash receipts journals will affect the accounts receivable subsidiary ledger. Likewise, transactions that are recorded in the purchases and cash payments journals will affect the accounts payable subsidiary ledger.

We will assume that NetSolutions had the following selected general ledger balances on March 1, 2010:

Account Number	Account	Balance
11	Cash	$6,200
12	Accounts Receivable	3,400
14	Supplies	2,500
18	Office Equipment	2,500
21	Accounts Payable	1,230

Revenue Journal

Fees earned on account would be recorded in the **revenue journal**. *Cash fees earned* would be recorded in the cash receipts journal.

To illustrate the efficiency of using a revenue journal, an example for NetSolutions is used. Specifically, assume that NetSolutions recorded the following four revenue transactions for March in its general journal:

2010					
Mar.	2	Accounts Receivable—Accessories By Claire	12/✓	2,200	
		Fees Earned	41		2,200
	6	Accounts Receivable—RapZone	12/✓	1,750	
		Fees Earned	41		1,750
	18	Accounts Receivable—Web Cantina	12/✓	2,650	
		Fees Earned	41		2,650
	27	Accounts Receivable—Accessories By Claire	12/✓	3,000	
		Fees Earned	41		3,000

For the above entries, NetSolutions recorded eight account titles and eight amounts. In addition, NetSolutions made twelve postings to the ledgers—four to Accounts Receivable in the general ledger, four to the accounts receivable subsidiary ledger (indicated by each check mark), and four to Fees Earned in the general ledger.

The preceding revenue transactions could be recorded more efficiently in a revenue journal, as shown in Exhibit 2. In each revenue transaction, the amount of the debit to Accounts Receivable is the same as the amount of the credit to Fees Earned. Thus, only a single amount column is necessary. The date, invoice number, customer name, and amount are entered separately for each transaction.

Revenues are normally recorded in the revenue journal when the company sends an invoice to the customer. An **invoice** is the bill that is sent to the customer by the company. Each invoice is normally numbered in sequence for future reference.

To illustrate, assume that on March 2 NetSolutions issued Invoice No. 615 to Accessories By Claire for fees earned of $2,200. This transaction is entered in the revenue journal, shown in Exhibit 2, by entering the following items:

1. Date column: *Mar. 2*
2. Invoice No. column: *615*
3. Account Debited column: *Accessories By Claire*
4. Accts. Rec. Dr./Fees Earned Cr. column: *2,200*

The process of posting from a revenue journal, shown in Exhibit 3, is as follows:

1. Each transaction is posted individually to a customer account in the accounts receivable subsidiary ledger. Postings to customer accounts should be made on a

Exhibit 2

Revenue Journal

		Revenue Journal			Page *35*
Date	**Invoice No.**	**Account Debited**	**Post. Ref.**	**Accts. Rec. Dr. Fees Earned Cr.**	
2010 Mar. 2	615	Accessories By Claire		2,200	
6	616	RapZone		1,750	
18	617	Web Cantina		2,650	
27	618	Accessories By Claire		3,000	
31				9,600	

Exhibit 3

Revenue Journal and Postings

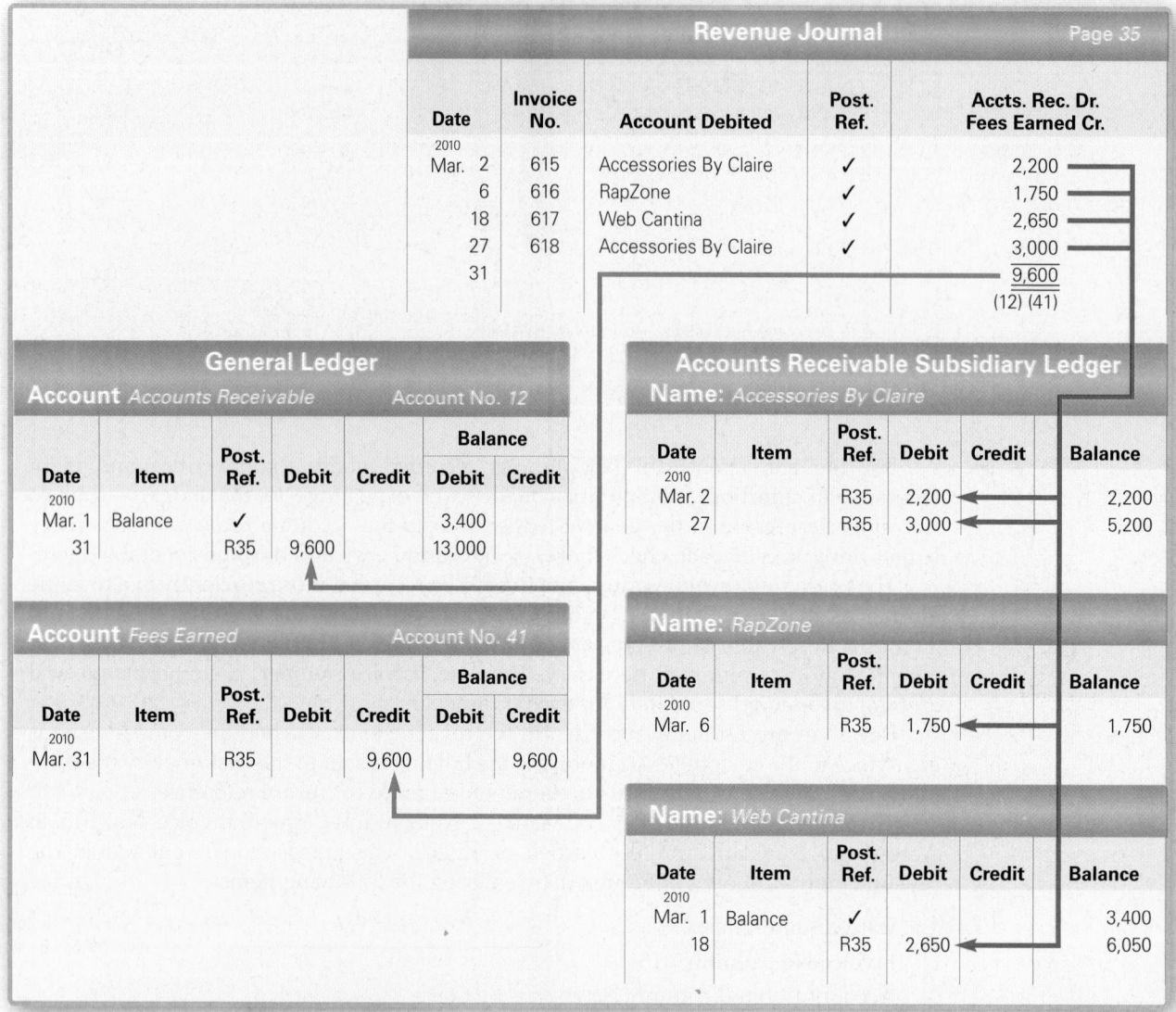

regular basis. In this way, the customer's account will show a current balance. Since the balances in the customer accounts are usually debit balances, the three-column account form is shown in Exhibit 3.

To illustrate, Exhibit 3 shows the posting of the $2,200 debit to Accessories By Claire in the accounts receivable subsidiary ledger. After the posting, Accessories By Claire has a debit balance of $2,200.

2. To provide a trail of the entries posted to the subsidiary and general ledger, the source of these entries is indicated in the Posting Reference column of each account by inserting the letter R (for revenue journal) and the page number of the revenue journal.

    To illustrate, Exhibit 3 shows that after $2,200 is posted to Accessories By Claire's account, R35 is inserted into the Post. Ref. column of the account.

3. To indicate that the transaction has been posted to the accounts receivable subsidiary ledger, a check mark (✓) is inserted in the Post. Ref. column of the revenue journal, as shown in Exhibit 3.

To illustrate, Exhibit 3 shows that a check mark (✓) has been inserted in the Post. Ref. column next to Accessories By Claire in the revenue journal to indicate that the $2,200 has been posted.

4. A single monthly total is posted to Accounts Receivable and Fees Earned in the general ledger. This total is equal to the sum of the month's debits to the individual accounts in the subsidiary ledger. It is posted in the general ledger as a debit to Accounts Receivable and a credit to Fees Earned, as shown in Exhibit 3. The accounts receivable account number (12) and the fees earned account number (41) are then inserted below the total in the revenue journal to indicate that the posting is completed.

To illustrate, Exhibit 3 shows the monthly total of $9,600 was posted as a debit to Accounts Receivable (12) and as a credit to Fees Earned (41).

Exhibit 3 illustrates the efficiency gained by using the revenue journal rather than the general journal. Specifically, all of the transactions for fees earned during the month are posted to the general ledger only once—at the end of the month.

Example Exercise 5-1   Revenue Journal

The following revenue transactions occurred during December:

Dec. 5   Issued Invoice No. 302 to Butler Company for services provided on account, $5,000.
   9   Issued Invoice No. 303 to JoJo Enterprises for services provided on account, $2,100.
   15   Issued Invoice No. 304 to Double D Inc. for services provided on account, $3,250.

Record these transactions in a revenue journal as illustrated in Exhibit 2.

Follow My Example 5-1

REVENUE JOURNAL

Date	Invoice No.	Account Debited	Post. Ref.	Accts. Rec. Dr. Fees Earned Cr.
Dec. 5	302	Butler Company		5,000
9	303	JoJo Enterprises		2,100
15	304	Double D Inc.		3,250

For Practice: PE 5-1A, PE 5-1B

Cash Receipts Journal

All transactions that involve the receipt of cash are recorded in a **cash receipts journal**. The cash receipts journal for NetSolutions is shown in Exhibit 4.

The cash receipts journal shown in Exhibit 4 has a Cash Dr. column. The kinds of transactions in which cash is received and how often they occur determine the titles of the other columns. For example, NetSolutions often receives cash from customers on account. Thus, the cash receipts journal in Exhibit 4 has an Accounts Receivable Cr. column.

To illustrate, on March 28 Accessories By Claire made a payment of $2,200 on its account. This transaction is recorded in the cash receipts journal, shown in Exhibit 4, by entering the following items:

1. Date column: *Mar. 28*
2. Account Credited column: *Accessories By Claire*
3. Accounts Receivable Cr. column: *2,200*
4. Cash Dr. column: *2,200*

Exhibit 4

Cash Receipts Journal and Postings

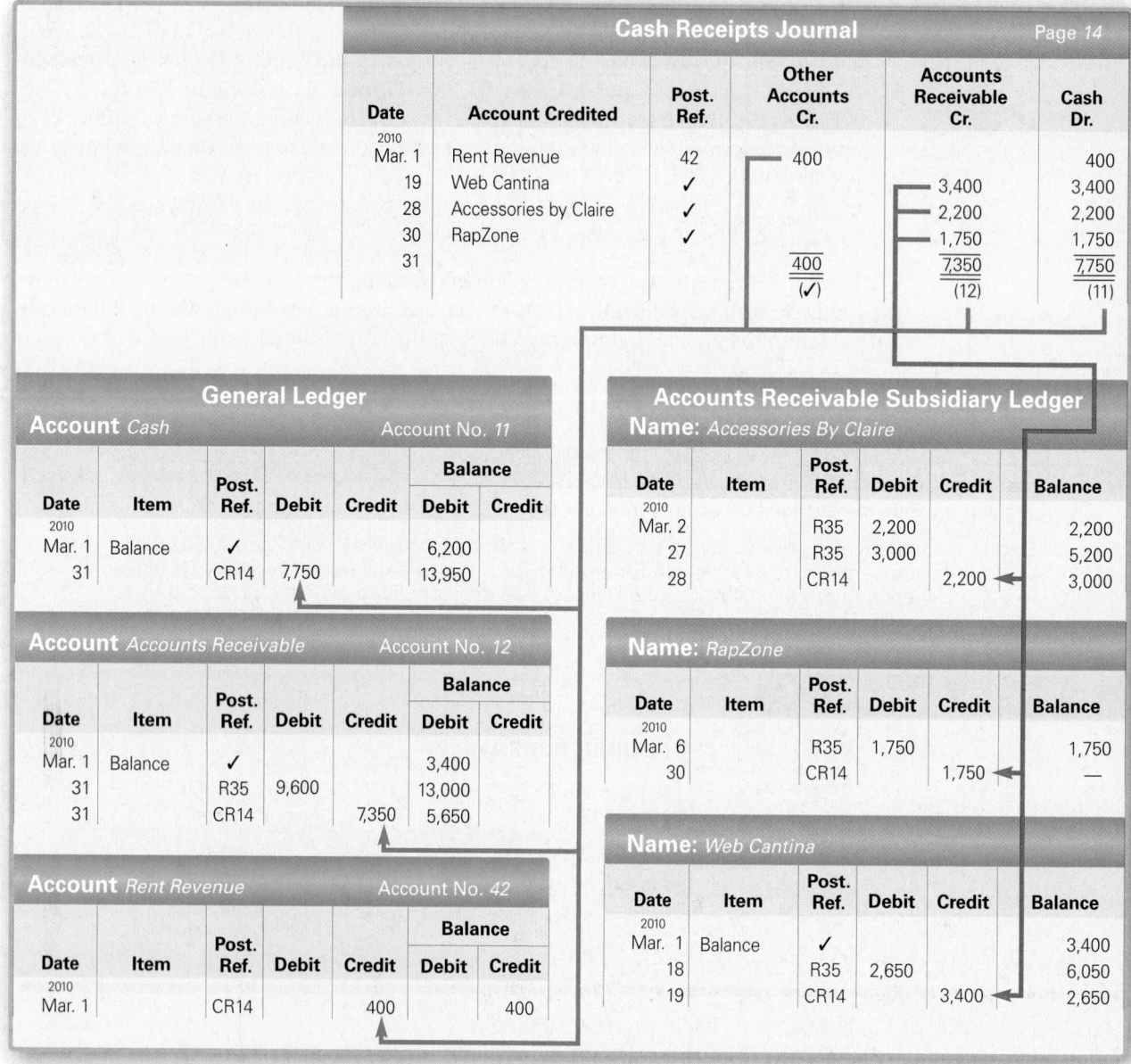

The Other Accounts Cr. column in Exhibit 4 is used for recording credits to any account for which there is no special credit column. For example, NetSolutions received cash on March 1 for rent. Since no special column exists for Rent Revenue, Rent Revenue is entered in the Account Credited column. Thus, this transaction is recorded in the cash receipts journal, shown in Exhibit 4, by entering the following items:

1. Date column: *Mar. 1*
2. Account Credited column: *Rent Revenue*
3. Other Accounts Cr. column: *400*
4. Cash Dr. column: *400*

At the end of the month, all of the amount columns are totaled. The debits must equal the credits. If the debits do not equal the credits, an error has occurred. Before proceeding further, the error must be found and corrected.

The process of posting from the cash receipts journal, shown in Exhibit 4, is as follows:

1. Each transaction involving the receipt of cash on account is posted individually to a customer account in the accounts receivable subsidiary ledger. Postings to customer accounts should be made on a regular basis. In this way, the customer's account will show a current balance.

   To illustrate, Exhibit 4 shows on March 19 the receipt of $3,400 on account from Web Cantina. The posting of the $3,400 credit to Web Cantina in the accounts receivable subsidiary ledger is shown in Exhibit 4. After the posting, Web Cantina has a debit balance of $2,650. If a posting results in a customer's account with a credit balance, the credit balance is indicated by an asterisk or parentheses in the Balance column. If an account's balance is zero, a line may be drawn in the Balance column.

2. To provide a trail of the entries posted to the subsidiary ledger, the source of these entries is indicated in the Posting Reference column of each account by inserting the letter CR (for cash receipts journal) and the page number of the cash receipts journal.

   To illustrate, Exhibit 4 shows that after $3,400 is posted to Web Cantina's account in the accounts receivable subsidiary ledger, CR14 is inserted into the Post. Ref. column of the account.

3. To indicate that the transaction has been posted to the accounts receivable subsidiary ledger, a check mark (✓) is inserted in the Posting Reference column of the cash receipts journal, as shown in Exhibit 4.

   To illustrate, Exhibit 4 shows that a check mark (✓) has been inserted in the Post. Ref. column next to Web Cantina to indicate that the $3,400 has been posted.

4. A single monthly total of the Accounts Receivable Cr. column is posted to the accounts receivable general ledger account. This is the total cash received on account and is posted as a credit to Accounts Receivable. The accounts receivable account number (12) is then inserted below the Accounts Receivable Cr. column to indicate that the posting is complete.

   To illustrate, Exhibit 4 shows the monthly total of $7,350 was posted as a credit to Accounts Receivable (12).

5. A single monthly total of the Cash Dr. column is posted to the cash general ledger account. This is the total cash received during the month and is posted as a debit to Cash. The cash account number (11) is then inserted below the Cash Dr. column to indicate that the posting is complete.

   To illustrate, Exhibit 4 shows the monthly total of $7,750 was posted as a debit to Cash (11).

6. The accounts listed in the Other Accounts Cr. column are posted on a regular basis as a separate credit to each account. The account number is then inserted in the Post. Ref. column to indicate that the posting is complete. Because accounts in the Other Accounts Cr. column are posted individually, a check mark is placed below the column total at the end of the month to show that no further action is needed.

   To illustrate, Exhibit 4 shows that $400 was posted as a credit to Rent Revenue (42). Also, at the end of the month a check mark (✓) is entered below the Other Accounts Cr. column to indicate that no further action is needed.

Accounts Receivable Control Account and Subsidiary Ledger

After all posting has been completed for the month, the balances in the accounts receivable subsidiary ledger should be totaled. This total should then be compared with the balance of the accounts receivable controlling account in the general ledger. If the controlling account and the subsidiary ledger do not agree, an error has occurred. Before proceeding further, the error must be located and corrected.

The total of NetSolutions' accounts receivable subsidiary ledger is $5,650. This total agrees with the balance of its accounts receivable control account on March 31, 2010, as shown below.

	Accounts Receivable (Control)		NetSolutions Accounts Receivable Subsidiary Ledger March 31, 2010	
Balance, March 1, 2010	$ 3,400		Accessories By Claire	$3,000
Total debits (from revenue journal)	9,600		RapZone	0
Total credits (from cash receipts journal)	(7,350)		Web Cantina	2,650
Balance, March 31, 2010	$ 5,650		Total accounts receivable	$5,650

Example Exercise 5-2   Accounts Receivable Subsidiary Ledger   •••••••• 2

The debits and credits from two transactions are presented in the following customer account:

NAME   *Sweet Tooth Confections*
ADDRESS   *1212 Lombard St.*

Date	Item	Post. Ref.	Debit	Credit	Balance
July 1	Balance				625
7	Invoice 35	R12	86		711
31	Invoice 31	CR4		122	589

Describe each transaction and the source of each posting.

Follow My Example 5-2

July 7   Provided $86 of services on account to Sweet Tooth Confections, itemized on Invoice No. 35. Amount posted from page 12 of the revenue journal.

     31   Collected cash of $122 from Sweet Tooth Confections (Invoice No. 31). Amount posted from page 4 of the cash receipts journal.

For Practice: PE 5-2A, PE 5-2B

Purchases Journal

All *purchases on account* are recorded in the **purchases journal**. *Cash purchases would be recorded in the cash payments journal*. The purchases journal for NetSolutions is shown in Exhibit 5.

The amounts purchased on account are recorded in the purchases journal in an Accounts Payable Cr. column. The items most often purchased on account determine the titles of the other columns. For example, NetSolutions often purchases supplies on account. Thus, the purchases journal in Exhibit 5 has a Supplies Dr. column.

To illustrate, on March 3 NetSolutions purchased $600 of supplies on account from Howard Supplies. This transaction is recorded in the purchases journal, shown in Exhibit 5, by entering the following items:

1. Date column: *Mar. 3*
2. Account Credited column: *Howard Supplies*
3. Accounts Payable Cr. column: *600*
4. Supplies Dr. column: *600*

The Other Accounts Dr. column in Exhibit 5 is used to record purchases, on account, of any item for which there is no debit column. The title of the account to be debited is entered in the Other Accounts Dr. column, and the amount is entered in the Amount column.

Exhibit 5

Purchases Journal and Postings

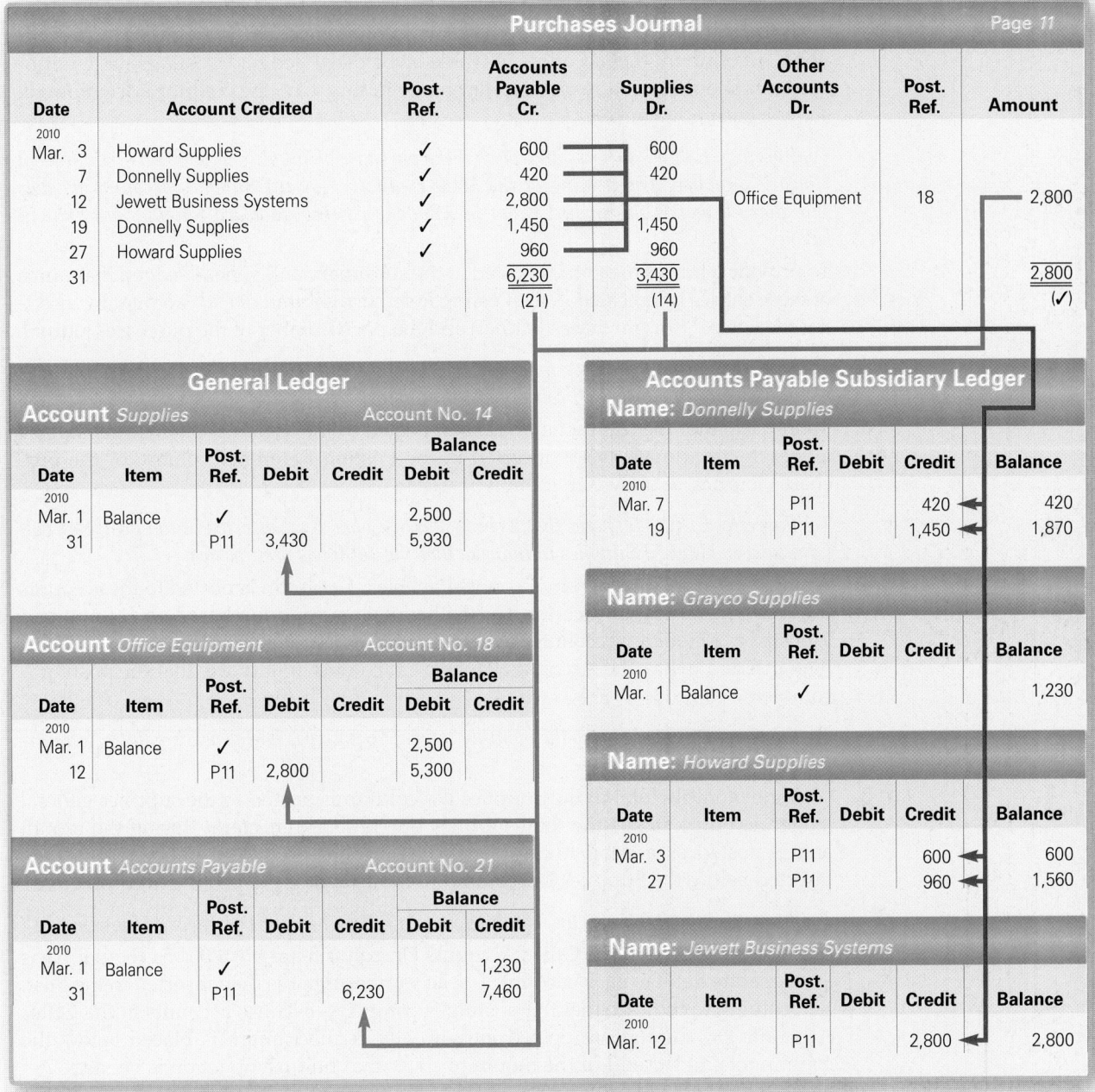

To illustrate, on March 12 NetSolutions purchased office equipment on account from Jewett Business Systems for $2,800. This transaction is recorded in the purchases journal shown in Exhibit 5 by entering the following items:

1. Date column: *Mar. 12*
2. Account Credited column: *Jewett Business Systems*
3. Accounts Payable Cr. column: *2,800*
4. Other Accounts Dr. column: *Office Equipment*
5. Amount column: *2,800*

At the end of the month, all of the amount columns are totaled. The debits must equal the credits. If the debits do not equal the credits, an error has occurred. Before proceeding further, the error must be found and corrected.

The process of posting from the purchases journal shown in Exhibit 5 is as follows:

1. Each transaction involving a purchase on account is posted individually to a creditor's account in the accounts payable subsidiary ledger. Postings to creditor accounts should be made on a regular basis. In this way, the creditor's account will show a current balance.

    To illustrate, Exhibit 5 shows on March 3 the purchase of supplies of $600 on account from Howard Supplies. The posting of the $600 credit to Howard Supplies accounts payable subsidiary ledger is shown in Exhibit 5. After the posting, Howard Supplies has a credit balance of $600.

2. To provide a trail of the entries posted to the subsidiary and general ledger, the source of these entries is indicated in the Posting Reference column of each account by inserting the letter P (for purchases journal) and the page number of the purchases journal.

    To illustrate, Exhibit 5 shows that after $600 is posted to Howard Supplies' account, P11 is inserted into the Post. Ref. column of the account.

3. To indicate that the transaction has been posted to the accounts payable subsidiary ledger, a check mark (✓) is inserted in the Posting Reference column of the purchases journal, as shown in Exhibit 5.

    To illustrate, Exhibit 5 shows that a check mark (✓) has been inserted in the Post. Ref. column next to Howard Supplies to indicate that the $600 has been posted.

4. A single monthly total of the Accounts Payable Cr. column is posted to the accounts payable general ledger account. This is the total amount purchased on account and is posted as a credit to Accounts Payable. The accounts payable account number (21) is then inserted below the Accounts Payable Cr. column to indicate that the posting is complete.

    To illustrate, Exhibit 5 shows the monthly total of $6,230 was posted as a credit to Accounts Payable (21).

5. A single monthly total of the Supplies Dr. column is posted to the supplies general ledger account. This is the total supplies purchased on account during the month and is posted as a debit to Supplies. The supplies account number (14) is then inserted below the Supplies Dr. column to indicate that the posting is complete.

    To illustrate, Exhibit 5 shows the monthly total of $3,430 was posted as a debit to Supplies (14).

6. The accounts listed in the Other Accounts Dr. column are posted on a regular basis as a separate debit to each account. The account number is then inserted in the Post. Ref. column to indicate that the posting is complete. Because accounts in the Other Accounts Dr. column are posted individually, a check mark is placed below the column total at the end of the month to show that no further action is needed.

    To illustrate, Exhibit 5 shows that $2,800 was posted as a debit to Office Equipment (18). Also, at the end of the month, a check mark (✓) is entered below the Amount column to indicate that no further action is needed.

Example Exercise 5-3 Purchases Journal ••••••• 2

The following purchase transactions occurred during October for Helping Hand Cleaners:

Oct. 11 Purchased cleaning supplies for $235, on account, from General Supplies.
   19 Purchased cleaning supplies for $110, on account, from Hubble Supplies.
   24 Purchased office equipment for $850, on account, from Office Warehouse.

Record these transactions in a purchases journal as illustrated at the top of Exhibit 5.

(continued)

Follow My Example 5-3

PURCHASES JOURNAL

Date	Account Credited	Post. Ref.	Accounts Payable Cr.	Cleaning Supplies Dr.	Other Accounts Dr.	Post. Ref.	Amount
Oct. 11	General Supplies		235	235			
19	Hubble Supplies		110	110			
24	Office Warehouse		850		Office Equipment		850

For Practice: PE 5-3A, PE 5-3B

Cash Payments Journal

All transactions that involve the payment of cash are recorded in a **cash payments journal**. The cash payments journal for NetSolutions is shown in Exhibit 6.

The cash payments journal shown in Exhibit 6 has a Cash Cr. column. The kinds of transactions in which cash is paid and how often they occur determine the titles of the other columns. For example, NetSolutions often pays cash to creditors on account. Thus, the cash payments journal in Exhibit 6 has an Accounts Payable Dr. column. In addition, NetSolutions makes all payments by check. Thus, a check number is entered for each payment in the Ck. No. (Check Number) column to the right of the Date column. The check numbers are helpful in controlling cash payments and provide a useful cross-reference.

To illustrate, on March 15 NetSolutions issued Check No. 151 for $1,230 to Grayco Supplies for payment on its account. This transaction is recorded in the cash payments journal shown in Exhibit 6 by entering the following items:

1. Date column: *Mar. 15*
2. Ck. No. column: *151*
3. Account Debited column: *Grayco Supplies*
4. Accounts Payable Dr. column: *1,230*
5. Cash Cr. column: *1,230*

The Other Accounts Dr. column in Exhibit 6 is used for recording debits to any account for which there is no special debit column. For example, NetSolutions issued Check No. 150 on March 2 for $1,600 in payment of the March rent. This transaction is recorded in the cash payments journal, shown in Exhibit 6, by entering the following items:

1. Date column: *Mar. 2*
2. Ck. No. column: *150*
3. Account Debited column: *Rent Expense*
4. Other Accounts Dr. column: *1,600*
5. Cash Cr. column: *1,600*

At the end of the month, all of the amount columns are totaled. The debits must equal the credits. If the debits do not equal the credits, an error has occurred. Before proceeding further, the error must be found and corrected.

The process of posting from the cash payments journal, shown in Exhibit 6, is as follows:

1. Each transaction involving the payment of cash on account is posted individually to a creditor account in the accounts payable subsidiary ledger. Postings to creditor accounts should be made on a regular basis. In this way, the creditor's account will show a current balance.

Exhibit 6

Cash Payments Journal and Postings

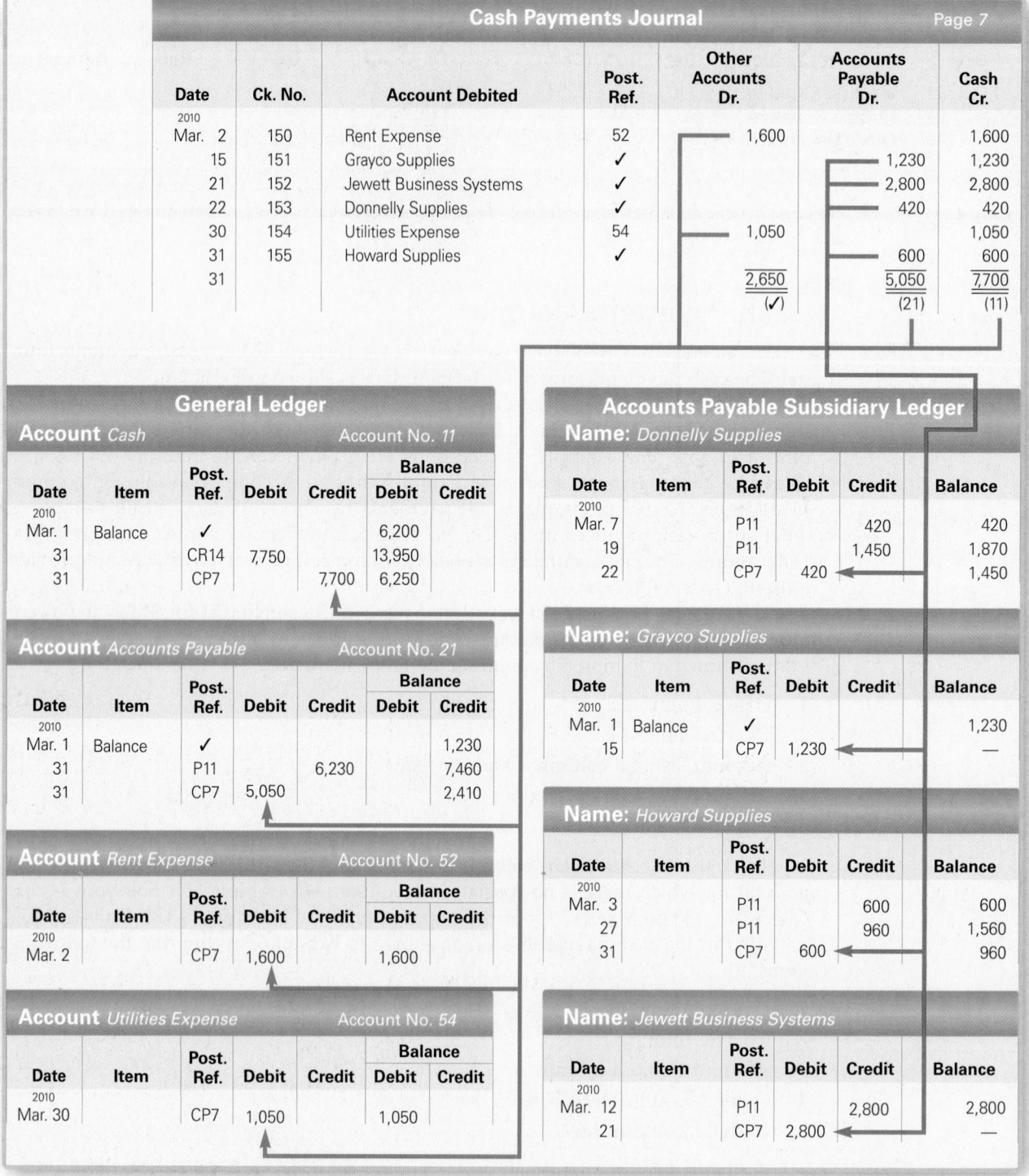

To illustrate, Exhibit 6 shows on March 22 the payment of $420 on account to Donnelly Supplies. The posting of the $420 debit to Donnelly Supplies in the accounts payable subsidiary ledger is shown in Exhibit 6. After the posting, Donnelly Supplies has a credit balance of $1,450.

2. To provide a trail of the entries posted to the subsidiary and general ledger, the source of these entries is indicated in the Posting Reference column of each account

by inserting the letter CP (for cash payments journal) and the page number of the cash payments journal.

To illustrate, Exhibit 6 shows that after $420 is posted to Donnelly Supplies' account, CP7 is inserted into the Post. Ref. column of the account.

3. To indicate that the transaction has been posted to the accounts payable subsidiary ledger, a check mark (✓) is inserted in the Posting Reference column of the cash payments journal, as shown in Exhibit 6.

    To illustrate, Exhibit 6 shows that a check mark (✓) has been inserted in the Post. Ref. column next to Donnelly Supplies to indicate that the $420 has been posted.

4. A single monthly total of the Accounts Payable Dr. column is posted to the accounts payable general ledger account. This is the total cash paid on account and is posted as a debit to Accounts Payable. The accounts payable account number (21) is then inserted below the Accounts Payable Dr. column to indicate that the posting is complete.

    To illustrate, Exhibit 6 shows the monthly total of $5,050 was posted as a debit to Accounts Payable (21).

5. A single monthly total of the Cash Cr. column is posted to the cash general ledger account. This is the total cash payments during the month and is posted as a credit to Cash. The cash account number (11) is then inserted below the Cash Cr. column to indicate that the posting is complete.

    To illustrate, Exhibit 6 shows the monthly total of $7,700 was posted as a credit to Cash (11).

6. The accounts listed in the Other Accounts Dr. column are posted on a regular basis as a separate debit to each account. The account number is then inserted in the Post. Ref. column to indicate that the posting is complete. Because accounts in the Other Accounts Dr. column are posted individually, a check mark is placed below the column total at the end of the month to show that no further action is needed.

    To illustrate, Exhibit 6 shows that $1,600 was posted as a debit to Rent Expense (52) and $1,050 was posted as a debit to Utilities Expense (54). Also, at the end of the month, a check mark (✓) is entered below the Other Accounts Dr. column to indicate that no further action is needed.

Accounts Payable Control Account and Subsidiary Ledger

After all posting has been completed for the month, the balances in the accounts payable subsidiary ledger should be totaled. This total should then be compared with the balance of the accounts payable controlling account in the general ledger. If the controlling account and the subsidiary ledger do not agree, an error has occurred. Before proceeding, the error must be located and corrected.

The total of NetSolutions' accounts payable subsidiary ledger is $2,410. This total agrees with the balance of its accounts payable control account on March 31, 2010, as shown below.

Accounts Payable (Control)		NetSolutions Accounts Payable Subsidiary Ledger March 31, 2010	
Balance, March 1, 2010	$ 1,230	Donnelly Supplies	$1,450
Total credits (from purchases journal)	6,230	Grayco Supplies	0
Total debits		Howard Supplies	960
(from cash payments journal)	(5,050)	Jewett Business Systems	0
Balance, March 31, 2010	$ 2,410	Total	$2,410

Example Exercise 5-4 Accounts Payable Subsidiary Ledger   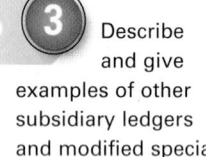 2

The debits and credits from two transactions are presented in the following creditor's (supplier's) account:

NAME   *Lassiter Services Inc.*
ADDRESS *301 St. Bonaventure Ave.*

Date	Item	Post. Ref.	Debit	Credit	Balance
Aug. 1	Balance				320
12	Invoice No. 101	CP36	200		120
22	Invoice No. 106	P16		140	260

Describe each transaction and the source of each posting.

Follow My Example 5-4

Aug. 12 Paid $200 to Lassiter Services Inc. on account (Invoice No. 101). Amount posted from page 36 of the cash payments journal.
   22 Purchased $140 of services on account from Lassiter Services Inc. itemized on Invoice No. 106. Amount posted from page 16 of the purchases journal.

For Practice: PE 5-4A, PE 5-4B

3 Describe and give examples of other subsidiary ledgers and modified special journals.

Adapting Manual Accounting Systems

In the prior sections of this chapter, we illustrated subsidiary ledgers and special journals that are common for small businesses. Many businesses use subsidiary ledgers for other accounts, in addition to Accounts Receivable and Accounts Payable. Also, special journals are often adapted or modified in practice.

Additional Subsidiary Ledgers

Subsidiary ledgers are often used for accounts that consist of a large number of individual items. For example, businesses often use a subsidiary equipment ledger to keep track of each item of equipment purchased, its cost, location, and other data. Such ledgers are similar to the accounts receivable and accounts payable subsidiary ledgers illustrated in this chapter.

Modified Special Journals

A business may modify its special journals by adding one or more columns for recording transactions that occur frequently. For example, a business may collect sales taxes that must be remitted to taxing authorities. Thus, the business may add a special column for *Sales Taxes Payable Cr.* in its revenue journal, as shown below.

Revenue Journal						Page 40
Date	Invoice No.	Account Debited	Post. Ref.	Accts. Rec. Dr.	Fees Earned Cr.	Sales Taxes Payable Cr.
2010 Nov. 2	842	Litten Co.	✓	4,770	4,500	270
3	843	Kauffman Supply Co.	✓	1,166	1,100	66

Other examples of how special journals may be modified for different types of businesses include the following:

- **Farm**—The purchases journal may be modified to include columns for various types of seeds (corn, wheat), livestock (cows, hogs, sheep), fertilizer, and fuel.

- **Automobile Repair Shop**—The revenue journal may be modified to include columns for each major type of repair service. In addition, columns for warranty repairs, credit card charges, and sales taxes may be added.
- **Hospital**—The cash receipts journal may be modified to include columns for receipts from patients on account, from Blue Cross/Blue Shield or other major insurance reimbursers, and Medicare.
- **Movie Theater**—The cash receipts journal may be modified to include columns for revenues from admissions, arcade, and concession sales.
- **Restaurant**—The purchases journal may be modified to include columns for food, linen, silverware and glassware, and kitchen supplies.

Regardless of how a special journal is modified, the basic procedures discussed in this chapter apply. For example, the columns in special journals are normally totaled at periodic intervals. The totals of the debit and credit columns are then compared to verify their equality before the totals are posted to the general ledger accounts.

Example Exercise 5-5 Modified Revenue Journal 3

The state of Tennessee has a 7% sales tax. Volunteer Services, Inc., a Tennessee company, had two revenue transactions as follows:

Aug. 3 Issued Invoice No. 58 to Helena Company for services provided on account, $1,400, plus sales tax.
   19   Issued Invoice No. 59 to K-Jam Enterprises for services provided on account, $900, plus sales tax.

Record these transactions in a revenue journal as illustrated in this section.

Follow My Example 5-5

REVENUE JOURNAL

Date	Invoice No.	Account Debited	Post. Ref.	Accts. Rec. Dr.	Fees Earned Cr.	Sales Taxes Payable Cr.
Aug. 3	58	Helena Company		1,498	1,400	98*
19	59	K-Jam Enterprises		963	900	63**

* 98 = 1,400 × 7%
** 63 = 900 × 7%

For Practice: PE 5-5A, PE 5-5B

4 Describe and illustrate the use of a computerized accounting system.

Computerized Accounting Systems

Computerized accounting systems are widely used by even the smallest of companies. Computerized accounting systems have the following three main advantages over manual systems:

1. Computerized systems simplify the record-keeping process in that transactions are recorded in electronic forms and, at the same time, posted electronically to general and subsidiary ledger accounts.
2. Computerized systems are generally more accurate than manual systems.

3. Computerized systems provide management with current account balance information to support decision making, since account balances are posted as the transactions occur.

@netsolutions

The popular QuickBooks® accounting software for small- to medium-sized businesses is used to illustrate a computerized accounting system for NetSolutions. To simplify, the illustration is limited to transactions involving the earning of revenue on account and the subsequent recording of cash collections. Exhibit 7 illustrates the use of QuickBooks® for NetSolutions to record transactions as follows:

Step 1. Record fees by completing an electronic invoice form.

Sales transactions are entered onto the computer screen using an electronic invoice form. The electronic form appears like a paper form with spaces, or fields, to input transaction data. The data spaces may have pull-down lists to ease data entry. After the form is completed, it is printed out and mailed, or e-mailed, to the customer.

To illustrate, on March 2, NetSolutions earned $2,200 on account from Accessories By Claire. As shown in Exhibit 7, Invoice No. 615 was created using an electronic form. Upon submitting the invoice form, QuickBooks® automatically posts a $2,200 debit to the Accessories By Claire customer account and the credit to Fees Earned. An invoice is also printed for mailing to Accessories By Claire.

Step 2. Record collection of payment by completing a "receive payment" form.

Upon collection from the customer, a "receive payment" electronic form is opened and completed. As with the "invoice form," data are input into the various spaces directly or by using pull-down lists.

To illustrate, a $2,200 payment was collected from Accessories By Claire on March 28. As shown in Exhibit 7, the $2,200 was applied to Invoice No. 615, as shown by the check mark (✓) next to the March 2 date at the bottom of the form. As shown at the bottom of the form, the March 27 invoice of $3,000 remains uncollected. When the screen is completed, a debit of $2,200 is automatically posted to the cash account, and a credit for $2,200 is posted to the Accessories By Claire account. This causes the balance of the Accessories By Claire account to be reduced from $5,200 to $3,000.

Step 3. Prepare reports.

At any time, managers may request reports from the software. Three such reports include the following:

1. "Accounts Receivable Subsidiary Ledger" lists as of a specific date the accounts receivable balances by customer.

   To illustrate, the Accounts Receivable Subsidiary Ledger shown in Exhibit 7 for NetSolutions was generated as of March 31, 2010. The total of the Accounts Receivable Subsidiary Ledger of $5,650 agrees with the accounts receivable subsidiary balance total we illustrated using a manual system for NetSolutions on page 211.

2. "Fees Earned by Customer" lists revenue by customer for the month. This is similar to the revenue journal in the manual system. It is created from the electronic invoice form used in step 1.

   To illustrate, the Fees Earned by Customer shown in Exhibit 7 for NetSolutions is for the month of March 2010. The total of the Fees Earned by Customer of $9,600 agrees with the total of the revenue journal we illustrated using a manual system for NetSolutions in Exhibits 2 and 3.

Exhibit 7

Revenue and Cash Receipts in QuickBooks®

1. Record fees by completing an electronic invoice form.

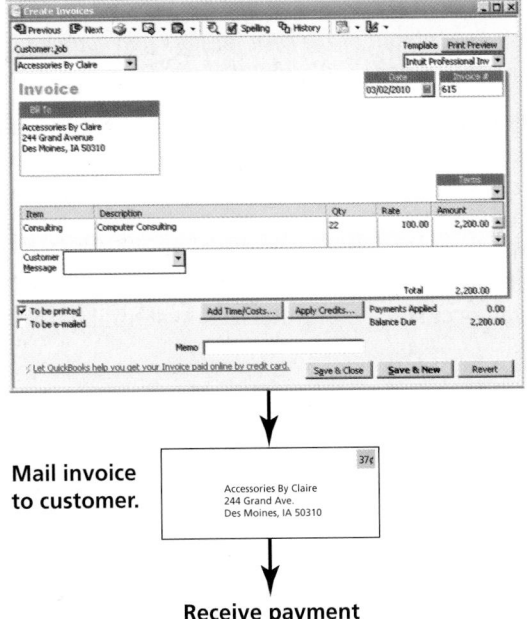

Automatic Postings	Dr.	Cr.
Accounts Receivable—		
Accessories By Claire	2,200	
Fees Earned		2,200

Mail invoice to customer.

Accessories By Claire
244 Grand Ave.
Des Moines, IA 50310

Receive payment

2. Record collection of payment by completing a "receive payment" form.

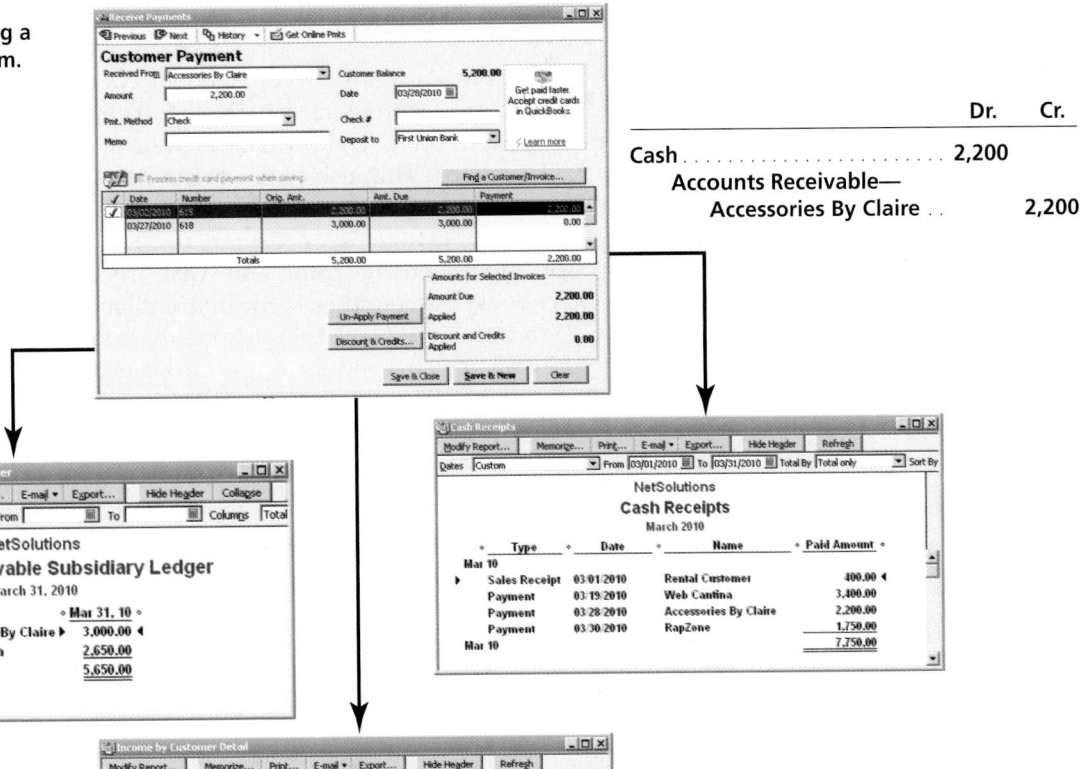

	Dr.	Cr.
Cash	2,200	
Accounts Receivable—		
Accessories By Claire		2,200

3. Prepare reports.

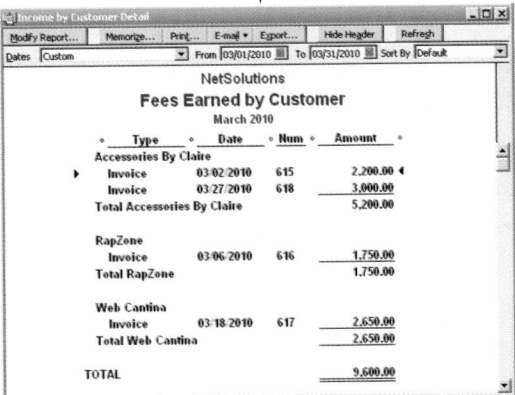

3. *"Cash Receipts"* lists the cash receipts during the month. This report is similar to the cash receipts journal in the manual system.

> *To illustrate, the Cash Receipts shown in Exhibit 7 for NetSolutions is for the month of March 2010. The total of the Cash Receipts of $7,750 agrees with the total of the Cash Dr. column of the cash receipts journal we illustrated using a manual system for NetSolutions in Exhibit 4.*

The computer does not make journalizing, posting, and mathematical errors. For example, a computerized accounting system will not process a transaction unless the total debits for the transaction equal the total credits for a transaction. Instead, an error screen will notify the user that the transaction data must be corrected. Likewise, the computer will not make posting or mathematical errors.

The discovery and correction of errors, however, is important in a computerized system. Errors that can occur in a computerized system include the following:

1. Failing to record a transaction.
2. Recording a transaction more than once.
3. Recording a transaction in incorrect accounts.
4. Entering an incorrect number in both the debit and credit parts of the transaction.

The preceding errors are often discovered by reviewing the computerized trial balance for any account balances that are unusual or unreasonable. For example, a credit balance for Supplies indicates that an error has occurred. In addition, errors are often discovered when parties affected by the incorrect transaction complain. For example, an employee would likely complain about a missed or incorrect payroll check.

Incorrectly recorded transactions can be corrected in computerized accounting systems by deleting the incorrect entries and replacing them with correct entries. When a transaction is deleted in a computerized system, the postings to the accounts are automatically deleted. This also removes the effect of the incorrect entry from the accounts. Alternatively, correcting entries may also be used as described in Chapter 2.

In this section, we illustrated revenue and cash receipt transactions for NetSolutions using QuickBooks® accounting software. Similar illustrations could be provided for purchases and cash payment transactions. A complete illustration of a computerized accounting system is beyond the scope of this text. However, this chapter provides a solid foundation for applying accounting system concepts in either a manual or a computerized system.

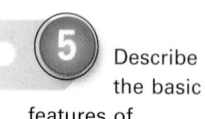

5 Describe the basic features of e-commerce.

E-Commerce

The U.S. Census Bureau indicates that e-commerce sales are growing at a rate of 21% per year to over $120 billion in retail sales. This represents over 3% of all retail sales.[1] Using the Internet to perform business transactions is termed **e-commerce**. When trans-

---

Integrity, Objectivity, and Ethics in Business

ONLINE FRAUD

Fraud accounted for over $3.6 billion in e-commerce losses in 2007, or approximately 1.4% of all online revenue. As a result, online retailers are using address verification and credit card security codes as additional security measures. Address verification matches the customer's address to the address on file with the credit card company, while the security code is the additional four-digit code designed to reduce fictitious credit card transactions.

Source: 9th Annual CyberSource fraud survey, *CyberSource*, November 13, 2007.

actions are between a company and a consumer, it is termed B2C (business-to-consumer) e-commerce. Examples of companies engaged in B2C e-commerce include Amazon.com, Priceline.com Inc., and Dell Inc.

The B2C business allows consumers to shop and receive goods at home, rather than going to the store. For example, Whirlpool Corporation allows consumers to use its Web site to order appliances, selecting color and other features. After paying with a credit card, customers can receive delivery of the appliance from the Whirlpool factory.

When transactions are conducted between two companies, it is termed B2B (business-to-business) e-commerce. Examples of companies engaged in B2B e-commerce include Cisco Systems, Inc., an Internet equipment manufacturer, and Bristol-Myers Squibb Company (BMS), a pharmaceutical company. BMS, for example, uses e-commerce to purchase supplies and equipment from its suppliers. E-commerce streamlines purchases and payments by automating transactions and eliminating paperwork. BMS claims over $90 million in savings by placing its purchase/payment cycle on the Internet.

The Internet creates opportunities for improving the speed and efficiency of transactions. Many companies are realizing these benefits of using e-commerce as illustrated above. Three additional areas where the Internet is being used for business purposes are as follows:

1. **Supply chain management (SCM):** Internet applications to plan and coordinate suppliers.
2. **Customer relationship management (CRM):** Internet applications to plan and coordinate marketing and sales effort.
3. **Product life-cycle management (PLM):** Internet applications to plan and coordinate the product development and design process.

E-commerce also provides opportunities for faster business processes that operate at lower costs. New Internet applications are continually being introduced as the Internet develops into a preferred method of conducting business.

A new trend is toward application service provider (ASP) software solutions whereby the accounting system is managed and distributed over the Internet by a third party. Under this model, the software is "rented," while analysis, design, and implementation are largely provided by the ASP vendor.

Financial Analysis and Interpretation

Accounting systems often use computers to collect, classify, summarize, and report financial and operating information in many different ways. One way is to report revenue earned by different *segments* of business. A segment of business may include regions, products or services, or customers. For example, Delta Air Lines uses the accounting system to determine the amount of revenue earned by different regions, shown as follows from the notes to its financial statements:

	2006 (in millions)	2005 (in millions)
North America	$12,931	$13,030
Trans Atlantic	2,997	2,255
Trans Pacific	164	150
Latin America	1,079	756
Total revenues	$17,171	$16,191

This regional information can be used to perform a horizontal analysis using 2005 for the base year, as illustrated in Chapter 2, as follows:

	2006 (in millions)	2005 (in millions)	Increase (Decrease) Amount	Percent
North America	$12,931	$13,030	$ (99)	−0.8%
Trans Atlantic	2,997	2,255	742	32.9
Trans Pacific	164	150	14	9.3
Latin America	1,079	756	323	42.7
Total revenues	$17,171	$16,191	$980	6.1

As can be seen from this analysis, Delta Air Lines increased total revenue by 6.1% from 2005 to 2006. However, this increase came mostly from increases in Trans Atlantic (32.9%) and Latin America (42.7%) revenues. The domestic North America revenues actually declined during the period.

In addition, a vertical analysis as shown in Chapter 3 could also be performed on the segment disclosures as follows:

	2006 Amount (in millions)	Percent	2005 Amount (in millions)	Percent
North America	$12,931	75.3%	$13,030	80.5%
Trans Atlantic	2,997	17.4	2,255	13.9
Trans Pacific	164	1.0	150	0.9
Latin America	1,079	6.3	756	4.7
Total	$17,171	100.0%	$16,191	100.0%

This analysis shows that revenue of North America flights declined from 80.5% of total revenue in 2005 to 75.3% of total revenue in 2006. Both the Trans Atlantic and Latin America revenues as a percent of the total revenues increased during the two-year period. Both analyses together indicate that Delta is benefiting from revenue growth in the Trans Atlantic and Latin America markets.

At a Glance 5

1   Define and describe an accounting system.

Key Points	Key Learning Outcomes	Example Exercises	Practice Exercises
An accounting system is the methods and procedures for collecting, classifying, summarizing, and reporting a business's financial information. The three steps through which an accounting system evolves are: (1) analysis of information needs, (2) design of the system, and (3) implementation of the system design.	• Define an accounting system. • Describe the three steps for designing an accounting system: (1) analysis, (2) design, and (3) implementation.		

2 Journalize and post transactions in a manual accounting system that uses subsidiary ledgers and special journals.

Key Points	Key Learning Outcomes	Example Exercises	Practice Exercises
Subsidiary ledgers may be used to maintain separate records for customers and creditors (vendors). A controlling account summarizes the subsidiary ledger accounts. The sum of the subsidiary ledger must agree with the balance in the related controlling account.	• Define subsidiary ledger accounts for customers and creditors.		
Special journals efficiently summarize a large number of similar transactions as follows:			
The revenue journal is used to record the sale of services on account.	• Prepare a revenue journal and post services provided on account to individual customer accounts and the accounts receivable control account.	5-1	5-1A, 5-1B
The cash receipts journal is used to record the collection of accounts and other cash receipts.	• Prepare a cash receipts journal and post collections to individual customer accounts and the accounts receivable control account.	5-2	5-2A, 5-2B
The purchases journal is used to record purchases on account.	• Prepare a purchases journal and post amounts owed to individual creditor accounts and the accounts payable control account.	5-3	5-3A, 5-3B
The cash payments journal is used to record the payments of creditor accounts and other cash payments.	• Prepare a cash payments journal and post the amounts paid to individual creditor accounts and the accounts payable control account.	5-4	5-4A, 5-4B

3 Describe and give examples of other subsidiary ledgers and modified special journals.

Key Points	Key Learning Outcomes	Example Exercises	Practice Exercises
Subsidiary ledgers may be maintained for a variety of accounts, such as fixed assets, accounts receivable, and accounts payable. Special journals may be modified by adding columns for frequently occurring transactions.	• Prepare modified special journals that incorporate additional columns for frequently occurring transactions.	5-5	5-5A, 5-5B

4 Describe and illustrate the use of a computerized accounting system.

Key Points	Key Learning Outcomes	Example Exercises	Practice Exercises
Computerized accounting systems are similar to manual systems. The main advantages of a computerized accounting system are the simultaneous recording and posting of transactions, high degree of accuracy, and timeliness of reporting.	• Differentiate between a manual and a computerized accounting system. • Illustrate revenue and cash receipts transactions using QuickBooks®.		

Key Points	Key Learning Outcomes	Example Exercises	Practice Exercises
Using the Internet to perform business transactions is termed e-commerce. B2C e-commerce involves Internet transactions between a business and consumer, while B2B e-commerce involves Internet transactions between businesses. More elaborate e-commerce involves planning and coordinating suppliers, customers, and product design.	• Define e-commerce and describe the major trends in e-commerce.		

Key Terms

accounting system (205)

accounts payable subsidiary ledger (206)

accounts receivable subsidiary ledger (206)

cash payments journal (217)

cash receipts journal (211)

controlling account (206)

e-commerce (224)

general journal (208)

general ledger (206)

internal controls (206)

invoice (209)

purchases journal (214)

revenue journal (208)

special journals (207)

subsidiary ledger (206)

Illustrative Problem

Selected transactions of O'Malley Co. for the month of May are as follows:

a. May 1. Issued Check No. 1001 in payment of rent for May, $1,200.
b.   2. Purchased office supplies on account from McMillan Co., $3,600.
c.   4. Issued Check No. 1003 in payment of freight charges on the supplies purchased on May 2, $320.
d.   8. Provided services on account to Waller Co., Invoice No. 51, $4,500.
e.   9. Issued Check No. 1005 for office supplies purchased, $450.
f.   10. Received cash for office supplies sold to employees at cost, $120.
g.   11. Purchased office equipment on account from Fender Office Products, $15,000.
h.   12. Issued Check No. 1010 in payment of the supplies purchased from McMillan Co. on May 2, $3,600.
i.   16. Provided services on account to Riese Co., Invoice No. 58, $8,000.
j.   18. Received $4,500 from Waller Co. in payment of May 8 invoice.
k.   20. Invested additional cash in the business, $10,000.
l.   25. Provided services for cash, $15,900.
m.   30. Issued Check No. 1040 for withdrawal of cash for personal use, $1,000.
n.   30. Issued Check No. 1041 in payment of electricity and water invoices, $690.
o.   30. Issued Check No. 1042 in payment of office and sales salaries for May, $15,800.
p.   31. Journalized adjusting entries from the work sheet prepared for the fiscal year ended May 31.

O'Malley Co. maintains a revenue journal, a cash receipts journal, a purchases journal, a cash payments journal, and a general journal. In addition, accounts receivable and accounts payable subsidiary ledgers are used.

Instructions

1. Indicate the journal in which each of the preceding transactions, (a) through (p), would be recorded.
2. Indicate whether an account in the accounts receivable or accounts payable subsidiary ledgers would be affected for each of the preceding transactions.
3. Journalize transactions (b), (c), (d), (h), and (j) in the appropriate journals.

Solution

1. Journal	2. Subsidiary Ledger
a. Cash payments journal	
b. Purchases journal	Accounts payable ledger
c. Cash payments journal	
d. Revenue journal	Accounts receivable ledger
e. Cash payments journal	
f. Cash receipts journal	
g. Purchases journal	Accounts payable ledger
h. Cash payments journal	Accounts payable ledger
i. Revenue journal	Accounts receivable ledger
j. Cash receipts journal	Accounts receivable ledger
k. Cash receipts journal	
l. Cash receipts journal	
m. Cash payments journal	
n. Cash payments journal	
o. Cash payments journal	
p. General journal	

3.
Transaction (b):

Purchases Journal

Date	Account Credited	Post. Ref.	Accounts Payable Cr.	Office Supplies Dr.	Other Accounts Dr.	Post. Ref.	Amount
May 2	McMillan Co.		3,600	3,600			

Transactions (c) and (h):

Cash Payments Journal

Date	Ck. No.	Account Debited	Post. Ref.	Other Accounts Dr.	Accounts Payable Dr.	Cash Cr.
May 4	1003	Freight Expense		320		320
12	1010	McMillan Co.			3,600	3,600

Transaction (d):

		Revenue Journal		
Date	Invoice No.	Account Debited	Post. Ref.	Accts. Rec. Dr. Fees Earned Cr.
May 8	51	Waller Co.		4,500

Transaction (j):

		Cash Receipts Journal			
Date	Account Credited	Post. Ref.	Other Accounts Cr.	Accounts Receivable Cr.	Cash Dr.
May 18	Waller Co.			4,500	4,500

Self-Examination Questions (Answers at End of Chapter)

1. The initial step in the process of developing an accounting system is called:
   A. analysis.
   B. design.
   C. implementation.
   D. feedback.

2. The policies and procedures used by management to protect assets from misuse, ensure accurate business information, and ensure compliance with laws and regulations are called:
   A. internal controls.
   B. systems analysis.
   C. systems design.
   D. systems implementation.

3. A payment of cash for the purchase of services should be recorded in the:
   A. purchases journal.
   B. cash payments journal.
   C. revenue journal.
   D. cash receipts journal.

4. When there are a large number of individual accounts with a common characteristic, it is common to place them in a separate ledger called a(n):
   A. subsidiary ledger.
   B. creditors ledger.
   C. accounts payable ledger.
   D. accounts receivable ledger.

5. Which of the following would be used in a computerized accounting system?
   A. Special journals
   B. Accounts receivable control accounts
   C. Electronic invoice form
   D. Month-end postings to the general ledger

Eye Openers

1. Why would a company maintain separate accounts receivable ledgers for each customer, as opposed to maintaining a single accounts receivable ledger for all customers?
2. What are the major advantages of the use of special journals?
3. In recording 400 fees earned on account during a single month, how many times will it be necessary to write Fees Earned (a) if each transaction, including fees earned, is recorded individually in a two-column general journal; (b) if each transaction for fees earned is recorded in a revenue journal?

4. How many postings to Fees Earned for the month would be needed in Eye Opener 3 if the procedure described in (a) had been used; if the procedure described in (b) had been used?
5. During the current month, the following errors occurred in recording transactions in the purchases journal or in posting from it.
   a. An invoice for $1,875 of supplies from Kelly Co. was recorded as having been received from Kelley Co., another supplier.
   b. A credit of $420 to Blackstone Company was posted as $240 in the subsidiary ledger.
   c. An invoice for equipment of $4,800 was recorded as $4,000.
   d. The Accounts Payable column of the purchases journal was overstated by $3,600.
   How will each error come to the bookkeeper's attention, other than by chance discovery?
6. The Accounts Payable and Cash columns in the cash payments journal were unknowingly overstated by $900 at the end of the month. (a) Assuming no other errors in recording or posting, will the error cause the trial balance totals to be unequal? (b) Will the creditors ledger agree with the accounts payable control account?
7. Assuming the use of a two-column general journal, a purchases journal, and a cash payments journal as illustrated in this chapter, indicate the journal in which each of the following transactions should be recorded:
   a. Purchase of office supplies on account.
   b. Purchase of supplies for cash.
   c. Purchase of store equipment on account.
   d. Payment of cash on account to creditor.
   e. Payment of cash for office supplies.
8. What is an electronic form, and how is it used in a computerized accounting system?
9. Do computerized systems use controlling accounts to verify the accuracy of the subsidiary accounts?
10. What happens to the special journal in a computerized accounting system that uses electronic forms?
11. How would e-commerce improve the revenue/collection cycle?

Practice Exercises

PE 5-1A
Revenue journal

obj. 2

EE 5-1   p. 211

The following revenue transactions occurred during February:

Feb. 6. Issued Invoice No. 78 to Howard Co. for services provided on account, $490.
     9. Issued Invoice No. 79 to Hitchcock Inc. for services provided on account, $240.
    15. Issued Invoice No. 80 to David Inc. for services provided on account, $515.

Record these three transactions into the following revenue journal format:

REVENUE JOURNAL

Date	Invoice No.	Account Debited	Post. Ref.	Accts. Rec. Dr. Fees Earned Cr.

PE 5-1B
Revenue journal

obj. 2

EE 5-1   p. 211

The following revenue transactions occurred during August:

Aug. 7. Issued Invoice No. 121 to Lincoln Co. for services provided on account, $5,410.
    15. Issued Invoice No. 122 to Triple A Inc. for services provided on account, $2,360.
    21. Issued Invoice No. 123 to Bailey Co. for services provided on account, $4,140.

Record these three transactions into the following revenue journal format:

REVENUE JOURNAL

Date	Invoice No.	Account Debited	Post. Ref.	Accts. Rec. Dr. Fees Earned Cr.

PE 5-2A
Accounts receivable
subsidiary ledger
obj. 2

EE 5-2 p. 214

The debits and credits from two transactions are presented in the following customer account:

NAME   XTREME Products Inc.
ADDRESS 46 W. Main St.

Date	Item	Post. Ref.	Debit	Credit	Balance
Mar. 1	Balance	✓			1,200
10	Invoice 127	R29	920		2,120
19	Invoice 106	CR52		690	1,430

Describe each transaction and the source of each posting.

PE 5-2B
Accounts receivable
subsidiary ledger
obj. 2

EE 5-2 p. 214

The debits and credits from two transactions are presented in the following customer account:

NAME   Airwave Communications Inc.
ADDRESS 76 Oak Ridge Rd.

Date	Item	Post. Ref.	Debit	Credit	Balance
May 1	Balance	✓			280
14	Invoice 564	CR92		125	155
22	Invoice 527	R127	90		245

Describe each transaction and the source of each posting.

PE 5-3A
Purchases journal
obj. 2

EE 5-3 p. 216

The following purchase transactions occurred during October for Rehoboth Inc.:

Oct. 4. Purchased office supplies for $105, on account from Office-to-Go Inc.
16. Purchased office equipment for $2,460, on account from Zell Computer Inc.
23. Purchased office supplies for $190, on account from Office Mate Inc.

Record these transactions in the following purchases journal format:

PURCHASES JOURNAL

Date	Account Credited	Post. Ref.	Accounts Payable Cr.	Office Supplies Dr.	Other Accounts Dr.	Post. Ref.	Amount

PE 5-3B
Purchases journal
obj. 2

EE 5-3 p. 216

The following purchase transactions occurred during May for Amy's Catering Service:

May 11. Purchased party supplies for $420, on account from Party Zone Supplies Inc.
19. Purchased party supplies for $290, on account from Party Time Supplies Inc.
21. Purchased office furniture for $2,160, on account from Office Space Inc.

Record these transactions in the following purchases journal format:

PURCHASES JOURNAL

Date	Account Credited	Post. Ref.	Accounts Payable Cr.	Party Supplies Dr.	Other Accounts Dr.	Post. Ref.	Amount

PE 5-4A
Accounts payable
subsidiary ledger
obj. 2

EE 5-4 p. 220

The debits and credits from two transactions are presented in the following supplier's (creditor's) account:

NAME   Carnation Inc.
ADDRESS 5000 Grand Ave.

Date	Item	Post. Ref.	Debit	Credit	Balance
Nov. 1	Balance				92
11	Invoice 128	CP71	47		45
18	Invoice 139	P43		88	133

Describe each transaction and the source of each posting.

PE 5-4B
Accounts payable
subsidiary ledger

obj. 2

EE 5-4   p. 220

The debits and credits from two transactions are presented in the following supplier's (creditor's) account:

NAME   *Da Vinci Computer Services Inc.*
ADDRESS   *2199 Technology Avenue*

Date		Item	Post. Ref.	Debit	Credit	Balance
July	1	Balance				9,400
	19	Invoice 75	P21		3,520	12,920
	21	Invoice 43	CP46	5,960		6,960

Describe each transaction and the source of each posting.

PE 5-5A
Modified revenue
journal

obj. 3

EE 5-5   p. 221

The state of Ohio has a 5.5% sales tax. Buckeye Services Inc., an Ohio company, had two revenue transactions as follows:

Aug.   7.   Issued Invoice No. 121 to Manly Inc. for services provided on account, $1,200, plus sales tax.
        21.   Issued Invoice No. 122 to Tel Optics Inc. for services provided on account, $2,200, plus sales tax.

Record these transactions in a revenue journal using the following format:

REVENUE JOURNAL

Date	Invoice No.	Account Debited	Post. Ref.	Accts. Rec. Dr.	Fees Earned Cr.	Sales Tax Payable Cr.

PE 5-5B
Modified revenue
journal

obj. 3

EE 5-5   p. 221

Armor Security Services Inc. provides both commercial and residential security services on account. Two transactions are identified below.

Dec.   1.   Issued Invoice No. 862 to Matrix Inc. for security services provided on account, $425.
        3.   Issued Invoice No. 863 to James Lawhorn, a residential customer, for services provided on account, $85.

Record these transactions in a revenue journal using the following format:

REVENUE JOURNAL

Date	Invoice No.	Account Debited	Post. Ref.	Accts. Rec. Dr.	Fees Earned— Commercial Cr.	Fees Earned— Residential Cr.

Exercises

EX 5-1
Identify postings
from revenue journal

obj. 2

Using the following revenue journal for Alpha Services Inc., identify each of the posting references, indicated by a letter, as representing (1) posting to general ledger accounts or (2) posting to subsidiary ledger accounts.

REVENUE JOURNAL

Date	Invoice No.	Account Debited	Post. Ref.	Accounts Rec. Dr. Fees Earned Cr.
2010				
Nov. 1	112	Environmental Safety Co.	(a)	$2,625
10	113	Jenkins Co.	(b)	1,050
18	114	Eco-Systems	(c)	1,600
27	115	TEK Corp.	(d)	965
30				$6,240
				(e)

EX 5-2
Accounts receivable ledger

obj. 2

✔ d. Total accounts receivable, $6,860

Based on the data presented in Exercise 5-1, assume that the beginning balances for the customer accounts were zero, except for TEK Corp., which had a $620 beginning balance. In addition, there were no collections during the period.

a. Set up a T account for Accounts Receivable and T accounts for the four accounts needed in the customer ledger.
b. Post to the T accounts.
c. Determine the balance in the accounts.
d. Prepare an accounts receivable subsidiary ledger at November 30, 2010.

EX 5-3
Identify journals

obj. 2

Assuming the use of a two-column (all-purpose) general journal, a revenue journal, and a cash receipts journal as illustrated in this chapter, indicate the journal in which each of the following transactions should be recorded:

a. Receipt of cash from sale of office equipment.
b. Sale of office supplies on account, at cost, to a neighboring business.
c. Providing services for cash.
d. Closing of drawing account at the end of the year.
e. Adjustment to record accrued salaries at the end of the year.
f. Receipt of cash refund from overpayment of taxes.
g. Receipt of cash on account from a customer.
h. Receipt of cash for rent.
i. Investment of additional cash in the business by the owner.
j. Providing services on account.

EX 5-4
Identify journals

obj. 2

Assuming the use of a two-column (all-purpose) general journal, a purchases journal, and a cash payments journal as illustrated in this chapter, indicate the journal in which each of the following transactions should be recorded:

a. Payment of six months' rent in advance.
b. Adjustment to record depreciation at the end of the month.
c. Adjustment to prepaid insurance at the end of the month.
d. Purchase of office equipment for cash.
e. Advance payment of a one-year fire insurance policy on the office.
f. Purchase of office supplies for cash.
g. Adjustment to record accrued salaries at the end of the period.
h. Adjustment to prepaid rent at the end of the month.
i. Purchase of office supplies on account.
j. Purchase of services on account.
k. Purchase of an office computer on account.

EX 5-5
Identify transactions in accounts receivable ledger

obj. 2

The debits and credits from three related transactions are presented in the following customer's account taken from the accounts receivable subsidiary ledger.

NAME   *Insite Design*
ADDRESS   *1319 Elm Street*

Date	Item	Post. Ref.	Debit	Credit	Balance
2010					
Nov. 3		R36	740		740
6		J11		80	660
13		CR47		660	—

Describe each transaction, and identify the source of each posting.

EX 5-6
Prepare journal
entries in a revenue
journal

obj. 2

Patton Services Company had the following transactions during the month of June:

June 2. Issued Invoice No. 201 to Thomas Corp. for services rendered on account, $290.
3. Issued Invoice No. 202 to Mid States Inc. for services rendered on account, $410.
12. Issued Invoice No. 203 to Thomas Corp. for services rendered on account, $145.
22. Issued Invoice No. 204 to Parker Co. for services rendered on account, $605.
28. Collected Invoice No. 201 from Thomas Corp.

a. Prepare a revenue journal with the following headings to record the June revenue transactions for Patton Services Company.

REVENUE JOURNAL

Date	Invoice No.	Account Debited	Post. Ref.	Accts. Rec. Dr. Fees Earned Cr.

b. What is the total amount posted to the accounts receivable control and fees earned accounts from the revenue journal for June?
c. What is the June 30 balance of the Thomas Corp. customer account assuming a zero balance on June 1?

EX 5-7
Posting a revenue
journal

obj. 2

The revenue journal for Hi Performance Consulting Inc. is shown below. The accounts receivable control account has a February 1, 2010, balance of $1,050 consisting of an amount due from Arnott Co. There were no collections during February.

REVENUE JOURNAL   Page *12*

Date	Invoice No.	Account Debited	Post. Ref.	Accts. Rec. Dr. Fees Earned Cr.
2010				
Feb. 4	355	Brown Co.		2,430
9	356	Life Star Inc.		3,640
16	357	Arnott Co.		1,710
22	359	Brown Co.		2,650
				10,430

a. Prepare a T account for the accounts receivable customer accounts.
b. Post the transactions from the revenue journal to the customer accounts, and determine their ending balances.
c. Prepare T accounts for the accounts receivable control and fees earned accounts. Post control totals to the two accounts, and determine the ending balances.
d. Verify the equality of the sum of the customer account balances and the accounts receivable control account balance.

EX 5-8
Accounts receivable
subsidiary ledger

obj. 2

✔ Accounts
Receivable balance,
April 30, $5,740

The revenue and cash receipts journals for Eclipse Productions Inc. are shown below. The accounts receivable control account has an April 1, 2010, balance of $4,710, consisting of an amount due from Best Studios Inc.

REVENUE JOURNAL   Page *16*

Date	Invoice No.	Account Debited	Post. Ref.	Accts. Rec. Dr. Fees Earned Cr.
2010				
Apr. 6	1	Crown Broadcasting Co.	✓	1,400
14	2	Gold Coast Media Inc.	✓	5,500
22	3	Crown Broadcasting Co.	✓	2,450
27	4	Best Studios Inc.	✓	1,250
28	5	Alpha Communications Inc.	✓	2,040
30				12,640
				(12) (41)

CASH RECEIPTS JOURNAL					Page *36*
Date	Account Credited	Post. Ref.	Fees Earned Cr.	Accts. Rec. Cr.	Cash Dr.
2010					
Apr. 6	Best Studios Inc.	✓	—	4,710	4,710
11	Fees Earned		3,200		3,200
18	Crown Broadcasting Co.	✓	—	1,400	1,400
28	Gold Coast Media Inc..	✓	—	5,500	5,500
30			3,200	11,610	14,810
			(41)	(12)	(11)

Prepare the accounts receivable subsidiary ledger, and determine that the total agrees with the ending balance of the accounts receivable control account.

EX 5-9
Revenue and cash receipts journals

obj. 2

Transactions related to revenue and cash receipts completed by Tex Max Inc. during the month of March 2010 are as follows:

Mar. 2. Issued Invoice No. 512 to Browne Co., $820.
4. Received cash from CMI Inc., on account, for $195.
8. Issued Invoice No. 513 to Gabriel Co., $265.
12. Issued Invoice No. 514 to Deacon Inc., $690.
19. Received cash from Deacon Inc., on account, $610.
22. Issued Invoice No. 515 to Electronic Central Inc., $150.
27. Received cash from Marshall Inc. for services provided, $90.
29. Received cash from Browne Co. for invoice of March 2.
31. Received cash from McCleary Co. for services provided, $75.

Prepare a single-column revenue journal and a cash receipts journal to record these transactions. Use the following column headings for the cash receipts journal: Fees Earned Cr., Accounts Receivable Cr., and Cash Dr. Place a check mark (✓) in the Post. Ref. column to indicate when the accounts receivable subsidiary ledger should be posted.

EX 5-10
Revenue and cash receipts journals

obj. 2

✔ Revenue journal total, $10,660

Leo Corp. has $2,050 in the October 1 balance of the accounts receivable account consisting of $940 from Charles Co. and $1,110 from Tower Co. Transactions related to revenue and cash receipts completed by Leo Corp. during the month of October 2010 are as follows:

Oct. 3. Issued Invoice No. 622 for services provided to Phillips Corp., $2,150.
5. Received cash from Charles Co., on account, for $940.
10. Issued Invoice No. 623 for services provided to Sunstream Aviation Inc., $3,720.
15. Received cash from Tower Co., on account, for $1,110.
18. Issued Invoice No. 624 for services provided to Amex Services Inc., $2,600.
23. Received cash from Phillips Corp. for Invoice No. 622.
28. Issued Invoice No. 625 to Tower Co., on account, for $2,190.
30. Received cash from Rogers Co. for services provided, $90.

a. Prepare a single-column revenue journal and a cash receipts journal to record these transactions. Use the following column headings for the cash receipts journal: Fees Earned Cr., Accounts Receivable Cr., and Cash Dr. Place a check mark (✓) in the Post. Ref. column to indicate when the accounts receivable subsidiary ledger should be posted.

b. Prepare an accounts receivable subsidiary ledger on October 31, 2010. Verify that the total of the accounts receivable subsidiary ledger equals the balance of the accounts receivable control account on October 31, 2010.

EX 5-11
Identify postings from purchases journal
obj. 2

Using the following purchases journal, identify each of the posting references, indicated by a letter, as representing (1) a posting to a general ledger account, (2) a posting to a subsidiary ledger account, or (3) that no posting is required.

PURCHASES JOURNAL   Page *49*

Date	Account Credited	Post. Ref.	Accounts Payable Cr.	Store Supplies Dr.	Office Supplies Dr.	Other Accounts Dr.	Post. Ref.	Amount
2010								
Sept. 4	Amex Supply Co.	(a)	4,000		4,000			
6	Coastal Equipment Co.	(b)	5,325			Warehouse Equipment	(c)	5,325
11	Office Warehouse	(d)	2,000			Office Equipment	(e)	2,000
13	Taylor Products	(f)	1,875	1,600	275			
20	Office Warehouse	(g)	6,000			Store Equipment	(h)	6,000
27	Miller Supply Co.	(i)	2,740	2,740				
30			21,940	4,340	4,275			13,325
			(j)	(k)	(l)			(m)

EX 5-12
Identify postings from cash payments journal
obj. 2

Using the following cash payments journal, identify each of the posting references, indicated by a letter, as representing (1) a posting to a general ledger account, (2) a posting to a subsidiary ledger account, or (3) that no posting is required.

CASH PAYMENTS JOURNAL   Page *46*

Date	Ck. No.	Account Debited	Post. Ref.	Other Accounts Dr.	Accounts Payable Dr.	Cash Cr.
2010						
Jan. 3	611	Aquatic Systems Co.	(a)		4,000	4,000
5	612	Utilities Expense	(b)	310		310
10	613	Prepaid Rent	(c)	3,200		3,200
17	614	Advertising Expense	(d)	640		640
20	615	Flowers to Go, Inc.	(e)		1,250	1,250
22	616	Office Equipment	(f)	3,600		3,600
25	617	Office Supplies	(g)	250		250
27	618	Evans Co.	(h)		5,500	5,500
31	619	Salaries Expense	(i)	1,750		1,750
31				9,750	10,750	20,500
				(j)	(k)	(l)

EX 5-13
Identify transactions in accounts payable ledger account
obj. 2

The debits and credits from three related transactions are presented in the following creditor's account taken from the accounts payable ledger.

NAME   *Madison Co.*
ADDRESS *101 W. Stratford Ave.*

Date	Item	Post. Ref.	Debit	Credit	Balance
2010					
Oct. 6		P39		11,900	11,900
11		J12	300		11,600
16		CP56	11,600		—

Describe each transaction, and identify the source of each posting.

EX 5-14
Prepare journal entries in a purchases journal
obj. 2

Shield Security Company had the following transactions during the month of November:

Nov. 4.   Purchased office supplies from Office Universe Inc. on account, $480.

8.   Purchased office equipment on account from Best Equipment, Inc., $1,900.

Nov. 12. Purchased office supplies from Office Universe Inc. on account, $130.
21. Purchased office supplies from Paper-to-Go Inc. on account, $195.
27. Paid invoice on November 4 purchase from Office Universe Inc.

a. Prepare a purchases journal with the following headings to record the November purchase transactions for Shield Security Company.

PURCHASES JOURNAL

Date	Account Credited	Post. Ref.	Accts. Payable Cr.	Office Supplies Dr.	Other Accounts Dr.	Post. Ref.	Amount

b. What is the total amount posted to the accounts payable control and office supplies accounts from the purchases journal for November?
c. What is the November 30 balance of the Office Universe Inc. creditor account assuming a zero balance on November 1?

EX 5-15
Posting a purchases journal
obj. 2

✔ d. Total, $3,650

The purchases journal for See-Thru Window Cleaners Inc. is shown below. The accounts payable control account has a January 1, 2010, balance of $295 of an amount due from Lawson Co. There were no payments made on creditor invoices during January.

PURCHASES JOURNAL — Page 16

Date	Account Credited	Post. Ref.	Accts. Payable Cr.	Cleaning Supplies Dr.	Other Accounts Dr.	Post. Ref.	Amount
2010							
Jan. 4	Crystal Cleaning Supplies Inc.		375	375			
15	Lawson Co.		250	250			
21	Office Mate Inc.		2,400		Office Equipment		2,400
26	Crystal Cleaning Supplies Inc.		330	330			
31			3,355	955			2,400

a. Prepare a T account for the accounts payable creditor accounts.
b. Post the transactions from the purchases journal to the creditor accounts, and determine their ending balances.
c. Prepare T accounts for the accounts payable control and cleaning supplies accounts. Post control totals to the two accounts, and determine their ending balances.
d. Verify the equality of the sum of the creditor account balances and the accounts payable control account balance.

EX 5-16
Accounts payable subsidiary ledger

✔ Accts. Pay., April 30, $11,905

The cash payments and purchases journals for Natural Creation Landscaping Co. are shown below. The accounts payable control account has an April 1, 2010, balance of $3,140, consisting of an amount owed to Augusta Sod Co.

CASH PAYMENTS JOURNAL — Page 31

Date	Ck. No.	Account Debited	Post. Ref.	Other Accounts Dr.	Accounts Payable Dr.	Cash Cr.
2010						
Apr. 4	203	Augusta Sod Co.	✓		3,140	3,140
5	204	Utilities Expense	54	410		410
15	205	Kimble Lumber Co.	✓		5,135	5,135
27	206	Schott's Fertilizer	✓		910	910
30				410	9,185	9,595
				(✓)	(21)	(11)

			PURCHASES JOURNAL				Page *22*	
Date	Account Credited	Post. Ref.	Accounts Payable Cr.	Landscaping Supplies Dr.	Other Accounts Dr	Post. Ref.	Amount	
2010								
Apr. 3	Kimble Lumber Co.	✓	5,135	5,135				
7	Cooke Equipment Co.	✓	2,400		Equipment	18	2,400	
14	Schott's Fertilizer	✓	910	910				
24	Augusta Sod Co.	✓	6,310	6,310				
29	Kimble Lumber Co.	✓	3,195	3,195				
30			17,950	15,550			2,400	
			(21)	(14)			(✓)	

Prepare the accounts payable subsidiary ledger, and determine that the total agrees with the ending balance of the accounts payable control account.

EX 5-17
Purchases and cash payments journals

obj. 2

✔ Purchases journal, Accts. Pay., Total, $710

Transactions related to purchases and cash payments completed by Lake County Cleaning Services Inc. during the month of May 2010 are as follows:

May 1. Issued Check No. 57 to Liquid Klean Supplies Inc. in payment of account, $235.

3. Purchased cleaning supplies on account from Industrial Products Inc., $140.

8. Issued Check No. 58 to purchase equipment from Jefferson Equipment Sales, $2,400.

12. Purchased cleaning supplies on account from Porter Products Inc., $205.

15. Issued Check No. 59 to Maryville Laundry Service in payment of account, $120.

17. Purchased supplies on account from Liquid Klean Supplies Inc., $265.

20. Purchased laundry services from Maryville Laundry Service on account, $100.

25. Issued Check No. 60 to Industrial Products Inc. in payment of May 3 invoice.

31. Issued Check No. 61 in payment of salaries, $4,600.

Prepare a purchases journal and a cash payments journal to record these transactions. The forms of the journals are similar to those illustrated in the text. Place a check mark (✓) in the Post. Ref. column to indicate when the accounts payable subsidiary ledger should be posted. Lake County Cleaning Services Inc. uses the following accounts:

Cleaning Supplies	14
Equipment	18
Salary Expense	51
Laundry Service Expense	53

EX 5-18
Purchases and cash payments journals

obj. 2

Happy Tails Inc. has $615 in the December 1 balance of the accounts payable control account. Transactions related to purchases and cash payments completed by Happy Tails Inc. during the month of December 2010 are as follows:

Dec. 4. Purchased pet supplies from Best Friend Supplies Inc. on account, $250.

6. Issued Check No. 345 to Larrimore Inc. in payment of account, $405.

11. Purchased pet supplies from Poodle Pals Inc., $660.

18. Issued Check No. 346 to Pets Mart Inc. in payment of account, $210.

19. Purchased office equipment from Office Helper Inc. on account, $2,000.

23. Issued Check No. 347 to Best Friend Supplies Inc. in payment of account from purchase made on December 4.

27. Purchased pet supplies from Pets Mart Inc. on account, $380.

30. Issued Check No. 348 to Sanders Inc. for cleaning expenses, $50.

a. Prepare a purchases journal and a cash payments journal to record these transactions. The forms of the journals are similar to those used in the text. Place a check mark (✓) in the Post. Ref. column to indicate when the accounts payable subsidiary ledger should be posted. Happy Tails Inc. uses the following accounts:

Office Equipment	13
Pet Supplies	14
Cleaning Expense	54

b. Prepare an accounts payable subsidiary ledger on December 31, 2010. Verify that the total of the accounts payable subsidiary ledger equals the balance of the accounts payable control account on December 31, 2010.

EX 5-19
Error in accounts payable ledger and accounts payable subsidiary ledger

obj. 2

After Sierra Assay Services Inc. had completed all postings for July in the current year (2010), the sum of the balances in the following accounts payable ledger did not agree with the $36,950 balance of the controlling account in the general ledger.

NAME   C. D. Greer and Son
ADDRESS   972 S. Tenth Street

Date	Item	Post. Ref.	Debit	Credit	Balance
2010					
July 17		P30		3,750	3,750
27		P31		10,000	13,750

NAME   Cheyenne Minerals Inc.
ADDRESS   1170 Mattis Avenue

Date	Item	Post. Ref.	Debit	Credit	Balance
2010					
July 1	Balance	✓			8,300
7		P30		5,800	14,200
12		J7	300		13,900
20		CP23	5,800		8,100

NAME   Cutler and Powell
ADDRESS   717 Elm Street

Date	Item	Post. Ref.	Debit	Credit	Balance
2010					
July 1	Balance	✓			6,100
18		CP23	6,100		—
29		P31		9,100	9,100

NAME   Perez Mining Co.
ADDRESS   1240 W. Main Street

Date	Item	Post. Ref.	Debit	Credit	Balance
2010					
July 1	Balance	✓			4,750
10		CP22	4,750		—
17		P30		3,700	3,700
27		J7	750		1,950

NAME   Valley Power
ADDRESS   915 E. Walnut Street

Date	Item	Post. Ref.	Debit	Credit	Balance
2010					
July 5		P30		3,150	3,150

Assuming that the controlling account balance of $36,950 has been verified as correct, (a) determine the error(s) in the preceding accounts and (b) prepare an accounts payable subsidiary ledger report (from the corrected accounts payable subsidiary ledger.

EX 5-20
Identify postings from special journals

obj. 2

Total Solutions Consulting Company makes most of its sales and purchases on credit. It uses the five journals described in this chapter (revenue, cash receipts, purchases, cash payments, and general journals). Identify the journal most likely used in recording the postings for selected transactions indicated by letter in the T accounts on the following page:

Cash		
a.	11,190	b.	6,500

Prepaid Rent		
		c.	400

Account Receivable		
d.	12,410	e.	11,190

Accounts Payable		
f.		6,500	g.	7,600

Office Supplies	
h.	7,600	

Fees Earned	
		i.	12,410

Rent Expense	
j.	400	

EX 5-21
Cash receipts journal
obj. 2

The following cash receipts journal headings have been suggested for a small service firm. List the errors you find in the headings.

						Page *12*
CASH RECEIPTS JOURNAL						
Date	Account Credited	Post. Ref.	Fees Earned Cr.	Accts. Rec. Cr.	Cash Cr.	Other Accounts Dr.

EX 5-22
Modified special journals
objs. 2, 3

✔ c. 2. $1,113

Steinway Technical Services Inc. was established on June 15, 2010. The clients for whom Steinway provided technical services during the remainder of June are listed below. These clients pay Steinway the amount indicated plus a 5% sales tax.

June 16. Issued Invoice No. 1 to A. Sommerfeld for $360 plus tax on account.
     19. Issued Invoice No. 2 to R. Mendoza for $160 plus tax.
     21. Issued Invoice No. 3 to J. Knight for $80 plus tax.
     22. Issued Invoice No. 4 to D. Jeffries for $140 plus tax.
     24. Provided services to K. Sallinger, in exchange for office supplies having a value of $100, plus tax.
     26. Issued Invoice No. 5 to J. Knight for $260 plus tax.
     28. Issued Invoice No. 6 to R. Mendoza for $60 plus tax.

a. Journalize the transactions for June, using a three-column revenue journal and a two-column general journal. Post the customer accounts in the accounts receivable subsidiary ledger, and insert the balance immediately after recording each entry.
b. Post the general journal and the revenue journal to the following general ledger accounts, inserting account balances only after the last postings:

     12   Accounts Receivable
     14   Office Supplies
     22   Sales Tax Payable
     41   Fees Earned

c. 1. What is the sum of the balances in the accounts receivable subsidiary ledger at June 30?
   2. What is the balance of the controlling account at June 30?

EX 5-23
Computerized accounting systems
obj. 4

Most computerized accounting systems use electronic forms to record transaction information, such as the invoice form illustrated at the top of Exhibit 7.

a. Identify the key input fields (spaces) in an electronic invoice form.
b. What accounts are posted from an electronic invoice form?
c. Why aren't special journal totals posted to control accounts at the end of the month in an electronic accounting system?

EX 5-24
E-commerce

obj. 5

For each of the following companies, determine if their e-commerce strategy is primarily business-to-consumer (B2C), business-to-business (B2B), or both. Use the Internet to investigate each company's site in conducting your research.

a. Amazon.com
b. Dell Inc.
c. W.W. Grainger, Inc.
d. L.L. Bean, Inc.
e. Smurfit-Stone Container Corporation
f. Intuit Inc.

EX 5-25
Segment revenue
analysis

obj. 5

Starbucks Corporation reported the following geographical segment revenues for fiscal years 2007 and 2006:

	2007 (in millions)	2006 (in millions)
United States	$7,679	$6,478
Other countries	1,733	1,309
Total revenues	$9,412	$7,787

a. Prepare a horizontal analysis of the segment data using 2006 as the base year.
b. Prepare a vertical analysis of the segment data.
c. What conclusions can be drawn from your analyses?

EX 5-26
Segment revenue
analysis

obj. 7

News Corporation is one of the world's largest entertainment companies that includes Twentieth Century Fox films, Fox Broadcasting, Fox News, the FX, and various satellite, cable, and publishing properties. The company provided revenue disclosures by its major product segments in the notes to its financial statements as follows:

Major Product Segments	For the Year Ended June 30, 2007 (in millions)
Filmed Entertainment	$ 6,734
Television	5,705
Cable Network Programming	3,902
Direct Broadcast Satellite Television	3,076
Magazines and Inserts	1,119
Newspapers	4,486
Book Publishing	1,347
Other	2,286
Total revenues	$28,655

a. Provide a vertical analysis of the product segment revenues.
b. Are the revenues of News Corporation diversified or concentrated within a product segment? Explain.

Problems Series A

PR 5-1A
Revenue journal;
accounts receivable
and general ledgers

obj. 2

Guardian Security Services was established on August 15, 2010, to provide security services. The services provided during the remainder of the month are listed below.

Aug. 18. Issued Invoice No. 1 to Jacob Co. for $325 on account.
      20. Issued Invoice No. 2 to Qwik-Mart Co. for $260 on account.
      22. Issued Invoice No. 3 to Hawke Co. for $545 on account.
      27. Issued Invoice No. 4 to Carson Co. for $450 on account.

Aug. 28. Issued Invoice No. 5 to Bower Co. for $100 on account.
     28. Provided security services, $80, to Qwik-Mart Co. in exchange for supplies.
     30. Issued Invoice No. 6 to Qwik-Mart Co. for $115 on account.
     31. Issued Invoice No. 7 to Hawke Co. for $230 on account.

Instructions

1. Journalize the transactions for August, using a single-column revenue journal and a two-column general journal. Post to the following customer accounts in the accounts receivable ledger, and insert the balance immediately after recording each entry: Bower Co.; Carson Co.; Hawke Co.; Jacob Co.; Qwik-Mart Co.
2. Post the revenue journal to the following accounts in the general ledger, inserting the account balances only after the last postings:

12	Accounts Receivable
14	Supplies
41	Fees Earned

3. a. What is the sum of the balances of the accounts in the subsidiary ledger at August 31?
   b. What is the balance of the controlling account at August 31?
4. Assume that on September 1, the state in which Guardian operates begins requiring that sales tax be collected on accounting services. Briefly explain how the revenue journal may be modified to accommodate sales of services on account requiring the collection of a state sales tax.

PR 5-2A
Revenue and cash receipts journals; accounts receivable and general ledgers

obj. 2

Transactions related to revenue and cash receipts completed by Sterling Engineering Services during the period November 2–30, 2010, are as follows:

Nov. 2. Issued Invoice No. 717 to Yee Co., $810.
     3. Received cash from AGI Co. for the balance owed on its account.
     7. Issued Invoice No. 718 to Phoenix Development Co., $400.
   10. Issued Invoice No. 719 to Ridge Communities, $1,940.
        Post revenue and collections to the accounts receivable subsidiary ledger.
   14. Received cash from Phoenix Development Co. for the balance owed on November 1.
   16. Issued Invoice No. 720 to Phoenix Development Co., $275.
        Post revenue and collections to the accounts receivable subsidiary ledger.
   19. Received cash from Yee Co. for the balance due on invoice of November 2.
   20. Received cash from Phoenix Development Co. for invoice of November 7.
   23. Issued Invoice No. 721 to AGI Co., $670.
   30. Recorded cash fees earned, $3,400.
   30. Received office equipment of $1,500 in partial settlement of balance due on the Ridge Communities account.
        Post revenue and collections to the accounts receivable subsidiary ledger.

Instructions

1. Insert the following balances in the general ledger as of November 1:

11	Cash	$17,240
12	Accounts Receivable	2,020
18	Office Equipment	31,500
41	Fees Earned	—

2. Insert the following balances in the accounts receivable subsidiary ledger as of November 1:

AGI Co.	$1,340
Phoenix Development Co.	680
Ridge Communities	—
Yee Co.	—

3. Prepare a single-column revenue journal and a cash receipts journal. Use the following column headings for the cash receipts journal: Fees Earned Cr., Accounts Receivable Cr., and Cash Dr. The Fees Earned column is used to record cash fees. Insert a check mark (✓) in the Post. Ref. column.
4. Using the two special journals and the two-column general journal, journalize the transactions for November. Post to the accounts receivable subsidiary ledger, and insert the balances at the points indicated in the narrative of transactions. Determine the balance in the customer's account before recording a cash receipt.
5. Total each of the columns of the special journals, and post the individual entries and totals to the general ledger. Insert account balances after the last posting.
6. Determine that the subsidiary ledger agrees with the controlling account in the general ledger.

PR 5-3A

Purchases, accounts payable account, and accounts payable ledger

objs. 2, 3

✔ 3. Total accounts payable credit, $20,950

GW Surveyors provides survey work for construction projects. The office staff use office supplies, while surveying crews use field supplies. Purchases on account completed by GW Surveyors during October 2010 are as follows:

Oct. 1. Purchased field supplies on account from Wendell Co., $2,505.
 3. Purchased office supplies on account from Lassiter Co., $260.
 8. Purchased field supplies on account from Sure Measure Supplies, $3,600.
 12. Purchased field supplies on account from Wendell Co., $2,850.
 15. Purchased office supplies on account from J-Mart Co., $375.
 19. Purchased office equipment on account from Eskew Co., $6,780.
 23. Purchased field supplies on account from Sure Measure Supplies, $1,910.
 26. Purchased office supplies on account from J-Mart Co., $170.
 30. Purchased field supplies on account from Sure Measure Supplies, $2,500.

Instructions
1. Insert the following balances in the general ledger as of October 1:

14	Field Supplies	$ 5,100
15	Office Supplies	1,170
18	Office Equipment	17,200
21	Accounts Payable	4,375

2. Insert the following balances in the accounts payable subsidiary ledger as of October 1:

Eskew Co.	$3,400
J-Mart Co.	580
Lassiter Co.	395
Sure Measure Supplies	—
Wendell Co.	—

3. Journalize the transactions for October, using a purchases journal similar to the one illustrated in this chapter. Prepare the purchases journal with columns for Accounts Payable, Field Supplies, Office Supplies, and Other Accounts. Post to the creditor accounts in the accounts payable ledger immediately after each entry.
4. Post the purchases journal to the accounts in the general ledger.
5. a. What is the sum of the balances in the subsidiary ledger at October 31?
   b. What is the balance of the controlling account at October 31?

PR 5-4A

Purchases and cash payments journals; accounts payable and general ledgers

objs. 2, 3

Black Gold Tea Exploration Co. was established on March 15, 2010, to provide oil-drilling services. Black Gold Tea uses field equipment (rigs and pipe) and field supplies (drill bits and lubricants) in its operations. Transactions related to purchases and cash payments during the remainder of March are as follows:

Mar. 16. Issued Check No. 1 in payment of rent for the remainder of March, $5,000.
 16. Purchased field equipment on account from PMI Sales Inc., $29,400.
 17. Purchased field supplies on account from Culver Supply Co., $9,320.

Mar. 18. Issued Check No. 2 in payment of field supplies, $2,180, and office supplies, $450.
20. Purchased office supplies on account from A-One Office Supply Co., $1,110. *Post the journals to the accounts payable subsidiary ledger.*
24. Issued Check No. 3 to PMI Sales Inc., in payment of March 16 invoice.
26. Issued Check No. 4 to Culver Supply Co. in payment of March 17 invoice.
28. Issued Check No. 5 to purchase land, $170,000.
28. Purchased office supplies on account from A-One Office Supply Co., $2,670. *Post the journals to the accounts payable subsidiary ledger.*
30. Purchased the following from PMI Sales Inc. on account: field supplies, $22,340 and office equipment, $12,200.
30. Issued Check No. 6 to A-One Office Supply Co. in payment of March 20 invoice.
30. Purchased field supplies on account from Culver Supply Co., $11,900.
31. Issued Check No. 7 in payment of salaries, $26,000.
31. Rented building for one year in exchange for field equipment having a cost of $12,000.
Post the journals to the accounts payable subsidiary ledger.

Instructions.
1. Journalize the transactions for March. Use a purchases journal and a cash payments journal, similar to those illustrated in this chapter, and a two-column general journal. Set debit columns for Field Supplies, Office Supplies, and Other Accounts in the purchases journal. Refer to the following partial chart of accounts:

11	Cash	18	Office Equipment
14	Field Supplies	19	Land
15	Office Supplies	21	Accounts Payable
16	Prepaid Rent	61	Salary Expense
17	Field Equipment	71	Rent Expense

At the points indicated in the narrative of transactions, post to the following accounts in the accounts payable ledger:

A-One Office Supply Co.
Culver Supply Co.
PMI Sales Inc.

2. Post the individual entries (Other Accounts columns of the purchases journal and the cash payments journal; both columns of the general journal) to the appropriate general ledger accounts.
3. Total each of the columns of the purchases journal and the cash payments journal, and post the appropriate totals to the general ledger. (Because the problem does not include transactions related to cash receipts, the cash account in the ledger will have a credit balance.)
4. Prepare an accounts payable subsidiary ledger.

PR 5-5A
All journals and general ledger; trial balance

obj. 2

The transactions completed by Over-Nite Express Company during May 2010, the first month of the fiscal year, were as follows:

May 1. Issued Check No. 205 for May rent, $1,000.
2. Purchased a vehicle on account from McIntyre Sales Co., $22,300.
3. Purchased office equipment on account from Office Mate Inc., $520.
5. Issued Invoice No. 91 to Martin Co., $5,200.
6. Received check for $5,610 from Baker Co. in payment of invoice.
7. Issued Invoice No. 92 to Trent Co., $8,150.
9. Issued Check No. 206 for fuel expense, $670.
10. Received check for $8,920 from Sanchez Co. in payment of invoice.
10. Issued Check No. 207 to Office City in payment of $490 invoice.

May 10. Issued Check No. 208 to Bastille Co. in payment of $1,350 invoice.
11. Issued Invoice No. 93 to Jarvis Co., $6,540.
11. Issued Check No. 209 to Porter Co. in payment of $325 invoice.
12. Received check for $5,200 from Martin Co. in payment of invoice.
13. Issued Check No. 210 to McIntyre Sales Co. in payment of $22,300 invoice.
16. Cash fees earned for May 1–16, $18,900.
16. Issued Check No. 211 for purchase of a vehicle, $22,400.
17. Issued Check No. 212 for miscellaneous administrative expense, $4,100.
18. Purchased maintenance supplies on account from Bastille Co., $1,680.
18. Received check for rent revenue on office space, $2,000.
19. Purchased the following on account from Master Supply Co.: maintenance supplies, $1,950, and office supplies, $2,050.
20. Issued Check No. 213 in payment of advertising expense, $7,250.
20. Used maintenance supplies with a cost of $2,400 to repair vehicles.
21. Purchased office supplies on account from Office City, $710.
24. Issued Invoice No. 94 to Sanchez Co., $7,890.
25. Received check for $11,900 from Baker Co. in payment of invoice.
25. Issued Invoice No. 95 to Trent Co., $5,030.
26. Issued Check No. 214 to Office Mate Inc. in payment of $520 invoice.
27. Issued Check No. 215 to J. Li as a personal withdrawal, $3,240.
30. Issued Check No. 216 in payment of driver salaries, $27,690.
31. Issued Check No. 217 in payment of office salaries, $18,600.
31. Issued Check No. 218 for office supplies, $450.
31. Cash fees earned for May 17–31, $20,700.

Instructions

1. Enter the following account balances in the general ledger as of May 1:

11	Cash	$ 61,300	32	J. Li, Drawing	—
12	Accounts Receivable	26,430	41	Fees Earned	—
14	Maintenance Supplies	6,580	42	Rent Revenue	—
15	Office Supplies	3,150	51	Driver Salaries Expense	—
16	Office Equipment	15,390	52	Maintenance Supplies Expense	—
17	Accum. Depr.—Office Equip.	3,450	53	Fuel Expense	—
18	Vehicles	57,000	61	Office Salaries Expense	—
19	Accum. Depr.—Vehicles	15,460	62	Rent Expense	—
21	Accounts Payable	2,165	63	Advertising Expense	—
31	J. Li, Capital	148,775	64	Miscellaneous Administrative Exp.	—

2. Journalize the transactions for May 2010, using the following journals similar to those illustrated in this chapter: single-column revenue journal, cash receipts journal, purchases journal (with columns for Accounts Payable, Maintenance Supplies, Office Supplies, and Other Accounts), cash payments journal, and two-column general journal. Assume that the daily postings to the individual accounts in the accounts payable ledger and the accounts receivable ledger have been made.

3. Post the appropriate individual entries to the general ledger.

4. Total each of the columns of the special journals, and post the appropriate totals to the general ledger; insert the account balances.

5. Prepare a trial balance.

6. Verify the agreement of each subsidiary ledger with its controlling account. The sum of the balances of the accounts in the subsidiary ledgers as of May 31 are as follows:

Accounts Receivable	$27,610
Accounts Payable	6,390

Problems Series B

PR 5-1B

**Revenue journal;
accounts receivable
and general ledgers**

obj. 2

✔ 1. Revenue
journal, total fees
earned, $960

Sage Learning Centers was established on January 20, 2010, to provide educational services. The services provided during the remainder of the month are as follows:

Jan. 21. Issued Invoice No. 1 to J. Dunlop for $75 on account.
22. Issued Invoice No. 2 to K. Todd for $280 on account.
24. Issued Invoice No. 3 to T. Morris for $65 on account.
25. Provided educational services, $100, to K. Todd in exchange for educational supplies.
27. Issued Invoice No. 4 to F. Mintz for $180 on account.
28. Issued Invoice No. 5 to D. Bennett for $155 on account.
30. Issued Invoice No. 6 to K. Todd for $120 on account.
31. Issued Invoice No. 7 to T. Morris for $85 on account.

Instructions

1. Journalize the transactions for January, using a single-column revenue journal and a two-column general journal. Post to the following customer accounts in the accounts receivable ledger, and insert the balance immediately after recording each entry: D. Bennett; J. Dunlop; F. Mintz; T. Morris; K. Todd.
2. Post the revenue journal and the general journal to the following accounts in the general ledger, inserting the account balances only after the last postings:

12	Accounts Receivable
13	Supplies
41	Fees Earned

3. a. What is the sum of the balances of the accounts in the subsidiary ledger at January 31?
   b. What is the balance of the controlling account at January 31?
4. Assume that on February 1, the state in which Sage operates begins requiring that sales tax be collected on educational services. Briefly explain how the revenue journal may be modified to accommodate sales of services on account that require the collection of a state sales tax.

PR 5-2B

**Revenue and cash
receipts journals;
accounts receivable
and general ledgers**

obj. 2

✔ 3. Total cash
receipts, $33,210

Transactions related to revenue and cash receipts completed by Bel-Aire Architects Co. during the period September 2–30, 2010, are as follows:

Sept. 2. Issued Invoice No. 793 to Morton Co., $5,200.
5. Received cash from Mendez Co. for the balance owed on its account.
6. Issued Invoice No. 794 to Pinnacle Co., $1,870.
13. Issued Invoice No. 795 to Shilo Co., $2,710.
   Post revenue and collections to the accounts receivable subsidiary ledger.
15. Received cash from Pinnacle Co. for the balance owed on September 1.
16. Issued Invoice No. 796 to Pinnacle Co., $6,000.
   Post revenue and collections to the accounts receivable subsidiary ledger.
19. Received cash from Morton Co. for the balance due on invoice of September 2.
20. Received cash from Pinnacle Co. for invoice of September 6.
22. Issued Invoice No. 797 to Mendez Co., $7,830.
25. Received $1,800 note receivable in partial settlement of the balance due on the Shilo Co. account.
30. Recorded cash fees earned, $11,570.
   Post revenue and collections to the accounts receivable subsidiary ledger.

Instructions

1. Insert the following balances in the general ledger as of September 1:

11	Cash	$12,970
12	Accounts Receivable	14,570
14	Notes Receivable	5,000
41	Fees Earned	—

2. Insert the following balances in the accounts receivable subsidiary ledger as of September 1:

Mendez Co.	8,420
Morton Co.	—
Pinnacle Co.	6,150
Shilo Co.	—

3. Prepare a single-column revenue journal and a cash receipts journal. Use the following column headings for the cash receipts journal: Fees Earned Cr., Accounts Receivable Cr., and Cash Dr. The Fees Earned column is used to record cash fees. Insert a check mark (✓) in the Post. Ref. column.
4. Using the two special journals and the two-column general journal, journalize the transactions for September. Post to the accounts receivable subsidiary ledger, and insert the balances at the points indicated in the narrative of transactions. Determine the balance in the customer's account before recording a cash receipt.
5. Total each of the columns of the special journals, and post the individual entries and totals to the general ledger. Insert account balances after the last posting.
6. Determine that the subsidiary ledger agrees with the controlling account in the general ledger.

PR 5-3B
Purchases, accounts payable account, and accounts payable ledger

objs. 2, 3

✔ 3. Total accounts payable credit, $17,415

Green Thumb Landscaping designs and installs landscaping. The landscape designers and office staff use office supplies, while field supplies (rock, bark, etc.) are used in the actual landscaping. Purchases on account completed by Green Thumb Landscaping during May 2010 are as follows:

May 2. Purchased office supplies on account from Lawson Co., $380.
    5. Purchased office equipment on account from Peach Computers Co., $5,340.
    9. Purchased office supplies on account from Executive Office Supply Co., $325.
  13. Purchased field supplies on account from Yamura Co., $1,390.
  14. Purchased field supplies on account from Nickle Co., $3,210.
  17. Purchased field supplies on account from Yamura Co., $1,445.
  24. Purchased field supplies on account from Nickle Co., $3,950.
  29. Purchased office supplies on account from Executive Office Supply Co., $275.
  31. Purchased field supplies on account from Nickle Co., $1,100.

Instructions

1. Insert the following balances in the general ledger as of May 1:

14	Field Supplies	$ 6,450
15	Office Supplies	890
18	Office Equipment	14,900
21	Accounts Payable	1,165

2. Insert the following balances in the accounts payable subsidiary ledger as of May 1:

Executive Office Supply Co.	$390
Lawson Co.	775
Nickle Co.	—
Peach Computers Co.	—
Yamura Co.	—

3. Journalize the transactions for May, using a purchases journal similar to the one illustrated in this chapter. Prepare the purchases journal with columns for Accounts Payable, Field Supplies, Office Supplies, and Other Accounts. Post to the creditor accounts in the accounts payable subsidiary ledger immediately after each entry.
4. Post the purchases journal to the accounts in the general ledger.
5. a. What is the sum of the balances in the subsidiary ledger at May 31?
   b. What is the balance of the controlling account at May 31?

PR 5-4B
Purchases and cash payments journals; accounts payable and general ledgers

objs. 2, 3

✔ 1. Total cash payments, $77,550

Tellico Springs Water Testing Service was established on September 16, 2010. Tellico uses field equipment and field supplies (chemicals and other supplies) to analyze water for unsafe contaminants in streams, lakes, and ponds. Transactions related to purchases and cash payments during the remainder of September are as follows:

Sept. 16. Issued Check No. 1 in payment of rent for the remainder of September, $1,400.
16. Purchased field supplies on account from Hydro Supply Co., $4,130.
16. Purchased field equipment on account from Test-Rite Equipment Co., $15,400.
17. Purchased office supplies on account from Baker Supply Co., $265.
19. Issued Check No. 2 in payment of field supplies, $2,380, and office supplies, $275.
Post the journals to the accounts payable subsidiary ledger.
23. Purchased office supplies on account from Baker Supply Co., $400.
23. Issued Check No. 3 to purchase land, $33,000.
24. Issued Check No. 4 to Hydro Supply Co. in payment of invoice, $4,130.
26. Issued Check No. 5 to Test-Rite Equipment Co. in payment of invoice, $15,400.
Post the journals to the accounts payable subsidiary ledger.
30. Acquired land in exchange for field equipment having a cost of $6,500.
30. Purchased field supplies on account from Hydro Supply Co., $5,100.
30. Issued Check No. 6 to Baker Supply Co. in payment of invoice, $265.
30. Purchased the following from Test-Rite Equipment Co. on account: field supplies, $700, and field equipment, $3,500.
30. Issued Check No. 7 in payment of salaries, $20,700.
Post the journals to the accounts payable subsidiary ledger.

Instructions
1. Journalize the transactions for September. Use a purchases journal and a cash payments journal, similar to those illustrated in this chapter, and a two-column general journal. Use debit columns for Field Supplies, Office Supplies, and Other Accounts in the purchases journal. Refer to the following partial chart of accounts:

11	Cash	19	Land
14	Field Supplies	21	Accounts Payable
15	Office Supplies	61	Salary Expense
17	Field Equipment	71	Rent Expense

At the points indicated in the narrative of transactions, post to the following accounts in the accounts payable subsidiary ledger:

Baker Supply Co.
Hydro Supply Co.
Test-Rite Equipment Co.

2. Post the individual entries (Other Accounts columns of the purchases journal and the cash payments journal and both columns of the general journal) to the appropriate general ledger accounts.
3. Total each of the columns of the purchases journal and the cash payments journal, and post the appropriate totals to the general ledger. (Because the problem does not include transactions related to cash receipts, the cash account in the ledger will have a credit balance.)
4. Prepare an accounts payable subsidiary ledger.

PR 5-5B
All journals and general ledger; trial balance

obj. 2

The transactions completed by Courtesy Courier Delivery Company during July 2010, the first month of the fiscal year, were as follows:

July 1. Issued Check No. 610 for July rent, $6,200.
2. Issued Invoice No. 940 to Capps Co., $2,340.
3. Received check for $5,150 from Perkins Co. in payment of account.
5. Purchased a vehicle on account from Browning Transportation, $30,200.

✔ 2. Total cash
receipts, $48,030

July 6. Purchased office equipment on account from Austin Computer Co., $4,100.
6. Issued Invoice No. 941 to Darr Co., $5,240.
9. Issued Check No. 611 for fuel expense, $810.
10. Received check from Sing Co. in payment of $3,720 invoice.
10. Issued Check No. 612 for $880 to Office To Go Inc. in payment of invoice.
10. Issued Invoice No. 942 to Joy Co., $1,210.
11. Issued Check No. 613 for $3,520 to Crowne Supply Co. in payment of account.
11. Issued Check No. 614 for $725 to Porter Co. in payment of account.
12. Received check from Capps Co. in payment of $2,340 invoice.
13. Issued Check No. 615 to Browning Transportation in payment of $30,200 balance.
16. Issued Check No. 616 for $37,300 for cash purchase of a vehicle.
16. Cash fees earned for July 1–16, $16,300.
17. Issued Check No. 617 for miscellaneous administrative expense, $245.
18. Purchased maintenance supplies on account from Crowne Supply Co., $1,630.
19. Purchased the following on account from McClain Co.: maintenance supplies, $1,820; office supplies, $430.
20. Issued Check No. 618 in payment of advertising expense, $1,625.
20. Used $3,000 maintenance supplies to repair delivery vehicles.
23. Purchased office supplies on account from Office To Go Inc., $500.
24. Issued Invoice No. 943 to Sing Co., $5,000.
24. Issued Check No. 619 to J. Bourne as a personal withdrawal, $2,500.
25. Issued Invoice No. 944 to Darr Co., $6,080.
25. Received check for $3,820 from Perkins Co. in payment of balance.
26. Issued Check No. 620 to Austin Computer Co. in payment of $4,100 invoice of July 6.
30. Issued Check No. 621 for monthly salaries as follows: driver salaries, $16,150; office salaries, $7,880.
31. Cash fees earned for July 17–31, $16,700.
31. Issued Check No. 622 in payment for office supplies, $750.

Instructions

1. Enter the following account balances in the general ledger as of July 1:

11	Cash	$155,300		32	J. Bourne, Drawing	—
12	Accounts Receivable	12,690		41	Fees Earned	—
14	Maintenance Supplies	9,150		51	Driver Salaries Expense	—
15	Office Supplies	4,200		52	Maintenance Supplies Exp.	—
16	Office Equipment	24,000		53	Fuel Expense	—
17	Accum. Depr.—Office Equip.	5,800		61	Office Salaries Expense	—
18	Vehicles	82,300		62	Rent Expense	—
19	Accum. Depr.—Vehicles	11,700		63	Advertising Expense	—
21	Accounts Payable	5,125		64	Miscellaneous Administrative Expense	—
31	J. Bourne, Capital	265,015				

2. Journalize the transactions for July 2010, using the following journals similar to those illustrated in this chapter: cash receipts journal, purchases journal (with columns for Accounts Payable, Maintenance Supplies, Office Supplies, and Other Accounts), single-column revenue journal, cash payments journal, and two-column general journal. Assume that the daily postings to the individual accounts in the accounts payable ledger and the accounts receivable ledger have been made.
3. Post the appropriate individual entries to the general ledger.
4. Total each of the columns of the special journals, and post the appropriate totals to the general ledger; insert the account balances.
5. Prepare a trial balance.
6. Verify the agreement of each subsidiary ledger with its control account. The sum of the balances of the accounts in the subsidiary ledgers as of July 31 are:

Accounts Receivable	$17,530
Accounts Payable	4,380

Special Activities

You can access the special activities online at **www.cengage.com/accounting/reeve**.

Answers to Self-Examination Questions

1. **A** Analysis (answer A) is the initial step of determining the informational needs and how the system provides this information. Design (answer B) is the step in which proposals for changes are developed. Implementation (answer C) is the final step involving carrying out or implementing the proposals for changes. Feedback (answer D) is not a separate step but is considered part of the systems implementation.

2. **A** The policies and procedures that are established to safeguard assets, ensure accurate business information, and ensure compliance with laws and regulations are called internal controls (answer A). The three steps in setting up an accounting system are (1) analysis (answer B), (2) design (answer C), and (3) implementation (answer D).

3. **B** All payments of cash for any purpose are recorded in the cash payments journal (answer B). Only purchases of services or other items on account are recorded in the purchases journal (answer A). All sales of services on account are recorded in the revenue journal (answer C), and all receipts of cash are recorded in the cash receipts journal (answer D).

4. **A** The general term used to describe the type of separate ledger that contains a large number of individual accounts with a common characteristic is a subsidiary ledger (answer A). The creditors ledger (answer B), sometimes called the accounts payable ledger (answer C), is a specific subsidiary ledger containing only individual accounts with creditors. Likewise, the accounts receivable ledger (answer D), also called the customers ledger, is a specific subsidiary ledger containing only individual accounts with customers.

5. **C** Both special journals (answer A) and accounts receivable control accounts (answer B) are generally not used in a computerized accounting system. Rather, electronic forms, such as an electronic invoice form (answer C), are used to record original transactions. The computer automatically posts transactions from electronic forms to the general ledger and individual accounts at the time the transactions are recorded. Therefore, month-end postings to the general ledger (answer D) are not necessary in a computerized accounting system.

Accounting for Merchandising Businesses

D O L L A R   T R E E   S T O R E S ,   I N C .

When you are low on cash but need to pick up party supplies, housewares, or other consumer items, where do you go? Many shoppers are turning to Dollar Tree Stores, Inc., the nation's largest single price point dollar retailer with over 3,400 stores in 48 states. For the fixed price of $1 on all merchandise in its stores, this retailer has worked hard on its concept to provide "new treasures" every week for the entire family.

Despite the fact that every item costs only $1, the accounting for a merchandiser, like Dollar Tree, is more complex than for a service company. This is because a service company sells only services and has no inventory. With Dollar Tree's locations and merchandise, the company must design its accounting system to not only record the receipt of goods for resale, but also to keep track of

what merchandise is available for sale as well as where the merchandise is located. In addition, Dollar Tree must record the sales and costs of the goods sold for each of its stores. Finally, Dollar Tree must record such data as delivery costs, merchandise discounts, and merchandise returns.

In this chapter, we focus on the accounting principles and concepts for a merchandising business. In doing so, we highlight the basic differences between merchandiser and service company activities. We then describe and illustrate the financial statements of a merchandising business and accounting for merchandise transactions.

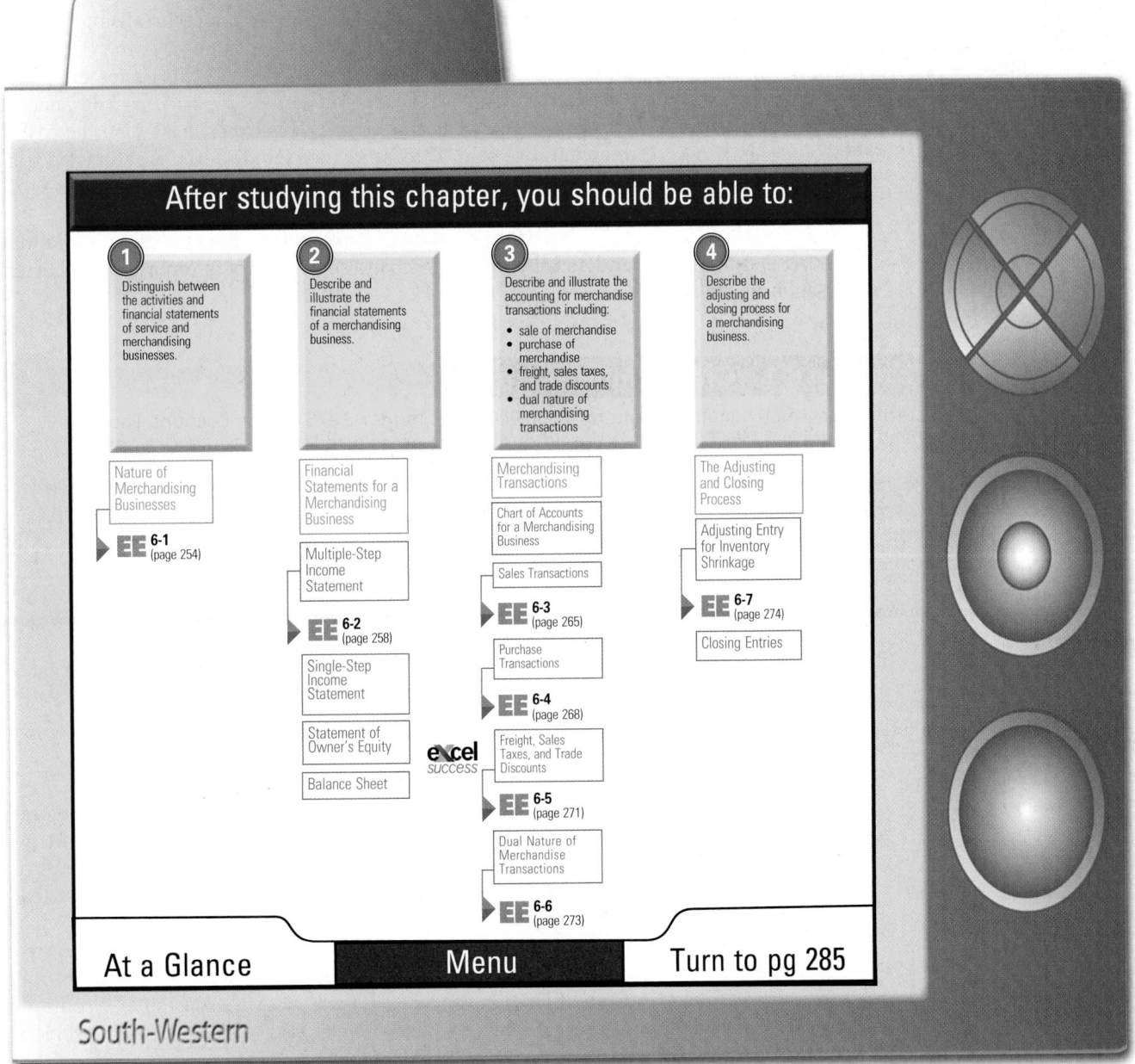

After studying this chapter, you should be able to:

1 Distinguish between the activities and financial statements of service and merchandising businesses.

Nature of Merchandising Businesses

EE 6-1 (page 254)

2 Describe and illustrate the financial statements of a merchandising business.

Financial Statements for a Merchandising Business

Multiple-Step Income Statement

EE 6-2 (page 258)

Single-Step Income Statement

Statement of Owner's Equity

Balance Sheet

3 Describe and illustrate the accounting for merchandise transactions including:
- sale of merchandise
- purchase of merchandise
- freight, sales taxes, and trade discounts
- dual nature of merchandising transactions

Merchandising Transactions

Chart of Accounts for a Merchandising Business

Sales Transactions

EE 6-3 (page 265)

Purchase Transactions

EE 6-4 (page 268)

excel success

Freight, Sales Taxes, and Trade Discounts

EE 6-5 (page 271)

Dual Nature of Merchandise Transactions

EE 6-6 (page 273)

4 Describe the adjusting and closing process for a merchandising business.

The Adjusting and Closing Process

Adjusting Entry for Inventory Shrinkage

EE 6-7 (page 274)

Closing Entries

At a Glance | Menu | Turn to pg 285

South-Western

Nature of Merchandising Businesses

1 Distinguish between the activities and financial statements of service and merchandising businesses.

The activities of a service business differ from those of a merchandising business. These differences are illustrated in the following condensed income statements:

Service Business	
Fees earned	$XXX
Operating expenses	−XXX
Net income	$XXX

Merchandising Business	
Sales	$XXX
Cost of merchandise sold	−XXX
Gross profit	$XXX
Operating expenses	−XXX
Net income	$XXX

The revenue activities of a service business involve providing services to customers. On the income statement for a service business, the revenues from services are reported as *fees earned*. The operating expenses incurred in providing the services are subtracted from the fees earned to arrive at *net income*.

Sales	–	Cost of Merchandise Sold	=	Gross Profit

Gross Profit	–	Operating Expenses	=	Net Income

In contrast, the revenue activities of a merchandising business involve the buying and selling of merchandise. A merchandising business first purchases merchandise to sell to its customers. When this merchandise is sold, the revenue is reported as sales, and its cost is recognized as an expense. This expense is called the **cost of merchandise sold**. The cost of merchandise sold is subtracted from sales to arrive at gross profit. This amount is called **gross profit** because it is the profit *before* deducting operating expenses.

Merchandise on hand (not sold) at the end of an accounting period is called **merchandise inventory**. Merchandise inventory is reported as a current asset on the balance sheet.

Example Exercise 6-1 Gross Profit

> 1

During the current year, merchandise is sold for $250,000 cash and for $975,000 on account. The cost of the merchandise sold is $735,000. What is the amount of the gross profit?

Follow My Example 6-1

The gross profit is $490,000 (250,000 + $975,000 − $735,000).

For Practice: PE 6-1A, PE 6-1B

---

2 Describe and illustrate the financial statements of a merchandising business.

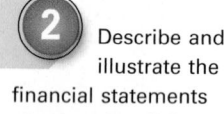

Financial Statements for a Merchandising Business

In this section, we illustrate the financial statements for NetSolutions after it becomes a retailer of computer hardware and software. During 2009, Chris Clark implemented the second phase of NetSolutions' business plan. In doing so, Chris notified clients that beginning July 1, 2010, NetSolutions would no longer offer consulting services. Instead, it would become a retailer.

NetSolutions' business strategy is to offer personalized service to individuals and small businesses who are upgrading or purchasing new computer systems. NetSolutions' personal service includes a no-obligation, on-site assessment of the customer's computer needs. By providing personalized service and follow-up, Chris feels that NetSolutions can compete effectively against such retailers as Best Buy and Office Depot, Inc.

Multiple-Step Income Statement

The 2011 income statement for NetSolutions is shown in Exhibit 1.[1] This form of income statement, called a **multiple-step income statement**, contains several sections, subsections, and subtotals.

Revenue from Sales This section of the multiple-step income statement consists of sales, sales returns and allowances, sales discounts, and net sales. This section, as shown in Exhibit 1, is as follows:

Revenue from sales:			
Sales			$720,185
Less: Sales returns and allowances	$6,140		
Sales discounts	5,790	11,930	
Net sales			$708,255

Sales is the total amount charged customers for merchandise sold, including cash sales and sales on account. During 2011, NetSolutions sold merchandise of $720,185 for cash or on account.

1 We use the NetSolutions income statement for 2011 as a basis for illustration because, as will be shown, it allows us to better illustrate the computation of the cost of merchandise sold.

Exhibit 1

**Multiple-Step
Income
Statement**

NetSolutions
Income Statement
For the Year Ended December 31, 2011

Revenue from sales:			
Sales		$720,185	
Less: Sales returns and allowances	$ 6,140		
Sales discounts	5,790	11,930	
Net sales			$708,255
Cost of merchandise sold			525,305
Gross profit			$182,950
Operating expenses:			
Selling expenses:			
Sales salaries expense	$53,430		
Advertising expense	10,860		
Depreciation expense—store equipment	3,100		
Delivery expense	2,800		
Miscellaneous selling expense	630		
Total selling expenses		$ 70,820	
Administrative expenses:			
Office salaries expense	$21,020		
Rent expense	8,100		
Depreciation expense—office equipment	2,490		
Insurance expense	1,910		
Office supplies expense	610		
Misc. administrative expense	760		
Total administrative expenses		34,890	
Total operating expenses			105,710
Income from operations			$ 77,240
Other income and expense:			
Rent revenue		$ 600	
Interest expense..................................		(2,440)	(1,840)
Net income			$ 75,400

Sales returns and allowances are granted by the seller to customers for damaged or defective merchandise. In such cases, the customer may either return the merchandise or accept an allowance from the seller. NetSolutions reported $6,140 of sales returns and allowances during 2011.

Sales discounts are granted by the seller to customers for early payment of amounts owed. For example, a seller may offer a customer a 2% discount on a sale of $10,000 if the customer pays within 10 days. If the customer pays within the 10-day period, the seller receives cash of $9,800, and the buyer receives a discount of $200 ($10,000 $\times$ 2%). NetSolutions reported $5,790 of sales discounts during 2011.

Net sales is determined by subtracting sales returns and allowances and sales discounts from sales. As shown above, NetSolutions reported $708,255 of net sales during 2011. Some companies report only net sales and report sales, sales returns and allowances, and sales discounts in notes to the financial statements.

Cost of Merchandise Sold The cost of merchandise sold is the cost of the merchandise sold to customers. NetSolutions reported cost of merchandise sold of $525,305 during 2011. To illustrate how cost of merchandise sold is determined, we use data from when NetSolutions began its merchandising operations on July 1, 2010.

Purchases July 1–December 31, 2010	$340,000
Merchandise inventory on December 31, 2010	59,700

Since NetSolutions had only $59,700 of merchandise left on December 31, 2010, it must have sold merchandise that cost $280,300 during 2010, as shown below.

Purchases	$340,000
Less merchandise inventory, December 31, 2010	59,700
Cost of merchandise sold	$280,300

To continue, assume the following 2011 data for NetSolutions:

Purchases of merchandise	$521,980
Purchases returns and allowances	9,100
Purchases discounts	2,525
Freight in on merchandise purchased	17,400

Sellers may grant a buyer sales returns and allowances for returned or damaged merchandise. From a buyer's perspective, such allowances are called **purchases returns and allowances**. Likewise, sellers may grant a buyer a sales discount for early payment of the amount owed. From a buyer's perspective, such discounts are called **purchases discounts**. Purchases returns and allowances and purchases discounts are subtracted from purchases to arrive at **net purchases,** as shown below for NetSolutions.

Purchases		$521,980
Less: Purchases returns and allowances	$9,100	
Purchases discounts	2,525	11,625
Net purchases		$510,355

Freight costs incurred in obtaining the merchandise increase the cost of the merchandise purchased. These costs are called **freight in**. Adding freight in to net purchases yields the **cost of merchandise purchased** as shown below for NetSolutions.

Net purchases	$510,355
Add freight in	17,400
Cost of merchandise purchased	$527,755

The beginning inventory is added to the cost of merchandise purchased to determine the **merchandise available for sale** for the period. The ending inventory of NetSolutions on December 31, 2010, $59,700, becomes the beginning (January 1, 2011) inventory for 2011. Thus, the merchandise available for sale for NetSolutions during 2011 is $587,455, as shown below.

Merchandise inventory, January 1, 2011	$ 59,700
Cost of merchandise purchased	527,755
Cost of merchandise available for sale	$587,455

The ending inventory is then subtracted from the merchandise available for sale to yield the cost of merchandise sold. Assuming the ending inventory on December 31, 2011, is $62,150, then the cost of merchandise sold for NetSolutions is $525,305, as shown in Exhibit 1 and below.

Cost of merchandise available for sale	$587,455
Less merchandise inventory, December 31, 2011	62,150
Cost of merchandise sold	$525,305

In the preceding computation, merchandise inventory at the end of the period is subtracted from the merchandise available for sale to determine the cost of merchandise sold. The merchandise inventory at the end of the period is determined by taking a physical count of inventory on hand. This method of determining the cost of merchandise sold and the amount of merchandise on hand is called the **periodic inventory system**. Under the periodic inventory system, the inventory records do not show the amount available for sale or the amount sold during the period. Instead, the cost of merchandise sold is computed and reported as shown in Exhibit 2.

Exhibit 2				

Cost of Merchandise Sold

Merchandise inventory, January 1, 2011			$ 59,700
Purchases		$521,980	
Less: Purchases returns and allowances	$9,100		
Purchases discounts	2,525	11,625	
Net purchases		$510,355	
Add freight in		17,400	
Cost of merchandise purchased			527,755
Merchandise available for sale			$587,455
Less merchandise inventory, December 31, 2011 . .			62,150
Cost of merchandise sold			$525,305

Retailers, such as Best Buy, Sears Holding Corporation, and Wal-Mart, and grocery store chains, such as Winn-Dixie Stores, Inc. and Kroger, use bar codes and optical scanners as part of their computerized inventory systems.

Under the **perpetual inventory system** of accounting, each purchase and sale of merchandise is recorded in the inventory and the cost of merchandise sold accounts. As a result, the amounts of merchandise available for sale and sold are continuously (perpetually) updated in the inventory records. Because many retailers use computerized systems, the perpetual inventory system is widely used. For example, such systems may use bar codes, such as the one on the back of this textbook. An optical scanner reads the bar code to record merchandise purchased and sold.

Businesses using a perpetual inventory system report the cost of merchandise sold as a single line on the income statement. An example of such reporting is illustrated in Exhibit 1 for NetSolutions.

Because of its wide use, we use the perpetual inventory system in the remainder of this chapter. The periodic inventory system is described and illustrated in Appendix 2 of this chapter.

Gross Profit Gross profit is computed by subtracting the cost of merchandise sold from net sales, as shown below.

Net sales	$708,255
Cost of merchandise sold	525,305
Gross profit	$182,950

As shown above and in Exhibit 1, NetSolutions has gross profit of $182,950 in 2011.

Income from Operations **Income from operations**, sometimes called **operating income**, is determined by subtracting operating expenses from gross profit. Operating expenses are normally classified as either selling expenses or administrative expenses.

Selling expenses are incurred directly in the selling of merchandise. Examples of selling expenses include sales salaries, store supplies used, depreciation of store equipment, delivery expense, and advertising.

Administrative expenses, sometimes called **general expenses**, are incurred in the administration or general operations of the business. Examples of administrative expenses include office salaries, depreciation of office equipment, and office supplies used.

Each selling and administrative expense may be reported separately, as shown in Exhibit 1. However, many companies report selling, administrative, and operating expenses as single line items as shown below for NetSolutions.

Gross profit		$182,950
Operating expenses:		
Selling expenses	$70,820	
Administrative expenses	34,890	
Total operating expenses		105,710
Income from operations		$ 77,240

Other Income and Expense Other income and expense items are not related to the primary operations of the business. **Other income** is revenue from sources other than the primary operating activity of a business. Examples of other income include income from interest, rent, and gains resulting from the sale of fixed assets. **Other expense** is an expense that cannot be traced directly to the normal operations of the business. Examples of other expenses include interest expense and losses from disposing of fixed assets.

Other income and other expense are offset against each other on the income statement. If the total of other income exceeds the total of other expense, the difference is added to income from operations to determine net income. If the reverse is true, the difference is subtracted from income from operations. The other income and expense items of NetSolutions are reported as shown below and in Exhibit 1.

Income from operations		$77,240
Other income and expense:		
Rent revenue	$ 600	
Interest expense	(2,440)	(1,840)
Net income		$75,400

Example Exercise 6-2   Cost of Merchandise Sold   •••••••• 2

Based on the following data, determine the cost of merchandise sold for May. Follow the format used in Exhibit 2.

Merchandise inventory, May 1	$121,200
Merchandise inventory, May 31	142,000
Purchases	985,000
Purchases returns and allowances	23,500
Purchases discounts	21,000
Freight in	11,300

Follow My Example 6-2

Cost of merchandise sold:

Merchandise inventory, May 1			$ 121,200
Purchases		$985,000	
Less: Purchases returns and allowances	$23,500		
Purchases discounts	21,000	44,500	
Net purchases		$940,500	
Add freight in		11,300	
Cost of merchandise purchased			951,800
Merchandise available for sale			$1,073,000
Less merchandise inventory, May 31			142,000
Cost of merchandise sold			$ 931,000

For Practice: PE 6-2A, PE 6-2B

Single-Step Income Statement

An alternate form of income statement is the **single-step income statement.** As shown in Exhibit 3, the income statement for NetSolutions deducts the total of all expenses *in one step* from the total of all revenues.

The single-step form emphasizes total revenues and total expenses in determining net income. A criticism of the single-step form is that gross profit and income from operations are not reported.

Statement of Owner's Equity

The statement of owner's equity for NetSolutions is shown in Exhibit 4. This statement is prepared in the same manner as for a service business.

Exhibit 3

**Single-Step
Income
Statement**

NetSolutions
Income Statement
For the Year Ended December 31, 2011

Revenues:		
Net sales		$708,255
Rent revenue		600
Total revenues		$708,855
Expenses:		
Cost of merchandise sold	$525,305	
Selling expenses	70,820	
Administrative expenses	34,890	
Interest expense	2,440	
Total expenses		633,455
Net income		$ 75,400

Exhibit 4

**Statement
of Owner's
Equity for
Merchandising
Business**

NetSolutions
Statement of Owner's Equity
For the Year Ended December 31, 2011

Chris Clark, capital, January 1, 2011		$153,800
Net income for the year	$75,400	
Less withdrawals	18,000	
Increase in owner's equity		57,400
Chris Clark, capital, December 31, 2011		$211,200

Balance Sheet

The balance sheet may be presented with assets on the left-hand side and the liabilities and owner's equity on the right-hand side. This form of the balance sheet is called the **account form.** The balance sheet may also be presented in a downward sequence in three sections. This form of balance sheet is called the **report form.** The report form of balance sheet for NetSolutions is shown in Exhibit 5. In Exhibit 5, merchandise inventory is reported as a current asset and the current portion of the note payable of $5,000 is reported as a current liability.

3 Describe and illustrate the accounting for merchandise transactions including:
- sale of merchandise
- purchase of merchandise
- freight, sales taxes, and trade discounts
- dual nature of merchandising transactions

Merchandising Transactions

In the prior section, we described and illustrated the financial statements of a merchandising business, NetSolutions. In this section, we describe and illustrate the recording of merchandise transactions. We begin by describing the chart of accounts for a merchandising business.

Chart of Accounts for a Merchandising Business

The chart of accounts for a merchandising business should reflect the elements of the financial statements. The chart of accounts for NetSolutions is shown in Exhibit 6. The accounts related to merchandising transactions are shown in color.

Exhibit 5

**Report Form of
Balance Sheet**

**NetSolutions
Balance Sheet
December 31, 2011**

Assets

Current assets:			
Cash		$52,950	
Accounts receivable		91,080	
Merchandise inventory		62,150	
Office supplies		480	
Prepaid insurance		2,650	
Total current assets			$209,310
Property, plant, and equipment:			
Land		$20,000	
Store equipment	$27,100		
Less accumulated depreciation	5,700	21,400	
Office equipment	$15,570		
Less accumulated depreciation	4,720	10,850	
Total property, plant, and equipment			52,250
Total assets			$261,560

Liabilities

Current liabilities:			
Accounts payable		$22,420	
Note payable (current portion)		5,000	
Salaries payable		1,140	
Unearned rent		1,800	
Total current liabilities			$ 30,360
Long-term liabilities:			
Note payable (final payment due 2021)			20,000
Total liabilities			$ 50,360

Owner's Equity

Chris Clark, capital			211,200
Total liabilities and owner's equity			$261,560

As shown in Exhibit 6, NetSolutions' chart of accounts consists of three-digit account numbers. The first digit indicates the major financial statement classification (1 for assets, 2 for liabilities, and so on). The second digit indicates the subclassification (e.g., 11 for current assets, 12 for noncurrent assets). The third digit identifies the specific account (e.g., 110 for Cash, 123 for Store Equipment). Using a three-digit numbering system makes it easier to add new accounts as they are needed.

Sales Transactions

Merchandise transactions are recorded using the rules of debit and credit that we described and illustrated in Chapter 2. Exhibit 3, shown on page 50 of Chapter 2, summarizes these rules.

Special journals may be used, or transactions may be entered, recorded, and posted using a computerized accounting system. To simplify, we will use a two-column general journal in this chapter.[2]

Cash Sales   A business may sell merchandise for cash. Cash sales are normally entered (rung up) on a cash register and recorded in the accounts. To illustrate, assume

---

2 Special journals and computerized accounting systems for merchandising businesses are described in Appendix 1 at the end of this chapter.

Exhibit 6

Chart of Accounts for NetSolutions, a Merchandising Business

Balance Sheet Accounts	Income Statement Accounts
100 Assets	**400 Revenues**
110 Cash	410 Sales
112 Accounts Receivable	411 Sales Returns and Allowances
115 Merchandise Inventory	412 Sales Discounts
116 Office Supplies	**500 Costs and Expenses**
117 Prepaid Insurance	510 Cost of Merchandise Sold
120 Land	520 Sales Salaries Expense
123 Store Equipment	521 Advertising Expense
124 Accumulated Depreciation—	522 Depreciation Expense—Store
Store Equipment	Equipment
125 Office Equipment	523 Delivery Expense
126 Accumulated Depreciation—	529 Miscellaneous Selling Expense
Office Equipment	530 Office Salaries Expense
	531 Rent Expense
200 Liabilities	532 Depreciation Expense—Office
210 Accounts Payable	Equipment
211 Salaries Payable	533 Insurance Expense
212 Unearned Rent	534 Office Supplies Expense
215 Notes Payable	539 Misc. Administrative Expense
300 Owner's Equity	**600 Other Income**
310 Chris Clark, Capital	610 Rent Revenue
311 Chris Clark, Drawing	**700 Other Expense**
312 Income Summary	710 Interest Expense

that on January 3, NetSolutions sells merchandise for $1,800. These cash sales are recorded as follows:

		Journal			Page 25
Date		**Description**	**Post. Ref.**	**Debit**	**Credit**
2011 Jan.	3	Cash		1,800	
		Sales			1,800
		To record cash sales.			

Using the perpetual inventory system, the cost of merchandise sold and the decrease in merchandise inventory are also recorded. In this way, the merchandise inventory account indicates the amount of merchandise on hand (not sold).

To illustrate, assume that the cost of merchandise sold on January 3 is $1,200. The entry to record the cost of merchandise sold and the decrease in the merchandise inventory is as follows:

Jan.	3	Cost of Merchandise Sold		1,200	
		Merchandise Inventory			1,200
		To record the cost of merchandise sold.			

Sales may be made to customers using credit cards such as MasterCard or VISA. Such sales are recorded as cash sales. This is because these sales are normally processed by a clearing-house that contacts the bank that issued the card. The issuing bank then electronically transfers cash directly to the retailer's bank account.[3] Thus, the retailer normally receives cash within a few days of making the credit card sale.

If the customers in the preceding sales had used MasterCards to pay for their purchases, the sales would be recorded exactly as shown in the preceding entry. Any processing fees charged by the clearing-house or issuing bank are periodically recorded as an expense. This expense is normally reported on the income statement as an administrative expense. To illustrate, assume that NetSolutions paid credit card processing fees of $48 on January 31. These fees would be recorded as follows:

Jan.	31	Credit Card Expense	48	
		Cash		48
		To record service charges on credit card sales for the month.		

Instead of using MasterCard or VISA, a customer may use a credit card that is not issued by a bank. For example, a customer might use an American Express card. If the seller uses a clearing-house, the clearing-house will collect the receivable and transfer the cash to the retailer's bank account similar to the way it would have if the customer had used MasterCard or VISA. Large businesses, however, may not use a clearing-house. In such cases, nonbank credit card sales must first be reported to the card company before cash is received. Thus, a receivable is created with the nonbank credit card company. However, since most retailers use clearing-houses to process both bank and nonbank credit cards, we will record all credit card sales as cash sales.

A retailer may accept MasterCard or VISA but not American Express. Why? The service fees that credit card companies charge retailers are the primary reason that some businesses do not accept all credit cards. For example, American Express Co.'s service fees are normally higher than MasterCard's or VISA's. As a result, some retailers choose not to accept American Express cards. The disadvantage of this practice is that the retailer may lose customers to competitors who do accept American Express cards.

Sales on Account A business may sell merchandise on account. The seller records such sales as a debit to Accounts Receivable and a credit to Sales. An example of an entry for a NetSolutions sale on account of $510 follows. The cost of merchandise sold was $280.

Jan.	12	Accounts Receivable—Sims Co.	510	
		Sales		510
		Invoice No. 7172.		
	12	Cost of Merchandise Sold	280	
		Merchandise Inventory		280
		Cost of merch. sold on Invoice No. 7172.		

Sales Discounts The terms of a sale are normally indicated on the **invoice** or bill that the seller sends to the buyer. An example of a sales invoice for NetSolutions is shown in Exhibit 7.

---

3 CyberSource is one of the major credit card clearing-houses. For a more detailed description of how credit card sales are processed, see the following CyberSource Web page: **http://www.cybersource.com/products_and_services/global_payment_services/credit_card_processing/howitworks.xml**.

Invoice

NetSolutions				106-8

5101 Washington Ave.
Cincinnati, OH 45227-5101

Invoice   Made in U.S.A.

SOLD TO		**CUSTOMER'S ORDER NO. & DATE**	
Omega Technologies		412 Jan.10, 2011	
1000 Matrix Blvd.			
San Jose, CA. 95116–1000			

DATE SHIPPED	**HOW SHIPPED AND ROUTE**	**TERMS**	**INVOICE DATE**
Jan. 12, 2011	US Express Trucking Co.	2/10, n/30	Jan. 12, 2011

FROM	**F.O.B.**
Cincinnati	Cincinnati

QUANTITY	**DESCRIPTION**	**UNIT PRICE**	**AMOUNT**
10	3COM Megahertz	150.00	1,500.00
10	3COM Wireless PC Card		

The terms for when payments for merchandise are to be made are called the **credit terms.** If payment is required on delivery, the terms are *cash* or *net cash*. Otherwise, the buyer is allowed an amount of time, known as the **credit period,** in which to pay.

The credit period usually begins with the date of the sale as shown on the invoice. If payment is due within a stated number of days after the invoice date, such as 30 days, the terms are *net 30 days*. These terms may be written as *n/30*.[4] If payment is due by the end of the month in which the sale was made, the terms are written as *n/eom.*

To encourage the buyer to pay before the end of the credit period, the seller may offer a discount. For example, a seller may offer a 2% discount if the buyer pays within 10 days of the invoice date. If the buyer does not take the discount, the total amount is due within 30 days. These terms are expressed as *2/10, n/30* and are read as *2% discount if paid within 10 days, net amount due within 30 days.* The credit terms of 2/10, n/30 are summarized in Exhibit 8, using the invoice in Exhibit 7.

Credit Terms

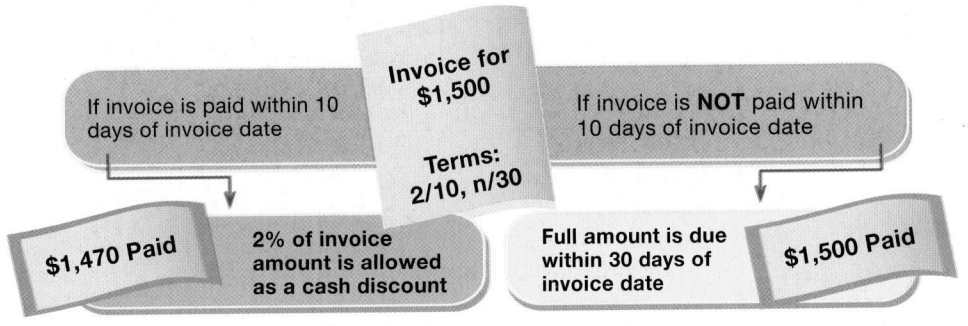

[4] The word *net* as used here does not have the usual meaning of a number after deductions have been subtracted, as in *net income.*

Discounts taken by the buyer for early payment are recorded as sales discounts by the seller. Managers usually want to know the amount of the sales discounts for a period. For this reason, sales discounts are recorded in a separate sales discounts account, which is a *contra* (or *offsetting*) account to Sales.

To illustrate, assume that NetSolutions receives $1,470 on January 22 for the invoice shown in Exhibit 7. Since the invoice was paid within the discount period (10 days), the buyer deducted $30 ($1,500 × 2%) from the invoice amount. NetSolutions would record the receipt of the cash as follows:

Jan.	22	Cash	1,470	
		Sales Discounts	30	
		Accounts Receivable—Omega Technologies		1,500
		Collection on Invoice No. 106-8, less		
		2% discount.		

Book publishers often experience large returns if a book is not immediately successful. For example, 35% of adult hardcover books shipped to retailers are returned to publishers, according to the Association of American Publishers.

Sales Returns and Allowances Merchandise sold may be returned to the seller (sales return). In other cases, the seller may reduce the initial selling price (sales allowance). This might occur if the merchandise is defective, damaged during shipment, or does not meet the buyer's expectations.

If the return or allowance is for a sale on account, the seller usually issues the buyer a **credit memorandum**, often called a **credit memo**. A credit memo authorizes a credit to (decreases) the buyer's account receivable. A credit memo indicates the amount and reason for the credit. An example of a credit memo issued by NetSolutions is shown in Exhibit 9.

Like sales discounts, sales returns and allowances reduce sales revenue. Also, returns often result in additional shipping and handling expenses. Thus, managers usually want to know the amount of returns and allowances for a period. For this reason, sales returns and allowances are recorded in a separate sales returns and allowances account, which is is a *contra* (or *offsetting*) account to Sales.

The seller debits Sales Returns and Allowances for the amount of the return or allowance. If the sale was on account, the seller credits Accounts Receivable. Using a perpetual inventory system, the seller must also debit (increase) Merchandise Inventory and decrease (credit) Cost of Merchandise Sold for the cost of the returned merchandise.

To illustrate, we use the credit memo shown in Exhibit 9. The selling price of the merchandise returned in Exhibit 9 is $225. Assuming that the cost of the

Exhibit 9

Credit Memo

NetSolutions			**No. 32**
5101 Washington Ave.			
Cincinnati, OH 45227-5101			

CREDIT MEMO

TO	**DATE**
Krier Company	January 13, 2011
7608 Melton Avenue	
Los Angeles, CA 90025-3942	

WE CREDIT YOUR ACCOUNT AS FOLLOWS	
1 Graphic Video Card	225.00

merchandise returned is $140, the sales return and allowance would be recorded as follows:

Jan.	13	Sales Returns and Allowances	225	
		Accounts Receivable—Krier Company		225
		Credit Memo No. 32.		

Jan.	13	Merchandise Inventory	140	
		Cost of Merchandise Sold		140
		Cost of merchandise returned, Credit		
		Memo No. 32.		

A buyer may pay for merchandise and then later return it. In this case, the seller may do one of the following:

1. Issue a credit that is applied against the buyer's other receivables.
2. Issue a cash refund.

If the credit is applied against the buyer's other receivables, the seller records the credit with entries similar to those shown above. If cash is refunded, the seller debits Sales Returns and Allowances and credits Cash.

Example Exercise 6-3 Sales Transactions 3

Journalize the following merchandise transactions:
a. Sold merchandise on account, $7,500 with terms 2/10, n/30. The cost of the merchandise sold was $5,625.
b. Received payment less the discount.

Follow My Example 6-3

a.	Accounts Receivable.	7,500	
	Sales		7,500
	Cost of Merchandise Sold.	5,625	
	Merchandise Inventory		5,625
b.	Cash	7,350	
	Sales Discounts	150	
	Accounts Receivable.		7,500

For Practice: PE 6-3A, PE 6-3B

Integrity, Objectivity, and Ethics in Business

THE CASE OF THE FRAUDULENT PRICE TAGS

One of the challenges for a retailer is policing its sales return policy. There are many ways in which customers can unethically or illegally abuse such policies. In one case, a couple was accused of attaching Marshalls' store price tags to cheaper merchandise bought or obtained elsewhere. The couple then returned the cheaper goods and received the substantially higher refund amount. Company security officials discovered the fraud and had the couple arrested after they had allegedly bilked the company for over $1 million.

Purchase Transactions

Under the perpetual inventory system, cash purchases of merchandise are recorded as follows:

		Journal			Page 24
Date		**Description**	**Post. Ref.**	**Debit**	**Credit**
2011 Jan. 3		Merchandise Inventory		2,510	
		Cash			2,510
		Purchased inventory from Bowen Co.			

Purchases of merchandise on account are recorded as follows:

Jan.	4	Merchandise Inventory		9,250	
		Accounts Payable—Thomas Corporation			9,250
		Purchased inventory on account.			

Purchases Discounts Purchases discounts taken by a buyer reduce the cost of the merchandise purchased. Even if the buyer has to borrow to pay within a discount period, it is normally to the buyer's advantage to do so. For this reason, accounting systems are normally designed so that all available discounts are taken.

To illustrate, assume that NetSolutions purchased merchandise from Alpha Technologies as follows:

Invoice Date	Invoice Amount	Terms
March 12	$3,000	2/10, n/30

The last day of the discount period is March 22 (March 12 + 10 days). Assume that in order to pay the invoice on March 22, NetSolutions borrows $2,940, which is $3,000 less the discount of $60 ($3,000 × 2%). If we also assume an annual interest rate of 6% and a 360-day year, the interest on the loan of $2,940 for the remaining 20 days of the credit period is $9.80 ($2,940 × 6% × 20/360).

The net savings to NetSolutions of taking the discount is $50.20, computed as follows:

Discount of 2% on $3,000	$60.00
Interest for 20 days at a rate of 6% on $2,940	9.80
Savings from taking the discount	$50.20

The savings can also be seen by comparing the interest rate on the money *saved* by taking the discount and the interest rate on the money *borrowed* to take the discount. The interest rate on the money saved in the prior example is estimated by converting 2% for 20 days to a yearly rate, as follows:

$$2\% \times \frac{360 \text{ days}}{20 \text{ days}} = 2\% \times 18 = 36\%$$

NetSolutions borrowed $2,940 at 6% to take the discount. If NetSolutions does not take the discount, it *pays* an estimated interest rate of 36% for using the $2,940 for the remaining 20 days of the credit period. Thus, buyers should normally take all available purchase discounts.

Under the perpetual inventory system, the buyer initially debits Merchandise Inventory for the amount of the invoice. When paying the invoice within the discount period, the buyer credits Merchandise Inventory for the amount of the discount. In this way, Merchandise Inventory shows the *net* cost to the buyer.

To illustrate, NetSolutions would record the Alpha Technologies invoice and its payment at the end of the discount period as follows:

Mar.	12	Merchandise Inventory	3,000	
		Accounts Payable—Alpha Technologies		3,000
	22	Accounts Payable—Alpha Technologies	3,000	
		Cash		2,940
		Merchandise Inventory		60

Assume that NetSolutions does not take the discount, but instead pays the invoice on April 11. In this case, NetSolutions would record the payment on April 11 as follows:

Apr.	11	Accounts Payable—Alpha Technologies	3,000	
		Cash		3,000

Purchases Returns and Allowances A buyer may return merchandise (purchases return) or request a price allowance (purchases allowance) from the seller. In both cases, the buyer normally sends the seller a debit memorandum. A **debit memorandum**, often called a **debit memo**, is shown in Exhibit 10. A debit memo informs the seller of the amount the buyer proposes to *debit* to the account payable due the seller. It also states the reasons for the return or the request for the price allowance.

The buyer may use the debit memo as the basis for recording the return or allowance or wait for approval from the seller (creditor). In either case, the buyer debits Accounts Payable and credits Merchandise Inventory.

Exhibit 10

Debit Memo

NetSolutions
5101 Washington Ave.
Cincinnati, OH 45227-5101

No. 18

DEBIT MEMO

TO
Maxim Systems
7519 East Willson Ave.
Seattle, WA 98101–7519

DATE
March 7, 2011

WE DEBIT YOUR ACCOUNT AS FOLLOWS
10 Server Network Interface Cards, your Invoice No. 7291, are being returned via parcel post. Our order specified No. 825X.   @ 90.00   900.00

To illustrate, NetSolutions records the return of the merchandise indicated in the debit memo in Exhibit 10 as follows:

Mar.	7	Accounts Payable—Maxim Systems	900	
		Merchandise Inventory		900
		Debit Memo No. 18.		

A buyer may return merchandise or be granted a price allowance before paying an invoice. In this case, the amount of the debit memo is deducted from the invoice. The amount is deducted before the purchase discount is computed.

To illustrate, assume the following data concerning a purchase of merchandise by NetSolutions on May 2:

May 2. Purchased $5,000 of merchandise on account from Delta Data Link, terms 2/10, n/30.
4. Returned $3,000 of the merchandise purchased on March 2.
12. Paid for the purchase of May 2 less the return and discount.

NetSolutions would record these transactions as follows:

May	2	Merchandise Inventory	5,000	
		Accounts Payable—Delta Data Link		5,000
		Purchased merchandise.		
	4	Accounts Payable—Delta Data Link	3,000	
		Merchandise Inventory		3,000
		Returned portion of merch. purchased.		
	12	Accounts Payable—Delta Data Link	2,000	
		Cash		1,960
		Merchandise Inventory		40
		Paid invoice [($5,000 − $3,000) × 2%		
		= $40; $2,000 − $40 = $1,960].		

Example Exercise 6-4 Purchase Transactions 3

Rofles Company purchased merchandise on account from a supplier for $11,500, terms 2/10, n/30. Rofles Company returned $3,000 of the merchandise and received full credit.

a. If Rofles Company pays the invoice within the discount period, what is the amount of cash required for the payment?
b. Under a perpetual inventory system, what account is credited by Rofles Company to record the return?

Follow My Example 6-4

a. $8,330. Purchase of $11,500 less the return of $3,000 less the discount of $170 [($11,500 − $3,000) × 2%].
b. Merchandise Inventory

For Practice: PE 6-4A, PE 6-4B

Freight, Sales Taxes, and Trade Discounts

Purchases and sales of merchandise often involve freight and sales taxes. Also, the seller may offer buyers trade discounts.

Freight The terms of a sale indicate when ownership (title) of the merchandise passes from the seller to the buyer. This point determines whether the buyer or the seller pays the freight costs.[5]

The ownership of the merchandise may pass to the buyer when the seller delivers the merchandise to the freight carrier. In this case, the terms are said to be **FOB (free on board) shipping point**. This term means that the buyer pays the freight costs from the shipping point to the final destination. Such costs are part of the buyer's total cost of purchasing inventory and are added to the cost of the inventory by debiting Merchandise Inventory.

To illustrate, assume that on June 10, NetSolutions purchased merchandise as follows:

June 10.   Purchased merchandise from Magna Data, $900, terms FOB shipping point.
    10.   Paid freight of $50 on June 10 purchase from Magna Data.

NetSolutions would record these two transactions as follows:

Sometimes FOB shipping point and FOB destination are expressed in terms of the location at which the title to the merchandise passes to the buyer. For example, if Toyota Motor Corporation's assembly plant in Osaka, Japan, sells automobiles to a dealer in Chicago, FOB shipping point could be expressed as FOB Osaka. Likewise, FOB destination could be expressed as FOB Chicago.

June	10	Merchandise Inventory	900	
		Accounts Payable—Magna Data		900
		Purchased merchandise, terms FOB shipping point.		
	10	Merchandise Inventory	50	
		Cash		50
		Paid shipping cost on merchandise purchased.		

The ownership of the merchandise may pass to the buyer when the buyer receives the merchandise. In this case, the terms are said to be **FOB (free on board) destination**. This term means that the seller pays the freight costs from the shipping point to the buyer's final destination. When the seller pays the delivery charges, the seller debits Delivery Expense or Freight Out. Delivery Expense is reported on the seller's income statement as a selling expense.

To illustrate, assume that NetSolutions sells merchandise as follows:

June 15.   Sold merchandise to Kranz Company on account, $700, terms FOB destination. The cost of the merchandise sold is $480.
    15.   NetSolutions pays freight of $40 on the sale of June 15.

NetSolutions records the sale, the cost of the sale, and the freight cost as follows:

5 The passage of title also determines whether the buyer or seller must pay other costs, such as the cost of insurance, while the merchandise is in transit.

June	15	Accounts Receivable—Kranz Company	700	
		Sales		700
		Sold merchandise, terms FOB		
		destination.		
	15	Cost of Merchandise Sold	480	
		Merchandise Inventory		480
		Recorded cost of merchandise sold to		
		Kranz Company.		
	15	Delivery Expense	40	
		Cash		40
		Paid shipping cost on merch. sold.		

The seller may prepay the freight, even though the terms are FOB shipping point. The seller will then add the freight to the invoice. The buyer debits Merchandise Inventory for the total amount of the invoice, including the freight. Any discount terms would not apply to the prepaid freight.

To illustrate, assume that NetSolutions sells merchandise as follows:

June 20. Sold merchandise to Planter Company on account, $800, terms FOB shipping point. NetSolutions paid freight of $45, which was added to the invoice. The cost of the merchandise sold is $360.

NetSolutions records the sale, the cost of the sale, and the freight as follows:

June	20	Accounts Receivable—Planter Company	800	
		Sales		800
		Sold merch., terms FOB shipping point.		
	20	Cost of Merchandise Sold	360	
		Merchandise Inventory		360
		Recorded cost of merchandise sold to		
		Planter Company.		
	20	Accounts Receivable—Planter Company	45	
		Cash		45
		Prepaid shipping cost on merch. sold.		

Shipping terms, the passage of title, and whether the buyer or seller is to pay the freight costs are summarized in Exhibit 11.

Exhibit 11

Freight Terms

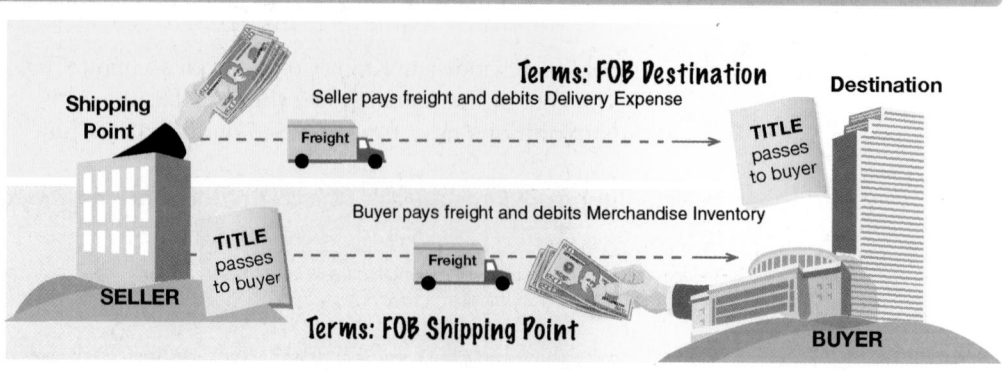

Example Exercise 6-5 Freight Terms

> 3

Determine the amount to be paid in full settlement of each of invoices (a) and (b), assuming that credit for returns and allowances was received prior to payment and that all invoices were paid within the discount period.

	Merchandise	Freight Paid by Seller	Freight Terms	Returns and Allowances
a.	$4,500	$200	FOB shipping point, 1/10, n/30	$ 800
b.	5,000	60	FOB destination, 2/10, n/30	2,500

Follow My Example 6-5

a. $3,863. Purchase of $4,500 less return of $800 less the discount of $37 [($4,500 − $800) × 1%] plus $200 of shipping.

b. $2,450. Purchase of $5,000 less return of $2,500 less the discount of $50 [($5,000 − $2,500) × 2%].

For Practice: PE 6-5A, PE 6-5B

The six states with the highest state sales tax (including the local option) are Tennessee, Louisiana, Washington, New York, Arkansas, and Alabama. Some states have no sales tax, including Alaska, Delaware, Montana, New Hampshire, and Oregon.

Sales Taxes Almost all states levy a tax on sales of merchandise.[6] The liability for the sales tax is incurred when the sale is made.

At the time of a cash sale, the seller collects the sales tax. When a sale is made on account, the seller charges the tax to the buyer by debiting Accounts Receivable. The seller credits the sales account for the amount of the sale and credits the tax to Sales Tax Payable. For example, the seller would record a sale of $100 on account, subject to a tax of 6%, as follows:

Aug.	12	Accounts Receivable—Lemon Co.	106	
		Sales		100
		Sales Tax Payable		6
		Invoice No. 339.		

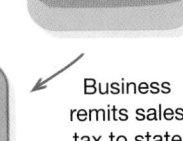

Business collects sales tax from customers

Business remits sales tax to state

On a regular basis, the seller pays to the taxing authority (state) the amount of the sales tax collected. The seller records such a payment as follows:

Sep.	15	Sales Tax Payable	2,900	
		Cash		2,900
		Payment for sales taxes collected during August.		

excel *success*

The calculation for sales tax can be accomplished within a spreadsheet. A spreadsheet is often used if there are sales from many different states with different sales tax rates. We will simplify by illustrating the calculation for only one state.

	A	B	
1	*Inputs:*		
2	Sales tax rate	6%	◄── **a.**
3	Total sales	$ 100	◄── **b.**
4			
5	*Output:*		
6	Sales tax	=B2*B3	◄── **c.**
7			

6 Businesses that purchase merchandise for resale to others are normally exempt from paying sales taxes on their purchases. Only final buyers of merchandise normally pay sales taxes.

The spreadsheet is developed with two inputs and one output. The sales tax rate is entered in cell B2 as .06, and then formatted as a percent. You can't simply type 6%, because that won't be interpreted as a number.

a.   Insert the sales tax rate .06, and format as a percent, in B2.
b.   Insert the total sales, and format as currency, in B3.
c.   Insert the formula for the sales tax calculation in B6, =B2*B3. Note that Excel uses the asterisk (*) to denote multiplication.

 Go to the hands-on *Excel Tutor* for this example!

Trade Discounts *Wholesalers* are companies that sell merchandise to other businesses rather than to the public. Many wholesalers publish sales catalogs. Rather than updating their catalogs, wholesalers may publish price updates. These updates may include large discounts from the catalog list prices. In addition, wholesalers often offer special discounts to government agencies or businesses that order large quantities. Such discounts are called **trade discounts**.

Sellers and buyers do not normally record the list prices of merchandise and trade discounts in their accounts. For example, assume that an item has a list price of $1,000 and a 40% trade discount. The seller records the sale of the item at $600 [$1,000 less the trade discount of $400 ($1,000 × 40%)]. Likewise, the buyer records the purchase at $600.

Dual Nature of Merchandise Transactions

Each merchandising transaction affects a buyer and a seller. In the illustration below, we show how the same transactions would be recorded by the seller and the buyer. In this example, the seller is Scully Company and the buyer is Burton Co.

Transaction	Scully Company (Seller)		Burton Co. (Buyer)	
July 1. Scully Company sold merchandise on account to Burton Co., $7,500, terms FOB shipping point, n/45. The cost of the merchandise sold was $4,500.	Accounts Receivable—Burton Co. . 7,500 　Sales . . . . Cost of Merchandise Sold . . . . . 4,500 　Merchandise Inventory	7,500 4,500	Merchandise Inventory . . . . . . .7,500 　Accounts Payable—Scully Co.	7,500
July 2. Burton Co. paid freight of $150 on July 1 purchase from Scully Company.	No entry.		Merchandise Inventory . . . . 150 　Cash	150
July 5. Scully Company sold merchandise on account to Burton Co., $5,000, terms FOB destination, n/30. The cost of the merchandise sold was $3,500.	Accounts Receivable—Burton Co. . . 5,000 　Sales . . . . Cost of Merchandise Sold . . . . . 3,500 　Merchandise Inventory	5,000 3,500	Merchandise Inventory . . . . . . .5,000 　Accounts Payable—Scully Co.	5,000
July 7. Scully Company paid freight of $250 for delivery of merchandise sold to Burton Co. on July 5.	Delivery Expense . . . . 250 　Cash	250	No entry.	

(continued)

Transaction	Scully Company (Seller)	Burton Co. (Buyer)

July 13. Scully Company issued Burton Co. a credit memo for merchandise returned, $1,000. The merchandise had been purchased by Burton Co. on account on July 5. The cost of the merchandise returned was $700.	Sales Returns and Allowances . . . 1,000
	   Accounts Receivable—Burton Co. 1,000
	
	Merchandise Inventory 700
	   Cost of Merchandise Sold 700
		Accounts Payable—Scully Co. . . 1,000
		   Merchandise Inventory 1,000

July 15. Scully Company received payment from Burton Co. for purchase of July 5.	Cash 4,000
	   Accounts Receivable—Burton Co. 4,000
		Accounts Payable—Scully Co. 4,000
		   Cash 4,000

July 18. Scully Company sold merchandise on account to Burton Co., $12,000, terms FOB shipping point, 2/10, n/eom. Scully Company prepaid freight of $500, which was added to the invoice. The cost of the merchandise sold was $7,200.	Accounts Receivable—Burton Co. 12,000
	   Sales 12,000
	
	Accounts Receivable—Burton Co. . . 500
	   Cash 500
	
	Cost of Merchandise Sold 7,200
	   Merchandise Inventory 7,200
		Merchandise Inventory 12,500
		   Accounts Payable—Scully Co. 12,500

July 28. Scully Company received payment from Burton Co. for purchase of July 18, less discount (2% × $12,000).	Cash 12,260
	Sales Discounts 240
	   Accounts Receivable—Burton Co. 12,500
		Accounts Payable—Scully Co. . .12,500
		   Merchandise Inventory 240
		   Cash 12,260

Example Exercise 6-6   Transactions for Buyer and Seller   • • • • • • • ➤ ③

Sievert Co. sold merchandise to Bray Co. on account, $11,500, terms 2/15, n/30. The cost of the merchandise sold is $6,900. Sievert Co. issued a credit memo for $900 for merchandise returned and later received the amount due within the discount period. The cost of the merchandise returned was $540. Journalize Sievert Co.'s and Bray Co.'s entries for the payment of the amount due.

Follow My Example 6-6

Sievert Co. journal entries:

Cash ($11,500 − $900 − $212)   10,388
Sales Discounts [($11,500 − $900) × 2%]   212
   Accounts Receivable—Bray Co. ($11,500 − $900)   10,600

Bray Co. journal entries:

Accounts Payable—Sievert Co. ($11,500 − $900)   10,600
   Merchandise Inventory [($11,500 − $900) × 2%]   212
   Cash ($11,500 − $900 − $212)   10,388

For Practice: PE 6-6A, PE 6-6B

The Adjusting and Closing Process

We have described and illustrated the chart of accounts and the recording of transactions for a merchandising business, NetSolutions. We have also illustrated the preparation of financial statements. In the remainder of this chapter, we describe the adjusting and closing process for a merchandising business. In this discussion, we will focus on the elements of the accounting cycle that differ from those of a service business.

Adjusting Entry for Inventory Shrinkage

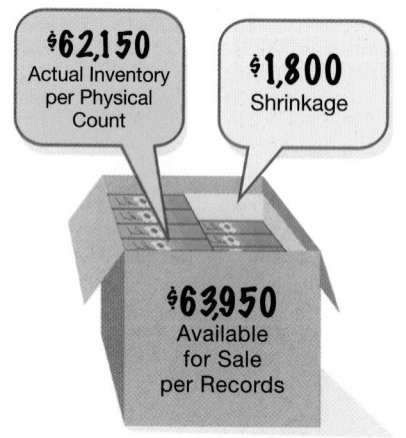

$62,150
Actual Inventory per Physical Count

$1,800
Shrinkage

$63,950
Available for Sale per Records

Under the perpetual inventory system, the merchandise inventory account is continually updated for purchase and sales transactions. As a result, the balance of the merchandise inventory account is the amount of merchandise available for sale at that point in time. However, retailers normally experience some loss of inventory due to shoplifting, employee theft, or errors. Thus, the physical inventory on hand at the end of the accounting period is usually less than the balance of Merchandise Inventory. This difference is called **inventory shrinkage** or **inventory shortage**.

To illustrate, NetSolutions' inventory records indicate the following on December 31, 2011:

	Dec. 31, 2011
Account balance of Merchandise Inventory	$63,950
Physical merchandise inventory on hand	62,150
Inventory shrinkage	$ 1,800

At the end of the accounting period, inventory shrinkage is recorded by the following adjusting entry:

Retailers lose an estimated $30 billion to inventory shrinkage. The primary causes of the shrinkage are employee theft and shoplifting.

		Adjusting Entry		
Dec.	31	Cost of Merchandise Sold	1,800	
		Merchandise Inventory		1,800
		Inventory shrinkage ($63,950 – $62,150).		

After the preceding entry is recorded, the balance of Merchandise Inventory agrees with the physical inventory on hand at the end of the period. Since inventory shrinkage cannot be totally eliminated, it is considered a normal cost of operations. If, however, the amount of the shrinkage is unusually large, it may be disclosed separately on the income statement. In such cases, the shrinkage may be recorded in a separate account, such as Loss from Merchandise Inventory Shrinkage.[7]

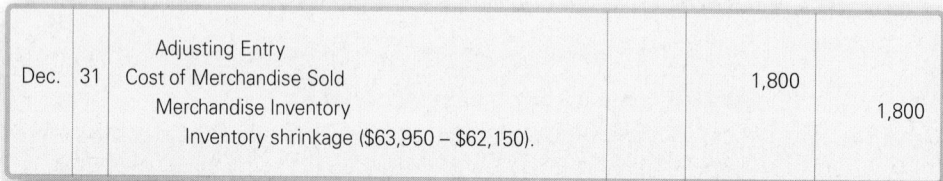

Example Exercise 6-7   Inventory Shrinkage   4

Pulmonary Company's perpetual inventory records indicate that $382,800 of merchandise should be on hand on March 31, 2010. The physical inventory indicates that $371,250 of merchandise is actually on hand. Journalize the adjusting entry for the inventory shrinkage for Pulmonary Company for the year ended March 31, 2010. Assume that the inventory shrinkage is a normal amount.

Follow My Example 6-7

Mar. 31	Cost of Merchandise Sold	11,550	
	Merchandise Inventory		11,550
	Inventory shrinkage ($382,800 – $371,250).		

For Practice: PE 6-7A, PE 6-7B

7 The adjusting process for a merchandising business may be aided by preparing an end-of-period spreadsheet (work sheet). An end-of-period spreadsheet (work sheet) for a merchandising business is described and illustrated in Appendix C.

Closing Entries

The closing entries for a merchandising business are similar to those for a service business. The four closing entries for a merchandising business are as follows:

1. Debit each temporary account with a credit balance, such as Sales, for its balance and credit Income Summary.
2. Credit each temporary account with a debit balance, such as the various expenses, and credit Income Summary. Since Sales Returns and Allowances, Sales Discounts, and Cost of Merchandise Sold are temporary accounts with debit balances, they are credited for their balances.
3. Debit Income Summary for the amount of its balance (net income) and credit the owner's capital account. The accounts debited and credited are reversed if there is a net loss.
4. Debit the owner's capital account for the balance of the drawing account and credit the drawing account.

The four closing entries for NetSolutions are shown at the top of the following page.

NetSolutions' income summary account after the closing entries have been posted is as follows:

Account *Income Summary*						Account No. *312*
					Balance	
Date	**Item**	**Post. Ref.**	**Debit**	**Credit**	**Debit**	**Credit**
2011 Dec. 31	Revenues	29		720,785		720,785
31	Expenses	29	645,385			75,400
31	Net income	29	75,400		—	—

After the closing entries are posted to the accounts, a post-closing trial balance is prepared. The only accounts that should appear on the post-closing trial balance are the asset, contra asset, liability, and owner's capital accounts with balances. These are the same accounts that appear on the end-of-period balance sheet. If the two totals of the trial balance columns are not equal, an error has occurred that must be found and corrected.

Journal					Page 29
Date		**Item**	**Post. Ref.**	**Debit**	**Credit**
2011		Closing Entries			
Dec.	31	Sales	410	720,185	
		Rent Revenue	610	600	
		Income Summary	312		720,785
	31	Income Summary	312	645,385	
		Sales Returns and Allowances	411		6,140
		Sales Discounts	412		5,790
		Cost of Merchandise Sold	510		525,305
		Sales Salaries Expense	520		53,430
		Advertising Expense	521		10,860
		Depr. Expense—Store Equipment	522		3,100
		Delivery Expense	523		2,800
		Miscellaneous Selling Expense	529		630
		Office Salaries Expense	530		21,020
		Rent Expense	531		8,100
		Depr. Expense—Office Equipment	532		2,490
		Insurance Expense	533		1,910
		Office Supplies Expense	534		610
		Misc. Administrative Expense	539		760
		Interest Expense	710		2,440
	31	Income Summary	312	75,400	
		Chris Clark, Capital	310		75,400
	31	Chris Clark, Capital	310	18,000	
		Chris Clark, Drawing	311		18,000

Financial Analysis and Interpretation

The ratio of net sales to assets measures how effectively a business is using its assets to generate sales. A high ratio indicates an effective use of assets. The assets used in computing the ratio may be the total assets at the end of the year, the average of the total assets at the beginning and end of the year, or the average of the monthly assets. For our purposes, we will use the average of the total assets at the beginning and end of the year. The ratio is computed as follows:

$$\text{Ratio of Net Sales to Assets} = \frac{\text{Net Sales}}{\text{Average Total Assets}}$$

To illustrate the use of this ratio, the following data (in millions) are taken from annual reports of Sears Holding Corporation and JCPenney:

	Sears	JCPenney
Total revenues (net sales)	$50,703	$19,903
Total assets:		
Beginning of year	27,397	12,673
End of year	30,066	12,461

The ratio of net sales to assets for each company is as follows:

	Sears	JCPenney
Ratio of net sales to assets	1.76*	1.58**

*$50,703/[($27,397 + $30,066)/2]
**$19,903/[($12,673 + $12,461)/2]

Based on these ratios, Sears appears better than JCPenney in utilizing its assets to generate sales. Comparing this ratio over time for both Sears and JCPenney, as well as comparing it with industry averages, would provide a better basis for interpreting the financial performance of each company.

A P P E N D I X   1

Accounting Systems for Merchandisers

Merchandising companies may use either manual or computerized accounting systems, similar to those used by service businesses. In this appendix, we describe and illustrate special journals and electronic forms that may be used in these systems.

Manual Accounting System

In a manual accounting system, a merchandise business normally uses the following four special journals:

Special Journal	Type of Transaction
Sales journal	Sales on account
Purchases journal	Purchases on account
Cash receipts journal	Cash receipts
Cash payments journal	Cash payments

enetsolutions

These journals can be adapted from the special journals that we illustrated in Chapter 5 for a service business.

Exhibit 12 illustrates NetSolutions' sales journal, which is modified from a revenue journal. In a sales journal, each transaction is recorded by entering the sales amount in the *Accounts Receivable Dr./Sales Cr.* column. The cost of the merchandise sold amount is entered in the *Cost of Merchandise Sold Dr./Merchandise Inventory Cr.* column. The totals of the two columns are posted to the general ledger accounts at the end of the month. The inventory and accounts receivable subsidiary ledgers are updated when each transaction is recorded.

Exhibit 12

Sales Journal for a Merchandising Business

Sales Journal — Page 35

Date	Invoice No.	Account Debited	Post. Ref.	Accts. Rec. Dr. Sales Cr.	Cost of Merchandise Sold Dr. Merchandise Inventory Cr.
2011 Mar. 2	810	Berry Co.	✓	2,750	2,000
14	811	Handler Co.	✓	4,260	3,470
19	812	Jordan Co.	✓	5,800	4,650
26	813	Kenner Co.	✓	4,500	3,840
				17,310	13,960
				(112) (410)	(510) (115)

Exhibit 13 illustrates a purchases journal for NetSolutions' merchandising business. This journal is similar to the purchases journal for NetSolutions' service business illustrated in Chapter 5. It includes an *Accounts Payable Cr.* column and a *Merchandise Inventory Dr.* column, rather than a *Supplies Dr.* column. At the end of the month, these two column totals are posted to the general ledger controlling accounts, Accounts Payable and Merchandise Inventory. The amounts in *Other Accounts Dr.* are posted individually. The inventory and accounts payable subsidiary ledgers are updated when each transaction is recorded.

Exhibit 13

Purchases Journal for a Merchandising Business

Purchases Journal — Page 11

Date		Account Credited	Post. Ref.	Accounts Payable Cr.	Merchandise Inventory Dr.	Other Accounts Dr.	Post. Ref.	Amount
2011 Mar.	4	Compu-Tek	✓	13,880	13,880			
	7	Omega Technologies	✓	4,650	4,650			
	15	Dale Furniture Co.	✓	5,700		Store Equipment	123	5,700
	22	Delta Data Link	✓	3,840	3,840			
	29	Power Electronics	✓	3,200	3,200			
				31,270	25,570			5,700
				(210)	(115)			(✓)

Exhibit 14 illustrates NetSolutions' cash receipts journal. Cash sales are recorded in a *Sales Cr.* column rather than a *Fees Earned Cr.* column. In addition, the cost of merchandise sold for cash sales is recorded in a *Cost of Merchandise Sold Dr./Merchandise Inventory Cr.* column. Sales discounts are recorded in a *Sales Discounts Dr.* column. At the end of the month, all the column totals except for *Other Accounts Cr.* are posted to the general ledger. The inventory and accounts receivable subsidiary ledgers are updated when each transaction is recorded.

Exhibit 14

Cash Receipts Journal for Merchandising Business

Cash Reciepts Journal — Page 14

Date		Account Credited	Post. Ref.	Other Accounts Cr.	Cost of Merchandise Sold Dr. Merchandise Inventory Cr.	Sales Cr.	Accounts Receivable Cr.	Sales Discounts Dr.	Cash Dr.
2011 Mar.	3	Sales	✓		400	600			600
	12	Berry Co.	✓				2,750	55	2,695

Exhibit 15 illustrates NetSolutions' cash payments journal. This journal is modified for a merchandising business by adding a *Merchandise Inventory Cr.* column for recording discounts on purchases paid within the discount period. The inventory and accounts payable subsidiary ledger are updated when each transaction is recorded. At the end of the month, all the column totals except for *Other Accounts Dr.* are posted to the general ledger.

Exhibit 15

Cash Payments Journal for Merchandising Business

						Cash Payments Journal		Page 7
Date	Ck. No.	Account Debited	Post. Ref.	Other Accounts Dr.	Accounts Payable Dr.	Merchandise Inventory Cr.	Cash Cr.
2011 Mar. 16	210	Compu-Tek	✓		13,880		13,880
17	211	Omega Technologies	✓		4,650	93	4,557

Computerized Accounting Systems

In computerized accounting systems, special journals are replaced by electronic forms. Electronic forms collect transaction data that are used for making computerized entries. In QuickBooks®, purchases and sales transactions are recorded using electronic bill and invoice forms.

To illustrate, NetSolutions purchased four LT-1000 servers for $13,880 on March 4, 2011 from Compu-Tek. This transaction was illustrated in the purchases journal in Exhibit 13. The "Enter Bills" form, shown in Exhibit 16, is used to record the purchase. The form is completed by entering the following data:

- Vendor: *Compu-Tek*
- Item purchased: *LT-1000 network server*
- Number purchased: *4*
- Cost per unit: *$3,470*
- Total amount of the purchase: *$13,880*

After the Enter Bills form has been completed and submitted (Save), QuickBooks® debits the cost of four LT-1000s to NetSolutions' Inventory and credits Accounts Payable to Compu-Tek for $13,880.

Assume that on March 14, 2011, NetSolutions invoices Handler Co. for the sale of one of the network servers. This transaction was illustrated in the sales journal in Exhibit 12.

Exhibit 16

Enter Bills Form

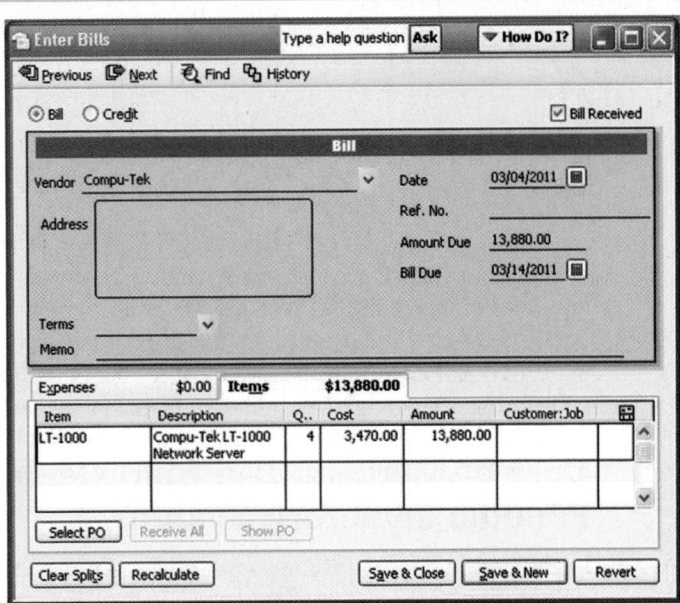

Exhibit 17

Create Invoice Form

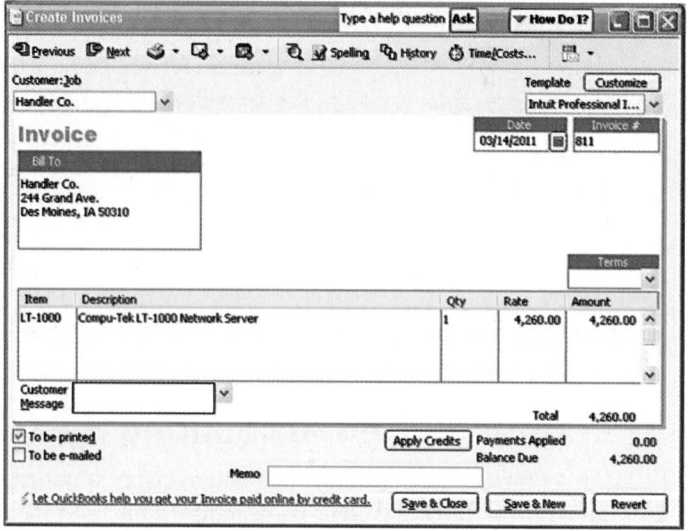

The sale can be entered in QuickBooks® using the "Create Invoices" form in QuickBooks®, as shown in Exhibit 17. The form is completed by entering the following data:

- Customer: *Handler Co*
- Item sold: *Compu-Tek LT-1000 network server*
- Quantity sold: *1*
- Price per item: *$4,260*
- Total invoice amount of the sale: *$4,260*

After the Create Invoice form has been completed and submitted to the system (Save), QuickBooks® debits Accounts Receivable for Handler Co. and credits Sales for $4,260. In addition, QuickBooks® debits Cost of Goods Sold and credits Inventory for the $3,470 cost of one LT-1000. This latter transaction is recorded automatically and is not shown on the Create Invoices form. The inventory and accounts receivable subsidiary ledgers are also automatically updated when the transaction is recorded.

An income statement prepared after these forms have been completed would show sales of $4,260, cost of goods sold of $3,470, and gross profit of $790. A balance sheet would show accounts receivable of $4,260, inventory of $10,410 (3 units × $3,470), accounts payable of $13,880, and retained earnings of $790.

A P P E N D I X   2

The Periodic Inventory System

Throughout this chapter, the perpetual inventory system was used to record purchases and sales of merchandise. Not all merchandise businesses, however, use the perpetual inventory system. For example, small merchandise businesses, such as a local hardware store, may use a manual accounting system. A manual perpetual inventory system is time consuming and costly to maintain. In this case, the periodic inventory system may be used.

Cost of Merchandise Sold Using the Periodic Inventory System

In the periodic inventory system, sales are recorded in the same manner as in the perpetual inventory system. However, cost of merchandise sold is not recorded on the

@netsolutions

Exhibit 18

Exhibit 18

Determining Cost of Merchandise Sold Using the Periodic System

Merchandise inventory, January 1, 2011			$ 59,700
Purchases		$521,980	
Less: Purchases returns and allowances	$9,100		
Purchases discounts	2,525	11,625	
Net purchases		$510,355	
Add freight in		17,400	
Cost of merchandise purchased			527,755
Merchandise available for sale			$587,455
Less merchandise inventory, December 31, 2011			62,150
Cost of merchandise sold			$525,305

date of sale. Instead, cost of merchandise sold is determined as shown in Exhibit 18 for NetSolutions.

Chart of Accounts Under the Periodic Inventory System

The chart of accounts under a periodic inventory system is shown in Exhibit 19. The accounts used to record transactions under the periodic inventory system are highlighted in Exhibit 19.

Exhibit 19

Chart of Accounts Under the Periodic Inventory System

Balance Sheet Accounts	Income Statement Accounts
100 Assets	**400 Revenues**
110 Cash	410 Sales
111 Notes Receivable	411 Sales Returns and Allowances
112 Accounts Receivable	412 Sales Discounts
115 Merchandise Inventory	**500 Costs and Expenses**
116 Office Supplies	510 Purchases
117 Prepaid Insurance	511 Purchases Returns and
120 Land	Allowances
123 Store Equipment	512 Purchases Discounts
124 Accumulated Depreciation—	513 Freight In
Store Equipment	520 Sales Salaries Expense
125 Office Equipment	521 Advertising Expense
126 Accumulated Depreciation—	522 Depreciation Expense—Store
Office Equipment	Equipment
	523 Delivery Expense
200 Liabilities	529 Miscellaneous Selling Expense
210 Accounts Payable	530 Office Salaries Expense
211 Salaries Payable	531 Rent Expense
212 Unearned Rent	532 Depreciation Expense—Office
215 Notes Payable	Equipment
	533 Insurance Expense
300 Owner's Equity	534 Office Supplies Expense
310 Chris Clark, Capital	539 Misc. Administrative Expense
311 Chris Clark, Drawing	**600 Other Income**
312 Income Summary	610 Rent Revenue
	700 Other Expense
	710 Interest Expense

Recording Merchandise Transactions Under the Periodic Inventory System

Using the periodic inventory system, purchases of inventory are not recorded in the merchandise inventory account. Instead, purchases, purchases discounts, and purchases returns and allowances accounts are used. In addition, the sales of merchandise are not recorded in the inventory account. Thus, there is no detailed record of the amount of inventory on hand at any given time. At the end of the period, a physical count of merchandise inventory on hand is taken. This physical count is used to determine the cost of merchandise sold as shown in Exhibit 18.

The use of purchases, purchases discounts, purchases returns and allowances, and freight in accounts are described below.

Purchases Purchases of inventory are recorded in a purchases account rather than in the merchandise inventory account. Purchases is debited for the invoice amount of a purchase.

Purchases Discounts Purchases discounts are normally recorded in a separate purchases discounts account. The balance of the purchases discounts account is reported as a deduction from Purchases for the period. Thus, Purchases Discounts is a contra (or offsetting) account to Purchases.

Purchases Returns and Allowances Purchases returns and allowances are recorded in a similar manner as purchases discounts. A separate purchases returns and allowances account is used to record returns and allowances. Purchases returns and allowances are reported as a deduction from Purchases for the period. Thus, Purchases Returns and Allowances is a contra (or offsetting) account to Purchases.

Freight In When merchandise is purchased FOB shipping point, the buyer pays for the freight. Under the periodic inventory system, freight paid when purchasing merchandise FOB shipping point is debited to Freight In, Transportation In, or a similar account.

The preceding periodic inventory accounts and their effect on the cost of merchandise purchased are summarized below.

Account	Entry to Increase (Decrease)	Normal Balance	Effect on Cost of Merchandise Purchased
Purchases	Debit	Debit	Increases
Purchases Discounts	Credit	Credit	Decreases
Purchases Returns and Allowances	Credit	Credit	Decreases
Freight In	Debit	Debit	Increases

Exhibit 20 illustrates the recording of merchandise transactions using the periodic system. As a review, Exhibit 20 also illustrates how each transaction would have been recorded using the perpetual system.

Adjusting Process Under the Periodic Inventory System

The adjusting process is the same under the periodic and perpetual inventory systems except for the inventory shrinkage adjustment. The ending merchandise inventory is determined by a physical count under both systems.

Under the perpetual inventory system, the ending inventory physical count is compared to the balance of Merchandise Inventory. The difference is the amount of inventory shrinkage. The inventory shrinkage is then recorded as a debit to Cost of Merchandise Sold and a credit to Merchandise Inventory.

Under the periodic inventory system, the merchandise inventory account is not kept up to date for purchases and sales. As a result, the inventory shrinkage cannot be directly determined. Instead, any inventory shrinkage is included indirectly in the computation of cost of merchandise sold as shown in Exhibit 18. This is a major disadvantage of the periodic inventory system. That is, under the periodic inventory system, inventory shrinkage is not separately determined.

Exhibit 20

Transactions Using the Periodic and Perpetual Inventory Systems

Transaction	Periodic Inventory System		Perpetual Inventory System	

June 5. Purchased $30,000 of merchandise on account, terms 2/10, n/30.	Purchases 30,000
	  Accounts Payable. . . . . . .
		30,000	Merchandise Inventory 30,000
			  Accounts Payable. . . . .
				30,000

June 8. Returned merchandise purchased on account on June 5, $500.	Accounts Payable 500
	  Purchases Returns and Allowances
		500	Accounts Payable. 500
			  Merchandise Inventory . . . .
				500

June 15. Paid for purchase of June 5, less return of $500 and discount of $590 [($30,000 − $500) × 2%].	Accounts Payable. 29,500
	  Cash . . . .
	  Purchases Discounts . . . .
		
		28,910
		590
			Accounts Payable 29,500
			  Cash . . . .
			  Merchandise Inventory . . . .
				
				28,910
				590

June 18. Sold merchandise on account, $12,500, 1/10, n/30. The cost of the merchandise sold was $9,000.	Accounts Receivable 12,500
	  Sales . . . .
		12,500	Accounts Receivable 12,500
			  Sales. . . . .
			Cost of Merchandise Sold 9,000
			  Merchandise Inventory . . . .
				
				12,500
				
				9,000

June 21. Received merchandise returned on account, $4,000. The cost of the merchandise returned was $2,800.	Sales Returns and Allowances . . 4,000
	  Accounts Receivable . . . .
		4,000	Sales Returns and Allowances . . 4,000
			  Accounts Receivable . . . .
			Merchandise Inventory 2,800
			  Cost of Merchandise Sold . .
				
				4,000
				
				2,800

June 22. Purchased merchandise, $15,000, terms FOB shipping point, 2/15, n/30, with prepaid freight of $750 added to the invoice.	Purchases 15,000
	Freight In. 750
	  Accounts Payable . . . .
		
		15,750
			Merchandise Inventory. 15,750
			  Accounts Payable . . . .
				15,750

June 28. Received $8,415 as payment on account from June 18 sale less return of June 21 and less discount of $85 [($12,500 − $4,000) × 1%].	Cash 8,415
	Sales Discounts. 85
	  Accounts Receivable . . . .
		
		8,500
			Cash 8,415
			Sales Discounts 85
			  Accounts Receivable. . . . . . .
				
				8,500

June 29. Received $19,600 from cash sales. The cost of the merchandise sold was $13,800.	Cash. 19,600
	  Sales. . . . .
		19,600	Cash. 19,600
			  Sales . . . .
			Cost of Merchandise Sold. . . . 13,800
			  Merchandise Inventory . . . .
				
				19,600
				
				13,800

Financial Statements Under the Periodic Inventory System

The financial statements are similar under the perpetual and periodic inventory systems. When a multiple-step income statement is prepared, cost of merchandise sold may be reported as shown in Exhibit 18.

Closing Entries Under the Periodic Inventory System

The closing entries differ in the periodic inventory system in that there is no cost of merchandise sold account to close to Income Summary. Instead, the purchases, purchases discounts, purchases returns and allowances, and freight in accounts are closed to Income Summary. In addition, the merchandise inventory account is adjusted to the end-of-period physical inventory count during the closing process.

The four closing entries under the periodic inventory system are as follows:

1. Debit each temporary account with a credit balance, such as Sales, for its balance and credit Income Summary. Since Purchases Discounts and Purchases Returns and Allowances are temporary accounts with credit balances, they are debited for their balances. In addition, Merchandise Inventory is debited for its end-of-period balance based on the end-of-period physical inventory.

2. Credit each temporary account with a debit balance, such as the various expenses, and debit Income Summary. Since Sales Returns and Allowances, Sales Discounts, Purchases, and Freight In are temporary accounts with debit balances, they are credited for their balances. In addition, Merchandise Inventory is credited for its balance as of the beginning of the period.

3. Debit Income Summary for the amount of its balance (net income) and credit the owner's capital account. The accounts debited and credited are reversed if there is a net loss.

4. Debit the owner's capital account for the balance of the drawing account and credit the drawing account.

The four closing entries for NetSolutions under the periodic inventory system are:

Journal

Date		Item	Post. Ref.	Debit	Credit
2011		Closing Entries			
Dec.	31	Merchandise Inventory	115	62,150	
		Sales	410	720,185	
		Purchases Returns and Allowances	511	9,100	
		Purchases Discounts	512	2,525	
		Rent Revenue	610	600	
		Income Summary	312		794,560
	31	Income Summary	312	719,160	
		Merchandise Inventory	115		59,700
		Sales Returns and Allowances	411		6,140
		Sales Discounts	412		5,790
		Purchases	510		521,980
		Freight In	513		17,400
		Sales Salaries Expense	520		53,430
		Advertising Expense	521		10,860
		Depreciation Expense—Store Equipment	522		3,100
		Delivery Expense	523		2,800
		Miscellaneous Selling Expense	529		630
		Office Salaries Expense	530		21,020
		Rent Expense	531		8,100
		Depreciation Expense—Office Equipment	532		2,490
		Insurance Expense	533		1,910
		Office Supplies Expense	534		610
		Miscellaneous Administrative Expense	539		760
		Interest Expense	710		2,440
	31	Income Summary	312	75,400	
		Chris Clark, Capital	310		75,400
	31	Chris Clark, Capital	310	18,000	
		Chris Clark, Drawing	311		18,000

In the first closing entry, Merchandise Inventory is debited for $62,150. This is the ending physical inventory count on December 31, 2011. In the second closing entry,

Merchandise Inventory is credited for its January 1, 2011, balance of $59,700. In this way, the closing entries highlight the importance of the beginning and ending balances of Merchandise Inventory in determining cost of merchandise sold, as shown in Exhibit 18. After the closing entries are posted, Merchandise Inventory will have a balance of $62,150. This is the amount reported on the December 31, 2011, balance sheet.

In the preceding closing entries, the periodic accounts are highlighted in color. Under the perpetual inventory system, the highlighted periodic inventory accounts are replaced by the cost of merchandise sold account.

At a Glance 6

1 Distinguish between the activities and financial statements of service and merchandising businesses.

Key Points	Key Learning Outcomes	Example Exercises	Practice Exercises
The primary differences between a service business and a merchandising business relate to revenue activities. Merchandising businesses purchase merchandise for selling to customers. On a merchandising business's income statement, revenue from selling merchandise is reported as sales. The cost of the merchandise sold is subtracted from sales to arrive at gross profit. The operating expenses are subtracted from gross profit to arrive at net income. Merchandise inventory, which is merchandise not sold, is reported as a current asset on the balance sheet.	• Describe how the activities of a service and a merchandising business differ. • Describe the differences between the income statements of a service and a merchandising business. • Compute gross profit. • Describe how merchandise inventory is reported on the balance sheet.	 6-1	 6-1A, 6-1B

2 Describe and illustrate the financial statements of a merchandising business.

Key Points	Key Learning Outcomes	Example Exercises	Practice Exercises
The multiple-step income statement of a merchandiser reports sales, sales returns and allowances, sales discounts, and net sales. The cost of the merchandise sold is subtracted from net sales to determine the gross profit. The cost of merchandise sold is determined by using either the periodic or perpetual inventory system. Operating income is determined by subtracting operating expenses from gross profit. Operating expenses are normally classified as selling or administrative expenses. Net income is determined by adding or subtracting the net of other income and expense. The income statement may also be reported in a single-step form. The statement of owner's equity is similar to that for a service business. The balance sheet reports merchandise inventory at the end of the period as a current asset.	• Prepare a multiple-step income statement for a merchandising business. • Describe how cost of merchandise sold is determined under a periodic inventory system. • Compute cost of merchandise sold under a periodic inventory system as shown in Exhibit 2. • Prepare a single-step income statement. • Prepare a statement of owner's equity for a merchandising business. • Prepare a balance sheet for a merchandising business.	 6-2	 6-2A, 6-2B

Describe and illustrate the accounting for merchandise transactions including:

- sale of merchandise
- purchase of merchandise
- freight, sales taxes, and trade discounts
- dual nature of merchandising transactions

Key Points	Key Learning Outcomes	Example Exercises	Practice Exercises
Sales of merchandise for cash or on account are recorded by crediting Sales. Under the perpetual inventory system, the cost of merchandise sold and the reduction in merchandise inventory are also recorded for the sale. For sales of merchandise on account, the credit terms may allow discounts for early payment. Such discounts are recorded by the seller as a debit to Sales Discounts. Sales discounts are reported as a deduction from the amount initially recorded in Sales. Likewise, when merchandise is returned or a price adjustment is granted, the seller debits Sales Returns and Allowances.	• Prepare journal entries to record sales of merchandise for cash or using a credit card.		
	• Prepare journal entries to record sales of merchandise on account.	**6-3**	6-3A, 6-3B
	• Prepare journal entries to record sales discounts and sales returns and allowances.	**6-3**	6-3A, 6-3B
Purchases of merchandise for cash or on account are recorded by debiting Merchandise Inventory. For purchases of merchandise on account, the credit terms may allow cash discounts for early payment. Such purchases discounts are viewed as a reduction in the cost of the merchandise purchased. When merchandise is returned or a price adjustment is granted, the buyer credits Merchandise Inventory.	• Prepare journal entries to record the purchase of merchandise for cash.		
	• Prepare journal entries to record the purchase of merchandise on account.	**6-4**	6-4A, 6-4B
	• Prepare journal entries to record purchases discounts and purchases returns and allowances.	**6-4**	6-4A, 6-4B
When merchandise is shipped FOB shipping point, the buyer pays the freight and debits Merchandise Inventory. When merchandise is shipped FOB destination, the seller pays the freight and debits Delivery Expense or Freight Out. If the seller prepays freight as a convenience to the buyer, the seller debits Accounts Receivable for the costs.	• Prepare journal entries for freight from the point of view of the buyer and seller.		
	• Determine the total cost of the purchase of merchandise under differing freight terms.	**6-5**	6-5A, 6-5B
The liability for sales tax is incurred when the sale is made and is recorded by the seller as a credit to the sales tax payable account. When the amount of the sales tax is paid to the taxing unit, Sales Tax Payable is debited and Cash is credited.	• Prepare journal entries for the collection and payment of sales taxes by the seller.		
Many wholesalers offer trade discounts, which are discounts off the list prices of merchandise. Normally, neither the seller nor the buyer records the list price and the related trade discount in the accounts.	• Determine the cost of merchandise purchased when a trade discount is offered by the seller.		
Each merchandising transaction affects a buyer and a seller. The illustration in this chapter shows how the same transactions would be recorded by both.	• Record the same merchandise transactions for the buyer and seller.	**6-6**	6-6A, 6-6B

Key Points	Key Learning Outcomes	Example Exercises	Practice Exercises
The accounting cycle for a merchandising business is similar to that of a service business. However, a merchandiser is likely to experience inventory shrinkage, which must be recorded. The normal adjusting entry is to debit Cost of Merchandise Sold and credit Merchandise Inventory for the amount of the shrinkage.	• Prepare the adjusting journal entry for inventory shrinkage.	6-7	6-7A, 6-7B
The closing entries for a merchandising business are similar to those for a service business. The first entry closes sales and other revenue to Income Summary. The second entry closes cost of merchandise sold, sales discounts, sales returns and allowances, and other expenses to Income Summary. The third entry closes the balance of Income Summary (the net income or net loss) to the owner's capital account. The fourth entry closes the owner's drawing account to the owner's capital account.	• Prepare the closing entries for a merchandising business.		

Key Terms

account form (259)

administrative expenses (general expenses) (257)

cost of merchandise purchased (256)

cost of merchandise sold (254)

credit memorandum (credit memo) (264)

credit period (263)

credit terms (263)

debit memorandum (debit memo) (267)

FOB (free on board) destination (269)

FOB (free on board) shipping point (269)

freight in (256)

gross profit (254)

income from operations (operating income) (257)

inventory shrinkage (inventory shortage) (274)

invoice (262)

merchandise available for sale (256)

merchandise inventory (254)

multiple-step income statement (254)

net purchases (256)

net sales (255)

other expense (258)

other income (258)

periodic inventory system (256)

perpetual inventory system (257)

purchases returns and allowance (256)

purchases discounts (256)

report form (259)

sales (254)

sales discounts (255)

sales returns and allowances (255)

selling expenses (257)

single-step income statement (258)

trade discounts (272)

Illustrative Problem

The following transactions were completed by Montrose Company during May of the current year. Montrose Company uses a perpetual inventory system.

May 3. Purchased merchandise on account from Floyd Co., $4,000, terms FOB shipping point, 2/10, n/30, with prepaid freight of $120 added to the invoice.

May 5. Purchased merchandise on account from Kramer Co., $8,500, terms FOB destination, 1/10, n/30.

6. Sold merchandise on account to C. F. Howell Co., list price $4,000, trade discount 30%, terms 2/10, n/30. The cost of the merchandise sold was $1,125.

8. Purchased office supplies for cash, $150.

10. Returned merchandise purchased on May 5 from Kramer Co., $1,300.

13. Paid Floyd Co. on account for purchase of May 3, less discount.

14. Purchased merchandise for cash, $10,500.

15. Paid Kramer Co. on account for purchase of May 5, less return of May 10 and discount.

16. Received cash on account from sale of May 6 to C. F. Howell Co., less discount.

19. Sold merchandise on MasterCard credit cards, $2,450. The cost of the merchandise sold was $980.

22. Sold merchandise on account to Comer Co., $3,480, terms 2/10, n/30. The cost of the merchandise sold was $1,400.

24. Sold merchandise for cash, $4,350. The cost of the merchandise sold was $1,750.

25. Received merchandise returned by Comer Co. from sale on May 22, $1,480. The cost of the returned merchandise was $600.

31. Paid a service processing fee of $140 for MasterCard sales.

Instructions

1. Journalize the preceding transactions.
2. Journalize the adjusting entry for merchandise inventory shrinkage, $3,750.

Solution

1.

May	3	Merchandise Inventory		4,120	
		Accounts Payable—Floyd Co.			4,120
	5	Merchandise Inventory		8,500	
		Accounts Payable—Kramer Co.			8,500
	6	Accounts Receivable—C. F. Howell Co.		2,800	
		Sales			2,800
		[$4,000 − (30% × $4,000)].			
	6	Cost of Merchandise Sold		1,125	
		Merchandise Inventory			1,125
	8	Office Supplies		150	
		Cash			150
	10	Accounts Payable—Kramer Co.		1,300	
		Merchandise Inventory			1,300
	13	Accounts Payable—Floyd Co.		4,120	
		Merchandise Inventory			80
		Cash			4,040
		[$4,000 − (2% × $4,000) + $120].			
	14	Merchandise Inventory		10,500	
		Cash			10,500
	15	Accounts Payable—Kramer Co.		7,200	
		Merchandise Inventory			72
		Cash			7,128
		[($8,500 − $1,300) × 1% = $72;			
		$8,500 − $1,300 − $72 = $7,128].			
	16	Cash		2,744	
		Sales Discounts		56	
		Accounts Receivable—C. F. Howell Co.			2,800
	19	Cash		2,450	
		Sales			2,450
	19	Cost of Merchandise Sold		980	
		Merchandise Inventory			980
	22	Accounts Receivable—Comer Co.		3,480	
		Sales			3,480
	22	Cost of Merchandise Sold		1,400	
		Merchandise Inventory			1,400

May 24	Cash		4,350	
	Sales			4,350
24	Cost of Merchandise Sold		1,750	
	Merchandise Inventory			1,750
25	Sales Returns and Allowances		1,480	
	Accounts Receivable—Comer Co.			1,480
25	Merchandise Inventory		600	
	Cost of Merchandise Sold			600
31	Credit Card Expense		140	
	Cash			140
2. May 31	Cost of Merchandise Sold		3,750	
	Merchandise Inventory			3,750
	Inventory shrinkage.			

Self-Examination Questions (Answers at End of Chapter)

1. If merchandise purchased on account is returned, the buyer may inform the seller of the details by issuing a(n):
   A. debit memo.   C. invoice.
   B. credit memo.   D. bill.

2. If merchandise is sold on account to a customer for $1,000, terms FOB shipping point, 1/10, n/30, and the seller prepays $50 in freight, the amount of the discount for early payment would be:
   A. $0.   C. $10.00.
   B. $5.00.   D. $10.50.

3. The income statement in which the total of all expenses is deducted from the total of all revenues is termed the:
   A. multiple-step form.   C. account form.
   B. single-step form.   D. report form.

4. On a multiple-step income statement, the excess of net sales over the cost of merchandise sold is called:
   A. operating income.
   B. income from operations.
   C. gross profit.
   D. net income.

5. Which of the following expenses would normally be classified as other expense on a multiple-step income statement?
   A. Depreciation expense—office equipment
   B. Sales salaries expense
   C. Insurance expense
   D. Interest expense

Eye Openers

1. What distinguishes a merchandising business from a service business?
2. Can a business earn a gross profit but incur a net loss? Explain.
3. In computing the cost of merchandise sold, does each of the following items increase or decrease that cost? (a) freight, (b) beginning merchandise inventory, (c) purchase discounts, (d) ending merchandise inventory
4. Describe how the periodic system differs from the perpetual system of accounting for merchandise inventory.
5. Differentiate between the multiple-step and the single-step forms of the income statement.
6. What are the major advantages and disadvantages of the single-step form of income statement compared to the multiple-step statement?
7. What type of revenue is reported in the other income section of the multiple-step income statement?
8. Name at least three accounts that would normally appear in the chart of accounts of a merchandising business but would not appear in the chart of accounts of a service business.

9. How are sales to customers using MasterCard and VISA recorded?
10. The credit period during which the buyer of merchandise is allowed to pay usually begins with what date?
11. What is the meaning of (a) 1/15, n/60; (b) n/30; (c) n/eom?
12. What is the nature of (a) a credit memo issued by the seller of merchandise, (b) a debit memo issued by the buyer of merchandise?
13. Who bears the freight when the terms of sale are (a) FOB shipping point, (b) FOB destination?
14. Business Outfitters Inc., which uses a perpetual inventory system, experienced a normal inventory shrinkage of $9,175. What accounts would be debited and credited to record the adjustment for the inventory shrinkage at the end of the accounting period?
15. Assume that Business Outfitters Inc. in Eye Opener 14 experienced an abnormal inventory shrinkage of $80,750. Business Outfitters Inc. has decided to record the abnormal inventory shrinkage so that it would be separately disclosed on the income statement. What account would be debited for the abnormal inventory shrinkage?

Practice Exercises

PE 6-1A
Gross profit

obj. 1

EE 6-1   p. 254

During the current year, merchandise is sold for $32,800 cash and $379,500 on account. The cost of the merchandise sold is $250,000. What is the amount of the gross profit?

PE 6-1B
Gross profit

obj. 1

EE 6-1   p. 254

During the current year, merchandise is sold for $375,000 cash and $815,000 on account. The cost of the merchandise sold is $700,000. What is the amount of the gross profit?

PE 6-2A
Cost of merchandise sold

obj. 2

EE 6-2   p. 258

Based on the following data, determine the cost of merchandise sold for June:

Merchandise inventory, June 1	$ 35,500
Merchandise inventory, June 30	40,500
Purchases	384,000
Purchases returns and allowances	11,000
Purchases discounts	3,000
Freight in	6,000

PE 6-2B
Cost of merchandise sold

obj. 2

EE 6-2   p. 258

Based on the following data, determine the cost of merchandise sold for August:

Merchandise inventory, August 1	$120,000
Merchandise inventory, August 31	150,000
Purchases	780,000
Purchases returns and allowances	20,000
Purchases discounts	10,000
Freight in	5,000

PE 6-3A
Sales transactions

obj. 3

EE 6-3   p. 265

Journalize the following merchandise transactions:

a. Sold merchandise on account, $41,000 with terms 1/10, n/30. The cost of the merchandise sold was $22,500.
b. Received payment less the discount.

PE 6-3B
Sales transactions
obj. 3
EE 6-3   p. 265

Journalize the following merchandise transactions:
a. Sold merchandise on account, $16,000 with terms 2/10, n/30. The cost of the merchandise sold was $9,600.
b. Received payment less the discount.

PE 6-4A
Purchase transactions
obj. 3
EE 6-4   p. 268

Kosmos Company purchased merchandise on account from a supplier for $21,500, terms 1/10, n/30. Kosmos Company returned $1,500 of the merchandise and received full credit.
a. If Kosmos Company pays the invoice within the discount period, what is the amount of cash required for the payment?
b. Under a perpetual inventory system, what account is debited by Kosmos Company to record the return?

PE 6-4B
Purchase transactions
obj. 3
EE 6-4   p. 268

Enduro Tile Company purchased merchandise on account from a supplier for $8,000, terms 2/10, n/30. Enduro Tile Company returned $3,500 of the merchandise and received full credit.
a. If Enduro Tile Company pays the invoice within the discount period, what is the amount of cash required for the payment?
b. Under a perpetual inventory system, what account is credited by Enduro Tile Company to record the return?

PE 6-5A
Freight terms
obj. 3
EE 6-5   p. 271

Determine the amount to be paid in full settlement of each of invoices (a) and (b), assuming that credit for returns and allowances was received prior to payment and that all invoices were paid within the discount period.

	Merchandise	Freight Paid by Seller	Freight Terms	Returns and Allowances
a.	$13,150	$450	FOB destination, 1/10, n/30	$4,150
b.	32,100	900	FOB shipping point, 2/10, n/30	5,000

PE 6-5B
Freight terms
obj. 3
EE 6-5   p. 271

Determine the amount to be paid in full settlement of each of invoices (a) and (b), assuming that credit for returns and allowances was received prior to payment and that all invoices were paid within the discount period.

	Merchandise	Freight Paid by Seller	Freight Terms	Returns and Allowances
a.	$9,000	$300	FOB shipping point, 1/10, n/30	$2,500
b.	7,500	200	FOB destination, 2/10, n/30	400

PE 6-6A
Transactions for buyer and seller
obj. 3
EE 6-6   p. 273

Saddlebag Co. sold merchandise to Bioscan Co. on account, $17,500, terms FOB shipping point, 2/10, n/30. The cost of the merchandise sold is $10,000. Saddlebag Co. paid freight of $600 and later received the amount due within the discount period. Journalize Saddlebag Co.'s and Bioscan Co.'s entries for the payment of the amount due.

PE 6-6B
Transactions for buyer and seller
obj. 3
EE 6-6   p. 273

Santana Co. sold merchandise to Birch Co. on account, $6,000, terms 2/15, n/30. The cost of the merchandise sold is $4,000. Santana Co. issued a credit memo for $800 for merchandise returned and later received the amount due within the discount period. The cost of the merchandise returned was $550. Journalize Santana Co.'s and Birch Co.'s entries for the payment of the amount due.

PE 6-7A
Inventory shrinkage
obj. 4
EE 6-7   p. 274

Retro Company's perpetual inventory records indicate that $975,000 of merchandise should be on hand on October 31, 2010. The physical inventory indicates that $894,750 of merchandise is actually on hand. Journalize the adjusting entry for the inventory shrinkage for Retro Company for the year ended October 31, 2010. Assume that the inventory shrinkage is a normal amount.

PE 6-7B
Inventory shrinkage

obj. 4

EE 6-7 p. 274

Hairology Company's perpetual inventory records indicate that $120,500 of merchandise should be on hand on April 30, 2010. The physical inventory indicates that $115,850 of merchandise is actually on hand. Journalize the adjusting entry for the inventory shrinkage for Hairology Company for the year ended April 30, 2010. Assume that the inventory shrinkage is a normal amount.

Exercises

EX 6-1
Determining gross profit

obj. 1

During the current year, merchandise is sold for $795,000. The cost of the merchandise sold is $477,000.

a. What is the amount of the gross profit?
b. Compute the gross profit percentage (gross profit divided by sales).
c. ━━━━▶ Will the income statement necessarily report a net income? Explain.

EX 6-2
Determining cost of merchandise sold

obj. 1

In 2007, Best Buy reported revenue of $35,934 million. Its gross profit was $8,769 million. What was the amount of Best Buy's cost of merchandise sold?

EX 6-3
Identify items missing in determining cost of merchandise sold

obj. 2

For (a) through (d), identify the items designated by "X" and "Y."

a. Purchases − (X + Y) = Net purchases.
b. Net purchases + X = Cost of merchandise purchased.
c. Merchandise inventory (beginning) + Cost of merchandise purchased = X.
d. Merchandise available for sale − X = Cost of merchandise sold.

EX 6-4
Cost of merchandise sold and related items

obj. 2

✔ a. Cost of merchandise sold, $1,400,600

The following data were extracted from the accounting records of Wedgeforth Company for the year ended November 30, 2010:

Merchandise inventory, December 1, 2009	$ 210,000
Merchandise inventory, November 30, 2010	185,000
Purchases	1,400,000
Purchases returns and allowances	20,000
Purchases discounts	18,500
Sales	2,250,000
Freight in	14,100

a. Prepare the cost of merchandise sold section of the income statement for the year ended November 30, 2010, using the periodic inventory system.
b. Determine the gross profit to be reported on the income statement for the year ended November 30, 2010.

EX 6-5

Cost of merchandise sold

obj. 2

✔ Correct cost of merchandise sold, $953,500

Identify the errors in the following schedule of cost of merchandise sold for the current year ended July 31, 2010:

Cost of merchandise sold:			
Merchandise inventory, July 31, 2010			$ 140,000
Purchases		$975,000	
Plus: Purchases returns and allowances	$12,000		
Purchases discounts	8,000	20,000	
Gross purchases		$995,000	
Less freight in		13,500	
Cost of merchandise purchased			981,500
Merchandise available for sale			$1,121,500
Less merchandise inventory, August 1, 2009			125,000
Cost of merchandise sold			$ 996,500

EX 6-6

Income statement for merchandiser

obj. 2

For the fiscal year, sales were $5,280,000, sales discounts were $100,000, sales returns and allowances were $75,000, and the cost of merchandise sold was $3,000,000.

a. What was the amount of net sales?

b. What was the amount of gross profit?

EX 6-7

Income statement for merchandiser

obj. 2

The following expenses were incurred by a merchandising business during the year. In which expense section of the income statement should each be reported: (a) selling, (b) administrative, or (c) other?

1. Advertising expense
2. Depreciation expense on store equipment
3. Insurance expense on office equipment
4. Interest expense on notes payable
5. Rent expense on office building
6. Salaries of office personnel
7. Salary of sales manager
8. Sales supplies used

EX 6-8

Single-step income statement

obj. 2

✔ Net income: $1,320,000

Summary operating data for Paper Plus Company during the current year ended June 30, 2010, are as follows: cost of merchandise sold, $4,000,000; administrative expenses, $500,000; interest expense, $30,000; rent revenue, $100,000; net sales, $6,500,000; and selling expenses, $750,000. Prepare a single-step income statement.

EX 6-9

Multiple-step income statement

obj. 2

Identify the errors in the following income statement:

Armortec Company
Income Statement
For the Year Ended February 28, 2010

Revenue from sales:			
Sales		$5,345,800	
Add: Sales returns and allowances	$120,000		
Sales discounts	60,000	180,000	
Gross sales			$5,525,800
Cost of merchandise sold			3,100,800
Income from operations			$2,425,000
Expenses:			
Selling expenses		$ 800,000	
Administrative expenses		600,000	
Delivery expense		50,000	
Total expenses			1,450,000
			$ 975,000
Other expense:			
Interest revenue			40,000
Gross profit			$ 935,000

EX 6-10
Determining amounts for items omitted from income statement

obj. 2

✔ a. $15,000
✔ h. $520,000

Two items are omitted in each of the following four lists of income statement data. Determine the amounts of the missing items, identifying them by letter.

Sales	$250,000	$600,000	$1,000,000	$ (g)
Sales returns and allowances	(a)	30,000	(e)	7,500
Sales discounts	10,000	18,000	40,000	11,500
Net sales	225,000	(c)	910,000	(h)
Cost of merchandise sold	(b)	330,000	(f)	400,000
Gross profit	90,000	(d)	286,500	120,000

EX 6-11
Multiple-step income statement

obj. 2

✔ a. Net income: $275,000

On March 31, 2010, the balances of the accounts appearing in the ledger of El Dorado Furnishings Company, a furniture wholesaler, are as follows:

Administrative Expenses	$ 250,000	Ricardo Cepeda, Capital	$1,137,600
Building	1,025,000	Ricardo Cepeda, Drawing	50,000
Cash	97,000	Salaries Payable	6,000
Cost of Merchandise Sold	1,400,000	Sales	2,550,000
Interest Expense	15,000	Sales Discounts	40,000
Merchandise Inventory	260,000	Sales Returns and Allowances	160,000
Notes Payable	59,000	Selling Expenses	410,000
Office Supplies	21,200	Store Supplies	15,400

a. Prepare a multiple-step income statement for the year ended March 31, 2010.
b. Compare the major advantages and disadvantages of the multiple-step and single-step forms of income statements.

EX 6-12
Chart of accounts

obj. 3

Frazee Paints Co. is a newly organized business with a list of accounts arranged in alphabetical order below.

Accounts Payable	Miscellaneous Administrative Expense
Accounts Receivable	Miscellaneous Selling Expense
Accumulated Depreciation—Office Equipment	Notes Payable
Accumulated Depreciation—Store Equipment	Office Equipment
Advertising Expense	Office Salaries Expense
Cash	Office Supplies
Cost of Merchandise Sold	Office Supplies Expense
Delivery Expense	Prepaid Insurance
Depreciation Expense—Office Equipment	Rent Expense
Depreciation Expense—Store Equipment	Salaries Payable
Income Summary	Sales
Insurance Expense	Sales Discounts
Interest Expense	Sales Returns and Allowances
Jim Frazee, Capital	Sales Salaries Expense
Jim Frazee, Drawing	Store Equipment
Land	Store Supplies
Merchandise Inventory	Store Supplies Expense

Construct a chart of accounts, assigning account numbers and arranging the accounts in balance sheet and income statement order, as illustrated in Exhibit 6. Each account number is three digits: the first digit is to indicate the major classification ("1" for assets, and so on); the second digit is to indicate the subclassification ("11" for current assets, and so on); and the third digit is to identify the specific account ("110" for Cash, and so on).

EX 6-13
Sales-related transactions, including the use of credit cards

obj. 3

Journalize the entries for the following transactions:

a. Sold merchandise for cash, $18,500. The cost of the merchandise sold was $11,000.
b. Sold merchandise on account, $12,000. The cost of the merchandise sold was $7,200.
c. Sold merchandise to customers who used MasterCard and VISA, $115,200. The cost of the merchandise sold was $70,000.
d. Sold merchandise to customers who used American Express, $45,000. The cost of the merchandise sold was $27,000.
e. Received an invoice from National Credit Co. for $5,600, representing a service fee paid for processing MasterCard, VISA, and American Express sales.

EX 6-14
Sales returns and allowances
obj. 3

During the year, sales returns and allowances totaled $65,900. The cost of the merchandise returned was $40,000. The accountant recorded all the returns and allowances by debiting the sales account and crediting Cost of Merchandise Sold for $65,900. ———➤ Was the accountant's method of recording returns acceptable? Explain. In your explanation, include the advantages of using a sales returns and allowances account.

EX 6-15
Sales-related transactions
obj. 3

After the amount due on a sale of $25,000, terms 1/10, n/eom, is received from a customer within the discount period, the seller consents to the return of the entire shipment. The cost of the merchandise returned was $15,000. (a) What is the amount of the refund owed to the customer? (b) Journalize the entries made by the seller to record the return and the refund.

EX 6-16
Sales-related transactions
obj. 3

The debits and credits for three related transactions are presented in the following T accounts. Describe each transaction.

Cash				Sales		
(5)	17,640				(1)	20,000

Accounts Receivable				Sales Discounts		
(1)	20,000	(3)	2,000	(5)	360	
		(5)	18,000			

Merchandise Inventory				Sales Returns and Allowances		
(4)	1,000	(2)	12,000	(3)	2,000	

				Cost of Merchandise Sold		
				(2)	12,000	(4)	1,000

EX 6-17
Sales-related transactions
obj. 3
✔ d. $12,775

Merchandise is sold on account to a customer for $12,500, terms FOB shipping point, 1/10, n/30. The seller paid the freight of $400. Determine the following: (a) amount of the sale, (b) amount debited to Accounts Receivable, (c) amount of the discount for early payment, and (d) amount due within the discount period.

EX 6-18
Purchase-related transaction
obj. 3

Newgen Company purchased merchandise on account from a supplier for $9,000, terms 2/10, n/30. Newgen Company returned $1,200 of the merchandise and received full credit.

a. If Newgen Company pays the invoice within the discount period, what is the amount of cash required for the payment?
b. Under a perpetual inventory system, what account is credited by Newgen Company to record the return?

EX 6-19
Purchase-related transactions
obj. 3

A retailer is considering the purchase of 100 units of a specific item from either of two suppliers. Their offers are as follows:

A: $200 a unit, total of $20,000, 2/10, n/30, no charge for freight.
B: $195 a unit, total of $19,500, 1/10, n/30, plus freight of $400.

Which of the two offers, A or B, yields the lower price?

EX 6-20
Purchase-related transactions

obj. 3

The debits and credits from four related transactions are presented in the following T accounts. Describe each transaction.

Cash				Accounts Payable			
	(2)	250	(3)	500	(1)		8,000
	(4)	7,350	(4)	7,500			

Merchandise Inventory			
(1)	8,000	(3)	500
(2)	250	(4)	150

EX 6-21
Purchase-related transactions

obj. 3

✔ (c) Cash, cr.
$14,700

Versailles Co., a women's clothing store, purchased $18,000 of merchandise from a supplier on account, terms FOB destination, 2/10, n/30. Versailles Co. returned $3,000 of the merchandise, receiving a credit memo, and then paid the amount due within the discount period. Journalize Versailles Co.'s entries to record (a) the purchase, (b) the merchandise return, and (c) the payment.

EX 6-22
Purchase-related transactions

obj. 3

✔ (e) Cash, dr. $900

Journalize entries for the following related transactions of Westcoast Diagnostic Company:
a. Purchased $25,000 of merchandise from Presidio Co. on account, terms 2/10, n/30.
b. Paid the amount owed on the invoice within the discount period.
c. Discovered that $5,000 of the merchandise was defective and returned items, receiving credit.
d. Purchased $4,000 of merchandise from Presidio Co. on account, terms n/30.
e. Received a check for the balance owed from the return in (c), after deducting for the purchase in (d).

EX 6-23
Determining amounts to be paid on invoices

obj. 3

✔ a. $14,200

Determine the amount to be paid in full settlement of each of the following invoices, assuming that credit for returns and allowances was received prior to payment and that all invoices were paid within the discount period.

	Merchandise	Freight Paid by Seller		Returns and Allowances
a.	$15,000	—	FOB destination, n/30	$ 800
b.	10,000	$400	FOB shipping point, 2/10, n/30	1,200
c.	8,250	—	FOB shipping point, 1/10, n/30	750
d.	2,900	125	FOB shipping point, 2/10, n/30	400
e.	3,850	—	FOB destination, 2/10, n/30	—

EX 6-24
Sales tax

obj. 3

✔ c. $14,850

A sale of merchandise on account for $13,750 is subject to an 8% sales tax. (a) Should the sales tax be recorded at the time of sale or when payment is received? (b) What is the amount of the sale? (c) What is the amount debited to Accounts Receivable? (d) What is the title of the account to which the $1,100 ($13,750 × 8%) is credited?

EX 6-25
Sales tax transactions

obj. 3

Journalize the entries to record the following selected transactions:
a. Sold $3,400 of merchandise on account, subject to a sales tax of 5%. The cost of the merchandise sold was $2,000.
b. Paid $41,950 to the state sales tax department for taxes collected.

EX 6-26
Sales-related transactions

obj. 3

Summit Co., a furniture wholesaler, sells merchandise to Bitone Co. on account, $23,400, terms 2/10, n/30. The cost of the merchandise sold is $14,000. Summit Co. issues a credit memo for $4,400 for merchandise returned and subsequently receives the amount due within the discount period. The cost of the merchandise returned is $2,600. Journalize Summit Co.'s entries for (a) the sale, including the cost of the merchandise sold, (b) the credit memo, including the cost of the returned merchandise, and (c) the receipt of the check for the amount due from Bitone Co.

EX 6-27
Purchase-related transactions
obj. 3

Based on the data presented in Exercise 6-26, journalize Bitone Co.'s entries for (a) the purchase, (b) the return of the merchandise for credit, and (c) the payment of the invoice within the discount period.

EX 6-28
Normal balances of merchandise accounts
obj. 3

What is the normal balance of the following accounts: (a) Cost of Merchandise Sold, (b) Delivery Expense, (c) Merchandise Inventory, (d) Sales, (e) Sales Discounts, (f) Sales Returns and Allowances, (g) Sales Tax Payable?

EX 6-29
Adjusting entry for merchandise inventory shrinkage
obj. 4

Iverson Tile Co.'s perpetual inventory records indicate that $675,150 of merchandise should be on hand on December 31, 2010. The physical inventory indicates that $649,780 of merchandise is actually on hand. Journalize the adjusting entry for the inventory shrinkage for Iverson Tile Co. for the year ended December 31, 2010.

EX 6-30
Closing the accounts of a merchandiser
obj. 4

From the following list, identify the accounts that should be closed to Income Summary at the end of the fiscal year under a perpetual inventory system: (a) Accounts Payable, (b) Advertising Expense, (c) Cost of Merchandise Sold, (d) Merchandise Inventory, (e) Sales, (f) Sales Discounts, (g) Sales Returns and Allowances, (h) Supplies, (i) Supplies Expense, (j) Talia Greenly, Drawing, (k) Wages Payable.

EX 6-31
Closing entries; net income
obj. 4

Based on the data presented in Exercise 6-11, journalize the closing entries.

EX 6-32
Closing entries
obj. 4

On May 31, 2010, the balances of the accounts appearing in the ledger of Champion Interiors Company, a furniture wholesaler, are as follows:

Accumulated Depr.—Building	$ 30,460	Notes Payable	$ 24,000
Administrative Expenses	65,300	Salaries Payable	680
Building	55,680	Sales	313,540
Cash	8,840	Sales Discounts	18,000
Cost of Merchandise Sold	188,000	Sales Returns and Allow.	12,000
Interest Expense	1,920	Sales Tax Payable	4,900
Jessica Duerr, Capital	141,155	Selling Expenses	124,000
Jessica Duerr, Drawing	7,950	Store Supplies	4,580
Merchandise Inventory	26,000	Store Supplies Expenses	2,465

Prepare the May 31, 2010, closing entries for Champion Interiors Company.

Appendix 1
EX 6-33
Merchandising special journals

Crown Rug Company had the following credit sales transactions during August 2010:

Date	Customer	Quantity	Rug Style	Sales
Aug. 7	Wes McGill	1	10 by 8 Chinese	$15,500
12	Joan Felt	1	8 by 12 Persian	11,000
23	Paula Larkin	1	8 by 10 Indian	11,500
30	Rajiv Kumar	1	10 by 12 Persian	23,000

✔ d. $79,000

The August 1 inventory was $44,500, consisting of:

Quantity	Style	Cost per Rug	Total Cost
3	10 by 8 Chinese	$7,500	$22,500
4	8 by 12 Persian	5,500	22,000

During August, Crown Rug Company purchased the following rugs from Royal Importers:

Date	Quantity	Rug Style	Cost per Rug	Amount
Aug. 10	3	8 by 10 Indian	$ 6,000	$18,000
12	1	10 by 8 Chinese	8,500	8,500
19	3	10 by 12 Persian	13,500	40,500

The general ledger includes the following accounts:

Account Number	Account
11	Accounts Receivable
12	Merchandise Inventory
21	Accounts Payable
41	Sales
51	Cost of Merchandise Sold

a. Record the sales in a two-column sales journal. Use the sales journal form shown in Appendix 1 at the end of this chapter. Begin with Invoice No. 93.
b. Record the purchases in a purchases journal. Use the purchases journal form shown in Appendix 1 at the end of this chapter.
c. Assume that you have posted the journal entries to the appropriate ledgers. Insert the correct posting references in the sales and purchases journals.
d. Determine the August 31 balance of Merchandise Inventory.

Appendix 2
EX 6-34
Accounts for periodic and perpetual inventory systems

Indicate which of the following accounts would be included in the chart of accounts of a merchandising company using either the (a) periodic inventory system or (b) perpetual inventory system. If the account would be included in the chart of accounts of a company using the periodic and perpetual systems, indicate (c) for both.

(1)	Cost of Merchandise Sold	(6)	Purchases Returns and Allowances
(2)	Delivery Expense	(7)	Sales
(3)	Merchandise Inventory	(8)	Sales Discounts
(4)	Purchases	(9)	Sales Returns and Allowances
(5)	Purchases Discounts	(10)	Freight In

Appendix 2
EX 6-35
Rules of debit and credit for periodic inventory accounts

Complete the following table by indicating for (a) through (g) whether the proper answer is debit or credit.

Account	Increase	Decrease	Normal Balance
Purchases	debit	(a)	(b)
Purchases Discounts	(c)	debit	credit
Purchases Returns and Allowances	credit	(d)	(e)
Freight In	(f)	credit	(g)

Appendix 2
EX 6-36
Journal entries using the periodic inventory system

The following selected transactions were completed by Artic Company during February of the current year. Artic Company uses the periodic inventory system.

Feb. 2. Purchased $17,500 of merchandise on account, FOB shipping point, terms 2/15, n/30.
    5. Paid freight of $300 on the February 2 purchase.
    6. Returned $2,000 of the merchandise purchased on February 2.

Feb. 13. Sold merchandise on account, $9,000, FOB destination, 2/10, n/30. The cost of merchandise sold was $6,600.

　　15. Paid freight of $100 for the merchandise sold on February 13.

　　17. Paid for the purchase of February 2 less the return and discount.

　　23. Received payment on account for the sale of February 13 less the discount.

Journalize the entries to record the transactions of Artic Company.

Appendix 2
EX 6-37
Journal entries using perpetual inventory system

Using the data shown in Exercise 6-38, journalize the entries for the transactions assuming that Artic Company uses the perpetual inventory system.

Appendix 2
EX 6-38
Closing entries using periodic inventory system

Aladdin Company is a small rug retailer owned and operated by Lin Endsley. After the accounts have been adjusted on October 31, the following account balances were taken from the ledger:

Advertising Expense	$ 16,500
Depreciation Expense	4,000
Freight In	8,000
Lin Endsley, Drawing	30,000
Merchandise Inventory, October 1	43,800
Merchandise Inventory, October 31	35,750
Miscellaneous Expense	1,750
Purchases	560,000
Purchases Discounts	12,000
Purchases Returns and Allowances	6,000
Sales	890,000
Sales Discounts	5,000
Sales Returns and Allowances	10,000
Salaries Expense	80,000

Journalize the closing entries on October 31.

EX 6-39
Ratio of net sales to total assets

The Home Depot reported the following data (in millions) in its financial statements:

	2007	2006
Net sales	$90,837	$81,511
Total assets at the end of the year	52,263	44,482
Total assets at the beginning of the year	44,482	38,907

a. Determine the ratio of net sales to average total assets for The Home Depot for 2007 and 2006. Round to two decimal places.

b. What conclusions can be drawn from these ratios concerning the trend in the ability of The Home Depot to effectively use its assets to generate sales?

EX 6-40
Ratio of net sales to total assets

Kroger, a national supermarket chain, reported the following data (in millions) in its financial statements for 2007:

Total revenue	$66,111
Total assets at end of year	21,215
Total assets at beginning of year	20,482

a. Compute the ratio of net sales to assets for 2007. Round to two decimal places.

b. ➤ Would you expect the ratio of net sales to assets for Kroger to be similar to or different from that of Tiffany & Co.? Tiffany is the large North American retailer of jewelry, with a ratio of net sales to average total assets of 0.94.

Problems Series A

PR 6-1A
Multiple-step income statement and report form of balance sheet

obj. 2

✔ 1. Net income:
$120,000

The following selected accounts and their current balances appear in the ledger of Case-It Co. for the fiscal year ended November 30, 2010:

Cash	$ 37,700	Sales Returns and Allowances	$ 37,800
Accounts Receivable	111,600	Sales Discounts	19,800
Merchandise Inventory	180,000	Cost of Merchandise Sold	1,926,000
Office Supplies	5,000	Sales Salaries Expense	378,000
Prepaid Insurance	12,000	Advertising Expense	50,900
Office Equipment	115,200	Depreciation Expense—	
Accumulated Depreciation—		Store Equipment	8,300
Office Equipment	49,500	Miscellaneous Selling Expense	2,000
Store Equipment	311,500	Office Salaries Expense	73,800
Accumulated Depreciation—		Rent Expense	39,900
Store Equipment	87,500	Insurance Expense	22,950
Accounts Payable	48,600	Depreciation Expense—	
Salaries Payable	3,600	Office Equipment	16,200
Note Payable	54,000	Office Supplies Expense	1,650
(final payment due 2025)		Miscellaneous Administrative	
Gina Hennessy, Capital	454,800	Expense	1,900
Gina Hennessy, Drawing	45,000	Interest Expense	4,400
Sales	2,703,600		

Instructions

1. Prepare a multiple-step income statement.
2. Prepare a statement of owner's equity.
3. Prepare a report form of balance sheet, assuming that the current portion of the note payable is $8,000.
4. Briefly explain (a) how multiple-step and single-step income statements differ and (b) how report-form and account-form balance sheets differ.

PR 6-2A
Single-step income statement and account form of balance sheet

objs. 2, 4

✔ 3. Total assets:
$636,000

Selected accounts and related amounts for Case-It Co. for the fiscal year ended November 30, 2010, are presented in Problem 6-1A.

Instructions

1. Prepare a single-step income statement in the format shown in Exhibit 3.
2. Prepare a statement of owner's equity.
3. Prepare an account form of balance sheet, assuming that the current portion of the note payable is $8,000.
4. Prepare closing entries as of November 30, 2010.

PR 6-3A
Sales-related transactions

obj. 3

The following selected transactions were completed by Rayne Supplies Co., which sells irrigation supplies primarily to wholesalers and occasionally to retail customers:

Aug. 1. Sold merchandise on account to Tomahawk Co., $12,500, terms FOB shipping point, n/eom. The cost of merchandise sold was $7,500.

2. Sold merchandise for $20,000 plus 7% sales tax to retail cash customers. The cost of merchandise sold was $13,100.

5. Sold merchandise on account to Epworth Company, $30,000, terms FOB destination, 1/10, n/30. The cost of merchandise sold was $19,500.

8. Sold merchandise for $11,500 plus 7% sales tax to retail customers who used VISA cards. The cost of merchandise sold was $7,000.

13. Sold merchandise to customers who used MasterCard cards, $8,000. The cost of merchandise sold was $5,000.

Aug. 14. Sold merchandise on account to Osgood Co., $11,800, terms FOB shipping point, 1/10, n/30. The cost of merchandise sold was $7,000.

15. Received check for amount due from Epworth Company for sale on August 5.

16. Issued credit memo for $1,800 to Osgood Co. for merchandise returned from sale on August 14. The cost of the merchandise returned was $1,000.

18. Sold merchandise on account to Horton Company, $6,850, terms FOB shipping point, 2/10, n/30. Paid $210 for freight and added it to the invoice. The cost of merchandise sold was $4,100.

24. Received check for amount due from Osgood Co. for sale on August 14 less credit memo of August 16 and discount.

28. Received check for amount due from Horton Company for sale of August 18.

31. Paid Piper Delivery Service $2,100 for merchandise delivered during August to customers under shipping terms of FOB destination.

31. Received check for amount due from Tomahawk Co. for sale of August 1.

Sept. 3. Paid First Federal Bank $980 for service fees for handling MasterCard and VISA sales during August.

10. Paid $1,750 to state sales tax division for taxes owed on sales.

Instructions
Journalize the entries to record the transactions of Rayne Supplies Co.

PR 6-4A
Purchase-related transactions

obj. **3**

The following selected transactions were completed by Padre Co. during October of the current year:

Oct. 1. Purchased merchandise from Wood Co., $15,500, terms FOB shipping point, 2/10, n/eom. Prepaid freight of $400 was added to the invoice.

5. Purchased merchandise from Davis Co., $14,150, terms FOB destination, n/30.

10. Paid Wood Co. for invoice of October 1, less discount.

13. Purchased merchandise from Folts Co., $8,000, terms FOB destination, 1/10, n/30.

14. Issued debit memo to Folts Co. for $1,500 of merchandise returned from purchase on October 13.

18. Purchased merchandise from Lakey Company, $12,250, terms FOB shipping point, n/eom.

18. Paid freight of $180 on October 18 purchase from Lakey Company.

19. Purchased merchandise from Noman Co., $11,150, terms FOB destination, 2/10, n/30.

23. Paid Folts Co. for invoice of October 13, less debit memo of October 14 and discount.

29. Paid Noman Co. for invoice of October 19, less discount.

31. Paid Lakey Company for invoice of October 18.

31. Paid Davis Co. for invoice of October 5.

Instructions
Journalize the entries to record the transactions of Padre Co. for October.

PR 6-5A
Sales-related and purchase-related transactions

obj. **3**

The following were selected from among the transactions completed by Sandusky Company during December of the current year:

Dec. 3. Purchased merchandise on account from Hillsboro Co., list price $38,000, trade discount 25%, terms FOB shipping point, 2/10, n/30, with prepaid freight of $900 added to the invoice.

5. Purchased merchandise on account from Deepwater Co., $18,750, terms FOB destination, 2/10, n/30.

Dec. 6. Sold merchandise on account to Zion Co., list price $27,000, trade discount 35%, terms 2/10, n/30. The cost of the merchandise sold was $14,000.

7. Returned $3,000 of merchandise purchased on December 5 from Deepwater Co.

13. Paid Hillsboro Co. on account for purchase of December 3, less discount.

15. Paid Deepwater Co. on account for purchase of December 5, less return of December 7 and discount.

16. Received cash on account from sale of December 6 to Zion Co., less discount.

19. Sold merchandise on MasterCard, $58,000. The cost of the merchandise sold was $34,800.

22. Sold merchandise on account to Smith River Co., $15,400, terms 2/10, n/30. The cost of the merchandise sold was $9,000.

23. Sold merchandise for cash, $33,600. The cost of the merchandise sold was $20,000.

28. Received merchandise returned by Smith River Co. from sale on December 22, $2,400. The cost of the returned merchandise was $1,400.

31. Paid MasterCard service fee of $1,750.

Instructions

Journalize the transactions.

PR 6-6A
Sales-related and purchase-related transactions for seller and buyer

obj. 3

The following selected transactions were completed during November between Sycamore Company and Bonita Company:

Nov. 2. Sycamore Company sold merchandise on account to Bonita Company, $16,000, terms FOB shipping point, 2/10, n/30. Sycamore Company paid freight of $375, which was added to the invoice. The cost of the merchandise sold was $10,000.

8. Sycamore Company sold merchandise on account to Bonita Company, $24,750, terms FOB destination, 1/15, n/eom. The cost of the merchandise sold was $14,850.

8. Sycamore Company paid freight of $640 for delivery of merchandise sold to Bonita Company on November 8.

12. Bonita Company returned $5,750 of merchandise purchased on account on November 8 from Sycamore Company. The cost of the merchandise returned was $3,000.

12. Bonita Company paid Sycamore Company for purchase of November 2, less discount.

23. Bonita Company paid Sycamore Company for purchase of November 8, less discount and less return of November 12.

24. Sycamore Company sold merchandise on account to Bonita Company, $13,200, terms FOB shipping point, n/eom. The cost of the merchandise sold was $8,000.

26. Bonita Company paid freight of $290 on November 24 purchase from Sycamore Company.

30. Bonita Company paid Sycamore Company on account for purchase of November 24.

Instructions

Journalize the November transactions for (1) Sycamore Company and (2) Bonita Company.

Appendix 2
PR 6-7A
Purchase-related transactions using periodic inventory system

Selected transactions for Padre Co. during October of the current year are listed in Problem 6-4A.

Instructions

Journalize the entries to record the transactions of Padre Co. for October using the periodic inventory system.

Appendix 2
PR 6-8A
Sales-related and purchase-related transactions using periodic inventory system

Selected transactions for Sandusky Company during December of the current year are listed in Problem 6-5A.

Instructions

Journalize the entries to record the transactions of Sandusky Company for December using the periodic inventory system.

Appendix 2
PR 6-9A
Sales-related and purchase-related transactions for buyer and seller using periodic inventory system

Selected transactions during November between Sycamore Company and Bonita Company are listed in Problem 6-6A.

Instructions

Journalize the entries to record the transactions for (1) Sycamore Company and (2) Bonita Company assuming that both companies use the periodic inventory system.

Appendix 2
PR 6-10A
Periodic inventory accounts, multiple-step income statement, closing entries

obj. 2

✔ 2. Net income, $362,600

On June 30, 2010, the balances of the accounts appearing in the ledger of Andover Company are as follows:

Cash	$ 36,600	Sales Discounts	$ 18,750
Accounts Receivable	144,250	Purchases	1,073,000
Merchandise Inventory, July 1, 2009	175,450	Purchases Returns and Allowances	12,000
Office Supplies	6,050	Purchases Discounts	9,000
Prepaid Insurance	9,000	Freight In	21,800
Land	70,000	Sales Salaries Expense	312,500
Store Equipment	341,550	Advertising Expense	110,000
Accumulated Depreciation—		Delivery Expense	18,000
Store Equipment	11,800	Depreciation Expense—	
Office Equipment	157,000	Store Equipment	11,800
Accumulated Depreciation—		Miscellaneous Selling Expense	21,400
Office Equipment	32,500	Office Salaries Expense	200,000
Accounts Payable	55,650	Rent Expense	62,500
Salaries Payable	5,900	Insurance Expense	6,000
Unearned Rent	16,600	Office Supplies Expense	4,600
Notes Payable	25,000	Depreciation Expense—	
Vanessa Andover, Capital	380,100	Office Equipment	3,000
Vanessa Andover, Drawing	37,500	Miscellaneous Administrative Expense	11,700
Sales	2,212,900	Rent Revenue	12,500
Sales Returns and Allowances	20,000	Interest Expense	1,500

Instructions

1. Does Andover Company use a periodic or perpetual inventory system? Explain.
2. Prepare a multiple-step income statement for Andover Company for the year ended June 30, 2010. The merchandise inventory as of June 30, 2010, was $188,200.
3. Prepare the closing entries for Andover Company as of June 30, 2010.

Problems Series B

PR 6-1B
Multiple-step income
statement and report
form of balance sheet

obj. 2

✔ 1. Net income:
$300,000

The following selected accounts and their current balances appear in the ledger of Drapery Land Co. for the fiscal year ended July 31, 2010:

Cash	$ 161,250	Sales Returns and Allowances	$ 69,300
Accounts Receivable	363,000	Sales Discounts	65,700
Merchandise Inventory	525,000	Cost of Merchandise Sold	2,325,000
Office Supplies	16,800	Sales Salaries Expense	519,600
Prepaid Insurance	10,200	Advertising Expense	131,400
Office Equipment	255,000	Depreciation Expense—	
Accumulated Depreciation—		Store Equipment	19,200
Office Equipment	138,400	Miscellaneous Selling Expense	4,800
Store Equipment	759,000	Office Salaries Expense	252,450
Accumulated Depreciation—		Rent Expense	94,050
Store Equipment	102,600	Depreciation Expense—	
Accounts Payable	166,800	Office Equipment	38,100
Salaries Payable	7,200	Insurance Expense	11,700
Note Payable		Office Supplies Expense	3,200
(final payment due 2020)	168,000	Miscellaneous Administrative	
Tanya Xavier, Capital	1,312,250	Expense	5,500
Tanya Xavier, Drawing	105,000	Interest Expense	15,000
Sales	3,855,000		

Instructions

1. Prepare a multiple-step income statement.
2. Prepare a statement of owner's equity.
3. Prepare a report form of balance sheet, assuming that the current portion of the note payable is $16,800.
4. Briefly explain (a) how multiple-step and single-step income statements differ and (b) how report-form and account-form balance sheets differ.

PR 6-2B
Single-step income
statement and
account form of
balance sheet

objs. 2, 4

✔ 3. Total assets:
$1,849,250

Selected accounts and related amounts for Drapery Land Co. for the fiscal year ended July 31, 2010, are presented in Problem 6-1B.

Instructions

1. Prepare a single-step income statement in the format shown in Exhibit 3.
2. Prepare a statement of owner's equity.
3. Prepare an account form of balance sheet, assuming that the current portion of the note payable is $16,800.
4. Prepare closing entries as of July 31, 2010.

PR 6-3B
Sales-related
transactions

obj. 3

The following selected transactions were completed by Yukon Supply Co., which sells office supplies primarily to wholesalers and occasionally to retail customers:

Jan. 2. Sold merchandise on account to Oakley Co., $8,000, terms FOB destination, 1/10, n/30. The cost of the merchandise sold was $4,500.

3. Sold merchandise for $21,800 plus 8% sales tax to retail cash customers. The cost of merchandise sold was $13,000.

4. Sold merchandise on account to Rawlins Co., $7,500, terms FOB shipping point, n/eom. The cost of merchandise sold was $4,200.

5. Sold merchandise for $10,000 plus 8% sales tax to retail customers who used MasterCard. The cost of merchandise sold was $6,000.

12. Received check for amount due from Oakley Co. for sale on January 2.

14. Sold merchandise to customers who used American Express cards, $6,000. The cost of merchandise sold was $3,200.

Jan. 16. Sold merchandise on account to Keystone Co., $16,500, terms FOB shipping point, 1/10, n/30. The cost of merchandise sold was $10,000.

18. Issued credit memo for $2,000 to Keystone Co. for merchandise returned from sale on January 16. The cost of the merchandise returned was $1,200.

19. Sold merchandise on account to Cooney Co., $15,750, terms FOB shipping point, 2/10, n/30. Added $400 to the invoice for prepaid freight. The cost of merchandise sold was $9,500.

26. Received check for amount due from Keystone Co. for sale on January 16 less credit memo of January 18 and discount.

28. Received check for amount due from Cooney Co. for sale of January 19.

31. Received check for amount due from Rawlins Co. for sale of January 4.

31. Paid Black Hawk Delivery Service $3,875 for merchandise delivered during January to customers under shipping terms of FOB destination.

Feb. 3. Paid City Bank $1,150 for service fees for handling MasterCard and American Express sales during January.

15. Paid $3,600 to state sales tax division for taxes owed on sales.

Instructions

Journalize the entries to record the transactions of Yukon Supply Co.

PR 6-4B
Purchase-related transactions

obj. 3

The following selected transactions were completed by Silvertree Company during January of the current year:

Jan. 1. Purchased merchandise from Guinn Co., $13,600, terms FOB destination, n/30.

3. Purchased merchandise from Cybernet Co., $18,000, terms FOB shipping point, 2/10, n/eom. Prepaid freight of $300 was added to the invoice.

4. Purchased merchandise from Berry Co., $22,000, terms FOB destination, 2/10, n/30.

6. Issued debit memo to Berry Co. for $3,500 of merchandise returned from purchase on January 4.

13. Paid Cybernet Co. for invoice of January 3, less discount.

14. Paid Berry Co. for invoice of January 4, less debit memo of January 6 and discount.

19. Purchased merchandise from Cleghorne Co., $18,000, terms FOB shipping point, n/eom.

19. Paid freight of $500 on January 19 purchase from Cleghorne Co.

20. Purchased merchandise from Lenn Co., $10,000, terms FOB destination, 1/10, n/30.

30. Paid Lenn Co. for invoice of January 20, less discount.

31. Paid Guinn Co. for invoice of January 1.

31. Paid Cleghorne Co. for invoice of January 19.

Instructions

Journalize the entries to record the transactions of Silvertree Company for January.

PR 6-5B
Sales-related and purchase-related transactions

obj. 3

The following were selected from among the transactions completed by Calworks Company during April of the current year:

Apr. 3. Purchased merchandise on account from Prescott Co., list price $42,000, trade discount 40%, terms FOB destination, 2/10, n/30.

4. Sold merchandise for cash, $18,200. The cost of the merchandise sold was $11,000.

5. Purchased merchandise on account from Stafford Co., $21,300, terms FOB shipping point, 2/10, n/30, with prepaid freight of $600 added to the invoice.

6. Returned $6,000 of merchandise purchased on April 3 from Prescott Co.

11. Sold merchandise on account to Logan Co., list price $8,500, trade discount 20%, terms 1/10, n/30. The cost of the merchandise sold was $4,500.

13. Paid Prescott Co. on account for purchase of April 3, less return of April 6 and discount.

14. Sold merchandise on VISA, $60,000. The cost of the merchandise sold was $36,000.

Apr. 15. Paid Stafford Co. on account for purchase of April 5, less discount.
21. Received cash on account from sale of April 11 to Logan Co., less discount.
24. Sold merchandise on account to Alma Co., $9,200, terms 1/10, n/30. The cost of the merchandise sold was $5,500.
28. Paid VISA service fee of $1,800.
30. Received merchandise returned by Alma Co. from sale on April 24, $1,200. The cost of the returned merchandise was $720.

Instructions
Journalize the transactions.

PR 6-6B
Sales-related and purchase-related transactions for seller and buyer

obj. 3

The following selected transactions were completed during August between Salem Company and Boulder Co.:

Aug. 1. Salem Company sold merchandise on account to Boulder Co., $28,600, terms FOB destination, 2/15, n/eom. The cost of the merchandise sold was $17,000.
2. Salem Company paid freight of $500 for delivery of merchandise sold to Boulder Co. on August 1.
5. Salem Company sold merchandise on account to Boulder Co., $18,000, terms FOB shipping point, n/eom. The cost of the merchandise sold was $10,800.
6. Boulder Co. returned $1,600 of merchandise purchased on account on August 1 from Salem Company. The cost of the merchandise returned was $960.
9. Boulder Co. paid freight of $350 on August 5 purchase from Salem Company.
15. Salem Company sold merchandise on account to Boulder Co., $36,200, terms FOB shipping point, 1/10, n/30. Salem Company paid freight of $900, which was added to the invoice. The cost of the merchandise sold was $19,600.
16. Boulder Co. paid Salem Company for purchase of August 1, less discount and less return of August 6.
25. Boulder Co. paid Salem Company on account for purchase of August 15, less discount.
31. Boulder Co. paid Salem Company on account for purchase of August 5.

Instructions
Journalize the August transactions for (1) Salem Company and (2) Boulder Co.

Appendix 2
PR 6-7B
Purchase-related transactions using periodic inventory system

Selected transactions for Silvertree Company during January of the current year are listed in Problem 6-4B.

Instructions
Journalize the entries to record the transactions of Silvertree Company for January using the periodic inventory system.

Appendix 2
PR 6-8B
Sales-related and purchase-related transactions using periodic inventory system

Selected transactions for Calworks Company during April of the current year are listed in Problem 6-5B.

Instructions
Journalize the entries to record the transactions of Calworks Company for April using the periodic inventory system.

Appendix 2
PR 6-9B
Sales-related and purchase-related transactions for buyer and seller using periodic inventory system

Selected transactions during August between Salem Company and Boulder Co. are listed in Problem 6-6B.

Instructions
Journalize the entries to record the transactions for (1) Salem Company and (2) Boulder Co. assuming that both companies use the periodic inventory system.

**Appendix 2
PR 6-10B**

Periodic inventory accounts, multiple-step income statement, closing entries

✔ 2. Net income, $181,350

On October 31, 2010, the balances of the accounts appearing in the ledger of Triple Creek Company are as follows:

Cash	$ 18,300	Sales Discounts	$ 9,300
Accounts Receivable	72,000	Purchases	536,500
Merchandise Inventory,		Purchases Returns and Allowances	6,000
November 1, 2009	87,700	Purchases Discounts	4,500
Office Supplies	3,000	Freight In	10,900
Prepaid Insurance	4,500	Sales Salaries Expense	156,250
Land	35,000	Advertising Expense	55,000
Store Equipment	170,000	Delivery Expense	9,000
Accumulated Depreciation—		Depreciation Expense—	
Store Equipment	55,900	Store Equipment	5,900
Office Equipment	78,500	Miscellaneous Selling Expense	10,700
Accumulated Depreciation—		Office Salaries Expense	100,000
Office Equipment	16,250	Rent Expense	31,250
Accounts Payable	27,800	Insurance Expense	3,000
Salaries Payable	3,000	Office Supplies Expense	2,300
Unearned Rent	8,300	Depreciation Expense—	
Notes Payable	12,500	Office Equipment	1,500
Shawn Hayes, Capital	189,050	Miscellaneous Administrative Expense	5,850
Shawn Hayes, Drawing	18,750	Rent Revenue	6,250
Sales	1,106,400	Interest Expense	750
Sales Returns and Allowances	10,000		

Instructions

1. Does Triple Creek Company use a periodic or perpetual inventory system? Explain.

2. Prepare a multiple-step income statement for Triple Creek Company for the year ended October 31, 2010. The merchandise inventory as of October 31, 2010, was $94,100.

3. Prepare the closing entries for Triple Creek Company as of October 31, 2010.

Comprehensive Problem 2

✔ 8. Net income: $693,800

South Coast Boards Co. is a merchandising business. The account balances for South Coast Boards Co. as of July 1, 2010 (unless otherwise indicated), are as follows:

110	Cash	$ 63,600
112	Accounts Receivable	153,900
115	Merchandise Inventory	602,400
116	Prepaid Insurance	16,800
117	Store Supplies	11,400
123	Store Equipment	469,500
124	Accum. Depreciation—Store Equipment	56,700
210	Accounts Payable	96,600
211	Salaries Payable	—
310	Rocky Hansen, Capital, Aug. 1, 2009	555,300
311	Rocky Hansen, Drawing	135,000
312	Income Summary	—
410	Sales	3,221,100
411	Sales Returns and Allowances	92,700
412	Sales Discounts	59,400
510	Cost of Merchandise Sold	1,623,000
520	Sales Salaries Expense	334,800
521	Advertising Expense	81,000
522	Depreciation Expense	—
523	Store Supplies Expense	—
529	Miscellaneous Selling Expense	12,600
530	Office Salaries Expense	182,100
531	Rent Expense	83,700
532	Insurance Expense	—
539	Misc. Administrative Expense	7,800

During July, the last month of the fiscal year, the following transactions were completed:

July 1. Paid rent for July, $5,000.
  3. Purchased merchandise on account from Belmont Co., terms 2/10, n/30, FOB shipping point, $40,000.
  4. Paid freight on purchase of July 3, $600.
  6. Sold merchandise on account to Modesto Co., terms 2/10, n/30, FOB shipping point, $25,000. The cost of the merchandise sold was $15,000.
  7. Received $26,500 cash from Yuba Co. on account, no discount.
  10. Sold merchandise for cash, $80,000. The cost of the merchandise sold was $50,000.
  13. Paid for merchandise purchased on July 3, less discount.
  14. Received merchandise returned on sale of July 6, $6,000. The cost of the merchandise returned was $4,500.
  15. Paid advertising expense for last half of July, $7,500.
  16. Received cash from sale of July 6, less return of July 14 and discount.
  19. Purchased merchandise for cash, $36,000.
  19. Paid $18,000 to Bakke Co. on account, no discount.
  20. Sold merchandise on account to Reedley Co., terms 1/10, n/30, FOB shipping point, $40,000. The cost of the merchandise sold was $25,000.
  21. For the convenience of the customer, paid freight on sale of July 20, $1,100.
  21. Received $17,600 cash from Owen Co. on account, no discount.
  21. Purchased merchandise on account from Nye Co., terms 1/10, n/30, FOB destination, $20,000.
  24. Returned $2,000 of damaged merchandise purchased on July 21, receiving credit from the seller.
  26. Refunded cash on sales made for cash, $3,000. The cost of the merchandise returned was $1,800.
  28. Paid sales salaries of $22,800 and office salaries of $15,200.
  29. Purchased store supplies for cash, $2,400.
  30. Sold merchandise on account to Whitetail Co., terms 2/10, n/30, FOB shipping point, $18,750. The cost of the merchandise sold was $11,250.
  30. Received cash from sale of July 20, less discount, plus freight paid on July 21.
  31. Paid for purchase of July 21, less return of July 24 and discount.

Instructions

1. Enter the balances of each of the accounts in the appropriate balance column of a four-column account. Write *Balance* in the item section, and place a check mark (✓) in the Posting Reference column. Journalize the transactions for July.
2. Post the journal to the general ledger, extending the month-end balances to the appropriate balance columns after all posting is completed. In this problem, you are not required to update or post to the accounts receivable and accounts payable subsidiary ledgers.
3. Prepare an unadjusted trial balance.
4. At the end of July, the following adjustment data were assembled. Analyze and use these data to complete (5) and (6).

a. Merchandise inventory on July 31		$589,850
b. Insurance expired during the year		12,500
c. Store supplies on hand on July 31		4,700
d. Depreciation for the current year		18,800
e. Accrued salaries on July 31:		
Sales salaries	$4,400	
Office salaries	2,700	7,100

5. **Optional:** Enter the unadjusted trial balance on a 10-column end-of-period spreadsheet (work sheet), and complete the spreadsheet. See Appendix C for how to prepare an end-of-period spreadsheet (work sheet) for a merchandising business.
6. Journalize and post the adjusting entries.

7. Prepare an adjusted trial balance.
8. Prepare an income statement, a statement of owner's equity, and a balance sheet.
9. Prepare and post the closing entries. Indicate closed accounts by inserting a line in both the Balance columns opposite the closing entry. Insert the new balance in the owner's capital account.
10. Prepare a post-closing trial balance.

Special Activities

You can access the special activities online at **www.cengage.com/accounting/reeve**.

Excel Success Special Activities

SA 6-1
Computing sales tax, multiple states

Jerrod Corporation had sales in several states. The sales and assumed sales tax rate for each state are summarized in a spreadsheet as follows:

	A	B	C	D
1		Total Sales	Sales Tax Rate	Sales Tax
2	Illinois	$ 318,000	6.5%	
3	Iowa	194,100	6.0%	
4	Missouri	241,200	4.0%	
5	Nebraska	86,200	5.5%	
6	Total	$ 839,500		
7				

a. Open the Excel file *SA6-1*.
b. Finalize the spreadsheet by determining the sales tax for each state and the total sales tax liability for Jerrod Corporation in Column D.
   Use percent formatting for the sales tax rates. For example, cell C2 is entered as .065 and formatted using the percent format with one decimal place.
c. When you have completed the sales tax table, perform a "save as," replacing the entire file name with the following:

   SA6-1_[your first name initial]_[your last name]

SA 6-2
Computing sales tax, multiple locations

U Store It, Inc., has multiple storage locations throughout the state of Colorado. The sales from each storage location are summarized in a spreadsheet as follows:

	A	B	C	D
1	Sales tax rate	3.5%		
2				
3		Total Sales	Sales Tax Rate	Sales Tax
4	North Denver	$ 24,200		
5	Central Denver	17,800		
6	Colorado Springs	8,400		
7	Ft. Collins	12,000		
8	Boulder	6,400		
9	Total	$ 68,800		
10				

a. Open the Excel file *SA6-2*.
b. Assume the sales tax rate for Colorado is 3.5%. Insert .035. Format as a percentage amount rounded to one decimal place in the cells C4:C8.
c. Finalize the spreadsheet by determining the sales tax for each location and total sales tax for U Store It, Inc. Use column C for the sales tax rate and column D for the total sales tax.

d. When you have completed the sales tax table, perform a "save as," replacing the entire file name with the following:

SA6-1_[your first name initial]_[your last name]

SA 6-3
Computing sales tax, multiple cities

Cities in many states may add an additional city sales tax rate to the state tax rate. Assume that cities in the state of New York can add an additional sales tax. Timely Blessings, Inc., has sales in various cities in New York. The sales and assumed total sales tax rate (city plus state rates) are summarized in a spreadsheet as follows:

	A	B	C	D
1		Total Sales	Sales Tax Rate	Sales Tax
2	New York City	$ 243,200	8.0%	
3	Rochester	98,200	7.5%	
4	White Plains	31,400	7.0%	
5	Buffalo	54,000	7.2%	
6	Albany	14,200	6.5%	
7	Total	$ 441,000		
8				
9				

a. Open the Excel file *SA6-3*.
b. Finalize the spreadsheet by determining the sales tax for each city and total sales tax Column D. Use percent format for the sales tax rates. For example, cell C2 is entered as .08 and formatted using the percent format with one decimal place.
c. When you have completed the sales tax table, perform a "save as," replacing the entire file name with the following:

SA6-3_[your first name initial]_[your last name]

Answers to Self-Examination Questions

1. **A** A debit memo (answer A), issued by the buyer, indicates the amount the buyer proposes to debit to the accounts payable account. A credit memo (answer B), issued by the seller, indicates the amount the seller proposes to credit to the accounts receivable account. An invoice (answer C) or a bill (answer D), issued by the seller, indicates the amount and terms of the sale.

2. **C** The amount of discount for early payment is $10 (answer C), or 1% of $1,000. Although the $50 of freight paid by the seller is debited to the customer's account, the customer is not entitled to a discount on that amount.

3. **B** The single-step form of income statement (answer B) is so named because the total of all expenses is deducted in one step from the total of all revenues. The multiple-step form (answer A) includes numerous sections and subsections with several subtotals. The account form (answer C) and the report form (answer D) are two common forms of the balance sheet.

4. **C** Gross profit (answer C) is the excess of net sales over the cost of merchandise sold. Operating income (answer A) or income from operations (answer B) is the excess of gross profit over operating expenses. Net income (answer D) is the final figure on the income statement after all revenues and expenses have been reported.

5. **D** Expenses such as interest expense (answer D) that cannot be associated directly with operations are identified as *other expense* or *nonoperating expense*. Depreciation expense—office equipment (answer A) is an administrative expense. Sales salaries expense (answer B) is a selling expense. Insurance expense (answer C) is a mixed expense with elements of both selling expense and administrative expense. For small businesses, insurance expense is usually reported as an administrative expense.

Inventories

© Ryan McVay/Photodisc/Getty Images

B E S T   B U Y

Assume that in September you purchased a Philips HDTV plasma television from Best Buy. At the same time, you purchased a Sony surround sound system for $299.99. You liked your surround sound so well that in November you purchased an identical Sony system on sale for $249.99 for your bedroom TV. Over the holidays, you moved to a new apartment and in the process of unpacking discovered that one of the Sony surround sound systems was missing. Luckily, your renters/homeowners insurance policy will cover the theft, but the insurance company needs to know the cost of the system that was stolen.

The Sony systems were identical. However, to respond to the insurance company, you will need to identify which system was stolen. Was it the first system, which cost $299.99, or was it the second system, which cost $249.99? Whichever assumption you make may determine the amount that you receive from the insurance company.

Merchandising businesses such as Best Buy make similar assumptions when identical merchandise is purchased at different costs. For example, Best Buy may have purchased thousands of Sony surround sound systems over the past year at different costs. At the end of a period, some of the Sony systems will still be in inventory, and some will have been sold. But which costs relate to the sold systems, and which costs relate to the Sony systems still in inventory? Best Buy's assumption about inventory costs can involve large dollar amounts and, thus, can have a significant impact on the financial statements. For example, Best Buy reported $4,028 million of inventory on March 3, 2007, and net income of $1,377 million for the year.

In this chapter, we will discuss such issues as how to determine the cost of merchandise in inventory and the cost of merchandise sold. However, we begin this chapter by discussing the importance of control over inventory.

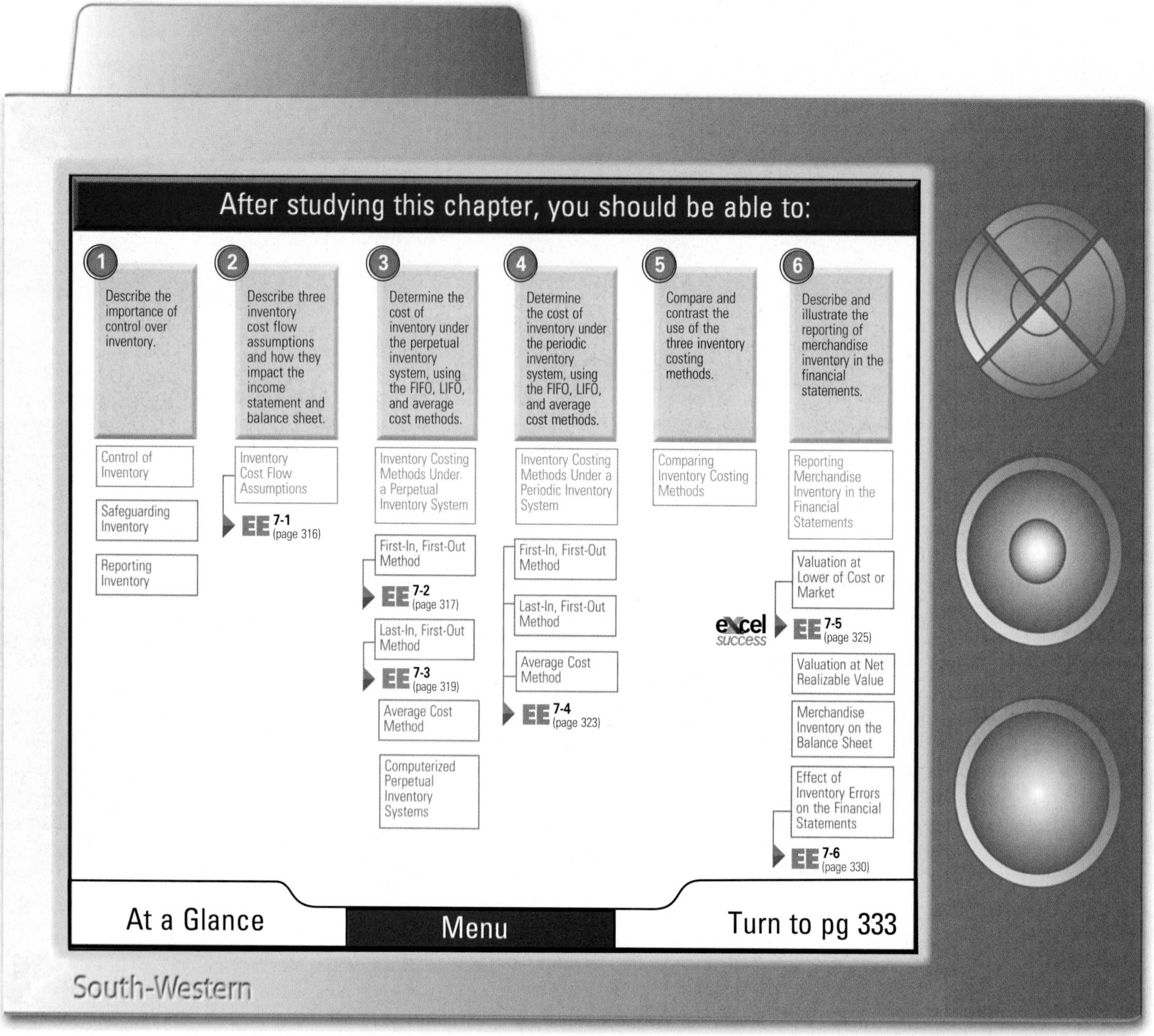

After studying this chapter, you should be able to:

1 Describe the importance of control over inventory.

2 Describe three inventory cost flow assumptions and how they impact the income statement and balance sheet.

3 Determine the cost of inventory under the perpetual inventory system, using the FIFO, LIFO, and average cost methods.

4 Determine the cost of inventory under the periodic inventory system, using the FIFO, LIFO, and average cost methods.

5 Compare and contrast the use of the three inventory costing methods.

6 Describe and illustrate the reporting of merchandise inventory in the financial statements.

Control of Inventory

Safeguarding Inventory

Reporting Inventory

Inventory Cost Flow Assumptions

EE 7-1 (page 316)

Inventory Costing Methods Under a Perpetual Inventory System

First-In, First-Out Method

EE 7-2 (page 317)

Last-In, First-Out Method

EE 7-3 (page 319)

Average Cost Method

Computerized Perpetual Inventory Systems

Inventory Costing Methods Under a Periodic Inventory System

First-In, First-Out Method

Last-In, First-Out Method

Average Cost Method

EE 7-4 (page 323)

Comparing Inventory Costing Methods

Reporting Merchandise Inventory in the Financial Statements

Valuation at Lower of Cost or Market

e**x**cel *success* **EE** 7-5 (page 325)

Valuation at Net Realizable Value

Merchandise Inventory on the Balance Sheet

Effect of Inventory Errors on the Financial Statements

EE 7-6 (page 330)

At a Glance   Menu   Turn to pg 333

South-Western

1 Describe the importance of control over inventory.

Control of Inventory

Two primary objectives of control over inventory are as follows:[1]

1. Safeguarding the inventory from damage or theft.
2. Reporting inventory in the financial statements.

Safeguarding Inventory

Controls for safeguarding inventory begin as soon as the inventory is ordered. The following documents are often used for inventory control:

Purchase order
Receiving report
Vendor's invoice

1 Additional controls used by businesses are described and illustrated in Chapter 8, "Sarbanes-Oxley, Internal Control, and Cash."

The **purchase order** authorizes the purchase of the inventory from an approved vendor. As soon as the inventory is received, a receiving report is completed. The **receiving report** establishes an initial record of the receipt of the inventory. To make sure the inventory received is what was ordered, the receiving report is compared with the company's purchase order. The price, quantity, and description of the item on the purchase order and receiving report are then compared to the vendor's invoice. If the receiving report, purchase order, and vendor's invoice agree, the inventory is recorded in the accounting records. If any differences exist, they should be investigated and reconciled.

Recording inventory using a perpetual inventory system is also an effective means of control. The amount of inventory is always available in the **subsidiary inventory ledger**. This helps keep inventory quantities at proper levels. For example, comparing inventory quantities with maximum and minimum levels allows for the timely reordering of inventory and prevents ordering excess inventory.

Finally, controls for safeguarding inventory should include security measures to prevent damage and customer or employee theft. Some examples of security measures include the following:

Best Buy uses scanners to screen customers as they leave the store for merchandise that has not been purchased. In addition, Best Buy stations greeters at the store's entrance to keep customers from bringing in bags that can be used to shoplift merchandise.

1. Storing inventory in areas that are restricted to only authorized employees.
2. Locking high-priced inventory in cabinets.
3. Using two-way mirrors, cameras, security tags, and guards.

Reporting Inventory

A **physical inventory** or count of inventory should be taken near year-end to make sure that the quantity of inventory reported in the financial statements is accurate. After the quantity of inventory on hand is determined, the cost of the inventory is assigned for reporting in the financial statements. Most companies assign costs to inventory using one of three inventory cost flow assumptions.

2 Describe three inventory cost flow assumptions and how they impact the income statement and balance sheet.

Inventory Cost Flow Assumptions

An accounting issue arises when identical units of merchandise are acquired at different unit costs during a period. In such cases, when an item is sold, it is necessary to determine its cost using a cost flow assumption and related inventory cost flow method. Three common cost flow assumptions and related inventory cost flow methods are shown below.

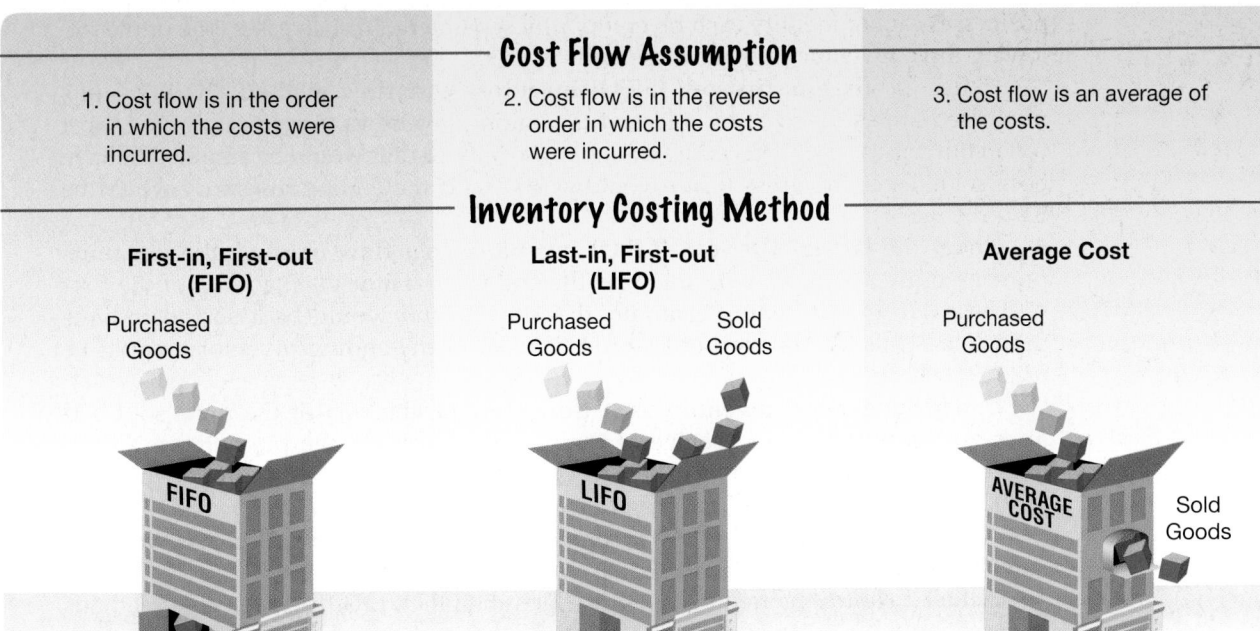

To illustrate, assume that three identical units of merchandise are purchased during May, as follows:

			Units	Cost
May	10	Purchase	1	$ 9
	18	Purchase	1	13
	24	Purchase	1	14
Total			3	$36

Average cost per unit: $12 ($36 ÷ 3 units)

Assume that one unit is sold on May 30 for $20. Depending on which unit was sold, the gross profit varies from $11 to $6, as shown below.

	May 10 Unit Sold	May 18 Unit Sold	May 24 Unit Sold
Sales	$20	$20	$20
Cost of merchandise sold	9	13	14
Gross profit	$11	$ 7	$ 6
Ending inventory	$27	$23	$22
	($13 + $14)	($9 + $14)	($9 + $13)

The specific identification method is normally used by automobile dealerships, jewelry stores, and art galleries.

Under the **specific identification inventory cost flow method**, the unit sold is identified with a specific purchase. The ending inventory is made up of the remaining units on hand. Thus, the gross profit, cost of merchandise sold, and ending inventory can vary as shown above. For example, if the May 18 unit was sold, the cost of merchandise sold is $13, the gross profit is $7, and the ending inventory is $23.

The specific identification method is not practical unless each inventory unit can be separately identified. For example, an automobile dealer may use the specific identification method since each automobile has a unique serial number. However, most businesses cannot identify each inventory unit separately. In such cases, one of the following three inventory cost flow methods is used.

Under the **first-in, first-out (FIFO) inventory cost flow method**, the first units purchased are assumed to be sold and the ending inventory is made up of the most recent purchases. In the preceding example, the May 10 unit would be assumed to have been sold. Thus, the gross profit would be $11, and the ending inventory would be $27 ($13 + $14).

Under the **last-in, first-out (LIFO) inventory cost flow method**, the last units purchased are assumed to be sold and the ending inventory is made up of the first purchases. In the preceding example, the May 24 unit would be assumed to have been sold. Thus, the gross profit would be $6, and the ending inventory would be $22 ($9 + $13).

Under the **average inventory cost flow method**, the cost of the units sold and in ending inventory is an average of the purchase costs. In the preceding example, the cost of the unit sold would be $12 ($36 ÷ 3 units), the gross profit would be $8 ($20 − $12), and the ending inventory would be $24 ($12 × 2 units).

The three inventory cost flow methods, FIFO, LIFO, and average, are shown in Exhibit 1.

Exhibit 2 shows the frequency with which the FIFO, LIFO, and average methods are used.

Exhibit 1

Inventory Costing Methods

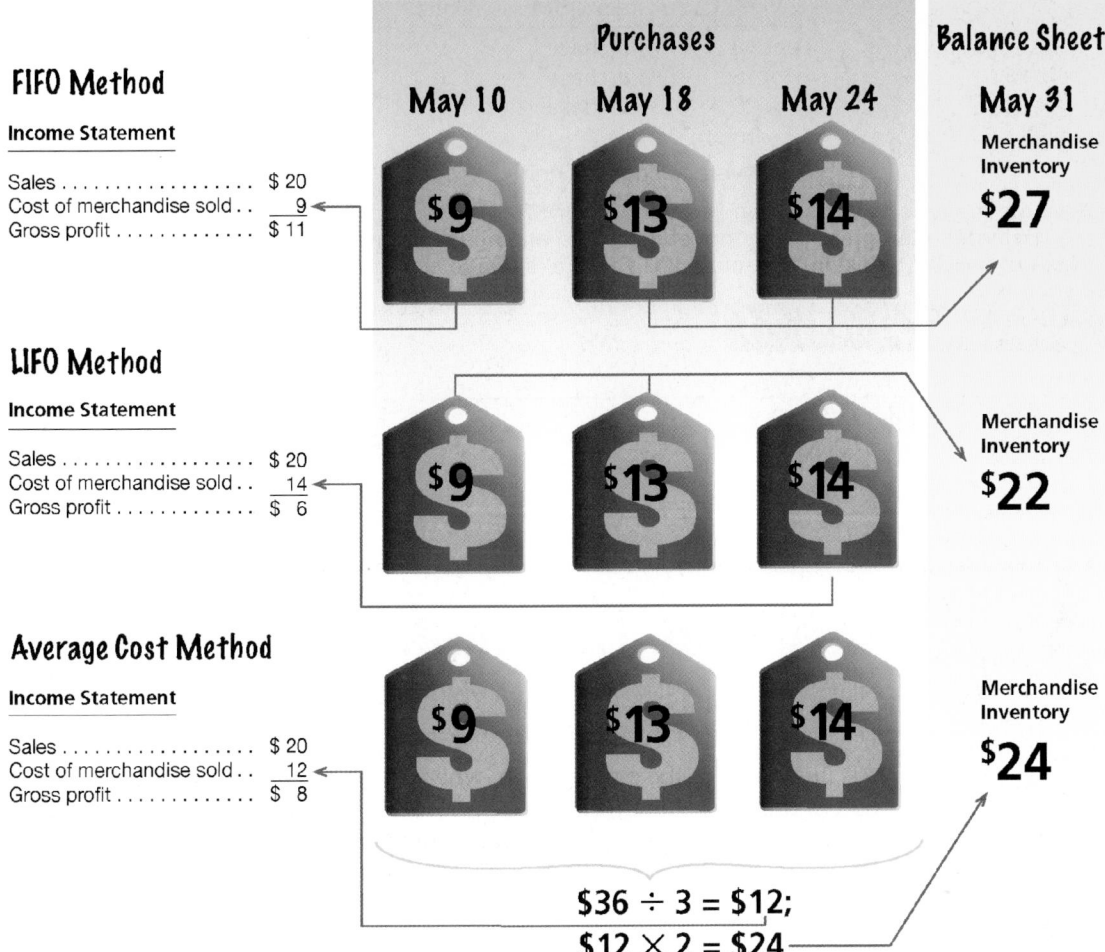

FIFO Method

Income Statement

Sales	$ 20
Cost of merchandise sold . .	9
Gross profit	$ 11

LIFO Method

Income Statement

Sales	$ 20
Cost of merchandise sold . .	14
Gross profit	$ 6

Average Cost Method

Income Statement

Sales	$ 20
Cost of merchandise sold . .	12
Gross profit	$ 8

Purchases

May 10 — $9
May 18 — $13
May 24 — $14

Balance Sheet

May 31
Merchandise Inventory $27

Merchandise Inventory $22

Merchandise Inventory $24

$36 ÷ 3 = $12;
$12 × 2 = $24

Exhibit 2

Use of Inventory Costing Methods*

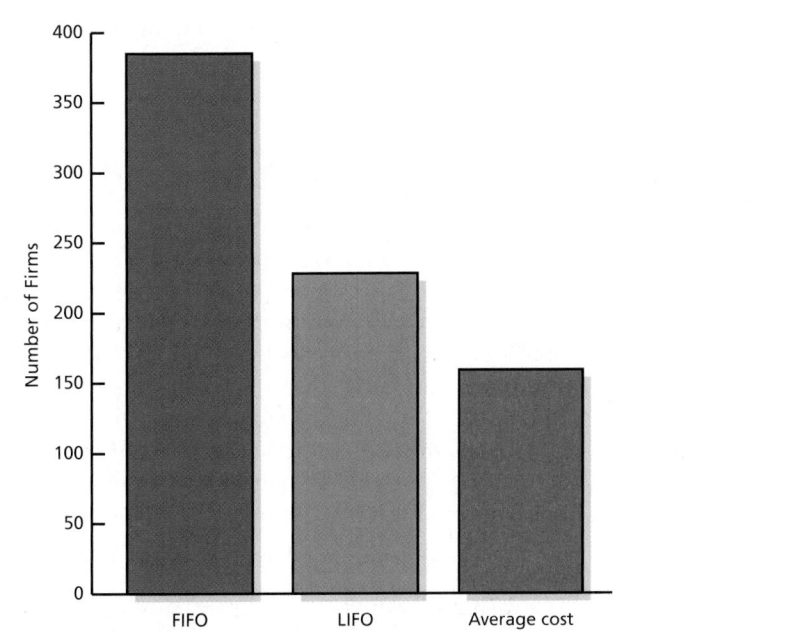

Source: *Accounting Trends and Techniques*, 61st edition, 2007 (New York: American Institute of Certified Public Accountants).

*Firms may be counted more than once for using multiple methods.

Example Exercise 7-1 Cost Flow Methods

Three identical units of Item QBM are purchased during February, as shown below.

	Item QBM	Units	Cost
Feb. 8	Purchase	1	$ 45
15	Purchase	1	48
26	Purchase	1	51
	Total	3	$144
	Average cost per unit		$ 48 ($144 ÷ 3 units)

Assume that one unit is sold on February 27 for $70.

Determine the gross profit for February and ending inventory on February 28 using the (a) first-in, first-out (FIFO); (b) last-in, first-out (LIFO); and (c) average cost methods.

Follow My Example 7-1

		Gross Profit	Ending Inventory
a.	First-in, first-out (FIFO)	$25 ($70 − $45)	$99 ($48 + $51)
b.	Last-in, first-out (LIFO)	$19 ($70 − $51)	$93 ($45 + $48)
c.	Average cost	$22 ($70 − $48)	$96 ($48 × 2)

For Practice: PE 7-1A, PE 7-1B

Inventory Costing Methods Under a Perpetual Inventory System

3 Determine the cost of inventory under the perpetual inventory system, using the FIFO, LIFO, and average cost methods.

Although e-tailers, such as eToys Direct, Inc., Amazon.com, and Furniture.com, Inc., don't have retail stores, they still take possession of inventory in warehouses. Thus, they must account for inventory as illustrated in this chapter.

As illustrated in the prior section, when identical units of an item are purchased at different unit costs, an inventory cost flow method must be used. This is true regardless of whether the perpetual or periodic inventory system is used.

In this section, the FIFO, LIFO, and average cost methods are illustrated under a perpetual inventory system. For purposes of illustration, the data for Item 127B is used, as shown below.

	Item 127B	Units	Cost
Jan. 1	Inventory	100	$20
4	Sale	70	
10	Purchase	80	21
22	Sale	40	
28	Sale	20	
30	Purchase	100	22

First-In, First-Out Method

When the FIFO method is used, costs are included in cost of merchandise sold in the order in which they were purchased. This is often the same as the physical flow of the merchandise. Thus, the FIFO method often provides results that are about the same as those that would have been obtained using the specific identification method. For example, grocery stores shelve milk and other perishable products by expiration dates. Products with early expiration dates are stocked in front. In this way, the oldest products (earliest purchases) are sold first.

To illustrate, Exhibit 3 shows use of FIFO under a perpetual inventory system for Item 127B. The journal entries and the subsidiary inventory ledger for Item 127B are shown in Exhibit 3 as follows:

1. The beginning balance on January 1 is $2,000 (100 units at a unit cost of $20).
2. On January 4, 70 units were sold at a price of $30 each for sales of $2,100 (70 units × $30). The cost of merchandise sold is $1,400 (70 units at a unit cost of $20). After the sale, there remains $600 of inventory (30 units at a unit cost of $20).

Exhibit 3

Entries and Perpetual Inventory Account (FIFO)

Jan. 4	Accounts Receivable	2,100	
	Sales		2,100
4	Cost of Merchandise Sold	1,400	
	Merchandise Inventory		1,400

| 10 | Merchandise Inventory | 1,680 | |
| | Accounts Payable | | 1,680 |

22	Accounts Receivable	1,200	
	Sales		1,200
22	Cost of Merchandise Sold	810	
	Merchandise Inventory		810

28	Accounts Receivable	600	
	Sales		600
28	Cost of Merchandise Sold	420	
	Merchandise Inventory		420

| 30 | Merchandise Inventory | 2,200 | |
| | Accounts Payable | | 2,200 |

Item 127B

	Purchases			Cost of Merchandise Sold			Inventory		
Date	Quantity	Unit Cost	Total Cost	Quantity	Unit Cost	Total Cost	Quantity	Unit Cost	Total Cost
Jan. 1							100	20	2,000
4				70	20	1,400	30	20	600
10	80	21	1,680				30	20	600
							80	21	1,680
22				30	20	600			
				10	21	210	70	21	1,470
28				20	21	420	50	21	1,050
30	100	22	2,200				50	21	1,050
							100	22	2,200
31	Balances					2,630			3,250

Cost of merchandise sold

January 31 inventory

3. On January 10, $1,680 is purchased (80 units at a unit cost of $21). After the purchase, the inventory is reported on two lines, $600 (30 units at a unit cost of $20) from the beginning inventory and $1,680 (80 units at a unit cost of $21) from the January 10 purchase.

4. On January 22, 40 units are sold at a price of $30 each for sales of $1,200 (40 units × $30). Using FIFO, the cost of merchandise sold of $810 consists of $600 (30 units at a unit cost of $20) from the beginning inventory plus $210 (10 units at a unit cost of $21) from the January 10 purchase. After the sale, there remains $1,470 of inventory (70 units at a unit cost of $21) from the January 10 purchase.

5. The January 28 sale and January 30 purchase are recorded in a similar manner.

6. The ending balance on January 31 is $3,250. This balance is made up of two layers of inventory as follows:

	Date of Purchase	Quantity	Unit Cost	Total Cost
Layer 1:	Jan. 10	50	$21	$1,050
Layer 2:	Jan. 30	100	22	2,200
Total		150		$3,250

Example Exercise 7-2 Perpetual Inventory Using FIFO 3

Beginning inventory, purchases, and sales for Item ER27 are as follows:

Nov. 1	Inventory	40 units at $5
5	Sale	32 units
11	Purchase	60 units at $7
21	Sale	45 units

Assuming a perpetual inventory system and using the first-in, first-out (FIFO) method, determine (a) the cost of merchandise sold on November 21 and (b) the inventory on November 30.

(continued)

Follow My Example 7-2

a. Cost of merchandise sold (November 21):

8 units at $5	$ 40
37 units at $7	259
45 units	$299

b. Inventory, November 30:

$161 = (23 units × $7)

For Practice: PE 7-2A, PE 7-2B

Last-In, First-Out Method

When the LIFO method is used, the cost of the units sold is the cost of the most recent purchases. The LIFO method was originally used in those rare cases where the units sold were taken from the most recently purchased units. However, for tax purposes, LIFO is now widely used even when it does not represent the physical flow of units. The tax impact of LIFO is discussed later in this chapter.

To illustrate, Exhibit 4 shows use of LIFO under a perpetual inventory system for Item 127B. The journal entries and the subsidiary inventory ledger for Item 127B are shown in Exhibit 4 as follows:

1. The beginning balance on January 1 is $2,000 (100 units at a unit of cost of $20).
2. On January 4, 70 units were sold at a price of $30 each for sales of $2,100 (70 units × $30). The cost of merchandise sold is $1,400 (70 units at a unit cost of $20). After the sale, there remains $600 of inventory (30 units at a unit cost of $20).
3. On January 10, $1,680 is purchased (80 units at a unit cost of $21). After the purchase, the inventory is reported on two lines, $600 (30 units at a unit cost of $20) from the beginning inventory and $1,680 (80 units at $21 per unit) from the January 10 purchase.
4. On January 22, 40 units are sold at a price of $30 each for sales of $1,200 (40 units × $30). Using LIFO, the cost of merchandise sold is $840 (40 units at unit cost of $21) from the January 10 purchase. After the sale, there remains $1,440 of inventory

Exhibit 4

Entries and Perpetual Inventory Account (LIFO)

Jan. 4	Accounts Receivable	2,100
	Sales	2,100
4	Cost of Merchandise Sold	1,400
	Merchandise Inventory	1,400
10	Merchandise Inventory	1,680
	Accounts Payable	1,680
22	Accounts Receivable	1,200
	Sales	1,200
22	Cost of Merchandise Sold	840
	Merchandise Inventory	840
28	Accounts Receivable	600
	Sales	600
28	Cost of Merchandise Sold	420
	Merchandise Inventory	420
30	Merchandise Inventory	2,200
	Accounts Payable	2,200

Item 127B

	Purchases			Cost of Merchandise Sold			Inventory		
Date	Quantity	Unit Cost	Total Cost	Quantity	Unit Cost	Total Cost	Quantity	Unit Cost	Total Cost
Jan. 1							100	20	2,000
4				70	20	1,400	30	20	600
10	80	21	1,680				30	20	600
							80	21	1,680
22				40	21	840	30	20	600
							40	21	840
28				20	21	420	30	20	600
							20	21	420
30	100	22	2,200				30	20	600
							20	21	420
							100	22	2,200
31	Balances					2,660			3,220

Cost of merchandise sold

January 31 inventory

consisting of $600 (30 units at a unit cost of $20) from the beginning inventory and $840 (40 units at a unit cost of $21) from the January 10 purchase.

5. The January 28 sale and January 30 purchase are recorded in a similar manner.
6. The ending balance on January 31 is $3,220. This balance is made up of three layers of inventory as follows:

	Date of Purchase	Quantity	Unit Cost	Total Cost
Layer 1:	Beg. inv. (Jan. 1)	30	$20	$ 600
Layer 2:	Jan. 10	20	21	420
Layer 3:	Jan. 30	100	22	2,200
Total		150		$3,220

When the LIFO method is used, the subsidiary inventory ledger is sometimes maintained in units only. The units are converted to dollars when the financial statements are prepared at the end of the period.

Example Exercise 7-3   Perpetual Inventory Using LIFO   3

Beginning inventory, purchases, and sales for Item ER27 are as follows:

Nov.	1	Inventory	40 units at $5
	5	Sale	32 units
	11	Purchase	60 units at $7
	21	Sale	45 units

Assuming a perpetual inventory system and using the last-in, first-out (LIFO) method, determine (a) the cost of the merchandise sold on November 21 and (b) the inventory on November 30.

Follow My Example 7-3

a. Cost of merchandise sold (November 21):
   $315 = (45 units × $7)

b. Inventory, November 30:
   8 units at $5 $ 40
   15 units at $7   105
   23 units $145

For Practice: PE 7-3A, PE 7-3B

Average Cost Method

When the average cost method is used in a perpetual inventory system, an average unit cost for each item is computed each time a purchase is made. This unit cost is then used to determine the cost of each sale until another purchase is made and a new average is computed. This averaging technique is called a *moving average*. Since the average cost method is rarely used in a perpetual inventory system, it is not illustrated.

Computerized Perpetual Inventory Systems

A perpetual inventory system may be used in a manual accounting system. However, if there are many inventory transactions, such a system is costly and time consuming. In most cases, perpetual inventory systems are computerized.

A computerized perpetual inventory system for a retail store could be used as follows:

1. Each inventory item, including description, quantity, and unit size, is stored electronically in an inventory file. The total of the file equals the balance of Merchandise Inventory in the general ledger.

2. Each time an item is purchased or returned by a customer, the inventory file is updated by scanning the item's bar code.

3. Each time an item is sold, the item's bar code is scanned at the cash register and the inventory files are updated.

4. After a physical inventory is taken, the inventory count data are used to update the inventory file. A listing of inventory overages and shortages is printed, and any unusual amounts are investigated.

Computerized perpetual inventory systems are useful to managers in controlling and managing inventory. For example, fast selling items can be reordered before the stock runs out. Sales patterns can also be analyzed to determine when to mark down merchandise or when to restock seasonal merchandise. Finally, inventory data can be used in evaluating advertising campaigns and sales promotions.

4 Determine the cost of inventory under the periodic inventory system, using the FIFO, LIFO, and average cost methods.

Inventory Costing Methods Under a Periodic Inventory System

When the periodic inventory system is used, only revenue is recorded each time a sale is made. No entry is made at the time of the sale to record the cost of the merchandise sold. At the end of the accounting period, a physical inventory is taken to determine the cost of the inventory and the cost of the merchandise sold.[2]

Like the perpetual inventory system, a cost flow assumption must be made when identical units are acquired at different unit costs during a period. In such cases, the FIFO, LIFO, or average cost method is used.

First-In, First-Out Method

To illustrate the use of the FIFO method in a periodic inventory system, we use the same data for Item 127B as in the perpetual inventory example. The beginning inventory entry and purchases of Item 127B in January are as follows:

Jan. 1	Inventory	100 units at	$20	$2,000
10	Purchase	80 units at	21	1,680
30	Purchase	100 units at	22	2,200
Available for sale during month		280		$5,880

The physical count on January 31 shows that 150 units are on hand. Using the FIFO method, the cost of the merchandise on hand at the end of the period is made up of the most recent costs. The cost of the 150 units in ending inventory on January 31 is determined as follows:

Most recent costs, January 30 purchase	100 units at	$22	$2,200
Next most recent costs, January 10 purchase	50 units at	$21	1,050
Inventory, January 31	150 units		$3,250

Deducting the cost of the January 31 inventory of $3,250 from the cost of merchandise available for sale of $5,880 yields the cost of merchandise sold of $2,630, as shown below.

Beginning inventory, January 1	$2,000
Purchases ($1,680 + $2,200)	3,880
Cost of merchandise available for sale in January	$5,880
Less ending inventory, January 31	3,250
Cost of merchandise sold	$2,630

---

2 Determining the cost of merchandise sold using the periodic system was illustrated in Chapter 6.

The $3,250 cost of the ending merchandise inventory on January 31 is made up of the most recent costs. The $2,630 cost of merchandise sold is made up of the beginning inventory and the earliest costs. Exhibit 5 shows the relationship of the cost of merchandise sold for January and the ending inventory on January 31.

Exhibit 5

First-In, First-Out Flow of Costs

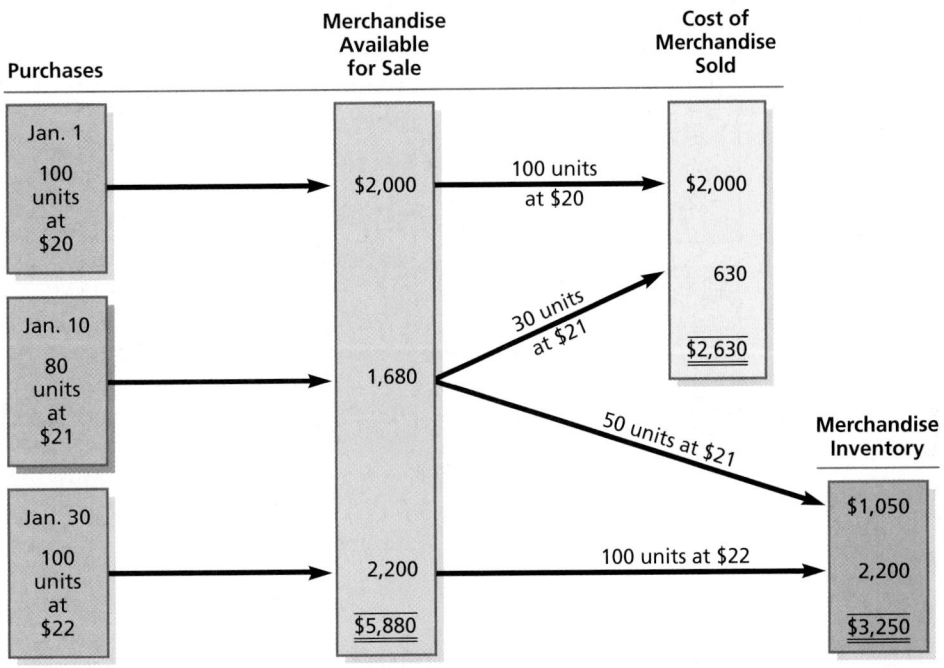

Last-In, First-Out Method

When the LIFO method is used, the cost of merchandise on hand at the end of the period is made up of the earliest costs. Based on the same data as in the FIFO example, the cost of the 150 units in ending inventory on January 31 is determined as follows:

Beginning inventory, January 1	100 units at	$20	$2,000
Next earliest costs, January 10	50 units at	$21	1,050
Inventory, January 31	150 units		$3,050

Deducting the cost of the January 31 inventory of $3,050 from the cost of merchandise available for sale of $5,880 yields the cost of merchandise sold of $2,830, as shown below.

Beginning inventory, January 1	$2,000
Purchases ($1,680 + $2,200)	3,880
Cost of merchandise available for sale in January	$5,880
Less ending inventory, January 31	3,050
Cost of merchandise sold	$2,830

The $3,050 cost of the ending merchandise inventory on January 31 is made up of the earliest costs. The $2,830 cost of merchandise sold is made up of the most recent costs. Exhibit 6 shows the relationship of the cost of merchandise sold for January and the ending inventory on January 31.

Exhibit 6

Last-In, First-Out Flow of Costs

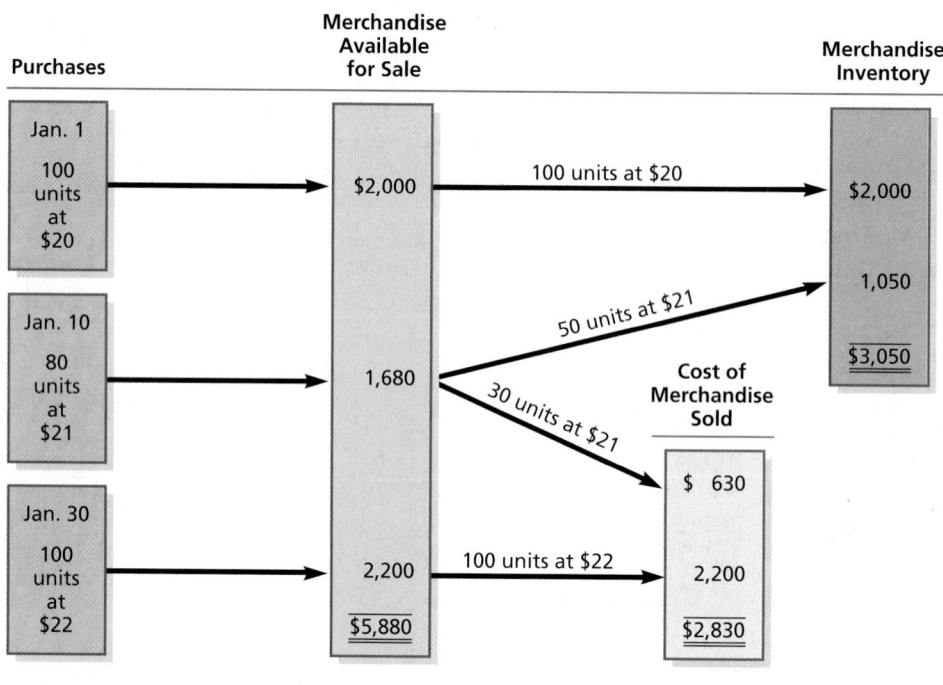

Average Cost Method

The average cost method is sometimes called the *weighted average method*. The average cost method uses the average unit cost for determining cost of merchandise sold and the ending merchandise inventory. If purchases are relatively uniform during a period, the average cost method provides results that are similar to the physical flow of goods.

The weighted average unit cost is determined as follows:

$$\text{Average Unit Cost} = \frac{\text{Total Cost of Units Available for Sale}}{\text{Units Available for Sale}}$$

To illustrate, we use the data for Item 127B as follows:

$$\text{Average Unit Cost} = \frac{\text{Total Cost of Units Available for Sale}}{\text{Units Available for Sale}} = \frac{\$5,880}{280 \text{ units}}$$

$$\text{Average Unit Cost} = \$21 \text{ per unit}$$

The cost of the January 31 ending inventory is as follows:

$$\text{Inventory, January 31: } \$3,150 \text{ (150 units} \times \$21)$$

Deducting the cost of the January 31 inventory of $3,150 from the cost of merchandise available for sale of $5,880 yields the cost of merchandise sold of $2,730, as shown below.

Beginning inventory, January 1	$2,000
Purchases ($1,680 + $2,200)	3,880
Cost of merchandise available for sale in January	$5,880
Less ending inventory, January 31	3,150
Cost of merchandise sold	$2,730

The cost of merchandise sold could also be computed by multiplying the number of units sold by the average cost as follows:

Cost of merchandise sold: $2,730 (130 units × $21)

Example Exercise 7-4 Periodic Inventory Using FIFO, LIFO, Average Cost Methods ••••••••⟩ 4

The units of an item available for sale during the year were as follows:

Jan. 1	Inventory	6 units at $50	$ 300
Mar. 20	Purchase	14 units at $55	770
Oct. 30	Purchase	20 units at $62	1,240
	Available for sale	40 units	$2,310

There are 16 units of the item in the physical inventory at December 31. The periodic inventory system is used. Determine the inventory cost using (a) the first-in, first-out (FIFO) method, (b) the last-in, first-out (LIFO) method, and (c) the average cost method.

Follow My Example 7-4

a. First-in, first-out (FIFO) method: $992 = (16 units × $62)

b. Last-in, first-out (LIFO) method: $850 = (6 units × $50) + (10 units × $55)

c. Average cost method: $924 (16 units × $57.75), where average cost = $57.75 = $2,310/40 units

For Practice: PE 7-4A, PE 7-4B

Compare and contrast the use of the three inventory costing methods.

Comparing Inventory Costing Methods

A different cost flow is assumed for the FIFO, LIFO, and average inventory cost flow methods. As a result, the three methods normally yield different amounts for the following:

1. Cost of merchandise sold
2. Gross profit
3. Net income
4. Ending merchandise inventory

Using the periodic inventory system illustration with sales of $3,900 (130 units × $30), these differences are illustrated below.[3]

Ford Motor Company reported LIFO inventories of $10,121 million along with the fact that FIFO inventories would have been $11,221 million.

Partial Income Statements

	First-In, First-Out		Average Cost		Last-In, First-Out	
Net sales		$3,900		$3,900		$3,900
Cost of merchandise sold:						
Beginning inventory	$2,000		$2,000		$2,000	
Purchases	3,880		3,880		3,880	
Merchandise available for sale	$5,880		$5,880		$5,880	
Less ending inventory	3,250		3,150		3,050	
Cost of merchandise sold		2,630		2,730		2,830
Gross profit		$1,270		$1,170		$1,070

The preceding differences show the effect of increasing costs (prices). If costs (prices) remain the same, all three methods would yield the same results. However, costs (prices) normally do change. The effects of changing costs (prices) on the FIFO and LIFO methods are summarized in Exhibit 7. The average cost method will always yield results between those of FIFO and LIFO.

3 Similar results would also occur when comparing inventory costing methods under a perpetual inventory system.

| Exhibit 7 |

Effects of Changing Costs (Prices): FIFO and LIFO Cost Methods

	Increasing Costs (Prices)		Decreasing Costs (Prices)	
	Highest Amount	Lowest Amount	Highest Amount	Lowest Amount
Cost of merchandise sold	LIFO	FIFO	FIFO	LIFO
Gross profit	FIFO	LIFO	LIFO	FIFO
Net income	FIFO	LIFO	LIFO	FIFO
Ending merchandise inventory	FIFO	LIFO	LIFO	FIFO

Chrysler's reason for changing from the FIFO method to the LIFO method was stated in the following note that accompanied its financial statements: *Chrysler changed its method of accounting from first-in, first-out (FIFO) to last-in, first-out (LIFO) for substantially all of its domestic productive inventories. The change to LIFO was made to more accurately match current costs with current revenues.*

FIFO reports higher gross profit and net income than the LIFO method when costs (prices) are increasing, as shown in Exhibit 7. However, in periods of rapidly rising costs, the inventory that is sold must be replaced at increasingly higher costs. In such cases, the larger FIFO gross profit and net income are sometimes called *inventory profits* or *illusory profits*.

During a period of increasing costs, LIFO matches more recent costs against sales on the income statement. Thus, it can be argued that the LIFO method more nearly matches current costs with current revenues. LIFO also offers an income tax savings during periods of increasing costs. This is because LIFO reports the lowest amount of gross profit and, thus, taxable net income. However, under LIFO, the ending inventory on the balance sheet may be quite different from its current replacement cost. In such cases, the financial statements normally include a note that estimates what the inventory would have been if FIFO had been used.

The average cost method is, in a sense, a compromise between FIFO and LIFO. The effect of cost (price) trends is averaged in determining the cost of merchandise sold and the ending inventory. For a series of purchases, the average cost will be the same, regardless of whether costs are increasing or decreasing. For example, reversing the sequence of unit costs presented in the prior illustration does not affect the average unit cost nor the amounts reported for cost of merchandise sold, gross profit, or ending inventory.

Integrity, Objectivity, and Ethics in Business

WHERE'S THE BONUS?

Managers are often given bonuses based on reported earnings numbers. This can create a conflict. LIFO can improve the value of the company through lower taxes. However, in periods of rising costs (prices), LIFO also produces a lower earnings number and, therefore, lower management bonuses. Ethically, managers should select accounting procedures that will maximize the value of the firm, rather than their own compensation. Compensation specialists can help avoid this ethical dilemma by adjusting the bonus plan for the accounting procedure differences.

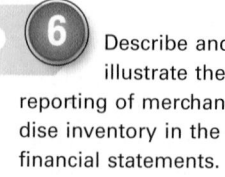

6 Describe and illustrate the reporting of merchandise inventory in the financial statements.

Reporting Merchandise Inventory in the Financial Statements

Cost is the primary basis for valuing and reporting inventories in the financial statements. However, inventory may be valued at other than cost in the following cases:

1. The cost of replacing items in inventory is below the recorded cost.
2. The inventory cannot be sold at normal prices due to imperfections, style changes, or other causes.

Valuation at Lower of Cost or Market

If the cost of replacing inventory is lower than its recorded purchase cost, the **lower-of-cost-or-market (LCM) method** is used to value the inventory. *Market,* as used in *lower of cost or market,* is the cost to replace the inventory. The market value is based on normal quantities that would be purchased from suppliers.

The lower-of-cost-or-market method can be applied in one of three ways. The cost, market price, and any declines could be determined for the following:

1. Each item in the inventory.
2. Each major class or category of inventory.
3. Total inventory as a whole.

The amount of any price decline is included in the cost of merchandise sold. This, in turn, reduces gross profit and net income in the period in which the price declines occur. This matching of price declines to the period in which they occur is the primary advantage of using the lower-of-cost-or-market method.

To illustrate, assume the following data for 400 identical units of Item A in inventory on December 31, 2010:

Unit purchased cost	$10.25
Replacement cost on December 31, 2010	9.50

Since Item A could be replaced at $9.50 a unit, $9.50 is used under the lower-of-cost-or-market method.

Exhibit 8 illustrates applying the lower-of-cost-or-market method to each inventory item (A, B, C, and D). As applied on an item-by-item basis, the total lower-of-cost-or-market is $15,070, which is a market decline of $450 ($15,520 − $15,070). This market decline of $450 is included in the cost of merchandise sold.

In Exhibit 8, Items A, B, C, and D could be viewed as a class of inventory items. If the lower-of-cost-or-market method is applied to the class, the inventory would be valued at $15,472, which is a market decline of $48 ($15,520 − $15,472). Likewise, if Items A, B, C, and D make up the total inventory, the lower-of-cost-or-market method as applied to the total inventory would be the same amount, $15,472.

Exhibit 8

Determining Inventory at Lower of Cost or Market

	A	B	C	D	E	F	G
1			Unit	Unit		Total	
2		Inventory	Cost	Market			Lower
3	Item	Quantity	Price	Price	Cost	Market	of C or M
4	A	400	$10.25	$ 9.50	$ 4,100	$ 3,800	$ 3,800
5	B	120	22.50	24.10	2,700	2,892	2,700
6	C	600	8.00	7.75	4,800	4,650	4,650
7	D	280	14.00	14.75	3,920	4,130	3,920
8	Total				$15,520	$15,472	$15,070
9							

Example Exercise 7-5   Lower-of-Cost-or-Market Method   ⬤⬤⬤⬤⬤⬤⬤⬤➤ 6

On the basis of the following data, determine the value of the inventory at the lower of cost or market. Apply lower of cost or market to each inventory item as shown in Exhibit 8.

Item	Inventory Quantity	Unit Cost Price	Unit Market Price
C17Y	10	$ 39	$40
B563	7	110	98

(continued)

Follow My Example 7-5

	A	B	C	D	E	F	G
1			Unit	Unit		Total	
2		Inventory	Cost	Market			Lower
3	Item	Quantity	Price	Price	Cost	Market	of C or M
4	C17Y	10	$ 39	$ 40	$ 390	$ 400	$ 390
5	B563	7	110	98	770	686	686
6	Total				$1,160	$1,086	$1,076
7							
8							
9							

For Practice: PE 7-5A, PE 7-5B

success

The lower of cost or market inventory schedule from Exhibit 8 can be developed on a spreadsheet as follows:

	A	B	C	D	E	F	G
					a.	b.	c.
1							
2						Total	
3	Item	Inventory Quantity	Unit Cost Price	Unit Market Price	Cost	Market	Lower of C or M
4	A	400	$ 10.25	$ 9.50	=B4*C4	=B4*D4	=MIN(E4:F4)
5	B	120	22.50	24.10	=B5*C5	=B5*D5	=MIN(E5:F5)
6	C	600	8.00	7.75	=B6*C6	=B6*D6	=MIN(E6:F6)
7	D	280	14.00	14.75	=B7*C7	=B7*D7	=MIN(E7:F7)
8	Total				=SUM(E4:E7)	=SUM(F4:F7)	=SUM(G4:G7)
9					e.	f.	

Develop the formulas by the following steps:

a. Enter in cell E4 the formula for the total cost, =B4*C4.
b. Enter in cell F4 the formula for the total market, =B4*D4.
c. Enter in cell G4 a =MIN function to calculate the lower of cost or market, as follows:

=MIN(E4:F4)

This function will return the minimum value within the range of cells from E4 to F4.

d. Copy E4:G4 to E5:G7.
e. Enter in E8 a formula to sum the column, =SUM(E4:E7)
f. Copy E8 to F8:G8

Copy cells by using the fill handle in the corner of the cell to be copied and dragging to the target cells.

 Go to the hands-on **Excel Tutor** for this example!

Digital Theater Systems Inc. reported the following inventory write-downs: "...an inventory write-down of $3,871,000 (was recorded) due to ... technological obsolescence."

Valuation at Net Realizable Value

Merchandise that is out of date, spoiled, or damaged can often be sold only at a price below its original cost. Such merchandise should be valued at its **net realizable value**. Net realizable value is determined as follows:

Net Realizable Value = Estimated Selling Price − Direct Costs of Disposal

Direct costs of disposal include selling expenses such as special advertising or sales commissions on sale. To illustrate, assume the following data about an item of damaged merchandise:

Original cost	$1,000
Estimated selling price	800
Selling expenses	150

The merchandise should be valued at its net realizable value of $650 as shown below.

Net Realizable Value = $800 − $150 = $650

Merchandise Inventory on the Balance Sheet

Merchandise inventory is usually reported in the Current Assets section of the balance sheet. In addition to this amount, the following are reported:

1. The method of determining the cost of the inventory (FIFO, LIFO, or average)
2. The method of valuing the inventory (cost or the lower of cost or market)

The financial statement reporting for the topics covered in Chapters 7–15 are illustrated using excerpts from the financial statements of Mornin' Joe. Mornin' Joe is a fictitious company that offers drip and espresso coffee in a coffeehouse setting. The complete financial statements of Mornin' Joe are illustrated at the end of Chapter 15 (pages 700–702).

The balance sheet presentation for merchandise inventory for Mornin' Joe is as follows:

Mornin' Joe
Balance Sheet
December 31, 2010

Current assets:		
Cash and cash equivalents		$235,000
Trading investments (at cost)	$420,000	
Plus valuation allowance on trading investments	45,000	465,000
Accounts receivable	$305,000	
Less allowance for doubtful accounts	12,300	292,700
Merchandise inventory—at lower of cost		
(first-in, first-out method) or market		120,000

It is not unusual for a large business to use different costing methods for segments of its inventories. Also, a business may change its inventory costing method. In such cases, the effect of the change and the reason for the change are disclosed in the financial statements.

Effect of Inventory Errors on the Financial Statements

Any errors in merchandise inventory will affect the balance sheet and income statement. Some reasons that inventory errors may occur include the following:

1. Physical inventory on hand was miscounted.
2. Costs were incorrectly assigned to inventory. For example, the FIFO, LIFO, or average cost method was incorrectly applied.
3. Inventory in transit was incorrectly included or excluded from inventory.
4. Consigned inventory was incorrectly included or excluded from inventory.

Inventory errors often arise from merchandise that is in transit at year-end. As discussed in Chapter 6, shipping terms determine when the title to merchandise passes. When goods are purchased or sold *FOB shipping point*, title passes to the buyer when the goods are shipped. When the terms are *FOB destination*, title passes to the buyer when the goods are received.

To illustrate, assume that SysExpress ordered the following merchandise from American Products:

Date ordered:	December 27, 2009
Amount:	$10,000
Terms:	FOB shipping point, 2/10, n/30
Date shipped by seller:	December 30
Date delivered:	January 3, 2010

When SysExpress counts its physical inventory on December 31, 2009, the merchandise is still in transit. In such cases, it would be easy for SysExpress to not include the $10,000 of merchandise in its December 31 physical inventory. However, since the merchandise was purchased *FOB shipping point*, SysExpress owns the merchandise. Thus, it should be included in the ending December 31 inventory even though it is not on hand. Likewise, any merchandise *sold* by SysExpress *FOB destination* is still SysExpress's inventory even if it is in transit to the buyer on December 31.

Inventory errors often arise from **consigned inventory**. Manufacturers sometimes ship merchandise to retailers who act as the manufacturer's selling agent. The manufacturer, called the **consignor**, retains title until the goods are sold. Such merchandise is said to be shipped *on consignment* to the retailer, called the **consignee**. Any unsold merchandise at year-end is a part of the manufacturer's (consignor's) inventory, even though the merchandise is in the hands of the retailer (consignee). At year-end, it would be easy for the retailer (consignee) to incorrectly include the consigned merchandise in its physical inventory. Likewise, the manufacturer (consignor) should include consigned inventory in its physical inventory even though the inventory is not on hand.

Income Statement Effects Inventory errors will misstate the income statement amounts for cost of merchandise sold, gross profit, and net income. The effects of inventory errors on the current period's income statement are summarized in Exhibit 9.

Exhibit 9

Effect of Inventory Errors on Current Period's Income Statement

	Income Statement Effect		
Inventory Error	**Cost of Merchandise Sold**	**Gross Profit**	**Net Income**
Beginning inventory is:			
Understated	*Understated*	*Overstated*	*Overstated*
Overstated	*Overstated*	*Understated*	*Understated*
Ending inventory is:			
Understated	*Overstated*	*Understated*	*Understated*
Overstated	*Understated*	*Overstated*	*Overstated*

To illustrate, we use the income statements of SysExpress shown in Exhibit 10.[4]

On December 31, 2009, assume that SysExpress incorrectly records its physical inventory as $50,000 instead of the correct amount of $60,000. Thus, the December 31, 2009, inventory is understated by $10,000 ($60,000 − $50,000). As a result, the cost of merchandise sold is overstated by $10,000. The gross profit and the net income for the year will also be understated by $10,000.

The December 31, 2009, merchandise inventory becomes the January 1, 2010, inventory. Thus, the beginning inventory for 2010 is understated by $10,000. As a result, the cost of merchandise sold is understated by $10,000 for 2010. The gross profit and net income for 2010 will be overstated by $10,000.

As shown in Exhibit 10, since the ending inventory of one period is the beginning inventory of the next period, the effects of inventory errors carry forward to the next period. Specifically, if uncorrected, the effects of inventory errors reverse themselves in the next period. In Exhibit 10, the combined net income for the two years of $525,000 is correct even though the 2009 and 2010 income statements were incorrect.

Balance Sheet Effects Inventory errors misstate the merchandise inventory, current assets, total assets, and owner's equity on the balance sheet. The effects of inventory errors on the current period's balance sheet are summarized in Exhibit 11.

For the SysExpress illustration shown in Exhibit 10, the December 31, 2009, ending inventory was understated by $10,000. As a result, the merchandise inventory, current assets, and total assets would be understated by $10,000 on the December 31, 2009, balance sheet. Because the ending physical inventory is understated, the cost of merchandise sold for 2009 will be overstated by $10,000. Thus, the gross profit and the net

4 We will illustrate the effect of inventory errors using the periodic system. This is because it is easier to see the impact of inventory errors on the income statement using the periodic system. The effect of inventory errors would be the same under the perpetual inventory system.

Exhibit 10

Effects of Inventory Errors on Two Years' Income Statements

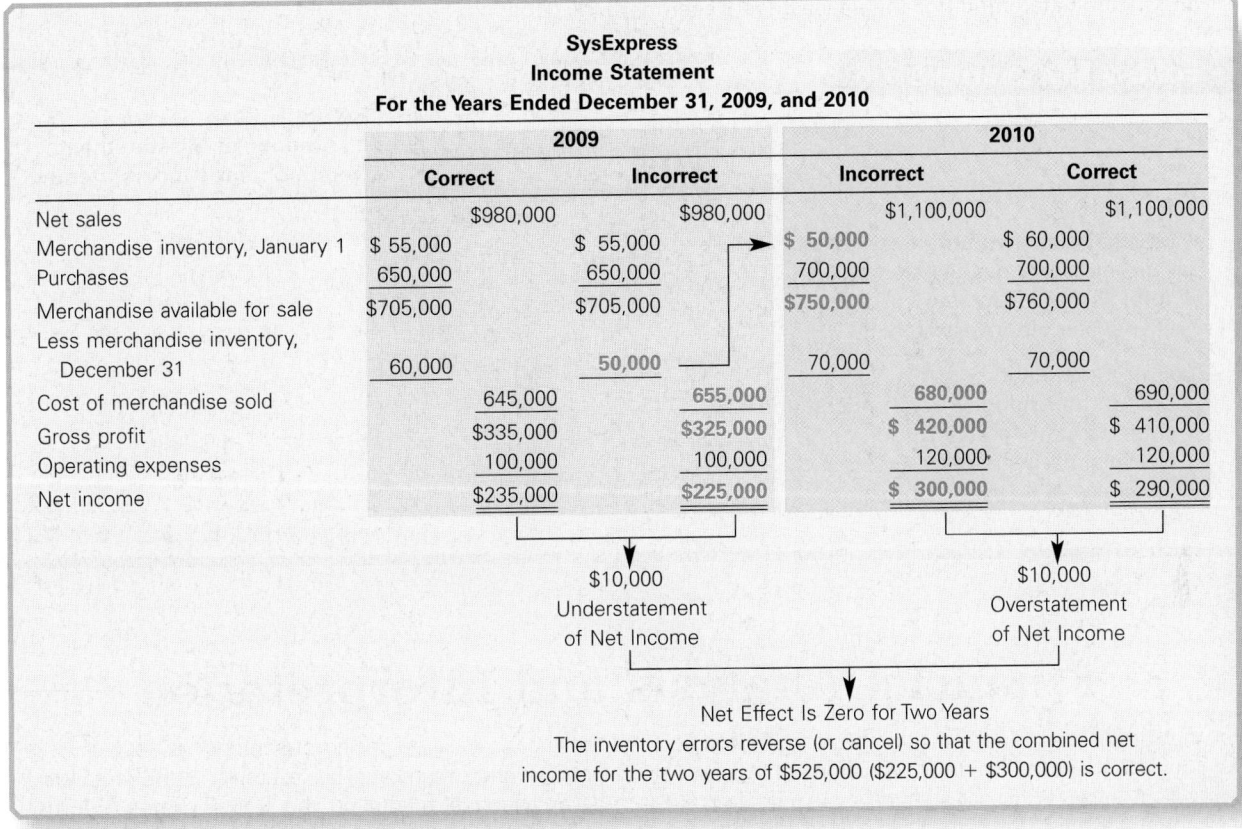

income for 2009 are understated by $10,000. Since the net income is closed to owner's equity (capital) at the end of the period, the owner's equity on the December 31, 2009, balance sheet is also understated by $10,000.

As just discussed, inventory errors reverse themselves within two years. As a result, the balance sheet will be correct as of December 31, 2010. Using the SysExpress illustration from Exhibit 10, these effects are summarized below.

	Amount of Misstatement	
	December 31, 2009	December 31, 2010
Balance Sheet:		
Merchandise inventory overstated (understated)	$(10,000)	Correct
Current assets overstated (understated)	(10,000)	Correct
Total assets overstated (understated)	(10,000)	Correct
Owner's equity overstated (understated)	(10,000)	Correct
Income Statement:	2009	2010
Cost of merchandise sold overstated (understated)	$ 10,000	$(10,000)
Gross profit overstated (understated)	(10,000)	10,000
Net income overstated (understated)	(10,000)	10,000

Exhibit 11

Effect of Inventory Errors on Current Period's Balance Sheet

	Balance Sheet Effect			
Ending Inventory Error	Merchandise Inventory	Current Assets	Total Assets	Owner's Equity (Capital)
Understated	Understated	Understated	Understated	Understated
Overstated	Overstated	Overstated	Overstated	Overstated

Example Exercise 7-6 Effect of Inventory Errors

Zula Repair Shop incorrectly counted its December 31, 2010, inventory as $250,000 instead of the correct amount of $220,000. Indicate the effect of the misstatement on Zula's December 31, 2010, balance sheet and income statement for the year ended December 31, 2010.

Follow My Example 7-6

	Amount of Misstatement Overstatement (Understatement)
Balance Sheet:	
Merchandise inventory overstated	$ 30,000
Current assets overstated	30,000
Total assets overstated	30,000
Owner's equity overstated	30,000
Income Statement:	
Cost of merchandise sold understated	$ (30,000)
Gross profit overstated	30,000
Net income overstated	30,000

For Practice: PE 7-6A, PE 7-6B

Financial Analysis and Interpretation

A merchandising business should keep enough inventory on hand to meet the needs of its customers. A failure to do so may result in lost sales. At the same time, too much inventory ties up funds that could be used to improve operations. In addition, excess inventory increases expenses such as storage, insurance, and property taxes. Finally, excess inventory increases the risk of losses due to price declines, damage, or changes in customers' tastes.

Two measures to analyze the efficiency and effectiveness of inventory are the inventory turnover and the number of days' sales in inventory.

Inventory turnover measures the relationship between cost of merchandise sold and the amount of inventory carried during the period. It is computed as follows:

$$\text{Inventory Turnover} = \frac{\text{Cost of Merchandise Sold}}{\text{Average Inventory}}$$

To illustrate, the following data (in thousands) have been taken from annual reports for SUPERVALU Inc. and Zale Corporation:

	SUPERVALU	Zale
Cost of merchandise sold	$29,267,000	$1,194,399
Inventories:		
Beginning of year	$ 954,200	$ 903,294
End of year	$ 2,749,000	$1,021,164
Average	$ 1,851,600	$ 962,229
Inventory turnover	15.8	1.2

The inventory turnover is 15.8 for SUPERVALU and 1.2 for Zale. Generally, the larger the inventory turnover, the more efficient and effective the management of inventory. However, differences in companies and industries may be too great to allow specific statements as to what is a good inventory turnover. For example, SUPERVALU is a leading food distributor in the United States. Because SUPERVALU's inventory is perishable, we would expect it to have a high inventory turnover. In contrast, Zale Corporation is a large retailer of fine jewelry in the United States. Thus, we would expect Zale to have a lower inventory turnover than SUPERVALU.

The **number of days' sales in inventory** is a rough measure of the length of time it takes to acquire, sell, and replace the inventory. It is computed as follows:

$$\text{Number of Days' Sales in Inventory} = \frac{\text{Average Inventory}}{\text{Average Daily Cost of Merchandise Sold}}$$

The average daily cost of merchandise sold is determined by dividing the cost of merchandise sold by 365. The number of days' sales in inventory for SUPERVALU and Zale is computed as shown below.

	SUPERVALU	Zale
Average daily cost of merchandise sold:		
$29,267,000/365	$ 80,184	
$1,194,399/365		$ 3,272
Average inventory	$1,851,600	$962,229
Number of days' sales in inventory	23.1 days	294.1 days

Generally, the lower the number of days' sales in inventory, the better. As with inventory turnover, we should expect differences among industries, such as those for SUPERVALU and Zale.

A P P E N D I X

Estimating Inventory Cost

A business may need to estimate the amount of inventory for the following reasons:

1. Perpetual inventory records are not maintained.
2. A disaster such as a fire or flood has destroyed the inventory records and the inventory.
3. Monthly or quarterly financial statements are needed, but a physical inventory is taken only once a year.

This appendix describes and illustrates two widely used methods of estimating inventory cost.

Retail Method of Inventory Costing

The **retail inventory method** of estimating inventory cost requires costs and retail prices to be maintained for the merchandise available for sale. A ratio of cost to retail price is then used to convert ending inventory at retail to estimate the ending inventory cost.

The retail inventory method is applied as follows:

Step 1. Determine the total merchandise available for sale at cost and retail.
Step 2. Determine the ratio of the cost to retail of the merchandise available for sale.
Step 3. Determine the ending inventory at retail by deducting the net sales from the merchandise available for sale at retail.
Step 4. Estimate the ending inventory cost by multiplying the ending inventory at retail by the cost to retail ratio.

Exhibit 12 illustrates the retail inventory method.

Exhibit 12

Determining Inventory by the Retail Method

A	B Cost	C Retail
Step 1 → 4 Merchandise inventory, January 1	$19,400	$ 36,000
Purchases in January (net)	42,600	64,000
Merchandise available for sale	$62,000	$100,000
Step 2 → 5 Ratio of cost to retail price: $\frac{\$62,000}{\$100,000} = 62\%$		
Sales for January (net)		70,000
Step 3 → 7 Merchandise inventory, January 31, at retail		$ 30,000
Step 4 → 8 Merchandise inventory, January 31, at estimated cost		
($30,000 × 62%)		$ 18,600

When estimating the cost to retail ratio, the mix of items in the ending inventory is assumed to be the same as the merchandise available for sale. If the ending inventory is made up of different classes of merchandise, cost to retail ratios may be developed for each class of inventory.

An advantage of the retail method is that it provides inventory figures for preparing monthly statements. Department stores and similar retailers often determine gross profit and operating income each month, but may take a physical inventory only once or twice a year. Thus, the retail method allows management to monitor operations more closely.

The retail method may also be used as an aid in taking a physical inventory. In this case, the items are counted and recorded at their retail (selling) prices instead of their costs. The physical inventory at retail is then converted to cost by using the cost to retail ratio.

Gross Profit Method of Inventory Costing

The **gross profit method** uses the estimated gross profit for the period to estimate the inventory at the end of the period. The gross profit is estimated from the preceding year, adjusted for any current-period changes in the cost and sales prices.

The gross profit method is applied as follows:

Step 1. Determine the merchandise available for sale at cost.

Step 2. Determine the estimated gross profit by multiplying the net sales by the gross profit percentage.

Step 3. Determine the estimated cost of merchandise sold by deducting the estimated gross profit from the net sales.

Step 4. Estimate the ending inventory cost by deducting the estimated cost of merchandise sold from the merchandise available for sale.

Exhibit 13 illustrates the gross profit method.

Exhibit 13

Estimating Inventory by Gross Profit Method

	A	B	C
1			Cost
2	Merchandise inventory, January 1		$ 57,000
3	Purchases in January (net)		180,000
Step 1 → 4	Merchandise available for sale		$237,000
5	Sales for January (net)	$250,000	
Step 2 → 6	Less estimated gross profit ($250,000 × 30%)	75,000	
Step 3 → 7	Estimated cost of merchandise sold		175,000
Step 4 → 8	Estimated merchandise inventory, January 31		$ 62,000
9			

The gross profit method is useful for estimating inventories for monthly or quarterly financial statements. It is also useful in estimating the cost of merchandise destroyed by fire or other disasters.

1 Describe the importance of control over inventory.

Key Points	Key Learning Outcomes	Example Exercises	Practice Exercises
Two primary objectives of control over inventory are safeguarding the inventory and properly reporting it in the financial statements. The perpetual inventory system enhances control over inventory. In addition, a physical inventory count should be taken periodically to detect shortages as well as to deter employee thefts.	• Describe controls for safeguarding inventory. • Describe how a perpetual inventory system enhances control over inventory. • Describe why taking a physical inventory enhances control over inventory.		

2 Describe three inventory cost flow assumptions and how they impact the income statement and balance sheet.

Key Points	Key Learning Outcomes	Example Exercises	Practice Exercises
The three common inventory cost flow assumptions used in business are the (1) first-in, first-out method (FIFO); (2) last-in, first-out method (LIFO); and (3) average cost method. The choice of a cost flow assumption directly affects the income statement and balance sheet.	• Describe the FIFO, LIFO, and average cost flow methods. • Describe how choice of a cost flow method affects the income statement and balance sheet.	**7-1**	7-1A, 7-1B

3 Determine the cost of inventory under the perpetual inventory system, using the FIFO, LIFO, and average cost methods.

Key Points	Key Learning Outcomes	Example Exercises	Practice Exercises
In a perpetual inventory system, the number of units and the cost of each type of merchandise are recorded in a subsidiary inventory ledger, with a separate account for each type of merchandise.	• Determine the cost of inventory and cost of merchandise sold using a perpetual inventory system under the FIFO method.	**7-2**	7-2A, 7-2B
	• Determine the cost of inventory and cost of merchandise sold using a perpetual inventory system under the LIFO method.	**7-3**	7-3A, 7-3B

4 Determine the cost of inventory under the periodic inventory system, using the FIFO, LIFO, and average cost methods.

Key Points	Key Learning Outcomes	Example Exercises	Practice Exercises
In a periodic inventory system, a physical inventory is taken to determine the cost of the inventory and the cost of merchandise sold.	• Determine the cost of inventory and cost of merchandise sold using a periodic inventory system under the FIFO method.	7-4	7-4A, 7-4B
	• Determine the cost of inventory and cost of merchandise sold using a periodic inventory system under the LIFO method.	7-4	7-4A, 7-4B
	• Determine the cost of inventory and cost of merchandise sold using a periodic inventory system under the average cost method.	7-4	7-4A, 7-4B

5 Compare and contrast the use of the three inventory costing methods.

Key Points	Key Learning Outcomes	Example Exercises	Practice Exercises
The three inventory costing methods will normally yield different amounts for (1) the ending inventory, (2) the cost of merchandise sold for the period, and (3) the gross profit (and net income) for the period.	• Indicate which inventory cost flow method will yield the highest and lowest ending inventory and net income during periods of increasing prices.		
	• Indicate which inventory cost flow method will yield the highest and lowest ending inventory and net income during periods of decreasing prices.		

6 Describe and illustrate the reporting of merchandise inventory in the financial statements.

Key Points	Key Learning Outcomes	Example Exercises	Practice Exercises
The lower of cost or market is used to value inventory. Inventory that is out of date, spoiled, or damaged is valued at its net realizable value.	• Determine inventory using lower of cost or market.	7-5	7-5A, 7-5B
Merchandise inventory is usually presented in the Current Assets section of the balance sheet, following receivables. The method of determining the cost and valuing the inventory is reported.	• Illustrate the use of net realizable value for spoiled or damaged inventory.		
	• Prepare the Current Assets section of the balance sheet that includes inventory.		
Errors in reporting inventory based on the physical inventory will affect the balance sheet and income statement.	• Determine the effect of inventory errors on the balance sheet and income statement.	7-6	7-6A, 7-6B

Key Terms

average inventory cost flow
  method (314)
consigned inventory (328)
consignee (328)
consignor (328)
first-in, first-out (FIFO)
  inventory cost flow
  method (314)
gross profit method (332)
inventory turnover (330)

last-in, first-out (LIFO)
  inventory cost flow
  method (314)
lower-of-cost-or-market (LCM)
  method (325)
net realizable value (326)
number of days' sales in
  inventory (330)
physical inventory (313)
purchase order (313)

receiving report (313)
retail inventory
  method (331)
specific identification
  inventory cost flow
  method (314)
subsidiary inventory
  ledger (313)

Illustrative Problem

Stewart Co.'s beginning inventory and purchases during the year ended December 31, 2010, were as follows:

		Units	Unit Cost	Total Cost
January 1	Inventory	1,000	$50.00	$ 50,000
March 10	Purchase	1,200	52.50	63,000
June 25	Sold 800 units			
August 30	Purchase	800	55.00	44,000
October 5	Sold 1,500 units			
November 26	Purchase	2,000	56.00	112,000
December 31	Sold 1,000 units			
Total		5,000		$269,000

Instructions

1. Determine the cost of inventory on December 31, 2010, using the perpetual inventory system and each of the following inventory costing methods:
   a. first-in, first-out
   b. last-in, first-out
2. Determine the cost of inventory on December 31, 2010, using the periodic inventory system and each of the following inventory costing methods:
   a. first-in, first-out
   b. last-in, first-out
   c. average cost
3. Appendix: Assume that during the fiscal year ended December 31, 2010, sales were $290,000 and the estimated gross profit rate was 40%. Estimate the ending inventory at December 31, 2010, using the gross profit method.

Solution

1. a. First-in, first-out method: $95,200 (shown on page 336)
   b. Last-in, first-out method: $91,000 ($35,000 + $56,000) (shown on page 336)
2. a. First-in, first-out method:
      1,700 units at $56 = $95,200
   b. Last-in, first-out method:

1,000 units at $50.00	$50,000
700 units at $52.50	36,750
1,700 units	$86,750

1. a. First-in, first-out method: $95,200

Date	Purchases Quantity	Unit Cost	Total Cost	Cost of Merchandise Sold Quantity	Unit Cost	Total Cost	Inventory Quantity	Unit Cost	Total Cost
2010 Jan. 1							1,000	50.00	50,000
Mar. 10	1,200	52.50	63,000				1,000	50.00	50,000
							1,200	52.50	63,000
June 25				800	50.00	40,000	200	50.00	10,000
							1,200	52.50	63,000
Aug. 30	800	55.00	44,000				200	50.00	10,000
							1,200	52.50	63,000
							800	55.00	44,000
Oct. 5				200	50.00	10,000	700	55.00	38,500
				1,200	52.50	63,000			
				100	55.00	5,500			
Nov. 26	2,000	56.00	112,000				700	55.00	38,500
							2,000	56.00	112,000
Dec. 31				700	55.00	38,500	1,700	56.00	95,200
				300	56.00	16,800			
31 Balances						173,800			95,200

b. Last-in, first-out method: $91,000 ($35,000 + $56,000)

Date	Purchases Quantity	Unit Cost	Total Cost	Cost of Merchandise Sold Quantity	Unit Cost	Total Cost	Inventory Quantity	Unit Cost	Total Cost
2010 Jan. 1							1,000	50.00	50,000
Mar. 10	1,200	52.50	63,000				1,000	50.00	50,000
							1,200	52.50	63,000
June 25				800	52.50	42,000	1,000	50.00	50,000
							400	52.50	21,000
Aug. 30	800	55.00	44,000				1,000	50.00	50,000
							400	52.50	21,000
							800	55.00	44,000
Oct. 5				800	55.00	44,000	700	50.00	35,000
				400	52.50	21,000			
				300	50.00	15,000			
Nov. 26	2,000	56.00	112,000				700	50.00	35,000
							2,000	56.00	112,000
Dec. 31				1,000	56.00	56,000	700	50.00	35,000
							1,000	56.00	56,000
31 Balances						178,000			91,000

c. Average cost method:

Average cost per unit: $269,000/5,000 units = $53.80

Inventory, December 31, 2010: 1,700 units at $53.80 = $91,460

3. Appendix:

Merchandise inventory, January 1, 2010	$ 50,000
Purchases (net)	219,000
Merchandise available for sale	$269,000
Sales (net) $290,000	
Less estimated gross profit ($290,000 × 40%) ... 116,000	
Estimated cost of merchandise sold	174,000
Estimated merchandise inventory, December 31, 2010	$ 95,000

Self-Examination Questions (Answers at End of Chapter)

1. The inventory costing method that is based on the assumption that costs should be charged against revenue in the order in which they were incurred is:
   A. FIFO.
   B. LIFO.
   C. average cost.
   D. perpetual inventory.

2. The following units of a particular item were purchased and sold during the period:

Beginning inventory	40 units at $20
First purchase	50 units at $21
Second purchase	50 units at $22
First sale	110 units
Third purchase	50 units at $23
Second sale	45 units

   What is the cost of the 35 units on hand at the end of the period as determined under the perpetual inventory system by the LIFO costing method?
   A. $715
   B. $705
   C. $700
   D. $805

3. The following units of a particular item were available for sale during the period:

Beginning inventory	40 units at $20
First purchase	50 units at $21
Second purchase	50 units at $22
Third purchase	50 units at $23

   What is the unit cost of the 35 units on hand at the end of the period as determined under the periodic inventory system by the FIFO costing method?
   A. $20
   B. $21
   C. $22
   D. $23

4. If merchandise inventory is being valued at cost and the price level is steadily rising, the method of costing that will yield the highest net income is:
   A. LIFO.
   B. FIFO.
   C. average.
   D. periodic.

5. If the inventory at the end of the year is understated by $7,500, the error will cause an:
   A. understatement of cost of merchandise sold for the year by $7,500.
   B. overstatement of gross profit for the year by $7,500.
   C. overstatement of merchandise inventory for the year by $7,500.
   D. understatement of net income for the year by $7,500.

Eye Openers

1. Before inventory purchases are recorded, the receiving report should be reconciled to what documents?
2. What security measures may be used by retailers to protect merchandise inventory from customer theft?
3. Which inventory system provides the more effective means of controlling inventories (perpetual or periodic)? Why?
4. Why is it important to periodically take a physical inventory if the perpetual system is used?
5. Do the terms *FIFO* and *LIFO* refer to techniques used in determining quantities of the various classes of merchandise on hand? Explain.
6. Does the term *last-in* in the LIFO method mean that the items in the inventory are assumed to be the most recent (last) acquisitions? Explain.
7. If merchandise inventory is being valued at cost and the price level is decreasing, which of the three methods of costing—FIFO, LIFO, or average cost—will yield (a) the highest inventory cost, (b) the lowest inventory cost, (c) the highest gross profit, and (d) the lowest gross profit?
8. Which of the three methods of inventory costing—FIFO, LIFO, or average cost—will in general yield an inventory cost most nearly approximating current replacement cost?
9. If inventory is being valued at cost and the price level is steadily rising, which of the three methods of costing—FIFO, LIFO, or average cost—will yield the lowest annual income tax expense? Explain.
10. Can a company change its method of costing inventory? Explain.
11. Because of imperfections, an item of merchandise cannot be sold at its normal selling price. How should this item be valued for financial statement purposes?

12. How is the method of determining the cost of the inventory and the method of valuing it disclosed in the financial statements?
13. The inventory at the end of the year was understated by $12,750. (a) Did the error cause an overstatement or an understatement of the gross profit for the year? (b) Which items on the balance sheet at the end of the year were overstated or understated as a result of the error?
14. Funtime Co. sold merchandise to Jaffe Company on December 31, FOB shipping point. If the merchandise is in transit on December 31, the end of the fiscal year, which company would report it in its financial statements? Explain.
15. A manufacturer shipped merchandise to a retailer on a consignment basis. If the merchandise is unsold at the end of the period, in whose inventory should the merchandise be included?

Practice Exercises

PE 7-1A
Cost flow methods

obj. 2

EE 7-1   p. 316

Three identical units of Item WH4 are purchased during June, as shown below.

Item WH4		Units	Cost
June 3	Purchase	1	$ 30
10	Purchase	1	36
19	Purchase	1	42
Total		3	$108
Average cost per unit			$ 36 ($108 ÷ 3 units)

Assume that one unit is sold on June 23 for $53.

Determine the gross profit for June and ending inventory on June 30 using the (a) first-in, first-out (FIFO); (b) last-in, first-out (LIFO); and (c) average cost methods.

PE 7-1B
Cost flow methods

obj. 2

EE 7-1   p. 316

Three identical units of Item JC07 are purchased during August, as shown below.

Item JC07		Units	Cost
Aug. 7	Purchase	1	$ 80
13	Purchase	1	84
25	Purchase	1	88
Total		3	$252
Average cost per unit			$ 84 ($252 ÷ 3 units)

Assume that one unit is sold on August 30 for $125.

Determine the gross profit for August and ending inventory on August 31 using the (a) first-in, first-out (FIFO); (b) last-in, first-out (LIFO); and (c) average cost methods.

PE 7-2A
Perpetual inventory using FIFO

obj. 3

EE 7-2   p. 317

Beginning inventory, purchases, and sales for Item VX48 are as follows:

July 1	Inventory	100 units at $8
8	Sale	90 units
15	Purchase	125 units at $12
25	Sale	60 units

Assuming a perpetual inventory system and using the first-in, first-out (FIFO) method, determine (a) the cost of merchandise sold on July 25 and (b) the inventory on July 31.

PE 7-2B
Perpetual inventory using FIFO

obj. 3

EE 7-2   p. 317

Beginning inventory, purchases, and sales for Item CJ10 are as follows:

Apr. 1	Inventory	30 units at $70
8	Sale	18 units
15	Purchase	25 units at $72
24	Sale	15 units

Assuming a perpetual inventory system and using the first-in, first-out (FIFO) method, determine (a) the cost of merchandise sold on April 24 and (b) the inventory on April 30.

PE 7-3A
Perpetual inventory
using LIFO

obj. 3

EE 7-3   p. 319

Beginning inventory, purchases, and sales for Item VX48 are as follows:

July 1	Inventory	100 units at $8
8	Sale	90 units
15	Purchase	125 units at $12
25	Sale	60 units

Assuming a perpetual inventory system and using the last-in, first-out (LIFO) method, determine (a) the cost of merchandise sold on July 25 and (b) the inventory on July 31.

PE 7-3B
Perpetual inventory
using LIFO

obj. 3

EE 7-3   p. 319

Beginning inventory, purchases, and sales for Item CJ10 are as follows:

Apr. 1	Inventory	30 units at $70
8	Sale	18 units
15	Purchase	25 units at $72
24	Sale	15 units

Assuming a perpetual inventory system and using the last-in, first-out (LIFO) method, determine (a) the cost of merchandise sold on April 24 and (b) the inventory on April 30.

PE 7-4A
Periodic inventory
using FIFO, LIFO,
average cost
methods

obj. 4

EE 7-4   p. 323

The units of an item available for sale during the year were as follows:

Jan. 1	Inventory	5 units at $120	$ 600
Feb. 13	Purchase	65 units at $114	7,410
Oct. 30	Purchase	10 units at $119	1,190
	Available for sale	80 units	$9,200

There are 24 units of the item in the physical inventory at December 31. The periodic inventory system is used. Determine the inventory cost using (a) the first-in, first-out (FIFO) method; (b) the last-in, first-out (LIFO) method; and (c) the average cost method.

PE 7-4B
Periodic inventory
using FIFO, LIFO,
average cost
methods

obj. 4

EE 7-4   p. 323

The units of an item available for sale during the year were as follows:

Jan. 1	Inventory	60 units at $45	$ 2,700
Apr. 20	Purchase	90 units at $50	4,500
Nov. 30	Purchase	75 units at $54	4,050
	Available for sale	225 units	$11,250

There are 48 units of the item in the physical inventory at December 31. The periodic inventory system is used. Determine the inventory cost using (a) the first-in, first-out (FIFO) method; (b) the last-in, first-out (LIFO) method; and (c) the average cost method.

PE 7-5A
Lower of cost or
market method

obj. 6

EE 7-5   p. 325

On the basis of the following data, determine the value of the inventory at the lower of cost or market. Apply lower of cost or market to each inventory item as shown in Exhibit 8.

Item	Inventory Quantity	Unit Cost Price	Unit Market Price
Alpha	400	$ 6	$ 5
Beta	350	12	14

PE 7-5B
Lower of cost or
market method

obj. 6

EE 7-5   p. 325

On the basis of the following data, determine the value of the inventory at the lower of cost or market. Apply lower of cost or market to each inventory item as shown in Exhibit 8.

Item	Inventory Quantity	Unit Cost Price	Unit Market Price
Widget	100	$30	$27
Gidget	75	24	25

PE 7-6A
Effect of inventory
errors

obj. 6

EE 7-6   p. 330

During the taking of its physical inventory on December 31, 2010, Euro Bath Company incorrectly counted its inventory as $496,000 instead of the correct amount of $480,000. Indicate the effect of the misstatement on Euro Bath's December 31, 2010, balance sheet and income statement for the year ended December 31, 2010.

PE 7-6B
Effect of inventory errors

obj. 6

EE 7-6 p. 330

During the taking of its physical inventory on December 31, 2010, Best Interiors Company incorrectly counted its inventory as $145,000 instead of the correct amount of $175,000. Indicate the effect of the misstatement on Best Interiors' December 31, 2010, balance sheet and income statement for the year ended December 31, 2010.

Exercises

EX 7-1
Control of inventories

obj. 1

Hammer & Nails Hardware Store currently uses a periodic inventory system. Alice Asaki, the owner, is considering the purchase of a computer system that would make it feasible to switch to a perpetual inventory system.

Alice is unhappy with the periodic inventory system because it does not provide timely information on inventory levels. Alice has noticed on several occasions that the store runs out of good-selling items, while too many poor-selling items are on hand.

Alice is also concerned about lost sales while a physical inventory is being taken. Hammer & Nails Hardware currently takes a physical inventory twice a year. To minimize distractions, the store is closed on the day inventory is taken. Alice believes that closing the store is the only way to get an accurate inventory count.

➡ Will switching to a perpetual inventory system strengthen Hammer & Nails Hardware's control over inventory items? Will switching to a perpetual inventory system eliminate the need for a physical inventory count? Explain.

EX 7-2
Control of inventories

obj. 1

Fly Away Luggage Shop is a small retail establishment located in a large shopping mall. This shop has implemented the following procedures regarding inventory items:

a. Whenever Fly Away receives a shipment of new inventory, the items are taken directly to the stockroom. Fly Away's accountant uses the vendor's invoice to record the amount of inventory received.

b. Since the shop carries mostly high-quality, designer luggage, all inventory items are tagged with a control device that activates an alarm if a tagged item is removed from the store.

c. Since the display area of the store is limited, only a sample of each piece of luggage is kept on the selling floor. Whenever a customer selects a piece of luggage, the salesclerk gets the appropriate piece from the store's stockroom. Since all salesclerks need access to the stockroom, it is not locked. The stockroom is adjacent to the break room used by all mall employees.

➡ State whether each of these procedures is appropriate or inappropriate. If it is inappropriate, state why.

EX 7-3
Perpetual inventory using FIFO

objs. 2, 3

✔ Inventory balance, April 30, $3,750

Beginning inventory, purchases, and sales data for portable video CD players are as follows:

Apr. 1	Inventory	50 units at $35
5	Sale	40 units
14	Purchase	60 units at $36
21	Sale	35 units
23	Sale	10 units
30	Purchase	75 units at $38

The business maintains a perpetual inventory system, costing by the first-in, first-out method. Determine the cost of the merchandise sold for each sale and the inventory balance after each sale, presenting the data in the form illustrated in Exhibit 3.

EX 7-4
Perpetual inventory using LIFO
objs. 2, 3

✔ Inventory balance, April 30, $3,740

Assume that the business in Exercise 7-3 maintains a perpetual inventory system, costing by the last-in, first-out method. Determine the cost of merchandise sold for each sale and the inventory balance after each sale, presenting the data in the form illustrated in Exhibit 4.

EX 7-5
Perpetual inventory using LIFO
objs. 2, 3

✔ Inventory balance, March 31, $14,600

Beginning inventory, purchases, and sales data for cell phones for March are as follows:

Inventory		Purchases		Sales	
March 1	1,000 units at $40	March 5	500 units at $42	March 8	700 units
		20	450 units at $44	14	600 units
				31	300 units

Assuming that the perpetual inventory system is used, costing by the LIFO method, determine the cost of merchandise sold for each sale and the inventory balance after each sale, presenting the data in the form illustrated in Exhibit 4.

EX 7-6
Perpetual inventory using FIFO
objs. 2, 3

✔ Inventory balance, March 31, $15,400

Assume that the business in Exercise 7-5 maintains a perpetual inventory system, costing by the first-in, first-out method. Determine the cost of merchandise sold for each sale and the inventory balance after each sale, presenting the data in the form illustrated in Exhibit 3.

EX 7-7
FIFO, LIFO costs under perpetual inventory system
objs. 2, 3

✔ a. $19,200

The following units of a particular item were available for sale during the year:

Beginning inventory	150 units at $75
Sale	120 units at $125
First purchase	400 units at $78
Sale	200 units at $125
Second purchase	300 units at $80
Sale	290 units at $125

The firm uses the perpetual inventory system, and there are 240 units of the item on hand at the end of the year. What is the total cost of the ending inventory according to (a) FIFO, (b) LIFO?

EX 7-8
Periodic inventory by three methods
objs. 2, 4

✔ b. $6,414

The units of an item available for sale during the year were as follows:

Jan. 1	Inventory	27 units at $120
Feb. 17	Purchase	54 units at $138
July 21	Purchase	63 units at $156
Nov. 23	Purchase	36 units at $165

There are 50 units of the item in the physical inventory at December 31. The periodic inventory system is used. Determine the inventory cost by (a) the first-in, first-out method, (b) the last-in, first-out method, and (c) the average cost method.

EX 7-9

Periodic inventory by three methods; cost of merchandise sold

objs. 2, 4

✔ a. Inventory, $2,508

The units of an item available for sale during the year were as follows:

Jan. 1	Inventory	42 units at $60
Mar. 10	Purchase	58 units at $65
Aug. 30	Purchase	20 units at $68
Dec. 12	Purchase	30 units at $70

There are 36 units of the item in the physical inventory at December 31. The periodic inventory system is used. Determine the inventory cost and the cost of merchandise sold by three methods, presenting your answers in the following form:

	Cost	
Inventory Method	**Merchandise Inventory**	**Merchandise Sold**
a. First-in, first-out	$	$
b. Last-in, first-out		
c. Average cost		

EX 7-10

Comparing inventory methods

obj. 5

Assume that a firm separately determined inventory under FIFO and LIFO and then compared the results.

1. In each space below, place the correct sign [less than (<), greater than (>), or equal (=)] for each comparison, assuming periods of rising prices.

a. FIFO inventory	_____	LIFO inventory
b. FIFO cost of goods sold	_____	LIFO cost of goods sold
c. FIFO net income	_____	LIFO net income
d. FIFO income tax	_____	LIFO income tax

2. Why would management prefer to use LIFO over FIFO in periods of rising prices?

EX 7-11

Lower-of-cost-or-market inventory

obj. 6

✔ LCM: $16,990

On the basis of the following data, determine the value of the inventory at the lower of cost or market. Assemble the data in the form illustrated in Exhibit 8.

Commodity	Inventory Quantity	Unit Cost Price	Unit Market Price
Aquarius	20	$ 80	$ 92
Capricorn	50	70	65
Leo	8	300	280
Scorpio	30	40	30
Taurus	100	90	94

EX 7-12

Merchandise inventory on the balance sheet

obj. 6

Based on the data in Exercise 7-11 and assuming that cost was determined by the FIFO method, show how the merchandise inventory would appear on the balance sheet.

EX 7-13

Effect of errors in physical inventory

obj. 6

Montana White Water Co. sells canoes, kayaks, whitewater rafts, and other boating supplies. During the taking of its physical inventory on December 31, 2010, Montana White Water incorrectly counted its inventory as $315,600 instead of the correct amount of $325,000.

a. State the effect of the error on the December 31, 2010, balance sheet of Montana White Water.

b. State the effect of the error on the income statement of Montana White Water for the year ended December 31, 2010.

EX 7-14

Effect of errors in physical inventory

obj. 6

Boss Motorcycle Shop sells motorcycles, ATVs, and other related supplies and accessories. During the taking of its physical inventory on December 31, 2010, Boss Motorcycle Shop incorrectly counted its inventory as $195,750 instead of the correct amount of $188,200.

a. State the effect of the error on the December 31, 2010, balance sheet of Boss Motorcycle Shop.

b. State the effect of the error on the income statement of Boss Motorcycle Shop for the year ended December 31, 2010.

EX 7-15
Error in inventory
obj. 6

During 2010, the accountant discovered that the physical inventory at the end of 2009 had been understated by $11,900. Instead of correcting the error, however, the accountant assumed that an $11,900 overstatement of the physical inventory in 2010 would balance out the error.

➤ Are there any flaws in the accountant's assumption? Explain.

Appendix
EX 7-16
Retail inventory
method

A business using the retail method of inventory costing determines that merchandise inventory at retail is $950,000. If the ratio of cost to retail price is 66%, what is the amount of inventory to be reported on the financial statements?

Appendix
EX 7-17
Retail inventory
method

A business using the retail method of inventory costing determines that merchandise inventory at retail is $880,000. If the ratio of cost to retail price is 65%, what is the amount of inventory to be reported on the financial statements?

Appendix
EX 7-18
Retail inventory
method

A business using the retail method of inventory costing determines that merchandise inventory at retail is $375,000. If the ratio of cost to retail price is 60%, what is the amount of inventory to be reported on the financial statements?

Appendix
EX 7-19
Retail inventory
method

✔ Inventory, April
30: $165,000

On the basis of the following data, estimate the cost of the merchandise inventory at April 30 by the retail method:

		Cost	Retail
April 1	Merchandise inventory	$ 180,000	$ 300,000
April 1–30	Purchases (net)	1,200,000	2,000,000
April 1–30	Sales (net)		2,025,000

Appendix
EX 7-20
Gross profit
inventory method

The merchandise inventory was destroyed by fire on October 11. The following data were obtained from the accounting records:

Jan. 1	Merchandise inventory	$ 260,000
Jan. 1–Oct. 11	Purchases (net)	1,900,000
	Sales (net)	3,200,000
	Estimated gross profit rate	40%

a. Estimate the cost of the merchandise destroyed.
b. Briefly describe the situations in which the gross profit method is useful.

Appendix
EX 7-21
Gross profit
method

Based on the following data, estimate the cost of ending merchandise inventory:

Sales (net)	$4,800,000
Estimated gross profit rate	40%
Beginning merchandise inventory	$ 250,000
Purchases (net)	2,900,000
Merchandise available for sale	$3,150,000

Appendix
EX 7-22
Gross profit
method

Based on the following data, estimate the cost of ending merchandise inventory:

Sales (net)	$1,500,000
Estimated gross profit rate	38%
Beginning merchandise inventory	$ 80,000
Purchases (net)	948,000
Merchandise available for sale	$1,028,000

EX 7-23
Inventory turnover

The following data were taken from recent annual reports of Apple Computer, Inc., a manufacturer of personal computers and related products, and American Greetings Corporation, a manufacturer and distributor of greeting cards and related products:

	Apple	American Greetings
Cost of goods sold	$13,717,000,000	$826,791,000
Inventory, end of year	270,000,000	187,817,000
Inventory, beginning of the year	165,000,000	230,308,000

a. Determine the inventory turnover for Apple and American Greetings. Round to one decimal place.
b. Would you expect American Greetings' inventory turnover to be higher or lower than Apple's? Why?

EX 7-24
Inventory turnover and number of days' sales in inventory

✔ a. Kroger, 33 days' sales in inventory

Kroger, Safeway Inc., and Winn-Dixie Stores Inc. are three grocery chains in the United States. Inventory management is an important aspect of the grocery retail business. Recent balance sheets for these three companies indicated the following merchandise inventory information:

	Merchandise Inventory	
	End of Year (in millions)	Beginning of Year (in millions)
Kroger	$4,609	$4,486
Safeway	2,643	2,766
Winn-Dixie	523	798

The cost of goods sold for each company were:

	Cost of Goods Sold (in millions)
Kroger	$50,115
Safeway	28,604
Winn-Dixie	5,327

a. Determine the number of days' sales in inventory and inventory turnover for the three companies. Round to the nearest day and one decimal place.
b. Interpret your results in (a).
c. If Safeway had Kroger's number of days' sales in inventory, how much additional cash flow (round to nearest million) would have been generated from the smaller inventory relative to its actual average inventory position?

Problems Series A

PR 7-1A
FIFO perpetual inventory

objs. 2, 3

✔ 3. $1,413,500

The beginning inventory of merchandise at Waldo Co. and data on purchases and sales for a three-month period are as follows:

Date	Transaction	Number of Units	Per Unit	Total
March 3	Inventory	60	$1,500	$ 90,000
8	Purchase	120	1,800	216,000
11	Sale	80	5,000	400,000
30	Sale	50	5,000	250,000
April 8	Purchase	100	2,000	200,000
10	Sale	60	5,000	300,000
19	Sale	30	5,000	150,000
28	Purchase	100	2,200	220,000
May 5	Sale	60	5,250	315,000
16	Sale	80	5,250	420,000
21	Purchase	180	2,400	432,000
28	Sale	90	5,250	472,500

Instructions
1. Record the inventory, purchases, and cost of merchandise sold data in a perpetual inventory record similar to the one illustrated in Exhibit 3, using the first-in, first-out method.
2. Determine the total sales and the total cost of merchandise sold for the period. Journalize the entries in the sales and cost of merchandise sold accounts. Assume that all sales were on account.
3. Determine the gross profit from sales for the period.
4. Determine the ending inventory cost.

PR 7-2A
LIFO perpetual inventory

objs. 2, 3

✔ 2. Gross profit,
$1,395,500

The beginning inventory for Waldo Co and data on purchases and sales for a three-month period are shown in Problem 7-1A.

Instructions
1. Record the inventory, purchases, and cost of merchandise sold data in a perpetual inventory record similar to the one illustrated in Exhibit 4, using the last-in, first-out method.
2. Determine the total sales, the total cost of merchandise sold, and the gross profit from sales for the period.
3. Determine the ending inventory cost.

PR 7-3A
Periodic inventory by three methods

objs. 2, 4

✔ 1. $15,583

Artic Appliances uses the periodic inventory system. Details regarding the inventory of appliances at January 1, 2010, purchases invoices during the year, and the inventory count at December 31, 2010, are summarized as follows:

Model	Inventory, January 1	Purchases Invoices 1st	2nd	3rd	Inventory Count, December 31
BB900	27 at $213	21 at $215	18 at $222	18 at $225	30
C911	10 at 60	6 at 65	2 at 65	2 at 70	4
L100	6 at 305	3 at 310	3 at 316	4 at 317	4
N201	2 at 520	2 at 527	2 at 530	2 at 535	4
Q73	6 at 520	8 at 531	4 at 549	6 at 542	7
Z120	—	4 at 222	4 at 232	—	2
ZZRF	8 at 70	12 at 72	16 at 74	14 at 78	12

Instructions
1. Determine the cost of the inventory on December 31, 2010, by the first-in, first-out method. Present data in columnar form, using the following headings:

Model	Quantity	Unit Cost	Total Cost

If the inventory of a particular model comprises one entire purchase plus a portion of another purchase acquired at a different unit cost, use a separate line for each purchase.
2. Determine the cost of the inventory on December 31, 2010, by the last-in, first-out method, following the procedures indicated in (1).
3. Determine the cost of the inventory on December 31, 2010, by the average cost method, using the columnar headings indicated in (1).
4. ➡ Discuss which method (FIFO or LIFO) would be preferred for income tax purposes in periods of (a) rising prices and (b) declining prices.

PR 7-4A
Lower-of-cost-or-market inventory

obj. 6

✔ Total LCM,
$43,096

If the working papers correlating with this textbook are not used, omit Problem 7-4A.
Data on the physical inventory of Winesap Co. as of December 31, 2010, are presented in the working papers. The quantity of each commodity on hand has been determined and recorded on the inventory sheet. Unit market prices have also been determined as of December 31 and recorded on the sheet. The inventory is to be determined at cost and also at the lower of cost or market, using the first-in, first-out method. Quantity and cost data from the last purchases invoice of the year and the next-to-the-last purchases invoice are summarized as follows:

Description	Last Purchases Invoice		Next-to-the-Last Purchases Invoice	
	Quantity Purchased	Unit Cost	Quantity Purchased	Unit Cost
Alpha 10	30	$ 60	40	$ 59
Beta 30	25	170	15	180
Charlie 4	20	132	15	131
Echo 9	150	25	100	27
Frank 6	6	550	15	540
George 15	90	16	100	15
Killo 6	8	400	4	398
Quebec 12	500	6	500	7
Romeo 7	75	25	80	26
Sierra 3	5	250	4	260
Washburn 2	100	15	115	14
X-Ray 4	10	750	8	740

Instructions

Record the appropriate unit costs on the inventory sheet, and complete the pricing of the inventory. When there are two different unit costs applicable to an item:

1. Draw a line through the quantity, and insert the quantity and unit cost of the last purchase.
2. On the following line, insert the quantity and unit cost of the next-to-the-last purchase.
3. Total the cost and market columns and insert the lower of the two totals in the Lower of C or M column. The first item on the inventory sheet has been completed as an example.

Appendix
PR 7-5A

Retail method; gross profit method

✔ 1. $351,500

Selected data on merchandise inventory, purchases, and sales for Clairemont Co. and Malibu Co. are as follows:

	Cost	Retail
Clairemont Co.		
Merchandise inventory, July 1	$ 300,000	$ 400,000
Transactions during July:		
Purchases (net)	3,400,000	4,600,000
Sales		4,715,000
Sales returns and allowances		190,000
Malibu Co.		
Merchandise inventory, February 1	$ 225,000	
Transactions during February and March:		
Purchases (net)	3,200,000	
Sales	5,200,000	
Sales returns and allowances	95,000	
Estimated gross profit rate	38%	

Instructions

1. Determine the estimated cost of the merchandise inventory of Clairemont Co. on July 31 by the retail method, presenting details of the computations.
2. a. Estimate the cost of the merchandise inventory of Malibu Co. on March 31 by the gross profit method, presenting details of the computations.
   b. Assume that Malibu Co. took a physical inventory on March 31 and discovered that $243,250 of merchandise was on hand. What was the estimated loss of inventory due to theft or damage during February and March?

Problems Series B

PR 7-1B
FIFO perpetual inventory

The beginning inventory at Thoreau Office Supplies and data on purchases and sales for a three-month period are as follows:

objs. 2, 3

✔ 3. $13,270

Date	Transaction	Number of Units	Per Unit	Total
Jan. 1	Inventory	75	$20	$1,500
10	Purchase	200	21	4,200
28	Sale	100	40	4,000
30	Sale	110	40	4,400
Feb. 5	Sale	20	44	880
10	Purchase	120	22	2,640
16	Sale	90	42	3,780
28	Sale	50	45	2,250
Mar. 5	Purchase	175	24	4,200
14	Sale	120	50	6,000
25	Purchase	150	25	3,750
30	Sale	100	50	5,000

Instructions

1. Record the inventory, purchases, and cost of merchandise sold data in a perpetual inventory record similar to the one illustrated in Exhibit 3, using the first-in, first-out method.
2. Determine the total sales and the total cost of merchandise sold for the period. Journalize the entries in the sales and cost of merchandise sold accounts. Assume that all sales were on account.
3. Determine the gross profit from sales for the period.
4. Determine the ending inventory cost.

PR 7-2B
LIFO perpetual inventory

objs. 2, 3

✔ 2. Gross profit, $13,090

The beginning inventory at Thoreau Office Supplies and data on purchases and sales for a three-month period are shown in Problem 7-1B.

Instructions

1. Record the inventory, purchases, and cost of merchandise sold data in a perpetual inventory record similar to the one illustrated in Exhibit 4, using the last-in, first-out method.
2. Determine the total sales, the total cost of merchandise sold, and the gross profit from sales for the period.
3. Determine the ending inventory cost.

PR 7-3B
Periodic inventory by three methods

objs. 2, 4

✔ 1. $7,581

Bulldog Appliances uses the periodic inventory system. Details regarding the inventory of appliances at August 1, 2009, purchases invoices during the year, and the inventory count at July 31, 2010, are summarized as follows:

Model	Inventory, August 1	Purchases Invoices 1st	Purchases Invoices 2nd	Purchases Invoices 3rd	Inventory Count, July 31
ALN3	16 at $ 88	8 at $ 79	6 at $ 85	12 at $ 92	16
UGA1	1 at 75	1 at 65	5 at 68	3 at 70	4
SL89	7 at 242	6 at 250	5 at 260	10 at 259	9
F69	6 at 80	5 at 82	8 at 89	8 at 90	6
H60W	2 at 108	2 at 110	3 at 128	3 at 130	5
J600T	5 at 160	4 at 170	4 at 175	7 at 180	8
ZZH0	—	7 at 75	7 at 100	7 at 101	9

Instructions

1. Determine the cost of the inventory on July 31, 2010, by the first-in, first-out method. Present data in columnar form, using the following headings:

Model	Quantity	Unit Cost	Total Cost

If the inventory of a particular model comprises one entire purchase plus a portion of another purchase acquired at a different unit cost, use a separate line for each purchase.

2. Determine the cost of the inventory on July 31, 2010, by the last-in, first-out method, following the procedures indicated in (1).
3. Determine the cost of the inventory on July 31, 2010, by the average cost method, using the columnar headings indicated in (1).
4. ➤ Discuss which method (FIFO or LIFO) would be preferred for income tax purposes in periods of (a) rising prices and (b) declining prices.

PR 7-4B

Lower-of-cost-or-market inventory

obj. 6

✔ Total LCM, $44,146

If the working papers correlating with this textbook are not used, omit Problem 7-4B.

Data on the physical inventory of Zircon Company as of December 31, 2010, are presented in the working papers. The quantity of each commodity on hand has been determined and recorded on the inventory sheet. Unit market prices have also been determined as of December 31 and recorded on the sheet. The inventory is to be determined at cost and also at the lower of cost or market, using the first-in, first-out method. Quantity and cost data from the last purchases invoice of the year and the next-to-the-last purchases invoice are summarized as follows:

Description	Last Purchases Invoice		Next-to-the-Last Purchases Invoice	
	Quantity Purchased	Unit Cost	Quantity Purchased	Unit Cost
Alpha 10	30	$ 60	30	$ 59
Beta 30	35	175	20	180
Charlie 4	20	130	25	129
Echo 9	150	26	100	27
Frank 6	10	565	10	560
George 15	100	15	100	14
Killo 6	10	385	5	384
Quebec 12	400	7	500	6
Romeo 7	80	22	50	21
Sierra 3	5	250	4	260
Washburn 2	90	24	80	22
X-Ray 4	10	750	9	745

Instructions

Record the appropriate unit costs on the inventory sheet, and complete the pricing of the inventory. When there are two different unit costs applicable to an item, proceed as follows:

1. Draw a line through the quantity, and insert the quantity and unit cost of the last purchase.
2. On the following line, insert the quantity and unit cost of the next-to-the-last purchase.
3. Total the cost and market columns and insert the lower of the two totals in the Lower of C or M column. The first item on the inventory sheet has been completed as an example.

Appendix
PR 7-5B

Retail method; gross profit method

✔ 1. $340,000

Selected data on merchandise inventory, purchases, and sales for Gainesville Co. and Tallahassee Co. are as follows:

	Cost	Retail
Gainesville Co.		
Merchandise inventory, April 1	$ 200,000	$ 300,000
Transactions during April:		
Purchases (net)	2,520,000	3,700,000
Sales		3,550,000
Sales returns and allowances		50,000
Tallahassee Co.		
Merchandise inventory, October 1	$ 300,000	
Transactions during October through December:		
Purchases (net)	1,800,000	
Sales	2,796,000	
Sales returns and allowances	96,000	
Estimated gross profit rate	36%	

Instructions
1. Determine the estimated cost of the merchandise inventory of Gainesville Co. on April 30 by the retail method, presenting details of the computations.
2. a. Estimate the cost of the merchandise inventory of Tallahassee Co. on December 31 by the gross profit method, presenting details of the computations.
   b. Assume that Tallahassee Co. took a physical inventory on December 31 and discovered that $358,500 of merchandise was on hand. What was the estimated loss of inventory due to theft or damage during October through December?

Special Activities

You can access the special activities online at **www.cengage.com/accounting/reeve**.

Excel Success Special Activities

SA 7-1
Lower of cost or market

All-Tech, Inc., has five inventory items with the following quantities, unit costs, and unit market values:

	A	B	C	D
1			Unit	Unit
2		Inventory	Cost	Market
3	Item	Quantity	Price	Price
4	A	250	$ 4.50	$ 4.20
5	B	340	9.20	8.90
6	C	90	12.90	13.50
7	D	125	18.90	21.80
8	E	440	11.30	11.40
9	Total			
10				

a. Open the Excel file *SA7-1*.
b. Complete the spreadsheet by determining the lower of cost or market valuation for inventory.
c. When you have completed the inventory table, perform a "save as," replacing the entire file name with the following:

   SA7-1_[your first nameinitial]_[your last name]

SA 7-2
Lower of cost or market

Net Way Industries, Inc., has the following inventory items and quantities:

Item	Inventory Quantity
DJ-12	15
KB-10	32
MM-1	65
PD-16	50
QR-5	120

The unit cost and market value information for the inventory items is as follows:

	DJ-12	KB-10	MM-1	PD-16	QR-5
Unit cost price	$145	$225	$90	$235	$32
Unit market price	150	208	94	244	30

a. Open the Excel file *SA7-2*.
b. Prepare a spreadsheet to determine the lower of cost or market valuation for inventory, as illustrated in Exhibit 8 and the associated Excel Success example.
c. When you have completed the inventory table, perform a "save as," replacing the entire file name with the following:

   SA7-2_[your first name initial]_[your last name]

Answers to Self-Examination Questions

1. **A** The FIFO method (answer A) is based on the assumption that costs are charged against revenue in the order in which they were incurred. The LIFO method (answer B) charges the most recent costs incurred against revenue, and the average cost method (answer C) charges a weighted average of unit costs of items sold against revenue. The perpetual inventory system (answer D) is a system and not a method of costing.

2. **A** The LIFO method of costing is based on the assumption that costs should be charged against revenue in the reverse order in which costs were incurred. Thus, the oldest costs are assigned to inventory. Thirty of the 35 units would be assigned a unit cost of $20 (since 10 of the beginning inventory units were sold on the first sale), and the remaining 5 units would be assigned a cost of $23, for a total of $715 (answer A).

3. **D** The FIFO method of costing is based on the assumption that costs should be charged against revenue in the order in which they were incurred (first-in, first-out). Thus, the most recent costs are assigned to inventory. The 35 units would be assigned a unit cost of $23 (answer D).

4. **B** When the price level is steadily rising, the earlier unit costs are lower than recent unit costs. Under the FIFO method (answer B), these earlier costs are matched against revenue to yield the highest possible net income. The periodic inventory system (answer D) is a system and not a method of costing.

5. **D** The understatement of inventory by $7,500 at the end of the year will cause the cost of merchandise sold for the year to be overstated by $7,500, the gross profit for the year to be understated by $7,500, the merchandise inventory to be understated by $7,500, and the net income for the year to be understated by $7,500 (answer D).

CHAPTER 8

Sarbanes-Oxley, Internal Control, and Cash

© Kemie Guaida/iStockphoto Inc.

e B A Y   I N C.

Controls are a part of your everyday life. At one extreme, laws are used to limit your behavior. For example, the speed limit is a control on your driving, designed for traffic safety. In addition, you are also affected by many nonlegal controls. For example, you can keep credit card receipts in order to compare your transactions to the monthly credit card statement. Comparing receipts to the monthly statement is a control designed to catch mistakes made by the credit card company. Likewise, recording checks in your checkbook is a control that you can use at the end of the month to verify the accuracy of your bank statement. In addition, banks give you a personal identification number (PIN) as a control against unauthorized access to your cash if you lose your automated teller machine (ATM) card. Dairies use freshness dating on their milk containers as a control to prevent the purchase or sale of soured milk. As you can see, you use and encounter controls every day.

Just as there are many examples of controls throughout society, businesses must also implement controls to help guide the behavior of their managers, employees, and customers. For example, eBay Inc. maintains an Internet-based marketplace for the sale of goods and services. Using eBay's online platform, buyers and sellers can browse, buy, and sell a wide variety of items including antiques and used cars. However, in order to maintain the integrity and trust of its buyers and sellers, eBay must have controls to ensure that buyers pay for their items and sellers don't misrepresent their items or fail to deliver sales. One such control eBay uses is a feedback forum that estabilishes buyer and seller reputations. A prospective buyer or seller can view the member's reputation and feedback comments before completing a transaction. Dishonest or unfair trading can lead to a negative reputation and even suspension or cancellation of the member's ability to trade on eBay.

In this chapter, we will discuss controls that can be included in accounting systems to provide reasonable assurance that the financial statements are reliable. We also discuss controls over cash that you can use to determine whether your bank has made any errors in your account. We begin this chapter by discussing the Sarbanes-Oxley Act of 2002 and its impact on controls and financial reporting.

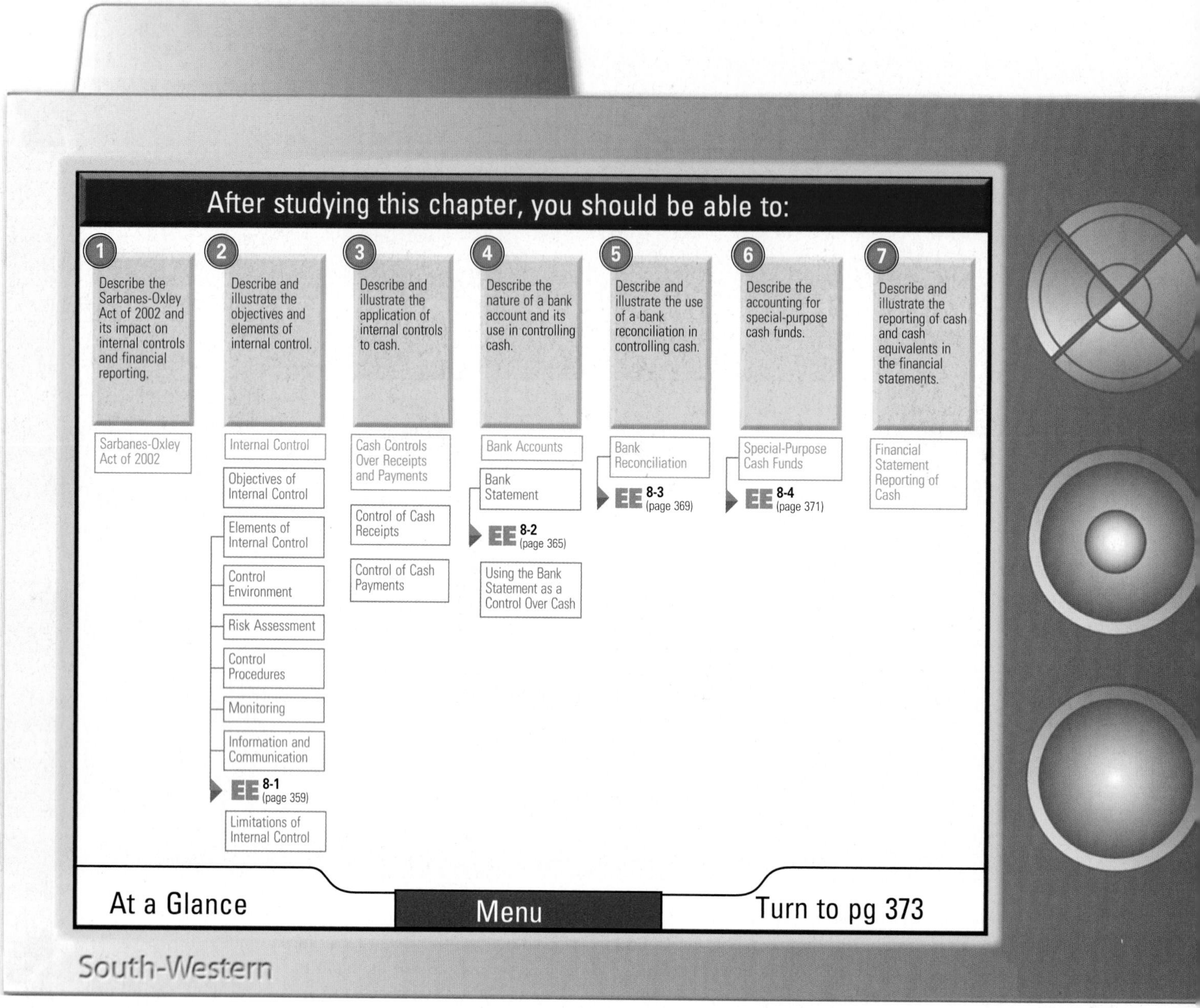

After studying this chapter, you should be able to:

1 Describe the Sarbanes-Oxley Act of 2002 and its impact on internal controls and financial reporting.

Sarbanes-Oxley Act of 2002

2 Describe and illustrate the objectives and elements of internal control.

Internal Control

Objectives of Internal Control

Elements of Internal Control

Control Environment

Risk Assessment

Control Procedures

Monitoring

Information and Communication

▶ **EE** 8-1 (page 359)

Limitations of Internal Control

3 Describe and illustrate the application of internal controls to cash.

Cash Controls Over Receipts and Payments

Control of Cash Receipts

Control of Cash Payments

4 Describe the nature of a bank account and its use in controlling cash.

Bank Accounts

Bank Statement

▶ **EE** 8-2 (page 365)

Using the Bank Statement as a Control Over Cash

5 Describe and illustrate the use of a bank reconciliation in controlling cash.

Bank Reconciliation

▶ **EE** 8-3 (page 369)

6 Describe the accounting for special-purpose cash funds.

Special-Purpose Cash Funds

▶ **EE** 8-4 (page 371)

7 Describe and illustrate the reporting of cash and cash equivalents in the financial statements.

Financial Statement Reporting of Cash

| At a Glance | Menu | Turn to pg 373 |

South-Western

---

1 Describe the Sarbanes-Oxley Act of 2002 and its impact on internal controls and financial reporting.

The ex-CEO of WorldCom, Bernard Ebbers, was sentenced to 25 years in prison.

Sarbanes-Oxley Act of 2002

During the financial scandals of the early 2000s, stockholders, creditors, and other investors lost billions of dollars.[1] As a result, the United States Congress passed the **Sarbanes-Oxley Act of 2002**. This act, often referred to as *Sarbanes-Oxley*, is one of the most important laws affecting U.S. companies in recent history. The purpose of Sarbanes-Oxley is to restore public confidence and trust in the financial reporting of companies.

Sarbanes-Oxley applies only to companies whose stock is traded on public exchanges, referred to as *publicly held companies*. However, Sarbanes-Oxley highlighted the importance of assessing the financial controls and reporting of all companies. As a result, companies of all sizes have been influenced by Sarbanes-Oxley.

Sarbanes-Oxley emphasizes the importance of effective internal control.[2] **Internal control** is defined as the procedures and processes used by a company to:

1 Exhibit 2 in Chapter 1 briefly summarizes these scandals.

2 Sarbanes-Oxley also has important implications for corporate governance and the regulation of the public accounting profession. This chapter, however, focuses on the internal control implications of Sarbanes-Oxley.

1. Safeguard its assets.
2. Process information accurately.
3. Ensure compliance with laws and regulations.

Sarbanes-Oxley requires companies to maintain effective internal controls over the recording of transactions and the preparing of financial statements. Such controls are important because they deter fraud and prevent misleading financial statements as shown below.

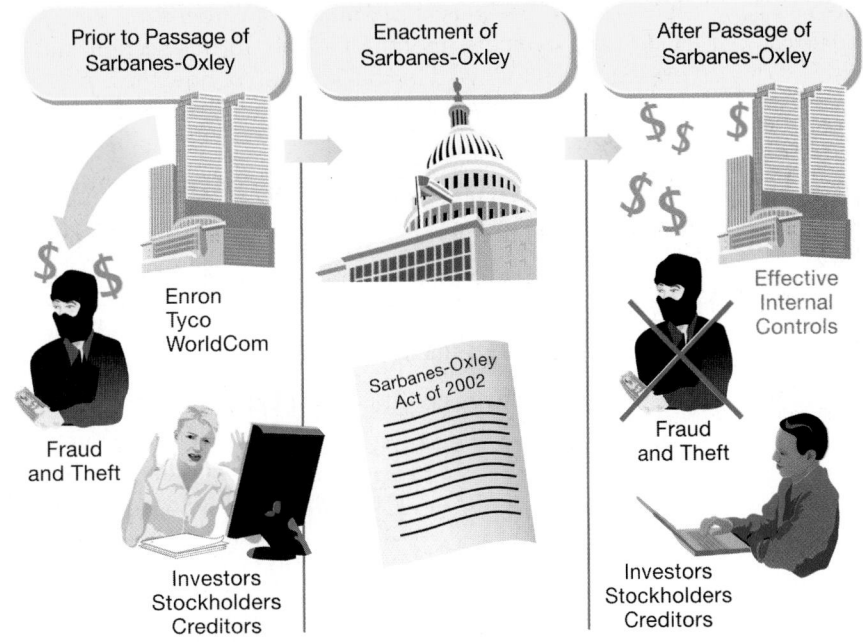

It is estimated that companies spend millions each year to comply with the requirements of Sarbanes-Oxley.

Sarbanes-Oxley also requires companies and their independent accountants to report on the effectiveness of the company's internal controls.[3] These reports are required to be filed with the company's annual 10-K report with the Securities and Exchange Commission. Companies are also encouraged to include these reports in their annual reports to stockholders. An example of such a report by the management of Nike is shown in Exhibit 1.

Exhibit 1

Sarbanes-Oxley Report of Nike

Management's Annual Report on Internal Control Over Financial Reporting

Management is responsible for establishing and maintaining adequate internal control over financial reporting . . . , Under the supervision and with the participation of our Chief Executive Officer and Chief Financial Officer, our management conducted an evaluation of the effectiveness of our internal control over financial reporting based upon the framework in *Internal Control—Integrated Framework* issued by the Committee of Sponsoring Organizations of the Treadway Commission. Based on that evaluation, our management concluded that our internal control over financial reporting is effective as of May 31, 2007. . . .

PricewaterhouseCoopers LLP, an independent registered public accounting firm, has audited . . . management's assessment of the effectiveness of our internal control over financial reporting . . . and . . . the effectiveness of our internal control over financial reporting . . . as stated in their report . . . .

MARK G. PARKER
Chief Executive Officer and President

DONALD W. BLAIR
Chief Financial Officer

3 These reporting requirements are required under Section 404 of the act. As a result, these requirements and reports are often referred to as 404 requirements and 404 reports.

Exhibit 1 indicates that Nike based its evaluation of internal controls on *Internal Control—Integrated Framework*, which was issued by the Committee of Sponsoring Organizations (COSO) of the Treadway Commission. This framework is the standard by which companies design, analyze, and evaluate internal controls. For this reason, this framework is used as the basis for discussing internal controls.

2 Describe and illustrate the objectives and elements of internal control.

Internal Control

Internal Control—Integrated Framework is the standard by which companies design, analyze, and evaluate internal control.[4] In this section, the objectives of internal control are described followed by a discussion of how these objectives can be achieved through the *Integrated Framework's* five elements of internal control.

Objectives of Internal Control

The objectives of internal control are to provide reasonable assurance that:

1. Assets are safeguarded and used for business purposes.
2. Business information is accurate.
3. Employees and managers comply with laws and regulations.

These objectives are illustrated below.

Information on *Internal Control—Integrated Framework* can be found on COSO's Web site at http://www.coso.org/.

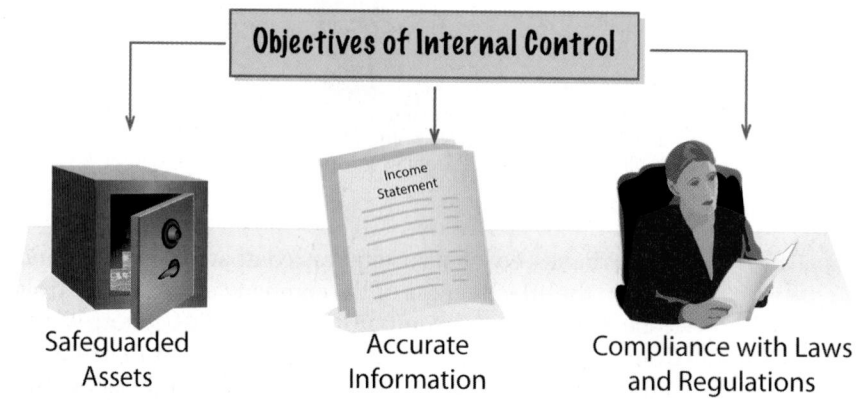

| | Safeguarded Assets | Accurate Information | Compliance with Laws and Regulations |

The Association of Certified Fraud Examiners has estimated that businesses will lose over $650 billion, or around 5% of revenue, to employee fraud.

Source: *2006 Report to the Nation: Occupational Fraud and Abuse*, Association of Certified Fraud Examiners.

Internal control can safeguard assets by preventing theft, fraud, misuse, or misplacement. A serious concern of internal control is preventing employee fraud. **Employee fraud** is the intentional act of deceiving an employer for personal gain. Such fraud may range from minor overstating of a travel expense report to stealing millions of dollars. Employees stealing from a business often adjust the accounting records in order to hide their fraud. Thus, employee fraud usually affects the accuracy of business information.

Accurate information is necessary to successfully operate a business. Businesses must also comply with laws, regulations, and financial reporting standards. Examples of such standards include environmental regulations, safety regulations, and generally accepted accounting principles (GAAP).

Elements of Internal Control

The three internal control objectives can be achieved by applying the five **elements of internal control** set forth by the *Integrated Framework*.[5] These elements are as follows:

1. Control environment
2. Risk assessment

---

4 *Internal Control—Integrated Framework* by the Committee of Sponsoring Organizations of the Treadway Commission, 1992.
5 Ibid., 12–14.

3. Control procedures
4. Monitoring
5. Information and communication

The elements of internal control are illustrated in Exhibit 2.

Exhibit 2

**Elements of
Internal Control**

In Exhibit 2, the elements of internal control form an umbrella over the business to protect it from control threats. The control environment is the size of the umbrella. Risk assessment, control procedures, and monitoring are the fabric of the umbrella, which keep it from leaking. Information and communication connect the umbrella to management.

Control Environment

The **control environment** is the overall attitude of management and employees about the importance of controls. Three factors influencing a company's control environment are as follows:

1. Management's philosophy and operating style
2. The company's organizational structure
3. The company's personnel policies

Control Environment

Management's philosophy and operating style relates to whether management emphasizes the importance of internal controls. An emphasis on controls and adherence to control policies creates an effective control environment. In contrast, overemphasizing operating goals and tolerating deviations from control policies creates an ineffective control environment.

The business's organizational structure is the framework for planning and controlling operations. For example, a retail store chain might organize each of its stores as separate business units. Each store manager has full authority over pricing and other operating activities. In such a structure, each store manager has the responsibility for establishing an effective control environment.

The business's personnel policies involve the hiring, training, evaluation, compensation, and promotion of employees. In addition, job descriptions, employee codes of ethics, and conflict-of-interest policies are part of the personnel policies. Such policies can enhance the internal control environment if they provide reasonable assurance that only competent, honest employees are hired and retained.

Risk Assessment

All businesses face risks such as changes in customer requirements, competitive threats, regulatory changes, and changes in economic factors. Management should identify such risks, analyze their significance, assess their likelihood of occurring, and take any necessary actions to minimize them.

A bank officer who was not required to take vacations stole almost $5 million by printing fake certificates of deposit. The theft was discovered when the bank began requiring all employees to take vacations.

Control Procedures

Control procedures provide reasonable assurance that business goals will be achieved, including the prevention of fraud. Control procedures, which constitute one of the most important elements of internal control, include the following as shown in Exhibit 3.

1. Competent personnel, rotating duties, and mandatory vacations
2. Separating responsibilities for related operations
3. Separating operations, custody of assets, and accounting
4. Proofs and security measures

Exhibit 3

Internal Control Procedures

Control Threats

Control Procedures
Competent personnel, rotating duties, and mandatory vacations
Separating responsibilities for related operations
Separating operations, custody of assets, and accounting
Proofs and security measures

Management

Business

Competent Personnel, Rotating Duties, and Mandatory Vacations

A successful company needs competent employees who are able to perform the duties that they are assigned. Procedures should be established for properly training and supervising employees. It is also advisable to rotate duties of accounting personnel and mandate vacations for all employees. In this way, employees are encouraged to adhere to procedures. Cases of employee fraud are often discovered when a long-term employee, who never took vacations, missed work because of an illness or another unavoidable reason.

An accounting clerk for the Grant County (Washington) Alcoholism Program was in charge of collecting money, making deposits, and keeping the records. While the clerk was away on maternity leave, the replacement clerk discovered a fraud: $17,800 in fees had been collected but had been hidden for personal gain.

Separating Responsibilities for Related Operations

The responsibility for related operations should be divided among two or more persons. This decreases the possibility of errors and fraud. For example, if the same person orders supplies, verifies the receipt of the supplies, and pays the supplier, the following abuses may occur:

1. Orders may be placed on the basis of friendship with a supplier, rather than on price, quality, and other objective factors.
2. The quantity and quality of supplies received may not be verified; thus, the company may pay for supplies not received or that are of poor quality.
3. Supplies may be stolen by the employee.
4. The validity and accuracy of invoices may not be verified; hence, the company may pay false or inaccurate invoices.

For the preceding reasons, the responsibilities for purchasing, receiving, and paying for supplies should be divided among three persons or departments.

An accounts payable clerk created false invoices and submitted them for payment. The clerk obtained the checks, cashed them, and stole thousands of dollars.

Separating Operations, Custody of Assets, and Accounting

The responsibilities for operations, custody of assets, and accounting should be separated. In this way, the accounting records serve as an independent check on the operating managers and the employees who have custody of assets.

To illustrate, employees who handle cash receipts should not record cash receipts in the accounting records. To do so would allow employees to borrow or steal cash and hide the theft in the accounting records. Likewise, operating managers should not also record the results of operations. To do so would allow the managers to distort the accounting reports to show favorable results, which might allow them to receive larger bonuses.

Proofs and Security Measures

Proofs and security measures are used to safeguard assets and ensure reliable accounting data. Proofs involve procedures such as authorization, approval, and reconciliation. For example, an employee planning to travel on company business may be required to complete a "travel request" form for a manager's authorization and approval.

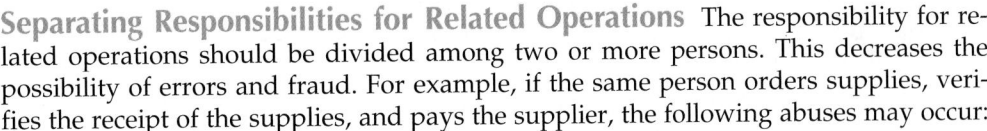

Integrity, Objectivity, and Ethics in Business

TIPS ON PREVENTING EMPLOYEE FRAUD IN SMALL COMPANIES

- Do not have the same employee write company checks and keep the books. Look for payments to vendors you don't know or payments to vendors whose names appear to be misspelled.
- If your business has a computer system, restrict access to accounting files as much as possible. Also, keep a backup copy of your accounting files and store it at an off-site location.
- Be wary of anybody working in finance who declines to take vacations. The employee may be afraid that a replacement will uncover fraud.

- Require and monitor supporting documentation (such as vendor invoices) before signing checks.
- Track the number of credit card bills you sign monthly.
- Limit and monitor access to important documents and supplies, such as blank checks and signature stamps.
- Check W-2 forms against your payroll annually to make sure you're not carrying any fictitious employees.
- Rely on yourself, not on your accountant, to spot fraud.

Source: Steve Kaufman, "Embezzlement Common at Small Companies," Knight-Ridder Newspapers, reported in *Athens Daily News/Athens Banner-Herald*, March 10, 1996, p. 4D.

Documents used for authorization and approval should be prenumbered, accounted for, and safeguarded. Prenumbering of documents helps prevent transactions from being recorded more than once or not at all. In addition, accounting for and safeguarding prenumbered documents helps prevent fraudulent transactions from being recorded. For example, blank checks are prenumbered and safeguarded. Once a payment has been properly authorized and approved, the checks are filled out and issued.

Reconciliations are also an important control. Later in this chapter, the use of bank reconciliations as an aid in controlling cash is described and illustrated.

Security measures involve measures to safeguard assets. For example, cash on hand should be kept in a cash register or safe. Inventory not on display should be stored in a locked storeroom or warehouse. Accounting records such as the accounts receivable subsidiary ledger should also be safeguarded to prevent their loss. For example, electronically maintained accounting records should be safeguarded with access codes and backed up so that any lost or damaged files could be recovered if necessary.

A 24-hour convenience store could use a security guard, video cameras, and an alarm system to deter robberies.

Monitoring

Monitoring the internal control system is used to locate weaknesses and improve controls. Monitoring often includes observing employee behavior and the accounting system for indicators of control problems. Some such indicators are shown in Exhibit 4.[6]

Evaluations of controls are often performed when there are major changes in strategy, senior management, business structure, or operations. Internal auditors, who are independent of operations, usually perform such evaluations. Internal auditors are also responsible for day-to-day monitoring of controls. External auditors also evaluate and report on internal control as part of their annual financial statement audit.

Exhibit 4

Warning Signs of Internal Control Problems

Warning signs with regard to people

1. Abrupt change in lifestyle (without winning the lottery).
2. Close social relationships with suppliers.
3. Refusing to take a vacation.
4. Frequent borrowing from other employees.
5. Excessive use of alcohol or drugs.

Warning signs from the accounting system

1. Missing documents or gaps in transaction numbers (could mean documents are being used for fraudulent transactions).
2. An unusual increase in customer refunds (refunds may be phony).
3. Differences between daily cash receipts and bank deposits (could mean receipts are being pocketed before being deposited).
4. Sudden increase in slow payments (employee may be pocketing the payments).
5. Backlog in recording transactions (possibly an attempt to delay detection of fraud).

6 Edwin C. Bliss, "Employee Theft," *Boardroom Reports*, July 15, 1994, pp. 5–6.

Information and Communication

Information and communication is an essential element of internal control. Information about the control environment, risk assessment, control procedures, and monitoring is used by management for guiding operations and ensuring compliance with reporting, legal, and regulatory requirements. Management also uses external information to assess events and conditions that impact decision making and external reporting. For example, management uses pronouncements of the Financial Accounting Standards Board (FASB) to assess the impact of changes in reporting standards on the financial statements.

Example Exercise 8-1   Internal Control Elements   2

Identify each of the following as relating to (a) the control environment, (b) risk assessment, or (c) control procedures.

1. Mandatory vacations
2. Personnel policies
3. Report of outside consultants on future market changes

Follow My Example 8-1

1. (c) control procedures
2. (a) the control environment
3. (b) risk assessment

For Practice: PE 8-1A, PE 8-1B

Limitations of Internal Control

Internal control systems can provide only reasonable assurance for safeguarding assets, processing accurate information, and compliance with laws and regulations. In other words, internal controls are not a guarantee. This is due to the following factors:

1. The human element of controls
2. Cost-benefit considerations

The *human element* recognizes that controls are applied and used by humans. As a result, human errors can occur because of fatigue, carelessness, confusion, or misjudgment. For example, an employee may unintentionally shortchange a customer or miscount the amount of inventory received from a supplier. In addition, two or more employees may collude to defeat or circumvent internal controls. This latter case often involves fraud and the theft of assets. For example, the cashier and the accounts receivable clerk might collude to steal customer payments on account.

Cost-benefit considerations recognize that cost of internal controls should not exceed their benefits. For example, retail stores could eliminate shoplifting by searching all customers before they leave the store. However, such a control procedure would upset customers and result in lost sales. Instead, retailers use cameras or signs saying *We prosecute all shoplifters.*

Cash Controls over Receipts and Payments

3 Describe and illustrate the application of internal controls to cash.

Cash includes coins, currency (paper money), checks, and money orders. Money on deposit with a bank or other financial institution that is available for withdrawal is also considered cash. Normally, you can think of cash as anything that a bank would accept

The Internet has given rise to a form of cash called "cybercash," which is used for Internet transactions, such as being used in conjunction with PayPal.

for deposit in your account. For example, a check made payable to you could normally be deposited in a bank and, thus, is considered cash.

Businesses usually have several bank accounts. For example, a business might have one bank account for general cash payments and another for payroll. A separate ledger account is normally used for each bank account. For example, a bank account at City Bank could be identified in the ledger as *Cash in Bank—City Bank*. To simplify, we will assume in this chapter that a company has only *one* bank account, which is identified in the ledger as *Cash*.

Cash is the asset most likely to be stolen or used improperly in a business. For this reason, businesses must carefully control cash and cash transactions.

Control of Cash Receipts

To protect cash from theft and misuse, a business must control cash from the time it is received until it is deposited in a bank. Businesses normally receive cash from two main sources.

1. Customers purchasing products or services
2. Customers making payments on account

Fast-food restaurants, such as McDonald's, receive cash primarily from over-the-counter sales. Internet retailers, such Amazon.com, receive cash primarily through electronic funds transfers from credit card companies.

Cash Received from Cash Sales An important control to protect cash received in over-the-counter sales is a cash register. The use of a cash register to control cash is shown below.

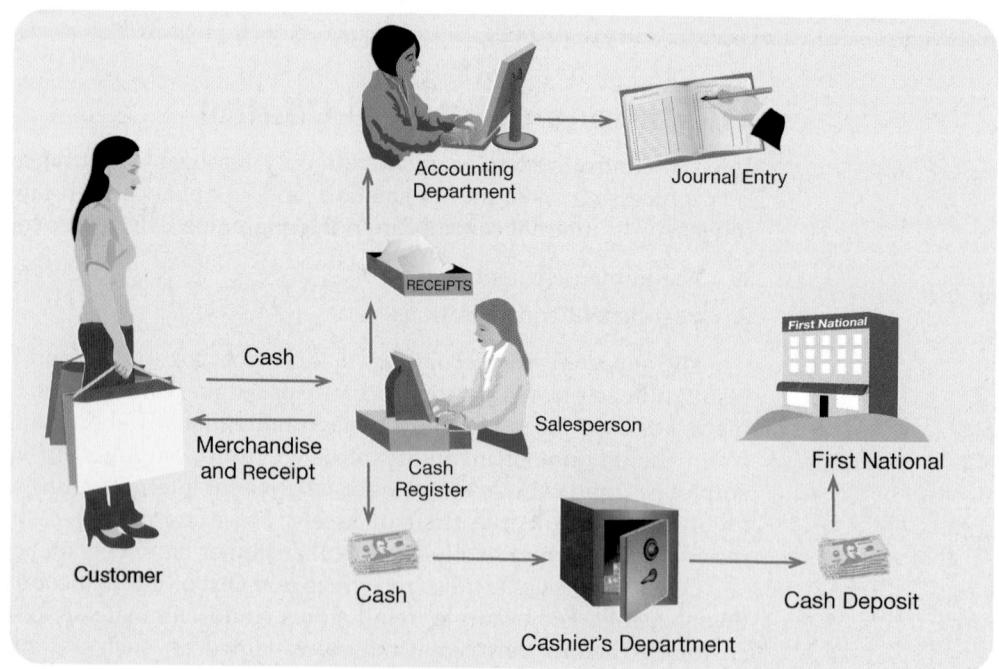

A cash register controls cash as follows:

1. At the beginning of every work shift, each cash register clerk is given a cash drawer containing a predetermined amount of cash. This amount is used for making change for customers and is sometimes called a *change fund*.
2. When a salesperson enters the amount of a sale, the cash register displays the amount to the customer. This allows the customer to verify that the clerk has charged the correct amount. The customer also receives a cash receipt.

3. At the end of the shift, the clerk and the supervisor count the cash in the clerk's cash drawer. The amount of cash in each drawer should equal the beginning amount of cash plus the cash sales for the day.

4. The supervisor takes the cash to the Cashier's Department, where it is placed in a safe.

5. The supervisor forwards the clerk's cash register receipts to the Accounting Department.

6. The cashier prepares a bank deposit ticket.

7. The cashier deposits the cash in the bank, or the cash is picked up by an armored car service, such as Wells Fargo.

8. The Accounting Department summarizes the cash receipts and records the day's cash sales.

9. When cash is deposited in the bank, the bank normally stamps a duplicate copy of the deposit ticket with the amount received. This bank receipt is returned to the Accounting Department, where it is compared to the total amount that should have been deposited. This control helps ensure that all the cash is deposited and that no cash is lost or stolen on the way to the bank. Any shortages are thus promptly detected.

Salespersons may make errors in making change for customers or in ringing up cash sales. As a result, the amount of cash on hand may differ from the amount of cash sales. Such differences are recorded in a **cash short and over account**.

To illustrate, assume the following cash register data for May 3:

Cash register total for cash sales	$35,690
Cash receipts from cash sales	35,668

The cash sales, receipts, and shortage of $22 ($35,690 − $35,668) would be recorded as follows:

May	3	Cash		35,668	
		Cash Short and Over		22	
		Sales			35,690

If there had been cash over, Cash Short and Over would have been credited for the overage. At the end of the accounting period, a debit balance in Cash Short and Over is included in Miscellaneous expense on the income statement. A credit balance is included in the Other income section. If a salesperson consistently has large cash short and over amounts, the supervisor may require the clerk to take additional training.

Cash Received in the Mail   Cash is received in the mail when customers pay their bills. This cash is usually in the form of checks and money orders. Most companies design their invoices so that customers return a portion of the invoice, called a *remittance advice*, with their payment. Remittance advices may be used to control cash received in the mail as follows:

1. An employee opens the incoming mail and compares the amount of cash received with the amount shown on the remittance advice. If a customer does not return a remittance advice, the employee prepares one. The remittance advice serves as a record of the cash initially received. It also helps ensure that the posting to the customer's account is for the amount of cash received.

2. The employee opening the mail stamps checks and money orders "For Deposit Only" in the bank account of the business.

3. The remittance advices and their summary totals are delivered to the Accounting Department.

4. All cash and money orders are delivered to the Cashier's Department.

5. The cashier prepares a bank deposit ticket.

6. The cashier deposits the cash in the bank, or the cash is picked up by an armored car service, such as Wells Fargo.

7. An accounting clerk records the cash received and posts the amounts to the customer accounts.

8. When cash is deposited in the bank, the bank normally stamps a duplicate copy of the deposit ticket with the amount received. This bank receipt is returned to the Accounting Department, where it is compared to the total amount that should have been deposited. This control helps ensure that all cash is deposited and that no cash is lost or stolen on the way to the bank. Any shortages are thus promptly detected.

Separating the duties of the Cashier's Department, which handles cash, and the Accounting Department, which records cash, is a control. If Accounting Department employees both handle and record cash, an employee could steal cash and change the accounting records to hide the theft.

Cash Received by EFT Cash may also be received from customers through **electronic funds transfer (EFT)**. For example, customers may authorize automatic electronic transfers from their checking accounts to pay monthly bills for such items as cell phone, Internet, and electric services. In such cases, the company sends the customer's bank a signed form from the customer authorizing the monthly electronic transfers. Each month, the company notifies the customer's bank of the amount of the transfer and the date the transfer should take place. On the due date, the company records the electronic transfer as a receipt of cash to its bank account and posts the amount paid to the customer's account.

Companies encourage customers to use EFT for the following reasons:

1. EFTs cost less than receiving cash payments through the mail.

2. EFTs enhance internal controls over cash since the cash is received directly by the bank without any employees handling cash.

3. EFTs reduce late payments from customers and speed up the processing of cash receipts.

Howard Schultz & Associates (HS&A) specializes in reviewing cash payments for its clients. HS&A searches for errors, such as duplicate payments, failures to take discounts, and inaccurate computations. Amounts recovered for clients range from thousands to millions of dollars.

Control of Cash Payments

The control of cash payments should provide reasonable assurance that:

1. Payments are made for only authorized transactions.

2. Cash is used effectively and efficiently. For example, controls should ensure that all available purchase discounts are taken.

In a small business, an owner/manager may authorize payments based on personal knowledge. In a large business, however, purchasing goods, inspecting the goods received, and verifying the invoices are usually performed by different employees. These duties must be coordinated to ensure that proper payments are made to creditors. One system used for this purpose is the voucher system.

Voucher System A **voucher system** is a set of procedures for authorizing and recording liabilities and cash payments. A **voucher** is any document that serves as proof of authority to pay cash or issue an electronic funds transfer. An invoice that has been approved for payment could be considered a voucher. In many businesses, however, a voucher is a special form used to record data about a liability and the details of its payment.

In a manual system, a voucher is normally prepared after all necessary supporting documents have been received. For the purchase of goods, a voucher is supported by the supplier's invoice, a purchase order, and a receiving report. After a voucher is prepared, it is submitted for approval. Once approved, the voucher is recorded in the accounts and filed by due date. Upon payment, the voucher is recorded in the same manner as the payment of an account payable.

Many businesses and individuals are now using Internet banking services, which provide for the payment of funds electronically.

In a computerized system, data from the supporting documents (such as purchase orders, receiving reports, and suppliers' invoices) are entered directly into computer files. At the due date, the checks are automatically generated and mailed to creditors. At that time, the voucher is electronically transferred to a paid voucher file.

Cash Paid by EFT   Cash can also be paid by electronic funds transfer systems. For example, many companies pay their employees by EFT. Under such a system, employees authorize the deposit of their payroll checks directly into their checking accounts. Each pay period, the company transfers the employees' net pay to their checking accounts through the use of EFT. Many companies also use EFT systems to pay their suppliers and other vendors.

4   Describe the nature of a bank account and its use in controlling cash.

Bank Accounts

A major reason that companies use bank accounts is for internal control. Some of the control advantages of using bank accounts are as follows:

1. Bank accounts reduce the amount of cash on hand.
2. Bank accounts provide an independent recording of cash transactions. Reconciling the balance of the cash account in the company's records with the cash balance according to the bank is an important control.
3. Use of bank accounts facilitates the transfer of funds using EFT systems.

Bank Statement

Banks usually maintain a record of all checking account transactions. A summary of all transactions, called a **bank statement**, is mailed to the company (depositor) or made available online, usually each month. The bank statement shows the beginning balance, additions, deductions, and the ending balance. A typical bank statement is shown in Exhibit 5.

Checks or copies of the checks listed in the order that they were paid by the bank may accompany the bank statement. If paid checks are returned, they are stamped "Paid," together with the date of payment. Many banks no longer return checks or check copies. Instead, the check payment information is available online.

The company's checking account balance *in the bank records* is a liability. Thus, in the bank's records, the company's account has a credit balance. Since the bank statement is prepared from the bank's point of view, a credit memo entry on the bank statement indicates an increase (a credit) to the company's account. Likewise, a debit memo entry on the bank statement indicates a decrease (a debit) in the company's account. This relationship is shown below.

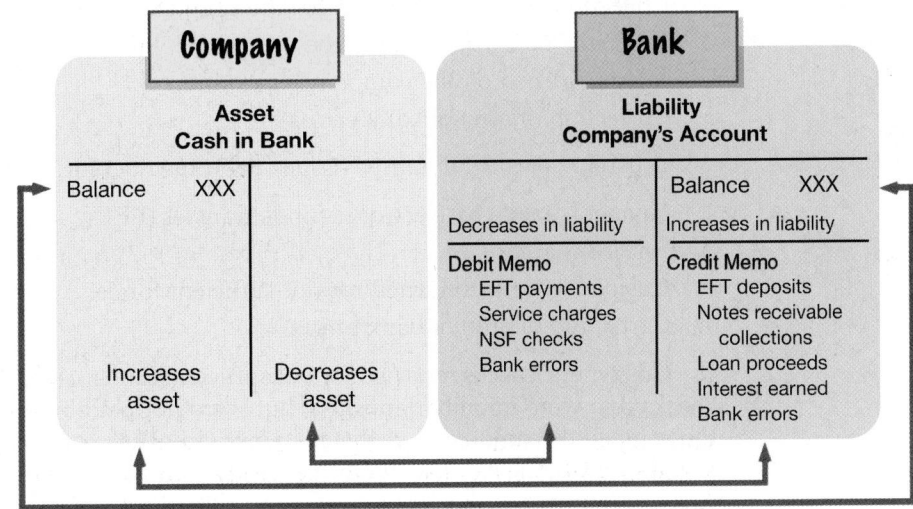

Exhibit 5

Bank Statement

```
                                    MEMBER FDIC                              PAGE    1

        VALLEY NATIONAL BANK                     ACCOUNT NUMBER   1627042
        OF LOS ANGELES
                                                 FROM  6/30/09   TO  7/31/09
        LOS ANGELES, CA 90020-4253   (310)555-5151
                                                 BALANCE              4,218.60

                                              22 DEPOSITS           13,749.75

                                              52 WITHDRAWALS        14,698.57
            POWER NETWORKING
            1000 Belkin Street                 3 OTHER DEBITS
            Los Angeles, CA 90014-1000           AND CREDITS          90.00CR

                                                 NEW BALANCE         3,359.78
```

* -- CHECKS AND OTHER DEBITS						DEPOSITS -*-DATE * BALANCE *
No. 850 819.40	No. 852 122.54			585.75	07/01	3,862.41
No. 854 369.50	No. 853 20.15			421.53	07/02	3,894.29
No. 851 600.00	No. 856 190.70	No. 857 52.50		781.30	07/03	3,832.39
No. 855 25.93	No. 858 160.00			662.50	07/05	4,308.96
No. 860 921.20	NSF 300.00			503.18	07/07	3,590.94

No. 880 32.26	No. 877 535.09			ACH 932.00	07/29	4,136.66
No. 881 21.10	No. 879 732.26	No. 882 126.20		705.21	07/30	3,962.31
	SC 18.00			MS 408.00	07/30	4,352.31
No. 874 26.12	ACH 1,615.13			648.72	07/31	3,359.78

```
        EC — ERROR CORRECTION          ACH — AUTOMATED CLEARING HOUSE
        MS — MISCELLANEOUS
        NSF — NOT SUFFICIENT FUNDS     SC — SERVICE CHARGE

 * * *                     * * *                          * * *

        THE RECONCILEMENT OF THIS STATEMENT WITH YOUR RECORDS IS ESSENTIAL.
        ANY ERROR OR EXCEPTION SHOULD BE REPORTED IMMEDIATELY.
```

A bank makes credit entries (issues credit memos) for the following:

1. Deposits made by electronic funds transfer (EFT)
2. Collections of note receivable for the company
3. Proceeds for a loan made to the company by the bank
4. Interest earned on the company's account
5. Correction (if any) of bank errors

A bank makes debit entries (issues debit memos) for the following:

1. Payments made by electronic funds transfer (EFT)
2. Service charges
3. Customer checks returned for not sufficient funds
4. Correction (if any) of bank errors

Customers' checks returned for not sufficient funds, called *NSF checks*, are customer checks that were initially deposited, but were not paid by the customer's bank. Since the company's bank credited the customer's check to the company's account when it was deposited, the bank debits the company's account (issues a debit memo) when the check is returned without payment.

The reason for a credit or debit memo entry is indicated on the bank statement. Exhibit 5 identifies the following types of credit and debit memo entries:

EC: Error correction to correct bank error
NSF: Not sufficient funds check
SC: Service charge
ACH: Automated clearing house entry for electronic funds transfer
MS: Miscellaneous item such as collection of a note receivable on behalf of the company or receipt of a loan by the company from the bank

The above list includes the notation "ACH" for electronic funds transfers. ACH is a network for clearing electronic funds transfers among individuals, companies, and banks.[7] Because electronic funds transfers may be either deposits or payments, ACH entries may indicate either a debit or credit entry to the company's account. Likewise, entries to correct bank errors and miscellaneous items may indicate a debit or credit entry to the company's account.

Example Exercise 8-2   Items on Company's Bank Statement   •••••••• 4

The following items may appear on a bank statement:

1. NSF check
2. EFT deposit
3. Service charge
4. Bank correction of an error from recording a $400 check as $40

Using the format shown below, indicate whether the item would appear as a debit or credit memo on the bank statement and whether the item would increase or decrease the balance of the company's account.

Item No.	Appears on the Bank Statement as a Debit or Credit Memo	Increases or Decreases the Balance of the Company's Bank Account

Follow My Example 8-2

Item No.	Appears on the Bank Statement as a Debit or Credit Memo	Increases or Decreases the Balance of the Company's Bank Account
1	debit memo	decreases
2	credit memo	increases
3	debit memo	decreases
4	debit memo	decreases

For Practice: PE 8-2A, PE 8-2B

Using the Bank Statement as a Control Over Cash

The bank statement is a primary control that a company uses over cash. A company uses the bank's statement as a control by comparing the company's recording of cash transactions to those recorded by the bank.

The cash balance shown by a bank statement is usually different from the company's cash balance, as shown in Exhibit 6.

---

7 For further information on ACH, go to **http://www.nacha.org/**. Click on "About Us," and then click on "What is ACH?"

Exhibit 6

Power Networking's Records and Bank Statement

Bank Statement		
Beginning balance		$ 4,218.60
Additions:		
Deposits	$13,749.75	
Miscellaneous	408.00	14,157.75
Deductions:		
Checks	$14,698.57	
NSF check	300.00	
Service charge	18.00	(15,016.57)
Ending balance		$ 3,359.78

Power Networking Records	
Beginning balance	$ 4,227.60
Deposits	14,565.95
Checks	(16,243.56)
Ending balance	$ 2,549.99

Power Networking should determine the reason for the difference in these two amounts.

Differences between the company and bank balance may arise because of a delay by either the company or bank in recording transactions. For example, there is normally a time lag of one or more days between the date a check is written and the date that it is paid by the bank. Likewise, there is normally a time lag between when the company mails a deposit to the bank (or uses the night depository) and when the bank receives and records the deposit.

Differences may also arise because the bank has debited or credited the company's account for transactions that the company will not know about until the bank statement is received. Finally, differences may arise from errors made by either the company or the bank. For example, the company may incorrectly post to Cash a check written for $4,500 as $450. Likewise, a bank may incorrectly record the amount of a check.

Integrity, Objectivity, and Ethics in Business

CHECK FRAUD

Check fraud involves counterfeiting, altering, or otherwise manipulating the information on checks in order to fraudulently cash a check. According to the National Check Fraud Center, check fraud and counterfeiting are among the fastest growing problems affecting the financial system, generating over $10 billion in losses annually. Criminals perpetrate the fraud by taking blank checks from your checkbook, finding a canceled check in the garbage, or removing a check you have mailed to pay bills. Consumers can prevent check fraud by carefully storing blank checks, placing outgoing mail in postal mailboxes, and shredding canceled checks.

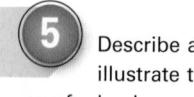

Bank Reconciliation

5 Describe and illustrate the use of a bank reconciliation in controlling cash.

A **bank reconciliation** is an analysis of the items and amounts that result in the cash balance reported in the bank statement to differ from the balance of the cash account in the ledger. The adjusted cash balance determined in the bank reconciliation is reported on the balance sheet.

A bank reconciliation is usually divided into two sections as follows:

1. The *bank section* begins with the cash balance according to the bank statement and ends with the *adjusted balance*.

2. The *company section* begins with the cash balance according to the company's records and ends with the *adjusted balance*.

The *adjusted balance* from bank and company sections must be equal. The format of the bank reconciliation is shown below.

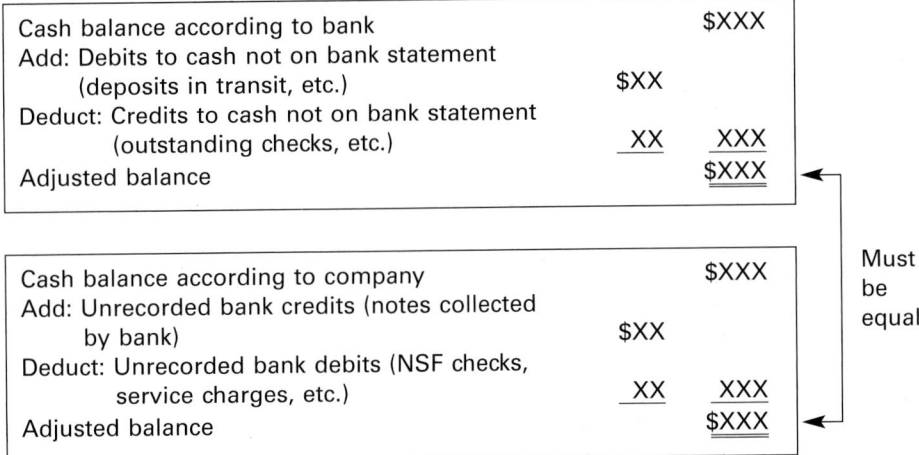

A bank reconciliation is prepared using the following steps:

Bank Section of Reconciliation

Step 1.   Enter the *Cash balance according to bank* from the ending cash balance according to the bank statement.

Step 2.   *Add deposits not recorded by the bank.*
Identify deposits not recorded by the bank by comparing each deposit listed on the bank statement with unrecorded deposits appearing in the preceding period's reconciliation and with the current period's deposits.

Examples: Deposits in transit at the end of the period.

Step 3.   *Deduct outstanding checks that have not been paid by the bank.*
Identify outstanding checks by comparing paid checks with outstanding checks appearing on the preceding period's reconciliation and with recorded checks.

Examples: Outstanding checks at the end of the period.

Step 4.   Determine the *Adjusted balance* by adding Step 2 and deducting Step 3.

Company Section of Reconciliation

Step 5.   Enter the *Cash balance according to company* from the ending cash balance in the ledger.

Step 6.   *Add credit memos that have not been recorded.*
Identify the bank credit memos that have not been recorded by comparing the bank statement credit memos to entries in the journal.

Examples: A note receivable and interest that the bank has collected for the company.

Step 7.   *Deduct debit memos that have not been recorded.*
Identify the bank debit memos that have not been recorded by comparing the bank statement debit memos to entries in the journal.

Examples: Customers' not sufficient funds (NSF) checks; bank service charges.

Step 8.   Determine the *Adjusted balance* by adding Step 6 and deducting Step 7.

Step 9.   Verify that the Adjusted balances determined in Steps 4 and 8 are equal.

The adjusted balances in the bank and company sections of the reconciliation must be equal. If the balances are not equal, an item has been overlooked and must be found.

Sometimes, the adjusted balances are not equal because either the company or the bank has made an error. In such cases, the error is often discovered by comparing the amount of each item (deposit and check) on the bank statement with that in the company's records.

Any bank or company errors discovered should be added or deducted from the bank or company section of the reconciliation depending on the nature of the error. For example, assume that the bank incorrectly recorded a company check for $50 as $500. This bank error of $450 ($500 − $50) would be added to the bank balance in the bank section of the reconciliation. In addition, the bank would be notified of the error so that it could be corrected. On the other hand, assume that the company recorded a deposit of $1,200 as $2,100. This company error of $900 ($2,100 − $1,200) would be deducted from the cash balance in the company section of the bank reconciliation. The company would later correct the error using a journal entry.

To illustrate, we will use the bank statement for Power Networking in Exhibit 5. This bank statement shows a balance of $3,359.78 as of July 31. The cash balance in Power Networking's ledger on the same date is $2,549.99. Using the preceding steps, the following reconciling items were identified:

Step 2. Deposit of July 31, not recorded on bank statement: $816.20
Step 3. Outstanding checks:

Check No. 812	$1,061.00
Check No. 878	435.39
Check No. 883	48.60
Total	$1,544.99

Step 6. Note receivable of $400 plus interest of $8 collected by bank not recorded in the journal as indicated by a credit memo of $408.
Step 7. Check from customer (Thomas Ivey) for $300 returned by bank because of insufficient funds (NSF) as indicated by a debit memo of $300.00.
Bank service charges of $18, not recorded in the journal as indicated by a debit memo of $18.00.

In addition, an error of $9 was discovered. This error occurred when Check No. 879 for $732.26 to Taylor Co., on account, was recorded in the company's journal as $723.26.

The bank reconciliation, based on the Exhibit 5 bank statement and the preceding reconciling items, is shown in Exhibit 7.

The company's records do not need to be updated for any items in the *bank section* of the reconciliation. This section begins with the cash balance according to the bank statement. However, the bank should be notified of any errors that need to be corrected.

The company's records do need to be updated for any items in the *company section* of the bank reconciliation. The company's records are updated using journal entries. For example, journal entries should be made for any unrecorded bank memos and any company errors.

The journal entries for Power Networking, based on the bank reconciliation shown in Exhibit 7, are as follows:

July	31	Cash	408	
		Notes Receivable		400
		Interest Revenue		8
	31	Accounts Receivable—Thomas Ivey	300	
		Miscellaneous Expense	18	
		Accounts Payable—Taylor Co.	9	
		Cash		327

Exhibit 7

Bank Reconciliation for Power Networking

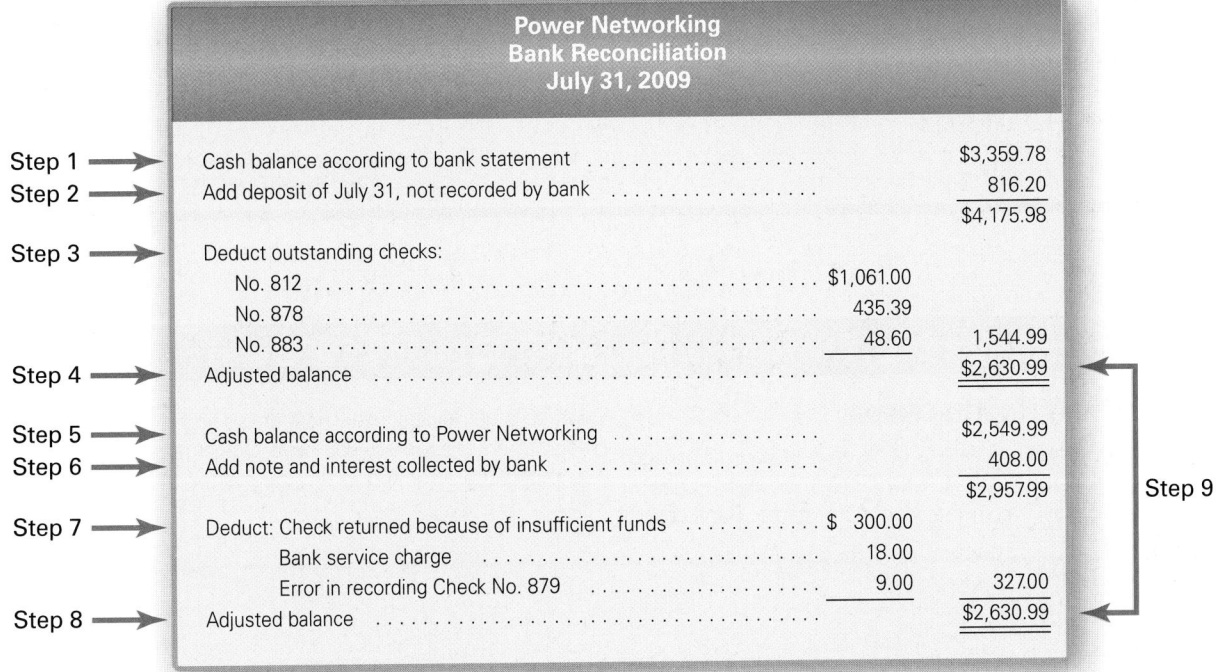

Step 1 → Cash balance according to bank statement	$3,359.78
Step 2 → Add deposit of July 31, not recorded by bank	816.20
	$4,175.98
Step 3 → Deduct outstanding checks:	
No. 812 .... $1,061.00	
No. 878 .... 435.39	
No. 883 .... 48.60	1,544.99
Step 4 → Adjusted balance	$2,630.99
Step 5 → Cash balance according to Power Networking	$2,549.99
Step 6 → Add note and interest collected by bank	408.00
	$2,957.99
Step 7 → Deduct: Check returned because of insufficient funds .... $ 300.00	
Bank service charge 18.00	
Error in recording Check No. 879 .... 9.00	327.00
Step 8 → Adjusted balance	$2,630.99

Power Networking
Bank Reconciliation
July 31, 2009

Step 9

After the preceding journal entries are recorded and posted, the cash account will have a debit balance of $2,630.99. This cash balance agrees with the adjusted balance shown on the bank reconciliation. This is the amount of cash on July 31 and is the amount that is reported on Power Networking's July 31 balance sheet.

Businesses may reconcile their bank accounts in a slightly different format from that shown in Exhibit 7. Regardless, the objective is to control cash by reconciling the company's records with the bank statement. In doing so, any errors or misuse of cash may be detected.

To enhance internal control, the bank reconciliation should be prepared by an employee who does not take part in or record cash transactions. Otherwise, mistakes may occur, and it is more likely that cash will be stolen or misapplied. For example, an employee who handles cash and also reconciles the bank statement could steal a cash deposit, omit the deposit from the accounts, and omit it from the reconciliation.

Bank reconciliations are also important computerized systems where deposits and checks are stored in electronic files and records. Some systems use computer software to determine the difference between the bank statement and company cash balances. The software then adjusts for deposits in transit and outstanding checks. Any remaining differences are reported for further analysis.

Example Exercise 8-3   Bank Reconciliation   ●●●●●●●● ❯ 5

The following data were gathered to use in reconciling the bank account of Photo Op:

Balance per bank.....................................	$14,500
Balance per company records	13,875
Bank service charges..................................	75
Deposit in transit....................................	3,750
NSF check..	800
Outstanding checks	5,250

a. What is the adjusted balance on the bank reconciliation?

b. Journalize any necessary entries for Photo Op based on the bank reconciliation.

(continued)

Follow My Example 8-3

a. $13,000, as shown below.

Bank section of reconciliation: $14,500 + $3,750 − $5,250 = $13,000
Company section of reconciliation: $13,875 − $75 − $800 = $13,000

b. Accounts Receivable 800
   Miscellaneous Expense 75
   Cash. 875

For Practice: PE 8-3A, PE 8-3B

Integrity, Objectivity, and Ethics in Business

BANK ERROR IN YOUR FAVOR

You may sometime have a bank error in your favor, such as a misposted deposit. Such errors are not a case of "found money," as in the Monopoly® game. Bank control systems quickly discover most errors and make automatic adjustments. Even so, you have a legal responsibility to report the error and return the money to the bank.

6 Describe the accounting for special-purpose cash funds.

Special-Purpose Cash Funds

A company often has to pay small amounts for such items as postage, office supplies, or minor repairs. Although small, such payments may occur often enough to total a significant amount. Thus, it is desirable to control such payments. However, writing a check for each small payment is not practical. Instead, a special cash fund, called a **petty cash fund**, is used.

A petty cash fund is established by estimating the amount of payments needed from the fund during a period, such as a week or a month. A check is then written and cashed for this amount. The money obtained from cashing the check is then given to an employee, called the *petty cash custodian*. The petty cash custodian disburses monies from the fund as needed. For control purposes, the company may place restrictions on the maximum amount and the types of payments that can be made from the fund. Each time money is paid from petty cash, the custodian records the details on a petty cash receipts form.

The petty cash fund is normally replenished at periodic intervals, when it is depleted, or reaches a minimum amount. When a petty cash fund is replenished, the accounts debited are determined by summarizing the petty cash receipts. A check is then written for this amount, payable to Petty Cash.

To illustrate, assume that a petty cash fund of $500 is established on August 1. The entry to record this transaction is as follows:

Aug.	1	Petty Cash		500	
		Cash			500

The only time Petty Cash is debited is when the fund is initially established, as shown in the preceding entry, or when the fund is being increased. The only time Petty Cash is credited is when the fund is being decreased.

At the end of August, the petty cash receipts indicate expenditures for the following items:

Office supplies	$380
Postage (debit Office Supplies)	22
Store supplies	35
Miscellaneous administrative expense	30
Total	$467

The entry to replenish the petty cash fund on August 31 is as follows:

Aug.	31	Office Supplies	402	
		Store Supplies	35	
		Miscellaneous Administrative Expense	30	
		Cash		467

Petty Cash is not debited when the fund is replenished. Instead, the accounts affected by the petty cash disbursements are debited, as shown in the preceding entry. Replenishing the petty cash fund restores the fund to its original amount of $500.

Companies often use other cash funds for special needs, such as payroll or travel expenses. Such funds are called **special-purpose funds**. For example, each salesperson might be given $1,000 for travel-related expenses. Periodically, each salesperson submits an expense report, and the fund is replenished. Special-purpose funds are established and controlled in a manner similar to that of the petty cash fund.

Example Exercise 8-4   Petty Cash Fund   •••••••• 6

Prepare journal entries for each of the following:

a.   Issued a check to establish a petty cash fund of $500.

b.   The amount of cash in the petty cash fund is $120. Issued a check to replenish the fund, based on the following summary of petty cash receipts: office supplies, $300 and miscellaneous administrative expense, $75. Record any missing funds in the cash short and over account.

Follow My Example 8-4

a.	Petty Cash	500	
	Cash		500
b.	Office Supplies.	300	
	Miscellaneous Administrative Expense.	75	
	Cash Short and Over	5	
	Cash		380

For Practice: PE 8-4A, PE 8-4B

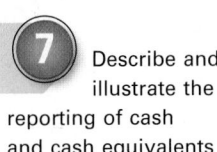

7   Describe and illustrate the reporting of cash and cash equivalents in the financial statements.

Financial Statement Reporting of Cash

Cash is normally listed as the first asset in the Current Assets section of the balance sheet. Most companies present only a single cash amount on the balance sheet by combining all their bank and cash fund accounts.

A company may temporarily have excess cash. In such cases, the company normally invests in highly liquid investments in order to earn interest. These investments are called **cash equivalents**.[8] Examples of cash equivalents include U.S. Treasury bills, notes issued by major corporations (referred to as commercial paper), and money market funds. In such cases, companies usually report *Cash and cash equivalents* as one amount on the balance sheet.

The balance sheet presentation for cash for Mornin' Joe is shown below.

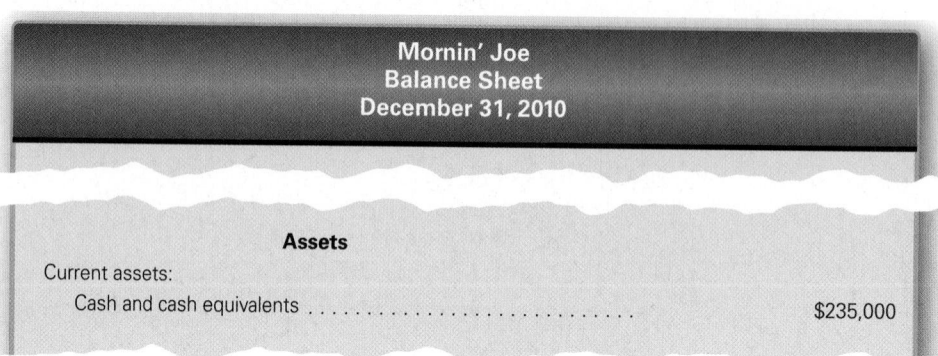

Mornin' Joe
Balance Sheet
December 31, 2010

Assets

Current assets:

Cash and cash equivalents $235,000

Banks may require that companies maintain minimum cash balances in their bank accounts. Such a balance is called a **compensating balance**. This is often required by the bank as part of a loan agreement or line of credit. A *line of credit* is a preapproved amount the bank is willing to lend to a customer upon request. Compensating balance requirements are normally disclosed in notes to the financial statements.

Financial Analysis and Interpretation

For companies that are either starting up or in financial distress, cash is critical for their survival. In their first few years of operations, startup companies often report losses and negative net cash flows. In these cases, the ratio of cash to monthly cash expenses (negative cash flow for operating activities) is useful for assessing how long a company can continue to operate without additional financing or without generating positive cash flows from operations. Likewise, this ratio can be used to assess how long a business may continue to operate when experiencing financial distress. In computing cash to monthly cash expenses, the amount of cash on hand can be taken from the balance sheet, while the monthly cash expenses can be estimated from the operating activities section of the statement of cash flows.

The ratio of cash to monthly cash expenses is computed by first determining the monthly cash expenses. The monthly cash expenses are determined as follows:

$$\text{Monthly Cash Expenses} = \frac{\text{Negative Cash Flows from Operations}}{12}$$

The ratio of cash to monthly cash expenses can then be computed as follows:

$$\text{Ratio of Cash to Monthly Cash Expenses} = \frac{\text{Cash and Cash Equivalents as of Year-End}}{\text{Monthly Cash Expenses}}$$

To illustrate these ratios, we use Northwest Airlines Corporation, a major carrier of passengers and cargo with service to approximately 900 cities in 160 countries. For the year ending December 31, 2005, Northwest Airlines reported the following data (in millions):

Negative cash flows from operations	$ (436)
Cash and cash equivalents as of December 31, 2005	1,284

Based on the preceding data, the monthly cash expenses, sometimes referred to as cash burn, were $36.3 million per month ($436/12). Thus, as of December 31, 2005, the cash to monthly cash expenses ratio was 35.4 ($1,284/$36.3). That is, as of December 31, 2005, Northwest would run out of cash in less than three years unless it changes its operations, sells investments, or raises additional financing. Northwest Airlines was able to reorganize and for the year ending December 31, 2006, generated $1,245 million in positive cash flows from operations.

---

8 To be classified a cash equivalent, according to FASB Statement No. 95, the investment is expected to be converted to cash within 90 days.

Business Connection

MICROSOFT CORPORATION

Microsoft Corporation develops, manufactures, licenses, and supports software products for computing devices. Microsoft software products include computer operating systems, such as Windows, and application software, such as Microsoft Word™ and Excel.™ Microsoft is actively involved in the video game market through its Xbox and is also involved in online products and services.

Microsoft is known for its strong cash position. Microsoft's June 30, 2007, balance sheet reported over $23 billion of cash and short-term investments, as shown below.

Balance Sheet
June 30, 2007
(In millions)
Assets

Current assets:	
Cash and equivalents	$ 6,111
Short-term investments	17,300
Total cash and short-term investments	$23,411

The cash and cash equivalents of $6,111 million are further described in the notes to the financial statements, as shown below.

Cash and equivalents:	
Cash	$3,040
Mutual funds	132
Commercial paper	179
U.S. government and agency securities	1
Corporate notes and bonds	2,425
Municipal securities	334
Total cash and equivalents	$6,111

At a Glance   8 ● ● ●

1 Describe the Sarbanes-Oxley Act of 2002 and its impact on internal controls and financial reporting.

Key Points	Key Learning Outcomes	Example Exercises	Practice Exercises
The purpose of the Sarbanes-Oxley Act of 2002 is to restore public confidence and trust in the financial statements of companies. Sarbanes-Oxley requires companies to maintain strong and effective internal controls and to report on the effectiveness of the internal controls.	• Describe why Congress passed Sarbanes-Oxley. • Describe the purpose of Sarbanes-Oxley. • Define *internal control*.		

2 Describe and illustrate the objectives and elements of internal control.

Key Points	Key Learning Outcomes	Example Exercises	Practice Exercises
The objectives of internal control are to provide reasonable assurance that (1) assets are safeguarded and used for business purposes, (2) business information is accurate, and (3) laws and regulations are complied with. The elements of internal control are the control environment, risk assessment, control procedures, monitoring, and information and communication.	• List the objectives of internal control. • List the elements of internal control. • Describe each element of internal control and factors influencing each element.	8-1	8-1A, 8-1B

3 Describe and illustrate the application of internal controls to cash.

Key Points	Key Learning Outcomes	Example Exercises	Practice Exercises
A cash register is one of the most important controls to protect cash received in over-the-counter sales. A remittance advice is a control for cash received through the mail. Separating the duties of handling cash and recording cash is also a control. A voucher system is a control system for cash payments that uses a set of procedures for authorizing and recording liabilities and cash payments. Many companies use electronic funds transfers to enhance their control over cash receipts and cash payments.	• Describe and give examples of controls for cash received from cash sales, cash received in the mail, and cash received by EFT. • Describe and give examples of controls for cash payments made using a voucher system and cash payments made by EFT.		

4 Describe the nature of a bank account and its use in controlling cash.

Key Points	Key Learning Outcomes	Example Exercises	Practice Exercises
Bank accounts help control cash by reducing the amount of cash on hand and facilitating the transfer of cash between businesses and locations. In addition, the bank statement allows a business to reconcile the cash transactions recorded in the accounting records to those recorded by the bank.	• Describe how the use of bank accounts helps control cash. • Describe a bank statement and provide examples of items that appear on a bank statement as debit and credit memos.	8-2	8-2A, 8-2B

5 Describe and illustrate the use of a bank reconciliation in controlling cash.

Key Points	Key Learning Outcomes	Example Exercises	Practice Exercises
The bank reconciliation begins with the cash balance according to the bank statement. This balance is adjusted for the company's changes in cash that do not appear on the bank statement and for any bank errors. The second section begins with the cash balance according to the company's records. This balance is adjusted for the bank's changes in cash that do not appear on the company's records and for any company errors. The adjusted balances for the two sections must be equal. The items in the company section must be journalized on the company's records.	• Describe a bank reconciliation. • Prepare a bank reconciliation. • Journalize any necessary entries on the company's records based on the bank reconciliation.	 8-3 8-3	 8-3A, 8-3B 8-3A, 8-3B

6 Describe the accounting for special-purpose cash funds.

Key Points	Key Learning Outcomes	Example Exercises	Practice Exercises
Special-purpose cash funds, such as a petty cash fund or travel funds, are used by businesses to meet specific needs. Each fund is established by cashing a check for the amount of cash needed. At periodic intervals, the fund is replenished and the disbursements recorded.	• Describe the use of special-purpose cash funds.		
	• Journalize the entry to establish a petty cash fund.	8-4	8-4A, 8-4B
	• Journalize the entry to replenish a petty cash fund.	8-4	8-4A, 8-4B

7 Describe and illustrate the reporting of cash and cash equivalents in the financial statements.

Key Points	Key Learning Outcomes	Example Exercises	Practice Exercises
Cash is listed as the first asset in the Current Assets section of the balance sheet. Companies that have invested excess cash in highly liquid investments usually report *Cash and cash equivalents* on the balance sheet.	• Describe the reporting of cash and cash equivalents in the financial statements.		
	• Illustrate the reporting of cash and cash equivalents in the financial statements.		

Key Terms

bank reconciliation (366)
bank statement (363)
cash (359)
cash equivalents (372)
cash short and over
   account (361)

compensating balance (372)
control environment (355)
electronic funds transfer
  (EFT) (362)
elements of internal control (354)
employee fraud (354)

internal control (352)
petty cash fund (370)
Sarbanes-Oxley Act of 2002 (352)
special-purpose funds (371)
voucher (362)
voucher system (362)

Illustrative Problem

The bank statement for Urethane Company for June 30, 2009, indicates a balance of $9,143.11. All cash receipts are deposited each evening in a night depository, after banking hours. The accounting records indicate the following summary data for cash receipts and payments for June:

Cash balance as of June 1	$ 3,943.50
Total cash receipts for June	28,971.60
Total amount of checks issued in June	28,388.85

Comparing the bank statement and the accompanying canceled checks and memos with the records reveals the following reconciling items:

a. The bank had collected for Urethane Company $1,030 on a note left for collection. The face amount of the note was $1,000.
b. A deposit of $1,852.21, representing receipts of June 30, had been made too late to appear on the bank statement.
c. Checks outstanding totaled $5,265.27.
d. A check drawn for $139 had been incorrectly charged by the bank as $157.
e. A check for $30 returned with the statement had been recorded in the company's records as $240. The check was for the payment of an obligation to Avery Equipment Company for the purchase of office supplies on account.
f. Bank service charges for June amounted to $18.20.

Instructions

1. Prepare a bank reconciliation for June.
2. Journalize the entries that should be made by Urethane Company.

Solution

1.

Urethane Company
Bank Reconciliation
June 30, 2009

Cash balance according to bank statement		$ 9,143.11
Add: Deposit of June 30 not recorded by bank	$1,852.21	
Bank error in charging check as $157		
instead of $139	18.00	1,870.21
		$11,013.32
Deduct: Outstanding checks		5,265.27
Adjusted balance		$ 5,748.05
Cash balance according to company's records		$ 4,526.25*
Add: Proceeds of note collected by bank,		
including $30 interest	$1,030.00	
Error in recording check	210.00	1,240.00
		$ 5,766.25
Deduct: Bank service charges		18.20
Adjusted balance		$ 5,748.05

*$3,943.50 + $28,971.60 − $28,388.85

2.

June	30	Cash	1,240.00	
		Notes Receivable		1,000.00
		Interest Revenue		30.00
		Accounts Payable—Avery Equipment Company		210.00
	30	Miscellaneous Administrative Expense	18.20	
		Cash		18.20

Self-Examination Questions (Answers at End of Chapter)

1. Which of the following is *not* an element of internal control?
   A. Control environment
   B. Monitoring
   C. Compliance with laws and regulations
   D. Control procedures

2. The bank erroneously charged Tropical Services' account for $450.50 for a check that was correctly written and recorded by Tropical Services as $540.50. To reconcile the bank account of Tropical Services at the end of the month, you would:
   A. add $90 to the cash balance according to the bank statement.
   B. add $90 to the cash balance according to Tropical Services' records.
   C. deduct $90 from the cash balance according to the bank statement.
   D. deduct $90 from the cash balance according to Tropical Services' records.

3. In preparing a bank reconciliation, the amount of checks outstanding would be:
   A. added to the cash balance according to the bank statement.
   B. deducted from the cash balance according to the bank statement.
   C. added to the cash balance according to the company's records.
   D. deducted from the cash balance according to the company's records.

4. Journal entries based on the bank reconciliation are required for:
   A. additions to the cash balance according to the company's records.
   B. deductions from the cash balance according to the company's records.
   C. both A and B.
   D. neither A nor B.

5. A petty cash fund is:
   A. used to pay relatively small amounts.
   B. established by estimating the amount of cash needed for disbursements of relatively small amounts during a specified period.
   C. reimbursed when the amount of money in the fund is reduced to a predetermined minimum amount.
   D. all of the above.

Eye Openers

1. (a) Why did Congress pass the Sarbanes-Oxley Act of 2002? (b) What is the purpose of the Sarbanes-Oxley Act of 2002?
2. Define *internal control.*
3. (a) Name and describe the five elements of internal control. (b) Is any one element of internal control more important than another?
4. How does a policy of rotating clerical employees from job to job aid in strengthening the control procedures within the control environment? Explain.
5. Why should the responsibility for a sequence of related operations be divided among different persons? Explain.
6. Why should the employee who handles cash receipts not have the responsibility for maintaining the accounts receivable records? Explain.
7. In an attempt to improve operating efficiency, one employee was made responsible for all purchasing, receiving, and storing of supplies. Is this organizational change wise from an internal control standpoint? Explain.
8. The ticket seller at a movie theater doubles as a ticket taker for a few minutes each day while the ticket taker is on a break. Which control procedure of a business's system of internal control is violated in this situation?
9. Why should the responsibility for maintaining the accounting records be separated from the responsibility for operations? Explain.
10. Assume that Yvonne Dauphin, accounts payable clerk for Bedell Inc., stole $73,250 by paying fictitious invoices for goods that were never received. The clerk set up accounts in the names of the fictitious companies and cashed the checks at a local bank. Describe a control procedure that would have prevented or detected the fraud.
11. Before a voucher for the purchase of merchandise is approved for payment, supporting documents should be compared to verify the accuracy of the liability. Give an example of supporting documents for the purchase of merchandise.

12. The accounting clerk pays all obligations by prenumbered checks. What are the strengths and weaknesses in the internal control over cash payments in this situation?
13. The balance of Cash is likely to differ from the bank statement balance. What two factors are likely to be responsible for the difference?
14. What is the purpose of preparing a bank reconciliation?
15. Do items reported as credits on the bank statement represent (a) additions made by the bank to the company's balance or (b) deductions made by the bank from the company's balance? Explain.
16. Oak Grove Inc. has a petty cash fund of $1,500. (a) Since the petty cash fund is only $1,500, should Oak Grove Inc. implement controls over petty cash? (b) What controls, if any, could be used for the petty cash fund?
17. (a) How are cash equivalents reported in the financial statements? (b) What are some examples of cash equivalents?

Practice Exercises

PE 8-1A
Internal control elements

obj. 2

EE 8-1   p. 359

Identify each of the following as relating to (a) the control environment, (b) control procedures, or (c) monitoring.
1. Hiring of external auditors to review the adequacy of controls
2. Personnel policies
3. Safeguarding inventory in a locked warehouse

PE 8-1B
Internal control elements

obj. 2

EE 8-1   p. 359

Identify each of the following as relating to (a) the control environment, (b) control procedures, or (c) information and communication.
1. Management's philosophy and operating style
2. Report of internal auditors
3. Separating related operations

PE 8-2A
Items on company's bank statement

obj. 4

EE 8-2   p. 365

The following items may appear on a bank statement:
1. Bank correction of an error from posting another customer's check to the company's account
2. EFT deposit
3. Loan proceeds
4. NSF check

Using the format shown below, indicate whether each item would appear as a debit or credit memo on the bank statement and whether the item would increase or decrease the balance of the company's account.

Item No.	Appears on the Bank Statement as a Debit or Credit Memo	Increases or Decreases the Balance of the Company's Bank Account

PE 8-2B
Items on company's bank statement

obj. 4

EE 8-2   p. 365

The following items may appear on a bank statement:
1. Bank correction of an error from recording a $3,200 deposit as $2,300
2. EFT payment
3. Note collected for company
4. Service charge

Using the format shown below, indicate whether each item would appear as a debit or credit memo on the bank statement and whether the item would increase or decrease the balance of the company's account.

Item No.	Appears on the Bank Statement as a Debit or Credit Memo	Increases or Decreases the Balance of the Company's Bank Account

PE 8-3A
Bank reconciliation

obj. 5

EE 8-3   p. 369

The following data were gathered to use in reconciling the bank account of East Meets West Company:

Balance per bank	$19,340
Balance per company records	6,480
Bank service charges	50
Deposit in transit	2,500
Note collected by bank with $250 interest	8,250
Outstanding checks	7,160

a. What is the adjusted balance on the bank reconciliation?
b. Journalize any necessary entries for East Meets West Company based on the bank reconciliation.

PE 8-3B
Bank reconciliation

obj. 5

EE 8-3   p. 369

The following data were gathered to use in reconciling the bank account of Crescent Moon Company:

Balance per bank	$11,200
Balance per company records	9,295
Bank service charges	25
Deposit in transit	1,650
NSF check	600
Outstanding checks	4,180

a. What is the adjusted balance on the bank reconciliation?
b. Journalize any necessary entries for Crescent Moon Company based on the bank reconciliation.

PE 8-4A
Petty cash fund

obj. 6

EE 8-4   p. 371

Prepare journal entries for each of the following:
a. Issued a check to establish a petty cash fund of $300.
b. The amount of cash in the petty cash fund is $95. Issued a check to replenish the fund, based on the following summary of petty cash receipts: store supplies, $120 and miscellaneous selling expense, $75. Record any missing funds in the cash short and over account.

PE 8-4B
Petty cash fund

obj. 6

EE 8-4   p. 371

Prepare journal entries for each of the following:
a. Issued a check to establish a petty cash fund of $500.
b. The amount of cash in the petty cash fund is $140. Issued a check to replenish the fund, based on the following summary of petty cash receipts: repair expense, $260 and miscellaneous selling expense, $84. Record any missing funds in the cash short and over account.

Exercises

EX 8-1
Sarbanes-Oxley internal control report

obj. 1

Using Wikpedia (**www.wikpedia.com**), look up the entry for Sarbanes-Oxley Act. Look over the table of contents and find the section that describes Section 404.
➤ What does Section 404 require of management's internal control report?

EX 8-2
Internal controls

objs. 2, 3

Blake Gable has recently been hired as the manager of Jittery Jim's Canyon Coffee. Jittery Jim's Canyon Coffee is a national chain of franchised coffee shops. During his first month as store manager, Blake encountered the following internal control situations:

a. Blake caught an employee putting a case of 100 single-serving tea bags in her car. Not wanting to create a scene, Blake smiled and said, "I don't think you're putting those tea bags on the right shelf. Don't they belong inside the coffee shop?" The employee returned the tea bags to the stockroom.

b. Jittery Jim's Canyon Coffee has one cash register. Prior to Blake's joining the coffee shop, each employee working on a shift would take a customer order, accept payment, and then prepare the order. Blake made one employee on each shift responsible for taking orders and accepting the customer's payment. Other employees prepare the orders.

c. Since only one employee uses the cash register, that employee is responsible for counting the cash at the end of the shift and verifying that the cash in the drawer matches the amount of cash sales recorded by the cash register. Blake expects each cashier to balance the drawer to the penny *every* time—no exceptions.

➤ State whether you agree or disagree with Blake's method of handling each situation and explain your answer.

EX 8-3
Internal controls

objs. 2, 3

Anasazi Earth Clothing is a retail store specializing in women's clothing. The store has established a liberal return policy for the holiday season in order to encourage gift purchases. Any item purchased during November and December may be returned through January 31, with a receipt, for cash or exchange. If the customer does not have a receipt, cash will still be refunded for any item under $100. If the item is more than $100, a check is mailed to the customer.

Whenever an item is returned, a store clerk completes a return slip, which the customer signs. The return slip is placed in a special box. The store manager visits the return counter approximately once every two hours to authorize the return slips. Clerks are instructed to place the returned merchandise on the proper rack on the selling floor as soon as possible.

This year, returns at Anasazi Earth Clothing have reached an all-time high. There are a large number of returns under $100 without receipts.

a. ➤ How can sales clerks employed at Anasazi Earth Clothing use the store's return policy to steal money from the cash register?

b. ➤ What internal control weaknesses do you see in the return policy that make cash thefts easier?

c. ➤ Would issuing a store credit in place of a cash refund for all merchandise returned without a receipt reduce the possibility of theft? List some advantages and disadvantages of issuing a store credit in place of a cash refund.

d. ➤ Assume that Anasazi Earth Clothing is committed to the current policy of issuing cash refunds without a receipt. What changes could be made in the store's procedures regarding customer refunds in order to improve internal control?

EX 8-4
Internal controls for bank lending

objs. 2, 3

First Kenmore Bank provides loans to businesses in the community through its Commercial Lending Department. Small loans (less than $100,000) may be approved by an individual loan officer, while larger loans (greater than $100,000) must be approved by a board of loan officers. Once a loan is approved, the funds are made available to the loan applicant under agreed-upon terms. The president of First Kenmore Bank has instituted a policy whereby he has the individual authority to approve loans up to $5,000,000. The president believes that this policy will allow flexibility to approve loans to valued clients much quicker than under the previous policy.

➤ As an internal auditor of First Kenmore Bank, how would you respond to this change in policy?

EX 8-5
Internal controls
objs. 2, 3

One of the largest losses in history from unauthorized securities trading involved a securities trader for the French bank, Societe Generale. The trader was able to circumvent internal controls and create over $7 billion in trading losses in six months. The trader apparently escaped detection by using knowledge of the bank's internal control systems learned from a previous back-office monitoring job. Much of this monitoring involved the use of software to monitor trades. In addition, traders are usually kept to tight spending limits. Apparently, these controls failed in this case.

➤ What general weaknesses in Societe Generale's internal controls contributed to the occurrence and size of the losses?

EX 8-6
Internal controls
objs. 2, 3

An employee of JHT Holdings, Inc., a trucking company, was responsible for resolving roadway accident claims under $25,000. The employee created fake accident claims and wrote settlement checks of between $5,000 and $25,000 to friends or acquaintances acting as phony "victims." One friend recruited subordinates at his place of work to cash some of the checks. Beyond this, the JHT employee also recruited lawyers, who he paid to represent both the trucking company and the fake victims in the bogus accident settlements. When the lawyers cashed the checks, they allegedly split the money with the corrupt JHT employee. This fraud went undetected for two years.

➤ Why would it take so long to discover such a fraud?

EX 8-7
Internal controls
objs. 2, 3

Bizarro Sound Co. discovered a fraud whereby one of its front office administrative employees used company funds to purchase goods, such as computers, digital cameras, compact disk players, and other electronic items for her own use. The fraud was discovered when employees noticed an increase in delivery frequency from vendors and the use of unusual vendors. After some investigation, it was discovered that the employee would alter the description or change the quantity on an invoice in order to explain the cost on the bill.

➤ What general internal control weaknesses contributed to this fraud?

EX 8-8
Financial statement fraud
objs. 2, 3

A former chairman, CFO, and controller of Donnkenny, Inc., an apparel company that makes sportswear for Pierre Cardin and Victoria Jones, pleaded guilty to financial statement fraud. These managers used false journal entries to record fictitious sales, hid inventory in public warehouses so that it could be recorded as "sold," and required sales orders to be backdated so that the sale could be moved back to an earlier period. The combined effect of these actions caused $25 million out of $40 million in quarterly sales to be phony.

a. ➤ Why might control procedures listed in this chapter be insufficient in stopping this type of fraud?
b. ➤ How could this type of fraud be stopped?

EX 8-9
Internal control of cash receipts
objs. 2, 3

The procedures used for over-the-counter receipts are as follows. At the close of each day's business, the sales clerks count the cash in their respective cash drawers, after which they determine the amount recorded by the cash register and prepare the memo cash form, noting any discrepancies. An employee from the cashier's office counts the cash, compares the total with the memo, and takes the cash to the cashier's office.

a. ➤ Indicate the weak link in internal control.
b. ➤ How can the weakness be corrected?

EX 8-10
Internal control of cash receipts
objs. 2, 3

Victor Blackmon works at the drive-through window of Buffalo Bob's Burgers. Occasionally, when a drive-through customer orders, Victor fills the order and pockets the customer's money. He does not ring up the order on the cash register.

➤ Identify the internal control weaknesses that exist at Buffalo Bob's Burgers, and discuss what can be done to prevent this theft.

EX 8-11
Internal control of
cash receipts
objs. 2, 3

The mailroom employees send all remittances and remittance advices to the cashier. The cashier deposits the cash in the bank and forwards the remittance advices and duplicate deposit slips to the Accounting Department.

a. ➤ Indicate the weak link in internal control in the handling of cash receipts.
b. ➤ How can the weakness be corrected?

EX 8-12
Entry for cash sales;
cash short
objs. 2, 3

The actual cash received from cash sales was $36,183, and the amount indicated by the cash register total was $36,197. Journalize the entry to record the cash receipts and cash sales.

EX 8-13
Entry for cash sales;
cash over
objs. 2, 3

The actual cash received from cash sales was $11,279, and the amount indicated by the cash register total was $11,256. Journalize the entry to record the cash receipts and cash sales.

EX 8-14
Internal control of
cash payments
objs. 2, 3

El Cordova Co. is a small merchandising company with a manual accounting system. An investigation revealed that in spite of a sufficient bank balance, a significant amount of available cash discounts had been lost because of failure to make timely payments. In addition, it was discovered that the invoices for several purchases had been paid twice. ➤ Outline procedures for the payment of vendors' invoices, so that the possibilities of losing available cash discounts and of paying an invoice a second time will be minimized.

EX 8-15
Internal control of
cash payments
objs. 2, 3

Digital Com Company, a communications equipment manufacturer, recently fell victim to a fraud scheme developed by one of its employees. To understand the scheme, it is necessary to review Digital Com's procedures for the purchase of services.

The purchasing agent is responsible for ordering services (such as repairs to a photocopy machine or office cleaning) after receiving a service requisition from an authorized manager. However, since no tangible goods are delivered, a receiving report is not prepared. When the Accounting Department receives an invoice billing Digital Com for a service call, the accounts payable clerk calls the manager who requested the service in order to verify that it was performed.

The fraud scheme involves Matt DuBois, the manager of plant and facilities. Matt arranged for his uncle's company, Urban Industrial Supply and Service, to be placed on Digital Com's approved vendor list. Matt did not disclose the family relationship.

On several occasions, Matt would submit a requisition for services to be provided by Urban Industrial Supply and Service. However, the service requested was really not needed, and it was never performed. Urban would bill Digital Com for the service and then split the cash payment with Matt.

➤ Explain what changes should be made to Digital Com's procedures for ordering and paying for services in order to prevent such occurrences in the future.

EX 8-16
Bank reconciliation
obj. 5

Identify each of the following reconciling items as: (a) an addition to the cash balance according to the bank statement, (b) a deduction from the cash balance according to the bank statement, (c) an addition to the cash balance according to the company's records, or (d) a deduction from the cash balance according to the company's records. (None of the transactions reported by bank debit and credit memos have been recorded by the company.)

1. Bank service charges, $15.
2. Check drawn by company for $160 but incorrectly recorded as $610.

3. Check for $500 incorrectly charged by bank as $5,000.
4. Check of a customer returned by bank to company because of insufficient funds, $3,000.
5. Deposit in transit, $15,500.
6. Outstanding checks, $9,600.
7. Note collected by bank, $10,000.

EX 8-17
Entries based on bank reconciliation

obj. 5

Which of the reconciling items listed in Exercise 8-16 require an entry in the company's accounts?

EX 8-18
Bank reconciliation

obj. 5

✔ Adjusted balance:
$13,680

The following data were accumulated for use in reconciling the bank account of Commander Co. for March:

a. Cash balance according to the company's records at March 31, $13,065.
b. Cash balance according to the bank statement at March 31, $12,750.
c. Checks outstanding, $4,170.
d. Deposit in transit, not recorded by bank, $5,100.
e. A check for $180 in payment of an account was erroneously recorded in the check register as $810.
f. Bank debit memo for service charges, $15.

Prepare a bank reconciliation, using the format shown in Exhibit 7.

EX 8-19
Entries for bank reconciliation

obj. 5

Using the data presented in Exercise 8-18, journalize the entry or entries that should be made by the company.

EX 8-20
Entries for note collected by bank

obj. 5

Accompanying a bank statement for Euthenics Company is a credit memo for $18,270, representing the principal ($18,000) and interest ($270) on a note that had been collected by the bank. The company had been notified by the bank at the time of the collection, but had made no entries. Journalize the entry that should be made by the company to bring the accounting records up to date.

EX 8-21
Bank reconciliation

obj. 5

✔ Adjusted balance:
$11,740

An accounting clerk for Grebe Co. prepared the following bank reconciliation:

Grebe Co.
Bank Reconciliation
August 31, 2010

Cash balance according to company's records		$ 4,690
Add: Outstanding checks	$3,110	
Error by Grebe Co. in recording Check		
No. 1115 as $940 instead of $490	450	
Note for $6,500 collected by bank, including interest	6,630	10,190
Deduct: Deposit in transit on August 31	$4,725	$14,880
Bank service charges	30	4,755
Cash balance according to bank statement		$10,125

a. From the data in the above bank reconciliation, prepare a new bank reconciliation for Grebe Co., using the format shown in the illustrative problem.
b. If a balance sheet were prepared for Grebe Co. on August 31, 2010, what amount should be reported for cash?

EX 8-22
Bank reconciliation

obj. 5

✔ Corrected
adjusted balance:
$11,960

Identify the errors in the following bank reconciliation:

Rakestraw Co.
Bank Reconciliation
For the Month Ended April 30, 2010

Cash balance according to bank statement.			$11,320
Add outstanding checks:			
No. 315		$450	
360		615	
364		850	
365		775	2,690
			$14,010
Deduct deposit of April 30, not recorded by bank.			3,330
Adjusted balance			$10,680
Cash balance according to company's records.			$ 7,003
Add: Proceeds of note collected by bank:			
Principal	$4,000		
Interest	120	$4,120	
Service charges		18	4,138
			$11,141
Deduct: Check returned because of insufficient funds		$ 945	
Error in recording April 20 deposit of $5,300 as $3,500 .		1,800	2,745
Adjusted balance			$ 8,396

EX 8-23
Using bank reconcili-
ation to determine
cash receipts stolen

objs. 2, 3, 5

First Impressions Co. records all cash receipts on the basis of its cash register tapes. First Impressions Co. discovered during June 2010 that one of its sales clerks had stolen an undetermined amount of cash receipts when she took the daily deposits to the bank. The following data have been gathered for June:

Cash in bank according to the general ledger	$ 7,865
Cash according to the June 30, 2010, bank statement	18,175
Outstanding checks as of June 30, 2010	5,190
Bank service charge for June	25
Note receivable, including interest collected by bank in June	8,400

No deposits were in transit on June 30.

a. Determine the amount of cash receipts stolen by the sales clerk.
b. ➡ What accounting controls would have prevented or detected this theft?

EX 8-24
Petty cash fund
entries

obj. 6

Journalize the entries to record the following:

a. Check No. 8193 is issued to establish a petty cash fund of $800.
b. The amount of cash in the petty cash fund is now $294. Check No. 8336 is issued to replenish the fund, based on the following summary of petty cash receipts: office supplies, $295; miscellaneous selling expense, $120; miscellaneous administrative expense, $75. (Since the amount of the check to replenish the fund plus the balance in the fund do not equal $800, record the discrepancy in the cash short and over account.)

EX 8-25
Variation in cash
flows

obj. 7

Mattel, Inc., designs, manufactures, and markets toy products worldwide. Mattel's toys include Barbie™ fashion dolls and accessories, Hot Wheels™, and Fisher-Price brands. For a recent year, Mattel reported the following net cash flows from operating activities (in thousands):

First quarter ending March 31	$ (326,536)
Second quarter ending June 30	(165,047)
Third quarter ending September 30	(9,738)
Fourth quarter December 31	1,243,603

➡ Explain why Mattel reports negative net cash flows from operating activities during the first three quarters yet reports positive cash flows for the fourth quarter and net positive cash flows for the year.

EX 8-26
Cash to monthly
cash expenses ratio

During 2010, Bezel Inc. has monthly cash expenses of $250,000. On December 31, 2010, the cash balance is $1,750,000.

a. Compute the ratio of cash to monthly cash expenses.
b. ━━━▶ Based on (a), what are the implications for Bezel Inc.?

EX 8-27
Cash to monthly
cash expenses ratio

Delta Air Lines is one of the major airlines in the United States and the world. It provides passenger and cargo services for over 200 domestic U.S. cities as well as 70 international cities. It operates a fleet of over 800 aircraft and is headquartered in Atlanta, Georgia. Delta reported the following financial data (in millions) for the year ended December 31, 2004:

Net cash flows from operating activities	$(1,123)
Cash, December 31, 2004	1,811

a. Determine the monthly cash expenses. Round to one decimal place.
b. Determine the ratio of cash to monthly expenses. Round to one decimal place.
c. ━━━▶ Based on your analysis, do you believe that Delta will remain in business?

EX 8-28
Cash to monthly
cash expenses ratio

Acusphere, Inc., is a specialty pharmaceutical company that develops new drugs and improved formulations of existing drugs using its proprietary microparticle technology. Currently, the company has three products in development in the areas of cardiology, oncology, and asthma. Acusphere reported the following data (in thousands) for the years ending December 31, 2006, 2005, 2004, and 2003:

	2006	2005	2004	2003
Cash as of December 31*	$ 59,750	$ 51,112	$ 45,180	$ 54,562
Net cash flows from operating activities	(48,089)	(30,683)	(19,319)	(15,507)

*Includes cash equivalents and short-term investments.

1. Determine the monthly cash expenses for 2006, 2005, 2004, and 2003. Round to one decimal place.
2. Determine the ratio of cash to monthly expenses as of December 31, 2006, 2005, 2004, and 2003. Round to one decimal place.
3. ━━━▶ Based on (1) and (2), comment on Acusphere's ratio of cash to monthly operating expenses for 2006, 2005, 2004, and 2003.

Problems Series A ● ● ● ● ●

PR 8-1A
Evaluate internal
control of cash

objs. 2, 3

The following procedures were recently installed by The Louver Shop:

a. Each cashier is assigned a separate cash register drawer to which no other cashier has access.
b. At the end of a shift, each cashier counts the cash in his or her cash register, unlocks the cash register record, and compares the amount of cash with the amount on the record to determine cash shortages and overages.
c. Vouchers and all supporting documents are perforated with a PAID designation after being paid by the treasurer.
d. Disbursements are made from the petty cash fund only after a petty cash receipt has been completed and signed by the payee.
e. All sales are rung up on the cash register, and a receipt is given to the customer. All sales are recorded on a record locked inside the cash register.
f. Checks received through the mail are given daily to the accounts receivable clerk for recording collections on account and for depositing in the bank.
g. The bank reconciliation is prepared by the accountant.

Instructions

➤ Indicate whether each of the procedures of internal control over cash represents (1) a strength or (2) a weakness. For each weakness, indicate why it exists.

PR 8-2A
Transactions for
petty cash, cash
short and over

objs. 3, 6

Hallihan Company completed the following selected transactions during June 2010:

June 1. Established a petty cash fund of $500.

12. The cash sales for the day, according to the cash register records, totaled $13,115. The actual cash received from cash sales was $13,129.

30. Petty cash on hand was $38. Replenished the petty cash fund for the following disbursements, each evidenced by a petty cash receipt:

June 2. Store supplies, $55.

10. Express charges on merchandise purchased, $80 (Merchandise Inventory).

14. Office supplies, $35.

15. Office supplies, $40.

18. Postage stamps, $42 (Office Supplies).

20. Repair to fax, $100 (Miscellaneous Administrative Expense).

21. Repair to office door lock, $35 (Miscellaneous Administrative Expense).

22. Postage due on special delivery letter, $27 (Miscellaneous Administrative Expense).

28. Express charges on merchandise purchased, $40 (Merchandise Inventory).

30. The cash sales for the day, according to the cash register records, totaled $16,850. The actual cash received from cash sales was $16,833.

30. Increased the petty cash fund by $125.

Instructions
Journalize the transactions.

PR 8-3A
Bank reconciliation
and entries

obj. 5

✔ 1. Adjusted
balance: $13,445

The cash account for Interactive Systems at February 28, 2010, indicated a balance of $7,635. The bank statement indicated a balance of $13,333 on February 28, 2010. Comparing the bank statement and the accompanying canceled checks and memos with the records reveals the following reconciling items:

a. Checks outstanding totaled $4,118.
b. A deposit of $4,500, representing receipts of February 28, had been made too late to appear on the bank statement.
c. The bank had collected $5,200 on a note left for collection. The face of the note was $5,000.
d. A check for $290 returned with the statement had been incorrectly recorded by Interactive Systems as $920. The check was for the payment of an obligation to Busser Co. for the purchase of office supplies on account.
e. A check drawn for $415 had been incorrectly charged by the bank as $145.
f. Bank service charges for February amounted to $20.

Instructions
1. Prepare a bank reconciliation.
2. Journalize the necessary entries. The accounts have not been closed.

PR 8-4A
Bank reconciliation
and entries

obj. 5

✔ 1. Adjusted
balance: $15,430

The cash account for Fred's Sports Co. on June 1, 2010, indicated a balance of $16,515. During June, the total cash deposited was $40,150, and checks written totaled $43,600. The bank statement indicated a balance of $18,175 on June 30, 2010. Comparing the bank statement, the canceled checks, and the accompanying memos with the records revealed the following reconciling items:

a. Checks outstanding totaled $6,840.
b. A deposit of $4,275, representing receipts of June 30, had been made too late to appear on the bank statement.

c. A check for $640 had been incorrectly charged by the bank as $460.

d. A check for $80 returned with the statement had been recorded by Fred's Sports Co. as $800. The check was for the payment of an obligation to Miliski Co. on account.

e. The bank had collected for Fred's Sports Co. $3,240 on a note left for collection. The face of the note was $3,000.

f. Bank service charges for June amounted to $35.

g. A check for $1,560 from ChimTech Co. was returned by the bank because of insufficient funds.

Instructions

1. Prepare a bank reconciliation as of June 30.

2. Journalize the necessary entries. The accounts have not been closed.

PR 8-5A
Bank reconciliation and entries

obj. 5

✔ 1. Adjusted balance: $11,178.59

Rocky Mountain Interiors deposits all cash receipts each Wednesday and Friday in a night depository, after banking hours. The data required to reconcile the bank statement as of July 31 have been taken from various documents and records and are reproduced as follows. The sources of the data are printed in capital letters. All checks were written for payments on account.

BANK RECONCILIATION FOR PRECEDING MONTH (DATED JUNE 30):

Cash balance according to bank statement.		$ 9,422.80
Add deposit of June 30, not recorded by bank		780.80
		$10,203.60
Deduct outstanding checks:		
No. 580	$310.10	
No. 602	85.50	
No. 612	92.50	
No. 613	137.50	625.60
Adjusted balance		$ 9,578.00
Cash balance according to company's records		$ 9,605.70
Deduct service charges		27.70
Adjusted balance		$ 9,578.00

CASH ACCOUNT:

Balance as of July 1	$ 9,578.00

CHECKS WRITTEN:
   Number and amount of each check issued in July:

Check No.	Amount	Check No.	Amount	Check No.	Amount
614	$243.50	621	$309.50	628	$ 837.70
615	350.10	622	Void	629	329.90
616	279.90	623	Void	630	882.80
617	395.50	624	707.01	631	1,081.56
618	435.40	625	158.63	632	62.40
619	320.10	626	550.03	633	310.08
620	328.87	627	318.73	634	503.30

Total amount of checks issued in July $8,405.01

```
                                                                    PAGE   1
   A              MEMBER FDIC
   ⅃ B  AMERICAN NATIONAL BANK      ACCOUNT NUMBER
         OF DETROIT
                                     FROM  7/01/20–  TO  7/31/20–
   DETROIT, MI 48201-2500  (313)933-8547
                                     BALANCE           9,422.80

                                   9 DEPOSITS          6,086.35

                                  20 WITHDRAWALS       8,237.41

         ROCKY MOUNTAIN INTERIORS  4 OTHER DEBITS
                                     AND CREDITS        3,685.00CR

                                     NEW BALANCE       10,956.74
```

* – – – – CHECKS AND OTHER DEBITS – – – – – *				– DEPOSITS – *	– DATE – *	– BALANCE – *
No.580	310.10	No.612	92.50	780.80	07/01	9,801.00
No.602	85.50	No.614	243.50	569.50	07/03	10,041.50
No.615	350.10	No.616	279.90	701.80	07/06	10,113.30
No.617	395.50	No.618	435.40	819.24	07/11	10,101.64
No.619	320.10	No.620	238.87	580.70	07/13	10,123.37
No.621	309.50	No.624	707.01	MS 4,000.00	07/14	13,106.86
No.625	158.63	No.626	550.03	MS 160.00	07/14	12,558.20
No.627	318.73	No.629	329.90	600.10	07/17	12,509.67
No.630	882.80	No.631	1,081.56 NSF 450.00		07/20	10,095.31
No.628	837.70	No.633	310.08	701.26	07/21	9,648.79
				731.45	07/24	10,380.24
				601.50	07/28	10,981.74
		SC	25.00		07/31	10,956.74

```
   EC — ERROR CORRECTION          OD — OVERDRAFT
   MS — MISCELLANEOUS             PS — PAYMENT STOPPED
   NSF — NOT SUFFICIENT FUNDS     SC — SERVICE CHARGE
   * * *              * * *                        * * *
```

THE RECONCILEMENT OF THIS STATEMENT WITH YOUR RECORDS IS ESSENTIAL.
ANY ERROR OR EXCEPTION SHOULD BE REPORTED IMMEDIATELY.

CASH RECEIPTS FOR MONTH OF JULY   6,158.60

DUPLICATE DEPOSIT TICKETS:
  Date and amount of each deposit in July:

Date	Amount	Date	Amount	Date	Amount
July 2	$569.50	July 12	$508.70	July 23	$731.45
5	701.80	16	600.10	26	601.50
9	819.24	19	701.26	31	925.05

Instructions

1. Prepare a bank reconciliation as of July 31. If errors in recording deposits or checks are discovered, assume that the errors were made by the company. Assume that all deposits are from cash sales. All checks are written to satisfy accounts payable.
2. Journalize the necessary entries. The accounts have not been closed.
3. What is the amount of cash that should appear on the balance sheet as of July 31?
4. ➤ Assume that a canceled check for $125 has been incorrectly recorded by the bank as $1,250. Briefly explain how the error would be included in a bank reconciliation and how it should be corrected.

Problems Series B

PR 8-1B
Evaluating internal control of cash

objs. 2, 3

The following procedures were recently installed by C&G Hydraulics Company:

a. The bank reconciliation is prepared by the cashier, who works under the supervision of the treasurer.
b. All mail is opened by the mail clerk, who forwards all cash remittances to the cashier. The cashier prepares a listing of the cash receipts and forwards a copy of the list to the accounts receivable clerk for recording in the accounts.
c. At the end of the day, cash register clerks are required to use their own funds to make up any cash shortages in their registers.
d. At the end of each day, all cash receipts are placed in the bank's night depository.
e. At the end of each day, an accounting clerk compares the duplicate copy of the daily cash deposit slip with the deposit receipt obtained from the bank.
f. The accounts payable clerk prepares a voucher for each disbursement. The voucher along with the supporting documentation is forwarded to the treasurer's office for approval.
g. After necessary approvals have been obtained for the payment of a voucher, the treasurer signs and mails the check. The treasurer then stamps the voucher and supporting documentation as paid and returns the voucher and supporting documentation to the accounts payable clerk for filing.
h. Along with petty cash expense receipts for postage, office supplies, etc., several post-dated employee checks are in the petty cash fund.

Instructions
➤ Indicate whether each of the procedures of internal control over cash represents (1) a strength or (2) a weakness. For each weakness, indicate why it exists.

PR 8-2B
Transactions for petty cash, cash short and over

objs. 3, 6

Padilla's Restoration Company completed the following selected transactions during March 2010:

Mar. 1. Established a petty cash fund of $800.
   10. The cash sales for the day, according to the cash register records, totaled $11,368. The actual cash received from cash sales was $11,375.
   31. Petty cash on hand was $193. Replenished the petty cash fund for the following disbursements, each evidenced by a petty cash receipt:
      Mar. 3. Store supplies, $275.
           7. Express charges on merchandise sold, $120 (Delivery Expense).
           9. Office supplies, $18.
          13. Office supplies, $13.
          19. Postage stamps, $9 (Office Supplies).
          21. Repair to office file cabinet lock, $40 (Miscellaneous Administrative Expense).
          22. Postage due on special delivery letter, $18 (Miscellaneous Administrative Expense).
          24. Express charges on merchandise sold, $90 (Delivery Expense).
          30. Office supplies, $16.
   31. The cash sales for the day, according to the cash register records, totaled $14,690. The actual cash received from cash sales was $14,675.
   31. Decreased the petty cash fund by $50.

Instructions
Journalize the transactions.

PR 8-3B
Bank reconciliation and entries

obj. 5

✔ 1. Adjusted balance: $8,613

The cash account for Discount Medical Co. at April 30, 2010, indicated a balance of $4,604. The bank statement indicated a balance of $9,158 on April 30, 2010. Comparing the bank statement and the accompanying canceled checks and memos with the records revealed the following reconciling items:

a. Checks outstanding totaled $5,225.
b. A deposit of $3,150, representing receipts of April 30, had been made too late to appear on the bank statement.
c. The bank had collected $4,120 on a note left for collection. The face of the note was $4,000.
d. A check for $2,490 returned with the statement had been incorrectly recorded by Discount Medical Co. as $2,409. The check was for the payment of an obligation to Goldstein Co. for the purchase of office equipment on account.
e. A check drawn for $170 had been erroneously charged by the bank as $1,700.
f. Bank service charges for April amounted to $30.

Instructions
1. Prepare a bank reconciliation.
2. Journalize the necessary entries. The accounts have not been closed.

PR 8-4B
Bank reconciliation and entries

obj. 5

✔ 1. Adjusted balance: $9,360

The cash account for Inky's Bike Co. at July 1, 2010, indicated a balance of $12,470. During July, the total cash deposited was $26,680, and checks written totaled $31,500. The bank statement indicated a balance of $16,750 on July 31. Comparing the bank statement, the canceled checks, and the accompanying memos with the records revealed the following reconciling items:

a. Checks outstanding totaled $12,850.
b. A deposit of $5,100, representing receipts of July 31, had been made too late to appear on the bank statement.
c. The bank had collected for Inky's Bike Co. $2,675 on a note left for collection. The face of the note was $2,500.
d. A check for $370 returned with the statement had been incorrectly charged by the bank as $730.
e. A check for $320 returned with the statement had been recorded by Inky's Bike Co. as $230. The check was for the payment of an obligation to Ranchwood Co. on account.
f. Bank service charges for July amounted to $25.
g. A check for $850 from Hallock Co. was returned by the bank because of insufficient funds.

Instructions
1. Prepare a bank reconciliation as of July 31.
2. Journalize the necessary entries. The accounts have not been closed.

PR 8-5B
Bank reconciliation and entries

obj. 5

✔ 1. Adjusted balance: $13,893.32

Reydell Furniture Company deposits all cash receipts each Wednesday and Friday in a night depository, after banking hours. The data required to reconcile the bank statement as of June 30 have been taken from various documents and records and are reproduced as follows. The sources of the data are printed in capital letters. All checks were written for payments on account.

JUNE BANK STATEMENT:

		MEMBER FDIC			PAGE	1

AMERICAN NATIONAL BANK OF DETROIT

DETROIT, MI 48201-2500   (313)933-8547

REYDELL FURNITURE COMPANY

ACCOUNT NUMBER	
FROM 6/01/20–	TO 6/30/20–
BALANCE	9,447.20
9 DEPOSITS	8,691.77
20 WITHDRAWALS	8,014.37
4 OTHER DEBITS AND CREDITS	3,370.00CR
NEW BALANCE	13,494.60

* – – – CHECKS AND OTHER DEBITS – – – * – – DEPOSITS – – * – DATE – * – – BALANCE– – *

				DEPOSITS	DATE	BALANCE
No.731	162.15	No.736	345.95	690.25	6/01	9,629.35
No.739	60.55	No.740	237.50	1,080.50	6/02	10,411.80
No.741	495.15	No.742	501.90	854.17	6/04	10,268.92
No.743	671.30	No.744	506.88	840.50	6/09	9,931.24
No.745	117.25	No.746	298.66	MS 3,500.00	6/09	13,015.33
No.748	450.90	No.749	640.13	MS 210.00	6/09	12,134.30
No.750	276.77	No.751	299.37	896.61	6/11	12,454.77
No.752	537.01	No.753	380.95	882.95	6/16	12,419.76
No.754	449.75	No.755	272.75	1,606.74	6/18	13,304.00
No.757	407.95	No.759	901.50	897.34	6/23	12,891.89
				942.71	6/25	13,834.60
			NSF 300.00		6/28	13,534.60
			SC 40.00		6/30	13,494.60

EC — ERROR CORRECTION   OD — OVERDRAFT
MS — MISCELLANEOUS   PS — PAYMENT STOPPED
NSF — NOT SUFFICIENT FUNDS   SC — SERVICE CHARGE

* * *   * * *   * * *

THE RECONCILEMENT OF THIS STATEMENT WITH YOUR RECORDS IS ESSENTIAL.
ANY ERROR OR EXCEPTION SHOULD BE REPORTED IMMEDIATELY.

CASH ACCOUNT:
  Balance as of June 1 $9,317.40

CASH RECEIPTS FOR MONTH OF JUNE $9,601.58

DUPLICATE DEPOSIT TICKETS:
  Date and amount of each deposit in June:

Date	Amount	Date	Amount	Date	Amount
June 1	$1,080.50	June 10	$ 896.61	June 22	$ 987.34
3	854.17	15	882.95	24	942.71
8	840.50	17	1,606.74	30	1,510.06

CHECKS WRITTEN:
  Number and amount of each check issued in June:

Check No.	Amount	Check No.	Amount	Check No.	Amount
740	$237.50	747	Void	754	$ 449.75
741	495.15	748	$ 450.90	755	272.75
742	501.90	749	640.13	756	113.95
743	671.30	750	276.77	757	407.95
744	506.88	751	299.37	758	259.60
745	117.25	752	537.01	759	901.50
746	298.66	753	830.95	760	486.39

Total amount of checks issued in June $8,755.66

392 Chapter 8   Sarbanes-Oxley, Internal Control, and Cash

BANK RECONCILIATION FOR PRECEDING MONTH:

Reydell Furniture Company
Bank Reconciliation
May 31, 20—

Cash balance according to bank statement.		$ 9,447.20
Add deposit for May 31, not recorded by bank		690.25
		$10,137.45
Deduct outstanding checks:		
No. 731	$162.15	
736	345.95	
738	251.40	
739	60.55	820.05
Adjusted balance		$ 9,317.40
Cash balance according to company's records		$ 9,352.50
Deduct service charges		35.10
Adjusted balance		$ 9,317.40

Instructions
1. Prepare a bank reconciliation as of June 30. If errors in recording deposits or checks are discovered, assume that the errors were made by the company. Assume that all deposits are from cash sales. All checks are written to satisfy accounts payable.
2. Journalize the necessary entries. The accounts have not been closed.
3. What is the amount of Cash that should appear on the balance sheet as of June 30?
4. ━━━━▶ Assume that a canceled check for $260 has been incorrectly recorded by the bank as $620. Briefly explain how the error would be included in a bank reconciliation and how it should be corrected.

Special Activities

You can access the special activities online at **www.cengage.com/accounting/reeve**.

Answers to Self-Examination Questions

1. **C** Compliance with laws and regulations (answer C) is an objective, not an element, of internal control. The control environment (answer A), monitoring (answer B), control procedures (answer D), risk assessment, and information and communication are the five elements of internal control.
2. **C** The error was made by the bank, so the cash balance according to the bank statement needs to be adjusted. Since the bank deducted $90 ($540.50 — $450.50) too little, the error of $90 should be deducted from the cash balance according to the bank statement (answer C).
3. **B** On any specific date, the cash account in a company's ledger may not agree with the account in the bank's ledger because of delays and/or errors by either party in recording transactions. The purpose of a bank reconciliation, therefore, is to determine the reasons for any differences between the two account balances. All errors should then be corrected by the company or the bank, as appropriate. In arriving at the adjusted cash

balance according to the bank statement, outstanding checks must be deducted (answer B) to adjust for checks that have been written by the company but that have not yet been presented to the bank for payment.
4. **C** All reconciling items that are added to and deducted from the cash balance according to the company's records on the bank reconciliation (answer C) require that journal entries be made by the company to correct errors made in recording transactions or to bring the cash account up to date for delays in recording transactions.
5. **D** To avoid the delay, annoyance, and expense that is associated with paying all obligations by check, relatively small amounts (answer A) are paid from a petty cash fund. The fund is established by estimating the amount of cash needed to pay these small amounts during a specified period (answer B), and it is then reimbursed when the amount of money in the fund is reduced to a predetermined minimum amount (answer C).

CHAPTER 9

Receivables

©Tetra Images/Jupiter Images

OAKLEY, INC.

The sale and purchase of merchandise involves the exchange of goods for cash. However, the point at which cash actually changes hands varies with the transaction. Consider transactions by Oakley, Inc., a worldwide leader in the design, development, manufacture, and distribution of premium sunglasses, goggles, prescription eyewear, apparel, footwear, and accessories. Not only does the company sell its products through three different company-owned retail chains, but it also has approximately 10,000 independent distributors.

If you were to buy a pair of sunglasses at an Oakley Vault, which is one of the company's retail outlet stores, you would have to pay cash or use a credit card to pay for the glasses before you left the store. However, Oakley allows its distributors to purchase sunglasses "on account." These sales on account are recorded as receivables due from the distributors.

As an individual, you also might build up a trusted financial history with a local company or department store that would allow you to purchase merchandise on account. Like Oakley's distributors, your purchase on account would be recorded as an account receivable. Such credit transactions facilitate sales and are a significant current asset for many businesses. In this chapter, we will describe common classifications of receivables, illustrate how to account for uncollectible receivables, and demonstrate the reporting of receivables on the balance sheet.

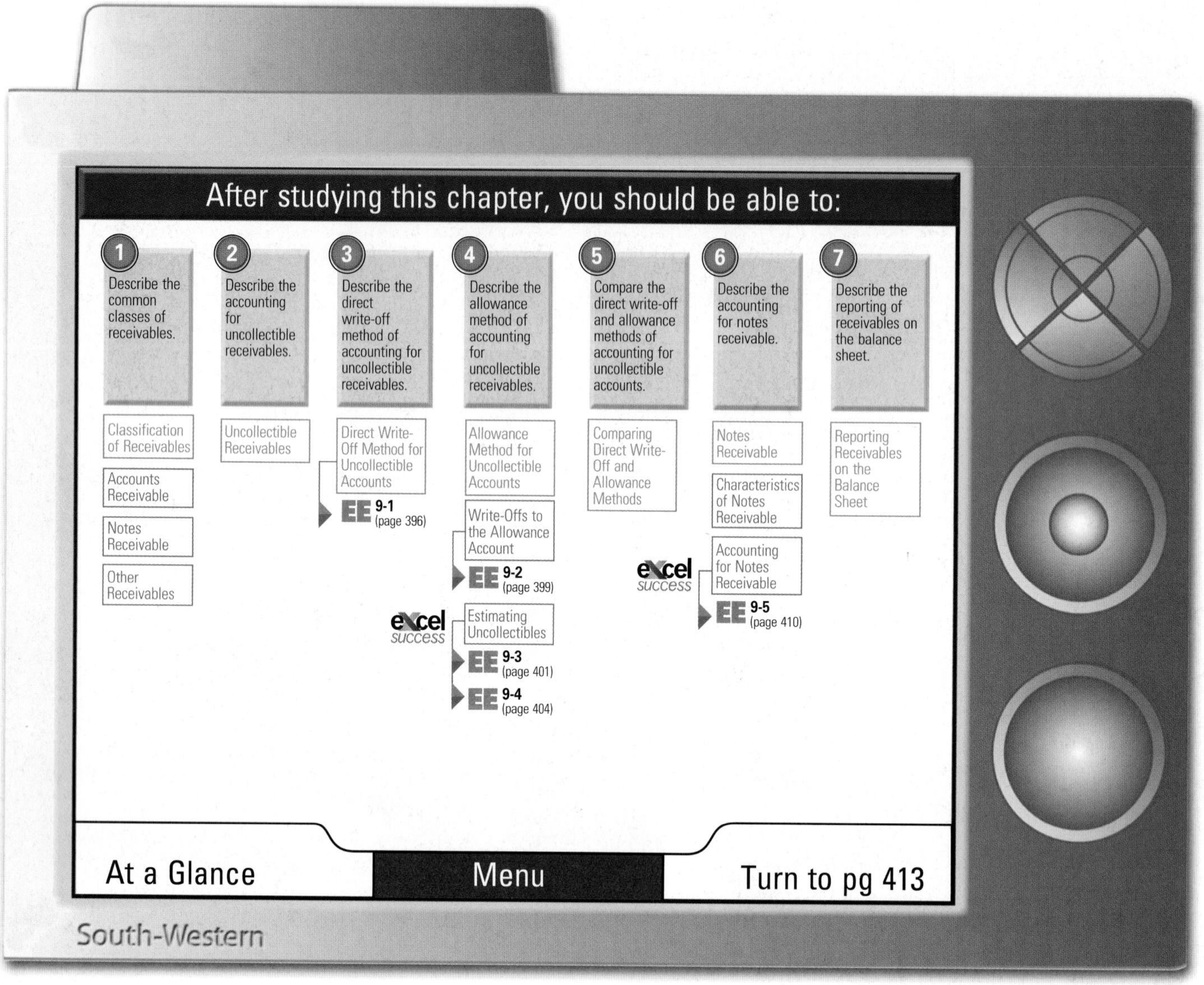

After studying this chapter, you should be able to:

1 Describe the common classes of receivables.

2 Describe the accounting for uncollectible receivables.

3 Describe the direct write-off method of accounting for uncollectible receivables.

4 Describe the allowance method of accounting for uncollectible receivables.

5 Compare the direct write-off and allowance methods of accounting for uncollectible accounts.

6 Describe the accounting for notes receivable.

7 Describe the reporting of receivables on the balance sheet.

Classification of Receivables

Accounts Receivable

Notes Receivable

Other Receivables

Uncollectible Receivables

Direct Write-Off Method for Uncollectible Accounts
EE 9-1 (page 396)

Allowance Method for Uncollectible Accounts

Write-Offs to the Allowance Account
EE 9-2 (page 399)

e**x**cel *success*

Estimating Uncollectibles
EE 9-3 (page 401)
EE 9-4 (page 404)

Comparing Direct Write-Off and Allowance Methods

e**x**cel *success*

Notes Receivable

Characteristics of Notes Receivable

Accounting for Notes Receivable
EE 9-5 (page 410)

Reporting Receivables on the Balance Sheet

At a Glance | **Menu** | **Turn to pg 413**

South-Western

---

1 Describe the common classes of receivables.

Classification of Receivables

The receivables that result from sales on account are normally accounts receivable or notes receivable. The term **receivables** includes all money claims against other entities, including people, companies, and other organizations. Receivables are usually a significant portion of the total current assets.

Accounts Receivable

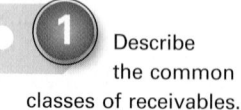

An annual report of La-Z-Boy Incorporated reported that receivables made up over 48% of La-Z-Boy's current assets.

The most common transaction creating a receivable is selling merchandise or services on account (on credit). The receivable is recorded as a debit to Accounts Receivable. Such **accounts receivable** are normally collected within a short period, such as 30 or 60 days. They are classified on the balance sheet as a current asset.

Notes Receivable

Notes receivable are amounts that customers owe for which a formal, written instrument of credit has been issued. If notes receivable are expected to be collected within a year, they are classified on the balance sheet as a current asset.

Notes are often used for credit periods of more than 60 days. For example, an automobile dealer may require a down payment at the time of sale and accept a note or a series of notes for the remainder. Such notes usually provide for monthly payments.

Notes may also be used to settle a customer's account receivable. Notes and accounts receivable that result from sales transactions are sometimes called *trade receivables*. We assume that all notes and accounts receivable in this chapter are from sales transactions.

Other Receivables

If you have purchased an automobile on credit, you probably signed a note. From your viewpoint, the note is a note payable. From the creditor's viewpoint, the note is a note receivable.

Other receivables include interest receivable, taxes receivable, and receivables from officers or employees. Other receivables are normally reported separately on the balance sheet. If they are expected to be collected within one year, they are classified as current assets. If collection is expected beyond one year, they are classified as noncurrent assets and reported under the caption *Investments*.

2 Describe the accounting for uncollectible receivables.

Uncollectible Receivables

In prior chapters, the accounting for sales of merchandise or services on account (on credit) was described and illustrated. A major issue that has not yet been discussed is that some customers will not pay their accounts. That is, some accounts receivable will be uncollectible.

Companies may shift the risk of uncollectible receivables to other companies. For example, some retailers do not accept sales on account, but will only accept cash or credit cards. Such policies shift the risk to the credit card companies.

Companies may also sell their receivables. This is often the case when a company issues its own credit card. For example, Macy's and JCPenney issue their own credit cards. Selling receivables is called *factoring* the receivables. The buyer of the receivables is called a *factor*. An advantage of factoring is that the company selling its receivables immediately receives cash for operating and other needs. Also, depending on the factoring agreement, some of the risk of uncollectible accounts is shifted to the factor.

Regardless of how careful a company is in granting credit, some credit sales will be uncollectible. The operating expense recorded from uncollectible receivables is called **bad debt expense**, *uncollectible accounts expense*, or *doubtful accounts expense*.

There is no general rule for when an account becomes uncollectible. Some indications that an account may be uncollectible include the following:

Adams, Stevens & Bradley, Ltd. is a collection agency that operates on a contingency basis. That is, its fees are based on what it collects.

1. The receivable is past due.
2. The customer does not respond to the company's attempts to collect.
3. The customer files for bankruptcy.
4. The customer closes its business.
5. The company cannot locate the customer.

If a customer doesn't pay, a company may turn the account over to a collection agency. After the collection agency attempts to collect payment, any remaining balance in the account is considered worthless.

The two methods of accounting for uncollectible receivables are as follows:

1. The **direct write-off method** records bad debt expense only when an account is determined to be worthless.
2. The **allowance method** records bad debt expense by estimating uncollectible accounts at the end of the accounting period.

The direct write-off method is often used by small companies and companies with few receivables.[1] Generally accepted accounting principles (GAAP), however, require companies with a large amount of receivables to use the allowance method. As a result, most well-known companies such as General Electric, Pepsi, Intel, and FedEx use the allowance method.

---

1 The direct write-off method is also required for federal income tax purposes.

3 Describe the direct write-off method of accounting for uncollectible receivables.

Direct Write-Off Method for Uncollectible Accounts

Under the direct write-off method, Bad Debt Expense is not recorded until the customer's account is determined to be worthless. At that time, the customer's account receivable is written off.

To illustrate, assume that a $4,200 account receivable from D. L. Ross has been determined to be uncollectible. The entry to write off the account is as follows:

May	10	Bad Debt Expense	4,200	
		Accounts Receivable—D. L. Ross		4,200

An account receivable that has been written off may be collected later. In such cases, the account is reinstated by an entry that reverses the write-off entry. The cash received in payment is then recorded as a receipt on account.

To illustrate, assume that the D. L. Ross account of $4,200 written off on May 10 is later collected on November 21. The reinstatement and receipt of cash is recorded as follows:

Nov.	21	Accounts Receivable—D. L. Ross	4,200	
		Bad Debt Expense		4,200
	21	Cash	4,200	
		Accounts Receivable—D. L. Ross		4,200

The direct write-off method is used by businesses that sell most of their goods or services for cash or accept only MasterCard or VISA, which are recorded as cash sales. In such cases, receivables are a small part of the current assets and any bad debt expense is small. Examples of such businesses are a restaurant, a convenience store, and a small retail store.

Example Exercise 9-1   Direct Write-Off Method   •••••••• 3

Journalize the following transactions using the direct write-off method of accounting for uncollectible receivables:

July 9 Received $1,200 from Jay Burke and wrote off the remainder owed of $3,900 as uncollectible.
Oct. 11 Reinstated the account of Jay Burke and received $3,900 cash in full payment.

Follow My Example 9-1

July 9	Cash		1,200	
	Bad Debt Expense		3,900	
	Accounts Receivable—Jay Burke			5,100
Oct. 11	Accounts Receivable—Jay Burke		3,900	
	Bad Debt Expense			3,900
11	Cash		3,900	
	Accounts Receivable—Jay Burke			3,900

For Practice: PE 9-1A, PE 9-1B

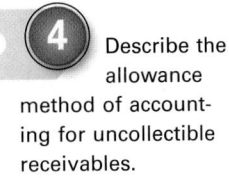

Describe the
allowance
method of account-
ing for uncollectible
receivables.

Allowance Method for Uncollectible Accounts

The allowance method estimates the uncollectible accounts receivable at the end of the accounting period. Based on this estimate, Bad Debt Expense is recorded by an adjusting entry.

To illustrate, assume that ExTone Company began operations August 1. As of the end of its accounting period on December 31, 2009, ExTone has an accounts receivable balance of $200,000. This balance includes some past due accounts. Based on industry averages, ExTone estimates that $30,000 of the December 31 accounts receivable will be uncollectible. However, on December 31, ExTone doesn't know which customer accounts will be uncollectible. Thus, specific customer accounts cannot be decreased or credited. Instead, a contra asset account, **Allowance for Doubtful Accounts**, is credited for the estimated bad debts.

Using the $30,000 estimate, the following adjusting entry is made on December 31:

2009				
Dec.	31	Bad Debt Expense	30,000	
		Allowance for Doubtful Accounts		30,000
		Uncollectible accounts estimate.		

The preceding adjusting entry affects the income statement and balance sheet. On the income statement, the $30,000 of Bad Debt Expense will be matched against the related revenues of the period. On the balance sheet, the value of the receivables is reduced to the amount that is expected to be collected or realized. This amount, $170,000 ($200,000 − $30,000), is called the **net realizable value** of the receivables.

After the preceding adjusting entry is recorded, Accounts Receivable still has a debit balance of $200,000. This balance is the total amount owed by customers on account on December 31 as supported by the accounts receivable subsidiary ledger. The accounts receivable contra account, Allowance for Doubtful Accounts, has a credit balance of $30,000.

Write-Offs to the Allowance Account

When a customer's account is identified as uncollectible, it is written off against the allowance account. This requires the company to remove the specific accounts receivable and an equal amount from the allowance account.

To illustrate, on January 21, 2010, John Parker's account of $6,000 with ExTone Company is written off as follows:

2010				
Jan.	21	Allowance for Doubtful Accounts	6,000	
		Accounts Receivable—John Parker		6,000

At the end of a period, Allowance for Doubtful Accounts will normally have a balance. This is because Allowance for Doubtful Accounts is based on an estimate. As a result, the total write-offs to the allowance account during the period will rarely equal the balance of the account at the beginning of the period. The allowance account will have a credit balance at the end of the period if the write-offs during the period are less than the beginning balance. It will have a debit balance if the write-offs exceed the beginning balance.

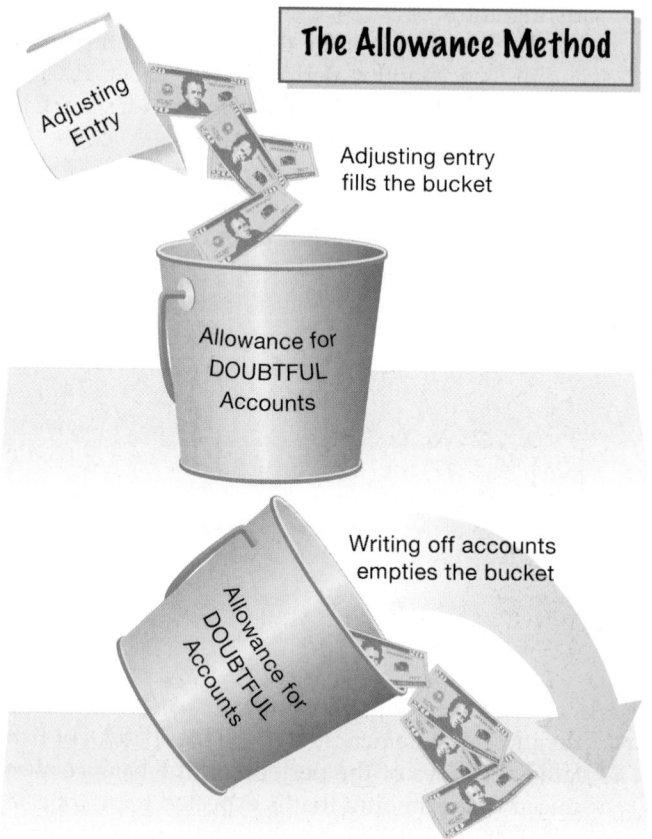

The Allowance Method

Adjusting entry fills the bucket

Allowance for DOUBTFUL Accounts

Writing off accounts empties the bucket

Allowance for DOUBTFUL Accounts

To illustrate, assume that during 2010 ExTone Company writes off $26,750 of uncollectible accounts, including the $6,000 account of John Parker recorded on January 21. Allowance for Doubtful Accounts will have a credit balance of $3,250 ($30,000 − $26,750), as shown below.

ALLOWANCE FOR DOUBTFUL ACCOUNTS

	Jan. 21 6,000	Jan. 1, 2010 Balance	30,000
Total accounts written off $26,750	Feb. 2 3,900		
	⋮ ⋮		
		Dec. 31, 2010 Unadjusted balance	3,250

If ExTone Company had written off $32,100 in accounts receivable during 2010, Allowance for Doubtful Accounts would have a debit balance of $2,100, as shown below.

ALLOWANCE FOR DOUBTFUL ACCOUNTS

	Jan. 21 6,000	Jan. 1, 2010 Balance	30,000
Total accounts written off $32,100	Feb. 2 3,900		
	⋮ ⋮		
Dec. 31, 2010 Unadjusted balance 2,100			

The allowance account balances (credit balance of $3,250 and debit balance of $2,100) in the preceding illustrations are *before* the end-of-period adjusting entry. After the end-of-period adjusting entry is recorded, Allowance for Doubtful Accounts should always have a credit balance.

An account receivable that has been written off against the allowance account may be collected later. Like the direct write-off method, the account is reinstated by an entry that reverses the write-off entry. The cash received in payment is then recorded as a receipt on account.

To illustrate, assume that Nancy Smith's account of $5,000 which was written off on April 2 is collected later on June 10. ExTone Company records the reinstatement and the collection as follows:

June	10	Accounts Receivable—Nancy Smith	5,000	
		Allowance for Doubtful Accounts		5,000
	10	Cash	5,000	
		Accounts Receivable—Nancy Smith		5,000

Example Exercise 9-2   Allowance Method

Journalize the following transactions using the allowance method of accounting for uncollectible receivables.

July 9   Received $1,200 from Jay Burke and wrote off the remainder owed of $3,900 as uncollectible.
Oct. 11   Reinstated the account of Jay Burke and received $3,900 cash in full payment.

Follow My Example 9-2

July 9	Cash	1,200	
	Allowance for Doubtful Accounts	3,900	
	Accounts Receivable—Jay Burke		5,100
Oct. 11	Accounts Receivable—Jay Burke	3,900	
	Allowance for Doubtful Accounts		3,900
11	Cash	3,900	
	Accounts Receivable—Jay Burke		3,900

For Practice: PE 9-2A, PE 9-2B

Estimating Uncollectibles

The allowance method requires an estimate of uncollectible accounts at the end of the period. This estimate is normally based on past experience, industry averages, and forecasts of the future.

The two methods used to estimate uncollectible accounts are as follows:

1. Percent of sales method.
2. Analysis of the receivables method.

Percent of Sales Method Since accounts receivable are created by credit sales, uncollectible accounts can be estimated as a percent of credit sales. If the portion of credit sales to sales is relatively constant, the percent may be applied to total sales or net sales.

To illustrate, assume the following data for ExTone Company on December 31, 2010, before any adjustments:

Balance of Accounts Receivable	$240,000
Balance of Allowance for Doubtful Accounts	3,250 (Cr.)
Total credit sales	3,000,000
Bad debt as a percent of credit sales	$\frac{3}{4}$%

Bad Debt Expense of $22,500 is estimated as follows:

Bad Debt Expense = Credit Sales × Bad Debt as a Percent of Credit Sales
Bad Debt Expense = $3,000,000 × $\frac{3}{4}$% = $22,500

The adjusting entry for uncollectible accounts on December 31, 2010, is as follows:

Dec.	31	Bad Debt Expense	22,500	
		Allowance for Doubtful Accounts		22,500
		Uncollectible accounts estimate.		
		($3,000,000 × 0.0075 = $22,500)		

After the adjusting entry is posted to the ledger, Bad Debt Expense will have an adjusted balance of $22,500. Allowance for Doubtful Accounts will have an adjusted balance of $25,750 ($3,250 + $22,500). Both T accounts are shown below.

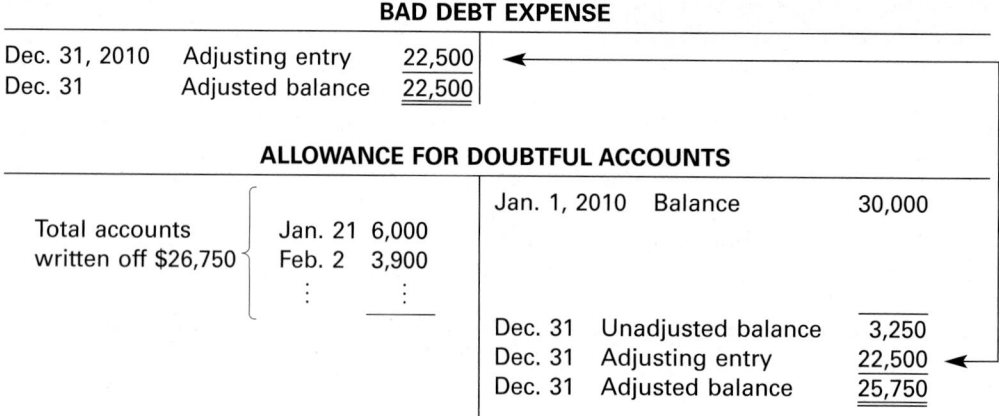

Under the percent of sales method, the amount of the adjusting entry is the amount estimated for Bad Debt Expense. This estimate is credited to whatever the unadjusted balance is for Allowance for Doubtful Accounts.

To illustrate, assume that in the preceding example the unadjusted balance of Allowance for Doubtful Accounts on December 31, 2010, had been a $2,100 debit balance instead of a $3,250 credit balance. The adjustment would still have been $22,500. However, the December 31, 2010, ending adjusted balance of Allowance for Doubtful Accounts would have been $20,400 ($22,500 − $2,100).

Example Exercise 9-3   Percent of Sales Method

At the end of the current year, Accounts Receivable has a balance of $800,000; Allowance for Doubtful Accounts has a credit balance of $7,500; and net sales for the year total $3,500,000. Bad debt expense is estimated at ½ of 1% of net sales.

Determine (a) the amount of the adjusting entry for uncollectible accounts; (b) the adjusted balances of Accounts Receivable, Allowance for Doubtful Accounts, and Bad Debt Expense; and (c) the net realizable value of accounts receivable.

Follow My Example 9-3

a. $17,500 ($3,500,000 × 0.005)

	Adjusted Balance
b. Accounts Receivable	$800,000
Allowance for Doubtful Accounts ($7,500 + $17,500)	25,000
Bad Debt Expense	17,500

c. $775,000 ($800,000 − $25,000)

For Practice: PE 9-3A, PE 9-3B

The percentage of uncollectible accounts will vary across companies and industries. For example, in their recent annual reports, JCPenney reported 1.7% of its receivables as uncollectible, Deere & Company (manufacturer of John Deere tractors, etc.) reported only 1.0% of its dealer receivables as uncollectible, and HCA Inc., a hospital management company, reported 42% of its receivables as uncollectible.

Analysis of Receivables Method   The analysis of receivables method is based on the assumption that the longer an account receivable is outstanding, the less likely that it will be collected. The analysis of receivables method is applied as follows:

Step 1.   The due date of each account receivable is determined.

Step 2.   The number of days each account is past due is determined. This is the number of days between the due date of the account and the date of the analysis.

Step 3.   Each account is placed in an aged class according to its days past due. Typical aged classes include the following:

> Not past due
> 1–30 days past due
> 31–60 days past due
> 61–90 days past due
> 91–180 days past due
> 181–365 days past due
> Over 365 days past due

Step 4.   The totals for each aged class are determined.

Step 5.   The total for each aged class is multiplied by an estimated percentage of uncollectible accounts for that class.

Step 6.   The estimated total of uncollectible accounts is determined as the sum of the uncollectible accounts for each aged class.

The preceding steps are summarized in an aging schedule, and this overall process is called **aging the receivables**.

To illustrate, assume that ExTone Company uses the analysis of receivables method instead of the percent of sales method. ExTone prepared an aging schedule for its accounts receivable of $240,000 as of December 31, 2010, as shown in Exhibit 1.

Exhibit 1

Aging of Receivables Schedule
December 31, 2010

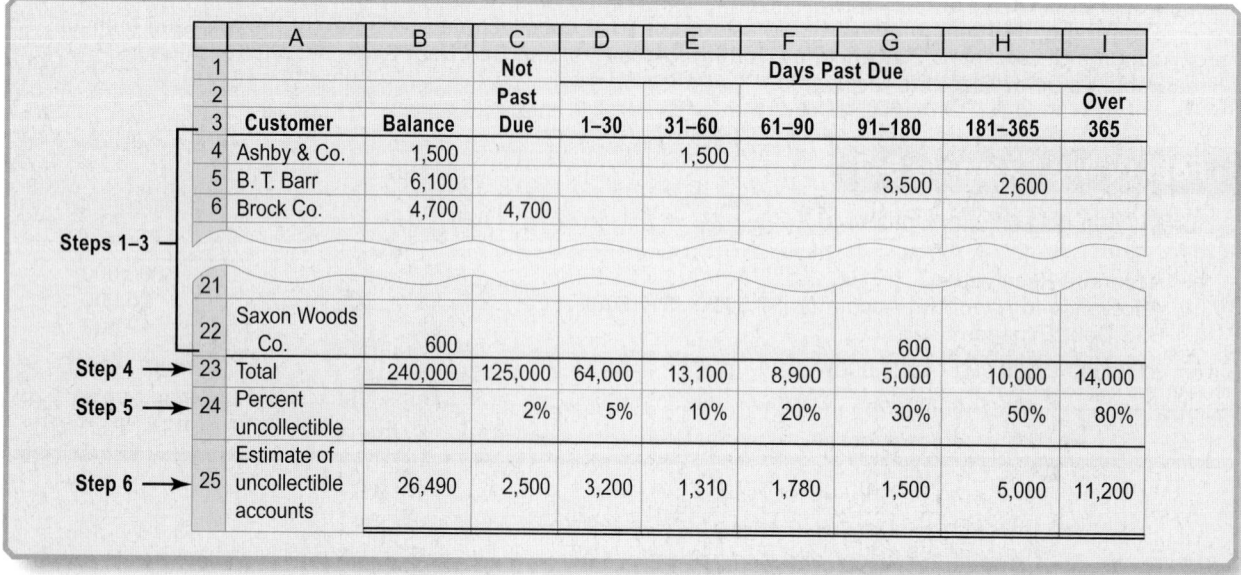

		A	B	C	D	E	F	G	H	I
	1			Not			Days Past Due			
	2			Past						Over
	3	Customer	Balance	Due	1–30	31–60	61–90	91–180	181–365	365
Steps 1–3	4	Ashby & Co.	1,500			1,500				
	5	B. T. Barr	6,100					3,500	2,600	
	6	Brock Co.	4,700	4,700						
	21									
	22	Saxon Woods Co.	600					600		
Step 4 →	23	Total	240,000	125,000	64,000	13,100	8,900	5,000	10,000	14,000
Step 5 →	24	Percent uncollectible		2%	5%	10%	20%	30%	50%	80%
Step 6 →	25	Estimate of uncollectible accounts	26,490	2,500	3,200	1,310	1,780	1,500	5,000	11,200

Assume that ExTone Company sold merchandise to Saxon Woods Co. on August 29 with terms 2/10, n/30. Thus, the due date (Step 1) of Saxon Woods' account is September 28, as shown below.

Credit terms, net	30 days
Less: Aug. 29 to Aug. 30	2 days
Days in September	28 days

As of December 31, Saxon Woods' account is 94 days past due (Step 2), as shown below.

Number of days past due in September	2 days (30 − 28)
Number of days past due in October	31 days
Number of days past due in November	30 days
Number of days past due in December	31 days
Total number of days past due	94 days

Exhibit 1 shows that the $600 account receivable for Saxon Woods Co. was placed in the 91–180 days past due class (Step 3).

The total for each of the aged classes is determined (Step 4). Exhibit 1 shows that $125,000 of the accounts receivable are not past due, while $64,000 are 1–30 days past due. ExTone Company applies a different estimated percentage of uncollectible accounts to the totals of each of the aged classes (Step 5). As shown in Exhibit 1, the percent is 2% for accounts not past due, while the percent is 80% for accounts over 365 days past due.

The sum of the estimated uncollectible accounts for each aged class (Step 6) is the estimated uncollectible accounts on December 31, 2010. This is the desired adjusted balance for Allowance for Doubtful Accounts. For ExTone Company, this amount is $26,490, as shown in Exhibit 1.

Comparing the estimate of $26,490 with the unadjusted balance of the allowance account determines the amount of the adjustment for Bad Debt Expense. For ExTone, the unadjusted balance of the allowance account is a credit balance of $3,250. The amount to be added to this balance is therefore $23,240 ($26,490 − $3,250). The adjusting entry is as follows:

After the preceding adjusting entry is posted to the ledger, Bad Debt Expense will have an adjusted balance of $23,240. Allowance for Doubtful Accounts will have an adjusted balance of $26,490, and the net realizable value of the receivables is $213,510 ($240,000 − $26,490). Both T accounts are shown as follows.

Dec.	31	Bad Debt Expense	23,240	
		Allowance for Doubtful Accounts		23,240
		Uncollectible accounts estimate.		
		($26,490 – $3,250)		

The Commercial Collection Agency Section of the Commercial Law League of America reported the following collection rates by number of months past due:

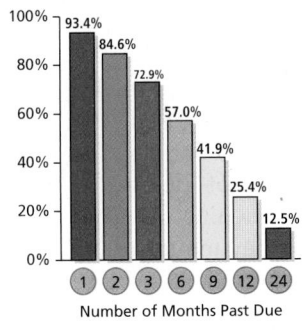

Number of Months Past Due

BAD DEBT EXPENSE

Dec. 31, 2010	Adjusting entry	23,240
Dec. 31	Adjusting balance	23,240

ALLOWANCE FOR DOUBTFUL ACCOUNTS

	Dec. 31, 2010	Unadjusted balance	3,250
	Dec. 31	Adjusting entry	23,240
	Dec. 31	Adjusted balance	26,490

Under the analysis of receivables method, the amount of the adjusting entry is the amount that will yield an adjusted balance for Allowance for Doubtful Accounts equal to that estimated by the aging schedule.

To illustrate, if the unadjusted balance of the allowance account had been a debit balance of $2,100, the amount of the adjustment would have been $28,590 ($26,490 + $2,100). In this case, Bad Debt Expense would have an adjusted balance of $28,590. However, the adjusted balance of Allowance for Doubtful Accounts would still have been $26,490. After the adjusting entry is posted, both T accounts are shown below.

BAD DEBT EXPENSE

Dec. 31, 2010	Adjusting entry	28,590
Dec. 31	Adjusting balance	28,590

ALLOWANCE FOR DOUBTFUL ACCOUNTS

Dec. 31, 2010	Unadjusted balance	2,100			
			Aug. 31	Adjusted entry	28,590
			Aug. 31	Adjusted balance	26,490

excel *success*

The aging of receivables schedule from *Exhibit 1* can be developed using spreadsheet software as follows:

	A	B	C	D	E	F	G	H	I
1						Days Past Due			
2	Customer	Balance	Not Past Due	1-30	31-60	61-90	91-180	181-365	Over 365
3	Ashby & Co.	1,500	-		1,500				
4	B.T. Barr	6,100	-					3,500	2,600
5	Brock Co.	4,700	4,700						
21	Saxon Woods Co.	600		-	-	600			
22	Total a.	=SUM(B3:B21)	=SUM(C3:C21)	=SUM(D3:D21)	=SUM(E3:E21) b.	=SUM(F3:F21)	=SUM(G3:G21)	=SUM(H3:H21)	=SUM(I3:I21)
23	Percent uncollectible		2%	5%	10%	20%	30%	50%	80%
24	Estimate of uncollectible accounts	=SUM(C24:I24)	=C22*C23	=D22*D23	=E22*E23	=F22*F23	=G22*G23	=H22*H23	=I22*I23
25									

c.

d.

A spreadsheet uses the asterisk symbol (*) for multiplication.

Develop the formulas by the following steps:

a. Enter a formula in B22 to sum the "Balance" column, =SUM(B3:B21).
b. Copy the formula from B22 to C22:I22 so that the sum formula applies to all *Days Past Due* categories.
c. Enter a formula in C24 to multiply the sum in C22 by the percent uncollectible in C23, =C22*C23.
d. Copy the formula from C24 to D24:I24 so that the multiplication formula applies to all *Days Past Due* categories.
e. Enter a formula in B24 to sum the total estimated uncollectible for each period, =SUM(C24:I24).

 Go to the hands-on *Excel Tutor* for this example!

Example Exercise 9-4 Analysis of Receivables Method

········➤ 4

At the end of the current year, Accounts Receivable has a balance of $800,000; Allowance for Doubtful Accounts has a credit balance of $7,500; and net sales for the year total $3,500,000. Using the aging method, the balance of Allowance for Doubtful Accounts is estimated as $30,000.

　　Determine (a) the amount of the adjusting entry for uncollectible accounts; (b) the adjusted balances of Accounts Receivable, Allowance for Doubtful Accounts, and Bad Debt Expense; and (c) the net realizable value of accounts receivable.

Follow My Example 9-4

a.　$22,500 ($30,000 − $7,500)

		Adjusted Balance
b.	Accounts Receivable	$800,000
	Allowance for Doubtful Accounts	30,000
	Bad Debt Expense	22,500

c.　$770,000 ($800,000 − $30,000)

For Practice: PE 9-4A, PE 9-4B

Comparing Estimation Methods Both the percent of sales and analysis of receivables methods estimate uncollectible accounts. However, each method has a slightly different focus and financial statement emphasis.

　　Under the percent of sales method, Bad Debt Expense is the focus of the estimation process. The percent of sales method places more emphasis on matching revenues and expenses and, thus, emphasizes the income statement. That is, the amount of the adjusting entry is based on the estimate of Bad Debt Expense for the period. Allowance for Doubtful Accounts is then credited for this amount.

　　Under the analysis of receivables method, Allowance for Doubtful Accounts is the focus of the estimation process. The analysis of receivables method places more emphasis on the net realizable value of the receivables and, thus, emphasizes the balance sheet. That is, the amount of the adjusting entry is the amount that will yield an adjusted balance for Allowance for Doubtful Accounts equal to that estimated by the aging schedule. Bad Debt Expense is then debited for this amount.

　　Exhibit 2 summarizes these differences between the percent of sales and the analysis of receivables methods. Exhibit 2 also shows the results of the ExTone

Exhibit 2

·········

Differences Between Estimation Methods

	Focus of Method	Financial Statement Emphasis	ExTone Company Example	
			Bad Debt Expense Estimate **	Allowance for Doubtful Accounts Estimate
Percent of Sales Method	Bad Debt Expense Estimate	Income Statement	$22,500	$25,750* ($22,500 + $3,250)
Analysis of Receivables Method	Allowance for Doubtful Accounts Estimate	Balance Sheet	$23,240* ($26,490 − $3,250)	$26,490

*Indicates that the estimate was derived (sometimes called plugged) from the estimate on which this method focuses.
** Amount of adjusting entry.

Company illustration for the percent of sales and analysis of receivables methods. The amounts shown in Exhibit 2 assume that an unadjusted credit balance of $3,250 for Allowance for Doubtful Accounts. While the methods normally yield different amounts for any one period, over several periods the amounts should be similar.

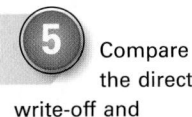

Compare the direct write-off and allowance methods of accounting for uncollectible accounts.

Comparing Direct Write-Off and Allowance Methods

The journal entries for the direct write-off and allowance methods are illustrated and compared in this section. As a basis for our illustration, the following selected transactions, taken from the records of Hobbs Company for the year ending December 31, 2009, are used:

Mar. 1. Wrote off account of C. York, $3,650.

Apr. 12. Received $2,250 as partial payment on the $5,500 account of Cary Bradshaw. Wrote off the remaining balance as uncollectible.

June 22. Received the $3,650 from C. York, which had been written off on March 1. Reinstated the account and recorded the cash receipt.

Sept. 7. Wrote off the following accounts as uncollectible (record as one journal entry):

Jason Bigg	$1,100	Stanford Noonan	$1,360
Steve Bradey	2,220	Aiden Wyman	990
Samantha Neeley	775		

Dec. 31. Hobbs Company uses the percent of credit sales method of estimating uncollectible expenses. Based on past history and industry averages, 1.25% of credit sales are expected to be uncollectible. Hobbs recorded $3,400,000 of credit sales during 2009.

Exhibit 3 illustrates the journal entries for Hobbs Company using the direct write-off and allowance methods. Using the direct write-off method, there is no adjusting entry on December 31 for uncollectible accounts. In contrast, the allowance method records an adjusting entry for estimated uncollectible accounts of $42,500.

The primary differences between the direct write-off and allowance methods are summarized below.

COMPARING THE DIRECT WRITE-OFF AND ALLOWANCE METHODS

	Direct Write-Off Method	Allowance Method
Bad debt expense is recorded	When the specific customer accounts are determined to be uncollectible.	Using estimate based on (1) a percent of sales or (2) an analysis of receivables.
Allowance account	No allowance account is used.	The allowance account is used.
Primary users	Small companies and companies with few receivables.	Large companies and those with a large amount of receivables.

Comparing Direct Write-Off and Allowance Methods

		Direct Write-Off Method			Allowance Method		
2009							
Mar.	1	Bad Debt Expense	3,650		Allowance for Doubtful Accounts	3,650	
		Accounts Receivable—C. York		3,650	Accounts Receivable—C. York		3,650
Apr.	12	Cash	2,250		Cash	2,250	
		Bad Debt Expense	3,250		Allowance for Doubtful Accounts	3,250	
		Accounts Receivable—Cary Bradshaw		5,500	Accounts Receivable—Cary Bradshaw		5,500
June	22	Accounts Receivable—C. York	3,650		Accounts Receivable—C. York	3,650	
		Bad Debt Expense		3,650	Allowance for Doubtful Accounts		3,650
	22	Cash	3,650		Cash	3,650	
		Accounts Receivable—C. York		3,650	Accounts Receivable—C. York		3,650
Sept.	7	Bad Debt Expense	6,445		Allowance for Doubtful Accounts	6,445	
		Accounts Receivable—Jason Bigg		1,100	Accounts Receivable—Jason Bigg		1,100
		Accounts Receivable—Steve Bradey		2,220	Accounts Receivable—Steve Bradey		2,220
		Accounts Receivable—Samantha Neeley		775	Accounts Receivable—Samantha Neeley		775
		Accounts Receivable—Stanford Noonan		1,360	Accounts Receivable—Stanford Noonan		1,360
		Accounts Receivable—Aiden Wyman		990	Accounts Receivable—Aiden Wyman		990
Dec.	31	No Entry			Bad Debt Expense	42,500	
					Allowance for Doubtful Accounts		42,500
					Uncollectible accounts estimate.		
					($3,400,000 × 0.0125 = $42,500)		

Integrity, Objectivity, and Ethics in Business

RECEIVABLES FRAUD

Financial reporting frauds are often tied to accounts receivable, because receivables allow companies to record revenue before cash is received. Take, for example, the case of entrepreneur Michael Weinstein, who acquired Coated Sales, Inc. with the dream of growing the small specialty company into a major corporation. To acquire funding that would facilitate this growth, Weinstein had to artificially boost the company's sales. He accomplished this by adding millions in false accounts receivable to existing customer accounts.

The company's auditors began to sense a problem when they called one of the company's customers to confirm a large order. When the customer denied placing the order, the auditors began to investigate the company's receivables more closely. Their analysis revealed a fraud which overstated profits by $55 million and forced the company into bankruptcy, costing investors and creditors over $160 million.

Source: Joseph T. Wells, "Follow Fraud to the Likely Perpetrator," *The Journal of Accountancy*, March 2001.

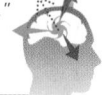

 **6** Describe the accounting for notes receivable.

Notes Receivable

A note has some advantages over an account receivable. By signing a note, the debtor recognizes the debt and agrees to pay it according to its terms. Thus, a note is a stronger legal claim.

Characteristics of Notes Receivable

A promissory note is a written promise to pay the face amount, usually with interest, on demand or at a date in the future.[2] Characteristics of a promissory note are as follows:

2 You may see references to non-interest-bearing notes. Such notes are not widely used and carry an assumed or implicit interest rate.

1. The *maker* is the party making the promise to pay.
2. The *payee* is the party to whom the note is payable.
3. The *face amount* is the amount the note is written for on its face.
4. The *issuance date* is the date a note is issued.
5. The *due date* or *maturity date* is the date the note is to be paid.
6. The *term* of a note is the amount of time between the issuance and due dates.
7. The *interest rate* is that rate of interest that must be paid on the face amount for the term of the note.

Exhibit 4 illustrates a promissory note. The maker of the note is Selig Company, and the payee is Pearland Company. The face value of the note is $2,000, and the issuance date is March 16, 2009. The term of the note is 90 days, which results in a due date of June 14, 2009, as shown below.

Days in March	31 days
Minus issuance date of note	16
Days remaining in March	15 days
Add days in April	30
Add days in May	31
Add days in June (due date of June 14)	14
Term of note	90 days

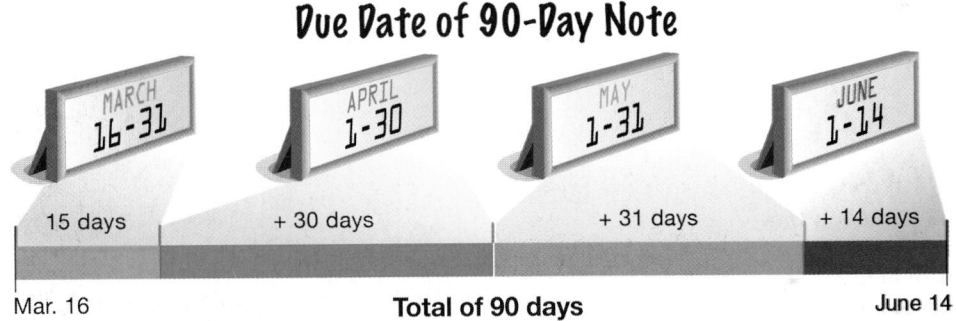

Due Date of 90-Day Note

In Exhibit 4, the term of the note is 90 days and has an interest rate of 10%.

Exhibit 4

Promissory Note

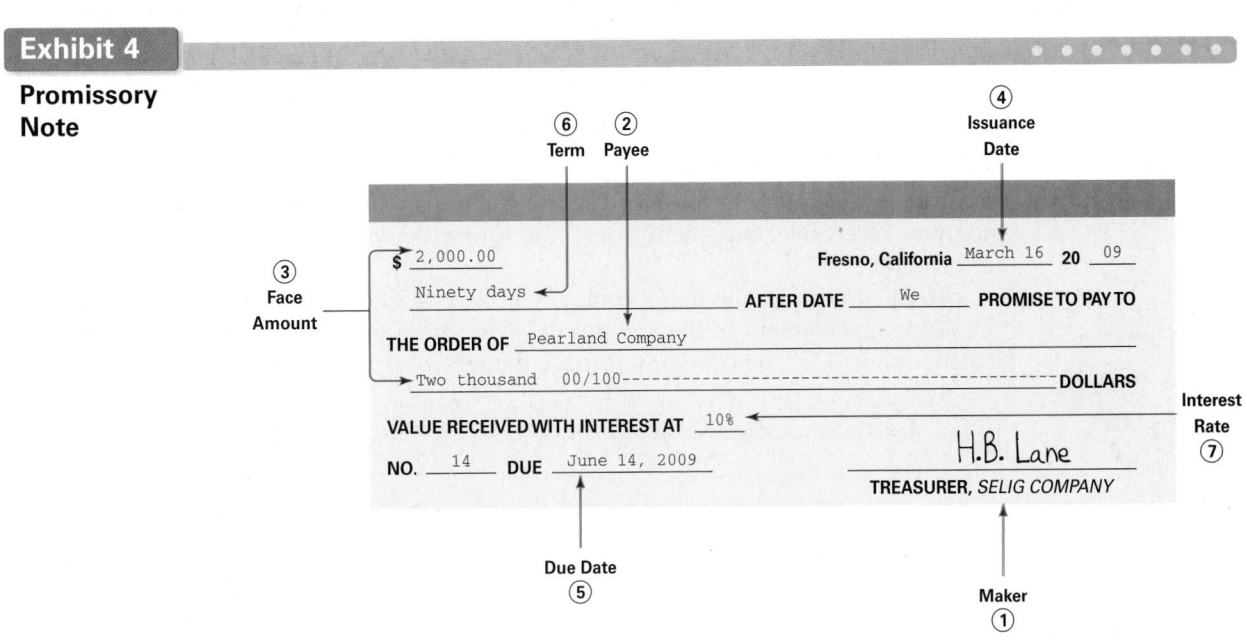

The interest on a note is computed as follows:

$$\text{Interest} = \text{Face Amount} \times \text{Interest Rate} \times (\text{Term}/360 \text{ days})$$

The interest rate is stated on an annual (yearly) basis, while the term is expressed as days. Thus, the interest on the note in Exhibit 4 is computed as follows:

$$\text{Interest} = \$2{,}000 \times 10\% \times (90/360) = \$50$$

To simplify, we will use 360 days per year. In practice, companies such as banks and mortgage companies use the exact number of days in a year, 365.

The **maturity value** is the amount that must be paid at the due date of the note, which is the sum of the face amount and the interest. The maturity value of the note in Exhibit 4 is $2,050 ($2,000 + $50).

The interest on a note can be computed using a simple spreadsheet formula shown as follows:

	A	B	C
1			
2	*Inputs*		
3	Face amount	$ 2,000	← a.
4	Interest rate	10%	← b.
5	Term	90	days ← c.
6			
7	*Output*		← d.
8	Interest	=B3*B4*(B5/360)	
9			
10			

Also, although the parentheses are not required, it is good programming practice.

There are three *inputs* to enter as follows:

a. Enter the face amount in cell B3 (in this example, 2,000).
b. Enter the interest rate in cell B4 (in this example, 10%).
c. Enter the term in cell B5 (in this example, 90, expressed in days).
d. The output is a formula entered in B8 that determines the interest, =B3*B4*(B5/360).

 Go to the hands-on *Excel Tutor* for this example!

Accounting for Notes Receivable

A promissory note may be received by a company from a customer to replace an account receivable. In such cases, the promissory note is recorded as a note receivable.[3]

To illustrate, assume that a company accepts a 30-day, 12% note dated November 21, 2010, in settlement of the account of W. A. Bunn Co., which is past due and has a balance of $6,000. The company records the receipt of the note as follows:

Nov.	21	Notes Receivable—W. A. Bunn Co.	6,000	
		Accounts Receivable—W. A. Bunn Co.		6,000

---

3 The accounting for notes payable is described and illustrated in Chapter 14.

At the due date, the company records the receipt of $6,060 ($6,000 face amount plus $60 interest) as follows:

Dec.	21	Cash	6,060	
		Notes Receivable—W. A. Bunn Co.		6,000
		Interest Revenue		60
		$6,060 = [$6,000 + ($6,000 × 12% × 30/360)].		

If the maker of a note fails to pay the note on the due date, the note is a **dishonored note receivable**. A company that holds a dishonored note transfers the face amount of the note plus any interest due back to an accounts receivable account. For example, assume that the $6,000, 30-day, 12% note received from W. A. Bunn Co. and recorded on November 21 is dishonored. The company holding the note transfers the note and interest back to the customer's account as follows:

Dec.	21	Accounts Receivable—W. A. Bunn Co.	6,060	
		Notes Receivable—W. A. Bunn Co.		6,000
		Interest Revenue		60

The company has earned the interest of $60, even though the note is dishonored. If the account receivable is uncollectible, the company will write off $6,060 against Allowance for Doubtful Accounts.

A company receiving a note should record an adjusting entry for any accrued interest at the end of the period. For example, assume that Crawford Company issues a $4,000, 90-day, 12% note dated December 1, 2010, to settle its account receivable. If the accounting period ends on December 31, the company receiving the note would record the following entries:

2010 Dec.	1	Notes Receivable—Crawford Company	4,000	
		Accounts Receivable—Crawford Company		4,000
	31	Interest Receivable	40	
		Interest Revenue		40
		Accrued interest.		
		($4,000 × 12% × 30/360)		
2011 Mar.	1	Cash	4,120	
		Notes Receivable—Crawford Company		4,000
		Interest Receivable		40
		Interest Revenue		80
		Total interest of $120.		
		($4,000 × 12% × 90/360)		

The interest revenue account is closed at the end of each accounting period. The amount of interest revenue is normally reported in the Other income section of the income statement.

Example Exercise 9-5   Note Receivable

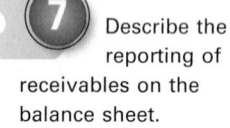

Same Day Surgery Center received a 120-day, 6% note for $40,000, dated March 14 from a patient on account.

a. Determine the due date of the note.
b. Determine the maturity value of the note.
c. Journalize the entry to record the receipt of the payment of the note at maturity.

Follow My Example 9-5

a. The due date of the note is July 12, determined as follows:

March	17 days (31 − 14)
April	30 days
May	31 days
June	30 days
July	12 days
Total	120 days

b. $40,800 [$40,000 + ($40,000 × 6% × 120/360)]

c. July 12   Cash 40,800
   Notes Receivable 40,000
   Interest Revenue 800

For Practice: PE 9-5A, PE 9-5B

---

7 Describe the reporting of receivables on the balance sheet.

Reporting Receivables on the Balance Sheet

All receivables that are expected to be realized in cash within a year are reported in the Current Assets section of the balance sheet. Current assets are normally reported in the order of their liquidity, beginning with cash and cash equivalents.

The balance sheet presentation for receivables for Mornin' Joe is shown below.

Mornin' Joe
Balance Sheet
December 31, 2010

Assets

Current assets:		
Cash and cash equivalents		$235,000
Trading investments (at cost)	$420,000	
Plus valuation allowance for trading investments	45,000	465,000
Accounts receivable	$305,000	
Less allowance for doubtful accounts	12,300	292,700

In Mornin Joe's financial statements, the allowance for doubtful accounts is subtracted from accounts receivable. Some companies report receivables at their net realizable value with a note showing the amount of the allowance.

Other disclosures related to receivables are reported either on the face of the financial statements or in the financial statement notes. Such disclosures include the market (fair) value of the receivables. In addition, if unusual credit risks exist within the receivables, the nature of the risks are disclosed. For example, if the majority of the receivables are due from one customer or are due from customers located in one area of the country or one industry, these facts are disclosed.[4]

Financial Analysis and Interpretation

Two financial measures that are especially useful in evaluating efficiency in collecting receivables are (1) the accounts receivable turnover and (2) the number of days' sales in receivables.

The **accounts receivable turnover** measures how frequently during the year the accounts receivable are being converted to cash. For example, with credit terms of 2/10, n/30, the accounts receivable should turn over more than 12 times per year. The accounts receivable turnover is computed as follows:[5]

$$\text{Accounts Receivable Turnover} = \frac{\text{Net Sales}}{\text{Average Accounts Receivable}}$$

The average accounts receivable can be determined by using monthly data or by simply adding the beginning and ending accounts receivable balances and dividing by two. For example, using the following financial data (in millions) for FedEx, the 2007 and 2006 accounts receivable turnover is computed as 10.5 and 7.7, respectively.

	2007		2006		2005
Net sales	$22,527		$21,296		—
Accounts receivable	1,429		2,860		$2,703
Average accounts receivable	2,145	[($1,429 + $2,860)/2]	2,782	[($2,860 + $2,703)/2]	
Accounts receivable turnover	10.5	($22,527/$2,145)	7.7	($21,296/$2,782)	

Comparing 2007 and 2006 indicates that the accounts receivable turnover has increased from 7.7 to 10.5. Thus, FedEx's management of accounts receivable has improved in 2007.

The **number of days' sales in receivables** is an estimate of the length of time the accounts receivable have been outstanding. With credit terms of 2/10, n/30, the number of days' sales in receivables should be less than 20 days. It is computed as follows:

$$\text{Number of Days' Sales in Receivables} = \frac{\text{Average Accounts Receivable}}{\text{Average Daily Sales}}$$

Average daily sales are determined by dividing net sales by 365 days. For example, using the preceding data for FedEx, the number of days' sales in receivables is 34.8 and 47.7 for 2007 and 2006, respectively, as shown below.

	2007		2006	
Net sales	$22,527		$21,296	
Average accounts receivable	2,145	[($1,429 + $2,860)/2]	2,782	[($2,860 + $2,703)/2]
Average daily sales	61.7	($22,527/365)	58.3	($21,296/365)
Days' sales in receivables	34.8	($2,145/61.7)	47.7	($2,782/58.3)

The number of days' sales in receivables confirms an improvement in managing accounts receivable during 2007. That is, the efficiency in collecting accounts receivable has improved when the number of days' sales in receivables decreases. During 2007, FedEx's days in receivables decreased from 47.7 in 2006 to 34.8. However, these measures should also be compared with similar companies within the industry.

---

4 *Statement of Financial Accounting Standards No. 105*, "Disclosures of Information about Financial Instruments with Off-Balance Sheet Risk and Financial Instruments with Concentrations of Credit Risk," and *No. 107*, "Disclosures about Fair Value of Financial Instruments" (Norwalk, CT: Financial Accounting Standards Board).

5 If known, credit sales can be used in the numerator. However, because credit sales are not normally disclosed to external users, most analysts use net sales in the numerator.

A P P E N D I X

Discounting Notes Receivable

A company may endorse a note receivable and transfer it to a bank in return for cash. This is called *discounting notes receivable*. The bank pays cash (the *proceeds*) to the company after deducting a *discount* (interest). The discount is computed using a *discount rate* on the maturity value of the note for the discount period. The *discount period* is the time that the bank must hold the note before it becomes due.

To illustrate, assume that on May 3 a note receivable from Pryor & Co is discounted by Deacon Company at its bank. The related data are as follows:

Face amount of note $1,800
Issuance date of note . . . . April 8
Interest rate on note 12%
Term of note . . . . 90 days
Due date of note . . . . July 7
Maturity value of note . . . . $1,854 [$1,800 + ($1,800 × 12% × 90/360)]
Discount date . . . . May 3
Discount period . . . . 65 days (May 3 to July 7)
Discount rate 14%
Discount . . . . $46.87 ($1,854 × 14% × 65/360)
Discount proceeds . . . . $1,807.13 ($1,854.00 − $46.87)

Deacon Company records the receipt of the proceeds as follows:

May	3	Cash		1,807.13	
		Notes Receivable			1,800.00
		Interest Revenue			7.13
		Discounted $1,800, 90-day, 12% note at 14%.			

If the proceeds had been less than the face amount, Deacon Company would have recorded the excess of the face amount over the proceeds as interest expense. For example, if the proceeds had been $1,785, Deacon Company would have recorded interest expense of $15 ($1,800 − $1,785). The length of the discount period, interest rate, and discount rate determine whether interest expense or interest revenue is recorded.

Without a statement limiting responsibility, Deacon Company must pay the maturity value of the note if the maker defaults. This potential liability is called a *contingent liability*. If the maker pays the maturity value, the contingent liability ceases to exist. If, however, the maker dishonors the note, the contingent liability becomes a liability that must be paid.

If a discounted note receivable is dishonored, the bank notifies the company and asks for payment. In some cases, the bank may charge a *protest fee* on dishonored notes. The entire amount paid to the bank, including the maturity value and protest fee, is debited to the account receivable of the maker.

To illustrate, assume that Pryor & Co. dishonors the $1,800, 90-day, 12% note that was discounted on May 3. The bank charges a protest fee of $12. Deacon Company's entry to record the payment to the bank is as follows:

July	7	Accounts Receivable—Pryor & Co.	1,866	
		Cash		1,866
		Paid dishonored, discounted note (maturity value of $1,854 plus protest fee of $12).		

At a Glance 9

1 Describe the common classes of receivables.

Key Points	Key Learning Outcomes	Example Exercises	Practice Exercises
The term *receivables* includes all money claims against other entities, including people, business firms, and other organizations. Receivables are normally classified as accounts receivable, notes receivable, or other receivables.	• Define the term *receivables*. • List some common classifications of receivables.		

2 Describe the accounting for uncollectible receivables.

Key Points	Key Learning Outcomes	Example Exercises	Practice Exercises
Regardless of the care used in granting credit and the collection procedures used, a part of the credit sales will not be collectible. The operating expense recorded from uncollectible receivables is called *bad debt expense*. The two methods of accounting for uncollectible receivables are the direct write-off method and the allowance method.	• Describe how a company may shift the risk of uncollectible receivables to other companies. • List factors that indicate an account receivable is uncollectible. • Describe two methods of accounting for uncollectible accounts receivable.		

3 Describe the direct write-off method of accounting for uncollectible receivables.

Key Points	Key Learning Outcomes	Example Exercises	Practice Exercises
Under the direct write-off method, the entry to write off an account debits Bad Debt Expense and credits Accounts Receivable. Neither an allowance account nor an adjusting entry is needed at the end of the period.	• Prepare journal entries to write off an account using the direct method.	9-1	9-1A, 9-1B
	• Prepare journal entries for the reinstatement and collection of an account previously written off.	9-1	9-1A, 9-1B

4 Describe the allowance method of accounting for uncollectible receivables.

Key Points	Key Learning Outcomes	Example Exercises	Practice Exercises
Under the allowance method, an adjusting entry is made for uncollectible accounts. When an account is determined to be uncollectible, it is written off against the allowance account. The allowance account normally has a credit balance after the adjusting entry has been posted and is a contra asset account.	• Prepare journal entries to write off an account using the allowance method.	9-2	9-2A, 9-2B
	• Prepare journal entries for the reinstatement and collection of an account previously written off.	9-2	9-2A, 9-2B
The estimate of uncollectibles may be based on a percent of sales or an analysis of receivables. Using the percent of sales, the adjusting entry is made without regard to the balance of the allowance account. Using the analysis of receivables, the adjusting entry is made so that the balance of the allowance account will equal the estimated uncollectibles at the end of the period.	• Determine the adjustment, bad debt expense, and net realizable value of accounts receivable using the percent of sales method.	9-3	9-3A, 9-3B
	• Determine the adjustment, bad debt expense, and net realizable value of accounts receivable using the analysis of receivables method.	9-4	9-4A, 9-4B

5 Compare the direct write-off and allowance methods of accounting for uncollectible accounts.

Key Points	Key Learning Outcomes	Example Exercises	Practice Exercises
The direct write-off and allowance methods of accounting for uncollectible accounts are recorded differently in the accounts and presented differently in the financial statements. Exhibit 3 illustrates both methods of accounting for uncollectible accounts.	• Describe the differences in accounting for uncollectible accounts under the direct write-off and allowance methods.		
	• Record journal entries using the direct write-off and allowance methods.		

6 Describe the accounting for notes receivable.

Key Points	Key Learning Outcomes	Example Exercises	Practice Exercises
A note received in settlement of an account receivable is recorded as a debit to Notes Receivable and a credit to Accounts Receivable. When a note matures, Cash is debited, Notes Receivable is credited, and Interest Revenue is credited. If the maker of a note fails to pay the debt on the due date, the dishonored note is recorded by debiting an accounts receivable account for the amount of the claim against the maker of the note.	• Describe the characteristics of a note receivable. • Determine the due date and maturity value of a note receivable.	9-5	9-5A, 9-5B
	• Prepare journal entries for the receipt of the payment of a note receivable.	9-5	9-5A, 9-5B
	• Prepare a journal entry for the dishonored note receivable.		

7 Describe the reporting of receivables on the balance sheet.

Key Points	Key Learning Outcomes	Example Exercises	Practice Exercises
All receivables that are expected to be realized in cash within a year are reported in the Current Assets section of the balance sheet in the order in which they can be converted to cash in normal operations. In addition to the allowance for doubtful accounts, additional receivable disclosures include the market (fair) value and unusual credit risks.	• Describe how receivables are reported in the Current Assets section of the balance sheet. • Describe disclosures related to receivables that should be reported in the financial statements.		

Key Terms

accounts receivable (394)
accounts receivable
 turnover (411)
aging the receivables (401)
Allowance for Doubtful
 Accounts (397)

allowance method (395)
bad debt expense (395)
direct write-off method (395)
dishonored note
 receivable (409)
maturity value (408)

net realizable value (397)
notes receivable (394)
number of days' sales
 in receivables (411)
receivables (394)

Illustrative Problem

Ditzler Company, a construction supply company, uses the allowance method of accounting for uncollectible accounts receivable. Selected transactions completed by Ditzler Company are as follows:

Feb.	1.	Sold merchandise on account to Ames Co., $8,000. The cost of the merchandise sold was $4,500.
Mar.	15.	Accepted a 60-day, 12% note for $8,000 from Ames Co. on account.
Apr.	9.	Wrote off a $2,500 account from Dorset Co. as uncollectible.
	21.	Loaned $7,500 cash to Jill Klein, receiving a 90-day, 14% note.
May	14.	Received the interest due from Ames Co. and a new 90-day, 14% note as a renewal of the loan. (Record both the debit and the credit to the notes receivable account.)
June	13.	Reinstated the account of Dorset Co., written off on April 9, and received $2,500 in full payment.
July	20.	Jill Klein dishonored her note.
Aug.	12.	Received from Ames Co. the amount due on its note of May 14.
	19.	Received from Jill Klein the amount owed on the dishonored note, plus interest for 30 days at 15%, computed on the maturity value of the note.
Dec.	16.	Accepted a 60-day, 12% note for $12,000 from Global Company on account.
	31.	It is estimated that 3% of the credit sales of $1,375,000 for the year ended December 31 will be uncollectible.

Instructions

1. Journalize the transactions.
2. Journalize the adjusting entry to record the accrued interest on December 31 on the Global Company note.

Solution

1.

Feb.	1	Accounts Receivable—Ames Co.	8,000.00	
		Sales		8,000.00
	1	Cost of Merchandise Sold	4,500.00	
		Merchandise Inventory		4,500.00
Mar.	15	Notes Receivable—Ames Co.	8,000.00	
		Accounts Receivable—Ames Co.		8,000.00
Apr.	9	Allowance for Doubtful Accounts	2,500.00	
		Accounts Receivable—Dorset Co.		2,500.00
	21	Notes Receivable—Jill Klein	7,500.00	
		Cash		7,500.00
May	14	Notes Receivable—Ames Co.	8,000.00	
		Cash	160.00	
		Notes Receivable—Ames Co.		8,000.00
		Interest Revenue		160.00
June	13	Accounts Receivable—Dorset Co.	2,500.00	
		Allowance for Doubtful Accounts		2,500.00
	13	Cash	2,500.00	
		Accounts Receivable—Dorset Co.		2,500.00
July	20	Accounts Receivable—Jill Klein	7,762.50	
		Notes Receivable—Jill Klein		7,500.00
		Interest Revenue		262.50
Aug.	12	Cash	8,280.00	
		Notes Receivable—Ames Co.		8,000.00
		Interest Revenue		280.00
	19	Cash	7,859.53	
		Accounts Receivable—Jill Klein		7,762.50
		Interest Revenue		97.03
		($7,762.50 × 15% × 30/360).		
Dec.	16	Notes Receivable—Global Company	12,000.00	
		Accounts Receivable—Global Company		12,000.00
	31	Bad Debt Expense	41,250.00	
		Allowance for Doubtful Accounts		41,250.00
		Uncollectible accounts estimate.		
		($1,375,000 × 3%)		

2.

Dec.	31	Interest Receivable	60.00	
		Interest Revenue		60.00
		Accrued interest.		
		($12,000 × 12% × 15/360)		

Self-Examination Questions (Answers at End of Chapter)

1. At the end of the fiscal year, before the accounts are adjusted, Accounts Receivable has a balance of $200,000 and Allowance for Doubtful Accounts has a credit balance of $2,500. If the estimate of uncollectible accounts determined by aging the receivables is $8,500, the amount of bad debt expense is:
   A. $2,500.   C. $8,500.
   B. $6,000.   D. $11,000.

2. At the end of the fiscal year, Accounts Receivable has a balance of $100,000 and Allowance for Doubtful Accounts has a balance of $7,000. The expected net realizable value of the accounts receivable is:
   A. $7,000.   C. $100,000.
   B. $93,000.   D. $107,000.

3. What is the maturity value of a 90-day, 12% note for $10,000?
   A. $8,800   C. $10,300
   B. $10,000   D. $11,200

4. What is the due date of a $12,000, 90-day, 8% note receivable dated August 5?
   A. October 31   C. November 3
   B. November 2   D. November 4

5. When a note receivable is dishonored, Accounts Receivable is debited for what amount?
   A. The face value of the note
   B. The maturity value of the note
   C. The maturity value of the note less accrued interest
   D. The maturity value of the note plus accrued interest

Eye Openers

1. What are the three classifications of receivables?
2. What types of transactions give rise to accounts receivable?
3. In what section of the balance sheet should a note receivable be listed if its term is (a) 90 days, (b) six years?
4. Give two examples of other receivables.
5. Gallatin Hardware is a small hardware store in the rural township of Willow Creek that rarely extends credit to its customers in the form of an account receivable. The few customers that are allowed to carry accounts receivable are long-time residents of Willow Creek and have a history of doing business at Gallatin Hardware. What method of accounting for uncollectible receivables should Gallatin Hardware use? Why?
6. Which of the two methods of accounting for uncollectible accounts provides for the recognition of the expense at the earlier date?
7. What kind of an account (asset, liability, etc.) is Allowance for Doubtful Accounts, and is its normal balance a debit or a credit?
8. After the accounts are adjusted and closed at the end of the fiscal year, Accounts Receivable has a balance of $298,150 and Allowance for Doubtful Accounts has a balance of $31,200. Describe how the accounts receivable and the allowance for doubtful accounts are reported on the balance sheet.
9. A firm has consistently adjusted its allowance account at the end of the fiscal year by adding a fixed percent of the period's net sales on account. After seven years, the balance in Allowance for Doubtful Accounts has become very large in relationship to the balance in Accounts Receivable. Give two possible explanations.
10. Which of the two methods of estimating uncollectibles provides for the most accurate estimate of the current net realizable value of the receivables?
11. For a business, what are the advantages of a note receivable in comparison to an account receivable?
12. Blanchard Company issued a note receivable to Tucker Company. (a) Who is the payee? (b) What is the title of the account used by Tucker Company in recording the note?
13. If a note provides for payment of principal of $90,000 and interest at the rate of 7%, will the interest amount to $6,300? Explain.

14. The maker of a $10,000, 8%, 90-day note receivable failed to pay the note on the due date of June 30. What accounts should be debited and credited by the payee to record the dishonored note receivable?

15. The note receivable dishonored in Eye Opener 14 is paid on July 30 by the maker, plus interest for 30 days, 10%. What entry should be made to record the receipt of the payment?

16. Under what section should accounts receivable be reported on the balance sheet?

Practice Exercises

PE 9-1A
Direct write-off method
obj. 3
EE 9-1   p. 396

Journalize the following transactions using the direct write-off method of accounting for uncollectible receivables:

Sept. 19. Received $100 from Pat Roark and wrote off the remainder owed of $500 as uncollectible.

Dec. 20. Reinstated the account of Pat Roark and received $500 cash in full payment.

PE 9-1B
Direct write-off method
obj. 3
EE 9-1   p. 396

Journalize the following transactions using the direct write-off method of accounting for uncollectible receivables:

Feb. 25. Received $500 from Jason Wilcox and wrote off the remainder owed of $4,000 as uncollectible.

May 9. Reinstated the account of Jason Wilcox and received $4,000 cash in full payment.

PE 9-2A
Allowance method
obj. 4
EE 9-2   p. 399

Journalize the following transactions using the allowance method of accounting for uncollectible receivables:

Sept. 19. Received $100 from Pat Roark and wrote off the remainder owed of $500 as uncollectible.

Dec. 20. Reinstated the account of Pat Roark and received $500 cash in full payment.

PE 9-2B
Allowance method
obj. 4
EE 9-2   p. 399

Journalize the following transactions using the allowance method of accounting for uncollectible receivables:

Feb. 25. Received $500 from Jason Wilcox and wrote off the remainder owed of $4,000 as uncollectible.

May 9. Reinstated the account of Jason Wilcox and received $4,000 cash in full payment.

PE 9-3A
Percent of sales method
obj. 4
EE 9-3   p. 401

At the end of the current year, Accounts Receivable has a balance of $1,400,000; Allowance for Doubtful Accounts has a debit balance of $2,250; and net sales for the year total $9,500,000. Bad debt expense is estimated at ¼ of 1% of net sales.

Determine (1) the amount of the adjusting entry for uncollectible accounts; (2) the adjusted balances of Accounts Receivable, Allowance for Doubtful Accounts, and Bad Debt Expense; and (3) the net realizable value of accounts receivable.

PE 9-3B
Percent of sales method
obj. 4

At the end of the current year, Accounts Receivable has a balance of $750,000; Allowance for Doubtful Accounts has a credit balance of $11,250; and net sales for the year total $4,100,000. Bad debt expense is estimated at ½ of 1% of net sales.

EE 9-3   p. 401

Determine (1) the amount of the adjusting entry for uncollectible accounts; (2) the adjusted balances of Accounts Receivable, Allowance for Doubtful Accounts, and Bad Debt Expense; and (3) the net realizable value of accounts receivable.

PE 9-4A
Analysis of
receivables method

obj. 4

EE 9-4   p. 404

At the end of the current year, Accounts Receivable has a balance of $1,400,000; Allowance for Doubtful Accounts has a debit balance of $2,250; and net sales for the year total $9,500,000. Using the aging method, the balance of Allowance for Doubtful Accounts is estimated as $24,000.

Determine (1) the amount of the adjusting entry for uncollectible accounts; (2) the adjusted balances of Accounts Receivable, Allowance for Doubtful Accounts, and Bad Debt Expense; and (3) the net realizable value of accounts receivable.

PE 9-4B
Analysis of
receivables method

obj. 4

EE 9-4   p. 404

At the end of the current year, Accounts Receivable has a balance of $750,000; Allowance for Doubtful Accounts has a credit balance of $11,250; and net sales for the year total $4,150,000. Using the aging method, the balance of Allowance for Doubtful Accounts is estimated as $30,000.

Determine (1) the amount of the adjusting entry for uncollectible accounts; (2) the adjusted balances of Accounts Receivable, Allowance for Doubtful Accounts, and Bad Debt Expense; and (3) the net realizable value of accounts receivable.

PE 9-5A
Note receivable

obj. 6

EE 9-5   p. 410

Cannondale Supply Company received a 120-day, 9% note for $200,000, dated March 13 from a customer on account.

a. Determine the due date of the note.
b. Determine the maturity value of the note.
c. Journalize the entry to record the receipt of the payment of the note at maturity.

PE 9-5B
Note receivable

obj. 6

EE 9-5   p. 410

Northrop Supply Company received a 30-day, 6% note for $40,000, dated September 23 from a customer on account.

a. Determine the due date of the note.
b. Determine the maturity value of the note.
c. Journalize the entry to record the receipt of the payment of the note at maturity.

Exercises

EX 9-1
Classifications of
receivables

obj. 1

Boeing is one of the world's major aerospace firms, with operations involving commercial aircraft, military aircraft, missiles, satellite systems, and information and battle management systems. As of December 31, 2007, Boeing had $2,838 million of receivables involving U.S. government contracts and $1,232 million of receivables involving commercial aircraft customers, such as Delta Air Lines and United Airlines.
Should Boeing report these receivables separately in the financial statements, or combine them into one overall accounts receivable amount? Explain.

EX 9-2
Nature of
uncollectible
accounts

The MGM Mirage owns and operates casinos including the MGM Grand and the Bellagio in Las Vegas, Nevada. As of December 31, 2007, the MGM Mirage reported accounts and notes receivable of $452,945,000 and allowance for doubtful accounts of $90,024,000.

obj. 2

✔ a. 19.9%

Johnson & Johnson manufactures and sells a wide range of health care products including Band-Aids and Tylenol. As of December 31, 2006, Johnson & Johnson reported accounts receivable of $8,872,000,000 and allowance for doubtful accounts of $160,000,000.

a. Compute the percentage of the allowance for doubtful accounts to the accounts and notes receivable as of December 31, 2006, for The MGM Mirage.

b. Compute the percentage of the allowance for doubtful accounts to the accounts receivable as of December 31, 2006, for Johnson & Johnson.

c. ━━━▶ Discuss possible reasons for the difference in the two ratios computed in (a) and (b).

EX 9-3
Entries for uncollectible accounts, using direct write-off method

obj. 3

Journalize the following transactions in the accounts of Laser Tech Co., a medical equipment company that uses the direct write-off method of accounting for uncollectible receivables:

Feb. 23. Sold merchandise on account to Dr. Judith Salazar, $41,500. The cost of the merchandise sold was $22,300.

May 10. Received $10,000 from Dr. Judith Salazar and wrote off the remainder owed on the sale of February 23 as uncollectible.

Dec. 2. Reinstated the account of Dr. Judith Salazar that had been written off on May 10 and received $31,500 cash in full payment.

EX 9-4
Entries for uncollectible receivables, using allowance method

obj. 4

Journalize the following transactions in the accounts of Food Unlimited Company, a restaurant supply company that uses the allowance method of accounting for uncollectible receivables:

Jan. 18. Sold merchandise on account to Wings Co., $13,200. The cost of the merchandise sold was $9,500.

Mar. 31. Received $5,000 from Wings Co. and wrote off the remainder owed on the sale of January 18 as uncollectible.

Sept. 3. Reinstated the account of Wings Co. that had been written off on March 31 and received $8,200 cash in full payment.

EX 9-5
Entries to write off accounts receivable

objs. 3, 4

Tech Savvy, a computer consulting firm, has decided to write off the $8,375 balance of an account owed by a customer, Nick Wadle. Journalize the entry to record the write-off, assuming that (a) the direct write-off method is used and (b) the allowance method is used.

EX 9-6
Providing for doubtful accounts

obj. 4

✔ a. $23,500
✔ b. $24,800

At the end of the current year, the accounts receivable account has a debit balance of $825,000 and net sales for the year total $9,400,000. Determine the amount of the adjusting entry to provide for doubtful accounts under each of the following assumptions:

a. The allowance account before adjustment has a credit balance of $11,200. Bad debt expense is estimated at ¼ of 1% of net sales.

b. The allowance account before adjustment has a credit balance of $11,200. An aging of the accounts in the customer ledger indicates estimated doubtful accounts of $36,000.

c. The allowance account before adjustment has a debit balance of $6,000. Bad debt expense is estimated at ½ of 1% of net sales.

d. The allowance account before adjustment has a debit balance of $6,000. An aging of the accounts in the customer ledger indicates estimated doubtful accounts of $49,500.

EX 9-7
Number of days past due

Bubba's Auto Supply distributes new and used automobile parts to local dealers throughout the Southeast. Bubba's credit terms are n/30. As of the end of business on July 31, the following accounts receivable were past due:

obj. 4

✔ AAA Pickup
Shop, 62 days

Account	Due Date	Amount
AAA Pickup Shop	May 30	$6,000
Best Auto	July 14	3,000
Downtown Repair	March 18	2,000
Luke's Auto Repair	June 1	5,000
New or Used Auto	June 18	750
Sally's	April 12	2,800
Trident Auto	May 31	1,500
Washburn Repair & Tow	March 13	7,500

Determine the number of days each account is past due.

EX 9-8
**Aging of receivables
schedule**

obj. 4

The accounts receivable clerk for Summit Industries prepared the following partially completed aging of receivables schedule as of the end of business on November 30:

	A	B	C	D	E	F	G
1			Not		Days Past Due		
2			Past				Over
3	Customer	Balance	Due	1–30	31–60	61–90	90
4	Abbott Brothers Inc.	2,000	2,000				
5	Alonso Company	1,500		1,500			
21	Ziel Company	5,000			5,000		
22	Subtotals	807,500	475,000	180,000	78,500	42,300	31,700

The following accounts were unintentionally omitted from the aging schedule and not included in the subtotals above:

Customer	Balance	Due Date
Cottonwood Industries	$14,300	July 6
Fargo Company	17,700	September 17
Garfield Inc.	8,500	October 17
Sadler Company	10,000	November 2
Twitty Company	25,000	December 23

a. Determine the number of days past due for each of the preceding accounts.
b. Complete the aging-of-receivables schedule by including the omitted accounts.

EX 9-9
**Estimating allowance
for doubtful accounts**

obj. 4

✔ $77,800

Summit Industries has a past history of uncollectible accounts, as shown below. Estimate the allowance for doubtful accounts, based on the aging of receivables schedule you completed in Exercise 9-8.

Age Class	Percent Uncollectible
Not past due	1%
1–30 days past due	6
31–60 days past due	20
61–90 days past due	35
Over 90 days past due	50

EX 9-10
**Adjustment for
uncollectible accounts**

obj. 4

Using data in Exercise 9-8, assume that the allowance for doubtful accounts for Summit Industries has a credit balance of $16,175 before adjustment on November 30. Journalize the adjusting entry for uncollectible accounts as of November 30.

EX 9-11
Estimating doubtful accounts

obj. **4**

Fonda Bikes Co. is a wholesaler of motorcycle supplies. An aging of the company's accounts receivable on December 31, 2010, and a historical analysis of the percentage of uncollectible accounts in each age category are as follows:

Age Interval	Balance	Percent Uncollectible
Not past due	$567,000	$\frac{1}{2}$%
1–30 days past due	58,000	3
31–60 days past due	29,000	7
61–90 days past due	20,500	15
91–180 days past due	15,000	40
Over 180 days past due	10,500	75
	$700,000	

Estimate what the proper balance of the allowance for doubtful accounts should be as of December 31, 2010.

EX 9-12
Entry for uncollectible accounts

obj. **4**

Using the data in Exercise 9-11, assume that the allowance for doubtful accounts for Fonda Bikes Co. had a debit balance of $4,145 as of December 31, 2010.
Journalize the adjusting entry for uncollectible accounts as of December 31, 2010.

EX 9-13
Entries for bad debt expense under the direct write-off and allowance methods

obj. **5**

✔ c. $6,025 higher

The following selected transactions were taken from the records of Lights of the West Company for the first year of its operations ending December 31, 2010:

Jan. 24. Wrote off account of J. Huntley, $3,000.
Feb. 17. Received $1,500 as partial payment on the $4,000 account of Karlene Solomon. Wrote off the remaining balance as uncollectible.
May 29. Received $3,000 from J. Huntley, which had been written off on January 24. Reinstated the account and recorded the cash receipt.
Nov. 30. Wrote off the following accounts as uncollectible (record as one journal entry):

Don O'Leary	$2,000
Kim Snider	1,500
Jennifer Kerlin	900
Tracy Lane	1,250
Lynn Fuqua	450

Dec. 31. Lights of the West Company uses the percent of credit sales method of estimating uncollectible accounts expense. Based on past history and industry averages, 1½% of credit sales are expected to be uncollectible. Lights of the West Company recorded $975,000 of credit sales during 2010.

a. Journalize the transactions for 2010 under the direct write-off method.
b. Journalize the transactions for 2010 under the allowance method.
c. ━━━▶ How much higher (lower) would Lights of the West Company's net income have been under the direct write-off method than under the allowance method?

EX 9-14
Entries for bad debt expense under the direct write-off and allowance methods

obj. **5**

✔ c. $17,200 higher

The following selected transactions were taken from the records of Burrito Company for the year ending December 31, 2010:

Mar. 13. Wrote off account of B. Hall, $4,200.
Apr. 19. Received $3,000 as partial payment on the $7,500 account of M. Rainey. Wrote off the remaining balance as uncollectible.
July 9. Received the $4,200 from B. Hall, which had been written off on March 13. Reinstated the account and recorded the cash receipt.
Nov. 23. Wrote off the following accounts as uncollectible (record as one journal entry):

Rai Quinn	$1,200
P. Newman	750
Ned Berry	2,900
Mary Adams	1,675
Nichole Chapin	480

Dec. 31.   The company prepared the following aging schedule for its accounts receivable:

Aging Class (Number of Days Past Due)	Receivables Balance on December 31	Estimated Percent of Uncollectible Accounts
0–30 days	$200,000	2%
31–60 days	75,000	8
61–90 days	24,000	25
91–120 days	9,000	40
More than 120 days	12,000	80
Total receivables	$320,000	

a. Journalize the transactions for 2010 under the direct write-off method.
b. Journalize the transactions for 2010 under the allowance method, assuming that the allowance account had a beginning balance of $12,000 on January 1, 2010, and the company uses the analysis of receivables method.
c. ━━━━▶ How much higher (lower) would Burrito's 2010 net income have been under the direct write-off method than under the allowance method?

EX 9-15
Effect of doubtful accounts on net income
obj. 5

During its first year of operations, Master Plumbing Supply Co. had net sales of $3,500,000, wrote off $50,000 of accounts as uncollectible using the direct write-off method, and reported net income of $390,500. Determine what the net income would have been if the allowance method had been used, and the company estimated that 1¾% of net sales would be uncollectible.

EX 9-16
Effect of doubtful accounts on net income
obj. 5

✔ b. $24,750 credit balance

Using the data in Exercise 9-15, assume that during the second year of operations Master Plumbing Supply Co. had net sales of $4,200,000, wrote off $60,000 of accounts as uncollectible using the direct write-off method, and reported net income of $425,000.

a. Determine what net income would have been in the second year if the allowance method (using 1¾% of net sales) had been used in both the first and second years.
b. Determine what the balance of the allowance for doubtful accounts would have been at the end of the second year if the allowance method had been used in both the first and second years.

EX 9-17
Entries for bad debt expense under the direct write-off and allowance methods
obj. 5

✔ c. $7,000 higher

Isner Company wrote off the following accounts receivable as uncollectible for the first year of its operations ending December 31, 2010:

Customer	Amount
L. Hearn	$10,000
Carrie Murray	9,500
Kelly Salkin	13,100
Shana Wagnon	2,400
Total	$35,000

a. Journalize the write-offs for 2010 under the direct write-off method.
b. Journalize the write-offs for 2010 under the allowance method. Also, journalize the adjusting entry for uncollectible accounts. The company recorded $2,400,000 of credit sales during 2010. Based on past history and industry averages, 1¾% of credit sales are expected to be uncollectible.
c. How much higher (lower) would Isner Company's 2010 net income have been under the direct write-off method than under the allowance method?

EX 9-18
Entries for bad debt
expense under the
direct write-off and
allowance methods

obj. 5

OK International wrote off the following accounts receivable as uncollectible for the year ending December 31, 2010:

Customer	Amount
Eva Fry	$ 6,500
Lance Landau	11,200
Marcie Moffet	3,800
Jose Reis	3,500
Total	$25,000

The company prepared the following aging schedule for its accounts receivable on December 31, 2010:

Aging Class (Number of Days Past Due)	Receivables Balance on December 31	Estimated Percent of Uncollectible Accounts
0–30 days	$480,000	1%
31–60 days	100,000	3
61–90 days	40,000	20
91–120 days	25,000	30
More than 120 days	5,000	40
Total receivables	$650,000	

a. Journalize the write-offs for 2010 under the direct write-off method.
b. Journalize the write-offs and the year-end adjusting entry for 2010 under the allowance method, assuming that the allowance account had a beginning balance of $22,500 on January 1, 2010, and the company uses the analysis of receivables method.

EX 9-19
Determine due date
and interest on notes

obj. 6

✔ d. May 5, $225

Determine the due date and the amount of interest due at maturity on the following notes:

	Date of Note	Face Amount	Interest Rate	Term of Note
a.	October 1	$10,500	8%	60 days
b.	August 30	18,000	10	120 days
c.	May 30	12,000	12	90 days
d.	March 6	15,000	9	60 days
e.	May 23	9,000	10	60 days

EX 9-20
Entries for notes
receivable

obj. 6

✔ b. $40,600

South Bay Interior Decorators issued a 90-day, 6% note for $40,000, dated April 15, to Miami Furniture Company on account.

a. Determine the due date of the note.
b. Determine the maturity value of the note.
c. Journalize the entries to record the following: (1) receipt of the note by Miami Furniture and (2) receipt of payment of the note at maturity.

EX 9-21
Entries for notes
receivable

obj. 6

The series of seven transactions recorded in the following T accounts were related to a sale to a customer on account and the receipt of the amount owed. Briefly describe each transaction.

CASH			NOTES RECEIVABLE		
(7)	30,955		(5)	30,000	(6) 30,000

ACCOUNTS RECEIVABLE			SALES RETURNS AND ALLOWANCES	
(1)	35,000	(3) 5,000	(3)	5,000
(6)	30,750	(5) 30,000		
		(7) 30,750		

MERCHANDISE INVENTORY			COST OF MERCHANDISE SOLD		
(4)	3,000	(2) 21,000	(2)	21,000	(4) 3,000

SALES			INTEREST REVENUE	
		(1) 35,000		(6) 750
				(7) 205

EX 9-22
Entries for notes receivable, including year-end entries
obj. 6

The following selected transactions were completed by Alcor Co., a supplier of Velcro™ for clothing:

2009

Dec. 13.   Received from Penick Clothing & Bags Co., on account, an $84,000, 90-day, 9% note dated December 13.
    31.   Recorded an adjusting entry for accrued interest on the note of December 13.
    31.   Recorded the closing entry for interest revenue.

2010

Mar. 12.   Received payment of note and interest from Penick Clothing & Bags Co.

Journalize the transactions.

EX 9-23
Entries for receipt and dishonor of note receivable
obj. 6

Journalize the following transactions of Funhouse Productions:

July   8.   Received a $120,000, 90-day, 8% note dated July 8 from Mystic Mermaid Company on account.
Oct.   6.   The note is dishonored by Mystic Mermaid Company.
Nov. 5.   Received the amount due on the dishonored note plus interest for 30 days at 10% on the total amount charged to Mystic Mermaid Company on October 6.

EX 9-24
Entries for receipt and dishonor of notes receivable
objs. 4, 6

Journalize the following transactions in the accounts of Lemon Grove Co., which operates a riverboat casino:

Mar. 1.   Received a $30,000, 60-day, 6% note dated March 1 from Bradshaw Co. on account.
    18.   Received a $25,000, 60-day, 9% note dated March 18 from Soto Co. on account.
Apr. 30.   The note dated March 1 from Bradshaw Co. is dishonored, and the customer's account is charged for the note, including interest.
May 17.   The note dated March 18 from Soto Co. is dishonored, and the customer's account is charged for the note, including interest.
July 29.   Cash is received for the amount due on the dishonored note dated March 1 plus interest for 90 days at 8% on the total amount debited to Bradshaw Co. on April 30.
Aug. 23.   Wrote off against the allowance account the amount charged to Soto Co. on May 17 for the dishonored note dated March 18.

EX 9-25
Receivables on the balance sheet
obj. 7

List any errors you can find in the following partial balance sheet:

Jennett Company
Balance Sheet
December 31, 2010

Assets		
Current assets:		
Cash		$ 95,000
Notes receivable	$250,000	
Less interest receivable	15,000	235,000
Accounts receivable	$398,000	
Plus allowance for doubtful accounts	36,000	434,000

Appendix
EX 9-26
Discounting notes receivable

✔ a. $61,800

D. Stoner Co., a building construction company, holds a 120-day, 9% note for $60,000, dated August 7, which was received from a customer on account. On October 6, the note is discounted at the bank at the rate of 12%.

a. Determine the maturity value of the note.
b. Determine the number of days in the discount period.
c. Determine the amount of the discount.
d. Determine the amount of the proceeds.
e. Journalize the entry to record the discounting of the note on October 6.

Appendix
EX 9-27
Entries for receipt
and discounting of
note receivable and
dishonored notes

Journalize the following transactions in the accounts of Zion Theater Productions:

Mar. 1.   Received a $40,000, 90-day, 8% note dated March 1 from Gymboree Company on account.

31.   Discounted the note at Security Credit Bank at 10%.

May 30.   The note is dishonored by Gymboree Company; paid the bank the amount due on the note, plus a protest fee of $200.

June 29.   Received the amount due on the dishonored note plus interest for 30 days at 12% on the total amount charged to Gymboree Company on May 30.

EX 9-28
Accounts receivable
turnover and days'
sales in receivables

✔ a. 2007: 8.4

Polo Ralph Lauren Corporation designs, markets, and distributes a variety of apparel, home decor, accessory, and fragrance products. The company's products include such brands as Polo by Ralph Lauren, Ralph Lauren Purple Label, Ralph Lauren, Polo Jeans Co., and Chaps. Polo Ralph Lauren reported the following (in thousands):

	For the Period Ending	
	March 31, 2007	April 1, 2006
Net sales	$4,295,400	$3,746,300
Accounts receivable	511,900	516,600

Assume that accounts receivable (in millions) were $530,503 at the beginning of the 2006 fiscal year.

a. Compute the accounts receivable turnover for 2007 and 2006. Round to one decimal place.
b. Compute the days' sales in receivables for 2007 and 2006. Round to one decimal place.
c. What conclusions can be drawn from these analyses regarding Ralph Lauren's efficiency in collecting receivables?

EX 9-29
Accounts receivable
turnover and days'
sales in receivables

✔ a. 2007: 9.0

H.J. Heinz Company was founded in 1869 at Sharpsburg, Pennsylvania, by Henry J. Heinz. The company manufactures and markets food products throughout the world, including ketchup, condiments and sauces, frozen food, pet food, soups, and tuna. For the fiscal years 2007 and 2006, H.J. Heinz reported the following (in thousands):

	Year Ending	
	May 2, 2007	May 3, 2006
Net sales	$9,001,630	$8,643,438
Accounts receivable	996,852	1,002,125

Assume that the accounts receivable (in thousands) were $1,092,394 at the beginning of 2006.

a. Compute the accounts receivable turnover for 2007 and 2006. Round to one decimal place.
b. Compute the days' sales in receivables at the end of 2007 and 2006. Round to one decimal place.
c. What conclusions can be drawn from these analyses regarding Heinz's efficiency in collecting receivables?

EX 9-30
Accounts receivable
turnover and days'
sales in receivables

The Limited, Inc., sells women's and men's clothing through specialty retail stores. The Limited sells women's intimate apparel and personal care products through Victoria's Secret and Bath & Body Works stores. The Limited reported the following (in millions):

	For the Period Ending	
	Feb. 3, 2007	Jan. 28, 2006
Net sales	$10,671	$9,699
Accounts receivable	176	182

Assume that accounts receivable (in millions) were $128 on January 29, 2005.

a. Compute the accounts receivable turnover for 2007 and 2006. Round to one decimal place.
b. Compute the day's sales in receivables for 2007 and 2006. Round to one decimal place.
c. 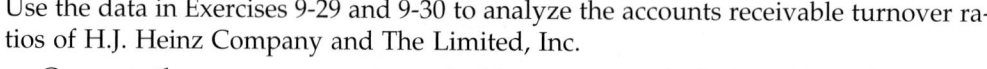 What conclusions can be drawn from these analyses regarding The Limited's efficiency in collecting receivables?

EX 9-31
Accounts receivable turnover

Use the data in Exercises 9-29 and 9-30 to analyze the accounts receivable turnover ratios of H.J. Heinz Company and The Limited, Inc.

a. Compute the average accounts receivable turnover ratio for The Limited, Inc., and H.J. Heinz Company for the years shown in Exercises 9-29 and 9-30.
b. ━━━ Does The Limited or H.J. Heinz Company have the higher average accounts receivable turnover ratio?
c. ━━━ Explain the logic underlying your answer in (b).

Problems Series A ● ● ● ● ● 》

PR 9-1A
Entries related to uncollectible accounts

obj. 4

KLOOSTER & ALLEN

✔ 3. $918,750

The following transactions were completed by The Bronze Gallery during the current fiscal year ended December 31:

June 6. Reinstated the account of Ian Netti, which had been written off in the preceding year as uncollectible. Journalized the receipt of $1,945 cash in full payment of Ian's account.

July 19. Wrote off the $11,150 balance owed by Rancho Rigging Co., which is bankrupt.

Aug. 13. Received 35% of the $20,000 balance owed by Santori Co., a bankrupt business, and wrote off the remainder as uncollectible.

Sept. 2. Reinstated the account of Sheryl Capers, which had been written off two years earlier as uncollectible. Recorded the receipt of $3,170 cash in full payment.

Dec. 31. Wrote off the following accounts as uncollectible (compound entry): Jacoba Co., $8,390; Garcia Co., $2,500; Summit Furniture, $6,400; Jill DePuy, $1,800.

31. Based on an analysis of the $960,750 of accounts receivable, it was estimated that $42,000 will be uncollectible. Journalized the adjusting entry.

Instructions
1. Record the January 1 credit balance of $40,000 in a T account for Allowance for Doubtful Accounts.
2. Journalize the transactions. Post each entry that affects the following T accounts and determine the new balances:

Allowance for Doubtful Accounts
Bad Debt Expense

3. Determine the expected net realizable value of the accounts receivable as of December 31.
4. Assuming that instead of basing the provision for uncollectible accounts on an analysis of receivables, the adjusting entry on December 31 had been based on an estimated expense of $3/4$ of 1% of the net sales of $6,000,000 for the year, determine the following:
a. Bad debt expense for the year.
b. Balance in the allowance account after the adjustment of December 31.
c. Expected net realizable value of the accounts receivable as of December 31.

PR 9-2A

Aging of receivables; estimating allowance for doubtful accounts

obj. 4

✔ 3. $67,210

Wigs Plus Company supplies wigs and hair care products to beauty salons throughout California and the Pacific Northwest. The accounts receivable clerk for Wigs Plus prepared the following partially completed aging of receivables schedule as of the end of business on December 31, 2009:

	A	B	C	D	E	F	G	H
1			Not		Days Past Due			
2			Past					
3	Customer	Balance	Due	1–30	31–60	61–90	91–120	Over 120
4	Alpha Beauty	20,000	20,000					
5	Blonde Wigs	11,000			11,000			
30	Zahn's Beauty	2,900		2,900				
31	Subtotals	900,000	498,600	217,250	98,750	33,300	29,950	22,150

The following accounts were unintentionally omitted from the aging schedule:

Customer	Due Date	Balance
Sun Coast Beauty	May 30, 2009	$2,850
Paradise Beauty Store	Sept. 15, 2009	6,050
Helix Hair Products	Oct. 17, 2009	800
Hairy's Hair Care	Oct. 20, 2009	2,000
Surf Images	Nov. 18, 2009	700
Oh The Hair	Nov. 29, 2009	3,500
Mountain Coatings	Dec. 1, 2009	2,250
Lasting Images	Jan. 9, 2010	7,400

Wigs Plus has a past history of uncollectible accounts by age category, as follows:

Age Class	Percent Uncollectible
Not past due	2%
1–30 days past due	4
31–60 days past due	10
61–90 days past due	15
91–120 days past due	35
Over 120 days past due	80

Instructions

1. Determine the number of days past due for each of the preceding accounts.
2. Complete the aging of receivables schedule.
3. Estimate the allowance for doubtful accounts, based on the aging of receivables schedule.
4. Assume that the allowance for doubtful accounts for Wigs Plus has a credit balance of $1,710 before adjustment on December 31, 2009. Journalize the adjustment for uncollectible accounts.

PR 9-3A

Compare two methods of accounting for uncollectible receivables

objs. 3, 4, 5

✔ 1. Year 4: Balance of allowance account, end of year, $13,350

J. J. Technology Company, which operates a chain of 30 electronics supply stores, has just completed its fourth year of operations. The direct write-off method of recording bad debt expense has been used during the entire period. Because of substantial increases in sales volume and the amount of uncollectible accounts, the firm is considering changing to the allowance method. Information is requested as to the effect that an annual provision of $\frac{1}{2}\%$ of sales would have had on the amount of bad debt expense reported for each of the past four years. It is also considered desirable to know what the balance of Allowance for Doubtful Accounts would have been at the end of each year. The following data have been obtained from the accounts:

			Year of Origin of Accounts Receivable Written Off as Uncollectible			
Year	Sales	Uncollectible Accounts Written Off	1st	2nd	3rd	4th
1st	$1,300,000	$ 1,200	$1,200			
2nd	$1,750,000	3,000	1,400	$1,600		
3rd	$3,000,000	13,000	3,800	3,000	$6,200	
4th	$3,600,000	17,700		4,000	6,100	$7,600

Instructions

1. Assemble the desired data, using the following column headings:

	Bad Debt Expense			
Year	Expense Actually Reported	Expense Based on Estimate	Increase (Decrease) in Amount of Expense	Balance of Allowance Account, End of Year

2. ➤ Experience during the first four years of operations indicated that the receivables were either collected within two years or had to be written off as uncollectible. Does the estimate of $\frac{1}{2}$% of sales appear to be reasonably close to the actual experience with uncollectible accounts originating during the first two years? Explain.

PR 9-4A
Details of notes receivable and related entries

obj. 6

✔1. Note 2: Due date, Sept. 13; Interest due at maturity, $150

Boutique Ads Co. produces advertising videos. During the last six months of the current fiscal year, Boutique Ads Co. received the following notes:

	Date	Face Amount	Term	Interest Rate
1.	May 9	$19,200	45 days	9%
2.	July 15	11,250	60 days	8
3.	Aug. 1	43,200	90 days	7
4.	Sept. 4	20,000	90 days	6
5.	Nov. 26	13,500	60 days	8
6.	Dec. 16	21,600	60 days	13

Instructions

1. Determine for each note (a) the due date and (b) the amount of interest due at maturity, identifying each note by number.
2. Journalize the entry to record the dishonor of Note (3) on its due date.
3. Journalize the adjusting entry to record the accrued interest on Notes (5) and (6) on December 31.
4. Journalize the entries to record the receipt of the amounts due on Notes (5) and (6) in January and February.

PR 9-5A
Notes receivable entries

obj. 6

The following data relate to notes receivable and interest for Vidovich Co., a financial services company. (All notes are dated as of the day they are received.)

Mar. 3.   Received a $72,000, 9%, 60-day note on account.
      25.   Received a $10,000, 8%, 90-day note on account.
May   2.   Received $73,080 on note of March 3.
      16.   Received a $40,000, 7%, 90-day note on account.
      31.   Received a $25,000, 6%, 30-day note on account.
June 23.   Received $10,200 on note of March 25.
      30.   Received $25,125 on note of May 31.
July   1.   Received a $7,500, 12%, 30-day note on account.
      31.   Received $7,575 on note of July 1.
Aug. 14.   Received $40,700 on note of May 16.

Instructions

Journalize the entries to record the transactions.

PR 9-6A
Sales and notes receivable transactions

obj. 6

The following were selected from among the transactions completed during the current year by Bonita Co., an appliance wholesale company:

Jan. 20.   Sold merchandise on account to Wilding Co., $30,750. The cost of merchandise sold was $18,600.
Mar. 3.   Accepted a 60-day, 8% note for $30,750 from Wilding Co. on account.
May   2.   Received from Wilding Co. the amount due on the note of March 3.
June 10.   Sold merchandise on account to Foyers for $13,600. The cost of merchandise sold was $8,200.

June 15.   Loaned $18,000 cash to Michele Hobson, receiving a 30-day, 6% note.

20.   Received from Foyers the amount due on the invoice of June 10, less 2% discount.

July 15.   Received the interest due from Michele Hobson and a new 60-day, 9% note as a renewal of the loan of June 15. (Record both the debit and the credit to the notes receivable account.)

Sept. 13.   Received from Michele Hobson the amount due on her note of July 15.

13.   Sold merchandise on account to Rainbow Co., $20,000. The cost of merchandise sold was $11,500.

Oct. 12.   Accepted a 60-day, 6% note for $20,000 from Rainbow Co. on account.

Dec. 11.   Rainbow Co. dishonored the note dated October 12.

26.   Received from Rainbow Co. the amount owed on the dishonored note, plus interest for 15 days at 12% computed on the maturity value of the note.

Instructions
Journalize the transactions.

Problems Series B

PR 9-1B
Entries related to uncollectible accounts

obj. 4

KLOOSTER
& ALLEN

✔ 3. $750,375

The following transactions were completed by Interia Management Company during the current fiscal year ended December 31:

Feb. 24.   Received 40% of the $18,000 balance owed by Broudy Co., a bankrupt business, and wrote off the remainder as uncollectible.

May 3.   Reinstated the account of Irma Alonso, which had been written off in the preceding year as uncollectible. Journalized the receipt of $1,725 cash in full payment of Alonso's account.

Aug. 9.   Wrote off the $3,600 balance owed by Tux Time Co., which has no assets.

Nov. 20.   Reinstated the account of Pexis Co., which had been written off in the preceding year as uncollectible. Journalized the receipt of $6,140 cash in full payment of the account.

Dec. 31.   Wrote off the following accounts as uncollectible (compound entry): Siena Co., $2,400; Kommers Co., $1,800; Butte Distributors, $6,000; Ed Ballantyne, $1,750.

31.   Based on an analysis of the $768,375 of accounts receivable, it was estimated that $18,000 will be uncollectible. Journalized the adjusting entry.

Instructions
1. Record the January 1 credit balance of $15,500 in a T account for Allowance for Doubtful Accounts.
2. Journalize the transactions. Post each entry that affects the following selected T accounts and determine the new balances:

Allowance for Doubtful Accounts
Bad Debt Expense

3. Determine the expected net realizable value of the accounts receivable as of December 31.
4. Assuming that instead of basing the provision for uncollectible accounts on an analysis of receivables, the adjusting entry on December 31 had been based on an estimated expense of ½ of 1% of the net sales of $4,100,000 for the year, determine the following:
    a. Bad debt expense for the year.
    b. Balance in the allowance account after the adjustment of December 31.
    c. Expected net realizable value of the accounts receivable as of December 31.

PR 9-2B
Aging of receivables; estimating allowance for doubtful accounts

obj. 4

✔ 3. $72,270

Cutthroat Company supplies flies and fishing gear to sporting goods stores and outfitters throughout the western United States. The accounts receivable clerk for Cutthroat prepared the following partially completed aging of receivables schedule as of the end of business on December 31, 2009:

	A	B	C	D	E	F	G	H
1			Not		Days Past Due			
2			Past					
3	Customer	Balance	Due	1–30	31–60	61–90	91–120	Over 120
4	Alder Fishery	15,000	15,000					
5	Brown Trout	5,500			5,500			
30	Zug Bug Sports	2,900		2,900				
31	Subtotals	850,000	422,450	247,250	103,850	33,300	25,000	18,150

The following accounts were unintentionally omitted from the aging schedule:

Customer	Due Date	Balance
AAA Sports & Flies	June 14, 2009	$2,850
Blackmon Flies	Aug. 30, 2009	1,200
Charlie's Fish Co.	Sept. 30, 2009	1,800
Firehole Sports	Oct. 17, 2009	600
Green River Sports	Nov. 7, 2009	950
Smith River Co.	Nov. 28, 2009	2,200
Wintson Company	Dec. 1, 2009	2,250
Wolfe Bug Sports	Jan. 6, 2010	6,550

Cutthroat Company has a past history of uncollectible accounts by age category, as follows:

Age Class	Percent Uncollectible
Not past due	2%
1–30 days past due	5
31–60 days past due	10
61–90 days past due	25
91–120 days past due	45
Over 120 days past due	90

Instructions
1. Determine the number of days past due for each of the preceding accounts.
2. Complete the aging of receivables schedule.
3. Estimate the allowance for doubtful accounts, based on the aging of receivables schedule.
4. Assume that the allowance for doubtful accounts for Cutthroat Company has a debit balance of $1,370 before adjustment on December 31, 2009. Journalize the adjusting entry for uncollectible accounts.

PR 9-3B
Compare two methods of accounting for uncollectible receivables

objs. 3, 4, 5

✔ 1. Year 4: Balance of allowance account, end of year, $13,700

Maywood Company, a telephone service and supply company, has just completed its fourth year of operations. The direct write-off method of recording bad debt expense has been used during the entire period. Because of substantial increases in sales volume and the amount of uncollectible accounts, the firm is considering changing to the allowance method. Information is requested as to the effect that an annual provision of $^3/_4$% of sales would have had on the amount of bad debt expense reported for each of the past four years. It is also considered desirable to know what the balance of Allowance for Doubtful Accounts would have been at the end of each year. The following data have been obtained from the accounts:

Year	Sales	Uncollectible Accounts Written off	Year of Origin of Accounts Receivable Written Off as Uncollectible: 1st	2nd	3rd	4th
1st	$ 680,000	$2,600	$2,600			
2nd	800,000	3,100	2,000	$1,100		
3rd	1,000,000	6,000	750	4,200	$1,050	
4th	2,000,000	8,200		1,260	2,700	$4,240

Instructions

1. Assemble the desired data, using the following column headings:

	Bad Debt Expense			
Year	Expense Actually Reported	Expense Based on Estimate	Increase (Decrease) in Amount of Expense	Balance of Allowance Account, End of Year

2. Experience during the first four years of operations indicated that the receivables were either collected within two years or had to be written off as uncollectible. Does the estimate of ¾% of sales appear to be reasonably close to the actual experience with uncollectible accounts originating during the first two years? Explain.

PR 9-4B
Details of notes receivable and related entries

obj. 6

✔ 1. Note 2: Due date, July 26; Interest due at maturity, $185

Hauser Co. wholesales bathroom fixtures. During the current fiscal year, Hauser Co. received the following notes:

	Date	Face Amount	Term	Interest Rate
1.	Apr. 4	$30,000	60 days	8%
2.	June 26	18,500	30 days	12
3.	July 5	16,200	120 days	6
4.	Oct. 31	36,000	60 days	9
5.	Nov. 23	21,000	60 days	6
6.	Dec. 27	40,500	30 days	12

Instructions

1. Determine for each note (a) the due date and (b) the amount of interest due at maturity, identifying each note by number.
2. Journalize the entry to record the dishonor of Note (3) on its due date.
3. Journalize the adjusting entry to record the accrued interest on Notes (5) and (6) on December 31.
4. Journalize the entries to record the receipt of the amounts due on Notes (5) and (6) in January.

PR 9-5B
Notes receivable entries

obj. 6

The following data relate to notes receivable and interest for Optic Co., a cable manufacturer and supplier. (All notes are dated as of the day they are received.)

June 10.	Received a $15,000, 9%, 60-day note on account.
July 13.	Received a $54,000, 10%, 120-day note on account.
Aug. 9.	Received $15,225 on note of June 10.
Sept. 4.	Received a $24,000, 9%, 60-day note on account.
Nov. 3.	Received $24,360 on note of September 4.
5.	Received a $24,000, 7%, 30-day note on account.
10.	Received $55,800 on note of July 13.
30.	Received a $15,000, 10%, 30-day note on account.
Dec. 5.	Received $24,140 on note of November 5.
30.	Received $15,125 on note of November 30.

Instructions

Journalize entries to record the transactions.

PR 9-6B
Sales and notes receivable transactions

obj. 6

The following were selected from among the transactions completed by Mair Co. during the current year. Mair Co. sells and installs home and business security systems.

Jan. 10. Loaned $12,000 cash to Jas Caudel, receiving a 90-day, 8% note.

Feb. 4. Sold merchandise on account to Periman & Co., $28,000. The cost of the merchandise sold was $16,500.

13. Sold merchandise on account to Centennial Co., $30,000. The cost of merchandise sold was $17,600.

Mar. 6. Accepted a 60-day, 6% note for $28,000 from Periman & Co. on account.

14. Accepted a 60-day, 12% note for $30,000 from Centennial Co. on account.

Apr. 10. Received the interest due from Jas Caudel and a new 90-day, 10% note as a renewal of the loan of January 10. (Record both the debit and the credit to the notes receivable account.)

May 5. Received from Periman & Co. the amount due on the note of March 6.

13. Centennial Co. dishonored its note dated March 14.

June 12. Received from Centennial Co. the amount owed on the dishonored note, plus interest for 30 days at 12% computed on the maturity value of the note.

July 9. Received from Jas Caudel the amount due on his note of April 10.

Aug. 10. Sold merchandise on account to Lindenfield Co., $13,600. The cost of the merchandise sold was $8,000.

20. Received from Lindenfield Co. the amount of the invoice of August 10, less 1% discount.

Instructions
Journalize the transactions.

Special Activities

You can access the special activities online at **www.cengage.com/accounting/reeve**.

Excel Success Special Activities

SA 9-1
Aging of receivables schedule

Brandy Company wholesales grocery food products to grocery stores. The accounts receivable clerk for Brandy Company prepared the following partially completed aging of receivables schedule on December 31, 2011.

	A	B	C	D	E	F	G	H
1			Not	Days Past Due				
2			Past					Over
3	Customer	Balance	Due	1-30	31-60	61-90	91-180	180
4	Aslan, T.L.	580	500	80				
5	Cheney, M.	930	130			800		
6	Field Stores Inc.	2,400	2,000	400				
7	Oakland City Stores	1,500	1,250	50	50			150
8	River Grocery	1,480	580	500	400			
9	Whitley, D.	960	300				660	
10	Total							

Brandy Company has a past history of uncollectible accounts by age category, as follows:

Age Class	Percent Uncollectible
Not past due	1%
1–30 days past due	3%
31–60 days past due	7%
61–90 days past due	10%
91–180 days past due	15%
Over 180 days past due	20%

a. Open the Excel file *SA9-1*.
b. Complete the aging of receivables schedule by using spreadsheet software.
c. Estimate the allowance for doubtful accounts, based on the aging of receivables schedule.
d. Assume that after additional historical analysis, the accounts receivable clerk revised the percent uncollectible as follows:

Age Class	Percent Uncollectible
Not past due	1%
1–30 days past due	2%
31–60 days past due	7%
61–90 days past due	12%
91–180 days past due	20%
Over 180 days past due	40%

e. Determine the estimate for the allowance for doubtful accounts under the revised percent uncollectible assumptions.
f. When you have completed the receivables aging schedule, perform a "save as," replacing the entire file name with the following:

SA9-1_[your first name initial]_[your last name]

SA 9-2

Aging of receivables schedule

e**X**cel
success

The Lawson Company accounts receivable clerk assembled customer data at year-end as follows:

Customer Name	Accounts Receivable Balance	Number of Days Past Due
Kress, T.	$2,400	Not past due
Bradley, V.	1,580	14
Silver, K.	500	123
Ng, N.	950	75
Horowitz, S.	670	41
Stevens, K.	3,100	Not past due
Wilde, P.	240	68
Total	$9,440	

A past history of uncollectible accounts was used to develop the following:

Age Class	Percent Uncollectible
Not past due	3%
1–30 days past due	8%
31–60 days past due	14%
61–90 days past due	20%
Over 90 days past due	30%

a. Open the Excel file *SA9-2*.
b. Prepare an aging of receivables schedule using spreadsheet software. Use the Data-Sort command to alphabetize the input data in the customer balance table.
c. Estimate the allowance for doubtful accounts, based on the aging of receivables schedule.
d. When you have completed the receivables aging schedule, perform a "save as," replacing the entire file name with the following:

SA9-2_[your first name initial]_[your last name]

SA 9-3

Determine interest on notes

Determine the amount of interest due at maturity on the following notes:

	Face Amount	Interest Rate	Term of Note
a.	$24,000	5%	60 days
b.	94,000	4%	45 days
c.	49,000	6%	90 days
d.	16,000	7%	36 days
e.	55,000	6%	30 days

a. Open the Excel file *SA9-3*.

b. When you have determined the interest calculation, perform a "save as," replacing the entire file name with the following:

SA9-3_[your first name initial]_[your last name]

SA 9-4

Entries for notes receivable, including year-end interest adjustment, is as follows:

2011

Dec. 11. Received a $56,000, 45-day, 4.5% noted dated Dec. 11 from Kimberly Co. on account.

31. Recorded an adjusting entry for accrued interest on the note of December 11.

31. Recorded the closing entry for interest revenue.

2012

Jan. 25. Received payment of note and interest from Kimberly Co.

a. Open the Excel file *SA9-4*.

b. Prepare a spreadsheet to determine the accrued interest on December 31, 2011, and interest earned on January 25, 2012.

c. When you have determined the interest calculation, perform a "save as," replacing the entire file name with the following:

SA9-4_[your first name initial]_[your last name]

Answers to Self-Examination Questions

1. **B** The estimate of uncollectible accounts, $8,500 (answer C), is the amount of the desired balance of Allowance for Doubtful Accounts after adjustment. The amount of the current provision to be made for uncollectible accounts expense is thus $6,000 (answer B), which is the amount that must be added to the Allowance for Doubtful Accounts credit balance of $2,500 (answer A) so that the account will have the desired balance of $8,500.

2. **B** The amount expected to be realized from accounts receivable is the balance of Accounts Receivable, $100,000, less the balance of Allowance for Doubtful Accounts, $7,000, or $93,000 (answer B).

3. **C** Maturity value is the amount that is due at the maturity or due date. The maturity value of $10,300 (answer C) is determined as follows:

Face amount of note	$10,000
Plus interest ($10,000 × 0.12 × 90/360)	300
Maturity value of note	$10,300

4. **C** November 3 is the due date of a $12,000, 90-day, 8% note receivable dated August 5 [26 days in August (31 days − 5 days) + 30 days in September + 31 days in October + 3 days in November].

5. **B** If a note is dishonored, Accounts Receivable is debited for the maturity value of the note (answer B). The maturity value of the note is its face value (answer A) plus the accrued interest. The maturity value of the note less accrued interest (answer C) is equal to the face value of the note. The maturity value of the note plus accrued interest (answer D) is incorrect, since the interest would be added twice.

Fixed Assets and Intangible Assets

F A T B U R G E R   I N C.

Do you remember purchasing your first car? You probably didn't buy your first car like you would buy a CD. Purchasing a new or used car is expensive. In addition, you would drive (use) the car for the next 3–5 years or longer. As a result, you might spend hours or weeks considering different makes and models, safety ratings, warranties, and operating costs before deciding on the final purchase.

Like buying her first car, Lovie Yancey spent a lot of time before deciding to open her first restaurant. In 1952, she created the biggest, juiciest hamburger that anyone had ever seen. She called it a Fatburger. The restaurant initially started as a 24-hour operation to cater to the schedules of professional musicians. As a fan of popular music and its performers, Yancey played rhythm and blues, jazz, and blues recordings for her customers. Fatburger's popularity with entertainers was illustrated when its name was used in a 1992 rap by Ice Cube. "Two in the mornin' got the Fatburger," Cube said, in "It Was a Good Day," a track on his *Predator* album.

The demand for this incredible burger was such that, in 1980, Ms. Yancey decided to offer Fatburger franchise opportunities. In 1990, with the goal of expanding Fatburger throughout the world, Fatburger Inc. purchased the business from Ms. Yancey. Today, Fatburger has grown to a multi-restaurant chain with owners and investors such as talk show host Montel Williams, Cincinnati Bengals' tackle Willie Anderson, comedian David Spade, and musicians Cher, Janet Jackson, and Pharrell.

So, how much would it cost you to open a Fatburger restaurant? The total investment begins at over $750,000 per restaurant. Thus, in starting a Fatburger restaurant, you would be making a significant investment that would affect your life for years to come. In this chapter, we discuss the accounting for investments in fixed assets such as those used to open a Fatburger restaurant. We also explain how to determine the portion of the fixed asset that becomes an expense over time. Finally, we discuss the accounting for the disposal of fixed assets and accounting for intangible assets such as patents and copyrights. **http://www .fatburger.com**

After studying this chapter, you should be able to:

1 Define, classify, and account for the cost of fixed assets.

2 Compute depreciation, using the following methods: straight-line method, units-of-production method, and double-declining-balance method.

3 Journalize entries for the disposal of fixed assets.

4 Compute depletion and journalize the entry for depletion.

5 Describe the accounting for intangible assets, such as patents, copyrights, and goodwill.

6 Describe how depreciation expense is reported in an income statement and prepare a balance sheet that includes fixed assets and intangible assets.

Nature of Fixed Assets

Classifying Costs

The Cost of Fixed Assets

Capital and Revenue Expenditures

EE 10-1 (page 442)

Leasing Fixed Assets

Accounting for Depreciation

Factors in Computing Depreciation Expense

Straight-Line Method
EE 10-2 (page 446)

Units-of-Production Method
EE 10-3 (page 447)

Double-Declining-Balance Method
EE 10-4 (page 448)

Comparing Depreciation Methods

Depreciation for Federal Income Tax

Revising Depreciation Estimates
EE 10-5 (page 451)

Disposal of Fixed Assets

Discarding Fixed Assets

Selling Fixed Assets
EE 10-6 (page 454)

Natural Resources
EE 10-7 (page 455)

Intangible Assets

Patents

Copyrights and Trademarks

Goodwill
EE 10-8 (page 458)

Financial Reporting for Fixed Assets and Intangible Assets

At a Glance | Menu | Turn to pg 462

South-Western

1 Define, classify, and account for the cost of fixed assets.

Nature of Fixed Assets

Fixed assets are long-term or relatively permanent assets such as equipment, machinery, buildings, and land. Other descriptive titles for fixed assets are *plant assets* or *property, plant, and equipment*. Fixed assets have the following characteristics:

1. They exist physically and, thus, are *tangible* assets.
2. They are owned and used by the company in its normal operations.
3. They are not offered for sale as part of normal operations.

Exhibit 1 shows the percent of fixed assets to total assets for some select companies. As shown in Exhibit 1, fixed assets are often a significant portion of the total assets of a company.

Exhibit 1

Fixed Assets as a Percent of Total Assets— Selected Companies

	Fixed Assets as a Percent of Total Assets
Alcoa Inc.	40%
ExxonMobil Corporation	60
Ford Motor Company	35
Kroger	55
Marriott International, Inc.	31
United Parcel Service, Inc.	53
Verizon Communications	45
Walgreen Co.	46
Wal-Mart	53

Classifying Costs

A cost that has been incurred may be classified as a fixed asset, an investment, or an expense. Exhibit 2 shows how to determine the proper classification of a cost and, thus, how it should be recorded. As shown in Exhibit 2, classifying a cost involves the following steps:

Step 1. Is the purchased item (cost) long-lived?

If *yes*, the item is capitalized as an asset on the balance sheet as either a fixed asset or an investment. Proceed to Step 2.

If *no*, the item is classified and recorded as an *expense*.

Step 2. Is the asset used in normal operations?

If *yes*, the asset is classified and recorded as a *fixed asset*.

If *no*, the asset is classified and recorded as an *investment*.

Costs that are classified and recorded as fixed assets include the purchase of land, buildings, or equipment. Such assets normally last more than a year and are used in

Exhibit 2

Classifying Costs

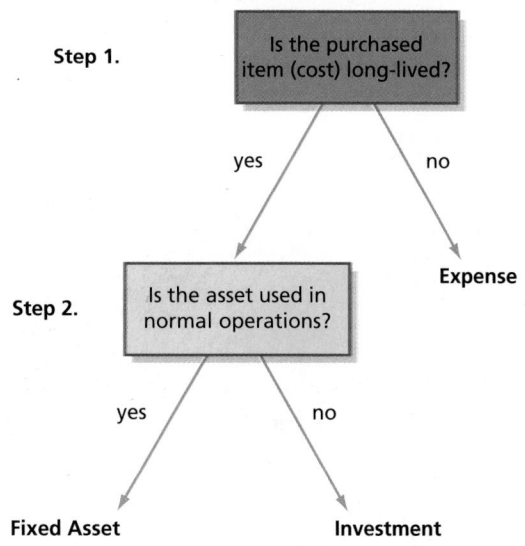

Step 1.   Is the purchased item (cost) long-lived?

yes   no

Expense

Step 2.   Is the asset used in normal operations?

yes   no

Fixed Asset   Investment

the normal operations. However, standby equipment for use during peak periods or when other equipment breaks down is still classified as a fixed asset even though it is not used very often. In contrast, fixed assets that have been abandoned or are no longer used in operations are not fixed assets.

Although fixed assets may be sold, they should not be offered for sale as part of normal operations. For example, cars and trucks offered for sale by an automotive dealership are not fixed assets of the dealership. On the other hand, a tow truck used in the normal operations of the dealership is a fixed asset of the dealership.

Investments are long-lived assets that are not used in the normal operations and are held for future resale. Such assets are reported on the balance sheet in a section entitled *Investments*. For example, undeveloped land acquired for future resale would be classified and reported as an investment, not land.

The Cost of Fixed Assets

The costs of acquiring fixed assets include all amounts spent to get the asset in place and ready for use. For example, freight costs and the costs of installing equipment are part of the asset's total cost.

Exhibit 3 summarizes some of the common costs of acquiring fixed assets. These costs are recorded by debiting the related fixed asset account, such as Land,[1] Building, Land Improvements, or Machinery and Equipment.

Exhibit 3

Costs of Acquiring Fixed Assets

Building	Machinery & Equipment	Land
• Architects' fees	• Sales taxes	• Purchase price
• Engineers' fees	• Freight	• Sales taxes
• Insurance costs incurred during construction	• Installation	• Permits from government agencies
• Interest on money borrowed to finance construction	• Repairs (purchase of used equipment)	• Broker's commissions
• Walkways to and around the building	• Reconditioning (purchase of used equipment)	• Title fees
• Sales taxes	• Insurance while in transit	• Surveying fees
• Repairs (purchase of existing building)	• Assembly	• Delinquent real estate taxes
• Reconditioning (purchase of existing building)	• Modifying for use	• Removing unwanted building less any salvage
• Modifying for use	• Testing for use	• Grading and leveling
• Permits from government agencies	• Permits from government agencies	• Paving a public street bordering the land

Land Improvements

• Trees and shrubs
• Fences
• Outdoor lighting
• Paved parking areas

---

1 As discussed here, land is assumed to be used only as a location or site and not for its mineral deposits or other natural resources.

Only costs necessary for preparing the fixed asset for use are included as a cost of the asset. Unnecessary costs that do not increase the asset's usefulness are recorded as an expense. For example, the following costs are included as an expense:

1. Vandalism
2. Mistakes in installation
3. Uninsured theft
4. Damage during unpacking and installing
5. Fines for not obtaining proper permits from governmental agencies

Intel Corporation recently reported almost $3 billion of construction in progress, which was 7% of its total fixed assets.

A company may incur costs associated with constructing a fixed asset such as a new building. The direct costs incurred in the construction, such as labor and materials, should be capitalized as a debit to an account entitled Construction in Progress. When the construction is complete, the costs are reclassified by crediting Construction in Progress and debiting the proper fixed asset account such as Building. For some companies, construction in progress can be significant.

Capital and Revenue Expenditures

Once a fixed asset has been acquired and placed in service, costs may be incurred for ordinary maintenance and repairs. In addition, costs may be incurred for improving an asset or for extraordinary repairs that extend the asset's useful life. Costs that benefit only the current period are called **revenue expenditures**. Costs that improve the asset or extend its useful life are **capital expenditures**.

Ordinary Maintenance and Repairs Costs related to the ordinary maintenance and repairs of a fixed asset are recorded as an expense of the current period. Such expenditures are *revenue expenditures* and are recorded as increases to Repairs and Maintenance Expense. For example, $300 paid for a tune-up of a delivery truck is recorded as follows:

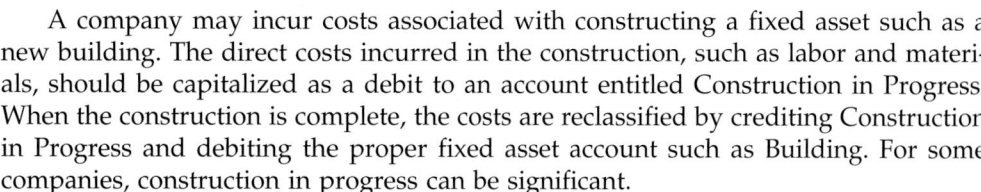

	Repairs and Maintenance Expense	300	
	Cash		300

Asset Improvements After a fixed asset has been placed in service, costs may be incurred to improve the asset. For example, the service value of a delivery truck might be improved by adding a $5,500 hydraulic lift to allow for easier and quicker loading of cargo. Such costs are *capital expenditures* and are recorded as increases to the fixed asset account. In the case of the hydraulic lift, the expenditure is recorded as follows:

	Delivery Truck	5,500	
	Cash		5,500

Because the cost of the delivery truck has increased, depreciation for the truck would also change over its remaining useful life.

Extraordinary Repairs After a fixed asset has been placed in service, costs may be incurred to extend the asset's useful life. For example, the engine of a forklift that is near the end of its useful life may be overhauled at a cost of $4,500, extending its useful life by eight years. Such costs are *capital expenditures* and are recorded as a decrease in an accumulated depreciation account. In the case of the fork-lift, the expenditure is recorded as follows:

	Accumulated Depreciation—Forklift	4,500	
	Cash		4,500

Integrity, Objectivity, and Ethics in Business

CAPITAL CRIME

One of the largest alleged accounting frauds in history involved the improper accounting for capital expenditures. WorldCom, the second largest telecommunications company in the United States at the time, improperly treated maintenance expenditures on its telecommunications network as capital expenditures. As a result, the company had to restate its prior years' earnings downward by nearly $4 billion to correct this error. The company declared bankruptcy within months of disclosing the error, and the CEO was sentenced to 25 years in prison.

Because the forklift's remaining useful life has changed, depreciation for the forklift would also change based on the new book value of the forklift.

The accounting for revenue and capital expenditures is summarized below.

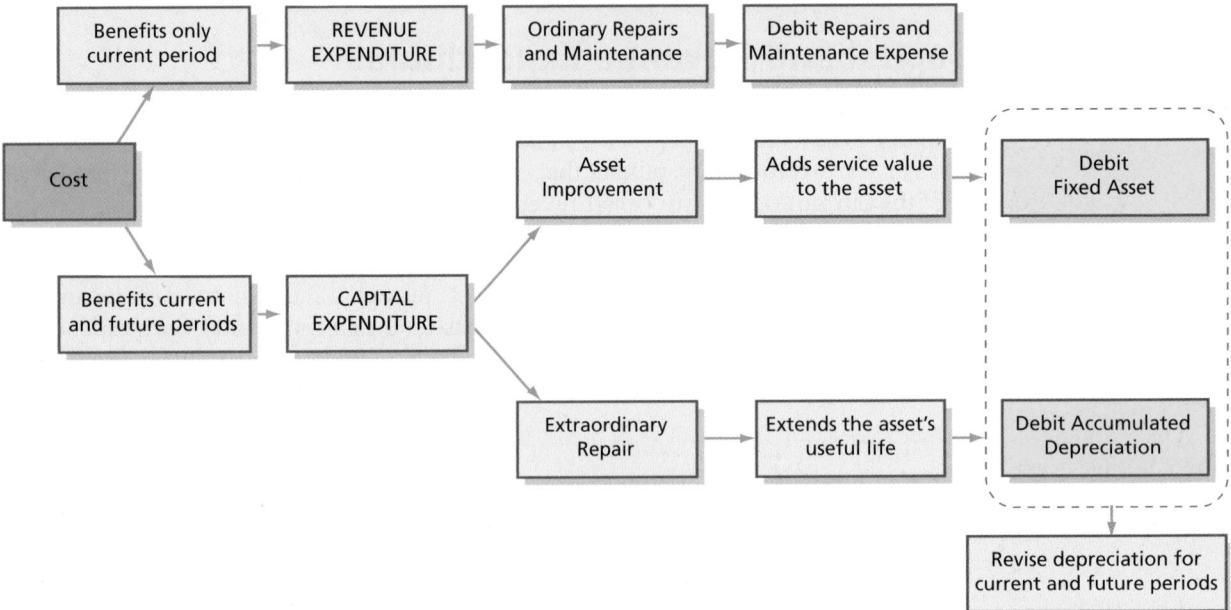

Example Exercise 10-1   Capital and Revenue Expenditures

On June 18, GTS Co. paid $1,200 to upgrade a hydraulic lift and $45 for an oil change for one of its delivery trucks. Journalize the entries for the hydraulic lift upgrade and oil change expenditures.

Follow My Example 10-1

June 18	Delivery Truck	1,200	
	Cash		1,200
18	Repairs and Maintenance Expense	45	
	Cash		45

For Practice: PE 10-1A, PE 10-1B

Leasing Fixed Assets

A *lease* is a contract for the use of an asset for a period of time. Leases are often used in business. For example, automobiles, computers, medical equipment, buildings, and airplanes are often leased.

On December 31, 2007, Delta Air Lines operated 137 aircraft under operating leases and 48 aircraft under capital leases with future lease commitments of over $8 billion.

The two parties to a lease contract are as follows:

1.   The *lessor* is the party who owns the asset.
2.   The *lessee* is the party to whom the rights to use the asset are granted by the lessor.

Under a lease contract, the lessee pays rent on a periodic basis for the lease term. The lessee accounts for a lease contract in one of two ways depending on how the lease contract is classified. A lease contract can be classified as either a:

1.   *Capital lease* or
2.   *Operating lease*

A **capital lease** is accounted for as if the lessee has purchased the asset. The lessee debits an asset account for the fair market value of the asset and credits a long-term lease liability account. The asset is then written off as an expense (amortized) over the life of the capital lease. The accounting for capital leases is discussed in more advanced accounting texts.

An **operating lease** is accounted for as if the lessee is renting the asset for the lease term. The lessee records operating lease payments by debiting *Rent Expense* and crediting *Cash*. The lessee's future lease obligations are not recorded in the accounts. However, such obligations are disclosed in notes to the financial statements.

The asset rentals described in earlier chapters of this text were accounted for as operating leases. To simplify, all leases are assumed to be operating leases throughout this text.

Compute depreciation, using the following methods: straight-line method, units-of-production method, and double-declining-balance method.

Accounting for Depreciation

Fixed assets, with the exception of land, lose their ability, over time, to provide services. Thus, the costs of fixed assets such as equipment and buildings should be recorded as an expense over their useful lives. This periodic recording of the cost of fixed assets as an expense is called **depreciation**. Because land has an unlimited life, it is not depreciated.

The adjusting entry to record depreciation debits *Depreciation Expense* and credits a *contra asset* account entitled *Accumulated Depreciation* or *Allowance for Depreciation*. The use of a contra asset account allows the original cost to remain unchanged in the fixed asset account.

Depreciation can be caused by physical or functional factors.

1.   *Physical depreciation* factors include wear and tear during use or from exposure to weather.
2.   *Functional depreciation* factors include obsolescence and changes in customer needs that cause the asset to no longer provide services for which it was intended. For example, equipment may become obsolete due to changing technology.

Two common misunderstandings exist about *depreciation* as used in accounting include:

Would you have more cash if you depreciated your car? The answer is no. Depreciation does not affect your cash flows. Likewise, depreciation does not affect the cash flows of a business. However, depreciation is subtracted in determining net income.

1.   Depreciation does not measure a decline in the market value of a fixed asset. Instead, depreciation is an allocation of a fixed asset's cost to expense over the asset's useful life. Thus, the book value of a fixed asset (cost less accumulated depreciation) usually does not agree with the asset's market value. This is justified in accounting because a fixed asset is for use in a company's operations rather than for resale.
2.   Depreciation does not provide cash to replace fixed assets as they wear out. This misunderstanding may occur because depreciation, unlike most expenses, does not require an outlay of cash when it is recorded.

Factors in Computing Depreciation Expense

Three factors determine the depreciation expense for a fixed asset. These three factors are as follows:

1. The asset's initial cost
2. The asset's expected useful life
3. The asset's estimated residual value

The initial *cost* of a fixed asset is determined using the concepts discussed and illustrated earlier in this chapter.

JCPenney depreciates buildings over 50 years, while Tandy Corporation depreciates buildings over 10–40 years.

The *expected useful life* of a fixed asset is estimated at the time the asset is placed into service. Estimates of expected useful lives are available from industry trade associations. The Internal Revenue Service also publishes guidelines for useful lives, which may be helpful for financial reporting purposes. However, it is not uncommon for different companies to use a different useful life for similar assets.

The **residual value** of a fixed asset at the end of its useful life is estimated at the time the asset is placed into service. Residual value is sometimes referred to as *scrap value*, *salvage value*, or *trade-in value*. The difference between a fixed asset's initial cost and its residual value is called the asset's *depreciable cost*. The depreciable cost is the amount of the asset's cost that is allocated over its useful life as depreciation expense. If a fixed asset has no residual value, then its entire cost should be allocated to depreciation.

Exhibit 4 shows the relationship between depreciation expense and a fixed asset's initial cost, expected useful life, and estimated residual value.

Exhibit 4

Depreciation Expense Factors

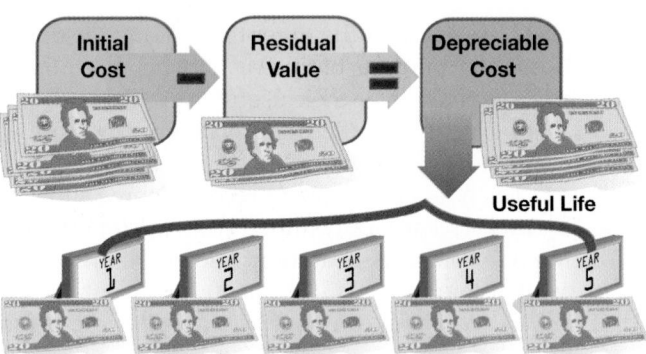

Periodic Depreciation Expense

For an asset placed into or taken out of service during the first half of a month, many companies compute depreciation on the asset for the entire month. That is, the asset is treated as having been purchased or sold on the first day of *that* month. Likewise, purchases and sales during the second half of a month are treated as having occurred on the first day of the *next* month. To simplify, this practice is used in this chapter.

The three depreciation methods used most often are as follows:[2]

1. Straight-line depreciation
2. Units-of-production depreciation
3. Double-declining-balance depreciation

Exhibit 5 shows how often these methods are used in financial statements.

It is not necessary that a company use one method of computing depreciation for all of its fixed assets. For example, a company may use one method for depreciating

---

2 Another method not often used today, called the *sum-of-the-years-digits method*, is described and illustrated in Appendix 1 at the end of this chapter.

Exhibit 5	

Use of Depreciation Methods

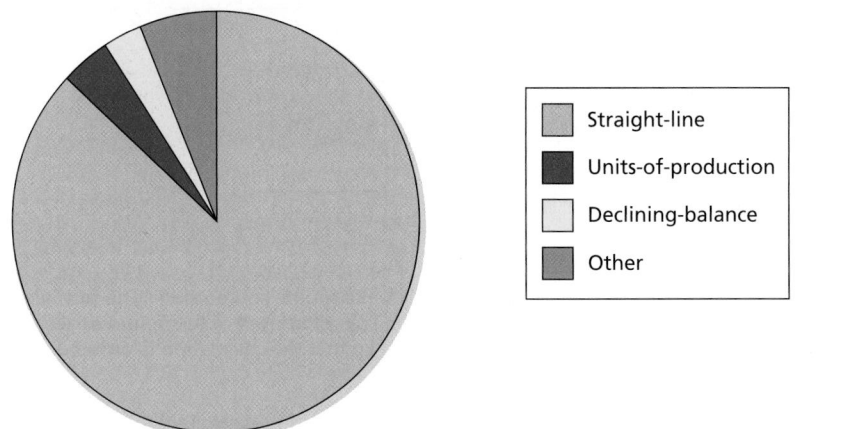

- Straight-line
- Units-of-production
- Declining-balance
- Other

Source: Accounting Trends & Techniques, 61st ed., American Institute of Certified Public Accountants, New York, 2007.

equipment and another method for depreciating buildings. A company may also use different methods for determining income and property taxes.

Straight-Line Method

The **straight-line method** provides for the same amount of depreciation expense for each year of the asset's useful life. As shown in Exhibit 5, the straight-line method is the most widely used depreciation method.

To illustrate, assume that equipment was purchased on January 1 as follows:

Initial cost	$24,000
Expected useful life	5 years
Estimated residual value	$2,000

The annual straight-line depreciation of $4,400 is computed below.

$$\text{Annual Depreciation} = \frac{\text{Cost} - \text{Residual Value}}{\text{Useful Life}} = \frac{\$24,000 - \$2,000}{5 \text{ Years}} = \$4,400$$

If an asset is used for only part of a year, the annual depreciation is prorated. For example, assume that the preceding equipment was purchased and placed into service on October 1. The depreciation for the year ending December 31 would be **$1,100,** computed as follows:

First-Year Partial Depreciation = $4,400 × 3/12 = $1,100

The computation of straight-line depreciation may be simplified by converting the annual depreciation to a percentage of depreciable cost.[3] The straight-line percentage is determined by dividing 100% by the number of years of expected useful life, as shown below.

Expected Years of Useful Life	Straight-Line Percentage
5 years	20% (100%/5)
8 years	12.5% (100%/8)
10 years	10% (100%/10)
20 years	5% (100%/20)
25 years	4% (100%/25)

For the preceding equipment, the annual depreciation of $4,400 can be computed by multiplying the depreciable cost of $22,000 by 20% (100%/5).

As shown above, the straight-line method is simple to use. When an asset's revenues are about the same from period to period, straight-line depreciation provides a good matching of depreciation expense with the asset's revenues.

3 The depreciation rate may also be expressed as a fraction. For example, the annual straight-line rate for an asset with a three-year useful life is 1/3.

Rather than using a formula, periodic depreciation can also be calculated using Excel depreciation functions. For example, straight-line depreciation can be determined using the =SLN function.

The straight-line method of depreciation can be calculated on a spreadsheet as follows:

	A	B	C
1	*Inputs*		
2	Initial cost	$ 24,000	
3	Expected useful life	5	years
4	Estimated residual value	$ 2,000	
5			
6	*Output*		
7	Annual depreciation	=(B2–B4)/B3	
8			

Inputs } rows 1-4
Outputs } row 7

The spreadsheet is divided into inputs and outputs. The formula in B7 is the straight-line depreciation formula using cell references of the input variables, =(B2-B4)/B3. Use parentheses as shown here so that the calculation is ordered properly.

tr✗*it*   Go to the hands-on *Excel Tutor* for this example!

Example Exercise 10-2   Straight-Line Depreciation   •••••••• 2

Equipment acquired at the beginning of the year at a cost of $125,000 has an estimated residual value of $5,000 and an estimated useful life of 10 years. Determine (a) the depreciable cost, (b) the straight-line rate, and (c) the annual straight-line depreciation.

Follow My Example 10-2

a. $120,000 ($125,000 − $5,000)

b. 10% = 1/10

c. $12,000 ($120,000 × 10%), or ($120,000/10 years)

For Practice: PE 10-2A, PE 10-2B

Norfolk Southern Corporation depreciates its train engines based on hours of operation.

Units-of-Production Method

The **units-of-production method** provides the same amount of depreciation expense for each unit of production. Depending on the asset, the units of production can be expressed in terms of hours, miles driven, or quantity produced.

The units-of-production method is applied in two steps.

Step 1. Determine the depreciation per unit as:

$$\text{Depreciation per Unit} = \frac{\text{Cost} - \text{Residual Value}}{\text{Total Units of Production}}$$

Step 2. Compute the depreciation expense as:

Depreciation Expense = Depreciation per Unit × Total Units of Production Used

To illustrate, assume that the equipment in the preceding example is expected to have a useful life of 10,000 operating hours. During the year, the equipment was operated 2,100 hours. The units-of-production depreciation for the year is $4,620, as shown below.

Step 1. Determine the depreciation per hour as:

$$\text{Depreciation per Hour} = \frac{\text{Cost} - \text{Residual Value}}{\text{Total Units of Production}} = \frac{\$24,000 - \$2,000}{10,000 \text{ Hours}} = \$2.20 \text{ per Hour}$$

Step 2. Compute the depreciation expense as:

Depreciation Expense = Depreciation per Unit × Total Units of Production Used

Depreciation Expense = $2.20 per Hour × 2,100 Hours = $4,620

The units-of-production method is often used when a fixed asset's in-service time (or use) varies from year to year. In such cases, the units-of-production method matches depreciation expense with the asset's revenues.

The units of production method of depreciation can be calculated on a spreadsheet as follows:

	A	B	C
1	*Inputs:*		
2	Initial cost	$ 24,000	
3	Estimated residual value	$ 2,000	
4	Total units of production	10,000	hours
5	Total units of production used during the period	2,100	hours
6			
7	*Outputs*		
8	Depreciation per unit	=(B2–B3)/B4	← a.
9	Depreciation expense for the period	=B8*B5	← b.
10			

a. Enter the formula for the depreciation per unit in cell B8, =(B2-B3)/B4. Use parentheses as shown here so that the calculation is ordered properly.

b. Enter in B9 the formula for determining the depreciation for the period. The formula multiplies the rate in B8 by the units of production used during the period in B5, =B8*B5.

   Go to the hands-on *Excel Tutor* for this example!

Example Exercise 10-3   Units-of-Production Depreciation   •••••••> 2

Equipment acquired at a cost of $180,000 has an estimated residual value of $10,000, has an estimated useful life of 40,000 hours, and was operated 3,600 hours during the year. Determine (a) the depreciable cost, (b) the depreciation rate, and (c) the units-of-production depreciation for the year.

Follow My Example 10-3

a. $170,000 ($180,000 − $10,000)

b. $4.25 per hour ($170,000/40,000 hours)

c. $15,300 (3,600 hours × $4.25)

For Practice: PE 10-3A, PE 10-3B

Double-Declining-Balance Method

The **double-declining-balance method** provides for a declining periodic expense over the expected useful life of the asset. The double-declining-balance method is applied in three steps.

Step 1. Determine the straight-line percentage using the expected useful life.

Step 2. Determine the double-declining-balance rate by multiplying the straight-line rate from Step 1 by two.

Step 3. Compute the depreciation expense by multiplying the double-declining-balance rate from Step 2 times the book value of the asset.

To illustrate, the equipment purchased in the preceding example is used to compute double-declining-balance depreciation. For the first year, the depreciation is **$9,600,** as shown below.

Step 1. Straight-line percentage = 20% (100%/5)

Step 2. Double-declining-balance rate = 40% (20% × 2)

Step 3. Depreciation expense = $9,600 ($24,000 × 40%)

For the first year, the book value of the equipment is its initial cost of $24,000. After the first year, the **book value** (cost minus accumulated depreciation) declines and, thus, the depreciation also declines. The double-declining-balance depreciation for the full five-year life of the equipment is shown below.

Year	Cost	Acc. Depr. at Beginning of Year	Book Value at Beginning of Year	Double-Declining-Balance Rate	Depreciation for Year	Book Value at End of Year
1	$24,000		$24,000.00 ×	40%	$9,600.00	$14,400.00
2	24,000	$ 9,600.00	14,400.00 ×	40%	5,760.00	8,640.00
3	24,000	15,360.00	8,640.00 ×	40%	3,456.00	5,184.00
4	24,000	18,816.00	5,184.00 ×	40%	2,073.60	3,110.40
5	24,000	20,889.60	3,110.40	—	1,110.40	2,000.00

When the double-declining-balance method is used, the estimated residual value is *not* considered. However, the asset should not be depreciated below its estimated residual value. In the above example, the estimated residual value was $2,000. Therefore, the depreciation for the fifth year is $1,110.40 ($3,110.40 − $2,000.00) instead of $1,244.16 (40% × $3,110.40).

Like straight-line depreciation, if an asset is used for only part of a year, the annual depreciation is prorated. For example, assume that the preceding equipment was purchased and placed into service on October 1. The depreciation for the year ending December 31 would be $2,400, computed as follows:

First-Year Partial Depreciation = $9,600 × 3/12 = $2,400

The depreciation for the second year would then be $8,640, computed as follows:

Second-Year Depreciation = $8,640 = [40% × ($24,000 − $2,400)]

The double-declining-balance method provides a higher depreciation in the first year of the asset's use, followed by declining depreciation amounts. For this reason, the double-declining-balance method is called an **accelerated depreciation method**.

An asset's revenues are often greater in the early years of its use than in later years. In such cases, the double-declining-balance method provides a good matching of depreciation expense with the asset's revenues.

Example Exercise 10-4 Double-Declining-Balance Depreciation ••••••➤ ❷

Equipment acquired at the beginning of the year at a cost of $125,000 has an estimated residual value of $5,000 and an estimated useful life of 10 years. Determine (a) the double-declining-balance rate and (b) the double-declining-balance depreciation for the first year.

Follow My Example 10-4

a. 20% [(1/10) × 2]
b. $25,000 ($125,000 × 20%)

....

For Practice: PE 10-4A, PE 10-4B

Comparing Depreciation Methods

The three depreciation methods are summarized in Exhibit 6. All three methods allocate a portion of the total cost of an asset to an accounting period, while never depreciating an asset below its residual value.

Exhibit 6

Summary of Depreciation Methods

Method	Useful Life	Depreciable Cost	Depreciation Rate	Depreciation Expense
Straight-line	Years	Cost less residual value	Straight-line rate*	Constant
Units-of-production	Total units of production	Cost less residual value	(Cost − Residual value)/Total units of production	Variable
Double-declining-balance	Years	Declining book value, but not below residual value	Straight-line rate* × 2	Declining

*Straight-line rate = (1/Useful life)

The straight-line method provides for the same periodic amounts of depreciation expense over the life of the asset. The units-of-production method provides for periodic amounts of depreciation expense that vary, depending on the amount the asset is used. The double-declining-balance method provides for a higher depreciation amount in the first year of the asset's use, followed by declining amounts.

The depreciation for the straight-line, units-of-production, and double-declining-balance methods is shown in Exhibit 7. The depreciation in Exhibit 7 is based on the equipment purchased in our prior illustrations. For the units-of-production method, we assume that the equipment was used as follows:

Year 1	2,100 hours
Year 2	1,500
Year 3	2,600
Year 4	1,800
Year 5	2,000
Total	10,000 hours

Exhibit 7

Comparing Depreciation Methods

	Depreciation Expense		
Year	Straight-Line Method	Units-of-Production Method	Double-Declining-Balance Method
1	$ 4,400*	$ 4,620 ($2.20 × 2,100 hrs)	$ 9,600.00 ($24,000 × 40%)
2	4,400	3,300 ($2.20 × 1,500 hrs.)	5,760.00 ($14,400 × 40%)
3	4,400	5,720 ($2.20 × 2,600 hrs.)	3,456.00 ($8,640 × 40%)
4	4,400	3,960 ($2.20 × 1,800 hrs.)	2,073.60 ($5,184 × 40%)
5	4,400	4,400 ($2.20 × 2,000 hrs.)	1,110.40**
Total	$22,000	$22,000	$22,000.00

*$4,400 = ($24,000 − $2,000)/5 years
**$3,110.40 − $2,000.00 because the equipment cannot be depreciated below its residual value of $2,000.

Tax Code Section 179 allows a business to deduct a portion of the cost of qualified property in the year it is placed into service.

Depreciation for Federal Income Tax

The Internal Revenue Code uses the *Modified Accelerated Cost Recovery System (MACRS)* to compute depreciation for tax purposes. MACRS has eight classes of useful life and depreciation rates for each class. Two of the most common classes are the five-year class and the seven-year class.[4] The five-year class includes automobiles and light-duty trucks. The seven-year class includes most machinery and equipment. Depreciation for these two classes is similar to that computed using the double-declining-balance method.

In using the MACRS rates, residual value is ignored. Also, all fixed assets are assumed to be put in and taken out of service in the middle of the year. For the five-year-class assets, depreciation is spread over six years, as shown below.

Year	MACRS 5-Year-Class Depreciation Rates
1	20.0%
2	32.0
3	19.2
4	11.5
5	11.5
6	5.8
	100.0%

To simplify, a company will sometimes use MACRS for both financial statement and tax purposes. This is acceptable if MACRS does not result in significantly different amounts than would have been reported using one of the three depreciation methods discussed in this chapter.

St. Paul Companies recently shortened the useful life of its application software at its data center.

Revising Depreciation Estimates

Estimates of residual values and useful lives of fixed assets may change due to abnormal wear and tear or obsolescence. When new estimates are determined, they are used to determine the depreciation expense in future periods. The depreciation expense recorded in earlier years is not affected.[5]

To illustrate, assume the following data for a machine that was purchased on January 1, 2009.

Initial machine cost	$140,000
Expected useful life	5 years
Estimated residual value	$10,000
Annual depreciation using the straight-line method	
[($140,000 − $10,000)/5 years]	$26,000

At the end of 2010, the machine's book value (undepreciated cost) is $88,000, as shown below.

Initial machine cost	$140,000
Less accumulated depreciation ($26,000 per year × 2 years)	52,000
Book value (undepreciated cost), end of second year	$ 88,000

---

4 Real estate is in either a 27½-year or a 31½-year class and is depreciated by the straight-line method.

5 *Statement of Financial Accounting Standards No. 154,* "Accounting Changes and Error Corrections" (Financial Accounting Standards Board, Norwalk, CT: 2005).

During 2011, the company estimates that the machine's remaining useful life is eight years (instead of three) and that its residual value is $8,000 (instead of $10,000). The depreciation expense for each of the remaining eight years is $10,000, computed as follows:

Book value (undepreciated cost), end of second year	$88,000
Less revised estimated residual value	8,000
Revised remaining depreciable cost	$80,000
Revised annual depreciation expense	
[($88,000 − $8,000)/8 years]	$10,000

Exhibit 8 shows the book value of the asset over its original and revised lives. After the depreciation is revised at the end of 2010, book value declines at a slower rate. At the end of year 2018, the book value reaches the revised residual value of $8,000.

Exhibit 8

Book Value of Asset with Change in Estimate

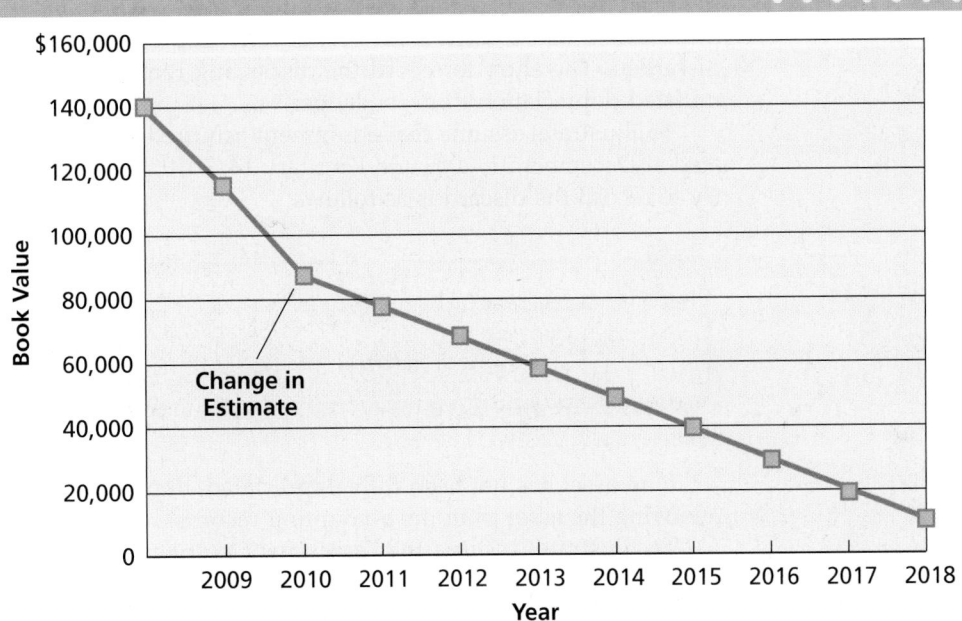

Example Exercise 10-5   Revision of Depreciation   2

A warehouse with a cost of $500,000 has an estimated residual value of $120,000, has an estimated useful life of 40 years, and is depreciated by the straight-line method. (a) Determine the amount of the annual depreciation. (b) Determine the book value at the end of the twentieth year of use. (c) Assuming that at the start of the twenty-first year the remaining life is estimated to be 25 years and the residual value is estimated to be $150,000, determine the depreciation expense for each of the remaining 25 years.

Follow My Example 10-5

a. $9,500 [($500,000 − $120,000)/40]

b. $310,000 [$500,000 − ($9,500 × 20)]

c. $6,400 [($310,000 − $150,000)/25]

For Practice: PE 10-5A, PE 10-5B

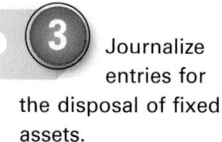

3 Journalize entries for the disposal of fixed assets.

Disposal of Fixed Assets

Fixed assets that are no longer useful may be discarded or sold.[6] In such cases, the fixed asset is removed from the accounts. Just because a fixed asset is fully depreciated, however, does not mean that it should be removed from the accounts.

The entry to record the disposal of a fixed asset removes the cost of the asset and its accumulated depreciation from the accounts.

If a fixed asset is still being used, its cost and accumulated depreciation should remain in the ledger even if the asset is fully depreciated. This maintains accountability for the asset in the ledger. If the asset was removed from the ledger, the accounts would contain no evidence of the continued existence of the asset. In addition, cost and accumulated depreciation data on such assets are often needed for property tax and income tax reports.

Discarding Fixed Assets

If a fixed asset is no longer used and has no residual value, it is discarded. For example, assume that a fixed asset that is fully depreciated and has no residual value is discarded. The entry to record the discarding removes the asset and its related accumulated depreciation from the ledger.

To illustrate, assume that equipment acquired at a cost of $25,000 is fully depreciated at December 31, 2009. On February 14, 2010, the equipment is discarded. The entry to record the discard is as follows:

Feb.	14	Accumulated Depreciation—Equipment	25,000	
		Equipment		25,000
		To write off equipment discarded.		

If an asset has not been fully depreciated, depreciation should be recorded before removing the asset from the accounting records.

To illustrate, assume that equipment costing $6,000 with no estimated residual value is depreciated at a straight-line rate of 10%. On December 31, 2009, the accumulated depreciation balance, after adjusting entries, is $4,750. On March 24, 2010, the asset is removed from service and discarded. The entry to record the depreciation for the three months of 2010 before the asset is discarded is as follows:

Mar.	24	Depreciation Expense—Equipment	150	
		Accumulated Depreciation—Equipment		150
		To record current depreciation on		
		equipment discarded ($600 × $^3/_{12}$).		

The discarding of the equipment is then recorded as follows:

Mar.	24	Accumulated Depreciation—Equipment	4,900	
		Loss on Disposal of Equipment	1,100	
		Equipment		6,000
		To write off equipment discarded.		

6 The accounting for the exchange of fixed assets is described and illustrated in Appendix 2 at the end of this chapter.

The loss of $1,100 is recorded because the balance of the accumulated depreciation account ($4,900) is less than the balance in the equipment account ($6,000). Losses on the discarding of fixed assets are nonoperating items and are normally reported in the Other expense section of the income statement.

Selling Fixed Assets

The entry to record the sale of a fixed asset is similar to the entries for discarding an asset. The only difference is that the receipt of cash is also recorded. If the selling price is more than the book value of the asset, a gain is recorded. If the selling price is less than the book value, a loss is recorded.

To illustrate, assume that equipment is purchased at a cost of $10,000 with no estimated residual value and is depreciated at a straight-line rate of 10%. The equipment is sold for cash on October 12 of the eighth year of its use. The balance of the accumulated depreciation account as of the preceding December 31 is $7,000. The entry to update the depreciation for the nine months of the current year is as follows:

Oct.	12	Depreciation Expense—Equipment	750	
		Accumulated Depreciation—Equipment		750
		To record current depreciation on		
		equipment sold ($10,000 × 9/12 × 10%).		

After the current depreciation is recorded, the book value of the asset is $2,250 ($10,000 − $7,750). The entries to record the sale, assuming three different selling prices, are as follows:

Sold at book value, for $2,250. No gain or loss.

Oct.	12	Cash	2,250	
		Accumulated Depreciation—Equipment	7,750	
		Equipment		10,000

Sold below book value, for $1,000. Loss of $1,250.

Oct.	12	Cash	1,000	
		Accumulated Depreciation—Equipment	7,750	
		Loss on Sale of Equipment	1,250	
		Equipment		10,000

Sold above book value, for $2,800. Gain of $550.

Oct.	12	Cash	2,800	
		Accumulated Depreciation—Equipment	7,750	
		Equipment		10,000
		Gain on Sale of Equipment		550

Example Exercise 10-6   Sale of Equipment

Equipment was acquired at the beginning of the year at a cost of $91,000. The equipment was depreciated using the straight-line method based on an estimated useful life of nine years and an estimated residual value of $10,000..

a. What was the depreciation for the first year?

b. Assuming the equipment was sold at the end of the second year for $78,000, determine the gain or loss on sale of the equipment.

c. Journalize the entry to record the sale.

Follow My Example 10-6

a. $9,000 [($91,000 − $10,000)/9]

b. $5,000 gain {$78,000 − [$91,000 − ($9,000 × 2)]}

c. Cash   78,000
    Accumulated Depreciation—Equipment   18,000
        Equipment   91,000
        Gain on Sale of Equipment   5,000

For Practice: PE 10-6A, PE 10-6B

Compute depletion and journalize the entry for depletion.

Natural Resources

The fixed assets of some companies include timber, metal ores, minerals, or other natural resources. As these resources are harvested or mined and then sold, a portion of their cost is debited to an expense account. This process of transferring the cost of natural resources to an expense account is called **depletion**.

Depletion is determined as follows:[7]

Step 1. Determine the depletion rate as:

$$\text{Depletion Rate} = \frac{\text{Cost of Resource}}{\text{Estimated Total Units of Resource}}$$

Step 2. Multiply the depletion rate by the quantity extracted from the resource during the period.

$$\text{Depletion Expense} = \text{Depletion Rate} \times \text{Quantity Extracted}$$

To illustrate, assume that Karst Company purchased mining rights as follows:

Cost of mineral deposit	$400,000
Estimated total units of resource	1,000,000 tons
Tons mined during year	90,000 tons

The depletion expense of $36,000 for the year is computed, as shown below.

Step 1.

$$\text{Depletion Rate} = \frac{\text{Cost of Resource}}{\text{Estimated Total Units of Resource}} = \frac{\$400,000}{1,000,000 \text{ Tons}} = \$0.40 \text{ per Ton}$$

Step 2.

$$\text{Depletion Expense} = \$0.40 \text{ per Ton} \times 90,000 \text{ Tons} = \$36,000$$

---

7 We assume that there is no significant residual value left after all the natural resource is extracted.

The adjusting entry to record the depletion is shown below.

Dec.	31	Depletion Expense	36,000	
		Accumulated Depletion		36,000
		Depletion of mineral deposit.		

Like the accumulated depreciation account, Accumulated Depletion is a *contra asset* account. It is reported on the balance sheet as a deduction from the cost of the mineral deposit.

Example Exercise 10-7   Depletion

•••••••• 4

Earth's Treasures Mining Co. acquired mineral rights for $45,000,000. The mineral deposit is estimated at 50,000,000 tons. During the current year, 12,600,000 tons were mined and sold.

a. Determine the depletion rate.

b. Determine the amount of depletion expense for the current year.

c. Journalize the adjusting entry on December 31 to recognize the depletion expense.

Follow My Example 10-7

a. $0.90 per ton ($45,000,000/50,000,000 tons)

b. $11,340,000 (12,600,000 tons × $0.90 per ton)

c. Dec. 31   Depletion Expense   11,340,000
                   Accumulated Depletion.   11,340,000
                   Depletion of mineral deposit.

For Practice: PE 10-7A, PE 10-7B

 5   Describe the accounting for intangible assets, such as patents, copyrights, and goodwill.

Intangible Assets

Patents, copyrights, trademarks, and goodwill are long-lived assets that are used in the operations of a business and are not held for sale. These assets are called **intangible assets** because they do not exist physically.

The accounting for intangible assets is similar to that for fixed assets. The major issues are:

1. Determining the initial cost.

2. Determining the **amortization**, which is the amount of cost to transfer to expense.

Amortization results from the passage of time or a decline in the usefulness of the intangible asset.

Patents

Manufacturers may acquire exclusive rights to produce and sell goods with one or more unique features. Such rights are granted by **patents,** which the federal government issues to inventors. These rights continue in effect for 20 years. A business may purchase patent rights from others, or it may obtain patents developed by its own research and development.

The initial cost of a purchased patent, including any legal fees, is debited to an asset account. This cost is written off, or amortized, over the years of the patent's expected useful life. The expected useful life of a patent may be less than its legal life. For example, a patent may become worthless due to changing technology or consumer tastes.

Apple Computer, Inc., amortizes intangible assets over 3–10 years.

Patent amortization is normally computed using the straight-line method. The amortization is recorded by debiting an amortization expense account and crediting the patents account. A separate contra asset account is usually *not* used for intangible assets.

To illustrate, assume that at the beginning of its fiscal year, a company acquires patent rights for $100,000. Although the patent will not expire for 14 years, its remaining useful life is estimated as five years. The adjusting entry to amortize the patent at the end of the year is as follows:

Dec.	31	Amortization Expense—Patents	20,000	
		Patents		20,000
		Patent amortization ($100,000/5).		

Some companies develop their own patents through research and development. In such cases, any *research and development costs* are usually recorded as current operating expenses in the period in which they are incurred. This accounting for research and development costs is justified on the basis that any future benefits from research and development are highly uncertain.

Copyrights and Trademarks

Coke® is one of the world's most recognizable trademarks. As stated in *LIFE*, "Two-thirds of the earth is covered by water; the rest is covered by Coke. If the French are known for wine and the Germans for beer, America achieved global beverage dominance with fizzy water and caramel color."

The exclusive right to publish and sell a literary, artistic, or musical composition is granted by a **copyright**. Copyrights are issued by the federal government and extend for 70 years beyond the author's death. The costs of a copyright include all costs of creating the work plus any other costs of obtaining the copyright. A copyright that is purchased is recorded at the price paid for it. Copyrights are amortized over their estimated useful lives.

A **trademark** is a name, term, or symbol used to identify a business and its products. Most businesses identify their trademarks with ® in their advertisements and on their products.

Under federal law, businesses can protect their trademarks by registering them for 10 years and renewing the registration for 10-year periods. Like a copyright, the legal costs of registering a trademark are recorded as an asset.

If a trademark is purchased from another business, its cost is recorded as an asset. In such cases, the cost of the trademark is considered to have an indefinite useful life. Thus, trademarks are not amortized. Instead, trademarks are reviewed periodically for impaired value. When a trademark is impaired, the trademark should be written down and a loss recognized.

Goodwill

eBay recorded an impairment of $1.39 billion in the goodwill created from its purchase of Skype.

Goodwill refers to an intangible asset of a business that is created from such favorable factors as location, product quality, reputation, and managerial skill. Goodwill allows a business to earn a greater rate of return than normal.

Generally accepted accounting principles (GAAP) allow goodwill to be recorded only if it is objectively determined by a transaction. An example of such a transaction is the purchase of a business at a price in excess of the fair value of its net assets (assets − liabilities). The excess is recorded as goodwill and reported as an intangible asset.

Unlike patents and copyrights, goodwill is not amortized. However, a loss should be recorded if the future prospects of the purchased firm become impaired. This loss would normally be disclosed in the Other expense section of the income statement.

To illustrate, assume that on December 31 FaceCard Company has determined that $250,000 of the goodwill created from the purchase of electronic Systems is impaired. The entry to record the impairment is as follows:

Dec.	31	Loss from Impaired Goodwill	250,000	
		Goodwill		250,000
		Impaired goodwill.		

Exhibit 9 shows intangible asset disclosures for 600 large firms. Goodwill is the most often reported intangible asset. This is because goodwill arises from merger transactions, which are common.

Exhibit 9

Frequency of Intangible Asset Disclosures for 600 Firms

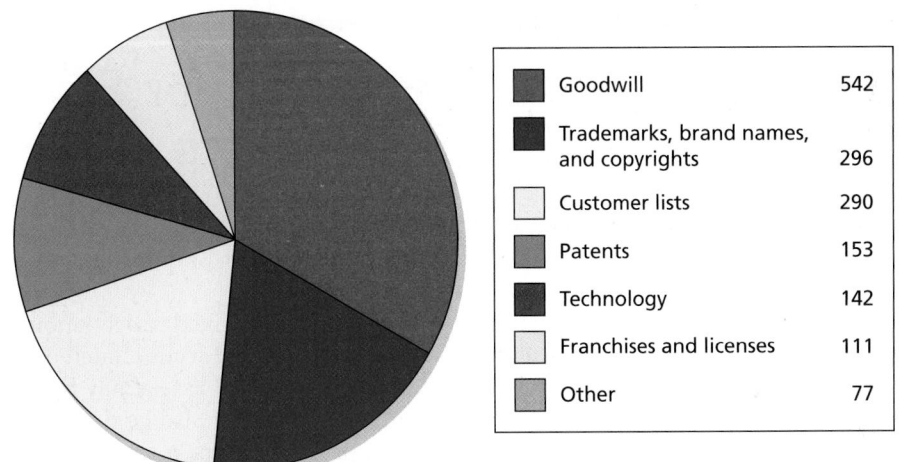

Goodwill	542
Trademarks, brand names, and copyrights	296
Customer lists	290
Patents	153
Technology	142
Franchises and licenses	111
Other	77

Source: Accounting Trends & Techniques, 61st ed., American Institute of Certified Public Accountants, New York, 2007.
Note: Some firms have multiple disclosures.

Exhibit 10 summarizes the characteristics of intangible assets.

Exhibit 10

Comparison of Intangible Assets

Intangible Asset	Description	Amortization Period	Periodic Expense
Patent	Exclusive right to benefit from an innovation.	Estimated useful life not to exceed legal life.	Amortization expense.
Copyright	Exclusive right to benefit from a literary, artistic, or musical composition.	Estimated useful life not to exceed legal life.	Amortization expense.
Trademark	Exclusive use of a name, term, or symbol.	None	Impairment loss if fair value less than carrying value (impaired).
Goodwill	Excess of purchase price of a business over the fair value of its net assets (assets − liabilities).	None	Impairment loss if fair value less than carrying value (impaired).

Example Exercise 10-8 Impaired Goodwill and Amortization of Patent

On December 31, it was estimated that goodwill of $40,000 was impaired. In addition, a patent with an estimated useful economic life of 12 years was acquired for $84,000 on July 1.

a. Journalize the adjusting entry on December 31 for the impaired goodwill.

b. Journalize the adjusting entry on December 31 for the amortization of the patent rights.

Follow My Example 10-8

a.	Dec. 31	Loss from Impaired Goodwill	40,000	
		Goodwill		40,000
		Impaired goodwill.		
b.	Dec. 31	Amortization Expense—Patents.................	3,500	
		Patents...............................		3,500
		Amortized patent rights [($84,000/12) × (6/12)].		

For Practice: PE 10-8A, PE 10-8B

6 Describe how depreciation expense is reported in an income statement and prepare a balance sheet that includes fixed assets and intangible assets.

Financial Reporting for Fixed Assets and Intangible Assets

In the income statement, depreciation and amortization expense should be reported separately or disclosed in a note. A description of the methods used in computing depreciation should also be reported.

In the balance sheet, each class of fixed assets should be disclosed on the face of the statement or in the notes. The related accumulated depreciation should also be disclosed, either by class or in total. The fixed assets may be shown at their *book value* (cost less accumulated depreciation), which can also be described as their *net* amount.

If there are many classes of fixed assets, a single amount may be presented in the balance sheet, supported by a note with a separate listing. Fixed assets may be reported under the more descriptive caption of property, plant, and equipment.

Intangible assets are usually reported in the balance sheet in a separate section following fixed assets. The balance of each class of intangible assets should be disclosed net of any amortization.

The balance sheet presentation for Mornin' Joe's fixed and intangible assets is shown below.

**Mornin' Joe
Balance Sheet
December 31, 2010**

Property, plant, and equipment:			
Land		$1,850,000	
Buildings	$2,650,000		
Less accumulated depreciation	420,000	2,230,000	
Office equipment	$ 350,000		
Less accumulated depreciation	102,000	248,000	
Total property, plant, and equipment			$4,328,000
Intangible assets:			
Patents			140,000

The cost and related accumulated depletion of mineral rights are normally shown as part of the Fixed Assets section of the balance sheet. The mineral rights may be shown net of depletion on the face of the balance sheet. In such cases, a supporting note discloses the accumulated depletion.

Financial Analysis and Interpretation

Fixed assets can be evaluated by their ability to generate revenue. One measure of the revenue-generating ability of fixed assets is the fixed asset turnover ratio. The **fixed asset turnover ratio** measures the number of dollars of revenue earned per dollar of fixed assets and is computed as follows:

Fixed Asset Turnover Ratio

$$= \frac{\text{Revenue}}{\text{Average Book Value of Fixed Assets}}$$

To illustrate, the following fixed asset balance sheet information is used for Marriott International, Inc.:

	December 29, 2006 (in millions)	December 30, 2005 (in millions)
Property and equipment (net)	$1,238	$2,341

Marriott reported revenue of $12,160 million for 2006. Thus, the fixed asset turnover ratio is calculated as follows:

$$\text{Fixed Asset Turnover Ratio} = \frac{\$12,160}{(1,238 + 2,341)/2} = 6.80$$

For every dollar of fixed assets, Marriott earns $6.80 of revenue. The larger this ratio, the more efficiently a business is using its fixed assets. This ratio can be compared across time within a single firm or to other companies in the industry to evaluate overall fixed asset turnover performance.

The fixed asset turnover ratio for a number of different companies is shown below. The smaller ratios are associated with companies that require large fixed asset investments. The larger fixed asset turnover ratios are associated with firms that are more labor-intensive and require smaller fixed asset investments.

Company (industry)	Fixed Asset Turnover Ratio
Comcast Corporation (cable)	1.25
Google (Internet)	6.32
Manpower Inc. (temporary employment)	88.14
Norfolk Southern Corporation (railroad)	0.45
Ruby Tuesday, Inc. (restaurant)	1.40
Southwest Airlines Co. (airline)	0.93

A P P E N D I X   1

A recent edition of *Accounting Trends & Techniques* reported that only 1%–2% of the surveyed companies now use this method for financial reporting purposes.

Sum-of-the-Years-Digits Depreciation

Under the *sum-of-the-years-digits method*, depreciation expense is determined by multiplying the original cost of the asset less its estimated residual value by a smaller fraction each year. Thus, the sum-of-the-years-digits method is similar to the double-declining-balance method in that the depreciation expense declines each year.

The denominator of the fraction used in determining the depreciation expense is the sum of the digits of the years of the asset's useful life. For example, an asset with a useful life of five years would have a denominator of 15 (5 + 4 + 3 + 2 + 1). The denominator can also be determined using the following formula where N is the useful life of the assest:

$$\text{Sum of Years of Useful Life} = \frac{N(N + 1)}{2} = \frac{5(5 + 1)}{2} = 15$$

The numerator of the fraction is the number of years of useful life remaining at the beginning of each year for which depreciation is being computed. Thus, the numerator decreases each year by 1. For a useful life of five years, the numerator is 5 the first year, 4 the second year, 3 the third year, and so on.

To illustrate, the equipment example from the illustrations for the straight-line, units-of-production, and double-declining-balance methods is used. This equipment was purchased on January 1 as follows:

Initial cost	$24,000
Expected useful life	5 years
Estimated residual value	$2,000

Using the sum-of-the-years-digits method, the depreciation is computed as shown below.

Year	Cost Less Residual Value	Rate	Depreciation for Year	Acc. Dep. at End of Year	Book Value at End of Year
1	$22,000	5/15	$7,333.33	$ 7,333.33	$16,666.67
2	22,000	4/15	5,866.67	13,200.00	10,800.00
3	22,000	3/15	4,400.00	17,600.00	6,400.00
4	22,000	2/15	2,933.33	20,533.33	3,466.67
5	22,000	1/15	1,466.67	22,000.00	2,000.00

If an asset is used for only part of a year, the annual depreciation is prorated. For example, assume that the preceding equipment was purchased and placed into service on October 1. The depreciation for the year ending December 31 would be **$1,833.33**, computed as follows:

First-Year Partial Depreciation = $7,333.33 × 3/12 = $1,833.33

The depreciation for the second year would then be **$6,966.67**, computed as follows:

Second-Year Depreciation = ($9/12$ × 5/15 × $22,000) + ($3/12$ × 4/15 × $22,000)

Second-Year Depreciation = $5,500.00 + $1,466.67 = $6,966.67

At one time, the sum-of-the-years-digits method of depreciation was widely used. However, MACRS and current tax law changes have limited its use.

APPENDIX 2

Exchanging Similar Fixed Assets

Old equipment is often traded in for new equipment having a similar use. In such cases, the seller allows the buyer an amount for the old equipment traded in. This amount, called the **trade-in allowance**, may be either greater or less than the book value of the old equipment. The remaining balance—the amount owed—is either paid in cash or recorded as a liability. It is normally called **boot**, which is its tax name.

Accounting for the exchange of similar assets depends on whether the transaction has *commercial substance*.[9] An exchange has commercial substance if future cash flows change as a result of the exchange. If an exchange of similar assets has commercial substance, a gain or loss is recognized based on the difference between the book value of the asset given up (exchanged) and the fair market value of the asset received. In such cases, the exchange is accounted for similar to that of a sale of a fixed asset.

9 *Statement of Financial Accounting Standards No. 153,* "Exchanges of Nonmonetary Assets" (Financial Accounting Standards Board, Norwalk, CT: 2004).

Gain on Exchange

To illustrate a gain on an exchange of similar assets, assume the following:

Similar equipment acquired (new):

Price (fair market value) of new equipment	$5,000
Trade-in allowance on old equipment	1,100
Cash paid at June 19, date of exchange	$3,900

Equipment traded in (old):

Cost of old equipment	$4,000
Accumulated depreciation at date of exchange	3,200
Book value at June 19, date of exchange	$ 800

The entry to record this exchange and payment of cash is as follows:

June 19	Accumulated Depreciation—Equipment	3,200	
	Equipment (new equipment)	5,000	
	Equipment (old equipment)		4,000
	Cash		3,900
	Gain on Exchange of Equipment		300

The gain on the exchange, $300, is the difference between the fair market value of the new asset of $5,000 and the book value of the old asset traded in of $800 plus the cash paid of $3,900 as shown below.

Price (fair market value) of new equipment		$5,000
Less assets given up in exchange:		
Book value of old equipment ($4,000 − $3,200) . . .	$ 800	
Cash paid on the exchange	3,900	4,700
Gain on exchange of assets		$ 300

Loss on Exchange

To illustrate a loss on an exchange of similar assets, assume that instead of a trade-in allowance of $1,100, a trade-in allowance of only $675 was allowed in the preceding example. In this case, the cash paid on the exchange is $4,325 as shown below.

Price (fair market value) of new equipment	$5,000
Trade-in allowance of old equipment	675
Cash paid at June 19, date of exchange	$4,325

The entry to record this exchange and payment of cash is as follows:

June 19	Accumulated Depreciation—Equipment	3,200	
	Equipment (new equipment)	5,000	
	Loss on Exchange of Equipment	125	
	Equipment (old equipment)		4,000
	Cash		4,325

The loss on the exchange, $125, is the difference between the fair market value of the new asset of $5,000 and the book value of the old asset traded in of $800 plus the cash paid of $4,325 as shown below.

Price (fair market value) of new equipment		$5,000
Less assets given up in exchange:		
Book value of old equipment ($4,000 − $3,200) . . .	$ 800	
Cash paid on the exchange	4,325	5,125
Loss on exchange of assets		$ (125)

In those cases where an asset exchange *lacks commercial substance*, no gain is recognized on the exchange. Instead, the cost of the new asset is adjusted for any gain. For example, in the first illustration, the gain of $300 would be subtracted from the purchase price of $5,000 and the new asset would be recorded at $4,700. Accounting for the exchange of assets that lack commercial substance is discussed in more advanced accounting texts.[10]

10 The exchange of similar assets also involves complex tax issues that are discussed in advanced accounting courses.

1 Define, classify, and account for the cost of fixed assets.

Key Points	Key Learning Outcomes	Example Exercises	Practice Exercises
Fixed assets are long-term tangible assets that are owned by the business and are used in the normal operations of the business such as equipment, buildings, and land. The initial cost of a fixed asset includes all amounts spent to get the asset in place and ready for use. Once an asset is placed into service, revenue and capital expenditures may be incurred. Revenue expenditures include ordinary repairs and maintenance. Capital expenditures include asset improvements and extraordinary repairs. Fixed assets may also be leased and accounted for as capital or operating leases.	• Define *fixed assets*. • List types of costs that should and should not be included in the cost of a fixed asset. • Provide examples of ordinary repairs, asset improvements, and extraordinary repairs. • Prepare journal entries for ordinary repairs, asset improvements, and extraordinary repairs.	 **10-1**	 10-1A, 10-1B

2 Compute depreciation, using the following methods: straight-line method, units-of-production method, and double-declining-balance method.

Key Points	Key Learning Outcomes	Example Exercises	Practice Exercises
All fixed assets except land lose their ability to provide services and should be depreciated over time. Three factors are considered in determining depreciation: (1) the fixed asset's initial cost, (2) the useful life of the asset, and (3) the residual value of the asset. The straight-line method spreads the initial cost less the residual value equally over the useful life. The units-of-production method spreads the initial cost less the residual value equally over the units expected to be produced by the asset during its useful life. The double-declining-balance method is applied by multiplying the declining book value of the asset by twice the straight-line rate. Depreciation may be revised for changes in an asset's useful life or residual value. Such changes affect future depreciation.	• Define and describe *depreciation*. • List the factors used in determining depreciation. • Compute straight-line depreciation. • Compute units-of-production depreciation. • Compute double-declining-balance depreciation. • Compute revised depreciation for a change in an asset's useful life and residual value.	 **10-2** **10-3** **10-4** **10-5**	 10-2A, 10-2B 10-3A, 10-3B 10-4A, 10-4B 10-5A, 10-5B

3 Journalize entries for the disposal of fixed assets.

Key Points	Key Learning Outcomes	Example Exercises	Practice Exercises
To record disposals of fixed assets, any depreciation for the current period should be recorded, and the book value of the asset is then removed from the accounts. For assets discarded from service, a loss may be recorded for any remaining book value of the asset.	• Prepare the journal entry for discarding a fixed asset.		
When a fixed asset is sold, the book value is removed, and the cash or other asset received is recorded. If the selling price is more than the book value of the asset, the transaction results in a gain. If the selling price is less than the book value, there is a loss.	• Prepare journal entries for the sale of a fixed asset.	10-6	10-6A, 10-6B

4 Compute depletion and journalize the entry for depletion.

Key Points	Key Learning Outcomes	Example Exercises	Practice Exercises
The amount of periodic depletion is computed by multiplying the quantity of minerals extracted during the period by a depletion rate. The depletion rate is computed by dividing the cost of the mineral deposit by its estimated total units of resource. The entry to record depletion debits a depletion expense account and credits an accumulated depletion account.	• Define and describe *depletion*.		
	• Compute a depletion rate.	10-7	10-7A, 10-7B
	• Prepare the journal entry to record depletion.	10-7	10-7A, 10-7B

5 Describe the accounting for intangible assets, such as patents, copyrights, and goodwill.

Key Points	Key Learning Outcomes	Example Exercises	Practice Exercises
Long-term assets such as patents, copyrights, trademarks, and goodwill that are without physical attributes but are used in the business are intangible assets. The initial cost of an intangible asset should be debited to an asset account. The cost of patents and copyrights should be amortized over the years of the asset's expected usefulness by debiting an expense account and crediting the intangible asset account. Trademarks and goodwill are not amortized, but are written down only upon impairment.	• Define, describe, and provide examples of intangible assets.		
	• Prepare a journal entry for the purchase of an intangible asset.		
	• Prepare a journal entry to amortize the costs of patents and copyrights.	10-8	10-8A, 10-8B
	• Prepare the journal entry to record the impairment of goodwill.	10-8	10-8A, 10-8B

6

Describe how depreciation expense is reported in an income statement and prepare a balance sheet that includes fixed assets and intangible assets.

Key Points	Key Learning Outcomes	Example Exercises	Practice Exercises
The amount of depreciation expense and the method or methods used in computing depreciation should be disclosed in the financial statements. In addition, each major class of fixed assets should be disclosed, along with the related accumulated depreciation. Intangible assets are usually presented in the balance sheet in a separate section immediately following fixed assets. Each major class of intangible assets should be disclosed at an amount net of the amortization recorded to date.	• Describe and illustrate how fixed assets are reported in the income statement and balance sheet. • Describe and illustrate how intangible assets are reported in the income statement and balance sheet.		

Key Terms ● ● ● ● ●

accelerated depreciation method (448)
amortization (455)
book value (448)
boot (460)
capital expenditures (441)
capital lease (443)
copyright (456)

depletion (454)
depreciation (443)
double-declining-balance method (447)
fixed asset turnover ratio (459)
fixed assets (438)
goodwill (456)
intangible assets (455)

operating lease (443)
patents (455)
residual value (444)
revenue expenditures (441)
straight-line method (445)
trade-in allowance (460)
trademark (456)
units-of-production method (446)

Illustrative Problem ● ● ● ● ●

McCollum Company, a furniture wholesaler, acquired new equipment at a cost of $150,000 at the beginning of the fiscal year. The equipment has an estimated life of five years and an estimated residual value of $12,000. Ellen McCollum, the president, has requested information regarding alternative depreciation methods.

Instructions

1. Determine the annual depreciation for each of the five years of estimated useful life of the equipment, the accumulated depreciation at the end of each year, and the book value of the equipment at the end of each year by (a) the straight-line method and (b) the double-declining-balance method.
2. Assume that the equipment was depreciated under the double-declining-balance method. In the first week of the fifth year, the equipment was sold for $10,000. Journalize the entry to record the sale.

Solution

1.

	Year	Depreciation Expense	Accumulated Depreciation, End of Year	Book Value, End of Year
a.	1	$27,600*	$ 27,600	$122,400
	2	27,600	55,200	94,800
	3	27,600	82,800	67,200
	4	27,600	110,400	39,600
	5	27,600	138,000	12,000

*$27,600 = ($150,000 − $12,000) ÷ 5

	Year	Depreciation Expense	Accumulated Depreciation, End of Year	Book Value, End of Year
b.	1	$60,000**	$ 60,000	$ 90,000
	2	36,000	96,000	54,000
	3	21,600	117,600	32,400
	4	12,960	130,560	19,440
	5	7,440***	138,000	12,000

**$60,000 = $150,000 × 40%
***The asset is not depreciated below the estimated residual value of $12,000.
$7,440 = $150,000 − $130,560 − $12,000

Cash	10,000	
Accumulated Depreciation—Equipment	130,560	
Loss on Sale of Equipment	9,440	
Equipment		150,000

Self-Examination Questions (Answers at End of Chapter)

1. Which of the following expenditures incurred in connection with acquiring machinery is a proper charge to the asset account?
   A. Freight
   B. Installation costs
   C. Both A and B
   D. Neither A nor B

2. What is the amount of depreciation, using the double-declining-balance method for the second year of use for equipment costing $9,000, with an estimated residual value of $600 and an estimated life of three years?
   A. $6,000
   B. $3,000
   C. $2,000
   D. $400

3. An example of an accelerated depreciation method is:
   A. straight-line.
   B. double-declining-balance.
   C. units-of-production.
   D. depletion.

4. Equipment purchased on January 3, 2008, for $80,000 was depreciated using the straight-line method based upon a 5-year life and $7,500 residual value. The equipment was sold on December 31, 2010, for $40,000. What is the gain on the sale of the equipment?
   A. $3,500
   B. $14,500
   C. $36,500
   D. $43,500

5. Which of the following is an example of an intangible asset?
   A. Patents
   B. Goodwill
   C. Copyrights
   D. All of the above

Eye Openers

1. Which of the following qualities are characteristic of fixed assets? (a) tangible, (b) capable of repeated use in the operations of the business, (c) held for sale in the normal course of business, (d) used rarely in the operations of the business, (e) long-lived.

2. Mancini Office Supplies has a fleet of automobiles and trucks for use by salespersons and for delivery of office supplies and equipment. East Village Auto Sales Co. has automobiles and trucks for sale. Under what caption would the automobiles and trucks be reported in the balance sheet of (a) Mancini Office Supplies, (b) East Village Auto Sales Co.?

3. Just Animals Co. acquired an adjacent vacant lot with the hope of selling it in the future at a gain. The lot is not intended to be used in Just Animals' business operations. Where should such real estate be listed in the balance sheet?

4. My Mother's Closet Company solicited bids from several contractors to construct an addition to its office building. The lowest bid received was for $375,000. My Mother's Closet Company decided to construct the addition itself at a cost of $298,500. What amount should be recorded in the building account?

5. Distinguish between the accounting for capital expenditures and revenue expenditures.

6. Immediately after a used truck is acquired, a new motor is installed at a total cost of $3,175. Is this a capital expenditure or a revenue expenditure?

7. How does the accounting for a capital lease differ from the accounting for an operating lease?

8. Are the amounts at which fixed assets are reported in the balance sheet their approximate market values as of the balance sheet date? Discuss.

9. a. Does the recognition of depreciation in the accounts provide a special cash fund for the replacement of fixed assets? Explain.
   b. Describe the nature of depreciation as the term is used in accounting.

10. Pac Vac Company purchased a machine that has a manufacturer's suggested life of 15 years. The company plans to use the machine on a special project that will last 12 years. At the completion of the project, the machine will be sold. Over how many years should the machine be depreciated?

11. Is it necessary for a business to use the same method of computing depreciation (a) for all classes of its depreciable assets, (b) for financial statement purposes and in determining income taxes?

12. a. Under what conditions is the use of an accelerated depreciation method most appropriate?
    b. Why is an accelerated depreciation method often used for income tax purposes?
    c. What is the Modified Accelerated Cost Recovery System (MACRS), and under what conditions is it used?

13. A company revised the estimated useful lives of its fixed assets, which resulted in an increase in the remaining lives of several assets. Can the company include, as income of the current period, the cumulative effect of the changes, which reduces the depreciation expense of past periods? Discuss.

14. For some of the fixed assets of a business, the balance in Accumulated Depreciation is exactly equal to the cost of the asset. (a) Is it permissible to record additional depreciation on the assets if they are still useful to the business? Explain. (b) When should an entry be made to remove the cost and the accumulated depreciation from the accounts?

15. a. Over what period of time should the cost of a patent acquired by purchase be amortized?
    b. In general, what is the required accounting treatment for research and development costs?
    c. How should goodwill be amortized?

Practice Exercises

PE 10-1A
Capital and revenue
expenditures
obj. 1
EE 10-1   p. 442

On May 27, Linoleum Associates Co. paid $950 to repair the transmission on one of its delivery vans. In addition, Linoleum Associates paid $450 to install a GPS system in its van. Journalize the entries for the transmission and GPS system expenditures.

PE 10-1B
Capital and revenue
expenditures
obj. 1
EE 10-1   p. 442

On October 9, Wonder Inflatables Co. paid $1,150 to install a hydraulic lift and $40 for an air filter for one of its delivery trucks. Journalize the entries for the new lift and air filter expenditures.

PE 10-2A
Straight-line
depreciation
obj. 2
EE 10-2   p. 446

A building acquired at the beginning of the year at a cost of $485,000 has an estimated residual value of $75,000 and an estimated useful life of 25 years. Determine (a) the depreciable cost, (b) the straight-line rate, and (c) the annual straight-line depreciation.

PE 10-2B
Straight-line
depreciation
obj. 2
EE 10-2   p. 446

Equipment acquired at the beginning of the year at a cost of $125,000 has an estimated residual value of $5,000 and an estimated useful life of eight years. Determine (a) the depreciable cost, (b) the straight-line rate, and (c) the annual straight-line depreciation.

PE 10-3A
Units-of-production
depreciation
obj. 2
EE 10-3   p. 447

A truck acquired at a cost of $134,000 has an estimated residual value of $35,000, has an estimated useful life of 300,000 miles, and was driven 52,000 miles during the year. Determine (a) the depreciable cost, (b) the depreciation rate, and (c) the units-of-production depreciation for the year.

PE 10-3B
Units-of-production
depreciation
obj. 2
EE 10-3   p. 447

A tractor acquired at a cost of $95,000 has an estimated residual value of $15,000, has an estimated useful life of 40,000 hours, and was operated 5,100 hours during the year. Determine (a) the depreciable cost, (b) the depreciation rate, and (c) the units-of-production depreciation for the year.

PE 10-4A
Double-declining-
balance depreciation
obj. 2
EE 10-4   p. 448

A building acquired at the beginning of the year at a cost of $650,000 has an estimated residual value of $125,000 and an estimated useful life of 40 years. Determine (a) the double-declining-balance rate and (b) the double-declining-balance depreciation for the first year.

PE 10-4B
Double-declining-
balance depreciation
obj. 2
EE 10-4   p. 448

Equipment acquired at the beginning of the year at a cost of $145,000 has an estimated residual value of $18,000 and an estimated useful life of five years. Determine (a) the double-declining-balance rate and (b) the double-declining-balance depreciation for the first year.

PE 10-5A
Revision of
depreciation

obj. 2

EE 10-5   p. 451

Equipment with a cost of $250,000 has an estimated residual value of $34,000, has an estimated useful life of 18 years, and is depreciated by the straight-line method. (a) Determine the amount of the annual depreciation. (b) Determine the book value at the end of the tenth year of use. (c) Assuming that at the start of the eleventh year the remaining life is estimated to be eight years and the residual value is estimated to be $6,000, determine the depreciation expense for each of the remaining eight years.

PE 10-5B
Revision of
depreciation

obj. 2

EE 10-5   p. 451

A truck with a cost of $80,000 has an estimated residual value of $15,000, has an estimated useful life of eight years, and is depreciated by the straight-line method. (a) Determine the amount of the annual depreciation. (b) Determine the book value at the end of the fourth year of use. (c) Assuming that at the start of the fifth year the remaining life is estimated to be five years and the residual value is estimated to be $10,000, determine the depreciation expense for each of the remaining five years.

PE 10-6A
Sale of equipment

obj. 3

EE 10-6   p. 454

Equipment was acquired at the beginning of the year at a cost of $324,000. The equipment was depreciated using the double-declining-balance method based on an estimated useful life of eight years and an estimated residual value of $43,000.

a. What was the depreciation for the first year?
b. Assuming the equipment was sold at the end of the second year for $200,000, determine the gain or loss on the sale of the equipment.
c. Journalize the entry to record the sale.

PE 10-6B
Sale of equipment

obj. 3

EE 10-6   p. 454

Equipment was acquired at the beginning of the year at a cost of $160,000. The equipment was depreciated using the straight-line method based on an estimated useful life of 15 years and an estimated residual value of $17,500.

a. What was the depreciation for the first year?
b. Assuming the equipment was sold at the end of the sixth year for $90,000, determine the gain or loss on the sale of the equipment.
c. Journalize the entry to record the sale.

PE 10-7A
Depletion

obj. 4

EE 10-7   p. 455

Montana Mining Co. acquired mineral rights for $120,000,000. The mineral deposit is estimated at 200,000,000 tons. During the current year, 31,155,000 tons were mined and sold.

a. Determine the depletion rate.
b. Determine the amount of depletion expense for the current year.
c. Journalize the adjusting entry on December 31 to recognize the depletion expense.

PE 10-7B
Depletion

obj. 4

EE 10-7   p. 455

Cooke City Mining Co. acquired mineral rights for $50,000,000. The mineral deposit is estimated at 125,000,000 tons. During the current year, 42,385,000 tons were mined and sold.

a. Determine the depletion rate.
b. Determine the amount of depletion expense for the current year.
c. Journalize the adjusting entry on December 31 to recognize the depletion expense.

PE 10-8A
Impaired goodwill
and amortization of
patent

obj. 5

EE 10-8   p. 458

On December 31, it was estimated that goodwill of $500,000 was impaired. In addition, a patent with an estimated useful economic life of eight years was acquired for $388,000 on July 1.

a. Journalize the adjusting entry on December 31 for the impaired goodwill.
b. Journalize the adjusting entry on December 31 for the amortization of the patent rights.

PE 10-8B
Impaired goodwill and amortization of patent

obj. 5

EE 10-8   p. 458

On December 31, it was estimated that goodwill of $875,000 was impaired. In addition, a patent with an estimated useful economic life of 17 years was acquired for $425,000 on April 1.

a. Journalize the adjusting entry on December 31 for the impaired goodwill.
b. Journalize the adjusting entry on December 31 for the amortization of the patent rights.

Exercises

EX 10-1
Costs of acquiring fixed assets

obj. 1

Catherine Simpkins owns and operates Speedy Print Co. During February, Speedy Print Co. incurred the following costs in acquiring two printing presses. One printing press was new, and the other was used by a business that recently filed for bankruptcy.

Costs related to new printing press:

1. Sales tax on purchase price
2. Freight
3. Special foundation
4. Insurance while in transit
5. New parts to replace those damaged in unloading
6. Fee paid to factory representative for installation

Costs related to used printing press:

7. Fees paid to attorney to review purchase agreement
8. Freight
9. Installation
10. Repair of vandalism during installation
11. Replacement of worn-out parts
12. Repair of damage incurred in reconditioning the press

a. Indicate which costs incurred in acquiring the new printing press should be debited to the asset account.
b. Indicate which costs incurred in acquiring the used printing press should be debited to the asset account.

EX 10-2
Determine cost of land

obj. 1

Bridger Ski Co. has developed a tract of land into a ski resort. The company has cut the trees, cleared and graded the land and hills, and constructed ski lifts. (a) Should the tree cutting, land clearing, and grading costs of constructing the ski slopes be debited to the land account? (b) If such costs are debited to Land, should they be depreciated?

EX 10-3
Determine cost of land

obj. 1

✔ $327,425

Fastball Delivery Company acquired an adjacent lot to construct a new warehouse, paying $30,000 and giving a short-term note for $270,000. Legal fees paid were $1,425, delinquent taxes assumed were $12,000, and fees paid to remove an old building from the land were $18,500. Materials salvaged from the demolition of the building were sold for $4,500. A contractor was paid $910,000 to construct a new warehouse. Determine the cost of the land to be reported on the balance sheet.

EX 10-4
Capital and revenue expenditures

obj. 1

Connect Lines Co. incurred the following costs related to trucks and vans used in operating its delivery service:

1. Replaced a truck's suspension system with a new suspension system that allows for the delivery of heavier loads.
2. Installed a hydraulic lift to a van.

3. Repaired a flat tire on one of the vans.
4. Overhauled the engine on one of the trucks purchased three years ago.
5. Removed a two-way radio from one of the trucks and installed a new radio with a greater range of communication.
6. Rebuilt the transmission on one of the vans that had been driven 40,000 miles. The van was no longer under warranty.
7. Changed the radiator fluid on a truck that had been in service for the past four years.
8. Tinted the back and side windows of one of the vans to discourage theft of contents.
9. Changed the oil and greased the joints of all the trucks and vans.
10. Installed security systems on four of the newer trucks.

Classify each of the costs as a capital expenditure or a revenue expenditure.

EX 10-5
Capital and revenue expenditures

obj. 1

Jaime Baldwin owns and operates Love Transport Co. During the past year, Jaime incurred the following costs related to an 18-wheel truck:

1. Changed engine oil.
2. Installed a wind deflector on top of the cab to increase fuel mileage.
3. Replaced fog and cab light bulbs.
4. Modified the factory-installed turbo charger with a special-order kit designed to add 50 more horsepower to the engine performance.
5. Replaced a headlight that had burned out.
6. Removed the old CB radio and replaced it with a newer model with a greater range.
7. Replaced the old radar detector with a newer model that detects the KA frequencies now used by many of the state patrol radar guns. The detector is wired directly into the cab, so that it is partially hidden. In addition, Jaime fastened the detector to the truck with a locking device that prevents its removal.
8. Replaced the hydraulic brake system that had begun to fail during his latest trip through the Rocky Mountains.
9. Installed a television in the sleeping compartment of the truck.
10. Replaced a shock absorber that had worn out.

Classify each of the costs as a capital expenditure or a revenue expenditure.

EX 10-6
Capital and revenue expenditures

obj. 1

Easy Move Company made the following expenditures on one of its delivery trucks:

Feb. 16.   Replaced transmission at a cost of $3,150.
July 15.   Paid $1,100 for installation of a hydraulic lift.
Oct.   3.   Paid $72 to change the oil and air filter.

Prepare journal entries for each expenditure.

EX 10-7
Nature of depreciation

obj. 2

Legacy Ironworks Co. reported $3,175,000 for equipment and $2,683,000 for accumulated depreciation—equipment on its balance sheet.
➤ Does this mean (a) that the replacement cost of the equipment is $3,175,000 and (b) that $2,683,000 is set aside in a special fund for the replacement of the equipment? Explain.

EX 10-8
Straight-line depreciation rates

obj. 2

✔ c. 10%

Convert each of the following estimates of useful life to a straight-line depreciation rate, stated as a percentage, assuming that the residual value of the fixed asset is to be ignored: (a) 2 years, (b) 8 years, (c) 10 years, (d) 20 years, (e) 25 years, (f) 40 years, (g) 50 years.

EX 10-9
Straight-line depreciation

obj. 2

✔ $3,350

A refrigerator used by a meat processor has a cost of $93,750, an estimated residual value of $10,000, and an estimated useful life of 25 years. What is the amount of the annual depreciation computed by the straight-line method?

EX 10-10

Depreciation by units-of-production method

obj. 2

✔ $276

A diesel-powered tractor with a cost of $145,000 and estimated residual value of $7,000 is expected to have a useful operating life of 75,000 hours. During July, the generator was operated 150 hours. Determine the depreciation for the month.

EX 10-11

Depreciation by units-of-production method

obj. 2

✔ a. Truck #1, credit Accumulated Depreciation, $6,670

Prior to adjustment at the end of the year, the balance in Trucks is $250,900 and the balance in Accumulated Depreciation—Trucks is $88,200. Details of the subsidiary ledger are as follows:

Truck No.	Cost	Estimated Residual Value	Estimated Useful Life	Accumulated Depreciation at Beginning of Year	Miles Operated During Year
1	$50,000	$ 6,500	150,000 miles	—	23,000 miles
2	72,900	9,900	300,000	$60,000	25,000
3	38,000	3,000	200,000	8,050	36,000
4	90,000	13,000	200,000	20,150	40,000

a. Determine the depreciation rates per mile and the amount to be credited to the accumulated depreciation section of each of the subsidiary accounts for the miles operated during the current year.
b. Journalize the entry to record depreciation for the year.

EX 10-12

Depreciation by two methods

obj. 2

✔ a. $3,750

A Kubota tractor acquired on January 9 at a cost of $75,000 has an estimated useful life of 20 years. Assuming that it will have no residual value, determine the depreciation for each of the first two years (a) by the straight-line method and (b) by the double-declining-balance method.

EX 10-13

Depreciation by two methods

obj. 2

✔ a. $19,000

A storage tank acquired at the beginning of the fiscal year at a cost of $172,000 has an estimated residual value of $20,000 and an estimated useful life of eight years. Determine the following: (a) the amount of annual depreciation by the straight-line method and (b) the amount of depreciation for the first and second years computed by the double-declining-balance method.

EX 10-14

Partial-year depreciation

obj. 2

✔ a. First year, $2,000

Sandblasting equipment acquired at a cost of $85,000 has an estimated residual value of $5,000 and an estimated useful life of 10 years. It was placed in service on October 1 of the current fiscal year, which ends on December 31. Determine the depreciation for the current fiscal year and for the following fiscal year by (a) the straight-line method and (b) the double-declining-balance method.

EX 10-15

Revision of depreciation

obj. 2

✔ a. $17,500

A building with a cost of $1,050,000 has an estimated residual value of $420,000, has an estimated useful life of 36 years, and is depreciated by the straight-line method. (a) What is the amount of the annual depreciation? (b) What is the book value at the end of the twentieth year of use? (c) If at the start of the twenty-first year it is estimated that the remaining life is 20 years and that the residual value is $300,000, what is the depreciation expense for each of the remaining 20 years?

EX 10-16

Capital expenditure and depreciation

objs. 1, 2

✔ b. Depreciation Expense, $600

Crane Company purchased and installed carpet in its new general offices on March 30 for a total cost of $12,000. The carpet is estimated to have a 15-year useful life and no residual value.

a. Prepare the journal entries necessary for recording the purchase of the new carpet.
b. Record the December 31 adjusting entry for the partial-year depreciation expense for the carpet, assuming that Crane Company uses the straight-line method.

EX 10-17

Entries for sale of fixed asset

obj. 3

Equipment acquired on January 3, 2007, at a cost of $504,000, has an estimated useful life of 12 years, has an estimated residual value of $42,000, and is depreciated by the straight-line method.

a. What was the book value of the equipment at December 31, 2010, the end of the year?
b. Assuming that the equipment was sold on April 1, 2011, for $315,000, journalize the entries to record (1) depreciation for the three months until the sale date, and (2) the sale of the equipment.

EX 10-18

Disposal of fixed asset

obj. 3

✔ b. $177,750

Equipment acquired on January 3, 2007, at a cost of $265,500, has an estimated useful life of eight years and an estimated residual value of $31,500.

a. What was the annual amount of depreciation for the years 2007, 2008, and 2009, using the straight-line method of depreciation?
b. What was the book value of the equipment on January 1, 2010?
c. Assuming that the equipment was sold on January 4, 2010, for $168,500, journalize the entry to record the sale.
d. Assuming that the equipment had been sold on January 4, 2010, for $180,000 instead of $168,500, journalize the entry to record the sale.

EX 10-19

Depletion entries

obj. 4

✔ a. $2,475,000

Cikan Mining Co. acquired mineral rights for $16,200,000. The mineral deposit is estimated at 90,000,000 tons. During the current year, 13,750,000 tons were mined and sold.

a. Determine the amount of depletion expense for the current year.
b. Journalize the adjusting entry to recognize the depletion expense.

EX 10-20

Amortization entries

obj. 5

✔ a. $57,500

Isolution Company acquired patent rights on January 4, 2007, for $750,000. The patent has a useful life equal to its legal life of 15 years. On January 7, 2010, Isolution successfully defended the patent in a lawsuit at a cost of $90,000.

a. Determine the patent amortization expense for the current year ended December 31, 2010.
b. Journalize the adjusting entry to recognize the amortization.

EX 10-21

Book value of fixed assets

obj. 6

Apple Computer, Inc., designs, manufactures, and markets personal computers and related software. Apple also manufactures and distributes music players (Ipod) along with related accessories and services including the online distribution of third-party music. The following information was taken from a recent annual report of Apple:

Property, Plant, and Equipment (in millions):

	Current Year	Preceding Year
Land and buildings	$626	$361
Machinery, equipment, and internal-use software	595	470
Office furniture and equipment	94	81
Other fixed assets related to leases	760	569
Accumulated depreciation and amortization	794	664

a. Compute the book value of the fixed assets for the current year and the preceding year and explain the differences, if any.
b. ━━━▶ Would you normally expect the book value of fixed assets to increase or decrease during the year?

EX 10-22
Balance sheet presentation

obj. 6

List the errors you find in the following partial balance sheet:

Hobart Company
Balance Sheet
December 31, 2010

Assets

~~~~~~

Total current assets $350,000

	Replacement Cost	Accumulated Depreciation	Book Value
Property, plant, and equipment:			
Land	$ 60,000	$ 12,000	$ 48,000
Buildings	156,000	45,600	110,400
Factory equipment	330,000	175,200	154,800
Office equipment	72,000	48,000	24,000
Patents	48,000	—	48,000
Goodwill	27,000	3,000	24,000
Total property, plant, and equipment	$693,000	$283,800	409,200

Appendix 1
EX 10-23
Sum-of-the-years-digits depreciation

✔ First year: $7,143

Based on the data in Exercise 10-12, determine the depreciation for the Kubota tractor for each of the first two years, using the sum-of-the-years-digits depreciation method. Round to the nearest dollar.

Appendix 1
EX 10-24
Sum-of-the-years-digits depreciation

✔ First year: $33,778

Based on the data in Exercise 10-13, determine the depreciation for the storage tank for each of the first two years, using the sum-of-the-years-digits depreciation method. Round to the nearest dollar.

Appendix 1
EX 10-25
Partial-year depreciation

✔ First year: $3,636

Based on the data in Exercise 10-14, determine the depreciation for the sandblasting equipment for each of the first two years, using the sum-of-the-years-digits depreciation method. Round to the nearest dollar.

Appendix 2
EX 10-26
Asset traded for similar asset

✔ a. $180,000

A printing press priced at a fair market value of $300,000 is acquired in a transaction that has commercial substance by trading in a similar press and paying cash for the difference between the trade-in allowance and the price of the new press.

a. Assuming that the trade-in allowance is $120,000, what is the amount of cash given?
b. Assuming that the book value of the press traded in is $115,500, what is the gain or loss on the exchange?

Appendix 2
EX 10-27
Asset traded for similar asset

✔ a. $180,000

Assume the same facts as in Exercise 10-26, except that the book value of the press traded in is $127,750. (a) What is the amount of cash given? (b) What is the gain or loss on the exchange?

Appendix 2
EX 10-28
Entries for trade of fixed asset

On October 1, Hot Springs Co., a water distiller, acquired new bottling equipment with a list price (fair market value) of $462,000. Hot Springs received a trade-in allowance of $96,000 on the old equipment of a similar type and paid cash of $366,000. The following information about the old equipment is obtained from the account in the equipment ledger: cost, $336,000; accumulated depreciation on December 31, the end of the preceding fiscal year, $220,000; annual depreciation, $20,000. Assuming the exchange has commercial substance, journalize the entries to record (a) the current depreciation of the old equipment to the date of trade-in and (b) the exchange transaction on October 1.

Appendix 2
EX 10-29
Entries for trade of fixed asset

On April 1, Gyminny Delivery Services acquired a new truck with a list price (fair market value) of $150,000. Gyminny received a trade-in allowance of $30,000 on an old truck of similar type and paid cash of $120,000. The following information about the old truck is obtained from the account in the equipment ledger: cost, $96,000; accumulated depreciation on December 31, the end of the preceding fiscal year, $64,000; annual depreciation, $16,000. Assuming the exchange has commercial substance, journalize the entries to record (a) the current depreciation of the old truck to the date of trade-in and (b) the transaction on April 1.

EX 10-30
Fixed asset turnover ratio

Verizon Communications is a major telecommunications company in the United States. Verizon's balance sheet disclosed the following information regarding fixed assets:

	Dec. 31, 2007 (in millions)	Dec. 31, 2006 (in millions)
Plant, property, and equipment	$ 213,994	$204,109
Less accumulated depreciation	128,700	121,753
	$ 85,294	$ 82,356

Verizon's revenue for 2007 was $93,469 million. The fixed asset turnover for the telecommunications industry averages 1.10.

a. Determine Verizon's fixed asset turnover ratio. Round to two decimal places.
b. ➤ Interpret Verizon's fixed asset turnover ratio.

EX 10-31
Fixed asset turnover ratio

The following table shows the revenue and average net fixed assets (in millions) for a recent fiscal year for Best Buy and Circuit City Stores, Inc.:

	Revenue	Average Net Fixed Assets
Best Buy	35,934	2,825
Circuit City Stores, Inc.	12,430	880

a. Compute the fixed asset turnover for each company. Round to two decimal places.
b. ➤ Which company uses its fixed assets more efficiently? Explain.

Problems Series A

PR 10-1A
Allocate payments and receipts to fixed asset accounts

obj. 1

✔ Land, $469,450

The following payments and receipts are related to land, land improvements, and buildings acquired for use in a wholesale apparel business. The receipts are identified by an asterisk.

a. Finder's fee paid to real estate agency	....	$ 4,000
b. Cost of real estate acquired as a plant site: Land	....	375,000
	Building	25,000
c. Fee paid to attorney for title search	....	2,500
d. Delinquent real estate taxes on property, assumed by purchaser	...	31,750
e. Architect's and engineer's fees for plans and supervision	....	36,000
f. Cost of removing building purchased with land in (b)	....	10,000
g. Proceeds from sale of salvage materials from old building	....	3,000*

h. Cost of filling and grading land	15,200
i Premium on one-year insurance policy during construction	5,400
j. Money borrowed to pay building contractor	600,000*
k. Special assessment paid to city for extension of water main to the	
property	9,000
l. Cost of repairing windstorm damage during construction	3,000
m. Cost of repairing vandalism damage during construction	1,800
n. Cost of trees and shrubbery planted	12,000
o. Cost of paving parking lot to be used by customers	14,500
p. Interest incurred on building loan during construction	33,000
q. Proceeds from insurance company for windstorm and vandalism	
damage	4,500*
r. Payment to building contractor for new building . . . . . :	700,000
s. Refund of premium on insurance policy (j) canceled after	
10 months	450*

Instructions

1. Assign each payment and receipt to Land (unlimited life), Land Improvements (limited life), Building, or Other Accounts. Indicate receipts by an asterisk. Identify each item by letter and list the amounts in columnar form, as follows:

Item	Land	Land Improvements	Building	Other Accounts

2. Determine the amount debited to Land, Land Improvements, and Building.
3. ━━━▶ The costs assigned to the land, which is used as a plant site, will not be depreciated, while the costs assigned to land improvements will be depreciated. Explain this seemingly contradictory application of the concept of depreciation.

PR 10-2A
Compare three depreciation methods

obj. 2

✔ a. 2009: straight-line depreciation, $86,000

Newbirth Coatings Company purchased waterproofing equipment on January 2, 2009, for $380,000. The equipment was expected to have a useful life of four years, or 8,000 operating hours, and a residual value of $36,000. The equipment was used for 3,000 hours during 2009, 2,500 hours in 2010, 1,400 hours in 2011, and 1,100 hours in 2012.

Instructions

Determine the amount of depreciation expense for the years ended December 31, 2009, 2010, 2011, and 2012, by (a) the straight-line method, (b) the units-of-production method, and (c) the double-declining-balance method. Also determine the total depreciation expense for the four years by each method. The following columnar headings are suggested for recording the depreciation expense amounts:

	Depreciation Expense		
Year	Straight-Line Method	Units-of-Production Method	Double-Declining-Balance Method

---

PR 10-3A
Depreciation by three methods; partial years

obj. 2

✔ a. 2008, $7,600

Razar Sharp Company purchased tool sharpening equipment on July 1, 2008, for $48,600. The equipment was expected to have a useful life of three years, or 7,500 operating hours, and a residual value of $3,000. The equipment was used for 1,800 hours during 2008, 2,600 hours in 2009, 2,000 hours in 2010, and 1,100 hours in 2011.

Instructions

Determine the amount of depreciation expense for the years ended December 31, 2008, 2009, 2010, and 2011, by (a) the straight-line method, (b) the units-of-production method, and (c) the double-declining-balance method.

PR 10-4A
Depreciation by two methods; sale of fixed asset

objs. 2, 3

New tire retreading equipment, acquired at a cost of $144,000 at the beginning of a fiscal year, has an estimated useful life of four years and an estimated residual value of $10,800. The manager requested information regarding the effect of alternative methods on the amount of depreciation expense each year. On the basis of the data presented to the manager, the double-declining-balance method was selected.

✔ 1. b. Year 1,
$72,000 depreciation
expense

In the first week of the fourth year, the equipment was sold for $19,750.

Instructions

1. Determine the annual depreciation expense for each of the estimated four years of use, the accumulated depreciation at the end of each year, and the book value of the equipment at the end of each year by (a) the straight-line method and (b) the double-declining-balance method. The following columnar headings are suggested for each schedule:

Year	Depreciation Expense	Accumulated Depreciation, End of Year	Book Value, End of Year

2. Journalize the entry to record the sale.
3. Journalize the entry to record the sale, assuming that the equipment sold for $14,900 instead of $19,750.

PR 10-5A
Transactions for fixed assets, including sale
objs. **1, 2, 3**

The following transactions, adjusting entries, and closing entries were completed by King Furniture Co. during a three-year period. All are related to the use of delivery equipment. The double-declining-balance method of depreciation is used.

2008
Jan. 7. Purchased a used delivery truck for $45,600, paying cash.
Feb. 27. Paid garage $130 for changing the oil, replacing the oil filter, and tuning the engine on the delivery truck.
Dec. 31. Recorded depreciation on the truck for the fiscal year. The estimated useful life of the truck is eight years, with a residual value of $10,000 for the truck.

2009
Jan. 8. Purchased a new truck for $75,000, paying cash.
Mar. 13. Paid garage $200 to tune the engine and make other minor repairs on the used truck.
Apr. 30. Sold the used truck for $30,000. (Record depreciation to date in 2009 for the truck.)
Dec. 31. Record depreciation for the new truck. It has an estimated trade-in value of $13,500 and an estimated life of 10 years.

2010
July 1. Purchased a new truck for $82,000, paying cash.
Oct. 4. Sold the truck purchased January 8, 2009, for $53,000. (Record depreciation for the year.)
Dec. 31. Recorded depreciation on the remaining truck. It has an estimated residual value of $15,000 and an estimated useful life of 10 years.

Instructions
Journalize the transactions and the adjusting entries.

PR 10-6A
Amortization and depletion entries
objs. **4, 5**
✔ b. $33,750

Data related to the acquisition of timber rights and intangible assets during the current year ended December 31 are as follows:

a. On December 31, the company determined that $20,000,000 of goodwill was impaired.
b. Governmental and legal costs of $675,000 were incurred on June 30 in obtaining a patent with an estimated economic life of 10 years. Amortization is to be for one-half year.
c. Timber rights on a tract of land were purchased for $1,665,000 on February 16. The stand of timber is estimated at 9,000,000 board feet. During the current year, 2,400,000 board feet of timber were cut and sold.

Instructions
1. Determine the amount of the amortization, depletion, or impairment for the current year for each of the foregoing items.
2. Journalize the adjusting entries to record the amortization, depletion, or impairment for each item.

Problems Series B

PR 10-1B
Allocate payments and receipts to fixed asset accounts

obj. 1

✔ Land, $356,200

The following payments and receipts are related to land, land improvements, and buildings acquired for use in a wholesale ceramic business. The receipts are identified by an asterisk.

a.	Fee paid to attorney for title search	$ 1,500
b.	Cost of real estate acquired as a plant site: Land	270,000
	Building	30,000
c.	Special assessment paid to city for extension of water main to the property	20,000
d.	Cost of razing and removing building	5,000
e.	Proceeds from sale of salvage materials from old building	3,600*
f.	Delinquent real estate taxes on property, assumed by purchaser	15,800
g.	Premium on one-year insurance policy during construction	4,200
h.	Cost of filling and grading land	17,500
i.	Architect's and engineer's fees for plans and supervision	18,000
j.	Money borrowed to pay building contractor	750,000*
k.	Cost of repairing windstorm damage during construction	4,500
l.	Cost of paving parking lot to be used by customers	15,000
m.	Cost of trees and shrubbery planted	9,000
n.	Cost of floodlights installed on parking lot	1,100
o.	Cost of repairing vandalism damage during construction	1,500
p.	Proceeds from insurance company for windstorm and vandalism damage	6,000*
q.	Payment to building contractor for new building	800,000
r.	Interest incurred on building loan during construction	45,000
s.	Refund of premium on insurance policy (g) canceled after 11 months	350*

Instructions
1. Assign each payment and receipt to Land (unlimited life), Land Improvements (limited life), Building, or Other Accounts. Indicate receipts by an asterisk. Identify each item by letter and list the amounts in columnar form, as follows:

Item	Land	Land Improvements	Building	Other Accounts

2. Determine the amount debited to Land, Land Improvements, and Building.
3. ➤ The costs assigned to the land, which is used as a plant site, will not be depreciated, while the costs assigned to land improvements will be depreciated. Explain this seemingly contradictory application of the concept of depreciation.

PR 10-2B
Compare three depreciation methods

obj. 2

✔ a. 2008: straight-line depreciation, $21,000

Mammoth Company purchased packaging equipment on January 3, 2008, for $67,500. The equipment was expected to have a useful life of three years, or 25,000 operating hours, and a residual value of $4,500. The equipment was used for 12,000 hours during 2008, 9,000 hours in 2009, and 4,000 hours in 2010.

Instructions
Determine the amount of depreciation expense for the years ended December 31, 2008, 2009, and 2010, by (a) the straight-line method, (b) the units-of-production method, and (c) the double-declining-balance method. Also determine the total depreciation expense for the three years by each method. The following columnar headings are suggested for recording the depreciation expense amounts:

	Depreciation Expense		
Year	Straight-Line Method	Units-of-Production Method	Double-Declining-Balance Method

PR 10-3B

Depreciation by three methods; partial years

obj. 2

✔ a. 2008: $2,510

Quality IDs Company purchased plastic laminating equipment on July 1, 2008, for $15,660. The equipment was expected to have a useful life of three years, or 18,825 operating hours, and a residual value of $600. The equipment was used for 3,750 hours during 2008, 7,500 hours in 2009, 5,000 hours in 2010, and 2,575 hours in 2011.

Instructions

Determine the amount of depreciation expense for the years ended December 31, 2008, 2009, 2010, and 2011, by (a) the straight-line method, (b) the units-of-production method, and (c) the double-declining-balance method. Round to the nearest dollar.

PR 10-4B

Depreciation by two methods; sale of fixed asset

objs. 2, 3

✔ b. Year 1: $52,500 depreciation expense

New lithographic equipment, acquired at a cost of $131,250 at the beginning of a fiscal year, has an estimated useful life of five years and an estimated residual value of $11,250. The manager requested information regarding the effect of alternative methods on the amount of depreciation expense each year. On the basis of the data presented to the manager, the double-declining-balance method was selected.

In the first week of the fifth year, the equipment was sold for $21,500.

Instructions

1. Determine the annual depreciation expense for each of the estimated five years of use, the accumulated depreciation at the end of each year, and the book value of the equipment at the end of each year by (a) the straight-line method and (b) the double-declining-balance method. The following columnar headings are suggested for each schedule:

Year	Depreciation Expense	Accumulated Depreciation, End of Year	Book Value, End of Year

2. Journalize the entry to record the sale.
3. Journalize the entry to record the sale, assuming that the equipment was sold for $12,500 instead of $21,500.

PR 10-5B

Transactions for fixed assets, including sale

objs. 1, 2, 3

The following transactions, adjusting entries, and closing entries were completed by Trail Creek Furniture Co. during a three-year period. All are related to the use of delivery equipment. The double-declining-balance method of depreciation is used.

2008

Jan. 6.   Purchased a used delivery truck for $24,000, paying cash.

July 19.   Paid garage $500 for miscellaneous repairs to the truck.

Dec. 31.   Recorded depreciation on the truck for the year. The estimated useful life of the truck is four years, with a residual value of $4,000 for the truck.

2009

Jan. 2.   Purchased a new truck for $69,000, paying cash.

Aug. 1.   Sold the used truck for $10,250. (Record depreciation to date in 2009 for the truck.)

Oct. 24.   Paid garage $415 for miscellaneous repairs to the truck.

Dec. 31.   Record depreciation for the new truck. It has an estimated residual value of $15,000 and an estimated life of five years.

2010

July 1.   Purchased a new truck for $70,000, paying cash.

Oct. 1.   Sold the truck purchased January 2, 2009, for $25,000. (Record depreciation for the year.)

Dec. 31.   Recorded depreciation on the remaining truck. It has an estimated residual value of $18,000 and an estimated useful life of eight years.

Instructions

Journalize the transactions and the adjusting entries.

PR 10-6B
Amortization and
depletion entries

objs. **4, 5**

✔ 1. a. $356,200

Data related to the acquisition of timber rights and intangible assets during the current year ended December 31 are as follows:

a. Timber rights on a tract of land were purchased for $1,170,000 on July 5. The stand of timber is estimated at 4,500,000 board feet. During the current year, 1,370,000 board feet of timber were cut and sold.

b. On December 31, the company determined that $5,000,000 of goodwill was impaired.

c. Governmental and legal costs of $234,000 were incurred on April 4 in obtaining a patent with an estimated economic life of 12 years. Amortization is to be for three-fourths of a year.

Instructions

1. Determine the amount of the amortization, depletion, or impairment for the current year for each of the foregoing items.

2. Journalize the adjusting entries required to record the amortization, depletion, or impairment for each item.

Special Activities

You can access the special activities online at **www.cengage.com/accounting/reeve**.

Excel Success Special Activities

SA 10-1
Straight-line depreciation, multiple assets

The fixed asset details for Hydro-Link, Inc., are as follows:

Asset	Initial Cost	Estimated Residual Value	Estimated Useful Life (in years)
Computers	$36,000	$ 5,800	4
Conveyors	58,000	16,000	12
Cutting machine	7,600	1,200	8
Extruding machine	9,000	1,500	10
Forklift	16,000	3,400	7
Furnace	22,000	4,500	20

a. Open the Excel file *SA10-1.*

b. Develop a spreadsheet to determine the annual straight-line depreciation for each asset.

c. When you have completed the depreciation table, perform a "save as," replacing the entire file name with the following:

SA10-1_[your first name initial]_[your last name]

SA 10-2
Straight-line
depreciation, revised
estimates

The Better Bakery Company has a baking oven that has a book value at the beginning of the current year of $95,000 and an estimated residual value of $3,000. The remaining useful life of the baking oven is estimated to be five years.

a. Open the Excel file *SA10-2.*

b. Prepare a spreadsheet to determine the depreciation expense under the straight-line method for the current year.

c. When you have completed the depreciation table, perform a "save as," replacing the entire file name with the following:

SA10-2_[your first name initial]_[your last name]

SA 10-3
Units-of-production
method, multiple
assets

Details of the subsidiary ledger for the delivery trucks of Klondike Delivery, Inc., are as follows:

Truck No.	Initial Cost	Estimated Residual Value	Estimated Useful Life (in miles)	Miles Operated in the Current Year
1	$37,500	$1,100	140,000	35,000
2	29,650	900	125,000	32,000
3	32,800	1,300	150,000	40,000
4	45,900	900	180,000	38,000
5	36,700	1,500	160,000	28,000
6	48,400	2,400	200,000	42,000

a. Open the Excel file *SA10-3*.
b. Develop a spreadsheet to determine the deprecation per mile and the current year depreciation expense for each truck using the units-of-production method.
c. When you have completed the depreciation table, perform a "save as," replacing the entire file name with the following:

   SA10-3_[your first name initial]_[your last name]

SA 10-4
Units-of-production
method, multiple
assets

Daniels Construction Company purchased a bulldozer, backhoe, and grader at the beginning of the current year. The bulldozer has an initial cost of $120,000 with an estimated salvage value of $12,000. The backhoe has an initial cost of $62,000 and an estimated salvage value of $6,000. Lastly, the grader has an initial cost of $75,000 and an estimated salvage value of $8,000. The estimated useful life and hours operated in the current year are as follows:

Equipment	Estimated Useful Life (in hours)	Hours Operated in the Current Year
Bulldozer	24,000	2,200
Backhoe	22,400	1,850
Grader	20,000	2,160

a. Open the Excel file *SA10-4*.
b. Develop a spreadsheet to determine the depreciation per hour and the current year depreciation expense for each piece of equipment using the units-of-production method.
c. When you have completed the depreciation table, perform a "save as," replacing the entire file name with the following:

   SA10-4_[your first name initial]_[your last name]

Self-Examination Questions

1. **C**   All amounts spent to get a fixed asset (such as machinery) in place and ready for use are proper charges to the asset account. In the case of machinery acquired, the freight (answer A) and the installation costs (answer B) are both (answer C) proper charges to the machinery account.

2. **C**   The periodic charge for depreciation under the double-declining-balance method for the second year is determined by first computing the depreciation charge for the first year. The depreciation for the first year of $6,000 (answer A) is computed by multiplying the cost of the equipment, $9,000, by 2/3 (the straight-line rate of 1/3 multiplied by 2). The depreciation for the second year of $2,000 (answer C) is then determined by multiplying the book value at the end of the first year, $3,000 (the

cost of $9,000 minus the first-year depreciation of $6,000), by 2/3. The third year's depreciation is $400 (answer D). It is determined by multiplying the book value at the end of the second year, $1,000, by 2/3, thus yielding $667. However, the equipment cannot be depreciated below its residual value of $600; thus, the third-year depreciation is $400 ($1,000 − $600).

3. **B**   A depreciation method that provides for a higher depreciation amount in the first year of the use of an asset and a gradually declining periodic amount thereafter is called an accelerated depreciation method. The double-declining-balance method (answer B) is an example of such a method.

4. **A**   A gain of $3,500 was recognized on the sale of the equipment as shown on the next page.

Annual depreciation [($80,000 − $7,500)/5 years]................	$14,500 (Answer B)
Cost of equipment	$80,000
Accumulated depreciation on December 31, 2010 ($14,500 × 3)	43,500 (Answer D)
Book value of equipment on December 31, 2010	$36,500 (Answer C)
Selling price	$40,000
Book value of equipment on December 31, 2010	36,500
Gain on sale of equipment	$ 3,500

5. **D**   Long-lived assets that are useful in operations, not held for sale, and without physical qualities are called intangible assets. Patents, goodwill, and copyrights are examples of intangible assets (answer D).

Current Liabilities and Payroll

PANERA BREAD

anks and other financial institutions provide loans or credit to buyers for purchases of various items. Using credit to purchase items is probably as old as commerce itself. In fact, the Babylonians were lending money to support trade as early as 1300 B.C. The use of credit provides *individuals* convenience and buying power. Credit cards provide individuals convenience over writing checks and make purchasing over the Internet easier. Credit cards also provide individuals control over cash by providing documentation of their purchases through receipt of monthly credit card statements and by allowing them to avoid carrying large amounts of cash and to purchase items before they are paid.

Short-term credit is also used by *businesses* to provide convenience in purchasing items for manufacture or resale. More importantly, short-term credit gives a business control over the payment for goods and services. For example, Panera Bread, a chain of bakery-cafés located throughout the United States, uses short-term trade credit, or accounts payable, to purchase ingredients for making bread products in its bakeries. Short-term trade credit gives Panera control over cash payments by separating the purchase function from the payment function. Thus, the employee responsible for purchasing the bakery ingredients is separated from the employee responsible for paying for the purchase. This separation of duties can help prevent unauthorized purchases or payments.

In addition to accounts payable, a business like Panera Bread can also have current liabilities related to payroll, payroll taxes, employee benefits, short-term notes, unearned revenue, and contingencies. We will discuss each of these types of current liabilities in this chapter.

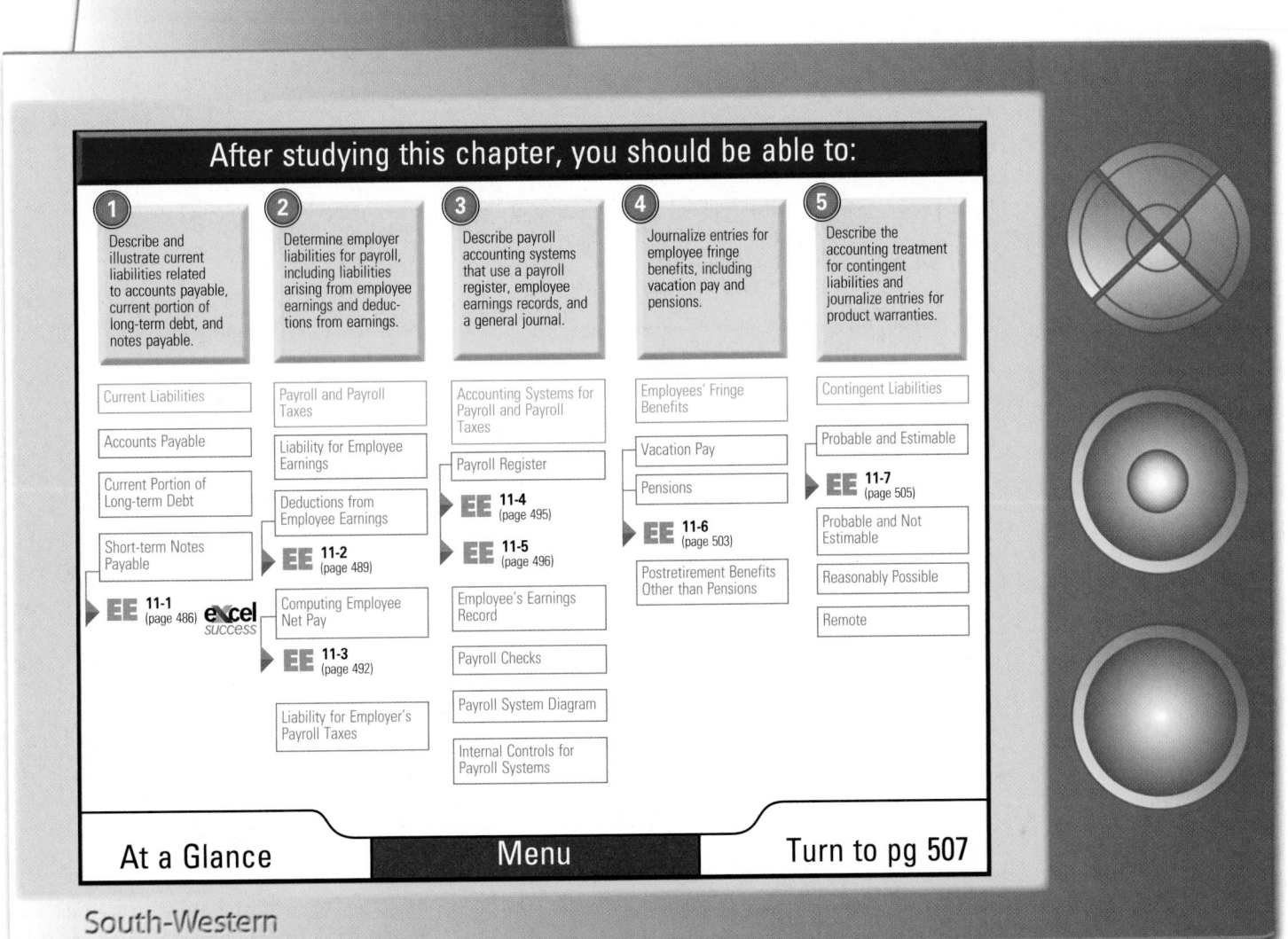

After studying this chapter, you should be able to:

1 Describe and illustrate current liabilities related to accounts payable, current portion of long-term debt, and notes payable.

Current Liabilities

Accounts Payable

Current Portion of Long-term Debt

Short-term Notes Payable

EE 11-1 (page 486) excel success

2 Determine employer liabilities for payroll, including liabilities arising from employee earnings and deductions from earnings.

Payroll and Payroll Taxes

Liability for Employee Earnings

Deductions from Employee Earnings

EE 11-2 (page 489)

Computing Employee Net Pay

EE 11-3 (page 492)

Liability for Employer's Payroll Taxes

3 Describe payroll accounting systems that use a payroll register, employee earnings records, and a general journal.

Accounting Systems for Payroll and Payroll Taxes

Payroll Register

EE 11-4 (page 495)

EE 11-5 (page 496)

Employee's Earnings Record

Payroll Checks

Payroll System Diagram

Internal Controls for Payroll Systems

4 Journalize entries for employee fringe benefits, including vacation pay and pensions.

Employees' Fringe Benefits

Vacation Pay

Pensions

EE 11-6 (page 503)

Postretirement Benefits Other than Pensions

5 Describe the accounting treatment for contingent liabilities and journalize entries for product warranties.

Contingent Liabilities

Probable and Estimable

EE 11-7 (page 505)

Probable and Not Estimable

Reasonably Possible

Remote

At a Glance   Menu   Turn to pg 507

South-Western

Current Liabilities

1 Describe and illustrate current liabilities related to accounts payable, current portion of long-term debt, and notes payable.

When a company or a bank advances *credit*, it is making a loan. The company or bank is called a *creditor* (or *lender*). The individuals or companies receiving the loan are called *debtors* (or *borrowers*).

Debt is recorded as a liability by the debtor. *Long-term liabilities* are debt due beyond one year. Thus, a 30-year mortgage used to purchase property is a long-term liability. *Current liabilities* are debt that will be paid out of current assets and are due within one year.

Three types of current liabilities are discussed in this section—accounts payable, current portion of long-term debt, and notes payable.

Accounts Payable

Accounts payable transactions have been described and illustrated in earlier chapters. These transactions involved a variety of purchases on account, including the purchase of merchandise and supplies. For most companies, accounts payable is the largest current liability. Exhibit 1 shows the accounts payable balance as a percent of total current liabilities for a number of companies.

Exhibit 1

Accounts Payable as a Percent of Total Current Liabilities

Company	Accounts Payable as a Percent of Total Current Liabilities
Alcoa Inc.	39%
AT&T	16
Gap Inc.	47
IBM	22
Nissan Motor Co. Ltd.	25
Rite Aid Corp.	51
ChevronTexaco	54

Current Portion of Long-Term Debt

Long-term liabilities are often paid back in periodic payments, called *installments*. Such installments that are due *within* the coming year are classified as a current liability. The installments due *after* the coming year are classified as a long-term liability.

To illustrate, Starbucks Corporation reported the following debt payments schedule in its September 30, 2007, annual report to shareholders:

Fiscal year ending	
2008	$ 775,000
2009	789,000
2010	337,000
2011	56,000
2012	0
Thereafter	550,000,000
Total principal payments	$551,957,000

The debt of $775,000 due in 2008 would be reported as a current liability on the September 30, 2007, balance sheet. The remaining debt of $551,182,000 ($551,957,000 − $775,000) would be reported as a long-term liability on the balance sheet.

Short-Term Notes Payable

Notes may be issued to purchase merchandise or other assets. Notes may also be issued to creditors to satisfy an account payable created earlier.[1]

To illustrate, assume that Nature's Sunshine Company issued a 90-day, 12% note for $1,000, dated August 1, 2009, to Murray Co. for a $1,000 overdue account. The entry to record the issuance of the note is as follows:

Aug.	1	Accounts Payable—Murray Co.	1,000	
		Notes Payable		1,000
		Issued a 90-day, 12% note on account.		

---

1 The accounting for notes received to satisfy an account receivable was described and illustrated in Chapter 9, Receivables.

When the note matures, the entry to record the payment of $1,000 plus $30 interest ($1,000 × 12% × 90/360) is as follows:

Oct.	30	Notes Payable	1,000	
		Interest Expense	30	
		Cash		1,030
		Paid principal and interest due on note.		

The interest expense is reported in the Other expense section of the income statement for the year ended December 31, 2009. The interest expense account is closed at December 31.

Each note transaction affects a debtor (borrower) and creditor (lender). The following illustration shows how the same transactions are recorded by the debtor and creditor. In this illustration, the debtor (borrower) is Bowden Co., and the creditor (lender) is Coker Co.

	Bowden Co. (Borrower)			Coker Co. (Creditor)		

May 1. Bowden Co. purchased merchandise on account from Coker Co., $10,000, 2/10, n/30. The merchandise cost Coker Co. $7,500.	Merchandise Inventory
	  Accounts Payable
		10,000	10,000	Accounts Receivable
				  Sales
				
				Cost of Merchandise Sold
				  Merchandise Inventory
					10,000
					
					7,500
						10,000
						
						7,500

May 31. Bowden Co. issued a 60-day, 12% note for $10,000 to Coker Co. on account.	Accounts Payable
	  Notes Payable
		10,000	10,000	Notes Receivable
				  Accounts Receivable
					10,000	10,000

July 30. Bowden Co. paid Coker Co. the amount due on the note of May 31. Interest: $10,000 × 12% × 60/360.	Notes Payable
	Interest Expense
	  Cash
		10,000
		200
			10,200	Cash
				  Interest Revenue
				  Notes Receivable
					10,200	200
						10,000

A company may borrow from a bank by issuing a note. To illustrate, assume that on September 19 Iceburg Company issues a $4,000, 90-day, 15% note to First National Bank. The entry to record the issuance of the note is as follows:

Sept.	19	Cash	4,000	
		Notes Payable		4,000
		Issued a 90-day, 15% note to First National Bank.		

On the due date of the note (December 18), Iceburg Company owes $4,000 plus interest of $150 ($4,000 × 15% × 90/360). The entry to record the payment of the note is as follows:

Dec.	18	Notes Payable	4,000	
		Interest Expense	150	
		Cash		4,150
		Paid principal and interest due on note.		

The U.S. Treasury issues short-term treasury bills to investors at a discount.

In some cases, a *discounted note* may be issued rather than an interest-bearing note. A discounted note has the following characteristics:

1. The creditor (lender) requires an interest rate, called the *discount rate*.
2. Interest, called the *discount*, is computed on the face amount of the note.
3. The debtor (borrower) receives the face amount of the note less the discount, called the *proceeds*.
4. The debtor pays the face amount of the note on the due date.

To illustrate, assume that on August 10, Cary Company issues a $20,000, 90-day discounted note to Western National Bank. The discount rate is 15%, and the amount of the discount is $750 ($20,000 × 15% × 90/360). Thus, the proceeds received by Cary Company are $19,250. The entry by Cary Company is as follows:

Aug.	10	Cash	19,250	
		Interest Expense	750	
		Notes Payable		20,000
		Issued a 90-day discounted note to Western National Bank at a 15% discount rate.		

The entry when Cary Company pays the discounted note on November 8 is as follows:[2]

Nov.	8	Notes Payable	20,000	
		Cash		20,000
		Paid note due.		

Other current liabilities that have been discussed in earlier chapters include accrued expenses, unearned revenue, and interest payable. The accounting for wages and salaries, termed *payroll accounting*, is discussed next.

Example Exercise 11-1 Proceeds from Notes Payable   1

On July 1, Bella Salon Company issued a 60-day note with a face amount of $60,000 to Delilah Hair Products Company for merchandise inventory.

a. Determine the proceeds of the note, assuming the note carries an interest rate of 6%.
b. Determine the proceeds of the note, assuming the note is discounted at 6%.

Follow My Example 11-1

a. $60,000.
b. $59,400 [$60,000 − ($60,000 × 6% × 60/360)].

For Practice: PE 11-1A, PE 11-1B

2 If the accounting period ends before a discounted note is paid, an adjusting entry should record the prepaid (deferred) interest that is not yet an expense. This deferred interest would be deducted from Notes Payable in the Current Liabilities section of the balance sheet.

Determine employer liabilities for payroll, including liabilities arising from employee earnings and deductions from earnings.

Payroll and Payroll Taxes

In accounting, **payroll** refers to the amount paid employees for services they provided during the period. A company's payroll is important for the following reasons:

1. Employees are sensitive to payroll errors and irregularities.
2. Good employee morale requires payroll to be paid timely and accurately.
3. Payroll is subject to federal and state regulations.
4. Payroll and related payroll taxes significantly affect the net income of most companies.

Liability for Employee Earnings

Salary usually refers to payment for managerial and administrative services. Salary is normally expressed in terms of a month or a year. *Wages* usually refers to payment for employee manual labor. The rate of wages is normally stated on an hourly or a weekly basis. The salary or wage of an employee may be increased by bonuses, commissions, profit sharing, or cost-of-living adjustments.

Companies engaged in interstate commerce must follow the Fair Labor Standards Act. This act, sometimes called the Federal Wage and Hour Law, requires employers to pay a minimum rate of $1\frac{1}{2}$ times the regular rate for all hours worked in excess of 40 hours per week. Exemptions are provided for executive, administrative, and some supervisory positions. Increased rates for working overtime, nights, or holidays are common, even when not required by law. These rates may be as much as twice the regular rate.

To illustrate computing an employee's earnings, assume that John T. McGrath is a salesperson employed by McDermott Supply Co. McGrath's regular rate is $34 per hour, and any hours worked in excess of 40 hours per week are paid at $1\frac{1}{2}$ times the regular rate. McGrath worked 42 hours for the week ended December 27. His earnings of **$1,462** for the week are computed as follows:

Earnings at regular rate (40 hrs. × $34)	$1,360
Earnings at overtime rate [2 hrs. × ($34 × $1\frac{1}{2}$)]	102
Total earnings	**$1,462**

Deductions from Employee Earnings

The total earnings of an employee for a payroll period, including any overtime pay, are called **gross pay**. From this amount is subtracted one or more *deductions* to arrive at the **net pay**. Net pay is the amount paid the employee. The deductions normally include federal, state, and local income taxes, medical insurance, and pension contributions.

Income Taxes   Employers normally withhold a portion of employee earnings for payment of the employees' federal income tax. Each employee authorizes the amount to be withheld by completing an "Employee's Withholding Allowance Certificate," called a W-4. Exhibit 2 is the W-4 form submitted by John T. McGrath.

On the W-4, an employee indicates marital status and the number of withholding allowances. A single employee may claim one withholding allowance. A married employee may claim an additional allowance for a spouse. An employee may also claim an allowance for each dependent other than a spouse. Each allowance reduces the federal income tax withheld from the employee's check. Exhibit 2 indicates that John T. McGrath is single and, thus, claimed one withholding allowance.

The federal income tax withheld depends on each employee's gross pay and W-4 allowance. Withholding tables issued by the Internal Revenue Service (IRS) are used to determine amounts to withhold. Exhibit 3 is an example of an IRS wage withholding table for a single person who is paid weekly.[3]

---

3 IRS withholding tables are also available for married employees and for pay periods other than weekly.

Exhibit 2

Employee's Withholding Allowance Certificate (W-4 Form)

```
------------   Cut here and give Form W-4 to your employer. Keep the top part for your records.   ---------------

Form  W-4              Employee's Withholding Allowance Certificate            OMB No. 1545-0074
Department of the Treasury    ▶ Whether you are entitled to claim a certain number of allowances or exemption from withholding is     2008
Internal Revenue Service        subject to review by the IRS. Your employer may be required to send a copy of this form to the IRS.

1  Type or print your first name and middle initial.   Last name                    2  Your social security number
   John T.                                             McGrath                          381  48  9120
   Home address (number and street or rural route)      3  ☒ Single ☐ Married ☐ Married, but withhold at higher Single rate.
   1830 4th Street                                      Note. If married, but legally separated, or spouse is a nonresident alien, check the "Single" box.
   City or town, state, and ZIP code                    4  If your last name differs from that shown on your social security
   Clinton, Iowa 52732-6142                                card, check here. You must call 1-800-772-1213 for a new card. ▶ ☐

5  Total number of allowances you are claiming (from line H above or from the applicable worksheet on page 2)  5  | 1
6  Additional amount, if any, you want withheld from each paycheck  . . . . . . . . . . . .  6  $
7  I claim exemption from withholding for 2008, and I certify that I meet both of the following conditions for exemption.
   • Last year I had a right to a refund of all federal income tax withheld because I had no tax liability and
   • This year I expect a refund of all federal income tax withheld because I expect to have no tax liability.
   If you meet both conditions, write "Exempt" here  . . . . . . . . . . . . . ▶ | 7 |

Under penalties of perjury, I declare that I have examined this certificate and to the best of my knowledge and belief, it is true, correct, and complete.
Employee's signature
(Form is not valid
unless you sign it.) ▶  John T. McGrath               Date ▶ June 2, 2008

8  Employer's name and address (Employer: Complete lines 8 and 10 only if sending to the IRS.)  9 Office code  10 Employer identification number (EIN)
                                                                                                    (optional)

                                                                Cat. No. 10220Q            Form W-4 (2008)
```

In Exhibit 3, each row is the employee's wages after deducting the employee's withholding allowances. Each year, the amount of the standard withholding allowance is determined by the IRS. For a single person paid weekly, we assume the standard withholding allowance to be deducted in Exhibit 3 is $67.[4] Thus, if two withholding allowances are claimed, $134 ($67 × 2) is deducted.

To illustrate, John T. McGrath made $1,462 for the week ended December 27. McGrath's W-4 claims one withholding allowance of $67. Thus, the wages used in determining McGrath's withholding bracket in Exhibit 3 are $1,395 ($1,462 − $67).

After the person's withholding wage bracket has been computed, the federal income tax to be withheld is determined as follows:

Step 1. Locate the proper withholding wage bracket in Exhibit 3.

> *McGrath's wages after deducting one standard IRS withholding allowance are $1,395 ($1,462 − $67). Therefore, the wage bracket for McGrath is $653–$1,533.*

Step 2. Compute the withholding for the proper wage bracket using the directions in the two right-hand columns in Exhibit 3.

> *For McGrath's wage bracket, the withholding is computed as "$82.95 plus 25% of the excess over $653." Hence, McGrath's withholding is $268.45, as shown below.*

Initial withholding from wage bracket	$ 82.95
Plus [25% × ($1,395 − $653)]	185.50
Total withholding	$268.45

Exhibit 3

Wage Bracket Withholding Table

Table for Percentage Method of Withholding WEEKLY Payroll Period

(a) SINGLE person (including head of household) —

If the amount of wages (after subtracting withholding allowances) is:	The amount of income tax to withhold is:
Not over $51	$0

Over—	But not over—		of excess over—
$51	—$198	10%	—$51
$198	—$653	$14.70 plus 15%	—$198
$653	—$1,533	$82.95 plus 25%	—$653 ◀— McGrath wage bracket
$1,533	—$3,202	$302.95 plus 28%	—$1,533
$3,202	—$6,916	$770.27 plus 33%	—$3,202
$6,916	. . . .	$1,995.89 plus 35%	—$6,916

Source: Publication 15, *Employer's Tax Guide,* Internal Revenue Service, 2008.

4 The actual IRS standard withholding allowance changes every year and was $67.31 for 2008.

Residents of New York City must pay federal, state, and city income taxes.

Employers may also be required to withhold state or city income taxes. The amounts to be withheld are determined on state-by-state and city-by-city bases.

Example Exercise 11-2   Federal Income Tax Withholding   ● ● ● ● ● ● ● ●▶ ②

Karen Dunn's weekly gross earnings for the present week were $2,250. Dunn has two exemptions. Using the wage bracket withholding table in Exhibit 3 with a $67 standard withholding allowance for each exemption, what is Dunn's federal income tax withholding?

Follow My Example 11-2

Total wage payment		$ 2,250
One allowance (provided by IRS)	$67	
Multiplied by allowances claimed on Form W-4	× 2	134
Amount subject to withholding		$ 2,116
Initial withholding from wage bracket in Exhibit 3		$302.95
Plus additional withholding: 28% of excess over $1,533		163.24*
Federal income tax withholding		$466.19

*28% × ($2,116 − $1,533)

For Practice: PE 11-2A, PE 11-2B

FICA Tax Employers are required by the Federal Insurance Contributions Act (FICA) to withhold a portion of the earnings of each employee. The **FICA tax** withheld contributes to the following two federal programs:

1. *Social security*, which provides payments for retirees, survivors, and disability insurance (OASDI).
2. *Medicare*, which provides health insurance for senior citizens.

The amount withheld from each employee is based on the employee's earnings *paid* in the *calendar* year. The withholding tax rates and maximum earnings subject to tax are often revised by Congress. To simplify, this chapter assumes the following rates and earnings subject to tax:

1. Social security: 6% on the first $100,000 of annual earnings
2. Medicare: 1.5% on all earnings

To illustrate, assume that John T. McGrath's annual earnings prior to the payroll period ending on December 27 total $99,038. Since McGrath's earnings for the week are $1,462, the total FICA tax to be withheld is **$79.65**, as shown below.

Earnings subject to 6% social security tax		
($100,000 − $99,038)	$ 962	
Social security tax rate	× 6%	
Social security tax		$57.72
Earnings subject to 1.5% Medicare tax	$1,462	
Medicare tax rate	× 1.5%	
Medicare tax		21.93
Total FICA tax		$79.65

Other Deductions Employees may choose to have additional amounts deducted from their gross pay. For example, an employee may authorize deductions for retirement savings, for charitable contributions, or life insurance. A union contract may also require the deduction of union dues.

Computing Employee Net Pay

Gross earnings less payroll deductions equals *net pay*, sometimes called *take-home pay*. Assuming that John T. McGrath authorized deductions for retirement savings and for a United Fund contribution, McGrath's net pay for the week ended December 27 is $1,088.90, as shown below.

Gross earnings for the week			$1,462.00
Deductions:			
Social security tax		$ 57.72	
Medicare tax		21.93	
Federal income tax		268.45	
Retirement savings		20.00	
United Fund		5.00	
Total deductions			373.10
Net pay			$1,088.90

Employee net pay can be computed using a spreadsheet, as follows.

	A	B	C	
1	*Inputs:*	*T. McGrath*		
2	Hours worked straight-time	40		
3	Hours worked overtime	2		
4	Hourly rate	$ 34.00		
5	Overtime premium	150%		
6	Federal income tax (weekly withholding)	$ 268.45		
7	Earnings prior to payroll period	$ 99,038		
8	Social security rate	6%		
9	Medicare rate	1.5%		
10	Social security maximum earnings	$ 100,000.00		
11	Retirement savings (weekly)	$ 20.00		
12	United Way	$ 5.00		
13				
14	*Outputs:*			
15	Gross earnings for the week		=(B2*B4)+(B3*B4*B5)	◄— a.
16	Deductions:			
17	Social security tax	=(B10-B7)*B8	◄— b.	
18	Medicare tax	=C15*B9	◄— c.	
19	Federal income tax	=B6		
20	Retirement savings (weekly)	=B11	◄— d.	
21	United Way	=B12		
22	Total deductions		=SUM(B17:B21)	◄— e.
23	Net Pay		=C15-C22	◄— f.
24				

The spreadsheet should be developed with an input and output section. The outputs build formulas based on the inputs.

a.   Enter in C15 the gross earnings:
=(B2*B4)+(B3*B4*B5)

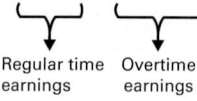

Regular time   Overtime
earnings   earnings

b.   McGrath's weekly earnings will cause the annual salary to exceed the maximum salary subject to social security tax of $100,000. Thus, enter in B17 the formula for social security tax.

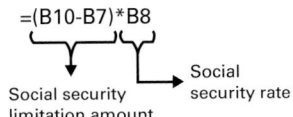

=(B10-B7)*B8

Social security
limitation amount

Social
security rate

    c.   Enter in B18 the formula for the Medicare tax, =C15*B9.

    d.   Enter in B19, B20, and B21 the cell references for the federal income tax, retirement savings, and United Way, respectively.

    e.   Enter in C22 the formula to sum the deductions, =Sum(B17:B21).

    f.   Enter in C23 the formula for the net pay, =C15-C22.

Absolute Cell References

Many employers have more than one employee. Spreadsheets are very useful for summarizing payroll information for many employees. We will illustrate multiple employees in order to introduce the Excel concept of absolute cell references. Absolute cell references are often used in Excel formula design. For example, assume Dandridge Company has three employees who are paid $15 per hour with an overtime premium of 150% for hours in excess of 40 hours per week. Payroll information for a recent week is as follows:

	A	B	C	D
1	*Inputs:*			
2	Hourly rate	$ 15.00		
3	Overtime premium	150%		
4	Regular time hours	40		
5				
6		Chambers, T.	Knox, J.	Little, B.
7	Hours worked	42	45	48
8				

The inputs include three columns of hours worked information for three employees. The formula for the straight-time, overtime, and gross earnings are first determined for T. Chambers as follows:

9	*Output:*			
10		Chambers, T.	Knox, J	Little, B.
11	Straight-time earnings	=$B4*$B2	Copied to	
12	Overtime earnings	=(B7-$B4)*$B2*$B3	two remaining	
13	Gross earnings	=SUM(B11:B12)	employees	
14				

The straight-time earnings formula is entered as,

=$B4*$B2

The dollar sign in front of both lettered columns indicates that the column references is to remain fixed when copying across the columns. That is, the formula is the same for all three employees, and the columns don't adjust during copying.

The overtime earnings formula is entered as:

=(B7-$B4)*$B2*$B3

In this case, the column reference for B4, B2, and B3 remains fixed in copying. However, B7 does adjust the column reference when copied. The sum formula is entered last. This formula requires no absolute cell references because the columns adjust in copying.

Once the three formulas are entered, they are copied to the two other employees. The formulas for all three employees after copying would appear as follows:

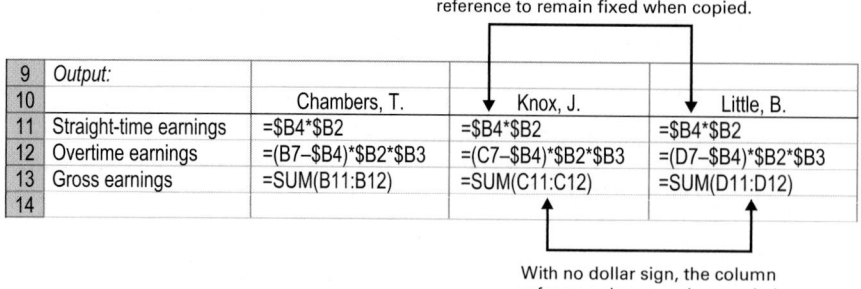

The dollar sign causes the column reference to remain fixed when copied.

9	Output:			
10		Chambers, T.	Knox, J.	Little, B.
11	Straight-time earnings	=$B4*$B2	=$B4*$B2	=$B4*$B2
12	Overtime earnings	=(B7−$B4)*$B2*$B3	=(C7−$B4)*$B2*$B3	=(D7−$B4)*$B2*$B3
13	Gross earnings	=SUM(B11:B12)	=SUM(C11:C12)	=SUM(D11:D12)
14				

With no dollar sign, the column reference changes when copied.

In the same way that the dollar sign is used in front of columns, the dollar sign can also be placed in front of the row reference when the row is to remain fixed when copying down rows. The use of absolute cell references ($ sign) is an important Excel formula design concept. You will use them often.

tr*it*   Go to the hands-on **Excel Tutor** for this example!

tr*it*   This Excel Success example uses an Excel function referred to as cell referencing. Go to the **Excel Tutor** titled **Absolute & Relative Cell References** for additional help on this useful Excel function!

Example Exercise 11-3   Employee Net Pay   •••••••▶ ②

Karen Dunn's weekly gross earnings for the week ending December 3 were $2,250, and her federal income tax withholding was $466.19. Prior to this week, Dunn had earned $98,000 for the year. Assuming the social security rate is 6% on the first $100,000 of annual earnings and Medicare is 1.5% of all earnings, what is Dunn's net pay?

Follow My Example 11-3

Total wage payment			$2,250.00
Less: Federal income tax withholding		$466.19	
Earnings subject to social security tax ($100,000 − $98,000)	$2,000		
Social security tax rate	× 6%		
Social security tax		120.00	
Medicare tax ($2,250 × 1.5%)		33.75	619.94
Net pay			$1,630.06

For Practice: PE 11-3A, PE 11-3B

Liability for Employer's Payroll Taxes

Employers are subject to the following payroll taxes for amounts paid their employees:

1. *FICA Tax*: Employers must match the employee's FICA tax contribution.
2. *Federal Unemployment Compensation Tax (FUTA)*: This employer tax provides for temporary payments to those who become unemployed. The tax collected by the federal government is allocated among the states for use in state programs rather than paid directly to employees. Congress often revises the FUTA tax rate and maximum earnings subject to tax. In this chapter, the FUTA rate and earnings subject to tax are assumed to be 6.2% rate on first $7,000 of annual earnings paid each employee during the calendar year.

3. *State Unemployment Compensation Tax (SUTA):* This employer tax also provides temporary payments to those who become unemployed. The FUTA and SUTA programs are closely coordinated, with the states distributing the unemployment checks.[5] SUTA tax rates and earnings subject to tax vary by state.[6]

The preceding employer taxes are an operating expense of the company. Exhibit 4 summarizes the responsibility for employee and employer payroll taxes.

Exhibit 4

Responsibility for Tax Payments

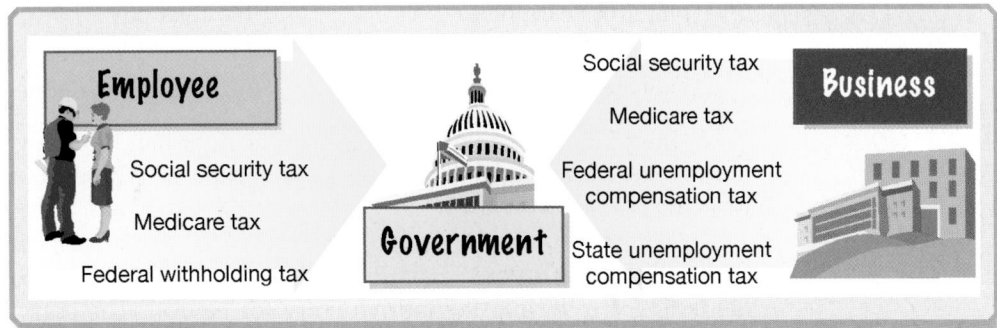

Integrity, Objectivity, and Ethics in Business

RESUMÉ PADDING

Misrepresenting your accomplishments on your resumé could come back to haunt you. In one case, the chief financial officer (CFO) of Veritas Software was forced to resign his position when it was discovered that he had lied about earning an MBA from Stanford University, when in actuality he had earned only an undergraduate degree from Idaho State University.

Source: Reuters News Service, October 4, 2002.

---

3 Describe payroll accounting systems that use a payroll register, employee earnings records, and a general journal.

Accounting Systems for Payroll and Payroll Taxes

Payroll systems should be designed to:

1. Pay employees accurately and timely.
2. Meet regulatory requirements of federal, state, and local agencies.
3. Provide useful data for management decision-making needs.

Although payroll systems differ among companies, the major elements of most payroll systems are:

1. Payroll register
2. Employee's earnings record
3. Payroll checks

---

5 This rate may be reduced to 0.8% for credits for state unemployment compensation tax.

6 As of January 1, 2008, the maximum state rate credited against the federal unemployment rate was 5.4% of the first $7,000 of each employee's earnings during a calendar year.

Payroll Register

The **payroll register** is a multicolumn report used for summarizing the data for each payroll period. Although payroll registers vary by company, a payroll register normally includes the following columns:

1. Employee name
2. Total hours worked
3. Regular earnings
4. Overtime earnings
5. Total gross earnings
6. Social security tax withheld
7. Medicare tax withheld

8. Federal income tax withheld
9. Retirement savings withheld
10. Miscellaneous items withheld
11. Total withholdings
12. Net pay
13. Check number of payroll check issued
14. Accounts debited for payroll expense

Exhibit 5 illustrates a payroll register. The right-hand columns of the payroll register indicate the accounts debited for the payroll expense. These columns are often referred to as the *payroll distribution*.

Recording Employees' Earnings The column totals of the payroll register provide the basis for recording the journal entry for payroll. The entry based on the payroll register in Exhibit 5 is shown below.

Dec.	27	Sales Salaries Expense	11,122.00	
		Office Salaries Expense	2,780.00	
		Social Security Tax Payable		643.07
		Medicare Tax Payable		208.53
		Employees Federal Income Tax Payable		3,332.00
		Retirement Savings Deductions Payable		680.00
		United Fund Deductions Payable		470.00
		Accounts Receivable—Fred G. Elrod (emp.)		50.00
		Salaries Payable		8,518.40
		Payroll for week ended December 27.		

Exhibit 5

Payroll Register

	Employee Name	Total Hours	Earnings			
			Regular	Overtime	Total	
1	Abrams, Julie S.	40	500.00		500.00	1
2	Elrod, Fred G.	44	392.00	58.80	450.80	2
3	Gomez, Jose C.	40	840.00		840.00	3
4	McGrath, John T.	42	1,360.00	102.00	1,462.00	4
25	Wilkes, Glenn K.	40	480.00		480.00	25
26	Zumpano, Michael W.	40	600.00		600.00	26
27	Total		13,328.00	574.00	13,902.00	27
28						28

Example Exercise 11-4   Journalize Period Payroll   ● ● ● ● ● ● ● ● ▶ ③

The payroll register of Chen Engineering Services indicates $900 of social security withheld and $225 of Medicare tax withheld on total salaries of $15,000 for the period. Federal withholding for the period totaled $2,925.

Provide the journal entry for the period's payroll.

Follow My Example 11-4

Salaries Expense	15,000	
Social Security Tax Payable		900
Medicare Tax Payable		225
Employees Federal Withholding Tax Payable		2,925
Salaries Payable		10,950

For Practice: PE 11-4A, PE 11-4B

Recording and Paying Payroll Taxes   Payroll taxes are recorded as liabilities when the payroll is *paid* to employees. In addition, employers compute and report payroll taxes on a *calendar-year* basis, which may differ from the company's fiscal year.

To illustrate, assume that Everson Company's fiscal year ends on April 30. Also, assume the following payroll data on December 31, 2009:

Wages owed employees on December 31	$26,000
Wages subject to payroll taxes:	
Social security tax (6.0%)	$18,000
Medicare tax (1.5%).	26,000
State (5.4%) and federal (0.8%)	
unemployment compensation tax	1,000

If the payroll is paid on December 31, the payroll taxes are computed as follows:

Social security	$1,080 ($18,000 × 6.0%)
Medicare tax	390 ($26,000 × 1.5%)
State unemployment compensation tax (SUTA)	54 ($1,000 × 5.4%)
Federal unemployment compensation tax (FUTA)	8 ($1,000 × 0.8%)
Total payroll taxes	$1,532

Exhibit 5   ● ● ● ● ● ● ● ●

(Concluded)

	Social Security Tax	Medicare Tax	Federal Income Tax	Retirement Savings	Misc.		Total	Net Pay	Check No.	Sales Salaries Expense	Office Salaries Expense	
	Deductions							**Paid**		**Accounts Debited**		
1	30.00	7.50	74.00	20.00	UF	10.00	141.50	358.50	6857	500.00		1
2	27.05	6.76	62.00		AR	50.00	145.81	304.99	6858		450.80	2
3	50.40	12.60	131.00	25.00	UF	10.00	229.00	611.00	6859	840.00		3
4	57.72	21.93	268.45	20.00	UF	5.00	373.10	1,088.90	6860	1,462.00		4
25	28.80	7.20	69.00	10.00			115.00	365.00	6880	480.00		25
26	36.00	9.00	79.00	5.00	UF	2.00	131.00	469.00	6881		600.00	26
27	643.07	208.53	3,332.00	680.00	UF	470.00	5,383.60	8,518.40		11,122.00	2,780.00	27
28					AR	50.00						28

Miscellaneous Deductions: UF—United Fund; AR—Accounts Receivable

If the payroll is paid on January 2, however, the *entire* $26,000 is subject to *all* payroll taxes. This is because the maximum earnings limit for social security and unemployment taxes starts on January 1 of each year. Thus, if the payroll is paid on January 2, the payroll taxes are computed as follows:

Social security	$1,560 ($26,000 × 6.0%)
Medicare tax	390 ($26,000 × 1.5%)
State unemployment compensation tax (SUTA)	1,404 ($26,000 × 5.4%)
Federal unemployment compensation tax (FUTA)	208 ($26,000 × 0.8%)
Total payroll taxes	$3,562

The payroll register in Exhibit 5 indicates that social security tax of $643.07 and Medicare tax of $208.53 were withheld. Employers must match the employees' FICA contributions. Thus, the employer's social security and Medicare payroll tax will also be $643.07 and $208.53, respectively.

Assume that in Exhibit 5 the earnings subject to state and federal unemployment compensation taxes are $2,710. In addition, assume a SUTA rate of 5.4% and a FUTA rate of 0.8%. The payroll taxes based on Exhibit 5 are $1,019.62, as shown below.

Social security	$ 643.07 (from Social Security Tax column of Exhibit 5)
Medicare tax	208.53 (from Medicare Tax column of Exhibit 5)
SUTA	146.34 ($2,710 × 5.4%)
FUTA	21.68 ($2,710 × 0.8%)
Total payroll taxes	$1,019.62

The entry to journalize the payroll tax expense for Exhibit 5 is shown below.

Dec.	27	Payroll Tax Expense	1,019.62	
		Social Security Tax Payable		643.07
		Medicare Tax Payable		208.53
		State Unemployment Tax Payable		146.34
		Federal Unemployment Tax Payable		21.68
		Payroll taxes for week ended December 27.		

The preceding entry records a liability for each payroll tax. When the payroll taxes are paid, an entry is recorded debiting the payroll tax liability accounts and crediting Cash.

Example Exercise 11-5   Journalize Payroll Tax   ••••••• 3

The payroll register of Chen Engineering Services indicates $900 of social security withheld and $225 of Medicare tax withheld on total salaries of $15,000 for the period. Assume earnings subject to state and federal unemployment compensation taxes are $5,250, at the federal rate of 0.8% and the state rate of 5.4%.

Provide the journal entry to record the payroll tax expense for the period.

Follow My Example 11-5

Payroll Tax Expense	1,450.50	
Social Security Tax Payable		900.00
Medicare Tax Payable		225.00
State Unemployment Tax Payable		283.50*
Federal Unemployment Tax Payable		42.00**

  *$5,250 × 5.4%
 **$5,250 × 0.8%

For Practice: PE 11-5A, PE 11-5B

Employee's Earnings Record

Each employee's earnings to date must be determined at the end of each payroll period. This total is necessary for computing the employee's social security tax withholding and the employer's payroll taxes. Thus, detailed payroll records must be kept for each employee. This record is called an **employee's earnings record**.

Exhibit 6, on pages 498–499, shows a portion of John T. McGrath's employee's earnings record. An employee's earnings record and the payroll register are interrelated. For example, McGrath's earnings record for December 27 can be traced to the fourth line of the payroll register in Exhibit 5.

As shown in Exhibit 6, an employee's earnings record has quarterly and yearly totals. These totals are used for tax, insurance, and other reports. For example, one such report is the Wage and Tax Statement, commonly called a *W-2*. This form is provided annually to each employee as well as to the Social Security Administration. The W-2 shown below is based on John T. McGrath's employee's earnings record shown in Exhibit 6.

22222 Void ☐	a Employee's social security number 381-48-9120	For Office Use Only ▶ OMB No. 1545–0008		
b Employer identification number (EIN) 61-8436524			1 Wages, tips, other compensation 100,500.00	2 Federal income tax withheld 21,387.65
c Employer's name, address, and ZIP code McDermott Supply Co. 415 5th Ave. So. Dubuque, IA 52736-0142			3 Social security wages 100,000.00	4 Social security tax withheld 6,000.00
			5 Medical wages and tips 100,500.00	6 Medicare tax withheld 1,507.50
			7 Social security tips	8 Allocated tips
d Control number			9 Advance EIC payment	10 Dependent care benefits
e Employee's first name and initial Last name Suff. John T. McGrath			11 Nonqualified plans	12a See instructions for box 12
1830 4th St. Clinton, IA 52732-6142			13 Statutory employee ☐ Retirement plan ☐ Third party sick pay ☐	12b
			14 Other	12c
				12d
f Employee's address, and ZIP code				
15 State Employer's state ID number IA	16 State wages, tips, etc.	17 State income tax	18 Local wages, tips, etc. 19 Local income tax	20 Locality name Dubuque

Form **W-2**   **Wage and Tax Statement**   **2009**   Department of the Treasury—Internal Revenue Service
For Privacy Act and Paperwork Reduction Act Notice, see back of Copy D.
Copy A For Social Security Administration — Send this entire page with Form W-3 to the Social Security Administration; photocopies are **not** acceptable.   Cat. No. 10134D

Do Not Cut, Fold, or Staple Forms on This Page — Do Not Cut, Fold, or Staple Forms on This Page

Payroll Checks

Companies may pay employees, especially part-time employees, by issuing *payroll checks*. Each check includes a detachable statement showing how the net pay was computed. Exhibit 7, on page 500, illustrates a payroll check for John T. McGrath.

Exhibit 6

Employee's Earnings Record

John T. McGrath
1830 4th St.
Clinton, IA 52732-6142   PHONE: 555-3148

SINGLE	NUMBER OF WITHHOLDING ALLOWANCES: 1	PAY RATE: $1,360.00 Per Week

OCCUPATION: Salesperson   EQUIVALENT HOURLY RATE: $34

	Period Ending	Total Hours	Regular Earnings	Overtime Earnings	Total Earnings	Total	
42	SEPT. 27	53	1,360.00	663.00	2,023.00	75,565.00	42
43	THIRD QUARTER		17,680.00	7,605.00	25,285.00		43
44	OCT. 4	51	1,360.00	561.00	1,921.00	77,486.00	44
50	NOV. 15	50	1,360.00	510.00	1,870.00	89,382.00	50
51	NOV. 22	53	1,360.00	663.00	2,023.00	91,405.00	51
52	NOV. 29	47	1,360.00	357.00	1,717.00	93,122.00	52
53	DEC. 6	53	1,360.00	663.00	2,023.00	95,145.00	53
54	DEC.13	52	1,360.00	612.00	1,972.00	97,117.00	54
55	DEC. 20	51	1,360.00	561.00	1,921.00	99,038.00	55
56	DEC. 27	42	1,360.00	102.00	1,462.00	100,500.00	56
57	FOURTH QUARTER		17,680.00	7,255.00	24,935.00		57
58	YEARLY TOTAL		70,720.00	29,780.00	100,500.00		58

Most companies issuing payroll checks use a special payroll bank account. In such cases, payroll is processed as follows:

1. The total net pay for the period is determined from the payroll register.
2. The company authorizes an electronic funds transfer (EFT) from its regular bank account to the special payroll bank account for the total net pay.
3. Individual payroll checks are written from the payroll account.
4. The numbers of the payroll checks are inserted in the payroll register.

An advantage of using a separate payroll bank account is that reconciling the bank statements is simplified. In addition, a payroll bank account establishes control over payroll checks and, thus, prevents their theft or misuse.

Many companies use electronic funds transfer to pay their employees. In such cases, each pay period an employee's net pay is deposited directly into the employee checking account. Later, employees receive a payroll statement summarizing how the net pay was computed.

Payroll System Diagram

Exhibit 8, on page 500, shows the flow of data and the interactions among the elements of a payroll system. As shown in Exhibit 8, the inputs into a payroll system may be classified as:

1. Constants, which are data that remain unchanged from payroll to payroll.

   Examples: Employee names, social security numbers, marital status, number of income tax withholding allowances, rates of pay, tax rates, and withholding tables.

Exhibit 6
(Concluded)

SOC. SEC. NO.: 381-48-9120								EMPLOYEE NO.: 814	

DATE OF BIRTH: February 15, 1982

DATE EMPLOYMENT TERMINATED:

	Deductions							Paid		
	Social Security Tax	Medicare Tax	Federal Income Tax	Retirement Savings		Other	Total	Net Amount	Check No.	
42	121.38	30.35	429.83	20.00			601.56	1,421.44	6175	42
43	1,517.10	379.28	5,391.71	260.00	UF	40.00	7,588.09	17,696.91		43
44	115.26	28.82	401.27	20.00			565.35	1,355.65	6225	44
50	112.20	28.05	386.99	20.00			547.24	1,322.76	6530	50
51	121.38	30.35	429.83	20.00			601.56	1,421.44	6582	51
52	103.02	25.76	344.15	20.00			492.93	1,224.07	6640	52
53	121.38	30.35	429.83	20.00	UF	5.00	606.56	1,416.44	6688	53
54	118.32	29.58	415.55	20.00			583.45	1,388.55	6743	54
55	115.26	28.82	401.27	20.00			565.35	1,355.65	6801	55
56	57.72	21.93	268.45	20.00	UF	5.00	373.10	1,088.90	6860	56
57	1,466.10	374.03	5,293.71	260.00	UF	15.00	7,408.84	17,526.16		57
58	6,000.00	1,507.50	21,387.65	1,040.00	UF	100.00	30,035.15	70,464.85		58

Many computerized payroll systems are offered on the Internet for a monthly fee. Internet-based payroll systems have the advantage of maintaining current federal and state tax rates.

2. Variables, which are data that change from payroll to payroll.

   Examples: Number of hours or days worked for each employee, accrued days of sick leave, vacation credits, total earnings to date, and total taxes withheld.

   In a computerized accounting system, constants are stored within a payroll file. The variables are input each pay period by a payroll clerk. In some systems, employees swipe their identification (ID) cards when they report for and leave work. In such cases, the hours worked by each employee are automatically updated.

   A computerized payroll system also maintains electronic versions of the payroll register and employee earnings records. Payroll system outputs, such as payroll checks, EFTs, and tax records, are automatically produced each pay period.

Internal Controls for Payroll Systems

Payroll frauds often involve a supervisor who cashes the payroll checks of fictitious employees or fired employees who are kept on the payroll.

The cash payment controls described in Chapter 8, *Sarbanes-Oxley, Internal Control, and Cash*, also apply to payrolls. Some examples of payroll controls include the following:

1. If a check-signing machine is used, blank payroll checks and access to the machine should be restricted to prevent their theft or misuse.

2. The hiring and firing of employees should be properly authorized and approved in writing.

3. All changes in pay rates should be properly authorized and approved in writing.

Exhibit 7

Payroll Check

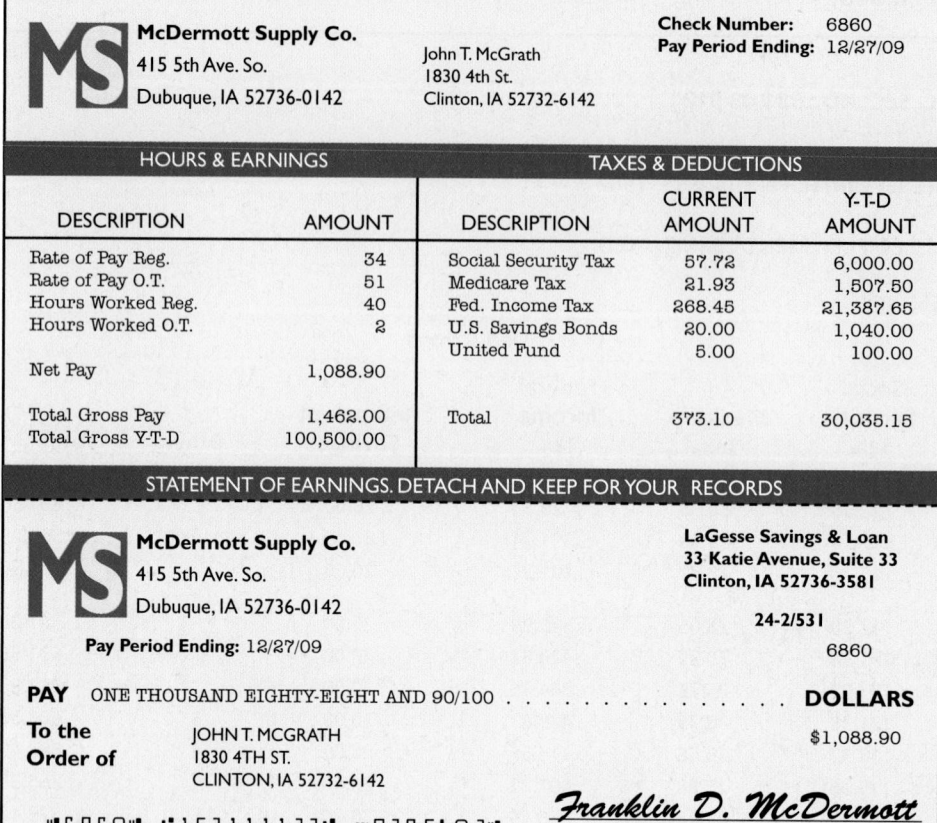

McDermott Supply Co.		John T. McGrath	**Check Number:** 6860	
415 5th Ave. So.		1830 4th St.	**Pay Period Ending:** 12/27/09	
Dubuque, IA 52736-0142		Clinton, IA 52732-6142		

HOURS & EARNINGS		TAXES & DEDUCTIONS		
DESCRIPTION	AMOUNT	DESCRIPTION	CURRENT AMOUNT	Y-T-D AMOUNT
Rate of Pay Reg.	34	Social Security Tax	57.72	6,000.00
Rate of Pay O.T.	51	Medicare Tax	21.93	1,507.50
Hours Worked Reg.	40	Fed. Income Tax	268.45	21,387.65
Hours Worked O.T.	2	U.S. Savings Bonds	20.00	1,040.00
		United Fund	5.00	100.00
Net Pay	1,088.90			
Total Gross Pay	1,462.00	Total	373.10	30,035.15
Total Gross Y-T-D	100,500.00			

STATEMENT OF EARNINGS. DETACH AND KEEP FOR YOUR RECORDS

McDermott Supply Co.
415 5th Ave. So.
Dubuque, IA 52736-0142

LaGesse Savings & Loan
33 Katie Avenue, Suite 33
Clinton, IA 52736-3581

24-2/531

6860

Pay Period Ending: 12/27/09

PAY ONE THOUSAND EIGHTY-EIGHT AND 90/100 . . . . **DOLLARS**

To the Order of JOHN T. MCGRATH
1830 4TH ST.
CLINTON, IA 52732-6142

$1,088.90

Franklin D. McDermott

⑈6860⑈ ⑆153111123⑆ ⑈938540 2⑈

4. Employees should be observed when arriving for work to verify that employees are "checking in" for work only once and only for themselves. Employees may "check in" for work by using a time card or by swiping their employee ID card.

5. Payroll checks should be distributed by someone other than employee supervisors.

6. A special payroll bank account should be used.

Exhibit 8

Flow of Data in a Payroll System

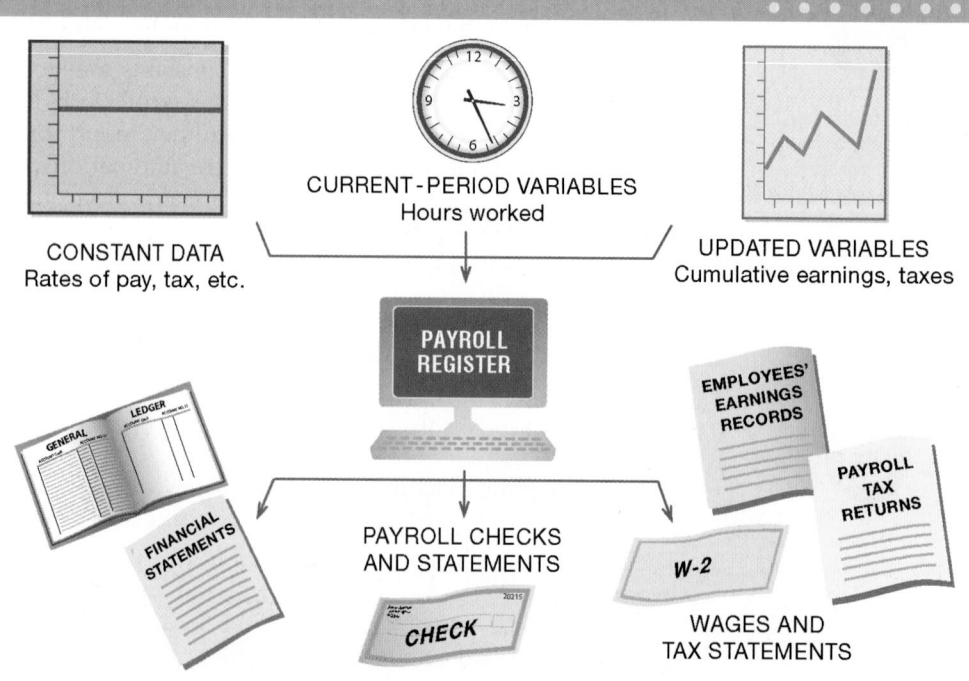

CONSTANT DATA
Rates of pay, tax, etc.

CURRENT-PERIOD VARIABLES
Hours worked

UPDATED VARIABLES
Cumulative earnings, taxes

PAYROLL REGISTER

GENERAL LEDGER

FINANCIAL STATEMENTS

PAYROLL CHECKS AND STATEMENTS

CHECK

EMPLOYEES' EARNINGS RECORDS

PAYROLL TAX RETURNS

W-2

WAGES AND TAX STATEMENTS

Integrity, Objectivity, and Ethics in Business

$8 MILLION FOR 18 MINUTES OF WORK

Computer system controls can be very important in issuing payroll checks. In one case, a Detroit school-teacher was paid $4,015,625 after deducting $3,884,375 in payroll deductions for 18 minutes of overtime work. The error was caused by a computer glitch when the teacher's employee identification number was substituted incorrectly in the "hourly wage" field and wasn't caught by the payroll software. After six days, the error was discovered and the money was returned. "One of the things that came with (the software) is a fail-safe that prevents that. It doesn't work," a financial officer said. The district has since installed a program to flag any paycheck exceeding $10,000.

Source: Associated Press, September 27, 2002.

4 Journalize entries for employee fringe benefits, including vacation pay and pensions.

Employees' Fringe Benefits

Many companies provide their employees benefits in addition to salary and wages earned. Such **fringe benefits** may include vacation, medical, and retirement benefits. Exhibit 9 shows these three fringe benefits as a percent of total payroll costs.[7]

Exhibit 9

Benefit Dollars as a Percent of Payroll Costs

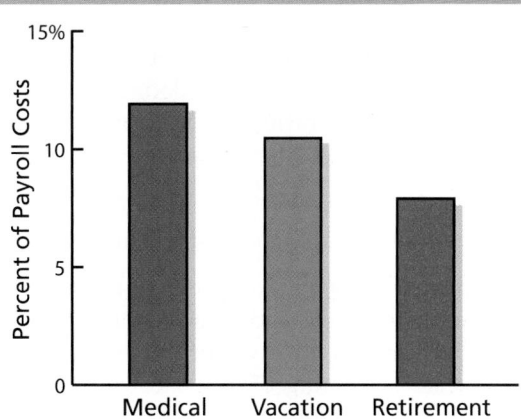

The U.S. Chamber of Commerce estimates that fringe benefits, excluding FICA, average about 33% of gross pay.

The cost of employee fringe benefits is recorded as an expense by the employer. To match revenues and expenses, the estimated cost of fringe benefits is recorded as an expense during the period in which the employees earn the benefits.

Vacation Pay

Most employers provide employees vacations, sometimes called *compensated absences*. The liability to pay for employee vacations could be accrued as a liability at the end of each pay period. However, many companies wait and record an adjusting entry for accrued vacation at the end of the year.

To illustrate, assume that employees earn one day of vacation for each month worked. The estimated vacation pay for the year ending December 31 is $325,000. The adjusting entry for the accrued vacation is shown below.

Dec.	31	Vacation Pay Expense	325,000	
		Vacation Pay Payable		325,000
		Accrued vacation pay for the year.		

7 *2005 Employee Benefits Study*, U.S. Chamber of Commerce, 2006.

Employees may be required to take all their vacation time within one year. In such cases, any accrued vacation pay will be paid within one year. Thus, the vacation pay payable is reported as a current liability on the balance sheet. If employees are allowed to accumulate their vacation pay, the estimated vacation pay payable that will *not* be taken within a year is reported as a long-term liability.

When employees take vacations, the liability for vacation pay is decreased by debiting Vacation Pay Payable. Salaries or Wages Payable and the other related payroll accounts for taxes and withholdings are credited.

Pensions

A **pension** is a cash payment to retired employees. Pension rights are accrued by employees as they work, based on the employer's pension plan. Two basic types of pension plans are:

1. Defined contribution plan
2. Defined benefit plan

In 90% of 401k plans, the employer matches some portion of the employee's contribution. As a result, nearly 70% of eligible employees elect to enroll in a 401k.

Source: "Employees Sluggish in Interacting with 401k Plans," Hewitt Associates, December 26, 2005.

In a **defined contribution plan**, the company invests contributions on behalf of the employee during the employee's working years. Normally, the employee and employer contribute to the plan. The employee's pension depends on the total contributions and the investment returns earned on those contributions.

One of the more popular defined contribution plans is the 401k plan. Under this plan, employees contribute a portion of their gross pay to investments, such as mutual funds. A 401k plan offers employees two advantages.

1. The employee contribution is deducted before taxes.
2. The contributions and related earnings are not taxed until withdrawn at retirement.

In most cases, the employer matches some portion of the employee's contribution. The employer's cost is debited to *Pension Expense*. To illustrate, assume that Heaven Scent Perfumes Company contributes 10% of employee monthly salaries to an employee 401k plan. Assuming $500,000 of monthly salaries, the journal entry to record the monthly contribution is shown below.

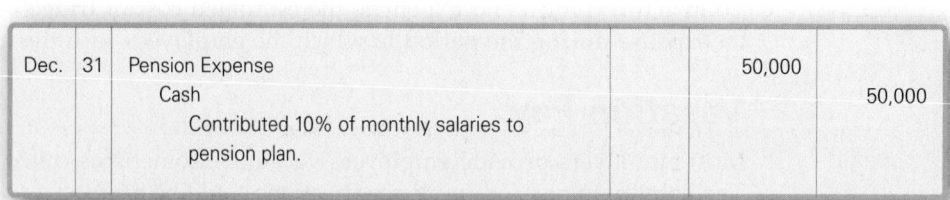

Dec.	31	Pension Expense	50,000	
		Cash		50,000
		Contributed 10% of monthly salaries to pension plan.		

Twenty percent of private industry uses defined benefit plans, while 43% uses defined contribution plans.

Source: Bureau of Labor Statistics, "Employee Benefits in Private Industry," 2007.

In a **defined benefit plan**, the company pays the employee a fixed annual pension based on a formula. The formula is normally based on such factors as the employee's years of service, age, and past salary.

Annual Pension = 1.5% × Years of Service × Highest 3-Year Average Salary

In a defined benefit plan, the employer is obligated to pay for (fund) the employee's future pension benefits. As a result, many companies are replacing their defined benefit plans with defined contribution plans.

The pension cost of a defined benefit plan is debited to *Pension Expense*. Cash is credited for the amount contributed (funded) by the employer. Any unfunded amount is credited to *Unfunded Pension Liability*.

To illustrate, assume that the defined benefit plan of Hinkle Co. requires an annual pension cost of $80,000. This annual contribution is based on estimates of Hinkle's future pension liabilities. On December 31, Hinkle Co. pays $60,000 to the pension fund. The entry to record the payment and unfunded liability is shown below.

Dec.	31	Pension Expense	80,000	
		Cash		60,000
		Unfunded Pension Liability		20,000
		Annual pension cost and contribution.		

If the unfunded pension liability is to be paid within one year, it is reported as a current liability on the balance sheet. Any portion of the unfunded pension liability that will be paid beyond one year is a long-term liability.

The accounting for pensions is complex due to the uncertainties of estimating future pension liabilities. These estimates depend on such factors as employee life expectancies, employee turnover, expected employee compensation levels, and investment income on pension contributions. Additional accounting and disclosures related to pensions are covered in advanced accounting courses.

Example Exercise 11-6   Vacation Pay and Pension Benefits   ••••••••⟩ 4

Manfield Services Company provides its employees vacation benefits and a defined contribution pension plan. Employees earned vacation pay of $44,000 for the period. The pension plan requires a contribution to the plan administrator equal to 8% of employee salaries. Salaries were $450,000 during the period.
   Provide the journal entry for the (a) vacation pay and (b) pension benefit.

Follow My Example 11-6

a.   Vacation Pay Expense   44,000
        Vacation Pay Payable   44,000
           Vacation pay accrued for the period.

b.   Pension Expense   36,000
        Cash   36,000
           Pension contribution, 8% of $450,000 salary.

For Practice: PE 11-6A, PE 11-6B

Postretirement Benefits Other than Pensions

Employees may earn rights to other postretirement benefits from their employer. Such benefits may include dental care, eye care, medical care, life insurance, tuition assistance, tax services, and legal services.

The accounting for other postretirement benefits is similar to that of defined benefit pension plans. The estimate of the annual benefits expense is recorded by debiting *Postretirement Benefits Expense.* If the benefits are fully funded, Cash is credited for the same amount. If the benefits are not fully funded, a postretirement benefits plan liability account is also credited.

The financial statements should disclose the nature of the postretirement benefit liabilities. These disclosures are usually included as notes to the financial statements. Additional accounting and disclosures for postretirement benefits are covered in advanced accounting courses.

Current Liabilities on the Balance Sheet

Accounts payable, the current portion of long-term debt, notes payable, and any other debts that are due within one year are reported as current liabilities on the balance sheet. The balance sheet presentation of current liabilities for Mornin' Joe is as follows:

Mornin' Joe
Balance Sheet
December 31, 2010

Liabilities

Current liabilities:		
Accounts payable	$133,000	
Notes payable (current portion)	200,000	
Salaries and wages payable	42,000	
Payroll taxes payable	16,400	
Interest payable	40,000	
Total current liabilities		$431,400

⑤ Describe the accounting treatment for contingent liabilities and journalize entries for product warranties.

Contingent Liabilities

Some liabilities may arise from past transactions if certain events occur in the future. These *potential* liabilities are called **contingent liabilities**.

The accounting for contingent liabilities depends on the following two factors:

1. Likelihood of occurring: Probable, reasonably possible, or remote
2. Measurement: Estimable or not estimable

The likelihood that the event creating the liability occurring is classified as *probable, reasonably possible,* or *remote.* The ability to estimate the potential liability is classified as *estimable* or *not estimable.*

Probable and Estimable

If a contingent liability is *probable* and the amount of the liability can be *reasonably estimated,* it is recorded and disclosed. The liability is recorded by debiting an expense and crediting a liability.

To illustrate, assume that during June a company sold a product for $60,000 that includes a 36-month warranty for repairs. The average cost of repairs over the warranty period is 5% of the sales price. The entry to record the estimated product warranty expense for June is as shown below.

The estimated costs of warranty work on new car sales are a contingent liability for Ford Motor Company.

June	30	Product Warranty Expense		3,000	
		Product Warranty Payable			3,000
		Warranty expense for June, 5% × $60,000.			

The preceding entry records warranty expense in the same period in which the sale is recorded. In this way, warranty expense is matched with the related revenue (sales).

If the product is repaired under warranty, the repair costs are recorded by debiting *Product Warranty Payable* and crediting *Cash, Supplies, Wages Payable*, or other appropriate accounts. Thus, if a $200 part is replaced under warranty on August 16, the entry is as follows:

Aug.	16	Product Warranty Payable	200	
		Supplies		200
		Replaced defective part under warranty.		

Example Exercise 11-7   Estimated Warranty Liability   • • • • • • • • ▶ 5

Cook-Rite Co. sold $140,000 of kitchen appliances during August under a six-month warranty. The cost to repair defects under the warranty is estimated at 6% of the sales price. On September 11, a customer required a $200 part replacement, plus $90 of labor under the warranty.

Provide the journal entry for (a) the estimated warranty expense on August 31 and (b) the September 11 warranty work.

Follow My Example 11-7

a. Product Warranty Expense 8,400
    Product Warranty Payable 8,400
      To record warranty expense for August, 6% × $140,000.

b. Product Warranty Payable 290
    Supplies 200
    Wages Payable 90
      Replaced defective part under warranty.

For Practice: PE 11-7A, PE 11-7B

Probable and Not Estimable

A contingent liability may be probable, but cannot be estimated. In this case, the contingent liability is disclosed in the notes to the financial statements. For example, a company may have accidentally polluted a local river by dumping waste products. At the end of the period, the cost of the cleanup and any fines may not be able to be estimated.

Reasonably Possible

A contingent liability may be only possible. For example, a company may have lost a lawsuit for infringing on another company's patent rights. However, the verdict is under appeal and the company's lawyers feel that the verdict will be reversed or significantly reduced. In this case, the contingent liability is disclosed in the notes to the financial statements.

Remote

A contingent liability may be remote. For example, a ski resort may be sued for injuries incurred by skiers. In most cases, the courts have found that a skier accepts the risk of injury when participating in the activity. Thus, unless the ski resort is grossly negligent, the resort will not incur a liability for ski injuries. In such cases, no disclosure needs to be made in the notes to the financial statements.

The accounting treatment of contingent liabilities is summarized in Exhibit 10.

Exhibit 10

Accounting Treatment of Contingent Liabilities

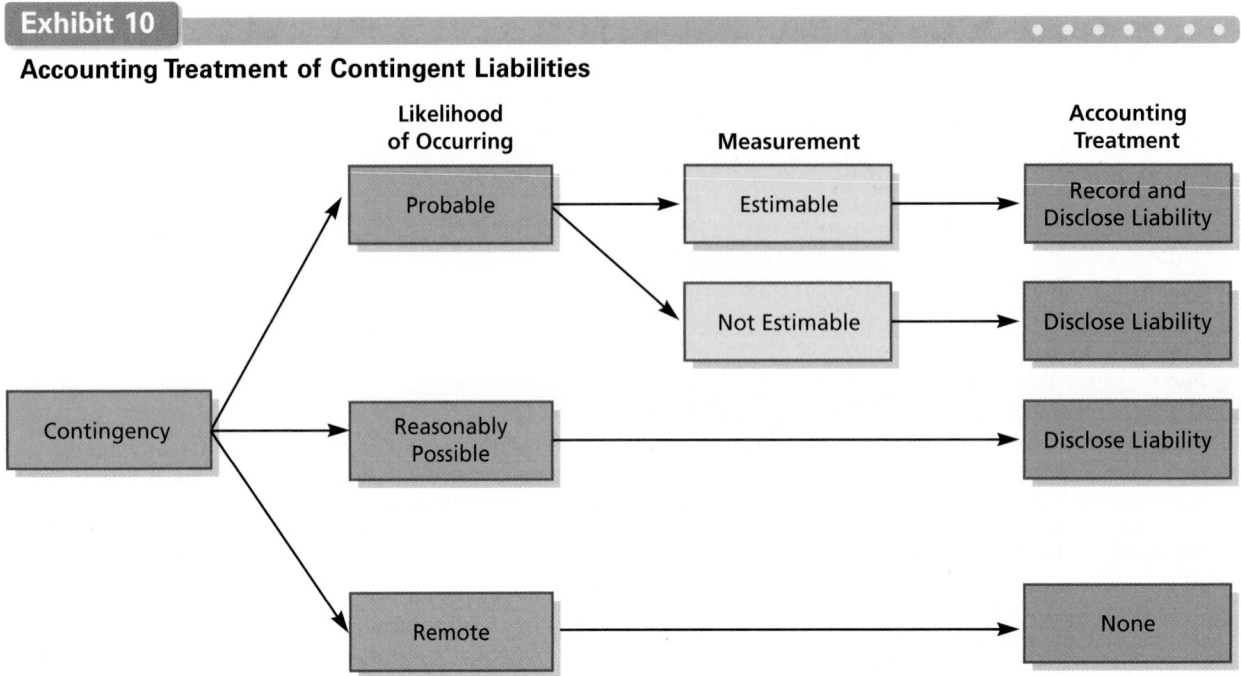

Common examples of contingent liabilities disclosed in notes to the financial statements are litigation, environmental matters, guarantees, and contingencies from the sale of receivables.

An example of a contingent liability disclosure from a recent annual report of Google Inc. is shown below.

> —*Certain entities have also filed copyright claims against us, alleging that certain of our products, including Google Web Search, Google News, Google Image Search, and Google Book Search, infringe their rights. Adverse results in these lawsuits may include awards of damages and may also result in, or even compel, a change in our business practices, which could result in a loss of revenue for us or otherwise harm our business.*

> —*Although the results of litigation and claims cannot be predicted with certainty, we believe that the final outcome of the matters discussed above will not have a material adverse effect on our business. . . .*

Professional judgment is necessary in distinguishing between classes of contingent liabilities. This is especially the case when distinguishing between probable and reasonably possible contingent liabilities.

Financial Analysis and Interpretation

The Current Assets and Current Liabilities sections of the balance sheet for Noble Co. and Hart Co. are illustrated as follows:

	Noble Co.	Hart Co.
Current assets:		
Cash	$147,000	$120,000
Accounts receivable (net)	84,000	472,000
Inventory	150,000	200,000
Total current assets	$381,000	$792,000
Current liabilities:		
Accounts payable	$ 75,000	$227,000
Wages payable	30,000	193,000
Notes payable	115,000	320,000
Total current liabilities	$220,000	$740,000

We can use this information to evaluate Noble's and Hart's ability to pay their current liabilities within a short period of time, using the **quick ratio** or *acid-test ratio*. The quick ratio is computed as follows:

$$\text{Quick Ratio} = \frac{\text{Quick Assets}}{\text{Current Liabilities}}$$

The quick ratio measures the "instant" debt-paying ability of a company, using quick assets. **Quick assets** are cash, receivables, and other current assets that can quickly be converted into cash. It is often considered desirable to have a quick ratio exceeding 1.0. A ratio less than 1.0 would indicate that current liabilities cannot be covered by cash and "near cash" assets.

To illustrate, the quick ratios for both companies would be as follows:

$$\text{Noble Co: } \frac{\$147,000 + \$84,000}{\$220,000} = 1.05$$

$$\text{Hart Co: } \frac{\$120,000 + \$472,000}{\$740,000} = 0.80$$

As you can see, Noble Co. has quick assets in excess of current liabilities, or a quick ratio of 1.05. The ratio exceeds 1.0, indicating that the quick assets should be sufficient to meet current liabilities. Hart Co. , however, has a quick ratio of 0.8. Its quick assets will not be sufficient to cover the current liabilities. Hart could solve this problem by working with a bank to convert its short-term debt of $320,000 into a long-term obligation. This would remove the notes payable from current liabilities. If Hart did this, then its quick ratio would improve to 1.4 ($592,000/ $420,000), which would be sufficient for quick assets to cover current liabilities.

 f·a·i

At a Glance **11** ● ● ● ▶

1 Describe and illustrate current liabilities related to accounts payable, current portion of long-term debt, and notes payable.

Key Points	Key Learning Outcomes	Example Exercises	Practice Exercises
Current liabilities are obligations that are to be paid out of current assets and are due within a short time, usually within one year. The three primary types of current liabilities are accounts payable, notes payable, and current portion of long-term debt.	• Identify and define the most frequently reported current liabilities on the balance sheet.		
	• Determine the interest from interest-bearing and discounted notes payable.	**11-1**	11-1A, 11-1B

2 Determine employer liabilities for payroll, including liabilities arising from employee earnings and deductions from earnings.

Key Points	Key Learning Outcomes	Example Exercises	Practice Exercises
An employer's liability for payroll is determined from employee total earnings, including overtime pay. From this amount, employee deductions are subtracted to arrive at the net pay to be paid to each employee. Most employers also incur liabilities for payroll taxes, such as social security tax, Medicare tax, federal unemployment compensation tax, and state unemployment compensation tax.	• Compute the federal withholding tax from a wage bracket withholding table.	**11-2**	11-2A, 11-2B
	• Compute employee net pay, including deductions for social security and Medicare tax.	**11-3**	11-3A, 11-3B

3 Describe payroll accounting systems that use a payroll register, employee earnings records, and a general journal.

Key Points	Key Learning Outcomes	Example Exercises	Practice Exercises
The payroll register is used in assembling and summarizing the data needed for each payroll period. The payroll register is supported by a detailed payroll record for each employee, called an *employee's earnings record*.	• Journalize the employee's earnings, net pay, and payroll liabilities from the payroll register.	**11-4**	11-4A, 11-4B
	• Journalize the payroll tax expense.	**11-5**	11-5A, 11-5B
	• Describe elements of a payroll system, including the employee's earnings record, payroll checks, and internal controls.		

4 Journalize entries for employee fringe benefits, including vacation pay and pensions.

Key Points	Key Learning Outcomes	Example Exercises	Practice Exercises
Fringe benefits are expenses of the period in which the employees earn the benefits. Fringe benefits are recorded by debiting an expense account and crediting a liability account.	• Journalize vacation pay.	**11-6**	11-6A, 11-6B
	• Distinguish and journalize defined contribution and defined benefit pension plans.	**11-6**	11-6A, 11-6B

5 Describe the accounting treatment for contingent liabilities and journalize entries for product warranties.

Key Points	Key Learning Outcomes	Example Exercises	Practice Exercises
A contingent liability is a potential obligation that results from a past transaction but depends on a future event. The accounting for contingent liabilities is summarized in Exhibit 10.	• Describe the accounting for contingent liabilities.		
	• Journalize estimated warranty obligations and services granted under warranty.	**11-7**	11-7A, 11-7B

Key Terms

contingent liabilities (504)
defined benefit plan (502)
defined contribution plan (502)
employee's earnings record (497)
FICA tax (489)

fringe benefits (501)
gross pay (487)
net pay (487)
payroll (487)
payroll register (494)

pension (502)
quick assets (507)
quick ratio (507)

Illustrative Problem

Selected transactions of Taylor Company, completed during the fiscal year ended December 31, are as follows:

Mar. 1. Purchased merchandise on account from Kelvin Co., $20,000.
Apr. 10. Issued a 60-day, 12% note for $20,000 to Kelvin Co. on account.
June 9. Paid Kelvin Co. the amount owed on the note of April 10.
Aug. 1. Issued a $50,000, 90-day note to Harold Co. in exchange for a building. Harold Co. discounted the note at 15%.
Oct. 30. Paid Harold Co. the amount due on the note of August 1.
Dec. 27. Journalized the entry to record the biweekly payroll. A summary of the payroll record follows:

Salary distribution:		
Sales	$63,400	
Officers	36,600	
Office	10,000	$110,000
Deductions:		
Social security tax	$ 5,050	
Medicare tax	1,650	
Federal income tax withheld	17,600	
State income tax withheld	4,950	
Savings bond deductions	850	
Medical insurance deductions	1,120	31,220
Net amount		$ 78,780

27. Journalized the entry to record payroll taxes for social security and Medicare from the biweekly payroll.
30. Issued a check in payment of liabilities for employees' federal income tax of $17,600, social security tax of $10,100, and Medicare tax of $3,300.
31. Issued a check for $9,500 to the pension fund trustee to fully fund the pension cost for December.
31. Journalized an entry to record the employees' accrued vacation pay, $36,100.
31. Journalized an entry to record the estimated accrued product warranty liability, $37,240.

Instructions

Journalize the preceding transactions.

Solution

Mar.	1	Merchandise Inventory	20,000	
		Accounts Payable—Kelvin Co.		20,000
Apr.	10	Accounts Payable—Kelvin Co.	20,000	
		Notes Payable		20,000
June	9	Notes Payable	20,000	
		Interest Expense	400	
		Cash		20,400
Aug.	1	Building	48,125	
		Interest Expense	1,875	
		Notes Payable		50,000
Oct.	30	Notes Payable	50,000	
		Cash		50,000
Dec.	27	Sales Salaries Expense	63,400	
		Officers Salaries Expense	36,600	
		Office Salaries Expense	10,000	
		Social Security Tax Payable		5,050
		Medicare Tax Payable		1,650
		Employees Federal Income Tax Payable		17,600
		Employees State Income Tax Payable		4,950
		Bond Deductions Payable		850
		Medical Insurance Payable		1,120
		Salaries Payable		78,780
	27	Payroll Tax Expense	6,700	
		Social Security Tax Payable		5,050
		Medicare Tax Payable		1,650
	30	Employees Federal Income Tax Payable	17,600	
		Social Security Tax Payable	10,100	
		Medicare Tax Payable	3,300	
		Cash		31,000
	31	Pension Expense	9,500	
		Cash		9,500
		Fund pension cost.		
	31	Vacation Pay Expense	36,100	
		Vacation Pay Payable		36,100
		Accrue vacation pay.		
	31	Product Warranty Expense	37,240	
		Product Warranty Payable		37,240
		Accrue warranty expense.		

Self-Examination Questions (Answers at End of Chapter)

1. A business issued a $5,000, 60-day, 12% note to the bank. The amount due at maturity is:
   A. $4,900. C. $5,100.
   B. $5,000. D. $5,600.

2. A business issued a $5,000, 60-day note to a supplier, which discounted the note at 12%. The proceeds are:
   A. $4,400. C. $5,000.
   B. $4,900. D. $5,100.

3. Which of the following taxes are employers usually not required to withhold from employees?
   A. Federal income tax
   B. Federal unemployment compensation tax
   C. Medicare tax
   D. State and local income tax

4. An employee's rate of pay is $40 per hour, with time and a half for all hours worked in excess of 40 during a week. The social security rate is 6.0% on the first $100,000 of annual earnings, and the Medicare rate is 1.5% on all earnings. The following additional data are available:

Hours worked during current week	45
Year's cumulative earnings prior to current week	$99,400
Federal income tax withheld	$450

   Based on these data, the amount of the employee's net pay for the current week is:
   A. $1,307.50. C. $1,450.00.
   B. $1,405.00. D. $1,385.50.

5. Within limitations on the maximum earnings subject to the tax, employers do not incur an expense for which of the following payroll taxes?
   A. Social security tax
   B. Federal unemployment compensation tax
   C. State unemployment compensation tax
   D. Employees' federal income tax

Eye Openers

1. Does a discounted note payable provide credit without interest? Discuss.
2. Employees are subject to taxes withheld from their paychecks.
   a. List the federal taxes withheld from most employee paychecks.
   b. Give the title of the accounts credited by amounts withheld.
3. For each of the following payroll-related taxes, indicate whether there is a ceiling on the annual earnings subject to the tax: (a) federal income tax, (b) Medicare tax, (c) social security tax, (d) federal unemployment compensation tax.
4. Why are deductions from employees' earnings classified as liabilities for the employer?
5. Taylor Company, with 20 employees, is expanding operations. It is trying to decide whether to hire one full-time employee for $25,000 or two part-time employees for a total of $25,000. Would any of the employer's payroll taxes discussed in this chapter have a bearing on this decision? Explain.
6. For each of the following payroll-related taxes, indicate whether they generally apply to (a) employees only, (b) employers only, or (c) both employees and employers:
   1. Federal income tax
   2. Medicare tax
   3. Social security tax
   4. Federal unemployment compensation tax
   5. State unemployment compensation tax
7. What are the principal reasons for using a special payroll checking account?
8. In a payroll system, what types of input data are referred to as (a) constants and (b) variables?
9. Explain how a payroll system that is properly designed and operated tends to ensure that (a) wages paid are based on hours actually worked and (b) payroll checks are not issued to fictitious employees.
10. To match revenues and expenses properly, should the expense for employee vacation pay be recorded in the period during which the vacation privilege is earned or during the period in which the vacation is taken? Discuss.

11. Identify several factors that influence the future pension obligation of an employer under a defined benefit pension plan.

12. When should the liability associated with a product warranty be recorded? Discuss.

13. General Motors Corporation reported $10.1 billion of product warranties in the Current Liabilities section of a recent balance sheet. How would costs of repairing a defective product be recorded?

14. The "Questions and Answers Technical Hotline" in the *Journal of Accountancy* included the following question:

Several years ago, Company B instituted legal action against Company A. Under a memorandum of settlement and agreement, Company A agreed to pay Company B a total of $17,500 in three installments—$5,000 on March 1, $7,500 on July 1, and the remaining $5,000 on December 31. Company A paid the first two installments during its fiscal year ended September 30. Should the unpaid amount of $5,000 be presented as a current liability at September 30?

How would you answer this question?

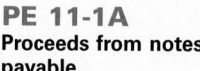

Practice Exercises

PE 11-1A
Proceeds from notes payable
obj. 1
EE 11-1   p. 486

On September 1, Klondike Co. issued a 60-day note with a face amount of $100,000 to Arctic Apparel Co. for merchandise inventory.

a. Determine the proceeds of the note, assuming the note carries an interest rate of 6%.
b. Determine the proceeds of the note, assuming the note is discounted at 6%.

PE 11-1B
Proceeds from notes payable
obj. 1
EE 11-1   p. 486

On February 1, Electronic Warehouse Co. issued a 45-day note with a face amount of $80,000 to Yamura Products Co. for cash.

a. Determine the proceeds of the note, assuming the note carries an interest rate of 10%.
b. Determine the proceeds of the note, assuming the note is discounted at 10%.

PE 11-2A
Federal income tax withholding
obj. 2
EE 11-2   p. 489

Todd Hackworth's weekly gross earnings for the present week were $2,000. Hackworth has two exemptions. Using the wage bracket withholding table in Exhibit 3 with a $67 standard withholding allowance for each exemption, what is Hackworth's federal income tax withholding?

PE 11-2B
Federal income tax withholding
obj. 2
EE 11-2   p. 489

Robert Clowney's weekly gross earnings for the present week were $800. Clowney has one exemption. Using the wage bracket withholding table in Exhibit 3 with a $67 standard withholding allowance for each exemption, what is Clowney's federal income tax withholding?

PE 11-3A
Employee net pay
obj. 2
EE 11-3   p. 492

Todd Hackworth's weekly gross earnings for the week ending December 18 were $2,000, and his federal income tax withholding was $396.19. Prior to this week, Hackworth had earned $98,500 for the year. Assuming the social security rate is 6% on the first $100,000 of annual earnings and Medicare is 1.5% of all earnings, what is Hackworth's net pay?

PE 11-3B
Employee net pay
obj. 2
EE 11-3 p. 492

Robert Clowney's weekly gross earnings for the week ending September 5 were $800, and his federal income tax withholding was $102.95. Prior to this week, Clowney had earned $24,000 for the year. Assuming the social security rate is 6% on the first $100,000 of annual earnings and Medicare is 1.5% of all earnings, what is Clowney's net pay?

PE 11-4A
Journalize period payroll
obj. 3
EE 11-4 p. 495

The payroll register of Woodard Construction Co. indicates $2,552 of social security withheld and $660 of Medicare tax withheld on total salaries of $44,000 for the period. Federal withholding for the period totaled $8,712.
　　Provide the journal entry for the period's payroll.

PE 11-4B
Journalize period payroll
obj. 3
EE 11-4 p. 495

The payroll register of Salem Communications Co. indicates $29,580 of social security withheld and $7,650 of Medicare tax withheld on total salaries of $510,000 for the period. Retirement savings withheld from employee paychecks were $30,600 for the period. Federal withholding for the period totaled $100,980.
　　Provide the journal entry for the period's payroll.

PE 11-5A
Journalize payroll tax
obj. 3
EE 11-5 p. 496

The payroll register of Woodard Construction Co. indicates $2,552 of social security withheld and $660 of Medicare tax withheld on total salaries of $44,000 for the period. Assume earnings subject to state and federal unemployment compensation taxes are $10,500, at the federal rate of 0.8% and the state rate of 5.4%.
　　Provide the journal entry to record the payroll tax expense for the period.

PE 11-5B
Journalize payroll tax
obj. 3
EE 11-5 p. 496

The payroll register of Salem Communications Co. indicates $29,580 of social security withheld and $7,650 of Medicare tax withheld on total salaries of $510,000 for the period. Assume earnings subject to state and federal unemployment compensation taxes are $16,000, at the federal rate of 0.8% and the state rate of 5.4%.
　　Provide the journal entry to record the payroll tax expense for the period.

PE 11-6A
Vacation pay and pension benefits
obj. 4
EE 11-6 p. 503

Blount Company provides its employees with vacation benefits and a defined contribution pension plan. Employees earned vacation pay of $30,000 for the period. The pension plan requires a contribution to the plan administrator equal to 10% of employee salaries. Salaries were $400,000 during the period.
　　Provide the journal entry for the (a) vacation pay and (b) pension benefit.

PE 11-6B
Vacation pay and pension benefits
obj. 4
EE 11-6 p. 503

Hobson Equipment Company provides its employees vacation benefits and a defined benefit pension plan. Employees earned vacation pay of $20,000 for the period. The pension formula calculated a pension cost of $140,000. Only $106,000 was contributed to the pension plan administrator.
　　Provide the journal entry for the (a) vacation pay and (b) pension benefit.

PE 11-7A
Estimated warranty liability

obj. 5

EE 11-7   p. 505

Akine Co. sold $600,000 of equipment during April under a one-year warranty. The cost to repair defects under the warranty is estimated at 6% of the sales price. On August 4, a customer required a $140 part replacement, plus $80 of labor under the warranty.
   Provide the journal entry for (a) the estimated warranty expense on April 30 and (b) the August 4 warranty work.

PE 11-7B
Estimated warranty liability

obj. 5

EE 11-7   p. 505

Robin Industries sold $350,000 of consumer electronics during May under a nine-month warranty. The cost to repair defects under the warranty is estimated at 3% of the sales price. On July 16, a customer was given $140 cash under terms of the warranty.
   Provide the journal entry for (a) the estimated warranty expense on May 31 and (b) the July 16 cash payment.

Exercises

EX 11-1
Current liabilities

obj. 1

✔ Total current liabilities, $790,000

I-Generation Co. sold 14,000 annual subscriptions of *Climber's World* for $60 during December 2010. These new subscribers will receive monthly issues, beginning in January 2011. In addition, the business had taxable income of $400,000 during the first calendar quarter of 2011. The federal tax rate is 40%. A quarterly tax payment will be made on April 7, 2011.
   Prepare the Current Liabilities section of the balance sheet for I-Generation Co. on March 31, 2011.

EX 11-2
Entries for discounting notes payable

obj. 1

U-Build It Warehouse issues a 45-day note for $800,000 to Thomson Home Furnishings Co. for merchandise inventory. Thomson Home Furnishings Co. discounts the note at 7%.
   a. Journalize U-Build It Warehouse's entries to record:
      1. the issuance of the note.
      2. the payment of the note at maturity.
   b. Journalize Thomson Home Furnishings Co.'s entries to record:
      1. the receipt of the note.
      2. the receipt of the payment of the note at maturity.

EX 11-3
Evaluate alternative notes

obj. 1

A borrower has two alternatives for a loan: (1) issue a $240,000, 60-day, 8% note or (2) issue a $240,000, 60-day note that the creditor discounts at 8%.
   a. Calculate the amount of the interest expense for each option.
   b. Determine the proceeds received by the borrower in each situation.
   c. ▬▬▶ Which alternative is more favorable to the borrower? Explain.

EX 11-4
Entries for notes payable

obj. 1

A business issued a 30-day, 4% note for $60,000 to a creditor on account. Journalize the entries to record (a) the issuance of the note and (b) the payment of the note at maturity, including interest.

EX 11-5
Entries for discounted note payable

obj. 1

A business issued a 60-day note for $45,000 to a creditor on account. The note was discounted at 6%. Journalize the entries to record (a) the issuance of the note and (b) the payment of the note at maturity.

EX 11-6
Fixed asset purchases with note
obj. 1

On June 30, Rioux Management Company purchased land for $400,000 and a building for $600,000, paying $500,000 cash and issuing a 6% note for the balance, secured by a mortgage on the property. The terms of the note provide for 20 semiannual payments of $25,000 on the principal plus the interest accrued from the date of the preceding payment. Journalize the entry to record (a) the transaction on June 30, (b) the payment of the first installment on December 31, and (c) the payment of the second installment the following June 30.

EX 11-7
Current portion of long-term debt
obj. 1

P.F. Chang's China Bistro, Inc., the operator of P.F. Chang restaurants, reported the following information about its long-term debt in the notes to a recent financial statement:

Long-term debt is comprised of the following:

	December 31,	
	2006	**2005**
Notes payable	$19,210,000	$10,470,000
Less current portion	(5,487,000)	(5,110,000)
Long-term debt	$13,723,000	$ 5,360,000

a. How much of the notes payable was disclosed as a current liability on the December 31, 2006, balance sheet?
b. How much did the total current liabilities change between 2005 and 2006 as a result of the current portion of long-term debt?
c. If P.F. Chang's did not issue additional notes payable during 2007, what would be the total notes payable on December 31, 2007?

EX 11-8
Calculate payroll
obj. 2

✔ b. Net pay, $2,061.00

An employee earns $40 per hour and 1.75 times that rate for all hours in excess of 40 hours per week. Assume that the employee worked 60 hours during the week, and that the gross pay prior to the current week totaled $58,000. Assume further that the social security tax rate was 6.0% (on earnings up to $100,000), the Medicare tax rate was 1.5%, and federal income tax to be withheld was $714.

a. Determine the gross pay for the week.
b. Determine the net pay for the week.

EX 11-9
Calculate payroll
obj. 2

✔ Administrator net pay, $1,423.57

Reaves Professional Services has three employees—a consultant, a computer programmer, and an administrator. The following payroll information is available for each employee:

	Consultant	Computer Programmer	Administrator
Regular earnings rate	$3,000 per week	$24 per hour	$36 per hour
Overtime earnings rate	Not applicable	2 times hourly rate	2 times hourly rate
Gross pay prior to current pay period	$118,000	$45,000	$99,000
Number of withholding allowances	2	1	2

For the current pay period, the computer programmer worked 50 hours and the administrator worked 46 hours. The federal income tax withheld for all three employees, who are single, can be determined from the wage bracket withholding table in Exhibit 3 in the chapter. Assume further that the social security tax rate was 6.0% on the first $100,000 of annual earnings, the Medicare tax rate was 1.5%, and one withholding allowance is $67.

Determine the gross pay and the net pay for each of the three employees for the current pay period.

EX 11-10
Summary payroll
data

objs. 2, 3

✔ a. (3) Total
earnings, $400,000

In the following summary of data for a payroll period, some amounts have been intentionally omitted:

Earnings:	
1. At regular rate	?
2. At overtime rate	$ 60,000
3. Total earnings	?
Deductions:	
4. Social security tax	23,200
5. Medicare tax	6,000
6. Income tax withheld	99,600
7. Medical insurance	14,000
8. Union dues	?
9. Total deductions	147,800
10. Net amount paid	252,200
Accounts debited:	
11. Factory Wages	210,000
12. Sales Salaries	?
13. Office Salaries	80,000

a. Calculate the amounts omitted in lines (1), (3), (8), and (12).
b. Journalize the entry to record the payroll accrual.
c. Journalize the entry to record the payment of the payroll.
d. ━━━▶ From the data given in this exercise and your answer to (a), would you conclude that this payroll was paid sometime during the first few weeks of the calendar year? Explain.

EX 11-11
Payroll tax entries

obj. 3

According to a summary of the payroll of Scofield Industries Co., $600,000 was subject to the 6.0% social security tax and $740,000 was subject to the 1.5% Medicare tax. Also, $20,000 was subject to state and federal unemployment taxes.

a. Calculate the employer's payroll taxes, using the following rates: state unemployment, 4.2%; federal unemployment, 0.8%.
b. Journalize the entry to record the accrual of payroll taxes.

EX 11-12
Payroll entries

obj. 3

The payroll register for Gentry Company for the week ended December 17 indicated the following:

Salaries	$540,000
Social security tax withheld	25,380
Medicare tax withheld	8,100
Federal income tax withheld	108,000

In addition, state and federal unemployment taxes were calculated at the rate of 5.2% and 0.8%, respectively, on $10,000 of salaries.

a. Journalize the entry to record the payroll for the week of December 17.
b. Journalize the entry to record the payroll tax expense incurred for the week of December 17.

EX 11-13
Payroll entries

obj. 3

Thorup Company had gross wages of $200,000 during the week ended December 10. The amount of wages subject to social security tax was $180,000, while the amount of wages subject to federal and state unemployment taxes was $25,000. Tax rates are as follows:

Social security	6.0%
Medicare	1.5%
State unemployment	5.3%
Federal unemployment	0.8%

The total amount withheld from employee wages for federal taxes was $40,000.

a. Journalize the entry to record the payroll for the week of December 10.
b. Journalize the entry to record the payroll tax expense incurred for the week of December 10.

EX 11-14
Payroll internal control procedures
obj. 3

Hillman Pizza is a pizza restaurant specializing in the sale of pizza by the slice. The store employs 7 full-time and 13 part-time workers. The store's weekly payroll averages $3,800 for all 20 workers.

Hillman Pizza uses a personal computer to assist in preparing paychecks. Each week, the store's accountant collects employee time cards and enters the hours worked into the payroll program. The payroll program calculates each employee's pay and prints a paycheck. The accountant uses a check-signing machine to sign the paychecks. Next, the restaurant's owner authorizes the transfer of funds from the restaurant's regular bank account to the payroll account.

For the week of July 11, the accountant accidentally recorded 250 hours worked instead of 40 hours for one of the full-time employees.

➡ Does Hillman Pizza have internal controls in place to catch this error? If so, how will this error be detected?

EX 11-15
Internal control procedures
obj. 3

Kailua Motors is a small manufacturer of specialty electric motors. The company employs 26 production workers and 7 administrative persons. The following procedures are used to process the company's weekly payroll:

a. All employees are required to record their hours worked by clocking in and out on a time clock. Employees must clock out for lunch break. Due to congestion around the time clock area at lunch time, management has not objected to having one employee clock in and out for an entire department.

b. Whenever a salaried employee is terminated, Personnel authorizes Payroll to remove the employee from the payroll system. However, this procedure is not required when an hourly worker is terminated. Hourly employees only receive a paycheck if their time cards show hours worked. The computer automatically drops an employee from the payroll system when that employee has six consecutive weeks with no hours worked.

c. Whenever an employee receives a pay raise, the supervisor must fill out a wage adjustment form, which is signed by the company president. This form is used to change the employee's wage rate in the payroll system.

d. Kailua Motors maintains a separate checking account for payroll checks. Each week, the total net pay for all employees is transferred from the company's regular bank account to the payroll account.

e. Paychecks are signed by using a check-signing machine. This machine is located in the main office so that it can be easily accessed by anyone needing a check signed.

➡ State whether each of the procedures is appropriate or inappropriate after considering the principles of internal control. If a procedure is inappropriate, describe the appropriate procedure.

EX 11-16
Payroll procedures
obj. 3

The fiscal year for Grain-Crop Stores Inc. ends on June 30. In addition, the company computes and reports payroll taxes on a fiscal-year basis. Thus, it applies social security and FUTA maximum earnings limitations to the fiscal-year payroll.

➡ What is wrong with these procedures for accounting for payroll taxes?

EX 11-17
Accrued vacation pay
obj. 4

A business provides its employees with varying amounts of vacation per year, depending on the length of employment. The estimated amount of the current year's vacation pay is $80,400. Journalize the adjusting entry required on January 31, the end of the first month of the current year, to record the accrued vacation pay.

EX 11-18
Pension plan entries
obj. 4

Washington Co. operates a chain of bookstores. The company maintains a defined contribution pension plan for its employees. The plan requires quarterly installments to be paid to the funding agent, Hamilton Funds, by the fifteenth of the month following the end of each quarter. Assuming that the pension cost is $124,600 for the quarter ended December 31, journalize entries to record (a) the accrued pension liability on December 31 and (b) the payment to the funding agent on January 15.

EX 11-19
Defined benefit pension plan terms
obj. 4

In a recent year's financial statements, Procter & Gamble showed an unfunded pension liability of $2,637 million and a periodic pension cost of $183 million.

Explain the meaning of the $2,637 million unfunded pension liability and the $183 million periodic pension cost.

EX 11-20
Accrued product warranty
obj. 5

Lachgar Industries warrants its products for one year. The estimated product warranty is 4% of sales. Assume that sales were $210,000 for June. In July, a customer received warranty repairs requiring $140 of parts and $95 of labor.

a. Journalize the adjusting entry required at June 30, the end of the first month of the current fiscal year, to record the accrued product warranty.
b. Journalize the entry to record the warranty work provided in July.

EX 11-21
Accrued product warranty
obj. 5

Ford Motor Company disclosed estimated product warranty payable for comparative years as follows:

	(in millions)	
	12/31/06	**12/31/05**
Current estimated product warranty payable	$13,644	$13,074
Noncurrent estimated product warranty payable	8,289	7,359
Total	$21,933	$20,433

Ford's sales were $160,123 million in 2005 and increased to $176,896 million in 2006. Assume that the total paid on warranty claims during 2006 was $14,000 million.

a. ➡ Why are short- and long-term estimated warranty liabilities separately disclosed?
b. Provide the journal entry for the 2006 product warranty expense.

EX 11-22
Contingent liabilities
obj. 5

Several months ago, Welker Chemical Company experienced a hazardous materials spill at one of its plants. As a result, the Environmental Protection Agency (EPA) fined the company $410,000. The company is contesting the fine. In addition, an employee is seeking $400,000 damages related to the spill. Lastly, a homeowner has sued the company for $260,000. The homeowner lives 30 miles from the plant, but believes that the incident has reduced the home's resale value by $260,000.

Welker's legal counsel believes that it is probable that the EPA fine will stand. In addition, counsel indicates that an out-of-court settlement of $170,000 has recently been reached with the employee. The final papers will be signed next week. Counsel believes that the homeowner's case is much weaker and will be decided in favor of Welker. Other litigation related to the spill is possible, but the damage amounts are uncertain.

a. Journalize the contingent liabilities associated with the hazardous materials spill. Use the account "Damage Awards and Fines" to recognize the expense for the period.
b. ➡ Prepare a note disclosure relating to this incident.

EX 11-23
Quick ratio

✔ a. 2010: 1.10

Austin Technology Co. had the following current assets and liabilities for two comparative years:

	Dec. 31, 2010	Dec. 31, 2009
Current assets:		
Cash	$370,000	$ 448,000
Accounts receivable	400,000	410,000
Inventory	220,000	180,000
Total current assets	$990,000	$1,038,000

	Dec. 31, 2010	Dec. 31, 2009
Current liabilities:		
Current portion of long-term debt	$110,000	$100,000
Accounts payable	220,000	200,000
Accrued and other current liabilities	370,000	360,000
Total current liabilities	$700,000	$660,000

a. Determine the quick ratio for December 31, 2010 and 2009.
b. ━━━▶ Interpret the change in the quick ratio between the two balance sheet dates.

EX 11-24
Quick ratio

The current assets and current liabilities for Apple Computer, Inc., and Dell Inc. are shown as follows at the end of a recent fiscal period:

	Apple Computer, Inc. (In millions) Sept. 29, 2007	Dell Inc. (In millions) Feb. 2, 2007
Current assets:		
Cash and cash equivalents	$ 9,352	$ 9,546
Short-term investments	6,034	752
Accounts receivable	4,029	6,152
Inventories	346	660
Other current assets*	2,195	2,829
Total current assets	$21,956	$19,939
Current liabilities:		
Accounts payable	$ 4,970	$10,430
Accrued and other current liabilities	4,329	7,361
Total current liabilities	$ 9,299	$17,791

*These represent prepaid expense and other nonquick current assets.

a. Determine the quick ratio for both companies.
b. ━━━▶ Interpret the quick ratio difference between the two companies.

Problems Series A

PR 11-1A
Liability transactions
objs. 1, 5

The following items were selected from among the transactions completed by Emerald Bay Stores Co. during the current year:

Jan. 15. Purchased merchandise on account from Hood Co., $220,000, terms n/30.

Feb. 14. Issued a 60-day, 6% note for $220,000 to Hood Co., on account.

Apr. 15. Paid Hood Co. the amount owed on the note of February 14.

June 2. Borrowed $187,500 from Acme Bank, issuing a 60-day, 8% note.

July 10. Purchased tools by issuing a $190,000, 90-day note to Columbia Supply Co., which discounted the note at the rate of 6%.

Aug. 1. Paid Acme Bank the interest due on the note of June 2 and renewed the loan by issuing a new 60-day, 10% note for $187,500. (Journalize both the debit and credit to the notes payable account.)

Sept. 30. Paid Acme Bank the amount due on the note of August 1.

Oct. 8. Paid Columbia Supply Co. the amount due on the note of July 10.

Dec. 1. Purchased office equipment from Mountain Equipment Co. for $120,000, paying $20,000 and issuing a series of ten 6% notes for $10,000 each, coming due at 30-day intervals.

5. Settled a product liability lawsuit with a customer for $76,000, payable in January. Emerald Bay accrued the loss in a litigation claims payable account.

31. Paid the amount due Mountain Equipment Co. on the first note in the series issued on December 1.

Instructions

1. Journalize the transactions.
2. Journalize the adjusting entry for each of the following accrued expenses at the end of the current year: (a) product warranty cost, $16,400; (b) interest on the nine remaining notes owed to Mountain Equipment Co.

PR 11-2A
Entries for payroll and payroll taxes

objs. 2, 3

KLOOSTER & ALLEN

✔ 1. (b) Dr. Payroll Tax Expense, $36,026

The following information about the payroll for the week ended December 30 was obtained from the records of Arnsparger Equipment Co.:

Salaries:		Deductions:	
Sales salaries	$244,000	Income tax withheld	$ 88,704
Warehouse salaries	135,000	Social security tax withheld	27,216
Office salaries	125,000	Medicare tax withheld	7,560
	$504,000	U.S. savings bonds	11,088
		Group insurance	9,072
			$143,640

Tax rates assumed:
Social security, 6% on first $100,000 of employee annual earnings
Medicare, 1.5%
State unemployment (employer only), 4.2%
Federal unemployment (employer only), 0.8%

Instructions

1. Assuming that the payroll for the last week of the year is to be paid on December 31, journalize the following entries:
   a. December 30, to record the payroll.
   b. December 30, to record the employer's payroll taxes on the payroll to be paid on December 31. Of the total payroll for the last week of the year, $25,000 is subject to unemployment compensation taxes.
2. Assuming that the payroll for the last week of the year is to be paid on January 5 of the following fiscal year, journalize the following entries:
   a. December 30, to record the payroll.
   b. January 5, to record the employer's payroll taxes on the payroll to be paid on January 5.

PR 11-3A
Wage and tax statement data on employer FICA tax

objs. 2, 3

✔ 2. (e) $28,503

Gridiron Concepts Co. began business on January 2, 2009. Salaries were paid to employees on the last day of each month, and social security tax, Medicare tax, and federal income tax were withheld in the required amounts. An employee who is hired in the middle of the month receives half the monthly salary for that month. All required payroll tax reports were filed, and the correct amount of payroll taxes was remitted by the company for the calendar year. Early in 2010, before the Wage and Tax Statements (Form W-2) could be prepared for distribution to employees and for filing with the Social Security Administration, the employees' earnings records were inadvertently destroyed.

None of the employees resigned or were discharged during the year, and there were no changes in salary rates. The social security tax was withheld at the rate of 6.0% on the first $100,000 of salary and Medicare tax at the rate of 1.5% on salary. Data on dates of employment, salary rates, and employees' income taxes withheld, which are summarized as follows, were obtained from personnel records and payroll records:

Employee	Date First Employed	Monthly Salary	Monthly Income Tax Withheld
Brooks	Jan. 2	$ 3,400	$ 502
Croom	June 16	5,600	1,052
Fulmer	Apr. 1	2,500	310
Johnson	Oct. 1	2,500	310
Nutt	Jan. 2	10,000	2,253
Richt	Jan. 16	3,600	552
Spurrier	Mar. 1	8,600	1,861

Instructions

1. Calculate the amounts to be reported on each employee's Wage and Tax Statement (Form W-2) for 2009, arranging the data in the following form:

Employee	Gross Earnings	Federal Income Tax Withheld	Social Security Tax Withheld	Medicare Tax Withheld

2. Calculate the following employer payroll taxes for the year: (a) social security; (b) Medicare; (c) state unemployment compensation at 4.8% on the first $8,000 of each employee's earnings; (d) federal unemployment compensation at 0.8% on the first $8,000 of each employee's earnings; (e) total.

PR 11-4A
Payroll register

objs. 2, 3

✔ 3. Dr. Payroll Tax
Expense, $773.71

If the working papers correlating with this textbook are not used, omit Problem 11-4A.

The payroll register for Namesake Co. for the week ended September 12, 2010, is presented in the working papers.

Instructions

1. Journalize the entry to record the payroll for the week.
2. Journalize the entry to record the issuance of the checks to employees.
3. Journalize the entry to record the employer's payroll taxes for the week. Assume the following tax rates: state unemployment, 3.2%; federal unemployment, 0.8%. Of the earnings, $1,500 is subject to unemployment taxes.
4. Journalize the entry to record a check issued on September 15 to Fourth National Bank in payment of employees' income taxes, $1,944.78, social security taxes, $1,084.32, and Medicare taxes, $343.10.

PR 11-5A
Payroll register

objs. 2, 3

✔ 1. Total net
amount payable,
$9,260.56

The following data for Enrichment Industries, Inc. relate to the payroll for the week ended December 10, 2010:

Employee	Hours Worked	Hourly Rate	Weekly Salary	Federal Income Tax	U.S. Savings Bonds	Accumulated Earnings, Dec. 3
Beilein	32	$16.00		$102.40	10	$ 24,576
Calhoun	50	32.00		369.60	10	84,480
Calipari	40	28.00		240.80	20	53,760
Knight	42	32.00		316.48		66,048
Odom			$3,400	748.00	90	163,200
Olson			1,600	384.00		76,800
Pitino	34	18.00		91.80		29,376
Ryan	44	34.00		297.16	20	75,072
Thompson	40	26.00		218.40	35	49,920

Employees Olson and Odom are office staff, and all of the other employees are sales personnel. All sales personnel are paid 1½ times the regular rate for all hours in excess of 40 hours per week. The social security tax rate is 6.0% on the first $100,000 of each employee's annual earnings, and Medicare tax is 1.5% of each employee's annual earnings. The next payroll check to be used is No. 345.

Instructions

1. Prepare a payroll register for Enrichment Industries, Inc. for the week ended December 10, 2010. Use the following columns for the payroll register: Name, Total Hours, Regular Earnings, Overtime Earnings, Total Earnings, Social Security Tax, Medicare Tax, Federal Income Tax, U.S. Savings Bonds, Total Deductions, Net Pay, Ck. No., Sales Salaries Expense, and Office Salaries Expense.
2. Journalize the entry to record the payroll sales for the week.

PR 11-6A
Payroll accounts and year-end entries

objs. 2, 3, 4

The following accounts, with the balances indicated, appear in the ledger of Wadsley Gifts Co. on December 1 of the current year:

211	Salaries Payable	—
212	Social Security Tax Payable	$ 7,234
213	Medicare Tax Payable	1,904
214	Employees Federal Income Tax Payable	11,739
215	Employees State Income Tax Payable	11,422
216	State Unemployment Tax Payable	1,200
217	Federal Unemployment Tax Payable	400

218	Bond Deductions Payable	$ 2,800
219	Medical Insurance Payable	22,000
611	Operations Salaries Expense	766,000
711	Officers Salaries Expense	504,000
712	Office Salaries Expense	126,000
719	Payroll Tax Expense	109,318

The following transactions relating to payroll, payroll deductions, and payroll taxes occurred during December:

Dec. 2. Issued Check No. 321 for $2,800 to Johnson Bank to purchase U.S. savings bonds for employees.

3. Issued Check No. 322 to Johnson Bank for $20,877, in payment of $7,234 of social security tax, $1,904 of Medicare tax, and $11,739 of employees' federal income tax due.

14. Journalized the entry to record the biweekly payroll. A summary of the payroll record follows:

Salary distribution:		
Operations	$34,800	
Officers	22,900	
Office	5,700	$63,400
Deductions:		
Social security tax	$ 3,550	
Medicare tax	951	
Federal income tax withheld	11,285	
State income tax withheld	2,853	
Savings bond deductions	1,400	
Medical insurance deductions	3,667	23,706
Net amount		$39,694

14. Issued Check No. 331 in payment of the net amount of the biweekly payroll.

14. Journalized the entry to record payroll taxes on employees' earnings of December 14: social security tax, $3,550; Medicare tax, $951; state unemployment tax, $300; federal unemployment tax, $100.

17. Issued Check No. 335 to Johnson Bank for $20,287, in payment of $7,100 of social security tax, $1,902 of Medicare tax, and $11,285 of employees' federal income tax due.

18. Issued Check No. 340 to Tidy Insurance Company for $22,000, in payment of the semiannual premium on the group medical insurance policy.

28. Journalized the entry to record the biweekly payroll. A summary of the payroll record follows:

Salary distribution:		
Operations	$34,200	
Officers	22,400	
Office	5,400	$62,000
Deductions:		
Social security tax	$ 3,348	
Medicare tax	930	
Federal income tax withheld	11,036	
State income tax withheld	2,790	
Savings bond deductions	1,400	19,504
Net amount		$42,496

28. Issued Check No. 352 in payment of the net amount of the biweekly payroll.

28. Journalized the entry to record payroll taxes on employees' earnings of December 28: social security tax, $3,348; Medicare tax, $930; state unemployment tax, $150; federal unemployment tax, $50.

30. Issued Check No. 354 to Johnson Bank for $2,800 to purchase U.S. savings bonds for employees.

30. Issued Check No. 356 for $17,065 to Johnson Bank in payment of employees' state income tax due on December 31.

Dec. 31.   Paid $34,000 to the employee pension plan. The annual pension cost is $40,000. (Record both the payment and unfunded pension liability.)

Instructions
1. Journalize the transactions.
2. Journalize the following adjusting entries on December 31:
   a. Salaries accrued: operations salaries, $3,420; officers salaries, $2,240; office salaries, $540. The payroll taxes are immaterial and are not accrued.
   b. Vacation pay, $11,500.

Problems Series B

PR 11-1B
Liability transactions

objs. **1, 5**

The following items were selected from among the transactions completed by Paulson, Inc. during the current year:

Apr. 1.   Borrowed $60,000 from McCaw Company, issuing a 45-day, 6% note for that amount.
    26.   Purchased equipment by issuing a $160,000, 180-day note to Houston Manufacturing Co., which discounted the note at the rate of 8%.
May 16.   Paid McCaw Company the interest due on the note of April 1 and renewed the loan by issuing a new 30-day, 10% note for $60,000. (Record both the debit and credit to the notes payable account.)
June 15.   Paid McCaw Company the amount due on the note of May 16.
Sept. 3.   Purchased merchandise on account from Oatley Co., $42,000, terms, n/30.
Oct. 3.   Issued a 30-day, 9% note for $42,000 to Oatley Co., on account.
    23.   Paid Houston Manufacturing Co. the amount due on the note of April 26.
Nov. 2.   Paid Oatley Co. the amount owed on the note of October 3.
    10.   Purchased store equipment from Biden Technology Co. for $200,000, paying $60,000 and issuing a series of seven 9% notes for $20,000 each, coming due at 30-day intervals.
Dec. 10.   Paid the amount due Biden Technology Co. on the first note in the series issued on November 10.
    16.   Settled a personal injury lawsuit with a customer for $42,500, to be paid in January. Paulson, Inc. accrued the loss in a litigation claims payable account.

Instructions
1. Journalize the transactions.
2. Journalize the adjusting entry for each of the following accrued expenses at the end of the current year:
   a. Product warranty cost, $10,400.
   b. Interest on the six remaining notes owed to Biden Technology Co.

PR 11-2B
Entries for payroll and payroll taxes

objs. **2, 3**

✔ 1. (b) Dr. Payroll Tax Expense, $68,304

The following information about the payroll for the week ended December 30 was obtained from the records of Vienna Co.:

Salaries:		Deductions:	
Sales salaries	$ 670,000	Income tax withheld	$198,744
Warehouse salaries	110,000	Social security tax withheld	51,714
Office salaries	234,000	Medicare tax withheld	15,210
	$1,014,000	U.S. savings bonds	30,420
		Group insurance	45,630
			$341,718

Tax rates assumed:
  Social security, 6% on first $100,000 of employee annual earnings
  Medicare, 1.5%
  State unemployment (employer only), 3.8%
  Federal unemployment (employer only), 0.8%

Instructions

1. Assuming that the payroll for the last week of the year is to be paid on December 31, journalize the following entries:
   a. December 30, to record the payroll.
   b. December 30, to record the employer's payroll taxes on the payroll to be paid on December 31. Of the total payroll for the last week of the year, $30,000 is subject to unemployment compensation taxes.
2. Assuming that the payroll for the last week of the year is to be paid on January 4 of the following fiscal year, journalize the following entries:
   a. December 30, to record the payroll.
   b. January 4, to record the employer's payroll taxes on the payroll to be paid on January 4.

PR 11-3B
Wage and tax statement data and employer FICA tax

objs. 2, 3

✔ 2. (e) $26,019.00

CTU Industries, Inc., began business on January 2, 2009. Salaries were paid to employees on the last day of each month, and social security tax, Medicare tax, and federal income tax were withheld in the required amounts. An employee who is hired in the middle of the month receives half the monthly salary for that month. All required payroll tax reports were filed, and the correct amount of payroll taxes was remitted by the company for the calendar year. Early in 2010, before the Wage and Tax Statements (Form W-2) could be prepared for distribution to employees and for filing with the Social Security Administration, the employees' earnings records were inadvertently destroyed.

None of the employees resigned or were discharged during the year, and there were no changes in salary rates. The social security tax was withheld at the rate of 6.0% on the first $100,000 of salary and Medicare tax at the rate of 1.5% on salary. Data on dates of employment, salary rates, and employees' income taxes withheld, which are summarized as follows, were obtained from personnel records and payroll records:

Employee	Date First Employed	Monthly Salary	Monthly Income Tax Withheld
Brown	Aug. 1	$3,600	$ 552
Carroll	Jan. 2	9,500	2,113
Grobe	May 1	6,500	1,277
Meyer	July 1	4,200	702
Saban	Jan. 2	5,100	927
Tressel	Apr. 16	3,200	452
Weis	Oct. 1	3,000	402

Instructions

1. Calculate the amounts to be reported on each employee's Wage and Tax Statement (Form W-2) for 2009, arranging the data in the following form:

Employee	Gross Earnings	Federal Income Tax Withheld	Social Security Tax Withheld	Medicare Tax Withheld

2. Calculate the following employer payroll taxes for the year: (a) social security; (b) Medicare; (c) state unemployment compensation at 4.8% on the first $10,000 of each employee's earnings; (d) federal unemployment compensation at 0.8% on the first $10,000 of each employee's earnings; (e) total.

PR 11-4B
Payroll register

objs. 2, 3

✔ 3. Dr. Payroll Tax Expense, $788.40

If the working papers correlating with this textbook are not used, omit Problem 11-4B.

The payroll register for Gogol Manufacturing Co. for the week ended September 12, 2010, is presented in the working papers.

Instructions

1. Journalize the entry to record the payroll for the week.
2. Journalize the entry to record the issuance of the checks to employees.
3. Journalize the entry to record the employer's payroll taxes for the week. Assume the following tax rates: state unemployment, 3.2%; federal unemployment, 0.8%. Of the earnings, $1,800 is subject to unemployment taxes.
4. Journalize the entry to record a check issued on September 15 to Third National Bank in payment of employees' income taxes, $2,337.88, social security taxes, $1,021.44, and Medicare taxes, $411.36.

PR 11-5B
Payroll register

objs. 2, 3

✔ 1. Total net amount payable, $8,610.31

The following data for Burtard Industries, Inc., relate to the payroll for the week ended December 10, 2010:

Employee	Hours Worked	Hourly Rate	Weekly Salary	Federal Income Tax	U.S. Savings Bonds	Accumulated Earnings, Dec. 3
Barnes			$3,000	$645.00		$144,000
Calhoun	50	$32.00		369.60	20	84,480
Crean			1,800	432.00	50	86,400
Donovan	34	20.00		136.00		32,640
Izzo	45	25.00		178.13		57,000
Matta	46	24.00		223.44	25	56,448
Self	40	23.00		193.20	40	44,160
Smith	40	22.00		202.40	30	42,240
Williams	36	18.00		142.56	30	31,104

Employees Barnes and Crean are office staff, and all of the other employees are sales personnel. All sales personnel are paid $1\frac{1}{2}$ times the regular rate for all hours in excess of 40 hours per week. The social security tax rate is 6.0% on the first $100,000 of each employee's annual earnings, and Medicare tax is 1.5% of each employee's annual earnings. The next payroll check to be used is No. 652.

Instructions
1. Prepare a payroll register for Burtard Industries, Inc. for the week ended December 10, 2010. Use the following columns for the payroll register: Name, Total Hours, Regular Earnings, Overtime Earnings, Total Earnings, Social Security Tax, Medicare Tax, Federal Income Tax, U.S. Savings Bonds, Total Deductions, Net Pay, Ck. No., Sales Salaries Expense, and Office Salaries Expense.
2. Journalize the entry to record the payroll sales for the week.

PR 11-6B
Payroll accounts and year-end entries

objs. 2, 3, 4

The following accounts, with the balances indicated, appear in the ledger of Yukon Kayak Co. on December 1 of the current year:

211	Salaries Payable	—	218	Bond Deductions Payable	$ 1,800
212	Social Security Tax Payable	$4,880	219	Medical Insurance Payable	2,000
213	Medicare Tax Payable	1,236	611	Sales Salaries Expense	556,000
214	Employees Federal Income Tax Payable	7,540	711	Officers Salaries Expense	266,400
215	Employees State Income Tax Payable	7,038	712	Office Salaries Expense	99,200
216	State Unemployment Tax Payable	1,000	719	Payroll Tax Expense	74,316
217	Federal Unemployment Tax Payable	280			

The following transactions relating to payroll, payroll deductions, and payroll taxes occurred during December:

Dec. 1. Issued Check No. 510 to Tidy Insurance Company for $2,000, in payment of the semiannual premium on the group medical insurance policy.

2. Issued Check No. 511 to Johnson Bank for $13,656, in payment for $4,880 of social security tax, $1,236 of Medicare tax, and $7,540 of employees' federal income tax due.

3. Issued Check No. 512 for $1,800 to Johnson Bank to purchase U.S. savings bonds for employees.

14. Journalized the entry to record the biweekly payroll. A summary of the payroll record follows:

Salary distribution:		
Sales	$25,000	
Officers	12,100	
Office	4,500	$41,600

Deductions:		
Social security tax	$ 2,288	
Medicare tax	624	
Federal income tax withheld	7,405	
State income tax withheld	1,872	
Savings bond deductions	900	
Medical insurance deductions	333	13,422
Net amount		$28,178

Dec. 14.   Issued Check No. 520 in payment of the net amount of the biweekly payroll.

14.   Journalized the entry to record payroll taxes on employees' earnings of December 14: social security tax, $2,288; Medicare tax, $624; state unemployment tax, $250; federal unemployment tax, $60.

17.   Issued Check No. 528 to Johnson Bank for $13,229, in payment for $4,576 of social security tax, $1,248 of Medicare tax, and $7,405 of employees' federal income tax due.

28.   Journalized the entry to record the biweekly payroll. A summary of the payroll record follows:

Salary distribution:		
Sales	$25,400	
Officers	12,400	
Office	4,800	$42,600
Deductions:		
Social security tax	$ 2,300	
Medicare tax	639	
Federal income tax withheld	7,583	
State income tax withheld	1,917	
Savings bond deductions	900	13,339
Net amount		$29,261

28.   Issued Check No. 540 for the net amount of the biweekly payroll.

28.   Journalized the entry to record payroll taxes on employees' earnings of December 28: social security tax, $2,300; Medicare tax, $639; state unemployment tax, $120; federal unemployment tax, $30.

30.   Issued Check No. 551 for $10,827 to Johnson Bank, in payment of employees' state income tax due on December 31.

30.   Issued Check No. 552 to Johnson Bank for $1,800 to purchase U.S. savings bonds for employees.

31.   Paid $44,000 to the employee pension plan. The annual pension cost is $52,000. (Record both the payment and the unfunded pension liability.)

Instructions
1. Journalize the transactions.
2. Journalize the following adjusting entries on December 31:
   a. Salaries accrued: sales salaries, $2,540; officers salaries, $1,240; office salaries, $480. The payroll taxes are immaterial and are not accrued.
   b. Vacation pay, $10,600.

Comprehensive Problem 3

✔ 5. Total assets, $1,567,300

Selected transactions completed by Blackwell Company during its first fiscal year ending December 31 were as follows:

Jan. 2.   Issued a check to establish a petty cash fund of $2,000.

Mar. 4.   Replenished the petty cash fund, based on the following summary of petty cash receipts: office supplies, $789; miscellaneous selling expense, $256; miscellaneous administrative expense, $378.

Apr. 5.   Purchased $14,000 of merchandise on account, terms 1/10, n/30. The perpetual inventory system is used to account for inventory.

May 7.   Paid the invoice of April 5 after the discount period had passed.

10.   Received cash from daily cash sales for $9,455. The amount indicated by the cash register was $9,545.

June 2.   Received a 60-day, 9% note for $80,000 on the Stevens account.

Aug. 1.   Received amount owed on June 2 note, plus interest at the maturity date.

8.   Received $3,400 on the Jacobs account and wrote off the remainder owed on a $4,000 accounts receivable balance. (The allowance method is used in accounting for uncollectible receivables.)

Aug. 25.   Reinstated the Jacobs account written off on August 8 and received $600 cash in full payment.

Sept. 2.   Purchased land by issuing a $300,000, 90-day note to Ace Development Co., which discounted it at 10%.

Oct. 2.   Sold office equipment in exchange for $60,000 cash plus receipt of a $40,000, 120-day, 6% note. The equipment had cost $140,000 and had accumulated depreciation of $25,000 as of October 1.

Nov. 30.   Journalized the monthly payroll for November, based on the following data:

Salaries		Deductions	
Sales salaries	$60,400	Income tax withheld	$17,082
Office salaries	34,500	Social security tax withheld	5,450
	$94,900	Medicare tax withheld	1,424

Unemployment tax rates:	
State unemployment	4.0%
Federal unemployment	0.8%
Amount subject to unemployment taxes:	
State unemployment	$4,000
Federal unemployment	4,000

30.   Journalized the employer's payroll taxes on the payroll.

Dec. 1.   Journalized the payment of the September 2 note at maturity.

31.   The pension cost for the year was $85,000, of which $62,400 was paid to the pension plan trustee.

Instructions

1. Journalize the selected transactions.
2. Based on the following data, prepare a bank reconciliation for December of the current year:
   a. Balance according to the bank statement at December 31, $126,400.
   b. Balance according to the ledger at December 31, $109,650.
   c. Checks outstanding at December 31, $30,600.
   d. Deposit in transit, not recorded by bank, $13,200.
   e. Bank debit memo for service charges, $350.
   f. A check for $530 in payment of an invoice was incorrectly recorded in the accounts as $230.
3. Based on the bank reconciliation prepared in (2), journalize the entry or entries to be made by Blackwell Company.
4. Based on the following selected data, journalize the adjusting entries as of December 31 of the current year:
   a. Estimated uncollectible accounts at December 31, $7,200, based on an aging of accounts receivable. The balance of Allowance for Doubtful Accounts at December 31 was $750 (debit).
   b. The physical inventory on December 31 indicated an inventory shrinkage of $1,480.
   c. Prepaid insurance expired during the year, $10,200.
   d. Office supplies used during the year, $1,760.
   e. Depreciation is computed as follows:

Asset	Cost	Residual Value	Acquisition Date	Useful Life in Years	Depreciation Method Used
Buildings	$400,000	$ 0	January 2	40	Straight-line
Office Equip.	110,000	10,000	July 1	4	Straight-line
Store Equip.	50,000	5,000	January 3	8	Double-declining-balance (at twice the straight-line rate)

   f. A patent costing $22,500 when acquired on January 2 has a remaining legal life of 10 years and is expected to have value for five years.
   g. The cost of mineral rights was $220,000. Of the estimated deposit of 400,000 tons of ore, 24,000 tons were mined and sold during the year.

h. Vacation pay expense for December, $4,800.

i. A product warranty was granted beginning December 1 and covering a one-year period. The estimated cost is 2.5% of sales, which totaled $840,000 in December.

j. Interest was accrued on the note receivable received on October 2.

5. Based on the following information and the post-closing trial balance shown below, prepare a balance sheet in report form at December 31 of the current year.

The merchandise inventory is stated at cost by the LIFO method.

The product warranty payable is a current liability.

Vacation pay payable:
Current liability $3,200
Long-term liability   1,600

The unfunded pension liability is a long-term liability.

Notes payable:
Current liability $25,000
Long-term liability   75,000

Blackwell Company
Post-Closing Trial Balance
December 31, 2010

	Debit Balances	Credit Balances
Petty Cash	2,000	
Cash	109,000	
Notes Receivable	40,000	
Accounts Receivable	210,000	
Allowance for Doubtful Accounts		7,200
Merchandise Inventory	144,200	
Interest Receivable	600	
Prepaid Insurance	20,400	
Office Supplies	6,000	
Land	292,500	
Buildings	400,000	
Accumulated Depreciation—Buildings		10,000
Office Equipment	110,000	
Accumulated Depreciation—Office Equipment		12,500
Store Equipment	50,000	
Accumulated Depreciation—Store Equipment		12,500
Mineral Rights	220,000	
Accumulated Depletion		13,200
Patents	18,000	
Social Security Tax Payable		10,420
Medicare Tax Payable		2,550
Employees Federal Income Tax Payable		17,260
State Unemployment Tax Payable		100
Federal Unemployment Tax Payable		20
Salaries Payable		85,000
Accounts Payable		140,000
Interest Payable		3,200
Product Warranty Payable		21,000
Vacation Pay Payable		4,800
Unfunded Pension Liability		22,600
Notes Payable		100,000
J. Crane, Capital		1,160,350
	1,622,700	1,622,700

6. On February 7 of the following year, the merchandise inventory was destroyed by fire. Based on the following data obtained from the accounting records, estimate the cost of the merchandise destroyed:

Jan. 1 Merchandise inventory $144,200
Jan. 1–Feb. 7 Purchases (net)   40,000
Jan. 1–Feb. 7 Sales (net)   70,000
Estimated gross profit rate   40%

Special Activities

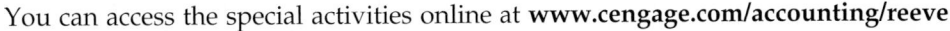

You can access the special activities online at **www.cengage.com/accounting/reeve**.

Excel Success Special Activities

SA 11-1
Computing employee net pay

JK Flowers Corporation has a single employee, S. Singh. Singh worked for 47 hours during the week, of which seven hours were overtime. Singh is paid $19.40 per hour. Overtime hours are paid at a rate of 150% of straight time. Additional information for Singh is as follows:

Federal income tax (weekly withholding)	$201.30
Retirement savings (weekly)	75.00
Earnings prior to payroll period	27,950

The social security tax rate is assumed to be 6% on the first $100,000 of employee earnings per year. The Medicare rate is assumed to be 1.5% on all employee earnings. All of Singh's earnings were under the social security maximum earnings threshold.

a. Open the Excel file *SA11-1.*
b. Prepare a spreadsheet to compute the weekly gross pay, deductions, and net pay for S. Singh.
c. When you have completed the pay calculations, perform a "save as," replacing the entire file name with the following:

   SA11-1_[your first name initial]_[your last name]

SA 11-2
Computing employee net pay, multiple employees

The Myatt Companies prepared the following weekly schedule for its three employees:

	A	B	C	D
		M. Todd	J. Kress	V. Johns
1	*Inputs:*			
2	Hours worked straight-time	40	40	40
3	Hours worked overtime	6	12	0
4	Hourly rate	$ 24.00	$ 30.00	$ 16.50
5	Overtime premium	200%	150%	150%
6	Weekly withholding	$ 218.42	$ 278.32	$ 186.45
7	Earnings prior to payroll period	$ 68,915	$ 91,725	$ 32,710
8	Retirement savings	$ 60.00	$ 150.00	$ 50.00
9				

The social security rate is assumed to be 6%, limited to the first $100,000 of annual earnings. The Medicare rate is assumed to be 1.5%.

a. Open the Excel file *SA11-2.*
b. Prepare a spreadsheet to compute the weekly gross pay, deductions, and net pay for each employee.
c. When you have completed the pay calculations, perform a "save as," replacing the entire file name with the following:

   SA11-2_[your first name initial]_[your last name]

SA 11-3
Computing employee net pay, multiple time periods

excel
success

Repair-It-for-U has a single employee, Josh Reed, who has the following weekly payroll information for four weeks:

	A	B	C	D	E
1		Week 1	Week 2	Week 3	Week 4
2	Hours worked straight-time	40	39	40	36
3	Hours worked overtime	5	0	3	0
4	Weekly withholding	$ 145.00	$ 121.00	$ 138.00	$ 109.00
5					

Reed had a pay rate of $16 per hour and an overtime premium of 150%. The social security tax rate is assumed to be 6%. The Medicare tax rate is assumed to be 1.5%. All of Reed's earnings were under the social security maximum earnings threshold.

a. Open the Excel file *SA11-3*.

b. Prepare a spreadsheet to compute the weekly gross pay, deductions, and net pay for each week.

c. When you have completed the pay calculations, perform a "save as," replacing the entire file name with the following:

   SA11-3_[your first name initial]_[your last name]

Answers to Self-Examination Questions

1. **C** The maturity value is $5,100, determined as follows:

Face amount of note	$5,000
Plus interest ($5,000 × 12% × 60/360)	100
Maturity value	$5,100

2. **B** The net amount available to a borrower from discounting a note payable is called the proceeds. The proceeds of $4,900 (answer B) is determined as follows:

Face amount of note	$5,000
Less discount ($5,000 × 12% × 60/360)	100
Proceeds	$4,900

3. **B** Employers are usually required to withhold a portion of their employees' earnings for payment of federal income taxes (answer A), Medicare tax (answer C), and state and local income taxes (answer D). Generally, federal unemployment compensation taxes (answer B) are levied against the employer only and thus are not deducted from employee earnings.

4. **D** The amount of net pay of $1,385.50 (answer D) is determined as follows:

Gross pay:			
40 hours at $40		$1,600.00	
5 hours at $60		300.00	$1,900.00
Deductions:			
Federal income tax withheld		$ 450.00	
FICA:			
Social security tax ($600 × 0 .06)	$ 36.00		
Medicare tax ($1,900 × 0 .015)	28.50	64.50	514.50
			$1,385.50

5. **D** The employer incurs an expense for social security tax (answer A), federal unemployment compensation tax (answer B), and state unemployment compensation tax (answer C). The employees' federal income tax (answer D) is not an expense of the employer. It is withheld from the employees' earnings.

Accounting for Partnerships and Limited Liability Companies

Courtesy: AgentBlaze, LLC. Photograph: Jerry Headrick, Charles Brooks Photography

A G E N T B L A Z E , L L C

If you were to start up any type of business, you would want to separate the business's affairs from your personal affairs. Keeping business transactions separate from personal transactions aids business analysis and simplifies tax reporting. For example, Brad Roberts, the founder of AgentBlaze, LLC, began his business in his home, designing Web sites for real estate agents. Even when he operated as a simple sole proprietorship, Brad maintained a separate business checking account for depositing receipts from sales and writing checks for expenses. Thus, at the end of the year, he would have the information necessary for determining the earnings of the business and completing tax returns.

As a business grows in size and complexity, the form of the business entity becomes an important consideration. For example, as Brad's home-based Web business grew, he needed partners to help with graphics design and additional funding. Thus was born AgentBlaze, LLC. The "LLC" means limited liability company and is a business form that frequently involves more than a single person as an owner.

The entity form has an important impact on the owners' legal liability, taxation, and ability to raise money. The four major forms of business entities discussed in this text are the proprietorship, partnership, limited liability company, and corporation. We have already introduced the proprietorship. Partnerships and limited liability companies will be discussed in this chapter, and corporations will be introduced in the next chapter.

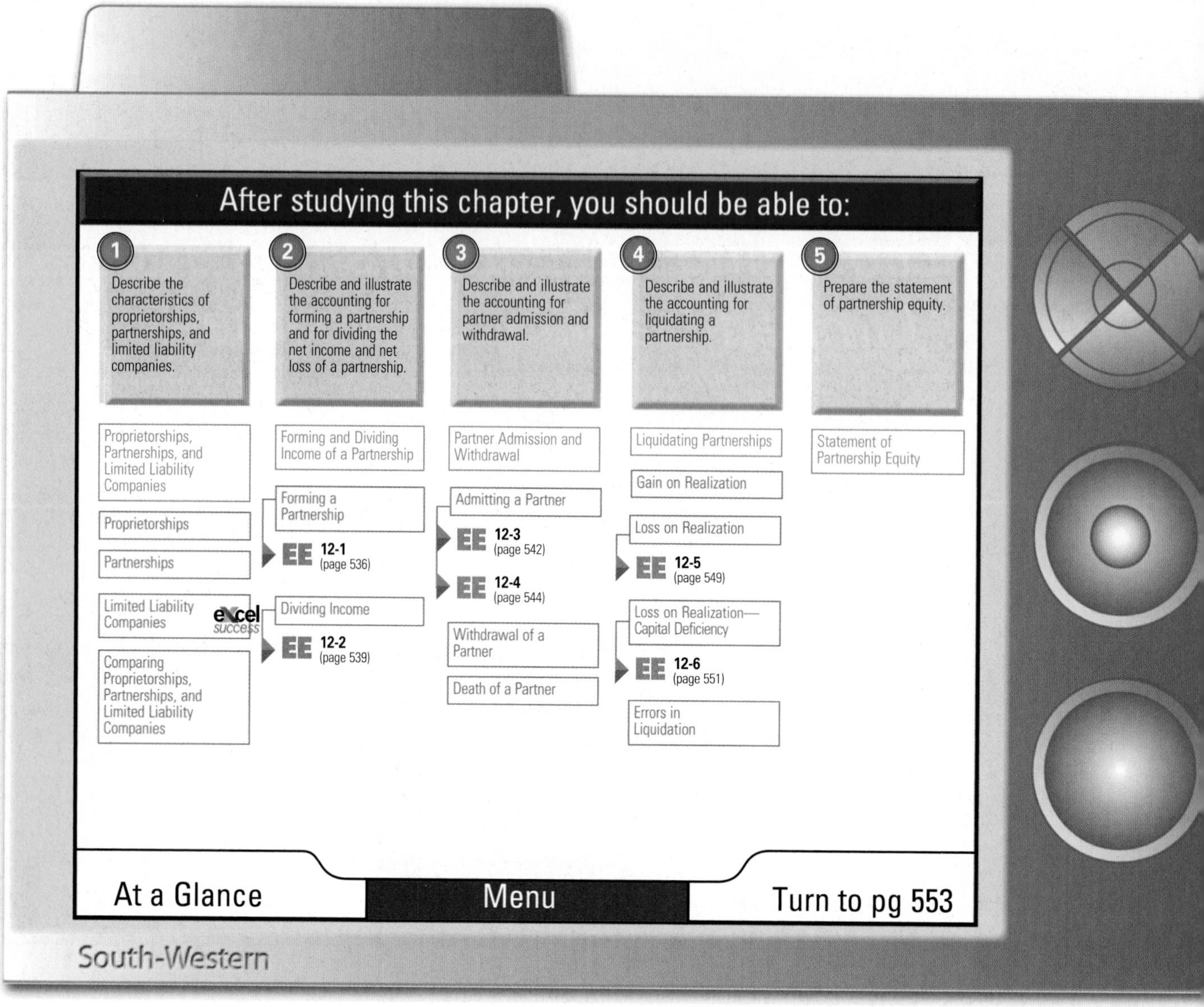

After studying this chapter, you should be able to:

1 Describe the characteristics of proprietorships, partnerships, and limited liability companies.

2 Describe and illustrate the accounting for forming a partnership and for dividing the net income and net loss of a partnership.

3 Describe and illustrate the accounting for partner admission and withdrawal.

4 Describe and illustrate the accounting for liquidating a partnership.

5 Prepare the statement of partnership equity.

Proprietorships, Partnerships, and Limited Liability Companies

Proprietorships

Partnerships

Limited Liability Companies

Comparing Proprietorships, Partnerships, and Limited Liability Companies

Forming and Dividing Income of a Partnership

Forming a Partnership

EE 12-1 (page 536)

Dividing Income

EE 12-2 (page 539)

Partner Admission and Withdrawal

Admitting a Partner

EE 12-3 (page 542)

EE 12-4 (page 544)

Withdrawal of a Partner

Death of a Partner

Liquidating Partnerships

Gain on Realization

Loss on Realization

EE 12-5 (page 549)

Loss on Realization— Capital Deficiency

EE 12-6 (page 551)

Errors in Liquidation

Statement of Partnership Equity

At a Glance | Menu | Turn to pg 553

South-Western

---

1 Describe the characteristics of proprietorships, partnerships, and limited liability companies.

Proprietorships, Partnerships, and Limited Liability Companies

The four most common legal forms for organizing and operating a business are as follows:

1. Proprietorship
2. Corporation
3. Partnership
4. Limited liability company

In this section, the characteristics of proprietorships, partnerships, and limited liability companies are described. The characteristics of corporations are described in Chapter 13.

Proprietorships

A proprietorship is a company owned by a single individual. The most common type of proprietorships are professional service providers, such as lawyers, architects, realtors, and physicians.

Characteristics of proprietorships include the following:

1. *Simple to form.* There are no legal restrictions or forms to file.
2. *No limitation on legal liability.* The owner is personally liable for any debts or legal claims against the company. Thus, creditors can take the personal assets of the owner if the business debts exceed the owner's investment in the company.
3. *Not taxable.* For federal income tax purposes, a proprietorship is not taxed. Instead, the company's income or loss is "passed through" to the owner's individual income tax return.[1]
4. *Limited life.* When the owner dies or retires, the proprietorship ceases to exist.
5. *Limited ability to raise capital (funds).* The ability to raise capital (funds) is limited to what the owner can provide from personal resources or through borrowing.

The Internal Revenue Service (IRS) estimates that proprietorships file 70% of business tax returns, but earn only 5% of all business revenues.

Partnerships

A **partnership** is an association of two or more persons who own and manage a company for profit.[2] Partnerships are less widely used than proprietorships.

Characteristics of a partnership include the following:

1. *Moderate to form.* A partnership requires only an agreement between two or more persons to organize. However, the **partnership agreement**, sometimes called the *articles of partnership*, includes matters such as amounts to be invested, limits on withdrawals, distributions of income and losses, and admission and withdrawal of partners. Thus, an attorney is often used in forming a partnership.
2. *No limitation on legal liability.* The partners are personally liable for any debts or legal claims against the company. Therefore, creditors can take the personal assets of the partners if the business debts exceed the partners' investment in the company.
3. *Not taxable.* For federal income tax purposes, a partnership is not taxed. Instead, the company's income or loss is "passed through" to the partners' individual income tax returns. However, partnerships must still report revenues, expenses, and income or loss annually to the Internal Revenue Service.
4. *Limited life.* When a partner dies or retires, the partnership ceases to exist. Likewise, the admission of a new partner dissolves the old partnership, and a new partnership must be formed if operations are to continue.
5. *Limited ability to raise capital (funds).* The ability to raise capital (funds) for the company is limited to what the partners can provide from personal resources or through borrowing.

In addition to the above characteristics, some unique aspects of partnerships are as follows:

1. *Co-ownership of partnership property.* The property invested in a partnership by a partner becomes the joint property of all the partners. When a partnership is dissolved, each partner's share of the partnership assets is the balance in their capital account.
2. *Mutual agency.* Each partner is an agent of the partnership and may act on behalf of the entire partnership. Thus, any liabilities created by one partner become liabilities of all the partners.
3. *Participation in income.* Net income and net loss are distributed among the partners according to their partnership agreement. If the partnership agreement does not provide for distribution of income and losses, then income and losses are divided equally among the partners.

---

1 The proprietor's statement of income is included on Schedule C of the individual 1040 tax return.
2 The definition of a partnership is included in the Uniform Partnership Act, which has been adopted by most states.

A partnership may be organized as a limited partnership. A *limited partnership* is a unique legal form that provides partners who are not involved in the operations of the partnership with limited liability. In such a form, at least one *general partner* operates the partnership and has unlimited liability. The remaining partners are considered *limited partners*.

Limited Liability Companies

CBS Corp. uses regionally placed joint ventures organized as partnerships and LLCs to broadcast MTV, VH1, Nickelodeon, and TV Land around the world. CBS's joint venture partners bring local customs, language, and culture to the broadcast offerings.

A **limited liability company (LLC)** is a form of legal entity that provides limited liability to its owners, but is treated as a partnership for tax purposes. The LLC is a relatively new form of business entity that has become widely used for small companies. LLCs, which may be owned by one or more persons or entities, are designed to overcome some of the disadvantages of a partnership.

Characteristics of an LLC include the following:

1. *Moderate to form.* An LLC requires an agreement among the owners who are called *members*. The *operating agreement*, sometimes called *articles of organization*, includes matters such as amounts to be invested, limits on withdrawals, distributions of income and losses, and admission and withdrawal of members. An attorney is normally used in forming an LCC.

2. *Limited legal liability.* The members have *limited liability* even if they are active in the company. Thus, the members' personal assets are legally protected against creditor claims made against the LLC. That is, only the members' investments in the company are subject to claims of creditors.

3. *Not taxable.* An LLC may elect to be treated as a partnership for tax purposes. In this way, income passes through the LLC and is taxed on the individual members' tax returns.[3]

4. *Unlimited life.* Most LLC operating agreements specify continuity of life for the LLC, even when a member withdraws or new members join the LLC.

5. *Moderate ability to raise capital (funds).* Because of their limited liability, LLCs are attractive to many investors, thus, allowing for greater access to capital (funds) than is normally the case in a partnership.

An LLC may elect to operate as a *member-managed* or a *manager-managed* company. In a member-managed LLC, individual members may legally bind the LLC, like partners bind a partnership. In a manager-managed LLC, only authorized members may legally bind the LLC. Thus, in a manager-managed LLC, members may share in the income of the LLC without concern for managing the company. As a result, manager-managed LLCs are attractive to many investors.

Comparing Proprietorships, Partnerships, and Limited Liability Companies

Exhibit 1 summarizes the characteristics of proprietorships, partnerships, and limited liability companies.

2 Describe and illustrate the accounting for forming a partnership and for dividing the net income and net loss of a partnership.

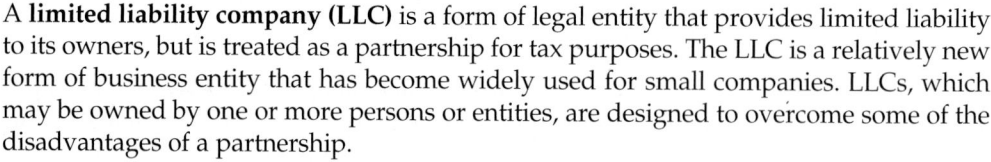

Forming and Dividing Income of a Partnership

Most of the day-to-day accounting for a partnership or an LLC is similar to that illustrated in earlier chapters. However, the formation, division of net income or net loss, dissolution, and liquidation of partnerships and LLCs give rise to unique transactions.

---

3 An LLC may also be taxed as a separate entity. However, doing so would remove these tax benefits, making this a less common election.

Characteristics of Proprietorships, Partnerships, and Limited Liability Companies

Organizational Form	Ease of Formation	Legal Liability	Taxation	Limitation on Life of Entity	Access to Capital
Proprietorship	Simple	No limitation	Nontaxable (pass-through) entity	Limited	Limited
Partnership	Moderate	No limitation	Nontaxable (pass-through) entity	Limited	Limited
Limited Liability Company	Moderate	Limited liability	Nontaxable (pass-through) entity by election	Unlimited	Moderate

In the remainder of this chapter, the unique transactions for partnerships and LLCs are described and illustrated. The accounting for an LLC is the same as a partnership, except that the terms "member" and "members' equity" are used rather than "partner" or "owners' capital." For this reason, the journal entries for an LLC are shown in the margin alongside the partnership entries.

Forming a Partnership

In forming a partnership, the investments of each partner are recorded in separate entries. The assets contributed by a partner are debited to the partnership asset accounts. If any liabilities are assumed by the partnership, the partnership liability accounts are credited. The partner's capital account is credited for the net amount.

To illustrate, assume that Joseph Stevens and Earl Foster, owners of competing hardware stores, agree to combine their businesses in a partnership. Stevens agrees to contribute the following:

Cash	$ 7,200	Office equipment	$2,500
Accounts receivable	16,300	Allowance for doubtful accounts	1,500
Merchandise inventory	28,700	Accounts payable	2,600
Store equipment	5,400		

The entry to record the assets and liabilities contributed by Stevens is as follows:

LLC

Cash	7,200	
Accounts Receivable	16,300	
Merchandise Inventory	28,700	
Store Equipment	5,400	
Office Equipment	2,500	
Allowance for Doubtful Accounts		1,500
Accounts Payable		2,600
Joseph Stevens, Member Equity		56,000

Apr.	1	Cash	7,200	
		Accounts Receivable	16,300	
		Merchandise Inventory	28,700	
		Store Equipment	5,400	
		Office Equipment	2,500	
		Allowance for Doubtful Accounts		1,500
		Accounts Payable		2,600
		Joseph Stevens, Capital		56,000

In the preceding entry, the noncash assets are recorded at values agreed upon by the partners. These values are normally based on current market values. As a result, the book value of the assets contributed by the partners normally differs from that recorded by the new partnership.

To illustrate, the store equipment contributed by Stevens may have had a book value of $3,500 in Stevens's ledger (cost of $10,000 less accumulated depreciation of $6,500). However, the store equipment is recorded at its current market value of $5,400 in the preceding entry. The contributions of Foster would be recorded in an entry similar to the entry for Stevens.

Example Exercise 12-1   Journalize Partner's Original Investment

Reese Howell contributed equipment, inventory, and $34,000 cash to a partnership. The equipment had a book value of $23,000 and a market value of $29,000. The inventory had a book value of $60,000, but only had a market value of $15,000, due to obsolescence. The partnership also assumed a $12,000 note payable owed by Howell that was used originally to purchase the equipment.

Provide the journal entry for Howell's contribution to the partnership.

Follow My Example 12-1

Cash	34,000	
Inventory.	15,000	
Equipment	29,000	
Notes Payable		12,000
Reese Howell, Capital		66,000

For Practice: PE 12-1A, PE 12-1B

Dividing Income

Income or losses of the partnership are divided *equally* if no partnership agreement exists or the partnership agreement does not specify how the division is to occur. Most partnership agreements, however, do specify how income or losses are to be divided.

Common methods of dividing partnership income are based on:

1. Services of the partners
2. Services and investments of the partners

Dividing Income—Services of Partners One method of dividing partnership income is based on the services provided by each partner to the partnership. These services are often recognized by partner salary allowances. Such allowances reflect differences in partners' abilities and time devoted to the partnership. Since partners are not employees, such allowances are recorded as divisions of net income and are credited to the partners' capital accounts.

To illustrate, assume that the partnership agreement of Jennifer Stone and Crystal Mills provides for the following:

	Monthly Salary Allowance
Jennifer Stone	$5,000
Crystal Mills	4,000
Remaining net income:	Divided Equally

The division of income may be reported at the bottom of the partnership income statement. Using this format, the division of $150,000 of net income would be reported on the bottom of the partnership income statement as follows:

Net income $150,000

Division of net income:

	J. Stone	C. Mills	Total
Annual salary allowance	$60,000	$48,000	$108,000
Remaining income	21,000	21,000	42,000
Net income	$81,000	$69,000	$150,000

The division of net income may also be reported as a separate statement accompanying the balance sheet and the income statement or in a statement of partnership capital.

The net income division is recorded as a closing entry, even if the partners do not withdraw the amounts of their salary allowances. The entry for closing Income Summary and dividing net income is as follows:

LLC

Income Summary	150,000	
Jennifer Stone, Member Equity		81,000
Crystal Mills, Member Equity		69,000

Dec. 31	Income Summary		150,000	
	Jennifer Stone, Capital			81,000
	Crystal Mills, Capital			69,000

If Stone and Mills withdraw their salary allowances monthly, the withdrawals are debited to their drawing accounts. At the end of the year, the drawing account debit balances of $60,000 and $48,000 are then closed to the partners' capital accounts.

Dividing Income—Services of Partners and Investments A partnership agreement may divide income not only based on services, but also based on the amount invested by each partner. In doing so, the partnership may pay interest on the capital balance of each partner. In this way, partners with more invested in the partnership are rewarded by receiving more of the partnership income. One such method of dividing partnership income would be as follows:

1. Partner salary allowances
2. Interest on capital investments
3. Any remaining income equally

To illustrate, assume that the partnership agreement for Stone and Mills provides for the following:

1.

	Monthly Salary Allowance
Jennifer Stone	$5,000
Crystal Mills	4,000

2. Interest of 12% on each partner's capital balance as of January 1.

Capital, Jennifer Stone, January 1	$160,000
Capital, Crystal Mills, January 1	120,000

3. Remaining income: Divided Equally

The $150,000 net income for the year is divided as follows:

Net income. $150,000

Division of net income:

	J. Stone	C. Mills	Total
Annual salary allowance	$60,000	$48,000	$108,000
Interest allowance	19,200[1]	14,400[2]	33,600
Remaining income	4,200	4,200	8,400
Net income	$83,400	$66,600	$150,000

[1]12% × $160,000
[2]12% × $120,000

The entry for closing Income Summary and dividing net income is as follows:

LLC

Income Summary	150,000	
Jennifer Stone, Member Equity		83,400
Crystal Mills, Member Equity		66,600

Dec. 31	Income Summary		150,000	
	Jennifer Stone, Capital			83,400
	Crystal Mills, Capital			66,600

Integrity, Objectivity, and Ethics in Business

TYRANNY OF THE MAJORITY

Some partnerships involve the contribution of money by one partner and the contribution of effort and expertise by another. This can create a conflict between the two partners, since one works and the other doesn't. Without a properly developed partnership agreement, the working partner could take income in the form of a salary allowance, leaving little for the investor partner. Thus, partnership agreements often require all partners to agree on salary allowances provided to working partners.

Dividing Income—Allowances Exceed Net Income

In the preceding example, the net income is $150,000. The total of the salary ($108,000) and interest ($33,600) allowances is $141,600. Thus, the net income exceeds the salary and interest allowances. In some cases, however, the net income may be less than the total of the allowances. In this case, the remaining net income to divide is a *negative* amount. This negative amount is divided among the partners as though it were a net loss.

To illustrate, assume the same salary and interest allowances as in the preceding example, but that the net income is $100,000. In this case, the total of the allowances of $141,600 exceeds the net income by $41,600 ($100,000 − $141,600). This amount is divided equally between Stone and Mills. Thus, $20,800 ($41,600/2) is deducted from each partner's share of the allowances. The final division of net income between Stone and Mills is shown below.

Net income. $100,000

Division of net income:

	J. Stone	C. Mills	Total
Annual salary allowance	$60,000	$48,000	$108,000
Interest allowance	19,200	14,400	33,600
Total	$79,200	$62,400	$141,600
Deduct excess of allowances over income	20,800	20,800	41,600
Net income	$58,400	$41,600	$100,000

The entry for closing Income Summary and dividing net income is as follows:[4]

LLC

Income Summary	100,000	
Jennifer Stone, Member Equity		58,400
Crystal Mills, Member Equity		41,600

Dec.	31	Income Summary		100,000	
		Jennifer Stone, Capital			58,400
		Crystal Mills, Capital			41,600

The income of a partnership can be divided using spreadsheet software. The spreadsheet solution for Stone and Mills is as follows:

	A	B	C	D
1	Inputs:			
2		J. Stone	C. Mills	
3	Monthly salary allowance	$ 5,000	$ 4,000	
4	Beginning Capital account balance	160,000	120,000	
5	Income-sharing ratio	1	1	=B5+C5
6				
7	Net income of the partnership	$ 100,000		
8	Interest on partnership Capital	12%		
9				
10				

The spreadsheet is developed by creating an input area where partnership income information is provided. The income-sharing ratio is presented as a number for each partner, such as 1:1 in this case, which is totaled in cell D5. If the partners shared income in the ratio of 2:1, then the numbers in row 5 would be 2 for Stone, 1 for Mills, totaling to 3.

4 In the event of a net loss, the amount deducted from the total allowances would be the "excess of allowances over loss" or the sum of the net loss and the allowances, divided according to the sharing ratio.

	A	B	C	D
11	*Output: Division of Net Income*			
12		J. Stone	C. Mills	Total
13	Annual salary allowance	**a.** ⟶ =B3*12	=C3*12	=B13+C13
14	Interest allowance	**b.** ⟶ =B4*$B$8	=C4*$B$8	=B14+C14
15	Total	**c.** ⟶ =SUM(B13:B14)	=SUM(C13:C14)	=B15+C15
16	Deduct excess of income over allowances	**d.** ⟶ =($D$15-$B$7)*(B5/$D$5)	=($D$15-$B$7)*(C5/$D$5)	=B16+C16
17	Net income	**e.** ⟶ =B15-B16	=C15-C16	=B17+C17
18				

The formulas for the output space would be developed as follows:

a.   Enter in cell B13 the formula for the annual salary allowance, =B3*12. (The monthly salary allowance must be multiplied by 12 to annualize the salary.)

b.   Enter in cell B14 the formula for the interest allowance on partner capital,

=B4*$B$8 ⟵ The dollar signs in this formula keeps the cell reference fixed when copying the cell. (See the Absolute / Relative tutorial for more information.)

c.   Enter in cell B15 the sum function, =SUM(B13:B14).

d.   Enter in cell B16 the formula for the excess of allowances over income that must be deducted in determining partnership capital, as follows:

=($D$15-$B$7)*(B5/$D$5)

This term is the total excess of allowances over income. The dollar signs fix the column and row references.

This term is the income-sharing ratio. The denominator of the ratio is an absolute cell reference.

e.   Enter the formula for the net income to the partner in cell B17, =B15-B16. Copy the formulas in cells B13:B17 to C13:C17. If you entered the dollar signs correctly in all the formulas, the copy command can copy the specified cell references during copying.

The output table for determining the share of partnership income when the total income exceeds total allowances would be formulated so that the excess would be multiplied by the income-sharing ratio. This would be similar to the equation in d. above, except the difference in the first term would be reversed.

 Go to the hands-on *Excel Tutor* for this example!

 This Excel Success example uses an Excel function referred to as cell referencing. Go to the *Excel Tutor* titled **Absolute & Relative Cell References** for additional help on this useful Excel function!

Example Exercise 12-2   Dividing Partnership Net Income   •••••••⟩ 2

Steve Prince and Chelsy Bernard formed a partnership, dividing income as follows:

1. Annual salary allowance to Prince of $42,000.
2. Interest of 9% on each partner's capital balance on January 1.
3. Any remaining net income divided equally.

Prince and Bernard had $20,000 and $150,000 in their January 1 capital balances, respectively. Net income for the year was $240,000.
    How much net income should be distributed to Prince?

Follow My Example 12-2

	Steve Prince	Chelsy Bernard	Total
Annual salary..............................	$ 42,000	$ 0	$ 42,000
Interest......................................	1,800[1]	13,500[2]	15,300
Remaining income..........................	91,350[3]	91,350	182,700
Total distributed to Prince.................	$135,150	$104,850	$240,000

[1] $20,000 × 9%
[2] $150,000 × 9%
[3] ($240,000 − $42,000 − $15,300) × 50%

For Practice: PE 12-2A, PE 12-2B

3 Describe and illustrate the accounting for partner admission and withdrawal.

Partner Admission and Withdrawal

Many partnerships provide for admitting new partners and for partner withdrawals by amending the existing partnership agreement. In this way, the company may continue operating without having to form a new partnership and prepare a new partnership agreement.

Admitting a Partner

As shown in Exhibit 2, a person may be admitted to a partnership by either of the following:

1. Purchasing an interest from one or more of the existing partners
2. Contributing assets to the partnership

Exhibit 2

Two Methods for Admitting a Partner

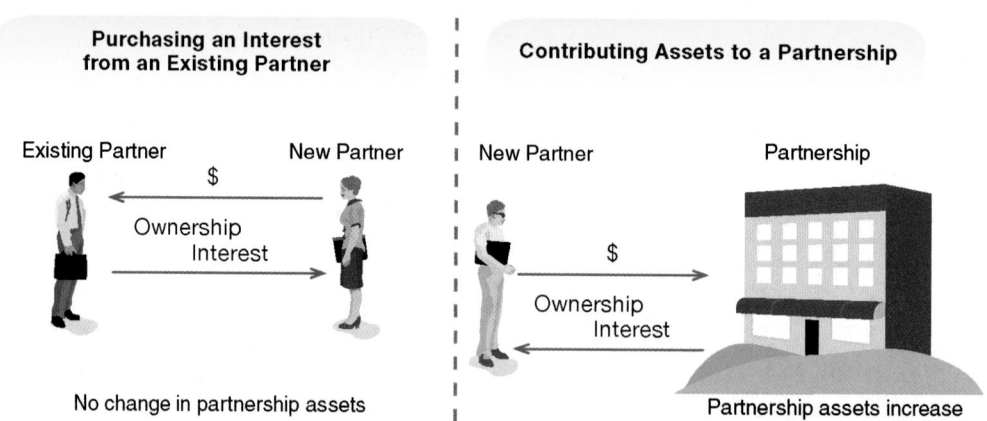

When a new partner is admitted by *purchasing an interest* from one or more of the existing partners, the total assets and the total owners' equity of the partnership are not affected. The capital (equity) of the new partner is recorded by transferring capital (equity) from the existing partners.

When a new partner is admitted by *contributing assets* to the partnership, the total assets and the total owners' equity of the partnership are increased. The capital (equity) of the new partner is recorded as the amount of assets contributed to the partnership by the new partner.

Purchasing an Interest from Existing Partners When a new partner is admitted by purchasing an interest from one or more of the existing partners, the transaction is between the new and existing partners acting as individuals. The admission of the new partner is recorded by transferring owners' equity amounts from the capital accounts of the selling partners to the capital account of the new partner.

To illustrate, assume that on June 1 Tom Andrews and Nathan Bell each sell one-fifth of their partnership equity of Bring It Consulting to Joe Canter for $10,000 in cash. On June 1, the partnership has net assets of $100,000 and both existing partners have capital balances of $50,000 each. This transaction is between Andrews, Bell, and Canter. The only entry required by Bring It Consulting is to record the transfer of capital (equity) from Andrews and Bell to Canter, as shown below.

LLC

Tom Andrews, Member Equity	*10,000*	
Nathan Bell, Member Equity	*10,000*	
Joe Canter, Member Equity		*20,000*

June	1	Tom Andrews, Capital	10,000	
		Nathan Bell, Capital	10,000	
		Joe Canter, Capital		20,000

The effect of the transaction on the partnership accounts is shown in the following diagram:

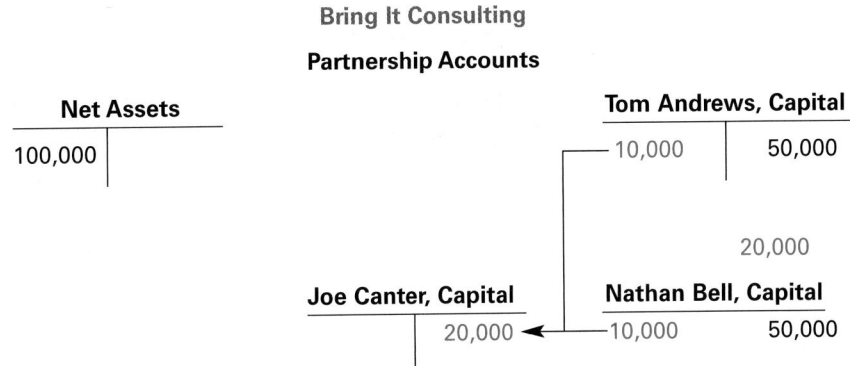

After Canter is admitted to Bring It Consulting, the total owners' equity is still $100,000. Canter has a one-fifth (20%) interest and a capital balance of $20,000. Andrews and Bell each own two-fifths (40%) interest and have capital balances of $40,000 each.

Even though Canter has a one-fifth (20%) interest in the partnership, he may not be entitled to a one-fifth share of the partnership net income. The division of the net income or net loss is made according to the new or amended partnership agreement.

The preceding entry is not affected by the amount paid by Canter for the one-fifth interest. For example, if Canter had paid $15,000 to Andrews and Bell instead of $10,000, the entry would still be the same. This is because the transaction is between Andrews, Bell, and Canter, rather than the partnership. Any gain or loss by Andrews and Bell on the sale of their partnership interest is theirs as individuals and does not affect the partnership.

Contributing Assets to a Partnership When a new partner is admitted by contributing assets to the partnership, the total assets and the total owners' equity of the partnership are increased. This is because the transaction is between the new partner and the partnership.

To illustrate, assume that instead of purchasing a one-fifth ownership in Bring It Consulting directly from Tom Andrews and Nathan Bell, Joe Canter contributes $20,000 cash to Bring It Consulting for ownership equity of $20,000. The entry to record this transaction is as follows:

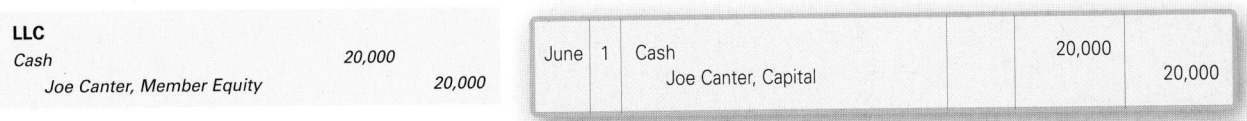

The effect of the transaction on the partnership accounts is shown in the following diagram:

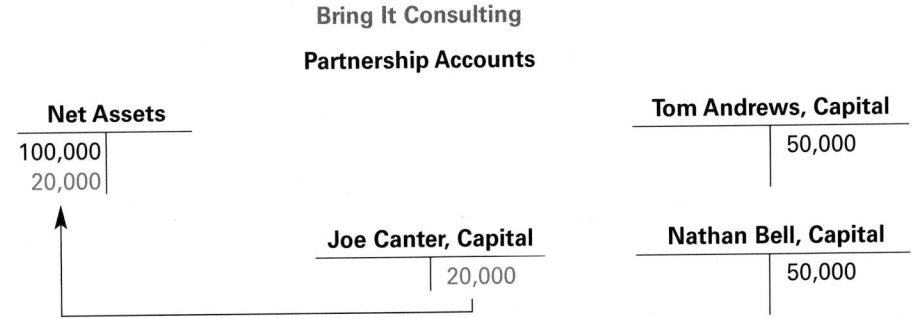

After the admission of Canter, the net assets and total owners' equity of Bring It Consulting increase to $120,000, of which Joe Canter has a $20,000 interest. In contrast, in the prior example, the net assets and total owners' equity of Bring It Consulting did not change from $100,000.

Revaluation of Assets Before a new partner is admitted, the balances of a partnership's asset accounts should be stated at current values. If necessary, the accounts should be adjusted. Any net adjustment (increase or decrease) in asset values is divided among the capital accounts of the existing partners similar to the division of income.

To illustrate, assume that in the preceding example the balance of the merchandise inventory account is $14,000 and the current replacement value is $17,000. If Andrews and Bell share net income equally, the revaluation is recorded as follows:

LLC

Merchandise Inventory	3,000	
Tom Andrews, Member Equity		1,500
Nathan Bell, Member Equity		1,500

June	1	Merchandise Inventory	3,000	
		Tom Andrews, Capital		1,500
		Nathan Bell, Capital		1,500

Failure to adjust the partnership accounts for current values before admission of a new partner may result in the new partner sharing in asset gains or losses that arose in prior periods.

Example Exercise 12-3 Revaluing and Contributing Assets to a Partnership

Blake Nelson invested $45,000 in the Lawrence & Kerry partnership for ownership equity of $45,000. Prior to the investment, land was revalued to a market value of $260,000 from a book value of $200,000. Lynne Lawrence and Tim Kerry share net income in a 1:2 ratio.

a. Provide the journal entry for the revaluation of land.

b. Provide the journal entry to admit Nelson.

Follow My Example 12-3

a. Land	60,000	
Lynne Lawrence, Capital		20,000[1]
Tim Kerry, Capital.		40,000[2]

[1] $60,000 × 1/3
[2] $60,000 × 2/3

b. Cash	45,000	
Blake Nelson, Capital.		45,000

For Practice: PE 12-3A, PE 12-3B

Partner Bonuses A new partner may pay existing partners a bonus to join a partnership. In other cases, existing partners may pay a new partner a bonus to join the partnership.

Bonuses are usually paid because of higher than normal profits the new or existing partners are expected to contribute in the future. For example, a new partner may bring special qualities or skills to the partnership. Celebrities such as actors, musicians, or sports figures often provide name recognition that is expected to increase a partnership's profits.

Partner bonuses are illustrated in Exhibit 3. Existing partners receive a bonus when the ownership interest received by the new partner is less than the amount paid. In contrast, the new partner receives a bonus when the ownership interest received by the new partner is greater than the amount paid.

Exhibit 3

Partner Bonuses

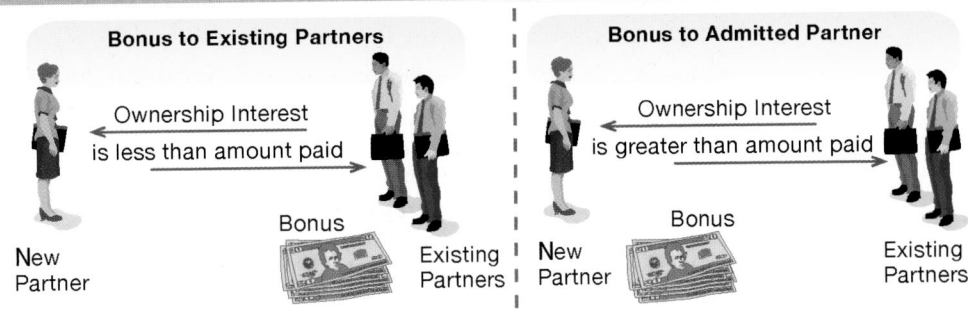

To illustrate, assume that on March 1 the partnership of Marsha Jenkins and Helen Kramer is considering a new partner, Alex Diaz. After the assets of the partnership have been adjusted to current market values, the capital balances of Jenkins and Kramer are as follows:

Marsha Jenkins, Capital	$20,000
Helen Kramer, Capital	24,000
Total owners' equity *before* admitting Diaz	$44,000

Jenkins and Kramer agree to admit Diaz to the partnership for $31,000. In return, Diaz will receive a one-third equity in the partnership and will share equally with Jenkins and Kramer in partnership income or losses. In this case, Diaz is paying Jenkins and Kramer a $6,000 bonus to join the partnership, computed as follows:

Marsha Jenkins, Capital	$20,000
Helen Kramer, Capital	24,000
Diaz's contribution	31,000
Total owners' equity *after* admitting Diaz	$75,000
Diaz's equity interest after admission	× 1/3
Alex Diaz, Capital	$25,000
Diaz's contribution	$31,000
Alex Diaz, Capital	25,000
Bonus paid to Jenkins and Kramer	$ 6,000

The $6,000 bonus paid by Diaz increases Jenkins's and Kramer's capital accounts. It is distributed to the capital accounts of Jenkins and Kramer according to their income-sharing ratio.[5] Assuming that Jenkins and Kramer share profits and losses equally, the entry to record the admission of Diaz to the partnership is as follows:

LLC

Cash	31,000	
Alex Diaz, Member Equity		25,000
Marsha Jenkins, Member Equity		3,000
Helen Kramer, Member Equity		3,000

Mar.	1	Cash	31,000	
		Alex Diaz, Capital		25,000
		Marsha Jenkins, Capital		3,000
		Helen Kramer, Capital		3,000

Existing partners may agree to pay the new partner a bonus to join a partnership. To illustrate, assume that after adjusting assets to market values, the capital balances of Janice Cowen and Steve Dodd are as follows:

Janice Cowen, Capital	$ 80,000
Steve Dodd, Capital	40,000
Total owners' equity *before* admitting Chou	$120,000

5 Another method used to record the admission of partners attributes goodwill rather than a bonus to the partners. This method is discussed in advanced accounting textbooks.

Cowen and Dodd agree to admit Ellen Chou to the partnership on June 1 for an investment of $30,000. In return, Chou will receive a one-fourth equity interest in the partnership and will share in one-fourth of the profits and losses. In this case, Cowen and Dodd are paying Chou a $7,500 bonus to join the partnership, computed as follows:

Janice Cowen, Capital	$ 80,000
Steve Dodd, Capital	40,000
Chou's contribution	30,000
Total owners' equity *after* admitting Chou	$150,000
Chou's equity interest after admission	× 1/4
Ellen Chou, Capital	$ 37,500
Ellen Chou, Capital	$ 37,500
Chou's contribution	30,000
Bonus paid to Chou	$ 7,500

The $7,500 bonus paid to Chou decreases Cowen's and Dodd's capital accounts. It is distributed to the capital accounts of Cowen and Dodd according to their income-sharing ratio. Assuming that the income-sharing ratio of Cowen and Dodd was 2:1 before the admission of Chou, the entry to record the admission of Chou to the partnership is as follows:

LLC

Cash	30,000	
Janice Cowen, Member Equity	5,000[1]	
Steve Dodd, Member Equity	2,500[2]	
Ellen Chou, Member Equity		37,500

June	1	Cash		30,000	
		Janice Cowen, Capital		5,000[1]	
		Steve Dodd, Capital		2,500[2]	
		Ellen Chou, Capital			37,500

[1] $7,500 × 2/3
[2] $7,500 × 1/3

Example Exercise 12-4   Partner Bonus ••••••••▷ 3

Lowman has a capital balance of $45,000 after adjusting assets to fair market value. Conrad contributes $26,000 to receive a 30% interest in a new partnership with Lowman.
    Determine the amount and recipient of the partner bonus.

Follow My Example 12-4

Equity of Lowman	$45,000
Conrad's contribution	26,000
Total equity after admitting Conrad.	$71,000
Conrad's equity interest.	× 30%
Conrad's equity after admission	$21,300
Conrad's contribution	$26,000
Conrad's equity after admission	21,300
Bonus paid to Lowman	$ 4,700

For Practice: PE 12-4A, PE 12-4B

Withdrawal of a Partner

A partner generally cannot withdraw without permission of the remaining partners, nor can a partner be forced to withdraw by the other partners. In this sense, a partnership is like a marriage, "for better or for worse."

A partner may retire or withdraw from a partnership. In such cases, the withdrawing partner's interest is normally sold to the:

1. Existing partners or
2. Partnership

If the *existing partners purchase* the withdrawing partner's interest, the purchase and sale of the partnership interest is between the partners as individuals. The only entry on the partnership's records is to debit the capital account of the partner withdrawing and to credit the capital account of the partner or partners buying the additional interest.

If the *partnership purchases* the withdrawing partner's interest, the assets and the owners' equity of the partnership are reduced by the purchase price. Before the purchase, the asset accounts should be adjusted to current values. The net amount of any adjustment should be divided among the capital accounts of the partners according to their income-sharing ratio.

The entry to record the purchase debits the capital account of the withdrawing partner and credits Cash for the amount of the purchase. If not enough partnership cash is available to pay the withdrawing partner, a liability may be created (credited) for the amount owed the withdrawing partner.

Death of a Partner

When a partner dies, the partnership accounts should be closed as of the date of death. The net income for the current period should then be determined and divided among the partners' capital accounts. The asset accounts should also be adjusted to current values and the amount of any adjustment divided among the capital accounts of the partners.

After the income is divided and any assets revalued, an entry is recorded to close the deceased partner's capital account. The entry debits the deceased partner's capital account for its balance and credits a liability account, which is payable to the deceased's estate. The remaining partner or partners may then decide to continue the business or liquidate it.

4 Describe and illustrate the accounting for liquidating a partnership.

Liquidating Partnerships

When a partnership goes out of business, it sells the assets, pays the creditors, and distributes the remaining cash or other assets to the partners. This winding-up process is called the **liquidation** of the partnership. Although *liquidating* refers to the payment of liabilities, it includes the entire winding-up process.

When the partnership goes out of business and the normal operations are discontinued, the accounts should be adjusted and closed. The only accounts remaining open will be the asset, contra asset, liability, and owners' equity accounts.

The liquidation process is illustrated in Exhibit 4. The steps in the liquidation process are as follows:

Step 1. Sell the partnership assets. This step is called **realization**.

Step 2. Distribute any gains or losses from realization to the partners based on their income-sharing ratio.

Step 3. Pay the claims of creditors using the cash from step 1 realization.

Step 4. Distribute the remaining cash to the partners based on the balances in their capital accounts.

Exhibit 4

Steps in Liquidating a Partnership

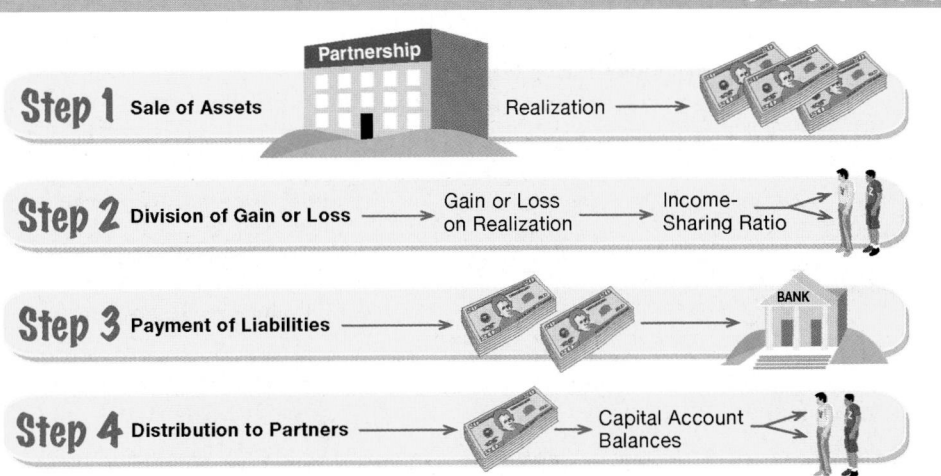

To illustrate, assume that Farley, Green, and Hall decide to liquidate their partnership. On April 9, after discontinuing business operations of the partnership and closing the accounts, the following trial balance is prepared:

Farley, Green, and Hall
Post-Closing Trial Balance
April 9, 2010

	Debit Balances	Credit Balances
Cash	11,000	
Noncash Assets	64,000	
Liabilities		9,000
Jean Farley, Capital		22,000
Brad Green, Capital		22,000
Alice Hall, Capital		22,000
	75,000	75,000

Farley, Green, and Hall share income and losses in a ratio of 5:3:2 (50%, 30%, 20%). To simplify, assume that all noncash assets are sold in a single transaction and that all liabilities are paid at one time. In addition, Noncash Assets and Liabilities will be used as account titles in place of the various asset, contra asset, and liability accounts.

Gain on Realization

Assume that Farley, Green, and Hall sell all noncash assets for $72,000. Thus, a gain of $8,000 ($72,000 − $64,000) is realized. The partnership is liquidated during April as follows:

Step 1. Sale of assets: $72,000 is realized from sale of all the noncash assets.

Step 2. Division of gain: The gain of $8,000 is distributed to Farley, Green, and Hall in the income-sharing ratio of 5:3:2. Thus, the partner capital accounts are credited as follows:

Farley $4,000 ($8,000 × 50%)
Green   2,400 ($8,000 × 30%)
Hall   1,600 ($8,000 × 20%)

Step 3. Payment of liabilities: Creditors are paid $9,000.

Step 4. Distribution of cash to partners: The remaining cash of $74,000 is distributed to the partners according to their capital balances as follows:

Farley $26,000
Green   24,400
Hall   23,600

A **statement of partnership liquidation**, which summarizes the liquidation process, is shown in Exhibit 5.
The entries to record the steps in the liquidating process are as follows:

Sale of assets (Step 1):

LLC

Cash	72,000	
Noncash Assets		64,000
Gain on Realization		8,000

Cash	72,000	
Noncash Assets		64,000
Gain on Realization		8,000

Division of gain (Step 2):

LLC

Gain on Realization	8,000	
Jean Farley, Member Equity		4,000
Brad Green, Member Equity		2,400
Alice Hall, Member Equity		1,600

Gain on Realization	8,000	
Jean Farley, Capital		4,000
Brad Green, Capital		2,400
Alice Hall, Capital		1,600

Exhibit 5

Statement of Partnership Liquidation: Gain on Realization

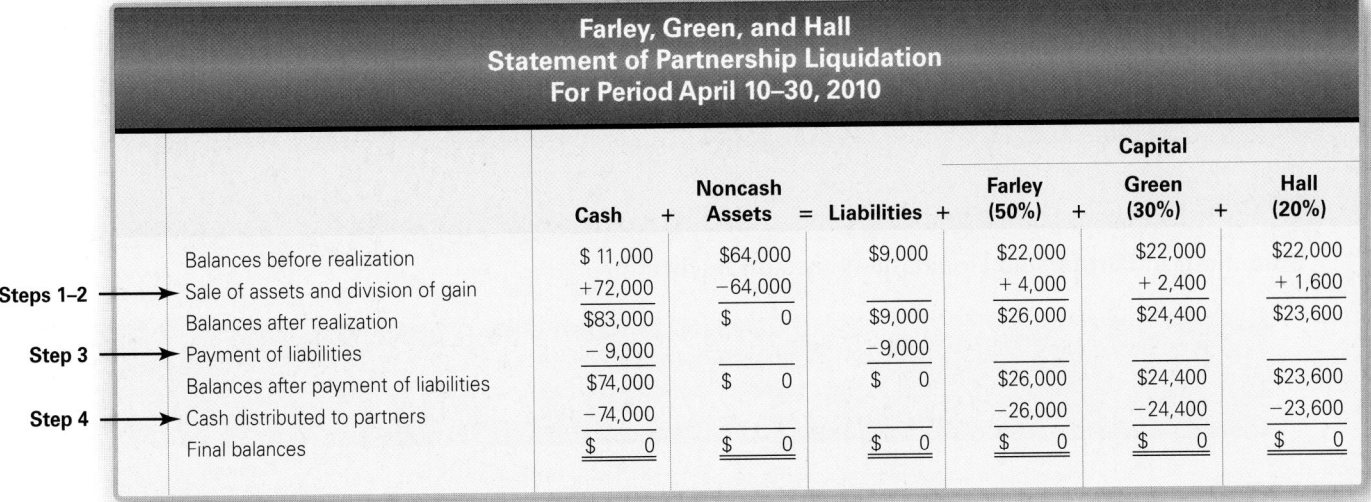

Farley, Green, and Hall
Statement of Partnership Liquidation
For Period April 10–30, 2010

	Cash +	Noncash Assets =	Liabilities +	Capital Farley (50%) +	Green (30%) +	Hall (20%)
Balances before realization	$ 11,000	$64,000	$9,000	$22,000	$22,000	$22,000
Steps 1–2 → Sale of assets and division of gain	+72,000	−64,000		+ 4,000	+ 2,400	+ 1,600
Balances after realization	$83,000	$ 0	$9,000	$26,000	$24,400	$23,600
Step 3 → Payment of liabilities	− 9,000		−9,000			
Balances after payment of liabilities	$74,000	$ 0	$ 0	$26,000	$24,400	$23,600
Step 4 → Cash distributed to partners	−74,000			−26,000	−24,400	−23,600
Final balances	$ 0	$ 0	$ 0	$ 0	$ 0	$ 0

Payment of liabilities (Step 3):

LLC		
Liabilities	9,000	
Cash		9,000

Liabilities	9,000	
Cash		9,000

Distribution of cash to partners (Step 4):

LLC		
Jean Farley, Member Equity	26,000	
Brad Green, Member Equity	24,400	
Alice Hall, Member Equity	23,600	
Cash		74,000

Jean Farley, Capital	26,000	
Brad Green, Capital	24,400	
Alice Hall, Capital	23,600	
Cash		74,000

As shown in Exhibit 5, the *cash is distributed to the partners based on the balances of their capital accounts.* These balances are determined after the gain on realization has been divided among the partners and the liabilities paid. The *income-sharing ratio should not be used as a basis for distributing the cash to partners.*

Loss on Realization

Assume that Farley, Green, and Hall sell all noncash assets for $44,000. Thus, a loss of $20,000 ($64,000 − $44,000) is realized. The liquidation of the partnership is as follows:

Step 1. Sale of assets: $44,000 is realized from the sale of all the noncash assets.

Step 2. Division of loss: The loss of $20,000 is distributed to Farley, Green, and Hall in the income-sharing ratio of 5:3:2. Thus, the partner capital accounts are debited as follows:

Farley	$10,000 ($20,000 × 50%)
Green	6,000 ($20,000 × 30%)
Hall	4,000 ($20,000 × 20%)

Step 3. Payment of liabilities: Creditors are paid $9,000.

Step 4. Distribution of cash to partners: The remaining cash of $46,000 is distributed to the partners according to their capital balances as follows:

Farley	$12,000
Green	16,000
Hall	18,000

The steps in liquidating the partnership are summarized in the statement of partnership liquidation shown in Exhibit 6.

Exhibit 6

Statement of Partnership Liquidation: Loss on Realization

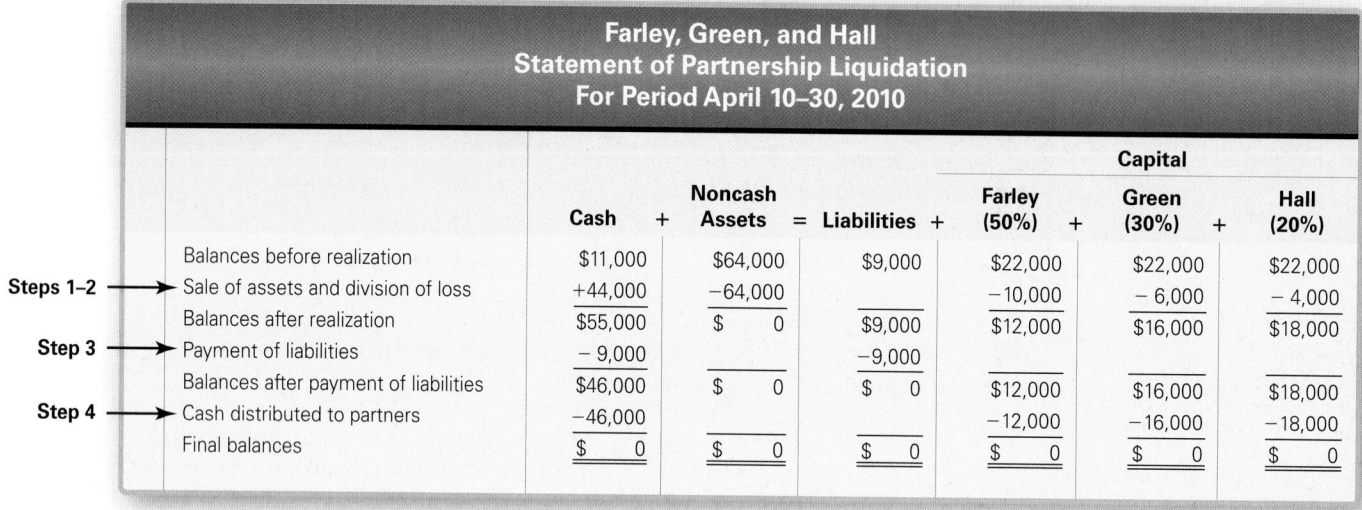

	Cash +	Noncash Assets =	Liabilities +	Farley (50%) +	Green (30%) +	Hall (20%)
Balances before realization	$11,000	$64,000	$9,000	$22,000	$22,000	$22,000
Sale of assets and division of loss	+44,000	−64,000		−10,000	−6,000	−4,000
Balances after realization	$55,000	$ 0	$9,000	$12,000	$16,000	$18,000
Payment of liabilities	−9,000		−9,000			
Balances after payment of liabilities	$46,000	$ 0	$ 0	$12,000	$16,000	$18,000
Cash distributed to partners	−46,000			−12,000	−16,000	−18,000
Final balances	$ 0	$ 0	$ 0	$ 0	$ 0	$ 0

The entries to liquidate the partnership are as follows:

Sale of assets (Step 1):

LLC		
Cash	44,000	
Loss on Realization	20,000	
Noncash Assets		64,000

Cash	44,000	
Loss on Realization	20,000	
Noncash Assets		64,000

Division of loss (Step 2):

LLC		
Jean Farley, Member Equity	10,000	
Brad Green, Member Equity	6,000	
Alice Hall, Member Equity	4,000	
Loss on Realization		20,000

Jean Farley, Capital	10,000	
Brad Green, Capital	6,000	
Alice Hall, Capital	4,000	
Loss on Realization		20,000

Payment of liabilities (Step 3):

LLC		
Liabilities	9,000	
Cash		9,000

Liabilities	9,000	
Cash		9,000

Distribution of cash to partners (Step 4):

LLC

Jean Farley, Member Equity	12,000	
Brad Green, Member Equity	16,000	
Alice Hall, Member Equity	18,000	
Cash		46,000

Jean Farley, Capital	12,000	
Brad Green, Capital	16,000	
Alice Hall, Capital	18,000	
Cash		46,000

Example Exercise 12-5   Liquidating Partnerships   ••••••• 4

Prior to liquidating their partnership, Todd and Gentry had capital accounts of $50,000 and $100,000, respectively. Prior to liquidation, the partnership had no other cash assets than what was realized from the sale of assets. These assets were sold for $220,000. The partnership had $20,000 of liabilities. Todd and Gentry share income and losses equally. Determine the amount received by Gentry as a final distribution from the liquidation of the partnership.

Follow My Example 12-5

Gentry's equity prior to liquidation.		$100,000
Realization of asset sale	$220,000	
Book value of assets ($50,000 + $100,000 + $20,000)	170,000	
Gain on liquidation	$ 50,000	
Gentry's share of gain (50% × $50,000)		25,000
Gentry's cash distribution		$125,000

For Practice: PE 12-5A, PE 12-5B

Loss on Realization—Capital Deficiency

The share of a loss on realization may be greater than the balance in a partner's capital account. The resulting debit balance in the capital account is called a **deficiency**. It represents a claim of the partnership against the partner.

To illustrate, assume that Farley, Green, and Hall sell all noncash assets for $10,000. Thus, a loss of $54,000 ($64,000 − $10,000) is realized. The liquidation of the partnership is as follows:

Step 1. Sale of assets: $10,000 is realized from the sale of all the noncash assets.

Step 2. Division of loss: The loss of $54,000 is distributed to Farley, Green, and Hall in the income-sharing ratio of 5:3:2. The partner capital accounts are debited as follows:

Farley	$27,000 ($54,000 × 50%)
Green	16,200 ($54,000 × 30%)
Hall	10,800 ($54,000 × 20%)

Step 3. Payment of liabilities: Creditors are paid $9,000.

Step 4. Distribution of cash to partners: The share of the loss allocated to Farley, $27,000 (50% × $54,000), exceeds the $22,000 balance in her capital account. This $5,000 deficiency represents an amount that Farley owes the partnership. Assuming that Farley pays the deficiency, the cash of $17,000 is distributed to the partners according to their capital balances as follows:

Farley	$ 0
Green	5,800
Hall	11,200

The steps in liquidating the partnership are summarized in the statement of partnership liquidation shown in Exhibit 7.

The entries to liquidate the partnership are as follows:

Sale of assets (Step 1):

LLC		
Cash	10,000	
Loss on Realization	54,000	
Noncash Assets		64,000

Cash	10,000	
Loss on Realization	54,000	
Noncash Assets		64,000

Exhibit 7

Statement of Partnership Liquidation: Loss on Realization—Capital Deficiency

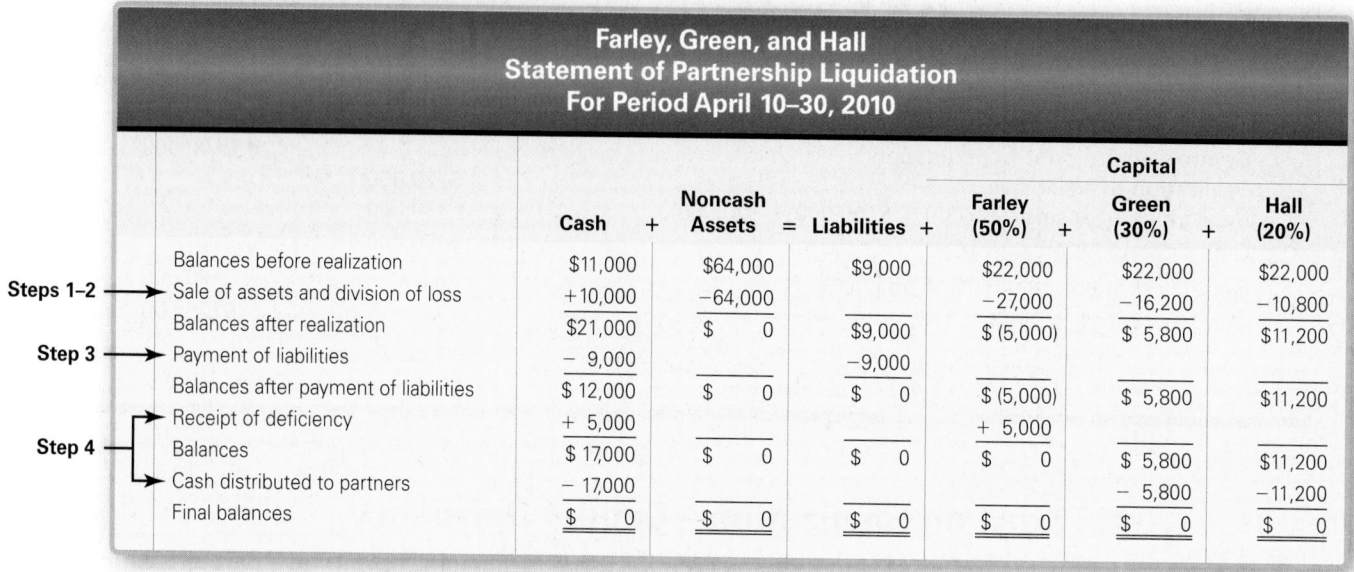

Farley, Green, and Hall
Statement of Partnership Liquidation
For Period April 10–30, 2010

	Cash	+	Noncash Assets	=	Liabilities	+	Farley (50%)	+	Green (30%)	+	Hall (20%)
Balances before realization	$11,000		$64,000		$9,000		$22,000		$22,000		$22,000
Sale of assets and division of loss	+10,000		−64,000				−27,000		−16,200		−10,800
Balances after realization	$21,000		$ 0		$9,000		$ (5,000)		$ 5,800		$11,200
Payment of liabilities	− 9,000				−9,000						
Balances after payment of liabilities	$ 12,000		$ 0		$ 0		$ (5,000)		$ 5,800		$11,200
Receipt of deficiency	+ 5,000						+ 5,000				
Balances	$ 17,000		$ 0		$ 0		$ 0		$ 5,800		$11,200
Cash distributed to partners	− 17,000								− 5,800		−11,200
Final balances	$ 0		$ 0		$ 0		$ 0		$ 0		$ 0

Steps 1–2 → Sale of assets and division of loss
Step 3 → Payment of liabilities
Step 4 → Receipt of deficiency / Cash distributed to partners

Division of loss (Step 2):

LLC		
Jean Farley, Member Equity	27,000	
Brad Green, Member Equity	16,200	
Alice Hall, Member Equity	10,800	
Loss on Realization		54,000

Jean Farley, Capital	27,000	
Brad Green, Capital	16,200	
Alice Hall, Capital	10,800	
Loss on Realization		54,000

Payment of liabilities (Step 3):

LLC		
Liabilities	9,000	
Cash		9,000

Liabilities	9,000	
Cash		9,000

Receipt of deficiency (Step 4):

LLC		
Cash	5,000	
Jean Farley, Member Equity		5,000

Cash	5,000	
Jean Farley, Capital		5,000

Distribution of cash to partners (Step 4):

LLC		
Brad Green, Member Equity	5,800	
Alice Hall, Member Equity	11,200	
Cash		17,000

Brad Green, Capital		5,800	
Alice Hall, Capital		11,200	
Cash			17,000

If the deficient partner does not pay the partnership their deficiency, there will not be sufficient partnership cash to pay the remaining partners in full. Any uncollected deficiency becomes a loss to the partnership and is divided among the remaining partners' capital balances based on their income-sharing ratio. The cash balance will then equal the sum of the capital account balances. The cash can then be distributed to the remaining partners, based on the balances of their capital accounts.

To illustrate, assume that in the preceding example Farley could not pay her deficiency. The deficiency would be allocated to Green and Hall based on their income-sharing ratio of 3:2. The remaining cash of $12,000 would then be distributed to Green ($2,800) and Hall ($9,200), as shown below.

	Capital Balances *Before* (Deficiency)	Allocated (Deficiency)	Capital Balances *After* Deficiency
Farley	$(5,000)	$5,000	$ 0
Green	5,800	(3,000)*	2,800
Hall	11,200	(2,000)**	9,200
Total	$12,000		$12,000

*$3,000 = [$5,000 × (3/5)] or ($5,000 × 60%)
**$2,000 = [$5,000 × (2/5)] or ($5,000 × 40%)

The entries to allocate Farley's deficiency and distribute the cash are as follows:

Allocation of deficiency:

LLC		
Brad Green, Member Equity	3,000	
Alice Hall, Member Equity	2,000	
Jean Farley, Member Equity		5,000

Brad Green, Capital		3,000	
Alice Hall, Capital		2,000	
Jean Farley, Capital			5,000

Distribution of cash to partners:

LLC		
Brad Green, Member Equity	2,800	
Alice Hall, Member Equity	9,200	
Cash		12,000

Brad Green, Capital		2,800	
Alice Hall, Capital		9,200	
Cash			12,000

Example Exercise 12-6   Liquidating Partnerships—Deficiency

Prior to liquidating their partnership, Short and Bain had capital accounts of $20,000 and $80,000, respectively. The partnership assets were sold for $40,000. The partnership had no liabilities. Short and Bain share income and losses equally.

a. Determine the amount of Short's deficiency.

b. Determine the amount distributed to Bain, assuming Short is unable to satisfy the deficiency.

(continued)

Follow My Example 12-6

a. Short's equity prior to liquidation . . . . $ 20,000
   Realization of asset sale . . . . $ 40,000
   Book value of assets ($20,000 + $80,000) 100,000
   Loss on liquidation . . . . $ 60,000
   Short's share of loss (50% × $60,000) 30,000
   Short's deficiency . . . . $ (10,000)

b. $40,000. $80,000 − $30,000 share of loss − $10,000 Short deficiency.

For Practice: PE 12-6A, PE 12-6B

Errors in Liquidation

Incorrectly distributing cash to partners is an error that may occur in liquidating a partnership. Such errors occur if distributing cash to partners is confused with the dividing of gains and losses on realization.

Realized gains and losses on the sale of assets should be divided among the partners' capital accounts in the same manner as the net income or net loss from normal business operations—using the income-sharing ratio. In contrast, the distribution of cash to partners in liquidation is the reverse of the contribution of assets by partners. Thus, distributing cash to partners in liquidation is based on the credit balances in the partners' capital accounts after all gains and losses on realization have been divided and any partner deficiencies have been paid or allocated.

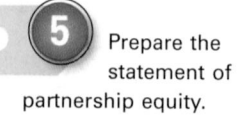

5 Prepare the statement of partnership equity.

Statement of Partnership Equity

Reporting changes in partnership capital accounts is similar to that for a proprietorship. The primary difference is that there is a capital account for each partner. The changes in partner capital accounts for a period of time are reported in a **statement of partnership equity**.

Exhibit 8 illustrates a statement of partnership equity for Investors Associates, a partnership of Dan Cross and Kelly Baker. Each partner's capital account is shown as a separate column. The partner capital accounts may change due to capital additions, net income, or withdrawals.

Exhibit 8

Statement of Partnership Equity

Investors Associates Statement of Partnership Equity For the Year Ended December 31, 2010			
	Dan Cross, Capital	Kelly Baker, Capital	Total Partnership Capital
Balance, January 1, 2010	$245,000	$365,000	$610,000
Capital additions	50,000		50,000
Net income for the year	40,000	80,000	120,000
Less partner withdrawals	(5,000)	(45,000)	(50,000)
Balance, December 31, 2010	$330,000	$400,000	$730,000

The equity reporting for an LLC is similar to that of a partnership. Instead of a statement of partnership capital, a statement of members' equity is prepared. The **statement of members' equity** reports the changes in member equity for a period. The statement is similar to Exhibit 8, except that the columns represent member equity rather than partner equity.

Financial Analysis and Interpretation

Some partnerships (LLCs) are service-oriented enterprises. This is the case for some professions, such as accounting. The performance of such firms can be measured by the amount of net income per partner, as illustrated in this chapter. Another measure used to assess the performance of service-oriented partnerships (LLCs) is *revenue per employee*. The definition of "employee" can be adjusted to suit the analysis, but often includes the partners of the firm. Revenue per employee may be used as a measure of partnership (LLC) efficiency. Revenues are a measure of "outcomes." The number of people in a service firm is a measure of the critical "effort" in earning those revenues. Thus, the ratio of the two is a type of outcome-to-effort, or efficiency, ratio. To illustrate, assume that Washburn & Lovett, CPAs, has the following information for the last two years:

	2011	2010
Revenues	$220,000,000	$180,000,000
Number of employees	1,600	1,500

For Washburn & Lovett, this ratio can be computed for 2011 and 2010 as follows:

Revenue per employee, 2011:

$$\frac{\$220,000,000}{1,600} = \$137,500$$

Revenue per employee, 2010:

$$\frac{\$180,000,000}{1,500} = \$120,000$$

Washburn & Lovett improved revenues from $180 million in 2010, to $220 million in 2011. The revenue per employee showed improvement, from $120,000 to $137,500 per employee. This suggests that the firm increased revenues at a faster rate than the increase in employees. Thus, each employee is producing more revenues in 2011 than in 2010, which may indicate improved productivity. Overall, it appears that the firm is properly managing the growth in staff.

At a Glance **12** ● ● ● ●

Describe the characteristics of proprietorships, partnerships, and limited liability companies.

	Example Exercises	Practice Exercises
Key Points / **Key Learning Outcomes**		

Key Points

The advantages and disadvantages of proprietorships, partnerships, and limited liability companies with regard to ease of formation, legal liability, taxation, limitation on life of entity, and access to capital were discussed. These characteristics are summarized in Exhibit 1.

Key Learning Outcomes

• Identify the advantages and disadvantages of proprietorships, partnerships, and limited liability companies.

② Describe and illustrate the accounting for forming a partnership and for dividing the net income and net loss of a partnership.

Key Points	**Key Learning Outcomes**	Example Exercises	Practice Exercises
When a partnership is formed, accounts are debited for contributed assets and credited for assumed liabilities, and the partner's capital account is credited for the net amount. The net income of a partnership may be divided among the partners on the basis of services rendered, interest earned on the capital account balance, and the income-sharing ratio.	• Journalize the initial formation of a partnership and establish partner capital.	12-1	12-1A, 12-1B
	• Determine and journalize the income distributed to each partner.	12-2	12-2A, 12-2B

3 Describe and illustrate the accounting for partner admission and withdrawal.

Key Points	Key Learning Outcomes	Example Exercises	Practice Exercises
Partnership assets should be restated to current values prior to admission or withdrawal of a partner. A new partner may be admitted into a partnership by either purchasing an interest from an existing partner or by purchasing an interest directly from the partnership.	• Prepare for partner admission by revaluing assets to approximate current values.	**12-3**	12-3A, 12-3B
	• Distinguish between partner admission through purchase from an existing partner or purchase from the partnership.	**12-3**	12-3A, 12-3B
	• Determine partner bonuses.	**12-4**	12-4A, 12-4B

4 Describe and illustrate the accounting for liquidating a partnership.

Key Points	Key Learning Outcomes	Example Exercises	Practice Exercises
A partnership is liquidated by the (1) sale of partnership assets (realization), (2) distribution of gain or loss on realization to the partners, (3) payments to creditors, and (4) distribution of the remaining cash to partners according to their capital account balances. A partner may be deficient when the amount of loss distribution exceeds the capital balance.	• Apply the four steps of liquidating a partnership for either gain or loss on realization.	**12-5**	12-5A, 12-5B
	• Apply the four steps of partnership liquidation when there is a partner deficiency.	**12-6**	12-6A, 12-6B

5 Prepare the statement of partnership equity.

Key Points	Key Learning Outcomes	Example Exercises	Practice Exercises
A statement of partnership equity reports the changes in partnership equity from capital additions, net income, and withdrawals. Net income is added based on the income distribution method identified in the partnership agreement, regardless of whether or not the net income is distributed in cash.	• Prepare a statement of partnership equity.		

Key Terms

deficiency (549)
limited liability company (LLC) (534)
liquidation (545)
partnership (533)

partnership agreement (533)
realization (545)
statement of members' equity (552)

statement of partnership equity (552)
statement of partnership liquidation (546)

Illustrative Problem

Radcliffe, Sonders, and Towers, who share in income and losses in the ratio of 2:3:5, decided to discontinue operations as of April 30, 2010, and liquidate their partnership. After the accounts were closed on April 30, 2010, the following trial balance was prepared:

Radcliffe, Sonders, and Towers
Post-Closing Trial Balance
April 30, 2010

	Debit Balances	Credit Balances
Cash	5,900	
Noncash Assets	109,900	
Liabilities		26,800
Radcliffe, Capital		14,600
Sonders, Capital		27,900
Towers, Capital		46,500
	115,800	115,800

Between May 1 and May 18, the noncash assets were sold for $27,400, and the liabilities were paid.

Instructions

1. Assuming that the partner with the capital deficiency pays the entire amount owed to the partnership, prepare a statement of partnership liquidation.
2. Journalize the entries to record (a) the sale of the assets, (b) the division of loss on the sale of the assets, (c) the payment of the liabilities, (d) the receipt of the deficiency, and (e) the distribution of cash to the partners.

Solution

1.

Radcliffe, Sonders, and Towers
Statement of Partnership Liquidation
For Period May 1–18, 2010

	Cash +	Noncash Assets =	Liabilities +	Capital Radcliffe (20%) +	Sonders (30%) +	Towers (50%)
Balances before realization	$ 5,900	$109,900	$26,800	$14,600	$27,900	$46,500
Sale of assets and division of loss	+27,400	−109,900		−16,500	−24,750	−41,250
Balances after realization	$33,300	$ 0	$26,800	$ (1,900)	$ 3,150	$ 5,250
Payment of liabilities	−26,800		−26,800			
Balances after payment of liabilities	$ 6,500	$ 0	$ 0	$ (1,900)	$ 3,150	$ 5,250
Receipt of deficiency	+ 1,900			+ 1,900		
Balances	$ 8,400	$ 0	$ 0	$ 0	$ 3,150	$ 5,250
Cash distributed to partners	− 8,400				− 3,150	− 5,250
Final balances	$ 0	$ 0	$ 0	$ 0	$ 0	$ 0

2. a.

Cash	27,400	
Loss on Realization	82,500	
Noncash Assets		109,900

b.

Radcliffe, Capital	16,500	
Sonders, Capital	24,750	
Towers, Capital	41,250	
Loss on Realization		82,500

c.

Liabilities	26,800	
Cash		26,800

d.

Cash	1,900	
Radcliffe, Capital		1,900

e.

Sonders, Capital	3,150	
Towers, Capital	5,250	
Cash		8,400

Self-Examination Questions (Answers at End of Chapter)

1. As part of the initial investment, a partner contributes office equipment that had cost $20,000 and on which accumulated depreciation of $12,500 had been recorded. If the partners agree on a valuation of $9,000 for the equipment, what amount should be debited to the office equipment account?
   A. $7,500
   B. $9,000
   C. $12,500
   D. $20,000

2. Chip and Dale agree to form a partnership. Chip is to contribute $50,000 in assets and to devote one-half time to the partnership. Dale is to contribute $20,000 and to devote full time to the partnership. How will Chip and Dale share in the division of net income or net loss?
   A. 5:2
   B. 1:2
   C. 1:1
   D. 2.5:1

3. Tracey and Hepburn invest $100,000 and $50,000, respectively, in a partnership and agree to a division of net income that provides for an allowance of interest at 10% on original investments, salary allowances of $12,000 and $24,000, respectively, with the remainder divided equally. What would be Tracey's share of a net income of $45,000?
   A. $22,500
   B. $22,000
   C. $19,000
   D. $10,000

4. Lee and Stills are partners who share income in the ratio of 2:1 and who have capital balances of $65,000 and $35,000, respectively. If Morr, with the consent of Stills, acquired one-half of Lee's interest for $40,000, for what amount would Morr's capital account be credited?
   A. $32,500
   B. $40,000
   C. $50,000
   D. $72,500

5. Pavin and Abdel share gains and losses in the ratio of 2:1. After selling all assets for cash, dividing the losses on realization, and paying liabilities, the balances in the capital accounts were as follows: Pavin, $10,000 Cr.; Abdel, $2,000 Cr. How much of the cash of $12,000 would be distributed to Pavin?
   A. $2,000
   B. $8,000
   C. $10,000
   D. $12,000

Eye Openers

1. What are the main advantages of (a) proprietorships, (b) partnerships, and (c) limited liability companies?
2. What are the disadvantages of a partnership over a limited liability company form of organization for a profit-making business?

3. Emilio Alvarez and Graciela Zavala joined together to form a partnership. Is it possible for them to lose a greater amount than the amount of their investment in the partnership? Explain.

4. What are the major features of a partnership agreement for a partnership, or an operating agreement for a limited liability company?

5. In the absence of an agreement, how will the net income be distributed between Ethan Arnold and Tessa Winthrop, partners in the firm of A and W Environmental Engineering?

6. Josiah Barlow, Patty DuMont, and Owen Maholic are contemplating the formation of a partnership. According to the partnership agreement, Barlow is to invest $60,000 and devote one-half time, DuMont is to invest $40,000 and devote three-fourths time, and Maholic is to make no investment and devote full time. Would Maholic be correct in assuming that, since he is not contributing any assets to the firm, he is risking nothing? Explain.

7. As a part of the initial investment, a partner contributes delivery equipment that had originally cost $50,000 and on which accumulated depreciation of $37,500 had been recorded. The partners agree on a valuation of $10,000. How should the delivery equipment be recorded in the accounts of the partnership?

8. All partners agree that $150,000 of accounts receivable invested by a partner will be collectible to the extent of 90%. How should the accounts receivable be recorded in the general ledger of the partnership?

9. During the current year, Marsha Engles withdrew $4,000 monthly from the partnership of Engles and Cox Water Management Consultants. Is it possible that her share of partnership net income for the current year might be more or less than $48,000? Explain.

10. a. What accounts are debited and credited to record a partner's cash withdrawal in lieu of salary?

    b. The articles of partnership provide for a salary allowance of $6,000 per month to partner C. If C withdrew only $4,000 per month, would this affect the division of the partnership net income?

    c. At the end of the fiscal year, what accounts are debited and credited to record the division of net income among partners?

11. Explain the difference between the admission of a new partner to a partnership (a) by purchase of an interest from another partner and (b) by contribution of assets to the partnership.

12. Why is it important to state all partnership assets in terms of current prices at the time of the admission of a new partner?

13. Why might a partnership pay a bonus to a newly admitted partner?

14. In the liquidation process, (a) how are losses and gains on realization divided among the partners, and (b) how is cash distributed among the partners?

15. How is the statement of members' equity similar to the statement of partners' equity?

Practice Exercises

PE 12-1A
Journalize partner's original investment
obj. 2
EE 12-1   p. 536

Josh Beach contributed land, inventory, and $24,000 cash to a partnership. The land had a book value of $65,000 and a market value of $114,000. The inventory had a book value of $60,000 and a market value of $56,000. The partnership also assumed a $50,000 note payable owed by Beach that was used originally to purchase the land.
    Provide the journal entry for Beach's contribution to the partnership.

PE 12-1B
Journalize partner's original investment
obj. 2
EE 12-1   p. 536

Jen Hall contributed a patent, accounts receivable, and $22,000 cash to a partnership. The patent had a book value of $56,000. However, the technology covered by the patent appeared to have significant market potential. Thus, the patent was appraised at $150,000. The accounts receivable control account was $32,000, with an allowance for doubtful accounts of $2,000. The partnership also assumed a $12,000 account payable from Hall.
    Provide the journal entry for Hall's contribution to the partnership.

PE 12-2A
Dividing partnership net income

obj. 2

EE 12-2   p. 539

Brandon Smithson and Lakendra Mooney formed a partnership, dividing income as follows:

1. Annual salary allowance to Mooney of $53,000.
2. Interest of 14% on each partner's capital balance on January 1.
3. Any remaining net income divided equally.

Smithson and Mooney had $50,000 and $150,000, respectively, in their January 1 capital balances. Net income for the year was $240,000.

How much net income should be distributed to Mooney?

PE 12-2B
Dividing partnership net income

obj. 2

EE 12-2   p. 539

Alex Hutchins and Caitlin Jenkins formed a partnership, dividing income as follows:

1. Annual salary allowance to Hutchins of $24,000.
2. Interest of 12% on each partner's capital balance on January 1.
3. Any remaining net income divided to Hutchins and Jenkins, 2:1.

Hutchins and Jenkins had $60,000 and $80,000, respectively, in their January 1 capital balances. Net income for the year was $36,000.

How much net income should be distributed to Hutchins?

PE 12-3A
Revaluing and contributing assets to a partnership

obj. 3

EE 12-3   p. 542

Brandon Tarr invested $64,000 in the Garmon and Miller partnership for ownership equity of $64,000. Prior to the investment, equipment was revalued to a market value of $45,000 from a book value of $33,000. Jordon Garmon and Kali Miller share net income in a 2:1 ratio.

a. Provide the journal entry for the revaluation of equipment.
b. Provide the journal entry to admit Tarr.

PE 12-3B
Revaluing and contributing assets to a partnership

obj. 3

EE 12-3   p. 542

Jamarcus Webster purchased one-half of Drew Akins's interest in the Perry and Akins partnership for $25,000. Prior to the investment, land was revalued to a market value of $100,000 from a book value of $84,000. Weston Perry and Drew Akins share net income equally. Akins had a capital balance of $25,000 prior to these transactions.

a. Provide the journal entry for the revaluation of land.
b. Provide the journal entry to admit Webster.

PE 12-4A
Partner bonus

obj. 3

EE 12-4   p. 544

Maples has a capital balance of $65,000 after adjusting assets to fair market value. Baker contributes $25,000 to receive a 30% interest in a new partnership with Maples.

Determine the amount and recipient of the partner bonus.

PE 12-4B
Partner bonus

obj. 3

EE 12-4   p. 544

Amory has a capital balance of $340,000 after adjusting assets to fair market value. Perez contributes $550,000 to receive a 60% interest in a new partnership with Amory.

Determine the amount and recipient of the partner bonus.

PE 12-5A
Liquidating partnerships

obj. 4

EE 12-5   p. 549

Prior to liquidating their partnership, Penn and Ryan had capital accounts of $160,000 and $100,000, respectively. Prior to liquidation, the partnership had no cash assets other than what was realized from the sale of assets. These partnership assets were sold for $250,000. The partnership had $15,000 of liabilities. Penn and Ryan share income and losses equally. Determine the amount received by Penn as a final distribution from liquidation of the partnership.

PE 12-5B
Liquidating partnerships

obj. 4

EE 12-5   p. 549

Prior to liquidating their partnership, Myers and Baird had capital accounts of $22,000 and $30,000, respectively. Prior to liquidation, the partnership had no cash assets other than what was realized from the sale of assets. These partnership assets were sold for $65,000. The partnership had $6,000 of liabilities. Myers and Baird share income and losses equally. Determine the amount received by Myers as a final distribution from liquidation of the partnership.

PE 12-6A
Liquidating partnerships— deficiency

obj. 4

EE 12-6   p. 551

Prior to liquidating their partnership, Min and Alvarez had capital accounts of $120,000 and $200,000, respectively. The partnership assets were sold for $60,000. The partnership had no liabilities. Min and Alvarez share income and losses equally.

a. Determine the amount of Min's deficiency.
b. Determine the amount distributed to Alvarez, assuming Min is unable to satisfy the deficiency.

PE 12-6B
Liquidating partnerships— deficiency

obj. 4

EE 12-6   p. 551

Prior to liquidating their partnership, Greer and Murphy had capital accounts of $70,000 and $30,000, respectively. The partnership assets were sold for $25,000. The partnership had no liabilities. Greer and Murphy share income and losses equally.

a. Determine the amount of Murphy's deficiency.
b. Determine the amount distributed to Greer, assuming Murphy is unable to satisfy the deficiency.

Exercises

EX 12-1
Record partner's original investment

obj. 2

Gwen Delk and Alliesha Johnson decide to form a partnership by combining the assets of their separate businesses. Delk contributes the following assets to the partnership: cash, $13,000; accounts receivable with a face amount of $136,000 and an allowance for doubtful accounts of $8,400; merchandise inventory with a cost of $90,000; and equipment with a cost of $155,000 and accumulated depreciation of $100,000.

The partners agree that $6,000 of the accounts receivable are completely worthless and are not to be accepted by the partnership, that $10,200 is a reasonable allowance for the uncollectibility of the remaining accounts, that the merchandise inventory is to be recorded at the current market price of $84,700, and that the equipment is to be valued at $69,500.

Journalize the partnership's entry to record Delk's investment.

EX 12-2
Record partner's original investment

obj. 2

Brandi Bonds and Cesar Ruiz form a partnership by combining assets of their former businesses. The following balance sheet information is provided by Bonds, sole proprietorship:

Cash		$ 40,000
Accounts receivable	$75,000	
Less: Allowance for doubtful accounts	4,100	70,900
Land		180,000
Equipment	$70,000	
Less: Accumulated depreciation—equipment	43,000	27,000
Total assets		$317,900
Accounts payable		$ 22,500
Notes payable		65,000
Brandi Bonds, capital		230,400
Total liabilities and owner's equity		$317,900

Bonds obtained appraised values for the land and equipment as follows:

Land	$250,000
Equipment	21,000

An analysis of the accounts receivable indicated that the allowance for doubtful accounts should be increased to $6,000.

Journalize the partnership's entry for Bonds's investment.

EX 12-3
Dividing partnership income
obj. 2

✔ b. Hassell, $150,000

Candace Hassell and Abby Lawson formed a partnership, investing $240,000 and $80,000, respectively. Determine their participation in the year's net income of $200,000 under each of the following independent assumptions: (a) no agreement concerning division of net income; (b) divided in the ratio of original capital investment; (c) interest at the rate of 15% allowed on original investments and the remainder divided in the ratio of 2:3; (d) salary allowances of $50,000 and $70,000, respectively, and the balance divided equally; (e) allowance of interest at the rate of 15% on original investments, salary allowances of $50,000 and $70,000, respectively, and the remainder divided equally.

EX 12-4
Dividing partnership income
obj. 2

✔ c. Hassell, $168,800

Determine the income participation of Hassell and Lawson, according to each of the five assumptions as to income division listed in Exercise 12-3 if the year's net income is $380,000.

EX 12-5
Dividing partnership net loss
obj. 2

Casey Fisher and Logan Baylor formed a partnership in which the partnership agreement provided for salary allowances of $40,000 and $35,000, respectively. Determine the division of a $20,000 net loss for the current year.

EX 12-6
Negotiating income-sharing ratio
obj. 2

Sixty-year-old Jasmine Howard retired from her computer consulting business in Boston and moved to Florida. There she met 27-year-old Dawn Patel, who had just graduated from Eldon Community College with an associate degree in computer science. Jasmine and Dawn formed a partnership called J&D Computer Consultants. Jasmine contributed $25,000 for startup costs and devoted one-half time to the business. Dawn devoted full time to the business. The monthly drawings were $2,000 for Jasmine and $4,000 for Dawn.

At the end of the first year of operations, the two partners disagreed on the division of net income. Jasmine reasoned that the division should be equal. Although she devoted only one-half time to the business, she contributed all of the startup funds. Dawn reasoned that the income-sharing ratio should be 2:1 in her favor because she devoted full time to the business and her monthly drawings were twice those of Jasmine.

Can you identify any flaws in the partners' reasoning regarding the income-sharing ratio?

EX 12-7
Dividing LLC income
obj. 2

✔ a. Bowman, $106,800

Ben Bowman and Savannah Mapes formed a limited liability company with an operating agreement that provided a salary allowance of $75,000 and $60,000 to each member, respectively. In addition, the operating agreement specified an income-sharing ratio of 3:2. The two members withdrew amounts equal to their salary allowances.

a. Determine the division of $188,000 net income for the year.

b. Provide journal entries to close the (1) income summary and (2) drawing accounts for the two members.

EX 12-8
Dividing LLC net income and statement of members' equity
objs. 2, 5

✔ a. Wilson, $268,600

Intermedia, LLC, has three members: WYXT Partners, Lindsey Wilson, and Daily Sun Newspaper, LLC. On January 1, 2010, the three members had equity of $200,000, $50,000, and $120,000, respectively. WYXT Partners contributed an additional $50,000 to Intermedia, LLC, on June 1, 2010. Lindsey Wilson received an annual salary allowance of $115,600 during 2010. The members' equity accounts are also credited with 12% interest on each member's January 1 capital balance. Any remaining income is to be shared in the ratio of 4:3:3 among the three members. The net income for Intermedia, LLC, for 2010 was $650,000. The salary and interest allowances were distributed to the members.

a. Determine the division of income among the three members.
b. Prepare the journal entry to close the net income and withdrawals to the individual member equity accounts.
c. Prepare a statement of members' equity for 2010.

EX 12-9
Partner income and withdrawal journal entries
objs. 2, 3

The notes to the annual report for KPMG LLP (U.K.) indicated the following policies regarding the partners' capital:

The allocation of profits to those who were partners during the financial year occurs following the finalization of the annual financial statements. During the year, partners receive monthly drawings and, from time to time, additional profit distributions. Both the monthly drawings and profit distributions represent payments on account of current-year profits and are reclaimable from partners until profits have been allocated.

Assume that the partners draw £30 million per month for 2010 and the net income for the year is £400 million. Journalize the partner capital and partner drawing control accounts in the following requirements:

a. Provide the journal entry for the monthly partner drawing for January.
b. Provide the journal entry to close the income summary account at the end of the year.
c. Provide the journal entry to close the drawing account at the end of the year.

EX 12-10
Admitting new partners
obj. 3

Lia Wu and Becca Sims are partners who share in the income equally and have capital balances of $150,000 and $62,500, respectively. Wu, with the consent of Sims, sells one-third of her interest to Kara Oliver. What entry is required by the partnership if the sales price is (a) $40,000? (b) $60,000?

EX 12-11
Admitting new partners
obj. 3

The public accounting firm of Grant Thornton LLP disclosed U.S. revenues of $940 million for a recent year. The revenues were attributable to 489 active partners.

a. What was the average revenue per partner? Round to the nearest $1,000.
b. Assuming that the total partners' capital is $195,600,000 and that it approximates the fair market value of the firm's net assets, what would be considered a minimum contribution for admitting a new partner to the firm, assuming no bonus is paid to the new partner? Round to the nearest $1,000.
c. Why might the amount to be contributed by a new partner for admission to the firm exceed the amount determined in (b)?

EX 12-12
Admitting new partners who buy an interest and contribute assets
obj. 3

✔ b. Hughes, $96,000

The capital accounts of Brad Hughes and Mitchell Isaacs have balances of $120,000 and $100,000, respectively. Leah Craft and Jayme Clark are to be admitted to the partnership. Craft buys one-fifth of Hughes's interest for $30,000 and one-fourth of Isaacs' interest for $20,000. Clark contributes $50,000 cash to the partnership, for which she is to receive an ownership equity of $50,000.

a. Journalize the entries to record the admission of (1) Craft and (2) Clark.
b. What are the capital balances of each partner after the admission of the new partners?

EX 12-13
Admitting new partner who contributes assets

obj. 3

✔ b. Flores, $60,000

After the tangible assets have been adjusted to current market prices, the capital accounts of Travis Harris and Keelyn Kidd have balances of $60,000 and $90,000, respectively. Felix Flores is to be admitted to the partnership, contributing $45,000 cash to the partnership, for which he is to receive an ownership equity of $60,000. All partners share equally in income.

a. Journalize the entry to record the admission of Flores, who is to receive a bonus of $15,000.
b. What are the capital balances of each partner after the admission of the new partner?

EX 12-14
Admitting a new LLC member

obj. 3

✔ b. (2) Bonus paid to Koster, $15,000

Excel Medical, LLC, consists of two doctors, Douglass and Finn, who share in all income and losses according to a 2:3 income-sharing ratio. Dr. Lindsey Koster has been asked to join the LLC. Prior to admitting Koster, the assets of Excel Medical were revalued to reflect their current market values. The revaluation resulted in medical equipment being increased by $25,000. Prior to the revaluation, the equity balances for Douglass and Finn were $240,000 and $275,000, respectively.

a. Provide the journal entry for the asset revaluation.
b. Provide the journal entry for the bonus under the following independent situations:
   1. Koster purchased a 30% interest in Excel Medical, LLC, for $310,000.
   2. Koster purchased a 25% interest in Excel Medical, LLC, for $160,000.

EX 12-15
Admitting new partner with bonus

obj. 3

✔ b. (1) Bonus paid to Harris, $6,200

J. Taylor and K. Garcia are partners in Green Earth Consultants. Taylor and Garcia share income equally. L. Harris will be admitted to the partnership. Prior to the admission, equipment was revalued downward by $8,000. The capital balances of each partner are $100,000 and $139,000, respectively, prior to the revaluation.

a. Provide the journal entry for the asset revaluation.
b. Provide the journal entry for Harris's admission under the following independent situations:
   1. Harris purchased a 20% interest for $50,000.
   2. Harris purchased a 30% interest for $125,000.

EX 12-16
Partner bonuses, statement of partners' equity

objs. 2, 3, 5

✔ Wilson capital, Dec. 31, 2010, $83,400

The partnership of Angel Investor Associates began operations on January 1, 2010, with contributions from two partners as follows:

Jen Wilson	$45,000
Teresa McDonald	55,000

The following additional partner transactions took place during the year:

1. In early January, Jaime Holden is admitted to the partnership by contributing $25,000 cash for a 20% interest.
2. Net income of $160,000 was earned in 2010. In addition, Jen Wilson received a salary allowance of $30,000 for the year. The three partners agree to an income-sharing ratio equal to their capital balances after admitting Holden.
3. The partners' withdrawals are equal to half of the increase in their capital balances from income.

Prepare a statement of partnership equity for the year ended December 31, 2010.

EX 12-17
Withdrawal of partner

obj. 3

Luke Gilbert is to retire from the partnership of Gilbert and Associates as of March 31, the end of the current fiscal year. After closing the accounts, the capital balances of the partners are as follows: Luke Gilbert, $245,000; Marissa Cohen, $125,000; and Tyrone Cobb, $140,000. They have shared net income and net losses in the ratio of 3:2:2. The partners agree that the merchandise inventory should be increased by $24,000, and the allowance for doubtful accounts should be increased by $5,800. Gilbert agrees to accept a note for $200,000 in partial settlement of his ownership equity. The remainder of his claim is to be paid in cash. Cohen and Cobb are to share equally in the net income or net loss of the new partnership.

Journalize the entries to record (a) the adjustment of the assets to bring them into agreement with current market prices and (b) the withdrawal of Gilbert from the partnership.

EX 12-18
Statement of
members' equity,
admitting new
member

objs. 2, 3, 5

✔ a. 3:7

The statement of members' equity for Yellow Mountain Mines, LLC, is shown below.

Yellow Mountain Mines, LLC
Statement of Members' Equity
For the Years Ended December 31, 2010 and 2011

	Nevada Properties, LLC, Member Equity	Star Holdings, LLC, Member Equity	Randy Reed, Member Equity	Total Members' Equity
Members' equity, January 1, 2010	$450,000	$310,000		$ 760,000
Net income	90,000	210,000		300,000
Members' equity, December 31, 2010	$540,000	$520,000		$1,060,000
Reed contribution	6,000	14,000	$270,000	290,000
Net income	100,000	220,000	80,000	400,000
Less member withdrawals	(32,000)	(48,000)	(50,000)	(130,000)
Members' equity, December 31, 2011	$614,000	$706,000	$300,000	$1,620,000

a. What was the income-sharing ratio in 2010?
b. What was the income-sharing ratio in 2011?
c. How much cash did Randy Reed contribute to Yellow Mountain Mines, LLC, for his interest?
d. Why do the member equity accounts of Nevada Properties, LLC, and Star Holdings, LLC, have positive entries for Randy Reed's contribution?
e. What percentage interest of Yellow Mountain Mines did Randy Reed acquire?

EX 12-19
Distribution of cash
upon liquidation

obj. 4

✔ a. $4,000 loss

Pryor and Lester are partners, sharing gains and losses equally. They decide to terminate their partnership. Prior to realization, their capital balances are $12,000 and $8,000, respectively. After all noncash assets are sold and all liabilities are paid, there is a cash balance of $16,000.

a. What is the amount of a gain or loss on realization?
b. How should the gain or loss be divided between Pryor and Lester?
c. How should the cash be divided between Pryor and Lester?

EX 12-20
Distribution of cash
upon liquidation

obj. 4

✔ Bradley, $33,500

Jason Bradley and Abdul Barak, with capital balances of $26,000 and $35,000, respectively, decide to liquidate their partnership. After selling the noncash assets and paying the liabilities, there is $76,000 of cash remaining. If the partners share income and losses equally, how should the cash be distributed?

EX 12-21
Liquidating
partnerships—
capital deficiency

obj. 4

✔ b. $72,500

Matthews, Williams, and Shen share equally in net income and net losses. After the partnership sells all assets for cash, divides the losses on realization, and pays the liabilities, the balances in the capital accounts are as follows: Matthews, $28,000 Cr.; Williams, $62,500 Cr.; Shen, $18,000 Dr.

a. What term is applied to the debit balance in Shen's capital account?
b. What is the amount of cash on hand?
c. Journalize the transaction that must take place for Matthews and Williams to receive cash in the liquidation process equal to their capital account balances.

EX 12-22
Distribution of cash upon liquidation
obj. **4**

✔ a. Houston, $380

Bianca Houston, Jana Alsup, and KeKe Cross arranged to import and sell orchid corsages for a university dance. They agreed to share equally the net income or net loss of the venture. Houston and Alsup advanced $250 and $380 of their own respective funds to pay for advertising and other expenses. After collecting for all sales and paying creditors, the partnership has $1,020 in cash.

a. How should the money be distributed?
b. Assuming that the partnership has only $540 instead of $1,020, do any of the three partners have a capital deficiency? If so, how much?

EX 12-23
Liquidating partnerships—capital deficiency
obj. **4**

Hilliard, Downey, and Petrov are partners sharing income 3:2:1. After the firm's loss from liquidation is distributed, the capital account balances were: Hilliard, $24,000 Dr.; Downey, $90,000 Cr.; and Petrov, $64,000 Cr. If Hilliard is personally bankrupt and unable to pay any of the $24,000, what will be the amount of cash received by Downey and Petrov upon liquidation?

EX 12-24
Statement of partnership liquidation
obj. **4**

After closing the accounts on July 1, prior to liquidating the partnership, the capital account balances of Dover, Goll, and Chamberland are $35,000, $50,000, and $22,000, respectively. Cash, noncash assets, and liabilities total $55,000, $92,000, and $40,000, respectively. Between July 1 and July 29, the noncash assets are sold for $74,000, the liabilities are paid, and the remaining cash is distributed to the partners. The partners share net income and loss in the ratio of 3:2:1. Prepare a statement of partnership liquidation for the period July 1–29, 2010.

EX 12-25
Statement of LLC liquidation
obj. **4**

Gordon, Hightower, and Mills are members of Capital Sales, LLC, sharing income and losses in the ratio of 2:2:1, respectively. The members decide to liquidate the limited liability company. The members' equity prior to liquidation and asset realization on May 1, 2010, are as follows:

Gordon	$15,000
Hightower	35,000
Mills	22,000
Total	$72,000

In winding up operations during the month of May, noncash assets with a book value of $94,000 are sold for $116,500, and liabilities of $30,000 are satisfied. Prior to realization, Capital Sales has a cash balance of $8,000.

a. Prepare a statement of LLC liquidation.
b. Provide the journal entry for the final cash distribution to members.

EX 12-26
Partnership entries and statement of partners' equity
objs. **2, 5**

✔ b. Abdel-Raja, capital, Dec. 31, $114,000

The capital accounts of Hossam Abdel-Raja and Aly Meyer have balances of $90,000 and $65,000, respectively, on January 1, 2010, the beginning of the current fiscal year. On April 10, Abdel-Raja invested an additional $10,000. During the year, Abdel-Raja and Meyer withdrew $48,000 and $39,000, respectively, and net income for the year was $124,000. The articles of partnership make no reference to the division of net income.

a. Journalize the entries to close (1) the income summary account and (2) the drawing accounts.
b. Prepare a statement of partners' equity for the current year for the partnership of Abdel-Raja and Meyer.

EX 12-27
Revenue per professional staff

The accounting firm of Deloitte & Touche is the largest international accounting firm in the world as ranked by total revenues. For the last two years, Deloitte & Touche reported the following for its U.S. operations:

	2007	2006
Revenue (in millions)	$ 9,850	$ 8,770
Number of professional staff (including partners)	32,483	29,614

a. For 2007 and 2006, determine the revenue per professional staff. Round to the nearest thousand dollars.
b. Interpret the trend between the two years.

EX 12-28
Revenue per employee

Office-Brite Cleaning Services, LLC, provides cleaning services for office buildings. The firm has 10 members in the LLC, which did not change between 2008 and 2009. During 2009, the business expanded into four new cities. The following revenue and employee information is provided:

	2009	2008
Revenues (in thousands)	$38,500	$33,750
Number of employees (excluding members)	350	250

a. For 2009 and 2008, determine the revenue per employee (excluding members).
b. Interpret the trend between the two years.

Problems Series A

PR 12-1A
Entries and balance sheet for partnership

obj. 2

✔ 3. Schmidt net income, $47,200

On June 1, 2009, Kevin Schmidt and David Cohen form a partnership. Schmidt agrees to invest $12,000 cash and merchandise inventory valued at $32,000. Cohen invests certain business assets at valuations agreed upon, transfers business liabilities, and contributes sufficient cash to bring his total capital to $80,000. Details regarding the book values of the business assets and liabilities, and the agreed valuations, follow:

	Cohen's Ledger Balance	Agreed-Upon Balance
Accounts Receivable	$18,400	$14,900
Allowance for Doubtful Accounts	800	1,000
Merchandise Inventory	21,400	28,600
Equipment	36,000 ⎱	35,000
Accumulated Depreciation—Equipment	12,000 ⎰	
Accounts Payable	6,500	6,500
Notes Payable	4,000	4,000

The partnership agreement includes the following provisions regarding the division of net income: interest of 10% on original investments, salary allowances of $36,000 (Schmidt) and $22,000 (Cohen), and the remainder equally.

Instructions
1. Journalize the entries to record the investments of Schmidt and Cohen in the partnership accounts.
2. Prepare a balance sheet as of June 1, 2009, the date of formation of the partnership of Schmidt and Cohen.
3. After adjustments and the closing of revenue and expense accounts at May 31, 2010, the end of the first full year of operations, the income summary account has a credit balance of $84,000, and the drawing accounts have debit balances of $30,000 (Schmidt) and $25,000 (Cohen). Journalize the entries to close the income summary account and the drawing accounts at May 31, 2010.

PR 12-2A

Dividing partnership income

obj. 3

✔ 1. f. Drury net income, $92,900

Desmond Drury and Ty Wilkins have decided to form a partnership. They have agreed that Drury is to invest $20,000 and that Wilkins is to invest $30,000. Drury is to devote full time to the business, and Wilkins is to devote one-half time. The following plans for the division of income are being considered:

a. Equal division.
b. In the ratio of original investments.
c. In the ratio of time devoted to the business.
d. Interest of 10% on original investments and the remainder in the ratio of 3:2.
e. Interest of 10% on original investments, salary allowances of $34,000 to Drury and $17,000 to Wilkins, and the remainder equally.
f. Plan (e), except that Drury is also to be allowed a bonus equal to 20% of the amount by which net income exceeds the salary allowances.

Instructions

For each plan, determine the division of the net income under each of the following assumptions: (1) net income of $150,000 and (2) net income of $66,000. Present the data in tabular form, using the following columnar headings:

	$150,000		$66,000	
Plan	Drury	Wilkins	Drury	Wilkins

PR 12-3A

Financial statements for partnerships

objs. 2, 5

✔ 2. Dec. 31 capital—Weekley, $182,400

The ledger of Amid Moshref and Alex Weekley, attorneys-at-law, contains the following accounts and balances after adjustments have been recorded on December 31, 2010:

	Debit Balances	Credit Balances
Cash	24,200	
Accounts Receivable	41,300	
Supplies	6,700	
Land	120,000	
Building	160,000	
Accumulated Depreciation—Building		52,300
Office Equipment	53,000	
Accumulated Depreciation—Office Equipment		21,300
Accounts Payable		3,400
Salaries Payable		5,200
Amid Moshref, Capital		125,000
Amid Moshref, Drawing	50,000	
Alex Weekley, Capital		160,000
Alex Weekley, Drawing	60,000	
Professional Fees		562,200
Salary Expense	312,300	
Depreciation Expense—Building	75,000	
Property Tax Expense	3,500	
Heating and Lighting Expense	11,200	
Supplies Expense	3,400	
Depreciation Expense—Office Equipment	6,700	
Miscellaneous Expense	2,100	
	929,400	929,400

The balance in Weekley's capital account includes an additional investment of $20,000 made on April 5, 2010.

Instructions

1. Prepare an income statement for the current fiscal year, indicating the division of net income. The articles of partnership provide for salary allowances of $60,000 to Moshref and $75,000 to Weekley, allowances of 12% on each partner's capital balance at the beginning of the fiscal year, and equal division of the remaining net income or net loss.
2. Prepare a statement of partners' equity for 2010.
3. Prepare a balance sheet as of the end of 2010.

PR 12-4A
Admitting new partner

obj. 3

✔ 3. Total assets, $220,200

Jordan Cates and LaToya Orr have operated a successful firm for many years, sharing net income and net losses equally. Caleb Webster is to be admitted to the partnership on June 1 of the current year, in accordance with the following agreement:

a. Assets and liabilities of the old partnership are to be valued at their book values as of May 31, except for the following:
- Accounts receivable amounting to $2,000 are to be written off, and the allowance for doubtful accounts is to be increased to 5% of the remaining accounts.
- Merchandise inventory is to be valued at $63,870.
- Equipment is to be valued at $90,000.

b. Webster is to purchase $30,000 of the ownership interest of Orr for $37,500 cash and to contribute $35,000 cash to the partnership for a total ownership equity of $65,000.

c. The income-sharing ratio of Cates, Orr, and Webster is to be 2:1:1.

The post-closing trial balance of Cates and Orr as of May 31 follows.

Cates and Orr
Post-Closing Trial Balance
May 31, 2010

	Debit Balances	Credit Balances
Cash	9,400	
Accounts Receivable	21,400	
Allowance for Doubtful Accounts		500
Merchandise Inventory	58,600	
Prepaid Insurance	3,500	
Equipment	95,000	
Accumulated Depreciation—Equipment		25,700
Accounts Payable		14,700
Notes Payable		12,000
Jordan Cates, Capital		75,000
LaToya Orr, Capital		60,000
	187,900	187,900

Instructions

1. Journalize the entries as of May 31 to record the revaluations, using a temporary account entitled Asset Revaluations. The balance in the accumulated depreciation account is to be eliminated.
2. Journalize the additional entries to record the remaining transactions relating to the formation of the new partnership. Assume that all transactions occur on June 1.
3. Present a balance sheet for the new partnership as of June 1, 2010.

PR 12-5A
Statement of partnership liquidation

obj. 4

After the accounts are closed on September 10, 2010, prior to liquidating the partnership, the capital accounts of Kris Harken, Brett Sedlacek, and Amy Eldridge are $31,000, $5,700, and $24,500, respectively. Cash and noncash assets total $7,800 and $61,400, respectively. Amounts owed to creditors total $8,000. The partners share income and losses in the ratio of 1:1:2. Between September 10 and September 30, the noncash assets are sold for $32,600, the partner with the capital deficiency pays his or her deficiency to the partnership, and the liabilities are paid.

Instructions

1. Prepare a statement of partnership liquidation, indicating (a) the sale of assets and division of loss, (b) the payment of liabilities, (c) the receipt of the deficiency (from the appropriate partner), and (d) the distribution of cash.
2. Assume the partner with the capital deficiency declares bankruptcy and is unable to pay the deficiency. Journalize the entries to (a) allocate the partner's deficiency and (b) distribute the remaining cash.

PR 12-6A
Statement of partnership liquidation
obj. 4

On June 3, 2010, the firm of McAdams, Cooper, and Zhang decided to liquidate their partnership. The partners have capital balances of $14,000, $84,000, and $118,000, respectively. The cash balance is $29,000, the book values of noncash assets total $242,000, and liabilities total $55,000. The partners share income and losses in the ratio of 1:2:2.

1. Prepare a statement of partnership liquidation, covering the period June 3–29, 2010, for each of the following independent assumptions:
   a. All of the noncash assets are sold for $290,000 in cash, the creditors are paid, and the remaining cash is distributed to the partners.
   b. All of the noncash assets are sold for $132,000 in cash, the creditors are paid, the partner with the debit capital balance pays the amount owed to the firm, and the remaining cash is distributed to the partners.
2. Assume the partner with the capital deficiency in part (b) above declares bankruptcy and is unable to pay the deficiency. Journalize the entries to (a) allocate the partner's deficiency and (b) distribute the remaining cash.

Problems Series B

PR 12-1B
Entries and balance sheet for partnership
obj. 2

✔ 3. Walker net income, $36,400

On August 1, 2010, Jarius Walker and Rae King form a partnership. Walker agrees to invest $18,200 in cash and merchandise inventory valued at $48,800. King invests certain business assets at valuations agreed upon, transfers business liabilities, and contributes sufficient cash to bring her total capital to $60,000. Details regarding the book values of the business assets and liabilities, and the agreed valuations, follow:

	King's Ledger Balance	Agreed-Upon Valuation
Accounts Receivable	$25,300	$24,100
Allowance for Doubtful Accounts	1,500	1,800
Equipment	92,300	55,100
Accumulated Depreciation—Equipment	35,600	
Accounts Payable	15,000	15,000
Notes Payable	25,000	25,000

The partnership agreement includes the following provisions regarding the division of net income: interest on original investments at 10%, salary allowances of $22,500 (Walker) and $30,400 (King), and the remainder equally.

Instructions

1. Journalize the entries to record the investments of Walker and King in the partnership accounts.
2. Prepare a balance sheet as of August 1, 2010, the date of formation of the partnership of Walker and King.
3. After adjustments and the closing of revenue and expense accounts at July 31, 2011, the end of the first full year of operations, the income summary account has a credit balance of $80,000, and the drawing accounts have debit balances of $22,500 (Walker) and $30,400 (King). Journalize the entries to close the income summary account and the drawing accounts at July 31, 2011.

PR 12-2B
Dividing partnership income
obj. 2

✔ 1. f. Larson net income, $41,600

Larson and Alvarez have decided to form a partnership. They have agreed that Larson is to invest $150,000 and that Alvarez is to invest $50,000. Larson is to devote one-half time to the business and Alvarez is to devote full time. The following plans for the division of income are being considered:

a. Equal division.
b. In the ratio of original investments.
c. In the ratio of time devoted to the business.
d. Interest of 12% on original investments and the remainder equally.

e. Interest of 12% on original investments, salary allowances of $32,000 to Larson and $64,000 to Alvarez, and the remainder equally.

f. Plan (e), except that Alvarez is also to be allowed a bonus equal to 20% of the amount by which net income exceeds the salary allowances.

Instructions

For each plan, determine the division of the net income under each of the following assumptions: (1) net income of $105,000 and (2) net income of $180,000. Present the data in tabular form, using the following columnar headings:

Plan	$105,000		$180,000	
	Larson	Alvarez	Larson	Alvarez

PR 12-3B

Financial statements for partnership

objs. 2, 5

✔ 2. Dec. 31 capital—Forte, $87,250

The ledger of Dan Yamada and Courtney Forte, attorneys-at-law, contains the following accounts and balances after adjustments have been recorded on December 31, 2010:

	Debit Balances	Credit Balances
Cash	32,000	
Accounts Receivable	42,300	
Supplies	1,500	
Land	75,000	
Building	128,100	
Accumulated Depreciation—Building		62,500
Office Equipment	46,000	
Accumulated Depreciation—Office Equipment		19,400
Accounts Payable		4,800
Salaries Payable		3,200
Dan Yamada, Capital		120,000
Dan Yamada, Drawing	45,000	
Courtney Forte, Capital		75,000
Courtney Forte, Drawing	65,000	
Professional Fees		340,300
Salary Expense	146,800	
Depreciation Expense—Building	14,500	
Property Tax Expense	9,000	
Heating and Lighting Expense	7,200	
Supplies Expense	5,200	
Depreciation Expense—Office Equipment	4,500	
Miscellaneous Expense	3,100	
	625,200	625,200

The balance in Forte's capital account includes an additional investment of $10,000 made on August 10, 2010.

Instructions

1. Prepare an income statement for 2010, indicating the division of net income. The articles of partnership provide for salary allowances of $40,000 to Yamada and $50,000 to Forte, allowances of 10% on each partner's capital balance at the beginning of the fiscal year, and equal division of the remaining net income or net loss.

2. Prepare a statement of partners' equity for 2010.

3. Prepare a balance sheet as of the end of 2010.

PR 12-4B

Admitting new partner

obj. 3

✔ 3. Total assets, $333,000

Sadhil Rao and Lauren Sails have operated a successful firm for many years, sharing net income and net losses equally. Paige Hancock is to be admitted to the partnership on May 1 of the current year, in accordance with the following agreement:

a. Assets and liabilities of the old partnership are to be valued at their book values as of April 30, except for the following:
   • Accounts receivable amounting to $2,800 are to be written off, and the allowance for doubtful accounts is to be increased to 5% of the remaining accounts.
   • Merchandise inventory is to be valued at $65,480.
   • Equipment is to be valued at $194,000.

b. Hancock is to purchase $55,000 of the ownership interest of Sails for $60,000 cash and to contribute another $30,000 cash to the partnership for a total ownership equity of $85,000.

c. The income-sharing ratio of Rao, Sails, and Hancock is to be 2:1:1.

The post-closing trial balance of Rao and Sails as of April 30 is as follows:

Rao and Sails
Post-Closing Trial Balance
April 30, 2010

	Debit Balances	Credit Balances
Cash	7,500	
Accounts Receivable	38,400	
Allowance for Doubtful Accounts		1,400
Merchandise Inventory	59,000	
Prepaid Insurance	2,200	
Equipment	165,000	
Accumulated Depreciation—Equipment		51,700
Accounts Payable		9,000
Notes Payable		10,000
Sadhil Rao, Capital		110,000
Lauren Sails, Capital		90,000
	272,100	272,100

Instructions

1. Journalize the entries as of April 30 to record the revaluations, using a temporary account entitled Asset Revaluations. The balance in the accumulated depreciation account is to be eliminated.

2. Journalize the additional entries to record the remaining transactions relating to the formation of the new partnership. Assume that all transactions occur on May 1.

3. Present a balance sheet for the new partnership as of May 1, 2010.

PR 12-5B
Statement of partnership liquidation

obj. 4

After the accounts are closed on July 3, 2010, prior to liquidating the partnership, the capital accounts of Whitney Lacy, Eli Oliver, and Alberto Diaz are $28,200, $7,800, and $37,200, respectively. Cash and noncash assets total $5,800 and $82,400, respectively. Amounts owed to creditors total $15,000. The partners share income and losses in the ratio of 2:1:1. Between July 3 and July 29, the noncash assets are sold for $33,200, the partner with the capital deficiency pays his deficiency to the partnership, and the liabilities are paid.

Instructions

1. Prepare a statement of partnership liquidation, indicating (a) the sale of assets and division of loss, (b) the payment of liabilities, (c) the receipt of the deficiency (from the appropriate partner), and (d) the distribution of cash.

2. Assume the partner with the capital deficiency declares bankruptcy and is unable to pay the deficiency. Journalize the entries to (a) allocate the partner's deficiency and (b) distribute the remaining cash.

PR 12-6B
Statement of partnership liquidation

obj. 4

On October 1, 2010, the firm of Orson, Dorr, and Killough decided to liquidate their partnership. The partners have capital balances of $48,000, $63,000, and $11,000, respectively. The cash balance is $9,000, the book values of noncash assets total $155,000, and liabilities total $42,000. The partners share income and losses in the ratio of 2:2:1.

1. Prepare a statement of partnership liquidation, covering the period October 1–30 2010, for each of the following independent assumptions:

a. All of the noncash assets are sold for $195,000 in cash, the creditors are paid, and the remaining cash is distributed to the partners.

b. All of the noncash assets are sold for $85,000 in cash, the creditors are paid, the partner with the debit capital balance pays the amount owed to the firm, and the remaining cash is distributed to the partners.

2. Assume the partner with the capital deficiency in part (b) above declares bankruptcy and is unable to pay the deficiency. Journalize the entries to (a) allocate the partner's deficiency and (b) distribute the remaining cash.

Special Activities

You can access the special activities online at **www.cengage.com/accounting/reeve**.

Excel Success Special Activities

SA 12-1
Division of partnership income

Dr. Preston and Dr. Patel are partners in a medical practice. The partnership agreement provides for annual salary allowances of $100,000 to Preston and $200,000 to Patel, along with a 10% interest allowance based on each partner's January 1 capital balance. Remaining profits or losses are to be shared equally. Open file *SA12-1* and determine the division of the partnership income in each of the following independent cases:

Case 1: Partnership income totaled $650,000. Preston's beginning Capital account balance was $1,200,000, and Patel's was $2,000,000.

Case 2: Partnership income totaled $650,000. Preston's beginning Capital account balance was $2,500,000, and Patel's was $700,000.

When you have completed the division of partnership income for both cases 1 and 2, perform a "save as," replacing the entire file name with the following:

SA12-1_[your first name initial]_[your last name]

SA 12-2
Division of partnership income

Jill Ahmad and Ramon Garcia are partners in an auto repair business. They have agreed to share profits and losses in the following manner. Jill, who is a better mechanic than Ramon, will receive a $1,000 per month salary allowance. Ramon will not receive a salary allowance, but both partners will be given a 12% interest allowance on their beginning capital account balances. Remaining profits and losses will be shared in the ratio of 1:2 (one third to Jill, and two thirds to Ramon).

Jill's beginning Capital account balance is $25,000, Ramon's beginning Capital account balance is $200,000, and the annual net income is $90,000.

Open file *SA12-2* to determine the division of the partnership income.

When you have completed the division of partnership income, perform a "save as," replacing the entire file name with the following:

SA12-2_[your first name initial]_[your last name]

SA 12-3
Division of partnership income

Information taken from the partnership records of Kuwanti and Carlita, attorneys-at-law, is presented below.

	Kuwanti	Carlita	Total
Beginning capital balance	$800,000	$700,000	$1,500,000
Monthly salary allowance	$ 12,500	$ 6,250	$ 18,750
Profit and loss sharing ratio	2	1	3

The partners have agreed to the monthly salary allowances shown above and to interest allowances equal to 15% of each partner's beginning capital account balance. Remaining profits and losses are to be divided in the ratio of 2:1.

Scenario 1: Open file *SA12-3* to determine the amount each partner will receive if the annual partnership income is $600,000.

Scenario 2: Create a new spreadsheet that determines the amount each partner will receive if the annual partnership income is $150,000.

When you have completed the division of partnership income, perform a "save as," replacing the entire file name with the following:

SA12-3_[your first name initial]_[your last name]

Answers to Self-Examination Questions

1. **B** Noncash assets contributed to a partnership should be recorded at the amounts agreed upon by the partners. The preferred practice is to record the office equipment at $9,000 (answer B).

2. **C** Net income and net loss are divided among the partners in accordance with their agreement. In the absence of any agreement, all partners share equally (answer C).

3. **C** Tracey's share of the $45,000 of net income is $19,000 (answer C), determined as follows:

	Tracey	Hepburn	Total
Interest allowance	$10,000	$ 5,000	$15,000
Salary allowance	12,000	24,000	36,000
Total	$22,000	$29,000	$51,000
Excess of allowances over income	3,000	3,000	6,000
Net income distribution	$19,000	$26,000	$45,000

4. **A** When an additional person is admitted to a partnership by purchasing an interest from one or more of the partners, the purchase price is paid directly to the selling partner(s). The amount of capital transferred from the capital account(s) of the selling partner(s) to the capital account of the incoming partner is the capital interest acquired from the selling partner(s). In the question, the amount is $32,500 (answer A), which is one-half of Lee's capital balance of $65,000.

5. **C** Partnership cash would be distributed in accordance with the credit balances in the partners' capital accounts. Therefore, $10,000 (answer C) would be distributed to Pavin (Pavin's $10,000 capital balance).

Corporations: Organization, Stock Transactions, and Dividends

© Susan Van Etten

H A S B R O

If you purchase a share of stock from Hasbro, you own a small interest in the company. You may request a Hasbro stock certificate as an indication of your ownership.

As you may know, Hasbro is one of the world's largest toy manufacturers and produces popular children's toys such as G.I. Joe, Play-Doh, Tonka toys, Mr. Potato Head, and Nerf balls. In addition, Hasbro manufactures family entertainment products such as Monopoly, Scrabble, and Trivial Pursuit under the Milton Bradley and Parker Brothers labels. In fact, the stock certificate of Hasbro has a picture of Uncle Pennybags, the Monopoly game icon, printed on it.

Purchasing a share of stock from Hasbro may be a great gift idea for the "hard-to-shop-for person." However, a stock certificate represents more than just a picture that you can frame. In fact, the stock certificate is a document that reflects legal ownership of the future financial prospects of Hasbro. In addition, as a shareholder, it represents your claim against the assets and earnings of the corporation.

If you are purchasing Hasbro stock as an investment, you should analyze Hasbro's financial statements and management's plans for the future. For example, Hasbro has a unique relationship with Disney that allows it to produce and sell licensed Disney products. Should this Disney relationship affect how much you are willing to pay for the stock? Also, you might want to know if Hasbro plans to pay cash dividends or whether management is considering issuing additional shares of stock.

In this chapter, we describe and illustrate the nature of corporations including the accounting for stock and dividends. This discussion will aid you in making decisions such as whether or not to buy Hasbro stock.

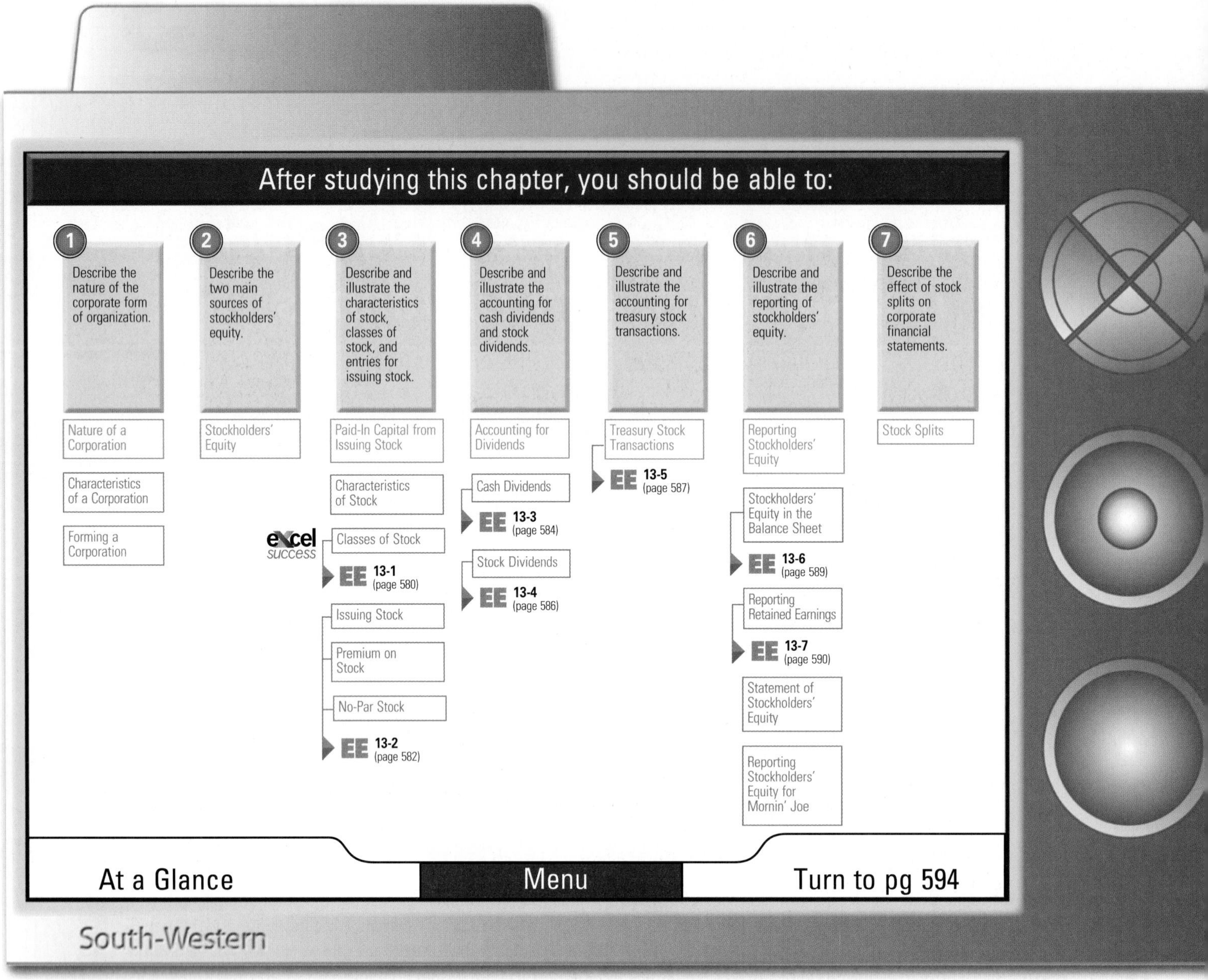

After studying this chapter, you should be able to:

1 Describe the nature of the corporate form of organization.

- Nature of a Corporation
- Characteristics of a Corporation
- Forming a Corporation

2 Describe the two main sources of stockholders' equity.

- Stockholders' Equity

3 Describe and illustrate the characteristics of stock, classes of stock, and entries for issuing stock.

- Paid-In Capital from Issuing Stock
- Characteristics of Stock
- Classes of Stock

excel success

  EE **13-1** (page 580)
- Issuing Stock
- Premium on Stock
- No-Par Stock

  EE **13-2** (page 582)

4 Describe and illustrate the accounting for cash dividends and stock dividends.

- Accounting for Dividends
- Cash Dividends

  EE **13-3** (page 584)
- Stock Dividends

  EE **13-4** (page 586)

5 Describe and illustrate the accounting for treasury stock transactions.

- Treasury Stock Transactions

  EE **13-5** (page 587)

6 Describe and illustrate the reporting of stockholders' equity.

- Reporting Stockholders' Equity
- Stockholders' Equity in the Balance Sheet

  EE **13-6** (page 589)
- Reporting Retained Earnings

  EE **13-7** (page 590)
- Statement of Stockholders' Equity
- Reporting Stockholders' Equity for Mornin' Joe

7 Describe the effect of stock splits on corporate financial statements.

- Stock Splits

At a Glance   Menu   Turn to pg 594

South-Western

---

1 Describe the nature of the corporate form of organization.

A corporation was defined in the Dartmouth College case of 1819, in which Chief Justice Marshall of the United States Supreme Court stated: "A corporation is an artificial being, invisible, intangible, and existing only in contemplation of the law."

Nature of a Corporation

Most large businesses are organized as corporations. As a result, corporations generate more than 90% of the total business dollars in the United States. In contrast, most small businesses are organized as proprietorships, partnerships, or limited liability companies.

Characteristics of a Corporation

A *corporation* is a legal entity, distinct and separate from the individuals who create and operate it. As a legal entity, a corporation may acquire, own, and dispose of property in its own name. It may also incur liabilities and enter into contracts. Most importantly, it can sell shares of ownership, called **stock**. This characteristic gives corporations the ability to raise large amounts of capital.

The **stockholders** or *shareholders* who own the stock own the corporation. They can buy and sell stock without affecting the corporation's operations or continued

The Coca-Cola Company is a well-known public corporation. Mars, Incorporated, which is owned by family members, is a well-known private corporation.

existence. Corporations whose shares of stock are traded in public markets are called *public corporations*. Corporations whose shares are not traded publicly are usually owned by a small group of investors and are called *nonpublic* or *private corporations*.

The stockholders of a corporation have *limited liability*. This means that creditors usually may not go beyond the assets of the corporation to satisfy their claims. Thus, the financial loss that a stockholder may suffer is limited to the amount invested.

The stockholders control a corporation by electing a *board of directors*. This board meets periodically to establish corporate policies. It also selects the chief executive officer (CEO) and other major officers to manage the corporation's day-to-day affairs. Exhibit 1 shows the organizational structure of a corporation.

Exhibit 1

Organizational Structure of a Corporation

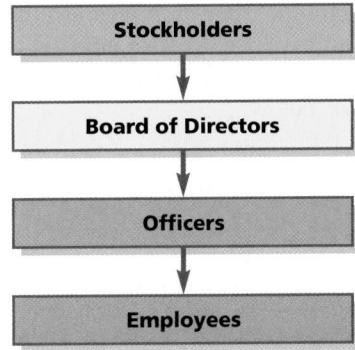

As a separate entity, a corporation is subject to taxes. For example, corporations must pay federal income taxes on their income.[1] Thus, corporate income that is distributed to stockholders in the form of *dividends* has already been taxed. In turn, stockholders must pay income taxes on the dividends they receive. This *double taxation* of corporate earnings is a major disadvantage of the corporate form.[2] The advantages and disadvantages of the corporate form are listed in Exhibit 2.

Exhibit 2

Advantages and Disadvantages of the Corporate Form

Advantages	Explanation
Separate legal existence	A corporation exists separately from its owners.
Continuous life	A corporation's life is separate from its owners; therefore, it exists indefinitely.
Raising large amounts of capital	The corporate form is suited for raising large amounts of money from shareholders.
Ownership rights are easily transferable	A corporation sells shares of ownership, called *stock*. The stockholders of a public company can transfer their shares of stock to other stockholders through stock markets, such as the New York Stock Exchange.
Limited liability	A corporation's creditors usually may not go beyond the assets of the corporation to satisfy their claims. Thus, the financial loss that a stockholder may suffer is limited to the amount invested.
Disadvantages	
Owner is separate from management	Stockholders control management through a board of directors. The board of directors should represent shareholder interests; however, the board is often more closely tied to management than to shareholders. As a result, the board of directors and management may not always behave in the best interests of stockholders.
Double taxation of dividends	As a separate legal entity, a corporation is subject to taxation. Thus, net income distributed as dividends will be taxed once at the corporation level, and then again at the individual level.
Regulatory costs	Corporations must satisfy many requirements such as those required by the Sarbanes-Oxley Act of 2002.

1 A majority of states also require corporations to pay income taxes.
2 Dividends presently receive a preferential individual tax rate of 15% to reduce the impact of double taxation.

Forming a Corporation

The first step in forming a corporation is to file an *application of incorporation* with the state. State incorporation laws differ, and corporations often organize in those states with the more favorable laws. For this reason, more than half of the largest companies are incorporated in Delaware. Exhibit 3 lists some corporations, their states of incorporation, and the location of their headquarters.

After the application of incorporation has been approved, the state grants a *charter* or *articles of incorporation*. The articles of incorporation formally create the corporation.[3] The corporate management and board of directors then prepare a set of *bylaws*, which are the rules and procedures for conducting the corporation's affairs.

Costs may be incurred in organizing a corporation. These costs include legal fees, taxes, state incorporation fees, license fees, and promotional costs. Such costs are debited to an expense account entitled *Organizational Expenses*.

To illustrate, a corporation's organizing costs of $8,500 on January 5 are recorded as shown below.

A Financial Executives International survey estimated that Sarbanes-Oxley costs the average public company over $3 million per year.

Jan.	5	Organizational Expenses	8,500	
		Cash		8,500
		Paid costs of organizing the corporation.		

Exhibit 3

Examples of Corporations and Their States of Incorporation

Corporation	State of Incorporation	Headquarters
Caterpillar	Delaware	Peoria, Ill.
Delta Air Lines	Delaware	Atlanta, Ga.
The Dow Chemical Company	Delaware	Midland, Mich.
General Electric Company	New York	Fairfield, Conn.
The Home Depot	Delaware	Atlanta, Ga.
Kellogg Company	Delaware	Battle Creek, Mich.
3M	Delaware	St. Paul, Minn.
R.J. Reynolds Tobacco Company	Delaware	Winston-Salem, N.C.
Starbucks Corporation	Washington	Seattle, Wash.
Sun Microsystems, Inc.	Delaware	Palo Alto, Calif.
The Washington Post Company	Delaware	Washington, D.C.
Whirlpool Corporation	Delaware	Benton Harbor, Mich.

Integrity, Objectivity, and Ethics in Business

NOT-FOR-PROFIT, OR NOT?

Corporations can be formed for not-for-profit purposes by making a request to the Internal Revenue Service under *Internal Revenue Code* section 501(c)3. Such corporations, such as the Sierra Club and the National Audubon Society, are exempt from federal taxes. Forming businesses inside a 501(c)3 exempt organization that competes with profit-making (and hence, tax-paying) businesses is very controversial. For example, should the local YMCA receive a tax exemption for providing similar services as the local health club business? The IRS is now challenging such businesses and is withholding 501(c)3 status to many organizations due to this issue.

3 The articles of incorporation may also restrict a corporation's activities in certain areas, such as owning certain types of real estate, conducting certain types of business activities, or purchasing its own stock.

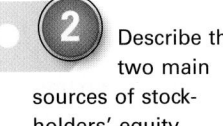

2 Describe the two main sources of stockholders' equity.

Stockholders' Equity

The owners' equity in a corporation is called **stockholders' equity**, *shareholders' equity*, *shareholders' investment*, or *capital*. In the balance sheet, stockholders' equity is reported by its two main sources.

1. Capital contributed to the corporation by the stockholders, called **paid-in capital** or *contributed capital*.
2. Net income retained in the business, called **retained earnings**.

A Stockholders' Equity section of a balance sheet is shown below.[4]

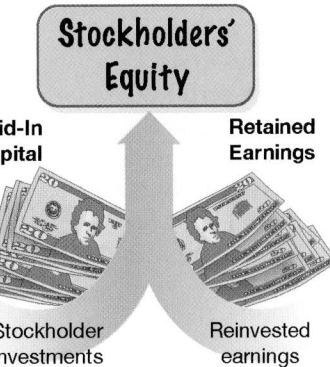

Stockholders' Equity

Pid-In pital   Retained Earnings

Stockholder nvestments   Reinvested earnings

Stockholders' Equity

Paid-in capital:		
Common stock	$330,000	
Retained earnings	80,000	
Total stockholders' equity		$410,000

The paid-in capital contributed by the stockholders is recorded in separate accounts for each class of stock. If there is only one class of stock, the account is entitled *Common Stock* or *Capital Stock*.

Retained earnings is a corporation's cumulative net income that has not been distributed as dividends. **Dividends** are distributions of a corporation's earnings to stockholders. Sometimes retained earnings that are not distributed as dividends are referred to in the financial statements as *earnings retained for use in the business* and *earnings reinvested in the business*.

Net income increases retained earnings, while a net loss and dividends decrease retained earnings. The net increase or decrease in retained earnings for a period is recorded by the following closing entries:

1. The balance of Income Summary (the net income or net loss) is transferred to Retained Earnings. For *net income*, Income Summary is debited and Retained Earnings is credited. For a *net loss*, Retained Earnings is debited and Income Summary is credited.
2. The balance of the dividends account, which is similar to the drawing account for a proprietorship, is transferred to Retained Earnings. Retained Earnings is debited and Dividends is credited for the balance of the dividends account.

Most companies generate net income. In addition, most companies do not pay out all of their net income in dividends. As a result, Retained Earnings normally has a credit balance. However, in some cases, a debit balance in Retained Earnings may occur. A debit balance in Retained Earnings is called a **deficit**. Such a balance often results from accumulated net losses. In the Stockholders' Equity section, a deficit is deducted from paid-in capital in determining total stockholders' equity.

The balance of Retained Earnings does not represent surplus cash or cash left over for dividends. This is because cash generated from operations is normally used to improve or expand operations. As cash is used, its balance decreases; however, the balance of the retained earnings account is unaffected. As a result, over time the balance in Retained Earnings becomes less and less related to the balance of Cash.

3 Describe and illustrate the characteristics of stock, classes of stock, and entries for issuing stock.

Paid-In Capital from Issuing Stock

The two main sources of stockholders' equity are paid-in capital (or contributed capital) and retained earnings. The main source of paid-in capital is from issuing stock.

4 The reporting of stockholders' equity is further discussed and illustrated later in this chapter.

Characteristics of Stock

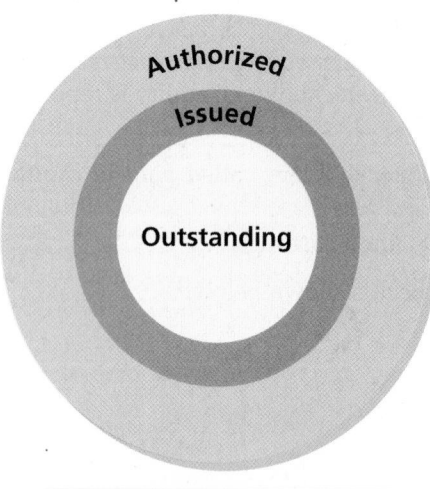

Number of shares authorized, issued, and outstanding

The number of shares of stock that a corporation is *authorized* to issue is stated in its charter. The term *issued* refers to the shares issued to the stockholders. A corporation may reacquire some of the stock that it has issued. The stock remaining in the hands of stockholders is then called **outstanding stock**. The relationship between authorized, issued, and outstanding stock is shown in the graphic at the left.

Upon request, corporations may issue stock certificates to stockholders to document their ownership. Printed on a stock certificate is the name of the company, the name of the stockholder, and the number of shares owned. The stock certificate may also indicate a dollar amount assigned to each share of stock, called **par** value. Stock may be issued without par, in which case it is called *no-par stock*. In some states, the board of directors of a corporation is required to assign a *stated value* to no-par stock.

Corporations have limited liability and, thus, creditors have no claim against stockholders' personal assets. To protect creditors, however, some states require corporations to maintain a minimum amount of paid-in capital. This minimum amount, called *legal capital,* usually includes the par or stated value of the shares issued.

The major rights that accompany ownership of a share of stock are as follows:

1. The right to vote in matters concerning the corporation.
2. The right to share in distributions of earnings.
3. The right to share in assets on liquidation.

These stock rights normally vary with the class of stock.

Some corporations have stopped issuing stock certificates except on special request. In these cases, the corporation maintains records of ownership.

Classes of Stock

When only one class of stock is issued, it is called **common stock**. Each share of common stock has equal rights.

A corporation may also issue one or more classes of stock with various preference rights such as a preference to dividends. Such a stock is called a **preferred stock**. The dividend rights of preferred stock are stated either as dollars per share or as a percent of par. For example, a $50 par value preferred stock with a $4 per share dividend may be described as either:[5]

$4 preferred stock, $50 par

or

8% preferred stock, $50 par

Because they have first rights (preference) to any dividends, preferred stockholders have a greater chance of receiving dividends than common stockholders. However, since dividends are normally based on earnings, a corporation cannot guarantee dividends even to preferred stockholders.

The payment of dividends is authorized by the corporation's board of directors. When authorized, the directors are said to have *declared* a dividend.

Cumulative preferred stock has a right to receive regular dividends that were not declared (paid) in prior years. Noncumulative preferred stock does not have this right.

Cumulative preferred stock dividends that have not been paid in prior years are said to

5 In some cases, preferred stock may receive additional dividends if certain conditions are met. Such stock, called *participating preferred stock,* is not often used.

be **in arrears**. Any preferred dividends in arrears must be paid before any common stock dividends are paid. In addition, any dividends in arrears are normally disclosed in notes to the financial statements.

To illustrate, assume that a corporation has issued the following preferred and common stock:

1,000 shares of $4 cumulative preferred stock, $50 par
4,000 shares of common stock, $15 par

The corporation was organized on January 1, 2008, and paid no dividends in 2008 and 2009. In 2010, the corporation paid dividends of $22,000. Exhibit 4 shows how the $22,000 of dividends paid in 2010 is distributed between the preferred and common stockholders.

In addition to dividend preference, preferred stock may be given preferences to assets if the corporation goes out of business and is liquidated. However, claims of creditors must be satisfied first. Preferred stockholders are next in line to receive any remaining assets, followed by the common stockholders.

Exhibit 4

Dividends to Cumulative Preferred Stock

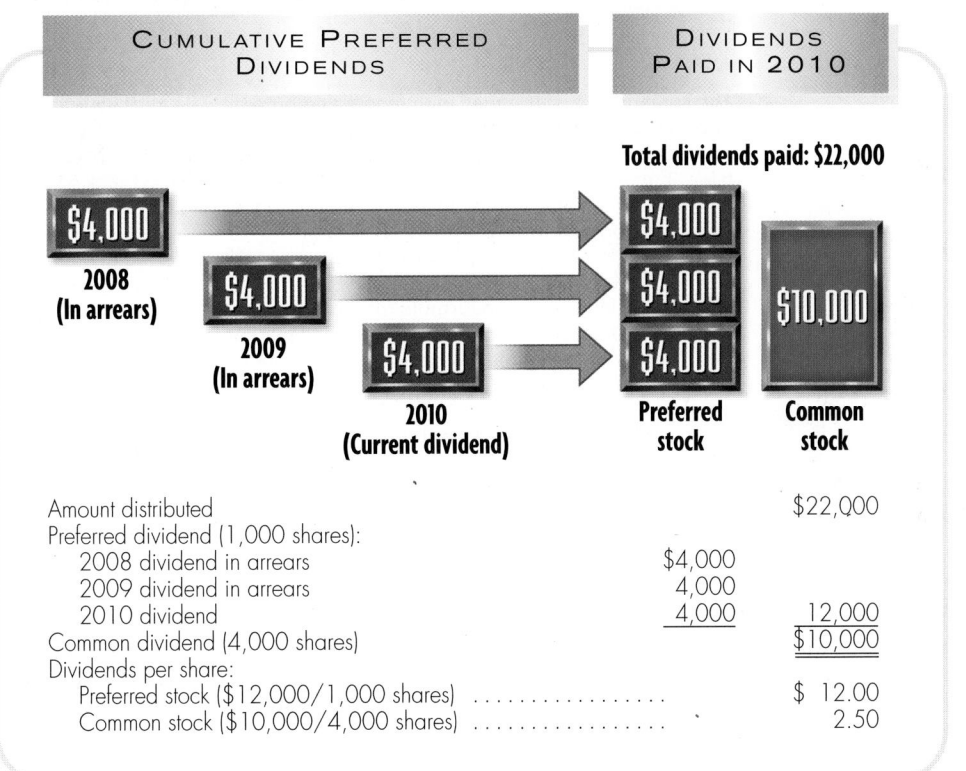

Amount distributed		$22,000
Preferred dividend (1,000 shares):		
2008 dividend in arrears	$4,000	
2009 dividend in arrears	4,000	
2010 dividend	4,000	12,000
Common dividend (4,000 shares)		$10,000
Dividends per share:		
Preferred stock ($12,000/1,000 shares)		$ 12.00
Common stock ($10,000/4,000 shares)		2.50

Issuing Stock

A separate account is used for recording the amount of each class of stock issued to investors in a corporation. For example, assume that a corporation is authorized to issue 10,000 shares of $100 par preferred stock and 100,000 shares of $20 par common stock. The corporation issued 5,000 shares of preferred stock and 50,000 shares of common stock at par for cash. The corporation's entry to record the stock issue is as follows:[6]

Cash		1,500,000	
Preferred Stock			500,000
Common Stock			1,000,000
Issued preferred stock and common stock at par for cash.			

6 The accounting for investments in stocks from the point of view of the investor is discussed in Chapter 15.

The calculation for the dividends per share can be accomplished using a spreadsheet as follows:

	A	B	C	
1	Inputs:			
2		Number of shares	Dividend per share	
3	Preferred stock	1,000	$ 4.00	
4	Common stock	4,000		
5				
6	Preferred dividends in arrears:	2008 and 2009		
7				
8	Dividend paid in 2010:	$ 22,000		
9				
10	Outputs:			
11				
12	Total amount to be distributed:		=B8 ←	a.
13	Preferred dividend:			
14	2008 dividend in arrears	=$B$3*$C$3 ←		b.
15	2009 dividend in arrears	=$B$3*$C$3		
16	2010 dividend	=$B$3*$C$3	=SUM(B14:B16) ←	c.
17	Common dividend		=C12-C16 ←	d.
18	Dividends per share			
19	Preferred stock		=C16/B3 ⎤	e.
20	Common stock		=C17/B4 ⎦	
21				

The spreadsheet is designed with inputs and outputs. The inputs are the stock and dividend information, and the output is the distribution of the dividend to the two classes of stock.

a. Enter in cell C12 the cell reference for the dividend paid in 2010, =B8.
b. Enter in cell B14 the formula for the 2008 dividend in arrears, =$B$3*$C$3. Use the dollar sign ($) to fix the cell reference. This will allow you to copy this formula from B14 to B15:B16.
c. Enter in cell C16 the formula for the sum of the preferred dividends to be distributed, =SUM(B14:B16).
d. Enter in cell C17 the formula for the remaining common dividend, =C12-C16.
e. Enter in cells C19 and 20 the dividends per share for the two classes of stock by dividing the total dividend by the number of shares. The formula from C19 can be copied to C20.

 Go to the hands-on **Excel Tutor** for this example!

 This Excel Success example uses an Excel function referred to as cell referencing. Go to the **Excel Tutor** titled **Absolute & Relative Cell References** for additional help on this useful Excel function!

Example Exercise 13-1 Dividends per Share ●●●●●●●●▶ ③

Sandpiper Company has 20,000 shares of 1% cumulative preferred stock of $100 par and 100,000 shares of $50 par common stock. The following amounts were distributed as dividends:

Year 1 $10,000
Year 2   45,000
Year 3   80,000

Determine the dividends per share for preferred and common stock for each year.

Follow My Example 13-1

	Year 1	Year 2	Year 3
Amount distributed	$10,000	$45,000	$80,000
Preferred dividend (20,000 shares)	10,000	30,000*	20,000
Common dividend (100,000 shares)	$ 0	$15,000	$60,000
*($10,000 + $20,000)			
Dividends per share:			
Preferred stock	$0.50	$1.50	$1.00
Common stock	None	$0.15	$0.60

For Practice: PE 13-1A, PE 13-1B

Stock is often issued by a corporation at a price other than its par. The price at which stock is sold depends on a variety of factors, such as the following:

1. The financial condition, earnings record, and dividend record of the corporation.
2. Investor expectations of the corporation's potential earning power.
3. General business and economic conditions and expectations.

If stock is issued (sold) for a price that is more than its par, the stock has been sold at a **premium**. For example, if common stock with a par of $50 is sold for $60 per share, the stock has sold at a premium of $10.

If stock is issued (sold) for a price that is less than its par, the stock has been sold at a **discount**. For example, if common stock with a par of $50 is sold for $45 per share, the stock has sold at a discount of $5. Many states do not permit stock to be sold at a discount. In other states, stock may be sold at a discount in only unusual cases. Since stock is rarely sold at a discount, it is not illustrated.

In order to distribute dividends, financial statements, and other reports, a corporation must keep track of its stockholders. Large public corporations normally use a financial institution, such as a bank, for this purpose.[7] In such cases, the financial institution is referred to as a *transfer agent* or *registrar*.

Premium on Stock

When stock is issued at a premium, Cash is debited for the amount received. Common Stock or Preferred Stock is credited for the par amount. The excess of the amount paid over par is part of the paid-in capital. An account entitled *Paid-In Capital in Excess of Par* is credited for this amount.

To illustrate, assume that Caldwell Company issues 2,000 shares of $50 par preferred stock for cash at $55. The entry to record this transaction is as follows:

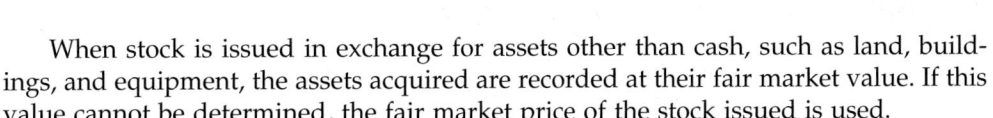

Cash	110,000	
Preferred Stock		100,000
Paid-In Capital in Excess of Par— Preferred Stock		10,000
Issued $50 par preferred stock at $55.		

The transfer agent and registrar for The Coca-Cola Company is First Chicago Trust Company of New York.

When stock is issued in exchange for assets other than cash, such as land, buildings, and equipment, the assets acquired are recorded at their fair market value. If this value cannot be determined, the fair market price of the stock issued is used.

To illustrate, assume that a corporation acquired land with a fair market value that cannot be determined. In exchange, the corporation issued 10,000 shares of its $10 par common. If the stock has a market price of $12 per share, the transaction is recorded as follows:

Land	120,000	
Common Stock		100,000
Paid-In Capital in Excess of Par		20,000
Issued $10 par common stock, valued		
at $12 per share, for land.		

7 Small corporations may use a subsidiary ledger, called a *stockholders ledger*. In this case, the stock accounts (Preferred Stock and Common Stock) are controlling accounts for the subsidiary ledger.

No-Par Stock

In most states, no-par preferred and common stock may be issued. When no-par stock is issued, Cash is debited and Common Stock is credited for the proceeds. As no-par stock is issued over time, this entry is the same even if the issuing price varies.

To illustrate, assume that on January 9 a corporation issues 10,000 shares of no-par common stock at $40 a share. On June 27, the corporation issues an additional 1,000 shares at $36. The entries to record these issuances of the no-par stock are as follows:

Jan.	9	Cash	400,000	
		Common Stock		400,000
		Issued 10,000 shares of no-par common at $40.		
June	27	Cash	36,000	
		Common Stock		36,000
		Issued 1,000 shares of no-par common at $36.		

In some states, no-par stock may be assigned a *stated value per share*. The stated value is recorded like a par value. Any excess of the proceeds over the stated value is credited to *Paid-in Capital in Excess of Stated Value*.

To illustrate, assume that in the preceding example the no-par common stock is assigned a stated value of $25. The issuance of the stock on January 9 and June 27 is recorded as follows:

Jan.	9	Cash	400,000	
		Common Stock		250,000
		Paid-In Capital in Excess of Stated Value		150,000
		Issued 10,000 shares of no-par common at $40; stated value, $25.		
June	27	Cash	36,000	
		Common Stock		25,000
		Paid-In Capital in Excess of Stated Value		11,000
		Issued 1,000 shares of no-par common at $36; stated value, $25.		

Example Exercise 13-2   Entries for Issuing Stock   •••••••> 3

On March 6, Limerick Corporation issued for cash 15,000 shares of no-par common stock at $30. On April 13, Limerick issued at par 1,000 shares of 4%, $40 par preferred stock for cash. On May 19, Limerick issued for cash 15,000 shares of 4%, $40 par preferred stock at $42.

Journalize the entries to record the March 6, April 13, and May 19 transactions.

(continued)

Follow My Example 13-2

Mar. 6	Cash	450,000	
	Common Stock		450,000
	(15,000 shares × $30).		
Apr. 13	Cash	40,000	
	Preferred Stock		40,000
	(1,000 shares × $40).		
May 19	Cash	630,000	
	Preferred Stock		600,000
	Paid-In Capital in Excess of Par		30,000
	(15,000 shares × $42).		

For Practice: PE 13-2A, PE 13-2B

Accounting for Dividends

4 Describe and illustrate the accounting for cash dividends and stock dividends.

When a board of directors declares a cash dividend, it authorizes the distribution of cash to stockholders. When a board of directors declares a stock dividend, it authorizes the distribution of its stock. In both cases, declaring a dividend reduces the retained earnings of the corporation.[8]

Cash Dividends

A cash distribution of earnings by a corporation to its shareholders is a **cash dividend**. Although dividends may be paid in other assets, cash dividends are the most common.

Three conditions for a cash dividend are as follows:

1. Sufficient retained earnings
2. Sufficient cash
3. Formal action by the board of directors

Date of Declaration	Date of Record	Date of Payment
October 1	November 10	December 2
Board of Directors takes action to declare dividends.	Owners of the shares on this date receive dividends.	Dividend is paid.
ENTRY	**NO ENTRY**	**ENTRY**

Oct. 1	Cash Dividends	42,500	
	Dividends Payable		42,500
Nov. 10	No entry		
Dec. 2	Dividends Payable	42,500	
	Cash		42,500

There must be a sufficient (large enough) balance in Retained Earnings to declare a cash dividend. That is, the balance of Retained Earnings must be large enough so that the dividend does not create a debit balance in the retained earnings account. However, a large Retained Earnings balance does not mean that there is cash available to pay dividends. This is because the balances of Cash and Retained Earnings are often unrelated.

Even if there are sufficient retained earnings and cash, a corporation's board of directors is not required to pay dividends. Nevertheless, many corporations pay quarterly cash dividends to make their stock more attractive to investors. *Special* or *extra* dividends may also be paid when a corporation experiences higher than normal profits.

Three dates included in a dividend announcement are as follows:

1. Date of declaration
2. Date of record
3. Date of payment

The *date of declaration* is the date the board of directors formally authorizes the payment of the dividend. On this date, the corporation incurs the liability to pay the amount of the dividend.

The *date of record* is the date the corporation uses to determine which stockholders will receive the dividend. During the period of time between the date of declaration and the date of record, the stock price is quoted as

[8] In rare cases, when a corporation is reducing its operations or going out of business, a dividend may be a distribution of paid-in capital. Such a dividend is called a *liquidating dividend*.

selling *with-dividends.* This means that any investors purchasing the stock before the date of record will receive the dividend.

The *date of payment* is the date the corporation will pay the dividend to the stockholders who owned the stock on the date of record. During the period of time between the record date and the payment date, the stock price is quoted as selling *ex-dividends.* This means that since the date of record has passed, any new investors will not receive the dividend.

To illustrate, assume that on October 1 Hiber Corporation declares the cash dividends shown below with a date of record of November 10 and a date of payment of December 2.

The Campbell Soup Company declared on March 27 a quarterly cash dividend of $0.22 to common stockholders of record as of the close of business on April 17, payable on April 28.

	Dividend per Share	Total Dividends
Preferred stock, $100 par, 5,000 shares outstanding	$2.50	$12,500
Common stock, $10 par, 100,000 shares outstanding	$0.30	30,000
Total		$42,500

On October 1, the declaration date, Hiber Corporation records the following entry:

Oct.	1	Cash Dividends	42,500	
		Cash Dividends Payable		42,500
		Declared cash dividends.		

On November 10, the date of record, no entry is necessary. This date merely determines which stockholders will receive the dividends.

On December 2, the date of payment, Hiber Corporation records the payment of the dividends as follows:

Dec.	2	Cash Dividends Payable	42,500	
		Cash		42,500
		Paid cash dividends.		

At the end of the accounting period, the balance in Cash Dividends will be transferred to Retained Earnings as part of the closing process. This closing entry debits Retained Earnings and credits Cash Dividends for the balance of the cash dividends account. If the cash dividends have not been paid by the end of the period, Cash Dividends Payable will be reported on the balance sheet as a current liability.

Example Exercise 13-3   Entries for Cash Dividends   • • • • • • • ▶ ④

The important dates in connection with a cash dividend of $75,000 on a corporation's common stock are February 26, March 30, and April 2. Journalize the entries required on each date.

Follow My Example 13-3

Feb. 26	Cash Dividends	75,000	
	Cash Dividends Payable		75,000
Mar. 30	No entry required.		
Apr. 2	Cash Dividends Payable	75,000	
	Cash		75,000

For Practice: PE 13-3A, PE 13-3B

Stock Dividends

A **stock dividend** is a distribution of shares of stock to stockholders. Stock dividends are normally declared only on common stock and issued to common stockholders.

The recording of a stock dividend affects only stockholders' equity. Specifically, the amount of the stock dividend is transferred from Retained Earnings to Paid-in Capital. The amount transferred is normally the fair value (market price) of the shares issued in the stock dividend.[9]

To illustrate, assume that the stockholders' equity accounts of Hendrix Corporation as of December 15 are as follows:

Common Stock, $20 par (2,000,000 shares issued)	$40,000,000
Paid-In Capital in Excess of Par—Common Stock	9,000,000
Retained Earnings	26,600,000

On December 15, Hendrix Corporation declares a stock dividend of 5% or 100,000 shares (2,000,000 shares × 5%) to be issued on January 10 to stockholders of record on December 31. The market price of the stock on December 15 (the date of declaration) is $31 per share.

The entry to record the stock dividend is as follows:

Dec.	15	Stock Dividends	3,100,000	
		Stock Dividends Distributable		2,000,000
		Paid-In Capital in Excess of Par—Common Stock		1,100,000
		Declared 5% (100,000 share) stock		
		dividend on $20 par common stock		
		with a market price of $31 per share.		

After the preceding entry is recorded, Stock Dividends will have a debit balance of $3,100,000. Like cash dividends, the stock dividends account is closed to Retained Earnings at the end of the accounting period. This closing entry debits Retained Earnings and credits Stock Dividends.

At the end of the period, the *stock dividends distributable* and *paid-in capital in excess of par—common stock* accounts are reported in the Paid-in Capital section of the balance sheet. Thus, the effect of the preceding stock dividend is to transfer $3,100,000 of retained earnings to paid-in capital.

On January 10, the stock dividend is distributed to stockholders by issuing 100,000 shares of common stock. The issuance of the stock is recorded by the following entry:

Jan.	10	Stock Dividends Distributable	2,000,000	
		Common Stock		2,000,000
		Issued stock as stock dividend.		

A stock dividend does not change the assets, liabilities, or total stockholders' equity of a corporation. Likewise, a stock dividend does not change an individual stockholder's proportionate interest (equity) in the corporation.

---

9 The use of fair market value is justified as long as the number of shares issued for the stock dividend is small (less than 25% of the shares outstanding).

To illustrate, assume a stockholder owns 1,000 of a corporation's 10,000 shares outstanding. If the corporation declares a 6% stock dividend, the stockholder's proportionate interest will not change, as shown below.

	Before Stock Dividend	After Stock Dividend
Total shares issued	10,000	10,600 [10,000 + (10,000 × 6%)]
Number of shares owned	1,000	1,060 [1,000 + (1,000 × 6%)]
Proportionate ownership	10% (1,000/10,000)	10% (1,060/10,600)

Example Exercise 13-4   Entries for Stock Dividends

Vienna Highlights Corporation has 150,000 shares of $100 par common stock outstanding. On June 14, Vienna Highlights declared a 4% stock dividend to be issued August 15 to stockholders of record on July 1. The market price of the stock was $110 per share on June 14.
    Journalize the entries required on June 14, July 1, and August 15.

Follow My Example 13-4

June 14	Stock Dividends (150,000 × 4% × $110)	660,000	
	Stock Dividends Distributable (6,000 × $100)		600,000
	Paid-In Capital in Excess of Par—Common Stock		
	($660,000 − $600,000)		60,000
July 1	No entry required.		
Aug. 15	Stock Dividends Distributable	600,000	
	Common Stock		600,000

For Practice: PE 13-4A, PE 13-4B

Treasury Stock Transactions

The 2007 edition of *Accounting Trends & Techniques* indicated that over 66% of the companies surveyed reported treasury stock.

⑤ Describe and illustrate the accounting for treasury stock transactions.

Treasury stock is stock that a corporation has issued and then reacquired. A corporation may reacquire (purchase) its own stock for a variety of reasons including the following:

1. To provide shares for resale to employees
2. To reissue as bonuses to employees, or
3. To support the market price of the stock

The *cost method* is normally used for recording the purchase and resale of treasury stock.[10] Using the cost method, *Treasury Stock* is debited for the cost (purchase price) of the stock. When the stock is resold, Treasury Stock is credited for its cost. Any difference between the cost and the selling price is debited or credited to *Paid-In Capital from Sale of Treasury Stock*.

To illustrate, assume that a corporation has the following paid-in capital on January 1:

Common stock, $25 par (20,000 shares authorized and issued)	$500,000
Excess of issue price over par	150,000
	$650,000

On February 13, the corporation purchases 1,000 shares of its common stock at $45 per share. The entry to record the purchase of the treasury stock is as follows:

Feb.	13	Treasury Stock	45,000	
		Cash		45,000
		Purchased 1,000 shares of treasury stock at $45.		

10 Another method that is infrequently used, called the *par value method*, is discussed in advanced accounting texts.

On April 29, the corporation sells 600 shares of the treasury stock for $60. The entry to record the sale is as follows:

Apr.	29	Cash	36,000	
		Treasury Stock		27,000
		Paid-In Capital from Sale of Treasury Stock		9,000
		Sold 600 shares of treasury stock at $60.		

A sale of treasury stock may result in a decrease in paid-in capital. To the extent that Paid-In Capital from Sale of Treasury Stock has a credit balance, it is debited for any such decrease. Any remaining decrease is then debited to the retained earnings account.

To illustrate, assume that on October 4, the corporation sells the remaining 400 shares of treasury stock for $40 per share. The entry to record the sale is as follows:

Oct.	4	Cash	16,000	
		Paid-In Capital from Sale of Treasury Stock	2,000	
		Treasury Stock		18,000
		Sold 400 shares of treasury stock at $40.		

The October 4 entry shown above decreases paid-in capital by $2,000. Since Paid-In Capital from Sale of Treasury Stock has a credit balance of $9,000, the entire $2,000 was debited to Paid-In Capital from Sale of Treasury Stock.

No dividends (cash or stock) are paid on the shares of treasury stock. To do so would result in the corporation earning dividend revenue from itself.

Example Exercise 13-5   Entries for Treasury Stock   •••••••> 5

On May 3, Buzz Off Corporation reacquired 3,200 shares of its common stock at $42 per share. On July 22, Buzz Off sold 2,000 of the reacquired shares at $47 per share. On August 30, Buzz Off sold the remaining shares at $40 per share.
 Journalize the transactions of May 3, July 22, and August 30.

Follow My Example 13-5

May 3	Treasury Stock (3,200 × $42)	134,400	
	Cash		134,400
July 22	Cash (2,000 × $47)	94,000	
	Treasury Stock (2,000 × $42)		84,000
	Paid-In Capital from Sale of Treasury Stock		
	[2,000 × ($47 − $42)]		10,000
Aug. 30	Cash (1,200 × $40)	48,000	
	Paid-In Capital from Sale of Treasury Stock [1,200 × ($42 − $40)]	2,400	
	Treasury Stock (1,200 × $42)		50,400

For Practice: PE 13-5A, PE 13-5B

6 Describe and illustrate the reporting of stockholders' equity.

Reporting Stockholders' Equity

As with other sections of the balance sheet, alternative terms and formats may be used in reporting stockholders' equity. Also, changes in retained earnings and paid-in capital may be reported in separate statements or notes to the financial statements.

Stockholders' Equity in the Balance Sheet

Exhibit 5 shows two methods for reporting stockholders' equity for the December 31, 2010, balance sheet for Telex Inc.

Method 1. Each class of stock is reported, followed by its related paid-in capital accounts. Retained earnings is then reported followed by a deduction for treasury stock.

Method 2. The stock accounts are reported, followed by the paid-in capital reported as a single item, Additional paid-in capital. Retained earnings is then reported followed by a deduction for treasury stock.

Exhibit 5

Stockholders' Equity Section of a Balance Sheet

**Telex Inc.
Balance Sheet
December 31, 2010**

Method 1

Stockholders' Equity

Paid-in capital:			
Preferred 10% stock, $50 par (2,000 shares authorized and issued)	$100,000		
Excess of issue price over par	10,000	$ 110,000	
Common stock, $20 par (50,000 shares authorized, 45,000 shares issued)	$900,000		
Excess of issue price over par	190,000	1,090,000	
From sale of treasury stock		2,000	
Total paid-in capital			$1,202,000
Retained earnings			350,000
Total			$1,552,000
Deduct treasury stock (600 shares at cost)			27,000
Total stockholders' equity			$1,525,000

**Telex Inc.
Balance Sheet
December 31, 2010**

Method 2

Stockholders' Equity

Contributed capital:		
Preferred 10% stock, $50 par (2,000 shares authorized and issued)	$100,000	
Common stock, $20 par (50,000 shares authorized, 45,000 shares issued)	900,000	
Additional paid-in capital	202,000	
Total contributed capital		$1,202,000
Retained earnings		350,000
Total		$1,552,000
Deduct treasury stock (600 shares at cost)		27,000
Total stockholders' equity		$1,525,000

Significant changes in stockholders' equity during a period may also be presented in a statement of stockholders' equity or in the notes to the financial statements. The statement of stockholders' equity is illustrated later in this section.

Relevant rights and privileges of the various classes of stock outstanding should also be reported.[11] Examples include dividend and liquidation preferences, conversion rights, and redemption rights. Such information may be disclosed on the face of the balance sheet or in the notes to the financial statements.

Example Exercise 13-6   Reporting Stockholders' Equity • • • • • • • •▶ **6**

Using the following accounts and balances, prepare the Stockholders' Equity section of the balance sheet. Forty thousand shares of common stock are authorized, and 5,000 shares have been reacquired.

Common Stock, $50 par	$1,500,000	Retained Earnings	$4,395,000
Paid-In Capital in Excess of Par	160,000	Treasury Stock	120,000
Paid-In Capital from Sale of Treasury Stock	44,000		

Follow My Example 13-6

Stockholders' Equity

Paid-in capital:		
Common stock, $50 par		
(40,000 shares authorized, 30,000 shares issued)	$1,500,000	
Excess of issue price over par	160,000	$1,660,000
From sale of treasury stock		44,000
Total paid-in capital		$1,704,000
Retained earnings		4,395,000
Total.		$6,099,000
Deduct treasury stock (5,000 shares at cost).		120,000
Total stockholders' equity		$5,979,000

For Practice: PE 13-6A, PE 13-6B

Reporting Retained Earnings

Changes in retained earnings may be reported using one of the following:

1. Separate retained earnings statement
2. Combined income and retained earnings statement
3. Statement of stockholders' equity

Changes in retained earnings may be reported in a separate retained earnings statement. When a separate **retained earnings statement** is prepared, the beginning balance of retained earnings is reported. The net income is then added (or net loss is subtracted) and any dividends are subtracted to arrive at the ending retained earnings for the period. To illustrate, a retained earnings statement for Telex Inc. is shown in Exhibit 6.

Exhibit 6

Retained Earnings Statement

Telex Inc.
Retained Earnings Statement
For the Year Ended December 31, 2010

Retained earnings, January 1, 2010			$245,000
Net income		$180,000	
Less dividends:			
Preferred stock	$10,000		
Common stock	65,000	75,000	
Increase in retained earnings			105,000
Retained earnings, December 31, 2010			$350,000

---

11 *Statement of Financial Accounting Standards No. 129*, "Disclosure Information about Capital Structure" (Financial Accounting Standards Board, Norwalk, CT: 1997).

Changes in retained earnings may also be reported in combination with the income statement. This format emphasizes net income as the connecting link between the income statement and ending retained earnings. Since this format is not often used, we do not illustrate it.

Changes in retained earnings may also be reported in a statement of stockholders' equity. An example of reporting changes in retained earnings in a statement of stockholders' equity for Telex Inc. is shown in Exhibit 7.

Exhibit 7

Statement of Stockholders' Equity

	Telex Inc. Statement of Stockholders' Equity For the Year Ended December 31, 2010					
	Preferred Stock	Common Stock	Additional Paid-In Capital	Retained Earnings	Treasury Stock	Total
Balance, January 1, 2010	$100,000	$850,000	$177,000	$245,000	$ (17,000)	$1,355,000
Net income				180,000		180,000
Dividends on preferred stock				(10,000)		(10,000)
Dividends on common stock				(65,000)		(65,000)
Issuance of additional common stock..		50,000	25,000			75,000
Purchase of treasury stock					(10,000)	(10,000)
Balance, December 31, 2010	$100,000	$900,000	$202,000	$350,000	$ (27,000)	$1,525,000

The 2007 edition of *Accounting Trends & Techniques* indicated that 0.5% of the companies surveyed presented a separate statement of retained earnings, 0.5% presented a combined income and retained earnings statement, and 1% presented changes in retained earnings in the notes to the financial statements. The other 98% of the companies presented changes in retained earnings in a statement of stockholders' equity.

Restrictions The use of retained earnings for payment of dividends may be restricted by action of a corporation's board of directors. Such **restrictions,** sometimes called *appropriations,* remain part of the retained earnings.

Restrictions of retained earnings are classified as:

1. *Legal.* State laws may require a restriction of retained earnings.

   Example: States may restrict retained earnings by the amount of treasury stock purchased. In this way, legal capital cannot be used for dividends.

2. *Contractual.* A corporation may enter into contracts that require restrictions of retained earnings.

   Example: A bank loan may restrict retained earnings so that money for repaying the loan cannot be used for dividends.

3. *Discretionary.* A corporation's board of directors may restrict retained earnings voluntarily.

   Example: The board may restrict retained earnings and, thus, limit dividend distributions so that more money is available for expanding the business.

Restrictions of retained earnings must be disclosed in the financial statements. Such disclosures are usually included in the notes to the financial statements.

Example Exercise 13-7 Retained Earnings Statement

Dry Creek Cameras Inc. reported the following results for the year ending March 31, 2010:

Retained earnings, April 1, 2009	$3,338,500
Net income	461,500
Cash dividends declared	80,000
Stock dividends declared	120,000

Prepare a retained earnings statement for the fiscal year ended March 31, 2010.

(continued)

Follow My Example 13-7

DRY CREEK CAMERAS INC.
RETAINED EARNINGS STATEMENT
For the Year Ended March 31, 2010

Retained earnings, April 1, 2009		$3,338,500
Net income	$461,500	
Less dividends declared	200,000	
Increase in retained earnings		261,500
Retained earnings, March 31, 2010		$3,600,000

For Practice: PE 13-7A, PE 13-7B

Prior Period Adjustments An error may arise from a mathematical mistake or from a mistake in applying accounting principles. Such errors may not be discovered within the same period in which they occur. In such cases, the effect of the error should not affect the current period's net income. Instead, the correction of the error, called a **prior period adjustment**, is reported in the retained earnings statement. Such corrections are reported as an adjustment to the beginning balance of retained earnings.[12]

Statement of Stockholders' Equity

When the only change in stockholders' equity is due to net income or net loss and dividends, a retained earnings statement is sufficient. However, when a corporation also has changes in stock and paid-in capital accounts, a **statement of stockholders' equity** is normally prepared.

A statement of stockholders' equity is normally prepared in a columnar format. Each column is a major stockholders' equity classification. Changes in each classification are then described in the left-hand column. Exhibit 7 illustrates a statement of stockholders' equity for Telex Inc.

Reporting Stockholders' Equity for Mornin' Joe

Mornin' Joe reports stockholders' equity in its balance sheet. Mornin' Joe also includes a retained earnings statement and statement of stockholders' equity in its financial statements.

The Stockholders' Equity section of Mornin' Joe's balance sheet as of December 31, 2010, is shown below.

Mornin' Joe
Balance Sheet
December 31, 2010

Stockholders' Equity

Paid-in capital:		
Preferred 10% stock, $50 par (6,000 shares authorized and issued)	$ 300,000	
Excess of issue price over par	50,000	$ 350,000
Common stock, $20 par (50,000 shares authorized, 45,000 shares issued)	$ 900,000	
Excess of issue price over par	1,450,000	2,350,000
Total paid-in capital		$2,700,000
Retained earnings		1,200,300
Total		$3,900,300
Deduct treasury stock (1,000 shares at cost)		46,000
Total stockholders' equity		$3,854,300
Total liabilities and stockholders' equity		$6,169,700

12 Prior period adjustments are illustrated in advanced texts.

Mornin' Joe's retained earnings statement for the year ended December 31, 2010, is as follows:

Mornin' Joe Retained Earnings Statment For the Year Ended December 31, 2010			
Retained earnings, January 1, 2010			$ 852,700
Net income		$421,600	
Less dividends:			
Preferred stock	$30,000		
Common stock	44,000	74,000	
Increase in retained earnings			347,600
Retained earnings, December 31, 2010			$1,200,300

The statement of stockholders' equity for Mornin' Joe is shown below.

Mornin' Joe Statement of Stockholders' Equity For the Year Ended December 31, 2010						
	Preferred Stock	Common Stock	Additional Paid-In Capital	Retained Earnings	Treasury Stock	Total
Balance, January 1, 2010	$300,000	$800,000	$1,325,000	$852,700	$ (36,000)	$3,241,700
Net income				421,600		421,600
Dividends on preferred stock				(30,000)		(30,000)
Dividends on common stock				(44,000)		(44,000)
Issuance of additional common stock		100,000	175,000			275,000
Purchase of treasury stock					(10,000)	(10,000)
Balance, December 31, 2010	$300,000	$900,000	$1,500,000	$1,200,300	$ (46,000)	$3,854,300

Stock Splits

7 Describe the effect of stock splits on corporate financial statements.

When Nature's Sunshine Products, Inc., declared a 2-for-1 stock split, the company president said:

We believe the split will place our stock price in a range attractive to both individual and institutional investors, broadening the market for the stock.

A **stock split** is a process by which a corporation reduces the par or stated value of its common stock and issues a proportionate number of additional shares. A stock split applies to all common shares including the unissued, issued, and treasury shares.

A major objective of a stock split is to reduce the market price per share of the stock. This, in turn, attracts more investors to the stock and broadens the types and numbers of stockholders.

To illustrate, assume that Rojek Corporation has 10,000 shares of $100

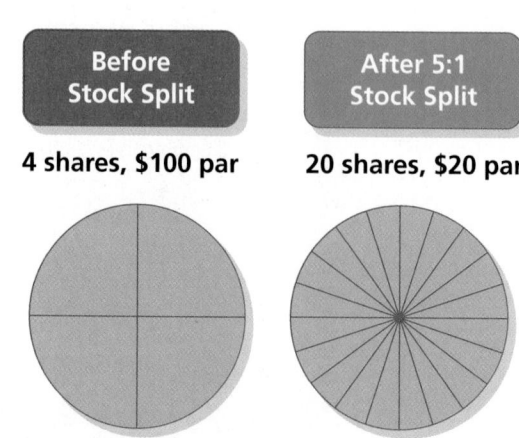

Before Stock Split — 4 shares, $100 par — $400 total par value

After 5:1 Stock Split — 20 shares, $20 par — $400 total par value

par common stock outstanding with a current market price of $150 per share. The board of directors declares the following stock split:

1. Each common shareholder will receive 5 shares for each share held. This is called a 5-for-l stock split. As a result, 50,000 shares (10,000 shares × 5) will be outstanding.
2. The par of each share of common stock will be reduced to $20 ($100/5).

The par value of the common stock outstanding is $1,000,000 both before and after the stock split as shown below.

	Before Split	After Split
Number of shares	10,000	50,000
Par value per share	× $100	× $20
Total	$1,000,000	$1,000,000

In addition, each Rojek Corporation shareholder owns the same total par amount of stock before and after the stock split. For example, a stockholder who owned 4 shares of $100 par stock before the split (total par of $400) would own 20 shares of $20 par stock after the split (total par of $400). Only the number of shares and the par value per share have changed.

Since there are more shares outstanding after the stock split, the market price of the stock should decrease. For example, in the preceding example, there would be 5 times as many shares outstanding after the split. Thus, the market price of the stock would be expected to fall from $150 to about $30 ($150/5).

Stock splits do not require a journal entry since only the par (or stated) value and number of shares outstanding have changed. However, the details of stock splits are normally disclosed in the notes to the financial statements.

Financial Analysis and Interpretation

The amount of net income is often used by investors and creditors in evaluating a company's profitability. However, net income by itself is difficult to use in comparing companies of different sizes. Also, trends in net income may be difficult to evaluate if there have been significant changes in a company's stockholders' equity. Thus, the profitability of companies is often expressed as earnings per share. **Earnings per common share (EPS)**, sometimes called *basic earnings per share,* is the net income per share of common stock outstanding during a period. Corporations whose stock is traded in a public market must report earnings per common share on their income statements.

The earnings per share is calculated as follows:

Earnings per Share

$$= \frac{\text{Net Income} - \text{Preferred Dividends}}{\text{Number of Common Shares Outstanding}}$$

If a company has preferred stock outstanding, the net income must be reduced by the amount of any preferred dividends since the numerator represents only those earnings available to the common shareholders. When the number of common shares outstanding has changed during the period, a weighted average number of shares outstanding is used in the denominator.

Earnings per share can be used to compare two companies with different net incomes. For example, the following data are available for a recent year for Blockbuster

Inc. and Netflix, Inc., which are two companies in the video rental business:

	Blockbuster Inc. (in millions)	Netflix, Inc. (in millions)
Net income	$54.7	$49.1
Preferred dividends	$11.3	$ 0.0
Number of common shares outstanding	187.1	62.6

The earnings per share for both companies can be calculated as follows:

Blockbuster Inc: $\dfrac{\$54.7 - \$11.3}{187.1 \text{ common shares outstanding}}$

$= \$0.23$ per common share

Netflix, Inc.: $\dfrac{\$49.1}{62.6 \text{ common shares outstanding}}$

$= \$0.78$ per common share

Thus, while the net income of Blockbuster exceeds that of Netflix, the earnings per share of Netflix is more than three times as great as Blockbuster. This results from Blockbuster's preferred dividends and Netflix's much fewer shares outstanding. Not surprisingly, the stock price of Netflix ($21.60) is greater than Blockbuster's ($3.25), reflecting the superior earnings per share performance.

f·a·i

1 Describe the nature of the corporate form of organization.

Key Points	Key Learning Outcomes	Example Exercises	Practice Exercises
Corporations have a separate legal existence, transferable units of stock, unlimited life, and limited stockholders' liability. The advantages and disadvantages of the corporate form are summarized in Exhibit 2. Costs incurred in organizing a corporation are debited to Organizational Expenses.	• Describe the characteristics of corporations. • List the advantages and disadvantages of the corporate form. • Prepare a journal entry for the costs of organizing a corporation.		

2 Describe the two main sources of stockholders' equity.

Key Points	Key Learning Outcomes	Example Exercises	Practice Exercises
The two main sources of stockholders' equity are (1) capital contributed by the stockholders and others, called *paid-in capital*, and (2) net income retained in the business, called *retained earnings*. Stockholders' equity is reported in a corporation balance sheet according to these two sources.	• Describe what is meant by paid-in capital. • Describe what is meant by net income retained in the business. • Prepare a simple Stockholders' Equity section of the balance sheet.		

3 Describe and illustrate the characteristics of stock, classes of stock, and entries for issuing stock.

Key Points	Key Learning Outcomes	Example Exercises	Practice Exercises
The main source of paid-in capital is from issuing common and preferred stock. Stock issued at par is recorded by debiting Cash and crediting the class of stock issued for its par amount. Stock issued for more than par is recorded by debiting Cash, crediting the class of stock for its par, and crediting Paid-In Capital in Excess of Par for the difference. When stock is issued in exchange for assets other than cash, the assets acquired are recorded at their fair market value. When no-par stock is issued, the entire proceeds are credited to the stock account. No-par stock may be assigned a stated value per share, and the excess of the proceeds over the stated value may be credited to Paid-In Capital in Excess of Stated Value.	• Describe the characteristics of common and preferred stock including rights to dividends.	13-1	13-1A, 13-1B
	• Journalize the entry for common and preferred stock issued at par.	13-2	13-2A, 13-2B
	• Journalize the entry for common and preferred stock issued at more than par.	13-2	13-2A, 13-2B
	• Journalize the entry for issuing no-par stock.	13-2	13-2A, 13-2B

4   Describe and illustrate the accounting for cash dividends and stock dividends.

Key Points	Key Learning Outcomes	Example Exercises	Practice Exercises
The entry to record a declaration of cash dividends debits Dividends and credits Dividends Payable. When a stock dividend is declared, Stock Dividends is debited for the fair value of the stock to be issued. Stock Dividends Distributable is credited for the par or stated value of the common stock to be issued. The difference between the fair value of the stock and its par or stated value is credited to Paid-In Capital in Excess of Par—Common Stock. When the stock is issued on the date of payment, Stock Dividends Distributable is debited and Common Stock is credited for the par or stated value of the stock issued.	• Journalize the entries for the declaration and payment of cash dividends.	13-3	13-3A, 13-3B
	• Journalize the entries for the declaration and payment of stock dividends.	13-4	13-4A, 13-4B

5   Describe and illustrate the accounting for treasury stock transactions.

Key Points	Key Learning Outcomes	Example Exercises	Practice Exercises
When a corporation buys its own stock, the cost method of accounting is normally used. Treasury Stock is debited for its cost, and Cash is credited. If the stock is resold, Treasury Stock is credited for its cost and any difference between the cost and the selling price is normally debited or credited to Paid-In Capital from Sale of Treasury Stock.	• Define *treasury stock*. • Describe the accounting for treasury stock. • Journalize entries for the purchase and sale of treasury stock.	13-5	13-5A, 13-5B

6   Describe and illustrate the reporting of stockholders' equity.

Key Points	Key Learning Outcomes	Example Exercises	Practice Exercises
Two alternatives for reporting stockholders' equity are shown in Exhibit 5. Changes in retained earnings are reported in a retained earnings statement, as shown in Exhibit 6. Restrictions to retained earnings should be disclosed. Any prior period adjustments are reported in the retained earnings statement. Changes in stockholders' equity may be reported on a statement of stockholders' equity, as shown in Exhibit 7.	• Prepare the Stockholders' Equity section of the balance sheet.	13-6	13-6A, 13-6B
	• Prepare a retained earnings statement.	13-7	13-7A, 13-7B
	• Describe retained earnings restrictions and prior period adjustments.		
	• Prepare a statement of stockholders' equity.		

7 Describe the effect of stock splits on corporate financial statements.

Key Points	Key Learning Outcomes	Example Exercises	Practice Exercises
When a corporation reduces the par or stated value of its common stock and issues a proportionate number of additional shares, a stock split has occurred. There are no changes in the balances of any accounts, and no entry is required for a stock split.	• Define and give an example of a stock split. • Describe the accounting for and effects of a stock split on the financial statements.		

Key Terms

cash dividend (583)
common stock (578)
cumulative preferred stock (578)
deficit (577)
discount (581)
dividends (577)
earnings per common share (EPS) (593)
in arrears (579)

outstanding stock (578)
paid-in capital (577)
par (578)
preferred stock (578)
premium (581)
prior period adjustments (591)
restrictions (590)
retained earnings (577)
retained earnings statement (589)

statement of stockholders' equity (591)
stock (574)
stock dividend (585)
stock split (592)
stockholders (574)
stockholders' equity (577)
treasury stock (586)

Illustrative Problem

Altenburg Inc. is a lighting fixture wholesaler located in Arizona. During its current fiscal year, ended December 31, 2010, Altenburg Inc. completed the following selected transactions:

Feb. 3. Purchased 2,500 shares of its own common stock at $26, recording the stock at cost. (Prior to the purchase, there were 40,000 shares of $20 par common stock outstanding.)

May 1. Declared a semiannual dividend of $1 on the 10,000 shares of preferred stock and a 30¢ dividend on the common stock to stockholders of record on May 31, payable on June 15.

June 15. Paid the cash dividends.

Sept. 23. Sold 1,000 shares of treasury stock at $28, receiving cash.

Nov. 1. Declared semiannual dividends of $1 on the preferred stock and 30¢ on the common stock. In addition, a 5% common stock dividend was declared on the common stock outstanding, to be capitalized at the fair market value of the common stock, which is estimated at $30.

Dec. 1. Paid the cash dividends and issued the certificates for the common stock dividend.

Instructions

Journalize the entries to record the transactions for Altenburg Inc.

Solution

2010				
Feb.	3	Treasury Stock	65,000	
		Cash		65,000
May	1	Cash Dividends	21,250	
		Cash Dividends Payable		21,250
		(10,000 × $1) + [(40,000 − 2,500) × $0.30].		
June	15	Cash Dividends Payable	21,250	
		Cash		21,250
Sept.	23	Cash	28,000	
		Treasury Stock		26,000
		Paid-In Capital from Sale of Treasury Stock		2,000
Nov.	1	Cash Dividends	21,550	
		Cash Dividends Payable		21,550
		(10,000 × $1) + [(40,000 − 1,500) × $0.30].		
	1	Stock Dividends	57,750*	
		Stock Dividends Distributable		38,500
		Paid-In Capital in Excess of		
		Par—Common Stock		19,250
		*(40,000 − 1,500) × 5% × $30.		
Dec.	1	Cash Dividends Payable	21,550	
		Stock Dividends Distributable	38,500	
		Cash		21,550
		Common Stock		38,500

Self-Examination Questions (Answers at End of Chapter)

1. Which of the following is a disadvantage of the corporate form of organization?
   A. Limited liability
   B. Continuous life
   C. Owner is separate from management
   D. Ability to raise capital

2. Paid-in capital for a corporation may arise from which of the following sources?
   A. Issuing preferred stock
   B. Issuing common stock
   C. Selling the corporation's treasury stock
   D. All of the above

3. The Stockholders' Equity section of the balance sheet may include:
   A. Common Stock.
   B. Stock Dividends Distributable.
   C. Preferred Stock.
   D. All of the above.

4. If a corporation reacquires its own stock, the stock is listed on the balance sheet in the:
   A. Current Assets section.
   B. Long-Term Liabilities section.
   C. Stockholders' Equity section.
   D. Investments section.

5. A corporation has issued 25,000 shares of $100 par common stock and holds 3,000 of these shares as treasury stock. If the corporation declares a $2 per share cash dividend, what amount will be recorded as cash dividends?
   A. $22,000   C. $44,000
   B. $25,000   D. $50,000

Eye Openers

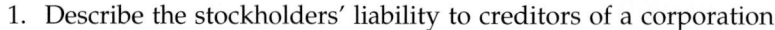

1. Describe the stockholders' liability to creditors of a corporation.
2. Why are most large businesses organized as corporations?
3. Of two corporations organized at approximately the same time and engaged in competing businesses, one issued $100 par common stock, and the other issued $0.01 par common stock. Do the par designations provide any indication as to which stock is preferable as an investment? Explain.
4. A stockbroker advises a client to "buy preferred stock. . . . With that type of stock, . . . [you] will never have to worry about losing the dividends." Is the broker right?
5. What are some of the factors that influence the market price of a corporation's stock?
6. When a corporation issues stock at a premium, is the premium income? Explain.
7. (a) What are the three conditions for the declaration and payment of a cash dividend? (b) The dates in connection with the declaration of a cash dividend are February 16, March 18, and April 17. Identify each date.
8. A corporation with both preferred stock and common stock outstanding has a substantial credit balance in its retained earnings account at the beginning of the current fiscal year. Although net income for the current year is sufficient to pay the preferred dividend of $125,000 each quarter and a common dividend of $300,000 each quarter, the board of directors declares dividends only on the preferred stock. Suggest possible reasons for passing the dividends on the common stock.
9. An owner of 500 shares of Microshop Company common stock receives a stock dividend of 5 shares. (a) What is the effect of the stock dividend on the stockholder's proportionate interest (equity) in the corporation? (b) How does the total equity of 505 shares compare with the total equity of 500 shares before the stock dividend?
10. a. Where should a declared but unpaid cash dividend be reported on the balance sheet?
    b. Where should a declared but unissued stock dividend be reported on the balance sheet?
11. a. In what respect does treasury stock differ from unissued stock?
    b. How should treasury stock be presented on the balance sheet?
12. A corporation reacquires 10,000 shares of its own $25 par common stock for $450,000, recording it at cost. (a) What effect does this transaction have on revenue or expense of the period? (b) What effect does it have on stockholders' equity?
13. The treasury stock in Eye Opener 12 is resold for $615,000. (a) What is the effect on the corporation's revenue of the period? (b) What is the effect on stockholders' equity?
14. What is the primary advantage of combining the retained earnings statement with the income statement?
15. What are the three classifications of restrictions of retained earnings, and how are such restrictions normally reported in the financial statements?
16. Indicate how prior period adjustments would be reported on the financial statements presented only for the current period.
17. When is a statement of stockholders' equity normally prepared?
18. What is the primary purpose of a stock split?

Practice Exercises

PE 13-1A
Dividends per share
obj. **3**

EE 13-1   p. 580

Taiwanese Company has 5,000 shares of 4% cumulative preferred stock of $40 par and 10,000 shares of $90 par common stock. The following amounts were distributed as dividends:

Year 1	$15,000
Year 2	5,000
Year 3	62,000

Determine the dividends per share for preferred and common stock for each year.

PE 13-1B
Dividends per share
obj. **3**

EE 13-1   p. 580

Master Craftmen Company has 10,000 shares of 2% cumulative preferred stock of $50 par and 25,000 shares of $75 par common stock. The following amounts were distributed as dividends:

Year 1	$30,000
Year 2	6,000
Year 3	80,000

Determine the dividends per share for preferred and common stock for each year.

PE 13-2A
Entries for issuing stock
obj. **3**

EE 13-2   p. 582

On July 3, Hanoi Artifacts Corporation issued for cash 450,000 shares of no-par common stock at $2.50. On September 1, Hanoi Artifacts issued 10,000 shares of 2%, $25 preferred stock at par for cash. On October 30, Hanoi Artifacts issued for cash 7,500 shares of 2%, $25 par preferred stock at $30.

Journalize the entries to record the July 3, September 1, and October 30 transactions.

PE 13-2B
Entries for issuing stock
obj. **3**

EE 13-2   p. 582

On February 13, Elman Corporation issued for cash 75,000 shares of no-par common stock (with a stated value of $125) at $140. On September 9, Elman issued 15,000 shares of 1%, $60 preferred stock at par for cash. On November 23, Elman issued for cash 8,000 shares of 1%, $60 par preferred stock at $70.

Journalize the entries to record the February 13, September 9, and November 23 transactions.

PE 13-3A
Entries for cash dividends
obj. **4**

EE 13-3   p. 584

The important dates in connection with a cash dividend of $112,750 on a corporation's common stock are October 6, November 5, and December 5. Journalize the entries required on each date.

PE 13-3B
Entries for cash dividends
obj. **4**

EE 13-3   p. 584

The important dates in connection with a cash dividend of $61,500 on a corporation's common stock are July 1, August 1, and September 30. Journalize the entries required on each date.

PE 13-4A
Entries for stock dividends
obj. **4**

EE 13-4   p. 586

Self Storage Corporation has 100,000 shares of $40 par common stock outstanding. On May 10, Self Storage Corporation declared a 2% stock dividend to be issued August 1 to stockholders of record on June 9. The market price of the stock was $48 per share on May 10.

Journalize the entries required on May 10, June 9, and August 1.

PE 13-4B
Entries for stock dividends
obj. **4**

EE 13-4   p. 586

Spectrum Corporation has 600,000 shares of $75 par common stock outstanding. On February 13, Spectrum Corporation declared a 4% stock dividend to be issued April 30 to stockholders of record on March 14. The market price of the stock was $90 per share on February 13.

Journalize the entries required on February 13, March 14, and April 30.

PE 13-5A
Entries for treasury stock

obj. 5

EE 13-5   p. 587

On October 3, Valley Clothing Inc. reacquired 10,000 shares of its common stock at $9 per share. On November 15, Valley Clothing sold 6,800 of the reacquired shares at $12 per share. On December 22, Valley Clothing sold the remaining shares at $7 per share.
    Journalize the transactions of October 3, November 15, and December 22.

PE 13-5B
Entries for treasury stock

obj. 5

EE 13-5   p. 587

On February 1, Motorsports Inc. reacquired 7,500 shares of its common stock at $30 per share. On March 15, Motorsports sold 4,500 of the reacquired shares at $34 per share. On June 2, Motorsports sold the remaining shares at $28 per share.
    Journalize the transactions of February 1, March 15, and June 2.

PE 13-6A
Reporting stock-holders' equity

obj. 6

EE 13-6   p. 589

Using the following accounts and balances, prepare the Stockholders' Equity section of the balance sheet. Seventy thousand shares of common stock are authorized, and 7,500 shares have been reacquired.

Common Stock, $75 par	$4,725,000
Paid-In Capital in Excess of Par	679,000
Paid-In Capital from Sale of Treasury Stock	25,200
Retained Earnings	2,032,800
Treasury Stock	588,000

PE 13-6B
Reporting stock-holders' equity

obj. 6

EE 13-6   p. 589

Using the following accounts and balances, prepare the Stockholders' Equity section of the balance sheet. Sixty thousand shares of common stock are authorized, and 4,000 shares have been reacquired.

Common Stock, $80 par	$4,000,000
Paid-In Capital in Excess of Par	630,000
Paid-In Capital from Sale of Treasury Stock	66,000
Retained Earnings	2,220,000
Treasury Stock	360,000

PE 13-7A
Retained earnings statement

obj. 6

EE 13-7   p. 590

Hornblower Cruises Inc. reported the following results for the year ending October 31, 2010:

Retained earnings, November 1, 2009	$1,500,000
Net income	475,000
Cash dividends declared	50,000
Stock dividends declared	300,000

Prepare a retained earnings statement for the fiscal year ended October 31, 2010.

PE 13-7B
Retained earnings statement

obj. 6

EE 13-7   p. 590

Frontier Leaders Inc. reported the following results for the year ending July 31, 2010:

Retained earnings, August 1, 2009	$875,000
Net income	260,000
Cash dividends declared	20,000
Stock dividends declared	100,000

Prepare a retained earnings statement for the fiscal year ended July 31, 2010.

Exercises

EX 13-1
Dividends per share

obj. 3

✔ Preferred stock,
1st year: $2.00

Fairmount Inc., a developer of radiology equipment, has stock outstanding as follows: 15,000 shares of cumulative 2%, preferred stock of $150 par, and 50,000 shares of $5 par common. During its first four years of operations, the following amounts were distributed as dividends: first year, $30,000; second year, $42,000; third year, $90,000; fourth year, $120,000. Calculate the dividends per share on each class of stock for each of the four years.

EX 13-2
Dividends per share
obj. 3

✔ Preferred stock,
1st year: $0.15

Michelangelo Inc., a software development firm, has stock outstanding as follows: 20,000 shares of cumulative 1%, preferred stock of $25 par, and 25,000 shares of $100 par common. During its first four years of operations, the following amounts were distributed as dividends: first year, $3,000; second year, $4,000; third year, $30,000; fourth year, $80,000. Calculate the dividends per share on each class of stock for each of the four years.

EX 13-3
Entries for issuing
par stock
obj. 3

On February 10, Peerless Rocks Inc., a marble contractor, issued for cash 40,000 shares of $10 par common stock at $34, and on May 9, it issued for cash 100,000 shares of $5 par preferred stock at $7.

a. Journalize the entries for February 10 and May 9.
b. What is the total amount invested (total paid-in capital) by all stockholders as of May 9?

EX 13-4
Entries for issuing
no-par stock
obj. 3

On June 4, Magic Carpet Inc., a carpet wholesaler, issued for cash 250,000 shares of no-par common stock (with a stated value of $3) at $12, and on October 9, it issued for cash 25,000 shares of $75 par preferred stock at $80.

a. Journalize the entries for June 4 and October 9, assuming that the common stock is to be credited with the stated value.
b. What is the total amount invested (total paid-in capital) by all stockholders as of October 9?

EX 13-5
Issuing stock for
assets other than cash
obj. 3

On January 30, Lift Time Corporation, a wholesaler of hydraulic lifts, acquired land in exchange for 18,000 shares of $10 par common stock with a current market price of $15. Journalize the entry to record the transaction.

EX 13-6
Selected stock
transactions
obj. 3

Rocky Mountain Sounds Corp., an electric guitar retailer, was organized by Cathy Dewitt, Melody Leimbach, and Mario Torres. The charter authorized 250,000 shares of common stock with a par of $40. The following transactions affecting stockholders' equity were completed during the first year of operations:

a. Issued 10,000 shares of stock at par to Cathy Dewitt for cash.
b. Issued 750 shares of stock at par to Mario Torres for promotional services provided in connection with the organization of the corporation, and issued 20,000 shares of stock at par to Mario Torres for cash.
c. Purchased land and a building from Melody Leimbach. The building is mortgaged for $400,000 for 20 years at 7%, and there is accrued interest of $7,000 on the mortgage note at the time of the purchase. It is agreed that the land is to be priced at $125,000 and the building at $600,000, and that Melody Leimbach's equity will be exchanged for stock at par. The corporation agreed to assume responsibility for paying the mortgage note and the accrued interest.

Journalize the entries to record the transactions.

EX 13-7
Issuing stock
obj. 3

Cashman Nursery, with an authorization of 25,000 shares of preferred stock and 300,000 shares of common stock, completed several transactions involving its stock on July 30, the first day of operations. The trial balance at the close of the day follows:

Cash	475,000	
Land	125,000	
Buildings	200,000	
Preferred 2% Stock, $100 par		250,000
Paid-In Capital in Excess of Par—Preferred Stock		75,000
Common Stock, $40 par		300,000
Paid-In Capital in Excess of Par—Common Stock		175,000
	800,000	800,000

All shares within each class of stock were sold at the same price. The preferred stock was issued in exchange for the land and buildings.

Journalize the two entries to record the transactions summarized in the trial balance.

EX 13-8

Issuing stock

obj. 3

Newgen Products Inc., a wholesaler of office products, was organized on February 20 of the current year, with an authorization of 75,000 shares of 2% preferred stock, $50 par and 400,000 shares of $15 par common stock. The following selected transactions were completed during the first year of operations:

Feb. 20. Issued 150,000 shares of common stock at par for cash.
       26. Issued 500 shares of common stock at par to an attorney in payment of legal fees for organizing the corporation.
Mar. 6. Issued 18,000 shares of common stock in exchange for land, buildings, and equipment with fair market prices of $50,000, $275,000, and $60,000, respectively.
Apr. 30. Issued 20,000 shares of preferred stock at $60 for cash.

Journalize the transactions.

EX 13-9

Entries for cash dividends

obj. 4

The important dates in connection with a cash dividend of $69,500 on a corporation's common stock are May 3, June 17, and August 1. Journalize the entries required on each date.

EX 13-10

Entries for stock dividends

obj. 4

✔ b. (1) $12,000,000
    (3) $57,000,000

Organic Health Co. is an HMO for businesses in the Chicago area. The following account balances appear on the balance sheet of Organic Health Co.: Common stock (300,000 shares authorized), $100 par, $10,000,000; Paid-in capital in excess of par—common stock, $2,000,000; and Retained earnings, $45,000,000. The board of directors declared a 2% stock dividend when the market price of the stock was $125 a share. Organic Health Co. reported no income or loss for the current year.

a. Journalize the entries to record (1) the declaration of the dividend, capitalizing an amount equal to market value, and (2) the issuance of the stock certificates.
b. Determine the following amounts before the stock dividend was declared: (1) total paid-in capital, (2) total retained earnings, and (3) total stockholders' equity.
c. Determine the following amounts after the stock dividend was declared and closing entries were recorded at the end of the year: (1) total paid-in capital, (2) total retained earnings, and (3) total stockholders' equity.

EX 13-11

Treasury stock transactions

obj. 5

✔ b. $32,000 credit

Beaverhead Creek Inc. bottles and distributes spring water. On March 4 of the current year, Beaverhead Creek reacquired 5,000 shares of its common stock at $90 per share. On August 7, Beaverhead Creek sold 3,500 of the reacquired shares at $100 per share. The remaining 1,500 shares were sold at $88 per share on November 29.

a. Journalize the transactions of March 4, August 7, and November 29.
b. What is the balance in Paid-In Capital from Sale of Treasury Stock on December 31 of the current year?
c. ▬▬▶ For what reasons might Beaverhead Creek have purchased the treasury stock?

EX 13-12

Treasury stock transactions

objs. 5, 6

✔ b. $54,000 credit

Augusta Gardens Inc. develops and produces spraying equipment for lawn maintenance and industrial uses. On August 30 of the current year, Augusta Gardens Inc. reacquired 17,500 shares of its common stock at $42 per share. On October 31, 14,000 of the reacquired shares were sold at $45 per share, and on November 10, 2,000 of the reacquired shares were sold at $48.

a. Journalize the transactions of August 30, October 31, and November 10.
b. What is the balance in Paid-In Capital from Sale of Treasury Stock on December 31 of the current year?
c. What is the balance in Treasury Stock on December 31 of the current year?
d. How will the balance in Treasury Stock be reported on the balance sheet?

EX 13-13
Treasury stock
transactions

objs. 5, 6

✔ b. $37,000 credit

Sweet Water Inc. bottles and distributes spring water. On July 15 of the current year, Sweet Water Inc. reacquired 24,000 shares of its common stock at $60 per share. On August 10, Sweet Water Inc. sold 19,000 of the reacquired shares at $63 per share. The remaining 5,000 shares were sold at $56 per share on December 18.

a. Journalize the transactions of July 15, August 10, and December 18.
b. What is the balance in Paid-In Capital from Sale of Treasury Stock on December 31 of the current year?
c. Where will the balance in Paid-In Capital from Sale of Treasury Stock be reported on the balance sheet?
d. ━━━▶ For what reasons might Sweet Water Inc. have purchased the treasury stock?

EX 13-14
Reporting paid-in
capital

obj. 6

✔ Total paid-in
capital, $2,225,000

The following accounts and their balances were selected from the unadjusted trial balance of REO Inc., a freight forwarder, at October 31, the end of the current fiscal year:

Preferred 2% Stock, $100 par	$ 750,000
Paid-In Capital in Excess of Par—Preferred Stock	90,000
Common Stock, no par, $5 stated value	400,000
Paid-In Capital in Excess of Stated Value—Common Stock	960,000
Paid-In Capital from Sale of Treasury Stock	25,000
Retained Earnings	3,150,000

Prepare the Paid-In Capital portion of the Stockholders' Equity section of the balance sheet. There are 250,000 shares of common stock authorized and 20,000 shares of preferred stock authorized.

EX 13-15
Stockholders' Equity
section of balance
sheet

obj. 6

✔ Total stockholders'
equity, $4,350,000

The following accounts and their balances appear in the ledger of Newberry Properties Inc. on June 30 of the current year:

Common Stock, $75 par	$1,350,000
Paid-In Capital in Excess of Par	108,000
Paid-In Capital from Sale of Treasury Stock	12,000
Retained Earnings	2,950,000
Treasury Stock	70,000

Prepare the Stockholders' Equity section of the balance sheet as of June 30. Forty thousand shares of common stock are authorized, and 875 shares have been reacquired.

EX 13-16
Stockholders' Equity
section of balance
sheet

obj. 6

✔ Total stockholders'
equity, $5,985,000

Race Car Inc. retails racing products for BMWs, Porsches, and Ferraris. The following accounts and their balances appear in the ledger of Race Car Inc. on April 30, the end of the current year:

Common Stock, $10 par	$ 400,000
Paid-In Capital in Excess of Par—Common Stock	120,000
Paid-In Capital in Excess of Par—Preferred Stock	90,000
Paid-In Capital from Sale of Treasury Stock—Common	30,000
Preferred 4% Stock, $50 par	1,500,000
Retained Earnings	3,900,000
Treasury Stock—Common	55,000

Fifty thousand shares of preferred and 200,000 shares of common stock are authorized. There are 5,000 shares of common stock held as treasury stock.

Prepare the Stockholders' Equity section of the balance sheet as of April 30, the end of the current year.

EX 13-17
Retained earnings
statement

obj. 6

✔ Retained earn-
ings, January 31,
$3,375,000

Bancroft Corporation, a manufacturer of industrial pumps, reports the following results for the year ending January 31, 2010:

Retained earnings, February 1, 2009	$3,175,500
Net income	415,000
Cash dividends declared	75,500
Stock dividends declared	140,000

Prepare a retained earnings statement for the fiscal year ended January 31, 2010.

EX 13-18
Stockholders' Equity section of balance sheet

obj. **6**

✔ Corrected total stockholders' equity, $16,758,000

List the errors in the following Stockholders' Equity section of the balance sheet prepared as of the end of the current year.

Stockholders' Equity

Paid-in capital:		
Preferred 2% stock, $150 par		
(10,000 shares authorized and issued)	$1,500,000	
Excess of issue price over par	250,000	$ 1,750,000
Retained earnings		1,450,000
Treasury stock (6,000 shares at cost)		432,000
Dividends payable....................................		135,000
Total paid-in capital		$ 3,767,000
Common stock, $75 par (250,000 shares		
authorized, 180,000 shares issued)....................		14,040,000
Organizing costs		50,000
Total stockholders' equity		$17,857,000

EX 13-19
Statement of stockholders' equity

obj. **6**

✔ Total stockholders' equity, Dec. 31, $7,182,000

The stockholders' equity T accounts of For All Occasions Greeting Cards Inc. for the current fiscal year ended December 31, 2010, are as follows. Prepare a statement of stockholders' equity for the fiscal year ended December 31, 2010.

COMMON STOCK

	Jan. 1	Balance	2,000,000
	Feb. 20	Issued	
		18,000 shares	900,000
	Dec. 31	Balance	2,900,000

PAID-IN CAPITAL IN EXCESS OF PAR

	Jan. 1	Balance	320,000
	Feb. 20	Issued	
		18,000 shares	216,000
	Dec. 31	Balance	536,000

TREASURY STOCK

July 19	Purchased		
	3,000 shares	144,000	

RETAINED EARNINGS

June 30	Dividend	50,000	Jan. 1	Balance	3,480,000
Dec. 30	Dividend	50,000	Dec. 31	Closing	
				(net income)	510,000
			Dec. 31	Balance	3,890,000

EX 13-20
Effect of stock split

obj. **7**

Mia Restaurant Corporation wholesales ovens and ranges to restaurants throughout the Southwest. Mia Restaurant Corporation, which had 40,000 shares of common stock outstanding, declared a 4-for-1 stock split (3 additional shares for each share issued).

a. What will be the number of shares outstanding after the split?

b. If the common stock had a market price of $300 per share before the stock split, what would be an approximate market price per share after the split?

EX 13-21
Effect of cash
dividend and stock
split
objs. 4, 7

Indicate whether the following actions would (+) increase, (−) decrease, or (0) not affect Indigo Inc.'s total assets, liabilities, and stockholders' equity:

	Assets	Liabilities	Stockholders' Equity
(1) Declaring a cash dividend	_____	_____	_____
(2) Paying the cash dividend declared in (1)	_____	_____	_____
(3) Authorizing and issuing stock certificates in a stock split	_____	_____	_____
(4) Declaring a stock dividend	_____	_____	_____
(5) Issuing stock certificates for the stock dividend declared in (4)	_____	_____	_____

EX 13-22
Selected dividend
transactions, stock
split
objs. 4, 7

Selected transactions completed by Hartwell Boating Supply Corporation during the current fiscal year are as follows:

Feb. 3. Split the common stock 2 for 1 and reduced the par from $40 to $20 per share. After the split, there were 250,000 common shares outstanding.

Apr. 10. Declared semiannual dividends of $1.50 on 18,000 shares of preferred stock and $0.08 on the common stock to stockholders of record on May 10, payable on June 9.

June 9. Paid the cash dividends.

Oct. 10. Declared semiannual dividends of $1.50 on the preferred stock and $0.04 on the common stock (before the stock dividend). In addition, a 2% common stock dividend was declared on the common stock outstanding. The fair market value of the common stock is estimated at $36.

Dec. 9. Paid the cash dividends and issued the certificates for the common stock dividend.

Journalize the transactions.

EX 13-23
EPS

Crystal Arts, Inc., had earnings of $160,000 for 2010. The company had 20,000 shares of common stock outstanding during the year. In addition, the company issued 2,000 shares of $100 par value preferred stock on January 3, 2010. The preferred stock has a dividend of $7 per share. There were no transactions in either common or preferred stock during 2010.
Determine the basic earnings per share for Crystal Arts.

EX 13-24
EPS

Procter & Gamble (P&G) is one of the largest consumer products companies in the world, famous for such brands as Crest® and Tide®. Financial information for the company for three recent years is as follows:

	Fiscal Years Ended (in millions)		
	2007	2006	2005
Net income	$10,340	$8,684	$6,923
Preferred dividends	$161	$148	$136
Common shares outstanding	3,159	3,055	2,515

a. Determine the earnings per share for fiscal years 2007, 2006, and 2005.
b. Evaluate the growth in earnings per share for the three years in comparison to the growth in net income for the three years.

EX 13-25
EPS

Staples and OfficeMax are two companies competing in the retail office supply business. OfficeMax had a net income of $91,721,000 for a recent year, while Staples had a net income of $973,577,000. OfficeMax had preferred stock of $54,735,000 with a preferred dividend of 7.375% on that amount. Staples had no preferred stock. The outstanding common shares for each company were as follows:

	Common Shares
OfficeMax	73,142,000
Staples	720,528,000

a. Determine the earnings per share for each company.
b. Evaluate the relative profitability of the two companies.

Problem Series A

PR 13-1A
Dividends on preferred and common stock

obj. 3

✔ 1. Common dividends in 2007: $8,000

Bridger Bike Corp. manufactures mountain bikes and distributes them through retail outlets in Montana, Idaho, Oregon, and Washington. Bridger Bike Corp. has declared the following annual dividends over a six-year period ending December 31 of each year: 2005, $5,000; 2006, $18,000; 2007, $45,000; 2008, $45,000; 2009, $60,000; and 2010, $67,000. During the entire period, the outstanding stock of the company was composed of 10,000 shares of 2% cumulative preferred stock, $100 par, and 25,000 shares of common stock, $1 par.

Instructions

1. Determine the total dividends and the per-share dividends declared on each class of stock for each of the six years. There were no dividends in arrears on January 1, 2005. Summarize the data in tabular form, using the following column headings:

Year	Total Dividends	Preferred Dividends		Common Dividends	
		Total	Per Share	Total	Per Share
2005	$ 5,000				
2006	18,000				
2007	45,000				
2008	45,000				
2009	60,000				
2010	67,000				

2. Determine the average annual dividend per share for each class of stock for the six-year period.
3. Assuming a market price of $125 for the preferred stock and $8 for the common stock, calculate the average annual percentage return on initial shareholders' investment, based on the average annual dividend per share (a) for preferred stock and (b) for common stock.

PR 13-2A
Stock transaction for corporate expansion

obj. 3

Sheldon Optics produces medical lasers for use in hospitals. The accounts and their balances appear in the ledger of Sheldon Optics on October 31 of the current year as follows:

Preferred 2% Stock, $80 par (50,000 shares authorized, 25,000 shares issued)	$ 2,000,000
Paid-In Capital in Excess of Par—Preferred Stock	75,000
Common Stock, $100 par (500,000 shares authorized, 50,000 shares issued)	5,000,000
Paid-In Capital in Excess of Par—Common Stock	600,000
Retained Earnings	16,750,000

At the annual stockholders' meeting on December 7, the board of directors presented a plan for modernizing and expanding plant operations at a cost of approximately $5,300,000. The plan provided (a) that the corporation borrow $2,000,000, (b) that 15,000 shares of the unissued preferred stock be issued through an underwriter, and (c) that a building, valued at $1,850,000, and the land on which it is located, valued at $162,500, be acquired in accordance with preliminary negotiations by the issuance of 17,500 shares of common stock. The plan was approved by the stockholders and accomplished by the following transactions:

Jan. 10. Borrowed $2,000,000 from Whitefish National Bank, giving a 7% mortgage note.

21. Issued 15,000 shares of preferred stock, receiving $84.50 per share in cash.

31. Issued 17,500 shares of common stock in exchange for land and a building, according to the plan.

No other transactions occurred during January.

Instructions

Journalize the entries to record the foregoing transactions.

PR 13-3A
Selected stock transactions

objs. **3, 4, 5**

KLOOSTER
& ALLEN

✔ f. Cash dividends,
$387,050

Coil Welding Corporation sells and services pipe welding equipment in California. The following selected accounts appear in the ledger of Coil Welding Corporation on February 1, 2010, the beginning of the current fiscal year:

Preferred 2% Stock, $25 par (50,000 shares authorized,	
40,000 shares issued)	$ 1,000,000
Paid-In Capital in Excess of Par—Preferred Stock	240,000
Common Stock, $5 par (1,000,000 shares authorized,	
750,000 shares issued)	3,750,000
Paid-In Capital in Excess of Par—Common Stock	6,000,000
Retained Earnings	36,785,000

During the year, the corporation completed a number of transactions affecting the stockholders' equity. They are summarized as follows:

a. Purchased 60,000 shares of treasury common for $540,000.

b. Sold 42,000 shares of treasury common for $462,000.

c. Issued 7,500 shares of preferred 2% stock at $38.

d. Issued 120,000 shares of common stock at $15, receiving cash.

e. Sold 13,000 shares of treasury common for $110,500.

f. Declared cash dividends of $0.50 per share on preferred stock and $0.42 per share on common stock.

g. Paid the cash dividends.

Instructions

Journalize the entries to record the transactions. Identify each entry by letter.

PR 13-4A
Entries for selected corporate transactions

objs. **3, 4, 5, 6**

KLOOSTER
& ALLEN

✔ 4. Total
stockholders' equity,
$11,407,975

Krisch Enterprises Inc. produces aeronautical navigation equipment. The stockholders' equity accounts of Krisch Enterprises Inc., with balances on January 1, 2010, are as follows:

Common Stock, $20 stated value (250,000 shares authorized,	
175,000 shares issued)	$3,500,000
Paid-In Capital in Excess of Stated Value	1,750,000
Retained Earnings	4,600,000
Treasury Stock (40,000 shares, at cost)	1,000,000

The following selected transactions occurred during the year:

Jan.   6. Paid cash dividends of $0.40 per share on the common stock. The dividend had been properly recorded when declared on November 29 of the preceding fiscal year for $54,000.

Mar.   9. Sold all of the treasury stock for $1,350,000.

Apr.   3. Issued 50,000 shares of common stock for $1,700,000.

July 30. Declared a 2% stock dividend on common stock, to be capitalized at the market price of the stock, which is $36 per share.

Aug. 30. Issued the certificates for the dividend declared on July 30.

Nov.   7. Purchased 25,000 shares of treasury stock for $800,000.

Dec. 30. Declared a $0.45-per-share dividend on common stock.

31. Closed the credit balance of the income summary account, $400,000.

31. Closed the two dividends accounts to Retained Earnings.

Instructions

1. Enter the January 1 balances in T accounts for the stockholders' equity accounts listed. Also prepare T accounts for the following: Paid-In Capital from Sale of Treasury Stock; Stock Dividends Distributable; Stock Dividends; Cash Dividends.
2. Journalize the entries to record the transactions, and post to the eight selected accounts.
3. Prepare a retained earnings statement for the year ended December 31, 2010.
4. Prepare the Stockholders' Equity section of the December 31, 2010, balance sheet.

PR 13-5A
Entries for selected corporate transactions

objs. 3, 4, 5, 7

KLOOSTER & ALLEN

✔ Sept. 1, Cash dividends, $165,750

Porto Bay Corporation manufactures and distributes leisure clothing. Selected transactions completed by Porto Bay during the current fiscal year are as follows:

Jan. 10. Split the common stock 4 for 1 and reduced the par from $100 to $25 per share. After the split, there were 500,000 common shares outstanding.

Mar. 1. Declared semiannual dividends of $1.20 on 80,000 shares of preferred stock and $0.24 on the 500,000 shares of $25 par common stock to stockholders of record on March 31, payable on April 30.

Apr. 30. Paid the cash dividends.

July 9. Purchased 75,000 shares of the corporation's own common stock at $26, recording the stock at cost.

Aug. 29. Sold 40,000 shares of treasury stock at $32, receiving cash.

Sept. 1. Declared semiannual dividends of $1.20 on the preferred stock and $0.15 on the common stock (before the stock dividend). In addition, a 1% common stock dividend was declared on the common stock outstanding, to be capitalized at the fair market value of the common stock, which is estimated at $30.

Oct. 31. Paid the cash dividends and issued the certificates for the common stock dividend.

Instructions
Journalize the transactions.

Problem Series B

PR 13-1B
Dividends on preferred and common stock

obj. 3

✔ 1. Common dividends in 2007: $16,500

Lone Star Theatre Inc. owns and operates movie theaters throughout Arizona and Texas. Lone Star Theatre has declared the following annual dividends over a six-year period: 2005, $7,500; 2006, $9,000; 2007, $30,000; 2008, $30,000; 2009, $40,000; and 2010, $48,500. During the entire period ending December 31 of each year, the outstanding stock of the company was composed of 10,000 shares of cumulative, 2% preferred stock, $50 par, and 50,000 shares of common stock, $1 par.

Instructions

1. Calculate the total dividends and the per-share dividends declared on each class of stock for each of the six years. There were no dividends in arrears on January 1, 2005. Summarize the data in tabular form, using the following column headings:

Year	Total Dividends	Preferred Dividends Total	Preferred Dividends Per Share	Common Dividends Total	Common Dividends Per Share
2005	$ 7,500				
2006	9,000				
2007	30,000				
2008	30,000				
2009	40,000				
2010	48,500				

2. Calculate the average annual dividend per share for each class of stock for the six-year period.
3. Assuming a market price per share of $40 for the preferred stock and $5 for the common stock, calculate the average annual percentage return on initial shareholders' investment, based on the average annual dividend per share (a) for preferred stock and (b) for common stock.

PR 13-2B
Stock transactions for corporate expansion

obj. 3

On February 28 of the current year, the following accounts and their balances appear in the ledger of Wild Things Corp., a meat processor:

Preferred 2% Stock, $25 par (75,000 shares authorized, 30,000 shares issued)	$ 750,000
Paid-In Capital in Excess of Par—Preferred Stock	120,000
Common Stock, $30 par (400,000 shares authorized, 250,000 shares issued)	7,500,000
Paid-In Capital in Excess of Par—Common Stock	500,000
Retained Earnings	12,180,000

At the annual stockholders' meeting on April 2, the board of directors presented a plan for modernizing and expanding plant operations at a cost of approximately $3,650,000. The plan provided (a) that a building, valued at $1,680,000, and the land on which it is located, valued at $420,000, be acquired in accordance with preliminary negotiations by the issuance of 65,000 shares of common stock, (b) that 21,000 shares of the unissued preferred stock be issued through an underwriter, and (c) that the corporation borrow $700,000. The plan was approved by the stockholders and accomplished by the following transactions:

June 9. Issued 65,000 shares of common stock in exchange for land and a building, according to the plan.
    13. Issued 21,000 shares of preferred stock, receiving $40 per share in cash.
    25. Borrowed $700,000 from Wasburn City Bank, giving an 8% mortgage note.

No other transactions occurred during June.

Instructions
Journalize the entries to record the foregoing transactions.

PR 13-3B
Selected stock transactions

objs. 3, 4, 5

f. Cash dividends, $73,200

The following selected accounts appear in the ledger of Okie Environmental Corporation on August 1, 2010, the beginning of the current fiscal year:

Preferred 2% Stock, $50 par (40,000 shares authorized, 20,000 shares issued)	$1,000,000
Paid-In Capital in Excess of Par—Preferred Stock	100,000
Common Stock, $75 par (100,000 shares authorized, 40,000 shares issued)	3,000,000
Paid-In Capital in Excess of Par—Common Stock	150,000
Retained Earnings	8,170,000

During the year, the corporation completed a number of transactions affecting the stockholders' equity. They are summarized as follows:

a. Issued 17,500 shares of common stock at $81, receiving cash.
b. Issued 8,000 shares of preferred 2% stock at $63.
c. Purchased 5,000 shares of treasury common for $390,000.
d. Sold 3,000 shares of treasury common for $240,000.
e. Sold 1,000 shares of treasury common for $75,000.
f. Declared cash dividends of $1 per share on preferred stock and $0.80 per share on common stock.
g. Paid the cash dividends.

Instructions
Journalize the entries to record the transactions. Identify each entry by letter.

PR 13-4B
Entries for selected corporate transactions

objs. 3, 4, 5, 6

✔ 4. Total stockholders' equity, $11,853,400

Ivy Enterprises Inc. manufactures bathroom fixtures. The stockholders' equity accounts of Ivy Enterprises Inc., with balances on January 1, 2010, are as follows:

Common Stock, $8 stated value (600,000 shares authorized, 400,000 shares issued)	$3,200,000
Paid-In Capital in Excess of Stated Value	600,000
Retained Earnings	7,100,000
Treasury Stock (30,000 shares, at cost)	240,000

The following selected transactions occurred during the year:

Jan. 7. Paid cash dividends of $0.18 per share on the common stock. The dividend had been properly recorded when declared on November 30 of the preceding fiscal year for $66,600.
Feb. 9. Issued 50,000 shares of common stock for $600,000.
May 21. Sold all of the treasury stock for $300,000.
July 1. Declared a 4% stock dividend on common stock, to be capitalized at the market price of the stock, which is $13 per share.
Aug. 15. Issued the certificates for the dividend declared on July 1.
Sept. 30. Purchased 10,000 shares of treasury stock for $100,000.
Dec. 27. Declared a $0.20-per-share dividend on common stock.
31. Closed the credit balance of the income summary account, $485,000.
31. Closed the two dividends accounts to Retained Earnings.

Instructions
1. Enter the January 1 balances in T accounts for the stockholders' equity accounts listed. Also prepare T accounts for the following: Paid-In Capital from Sale of Treasury Stock; Stock Dividends Distributable; Stock Dividends; Cash Dividends.
2. Journalize the entries to record the transactions, and post to the eight selected accounts.
3. Prepare a retained earnings statement for the year ended December 31, 2010.
4. Prepare the Stockholders' Equity section of the December 31, 2010, balance sheet.

PR 13-5B
Entries for selected corporate transactions

objs. 3, 4, 5, 7

✔ Nov. 15, cash dividends, $138,400

Selected transactions completed by Kearny Boating Corporation during the current fiscal year are as follows:

Jan. 8. Split the common stock 3 for 1 and reduced the par from $75 to $25 per share. After the split, there were 600,000 common shares outstanding.
Feb. 13. Purchased 30,000 shares of the corporation's own common stock at $27, recording the stock at cost.
May 1. Declared semiannual dividends of $0.80 on 25,000 shares of preferred stock and $0.18 on the common stock to stockholders of record on May 15, payable on June 1.
June 1. Paid the cash dividends.
Aug. 5. Sold 22,000 shares of treasury stock at $34, receiving cash.
Nov. 15. Declared semiannual dividends of $0.80 on the preferred stock and $0.20 on the common stock (before the stock dividend). In addition, a 2% common stock dividend was declared on the common stock outstanding. The fair market value of the common stock is estimated at $40.
Dec. 31. Paid the cash dividends and issued the certificates for the common stock dividend.

Instructions
Journalize the transactions.

Special Activities

You can access the special activities online at **www.cengage.com/accounting/reeve**.

Excel Success Special Activities

SA 13-1
Dividends per share

Truett Company issued 100,000 shares of $1 par value common stock and 12,000 shares of $100 par value cumulative preferred stock. The preferred stock has a dividend rate of $6.50 per share. The preferred dividend is in arrears for 2009 and 2010. Truett is able to pay a total dividend of $420,000 in 2011.

a. Open file *SA13-1* and determine the dividend and dividend per share for common and preferred stock in 2011.
b. When you have completed the dividend calculations, perform a "save as," replacing the entire file name with the following:

SA13-1_[your first name initial]_[your last name]

SA 13-2
Dividends per share

Daniels Company began business on January 1, 2008, by issuing 50,000 shares of $1 par value common stock. On January 1, 2009, Daniels issued 4,000 shares of $120 par value, 5% cumulative preferred stock. A dividend was paid on the preferred stock in 2009, but not in 2010. A total dividend of $68,000 was paid in 2011.

a. Open file *SA13-2* and determine the dividend and dividend per share for common and preferred stock in 2011.
b. When you have completed the dividend calculations, perform a "save as," replacing the entire file name with the following:

SA13-2_[your first name initial]_[your last name]

SA 13-3
Dividends per share

Sable Company has two classes of stock issued on January 1, 2009, as follows:

- Common stock, $1 par value, 150,000 issued and outstanding
- $2 cumulative preferred stock, $25 par value, 8,000 shares issued and outstanding

The cumulative preferred stock paid no dividends in 2009. The total dividends paid in 2010 and 2011 were $4,000 and $56,000, respectively.

a. Open file *SA13-3* and determine the dividend and dividend per share for common and preferred stock in 2011.
b. When you have completed the dividend calculations, perform a "save as," replacing the entire file name with the following:

SA13-3_[your first name initial]_[your last name]

Answers to Self-Examination Questions

1. **C** The separation of the owner from management (answer C) is a disadvantage of the corporate form of organization. This is because management may not always behave in the best interests of the owners. Limited liability (answer A), continuous life (answer B), and the ability to raise capital (answer D) are all advantages of the corporate form of organization.
2. **D** Paid-in capital is one of the two major subdivisions of the stockholders' equity of a corporation. It may result from many sources, including the issuance of preferred stock (answer A), issuing common stock (answer B), or the sale of a corporation's treasury stock (answer C).
3. **D** The Stockholders' Equity section of corporate balance sheets is divided into two principal subsections: (1) investments contributed by the stockholders and others and (2) net income

retained in the business. Included as part of the investments by stockholders and others is the par of common stock (answer A), stock dividends distributable (answer B), and the par of preferred stock (answer C).
4. **C** Reacquired stock, known as *treasury stock*, should be listed in the Stockholders' Equity section (answer C) of the balance sheet. The price paid for the treasury stock is deducted from the total of all the stockholders' equity accounts.
5. **C** If a corporation that holds treasury stock declares a cash dividend, the dividends are not paid on the treasury shares. To do so would place the corporation in the position of earning income through dealing with itself. Thus, the corporation will record $44,000 (answer C) as cash dividends [(25,000 shares issued less 3,000 shares held as treasury stock) × $2 per share dividend].

Long-Term Liabilities: Bonds and Notes

© UNDER ARMOUR®/PRNEWSFOTO (AP TOPIC GALLERY)

U N D E R   A R M O U R®

Most of us don't have enough money in our bank accounts to buy a house or a car by simply writing a check. Just imagine if you had to save the complete purchase price of a house before you could buy it! To help us make these types of purchases, banks will typically lend us the money, as long as we agree to repay the loan with interest in smaller future payments. Loans such as this, or long-term debt, allow us to purchase assets such as houses and cars today, which benefit us over the long term.

The use of debt can also help a business reach its objectives. Most businesses have to borrow money in order to acquire assets that they will use to generate income. For example, Under Armour®, a maker of performance athletic clothing, uses debt to acquire assets that it needs to manufacture and sell its products. Since it began in 1995, the company has used long-term debt to transform itself from a small business to a leading athletic wear company. The company now sells products in over 8,000 retail stores across the world. In addition, Under Armour® products are used by a number of teams in the National Football League, Major League Baseball, the National Hockey League, and in Olympic sports.

While debt can help companies like Under Armour® grow to achieve financial success, too much debt can be a financial burden that may even lead to bankruptcy. Just like individuals, businesses must manage debt wisely. In this chapter, we will discuss the nature of, accounting for, analysis of, and investments in long-term debt.

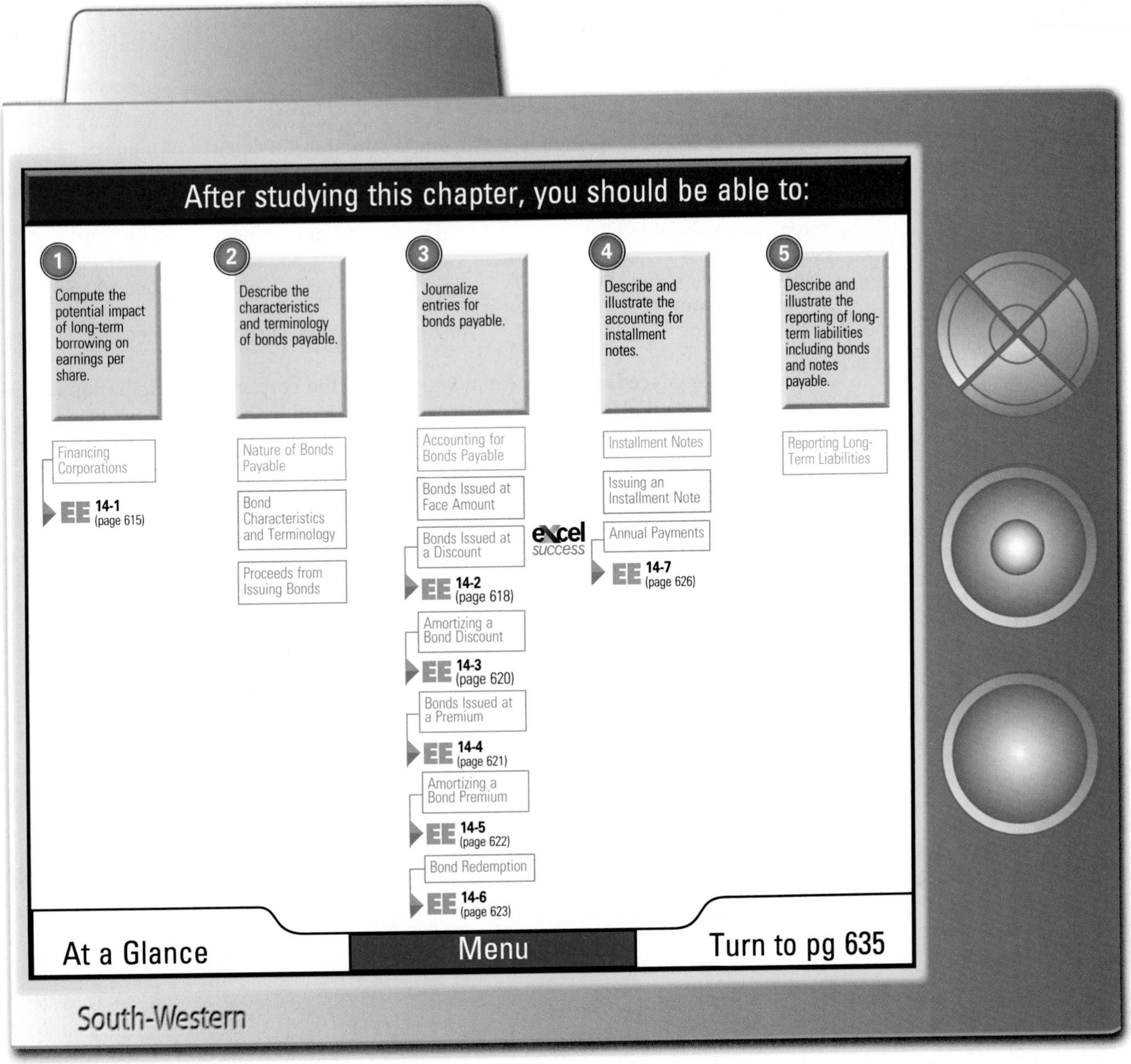

After studying this chapter, you should be able to:

1 Compute the potential impact of long-term borrowing on earnings per share.

2 Describe the characteristics and terminology of bonds payable.

3 Journalize entries for bonds payable.

4 Describe and illustrate the accounting for installment notes.

5 Describe and illustrate the reporting of long-term liabilities including bonds and notes payable.

Financing Corporations

EE **14-1** (page 615)

Nature of Bonds Payable

Bond Characteristics and Terminology

Proceeds from Issuing Bonds

Accounting for Bonds Payable

Bonds Issued at Face Amount

Bonds Issued at a Discount

e**X**cel *success*

EE **14-2** (page 618)

Amortizing a Bond Discount

EE **14-3** (page 620)

Bonds Issued at a Premium

EE **14-4** (page 621)

Amortizing a Bond Premium

EE **14-5** (page 622)

Bond Redemption

EE **14-6** (page 623)

Installment Notes

Issuing an Installment Note

Annual Payments

EE **14-7** (page 626)

Reporting Long-Term Liabilities

At a Glance | Menu | Turn to pg 635

South-Western

1 Compute the potential impact of long-term borrowing on earnings per share.

Financing Corporations

Corporations finance their operations using the following:

1. Debt such as purchasing on account or issuing bonds or notes payable
2. Equity such as issuing common stock and, in some cases, preferred stock

Purchasing on account and issuing short-term notes payable as well as issuing common and preferred stock have been discussed in earlier chapters. This chapter focuses on issuing long-term bonds and notes payable to finance a company's operations.

A **bond** is a form of an interest-bearing note. Like a note, a bond requires periodic interest payments with the face amount to be repaid at the maturity date. As creditors of the corporation, bondholder claims on the corporation's assets rank ahead of stockholders.

To illustrate the financing of long-term operations, assume Huckadee Corporation is considering the following plans to issue debt and equity:

	Plan 1		Plan 2		Plan 3	
	Amount	Percent	Amount	Percent	Amount	Percent
Issue 12% bonds	—	0%	—	0%	$2,000,000	50%
Issue 9% preferred stock, $50 par value	—	0	$2,000,000	50	1,000,000	25
Issue common stock, $10 par value	$4,000,000	100	2,000,000	50	1,000,000	25
Total amount of financing	$4,000,000	100%	$4,000,000	100%	$4,000,000	100%

Each of the preceding plans finances some of the corporation's operations by issuing common stock. However, the percentage financed by common stock varies from 100% (Plan 1) to 25% (Plan 3). In deciding among financing plans, the effect on earnings per share is often considered.

Earnings per share (EPS) measures the income earned by each share of common stock. It is computed as follows:[1]

$$\text{Earnings per Share} = \frac{\text{Net Income} - \text{Preferred Dividends}}{\text{Number of Common Shares Outstanding}}$$

To illustrate, assume the following data for Huckadee Corporation:

1. Earnings before interest and income taxes are $800,000.
2. The tax rate is 40%.
3. All bonds or stocks are issued at their par or face amount.

The effect of the preceding financing plans on Huckadee's net income and earnings per share is shown in Exhibit 1.

When interest rates are low, corporations usually finance their operations with debt. For example, as interest rates fell in recent years, corporations issued large amounts of new debt.

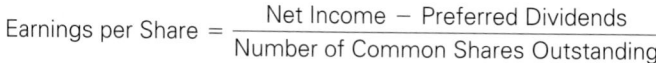

Exhibit 1

Effect of Alternative Financing Plans— $800,000 Earnings

	Plan 1	Plan 2	Plan 3
12% bonds	—	—	$2,000,000
Preferred 9% stock, $50 par	—	$2,000,000	1,000,000
Common stock, $10 par	$4,000,000	2,000,000	1,000,000
Total	$4,000,000	$4,000,000	$4,000,000
Earnings before interest and income tax	$ 800,000	$ 800,000	$ 800,000
Deduct interest on bonds	—	—	240,000
Income before income tax	$ 800,000	$ 800,000	$ 560,000
Deduct income tax	320,000	320,000	224,000
Net income	$ 480,000	$ 480,000	$ 336,000
Dividends on preferred stock	—	180,000	90,000
Available for dividends on common stock	$ 480,000	$ 300,000	$ 246,000
Shares of common stock outstanding	÷ 400,000	÷ 200,000	÷ 100,000
Earnings per share on common stock	$ 1.20	$ 1.50	$ 2.46

Exhibit 1 indicates that Plan 3 yields the highest earnings per share on common stock and, thus, is the most attractive for common stockholders. If the estimated earnings are more than $800,000, the difference between the earnings per share to common stockholders under Plans 1 and 3 is even greater.[2]

1 Earnings per share is also discussed in the *Financial Analysis and Interpretation* section of Chapter 13 and in Chapter 17.
2 The higher earnings per share under Plan 3 is due to a finance concept known as *leverage*. This concept is discussed further in Chapter 17.

If smaller earnings occur, however, Plans 1 and 2 become more attractive to common stockholders. To illustrate, the effect of earnings of $440,000 rather than $800,000 is shown in Exhibit 2.

Exhibit 2

Effect of Alternative Financing Plans— $440,000 Earnings

	Plan 1	Plan 2	Plan 3
12% bonds	—	—	$2,000,000
Preferred 9% stock, $50 par	—	$2,000,000	1,000,000
Common stock, $10 par..................	$4,000,000	2,000,000	1,000,000
Total	$4,000,000	$4,000,000	$4,000,000
Earnings before interest and income tax	$ 440,000	$ 440,000	$ 440,000
Deduct interest on bonds.................	—	—	240,000
Income before income tax	$ 440,000	$ 440,000	$ 200,000
Deduct income tax.....................	176,000	176,000	80,000
Net income	$ 264,000	$ 264,000	$ 120,000
Dividends on preferred stock..............	—	180,000	90,000
Available for dividends on common stock	$ 264,000	$ 84,000	$ 30,000
Shares of common stock outstanding	÷ 400,000	÷ 200,000	÷ 100,000
Earnings per share on common stock	$ 0.66	$ 0.42	$ 0.30

In addition to earnings per share, the corporation should consider other factors in deciding among the financing plans. For example, once bonds are issued, the interest and the face value of the bonds at maturity must be paid. If these payments are not made, the bondholders could seek court action and force the company into bankruptcy. In contrast, a corporation is not legally obligated to pay dividends on preferred or common stock.

Example Exercise 14-1   Alternative Financing Plans   1

Gonzales Co. is considering the following alternative plans for financing its company:

	Plan 1	Plan 2
Issue 10% bonds (at face value)	—	$2,000,000
Issue common stock, $10 par	$3,000,000	1,000,000

Income tax is estimated at 40% of income.
Determine the earnings per share of common stock under the two alternative financing plans, assuming income before bond interest and income tax is $750,000.

Follow My Example 14-1

	Plan 1	Plan 2
Earnings before bond interest and income tax	$750,000	$750,000
Bond interest	0	200,000[2]
Balance	$750,000	$550,000
Income tax	300,000[1]	220,000[3]
Net income	$450,000	$330,000
Dividends on preferred stock	0	0
Earnings available for common stock	$450,000	$330,000
Number of common shares	÷300,000	÷100,000
Earnings per share on common stock	$ 1.50	$ 3.30

[1]$750,000 × 40%   [2]$2,000,000 × 10%   [3]$550,000 × 40%

For Practice: PE 14-1A, PE 14-1B

Describe the characteristics and terminology of bonds payable.

Nature of Bonds Payable

Corporate bonds normally differ in face values, interest rates, interest payment dates, and maturity dates. Bonds also differ in other ways such as whether corporate assets are pledged in support of the bonds.

Bond Characteristics and Terminology

Time Warner, Inc., 7.625% bonds maturing in 2031 were listed as selling for 106.505 on February 1, 2008.

The underlying contract between the company issuing bonds and the bondholders is called a **bond indenture** or *trust indenture*. A bond issue is normally divided into a number of individual bonds. Usually, the face value of each bond, called the *principal*, is $1,000 or a multiple of $1,000. The interest on bonds may be payable annually, semiannually, or quarterly. Most bonds pay interest semiannually.

The price of a bond is quoted as a percentage of the bond's face value. For example, a $1,000 bond quoted at 98 could be purchased or sold for $980 ($1,000 × 0.98). Likewise, bonds quoted at 109 could be purchased or sold for $1,090 ($1,000 × 1.09).

When all bonds of an issue mature at the same time, they are called *term bonds*. If the bonds mature over several dates, they are called *serial bonds*. For example, one-tenth of an issue of $1,000,000 bonds, or $100,000, may mature 16 years from the issue date, another $100,000 in the 17th year, and so on.

Bonds that may be exchanged for other securities, such as common stock, are called *convertible bonds*. Bonds that a corporation reserves the right to redeem before their maturity are called *callable bonds*. Bonds issued on the basis of the general credit of the corporation are called *debenture bonds*.

Proceeds from Issuing Bonds

When a corporation issues bonds, the proceeds received for the bonds depend on the following:

1. The face amount of the bonds, which is the amount due at the maturity date.
2. The interest rate on the bonds.
3. The market rate of interest.

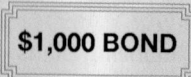

Market Rate = Contract Rate

Selling price of bond = $1,000

$1,000 BOND

The face amount and the interest rate on the bonds are identified in the bond indenture. The interest rate to be paid on the face amount of the bond is called the **contract rate** or *coupon rate*.

The **market rate of interest**, sometimes called the **effective rate of interest**, is the rate determined from sales and purchases of similar bonds. The market rate of interest is affected by a variety of factors, including investors' expectations of current and future economic conditions.

By comparing the market and contract rates of interest, it can be determined whether the selling price of a bond will be equal, less than, or more than the bond's face amount, as shown below.

1. Market Rate = Contract Rate
   Selling Price = Face Amount of Bonds

2. Market Rate > Contract Rate
   Selling Price < Face Amount of Bonds
   The face amount of bonds less the selling price is called a **discount**.

3. Market Rate < Contract Rate
   Selling Price > Face Amount of Bonds
   The selling price less the face amount of the bonds is called a **premium**.

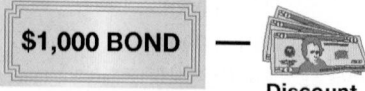

Market Rate > Contract Rate

Selling price of bond < $1,000

$1,000 BOND — Discount

Market Rate < Contract Rate

Selling price of bond > $1,000

$1,000 BOND + Premium

A bond sells at a discount because buyers are only willing to pay less than the face amount for bonds whose contract rate is less than the market rate. A bond sells at a premium because buyers are willing to pay more than the face amount for bonds whose contract rate is higher than the market rate.

Integrity, Objectivity, and Ethics in Business

CREDIT QUALITY

The market rate of interest for a corporate bond is influenced by a number of factors, including the credit quality of the issuer. During 2007 and 2008, subprime bonds became less secure due to falling house prices and

mortgage defaults. As a result, investors in these bonds lost billions of dollars, causing the eventual takeover of Bear Stearns & Co., a Wall Street investment company.

Journalize entries for bonds payable.

Accounting for Bonds Payable

Bonds may be issued at their face amount, a discount, or a premium. When bonds are issued at less or more than their face amount, the discount or premium must be amortized over the life of the bonds. A corporation may redeem bonds before their maturity date.

Bonds Issued at Face Amount

If the market rate of interest is equal to the contract rate of interest, the bonds will sell for their face amount or a price of 100. To illustrate, assume that on January 1, 2009, Eastern Montana Communications Inc. issued the following bonds:

Face amount	$100,000
Contract rate of interest	12%
Interest paid semiannually on June 30 and December 31.	
Term of bonds	5 years
Market rate of interest	12%

Since the contract rate of interest and the market rate of interest are the same, the bonds will sell at their face amount. The entry to record the issuance of the bonds is as follows:

2009					
Jan.	1	Cash		100,000	
		Bonds Payable			100,000
		Issued $100,000 bonds payable at			
		face amount.			

Every six months (on June 30 and December 31) after the bonds are issued, interest of $6,000 ($100,000 × 12% × ½) is paid. The first interest payment on June 30, 2009, is recorded as follows:

2009					
June	30	Interest Expense		6,000	
		Cash			6,000
		Paid six months' interest on bonds.			

At the maturity date, the payment of the principal of $100,000 is recorded as follows:

2013 Dec. 31	Bonds Payable	100,000	
	Cash		100,000
	Paid bond principal at maturity date.		

Bonds Issued at a Discount

If the market rate of interest is more than the contract rate of interest, the bonds will sell for less than their face amount. This is because investors are not willing to pay the full face amount for bonds that pay a lower contract rate of interest than the rate they could earn on similar bonds (market rate).[3]

To illustrate, assume that on January 1, 2009, Western Wyoming Distribution Inc. issued the following bonds:

Face amount	$100,000
Contract rate of interest	12%
Interest paid semiannually on June 30 and December 31.	
Term of bonds	5 years
Market rate of interest	13%

Since the contract rate of interest is less than the market rate of interest, the bonds will sell at less than their face amount. Assuming the bonds sell for $96,406, the entry to record the issuance of the bonds is as follows:

2009 Jan. 1	Cash	96,406	
	Discount on Bonds Payable	3,594	
	Bonds Payable		100,000
	Issued $100,000 bonds at discount.		

The $96,406 may be viewed as the amount investors are willing to pay for bonds that have a lower contract rate of interest (12%) than the market rate (13%). The discount is the market's way of adjusting the contract rate of interest to the higher market rate of interest.

The account, Discount on Bonds Payable, is a contra account to Bonds Payable and has a normal debit balance. It is subtracted from Bonds Payable to determine the carrying amount (or book value) of the bonds payable. Thus, after the preceding entry, the carrying amount of the bonds payable is $96,406 ($100,000 − $3,594).

Example Exercise 14-2   Issuing Bonds at a Discount   ▸ 3

On the first day of the fiscal year, a company issues a $1,000,000, 6%, five-year bond that pays semiannual interest of $30,000 ($1,000,000 × 6% × ½), receiving cash of $936,420. Journalize the entry to record the issuance of the bonds.

Follow My Example 14-2

Cash	936,420	
Discount on Bonds Payable	63,580	
Bonds Payable		1,000,000

For Practice: PE 14-2A, PE 14-2B

---

3 The price that investors are willing to pay for the bonds depends on present value concepts. Present value concepts, including the computation of bond prices, are described and illustrated in Appendix 1 at the end of this chapter.

Amortizing a Bond Discount

A bond discount must be amortized to interest expense over the life of the bond. The entry to amortize a bond discount is shown below.

| Interest Expense | XXX | |
| Discount on Bonds Payable | | XXX |

The preceding entry may be made annually as an adjusting entry, or it may be combined with the semiannual interest payment. In the latter case, the entry would be as follows:

Interest Expense	XXX	
Discount on Bonds Payable		XXX
Cash (amount of semiannual interest)		XXX

The two methods of computing the amortization of a bond discount are:

1. *Straight-line method*
2. *Effective interest rate method*, sometimes called the *interest method*

The **effective interest rate method** is required by generally accepted accounting principles. However, the straight-line method may be used if the results do not differ significantly from the interest method. The straight-line method is used in this chapter. The effective interest rate method is described and illustrated in Appendix 2 at the end of this chapter.

The straight-line method provides equal amounts of amortization. To illustrate, amortization of the Western Wyoming Distribution bond discount of $3,594 is computed below.

Discount on bonds payable . .	$3,594.00
Term of bonds	5 years
Semiannual amortization	$359.40 ($3,594/10 periods)

The combined entry to record the first interest payment and the amortization of the discount is as follows:

2009				
June	30	Interest Expense	6,359.40	
		Discount on Bonds Payable		359.40
		Cash		6,000.00
		Paid semiannual interest and		
		amortized ¹⁄₁₀ of bond discount.		

The preceding entry is made on each interest payment date. Thus, the amount of the semiannual interest expense on the bonds ($6,359.40) remains the same over the life of the bonds.

The effect of the discount amortization is to increase the interest expense from $6,000.00 to $6,359.40. In effect, this increases the contract rate of interest from 12% to a rate of interest that approximates the market rate of 13%. In addition, as the discount is amortized, the carrying amount of the bonds increases until it equals the face amount of the bonds on the maturity date.

Example Exercise 14-3 Discount Amortization

Using the bond from Example Exercise 14-2, journalize the first interest payment and the amortization of the related bond discount.

Follow My Example 14-3

Interest Expense	36,358	
Discount on Bonds Payable		6,358
Cash.		30,000
Paid interest and amortized the bond discount ($63,580/10).		

For Practice: PE 14-3A, PE 14-3B

Bonds Issued at a Premium

If the market rate of interest is less than the contract rate of interest (contract rate), the bonds will sell for more than their face amount. This is because investors are willing to pay more for bonds that pay a higher rate of interest (contract rate) than the rate they could earn on similar bonds (market rate).

To illustrate, assume that on January 1, 2009, Northern Idaho Transportation Inc. issued the following bonds:

Face amount	$100,000
Contract rate of interest	12%
Interest paid semiannually on	
June 30 and December 31.	
Term of bonds	5 years
Market rate of interest	11%

Since the contract rate of interest is more than the market rate of interest, the bonds will sell at more than their face amount. Assuming the bonds sell for $103,769, the entry to record the issuance of the bonds is as follows:

2009					
Jan.	1	Cash		103,769	
		Bonds Payable			100,000
		Premium on Bonds Payable			3,769
		Issued $100,000 bonds at a premium.			

The $3,769 premium may be viewed as the extra amount investors are willing to pay for bonds that have a higher rate of interest (12%) than the market rate (11%). The premium is the market's way of adjusting the contract rate of interest to the lower market rate of interest.

The account, Premium on Bonds Payable, has a normal credit balance. It is added to Bonds Payable to determine the carrying amount (or book value) of the bonds payable. Thus, after the preceding entry, the carrying amount of the bonds payable is $103,769 ($100,000 + $3,769).

Example Exercises 14-4   Issuing Bonds at a Premium

A company issues a $2,000,000, 12%, five-year bond that pays semiannual interest of $120,000 ($2,000,000 × 12% × ½), receiving cash of $2,154,440. Journalize the bond issuance.

Follow My Example 14-4

Cash.	2,154,440	
Premium on Bonds Payable		154,440
Bonds Payable		2,000,000

For Practice: PE 14-4A, PE 14-4B

Amortizing a Bond Premium

Like bond discounts, a bond premium must be amortized over the life of the bond. The amortization can be computed using either the straight-line or the effective interest rate method. The entry to amortize a bond premium is shown below.

Premium on Bonds Payable	XXX	
Interest Expense		XXX

The preceding entry may be made annually as an adjusting entry, or it may be combined with the semiannual interest payment. In the latter case, the entry would be as follows:

Interest Expense	XXX	
Discount on Bonds Payable		XXX
Cash (amount of semiannual interest)		XXX

To illustrate, amortization of the preceding premium of $3,769 is computed using the straight-line method, as shown below.

Premium on bonds payable . .	$3,769.00	
Term of bonds	5 years	
Semiannual amortization	$376.90	($3,769/10 periods)

The combined entry to record the first interest payment and the amortization of the discount is as follows:

2009					
June	30	Interest Expense		5,623.10	
		Premium on Bonds Payable		376.90	
		Cash			6,000.00
		Paid semiannual interest and			
		amortized ¹⁄₁₀ of bond premium.			

The preceding entry is made on each interest payment date. Thus, the amount of the semiannual interest expense ($5,623.10) on the bonds remains the same over the life of the bonds.

The effect of the premium amortization is to decrease the interest expense from $6,000.00 to $5,623.10. In effect, this decreases the contract rate of interest from 12% to a rate of interest that approximates the market rate of 11%. In addition, as the premium is amortized, the carrying amount of the bonds decreases until it equals the face amount of bonds on the maturity date.

Example Exercise 14-5   Premium Amortization

Using the bond from Example Exercise 14-4, journalize the first interest payment and the amortization of the related bond premium.

Follow My Example 14-5

Interest Expense.	104,556	
Premium on Bonds Payable	15,444	
Cash.		120,000
Paid interest and amortized the bond premium ($154,440/10).		

For Practice: PE 14-5A, PE 14-5B

Pacific Bell issued 7.5% bonds, maturing in 2033 but callable in 2023.

Bond Redemption

A corporation may redeem or call bonds before they mature. This is often done when the market rate of interest declines below the contract rate of interest. In such cases, the corporation may issue new bonds at a lower interest rate and use the proceeds to redeem the original bond issue.

Callable bonds can be redeemed by the issuing corporation within the period of time and at the price stated in the bond indenture. Normally, the call price is above the face value. A corporation may also redeem its bonds by purchasing them on the open market.[4]

A corporation usually redeems its bonds at a price different from the carrying amount (or book value) of the bonds. The **carrying amount** of bonds payable is the face amount of the bonds less any unamortized discount or plus any unamortized premium. A gain or loss may be realized on a bond redemption as follows:

1. A *gain* is recorded if the price paid for redemption is below the bond carrying amount.
2. A *loss* is recorded if the price paid for the redemption is above the carrying amount.

Gains and losses on the redemption of bonds are reported in the *Other income (loss)* section of the income statement.

To illustrate, assume that on June 30, 2009, a corporation has the following bond issue:

Face amount of bonds	$100,000
Premium on bonds payable	4,000

On June 30, 2009, the corporation redeemed one-fourth ($25,000) of these bonds in the market for $24,000. The entry to record the redemption is as follows:

2009				
June	30	Bonds Payable	25,000	
		Premium on Bonds Payable	1,000	
		Cash		24,000
		Gain on Redemption of Bonds		2,000
		Redeemed $25,000 bonds for $24,000.		

In the preceding entry, only the portion of the premium related to the redeemed bonds ($1,000) is written off. The difference between the carrying amount of the bonds redeemed, $26,000 ($25,000 + $1,000), and the redemption price, $24,000, is recorded as a gain.

4 Some bond indentures require the corporation issuing the bonds to transfer cash to a special cash fund, called a *sinking fund,* over the life of the bond. Such funds help assure investors that there will be adequate cash to pay the bonds at their maturity date.

Assume that the corporation calls the remaining $75,000 of outstanding bonds, which are held by a private investor, for $79,500 on July 1, 2009. The entry to record the redemption is as follows:

2009					
July	1	Bonds Payable		75,000	
		Premium on Bonds Payable		3,000	
		Loss on Redemption of Bonds		1,500	
		Cash			79,500
		Redeemed $75,000 bonds for $79,500.			

Example Exercise 14-6   Redemption of Bonds Payable   • • • • • • • •▸ 3

A $500,000 bond issue on which there is an unamortized discount of $40,000 is redeemed for $475,000. Journalize the redemption of the bonds.

Follow My Example 14-6

Bonds Payable.	500,000	
Loss on Redemption of Bonds	15,000	
Discount on Bonds Payable		40,000
Cash.		475,000

For Practice: PE 14-6A, PE 14-6B

---

4 Describe and illustrate the accounting for installment notes.

Installment Notes

Mortgage notes are used by individuals to buy a car or house.

Corporations often finance their operations by issuing bonds payable. Corporations may also issue installment notes. An **installment note** is a debt that requires the borrower to make equal periodic payments to the lender for the term of the note. Unlike bonds, each note payment consists of the following:

1. Payment of a portion of the amount initially borrowed, called the *principal*
2. Payment of interest on the outstanding balance

At the end of the note's term, the principal will have been repaid in full.

Installment notes are often used to purchase assets such as equipment and are usually issued by an individual bank. An installment note may be secured by a pledge of the borrower's assets. Such notes are called **mortgage notes**. If the borrower fails to pay a mortgage note, the lender has the right to take possession of the pledged asset and sell it to pay off the debt.

Issuing an Installment Note

When an installment note is issued, an entry is recorded debiting Cash and crediting Notes Payable. To illustrate, assume that Lewis Company issues the following installment note to City National Bank on January 1, 2008.

Principal amount of note.	$24,000
Interest rate	6%
Term of note.	5 years
Annual payments	$5,698[5]

5 The amount of the annual payment is calculated by using the present value concepts discussed in Appendix 1. The annual payment of $5,698 is computed by dividing the $24,000 loan amount by the present value of an annuity of $1 for 5 periods at 6% (4.21236) from Exhibit 5 (rounded to the nearest dollar).

The entry to record the issuance of the note is as follows:

2008					
Jan.	1	Cash		24,000	
		Notes Payable			24,000
		Issued installment note for cash.			

Annual Payments

The preceding note payable requires Lewis Company to repay the principal and interest in equal payments of $5,698 beginning December 31, 2008, for each of the next five years. Unlike bonds, however, each installment note payment includes an interest and principal payment.

The interest portion of an installment note payment is computed by multiplying the interest rate by the carrying amount (book value) of the note at the beginning of the period. The principal portion of the payment is then computed as the difference between the total payment (cash paid) and the interest. These computations are illustrated in Exhibit 3 as follows:

1. The January 1, 2008, carrying value (Column A) equals the amount borrowed from the bank. The January 1 balance in the following years equals the December 31 balance from the prior year.

2. The note payment (Column B) remains constant at $5,698, the annual cash payments required by the bank.

3. The interest expense (Column C) is computed at 6% of the installment note carrying amount at the beginning of each year. As a result, the interest expense decreases each year.

4. Notes payable (Column D) decreases each year by the amount of the principal repayment. The principal repayment is computed by subtracting the interest expense (Column C) from the total payment (Column B). The principal repayment increases each year as the interest expense decreases (Column C).

5. The carrying amount on December 31 (Column E) of the note decreases from $24,000, the initial amount borrowed, to $0 at the end of the five years.

Exhibit 3

Amortization of Installment Notes

For the Year Ending:	A January 1 Carrying Amount	B Note Payment (cash paid)	C Interest Expense (6% of January 1 Note Carrying Amount)			D Decrease in Notes Payable (B − C)	E December 31 Carrying Amount (A − D)
December 31, 2008	$24,000	$ 5,698	$1,440	(6% of	$24,000)	$ 4,258	$19,742
December 31, 2009	19,742	5,698	1,185	(6% of	$19,742)	4,513	15,229
December 31, 2010	15,229	5,698	914	(6% of	$15,229)	4,784	10,445
December 31, 2011	10,445	5,698	627	(6% of	$10,445)	5,071	5,374
December 31, 2012	5,374	5,698	324*	(6% of	$5,374)	5,374	0
		$28,490	$4,490			$24,000	

*Rounded.

The entry to record the first payment on December 31, 2008, is as follows:

2008 Dec.	31	Interest Expense	1,440	
		Notes Payable	4,258	
		Cash		5,698
		Paid principal and interest on installment note.		

The entry to record the second payment on December 31, 2009, is as follows:

2009 Dec.	31	Interest Expense	1,185	
		Notes Payable	4,513	
		Cash		5,698
		Paid principal and interest on installment note.		

As the prior entries show, the cash payment is the same in each year. The interest and principal repayment, however, change each year. This is because the carrying amount (book value) of the note decreases each year as principal is repaid, which decreases the interest.

The entry to record the final payment on December 31, 2012, is as follows:

2012 Dec.	31	Interest Expense	324	
		Notes Payable	5,374	
		Cash		5,698
		Paid principal and interest on installment notes.		

After the final payment, the carrying amount on the note is zero, indicating that the note has been paid in full. Any assets that secure the note would then be released by the bank.

excel success

Spreadsheet software can be used to develop an amortization table for installment notes as follows:

	A	B	C	D	E	F
1	*Inputs:*					
2	Principal amount on note	$ 24,000.00				
3	Interest rate	6%				
4	Term of note	5	years			
5	Annual payments	$ 5,698				
6						
7						
8	*Output:*	**b.**	**c.**	**d.**	**e.**	**f.**
9	For the year ending:	January 1 Carrying Amount	Note Payment (cash paid)	Interest Expense at 6%	Decrease in Notes Payable	December 31 Carrying Amount
10	December 31, 2008	=B2	=$B$5	=B$3*B10	=C10-D10	=B10-E10
11	December 31, 2009	=F10	=$B$5	=B$3*B11	=C11-D11	=B11-E11
12	December 31, 2010	=F11	=$B$5	=B$3*B12	=C12-D12	=B12-E12
13	December 31, 2011	=F12	=$B$5	=B$3*B13	=C13-D13	=B13-E13
14	December 31, 2012	=F13	=$B$5	=B$3*B14	=C14-D14	=B14-E14

a. **g.** **h.** **i.**

The spreadsheet is developed by creating input and output areas. The four inputs are the principal amount of the note, interest rate, term of note, and annual payments, as shown in the chapter illustration. Use the following steps in formulating the output table.

You can fill cells according to a sequence of numbers or dates by highlighting the cells containing the fill sequence, then using the fill handle to drag to the empty cells to be filled.

a. Enter the dates for December 31, 2008, and 2009 in cells A10 and A11. You may need to reformat the date in these two cells to appear as shown. Highlight these two cells, then drag the fill handle over the range that you want to fill, or A12:A14. The dates will automatically fill in with correct annual spacing.

b. Enter in cell B10 the cell reference for principal amount of the note, =B2.

c. Enter in cell C10 the cell reference for the annual payment, =$B$5. The dollar sign makes the cell absolute, so that the installment is fixed when copied.

d. Enter in cell D10 the formula for the interest expense, =B$3*B10. The interest rate row must also remain fixed (absolute) for copying.

e. Enter in cell E10 the formula for the decrease in notes payable, =C10-D10.

f. Enter in cell F10 the formula for the December 31 carrying amount, =B10-E10.

g. Enter in cell B11 the cell reference for the January 1 carrying amount, =F10.

h. Copy B11 to B12:B14.

i. Copy cells C10:F10 to C11:F14.

 Go to the hands-on **Excel Tutor** for this example!

 This Excel Success example shows the use of an Excel function referred to as cell referencing. Go to the **Excel Tutor** titled **Absolute & Relative Cell References** for additional help on this useful Excel function!

Example Exercise 14-7 Journalizing Installment Notes   ·······› 4

On the first day of the fiscal year, a company issues $30,000, 10%, five-year installment note that has annual payments of $7,914. The first note payment consists of $3,000 of interest and $4,914 of principal repayment.

a. Journalize the entry to record the issuance of the installment note.

b. Journalize the first annual note payment.

Follow My Example 14-7

a.

Cash		30,000	
Notes Payable			30,000
Issued $30,000 of installment note for cash.			

b.

Interest Expense		3,000	
Notes Payable		4,914	
Cash			7,914
Paid principal and interest on installment note.			

For Practice: PE 14-7A, PE 14-7B

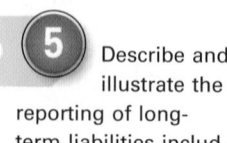 **5** Describe and illustrate the reporting of long-term liabilities including bonds and notes payable.

Reporting Long-Term Liabilities

Bonds payable and notes payable are reported as liabilities on the balance sheet. Any portion of the bonds or notes that is due within one year is reported as a current liability. Any remaining bonds or notes are reported as a long-term liability.

Any unamortized premium is reported as an addition to the face amount of the bonds. Any unamortized discount is reported as a deduction from the face amount of the bonds. A description of the bonds and notes should also be reported either on the face of the financial statements or in the accompanying notes.

The reporting of bonds and notes payable for Mornin' Joe is shown below.

Mornin' Joe
Balance Sheet
December 31, 2010

Current liabilities:		
Accounts payable	$133,000	
Notes payable (current portion)	200,000	
Salaries and wages payable	42,000	
Payroll taxes payable	16,400	
Interest payable	40,000	
Total current liabilities		$ 431,400
Long-term liabilities:		
Bonds payable, 8%, due December 31, 2030	$500,000	
Less unamortized discount	16,000	$ 484,000
Notes payable		1,400,000
Total long-term liabilities		$1,884,000
Total liabilities		$2,315,400

Financial Analysis and Interpretation

Analysts often assess the relative risk of the bondholders in terms of the **number of times interest charges are earned** during the year. The higher the ratio, the greater the chance that interest payments will continue to be made if earnings decrease.

The amount available to make interest payments is not affected by taxes on income. This is because interest is deductible in determining taxable income. To illustrate, the following data were taken from the 2006 annual report of Briggs & Stratton Corporation:

Interest expense	$ 42,091,000
Income before income tax	$152,366,000

The number of times interest charges are earned, 4.62, is computed at the top of the next column.

Number of Times Interest Charges Are Earned =

$$\frac{\text{Income Before Income Tax} + \text{Interest Expense}}{\text{Interest Expense}}$$

Number of Times Interest Charges Are Earned =

$$\frac{\$152,366,000 + \$42,091,000}{\$42,091,000} = 4.62$$

The number of times interest charges are earned indicates that the debtholders of Briggs & Stratton Corporation have adequate protection against a potential drop in earnings jeopardizing their receipt of interest payments. However, a final assessment should include a review of trends of past years and a comparison with industry averages.

f·a·i

A P P E N D I X 1

Present Value Concepts and Pricing Bonds Payable

When a corporation issues bonds, the price that investors are willing to pay for the bonds depends on the following:

1. The face amount of the bonds, which is the amount due at the maturity date
2. The periodic interest to be paid on the bonds
3. The market rate of interest

An investor determines how much to pay for the bonds by computing the present value of the bond's future cash receipts, using the market rate of interest. A bond's future cash receipts include its face value at maturity and the periodic interest.

Present Value Concepts

The concept of present value is based on the time value of money. The *time value of money concept* recognizes that cash received today is worth more than the same amount of cash to be received in the future.

To illustrate, what would you rather have: $1,000 today or $1,000 one year from now? You would rather have the $1,000 today because it could be invested to earn interest. For example, if the $1,000 could be invested to earn 10% per year, the $1,000 will accumulate to $1,100 ($1,000 plus $100 interest) in one year. In this sense, you can think of the $1,000 in hand today as the **present value** of $1,100 to be received a year from today. This present value is illustrated below.

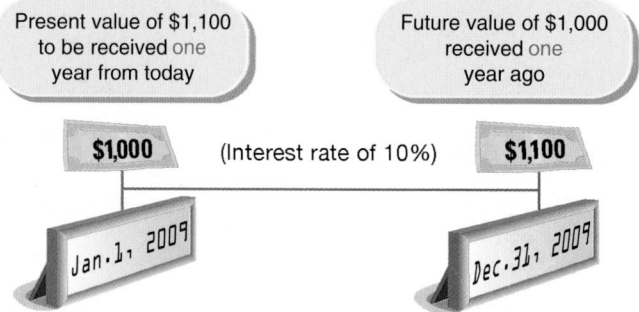

A related concept to present value is **future value**. To illustrate, using the preceding example, the $1,100 to be received on December 31, 2009, is the *future value* of $1,000 on January 1, 2009, assuming an interest rate of 10%.

Present Value of an Amount   To illustrate the present value of an amount, assume that $1,000 is to be received in one year. If the market rate of interest is 10%, the present value of the $1,000 is $909.09 ($1,000/1.10). This present value is illustrated below.

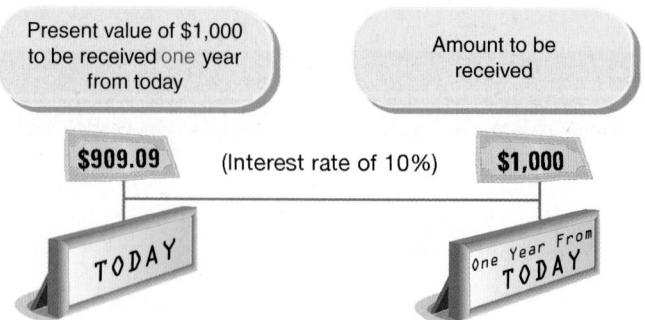

If the $1,000 is to be received in two years, with interest of 10% compounded at the end of the first year, the present value is $826.45 ($909.09/1.10).[6] This present value is illustrated at the top of the next page.

6 Note that the future value of $826.45 in two years, at an interest rate of 10% compounded annually, is $1,000.

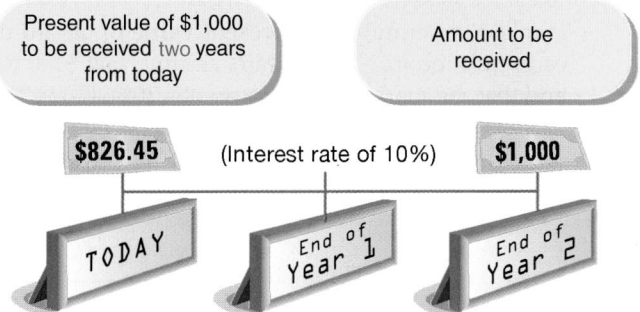

The present value of an amount to be received in the future can be determined by a series of divisions such as illustrated above. In practice, however, it is easier to use a table of present values.

The *present value of $1* table is used to find the present value factor for $1 to be received after a number of periods in the future. The amount to be received is then multiplied by this factor to determine its present value.

To illustrate, Exhibit 4 is a partial table of the present value of $1.[7] Exhibit 4 indicates that the present value of $1 to be received in two years with a market rate of interest of 10% a year is 0.82645. Multiplying $1,000 to be received in two years by 0.82645 yields $826.45 ($1,000 × 0.82645). This amount is the same amount computed above. In Exhibit 4, the Periods column represents the number of compounding periods, and the percentage columns represent the compound interest rate per period. Thus, the present value factor from Exhibit 4 for 12% for five years compounded *semiannually* is 0.55840. Since the interest is compounded semiannually, the interest rate is 6% (12% divided by 2), and the number of periods is 10 (5 years × 2 times per year). Some additional examples using Exhibit 4 are shown below.

Spreadsheet software with built-in present value functions can be used to calculate present values.

Exhibit 4

Present Value of $1 at Compound Interest

Periods	5%	5½%	6%	6½%	7%	10%	11%	12%	13%	14%
1	0.95238	0.94787	0.94340	0.93897	0.93458	0.90909	0.90090	0.89286	0.88496	0.87719
2	0.90703	0.89845	0.89000	0.88166	0.87344	0.82645	0.81162	0.79719	0.78315	0.76947
3	0.86384	0.85161	0.83962	0.82785	0.81630	0.75132	0.73119	0.71178	0.69305	0.67497
4	0.82270	0.80722	0.79209	0.77732	0.76290	0.68301	0.65873	0.63552	0.61332	0.59208
5	0.78353	0.76513	0.74726	0.72988	0.71299	0.62092	0.59345	0.56743	0.54276	0.51937
6	0.74622	0.72525	0.70496	0.68533	0.66634	0.56447	0.53464	0.50663	0.48032	0.45559
7	0.71068	0.68744	0.66506	0.64351	0.62275	0.51316	0.48166	0.45235	0.42506	0.39964
8	0.67684	0.65160	0.62741	0.60423	0.58201	0.46651	0.43393	0.40388	0.37616	0.35056
9	0.64461	0.61763	0.59190	0.56735	0.54393	0.42410	0.39092	0.36061	0.33288	0.30751
10	0.61391	0.58543	0.55840	0.53273	0.50835	0.38554	0.35218	0.32197	0.29459	0.26974

	Number of Periods	Interest Rate	Present Value of $1 Factor from Exhibit 4
10% for *two* years compounded *annually*	2	10%	0.82645
10% for *two* years compounded *semiannually*	4	5%	0.82270
10% for *three* years compounded *semiannually*	6	5%	0.74622
12% for *five* years compounded *semiannually*	10	6%	0.55840

7 To simplify the illustrations and homework assignments, the tables presented in this chapter are limited to 10 periods for a small number of interest rates, and the amounts are carried to only five decimal places. Computer programs are available for determining present value factors for any number of interest rates, decimal places, or periods. More complete interest tables are presented in Appendix A of the text.

Present Value of the Periodic Receipts A series of equal cash receipts at fixed intervals is called an **annuity**. The **present value of an annuity** is the sum of the present values of each cash receipt. To illustrate, assume that $100 is to be received annually for two years and that the market rate of interest is 10%. Using Exhibit 4, the present value of the receipt of the two amounts of $100 is $173.55, as shown below.

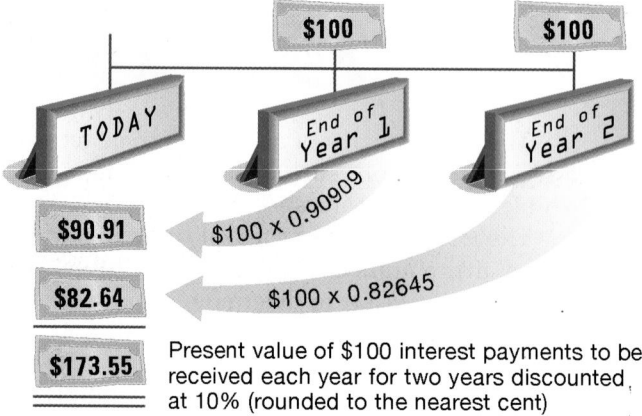

Instead of using present value of $1 tables, such as Exhibit 4, separate present value tables are normally used for annuities. Exhibit 5 is a partial table of the **present value of an annuity of $1** at compound interest. It shows the present value of $1 to be received at the end of each period for various compound rates of interest.

Exhibit 5

Present Value of Annuity of $1 at Compound Interest

Periods	5%	5½%	6%	6½%	7%	10%	11%	12%	13%	14%
1	0.95238	0.94787	0.94340	0.93897	0.93458	0.90909	0.90090	0.89286	0.88496	0.87719
2	1.85941	1.84632	1.83339	1.82063	1.80802	1.73554	1.71252	1.69005	1.66810	1.64666
3	2.72325	2.69793	2.67301	2.64848	2.62432	2.48685	2.44371	2.40183	2.36115	2.32163
4	3.54595	3.50515	3.46511	3.42580	3.38721	3.16987	3.10245	3.03735	2.97447	2.91371
5	4.32948	4.27028	4.21236	4.15568	4.10020	3.79079	3.69590	3.60478	3.51723	3.43308
6	5.07569	4.99553	4.91732	4.84101	4.76654	4.35526	4.23054	4.11141	3.99755	3.88867
7	5.78637	5.68297	5.58238	5.48452	5.38929	4.86842	4.71220	4.56376	4.42261	4.28830
8	6.46321	6.33457	6.20979	6.08875	5.97130	5.33493	5.14612	4.96764	4.79677	4.63886
9	7.10782	6.95220	6.80169	6.65610	6.51523	5.75902	5.53705	5.32825	5.13166	4.94637
10	7.72174	7.53763	7.36009	7.18883	7.02358	6.14457	5.88923	5.65022	5.42624	5.21612

To illustrate, the present value of $100 to be received at the end of each of the next two years at 10% compound interest per period is $173.55 ($100 × 1.73554). This amount is the same amount computed above.

Pricing Bonds

The selling price of a bond is the present value, using the current market rate of interest, of the following:

1. The face amount of the bonds due at the maturity date
2. The periodic interest to be paid on the bonds

To illustrate the pricing of bonds, assume that Southern Utah Communications Inc. issued the following bond on January 1, 2009:

Face amount $100,000
Contract rate of interest 12%
Interest paid semiannually on
   June 30 and December 31.
Term of bonds . . . .   5 years

Market Rate of Interest of 12%

Assuming a market rate of interest of 12%, the bonds would sell for $100,000, their face amount, as shown by the following present value computations.

Present value of face amount of $100,000 due in 5 years,
   at 12% compounded semiannually: $100,000 × 0.55840
   (present value of $1 for 10 periods at 6% from Exhibit 4) . . . . $ 55,840
Present value of 10 semiannual interest payments of $6,000,
   at 12% compounded semiannually: $6,000 × 7.36009
   (present value of annuity of $1 for 10 periods at 6% from Exhibit 5)   44,160
Total present value of bonds $100,000

Market Rate of Interest of 13%

Assuming a market rate of interest of 13%, the bonds would sell at a discount. As shown by the following present value computations, the bonds would sell for $96,406.[8]

Present value of face amount of $100,000 due in 5 years,
   at 13% compounded semiannually: $100,000 × 0.53273
   (present value of $1 for 10 periods at 6½% from Exhibit 4) . . . . $ 53,273
Present value of 10 semiannual interest payments of $6,000,
   at 13% compounded semiannually: $6,000 × 7.18883
   (present value of an annuity of $1 for 10 periods at 6½% from Exhibit 5) . .   43,133
Total present value of bonds . . . . $ 96,406

Market Rate of Interest of 11%

Assuming a market rate of interest of 11%, the bonds would sell at a premium. As shown by the following present value computations, the bonds would sell for $103,769.

Present value of face amount of $100,000 due in 5 years,
   at 11% compounded semiannually: $100,000 × 0.58543
   (present value of $1 for 10 periods at 5½% from Exhibit 4) . . . . $ 58,543
Present value of 10 semiannual interest payments of $6,000,
   at 11% compounded semiannually: $6,000 × 7.53763
   (present value of an annuity of $1 for 10 periods at 5½% from Exhibit 5) . .   45,226
Total present value of bonds $103,769

As shown above, the selling price of the bond varies with the present value of the bond's face amount at maturity, interest payments, and the market rate of interest.

---

8 Some corporations issue bonds called *zero-coupon bonds* that provide for only the payment of the face amount at maturity. Such bonds sell for large discounts. In this example, such a bond would sell for $53,273, which is the present value of the face amount.

APPENDIX 2

Effective Interest Rate Method of Amortization

The effective interest rate method of amortization provides for a constant *rate* of interest over the life of the bonds. As the discount or premium is amortized, the carrying amount of the bonds changes. As a result, interest expense also changes each period. This is in contrast to the straight-line method, which provides for a constant *amount* of interest expense each period.

The interest rate used in the effective interest rate method of amortization, sometimes called the *interest method*, is the market rate on the date the bonds are issued. The carrying amount of the bonds is multiplied by this interest rate to determine the interest expense for the period. The difference between the interest expense and the interest payment is the amount of discount or premium to be amortized for the period.

Amortization of Discount by the Interest Method

To illustrate, the following data taken from the chapter illustration of issuing bonds at a discount are used:

Face value of 12%, 5-year bonds, interest compounded semiannually	$100,000
Present value of bonds at effective (market) rate of interest of 13%	96,406
Discount on bonds payable	$ 3,594

Exhibit 6 illustrates the interest method for the preceding bonds. Exhibit 6 was prepared as follows:

Step 1. List the interest payments dates in the first column, which for the preceding bond are 10 interest payment dates (semiannual interest over five years). Also, list on the first line the initial amount of discount in Column D and the initial carrying amount (selling price) of the bonds in Column E.

Step 2. List in Column A the semiannual interest payments, which for the preceding bond is $6,000 ($100,000 × 6%).

Step 3. Compute the interest expense in Column B by multiplying the bond carrying amount at the beginning of each period times 6½%, which is the effective interest (market) rate.

Step 4. Compute the discount to be amortized each period in Column C by subtracting the interest payment in Column A ($6,000) from the interest expense for the period shown in Column B.

Step 5. Compute the remaining unamortized discount by subtracting the amortized discount in Column C for the period from the unamortized discount at the beginning of the period in Column D.

Step 6. Compute the bond carrying amount at the end of the period by subtracting the unamortized discount at the end of the period from the face amount of the bonds.

Steps 3–6 are repeated for each interest payment.

As shown in Exhibit 6, the interest expense increases each period as the carrying amount of the bond increases. Also, the unamortized discount decreases each period to zero at the maturity date. Finally, the carrying amount of the bonds increases from $96,406 to $100,000 (the face amount) at maturity.

Exhibit 6

Amortization of Discount on Bonds Payable

Interest Payment Date	A Interest Paid (6% of Face Amount)	B Interest Expense (6½% of Bond Carrying Amount)	C Discount Amortization (B − A)	D Unamortized Discount (D − C)	E Bond Carrying Amount ($100,000 − D)
				$3,594	$ 96,406
June 30, 2009	$6,000	$6,266 (6½% of $96,406)	$266	3,328	96,672
Dec. 31, 2009	6,000	6,284 (6½% of $96,672)	284	3,044	96,956
June 30, 2010	6,000	6,302 (6½% of $96,956)	302	2,742	97,258
Dec. 31, 2010	6,000	6,322 (6½% of $97,258)	322	2,420	97,580
June 30, 2011	6,000	6,343 (6½% of $97,580)	343	2,077	97,923
Dec. 31, 2011	6,000	6,365 (6½% of $97,923)	365	1,712	98,288
June 30, 2012	6,000	6,389 (6½% of $98,288)	389	1,323	98,677
Dec. 31, 2012	6,000	6,414 (6½% of $98,677)	414	909	99,091
June 30, 2013	6,000	6,441 (6½% of $99,091)	441	468	99,532
Dec. 31, 2013	6,000	6,470 (6½% of $99,532)	468*	—	100,000

*Cannot exceed unamortized discount.

The entry to record the first interest payment on June 30, 2009, and the related discount amortization is as follows:

2009 June	30	Interest Expense		6,266	
		Discount on Bonds Payable			266
		Cash			6,000
		Paid semiannual interest and amortized bond discount for ½ year.			

If the amortization is recorded only at the end of the year, the amount of the discount amortized on December 31, 2009, would be $550. This is the sum of the first two semiannual amortization amounts ($266 and $284) from Exhibit 6.

Amortization of Premium by the Interest Method

To illustrate, the following data taken from the chapter illustration of issuing bonds at a premium are used:

Present value of bonds at effective (market) rate of interest of 11%	$103,769
Face value of 12%, 5-year bonds, interest compounded semiannually . .	100,000
Premium on bonds payable	$ 3,769

Exhibit 7 illustrates the interest method for the preceding bonds. Exhibit 7 was prepared as follows:

Step 1. List the number of interest payments in the first column, which for the preceding bond are 10 interest payments (semiannual interest over 5 years). Also, list on the first line the initial amount of premium in Column D and the initial carrying amount of the bonds in Column E.

Step 2. List in Column A the semiannual interest payments, which for the preceding bond is $6,000 ($100,000 × 6%).

Step 3. Compute the interest expense in Column B by multiplying the bond carrying amount at the beginning of each period times 5½%, which is the effective interest (market) rate.

Step 4. Compute the premium to be amortized each period in Column C by subtracting the interest expense for the period shown in Column B from the interest payment in Column A ($6,000).

Step 5. Compute the remaining unamortized premium by subtracting the amortized premium in Column C for the period from the unamortized premium at the beginning of the period in Column D.

Step 6. Compute the bond carrying amount at the end of the period by adding the unamortized premium at the end of the period to the face amount of the bonds.

Steps 3–6 are repeated for each interest payment.

As shown in Exhibit 7, the interest expense decreases each period as the carrying amount of the bond decreases. Also, the unamortized premium decreases each period to zero at the maturity date. Finally, the carrying amount of the bonds decreases from $103,769 to $100,000 (the face amount) at maturity.

Exhibit 7

Amortization of Premium on Bonds Payable

Interest Payment Date	A Interest Paid (6% of Face Amount)	B Interest Expense (5½% of Bond Carrying Amount)	C Premium Amortization (A − B)	D Unamortized Premium (D − C)	E Bond Carrying Amount ($100,000 + D)
				$3,769	$103,769
June 30, 2009	$6,000	5,707 (5½% of $103,769)	$293	3,476	103,476
Dec. 31, 2009	6,000	5,691 (5½% of $103,476)	309	3,167	103,167
June 30, 2010	6,000	5,674 (5½% of $103,167)	326	2,841	102,841
Dec. 31, 2010	6,000	5,656 (5½% of $102,841)	344	2,497	102,497
June 30, 2011	6,000	5,637 (5½% of $102,497)	363	2,134	102,134
Dec. 31, 2011	6,000	5,617 (5½% of $102,134)	383	1,751	101,751
June 30, 2012	6,000	5,596 (5½% of $101,751)	404	1,347	101,347
Dec. 31, 2012	6,000	5,574 (5½% of $101,347)	426	921	100,921
June 30, 2013	6,000	5,551 (5½% of $100,921)	449	472	100,472
Dec. 31, 2013	6,000	5,526 (5½% of $100,472)	472*	—	100,000

*Cannot exceed unamortized premium.

The entry to record the first interest payment on June 30, 2009, and the related premium amortization is as follows:

2009				
June	30	Interest Expense	5,707	
		Premium on Bonds Payable	293	
		Cash		6,000
		Paid semiannual interest and amortized bond premium for ½ year.		

If the amortization is recorded only at the end of the year, the amount of the premium amortized on December 31, 2009, would be $602. This is the sum of the first two semiannual amortization amounts ($293 and $309) from Exhibit 7.

1 Compute the potential impact of long-term borrowing on earnings per share.

Key Points	Key Learning Outcomes	Example Exercises	Practice Exercises
Corporations can finance their operations by issuing bonds or additional equity. A bond is simply a form of an interest-bearing note. One of the many factors that influence a corporation's decision on whether it should issue debt or equity is the effect each alternative has on earnings per share.	• Define the concept of a bond.		
	• Calculate and compare the effect of alternative financing plans on earnings per share.	**14-1**	14-1A, 14-1B

2 Describe the characteristics and terminology of bonds payable.

Key Points	Key Learning Outcomes	Example Exercises	Practice Exercises
A corporation that issues bonds enters into a contract, or bond indenture. The characteristics of a bond depend on the type of bonds issued by a corporation.	• Define the characteristics of a bond.		
When a corporation issues bonds, the price that buyers are willing to pay for the bonds depends on (1) the face amount of the bonds, (2) the periodic interest to be paid on the bonds, and (3) the market rate of interest.	• Describe the various types of bonds.		
	• Describe the factors that determine the price of a bond.		

3 Journalize entries for bonds payable.

Key Points	Key Learning Outcomes	Example Exercises	Practice Exercises
The journal entry for issuing bonds payable debits Cash for the proceeds received and credits Bonds Payable for the face amount of the bonds. Any difference between the face amount of the bonds and the proceeds is debited to Discount on Bonds Payable or credited to Premium on Bonds Payable. A discount or premium on bonds payable is amortized to interest expense over the life of the bonds.	• Journalize the issuance of bonds at face value and the payment of periodic interest.		
	• Journalize the issuance of bonds at a discount.	**14-2**	14-2A, 14-2B
	• Journalize the amortization of a bond discount.	**14-3**	14-3A, 14-3B
At the maturity date, the entry to record the payment at face value of a bond is a debit to Bonds Payable and a credit to Cash.	• Journalize the issuance of bonds at a premium.	**14-4**	14-4A, 14-4B
	• Journalize the amortization of a bond premium.	**14-5**	14-5A, 14-5B
When a corporation redeems bonds, Bonds Payable is debited for the face amount of the bonds, the premium (discount) on bonds payable account is debited (credited) for its balance, Cash is credited, and any gain or loss on the redemption is recorded.	• Describe bond redemptions.		
	• Journalize the redemption of bonds payable.	**14-6**	14-6A, 14-6B

4 Describe and illustrate the accounting for installment notes.

Key Points	Key Learning Outcomes	Example Exercises	Practice Exercises
Companies issue installment notes as an alternative to issuing bonds. An installment note requires the borrower to make equal periodic payments to the lender for the term of the note. Unlike bonds, the annual payment in an installment note consists of both principal and interest. The journal entry for the annual payment debits Interest Expense and Notes Payable and credits Cash for the amount of the payment. After the final payment, the carrying amount on the note is zero.	• Define the characteristics of an installment note. • Journalize the issuance of installment notes. • Journalize the annual payment for an installment note.	**14-7**	14-7A, 14-7B

5 Describe and illustrate the reporting of long-term liabilities including bonds and notes payable.

Key Points	Key Learning Outcomes	Example Exercises	Practice Exercises
Bonds payable and notes payable are usually reported as long-term liabilities. If the balance sheet date is within one year, they are reported as a current liability. A discount on bonds should be reported as a deduction from the related bonds payable. A premium on bonds should be reported as an addition to related bonds payable.	• Illustrate the balance sheet presentation of bonds payable and notes payable.		

Key Terms

annuity (630)
bond (613)
bond indenture (616)
carrying amount (622)
contract rate (616)
discount (616)
earnings per share (EPS) (614)

effective interest rate method (619)
effective rate of interest (616)
future value (628)
installment note (623)
market rate of interest (616)
mortgage notes (623)

number of times interest charges are earned (627)
premium (616)
present value (628)
present value of an annuity (630)
present value of an annuity of $1 (630)

Illustrative Problem

The fiscal year of Russell Inc., a manufacturer of acoustical supplies, ends December 31. Selected transactions for the period 2009 through 2016, involving bonds payable issued by Russell Inc., are as follows:

2009
June 30. Issued $2,000,000 of 25-year, 7% callable bonds dated June 30, 2009, for cash of $1,920,000. Interest is payable semiannually on June 30 and December 31.

Dec. 31. Paid the semiannual interest on the bonds.
  31. Recorded straight-line amortization of $1,600 of discount on the bonds.
  31. Closed the interest expense account.

2010
June 30. Paid the semiannual interest on the bonds.
Dec. 31. Paid the semiannual interest on the bonds.
  31. Recorded straight-line amortization of $3,200 of discount on the bonds.
  31. Closed the interest expense account.

2016
June 30. Recorded the redemption of the bonds, which were called at 101.5. The balance in the bond discount account is $57,600 after the payment of interest and amortization of discount have been recorded. (Record the redemption only.)

Instructions

1. Journalize entries to record the preceding transactions.
2. Determine the amount of interest expense for 2009 and 2010.
3. Determine the carrying amount of the bonds as of December 31, 2010.

Solution

1.

2009				
June	30	Cash	1,920,000	
		Discount on Bonds Payable	80,000	
		Bonds Payable		2,000,000
Dec.	31	Interest Expense	70,000	
		Cash		70,000
	31	Interest Expense	1,600	
		Discount on Bonds Payable		1,600
		Amortization of discount from July 1 to December 31.		
	31	Income Summary	71,600	
		Interest Expense		71,600
2010				
June	30	Interest Expense	70,000	
		Cash		70,000
Dec.	31	Interest Expense	70,000	
		Cash		70,000
	31	Interest Expense	3,200	
		Discount on Bonds Payable		3,200
		Amortization of discount from January 1 to December 31.		
	31	Income Summary	143,200	
		Interest Expense		143,200
2016				
June	30	Bonds Payable	2,000,000	
		Loss on Redemption of Bonds Payable	87,600	
		Discount on Bonds Payable		57,600
		Cash		2,030,000

2. a. 2009—$71,600
   b. 2010—$143,200

3.	Initial carrying amount of bonds	$1,920,000
	Discount amortized on December 31, 2009	1,600
	Discount amortized on December 31, 2010	3,200
	Carrying amount of bonds, December 31, 2010	$1,924,800

Self-Examination Questions (Answers at End of Chapter)

1. Which of the following measures might a company use to compare alternative financing decisions?
   A. The price of the bond issue
   B. The discount on the bonds payable
   C. Earnings per share
   D. Interest expense

2. If a corporation plans to issue $1,000,000 of 12% bonds at a time when the market rate for similar bonds is 10%, the bonds can be expected to sell at:
   A. their face amount.
   B. a premium.
   C. a discount.
   D. a price below their face amount.

3. If the bonds payable account has a balance of $900,000 and the discount on bonds payable account has a balance of $72,000, what is the carrying amount of the bonds?
   A. $828,000   C. $972,000
   B. $900,000   D. $580,000

4. If a company borrows money from a bank as an installment note, the interest portion of each annual payment will:
   A. equal the interest rate on the note times the face amount.
   B. equal the interest rate on the note times the carrying amount of the note at the beginning of the period.
   C. increase over the term of the note.
   D. remain constant over the term of the note.

5. The balance in the discount on bonds payable account would usually be reported on the balance sheet in the:
   A. Current Assets section.
   B. Current Liabilities section.
   C. Long-Term Liabilities section.
   D. Investments section.

Eye Openers

1. Describe the two distinct obligations incurred by a corporation when issuing bonds.
2. Explain the meaning of each of the following terms as they relate to a bond issue: (a) convertible, (b) callable, and (c) debenture.
3. If you asked your broker to purchase for you a 10% bond when the market interest rate for such bonds was 11%, would you expect to pay more or less than the face amount for the bond? Explain.
4. A corporation issues $9,000,000 of 9% bonds to yield interest at the rate of 7%. (a) Was the amount of cash received from the sale of the bonds greater or less than $9,000,000? (b) Identify the following terms related to the bond issue: (1) face amount, (2) market or effective rate of interest, (3) contract rate of interest, and (4) maturity amount.
5. If bonds issued by a corporation are sold at a premium, is the market rate of interest greater or less than the contract rate?
6. The following data relate to a $100,000,000, 12% bond issue for a selected semiannual interest period:

Bond carrying amount at beginning of period	$112,085,373
Interest paid during period	6,000,000
Interest expense allocable to the period	5,623,113

(a) Were the bonds issued at a discount or at a premium? (b) What is the unamortized amount of the discount or premium account at the beginning of the period? (c) What account was debited to amortize the discount or premium?

7. Assume that Smith Co. amortizes premiums and discounts on bonds payable at the end of the year rather than when interest is paid. What accounts would be debited and credited to record (a) the amortization of a discount on bonds payable and (b) the amortization of a premium on bonds payable?
8. When a corporation issues bonds at a discount, is the discount recorded as income when the bonds are issued? Explain.
9. Assume that two 30-year, 10% bond issues are identical, except that one bond issue is callable at its face amount at the end of five years. Which of the two bond issues do you think will sell for a lower value?
10. Bonds Payable has a balance of $1,000,000, and Discount on Bonds Payable has a balance of $50,000. If the issuing corporation redeems the bonds at 98, is there a gain or loss on the bond redemption?
11. What is a mortgage note?
12. Fleeson Company needs additional funds to purchase equipment for a new production facility and is considering either issuing bonds payable or borrowing the money from a local bank in the form of an installment note. How does an installment note differ from a bond payable?
13. How would a bond payable be reported on the balance sheet if: (a) it is payable within one year and (b) it is payable beyond one year?
14. Sol Company issued $10,000,000 of bonds payable at a price of 102. How would the premium on the bonds payable be presented on the balance sheet?
15. What is meant by the phrase "time value of money"?
16. What has the higher present value: (a) $20,000 to be received at the end of two years, or (b) $10,000 to be received at the end of each of the next two years?

Practice Exercises

PE 14-1A
Alternative financing plans
obj. 1
EE 14-1 p. 615

Folmar Co. is considering the following alternative financing plans:

	Plan 1	Plan 2
Issue 10% bonds (at face value)	$2,000,000	$1,000,000
Issue preferred $1 stock, $5 par	—	1,500,000
Issue common stock, $5 par	2,000,000	1,500,000

Income tax is estimated at 40% of income.
Determine the earnings per share of common stock, assuming income before bond interest and income tax is $800,000.

PE 14-1B
Alternative financing plans
obj. 1
EE 14-1 p. 615

Simonelli Co. is considering the following alternative financing plans:

	Plan 1	Plan 2
Issue 8% bonds (at face value)	$5,000,000	4,000,000
Issue preferred $2.00 stock, $20 par	—	2,000,000
Issue common stock, $25 par	5,000,000	4,000,000

Income tax is estimated at 40% of income.
Determine the earnings per share of common stock, assuming income before bond interest and income tax is $1,000,000.

PE 14-2A
Issuing bonds at a discount
obj. 3
EE 14-2 p. 618

On the first day of the fiscal year, a company issues a $1,000,000, 11%, 10-year bond that pays semiannual interest of $55,000 ($1,000,000 × 11% × ½), receiving cash of $942,646. Journalize the bond issuance.

PE 14-2B
Issuing bonds at a discount

obj. 3

EE 14-2   p. 618

On the first day of the fiscal year, a company issues a $750,000, 7%, five-year bond that pays semiannual interest of $26,250 ($750,000 × 7% × ½), receiving cash of $663,128. Journalize the bond issuance.

PE 14-3A
Discount amortization

obj. 3

EE 14-3   p. 620

Using the bond from Practice Exercise 14-2A, journalize the first interest payment and the amortization of the related bond discount.

PE 14-3B
Discount amortization

obj. 3

EE 14-3   p. 620

Using the bond from Practice Exercise 14-2B, journalize the first interest payment and the amortization of the related bond discount.

PE 14-4A
Issuing bonds at a premium

obj. 3

EE 14-4   p. 621

A company issues a $5,000,000, 11%, five-year bond that pays semiannual interest of $275,000 ($5,000,000 × 11% × ½), receiving cash of $5,193,030. Journalize the bond issuance.

PE 14-4B
Issuing bonds at a premium

obj. 3

EE 14-4   p. 621

A company issues a $3,000,000, 12%, five-year bond that pays semiannual interest of $180,000 ($3,000,000 × 12% × ½), receiving cash of $3,146,200. Journalize the bond issuance.

PE 14-5A
Premium amortization

obj. 3

EE 14-5   p. 622

Using the bond from Practice Exercise 14-4A, journalize the first interest payment and the amortization of the related bond premium.

PE 14-5B
Premium amortization

obj. 3

EE 14-5   p. 622

Using the bond from Practice Exercise 14-4B, journalize the first interest payment and the amortization of the related bond premium.

PE 14-6A
Redemption of bonds payable

obj. 3

EE 14-6   p. 623

A $500,000 bond issue on which there is an unamortized discount of $50,000 is redeemed for $475,000. Journalize the redemption of the bonds.

PE 14-6B
Redemption of bonds payable

obj. **3**

EE 14-6   p. 623

A $200,000 bond issue on which there is an unamortized premium of $15,000 is redeemed for $195,000. Journalize the redemption of the bonds.

PE 14-7A
Journalizing installment notes

obj. **4**

EE 14-7   p. 626

On the first day of the fiscal year, a company issues $65,000, 10%, six-year installment notes that have annual payments of $14,924. The first note payment consists of $6,500 of interest and $8,424 of principal repayment.

a. Journalize the entry to record the issuance of the installment notes.
b. Journalize the first annual note payment.

PE 14-7B
Journalizing installment notes

obj. **4**

EE 14-7   p. 626

On the first day of the fiscal year, a company issues $35,000, 12%, five-year installment notes that have annual payments of $9,709. The first note payment consists of $4,200 of interest and $5,509 of principal repayment.

a. Journalize the entry to record the issuance of the installment notes.
b. Journalize the first annual note payment.

Exercises

EX 14-1
Effect of financing on earnings per share

obj. **1**

✔ a. $0.50

Miller Co., which produces and sells skiing equipment, is financed as follows:

Bonds payable, 10% (issued at face amount)	$10,000,000
Preferred $1 stock, $10 par	10,000,000
Common stock, $25 par	10,000,000

Income tax is estimated at 40% of income.
    Determine the earnings per share of common stock, assuming that the income before bond interest and income tax is (a) $3,000,000, (b) $4,000,000, and (c) $5,000,000.

EX 14-2
Evaluate alternative financing plans

obj. **1**

━━━► Based on the data in Exercise 14-1, discuss factors other than earnings per share that should be considered in evaluating such financing plans.

EX 14-3
Corporate financing

obj. **1**

The financial statements for Nike, Inc., are presented in Appendix E at the end of the text. What is the major source of financing for Nike?

EX 14-4
Bond price

obj. **3**

Procter and Gamble's 8% bonds due in 2024 were reported as selling for 126.987.
━━━► Were the bonds selling at a premium or at a discount? Explain.

EX 14-5
Entries for issuing bonds

obj. 3

Grodski Co. produces and distributes semiconductors for use by computer manufacturers. Grodski Co. issued $24,000,000 of 20-year, 10% bonds on April 1 of the current year, with interest payable on April 1 and October 1. The fiscal year of the company is the calendar year. Journalize the entries to record the following selected transactions for the current year:

Apr. 1.   Issued the bonds for cash at their face amount.
Oct. 1.   Paid the interest on the bonds.
Dec. 31. Recorded accrued interest for three months.

EX 14-6
Entries for issuing bonds and amortizing discount by straight-line method

obj. 3

✔ b. $5,130,648

On the first day of its fiscal year, Robbins Company issued $50,000,000 of five-year, 8% bonds to finance its operations of producing and selling home improvement products. Interest is payable semiannually. The bonds were issued at an effective interest rate of 11%, resulting in Robbins Company receiving cash of $44,346,760.

a. Journalize the entries to record the following:
   1. Sale of the bonds.
   2. First semiannual interest payment. (Amortization of discount is to be recorded annually.)
   3. Second semiannual interest payment.
   4. Amortization of discount at the end of the first year, using the straight-line method. (Round to the nearest dollar.)
b. Determine the amount of the bond interest expense for the first year.

EX 14-7
Entries for issuing bonds and amortizing premium by straight-line method

objs. 2, 3

Daan Corporation wholesales repair products to equipment manufacturers. On March 1, 2010, Daan Corporation issued $24,000,000 of five-year, 12% bonds at an effective interest rate of 10%, receiving cash of $25,853,146. Interest is payable semiannually on March 1 and September 1. Journalize the entries to record the following:

a. Sale of bonds on March 1, 2010.
b. First interest payment on September 1, 2010, and amortization of bond premium for six months, using the straight-line method. (Round to the nearest dollar.)

EX 14-8
Entries for issuing and calling bonds; loss

obj. 3

Polders Corp., a wholesaler of office equipment, issued $16,000,000 of 20-year, 11% callable bonds on April 1, 2010, with interest payable on April 1 and October 1. The fiscal year of the company is the calendar year. Journalize the entries to record the following selected transactions:

2010
Apr. 1.   Issued the bonds for cash at their face amount.
Oct. 1.   Paid the interest on the bonds.

2014
Oct. 1.   Called the bond issue at 102, the rate provided in the bond indenture. (Omit entry for payment of interest.)

EX 14-9
Entries for issuing and calling bonds; gain

obj. 3

Vidovich Corp. produces and sells soccer equipment. To finance its operations, Vidovich Corp. issued $15,000,000 of 30-year, 14% callable bonds on January 1, 2010, with interest payable on January 1 and July 1. The fiscal year of the company is the calendar year. Journalize the entries to record the following selected transactions:

2010
Jan. 1.   Issued the bonds for cash at their face amount.
July 1.   Paid the interest on the bonds.

2016
July 1.   Called the bond issue at 98, the rate provided in the bond indenture. (Omit entry for payment of interest.)

EX 14-10
Entries for issuing
installment note
transactions

obj. 4

On the first day of the fiscal year, Hammond Company obtained a $44,000, seven-year, 5% installment note from Vegas Bank. The note requires annual payments of $7,604, with the first payment occurring on the last day of the fiscal year. The first payment consists of interest of $2,200 and principal repayment of $5,404.

a. Journalize the entries to record the following:
　1. Issued the installment notes for cash on the first day of the fiscal year.
　2. Paid the first annual payment on the note.
b. Determine the amount of bond interest expense for the first year.

EX 14-11
Entries for issuing
installment note
transactions

obj. 4

On January 1, 2010, Guiado Company obtained a $140,000, 10-year, 11% installment note from Best Bank. The note requires annual payments of $23,772, beginning on December 31, 2010. Journalize the entries to record the following:

2010
Jan. 1.　Issued the notes for cash at their face amount.
Dec. 31.　Paid the annual payment on the note, which consisted of interest of $15,400 and principal of $8,372.

2019
Dec. 31.　Paid the annual payment on the note, which consisted of interest of $2,353 and principal of $21,419.

EX 14-12
Entries for issuing
installment note
transactions

obj. 4

On January 1, 2010, Zinn Company obtained a $52,000, four-year, 6.5% installment note from Fidelity Bank. The note requires annual payments of $15,179, beginning on December 31, 2011.

a. Prepare an amortization table for this installment note, similar to the one presented in Exhibit 3.
b. Journalize the entries for the issuance of the note and the four annual note payments.

EX 14-13
Reporting bonds

obj. 5

At the beginning of the current year, two bond issues (X and Y) were outstanding. During the year, bond issue X was redeemed and a significant loss on the redemption of bonds was reported as an extraordinary item on the income statement. At the end of the year, bond issue Y was reported as a noncurrent liability. The maturity date on the bonds was early in the following year.
　　　　Identify the flaws in the reporting practices related to the two bond issues.

Appendix 1
EX 14-14
Present value of
amounts due

Determine the present value of $400,000 to be received in three years, using an interest rate of 10%, compounded annually, as follows:

a. By successive divisions. (Round to the nearest dollar.)
b. By using the present value table in Exhibit 4.

Appendix 1
EX 14-15
Present value of an
annuity

Determine the present value of $100,000 to be received at the end of each of four years, using an interest rate of 6%, compounded annually, as follows:

a. By successive computations, using the present value table in Exhibit 4.
b. By using the present value table in Exhibit 5.

Appendix 1
EX 14-16
Present value of an
annuity

✔ $21,070,740

On January 1, 2010, you win $30,000,000 in the state lottery. The $30,000,000 prize will be paid in equal installments of $3,000,000 over 10 years. The payments will be made on December 31 of each year, beginning on December 31, 2010. If the current interest rate is 7%, determine the present value of your winnings. Use the present value tables in Appendix A.

Appendix 1
EX 14-17
Present value of an
annuity

Assume the same data as in Appendix 1 Exercise 14-16, except that the current interest rate is 14%.
━━━━▶ Will the present value of your winnings using an interest rate of 14% be one-half the present value of your winnings using an interest rate of 7%? Why or why not?

Appendix 1
EX 14-18
Present value of
bonds payable;
discount

Hi-Vis Co. produces and sells high resolution flat panel televisions. To finance its operations, Hi-Vis Co. issued $10,000,000 of five-year, 10% bonds with interest payable semi-annually at an effective interest rate of 12%. Determine the present value of the bonds payable, using the present value tables in Exhibits 4 and 5. Round to the nearest dollar.

Appendix 1
EX 14-19
Present value of
bonds payable;
premium

✔ $69,265,908

Mason Co. issued $60,000,000 of five-year, 14% bonds with interest payable semiannually, at an effective interest rate of 10%. Determine the present value of the bonds payable, using the present value tables in Exhibits 4 and 5. Round to the nearest dollar.

Appendix 2
EX 14-20
Amortize discount by
interest method

✔ b. $2,719,776

On the first day of its fiscal year, Simon Company issued $25,000,000 of 10-year, 10% bonds to finance its operations of producing and selling video equipment. Interest is payable semiannually. The bonds were issued at an effective interest rate of 13%, resulting in Simon Company receiving cash of $20,868,138.

a. Journalize the entries to record the following:
   1. Sale of the bonds.
   2. First semiannual interest payment, including amortization of discount.
   3. Second semiannual interest payment, including amortization of discount.
b. Compute the amount of the bond interest expense for the first year.

Appendix 2
EX 14-21
Amortize premium by
interest method

✔ b. $1,027,982

Gary Miller Corporation wholesales bike parts to bicycle manufacturers. On March 1, 2010, Gary Miller Corporation issued $8,000,000 of five-year, 14% bonds at an effective interest rate of 12%, receiving cash of $8,588,850. Interest is payable semiannually. Gary Miller Corporation's fiscal year begins on March 1.

a. Journalize the entries to record the following:
   1. Sale of the bonds.
   2. First semiannual interest payment, including amortization of premium.
   3. Second semiannual interest payment, including amortization of premium.
b. Determine the bond interest expense for the first year.

Appendix 2
EX 14-22
Compute bond
proceeds, amortizing
premium by interest
method, and interest
expense

✔ a. $16,078,384
✔ c. $85,099

Motocar Co. produces and sells automobile parts. On the first day of its fiscal year, Motocar Co. issued $15,000,000 of five-year, 15% bonds at an effective interest rate of 13%, with interest payable semiannually. Compute the following, presenting figures used in your computations.

a. The amount of cash proceeds from the sale of the bonds. (Use the tables of present values in Exhibits 4 and 5. Round to the nearest dollar.)
b. The amount of premium to be amortized for the first semiannual interest payment period, using the interest method. (Round to the nearest dollar.)
c. The amount of premium to be amortized for the second semiannual interest payment period, using the interest method. (Round to the nearest dollar.)
d. The amount of the bond interest expense for the first year.

Appendix 2
EX 14-23
Compute bond
proceeds, amortizing
discount by interest
method, and interest
expense

✔ a. $35,785,876
✔ b. $305,011

Seward Co. produces and sells restaurant equipment. On the first day of its fiscal year, Seward Co. issued $40,000,000 of five-year, 11% bonds at an effective interest rate of 14%, with interest payable semiannually. Compute the following, presenting figures used in your computations.

a. The amount of cash proceeds from the sale of the bonds. (Use the tables of present values in Exhibits 4 and 5.)
b. The amount of discount to be amortized for the first semiannual interest payment period, using the interest method. (Round to the nearest dollar.)
c. The amount of discount to be amortized for the second semiannual interest payment period, using the interest method. (Round to the nearest dollar.)
d. The amount of the bond interest expense for the first year.

EX 14-24
Number of times
interest charges
earned

The following data were taken from recent annual reports of Southwest Airlines, which operates a low-fare airline service to over 50 cities in the United States.

	Current Year	Preceding Year
Interest expense	$ 56,000,000	$ 60,000,000
Income before income tax	325,000,000	450,000,000

a. Determine the number of times interest charges were earned for the current and preceding years. Round to one decimal place.
b. ▬▬▶ What conclusions can you draw?

Problems Series A

PR 14-1A
Effect of financing on
earnings per share
obj. 1

✔ 1. Plan 3: $2.60

Three different plans for financing a $10,000,000 corporation are under consideration by its organizers. Under each of the following plans, the securities will be issued at their par or face amount, and the income tax rate is estimated at 40% of income.

	Plan 1	Plan 2	Plan 3
10% bonds	—	—	$ 5,000,000
Preferred 10% stock, $40 par	—	$ 5,000,000	2,500,000
Common stock, $10 par	$10,000,000	5,000,000	2,500,000
Total	$10,000,000	$10,000,000	$10,000,000

Instructions
1. Determine for each plan the earnings per share of common stock, assuming that the income before bond interest and income tax is $2,000,000.
2. Determine for each plan the earnings per share of common stock, assuming that the income before bond interest and income tax is $950,000.
3. ▬▬▶ Discuss the advantages and disadvantages of each plan.

PR 14-2A
Bond discount,
entries for bonds
payable transactions
obj. 3

KLOOSTER
& ALLEN

✔ 3. $2,008,143

On July 1, 2010, Brower Industries Inc. issued $32,000,000 of 10-year, 12% bonds at an effective interest rate of 13%, receiving cash of $30,237,139. Interest on the bonds is payable semiannually on December 31 and June 30. The fiscal year of the company is the calendar year.

Instructions
1. Journalize the entry to record the amount of cash proceeds from the sale of the bonds.
2. Journalize the entries to record the following:
   a. The first semiannual interest payment on December 31, 2010, and the amortization of the bond discount, using the straight-line method. (Round to the nearest dollar.)
   b. The interest payment on June 30, 2011, and the amortization of the bond discount, using the straight-line method. (Round to the nearest dollar.)
3. Determine the total interest expense for 2010.
4. Will the bond proceeds always be less than the face amount of the bonds when the contract rate is less than the market rate of interest?

5. (Appendix 1) Compute the price of $30,237,139 received for the bonds by using the tables of present value in Appendix A at end of text. (Round to the nearest dollar.)

PR 14-3A
Bond premium, entries for bonds payable transactions
obj. 3

KA
KLOOSTER & ALLEN

✔ 3. $164,627

Maui Blends, Inc. produces and sells organically grown coffee. On July 1, 2010, Maui Blends, Inc. issued $3,000,000 of 15-year, 12% bonds at an effective interest rate of 10%, receiving cash of $3,461,181. Interest on the bonds is payable semiannually on December 31 and June 30. The fiscal year of the company is the calendar year.

Instructions
1. Journalize the entry to record the amount of cash proceeds from the sale of the bonds.
2. Journalize the entries to record the following:
   a. The first semiannual interest payment on December 31, 2010, and the amortization of the bond premium, using the straight-line method. (Round to the nearest dollar.)
   b. The interest payment on June 30, 2011, and the amortization of the bond premium, using the straight-line method. (Round to the nearest dollar.)
3. Determine the total interest expense for 2010.
4. Will the bond proceeds always be greater than the face amount of the bonds when the contract rate is greater than the market rate of interest?
5. (Appendix 1) Compute the price of $3,461,181 received for the bonds by using the tables of present value in Appendix A at the end of the text. (Round to the nearest dollar.)

PR 14-4A
Entries for bonds payable and installment note transactions
objs. 3, 4

KLOOSTER & ALLEN

✔ 3. $17,072,630

The following transactions were completed by Hobson Inc., whose fiscal year is the calendar year:

2010
July 1. Issued $18,000,000 of five-year, 10% callable bonds dated July 1, 2010, at an effective rate of 12%, receiving cash of $16,675,184. Interest is payable semiannually on December 31 and June 30.
Oct. 1. Borrowed $400,000 as a 10-year, 7% installment note from Marble Bank. The note requires annual payments of $56,951, with the first payment occurring on September 30, 2011.
Dec. 31. Accrued $7,000 of interest on the installment note. The interest is payable on the date of the next installment note payment.
   31. Paid the semiannual interest on the bonds.
   31. Recorded bond discount amortization of $132,482, which was determined using the straight-line method.
   31. Closed the interest expense account.

2011
June 30. Paid the semiannual interest on the bonds.
Sept. 30. Paid the annual payment on the note, which consisted of interest of $28,000 and principal of $28,951.
Dec. 31. Accrued $6,493 of interest on the installment note. The interest is payable on the date of the next installment note payment.
   31. Paid the semiannual interest on the bonds.
   31. Recorded bond discount amortization of $264,964, which was determined using the straight-line method.
   31. Closed the interest expense account.

2012
June 30. Recorded the redemption of the bonds, which were called at 97. The balance in the bond discount account is $794,888 after payment of interest and amortization of discount have been recorded. (Record the redemption only.)
Sept. 30. Paid the second annual payment on the note, which consisted of interest of $25,973 and principal of $30,978.

Instructions
1. Journalize the entries to record the foregoing transactions.
2. Indicate the amount of the interest expense in (a) 2010 and (b) 2011.
3. Determine the carrying amount of the bonds as of December 31, 2011.

Appendix 2
PR 14-5A
Bond discount,
entries for bonds
payable transactions,
interest method of
amortizing bond
discount

✔ 3. $1,965,414

On July 1, 2010, Brower Industries, Inc. issued $32,000,000 of 10-year, 12% bonds at an effective interest rate of 13%, receiving cash of $30,237,139. Interest on the bonds is payable semiannually on December 31 and June 30. The fiscal year of the company is the calendar year.

Instructions
1. Journalize the entry to record the amount of cash proceeds from the sale of the bonds.
2. Journalize the entries to record the following:
   a. The first semiannual interest payment on December 31, 2010, and the amortization of the bond discount, using the interest method. (Round to the nearest dollar.)
   b. The interest payment on June 30, 2011, and the amortization of the bond discount, using the interest method. (Round to the nearest dollar.)
3. Determine the total interest expense for 2010.

Appendix 2
PR 14-6A
Bond premium,
entries for bonds
payable transactions,
interest method of
amortizing bond
discount

✔ 3. $173,059

Maui Blends, Inc. produces and sells organically grown coffee. On July 1, 2010, Maui Blends, Inc. issued $3,000,000 of 15-year, 12% bonds at an effective interest rate of 10%, receiving cash of $3,461,181. Interest on the bonds is payable semiannually on December 31 and June 30. The fiscal year of the company is the calendar year.

Instructions
1. Journalize the entry to record the amount of cash proceeds from the sale of the bonds.
2. Journalize the entries to record the following:
   a. The first semiannual interest payment on December 31, 2010, and the amortization of the bond discount, using the interest method. (Round to the nearest dollar.)
   b. The interest payment on June 30, 2011, and the amortization of the bond discount, using the interest method. (Round to the nearest dollar.)
3. Determine the total interest expense for 2010.

Problems Series B

PR 14-1B
Effect of financing on
earnings per share

obj. 1

✔ 1. Plan 3: $5.12

Three different plans for financing a $60,000,000 corporation are under consideration by its organizers. Under each of the following plans, the securities will be issued at their par or face amount, and the income tax rate is estimated at 40% of income.

	Plan 1	Plan 2	Plan 3
12% bonds	—	—	$40,000,000
Preferred $2 stock, $20 par	—	$30,000,000	10,000,000
Common stock, $10 par	$60,000,000	30,000,000	10,000,000
Total	$60,000,000	$60,000,000	$60,000,000

Instructions
1. Determine for each plan the earnings per share of common stock, assuming that the income before bond interest and income tax is $15,000,000.
2. Determine for each plan the earnings per share of common stock, assuming that the income before bond interest and income tax is $7,000,000.
3. ▬▬▶ Discuss the advantages and disadvantages of each plan.

PR 14-2B
Bond discount,
entries for bonds
payable transactions

obj. 3

✔ 3. $2,726,729

On July 1, 2010, Linux Corporation, a wholesaler of electronics equipment, issued $45,000,000 of 10-year, 10% bonds at an effective interest rate of 14%, receiving cash of $35,465,423. Interest on the bonds is payable semiannually on December 31 and June 30. The fiscal year of the company is the calendar year.

Instructions
1. Journalize the entry to record the amount of cash proceeds from the sale of the bonds.
2. Journalize the entries to record the following:
   a. The first semiannual interest payment on December 31, 2010, and the amortization of the bond discount, using the straight-line method. (Round to the nearest dollar.)
   b. The interest payment on June 30, 2011, and the amortization of the bond discount, using the straight-line method. (Round to the nearest dollar.)
3. Determine the total interest expense for 2010.

4. Will the bond proceeds always be less than the face amount of the bonds when the contract rate is less than the market rate of interest?
5. (Appendix 1) Compute the price of $35,465,423 received for the bonds by using the tables of present value in Appendix A at end of text. (Round to the nearest dollar.)

PR 14-3B

Bond premium, entries for bonds payable transactions

obj. 3

✔ 3. $2,280,494

Prosser Corporation produces and sells baseball cards. On July 1, 2010, Prosser Corporation issued $40,000,000 of 10-year, 12% bonds at an effective interest rate of 11%, receiving cash of $42,390,112. Interest on the bonds is payable semiannually on December 31 and June 30. The fiscal year of the company is the calendar year.

Instructions

1. Journalize the entry to record the amount of cash proceeds from the sale of the bonds.
2. Journalize the entries to record the following:
   a. The first semiannual interest payment on December 31, 2010, and the amortization of the bond premium, using the straight-line method. (Round to the nearest dollar.)
   b. The interest payment on June 30, 2011, and the amortization of the bond premium, using the straight-line method. (Round to the nearest dollar.)
3. Determine the total interest expense for 2010.
4. Will the bond proceeds always be greater than the face amount of the bonds when the contract rate is greater than the market rate of interest?
5. (Appendix 1) Compute the price of $42,390,112 received for the bonds by using the tables of present value in Appendix A at the end of the text. (Round to the nearest dollar.)

PR 14-4B

Entries for bonds payable and installment note transactions

objs. 3, 4

✔ 3. $12,031,573

The following transactions were completed by Hobson Inc., whose fiscal year is the calendar year:

2010
July 1. Issued $10,000,000 of 10-year, 15% callable bonds dated July 1, 2010, at an effective rate of 11%, receiving cash of $12,390,085. Interest is payable semiannually on December 31 and June 30.

Oct. 1. Borrowed $225,000 as a six-year, 8% installment note from Titan Bank. The note requires annual payments of $48,671, with the first payment occurring on September 30, 2011.

Dec. 31. Accrued $4,500 of interest on the installment note. The interest is payable on the date of the next installment note payment.
     31. Paid the semiannual interest on the bonds.
     31. Recorded bond premium amortization of $119,504, which was determined using the straight-line method.
     31. Closed the interest expense account.

2011
June 30. Paid the semiannual interest on the bonds.
Sept. 30. Paid the annual payment on the note, which consisted of interest of $18,000 and principal of $30,671.
Dec. 31. Accrued $3,887 of interest on the installment note. The interest is payable on the date of the next installment note payment.
     31. Paid the semiannual interest on the bonds.
     31. Recorded bond premium amortization of $239,008, which was determined using the straight-line method.
     31. Closed the interest expense account.

2012
June 30. Recorded the redemption of the bonds, which were called at 101.5. The balance in the bond premium account is $1,912,069 after payment of interest and amortization of premium have been recorded. (Record the redemption only.)
Sept. 30. Paid the second annual payment on the note, which consisted of interest of $15,546 and principal of $33,125.

Instructions

1. Journalize the entries to record the foregoing transactions.
2. Indicate the amount of the interest expense in (a) 2010 and (b) 2011.
3. Determine the carrying amount of the bonds as of December 31, 2011.

**Appendix 2
PR 14-5B**
Bond discount,
entries for bonds
payable transactions,
interest method of
amortizing bond
discount

✔ 3. $2,482,580

On July 1, 2010, Linux Corporation, a wholesaler of electronics equipment, issued $45,000,000 of 10-year, 10% bonds at an effective interest rate of 14%, receiving cash of $35,465,423. Interest on the bonds is payable semiannually on December 31 and June 30. The fiscal year of the company is the calendar year.

Instructions
1. Journalize the entry to record the amount of cash proceeds from the sale of the bonds.
2. Journalize the entries to record the following:
   a. The first semiannual interest payment on December 31, 2010, and the amortization of the bond discount, using the interest method. (Round to the nearest dollar.)
   b. The interest payment on June 30, 2011, and the amortization of the bond discount, using the interest method. (Round to the nearest dollar.)
3. Determine the total interest expense for 2010.

**Appendix 2
PR 14-6B**
Bond premium,
entries for bonds
payable transactions,
interest method of
amortizing bond
premium

✔ 3. $2,331,456

Prosser Corporation produces and sells baseball cards. On July 1, 2010, Prosser Corporation issued $40,000,000 of 10-year, 12% bonds at an effective interest rate of 11%, receiving cash of $42,390,112. Interest on the bonds is payable semiannually on December 31 and June 30. The fiscal year of the company is the calendar year.

Instructions
1. Journalize the entry to record the amount of cash proceeds from the sale of the bonds.
2. Journalize the entries to record the following:
   a. The first semiannual interest payment on December 31, 2010, and the amortization of the bond premium, using the interest method. (Round to the nearest dollar.)
   b. The interest payment on June 30, 2011, and the amortization of the bond premium, using the interest method. (Round to the nearest dollar.)
3. Determine the total interest expense for 2010.

Special Activities

You can access the special activities online at **www.cengage.com/accounting/reeve**.

Excel Success Special Activities

SA 14-1
Interest amortization
table

On July 1, 2009, the beginning of Egan Enterprises' fiscal year, the company borrowed $15,000 from Claymore Bank by signing a 6% installment note. The note calls for annual payments of $3,561 at the end of each calendar year during the note's 5-year term.

a. Open the Excel file *SA14-1*.
b. Use your spreadsheet program to prepare an amortization table for the note.
c. When you have completed the amortization table, perform a "save as," replacing the entire file name with the following:

   SA14-1_[your first name initial]_[your last name]

SA 14-2
Interest amortization
table

Amad Mosan is a realtor who is arranging for $35,000 of financing for the purchase of a new automobile. Amad is considering two financing options.

Option 1: A 7% 4-year installment note dated January 1, 2010, requiring 4 annual payments of $10,333 at the end of each of the four years.

Option 2: An 8% 6-year installment note dated January 1, 2010, requiring 6 annual payments of $7,571 at the end of each of the six years.

a. Open the Excel file *SA14-2*.
b. Use your spreadsheet program to prepare an amortization table for each of the installment notes described above.
c. When you have completed the amortization tables perform a "save as," replacing the entire file name with the following:

SA14-2_[your first name initial]_[your last name]

SA 14-3
Interest amortization table

success

Use your spreadsheet program to prepare interest amortization tables for each of the installment notes listed below.

	Principal Amount	Date of Note	Annual Interest Rate	Term (Years)	Annual Payment
Note A	$9,000	01/01/2010	10%	3	$3,619
Note B	4,500	07/01/2009	5%	4	1,269
Note C	3,800	07/01/2010	9%	7	755

a. Open the Excel file *SA14-3*.
b. Use your spreadsheet program to prepare an amortization table for each note.
c. When you have completed the amortization tables perform a "save as," replacing the entire file name with the following:

SA14-3_[your first name initial]_[your last name]

Answers to Self-Examination Questions

1. **C** Earnings per share is preferred for comparing financing decisions because it captures the effect of alternative decisions on the earnings available to individual shareholders (answer C). The price of the bond issue and the discount on the bond issue relate to the cost of borrowing, but do not reflect the individual shareholder impact (answers A and B). Interest expense reflects the cost of debt financing to the company, but does not capture the effect on individual shareholders (answer D).

2. **B** Since the contract rate on the bonds is higher than the prevailing market rate, a rational investor would be willing to pay more than the face amount, or a premium (answer B), for the bonds. If the contract rate and the market rate were equal, the bonds could be expected to sell at their face amount (answer A). Likewise, if the market rate is higher than the contract rate, the bonds would sell at a price below their face amount (answer D) or at a discount (answer C).

3. **A** The bond carrying amount is the face amount plus unamortized premium or less unamortized

discount. For this question, the carrying amount is $900,000 less $72,000, or $828,000 (answer A).

4. **B** The interest portion of an installment note payment is computed by multiplying the interest rate by the carrying amount of the note at the beginning of the period. The periodic interest on bonds payable is computed by multiplying the interest rate times the face amount of the bond (answer A). Because installment note payments include both principal and interest components, the amount of principal is reduced each period which, in turn, reduces the interest portion of each payment (answers C and D).

5. **C** The balance of Discount on Bonds Payable is usually reported as a deduction from Bonds Payable in the Long-Term Liabilities section (answer C) of the balance sheet. Likewise, a balance in a premium on bonds payable account would usually be reported as an addition to Bonds Payable in the Long-Term Liabilities section of the balance sheet.

Investments and Fair Value Accounting

N E W S   C O R P O R A T I O N

You invest cash to earn more cash. For example, you could deposit cash in a bank account to earn interest. You could also invest cash in preferred or common stocks and in corporate or U.S. government notes and bonds.

Preferred and common stock can be purchased through a stock exchange, such as the New York Stock Exchange (NYSE). Preferred stock is purchased primarily with the expectation of earning dividends. Common stock is purchased with the expectation of earning dividends or realizing gains from a price increase in the stock.

Corporate and U.S. government bonds can also be purchased through a bond exchange. Bonds are purchased with the primary expectation of earning interest revenue.

Companies make investments for many of the same reasons that you would as an individual. For example, News Corporation, a diversified media company, which

produces such popular television shows as *The Simpsons* and *American Idol*, has invested $636 million of available cash in stocks and bonds. These investments are held by News Corporation for interest, dividends, and expected price increases.

Companies, however, unlike most individuals, also purchase significant amounts of the outstanding common stock of other companies for strategic reasons. For example, to expand its online presence, News Corporation recently acquired all of the stock of MySpace, the popular social networking Web site.

Investments in debt and equity securities give rise to a number of accounting issues. These issues are described and illustrated in this chapter.

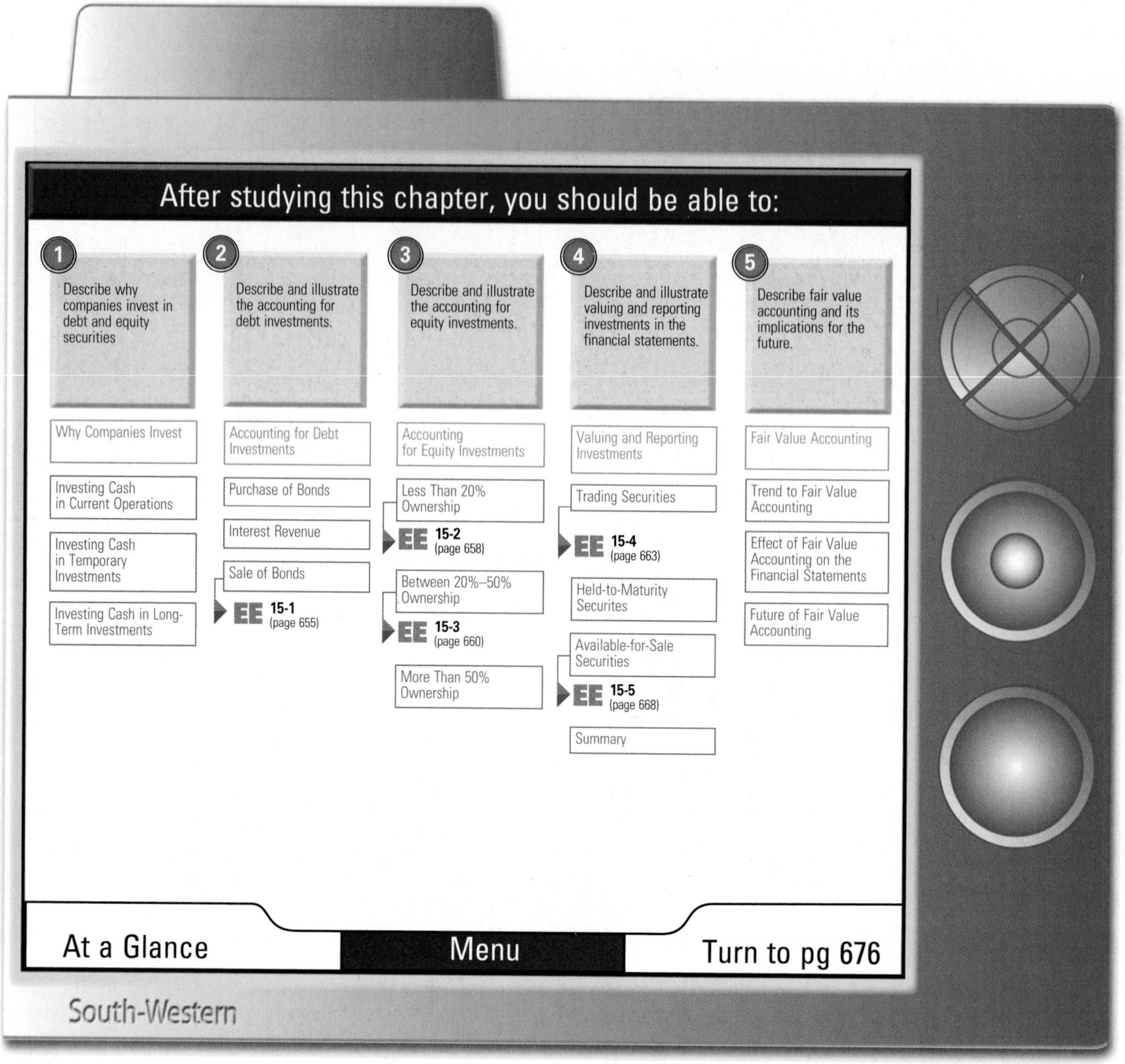

After studying this chapter, you should be able to:

1 Describe why companies invest in debt and equity securities

Why Companies Invest

Investing Cash in Current Operations

Investing Cash in Temporary Investments

Investing Cash in Long-Term Investments

2 Describe and illustrate the accounting for debt investments.

Accounting for Debt Investments

Purchase of Bonds

Interest Revenue

Sale of Bonds

EE 15-1 (page 655)

3 Describe and illustrate the accounting for equity investments.

Accounting for Equity Investments

Less Than 20% Ownership

EE 15-2 (page 658)

Between 20%–50% Ownership

EE 15-3 (page 660)

More Than 50% Ownership

4 Describe and illustrate valuing and reporting investments in the financial statements.

Valuing and Reporting Investments

Trading Securities

EE 15-4 (page 663)

Held-to-Maturity Securites

Available-for-Sale Securities

EE 15-5 (page 668)

Summary

5 Describe fair value accounting and its implications for the future.

Fair Value Accounting

Trend to Fair Value Accounting

Effect of Fair Value Accounting on the Financial Statements

Future of Fair Value Accounting

At a Glance   Menu   Turn to pg 676

South-Western

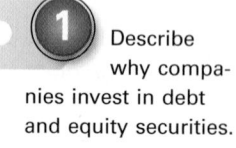

1 Describe why companies invest in debt and equity securities.

Why Companies Invest

Most companies generate cash from their operations. This cash can be used for the following purposes:

1. Investing in current operations
2. Investing in temporary investments to earn additional revenue
3. Investing in long-term investments in stock of other companies for strategic reasons

Investing Cash in Current Operations

Cash is often used to support the current operating activities of a company. For example, cash may be used to replace worn out equipment or to purchase new, more efficient, and productive equipment. In addition, cash may be reinvested in the company to expand its current operations. For example, a retailer based in the northwest United States might decide to expand by opening stores in the midwest.

To support its current level of operations, a company also uses cash to pay suppliers or other creditors. For example, suppliers must be paid to ensure that the company will be able to continue to purchase merchandise on account. The company may also have issued notes or bonds payable to finance its current operations. The interest on the notes or bonds must be paid.

Cash is also used to pay dividends to preferred or common stockholders. In order to maintain its ability to raise cash (capital), a company must reward (pay) investors for the use of their funds. For preferred stockholders, this reward is primarily the payment of dividends on a regular basis. For common stockholders, this reward may be in the form of an increasing stock price from improving prospects of the company. The reward for common stockholders may also take the form of cash dividends.

The accounting for the use of cash in current operations has been described and illustrated in earlier chapters. For example, Chapter 10, "Fixed Assets and Intangible Assets," illustrated the use of cash for purchasing property, plant, and equipment. In this chapter, we describe and illustrate the use of cash for investing in temporary investments and stock of other companies.

Investing Cash in Temporary Investments

A company may temporarily have excess cash that is not needed for use in its current operations. This is often the case when a company has a seasonal operating cycle. For example, a significant portion of the annual merchandise sales of a retailer occurs during the fall holiday season. As a result, retailers often experience a large increase in cash during this period, which is not needed until the spring buying season.

Instead of letting excess cash remain idle in a checking account, most companies invest their excess cash in temporary investments. In doing so, companies invest in securities such as:

1. **Debt securities**, which are notes and bonds that pay interest and have a fixed maturity date.
2. **Equity securities**, which are preferred and common stock that represent ownership in a company and do not have a fixed maturity date.

Investments in debt and equity securities, termed **Investments** or *Temporary Investments*, are reported in the Current Assets section of the balance sheet.

The primary objective of investing in temporary investments is to:

1. earn interest revenue
2. receive dividends
3. realize gains from increases in the market price of the securities.

Investments in certificates of deposit and other securities that do not normally change in value are disclosed on the balance sheet as *cash and cash equivalents*. Such investments are held primarily for their interest revenue.

Investing Cash in Long-Term Investments

SuperValu, a retail grocer, purchased Albertson's, another retail grocer, to form the third largest grocery retailing company in the United States.

The Walt Disney Company purchased Pixar Animation Studios to increase Disney's ability to produce and market animation movies.

A company may invest cash in the debt or equity of another company as a long-term investment. Long-term investments may be held for the same investment objectives as temporary investments. However, long-term investments often involve the purchase of a significant portion of the stock of another company. Such investments usually have a strategic purpose, such as:

1. *Reduction of costs*: When one company buys another company, the combined company may be able to reduce administrative expenses. For example, a combined company does not need two chief executive officers (CEOs) or chief financial officers (CFOs).
2. *Replacement of management*: If the purchased company has been mismanaged, the acquiring company may replace the company's management and, thus, improve operations and profits.
3. *Expansion*: The acquiring company may purchase a company because it has a complementary product line, territory, or customer base. The new combined company may be able to serve customers better than the two companies could separately.
4. *Integration*: A company may integrate operations by acquiring a supplier or customer. Acquiring a supplier may provide a more stable or uninterrupted supply of resources. Acquiring a customer may also provide a market for the company's products or services.

Accounting for Debt Investments

Debt securities include notes and bonds, issued by corporations and governmental organizations. Most companies invest excess cash in bonds as investments to earn interest revenue.

The accounting for bond investments[1] includes recording the following:

1. Purchase of bonds
2. Interest revenue
3. Sale of bonds

Purchase of Bonds

The purchase of bonds is recorded by debiting an investments account for the purchase price of the bonds, including any brokerage commissions. If the bonds are purchased between interest dates, the purchase price includes accrued interest since the last interest payment. This is because the seller has earned the accrued interest, but the buyer will receive the accrued interest when it is paid.

To illustrate, assume that Homer Company purchases $18,000 of U.S. Treasury bonds at their par value on March 17, 2010, plus accrued interest for 45 days. The bonds have an interest rate of 6%, payable on July 31 and January 31.

The entry to record the purchase of Treasury bonds is as follows:

2010				
Mar.	17	Investments—U.S. Treasury Bonds	18,000	
		Interest Receivable	135	
		Cash		18,135
		Purchased $18,000, 6% Treasury bonds.		

Since Homer Company purchased the bonds on March 17, it is also purchasing the accrued interest for 45 days (January 31 to March 17). The accrued interest of $135 is computed as follows:[2]

$$\text{Accrued Interest} = \$18{,}000 \times 6\% \times (45/360) = \$135$$

The accrued interest is recorded by debiting Interest Receivable for $135. Bond Investments is debited for the purchase price of the bonds of $18,000.

Interest Revenue

On July 31, Homer Company receives a semiannual interest payment of $540 ($18,000 × 6% × ½). The $540 interest includes the $135 accrued interest that Homer Company purchased with the bonds on March 17. Thus, Homer Company has earned $405 ($540 − $135) of interest revenue since purchasing the bonds.

The receipt of the interest on July 31 is recorded as follows:

2010				
July	31	Cash	540	
		Interest Receivable		135
		Interest Revenue		405
		Received semiannual interest.		

---

1 Debt investments may also include installment notes and short-term notes. The basic accounting for notes is similar to bonds and, thus, is not illustrated.
2 To simplify, a 360-day year is used to compute interest.

Homer Company's accounting period ends on December 31. Thus, an adjusting entry must be made to accrue interest for five months (August 1 to December 31) of $450 ($18,000 × 6% × ⁵⁄₁₂). The adjusting entry to record the accrued interest is as follows:

2010 Dec.	31	Interest Receivable	450	
		Interest Revenue		450
		Accrue interest.		

For the year ended December 31, 2010, Homer Company would report *Interest revenue* of $855 ($405 + $450) as part of *Other income* on its income statement.

The receipt of the semiannual interest of $540 on January 31, 2011, is recorded as follows:

2011 Jan.	31	Cash	540	
		Interest Revenue		90
		Interest Receivable		450
		Received interest on Treasury bonds.		

Sale of Bonds

The sale of a bond investment normally results in a gain or loss. If the proceeds from the sale exceed the book value (cost) of the bonds, then a gain is recorded. If the proceeds are less than the book value (cost) of the bonds, a loss is recorded.

To illustrate, on January 31, 2011, Homer Company sells the Treasury bonds at 98, which is a price equal to 98% of par value. The sale results in a loss of $360, as shown below.

Proceeds from sale	$17,640*
Less book value (cost) of the bonds	18,000
Loss on sale of bonds	$ (360)

*($18,000 × 98%)

The entry to record the sale is as follows:

2011 Jan.	31	Cash	17,640	
		Loss on Sale of Investment	360	
		Investments—U.S. Treasury Bonds		18,000
		Sale of U.S. Treasury bonds.		

There is no accrued interest upon the sale since the interest payment date is also January 31. If the sale were between interest dates, interest accrued since the last interest payment date would be added to the sale proceeds and credited to Interest Revenue. The loss on the sale of bond investments is reported as part of *Other income (loss)* on Homer Company's income statement.

Example Exercise 15-1   Bond Transactions

Journalize the entries to record the following selected bond investment transactions for Tyler Company:

1. Purchased for cash $40,000 of Tyler Company 10% bonds at 100 plus accrued interest of $320.
2. Received the first semiannual interest.
3. Sold $30,000 of the bonds at 102 plus accrued interest of $110.

(continued)

Follow My Example 15-1

1. Investments—Tyler Company Bonds	40,000	
Interest Receivable	320	
Cash		40,320
2. Cash	2,000*	
Interest Receivable		320
Interest Revenue		1,680
*$40,000 × 10% × ½		
3. Cash	30,710*	
Interest Revenue		110
Gain on Sale of Investments		600
Investments—Tyler Company Bonds		30,000
*Sale proceeds ($30,000 × 102%)	$30,600	
Accrued interest	110	
Total proceeds from sale	$30,710	

For Practice: PE 15-1A, PE 15-1B

---

3 Describe and illustrate the accounting for equity investments.

Accounting for Equity Investments

A company may invest in the preferred or common stock of another company. The company investing in another company's stock is the **investor**. The company whose stock is purchased is the **investee**.

The percent of the investee's outstanding stock purchased by the investor determines the degree of control that the investor has over the investee. This, in turn, determines the accounting method used to record the stock investment as shown in Exhibit 1.

Exhibit 1

Stock Investments

Percent of Outstanding Stock Owned by Investor	Degree of Control of Investor over Investee	Accounting Method
Less than 20%	No control	Cost method
Between 20% and 50%	Significant influence	Equity method
Greater than 50%	Control	Consolidation

Less Than 20% Ownership

If the investor purchases less than 20% of the outstanding stock of the investee, the investor is considered to have no control over the investee. In this case, it is assumed that the investor purchased the stock primarily to earn dividends or realize gains on price increases of the stock.

Investments of less than 20% of the investee's outstanding stock are accounted for using the **cost method**. Under the cost method, entries are recorded for the following transactions:

1. Purchase of stock
2. Receipt of dividends
3. Sale of stock

Purchase of Stock The purchase of stock is recorded at its cost. Any brokerage commissions are included as part of the cost.

To illustrate, assume that on May 1, Bart Company purchases 2,000 shares of Lisa Company common stock at $49.90 per share plus a brokerage fee of $200. The entry to record the purchase of the stock is as follows:

May	1	Investments—Lisa Company Stock	100,000	
		Cash		100,000
		Purchased 2,000 shares of Lisa Company		
		common stock [($49.90 × 2,000		
		shares) + $200].		

Receipt of Dividends On July 31, Bart Company receives a dividend of $0.40 per share from Lisa Company. The entry to record the receipt of the dividend is as follows:

July	31	Cash	800	
		Dividend Revenue		800
		Received dividend on Lisa Company		
		common stock (2,000 shares × $0.40).		

Dividend revenue is reported as part of *Other income* on Bart Company's income statement.

Sale of Stock The sale of a stock investment normally results in a gain or loss. A gain is recorded if the proceeds from the sale exceed the book value (cost) of the stock. A loss is recorded if the proceeds from the sale are less than the book value (cost).

To illustrate, on September 1, Bart Company sells 1,500 shares of Lisa Company stock for $54.50 per share, less a $160 commission. The sale results in a gain of $6,590, as shown below.

Proceeds from sale	$81,590*
Book value (cost) of the stock	75,000**
Gain on sale	$ 6,590

*[($54.50 × 1,500 shares) − $160
**($100,000/2,000 shares) × 1,500 shares

The entry to record the sale is as follows:

Sept.	1	Cash	81,590	
		Gain on Sale of Investments		6,590
		Investments—Lisa Company Stock		75,000
		Sale of 1,500 shares of Lisa Company		
		common stock.		

The gain on the sale of investments is reported as part of *Other income* on Bart Company's income statement.

Example Exercise 15-2 Stock Transactions

On September 1, 1,500 shares of Monroe Company are acquired at a price of $24 per share plus a $40 brokerage fee. On October 14, a $0.60 per share dividend was received on the Monroe Company stock. On November 11, 750 shares (half) of Monroe Company stock were sold for $20 per share, less a $45 brokerage fee. Prepare the journal entries for the original purchase, dividend, and sale.

Follow My Example 15-2

Sept. 1	Investments—Monroe Company Stock	36,040*	
	Cash		36,040
	*(1,500 shares × $24 per share) + $40		
Oct. 14	Cash	900*	
	Dividend Revenue		900
	*$0.60 per share × 1,500 shares		
Nov. 11	Cash	14,955*	
	Loss on Sale of Investments	3,065	
	Investments—Monroe Company Stock		18,020**
	*(750 shares × $20) − $45		
	**$36,040 × ½		

For Practice: PE 15-2A, PE 15-2B

Starbucks Corporation has a 40% ownership interest in Starbucks Coffee Japan, Ltd. Thus, Starbucks Corporation has significant influence over the operations of Starbucks Coffee Japan, Ltd.

Between 20%–50% Ownership

If the investor purchases between 20% and 50% of the outstanding stock of the investee, the investor is considered to have a significant influence over the investee. In this case, it is assumed that the investor purchased the stock primarily for strategic reasons such as developing a supplier relationship.

Investments of between 20% and 50% of the investee's outstanding stock are accounted for using the **equity method**. Under the equity method, the stock is recorded initially at its cost, including any brokerage commissions. This is the same as under the cost method.

Under the equity method, the investment account is adjusted for the investor's share of the *net income* and *dividends* of the investee. These adjustments are as follows:

1. *Net Income:* The investor records its share of the net income of the investee as an increase in the investment account. Its share of any net loss is recorded as a decrease in the investment account.
2. *Dividends:* The investor's share of cash dividends received from the investee decreases the investment account.

Purchase of Stock To illustrate, assume that Simpson Inc. purchased its 40% interest in Flanders Corporation's common stock on January 2, 2010, for $350,000. The entry to record the purchase is as follows:

2010					
Jan.	2	Investment in Flanders Corporation Stock		350,000	
		Cash			350,000
		Purchased 40% of Flanders			
		Corporation stock.			

Recording Investee Net Income For the year ended December 31, 2010, Flanders Corporation reported net income of $105,000. Under the equity method, Simpson Inc. (the investor) records its share of Flanders net income as follows:

2010				
Dec.	31	Investment in Flanders Corporation Stock	42,000	
		Income of Flanders Corporation		42,000
		Record 40% share of Flanders		
		Corporation net income.		

Income of Flanders Corporation is reported on Simpson Inc.'s income statement. Depending on its significance, it may be reported separately or as part of *Other income*.

Recording Investee Dividends During the year, Flanders declared and paid cash dividends of $45,000. Under the equity method, Simpson Inc. (the investor) records its share of Flanders dividends as follows:

2010				
Dec.	31	Cash	18,000	
		Investment in Flanders Corporation Stock		18,000
		Record 40% share of Flanders		
		Corporation dividends.		

The effect of recording 40% of Flanders Corporation's net income and dividends is to increase the investment account by $24,000 ($42,000 − $18,000). Thus, Investment in Flanders Corporation Stock increases from $350,000 to $374,000, as shown below.

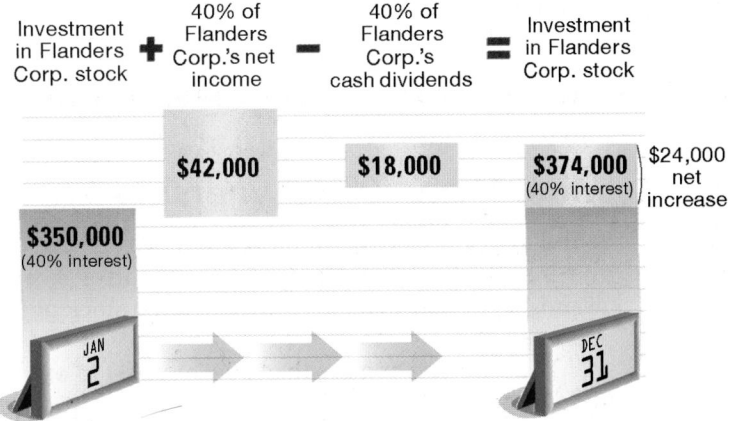

Investment and Dividends

Under the equity method, the investment account reflects the investor's proportional changes in the net book value of the investee. For example, Flanders Corporation's net book value increased by $60,000 (net income of $105,000 less dividends of $45,000) during the year. As a result, Simpson's share of Flanders' net book value increased by $24,000 ($60,000 × 40%).

Sale of Stock Under the equity method, a gain or loss is normally recorded from the sale of an investment. A gain is recorded if the proceeds exceed the *book value* of the investment. A loss is recorded if the proceeds are less than the *book value* of the investment.

To illlustrate, if Simpson Inc. sold Flanders Corporation's stock on January 1, 2011, for $400,000, a gain of $26,000 would be reported, as shown below.

Proceeds from sale	$400,000
Book value of stock investment	374,000
Gain on sale	$ 26,000

The entry to record the sale is as follows:

2011					
Jan.	1	Cash		400,000	
		Investment in Flanders Corporation Stock			374,000
		Gain on Sale of Flanders Corporation Stock			26,000
		Sale of Flanders Corporation stock.			

Example Exercise 15-3   Equity Method   ●●●●●●●●▷ ③

On January 2, Olson Company acquired 35% of the outstanding stock of Bryant Company for $140,000. For the year ending December 31, Bryant Company earned income of $44,000 and paid dividends of $20,000. Prepare the entries for Olson Company for the purchase of the stock, share of Bryant income, and dividends received from Bryant Company.

Follow My Example 15-3

Jan. 2	Investment in Bryant Company Stock	140,000	
	Cash		140,000
Dec. 31	Investment in Bryant Company Stock	15,400*	
	Income of Bryant Company		15,400
	*Record 35% of Bryant income, 35% × $44,000		
Dec. 31	Cash	7,000*	
	Investment in Bryant Company Stock		7,000
	*35% × $20,000		

For Practice: PE 15-3A, PE 15-3B

To expand its Internet presence, Google purchased 100% of YouTube's outstanding stock.

More Than 50% Ownership

If the investor purchases more than 50% of the outstanding stock of the investee, the investor is considered to have control over the investee. In this case, it is assumed that the investor purchased the stock of the investee primarily for strategic reasons.

The purchase of more than 50% ownership of the investee's stock is termed a **business combination**. Companies may combine in order to produce more efficiently, diversify product lines, expand geographically, or acquire know-how.

A corporation owning all or a majority of the voting stock of another corporation is called a **parent company**. The corporation that is controlled is called the **subsidiary company**.

Parent and subsidiary corporations often continue to maintain separate accounting records and prepare their own financial statements. In such cases, at the end of the year, the financial statements of the parent and subsidiary are combined and reported as a single company. These combined financial statements are called **consolidated financial statements**. Such statements are normally identified by adding *and Subsidiary(ies)* to the name of the parent corporation or by adding *Consolidated* to the statement title.

To the external stakeholders of the parent company, consolidated financial statements are more meaningful than separate statements for each corporation. This is because the parent company, in substance, controls the subsidiaries. The accounting for business combinations, including preparing consolidated financial statements, is decribed and illustrated in advanced accounting courses and textbooks.

Valuing and Reporting Investments

4 Describe and illustrate valuing and reporting investments in the financial statements.

Debt and equity securities are *financial assets* that are often traded on public exchanges such as the New York Stock Exchange. As a result, their market value can be observed and, thus, objectively determined.

For this reason, generally accepted accounting principles (GAAP) allow some debt and equity securities to be valued in the accounting records and financial statements at their fair market values. In contrast, GAAP requires tangible assets such as property, plant, and equipment to be valued and reported at their net book values (cost less accumulated depreciation).

For purposes of valuing and reporting, debt and equity securities are classified as follows:

1. Trading securities
2. Held-to-maturity securities
3. Available-for-sale securities

Trading Securities

Trading securities are debt and equity securities that are purchased and sold to earn short-term profits from changes in their market prices. Trading securities are often held by banks, mutual funds, insurance companies, and other financial institutions.

SunTrust Banks Inc. holds $2 billion in trading securities as current assets.

Since trading securities are held as a short-term investment, they are reported as a current asset on the balance sheet. Trading securities are valued as a portfolio (group) of securities using the securities' fair values. **Fair value** is the market price that the company would receive for a security if it were sold. Changes in fair value of the portfolio (group) of trading securities are recognized as an **unrealized gain or loss** for the period.

To illustrate, assume Maggie Company purchased a portfolio of trading securities during 2009. On December 31, 2009, the cost and fair values of the securities were as follows:

Name	Number of Shares	Total Cost	Total Fair Value
Armour Company	400	$ 5,000	$ 7,200
Maven, Inc.	500	11,000	7,500
Polaris Co.	200	8,000	10,600
Total		$24,000	$25,300

The portfolio of trading securities is reported at its fair value of $25,300. An adjusting entry is made to record the increase in fair value of $1,300 ($25,300 − $24,000). In order to maintain a record of the original cost of the securities, a valuation account, called *Valuation Allowance for Trading Investments*, is debited for $1,300 and *Unrealized Gain on Trading Investments* is credited for $1,300. The adjusting entry on December 31, 2009, to record the fair value of the portfolio of trading securities is shown below.

2009				
Dec.	31	Valuation Allowance for Trading Investments	1,300	
		Unrealized Gain on Trading Investments		1,300
		To record increase in fair value of		
		trading securities.		

The *Unrealized Gain on Trading Investments* is reported on the income statement. Depending on its significance, it may be reported separately or as *Other income* on the income statement. The valuation allowance is reported on the December 31, 2009, balance sheet as follows:

Maggie Company
Balance Sheet (selected items)
December 31, 2009

Current assets:		
Cash.		$120,000
Trading investments (at cost)	$24,000	
Plus valuation allowance for trading investments.	1,300	
Trading investments (at fair value)		25,300

On September 10, 2010, Maggie Company purchases 300 shares of Zane Inc. as a trading security for $12 per share, including a brokerage commission. The entry to record this transaction is as follows:

Sept.	10	Trading Investments—Zane Inc.	3,600	
		Cash		3,600

Assume that on December 31, 2010, the cost and fair valuation of the portfolio of trading securities are as follows:

Name	Number of Shares	Total Cost	Total Fair Value
Armour Company	400	$ 5,000	$ 5,500
Maven, Inc.	500	11,000	9,000
Polaris Co.	200	8,000	7,000
Zane Inc.	300	3,600	3,000
Total		$27,600	$24,500

The Valuation Allowance for Trading Investments should have a credit balance on December 31, 2010, of $3,100 ($27,600 − $24,500). *Before* adjustment, Valuation Allowance for Trading Investments has a debit balance of $1,300, which is its ending balance for the prior year (2009). On December 31, 2010, this prior year balance must be adjusted to a credit balance of $3,100. In order to do this, a credit adjustment of $4,400 is required as shown below.

Valuation allowance for trading investments, January 1, 2010		$1,300 Dr.
Trading investments at cost, December 31, 2010	$27,600	
Trading investments at fair value, December 31, 2010	24,500	
Valuation allowance for trading investments, December 31, 2010		3,100 Cr.
Adjustment		$4,400 Cr.

The adjusting entry on December 31, 2010, is as follows:

2010				
Dec.	31	Unrealized Loss on Trading Investments	4,400	
		Valuation Allowance for Trading Investments		4,400
		To record decrease in fair value of		
		trading investments.		

The valuation allowance for trading investments account after the December 31, 2010, adjusting entry is as follows:

Valuation Allowance for Trading Investments

2009				
Dec. 31 Adj.	1,300			
Dec. 31 Bal.	1,300			
2010		2010		
Jan. 1 Bal.	1,300	Dec. 31 Adj.	4,400	
		Dec. 31 Bal.	3,100	

A debit balance in Valuation Allowance for Trading Investments is added to the investment account, while a credit balance is subtracted from the investment account.

The *Unrealized Loss on Trading Investments* is reported on the income statement separately, or as part of *Other income (loss)*, depending on its significance. The valuation allowance is reported on the December 31, 2010, balance sheet as follows:

Maggie Company
Balance Sheet
December 31, 2010

Current assets:		
Cash		$146,000
Trading investments (at cost)	$27,600	
Less valuation allowance for trading investments	3,100	
Trading investments (at fair value)		24,500

Example Exercise 15-4   Valuing Trading Securities at Fair Value

On January 1, 2010, Valuation Allowance for Trading Investments has a debit balance of $23,500. On December 31, 2010, the cost of the trading securities portfolio was $79,200, and the fair value was $95,000. Prepare the December 31, 2010, adjusting journal entry to record the unrealized gain or loss on trading investments.

(continued)

Follow My Example 15-4

2010
Dec. 31   Unrealized Loss on Trading Investments   7,700
                  Valuation Allowance for Trading Investments 7,700*
                  To record decrease in fair value of trading investments.

Valuation allowance for trading investments, January 1, 2010		$23,500 Dr.
Trading investments at cost, December 31, 2010	$79,200	
Trading investments at fair value, December 31, 2010	95,000	
Valuation allowance for trading investments, December 31, 2010		15,800 Dr.
*Adjustment		$ 7,700 Cr.

For Practice: PE 15-4A, PE 15-4B

Integrity, Objectivity, and Ethics in Business

SUB-PRIME WOES

Many of the largest U.S. banks provided mortgages to marginally qualified borrowers. Such loans were termed "sub-prime" loans. These loans were then packaged into securities that were sold to investors. Often, the banks earned attractive fees for creating these financial products. Unfortunately, many weak borrowers were unable to make their mortgage payments, which resulted in defaults on the mortgages. These defaults caused the packaged securities that held these loans to fall in value. As a result, many investors, including the banks themselves, were required to recognize large losses from declines in fair value of these securities. Some of these losses were as follows:

UBS	$37 billion
Merrill Lynch & Co.	34 billion
Citigroup	30 billion

These losses were some of the largest in the history of these companies. Since the losses were immediately disclosed and recognized, they were never hidden from company stakeholders. This is because the accounting rules require such losses to be recognized even if the securities are not sold.

Held-to-Maturity Securities

Merrill Lynch & Co. reported $254 million in municipal bonds as held-to-maturity securities in its current assets.

Held-to-maturity securities are debt investments, such as notes or bonds, that a company intends to hold until their maturity date. Held-to-maturity securities are primarily purchased to earn interest revenue.

If a held-to-maturity security will mature within a year, it is reported as a current asset on the balance sheet. Held-to-maturity securities maturing beyond a year are reported as noncurrent assets.

Only securities with maturity dates such as corporate notes and bonds are classified as held-to-maturity securities. Equity securities are not held-to-maturity securities because they have no maturity date.

Held-to-maturity bond investments are recorded at their cost, including any brokerage commissions, as illustrated earlier in this chapter. If the interest rate on the bonds differs from the market rate of interest, the bonds may be purchased at a premium or discount. In such cases, the premium or discount is amortized over the life of the bonds.

Held-to-maturity bond investments are reported on the balance sheet at their amortized cost. The accounting for held-to-maturity bond investments, including premium and discount amortization, is described and illustrated in Appendix 1 at the end of this chapter.

Available-for-Sale Securities

Available-for-sale securities are debt and equity securities that are not classified as trading or held-to-maturity securities. For example, bonds that management does not intend to hold to maturity are classified as available-for-sale securities.

The accounting for available-for-sale securities is similar to the accounting for trading securities except for the reporting of changes in fair values. Specifically, changes in the fair values of trading securities are reported as an unrealized gain or loss on the income statement. In contrast, changes in the fair values of available-for-sale securities are reported as part of stockholders' equity and, thus, excluded from the income statement.

To illustrate, assume that Maggie Company purchased securities during 2009 as available-for-sale securities instead of trading securities. On December 31, 2009, the cost and fair values of the securities were as follows:

Name	Number of Shares	Total Cost	Total Fair Value
Armour Company	400	$ 5,000	$ 7,200
Maven, Inc.	500	11,000	7,500
Polaris Co.	200	8,000	10,600
Total		$24,000	$25,300

The portfolio of available-for-sale securities is reported at its fair value of $25,300. An adjusting entry is made to record the increase in fair value of $1,300 ($25,300 − $24,000). In order to maintain a record of the original cost of the securities, a valuation account, called *Valuation Allowance for Available-for-Sale Investments*, is debited for $1,300. This account is similar to the valuation account used for trading securities.

Unlike trading securities, the December 31, 2009, adjusting entry credits a stockholders' equity account instead of an income statement account.[3] The $1,300 gain is credited to *Unrealized Gain (Loss) on Available-for-Sale Investments*.

The adjusting entry on December 31, 2009, to record the fair value of the portfolio of available-for-sale securities is as follows:

2009				
Dec.	31	Valuation Allowance for Available-for-Sale Investments	1,300	
		Unrealized Gain (Loss) on Available-for-Sale Investments		1,300
		To record increase in fair value of available-for-sale investments.		

A credit balance in Unrealized Gain (Loss) on Available-for-Sale Investments is added to stockholders' equity, while a debit balance is subtracted from stockholders' equity.

---

3 This is a rare exception to the rule that every adjusting entry must affect an income statement and a balance sheet account.

The valuation allowance and the unrealized gain are reported on the December 31, 2009, balance sheet as follows:

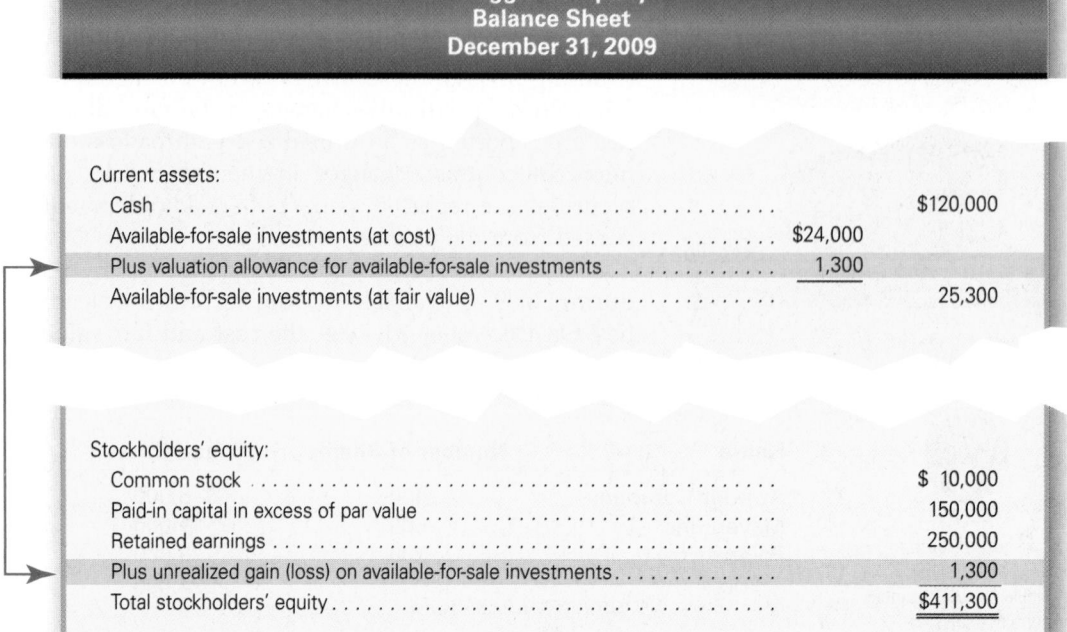

Maggie Company
Balance Sheet
December 31, 2009

Current assets:		
Cash		$120,000
Available-for-sale investments (at cost)	$24,000	
Plus valuation allowance for available-for-sale investments	1,300	
Available-for-sale investments (at fair value)		25,300

Stockholders' equity:	
Common stock	$ 10,000
Paid-in capital in excess of par value	150,000
Retained earnings	250,000
Plus unrealized gain (loss) on available-for-sale investments	1,300
Total stockholders' equity	$411,300

As shown above, Unrealized Gain (Loss) on Available-for-Sale Investments is reported as an addition to stockholders' equity. In future years, the cumulative effects of unrealized gains and losses are reported in this account. Since 2009 was the first year that Maggie Company purchased available-for-sale securities, the unrealized gain is reported as the balance of *Unrealized Gain (Loss) on Available-for-Sale Investments.*

On September 10, 2010, Maggie Company purchases 300 shares of Zane Inc. as an available-for-sale security for $12 per share, including brokerage commission. The entry to record this transaction would be as follows:

2010					
Sept.	10	Available-for-Sale Investments—Zane Inc.		3,600	
		Cash			3,600

On December 31, 2010, the cost and fair valuation of the portfolio of available-for-sale securities are as follows:

Name	Number of Shares	Total Cost	Total Fair Value
Armour Company	400	$ 5,000	$ 5,500
Maven, Inc.	500	11,000	9,000
Polaris Co.	200	8,000	7,000
Zane Inc.	300	3,600	3,000
Total		$27,600	$24,500

Valuation Allowance for Available-for-Sale Investments should have a credit balance on December 31, 2010, of $3,100 ($27,600 − $24,500). *Before* adjustment, Valuation Allowance for Available-for-Sale Investments has a debit balance of $1,300. Thus, Valuation Allowance for Available-for-Sale Investments must be adjusted on December 31, 2010, by a credit for $4,400 as shown at the top of the next page.

Valuation allowance for available-for-sale
   investments, January 1, 2010 .... $1,300   Dr.
   Available-for-sale investments at cost,
      December 31, 2010 .... $27,600
   Available-for-sale investments at fair value,
      December 31, 2010 24,500
Valuation allowance for available-for-sale investments,
   December 31, 2010   3,100   Cr.
Adjustment .... $4,400   Cr.

The adjusting entry on December 31, 2010, is as follows:

2010 Dec.	31	Unrealized Gain (Loss) on Available-for-Sale Investments	4,400	
		Valuation Allowance for Available-for-Sale Investments		4,400
		To record decrease in fair value of available-for-sale investments.		

The valuation allowance and unrealized gains and losses accounts after the December 31, 2010, adjusting entry are as follows:

Valuation Allowance for Available-for-Sale Investments

2009	
Dec. 31 Adj. 1,300	
Dec. 31 Bal. 1,300	
2010	2010
Jan. 1 Bal. 1,300	Dec. 31 Adj. 4,400
	Dec. 31 Bal. 3,100

Unrealized Gain (Loss) on Available-for-Sale Investments

	2009
	Dec. 31 Adj. 1,300
	Dec. 31 Bal. 1,300
2010	2010
Dec. 31 Adj. 4,400	Jan. 1 Bal. 1,300
Dec. 31 Bal. 3,100	

The valuation allowance and unrealized gain (loss) are reported on the December 31, 2010, balance sheet as follows:

Maggie Company
Balance Sheet
December 31, 2010

Current assets:
  Cash..................................... $146,000
  Available-for-sale investments (at cost)............ $27,600
  Less valuation allowance for available-for-sale investments 3,100
  Available-for-sale investments (at fair value)   24,500

Stockholders' equity:
  Common stock................ $ 10,000
  Paid-in capital in excess of par value   150,000
  Retained earnings   320,000
  Less unrealized gain (loss) on available-for-sale investments...........   (3,100)
  Total stockholders' equity $476,900

Example Exercise 15-5   Valuing Available-for-Sale Securities at Fair Value

On January 1, 2010, Valuation Allowance for Available-for-Sale Investments has a credit balance of $9,000. On December 31, 2010, the cost of the available-for-sale securities was $45,700, and the fair value was $37,200.

Prepare the adjusting entry to record the unrealized gain or loss for available-for-sale investments on December 31, 2010.

Follow My Example 15-5

2010			
Dec. 31	Valuation Allowance for Available-for-Sale Investments	500*	
	Unrealized Gain (Loss) on Available-for-Sale Investments		500
	To record increase in fair value of available-for-sale securities.		

Valuation allowance for available-for-sale investments, January 1, 2010		$9,000 Cr.
Available-for-sale investments at cost, December 31, 2010	$45,700	
Available-for-sale investments at fair value, December 31, 2010	37,200	
Valuation allowance for available-for-sale investments, December 31, 2010		8,500 Cr.
*Adjustment		$ 500 Dr.

For Practice: PE 15-5A, PE 15-5B

Summary

Exhibit 2 summarizes the valuation and balance sheet reporting of trading, held-to-maturity, and available-for-sale securities.

Exhibit 2

Summary of Valuing and Reporting of Investments

	Trading Securities	Held-to-Maturity Securities	Available-for-Sale Securities
Valued at:	**Fair Value**	**Amortized Cost**	**Fair Value**
Changes in valuation are reported as:	Unrealized gain or loss is reported on income statement as Other income (loss).	Premium or discount amortization is reported as part of interest revenue on the income statement.	Accumulated unrealized gain or loss is reported in stockholders' equity on the balance sheet.
Reported on the balance sheet as:	Cost of investments plus or minus valuation allowance.	Amortized cost of investment.	Cost of investments plus or minus valuation allowance.
Classified on balance sheet as:	A current asset.	Either as a current or noncurrent asset, depending on management's intent.	Either as a current or noncurrent asset, depending on management's intent.

Common stock investments in trading and available-for-sale securities are normally less than 20% of the outstanding common stock of the investee. The portfolios are reported at fair value using the valuation allowance account, while the individual securities are accounted for using the cost method. Investments between 20% and 50% of the outstanding common stock of the investee are accounted for using the equity method illustrated earlier in this chapter. Such investments, however, are permitted to be valued using fair values. To simplify, it is assumed that the investor does not elect this option.

Common stock investments of more than 50% of the outstanding stock of the investee are reported as part of the consolidated financial statements of the parent company. Thus, using fair values for such investments is not an option.

The balance sheet reporting for the investments of Mornin' Joe is shown below.

Mornin' Joe
Balance Sheet
December 31, 2010

Assets

Current assets:		
Cash and cash equivalents		$235,000
Trading investments (at cost)	$420,000	
Plus valuation allowance for trading investments	45,000	465,000
Accounts receivable	$305,000	
Less allowance for doubtful accounts	12,300	292,700
Merchandise inventory—at lower of cost		
(first-in, first-out method) or market		120,000
Prepaid insurance		24,000
Total current assets		$1,136,700
Investments:		
Investment in AM Coffee (equity method)		565,000
Property, plant, and equipment:		

Mornin' Joe invests in trading securities and does not have investments in held-to-maturity or available-for-sale securities. Mornin' Joe also owns 40% of AM Coffee Corporation, which is accounted for using the equity method. Mornin' Joe intends to keep its investment in AM Coffee indefinitely for strategic reasons; thus, its investment in AM Coffee is classified as a noncurrent asset. Such investments are normally reported before property, plant, and equipment.

Mornin' Joe reported an Unrealized Gain on Trading Investments of $5,000 and Equity Income in AM Coffee of $57,000 in the Other income and expense section of its income statement, as shown below.

Mornin' Joe
Income Statement
For the Year Ended December 31, 2010

Revenue from sales:			
Sales			$5,450,000
Less: Sales returns and allowances		$26,500	
Sales discounts		21,400	47,900
Net sales			$5,402,100
Cost of merchandise sold			2,160,000
Gross profit			$3,242,100
Total operating expenses			2,608,700
Income from operations			$ 633,400
Other income and expense:			
Interest revenue		$ 18,000	
Interest expense		(136,000)	
Loss on disposal of fixed asset		(23,000)	
Unrealized gain on trading investments		5,000	
Equity income in AM Coffee		57,000	(79,000)
Income before income taxes			$ 554,400
Income tax expense			132,800
Net income			$ 421,600

Mornin' Joe reports an *Unrealized Gain on Trading Investments* of $5,000 and *Equity Income in AM Coffee* of $57,000 in the *Other income* section of its income statement.

Describe fair value accounting and its implications for the future.

Fair Value Accounting

Fair value is the price that would be received for selling an asset or paying off a liability. Fair value assumes that the asset is sold or the liability paid off under *normal* rather than under distressed conditions.

As illustrated earlier, generally accepted accounting principles require the use of fair values for valuing and reporting debt and equity securities held as trading or available-for-sale investments. In addition, accounts receivable is recorded and reported at an amount that approximates its fair value. This is because accounts receivable is reported at its net realizable value. In addition, accounts receivable is a current asset that will be collected (converted to cash) within a relatively short period. Likewise, accounts payable are recorded and reported at approximately their fair value.

In contrast, many assets and liabilities are recorded and reported at amounts that differ significantly from their fair values. For example, when equipment or other property, plant, and equipment assets are purchased, they are initially recorded at their fair values. That is, they are recorded at their purchase price (initial cost). However, their initial cost, called *historical cost*, is not adjusted for changes in fair values. Instead, equipment is depreciated over its useful life. As a result, the book value of property, plant, and equipment normally differs significantly from its fair value. Likewise, held-to-maturity securities are valued at their amortized cost rather than at their fair values.

Trend to Fair Value Accounting

A current trend is for the Financial Accounting Standards Board (FASB) and other accounting regulators to adopt accounting principles using fair values for valuing and reporting assets and liabilities. Factors contributing to this trend include the following:

1. Current generally accepted accounting principles are a hybrid of varying measurement methods that often conflict with each other. For example, property, plant, and equipment are normally reported at their depreciated book values. However, GAAP require that if a fixed asset value is *impaired*, that it be written down to its fair value. Such conflicting accounting principles could confuse users of financial statements.
2. A greater percentage of the total assets of many companies consists of financial assets such as receivables and securities. Fair values for such assets can often be readily obtained from stock market quotations or computed using current interest rates and present values. Likewise, many liabilities can be readily valued using market quotations or current interest rates and present values.
3. The world economy has created pressure on accounting regulators to adopt a worldwide set of accounting principles and standards. *International Financial Reporting Standards (IFRSs)* are issued by the International Accounting Standards Board *(IASB)* and are used by the European Economic Union (EU). As a result, the FASB is under increasing pressure to conform U.S. standards with International Financial Reporting Standards. One area where differences exist is in the use of fair values, which are more often used by International Financial Reporting Standards.

While there is an increasing trend to fair value accounting, using fair values has several potential disadvantages. Some of these disadvantages include the following:

1. Fair values may not be readily obtainable for some assets or liabilities. As a result, accounting reports may become more subjective and less reliable. For example, fair

values (market quotations) are normally available for trading and available-for-sale securities. However, fair values may not be as available for assets such as property, plant, and equipment or intangible assets such as goodwill.

2. Fair values make it more difficult to compare companies if companies use different methods of determining (measuring) fair values. This would be especially true for assets and liabilities for which fair values are not readily available.

3. Using fair values could result in more fluctuations in accounting reports because fair values normally change from year to year. Such volatility may confuse users of the financial statements. It may also make it more difficult for users to determine current operating trends and to predict future trends.

Effect of Fair Value Accounting on the Financial Statements

The use of fair values for valuing assets and liabilities affects the financial statements. Specifically, the balance sheet and income statement could be affected.

Balance Sheet When an asset or a liability is reported at its fair value, any difference between the asset's original cost or prior period's fair value must be recorded. As we illustrated for trading and available-for-sale securities, one method for doing this is to use a valuation allowance. The account, *Valuation Allowance for Trading Investments*, was used earlier in this chapter to adjust trading securities to their fair values. Similar accounts could be used for the other assets and liabilities.

In addition, the unrealized gain or loss on changes in fair values must be recorded. One method reports these unrealized gains and losses as part of stockholders' equity. This method was illustrated earlier in this chapter for *available-for-sale* securities.

Income Statement Instead of recording the unrealized gain or loss on changes in fair values as part of stockholders' equity, the unrealized gains or losses may be reported on the income statement. This method was illustrated earlier in this chapter for *trading* securities.

As shown above, differences exist as to how to best report changes in fair values— that is, whether to report gains or losses on fair values on the income statement or the balance sheet.

In an attempt to bridge these differences, the FASB introduced the concepts of *comprehensive income* and *accumulated other comprehensive income*. These concepts are described in Appendix 2 to this chapter.

Future of Fair Value Accounting

The use of fair value accounting was described and illustrated in this chapter for trading and available-for-sale securities. The FASB and other accounting regulators are continuing to explore the use of fair value accounting for other assets and liabilities. For example, the FASB recently issued *Statement of Financial Accounting Standards No. 159*, "The Fair Value Option for Financial Assets and Financial Liabilities," which expands the use of fair value reporting for financial assets and liabilities.[4]

---

4 *Statement of Financial Accounting Standards No. 154*, "The Fair Value Option for Financial Assets and Liabilities" (Norwalk, CT: Financial Accounting Standards Board, 2007).

Financial Analysis and Interpretation

The dividend yield indicates the rate of return to stock-holders in terms of cash dividend distributions. Although the dividend yield can be computed for both preferred and common stock, it is most often computed for common stock. This is because most preferred stock has a stated dividend rate or amount. In contrast, the amount of common stock dividends normally varies with the profitability of the corporation.

The dividend yield is computed by dividing the annual dividends paid per share of common stock by the market price per share at a specific date, as shown below.

$$\text{Dividend Yield} = \frac{\text{Dividends per Share of Common Stock}}{\text{Market Price per Share of Common Stock}}$$

To illustrate, the market price of Mattel, Inc., common stock was $19.09 on April 29, 2008. During the preceding year, Mattel had paid dividends of $0.75 per share. Thus, the dividend yield of Mattel's common stock is 3.93% ($0.75/$19.09). Because the market price of a corporation's stock will vary from day to day, its dividend yield

will also vary from day to day. Fortunately, the dividend yield is provided with newspaper listings of market prices and most Internet quotation services, such as from Yahoo's Finance Web site.

The recent dividend yields for some selected companies are as follows:

Company	Dividend Yield (%)
Apple	None
Bank of America	6.76
Coca-Cola Company	2.59
General Motors	4.72
Hewlett-Packard	0.67
The Home Depot	3.07
Microsoft	1.54

As can be seen, the dividend yield varies widely across firms. Growth companies ofen do not pay dividends, but instead, reinvest their earnings in research and development, such as with Apple.

A P P E N D I X 1

Accounting for Held-to-Maturity Investments

Held-to-maturity securities are debt investments such as notes or bonds that a company intends to hold until their maturity date. This appendix describes and illustrates the accounting for bonds purchased as a held-to-maturity investment when the price of the bond differs from par value.

Purchase of Bonds

Bonds may be purchased directly from the issuing corporation or through a bond exchange such as the New York Bond Exchange. Daily bond quotations are available from bond exchanges that include the following:

1. Interest rate
2. Maturity date
3. Volume of sales
4. High, low, and closing prices for the day

Prices for bonds are quoted as a percentage of the face amount. Thus, the price of a $1,000 bond quoted at 99.5 would be $995, while the price of a $1,000 bond quoted at 104.25 would be $1,042.50.

The cost of a bond investment includes all costs related to the purchase including any brokerage commissions. When bonds are purchased between interest dates, the buyer normally pays the seller the interest accrued from the last interest payment date to the date of purchase. The accounting for the purchase of a bond, which included accrued interest, was illustrated in this chapter.

Bonds may be purchased at a price other than their face amount. Bonds are purchased at a premium or discount as follows:

1. If the coupon bond rate of interest is *more than* the market rate of interest for equivalent investments, bonds are purchased at a *premium*. That is, the bonds are purchased for more than their face amount.

2. If the coupon bond rate of interest is *less than* the market rate of interest for equivalent investments, bonds are purchased at a *discount*. That is, the bonds are purchased for less than their face amount.

The cost of a bond investment is recorded in an investment account, *Investment— Bonds*. The face amount of the bond and related premium or discount are normally not recorded in separate accounts. This is different from the accounting for bonds payable for which separate premium and discount accounts are used. However, like bonds payable, any premium or discount on a bond investment is amortized over the remaining life of the bonds.

Amortization of Premium or Discount

Any premium or discount on a bond investment should be amortized over the remaining life of the bond. The amortization affects the investment and interest revenue accounts as follows:

1. Bond *Premium* Amortization: Decreases Bond Investment and decreases Interest Revenue as shown in the following journal entry:

Interest Revenue	XXX	
Investment—Bonds		XXX
To amortize premium on bond investment.		

2. Bond *Discount* Amortization: Increases Bond Investment and increases Interest Revenue as shown in the following journal entry:

Investment—Bonds	XXX	
Interest Revenue		XXX
To amortize discount on bond investment.		

The amortization on bond investments is usually recorded at the end of the period as an adjusting entry. The amortization can be computed using the straight-line or interest methods.

To illustrate, assume that on April 1, 2010, Crenshaw Inc. purchases 10-year, 8% bonds on their issuance date directly from XPS Corporation as a held-to-maturity investment. The bonds pay semiannual interest and were purchased at a discount as follows:

Face amount of bonds	$50,000
Less discount on bonds	(6,000)
Purchase price of bonds	$44,000

The entries related to the bond investment during 2010 are as follows:

Purchase of bonds on April 1, 2010.

2010 Apr.	1	Investment—XPS Corporation Bonds	44,000	
		Cash		44,000
		Purchase of bonds as held-to-maturity investment.		

Receipt of semiannual interest on October 1.

Oct.	1	Cash	2,000	
		Interest Revenue		2,000
		Receipt of semiannual interest ($50,000 × 8% × ½).		

Adjusting entry for 3 months of accrued interest on December 31.

Dec.	31	Interest Receivable	1,000	
		Interest Revenue		1,000
		Accrued interest ($50,000 × 8% × ¼).		

Adjusting entry for amortization of discount on December 31 using the straight-line method.

Dec.	31	Investment—XPS Corporation Bonds	450	
		Interest Revenue		450
		Amortization of discount on bond investment ($6,000/120 months) = $50 per month $50 × 9 months = $450.		

Receipt of Maturity Value of Bond

At the maturity date of the bonds, any premium or discount will be fully amortized, and the book value (carrying value) of the bond investment account will equal the face amount of the bonds. At the maturity date, the investor will receive the face amount of the bonds.

To illustrate, the XPS Corporation bonds mature on April 1, 2020. At that date, the $6,000 discount will have been totally amortized, and Investment—XPS Corporation

Bonds will have a balance of $50,000. The receipt of the face amount of the bonds on April 1, 2020, is recorded as follows:

2020 Apr.	1	Cash	50,000	
		Investment—XPS Corporation Bonds		50,000
		Receipt of maturity value of		
		bond investment.		

A P P E N D I X   2

Comprehensive Income

Comprehensive income is defined as all changes in stockholders' equity during a period, except those resulting from dividends and stockholders' investments. Comprehensive income is computed by adding or subtracting *other comprehensive income* from net income as follows:

Net income	$XXX
Other comprehensive income	XXX
Comprehensive income	$XXX

Other comprehensive income items include unrealized gains and losses on available-for-sale securities as well as other items such as foreign currency and pension liability adjustments. The *cumulative* effect of other comprehensive income is reported on the balance sheet, as **accumulated other comprehensive income**.

Companies may report comprehensive income in the financial statements as follows:

1. On the income statement
2. In a separate statement of comprehensive income
3. In the statement of stockholders' equity

Companies may use terms other than comprehensive income, such as *total nonowner changes in equity*.

In the earlier illustration, Maggie Company had reported an unrealized gain on available-for-sale investments of $1,300. This unrealized gain would be reported in the Stockholders' Equity section of its 2009 balance sheet, as follows:

Maggie Company
Balance Sheet
December 31, 2009

Stockholders' equity:

Common stock	$ 10,000
Paid-in capital in excess of par value	150,000
Retained earnings	250,000
Plus unrealized gain (loss) on available-for-sale investments	1,300
Total stockholders' equity	$411,300

Alternatively, Maggie Company could have reported the unrealized gain as part of accumulated other comprehensive income as follows:

Maggie Company
Balance Sheet
December 31, 2009

Stockholders' equity:	
Common stock	$ 10,000
Paid-in capital in excess of par value	150,000
Retained earnings	250,000
Accumulated other comprehensive income:	
Unrealized gain on available-for-sale investments	1,300
Total stockholders' equity	$411,300

◀ ● ● ● *At a Glance* 15

1 Describe why companies invest in debt and equity securities.

Key Points	Key Learning Outcomes	Example Exercises	Practice Exercises
Cash can be used to (1) invest in current operations such as plant and equipment, (2) invest to earn additional revenue in marketable securities, or (3) invest in marketable securities for strategic reasons. Strategic investments are made to reduce costs, replace management, expand, or integrate operations.	• Describe the ways excess cash is used by a business. • Describe the purpose of temporary investments. • Describe the strategic purpose of long-term investments.		

2 Describe and illustrate the accounting for debt investments.

Key Points	Key Learning Outcomes	Example Exercises	Practice Exercises
The accounting for debt investments includes recording the purchase, interest revenue, and sale of the debt. Both the purchase and sale date may include accrued interest.	• Prepare journal entries to record the purchase of a debt investment, including accrued interest.	15-1	15-1A, 15-1B
	• Prepare journal entries for interest revenue from debt investments.	15-1	15-1A, 15-1B
	• Prepare journal entries to record the sale of a debt investment at a gain or loss.	15-1	15-1A, 15-1B

3 Describe and illustrate the accounting for equity investments.

Key Points

The accounting for equity investments differs depending on the degree of control. Accounting for investments of less than 20% of the outstanding stock (no control) of the investee includes recording the purchase of stock, receipt of dividends, and sale of stock at a gain or loss. Influential investments of 20%–50% of the outstanding stock of an investee are accounted for under the *equity method*. Under the equity method, the investment is debited for the proportional share of earnings of the investee and credited for dividends received. An investment for more than 50% of the outstanding stock of an investee is treated as a *business combination* and accounted for using *consolidated financial statements*.

Key Learning Outcomes	Example Exercises	Practice Exercises
• Describe the accounting for less than 20%, 20%–50%, and greater than 50% investments.		
• Prepare journal entries to record the purchase of a stock investment.	**15-2**	15-2A, 15-2B
• Prepare journal entries for receipt of dividends.	**15-2**	15-2A, 15-2B
• Prepare journal entries for the sale of a stock investment at a gain or loss.	**15-2**	15-2A, 15-2B
• Prepare journal entries for the equity earnings of an equity method investee.	**15-3**	15-3A, 15-3B
• Prepare journal entries for the dividends received from an equity method investee.	**15-3**	15-3A, 15-3B
• Describe a business combination, parent company, and subsidiary company.		
• Describe consolidated financial statements.		

4 Describe and illustrate valuing and reporting investments in the financial statements.

Key Points

Debt and equity securities are classified as (1) trading securities, (2) held-to-maturity securities, and (3) available-for-sale securities for reporting and valuation purposes. *Trading securities* are debt and equity securities purchased and sold to earn short-term profits. They are valued at *fair value*, which is the market price that a company would receive if the security were sold. Unrealized gains or losses from the change in fair value are reported on the income statement. *Held-to-maturity* investments are debt securities that are intended to be held until their maturity date. Held-to-maturity debt investments are valued at amortized cost. *Available-for-sale securities* are debt and equity securities that are not classified as trading or held-to-maturity. Available-for-sale securities are reported at fair value with unrealized gains or losses from changes in fair value being recognized in the Stockholders' Equity section of the balance sheet.

Key Learning Outcomes	Example Exercises	Practice Exercises
• Describe trading securities, held-to-maturity securities, and available-for-sale securities.		
• Prepare journal entries to record the change in the fair value of a trading security portfolio.	**15-4**	15-4A, 15-4B
• Describe and illustrate the reporting of trading securities on the balance sheet.		
• Describe the accounting for held-to-maturity debt securities.		
• Prepare journal entries to record the change in fair value of an available-for-sale security portfolio.	**15-5**	15-5A, 15-5B
• Describe and illustrate the reporting of available-for-sale securities on the balance sheet.		

5 Describe fair value accounting and its implications for the future.

Key Points	Key Learning Outcomes	Example Exercises	Practice Exercises
There is a trend toward fair value accounting in generally accepted accounting principles (GAAP). One advantage of this trend is a convergence of U.S. GAAP with International Accounting Standards. Some disadvantages of using fair value accounting are that fair values may not be obtainable for some items and fair values are difficult to compare across companies. Since fair value reporting affects the financial statements, using fair value accounting could create more fluctuations in valuations and earnings.	• Describe the reasons why there is a trend toward fair value accounting. • Describe the disadvantages of fair value accounting. • Describe how fair value accounting impacts the balance sheet and income statement. • Describe the future of fair value accounting.		

Key Terms

accumulated other comprehensive income (675)
available-for-sale securities (665)
business combination (660)
comprehensive income (675)
consolidated financial statements (660)
cost method (656)
debt securities (653)
equity method (658)
equity securities (653)
fair value (661)
held-to-maturity securities (664)
investee (656)
investments (653)
investor (656)
other comprehensive income (675)
parent company (660)
subsidiary company (660)
trading securities (661)
unrealized gain or loss (661)

Illustrative Problem

The following selected investment transactions were completed by Rosewell Company during 2010, its first year of operations:

2010
Jan. 11. Purchased 800 shares of Bryan Company stock as an available-for-sale security at $23 per share plus an $80 brokerage commission.
Feb. 6. Purchased $40,000 of 8% U.S. Treasury bonds at par value plus accrued interest for 36 days. The bonds pay interest on January 1 and July 1. The bonds were classified as held-to-maturity securities.
Mar. 3. Purchased 1,900 shares of Cohen Company stock as a trading security at $48 per share plus a $152 brokerage commission.
Apr. 5. Purchased 2,400 shares of Lyons Inc. stock as an available-for-sale security at $68 per share plus a $120 brokerage commission.

May 12. Purchased 200,000 shares of Myers Company at $37 per share plus an $8,000 brokerage commission. Myers Company has 800,000 common shares issued and outstanding. The equity method was used for this investment.

July 1. Received semiannual interest on bonds purchased on February 6.

Aug. 29. Sold 1,200 shares of Cohen Company stock at $61 per share less a $90 brokerage commission.

Oct. 5. Received an $0.80-per-share dividend on Bryan Company stock.

Nov. 11. Received a $1.10-per-share dividend on Myers Company stock.

16. Purchased 3,000 shares of Morningside Company stock as a trading security for $52 per share plus a $150 brokerage commission.

Dec. 31. Accrued interest on February 6 bonds.

31. Recorded Rosewell's share of Myers Company earnings of $146,000 for the year.

31. Prepared adjusting entries for the portfolios of trading and available-for-sale securities based upon the following fair values (stock prices):

Bryan Company	$21
Cohen Company	43
Lyons Inc.	88
Myers Company	40
Morningside Company	45

Instructions

1. Journalize the preceding transactions.
2. Prepare the balance sheet disclosure for Rosewell Company's investments on December 31, 2010.

Solution

1.

2010				
Jan.	11	Available-for-Sale Investments—Bryan Company	18,480*	
		Cash		18,480
		*(800 shares × $23 per share) + $80		

Feb.	6	Investments—U.S. Treasury Bonds	40,000	
		Interest Receivable	320*	
		Cash		40,320
		*$40,000 × 8% × (36 days/360 days)		

Mar.	3	Trading Investments—Cohen Company	91,352*	
		Cash		91,352
		*(1,900 shares × $48 per share) + $152		

Apr.	5	Available-for-Sale Investments—Lyons Inc.	163,320*	
		Cash		163,320
		*(2,400 shares × $68 per share) + $120		

2010				
May	12	Investment in Myers Company	7,408,000*	
		Cash		7,408,000
		*(200,000 shares × $37 per share) + $8,000		

July	1	Cash	1,600*	
		Interest Receivable		320
		Interest Revenue		1,280
		*$40,000 × 8% × ½		

Aug.	29	Cash	73,110*	
		Trading Investments—Cohen Company		57,696**
		Gain on Sale of Investments		15,414
		*(1,200 shares × $61 per share) − $90		
		**1,200 shares × ($91,352/1,900 shares)		

Oct.	5	Cash	640	
		Dividend Revenue		640
		*800 shares × $0.80 per share		

Nov.	11	Cash	220,000	
		Investment in Myers Company Stock		220,000
		*200,000 shares × $1.10 per share		

Nov.	16	Trading Investments—Morningside Company	156,150*	
		Cash		156,150
		*(3,000 shares × $52 per share) + $150		

Dec.	31	Interest Receivable	1,600	
		Interest Revenue		1,600
		Accrue interest, $40,000 × 8% × ½.		

Dec.	31	Investment in Myers Company Stock	36,500	
		Income of Myers Company		36,500
		Record equity income,		
		$146,000 × (200,000 shares/800,000 shares).		

2010 Dec.	31	Unrealized Loss on Trading Investments	24,706	
		Valuation Allowance for Trading Investments		24,706
		Record decease in fair value of trading investments, $165,100 − $189,806.		

Name	Number of Shares	Total Cost	Total Fair Value
Cohen Company	700	$ 33,656	$ 30,100*
Morningside Company	3,000	156,150	135,000**
Total		$189,806	$165,100

  * 700 shares × $43 per share
**3,000 shares × $45 per share

Note: Myers Company is valued using the equity method; thus, the fair value is not used.

Dec.	31	Valuation Allowance for Available-for-Sale Investments	46,200	
		Unrealized Gain (Loss) on Available-for-Sale Investments		46,200
		Record increase in fair value of available-for-sale investments, $228,000 − $181,800.		

Name	Number of Shares	Total Cost	Total Fair Value
Bryan Company	800	$ 18,480	$ 16,800*
Lyons Inc.	2,400	163,320	211,200**
Total		$181,800	$228,000

  * 800 shares × $21 per share
**2,400 shares × $88 per share

2.

Rosewell Company
Balance Sheet (Selected)
December 31, 2010

Current assets:		
Cash.		$XXX,XXX
Trading investments (at cost)	$189,806	
Less valuation allowance for trading investments	24,706	
Trading investments at fair value		165,100
Available-for-sale investments (at cost)	$181,800	
Plus valuation allowance for available-for-sale investments . .	46,200	
Available-for-sale investments at fair value		228,000

Stockholders' equity:	
Common stock	$ XX,XXX
Paid-in capital in excess of par value	XXX,XXX
Retained earnings	XXX,XXX
Plus unrealized gain (loss) on available-for-sale investments .	46,200
Total stockholders' equity	$XXX,XXX

Self-Examination Questions (Answers at End of Chapter)

1. An investment is made on May 24 for $50,000, 5% bonds at par value. Interest is payable on March 31 and September 30. What is the accrued interest on the purchase date?

   A. $167   C. $625
   B. $375   D. $875

2. On January 15 of the current year, Thomas Company purchased 1,400 shares of Dillon Company at a price of $23 per share plus a $70 brokerage commission. On April 10, Thomas Company subsequently sold 800 shares of Dillon Company for $20 per share less a $50 brokerage commission. Determine the loss on sale of investment.

   A. $2,400   C. $2,490
   B. $2,420   D. $2,520

3. Cole Company owns 40% of Barnwell Inc. During the current year, Barnwell reported net income of $200,000 and declared dividends of $60,000. How much would Cole Company increase Investment in Barnwell Inc. Stock for the current year?

   A. $24,000   C. $80,000
   B. $56,000   D. $104,000

4. On December 31, 2010, Southern Life Insurance Co. had investments in trading securities of $450,000 and a debit balance in Valuation Allowance for Trading Investments of $32,000. On December 31, 2011, the portfolio of trading securities had a cost of $500,000 and a fair value of $520,000. What was the unrealized gain or loss on the trading investments reported on the income statement for 2011?

   A. $12,000 unrealized loss
   B. $12,000 unrealized gain
   C. $20,000 unrealized gain
   D. $52,000 unrealized gain

5. On December 31, 2010, Naples Company had investments in available-for-sale securities of $200,000 and a credit balance in Valuation Allowance for Available-for-Sale Investments of $20,000. On December 31, 2011, the portfolio of available-for-sale securities had a cost of $215,000 and a fair value of $250,000. What was the unrealized gain or loss from available-for-sale securities reported on the income statement for 2011?

   A. $0
   B. $15,000 unrealized gain
   C. $20,000 unrealized gain
   D. $55,000 unrealized gain

Eye Openers

1. Why might a business invest in another company's stock?
2. If a bond is purchased between interest payment periods, how is the accrued interest treated?
3. Why would there be a gain or loss on the sale of a bond investment?
4. When is using the cost method the appropriate accounting for equity investments?
5. How does the accounting for a dividend received differ between the cost method and the equity method?
6. How are brokerage commissions treated under the cost method of accounting for equity investments?
7. How is the income of the investor impacted by equity method investments?
8. If an investor owns more than 50% of an investee, how is this treated on the investor's financial statements?

9. Google Inc. recently purchased all of the outstanding common stock of YouTube. Which is the parent company, and which is the subsidiary company in this transaction?
10. What is the major difference in the accounting for a portfolio of trading securities and a portfolio of available-for-sale securities?
11. If Valuation Allowance for Trading Investments has a credit balance, how is it treated on the balance sheet?
12. Are held-to-maturity securities (a) equity investments, (b) debt investments, or (c) both?
13. How would a debit balance in Unrealized Gain (Loss) on Available-for-Sale Investments be disclosed in the financial statements?
14. What would cause Unrealized Gain (Loss) on Available-for-Sale Investments to go from a $12,000 debit balance at the beginning of the year to a $1,000 credit balance at the end of the year?
15. What is the evidence of the trend toward fair value accounting?
16. What are some potential disadvantages of fair value accounting?

Practice Exercises

PE 15-1A
Bond transactions
obj. 2
EE 15-1   p. 655

Journalize the entries to record the following selected bond investment transactions for Olson Technologies:

a. Purchased for cash $90,000 of Hart Industries 7% bonds at 100 plus accrued interest of $1,050.
b. Received first semiannual interest.
c. Sold $60,000 of the bonds at 102 plus accrued interest of $750.

PE 15-1B
Bond transactions
obj. 2
EE 15-1   p. 655

Journalize the entries to record the following selected bond investment transactions for First Union:

a. Purchased for cash $400,000 of Medford City 5% bonds at 100 plus accrued interest of $4,500.
b. Received first semiannual interest.
c. Sold $250,000 of the bonds at 97 plus accrued interest of $1,800.

PE 15-2A
Stock transactions
obj. 3
EE 15-2   p. 658

On August 15, 2,500 shares of Collins Company are acquired at a price of $51 per share plus a $125 brokerage fee. On September 10, a $1.10-per-share dividend was received on the Collins Company stock. On October 5, 1,000 shares of the Collins Company stock were sold for $45 per share less a $50 brokerage fee. Prepare the journal entries for the original purchase, dividend, and sale.

PE 15-2B
Stock transactions
obj. 3
EE 15-2   p. 658

On February 12, 6,000 shares of Gilbert Company are acquired at a price of $22 per share plus a $240 brokerage fee. On April 22, a $0.42-per-share dividend was received on the Gilbert Company stock. On May 10, 4,000 shares of the Gilbert Company stock were sold for $28 per share less a $160 brokerage fee. Prepare the journal entries for the original purchase, dividend, and sale.

PE 15-3A
Equity method
obj. 3
EE 15-3   p. 660

On January 2, Leonard Company acquired 30% of the outstanding stock of Bristol Company for $350,000. For the year ending December 31, Bristol Company earned income of $90,000 and paid dividends of $28,000. Prepare the entries for Leonard Company for the purchase of the stock, share of Bristol income, and dividends received from Bristol Company.

PE 15-3B
Equity method
obj. 3
EE 15-3   p. 660

On January 2, Trey Company acquired 40% of the outstanding stock of Manning Company for $205,000. For the year ending December 31, Manning Company earned income of $48,000 and paid dividends of $14,000. Prepare the entries for Trey Company for the purchase of the stock, share of Manning income, and dividends received from Manning Company.

PE 15-4A
Valuing trading securities at fair value
obj. 4
EE 15-4   p. 663

On January 1, 2010, Valuation Allowance for Trading Investments has a credit balance of $8,700. On December 31, 2010, the cost of the trading securities portfolio was $52,400, and the fair value was $53,000. Prepare the December 31, 2010, adjusting journal entry to record the unrealized gain or loss on trading investments.

PE 15-4B
Valuing trading securities at fair value
obj. 4
EE 15-4   p. 663

On January 1, 2010, Valuation Allowance for Trading Investments has a credit balance of $1,200. On December 31, 2010, the cost of the trading securities portfolio was $99,600, and the fair value was $91,200. Prepare the December 31, 2010 adjusting journal entry to record the unrealized gain or loss on trading investments.

PE 15-5A
Valuing available-for-sale securities at fair value

obj. 4

EE 15-5   p. 668

On January 1, 2010, Valuation Allowance for Available-for-Sale Securities has a debit balance of $1,500. On December 31, 2010, the cost of the available-for-sale securities was $67,500, and the fair value was $69,200. Prepare the adjusting entry to record the unrealized gain or loss for available-for-sale securities on December 31, 2010.

PE 15-5B
Valuing available-for-sale securities at fair value

obj. 4

EE 15-5   p. 668

On January 1, 2010, Valuation Allowance for Available-for-Sale Securities has a credit balance of $3,400. On December 31, 2010, the cost of the available-for-sale securities was $35,700, and the fair value was $30,100. Prepare the adjusting entry to record the unrealized gain or loss for available-for-sale securities on December 31, 2010.

Exercises

EX 15-1
Entries for investments in bonds, interest, and sale of bonds

obj. 2

Mercer Investments acquired $120,000 Jericho Corp., 6% bonds at par value on September 1, 2010. The bonds pay interest on September 1 and March 1. On March 1, 2011, Mercer sold $40,000 par value Jericho Corp. bonds at 102.

Journalize the entries to record the following:

a. The initial acquisition of the Jericho Corp. bonds on September 1, 2010.
b. The adjusting entry for 4 months of accrued interest earned on the Jericho Corp. bonds on December 31, 2010.
c. The receipt of semiannual interest on March 1, 2011.
d. The sale of $40,000 Jericho Corp. bonds on March 1, 2011, at 102.

EX 15-2
Entries for investment in bonds, interest, and sale of bonds

obj. 2

✔ Dec. 1, Loss on sale of investments, $20

Lance Co. purchased $36,000 of 6%, 10-year Bergen County bonds on July 12, 2010, directly from the county at par value. The bonds pay semiannual interest on May 1 and November 1. On December 1, 2010, Lance Co. sold $14,000 of the Bergen County bonds at 102 plus $70 accrued interest, less a $300 brokerage commission.

Provide the journal entries for:

a. the purchase of the bonds on July 12, plus 72 days of accrued interest.
b. semiannual interest on May 1 and November 1.
c. sale of the bonds on December 1.
d. adjusting entry for accrued interest of $220 on December 31.

EX 15-3
Entries for investment in bonds, interest, and sale of bonds

obj. 2

The following bond investment transactions were completed during 2010 by Torrence Company:

Jan. 21. Purchased 30, $1,000 par value government bonds at 100 plus 20 days' accrued interest. The bonds pay 6% annual interest on June 30 and January 1.
June 30. Received semiannual interest on bond investment.
Sept. 5. Sold 12, $1,000 par value bonds at 98 plus $134 accrued interest.

a. Journalize the entries for these transactions.
b. Provide the December 31, 2010, adjusting journal entry for semiannual interest earned from the bond coupon.

EX 15-4
Interest on bond investments

obj. 2

On May 1, 2010, Carly Company purchased $84,000 of 5%, 12-year Baltimore Company bonds at par plus 2 months' accrued interest. The bonds pay interest on March 1 and September 1. On October 1, 2010, Carly Company sold $30,000 of the Baltimore Company bonds acquired on May 1, plus one month accrued interest. On December 31, 2010, four months' interest was accrued for the remaining bonds.

Determine the interest earned by Carly Company on Baltimore Company bonds for 2010.

EX 15-5
Entries for investment in stock, receipt of dividends, and sale of shares

obj. 3

✔ c. Gain on sale of investments, $6,875

On February 17, Asher Corporation acquired 3,000 shares of the 100,000 outstanding shares of Dan Co. common stock at $28.90 plus commission charges of $300. On July 11, a cash dividend of $0.95 per share was received. On December 4, 1,000 shares were sold at $36, less commission charges of $125.

Record the entries for (a) the purchase of stock, (b) the receipt of dividends, and (c) the sale of 1,000 shares.

EX 15-6
Entries for investment in stock, receipt of dividends, and sale of shares

obj. 3

✔ June 3, Loss on sale of investments, $12,725

The following equity investment-related transactions were completed by Lance Company in 2010:

Jan. 12. Purchased 1,800 shares of Baxter Company for a price of $56.50 per share plus a brokerage commission of $90.

Apr. 10. Received a quarterly dividend of $0.25 per share on the Baxter Company investment.

June 3. Sold 1,200 shares for a price of $46 per share less a brokerage commission of $65.

Journalize the entries for these transactions.

EX 15-7
Entries for stock investments, dividends, and sale of stock

obj. 3

✔ Nov. 14, Dividend revenue, $150

Plumbline Tech Corp. manufactures surveying equipment. Journalize the entries to record the following selected equity investment transactions completed by Plumbline during 2010:

Feb. 2. Purchased for cash 900 shares of Devon Inc. stock for $54 per share plus a $450 brokerage commission.

Apr. 16. Received dividends of $0.25 per share on Devon Inc. stock.

June 17. Purchased 600 shares of Devon Inc. stock for $65 per share plus a $300 brokerage commission.

Aug. 19. Sold 1,000 shares of Devon Inc. stock for $70 per share less a $500 brokerage commission. Plumbline assumes that the first investments purchased are the first investments sold.

Nov. 14. Received dividends of $0.30 per share on Devon Inc. stock.

EX 15-8
Entries for available-for-sale stock investments and dividends

obj. 3

During 2010, its first year of operations, LandStar Corporation purchased the following securities classified as available-for-sale securities:

Security	Shares Purchased	Cost	Cash Dividends Received
Tekniks Inc.	2,800	$78,400	$560
Lakeshore Corp.	1,200	16,800	240

a. Record the purchase of the investments for cash.
b. Record the receipt of the dividends.

EX 15-9
Equity method for stock investment

obj. 3

At a total cost of $710,000, Abbott Corporation acquired 50,000 shares of Costello Corp. common stock as a long-term investment. Abbott Corporation uses the equity method of accounting for this investment. Costello Corp. has 200,000 shares of common stock outstanding, including the shares acquired by Abbott Corporation.

Journalize the entries by Abbott Corporation to record the following information:

a. Costello Corp. reports net income of $1,280,000 for the current period.
b. A cash dividend of $1.40 per common share is paid by Costello Corp. during the current period.

EX 15-10
Equity method for stock investment

obj. 3

✔ b. $4,565,760

On January 15, 2010, National Star Inc. purchased 80,000 shares of Krypton Labs Inc. directly from one of the founders for a price of $55 per share. Krypton has 250,000 shares outstanding, including the National Star shares. On July 2, 2010, Krypton paid $217,000 in total dividends to its shareholders. On December 31, 2010, Krypton reported a net income of $735,000 for the year. National Star uses the equity method in accounting for its investment in Krypton Labs.

a. Provide the National Star Inc. journal entries for the transactions involving its investment in Krypton Labs Inc. during 2010.
b. Determine the December 31, 2010, balance of Investment in Krypton Labs Inc. Stock.

EX 15-11
Equity method for stock investment

obj. 3

Corvis Company's balance sheet disclosed its long-term investment in Mid-American Company under the equity method for comparative years as follows:

	Dec. 31, 2011	Dec. 31, 2010
Investment in Mid-American Company stock (in millions)	$98	$90

In addition, the 2011 Corvis Company income statement disclosed equity earnings in the Mid-American Company investment as $10 million. Corvis Company neither purchased nor sold Mid-American Company stock during 2011. The fair value of Mid-American Company stock investment on December 31, 2011, was $107.

Explain the change in the Investment in Mid-American Company Stock balance sheet account from December 31, 2010, to December 31, 2011.

EX 15-12
Missing statement items, trading investments

obj. 4

✔ g. $7,000

Lydell Capital, Inc., makes investments in trading securities. Selected income statement items for the years ended December 31, 2010, and 2011, plus selected items from comparative balance sheets, are as follows:

Lydell Capital, Inc.
Selected Income Statement Items
For the Years Ended December 31, 2010 and 2011

	2010	2011
Operating income	a.	e.
Unrealized gain (loss)	b.	$(2,000)
Net income	c.	14,000

Lydell Capital, Inc.
Selected Balance Sheet Items
December 31, 2009, 2010, and 2011

	Dec. 31, 2009	Dec. 31, 2010	Dec. 31, 2011
Trading investments, at cost	$123,000	$146,000	$172,000
Valuation allowance for trading investments	(6,000)	9,000	g.
Trading investments, at fair value	d.	f.	h.
Retained earnings	$145,000	$192,000	i.

There were no dividends.
Determine the missing lettered items.

EX 15-13
Fair value journal entries, trading investments

obj. 4

The investments of Commerce Bank Inc. include 12,000 shares of RadTek Inc. common stock purchased on February 21, 2010, for $16 per share. These shares were classified as trading securities. As of the December 31, 2010, balance sheet date, assume that the share price increased to $21 per share. As of the December 31, 2011, balance sheet date, assume that the share price declined to $20 per share. The investment was held through December 31, 2011.

a. Journalize the entries to record the adjustment of the RadTek Inc. investment to fair value on December 31, 2010, and December 31, 2011.
b. Where is the unrealized gain or unrealized loss for trading investments disclosed on the financial statements?

EX 15-14
Fair value journal entries, trading investments

objs. 3, 4

Horizon Bancorp Inc. purchased a portfolio of trading securities during 2009. The cost and fair value of this portfolio on December 31, 2009, was as follows:

Name	Number of Shares	Total Cost	Total Fair Value
Apex, Inc.	1,200	$16,000	$15,000
Evans Company	700	23,000	21,500
Poole Company	300	9,000	9,200
Total		$48,000	$45,700

On April 3, 2010, Horizon Bancorp Inc. purchased 500 shares of Cable, Inc., at $30 per share plus a $100 brokerage fee. On December 31, 2010, the trading security portfolio had the following cost and fair value:

Name	Number of Shares	Total Cost	Total Fair Value
Apex, Inc.	1,200	$16,000	$16,400
Cable, Inc.	500	15,100	17,500
Evans Company	700	23,000	22,000
Poole Company	300	9,000	12,400
Total		$63,100	$68,300

Provide the journal entries to record the following:
a. The adjustment of the trading security portfolio to fair value on December 31, 2009.
b. The April 3, 2010, purchase of Cable, Inc., stock.
c. The adjustment of the trading securities portfolio to fair value on December 31, 2010.

EX 15-15
Fair value journal entries, trading investments

obj. 4

✔ a. 2. Dec. 31, 2010, Unrealized loss on trading investments, $4,900

Union Financial Services, Inc., purchased the following trading securities during 2009, its first year of operations:

Name	Number of Shares	Cost
B&T Transportation, Inc.	3,400	$ 67,100
Citrus Foods, Inc.	1,800	29,700
Stuart Housewares, Inc.	800	19,700
Total		$116,500

The market price per share for the trading security portfolio on December 31, 2009, and December 31, 2010, was as follows:

	Market Price per Share	
	Dec. 31, 2009	Dec. 31, 2010
B&T Transportation, Inc.	$25.00	$24.00
Citrus Foods, Inc.	17.50	18.00
Stuart Housewares, Inc.	23.00	20.00

a. Provide the journal entry to adjust the trading security portfolio to fair value on:
1. December 31, 2009
2. December 31, 2010
b. Describe the income statement impact from the December 31, 2010, journal entry.

EX 15-16
Financial statement disclosure, trading investments

obj. 4

The income statement for Harris Company was as follows:

Harris Company
Income Statement (selected items)
For the Year Ended December 31, 2010

Income from operations	$345,000
Less unrealized loss on trading investments	23,000
Net income	$322,000

The balance sheet dated December 31, 2009, showed a Retained Earnings balance of $823,000 and a Valuation Allowance for Trading Investments debit balance of $68,000. The company paid $43,000 in dividends during 2010.

a. Determine the December 31, 2010, Retained Earnings balance.
b. Determine the December 31, 2010, Valuation Allowance for Trading Investments balance.

EX 15-17
Missing statement items, available-for-sale securities

obj. 4

✔ f. ($6,000)

Oceanic Airways makes investments in available-for-sale securities. Selected income statement items for the years ended December 31, 2010, and 2011, plus selected items from comparative balance sheets, are as follows:

Oceanic Airways
Selected Income Statement Items
For the Years Ended December 31, 2010, and 2011

	2010	2011
Operating income	a.	g.
Gain (loss) from sale of investments	$4,000	$ (8,000)
Net income	b.	(11,000)

Oceanic Airways
Selected Balance Sheet Items
December 31, 2009, 2010, and 2011

	Dec. 31, 2009	Dec. 31, 2010	Dec. 31, 2011
Assets			
Available-for-sale investments, at cost	$ 78,000	$ 68,000	$95,000
Valuation allowance for available-for-sale investments	5,000	(6,000)	h.
Available-for-sale investments, at fair value	c.	e.	i.
Stockholders' Equity			
Unrealized gain (loss) on available-for-sale investments	d.	f.	(7,000)
Retained earnings	$164,000	$232,000	j.

There were no dividends.
Determine the missing lettered items.

EX 15-18
Fair value journal entries, available-for-sale investments

obj. 4

✔ b. Dec. 31, 2010, Unrealized gain (loss) on available-for-sale investments, ($70,000)

The investments of Charter Inc. include 10,000 shares of Wallace Inc. common stock purchased on January 10, 2010, for $30 per share. These shares were classified as available-for-sale securities. As of the December 31, 2010, balance sheet date, assume that the share price declined to $23 per share. As of the December 31, 2011, balance sheet date, assume that the share price rose to $27 per share. The investment was held through December 31, 2011.

a. Journalize the entries to record the adjustment of the Wallace Inc. investment to fair value on December 31, 2010, and December 31, 2011.

b. What is the balance of Unrealized Gain (Loss) on Available-for-Sale Investments for December 31, 2010, and December 31, 2011?

c. Where is Unrealized Gain (Loss) on Available-for-Sale Investments disclosed on the financial statements?

EX 15-19
Fair value journal entries, available-for-sale investments

objs. 3, 4

Lipscomb Inc. purchased a portfolio of available-for-sale securities in 2009, its first year of operations. The cost and fair value of this portfolio on December 31, 2009, was as follows:

Name	Number of Shares	Total Cost	Total Fair Value
Loomis, Inc.	600	$ 9,000	$10,000
Parker Corp.	900	21,000	22,800
Smithfield Corp.	1,800	32,500	31,000
Total		$62,500	$63,800

On May 10, 2010, Lipscomb purchased 700 shares of Nova Inc. at $50 per share plus a $150 brokerage fee. On December 31, 2010, the available-for-sale security portfolio had the following cost and fair value:

Name	Number of Shares	Total Cost	Total Fair Value
Loomis, Inc.	600	$ 9,000	$ 12,300
Nova, Inc.	700	35,150	36,100
Parker Corp.	900	21,000	20,000
Smithfield Corp.	1,800	32,500	33,100
Total		$97,650	$101,500

Provide the journal entries to record the following:

a. The adjustment of the available-for-sale security portfolio to fair value on December 31, 2009.
b. The May 10, 2010, purchase of Nova Inc. stock.
c. The adjustment of the available-for-sale security portfolio to fair value on December 31, 2010.

EX 15-20
Fair value journal entries, available-for-sale investments

obj. 4

Nantahla, Inc., purchased the following available-for-sale securities during 2009, its first year of operations:

Name	Number of Shares	Cost
Barns Electronics, Inc.	1,500	$ 42,500
Ryan Co.	400	28,200
Sharon Co.	2,200	66,100
Total		$136,800

The market price per share for the available-for-sale security portfolio on December 31, 2009, and December 31, 2010, was as follows:

	Market Price per Share	
	Dec. 31, 2009	Dec. 31, 2010
Barns Electronics, Inc.	$31.00	$28.00
Ryan Co.	77.00	67.00
Sharon Co.	29.00	26.00

a. Provide the journal entry to adjust the available-for-sale security portfolio to fair value on:
   1. December 31, 2009
   2. December 31, 2010
b. Describe the income statement impact from the December 31, 2010, journal entry.

EX 15-21
Balance sheet presentation of available-for-sale investments

obj. 4

During 2010, its first year of operations, Myron Company purchased two available-for-sale investments as follows:

Security	Shares Purchased	Cost
Olson Products, Inc.	700	$29,000
Reynolds Co.	1,900	41,000

Assume that as of December 31, 2010, the Olson Products, Inc., stock had a market value of $49 per share and the Reynolds Co. stock had a market value of $20 per share. Myron Company had net income of $225,000, and paid no dividends for the year ending December 31, 2010.

a. Prepare the Current Assets section of the balance sheet presentation for the available-for-sale investments.
b. Prepare the Stockholders' Equity section of the balance sheet to reflect the earnings and unrealized gain (loss) for the available-for-sale investments.

EX 15-22
Balance sheet presentation of available-for-sale investments

obj. 4

During 2010, Toney Corporation held a portfolio of available-for-sale securities having a cost of $190,000. There were no purchases or sales of investments during the year. The market values at the beginning and end of the year were $225,000 and $180,000, respectively. The net income for 2010 was $175,000, and no dividends were paid during the year. The Stockholders' Equity section of the balance sheet was as follows on December 31, 2009:

Toney Corporation
Stockholders' Equity
December 31, 2009

Common stock	$ 40,000
Paid-in capital in excess of par value	300,000
Retained earnings	395,000
Unrealized gain (loss) on available-for- sale investments	35,000
Total	$770,000

Prepare the Stockholders' Equity section of the balance sheet for December 31, 2010.

Appendix 1
EX 15-23
Bond premium amortization

On January 2, 2010, Patel Company purchased $80,000, 10-year, 7%, government bonds at 104, including the brokerage commission. January 2 is an interest payment date.

a. Journalize the entry to record the bond purchase.
b. Journalize the entry to amortize the bond premium on December 31, 2010.
c. What is the relationship between the market rate of interest and the coupon rate on the bond investment acquisition date?

Appendix 1
EX 15-24
Bond discount amortization

On September 1, 2010, Longstreet Company purchased $150,000 of 20-year, 6%, Marvin Company bonds at 97, including the brokerage commission. September 1 is an interest payment date.

a. Journalize the entry to record the bond purchase.
b. Journalize the entry to amortize the bond discount on December 31, 2010.
c. What is the relationship between the market rate of interest and the coupon rate on the bond investment acquisition date?

Appendix 1
EX 15-25
Bond interest and premium amortization entries

On May 1, 2010, Starmaker Machinery, Inc., purchased $60,000 of 10-year, 5% government bonds at 103, including the brokerage commission. The interest is received semi-annually on May 1 and November 1.

a. Journalize the entry to record the May 1, 2010, bond purchase.
b. Journalize the semiannual interest received on November 1, 2010.
c. Journalize the accrued interest adjustment on December 31, 2010.
d. Journalize the premium amortization adjustment on December 31, 2010.
e. Journalize the receipt of the face amount of the bonds on the bond maturity date, May 1, 2020.

Appendix 1
EX 15-26
Bond interest and discount amortization entries

On June 1, 2010, Firefly, Inc., purchased $120,000 of 10-year, 6% Barron Company bonds at 98, including the brokerage commission. The interest is payable semiannually on June 1 and December 1.

a. Journalize the entry to record the June 1, 2010, bond purchase.
b. Journalize the semiannual interest received on December 1, 2010.
c. Journalize the accrued interest adjustment on December 31, 2010.
d. Journalize the discount amortization adjustment on December 31, 2010.
e. Journalize the receipt of the face amount of the bonds on the bond maturity date, June 1, 2020.

Appendix 2
EX 15-27
Comprehensive income

On April 23, 2010, Albert Co. purchased 1,500 shares of Conover, Inc., for $55 per share including the brokerage commission. The Conover investment was classified as an available-for-sale security. On December 31, 2010, the fair value of Conover, Inc., was $65 per share. The net income of Albert Co. was $70,000 for 2010.

Prepare a statement of comprehensive income for Albert Co. for the year ended December 31, 2010.

Appendix 2
EX 15-28
Comprehensive income

On December 31, 2009, Phoenix Co. had the following available-for-sale investment disclosure within the Current Assets section of the balance sheet:

Available-for-sale investments (at cost)	$105,000
Plus valuation allowance for available-for-sale investments	15,000
Available-for-sale investments (at fair value)	$120,000

There were no purchases or sales of available-for-sale investments during 2010. On December 31, 2010, the fair value of the available-for-sale investment portfolio was $101,000. The net income of Phoenix Co. was $135,000 for 2010.

Prepare a statement of comprehensive income for Phoenix Co. for the year ended December 31, 2010.

EX 15-29
Dividend yield

At the market close on January 29, 2008, Bank of America Corporation had a closing stock price of $41.84. In addition, Bank of America had a dividend per share of $2.40. Determine Bank of America's dividend yield. (Round to one decimal place.)

EX 15-30
Dividend yield

✔ a. Dec. 29, 2006, 1.24%

The market price for Microsoft Corporation closed at $29.86 and $35.60 on December 29, 2006, and December 31, 2007, respectively. The dividends per share were $0.37 for 2006 and $0.41 for 2007.

a. Determine the dividend yield for Microsoft on December 29, 2006, and December 31, 2007. (Round percentages to two decimal places.)
b. Interpret these measures.

EX 15-31
Dividend yield

eBay Inc. developed a Web-based marketplace at **http://www.ebay.com**, in which individuals can buy and sell a variety of items. eBay also acquired PayPal, an online payments system that allows businesses and individuals to send and receive online payments securely. In a recent annual report, eBay published the following dividend policy:

We have never paid cash dividends on our stock and currently anticipate that we will continue to retain any future earnings for the foreseeable future.

Given eBay's dividend policy, why would an investor be attracted to its stock?

Problems Series A

PR 15-1A
Stock investment transactions, equity method and available-for-sale securities

objs. 3, 4

Roman Products, Inc., is a wholesaler of men's hair products. The company began operations on January 1, 2010. The following transactions relate to securities acquired by Roman Products, Inc., which has a fiscal year ending on December 31:

2010
Jan. 3. Purchased 3,000 shares of Whalen Inc. as an available-for-sale investment at $46 per share, including the brokerage commission.
July 6. Split Whalen Inc. stock 2 for 1 and received the regular cash dividend of $0.60 per share on the Whalen Inc. stock after the split.
Oct. 14. Sold 900 shares of Whalen Inc. stock at $25 per share, less a brokerage commission of $50.
Dec. 9. Received the regular cash dividend of $0.60 per share.
     31. Whalen Inc. is classified as an available-for-sale investment and is adjusted to a fair value of $21 per share. Use the Valuation Allowance for Available-for-Sale Investments account in making the adjustment.

2011
Jan. 5. Purchased an influential interest in Tasmania Co. for $620,000 by purchasing 60,000 shares directly from the estate of the founder of Tasmania. There are 150,000 shares of Tasmania Co. stock outstanding.
July 8. Received the regular cash divided of $0.70 per share on Whalen Inc. stock.
Dec. 8. Received the regular cash dividend of $0.70 per share plus an extra dividend of $0.15 per share on Whalen Inc. stock.
     31. Received $18,000 of cash dividends on Tasmania Co. stock. Tasmania Co. reported net income of $74,000 in 2011. Roman Products uses the equity method of accounting for its investment in Tasmania Co.
     31. Whalen Inc. is classified as an available-for-sale investment and is adjusted to a fair value of $26 per share. Use the Valuation Allowance for Available-for-Sale Investments account in making the adjustment.

Instructions

1. Journalize the entries to record the preceding transactions.
2. Prepare the investment-related asset and stockholders' equity balance sheet disclosures for Roman Products, Inc., on December 31, 2011, assuming the Retained Earnings balance on December 31, 2011, is $455,000.

PR 15-2A
Stock investment transactions, trading securities

objs. 3, 4

Western Capital Inc. is a regional investment company that began operations on January 1, 2010. The following transactions relate to trading securities acquired by Western Capital Inc., which has a fiscal year ending on December 31:

2010

Feb.   3.   Purchased 2,500 shares of Titan Inc. as a trading security at $35 per share plus a brokerage commission of $500.
Mar. 12.   Purchased 1,200 shares of Quick Tyme Inc. as a trading security at $14 per share plus a brokerage commission of $240.
May 15.   Sold 600 shares of Titan Inc. for $36 per share less a $80 brokerage commission.
June 12.   Received an annual dividend of $0.12 per share on Titan Inc. stock.
Dec. 31.   The portfolio of trading securities was adjusted to fair values of $15 and $39 per share for Quick Tyme Inc. and Titan Inc., respectively.

2011

Apr.   9.   Purchased 1,100 shares of Aspire Inc. as a trading security at $41 per share plus a $165 brokerage commission.
June 15.   Received an annual dividend of $0.15 per share on Titan Inc. stock.
Aug. 20.   Sold 200 shares of Aspire Inc. for $35 per share less a $60 brokerage commission.
Dec. 31.   The portfolio of trading securities was adjusted to fair value using the following fair values per share for the trading securities:

Aspire Inc.	$31
Quick Tyme Inc.	16
Titan Inc.	37

The portfolio of trading securities was adjusted to fair value.

Instructions

1. Journalize the entries to record these transactions.
2. Prepare the investment-related current asset balance sheet disclosures for Western Capital Inc. on December 31, 2011.
3. How are unrealized gains or losses on trading investments disclosed on the financial statements of Western Capital Inc.?

PR 15-3A
Debt investment transactions, available-for-sale valuation

objs. 2, 4

✔ 2. Available-for-sale investment (at fair value), $147,640

Dollar-Mart Inc. is a general merchandise retail company that began operations on January 1, 2010. The following transactions relate to debt investments acquired by Dollar-Mart Inc., which has a fiscal year ending on December 31:

2010

May   1.   Purchased $60,000 of Elkin City 4%, 10-year bonds at face value plus accrued interest of $400. The bond is classified as an available-for-sale investment. The bonds pay interest semiannually on March 1 and September 1.
June 16.   Purchased $112,000 of Morgan Co. 6%, 12-year bonds at face value plus accrued interest of $280. The bond is classified as an available-for-sale investment. The bonds pay interest semiannually on June 1 and December 1.
Sept. 1.   Received semiannual interest on the Elkin City bonds.
Oct.   1.   Sold $24,000 of Elkin City bonds at 103 plus accrued interest of $80.
Dec.   1.   Received semiannual interest on Morgan Co. bonds.
       31.   Accrued $480 interest on Elkin City bonds.
       31.   Accrued $560 interest on Morgan Co. bonds.
       31.   The available-for-sale bond portfolio was adjusted to fair values of 102 and 101 for Elkin City and Morgan Co. bonds, respectively.

2011
Mar. 1. Received semiannual interest on the Elkin City bonds.
June 1. Received semiannual interest on the Morgan Co. bonds.
         (Assume that there are no more purchases or sales of bonds during 2011.
         Also assume all subsequent interest transactions for 2011 have been
         recorded properly.)
Dec. 31. The available-for-sale bond portfolio was adjusted to fair values of 99 and
         100 for Elkin City and Morgan Co. bonds, respectively.

Instructions
1. Journalize the entries to record these transactions.
2. Prepare the investment-related current asset and stockholders' equity balance sheet
    disclosures for Dollar-Mart Inc. on December 31, 2011, assuming the Retained
    Earnings balance on December 31, 2011, is $310,000.

PR 15-4A
Investment reporting

objs. 2, 3, 4

✔ 1. b. 6,115

Miranda, Inc., manufactures and sells commercial and residential security equipment.
The comparative unclassified balance sheets for December 31, 2011 and 2010 are provided below. Selected missing balances are shown by letters.

Miranda, Inc.
Balance Sheet
December 31, 2011, and 2010

	Dec. 31, 2011	Dec. 31, 2010
Cash	$104,000	$ 98,000
Accounts receivable (net)	71,000	67,500
Available-for-sale investments (at cost)—Note 1	a.	36,000
Plus valuation allowance for available-for-sale investments	b.	4,000
Available-for-sale investments (fair value)	$ c.	$ 40,000
Interest receivable	$ d.	—
Investment in Denver Co. stock—Note 2	e.	$ 48,000
Office equipment (net)	60,000	65,000
Total assets	$ f.	$318,500
Accounts payable	$ 56,900	$ 51,400
Common stock	50,000	50,000
Excess of issue price over par	160,000	160,000
Retained earnings	g.	53,100
Plus unrealized gain (loss) on available-for-sale investments	h.	4,000
Total liabilities and stockholders' equity	$ i.	$318,500

Note 1. Investments are classified as available for sale. The investments at cost and
fair value on December 31, 2010, are as follows:

	No. of Shares	Cost per Share	Total Cost	Total Fair Value
Tyndale Inc. Stock	600	$24	$14,400	$16,000
UR-Smart Inc. Stock	1,200	18	21,600	24,000
			$36,000	$40,000

Note 2. The Investment in Denver Co. stock is an equity method investment representing 36% of the outstanding shares of Denver Co.
The following selected investment transactions occurred during 2011:

2011
Apr. 21. Purchased 300 shares of Vegas Resorts, Inc., at $20 per share plus a $45
         brokerage commission.
June 12. Dividends of $1 per share are received on the UR-Smart Inc. stock investment.
Sept. 9. Dividends of $8,900 are received on the Denver Co. investment.

Oct. 1. Purchased $8,000 of Vita-Mighty Co. 7%, 10-year bonds at 100. The bonds are classified as available for sale. The bonds pay interest on Oct. 1 and Apr. 1.

Dec. 31. Denver Co. reported a total net income of $40,000 for 2011. Miranda recorded equity earnings for its share of Denver Co. net income.

31. Accrued interest on Vita-Mighty bonds purchased on October 1.

31. Adjusted the available-for-sale investment portfolio to fair value using the following fair value per share amounts:

Available-for-Sale Investments	Fair Value
Tyndale Inc. stock	$28 per share
UR-Smart, Inc., stock	$20 per share
Vegas Resorts, Inc., stock	$24 per share
Vita-Mighty Co. bonds	102 per $1,000 of face value

31. Closed the Miranda, Inc., net income of $18,685 for 2011. Miranda paid no dividends during 2011.

Instructions

Determine the missing letters in the unclassified balance sheet. Provide appropriate supporting calculations.

Problems Series B

PR 15-1B
Stock investment transactions, equity method and available-for-sale securities

objs. 3, 4

Broadway Arts Inc. produces and sells theater set designs and costumes. The company began operations on January 1, 2010. The following transactions relate to securities acquired by Broadway Arts Inc., which has a fiscal year ending on December 31:

2010

Jan. 10. Purchased 5,000 shares of Crystal Inc. as an available-for-sale security at $36 per share, including the brokerage commission.

Mar. 12. Received the regular cash dividend of $0.80 per share.

Sept. 9. Split Crystal Inc. stock 2 for 1 and received the regular cash dividend of $0.40 per share on the Crystal Inc. stock.

Oct. 14. Sold 1,000 shares of Crystal Inc. stock at $15 per share, less a brokerage commission of $100.

Dec. 31. Crystal Inc. is classified as an available-for-sale investment and is adjusted to a fair value of $19 per share. Use the Valuation Allowance for Available-for-Sale Investments account in making the adjustment.

2011

Jan. 5. Purchased an influential interest in Bulls Eye Inc. for $410,000 by purchasing 50,000 shares directly from the estate of the founder of Bulls Eye Inc. There are 200,000 shares of Bulls Eye Inc. stock outstanding.

Mar. 8. Received the regular cash divided of $0.45 per share on Crystal Inc. stock.

Sept. 10. Received the regular cash dividend of $0.45 per share plus an extra dividend of $0.10 per share on Crystal Inc. stock.

Dec. 31. Received $35,000 of cash dividends on Bulls Eye Inc. stock. Bulls Eye Inc. reported net income of $126,000 in 2011. Broadway Arts Inc. uses the equity method of accounting for its investment in Bulls Eye Inc.

31. Crystal Inc. is classified as an available-for-sale investment and is adjusted to a fair value of $15 per share. Use the Valuation Allowance for Available-for-Sale Investments account in making the adjustment.

Instructions

1. Journalize the entries to record these transactions.

2. Prepare the investment-related asset and stockholders' equity balance sheet disclosures for Broadway Arts Inc. on December 31, 2011, assuming the Retained Earnings balance on December 31, 2011, is $390,000.

PR 15-2B
Stock investment transactions, trading securities

objs. 3, 4

Jupiter Insurance Co. is a regional insurance company that began operations on January 1, 2010. The following transactions relate to trading securities acquired by Jupiter Insurance Co., which has a fiscal year ending on December 31:

2010
Feb. 21.   Purchased 3,000 shares of Loral Inc. as a trading security at $25 per share plus a brokerage commission of $600.
Mar. 2.   Purchased 900 shares of Monarch Inc. as a trading security at $52 per share plus a brokerage commission of $180.
May   3.   Sold 800 shares of Loral Inc. for $23.50 per share less a $80 brokerage commission.
June 8.   Received an annual dividend of $0.18 per share on Loral Inc. stock.
Dec. 31.   The portfolio of trading securities was adjusted to fair values of $24 and $48 per share for Loral Inc. and Monarch Inc., respectively.

2011
May 11.   Purchased 1,600 shares of Echelon Inc. as a trading security at $18 per share plus a $160 brokerage commission.
June 11.   Received an annual dividend of $0.20 per share on Loral Inc. stock.
Aug. 14.   Sold 400 shares of Echelon Inc. for $20 per share less a $80 brokerage commission.
Dec. 31.   The portfolio of trading securities was adjusted to fair value using the following fair values per share for the trading securities:

Echelon Inc.	$22
Loral Inc.	23
Monarch Inc.	49

The portfolio of trading securities was adjusted to fair value.

Instructions
1. Journalize the entries to record these transactions.
2. Prepare the investment-related current asset balance sheet disclosures for Jupiter Insurance Co. on December 31, 2011.
3. How are unrealized gains or losses on trading investments disclosed on the financial statements of Jupiter Insurance Co.?

PR 15-3B
Debt investment transactions, available-for-sale valuation

objs. 2, 4

✔ 2. Available-for-sale investments (at fair value), $156,000

Eclipse Inc. is an athletic footware company that began operations on January 1, 2010. The following transactions relate to debt investments acquired by Eclipse Inc., which has a fiscal year ending on December 31:

2010
Mar. 1.   Purchased $80,000 of Noble Co. 6%, 10-year bonds at face value plus accrued interest of $400. The bond is classified as an available-for-sale investment. The bonds pay interest semiannually on February 1 and August 1.
Apr. 16. Purchased $105,000 of Mason City 4%, 15-year bonds at face value plus accrued interest of $175. The bond is classified as an available-for-sale investment. The bonds pay interest semiannually on April 1 and October 1.
Aug. 1.   Received semiannual interest on the Noble Co. bonds.
Sept. 1. Sold $30,000 of Noble Co. bonds at 99 plus accrued interest of $150.
Oct. 1.   Received semiannual interest on Mason City bonds.
Dec. 31. Accrued $1,250 interest on Noble Co. bonds.
     31. Accrued $1,050 interest on Mason City bonds.
     31. The available-for-sale bond portfolio was adjusted to fair values of 98 and 99 for Mason City and Noble Co. bonds, respectively.

2011
Feb. 1. Received semiannual interest on the Noble Co. bonds.
Apr. 1. Received semiannual interest on the Mason City bonds.
(Assume that there are no more purchases or sales of bonds during 2011. Also assume all subsequent interest transactions for 2011 have been recorded properly.)
Dec. 31. The available-for-sale bond portfolio was adjusted to fair values of 100 and 102 for Mason City and Noble Co. bonds, respectively.

Instructions

1. Journalize the entries to record these transactions.
2. Prepare the investment-related current asset and stockholders' equity balance sheet disclosures for Eclipse Inc. on December 31, 2011, assuming the Retained Earnings balance on December 31, 2011, is $490,000.

PR 15-4B
Investment reporting
objs. 2, 3, 4

✔ 1. b. 6,040

Scholar House, Inc., is a book publisher. The comparative unclassified balance sheets for December 31, 2011, and 2010 are provided below. Selected missing balances are shown by letters.

Scholar House, Inc.
Balance Sheet
December 31, 2011, and 2010

	Dec. 31, 2011	Dec. 31, 2010
Cash	$178,000	$157,000
Accounts receivable (net)	106,000	98,000
Available-for-sale investments (at cost)—Note 1	a.	53,400
Less valuation allowance for available-for-sale investments	b.	2,400
Available-for-sale investments (fair value)	$ c.	$ 51,000
Interest receivable	$ d.	—
Investment in Nahum Co. stock—Note 2	e.	$ 64,000
Office equipment (net)	90,000	95,000
Total assets	$ f.	$465,000
Accounts payable	$ 56,900	$ 51,400
Common stock	50,000	50,000
Excess of issue price over par	160,000	160,000
Retained earnings	g.	206,000
Less unrealized gain (loss) on available-for-sale investments	h.	2,400
Total liabilities and stockholders' equity	$ i.	$465,000

Note 1. Investments are classified as available for sale. The investments at cost and fair value on December 31, 2010, are as follows:

	No. of Shares	Cost per Share	Total Cost	Total Fair Value
Barns Co. Stock	1,600	$12	$19,200	$18,000
Dynasty Co. Stock	900	38	34,200	33,000
			$53,400	$51,000

Note 2. The investment in Nahum Co. stock is an equity method investment representing 32% of the outstanding shares of Nahum Co.

The following selected investment transactions occurred during 2011:

2011
May 5. Purchased 500 shares of High-Star, Inc., at $29 per share plus a $100 brokerage commission.
June 12. Dividends of $1.25 per share are received on the Dynasty Co. stock investment.
Sept. 9. Dividends of $5,700 are received on the Nahum Co. investment.
Sept. 1. Purchased $18,000 of Opus Co. 5%, 10-year bonds at 100. The bonds are classified as available for sale. The bonds pay interest on September 1 and March 1.
Dec. 31. Nahum Co. reported a total net income of $60,000 for 2011. Scholar House recorded equity earnings for its share of Nahum Co. net income.
31. Accrued 4 months of interest on the Opus bonds.
31. Adjusted the available-for-sale investment portfolio to fair value using the following fair value per share amounts:

Available-for-Sale Investments	Fair Value
Barns Co. stock	$10 per share
Dynasty Co. stock	$35 per share
High-Star Inc. stock	$30 per share
Opus Co. bonds	97 per $1,000 of face value

Dec. 31. Closed the Scholar House Inc. net income of $64,900 for 2011. Miranda paid no dividends during 2011.

Instructions

Determine the missing letters in the unclassified balance sheet. Provide appropriate supporting calculations.

Comprehensive Problem 4

Selected transactions completed by Jordan Products Inc. during the fiscal year ending December 31, 2010, were as follows:

a. Issued 14,500 shares of $30 par common stock at $48, receiving cash.

b. Issued 8,000 shares of $120 par preferred 6% stock at $130, receiving cash.

c. Issued $8,000,000 of 10-year, 7% bonds at 110, with interest payable semiannually.

d. Declared a dividend of $0.65 per share on common stock and $1.80 per share on preferred stock. On the date of record, 120,000 shares of common stock were outstanding, no treasury shares were held, and 22,500 shares of preferred stock were outstanding.

e. Paid the cash dividends declared in (d).

f. Purchased 12,000 shares of Avocado Corp. at $31 per share, plus a $2,400 brokerage commission. The investment is classified as an available-for-sale investment.

g. Purchased 9,500 shares of treasury common stock at $52 per share.

h. Purchased 340,000 shares of Amigo Co. stock directly from the founders for $21 per share. Amigo has 1,000,000 shares issued and outstanding. Jordan Products Inc. treated the investment as an equity method investment.

i. Declared a 2% stock dividend on common stock and a $1.80 cash dividend per share on preferred stock. On the date of declaration, the market value of the common stock was $55 per share. On the date of record, 120,000 shares of common stock had been issued, 9,500 shares of treasury common stock were held, and 22,500 shares of preferred stock had been issued.

j. Issued the stock certificates for the stock dividends declared in (h) and paid the cash dividends to the preferred stockholders.

k. Received $272,000 dividend from Amigo Co. investment in (h).

l. Purchased $86,000 of Game Gear Inc. 10-year, 6% bonds, directly from the issuing company at par value, plus accrued interest of $950. The bonds are classifed as a held-to-maturity long-term investment.

m. Sold, at $59.50 per share, 3,800 shares of treasury common stock purchased in (g).

n. Received a dividend of $1.45 per share from the Avacodo Corp. investment in (f).

o. Sold 2,000 shares of Avocado Corp. at $32.80, including commission.

p. Recorded the payment of semiannual interest on the bonds issued in (c) and the amortization of the premium for six months. The amortization was determined using the straight-line method.

q. Accrued interest for three months on the Game Gear Inc. bonds purchased in (l).

r. Amigo Co. recorded total earnings of $478,000. Jordan Products recorded equity earnings for its share of Amigo Co. net income.

s. The fair value for Avocado Corp. stock was $28.50 per share on December 31, 2010. The investment is adjusted to fair value using a valuation allowance account. Assume the Valuation Allowance for Available-for-Sale Investments had a beginning balance of zero.

Instructions

1. Journalize the selected transactions.

2. After all of the transactions for the year ended December 31, 2010, had been posted [including the transactions recorded in part (1) and all adjusting entries], the data on the following page were taken from the records of Jordan Products Inc.

    a. Prepare a multiple-step income statement for the year ended December 31, 2010, concluding with earnings per share. In computing earnings per share, assume that the average number of common shares outstanding was 120,000 and pre-ferred dividends were $162,000. (Round earnings per share to the nearest cent.)

b. Prepare a retained earnings statement for the year ended December 31, 2010.

c. Prepare a balance sheet in report form as of December 31, 2010.

Income statement data:

Advertising expense	$ 125,000
Cost of merchandise sold	3,240,000
Delivery expense	29,000
Depreciation expense—office buildings and equipment	26,000
Depreciation expense—store buildings and equipment	95,000
Dividend revenue	17,400
Gain on sale of investment	3,200
Income from Amigo Co. investment	162,520
Income tax expense	306,700
Interest expense	384,000
Interest revenue	1,650
Miscellaneous administrative expense	7,500
Miscellaneous selling expense	13,750
Office rent expense	50,000
Office salaries expense	140,000
Office supplies expense	10,000
Sales	5,580,000
Sales commissions	182,000
Sales salaries expense	345,000
Store supplies expense	22,000

Retained earnings and balance sheet data:

Accounts payable	195,000
Accounts receivable	543,000
Accumulated depreciation—office buildings and equipment	1,580,000
Accumulated depreciation—store buildings and equipment	4,126,000
Allowance for doubtful accounts	8,150
Available-for-sale investments (at cost)	312,000
Bonds payable, 7%, due 2020	8,000,000
Cash	240,000
Common stock, $30 par (400,000 shares authorized; 122,210 shares issued, 116,510 outstanding)	3,666,300
Dividends:	
Cash dividends for common stock	316,310
Cash dividends for preferred stock	162,000
Stock dividends for common stock	121,550
Goodwill	510,000
Income tax payable	40,000
Interest receivable	1,290
Investment in Amigo Co. stock (equity method)	7,030,520
Investment in Game Gear Inc. bonds (long term)	86,000
Merchandise inventory (December 31, 2010), at lower of cost (FIFO) or market	780,000
Office buildings and equipment	4,320,000
Paid-in capital from sale of treasury stock	28,500
Paid-in capital in excess of par—common stock	842,000
Paid-in capital in excess of par—preferred stock	150,000
Preferred 6% stock, $120 par (30,000 shares authorized; 22,500 shares issued)	2,700,000
Premium on bonds payable	760,000
Prepaid expenses	26,500
Retained earnings, January 1, 2010	4,420,800
Store buildings and equipment	12,560,000
Treasury stock (5,700 shares of common stock at cost of $52 per share)	296,400
Unrealized gain (loss) on available-for-sale investments	(27,000)
Valuation allowance for available-for-sale investments	(27,000)

Special Activities

You can access the special activities online at **www.cengage.com/accounting/reeve**.

Answers to Self-Examination Questions

1. **B**   ($50,000 × 5% × 54/360)

2. **C**

Proceeds (800 shares × $20) − $50	$15,950
Cost (800 shares × $23.05*)	18,440
Loss on sale of investment	$ 2,490

$$\frac{*(1,400 \text{ shares} \times \$23) + \$70}{1,400 \text{ shares}}$$

3. **B**

Income from Barnwell Inc. ($200,000 × 40%)	$80,000
Barnwell Inc. dividend ($60,000 × 40%)	24,000
Increase in Investment in Barnwell Inc. Stock	$56,000

4. **A**   Answer C is the valuation allowance balance on December 31, 2010, but not the adjustment to arrive at the balance. Answer D incorrectly adds the beginning and ending debit balances of the valuation allowance. Answer B incorrectly interprets the credit adjustment as an unrealized gain. The adjustment is the net decrease in the debit balance, or answer A, as shown below.

Valuation allowance for trading investments, January 1, 2011		$32,000	Dr.
Trading investments at cost, December 31, 2011	$500,000		
Trading investments at fair value, December 31, 2011	520,000		
Valuation allowance for trading investments, December 31, 2011		20,000	Dr.
Adjustment		$12,000	Cr.

5. **A**   There is no income statement recognition of changes in the fair value of the available-for-sale portfolio; thus, Answers B, C, and D are incorrect. The accumulated change in fair value for the available-for-sale portfolio is recognized in the Stockholders' Equity section of the balance sheet.

Financial Statements for Mornin' Joe

The financial statements of Mornin' Joe are provided in the following pages. Mornin' Joe is a fictitious coffeehouse chain featuring drip and espresso coffee in a café setting. The financial statements of Mornin' Joe are provided to illustrate the complete financial statements of a corporation using the terms, formats, and reporting illustrated throughout this text. In addition, excerpts of the Mornin' Joe financial statements are used to illustrate the financial reporting presentation for the topics discussed in Chapters 7–15. Thus, you can refer to the complete financial statements shown here or the excerpts in Chapters 7–15. A set of real world financial statements by Nike, Inc., is provided in Appendix F.

Mornin' Joe
Income Statement
For the Year Ended December 31, 2010

Revenue from sales:			
Sales		$5,450,000	
Less: Sales returns and allowances	$ 26,500		
Sales discounts	21,400	47,900	
Net sales			$5,402,100
Cost of merchandise sold			2,160,000
Gross profit			$3,242,100
Operating expenses			
Selling expenses:			
Wages expense	$825,000		
Advertising expense	678,900		
Depreciation expense—buildings	124,300		
Miscellaneous selling expense	26,500		
Total selling expenses		$1,654,700	
Administrative expenses:			
Office salaries expense	$325,000		
Rent expense	425,600		
Payroll tax expense	110,000		
Depreciation expense—office equipment	68,900		
Bad debt expense	14,000		
Amortization expense	10,500		
Total administrative expenses		954,000	
Total operating expenses			2,608,700
Income from operations			$ 633,400
Other income and expense:			
Interest revenue		$ 18,000	
Interest expense		(136,000)	
Loss on disposal of fixed asset		(23,000)	
Unrealized gain on trading investments		5,000	
Equity income in AM Coffee		57,000	(79,000)
Income before income taxes			$ 554,400
Income tax expense			132,800
Net income			$ 421,600
Basic earnings per share [($421,600 − $30,000)/44,000 shares issued and outstanding]			$ 8.90

Mornin' Joe
Balance Sheet
December 31, 2010

Assets

Current assets:			
Cash and cash equivalents		$ 235,000	
Trading investments (at cost)	$ 420,000		
Plus valuation allowance for trading investments	45,000	465,000	
Accounts receivable	$ 305,000		
Less allowance for doubtful accounts	12,300	292,700	
Merchandise inventory—at lower of cost			
(first-in, first-out method) or market		120,000	
Prepaid insurance		24,000	
Total current assets			$1,136,700
Investments:			
Investment in AM Coffee (equity method)			565,000
Property, plant, and equipment:			
Land		$1,850,000	
Buildings	$2,650,000		
Less accumulated depreciation	420,000	2,230,000	
Office equipment	$ 350,000		
Less accumulated depreciation	102,000	248,000	
Total property, plant, and equipment			4,328,000
Intangible assets:			
Patents			140,000
Total assets			$6,169,700

Liabilities

Current liabilities:			
Accounts payable		$ 133,000	
Notes payable (current portion)		200,000	
Salaries and wages payable		42,000	
Payroll taxes payable		16,400	
Interest payable		40,000	
Total current liabilities			$ 431,400
Long-term liabilities:			
Bonds payable, 8%, due December 31, 2030	$ 500,000		
Less unamortized discount	16,000	$ 484,000	
Notes payable		1,400,000	
Total long-term liabilities		$1,884,000	
Total liabilities			$2,315,400

Stockholders' Equity

Paid-in capital:			
Preferred 10% stock, $50 par (6,000 shares			
authorized and issued)		$ 300,000	
Excess of issue price over par		50,000	$ 350,000
Common stock, $20 par (50,000 shares			
authorized, 45,000 shares issued)		$ 900,000	
Excess of issue price over par		1,450,000	2,350,000
Total paid-in capital			$2,700,000
Retained earnings			1,200,300
Total			$3,900,300
Deduct treasury stock (1,000 shares at cost)			46,000
Total stockholders' equity			$3,854,300
Total liabilities and stockholders' equity			$6,169,700

Mornin' Joe
Retained Earnings Statement
For the Year Ended December 31, 2010

Retained earnings, January 1, 2010			$ 852,700
Net income		$421,600	
Less dividends:			
Preferred stock	$30,000		
Common stock	44,000	74,000	
Increase in retained earnings			347,600
Retained earnings, December 31, 2010			$1,200,300

Mornin' Joe
Statement of Stockholders' Equity
For the Year Ended December 31, 2010

	Preferred Stock	Common Stock	Additional Paid-In Capital	Retained Earnings	Treasury Stock	Total
Balance, January 1, 2010	$300,000	$800,000	$1,325,000	$ 852,700	$(36,000)	$3,241,700
Net income				421,600		421,600
Dividends on preferred stock				(30,000)		(30,000)
Dividends on common stock				(44,000)		(44,000)
Issuance of additional common stock		100,000	175,000			275,000
Purchase of treasury stock					(10,000)	(10,000)
Balance, December 31, 2010	$300,000	$900,000	$1,500,000	$1,200,300	$(46,000)	$3,854,300

Statement of Cash Flows

J O N E S S O D A C O.

Suppose you were to receive $100 as a result of some event. Would it make a difference what the event was? Yes, it would! If you received $100 for your birthday, then it's a gift. If you received $100 as a result of working part time for a week, then it's the result of your effort. If you received $100 as a loan, then it's money that you will have to pay back in the future. If you received $100 as a result of selling your iPod, then it's the result of giving up something tangible. Thus, the same $100 received can be associated with different types of events, and these events have different meanings to you. You would much rather receive a $100 gift than take out a $100 loan. Likewise, company stakeholders would also view events such as these differently.

Companies are required to report information about the events causing a change in cash over a period time. This information is reported in the statement of cash flows. One such company is Jones Soda Co. Jones began in the late 1980s as an alternative beverage company, known for its customer-provided labels, unique flavors, and support for extreme sports. You have probably seen Jones Soda at Barnes & Noble, Panera Bread, or Starbucks, or maybe sampled some of its unique flavors, such as Fufu Berry®, Blue Bubblegum®, or Lemon Drop®. As with any company, cash is important to Jones Soda. Without cash, Jones would be unable to expand its brands, distribute its product, support extreme sports, or provide a return for its owners. Thus, its managers are concerned about the sources and uses of cash.

In previous chapters, we have used the income statement, balance sheet, retained earnings statement, and other information to analyze the effects of management decisions on a business's financial position and operating performance. In this chapter, we focus on the events causing a change in cash by presenting the preparation and use of the statement of cash flows.

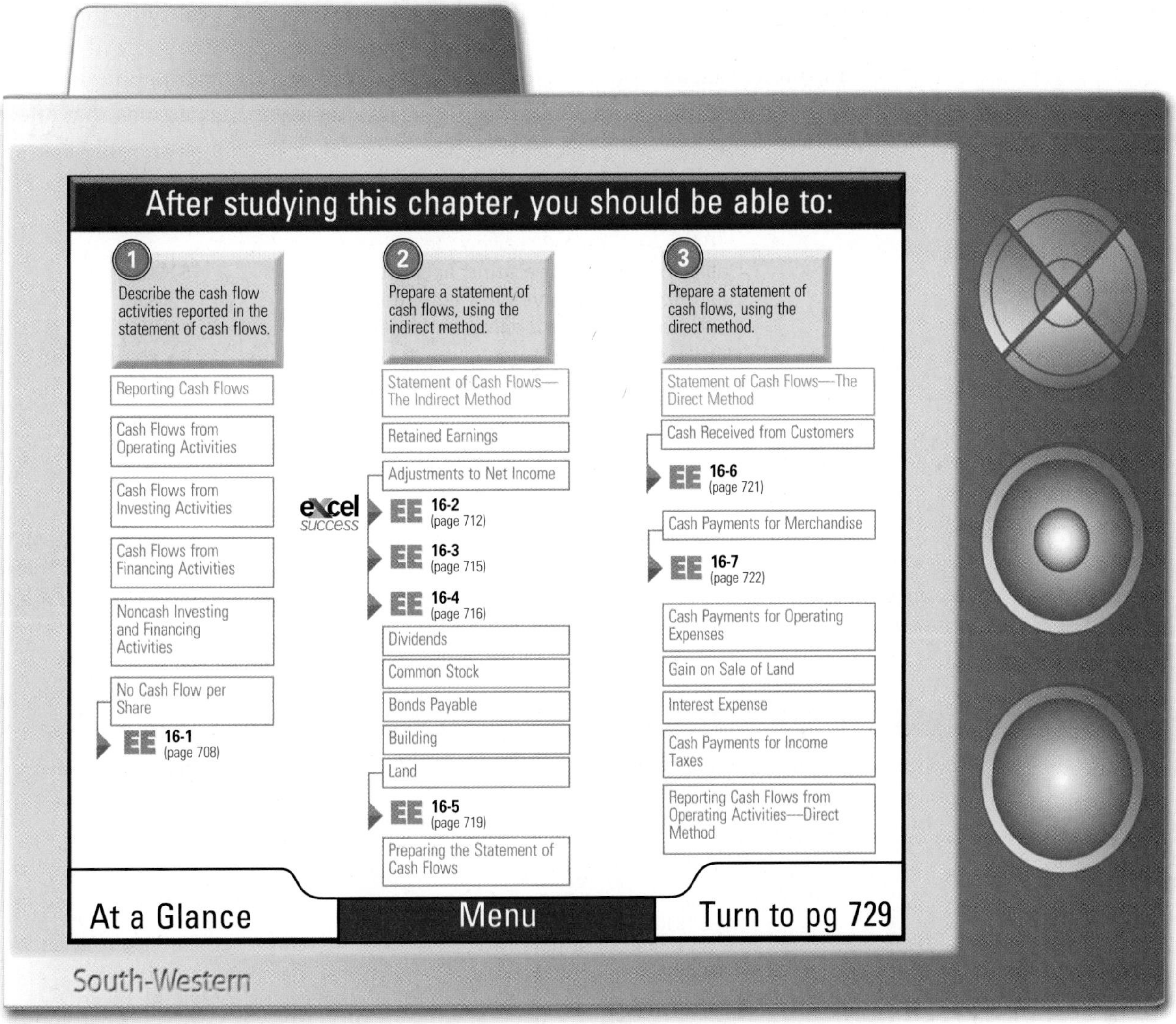

After studying this chapter, you should be able to:

1 Describe the cash flow activities reported in the statement of cash flows.

- Reporting Cash Flows
- Cash Flows from Operating Activities
- Cash Flows from Investing Activities
- Cash Flows from Financing Activities
- Noncash Investing and Financing Activities
- No Cash Flow per Share
  - **EE** 16-1 (page 708)

excel *success*

2 Prepare a statement of cash flows, using the indirect method.

- Statement of Cash Flows— The Indirect Method
- Retained Earnings
- Adjustments to Net Income
  - **EE** 16-2 (page 712)
  - **EE** 16-3 (page 715)
  - **EE** 16-4 (page 716)
- Dividends
- Common Stock
- Bonds Payable
- Building
- Land
  - **EE** 16-5 (page 719)
- Preparing the Statement of Cash Flows

3 Prepare a statement of cash flows, using the direct method.

- Statement of Cash Flows—The Direct Method
- Cash Received from Customers
  - **EE** 16-6 (page 721)
- Cash Payments for Merchandise
  - **EE** 16-7 (page 722)
- Cash Payments for Operating Expenses
- Gain on Sale of Land
- Interest Expense
- Cash Payments for Income Taxes
- Reporting Cash Flows from Operating Activities—Direct Method

At a Glance   **Menu**   **Turn to pg 729**

South-Western

---

1 Describe the cash flow activities reported in the statement of cash flows.

Reporting Cash Flows

The **statement of cash flows** reports a company's cash inflows and outflows for a period.[1] The statement of cash flows provides useful information about a company's ability to do the following:

1. Generate cash from operations
2. Maintain and expand its operating capacity
3. Meet its financial obligations
4. Pay dividends

The statement of cash flows is used by managers in evaluating past operations and in planning future investing and financing activities. It is also used by external users such as investors and creditors to assess a company's profit potential and ability to pay its debt and pay dividends.

The statement of cash flows reports three types of cash flow activities as follows:

1. **Cash flows from operating activities** are cash flows from transactions that affect the net income of the company.

   Example: Purchase and sale of merchandise by a retailer.

---

1 As used in this chapter, *cash* refers to cash and cash equivalents. Examples of cash equivalents include short-term, highly liquid investments, such as money market accounts, bank certificates of deposit, and U.S. Treasury bills.

2. **Cash flows from investing activities** are cash flows from transactions that affect investments in noncurrent assets of the company.

   Example: Sale and purchase of fixed assets, such as equipment and buildings.

3. **Cash flows from financing activities** are cash flows from transactions that affect the debt and equity of the company.

   Example: Issuing or retiring equity and debt securities.

The cash flows are reported in the statement of cash flows as follows:

Cash flows from operating activities	$XXX
Cash flows from investing activities	XXX
Cash flows from financing activities	XXX
Net increase or decrease in cash for the period	$XXX
Cash at the beginning of the period	XXX
Cash at the end of the period	$XXX

The ending cash on the statement of cash flows equals the cash reported on the company's balance sheet.

Exhibit 1 illustrates the sources (increases) and uses (decreases) of cash by each of the three cash flow activities. A *source* of cash causes the cash flow to increase and is called a *cash inflow*. A *use* of cash causes cash flow to decrease and is called *cash outflow*.

Exhibit 1

Cash Flows

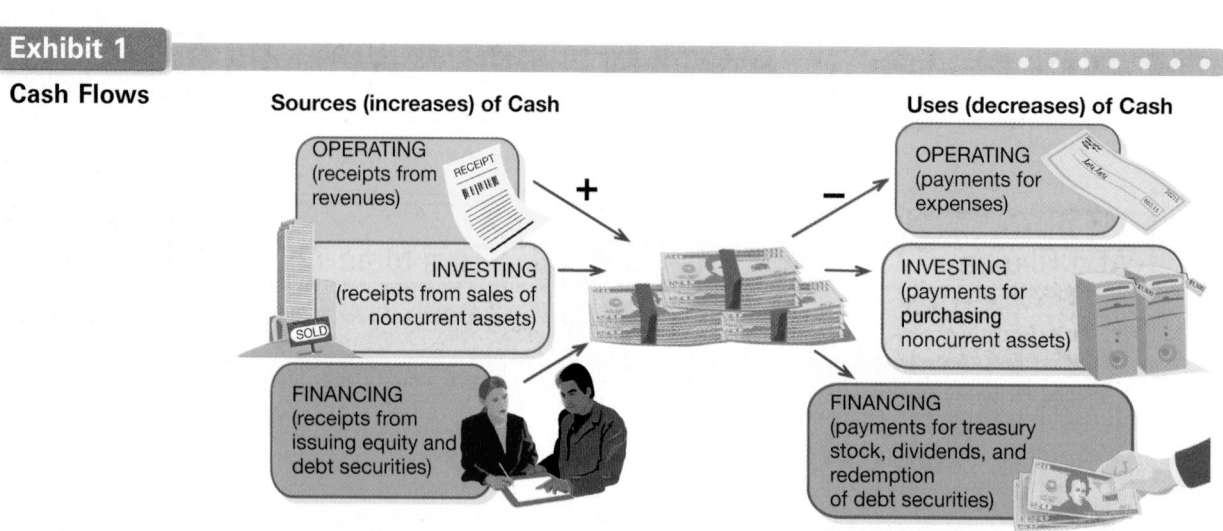

Cash Flows from Operating Activities

There are two methods for reporting cash flows from operating activities in the statement of cash flows. These methods are as follows:

1. Direct method
2. Indirect method

The **direct method** reports operating cash inflows (receipts) and cash outflows (payments) as follows:

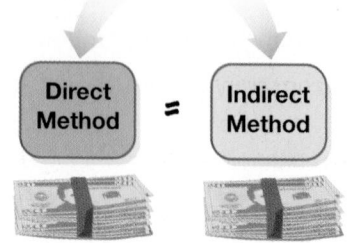

Cash flows from operating activities:		
Cash received from customers		$XXX
Less: Cash payments for merchandise	$XXX	
Cash payments for operating expenses	XXX	
Cash payments for interest	XXX	
Cash payments for income taxes	XXX	XXX
Net cash flows from operating activities		$XXX

The primary operating cash inflow is cash received from customers. The primary operating cash outflows are cash payments for merchandise, operating expenses, interest, and income tax payments. The cash received less the cash payments is the net cash flow from operating activities.

The primary advantage of the direct method is that it *directly* reports cash receipts and payments in the statement of cash flows. Its primary disadvantage is that these data may not be readily available in the accounting records. Thus, the direct method is normally more costly to use and, as a result, is used by less than 1% of companies.[2]

The **indirect method** reports operating cash flows by beginning with net income and adjusting it for revenues and expenses that do not involve the receipt or payment of cash as follows:

Cash flows from operating activities:		
Net income	$XXX	
Adjustments to reconcile net income to net cash flow from operating activities	XXX	
Net cash flow from operating activities		$XXX

The adjustments to reconcile net income to net cash flow from operating activities include such items as depreciation and gains (or losses) on fixed assets. Changes in current operating assets and liabilities such as accounts receivable or accounts payable are also added or deducted depending on their effect on cash flows. In effect, these additions and deductions adjust net income, which is reported on an accrual accounting basis, to cash flows from operating activities, which uses a cash basis.

A primary advantage of the indirect method is that it reconciles the differences between net income and net cash flows from operations. In doing so, it shows how net income is related to the ending cash balance that is reported on the balance sheet.

Because the data are readily available, the indirect method is less costly to use than the direct method. As a result, over 99% of companies use the indirect method of reporting cash flows from operations.

Exhibit 2 illustrates the Cash Flows from Operating Activities section of the statement of cash flows for **NetSolutions**. Exhibit 2 shows the direct and indirect methods using the **NetSolutions** data from Chapter 1. As Exhibit 2 illustrates, both methods report the same amount of net cash flow from operating activities, $2,900.

@netsolutions

Exhibit 2

Cash Flow from Operations: Direct and Indirect Methods—NetSolutions

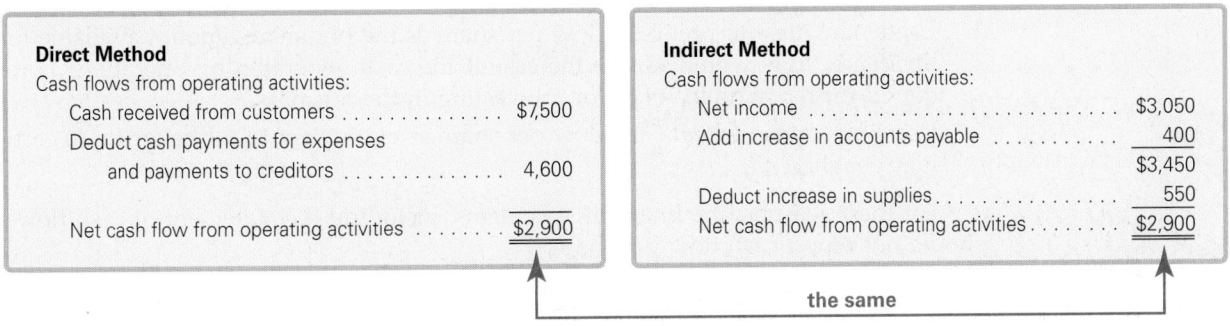

Direct Method

Cash flows from operating activities:	
Cash received from customers	$7,500
Deduct cash payments for expenses and payments to creditors	4,600
Net cash flow from operating activities	$2,900

Indirect Method

Cash flows from operating activities:	
Net income	$3,050
Add increase in accounts payable	400
	$3,450
Deduct increase in supplies	550
Net cash flow from operating activities	$2,900

the same

In Chapter 1, the direct method was used to report **NetSolutions'** statement of cash flows. This is because the indirect method requires an understanding of the accrual accounting concepts such as depreciation, which had yet to be covered in Chapter 1.

The Walt Disney Company recently invested $1.1 billion in parks, resorts, and other properties, including two new cruise ships and new attractions at Disneyland.

Cash Flows from Investing Activities

Cash flows from investing activities are reported on the statement of cash flows as follows:

Cash flows from investing activities:
Cash inflows from investing activities $XXX
Less cash used for investing activities   XXX
    Net cash flows from investing activities $XXX

Cash inflows from investing activities normally arise from selling fixed assets, investments, and intangible assets. Cash outflows normally include payments to purchase fixed assets, investments, and intangible assets.

Cash Flows from Financing Activities

Cash flows from financing activities are reported on the statement of cash flows as follows:

Cash flows from financing activities:
Cash inflows from financing activities $XXX
Less cash used for financing activities   XXX
    Net cash flows from financing activities $XXX

Cash inflows from financing activities normally arise from issuing debt or equity securities. For example, issuing bonds, notes payable, preferred stock, and common stock creates cash inflows from financing activities. Cash outflows from financing activities include paying cash dividends, repaying debt, and acquiring treasury stock.

Google disclosed the issuance of over $25 million in common stock for business acquisitions in its statement of cash flows as a noncash investing and financing activity.

Noncash Investing and Financing Activities

A company may enter into transactions involving investing and financing activities that do not *directly* affect cash. For example, a company may issue common stock to retire long-term debt. Although this transaction does not directly affect cash, it does eliminate future cash payments for interest and for paying the bonds when they mature. Because such transactions *indirectly* affect cash flows, they are reported in a separate section of the statement of cash flows. This section usually appears at the bottom of the statement of cash flows.

No Cash Flow per Share

Cash flow per share is sometimes reported in the financial press. As reported, cash flow per share is normally computed as *cash flow from operations per share*. However, such reporting may be misleading because of the following:

1. Users may misinterpret cash flow per share as the per-share amount available for dividends. This would not be the case if the cash generated by operations is required for repaying loans or for reinvesting in the business.
2. Users may misinterpret cash flow per share as equivalent to (or better than) earnings per share.

For these reasons, the financial statements, including the statement of cash flows, should not report cash flow per share.

Example Exercise 16-1   Classifying Cash Flows   •••••••• ❯ 1

Identify whether each of the following would be reported as an operating, investing, or financing activity in the statement of cash flows.

a. Purchase of patent   d. Cash sales

b. Payment of cash dividend   e. Purchase of treasury stock

c. Disposal of equipment   f. Payment of wages expense

(continued)

Chapter 16   Statement of Cash Flows   **709**

Follow My Example 16-1

a. Investing

b. Financing

c. Investing

d. Operating

e. Financing

f. Operating

For Practice: PE 16-1A, PE 16-1B

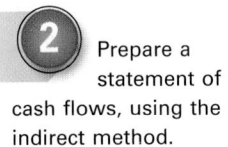

Prepare a statement of cash flows, using the indirect method.

Statement of Cash Flows— The Indirect Method

The indirect method of reporting cash flows from operating activities uses the logic that a change in any balance sheet account (including cash) can be analyzed in terms of changes in the other balance sheet accounts. Thus, by analyzing changes in noncash balance sheet accounts, any change in the cash account can be *indirectly* determined.

To illustrate, the accounting equation can be solved for cash, as shown below.

$$\text{Assets} = \text{Liabilities} + \text{Stockholders' Equity}$$
$$\text{Cash} + \text{Noncash Assets} = \text{Liabilities} + \text{Stockholders' Equity}$$
$$\text{Cash} = \text{Liabilities} + \text{Stockholders' Equity} - \text{Noncash Assets}$$

Therefore, any change in the cash account can be determined by analyzing changes in the liability, stockholders' equity, and noncash asset accounts, as shown below.

$$\textit{Change} \text{ in Cash} = \textit{Change} \text{ in Liabilities} + \textit{Change} \text{ in Stockholders' Equity}$$
$$- \textit{Change} \text{ in Noncash Assets}$$

Under the indirect method, there is no order in which the balance sheet accounts must be analyzed. However, net income (or net loss) is the first amount reported on the statement of cash flows. Since net income (or net loss) is a component of any change in Retained Earnings, the first account normally analyzed is Retained Earnings.

To illustrate the indirect method, the income statement and comparative balance sheets for Rundell Inc. shown in Exhibit 3 are used. Ledger accounts and other data supporting the income statement and balance sheet are presented as needed.[3]

Retained Earnings

The comparative balance sheet for Rundell Inc. shows that retained earnings increased $80,000 during the year. The retained earnings account shown below indicates how this change occurred.

Account *Retained Earnings*				Account No.	
				Balance	
Date	**Item**	**Debit**	**Credit**	**Debit**	**Credit**
2010 Jan. 1	Balance				202,300
Dec. 31	Net income		108,000		310,300
31	Cash dividends	28,000			282,300

The retained earnings account indicates that the $80,000 ($108,000 − $28,000) change resulted from net income of $108,000 and cash dividends of $28,000. The net income of $108,000 is the first amount reported in the Cash Flows from Operating Activities section.

---

3 An appendix that discusses using a spreadsheet (work sheet) as an aid in assembling data for the statement of cash flows is presented at the end of this chapter. This appendix illustrates the use of this spreadsheet in reporting cash flows from operating activities using the indirect method.

Exhibit 3

Income
Statement and
Comparative
Balance Sheet

Rundell Inc.
Income Statement
For the Year Ended December 31, 2010

Sales		$1,180,000
Cost of merchandise sold		790,000
Gross profit		$ 390,000
Operating expenses:		
Depreciation expense	$ 7,000	
Other operating expenses	196,000	
Total operating expenses		203,000
Income from operations		$ 187,000
Other income:		
Gain on sale of land	$ 12,000	
Other expense:		
Interest expense	8,000	4,000
Income before income tax		$ 191,000
Income tax expense		83,000
Net income		$ 108,000

Rundell Inc.
Comparative Balance Sheet
December 31, 2010 and 2009

	2010	2009	Increase Decrease*
Assets			
Cash	$ 97,500	$ 26,000	$ 71,500
Accounts receivable (net)	74,000	65,000	9,000
Inventories	172,000	180,000	8,000*
Land	80,000	125,000	45,000*
Building	260,000	200,000	60,000
Accumulated depreciation—building	(65,300)	(58,300)	7,000
Total assets	$618,200	$537,700	$ 80,500
Liabilities			
Accounts payable (merchandise creditors)	$ 43,500	$ 46,700	$ 3,200*
Accrued expenses payable (operating expenses)	26,500	24,300	2,200
Income taxes payable	7,900	8,400	500*
Dividends payable	14,000	10,000	4,000
Bonds payable	100,000	150,000	50,000*
Total liabilities	$191,900	$239,400	$ 47,500*
Stockholders' Equity			
Common stock ($2 par)	$ 24,000	$ 16,000	$ 8,000
Paid-in capital in excess of par	120,000	80,000	40,000
Retained earnings	282,300	202,300	80,000
Total stockholders' equity	$426,300	$298,300	$128,000
Total liabilities and stockholders' equity	$618,200	$537,700	$ 80,500

Adjustments to Net Income

The net income of $108,000 reported by Rundell Inc. does not equal the cash flows from operating activities for the period. This is because net income is determined using the accrual method of accounting.

Under the accrual method of accounting, revenues and expenses are recorded at different times from when cash is received or paid. For example, merchandise may be sold on account and the cash received at a later date. Likewise, insurance premiums may be paid in the current period, but expensed in a following period.

Thus, under the indirect method, adjustments to net income must be made to determine cash flows from operating activities. The typical adjustments to net income are shown in Exhibit 4.[4]

Net income is normally adjusted to cash flows from operating activities using the following steps:

Step 1. Expenses that do not affect cash are added. Such expenses decrease net income, but did not involve cash payments and, thus, are added to net income.

Examples: *Depreciation* of fixed assets and *amortization* of intangible assets are added to net income.

Step 2. Losses and gains on disposal of assets are added or deducted. The disposal (sale) of assets is an investing activity rather than an operating activity.

Exhibit 4

Adjustments to Net Income (Loss) Using the Indirect Method

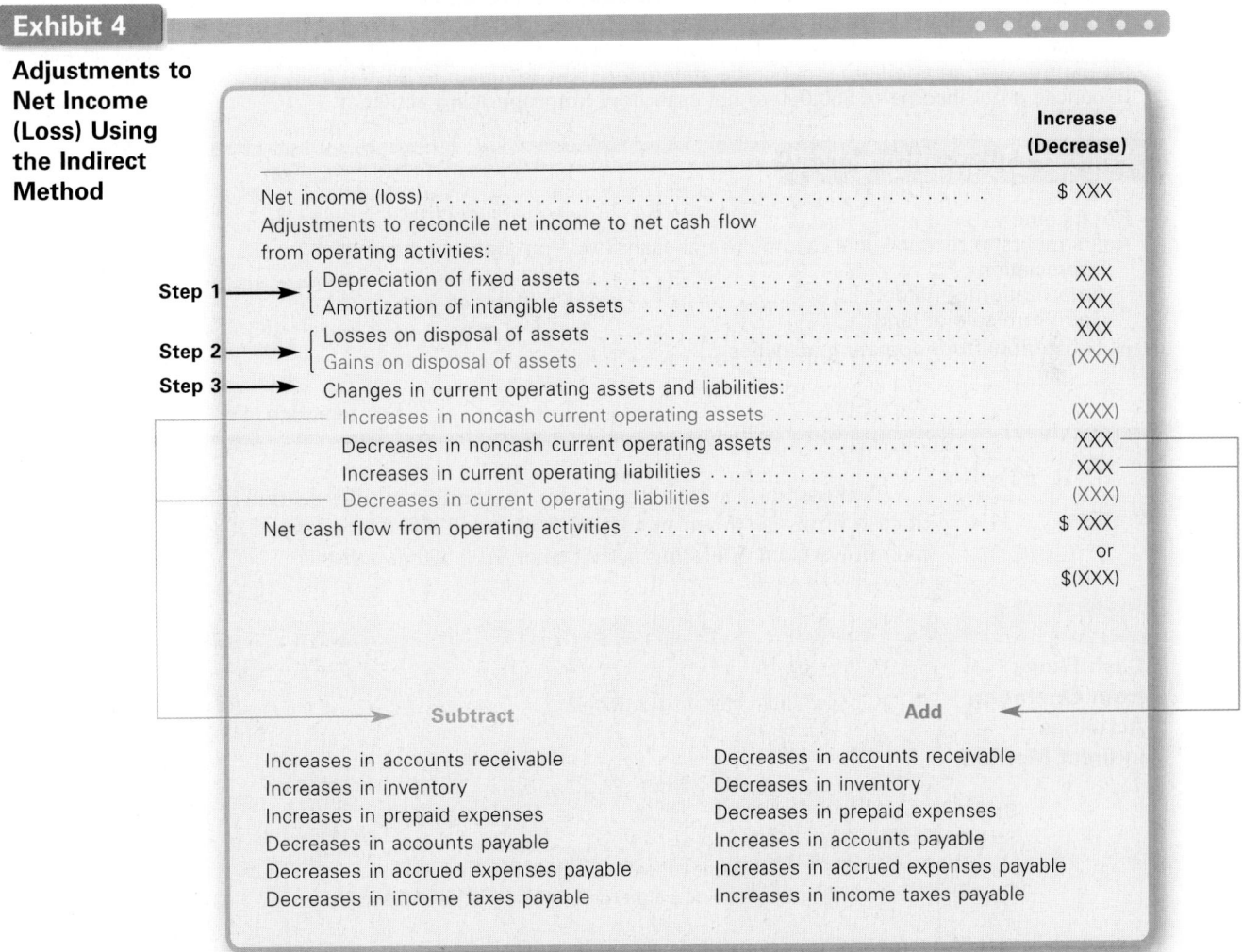

	Increase (Decrease)
Net income (loss)	$ XXX
Adjustments to reconcile net income to net cash flow from operating activities:	
Step 1 → Depreciation of fixed assets	XXX
Amortization of intangible assets	XXX
Step 2 → Losses on disposal of assets	XXX
Gains on disposal of assets	(XXX)
Step 3 → Changes in current operating assets and liabilities:	
Increases in noncash current operating assets	(XXX)
Decreases in noncash current operating assets	XXX
Increases in current operating liabilities	XXX
Decreases in current operating liabilities	(XXX)
Net cash flow from operating activities	$ XXX
	or
	$(XXX)

Subtract	Add
Increases in accounts receivable	Decreases in accounts receivable
Increases in inventory	Decreases in inventory
Increases in prepaid expenses	Decreases in prepaid expenses
Decreases in accounts payable	Increases in accounts payable
Decreases in accrued expenses payable	Increases in accrued expenses payable
Decreases in income taxes payable	Increases in income taxes payable

---

4 Other items that also require adjustments to net income to obtain cash flows from operating activities include amortization of bonds payable discounts (add), losses on debt retirement (add), amortization of bonds payable premiums (deduct), and gains on retirement of debt (deduct).

However, such losses and gains are reported as part of net income. As a result, any *losses* on disposal of assets are *added* back to net income. Likewise, any *gains* on disposal of assets are *deducted* from net income.

Example: Land costing $100,000 is sold for $90,000. The loss of $10,000 is added back to net income.

Step 3. Changes in current operating assets and liabilities are added or deducted as follows:

> Increases in noncash current operating assets are deducted.
> Decreases in noncash current operating assets are added.
> Increases in current operating liabilities are added.
> Decreases in current operating liabilities are deducted.

Example: A sale of $10,000 on account increases accounts receivable by $10,000. However, cash is not affected. Thus, an increase in accounts receivable of $10,000 is deducted. Similar adjustments are required for the changes in the other current asset and liability accounts such as inventory, prepaid expenses, accounts payable, accrued expenses payable, and income taxes payable as shown in Exhibit 4.

Example Exercise 16-2 Adjustments to Net Income— Indirect Method

Omni Corporation's accumulated depreciation increased by $12,000, while $3,400 of patents were amortized between balance sheet dates. There were no purchases or sales of depreciable or intangible assets during the year. In addition, the income statement showed a gain of $4,100 from the sale of land. Reconcile a net income of $50,000 to net cash flow from operating activities.

Follow My Example 16-2

Net income	$50,000
Adjustments to reconcile net income to net cash flow from operating activities:	
Depreciation	12,000
Amortization of patents	3,400
Gain from sale of land	(4,100)
Net cash flow from operating activities	$61,300

For Practice: PE 16-2A, PE 16-2B

To illustrate, the cash flows from operating activities section of Rundell's statement of cash flows is shown in Exhibit 5. Rundell's net income of $108,000 is converted to cash flows from operating activities of $100,500 as follows:

Exhibit 5

Cash Flows from Operating Activities— Indirect Method

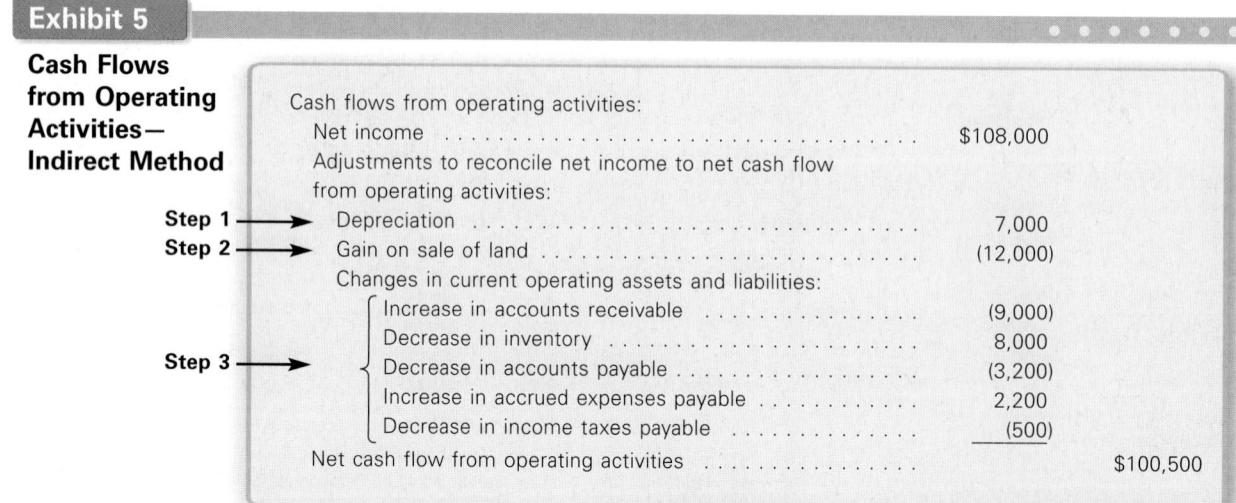

Cash flows from operating activities:	
Net income	$108,000
Adjustments to reconcile net income to net cash flow from operating activities:	
Depreciation	7,000
Gain on sale of land	(12,000)
Changes in current operating assets and liabilities:	
Increase in accounts receivable	(9,000)
Decrease in inventory	8,000
Decrease in accounts payable	(3,200)
Increase in accrued expenses payable	2,200
Decrease in income taxes payable	(500)
Net cash flow from operating activities	$100,500

Step 1 → Depreciation
Step 2 → Gain on sale of land
Step 3 → Changes in current operating assets and liabilities

Step 1. Add depreciation of $7,000.

Analysis: The comparative balance sheet in Exhibit 3 indicates that Accumulated Depreciation—Building increased by $7,000. The account, shown below, indicates that depreciation for the year was $7,000 for the building.

Account *Accumulated Depreciation—Building*   Account No.

Date		Item	Debit	Credit	Balance Debit	Balance Credit
2010						
Jan.	1	Balance				58,300
Dec.	31	Depreciation for year		7,000		65,300

Step 2. Deduct the gain on the sale of land of $12,000.

Analysis: The income statement in Exhibit 3 reports a gain from the sale of land of $12,000. The proceeds, which include the gain, are reported in the Investing section of the statement of cash flows.[5] Thus, the gain of $12,000 is deducted from net income in determining cash flows from operating activities.

Step 3. Add and deduct changes in current operating assets and liabilities.

Analysis: The increases and decreases in the current operating asset and current liability accounts are shown below.

Accounts	December 31 2010	December 31 2009	Increase Decrease*
Accounts Receivable (net)	$ 74,000	$ 65,000	$9,000
Inventories	172,000	180,000	8,000*
Accounts Payable (merchandise creditors)	43,500	46,700	3,200*
Accrued Expenses Payable (operating expenses)	26,500	24,300	2,200
Income Taxes Payable	7,900	8,400	500*

Accounts receivable (net): The $9,000 increase is deducted from net income. This is because the $9,000 increase in accounts receivable indicates that sales on account were $9,000 more than the cash received from customers. Thus, sales (and net income) includes $9,000 that was not received in cash during the year.

Inventories: The $8,000 decrease is added to net income. This is because the $8,000 decrease in inventories indicates that the cost of merchandise *sold* exceeds the cost of the merchandise *purchased* during the year by $8,000. In other words, cost of merchandise sold includes $8,000 that was not purchased (used cash) during the year.

Accounts payable (merchandise creditors): The $3,200 decrease is deducted from net income. This is because a decrease in accounts payable indicates that the cash *payments* to merchandise creditors exceeds the merchandise *purchased on account* by $3,200. Therefore, cost of merchandise sold is $3,200 less than the cash paid to merchandise creditors during the year.

Accrued expenses payable (operating expenses): The $2,200 increase is added to net income. This is because an increase in accrued expenses payable indicates that operating expenses exceed the cash payments for operating expenses by $2,200. In other words, operating expenses reported on the income statement include $2,200 that did not require a cash outflow during the year.

Ford Motor Company had a net loss of $12.6 billion but a positive cash flow from operating activities of $3.3 billion. This difference was mostly due to $16.5 billion of depreciation expenses.

---

5 The reporting of the proceeds (cash flows) from the sale of land as part of investing activities is discussed later in this chapter.

Income taxes payable: The $500 decrease is deducted from net income. This is because a decrease in income taxes payable indicates that taxes paid exceed the amount of taxes incurred during the year by $500. In other words, the amount reported on the income statement for income tax expense is less than the amount paid by $500.

Spreadsheet software can be used to develop the complete statement of cash flows using the worksheet approach illustrated in the appendix to this chapter. Here we illustrate the use of spreadsheet software for developing the cash flows from operating activities section of the statement of cash flows.

	A	B	C	D	E
1	Inputs:				
2					
3	Selected income statement items:				
4	Net income	$ 108,000			
5	Depreciation expense	7,000			
6	Gain on sale of land	12,000			
7					
8	Comparative noncash current assets and liabilities				
9					
10		December 31, 2010	December 31, 2009	Increase/ (Decrease)	1 = Current asset 2 = Current liability
11	Accounts receivable	$ 74,000	$ 65,000	=B11-C11	1
12	Inventories	172,000	180,000	=B12-C12	1
13	Accounts payable	43,500	46,700	=B13-C13	2
14	Accrued expenses	26,500	24,300	=B14-C14	2
15	Income taxes payable	7,900	8,400	=B15-C15	2
16				↑	↑
17					
18	Output:			a.	b.
19					
20	Cash flows from operating activities:				
21	Net income	=B4 ⎤			
22	Adjustments to reconcile net income to net cash flow:	⎬ c.			
23	Depreciation	=B5			
24	Gain on sale of land	=-B6 ⎦			
25	Changes in current operating assets and liabilities:				
26	Increase in accounts receivable	=IF(E11=1,-D11,D11) ← d.			
27	Decrease in inventory	=IF(E12=1,-D12,D12) ⎤			
28	Decrease in accounts payable	=IF(E13=1,-D13,D13) ⎬ e.			
29	Increase in accrued expense payable	=IF(E14=1,-D14,D14) ⎦			
30	Decrease in income taxes payable	=IF(E15=1,-D15,D15) ⎦			
31	Net cash flow from operating activities	=SUM(B21:B30) ← f.			

The **input** section of the spreadsheet includes the selected income statement items that are required on the cash flows from operating activities. These include the net income, depreciation expense, and gain on sale of land in this example, B4, B5, and B6.

The input section also contains the comparative noncash current assets and current liabilities from the balance sheet. Begin by computing the Increase/Decrease in current assets and current liabilities in the input section:

Indicator variables can be any number. For example, 0 or 1 would also work.

a. Enter in D11 the formula for the increase or decrease in accounts receivable, =B11-C11. Copy this formula for the remaining current assets and liabilities.

b. Enter into cells E11 through E16, a number "1" for current assets and a number "2" for current liabilities. This is termed an *indicator* variable, which we will use in a formula below.

The **output** section contains the cash flows from operating activities, which is the first section of the complete statement of cash flows. The output section is prepared using cell references from the input section. It is important to insert cell references with the correct sign.

c.   Enter in cell B21 the cell reference for net income, =B4. Enter in cell B23 the cell reference for depreciation, =B5. Enter in cell B24 the cell reference for gain on sale of land as a minus, =-B6.

d.   Enter in cell B26 a formula for calculating the impact of changes in current assets and current liabilities on net income in determining net cash flows from operating activities. We will use the =IF function to develop a formula that works for all current items, as follows:

The =IF function is used to program your spreadsheet to test for conditions. Complex =IF statements include multiple =IF functions nested inside each other.

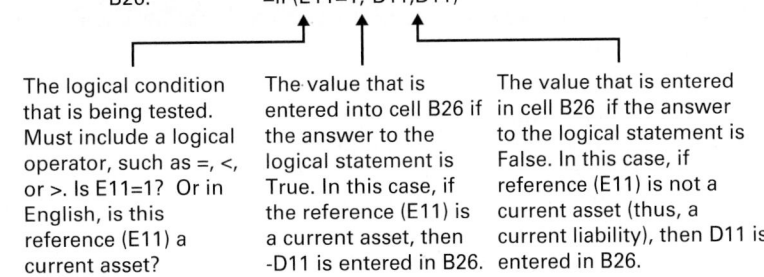

B26:   =IF(E11=1,-D11,D11)

The logical condition that is being tested. Must include a logical operator, such as =, <, or >. Is E11=1? Or in English, is this reference (E11) a current asset?

The value that is entered into cell B26 if the answer to the logical statement is True. In this case, if the reference (E11) is a current asset, then -D11 is entered in B26.

The value that is entered in cell B26 if the answer to the logical statement is False. In this case, if reference (E11) is not a current asset (thus, a current liability), then D11 is entered in B26.

After you enter this formula in cell B26, you should see that -D11, or (9,000), is entered in cell B26. This is what we want. For current assets, increases are subtracted and decreases are added, when adjusting net income to cash flows from operating activities. For the current liabilities, the increases and decreases keep their sign in adjusting net income to cash flows from operating activities. Thus, we have created a single formula that will work for all current assets and current liabilities. We only needed to add the indicator variable in the input section for the =IF function to work.

We can now copy this formula to the remaining current assets and liabilities:

e.   Copy B26 to B27:B30.

f.   Enter in C31 the formula to sum cells B21:B30, =SUM(B21:B30).

 Go to the hands-on **Excel Tutor** for this example!

Example Exercise 16-3   Changes in Current Operating Assets and Liabilities—Indirect Method   ● ● ● ● ● ● ● ● ▶ **2**

Victor Corporation's comparative balance sheet for current assets and liabilities was as follows:

	Dec. 31, 2011	Dec. 31, 2010
Accounts receivable	$ 6,500	$ 4,900
Inventory	12,300	15,000
Accounts payable	4,800	5,200
Dividends payable	5,000	4,000

Adjust net income of $70,000 for changes in operating assets and liabilities to arrive at cash flows from operating activities.

Follow My Example 16-3

Net income	$70,000

Adjustments to reconcile net income to net cash flow from operating activities:
Changes in current operating assets and liabilities:

Increase in accounts receivable	(1,600)
Decrease in inventory	2,700
Decrease in accounts payable	(400)
Net cash flow from operating activities	$70,700

For Practice: PE 16-3A, PE 16-3B

Using the preceding analyses, Rundell's net income of $108,000 is converted to cash flows from operating activities of $100,500 as shown in Exhibit 5, on page 712.

Exercise 16-4   Cash Flows from Operating Activities—Indirect Method

Omicron Inc. reported the following data:

Net income	$120,000
Depreciation expense	12,000
Loss on disposal of equipment	15,000
Increase in accounts receivable	5,000
Decrease in accounts payable	2,000

Prepare the Cash Flows from Operating Activities section of the statement of cash flows using the indirect method.

Follow My Example 16-4

Cash flows from operating activities:

Net income		$120,000
Adjustments to reconcile net income to net cash flow from operating activities:		
Depreciation expense		12,000
Loss on disposal of equipment		15,000
Changes in current operating assets and liabilities:		
Increase in accounts receivable		(5,000)
Decrease in accounts payable		(2,000)
Net cash flow from operating activities		$140,000

Note: The change in dividends payable impacts the cash paid for dividends, which is disclosed under financing activities.

For Practice: PE 16-4A, PE 16-4B

Integrity, Objectivity, and Ethics in Business

CREDIT POLICY AND CASH FLOW

One would expect customers to pay for products and services sold on account. Unfortunately, that is not always the case. Collecting accounts receivable efficiently is the key to turning a current asset into positive cash flow. Most entrepreneurs would rather think about the exciting aspects of their business—such as product development, marketing, sales, and advertising—rather than credit collection. This can be a mistake. Hugh McHugh of Overhill Flowers, Inc., decided that he would have no more trade accounts after dealing with Christmas orders that weren't paid for until late February, or sometimes not paid at all. As stated by one collection service, "One thing business owners always tell me is that they never thought about [collections] when they started their own business." To the small business owner, the collection of accounts receivable may mean the difference between succeeding and failing.

Source: Paulette Thomas, "Making Them Pay: The Last Thing Most Entrepreneurs Want to Think About Is Bill Collection; It Should Be One of the First Things," *The Wall Street Journal*, September 19, 2005, p. R6.

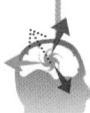

Dividends

The retained earnings account of Rundell Inc., shown on page 709, indicates cash dividends of $28,000 during the year. However, the dividends payable account, shown below, indicates that only $24,000 of the dividends was paid during the year.

Account *Dividends Payable*   Account No.

Date		Item	Debit	Credit	Balance Debit	Balance Credit
2010						
Jan.	1	Balance				10,000
	10	Cash paid	10,000		—	—
June	20	Dividends declared		14,000		14,000
July	10	Cash paid	14,000		—	—
Dec.	20	Dividends declared		14,000		14,000

Since dividend payments are a financing activity, the dividend payment of $24,000 is reported in the Financing Activities section of the statement of cash flows, as shown below.

Cash flows from financing activities:
Cash paid for dividends $24,000

Common Stock

The common stock account increased by $8,000, and the paid-in capital in excess of par—common stock account increased by $40,000, as shown below. These increases were from issuing 4,000 shares of common stock for $12 per share.

Account *Common Stock*   Account No.

Date		Item	Debit	Credit	Balance Debit	Balance Credit
2010						
Jan.	1	Balance				16,000
Nov.	1	4,000 shares issued for cash		8,000		24,000

Account *Paid-In Capital in Excess of Par—Common Stock*   Account No.

Date		Item	Debit	Credit	Balance Debit	Balance Credit
2010						
Jan.	1	Balance				80,000
Nov.	1	4,000 shares issued for cash		40,000		120,000

This cash inflow is reported in the Financing Activities section as follows:

Cash flows from financing activities:
Cash received from sale of common stock $48,000

Bonds Payable

The bonds payable account decreased by $50,000, as shown below. This decrease is from retiring the bonds by a cash payment for their face amount.

					Balance	
Account Bonds Payable					**Account No.**	
Date	**Item**	**Debit**	**Credit**	**Debit**	**Credit**	
2010						
Jan. 1	Balance				150,000	
June 30	Retired by payment of cash at face amount	50,000			100,000	

This cash outflow is reported in the Financing Activities section as follows:

Cash flows from financing activities:
Cash paid to retire bonds payable $50,000

Building

The building account increased by $60,000, and the accumulated depreciation—building account increased by $7,000, as shown below.

					Balance	
Account Building					**Account No.**	
Date	**Item**	**Debit**	**Credit**	**Debit**	**Credit**	
2010						
Jan. 1	Balance			200,000		
Dec. 27	Purchased for cash	60,000		260,000		

					Balance	
Account Accumulated Depreciation—Building					**Account No.**	
Date	**Item**	**Debit**	**Credit**	**Debit**	**Credit**	
2010						
Jan. 1	Balance				58,300	
Dec. 31	Depreciation for the year		7,000		65,300	

The purchase of a building for cash of $60,000 is reported as an outflow of cash in the Investing Activities section as follows:

Cash flows from investing activities:
Cash paid for purchase of building $60,000

The credit in the accumulated depreciation—building account represents depreciation expense for the year. This depreciation expense of $7,000 on the building was added to net income in determining cash flows from operating activities, as reported in Exhibit 5, on page 712.

Land

The $45,000 decline in the land account was from two transactions, as shown below.

Account *Land*					Account No.	
					Balance	
Date	**Item**	**Debit**	**Credit**	**Debit**	**Credit**	
2010						
Jan. 1	Balance			125,000		
June 8	Sold for $72,000 cash		60,000	65,000		
Oct. 12	Purchased for $15,000 cash	15,000		80,000		

The June 8 transaction is the sale of land with a cost of $60,000 for $72,000 in cash. The $72,000 proceeds from the sale are reported in the Investing Activities section, as follows:

```
Cash flows from investing activities:
  Cash received from sale of land  . . . . . . . . . . . . . . . . . .   $72,000
```

The proceeds of $72,000 include the $12,000 gain on the sale of land and the $60,000 cost (book value) of the land. As shown in Exhibit 5, on page 712, the $12,000 gain is deducted from net income in the Cash Flows from Operating Activities section. This is so that the $12,000 cash inflow related to the gain is not included twice as a cash inflow.

The October 12 transaction is the purchase of land for cash of $15,000. This transaction is reported as an outflow of cash in the Investing Activities section, as follows:

```
Cash flows from investing activities:
  Cash paid for purchase of land  . . . . . . . . . . . . . . . . . .   $15,000
```

Example Exercise 16-5   Land Transactions on the Statement of Cash Flows

 2

Alpha Corporation purchased land for $125,000. Later in the year, the company sold land with a book value of $165,000 for $200,000. How are the effects of these transactions reported on the statement of cash flows?

Follow My Example 16-5

The gain on sale of land is deducted from net income, as shown below.

```
  Gain on sale of land . . . . . . . . . . . . . . . . . . . . . . . . . . . . . . . . . . . . . . . . .   $ (35,000)
```

The purchase and sale of land is reported as part of cash flows from investing activities, as shown below.

```
  Cash received for sale of land . . . . . . . . . . . . . . . . . . . . . . . . . . . . . . . . .    200,000
  Cash paid for purchase of land . . . . . . . . . . . . . . . . . . . . . . . . . . . . . . . . .   (125,000)
```

For Practice: PE 16-5A, PE 16-5B

Preparing the Statement of Cash Flows

The statement of cash flows for Rundell Inc. using the indirect method is shown in Exhibit 6. The statement of cash flows indicates that cash increased by $71,500 during the year. The most significant increase in net cash flows ($100,500) was from operating activities. The most significant use of cash ($26,000) was for financing activities. The ending balance of cash on December 31, 2010, is $97,500. This ending cash balance is also reported on the December 31, 2010, balance sheet shown in Exhibit 3, on page 710.

Exhibit 6

Statement of Cash Flows— Indirect Method

Rundell Inc.
Statement of Cash Flows
For the Year Ended December 31, 2010

Cash flows from operating activities:			
Net income		$108,000	
Adjustments to reconcile net income to net			
cash flow from operating activities:			
Depreciation		7,000	
Gain on sale of land		(12,000)	
Changes in current operating assets and liabilities:			
Increase in accounts receivable		(9,000)	
Decrease in inventory		8,000	
Decrease in accounts payable		(3,200)	
Increase in accrued expenses payable		2,200	
Decrease in income taxes payable		(500)	
Net cash flow from operating activities			$100,500
Cash flows from investing activities:			
Cash from sale of land		$ 72,000	
Less: Cash paid to purchase land	$15,000		
Cash paid for purchase of building	60,000	75,000	
Net cash flow used for investing activities			(3,000)
Cash flows from financing activities:			
Cash received from sale of common stock		$ 48,000	
Less: Cash paid to retire bonds payable	$50,000		
Cash paid for dividends	24,000	74,000	
Net cash flow used for financing activities			(26,000)
Increase in cash			$ 71,500
Cash at the beginning of the year			26,000
Cash at the end of the year			$ 97,500

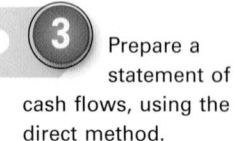

3 Prepare a statement of cash flows, using the direct method.

Statement of Cash Flows— The Direct Method

The direct method reports cash flows from operating activities as follows:

Cash flows from operating activities:		
Cash received from customers		$XXX
Less: Cash payments for merchandise	$XXX	
Cash payments for operating expenses	XXX	
Cash payments for interest	XXX	
Cash payments for income taxes	XXX	XXX
Net cash flows from operating activities		$XXX

The Cash Flows from Investing and Financing Activities sections of the statement of cash flows are the same under the direct and indirect methods. The amount of cash flows from operating activities is also the same.

Under the direct method, the income statement is adjusted to cash flows from operating activities as follows:

Income Statement	Adjusted to	Cash Flows from Operating Activities
Sales	→	Cash received from customers
Cost of merchandise sold	→	Cash payments for merchandise
Operating expenses:		
Depreciation expense	N/A	N/A
Other operating expenses	→	Cash payments for operating expenses
Gain on sale of land	N/A	N/A
Interest expense	→	Cash payments for interest
Income tax expense	→	Cash payments for income taxes
Net income	→	Cash flows from operating activities

N/A—Not applicable

    As shown above, depreciation expense is not adjusted or reported as part of cash flows from operating activities. This is because deprecation expense does not involve a cash outflow. The gain on sale of land is also not adjusted or reported as part of cash flows from operating activities. This is because the sale of land is reported as an investing activity rather than an operating activity.

    To illustrate the direct method, the income statement and comparative balance sheet for Rundell Inc. shown in Exhibit 3, on page 710, are used.

Cash Received from Customers

The income statement (shown in Exhibit 3) of Rundell Inc. reports sales of $1,180,000. To determine the *cash received from customers*, the $1,180,000 is adjusted for any increase or decrease in accounts receivable. The adjustment is summarized below.

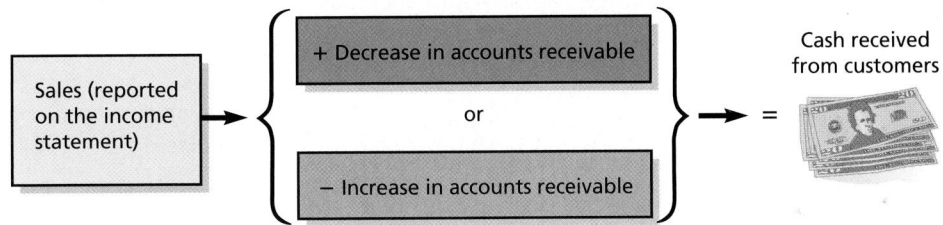

The cash received from customers is $1,171,000, computed as follows:

Sales	$1,180,000
Less increase in accounts receivable	9,000
Cash received from customers	$1,171,000

    The increase of $9,000 in accounts receivable (shown in Exhibit 3) during 2010 indicates that sales on account exceeded cash received from customers by $9,000. In other words, sales include $9,000 that did not result in a cash inflow during the year. Thus, $9,000 is deducted from sales to determine the *cash received from customers*.

Example Exercise 16-6   Cash Received from Customers— Direct Method •••••••▶ ③

Sales reported on the income statement were $350,000. The accounts receivable balance declined $8,000 over the year. Determine the amount of cash received from customers.

Follow My Example 16-6

Sales	$350,000
Add decrease in accounts receivable	8,000
Cash received from customers	$358,000

For Practice: PE 16-6A, PE 16-6B

Cash Payments for Merchandise

The income statement (shown in Exhibit 3) for Rundell Inc. reports cost of merchandise sold of $790,000. To determine the *cash payments for merchandise*, the $790,000 is adjusted for any increases or decreases in inventories and accounts payable. Assuming the accounts payable are owed to merchandise suppliers, the adjustment is summarized below.

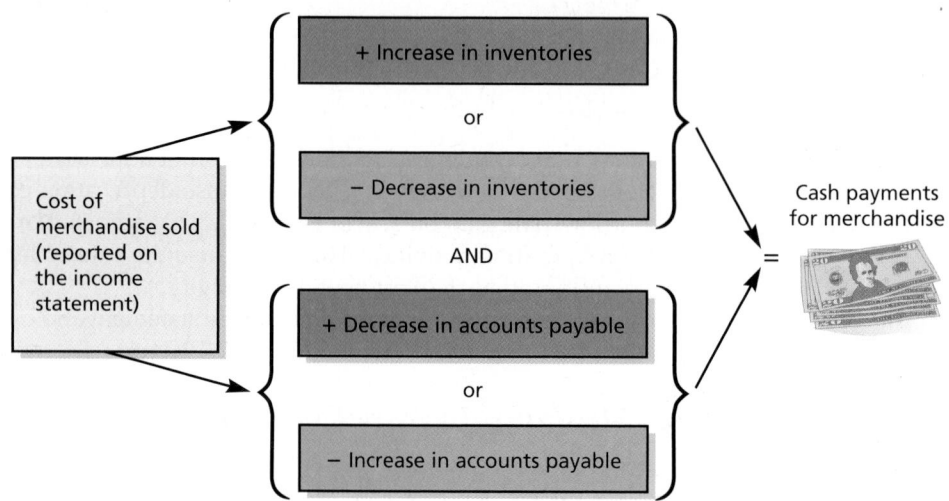

The cash payments for merchandise are $785,200, computed as follows:

Cost of merchandise sold	$790,000
Deduct decrease in inventories	(8,000)
Add decrease in accounts payable	3,200
Cash payments for merchandise	$785,200

The $8,000 decrease in inventories (from Exhibit 3) indicates that the merchandise sold exceeded the cost of the merchandise purchased by $8,000. In other words, cost of merchandise sold includes $8,000 that did not require a cash outflow during the year. Thus, $8,000 is deducted from the cost of merchandise sold in determining the *cash payments for merchandise*.

The $3,200 decrease in accounts payable (from Exhibit 3) indicates that cash payments for merchandise were $3,200 more than the purchases on account during 2010. Therefore, $3,200 is added to the cost of merchandise sold in determining the *cash payments for merchandise*.

Example Exercise 16-7 Cash Payments for Merchandise—Direct Method

Cost of merchandise sold reported on the income statement was $145,000. The accounts payable balance increased $4,000, and the inventory balance increased by $9,000 over the year. Determine the amount of cash paid for merchandise.

Follow My Example 16-7

Cost of merchandise sold	$145,000
Add increase in inventories.	9,000
Deduct increase in accounts payable	(4,000)
Cash paid for merchandise	$150,000

For Practice: PE 16-7A, PE 16-7B

Cash Payments for Operating Expenses

The income statement (from Exhibit 3) for Rundell Inc. reports total operating expenses of $203,000, which includes depreciation expense of $7,000. Since depreciation expense does not require a cash outflow, it is omitted from *cash payments for operating expenses*.

To determine the *cash payments for operating expenses*, the other operating expenses (excluding depreciation) of $196,000 ($203,000 − $7,000) are adjusted for any increase or decrease in accrued expenses payable. Assuming that the accrued expenses payable are all operating expenses, this adjustment is summarized below.

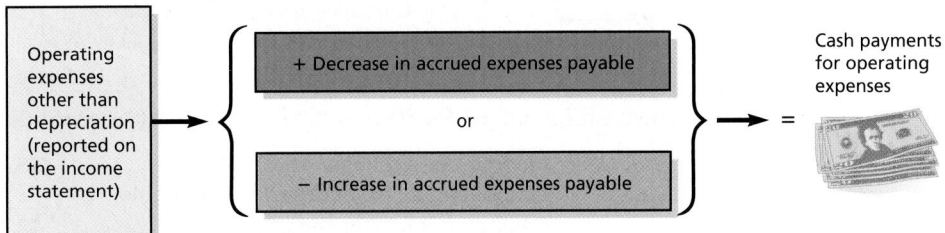

The cash payments for operating expenses is $193,800, computed as follows:

Operating expenses other than depreciation	$196,000
Deduct increase in accrued expenses payable	(2,200)
Cash payments for operating expenses	$193,800

The increase in accrued expenses payable (from Exhibit 3) indicates that the cash payments for operating expenses were $2,200 less than the amount reported for operating expenses during the year. Thus, $2,200 is deducted from the operating expenses in determining the *cash payments for operating expenses*.

Gain on Sale of Land

The income statement for Rundell Inc. (from Exhibit 3) reports a gain of $12,000 on the sale of land. The sale of land is an investing activity. Thus, the proceeds from the sale, which include the gain, are reported as part of the cash flows from investing activities.

Interest Expense

The income statement (from Exhibit 3) for Rundell Inc. reports interest expense of $8,000. To determine the *cash payments for interest*, the $8,000 is adjusted for any increases or decreases in interest payable. The adjustment is summarized below.

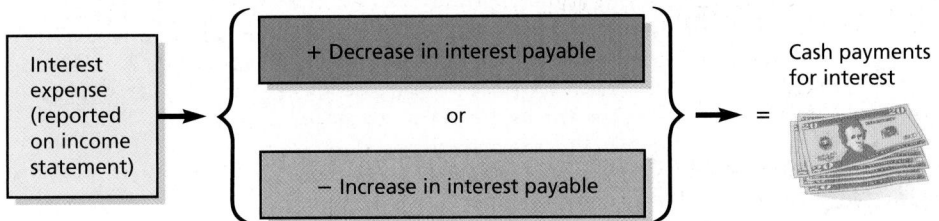

The comparative balance sheet of Rundell Inc. in Exhibit 3 indicates no interest payable. This is because the interest expense on the bonds payable is paid on June 1 and December 31. Since there is no interest payable, no adjustment of the interest expense of $8,000 is necessary.

Cash Payments for Income Taxes

The income statement (from Exhibit 3) for Rundell Inc. reports income tax expense of $83,000. To determine the *Cash payments for income taxes,* the $83,000 is adjusted for any increases or decreases in income taxes payable. The adjustment is summarized below.

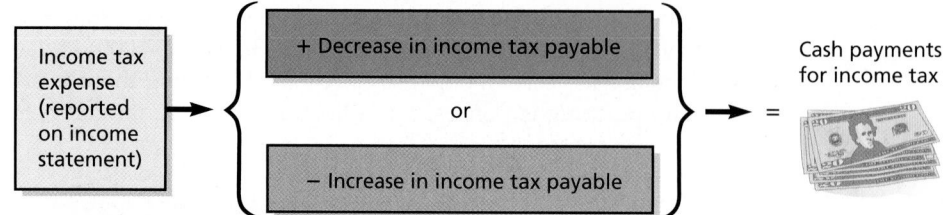

The cash payments for income taxes are $83,500, computed as follows:

Income tax expense	$83,000
Add decrease in income taxes payable	500
Cash payments for income taxes	$83,500

The $500 decrease in income taxes payable (from Exhibit 3) indicates that the cash payments for income taxes were $500 more than the amount reported for income tex expense during 2010. Thus, $500 is added to the income tax expense in determining the *cash payments for income taxes.*

Reporting Cash Flows from Operating Activities—Direct Method

The statement of cash flows for Rundell Inc. using the direct method for reporting cash flows from operating activities is shown in Exhibit 7. The portions of the

---

Exhibit 7

Statement of Cash Flows— Direct Method

Rundell Inc.
Statement of Cash Flows
For the Year Ended December 31, 2010

Cash flows from operating activities:			
Cash received from customers		$1,171,000	
Deduct: Cash payments for merchandise	$785,200		
Cash payments for operating expenses	193,800		
Cash payments for interest	8,000		
Cash payments for income taxes	83,500	1,070,500	
Net cash flow from operating activities			$100,500
Cash flows from investing activities:			
Cash from sale of land		$ 72,000	
Less: Cash paid to purchase land	$ 15,000		
Cash paid for purchase of building	60,000	75,000	
Net cash flow used for investing activities			(3,000)
Cash flows from financing activities:			
Cash received from sale of common stock		$ 48,000	
Less: Cash paid to retire bonds payable	$ 50,000		
Cash paid for dividends	24,000	74,000	
Net cash flow used for financing activities			(26,000)
Increase in cash			$ 71,500
Cash at the beginning of the year			26,000
Cash at the end of the year			$ 97,500

(continued)

(concluded)

Schedule Reconciling Net Income with Cash Flows from Operating Activities:

Cash flows from operating activities:	
Net income	$108,000
Adjustments to reconcile net income to net cash flow from operating activities:	
Depreciation	7,000
Gain on sale of land	(12,000)
Changes in current operating assets and liabilities:	
Increase in accounts receivable	(9,000)
Decrease in inventory	8,000
Decrease in accounts payable	(3,200)
Increase in accrued expenses payable	2,200
Decrease in income taxes payable	(500)
Net cash flow from operating activities	$100,500

statement that differ from those prepared under the indirect method are highlighted in color.

Exhibit 7 also includes the separate schedule reconciling net income and net cash flow from operating activities. This schedule is included in the statement of cash flows when the direct method is used. This schedule is similar to the Cash Flows from Operating Activities section prepared under the indirect method.

Financial Analysis and Interpretation

A valuable tool for evaluating the cash flows of a business is free cash flow. **Free cash flow** is a measure of operating cash flow available for corporate purposes after providing sufficient fixed asset additions to maintain current productive capacity. Thus, free cash flow can be calculated as follows:

Cash flow from operating activities	$XXX
Less: Investments in fixed assets to maintain current production	XXX
Free cash flow	$XXX

Analysts often use free cash flow, rather than cash flows from operating activities, to measure the financial strength of a business. Many high-technology firms must aggressively reinvest in new technology to remain competitive. This can reduce free cash flow. For example, Verizon Communications Inc.'s free cash flow is less than 30% of the cash flow from operating activities. In contrast, The Coca-Cola Company's free cash flow is approximately 75% of the cash flow from operating activities. Three nonfinancial companies with large free cash flows for a recent year were as follows:

	Free Cash Flow (in millions)
General Electric Company	$13,996
ExxonMobil Corporation	33,824
Microsoft Corporation	15,532

To illustrate, the cash flow from operating activities for Intuit Inc., the developer of TurboTax®, was $727 million in a recent fiscal year. The statement of cash flows indicated that the cash invested in property, plant, and equipment was $105 million. Assuming that the amount invested in property, plant, and equipment maintained existing operations, free cash flow would be calculated as follows (in millions):

Cash flow from operating activities	$727
Less: Investments in fixed assets to maintain current production	105
Free cash flow	$622

During this period, Intuit generated free cash flow in excess of $600 million, which was 86% of cash flows from operations and over 23% of sales.

Positive free cash flow is considered favorable. A company that has free cash flow is able to fund internal growth, retire debt, pay dividends, and enjoy financial flexibility. A company with no free cash flow is unable to maintain current productive capacity. Lack of free cash flow can be an early indicator of liquidity problems. As stated by one analyst, "Free cash flow gives the company firepower to reduce debt and ultimately generate consistent, actual income."[6]

Source: "CFO Free Cash Flow Scorecard," CFO Magazine, January 1, 2005.

6 Jill Krutick, *Fortune,* March 30, 1998, p. 106.

A P P E N D I X

Spreadsheet (Work Sheet) for Statement of Cash Flows— The Indirect Method

A spreadsheet (work sheet) may used in preparing the statement of cash flows. However, whether or not a spreadsheet (work sheet) is used, the concepts presented in this chapter are not affected.

The data for Rundell Inc., presented in Exhibit 3, are used as a basis for illustrating the spreadsheet (work sheet) for the indirect method. The steps in preparing this spreadsheet (work sheet), shown in Exhibit 8, are as follows:

Step 1. List the title of each balance sheet account in the Accounts column.
Step 2. For each balance sheet account, enter its balance as of December 31, 2009, in the first column and its balance as of December 31, 2010, in the last column. Place the credit balances in parentheses.
Step 3. Add the December 31, 2009 and 2010 column totals, which should total to zero.
Step 4. Analyze the change during the year in each noncash account to determine its net increase (decrease) and classify the change as affecting cash flows from operating activities, investing activities, financing activities, or noncash investing and financing activities.
Step 5. Indicate the effect of the change on cash flows by making entries in the Transactions columns.
Step 6. After all noncash accounts have been analyzed, enter the net increase (decrease) in cash during the period.
Step 7. Add the Debit and Credit Transactions columns. The totals should be equal.

Analyzing Accounts

In analyzing the noncash accounts (Step 4), try to determine the type of cash flow activity (operating, investing, or financing) that led to the change in account. As each noncash account is analyzed, an entry (Step 5) is made on the spreadsheet (work sheet) for the type of cash flow activity that caused the change. After all noncash accounts have been analyzed, an entry (Step 6) is made for the increase (decrease) in cash during the period.

The entries made on the spreadsheet are not posted to the ledger. They are only used in preparing and summarizing the data on the spreadsheet.

The order in which the accounts are analyzed is not important. However, it is more efficient to begin with Retained Earnings and proceed upward in the account listing.

Retained Earnings

The spreadsheet (work sheet) shows a Retained Earnings balance of $202,300 at December 31, 2009, and $282,300 at December 31, 2010. Thus, Retained Earnings increased $80,000 during the year. This increase is from the following:

1. Net income of $108,000
2. Declaring cash dividends of $28,000

To identify the cash flows from these activities, two entries are made on the spreadsheet.

The $108,000 is reported on the statement of cash flows as part of "cash flows from operating activities." Thus, an entry is made in the Transactions columns on the spreadsheet as follows:

(a)   Operating Activities—Net Income 108,000
        Retained Earnings   108,000

The preceding entry accounts for the net income portion of the change to Retained Earnings. It also identifies the cash flow in the bottom portion of the spreadsheet as related to operating activities.

Exhibit 8

End-of-Period Spreadsheet (Work Sheet) for Statement of Cash Flows—Indirect Method

Step 2

	Accounts	Balance, Dec. 31, 2009	Transactions Debit		Transactions Credit		Balance, Dec. 31, 2010
1	Rundell Inc.						
2	End-of-Period Spreadsheet (Work Sheet) for Statement of Cash Flows						
3	For the Year Ended December 31, 2010						
6	Cash	26,000	(o)	71,500			97,500
7	Accounts receivable (net)	65,000	(n)	9,000			74,000
8	Inventories	180,000			(m)	8,000	172,000
9	Land	125,000	(k)	15,000	(l)	60,000	80,000
10	Building	200,000	(j)	60,000			260,000
11	Accumulated depreciation—building	(58,300)			(i)	7,000	(65,300)
12	Accounts payable (merchandise creditors)	(46,700)	(h)	3,200			(43,500)
13	Accrued expenses payable (operating expenses)	(24,300)			(g)	2,200	(26,500)
14	Income taxes payable	(8,400)	(f)	500			(7,900)
15	Dividends payable	(10,000)			(e)	4,000	(14,000)
16	Bonds payable	(150,000)	(d)	50,000			(100,000)
17	Common stock	(16,000)			(c)	8,000	(24,000)
18	Paid-in capital in excess of par	(80,000)			(c)	40,000	(120,000)
19	Retained earnings	(202,300)	(b)	28,000	(a)	108,000	(282,300)
20	Totals	0		237,200		237,200	0
21	Operating activities:						
22	Net income		(a)	108,000			
23	Depreciation of building		(i)	7,000			
24	Gain on sale of land				(l)	12,000	
25	Increase in accounts receivable				(n)	9,000	
26	Decrease in inventories		(m)	8,000			
27	Decrease in accounts payable				(h)	3,200	
28	Increase in accrued expenses payable		(g)	2,200			
29	Decrease in income taxes payable				(f)	500	
30	Investing activities:						
31	Sale of land		(l)	72,000			
32	Purchase of land				(k)	15,000	
33	Purchase of building				(j)	60,000	
34	Financing activities:						
35	Issued common stock		(c)	48,000			
36	Retired bonds payable				(d)	50,000	
37	Declared cash dividends				(b)	28,000	
38	Increase in dividends payable		(e)	4,000			
39	Net increase in cash				(o)	71,500	
40	Totals			249,200		249,200	

Step 1

Step 3

Steps 4–7

The $28,000 of dividends is reported as a financing activity on the statement of cash flows. Thus, an entry is made in the Transactions columns on the spreadsheet as follows:

| (b) | Retained Earnings | 28,000 | |
| | Financing Activities—Declared Cash Dividends | | 28,000 |

The preceding entry accounts for the dividends portion of the change to Retained Earnings. It also identifies the cash flow in the bottom portion of the spreadsheet as related to financing activities. The $28,000 of declared dividends will be adjusted later for the actual amount of cash dividends paid during the year.

Other Accounts

The entries for the other noncash accounts are made in the spreadsheet in a manner similar to entries (a) and (b). A summary of these entries is as follows:

(c)	Financing Activities—Issued Common Stock	48,000	
	Common Stock		8,000
	Paid-In Capital in Excess of Par—Common Stock		40,000
(d)	Bonds Payable	50,000	
	Financing Activities—Retired Bonds Payable		50,000
(e)	Financing Activities—Increase in Dividends Payable	4,000	
	Dividends Payable		4,000
(f)	Income Taxes Payable	500	
	Operating Activities—Decrease in Income Taxes Payable		500
(g)	Operating Activities—Increase in Accrued Expenses Payable	2,200	
	Accrued Expenses Payable		2,200
(h)	Accounts Payable	3,200	
	Operating Activities—Decrease in Accounts Payable		3,200
(i)	Operating Activities—Depreciation of Building	7,000	
	Accumulated Depreciation—Building		7,000
(j)	Building	60,000	
	Investing Activities—Purchase of Building		60,000
(k)	Land	15,000	
	Investing Activities—Purchase of Land		15,000
(l)	Investing Activities—Sale of Land	72,000	
	Operating Activities—Gain on Sale of Land		12,000
	Land		60,000
(m)	Operating Activities—Decrease in Inventories	8,000	
	Inventories		8,000
(n)	Accounts Receivable	9,000	
	Operating Activities—Increase in Accounts Receivable		9,000
(o)	Cash	71,500	
	Net Increase in Cash		71,500

After all the balance sheet accounts are analyzed and the entries made on the spreadsheet (work sheet), all the operating, investing, and financing activities are identified in the bottom portion of the spread sheet. The accuracy of the entries is verified by totaling the Debit and Credit Transactions columns. The totals of the columns should be equal.

Preparing the Statement of Cash Flows

The statement of cash flows prepared from the spreadsheet is identical to the statement in Exhibit 6. The data for the three sections of the statement are obtained from the bottom portion of the spreadsheet.

1 Describe the cash flow activities reported in the statement of cash flows.

Key Points	Key Learning Outcomes	Example Exercises	Practice Exercises
The statement of cash flows reports cash receipts and cash payments by three types of activities: operating activities, investing activities, and financing activities. Investing and financing for a business may be affected by transactions that do not involve cash. The effect of such transactions should be reported in a separate schedule accompanying the statement of cash flows.	• Classify transactions that either provide or use cash into either operating, investing, or financing activities.	**16-1**	16-1A, 16-1B

2 Prepare a statement of cash flows, using the indirect method.

Key Points	Key Learning Outcomes	Example Exercises	Practice Exercises
The changes in the noncash balance sheet accounts are used to develop the statement of cash flows, beginning with the cash flows from operating activities.			
Determine the cash flows from operating activities using the indirect method by adjusting net income for expenses that do not require cash and for gains and losses from disposal of fixed assets.	• Adjust net income for noncash expenses and gains and losses from asset disposals under the indirect method.	**16-2**	16-2A, 16-2B
Determine the cash flows from operating activities using the indirect method by adjusting net income for changes in current operating assets and liabilities.	• Adjust net income for changes in current operating assets and liabilities under the indirect method.	**16-3**	16-3A, 16-3B
Report cash flows from operating activities under the indirect method.	• Prepare the cash flows from operating activities under the indirect method in proper form.	**16-4**	16-4A, 16-4B
Report investing and financing activities on the statement of cash flows.	• Prepare the remainder of the statement of cash flows by reporting investing and financing activities.	**16-5**	16-5A, 16-5B

3 Prepare a statement of cash flows, using the direct method.

Key Points	Key Learning Outcomes	Example Exercises	Practice Exercises
The direct method reports cash flows from operating activities by major classes of operating cash receipts and cash payments. The difference between the major classes of total operating cash receipts and total operating cash payments is the net cash flow from operating activities. The investing and financing activities sections of the statement are the same as under the indirect method.	• Prepare the cash flows from operating activities and the remainder of the statement of cash flows under the direct method.	**16-6** **16-7**	16-6A, 16-6B 16-7A, 16-7B

Key Terms

cash flow per share (708)
cash flows from financing
  activities (706)
cash flows from investing
  activities (706)

cash flows from operating
  activities (705)
direct method (706)
free cash flow (725)

indirect method (707)
statement of cash flows (705)

Illustrative Problem

The comparative balance sheet of Dowling Company for December 31, 2010, and 2009, is as follows:

Dowling Company
Comparative Balance Sheet
December 31, 2010, and 2009

	2010	2009
Assets		
Cash	$ 140,350	$ 95,900
Accounts receivable (net)	95,300	102,300
Inventories	165,200	157,900
Prepaid expenses	6,240	5,860
Investments (long-term)	35,700	84,700
Land	75,000	90,000
Buildings	375,000	260,000
Accumulated depreciation—buildings	(71,300)	(58,300)
Machinery and equipment	428,300	428,300
Accumulated depreciation—machinery and equipment	(148,500)	(138,000)
Patents	58,000	65,000
Total assets	$1,159,290	$1,093,660
Liabilities and Stockholders' Equity		
Accounts payable (merchandise creditors)	$ 43,500	$ 46,700
Accrued expenses payable (operating expenses)	14,000	12,500
Income taxes payable	7,900	8,400
Dividends payable	14,000	10,000
Mortgage note payable, due 2021	40,000	0
Bonds payable	150,000	250,000
Common stock, $30 par	450,000	375,000
Excess of issue price over par—common stock	66,250	41,250
Retained earnings	373,640	349,810
Total liabilities and stockholders' equity	$1,159,290	$1,093,660

The income statement for Dowling Company is shown here.

Dowling Company
Income Statement
For the Year Ended December 31, 2010

Sales		$1,100,000
Cost of merchandise sold		710,000
Gross profit		$ 390,000
Operating expenses:		
Depreciation expense	$ 23,500	
Patent amortization	7,000	
Other operating expenses	196,000	
Total operating expenses		226,500
Income from operations		$ 163,500
Other income:		
Gain on sale of investments	$ 11,000	
Other expense:		
Interest expense	26,000	(15,000)
Income before income tax		$ 148,500
Income tax expense		50,000
Net income		$ 98,500

An examination of the accounting records revealed the following additional information applicable to 2010:

a. Land costing $15,000 was sold for $15,000.
b. A mortgage note was issued for $40,000.
c. A building costing $115,000 was constructed.
d. 2,500 shares of common stock were issued at 40 in exchange for the bonds payable.
e. Cash dividends declared were $74,670.

Instructions

1. Prepare a statement of cash flows, using the indirect method of reporting cash flows from operating activities.
2. Prepare a statement of cash flows, using the direct method of reporting cash flows from operating activities.

Solution

1.

Dowling Company Statement of Cash Flows—Indirect Method For the Year Ended December 31, 2010			
Cash flows from operating activities:			
Net income		$ 98,500	
Adjustments to reconcile net income to net cash flow from operating activities:			
Depreciation		23,500	
Amortization of patents		7,000	
Gain on sale of investments		(11,000)	
Changes in current operating assets and liabilities:			
Decrease in accounts receivable		7,000	
Increase in inventories		(7,300)	
Increase in prepaid expenses		(380)	
Decrease in accounts payable		(3,200)	
Increase in accrued expenses payable		1,500	
Decrease in income taxes payable		(500)	
Net cash flow from operating activities			$115,120
Cash flows from investing activities:			
Cash received from sale of:			
Investments	$60,000		
Land	15,000	$ 75,000	
Less: Cash paid for construction of building		115,000	
Net cash flow used for investing activities			(40,000)
Cash flows from financing activities:			
Cash received from issuing mortgage note payable		$ 40,000	
Less: Cash paid for dividends		70,670*	
Net cash flow used for financing activities			(30,670)
Increase in cash			$ 44,450
Cash at the beginning of the year			95,900
Cash at the end of the year			$140,350
Schedule of Noncash Investing and Financing Activities:			
Issued common stock to retire bonds payable			$100,000
* $70,670 = $74,670 − $4,000 (increase in dividends)			

2.

Dowling Company Statement of Cash Flows—Direct Method For the Year Ended December 31, 2010			
Cash flows from operating activities:			
Cash received from customers[1]		$1,107,000	
Deduct: Cash paid for merchandise[2]	$720,500		
Cash paid for operating expenses[3]	194,880		
Cash paid for interest expense	26,000		
Cash paid for income tax[4]	50,500	991,880	
Net cash flow from operating activities			$115,120
Cash flows from investing activities:			
Cash received from sale of:			
Investments	$ 60,000		
Land	15,000	$ 75,000	
Less: Cash paid for construction of building		115,000	
Net cash flow used for investing activities			(40,000)
Cash flows from financing activities:			
Cash received from issuing mortgage note payable		$ 40,000	
Less: Cash paid for dividends[5]		70,670	
Net cash flow used for financing activities			(30,670)
Increase in cash			$ 44,450
Cash at the beginning of the year			95,900
Cash at the end of the year			$140,350

Schedule of Noncash Investing and Financing Activities:

Issued common stock to retire bonds payable	$100,000

Schedule Reconciling Net Income with Cash Flows from Operating Activities[6]

Computations:

[1]$1,100,000 + $7,000 = $1,107,000
[2]$710,000 + $3,200 + $7,300 = $720,500
[3]$196,000 + $380 − $1,500 = $194,880
[4]$50,000 + $500 = $50,500

[5]$74,670 + $10,000 − $14,000 = $70,670
[6]The content of this schedule is the same as the Operating Activities section of part (1) of this solution and is not reproduced here for the sake of brevity.

Self-Examination Questions (Answers at End of Chapter)

1. An example of a cash flow from an operating activity is:
   A. receipt of cash from the sale of stock.
   B. receipt of cash from the sale of bonds.
   C. payment of cash for dividends.
   D. receipt of cash from customers on account.

2. An example of a cash flow from an investing activity is:
   A. receipt of cash from the sale of equipment.
   B. receipt of cash from the sale of stock.
   C. payment of cash for dividends.
   D. payment of cash to acquire treasury stock.

3. An example of a cash flow from a financing activity is:
   A. receipt of cash from customers on account.
   B. receipt of cash from the sale of equipment.
   C. payment of cash for dividends.
   D. payment of cash to acquire land.

4. Which of the following methods of reporting cash flows from operating activities adjusts net income for revenues and expenses not involving the receipt or payment of cash?
   A. Direct method
   B. Purchase method
   C. Reciprocal method
   D. Indirect method

5. The net income reported on the income statement for the year was $55,000, and depreciation of fixed assets for the year was $22,000. The balances of the current asset and current liability accounts at the beginning and end of the year are shown below.

	End	Beginning
Cash	$ 65,000	$ 70,000
Accounts receivable	100,000	90,000
Inventories	145,000	150,000
Prepaid expenses	7,500	8,000
Accounts payable		
(merchandise creditors)	51,000	58,000

The total amount reported for cash flows from operating activities in the statement of cash flows, using the indirect method, is:

A. $33,000. C. $65,500.
B. $55,000. D. $77,000.

Eye Openers

1. What is the principal disadvantage of the direct method of reporting cash flows from operating activities?
2. What are the major advantages of the indirect method of reporting cash flows from operating activities?
3. A corporation issued $500,000 of common stock in exchange for $500,000 of fixed assets. Where would this transaction be reported on the statement of cash flows?
4. A retail business, using the accrual method of accounting, owed merchandise creditors (accounts payable) $300,000 at the beginning of the year and $340,000 at the end of the year. How would the $40,000 increase be used to adjust net income in determining the amount of cash flows from operating activities by the indirect method? Explain.
5. If salaries payable was $90,000 at the beginning of the year and $70,000 at the end of the year, should $20,000 be added to or deducted from income to determine the amount of cash flows from operating activities by the indirect method? Explain.
6. A long-term investment in bonds with a cost of $60,000 was sold for $72,000 cash. (a) What was the gain or loss on the sale? (b) What was the effect of the transaction on cash flows? (c) How should the transaction be reported in the statement of cash flows if cash flows from operating activities are reported by the indirect method?
7. A corporation issued $6,000,000 of 20-year bonds for cash at 104. How would the transaction be reported on the statement of cash flows?
8. Fully depreciated equipment costing $100,000 was discarded. What was the effect of the transaction on cash flows if (a) $24,000 cash is received, (b) no cash is received?
9. For the current year, Bearings Company decided to switch from the indirect method to the direct method for reporting cash flows from operating activities on the statement of cash flows. Will the change cause the amount of net cash flow from operating activities to be (a) larger, (b) smaller, or (c) the same as if the indirect method had been used? Explain.
10. Name five common major classes of operating cash receipts or operating cash payments presented on the statement of cash flows when the cash flows from operating activities are reported by the direct method.
11. In a recent annual report, eBay Inc. reported that during the year it issued stock of $128 million for acquisitions. How would this be reported on the statement of cash flows?

Practice Exercises

PE 16-1A
Classifying cash flows
obj. 1
EE 16-1   p. 708

Identify whether each of the following would be reported as an operating, investing, or financing activity in the statement of cash flows.

a. Issuance of common stock
b. Purchase of land
c. Payment of accounts payable

d. Retirement of bonds payable
e. Payment for administrative expenses
f. Cash received from customers

PE 16-1B
Classifying cash flows
obj. 1
EE 16-1   p. 708

Identify whether each of the following would be reported as an operating, investing, or financing activity in the statement of cash flows.

a. Payment for selling expenses
b. Issuance of bonds payable
c. Disposal of equipment

d. Cash sales
e. Purchase of investments
f. Collection of accounts receivable

PE 16-2A
Adjustments to net income—indirect method
obj. 2
EE 16-2   p. 712

Choi Corporation's accumulated depreciation—furniture increased by $7,000, while $2,600 of patents were amortized between balance sheet dates. There were no purchases or sales of depreciable or intangible assets during the year. In addition, the income statement showed a gain of $15,000 from the sale of land. Reconcile a net income of $140,000 to net cash flow from operating activities.

PE 16-2B
Adjustments to net income—indirect method
obj. 2
EE 16-2   p. 712

Singh Corporation's accumulated depreciation—equipment increased by $6,000, while $2,200 of patents were amortized between balance sheet dates. There were no purchases or sales of depreciable or intangible assets during the year. In addition, the income statement showed a loss of $3,200 from the sale of investments. Reconcile a net income of $86,000 to net cash flow from operating activities.

PE 16-3A
Changes in current operating assets and liabilities—indirect method
obj. 2
EE 16-3   p. 715

Watson Corporation's comparative balance sheet for current assets and liabilities was as follows:

	Dec. 31, 2010	Dec. 31, 2009
Accounts receivable	$30,000	$24,000
Inventory	58,000	49,500
Accounts payable	46,000	34,500
Dividends payable	14,000	18,000

Adjust net income of $320,000 for changes in operating assets and liabilities to arrive at net cash flow from operating activities.

PE 16-3B
Changes in current operating assets and liabilities—indirect method
obj. 2
EE 16-3   p. 715

Chopra Corporation's comparative balance sheet for current assets and liabilities was as follows:

	Dec. 31, 2010	Dec. 31, 2009
Accounts receivable	$15,000	$18,000
Inventory	10,000	8,600
Accounts payable	9,000	7,900
Dividends payable	27,500	29,500

Adjust net income of $115,000 for changes in operating assets and liabilities to arrive at net cash flow from operating activities.

PE 16-4A

Cash flows from
operating activities—
indirect method

obj. 2

EE 16-4   p. 716

Trahan Inc. reported the following data:

Net income	$175,000
Depreciation expense	30,000
Loss on disposal of equipment	12,200
Increase in accounts receivable	10,800
Increase in accounts payable	5,600

Prepare the Cash Flows from Operating Activities section of the statement of cash flows using the indirect method.

PE 16-4B

Cash flows from
operating activities—
indirect method

obj. 2

EE 16-4   p. 716

Daly Inc. reported the following data:

Net income	$225,000
Depreciation expense	25,000
Gain on disposal of equipment	20,500
Decrease in accounts receivable	14,000
Decrease in accounts payable	3,600

Prepare the Cash Flows from Operating Activities section of the statement of cash flows using the indirect method.

PE 16-5A

Land transactions on
the statement of
cash flows

obj. 2

EE 16-5   p. 719

Slocum Corporation purchased land for $600,000. Later in the year, the company sold land with a book value of $360,000 for $410,000. How are the effects of these transactions reported on the statement of cash flows?

PE 16-5B

Land transactions on
the statement of
cash flows

obj. 2

EE 16-5   p. 719

Verplank Corporation purchased land for $340,000. Later in the year, the company sold land with a book value of $145,000 for $110,000. How are the effects of these transactions reported on the statement of cash flows?

PE 16-6A

Cash received from
customers—direct
method

obj. 3

EE 16-6   p. 721

Sales reported on the income statement were $46,200. The accounts receivable balance decreased $3,400 over the year. Determine the amount of cash received from customers.

PE 16-6B

Cash received from
customers—direct
method

obj. 3

EE 16-6   p. 721

Sales reported on the income statement were $521,000. The accounts receivable balance increased $56,000 over the year. Determine the amount of cash received from customers.

PE 16-7A

Cash payments for
merchandise—direct
method

obj. 3

EE 16-7   p. 722

Cost of merchandise sold reported on the income statement was $130,000. The accounts payable balance increased $6,200, and the inventory balance increased by $11,400 over the year. Determine the amount of cash paid for merchandise.

PE 16-7B
Cash payments for merchandise — direct method

obj. 3

EE 16-7   p. 722

Cost of merchandise sold reported on the income statement was $420,000. The accounts payable balance decreased $22,500, and the inventory balance decreased by $26,000 over the year. Determine the amount of cash paid for merchandise.

Exercises

EX 16-1
Cash flows from operating activities — net loss

obj. 1

On its income statement for a recent year, Continental Airlines, Inc., reported a net *loss* of $68 million from operations. On its statement of cash flows, it reported $457 million of cash flows from operating activities.

➤ Explain this apparent contradiction between the loss and the positive cash flows.

EX 16-2
Effect of transactions on cash flows

obj. 1

✔ c. Cash receipt, $500,000

State the effect (cash receipt or payment and amount) of each of the following transactions, considered individually, on cash flows:

a. Sold a new issue of $200,000 of bonds at 99.
b. Purchased 4,000 shares of $35 par common stock as treasury stock at $70 per share.
c. Sold 10,000 shares of $20 par common stock for $50 per share.
d. Purchased a building by paying $60,000 cash and issuing a $100,000 mortgage note payable.
e. Retired $250,000 of bonds, on which there was $2,500 of unamortized discount, for $260,000.
f. Purchased land for $320,000 cash.
g. Paid dividends of $2.00 per share. There were 25,000 shares issued and 4,000 shares of treasury stock.
h. Sold equipment with a book value of $50,000 for $72,000.

EX 16-3
Classifying cash flows

obj. 1

Identify the type of cash flow activity for each of the following events (operating, investing, or financing):

a. Issued common stock.
b. Redeemed bonds.
c. Issued preferred stock.
d. Purchased patents.
e. Net income.
f. Paid cash dividends.

g. Purchased treasury stock.
h. Sold long-term investments.
i. Sold equipment.
j. Purchased buildings.
k. Issued bonds.

EX 16-4
Cash flows from operating activities — indirect method

obj. 2

Indicate whether each of the following would be added to or deducted from net income in determining net cash flow from operating activities by the indirect method:

a. Decrease in accounts receivable
b. Increase in notes payable due in 90 days to vendors
c. Decrease in salaries payable
d. Decrease in prepaid expenses
e. Gain on retirement of long-term debt
f. Decrease in accounts payable

g. Increase in notes receivable due in 90 days from customers
h. Depreciation of fixed assets
i. Increase in merchandise inventory
j. Amortization of patent
k. Loss on disposal of fixed assets

EX 16-5
Cash flows from operating activities— indirect method

obj. 2

✔ Net cash flow from operating activities, $153,920

The net income reported on the income statement for the current year was $132,000. Depreciation recorded on store equipment for the year amounted to $21,800. Balances of the current asset and current liability accounts at the beginning and end of the year are as follows:

	End of Year	Beginning of Year
Cash	$52,300	$48,200
Accounts receivable (net)	37,500	35,600
Merchandise inventory	51,200	54,220
Prepaid expenses	6,000	4,600
Accounts payable (merchandise creditors)	49,000	45,600
Wages payable	26,800	29,800

Prepare the Cash Flows from Operating Activities section of the statement of cash flows, using the indirect method.

EX 16-6
Cash flows from operating activities— indirect method

objs. 1, 2

✔ Cash flows from operating activities, $258,950

The net income reported on the income statement for the current year was $210,000. Depreciation recorded on equipment and a building amounted to $62,500 for the year. Balances of the current asset and current liability accounts at the beginning and end of the year are as follows:

	End of Year	Beginning of Year
Cash	$ 56,000	$ 59,500
Accounts receivable (net)	71,000	73,400
Inventories	140,000	126,500
Prepaid expenses	7,800	8,400
Accounts payable (merchandise creditors)	62,600	66,400
Salaries payable	9,000	8,250

a. Prepare the Cash Flows from Operating Activities section of the statement of cash flows, using the indirect method.
b. ━━━━━ If the direct method had been used, would the net cash flow from operating activities have been the same? Explain.

EX 16-7
Cash flows from operating activities— indirect method

objs. 1, 2

✔ Cash flows from operating activities, $328,700

The income statement disclosed the following items for 2010:

Depreciation expense	$ 36,000
Gain on disposal of equipment	21,000
Net income	317,500

Balances of the current assets and current liability accounts changed between December 31, 2009, and December 31, 2010, as follows:

Accounts receivable	$5,600
Inventory	3,200*
Prepaid insurance	1,200*
Accounts payable	3,800*
Income taxes payable	1,200
Dividends payable	850

*Decrease

Prepare the Cash Flows from Operating Activities section of the statement of cash flows, using the indirect method.

EX 16-8
Determining cash payments to stockholders

obj. 2

The board of directors declared cash dividends totaling $152,000 during the current year. The comparative balance sheet indicates dividends payable of $42,000 at the beginning of the year and $38,000 at the end of the year. What was the amount of cash payments to stockholders during the year?

EX 16-9

Reporting changes in equipment on statement of cash flows

obj. 2

An analysis of the general ledger accounts indicates that office equipment, which cost $67,000 and on which accumulated depreciation totaled $22,500 on the date of sale, was sold for $38,600 during the year. Using this information, indicate the items to be reported on the statement of cash flows.

EX 16-10

Reporting changes in equipment on statement of cash flows

obj. 2

An analysis of the general ledger accounts indicates that delivery equipment, which cost $96,000 and on which accumulated depreciation totaled $42,100 on the date of sale, was sold for $46,500 during the year. Using this information, indicate the items to be reported on the statement of cash flows.

EX 16-11

Reporting land transactions on statement of cash flows

obj. 2

On the basis of the details of the following fixed asset account, indicate the items to be reported on the statement of cash flows:

ACCOUNT *Land*   ACCOUNT NO.

Date		Item	Debit	Credit	Balance Debit	Balance Credit
2010						
Jan.	1	Balance			1,200,000	
Feb.	5	Purchased for cash	380,000		1,580,000	
Oct.	30	Sold for $210,000		180,000	1,400,000	

EX 16-12

Reporting stockholders' equity items on statement of cash flows

obj. 2

On the basis of the following stockholders' equity accounts, indicate the items, exclusive of net income, to be reported on the statement of cash flows. There were no unpaid dividends at either the beginning or the end of the year.

ACCOUNT *Common Stock, $20 par*   ACCOUNT NO.

Date		Item	Debit	Credit	Balance Debit	Balance Credit
2010						
Jan.	1	Balance, 60,000 shares				1,200,000
Feb.	11	15,000 shares issued for cash		300,000		1,500,000
June	30	2,200-share stock dividend		44,000		1,544,000

ACCOUNT *Paid-In Capital in Excess of Par—Common Stock*   ACCOUNT NO.

Date		Item	Debit	Credit	Balance Debit	Balance Credit
2010						
Jan.	1	Balance				200,000
Feb.	11	15,000 shares issued for cash		480,000		680,000
June	30	Stock dividend		79,200		759,200

ACCOUNT *Retained Earnings*   **ACCOUNT NO.**

Date		Item	Debit	Credit	Balance Debit	Balance Credit
2010						
Jan.	1	Balance				1,000,000
June	30	Stock dividend	123,200			876,800
Dec.	30	Cash dividend	115,800			761,000
	31	Net income		720,000		1,481,000

EX 16-13
Reporting land acquisition for cash and mortgage note on statement of cash flows

obj. 2

On the basis of the details of the following fixed asset account, indicate the items to be reported on the statement of cash flows:

ACCOUNT *Land*   **ACCOUNT NO.**

Date		Item	Debit	Credit	Balance Debit	Balance Credit
2010						
Jan.	1	Balance			260,000	
Feb.	10	Purchased for cash	410,000		670,000	
Nov.	20	Purchased with long-term mortgage note	540,000		1,210,000	

EX 16-14
Reporting issuance and retirement of long-term debt

obj. 2

On the basis of the details of the following bonds payable and related discount accounts, indicate the items to be reported in the Financing section of the statement of cash flows, assuming no gain or loss on retiring the bonds:

ACCOUNT *Bonds Payable*   **ACCOUNT NO.**

Date		Item	Debit	Credit	Balance Debit	Balance Credit
2010						
Jan.	1	Balance				500,000
	3	Retire bonds	100,000			400,000
July	30	Issue bonds		300,000		700,000

ACCOUNT *Discount on Bond Payable*   **ACCOUNT NO.**

Date		Item	Debit	Credit	Balance Debit	Balance Credit
2010						
Jan.	1	Balance			22,500	
	3	Retire bonds		8,000	14,500	
July	30	Issue bonds	20,000		34,500	
Dec.	31	Amortize discount		1,750	32,750	

EX 16-15

Determining net income from net cash flow from operating activities

obj. 2

✔ Net income, $155,350

Sanhueza, Inc., reported a net cash flow from operating activities of $162,500 on its statement of cash flows for the year ended December 31, 2010. The following information was reported in the Cash Flows from Operating Activities section of the statement of cash flows, using the indirect method:

Decrease in income taxes payable	$ 3,500
Decrease in inventories	8,700
Depreciation	13,400
Gain on sale of investments	6,000
Increase in accounts payable	2,400
Increase in prepaid expenses	1,350
Increase in accounts receivable	6,500

Determine the net income reported by Sanhueza, Inc., for the year ended December 31, 2010.

EX 16-16

Cash flows from operating activities— indirect method

obj. 2

✔ Net cash flow from operating activities, $3,048

Selected data derived from the income statement and balance sheet of Jones Soda Co. for a recent year are as follows:

Income statement data (in thousands):	
Net earnings	$4,574
Depreciation expense	256
Stock-based compensation expense (noncash)	1,196
Balance sheet data (in thousands):	
Increase in accounts receivable	$3,214
Increase in inventory	1,089
Increase in prepaid expenses	566
Increase in accounts payable	1,891

a. Prepare the Cash Flows from Operating Activities section of the statement of cash flows using the indirect method for Jones Soda Co. for the year.

b. ➡ Interpret your results in part (a).

EX 16-17

Statement of cash flows—indirect method

obj. 2

✔ Net cash flow from operating activities, $30

The comparative balance sheet of Tru-Built Construction Inc. for December 31, 2010 and 2009, is as follows:

	Dec. 31, 2010	Dec. 31, 2009
Assets		
Cash	$ 98	$ 32
Accounts receivable (net).	56	40
Inventories	35	22
Land	80	90
Equipment	45	35
Accumulated depreciation—equipment	(12)	(6)
Total.	$302	$213
Liabilities and Stockholders' Equity		
Accounts payable (merchandise creditors)	$ 35	$ 32
Dividends payable	6	—
Common stock, $1 par	20	10
Paid-in capital in excess of par—common stock	50	25
Retained earnings	191	146
Total.	$302	$213

The following additional information is taken from the records:

a. Land was sold for $25.

b. Equipment was acquired for cash.

c. There were no disposals of equipment during the year.

d. The common stock was issued for cash.

e. There was a $65 credit to Retained Earnings for net income.

f. There was a $20 debit to Retained Earnings for cash dividends declared.

Prepare a statement of cash flows, using the indirect method of presenting cash flows from operating activities.

EX 16-18
Statement of cash flows—indirect method

obj. 2

List the errors you find in the following statement of cash flows. The cash balance at the beginning of the year was $100,320. All other amounts are correct, except the cash balance at the end of the year.

Devon Inc.
Statement of Cash Flows
For the Year Ended December 31, 2010

Cash flows from operating activities:			
Net income			$148,080
Adjustments to reconcile net income to net cash flow			
from operating activities:			
Depreciation			42,000
Gain on sale of investements			7,200
Changes in current operating assets and liabilities:			
Increase in accounts receivable			11,400
Increase in inventories			(14,760)
Increase in accounts payable			(4,440)
Decrease in accrued expenses payable			(1,080)
Net cash flow from operating activities			$188,400
Cash flows from investing activities:			
Cash received from sale of investments			$102,000
Less: Cash paid for purchase of land		$108,000	
Cash paid for purchase of equipment		180,200	288,200
Net cash flow used for investing activities			(186,200)
Cash flows from financing activities:			
Cash received from sale of common stock			$128,400
Cash paid for dividends			54,000
Net cash flow provided by financing activities			182,400
Increase in cash			$184,600
Cash at the end of the year			126,300
Cash at the beginning of the year			$310,900

EX 16-19
Cash flows from operating activities—direct method

obj. 3

✔ a. $728,500

The cash flows from operating activities are reported by the direct method on the statement of cash flows. Determine the following:

a. If sales for the current year were $685,000 and accounts receivable decreased by $43,500 during the year, what was the amount of cash received from customers?

b. If income tax expense for the current year was $46,000 and income tax payable decreased by $5,200 during the year, what was the amount of cash payments for income tax?

EX 16-20
Cash paid for merchandise purchases

obj. 3

The cost of merchandise sold for Kohl's Corporation for a recent year was $9,891 million. The balance sheet showed the following current account balances (in millions):

	Balance, End of Year	Balance, Beginning of Year
Merchandise inventories	$2,588	$2,238
Accounts payable	934	830

Determine the amount of cash payments for merchandise.

EX 16-21
Determining selected amounts for cash flows from operating activities—direct method

obj. 3

✔ b. $77,870

Selected data taken from the accounting records of Lachgar Inc. for the current year ended December 31 are as follows:

	Balance, December 31	Balance, January 1
Accrued expenses payable (operating expenses)	$ 5,590	$ 6,110
Accounts payable (merchandise creditors)	41,730	46,020
Inventories	77,350	84,110
Prepaid expenses	3,250	3,900

During the current year, the cost of merchandise sold was $448,500, and the operating expenses other than depreciation were $78,000. The direct method is used for presenting the cash flows from operating activities on the statement of cash flows.

Determine the amount reported on the statement of cash flows for (a) cash payments for merchandise and (b) cash payments for operating expenses.

EX 16-22
Cash flows from operating activities— direct method

obj. 3

✔ Net cash flow from operating activities, $69,760

The income statement of Kodiak Industries Inc. for the current year ended June 30 is as follows:

Sales		$364,800
Cost of merchandise sold		207,200
Gross profit		$157,600
Operating expenses:		
Depreciation expense	$28,000	
Other operating expenses	73,920	
Total operating expenses		101,920
Income before income tax		$ 55,680
Income tax expense		15,440
Net income		$ 40,240

Changes in the balances of selected accounts from the beginning to the end of the current year are as follows:

	Increase Decrease*
Accounts receivable (net)	$8,400*
Inventories	2,800
Prepaid expenses	2,720*
Accounts payable (merchandise creditors)	5,760*
Accrued expenses payable (operating expenses) . .	880
Income tax payable	1,920*

Prepare the Cash Flows from Operating Activities section of the statement of cash flows, using the direct method.

EX 16-23
Cash flows from operating activities— direct method

obj. 3

✔ Net cash flow from operating activities, $56,490

The income statement for M2 Pizza Pie Company for the current year ended June 30 and balances of selected accounts at the beginning and the end of the year are as follows:

Sales		$202,400
Cost of merchandise sold		70,000
Gross profit		$132,400
Operating expenses:		
Depreciation expense	$17,500	
Other operating expenses	52,400	
Total operating expenses		69,900
Income before income tax		$ 62,500
Income tax expense		18,000
Net income		$ 44,500

	End of Year	Beginning of Year
Accounts receivable (net)	$16,300	$14,190
Inventories	41,900	36,410
Prepaid expenses	6,600	7,260
Accounts payable (merchandise creditors)	30,690	28,490
Accrued expenses payable (operating expenses) . .	8,690	9,460
Income tax payable	1,650	1,650

Prepare the Cash Flows from Operating Activities section of the statement of cash flows, using the direct method.

EX 16-24
Free cash flow

Morrocan Marble Company has cash flows from operating activities of $300,000. Cash flows used for investments in property, plant, and equipment totaled $65,000, of which 75% of this investment was used to replace existing capacity.

Determine the free cash flow for Morrocan Marble Company.

EX 16-25
Free cash flow

The financial statements for Nike, Inc., are provided in Appendix E at the end of the text.

Determine the free cash flow for the year ended May 31, 2007. Assume that 90% of additions to property, plant and equipment were used to maintain productive capacity.

Problems Series A

PR 16-1A
Statement of cash flows—indirect method

obj. 2

✔ Net cash flow from operating activities, $49,520

The comparative balance sheet of Mavenir Technologies Inc. for December 31, 2010 and 2009, is shown as follows:

	Dec. 31, 2010	Dec. 31, 2009
Assets		
Cash	$ 312,880	$ 292,960
Accounts receivable (net).	113,920	104,480
Inventories	320,880	308,560
Investments	0	120,000
Land	164,000	0
Equipment	352,560	276,560
Accumulated depreciation—equipment	(83,200)	(74,000)
	$1,181,040	$1,028,560
Liabilities and Stockholders' Equity		
Accounts payable (merchandise creditors)	$ 214,240	$ 202,480
Accrued expenses payable (operating expenses) . . .	21,120	26,320
Dividends payable	12,000	9,600
Common stock, $10 par	64,000	48,000
Paid-in capital in excess of par—common stock	240,000	140,000
Retained earnings	629,680	602,160
	$1,181,040	$1,028,560

The following additional information was taken from the records:

a. The investments were sold for $140,000 cash.
b. Equipment and land were acquired for cash.
c. There were no disposals of equipment during the year.
d. The common stock was issued for cash.
e. There was a $75,520 credit to Retained Earnings for net income.
f. There was a $48,000 debit to Retained Earnings for cash dividends declared.

Instructions

Prepare a statement of cash flows, using the indirect method of presenting cash flows from operating activities.

PR 16-2A
Statement of cash
flows—indirect
method

obj. 2

✔ Net cash flow
from operating
activities, $169,600

The comparative balance sheet of Amelia Enterprises, Inc., at December 31, 2010 and 2009, is as follows:

	Dec. 31, 2010	Dec. 31, 2009
Assets		
Cash	$ 73,300	$ 89,900
Accounts receivable (net)	112,300	121,000
Merchandise inventory	160,800	149,600
Prepaid expenses	6,700	4,800
Equipment	327,500	268,500
Accumulated depreciation—equipment	(85,400)	(66,100)
	$595,200	$567,700
Liabilities and Stockholders' Equity		
Accounts payable (merchandise creditors)	$125,100	$118,800
Mortgage note payable	0	168,000
Common stock, $1 par	24,000	12,000
Paid-in capital in excess of par—common stock	288,000	160,000
Retained earnings	158,100	108,900
	$595,200	$567,700

Additional data obtained from the income statement and from an examination of the accounts in the ledger for 2010 are as follows:

a. Net income, $126,000.
b. Depreciation reported on the income statement, $41,700.
c. Equipment was purchased at a cost of $81,400, and fully depreciated equipment costing $22,400 was discarded, with no salvage realized.
d. The mortgage note payable was not due until 2013, but the terms permitted earlier payment without penalty.
e. 7,000 shares of common stock were issued at $20 for cash.
f. Cash dividends declared and paid, $76,800.

Instructions
Prepare a statement of cash flows, using the indirect method of presenting cash flows from operating activities.

PR 16-3A
Statement of cash
flows—indirect
method

obj. 2

✔ Net cash flow
from operating
activities, ($92,000)

The comparative balance sheet of Putnam Cycle Co. at December 31, 2010 and 2009, is as follows:

	Dec. 31, 2010	Dec. 31, 2009
Assets		
Cash	$ 510,000	$ 536,000
Accounts receivable (net)	460,500	423,300
Inventories	704,700	646,100
Prepaid expenses	16,300	19,500
Land	175,500	266,500
Buildings	812,500	500,500
Accumulated depreciation—buildings	(227,000)	(212,400)
Equipment	284,600	252,600
Accumulated depreciation—equipment	(78,500)	(88,200)
	$2,658,600	$2,343,900
Liabilities and Stockholders' Equity		
Accounts payable (merchandise creditors)	$ 512,500	$ 532,400
Bonds payable	150,000	0
Common stock, $1 par	75,000	65,000
Paid-in capital in excess of par—common stock	520,000	310,000
Retained earnings	1,401,100	1,436,500
	$2,658,600	$2,343,900

The noncurrent asset, noncurrent liability, and stockholders' equity accounts for 2010 are as follows:

ACCOUNT *Land*   ACCOUNT NO.

Date		Item	Debit	Credit	Balance Debit	Balance Credit
2010						
Jan.	1	Balance			266,500	
Apr.	20	Realized $84,000 cash from sale		91,000	175,500	

ACCOUNT *Buildings*   ACCOUNT NO.

Date		Item	Debit	Credit	Balance Debit	Balance Credit
2010						
Jan.	1	Balance			500,500	
Apr.	20	Acquired for cash	312,000		812,500	

ACCOUNT *Accumulated Depreciation—Buildings*   ACCOUNT NO.

Date		Item	Debit	Credit	Balance Debit	Balance Credit
2010						
Jan.	1	Balance				212,400
Dec.	31	Depreciation for year		14,600		227,000

ACCOUNT *Equipment*   ACCOUNT NO.

Date		Item	Debit	Credit	Balance Debit	Balance Credit
2010						
Jan.	1	Balance			252,600	
	26	Discarded, no salvage		26,000	226,600	
Aug.	11	Purchased for cash	58,000		284,600	

ACCOUNT *Accumulated Depreciation—Equipment*   ACCOUNT NO.

Date		Item	Debit	Credit	Balance Debit	Balance Credit
2010						
Jan.	1	Balance				88,200
	26	Equipment discarded	26,000			62,200
Dec.	31	Depreciation for year		16,300		78,500

ACCOUNT *Bonds Payable*   ACCOUNT NO.

Date		Item	Debit	Credit	Balance Debit	Balance Credit
2010						
May	1	Issued 20-year bonds		150,000		150,000

ACCOUNT *Common Stock, $1 Par*   ACCOUNT NO.

Date		Item	Debit	Credit	Balance Debit	Balance Credit
2010						
Jan.	1	Balance				65,000
Dec.	7	Issued 10,000 shares of common stock for $22 per share		10,000		75,000

ACCOUNT *Paid-In Capital in Excess of Par—Common Stock*   ACCOUNT NO.

Date		Item	Debit	Credit	Balance Debit	Balance Credit
2010						
Jan.	1	Balance				310,000
Dec.	7	Issued 10,000 shares of common stock for $22 per share		210,000		520,000

ACCOUNT *Retained Earnings*   ACCOUNT NO.

Date		Item	Debit	Credit	Balance Debit	Balance Credit
2010						
Jan.	1	Balance				1,436,500
Dec.	31	Net loss	17,400			1,419,100
	31	Cash dividends	18,000			1,401,100

Instructions

Prepare a statement of cash flows, using the indirect method of presenting cash flows from operating activities.

PR 16-4A
Statement of cash flows—direct method

obj. 3

✔ Net cash flow from operating activities, $146,800

The comparative balance sheet of Rucker Photography Products Inc. for December 31, 2011 and 2010, is as follows:

	Dec. 31, 2011	Dec. 31, 2010
Assets		
Cash	$ 321,700	$ 339,700
Accounts receivable (net).	283,400	273,700
Inventories	505,500	491,400
Investments	0	120,000
Land	260,000	0
Equipment	440,000	340,000
Accumulated depreciation	(122,200)	(100,200)
	$1,688,400	$1,464,600

(continued)

Liabilities and Stockholders' Equity

Accounts payable (merchandise creditors)	$ 385,900	$ 374,200
Accrued expenses payable (operating expenses) . . .	31,700	35,400
Dividends payable	4,400	3,200
Common stock, $1 par	20,000	16,000
Paid-in capital in excess of par—common stock	208,000	96,000
Retained earnings	1,038,400	939,800
	$1,688,400	$1,464,600

The income statement for the year ended December 31, 2011, is as follows:

Sales		$2,990,000
Cost of merchandise sold		1,226,000
Gross profit		$1,764,000
Operating expenses:		
Depreciation expense	$ 22,000	
Other operating expenses	1,550,000	
Total operating expenses		1,572,000
Operating income		$ 192,000
Other expense:		
Loss on sale of investments		(32,000)
Income before income tax		$ 160,000
Income tax expense		51,400
Net income		$ 108,600

The following additional information was taken from the records:

a. Equipment and land were acquired for cash.
b. There were no disposals of equipment during the year.
c. The investments were sold for $88,000 cash.
d. The common stock was issued for cash.
e. There was a $10,000 debit to Retained Earnings for cash dividends declared.

Instructions

Prepare a statement of cash flows, using the direct method of presenting cash flows from operating activities.

PR 16-5A
Statement of cash flows—direct method applied to PR 16-1A

obj. 3

✔ Net cash flow from operating activities, $49,520

The comparative balance sheet of Mavenir Technologies Inc. for December 31, 2010 and 2009, is as follows:

	Dec. 31, 2010	Dec. 31, 2009
Assets		
Cash	$ 312,880	$ 292,960
Accounts receivable (net)	113,920	104,480
Inventories	320,880	308,560
Investments	0	120,000
Land	164,000	0
Equipment	352,560	276,560
Accumulated depreciation—equipment	(83,200)	(74,000)
	$1,181,040	$1,028,560
Liabilities and Stockholders' Equity		
Accounts payable (merchandise creditors)	$ 214,240	$ 202,480
Accrued expenses payable (operating expenses) . . .	21,120	26,320
Dividends payable	12,000	9,600
Common stock, $10 par	64,000	48,000
Paid-in capital in excess of par—common stock	240,000	140,000
Retained earnings	629,680	602,160
	$1,181,040	$1,028,560

The income statement for the year ended December 31, 2010, is as follows:

Sales		$1,950,699
Cost of merchandise sold		1,200,430
Gross profit		$ 750,269
Operating expenses:		
Depreciation expense	$ 9,200	
Other operating expenses	635,202	
Total operating expenses		644,402
Operating income		$ 105,867
Other income:		
Gain on sale of investments		20,000
Income before income tax		$ 125,867
Income tax expense		50,347
Net income		$ 75,520

The following additional information was taken from the records:

a. The investments were sold for $140,000 cash.
b. Equipment and land were acquired for cash.
c. There were no disposals of equipment during the year.
d. The common stock was issued for cash.
e. There was a $48,000 debit to Retained Earnings for cash dividends declared.

Instructions

Prepare a statement of cash flows, using the direct method of presenting cash flows from operating activities.

Problems Series B

PR 16-1B
Statement of cash flows—indirect method

obj. 2

✔ Net cash flow from operating activities, $86,600

The comparative balance sheet of House Construction Co. for June 30, 2010 and 2009, is as follows:

	June 30, 2010	June 30, 2009
Assets		
Cash	$ 41,600	$ 28,200
Accounts receivable (net)	121,900	110,700
Inventories	175,600	170,500
Investments	0	60,000
Land	174,000	0
Equipment	258,000	210,600
Accumulated depreciation	(58,300)	(49,600)
	$712,800	$530,400
Liabilities and Stockholders' Equity		
Accounts payable (merchandise creditors)	$121,000	$114,200
Accrued expenses payable (operating expenses)	18,000	15,800
Dividends payable	15,000	12,000
Common stock, $1 par	67,200	60,000
Paid-in capital in excess of par—common stock	264,000	120,000
Retained earnings	227,600	208,400
	$712,800	$530,400

The following additional information was taken from the records of House Construction Co.:

a. Equipment and land were acquired for cash.
b. There were no disposals of equipment during the year.
c. The investments were sold for $54,000 cash.
d. The common stock was issued for cash.
e. There was a $79,200 credit to Retained Earnings for net income.
f. There was a $60,000 debit to Retained Earnings for cash dividends declared.

Instructions

Prepare a statement of cash flows, using the indirect method of presenting cash flows from operating activities.

PR 16-2B
Statement of cash flows—indirect method

obj. 2

✔ Net cash flow from operating activities, $200,500

The comparative balance sheet of TorMax Technology, Inc., at December 31, 2010 and 2009, is as follows:

	Dec. 31, 2010	Dec. 31, 2009
Assets		
Cash	$ 158,300	$ 128,900
Accounts receivable (net)	237,600	211,500
Inventories	317,100	365,200
Prepaid expenses	11,300	9,000
Land	108,000	108,000
Buildings	612,000	405,000
Accumulated depreciation—buildings	(166,500)	(148,050)
Machinery and equipment	279,000	279,000
Accumulated depreciation—machinery & equipment	(76,500)	(68,400)
Patents	38,200	43,200
	$1,518,500	$1,333,350
Liabilities and Stockholders' Equity		
Accounts payable (merchandise creditors)	$ 299,100	$ 331,100
Dividends payable	11,700	9,000
Salaries payable	28,200	31,100
Mortgage note payable, due 2017	80,000	—
Bonds payable	—	140,000
Common stock, $1 par	23,000	18,000
Paid-in capital in excess of par—common stock	180,000	45,000
Retained earnings	896,500	759,150
	$1,518,500	$1,333,350

An examination of the income statement and the accounting records revealed the following additional information applicable to 2010:

a. Net income, $184,150.
b. Depreciation expense reported on the income statement: buildings, $18,450; machinery and equipment, $8,100.
c. Patent amortization reported on the income statement, $5,000.
d. A building was constructed for $207,000.
e. A mortgage note for $80,000 was issued for cash.
f. 5,000 shares of common stock were issued at $28 in exchange for the bonds payable.
g. Cash dividends declared, $46,800.

Instructions Prepare a statement of cash flows, using the indirect method of presenting cash flows from operating activities.

PR 16-3B
Statement of cash flows—indirect method

obj. 2

✔ Net cash flow from operating activities, $7,800

The comparative balance sheet of Cantor Industries, Inc., at December 31, 2010 and 2009, is as follows:

	Dec. 31, 2010	Dec. 31, 2009
Assets		
Cash	$ 50,100	$ 56,300
Accounts receivable (net)	117,400	101,600
Inventories	153,100	144,300
Prepaid expenses	3,100	4,400
Land	165,000	231,000
Buildings	330,000	165,000
Accumulated depreciation—buildings	(66,200)	(61,000)
Equipment	110,100	88,300
Accumulated depreciation—equipment	(22,200)	(27,000)
	$840,400	$702,900
Liabilities and Stockholders' Equity		
Accounts payable (merchandise creditors)	$ 99,000	$105,200
Income tax payable	4,400	3,600
Bonds payable	55,000	0
Common stock, $1 par	36,000	30,000
Paid-in capital in excess of par—common stock	195,000	135,000
Retained earnings	451,000	429,100
	$840,400	$702,900

The noncurrent asset, noncurrent liability, and stockholders' equity accounts for 2010 are as follows:

ACCOUNT *Land*   **ACCOUNT NO.**

Date		Item	Debit	Credit	Balance Debit	Balance Credit
2010						
Jan.	1	Balance			231,000	
Apr.	20	Realized $76,000 cash from sale		66,000	165,000	

ACCOUNT *Buildings*   **ACCOUNT NO.**

Date		Item	Debit	Credit	Balance Debit	Balance Credit
2010						
Jan.	1	Balance			165,000	
Apr.	20	Acquired for cash	165,000		330,000	

ACCOUNT *Accumulated Depreciation—Buildings*   **ACCOUNT NO.**

Date		Item	Debit	Credit	Balance Debit	Balance Credit
2010						
Jan.	1	Balance				61,000
Dec.	31	Depreciation for year		5,200		66,200

ACCOUNT *Equipment*   **ACCOUNT NO.**

Date		Item	Debit	Credit	Balance Debit	Balance Credit
2010						
Jan.	1	Balance			88,300	
	26	Discarded, no salvage		11,000	77,300	
Aug.	11	Purchased for cash	32,800		110,100	

ACCOUNT *Accumulated Depreciation—Equipment*   **ACCOUNT NO.**

Date		Item	Debit	Credit	Balance Debit	Balance Credit
2010						
Jan.	1	Balance				27,000
	26	Equipment discarded	11,000			16,000
Dec.	31	Depreciation for year		6,200		22,200

ACCOUNT *Bonds Payable*   **ACCOUNT NO.**

Date		Item	Debit	Credit	Balance Debit	Balance Credit
2010						
May	1	Issued 20-year bonds		55,000		55,000

ACCOUNT Common Stock, $1 par

ACCOUNT NO.

Date		Item	Debit	Credit	Balance Debit	Balance Credit
2010						
Jan.	1	Balance				30,000
Dec.	7	Issued 6,000 shares of common stock for $11 per share		6,000		36,000

ACCOUNT Paid-In Capital in Excess of Par—Common Stock

ACCOUNT NO.

Date		Item	Debit	Credit	Balance Debit	Balance Credit
2010						
Jan.	1	Balance				135,000
Dec.	7	Issued 6,000 shares of common stock for $11 per share		60,000		195,000

ACCOUNT Retained Earnings

ACCOUNT NO.

Date		Item	Debit	Credit	Balance Debit	Balance Credit
2010						
Jan.	1	Balance				429,100
Dec.	31	Net income		35,100		464,200
	31	Cash dividends	13,200			451,000

Instructions

Prepare a statement of cash flows, using the indirect method of presenting cash flows from operating activities.

PR 16-4B
Statement of cash flows—direct method
obj. 3

✔ Net cash flow from operating activities, $169,740

The comparative balance sheet of Lim Garden Supplies Inc. for December 31, 2010 and 2011, is as follows:

	Dec. 31, 2011	Dec. 31, 2010
Assets		
Cash	$ 220,640	$ 227,700
Accounts receivable (net).	330,880	304,800
Inventories	464,800	454,600
Investments	0	144,000
Land	320,000	0
Equipment	408,000	328,000
Accumulated depreciation	(160,500)	(122,800)
	$1,583,820	$1,336,300
Liabilities and Stockholders' Equity		
Accounts payable (merchandise creditors)	$ 360,000	$ 322,200
Accrued expenses payable (operating expenses) . . .	22,600	26,400
Dividends payable	33,600	30,400
Common stock, ...	16,000	8,000
Paid-in capital in excess of par—common stock	320,000	160,000
Retained earnings	831,620	789,300
	$1,583,820	$1,336,300

The income statement for the year ended December 31, 2011, is as follows:

Sales	$1,504,000
Cost of merchandise sold	784,000
Gross profit	$ 720,000
Operating expenses:	
Depreciation expense . . . . $ 37,700	
Other operating expenses 448,280	
Total operating expenses	485,980
Operating income	$ 234,020
Other income:	
Gain on sale of investments	52,000
Income before income tax	$ 286,020
Income tax expense	99,700
Net income	$ 186,320

The following additional information was taken from the records:

a. Equipment and land were acquired for cash.
b. There were no disposals of equipment during the year.
c. The investments were sold for $196,000 cash.
d. The common stock was issued for cash.
e. There was a $144,000 debit to Retained Earnings for cash dividends declared.

Instructions Prepare a statement of cash flows, using the direct method of presenting cash flows from operating activities.

PR 16-5B
Statement of cash flows—direct method applied to PR 16-1B

obj. 3

✔ Net cash flow from operating activities, $86,600

The comparative balance sheet of House Construction Co. for June 30, 2010 and 2009, is as follows:

	June 30, 2010	June 30, 2009
Assets		
Cash	$ 41,600	$ 28,200
Accounts receivable (net).	121,900	110,700
Inventories	175,600	170,500
Investments	0	60,000
Land	174,000	0
Equipment	258,000	210,600
Accumulated depreciation	(58,300)	(49,600)
	$712,800	$530,400
Liabilities and Stockholders' Equity		
Accounts payable (merchandise creditors)	$121,000	$114,200
Accrued expenses payable (operating expenses) . . .	18,000	15,800
Dividends payable	15,000	12,000
Common stock, $1 par	67,200	60,000
Paid-in capital in excess of par—common stock	264,000	120,000
Retained earnings	227,600	208,400
	$712,800	$530,400

The income statement for the year ended June 30, 2010, is as follows:

Sales	$1,134,900
Cost of merchandise sold	698,400
Gross profit	$ 436,500
Operating expenses:	
Depreciation expense . . . . $ 8,700	
Other operating expenses 289,800	
Total operating expenses	298,500
Operating income	$ 138,000
Other expenses:	
Loss on sale of investments	(6,000)
Income before income tax	$ 132,000
Income tax expense	52,800
Net income	$ 79,200

The following additional information was taken from the records:

a. Equipment and land were acquired for cash.
b. There were no disposals of equipment during the year.
c. The investments were sold for $54,000 cash.
d. The common stock was issued for cash.
e. There was a $60,000 debit to Retained Earnings for cash dividends declared.

Instructions Prepare a statement of cash flows, using the direct method of presenting cash flows from operating activities.

Special Activities

You can access the special activities online at **www.cengage.com/accounting/reeve**.

Excel Success Special Activities

SA 16-1
Cash flow from operating activities

Omar Company had the following selected income statement information for the year ended December 31, 2011:

Net income	$310,000
Depreciation expense	48,000
Loss on sale of land	21,000

Comparative noncash current assets and current liabilities for December 31, 2011, and 2010, are as follows:

	2011	2010
Accounts receivable	132,400	145,200
Inventories	256,000	231,900
Accounts payable	194,600	209,800
Accrued expenses	89,200	94,200
Interest payable	24,500	20,000

a. Open the Excel file *SA16-1*.
b. Use your spreadsheet to prepare the cash flows from operating activities section of the statement of cash flows.
c. When you have completed the section, perform a "save as," replacing the entire file name with the following:

   SA16-1_[your first name initial]_[your last name]

SA 16-2
Cash flow from operating activities

Troy Company had the following selected income statement information for the year ended December 31, 2011:

Net income	$79,000
Amortization expense	14,500
Gain on sale of land	5,600

Comparative noncash current assets and current liabilities at the end of the two latest years are as follows:

	2011	2010
Accounts receivable	57,300	68,900
Inventories	42,100	47,300
Prepaid expenses	12,300	10,100
Accounts payable	37,900	35,100
Accrued expenses	21,500	24,600
Income taxes payable	15,400	13,200

Use your spreadsheet to prepare the cash flows from operating activities section of the statement of cash flows.

a. Open the Excel file *SA16-2.*
b. Use your spreadsheet to prepare the cash flows from operating activities section of the statement of cash flows.
c. When you have completed the section, perform a "save as," replacing the entire file name with the following:

SA16-2_[your first name initial]_[your last name]

SA 16-3
Cash flow from operating activities

The income statement for the McIntyre Company is as follows for the year ended December 31, 2011:

McIntyre Company
Income Statement
For the Year Ended December 31, 2011

Sales	$325,000
Cost of merchandise sold	143,000
Gross profit	$182,000
Operating expenses:	
Salaries expense	$45,600
Sales expenses	34,100
Depreciation expense	13,200
Total operating expenses	92,900
Income from operations	$ 89,100
Other expense	
Loss on sale of investments	22,000
Income before income tax	$ 67,100
Income tax expense	25,000
Net income	$ 42,100

Increases and decreases in noncash current assets and liabilities for the comparative balances sheets dated December 31, 2011 and 2010, are as follows:

	Increase/(Decrease)
Accounts receivable	$ (2,900)
Inventories	5,800
Prepaid expenses	(2,100)
Accounts payable	(12,400)
Accrued expenses	(3,400)
Income taxes payable	1,500

a. Open the Excel file *SA16-3.*
b. Use your spreadsheet to prepare the cash flows from operating activities section of the statement of cash flows.
c. When you have completed the section, perform a "save as," replacing the entire file name with the following:

SA16-3_[your first name initial]_[your last name]

Answers to Self-Examination Questions ● ● ● ●

1. **D** Cash flows from operating activities affect transactions that enter into the determination of net income, such as the receipt of cash from customers on account (answer D). Receipts of cash from the sale of stock (answer A) and the sale of bonds (answer B) and payments of cash for dividends (answer C) are cash flows from financing activities.

2. **A** Cash flows from investing activities include receipts from the sale of noncurrent assets, such as equipment (answer A), and payments to acquire noncurrent assets. Receipts of cash from the sale of stock (answer B) and payments of cash for dividends (answer C) and to acquire treasury stock (answer D) are cash flows from financing activities.

3. **C** Payment of cash for dividends (answer C) is an example of a financing activity. The receipt of cash from customers on account (answer A) is an operating activity. The receipt of cash from the sale of equipment (answer B) is an investing

activity. The payment of cash to acquire land (answer D) is an example of an investing activity.

4. **D** The indirect method (answer D) reports cash flows from operating activities by beginning with net income and adjusting it for revenues and expenses not involving the receipt or payment of cash.

5. **C** The Cash Flows from Operating Activities section of the statement of cash flows would report net cash flow from operating activities of $65,500, determined as follows:

Cash flows from operating activities:

Net income		$55,000
Adjustments to reconcile net income to net cash flow from operating activities:		
Depreciation		22,000
Changes in current operating assets and liabilities:		
Increase in accounts receivable		(10,000)
Decrease in inventories		5,000
Decrease in prepaid expenses		500
Decrease in accounts payable		(7,000)
Net cash flow from operating activities		$65,500

Financial Statement Analysis

© AP Photo/Matt York

N I K E ,   I N C.

"**J**ust do it." These three words identify one of the most recognizable brands in the world, Nike. While this phrase inspires athletes to "compete and achieve their potential," it also defines the company.

Nike began in 1964 as a partnership between University of Oregon track coach Bill Bowerman and one of his former student-athletes, Phil Knight. The two began by selling shoes imported from Japan out of the back of Knight's car to athletes at track and field events. As sales grew, the company opened retail outlets and began to develop its own shoes. In 1971 the company, originally named Blue Ribbon Sports, commissioned a graphic design student at Portland State University to develop the Nike Swoosh logo for a fee of $35. In 1978 the company changed its name to Nike, and in 1980, it sold its first shares of stock to the public.

Nike would have been a great company in which to have invested. If you had invested in Nike's common stock back in 1990, you would have paid $5.00 per share. Today Nike's stock sells for $56.75 per share. Unfortunately, you can't invest using hindsight.

How then should you select companies to invest in? Like any significant purchase, you should do some research to guide your investment decision. If you were buying a car, for example, you might go to Edmunds.com to obtain reviews, ratings, prices, specifications, options, and fuel economy across a number of vehicles. In deciding whether to invest in a company, you can use financial analysis to gain insight into a company's past performance and future prospects. This chapter describes and illustrates common financial data that can be analyzed to assist you in making investment decisions such as whether or not to invest in Nike's stock.

Source: http://www.nikebiz.com/

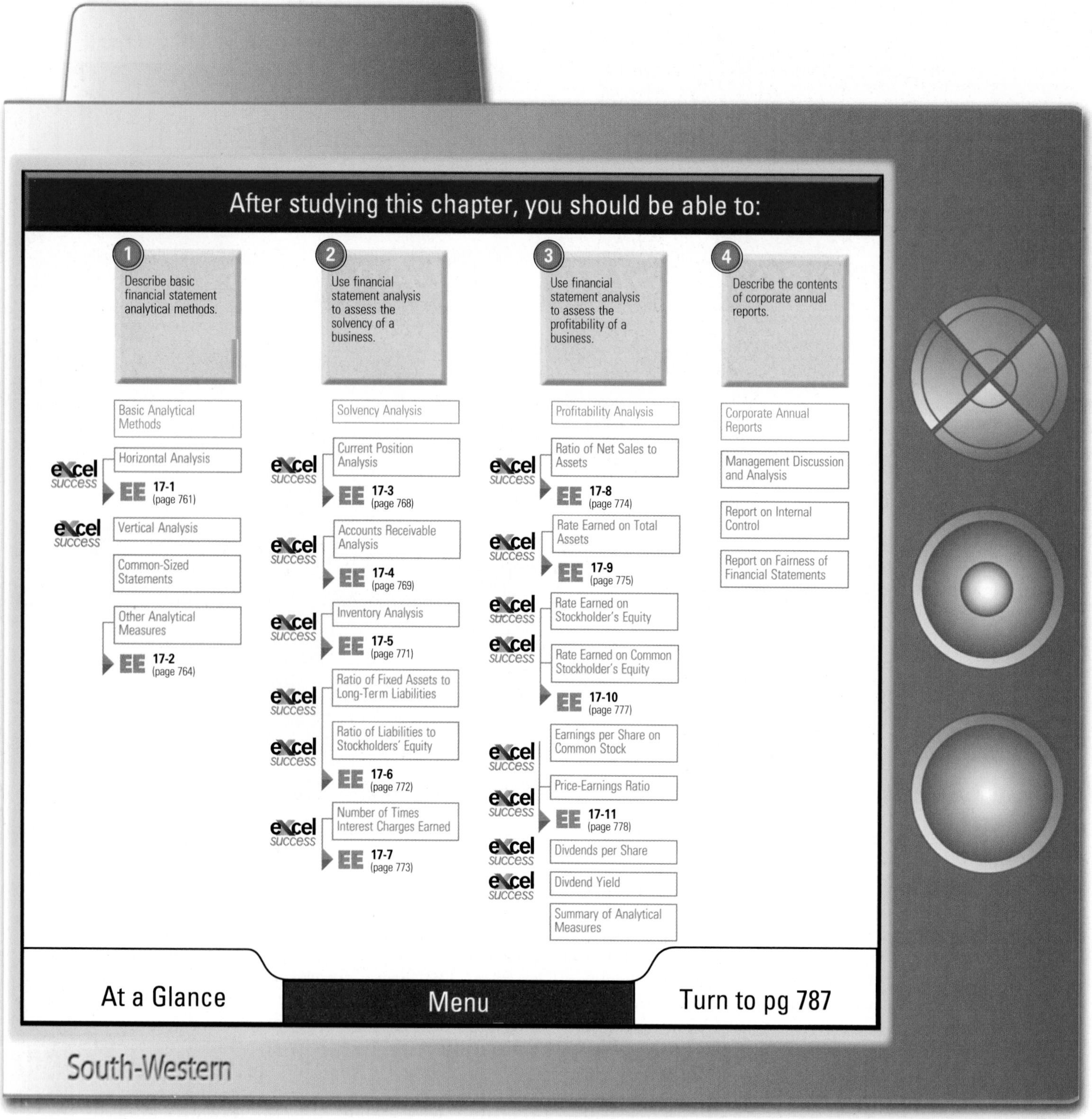

After studying this chapter, you should be able to:

1 Describe basic financial statement analytical methods.

Basic Analytical Methods

Horizontal Analysis

excel success
EE 17-1 (page 761)

Vertical Analysis

Common-Sized Statements

Other Analytical Measures

EE 17-2 (page 764)

2 Use financial statement analysis to assess the solvency of a business.

Solvency Analysis

Current Position Analysis

excel success
EE 17-3 (page 768)

Accounts Receivable Analysis

excel success
EE 17-4 (page 769)

Inventory Analysis

excel success
EE 17-5 (page 771)

Ratio of Fixed Assets to Long-Term Liabilities

excel success

Ratio of Liabilities to Stockholders' Equity

excel success
EE 17-6 (page 772)

Number of Times Interest Charges Earned

excel success
EE 17-7 (page 773)

3 Use financial statement analysis to assess the profitability of a business.

Profitability Analysis

Ratio of Net Sales to Assets

excel success
EE 17-8 (page 774)

Rate Earned on Total Assets

excel success
EE 17-9 (page 775)

Rate Earned on Stockholder's Equity

Rate Earned on Common Stockholder's Equity

EE 17-10 (page 777)

Earnings per Share on Common Stock

Price-Earnings Ratio

excel success
EE 17-11 (page 778)

Divdends per Share

excel success

Divdend Yield

excel success

Summary of Analytical Measures

4 Describe the contents of corporate annual reports.

Corporate Annual Reports

Management Discussion and Analysis

Report on Internal Control

Report on Fairness of Financial Statements

At a Glance | Menu | Turn to pg 787

South-Western

1 Describe basic financial statement analytical methods.

Basic Analytical Methods

Users analyze a company's financial statements using a variety of analytical methods. Three such methods are as follows:

1. Horizontal analysis
2. Vertical analysis
3. Common-sized statements

Horizontal Analysis

The percentage analysis of increases and decreases in related items in comparative financial statements is called **horizontal analysis**. Each item on the most recent statement is compared with the related item on one or more earlier statements in terms of the following:

1.   *Amount* of increase or decrease.
2.   *Percent* of increase or decrease.

When comparing statements, the earlier statement is normally used as the base for computing increases and decreases.

Exhibit 1 illustrates horizontal analysis for the December 31, 2010 and 2009, balance sheets of Lincoln Company. In Exhibit 1, the December 31, 2009, balance sheet (the earliest year presented) is used as the base.

Exhibit 1

Comparative Balance Sheet— Horizontal Analysis

Lincoln Company
Comparative Balance Sheet
December 31, 2010 and 2009

	Dec. 31, 2010	Dec. 31, 2009	Increase (Decrease) Amount	Increase (Decrease) Percent
Assets				
Current assets	$ 550,000	$ 533,000	$ 17,000	3.2%
Long-term investments	95,000	177,500	(82,500)	(46.5%)
Property, plant, and equipment (net)	444,500	470,000	(25,500)	(5.4%)
Intangible assets	50,000	50,000	—	—
Total assets	$1,139,500	$1,230,500	$ (91,000)	(7.4%)
Liabilities				
Current liabilities	$ 210,000	$ 243,000	$ (33,000)	(13.6%)
Long-term liabilities	100,000	200,000	(100,000)	(50.0%)
Total liabilities	$ 310,000	$ 443,000	$(133,000)	(30.0%)
Stockholders' Equity				
Preferred 6% stock, $100 par	$ 150,000	$ 150,000	—	—
Common stock, $10 par	500,000	500,000	—	—
Retained earnings	179,500	137,500	$ 42,000	30.5%
Total stockholders' equity	$ 829,500	$ 787,500	$ 42,000	5.3%
Total liabilities and stockholders' equity	$1,139,500	$1,230,500	$ (91,000)	(7.4%)

Exhibit 1 indicates that total assets decreased by $91,000 (7.4%), liabilities decreased by $133,000 (30.0%), and stockholders' equity increased by $42,000 (5.3%). It appears that most of the decrease in long-term liabilities of $100,000 was achieved through the sale of long-term investments.

The balance sheets in Exhibit 1 may be expanded or supported by a separate schedule that includes the individual asset and liability accounts. For example, Exhibit 2 is a supporting schedule of Lincoln's current asset accounts.

Exhibit 2 indicates that while cash and temporary investments increased, accounts receivable and inventories decreased. The decrease in accounts receivable could be caused by improved collection policies, which would increase cash. The decrease in inventories could be caused by increased sales.

Exhibit 2

Comparative Schedule of Current Assets— Horizontal Analysis

Lincoln Company
Comparative Schedule of Current Assets
December 31, 2010 and 2009

	Dec. 31, 2010	Dec. 31, 2009	Increase (Decrease) Amount	Percent
Cash	$ 90,500	$ 64,700	$ 25,800	39.9%
Temporary investments	75,000	60,000	15,000	25.0%
Accounts receivable (net)	115,000	120,000	(5,000)	(4.2%)
Inventories	264,000	283,000	(19,000)	(6.7%)
Prepaid expenses	5,500	5,300	200	3.8%
Total current assets	$550,000	$533,000	$ 17,000	3.2%

Exhibit 3 illustrates horizontal analysis for the 2010 and 2009 income statements of Lincoln Company. Exhibit 3 indicates an increase in sales of $296,500, or 24.0%. However, the percentage increase in sales of 24.0% was accompanied by an even greater percentage increase in the cost of goods (merchandise) sold of 27.2%.[1] Thus, gross profit increased by only 19.7% rather than by the 24.0% increase in sales.

Exhibit 3

Comparative Income Statement— Horizontal Analysis

Lincoln Company
Comparative Income Statement
For the Years Ended December 31, 2010 and 2009

	2010	2009	Increase (Decrease) Amount	Percent
Sales	$1,530,500	$1,234,000	$296,500	24.0%
Sales returns and allowances	32,500	34,000	(1,500)	(4.4%)
Net sales	$1,498,000	$1,200,000	$298,000	24.8%
Cost of goods sold	1,043,000	820,000	223,000	27.2%
Gross profit	$ 455,000	$ 380,000	$ 75,000	19.7%
Selling expenses	$ 191,000	$ 147,000	$ 44,000	29.9%
Administrative expenses	104,000	97,400	6,600	6.8%
Total operating expenses	$ 295,000	$ 244,400	$ 50,600	20.7%
Income from operations	$ 160,000	$ 135,600	$ 24,400	18.0%
Other income	8,500	11,000	(2,500)	(22.7%)
	$ 168,500	$ 146,600	$ 21,900	14.9%
Other expense (interest)	6,000	12,000	(6,000)	(50.0%)
Income before income tax	$ 162,500	$ 134,600	$ 27,900	20.7%
Income tax expense	71,500	58,100	13,400	23.1%
Net income	$ 91,000	$ 76,500	$ 14,500	19.0%

1 The term *cost of goods sold* is often used in practice in place of *cost of merchandise sold.* Such usage is followed in this chapter.

Exhibit 3 also indicates that selling expenses increased by 29.9%. Thus, the 24.0% increases in sales could have been caused by an advertising campaign, which increased selling expenses. Administrative expenses increased by only 6.8%, total operating expenses increased by 20.7%, and income from operations increased by 18.0%. Interest expense decreased by 50.0%. This decrease was probably caused by the 50.0% decrease in long-term liabilities (Exhibit 1). Overall, net income increased by 19.0%, a favorable result.

Exhibit 4 illustrates horizontal analysis for the 2010 and 2009 retained earnings statements of Lincoln Company. Exhibit 4 indicates that retained earnings increased by 30.5% for the year. The increase is due to net income of $91,000 for the year, less dividends of $49,000.

Exhibit 4

Comparative Retained Earnings Statement— Horizontal Analysis

Lincoln Company
Comparative Retained Earnings Statement
For the Years Ended December 31, 2010 and 2009

	2010	2009	Increase (Decrease) Amount	Increase (Decrease) Percent
Retained earnings, January 1	$ 137,500	$100,000	$ 37,500	37.5%
Net income for the year	91,000	76,500	14,500	19.0%
Total	$228,500	$176,500	$52,000	29.5%
Dividends:				
On preferred stock	$ 9,000	$ 9,000	—	—
On common stock	40,000	30,000	$10,000	33.3%
Total	$ 49,000	$ 39,000	$10,000	25.6%
Retained earnings, December 31	$179,500	$ 137,500	$42,000	30.5%

Example Exercise 17-1   Horizontal Analysis   ⟩ 1

The comparative cash and accounts receivable balances for a company are provided below.

	Dec. 31, 2010	Dec. 31, 2009
Cash	$62,500	$50,000
Accounts receivable (net)	74,400	80,000

Based on this information, what is the amount and percentage of increase or decrease that would be shown in a balance sheet with horizontal analysis?

Follow My Example 17-1

Cash	$12,500 increase ($62,500 − $50,000), or 25%
Accounts receivable	$5,600 decrease ($74,400 − $80,000), or (7%)

For Practice: PE 17-1A, PE 17-1B

Vertical Analysis

The percentage analysis of the relationship of each component in a financial statement to a total within the statement is called **vertical analysis**. Although vertical analysis is applied to a single statement, it may be applied on the same statement over time. This enhances the analysis by showing how the percentages of each item have changed over time.

In vertical analysis of the balance sheet, the percentages are computed as follows:

1. Each asset item is stated as a percent of the total assets.
2. Each liability and stockholders' equity item is stated as a percent of the total liabilities and stockholders' equity.

Exhibit 5 illustrates the vertical analysis of the December 31, 2010 and 2009, balance sheets of Lincoln Company. Exhibit 5 indicates that current assets have increased from 43.3% to 48.3% of total assets. Long-term investments decreased from 14.4% to 8.3% of total assets. Stockholders' equity increased from 64.0% to 72.8% with a comparable decrease in liabilities.

Exhibit 5

Comparative Balance Sheet— Vertical Analysis

Lincoln Company
Comparative Balance Sheet
December 31, 2010 and 2009

	Dec. 31, 2010		Dec. 31, 2009	
	Amount	Percent	Amount	Percent
Assets				
Current assets	$ 550,000	48.3%	$ 533,000	43.3%
Long-term investments	95,000	8.3	177,500	14.4
Property, plant, and equipment (net)	444,500	39.0	470,000	38.2
Intangible assets	50,000	4.4	50,000	4.1
Total assets	$1,139,500	100.0%	$1,230,500	100.0%
Liabilities				
Current liabilities	$ 210,000	18.4%	$ 243,000	19.7%
Long-term liabilities	100,000	8.8	200,000	16.3
Total liabilities	$ 310,000	27.2%	$ 443,000	36.0%
Stockholders' Equity				
Preferred 6% stock, $100 par	$ 150,000	13.2%	$ 150,000	12.2%
Common stock, $10 par	500,000	43.9	500,000	40.6
Retained earnings	179,500	15.7	137,500	11.2
Total stockholders' equity	$ 829,500	72.8%	$ 787,500	64.0%
Total liabilities and stockholders' equity	$1,139,500	100.0%	$1,230,500	100.0%

In a vertical analysis of the income statement, each item is stated as a percent of net sales. Exhibit 6 illustrates the vertical analysis of the 2010 and 2009 income statements of Lincoln Company.

Exhibit 6 indicates a decrease of the gross profit rate from 31.7% in 2009 to 30.4% in 2010. Although this is only a 1.3 percentage point (31.7% − 30.4%) decrease, in dollars of potential gross profit, it represents a decrease of about $19,500 (1.3% × $1,498,000). Thus, a small percentage decrease can have a large dollar effect.

Common-Sized Statements

In a **common-sized statement**, all items are expressed as percentages with no dollar amounts shown. Common-sized statements are often useful for comparing one company with another or for comparing a company with industry averages.

Exhibit 6

Comparative Income Statement— Vertical Analysis

Lincoln Company
Comparative Income Statement
For the Years Ended December 31, 2010 and 2009

	2010		2009	
	Amount	Percent	Amount	Percent
Sales	$1,530,500	102.2%	$1,234,000	102.8%
Sales returns and allowances	32,500	2.2	34,000	2.8
Net sales	$1,498,000	100.0%	$1,200,000	100.0%
Cost of goods sold	1,043,000	69.6	820,000	68.3
Gross profit	$ 455,000	30.4%	$ 380,000	31.7%
Selling expenses	$ 191,000	12.8%	$ 147,000	12.3%
Administrative expenses	104,000	6.9	97,400	8.1
Total operating expenses	$ 295,000	19.7%	$ 244,400	20.4%
Income from operations	$ 160,000	10.7%	$ 135,600	11.3%
Other income	8,500	0.6	11,000	0.9
	$ 168,500	11.3%	$ 146,600	12.2%
Other expense (interest)	6,000	0.4	12,000	1.0
Income before income tax	$ 162,500	10.9%	$ 134,600	11.2%
Income tax expense	71,500	4.8	58,100	4.8
Net income	$ 91,000	6.1%	$ 76,500	6.4%

Exhibit 7 illustrates common-sized income statements for Lincoln Company and Madison Corporation. Exhibit 7 indicates that Lincoln Company has a slightly higher rate of gross profit (30.4%) than Madison Corporation (30.0%). However, Lincoln has a higher percentage of selling expenses (12.8%) and administrative expenses (6.9%) than does Madison (11.5% and 4.1%). As a result, the income from operations of Lincoln (10.7%) is less than that of Madison (14.4%).

The unfavorable difference of 3.7 (14.4% − 10.7%) percentage points in income from operations would concern the managers and other stakeholders of Lincoln. The underlying causes of the difference should be investigated and possibly corrected. For example, Lincoln Company may decide to outsource some of its administrative duties so that its administrative expenses are more comparative to that of Madison Corporation.

Exhibit 7

Common-Sized Income Statement

	Lincoln Company	Madison Corporation
Sales	102.2%	102.3%
Sales returns and allowances	2.2	2.3
Net sales	100.0%	100.0%
Cost of goods sold	69.6	70.0
Gross profit	30.4%	30.0%
Selling expenses	12.8%	11.5%
Administrative expenses	6.9	4.1
Total operating expenses	19.7%	15.6%
Income from operations	10.7%	14.4%
Other income	0.6	0.6
	11.3%	15.0%
Other expense (interest)	0.4	0.5
Income before income tax	10.9%	14.5%
Income tax expense	4.8	5.5
Net income	6.1%	9.0%

All of the analyses illustrated in this objective are well suited to a spreadsheet solution approach because of the repetitive calculations across rows and columns. However, for brevity we will illustrate only the vertical analysis of comparative income statements. The formulas are as follows:

a.   b.

	A	B	C	D	E	F
1		Lincoln Company				
2		Comparative Income Statement				
3		For the Years Ended December 31, 2010 and 2009				
4						
5		2010			2009	
6		Amount	Percent		Amount	Percent
7	Sales	$ 1,530,500	=B7/B$9		$ 1,234,000	=E7/E$9
8	Sales returns and allowances	32,500	=B8/B$9		34,000	=E8/E$9
9	Net sales	=B7-B8	=B9/B$9		=E7-E8	=E9/E$9
10	Cost of goods sold	1,043,000	=B10/B$9		820,000	=E10/E$9
11	Gross profit	=B9-B10	=B11/B$9		=E9-E10	=E11/E$9
12	Selling expenses	191,000	=B12/B$9		147,000	=E12/E$9
13	Administrative expenses	104,000	=B13/B$9		97,400	=E13/E$9
14	Total operating expenses	=B12+B13	=B14/B$9		=E12+E13	=E14/E$9
15	Income from operations	=B11-B14	=B15/B$9		=E11-E14	=E15/E$9
16	Other income	8,500	=B16/B$9		11,000	=E16/E$9
17		=B15+B16	=B17/B$9		=E15+E16	=E17/E$9
18	Other expense (interest)	6,000	=B18/B$9		12,000	=E18/E$9
19	Income before income tax	=B17-B18	=B19/B$9		=E17-E18	=E19/E$9
20	Income tax expense	71,500	=B20/B$9		58,100	=E20/E$9
21	Net Income	=B19-B20	=B21/B$9		=E19-E20	=E21/E$9

c.   c.

a. Enter the formulas for the sub-totals and totals within the income statement at appropriate cell locations, such as B9. The formulas entered in column B can be copied into the adjacent cell location in column E, one-by-one, to save time. For example, the formula in B9 can be copied to E9; B11 copied to E11; and so on.

b. Insert the formula in cell C7 for the vertical percentage computation, =B7/B$9. The absolute cell address ($ sign) is placed in front of the row 9 number. This is because the sales denominator remains fixed when the formula is copied across the rows.

c. Copy the formula in cell C7 to C8:C21 and F7:F21. Column C and F calculations are formatted as a percent with one decimal place.

 Go to the hands-on *Excel Tutor* for this example!
(Note: The example here and throughout this chapter are contained in a **single** tutorial.)

 This Excel Success example uses an Excel function referred to as cell referencing. Go to the *Excel Tutor* titled **Absolute & Relative Cell References** for additional help with this useful Excel function!

Example Exercise 17-2   Vertical Analysis   ••••••••> ①

Income statement information for Lee Corporation is provided below.

Sales	$100,000
Cost of goods sold	65,000
Gross profit	$ 35,000

Prepare a vertical analysis of the income statement for Lee Corporation.

Follow My Example 17-2

	Amount	Percentage	
Sales	$100,000	100%	($100,000 ÷ $100,000)
Cost of goods sold	65,000	65	($65,000 ÷ $100,000)
Gross profit	$ 35,000	35%	($35,000 ÷ $100,000)

For Practice: PE 17-2A, PE 17-2B

Other Analytical Measures

Other relationships may be expressed in ratios and percentages. Often, these relationships are compared within the same statement and, thus, are a type of vertical analysis. Comparing these items with items from earlier periods is a type of horizontal analysis.

Analytical measures are not ends in themselves. They are only guides in evaluating financial and operating data. Many other factors, such as trends in the industry and general economic conditions, should also be considered when analyzing a company.

Solvency Analysis

2 Use financial statement analysis to assess the solvency of a business.

All users of financial statements are interested in the ability of a company to do the following:

1. Meet its financial obligations (debts), called **solvency**
2. Earn income, called **profitability**

Solvency and profitability are interrelated. For example, a company that cannot pay its debts will have difficulty obtaining credit. A lack of credit will, in turn, limit the company's ability to purchase merchandise or expand operations, which decreases its profitability.

Solvency analysis focuses on the ability of a company to pay its liabilities. It is normally assessed using the following:

One popular printed source for industry ratios is *Annual Statement Studies* from Risk Management Association. Online analysis is available from Zacks Investment Research site, which is linked to the text's Web site at **www.cengage.com/accounting/reeve**.

1. Current position analysis
    Working capital
    Current ratio
    Quick ratio

2. Accounts receivable analysis
    Accounts receivable turnover
    Number of days' sales in receivables

3. Inventory analysis
    Inventory turnover
    Number of days' sales in inventory

4. The ratio of fixed assets to long-term liabilities

5. The ratio of liabilities to stockholders' equity

6. The number of times interest charges are earned

The Lincoln Company financial statements presented earlier are used to illustrate the preceding analyses.

Current Position Analysis

A company's ability to pay its current liabilities is called **current position analysis**. It is of special interest to short-term creditors and includes the computation and analysis of the following:

1. Working capital
2. Current ratio
3. Quick ratio

Working Capital A company's **working capital** is computed as follows:

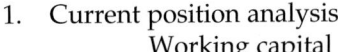

Working Capital = Current Assets − Current Liabilities

To illustrate, the working capital for Lincoln Company for 2010 and 2009 is computed below.

	2010	2009
Current assets	$550,000	$533,000
Less current liabilities	210,000	243,000
Working capital	$340,000	$290,000

The working capital is used to evaluate a company's ability to pay current liabilities. A company's working capital is often monitored monthly, quarterly, or yearly by creditors and other debtors. However, it is difficult to use working capital to compare companies of different sizes. For example, working capital of $250,000 may be adequate for a local hardware store, but it would be inadequate for The Home Depot.

Current Ratio The **current ratio**, sometimes called the *working capital ratio or banker's ratio*, is computed as follows:

$$\text{Current Ratio} = \frac{\text{Current Assets}}{\text{Current Liabilities}}$$

To illustrate, the current ratio for Lincoln Company is computed below.

	2010	2009
Current assets	$550,000	$533,000
Current liabilities	$210,000	$243,000
Current ratio	2.6 ($550,000/$210,000)	2.2 ($533,000/$243,000)

The current ratio is a more reliable indicator of the ability to pay current liabilities than is working capital. To illustrate, assume that as of December 31, 2010, the working capital of a competitor is much greater than $340,000, but its current ratio is only 1.3. Considering these facts alone, Lincoln Company, with its current ratio of 2.6, is in a more favorable position to obtain short-term credit than the competitor, which has the greater amount of working capital.

excel *SUCCESS*

The ratios illustrated in the chapter can all be computed using spreadsheet software. To simplify, we will illustrate only the use of spreadsheet software for the current ratio and rate earned on total assets in this chapter. At the end of the chapter a comprehensive spreadsheet illustration is provided to show the calculations of all of the ratios using spreadsheet software. The working capital and current ratio can be computed using spreadsheet software as follows:

	A	B	C
1	Inputs:		
2		2010	2009
3	Current assets	$ 550,000	$ 533,000
4	Current liabilities	210,000	243,000
5			
6	Outputs		
7	Working capital	=B3-B4	=C3-C4	→ a.
8			
9	Current ratio	=B3/B4	=C3/C4	→ b.
10			

The two calculations in column B can be copied simultaneously (B7:B9 to C7:C9) rather than copying one at a time.

The inputs could be the financial statements or a section of the financial statements. Here we illustrate just two separate lines, current assets and current liabilities. The outputs are two analyses, working capital and the current ratio.

a.   Enter the formula for working capital in B7, =B3-B4, then copy to C7.

b.   Enter the formula for the current ratio in B9, =B3/B4, then copy to C9.

      Format this ratio with one decimal place.

tr*it*   Go to the hands-on **Excel Tutor** for this example!
(Note: The example here and throughout this chapter are contained in a **single** tutorial.)

Quick Ratio One limitation of working capital and the current ratio is that they do not consider the makeup of the current assets. Because of this, two companies may have the same working capital and current ratios, but differ significantly in their ability to pay their current liabilities.

To illustrate, the current assets and liabilities for Lincoln Company and Jefferson Corporation as of December 31, 2010, are as follows:

	Lincoln Company	Jefferson Corporation
Current assets:		
Cash	$ 90,500	$ 45,500
Temporary investments	75,000	25,000
Accounts receivable (net)	115,000	90,000
Inventories	264,000	380,000
Prepaid expenses	5,500	9,500
Total current assets	$550,000	$550,000
Total current assets	$550,000	$550,000
Less current liabilities	210,000	210,000
Working capital	$340,000	$340,000
Current ratio ($550,000/$210,000)	2.6	2.6

Lincoln and Jefferson both have a working capital of $340,000 and current ratios of 2.6. Jefferson, however, has more of its current assets in inventories. These inventories must be sold and the receivables collected before all the current liabilities can be paid. This takes time. In addition, if the market for its product declines, Jefferson may have difficulty selling its inventory. This, in turn, could impair its ability to pay its current liabilities.

In contrast, Lincoln's current assets contain more cash, temporary investments, and accounts receivable, which can easily be converted to cash. Thus, Lincoln is in a stronger current position than Jefferson to pay its current liabilities.

A ratio that measures the "instant" debt-paying ability of a company is the **quick ratio**, sometimes called the *acid-test ratio*. The quick ratio is computed as follows:

$$\text{Quick Ratio} = \frac{\text{Quick Assets}}{\text{Current Liabilities}}$$

Quick assets are cash and other current assets that can be easily converted to cash. Quick assets normally include cash, temporary investments, and receivables.

To illustrate, the quick ratio for Lincoln Company is computed below.

	2010	2009
Quick assets:		
Cash	$ 90,500	$ 64,700
Temporary investments	75,000	60,000
Accounts receivable (net)	115,000	120,000
Total quick assets	$280,500	$244,700
Current liabilities	$210,000	$243,000
Quick ratio	1.3*	1.0**

*1.3 = $280,500 ÷ $210,000
**1.0 = $244,700 ÷ $243,000

Example Exercise 17-3   Current Position Analysis

The following items are reported on a company's balance sheet:

Cash	$300,000
Temporary investments	100,000
Accounts receivable (net)	200,000
Inventory	200,000
Accounts payable	400,000

Determine (a) the current ratio and (b) the quick ratio.

Follow My Example 17-3

a. Current Ratio = Current Assets ÷ Current Liabilities
    Current Ratio = ($300,000 + $100,000 + $200,000 + $200,000) ÷ $400,000
    Current Ratio = 2.0

b. Quick Ratio = Quick Assets ÷ Current Liabilities
    Quick Ratio = ($300,000 + $100,000 + $200,000) ÷ $400,000
    Quick Ratio = 1.5

For Practice: PE 17-3A, PE 17-3B

Accounts Receivable Analysis

A company's ability to collect its accounts receivable is called **accounts receivable analysis**. It includes the computation and analysis of the following:

1. Accounts receivable turnover
2. Number of days' sales in receivables

Collecting accounts receivable as quickly as possible improves a company's solvency. In addition, the cash collected from receivables may be used to improve or expand operations. Quick collection of receivables also reduces the risk of uncollectible accounts.

Accounts Receivable Turnover The **accounts receivable turnover** is computed as follows:

$$\text{Accounts Receivable Turnover} = \frac{\text{Net Sales}^2}{\text{Average Accounts Receivable}}$$

To illustrate, the accounts receivable turnover for Lincoln Company for 2010 and 2009 is computed below.

	2010	2009
Net sales	$1,498,000	$1,200,000
Accounts receivable (net):		
Beginning of year	$ 120,000	$ 140,000
End of year	115,000	120,000
Total	$ 235,000	$ 260,000
Average accounts receivable	$117,500 ($235,000 ÷ 2)	$130,000 ($260,000 ÷ 2)
Accounts receivable turnover	12.7 ($1,498,000 ÷ $117,500)	9.2 ($1,200,000 ÷ $130,000)

The increase in Lincoln's accounts receivable turnover from 9.2 to 12.7 indicates that the collection of receivables has improved during 2010. This may be due to a change in how credit is granted, collection practices, or both.

For Lincoln Company, the average accounts receivable was computed using the accounts receivable balance at the beginning and the end of the year. When sales are seasonal and, thus, vary throughout the year, monthly balances of receivables are often

---

2 If known, *credit* sales should be used in the numerator. Because credit sales are not normally known by external users, we use net sales in the numerator.

used. Also, if sales on account include notes receivable as well as accounts receivable, notes and accounts receivables are normally combined for analysis.

Number of Days' Sales in Receivables The **number of days' sales in receivables** is computed as follows:

$$\text{Number of Days' Sales in Receivables} = \frac{\text{Average Accounts Receivable}}{\text{Average Daily Sales}}$$

where

$$\text{Average Daily Sales} = \frac{\text{Net Sales}}{365 \text{ days}}$$

To illustrate, the number of days' sales in receivables for Lincoln Company is computed below.

	2010	2009
Average accounts receivable	$117,500 ($235,000 ÷ 2)	$130,000 ($260,000 ÷ 2)
Average daily sales	$4,104 ($1,498,000 ÷ 365)	$3,288 ($1,200,000 ÷ 365)
Number of days' sales in receivables	28.6 ($117,500 ÷ $4,104)	39.5 ($130,000 ÷ $3,288)

The number of days' sales in receivables is an estimate of the time (in days) that the accounts receivable have been outstanding. The number of days' sales in receivables is often compared with a company's credit terms to evaluate the efficiency of the collection of receivables.

To illustrate, if Lincoln's credit terms are 2/10, n/30, then Lincoln was very *inefficient* in collecting receivables in 2009. In other words, receivables should have been collected in 30 days or less, but were being collected in 39.5 days. Although collections improved during 2010 to 28.6 days, there is probably still room for improvement. On the other hand, if Lincoln's credit terms are n/45, then there is probably little room for improving collections.

Example Exercise 17-4   Accounts Receivable Analysis

A company reports the following:

Net sales	$960,000
Average accounts receivable (net)	48,000

Determine (a) the accounts receivable turnover and (b) the number of days' sales in receivables. Round to one decimal place.

Follow My Example 17-4

a.   Accounts Receivable Turnover = Sales ÷ Average Accounts Receivable
     Accounts Receivable Turnover = $960,000 ÷ $48,000
     Accounts Receivable Turnover = 20.0

b.   Number of Days' Sales in Receivables = Average Accounts Receivable ÷ Average Daily Sales
     Number of Days' Sales in Receivables = $48,000 ÷ ($960,000/365) = $48,000 ÷ $2,630
     Number of Days' Sales in Receivables = 18.3 days

For Practice: PE 17-4A, PE 17-4B

Inventory Analysis

A company's ability to manage its inventory effectively is evaluated using **inventory analysis**. It includes the computation and analysis of the following:

1. Inventory turnover
2. Number of days' sales in inventory

Excess inventory decreases solvency by tying up funds (cash) in inventory. In addition, excess inventory increases insurance expense, property taxes, storage costs, and other related expenses. These expenses further reduce funds that could be used elsewhere to improve or expand operations.

Excess inventory also increases the risk of losses because of price declines or obsolescence of the inventory. On the other hand, a company should keep enough inventory in stock so that it doesn't lose sales because of lack of inventory.

Inventory Turnover The **inventory turnover** is computed as follows:

$$\text{Inventory Turnover} = \frac{\text{Cost of Goods Sold}}{\text{Average Inventory}}$$

To illustrate, the inventory turnover for Lincoln Company for 2010 and 2009 is computed below.

	2010	2009
Cost of goods sold	$1,043,000	$820,000
Inventories:		
Beginning of year	$ 283,000	$311,000
End of year	264,000	283,000
Total	$ 547,000	$594,000
Average inventory	$273,500 ($547,000 ÷ 2)	$297,000 ($594,000 ÷ 2)
Inventory turnover	3.8 ($1,043,000 ÷ $273,500)	2.8 ($820,000 ÷ $297,000)

The increase in Lincoln's inventory turnover from 2.8 to 3.8 indicates that the management of inventory has improved in 2010. The inventory turnover improved because of an increase in the cost of goods sold, which indicates more sales, and a decrease in the average inventories.

What is considered a good inventory turnover varies by type of inventory, companies, and industries. For example, grocery stores have a higher inventory turnover than jewelers or furniture stores. Likewise, within a grocery store, perishable foods have a higher turnover than the soaps and cleansers.

Number of Days' Sales in Inventory The **number of days' sales in inventory** is computed as follows:

$$\text{Number of Days' Sales in Inventory} = \frac{\text{Average Inventory}}{\text{Average Daily Cost of Goods Sold}}$$

where

$$\text{Average Daily Cost of Goods Sold} = \frac{\text{Cost of Goods Sold}}{365 \text{ days}}$$

To illustrate, the number of days' sales in inventory for Lincoln Company is computed below.

	2010	2009
Average inventory	$273,500 ($547,000 ÷ 2)	$297,000 ($594,000 ÷ 2)
Average daily cost of goods sold	$2,858 ($1,043,000 ÷ 365)	$2,247 ($820,000 ÷ 365)
Number of days' sales in inventory	95.7 ($273,500 ÷ $2,858)	132.2 ($297,000 ÷ $2,247)

The number of days' sales in inventory is a rough measure of the length of time it takes to purchase, sell, and replace the inventory. Lincoln's number of days' sales in inventory improved from 132.2 days to 95.7 days during 2010. This is a major improvement in managing inventory.

Example Exercise 17-5   Inventory Analysis ·········▷ ②

A company reports the following:

Cost of goods sold	$560,000
Average inventory	112,000

Determine (a) the inventory turnover and (b) the number of days' sales in inventory. Round to one decimal place.

Follow My Example 17-5

a.   Inventory Turnover = Cost of Goods Sold ÷ Average Inventory
     Inventory Turnover = $560,000 ÷ $112,000
     Inventory Turnover = 5.0

b.   Number of Days' Sales in Inventory = Average Inventory ÷ Average Daily Cost of Goods Sold
     Number of Days' Sales in Inventory = $112,000 ÷ ($560,000/365) = $112,000 ÷ $1,534
     Number of Days' Sales in Inventory = 73.0 days

For Practice: PE 17-5A, PE 17-5B

Ratio of Fixed Assets to Long-Term Liabilities

The **ratio of fixed assets to long-term liabilities** provides a measure of whether note-holders or bondholders will be paid. Since fixed assets are often pledged as security for long-term notes and bonds, it is computed as follows:

$$\text{Ratio of Fixed Assets to Long-Term Liabilities} = \frac{\text{Fixed Assets (net)}}{\text{Long-Term Liabilities}}$$

To illustrate, the ratio of fixed assets to long-term liabilities for Lincoln Company is computed below.

	2010	2009
Fixed assets (net)	$444,500	$470,000
Long-term liabilities	$100,000	$200,000
Ratio of fixed assets to long-term liabilities	4.4 ($444,500 ÷ $100,000)	2.4 ($470,000 ÷ $200,000)

During 2010, Lincoln's ratio of fixed assets to long-term liabilities increased from 2.4 to 4.4. This increase was due primarily to Lincoln paying off one-half of its long-term liabilities in 2010.

Ratio of Liabilities to Stockholders' Equity

The **ratio of liabilities to stockholders' equity** measures how much of the company is financed by debt and equity. It is computed as follows:

The ratio of liabilities to stockholders' equity varies across industries as in the following examples:

Continental Airlines   31.6

Procter & Gamble   1.1

Circuit City Stores, Inc. 1.2

$$\text{Ratio of Liabilities to Stockholders' Equity} = \frac{\text{Total Liabilities}}{\text{Total Stockholders' Equity}}$$

To illustrate, the ratio of liabilities to stockholders' equity for Lincoln Company is computed below.

	2010	2009
Total liabilities	$310,000	$443,000
Total stockholders' equity	$829,500	$787,500
Ratio of liabilities to stockholders' equity	0.4 ($310,000 ÷ $829,500)	0.6 ($443,000 ÷ $787,500)

Lincoln's ratio of liabilities to stockholders' equity decreased from 0.6 to 0.4 during 2010. This is an improvement and indicates that Lincoln's creditors have an adequate margin of safety.

Example Exercise 17-6 Long-Term Solvency Analysis ••••••••> ②

The following information was taken from Acme Company's balance sheet:

Fixed assets (net)	$1,400,000
Long-term liabilities	400,000
Total liabilities	560,000
Total stockholders' equity	1,400,000

Determine the company's (a) ratio of fixed assets to long-term liabilities and (b) ratio of liabilities to total stockholders' equity.

Follow My Example 17-6

a. Ratio of Fixed Assets to Long-Term Liabilities = Fixed Assets ÷ Long-Term Liabilities
   Ratio of Fixed Assets to Long-Term Liabilities = $1,400,000 ÷ $400,000
   Ratio of Fixed Assets to Long-Term Liabilities = 3.5

b. Ratio of Liabilities to Total Stockholders' Equity = Total Liabilities ÷ Total Stockholders' Equity
   Ratio of Liabilities to Total Stockholders' Equity = $560,000 ÷ $1,400,000
   Ratio of Liabilities to Total Stockholders' Equity = 0.4

For Practice: PE 17-6A, PE 17-6B

Number of Times Interest Charges Earned

The **number of times interest charges are earned**, sometimes called the *fixed charge coverage ratio*, measures the risk that interest payments will not be made if earnings decrease. It is computed as follows:

$$\text{Number of Times Interest Charges Are Earned} = \frac{\text{Income Before Income Tax + Interest Expense}}{\text{Interest Expense}}$$

Interest expense is paid before income taxes. In other words, interest expense is deducted in determining taxable income and, thus, income tax. For this reason, income *before taxes* is used in computing the number of times interest charges are earned.

The *higher* the ratio the more likely interest payments will be paid if earnings decrease. To illustrate, the number of times interest charges are earned for Lincoln Company is computed below.

	2010	2009
Income before income tax	$162,500	$134,600
Add interest expense	6,000	12,000
Amount available to pay interest	$168,500	$146,600
Number of times interest charges earned	28.1 ($168,500 ÷ $6,000)	12.2 ($146,600 ÷ $12,000)

The number of times interest charges are earned improved from 12.2 to 28.1 during 2010. This indicates that Lincoln Company has sufficient earnings to pay interest expense.

The number of times interest charges are earned can be adapted for use with dividends on preferred stock. In this case, the *number of times preferred dividends are earned* is computed as follows:

$$\text{Number of Times Preferred Dividends Are Earned} = \frac{\text{Net Income}}{\text{Preferred Dividends}}$$

Since dividends are paid after taxes, net income is used in computing the number of times preferred dividends are earned. The *higher* the ratio, the more likely preferred dividends payments will be paid if earnings decrease.

Example Exercise 17-7   Times Interest Charges Are Earned

A company reports the following:

Income before income tax	$250,000
Interest expense	100,000

Determine the number of times interest charges are earned.

Follow My Example 17-7

Number of Times Interest Charges Are Earned = (Income Before Income Tax + Interest Expense)
÷ Interest Expense
Number of Times Interest Charges Are Earned = ($250,000 + $100,000) ÷ $100,000
Number of Times Interest Charges Are Earned = 3.5

For Practice: PE 17-7A, PE 17-7B

3 Use financial statement analysis to assess the profitability of a business.

Profitability Analysis

Profitability analysis focuses on the ability of a company to earn profits. This ability is reflected in the company's operating results, as reported in its income statement. The ability to earn profits also depends on the assets the company has available for use in its operations, as reported in its balance sheet. Thus, income statement and balance sheet relationships are often used in evaluating profitability.

Common profitability analyses include the following:

1. Ratio of net sales to assets
2. Rate earned on total assets
3. Rate earned on stockholders' equity
4. Rate earned on common stockholders' equity
5. Earnings per share on common stock
6. Price-earnings ratio
7. Dividends per share
8. Dividend yield

Ratio of Net Sales to Assets

The **ratio of net sales to assets** measures how effectively a company uses its assets. It is computed as follows:

$$\text{Ratio of Net Sales to Assets} = \frac{\text{Net Sales}}{\text{Average Total Assets}}$$
(excluding long-term investments)

As shown above, any long-term investments are excluded in computing the ratio of net sales to assets. This is because long-term investments are unrelated to normal operations and net sales.

To illustrate, the ratio of net sales to assets for Lincoln Company is computed below.

	2010	2009
Net sales	$1,498,000	$1,200,000
Total assets (excluding long-term investments):		
Beginning of year	$1,053,000	$1,010,000
End of year	1,044,500	1,053,000
Total	$2,097,500	$2,063,000
Average total assets	$1,048,750 ($2,097,500 ÷ 2)	$1,031,500 ($2,063,000 ÷ 2)
Ratio of net sales to assets	1.4 ($1,498,000 ÷ $1,048,750)	1.2 ($1,200,000 ÷ $1,031,500)

For Lincoln Company, the average total assets was computed using total assets (excluding long-term investments) at the beginning and the end of the year. The average total assets could also be based on monthly or quarterly averages.

The ratio of net sales to assets indicates that Lincoln's use of its operating assets has improved in 2010. This was due primarily due to the increase in net sales in 2010.

Example Exercise 17-8 Net Sales to Assets ·········▶ ③

A company reports the following:

Net sales	$2,250,000
Average total assets	1,500,000

Determine the ratio of net sales to assets.

Follow My Example 17-8

Ratio of Net Sales to Assets = Net Sales ÷ Average Total Assets
Ratio of Net Sales to Assets = $2,250,000 ÷ $1,500,000
Ratio of Net Sales to Assets = 1.5

....

For Practice: PE 17-8A, PE 17-8B

Rate Earned on Total Assets

The **rate earned on total assets** measures the profitability of total assets, without considering how the assets are financed. In other words, this rate is not affected by the portion of assets financed by creditors or stockholders. It is computed as follows:

$$\text{Rate Earned on Total Assets} = \frac{\text{Net Income} + \text{Interest Expense}}{\text{Average Total Assets}}$$

The rate earned on total assets is computed by adding interest expense to net income. By adding interest expense to net income, the effect of whether the assets are financed by creditors (debt) or stockholders (equity) is eliminated. Because net income includes any income earned from long-term investments, the average total assets includes long-term investments as well as the net operating assets.

To illustrate, the rate earned on total assets by Lincoln Company is computed below.

	2010	2009
Net income	$ 91,000	$ 76,500
Plus interest expense	6,000	12,000
Total	$ 97,000	$ 88,500
Total assets:		
Beginning of year	$ 1,230,500	$ 1,187,500
End of year	1,139,500	1,230,500
Total	$2,370,000	$2,418,000
Average total assets	$1,185,000 ($2,370,000 ÷ 2)	$1,209,000 ($2,418,000 ÷ 2)
Rate earned on total assets	8.2% ($97,000 ÷ $1,185,000)	7.3% ($88,500 ÷ $1,209,000)

The rate earned on total assets improved from 7.3% to 8.2% during 2010.

The *rate earned on operating assets* is sometimes computed when there are large amounts of nonoperating income and expense. It is computed as follows:

$$\text{Rate Earned on Operating Assets} = \frac{\text{Income from Operations}}{\text{Average Operating Assets}}$$

Since Lincoln Company does not have a significant amount of nonoperating income and expense, the rate earned on operating assets is not illustrated.

The rate earned on total assets can be computed using spreadsheet software as follows:

	A	B	C
1	Inputs:		
2		2010	2009
3	Net income	$ 91,000	$ 76,500
4	Interest expense	6,000	12,000
5			
6	Total assets:		
7	Beginning of year	$ 1,230,500	$ 1,187,500
8	End of year	1,139,500	1,230,500
9			
10	Outputs:		
11	Rate earned on total assets	=(B3+B4)/((B7+B8)/2)	=(C3+C4)/((C7+C8)/2)

a.   b.

The inputs could be the financial statements or a section of the financial statements. Here we illustrate only the data needed to compute the ratio. The output is the rate earned on total assets for the two years.

a.   Enter the formula for the rate earned on total assets in B11 as follows:

$$=(B3+B4)/((B7+B8)/2)$$

Numerator, using   Denominator, using
parentheses to force   parentheses to force
calculation order.   calculation order.

b.   Copy the formula from B11 to C11.

 Go to the hands-on **Excel Tutor** for this example!
(Note: The example here and throughout this chapter are contained in a **single** tutorial.)

 This Excel Success example shows the use of parentheses.
Go to the **Excel Tutor** titled **Using Parentheses** for additional help!

Example Exercise 17-9   Rate Earned on Total Assets    ③

A company reports the following income statement and balance sheet information for the current year:

Net income	$ 125,000
Interest expense	25,000
Average total assets	2,000,000

Determine the rate earned on total assets.

Follow My Example 17-9

Rate Earned on Total Assets = (Net Income + Interest Expense) ÷ Average Total Assets
Rate Earned on Total Assets = ($125,000 + $25,000) ÷ $2,000,000
Rate Earned on Total Assets = $150,000 ÷ $2,000,000
Rate Earned on Total Assets = 7.5%

For Practice: PE 17-9A, PE 17-9B

Rate Earned on Stockholders' Equity

The **rate earned on stockholders' equity** measures the rate of income earned on the amount invested by the stockholders. It is computed as follows:

$$\text{Rate Earned on Stockholders' Equity} = \frac{\text{Net Income}}{\text{Average Total Stockholders' Equity}}$$

To illustrate, the rate earned on stockholders' equity for Lincoln Company is:

	2010	2009
Net income	$ 91,000	$ 76,500
Stockholders' equity:		
Beginning of year	$ 787,500	$ 750,000
End of year	829,500	787,500
Total	$1,617,000	$1,537,500

Average stockholders' equity	$808,500 ($1,617,000 ÷ 2)	$768,750 ($1,537,500 ÷ 2)
Rate earned on stockholders' equity	11.3% ($91,000 ÷ $808,500)	10.0% ($76,500 ÷ $768,750)

The rate earned on stockholders' equity improved from 10.0% to 11.3% during 2010. Leverage involves using debt to increase the return on an investment. The rate earned on stockholders' equity is normally higher than the rate earned on total assets. This is because of the effect of leverage.

For Lincoln Company, the effect of leverage for 2010 is 3.1%, computed as follows:

Rate earned on stockholders' equity	11.3%
Less rate earned on total assets	8.2
Effect of leverage	3.1%

Exhibit 8 shows the 2010 and 2009 effects of leverage for Lincoln Company.

Exhibit 8

Effect of Leverage

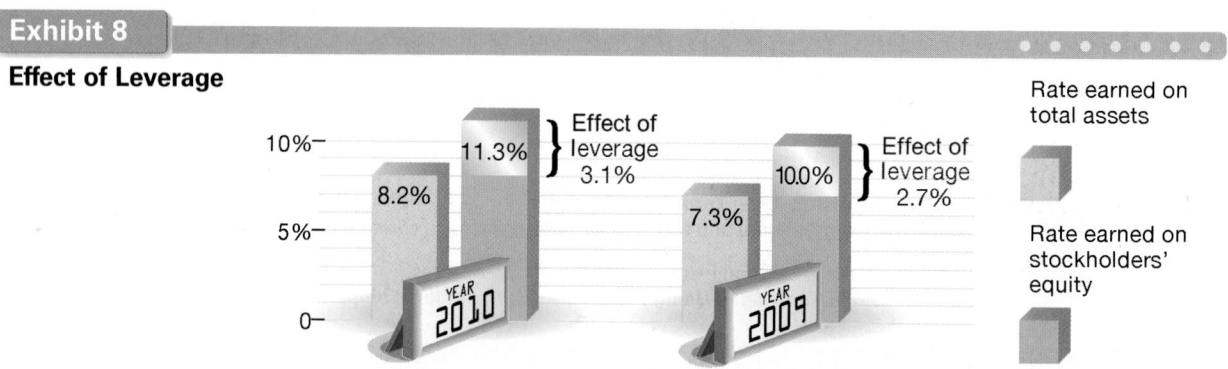

Rate Earned on Common Stockholders' Equity

The **rate earned on common stockholders' equity** measures the rate of profits earned on the amount invested by the common stockholders. It is computed as follows:

$$\text{Rate Earned on Common Stockholders' Equity} = \frac{\text{Net Income} - \text{Preferred Dividends}}{\text{Average Common Stockholders' Equity}}$$

Because preferred stockholders rank ahead of the common stockholders in their claim on earnings, any preferred dividends are subtracted from net income in computing the rate earned on common stockholders' equity.

To illustrate, the rate earned on common stockholders' equity for Lincoln Company is computed below.

	2010	2009
Net income	$ 91,000	$ 76,500
Less preferred dividends	9,000	9,000
Total	$ 82,000	$ 67,500
Common stockholders' equity:		
Beginning of year	$ 637,500	$ 600,000
End of year	679,500	637,500
Total	$1,317,000	$1,237,500
Average common stockholders' equity	$658,500 ($1,317,000 ÷ 2)	$618,750 ($1,237,500 ÷ 2)
Rate earned on common stockholders' equity	12.5% ($82,000 ÷ $658,500)	10.9% ($67,500 ÷ $618,750)

Lincoln Company had $150,000 of 6% preferred stock outstanding on December 31, 2010 and 2009. Thus, preferred dividends of $9,000 ($150,000 × 6%) were deducted from net income. Lincoln's common stockholders' equity was determined as follows:

	December 31		
	2010	**2009**	**2008**
Common stock, $10 par	$500,000	$500,000	$500,000
Retained earnings	179,500	137,500	100,000
Common stockholders' equity	$679,500	$637,500	$600,000

The retained earnings on December 31, 2008, of $100,000 is the same as the retained earnings on January 1, 2009, as shown in Lincoln's retained earnings statement in Exhibit 4.

Lincoln Company's rate earned on common stockholders' equity improved from 10.9% to 12.5% in 2010. This rate differs from the rates earned by Lincoln Company on total assets and stockholders' equity as shown below.

	2010	2009
Rate earned on total assets	8.2%	7.3%
Rate earned on stockholders' equity	11.3%	10.0%
Rate earned on common stockholders' equity	12.5%	10.9%

These rates differ because of leverage, as discussed in the preceding section.

Example Exercise 17-10   Common Stockholders' Profitability Analysis   ·········▶ ③

A company reports the following:

Net income	$ 125,000
Preferred dividends	5,000
Average stockholders' equity	1,000,000
Average common stockholders' equity	800,000

Determine (a) the rate earned on stockholders' equity and (b) the rate earned on common stockholders' equity.

Follow My Example 17-10

a. Rate Earned on Stockholders' Equity = Net Income ÷ Average Stockholders' Equity
    Rate Earned on Stockholders' Equity = $125,000 ÷ $1,000,000
    Rate Earned on Stockholders' Equity = 12.5%

b. Rate Earned on Common Stockholders' Equity = (Net Income − Preferred Dividends) ÷ Average
    Common Stockholders' Equity
    Rate Earned on Common Stockholders' Equity = ($125,000 − $5,000) ÷ $800,000
    Rate Earned on Common Stockholders' Equity = 15%

For Practice: PE 17-10A, PE 17-10B

Earnings Per Share on Common Stock

Earnings per share (EPS) on common stock measures the share of profits that are earned by a share of common stock. Generally accepted accounting principles (GAAP) require the reporting of earnings per share in the income statement.[3] As a result, earnings per share (EPS) is often reported in the financial press. It is computed as follows:

$$\text{Earnings per Share (EPS) on Common Stock} = \frac{\text{Net Income} - \text{Preferred Dividends}}{\text{Shares of Common Stock Outstanding}}$$

When preferred and common stock are outstanding, preferred dividends are subtracted from net income to determine the income related to the common shares.

To illustrate, the earnings per share (EPS) of common stock for Lincoln Company is computed below.

3 *Statement of Financial Accounting Standards No. 128*, "Earnings per Share" (Norwalk, CT: Financial Accounting Standards Board, 1997).

	2010	2009
Net income	$91,000	$76,500
Preferred dividends	9,000	9,000
Total	$82,000	$67,500
Shares of common stock outstanding	50,000	50,000
Earnings per share on common stock	$1.64 ($82,000 ÷ 50,000)	$1.35 ($67,500 ÷ 50,000)

Lincoln Company had $150,000 of 6% preferred stock outstanding on December 31, 2010 and 2009. Thus, preferred dividends of $9,000 ($150,000 × 6%) are deducted from net income in computing earnings per share on common stock.

Lincoln did not issue any additional shares of common stock in 2010. If Lincoln had issued additional shares in 2010, a weighted average of common shares outstanding during the year would have been used.

As shown on the previous page, Lincoln's earnings per share (EPS) on common stock improved from $1.35 to $1.64 during 2010.

Lincoln Company has a simple capital structure with only common stock and preferred stock outstanding. Many corporations, however, have complex capital structures with various types of equity securities outstanding, such as convertible preferred stock, stock options, and stock warrants. In such cases, the possible effects of such securities on the shares of common stock outstanding are considered in reporting earnings per share. These possible effects are reported separately as *earnings per common share assuming dilution* or *diluted earnings per share*.[4] This topic is described and illustrated in advanced accounting courses and textbooks.

Price-Earnings Ratio

The **price-earnings (P/E) ratio** on common stock measures a company's future earnings prospects. It is often quoted in the financial press and is computed as follows:

$$\text{Price-Earnings (P/E) Ratio} = \frac{\text{Market Price per Share of Common Stock}}{\text{Earnings per Share on Common Stock}}$$

To illustrate, the price-earnings (P/E) ratio for Lincoln Company is computed below.

	2010	2009
Market price per share of common stock	$41.00	$27.00
Earnings per share on common stock	$1.64	$1.35
Price-earnings ratio on common stock	25 ($41 ÷ $1.64)	20 ($27 ÷ $1.35)

The price-earnings ratio improved from 20 to 25 during 2010. In other words, a share of common stock of Lincoln Company was selling for 20 times earnings per share at the end of 2009. At the end of 2010, the common stock was selling for 25 times earnings per share. This indicates that the market expects Lincoln to experience favorable earnings in the future.

Example Exercise 17-11   Earnings per Share and Price-Earnings   •••••••• ❯ 3

A company reports the following:

Net income	$250,000
Preferred dividends	$15,000
Shares of common stock outstanding	20,000
Market price per share of common stock	$35.00

a. Determine the company's earnings per share on common stock.
b. Determine the company's price-earnings ratio. Round to one decimal place.

(continued)

4 Ibid. , pars. 11–39.

Follow My Example 17-11

a.   Earnings per Share on Common Stock = (Net Income − Preferred Dividends) ÷ Shares of Common
Stock Outstanding
Earnings per Share = ($250,000 − $15,000) ÷ 20,000
Earnings per Share = $11.75

b.   Price-Earnings Ratio = Market Price per Share of Common Stock ÷ Earnings per Share on Common
Stock
Price-Earnings Ratio = $35.00 ÷ $11.75
Price-Earnings Ratio = 3.0

For Practice: PE 17-11A, PE 17-11B

Dividends Per Share

Dividends per share measures the extent to which earnings are being distributed to common shareholders. It is computed as follows:

$$\text{Dividends per Share} = \frac{\text{Dividends}}{\text{Shares of Common Stock Outstanding}}$$

To illustrate, the dividends per share for Lincoln Company are computed below.

	2010	2009
Dividends	$40,000	$30,000
Shares of common stock outstanding	50,000	50,000
Dividends per share of common stock	$0.80 ($40,000 ÷ 50,000)	$0.60 ($30,000 ÷ 50,000)

The dividends per share of common stock increased from $0.60 to $0.80 during 2010.

Dividends per share are often reported with earnings per share. Comparing the two per-share amounts indicates the extent to which earnings are being retained for use in operations. To illustrate, the dividends and earnings per share for Lincoln Company are shown in Exhibit 9.

The dividends per share, dividend yield, and P/E ratio of a common stock are normally quoted on the daily listing of stock prices in *The Wall Street Journal* and on Yahoo!'s finance Web site.

Exhibit 9

Dividends and Earnings per Share of Common Stock

Dividend Yield

The **dividend yield** on common stock measures the rate of return to common stockholders from cash dividends. It is of special interest to investors whose objective is to earn revenue (dividends) from their investment. It is computed as follows:

$$\text{Dividend Yield} = \frac{\text{Dividends per Share of Common Stock}}{\text{Market Price per Share of Common Stock}}$$

To illustrate, the dividend yield for Lincoln Company is computed below.

	2010	2009
Dividends per share of common stock	$ 0.80	$ 0.60
Market price per share of common stock	$41.00	$27.00
Dividend yield on common stock	2.0% ($0.80 ÷ $41)	2.2% ($0.60 ÷ $27)

The dividend yield declined slightly from 2.2% to 2.0% in 2010. This decline was primarily due to the increase in the market price of Lincoln's common stock.

Summary of Analytical Measures

Exhibit 10 shows a summary of the solvency and profitability measures discussed in this chapter. The type of industry and the company's operations usually affect which measures are used. In many cases, additional measures are used for a specific industry. For example, airlines use *revenue per passenger mile* and *cost per available seat* as profitability measures. Likewise, hotels use *occupancy rates* as a profitability measure.

The analytical measures shown in Exhibit 10 are a useful starting point for analyzing a company's solvency and profitability. However, they are not a substitute for sound judgment. For example, the general economic and business environment should always be considered in analyzing a company's future prospects. In addition, any trends and interrelationships among the measures should be carefully studied.

Integrity, Objectivity, and Ethics in Business

ONE BAD APPLE

A recent survey by *CFO* magazine reported that 47% of chief financial officers have been pressured by the chief executive officer to use questionable accounting. In addition, only 38% of those surveyed feel less pressure to use aggressive accounting today than in years past, while 20% believe there is more pressure. Perhaps more troublesome is the chief financial officers' confidence in the quality of financial information, with only 27% being "very confident" in the quality of financial information presented by public companies.

Source: D. Durfee, "It's Better (and Worse) Than You Think," *CFO*, May 3, 2004.

Corporate Annual Reports

4 Describe the contents of corporate annual reports.

Public corporations issue annual reports summarizing their operating activities for the past year and plans for the future. Such annual reports include the financial statements and the accompanying notes. In addition, annual reports normally include the following sections:

1. Management discussion and analysis
2. Report on internal control
3. Report on fairness of the financial statements

Management Discussion and Analysis

Management's Discussion and Analysis (MD&A) is required in annual reports filed with the Securities and Exchange Commission. It includes management's analysis of current operations and its plans for the future. Typical items included in the MD&A include the following:

1. Management's analysis and explanations of any significant changes between the current and prior years' financial statements.

Exhibit 10

Summary of Analytical Measures

Solvency measures:	Method of Computation	Use
Working Capital	Current Assets − Current Liabilities	To indicate the ability to meet currently maturing obligations
Current Ratio	$\dfrac{\text{Current Assets}}{\text{Current Liabilities}}$	
Quick Ratio	$\dfrac{\text{Quick Assets}}{\text{Current Liabilities}}$	To indicate instant debt-paying ability
Accounts Receivable Turnover	$\dfrac{\text{Net Sales}}{\text{Average Accounts Receivable}}$	To assess the efficiency in collecting receivables and in the management of credit
Numbers of Days' Sales in Receivables	$\dfrac{\text{Average Accounts Receivable}}{\text{Average Daily Sales}}$	
Inventory Turnover	$\dfrac{\text{Cost of Goods Sold}}{\text{Average Inventory}}$	To assess the efficiency in the management of inventory
Number of Days' Sales in Inventory	$\dfrac{\text{Average Inventory}}{\text{Average Daily Cost of Goods Sold}}$	
Ratio of Fixed Assets to Long-Term Liabilities	$\dfrac{\text{Fixed Assets (net)}}{\text{Long-Term Liabilities}}$	To indicate the margin of safety to long-term creditors
Ratio of Liabilities to Stockholders' Equity	$\dfrac{\text{Total Liabilities}}{\text{Total Stockholders' Equity}}$	To indicate the margin of safety to creditors
Number of Times Interest Charges are Earned	$\dfrac{\text{Income Before Income Tax + Interest Expense}}{\text{Interest Expense}}$	To assess the risk to debtholders in terms of number of times interest charges were earned
Profitability measures:		
Ratio of Net Sales to Assets	$\dfrac{\text{Net Sales}}{\text{Average Total Assets (excluding long-term investments)}}$	To assess the effectiveness in the use of assets
Rate Earned on Total Assets	$\dfrac{\text{Net Income + Interest Expense}}{\text{Average Total Assets}}$	To assess the profitability of the assets
Rate Earned on Stockholders' Equity	$\dfrac{\text{Net Income}}{\text{Average Total Stockholders' Equity}}$	To assess the profitability of the investment by stockholders
Rate Earned on Common Stockholders' Equity	$\dfrac{\text{Net Income − Preferred Dividends}}{\text{Average Common Stockholders' Equity}}$	To assess the profitability of the investment by common stockholders
Earnings per Share on Common Stock	$\dfrac{\text{Net Income − Preferred Dividends}}{\text{Shares of Common Stock Outstanding}}$	
Price-Earnings Ratio	$\dfrac{\text{Market Price per Share of Common Stock}}{\text{Earnings per Share on Common Stock}}$	To indicate future earnings prospects, based on the relationship between market value of common stock and earnings
Dividends per Share	$\dfrac{\text{Dividends}}{\text{Shares of Common Stock Outstanding}}$	To indicate the extent to which earnings are being distributed to common stockholders
Dividend Yield	$\dfrac{\text{Dividends per Share of Common Stock}}{\text{Market Price per Share of Common Stock}}$	To indicate the rate of return to common stockholders in terms of dividends

2. Important accounting principles or policies that could affect interpretation of the financial statements, including the effect of changes in accounting principles or the adoption of new accounting principles.

3. Management's assessment of the company's liquidity and the availability of capital to the company.

4. Significant risk exposures that might affect the company.

5. Any "off-balance-sheet" arrangements such as leases not included directly in the financial statements. Such arrangements are discussed in advanced accounting courses and textbooks.

Report on Internal Control

The Sarbanes-Oxley Act of 2002 requires a report on internal control by management. The report states management's responsibility for establishing and maintaining internal control. In addition, management's assessment of the effectiveness of internal controls over financial reporting is included in the report.

Sarbanes-Oxley also requires a public accounting firm to verify management's conclusions on internal control. Thus, two reports on internal control, one by management and one by a public accounting firm, are included in the annual report. In some situations, these may be combined into a single report on internal control.

Report on Fairness of the Financial Statements

All publicly held corporations are required to have an independent audit (examination) of their financial statements. The Certified Public Accounting (CPA) firm that conducts the audit renders an opinion, called the *Report of Independent Registered Public Accounting Firm*, on the fairness of the statements.

An opinion stating that the financial statements present fairly the financial position, results of operations, and cash flows of the company is said to be an *unqualified opinion*, sometimes called a *clean opinion*. Any report other than an unqualified opinion raises a "red flag" for financial statement users and requires further investigation as to its cause.

The annual report of Nike Inc. is shown in Appendix E. The Nike report includes the financial statements as well as the MD&A Report on Internal Control, and Report on Fairness of the Financial Statements.

success

Comprehensive Spreadsheet Illustration:
Rainbow Paint Co.'s comparative financial statement for the years ending December 31, 2010 and 2009, in spreadsheet form are shown below. The market price of Rainbow Paint Co.'s common stock was $30 on December 31, 2010.

	A	B	C
1	Rainbow Paint Co.		
2	Comparative Income Statements		
3	For the Years Ended December 31, 2010 and 2009		
4			
5		2010	2009
6	Sales	$ 5,125,000	$ 3,257,600
7	Sales returns and allowances	125,000	57,600
8	Net sales	$ 5,000,000	$ 3,200,000
9	Cost of goods sold	3,400,000	2,080,000
10	Gross profit	$ 1,600,000	$ 1,120,000
11	Selling expenses	650,000	464,000
12	Administrative expenses	325,000	224,000
13	Total operating expenses	$ 975,000	$ 688,000
14	Income from operations	$ 625,000	$ 432,000
15	Other income	25,000	19,200
16		$ 650,000	$ 451,200
17	Other expense (interest)	105,000	64,000
18	Income before income tax	$ 545,000	$ 387,200
19	Income tax expense	300,000	176,000
20	Net Income	$ 245,000	$ 211,200
21			

	A	B	C
23		Rainbow Paint Co.	
24		Comparative Retained Earnings Statement	
25		For the Years Ended December 31, 2010 and 2009	
26			
27		2010	2009
28	Retained earnings, January 1	$ 723,000	$ 581,800
29	Add net income for year	245,000	211,200
30	Total	$ 968,000	$ 793,000
31	Deduct dividends:		
32	On preferred stock	$ 40,000	$ 40,000
33	On common stock	45,000	30,000
34	Total	$ 85,000	$ 70,000
35	Retained earnings, December 31	$ 883,000	$ 723,000

	A	B	C	
38		Rainbow Paint Co.		
39		Comparative Balance Sheet		
40		For the Years Ended December 31, 2010 and 2009		
41				
42		Dec. 31, 2010	Dec. 31, 2009	
43	Assets			
44	Current assets:			
45	Cash	$ 175,000	$ 125,000	
46	Temporary investments	150,000	50,000	
47	Accounts receivable (net)	425,000	325,000	
48	Inventories	720,000	480,000	
49	Prepaid expenses	30,000	20,000	
50	Total current assets	$ 1,500,000	$ 1,000,000	
51	Long-term investments	250,000	225,000	
52	Property, plant, and equipment	2,093,000	1,948,000	**Working**
53	Total assets	$ 3,843,000	$ 3,173,000	**Capital,**
54				**=B50-B56**
55	Liabilities			
56	Current liabilities	$ 750,000	$ 650,000	
57	Long-term liabilities:			
58	Mortgage note payable, 10% due 2013	410,000	-	
59	Bonds payable, 8%, due 2016	800,000	800,000	
60	Total long-term liabilities	$ 1,210,000	$ 800,000	
61	Total liabilities	$ 1,960,000	$ 1,450,000	
62				
63	Stockholders' Equity			
64	Preferred 8% stock, $100 par	$ 500,000	$ 500,000	
65	Common stock, $10 par	500,000	500,000	
66	Retained earnings	883,000	723,000	
67	Total stockholders' equity	$ 1,883,000	$ 1,723,000	
68	Total liabilities and stockholders' equity	$ 3,843,000	$ 3,173,000	
69				
70		Dec. 31, 2010		
71	Common stock market price	$ 25.00		
72	Number of common shares outstanding	$ 50,000		

Solution

Ratio formulas are illustrated for Rainbow Paint Co. for 2010. The Excel formulas refer to the cell references shown in the financial statements for Rainbow Paint Co. For example, the working capital is computed as the difference between cells B50 and B56, or =B50-B56. This formula is computed based on the balance sheet data. The remaining formulas reference fin statement cells for 2010.

The parentheses in the Excel formulas are required to force proper calculation order. Proper use of parenthesis is important when developing complex Excel formulas.

	A	B	C
1		**Ratio solution and numerical formula**	**Excel formula**
2	1.	Working capital: $750,000 $1,500,000 - $750,000	=B50-B56
3	2.	Current ratio: 2.0 $1,500,000 ÷ $750,000	=B50/B56
4	3.	Quick ratio: 1.0 $750,000 ÷ $750,000	=SUM(B45:B47)/B56
5	4.	Accounts receivable turnover: 13.3 $5,000,000 ÷ [($425,000 + 325,000) ÷ 2]	=B8/((B47+C47)/2)
6	5.	Number of days' sales in receivables: 27.4 days $5,000,000 ÷ 365 days = $13,699 $375,000 ÷ $13,699	=((B47+C47)/2)/(B8/365)
7	6.	Inventory turnover: 5.7 $3,400,000 ÷ [($720,000 + $480,000) ÷ 2]	=B9/((B48+C48)/2)
8	7.	Number of days' sales in inventory: 64.4 days $3,400,000 ÷ 365 days = $9,315 $600,000 ÷ $9,315	=((B48+C48)/2)/(B9/365)
9	8.	Ratio of fixed assets to long-term liabilities: 1.7 $2,093,000 ÷ $1,210,000	=B52/B60
10	9.	Ratio of liabilities to stockholders' equity: 1.0 $1,960,000 ÷ $1,883,000	=B61/B67
11	10.	Number of times interest charges are earned: 6.2 ($545,000 + $105,000) ÷ $105,000	=(B18+B17)/B17
12	11.	Number of times preferred dividends are earned: 6.1 $245,000 ÷ $40,000	=B20/B32
13	12.	Ratio of net sales to assets: 1.5 $5,000,000 ÷ [($3,593,000 + $2,948,000) ÷ 2]	=B8/(((B53-B51)+(C53-C51))/2)
14	13.	Rate earned on total assets: 10.0% ($245,000 + $105,000) ÷ [($3,843,000 + $3,173,000) ÷ 2)	=(B20+B17)/((B53+C53)/2)
15	14.	Rate earned on stockholders' equity: 13.6% $245,000 + [($1,883,000 + $1,723,000) ÷ 2]	=B20/((B67+C67)/2)
16	15.	Rate earned on common stockholders' equity: 15.7% ($245,000 - $40,000) ÷ [($1,383,000 + $1,223,000) ÷ 2]	=(B20-B32)/(((B67-B64)+(C67-C64))/2)
17	16.	Earnings per share on common stock: $4.10 ($245,000 - $40,000) ÷ 50,000 shares	=(B20-B32)/B72
18	17.	Price-earnings ratio: 6.1 $25 ÷ [($245,000 - $40,000) ÷ 50,000 shares]	=B71/((B20-B32)/B72)
19	18.	Dividends per share: $0.90 $45,000 ÷ 50,000 shares	=B33/B72
20	19.	Dividend yield: 3.6% (45,000 ÷ 50,000 shares) ÷ $25	=(B33/B72)/B71

tr✗it Reminder: Go to the *Excel Tutor* titled **Using Parentheses** for additional help!

A P P E N D I X

Unusual Items on the Income Statement

Generally accepted accounting principles require that unusual items be reported separately on the income statement. This is because such items do not occur frequently and often are unrelated to current operations. Without separate reporting of these items, users of the financial statements might be misled about current and future operations.

Unusual items on the income statement are classified as one of the following:

1. Affecting the *current period* income statement
2. Affecting a *prior period* income statement

Unusual Items Affecting the Current Period's Income Statement

Unusual items affecting the current period's income statement include the following:

1. Discontinued operations
2. Extraordinary items

Discontinued Operations A company may discontinue a segment of its operations by selling or abandoning the operations. For example, a retailer might decide to sell its product only online and, thus, discontinue selling its merchandise at its retail outlets (stores).

Any gain or loss on discontinued operations is reported on the income statement as a *Gain (or loss) from discontinued operations*. It is reported immediately following *Income from continuing operations*.[5]

To illustrate, assume that Jones Corporation produces and sells electrical products, hardware supplies, and lawn equipment. Because of lack of profits, Jones discontinues its electrical products operation and sells the remaining inventory and other assets at a loss of $100,000. Exhibit 11 illustrates the reporting of the loss on discontinued operations.[6]

Exhibit 11

Unusual Items in the Income Statement

Jones Corporation Income Statement For the Year Ended December 31, 2010	
Net sales	$12,350,000
Cost of merchandise sold	5,800,000
Gross profit	$ 6,550,000
Selling and administrative expenses	5,240,000
Income from continuing operations before income tax	$ 1,310,000
Income tax expense	620,000
Income from continuing operations	$ 690,000
Loss on discontinued operations	100,000
Income before extraordinary items	$ 590,000
Extraordinary items:	
Gain on condemnation of land	150,000
Net income	$ 740,000

In addition, a note accompanying the income statement should describe the operations sold including such details as the date operations were discontinued, the assets sold, and the effect (if any) on current and future operations.

Extraordinary Items An **extraordinary item** is defined as an event or transaction with the following characteristics:

1. Unusual in nature
2. Infrequent in occurrence

Gains and losses from natural disasters such as floods, earthquakes, and fires are normally reported as extraordinary items, provided that they occur infrequently. Gains or losses from land or buildings taken (condemned) for public use are also reported as extraordinary items.

5 *Statement of Financial Accounting Standards No. 144*, "Accounting for the Impairment or Disposal of Long-Lived Assets" (Norwalk, CT: Financial Accounting Standards Board, 2001).

6 The gain or loss on discontinued operations is reported net of any tax effects. To simplify, the tax effects are not specifically identified in Exhibit 11.

Any gain or loss from extraordinary items is reported on the income statement as *Gain (or loss) from extraordinary item*. It is reported immediately following *Income from continuing operations* and any *Gain (or loss) on discontinued operations*.

To illustrate, assume that land owned by Jones Corporation was condemned by the local government. The condemnation of the land resulted in a gain of $150,000. Exhibit 11 illustrates the reporting of the extraordinary gain.[7]

Reporting Earnings per Share Earnings per common share should be reported separately for discontinued operations and extraordinary items. To illustrate, a partial income statement for Jones Corporation is shown in Exhibit 12.

Exhibit 12 reports earnings per common share for income from continuing operations, discontinued operations, and extraordinary items. However, only earnings per share for income from continuing operations and net income are required by generally accepted accounting principles. The other per-share amounts may be presented in the notes to the financial statements.[8]

Exhibit 12

Income Statement with Earnings per Share

Jones Corporation Income Statement For the Year Ended December 31, 2010	
Earnings per common share:	
Income from continuing operations	$3.45
Loss on discontinued operations	0.50
Income before extraordinary items	$2.95
Extraordinary items:	
Gain on condemnation of land	0.75
Net income	$3.70

Unusual Items Affecting the Prior Period's Income Statement

An unusual item may occur that affects a prior period's income statement. Two such items are as follows:

1. Errors in applying generally accepted accounting principles
2. Changes from one generally accepted accounting principle to another[9]

If an error is discovered in a prior period's financial statement, the prior-period statement and all following statements are restated and thus corrected.

A company may change from one generally accepted accounting principle to another. In this case, the prior-period financial statements are restated as if the new accounting principle had always been used.[10]

For both of the preceding items, the current-period earnings are not affected. That is, only the earnings reported in prior periods are restated. However, because the prior earnings are restated, the beginning balance of Retained Earnings may also have to be restated. This, in turn, may cause the restatement of other balance sheet accounts. Illustrations of these types of adjustments and restatements are provided in advanced accounting courses.

7 The gain or loss on extraordinary operations is reported net of any tax effects..

8 *Statement of Financial Accounting Standards No. 128*, op. cit., pars. 36 and 37.

9 *Statement of Finanical Accounting Standards No. 154*, "Accounting Changes and Error Corrections" (Norwalk, CT: Finanical Accounting Standards Board, 2005).

10 Changes from one acceptable depreciation method to another acceptable depreciation method are an exception to this general rule and are to be treated prospectively as a change in estimate, as discussed in Chapter 10.

1 Describe basic financial statement analytical methods.

Key Points	Key Learning Outcomes	Example Exercises	Practice Exercises
The basic financial statements provide much of the information users need to make economic decisions. Analytical procedures are used to compare items on a current financial statement with related items on earlier statements, or to examine relationships within a financial statement.	• Prepare a horizontal analysis from a company's financial statements.	**17-1**	17-1A, 17-1B
	• Prepare a vertical analysis from a company's financial statements.	**17-2**	17-2A, 17-2B
	• Prepare common-sized financial statements.		

2 Use financial statement analysis to assess the solvency of a business.

Key Points	Key Learning Outcomes	Example Exercises	Practice Exercises
All users of financial statements are interested in the ability of a business to pay its debts (solvency) and earn income (profitability). Solvency and profitability are interrelated. Solvency analysis is normally assessed by examining the following balance sheet relationships: (1) current position analysis, (2) accounts receivable analysis, (3) inventory analysis, (4) the ratio of fixed assets to long-term liabilities, (5) the ratio of liabilities to stockholders' equity, and (6) the number of times interest charges are earned.	• Determine working capital.		
	• Compute and interpret the current ratio.	**17-3**	17-3A, 17-3B
	• Compute and interpret the quick ratio.	**17-3**	17-3A, 17-3B
	• Compute and interpret accounts receivable turnover.	**17-4**	17-4A, 17-4B
	• Compute and interpret number of days' sales in receivables.	**17-4**	17-4A, 17-4B
	• Compute and interpret inventory turnover.	**17-5**	17-5A, 17-5B
	• Compute and interpret number of days' sales in inventory.	**17-5**	17-5A, 17-5B
	• Compute and interpret the ratio of fixed assets to long-term liabilities.	**17-6**	17-6A, 17-6B
	• Compute and interpret the ratio of liabilities to stockholders' equity.	**17-6**	17-6A, 17-6B
	• Compute and interpret the number of times interest charges are earned.	**17-7**	17-7A, 17-7B

3 Use financial statement analysis to assess the profitability of a business.

Key Points	Key Learning Outcomes	Example Exercises	Practice Exercises
Profitability analysis focuses mainly on the relationship between operating results (income statement) and resources available (balance sheet). Major analyses include (1) the ratio of net sales to assets, (2) the rate earned on total assets, (3) the rate earned on stockholders' equity, (4) the rate earned on common stockholders' equity, (5) earnings per share on common stock, (6) the price-earnings ratio, (7) dividends per share, and (8) dividend yield.	• Compute and interpret the ratio of net sales to assets.	**17-8**	17-8A, 17-8B
	• Compute and interpret the rate earned on total assets.	**17-9**	17-9A, 17-9B
	• Compute and interpret the rate earned on stockholders' equity.	**17-10**	17-10A, 17-10B
	• Compute and interpret the rate earned on common stockholders' equity.	**17-10**	17-10A, 17-10B
	• Compute and interpret the earnings per share on common stock.	**17-11**	17-11A, 17-11B
	• Compute and interpret the price-earnings ratio.	**17-11**	17-11A, 17-11B
	• Compute and interpret the dividends per share and dividend yield.		
	• Describe the uses and limitations of analytical measures.		

4 Describe the contents of corporate annual reports.

Key Points	Key Learning Outcomes	Example Exercises	Practice Exercises
Corporations normally issue annual reports to their stockholders and other interested parties. Such reports summarize the corporation's operating activities for the past year and plans for the future.	• Describe the elements of a corporate annual report.		

Key Terms ● ● ● ● ●

accounts receivable analysis (768)
accounts receivable turnover (768)
common-sized statement (762)
current position analysis (765)
current ratio (766)
dividend yield (779)
dividends per share (779)
earnings per share (EPS) on common stock (777)
extraordinary item (785)
horizontal analysis (759)
inventory analysis (769)

inventory turnover (770)
Management's Discussion and Analysis (MD&A) (780)
number of days' sales in inventory (770)
number of days' sales in receivables (769)
number of times interest charges are earned (772)
price-earnings (P/E) ratio (778)
profitability (765)
quick assets (767)
quick ratio (767)

rate earned on common stockholders' equity (776)
rate earned on stockholders' equity (775)
rate earned on total assets (774)
ratio of fixed assets to long-term liabilities (771)
ratio of liabilities to stockholders' equity (771)
ratio of net sales to assets (773)
solvency (765)
vertical analysis (761)
working capital (765)

Self-Examination Questions (Answers at End of Chapter)

1. What type of analysis is indicated by the following?

	Amount	Percent
Current assets	$100,000	20%
Property, plant, and equipment	400,000	80
Total assets	$500,000	100%

   A. Vertical analysis C. Profitability analysis
   B. Horizontal analysis D. Contribution margin analysis

2. Which of the following measures indicates the ability of a firm to pay its current liabilities?
   A. Working capital C. Quick ratio
   B. Current ratio D. All of the above

3. The ratio determined by dividing total current assets by total current liabilities is the:
   A. current ratio. C. bankers' ratio.
   B. working capital ratio. D. all of the above.

4. The ratio of the quick assets to current liabilities, which indicates the "instant" debt-paying ability of a firm, is the:
   A. current ratio. C. quick ratio.
   B. working capital ratio. D. bankers' ratio.

5. A measure useful in evaluating efficiency in the management of inventories is the:
   A. working capital ratio.
   B. quick ratio.
   C. number of days' sales in inventory.
   D. ratio of fixed assets to long-term liabilities.

Eye Openers

1. What is the difference between horizontal and vertical analysis of financial statements?
2. What is the advantage of using comparative statements for financial analysis rather than statements for a single date or period?
3. The current year's amount of net income (after income tax) is 20% larger than that of the preceding year. Does this indicate an improved operating performance? Discuss.
4. How would you respond to a horizontal analysis that showed an expense increasing by over 80%?
5. How would the current and quick ratios of a service business compare?
6. For Gray Corporation, the working capital at the end of the current year is $10,000 more than the working capital at the end of the preceding year, reported as follows:

	Current Year	Preceding Year
Current assets:		
Cash, temporary investments, and receivables	$ 80,000	$ 84,000
Inventories	120,000	66,000
Total current assets	$200,000	$150,000
Current liabilities	100,000	60,000
Working capital	$100,000	$ 90,000

   Has the current position improved? Explain.

7. Why would the accounts receivable turnover ratio be different between Wal-Mart and Procter & Gamble?
8. A company that grants terms of n/45 on all sales has a yearly accounts receivable turnover, based on monthly averages, of 5. Is this a satisfactory turnover? Discuss.
9. a. Why is it advantageous to have a high inventory turnover?
   b. Is it possible for the inventory turnover to be too high? Discuss.
   c. Is it possible to have a high inventory turnover and a high number of days' sales in inventory? Discuss.
10. What do the following data taken from a comparative balance sheet indicate about the company's ability to borrow additional funds on a long-term basis in the current year as compared to the preceding year?

	Current Year	Preceding Year
Fixed assets (net)	$480,000	$540,000
Total long-term liabilities	120,000	180,000

11. a. How does the rate earned on total assets differ from the rate earned on stock-holders' equity?
    b. Which ratio is normally higher? Explain.

12. a. Why is the rate earned on stockholders' equity by a thriving business ordinarily higher than the rate earned on total assets?
    b. Should the rate earned on common stockholders' equity normally be higher or lower than the rate earned on total stockholders' equity? Explain.

13. The net income (after income tax) of McCants Inc. was $20 per common share in the latest year and $80 per common share for the preceding year. At the beginning of the latest year, the number of shares outstanding was doubled by a stock split. There were no other changes in the amount of stock outstanding. What were the earnings per share in the preceding year, adjusted for comparison with the latest year?

14. The price-earnings ratio for the common stock of Breeden Company was 12 at December 31, the end of the current fiscal year. What does the ratio indicate about the selling price of the common stock in relation to current earnings?

15. Why would the dividend yield differ significantly from the rate earned on common stockholders' equity?

16. Favorable business conditions may bring about certain seemingly unfavorable ratios, and unfavorable business operations may result in apparently favorable ratios. For example, Grochoske Company increased its sales and net income substantially for the current year, yet the current ratio at the end of the year is lower than at the beginning of the year. Discuss some possible causes of the apparent weakening of the current position, while sales and net income have increased substantially.

17. Describe two reports provided by independent auditors in the annual report to shareholders.

Practice Exercises

PE 17-1A
Horizontal analysis
obj. 1

EE 17-1   p. 761

The comparative accounts payable and long-term debt balances of a company are provided below.

	2010	2009
Accounts payable	$ 78,400	$70,000
Long-term debt	101,760	96,000

Based on this information, what is the amount and percentage of increase or decrease that would be shown in a balance sheet with horizontal analysis?

PE 17-1B
Horizontal analysis
obj. 1

EE 17-1   p. 761

The comparative temporary investments and inventory balances for a company are provided below.

	2010	2009
Temporary investments	$70,800	$ 60,000
Inventory	99,000	110,000

Based on this information, what is the amount and percentage of increase or decrease that would be shown in a balance sheet with horizontal analysis?

PE 17-2A
Vertical analysis

obj. 1

EE 17-2   p. 764

Income statement information for Sheaf Corporation is provided below.

Sales	$500,000
Gross profit	140,000
Net income	40,000

Prepare a vertical analysis of the income statement for Sheaf Corporation.

PE 17-2B
Vertical analysis

obj. 1

EE 17-2   p. 764

Income statement information for Beowulf Corporation is provided below.

Sales	$600,000
Cost of goods sold	480,000
Gross profit	$120,000

Prepare a vertical analysis of the income statement for Beowulf Corporation.

PE 17-3A
Current position
analysis

obj. 2

EE 17-3   p. 768

The following items are reported on a company's balance sheet:

Cash	$190,000
Temporary investments	150,000
Accounts receivable (net)	260,000
Inventory	300,000
Accounts payable	600,000

Determine (a) the current ratio and (b) the quick ratio. Round to one decimal place.

PE 17-3B
Current position
analysis

obj. 2

EE 17-3   p. 768

The following items are reported on a company's balance sheet:

Cash	$140,000
Temporary investments	60,000
Accounts receivable (net)	40,000
Inventory	80,000
Accounts payable	160,000

Determine (a) the current ratio and (b) the quick ratio. Round to one decimal place.

PE 17-4A
Accounts receivable
analysis

obj. 2

EE 17-4   p. 769

A company reports the following:

Net sales	$560,000
Average accounts receivable (net)	40,000

Determine (a) the accounts receivable turnover and (b) the number of days' sales in receivables. Round to one decimal place.

PE 17-4B
Accounts receivable
analysis

obj. 2

EE 17-4   p. 769

A company reports the following:

Net sales	$600,000
Average accounts receivable (net)	60,000

Determine (a) the accounts receivable turnover and (b) the number of days' sales in receivables. Round to one decimal place.

PE 17-5A
Inventory analysis

obj. 2

EE 17-5   p. 771

A company reports the following:

Cost of goods sold	$510,000
Average inventory	60,000

Determine (a) the inventory turnover and (b) the number of days' sales in inventory. Round to one decimal place.

PE 17-5B
Inventory analysis
obj. 2

EE 17-5   p. 771

A company reports the following:

Cost of goods sold	$480,000
Average inventory	80,000

Determine (a) the inventory turnover and (b) the number of days' sales in inventory. Round to one decimal place.

PE 17-6A
Long-term solvency analysis
obj. 2

EE 17-6   p. 772

The following information was taken from Grain Company's balance sheet:

Fixed assets (net)	$600,000
Long-term liabilities	400,000
Total liabilities	600,000
Total stockholders' equity	400,000

Determine the company's (a) ratio of fixed assets to long-term liabilities and (b) ratio of liabilities to stockholders' equity.

PE 17-6B
Long-term solvency analysis
obj. 2

EE 17-6   p. 772

The following information was taken from Shield Company's balance sheet:

Fixed assets (net)	$1,000,000
Long-term liabilities	500,000
Total liabilities	800,000
Total stockholders' equity	800,000

Determine the company's (a) ratio of fixed assets to long-term liabilities and (b) ratio of liabilities to stockholders' equity.

PE 17-7A
Times interest charges are earned
obj. 2

EE 17-7   p. 773

A company reports the following:

Income before income tax	$2,000,000
Interest expense	80,000

Determine the number of times interest charges are earned.

PE 17-7B
Times interest charges are earned
obj. 2

EE 17-7   p. 773

A company reports the following:

Income before income tax	$1,500,000
Interest expense	200,000

Determine the number of times interest charges are earned.

PE 17-8A
Net sales to assets
obj. 3

EE 17-8   p. 774

A company reports the following:

Net sales	$2,400,000
Average total assets	1,600,000

Determine the ratio of net sales to assets.

PE 17-8B
Net sales to assets
obj. 3

EE 17-8   p. 774

A company reports the following:

Net sales	$1,200,000
Average total assets	1,000,000

Determine the ratio of net sales to assets.

PE 17-9A
Rate earned on total assets
obj. 3

EE 17-9   p. 775

A company reports the following income statement and balance sheet information for the current year:

Net income	$ 400,000
Interest expense	20,000
Average total assets	3,500,000

Determine the rate earned on total assets.

PE 17-9B
Rate earned on total assets

obj. **3**

EE 17-9   p. 775

A company reports the following income statement and balance sheet information for the current year:

Net income	$ 600,000
Interest expense	75,000
Average total assets	4,500,000

Determine the rate earned on total assets.

PE 17-10A
Common stockholders' profitability analysis

obj. **3**

EE 17-10   p. 777

A company reports the following:

Net income	$120,000
Preferred dividends	20,000
Average stockholders' equity	600,000
Average common stockholders' equity	500,000

Determine (a) the rate earned on stockholders' equity and (b) the rate earned on common stockholders' equity. Round to one decimal place.

PE 17-10B
Common stockholders' profitability analysis

obj. **3**

EE 17-10   p. 777

A company reports the following:

Net income	$ 180,000
Preferred dividends	12,000
Average stockholders' equity	1,200,000
Average common stockholders' equity	800,000

Determine (a) the rate earned on stockholders' equity and (b) the rate earned on common stockholders' equity. Round to one decimal place.

PE 17-11A
Earnings per share and price-earnings

obj. **3**

EE 17-11   p. 778

A company reports the following:

Net income	$340,000
Preferred dividends	$40,000
Shares of common stock outstanding	40,000
Market price per share of common stock	$60.00

a. Determine the company's earnings per share on common stock.
b. Determine the company's price-earnings ratio.

PE 17-11B
Earnings per share and price-earnings

obj. **3**

EE 17-11   p. 778

A company reports the following:

Net income	$140,000
Preferred dividends	$20,000
Shares of common stock outstanding	60,000
Market price per share of common stock	$50.00

a. Determine the company's earnings per share on common stock.
b. Determine the company's price-earnings ratio.

Exercises

EX 17-1
Vertical analysis of income statement

obj. 1

✔ a. 2010 net income: $5,000; 1.0% of sales

Revenue and expense data for Rogan Technologies Co. are as follows:

	2010	2009
Sales	$500,000	$440,000
Cost of goods sold	325,000	242,000
Selling expenses	70,000	79,200
Administrative expenses	75,000	70,400
Income tax expense	25,000	26,400

a. Prepare an income statement in comparative form, stating each item for both 2010 and 2009 as a percent of sales. Round to one decimal place.
b. ➤ Comment on the significant changes disclosed by the comparative income statement.

EX 17-2
Vertical analysis of income statement

obj. 1

✔ a. Fiscal year 2006 income from continuing operations, 30.7% of revenues

The following comparative income statement (in thousands of dollars) for the fiscal years 2005 and 2006 was adapted from the annual report of Speedway Motorsports, Inc., owner and operator of several major motor speedways, such as the Atlanta, Texas, and Las Vegas Motor Speedways.

	Fiscal Year 2006	Fiscal Year 2005
Revenues:		
Admissions	$175,208	$177,352
Event-related revenue	183,404	168,359
NASCAR broadcasting revenue	162,715	140,956
Other operating revenue	46,038	57,401
Total revenue	$567,365	$544,068
Expenses and other:		
Direct expense of events	$ 95,990	$ 97,042
NASCAR purse and sanction fees	105,826	96,306
Other direct expenses	113,141	102,535
General and administrative	78,070	73,281
Total expenses and other	$393,027	$369,164
Income from continuing operations	$174,338	$174,904

a. Prepare a comparative income statement for fiscal years 2005 and 2006 in vertical form, stating each item as a percent of revenues. Round to one decimal place.
b. ➤ Comment on the significant changes.

EX 17-3
Common-sized income statement

obj. 1

✔ a. Sorenson net income: $44,000; 2.2% of sales

Revenue and expense data for the current calendar year for Sorenson Electronics Company and for the electronics industry are as follows. The Sorenson Electronics Company data are expressed in dollars. The electronics industry averages are expressed in percentages.

	Sorenson Electronics Company	Electronics Industry Average
Sales	$2,050,000	102.5%
Sales returns and allowances	50,000	2.5
Net sales	$2,000,000	100.0%
Cost of goods sold	1,100,000	61.0
Gross profit	$ 900,000	39.0%
Selling expenses	$ 560,000	23.0%
Administrative expenses	220,000	10.0
Total operating expenses	$ 780,000	33.0%
Operating income	$ 120,000	6.0%
Other income	44,000	2.2
	$ 164,000	8.2%
Other expense	20,000	1.0
Income before income tax	$ 144,000	7.2%
Income tax	60,000	5.0
Net income	$ 84,000	2.2%

a. Prepare a common-sized income statement comparing the results of operations for Hrothgar Electronics Company with the industry average. Round to one decimal place.

b. ➤ As far as the data permit, comment on significant relationships revealed by the comparisons.

EX 17-4
Vertical analysis of balance sheet

obj. 1

✔ Retained earnings, Dec. 31, 2010, 34.0%

Balance sheet data for Hanes Company on December 31, the end of the fiscal year, are shown below.

	2010	2009
Current assets	320,000	200,000
Property, plant, and equipment	560,000	560,000
Intangible assets	120,000	40,000
Current liabilities	210,000	120,000
Long-term liabilities	350,000	300,000
Common stock	100,000	100,000
Retained earnings	340,000	280,000

Prepare a comparative balance sheet for 2010 and 2009, stating each asset as a percent of total assets and each liability and stockholders' equity item as a percent of the total liabilities and stockholders' equity. Round to one decimal place.

EX 17-5
Horizontal analysis of the income statement

obj. 1

✔ a. Net income increase, 95.0%

Income statement data for Grendel Images Company for the years ended December 31, 2010, and 2009, are as follows:

	2010	2009
Sales	$196,000	$160,000
Cost of goods sold	170,100	140,000
Gross profit	$ 25,900	$ 20,000
Selling expenses	$ 12,200	$ 10,000
Administrative expenses	9,750	8,000
Total operating expenses	$ 21,950	$ 18,000
Income before income tax	$ 3,950	$ 2,000
Income tax expenses	2,000	1,000
Net income	$ 1,950	$ 1,000

a. Prepare a comparative income statement with horizontal analysis, indicating the increase (decrease) for 2010 when compared with 2009. Round to one decimal place.

b. ➤ What conclusions can be drawn from the horizontal analysis?

EX 17-6
Current position analysis

obj. 2

✔ a. 2010 working capital, $1,000,000

The following data were taken from the balance sheet of Bock Suppliers Company:

	Dec. 31, 2010	Dec. 31, 2009
Cash	$ 295,000	$ 210,000
Temporary investments	315,000	230,000
Accounts and notes receivable (net)	290,000	250,000
Inventories	405,000	309,000
Prepaid expenses	195,000	105,000
Total current assets	$1,500,000	$1,104,000
Accounts and notes payable (short-term)	$ 290,000	$ 320,000
Accrued liabilities	210,000	140,000
Total current liabilities	$ 500,000	$ 460,000

a. Determine for each year (1) the working capital, (2) the current ratio, and (3) the quick ratio. Round ratios to one decimal place.

b. ➤ What conclusions can be drawn from these data as to the company's ability to meet its currently maturing debts?

EX 17-7

Current position analysis

obj. 2

✔ a. (1) Dec. 31, 2005 current ratio, 1.1

PepsiCo, Inc., the parent company of Frito-Lay snack foods and Pepsi beverages, had the following current assets and current liabilities at the end of two recent years:

	Dec. 30, 2006 (in millions)	Dec. 31, 2005 (in millions)
Cash and cash equivalents	$1,651	$1,716
Short-term investments, at cost	1,171	3,166
Accounts and notes receivable, net	3,725	3,261
Inventories	1,926	1,693
Prepaid expenses and other current assets	657	618
Short-term obligations	274	2,889
Accounts payable and other current liabilities	6,496	5,971
Income taxes payable	90	546

a. Determine the (1) current ratio and (2) quick ratio for both years. Round to one decimal place.

b. ▬▬▶ What conclusions can you draw from these data?

EX 17-8

Current position analysis

obj. 2

The bond indenture for the 10-year, 10% debenture bonds dated January 2, 2009, required working capital of $142,000 a current ratio of 1.7, and a quick ratio of 1.2 at the end of each calendar year until the bonds mature. At December 31, 2010, the three measures were computed as follows:

1. Current assets:

Cash	$170,000	
Temporary investments	80,000	
Accounts and notes receivable (net)	200,000	
Inventories	60,000	
Prepaid expenses	40,000	
Intangible assets	208,000	
Property, plant and equipment	92,000	
Total current assets (net)		$850,000
Current liabilities:		
Accounts and short-term notes payable	$160,000	
Accrued liabilities	340,000	
Total current liabilities		500,000
Working capital		$350,000

2. Current Ratio	1.7	$850,000 ÷ $500,000
3. Quick Ratio	1.2	$192,000 ÷ $160,000

a. List the errors in the determination of the three measures of current position analysis.

b. ▬▬▶ Is the company satisfying the terms of the bond indenture?

EX 17-9

Accounts receivable analysis

obj. 2

✔ a. Accounts receivable turnover, 2010, 8.0

The following data are taken from the financial statements of McKee Technology Inc. Terms of all sales are 2/10, n/60.

	2010	2009	2008
Accounts receivable, end of year	$147,500	$158,000	$165,000
Net sales on account	975,000	900,000	

a. Determine for each year (1) the accounts receivable turnover and (2) the number of days' sales in receivables. Round to nearest dollar and one decimal place.

b. ▬▬▶ What conclusions can be drawn from these data concerning accounts receivable and credit policies?

EX 17-10

Accounts receivable analysis

obj. 2

Xavier Stores Company and Lestrade Stores, Inc., are large retail department stores. Both companies offer credit to their customers through their own credit card operations. Information from the financial statements for both companies for two recent years is as follows (all numbers are in millions):

	Xavier	Lestrade
Merchandise sales	$28,000	$65,000
Credit card receivables—beginning	2,750	15,000
Credit card receivables—ending	2,250	11,000

a. Determine the (1) accounts receivable turnover and (2) the number of days' sales in receivables for both companies. Round to one decimal place.

b. ➤ Compare the two companies with regard to their credit card policies.

EX 17-11
Inventory analysis

obj. 2

✔ a. Inventory turnover, current year, 7.4

The following data were extracted from the income statement of Brecca Systems Inc.:

	Current Year	Preceding Year
Sales	$1,139,600	$1,192,320
Beginning inventories	80,000	64,000
Cost of goods sold	569,800	662,400
Ending inventories	74,000	80,000

a. Determine for each year (1) the inventory turnover and (2) the number of days' sales in inventory. Round to nearest dollar and one decimal place.

b. ➤ What conclusions can be drawn from these data concerning the inventories?

EX 17-12
Inventory analysis

obj. 2

✔ a. Dell inventory turnover, 76.8

Dell Inc. and Hewlett-Packard Company (HP) compete with each other in the personal computer market. Dell's primary strategy is to assemble computers to customer orders, rather than for inventory. Thus, for example, Dell will build and deliver a computer within four days of a customer entering an order on a Web page. Hewlett-Packard, on the other hand, builds some computers prior to receiving an order, then sells from this inventory once an order is received. Below is selected financial information for both companies from a recent year's financial statements (in millions):

	Dell Inc.	Hewlett-Packard Company
Sales	$57,420	$73,557
Cost of goods sold	47,904	69,427
Inventory, beginning of period	588	6,877
Inventory, end of period	660	7,750

a. Determine for both companies (1) the inventory turnover and (2) the number of days' sales in inventory. Round to one decimal place.

b. ➤ Interpret the inventory ratios by considering Dell's and Hewlett-Packard's operating strategies.

EX 17-13
Ratio of liabilities to stockholders' equity and number of times interest charges earned

obj. 2

✔ a. Ratio of liabilities to stockholders' equity, Dec. 31, 2010, 0.6

The following data were taken from the financial statements of Weal Construction Inc. for December 31, 2010 and 2009:

	Dec. 31, 2010	Dec. 31, 2009
Accounts payable	$ 300,000	$ 280,000
Current maturities of serial bonds payable	400,000	400,000
Serial bonds payable, 10%, issued 2005, due 2015	2,000,000	2,400,000
Common stock, $1 par value	100,000	100,000
Paid-in capital in excess of par	1,000,000	1,000,000
Retained earnings	3,400,000	2,750,000

The income before income tax was $720,000 and $560,000 for the years 2010 and 2009, respectively.

a. Determine the ratio of liabilities to stockholders' equity at the end of each year. Round to one decimal place.

b. Determine the number of times the bond interest charges are earned during the year for both years. Round to one decimal place.

c. ➤ What conclusions can be drawn from these data as to the company's ability to meet its currently maturing debts?

EX 17-14
Ratio of liabilities to stockholders' equity and number of times interest charges earned

obj. 2

Hasbro and Mattel, Inc., are the two largest toy companies in North America. Condensed liabilities and stockholders' equity from a recent balance sheet are shown for each company as follows (in thousands):

	Hasbro	Mattel
Current liabilities	$ 905,873	$1,582,520
Long-term debt	494,917	635,714
Other liabilities	—	304,676
Total liabilities	$1,400,790	$2,522,910

(continued)

Shareholders' equity:		
Common stock	$ 104,847	$ 441,369
Additional paid in capital	322,254	1,613,307
Retained earnings	2,020,348	1,652,140
Accumulated other comprehensive loss and other equity items	11,186	(276,861)
Treasury stock, at cost	(920,475)	(996,981)
Total stockholders' equity	$1,538,160	$2,432,974
Total liabilities and stockholder's equity	$2,938,950	$4,955,884

The income from operations and interest expense from the income statement for both companies were as follows:

	Hasbro	Mattel
Income from operations	$376,363	$728,818
Interest expense	27,521	79,853

a. Determine the ratio of liabilities to stockholders' equity for both companies. Round to one decimal place.

b. Determine the number of times interest charges are earned for both companies. Round to one decimal place.

c. ━━━▶ Interpret the ratio differences between the two companies.

EX 17-15

Ratio of liabilities to stockholders' equity and ratio of fixed assets to long-term liabilities

obj. 2

Recent balance sheet information for two companies in the food industry, H.J. Heinz Company and The Hershey Company, are as follows (in thousands of dollars):

	H.J. Heinz	Hershey
Net property, plant, and equipment	$1,998,153	$1,651,300
Current liabilities	2,505,106	1,453,538
Long-term debt	4,413,641	1,248,128
Other long-term liabilities	1,272,596	486,473
Stockholders' equity	1,841,683	683,423

a. Determine the ratio of liabilities to stockholders' equity for both companies. Round to one decimal place.

b. Determine the ratio of fixed assets to long-term liabilities for both companies. Round to one decimal place.

c. ━━━▶ Interpret the ratio differences between the two companies.

EX 17-16

Ratio of net sales to assets

obj. 3

Three major segments of the transportation industry are motor carriers, such as YRC Worldwide; railroads, such as Union Pacific; and transportation arrangement services, such as C.H. Robinson Worldwide Inc. Recent financial statement information for these three companies is shown as follows (in thousands of dollars):

	YRC Worldwide	Union Pacific	C.H. Robinson Worldwide Inc.
Net sales	$9,918,690	$15,578,000	$6,566,194
Average total assets	5,829,713	36,067,500	1,513,381

a. Determine the ratio of net sales to assets for all three companies. Round to one decimal place.

b. ━━━▶ Assume that the ratio of net sales to assets for each company represents their respective industry segment. Interpret the differences in the ratio of net sales to assets in terms of the operating characteristics of each of the respective segments.

EX 17-17

Profitability ratios

obj. 3

The following selected data were taken from the financial statements of The Sigemund Group Inc. for December 31, 2010, 2009, and 2008:

	December 31		
	2010	2009	2008
Total assets	$3,000,000	$2,700,000	$2,400,000
Notes payable (10% interest) . .	1,000,000	1,000,000	1,000,000
Common stock	400,000	400,000	400,000
Preferred $6 stock, $100 par (no change during year)	200,000	200,000	200,000
Retained earnings	1,126,000	896,000	600,000

The 2010 net income was $242,000, and the 2009 net income was $308,000. No dividends on common stock were declared between 2008 and 2010.

a. Determine the rate earned on total assets, the rate earned on stockholders' equity, and the rate earned on common stockholders' equity for the years 2009 and 2010. Round to one decimal place.

b. ━━━▶ What conclusions can be drawn from these data as to the company's profitability?

EX 17-18
Profitability ratios

obj. 3

✔ a. 2006 rate earned on total assets, 9.5%

Ann Taylor Retail, Inc., sells professional women's apparel through company-owned retail stores. Recent financial information for Ann Taylor is provided below (all numbers in thousands).

	Fiscal Year Ended		
	February 3, 2007	**January 28, 2006**	
Net income	$142,982	$81,872	
Interest expense	2,230	2,083	
	February 3, 2007	**January 28, 2006**	**January 29, 2005**
Total assets	$1,568,503	$1,492,906	$1,327,338
Total stockholders' equity	1,049,911	1,034,482	926,744

Assume the apparel industry average rate earned on total assets is 8.2%, and the average rate earned on stockholders' equity is 10.0% for the year ended February 3, 2007 (fiscal year 2006).

a. Determine the rate earned on total assets for Ann Taylor for the fiscal years ended February 3, 2007, and January 28, 2006. Round to one digit after the decimal place.

b. Determine the rate earned on stockholders' equity for Ann Taylor for the fiscal years ended February 3, 2007, and January 28, 2006. Round to one decimal place.

c. ━━━▶ Evaluate the two-year trend for the profitability ratios determined in (a) and (b).

d. ━━━▶ Evaluate Ann Taylor's profit performance relative to the industry.

EX 17-19
Six measures of solvency or profitability

objs. 2, 3

✔ c. Ratio of net sales to assets, 5.0

The following data were taken from the financial statements of Heston Enterprises Inc. for the current fiscal year. Assuming that long-term investments totaled $2,100,000 throughout the year and that total assets were $4,000,000 at the beginning of the year, determine the following: (a) ratio of fixed assets to long-term liabilities, (b) ratio of liabilities to stockholders' equity, (c) ratio of net sales to assets, (d) rate earned on total assets, (e) rate earned on stockholders' equity, and (f) rate earned on common stockholders' equity. Round to one decimal place.

Property, plant, and equipment (net)			$ 1,600,000
Liabilities:			
Current liabilities		$ 200,000	
Mortgage note payable, 10%, issued 1999, due 2015		1,000,000	
Total liabilities			$ 1,200,000
Stockholders' equity:			
Preferred $10 stock, $100 par (no change during year)			$ 1,000,000
Common stock, $10 par (no change during year) . . .			1,000,000
Retained earnings:			
Balance, beginning of year	$800,000		
Net income	400,000	$1,200,000	
Preferred dividends	$100,000		
Common dividends	100,000	200,000	
Balance, end of year			1,000,000
Total stockholders' equity			$ 3,000,000
Net sales			$10,000,000
Interest expense			$ 100,000

EX 17-20

Six measures of solvency or profitability

objs. 2, 3

✔ d. Price-earnings ratio, 10.0

The balance sheet for Bearing Industries Inc. at the end of the current fiscal year indicated the following:

Bonds payable, 10% (issued in 2000, due in 2020)	$4,000,000
Preferred $5 stock, $100 par	1,000,000
Common stock, $10 par	2,000,000

Income before income tax was $1,000,000, and income taxes were $150,000, for the current year. Cash dividends paid on common stock during the current year totaled $200,000. The common stock was selling for $40 per share at the end of the year. Determine each of the following: (a) number of times bond interest charges are earned, (b) number of times preferred dividends are earned, (c) earnings per share on common stock, (d) price-earnings ratio, (e) dividends per share of common stock, and (f) dividend yield. Round to one decimal place except earnings per share, which should be rounded to two decimal places.

EX 17-21

Earnings per share, price-earnings ratio, dividend yield

obj. 3

✔ b. Price-earnings ratio, 12.5

The following information was taken from the financial statements of Finn Resources Inc. for December 31 of the current fiscal year:

Common stock, $20 par value (no change during the year)	$5,000,000
Preferred $10 stock, $40 par (no change during the year)	800,000

The net income was $600,000 and the declared dividends on the common stock were $125,000 for the current year. The market price of the common stock is $20 per share.

For the common stock, determine (a) the earnings per share, (b) the price-earnings ratio, (c) the dividends per share, and (d) the dividend yield. Round to one decimal place except earnings per share, which should be rounded to two decimal places.

Appendix EX 17-22

Price-earnings ratio; dividend yield

obj. 3

The table below shows the stock price, earnings per share, and dividends per share for three companies as of October 2007:

	Price	Earnings per Share	Dividends per Share
Bank of America Corporation	$52.99	$4.59	$2.12
eBay Inc.	33.51	0.57	0.00
The Coca-Cola Company	47.76	2.16	1.24

a. Determine the price-earnings ratio and dividend yield for the three companies. Round to one decimal place.
b. ⬤━━━▶ Explain the differences in these ratios across the three companies.

Appendix EX 17-23

Earnings per share

obj. 3

✔ b. Earnings per share on common stock, $23.40

The net income reported on the income statement of Goth Co. was $2,500,000. There were 100,000 shares of $10 par common stock and 40,000 shares of $4 preferred stock outstanding throughout the current year. The income statement included two extraordinary items: a $500,000 gain from condemnation of land and a $200,000 loss arising from flood damage, both after applicable income tax. Determine the per-share figures for common stock for (a) income before extraordinary items and (b) net income.

Appendix EX 17-24

Extraordinary item

Assume that the amount of each of the following items is material to the financial statements. Classify each item as either normally recurring (NR) or extraordinary (E).

a. Loss on the disposal of equipment considered to be obsolete because of the development of new technology.
b. Uncollectible accounts expense.
c. Gain on sale of land condemned by the local government for a public works project.
d. Interest revenue on notes receivable.
e. Uninsured loss on building due to hurricane damage. The building was purchased by the company in 1910 and had not previously incurred hurricane damage.
f. Loss on sale of investments in stocks and bonds.
g. Uninsured flood loss. (Flood insurance is unavailable because of periodic flooding in the area.)

**Appendix
EX 17-25**
**Income statement
and earnings per
share for extraordi-
nary items and dis-
continued operations**

Brady, Inc., reports the following for 2010:

Income from continuing operations before income tax	$500,000
Extraordinary property loss from hurricane	$60,000*
Loss from discontinued operations	$90,000*
Weighted average number of shares outstanding	40,000
Applicable tax rate	40%

*Net of any tax effect.

a. Prepare a partial income statement for Brady, Inc., beginning with income from continuing operations before income tax.
b. Calculate the earnings per common share for Brady, Inc., including per-share
amounts for unusual items.

**Appendix
EX 17-26**
Unusual items

Discuss whether Baxter Company correctly reported the following items in the financial statements:

a. In 2010, the company discovered a clerical error in the prior year's accounting
records. As a result, the reported net income for 2009 was overstated by
$20,000. The company corrected this error by restating the prior-year financial
statements.
b. In 2010, the company voluntarily changed its method of accounting for long-term
construction contracts from the percentage of completion method to the completed
contract method. Both methods are acceptable under generally acceptable accounting principles. The cumulative effect of this change was reported as a separate component of income in the 2010 income statement.

Problems Series A

PR 17-1A
**Horizontal analysis
for income statement**

obj. 1

✔ 1. Net sales
10.0% increase

For 2010, Wiglaf Technology Company reported its most significant decline in net
income in years. At the end of the year, C. S. Lewis, the president, is presented with the
following condensed comparative income statement:

Wiglaf Technology Company
Comparative Income Statement
For the Years Ended December 31, 2010 and 2009

	2010	2009
Sales	$560,000	$500,000
Sales returns and allowances	37,500	25,000
Net sales	$522,500	$475,000
Cost of goods sold	372,000	300,000
Gross profit	$150,500	$175,000
Selling expenses	$ 52,000	$ 40,000
Administrative expenses	30,500	25,000
Total operating expenses	$ 82,500	$ 65,000
Income from operations	$ 68,000	$110,000
Other income	3,000	2,000
Income before income tax	$ 71,000	$112,000
Income tax expense	5,500	5,000
Net income	$ 65,500	$107,000

Instructions
1. Prepare a comparative income statement with horizontal analysis for the two-year
period, using 2009 as the base year. Round to one decimal place.
2. ➡ To the extent the data permit, comment on the significant relationships
revealed by the horizontal analysis prepared in (1).

PR 17-2A

Vertical analysis for income statement

obj. 1

✔ 1. Net income, 2010, 16.0%

For 2010, Othere Technology Company initiated a sales promotion campaign that included the expenditure of an additional $20,000 for advertising. At the end of the year, George Wallace, the president, is presented with the following condensed comparative income statement:

Othere Technology Company
Comparative Income Statement
For the Years Ended December 31, 2010 and 2009

	2010	2009
Sales	$714,000	$612,000
Sales returns and allowances	14,000	12,000
Net sales	$700,000	$600,000
Cost of goods sold	322,000	312,000
Gross profit	$378,000	$288,000
Selling expenses	$154,000	$120,000
Administrative expenses	70,000	66,000
Total operating expenses	$224,000	$186,000
Income from operations	$154,000	$102,000
Other income	28,000	24,000
Income before income tax	$182,000	$126,000
Income tax	70,000	60,000
Net income	$112,000	$ 66,000

Instructions

1. Prepare a comparative income statement for the two-year period, presenting an analysis of each item in relationship to net sales for each of the years. Round to one decimal place.

2. ➞ To the extent the data permit, comment on the significant relationships revealed by the vertical analysis prepared in (1).

PR 17-3A

Effect of transactions on current position analysis

obj. 2

✔ 2. c. Current ratio, 2.6

Data pertaining to the current position of Boole Company are as follows:

Cash	$240,000
Temporary investments	120,000
Accounts and notes receivable (net)	360,000
Inventories	380,000
Prepaid expenses	20,000
Accounts payable	140,000
Notes payable (short-term)	200,000
Accrued expenses	60,000

Instructions

1. Compute (a) the working capital, (b) the current ratio, and (c) the quick ratio. Round to one decimal place.

2. List the following captions on a sheet of paper:

Transaction	Working Capital	Current Ratio	Quick Ratio

Compute the working capital, the current ratio, and the quick ratio after each of the following transactions, and record the results in the appropriate columns. Consider each transaction separately and assume that only that transaction affects the data given above. Round to one decimal place.

a. Sold temporary investments at no gain or loss, $45,000.
b. Paid accounts payable, $80,000.
c. Purchased goods on account, $50,000.
d. Paid notes payable, $100,000.
e. Declared a cash dividend, $80,000.
f. Declared a common stock dividend on common stock, $22,500.
g. Borrowed cash from bank on a long-term note, $200,000.
h. Received cash on account, $67,500.
i. Issued additional shares of stock for cash, $400,000.
j. Paid cash for prepaid expenses, $40,000.

PR 17-4A
Nineteen measures of solvency and profitability

objs. 2, 3

✔ 5. Number of days' sales in receivables, 53.7

The comparative financial statements of Optical Solutions Inc. are as follows. The market price of Optical Solutions Inc. common stock was $60.00 on December 31, 2010.

Optical Solutions Inc.
Comparative Retained Earnings Statement
For the Years Ended December 31, 2010 and 2009

	2010	2009
Retained earnings, January 1	$ 604,000	$306,000
Add net income for year	428,000	314,000
Total	$1,032,000	$620,000
Deduct dividends:		
On preferred stock	$ 4,000	$ 4,000
On common stock	12,000	12,000
Total	$ 16,000	$ 16,000
Retained earnings, December 31	$1,016,000	$604,000

Optical Solutions Inc.
Comparative Income Statement
For the Years Ended December 31, 2010 and 2009

	2010	2009
Sales	$1,608,000	$1,481,600
Sales returns and allowances	5,920	6,000
Net sales	$1,602,080	$1,475,600
Cost of goods sold	480,200	499,200
Gross profit	$1,121,880	$ 976,400
Selling expenses	$ 324,000	$ 352,000
Administrative expenses	234,000	211,200
Total operating expenses	$ 558,000	$ 563,200
Income from operations	$ 563,880	$ 413,200
Other income	24,000	19,200
	$ 587,880	$ 432,400
Other expense (interest)	110,720	80,000
Income before income tax	$ 477,160	$ 352,400
Income tax expense	49,160	38,400
Net income	$ 428,000	$ 314,000

Optical Solutions Inc.
Comparative Balance Sheet
December 31, 2010 and 2009

	Dec. 31, 2010	Dec. 31, 2009
Assets		
Current assets:		
Cash	$ 240,000	$ 162,400
Temporary investments	364,000	328,800
Accounts receivable (net)	260,000	211,200
Inventories	208,000	66,400
Prepaid expenses	44,000	23,200
Total current assets	$1,116,000	$ 792,000
Long-term investments	204,800	256,000
Property, plant, and equipment (net)	1,539,200	976,000
Total assets	$2,860,000	$2,024,000
Liabilities		
Current liabilities	$ 360,000	$ 320,000
Long-term liabilities:		
Mortgage note payable, 8%, due 2015	$ 384,000	—
Bonds payable, 10%, due 2019	800,000	$ 800,000
Total long-term liabilities	$1,184,000	$ 800,000
Total liabilities	$1,544,000	$1,120,000
Stockholders' Equity		
Preferred $2.00 stock, $50 par	$ 100,000	$ 100,000
Common stock, $5 par	200,000	200,000
Retained earnings	1,016,000	604,000
Total stockholders' equity	$1,316,000	$ 904,000
Total liabilities and stockholders' equity	$2,860,000	$2,024,000

Instructions

Determine the following measures for 2010, rounding to one decimal place:

1. Working capital
2. Current ratio
3. Quick ratio
4. Accounts receivable turnover
5. Number of days' sales in receivables
6. Inventory turnover
7. Number of days' sales in inventory
8. Ratio of fixed assets to long-term liabilities
9. Ratio of liabilities to stockholders' equity
10. Number of times interest charges earned
11. Number of times preferred dividends earned
12. Ratio of net sales to assets
13. Rate earned on total assets
14. Rate earned on stockholders' equity
15. Rate earned on common stockholders' equity
16. Earnings per share on common stock
17. Price-earnings ratio
18. Dividends per share of common stock
19. Dividend yield

PR 17-5A
Solvency and
profitability trend
analysis

objs. 2, 3

Lancelot Company has provided the following comparative information:

	2010	2009	2008	2007	2006
Net income	$ 1,930,500	$1,287,000	$ 975,000	$ 650,000	$ 500,000
Interest expense	400,200	345,000	300,000	240,000	200,000
Income tax expense	477,360	318,240	244,800	163,200	120,000
Total assets (ending balance)	11,498,760	8,845,200	6,804,000	5,040,000	4,200,000
Total stockholders' equity (ending balance)	6,742,500	4,812,000	3,525,000	2,550,000	1,900,000
Average total assets	10,171,980	7,824,600	5,922,000	4,620,000	3,600,000
Average stockholders' equity	5,777,250	4,168,500	3,037,500	2,225,000	1,650,000

You have been asked to evaluate the historical performance of the company over the last five years.

Selected industry ratios have remained relatively steady at the following levels for the last five years:

	2006–2010
Rate earned on total assets	15%
Rate earned on stockholders' equity	18%
Number of times interest charges earned	3.5
Ratio of liabilities to stockholders' equity	1.4

Instructions

1. Prepare four line graphs with the ratio on the vertical axis and the years on the horizontal axis for the following four ratios (rounded to one decimal place):
   a. Rate earned on total assets
   b. Rate earned on stockholders' equity
   c. Number of times interest charges earned
   d. Ratio of liabilities to stockholders' equity
   Display both the company ratio and the industry benchmark on each graph. That is, each graph should have two lines.
2. ▬▬▶ Prepare an analysis of the graphs in (1).

Problems Series B ● ● ● ● ●〉〉

PR 17-1B
Horizontal analysis
for income statement

obj. 1

For 2010, Egils Inc. reported its most significant increase in net income in years. At the end of the year, David Dickens, the president, is presented with the following condensed comparative income statement:

✔ 1. Net sales,
26.3% increase

Egils Inc.
Comparative Income Statement
For the Years Ended December 31, 2010 and 2009

	2010	2009
Sales	$126,200	$100,000
Sales returns and allowances	2,426	2,000
Net sales	$123,774	$ 98,000
Cost of goods sold	58,800	50,000
Gross profit	$ 64,974	$ 48,000
Selling expenses	$ 17,310	$ 15,000
Administrative expenses	13,464	12,000
Total operating expenses	$ 30,774	$ 27,000
Income from operations	$ 34,200	$ 21,000
Other income	1,000	1,000
Income before income tax	$ 35,200	$ 22,000
Income tax expense	12,000	6,000
Net income	$ 23,200	$ 16,000

Instructions
1. Prepare a comparative income statement with horizontal analysis for the two-year period, using 2009 as the base year. Round to one decimal place.
2. ▬▬▶ To the extent the data permit, comment on the significant relationships revealed by the horizontal analysis prepared in (1).

PR 17-2B
Vertical analysis for
income statement

obj. 1

✔ 1. Net income,
2009, 10.0%

For 2010, Einar Industries Inc. initiated a sales promotion campaign that included the expenditure of an additional $40,000 for advertising. At the end of the year, David Heaney, the president, is presented with the following condensed comparative income statement:

Einar Industries
Comparative Income Statement
For the Years Ended December 31, 2010 and 2009

	2010	2009
Sales	$525,000	$420,000
Sales returns and allowances	25,000	20,000
Net sales	$500,000	$400,000
Cost of goods sold	280,000	220,000
Gross profit	$220,000	$180,000
Selling expenses	$130,000	$ 80,000
Adminstrative expenses	65,000	56,000
Total operating expenses	$195,000	$136,000
Income from operations	$ 25,000	$ 44,000
Other income	30,000	24,000
Income before income tax	$ 55,000	$ 68,000
Income tax expense (benefit)	35,000	28,000
Net income (loss)	$ 20,000	$ 40,000

Instructions
1. Prepare a comparative income statement for the two-year period, presenting an analysis of each item in relationship to net sales for each of the years. Round to one decimal place.
2. ▬▬▶ To the extent the data permit, comment on the significant relationships revealed by the vertical analysis prepared in (1).

PR 17-3B
Effect of transactions
on current position
analysis

obj. 2

✔ 2. e. Quick
ratio, 0.8

Data pertaining to the current position of Newton Industries, Inc., are as follows:

Cash	$300,000
Temporary investments	250,000
Accounts and notes receivable (net)	350,000
Inventories	440,000
Prepaid expenses	60,000
Accounts payable	420,000
Notes payable (short-term)	460,000
Accrued expenses	120,000

Instructions

1. Compute (a) the working capital, (b) the current ratio, and (c) the quick ratio. Round to one decimal place.

2. List the following captions on a sheet of paper:

Transaction	Working Capital	Current Ratio	Quick Ratio

Compute the working capital, the current ratio, and the quick ratio after each of the following transactions, and record the results in the appropriate columns. Consider each transaction separately and assume that only that transaction affects the data given above. Round to one decimal place.

   a. Sold temporary investments at no gain or loss, $120,000.
   b. Paid accounts payable, $200,000.
   c. Purchased goods on account, $80,000.
   d. Paid notes payable, $200,000.
   e. Declared a cash dividend, $125,000.
   f. Declared a common stock dividend on common stock, $100,000.
   g. Borrowed cash from bank on a long-term note, $400,000.
   h. Received cash on account, $65,000.
   i. Issued additional shares of stock for cash, $800,000.
   j. Paid cash for prepaid expenses, $20,000.

PR 17-4B
Nineteen measures of solvency and profitability

objs. 2, 3

✔ 9. Ratio of liabilities to stockholders' equity, 0.6

The comparative financial statements of Caylay Technologies Inc. are as follows. The market price of Caylay Technologies Inc. common stock was $40 on December 31, 2010.

Caylay Technologies Inc.
Comparative Retained Earnings Statement
For the Years Ended December 31, 2010 and 2009

	2010	2009
Retained earnings, January 1	$1,453,600	$1,218,100
Add net income for year	482,850	307,500
Total	$1,936,450	$1,525,600
Deduct dividends:		
On preferred stock	$ 24,000	$ 24,000
On common stock	48,000	48,000
Total	$ 72,000	$ 72,000
Retained earnings, December 31	$1,864,450	$1,453,600

Caylay Technologies Inc.
Comparative Income Statement
For the Years Ended December 31, 2010 and 2009

	2010	2009
Sales (all on account)	$4,245,000	$3,675,000
Sales returns and allowances	35,000	22,500
Net sales	$4,210,000	$3,652,500
Cost of goods sold	1,866,150	1,725,000
Gross profit	$2,343,850	$1,927,500
Selling expenses	$ 907,500	$ 862,500
Administrative expenses	607,500	570,000
Total operating expenses	$1,515,000	$1,432,500
Income from operations	$ 828,850	$ 495,000
Other income	60,000	45,000
	$ 888,850	$ 540,000
Other expense (interest)	196,000	90,000
Income before income tax	$ 692,850	$ 450,000
Income tax expense	210,000	142,500
Net income	$ 482,850	$ 307,500

Caylay Technologies Inc.
Comparative Balance Sheet
December 31, 2010 and 2009

	Dec. 31, 2010	Dec. 31, 2009
Assets		
Current assets:		
Cash	$ 400,000	$ 180,000
Temporary investments	614,000	240,000
Accounts receivable (net)	390,000	283,600
Inventories	631,000	500,000
Prepaid expenses	45,000	52,500
Total current assets	$2,080,000	$1,256,100
Long-term investments	324,450	375,000
Property, plant, and equipment (net)	3,780,000	3,000,000
Total assets	$6,184,450	$4,631,100
Liabilities		
Current liabilities	$ 520,000	$ 427,500
Long-term liabilities:		
Mortgage note payable, 10%, due 2015	$1,000,000	—
Bonds payable, 12%, due 2019	800,000	$ 750,000
Total long-term liabilities	$1,800,000	$ 750,000
Total liabilities	$2,320,000	$1,177,500
Stockholders' Equity		
Preferred $3.00 stock, $100 par	$ 800,000	$ 800,000
Common stock, $10 par	1,200,000	1,200,000
Retained earnings	1,864,450	1,453,600
Total stockholders' equity	$3,864,450	$3,453,600
Total liabilities and stockholders' equity	$6,184,450	$4,631,100

Instructions

Determine the following measures for 2010, rounding to one decimal place:

1. Working capital
2. Current ratio
3. Quick ratio
4. Accounts receivable turnover
5. Number of days' sales in receivables
6. Inventory turnover
7. Number of days' sales in inventory
8. Ratio of fixed assets to long-term liabilities
9. Ratio of liabilities to stockholders' equity
10. Number of times interest charges earned
11. Number of times preferred dividends earned
12. Ratio of net sales to assets
13. Rate earned on total assets
14. Rate earned on stockholders' equity
15. Rate earned on common stockholders' equity
16. Earnings per share on common stock
17. Price-earnings ratio
18. Dividends per share of common stock
19. Dividend yield

PR 17-5B
Solvency and
profitability trend
analysis

objs. 2, 3

Merlin Company has provided the following comparative information:

	2010	2009	2008	2007	2006
Net income	$ 129,868	$ 174,788	$ 299,809	$ 419,900	$ 380,000
Interest expense	280,021	260,001	240,075	225,000	200,000
Income tax expense	20,002	33,617	67,234	100,800	126,000
Total assets (ending balance)	4,417,178	4,124,350	3,732,443	3,338,500	2,750,000
Total stockholders' equity (ending balance)	1,904,365	1,774,497	1,599,709	1,299,900	880,000
Average total assets	4,270,764	3,928,396	3,535,472	3,044,250	2,475,000
Average stockholders' equity	1,839,431	1,687,103	1,449,804	1,089,950	690,000

You have been asked to evaluate the historical performance of the company over the last five years.

Selected industry ratios have remained relatively steady at the following levels for the last five years:

	2006–2010
Rate earned on total assets	12%
Rate earned on stockholders' equity	18%
Number of times interest charges earned	2.8
Ratio of liabilities to stockholders' equity	1.6

Instructions

1. Prepare four line graphs with the ratio on the vertical axis and the years on the horizontal axis for the following four ratios (rounded to one decimal place):
   a. Rate earned on total assets
   b. Rate earned on stockholders' equity
   c. Number of times interest charges earned
   d. Ratio of liabilities to stockholders' equity
   Display both the company ratio and the industry benchmark on each graph. That is, each graph should have two lines.
2. ➤ Prepare an analysis of the graphs in (1).

Nike, Inc., Problem

Financial Statement Analysis

The financial statements for Nike, Inc., are presented in Appendix E at the end of the text. The following additional information (in thousands) is available:

Accounts receivable at May 31, 2005	$2,249.9
Inventories at May 31, 2005	1,811.1
Total assets at May 31, 2005	8,793.6
Stockholders' equity at May 31, 2005	5,644.2

Instructions

1. Determine the following measures for the fiscal years ended May 31, 2007, and May 31, 2006, rounding to one decimal place.
   a. Working capital
   b. Current ratio
   c. Quick ratio
   d. Accounts receivable turnover
   e. Number of days' sales in receivables
   f. Inventory turnover
   g. Number of days' sales in inventory
   h. Ratio of liabilities to stockholders' equity
   i. Ratio of net sales to average total assets
   j. Rate earned on average total assets, assuming interest expense is $20.495 million for the year ending May 31, 2007, and $20.956 million for the year ending May 31, 2006
   k. Rate earned on average common stockholders' equity
   l. Price-earnings ratio, assuming that the market price was $56.75 per share on May 31, 2007, and $40.16 per share on May 31, 2006
   m. Percentage relationship of net income to net sales
2. ➤ What conclusions can be drawn from these analyses?

Special Activities

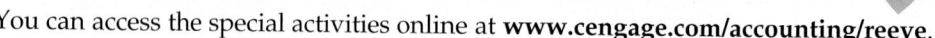

You can access the special activities online at **www.cengage.com/accounting/reeve**.

Excel Success Special Activities

SA 17-1
Horizontal analysis

The comparative income statement for Ironside, Inc., is provided below.

	A	B	C
1	Ironside, Inc.		
2	Comparative Income Statement		
3	For the Years Ended December 31, 2011 and 2010		
4			
5		2011	2010
6	Sales	$ 425,000	$ 460,000
7	Sales returns and allowances	25,000	30,000
8	Net sales	$ 400,000	$ 430,000
9	Cost of goods sold	205,000	227,000
10	Gross profit	$ 195,000	$ 203,000
11	Selling expenses	82,400	99,500
12	Administrative expenses	31,900	34,600
13	Total operating expenses	114,300	134,100
14	Income from operations	$ 80,700	$ 68,900
15	Other income	5,000	5,000
16		$ 85,700	$ 73,900
17	Other expense (interest)	10,000	12,000
18	Income before income tax	$ 75,700	$ 61,900
19	Income tax expense	25,700	31,400
20	Net Income	$ 50,000	$ 30,500
21			

a. Open the Excel file *SA17-1*.
b. Prepare a horizontal analysis using 2010 as the base year. Round percentages to one tenth of a percent (for example, 10.47% rounds to 10.5%).
c. When you have completed the horizontal analysis, perform a "save as," replacing the entire file name with the following:

   SA17-1_[your first name initial]_[your last name]

SA 17-2
Vertical analysis

The comparative balance sheet for Ironside, Inc., is provided below.

	A	B	C	D	E
1	Ironside, Inc.				
2	Comparative Balance Sheet				
3	For the Years Ended December 31, 2011 and 2010				
4					
5		Dec. 31, 2011	Percent	Dec. 31, 2010	Percent
6	Assets				
7	Current assets:				
8	Cash	$ 27,000		$ 25,000	
9	Temporary investments	32,000		35,000	
10	Accounts receivable (net)	55,000		50,000	
11	Inventories	51,000		55,000	
12	Prepaid expenses	5,000		5,000	
13	Total current assets	$ 170,000		$ 170,000	
14	Long-term investments	55,000		60,000	
15	Property, plant, and equipment (net)	305,000		290,000	
16	Total assets	$ 530,000		$ 520,000	
17					
18	Liabilities				
19	Current liabilities	$ 60,000		$ 70,000	
20	Bonds payable, 6%, due 2020	170,000		200,000	
21	Total liabilities	$ 230,000		$ 270,000	
22					
23	Stockholders' Equity				
24	Common stock, $10 par	$ 50,000		$ 50,000	
25	Retained earnings	250,000		200,000	
26	Total stockholders' equity	$ 300,000		$ 250,000	
27	Total liabilities and stockholders' equity	$ 530,000		$ 520,000	
28					

a. Open the Excel file *SA17-2*.
b. Prepare a vertical analysis for December 31, 2010 and 2011, balance sheets. Round percentages to one tenth of a percent (for example, 10.47% rounds to 10.5%).
c. When you have completed the vertical analysis, perform a "save as," replacing the entire file name with the following:

SA17-2_[your first name initial]_[your last name]

SA 17-3
Financial ratios

In addition to the financial statements in **SA 17-1** and **SA 17-2,** the following information is available for Ironside, Inc.

	A	B	C
50			
51		Dec. 31, 2011	Dec. 31, 2010
52	Common stock market price	$ 20.00	$ 15.00
53	Number of common shares outstanding	25,000	25,000
54			

a. Open the Excel file *SA17-3*.
b. Using the financial statements for Ironside, Inc., in the file provided, determine the following ratios for 2011:

- Working capital
- Current ratio
- Inventory turnover
- Number of days' sales in inventory
- Ratio of fixed assets to long-term liabilities
- Number of times interest charges are earned
- Rate earned on total assets
- Earnings per share

c. When you have completed computing the ratios listed, perform a "save as," replacing the entire file name with the following:

SA17-3_[your first name initial]_[your last name]

SA 17-4
Financial ratios

In addition to the financial statements in **SA 17-1** and **SA 17-2,** the following information is available for Ironside, Inc.

	A	B	C
50			
51		Dec. 31, 2011	Dec. 31, 2010
52	Common stock market price	$ 20.00	$ 15.00
53	Number of common shares outstanding	25,000	25,000
54			
55	Earnings per share on common stock	2.0	
56			

a. Open the Excel file *SA17-4*.
b. Using the financial statements for Ironside, Inc., in the file provided, determine the following ratios for 2011:

- Quick ratio
- Accounts receivable turnover
- Number of days' sales in receivables
- Ratio of liabilities to stockholders' equity
- Ratio of net sales to assets
- Rate earned on common stockholders' equity
- Price-earnings ratio

c. When you have completed computing the ratios listed, perform a "save as," replacing the entire file name with the following:

SA17-4_[your first name initial]_[your last name]

Answers to Self-Examination Questions

1. **A** Percentage analysis indicating the relationship of the component parts to the total in a financial statement, such as the relationship of current assets to total assets (20% to 100%) in the question, is called vertical analysis (answer A). Percentage analysis of increases and decreases in corresponding items in comparative financial statements is called horizontal analysis (answer B). An example of horizontal analysis would be the presentation of the amount of current assets in the preceding balance sheet, along with the amount of current assets at the end of the current year, with the increase or decrease in current assets between the periods expressed as a percentage. Profitability analysis (answer C) is the analysis of a firm's ability to earn income. Contribution margin analysis (answer D) is discussed in a later managerial accounting chapter.

2. **D** Various solvency measures, categorized as current position analysis, indicate a firm's ability to meet currently maturing obligations. Each measure contributes to the analysis of a firm's current position and is most useful when viewed with other measures and when compared with similar measures for other periods and for other firms. Working capital (answer A) is the excess of current assets over current liabilities; the current ratio (answer B) is the ratio of current assets

to current liabilities; and the quick ratio (answer C) is the ratio of the sum of cash, receivables, and temporary investments to current liabilities.

3. **D** The ratio of current assets to current liabilities is usually called the current ratio (answer A). It is sometimes called the working capital ratio (answer B) or bankers' ratio (answer C).

4. **C** The ratio of the sum of cash, receivables, and temporary investments (sometimes called quick assets) to current liabilities is called the quick ratio (answer C) or acid-test ratio. The current ratio (answer A), working capital ratio (answer B), and bankers' ratio (answer D) are terms that describe the ratio of current assets to current liabilities.

5. **C** The number of days' sales in inventory (answer C), which is determined by dividing the average inventory by the average daily cost of goods sold, expresses the relationship between the cost of goods sold and inventory. It indicates the efficiency in the management of inventory. The working capital ratio (answer A) indicates the ability of the business to meet currently maturing obligations (debt). The quick ratio (answer B) indicates the "instant" debt-paying ability of the business. The ratio of fixed assets to long-term liabilities (answer D) indicates the margin of safety for long-term creditors.

Managerial Accounting Concepts and Principles

© AP Photo/Greg Brown/Waterloo Courier

W A S H B U R N   G U I T A R S

Dan Donegan, guitarist for the rock band *Disturbed*, entertains millions of fans each year playing his guitar. His guitar was built by quality craftsmen at Washburn Guitars in Chicago. Washburn Guitars is well-known in the music industry and has been in business for over 120 years.

Staying in business for 120 years requires a thorough understanding of how to manufacture high-quality guitars. In addition, it requires knowledge of how to account for the costs of making guitars. For example, Washburn needs cost information to answer the following questions:

How much should be charged for its guitars?

How many guitars does it have to sell in a year to cover its costs and earn a profit?

How many employees should the company have working on each stage of the manufacturing process?

How would purchasing automated equipment affect the costs of its guitars?

This chapter introduces managerial accounting concepts that are useful in addressing the preceding questions.

This chapter begins by describing managerial accounting and its relationship to financial accounting. Following this overview, the management process is described along with the role of managerial accounting in this process. Finally, characteristics of managerial accounting reports, managerial accounting terms, and uses of managerial accounting information are described and illustrated.

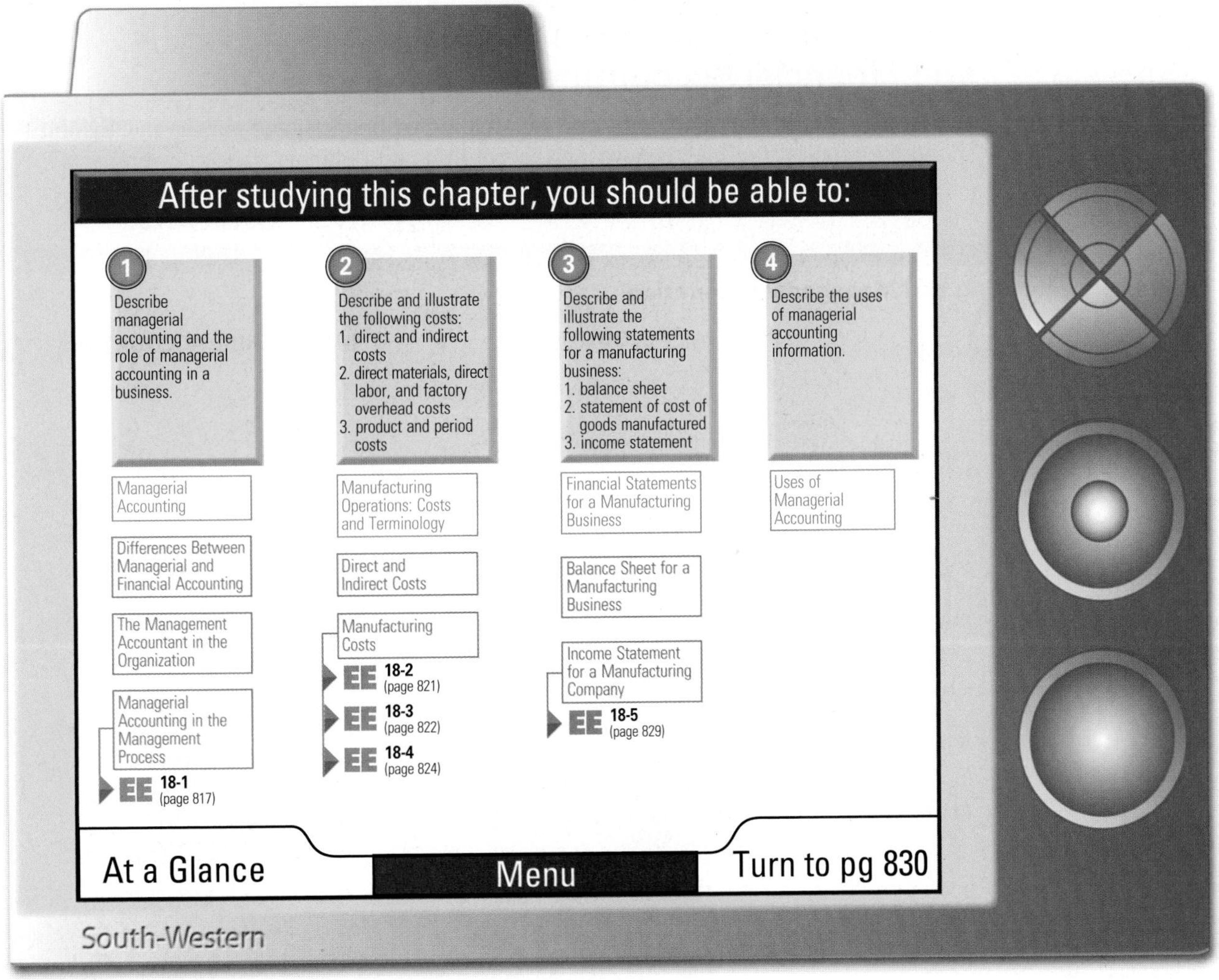

After studying this chapter, you should be able to:

1 Describe managerial accounting and the role of managerial accounting in a business.

2 Describe and illustrate the following costs:
1. direct and indirect costs
2. direct materials, direct labor, and factory overhead costs
3. product and period costs

3 Describe and illustrate the following statements for a manufacturing business:
1. balance sheet
2. statement of cost of goods manufactured
3. income statement

4 Describe the uses of managerial accounting information.

Managerial Accounting

Differences Between Managerial and Financial Accounting

The Management Accountant in the Organization

Managerial Accounting in the Management Process
EE 18-1 (page 817)

Manufacturing Operations: Costs and Terminology

Direct and Indirect Costs

Manufacturing Costs
EE 18-2 (page 821)
EE 18-3 (page 822)
EE 18-4 (page 824)

Financial Statements for a Manufacturing Business

Balance Sheet for a Manufacturing Business

Income Statement for a Manufacturing Company
EE 18-5 (page 829)

Uses of Managerial Accounting

At a Glance   **Menu**   **Turn to pg 830**

South-Western

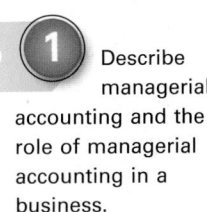

1 Describe managerial accounting and the role of managerial accounting in a business.

Managerial Accounting

Managers make numerous decisions during the day-to-day operations of a business and in planning for the future. Managerial accounting provides much of the information used for these decisions.

Some examples of managerial accounting information along with the chapter in which it is described and illustrated are listed below.

1. Classifying manufacturing and other costs and reporting them in the financial statements (Chapter 18)
2. Determining the cost of manufacturing a product or providing a service (Chapters 19 and 20)
3. Estimating the behavior of costs for various levels of activity and assessing cost-volume-profit relationships (Chapter 21)
4. Planning for the future by preparing budgets (Chapter 22)
5. Evaluating manufacturing costs by comparing actual with expected results (Chapter 23)
6. Evaluating decentralized operations by comparing actual and budgeted costs as well as computing various measures of profitability (Chapter 24)
7. Evaluating special decision-making situations by comparing differential revenues and costs (Chapter 25)
8. Evaluating alternative proposals for long-term investments in fixed assets (Chapter 26)

Differences Between Managerial and Financial Accounting

Accounting information is often divided into two types: financial and managerial. Exhibit 1 shows the relationship between financial accounting and managerial accounting.

Exhibit 1

Financial Accounting and Managerial Accounting

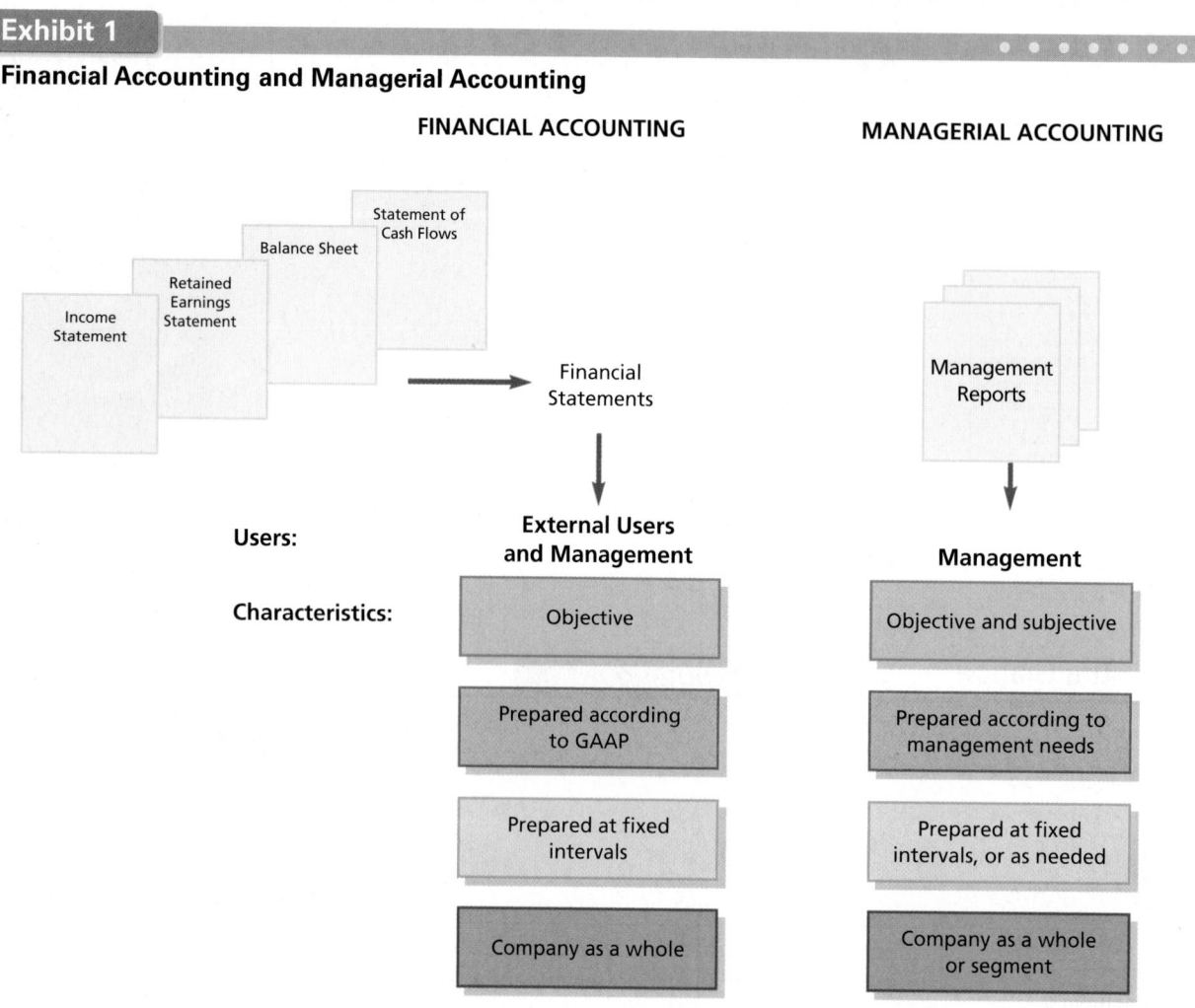

Financial accounting information is reported at fixed intervals (monthly, quarterly, yearly) in general-purpose financial statements. These financial statements—the income statement, retained earnings statement, balance sheet, and statement of cash flows—are prepared according to generally accepted accounting principles (GAAP). These statements are used by external users such as the following:

1. Shareholders
2. Creditors
3. Government agencies
4. The general public

Managers of a company also use general-purpose financial statements. For example, in planning future operations, managers often begin by evaluating the current income statement and statement of cash flows.

Managerial accounting information is designed to meet the specific needs of a company's management. This information includes the following:

1. Historical data, which provide *objective measures* of past operations
2. Estimated data, which provide *subjective estimates* about future decisions

Management uses both types of information in directing daily operations, planning future operations, and developing business strategies.

Unlike the financial statements prepared in financial accounting, managerial accounting reports do *not* always have to be:

1. Prepared according to generally accepted accounting principles. This is because *only* the company's management uses the information. Also, in many cases, GAAP are not relevant to the specific decision-making needs of management.

2. Prepared at fixed intervals (monthly, quarterly, yearly). Although some management reports are prepared at fixed intervals, most reports are prepared as management needs the information.

3. Prepared for the business as a whole. Most management reports are prepared for products, projects, sales territories, or other segments of the company.

The Management Accountant in the Organization

In most companies, departments or similar organizational units are assigned responsibilities for specific functions or activities. The operating structure of a company can be shown in an *organization chart*.

Exhibit 2 is a partial organization chart for Callaway Golf Company, the manufacturer and distributor of Hyper X® golf clubs.

Exhibit 2

Partial Organizational Chart for Callaway Golf Company

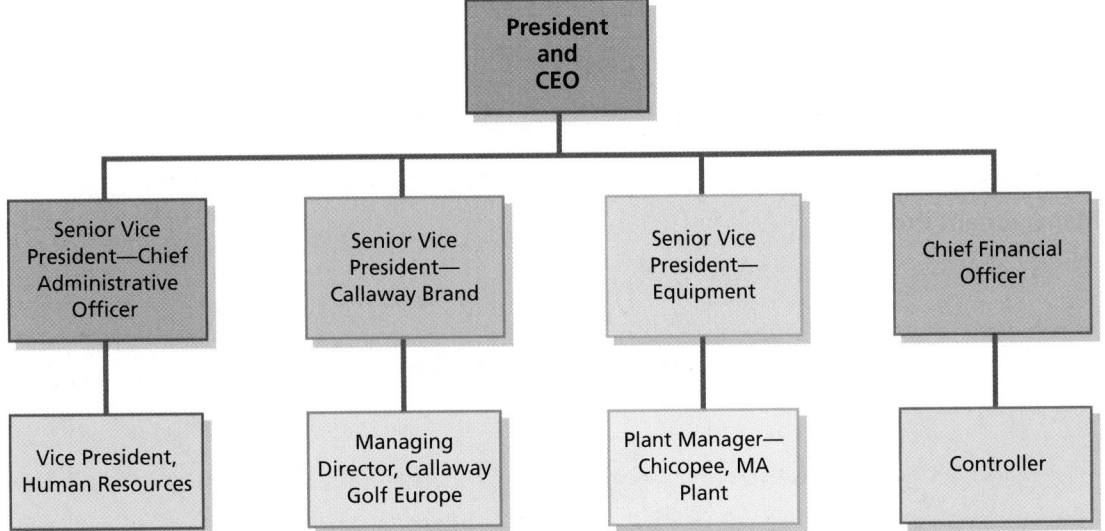

The departments in a company can be viewed as having either of the following:

1. Line responsibilities
2. Staff responsibilities

A **line department** is directly involved in providing goods or services to the customers of the company. For Callaway Golf (shown in Exhibit 2), the following occupy line positions:

1. Senior Vice President—Equipment
2. Plant Manager—Chicopee, MA Plant
3. Senior Vice President—Callaway Brand
4. Managing Director, Callaway Golf Europe

The preceding occupy line positions because they are responsible for manufacturing and selling Callaway's products.

The terms *line* and *staff* may be applied to service organizations. For example, the line positions in a hospital would be the nurses, doctors, and other caregivers. Staff positions would include admissions and records.

A **staff department** provides services, assistance, and advice to the departments with line or other staff responsibilities. A staff department has no direct authority over a line department. For Callaway Golf (shown in Exhibit 2), the following occupy staff positions:

1. Senior Vice President—Chief Administrative Officer
2. Vice President, Human Resources
3. Chief Financial Officer
4. Controller

As shown above, the chief financial officer (CFO) and the controller occupy staff positions. In most companies, the **controller** is the chief management accountant. The controller's staff consists of a variety of other accountants who are responsible for specialized accounting functions such as the following:

1. Systems and procedures
2. General accounting
3. Budgets and budget analysis
4. Special reports and analysis
5. Taxes
6. Cost accounting

Experience in managerial accounting is often an excellent training ground for senior management positions. This is not surprising, since accounting touches all phases of a company's operations.

Managerial Accounting in the Management Process

As a staff department, managerial accounting supports management and the management process. The **management process** has the following five basic phases, as shown in Exhibit 3.

1. Planning
2. Directing
3. Controlling
4. Improving
5. Decision making

As Exhibit 3 illustrates, the five phases interact with each other.

Exhibit 3

The Management Process

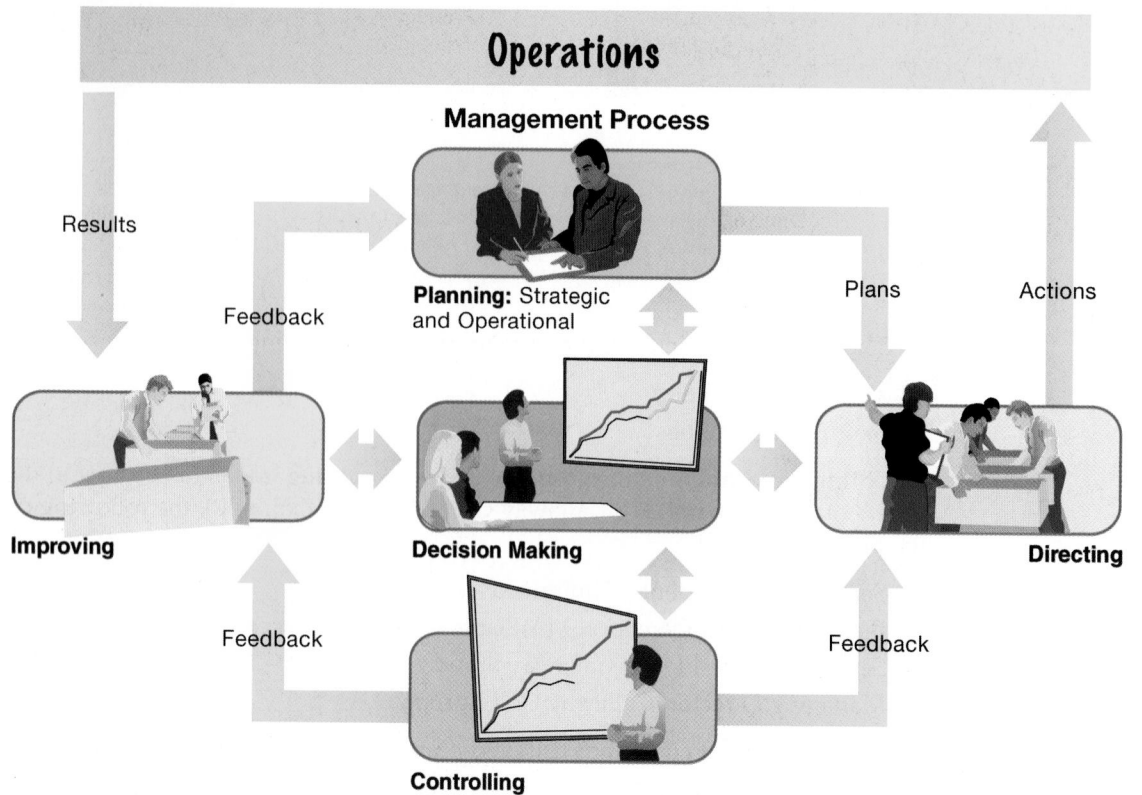

Planning Management uses **planning** in developing the company's **objectives (goals)** and translating these objectives into courses of action. For example, a company may set an objective to increase market share by 15 percent by introducing three new products. The actions to achieve this objective might be as follows:

1.   Increase the advertising budget
2.   Open a new sales territory
3.   Increase the research and development budget

Planning may be classified as follows:

1.   **Strategic planning**, which is developing long-term actions to achieve the company's objectives. These long-term actions are called **strategies**, which often involve periods of 5 to 10 years.
2.   **Operational planning**, which develops short-term actions for managing the day-to-day operations of the company.

Directing The process by which managers run day-to-day operations is called **directing**. An example of directing is a production supervisor's efforts to keep the production line moving without interruption (downtime). A credit manager's development of guidelines for assessing the ability of potential customers to pay their bills is also an example of directing.

Controlling Monitoring operating results and comparing actual results with the expected results is **controlling**. This **feedback** allows management to isolate areas for further investigation and possible remedial action. It may also lead to revising future plans. This philosophy of controlling by comparing actual and expected results is called **management by exception**.

Improving Feedback is also used by managers to support continuous process improvement. **Continuous process improvement** is the philosophy of continually improving employees, business processes, and products. The objective of continuous improvement is to eliminate the *source* of problems in a process. In this way, the right products (services) are delivered in the right quantities at the right time.

Decision Making Inherent in each of the preceding management processes is **decision making**. In managing a company, management must continually decide among alternative actions. For example, in directing operations, managers must decide on an operating structure, training procedures, and staffing of day-to-day operations.

Managerial accounting supports managers in all phases of the management process. For example, accounting reports comparing actual and expected operating results aid managers in planning and improving current operations. Such a report might compare the actual and expected costs of defective materials. If the cost of defective materials is unusually high, management might decide to change suppliers.

Example Exercise 18-1   Management Process   •••••••>  **1**

Three phases of the management process are planning, controlling, and improving. Match the following descriptions to the proper phase:

Phase of management process	Description
Planning	a. Monitoring the operating results of implemented plans and comparing the actual results with expected results.
Controlling	b. Rejects solving individual problems with temporary solutions that fail to address the root cause of the problem.
Improving	c. Used by management to develop the company's objectives.

(continued)

Follow My Example 18-1

Phase of management process

Planning (c)
Controlling (a)
Improving (b)

For Practice: PE 18-1A, PE 18-1B

Integrity, Objectivity, and Ethics in Business

ENVIRONMENTAL ACCOUNTING

In recent years, the environmental impact of a business has become an increasingly important issue. Multinational agreements such as the Montreal Protocol and Kyoto Protocol have acknowledged the impact that society has on the environment and raised public awareness of the impact that businesses have on the environment. As a result, environmental issues have become an important operational issue for most businesses. Managers must now consider the environmental impact of their decisions in the same way that they would consider other operational issues.

To help managers understand the environmental impact of their business decisions, new managerial accounting measures are being developed. The emerging field of environmental management accounting focuses on developing various measures of the environmental-related costs of a business. These measures can evaluate a variety of issues including the volume and level of emissions, the estimated costs of different levels of emissions, and the impact that environmental costs have on product cost. Thus, environmental managerial accounting can provide managers with important information to help them more clearly consider the environmental effects of their decisions.

2 Describe and illustrate the following costs:

1. direct and indirect costs
2. direct materials, direct labor, and factory overhead costs
3. product and period costs

Manufacturing Operations: Costs and Terminology

The operations of a business can be classified as service, merchandising, or manufacturing. The accounting for service and merchandising businesses has been described and illustrated in earlier chapters. For this reason, the remaining chapters of this text focus primarily on manufacturing businesses. Most of the managerial accounting concepts discussed, however, also apply to service and merchandising businesses.

As a basis for illustration of manufacturing operations, a guitar manufacturer, Legend Guitars, is used. Exhibit 4 is an overview of Legend's guitar manufacturing operations.

Exhibit 4

Guitar Making Operations of Legend Guitars

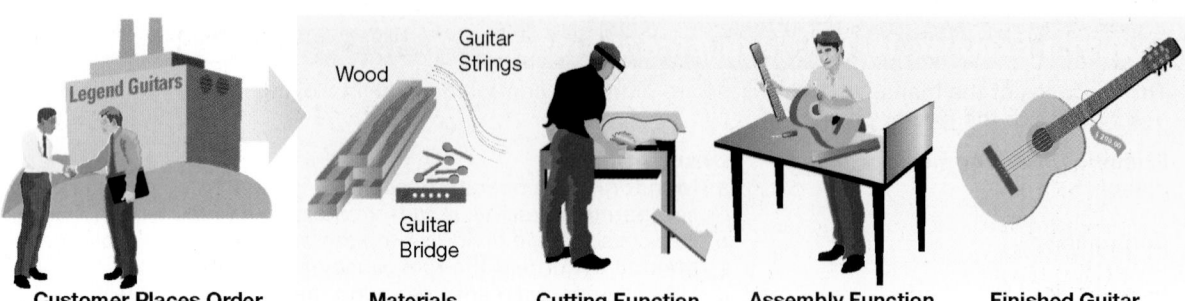

| Customer Places Order | Materials | Cutting Function | Assembly Function | Finished Guitar |

Legend's guitar making process begins when a customer places an order for a guitar. Once the order is accepted, the manufacturing process begins by obtaining the necessary materials. An employee then cuts the body and neck of the guitar out of raw lumber. Once the wood is cut, the body and neck of the guitar are assembled. When the assembly is complete, the guitar is painted and finished.

Direct and Indirect Costs

A **cost** is a payment of cash or the commitment to pay cash in the future for the purpose of generating revenues. For example, cash (or credit) used to purchase equipment is the cost of the equipment. If equipment is purchased by exchanging assets other than cash, the current market value of the assets given up is the cost of the equipment purchased.

In managerial accounting, costs are classified according to the decision-making needs of management. For example, costs are often classified by their relationship to a segment of operations, called a **cost object**. A cost object may be a product, a sales territory, a department, or an activity, such as research and development. Costs identified with cost objects are either direct costs or indirect costs.

Direct costs are identified with and can be traced to a cost object. For example, the cost of wood (materials) used by Legend Guitars in manufacturing a guitar is a direct cost of the guitar.

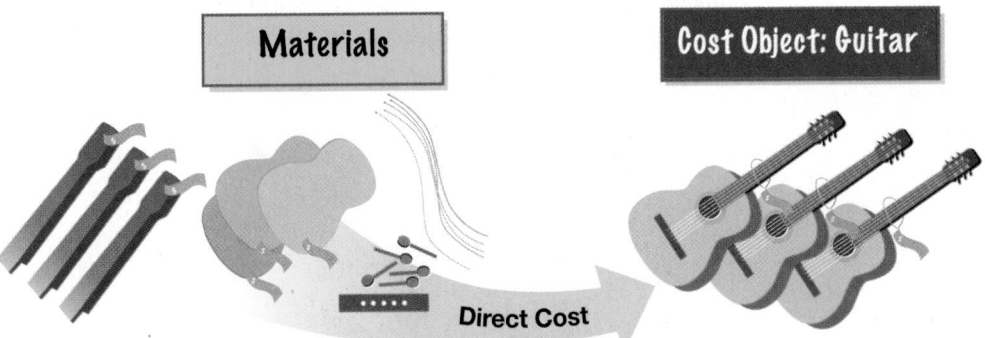

Indirect costs cannot be identified with or traced to a cost object. For example, the salaries of the Legend Guitars production supervisors are indirect costs of producing a guitar. While the production supervisors contribute to the production of a guitar, their salaries cannot be identified with or traced to any individual guitar.

Depending on the cost object, a cost may be either a direct or an indirect cost. For example, the salaries of production supervisors are indirect costs when the cost object is an individual guitar. If, however, the cost object is Legend Guitars' overall production process, then the salaries of production supervisors are direct costs.

This process of classifying a cost as direct or indirect is illustrated in Exhibit 5.

Exhibit 5

Classifying Direct and Indirect Costs

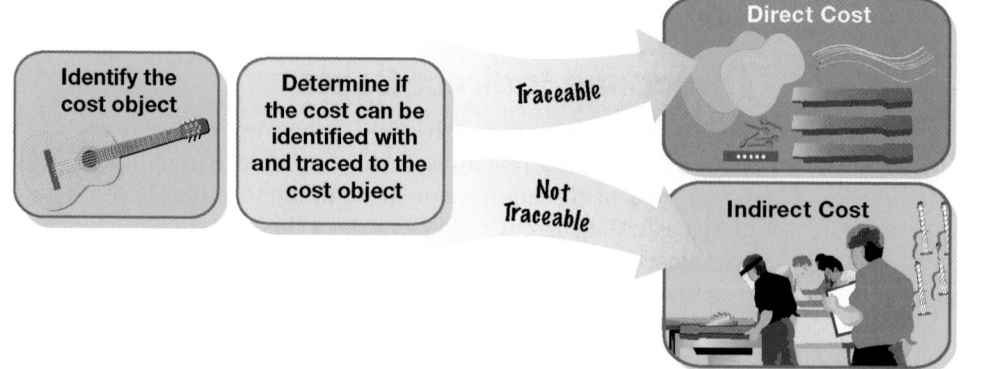

Manufacturing Costs

The cost of a manufactured product includes the cost of materials used in making the product. In addition, the cost of a manufactured product includes the cost of converting the materials into a finished product. For example, Legend Guitars uses employees and machines to convert wood (and other supplies) into finished guitars. Thus, the cost of a finished guitar (the cost object) includes the following:

1. Direct materials cost
2. Direct labor cost
3. Factory overhead cost

Direct Materials Cost Manufactured products begin with raw materials that are converted into finished products. The cost of any material that is an integral part of the finished product is classified as a **direct materials cost**. For Legend Guitars, direct materials cost includes the cost of the wood used in producing each guitar. Other examples of direct materials costs include the cost of electronic components for a television, silicon wafers for microcomputer chips, and tires for an automobile.

To be classified as a direct materials cost, the cost must be *both* of the following:

1. An integral part of the finished product
2. A significant portion of the total cost of the product

For Legend Guitars, the cost of the guitar strings is not a direct materials cost. This is because the cost of guitar strings is an insignificant part of the total cost of each guitar. Instead, the cost of guitar string is classified as a factory overhead cost, which is discussed later.

Direct Labor

Direct Labor Cost Most manufacturing processes use employees to convert materials into finished products. The cost of employee wages that is an integral part of the finished product is classified as **direct labor cost**. For Legend Guitars, direct labor cost includes the wages of the employees who cut each guitar out of raw lumber and assemble it. Other examples of direct labor costs include mechanics' wages for repairing an automobile, machine operators' wages for manufacturing tools, and assemblers' wages for assembling a laptop computer.

Like a direct materials cost, a direct labor cost must be *both* of the following:

1. An integral part of the finished product
2. A significant portion of the total cost of the product

For Legend Guitars, the wages of the janitors who clean the factory are not a direct labor cost. This is because janitorial costs are not an integral part or a significant cost of each guitar. Instead, janitorial costs are classified as a factory overhead cost, which is discussed next.

Factory Overhead

Factory Overhead Cost Costs other than direct materials cost and direct labor cost that are incurred in the manufacturing process are combined and classified as **factory overhead cost**. Factory overhead is sometimes called **manufacturing overhead** or **factory burden**.

All factory overhead costs are indirect costs of the product. Some factory overhead costs include the following:

1. Heating and lighting the factory
2. Repairing and maintaining factory equipment
3. Property taxes on factory buildings and land
4. Insurance on factory buildings
5. Depreciation on factory plant and equipment

As manufacturing processes have become more automated, direct labor costs have become so small that they are often included as part of factory overhead.

Factory overhead cost also includes materials and labor costs that do not enter directly into the finished product. Examples include the cost of oil used to lubricate machinery and the wages of janitorial and supervisory employees. Also, if the costs of direct materials or direct labor are not a significant portion of the total product cost, these costs may be classified as factory overhead costs.

For Legend Guitars, the costs of guitar strings and janitorial wages are factory overhead costs. Additional factory overhead costs of making guitars are as follows:

1. Sandpaper
2. Buffing compound
3. Glue

4. Power (electricity) to run the machines
5. Depreciation of the machines and building
6. Salaries of production supervisors

Example Exercise 18-2   Direct Materials, Direct Labor, and Factory Overhead   •••••••⟩ ②

Identify the following costs as direct materials (DM), direct labor (DL), or factory overhead (FO) for a baseball glove manufacturer.

a. Leather used to make a baseball glove
b. Coolants for machines that sew baseball gloves
c. Wages of assembly line employees
d. Ink used to print a player's autograph on a baseball glove

Follow My Example 18-2

a. DM
b. FO
c. DL
d. FO

....

For Practice: PE 18-2A, PE 18-2B

Prime Costs and Conversion Costs Direct materials, direct labor, and factory overhead costs may be grouped together for analysis and reporting. Two such common groupings are as follows:

1. **Prime costs**, which consist of direct materials and direct labor costs
2. **Conversion costs**, which consist of direct labor and factory overhead costs

Conversion costs are the costs of converting the materials into a finished product. Direct labor is both a prime cost and a conversion cost, as shown in Exhibit 6.

Exhibit 6

Prime Costs and Conversion Costs

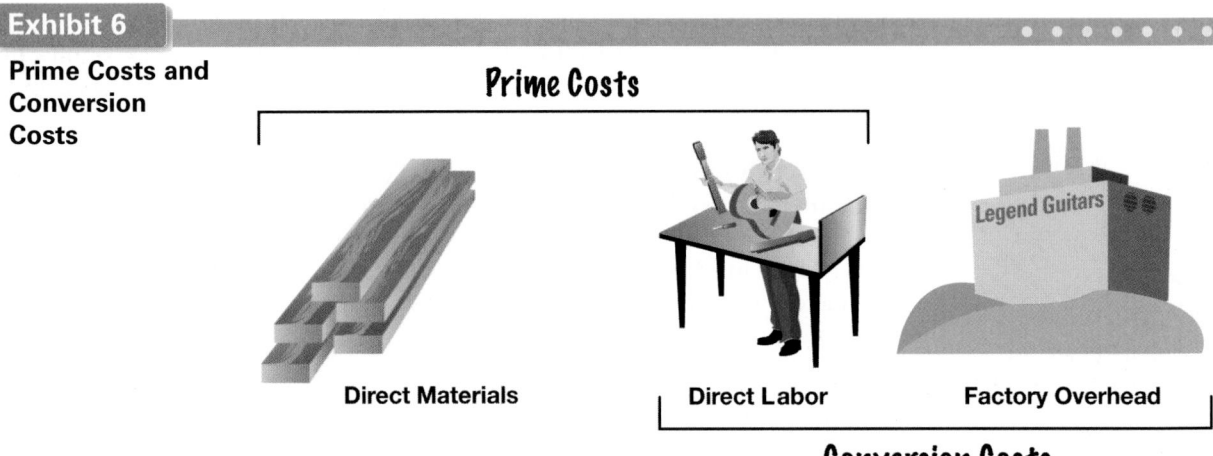

Example Exercise 18-3   Prime and Conversion Costs   2

Identify the following costs as a prime cost (P), conversion cost (C), or both (B) for a baseball glove manufacturer.

a. Leather used to make a baseball glove
b. Coolants for machines that sew baseball gloves
c. Wages of assembly line employees
d. Ink used to print a player's autograph on a baseball glove

Follow My Example 18-3

a. P
b. C
c. B
d. C

For Practice: PE 18-3A, PE 18-3B

Product Costs and Period Costs For financial reporting purposes, costs are classified as product costs or period costs.

1. **Product costs** consist of manufacturing costs: direct materials, direct labor, and factory overhead.
2. **Period costs** consist of selling and administrative expenses. *Selling expenses* are incurred in marketing the product and delivering the product to customers. *Administrative expenses* are incurred in managing the company and are not directly related to the manufacturing or selling functions.

Examples of product costs and period costs for Legend Guitars are presented in Exhibit 7.

Exhibit 7

Examples of Product Costs and Period Costs—Legend Guitars

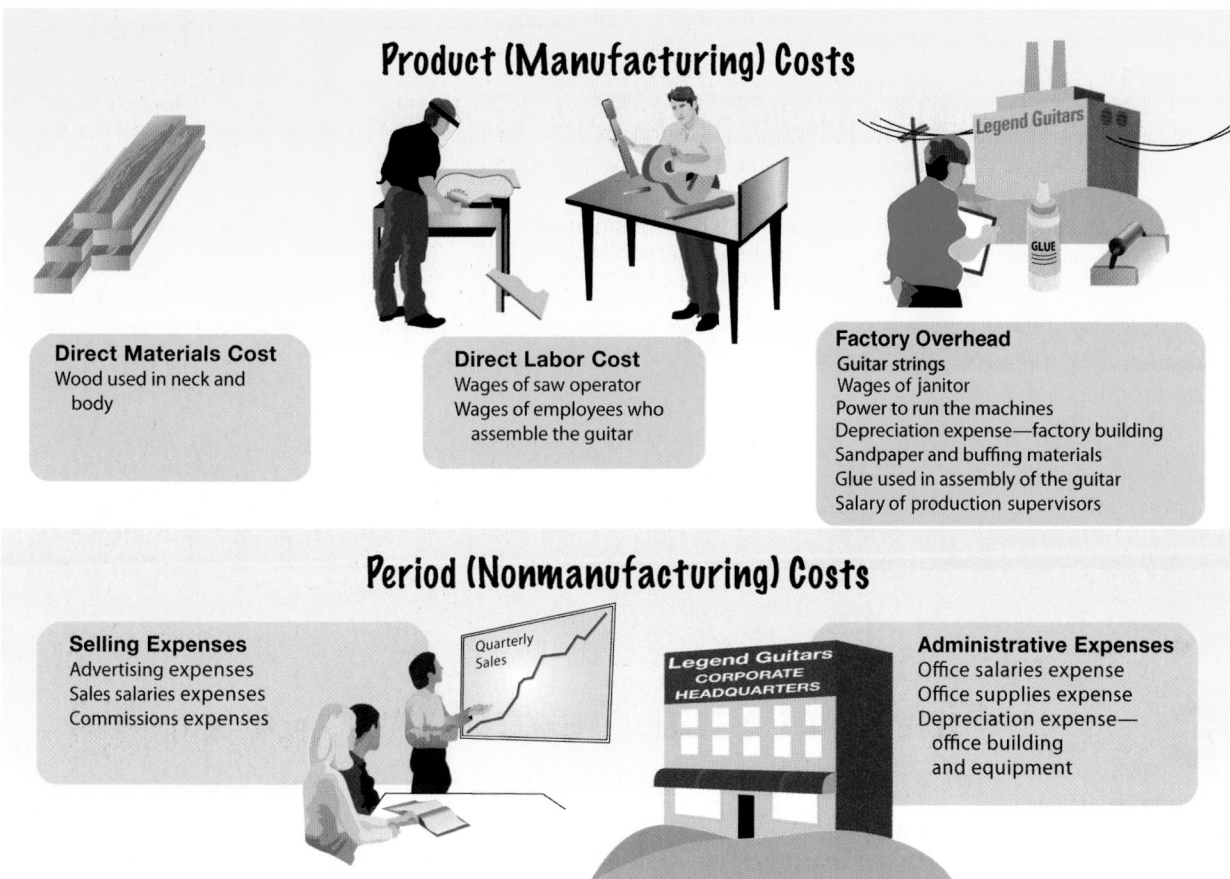

Product (Manufacturing) Costs

Direct Materials Cost
Wood used in neck and body

Direct Labor Cost
Wages of saw operator
Wages of employees who assemble the guitar

Factory Overhead
Guitar strings
Wages of janitor
Power to run the machines
Depreciation expense—factory building
Sandpaper and buffing materials
Glue used in assembly of the guitar
Salary of production supervisors

Period (Nonmanufacturing) Costs

Selling Expenses
Advertising expenses
Sales salaries expenses
Commissions expenses

Administrative Expenses
Office salaries expense
Office supplies expense
Depreciation expense—
office building
and equipment

To facilitate control, selling and administrative expenses may be reported by level of responsibility. For example, selling expenses may be reported by products, salespersons, departments, divisions, or territories. Likewise, administrative expenses may be reported by areas such as human resources, computer services, legal, accounting, or finance.

The impact on the financial statements of product and period costs is summarized in Exhibit 8. As product costs are incurred, they are recorded and reported on the balance sheet as *inventory*. When the inventory is sold, the cost of the manufactured product sold

Exhibit 8

Product Costs, Period Costs, and the Financial Statements

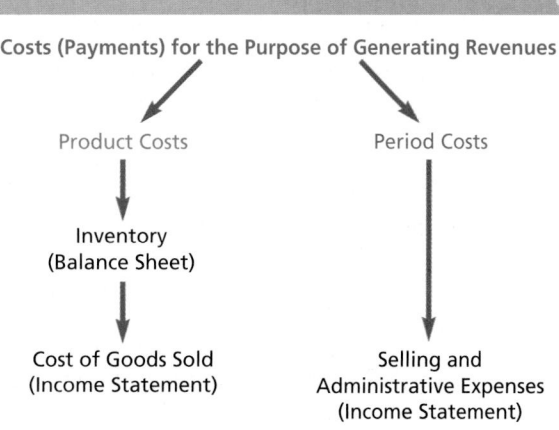

Costs (Payments) for the Purpose of Generating Revenues

Product Costs

Period Costs

Inventory
(Balance Sheet)

Cost of Goods Sold
(Income Statement)

Selling and
Administrative Expenses
(Income Statement)

is reported as *cost of goods sold* on the income statement. Period costs are reported as *expenses* on the income statement in the period in which they are incurred and, thus, never appear on the balance sheet.

Example Exercise 18-4 Product and Period Costs

Identify the following costs as a product cost or a period cost for a baseball glove manufacturer.

a. Leather used to make a baseball glove
b. Cost of endorsement from a professional baseball player
c. Office supplies used at the company headquarters
d. Ink used to print a player's autograph on the baseball glove

Follow My Example 18-4

a. Product cost
b. Period cost
c. Period cost
d. Product cost

For Practice: PE 18-4A, PE 18-4B

Describe and illustrate the following statements for a manufacturing business:

1. balance sheet
2. statement of cost of goods manufactured
3. income statement

Financial Statements for a Manufacturing Business

The retained earnings and cash flow statements for a manufacturing business are similar to those illustrated in earlier chapters for service and merchandising businesses. However, the balance sheet and income statement for a manufacturing business are more complex. This is because a manufacturer makes the products that it sells and, thus, must record and report product costs. The reporting of product costs primarily affects the balance sheet and the income statement.

Balance Sheet for a Manufacturing Business

A manufacturing business reports three types of inventory on its balance sheet as follows:

1. **Materials inventory** (sometimes called raw materials inventory). This inventory consists of the costs of the direct and indirect materials that have not entered the manufacturing process.

    Examples for Legend Guitars: Wood, guitar strings, glue, sandpaper

2. **Work in process inventory**. This inventory consists of the direct materials, direct labor, and factory overhead costs for products that have entered the manufacturing process, but are not yet completed (in process).

    Example for Legend Guitars: Unfinished (partially assembled) guitars

3. **Finished goods inventory**. This inventory consists of completed (or finished) products that have not been sold.

    Example for Legend Guitars: Unsold guitars

Exhibit 9 illustrates the reporting of inventory on the balance sheet for a merchandising and a manufacturing business. MusicLand Stores, Inc., a retailer of musical instruments, reports only *Merchandise Inventory*. In contrast, Legend

Exhibit 9

Balance Sheet Presentation of Inventory in Manufacturing and Merchandising Companies

MusicLand Stores, Inc. Balance Sheet December 31, 2010		
Current assests:		
Cash		$ 25,000
Accounts receivable (net)		85,000
Merchandise inventory		**142,000**
Supplies		10,000
Total current assets		$ 262,000

Legend Guitars Balance Sheet December 31, 2010		
Current assests:		
Cash		$ 21,000
Accounts receivable (net)		120,000
Inventories:		
Finished goods	**$62,500**	
Work in process	**24,000**	
Materials	**35,000**	**121,500**
Supplies		2,000
Total current assets		$ 264,500

Guitars, a manufacturer of guitars, reports *Finished Goods, Work in Process*, and *Materials* inventories. In both balance sheets, inventory is reported in the *Current Assets* section.

Income Statement for a Manufacturing Company

The income statements for merchandising and manufacturing businesses differ primarily in the reporting of the cost of merchandise (goods) *available for sale* and *sold* during the period. These differences are shown below.

Merchandising Business		
Sales		$XXX
Beginning merchandise inventory	$XXX	
Plus net purchases	XXX	
Merchandise available for sale	$XXX	
Less ending merchandise inventory	XXX	
Cost of merchandise sold		XXX
Gross profit		$XXX

Manufacturing Business		
Sales		$XXX
Beginning finished goods inventory	$XXX	
Plus **cost of goods manufactured**	XXX	
Cost of finished goods available for sale	$XXX	
Less ending finished goods inventory	XXX	
Cost of goods sold		XXX
Gross profit		$XXX

A merchandising business purchases merchandise ready for resale to customers. The total cost of the **merchandise available for sale** during the period is determined by adding the beginning merchandise inventory to the net purchases. The **cost of merchandise sold** is determined by subtracting the ending merchandise inventory from the cost of merchandise available for sale.

A manufacturer makes the products it sells, using direct materials, direct labor, and factory overhead. The total cost of making products that are available for sale during the period is called the **cost of goods manufactured**. The **cost of finished goods available** for sale is determined by adding the beginning finished goods inventory to the cost of goods manufactured during the period. The **cost of goods sold** is determined by subtracting the ending finished goods inventory from the cost of finished goods available for sale.

Cost of goods manufactured is required to determine the *cost of goods sold*, and thus to prepare the income statement. The cost of goods manufactured is often determined by preparing a **statement of cost of goods manufactured**.[1] This statement summarizes the cost of goods manufactured during the period as shown below.

Statement of Cost of Goods Manufactured

Beginning work in process inventory		$XXX
Direct materials:		
Beginning materials inventory	$XXX	
Purchases	XXX	
Cost of materials available for use	$XXX	
Less ending materials inventory	XXX	
Cost of direct materials used	$ XXX	
Direct labor	XXX	
Factory overhead	XXX	
Total manufacturing costs incurred		XXX
Total manufacturing costs		$XXX
Less ending work in process inventory		XXX
Cost of goods manufactured		$XXX

To illustrate, the following data for Legend Guitars are used:

	Jan. 1, 2010	Dec. 31, 2010
Inventories:		
Materials	$ 65,000	$ 35,000
Work in process	30,000	24,000
Finished goods	60,000	62,500
Total inventories	$155,000	$121,500
Manufacturing costs incurred during 2010:		
Materials purchased		$100,000
Direct labor		110,000
Factory overhead:		
Indirect labor	$ 24,000	
Depreciation on factory equipment	10,000	
Factory supplies and utility costs	10,000	44,000
Total		$254,000
Sales		$366,000
Selling expenses		20,000
Administrative expenses		15,000

---

[1] Chapters 19 and 20 describe and illustrate the use of job order and process cost systems. As will be discussed, these systems do not require a statement of cost of goods manufactured.

The statement of cost of goods manufactured is prepared using the following three steps:

Step 1. Determine the *cost of materials used.*
Step 2. Determine the *total manufacturing costs incurred*
Step 3. Determine the *cost of goods manufactured.*

Using the preceding data for Legend Guitars, the preparation of the statement of cost of goods manufactured is illustrated below.

Step 1. The *cost of materials used* in production is determined as follows:

Materials inventory, January 1, 2010	$ 65,000
Add materials purchased	100,000
Cost of materials available for use	$165,000
Less materials inventory, December 31, 2010	35,000
Cost of direct materials used	$130,000

The January 1, 2010 (beginning), materials inventory of $65,000 is added to the cost of materials purchased of $100,000 to yield the total cost of materials that are available for use during 2010 of $165,000. Deducting the December 31, 2010 (ending), materials inventory of $35,000 yields the cost of direct materials used in production of $130,000.

Step 2. The *total manufacturing costs incurred* is determined as follows:

Direct materials used in production (Step 1)	$130,000
Direct labor	110,000
Factory overhead	44,000
Total manufacturing costs incurred	$284,000

The total manufacturing costs incurred in 2010 of $284,000 are determined by adding the direct materials used in production (Step 1), the direct labor cost, and the factory overhead costs.

Step 3. The *cost of goods manufactured* is determined as follows:

Work in process inventory, January 1, 2010	$ 30,000
Total manufacturing costs incurred (Step 2)	284,000
Total manufacturing costs	$314,000
Less work in process inventory, December 31, 2010	24,000
Cost of goods manufactured	$290,000

The cost of goods manufactured of $290,000 is determined by adding the total manufacturing costs incurred (Step 2) to the January 1, 2010 (beginning), work in process inventory of $30,000. This yields total manufacturing costs of $314,000. The December 31, 2010 (ending), work in process of $24,000 is then deducted to determine the cost of goods manufactured of $290,000.

The income statement and statement of cost of goods manufactured for Legend Guitars is shown in Exhibit 10.

Exhibit 11, on page 829, summarizes how manufacturing costs flow to the income statement and balance sheet of a manufacturing business.

Uses of Managerial Accounting

4 Describe the uses of managerial accounting information.

As mentioned earlier, managerial accounting provides information and reports for managers to use in operating a business. Some examples of how managerial accounting could be used by Legend Guitars include the following:

1. The cost of manufacturing each guitar could be used to determine its selling price.
2. Comparing the costs of guitars over time can be used to monitor and control the cost of direct materials, direct labor, and factory overhead.

Exhibit 10

Manufacturing Company— Income Statement with Statement of Cost of Goods Manufactured

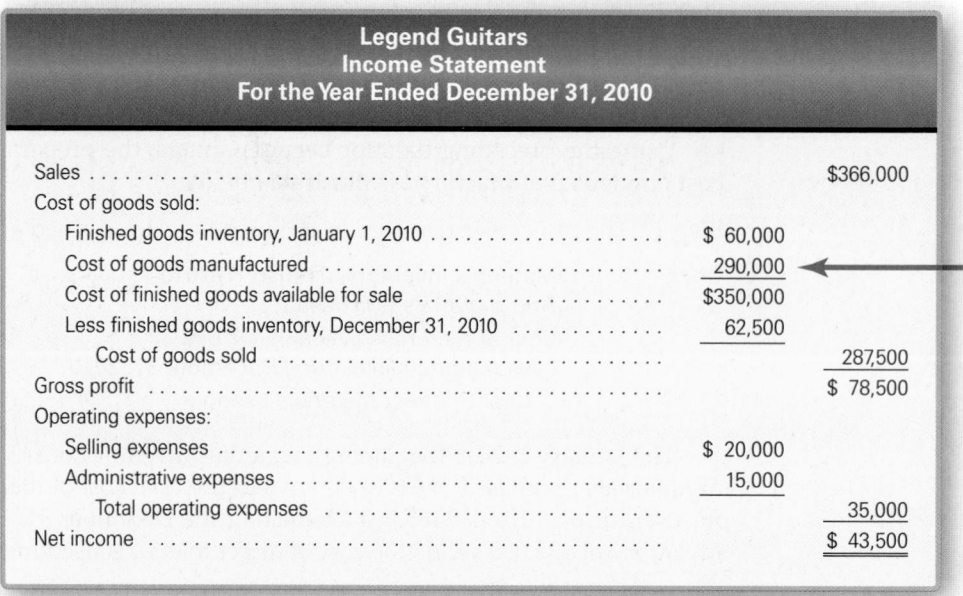

Legend Guitars
Income Statement
For the Year Ended December 31, 2010

Sales		$366,000
Cost of goods sold:		
Finished goods inventory, January 1, 2010	$ 60,000	
Cost of goods manufactured	290,000	
Cost of finished goods available for sale	$350,000	
Less finished goods inventory, December 31, 2010	62,500	
Cost of goods sold		287,500
Gross profit		$ 78,500
Operating expenses:		
Selling expenses	$ 20,000	
Administrative expenses	15,000	
Total operating expenses		35,000
Net income		$ 43,500

Legend Guitars
Statement of Cost of Goods Manufactured
For the Year Ended December 31, 2010

Work in process inventory, January 1, 2010			$ 30,000
Direct materials:			
Materials inventory, January 1, 2010	$ 65,000		
Purchases	100,000		
Cost of materials available for use	$165,000		
Less materials inventory, December 31, 2010	35,000		
Cost of direct materials used		$130,000	
Direct labor		110,000	
Factory overhead:			
Indirect labor	$ 24,000		
Depreciation on factory equipment	10,000		
Factory supplies and utility costs	10,000		
Total factory overhead		44,000	
Total manufacturing costs incurred			284,000
Total manufacturing costs			$314,000
Less work in process inventory, December 31, 2010			24,000
Cost of goods manufactured			$290,000

3. Performance reports could be used to identify any large amounts of scrap or employee downtime. For example, large amounts of unusable wood (scrap) after the cutting process should be investigated to determine the underlying cause. Such scrap may be caused by saws that have not been properly maintained.

4. A report could analyze the potential efficiencies and dollar savings of purchasing a new computerized saw to speed up the production process.

5. A report could analyze how many guitars need to be sold to cover operating costs and expenses. Such information could be used to set monthly selling targets and bonuses for sales personnel.

Exhibit 11

Flow of Manufacturing Costs

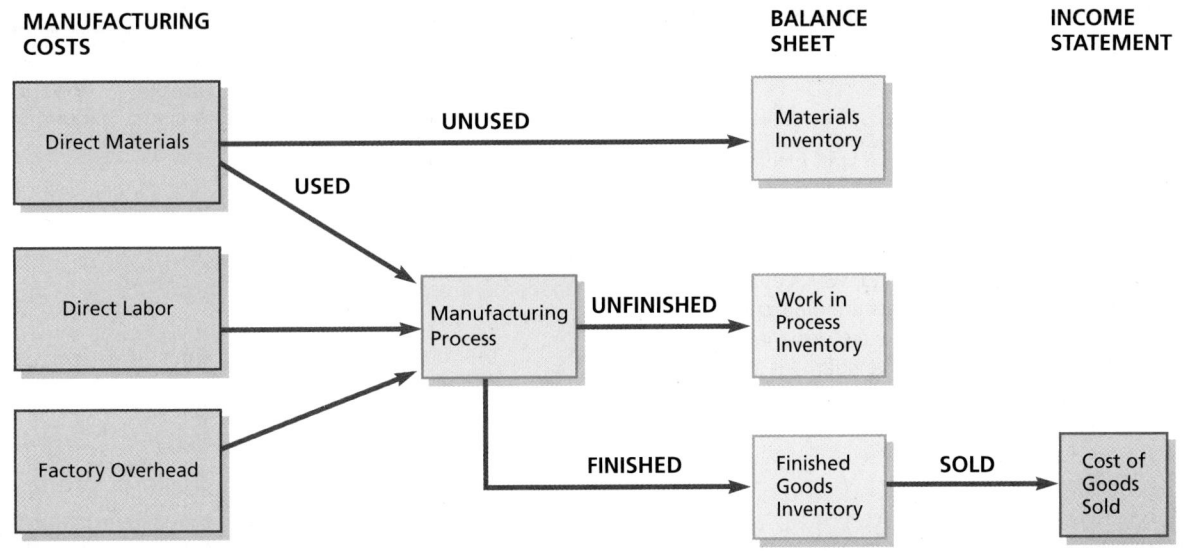

Example Exercise 18-5   Cost of Goods Sold, Cost of Goods Manufactured

> 3

Gauntlet Company has the following information for January:

Cost of direct materials used in production	$25,000
Direct labor	35,000
Factory overhead	20,000
Work in process inventory, January 1	30,000
Work in process inventory, January 31	25,000
Finished goods inventory, January 1	15,000
Finished goods inventory, January 31	12,000

For January, determine (a) the cost of goods manufactured and (b) the cost of goods sold.

Follow My Example 18-5

a.	Work in process inventory, January 1		$ 30,000
	Cost of direct materials used in production	$25,000	
	Direct labor	35,000	
	Factory overhead	20,000	
	Total manufacturing costs incurred during January		80,000
	Total manufacturing costs		$110,000
	Less work in process inventory, January 31		25,000
	Cost of goods manufactured		$ 85,000
b.	Finished goods inventory, January 1	$ 15,000	
	Cost of goods manufactured	85,000	
	Cost of finished goods available for sale	$100,000	
	Less finished goods inventory, January 31	12,000	
	Cost of goods sold	$ 88,000	

For Practice: PE 18-5A, PE 18-5B

As the prior examples illustrate, managerial accounting information can be used for a variety of purposes. In the remaining chapters of this text, we examine these and other areas of managerial accounting.

1 Describe managerial accounting and the role of managerial accounting in a business.

Key Points	Key Learning Outcomes	Example Exercises	Practice Exercises
Managerial accounting is a staff function that supports the management process by providing reports to aid management in planning, directing, controlling, improving, and decision making. This differs from financial accounting, which provides information to users outside of the organization. Managerial accounting reports are designed to meet the specific needs of management and aid management in planning long-term strategies and running the day-to-day operations.	• Describe the differences between financial accounting and managerial accounting. • Describe the role of the management accountant in the organization. • Describe the role of managerial accounting in the management process.	**18-1**	18-1A, 18-1B

2 Describe and illustrate the following costs: (1) direct and indirect costs; (2) direct materials, direct labor, and factory overhead costs; and (3) product and period costs.

Key Points	Key Learning Outcomes	Example Exercises	Practice Exercises
Manufacturing companies use machinery and labor to convert materials into a finished product. A direct cost can be directly traced to a finished product, while an indirect cost cannot. The cost of a finished product is made up of three components: (1) direct materials, (2) direct labor, and (3) factory overhead.	• Describe a cost object.		
	• Classify a cost as a direct or indirect cost for a cost object.		
	• Describe direct materials cost.	**18-2**	18-2A, 18-2B
	• Describe direct labor cost.	**18-2**	18-2A, 18-2B
These three manufacturing costs can be categorized into prime costs (direct material and direct labor) or conversion costs (direct labor and factory overhead). Product costs consist of the elements of manufacturing cost—direct materials, direct labor, and factory overhead—while period costs consist of selling and administrative expenses.	• Describe factory overhead cost.	**18-2**	18-2A, 18-2B
	• Describe prime costs and conversion costs.	**18-3**	18-3A, 18-3B
	• Describe product costs and period costs.	**18-4**	18-4A, 18-4B

3 Describe and illustrate the following statements for a manufacturing business: (1) balance sheet, (2) statement of cost of goods manufactured, (3) income statement .

Key Points	Key Learning Outcomes	Example Exercises	Practice Exercises
The financial statements of manufacturing companies differ from those of merchandising companies. Manufacturing company balance sheets report three types of inventory: materials, work in process, and finished goods. The income statement of manufacturing companies reports cost of goods sold, which is the total manufacturing cost of the goods sold. The income statement is supported by the statement of cost of goods manufactured, which provides the details of the cost of goods manufactured during the period.	• Describe materials inventory.		
	• Describe work in process inventory.		
	• Describe finished goods inventory.		
	• Describe the differences between merchandising and manufacturing company balance sheets.		
	• Prepare a statement of cost of goods manufactured.	**18-5**	18-5A, 18-5B
	• Prepare an income statement for a manufacturing company.	**18-5**	18-5A, 18-5B

Key Points	Key Learning Outcomes	Example Exercises	Practice Exercises
Managers need information to guide their decision making. Managerial accounting provides a variety of information and reports that help managers run the operations of their business.	• Describe examples of how managerial accounting aids managers in decision making.		

Key Terms

continuous process improvement (817)
controller (816)
controlling (817)
conversion costs (822)
cost (819)
cost object (819)
cost of finished goods available (826)
cost of goods manufactured (826)
cost of goods sold (826)
cost of merchandise sold (825)
decision making (817)
direct costs (819)
direct labor cost (821)

direct materials cost (820)
directing (817)
factory burden (821)
factory overhead cost (821)
feedback (817)
financial accounting (814)
finished goods inventory (824)
indirect costs (819)
line department (815)
management by exception (817)
management process (816)
managerial accounting (814)
manufacturing overhead (821)
materials inventory (824)

merchandise available for sale (825)
objectives (goals) (817)
operational planning (817)
period costs (822)
planning (817)
prime costs (822)
product costs (822)
staff department (816)
statement of cost of goods manufactured (826)
strategic planning (817)
strategies (817)
work in process inventory (824)

Illustrative Problem

The following is a list of costs that were incurred in producing this textbook:

a. Insurance on the factory building and equipment
b. Salary of the vice president of finance
c. Hourly wages of printing press operators during production
d. Straight-line depreciation on the printing presses used to manufacture the text
e. Electricity used to run the presses during the printing of the text
f. Sales commissions paid to textbook representatives for each text sold
g. Paper on which the text is printed
h. Book covers used to bind the pages
i. Straight-line depreciation on an office building
j. Salaries of staff used to develop artwork for the text
k. Glue used to bind pages to cover

Instructions

With respect to the manufacture and sale of this text, classify each cost as either a product cost or a period cost. Indicate whether each product cost is a direct materials cost, a direct labor cost, or a factory overhead cost. Indicate whether each period cost is a selling expense or an administrative expense.

Solution

Cost	Product Cost			Period Cost	
	Direct Materials Cost	Direct Labor Cost	Factory Overhead Cost	Selling Expense	Administrative Expense
a.			X		
b.					X
c.		X			
d.			X		
e.			X		
f.				X	
g.	X				
h.	X				
i.					X
j.			X		
k.			X		

Self-Examination Questions (Answers at End of Chapter)

1. Which of the following best describes the difference between financial and managerial accounting?
   A. Managerial accounting provides information to support decisions, while financial accounting does not.
   B. Managerial accounting is not restricted to generally accepted accounting principles, while financial accounting is restricted to GAAP.
   C. Managerial accounting does not result in financial reports, while financial accounting does result in financial reports.
   D. Managerial accounting is concerned solely with the future and does not record events from the past, while financial accounting records only events from past transactions.

2. Which of the following is *not* one of the five basic phases of the management process?
   A. Planning   C. Decision making
   B. Controlling D. Operating

3. Which of the following is *not* considered a cost of manufacturing a product?
   A. Direct materials cost
   B. Factory overhead cost
   C. Sales salaries
   D. Direct labor cost

4. Which of the following costs would be included as part of the factory overhead costs of a microcomputer manufacturer?
   A. The cost of memory chips
   B. Depreciation of testing equipment
   C. Wages of microcomputer assemblers
   D. The cost of disk drives

5. For the month of May, Latter Company has beginning finished goods inventory of $50,000, ending finished goods inventory of $35,000, and cost of goods manufactured of $125,000. What is the cost of goods sold for May?
   A. $90,000   C. $140,000
   B. $110,000   D. $170,000

Eye Openers

1. What are the major differences between managerial accounting and financial accounting?
2. a. Differentiate between a department with line responsibility and a department with staff responsibility.
   b. In an organization that has a Sales Department and a Personnel Department, among others, which of the two departments has (1) line responsibility and (2) staff responsibility?
3. a. What is the role of the controller in a business organization?
   b. Does the controller have a line or staff responsibility?

4. What are the five basic phases of the management process?
5. What is the term for a plan that encompasses a period ranging from five or more years and that serves as a basis for long-range actions?
6. What is the process by which management runs day-to-day operations?
7. What is the process by which management assesses how well a plan is working?
8. Describe what is meant by *management by exception*.
9. What term describes a payment in cash or the commitment to pay cash in the future for the purpose of generating revenues?
10. For a company that produces desktop computers, would memory chips be considered a direct or an indirect cost of each microcomputer produced?
11. What three costs make up the cost of manufacturing a product?
12. What manufacturing cost term is used to describe the cost of materials that are an integral part of the manufactured end product?
13. If the cost of wages paid to employees who are directly involved in converting raw materials into a manufactured end product is not a significant portion of the total product cost, how would the wages cost be classified as to type of manufacturing cost?
14. Distinguish between prime costs and conversion costs.
15. What is the difference between a product cost and a period cost?
16. Name the three inventory accounts for a manufacturing business, and describe what each balance represents at the end of an accounting period.
17. In what order should the three inventories of a manufacturing business be presented on the balance sheet?
18. What are the three categories of manufacturing costs included in the cost of finished goods and the cost of work in process?
19. For a manufacturer, what is the description of the amount that is comparable to a merchandising business's cost of merchandise sold?
20. For June, Fosina Company had beginning materials inventory of $50,000, ending materials inventory of $60,000, and materials purchases of $280,000. What is the cost of direct materials used in production?
21. How does the Cost of Goods Sold section of the income statement differ between merchandising and manufacturing companies?
22. Describe how an automobile manufacturer might use managerial accounting information to (a) evaluate the performance of the company and (b) make strategic decisions.

Practice Exercises

PE 18-1A
Management process
obj. 1
EE 18-1   p. 817

Three phases of the management process are controlling, planning, and decision making. Match the following descriptions to the proper phase.

Phase of management process	Description
Planning	a. Monitoring the operating results of implemented plans and comparing the actual results with expected results.
Controlling	
Decision making	b. Inherent in planning, directing, controlling, and improving.
	c. Long-range courses of action.

PE 18-1B
Management process
obj. 1
EE 18-1   p. 817

Three phases of the management process are planning, directing, and controlling. Match the following descriptions to the proper phase.

Phase of management process	Description
Directing	a. Process by which managers, given their assigned levels of responsibilities, run day-to-day operations.
Planning	
Controlling	b. Isolating significant departures from plans for further investigation and possible remedial action. It may lead to a revision of future plans.
	c. Developing long-range courses of action to achieve goals.

PE 18-2A
Direct materials, direct labor, and factory overhead

obj. 2

EE 18-2   p. 821

Identify the following costs as direct materials (DM), direct labor (DL), or factory overhead (FO) for an automobile manufacturer.
a. Oil used for assembly line machinery
b. Wages of the plant manager
c. Wages of employees that operate painting equipment
d. Steel

PE 18-2B
Direct materials, direct labor, and factory overhead

obj. 2

EE 18-2   p. 821

Identify the following costs as direct materials (DM), direct labor (DL), or factory overhead (FO) for a textbook publisher.
a. Wages of printing machine employees
b. Maintenance on printing machines
c. Paper used to make a textbook
d. Glue used to bind books

PE 18-3A
Prime and conversion costs

obj. 2

EE 18-3   p. 822

Identify the following costs as a prime cost (P), conversion cost (C), or both (B) for an automobile manufacturer.
a. Oil used for assembly line machinery
b. Wages of employees that operate painting equipment
c. Steel
d. Wages of the plant manager

PE 18-3B
Prime and conversion costs

obj. 2

EE 18-3   p. 822

Identify the following costs as a prime cost (P), conversion cost (C), or both (B) for a textbook publisher.
a. Glue used to bind books
b. Maintenance on printing machines
c. Paper used to make a textbook
d. Wages of printing machine employees

PE 18-4A
Product and period costs

obj. 2

EE 18-4   p. 824

Identify the following costs as a product cost or a period cost for an automobile manufacturer.
a. Rent on office building
b. Accounting staff salaries
c. Steel
d. Wages of employees that operate painting equipment

PE 18-4B
Product and period costs

obj. 2

EE 18-4   p. 824

Identify the following costs as a product cost or a period cost for a textbook publisher.
a. Paper used to make a textbook
b. Depreciation expense—corporate headquarters
c. Sales salaries
d. Maintenance on printing machines

PE 18-5A
Cost of goods sold, cost of goods manufactured

obj. 3

EE 18-5   p. 829

Siler Company has the following information for February:

Cost of direct materials used in production	$ 9,000
Direct labor	27,000
Factory overhead	18,000
Work in process inventory, February 1	25,000
Work in process inventory, February 28	26,000
Finished goods inventory, February 1	11,000
Finished goods inventory, February 28	13,000

For February, determine (a) the cost of goods manufactured and (b) the cost of goods sold.

PE 18-5B
Cost of goods
sold, cost of goods
manufactured

obj. 3

EE 18-5   p. 829

Davidson Company has the following information for August:

Cost of direct materials used in production	$60,000
Direct labor	90,000
Factory overhead	44,000
Work in process inventory, August 1	20,000
Work in process inventory, August 31	16,000
Finished goods inventory, August 1	36,000
Finished goods inventory, August 31	20,000

For August, determine (a) the cost of goods manufactured and (b) the cost of goods sold.

Exercises

EX 18-1
Classifying costs as
materials, labor, or
factory overhead

obj. 2

Indicate whether each of the following costs of an airplane manufacturer would be classified as direct materials cost, direct labor cost, or factory overhead cost:

a. Controls for flight deck
b. Aircraft engines
c. Depreciation of welding equipment
d. Welding machinery lubricants
e. Salary of test pilot
f. Steel used in landing gear
g. Wages of assembly line worker
h. Tires

EX 18-2
Classifying costs as
materials, labor, or
factory overhead

obj. 2

Indicate whether the following costs of Colgate-Palmolive Company would be classified as direct materials cost, direct labor cost, or factory overhead cost:

a. Wages paid to Packaging Department employees
b. Maintenance supplies
c. Plant manager salary for the Morristown, Tennessee, toothpaste plant
d. Packaging materials
e. Depreciation on production machinery
f. Salary of process engineers
g. Depreciation on the Clarksville, Indiana, soap plant
h. Resins for soap and shampoo products
i. Scents and fragrances
j. Wages of production line employees

EX 18-3
Classifying costs as
factory overhead

obj. 2

Which of the following items are properly classified as part of factory overhead for Caterpillar?

a. Factory supplies used in the Morganton, North Carolina, engine parts plant
b. Amortization of patents on new assembly process
c. Steel plate
d. Vice president of finance's salary
e. Sales incentive fees to dealers
f. Depreciation on Peoria, Illinois, headquarters building
g. Interest expense on debt
h. Plant manager's salary at Aurora, Illinois, manufacturing plant
i. Consultant fees for a study of production line employee productivity
j. Property taxes on the Danville, Kentucky, tractor tread plant

EX 18-4
**Classifying costs as
product or period
costs**

obj. 2

For apparel manufacturer Ann Taylor, Inc., classify each of the following costs as either a product cost or a period cost:

a. Travel costs of salespersons
b. Fabric used during production
c. Salaries of distribution center personnel
d. Factory janitorial supplies
e. Repairs and maintenance costs for sewing machines
f. Corporate controller's salary
g. Depreciation on office equipment
h. Advertising expenses
i. Utility costs for office building
j. Depreciation on sewing machines
k. Property taxes on factory building and equipment
l. Research and development costs
m. Sales commissions
n. Oil used to lubricate sewing machines
o. Factory supervisors' salaries
p. Wages of sewing machine operators
q. Salary of production quality control supervisor

EX 18-5
**Concepts and
terminology**

objs. 1, 2

From the choices presented in parentheses, choose the appropriate term for completing each of the following sentences:

a. Payments of cash or the commitment to pay cash in the future for the purpose of generating revenues are (costs, expenses).
b. The implementation of automatic, robotic factory equipment normally (increases, decreases) the direct labor component of product costs.
c. Feedback is often used to (improve, direct) operations.
d. A product, sales territory, department, or activity to which costs are traced is called a (direct cost, cost object).
e. The balance sheet of a manufacturer would include an account for (cost of goods sold, work in process inventory).
f. Factory overhead costs combined with direct labor costs are called (prime, conversion) costs.
g. Advertising costs are usually viewed as (period, product) costs.

EX 18-6
**Concepts and
terminology**

objs. 1, 2

From the choices presented in parentheses, choose the appropriate term for completing each of the following sentences:

a. Short-term plans are called (strategic, operational) plans.
b. The plant manager's salary would be considered (direct, indirect) to the product.
c. The phase of the management process that uses process information to eliminate the source of problems in a process so that the process delivers the correct product in the correct quantities is called (directing, improving).
d. The wages of an assembly worker are normally considered a (period, product) cost.
e. Materials for use in production are called (supplies, materials inventory).
f. Direct materials costs combined with direct labor costs are called (prime, conversion) costs.
g. An example of factory overhead is (sales office depreciation, plant depreciation).

EX 18-7
**Classifying costs in a
service company**

obj. 2

A partial list of the costs for Mountain Lakes Railroad, a short hauler of freight, is provided below. Classify each cost as either indirect or direct. For purposes of classifying each cost as direct or indirect, use the train as the cost object.

a. Wages of switch and classification yard personnel
b. Cost to lease (rent) railroad cars
c. Depreciation of terminal facilities
d. Payroll clerk salaries
e. Salaries of dispatching and communications personnel

f. Safety training costs
g. Cost to lease (rent) train locomotives.
h. Wages of train engineers
i. Cost of track and bed (ballast) replacement
j. Costs of accident cleanup
k. Fuel costs
l. Maintenance costs of right of way, bridges, and buildings

EX 18-8
Classifying costs
objs. 2, 3

The following report was prepared for evaluating the performance of the plant manager of Second Hand Inc. Evaluate and correct this report.

Second Hand Inc.
Manufacturing Costs
For the Quarter Ended March 31, 2010

Materials used in production (including $50,000 of indirect materials)	$ 540,000
Direct labor (including $75,000 maintenance salaries)	500,000
Factory overhead:	
Supervisor salaries	460,000
Heat, light, and power	125,000
Sales salaries	310,000
Promotional expenses	280,000
Insurance and property taxes—plant	135,000
Insurance and property taxes—corporate offices	195,000
Depreciation—plant and equipment	110,000
Depreciation—corporate offices	80,000
Total	$2,735,000

EX 18-9
Financial statements of a manufacturing firm
obj. 3

✔ a. Net income, $48,000

The following events took place for LAE Manufacturing Company during March, the first month of its operations as a producer of digital clocks:

a. Purchased $52,000 of materials.
b. Used $40,000 of direct materials in production.
c. Incurred $60,000 of direct labor wages.
d. Incurred $84,000 of factory overhead.
e. Transferred $140,000 of work in process to finished goods.
f. Sold goods with a cost of $110,000.
g. Earned revenues of $250,000.
h. Incurred $64,000 of selling expenses.
i. Incurred $28,000 of administrative expenses.

a. Prepare the March income statement for LAE Manufacturing Company.
b. Determine the inventory balances at the end of the first month of operations.

EX 18-10
Manufacturing company balance sheet
obj. 3

Partial balance sheet data for Lawson Company at December 31, 2010, are as follows:

Finished goods inventory	$10,000	Supplies	$18,000
Prepaid insurance	10,000	Materials inventory	22,000
Accounts receivable	26,000	Cash	28,000
Work in process inventory	40,000		

Prepare the Current Assets section of Lawson Company's balance sheet at December 31, 2010.

EX 18-11
Cost of direct materials used in production for a manufacturing company
obj. 3

Monterey Manufacturing Company reported the following materials data for the month ending October 31, 2010:

Materials purchased	$160,000
Materials inventory, October 1	50,000
Materials inventory, October 31	42,000

Determine the cost of direct materials used in production by Monterey during the month ended October 31, 2010.

EX 18-12

Cost of goods manufactured for a manufacturing company

obj. 3

✔ e. $6,000

Two items are omitted from each of the following three lists of cost of goods manufactured statement data. Determine the amounts of the missing items, identifying them by letter.

Work in process inventory, December 1	$ 2,000	$ 12,000	(e)
Total manufacturing costs incurred during December	14,000	(c)	70,000
Total manufacturing costs	(a)	$140,000	$76,000
Work in process inventory, December 31	3,000	30,000	(f)
Cost of goods manufactured	(b)	(d)	$62,000

EX 18-13

Cost of goods manufactured for a manufacturing company

obj. 3

The following information is available for O'Neal Manufacturing Company for the month ending January 31, 2010:

Cost of direct materials used in production	$132,000
Direct labor	158,000
Work in process inventory, January 1	60,000
Work in process inventory, January 31	80,000
Total factory overhead	72,000

Determine O'Neal's cost of goods manufactured for the month ended January 31, 2010.

EX 18-14

Income statement for a manufacturing company

obj. 3

✔ d. $160,000

Two items are omitted from each of the following three lists of cost of goods sold data from a manufacturing company income statement. Determine the amounts of the missing items, identifying them by letter.

Finished goods inventory, November 1	$ 60,000	$ 20,000	(e)
Cost of goods manufactured	300,000	(c)	260,000
Cost of finished goods available for sale	(a)	$190,000	$300,000
Finished goods inventory, November 30	70,000	30,000	(f)
Cost of goods sold	(b)	(d)	$275,000

EX 18-15

Statement of cost of goods manufactured for a manufacturing company

obj. 3

✔ a. Total manufacturing costs, $871,200

Cost data for F. Mills Manufacturing Company for the month ending April 30, 2010, are as follows:

Inventories	April 1	April 30
Materials	$175,000	$154,000
Work in process	119,000	133,000
Finished goods	91,000	105,000

Direct labor	$315,000
Materials purchased during April	336,000
Factory overhead incurred during April:	
Indirect labor	33,600
Machinery depreciation	20,000
Heat, light, and power	7,000
Supplies	5,600
Property taxes	4,900
Miscellaneous cost	9,100

a. Prepare a cost of goods manufactured statement for April 2010.
b. Determine the cost of goods sold for April 2010.

EX 18-16

Cost of goods sold, profit margin, and net income for a manufacturing company

obj. 3

✔ a. Cost of goods sold, $244,000

The following information is available for Gonzalez Manufacturing Company for the month ending March 31, 2010:

Cost of goods manufactured	$240,000
Selling expenses	76,500
Administrative expenses	40,500
Sales	486,000
Finished goods inventory, March 1	54,000
Finished goods inventory, March 31	50,000

For the month ended March 31, 2010, determine Gonzalez's (a) cost of goods sold, (b) gross profit, and (c) net income.

EX 18-17
Cost flow relationships

obj. **3**

✔ a. $150,000

The following information is available for the first month of operations of Zahorik Company, a manufacturer of mechanical pencils:

Sales	$360,000
Gross profit	210,000
Cost of goods manufactured	180,000
Indirect labor	78,000
Factory depreciation	12,000
Materials purchased	111,000
Total manufacturing costs for the period	207,000
Materials inventory	15,000

Using the above information, determine the following missing amounts:

a. Cost of goods sold
b. Finished goods inventory
c. Direct materials cost
d. Direct labor cost
e. Work in process inventory

Problems Series A

PR 18-1A
Classifying costs

obj. **2**

The following is a list of costs that were incurred in the production and sale of lawn mowers:

a. Attorney fees for drafting a new lease for headquarters offices.
b. Commissions paid to sales representatives, based on the number of lawn mowers sold.
c. Property taxes on the factory building and equipment.
d. Hourly wages of operators of robotic machinery used in production.
e. Salary of vice president of marketing.
f. Gasoline engines used for lawn mowers.
g. Factory cafeteria cashier's wages.
h. Electricity used to run the robotic machinery.
i. Maintenance costs for new robotic factory equipment, based on hours of usage.
j. License fees for use of patent for lawn mower blade, based on the number of lawn mowers produced.
k. Salary of factory supervisor.
l. Steel used in producing the lawn mowers.
m. Telephone charges for company controller's office.
n. Paint used to coat the lawn mowers.
o. Straight-line depreciation on the robotic machinery used to manufacture the lawn mowers.
p. Tires for lawn mowers.
q. Engine oil used in mower engines prior to shipment.
r. Cash paid to outside firm for janitorial services for factory.
s. Cost of advertising in a national magazine.
t. Salary of quality control supervisor who inspects each lawn mower before it is shipped.
u. Plastic for outside housing of lawn mowers.
v. Steering wheels for lawn mowers.
w. Filter for spray gun used to paint the lawn mowers.
x. Cost of boxes used in packaging lawn mowers.
y. Premiums on insurance policy for factory buildings.
z. Payroll taxes on hourly assembly line employees.

Instructions

Classify each cost as either a product cost or a period cost. Indicate whether each product cost is a direct materials cost, a direct labor cost, or a factory overhead cost. Indicate whether each period cost is a selling expense or an administrative expense.

(continued)

Use the following tabular headings for your answer, placing an "X" in the appropriate column.

	Product Costs			Period Costs	
Cost	Direct Materials Cost	Direct Labor Cost	Factory Overhead Cost	Selling Expense	Administrative Expense

PR 18-2A
Classifying costs
obj. 2

The following is a list of costs incurred by several businesses:

a. Costs for television advertisement.
b. Disk drives for a microcomputer manufacturer.
c. Executive bonus for vice president of marketing.
d. Packing supplies for products sold.
e. Protective glasses for factory machine operators.
f. Cost of telephone operators for a toll-free hotline to help customers operate products.
g. Entertainment expenses for sales representatives.
h. Wages of a machine operator on the production line.
i. Seed for grain farmer.
j. Tires for an automobile manufacturer.
k. Costs of operating a research laboratory.
l. Paper used by Computer Department in processing various managerial reports.
m. Hourly wages of warehouse laborers.
n. Wages of company controller's secretary.
o. Factory operating supplies.
p. First-aid supplies for factory workers.
q. Depreciation of factory equipment.
r. Salary of quality control supervisor.
s. Sales commissions.
t. Paper used by commercial printer.
u. Lumber used by furniture manufacturer.
v. Health insurance premiums paid for factory workers.
w. Cost of hogs for meat processor.
x. Maintenance and repair costs for factory equipment.

Instructions

Classify each of the preceding costs as a product cost or period cost. Indicate whether each product cost is a direct materials cost, a direct labor cost, or a factory overhead cost. Indicate whether each period cost is a selling expense or an administrative expense. Use the following tabular headings for preparing your answer. Place an "X" in the appropriate column.

	Product Costs			Period Costs	
Cost	Direct Materials Cost	Direct Labor Cost	Factory Overhead Cost	Selling Expense	Administrative Expense

PR 18-3A
Cost classifications—service company
obj. 2

A partial list of Frend Hotel's costs is provided below.

a. Champagne for guests.
b. Cost to mail a customer survey.
c. Training for hotel restaurant servers.
d. Cost to replace lobby furniture.
e. Cost of soaps and shampoos for rooms.
f. Cost of food.
g. Wages of desk clerks.
h. Cost to paint lobby.
i. Cost of advertising in local newspaper.
j. Cost of laundering towels and bedding.
k. Wages of kitchen employees.
l. Guest room telephone costs for long-distance calls.
m. Cost of room mini-bar supplies.

n. Utility cost.
o. Cost of valet service.
p. General maintenance supplies.
q. Wages of maids.
r. Salary of the hotel president.
s. Depreciation of the hotel.
t. Cost of new carpeting.
u. Wages of bellhops.
v. Wages of convention setup employees.
w. Pay per view movie rental costs (in rooms).

Instructions
1. What would be Frend's most logical definition for the final cost object?
2. Identify whether each of the costs is to be classified as direct or indirect. Define direct costs in terms of a hotel guest as the cost object.

PR 18-4A
Manufacturing income statement, statement of cost of goods manufactured

objs. 2, 3

✔ 1. b. Grant
$594,000

Several items are omitted from each of the following income statement and cost of goods manufactured statement data for the month of December 2010:

	Grant Company	McClellan Company
Materials inventory, December 1	$ 78,000	$ 102,000
Materials inventory, December 31	(a)	115,000
Materials purchased	198,000	230,000
Cost of direct materials used in production	209,000	(a)
Direct labor	294,000	(b)
Factory overhead	91,000	114,000
Total manufacturing costs incurred during December	(b)	660,000
Total manufacturing costs	744,000	906,000
Work in process inventory, December 1	150,000	246,000
Work in process inventory, December 31	126,000	(c)
Cost of goods manufactured	(c)	654,000
Finished goods inventory, December 1	132,000	114,000
Finished goods inventory, December 31	138,000	(d)
Sales	1,150,000	1,020,000
Cost of goods sold	(d)	660,000
Gross profit	(e)	(e)
Operating expenses	150,000	(f)
Net income	(f)	226,000

Instructions
1. Determine the amounts of the missing items, identifying them by letter.
2. Prepare a statement of cost of goods manufactured for McClellan Company.
3. Prepare an income statement for McClellan Company.

PR 18-5A
Statement of cost of goods manufactured and income statement for a manufacturing company

objs. 2, 3

The following information is available for Deutsch Corporation for 2010:

Inventories	January 1	December 31
Materials	$225,000	$280,000
Work in process	405,000	380,000
Finished goods	390,000	380,000

Advertising expense	$ 190,000
Depreciation expense—office equipment	27,000
Depreciation expense—factory equipment	36,000
Direct labor	430,000
Heat, light, and power—factory	14,400
Indirect labor	50,400
Materials purchased	423,000
Office salaries expense	147,500
Property taxes—factory	11,700
Property taxes—office building	24,300
Rent expense—factory	19,800
Sales	1,980,000
Sales salaries expense	243,000
Supplies—factory	9,900
Miscellaneous cost—factory	6,120

Instructions

1. Prepare the 2010 statement of cost of goods manufactured.
2. Prepare the 2010 income statement.

Problems Series B

PR 18-1B
Classifying costs

obj. 2

The following is a list of costs that were incurred in the production and sale of boats:

a. Cost of electrical wiring for boats.
b. Commissions to sales representatives, based upon the number of boats sold.
c. Salary of shop supervisor.
d. Salary of president of company.
e. Cost of boat for "grand prize" promotion in local bass tournament.
f. Power used by sanding equipment.
g. Hourly wages of assembly line workers.
h. Boat chairs.
i. Legal department costs for the year.
j. Memberships for key executives in the Bass World Association.
k. Cost of normal scrap from defective hulls.
l. Fiberglass for producing the boat hull.
m. Decals for boat hull.
n. Annual fee to pro-fisherman Jim Bo Wilks to promote the boats.
o. Yearly cost maintenance contract for robotic equipment.
p. Annual bonus paid to top executives of the company.
q. Masks for use by sanders in smoothing boat hulls.
r. Special advertising campaign in *Bass World*.
s. Cost of metal hardware for boats, such as ornaments and tie-down grasps.
t. Straight-line depreciation on factory equipment.
u. Oil to lubricate factory equipment.
v. Salary of chief financial officer.
w. Canvas top for boats.
x. Wood paneling for use in interior boat trim.
y. Cost of paving the headquarters employee parking lot.
z. Steering wheels.

Instructions

Classify each cost as either a product cost or a period cost. Indicate whether each product cost is a direct materials cost, a direct labor cost, or a factory overhead cost. Indicate whether each period cost is a selling expense or an administrative expense. Use the following tabular headings for your answer, placing an "X" in the appropriate column.

	Product Costs			Period Costs	
Cost	Direct Materials Cost	Direct Labor Cost	Factory Overhead Cost	Selling Expense	Administrative Expense

PR 18-2B
Classifying costs

obj. 2

The following is a list of costs incurred by several businesses:

a. Charitable contribution to United Fund.
b. Fees charged by collection agency on past-due customer accounts.
c. Maintenance costs for factory equipment.
d. Cost of fabric used by clothing manufacturer.
e. Salary of the vice president of manufacturing logistics.
f. Rent for a warehouse used to store finished products.
g. Wages of a machine operator on the production line.
h. Depreciation of tools used in production.

i.   Travel costs of marketing executives to annual sales meeting.
j.   Cost of sewing machine needles used by a shirt manufacturer.
k.   Depreciation of microcomputers used in the factory to coordinate and monitor the production schedules.
l.   Maintenance and repair costs for factory equipment.
m. Wages of production quality control personnel.
n.   Depreciation of robot used to assemble a product.
o.   Cost of a 30-second television commercial.
p.   Pens, paper, and other supplies used by the Accounting Department in preparing various managerial reports.
q.   Electricity used to operate factory machinery.
r.   Factory janitorial supplies.
s.   Oil lubricants for factory plant and equipment.
t.   Cost of plastic for a telephone being manufactured.
u.   Fees paid to lawn service for office grounds upkeep.
v.   Telephone charges by president's office.
w. Surgeon's fee for knee replacement.
x.   Depreciation of copying machines used by the Marketing Department.

Instructions

Classify each of the preceding costs as a product cost or period cost. Indicate whether each product cost is a direct materials cost, a direct labor cost, or a factory overhead cost. Indicate whether each period cost is a selling expense or an administrative expense. Use the following tabular headings for preparing your answer, placing an "X" in the appropriate column.

	Product Costs			Period Costs	
Cost	Direct Materials Cost	Direct Labor Cost	Factory Overhead Cost	Selling Expense	Administrative Expense

PR 18-3B
Cost classifications—service company

obj. 2

A partial list of Gaelic Medical Center's costs is provided below.

a. Operating room supplies used on patients (catheters, sutures, etc.).
b. Utility costs of the hospital.
c. Training costs for nurses.
d. Cost of maintaining the staff and visitors' cafeteria.
e. Cost of intravenous solutions.
f. Cost of blood tests.
g. Cost of improvements on the employee parking lot.
h. Salary of the nutritionist.
i.   General maintenance of the hospital.
j.   Cost of patient meals.
k.   Cost of laundry services for operating room personnel.
l.   Depreciation on patient rooms.
m. Depreciation of X-ray equipment.
n.   Cost of drugs used for patients.
o.   Doctor's fee.
p.   Nurses' salaries.
q.   Overtime incurred in the Records Department due to a computer failure.
r.   Salary of intensive care personnel.
s.   Cost of X-ray test.
t.   Cost of new heart wing.
u.   Cost of advertising hospital services on television.

Instructions
1. What would be Gaelic's most logical definition for the final cost object?
2. Identify whether each of the costs is to be classified as direct or indirect. Define direct costs in terms of a patient as a cost object.

PR 18-4B
Manufacturing
income statement,
statement of cost of
goods manufactured

objs. 2, 3

✔ 1. McCain, c.
$423,000

Several items are omitted from each of the following income statement and cost of goods manufactured statement data for the month of December 2010:

	McCain Company	Buffet Company
Materials inventory, December 1	$ 35,000	$ 45,000
Materials inventory, December 31	(a)	21,000
Materials purchased	150,000	(a)
Cost of direct materials used in production	168,000	(b)
Direct labor	205,000	133,000
Factory overhead	78,000	59,000
Total manufacturing costs incurred in December	(b)	350,000
Total manufacturing costs	514,000	398,000
Work in process inventory, December 1	63,000	48,000
Work in process inventory, December 31	91,000	(c)
Cost of goods manufactured	(c)	353,000
Finished goods inventory, December 1	118,000	62,000
Finished goods inventory, December 31	104,000	(d)
Sales	595,000	448,000
Cost of goods sold	(d)	356,000
Gross profit	(e)	(e)
Operating expenses	62,000	(f)
Net income	(f)	38,000

Instructions
1. Determine the amounts of the missing items, identifying them by letter.
2. Prepare a statement of cost of goods manufactured for McCain Company.
3. Prepare an income statement for McCain Company.

PR 18-5B
Statement of cost of
goods manufactured
and income
statement for a
manufacturing
company

objs. 2, 3

The following information is available for Rosetta Company for 2010:

Inventories	January 1	December 31
Materials	$59,500	$73,500
Work in process	84,000	73,500
Finished goods	87,500	77,000

Advertising expense	$ 52,500
Depreciation expense—office equipment	17,500
Depreciation expense—factory equipment	11,200
Direct labor	143,500
Heat, light, and power—factory	4,500
Indirect labor	18,200
Materials purchased	95,000
Office salaries expense	59,500
Property taxes—factory	3,150
Property taxes—headquarters building	10,500
Rent expense—factory	5,250
Sales	665,000
Sales salaries expense	105,000
Supplies—factory	2,500
Miscellaneous cost—factory	3,400

Instructions
1. Prepare the 2010 statement of cost of goods manufactured.
2. Prepare the 2010 income statement.

Special Activities ● ● ● ● ▶

You can access the special activities online at **www.cengage.com/accounting/reeve**.

Answers to Self-Examination Questions

1. **B** Managerial accounting is not restricted to generally accepted accounting principles, as is financial accounting (answer B). Both financial and managerial accounting support decision making (answer A). Financial accounting is mostly concerned with the decision making of external users, while managerial accounting supports decision making of management. Both financial and managerial accounting can result in financial reports (answer C). Managerial accounting reports are developed for internal use by managers at various levels in the organization. Both managerial and financial accounting record events from the past (answer D); however, managerial accounting can also include information about the future in the form of budgets and cash flow projections.

2. **D** The five basic phases of the management process are planning (answer A), directing (not listed), controlling (answer B), improving (not listed), and decision making (answer C). Operating (answer D) is not one of the five basic phases, but operations are the object of managers' attention.

3. **C** Sales salaries (answer C) is a selling expense and is not considered a cost of manufacturing a product. Direct materials cost (answer A), factory overhead cost (answer B), and direct labor cost (answer D) are costs of manufacturing a product.

4. **B** Depreciation of testing equipment (answer B) is included as part of the factory overhead costs of the microcomputer manufacturer. The cost of memory chips (answer A) and the cost of disk drives (answer D) are both considered a part of direct materials cost. The wages of microcomputer assemblers (answer C) are part of direct labor costs.

5. **C** Cost of goods sold is calculated as follows:

Beginning finished goods inventory	$ 50,000
Add: Cost of goods manufactured	125,000
Less: Ending finished goods inventory	(35,000)
Cost of goods sold	$140,000

Job Order Costing

DAN DONEGAN'S GUITAR

As we discussed in Chapter 18, Dan Donegan of the rock band *Disturbed* uses a custom-made guitar purchased from Washburn Guitars. In fact, Dan Donegan designed his guitar in partnership with Washburn Guitars, which contributed to Washburn's Maya Series of guitars. The Maya guitar is a precision instrument that amateurs and professionals are willing to pay between $1,400 and $7,000 to own. In order for Washburn to stay in business, the purchase price of the guitar must be greater than the cost of producing the guitar. So, how does Washburn determine the cost of producing a guitar?

Costs associated with creating a guitar include materials such as wood and strings, the wages of employees who build the guitar, and factory overhead. To determine the purchase price of Dan's Maya, Washburn identifies and records the costs that go into the guitar during each step of the manufacturing process. As the guitar moves through the production process, the costs of direct materials, direct labor, and factory overhead are recorded. When the guitar is complete, the costs that have been recorded are added up to determine the cost of Dan's unique Maya Series guitar. The company then prices the guitar to achieve a level of profit over the cost of the guitar. This chapter introduces the principles of accounting systems that accumulate costs in the same manner as they were for Dan Donegan's guitar.

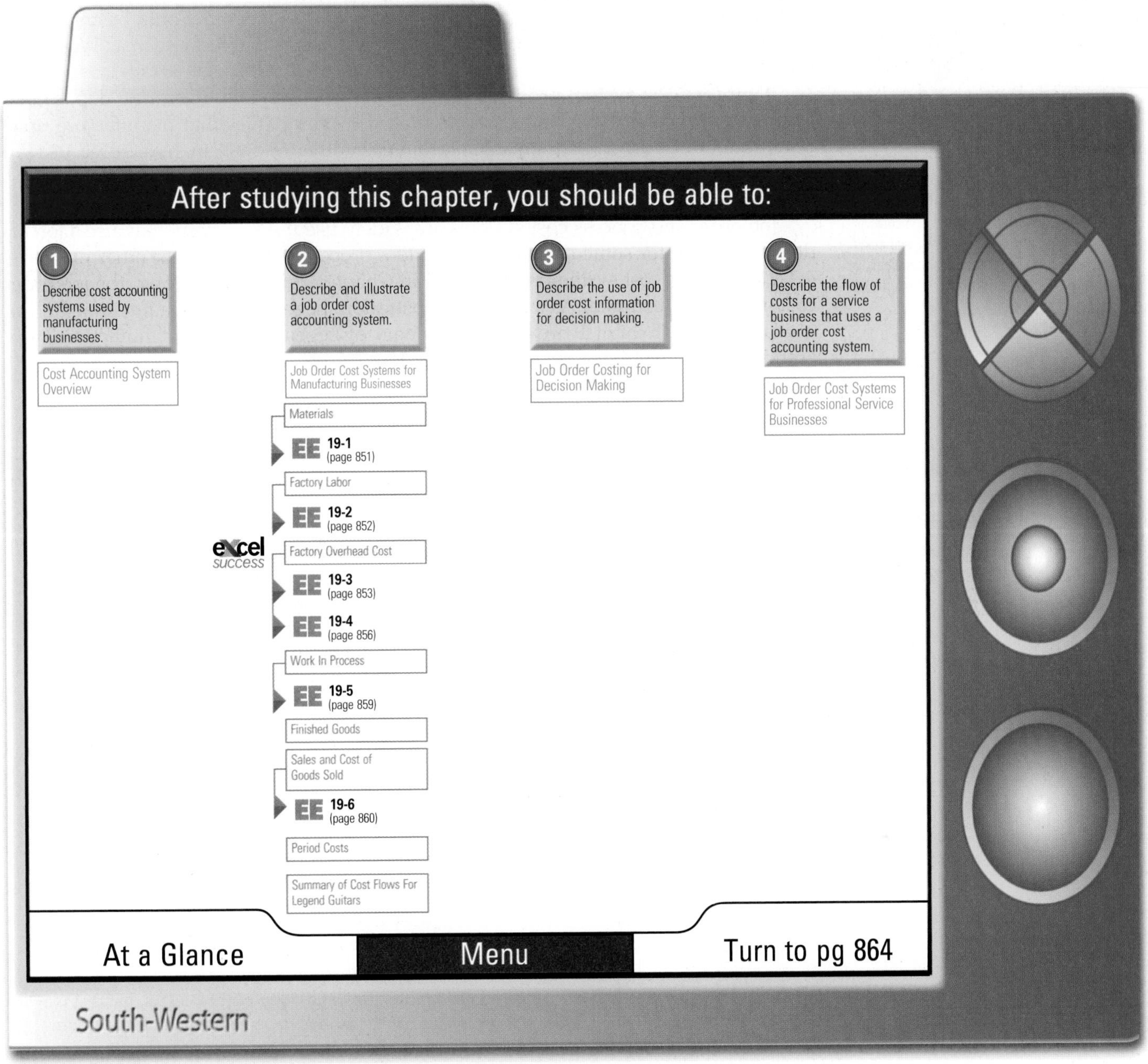

After studying this chapter, you should be able to:

1
Describe cost accounting systems used by manufacturing businesses.

Cost Accounting System Overview

2
Describe and illustrate a job order cost accounting system.

Job Order Cost Systems for Manufacturing Businesses

Materials

EE 19-1 (page 851)

Factory Labor

EE 19-2 (page 852)

e**x**cel *success*

Factory Overhead Cost

EE 19-3 (page 853)

EE 19-4 (page 856)

Work In Process

EE 19-5 (page 859)

Finished Goods

Sales and Cost of Goods Sold

EE 19-6 (page 860)

Period Costs

Summary of Cost Flows For Legend Guitars

3
Describe the use of job order cost information for decision making.

Job Order Costing for Decision Making

4
Describe the flow of costs for a service business that uses a job order cost accounting system.

Job Order Cost Systems for Professional Service Businesses

At a Glance   Menu   Turn to pg 864

South-Western

---

1 Describe cost accounting systems used by manufacturing businesses.

Cost Accounting System Overview

Cost accounting systems measure, record, and report product costs. Managers use product costs for setting product prices, controlling operations, and developing financial statements.

The two main types of cost accounting systems for manufacturing operations are:

1. Job order cost systems
2. Process cost systems

A **job order cost system** provides product costs for each quantity of product that is manufactured. Each quantity of product that is manufactured is called a *job*. Job order cost systems are often used by companies that manufacture custom products for customers or batches of similar products. Manufacturers that use a job order cost

system are sometimes called *job shops*. An example of a job shop would be an apparel manufacturer, such as Levi Strauss & Co., or a guitar manufacturer such as Washburn Guitars.

A **process cost system** provides product costs for each manufacturing department or process. Process cost systems are often used by companies that manufacture units of a product that are indistinguishable from each other and are manufactured using a continuous production process. Examples would be oil refineries, paper producers, chemical processors, and food processors.

Job order and process cost systems are widely used. A company may use a job order cost system for some of its products and a process cost system for other products.

The process cost system is illustrated in Chapter 20. In this chapter, the job order cost system is illustrated. As a basis for illustration, Legend Guitars, a manufacturer of guitars, is used. Exhibit 1 provides a summary of Legend Guitars' manufacturing operations, which were described in Chapter 18.

Exhibit 1

Summary of Legend Guitars' Manufacturing Operations

Manufacturing Operations	
Cutting	Employees cut the body and neck of the guitar out of wood.
Assembling	Employees assemble and finish the guitars.

Product Costs	
Direct materials	The cost of material that is an integral part of and a significant portion of the total cost of the final product. The cost of wood used in the neck and body of the guitars.
Direct labor	The cost of employee wages that is an integral part of and a significant portion of the total cost of the final product. The wages of the cutting and assembling employees.
Factory overhead	Costs other than direct materials and direct labor that are incurred in the manufacturing process. The cost of guitar strings, glue, sandpaper, buffing compound, paint, salaries of production supervisors, janitorial salaries, and factory utilities.

Inventories	
Materials	Includes the cost of direct and indirect materials used to produce the guitars. Direct materials include the cost of wood used in the neck and body of the guitars. Indirect materials include guitar strings, glue, sandpaper, buffing compound, varnish, and paint.
Work in process	Includes the product costs of units that have entered the manufacturing process, but have not been completed. The product costs of guitars for which the neck and body have been cut, but not yet assembled.
Finished goods	Includes the cost of completed (or finished) products that have not been sold. The product costs assigned to completed guitars that have not yet been sold.

Describe and illustrate a job order cost accounting system.

Job Order Cost Systems for Manufacturing Businesses

A job order cost system records and summarizes manufacturing costs by jobs. The flow of manufacturing costs in a job order system is illustrated in Exhibit 2.

Exhibit 2

Flow of Manufacturing Costs

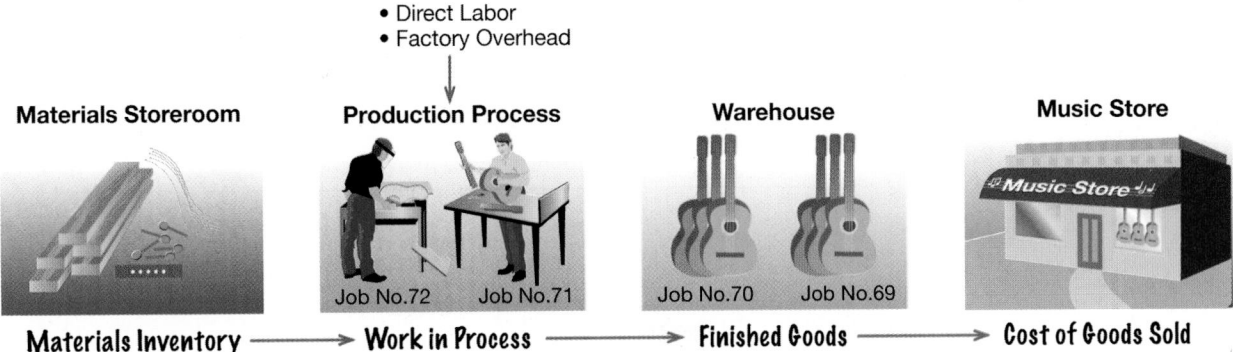

Exhibit 2 indicates that although the materials for Jobs 71 and 72 have been added, both jobs are still in the production process. Thus, Jobs 71 and 72 are part of *Work in Process Inventory*. In contrast, Exhibit 2 indicates that Jobs 69 and 70 have been completed. Thus, Jobs 69 and 70 are part of *Finished Goods Inventory*. Exhibit 2 also indicates that when finished guitars are sold to music stores, their costs become part of *Cost of Goods Sold*.

In a job order cost accounting system, perpetual inventory controlling accounts and subsidiary ledgers are maintained for materials, work in process, and finished goods inventories, as shown below.

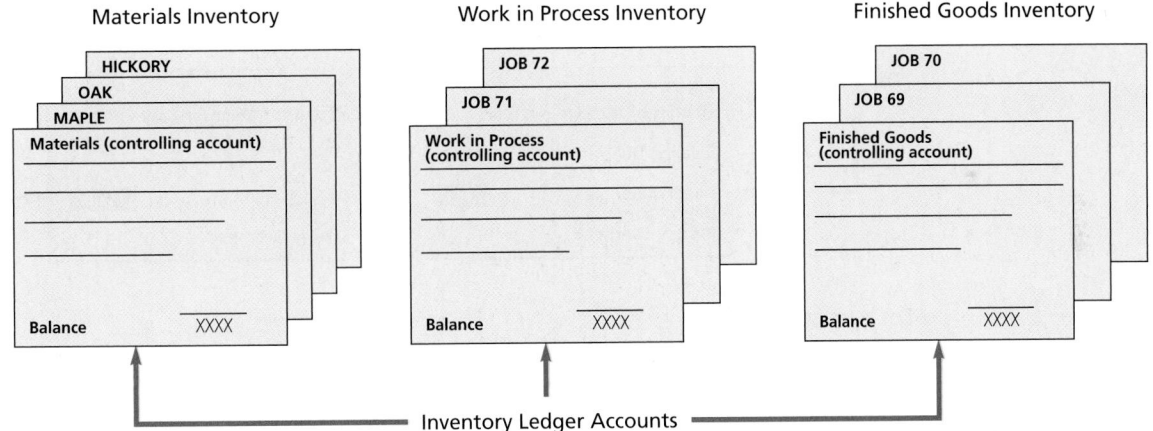

Materials

The materials account in the general ledger is a controlling account. A separate account for each type of material is maintained in a subsidiary **materials ledger**.

Exhibit 3 shows Legend Guitars' materials ledger account for maple. Increases (debits) and decreases (credits) to the account are as follows:

1. Increases (debits) are based on *receiving reports* such as Receiving Report No. 196 for $10,500, which is supported by the supplier's invoice.

2. Decreases (credits) are based on *materials requisitions* such as Requisition No. 672 for $2,000 for Job 71 and Requisition No. 704 for $11,000 for Job 72.

Many companies use bar code scanning devices in place of receiving reports to record and electronically transmit incoming materials data.

A **receiving report** is prepared when materials that have been ordered are received and inspected. The quantity received and the condition of the materials are entered on the receiving report. When the supplier's invoice is received, it is compared to the receiving report. If there are no discrepancies, a journal entry is made to record the

Exhibit 3

Materials Information and Cost Flows

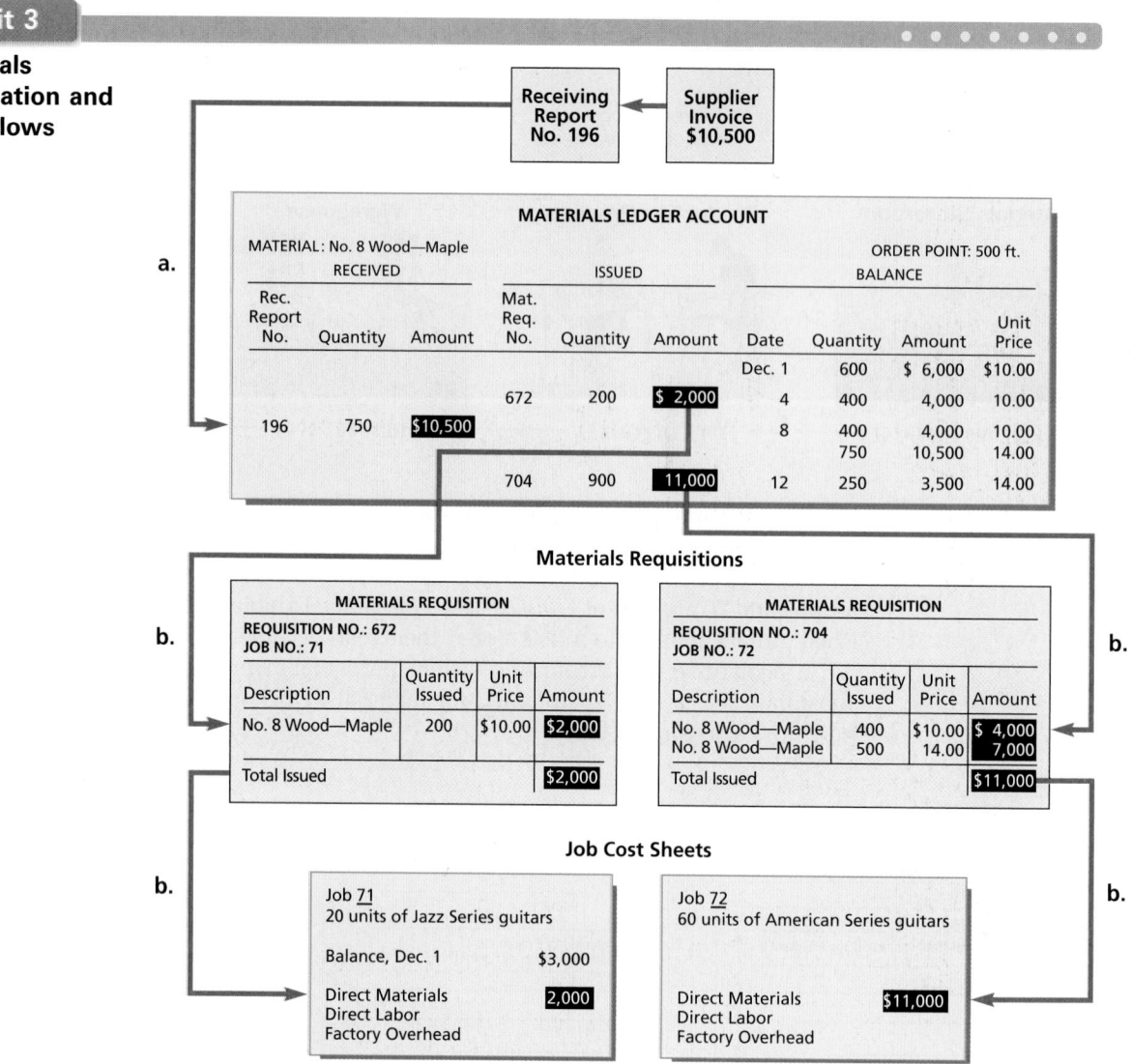

purchase. The journal entry to record the supplier's invoice related to Receiving Report No. 196 in Exhibit 3 is as follows:

a.	Materials		10,500	
	Accounts Payable			10,500
	Materials purchased during December.			

The storeroom releases materials for use in manufacturing when a **materials requisition** is received. An example of a materials requisition is shown in Exhibit 3.

The materials requisitions for each job serve as the basis for recording materials used. For direct materials, the quantities and amounts from the materials requisitions are posted to job cost sheets. **Job cost sheets**, which are illustrated in Exhibit 3, make up the work in process subsidiary ledger.

Exhibit 3 shows the posting of $2,000 of direct materials to Job 71 and $11,000 of direct materials to Job 72.[1] Job 71 is an order for 20 units of Jazz Series guitars, while Job 72 is an order for 60 units of American Series guitars.

A summary of the materials requisitions is used as a basis for the journal entry recording the materials used for the month. For direct materials, this entry increases (debits) Work in Process and decreases (credits) Materials, as shown below.

For many manufacturing firms, the direct materials cost can be greater than 50% of the total cost to manufacture a product. This is why controlling materials costs is very important.

b.	Work in Process	13,000	
	Materials		13,000
	Materials requisitioned to jobs ($2,000 + $11,000).		

Many companies use computerized information processes to record the use of materials. In such cases, storeroom employees electronically record the release of materials, which automatically updates the materials ledger and job cost sheets.

Example Exercise 19-1   Issuance of Materials

••••••• **2**

On March 5, Hatch Company purchased 400 units of raw materials at $14 per unit. On March 10, raw materials were requisitioned for production as follows: 200 units for Job 101 at $12 per unit and 300 units for Job 102 at $14 per unit. Journalize the entry on March 5 to record the purchase and on March 10 to record the requisition from the materials storeroom.

Follow My Example 19-1

Mar. 5	Materials..	5,600	
	Accounts Payable...............................		5,600
	$5,600 = 400 × $14.		
10	Work in Process..................................	6,600*	
	Materials		6,600

*Job 101	$2,400 = 200 × $12
Job 102	4,200 = 300 × $14
Total	$6,600

For Practice: PE 19-1A, PE 19-1B

Factory Labor

When employees report for work, they may use *clock cards*, *in-and-out cards*, or *electronic badges* to clock in. When employees work on an individual job, they use **time tickets**. Exhibit 4 illustrates time tickets for Jobs 71 and 72.

Exhibit 4 shows that on December 13, 2010, D. McInnis spent six hours working on Job 71 at an hourly rate of $10 for a cost of $60 (6 hrs. × $10). Exhibit 4 also indicates that a total of 350 hours was spent by employees on Job 71 during December for a total cost of $3,500. This total direct labor cost of $3,500 is posted to the job cost sheet for Job 71, as shown in Exhibit 4.

Likewise, Exhibit 4 shows that on December 26, 2010, S. Andrews spent eight hours on Job 72 at an hourly rate of $15 for a cost of $120 (8 hrs. × $15). A total of 500 hours

1 To simplify, Exhibit 3 and this chapter use the first-in, first-out cost flow method.

Exhibit 4

Labor Information and Cost Flows

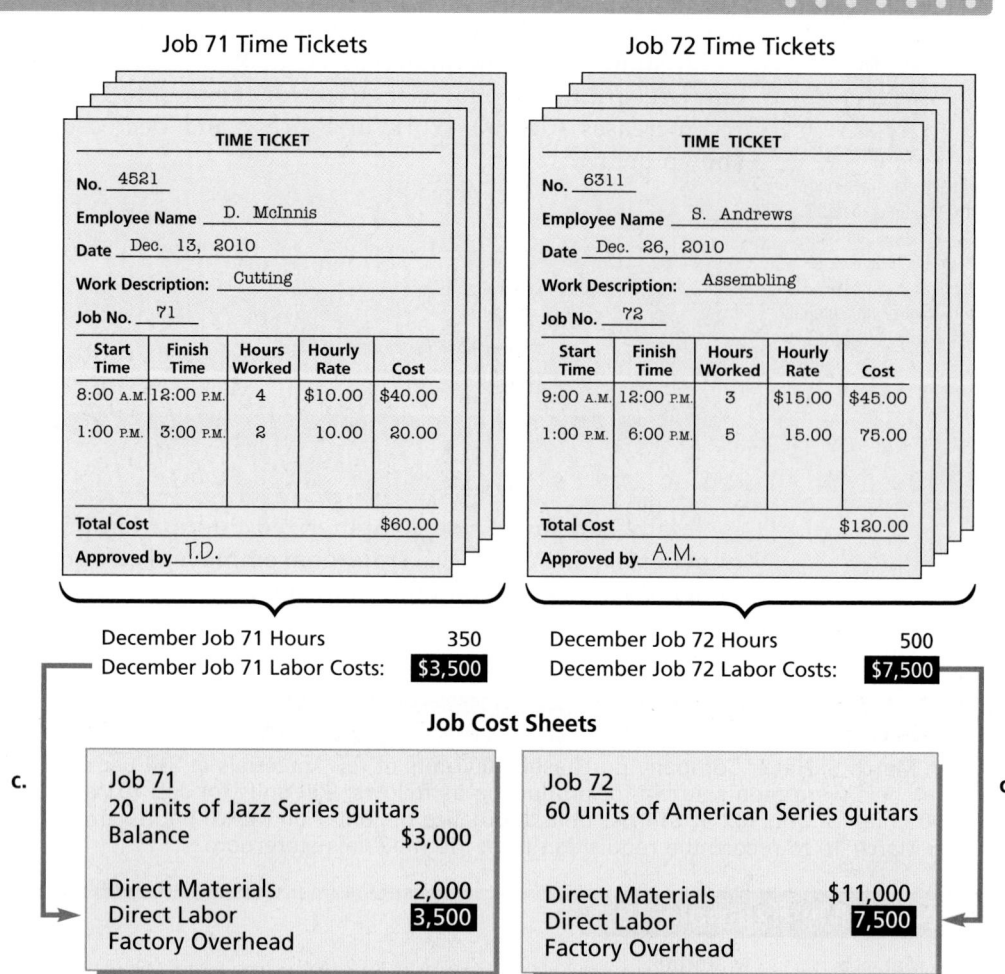

Job 71 Time Tickets

TIME TICKET

No. 4521
Employee Name D. McInnis
Date Dec. 13, 2010
Work Description: Cutting
Job No. 71

Start Time	Finish Time	Hours Worked	Hourly Rate	Cost
8:00 A.M.	12:00 P.M.	4	$10.00	$40.00
1:00 P.M.	3:00 P.M.	2	10.00	20.00

Total Cost $60.00
Approved by T.D.

Job 72 Time Tickets

TIME TICKET

No. 6311
Employee Name S. Andrews
Date Dec. 26, 2010
Work Description: Assembling
Job No. 72

Start Time	Finish Time	Hours Worked	Hourly Rate	Cost
9:00 A.M.	12:00 P.M.	3	$15.00	$45.00
1:00 P.M.	6:00 P.M.	5	15.00	75.00

Total Cost $120.00
Approved by A.M.

December Job 71 Hours 350
December Job 71 Labor Costs: $3,500

December Job 72 Hours 500
December Job 72 Labor Costs: $7,500

Job Cost Sheets

c.

Job 71
20 units of Jazz Series guitars
Balance $3,000

Direct Materials 2,000
Direct Labor 3,500
Factory Overhead

c.

Job 72
60 units of American Series guitars

Direct Materials $11,000
Direct Labor 7,500
Factory Overhead

was spent by employees on Job 72 during December for a total cost of $7,500. This total direct labor cost of $7,500 is posted to the job cost sheet for Job 72, as shown in Exhibit 4.

A summary of the time tickets is used as the basis for the journal entry recording direct labor for the month. This entry increases (debits) Work in Process and increases (credits) Wages Payable, as shown below.

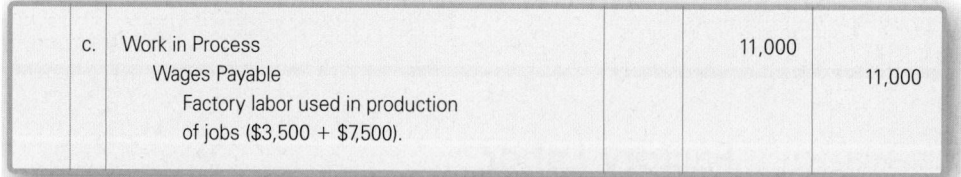

c.	Work in Process		11,000	
	Wages Payable			11,000
	Factory labor used in production of jobs ($3,500 + $7,500).			

Shell Group uses a magnetic card system to track the work of maintenance crews in its refinery operations.

As with direct materials, many businesses use computerized information processing to record direct labor. In such cases, employees may log their time directly into computer terminals at their workstations. In other cases, employees may be issued magnetic cards, much like credit cards, to log in and out of work assignments.

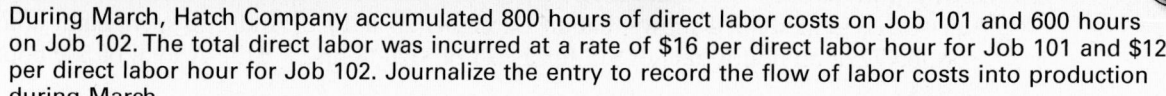

Example Exercise 19-2   Direct Labor Costs   2

During March, Hatch Company accumulated 800 hours of direct labor costs on Job 101 and 600 hours on Job 102. The total direct labor was incurred at a rate of $16 per direct labor hour for Job 101 and $12 per direct labor hour for Job 102. Journalize the entry to record the flow of labor costs into production during March.

(continued)

Follow My Example 19-2

Work in Process.	20,000*	
Wages Payable.		20,000

*Job 101	$12,800	= 800 hrs. × $16
Job 102	7,200	= 600 hrs. × $12
Total	$20,000	

For Practice: PE 19-2A, PE 19-2B

Integrity, Objectivity, and Ethics in Business

GHOST EMPLOYEES

Companies must guard against the fraudulent creation and cashing of payroll checks. Numerous payroll frauds involve supervisors adding fictitious employees to or failing to remove departing employees from the payroll and then cashing the check. This type of fraud can be minimized by requiring proper authorization and approval of employee additions, removals, or changes in pay rates.

Factory Overhead Cost

Factory overhead includes all manufacturing costs except direct materials and direct labor.

A summary of factory overhead costs comes from a variety of sources including the following:

1. *Indirect materials* comes from a summary of materials requisitions.
2. *Indirect labor* comes from the salaries of production supervisors and the wages of other employees such as janitors.
3. *Factory power* comes from utility bills.
4. *Factory depreciation* comes from Accounting Department computations of depreciation.

To illustrate the recording of factory overhead, assume that Legend Guitars incurred $4,600 of overhead in December. The entry to record the factory overhead is shown below.

d.	Factory Overhead		4,600	
	Materials			500
	Wages Payable			2,000
	Utilities Payable			900
	Accumulated Depreciation			1,200
	Factory overhead incurred in production.			

Example Exercise 19-3   Factory Overhead Costs    2

During March, Hatch Company incurred factory overhead costs as follows: indirect materials, $800; indirect labor, $3,400; utilities cost, $1,600; and factory depreciation, $2,500. Journalize the entry to record the factory overhead incurred during March.

Follow My Example 19-3

Factory Overhead.	8,300	
Materials.		800
Wages Payable		3,400
Utilities Payable		1,600
Accumulated Depreciation		2,500

For Practice: PE 19-3A, PE 19-3B

Allocating Factory Overhead Factory overhead is different from direct labor and direct materials in that it is *indirectly* related to the jobs. That is, factory overhead costs cannot be identified with or traced to specific jobs. For this reason, factory overhead costs are allocated to jobs. The process by which factory overhead or other costs are assigned to a cost object, such as a job, is called **cost allocation**.

The factory overhead costs are *allocated* to jobs using a common measure related to each job. This measure is called an **activity base**, *allocation base*, or *activity driver*. The activity base used to allocate overhead should reflect the consumption or use of factory overhead costs. For example, production supervisor salaries could be allocated on the basis of direct labor hours or direct labor cost of each job.

Predetermined Factory Overhead Rate Factory overhead costs are normally allocated or *applied* to jobs using a **predetermined factory overhead rate**. The predetermined factory overhead rate is computed as follows:

$$\text{Predetermined Factory Overhead Rate} = \frac{\text{Estimated Total Factory Overhead Costs}}{\text{Estimated Activity Base}}$$

To illustrate, assume that Legend Guitars estimates the total factory overhead cost as $50,000 for the year and the activity base as 10,000 direct labor hours. The predetermined factory overhead rate of $5 per direct labor hour is computed as follows:

$$\text{Predetermined Factory Overhead Rate} = \frac{\text{Estimated Total Factory Overhead Costs}}{\text{Estimated Activity Base}}$$

$$\text{Predetermined Factory Overhead Rate} = \frac{\$50,000}{10,000 \text{ direct labor hours}} = \$5 \text{ per direct labor hour}$$

As shown above, the predetermined overhead rate is computed using *estimated* amounts at the beginning of the period. This is because managers need timely information on the product costs of each job. If a company waited until all overhead costs were known at the end of the period, the allocated factory overhead would be accurate, but not timely. Only through timely reporting can managers adjust manufacturing methods or product pricing.

Many companies are using a method for accumulating and allocating factory overhead costs. This method, called **activity-based costing**, uses a different overhead rate for each type of factory overhead activity, such as inspecting, moving, and machining. Activity-based costing is discussed and illustrated in the appendix to Chapter 25.

A spreadsheet can be used to calculate the predetermined factory overhead rate, as follows:

	A	B	C	D
1	Inputs:			
2				
3	Estimated total factory overhead costs	$ 50,000		
4	Estimated activity base	10,000	*direct labor hours*	
5				
6	Output:			
7				
8	Predetermined factory overhead rate	=B3/B4	*per direct labor hour*	

↑
a.

a. The predetermined factory overhead rate is determined by dividing the two inputs, =B3/B4.

The spreadsheet might involve multiple factories, thus requiring the calculation of multiple rates across columns or rows. In addition, spreadsheets are particularly useful when determining multiple activity rates under activity-based costing.

 Go to the hands-on *Excel Tutor* for this example!

Applying Factory Overhead to Work in Process Legend Guitars applies factory overhead using a rate of $5 per direct labor hour. The factory overhead applied to each job is recorded in the job cost sheets, as shown in Exhibit 5.

Exhibit 5

Applying Factory Overhead to Jobs

Exhibit 5 shows that 850 direct labor hours were used in Legend Guitars' December operations. Based on the time tickets, 350 hours can be traced to Job 71, and 500 hours can be traced to Job 72.

Using a factory overhead rate of $5 per direct labor hour, $4,250 of factory overhead is applied as follows:

	Direct Labor Hours	Factory Overhead Rate	Factory Overhead Applied
Job 71	350	$5	$1,750 (350 hrs. × $5)
Job 72	500	$5	2,500 (500 hrs. × $5)
Total	850		$4,250

As shown in Exhibit 5, the applied overhead is posted to each job cost sheet. Factory overhead of $1,750 is posted to Job 71, which results in a total product cost on December 31, 2010, of $10,250. Factory overhead of $2,500 is posted to Job 72, which results in a total product cost on December 31, 2010, of $21,000.

The journal entry to apply factory overhead increases (debits) Work in Process and credits Factory Overhead. This journal entry to apply overhead to Jobs 71 and 72 is shown at the top of the next page.

e.	Work in Process		4,250	
	Factory Overhead			4,250
	Factory overhead applied to jobs			
	according to the predetermined			
	overhead rate (850 hrs. × $5).			

To summarize, the factory overhead account is:

1. Increased (debited) for the *actual overhead* costs incurred, as shown earlier for transaction (d) on page 853.
2. Decreased (credited) for the *applied overhead*, as shown above for transaction (e).

The actual and applied overhead usually differ because the actual overhead costs are normally different from the estimated overhead costs. Depending on whether actual overhead is greater or less than applied overhead, the factory overhead account will either have a debit or credit ending balance as follows:

1. If the applied overhead is *less than* the actual overhead incurred, the factory overhead account will have a debit balance. This debit balance is called **underapplied factory overhead** or *underabsorbed factory overhead*.
2. If the applied overhead is *more than* the actual overhead incurred, the factory overhead account will have a credit balance. This credit balance is called **overapplied factory overhead** or *overabsorbed factory overhead*.

The factory overhead account for Legend Guitars shown below illustrates both underapplied and overapplied factory overhead. Specifically, the December 1, 2010, credit balance of $200 represents overapplied factory overhead. In contrast, the December 31, 2010, debit balance of $150 represents underapplied factory overhead.

Account *Factory Overhead*						Account No.	
						Balance	
Date		**Item**	**Post. Ref.**	**Debit**	**Credit**	**Debit**	**Credit**
2010							
Dec.	1	Balance					200
	31	Factory overhead cost incurred		4,600		4,400	
	31	Factory overhead cost applied			4,250	150	

Underapplied balance ⟶

Overapplied balance ⟶

If the balance of factory overhead (either underapplied or overapplied) becomes large, the balance and related overhead rate should be investigated. For example, a large balance could be caused by changes in manufacturing methods. In this case, the factory overhead rate should be revised.

Example Exercise 19-4   Applying Factory Overhead ⸱⸱⸱⸱⸱⸱⸱> 2

Hatch Company estimates that total factory overhead costs will be $100,000 for the year. Direct labor hours are estimated to be 25,000. For Hatch Company, (a) determine the predetermined factory overhead rate, (b) determine the amount of factory overhead applied to Jobs 101 and 102 in March using the data on direct labor hours from Example Exercise 19-2, and (c) prepare the journal entry to apply factory overhead to both jobs in March according to the predetermined overhead rate.

(continued)

Follow My Example 19-4

a. $4.00 = $100,000/25,000 direct labor hours

b. Job 101 $3,200 = 800 hours × $4.00 per hour
   Job 102   2,400 = 600 hours × $4.00 per hour
   Total $5,600

c. Work in Process.   5,600
       Factory Overhead   5,600

For Practice: PE 19-4A, PE 19-4B

Disposal of Factory Overhead Balance During the year, the balance in the factory overhead account is carried forward and reported as a deferred debit or credit on the monthly (interim) balance sheets. However, any balance in the factory overhead account should not be carried over to the next year. This is because any such balance applies only to operations of the current year.

If the estimates for computing the predetermined overhead rate are reasonably accurate, the ending balance of Factory Overhead should be relatively small. For this reason, the balance of Factory Overhead at the end of the year is disposed of by transferring it to the cost of goods sold account as follows:[2]

1. If there is an ending debit balance (underapplied overhead) in the factory overhead account is disposed of by the entry shown below.

Cost of Goods Sold		XXX	
Factory Overhead			XXX
Transfer of underapplied			
overhead to cost of goods sold.			

2. If there is an ending credit balance (overapplied overhead) in the factory overhead account is disposed of by the entry shown below.

Factory Overhead		XXX	
Cost of Goods Sold			XXX
Transfer of overapplied			
overhead to cost of goods sold.			

To illustrate, the journal entry to dispose of Legend Guitars' December 31, 2010 underapplied overhead balance of $150 is as follows:

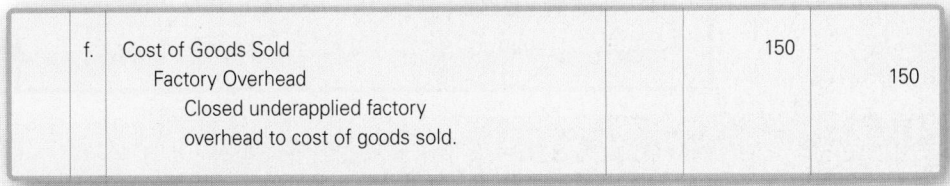

f.	Cost of Goods Sold		150	
	Factory Overhead			150
	Closed underapplied factory			
	overhead to cost of goods sold.			

2 An ending balance in the factory overhead account may also be allocated among the work in process, finished goods, and cost of goods sold accounts. This brings these accounts into agreement with the actual costs incurred. This approach is rarely used and is only required for large ending balances in the factory overhead account. For this reason, it will not be used in this text.

Work in Process

During the period, Work in Process is increased (debited) for the following:

1. Direct materials cost
2. Direct labor cost
3. Applied factory overhead cost

To illustrate, the work in process account for Legend Guitars is shown in Exhibit 6. The balance of Work in Process on December 1, 2010 (beginning balance), was $3,000. As shown in Exhibit 6, this balance relates to Job 71, which was the only job in process on this date. During December, Work in Process was debited for the following:

1. Direct materials cost of $13,000 [transaction (b)] based on materials requisitions.
2. Direct labor cost of $11,000 [transaction (c)] based on time tickets.
3. Applied factory overhead of $4,250 [transaction (e)] based on the predetermined overhead rate of $5 per direct labor hour.

The preceding Work in Process debits are supported by the detail postings to job cost sheets for Jobs 71 and 72, as shown in Exhibit 6.

Exhibit 6

Job Cost Sheets and the Work in Process Controlling Account

Job Cost Sheets

Job 71
20 units of Jazz Series guitars

Balance	$ 3,000
Direct Materials	2,000
Direct Labor	3,500
Factory Overhead	1,750
Total Job Cost	$10,250
Unit Cost	$512.50

Job 72
60 units of American Series guitars

Direct Materials	$11,000
Direct Labor	7,500
Factory Overhead	2,500
	$21,000

Account Work in Process   Account No.

Date		Item	Post. Ref.	Debit	Credit	Balance Debit	Balance Credit
2010 Dec.	1	Balance				3,000	
	31	Direct materials		13,000		16,000	
	31	Direct labor		11,000		27,000	
	31	Factory overhead		4,250		31,250	
	31	Jobs completed—Job 71			10,250	21,000	

g.

During December, Job 71 was completed. Upon completion, the product costs (direct materials, direct labor, factory overhead) are totaled. This total is divided by the number of units produced to determine the cost per unit. Thus, the 20 Jazz Series guitars produced as Job 71 cost $512.50 ($10,250/20) per guitar.

After completion, Job 71 is transferred from Work in Process to Finished Goods by the entry shown at the top of the next page.

				10,250	
g.	Finished Goods			10,250	
	Work in Process				10,250
	Job 71 completed in December.				

Job 72 was started in December, but was not completed by December 31, 2010. Thus, Job 72 is still part of work in process on December 31, 2010. As shown in Exhibit 6, the balance of the job cost sheet for Job 72 ($21,000) is also the December 31, 2010, balance of Work in Process.

Example Exercise 19-5 Job Costs

At the end of March, Hatch Company had completed Jobs 101 and 102. Job 101 is for 500 units, and Job 102 is for 1,000 units. Using the data from Example Exercises 19-1, 19-2, and 19-4, determine (a) the balance on the job cost sheets for Jobs 101 and 102 at the end of March and (b) the cost per unit for Jobs 101 and 102 at the end of March.

Follow My Example 19-5

a.
	Job 101	Job 102
Direct materials	$ 2,400	$ 4,200
Direct labor	12,800	7,200
Factory overhead	3,200	2,400
Total costs	$18,400	$13,800

b. Job 101 $36.80 = $18,400/500 units
    Job 102 $13.80 = $13,800/1,000 units

For Practice: PE 19-5A, PE 19-5B

Finished Goods

The finished goods account is a controlling account for the subsidiary **finished goods ledger** or *stock ledger*. Each account in the finished goods ledger contains cost data for the units manufactured, units sold, and units on hand.

Exhibit 7 illustrates the finished goods ledger account for Jazz Series guitars.

Exhibit 7

Finished Goods Ledger Account

ITEM: Jazz Series guitars								
Manufactured			**Shipped**			**Balance**		
Job Order No.	Quantity	Amount	Ship Order No.	Quantity	Amount	Date	Quantity	Amount	Unit Cost
						Dec. 1	40	$20,000	$500.00
			643	40	$20,000	9	—	—	—
71	20	$10,250				31	20	10,250	512.50

Exhibit 7 indicates that there were 40 Jazz Series guitars on hand on December 1, 2010. During the month, 20 additional Jazz guitars were completed and transferred to Finished Goods from the completion of Job 71. In addition, the beginning inventory of 40 Jazz guitars were sold during the month.

Sales and Cost of Goods Sold

During December, Legend Guitars sold 40 Jazz Series guitars for $850 each, generating total sales of $34,000 ($850 × 40 guitars). Exhibit 7 indicates that the cost of these guitars was $500 per guitar or a total cost of $20,000 ($500 × 40 guitars). The entries to record the sale and related cost of goods sold are as follows:

h.	Accounts Receivable	34,000	
	Sales		34,000
	Revenue received from guitars sold		
	on account.		

i.	Cost of Goods Sold	20,000	
	Finished Goods		20,000
	Cost of 40 Jazz Series guitars sold.		

In a job order cost accounting system, the preparation of a statement of cost of goods manufactured, which was discussed in Chapter 18, is not necessary. This is because job order costing uses the perpetual inventory system and, thus, the cost of goods sold can be directly determined from the finished goods ledger as illustrated in Exhibit 7.

Example Exercise 19-6 Cost of Goods Sold ·······▶ ②

Nejedly Company completed 80,000 units during the year at a cost of $680,000. The beginning finished goods inventory was 10,000 units at $80,000. Determine the cost of goods sold for 60,000 units, assuming a FIFO cost flow.

Follow My Example 19-6

$505,000 = $80,000 + (50,000 × $8.50*)

*Cost per unit of goods produced during the year = $8.50 = $680,000/80,000 units

For Practice: PE 19-6A, PE 19-6B

Period Costs

Service companies, such as telecommunications, insurance, banking, broadcasting, and hospitality, typically have a large portion of their total costs as period costs with few product costs.

Period costs are used in generating revenue during the current period, but are not involved in the manufacturing process. As discussed in Chapter 18, **period costs** are recorded as expenses of the current period as either selling or administrative expenses.

Selling expenses are incurred in marketing the product and delivering sold products to customers. Administrative expenses are incurred in managing the company, but are not related to the manufacturing or selling functions. During December, Legend Guitars recorded the following selling and administrative expenses:

j.	Sales Salaries Expense	2,000	
	Office Salaries Expense	1,500	
	Salaries Payable		3,500
	Recorded December period costs.		

Summary of Cost Flows for Legend Guitars

Exhibit 8 shows the cost flows through the manufacturing accounts of Legend Guitars for December.

Exhibit 8

Flow of Manufacturing Costs for Legend Guitars

Materials

Dec. 1	6,500	(b)	13,000	
(a)	10,500			

Factory Overhead

Dec. 1	500	(d)	200	
(d)	900			
(e)	1,200			
(f)	2,000			

Work in Process

Dec. 1	3,000	(g)	10,250	
(b)	13,000			
(e)	4,250			
(c)	11,000			

Finished Goods

Dec. 1	20,000	(i)	20,000	
(g)	10,250			

Cost of Goods Sold

(i)	20,000		
(f)	150		

Wages Payable

(d)	2,000	
(c)	11,000	

Job Cost Sheets

20 Units of Jazz Series Guitars, Job 71

Dec. 1	3,000
(b) Direct materials	2,000
(c) Direct labor	3,500
(e) Factory overhead	1,750
	10,250

60 Units of American Series Guitars, Job 72

(b) Direct materials	11,000
(c) Direct labor	7,500
(e) Factory overhead	2,500
	21,000

Materials Ledger

No. 8 Wood—Maple

Dec. 1	6,000	(b)	13,000	
(a)	10,500			

Glue

Dec. 1	200	(d)	200

Sandpaper

Dec. 1	300	(d)	300

Finished Goods Ledger

Jazz Series Guitars

Dec. 1	20,000	(i)	20,000	
(g)	10,250			

Transactions

a. Materials purchased during December
b. Materials requisitioned to jobs
c. Factory labor used in production of jobs
d. Factory overhead incurred in production
e. Factory overhead applied to jobs according to the predetermined overhead rate
f. Closed underapplied factory overhead to cost of goods sold
g. Job 71 completed in December
h. Sold 40 units of Jazz Series guitars (not shown)
i. Cost of 40 units of Jazz Series guitars sold

In addition, summary details of the following subsidiary ledgers are shown:

1. *Materials Ledger*—the subsidiary ledger for Materials.
2. *Job Cost Sheets*—the subsidiary ledger for Work in Process.
3. *Finished Goods Ledger*—the subsidiary ledger for Finished Goods.

Entries in the accounts shown in Exhibit 8 are identified by letters. These letters refer to the journal entries described and illustrated in the chapter. Entry (h) is not shown because it does not involve a cost flow.

As shown in Exhibit 8, the balances of Materials, Work in Process, and Finished Goods are supported by their subsidiary ledgers. These balances are as follows:

Controlling Account	Balance and Total of Related Subsidiary Ledger
Materials	$ 3,500
Work in Process	21,000
Finished Goods	10,250

The income statement for Legend Guitars is shown in Exhibit 9.

Exhibit 9

Income Statement of Legend Guitars

Legend Guitars
Income Statement
For the Month Ended December 31, 2010

Sales		$34,000
Cost of goods sold		20,150
Gross profit		$13,850
Selling and administrative expenses:		
Sales salaries expense	$2,000	
Office salaries expense	1,500	
Total selling and administrative expenses		3,500
Income from operations		$10,350

Job Order Costing for Decision Making

③ Describe the use of job order cost information for decision making.

A job order cost accounting system accumulates and records product costs by jobs. The resulting total and unit product costs can be compared to similar jobs, compared over time, or compared to expected costs. In this way, a job order cost system can be used by managers for cost evaluation and control.

Major electric utilities such as Tennessee Valley Authority, Consolidated Edison Inc., and Pacific Gas and Electric Company use job order accounting to control the costs associated with major repairs and overhauls that occur during maintenance shutdowns.

To illustrate, Exhibit 10 shows the direct materials used for Jobs 54 and 63 for Legend Guitars. The wood used in manufacturing guitars is measured in board feet. Since Jobs 54 and 63 produced the same type and number of guitars, the direct materials cost per unit should be about the same. However, the materials cost per guitar for Job 54 is $100, while for Job 63 it is $125. Thus, the materials costs are significantly more for Job 63.

The job cost sheets shown in Exhibit 10 can be analyzed for possible reasons for the increased materials cost for Job 63. Since the materials price did not change ($10 per board foot), the increased materials cost must be related to wood consumption.

Comparing wood consumed for Jobs 54 and 63 shows that 400 board feet were used in Job 54 to produce 40 guitars. In contrast, Job 63 used 500 board feet to produce the same number of guitars. Thus, an investigation should be undertaken to determine

Exhibit 10

Comparing Data from Job Cost Sheets

Job 54

Item: 40 Jazz Series guitars

	Materials Quantity (board feet)	Materials Price	Materials Amount
Direct materials:			
No. 8 Wood—Maple	400	$10.00	$4,000
Direct materials per guitar			$ 100

Job 63

Item: 40 Jazz Series guitars

	Materials Quantity (board feet)	Materials Price	Materials Amount
Direct materials:			
No. 8 Wood—Maple	500	$10.00	$5,000
Direct materials per guitar			$ 125

the cause of the extra 100 board feet used for Job 63. Possible explanations could include the following:

1. A new employee, who was not properly trained, cut the wood for Job 63. As a result, there was excess waste and scrap.

2. The wood used for Job 63 was purchased from a new supplier. The wood was of poor quality, which created excessive waste and scrap.

3. The cutting tools needed repair and were not properly maintained. As a result, the wood was miscut, which created excessive waste and scrap.

4. The instructions attached to the job were incorrect. The wood was cut according to the instructions. The incorrect instructions were discovered later in assembly. As a result, the wood had to be recut and the initial cuttings scrapped.

Job Order Cost Systems for Professional Service Businesses

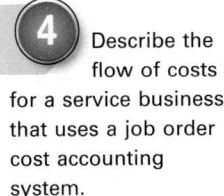

4 Describe the flow of costs for a service business that uses a job order cost accounting system.

A job order cost accounting system may be used for a professional service business. For example, an advertising agency, an attorney, and a physician provide services to individual customers, clients, or patients. In such cases, the customer, client, or patient can be viewed as a job for which costs are accumulated and reported.

The primary product costs for a service business are direct labor and overhead costs. Any materials or supplies used in rendering services are normally insignificant. As a result, materials and supply costs are included as part of the overhead cost.

Like a manufacturing business, direct labor and overhead costs of rendering services to clients are accumulated in a work in process account. *Work in Process* is supported by a cost ledger with a job cost sheet for each client.

When a job is completed and the client is billed, the costs are transferred to a cost of services account. *Cost of Services* is similar to the cost of merchandise sold account for a merchandising business or the cost of goods sold account for a manufacturing business. A finished goods account and related finished goods ledger are not necessary. This is because the revenues for the services are recorded only after the services are provided.

The flow of costs through a service business using a job order cost accounting system is shown in Exhibit 11.

Exhibit 11

Flow of Costs Through a Service Business

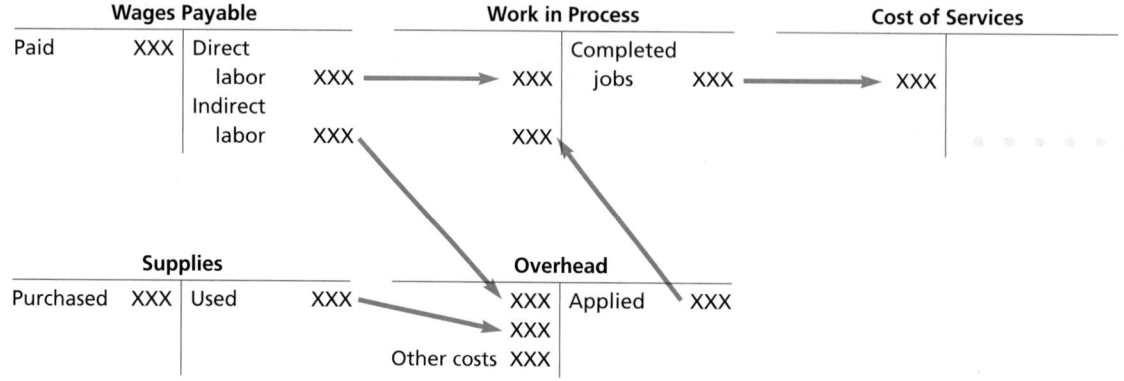

In practice, other considerations unique to service businesses may need to be considered. For example, a service business may bill clients on a weekly or monthly basis rather than when a job is completed. In such cases, a portion of the costs related to each billing is transferred from the work in process account to the cost of services account. A service business may also bill clients for services in advance, which would be accounted for as deferred revenue until the services are completed.

At a Glance 19

1 Describe cost accounting systems used by manufacturing businesses.

Key Points	Key Learning Outcomes	Example Exercises	Practice Exercises
A cost accounting system accumulates product costs. Management uses cost accounting systems to determine product cost, establish product prices, control operations, and develop financial statements. The two primary cost accounting systems are job order and process cost systems. Job order cost systems accumulate costs for each quantity of product that passes through the factory. Process cost systems accumulate costs for each department or process within the factory.	• Describe a cost accounting system. • Describe a job order cost system. • Describe a process cost system.		

2   Describe and illustrate a job order cost accounting system.

Key Points	Key Learning Outcomes	Example Exercises	Practice Exercises
A job order cost system accumulates costs for each quantity of product, or "job," that passes through the factory. Direct materials, direct labor, and factory overhead are accumulated on the job cost sheet, which is the subsidiary cost ledger for each job. Direct materials and direct labor are assigned to individual jobs based on the quantity used. Factory overhead costs are assigned to each job based on an activity base that reflects the use of factory overhead costs. As a job is finished, its costs are transferred to the finished goods ledger. When goods are sold, the cost is transferred from finished goods inventory to cost of goods sold.	• Describe the flow of materials and how materials costs are assigned in a job order cost system.		
	• Prepare the journal entry to record materials used in production.	19-1	19-1A, 19-1B
	• Describe how factory labor hours are recorded and how labor costs are assigned in a job order cost system.		
	• Prepare the journal entry to record factory labor used in production.	19-2	19-2A, 19-2B
	• Describe and illustrate how factory overhead costs are accumulated and assigned in a job order cost system.	19-3 19-4	19-3A, 19-3B 19-4A, 19-4B
	• Compute the predetermined overhead rate.	19-4	19-4A, 19-4B
	• Describe and illustrate how to dispose of the balance in the factory overhead account.		
	• Describe and illustrate how costs are accumulated for work in process and finished goods inventory and assigned to cost of goods sold in a job order cost system.	19-5 19-6	19-5A, 19-5B 19-6A, 19-6B
	• Describe and illustrate the flow of costs in a job order cost system.		

3   Describe the use of job order cost information for decision making.

Key Points	Key Learning Outcomes	Example Exercises	Practice Exercises
Job order cost systems can be used to evaluate cost performance. Unit costs can be compared over time to determine if product costs are staying within expected ranges.	• Describe and illustrate how job cost sheets can be used to investigate possible reasons for increased product costs.		

4 Describe the flow of costs for a service business that uses a job order cost accounting system.

Key Points	Key Learning Outcomes	Example Exercises	Practice Exercises
Job order cost accounting systems can be used by service businesses to plan and control operations. Since the product is a service, the focus is on direct labor and overhead costs. The costs of providing a service are accumulated in a work in process account and transferred to a cost of services account upon completion.	• Describe how service businesses use a job order cost system.		

Key Terms

activity base (854)
activity-based costing (854)
cost accounting systems (847)
cost allocation (854)
finished goods ledger (859)
job cost sheets (860)
job order cost system (847)

materials ledger (849)
materials requisition (850)
overapplied factory overhead (856)
period costs (860)
predetermined factory overhead rate (854)

process cost system (848)
receiving report (849)
time tickets (851)
underapplied factory overhead (856)

Illustrative Problem

Derby Music Company specializes in producing and packaging compact discs (CDs) for the music recording industry. Derby uses a job order cost system. The following data summarize the operations related to production for March, the first month of operations:

a. Materials purchased on account, $15,500.
b. Materials requisitioned and labor used:

	Materials	Factory Labor
Job No. 100	$2,650	$1,770
Job No. 101	1,240	650
Job No. 102	980	420
Job No. 103	3,420	1,900
Job No. 104	1,000	500
Job No. 105	2,100	1,760
For general factory use	450	650

c. Factory overhead costs incurred on account, $2,700.
d. Depreciation of machinery, $1,750.

e. Factory overhead is applied at a rate of 70% of direct labor cost.
f. Jobs completed: Nos. 100, 101, 102, 104.
g. Jobs 100, 101, and 102 were shipped, and customers were billed for $8,100, $3,800, and $3,500, respectively.

Instructions

1. Journalize the entries to record the transactions identified above.
2. Determine the account balances for Work in Process and Finished Goods.
3. Prepare a schedule of unfinished jobs to support the balance in the work in process account.
4. Prepare a schedule of completed jobs on hand to support the balance in the finished goods account.

Solution

1. a.	Materials		15,500	
	Accounts Payable			15,500
b.	Work in Process		11,390	
	Materials			11,390
	Work in Process		7,000	
	Wages Payable			7,000
	Factory Overhead		1,100	
	Materials			450
	Wages Payable			650
c.	Factory Overhead		2,700	
	Accounts Payable			2,700
d.	Factory Overhead		1,750	
	Accumulated Depreciation—Machinery			1,750
e.	Work in Process		4,900	
	Factory Overhead (70% of $7,000)			4,900
f.	Finished Goods		11,548	
	Work in Process			11,548

Computation of the cost of jobs finished:

Job	Direct Materials	Direct Labor	Factory Overhead	Total
Job No. 100	$2,650	$1,770	$1,239	$ 5,659
Job No. 101	1,240	650	455	2,345
Job No. 102	980	420	294	1,694
Job No. 104	1,000	500	350	1,850
				$11,548

g.	Accounts Receivable		15,400	
	Sales			15,400
	Cost of Goods Sold		9,698	
	Finished Goods			9,698

Cost of jobs sold computation:

Job No. 100	$5,659
Job No. 101	2,345
Job No. 102	1,694
	$9,698

2. Work in Process: $11,742 ($11,390 + $7,000 + $4,900 − $11,548)
    Finished Goods: $1,850 ($11,548 − $9,698)

3.

Schedule of Unfinished Jobs

Job	Direct Materials	Direct Labor	Factory Overhead	Total
Job No. 103	$3,420	$1,900	$1,330	$ 6,650
Job No. 105	2,100	1,760	1,232	5,092
Balance of Work in Process, March 31				$11,742

4.

Schedule of Completed Jobs

Job No. 104:

Direct materials	$1,000
Direct labor	500
Factory overhead	350
Balance of Finished Goods, March 31	$1,850

Self-Examination Questions (Answers at End of Chapter)

1. For which of the following would the job order cost system be appropriate?
   A. Antique furniture repair shop
   B. Rubber manufacturer
   C. Coal manufacturer
   D. Computer chip manufacturer

2. The journal entry to record the requisition of materials to the factory in a job order cost system is a debit to:
   A. Materials.
   B. Accounts Payable.
   C. Work in Process.
   D. Cost of Goods Sold.

3. Job order cost sheets accumulate all of the following costs *except* for:
   A. direct materials.
   B. indirect materials.
   C. direct labor.
   D. factory overhead applied.

4. A company estimated $420,000 of factory overhead cost and 16,000 direct labor hours for the period. During the period, a job was completed with $4,500 of direct materials and $3,000 of direct labor. The direct labor rate was $15 per hour. What is the factory overhead applied to this job?
   A. $2,100
   B. $5,250
   C. $78,750
   D. $420,000

5. If the factory overhead account has a credit balance, factory overhead is said to be:
   A. underapplied.
   B. overapplied.
   C. underabsorbed.
   D. in error.

Eye Openers

1. How is product cost information used by managers?
2. a. Name two principal types of cost accounting systems.
   b. Which system provides for a separate record of each particular quantity of product that passes through the factory?
   c. Which system accumulates the costs for each department or process within the factory?
3. What kind of firm would use a job order cost system?
4. Hewlett-Packard Company assembles ink jet printers in which a high volume of standardized units are assembled and tested. Is the job order cost system appropriate in this situation?
5. Which account is used in the job order cost system to accumulate direct materials, direct labor, and factory overhead applied to production costs for individual jobs?
6. How does the use of the materials requisition help control the issuance of materials from the storeroom?
7. What document is the source for (a) debiting the accounts in the materials ledger and (b) crediting the accounts in the materials ledger?
8. What is a job cost sheet?
9. a. Differentiate between the clock card and the time ticket.
   b. Why should the total time reported on an employee's time tickets for a payroll period be compared with the time reported on the employee's clock cards for the same period?
10. Describe the source of the data for debiting Work in Process for (a) direct materials, (b) direct labor, and (c) factory overhead.
11. Discuss how the predetermined factory overhead rate can be used in job order cost accounting to assist management in pricing jobs.

12. a. How is a predetermined factory overhead rate calculated?
    b. Name three common bases used in calculating the rate.
13. a. What is (1) overapplied factory overhead and (2) underapplied factory overhead?
    b. If the factory overhead account has a debit balance, was factory overhead underapplied or overapplied?
    c. If the factory overhead account has a credit balance at the end of the first month of the fiscal year, where will the amount of this balance be reported on the interim balance sheet?
14. At the end of the fiscal year, there was a relatively minor balance in the factory overhead account. What procedure can be used for disposing of the balance in the account?
15. What account is the controlling account for (a) the materials ledger, (b) the job cost sheets, and (c) the finished goods ledger?
16. How can job cost information be used to identify cost improvement opportunities?
17. Describe how a job order cost system can be used for professional service businesses.

Practice Exercises

PE 19-1A
Issuance of materials

obj. 2

EE 19-1   p. 851

On May 9, Thomson Company purchased 54,000 units of raw materials at $6 per unit. On May 21, raw materials were requisitioned for production as follows: 22,000 units for Job 70 at $5 per unit and 24,000 units for Job 71 at $6 per unit. Journalize the entry on May 9 to record the purchase and on May 21 to record the requisition from the materials storeroom.

PE 19-1B
Issuance of materials

obj. 2

EE 19-1   p. 851

On June 2, Lewis Company purchased 4,000 units of raw materials at $8 per unit. On June 12, raw materials were requisitioned for production as follows: 1,200 units for Job 30 at $6 per unit and 800 units for Job 32 at $8 per unit. Journalize the entry on June 2 to record the purchase and on June 12 to record the requisition from the materials storeroom.

PE 19-2A
Direct labor costs

obj. 2

EE 19-2   p. 852

During May, Thomson Company accumulated 10,000 hours of direct labor costs on Job 70 and 12,000 hours on Job 71. The total direct labor was incurred at a rate of $18 per direct labor hour for Job 70 and $20 per direct labor hour for Job 71. Journalize the entry to record the flow of labor costs into production during May.

PE 19-2B
Direct labor costs

obj. 2

EE 19-2   p. 852

During June, Lewis Company accumulated 1,200 hours of direct labor costs on Job 30 and 1,300 hours on Job 32. The total direct labor was incurred at a rate of $16 per direct labor hour for Job 30 and $14 per direct labor hour for Job 32. Journalize the entry to record the flow of labor costs into production during June.

PE 19-3A
Factory overhead costs

obj. 2

EE 19-3   p. 853

During May, Thomson Company incurred factory overhead costs as follows: indirect materials, $24,500; indirect labor, $64,500; utilities cost, $5,800; and factory depreciation, $45,200. Journalize the entry to record the factory overhead incurred during May.

PE 19-3B
Factory overhead costs
obj. 2
EE 19-3 p. 853

During June, Lewis Company incurred factory overhead costs as follows: indirect materials, $6,000; indirect labor, $7,600; utilities cost, $3,200; and factory depreciation $7,200. Journalize the entry to record the factory overhead incurred during June.

PE 19-4A
Applying factory overhead
obj. 2
EE 19-4 p. 856

Thomson Company estimates that total factory overhead costs will be $600,000 for the year. Direct labor hours are estimated to be 250,000. For Thomson Company, (a) determine the predetermined factory overhead rate, (b) determine the amount of factory overhead applied to Jobs 70 and 71 in May using the data on direct labor hours from Practice Exercise 19-2A, and (c) prepare the journal entry to apply factory overhead to both jobs in May according to the predetermined overhead rate.

PE 19-4B
Applying factory overhead
obj. 2
EE 19-4 p. 856

Lewis Company estimates that total factory overhead costs will be $200,000 for the year. Direct labor hours are estimated to be 25,000. For Lewis Company, (a) determine the predetermined factory overhead rate, (b) determine the amount of factory overhead applied to Jobs 30 and 32 in June using the data on direct labor hours from Practice Exercise 19-2B, and (c) prepare the journal entry to apply factory overhead to both jobs in June according to the predetermined overhead rate.

PE 19-5A
Job costs
obj. 2
EE 19-5 p. 859

At the end of May, Thomson Company had completed Jobs 70 and 71. Job 70 is for 8,000 units, and Job 71 is for 10,000 units. Using the data from Practice Exercises 19-1A, 19-2A, and 19-4A, determine (a) the balance on the job cost sheets for Jobs 70 and 71 at the end of May and (b) the cost per unit for Jobs 70 and 71 at the end of May.

PE 19-5B
Job costs
obj. 2
EE 19-5 p. 859

At the end of June, Lewis Company had completed Jobs 30 and 32. Job 30 is for 1,600 units, and Job 32 is for 1,750 units. Using the data from Practice Exercises 19-1B, 19-2B, and 19-4B, determine (a) the balance on the job cost sheets for Jobs 30 and 32 at the end of June and (b) the cost per unit for Jobs 30 and 32 at the end of June.

PE 19-6A
Cost of goods sold
obj. 2
EE 19-6 p. 860

Luek Company completed 60,000 units during the year at a cost of $900,000. The beginning finished goods inventory was 10,000 units at $140,000. Determine the cost of goods sold for 45,000 units, assuming a FIFO cost flow.

PE 19-6B
Cost of goods sold
obj. 2
EE 19-6 p. 860

Suo Company completed 20,000 units during the year at a cost of $120,000. The beginning finished goods inventory was 2,500 units at $14,000. Determine the cost of goods sold for 12,000 units, assuming a FIFO cost flow.

Exercises

EX 19-1
Transactions in a job order cost system
obj. 2

Five selected transactions for the current month are indicated by letters in the following T accounts in a job order cost accounting system:

Materials		Work in Process	
	(a)	(a)	(d)
		(b)	
		(c)	

Wages Payable		Finished Goods	
	(b)	(d)	(e)

Factory Overhead		Cost of Goods Sold	
(a)	(c)	(e)	
(b)			

Describe each of the five transactions.

EX 19-2
Cost flow relationships
obj. 2

✔ c. $630,000

The following information is available for the first month of operations of Url Inc., a manufacturer of art and craft items:

Sales	$1,200,000
Gross profit	320,000
Indirect labor	110,000
Indirect materials	45,000
Other factory overhead	20,000
Materials purchased	610,000
Total manufacturing costs for the period	1,325,000
Materials inventory, end of period	45,000

Using the above information, determine the following missing amounts:
a. Cost of goods sold
b. Direct materials cost
c. Direct labor cost

EX 19-3
Cost of materials issuances under the FIFO method
obj. 2

✔ b. $1,320

An incomplete subsidiary ledger of wire cable for May is as follows:

RECEIVED			ISSUED			BALANCE			
Receiving Report Number	Quantity	Unit Price	Materials Requisition Number	Quantity	Amount	Date	Quantity	Amount	Unit Price
						May 1	300	$2,400	$8.00
24	210	$10.00				May 2			
			101	340		May 6			
30	140	12.00				May 12			
			114	200		May 21			

a. Complete the materials issuances and balances for the wire cable subsidiary ledger under FIFO.
b. Determine the balance of wire cable at the end of May.
c. Journalize the summary entry to transfer materials to work in process.
d. ▬▬▶ Explain how the materials ledger might be used as an aid in maintaining inventory quantities on hand.

EX 19-4
Entry for issuing materials

obj. 2

Materials issued for the current month are as follows:

Requisition No.	Material	Job No.	Amount
101	Steel	210	$25,400
102	Plastic	215	19,600
103	Glue	Indirect	1,450
104	Rubber	222	1,200
105	Aluminum	231	52,400

Journalize the entry to record the issuance of materials.

EX 19-5
Entries for materials

obj. 2

✔ c. fabric, $33,500

Bullock Furniture Company manufactures furniture. Bullock uses a job order cost system. Balances on June 1 from the materials ledger are as follows:

Fabric	$25,000
Polyester filling	7,500
Lumber	56,000
Glue	2,400

The materials purchased during June are summarized from the receiving reports as follows:

Fabric	$126,000
Polyester filling	175,000
Lumber	345,000
Glue	12,000

Materials were requisitioned to individual jobs as follows:

	Fabric	Polyester Filling	Lumber	Glue	Total
Job 101	$ 47,500	$ 60,000	$160,000		$267,500
Job 102	36,500	54,000	140,000		230,500
Job 103	33,500	44,000	78,000		155,500
Factory overhead—indirect materials				$13,000	13,000
Total	$117,500	$158,000	$378,000	$13,000	$666,500

The glue is not a significant cost, so it is treated as indirect materials (factory overhead).

a. Journalize the entry to record the purchase of materials in June.
b. Journalize the entry to record the requisition of materials in June.
c. Determine the June 30 balances that would be shown in the materials ledger accounts.

EX 19-6
Entry for factory labor costs

obj. 2

A summary of the time tickets for the current month follows:

Job No.	Amount	Job No.	Amount
201	$ 2,100	220	$3,650
204	1,750	224	2,240
205	3,200	228	1,460
Indirect labor	11,200	236	9,875

Journalize the entry to record the factory labor costs.

EX 19-7
Entry for factory labor costs

obj. 2

The weekly time tickets indicate the following distribution of labor hours for three direct labor employees:

	Hours			
	Job 201	**Job 202**	**Job 203**	**Process Improvement**
John Washington	20	10	7	3
George Jefferson	10	15	13	2
Thomas Adams	12	14	10	4

The direct labor rate earned by the three employees is as follows:

Washington	$20.00
Jefferson	22.00
Adams	18.00

The process improvement category includes training, quality improvement, house-keeping, and other indirect tasks.

a. Journalize the entry to record the factory labor costs for the week.
b. Assume that Jobs 201 and 202 were completed but not sold during the week and that Job 203 remained incomplete at the end of the week. How would the direct labor costs for all three jobs be reflected on the financial statements at the end of the week?

EX 19-8
Entries for direct labor and factory overhead

obj. 2

Moura Industries Inc. manufactures recreational vehicles. Moura uses a job order cost system. The time tickets from August jobs are summarized below.

Job 410	$3,400
Job 411	1,700
Job 412	1,400
Job 413	2,500
Factory supervision	1,900

Factory overhead is applied to jobs on the basis of a predetermined overhead rate of $25 per direct labor hour. The direct labor rate is $15 per hour.

a. Journalize the entry to record the factory labor costs.
b. Journalize the entry to apply factory overhead to production for August.

EX 19-9
Factory overhead rates, entries, and account balance

obj. 2

✔ b. $40.00 per direct labor hour

Hudson Company operates two factories. The company applies factory overhead to jobs on the basis of machine hours in Factory 1 and on the basis of direct labor hours in Factory 2. Estimated factory overhead costs, direct labor hours, and machine hours are as follows:

	Factory 1	Factory 2
Estimated factory overhead cost for fiscal year beginning June 1	$475,000	$600,000
Estimated direct labor hours for year		15,000
Estimated machine hours for year	20,000	
Actual factory overhead costs for June	$38,000	$52,000
Actual direct labor hours for June		1,350
Actual machine hours for June	1,560	

a. Determine the factory overhead rate for Factory 1.
b. Determine the factory overhead rate for Factory 2.
c. Journalize the entries to apply factory overhead to production in each factory for June.
d. Determine the balances of the factory accounts for each factory as of June 30, and indicate whether the amounts represent overapplied or underapplied factory overhead.

EX 19-10
Predetermined factory overhead rate

obj. 2

Willies Engine Shop uses a job order cost system to determine the cost of performing engine repair work. Estimated costs and expenses for the coming period are as follows:

Engine parts	$ 875,000
Shop direct labor	640,000
Shop and repair equipment depreciation	45,000
Shop supervisor salaries	125,800
Shop property tax	22,600
Shop supplies	16,600
Advertising expense	17,800
Administrative office salaries	75,000
Administrative office depreciation expense	10,000
Total costs and expenses	$1,827,800

The average shop direct labor rate is $16 per hour.
Determine the predetermined shop overhead rate per direct labor hour.

EX 19-11
Predetermined factory overhead rate

obj. 2

✔ a. $205 per hour

The Medical Center has a single operating room that is used by local physicians to perform surgical procedures. The cost of using the operating room is accumulated by each patient procedure and includes the direct materials costs (drugs and medical devices), physician surgical time, and operating room overhead. On November 1 of the current year, the annual operating room overhead is estimated to be:

Disposable supplies	$150,000
Depreciation expense	27,000
Utilities	15,500
Nurse salaries	225,500
Technician wages	74,000
Total operating room overhead	$492,000

The overhead costs will be assigned to procedures based on the number of surgical room hours. The Medical Center expects to use the operating room an average of eight hours per day, six days per week. In addition, the operating room will be shut down two weeks per year for general repairs.

a. Determine the predetermined operating room overhead rate for the year.
b. Gretchen Kelton had a 6-hour procedure on November 10. How much operating room overhead would be charged to her procedure, using the rate determined in part (a)?
c. During November, the operating room was used 192 hours. The actual overhead costs incurred for November were $38,500. Determine the overhead under- or overapplied for the period.

EX 19-12
Entry for jobs completed; cost of unfinished jobs

obj. 2

✔ b. $13,500

The following account appears in the ledger after only part of the postings have been completed for January:

Work in Process

Balance, January 1	$ 14,200
Direct materials	115,400
Direct labor	124,500
Factory overhead	65,400

Jobs finished during January are summarized as follows:

Job 710	$62,500	Job 727	$ 35,400
Job 714	75,600	Job 732	132,500

a. Journalize the entry to record the jobs completed.
b. Determine the cost of the unfinished jobs at January 31.

EX 19-13
Entries for factory costs and jobs completed

obj. 2

✔ d. $31,160

Munch Printing Inc. began printing operations on July 1. Jobs 10 and 11 were completed during the month, and all costs applicable to them were recorded on the related cost sheets. Jobs 12 and 13 are still in process at the end of the month, and all applicable costs except factory overhead have been recorded on the related cost sheets. In addition to the materials and labor charged directly to the jobs, $1,200 of indirect materials and $14,500 of indirect labor were used during the month. The cost sheets for the four jobs entering production during the month are as follows, in summary form:

Job 10		Job 11	
Direct materials	12,400	Direct materials	5,800
Direct labor	4,750	Direct labor	2,450
Factory overhead	3,800	Factory overhead	1,960
Total	20,950	Total	10,210

Job 12		Job 13	
Direct materials	17,400	Direct materials	3,500
Direct labor	5,250	Direct labor	700
Factory overhead		Factory overhead	

Journalize the summary entry to record each of the following operations for July (one entry for each operation):

a. Direct and indirect materials used.
b. Direct and indirect labor used.
c. Factory overhead applied (a single overhead rate is used based on direct labor cost).
d. Completion of Jobs 10 and 11.

EX 19-14
Financial statements of a manufacturing firm

obj. 2

✔ a. Income from operations, $99,600

The following events took place for Salsa Inc. during May 2010, the first month of operations as a producer of road bikes:

• Purchased $244,000 of materials.
• Used $210,000 of direct materials in production.
• Incurred $180,000 of direct labor wages.
• Applied factory overhead at a rate of 75% of direct labor cost.
• Transferred $510,000 of work in process to finished goods.
• Sold goods with a cost of $485,000.
• Sold goods for $870,000.
• Incurred $210,000 of selling expenses.
• Incurred $75,400 of administrative expenses.

a. Prepare the May income statement for Salsa. Assume that Salsa uses the perpetual inventory method.
b. Determine the inventory balances at the end of the first month of operations.

EX 19-15
Decision making with job order costs

obj. 3

Letson Manufacturing Inc. is a job shop. The management of Letson Manufacturing uses the cost information from the job sheets to assess their cost performance. Information on the total cost, product type, and quantity of items produced is as follows:

Date	Job No.	Quantity	Product	Amount
Jan. 2	1	240	Alpha	$ 6,000
Jan. 15	22	1,100	Beta	8,800
Feb. 3	38	800	Beta	8,000
Mar. 7	56	400	Alpha	8,800
Mar. 24	65	1,500	Gamma	6,000
May 19	74	1,750	Gamma	10,500
June 12	87	350	Alpha	6,300
Aug. 18	92	2,200	Gamma	19,800
Sept. 2	100	600	Beta	4,800
Nov. 14	110	500	Alpha	7,000
Dec. 12	116	2,000	Gamma	24,000

a. Develop a graph for *each* product (three graphs), with Job No. (in date order) on the horizontal axis and unit cost on the vertical axis. Use this information to determine Letson Manufacturing's cost performance over time for the three products.

b. ➤ What additional information would you require to investigate Letson Manufacturing's cost performance more precisely?

EX 19-16
Decision making with job order costs

obj. 3

Duncan Trophies Inc. uses a job order cost system for determining the cost to manufacture award products (plaques and trophies). Among the company's products is an engraved plaque that is awarded to participants who complete an executive education program at a local university. The company sells the plaque to the university for $160 each.

Each plaque has a brass plate engraved with the name of the participant. Engraving requires approximately 20 minutes per name. Improperly engraved names must be redone. The plate is screwed to a walnut backboard. This assembly takes approximately 10 minutes per unit. Improper assembly must be redone using a new walnut backboard.

During the first half of the year, the university had two separate executive education classes. The job cost sheets for the two separate jobs indicated the following information:

Job 201   **April 12**

	Cost per Unit	Units	Job Cost
Direct materials:			
Wood	$32.00/unit	60 units	$ 1,920
Brass	24.00/unit	60 units	1,440
Engraving labor	60.00/hr.	20 hrs.	1,200
Assembly labor	45.00/hr.	10 hrs.	450
Factory overhead	35.00/hr.	30 hrs.	1,050
			$ 6,060
Plaques shipped			÷ 60
Cost per plaque			$ 101.00

Job 212   **May 6**

	Cost per Unit	Units	Job Cost
Direct materials:			
Wood	$32.00/unit	48 units	$ 1,536
Brass	24.00/unit	48 units	1,152
Engraving labor	60.00/hr.	28 hrs.	1,680
Assembly labor	45.00/hr.	14 hrs.	630
Factory overhead	35.00/hr.	42 hrs.	1,470
			$ 6,468
Plaques shipped			÷ 42
Cost per plaque			$ 154.00

a. Why did the cost per plaque increase from $101.00 to $154.00?
b. What improvements would you recommend for Duncan Trophies Inc.?

EX 19-17
Job order cost accounting entries for a service business

obj. 4

The consulting firm of Tilton and Henderson accumulates costs associated with individual cases, using a job order cost system. The following transactions occurred during June:

June 4. Charged 600 hours of professional (lawyer) time to the Rucker Co. breech of contract suit to prepare for the trial, at a rate of $200 per hour.
8. Reimbursed travel costs to employees for depositions related to the Rucker case, $21,000.
12. Charged 300 hours of professional time for the Rucker trial at a rate of $260 per hour.
16. Received invoice from consultants Wenzel and Lachgar for $64,000 for expert testimony related to the Rucker trial.
24. Applied office overhead at a rate of $55 per professional hour charged to the Rucker case.
30. Paid secretarial and administrative salaries of $35,000 for the month.
30. Used office supplies for the month, $12,000.

June 30. Paid professional salaries of $180,000 for the month.

    30. Billed Rucker $380,000 for successful defense of the case.

a. Provide the journal entries for each of these transactions.

b. How much office overhead is over- or underapplied?

c. Determine the gross profit on the Rucker case, assuming that over- or underapplied office overhead is closed monthly to cost of services.

EX 19-18

Job order cost accounting entries for a service business

obj. 4

✔ d. Dr. Cost of Services, $777,500

The Ad Guys Inc. provides advertising services for clients across the nation. The Ad Guys is presently working on four projects, each for a different client. The Ad Guys accumulates costs for each account (client) on the basis of both direct costs and allocated indirect costs. The direct costs include the charged time of professional personnel and media purchases (air time and ad space). Overhead is allocated to each project as a percentage of media purchases. The predetermined overhead rate is 50% of media purchases.

On June 1, the four advertising projects had the following accumulated costs:

	June 1 Balances
Clinton Bank	$80,000
Pryor Airlines	24,000
O'Ryan Hotels	56,000
Marshall Beverages	34,000

During June, The Ad Guys incurred the following direct labor and media purchase costs related to preparing advertising for each of the four accounts:

	Direct Labor	Media Purchases
Clinton Bank	$ 56,000	$210,000
Pryor Airlines	25,000	185,000
O'Ryan Hotels	110,000	135,000
Marshall Beverages	125,000	101,000
Total	$316,000	$631,000

At the end of June, both the Clinton Bank and Pryor Airlines campaigns were completed. The costs of completed campaigns are debited to the cost of services account. Journalize the summary entry to record each of the following for the month:

a. Direct labor costs

b. Media purchases

c. Overhead applied

d. Completion of Clinton Bank and Pryor Airlines campaigns

Problems Series A

PR 19-1A

Entries for costs in a job order cost system

obj. 2

Keltner Co. uses a job order cost system. The following data summarize the operations related to production for November:

a. Materials purchased on account, $350,000.

b. Materials requisitioned, $275,000, of which $35,000 was for general factory use.

c. Factory labor used, $324,500, of which $45,500 was indirect.

d. Other costs incurred on account were for factory overhead, $128,600; selling expenses, $116,400; and administrative expenses, $72,500.

e. Prepaid expenses expired for factory overhead were $14,500; for selling expenses, $12,300; and for administrative expenses, $8,900.

f. Depreciation of office building was $42,000; of office equipment, $21,500; and of factory equipment, $14,500.

g. Factory overhead costs applied to jobs, $256,400.

h. Jobs completed, $726,500.

i. Cost of goods sold, $715,000.

Instructions

Journalize the entries to record the summarized operations.

PR 19-2A

Entries and schedules for unfinished jobs and completed jobs

obj. 2

✔ 3. Work in Process balance, $22,290

Staircase Equipment Company uses a job order cost system. The following data summarize the operations related to production for April 2010, the first month of operations:

a. Materials purchased on account, $23,400.
b. Materials requisitioned and factory labor used:

Job	Materials	Factory Labor
No. 201	$2,350	$2,200
No. 202	2,875	2,970
No. 203	1,900	1,490
No. 204	6,450	5,460
No. 205	4,100	4,150
No. 206	2,980	2,650
For general factory use	860	3,250

c. Factory overhead costs incurred on account, $4,500.
d. Depreciation of machinery and equipment, $1,560.
e. The factory overhead rate is $50 per machine hour. Machine hours used:

Job	Machine Hours
No. 201	18
No. 202	30
No. 203	24
No. 204	75
No. 205	33
No. 206	20
Total	200

f. Jobs completed: 201, 202, 203, and 205.
g. Jobs were shipped and customers were billed as follows: Job 201, $6,540; Job 202, $8,820; Job 203, $11,880.

Instructions

1. Journalize the entries to record the summarized operations.
2. Post the appropriate entries to T accounts for Work in Process and Finished Goods, using the identifying letters as dates. Insert memo account balances as of the end of the month.
3. Prepare a schedule of unfinished jobs to support the balance in the work in process account.
4. Prepare a schedule of completed jobs on hand to support the balance in the finished goods account.

PR 19-3A

Job order cost sheet

objs. 2, 3

If the working papers correlating with the textbook are not used, omit Problem 19-3A.

Lynch Furniture Company refinishes and reupholsters furniture. Lynch uses a job order cost system. When a prospective customer asks for a price quote on a job, the estimated cost data are inserted on an unnumbered job cost sheet. If the offer is accepted, a number is assigned to the job, and the costs incurred are recorded in the usual manner on the job cost sheet. After the job is completed, reasons for the variances between the estimated and actual costs are noted on the sheet. The data are then available to management in evaluating the efficiency of operations and in preparing quotes on future jobs. On May 10, 2010, an estimate of $1,530.00 for reupholstering a chair and couch was given to Queen Mercury. The estimate was based on the following data:

Estimated direct materials:	
40 meters at $12 per meter	$ 480.00
Estimated direct labor:	
24 hours at $15 per hour	360.00
Estimated factory overhead (50% of direct labor cost)	180.00
Total estimated costs	$1,020.00
Markup (50% of production costs)	510.00
Total estimate	$1,530.00

On May 16, the chair and couch were picked up from the residence of Queen Mercury, 10 Rhapsody Lane, Lake Forest, with a commitment to return it on June 12. The job was completed on June 8.

The related materials requisitions and time tickets are summarized as follows:

Materials Requisition No.	Description	Amount
210	24 meters at $12	$288
212	21 meters at $12	252

Time Ticket No.	Description	Amount
H25	18 hours at $14.50	$261.00
H34	9 hours at $14.50	130.50

Instructions

1. Complete that portion of the job order cost sheet that would be prepared when the estimate is given to the customer.
2. ➡ Assign number 10-206 to the job, record the costs incurred, and complete the job order cost sheet. Comment on the reasons for the variances between actual costs and estimated costs. For this purpose, assume that five meters of materials were spoiled, the factory overhead rate has been proved to be satisfactory, and an inexperienced employee performed the work.

PR 19-4A
Analyzing manufacturing cost accounts
obj. 2

✔ G. $282,130

Big Wave Company manufactures surf boards in a wide variety of sizes and styles. The following incomplete ledger accounts refer to transactions that are summarized for July:

Materials

July	1	Balance	30,000	July 31	Requisitions	(A)
	31	Purchases	120,000			

Work in Process

July	1	Balance	(B)	July 31	Completed jobs	(F)
	31	Materials	(C)			
	31	Direct labor	(D)			
	31	Factory overhead applied	(E)			

Finished Goods

July	1	Balance	0	July 31	Cost of goods sold	(G)
	31	Completed jobs	(F)			

Wages Payable

				July 31	Wages incurred	120,000

Factory Overhead

July	1	Balance	22,000	July 31	Factory overhead applied	(E)
	31	Indirect labor	(H)			
	31	Indirect materials	16,000			
	31	Other overhead	95,000			

In addition, the following information is available:

a. Materials and direct labor were applied to six jobs in July:

Job No.	Style	Quantity	Direct Materials	Direct Labor
No. 21	X-10	200	$ 20,000	$15,000
No. 22	X-20	400	34,000	26,000
No. 23	X-50	200	14,000	8,000
No. 24	T-20	250	30,000	25,000
No. 25	X-40	180	22,000	17,500
No. 26	T-10	140	8,000	4,500
	Total	1,370	$128,000	$96,000

b. Factory overhead is applied to each job at a rate of 160% of direct labor cost.
c. The July 1 Work in Process balance consisted of two jobs, as follows:

Job No.	Style	Work in Process, July 1
Job 21	X-10	$ 6,000
Job 22	X-20	16,000
Total		$22,000

d. Customer jobs completed and units sold in July were as follows:

Job No.	Style	Completed in July	Units Sold in July
No. 21	X-10	X	160
No. 22	X-20	X	320
No. 23	X-50		0
No. 24	T-20	X	210
No. 25	X-40	X	150
No. 26	T-10		0

Instructions

1. Determine the missing amounts associated with each letter. Provide supporting calculations by completing a table with the following headings:

Job No.	Quantity	July 1 Work in Process	Direct Materials	Direct Labor	Factory Overhead	Total Cost	Unit Cost	Units Sold	Cost of Goods Sold

2. Determine the July 31 balances for each of the inventory accounts and factory overhead.

PR 19-5A
Flow of costs and income statement

obj. 2

✔ 1. Income from operations, $3,300,000

Digital Tunes Inc. is in the business of developing, promoting, and selling musical talent on compact disc (CD). The company signed a new group, called *Smashing Britney*, on January 1, 2010. For the first six months of 2010, the company spent $4,000,000 on a media campaign for *Smashing Britney* and $1,200,000 in legal costs. The CD production began on February 1, 2010.

Digital Tunes uses a job order cost system to accumulate costs associated with a CD title. The unit direct materials cost for the CD is:

Blank CD	$1.80
Jewel case	0.60
Song lyric insert	0.60

The production process is straightforward. First, the blank CDs are brought to a production area where the digital soundtrack is copied onto the CD. The copying machine requires one hour per 2,400 CDs.

After the CDs are copied, they are brought to an assembly area where an employee packs the CD with a jewel case and song lyric insert. The direct labor cost is $0.25 per unit.

The CDs are sold to record stores. Each record store is given promotional materials, such as posters and aisle displays. Promotional materials cost $40 per record store. In addition, shipping costs average $0.25 per CD.

Total completed production was 1,000,000 units during the year. Other information is as follows:

Number of customers (record stores)	42,500
Number of CDs sold	850,000
Wholesale price (to record store) per CD	$16

Factory overhead cost is applied to jobs at the rate of $1,200 per copy machine hour. There were an additional 25,000 copied CDs, packages, and inserts waiting to be assembled on December 31, 2010.

Instructions

1. Prepare an annual income statement for the *Smashing Britney* CD, including supporting calculations, from the information above.
2. Determine the balances in the work in process and finished goods inventory for the *Smashing Britney* CD on December 31, 2010.

Problems Series B

PR 19-1B
Entries for costs in a job order cost system

obj. 2

Dacher Company uses a job order cost system. The following data summarize the operations related to production for October:

a. Materials purchased on account, $450,000.
b. Materials requisitioned, $425,000, of which $4,500 was for general factory use.
c. Factory labor used, $385,000, of which $95,000 was indirect.
d. Other costs incurred on account were for factory overhead, $125,400; selling expenses, $87,500; and administrative expenses, $56,400.
e. Prepaid expenses expired for factory overhead were $12,500; for selling expenses, $14,500; and for administrative expenses, $8,500.
f. Depreciation of factory equipment was $25,300; of office equipment, $31,600; and of store equipment, $7,600.
g. Factory overhead costs applied to jobs, $261,500.
h. Jobs completed, $965,000.
i. Cost of goods sold, $952,400.

Instructions

Journalize the entries to record the summarized operations.

PR 19-2B
Entries and schedules for unfinished jobs and completed jobs

obj. 2

✔ 3. Work in Process balance, $59,925

Grand Valley Apparel Co. uses a job order cost system. The following data summarize the operations related to production for May 2010, the first month of operations:

a. Materials purchased on account, $68,000.
b. Materials requisitioned and factory labor used:

Job	Materials	Factory Labor
No. 401	$ 9,200	$ 9,250
No. 402	11,000	13,400
No. 403	6,400	5,000
No. 404	18,200	17,400
No. 405	8,600	7,400
No. 406	8,500	8,900
For general factory use	4,100	9,600

c. Factory overhead costs incurred on account, $2,750.
d. Depreciation of machinery and equipment, $1,870.
e. The factory overhead rate is $25 per machine hour. Machine hours used:

Job	Machine Hours
No. 401	108
No. 402	110
No. 403	86
No. 404	160
No. 405	109
No. 406	117
Total	690

f. Jobs completed: 401, 402, 403, and 405.
g. Jobs were shipped and customers were billed as follows: Job 401, $26,000; Job 402, $33,400; Job 405, $23,400.

Instructions

1. Journalize the entries to record the summarized operations.
2. Post the appropriate entries to T accounts for Work in Process and Finished Goods, using the identifying letters as dates. Insert memo account balances as of the end of the month.
3. Prepare a schedule of unfinished jobs to support the balance in the work in process account.
4. Prepare a schedule of completed jobs on hand to support the balance in the finished goods account.

PR 19-3B
Job order cost sheet

objs. 2, 3

If the working papers correlating with the textbook are not used, omit Problem 19-3B.

Terry Furniture Company refinishes and reupholsters furniture. Terry uses a job order cost system. When a prospective customer asks for a price quote on a job, the estimated cost data are inserted on an unnumbered job cost sheet. If the offer is accepted, a number is assigned to the job, and the costs incurred are recorded in the usual manner on the job cost sheet. After the job is completed, reasons for the variances between the estimated and actual costs are noted on the sheet. The data are then available to management in evaluating the efficiency of operations and in preparing quotes on future jobs. On June 1, 2010, an estimate of $1,087.80 for reupholstering two chairs and a couch was given to Ted Austin. The estimate was based on the following data:

Estimated direct materials:	
24 meters at $14 per meter.	$ 336.00
Estimated direct labor:	
14 hours at $18 per hour.	252.00
Estimated factory overhead (75% of direct labor cost)	189.00
Total estimated costs	$ 777.00
Markup (40% of production costs)	310.80
Total estimate	$1,087.80

On June 4, the chairs and couch were picked up from the residence of Ted Austin, 409 Patterson St., Vienna, with a commitment to return them on August 5. The job was completed on August 2.

The related materials requisitions and time tickets are summarized as follows:

Materials Requisition No.	Description	Amount
210	10 meters at $14	$140
212	16 meters at $14	224

Time Ticket No.	Description	Amount
H16	6 hours at $18	$108
H21	10 hours at $18	180

Instructions
1. Complete that portion of the job order cost sheet that would be prepared when the estimate is given to the customer.
2. ➡ Assign number 10-110 to the job, record the costs incurred, and complete the job order cost sheet. Comment on the reasons for the variances between actual costs and estimated costs. For this purpose, assume that two meters of materials were spoiled, the factory overhead rate has been proved to be satisfactory, and an inexperienced employee performed the work.

PR 19-4B
Analyzing manufacturing cost accounts

obj. 2

✔ G. $205,970

Davidson Outdoor Equipment Company manufactures kayaks in a wide variety of lengths and styles. The following incomplete ledger accounts refer to transactions that are summarized for August:

Materials

Aug. 1	Balance	32,000	Aug. 31	Requisitions		(A)
31	Purchases	150,000				

Work in Process

Aug. 1	Balance	(B)	Aug. 31	Completed jobs		(F)
31	Materials	(C)				
31	Direct labor	(D)				
31	Factory overhead applied	(E)				

Finished Goods

Aug. 1	Balance	0	Aug. 31	Cost of goods sold		(G)
31	Completed jobs	(F)				

Wages Payable

	Aug. 31	Wages incurred	120,000

Factory Overhead

Aug. 1	Balance	8,000	Aug. 31	Factory overhead applied	(E)
31	Indirect labor	(H)			
31	Indirect materials	4,500			
31	Other overhead	51,500			

In addition, the following information is available:

a. Materials and direct labor were applied to six jobs in August:

Job No.	Style	Quantity	Direct Materials	Direct Labor
No. 101	T-100	100	$ 25,000	$ 18,000
No. 102	T-300	125	32,000	22,000
No. 103	T-200	150	40,000	34,000
No. 104	S-100	125	20,000	12,500
No. 105	S-200	200	36,000	20,000
No. 106	T-400	100	18,000	9,600
	Total	800	$171,000	$116,100

b. Factory overhead is applied to each job at a rate of 50% of direct labor cost.

c. The August 1 Work in Process balance consisted of two jobs, as follows:

Job No.	Style	Work in Process, August 1
Job 101	T-100	$ 8,000
Job 102	T-300	14,000
	Total	$22,000

d. Customer jobs completed and units sold in August were as follows:

Job No.	Style	Completed in August	Units Sold in August
Job 101	T-100	X	80
Job 102	T-300	X	110
Job 103	T-200		0
Job 104	S-100	X	115
Job 105	S-200	X	160
Job 106	T-400		0

Instructions

1. Determine the missing amounts associated with each letter. Provide supporting calculations by completing a table with the following headings:

Job No.	Quantity	Aug. 1 Work in Process	Direct Materials	Direct Labor	Factory Overhead	Total Cost	Unit Cost	Units Sold	Cost of Goods Sold

2. Determine the August 31 balances for each of the inventory accounts and factory overhead.

PR 19-5B
Flow of costs and income statement

obj. 2

✔ 1. Income from operations, $2,400,000

My Way Software Inc. is a designer, manufacturer, and distributor of software for microcomputers. A new product, *Movie Design 2010*, was released for production and distribution in early 2010. In January, $1,400,000 was spent to design print advertisement. For the first six months of 2010, the company spent $1,380,000 promoting *Movie Design 2010* in trade magazines. The product was ready for manufacture on January 10, 2010.

My Way uses a job order cost system to accumulate costs associated with each software title. Direct materials unit costs are as follows:

Blank CD	$ 2.50
Packaging	4.00
Manual	12.00
Total	$18.50

The actual production process for the software product is fairly straightforward. First, blank CDs are brought to a CD copying machine. The copying machine requires 1 hour per 2,000 CDs.

After the program is copied onto the CD, the CD is brought to assembly, where assembly personnel pack the CD and manual for shipping. The direct labor cost for this work is $0.50 per unit.

The completed packages are then sold to retail outlets through a sales force. The sales force is compensated by a 15% commission on the wholesale price for all sales.

Total completed production was 100,000 units during the year. Other information is as follows:

Number of software units sold in 2010	80,000
Wholesale price per unit	$100

Factory overhead cost is applied to jobs at the rate of $2,500 per copy machine hour. There were an additional 4,000 copied CDs, packaging, and manuals waiting to be assembled on December 31, 2010.

Instructions
1. Prepare an annual income statement for the *Movie Design 2010* product, including supporting calculations, from the information above.
2. Determine the balances in the finished goods and work in process inventory for the *Movie Design 2010* product on December 31, 2010.

Special Activities

You can access the special activities online at **www.cengage.com/accounting/reeve**.

Excel Success Special Activities

SA 19-1
Calculation of predetermined overhead application rate

California Custom Design, LLC, is a business that customizes motorcycles and automobiles according to the customers' specifications. The company uses a job-order cost accounting system. Factory overhead is applied to production on the basis of direct labor hours. Estimated overhead costs for the coming year amount to $860,000. The company expects to operate at 80% of capacity, utilizing 16,000 direct labor hours.

a. Open the Excel file *SA19-1.*
b. Calculate the predetermined overhead application rate.
c. When you have completed determining the overhead application rate, perform a "save as," replacing the entire file name with the following:

   SA19-1_[your first name initial]_[your last name]

SA 19-2
Calculation of predetermined overhead application rate

Mendoza Home Builders, Inc., specializes in the construction of large family homes. The company applies overhead to each home it builds on the basis of the direct labor cost incurred on the job site. The budgeted total direct labor costs for the coming year amount to $5,000,000. A list of the budgeted overhead costs is presented below.

Budgeted Overhead Costs	
Indirect labor—hourly workers	$1,000,000
Indirect labor—supervisor salaries	400,000
Equipment repairs and maintenance	350,000
Indirect materials	250,000
Licenses, permits, and taxes	100,000
Waste disposal	75,000
Equipment depreciation	50,000
Materials and equipment storage	20,000
Small tools lost or broken	12,000
Other miscellaneous overhead	43,000

a. Open the Excel file *SA19-2.*
b. Calculate the predetermined overhead application rate for the coming year.
c. When you have completed determining the overhead application rate, perform a "save as," replacing the entire file name with the following:

   SA19-2_[your first name initial]_[your last name]

SA 19-3
Calculation of predetermined overhead application rate

Sandstone Manufacturing Company operates three production facilities in the state of New Mexico. Because manufacturing operations are heavily automated, the company uses machine hours as the factory overhead allocation base. The estimated annual overhead costs and the budgeted number of machine hours for each of these facilities are as follows:

	Manufacturing Facility		
	Santa Fe	Clovis	Roswell
Estimated annual factory overhead cost	$1,670,000	$1,394,000	$1,200,000
Estimated total machine hours	1,000,000	820,000	750,000

Calculate the predetermined factory overhead application rates that would be used in each of these manufacturing plants during the coming year.

a. Open the Excel file *SA19-3.*
b. Calculate the predetermined overhead rate for the coming year for each manufacturing plant.
c. When you have completed determining the overhead application rate, perform a "save as," replacing the entire file name with the following:

   SA19-3_[your first name initial]_[your last name]

Answers to Self-Examination Questions

1. **A** Job order cost systems are best suited to businesses manufacturing special orders from customers, such as would be the case for a repair shop for antique furniture (answer A). A process cost system is best suited for manufacturers of similar units of products such as rubber manufacturers (answer B), coal manufacturers (answer C), and computer chip manufacturers (answer D).

2. **C** The journal entry to record the requisition of materials to the factory in a job order cost system is a debit to Work in Process and a credit to Materials.

3. **B** The job cost sheet accumulates the cost of materials (answer A), direct labor (answer C), and factory overhead applied (answer D). Indirect materials are NOT accumulated on the job order cost sheets, but are included as part of factory overhead applied.

4. **B**

5. **B** If the amount of factory overhead applied during a particular period exceeds the actual overhead costs, the factory overhead account will have a credit balance and is said to be overapplied (answer B) or overabsorbed. If the amount applied is less than the actual costs, the account will have a debit balance and is said to be underapplied (answer A) or underabsorbed (answer C). Since an "estimated" predetermined overhead rate is used to apply overhead, a credit balance does not necessarily represent an error (answer D).

$$\frac{\text{Predetermined Factory}}{\text{Overhead Rate}} = \frac{\text{Estimated Total Factory Overhead Costs}}{\text{Estimated Activity Base}}$$

$$\frac{\text{Predetermined Factory}}{\text{Overhead Rate}} = \frac{\$420{,}000}{16{,}000 \text{ dlh}} = \$26.25$$

$$\text{Hours applied to the job: } \frac{\$3{,}000}{\$15 \text{ per hour}} = 200 \text{ hours}$$

Factory overhead applied to the job: 200 hours $\times$ $26.25 = $5,250

CHAPTER 20

Process Cost Systems

DREYER'S GRAND ICE CREAM, INC.

In making ice cream, an electric ice cream maker is used to mix ingredients, which include milk, cream, sugar, and flavoring. After the ingredients are added, the mixer is packed with ice and salt to cool the ingredients, and it is then turned on.

After mixing for half of the required time, would you have ice cream? Of course not, because the ice cream needs to mix longer to freeze. Now, assume that you ask the question:

What costs have I incurred so far in making ice cream?

The answer to this question requires knowing the cost of the ingredients and electricity. The ingredients are added at the beginning; thus, all the ingredient costs have been incurred. Since the mixing is only half complete, only 50% of the electricity costs has been incurred. Therefore, the answer to the preceding question is:

All the materials costs and half the electricity costs have been incurred.

The same cost concepts just described apply to larger ice cream processes like those of Dreyer's Grand Ice Cream, Inc., manufacturer of Häagen-Dazs®, Edys®, Dreyer's®, and Nestle® ice cream. Dreyer's mixes ingredients in 3,000-gallon vats in much the same way you would with an electric ice cream maker. Dreyer's also records the costs of the ingredients, labor, and factory overhead used in making ice cream. These costs are used by managers for decisions such as setting prices and improving operations.

This chapter describes and illustrates process cost systems that are used by manufacturers such as Dreyer's. In addition, the use of cost of production reports in decision making is described. Finally, just-in-time cost systems are discussed.

After studying this chapter, you should be able to:

1 Describe process cost systems.

Process Cost Systems

Comparing Job Order and Process Cost Systems

EE 20-1 (page 890)

Cost Flows for a Process Manufacturer

2 Prepare a cost of production report.

Cost of Production Report

Step 1: Determine the Units to Be Assigned Costs

EE 20-2 (page 895)

Step 2: Compute Equivalent Units of Production

EE 20-3 (page 896)

EE 20-4 (page 898)

e**x**cel *success*

Step 3: Determine the Cost per Equivalent Unit

EE 20-5 (page 900)

Step 4: Allocate Costs to Units Transferred Out and Partially Completed Units

EE 20-6 (page 902)

e**x**cel *success*

Preparing the Cost of Production Report

3 Journalize entries for transactions using a process cost system.

Journal Entries for a Process Cost System

EE 20-7 (page 906)

4 Describe and illustrate the use of cost of production reports for decision making.

Using the Cost of Production Report for Decision Making

Frozen Delight

Holland Beverage Company

EE 20-8 (page 908)

Yield

5 Compare just-in-time processing with traditional manufacturing processing.

Just-in-Time Processing

At a Glance   Menu   Turn to pg 915

South-Western

1 Describe process cost systems.

Process Cost Systems

A **process manufacturer** produces products that are indistinguishable from each other using a continuous production process. For example, an oil refinery processes crude oil through a series of steps to produce a barrel of gasoline. One barrel of gasoline, the product, cannot be distinguished from another barrel. Other examples of process manufacturers include paper producers, chemical processors, aluminum smelters, and food processors.

The cost accounting system used by process manufacturers is called the **process cost system.** A process cost system records product costs for each manufacturing department or process.

In contrast, a job order manufacturer produces custom products for customers or batches of similar products. For example, a custom printer produces wedding invitations, graduation announcements, or other special print items that are tailored to the specifications of each customer. Each item manufactured is unique to itself. Other examples of job order manufacturers include furniture manufacturers, shipbuilders, and home builders.

As described and illustrated in Chapter 19, the cost accounting system used by job order manufacturers is called the *job order cost system*. A job order cost system records product cost for each job using job cost sheets.

Some examples of process and job order manufacturers are shown below.

Process Manufacturers		**Job Order Manufacturers**	
Company	**Product**	**Company**	**Product**
Pepsi	soft drinks	Walt Disney	movies
Alcoa	aluminum	Nike, Inc.	athletic shoes
Intel	computer chip	Tiger Woods Design	golf courses
Apple	iPhone	Heritage Log Homes	log homes
Hershey Foods	chocolate bars	DDB Advertising Agency	advertising

Comparing Job Order and Process Cost Systems

Process and job order cost systems are similar in that each system:

1. Records and summarizes product costs.
2. Classifies product costs as direct materials, direct labor, and factory overhead.
3. Allocates factory overhead costs to products.
4. Uses perpetual inventory system for materials, work in process, and finished goods.
5. Provides useful product cost information for decision making.

Process and job costing systems are different in several ways. As a basis for illustrating these differences, the cost systems for Frozen Delight and Legend Guitars are used.

Exhibit 1 illustrates the process cost system for Frozen Delight, an ice cream manufacturer. As a basis for comparison, Exhibit 1 also illustrates the job order cost system for Legend Guitars, a custom guitar manufacturer. Legend Guitars was described and illustrated in Chapters 18 and 19.

Exhibit 1 indicates that Frozen Delight manufactures ice cream using two departments:

1. Mixing Department mixes the ingredients using large vats.
2. Packaging Department puts the ice cream into cartons for shipping to customers.

Exhibit 1

Process Cost and Job Order Cost Systems

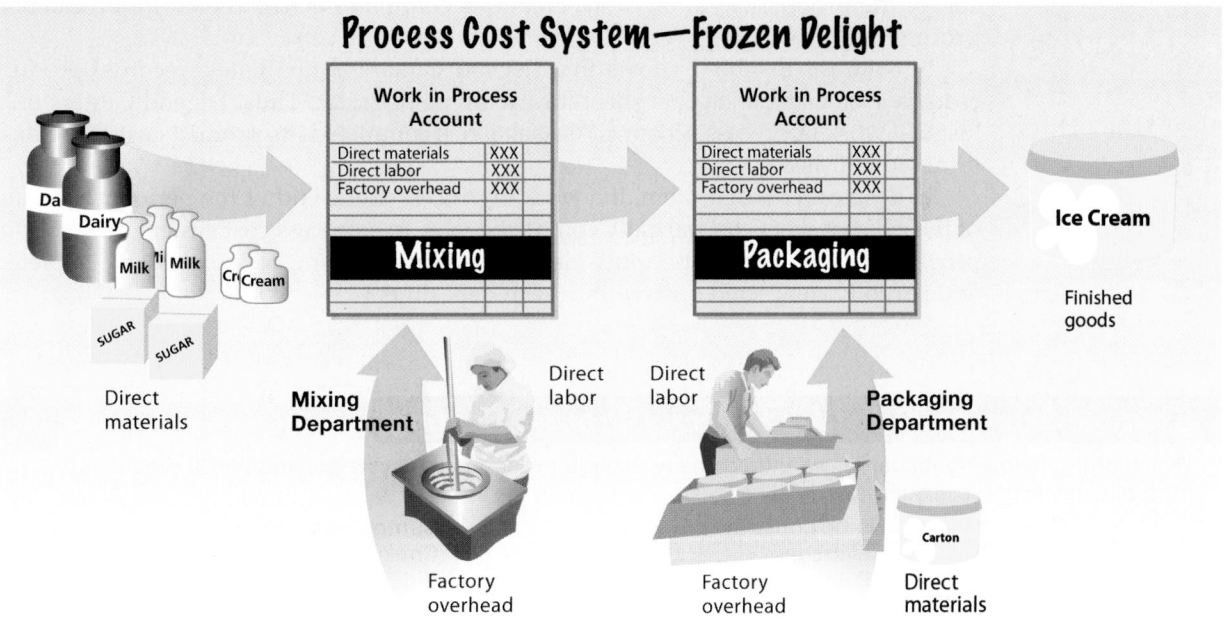

Process Cost System—Frozen Delight

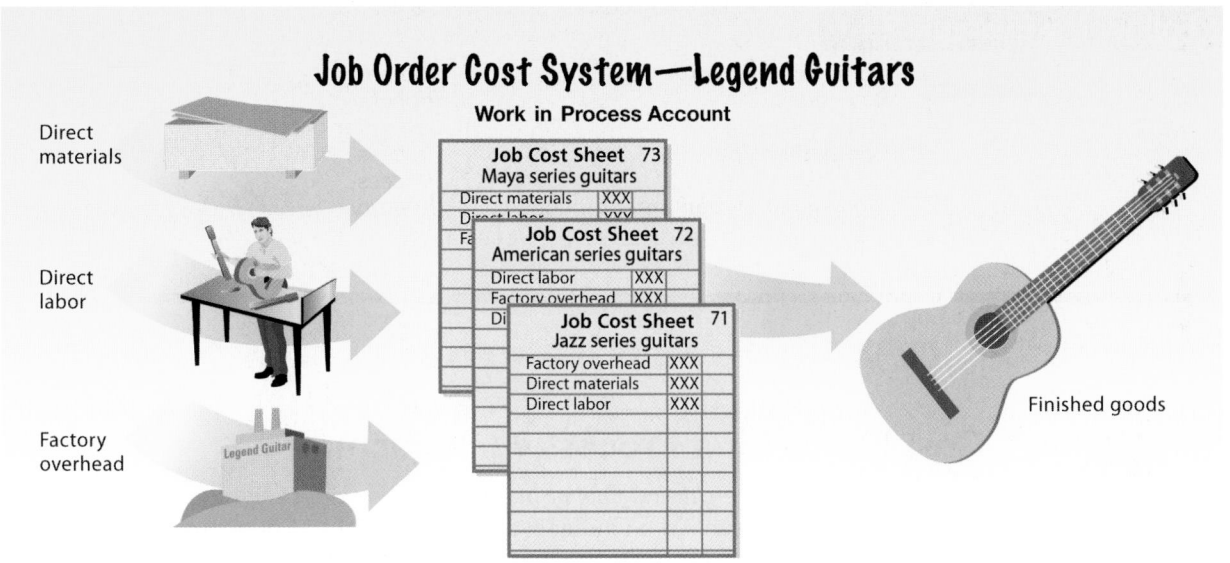

Job Order Cost System—Legend Guitars

Since each gallon of ice cream is similar, product costs are recorded in each department's work in process account. As shown in Exhibit 1, Frozen Delight accumulates (records) the cost of making ice cream in *work in process accounts* for the Mixing and Packaging departments. The product costs of making a gallon of ice cream include:

1. *Direct materials cost,* which include milk, cream, sugar, and packing cartons. All materials costs are added at the beginning of the process for both the Mixing Department and the Packaging Department.
2. *Direct labor cost,* which is incurred by employees in each department who run the equipment and load and unload product.
3. *Factory overhead costs,* which include the utility costs (power) and depreciation on the equipment.

When the Mixing Department completes the mixing process, its product costs are transferred to the Packaging Department. When the Packaging Department completes its process, the product costs are transferred to Finished Goods. In this way, the cost of the product (a gallon of ice cream) accumulates across the entire production process.

In contrast, Exhibit 1 shows that Legend Guitars accumulates (records) product costs by jobs using a job cost sheet for each type of guitar. Thus, Legend Guitars uses just one work in process account. As each job is completed, its product costs are transferred to Finished Goods.

In a job order cost system, the work in process at the end of the period is the sum of the job cost sheets for partially completed jobs. In a process cost system, the work in process at the end of the period is determined by allocating costs between completed and partially completed units within each department.

Example Exercise 20-1   Job Order vs. Process Costing   1

Which of the following industries would normally use job order costing systems, and which would normally use process costing systems?

Home construction	Computer chips
Beverages	Cookies
Military aircraft	Video game design and production

Follow My Example 20-1

Home construction	Job order
Beverages	Process
Military aircraft	Job order
Computer chips	Process
Cookies	Process
Video game design and production	Job order

For Practice: PE 20-1A, PE 20-1B

Cost Flows for a Process Manufacturer

Exhibit 2 illustrates the *physical flow* of materials for Frozen Delight. Ice cream is made in a manufacturing plant in a similar way as you would at home except on a larger scale.

In the Mixing Department, direct materials in the form of milk, cream, and sugar are placed into a vat. An employee (direct labor) fills each vat, sets the cooling temperature, and sets the mix speed. The vat is cooled (refrigerated) as the direct materials are being mixed by agitators (paddles). Factory overhead is incurred in the form of power to run the vat (electricity) and vat (equipment) depreciation.

In the Packaging Department, the ice cream is received from the Mixing Department in a form ready for packaging. The Packaging Department uses direct labor and factory overhead (conversion costs) to package the ice cream into one-gallon containers (direct materials). The ice cream is then transferred to finished goods where it is frozen and stored in refrigerators prior to shipment to customers (stores).

Exhibit 2

Physical Flows for a Process Manufacturer

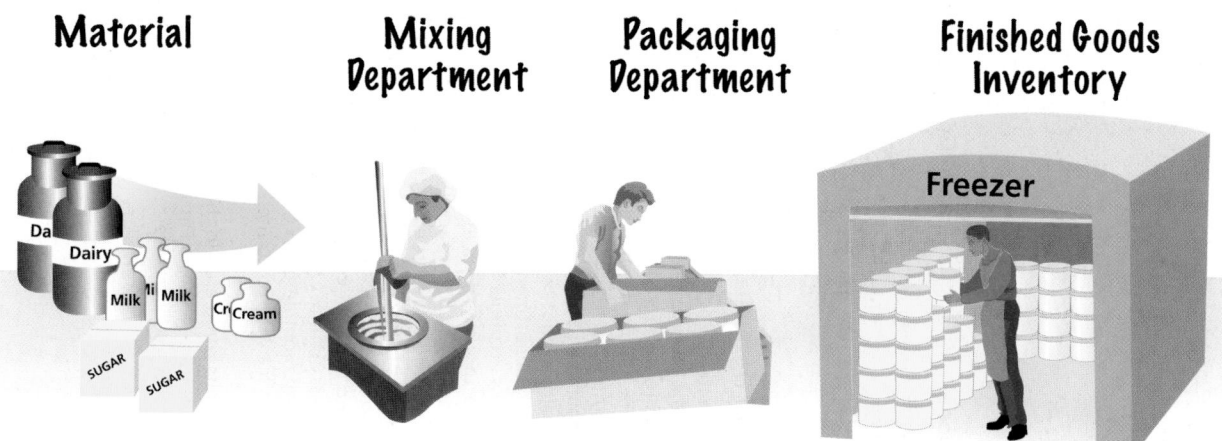

The *cost flows* in a process cost accounting system are similar to the *physical flow* of materials described above. The cost flows for Frozen Delight are illustrated in Exhibit 3 as follows:

a.   The cost of materials purchased is recorded in the materials account.

b.   The cost of direct materials used by the Mixing and Packaging departments are recorded in the work in process accounts for each department.

c.   The cost of direct labor used by the Mixing and Packaging departments is recorded in work in process accounts for each department.

d.   The cost of factory overhead incurred for indirect materials and other factory overhead such as depreciation is recorded in the factory overhead accounts for each department.

e.   The factory overhead incurred in the Mixing and Packaging departments is applied to the work in process accounts for each department.

f.   The cost of units completed in the Mixing Department is transferred to the Packaging Department.

g.   The cost of units completed in the Packaging Department is transferred to Finished Goods.

h.   The cost of units sold is transferred to Cost of Goods Sold.

As shown in Exhibit 3, the Mixing and Packaging Departments have separate factory overhead accounts. The factory overhead costs incurred for indirect materials, depreciation, and other overhead are debited to each department's factory overhead account. The overhead is applied to work in process by debiting each department's work in process account and crediting the department's factory overhead account.

Exhibit 3 illustrates how the Mixing and Packaging Departments have separate work in process accounts. Each work in process account is debited for the direct materials, direct labor, and applied factory overhead. In addition, the work in process account for the Packaging Department is debited for the cost of the units transferred in from the Mixing Department. Each work in process account is credited for the cost of the units transferred to the next department.

Lastly, Exhibit 3 shows that the finished goods account is debited for the cost of the units transferred from the Packaging Department. The finished goods account is credited for the cost of the units sold, which is debited to the cost of goods sold account.

Exhibit 3

Cost Flows for a Process Manufacturer—Frozen Delight

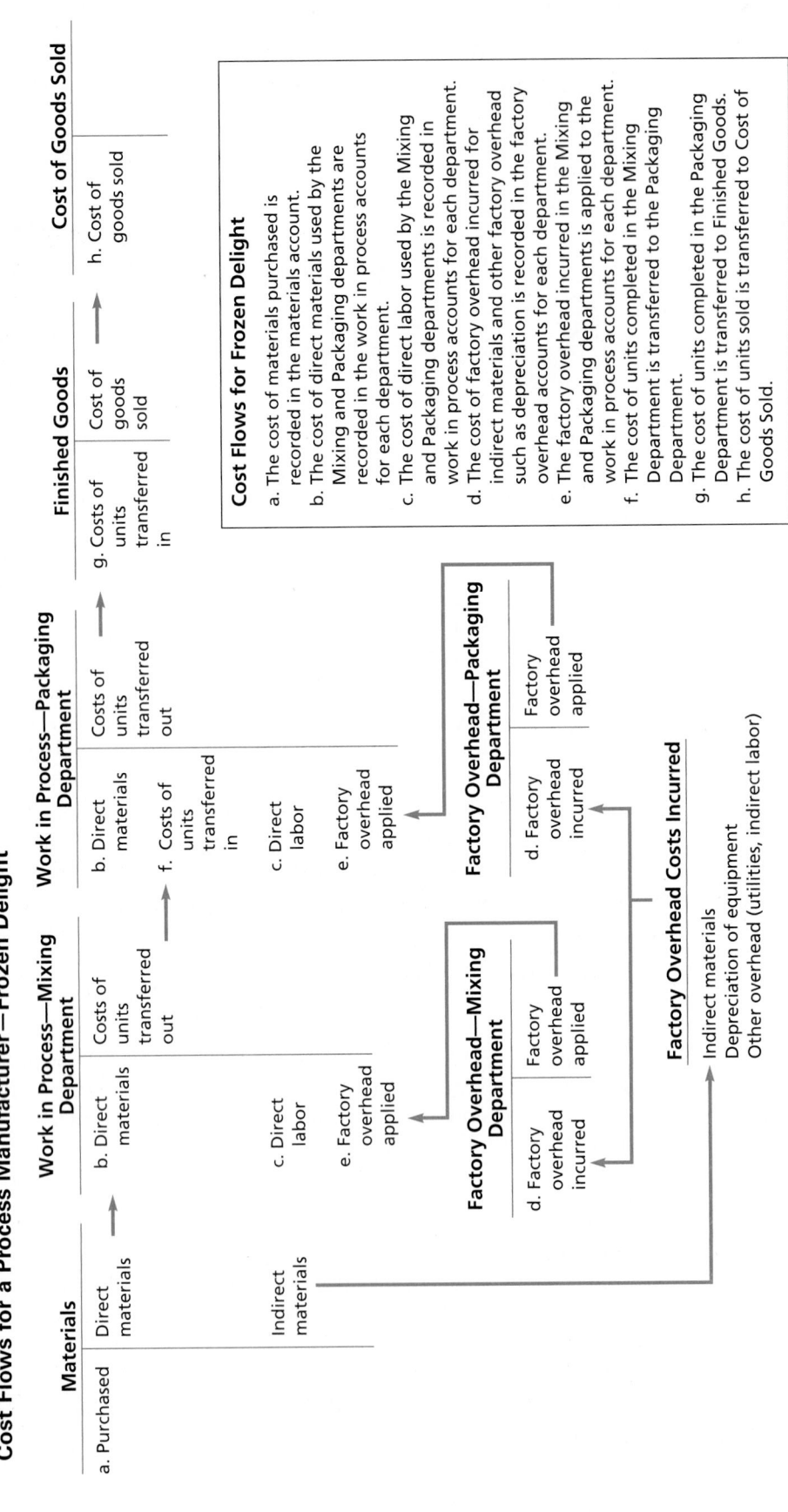

Materials

a. Purchased | Direct materials

Indirect materials

Work in Process—Mixing Department

b. Direct materials | Costs of units transferred out

c. Direct labor

e. Factory overhead applied

Work in Process—Packaging Department

b. Direct materials | Costs of units transferred out

f. Costs of units transferred in

c. Direct labor

e. Factory overhead applied

Finished Goods

g. Costs of units transferred in | Cost of goods sold

Cost of Goods Sold

h. Cost of goods sold

Factory Overhead—Mixing Department

d. Factory overhead incurred | Factory overhead applied

Factory Overhead—Packaging Department

d. Factory overhead incurred | Factory overhead applied

Factory Overhead Costs Incurred

Indirect materials
Depreciation of equipment
Other overhead (utilities, indirect labor)

Cost Flows for Frozen Delight

a. The cost of materials purchased is recorded in the materials account.

b. The cost of direct materials used by the Mixing and Packaging departments are recorded in the work in process accounts for each department.

c. The cost of direct labor used by the Mixing and Packaging departments is recorded in work in process accounts for each department.

d. The cost of factory overhead incurred for indirect materials and other factory overhead such as depreciation is recorded in the factory overhead accounts for each department.

e. The factory overhead incurred in the Mixing and Packaging departments is applied to the work in process accounts for each department.

f. The cost of units completed in the Mixing Department is transferred to the Packaging Department.

g. The cost of units completed in the Packaging Department is transferred to Finished Goods.

h. The cost of units sold is transferred to Cost of Goods Sold.

Prepare a
cost of
production report.

Cost of Production Report

In a process cost system, the cost of units transferred out of each processing department must be determined along with the cost of any partially completed units remaining in the department. The report that summarizes these costs is a cost of production report.

The **cost of production report** summarizes the production and cost data for a department as follows:

1.   The units the department is accountable for and the disposition of those units.
2.   The product costs incurred by the department and the allocation of those costs between completed (transferred out) and partially completed units.

A cost of production report is prepared using the following four steps:

Step 1.   Determine the units to be assigned costs.
Step 2.   Compute equivalent units of production.
Step 3.   Determine the cost per equivalent unit.
Step 4.   Allocate costs to units transferred out and partially completed units.

Preparing a cost of production report requires making a cost flow assumption. Like merchandise inventory, costs can be assumed to flow through the manufacturing process using the first-in, first-out (FIFO), last in, first-out (LIFO), or average cost methods. Because the **first-in, first-out (FIFO) method** is often the same as the physical flow of units, the FIFO method is used in this chapter.[1]

To illustrate, a cost of production report for the Mixing Department of Frozen Delight for July 2010 is prepared. The July data for the Mixing Department are as follows:

Inventory in process, July I, 5,000 gallons:		
Direct materials cost, for 5,000 gallons	$5,000	
Conversion costs, for 5,000 gallons, 70% completed	1,225	
Total inventory in process, July 1		$ 6,225
Direct materials cost for July, 60,000 gallons		66,000
Direct labor cost for July		10,500
Factory overhead applied for July		7,275
Total production costs to account for		$90,000
Gallons transferred to Packaging in July (includes units in		
process on July 1), 62,000 gallons		?
Inventory in process, July 31, 3,000 gallons,		
25% completed as to conversion costs		?

By preparing a cost of production report, the cost of the gallons transferred to the Packaging Department in July and the ending work in process inventory in the Mixing Department is determined. These amounts are indicated by question marks (?).

Step 1: Determine the Units to Be Assigned Costs

The first step is to determine the units to be assigned costs. A unit can be any measure of completed production, such as tons, gallons, pounds, barrels, or cases. For Frozen Delight, a unit is a gallon of ice cream.

---

1 The average cost method is illustrated in an appendix to this chapter.

The Mixing Department is accountable for 65,000 gallons of direct materials during July, as shown below.

Total units (gallons) charged to production:
In process, July 1 . . . .   5,000 gallons
Received from materials storage   60,000
    Total units (gallons) accounted for . . . .   65,000 gallons

For July, the following three groups of units (gallons) are assigned costs:

Group 1.   Units (gallons) in beginning work in process inventory on July 1.
Group 2.   Units (gallons) started and completed during July.
Group 3.   Units (gallons) in ending work in process inventory on July 31.

Exhibit 4 illustrates these groups of units (gallons) in the Mixing Department for July. The 5,000 gallons of beginning inventory were completed and transferred to the Packaging Department. During July, 60,000 gallons of material were started (entered into mixing). Of the 60,000 gallons started in July, 3,000 gallons were incomplete on July 31. Thus, 57,000 gallons (60,000 − 3,000) were started and completed in July.

The total units (gallons) to be assigned costs for July are summarized below.

Group 1   Inventory in process, July 1, completed in July . . . .   5,000 gallons
Group 2   Started and completed in July   57,000
                Transferred out to the Packaging Department in July. . . .   62,000 gallons
Group 3   Inventory in process, July 31   3,000
                Total units (gallons) to be assigned costs . . . .   65,000 gallons

The total gallons to be assigned costs (65,000) equal the total gallons accounted for (65,000) by the Mixing Department.

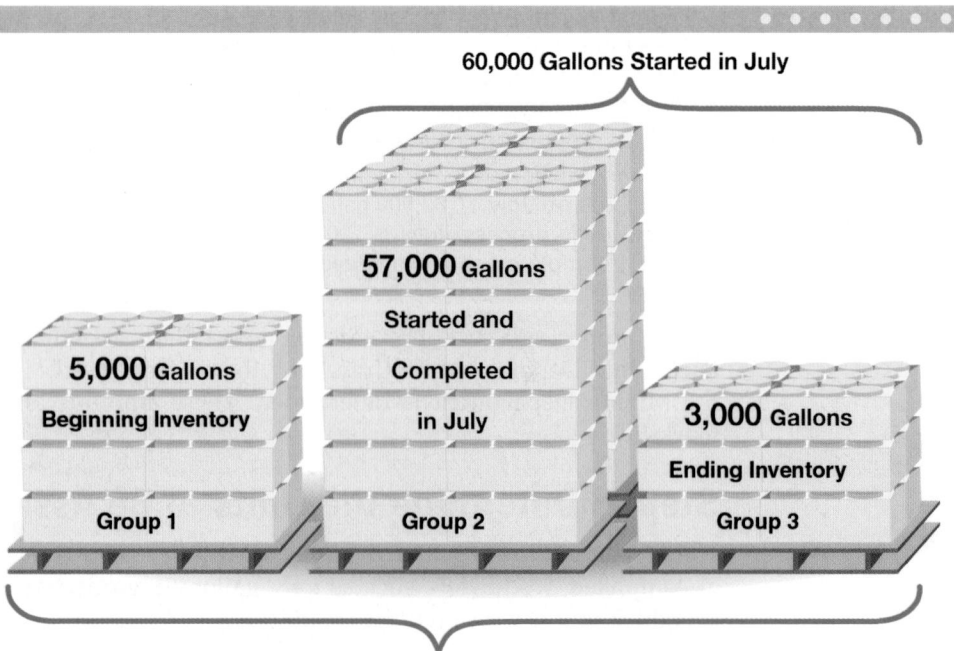

Exhibit 4

July Units to Be Costed—Mixing Department

60,000 Gallons Started in July

57,000 Gallons
Started and Completed in July

5,000 Gallons
Beginning Inventory

3,000 Gallons
Ending Inventory

Group 1

Group 2

Group 3

65,000 Gallons to Be Assigned Costs

Example Exercise 20-2   Units to Be Assigned Costs   ●●●●●●●● ⟩ 2

Rocky Springs Beverage Company has two departments, Blending and Bottling. The Bottling Department received 57,000 liters from the Blending Department. During the period, the Bottling Department completed 58,000 liters, including 4,000 liters of work in process at the beginning of the period. The ending work in process was 3,000 liters. How many liters were started and completed during the period?

Follow My Example 20-2

54,000 liters started and completed (58,000 completed − 4,000 beginning WIP), or (57,000 started − 3,000 WIP)

For Practice: PE 20-2A, PE 20-2B

Step 2: Compute Equivalent Units of Production

Whole units are the number of units in production during a period, whether completed or not. **Equivalent units of production** are the portion of whole units that are complete with respect to materials or conversion (direct labor and factory overhead) costs.

To illustrate, assume that a 1,000-gallon batch (vessel) of ice cream is only 40% complete in the mixing process on July 31. Thus, the batch is only 40% complete as to conversion costs such as power. In this case, the whole units and equivalent units of production are as follows:

	Whole Units	Equivalent Units
Materials costs	1,000 gallons	1,000 gallons
Conversion costs	1,000 gallons	400 gallons (1,000 × 40%)

Since the materials costs are all added at the beginning of the process, the materials costs are 100% complete for the 1,000-gallon batch of ice cream. Thus, the whole units and equivalent units for materials costs are 1,000 gallons. However, since the batch is only 40% complete as to conversion costs, the equivalent units for conversion costs are 400 gallons.

Equivalent units for materials and conversion costs are usually determined separately as shown above. This is because materials and conversion costs normally enter production at different times and rates. In contrast, direct labor and factory overhead normally enter production at the same time and rate. For this reason, direct labor and factory overhead are combined as conversion costs in computing equivalent units.

Materials Equivalent Units   To compute equivalent units for materials, it is necessary to know how materials are added during the manufacturing process. In the case of Frozen Delight, all the materials are added at the beginning of the mixing process. Thus, the equivalent units for materials in July are computed as follows:

		Total Whole Units	Percent Materials Added in July	Equivalent Units for Direct Materials
Group 1	Inventory in process, July 1	5,000	0%	0
Group 2	Started and completed in July (62,000 − 5,000)	57,000	100%	57,000
	Transferred out to Packaging Department in July	62,000	—	57,000
Group 3	Inventory in process, July 31	3,000	100%	3,000
	Total gallons to be assigned cost . . .	65,000		60,000

As shown on the previous page, the whole units for the three groups of units determined in Step 1 are listed in the first column. The percent of materials added in July is then listed. The equivalent units are determined by multiplying the whole units by the percent of materials added.

To illustrate, the July 1 inventory (Group 1) has 5,000 gallons of whole units, which are complete as to materials. That is, all the direct materials for the 5,000 gallons in process on July 1 were added in June. Thus, the percent of materials added in July is zero, and the equivalent units added in July are zero.

The 57,000 gallons started and completed in July (Group 2) are 100% complete as to materials. The 3,000 gallons in process on July 31 (Group 3) are also 100% complete as to materials since all materials are added at the beginning of the process. Thus, the equivalent units for the gallons started and completed in July are 57,000 (57,000 × 100%) gallons. For the inventory in process on July 31, the equivalent units is 3,000 (3,000 × 100%) gallons.

The equivalent units for direct materials are summarized in Exhibit 5.

Exhibit 5

Direct Materials Equivalent Units

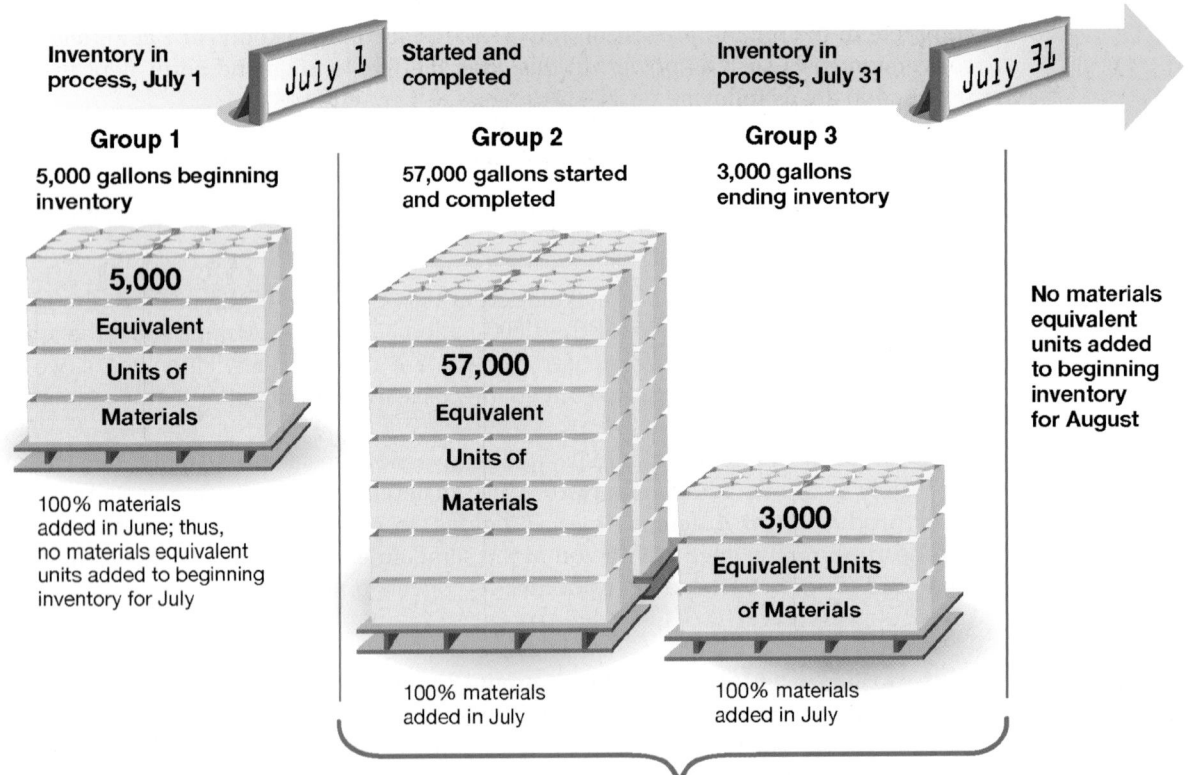

60,000 Total Equivalent Units of Materials Cost in July

Example Exercise 20-3   Equivalent Units of Materials Cost   2

The Bottling Department of Rocky Springs Beverage Company had 4,000 liters in beginning work in process inventory (30% complete). During the period, 58,000 liters were completed. The ending work in process inventory was 3,000 liters (60% complete). What are the total equivalent units for direct materials if materials are added at the beginning of the process?

(continued)

Follow My Example 20-3

Total equivalent units for direct materials is 57,000, computed as follows:

	Total Whole Units	Percent Materials Added in Period	Equivalent Units for Direct Materials
Inventory in process, beginning of period	4,000	0%	0
Started and completed during the period	54,000*	100%	54,000
Transferred out of Bottling (completed)	58,000	—	54,000
Inventory in process, end of period	3,000	100%	3,000
Total units to be assigned costs	61,000		57,000

*(58,000 − 4,000)

For Practice: PE 20-3A, PE 20-3B

Conversion Equivalent Units To compute equivalent units for conversion costs, it is necessary to know how direct labor and factory overhead enter the manufacturing process. Direct labor, utilities, and equipment depreciation are often incurred uniformly during processing. For this reason, it is assumed that Frozen Delight incurs conversion costs evenly throughout its manufacturing process. Thus, the equivalent units for conversion costs in July are computed as follows:

		Total Whole Units	Percent Conversion Completed in July	Equivalent Units for Conversion
Group 1	Inventory in process, July 1 (70% completed)	5,000	30%	1,500
Group 2	Started and completed in July (62,000 − 5,000)	57,000	100%	57,000
	Transferred out to Packaging Department in July	62,000	—	58,500
Group 3	Inventory in process, July 31 (25% completed)	3,000	25%	750
	Total gallons to be assigned cost	65,000		59,250

As shown above, the whole units for the three groups of units determined in Step 1 are listed in the first column. The percent of conversion costs added in July is then listed. The equivalent units are determined by multiplying the whole units by the percent of conversion costs added.

To illustrate, the July 1 inventory has 5,000 gallons of whole units (Group 1) are 70% complete as to conversion costs. During July, the remaining 30% (100% − 70%) of conversion costs was added. Therefore, the equivalent units of conversion costs added in July are 1,500 (5,000 × 30%) gallons.

The 57,000 gallons started and completed in July (Group 2) are 100% complete as to conversion costs. Thus, the equivalent units of conversion costs for the gallons started and completed in July are 57,000 (57,000 × 100%) gallons.

The 3,000 gallons in process on July 31 (Group 3) are 25% complete as to conversion costs. Hence, the equivalent units for the inventory in process on July 31 are 750 (3,000 × 25%) gallons.

The equivalent units for conversion costs are summarized in Exhibit 6.

Exhibit 6

Conversion Equivalent Units

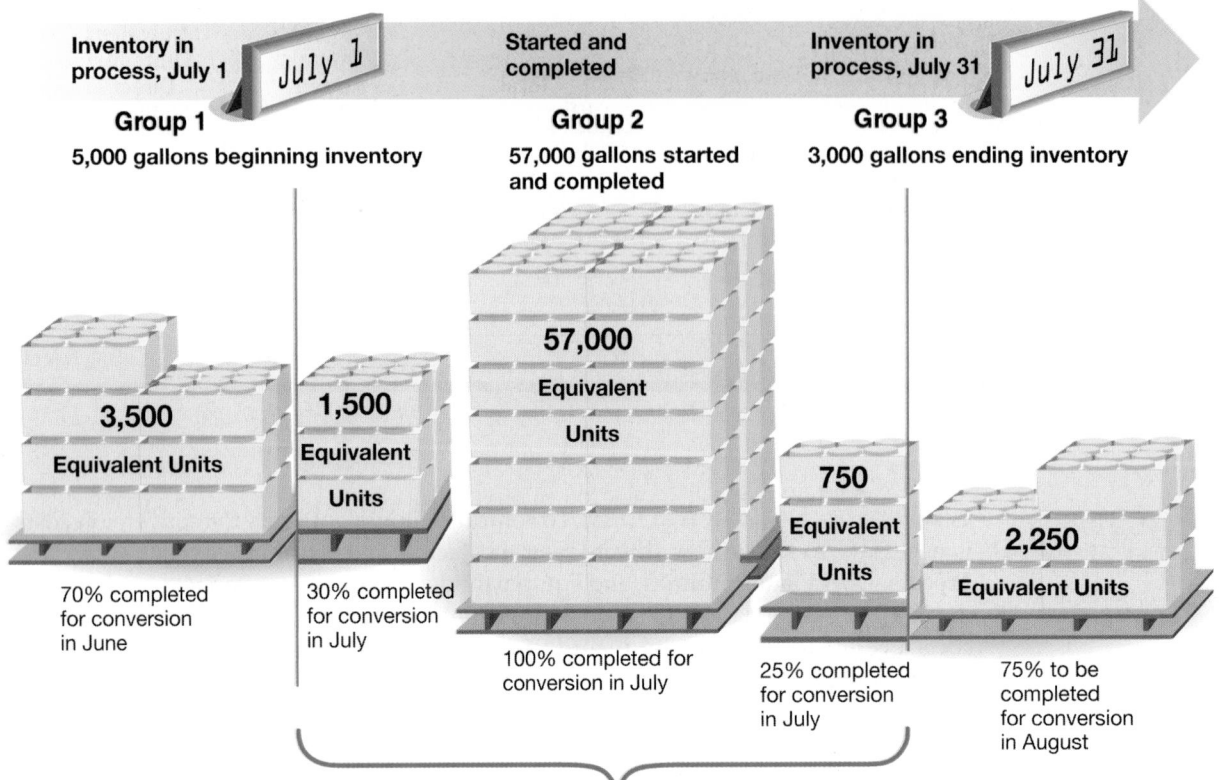

59,250 Total Equivalent Units of Conversion Costs in July

Example Exercise 20-4 Equivalent Units of Conversion Costs 2

The Bottling Department of Rocky Springs Beverage Company had 4,000 liters in beginning work in process inventory (30% complete). During the period, 58,000 liters were completed. The ending work in process inventory was 3,000 liters (60% complete). What are the total equivalent units for conversion costs?

Follow My Example 20-4

	Total Whole Units	Percent Conversion Completed in Period	Equivalent Units for Conversion
Inventory in process, beginning of period	4,000	70%	2,800
Started and completed during the period	54,000*	100%	54,000
Transferred out of Bottling (completed)	58,000	—	56,800
Inventory in process, end of period	3,000	60%	1,800
Total units to be assigned costs	61,000		58,600

*(58,000 − 4,000)

For Practice: PE 20-4A, PE 20-4B

Step 3: Determine the Cost per Equivalent Unit

The next step in preparing the cost of production report is to compute the cost per equivalent unit for direct materials and conversion costs. The **cost per equivalent unit** for direct materials and conversion costs is computed as follows:

$$\text{Direct Materials Cost per Equivalent Unit} = \frac{\text{Total Direct Materials Cost for the Period}}{\text{Total Equivalent Units of Direct Materials}}$$

$$\text{Conversion Cost per Equivalent Unit} = \frac{\text{Total Conversion Costs for the Period}}{\text{Total Equivalent Units of Conversion Costs}}$$

The July direct materials and conversion cost equivalent units for Frozen Delight's Mixing Department from Step 2 are shown below.

		Equivalent Units	
		Direct Materials	Conversion
Group 1	Inventory in process, July 1	0	1,500
Group 2	Started and completed in July (62,000 − 5,000)	57,000	57,000
	Transferred out to Packaging Department in July	57,000	58,500
Group 3	Inventory in process, July 31	3,000	750
	Total gallons to be assigned cost	60,000	59,250

The direct materials and conversion costs incurred by Frozen Delight in July are as follows:

Direct materials		$66,000
Conversion costs:		
Direct labor	$10,500	
Factory overhead	7,275	17,775
Total product costs incurred in July		$83,775

The direct materials and conversion costs per equivalent unit are $1.10 and $0.30 per gallon, as computed below.

$$\text{Direct Materials Cost per Equivalent Unit} = \frac{\text{Total Direct Materials Cost for the Period}}{\text{Total Equivalent Units of Direct Materials}}$$

$$\text{Direct Materials Cost per Equivalent Unit} = \frac{\$66,000}{60,000 \text{ gallons}} = \$1.10 \text{ per gallon}$$

$$\text{Conversion Cost per Equivalent Unit} = \frac{\text{Total Conversion Costs for the Period}}{\text{Total Equivalent Units of Conversion Costs}}$$

$$\text{Conversion Cost per Equivalent Unit} = \frac{\$17,775}{59,250 \text{ gallons}} = \$0.30 \text{ per gallon}$$

The preceding costs per equivalent unit are used in Step 4 to allocate the direct materials and conversion costs to the completed and partially completed units.

The cost per equivalent unit can be determined using a spreadsheet as follows:

	A	B	C	
1		Equivalent Units		
2		Direct Materials	Conversion	
3	Inventory in process, July 1	-	1,500	a.
4	Started and completed in July	57,000	57,000	
5	Transferred out to Packaging	=B3+B4	=C3+C4	
6	Inventory in process, July 31	3,000	750	b.
7	Total gallons to be assigned cost	=B5+B6	=C5+C6	
8				
9		Direct Materials	Conversion	
10	Costs	$ 66,000	$ 17,775	
11				
12		Direct Materials	Conversion	
13	Cost per Equivalent Unit c.	=B10/B7	=C10/C7	d.
14		per gallon	per gallon	

a. Arrange the equivalent units and cost information in two columns, one for direct materials and one for conversion. Doing so will facilitate copying the cost per equivalent unit formula in step d.

b. Insert the appropriate sum formulas to compute the totals and subtotals of the equivalent units.

c. Insert in cell B13 a formula that divides the direct materials costs by the total gallons to be assigned.

d. Copy this formula to C13 to determine the cost per equivalent unit of conversion.

 Go to the hands-on **Excel Tutor** for this example!

Example Exercise 20-5 Cost per Equivalent Unit

The cost of direct materials transferred into the Bottling Department of Rocky Springs Beverage Company is $22,800. The conversion cost for the period in the Bottling Department is $8,790. The total equivalent units for direct materials and conversion are 57,000 liters and 58,600 liters, respectively. Determine the direct materials and conversion costs per equivalent unit.

Follow My Example 20-5

$$\text{Direct materials cost per equivalent unit} = \frac{\$22,800}{57,000 \text{ liters}} = \$0.40 \text{ per liter}$$

$$\text{Conversion cost per equivalent unit} = \frac{\$8,790}{58,600 \text{ liters}} = \$0.15 \text{ per liter}$$

For Practice: PE 20-5A, PE 20-5B

Step 4: Allocate Costs to Units Transferred Out and Partially Completed Units

Product costs must be allocated to the units transferred out and the partially completed units on hand at the end of the period. The product costs are allocated using the costs per equivalent unit for materials and conversion costs that were computed in Step 3.

The total production costs to be assigned for Frozen Delight in July are $90,000, as shown below.

Inventory in process, July 1, 5,000 gallons:	
Direct materials cost, for 5,000 gallons	$ 5,000
Conversion costs, for 5,000 gallons, 70% completed	1,225
Total inventory in process, July 1	$ 6,225
Direct materials cost for July, 60,000 gallons	66,000
Direct labor cost for July	10,500
Factory overhead applied for July	7,275
Total production costs to account for	$90,000

The units to be assigned these costs are shown below. The costs to be assigned these units are indicated by question marks (?).

		Units	Total Cost
Group 1	Inventory in process, July 1, completed in July. .	5,000 gallons	?
Group 2	Started and completed in July	57,000	?
	Transferred out to the Packaging Department in July	62,000 gallons	?
Group 3	Inventory in process, July 31	3,000	?
	Total	65,000 gallons	$90,000

Group 1: Inventory in Process on July 1 The 5,000 gallons of inventory in process on July 1 (Group 1) were completed and transferred out to the Packaging Department in July. The cost of these units of $6,675 is determined as follows:

	Direct Materials Costs	Conversion Costs	Total Costs
Inventory in process, July 1 balance			$6,225
Equivalent units for completing the			
July 1 in-process inventory	0	1,500	
Cost per equivalent unit	× $1.10	× $0.30	
Cost of completed July 1 in-process inventory . . .	0	$ 450	450
Cost of July 1 in-process inventory			
transferred to Packaging Department			$6,675

As shown above, $6,225 of the cost of the July 1 in-process inventory of 5,000 gallons was carried over from June. This cost plus the cost of completing the 5,000 gallons in July was transferred to the Packaging Department during July. The cost of completing the 5,000 gallons during July is $450. The $450 represents the conversion costs necessary to complete the remaining 30% of the processing. There were no direct materials costs added in July because all the materials costs had been added in June. Thus, the cost of the 5,000 gallons in process on July 1 (Group 1) transferred to the Packaging Department is $6,675.

Group 2: Started and Completed The 57,000 units started and completed in July (Group 2) incurred all (100%) of their direct materials and conversion costs in July. Thus, the cost of the 57,000 gallons started and completed is $79,800 computed by multiplying 57,000 gallons by the costs per equivalent unit for materials and conversion costs, as shown below.

	Direct Materials Costs	Conversion Costs	Total Costs
Units started and completed in July. . . .	57,000 gallons	57,000 gallons	
Cost per equivalent unit	× $1.10	× $0.30	
Cost of the units started			
and completed in July.	$62,700	$17,100	$79,800

The total cost transferred to the Packaging Department in July of $86,475 is the sum of the beginning inventory cost and the costs of the units started and completed in July, as shown below.

Group 1	Cost of July 1 in-process inventory	$ 6,675
Group 2	Cost of the units started and completed in July	79,800
	Total costs transferred to Packaging Department in July	$86,475

Group 3: Inventory in Process on July 31 The 3,000 gallons in process on July 31 (Group 3) incurred all their direct materials costs and 25% of their conversion costs in July. The cost of these partially completed units of $3,525 is computed below.

	Direct Materials Costs	Conversion Costs	Total Costs
Equivalent units in ending inventory	3,000 gallons	750 gallons	
Cost per equivalent unit	× $1.10	× $0.30	
Cost of July 31 in-process inventory	$3,300	$225	$3,525

The 3,000 gallons in process on July 31 received all (100%) of their materials in July. Therefore, the direct materials cost incurred in July is $3,300 (3,000 × $1.10). The conversion costs of $225 represent the cost of the 750 (3,000 × 25%) equivalent gallons times the cost per equivalent unit for conversion costs of $0.30. The sum of the direct materials cost ($3,300) and the conversion costs ($225) equals the total cost of the July 31 work in process inventory of $3,525 ($3,300 + $225).

To summarize, the total manufacturing costs for Frozen Delight in July were assigned as shown below. In doing so, the question marks (?) on page 900 have been answered.

		Units	Total Cost
Group 1	Inventory in process, July 1, completed in July . .	5,000 gallons	$ 6,675
Group 2	Started and completed in July	57,000	79,800
	Transferred out to the Packaging		
	Department in July	62,000 gallons	$86,475
Group 3	Inventory in process, July 31.	3,000	3,525
	Total	65,000 gallons	$90,000

Example Exercise 20-6   Cost of Units Transferred Out and Ending Work in Process

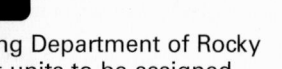

The costs per equivalent unit of direct materials and conversion in the Bottling Department of Rocky Springs Beverage Company are $0.40 and $0.15, respectively. The equivalent units to be assigned costs are as follows:

	Equivalent Units	
	Direct Materials	**Conversion**
Inventory in process, beginning of period	0	2,800
Started and completed during the period	54,000	54,000
Transferred out of Bottling (completed)	54,000	56,800
Inventory in process, end of period	3,000	1,800
Total units to be assigned costs	57,000	58,600

The beginning work in process inventory had a cost of $1,860. Determine the cost of units transferred out and the ending work in process inventory.

Follow My Example 20-6

	Direct Materials Costs		**Conversion Costs**	**Total Costs**
Inventory in process, beginning of period				$ 1,860
Inventory in process, beginning of period	0	+	2,800 × $0.15	420
Started and completed during the period	54,000 × $0.40	+	54,000 × $0.15	29,700
Transferred out of Bottling (completed)				$31,980
Inventory in process, end of period	3,000 × $0.40	+	1,800 × $0.15	1,470
Total costs assigned by the Bottling Department				$33,450
Completed and transferred out of production	$31,980			
Inventory in process, ending	$ 1,470			

For Practice: PE 20-6A, PE 20-6B

Preparing the Cost of Production Report

A cost of production report is prepared for each processing department at periodic intervals. The report summarizes the following production quantity and cost data:

1.   The units for which the department is accountable and the disposition of those units.
2.   The production costs incurred by the department and the allocation of those costs between completed (transferred out) and partially completed units.

Using Steps 1–4, the July cost of production report for Frozen Delight's Mixing Department is shown in Exhibit 7.

As shown in Exhibit 7, the Mixing Department was accountable for 65,000 units (gallons). Of these units, 62,000 units were completed and transferred to the Packaging Department. The remaining 3,000 units are partially completed and are part of in-process inventory as of July 31.

The Mixing Department was responsible for $90,000 of production costs during July. The cost of goods transferred to the Packaging Department in July was $86,475. The remaining cost of $3,525 is part of in-process inventory as of July 31.

The cost of production report on a spreadsheet is illustrated at the end of the chapter in a comprehensive spreadsheet illustration.

Exhibit 7

Cost of Production Report for Frozen Delight's Mixing Department—FIFO

	A	B	C	D	E
1		Frozen Delight			
2		Cost of Production Report—Mixing Department			
3		For the Month Ended July 31, 2010			
4					
5		Whole Units	Equivalent Units		
6	**UNITS**		Direct Materials	Conversion	
7	Units charged to production:				
8	Inventory in process, July 1	5,000			
9	Received from materials storeroom	60,000			
10	Total units accounted for by the Mixing Department	65,000			
11					
12	Units to be assigned costs:				
13	Inventory in process, July 1 (70% completed)	5,000	0	1,500	
14	Started and completed in July	57,000	57,000	57,000	
15	Transferred to Packaging Department in July	62,000	57,000	58,500	
16	Inventory in process, July 31 (25% completed)	3,000	3,000	750	
17	Total units to be assigned costs	65,000	60,000	59,250	
18					

Step 1 (under Whole Units column)   Step 2 (under Equivalent Units columns)

	A	B	C	D	E
19			Costs		
20	**COSTS**		Direct Materials	Conversion	Total
21					
22	Costs per equivalent unit:				
23	Total costs for July in Mixing Department		$ 66,000	$ 17,775	
24	Total equivalent units (from step 2 above)		÷60,000	÷59,250	
25	Cost per equivalent unit		$ 1.10	$ 0.30	
26					
27	Costs assigned to production:				
28	Inventory in process, July 1				$ 6,225
29	Costs incurred in July				83,775[a]
30	Total costs accounted for by the Mixing Department				$90,000
31					
32					
33	Cost allocated to completed and partially				
34	completed units:				
35	Inventory in process, July 1—balance				$ 6,225
36	To complete inventory in process, July 1		$ 0 +	$ 450[b] =	450
37	Cost of completed July 1 work in process				$ 6,675
38	Started and completed in July		62,700[c] +	17,100[d] =	79,800
39	Transferred to Packaging Department in July				$86,475
40	Inventory in process, July 31		$ 3,300[e] +	$ 225[f] =	3,525
41	Total costs assigned by the Mixing Department				$90,000
42					

Step 3 (rows 22–30), Step 4 (rows 33–42)

[a]$66,000 + $10,500 + $7,275 = $83,775 [b]1,500 units × $0.30 = $450 [c]57,000 units × $1.10 = $62,700 [d]57,000 units × $0.30 = $17,100
[e]3,000 units × $1.10 = $3,300 [f]750 units × $0.30 = $225

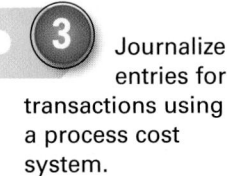 Journalize entries for transactions using a process cost system.

Journal Entries for a Process Cost System

The journal entries to record the cost flows and transactions for a process cost system are illustrated in this section. As a basis for illustration, the July transactions for Frozen Delight are used. To simplify, the entries are shown in summary form, even though many of the transactions would be recorded daily.

a. Purchased materials, including milk, cream, sugar, packaging, and indirect materials on account, $88,000.

Materials	88,000	
Accounts Payable		88,000

b. The Mixing Department requisitioned milk, cream, and sugar, $66,000. This is the amount indicated on page 893. Packaging materials of $8,000 were requisitioned by the Packaging Department. Indirect materials for the Mixing and Packaging departments were $4,125 and $3,000, respectively.

Work in Process—Mixing	66,000	
Work in Process—Packaging	8,000	
Factory Overhead—Mixing	4,125	
Factory Overhead—Packaging	3,000	
Materials		81,125

c. Incurred direct labor in the Mixing and Packaging departments of $10,500 and $12,000, respectively.

Work in Process—Mixing	10,500	
Work in Process—Packaging	12,000	
Wages Payable		22,500

d. Recognized equipment depreciation for the Mixing and Packaging departments of $3,350 and $1,000, respectively.

Factory Overhead—Mixing	3,350	
Factory Overhead—Packaging	1,000	
Accumulated Depreciation—Equipment		4,350

e. Applied factory overhead to Mixing and Packaging departments of $7,275 and $3,500, respectively.

Work in Process—Mixing	7,275	
Work in Process—Packaging	3,500	
Factory Overhead—Mixing		7,275
Factory Overhead—Packaging		3,500

f. Transferred costs of $86,475 from the Mixing Department to the Packaging Department per the cost of production report in Exhibit 7.

Work in Process—Packaging	86,475	
Work in Process—Mixing		86,475

g. Transferred goods of $106,000 out of the Packaging Department to Finished Goods according to the Packaging Department cost of production report (not illustrated).

Finished Goods—Ice Cream	106,000	
Work in Process—Packaging		106,000

h. Recorded cost of goods sold out of the finished goods inventory of $107,000.

Cost of Goods Sold	107,000	
Finished Goods—Ice Cream		107,000

Exhibit 8 shows the flow of costs for each transaction. The highlighted amounts in Exhibit 8 were determined from assigning the costs in the Mixing Department. These amounts were computed and are shown at the bottom of the cost of production report for the Mixing Department in Exhibit 7. Likewise, the amount transferred out of the Packaging Department to Finished Goods would have also been determined from a cost of production report for the Packaging Department.

Exhibit 8

Frozen Delight's Cost Flows

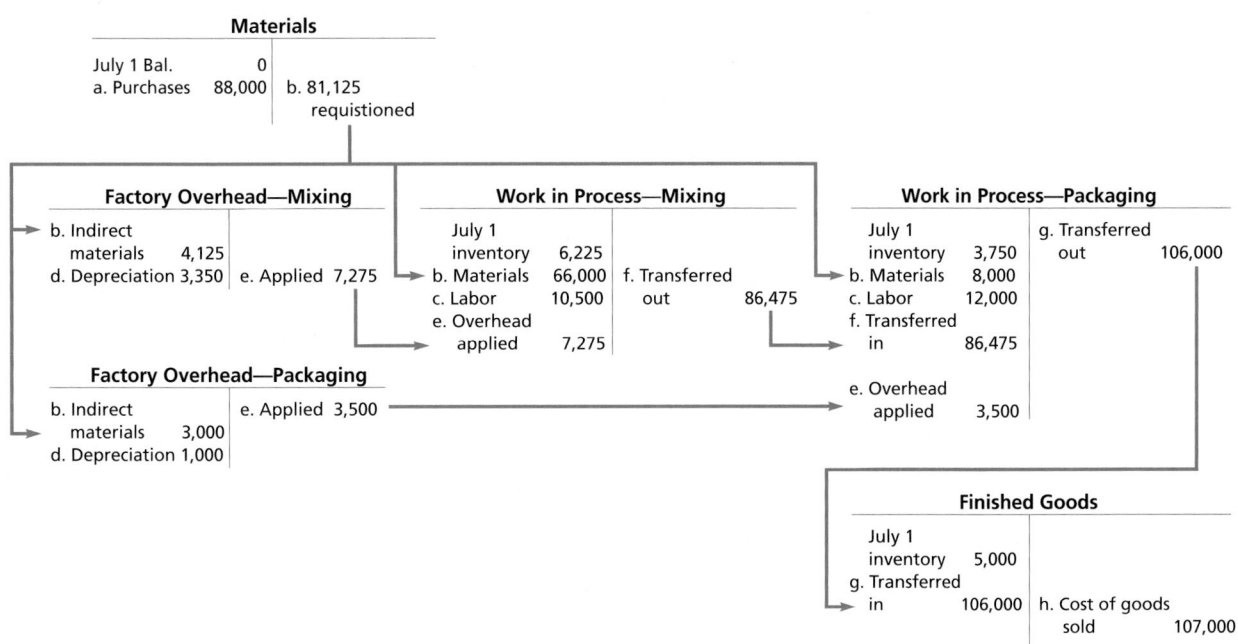

The ending inventories for Frozen Delight are reported on the July 31 balance sheet as follows:

Materials	$ 6,875
Work in Process—Mixing Department	3,525
Work in Process—Packaging Department	7,725
Finished Goods	4,000
Total inventories	$22,125

The $3,525 of Work in Process—Mixing Department is the amount determined from the bottom of the cost of production report in Exhibit 7.

Example Exercise 20-7   Process Cost Journal Entries   •••••••••> 3

The cost of materials transferred into the Bottling Department of Rocky Springs Beverage Company is $22,800, including $20,000 from the Blending Department and $2,800 from the materials storeroom. The conversion cost for the period in the Bottling Department is $8,790 ($3,790 factory overhead applied and $5,000 direct labor). The total cost transferred to Finished Goods for the period was $31,980. The Bottling Department had a beginning inventory of $1,860.

a. Journalize (1) the cost of transferred-in materials, (2) conversion costs, and (3) the costs transferred out to Finished Goods.
b. Determine the balance of Work in Process—Bottling at the end of the period.

Follow My Example 20-7

a. 1. Work in Process—Bottling	22,800	
Work in Process—Blending		20,000
Materials		2,800
2. Work in Process—Bottling	8,790	
Factory Overhead—Bottling		3,790
Wages Payable		5,000
3. Finished Goods	31,980	
Work in Process—Bottling		31,980
b. $1,470 ($1,860 + $22,800 + $8,790 − $31,980)		

For Practice: PE 20-7A, PE 20-7B

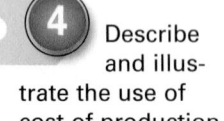
4 Describe and illus- trate the use of cost of production reports for decision making.

Using the Cost of Production Report for Decision Making

The cost of production report is often used by managers for decisions involving the control and improvement of operations. To illustrate, cost of production reports for Frozen Delight and Holland Beverage Company are used. Finally, the computation and use of yield is discussed.

Frozen Delight

The cost of production report for the Mixing Department is shown in Exhibit 7. The cost per equivalent unit for June can be determined from the beginning inventory. The Frozen Delight data on page 893 indicate that the July 1 inventory in process of $6,225 consists of the following costs:

Direct materials cost, 5,000 gallons	$5,000
Conversion costs, 5,000 gallons, 70% completed	1,225
Total inventory in process, July 1	$6,225

Using the preceding data, the June costs per equivalent unit of materials and conversion costs can be determined as follows:

$$\text{Direct Materials Cost per Equivalent Unit} = \frac{\text{Total Direct Materials Cost for the Period}}{\text{Total Equivalent Units of Direct Materials}}$$

$$\text{Direct Materials Cost per Equivalent Unit} = \frac{\$5{,}000}{5{,}000 \text{ gallons}} = \$1.00 \text{ per gallon}$$

$$\text{Conversion Cost per Equivalent Unit} = \frac{\text{Total Conversion Costs for the Period}}{\text{Total Equivalent Units of Conversion Costs}}$$

$$\text{Conversion Cost per Equivalent Unit} = \frac{\$1{,}225}{(5{,}000 \times 70\%) \text{ gallons}} = \$0.35 \text{ per gallon}$$

In July the cost per equivalent unit of materials increased by $0.10 per gallon, while the cost per equivalent unit for conversion costs decreased by $0.05 per gallon, as shown below.

	July	June	Increase (Decrease)
Cost per equivalent unit for direct materials	$1.10	$1.00	$0.10
Cost per equivalent unit for conversion costs	0.30	0.35	(0.05)

Frozen Delight's management could use the preceding analysis as a basis for investigating the increase in the direct materials cost per equivalent unit and the decrease in the conversion cost per equivalent unit.

Holland Beverage Company

A cost of production report may be prepared in greater detail than shown in Exhibit 7. This greater detail can help managers isolate problems and seek opportunities for improvement.

To illustrate, the Blending Department of Holland Beverage Company prepared cost of production reports for April and May. To simplify, assume that the Blending Department had no beginning or ending work in process inventory in either month. In other words, all units started were completed in each month. The cost of production reports for April and May in the Blending Department are as follows:

	A	B	C	D
1	Cost of Production Reports			
2	Holland Beverage Company—Blending Department			
3	For the Months Ended April 30 and May 31, 2010			
4		April	May	
5	Direct materials	$ 20,000	$ 40,600	
6	Direct labor	15,000	29,400	
7	Energy	8,000	20,000	
8	Repairs	4,000	8,000	
9	Tank cleaning	3,000	8,000	
10	Total	$ 50,000	$106,000	
11	Units completed	÷100,000	÷200,000	
12	Cost per unit	$ 0.50	$ 0.53	
13				

The May results indicate that total unit costs have increased from $0.50 to $0.53, or 6% from April. To determine the possible causes for this increase, the cost of production report is restated in per-unit terms by dividing the costs by the number of units completed, as shown below.

	A	B	C	D
1	Blending Department			
2	Per-Unit Expense Comparisons			
3		April	May	% Change
4	Direct materials	$0.200	$0.203	1.50%
5	Direct labor	0.150	0.147	−2.00%
6	Energy	0.080	0.100	25.00%
7	Repairs	0.040	0.040	0.00%
8	Tank cleaning	0.030	0.040	33.33%
9	Total	$0.500	$0.530	6.00%
10				

Both energy and tank cleaning per-unit costs have increased significantly in May. These increases should be further investigated. For example, the increase in energy may be due to the machines losing fuel efficiency. This could lead management to repair the machines. The tank cleaning costs could be investigated in a similar fashion.

Yield

In addition to unit costs, managers of process manufacturers are also concerned about yield. The **yield** is computed as follows:

$$\text{Yield} = \frac{\text{Quantity of Material Output}}{\text{Quantity of Material Input}}$$

To illustrate, assume that 1,000 pounds of sugar enter the Packaging Department, and 980 pounds of sugar were packed. The yield is 98%, as computed below.

$$\text{Yield} = \frac{\text{Quantity of Material Output}}{\text{Quantity of Material Input}} = \frac{980 \text{ pounds}}{1,000 \text{ pounds}} = 98\%$$

Thus, two percent (100% − 98%) or 20 pounds of sugar was lost or spilled during the packing process. Managers can investigate significant changes in yield over time or significant differences in yield from industry standards.

Example Exercise 20-8   Using Process Costs for Decision Making ••••••••▷ 4

The cost of energy consumed in producing good units in the Bottling Department of Rocky Springs Beverage Company was $4,200 and $3,700 for March and April, respectively. The number of equivalent units produced in March and April was 70,000 liters and 74,000 liters, respectively. Evaluate the cost of energy between the two months.

Follow My Example 20-8

$$\text{Energy cost per liter, March} = \frac{\$4,200}{70,000 \text{ liters}} = \$0.06$$

$$\text{Energy cost per liter, April} = \frac{\$3,700}{74,000 \text{ liters}} = \$0.05$$

The cost of energy has appeared to improve by 1 cent per liter between March and April.

For Practice: PE 20-8A, PE 20-8B

Compare just-in-time processing with traditional manufacturing processing.

Just-in-Time Processing

The objective of most manufacturers is to produce products with high quality, low cost, and instant availability. In attempting to achieve this objective, many manufacturers have implemented just-in-time processing. **Just-in-time (JIT) processing** is a management approach that focuses on reducing time and cost and eliminating poor quality. A JIT system obtains efficiencies and flexibility by reorganizing the traditional production process.

A traditional manufacturing process for a furniture manufacturer is shown in Exhibit 9. The product (chair) moves through seven processes. In each process, workers are assigned a specific job, which is performed repeatedly as unfinished products are received from the preceding department. The product moves from process to process as each function or step is completed.

EXHIBIT 9

Traditional Production Line

Furniture Manufacturer

Work in Progress

Direct Materials

Finished Goods

Cutting Department | Drilling Department | Sanding Department | Staining Department | Varnishing Department | Upholstery Department | Assembly Department

For the furniture maker in Exhibit 9, the product (chair) moves through the following processes:

1. In the Cutting Department, the wood is cut to design specifications.
2. In the Drilling Department, the wood is drilled to design specifications.
3. In the Sanding Department, the wood is sanded.
4. In the Staining Department, the wood is stained.
5. In the Varnishing Department, varnish and other protective coatings are applied.
6. In the Upholstery Department, fabric and other materials are added.
7. In the Assembly Department, the product (chair) is assembed.

In the traditional production process, supervisors enter materials into manufacturing so as to keep all the manufacturing departments (processes) operating. Some departments, however, may process materials more rapidly than others. In addition, if one department stops because of machine breakdowns, for example, the preceding departments usually continue production in order to avoid idle time. In such cases, a buildup of work in process inventories results in some departments.

In a just-in-time system, processing functions are combined into work centers, sometimes called **manufacturing cells**. For example, the seven departments illustrated in Exhibit 9 might be reorganized into the following three work centers:

1. Work Center 1 performs the cutting, drilling, and sanding functions.
2. Work Center 2 performs the staining and varnishing functions.
3. Work Center 3 performs the upholstery and assembly functions.

The preceding JIT manufacturing process is illustrated in Exhibit 10.

Exhibit 10

Just-in-Time Production Line

Furniture Manufacturer

Direct Materials	Work in Progress			Finished Goods

  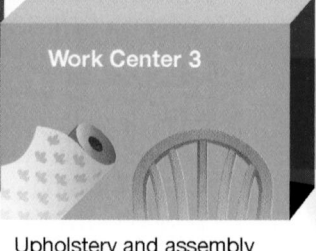 

Work Center 1 — Cutting, drilling, and sanding

Work Center 2 — Staining and varnishing

Work Center 3 — Upholstery and assembly

Before Caterpillar implemented JIT, a transmission traveled 10 miles through the factory and required 1,000 pieces of paper to support the manufacturing process. After implementing JIT, a transmission travels only 200 feet and requires only 10 pieces of paper.

The Internet complements a just-in-time processing strategy. Ford Motor Company states that the impact of the Internet is the equivalent of "the moving assembly line of the 21st Century." This is because the Internet will connect the whole supply chain—from customers to suppliers—to create a fast and efficient manufacturing system.

In traditional manufacturing, a worker typically performs only one function. However, in JIT manufacturing, work centers complete several functions. Thus, workers are often cross-trained to perform more than one function. Research has indicated that workers who perform several functions identify better with the end product. This creates pride in the product and improves quality and productivity.

The activities supporting the manufacturing process are called *service activities*. For example, repair and maintenance of manufacturing equipment are service activities. In a JIT manufacturing process, service activities may be assigned to individual work centers, rather than to centralized service departments. For example, each work center may be assigned responsibility for the repair and maintenance of its machinery and equipment. This creates an environment in which workers gain a better understanding of the production process and their machinery. In turn, workers tend to take better care of the machinery, which decreases repairs and maintenance costs, reduces machine downtime, and improves product quality.

In a JIT system, the product is often placed on a movable carrier that is centrally located in the work center. After the workers in a work center have completed their activities with the product, the entire carrier and any additional materials are moved just in time to satisfy the demand or need of the next work center. In this sense, the product is said to be "pulled through." Each work center is connected to other work centers through information contained on a Kanban, which is a Japanese term for cards.

In summary, the primary objective of JIT systems is to increase the efficiency of operations. This is achieved by eliminating waste and simplifying the production process. At the same time, JIT systems emphasize continually improving the manufacturing process and product quality.

Comprehensive Spreadsheet Illustration

Southern Aggregate Company manufactures concrete through a series of processes. All materials are introduced in Crushing. From Crushing, the materials pass through Sifting, Baking, and Mixing, emerging as finished concrete. All inventories are costed by the first-in, first-out method.

The following information has been prepared on a spreadsheet as follows:

	A	B	C	D
1	*Inputs:*			
2				
3	Work in Process–Mixing Department			
4		Units	Amount	Percent Complete
5	Work in Process, May 1, 2010	2,000	$ 13,700	25%
6	Direct materials transferred from Baking	15,200	98,800	
7	Direct labor		17,200	
8	Factory overhead		11,780	
9				
10	Work in Process, May 31, 2010	1,200		50%

Instructions

Using the input information, prepare a cost of production report for the Mixing Department in a spreadsheet.

Solution

	A	B	C	D	E
12	Output:				
13					
14	Southern Aggregate Company				
15	Cost of Production Report–Mixing Department				
16	For the Month Ended May 31, 2010				
17			Equivalent Units		
18	UNITS	Whole Units	Direct Materials	Conversion	
19	Units charged to production:				
20	Inventory in process, May 1	2,000			
21	Received from Baking	15,200			
22	Total units accounted for by the Mixing Department	17,200			
23					
24	Units to be assigned costs:				
25	Inventory in process, May 1 (25% completed)	2,000	-	1,500	
26	Started and completed in May	14,000	14,000	14,000	
27	Transferred to finished goods in May	16,000	14,000	15,500	
28	Inventory in process, May 31 (50% completed)	1,200	1,200	600	
29	Total units to be assigned costs	17,200	15,200	16,100	
30					
31				Costs	
32	COSTS		Direct Materials	Conversion	Total
33	Unit costs:				
34	Total costs for May in Mixing Department		$ 98,800	$ 28,980	
35	Total equivalent units (from row 29)		15,200	16,100	
36	Cost per equivalent unit		$ 6.50	$ 1.80	
37					
38	Costs assigned to production:				
39	Inventory in process, May 1				$ 13,700
40	Costs incurred in May				127,780
41	Total costs accounted for by the Mixing Department				$ 141,480
42					
43	Cost allocated to completed and partially completed				
44	units:				
45	Inventory in process, May 1–balance				$ 13,700
46	To complete inventory in process, May 1		$ –	$ 2,700	2,700
47	Cost of completed May 1 work in process				$ 16,400
48	Started and completed in May		91,000	25,200	116,200
49	Transferred to finished goods in May				$ 132,600
50	Inventory in process, May 31		7,800	1,080	8,880
51	Total costs assigned by the Mixing Department				$ 141,480

The formulas used to create the cost of production report are as follows:

	A	B	C	D	E
12	Output:				
13					
14	Southern Aggregate Company				
15	Cost of Production Report–Mixing Department				
16	For the Month Ended May 31, 2010				
17			Equivalent Units		
18	UNITS	Whole Units	Direct Materials	Conversion	
19	Units charged to production:				
20	Inventory in process, May 1	=B5			
21	Received from Baking	=B6			
22	Total units accounted for by the Mixing Department	=SUM(B20:B21)			
23					

24	Units to be assigned costs:				
25	Inventory in process, May 1 (25% completed)	=B20	–	=B25*(1–D5)	
26	Started and completed in May	=B6-B28	=B26	=B26	
27	Transferred to finished goods in May	=SUM(B25:B26)	=SUM(C25:C26)	=SUM(D25:D26)	
28	Inventory in process, May 31 (50% completed)	=B10	=B28	=B28*D10	
29	Total units to be assigned costs	=B27+B28	=C27+C28	=D27+D28	
30					
31				Costs	
32	COSTS		Direct Materials	Conversion	Total
33	Unit Costs:				
34	Total costs for May in Mixing		=C6	=C7+C8	
35	Total equivalent units (row 29)		=C29	=D29	
36	Cost per equivalent unit		=C34/C35	=D34/D35	
37					
38	Costs assigned to production:				
39	Inventory in process, May 1				=C5
40	Costs incurred in May				=SUM(C6:C8)
41	Total costs accounted for by the Mixing Department				=SUM(E39:E40)
42					
43	Cost allocated to completed and partially completed				
44	units:				
45	Inventory in process, May 1–balance				=E39
46	To complete inventory in process, May 1		=C25*C36	=D25*D36	=C46+D46
47	Cost of completed May 1 work in process				=SUM(E45:E46)
48	Started and completed in May		=C26*C36	=D26*D36	=C48+D48
49	Transferred to finished goods in May 31				=E47+E48
50	Inventory in proccess, May 31		=C28*C36	=D28*D36	=C50+D50
51	Total costs assigned by the Mixing Department				=E49+E50

The cell formulas follow the steps outlined within the chapter for developing the cost of production report. Note that the complete cost of production report uses cell references. There are no number inputs into the report. Rather, the report will work for any and all input combinations.

APPENDIX

Average Cost Method

A cost flow assumption must be used as product costs flow through manufacturing processes. In this chapter, the first-in, first-out cost flow method was used for the Mixing Department of Frozen Delight. In this appendix, the average cost flow method is illustrated for S&W Ice Cream Company (S&W).

Determining Costs Using the Average Cost Method

S&W's operations are similar to those of Frozen Delight. Like Frozen Delight, S&W mixes direct materials (milk, cream, sugar) in refrigerated vessels and has two manufacturing departments, Mixing and Packaging.

The manufacturing data for the Mixing Department for July 2010 are as follows:

Work in process inventory, July 1, 5,000 gallons (70% completed) . .	$ 6,200
Direct materials cost incurred in July, 60,000 gallons	66,000
Direct labor cost incurred in July	10,500
Factory overhead applied in July	6,405
Total production costs to account for	$89,105

Cost of goods transferred to Packaging in July (includes units in process on July 1), 62,000 gallons.	?
Cost of work in process inventory, July 31, 3,000 gallons, 25% completed as to conversion costs	?

Using the average cost method, the objective is to allocate the total costs of production of $89,105 to the following:

1. The 62,000 gallons completed and transferred to the Packaging Department
2. The 3,000 gallons in the July 31 (ending) work in process inventory

The preceding costs show two question marks. These amounts are determined by preparing a cost of production report using the following four steps:

Step 1. Determine the units to be assigned costs.
Step 2. Compute equivalent units of production.
Step 3. Determine the cost per equivalent unit.
Step 4. Allocate costs to transferred out and partially completed units.

Under the average cost method, all production costs (materials and conversion costs) are combined together for determining equivalent units and cost per equivalent unit. To simplify, this approach is used in this appendix.

Step 1: Determine the Units to Be Assigned Costs
The first step is to determine the units to be assigned costs. A unit can be any measure of completed production, such as tons, gallons, pounds, barrels, or cases. For S&W, a unit is a gallon of ice cream.

S&W's Mixing Department had 65,000 gallons of direct materials to account for during July, as shown here.

Total gallons to account for:	
Work in process, July	5,000 gallons
Received from materials storeroom	60,000
Total units to account for by the Packaging Department	65,000 gallons

There are two groups of units to be assigned costs for the period.

Group 1	Units completed and transferred out
Group 2	Units in the July 31 (ending) work in process inventory

During July, the Mixing Department completed and transferred 62,000 gallons to the Packaging Department. Of the 60,000 gallons started in July, 57,000 (60,000 − 3,000) gallons were completed and transferred to the Packaging Department. Thus, the ending work in process inventory consists of 3,000 gallons.

The total units (gallons) to be assigned costs for S&W can be summarized as follows:

Group 1	Units transferred out to the Packaging Department in July	62,000 gallons
Group 2	Work in process inventory, July 31	3,000
	Total gallons to be assigned costs	65,000 gallons

The total units (gallons) to be assigned costs (65,000 gallons) equal the total units to account for (65,000 gallons).

Step 2: Compute Equivalent Units of Production

S&W has 3,000 gallons of whole units in the work in process inventory for the Mixing Department on July 31. Since these units are 25% complete, the number of equivalent units in process in the Mixing Department on July 31 is 750 gallons (3,000 gallons × 25%). Since the units transferred to the Packaging Department have been completed, the whole units (62,000 gallons) transferred are the same as the equivalent units transferred.

The total equivalent units of production for the Mixing Department are determined by adding the equivalent units in the ending work in process inventory to the units transferred and completed during the period, as shown below.

Equivalent units completed and transferred to the Packaging Department during July	62,000 gallons
Equivalent units in ending work in process, July 31 . .	750
Total equivalent units	62,750 gallons

Step 3: Determine the Cost per Equivalent Unit

Since materials and conversion costs are combined under the average cost method, the cost per equivalent unit is determined by dividing the total production costs by the total equivalent units of production as follows:

$$\text{Cost per Equivalent Unit} = \frac{\text{Total Production Costs}}{\text{Total Equivalent Units}}$$

$$\text{Cost per Equivalent Unit} = \frac{\text{Total Production Costs}}{\text{Total Equivalent Units}} = \frac{\$89,105}{62,750 \text{ gallons}} = \$1.42$$

The cost per equivalent unit shown above is used in Step 4 to allocate the production costs to the completed and partially completed units.

Step 4: Allocate Costs to Transferred Out and Partially Completed Units

The cost of transferred and partially completed units is determined by multiplying the cost per equivalent unit times the equivalent units of production. For the Mixing Department, these costs are determined as follows:

Group 1	Transferred out to the Packaging Department (62,000 gallons × $1.42)	$88,040
Group 2	Work in process inventory, July 31 (3,000 gallons × 25% × $1.42) . .	1,065
	Total production costs assigned	$89,105

The Cost of Production Report

The July cost of production report for S&W's Mixing Department is shown in Exhibit 11. This cost of production report summarizes the following:

1. The units for which the department is accountable and the disposition of those units
2. The production costs incurred by the department and the allocation of those costs between completed and partially completed units

Exhibit 11

Cost of Production Report for S&W's Mixing Department— Average Cost

	A	B	C
1	S&W Ice Cream Company		
2	Cost of Production Report—Mixing Department		
3	For the Month Ended July 31, 2010		
4	**UNITS**		
5		Whole Units	Equivalent Units
6			of Production
7	Units to account for during production:		
8	Work in process inventory, July 1	5,000	
9	Received from materials storeroom	60,000	
10	Total units accounted for by the Mixing Department	65,000	
11			
12	Units to be assigned costs:		
13	Transferred to Packaging Department in July	62,000	62,000
14	Inventory in process, July 31 (25% completed)	3,000	750
15	Total units to be assigned costs	65,000	62,750
16			
17	**COSTS**		
18			
19	Cost per equivalent unit:		
20	Total production costs for July in Mixing Department		$89,105
21	Total equivalent units (from Step 2 above)		÷62,750
22	Cost per equivalent unit		$ 1.42
23			
24	Costs assigned to production:		
25	Inventory in process, July 1		$ 6,200
26	Direct materials, direct labor, and factory overhead incurred in July		82,905
27	Total costs accounted for by the Mixing Department		$89,105
28			
29			
30	Costs allocated to completed and partially completed units:		
31	Transferred to Packaging Department in July (62,000 gallons × $1.42)		$88,040
32	Inventory in process, July 31 (3,000 gallons × 25% × $1.42)		1,065
33	Total costs assigned by the Mixing Department		$89,105
34			

Step 1
Step 2
Step 3
Step 4

At a Glance 20

1 Describe process cost systems.

Key Points

The process cost system is best suited for industries that mass produce identical units of a product. Costs are charged to processing departments, rather than to jobs as with the job order cost system. These costs are transferred from one department to the next until production is completed.

Key Learning Outcomes	Example Exercises	Practice Exercises
• Identify the characteristics of a process manufacturer.		
• Compare and contrast the job order cost system with the process cost system.	20-1	20-1A, 20-1B
• Describe the physical and cost flows of a process manufacturer.		

2 Prepare a cost of production report.

Key Points	Key Learning Outcomes	Example Exercises	Practice Exercises
Manufacturing costs must be allocated between the units that have been completed and those that remain within the department. This allocation is accomplished by allocating costs using equivalent units of production during the period for the beginning inventory, units started and completed, and the ending inventory.	• Determine the whole units charged to production and to be assigned costs.	20-2	20-2A, 20-2B
	• Compute the equivalent units with respect to materials.	20-3	20-3A, 20-3B
	• Compute the equivalent units with respect to conversion.	20-4	20-4A, 20-4B
	• Compute the costs per equivalent unit.	20-5	20-5A, 20-5B
	• Allocate the costs to beginning inventory, units started and completed, and ending inventory.	20-6	20-6A, 20-6B
	• Prepare a cost of production report.		

3 Journalize entries for transactions using a process cost system.

Key Points	Key Learning Outcomes	Example Exercises	Practice Exercises
Prepare the summary journal entries for materials, labor, applied factory overhead, and transferred costs incurred in production.	• Prepare journal entries for process costing transactions.	20-7	20-7A, 20-7B
	• Summarize cost flows in T account form.		
	• Compute the ending inventory balances.		

4 Describe and illustrate the use of cost of production reports for decision making.

Key Points	Key Learning Outcomes	Example Exercises	Practice Exercises
The cost of production report provides information for controlling and improving operations. The report(s) can provide details of a department for a single period, or over a period of time.	• Prepare and evaluate a report showing the change in costs per unit by cost element for comparative periods.	20-8	20-8A, 20-8B
Yield measures the quantity of output of production relative to the inputs.	• Compute and interpret yield.		

5 Compare just-in-time processing with traditional manufacturing processing.

Key Points	Key Learning Outcomes	Example Exercises	Practice Exercises
The just-in-time processing philosophy focuses on reducing time, cost, and poor quality within the process.	• Identify the characteristics of a just-in-time process.		

Key Terms

cost of production report (893)
cost per equivalent unit (898)
equivalent units of
   production (895)

first-in, first-out (FIFO)
   method (893)
just-in-time (JIT) processing (909)
manufacturing cells (909)

process cost system (887)
process manufacturer (887)
whole units (895)
yield (908)

Self-Examination Questions (Answers at End of Chapter)

1. For which of the following businesses would the process cost system be most appropriate?
   A. Custom furniture manufacturer
   B. Commercial building contractor
   C. Crude oil refinery
   D. Automobile repair shop
2. There were 2,000 pounds in process at the beginning of the period in the Packing Department. Packing received 24,000 pounds from the Blending Department during the month, of which 3,000 pounds were in process at the end of the month. How many pounds were completed and transferred to finished goods from the Packing Department?
   A. 23,000   C. 26,000
   B. 21,000   D. 29,000
3. Information relating to production in Department A for May is as follows:

May 1 Balance, 1,000 units, ¾ completed $22,150
     31 Direct materials, 5,000 units   75,000
     31 Direct labor   32,500
     31 Factory overhead   16,250

If 500 units were one-fourth completed at May 31, 5,500 units were completed during May, and inventories are costed by the first-in, first-out method, what was the number of equivalent

units of production with respect to conversion costs for May?
   A. 4,500   C. 5,500
   B. 4,875   D. 6,000
4. Based on the data presented in Question 3, what is the conversion cost per equivalent unit?
   A. $10   C. $25
   B. $15   D. $32
5. Information from the accounting system revealed the following:

	Day 1	Day 2	Day 3	Day 4	Day 5
Materials	$20,000	$18,000	$22,000	$20,000	$20,000
Electricity	2,500	3,000	3,500	4,000	4,700
Maintenance	4,000	3,750	3,400	3,000	2,800
Total costs	$26,500	$24,750	$28,900	$27,000	$27,500
Pounds produced	÷10,000	÷9,000	÷11,000	÷10,000	÷10,000
Cost per unit	$ 2.65	$ 2.75	$ 2.63	$ 2.70	$ 2.75

Which of the following statements best interprets this information?
   A. The total costs are out of control.
   B. The product costs have steadily increased because of higher electricity costs.
   C. Electricity costs have steadily increased because of lack of maintenance.
   D. The unit costs reveal a significant operating problem.

Eye Openers

1. Which type of cost system, process or job order, would be best suited for each of the following: (a) TV assembler, (b) building contractor, (c) automobile repair shop, (d) paper manufacturer, (e) custom jewelry manufacturer? Give reasons for your answers.
2. In job order cost accounting, the three elements of manufacturing cost are charged directly to job orders. Why is it not necessary to charge manufacturing costs in process cost accounting to job orders?
3. In a job order cost system, direct labor and factory overhead applied are debited to individual jobs. How are these items treated in a process cost system and why?
4. What are transferred-out materials?
5. What are the four steps for determining the cost of goods completed and the ending inventory?
6. What is meant by the term *equivalent units*?

7. Why is the cost per equivalent unit often determined separately for direct materials and conversion costs?
8. What is the purpose for determining the cost per equivalent unit?
9. Rameriz Company is a process manufacturer with two production departments, Blending and Filling. All direct materials are introduced in Blending from the materials store area. What is included in the cost transferred to Filling?
10. How is actual factory overhead accounted for in a process manufacturer?
11. What is the most important purpose of the cost of production report?
12. How are cost of production reports used for controlling and improving operations?
13. How is "yield" determined for a process manufacturer?
14. What is just-in-time processing?
15. How does just-in-time processing differ from the conventional manufacturing process?

Practice Exercises

PE 20-1A Job order vs. process costing obj. 1 EE 20-1 p. 890	Which of the following industries would typically use job order costing, and which would typically use process costing? Designer clothes manufacturing Home construction Business consulting Plastic manufacturing CD manufacturing Steel manufacturing
PE 20-1B Job order vs. process costing obj. 1 EE 20-1 p. 890	Which of the following industries would typically use job order costing, and which would typically use process costing? Aluminum production Papermaking Gasoline refining Print shop Movie studio Web designer
PE 20-2A Units to be assigned costs obj. 2 EE 20-2 p. 895	Atlas Steel Company has two departments, Casting and Rolling. In the Rolling Department, ingots from the Casting Department are rolled into steel sheet. The Rolling Department received 86,200 tons from the Casting Department. During the period, the Rolling Department completed 83,580 tons, including 4,150 tons of work in process at the beginning of the period. The ending work in process inventory was 6,770 tons. How many tons were started and completed during the period?
PE 20-2B Units to be assigned costs obj. 2 EE 20-2 p. 895	Satin Skin Lotion Company consists of two departments, Blending and Filling. The Filling Department received 480,000 ounces from the Blending Department. During the period, the Filling Department completed 486,000 ounces, including 25,000 ounces of work in process at the beginning of the period. The ending work in process inventory was 19,000 ounces. How many ounces were started and completed during the period?
PE 20-3A Equivalent units of materials cost obj. 2 EE 20-3 p. 896	The Rolling Department of Atlas Steel Company had 4,150 tons in beginning work in process inventory (40% complete). During the period, 83,580 tons were completed. The ending work in process inventory was 6,770 tons (30% complete). What are the total equivalent units for direct materials if materials are added at the beginning of the process?

PE 20-3B
Equivalent units of materials cost
obj. 2
EE 20-3   p. 896

The Filling Department of Satin Skin Lotion Company had 25,000 ounces in beginning work in process inventory (70% complete). During the period, 486,000 ounces were completed. The ending work in process inventory was 19,000 ounces (25% complete). What are the total equivalent units for direct materials if materials are added at the beginning of the process?

PE 20-4A
Equivalent units of conversion costs
obj. 2
EE 20-4   p. 898

The Rolling Department of Atlas Steel Company had 4,150 tons in beginning work in process inventory (40% complete). During the period, 83,580 tons were completed. The ending work in process inventory was 6,770 tons (30% complete). What are the total equivalent units for conversion costs?

PE 20-4B
Equivalent units of conversion costs
obj. 2
EE 20-4   p. 898

The Filling Department of Satin Skin Lotion Company had 25,000 ounces in beginning work in process inventory (70% complete). During the period, 486,000 ounces were completed. The ending work in process inventory was 19,000 ounces (25% complete). What are the total equivalent units for conversion costs?

PE 20-5A
Cost per equivalent unit
obj. 2
EE 20-5   p. 900

The cost of direct materials transferred into the Rolling Department of Atlas Steel Company is $4,654,800. The conversion cost for the period in the Rolling Department is $1,091,363. The total equivalent units for direct materials and conversion are 86,200 tons and 83,951 tons, respectively. Determine the direct materials and conversion costs per equivalent unit.

PE 20-5B
Cost per equivalent unit
obj. 2
EE 20-5   p. 900

The cost of direct materials transferred into the Filling Department of Satin Skin Lotion Company is $216,000. The conversion cost for the period in the Filling Department is $47,325. The total equivalent units for direct materials and conversion are 480,000 ounces and 473,250 ounces, respectively. Determine the direct materials and conversion costs per equivalent unit.

PE 20-6A
Cost of units transferred out and ending work in process
obj. 2
EE 20-6   p. 902

The costs per equivalent unit of direct materials and conversion in the Rolling Department of Atlas Steel Company are $54 and $13, respectively. The equivalent units to be assigned costs are as follows:

	Equivalent Units	
	Direct Materials	Conversion
Inventory in process, beginning of period	0	2,490
Started and completed during the period	79,430	79,430
Transferred out of Rolling (completed)	79,430	81,920
Inventory in process, end of period	6,770	2,031
Total units to be assigned costs	86,200	83,951

The beginning work in process inventory had a cost of $246,000. Determine the cost of completed and transferred-out production and the ending work in process inventory.

PE 20-6B
Cost of units
transferred out
and ending work
in process

obj. 2

EE 20-6 p. 902

The costs per equivalent unit of direct materials and conversion in the Filling Department of Satin Skin Lotion Company are $0.45 and $0.10, respectively. The equivalent units to be assigned costs are as follows:

	Equivalent Units	
	Direct Materials	Conversion
Inventory in process, beginning of period	0	7,500
Started and completed during the period	461,000	461,000
Transferred out of Filling (completed)	461,000	468,500
Inventory in process, end of period	19,000	4,750
Total units to be assigned costs	480,000	473,250

The beginning work in process inventory had a cost of $13,000. Determine the cost of completed and transferred-out production and the ending work in process inventory.

PE 20-7A
Process cost journal
entries

obj. 3

EE 20-7 p. 906

The cost of materials transferred into the Rolling Department of Atlas Steel Company is $4,654,800 from the Casting Department. The conversion cost for the period in the Rolling Department is $1,091,363 ($666,563 factory overhead applied and $424,800 direct labor). The total cost transferred to Finished Goods for the period was $5,600,180. The Rolling Department had a beginning inventory of $246,000.

a. Journalize (1) the cost of transferred-in materials, (2) conversion costs, and (3) the costs transferred out to Finished Goods.
b. Determine the balance of Work in Process—Rolling at the end of the period.

PE 20-7B
Process cost journal
entries

obj. 3

EE 20-7 p. 906

The cost of materials transferred into the Filling Department of Satin Skin Lotion Company is $216,000, including $55,600 from the Blending Department and $160,400 from the materials storeroom. The conversion cost for the period in the Filling Department is $47,325 ($29,300 factory overhead applied and $18,025 direct labor). The total cost transferred to Finished Goods for the period was $267,300. The Filling Department had a beginning inventory of $13,000.

a. Journalize (1) the cost of transferred-in materials, (2) conversion costs, and (3) the costs transferred out to Finished Goods.
b. Determine the balance of Work in Process—Filling at the end of the period.

PE 20-8A
Using process costs
for decision making

obj. 4

EE 20-8 p. 908

The costs of materials consumed in producing good units in the Forming Department were $94,000 and $82,800 for May and June, respectively. The number of equivalent units produced in May and June was 500 tons and 450 tons, respectively. Evaluate the cost of materials between the two months.

PE 20-8B
Using process costs
for decision making

obj. 4

EE 20-8 p. 908

The costs of energy consumed in producing good units in the Baking Department were $162,000 and $160,000 for August and September, respectively. The number of equivalent units produced in August and September was 450,000 pounds and 400,000 pounds, respectively. Evaluate the cost of energy between the two months.

Exercises

EX 20-1
Entries for materials cost flows in a process cost system
objs. 1, 3

The Hershey Foods Company manufactures chocolate confectionery products. The three largest raw materials are cocoa beans, sugar, and dehydrated milk. These raw materials first go into the Blending Department. The blended product is then sent to the Molding Department, where the bars of candy are formed. The candy is then sent to the Packing Department, where the bars are wrapped and boxed. The boxed candy is then sent to the distribution center, where it is eventually sold to food brokers and retailers.

Show the accounts debited and credited for each of the following business events:

a. Materials used by the Blending Department.
b. Transfer of blended product to the Molding Department.
c. Transfer of chocolate to the Packing Department.
d. Transfer of boxed chocolate to the distribution center.
e. Sale of boxed chocolate.

EX 20-2
Flowchart of accounts related to service and processing departments
obj. 1

Alcoa Inc. is the world's largest producer of aluminum products. One product that Alcoa manufactures is aluminum sheet products for the aerospace industry. The entire output of the Smelting Department is transferred to the Rolling Department. Part of the fully processed goods from the Rolling Department are sold as rolled sheet, and the remainder of the goods are transferred to the Converting Department for further processing into sheared sheet.

Prepare a chart of the flow of costs from the processing department accounts into the finished goods accounts and then into the cost of goods sold account. The relevant accounts are as follows:

Cost of Goods Sold	Finished Goods—Rolled Sheet
Materials	Finished Goods—Sheared Sheet
Factory Overhead—Smelting Department	Work in Process—Smelting Department
Factory Overhead—Rolling Department	Work in Process—Rolling Department
Factory Overhead—Converting Department	Work in Process—Converting Department

EX 20-3
Entries for flow of factory costs for process cost system
objs. 1, 3

Domino Foods, Inc., manufactures a sugar product by a continuous process, involving three production departments—Refining, Sifting, and Packing. Assume that records indicate that direct materials, direct labor, and applied factory overhead for the first department, Refining, were $420,000, $148,000, and $97,300, respectively. Also, work in process in the Refining Department at the beginning of the period totaled $23,700, and work in process at the end of the period totaled $29,100.

Journalize the entries to record (a) the flow of costs into the Refining Department during the period for (1) direct materials, (2) direct labor, and (3) factory overhead, and (b) the transfer of production costs to the second department, Sifting.

EX 20-4
Factory overhead rate, entry for applying factory overhead, and factory overhead account balance
objs. 1, 3
✔ a. 130%

The chief cost accountant for Mountain Glade Beverage Co. estimated that total factory overhead cost for the Blending Department for the coming fiscal year beginning March 1 would be $546,000, and total direct labor costs would be $420,000. During March, the actual direct labor cost totaled $36,000, and factory overhead cost incurred totaled $45,000.

a. What is the predetermined factory overhead rate based on direct labor cost?
b. Journalize the entry to apply factory overhead to production for March.
c. What is the March 31 balance of the account Factory Overhead—Blending Department?
d. Does the balance in part (c) represent overapplied or underapplied factory overhead?

EX 20-5
Equivalent units of production
obj. 2
✔ Direct materials, 17,700 units

The Converting Department of Forever Fresh Towel and Tissue Company had 840 units in work in process at the beginning of the period, which were 75% complete. During the period, 17,600 units were completed and transferred to the Packing Department. There were 940 units in process at the end of the period, which were 25% complete. Direct materials are placed into the process at the beginning of production. Determine the number of equivalent units of production with respect to direct materials and conversion costs.

EX 20-6
Equivalent units of production

obj. 2

✔ a. Conversion, 74,095 units

Units of production data for the two departments of Continental Cable and Wire Company for April of the current fiscal year are as follows:

	Drawing Department	Winding Department
Work in process, April 1	5,400 units, 40% completed	2,200 units, 70% completed
Completed and transferred to next processing department during April	74,000 units	73,200 units
Work in process, April 30	4,100 units, 55% completed	3,000 units, 15% completed

If all direct materials are placed in process at the beginning of production, determine the direct materials and conversion equivalent units of production for April for (a) the Drawing Department and (b) the Winding Department.

EX 20-7
Equivalent units of production

obj. 2

✔ b. Conversion, 147,800

The following information concerns production in the Baking Department for March. All direct materials are placed in process at the beginning of production.

ACCOUNT *Work in Process—Baking Department*   ACCOUNT NO.

Date		Item	Debit	Credit	Balance Debit	Balance Credit
Mar.	1	Bal., 8,000 units, ⅖ completed			15,360	
	31	Direct materials, 145,000 units	232,000		247,360	
	31	Direct labor	66,400		313,760	
	31	Factory overhead	37,060		350,820	
	31	Goods finished, 148,000 units		340,720	10,100	
	31	Bal., units, ⅗ completed			10,100	

a. Determine the number of units in work in process inventory at the end of the month.
b. Determine the equivalent units of production for direct materials and conversion costs in March.

EX 20-8
Costs per equivalent unit

obj. 2

✔ a. 2. Conversion cost per equivalent unit, $0.70

a. Based upon the data in Exercise 20-7, determine the following:
   1. Direct materials cost per equivalent unit.
   2. Conversion cost per equivalent unit.
   3. Cost of the beginning work in process completed during March.
   4. Cost of units started and completed during March.
   5. Cost of the ending work in process.
b. Assuming that the direct materials cost is the same for February and March, did the conversion cost per equivalent unit increase, decrease, or remain the same in March?

EX 20-9
Equivalent units of production

obj. 2

Kellogg Company manufactures cold cereal products, such as *Frosted Flakes*. Assume that the inventory in process on October 1 for the Packing Department included 900 pounds of cereal in the packing machine hopper. In addition, there were 600 empty 24-oz. boxes held in the package carousel of the packing machine. During October, 32,800 boxes of 24-oz. cereal were packaged. Conversion costs are incurred when a box is filled with cereal. On October 31, the packing machine hopper held 1,125 pounds of cereal, and the package carousel held 750 empty 24-oz. (1½-pound) boxes. Assume that once a box is filled with cereal, it is immediately transferred to the finished goods warehouse.

Determine the equivalent units of production for cereal, boxes, and conversion costs for October. An equivalent unit is defined as "pounds" for cereal and "24-oz. boxes" for boxes and conversion costs.

EX 20-10
Costs per equivalent unit

obj. 2

✔ c. $3.10

Georgia Products Inc. completed and transferred 180,000 particle board units of production from the Pressing Department. There was no beginning inventory in process in the department. The ending in-process inventory was 15,000 units, which were ½ complete as to conversion cost. All materials are added at the beginning of the process. Direct materials cost incurred was $604,500, direct labor cost incurred was $99,500, and factory overhead applied was $23,350.

Determine the following for the Pressing Department:

a. Total conversion cost
b. Conversion cost per equivalent unit
c. Direct materials cost per equivalent unit

EX 20-11
Equivalent units of production and related costs

obj. 2

✔ a. 5,800 units

The charges to Work in Process—Assembly Department for a period, together with information concerning production, are as follows. All direct materials are placed in process at the beginning of production.

Work in Process—Assembly Department			
Bal., 4,000 units, 35% completed	9,590	To Finished Goods, 92,200 units	?
Direct materials, 94,000 units @ $1.75	164,500		
Direct labor	134,800		
Factory overhead	52,020		
Bal. ? units, 45% completed	?		

Determine the following:

a. The number of units in work in process inventory at the end of the period.
b. Equivalent units of production for direct materials and conversion.
c. Costs per equivalent unit for direct materials and conversion.
d. Cost of the units started and completed during the period.

EX 20-12
Cost of units completed and in process

objs. 2, 4

✔ 1. $14,790

a. Based on the data in Exercise 20-11, determine the following:
   1. Cost of beginning work in process inventory completed this period.
   2. Cost of units transferred to finished goods during the period.
   3. Cost of ending work in process inventory.
   4. Cost per unit of the completed beginning work in process inventory, rounded to the nearest cent.
b. Did the production costs change from the preceding period? Explain.
c. Assuming that the direct materials cost per unit did not change from the preceding period, did the conversion costs per equivalent unit increase, decrease, or remain the same for the current period?

EX 20-13
Errors in equivalent unit computation

obj. 2

Lone Star Refining Company processes gasoline. On September 1 of the current year, 4,000 units were ⅗ completed in the Blending Department. During September, 36,000 units entered the Blending Department from the Refining Department. During September, the units in process at the beginning of the month were completed. Of the 36,000 units entering the department, all were completed except 5,500 units that were ⅕ completed. The equivalent units for conversion costs for September for the Blending Department were computed as follows:

Equivalent units of production in September:	
To process units in inventory on September 1:	
4,000 × ⅗	2,400
To process units started and completed in September:	
36,000 − 4,000	32,000
To process units in inventory on September 30:	
5,500 × ⅕	1,100
Equivalent units of production	35,500

List the errors in the computation of equivalent units for conversion costs for the Blending Department for September.

EX 20-14
Cost per equivalent unit

obj. 2

✔ a. 69,500 units

The following information concerns production in the Forging Department for June. All direct materials are placed into the process at the beginning of production, and conversion costs are incurred evenly throughout the process. The beginning inventory consists of $86,250 of direct materials.

ACCOUNT *Work in Process—Forging Department*   **ACCOUNT NO.**

Date		Item	Debit	Credit	Balance Debit	Balance Credit
June	1	Bal., 7,500 units, 60% completed			98,850	
	30	Direct materials, 68,000 units	761,600		860,450	
	30	Direct labor	83,380		943,830	
	30	Factory overhead	117,300	?	1,061,130	
	30	Goods transferred, ? units			?	
	30	Bal., 6,000 units, 70% completed			?	

a. Determine the number of units transferred to the next department.
b. Determine the costs per equivalent unit of direct materials and conversion.
c. Determine the cost of units started and completed in June.

EX 20-15
Costs per equivalent unit and production costs

objs. 2, 4

✔ a. $107,550

Based on the data in Exercise 20-14, determine the following:

a. Cost of beginning work in process inventory completed in June.
b. Cost of units transferred to the next department during June.
c. Cost of ending work in process inventory on June 30.
d. Costs per equivalent unit of direct materials and conversion included in the June 1 beginning work in process.
e. The June increase or decrease in costs per equivalent unit for direct materials and conversion from the previous month.

EX 20-16
Cost of production report

obj. 2

✔ d. $2,211

The debits to Work in Process—Roasting Department for St. Arbucks Coffee Company for May 2010, together with information concerning production, are as follows:

Work in process, May 1, 800 pounds, 20% completed	$ 3,280*
*Direct materials (800 × $3.80) $3,040	
Conversion (800 × 20% × $1.50) 240	
$3,280	
Coffee beans added during May, 25,000 pounds	93,750
Conversion costs during May	40,560
Work in process, May 31, 500 pounds, 42% completed	?
Goods finished during May, 25,300 pounds	?

All direct materials are placed in process at the beginning of production. Prepare a cost of production report, presenting the following computations:

a. Direct materials and conversion equivalent units of production for May.
b. Direct materials and conversion costs per equivalent unit for May.
c. Cost of goods finished during May.
d. Cost of work in process at May 31, 2010.

EX 20-17
Cost of production report

obj. 2

✔ Conversion cost per equivalent unit, $3.50

Prepare a cost of production report for the Cutting Department of Perma-Wear Carpet Company for October 2010, using the following data and assuming that all materials are added at the beginning of the process:

Work in process, October 1, 6,000 units, 75% completed	$ 62,250*
*Direct materials (6,000 × $7.60) $45,600	
Conversion (6,000 × 75% × $3.70) 16,650	
$62,250	
Materials added during October from Weaving Department, 162,000 units	$1,215,000
Direct labor for October	362,080
Factory overhead for October	191,550
Goods finished during October (includes goods in process, October 1), 160,400 units	—
Work in process, October 31, 7,600 units, 30% completed	—

EX 20-18
Cost of production
and journal entries

objs. 1, 2, 3

✔ b. $72,930

Performance Castings Inc. casts blades for turbine engines. Within the Casting Department, alloy is first melted in a crucible, then poured into molds to produce the castings. On December 1, there were 800 pounds of alloy in process, which were 60% complete as to conversion. The Work in Process balance for these 800 pounds was $111,680, determined as follows:

Direct materials (800 × $130)	$104,000
Conversion (800 × 60% × $16)	7,680
	$111,680

During December, the Casting Department was charged $945,000 for 7,500 pounds of alloy and $45,072 for direct labor. Factory overhead is applied to the department at a rate of 150% of direct labor. The department transferred out 7,750 pounds of finished castings to the Machining Department. The December 31 inventory in process was 44% complete as to conversion.

a. Prepare the following December journal entries for the Casting Department:
   1. The materials charged to production.
   2. The conversion costs charged to production.
   3. The completed production transferred to the Machining Department.
b. Determine the Work in Process—Casting Department December 31 balance.

EX 20-19
Cost of production
and journal entries

objs. 1, 2, 3

✔ b. $37,914

Franklin Paper Company manufactures newsprint. The product is manufactured in two departments, Papermaking and Converting. Pulp is first placed into a vessel at the beginning of papermaking production. The following information concerns production in the Papermaking Department for January.

ACCOUNT *Work in Process—Papermaking Department*   **ACCOUNT NO.**

Date		Item	Debit	Credit	Balance Debit	Balance Credit
Jan.	1	Bal., 6,500 units, 35% completed			29,250	
	31	Direct materials, 102,000 units	397,800		427,050	
	31	Direct labor	107,600		534,650	
	31	Factory overhead	81,049		615,699	
	31	Goods transferred, 101,400 units		?	?	
	31	Bal., 7,100 units, 80% completed			?	

a. Prepare the following January journal entries for the Papermaking Department:
   1. The materials charged to production.
   2. The conversion costs charged to production.
   3. The completed production transferred to the Converting Department.
b. Determine the Work in Process—Papermaking Department January 31 balance.

EX 20-20
Decision making

obj. 4

Oasis Bottling Company bottles popular beverages in the Bottling Department. The beverages are produced by blending concentrate with water and sugar. The concentrate is purchased from a concentrate producer. The concentrate producer sets higher prices for the more popular concentrate flavors. Below is a simplified Bottling Department cost of production report separating the cost of bottling the four flavors.

	A	B	C	D	E
1		Orange	Cola	Lemon-Lime	Root Beer
2	Concentrate	$ 6,650	$135,000	$ 99,000	$3,600
3	Water	2,100	36,000	27,000	1,200
4	Sugar	3,500	60,000	45,000	2,000
5	Bottles	7,700	132,000	99,000	4,400
6	Flavor changeover	3,500	6,000	4,500	5,000
7	Conversion cost	2,625	24,000	18,000	1,500
8	Total cost transferred to finished goods	$26,075	$393,000	$292,500	$17,700
9	Number of cases	3,500	60,000	45,000	2,000
10					

Beginning and ending work in process inventories are negligible, so are omitted from the cost of production report. The flavor changeover cost represents the cost of cleaning the bottling machines between production runs of different flavors.

➤ Prepare a memo to the production manager analyzing this comparative cost information. In your memo, provide recommendations for further action, along with supporting schedules showing the total cost per case and cost per case by cost element.

EX 20-21
Decision making
obj. **4**

Instant Memories Inc. produces photographic paper for printing digital images. One of the processes for this operation is a coating (solvent spreading) operation, where chemicals are coated on to paper stock. There has been some concern about the cost performance of this operation. As a result, you have begun an investigation. You first discover that all materials and conversion prices have been stable for the last six months. Thus, increases in prices for inputs are not an explanation for increasing costs. However, you have discovered three possible problems from some of the operating personnel whose quotes follow:

Operator 1: "I've been keeping an eye on my operating room instruments. I feel as though our energy consumption is becoming less efficient."

Operator 2: "Every time the coating machine goes down, we produce waste on shutdown and subsequent startup. It seems like during the last half year we have had more unscheduled machine shutdowns than in the past. Thus, I feel as though our yields must be dropping."

Operator 3: "My sense is that our coating costs are going up. It seems to me like we are spreading a thicker coating than we should. Perhaps the coating machine needs to be recalibrated."

The Coating Department had no beginning or ending inventories for any month during the study period. The following data from the cost of production report are made available:

	A	B	C	D	E	F	G
1		January	February	March	April	May	June
2	Paper stock	$72,960	$69,120	$ 76,800	$69,120	$65,280	$61,440
3	Coating	$16,416	$17,280	$ 21,120	$21,600	$21,216	$23,040
4	Conversion cost (incl. energy)	$36,480	$34,560	$ 38,400	$34,560	$32,640	$30,720
5	Pounds input to the process	95,000	90,000	100,000	90,000	85,000	80,000
6	Pounds transferred out	91,200	86,400	96,000	86,400	81,600	76,800
7							

a. Prepare a table showing the paper cost per output pound, coating cost per output pound, conversion cost per output pound, and yield for each month.
b. Interpret your table results.

EX 20-22
Just-in-time
manufacturing
obj. **5**

The following are some quotes provided by a number of managers at Solaris Machining Company regarding the company's planned move toward a just-in-time manufacturing system:

Director of Sales: I'm afraid we'll miss some sales if we don't keep a large stock of items on hand just in case demand increases. It only makes sense to me to keep large inventories in order to assure product availability for our customers.

Director of Purchasing: I'm very concerned about moving to a just-in-time system for materials. What would happen if one of our suppliers were unable to make a shipment? A supplier could fall behind in production or have a quality problem. Without some safety stock in our materials, our whole plant would shut down.

Director of Manufacturing: If we go to just-in-time, I think our factory output will drop. We need in-process inventory in order to "smooth out" the inevitable problems that occur during manufacturing. For example, if a machine that is used to process a product breaks down, it would starve the next machine if I don't have in-process inventory between the two machines. If I have in-process inventory, then I can keep the next operation busy while I fix the broken machine. Thus, the in-process inventories give me a safety valve that I can use to keep things running when things go wrong.

➤ How would you respond to these managers?

**Appendix
EX 20-23**
Equivalent units of
production: average
cost method

✔ a. 26,300

The Converting Department of Osaka Napkin Company uses the average cost method and had 2,000 units in work in process that were 60% complete at the beginning of the period. During the period, 25,200 units were completed and transferred to the Packing Department. There were 1,100 units in process that were 30% complete at the end of the period.

a. Determine the number of whole units to be accounted for and to be assigned costs for the period.
b. Determine the number of equivalent units of production for the period.

**Appendix
EX 20-24**
Equivalent units of
production: average
cost method

✔ a. 92,500 units to
be accounted for

Units of production data for the two departments of Atlantic Cable and Wire Company for August of the current fiscal year are as follows:

	Drawing Department	Winding Department
Work in process, August 1	2,100 units, 50% completed	2,000 units, 30% completed
Completed and transferred to next processing department during August	90,000 units	89,200 units
Work in process, August 31	2,500 units, 55% completed	2,800 units, 25% completed

Each department uses the average cost method.

a. Determine the number of whole units to be accounted for and to be assigned costs and the equivalent units of production for the Drawing Department.
b. Determine the number of whole units to be accounted for and to be assigned costs and the equivalent units of production for the Winding Department.

**Appendix
EX 20-25**
Equivalent units of
production: average
cost method

✔ a. 16,500

The following information concerns production in the Finishing Department for March. The Finishing Department uses the average cost method.

ACCOUNT *Work in Process—Finishing Department*   **ACCOUNT NO.**

Date		Item	Debit	Credit	Balance Debit	Balance Credit
Mar.	1	Bal., 15,000 units, 40% completed			24,600	
	31	Direct materials, 144,000 units	345,000		369,600	
	31	Direct labor	163,200		532,800	
	31	Factory overhead	86,700		619,500	
	31	Goods transferred, 142,500 units		578,550	40,950	
	31	Bal., ? units, 60% completed			40,950	

a. Determine the number of units in work in process inventory at the end of the month.
b. Determine the number of whole units to be accounted for and to be assigned costs and the equivalent units of production for March.

**Appendix
EX 20-26**
Equivalent units of
production and
related costs

✔ b. 86,870 units

The charges to Work in Process—Baking Department for a period as well as information concerning production are as follows. The Baking Department uses the average cost method, and all direct materials are placed in process during production.

Work in Process—Baking Department

Bal., 8,000 units, 70% completed	12,900	To Finished Goods, 85,400 units	?
Direct materials, 82,300 units	161,000		
Direct labor	91,800		
Factory overhead	81,780		
Bal., 4,900 units, 30% completed	?		

Determine the following:

a. The number of whole units to be accounted for and to be assigned costs.
b. The number of equivalent units of production.
c. The cost per equivalent unit.
d. The cost of the units transferred to Finished Goods.
e. The cost of ending Work in Process.

**Appendix
EX 20-27
Cost per equivalent
unit: average cost
method**

✔ a. $11.50

The following information concerns production in the Forging Department for June. The Forging Department uses the average cost method.

			ACCOUNT *Work in Process—Forging Department*			ACCOUNT NO.	
						Balance	
Date			**Item**	**Debit**	**Credit**	**Debit**	**Credit**
June	1		Bal., 2,000 units, 40% completed			9,120	
	30		Direct materials, 46,200 units	324,800		333,920	
	30		Direct labor	137,045		470,965	
	30		Factory overhead	75,400		546,365	
	30		Goods transferred, 45,900 units		?	?	
	30		Bal., 2,300 units, 70% completed			?	

a. Determine the cost per equivalent unit.
b. Determine the cost of the units transferred to Finished Goods.
c. Determine the cost of ending Work in Process.

**Appendix
EX 20-28
Cost of production
report: average cost
method**

✔ Cost per equiva-
lent unit, $6.00

The increases to Work in Process—Roasting Department for Boston Coffee Company for December 2010 as well as information concerning production are as follows:

Work in process, December 1, 1,500 pounds, 40% completed	$ 3,600
Coffee beans added during December, 92,500 pounds	391,420
Conversion costs during December	167,900
Work in process, December 31, 900 pounds, 80% completed	—
Goods finished during December, 93,100 pounds	—

Prepare a cost of production report, using the average cost method.

**Appendix
EX 20-29
Cost of production
report: average cost
method**

✔ Cost per equiva-
lent unit, $11.00

Prepare a cost of production report for the Cutting Department of Chota Carpet Company for October 2010. Use the average cost method with the following data:

Work in process, October 1, 9,000 units, 75% completed	$ 75,000
Materials added during October from Weaving Department, 105,000 units	807,750
Direct labor for October	175,200
Factory overhead for October	92,100
Goods finished during October (includes goods in process, October 1), 103,500 units	—
Work in process, October 31, 10,500 units, 10% completed	—

Problems Series A

**PR 20-1A
Entries for process
cost system**

objs. 1, 3

✔ 2. Materials
December 31
balance, $14,120

Cincinnati Soap Company manufactures powdered detergent. Phosphate is placed in process in the Making Department, where it is turned into granulars. The output of Making is transferred to the Packing Department, where packaging is added at the beginning of the process. On December 1, Cincinnati Soap Company had the following inventories:

Finished Goods	$12,300
Work in Process—Making	4,780
Work in Process—Packing	6,230
Materials	2,700

Departmental accounts are maintained for factory overhead, which both have zero balances on December 1.

Manufacturing operations for December are summarized as follows:

a. Materials purchased on account	$153,200
b. Materials requisitioned for use:	
Phosphate—Making Department	$101,200
Packaging—Packing Department	35,200
Indirect materials—Making Department	3,960
Indirect materials—Packing Department	1,420
c. Labor used:	
Direct labor—Making Department	$72,300
Direct labor—Packing Department	48,800
Indirect labor—Making Department	14,000
Indirect labor—Packing Department	25,100
d. Depreciation charged on fixed assets:	
Making Department	$13,200
Packing Department	10,900
e. Expired prepaid factory insurance:	
Making Department	$2,500
Packing Department	1,000
f. Applied factory overhead:	
Making Department	$34,500
Packing Department	38,120
g. Production costs transferred from Making Department to Packing Department	$208,600
h. Production costs transferred from Packing Department to Finished Goods	$328,300
i. Cost of goods sold during the period	$329,500

Instructions
1. Journalize the entries to record the operations, identifying each entry by letter.
2. Compute the December 31 balances of the inventory accounts.
3. Compute the December 31 balances of the factory overhead accounts.

PR 20-2A
Cost of production report

objs. 2, 4

✔ 1. Conversion rate per equivalent unit, $0.80

Venus Chocolate Company processes chocolate into candy bars. The process begins by placing direct materials (raw chocolate, milk, and sugar) into the Blending Department. All materials are placed into production at the beginning of the blending process. After blending, the milk chocolate is then transferred to the Molding Department, where the milk chocolate is formed into candy bars. The following is a partial work in process account of the Blending Department at January 31, 2010:

ACCOUNT *Work in Process—Blending Department*					ACCOUNT NO.	
					Balance	
Date		Item	Debit	Credit	Debit	Credit
Jan.	1	Bal., 6,000 units, ⅗ completed			21,840	
	31	Direct materials, 240,000 units	768,000		789,840	
	31	Direct labor	153,200		943,040	
	31	Factory overhead	38,160		981,200	
	31	Goods transferred, 242,000 units		?		
	31	Bal., ? units, ⅕ completed			?	

Instructions
1. Prepare a cost of production report, and identify the missing amounts for Work in Process—Blending Department.
2. Assuming that the January 1 work in process inventory includes direct materials of $18,600, determine the increase or decrease in the cost per equivalent unit for direct materials and conversion between December and January.

PR 20-3A

Equivalent units and related costs; cost of production report; entries

objs. 2, 3, 4

✔ 2. Transferred to finished goods, $858,150

Wilmington Chemical Company manufactures specialty chemicals by a series of three processes, all materials being introduced in the Distilling Department. From the Distilling Department, the materials pass through the Reaction and Filling departments, emerging as finished chemicals.

The balance in the account Work in Process—Filling was as follows on December 1, 2010:

Work in Process—Filling Department
(2,800 units, 60% completed):
Direct materials (2,800 × $14.60)	$40,880
Conversion (2,800 × 60% × $9.25)	15,540
	$56,420

The following costs were charged to Work in Process—Filling during December:

Direct materials transferred from Reaction Department: 36,200 units at $14.40 a unit	$521,280
Direct labor	167,900
Factory overhead	166,025

During December, 35,900 units of specialty chemicals were completed. Work in Process—Filling Department on December 31 was 3,100 units, 30% completed.

Instructions
1. Prepare a cost of production report for the Filling Department for December.
2. Journalize the entries for costs transferred from Reaction to Filling and the cost transferred from filling to finished goods.
3. Determine the increase or decrease in the cost per equivalent unit from November to December for direct materials and conversion costs.
4. ━━━▶ Discuss the uses of the cost of production report and the results of part (3).

PR 20-4A

Work in process account data for two months; cost of production reports

objs. 1, 2, 3

✔ 1. c. Transferred to finished goods in June, $918,600

Pittsburgh Aluminum Company uses a process cost system to record the costs of manufacturing rolled aluminum, which requires a series of four processes. Materials are entered at the beginning of the Rolling process. The inventory of Work in Process—Rolling on June 1, 2010, and debits to the account during June were as follows:

Bal., 3,000 units, ¼ completed:
Direct materials (3,000 × $14.00)	$42,000
Conversion (3,000 × ¼ × $8.30)	6,225
	$48,225

From Smelting Department, 42,000 units	$596,400
Direct labor	212,435
Factory overhead	156,040

During June, 3,000 units in process on June 1 were completed, and of the 42,000 units entering the department, all were completed except 4,500 units that were ⅖ completed.

Charges to Work in Process—Rolling for July were as follows:

From Smelting Department, 45,000 units	$652,500
Direct labor	219,900
Factory overhead	160,800

During July, the units in process at the beginning of the month were completed, and of the 45,000 units entering the department, all were completed except 6,000 units that were ⅔ completed.

Instructions
1. Enter the balance as of June 1, 2010, in a four-column account for Work in Process—Rolling. Record the debits and the credits in the account for June. Construct a cost of production report and present computations for determining (a) equivalent units of production for materials and conversion, (b) costs per equivalent unit, (c) cost of goods finished, differentiating between units started in the prior period and units started and finished in June, and (d) work in process inventory.

2. Provide the same information for July by recording the July transactions in the four-column work in process account. Construct a cost of production report, and present the July computations (a through d) listed in part (1).

3. ➤ Comment on the change in costs per equivalent unit for May through July for direct materials and conversion cost.

Appendix
PR 20-5A
Equivalent units and related costs; cost of production report: average cost method

✔ Transferred to Packaging Dept., $74,000

Olde Stone Mill Flour Company manufactures flour by a series of three processes, beginning in the Milling Department. From the Milling Department, the materials pass through the Sifting and Packaging departments, emerging as packaged refined flour.

The balance in the account Work in Process—Sifting Department was as follows on December 1, 2010:

Work in Process—Sifting Department (1,200 units, 75% completed)	$4,500

The following costs were charged to Work in Process—Sifting Department during December:

Direct materials transferred from Milling Department: 14,500 units	$51,400
Direct labor	14,350
Factory overhead	7,125

During December, 14,800 units of flour were completed. Work in Process—Sifting Department on December 31 was 900 units, 75% completed.

Instructions
Prepare a cost of production report for the Sifting Department for December, using the average cost method.

Problems Series B

PR 20-1B
Entries for process cost system
objs. 1, 3

KA
KLOOSTER & ALLEN

✔ 2. Materials July 31 balance, $42,800

Floor Guard Carpet Company manufactures carpets. Fiber is placed in process in the Spinning Department, where it is spun into yarn. The output of the Spinning Department is transferred to the Tufting Department, where carpet backing is added at the beginning of the process and the process is completed. On July 1, Floor Guard Carpet Company had the following inventories:

Finished Goods	$51,200
Work in Process—Spinning Department	8,500
Work in Process—Tufting Department	23,600
Materials	41,100

Departmental accounts are maintained for factory overhead, and both have zero balances on July 1.

Manufacturing operations for July are summarized as follows:

a. Materials purchased on account	$825,300
b. Materials requisitioned for use:	
Fiber—Spinning Department	$547,200
Carpet backing—Tufting Department	215,300
Indirect materials—Spinning Department	44,200
Indirect materials—Tufting Department	16,900
c. Labor used:	
Direct labor—Spinning Department	$234,700
Direct labor—Tufting Department	189,900
Indirect labor—Spinning Department	124,200
Indirect labor—Tufting Department	110,000
d. Depreciation charged on fixed assets:	
Spinning Department	$56,700
Tufting Department	32,500
e. Expired prepaid factory insurance:	
Spinning Department	$12,000
Tufting Department	9,000
f. Applied factory overhead:	
Spinning Department	$235,600
Tufting Department	169,800

g. Production costs transferred from Spinning Department to Tufting Department $1,021,600
h. Production costs transferred from Tufting Department to Finished Goods $1,590,200
i. Cost of goods sold during the period $1,600,700

Instructions

1. Journalize the entries to record the operations, identifying each entry by letter.
2. Compute the July 31 balances of the inventory accounts.
3. Compute the July 31 balances of the factory overhead accounts.

PR 20-2B
Cost of production report
objs. 2, 4

✔ 1. Conversion cost per equivalent unit, $1.50

Ariba Coffee Company roasts and packs coffee beans. The process begins by placing coffee beans into the Roasting Department. From the Roasting Department, coffee beans are then transferred to the Packing Department. The following is a partial work in process account of the Roasting Department at March 31, 2010:

ACCOUNT Work in Process—Roasting Department				ACCOUNT NO.	
				Balance	
Date	**Item**	**Debit**	**Credit**	**Debit**	**Credit**
Mar. 1	Bal., 10,500 units, 30% completed			59,640	
31	Direct materials, 156,000 units	780,000		839,640	
31	Direct labor	142,225		981,865	
31	Factory overhead	92,990		1,074,855	
31	Goods transferred, 155,600 units		?		
31	Bal., ? units, 40% completed			?	

Instructions

1. Prepare a cost of production report, and identify the missing amounts for Work in Process—Roasting Department.
2. Assuming that the March 1 work in process inventory includes $54,600 of direct materials, determine the increase or decrease in the cost per equivalent unit for direct materials and conversion between February and March.

PR 20-3B
Equivalent units and related costs; cost of production report; entries
objs. 2, 3, 4

✔ 2. Transferred to Packaging Dept., $1,000,460

Angel White Flour Company manufactures flour by a series of three processes, beginning with wheat grain being introduced in the Milling Department. From the Milling Department, the materials pass through the Sifting and Packaging departments, emerging as packaged refined flour.

The balance in the account Work in Process—Sifting Department was as follows on August 1, 2010:

Work in Process—Sifting Department (12,000 units, ⅗ completed):
Direct materials (12,000 × $2.35) $28,200
Conversion (12,000 × ⅗ × $0.70)   5,040
                                       $33,240

The following costs were charged to Work in Process—Sifting Department during August:

Direct materials transferred from Milling Department:
320,000 units at $2.45 a unit $784,000
Direct labor   179,000
Factory overhead   30,950

During August, 323,000 units of flour were completed. Work in Process—Sifting Department on August 31 was 9,000 units, ⅘ completed.

Instructions

1. Prepare a cost of production report for the Sifting Department for August.
2. Journalize the entries for costs transferred from Milling to Sifting and the costs transferred from Sifting to Packaging.
3. Determine the increase or decrease in the cost per equivalent unit from July to August for direct materials and conversion costs.
4. ▬▬▶ Discuss the uses of the cost of production report and the results of part (3).

PR 20-4B
Work in process account data for two months; cost of production reports

objs. 1, 2, 3

✔ 1. c. Transferred to finished goods in February, $452,368

Hearty Soup Co. uses a process cost system to record the costs of processing soup, which requires a series of three processes. Materials are entered at the beginning of the Filling process. The inventory of Work in Process—Filling on February 1 and debits to the account during February 2010 were as follows:

Bal., 3,200 units, 30% completed:	
Direct materials (3,200 × $4.50)	$14,400
Conversion (3,200 × 30% × $2.00)	1,920
	$16,320
From Cooking Department, 65,900 units	$303,140
Direct labor	87,450
Factory overhead	61,908

During February, 3,200 units in process on February 1 were completed, and of the 65,900 units entering the department, all were completed except 2,500 units that were 90% completed.

Charges to Work in Process—Filling for March were as follows:

From Cooking Department, 73,500 units	$352,800
Direct labor	103,345
Factory overhead	74,530

During March, the units in process at the beginning of the month were completed, and of the 73,500 units entering the department, all were completed except 4,000 units that were 35% completed.

Instructions
1. Enter the balance as of February 1, 2010, in a four-column account for Work in Process—Filling. Record the debits and the credits in the account for February. Construct a cost of production report, and present computations for determining (a) equivalent units of production for materials and conversion, (b) costs per equivalent unit, (c) cost of goods finished, differentiating between units started in the prior period and units started and finished in February, and (d) work in process inventory.
2. Provide the same information for March by recording the March transactions in the four-column work in process account. Construct a cost of production report, and present the March computations (a through d) listed in part (1).
3. ➤ Comment on the change in costs per equivalent unit for January through March for direct materials and conversion costs.

Appendix
PR 20-5B
Cost of production report: average cost method

✔ Cost per equivalent unit, $4.90

Starburst Coffee Company roasts and packs coffee beans. The process begins in the Roasting Department. From the Roasting Department, the coffee beans are transferred to the Packing Department. The following is a partial work in process account of the Roasting Department at January 31, 2010:

ACCOUNT *Work in Process—Roasting Department*				ACCOUNT NO.		
					Balance	
Date		Item	Debit	Credit	Debit	Credit
Jan.	1	Bal., 9,400 units, 80% completed			37,600	
	31	Direct materials, 65,200 units	135,600		173,200	
	31	Direct labor	109,152		282,352	
	31	Factory overhead	67,900		350,252	
	31	Goods transferred, 66,800 units		?	?	
	31	Bal., ? units, 60% completed			?	

Instructions

Prepare a cost of production report, using the average cost method, and identify the missing amounts for Work in Process—Roasting Department.

Special Activities

You can access the special activities online at **www.cengage.com/accounting/reeve**.

Excel Success Special Activities

SA 20-1
Cost per equivalent unit

Brazil Aluminum, Inc., processes aluminum. The Smelting Department had the following equivalent units with respect to direct materials and conversion:

	Equivalent Units	
	Direct Materials	Conversion
Inventory in process, October 1	—	2,400
Started and completed in October	95,000	95,000
Transferred out to Rolling	95,000	97,400
Inventory in process, October 31	6,000	1,200
Total equivalent units to be assigned costs (tons)	101,000	98,600

	Direct Materials	Conversion
Costs	$1,727,100	$423,980

a. Open the Excel file *SA20-1*.
b. Develop a spreadsheet to determine the cost per equivalent unit for direct materials and for conversion.
c. When you have completed the spreadsheet, perform a "save as," replacing the entire file name with the following:

   SA20-1_[your first name initial]_[your last name]

SA 20-2
Cost per equivalent unit

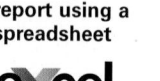

The Crumble Cookie Company makes cookies using two departments, Mixing and Baking. The Baking Department started and completed 56,000 units during August. The Baking Department had the following units of inventory on August 1 and August 31, 2011.

Aug. 1, 2011 Work in Process—Baking   3,200 units   (¾ complete as to conversion costs)

Aug. 31, 2011 Work in Process—Baking   1,600 units   (¼ complete as to conversion costs)

Total costs incurred during the month in the Baking Department were as follows:

Direct materials	$1,238,400
Conversion	280,220

a. Open the Excel file *SA20-2*.
b. Develop a spreadsheet to determine the cost per equivalent unit for direct materials and for conversion.
c. When you have completed the spreadsheet, perform a "save as," replacing the entire file name with the following:

   SA20-2_[your first name initial]_[your last name]

SA 20-3
Cost of production report using a spreadsheet

Atlantic Beverages, Inc., produces soft drinks. The Mixing Department had the following information with respect to the Work in Process—Mixing Department for June 2011:

	Units	Amount	Percent Complete
Work in Process, June 1, 2011	5,000	$ 41,000	60%
Direct materials received from Materials	36,000	198,000	
Direct labor		101,890	
Factory overhead		61,640	
Work in Process, June 30, 2011	3,500		30%

a. Open the Excel file *SA20-3*.
b. Prepare a cost of production report using spreadsheet software for the Mixing Department for June, 2011.
c. When you have completed the spreadsheet, perform a "save as," replacing the entire file name with the following:

SA20-3_[your first name initial]_[your last name]

SA 20-4
Cost of production report using a spreadsheet

Alberta Paper Company produces paper. The Converting Department had the following information with respect to the Work in Process—Converting for April 1, 2011:

Work in Process—Converting (1,200 units, ⅖ completed) $35,800

The following costs were charged to Work in Process—Converting during April:

Direct materials transferred from Rolling, 21,400 units $175,480
Direct labor   53,600
Factory overhead   71,920

During April, 21,100 units of paper were completed in the Converting Department and transferred to finished goods. Inventories for April 30, 2011, were 1,500 whole units that were 1/5 completed as to conversion costs.

Prepare a cost of production report using spreadsheet software for the Converting Department for April 2011.

a. Open the Excel file *SA20-4*.
b. Prepare a cost of production report using spreadsheet software for the Converting Department for April 2011.
c. When you have completed the spreadsheet, perform a "save as," replacing the entire file name with the following:

SA20-4_[your first name initial]_[your last name]

Answers to Self-Examination Questions

1. **C** The process cost system is most appropriate for a business where manufacturing is conducted by continuous operations and involves a series of uniform production processes, such as the processing of crude oil (answer C). The job order cost system is most appropriate for a business where the product is made to customers' specifications, such as custom furniture manufacturing (answer A), commercial building construction (answer B), or automobile repair shop (answer D).

2. **A** The total pounds transferred to finished goods (23,000) are the 2,000 in-process pounds at the beginning of the period plus the number of pounds started and completed during the month, 21,000 (24,000 − 3,000). Answer B incorrectly assumes that the beginning inventory is not transferred during the month. Answer C assumes that all 24,000 pounds started during the month are transferred to finished goods, instead of only the portion started and completed. Answer D incorrectly adds all the numbers together.

3. **B** The number of units that could have been produced from start to finish during a period is termed equivalent units. The 4,875 equivalent units (answer B) is determined as follows:

To process units in inventory on May 1	
(1,000 × ¼)	250
To process units started and completed	
in May (5,500 units − 1,000 units)	4,500
To process units in inventory on May 31	
(500 units × ¼)	125
Equivalent units of production in May	4,875

4. **A** The conversion costs (direct labor and factory overhead) totaling $48,750 are divided by the number of equivalent units (4,875) to determine the unit conversion cost of $10 (answer A).

5. **C** The electricity costs have increased, and maintenance costs have decreased. Answer C would be a reasonable explanation for these results. The total costs, materials costs, and costs per unit do not reveal any type of pattern over the time period. In fact, the materials costs have stayed at exactly $2.00 per pound over the time period. This demonstrates that aggregated numbers can sometimes hide underlying information that can be used to improve the process.

Cost Behavior and Cost-Volume-Profit Analysis

N E T F L I X

How do you decide whether you are going to buy or rent a video game? It probably depends on how much you think you are going to use the game. If you are going to play the game a lot, you are probably better off buying the game than renting. The one time cost of buying the game would be much less expensive than the cost of multiple rentals. If, on the other hand, you are uncertain about how frequently you are going to play the game, it may be less expensive to rent. The cost of an individual rental is much less than the cost of purchase. Understanding how the costs of rental and purchase behave affects your decision.

Understanding how costs behave is also important to companies like Netflix, an online DVD movie rental service. For a fixed monthly fee, Netflix customers can select DVDs from their own computer, and have the DVDs delivered to their home along with a prepaid return envelope. Customers can keep the DVDs as long as they want, but must return the DVDs before they rent additional movies. The number of DVDs that members can check out at one time varies between one and three, depending on their subscription plan.

In order to entice customers to subscribe, Netflix had to invest in a well-stocked library of DVD titles, and build a warehouse to hold and distribute these titles. These costs do not change with the number of subscriptions. But how many subscriptions does Netflix need in order to make a profit? That depends on the price of each subscription, the costs incurred with each DVD rental, and the costs associated with maintaining the DVD library.

As with Netflix, understanding how costs behave, and the relationship between costs, profits, and volume is important for all businesses. This chapter discusses commonly used methods for classifying costs according to how they change. Techniques that management can use to evaluate costs in order to make sound business decisions are also discussed.

After studying this chapter, you should be able to:

1 Classify costs as variable costs, fixed costs, or mixed costs.

2 Compute the contribution margin, the contribution margin ratio, and the unit contribution margin.

3 Determine the break-even point and sales necessary to achieve a target profit.

4 Using a cost-volume-profit chart and a profit-volume chart, determine the break-even point and sales necessary to achieve a target profit.

5 Compute the break-even point for a company selling more than one product, the operating leverage, and the margin of safety.

Cost Behavior
Variable Costs
Fixed Costs
Mixed Costs
EE 21-1 (page 943) excel SUCCESS
Summary of Cost Behavior Concepts

Cost-Volume-Profit Relationships
Contribution Margin
Contribution Margin Ratio
Unit Contribution Margin
EE 21-2 (page 946)

Mathematical Approach to Cost-Volume-Profit Analysis
Break-Even Point
EE 21-3 (page 950)
Target Profit
EE 21-4 (page 951)

Graphic Approach to Cost-Volume-Profit Analysis
Cost-Volume-Profit (Break-Even) Chart
Profit-Volume Chart
Use of Computers in Cost-Volume-Profit Analysis
Assumptions of Cost-Volume-Profit Analysis

Special Cost-Volume-Profit Relationships
Sales Mix Considerations
EE 21-5 (page 958)
Operating Leverage
EE 21-6 (page 960)
Margin of Safety
EE 21-7 (page 961)

At a Glance   Menu   Turn to pg 964

South-Western

1 Classify costs as variable costs, fixed costs, or mixed costs.

Cost Behavior

Cost behavior is the manner in which a cost changes as a related activity changes. The behavior of costs is useful to managers for a variety of reasons. For example, knowing how costs behave allows managers to predict profits as sales and production volumes change. Knowing how costs behave is also useful for estimating costs, which affects a variety of decisions such as whether to replace a machine.

Understanding the behavior of a cost depends on:

1. Identifying the activities that cause the cost to change. These activities are called **activity bases** (or *activity drivers*).
2. Specifying the range of activity over which the changes in the cost are of interest. This range of activity is called the **relevant range.**

To illustrate, assume that a hospital is concerned about planning and controlling patient food costs. A good activity base is number of patients who *stay* overnight in the hospital. The number of patients who are *treated* is not as good an activity base since some patients are outpatients and, thus, do not consume food. Once an activity base is identified, food costs can then be analyzed over the range of the number of patients who normally stay in the hospital (the relevant range).

Costs are normally classified as variable costs, fixed costs, or mixed costs.

Variable Costs

Variable costs are costs that vary in proportion to changes in the activity base. When the activity base is units produced, direct materials and direct labor costs are normally classified as variable costs.

To illustrate, assume that Jason Sound Inc. produces stereo systems. The parts for the stereo systems are purchased from suppliers for $10 per unit and are assembled by Jason Sound Inc. For Model JS-12, the direct materials costs for the relevant range of 5,000 to 30,000 units of production are shown below.

Number of Units of Model JS-12 Produced	Direct Materials Cost per Unit	Total Direct Materials Cost
5,000 units	$10	$ 50,000
10,000	10	100,000
15,000	10	150,000
20,000	10	200,000
25,000	10	250,000
30,000	10	300,000

As shown above, variable costs have the following characteristics:

1. *Cost per unit* remains the same regardless of changes in the activity base. For Model JS-12, the cost per unit is $10.

2. *Total cost* changes in proportion to changes in the activity base. For Model JS-12, the direct materials cost for 10,000 units ($100,000) is twice the direct materials cost for 5,000 units ($50,000).

Exhibit 1 illustrates how the variable costs for direct materials for Model JS-12 behave in total and on a per-unit basis as production changes.

Exhibit 1

Variable Cost Graphs

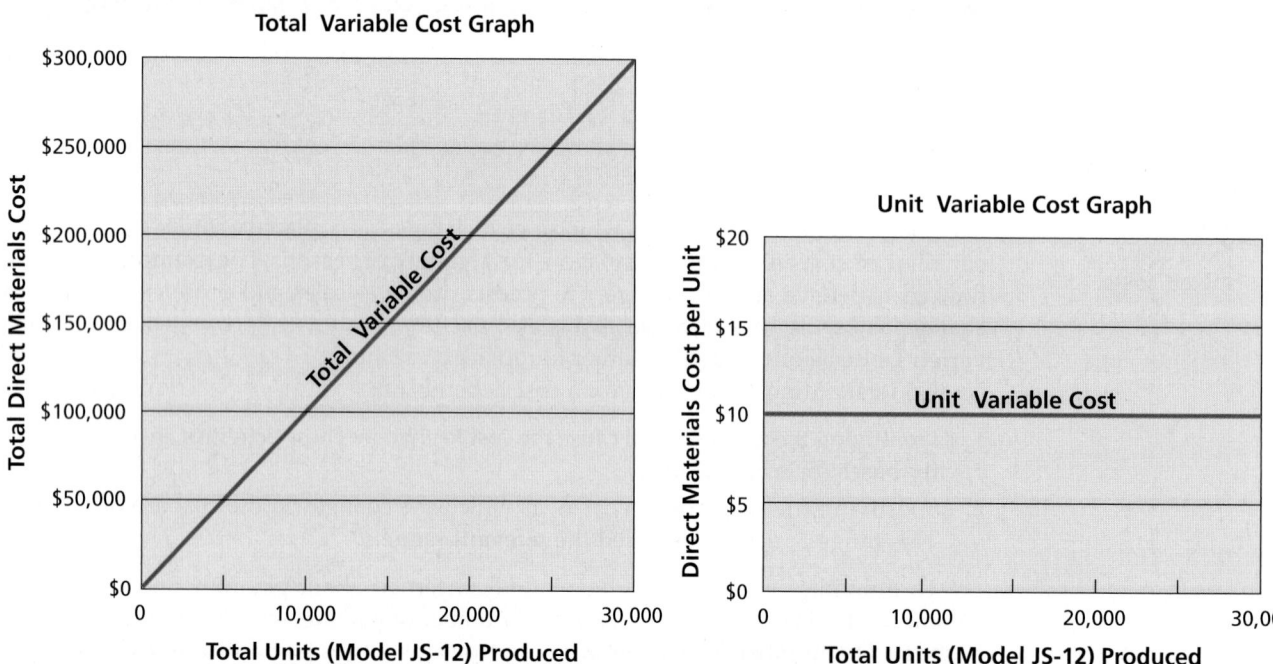

Some examples of variable costs and their related activity bases for various types of businesses are shown below.

Type of Business	Cost	Activity Base
University	Instructor salaries	Number of classes
Passenger airline	Fuel	Number of miles flown
Manufacturing	Direct materials	Number of units produced
Hospital	Nurse wages	Number of patients
Hotel	Maid wages	Number of guests
Bank	Teller wages	Number of banking transactions

Fixed Costs

Fixed costs are costs that remain the same in total dollar amount as the activity base changes. When the activity base is units produced, many factory overhead costs such as straight-line depreciation are classified as fixed costs.

To illustrate, assume that Minton Inc. manufactures, bottles, and distributes perfume. The production supervisor is Jane Sovissi, who is paid a salary of $75,000 per year. For the relevant range of 50,000 to 300,000 bottles of perfume, the total fixed cost of $75,000 does not vary as production increases. However, the fixed cost per bottle decreases as the units produced increase; thus, the fixed cost is spread over a larger number of bottles, as shown below.

Number of Bottles of Perfume Produced	Total Salary for Jane Sovissi	Salary per Bottle of Perfume Produced
50,000 bottles	$75,000	$1.500
100,000	75,000	0.750
150,000	75,000	0.500
200,000	75,000	0.375
250,000	75,000	0.300
300,000	75,000	0.250

As shown above, fixed costs have the following characteristics:

1. *Cost per unit* changes inversely to changes in the activity base. For Jane Sovissi's salary, the cost per unit decreased from $1.50 for 50,000 bottles produced to $0.25 for 300,000 bottles produced.

2. *Total cost* remains the same regardless of changes in the activity base. Jane Sovissi's salary of $75,000 remained the same regardless of whether 50,000 bottles or 300,000 bottles were produced.

Exhibit 2 illustrates how Jane Sovissi's salary (fixed cost) behaves in total and on a per-unit basis as production changes.

Some examples of fixed costs and their related activity bases for various types of businesses are shown below.

Type of Business	Fixed Cost	Activity Base
University	Building (straight-line) depreciation	Number of students
Passenger airline	Airplane (straight-line) depreciation	Number of miles flown
Manufacturing	Plant manager salary	Number of units produced
Hospital	Property insurance	Number of patients
Hotel	Property taxes	Number of guests
Bank	Branch manager salary	Number of customer accounts

Mixed Costs

Mixed costs are costs that have characteristics of both a variable and a fixed cost. Mixed costs are sometimes called *semivariable* or *semifixed* costs.

To illustrate, assume that Simpson Inc. manufactures sails, using rented machinery. The rental charges are as follows:

Rental Charge = $15,000 per year + $1 times each machine hour over 10,000 hours

A salesperson's compensation can be a mixed cost composed of a salary (fixed portion) plus a commission as a percent of sales (variable portion).

Exhibit 2

Fixed Cost Graphs

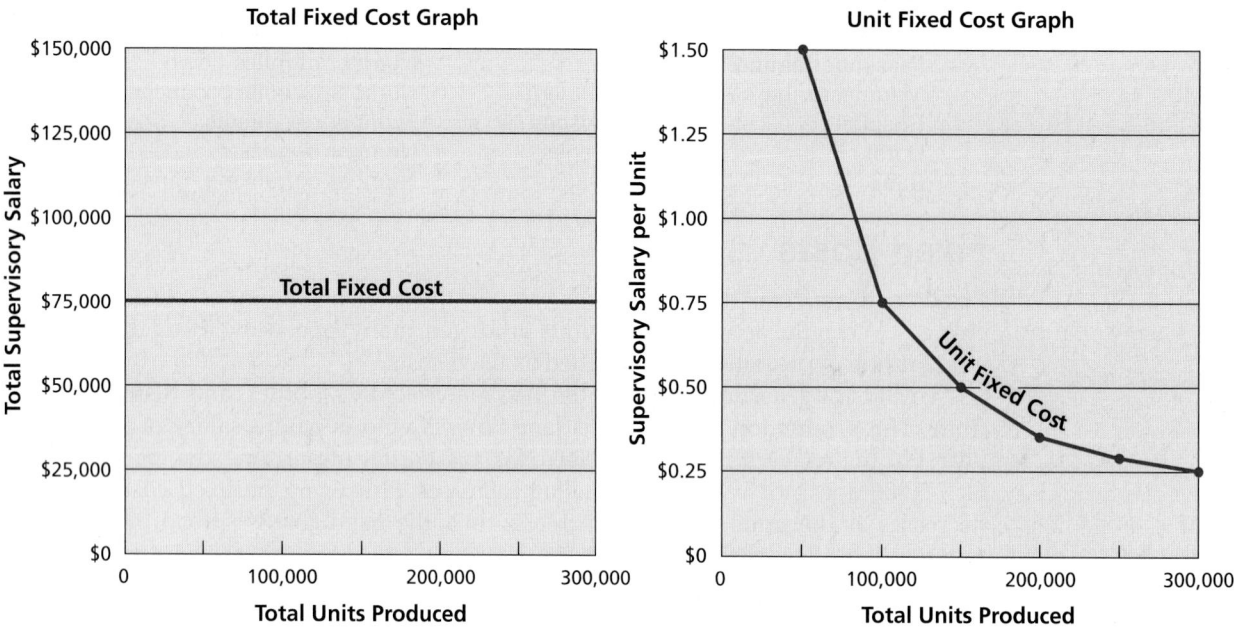

The rental charges for various hours used within the relevant range of 8,000 hours to 40,000 hours are as follows:

Hours Used	Rental Charge
8,000 hours	$15,000
12,000	$17,000 {$15,000 + [(12,000 hrs. − 10,000 hrs.) × $1]}
20,000	$25,000 {$15,000 + [(20,000 hrs. − 10,000 hrs.) × $1]}
40,000	$45,000 {$15,000 + [(40,000 hrs. − 10,000 hrs.) × $1]}

Exhibit 3 illustrates the preceding mixed cost behavior.

Exhibit 3

Mixed Costs

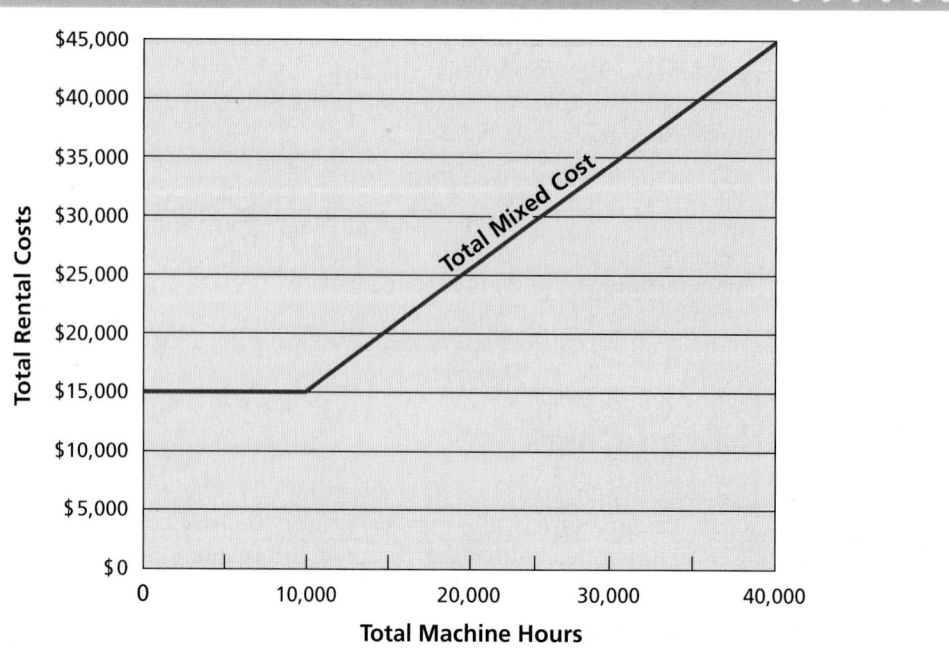

For purposes of analysis, mixed costs are usually separated into their fixed and variable components. The **high-low method** is a cost estimation method that may be used for this purpose.[1] The high-low method uses the highest and lowest activity levels and their related costs to estimate the variable cost per unit and the fixed cost.

To illustrate, assume that the Equipment Maintenance Department of Kason Inc. incurred the following costs during the past five months:

	Production	Total Cost
June	1,000 units	$45,550
July	1,500	52,000
August	2,100	61,500
September	1,800	57,500
October	750	41,250

The number of units produced is the activity base, and the relevant range is the units produced between June and October. For Kason Inc., the difference between the units produced and total costs at the highest and lowest levels of production are as follows:

	Production	Total Cost
Highest level	2,100 units	$61,500
Lowest level	750	41,250
Difference	1,350 units	$20,250

The total fixed cost does not change with changes in production. Thus, the $20,250 difference in the total cost is the change in the total variable cost. Dividing this difference of $20,250 by the difference in production is an estimate of the variable cost per unit. For Kason Inc., this estimate is $15, as computed below.

$$\text{Variable Cost per Unit} = \frac{\text{Difference in Total Cost}}{\text{Difference in Production}}$$

$$\text{Variable Cost per Unit} = \frac{\$20,250}{1,350 \text{ units}} = \$15 \text{ per unit}$$

The fixed cost is estimated by subtracting the total variable costs from the total costs for the units produced, as shown below.

$$\text{Fixed Cost} = \text{Total Costs} - (\text{Variable Cost per Unit} \times \text{Units Produced})$$

The fixed cost is the same at the highest and the lowest levels of production, as shown below for Kason Inc.

Highest level (2,100 units)

Fixed Cost = Total Costs − (Variable Cost per Unit × Units Produced)
Fixed Cost = $61,500 − ($15 × 2,100 units)
Fixed Cost = $61,500 − $31,500
Fixed Cost = $30,000

Lowest level (750 units)

Fixed Cost = Total Costs − (Variable Cost per Unit × Units Produced)
Fixed Cost = $41,250 − ($15 × 750 units)
Fixed Cost = $41,250 − $11,250
Fixed Cost = $30,000

Using the variable cost per unit and the fixed cost, the total equipment maintenance cost for Kason Inc. can be computed for various levels of production as follows:

$$\text{Total Cost} = (\text{Variable Cost per Unit} \times \text{Units Produced}) + \text{Fixed Costs}$$

$$\text{Total Cost} = (\$15 \times \text{Units Produced}) + \$30,000$$

1 Other methods of estimating costs, such as the scattergraph method and the least squares method, are discussed in cost accounting textbooks.

To illustrate, the estimated total cost of 2,000 units of production is $60,000, as computed below:

$$\text{Total Cost} = (\$15 \times \text{Units Produced}) + \$30,000$$
$$\text{Total Cost} = (\$15 \times 2,000 \text{ units}) + \$30,000 = \$30,000 + \$30,000$$
$$\text{Total Cost} = \$60,000$$

A spreadsheet can be used to determine the variable cost per unit and total fixed cost under the high-low method as follows:

	A	B	C	D	E
1					
2	*Inputs*	Production	Total Cost		
3	June	1,000	$ 45,550		
4	July	1,500	52,000		
5	August	2,100	61,500		
6	September	1,800	57,500		
7	October	750	41,250		
8					
9	*Outputs*	Production	Total Cost		
10	Highest level a. →	=MAX(B3:B7)	=VLOOKUP(B10,B$3:C$7,2,FALSE) ← d.		
11	Lowest level b. →	=MIN(B3:B7)	=VLOOKUP(B11,B$3:C$7,2,FALSE) ← e.		
12	Difference c. →	=B10-B11	=C10-C11 ← f.		
13					
14	Variable cost per unit	=C12/B12 ← g.			
15					
16	Fixed cost at the highest				
17	level of production	=C5-(B14*B10) ← h.			
18					

a. Enter in cell B10 the maximum production by using the =MAX function, =MAX(B3:B7). This function will return the maximum value in the stated range.

b. Enter in cell B11 the minimum production by using the =MIN function, =MIN(B3:B7). This function will return the minimum value in the stated range.

c. Enter in cell B12 the formula for the difference between the maximum and minimum, =B10-B11.

d. The total cost that is associated with the maximum value from the table must be inserted in C10. While you could do this by eye, there is a useful Excel function that can be used to find the matching cost. The VLOOKUP function finds a value in the first column and returns the value in the same row from the second column. For example, enter in C10 the following formula:

=VLOOKUP(B10,B$3:C$7,2,FALSE), where

> B10 is the value that is to be found in the first column of the production and total cost table. In this case, the maximum value is 2,100.

> B$3:C$7 is the table that contains the production and cost information. The dollar sign makes the rows absolute so that we can copy this formula when it is completed.

> "2" indicates the column number of the table from which the matching value is to be returned. We enter 2 for the second column, or Total Cost column. Thus, we want the function to return the number 61,500, which is the number in the second column that matches the maximum number from the first column, or 2,100.

> "False" tells Excel to find an exact match.

e. Copy the VLOOKUP function from cell C10 to C11.

f. Enter in cell C12 the difference, or copy from B12.

g. Enter in B14 the formula for the variable cost per unit, =C12/B12.

h. Enter in B16 the formula for the total fixed cost, =C5-(B14*B10) using the maximum level total cost and matching production level. The formula could also use the minimum cost and matching production level to yield the same result.

Go to the hands-on *Excel Tutor* for this example!

Example Exercise 21-1 High-Low Method

1

The manufacturing costs of Alex Industries for the first three months of the year are provided below.

	Total Cost	Production
January	$ 80,000	1,000 units
February	125,000	2,500
March	100,000	1,800

Using the high-low method, determine (a) the variable cost per unit and (b) the total fixed cost.

Follow My Example 21-1

a. $30 per unit = ($125,000 − $80,000)/(2,500 − 1,000)
b. $50,000 = $125,000 − ($30 × 2,500) or $80,000 − ($30 × 1,000)

For Practice: PE 21-1A, PE 21-1B

Summary of Cost Behavior Concepts

The cost behavior of variable costs and fixed costs is summarized below.

	Effect of Changing Activity Level	
Cost	**Total Amount**	**Per Unit Amount**
Variable	Increases and decreases proportionately with activity level.	Remains the same regardless of activity level.
Fixed	Remains the same regardless of activity level.	Increases and decreases inversely with activity level.

Mixed costs contain a fixed cost component that is incurred even if nothing is produced. For analysis, the fixed and variable cost components of mixed costs are separated using the high-low method.

Some examples of variable, fixed, and mixed costs for the activity base *units produced* are as follows:

Variable Cost	**Fixed Cost**	**Mixed Cost**
Direct materials	Straight-line depreciation	Quality Control Department salaries
Direct labor	Property taxes	Purchasing Department salaries
Electricity expense	Production supervisor salaries	Maintenance expenses
Supplies	Insurance expense	Warehouse expenses

One method of reporting variable and fixed costs is called **variable costing** or *direct costing*. Under variable costing, only the variable manufacturing costs (direct materials, direct labor, and variable factory overhead) are included in the product cost. The fixed factory overhead is treated as an expense of the period in which it is incurred. Variable costing is described and illustrated in the appendix to this chapter.

Cost-Volume-Profit Relationships

2 Compute the contribution margin, the contribution margin ratio, and the unit contribution margin.

Cost-volume-profit analysis is the examination of the relationships among selling prices, sales and production volume, costs, expenses, and profits. Cost-volume-profit analysis is useful for managerial decision making. Some of the ways cost-volume-profit analysis may be used include:

1. Analyzing the effects of changes in selling prices on profits
2. Analyzing the effects of changes in costs on profits
3. Analyzing the effects of changes in volume on profits
4. Setting selling prices
5. Selecting the mix of products to sell
6. Choosing among marketing strategies

Contribution Margin

Contribution margin is especially useful because it provides insight into the profit potential of a company. **Contribution margin** is the excess of sales over variable costs, as shown below.

$$\text{Contribution Margin} = \text{Sales} - \text{Variable Costs}$$

To illustrate, assume the following data for Lambert Inc.:

Sales	50,000 units
Sales price per unit	$20 per unit
Variable cost per unit	$12 per unit
Fixed costs	$300,000

Exhibit 4 illustrates an income statement for Lambert Inc. prepared in a contribution margin format.

Exhibit 4

Contribution Margin Income Statement

Sales (50,000 units x $20)	$1,000,000
Variable costs (50,000 units x $12)	600,000
Contribution margin (50,000 units x $8)	$ 400,000
Fixed costs	300,000
Income from operations	$ 100,000

Lambert's contribution margin of $400,000 is available to cover the fixed costs of $300,000. Once the fixed costs are covered, any additional contribution margin increases income from operations.

The graphic to the left illustrates the contribution margin and its effect on profits. The fixed costs are a bucket and the contribution margin is water filling the bucket. Once the bucket is filled, the overflow represents income from operations. Up until the point of overflow, the contribution margin contributes to fixed costs (filling the bucket).

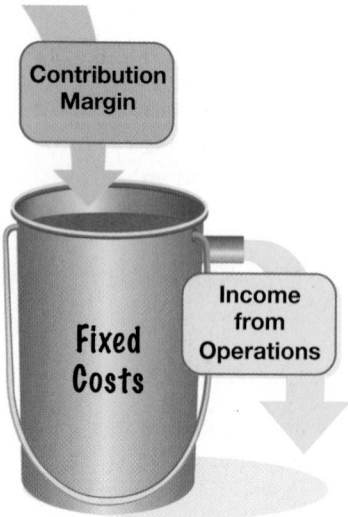

Contribution Margin Ratio

The contribution margin can also be expressed as a percentage. The **contribution margin ratio**, sometimes called the *profit-volume ratio*, indicates the percentage of each sales dollar available to cover fixed costs and to provide income from operations. The contribution margin ratio is computed as follows:

$$\text{Contribution Margin Ratio} = \frac{\text{Contribution Margin}}{\text{Sales}}$$

The contribution margin ratio is 40% for Lambert Inc., as computed below.

$$\text{Contribution Margin Ratio} = \frac{\text{Contribution Margin}}{\text{Sales}}$$

$$\text{Contribution Margin Ratio} = \frac{\$400,000}{\$1,000,000} = 40\%$$

The contribution margin ratio is most useful when the increase or decrease in sales volume is measured in sales *dollars*. In this case, the change in sales dollars multiplied by the contribution margin ratio equals the change in income from operations, as shown below.

Change in Income from Operations = Change in Sales Dollars × Contribution Margin Ratio

To illustrate, if Lambert Inc. adds $80,000 in sales orders, its income from operations will increase by $32,000, as computed below.

Change in Income from Operations = Change in Sales Dollars × Contribution Margin Ratio
Change in Income from Operations = $80,000 × 40% = $32,000

The preceding analysis is confirmed by the following contribution margin income statement of Lambert Inc.:

Sales	$1,080,000
Variable costs ($1,080,000 × 60%)	648,000
Contribution margin ($1,080,000 × 40%)	$ 432,000
Fixed costs	300,000
Income from operations	$ 132,000

Income from operations increased from $100,000 to $132,000 when sales increased from $1,000,000 to $1,080,000. Variable costs as a percentage of sales are equal to 100% minus the contribution margin ratio. Thus, in the above income statement, the variable costs are 60% (100% − 40%) of sales, or $648,000 ($1,080,000 × 60%). The total contribution margin, $432,000, can also be computed directly by multiplying the total sales by the contribution margin ratio ($1,080,000 × 40%).

In the preceding analysis, factors other than sales volume, such as variable cost per unit and sales price, are assumed to remain constant. If such factors change, their effect must also be considered.

The contribution margin ratio is also useful in developing business strategies. For example, assume that a company has a high contribution margin ratio and is producing below 100% of capacity. In this case, a large increase in income from operations can be expected from an increase in sales volume. Therefore, the company might consider implementing a special sales campaign to increase sales. In contrast, a company with a small contribution margin ratio will probably want to give more attention to reducing costs before attempting to promote sales.

Unit Contribution Margin

The unit contribution margin is also useful for analyzing the profit potential of proposed decisions. The **unit contribution margin** is computed as follows:

Unit Contribution Margin = Sales Price per Unit − Variable Cost per Unit

To illustrate, if Lambert Inc.'s unit selling price is $20 and its variable cost per unit is $12, the unit contribution margin is $8, as shown below.

Unit Contribution Margin = Sales Price per Unit − Variable Cost per Unit
Unit Contribution Margin = $20 − $12 = $8

The unit contribution margin is most useful when the increase or decrease in sales volume is measured in sales *units* (quantities). In this case, the change in sales volume (units) multiplied by the unit contribution margin equals the change in income from operations, as shown below.

Change in Income from Operations = Change in Sales Units × Unit Contribution Margin

To illustrate, assume that Lambert Inc.'s sales could be increased by 15,000 units, from 50,000 units to 65,000 units. Lambert's income from operations would increase by $120,000 (15,000 units × $8), as shown below.

Change in Income from Operations = Change in Sales Units × Unit Contribution Margin
Change in Income from Operations = 15,000 units × $8 = $120,000

The preceding analysis is confirmed by the following contribution margin income statement of Lambert Inc., which shows that income increased to $220,000 when 65,000 units are sold. The prior income statement on page 944 indicates income of $100,000 when 50,000 units are sold. Thus, selling an additional 15,000 units increases income by $120,000 ($220,000 − $100,000).

A room night at Hilton Hotels has a high contribution margin. The high contribution margin per room night is necessary to cover the high fixed costs for the hotel.

Sales (65,000 units × $20)	$1,300,000
Variable costs (65,000 units × $12)	780,000
Contribution margin (65,000 units × $8)	$ 520,000
Fixed costs	300,000
Income from operations	$ 220,000

Unit contribution margin analysis is useful information for managers. For example, in the preceding illustration, Lambert Inc. could spend up to $120,000 for special advertising or other product promotions to increase sales by 15,000 units and still increase income by $100,000 ($220,000 − $120,000).

Example Exercise 21-2 Contribution Margin ●●●●●●●> 2

Molly Company sells 20,000 units at $12 per unit. Variable costs are $9 per unit, and fixed costs are $25,000. Determine the (a) contribution margin ratio, (b) unit contribution margin, and (c) income from operations.

Follow My Example 21-2

a. 25% = ($12 − $9)/$12 or ($240,000 − $180,000)/$240,000
b. $3 per unit = $12 − $9
c.

	Sales	$240,000	(20,000 units × $12 per unit)
	Variable costs	180,000	(20,000 units × $9 per unit)
	Contribution margin	$ 60,000	[20,000 units × ($12 − $9)]
	Fixed costs	25,000	
	Income from operations	$ 35,000	

For Practice: PE 21-2A, PE 21-2B

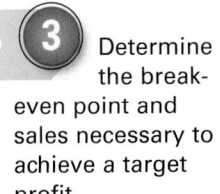

3 Determine the break-even point and sales necessary to achieve a target profit.

Mathematical Approach to Cost-Volume-Profit Analysis

The mathematical approach to cost-volume-profit analysis uses equations to determine the following:

1. Sales necessary to break even
2. Sales necessary to make a target or desired profit

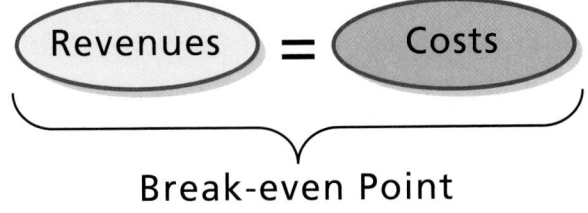

Revenues = Costs

Break-even Point

Break-Even Point

The **break-even point** is the level of operations at which a company's revenues and expenses are equal. At break-even, a company reports neither an income nor a loss from operations. The break-even point in *sales units* is computed as follows:

$$\text{Break-Even Sales (units)} = \frac{\text{Fixed Costs}}{\text{Unit Contribution Margin}}$$

To illustrate, assume the following data for Baker Corporation:

Fixed costs	$90,000
Unit selling price	$25
Unit variable cost	15
Unit contribution margin	$10

The break-even point is 9,000 units, as shown below.

$$\text{Break-Even Sales (units)} = \frac{\text{Fixed Costs}}{\text{Unit Contribution Margin}} = \frac{\$90,000}{\$10} = 9,000 \text{ units}$$

The following income statement verifies the break-even point of 9,000 units:

Sales (9,000 units × $25)	$225,000
Variable costs (9,000 units × $15)	135,000
Contribution margin	$ 90,000
Fixed costs	90,000
Income from operations	$ 0

As shown in the preceding income statement, the break-even point is $225,000 (9,000 units × $25) of sales. The break-even point in *sales dollars* can be determined directly as follows:

$$\text{Break-Even Sales (dollars)} = \frac{\text{Fixed Costs}}{\text{Contribution Margin Ratio}}$$

The contribution margin ratio can be computed using the unit contribution margin and unit selling price as follows:

$$\text{Contribution Margin Ratio} = \frac{\text{Unit Contribution Margin}}{\text{Unit Selling Price}}$$

The contribution margin ratio for Baker Corporation is 40%, as shown below.

$$\text{Contribution Margin Ratio} = \frac{\text{Unit Contribution Margin}}{\text{Unit Selling Price}} = \frac{\$10}{\$25} = 40\%$$

Thus, the break-even sales dollars for Baker Corporation of $225,000 can be computed directly as follows:

$$\text{Break-Even Sales (dollars)} = \frac{\text{Fixed Costs}}{\text{Contribution Margin Ratio}} = \frac{\$90,000}{40\%} = \$225,000$$

The break-even point is affected by changes in the fixed costs, unit variable costs, and the unit selling price.

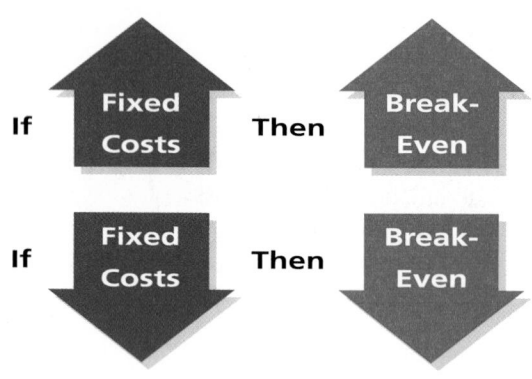

Effect of Changes in Fixed Costs Fixed costs do not change in total with changes in the level of activity. However, fixed costs may change because of other factors such as changes in property tax rates or factory supervisors' salaries.

Changes in fixed costs affect the break-even point as follows:

1. Increases in fixed costs increase the break-even point.
2. Decreases in fixed costs decrease the break-even point.

To illustrate, assume that Bishop Co. is evaluating a proposal to budget an additional $100,000 for advertising. The data for Bishop Co. are as follows:

	Current	Proposed
Unit selling price	$90	$90
Unit variable cost	70	70
Unit contribution margin	$20	$20
Fixed costs	$600,000	$700,000

Bishop Co.'s break-even point *before* the additional advertising expense of $100,000 is 30,000 units, as shown below.

$$\text{Break-Even Sales (units)} = \frac{\text{Fixed Costs}}{\text{Unit Contribution Margin}} = \frac{\$600,000}{\$20} = 30,000 \text{ units}$$

Bishop Co.'s break-even point *after* the additional advertising expense of $100,000 is 35,000 units, as shown below.

$$\text{Break-Even Sales (units)} = \frac{\text{Fixed Costs}}{\text{Unit Contribution Margin}} = \frac{\$700,000}{\$20} = 35,000 \text{ units}$$

As shown above, the $100,000 increase in advertising (fixed costs) requires an additional 5,000 units (35,000 − 30,000) of sales to break even.[2] In other words, an increase in sales of 5,000 units is required in order to generate an additional $100,000 of total contribution margin (5,000 units × $20) to cover the increased fixed costs.

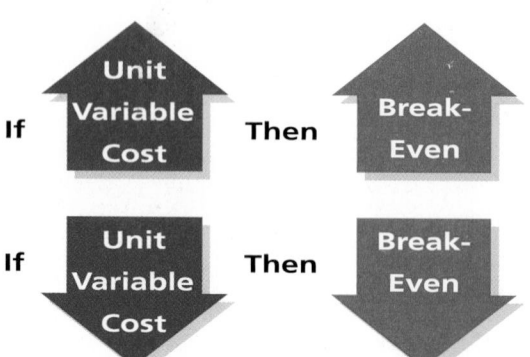

Effect of Changes in Unit Variable Costs Unit variable costs do not change with changes in the level of activity. However, unit variable costs may be affected by other factors such as changes in the cost per unit of direct materials.

Changes in unit variable costs affect the break-even point as follows:

1. Increases in unit variable costs increase the break-even point.
2. Decreases in unit variable costs decrease the break-even point.

---

2 The increase of 5,000 units can also be computed by dividing the increase in fixed costs of $100,000 by the unit contribution margin, $20, as follows: 5,000 units = $100,000/$20.

Increases in fuel prices increase the break-even freight load for the Union Pacific railroad.

To illustrate, assume that Park Co. is evaluating a proposal to pay an additional 2% commission on sales to its salespeople as an incentive to increase sales. The data for Park Co. are as follows:

	Current	Proposed
Unit selling price	$250	$250
Unit variable cost	145	150
Unit contribution margin	$105	$100
Fixed costs	$840,000	$840,000

Park Co.'s break-even point *before* the additional 2% commission is 8,000 units, as shown below.

$$\text{Break-Even Sales (units)} = \frac{\text{Fixed Costs}}{\text{Unit Contribution Margin}} = \frac{\$840,000}{\$105} = 8,000 \text{ units}$$

If the 2% sales commission proposal is adopted, unit variable costs will increase by $5 ($250 × 2%) from $145 to $150 per unit. This increase in unit variable costs will decrease the unit contribution margin from $105 to $100 ($250 − $150). Thus, Park Co.'s break-even point *after* the additional 2% commission is 8,400 units, as shown below.

$$\text{Break-Even Sales (units)} = \frac{\text{Fixed Costs}}{\text{Unit Contribution Margin}} = \frac{\$840,000}{\$100} = 8,400 \text{ units}$$

As shown above, an additional 400 units of sales will be required in order to break even. This is because if 8,000 units are sold, the new unit contribution margin of $100 provides only $800,000 (8,000 units × $100) of contribution margin. Thus, $40,000 more contribution margin is necessary to cover the total fixed costs of $840,000. This additional $40,000 of contribution margin is provided by selling 400 more units (400 units × $100).

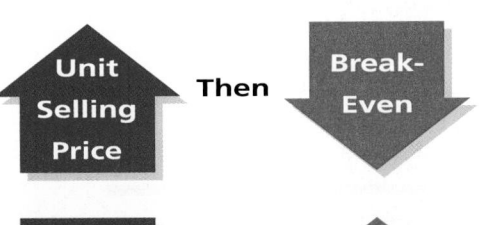

Effect of Changes in Unit Selling Price Changes in the unit selling price affect the unit contribution margin and, thus, the break-even point. Specifically, changes in the unit selling price affect the break-even point as follows:

1. Increases in the unit selling price decrease the break-even point.
2. Decreases in the unit selling price increase the break-even point.

To illustrate, assume that Graham Co. is evaluating a proposal to increase the unit selling price of its product from $50 to $60. The data for Graham Co. are as follows:

	Current	Proposed
Unit selling price	$50	$60
Unit variable cost	30	30
Unit contribution margin	$20	$30
Fixed costs	$600,000	$600,000

The Golf Channel went from a premium cable service price of $6.95 per month to a much lower basic cable price, causing its break-even point to increase from 6 million to 19 million subscribers. The price change was successful, however, since the subscriber numbers exceeded the new break-even point.

Graham Co.'s break-even point *before* the price increase is 30,000 units, as shown below.

$$\text{Break-Even Sales (units)} = \frac{\text{Fixed Costs}}{\text{Unit Contribution Margin}} = \frac{\$600,000}{\$20} = 30,000 \text{ units}$$

The increase of $10 per unit in the selling price increases the unit contribution margin by $10. Thus, Graham Co.'s break-even point *after* the price increase is 20,000 units, as shown below.

$$\text{Break-Even Sales (units)} = \frac{\text{Fixed Costs}}{\text{Unit Contribution Margin}} = \frac{\$600,000}{\$30} = 20,000 \text{ units}$$

As shown on the previous page, the price increase of $10 increased the unit contribution margin by $10, which decreased the break-even point by 10,000 units (30,000 units − 20,000 units).

Summary of Effects of Changes on Break-Even Point The break-even point in sales changes in the same direction as changes in the variable cost per unit and fixed costs. In contrast, the break-even point in sales changes in the opposite direction as changes in the unit selling price. These changes on the break-even point in sales are summarized below.

Type of Change	Direction of Change	Effect of Change on Break-Even Sales
Fixed cost	Increase	Increase
	Decrease	Decrease
Unit variable cost	Increase	Increase
	Decrease	Decrease
Unit selling price	Increase	Decrease
	Decrease	Increase

Example Exercise 21-3   Break-Even Point   •••••••• ❯ ③

Nicolas Enterprises sells a product for $60 per unit. The variable cost is $35 per unit, while fixed costs are $80,000. Determine the (a) break-even point in sales units and (b) break-even point if the selling price were increased to $67 per unit.

Follow My Example 21-3

a. 3,200 units = $80,000/($60 − $35)
b. 2,500 units = $80,000/($67 − $35)

....

For Practice: PE 21-3A, PE 21-3B

Target Profit

At the break-even point, sales and costs are exactly equal. However, the goal of most companies is to make a profit.

By modifying the break-even equation, the sales required to earn a target or desired amount of profit may be computed. For this purpose, target profit is added to the break-even equation, as shown below.

$$\text{Sales (units)} = \frac{\text{Fixed Costs} + \text{Target Profit}}{\text{Unit Contribution Margin}}$$

To illustrate, assume the following data for Waltham Co.:

Fixed costs	$200,000
Target profit	100,000
Unit selling price	$75
Unit variable cost	45
Unit contribution margin	$30

The sales necessary to earn the target profit of $100,000 would be 10,000 units, computed as follows:

$$\text{Sales (units)} = \frac{\text{Fixed Costs} + \text{Target Profit}}{\text{Unit Contribution Margin}} = \frac{\$200,000 + \$100,000}{\$30} = 10,000 \text{ units}$$

The following income statement verifies this computation:

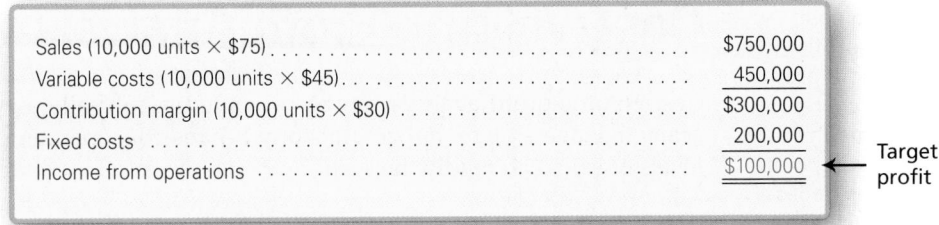

Sales (10,000 units × $75)	$750,000
Variable costs (10,000 units × $45)	450,000
Contribution margin (10,000 units × $30)	$300,000
Fixed costs	200,000
Income from operations	$100,000	← Target profit

As shown in the preceding income statement, sales of $750,000 (10,000 units × $75) are necessary to earn the target profit of $100,000. The sales of $750,000 needed to earn the target profit of $100,000 can be computed directly using the contribution margin ratio, as shown below.

$$\text{Contribution Margin Ratio} = \frac{\text{Unit Contribution Margin}}{\text{Unit Selling Price}} = \frac{\$30}{\$75} = 40\%$$

$$\text{Sales (dollars)} = \frac{\text{Fixed Costs} + \text{Target Profit}}{\text{Contribution Margin Ratio}}$$

$$= \frac{\$200,000 + \$100,000}{40\%} = \frac{\$300,000}{40\%} = \$750,000$$

Example Exercise 21-4   Target Profit   3

Forest Company sells a product for $140 per unit. The variable cost is $60 per unit, and fixed costs are $240,000. Determine the (a) break-even point in sales units and (b) break-even point in sales units if the company desires a target profit of $50,000.

Follow My Example 21-4

a. 3,000 units = $240,000/($140 − $60)
b. 3,625 units = ($240,000 + $50,000)/($140 − $60)

For Practice: PE 21-4A, PE 21-4B

Integrity, Objectivity, and Ethics in Business

ORPHAN DRUGS

Each year, pharmaceutical companies develop new drugs that cure a variety of physical conditions. In order to be profitable, drug companies must sell enough of a product to exceed break even for a reasonable selling price. Break-even points, however, create a problem for drugs targeted at rare diseases, called "orphan drugs." These drugs are typically expensive to develop and have low sales volumes, making it impossible to achieve break even. To ensure that orphan drugs are not overlooked, Congress passed the Orphan Drug Act that provides incentives for pharmaceutical companies to develop drugs for rare diseases that might not generate enough sales to reach break even. The program has been a great success. Since 1982, over 200 orphan drugs have come to market, including Jacobus Pharmaceuticals Company, Inc.'s drug for the treatment of tuberculosis and Novartis AG's drug for the treatment of Paget's disease.

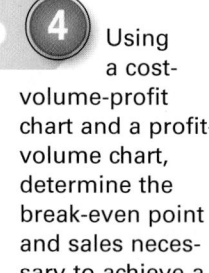

4 Using a cost-volume-profit chart and a profit-volume chart, determine the break-even point and sales necessary to achieve a target profit.

Graphic Approach to Cost-Volume-Profit Analysis

Cost-volume-profit analysis can be presented graphically as well as in equation form. Many managers prefer the graphic form because the operating profit or loss for different levels of sales can readily be seen.

Cost-Volume-Profit (Break-Even) Chart

A **cost-volume-profit chart**, sometimes called a *break-even chart*, graphically shows sales, costs, and the related profit or loss for various levels of units sold. It assists in understanding the relationship among sales, costs, and operating profit or loss.

To illustrate, the cost-volume-profit chart in Exhibit 5 is based on the following data:

Total fixed costs	$100,000
Unit selling price	$50
Unit variable cost	30
Unit contribution margin	$20

The cost-volume-profit chart in Exhibit 5 is constructed using the following steps:

Step 1. Volume in units of sales is indicated along the horizontal axis. The range of volume shown is the relevant range in which the company expects to operate. Dollar amounts of total sales and costs are indicated along the vertical axis.

Step 2. A sales line is plotted by beginning at zero on the left corner of the graph. A second point is determined by multiplying any units of sales on the horizontal axis by the unit sales price of $50. For example, for 10,000 units of sales, the total sales would be $500,000 (10,000 units × $50). The sales line is drawn upward to the right from zero through the $500,000 point.

Step 3. A cost line is plotted by beginning with total fixed costs, $100,000, on the vertical axis. A second point is determined by multiplying any units of sales on the horizontal axis by the unit variable costs and adding the fixed costs. For example, for 10,000 units of sales, the total estimated costs would be $400,000 [(10,000 units × $30) + $100,000]. The cost line is drawn upward to the right from $100,000 on the vertical axis through the $400,000 point.

Step 4. The break-even point is the intersection point of the total sales and total cost lines. A vertical dotted line drawn downward at the intersection point indicates the units of sales at the break-even point. A horizontal dotted line drawn to the left at the intersection point indicates the sales dollars and costs at the break-even point.

In Exhibit 5, the break-even point is $250,000 of sales, which represents sales of 5,000 units. Operating profits will be earned when sales levels are to the right of the break-even point (*operating profit area*). Operating losses will be incurred when sales levels are to the left of the break-even point (*operating loss area*).

Changes in the unit selling price, total fixed costs, and unit variable costs can be analyzed by using a cost-volume-profit chart. Using the data in Exhibit 5, assume that a proposal to reduce fixed costs by $20,000 is to be evaluated. In this case, the total fixed costs would be $80,000 ($100,000 − $20,000).

As shown in Exhibit 6, the total cost line is redrawn, starting at the $80,000 point (total fixed costs) on the vertical axis. A second point is determined by multiplying any

Exhibit 5

Cost-Volume-Profit Chart

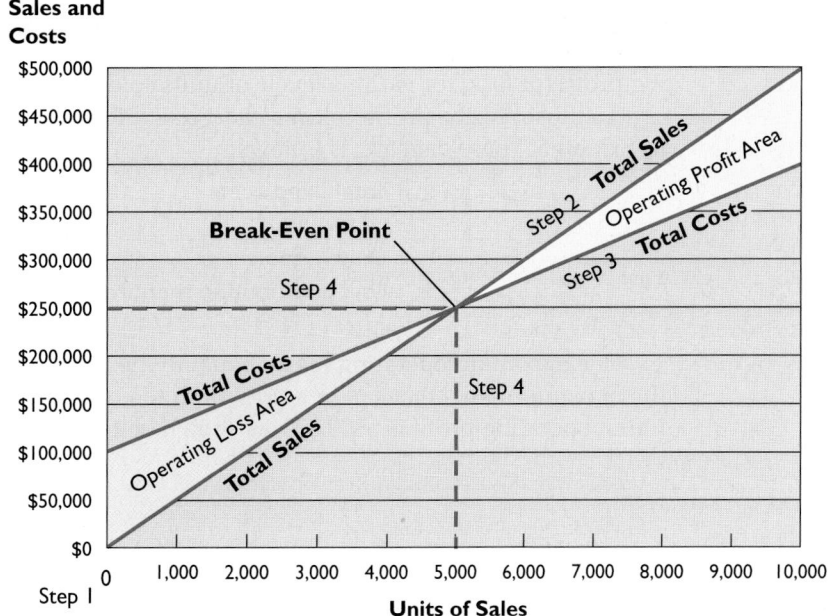

units of sales on the horizontal axis by the unit variable costs and adding the fixed costs. For example, for 10,000 units of sales, the total estimated costs would be $380,000 [(10,000 units × $30) + $80,000]. The cost line is drawn upward to the right from $80,000 on the vertical axis through the $380,000 point. The revised cost-volume-profit chart in Exhibit 6 indicates that the break-even point decreases to $200,000 and 4,000 units of sales.

Exhibit 6

Revised Cost-Volume-Profit Chart

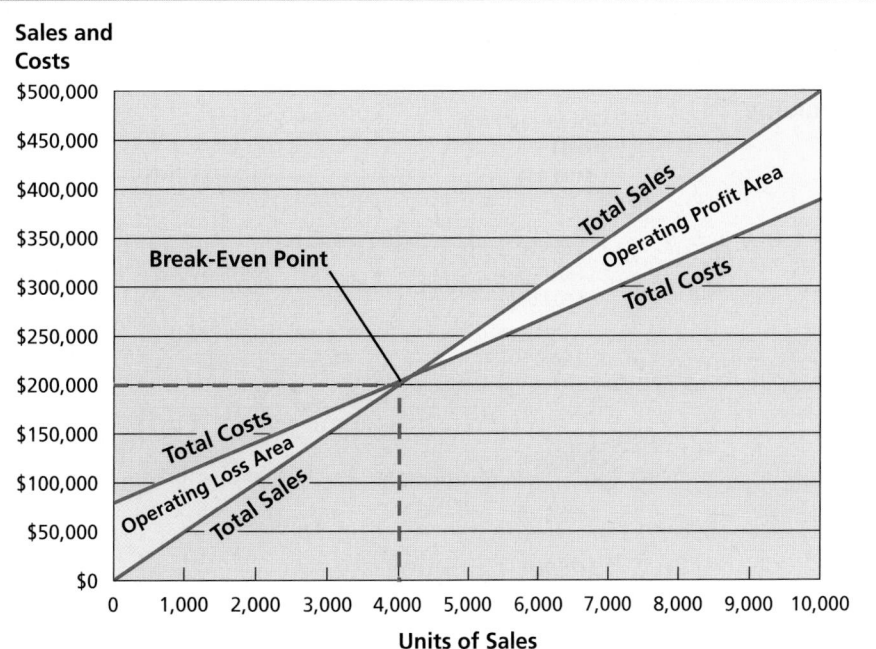

Profit-Volume Chart

Another graphic approach to cost-volume-profit analysis is the profit-volume chart. The **profit-volume chart** plots only the difference between total sales and total costs (or profits). In this way, the profit-volume chart allows managers to determine the operating profit (or loss) for various levels of units sold.

To illustrate, the profit-volume chart in Exhibit 7 is based on the same data as used in Exhibit 5. These data are as follows:

Total fixed costs	$100,000
Unit selling price	$50
Unit variable cost	30
Unit contribution margin	$20

The maximum operating loss is equal to the fixed costs of $100,000. Assuming that the maximum units that can be sold within the relevant range is 10,000 units, the maximum operating profit is $100,000, as shown below.

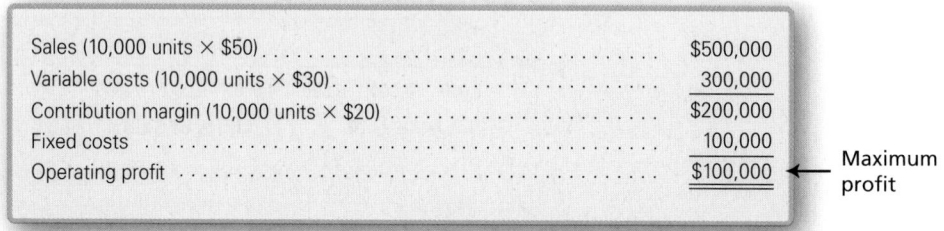

Sales (10,000 units × $50)	$500,000
Variable costs (10,000 units × $30)	300,000
Contribution margin (10,000 units × $20)	$200,000
Fixed costs	100,000
Operating profit	$100,000

Maximum profit

The profit-volume chart in Exhibit 7 is constructed using the following steps:

Step 1. Volume in units of sales is indicated along the horizontal axis. The range of volume shown is the relevant range in which the company expects to operate. In Exhibit 7, the maximum units of sales is 10,000 units. Dollar amounts indicating operating profits and losses are shown along the vertical axis.

Step 2. A point representing the maximum operating loss is plotted on the vertical axis at the left. This loss is equal to the total fixed costs at the zero level of sales. Thus, the maximum operating loss is equal to the fixed costs of $100,000.

Exhibit 7

Profit-Volume Chart

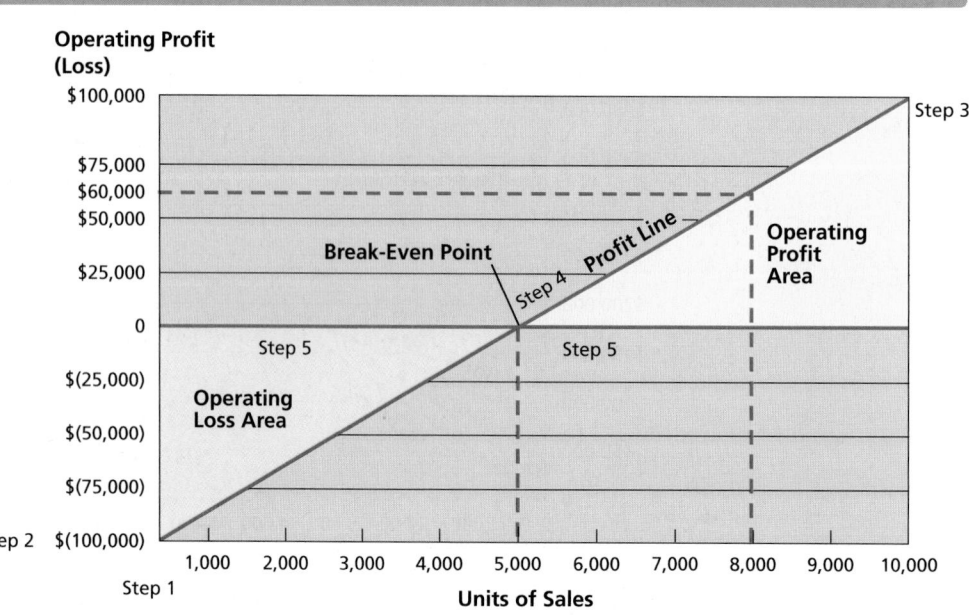

Step 3. A point representing the maximum operating profit within the relevant range is plotted on the right. Assuming that the maximum unit sales within the relevant range is 10,000 units, the maximum operating profit is $100,000.

Step 4. A diagonal profit line is drawn connecting the maximum operating loss point with the maximum operating profit point.

Step 5. The profit line intersects the horizontal zero operating profit line at the break-even point in units of sales. The area indicating an operating profit is identified to the right of the intersection, and the area indicating an operating loss is identified to the left of the intersection.

In Exhibit 7, the break-even point is 5,000 units of sales, which is equal to total sales of $250,000 (5,000 units × $50). Operating profit will be earned when sales levels are to the right of the break-even point (*operating profit area*). Operating losses will be incurred when sales levels are to the left of the break-even point (*operating loss area*). For example, at sales of 8,000 units, an operating profit of $60,000 will be earned, as shown in Exhibit 7.

Changes in the unit selling price, total fixed costs, and unit variable costs on profit can be analyzed using a profit-volume chart. Using the data in Exhibit 7, assume the effect on profit of an increase of $20,000 in fixed costs is to be evaluated. In this case, the total fixed costs would be $120,000 ($100,000 + $20,000), and the maximum operating loss would also be $120,000. At the maximum sales of 10,000 units, the maximum operating profit would be $80,000, as shown below.

Sales (10,000 units × $50)	$500,000
Variable costs (10,000 units × $30)	300,000
Contribution margin (10,000 units × $20)	$200,000
Fixed costs	120,000
Operating profit	$ 80,000

Revised maximum profit

A revised profit-volume chart is constructed by plotting the maximum operating loss and maximum operating profit points and drawing the revised profit line. The original and the revised profit-volume charts are shown in Exhibit 8.

The revised profit-volume chart indicates that the break-even point is 6,000 units of sales. This is equal to total sales of $300,000 (6,000 units × $50). The operating loss area of the chart has increased, while the operating profit area has decreased.

Use of Computers in Cost-Volume-Profit Analysis

With computers, the graphic approach and the mathematical approach to cost-volume-profit analysis are easy to use. Managers can vary assumptions regarding selling prices, costs, and volume and can observe the effects of each change on the break-even point and profit. Such an analysis is called a *"what if"* analysis or *sensitivity* analysis.

Assumptions of Cost-Volume-Profit Analysis

Cost-volume-profit analysis depends on several assumptions. The primary assumptions are listed below.

1. Total sales and total costs can be represented by straight lines.
2. Within the relevant range of operating activity, the efficiency of operations does not change.
3. Costs can be divided into fixed and variable components.
4. The sales mix is constant.
5. There is no change in the inventory quantities during the period.

Exhibit 8

Original Profit-Volume Chart and Revised Profit-Volume Chart

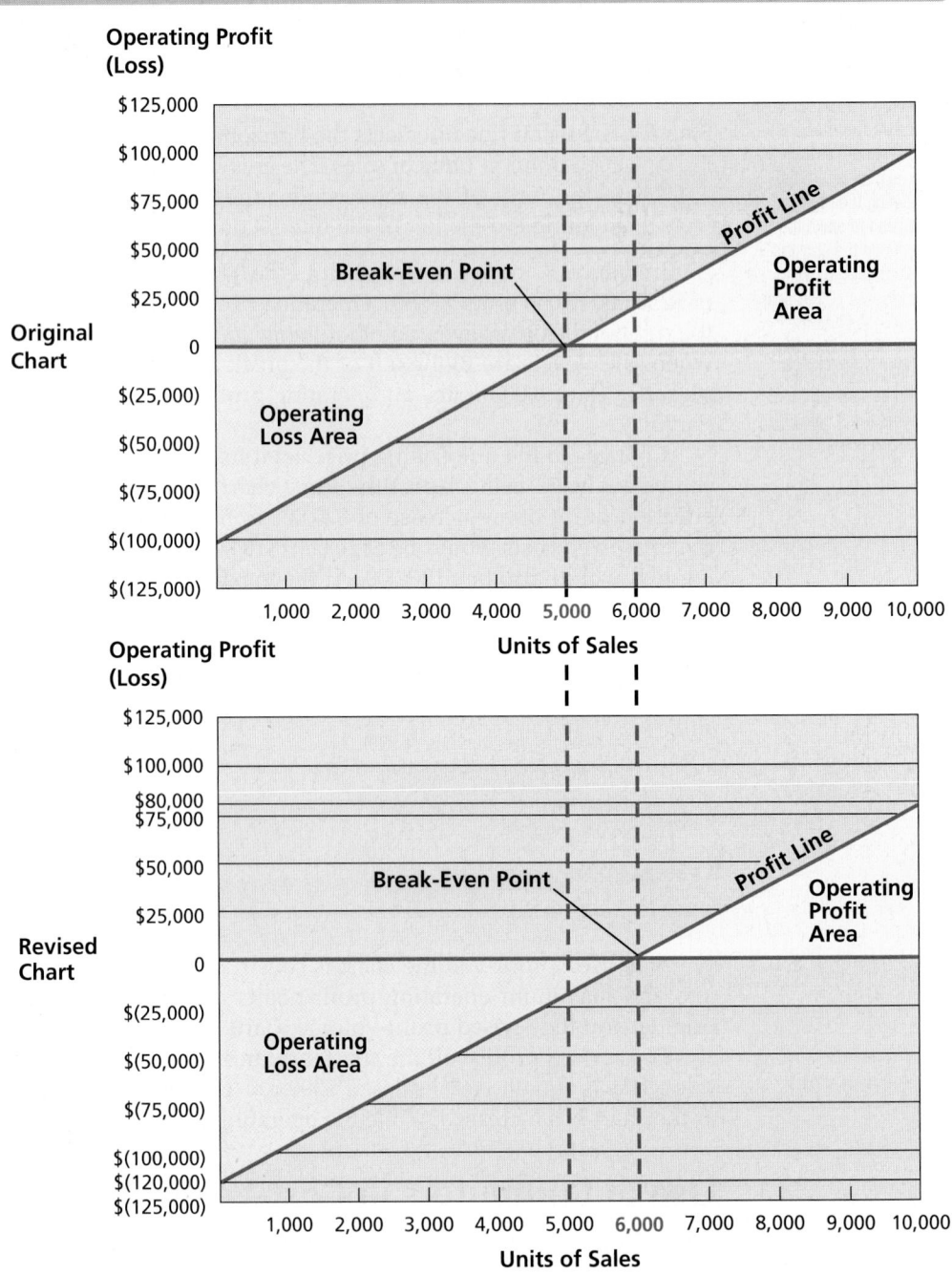

These assumptions simplify cost-volume-profit analysis. Since they are often valid for the relevant range of operations, cost-volume-profit analysis is useful for decision making.[3]

⑤ Compute the break-even point for a company selling more than one product, the operating leverage, and the margin of safety.

Special Cost-Volume-Profit Relationships

Cost-volume-profit analysis can also be used when a company sells several products with different costs and prices. In addition, operating leverage and the margin of safety are useful in analyzing cost-volume-profit relationships.

3 The impact of violating these assumptions is discussed in advanced accounting texts.

Sales Mix Considerations

Many companies sell more than one product at different selling prices. In addition, the products normally have different unit variable costs and, thus, different unit contribution margins. In such cases, break-even analysis can still be performed by considering the sales mix. The **sales mix** is the relative distribution of sales among the products sold by a company.

To illustrate, assume that Cascade Company sold Products A and B during the past year as follows:

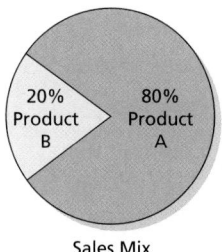

Sales Mix

	Product A	Product B
Total fixed costs	$200,000	
Unit selling price	$90	$140
Unit variable cost	70	95
Unit contribution margin ..	$20	$ 45
Units sold	8,000	2,000
Sales mix	80%	20%

The sales mix for Products A and B is expressed as a percentage of total units sold. For Cascade Company, a total of 10,000 (8,000 + 2,000) units were sold during the year. Therefore, the sales mix is 80% (8,000/10,000) for Product A and 20% for Product B (2,000/10,000), as shown above. The sales mix could also be expressed as the ratio 80:20.

For break-even analysis, it is useful to think of Products A and B as components of one overall enterprise product called E. The unit selling price of E equals the sum of the unit selling prices of each product multiplied by its sales mix percentage. Likewise, the unit variable cost and unit contribution margin of E equal the sum of the unit variable costs and unit contribution margins of each product multiplied by its sales mix percentage.

For Cascade Company, the unit selling price, unit variable cost, and unit contribution margin for E are computed as follows:

Product E		Product A		Product B
Unit selling price of E	$100 =	($90 × 0.8)	+	($140 × 0.2)
Unit variable cost of E	75 =	($70 × 0.8)	+	($95 × 0.2)
Unit contribution margin of E	$ 25 =	($20 × 0.8)	+	($45 × 0.2)

The break-even point of 8,000 units of E can be determined in the normal manner, as shown below.

$$\text{Break-Even Sales (units) for E} = \frac{\text{Fixed Costs}}{\text{Unit Contribution Margin}} = \frac{\$200,000}{\$25} = 8,000 \text{ units}$$

Since the sales mix for Products A and B is 80% and 20% respectively, the break-even quantity of A is 6,400 units (8,000 units × 80%) and B is 1,600 units (8,000 units × 20%). The preceding break-even analysis is verified by the following income statement:

The daily break-even attendance at Universal Studios theme areas depends on how many tickets were sold at an *advance purchase discount* rate vs. the full gate rate. Likewise, the break-even point for an overseas flight of Delta Air Lines will be influenced by the number of first class, business class, and economy class tickets sold for the flight.

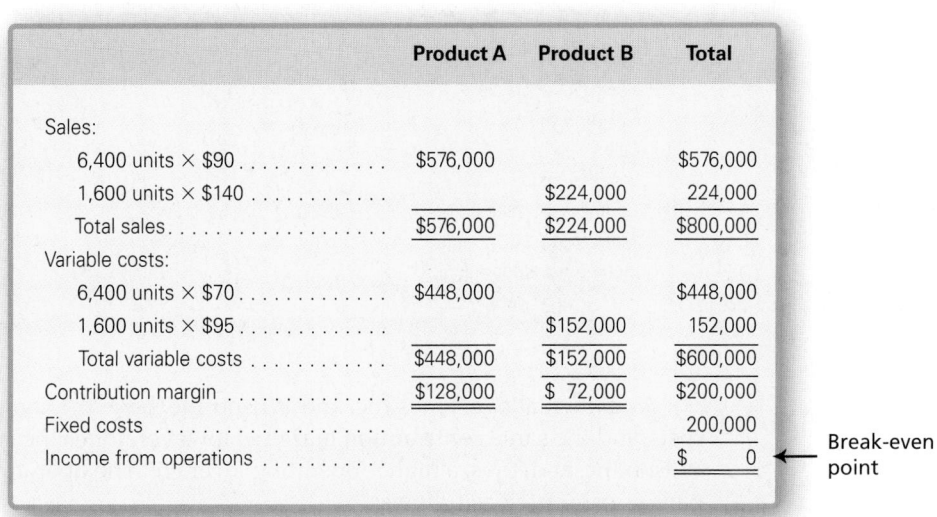

	Product A	Product B	Total
Sales:			
6,400 units × $90	$576,000		$576,000
1,600 units × $140		$224,000	224,000
Total sales...................	$576,000	$224,000	$800,000
Variable costs:			
6,400 units × $70	$448,000		$448,000
1,600 units × $95		$152,000	152,000
Total variable costs	$448,000	$152,000	$600,000
Contribution margin	$128,000	$ 72,000	$200,000
Fixed costs			200,000
Income from operations			$ 0	← Break-even point

The effects of changes in the sales mix on the break-even point can be determined by assuming a different sales mix. The break-even point of E can then be recomputed.

Example Exercise 21-5 Sales Mix and Break-Even Analysis •••••••• 5

Megan Company has fixed costs of $180,000. The unit selling price, variable cost per unit, and contribution margin per unit for the company's two products are provided below.

Product	Selling Price	Variable Cost per Unit	Contribution Margin per Unit
Q	$160	$100	$60
Z	100	80	20

The sales mix for products Q and Z is 75% and 25%, respectively. Determine the break-even point in units of Q and Z.

Follow My Example 21-5

Unit selling price of E: [($160 × 0.75) + ($100 × 0.25)] = $145
Unit variable cost of E: [($100 × 0.75) + ($80 × 0.25)] = 95
Unit contribution margin of E: $ 50

Break-Even Sales (units) = 3,600 units = $180,000/$50

For Practice: PE 21-5A, PE 21-5B

Operating Leverage

One type of business that has high operating leverage is what is called a "network" business—one in which service is provided over a network that moves either goods or information. Examples of network businesses include American Airlines, Verizon Communications, Yahoo!, and Google.

The relationship of a company's contribution margin to income from operations is measured by **operating leverage**. A company's operating leverage is computed as follows:

$$\text{Operating Leverage} = \frac{\text{Contribution Margin}}{\text{Income from Operations}}$$

The difference between contribution margin and income from operations is fixed costs. Thus, companies with high fixed costs will normally have a high operating leverage. Examples of such companies include airline and automotive companies. Low operating leverage is normal for companies that are labor intensive, such as professional service companies, which have low fixed costs.

To illustrate operating leverage, assume the following data for Jones Inc. and Wilson Inc.:

	Jones Inc.	Wilson Inc.
Sales	$400,000	$400,000
Variable costs	300,000	300,000
Contribution margin	$100,000	$100,000
Fixed costs	80,000	50,000
Income from operations	$ 20,000	$ 50,000

As shown above, Jones Inc. and Wilson Inc. have the same sales, the same variable costs, and the same contribution margin. However, Jones Inc. has larger fixed costs than Wilson Inc. and, thus, a higher operating leverage. The operating leverage for each company is computed as follows:

Jones Inc.

$$\text{Operating Leverage} = \frac{\text{Contribution Margin}}{\text{Income from Operations}} = \frac{\$100,000}{\$20,000} = 5$$

Wilson Inc.

$$\text{Operating Leverage} = \frac{\text{Contribution Margin}}{\text{Income from Operations}} = \frac{\$100,000}{\$50,000} = 2$$

Operating leverage can be used to measure the impact of changes in sales on income from operations. Using operating leverage, the effect of changes in sales on income from operations is computed as follows:

$$\text{Percent Change in Income from Operations} = \text{Percent Change in Sales} \times \text{Operating Leverage}$$

To illustrate, assume that sales increased by 10%, or $40,000 ($400,000 × 10%), for Jones Inc. and Wilson Inc. The percent increase in income from operations for Jones Inc. and Wilson Inc. is computed below.

Jones Inc.

$$\text{Percent Change in Income from Operations} = \text{Percent Change in Sales} \times \text{Operating Leverage}$$

$$\text{Percent Change in Income from Operations} = 10\% \times 5 = 50\%$$

Wilson Inc.

$$\text{Percent Change in Income from Operations} = \text{Percent Change in Sales} \times \text{Operating Leverage}$$

$$\text{Percent Change in Income from Operations} = 10\% \times 2 = 20\%$$

As shown above, Jones Inc.'s income from operations increases by 50%, while Wilson Inc.'s income from operations increases by only 20%. The validity of this analysis is shown in the following income statements for Jones Inc. and Wilson Inc. based on the 10% increase in sales:

	Jones Inc.	Wilson Inc.
Sales	$440,000	$440,000
Variable costs	330,000	330,000
Contribution margin	$ 110,000	$ 110,000
Fixed costs	80,000	50,000
Income from operations	$ 30,000	$ 60,000

The preceding income statements indicate that Jones Inc.'s income from operations increased from $20,000 to $30,000, a 50% increase ($10,000/$20,000). In contrast, Wilson Inc.'s income from operations increased from $50,000 to $60,000, a 20% increase ($10,000/$50,000).

Because even a small increase in sales will generate a large percentage increase in income from operations, Jones Inc. might consider ways to increase sales. Such actions could include special advertising or sales promotions. In contrast, Wilson Inc. might consider ways to increase operating leverage by reducing variable costs.

The impact of a change in sales on income from operations for companies with high and low operating leverage can be summarized as follows:

Operating Leverage	Percentage Impact on Income from Operations from a Change in Sales
High	Large
Low	Small

Example Exercise 21-6   Operating Leverage   •••••••• 5

Tucker Company reports the following data:

Sales	$750,000
Variable costs	500,000
Contribution margin	$250,000
Fixed costs	187,500
Income from operations	$ 62,500

Determine Tucker Company's operating leverage.

Follow My Example 21-6

$$\text{Operating Leverage} = \frac{\text{Contribution Margin}}{\text{Income from Operations}} = \frac{\$250,000}{\$62,500} = 4.0$$

$$4.0 = (\$750,000 - \$500,000)/(\$750,000 - \$500,000 - \$187,500) = \$250,000/\$62,500$$

For Practice: PE 21-6A, PE 21-6B

Margin of Safety

The **margin of safety** indicates the possible decrease in sales that may occur before an operating loss results. Thus, if the margin of safety is low, even a small decline in sales revenue may result in an operating loss.

The margin of safety may be expressed in the following ways:

1. Dollars of sales
2. Units of sales
3. Percent of current sales

To illustrate, assume the following data:

Sales	$250,000
Sales at the break-even point	200,000
Unit selling price	25

The margin of safety in dollars of sales is $50,000 ($250,000 − $200,000). The margin of safety in units is 2,000 units ($50,000/$25). The margin of safety expressed as a percent of current sales is 20%, as computed below.

$$\text{Margin of Safety} = \frac{\text{Sales} - \text{Sales at Break-Even Point}}{\text{Sales}}$$

$$= \frac{\$250,000 - \$200,000}{\$250,000} = \frac{\$50,000}{\$250,000} = 20\%$$

Therefore, the current sales may decline $50,000, 2,000 units, or 20% before an operating loss occurs.

Example Exercise 21-7   Margin of Safety •••••••• ▶ ⑤

The Rachel Company has sales of $400,000, and the break-even point in sales dollars is $300,000. Determine the company's margin of safety as a percent of current sales.

Follow My Example 21-7

25% = ($400,000 − $300,000)/$400,000

For Practice: PE 21-7A, PE 21-7B

A P P E N D I X

Absorption Costing

COST OF GOODS MANUFACTURED
INVENTORY
- Direct materials
- Direct labor
- Variable factory overhead
- Fixed factory overhead

Direct Costing

COST OF GOODS MANUFACTURED
INVENTORY
- Direct materials
- Direct labor
- Variable factory overhead

Variable Costing

The cost of manufactured products consists of direct materials, direct labor, and factory overhead. The reporting of all these costs in financial statements is called **absorption costing**. Absorption costing is required under generally accepted accounting principles for financial statements distributed to external users. However, alternative reports may be prepared for decision-making purposes by managers and other internal users. One such alternative reporting is *variable costing* or *direct costing*.

In *variable costing*, the cost of goods manufactured is composed only of variable costs. Thus, the cost of goods manufactured consists of the following:

1. Direct materials
2. Direct labor
3. *Variable* factory overhead

In a variable costing income statement, *fixed* factory overhead costs do not become a part of the cost of goods manufactured. Instead, fixed factory overhead costs are treated as a period expense.

The form of a variable costing income statement is as follows:

Sales		$XXX
Variable cost of goods sold		XXX
Manufacturing margin		$XXX
Variable selling and administrative expenses		XXX
Contribution margin		$XXX
Fixed costs:		
Fixed manufacturing costs	$XXX	
Fixed selling and administrative expenses	XXX	XXX
Income from operations		$XXX

Manufacturing margin is sales less variable cost of goods sold. *Variable cost of goods sold* consists of direct materials, direct labor, and variable factory overhead for the units sold. *Contribution margin* is manufacturing margin less variable selling and administrative expenses. Subtracting fixed costs from contribution margin yields *income from operations*.

The variable costing income statement facilitates managerial decision making since manufacturing margin and contribution margin are reported directly. As illustrated in this chapter, contribution margin is used in break-even analysis and other analyses.

To illustrate the variable costing income statement, assume that 15,000 units are manufactured and sold at a price of $50. The related costs and expenses are as follows:

	Total Cost	Number of Units	Unit Cost
Manufacturing costs:			
Variable	$375,000	15,000	$25
Fixed	150,000	15,000	10
Total	$525,000		$35
Selling and administrative expenses:			
Variable ($5 per unit sold)	$ 75,000		
Fixed	50,000		
Total	$125,000		

Exhibit 9 shows the variable costing income statement prepared from the above data. The computations are shown in parentheses.

Exhibit 9

Variable Costing Income Statement

Sales (15,000 × $50)		$750,000
Variable cost of goods sold (15,000 × $25)		375,000
Manufacturing margin		$375,000
Variable selling and administrative expenses (15,000 × $5)		75,000
Contribution margin		$300,000
Fixed costs:		
Fixed manufacturing costs	$150,000	
Fixed selling and administrative expenses	50,000	200,000
Income from operations		$100,000

Exhibit 10 illustrates the absorption costing income statement prepared from the same data. The absorption costing income statement does not distinguish between variable and fixed costs. All manufacturing costs are included in the cost of goods sold. Deducting the cost of goods sold from sales yields the *gross profit*. Deducting the selling and administrative expenses from gross profit yields the *income from operations*.

Exhibit 10

Absorption Costing Income Statement

Sales (15,000 × $50)	$750,000
Cost of goods sold (15,000 × $35)	525,000
Gross profit	$225,000
Selling and administrative expenses ($75,000 + $50,000)	125,000
Income from operations	$100,000

The relationship between variable and absorption costing *income from operations* is summarized on the next page.

Income from Operations

Units Sold = Units Manufactured	Variable Costing = Absorption Costing
Units Sold < Units Manufactured	Variable Costing < Absorption Costing
Units Sold > Units Manufactured	Variable Costing > Absorption Costing

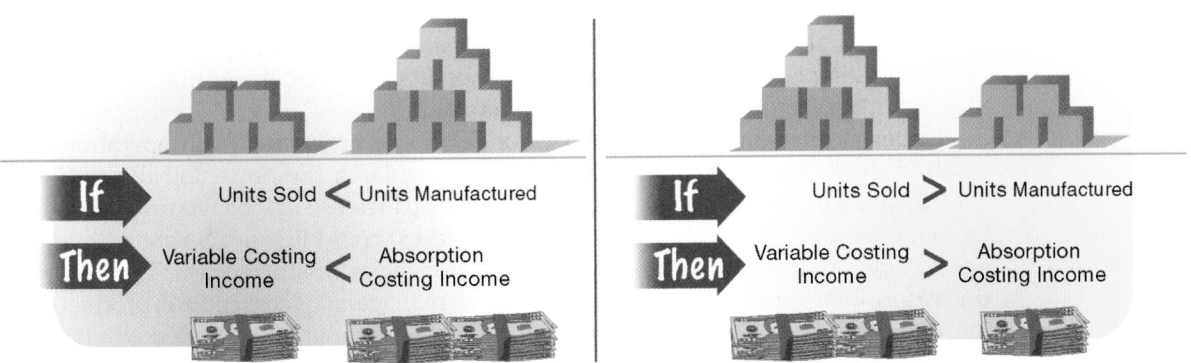

In Exhibits 9 and 10, 15,000 units were manufactured and sold. Thus, the variable and absorption costing income statements reported the same income from operations of $100,000. However, assume that in the preceding example only 12,000 units of the 15,000 units manufactured were sold. Exhibit 11 shows the related variable and absorption costing income statements.

Exhibit 11

Units Manufactured Exceed Units Sold

Variable Costing Income Statement

Sales (12,000 × $50)		$600,000
Variable cost of goods sold:		
Variable cost of goods manufactured (15,000 × $25)	$375,000	
Less ending inventory (3,000 × $25)	75,000	
Variable cost of goods sold		300,000
Manufacturing margin		$300,000
Variable selling and administrative expenses (12,000 × $5)		60,000
Contribution margin		$240,000
Fixed costs:		
Fixed manufacturing costs	$150,000	
Fixed selling and administrative expenses	50,000	200,000
Income from operations		$ 40,000

Absorption Costing Income Statement

Sales (12,000 × $50)		$600,000
Cost of goods sold:		
Cost of goods manufactured (15,000 × $35)	$525,000	
Less ending inventory (3,000 × $35)	105,000	
Cost of goods sold		420,000
Gross profit		$180,000
Selling and administrative expenses [(12,000 × $5) + $50,000]		110,000
Income from operations		$ 70,000

Exhibit 11 shows a $30,000 ($70,000 − $40,000) difference in income from operations. This difference is due to the fixed manufacturing costs. All of the $150,000 of fixed manufacturing costs is included as a period expense in the variable costing statement. However, the 3,000 units of ending inventory in the absorption costing statement includes $30,000 (3,000 units × $10) of fixed manufacturing costs. By being included in inventory, this $30,000 is thus excluded from the current cost of goods sold. Thus, the absorption costing income from operations is $30,000 higher than the income from operations for variable costing.

A similar analysis could be used to illustrate that income from operations under variable costing is greater than income from operations under absorption costing when the units manufactured are less than the units sold.

Under absorption costing, increases or decreases in income from operations can result from changes in inventory levels. For example, in the preceding illustration, a 3,000 increase in ending inventory created a $30,000 increase in income from operations under absorption costing. Such increases (decreases) could be misinterpreted by managers using absorption costing as operating efficiencies (inefficiencies). This is one of the reasons that variable costing is often used by managers for cost control, product pricing, and production planning. Such uses of variable costing are discussed in advanced accounting texts.

At a Glance 21

1 Classify costs as variable costs, fixed costs, or mixed costs.

Key Points	Key Learning Outcomes	Example Exercises	Practice Exercises
Cost behavior refers to the manner in which costs change as a related activity changes. Variable costs vary in proportion to changes in the level of activity. Fixed costs remain the same in total dollar amount as the level of activity changes. Mixed costs are comprised of both fixed and variable costs.	• Describe variable costs. • Describe fixed costs. • Describe mixed costs. • Separate mixed costs using the high-low method.	 21-1	 21-1A, 21-1B

2 Compute the contribution margin, the contribution margin ratio, and the unit contribution margin.

Key Points	Key Learning Outcomes	Example Exercises	Practice Exercises
Contribution margin is the excess of sales revenue over variable costs and can be expressed as a ratio (contribution margin ratio) or a dollar amount (unit contribution margin). The contribution margin concept is useful for business planning because it provides insight into the profit potential of the firm.	• Describe contribution margin. • Compute the contribution margin ratio. • Compute the unit contribution margin.	 21-2 21-2	 21-2A, 21-2B 21-2A, 21-2B

3 Determine the break-even point and sales necessary to achieve a target profit.

Key Points	Key Learning Outcomes	Example Exercises	Practice Exercises
The break-even point is the point at which a business's revenues exactly equal costs. The mathematical approach to cost-volume-profit analysis uses the unit contribution margin concept and mathematical equations to determine the break-even point and the volume necessary to achieve a target profit for a business.	• Compute the break-even point in units.	**21-3**	21-3A, 21-3B
	• Describe how changes in fixed costs affect the break-even point.		
	• Describe how changes in unit variable costs affect the break-even point.		
	• Describe how a change in the unit selling price affects the break-even point.	**21-3**	21-3A, 21-3B
	• Compute the break-even point to earn a target profit.	**21-4**	21-4A, 21-4B

4 Using a cost-volume-profit chart and a profit-volume chart, determine the break-even point and sales necessary to achieve a target profit.

Key Points	Key Learning Outcomes	Example Exercises	Practice Exercises
Graphical methods can be used to determine the break-even point and the volume necessary to achieve a target profit. A cost-volume-profit chart focuses on the relationship among costs, sales, and operating profit or loss. The profit-volume chart focuses on profits rather than on revenues and costs.	• Describe how to construct a cost-volume-profit chart.		
	• Determine the break-even point using a cost-volume-profit chart.		
	• Describe how to construct a profit-volume chart.		
	• Determine the break-even point using a profit-volume chart.		
	• Describe factors affecting the reliability of cost-volume-profit analysis.		

5 Compute the break-even point for a company selling more than one product, the operating leverage, and the margin of safety.

Key Points	Key Learning Outcomes	Example Exercises	Practice Exercises
Cost-volume-profit relationships can be used for analyzing (1) sales mix, (2) operating leverage, and (3) margin of safety. Sales mix computes the break-even point for a business selling more than one product. Operating leverage measures the impact of changes in sales on income from operations. The margin of safety measures the possible decrease in sales that may occur before an operating loss results.	• Compute the break-even point for more than one product.	**21-5**	21-5A, 21-5B
	• Compute operating leverage.	**21-6**	21-6A, 21-6B
	• Compute the margin of safety.	**21-7**	21-7A, 21-7B

Key Terms

absorption costing (961)
activity bases (drivers) (937)
break-even point (947)
contribution margin (944)
contribution margin ratio (944)
cost behavior (937)
cost-volume-profit analysis (943)

cost-volume-profit chart (952)
fixed costs (939)
high-low method (941)
margin of safety (960)
mixed costs (939)
operating leverage (958)
profit-volume chart (954)

relevant range (937)
sales mix (957)
unit contribution margin (945)
variable costing (943)
variable costs (938)

Illustrative Problem

Wyatt Inc. expects to maintain the same inventories at the end of the year as at the beginning of the year. The estimated fixed costs for the year are $288,000, and the estimated variable costs per unit are $14. It is expected that 60,000 units will be sold at a price of $20 per unit. Maximum sales within the relevant range are 70,000 units.

Instructions

1. What is (a) the contribution margin ratio and (b) the unit contribution margin?
2. Determine the break-even point in units.
3. Construct a cost-volume-profit chart, indicating the break-even point.
4. Construct a profit-volume chart, indicating the break-even point.
5. What is the margin of safety?

Solution

1. a. $\text{Contribution Margin Ratio} = \dfrac{\text{Sales} - \text{Variable Costs}}{\text{Sales}}$

$\text{Contribution Margin Ratio} = \dfrac{(60,000 \text{ units} \times \$20) - (60,000 \text{ units} \times \$14)}{(60,000 \text{ units} \times \$20)}$

$\text{Contribution Margin Ratio} = \dfrac{\$1,200,000 - \$840,000}{\$1,200,000} = \dfrac{\$360,000}{\$1,200,000}$

$\text{Contribution Margin Ratio} = 30\%$

   b. Unit Contribution Margin = Unit Selling Price − Unit Variable Costs
   Unit Contribution Margin = $20 − $14 = $6

2. $\text{Break-Even Sales (units)} = \dfrac{\text{Fixed Costs}}{\text{Unit Contribution Margin}}$

$\text{Break-Even Sales (units)} = \dfrac{\$288,000}{\$6} = 48,000 \text{ units}$

3. **Sales and Costs**

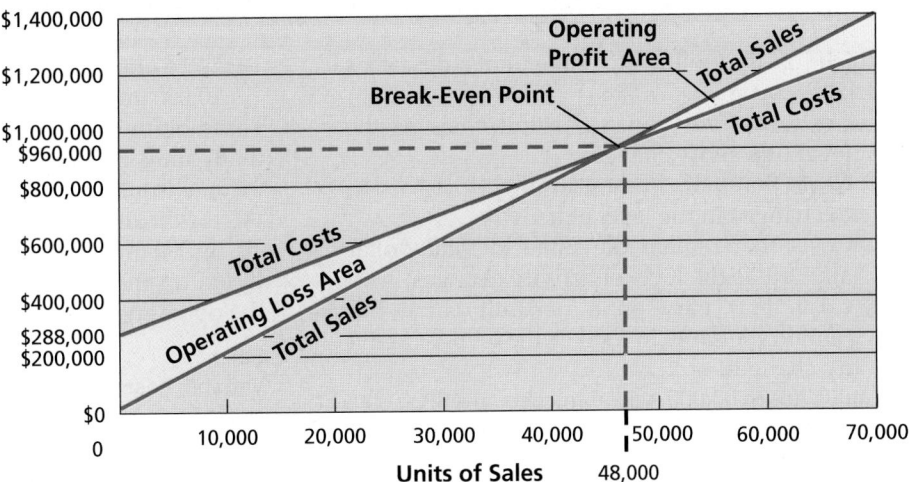

4. **Operating Profit (Loss)**

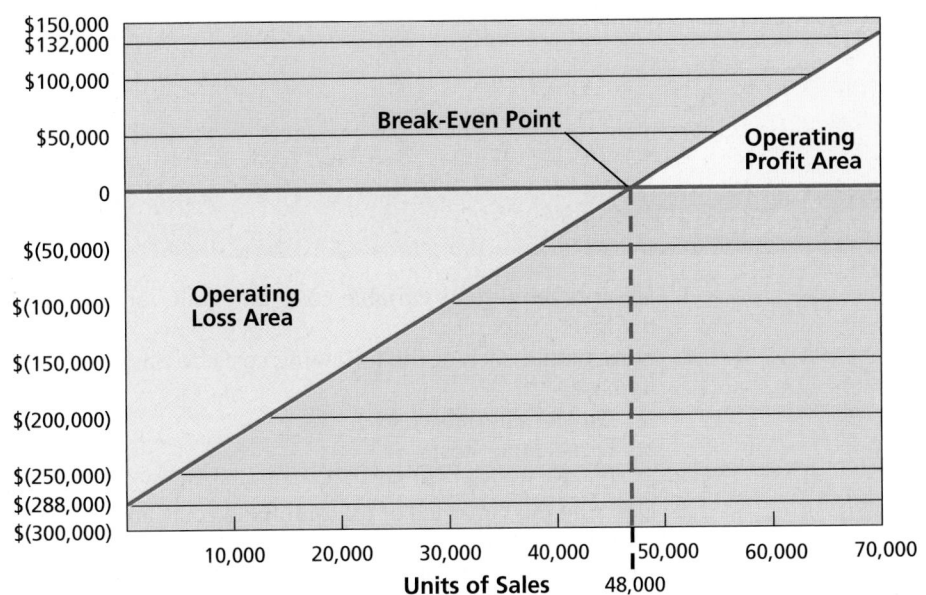

5. Margin of safety:

Expected sales (60,000 units × $20)	$1,200,000
Break-even point (48,000 units × $20)	960,000
Margin of safety	$ 240,000

or

$$\text{Margin of Safety (units)} = \frac{\text{Margin of Safety (dollars)}}{\text{Unit Contribution Margin}}$$

or

12,000 units ($240,000/$20)

or

$$\text{Margin of Safety} = \frac{\text{Sales} - \text{Sales at Break-Even Point}}{\text{Sales}}$$

$$\text{Margin of Safety} = \frac{\$240,000}{\$1,200,000} = 20\%$$

Self-Examination Questions (Answers at End of Chapter)

1. Which of the following statements describes variable costs?
   A. Costs that vary on a per-unit basis as the level of activity changes.
   B. Costs that vary in total in direct proportion to changes in the level of activity.
   C. Costs that remain the same in total dollar amount as the level of activity changes.
   D. Costs that vary on a per-unit basis, but remain the same in total as the level of activity changes.

2. If sales are $500,000, variable costs are $200,000, and fixed costs are $240,000, what is the contribution margin ratio?
   A. 40%   C. 52%
   B. 48%   D. 60%

3. If the unit selling price is $16, the unit variable cost is $12, and fixed costs are $160,000, what are the break-even sales (units)?

A. 5,714 units   C. 13,333 units
B. 10,000 units   D. 40,000 units

4. Based on the data presented in Question 3, how many units of sales would be required to realize income from operations of $20,000?
   A. 11,250 units   C. 40,000 units
   B. 35,000 units   D. 45,000 units

5. Based on the following operating data, what is the operating leverage?

Sales	$600,000
Variable costs	240,000
Contribution margin	$360,000
Fixed costs	160,000
Income from operations	$200,000

A. 0.8   C. 1.8
B. 1.2   D. 4.0

Eye Openers

1. Describe how total variable costs and unit variable costs behave with changes in the level of activity.
2. How would each of the following costs be classified if units produced is the activity base?
   a. Direct materials costs
   b. Direct labor costs
   c. Electricity costs of $0.35 per kilowatt-hour
3. Describe the behavior of (a) total fixed costs and (b) unit fixed costs as the level of activity increases.
4. How would each of the following costs be classified if units produced is the activity base?
   a. Salary of factory supervisor ($70,000 per year)
   b. Straight-line depreciation of plant and equipment
   c. Property rent of $6,000 per month on plant and equipment
5. In cost analyses, how are mixed costs treated?
6. Which of the following graphs illustrates how total fixed costs behave with changes in total units produced?

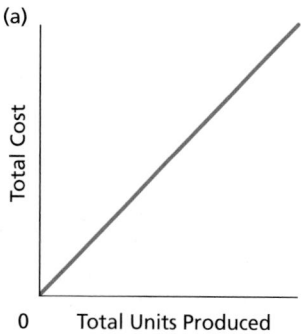

(a)

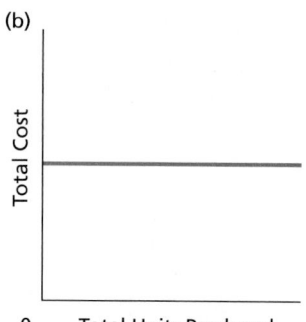

(b)

7. Which of the following graphs illustrates how unit variable costs behave with changes in total units produced?

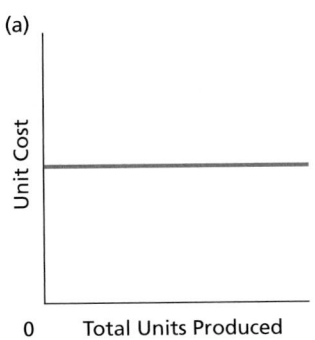

(a)

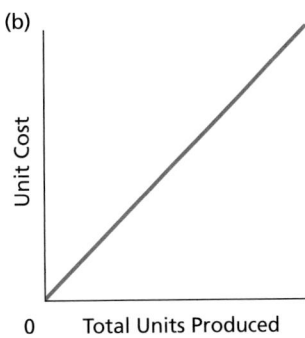

(b)

8. Which of the following graphs best illustrates fixed costs per unit as the activity base changes?

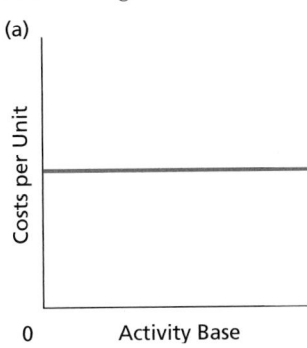

(a)

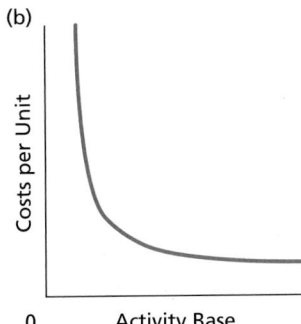

(b)

9. In applying the high-low method of cost estimation, how is the total fixed cost estimated?
10. If fixed costs increase, what would be the impact on the (a) contribution margin? (b) income from operations?
11. An examination of the accounting records of Clowney Company disclosed a high contribution margin ratio and production at a level below maximum capacity. Based on this information, suggest a likely means of improving income from operations. Explain.
12. If the unit cost of direct materials is decreased, what effect will this change have on the break-even point?
13. If insurance rates are increased, what effect will this change in fixed costs have on the break-even point?
14. Both Austin Company and Hill Company had the same sales, total costs, and income from operations for the current fiscal year; yet Austin Company had a lower break-even point than Hill Company. Explain the reason for this difference in break-even points.
15. The reliability of cost-volume-profit (CVP) analysis depends on several key assumptions. What are those primary assumptions?
16. How does the sales mix affect the calculation of the break-even point?
17. What does operating leverage measure, and how is it computed?

Practice Exercises

PE 21-1A
High-low method
obj. 1

EE 21-1   p. 943

The manufacturing costs of Nashbar Industries for three months of the year are provided below.

	Total Costs	Production
April	$140,000	6,000 units
May	300,000	16,000
June	380,000	18,000

Using the high-low method, determine (a) the variable cost per unit and (b) the total fixed cost.

PE 21-1B
High-low method
obj. 1
EE 21-1 p. 943

The manufacturing costs of Sige Enterprises for the first three months of the year are provided below.

	Total Costs	Production
January	$150,000	1,500 units
February	200,000	2,500
March	180,000	2,000

Using the high-low method, determine (a) the variable cost per unit and (b) the total fixed cost.

PE 21-2A
Contribution margin
obj. 2
EE 21-2 p. 946

Rumpza Company sells 8,000 units at $50 per unit. Variable costs are $40 per unit, and fixed costs are $20,000. Determine (a) the contribution margin ratio, (b) the unit contribution margin, and (c) income from operations.

PE 21-2B
Contribution margin
obj. 2
EE 21-2 p. 946

Carlin Company sells 14,000 units at $10 per unit. Variable costs are $9 per unit, and fixed costs are $5,000. Determine (a) the contribution margin ratio, (b) the unit contribution margin, and (c) income from operations.

PE 21-3A
Break-even point
obj. 3
EE 21-3 p. 950

Frankel Enterprises sells a product for $60 per unit. The variable cost is $40 per unit, while fixed costs are $30,000. Determine (a) the break-even point in sales units and (b) the break-even point if the selling price were increased to $65 per unit.

PE 21-3B
Break-even point
obj. 3
EE 21-3 p. 950

Grobe Inc. sells a product for $90 per unit. The variable cost is $75 per unit, while fixed costs are $45,000. Determine (a) the break-even point in sales units and (b) the break-even point if the selling price were decreased to $85 per unit.

PE 21-4A
Target profit
obj. 3
EE 21-4 p. 951

Steward Inc. sells a product for $40 per unit. The variable cost is $30 per unit, and fixed costs are $15,000. Determine (a) the break-even point in sales units and (b) the break-even point in sales units if the company desires a target profit of $15,000.

PE 21-4B
Target profit
obj. 3
EE 21-4 p. 951

Beets Company sells a product for $75 per unit. The variable cost is $65 per unit, and fixed costs are $100,000. Determine (a) the break-even point in sales units and (b) the break-even point in sales units if the company desires a target profit of $50,000.

PE 21-5A
Sales mix and break-even analysis
obj. 5
EE 21-5 p. 958

Dewi Inc. has fixed costs of $220,000. The unit selling price, variable cost per unit, and contribution margin per unit for the company's two products are provided below.

Product	Selling Price	Variable Cost per Unit	Contribution Margin per Unit
A	$120	$100	$20
B	75	45	30

The sales mix for products A and B is 80% and 20%, respectively. Determine the break-even point in units of A and B.

PE 21-5B
Sales mix and break-even analysis
obj. 5
EE 21-5 p. 958

Hackworth Company has fixed costs of $150,000. The unit selling price, variable cost per unit, and contribution margin per unit for the company's two products are provided below.

Product	Selling Price	Variable Cost per Unit	Contribution Margin per Unit
R	$40	$25	$15
S	60	50	10

The sales mix for products R and S is 40% and 60%, respectively. Determine the break-even point in units of R and S.

PE 21-6A
Operating leverage
obj. 5
EE 21-6 p. 960

Ruth Enterprises reports the following data:

Sales	$800,000
Variable costs	350,000
Contribution margin	$450,000
Fixed costs	225,000
Income from operations	$225,000

Determine Ruth Enterprises's operating leverage.

PE 21-6B
Operating leverage
obj. 5
EE 21-6 p. 960

Saik Co. reports the following data:

Sales	$750,000
Variable costs	300,000
Contribution margin	$450,000
Fixed costs	150,000
Income from operations	$300,000

Determine Saik Co.'s operating leverage.

PE 21-7A
Margin of safety
obj. 5
EE 21-7 p. 961

Rogan Inc. has sales of $750,000, and the break-even point in sales dollars is $675,000. Determine the company's margin of safety as a percent of current sales.

PE 21-7B
Margin of safety
obj. 5
EE 21-7 p. 961

Rejeski Company has sales of $400,000, and the break-even point in sales dollars is $240,000. Determine the company's margin of safety as a percent of current sales.

Exercises

EX 21-1
Classify costs
obj. 1

Following is a list of various costs incurred in producing toy robotic helicopters. With respect to the production and sale of these toy helicopters, classify each cost as either variable, fixed, or mixed.

1. Oil used in manufacturing equipment
2. Hourly wages of inspectors
3. Electricity costs, $0.20 per kilowatt-hour
4. Property insurance premiums, $1,500 per month plus $0.006 for each dollar of property over $2,000,000
5. Janitorial costs, $4,000 per month
6. Pension cost, $0.80 per employee hour on the job
7. Computer chip (purchased from a vendor)
8. Hourly wages of machine operators
9. Straight-line depreciation on the production equipment
10. Metal

(continued)

11. Packaging
12. Rent on warehouse, $10,000 per month plus $10 per square foot of storage used
13. Plastic
14. Property taxes, $100,000 per year on factory building and equipment
15. Salary of plant manager

EX 21-2
Identify cost graphs
obj. **1**

The following cost graphs illustrate various types of cost behavior:

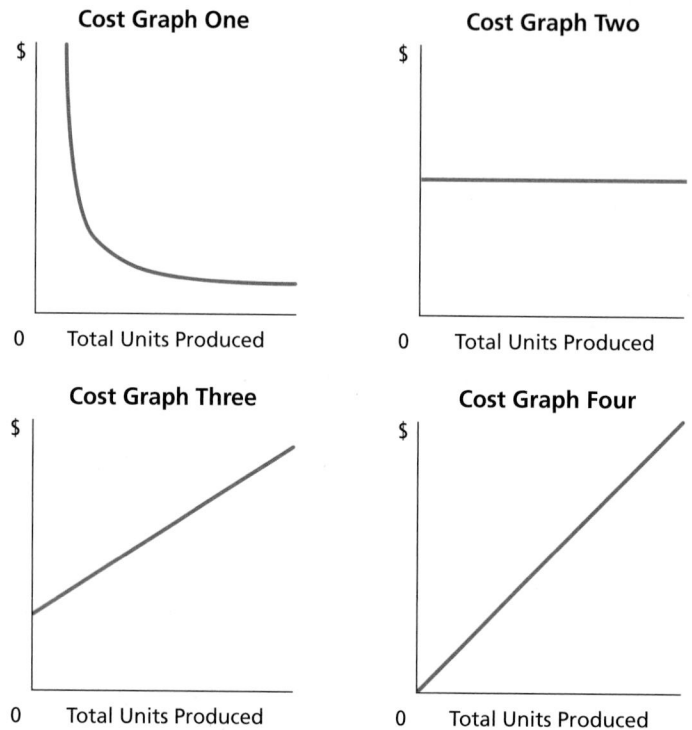

For each of the following costs, identify the cost graph that best illustrates its cost behavior as the number of units produced increases.

a. Total direct materials cost
b. Electricity costs of $2,000 per month plus $0.09 per kilowatt-hour
c. Per-unit direct labor cost
d. Salary of quality control supervisor, $10,000 per month
e. Per-unit cost of straight-line depreciation on factory equipment

EX 21-3
Identify activity bases
obj. **1**

For a major university, match each cost in the following table with the activity base most appropriate to it. An activity base may be used more than once, or not used at all.

Cost:
1. Housing personnel wages
2. Student records office salaries
3. Financial aid office salaries
4. School supplies
5. Instructor salaries
6. Admissions office salaries

Activity Base:
a. Number of financial aid applications
b. Number of enrolled students and alumni
c. Student credit hours
d. Number of student/athletes
e. Number of enrollment applications
f. Number of students living on campus

EX 21-4
Identify activity bases
obj. **1**

From the following list of activity bases for an automobile dealership, select the base that would be most appropriate for each of these costs: (1) preparation costs (cleaning, oil, and gasoline costs) for each car received, (2) salespersons' commission of 4% of the sales price for each car sold, and (3) administrative costs for ordering cars.

a. Dollar amount of cars sold	e. Dollar amount of cars ordered
b. Number of cars received	f. Dollar amount of cars received
c. Dollar amount of cars on hand	g. Number of cars ordered
d. Number of cars on hand	h. Number of cars sold

EX 21-5
Identify fixed and variable costs

obj. 1

Intuit Inc. develops and sells software products for the personal finance market, including popular titles such as Quicken® and TurboTax®. Classify each of the following costs and expenses for this company as either variable or fixed to the number of units produced and sold:

a. Shipping expenses
b. Property taxes on general offices
c. Straight-line depreciation of computer equipment
d. Salaries of human resources personnel
e. President's salary
f. Advertising
g. Sales commissions
h. CDs
i. Packaging costs
j. Salaries of software developers
k. Wages of telephone order assistants
l. User's guides

EX 21-6
Relevant range and fixed and variable costs

obj. 1

✔ a. $0.32

Robo-Tech Inc. manufactures components for computer games within a relevant range of 200,000 to 320,000 disks per year. Within this range, the following partially completed manufacturing cost schedule has been prepared:

Components produced	200,000	250,000	320,000
Total costs:			
Total variable costs	$ 64,000	(d)	(j)
Total fixed costs	80,000	(e)	(k)
Total costs	$144,000	(f)	(l)
Cost per unit:			
Variable cost per unit	(a)	(g)	(m)
Fixed cost per unit	(b)	(h)	(n)
Total cost per unit	(c)	(i)	(o)

Complete the cost schedule, identifying each cost by the appropriate letter (a) through (o).

EX 21-7
High-low method

obj. 1

✔ a. $16.00 per unit

Shatner Inc. has decided to use the high-low method to estimate the total cost and the fixed and variable cost components of the total cost. The data for various levels of production are as follows:

Units Produced	Total Costs
7,500	$600,000
12,500	725,000
20,000	800,000

a. Determine the variable cost per unit and the fixed cost.
b. Based on part (a), estimate the total cost for 10,000 units of production.

EX 21-8
High-low method for service company

obj. 1

Blowing Rock Railroad decided to use the high-low method and operating data from the past six months to estimate the fixed and variable components of transportation costs. The activity base used by Blowing Rock Railroad is a measure of railroad operating activity, termed "gross-ton miles," which is the total number of tons multiplied by the miles moved.

	Transportation Costs	Gross-Ton Miles
January	$760,000	275,000
February	850,000	310,000
March	600,000	200,000
April	810,000	300,000
May	680,000	240,000
June	875,000	325,000

✔ Fixed cost, $160,000

Determine the variable cost per gross-ton mile and the fixed cost.

EX 21-9

Contribution margin ratio

obj. 2

✔ a. 84%

a. Bert Company budgets sales of $1,250,000, fixed costs of $450,000, and variable costs of $200,000. What is the contribution margin ratio for Bert Company?

b. If the contribution margin ratio for Ernie Company is 40%, sales were $750,000, and fixed costs were $225,000, what was the income from operations?

EX 21-10

Contribution margin and contribution margin ratio

obj. 2

✔ b. 34.9%

For a recent year, McDonald's company-owned restaurants had the following sales and expenses (in millions):

Sales	$16,083
Food and packaging	$ 5,350
Payroll	4,185
Occupancy (rent, depreciation, etc.)	4,006
General, selling, and administrative expenses	2,340
	$15,881
Income from operations	$ 202

Assume that the variable costs consist of food and packaging, payroll, and 40% of the general, selling, and administrative expenses.

a. What is McDonald's contribution margin? Round to the nearest million.

b. What is McDonald's contribution margin ratio? Round to one decimal place.

c. How much would income from operations increase if same-store sales increased by $500 million for the coming year, with no change in the contribution margin ratio or fixed costs?

EX 21-11

Break-even sales and sales to realize income from operations

obj. 3

✔ b. 21,200 units

For the current year ending March 31, Jwork Company expects fixed costs of $440,000, a unit variable cost of $50, and a unit selling price of $75.

a. Compute the anticipated break-even sales (units).

b. Compute the sales (units) required to realize income from operations of $90,000.

EX 21-12

Break-even sales

obj. 3

✔ a. 76,149,219 barrels

Anheuser-Busch Companies, Inc., reported the following operating information for a recent year (in millions):

Net sales	$15,717.1
Cost of goods sold	$10,165.0
Marketing and distribution	2,832.5
	$12,997.5
Income from operations	$ 2,719.6*
*Before special items	

In addition, Anheuser-Busch sold 125 million barrels of beer during the year. Assume that variable costs were 75% of the cost of goods sold and 40% of marketing and distribution expenses. Assume that the remaining costs are fixed. For the following year, assume that Anheuser-Busch expects pricing, variable costs per barrel, and fixed costs to remain constant, except that new distribution and general office facilities are expected to increase fixed costs by $150 million.

Rounding to the nearest cent:

a. Compute the break-even sales (barrels) for the current year.

b. Compute the anticipated break-even sales (barrels) for the following year.

EX 21-13

Break-even sales

obj. **3**

✔ a. 10,500 units

Currently, the unit selling price of a product is $280, the unit variable cost is $230, and the total fixed costs are $525,000. A proposal is being evaluated to increase the unit selling price to $300.

a. Compute the current break-even sales (units).

b. Compute the anticipated break-even sales (units), assuming that the unit selling price is increased and all costs remain constant.

EX 21-14

Break-even analysis

obj. **3**

The Dash Club of Tampa, Florida, collected recipes from members and published a cookbook entitled *Life of the Party*. The book will sell for $25 per copy. The chairwoman of the cookbook development committee estimated that the club needed to sell 10,000 books to break even on its $90,000 investment. What is the variable cost per unit assumed in the Dash Club's analysis?

EX 21-15

Break-even analysis

obj. **3**

Media outlets such as ESPN and Fox Sports often have Web sites that provide in-depth coverage of news and events. Portions of these Web sites are restricted to members who pay a monthly subscription to gain access to exclusive news and commentary. These Web sites typically offer a free trial period to introduce viewers to the Web site. Assume that during a recent fiscal year, ESPN.com spent $1,800,000 on a promotional campaign for the ESPN.com Web site that offered two free months of service for new subscribers. In addition, assume the following information:

Number of months an average new customer stays with the service (including the two free months)	25 months
Revenue per month per customer subscription	$10.00
Variable cost per month per customer subscription	$2.00

Determine the number of new customer accounts needed to break even on the cost of the promotional campaign. In forming your answer, (1) treat the cost of the promotional campaign as a fixed cost, and (2) treat the revenue less variable cost per account for the subscription period as the unit contribution margin.

EX 21-16

Break-even analysis

obj. **3**

Sprint Nextel is one of the largest digital wireless service providers in the United States. In a recent year, it had approximately 41.5 million direct subscribers (accounts) that generated revenue of $40,146 million. Costs and expenses for the year were as follows (in millions):

Cost of revenue	$17,191
Selling, general, and administrative expenses	12,673
Depreciation	5,711

Assume that 75% of the cost of revenue and 35% of the selling, general, and administrative expenses are variable to the number of direct subscribers (accounts).

a. What is Sprint Nextel's break-even number of accounts, using the data and assumptions above? Round units to one decimal place (in millions).

b. How much revenue per account would be sufficient for Sprint Nextel to break even if the number of accounts remained constant?

EX 21-17

Cost-volume-profit chart

obj. **4**

✔ b. $360,000

For the coming year, Paladin Inc. anticipates fixed costs of $120,000, a unit variable cost of $60, and a unit selling price of $90. The maximum sales within the relevant range are $900,000.

a. Construct a cost-volume-profit chart.

b. Estimate the break-even sales (dollars) by using the cost-volume-profit chart constructed in part (a).

c. ➤ What is the main advantage of presenting the cost-volume-profit analysis in graphic form rather than equation form?

EX 21-18
Profit-volume chart
obj. **4**
✔ b. $180,000

Using the data for Paladin Inc. in Exercise 21-17, (a) determine the maximum possible operating loss, (b) compute the maximum possible income from operations, (c) construct a profit-volume chart, and (d) estimate the break-even sales (units) by using the profit-volume chart constructed in part (c).

EX 21-19
Break-even chart
obj. **4**

Name the following chart, and identify the items represented by the letters (a) through (f).

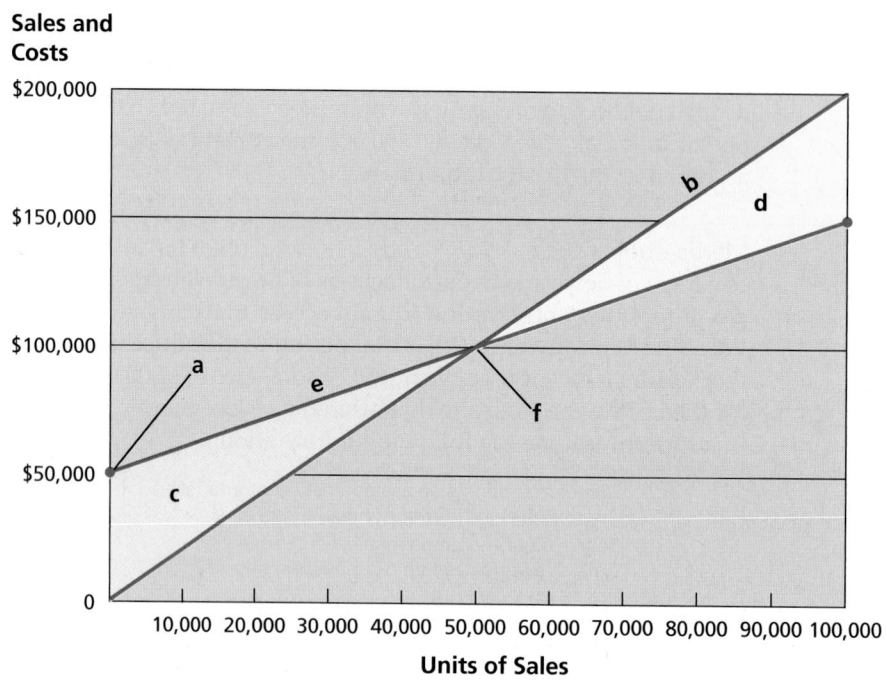

EX 21-20
Break-even chart
obj. **4**

Name the following chart, and identify the items represented by the letters (a) through (f).

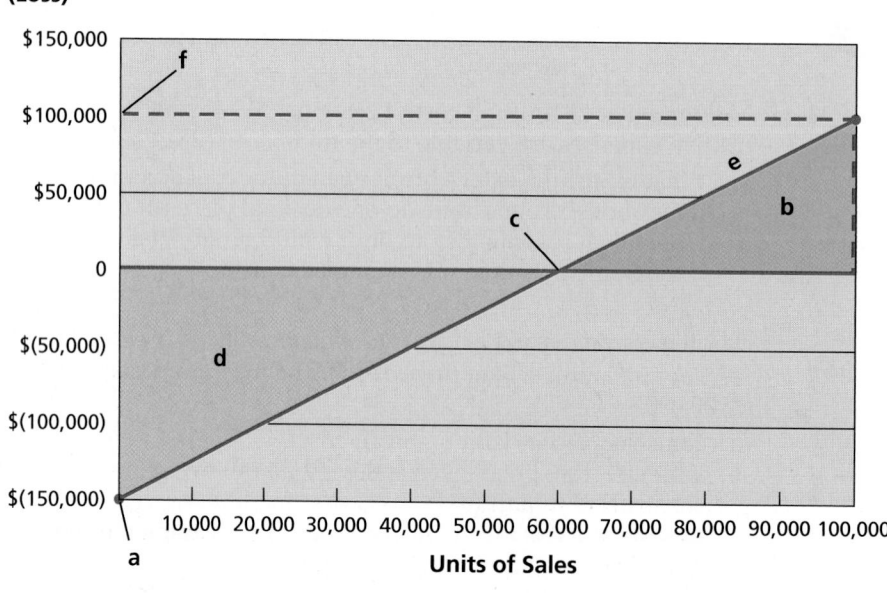

EX 21-21

Sales mix and break-even sales

obj. 5

✔ a. 10,000 units

New Wave Technology Inc. manufactures and sells two products, MP3 players and satellite radios. The fixed costs are $300,000, and the sales mix is 40% MP3 players and 60% satellite radios. The unit selling price and the unit variable cost for each product are as follows:

Products	Unit Selling Price	Unit Variable Cost
MP3 players	$ 60.00	$45.00
Satellite radios	100.00	60.00

a. Compute the break-even sales (units) for the overall product, E.

b. How many units of each product, MP3 players and satellite radios, would be sold at the break-even point?

EX 21-22

Break-even sales and sales mix for a service company

obj. 5

✔ a. 50 seats

Southwest Blue Airways provides air transportation services between Seattle and San Diego. A single Seattle to San Diego round-trip flight has the following operating statistics:

Fuel	$7,000
Flight crew salaries	5,400
Airplane depreciation	2,600
Variable cost per passenger—business class	50
Variable cost per passenger—economy class	40
Round-trip ticket price—business class	550
Round-trip ticket price—economy class	290

It is assumed that the fuel, crew salaries, and airplane depreciation are fixed, regardless of the number of seats sold for the round-trip flight.

a. Compute the break-even number of seats sold on a single round-trip flight for the overall product. Assume that the overall product is 20% business class and 80% economy class tickets.

b. How many business class and economy class seats would be sold at the break-even point?

EX 21-23

Margin of safety

obj. 5

✔ a. (2) 25%

a. If Fama Company, with a break-even point at $360,000 of sales, has actual sales of $480,000, what is the margin of safety expressed (1) in dollars and (2) as a percentage of sales?

b. If the margin of safety for Watkins Company was 25%, fixed costs were $1,200,000, and variable costs were 75% of sales, what was the amount of actual sales (dollars)? (*Hint:* Determine the break-even in sales dollars first.)

EX 21-24

Break-even and margin of safety relationships

obj. 5

At a recent staff meeting, the management of Guthold Gaming Technologies, Inc., was considering discontinuing the Evegi line of electronic games from the product line. The chief financial analyst reported the following current monthly data for the Evegi:

Units of sales	85,000
Break-even units	100,000
Margin of safety in units	7,000

➤ For what reason would you question the validity of these data?

EX 21-25

Operating leverage

obj. 5

✔ a. Varner, 3.00

Varner Inc. and King Inc. have the following operating data:

	Varner	King
Sales	$300,000	$600,000
Variable costs	120,000	360,000
Contribution margin	$180,000	$240,000
Fixed costs	120,000	80,000
Income from operations	$ 60,000	$160,000

a. Compute the operating leverage for Varner Inc. and King Inc.

b. How much would income from operations increase for each company if the sales of each increased by 20%?

c. ➤ Why is there a difference in the increase in income from operations for the two companies? Explain.

**Appendix
EX 21-26**

**Items on variable
costing income
statement**

In the following equations, based on the variable costing income statement, identify the items designated by "X":

a. Net Sales − X = Manufacturing Margin
b. Manufacturing Margin − X = Contribution Margin
c. Contribution Margin − X = Income from Operations

**Appendix
EX 21-27**

**Variable costing
income statement**

✔ Contribution
margin, $531,000

On July 31, 2010, the end of the first month of operations, Hilton Company prepared the following income statement, based on the absorption costing concept:

Sales (20,000 units)		$1,400,000
Cost of goods sold:		
Cost of goods manufactured	$1,050,000	
Less ending inventory (4,000 units)	175,000	
Cost of goods sold		875,000
Gross profit		$ 525,000
Selling and administrative expenses		75,000
Income from operations		$ 450,000

Prepare a variable costing income statement, assuming that the fixed manufacturing costs were $48,000 and the variable selling and administrative expenses were $34,000.

**Appendix
EX 21-28**

**Absorption costing
income statement**

✔ Gross profit,
$415,000

On June 30, 2010, the end of the first month of operations, Smithey Manufacturing Co. prepared the following income statement, based on the variable costing concept:

Sales (100,000 units)		$1,650,000
Variable cost of goods sold:		
Variable cost of goods manufactured (120,000 units ×		
$12 per unit)	$1,440,000	
Less ending inventory (20,000 units × $12 per unit)	240,000	
Variable cost of goods sold		1,200,000
Manufacturing margin		$ 450,000
Variable selling and administrative expenses		16,000
Contribution margin		$ 434,000
Fixed costs:		
Fixed manufacturing costs	$ 42,000	
Fixed selling and administrative expenses	28,000	70,000
Income from operations		$ 364,000

Prepare an absorption costing income statement.

Problem Series A

PR 21-1A

Classify costs

obj. 1

West Coast Apparel Co. manufactures a variety of clothing types for distribution to several major retail chains. The following costs are incurred in the production and sale of blue jeans:

a. Salary of production vice president
b. Property taxes on property, plant, and equipment
c. Electricity costs of $0.12 per kilowatt-hour
d. Salesperson's salary, $30,000 plus 2% of the total sales
e. Consulting fee of $100,000 paid to industry specialist for marketing advice
f. Shipping boxes used to ship orders
g. Dye
h. Thread
i. Salary of designers
j. Brass buttons
k. Janitorial supplies, $2,000 per month
l. Legal fees paid to attorneys in defense of the company in a patent infringement suit, $40,000 plus $150 per hour

m. Straight-line depreciation on sewing machines
n. Insurance premiums on property, plant, and equipment, $50,000 per year plus $4 per $20,000 of insured value over $10,000,000
o. Hourly wages of machine operators
p. Fabric
q. Rental costs of warehouse, $4,000 per month plus $3 per square foot of storage used
r. Rent on experimental equipment, $40,000 per year
s. Leather for patches identifying the brand on individual pieces of apparel
t. Supplies

Instructions

Classify the preceding costs as either fixed, variable, or mixed. Use the following tabular headings and place an "X" in the appropriate column. Identify each cost by letter in the cost column.

Cost	Fixed Cost	Variable Cost	Mixed Cost

PR 21-2A
Break-even sales under present and proposed conditions

objs. 2, 3

✔ 2. (a) $50.00

Battonkill Company, operating at full capacity, sold 112,800 units at a price of $150 per unit during 2010. Its income statement for 2010 is as follows:

Sales		$16,920,000
Cost of goods sold		6,000,000
Gross profit		$10,920,000
Expenses:		
Selling expenses	$3,000,000	
Administrative expenses	1,800,000	
Total expenses		4,800,000
Income from operations		$ 6,120,000

The division of costs between fixed and variable is as follows:

	Fixed	Variable
Cost of sales	40%	60%
Selling expenses	50%	50%
Administrative expenses	70%	30%

   Management is considering a plant expansion program that will permit an increase of $1,500,000 in yearly sales. The expansion will increase fixed costs by $200,000, but will not affect the relationship between sales and variable costs.

Instructions
1. Determine for 2010 the total fixed costs and the total variable costs.
2. Determine for 2010 (a) the unit variable cost and (b) the unit contribution margin.
3. Compute the break-even sales (units) for 2010.
4. Compute the break-even sales (units) under the proposed program.
5. Determine the amount of sales (units) that would be necessary under the proposed program to realize the $6,120,000 of income from operations that was earned in 2010.
6. Determine the maximum income from operations possible with the expanded plant.
7. If the proposal is accepted and sales remain at the 2010 level, what will the income or loss from operations be for 2011?
8. ━━━▶ Based on the data given, would you recommend accepting the proposal? Explain.

PR 21-3A
Break-even sales and cost-volume-profit chart

objs. 3, 4

✔ 1. 30,000 units

For the coming year, Tolstoy Company anticipates a unit selling price of $100, a unit variable cost of $30, and fixed costs of $2,100,000.

Instructions
1. Compute the anticipated break-even sales (units).
2. Compute the sales (units) required to realize income from operations of $350,000.
3. Construct a cost-volume-profit chart, assuming maximum sales of 50,000 units within the relevant range.
4. Determine the probable income (loss) from operations if sales total 40,000 units.

PR 21-4A
Break-even sales and cost-volume-profit chart
objs. 3, 4

✔ 1. 3,400 units

Last year, Douthett Inc. had sales of $2,400,000, based on a unit selling price of $600. The variable cost per unit was $440, and fixed costs were $544,000. The maximum sales within Douthett's relevant range are 5,000 units. Douthett is considering a proposal to spend an additional $80,000 on billboard advertising during the current year in an attempt to increase sales and utilize unused capacity.

Instructions
1. Construct a cost-volume-profit chart indicating the break-even sales for last year. Verify your answer, using the break-even equation.
2. Using the cost-volume-profit chart prepared in part (1), determine (a) the income from operations for last year and (b) the maximum income from operations that could have been realized during the year. Verify your answers arithmetically.
3. Construct a cost-volume-profit chart indicating the break-even sales for the current year, assuming that a noncancelable contract is signed for the additional billboard advertising. No changes are expected in the unit selling price or other costs. Verify your answer, using the break-even equation.
4. Using the cost-volume-profit chart prepared in part (3), determine (a) the income from operations if sales total 4,000 units and (b) the maximum income from operations that could be realized during the year. Verify your answers arithmetically.

PR 21-5A
Sales mix and break-even sales
obj. 5

✔ 1. 3,000 units

Data related to the expected sales of snowboards and skis for Winter Sports Inc. for the current year, which is typical of recent years, are as follows:

Products	Unit Selling Price	Unit Variable Cost	Sales Mix
Snowboards	$250.00	$170.00	40%
Skis	340.00	160.00	60%

The estimated fixed costs for the current year are $420,000.

Instructions
1. Determine the estimated units of sales of the overall product necessary to reach the break-even point for the current year.
2. Based on the break-even sales (units) in part (1), determine the unit sales of both snowboards and skis for the current year.
3. ━━━━▶ Assume that the sales mix was 60% snowboards and 40% skis. Compare the break-even point with that in part (1). Why is it so different?

PR 21-6A
Contribution margin, break-even sales, cost-volume-profit chart, margin of safety, and operating leverage
objs. 2, 3, 4, 5

✔ 2. 50%

Soldner Health Care Products Inc. expects to maintain the same inventories at the end of 2010 as at the beginning of the year. The total of all production costs for the year is therefore assumed to be equal to the cost of goods sold. With this in mind, the various department heads were asked to submit estimates of the costs for their departments during 2010. A summary report of these estimates is as follows:

	Estimated Fixed Cost	Estimated Variable Cost (per unit sold)
Production costs:		
Direct materials	—	$18.00
Direct labor	—	12.00
Factory overhead	$318,000	9.00
Selling expenses:		
Sales salaries and commissions	65,500	4.00
Advertising	22,500	—
Travel	5,000	—
Miscellaneous selling expense	5,500	3.50
Administrative expenses:		
Office and officers' salaries	65,000	—
Supplies	8,000	1.50
Miscellaneous administrative expense	10,500	2.00
Total	$500,000	$50.00

It is expected that 20,000 units will be sold at a price of $100 a unit. Maximum sales within the relevant range are 25,000 units.

Instructions

1. Prepare an estimated income statement for 2010.
2. What is the expected contribution margin ratio?
3. Determine the break-even sales in units.
4. Construct a cost-volume-profit chart indicating the break-even sales.
5. What is the expected margin of safety in dollars and as a percentage of sales?
6. Determine the operating leverage.

Problem Series B

PR 21-1B
Classify costs

obj. 1

New Age Furniture Company manufactures sofas for distribution to several major retail chains. The following costs are incurred in the production and sale of sofas:

a. Salary of production vice president
b. Rental costs of warehouse, $20,000 per month
c. Consulting fee of $100,000 paid to efficiency specialists
d. Janitorial supplies, $25 for each sofa produced
e. Employer's FICA taxes on controller's salary of $200,000
f. Hourly wages of sewing machine operators
g. Salary of designers
h. Foam rubber for cushion fillings
i. Straight-line depreciation on factory equipment
j. Cartons used to ship sofas
k. Legal fees paid to attorneys in defense of the company in a patent infringement suit, $20,000 plus $150 per hour
l. Property taxes on property, plant, and equipment
m. Springs
n. Electricity costs of $0.15 per kilowatt-hour
o. Sewing supplies
p. Fabric for sofa coverings
q. Salesperson's salary, $70,000 plus 5% of the selling price of each sofa sold
r. Insurance premiums on property, plant, and equipment, $20,000 per year plus $20 per $20,000 of insured value over $15,000,000
s. Rent on experimental equipment, $45 for every sofa produced
t. Wood for framing the sofas

Instructions

Classify the preceding costs as either fixed, variable, or mixed. Use the following tabular headings and place an "X" in the appropriate column. Identify each cost by letter in the Cost column.

Cost	Fixed Cost	Variable Cost	Mixed Cost

PR 21-2B
Break-even sales under present and proposed conditions

objs. 2, 3

✔ 3. 15,825 units

Gaelic Industries Inc., operating at full capacity, sold 22,350 units at a price of $150 per unit during 2010. Its income statement for 2010 is as follows:

Sales		$3,352,500
Cost of goods sold		2,200,000
Gross profit		$1,152,500
Expenses:		
Selling expenses	$250,000	
Administrative expenses	250,000	
Total expenses		500,000
Income from operations		$ 652,500

The division of costs between fixed and variable is as follows:

	Fixed	Variable
Cost of sales	60%	40%
Selling expenses	50%	50%
Administrative expenses	55%	45%

Management is considering a plant expansion program that will permit an increase of $900,000 in yearly sales. The expansion will increase fixed costs by $242,500, but will not affect the relationship between sales and variable costs.

Instructions
1. Determine for 2010 the total fixed costs and the total variable costs.
2. Determine for 2010 (a) the unit variable cost and (b) the unit contribution margin.
3. Compute the break-even sales (units) for 2010.
4. Compute the break-even sales (units) under the proposed program.
5. Determine the amount of sales (units) that would be necessary under the proposed program to realize the $652,500 of income from operations that was earned in 2010.
6. Determine the maximum income from operations possible with the expanded plant.
7. If the proposal is accepted and sales remain at the 2010 level, what will the income or loss from operations be for 2011?
8. ➤ Based on the data given, would you recommend accepting the proposal? Explain.

PR 21-3B
Break-even sales and cost-volume-profit chart

objs. 3, 4

✔ 1. 20,000 units

For the coming year, Favre Products Inc. anticipates a unit selling price of $160, a unit variable cost of $90, and fixed costs of $1,400,000.

Instructions
1. Compute the anticipated break-even sales (units).
2. Compute the sales (units) required to realize income from operations of $525,000.
3. Construct a cost-volume-profit chart, assuming maximum sales of 50,000 units within the relevant range.
4. Determine the probable income (loss) from operations if sales total 30,000 units.

PR 21-4B
Break-even sales and cost-volume-profit chart

objs. 3, 4

✔ 1. 3,250 units

Last year, Cul de sac Co. had sales of $740,000, based on a unit selling price of $200. The variable cost per unit was $120, and fixed costs were $260,000. The maximum sales within Cul de sac's relevant range are 5,000 units. Cul de sac is considering a proposal to spend an additional $30,000 on billboard advertising during the current year in an attempt to increase sales and utilize unused capacity.

Instructions
1. Construct a cost-volume-profit chart indicating the break-even sales for last year. Verify your answer, using the break-even equation.
2. Using the cost-volume-profit chart prepared in part (1), determine (a) the income from operations for last year and (b) the maximum income from operations that could have been realized during the year. Verify your answers arithmetically.
3. Construct a cost-volume-profit chart indicating the break-even sales for the current year, assuming that a noncancelable contract is signed for the additional billboard advertising. No changes are expected in the selling price or other costs. Verify your answer, using the break-even equation.
4. Using the cost-volume-profit chart prepared in part (3), determine (a) the income from operations if sales total 4,000 units and (b) the maximum income from operations that could be realized during the year. Verify your answers arithmetically.

PR 21-5B
Sales mix and break-even sales

obj. 5

✔ 1. 6,156 units

Data related to the expected sales of two types of flat panel TVs for Yan Electronics Inc. for the current year, which is typical of recent years, are as follows:

Products	Unit Selling Price	Unit Variable Cost	Sales Mix
18" Flat panel	$420.00	$300.00	75%
22" Flat panel	540.00	340.00	25%

The estimated fixed costs for the current year are $861,840.

Instructions
1. Determine the estimated units of sales of the overall product necessary to reach the break-even point for the current year.
2. Based on the break-even sales (units) in part (1), determine the unit sales of both the 18" flat panel TV and 22" flat panel TV for the current year.
3. ━━━━▶ Assume that the sales mix was 25% 18" flat panel TV and 75% 22" flat panel TV. Compare the break-even point with that in part (1). Why is it so different?

PR 21-6B
Contribution margin, break-even sales, cost-volume-profit chart, margin of safety, and operating leverage

objs. 2, 3, 4, 5

✔ 3. 15,000

Steamboat Co. expects to maintain the same inventories at the end of 2010 as at the beginning of the year. The total of all production costs for the year is therefore assumed to be equal to the cost of goods sold. With this in mind, the various department heads were asked to submit estimates of the costs for their departments during 2010. A summary report of these estimates is as follows:

	Estimated Fixed Cost	Estimated Variable Cost (per unit sold)
Production costs:		
Direct materials	—	$15.00
Direct labor	—	10.00
Factory overhead	$210,000	4.50
Selling expenses:		
Sales salaries and commissions	42,500	2.20
Advertising	14,500	—
Travel	3,500	—
Miscellaneous selling expense	2,500	1.80
Administrative expenses:		
Office and officers' salaries	70,000	—
Supplies	6,000	0.75
Miscellaneous administrative expense	11,000	1.75
Total	$360,000	$36.00

It is expected that 30,000 units will be sold at a price of $60 a unit. Maximum sales within the relevant range are 45,000 units.

Instructions
1. Prepare an estimated income statement for 2010.
2. What is the expected contribution margin ratio?
3. Determine the break-even sales in units.
4. Construct a cost-volume-profit chart indicating the break-even sales.
5. What is the expected margin of safety in dollars and as a percentage of sales?
6. Determine the operating leverage.

Special Activities ● ● ● ● ▶

You can access the special activities online at **www.cengage.com/accounting/reeve**.

Excel Success Special Activities ● ● ● ● ▶

SA 21-1
High-low method

success

Bi-Rize, Inc., incurred the following production volumes and costs for the last six months of the current year:

	Production Unit	Total Cost
July	3,000	$111,700
August	2,980	110,600
September	3,250	118,250
October	2,520	100,200
November	2,260	93,500
December	3,110	114,800

a. Open the Excel file *SA21-1*.
b. Prepare a spreadsheet to determine the variable cost per unit and total fixed cost using the high-low method. Use the VLOOKUP function to match the total cost to the minimum and maximum production in computing the variable cost per unit.
c. When you have completed the high-low analysis, perform a "save as," replacing the entire file name with the following:

SA21-1_[your first name initial]_[your last name]

SA 21-2
High-low method

Jeffries Industrial Products Company prepared production and total cost information for their Moline plant for seven months as follows:

	Production Unit	Total Cost
April	450	$32,485
May	525	35,100
June	590	36,700
July	680	38,650
August	820	43,240
September	910	45,825
October	750	41,710

a. Open the Excel file *SA21-2*.
b. Prepare a spreadsheet to determine the variable cost per unit and total fixed cost using the high-low method. Use the VLOOKUP function to match the total cost to the minimum and maximum production in computing the variable cost per unit.
c. When you have completed the high-low analysis, perform a "save as," replacing the entire file name with the following:

SA21-2_[your first name initial]_[your last name]

SA 21-3
High-low method

Barnstable Company prepared weekly production and total cost information for the Assembly Department for 12 weeks as follows:

	Production Unit	Total Cost
Week 1	1,930	$46,790
Week 2	1,240	33,710
Week 3	1,760	42,490
Week 4	980	28,740
Week 5	1,130	31,740
Week 6	1,520	39,400
Week 7	1,690	42,350
Week 8	1,420	37,240
Week 9	1,550	38,540
Week 10	1,300	34,990
Week 11	1,750	42,870
Week 12	1,890	46,320

a. Open the Excel file *SA21-3*.
b. Prepare a spreadsheet to determine the variable cost per unit and total fixed cost using the high-low method. Use the VLOOKUP function to match the total cost to the minimum and maximum production in computing the variable cost per unit.
c. When you have completed the high-low analysis, perform a "save as," replacing the entire file name with the following:

SA21-3_[your first name initial]_[your last name]

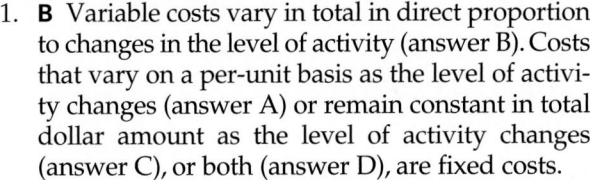

Answers to Self-Examination Questions

1. **B** Variable costs vary in total in direct proportion to changes in the level of activity (answer B). Costs that vary on a per-unit basis as the level of activity changes (answer A) or remain constant in total dollar amount as the level of activity changes (answer C), or both (answer D), are fixed costs.

2. **D** The contribution margin ratio indicates the percentage of each sales dollar available to cover the fixed costs and provide income from operations and is determined as follows:

$$\text{Contribution Margin Ratio} = \frac{\text{Sales} - \text{Variable Costs}}{\text{Sales}}$$

$$\text{Contribution Margin Ratio} = \frac{\$500,000 - \$200,000}{\$500,000}$$

$$= 60\%$$

3. **D** The break-even sales of 40,000 units (answer D) is computed as follows:

$$\text{Break-Even Sales (units)} = \frac{\text{Fixed Costs}}{\text{Unit Contribution Margin}}$$

$$\text{Break-Even Sales (units)} = \frac{\$160,000}{\$4} = 40,000 \text{ units}$$

4. **D** Sales of 45,000 units are required to realize income from operations of $20,000, computed as follows:

$$\text{Sales (units)} = \frac{\text{Fixed Costs} + \text{Target Profit}}{\text{Unit Contribution Margin}}$$

$$\text{Sales (units)} = \frac{\$160,000 + \$20,000}{\$4} = 45,000 \text{ units}$$

5. **C** The operating leverage is 1.8, computed as follows:

$$\text{Operating Leverage} = \frac{\text{Contribution Margin}}{\text{Income from Operations}}$$

$$\text{Operating Leverage} = \frac{\$360,000}{\$200,000} = 1.8$$

Budgeting

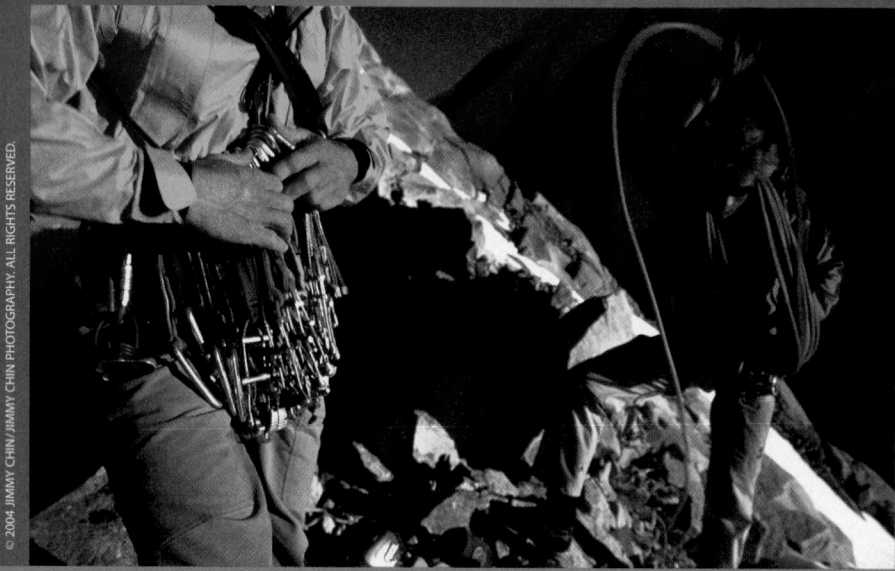

T H E   N O R T H   F A C E

You may have financial goals for your life. To achieve these goals, it is necessary to plan for future expenses. For example, you may consider taking a part-time job to save money for school expenses for the coming school year. How much money would you need to earn and save in order to pay these expenses? One way to find an answer to this question would be to prepare a budget. A budget would show an estimate of your expenses associated with school, such as tuition, fees, and books. In addition, you would have expenses for day-to-day living, such as rent, food, and clothing. You might also have expenses for travel and entertainment. Once the school year begins, you can use the budget as a tool for guiding your spending priorities during the year.

The budget is used in businesses in much the same way as it can be used in personal life. For example, The North Face sponsors mountain climbing expeditions throughout the year for professional and amateur climbers. These events require budgeting to plan trip expenses, much like you might use a budget to plan a vacation.

Budgeting is also used by The North Face to plan the manufacturing costs associated with its outdoor clothing and equipment production. For example, budgets would be used to determine the number of coats to be produced, number of people to be employed, and amount of material to be purchased. The budget provides the company with a "game plan" for the year. In this chapter, you will see how budgets can be used for financial planning and control.

After studying this chapter, you should be able to:

1 Describe budgeting, its objectives, and its impact on human behavior.

2 Describe the basic elements of the budget process, the two major types of budgeting, and the use of computers in budgeting.

3 Describe the master budget for a manufacturing company.

4 Prepare the basic income statement budgets for a manufacturing company.

5 Prepare balance sheet budgets for a manufacturing company.

Nature and Objectives of Budgeting

Objectives of Budgeting

Human Behavior and Budgeting

Budgeting Systems

Static Budget

Flexible Budget

EE 22-1 (page 992)

Computerized Budgeting Systems

Master Budget

Income Statement Budgets

excel *success*   Sales Budget

excel *success*   Production Budget

EE 22-2 (page 997)

excel *success*   Direct Materials Purchases Budget

EE 22-3 (page 998)

excel *success*   Direct Labor Cost Budget

EE 22-4 (page 999)

excel *success*   Factory Overhead Cost Budget

excel *success*   Cost of Goods Sold Budget

EE 22-5 (page 1001)

Selling and Administrative Expenses Budget

Budgeted Income Statement

Balance Sheet Budgets

Cash Budget

EE 22-6 (page 1006)

Capital Expenditures Budget

Budgeted Balance Sheet

At a Glance   Menu   Turn to pg 1010

South-Western

---

1 Describe budgeting, its objectives, and its impact on human behavior.

Nature and Objectives of Budgeting

Budgets play an important role for organizations of all sizes and forms. For example, budgets are used in managing the operations of government agencies, churches, hospitals, and other nonprofit organizations. Individuals and families also use budgeting in managing their financial affairs. This chapter describes and illustrates budgeting for a manufacturing company.

Objectives of Budgeting

Budgeting involves (1) establishing specific goals, (2) executing plans to achieve the goals, and (3) periodically comparing actual results with the goals. In doing so, budgeting affects the following managerial functions:

1. Planning
2. Directing
3. Controlling

The relationships of these activities are illustrated in Exhibit 1.

Planning involves setting goals as a guide for making decisions. Budgeting supports the planning process by requiring all departments and other organizational units to establish their goals for the future. These goals help motivate employees. In addition, the budgeting process often identifies areas where operations can be improved or inefficiencies eliminated.

Exhibit 1

Planning, Directing, and Controlling

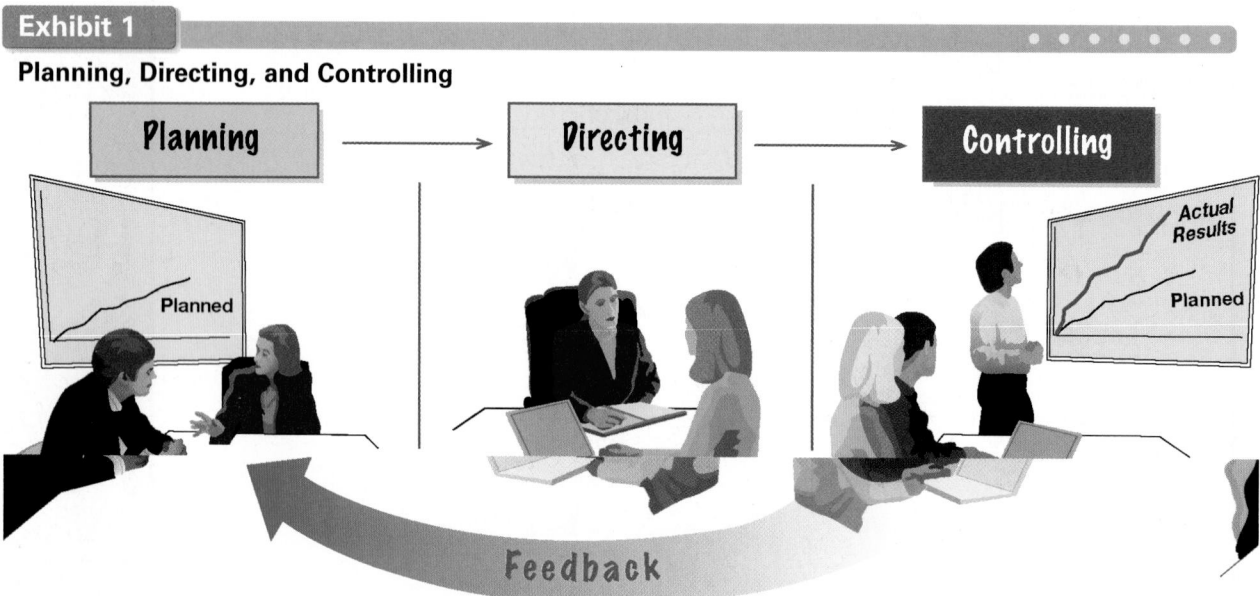

Directing involves decisions and actions to achieve budgeted goals. Budgeting aids in coordinating management's decisions and actions to achieve the company's budgeted goals. A budgetary unit of a company is called a **responsibility center**. Each responsibility center is led by a manager who has the authority and responsibility for achieving the center's budgeted goals.

Controlling involves comparing actual performance against the budgeted goals. Such comparisons provide feedback to managers and employees about their performance. If necessary, responsibility centers can use such feedback to adjust their activities in the future.

A budget is like a road map. It charts a future course for a company in financial terms and, thus, aids the company in navigating through the year to reach its destination.

Human Behavior and Budgeting

Human behavior problems can arise in the budgeting process in the following situations:

1. Budgeted goals are set too tight, which are very hard or impossible to achieve
2. Budgeted goals are set too loose, which are very easy to achieve
3. Budgeted goals conflict with the objectives of the company and employees

These behavior problems are illustrated in Exhibit 2.

Exhibit 2

Human Behavior Problems in Budgeting

Budget Goals Too Tight   Budget Goals Too Loose   Conflicting Budget Goals

Setting Budget Goals Too Tightly Employees and managers may become discouraged if budgeted goals are set too high. That is, if budgeted goals are viewed as unrealistic or unachievable, the budget may have a negative effect on the ability of the company to achieve its goals.

Reasonable, attainable goals are more likely to motivate employees and managers. For this reason, it is important that employees and managers be involved in the budgeting process. Involving employees in the budgeting process provides employees with a sense of control and, thus, more of a commitment in meeting budgeted goals. Finally, involving employees and managers also encourages cooperation across departments and responsibility centers. Such cooperation increases awareness of each department's importance to the overall goals of the company.

Setting Budget Goals Too Loosely Although it is desirable to establish attainable goals, it is undesirable to plan lower goals than may be possible. Such budget "padding" is termed **budgetary slack**. Managers may plan slack in the budget in order to provide a "cushion" for unexpected events or improve the appearance of operations. Budgetary slack can be reduced by properly training employees and managers in the importance of realistic, attainable budgets.

Slack budgets may cause a "spend it or lose it" mentality. This often occurs at the end of the budget period when actual spending is less than the budget. Employees and managers may spend the remaining budget on unnecessary purchases in order to avoid having their budget reduced for the next period.

Setting Conflicting Budget Goals **Goal conflict** occurs when the employees' or managers' self-interest differs from the company's objectives or goals. Goal conflict may also occur among responsibility centers such as departments.

To illustrate, assume that the sales department manager is given an increased sales goal and as a result accepts customers who are poor credit risks. This, in turn, causes bad debt expense to increase and profitability to decline. Likewise, a manufacturing department manager may be told to reduce costs. As a result, the manufacturing department manager might use lower-cost direct materials, which are also of lower quality. As a result, customer complaints and returns might increase significantly, which would adversely affect the company's profitability.

Integrity, Objectivity, and Ethics in Business

BUDGET GAMES

The budgeting system is designed to plan and control a business. However, it is common for the budget to be "gamed" by its participants. For example, managers may pad their budgets with excess resources. In this way, the managers have additional resources for unexpected events during the period. If the budget is being used to establish the incentive plan, then sales managers have incentives to understate the sales potential of a territory in order to ensure hitting their quotas. Other times, managers engage in "land grabbing," which occurs when they overstate the sales potential of a territory in order to guarantee access to resources. If managers believe that unspent resources will not roll over to future periods, then they may be encouraged to "spend it or lose it," causing wasteful expenditures. These types of problems can be partially overcome by separating the budget into planning and incentive components. This is why many organizations have two budget processes, one for resource planning and another, more challenging budget, for motivating managers.

2 Describe the basic elements of the budget process, the two major types of budgeting, and the use of computers in budgeting.

Budgeting Systems

Budgeting systems vary among companies and industries. For example, the budget system used by Ford Motor Company differs from that used by Delta Air Lines. However, the basic budgeting concepts discussed in this section apply to all types of businesses and organizations.

The budgetary period for operating activities normally includes the fiscal year of a company. A year is short enough that future operations can be estimated fairly accurately, yet long enough that the future can be viewed in a broad context. However, for control purposes, annual budgets are usually subdivided into shorter time periods, such as quarters of the year, months, or weeks.

A variation of fiscal-year budgeting, called **continuous budgeting**, maintains a 12-month projection into the future. The 12-month budget is continually revised by replacing the data for the month just ended with the budget data for the same month in the next year. A continuous budget is illustrated in Exhibit 3.

Developing an annual budget usually begins several months prior to the end of the current year. This responsibility is normally assigned to a budget committee. Such a committee often consists of the budget director, the controller, the treasurer, the production manager, and the sales manager. The budget process is monitored and summarized by the Accounting Department, which reports to the committee.

There are several methods of developing budget estimates. One method, termed **zero-based budgeting**, requires managers to estimate sales, production, and other operating data as though operations are being started for the first time. This approach has the benefit of taking a fresh view of operations each year. A more common approach is to start with last year's budget and revise it for actual results and expected changes for the coming year. Two major budgets using this approach are the static budget and the flexible budget.

Exhibit 3

Continuous Budgeting

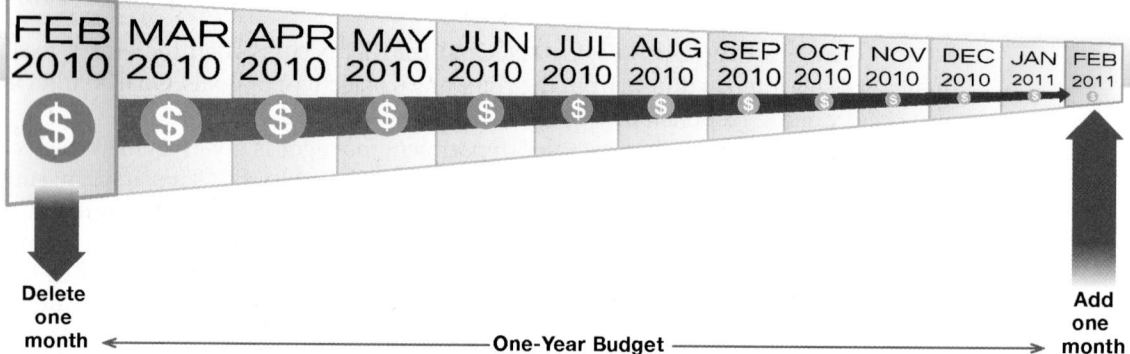

Static Budget

A **static budget** shows the expected results of a responsibility center for only one activity level. Once the budget has been determined, it is not changed, even if the activity changes. Static budgeting is used by many service companies and for some functions of manufacturing companies, such as purchasing, engineering, and accounting.

To illustrate, the static budget for the Assembly Department of Colter Manufacturing Company is shown in Exhibit 4.

Exhibit 4

Static Budget

	A	B
1	Colter Manufacturing Company	
2	Assembly Department Budget	
3	For the Year Ending July 31, 2010	
4	Direct labor	$40,000
5	Electric power	5,000
6	Supervisor salaries	15,000
7	Total department costs	$60,000
8		

A disadvantage of static budgets is that they do not adjust for changes in activity levels. For example, assume that the Assembly Department of Colter Manufacturing spent $70,800 for the year ended July 31, 2010. Thus, the Assembly Department spent $10,800 ($70,800 − $60,000), or 18% ($10,800/$60,000) more than budgeted. Is this good news or bad news?

The first reaction is that this is bad news and the Assembly Department was inefficient in spending more than budgeted. However, assume that the Assembly Department's budget was based on plans to assemble 8,000 units during the year. If 10,000 units were actually assembled, the additional $10,800 spent in excess of budget might be good news. That is, the Assembly Department assembled 25% (2,000 units/8,000 units) more than planned for only 18% more cost.

Flexible Budget

Unlike static budgets, **flexible budgets** show the expected results of a responsibility center for several activity levels. A flexible budget is, in effect, a series of static budgets for different levels of activity.

To illustrate, a flexible budget for the Assembly Department of Colter Manufacturing Company is shown in Exhibit 5.

Exhibit 5

Flexible Budget

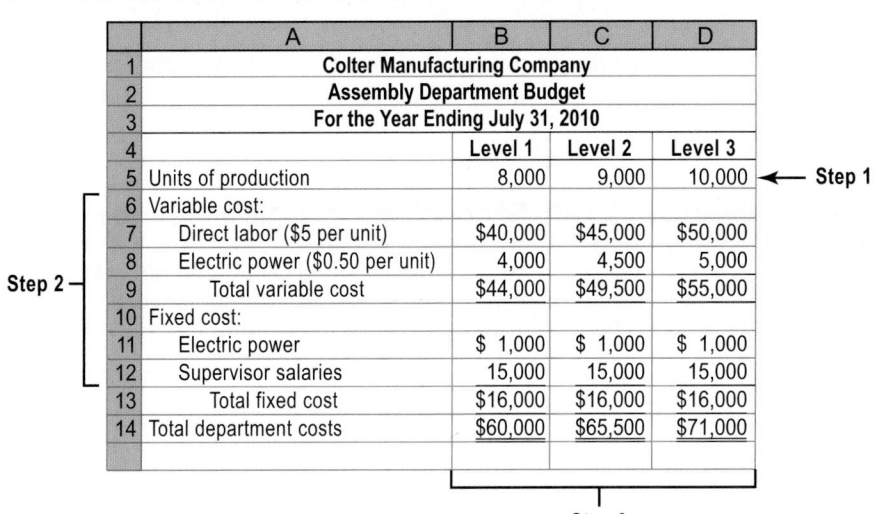

	A	B	C	D
1	Colter Manufacturing Company			
2	Assembly Department Budget			
3	For the Year Ending July 31, 2010			
4		Level 1	Level 2	Level 3
5	Units of production	8,000	9,000	10,000
6	Variable cost:			
7	Direct labor ($5 per unit)	$40,000	$45,000	$50,000
8	Electric power ($0.50 per unit)	4,000	4,500	5,000
9	Total variable cost	$44,000	$49,500	$55,000
10	Fixed cost:			
11	Electric power	$ 1,000	$ 1,000	$ 1,000
12	Supervisor salaries	15,000	15,000	15,000
13	Total fixed cost	$16,000	$16,000	$16,000
14	Total department costs	$60,000	$65,500	$71,000

Step 1

Step 2

Step 3

A flexible budget is constructed as follows:

Step 1. Identify the relevant activity levels. The relevant levels of activity could be expressed in units, machine hours, direct labor hours, or some other activity base. In Exhibit 5, the levels of activity are 8,000, 9,000, and 10,000 units of production.

Step 2. Identify the fixed and variable cost components of the costs being budgeted. In Exhibit 5, the electric power cost is separated into its fixed cost ($1,000 per year) and variable cost ($0.50 per unit). The direct labor is a variable cost, and the supervisor salaries are all fixed costs.

Step 3. Prepare the budget for each activity level by multiplying the variable cost per unit by the activity level and then adding the monthly fixed cost.

With a flexible budget, actual costs can be compared to the budgeted costs for actual activity. To illustrate, assume that the Assembly Department spent $70,800 to produce 10,000 units. Exhibit 5 indicates that the Assembly Department was *under* budget by $200 ($71,000 − $70,800).

Under the static budget in Exhibit 4, the Assembly Department was $10,800 *over* budget. This comparison is illustrated in Exhibit 6.

Many hospitals use flexible budgeting to plan the number of nurses for patient floors. These budgets use a measure termed "relative value units," which is a measure of nursing effort. The more patients and the more severe their illnesses, the higher the total relative value units, and thus the higher the staffing budget.

Exhibit 6

Static and Flexible Budgets

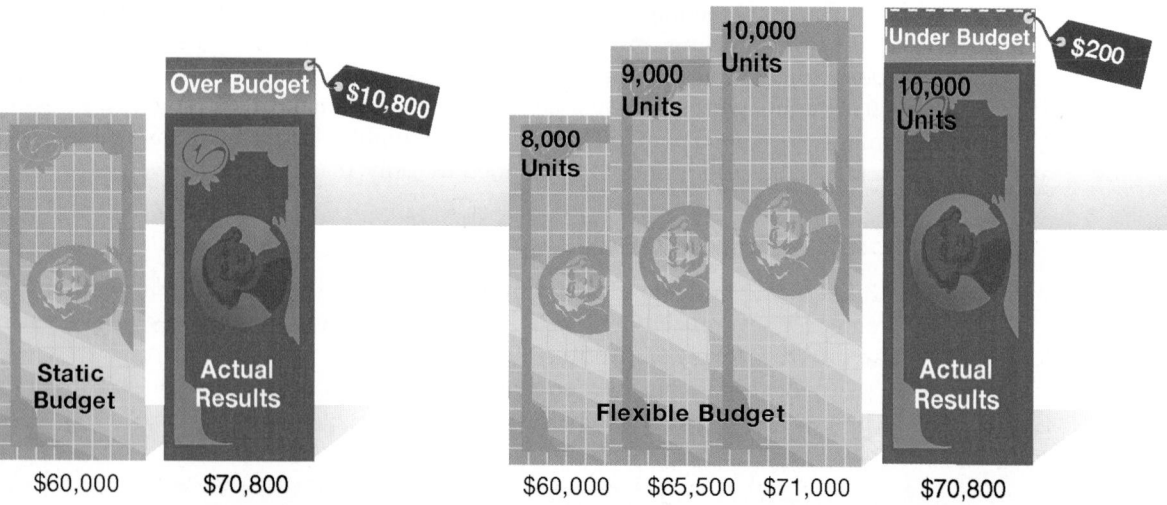

The flexible budget for the Assembly Department is much more accurate and useful than the static budget. This is because the flexible budget adjusts for changes in the level of activity.

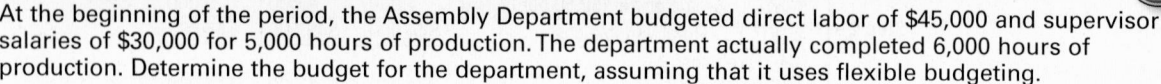

Example Exercise 22-1 Flexible Budgeting

At the beginning of the period, the Assembly Department budgeted direct labor of $45,000 and supervisor salaries of $30,000 for 5,000 hours of production. The department actually completed 6,000 hours of production. Determine the budget for the department, assuming that it uses flexible budgeting.

(continued)

Follow My Example 22-1

Variable cost:	
Direct labor (6,000 hours × $9* per hour)	$54,000
Fixed cost:	
Supervisor salaries	30,000
Total department costs	$84,000

*$45,000/5,000 hours

For Practice: PE 22-1A, PE 22-1B

Computerized Budgeting Systems

One survey reported that 67% of the companies relied on spreadsheets for budgeting and planning.

Source: Tim Reason, "Budgeting in the Real World," *CFO Magazine,* July 1, 2005.

In developing budgets, companies use a variety of computerized approaches. Two of the most popular computerized approaches use:

1. Spreadsheet software such as Microsoft Excel
2. Integrated budget and planning (B&P) software systems

Integrated computerized budget and planning systems speed up and reduce the cost of preparing the budget. This is especially true when large quantities of data need to be processed.

B&P software systems are also useful in continuous budgeting. For example, the latest B&P systems use the Web (Intranet) to link thousands of employees together during the budget process. Employees can input budget data onto Web pages that are integrated and summarized throughout the company. In this way, a company can quickly and consistently integrate top-level strategies and goals to lower-level operational goals. These latest B&P software systems are moving companies closer to the real-time budget, wherein the budget is being "rolled" every day.[1]

Fujitsu, a Japanese technology company, used B&P to reduce its budgeting process from 6–8 weeks down to 10–15 days.

Companies may also use computer simulation models to analyze the impact of various assumptions and operating alternatives on the budget. For example, the budget can be revised to show the impact of a proposed change in indirect labor wage rates. Likewise, the budgetary effect of a proposed product line can be determined.

3   Describe the master budget for a manufacturing company.

Master Budget

The **master budget** is an integrated set of operating, investing, and financing budgets for a period of time. Most companies prepare the master budget on a yearly basis.

For a manufacturing company, the master budget consists of the following integrated budgets:

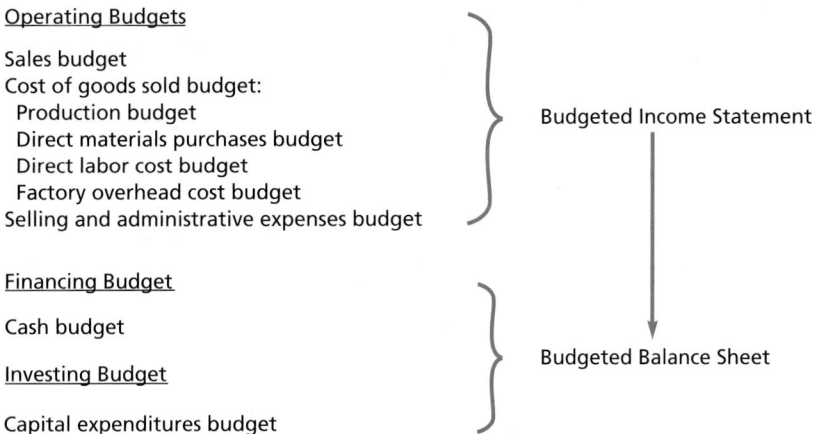

1 Janet Kersnar, "Rolling Along," *CFO Europe,* September 14, 2004.

As shown on page 993, the master budget is an integrated set of budgets that tie together a company's operating, financing, and investing activities into an integrated plan for the coming year.

The master budget begins with preparing the operating budgets, which form the budgeted income statement. The income statement budgets are normally prepared in the following order beginning with the sales budget:

1. Sales budget
2. Production budget
3. Direct materials purchases budget
4. Direct labor cost budget
5. Factory overhead cost budget
6. Cost of goods sold budget
7. Selling and administrative expenses budget
8. Budgeted income statement

After the budgeted income statement is prepared, the budgeted balance sheet is prepared. Two major budgets comprising the budgeted balance sheet are the cash budget and the capital expenditures budget.

Exhibit 7 shows the relationships among the income statement budgets.

Exhibit 7

Income Statement Budgets

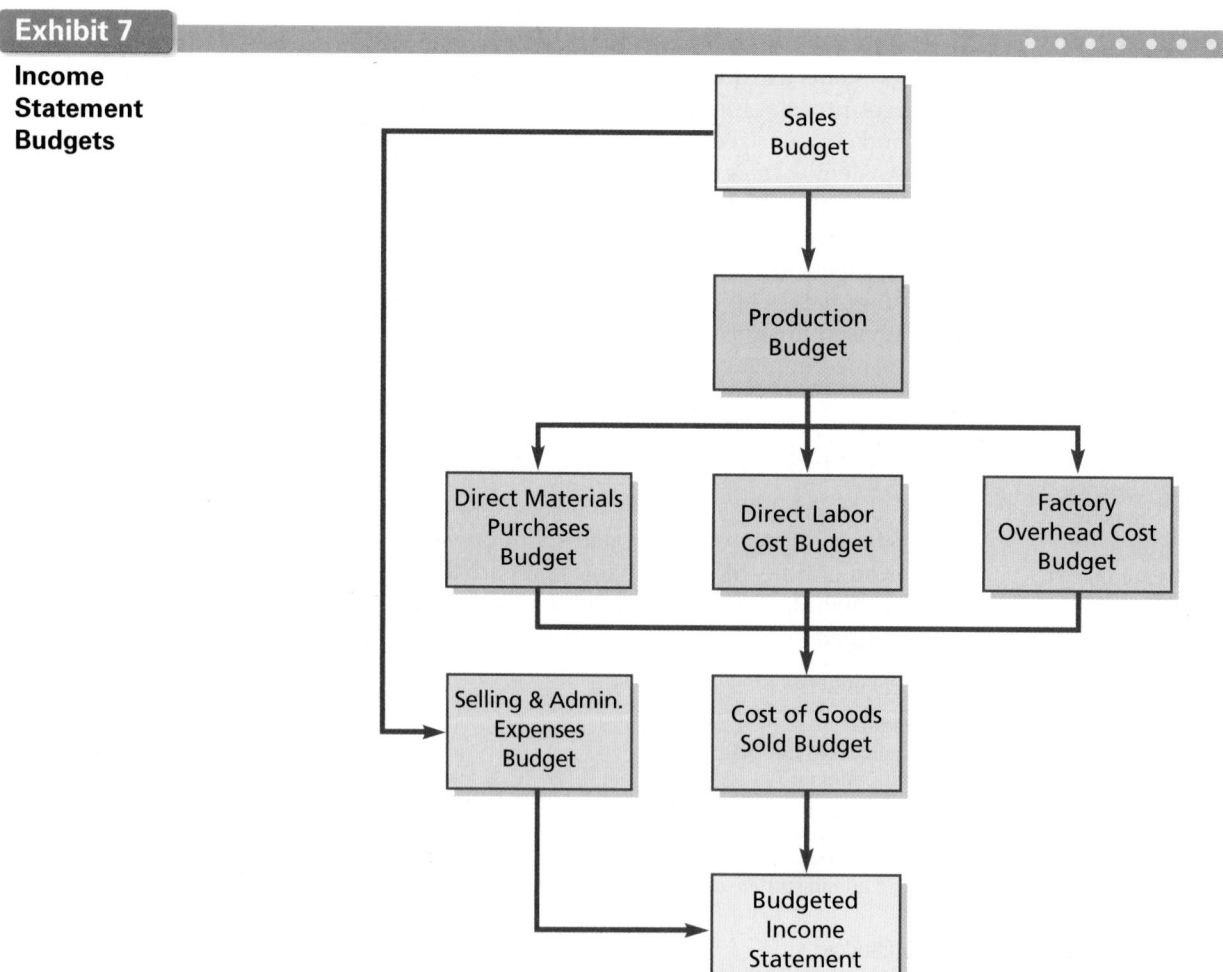

Income Statement Budgets

4 Prepare the basic income statement budgets for a manufacturing company.

The integrated budgets that support the income statement budget are described and illustrated in this section. Elite Accessories Inc., a small manufacturing company, is used as a basis for illustration.

Sales Budget

The **sales budget** begins by estimating the quantity of sales. As a starting point, the prior year's sales quantities are often used. These sales quantities are then revised for such factors as the following:

1.   Backlog of unfilled sales orders from the prior period
2.   Planned advertising and promotion
3.   Productive capacity
4.   Projected pricing changes
5.   Findings of market research studies
6.   Expected industry and general economic conditions

Once sales quantities are estimated, the expected sales revenue can be determined by multiplying the volume by the expected unit sales price.

To illustrate, Elite Accessories Inc. manufactures wallets and handbags that are sold in two regions, the East and West Regions. Elite Accessories estimates the following sales quantities and prices for 2010:

	East Region	West Region	Unit Selling Price
Wallets	287,000	241,000	$12
Handbags	156,400	123,600	25

Exhibit 8 illustrates the sales budget for Elite Accessories based on the preceding data.

Exhibit 8

Sales Budget

	A	B	C	D
1	Elite Accessories Inc.			
2	Sales Budget			
3	For the Year Ending December 31, 2010			
4		Unit Sales	Unit Selling	
5	Product and Region	Volume	Price	Total Sales
6	Wallet:	287,000	$12.00	$ 3,444,000
7	East	241,000	12.00	2,892,000
8	West	528,000		$ 6,336,000
9	Total			
10				
11	Handbag:			
12	East	156,400	$25.00	$ 3,910,000
13	West	123,600	25.00	3,090,000
14	Total	280,000		$ 7,000,000
15				
16	Total revenue from sales			$13,336,000

Production Budget

The production budget should be integrated with the sales budget to ensure that production and sales are kept in balance during the year. The **production budget** estimates the number of units to be manufactured to meet budgeted sales and desired inventory levels.

The budgeted units to be produced are determined as follows:

Expected units to be sold	XXX units
Plus desired units in ending inventory	+ XXX
Less estimated units in beginning inventory	− XXX
Total units to be produced	XXX units

Elite Accessories Inc. expects the following inventories of wallets and handbags:

	Estimated Inventory January 1, 2010	Desired Inventory December 31, 2010
Wallets	88,000	80,000
Handbags	48,000	60,000

Exhibit 9 illustrates the production budget for Elite Accessories Inc.

Exhibit 9

Production Budget

	A	B	C
1	Elite Accessories Inc.		
2	Production Budget		
3	For the Year Ending December 31, 2010		
4		Units	
5		Wallet	Handbag
6	Expected units to be sold (from Exhibit 8)	528,000	280,000
7	Plus desired ending inventory, December 31, 2010	80,000	60,000
8	Total	608,000	340,000
9	Less estimated beginning inventory, January 1, 2010	88,000	48,000
10	Total units to be produced	520,000	292,000

A spreadsheet can be used to create a sales budget, as illustrated below:

	A	B	C	D
1	Elite Accessories			
2	Sales Budget			
3	For the Year Ending December 31, 2010			
4				
5	Product and Region	Unit Sales Volume	Unit Selling Price	Total Sales
6	Wallet:			
7	East	287,000	$ 12.00	=B7*C7
8	West	241,000	12.00	=B8*C8
9	Total			=SUM(D7:D8)
10				
11	Handbag:			
12	East	156,400	$ 25.00	=B12*C12
13	West	123,600	25.00	=B13*C13
14	Total			=SUM(D12:D13)
15				
16	Total revenue from sales			=D9+D14

a. Format the budget in a spreadsheet, centering the heading in merged cells over four columns. Enter row text and data in the first three columns as shown.
b. Enter in cell D7 the formula for the total sales for the first line of data (East region, wallet), =B7*C7.
c. Copy cell D7 to D8, D12, and D13. Thus, the product of the units sales volume and unit selling price are now calculated for each region.
d. Enter in D9 the sum of D7 and D8, =SUM(D7:D8).
e. Copy D9 to D14.
f. Enter in D16 the formula to sum the two region subtotals, =D9+D14.

The remaining budgets illustrated in this chapter can also be constructed on a spreadsheet using appropriate formulas and cell references. The complete master budget is shown on a spreadsheet at the end of this chapter illustrating selected formula entries.

 Go to the hands-on **Excel Tutor** for this example!

Example Exercise 22-2   Production Budget   **4**

Landon Awards Co. projected sales of 45,000 brass plaques for 2010. The estimated January 1, 2010, inventory is 3,000 units, and the desired December 31, 2010, inventory is 5,000 units. What is the budgeted production (in units) for 2010?

Follow My Example 22-2

Expected units to be sold	45,000
Plus desired ending inventory, December 31, 2010	5,000
Total	50,000
Less estimated beginning inventory, January 1, 2010	3,000
Total units to be produced	47,000

For Practice: PE 22-2A, PE 22-2B

Direct Materials Purchases Budget

The direct materials purchases budget should be integrated with the production budget to ensure that production is not interrupted during the year. The **direct materials purchases budget** estimates the quantities of direct materials to be purchased to support budgeted production and desired inventory levels.

The direct materials to be purchased are determined as follows:

Materials required for production	XXX
Plus desired ending materials inventory	+ XXX
Less estimated beginning materials inventory	− XXX
Direct materials to be purchased	XXX

Elite Accessories Inc. uses leather and lining in producing wallets and handbags. The quantity of direct materials expected to be used for each unit of product is as follows:

Wallet	**Handbag**
Leather: 0.30 sq. yd. per unit	Leather: 1.25 sq. yds. per unit
Lining: 0.10 sq. yd. per unit	Lining: 0.50 sq. yd. per unit

Elite Accessories Inc. expects the following direct materials inventories of leather and lining:

	Estimated Direct Materials Inventory January 1, 2010	**Desired Direct Materials Inventory December 31, 2010**
Leather	18,000 sq. yds.	20,000 sq. yds.
Lining	15,000 sq. yds.	12,000 sq. yds.

The estimated price per square yard of leather and lining during 2010 is shown below.

	Price per Square Yard
Leather	$4.50
Lining	1.20

Exhibit 10 illustrates the direct materials purchases budget for Elite Accessories Inc.

Exhibit 10

Direct Materials Purchases Budget

	A	B	C	D	E
1		Elite Accessories Inc.			
2		Direct Materials Purchases Budget			
3		For the Year Ending December 31, 2010			
4			Direct Materials		
5			Leather	Lining	Total
6	Square yards required for production:				
7	Wallet (Note A)		156,000	52,000	
8	Handbag (Note B)		365,000	146,000	
9	Plus desired inventory, December 31, 2010		20,000	12,000	
10	Total		541,000	210,000	
11	Less estimated inventory, January 1, 2010		18,000	15,000	
12	Total square yards to be purchased		523,000	195,000	
13	Unit price (per square yard)		× $4.50	× $1.20	
14	Total direct materials to be purchased		$2,353,500	$234,000	$2,587,500
15					
16	Note A:	Leather: 520,000 units × 0.30 sq. yd. per unit = 156,000 sq. yds.			
17		Lining: 520,000 units × 0.10 sq. yd. per unit = 52,000 sq. yds.			
18					
19	Note B:	Leather: 292,000 units × 1.25 sq. yds. per unit = 365,000 sq. yds.			
20		Lining: 292,000 units × 0.50 sq. yd. per unit = 146,000 sq. yds.			

The timing of the direct materials purchases should be coordinated between the purchasing and production departments so that production is not interrupted.

Example Exercise 22-3 Direct Materials Purchases Budget ········▶ 4

Landon Awards Co. budgeted production of 47,000 brass plaques in 2010. Brass sheet is required to produce a brass plaque. Assume 96 square inches of brass sheet are required for each brass plaque. The estimated January 1, 2010, brass sheet inventory is 240,000 square inches. The desired December 31, 2010, brass sheet inventory is 200,000 square inches. If brass sheet costs $0.12 per square inch, determine the direct materials purchases budget for 2010.

Follow My Example 22-3

Square inches required for production:	
Brass sheet (47,000 × 96 sq. in.)	4,512,000
Plus desired ending inventory, December 31, 2010	200,000
Total	4,712,000
Less estimated beginning inventory, January 1, 2010	240,000
Total square inches to be purchased	4,472,000
Unit price (per square inch)	× $0.12
Total direct materials to be purchased	$ 536,640

For Practice: PE 22-3A, PE 22-3B

Direct Labor Cost Budget

The **direct labor cost budget** estimates the direct labor hours and related cost needed to support budgeted production.

Elite Accessories Inc. estimates that the following direct labor hours are needed to produce a wallet and handbag:

Wallet	**Handbag**
Cutting Department: 0.10 hr. per unit	Cutting Department: 0.15 hr. per unit
Sewing Department: 0.25 hr. per unit	Sewing Department: 0.40 hr. per unit

The estimated direct labor hourly rates for the Cutting and Sewing departments during 2010 are shown below.

	Hourly Rate
Cutting Department	$12
Sewing Department	15

Exhibit 11 illustrates the direct labor cost budget for Elite Accessories Inc.

Exhibit 11

Direct Labor Cost Budget

	A	B	C	D	E
1		Elite Accessories Inc.			
2		Direct Labor Cost Budget			
3		For the Year Ending December 31, 2010			
4			Cutting	Sewing	Total
5	Hours required for production:				
6	Wallet (Note A)		52,000	130,000	
7	Handbag (Note B)		43,800	116,800	
8	Total		95,800	246,800	
9	Hourly rate		× $12.00	× $15.00	
10	Total direct labor cost		$1,149,600	$3,702,000	$4,851,600
11					
12	Note A:	Cutting Department: 520,000 units × 0.10 hr. per unit = 52,000 hrs.			
13		Sewing Department: 520,000 units × 0.25 hr. per unit = 130,000 hrs.			
14					
15	Note B:	Cutting Department: 292,000 units × 0.15 hr. per unit = 43,800 hrs.			
16		Sewing Department: 292,000 units × 0.40 hr. per unit = 116,800 hrs.			

As shown in Exhibit 11, for Elite Accessories Inc. to produce 520,000 wallets, 52,000 hours (520,000 units × 0.10 hr. per unit) of labor are required in the Cutting Department. Likewise, to produce 292,000 handbags, 43,800 hours (292,000 units × 0.15 hour per unit) of labor are required in the Cutting Department. Thus, the estimated total direct labor cost for the Cutting Department is $1,149,600 [(52,000 hrs. + 43,800 hrs.) × $12 per hr.]. In a similar manner, the direct labor hours and cost for the Sewing Department are determined.

The direct labor needs should be coordinated between the production and personnel departments so that there will be enough labor available for production.

Example Exercise 22-4   Direct Labor Cost Budget   **4**

Landon Awards Co. budgeted production of 47,000 brass plaques in 2010. Each plaque requires engraving. Assume that 12 minutes are required to engrave each plaque. If engraving labor costs $11.00 per hour, determine the direct labor cost budget for 2010.

Follow My Example 22-4

Hours required for engraving:	
Brass plaque (47,000 × 12 min.)	564,000 min.
Convert minutes to hours	÷ 60 min.
Engraving hours	9,400 hrs.
Hourly rate	× $11.00
Total direct labor cost	$103,400

For Practice: PE 22-4A, PE 22-4B

Factory Overhead Cost Budget

The **factory overhead cost budget** estimates the cost for each item of factory overhead needed to support budgeted production.

Exhibit 12 illustrates the factory overhead cost budget for Elite Accessories Inc.

Exhibit 12

Factory Overhead Cost Budget

	A	B
1	Elite Accessories Inc.	
2	Factory Overhead Cost Budget	
3	For the Year Ending December 31, 2010	
4	Indirect factory wages	$ 732,800
5	Supervisor salaries	360,000
6	Power and light	306,000
7	Depreciation of plant and equipment	288,000
8	Indirect materials	182,800
9	Maintenance	140,280
10	Insurance and property taxes	79,200
11	Total factory overhead cost	$2,089,080

The factory overhead cost budget shown in Exhibit 12 may be supported by departmental schedules. Such schedules normally separate factory overhead costs into fixed and variable costs to better enable department managers to monitor and evaluate costs during the year.

The factory overhead cost budget should be integrated with the production budget to ensure that production is not interrupted during the year.

Cost of Goods Sold Budget

The **cost of goods sold budget** is prepared by integrating the following budgets:

1. Direct materials purchases budget (Exhibit 10)
2. Direct labor cost budget (Exhibit 11)
3. Factory overhead cost budget (Exhibit 12)

In addition, the estimated and desired inventories for direct materials, work in process, and finished goods must be integrated into the cost of goods sold budget.

Elite Accessories Inc. expects the following direct materials, work in process, and finished goods inventories:

	Estimated Inventory Jan. 1, 2010	Desired Inventory Dec. 31, 2010
Direct materials:		
Leather	$ 81,000 (18,000 sq. yds. × $4.50)	$ 90,000 (20,000 sq. yds. × $4.50)
Lining	18,000 (15,000 sq. yds. × $1.20)	14,400 (12,000 sq. yds. × $1.20)
Total direct materials	$ 99,000	$ 104,400
Work in process:	$ 214,400	$ 220,000
Finished goods:	$1,095,600	$1,565,000

Exhibit 13 illustrates the cost of goods sold budget for Elite Accessories Inc. It indicates that total manufacturing costs of $9,522,780 are budgeted to be incurred in 2010. Of this total, $2,582,100 is budgeted for direct materials, $4,851,600 is budgeted for direct labor, and $2,089,080 is budgeted for factory overhead. After considering work in process inventories, the total budgeted cost of goods manufactured and transferred to finished goods during 2010 is $9,517,180. Based on expected sales, the budgeted cost of goods sold is $9,047,780.

Exhibit 13

Cost of Goods Sold Budget

	A	B	C	D	E	F
1		Elite Accessories Inc.				
2		Cost of Goods Sold Budget				
3		For the Year Ending December 31, 2010				
4	Finished goods inventory, January 1, 2010					$ 1,095,600
5	Work in process inventory, January 1, 2010				$ 214,400	
6	Direct materials:					
7	Direct materials inventory,					
8	January 1, 2010			$ 99,000		
9	Direct materials purchases (from Exhibit 10)			2,587,500		
10	Cost of direct materials available for use			$2,686,500		
11	Less direct materials inventory,					
12	December 31, 2010			104,400		
13	Cost of direct materials placed in production			$2,582,100		
14	Direct labor (from Exhibit 11)			4,851,600		
15	Factory overhead (from Exhibit 12)			2,089,080		
16	Total manufacturing costs				9,522,780	
17	Total work in process during period				$9,737,180	
18	Less work in process inventory,					
19	December 31, 2010				220,000	
20	Cost of goods manufactured					9,517,180
21	Cost of finished goods available for sale					$10,612,780
22	Less finished goods inventory,					
23	December 31, 2010					1,565,000
24	Cost of goods sold					$ 9,047,780
25						

Direct materials purchases budget → (line 9)

Direct labor cost budget → (line 14)

Factory overhead cost budget → (line 15)

Example Exercise 22-5   Cost of Goods Sold Budget   ▶ 4

Prepare a cost of goods sold budget for Landon Awards Co. using the information in Example Exercises 22-3 and 22-4. Assume the estimated inventories on January 1, 2010, for finished goods and work in process were $54,000 and $47,000, respectively. Also assume the desired inventories on December 31, 2010, for finished goods and work in process were $50,000 and $49,000, respectively. Factory overhead was budgeted for $126,000.

Follow My Example 22-5

Finished goods inventory, January 1, 2010			$ 54,000
Work in process inventory, January 1, 2010		$ 47,000	
Direct materials:			
Direct materials inventory, January 1, 2010			
(240,000 × $0.12, from EE 22-3)	$ 28,800		
Direct materials purchases (from EE 22-3)	536,640		
Cost of direct materials available for use	$565,440		
Less direct materials inventory, December 31, 2010			
(200,000 × $0.12, from EE 22-3)	24,000		
Cost of direct materials placed in production	$541,440		
Direct labor (from EE 22-4)	103,400		
Factory overhead	126,000		
Total manufacturing costs		770,840	
Total work in process during period		$817,840	
Less work in process inventory, December 31, 2010		49,000	
Cost of goods manufactured			768,840
Cost of finished goods available for sale			$822,840
Less finished goods inventory, December 31, 2010			50,000
Cost of goods sold			$772,840

For Practice: PE 22-5A, PE 22-5B

Selling and Administrative Expenses Budget

The sales budget is often used as the starting point for the selling and administrative expenses budget. For example, a budgeted increase in sales may require more advertising expenses.

Exhibit 14 illustrates the selling and administrative expenses budget for Elite Accessories Inc.

Exhibit 14

Selling and Administrative Expenses Budget

	A	B	C
1	Elite Accessories Inc.		
2	Selling and Administrative Expenses Budget		
3	For the Year Ending December 31, 2010		
4	Selling expenses:		
5	Sales salaries expense	$715,000	
6	Advertising expense	360,000	
7	Travel expense	115,000	
8	Total selling expenses		$1,190,000
9	Administrative expenses:		
10	Officers' salaries expense	$360,000	
11	Office salaries expense	258,000	
12	Office rent expense	34,500	
13	Office supplies expense	17,500	
14	Miscellaneous administrative expenses	25,000	
15	Total administrative expenses		695,000
16	Total selling and administrative expenses		$1,885,000

The selling and administrative expenses budget shown in Exhibit 14 is normally supported by departmental schedules. For example, an advertising expense schedule for the Marketing Department could include the advertising media to be used (newspaper, direct mail, television), quantities (column inches, number of pieces, minutes), the cost per unit, and related costs per unit.

Budgeted Income Statement

The budgeted income statement is prepared by integrating the following budgets:

1. Sales budget (Exhibit 8)
2. Cost of goods sold budget (Exhibit 13)
3. Selling and administrative expenses budget (Exhibit 14)

In addition, estimates of other income, other expense, and income tax are also integrated into the budgeted income statement.

Exhibit 15 illustrates the budgeted income statement for Elite Accessories Inc. This budget summarizes the budgeted operating activities of the company. In doing so, the budgeted income statement allows management to assess the effects of estimated sales, costs, and expenses on profits for the year.

5 Prepare balance sheet budgets for a manufacturing company.

Balance Sheet Budgets

While the income statement budgets reflect the operating activities of the company, the balance sheet budgets reflect the financing and investing activities. In this section, the following balance sheet budgets are described and illustrated:

1. Cash budget (financing activity)
2. Capital expenditures budget (investing activity)

Exhibit 15

**Budgeted
Income
Statement**

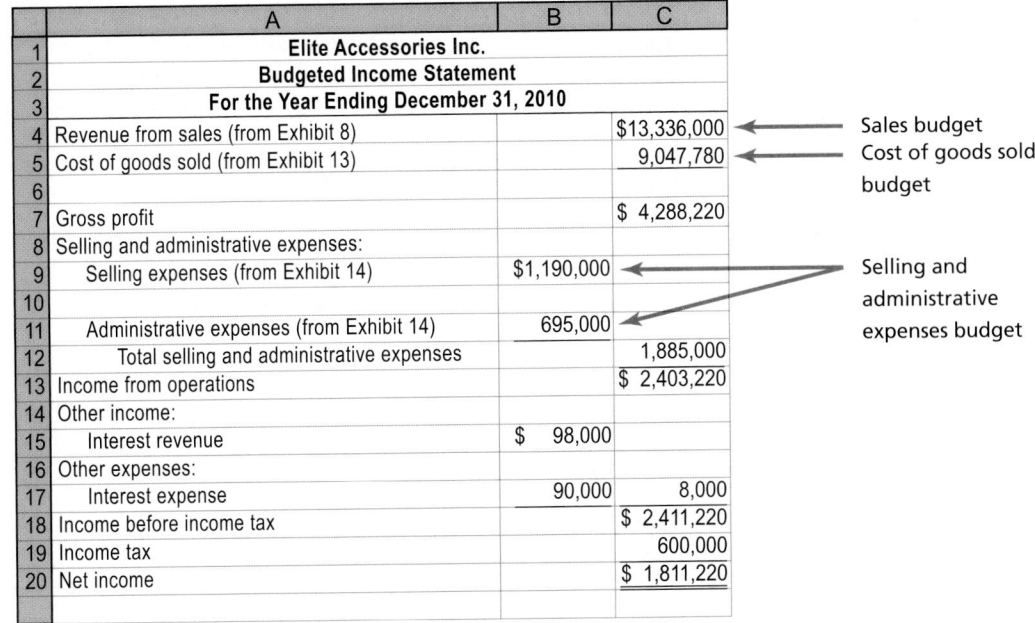

	A	B	C
1	Elite Accessories Inc.		
2	Budgeted Income Statement		
3	For the Year Ending December 31, 2010		
4	Revenue from sales (from Exhibit 8)		$13,336,000
5	Cost of goods sold (from Exhibit 13)		9,047,780
6			
7	Gross profit		$ 4,288,220
8	Selling and administrative expenses:		
9	Selling expenses (from Exhibit 14)	$1,190,000	
10			
11	Administrative expenses (from Exhibit 14)	695,000	
12	Total selling and administrative expenses		1,885,000
13	Income from operations		$ 2,403,220
14	Other income:		
15	Interest revenue	$ 98,000	
16	Other expenses:		
17	Interest expense	90,000	8,000
18	Income before income tax		$ 2,411,220
19	Income tax		600,000
20	Net income		$ 1,811,220

Sales budget

Cost of goods sold budget

Selling and administrative expenses budget

Cash Budget

The **cash budget** estimates the expected receipts (inflows) and payments (outflows) of cash for a period of time. The cash budget is integrated with the various operating budgets. In addition, the capital expenditures budget, dividends, and equity or long-term debt financing plans of the company affect the cash budget.

To illustrate, a monthly cash budget for January, February, and March 2010 for Elite Accessories Inc. is prepared. The preparation of the cash budget begins by estimating cash receipts.

Estimated Cash Receipts The primary source of estimated cash receipts is from cash sales and collections on account. In addition, cash receipts may be obtained from plans to issue equity or debt financing as well as other sources such as interest revenue.

To estimate cash receipts from cash sales and collections on account, a *schedule of collections from sales* is prepared. To illustrate, the following data for Elite Accessories Inc. are used:

	January	February	March
Sales:			
Budgeted sales	$1,080,000	$1,240,000	$970,000
Percent of cash sales	10%	10%	10%
Accounts receivable, January 1, 2010	$370,000		
Receipts from sales on account:			
From prior month's sales on account	40%		
From current month's sales on account	60		
	100%		

Using the preceding data, the schedule of collections from sales is prepared, as shown in Exhibit 16. Cash sales are determined by multiplying the percent of cash sales by the monthly budgeted sales. The cash receipts from sales on account are determined by adding the cash received from the prior month's sales on account (40%) and the cash received from the current month's sales on account (60%). To simplify, it is assumed that all accounts receivable are collected.

Exhibit 16

Schedule of Collections from Sales

	A	B	C	D	E
1		Elite Accessories Inc.			
2		Schedule of Collections from Sales			
3		For the Three Months Ending March 31, 2010			
4			January	February	March
5	Receipts from cash sales:				
6	Cash sales (10% × current month's sales—				
7	Note A)		$108,000	$ 124,000	$ 97,000
8					
9	Receipts from sales on account:				
10	Collections from prior month's sales (40% of				
11	previous month's credit sales—Note B)		$370,000	$ 388,800	$446,400
12	Collections from current month's sales (60%				
13	of current month's credit sales—Note C)		583,200	669,600	523,800
14	Total receipts from sales on account		$953,200	$1,058,400	$970,200
15					
16	Note A:	$108,000 = $1,080,000 × 10%			
17		$124,000 = $1,240,000 × 10%			
18		$ 97,000 = $ 970,000 × 10%			
19					
20	Note B:	$370,000, given as January 1, 2010, Accounts Receivable balance			
21		$388,800 = $1,080,000 × 90% × 40%			
22		$446,400 = $1,240,000 × 90% × 40%			
23					
24	Note C:	$583,200 = $1,080,000 × 90% × 60%			
25		$669,600 = $1,240,000 × 90% × 60%			
26		$523,800 = $ 970,000 × 90% × 60%			

Estimated Cash Payments Estimated cash payments must be budgeted for operating costs and expenses such as manufacturing costs, selling expenses, and administrative expenses. In addition, estimated cash payments may be planned for capital expenditures, dividends, interest payments, or long-term debt payments.

To estimate cash payments for manufacturing costs, a *schedule of payments for manufacturing costs* is prepared. To illustrate, the following data for Elite Accessories Inc. are used:

	January	February	March
Manufacturing Costs:			
Budgeted manufacturing costs	$840,000	$780,000	$812,000
Depreciation on machines included in manufacturing costs	24,000	24,000	24,000
Accounts Payable:			
Accounts payable, January 1, 1010	$190,000		
Payments of manufacturing costs on account:			
From prior month's manufacturing costs ...	25%		
From current month's manufacturing costs ...	75		
	100%		

Using the preceding data, the schedule of payments for manufacturing costs is prepared, as shown in Exhibit 17. The cash payments are determined by adding the cash paid on costs incurred from the prior month (25%) to the cash paid on costs incurred in the current month (75%). The $24,000 of depreciation is excluded from all computations, since depreciation does not require a cash payment.

Exhibit 17

Schedule of Payments for Manufacturing Costs

	A	B	C	D	E
1		Elite Accessories Inc.			
2		Schedule of Payments for Manufacturing Costs			
3		For the Three Months Ending March 31, 2010			
4			January	February	March
5	Payments of prior month's manufacturing costs				
6	{[25% × previous month's manufacturing costs				
7	(less depreciation)]—Note A}		$190,000	$204,000	$189,000
8	Payments of current month's manufacturing costs				
9	{[75% × current month's manufacturing costs				
10	(less depreciation)]—Note B}		612,000	567,000	591,000
11	Total payments		$802,000	$771,000	$780,000
12					
13	Note A:	$190,000, given as January 1, 2010, Accounts Payable balance			
14		$204,000 = ($840,000 − $24,000) × 25%			
15		$189,000 = ($780,000 − $24,000) × 25%			
16					
17	Note B:	$612,000 = ($840,000 − $24,000) × 75%			
18		$567,000 = ($780,000 − $24,000) × 75%			
19		$591,000 = ($812,000 − $24,000) × 75%			

Completing the Cash Budget Assume the additional data for Elite Accessories Inc. shown below.

Cash balance on January 1, 2010	$280,000
Quarterly taxes paid on March 31, 2010	150,000
Quarterly interest expense paid on January 10, 2010	22,500
Quarterly interest revenue received on March 21, 2010	24,500
Sewing equipment purchased in February 2010	274,000
Selling and administrative expenses (paid in month incurred):	

January	February	March
$160,000	$165,000	$145,000

Using the preceding data, the *cash budget* is prepared, as shown in Exhibit 18.

Exhibit 18

Cash Budget

	A	B	C	D	
1		Elite Accessories Inc.			
2		Cash Budget			
3		For the Three Months Ending March 31, 2010			
4		January	February	March	
5	Estimated cash receipts from:				
6	Cash sales (from Exhibit 16)	$ 108,000	$ 124,000	$ 97,000	← Schedule of
7	Collections of accounts receivable				collections
8	(from Exhibit 16)	953,200	1,058,400	970,200	from sales
9	Interest revenue			24,500	
10	Total cash receipts	$1,061,200	$1,182,400	$1,091,700	
11	Estimated cash payments for:				
12	Manufacturing costs (from Exhibit 17)	$ 802,000	$ 771,000	$ 780,000	← Schedule of cash
13	Selling and administrative expenses	160,000	165,000	145,000	payments for
14	Capital additions		274,000		manufacturing
15	Interest expense	22,500			costs
16	Income taxes			150,000	
17	Total cash payments	$ 984,500	$1,210,000	$1,075,000	
18	Cash increase (decrease)	$ 76,700	$ (27,600)	$ 16,700	
19	Cash balance at beginning of month	280,000	356,700	329,100	
20	Cash balance at end of month	$ 356,700	$ 329,100	$ 345,800	
21	Minimum cash balance	340,000	340,000	340,000	
22	Excess (deficiency)	$ 16,700	$ (10,900)	$ 5,800	

As shown in Exhibit 18, Elite Accessories Inc. has estimated that a *minimum cash balance* of $340,000 is required at the end of each month to support its operations. This minimum cash balance is compared to the estimated ending cash balance for each month. In this way, any expected cash excess or deficiency is determined.

Exhibit 18 indicates that Elite Accessories expects a cash excess at the end of January of $16,700. This excess could be invested in temporary income-producing securities such as U.S. Treasury bills or notes. In contrast, the estimated cash deficiency at the end of February of $10,900 might require Elite Accessories to borrow cash from its bank.

Example Exercise 22-6   Cash Budget   5

Landon Awards Co. collects 25% of its sales on account in the month of the sale and 75% in the month following the sale. If sales on account are budgeted to be $100,000 for March and $126,000 for April, what are the budgeted cash receipts from sales on account for April?

Follow My Example 22-6

	April
Collections from March sales (75% × $100,000)...........................	$ 75,000
Collections from April sales (25% × $126,000)............................	31,500
Total receipts from sales on account	$106,500

For Practice: PE 22-6A, PE 22-6B

Capital Expenditures Budget

The **capital expenditures budget** summarizes plans for acquiring fixed assets. Such expenditures are necessary as machinery and other fixed assets wear out or become obsolete. In addition, purchasing additional fixed assets may be necessary to meet increasing demand for the company's product.

To illustrate, a five-year capital expenditures budget for Elite Accessories Inc. is shown in Exhibit 19.

Exhibit 19

Capital Expenditures Budget

	A	B	C	D	E	F
1	Elite Accessories Inc.					
2	Capital Expenditures Budget					
3	For the Five Years Ending December 31, 2014					
4	Item	2010	2011	2012	2013	2014
5	Machinery—Cutting Department	$400,000			$280,000	$360,000
6	Machinery—Sewing Department	274,000	$260,000	$560,000	200,000	
7	Office equipment		90,000			60,000
8	Total	$674,000	$350,000	$560,000	$480,000	$420,000

As shown in Exhibit 19, capital expenditures budgets are often prepared for five to ten years into the future. This is necessary since fixed assets often must be ordered years in advance. Likewise, it could take years to construct new buildings or other production facilities.

The capital expenditures budget should be integrated with the operating and financing budgets. For example, depreciation of new manufacturing equipment affects

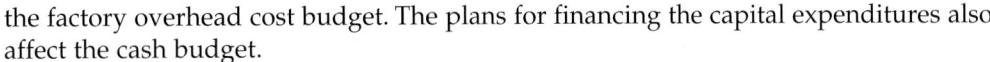

the factory overhead cost budget. The plans for financing the capital expenditures also affect the cash budget.

Budgeted Balance Sheet

The budgeted balance sheet is prepared based on the operating, financing, and investing budgets of the master budget. The budgeted balance sheet is dated as of the end of the budget period and is similar to a normal balance sheet except that estimated amounts are used. For this reason, a budgeted balance sheet for Elite Accessories Inc. is not illustrated.

Comprehensive Spreadsheet Illustration: Master Budget
The master budget is often developed on a spreadsheet. A spreadsheet to create the master budget is shown below. Spreadsheet formulas in selected cells are identified to illustrate the relationships.

Selected information concerning estimated sales and production for Cabot Co. for July 2010 are summarized in a spreadsheet as follows:

a.   Estimated sales:

	A	B	C
1			
2	**Estimated Sales**	**Units**	**Price**
3	Product K	40,000	$ 30
4	Product L	20,000	$ 65
5	Total		
6			

b.   Estimated inventories, July 1, 2010:

	A	B	C	D	E
7					
8	**Estimated Inventories, July 1, 2010**	**Pounds**		**Units**	**Price per Unit**
9	Material A	4,000	Product K	3,000	$ 17
10	Material B	3,500	Product L	2,700	$ 35
11					
12	There were no work-in-process inventories estimated for July 1, 2010				
13					

c.   Desired inventories, July 31, 2010:

	A	B	C	D	E
14					
15	**Desired Inventories, July 31, 2010**	**Pounds**		**Units**	**Price per Unit**
16	Material A	3,000	Product K	2,500	$ 17
17	Material B	2,500	Product L	2,000	$ 35
18					
19	There were no work-in-process inventories desired for July 31, 2010				
20					

d.   Direct materials used in production:

	A	B	C
21			
22	**Direct materials used in production (pounds per unit)**	**Product K**	**Product L**
23	Material A	0.7	3.5
24	Material B	1.2	1.8
25			

e.   Unit cost for direct materials (price per lb.):

	A	B
26		
27	**Unit costs for direct materials (per pound)**	
28	Material A	$ 4.00
29	Material B	$ 2.00
30		

f. Direct labor requirements per unit:

	A	B	C
31			
32	**Direct labor requirements (hours per unit)**	Department 1	Department 2
33	Product K	0.40	0.15
34	Product L	0.60	0.25
35			

g. Direct labor rate:

	A	B	C
36			
37		Department 1	Department 2
38	Direct labor rate (per hour)	$ 12.00	$ 16.00
39			

h. Estimated factory overhead costs for July:

	A	B
40		
41	Estimated factory overhead costs for July:	
42	Indirect factory wages	$ 200,000
43	Depreciation of plant and equipment	40,000
44	Power and light	25,000
45	Indirect materials	34,000
46	Total	$ 299,000
47		

Instructions:
1. Prepare a sales budget for July.
2. Prepare a production budget for July.
3. Prepare a direct materials budget for July.
4. Prepare a direct labor cost budget for July.
5. Prepare a cost of goods sold budget for July.

Note: Numbers correlate to the solutions outlined in the following pages.

Spreadsheet Solution

Formulas are provided for selected cells. Many formulas are provided for Product L. Use the Product L formulas as a pattern to determine the correct Product K cell references and formulas.

1. Sales Budget:

	A	B	C	D
50				
51	Cabot Co.			
52	Sales Budget			
53	For the Month Ending July 31, 2010			
54	**Product**	Unit Sales Volume	Unit Selling Price	Total Sales
55	Product K	40,000	$ 30	$ 1,200,000
56	Product L	=B4	=C4	=B56*C56
57	Total revenue from sales			=SUM(D55:D56)
58				

2. Production Budget:

	A	B	C
60			
61	Cabot Co.		
62	Sales Budget		
63	For the Month Ending July 31, 2010		
64		Product K	Product L
65	Expected units to be sold	40,000	=B4
66	Plus desired units of inventory, July 31, 2010	2,500	=D17
67	Total	42,500	=SUM(C65:C66)
68	Less estimated units of inventory, July 1, 2010	3,000	=D10
69	Total units to be produced	39,500	=C67-C68
70			

3. Direct Material Purchases Budget

	A	B	C	D
75				
76	Cabot Co.			
77	Direct Materials Purchases Budget			
78	For the Month Ending July 31, 2010			
79	Product	Material A	Material B	Total
80	Pounds required for production:			
81	Product K (39,500 × lbs. per unit)	27,650	=B69*B24	
82	Product L (19,300 × lbs. per unit)	67,550	C69*C24	
83	Plus desired pounds of inventory, July 31, 2010	3,000	=B17	
84	Total	98,200	=SUM(C81:C83)	
85	Less estimated pounds of inventory, July 1, 2010	4,000	=B10	
86	Total pounds to be purchased	94,200	=C84-C85	
87	Unit price (per pound)	$ 4.00	=B29	
88	Total direct materials purchases	$ 376,800	=C86*C87	=SUM(B88:C88)
89				

4. Direct Labor Cost Budget

	A	B	C	D
90				
91	Cabot Co.			
92	Direct Labor Cost Budget			
93	For the Month Ending July 31, 2010	Department	Department	
94		1	2	Total
95	Hours required for production:			
96	Product K	15,800	5,925	
97	Product L	11,580	=C69*C34	
98	Total	27,380	10,750	
99	Hourly rate	$ 12.00	$ 16.00	
100	Total direct labor cost	$ 328,560	=C38*C99	$ 500,560
101				

5. Cost of Goods Sold Budget

	A	B	C	D
102				
103	Cabot Co.			
104	Cost of Goods Sold Budget			
105	For the Month Ending July 31, 2010			
106	Finished goods inventory, July 1, 2010		$ 145,500	
107	Direct materials:			
108	Direct materials inventory, July 1, 2010 (*Note A*)	=D124		
109	Direct materials purchases	=D88		
110	Cost of direct materials available for use	=SUM(B108:B109)		
111	Less direct materials inventory, July 31, 2010 (*Note B*)	=D129		
112	Cost of direct materials placed in production	=B110-B111		
113	Direct labor	=D100		
114	Factory overhead	=B46		
115	Cost of goods manufactured		=SUM(B112:B114)	
116	Cost of finished goods available for sale		=SUM(C106:C115)	
117	Less finished goods inventory, July 31, 2010		=(D16*E16)+(D17*E17)	
118	Cost of goods sold		=C116-C117	
119				
120				
121	*Note A*:	Pounds	Price per lb.	
122	Material A	4,000	$ 4.00	$ 16,000
123	Material B	3,500	$ 2.00	7,000
124	Direct materials inventory, July 1, 2010			$ 23,000
125				
126	*Note B*:	Pounds	Price per lb.	
127	Material A	3,000	$ 4.00	$ 12,000
128	Material B	2,500	$ 2.00	5,000
129	Direct materials inventory, July 31, 2010			$ 17,000
130				

1 **Describe budgeting, its objectives, and its impact on human behavior.**

Key Points	Key Learning Outcomes	Example Exercises	Practice Exercises
Budgeting involves (1) establishing plans (planning), (2) directing operations (directing), and (3) evaluating performance (controlling). In addition, budgets should be established to avoid human behavior problems.	• Describe the planning, directing, controlling, and feedback elements of the budget process. • Describe the behavioral issues associated with tight goals, loose goals, and goal conflict.		

2 **Describe the basic elements of the budget process, the two major types of budgeting, and the use of computers in budgeting.**

Key Points	Key Learning Outcomes	Example Exercises	Practice Exercises
The budget process is often initiated by the budget committee. The budget estimates received by the committee should be carefully studied, analyzed, revised, and integrated. The static and flexible budgets are two major budgeting approaches. Computers can be used to make the budget process more efficient and organizationally integrated.	• Describe a static budget and explain when it might be used. • Describe and prepare a flexible budget and explain when it might be used. • Describe the role of computers in the budget process.	22-1	22-1A, 22-1B

3 **Describe the master budget for a manufacturing company.**

Key Points	Key Learning Outcomes	Example Exercises	Practice Exercises
The master budget consists of the budgeted income statement and budgeted balance sheet.	• Illustrate the connection between the major income statement and balance sheet budgets.		

4 **Prepare the basic income statement budgets for a manufacturing company.**

Key Points	Key Learning Outcomes	Example Exercises	Practice Exercises
The basic income statement budgets are the sales budget, production budget, direct materials purchases budget, direct labor cost budget, factory overhead cost budget, cost of goods sold budget, and selling and administrative expenses budget.	• Prepare a sales budget. • Prepare a production budget. • Prepare a direct materials purchases budget. • Prepare a direct labor cost budget. • Prepare a factory overhead cost budget. • Prepare a cost of goods sold budget. • Prepare a selling and administrative expenses budget.	22-2 22-3 22-4 22-5	22-2A, 22-2B 22-3A, 22-3B 22-4A, 22-4B 22-5A, 22-5B

Key Points	Key Learning Outcomes	Example Exercises	Practice Exercises
The cash budget and capital expenditures budget can be used in preparing the budgeted balance sheet.	• Prepare cash receipts and cash payments budgets. • Prepare a capital expenditures budget.	**22-6**	22-6A, 22-6B

Key Terms

budget (987)
budgetary slack (989)
capital expenditures
   budget (1006)
cash budget (1003)
continuous budgeting (990)
cost of goods sold budget (1000)

direct labor cost budget (998)
direct materials purchases
   budget (997)
factory overhead cost
   budget (999)
flexible budget (991)
goal conflict (989)

master budget (993)
production budget (995)
responsibility
   center (988)
sales budget (995)
static budget (991)
zero-based budgeting (990)

Self-Examination Questions (Answers at End of Chapter)

1. A tight budget may create:
   A. budgetary slack.
   B. discouragement.
   C. a flexible budget.
   D. a "spend it or lose it" mentality.
2. The first step of the budget process is:
   A. plan.   C. control.
   B. direct.   D. feedback.
3. Static budgets are often used by:
   A. production departments.
   B. administrative departments.
   C. responsibility centers.
   D. capital projects.
4. The total estimated sales for the coming year is 250,000 units. The estimated inventory at the beginning of the year is 22,500 units, and the desired inventory at the end of the year is 30,000 units. The total production indicated in the production budget is:
   A. 242,500 units.   C. 280,000 units.
   B. 257,500 units.   D. 302,500 units.
5. Dixon Company expects $650,000 of credit sales in March and $800,000 of credit sales in April. Dixon historically collects 70% of its sales in the month of sale and 30% in the following month. How much cash does Dixon expect to collect in April?
   A. $800,000   C. $755,000
   B. $560,000   D. $1,015,000

Eye Openers

1. What are the three major objectives of budgeting?
2. What is the manager's role in a responsibility center?
3. Briefly describe the type of human behavior problems that might arise if budget goals are set too tightly.
4. Give an example of budgetary slack.
5. What behavioral problems are associated with setting a budget too loosely?
6. What behavioral problems are associated with establishing conflicting goals within the budget?

7. When would a company use zero-based budgeting?
8. Under what circumstances would a static budget be appropriate?
9. How do computerized budgeting systems aid firms in the budgeting process?
10. What is the first step in preparing a master budget?
11. Why should the production requirements set forth in the production budget be carefully coordinated with the sales budget?
12. Why should the timing of direct materials purchases be closely coordinated with the production budget?
13. In preparing the budget for the cost of goods sold, what are the three budgets from which data on relevant estimates of quantities and costs are combined with data on estimated inventories?
14. a. Discuss the purpose of the cash budget.
    b. If the cash for the first quarter of the fiscal year indicates excess cash at the end of each of the first two months, how might the excess cash be used?
15. How does a schedule of collections from sales assist in preparing the cash budget?
16. Give an example of how the capital expenditures budget affects other operating budgets.

Practice Exercises

PE 22-1A
Flexible budgeting
obj. 2
EE 22-1   p. 992

At the beginning of the period, the Fabricating Department budgeted direct labor of $22,500 and equipment depreciation of $7,000 for 900 hours of production. The department actually completed 750 hours of production. Determine the budget for the department, assuming that it uses flexible budgeting.

PE 22-1B
Flexible budgeting
obj. 2
EE 22-1   p. 992

At the beginning of the period, the Assembly Department budgeted direct labor of $186,000 and property tax of $15,000 for 12,000 hours of production. The department actually completed 13,400 hours of production. Determine the budget for the department, assuming that it uses flexible budgeting.

PE 22-2A
Production budget
obj. 4
EE 22-2   p. 997

Soft Glow Candle Co. projected sales of 78,000 candles for 2010. The estimated January 1, 2010, inventory is 3,600 units, and the desired December 31, 2010, inventory is 4,500 units. What is the budgeted production (in units) for 2010?

PE 22-2B
Production budget
obj. 4
EE 22-2   p. 997

Day Timer Publishers Inc. projected sales of 205,000 schedule planners for 2010. The estimated January 1, 2010, inventory is 18,500 units, and the desired December 31, 2010, inventory is 15,000 units. What is the budgeted production (in units) for 2010?

PE 22-3A
Direct materials
purchases budget
obj. 4
EE 22-3   p. 998

Soft Glow Candle Co. budgeted production of 78,900 candles in 2010. Wax is required to produce a candle. Assume 8 ounces (one half of a pound) of wax is required for each candle. The estimated January 1, 2010, wax inventory is 2,000 pounds. The desired December 31, 2010, wax inventory is 2,400 pounds. If candle wax costs $3.20 per pound, determine the direct materials purchases budget for 2010.

PE 22-3B
Direct materials
purchases budget
obj. 4
EE 22-3   p. 998

Day Timer Publishers Inc. budgeted production of 201,500 schedule planners in 2010. Paper is required to produce a planner. Assume 80 square feet of paper are required for each planner. The estimated January 1, 2010, paper inventory is 250,000 square feet. The desired December 31, 2010, paper inventory is 210,000 square feet. If paper costs $0.10 per square foot, determine the direct materials purchases budget for 2010.

PE 22-4A
Direct labor cost budget
obj. 4
EE 22-4   p. 999

Soft Glow Candle Co. budgeted production of 78,900 candles in 2010. Each candle requires molding. Assume that 15 minutes are required to mold each candle. If molding labor costs $16.00 per hour, determine the direct labor cost budget for 2010.

PE 22-4B
Direct labor cost budget
obj. 4
EE 22-4   p. 999

Day Timer Publishers Inc. budgeted production of 201,500 schedule planners in 2010. Each planner requires assembly. Assume that 12 minutes are required to assemble each planner. If assembly labor costs $14 per hour, determine the direct labor cost budget for 2010.

PE 22-5A
Cost of goods sold budget
obj. 4
EE 22-5   p. 1001

Prepare a cost of goods sold budget for Soft Glow Candle Co. using the information in Practice Exercises 22-3A and 22-4A. Assume the estimated inventories on January 1, 2010, for finished goods and work in process were $12,000 and $4,000, respectively. Also assume the desired inventories on December 31, 2010, for finished goods and work in process were $11,200 and $5,000, respectively. Factory overhead was budgeted at $108,000.

PE 22-5B
Cost of goods sold budget
obj. 4
EE 22-5   p. 1001

Prepare a cost of goods sold budget for Day Timer Publishers Inc. using the information in Practice Exercises 22-3B and 22-4B. Assume the estimated inventories on January 1, 2010, for finished goods and work in process were $39,000 and $18,000, respectively. Also assume the desired inventories on December 31, 2010, for finished goods and work in process were $43,000 and $15,000, respectively. Factory overhead was budgeted at $240,000.

PE 22-6A
Cash budget
obj. 5
EE 22-6   p. 1006

Soft Glow Candle Co. pays 20% of its purchases on account in the month of the purchase and 80% in the month following the purchase. If purchases are budgeted to be $15,000 for October and $17,000 for November, what are the budgeted cash payments for purchases on account for November?

PE 22-6B
Cash budget
obj. 5
EE 22-6   p. 1006

Day Timer Publishers Inc. collects 25% of its sales on account in the month of the sale and 75% in the month following the sale. If sales on account are budgeted to be $390,000 for April and $360,000 for May, what are the budgeted cash receipts from sales on account for May?

Exercises

EX 22-1
Personal cash budget
objs. 2, 5

✔ a. December 31 cash balance, $3,500

At the beginning of the 2010 school year, Britney Logan decided to prepare a cash budget for the months of September, October, November, and December. The budget must plan for enough cash on December 31 to pay the spring semester tuition, which is the same as the fall tuition. The following information relates to the budget:

Cash balance, September 1 (from a summer job)	$7,000
Purchase season football tickets in September	100
Additional entertainment for each month	250
Pay fall semester tuition on September 3	3,800
Pay rent at the beginning of each month	350
Pay for food each month	200
Pay apartment deposit on September 2 (to be returned Dec. 15)	500
Part-time job earnings each month (net of taxes)	900

a. Prepare a cash budget for September, October, November, and December.
b. Are the four monthly budgets that are presented prepared as static budgets or flexible budgets?
c. ➤ What are the budget implications for Britney Logan?

EX 22-2

Flexible budget for selling and administrative expenses

objs. 2, 4

✔ Total selling and administrative expenses at $125,000 sales, $66,350

Agent Blaze uses flexible budgets that are based on the following data:

Sales commissions	8% of sales
Advertising expense	21% of sales
Miscellaneous selling expense	$2,250 plus 3% of sales
Office salaries expense	$15,000 per month
Office supplies expense	4% of sales
Miscellaneous administrative expense	$1,600 per month plus 2% of sales

Prepare a flexible selling and administrative expenses budget for January 2010 for sales volumes of $100,000, $125,000, and $150,000. (Use Exhibit 5 as a model.)

EX 22-3

Static budget vs. flexible budget

objs. 2, 4

✔ b. Excess of actual over budget for March, $53,000

The production supervisor of the Machining Department for Nell Company agreed to the following monthly static budget for the upcoming year:

Nell Company
Machining Department
Monthly Production Budget

Wages	$540,000
Utilities	36,000
Depreciation	60,000
Total	$636,000

The actual amount spent and the actual units produced in the first three months of 2010 in the Machining Department were as follows:

	Amount Spent	Units Produced
January	$600,000	110,000
February	570,000	100,000
March	545,000	90,000

The Machining Department supervisor has been very pleased with this performance, since actual expenditures have been less than the monthly budget. However, the plant manager believes that the budget should not remain fixed for every month but should "flex" or adjust to the volume of work that is produced in the Machining Department. Additional budget information for the Machining Department is as follows:

Wages per hour	$18.00
Utility cost per direct labor hour	$1.20
Direct labor hours per unit	0.25
Planned unit production	120,000

a. Prepare a flexible budget for the actual units produced for January, February, and March in the Machining Department. Assume depreciation is a fixed cost.
b. ➤ Compare the flexible budget with the actual expenditures for the first three months. What does this comparison suggest?

EX 22-4

Flexible budget for Fabrication Department

obj. 2

✔ Total department cost at 12,000 units, $1,029,000

Steelcase Inc. is one of the largest manufacturers of office furniture in the United States. In Grand Rapids, Michigan, it produces filing cabinets in two departments: Fabrication and Trim Assembly. Assume the following information for the Fabrication Department:

Steel per filing cabinet	45 pounds
Direct labor per filing cabinet	20 minutes
Supervisor salaries	$140,000 per month
Depreciation	$22,000 per month
Direct labor rate	$21 per hour
Steel cost	$1.45 per pound

Prepare a flexible budget for 12,000, 15,000, and 18,000 filing cabinets for the month of October 2010, similar to Exhibit 5, assuming that inventories are not significant.

EX 22-5
Production budget

obj. 4

✔ Small scale
budgeted produc-
tion, 51,600 units

Accu-Weight, Inc. produces a small and large version of its popular electronic scale. The anticipated unit sales for the scales by sales region are as follows:

	Small Scale	Large Scale
North Region unit sales	25,000	34,000
South Region unit sales	27,000	32,500
Total	52,000	66,500

The finished goods inventory estimated for May 1, 2011, for the small and large scale models is 1,500 and 2,300 units, respectively. The desired finished goods inventory for May 31, 2011, for the small and large scale models is 1,100 and 2,500 units, respectively.

Prepare a production budget for the small and large scales for the month ended May 31, 2011.

EX 22-6
Sales and production budgets

obj. 4

✔ b. Model DL
total production,
7,985 units

Harmony Audio Company manufactures two models of speakers, DL and XL. Based on the following production and sales data for September 2009, prepare (a) a sales budget and (b) a production budget.

	DL	XL
Estimated inventory (units), September 1	240	60
Desired inventory (units), September 30	275	52
Expected sales volume (units):		
East Region	3,700	3,250
West Region	4,250	3,700
Unit sales price	$125	$195

EX 22-7
Professional fees earned budget

obj. 4

✔ Total professional
fees earned,
$10,153,500

Roberts and Chou, CPAs, offer three types of services to clients: auditing, tax, and small business accounting. Based on experience and projected growth, the following billable hours have been estimated for the year ending December 31, 2010:

	Billable Hours
Audit Department:	
Staff	32,400
Partners	4,800
Tax Department:	
Staff	24,800
Partners	3,100
Small Business Accounting Department:	
Staff	4,500
Partners	630

The average billing rate for staff is $130 per hour, and the average billing rate for partners is $250 per hour. Prepare a professional fees earned budget for Roberts and Chou, CPAs, for the year ending December 31, 2010, using the following column headings and showing the estimated professional fees by type of service rendered:

Billable Hours	Hourly Rate	Total Revenue

EX 22-8
Professional labor cost budget

obj. 4

✔ Staff total labor
cost, $1,851,000

Based on the data in Exercise 22-7 and assuming that the average compensation per hour for staff is $30 and for partners is $125, prepare a professional labor cost budget for Roberts and Chou, CPAs, for the year ending December 31, 2010. Use the following column headings:

Staff	Partners

EX 22-9
Direct materials
purchases budget

obj. 4

✔ Total cheese
purchases, $123,163

Marino's Frozen Pizza Inc. has determined from its production budget the following estimated production volumes for 12" and 16" frozen pizzas for April 2010:

	Units	
	12" Pizza	16" Pizza
Budgeted production volume	15,100	22,700

There are three direct materials used in producing the two types of pizza. The quantities of direct materials expected to be used for each pizza are as follows:

	12" Pizza	16" Pizza
Direct materials:		
Dough	0.90 lb. per unit	1.50 lbs. per unit
Tomato	0.60	1.00
Cheese	0.75	1.25

In addition, Marino's has determined the following information about each material:

	Dough	Tomato	Cheese
Estimated inventory, April 1, 2010	580 lbs.	205 lbs.	325 lbs.
Desired inventory, April 30, 2010	610 lbs.	200 lbs.	355 lbs.
Price per pound	$1.20	$2.60	$3.10

Prepare April's direct materials purchases budget for Marino's Frozen Pizza Inc.

EX 22-10
Direct materials
purchases budget

obj. 4

✔ Concentrate
budgeted purchases,
$107,600

Coca-Cola Enterprises is the largest bottler of Coca-Cola® in North America. The company purchases Coke® and Sprite® concentrate from The Coca-Cola Company, dilutes and mixes the concentrate with carbonated water, and then fills the blended beverage into cans or plastic two-liter bottles. Assume that the estimated production for Coke and Sprite two-liter bottles at the Dallas, Texas, bottling plant are as follows for the month of March:

Coke	214,000 two-liter bottles
Sprite	163,000 two-liter bottles

In addition, assume that the concentrate costs $80 per pound for both Coke and Sprite and is used at a rate of 0.2 pound per 100 liters of carbonated water in blending Coke and 0.15 pound per 100 liters of carbonated water in blending Sprite. Assume that two-liter bottles cost $0.08 per bottle and carbonated water costs $0.06 per liter.

Prepare a direct materials purchases budget for March 2010, assuming no changes between beginning and ending inventories for all three materials.

EX 22-11
Direct materials
purchases budget

obj. 4

✔ Total steel belt
purchases,
$1,344,000

Anticipated sales for Sure Grip Tire Company were 42,000 passenger car tires and 15,000 truck tires. There were no anticipated beginning or ending finished goods inventories for either product. Rubber and steel belts are used in producing passenger car and truck tires according to the following table:

	Passenger Car	Truck
Rubber	30 lbs. per unit	70 lbs. per unit
Steel belts	4 lbs. per unit	10 lbs. per unit

The purchase prices of rubber and steel are $3.20 and $4.20 per pound, respectively. The desired ending inventories of rubber and steel belts are 40,000 and 10,000 pounds, respectively. The estimated beginning inventories for rubber and steel belts are 46,000 and 8,000 pounds, respectively.

Prepare a direct materials purchases budget for Sure Grip Tire Company for the year ended December 31, 2010.

EX 22-12
Direct labor cost budget

obj. **4**

✔ Total direct labor cost, Assembly, $208,860

Hammer Racket Company manufactures two types of tennis rackets, the Junior and Pro Striker models. The production budget for October for the two rackets is as follows:

	Junior	Pro Striker
Production budget	7,600 units	22,100 units

Both rackets are produced in two departments, Forming and Assembly. The direct labor hours required for each racket are estimated as follows:

	Forming Department	Assembly Department
Junior	0.25 hour per unit	0.40 hour per unit
Pro Striker	0.35 hour per unit	0.65 hour per unit

The direct labor rate for each department is as follows:

Forming Department	$16.00 per hour
Assembly Department	$12.00 per hour

Prepare the direct labor cost budget for October 2010.

EX 22-13
Direct labor budget—service business

obj. **4**

✔ Average weekday total, $1,712

Sleep-EZ Suites, Inc., operates a downtown hotel property that has 250 rooms. On average, 72% of Sleep-EZ Suites' rooms are occupied on weekdays, and 48% are occupied during the weekend. The manager has asked you to develop a direct labor budget for the housekeeping and restaurant staff for weekdays and weekends. You have determined that the housekeeping staff requires 40 minutes to clean each occupied room. The housekeeping staff is paid $10 per hour. The restaurant has five full-time staff (eight-hour day) on duty, regardless of occupancy. However, for every 60 occupied rooms, an additional person is brought in to work in the restaurant for the eight-hour day. The restaurant staff is paid $8 per hour.

Determine the estimated housekeeping, restaurant, and total direct labor cost for an average weekday and weekend day. Format the budget in two columns, labeled as weekday and weekend day.

EX 22-14
Production and direct labor cost budgets

obj. **4**

✔ a. Total production of 501 Jeans, 54,000

Levi Strauss & Co. manufactures slacks and jeans under a variety of brand names, such as Dockers® and 501 Jeans®. Slacks and jeans are assembled by a variety of different sewing operations. Assume that the sales budget for Dockers and 501 Jeans shows estimated sales of 24,700 and 53,600 pairs, respectively, for January 2010. The finished goods inventory is assumed as follows:

	Dockers	501 Jeans
January 1 estimated inventory	1,110	1,490
January 31 desired inventory	410	1,890

Assume the following direct labor data per 10 pairs of Dockers and 501 Jeans for four different sewing operations:

	Direct Labor per 10 Pairs	
	Dockers	501 Jeans
Inseam	18 minutes	12 minutes
Outerseam	22	15
Pockets	7	9
Zipper	10	6
Total	57 minutes	42 minutes

a. Prepare a production budget for January. Prepare the budget in two columns: Dockers® and 501 Jeans®.
b. Prepare the January direct labor cost budget for the four sewing operations, assuming a $12.50 wage per hour for the inseam and outerseam sewing operations and a $16 wage per hour for the pocket and zipper sewing operations. Prepare the direct labor cost budget in four columns: inseam, outerseam, pockets, and zipper.

EX 22-15
Factory overhead cost budget
obj. 4

✔ Total variable factory overhead costs, $264,000

Venus Candy Company budgeted the following costs for anticipated production for September 2010:

Advertising expenses	$275,000	Production supervisor wages	$132,000
Manufacturing supplies	15,000	Production control salaries	35,000
Power and light	44,000	Executive officer salaries	280,000
Sales commissions	300,000	Materials management salaries	38,000
Factory insurance	26,000	Factory depreciation	21,000

Prepare a factory overhead cost budget, separating variable and fixed costs. Assume that factory insurance and depreciation are the only factory fixed costs.

EX 22-16
Cost of goods sold budget
obj. 4

✔ Cost of goods sold, $2,334,000

Delaware Chemical Company uses oil to produce two types of plastic products, P1 and P2. Deleware budgeted 25,000 barrels of oil for purchase in September for $72 per barrel. Direct labor budgeted in the chemical process was $210,000 for September. Factory overhead was budgeted $325,000 during September. The inventories on September 1 were estimated to be:

Oil	$14,600
P1	9,800
P2	8,600
Work in process	12,100

The desired inventories on September 30 were:

Oil	$16,100
P1	9,100
P2	7,900
Work in process	13,000

Use the preceding information to prepare a cost of goods sold budget for September 2011.

EX 22-17
Cost of goods sold budget
obj. 4

✔ Cost of goods sold, $425,420

The controller of Swiss Ceramics Inc. wishes to prepare a cost of goods sold budget for June. The controller assembled the following information for constructing the cost of goods sold budget:

Direct materials:	Enamel	Paint	Porcelain	Total
Total direct materials purchases budgeted for June	$33,840	$5,340	$118,980	$158,160
Estimated inventory, June 1, 2010	1,150	2,800	4,330	8,280
Desired inventory, June 30, 2010	2,400	2,050	6,000	10,450

Direct labor cost:	Kiln Department	Decorating Department	Total
Total direct labor cost budgeted for June	$41,600	$142,400	$184,000

Finished goods inventories:	Dish	Bowl	Figurine	Total
Estimated inventory, June 1, 2010	$4,060	$2,970	$2,470	$ 9,500
Desired inventory, June 30, 2010	3,350	4,150	3,590	11,090

Work in process inventories:

Estimated inventory, June 1, 2010	$ 2,800
Desired inventory, June 30, 2010	1,880

Budgeted factory overhead costs for June:

Indirect factory wages	$64,900
Depreciation of plant and equipment	12,600
Power and light	4,900
Indirect materials	3,700
Total	$86,100

Use the preceding information to prepare a cost of goods sold budget for June 2010.

EX 22-18

Schedule of cash collections of accounts receivable

obj. 5

✔ Total cash collected in July, $520,350

Pet Joy Wholesale Inc., a pet wholesale supplier, was organized on May 1, 2010. Projected sales for each of the first three months of operations are as follows:

May	$360,000
June	450,000
July	600,000

The company expects to sell 10% of its merchandise for cash. Of sales on account, 50% are expected to be collected in the month of the sale, 35% in the month following the sale, and the remainder in the second month following the sale.

Prepare a schedule indicating cash collections from sales for May, June, and July.

EX 22-19

Schedule of cash collections of accounts receivable

obj. 5

✔ Total cash collected in August, $300,000

Office Mate Supplies Inc. has "cash and carry" customers and credit customers. Office Mate estimates that 25% of monthly sales are to cash customers, while the remaining sales are to credit customers. Of the credit customers, 20% pay their accounts in the month of sale, while the remaining 80% pay their accounts in the month following the month of sale. Projected sales for the first three months of 2010 are as follows:

August	$250,000
September	290,000
October	270,000

The Accounts Receivable balance on July 31, 2010, was $200,000.

Prepare a schedule of cash collections from sales for August, September, and October.

EX 22-20

Schedule of cash payments

obj. 5

✔ Total cash payments in August, $79,440

Excel Learning Systems Inc. was organized on May 31, 2010. Projected selling and administrative expenses for each of the first three months of operations are as follows:

June	$117,400
July	110,500
August	100,400

Depreciation, insurance, and property taxes represent $25,000 of the estimated monthly expenses. The annual insurance premium was paid on May 31, and property taxes for the year will be paid in December. Sixty percent of the remainder of the expenses are expected to be paid in the month in which they are incurred, with the balance to be paid in the following month.

Prepare a schedule indicating cash payments for selling and administrative expenses for June, July, and August.

EX 22-21

Schedule of cash payments

obj. 5

✔ Total cash payments in September, $123,300

Rejuvenation Physical Therapy Inc. is planning its cash payments for operations for the third quarter (July–September), 2011. The Accrued Expenses Payable balance on July 1 is $24,000. The budgeted expenses for the next three months are as follows:

	July	August	September
Salaries	$ 58,200	$ 63,500	$ 74,500
Utilities	5,300	5,600	7,100
Other operating expenses	48,500	52,700	58,200
Total	$112,000	$121,800	$139,800

Other operating expenses include $10,500 of monthly depreciation expense and $600 of monthly insurance expense that was prepaid for the year on March 1 of the current year. Of the remaining expenses, 70% are paid in the month in which they are incurred, with the remainder paid in the following month. The Accrued Expenses Payable balance on July 1 relates to the expenses incurred in June.

Prepare a schedule of cash payments for operations for July, August, and September.

EX 22-22
Capital expenditures budget

obj. 5

✔ Total capital expenditures in 2010, $7,000,000

On January 1, 2010, the controller of Gardeneer Tools Inc. is planning capital expenditures for the years 2010–2013. The following interviews helped the controller collect the necessary information for the capital expenditures budget:

Director of Facilities: A construction contract was signed in late 2009 for the construction of a new factory building at a contract cost of $13,000,000. The construction is scheduled to begin in 2010 and be completed in 2011.

Vice President of Manufacturing: Once the new factory building is finished, we plan to purchase $1.7 million in equipment in late 2011. I expect that an additional $200,000 will be needed early in the following year (2012) to test and install the equipment before we can begin production. If sales continue to grow, I expect we'll need to invest another million in equipment in 2013.

Vice President of Marketing: We have really been growing lately. I wouldn't be surprised if we need to expand the size of our new factory building in 2013 by at least 40%. Fortunately, we expect inflation to have minimal impact on construction costs over the next four years. Additionally, I would expect the cost of the expansion to be proportional to the size of the expansion.

Director of Information Systems: We need to upgrade our information systems to wireless network technology. It doesn't make sense to do this until after the new factory building is completed and producing product. During 2012, once the factory is up and running, we should equip the whole facility with wireless technology. I think it would cost us $1,600,000 today to install the technology. However, prices have been dropping by 25% per year, so it should be less expensive at a later date.

President: I am excited about our long-term prospects. My only short-term concern is financing the $7,000,000 of construction costs on the portion of the new factory building scheduled to be completed in 2010.

Use the interview information above to prepare a capital expenditures budget for Gardeneer Tools Inc. for the years 2010–2013.

Problems Series A

PR 22-1A
Forecast sales volume and sales budget

obj. 4

✔ 3. Total revenue from sales, $34,374,630

Guardian Devices Inc. prepared the following sales budget for the current year:

Guardian Devices Inc.
Sales Budget
For the Year Ending December 31, 2010

Product and Area	Unit Sales Volume	Unit Selling Price	Total Sales
Home Alert System:			
United States	24,300	$250	$ 6,075,000
Europe	6,700	250	1,675,000
Asia	5,900	250	1,475,000
Total	36,900		$ 9,225,000
Business Alert System:			
United States	14,900	$900	$13,410,000
Europe	6,400	900	5,760,000
Asia	4,200	900	3,780,000
Total	25,500		$22,950,000
Total revenue from sales			$32,175,000

At the end of December 2010, the following unit sales data were reported for the year:

	Unit Sales	
	Home Alert System	Business Alert System
United States	25,272	15,645
Europe	6,834	6,336
Asia	5,723	4,326

For the year ending December 31, 2011, unit sales are expected to follow the patterns established during the year ending December 31, 2010. The unit selling price for the Home Alert System is expected to increase to $270, and the unit selling price for the Business Alert System is expected to be decreased to $880, effective January 1, 2011.

Instructions

1. Compute the increase or decrease of actual unit sales for the year ended December 31, 2010, over budget. Place your answers in a columnar table with the following format:

	Unit Sales, Year Ended 2010		Increase (Decrease) Actual Over Budget	
	Budget	**Actual Sales**	**Amount**	**Percent**
Home Alert System:				
United States				
Europe				
Asia				
Business Alert System:				
United States				
Europe				
Asia				

2. Assuming that the trend of sales indicated in part (1) is to continue in 2011, compute the unit sales volume to be used for preparing the sales budget for the year ending December 31, 2011. Place your answers in a columnar table similar to that in part (1) above but with the following column heads. Round budgeted units to the nearest unit.

2010 Actual Units	Percentage Increase (Decrease)	2011 Budgeted Units (rounded)

3. Prepare a sales budget for the year ending December 31, 2011.

PR 22-2A

Sales, production, direct materials purchases, and direct labor cost budgets

obj. 4

✔ 3. Total direct materials purchases, $7,721,394

The budget director of Regal Furniture Company requests estimates of sales, production, and other operating data from the various administrative units every month. Selected information concerning sales and production for August 2010 is summarized as follows:

a. Estimated sales of King and Prince chairs for August by sales territory:

Northern Domestic:
King .... 5,500 units at $750 per unit
Prince .... 6,900 units at $520 per unit
Southern Domestic:
King .... 3,200 units at $690 per unit
Prince .... 4,000 units at $580 per unit
International:
King .... 1,450 units at $780 per unit
Prince .... 900 units at $600 per unit

b. Estimated inventories at August 1:

Direct materials:
Fabric .... 4,500 sq. yds.
Wood .... 6,000 lineal ft.
Filler .... 2,800 cu. ft.
Springs .... 6,700 units

Finished products:
King .... 950 units
Prince .... 280 units

c. Desired inventories at August 31:

Direct materials:
Fabric .... 4,300 sq. yds.
Wood .... 6,200 lineal ft.
Filler .... 3,100 cu. ft.
Springs .... 7,500 units

Finished products:
King .... 800 units
Prince .... 400 units

d. Direct materials used in production:

In manufacture of King:
Fabric .... 5.0 sq. yds. per unit of product
Wood .... 35 lineal ft. per unit of product
Filler .... 3.8 cu. ft. per unit of product
Springs .... 14 units per unit of product

In manufacture of Prince:

Fabric	3.5 sq. yds. per unit of product
Wood	25 lineal ft. per unit of product
Filler	3.2 cu. ft. per unit of product
Springs	10 units per unit of product

e. Anticipated purchase price for direct materials:

Fabric	$12.00 per sq. yd.	Filler	$3.50 per cu. ft.
Wood	8.00 per lineal ft.	Springs	4.50 per unit

f. Direct labor requirements:

King:

Framing Department	2.5 hrs. at $12 per hr.
Cutting Department	1.5 hrs. at $11 per hr.
Upholstery Department	2.4 hrs. at $14 per hr.

Prince:

Framing Department	1.8 hrs. at $12 per hr.
Cutting Department	0.5 hrs. at $11 per hr.
Upholstery Department	2.0 hrs. at $14 per hr.

Instructions

1. Prepare a sales budget for August.
2. Prepare a production budget for August.
3. Prepare a direct materials purchases budget for August.
4. Prepare a direct labor cost budget for August.

PR 22-3A
Budgeted income statement and supporting budgets

obj. 4

✔ 4. Total direct labor cost in Assembly Dept., $85,605

The budget director of Heads Up Athletic Co., with the assistance of the controller, treasurer, production manager, and sales manager, has gathered the following data for use in developing the budgeted income statement for January 2010:

a. Estimated sales for January:

Batting helmet	3,700 units at $70 per unit
Football helmet	7,200 units at $142 per unit

b. Estimated inventories at January 1:

Direct materials:		Finished products:	
Plastic	800 lbs.	Batting helmet	310 units at $33 per unit
Foam lining	520 lbs.	Football helmet	420 units at $57 per unit

c. Desired inventories at January 31:

Direct materials:		Finished products:	
Plastic	1,240 lbs.	Batting helmet	290 units at $34 per unit
Foam lining	450 lbs.	Football helmet	520 units at $58 per unit

d. Direct materials used in production:

In manufacture of batting helmet:

Plastic	1.20 lbs. per unit of product
Foam lining	0.50 lb. per unit of product

In manufacture of football helmet:

Plastic	2.80 lbs. per unit of product
Foam lining	1.40 lbs. per unit of product

e. Anticipated cost of purchases and beginning and ending inventory of direct materials:

Plastic	$7.50 per lb.
Foam lining	$5.00 per lb.

f. Direct labor requirements:

Batting helmet:

Molding Department	0.20 hr. at $15 per hr.
Assembly Department	0.50 hr. at $13 per hr.

Football helmet:

Molding Department	0.30 hr. at $15 per hr.
Assembly Department	0.65 hr. at $13 per hr.

g. Estimated factory overhead costs for January:

Indirect factory wages	$115,000	Power and light	$18,000
Depreciation of plant and equipment	32,000	Insurance and property tax	8,700

h. Estimated operating expenses for January:

Sales salaries expense	$275,300
Advertising expense	139,500
Office salaries expense	83,100
Depreciation expense—office equipment	5,800
Telephone expense—selling	3,200
Telephone expense—administrative	900
Travel expense—selling	46,200
Office supplies expense	4,900
Miscellaneous administrative expense	5,200

i. Estimated other income and expense for January:

Interest revenue	$14,500
Interest expense	17,400

j. Estimated tax rate: 30%

Instructions
1. Prepare a sales budget for January.
2. Prepare a production budget for January.
3. Prepare a direct materials purchases budget for January.
4. Prepare a direct labor cost budget for January.
5. Prepare a factory overhead cost budget for January.
6. Prepare a cost of goods sold budget for January. Work in process at the beginning of January is estimated to be $12,500, and work in process at the end of January is desired to be $13,500.
7. Prepare a selling and administrative expenses budget for January.
8. Prepare a budgeted income statement for January.

PR 22-4A
Cash budget

obj. 5

✔ 1. August
deficiency, $21,100

The controller of Dash Shoes Inc. instructs you to prepare a monthly cash budget for the next three months. You are presented with the following budget information:

	June	July	August
Sales	$120,000	$150,000	$200,000
Manufacturing costs	50,000	65,000	72,000
Selling and administrative expenses	35,000	40,000	45,000
Capital expenditures	—	—	48,000

The company expects to sell about 10% of its merchandise for cash. Of sales on account, 60% are expected to be collected in full in the month following the sale and the remainder the following month. Depreciation, insurance, and property tax expense represent $8,000 of the estimated monthly manufacturing costs. The annual insurance premium is paid in February, and the annual property taxes are paid in November. Of the remainder of the manufacturing costs, 80% are expected to be paid in the month in which they are incurred and the balance in the following month.

Current assets as of June 1 include cash of $45,000, marketable securities of $65,000, and accounts receivable of $143,400 ($105,000 from May sales and $38,400 from April sales). Sales on account in April and May were $96,000 and $105,000, respectively. Current liabilities as of June 1 include a $60,000, 12%, 90-day note payable due August 20 and $8,000 of accounts payable incurred in May for manufacturing costs. All selling and administrative expenses are paid in cash in the period they are incurred. It is expected that $3,500 in dividends will be received in June. An estimated income tax payment of $18,000 will be made in July. Dash Shoes' regular quarterly dividend of $8,000 is expected to be declared in July and paid in August. Management desires to maintain a minimum cash balance of $35,000.

Instructions
1. Prepare a monthly cash budget and supporting schedules for June, July, and August 2010.
2. ➤ On the basis of the cash budget prepared in part (1), what recommendation should be made to the controller?

PR 22-5A

Budgeted income statement and balance sheet

objs. 4, 5

✔ 1. Budgeted net income, $613,700

As a preliminary to requesting budget estimates of sales, costs, and expenses for the fiscal year beginning January 1, 2011, the following tentative trial balance as of December 31, 2010, is prepared by the Accounting Department of Webster Publishing Co.:

Cash.	$ 118,600	
Accounts Receivable.	232,400	
Finished Goods.	148,900	
Work in Process	32,700	
Materials	52,500	
Prepaid Expenses.	4,000	
Plant and Equipment	580,000	
Accumulated Depreciation—Plant and Equipment.		$ 251,000
Accounts Payable		182,500
Common Stock, $15 par		450,000
Retained Earnings.		285,600
	$1,169,100	$1,169,100

Factory output and sales for 2011 are expected to total 32,000 units of product, which are to be sold at $100 per unit. The quantities and costs of the inventories at December 31, 2011, are expected to remain unchanged from the balances at the beginning of the year.

Budget estimates of manufacturing costs and operating expenses for the year are summarized as follows:

	Estimated Costs and Expenses	
	Fixed **(Total for Year)**	**Variable** **(Per Unit Sold)**
Cost of goods manufactured and sold:		
Direct materials	—	$25.00
Direct labor.	—	7.80
Factory overhead:		
Depreciation of plant and equipment.	$ 32,000	—
Other factory overhead	10,000	4.50
Selling expenses:		
Sales salaries and commissions	115,000	12.80
Advertising	112,400	—
Miscellaneous selling expense	8,400	2.00
Administrative expenses:		
Office and officers salaries	75,400	6.25
Supplies	3,900	1.00
Miscellaneous administrative expense	2,000	1.50

Balances of accounts receivable, prepaid expenses, and accounts payable at the end of the year are not expected to differ significantly from the beginning balances. Federal income tax of $280,000 on 2011 taxable income will be paid during 2011. Regular quarterly cash dividends of $1.50 a share are expected to be declared and paid in March, June, September, and December on 30,000 shares of common stock outstanding. It is anticipated that fixed assets will be purchased for $170,000 cash in May.

Instructions
1. Prepare a budgeted income statement for 2011.
2. Prepare a budgeted balance sheet as of December 31, 2011, with supporting calculations.

Problems Series B

PR 22-1B
Forecast sales
volume and sales
budget

obj. **4**

✔ 3. Total revenue
from sales,
$2,447,424

Van Gogh Frame Company prepared the following sales budget for the current year:

Van Gogh Frame Company
Sales Budget
For the Year Ending December 31, 2010

Product and Area	Unit Sales Volume	Unit Selling Price	Total Sales
8" × 10" Frame:			
East	28,000	$15.00	$ 420,000
Central	24,000	15.00	360,000
West	32,500	15.00	487,500
Total	84,500		$1,267,500
12" × 16" Frame:			
East	15,000	$25.00	$ 375,000
Central	9,500	25.00	237,500
West	14,000	25.00	350,000
Total	38,500		$ 962,500
Total revenue from sales			$2,230,000

At the end of December 2010, the following unit sales data were reported for the year:

	Unit Sales	
	8" × 10" Frame	12" × 16" Frame
East	29,680	15,300
Central	23,040	9,405
West	33,150	14,700

For the year ending December 31, 2011, unit sales are expected to follow the patterns established during the year ending December 31, 2010. The unit selling price for the 8" × 10" frame is expected to increase to $16, and the unit selling price for the 12" × 16" frame is expected to increase to $26, effective January 1, 2011.

Instructions

1. Compute the increase or decrease of actual unit sales for the year ended December 31, 2010, over budget. Place your answers in a columnar table with the following format:

	Unit Sales, Year Ended 2010		Increase (Decrease) Actual Over Budget	
	Budget	Actual Sales	Amount	Percent
8" × 10" Frame:				
East				
Central				
West				
12" × 16" Frame:				
East				
Central				
West				

2. Assuming that the trend of sales indicated in part (1) is to continue in 2011, compute the unit sales volume to be used for preparing the sales budget for the year ending December 31, 2011. Place your answers in a columnar table similar to that in part (1) above but with the following column heads. Round budgeted units to the nearest unit.

2010 Actual Units	Percentage Increase (Decrease)	2011 Budgeted Units (rounded)

3. Prepare a sales budget for the year ending December 31, 2011.

PR 22-2B
Sales, production, direct materials purchases, and direct labor cost budgets

obj. 4

✔ 3. Total direct materials purchases, $10,383,800

The budget director of Outdoor Gourmet Grill Company requests estimates of sales, production, and other operating data from the various administrative units every month. Selected information concerning sales and production for July 2010 is summarized as follows:

a. Estimated sales for July by sales territory:

Maine:
Backyard Chef............... 5,000 units at $750 per unit
Master Chef................. 1,800 units at $1,500 per unit
Vermont:
Backyard Chef............... 4,200 units at $800 per unit
Master Chef................. 1,600 units at $1,600 per unit
New Hampshire:
Backyard Chef............... 4,600 units at $850 per unit
Master Chef................. 1,900 units at $1,700 per unit

b. Estimated inventories at July 1:

Direct materials:		Finished products:	
Grates.................	1,000 units	Backyard Chef......	1,400 units
Stainless steel..........	1,800 lbs.	Master Chef.......	600 units
Burner subassemblies.....	500 units		
Shelves...............	300 units		

c. Desired inventories at July 31:

Direct materials:		Finished products:	
Grates.................	800 units	Backyard Chef......	1,600 units
Stainless steel..........	2,100 lbs.	Master Chef.......	500 units
Burner subassemblies.....	550 units		
Shelves...............	350 units		

d. Direct materials used in production:

In manufacture of Backyard Chef:
Grates .... 3 units per unit of product
Stainless steel .... 20 lbs. per unit of product
Burner subassemblies......... 2 units per unit of product
Shelves.................... 5 units per unit of product

In manufacture of Master Chef:
Grates .... 6 units per unit of product
Stainless steel .... 45 lbs. per unit of product
Burner subassemblies......... 4 units per unit of product
Shelves.................... 6 units per unit of product

e. Anticipated purchase price for direct materials:

Grates................... $20 per unit   Burner subassemblies .... $105 per unit
Stainless steel............. $6 per lb.   Shelves .... $7 per unit

f. Direct labor requirements:

Backyard Chef:
Stamping Department......... 0.60 hr. at $18 per hr.
Forming Department.......... 0.80 hr. at $14 per hr.
Assembly Department .... 1.50 hr. at $12 per hr.

Master Chef:
Stamping Department......... 0.80 hr. at $18 per hr.
Forming Department.......... 1.50 hr. at $14 per hr.
Assembly Department .... 2.50 hr. at $12 per hr.

Instructions
1. Prepare a sales budget for July.
2. Prepare a production budget for July.
3. Prepare a direct materials purchases budget for July.
4. Prepare a direct labor cost budget for July.

PR 22-3B
Budgeted income statement and supporting budgets

obj. 4

✔ 4. Total direct labor cost in Fabrication Dept., $226,200

The budget director of Feathered Friends Inc., with the assistance of the controller, treasurer, production manager, and sales manager, has gathered the following data for use in developing the budgeted income statement for December 2010:

a. Estimated sales for December:

Bird House	32,500 units at $50 per unit
Bird Feeder	21,300 units at $85 per unit

b. Estimated inventories at December 1:

Direct materials:		Finished products:	
Wood	2,400 ft.	Bird House	3,100 units at $26 per unit
Plastic	3,600 lbs.	Bird Feeder	1,900 units at $40 per unit

c. Desired inventories at December 31:

Direct materials:		Finished products:	
Wood	2,900 ft.	Bird House	3,600 units at $27 per unit
Plastic	3,400 lbs.	Bird Feeder	1,800 units at $41 per unit

d. Direct materials used in production:

In manufacture of Bird House:		In manufacture of Bird Feeder:	
Wood	0.80 ft. per unit of product	Wood	1.20 ft. per unit of product
Plastic	0.50 lb. per unit of product	Plastic	0.75 lb. per unit of product

e. Anticipated cost of purchases and beginning and ending inventory of direct materials:

Wood	$6.00 per ft.	Plastic	$0.80 per lb.

f. Direct labor requirements:

Bird House:

Fabrication Department	0.20 hr. at $15 per hr.
Assembly Department	0.30 hr. at $11 per hr.

Bird Feeder:

Fabrication Department	0.40 hr. at $15 per hr.
Assembly Department	0.35 hr. at $11 per hr.

g. Estimated factory overhead costs for December:

Indirect factory wages	$750,000	Power and light	$47,000
Depreciation of plant and equipment	185,000	Insurance and property tax	15,400

h. Estimated operating expenses for December:

Sales salaries expense	$645,000
Advertising expense	149,700
Office salaries expense	211,100
Depreciation expense—office equipment	5,200
Telephone expense—selling	4,800
Telephone expense—administrative	1,500
Travel expense—selling	41,200
Office supplies expense	3,500
Miscellaneous administrative expense	5,000

i. Estimated other income and expense for December:

Interest revenue	$16,900
Interest expense	11,600

j. Estimated tax rate: 35%

Instructions
1. Prepare a sales budget for December.
2. Prepare a production budget for December.
3. Prepare a direct materials purchases budget for December.
4. Prepare a direct labor cost budget for December.
5. Prepare a factory overhead cost budget for December.
6. Prepare a cost of goods sold budget for December. Work in process at the beginning of December is estimated to be $27,000, and work in process at the end of December is estimated to be $32,400.

(continued)

7. Prepare a selling and administrative expenses budget for December.
8. Prepare a budgeted income statement for December.

PR 22-4B
Cash budget
obj. 5

✔ 1. May deficiency,
$30,340

The controller of Sedona Housewares Inc. instructs you to prepare a monthly cash budget for the next three months. You are presented with the following budget information:

	March	April	May
Sales	$650,000	$732,000	$850,000
Manufacturing costs	350,000	370,000	430,000
Selling and administrative expenses.	175,000	225,000	245,000
Capital expenditures			160,000

The company expects to sell about 10% of its merchandise for cash. Of sales on account, 70% are expected to be collected in full in the month following the sale and the remainder the following month. Depreciation, insurance, and property tax expense represent $25,000 of the estimated monthly manufacturing costs. The annual insurance premium is paid in July, and the annual property taxes are paid in November. Of the remainder of the manufacturing costs, 80% are expected to be paid in the month in which they are incurred and the balance in the following month.

Current assets as of March 1 include cash of $30,000, marketable securities of $105,000, and accounts receivable of $750,000 ($600,000 from February sales and $150,000 from January sales). Sales on account for January and February were $500,000 and $600,000, respectively. Current liabilities as of March 1 include a $120,000, 15%, 90-day note payable due May 20 and $60,000 of accounts payable incurred in February for manufacturing costs. All selling and administrative expenses are paid in cash in the period they are incurred. It is expected that $1,800 in dividends will be received in March. An estimated income tax payment of $46,000 will be made in April. Sedona's regular quarterly dividend of $12,000 is expected to be declared in April and paid in May. Management desires to maintain a minimum cash balance of $40,000.

Instructions
1. Prepare a monthly cash budget and supporting schedules for March, April, and May.
2. ━━━▶ On the basis of the cash budget prepared in part (1), what recommendation should be made to the controller?

PR 22-5B
Budgeted income statement and balance sheet
objs. 4, 5

✔ 1. Budgeted net income, $222,050

As a preliminary to requesting budget estimates of sales, costs, and expenses for the fiscal year beginning January 1, 2011, the following tentative trial balance as of December 31, 2010, is prepared by the Accounting Department of Spring Garden Soap Co.:

Cash.	$ 100,000	
Accounts Receivable.	112,300	
Finished Goods.	76,700	
Work in Process	24,300	
Materials	54,100	
Prepaid Expenses.	3,400	
Plant and Equipment	375,000	
Accumulated Depreciation—Plant and Equipment.		$140,400
Accounts Payable		59,000
Common Stock, $10 par		190,000
Retained Earnings.		356,400
	$745,800	$745,800

Factory output and sales for 2011 are expected to total 225,000 units of product, which are to be sold at $5.20 per unit. The quantities and costs of the inventories at December 31, 2011, are expected to remain unchanged from the balances at the beginning of the year.

Budget estimates of manufacturing costs and operating expenses for the year are summarized as follows:

	Estimated Costs and Expenses	
	Fixed (Total for Year)	Variable (Per Unit Sold)
Cost of goods manufactured and sold:		
Direct materials	—	$0.90
Direct labor	—	0.55
Factory overhead:		
Depreciation of plant and equipment	$48,000	—
Other factory overhead	8,000	0.35
Selling expenses:		
Sales salaries and commissions	42,000	0.40
Advertising	60,000	—
Miscellaneous selling expense	5,000	0.20
Administrative expenses:		
Office and officers salaries	69,200	0.15
Supplies	4,000	0.08
Miscellaneous administrative expense	3,000	0.12

Balances of accounts receivable, prepaid expenses, and accounts payable at the end of the year are not expected to differ significantly from the beginning balances. Federal income tax of $90,000 on 2011 taxable income will be paid during 2011. Regular quarterly cash dividends of $1.00 a share are expected to be declared and paid in March, June, September, and December on 19,000 shares of common stock outstanding. It is anticipated that fixed assets will be purchased for $75,000 cash in May.

Instructions
1. Prepare a budgeted income statement for 2011.
2. Prepare a budgeted balance sheet as of December 31, 2011, with supporting calculations.

Special Activities ● ● ● ● ❯

You can access the special activities online at **www.cengage.com/accounting/reeve**.

Excel Success Special Activities ● ● ● ● ❯

SA 22-1
Sales budget

Cramden Talent Agency, Inc., books musical performances for the bands that it has under contract. The booking agent has partially completed a sales budget for two of the bands:

	A	B	C	D
1	Cramden Talent Agency, Inc.			
2	Sales Budget			
3	For November and December 2011			
4				
5		Number	Fee	Total
6		of	per	Performance
7	Band and Month	Performances	Performance	Revenue
8	The Saturn Five:			
9	November	10	$ 1,000	$ 10,000
10	December	15	1,000	15,000
11	Total			$ 25,000
12				
13	Alice and the Heartbeats:			
14	November	8	$ 800	
15	December	12	800	
16	Total			
17				
18	Total Revenue from Performances			

a. Open Excel file *SA22-1* and complete the sales budget.
b. If the Christmas season is unusually active, the number of performances for each of the bands will increase. Revise the sales budget, assuming that the number of performances for each of the bands increases by two performances in November and by three in December.

   [*Hint:* Copy and paste the spreadsheet you created in part (a) into the Revised Sales Budget worksheet and then modify it.]
c. When you have completed the sales budget and revisions, perform a "save as," replacing the entire file name with the following:

   SA22-1_[your first name initial]_[your last name]

SA 22-2
Sales budget

Bluewater Sailing, Inc., manufactures and sells three cruising sailboats: the $200,000 *Nantucket,* the $350,000 *Circumnavigator,* and the $500,000 *Cape Horn.* Boats of this class require months to build; thus, long-range sales forecasts are critical in managing operations. The cruisers are manufactured in boatyards in California, North Carolina, and Italy. The estimated number of boats that will be delivered to customers during 2011 follows:

Product	West Coast	East Coast	Italy	Total
Nantucket	1	2	0	3
Circumnavigator	3	3	4	10
Cape Horn	2	2	2	6

a. Open Excel file *SA22-2* to complete the sales budget.
b. Using the sales volume data and your spreadsheet software, prepare a sales budget that displays total sales volume and revenue for 2011. Your budget should display total estimated sales volume and revenue for each vessel and for all three boatyards.
c. When you have completed the sales budget and revisions, perform a "save as," replacing the entire file name with the following:

   SA22-2_[your first name initial]_[your last name]

SA 22-3
Sales budget

Completely Fit, Inc., sells exercise equipment through three retail outlets in California. Among the fitness equipment items are two elliptical trainers: the Enduro (priced at $1,500 per unit) and the Marathon (priced at $2,500 per unit).

a. Open Excel file *SA22-3* to complete the sales budget.
b. Using the estimated sales volume data below and your spreadsheet software, prepare a sales budget that displays total estimated sales volume and revenue for the first quarter of 2011.

Completely Fit, Inc.
Projected Unit Sales
For the Quarter Ending March 31, 2011

Outlet and Model	Estimated Sales Volume (Units)
Northern California Outlet:	
Enduro	10
Marathon	7
Bay Area Outlet:	
Enduro	23
Marathon	18
Southern California Outlet:	
Enduro	40
Marathon	48
Total	146

c. The marketing department has recommended that the price of the Enduro model be reduced by $150 in order to stimulate sales. If this is done, Enduro sales will increase by an estimated 6 units per quarter in Northern California, by 12 units per quarter in the Bay Area, and by 15 units per quarter in Southern California. Prepare a revised sales budget for the quarter.

[*Hint:* Copy and save the spreadsheet created in part (a) to another worksheet and then modify it.]

d. When you have completed the sales budget and revisions, perform a "save as," replacing the entire file name with the following:

SA22-3_[your first name initial]_[your last name]

Answers to Self-Examination Questions

1. **B** Individuals can be discouraged with budgets that appear too tight or unobtainable. Flexible budgeting (answer C) provides a series of budgets for varying rates of activity and thereby builds into the budgeting system the effect of fluctuations in the level of activity. Budgetary slack (answer A) comes from a loose budget, not a tight budget. A "spend it or lose it" mentality (answer D) is often associated with loose budgets.

2. **A** The first step of the budget process is to develop a plan. Once plans are established, management may direct actions (answer B). The results of actions can be controlled (answer C) by comparing them to the plan. This feedback (answer D) can be used by management to change plans or redirect actions.

3. **B** Administrative departments (answer B), such as Purchasing or Human Resources, will often use static budgeting. Production departments (answer A) frequently use flexible budgets. Responsibility centers (answer C) can use either static or flexible budgeting. Capital expenditures budgets are used to plan capital projects (answer D).

4. **B** The total production indicated in the production budget is 257,500 units (answer B), which is computed as follows:

Sales	250,000 units
Plus desired ending inventory	30,000 units
Total	280,000 units
Less estimated beginning inventory	22,500 units
Total production	257,500 units

5. **C** Dixon expects to collect 70% of April sales ($560,000) plus 30% of the March sales ($195,000) in April, for a total of $755,000 (answer C). Answer A is 100% of April sales. Answer B is 70% of April sales. Answer D adds 70% of both March and April sales.

Performance Evaluation Using Variances from Standard Costs

B M W   G R O U P — M I N I   C O O P E R

When you play a sport, you are evaluated with respect to how well you perform compared to a standard or to a competitor. In bowling, for example, your score is compared to a perfect score of 300 or to the scores of your competitors. In this class, you are compared to performance standards. These standards are often described in terms of letter grades, which provide a measure of how well you achieved the class objectives. On your job, you are also evaluated according to performance standards.

Just as your class performance is evaluated, managers are evaluated according to goals and plans. For example, BMW Group uses manufacturing standards at its automobile assembly plants to guide performance. The Mini Cooper, a BMW Group car, is manufactured in a modern facility in Oxford, England. There are a number of performance targets used in this plant. For example, the bodyshell is welded by over 250 robots so as to be two to three times stiffer than rival cars. In addition, the bodyshell dimensions are tested to the accuracy of the width of a human hair. Such performance standards are not surprising given the automotive racing background of John W. Cooper, the designer of the original Mini Cooper.

If you want to take an online tour of the Oxford plant to see how a Mini Cooper is manufactured, go to **http://www.mini.com/com/en/ manufacturing.**

Performance is often measured as the difference between actual results and planned results. In this chapter, we will discuss and illustrate the ways in which business performance is evaluated.

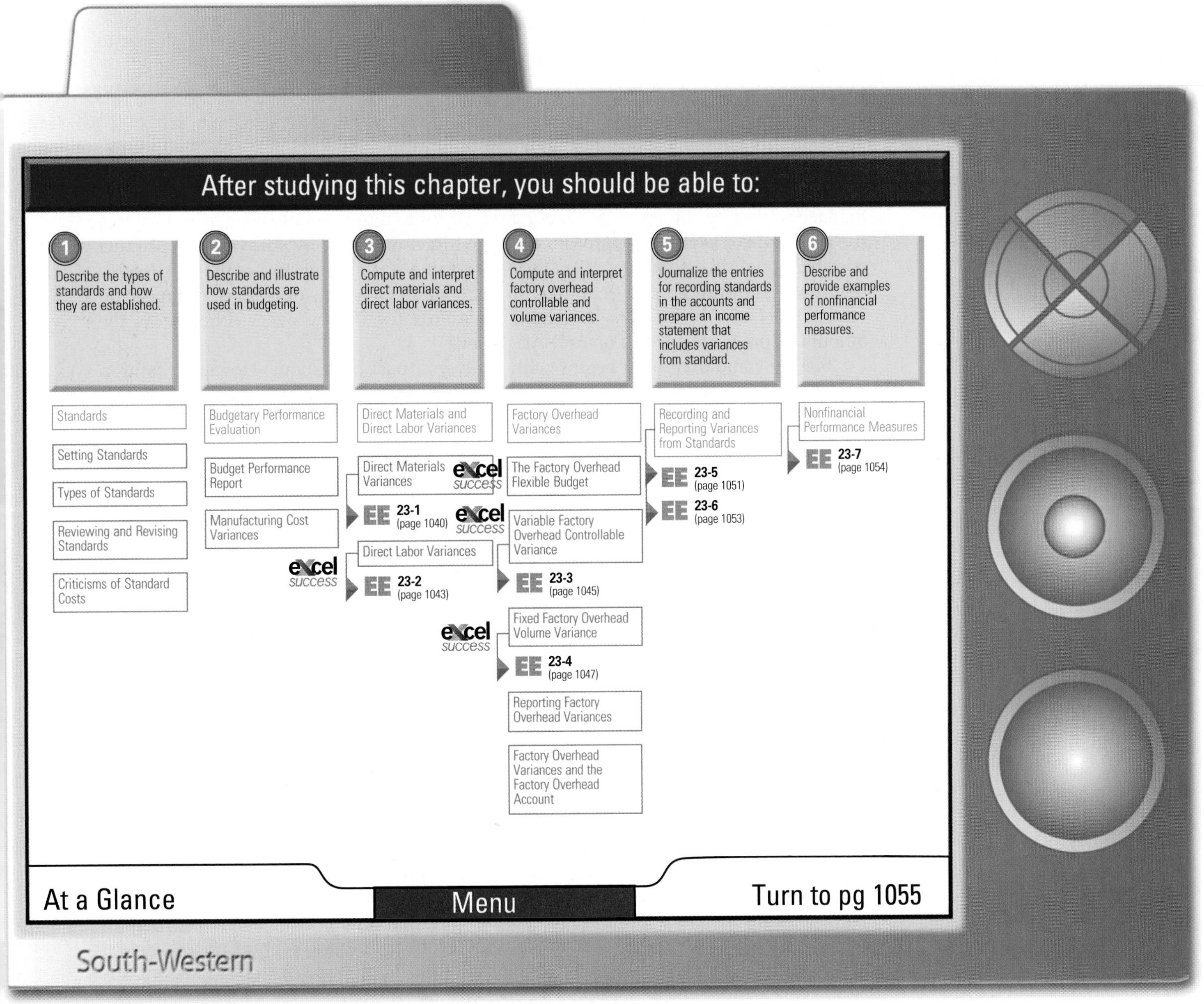

After studying this chapter, you should be able to:

1 Describe the types of standards and how they are established.

2 Describe and illustrate how standards are used in budgeting.

3 Compute and interpret direct materials and direct labor variances.

4 Compute and interpret factory overhead controllable and volume variances.

5 Journalize the entries for recording standards in the accounts and prepare an income statement that includes variances from standard.

6 Describe and provide examples of nonfinancial performance measures.

Standards

Setting Standards

Types of Standards

Reviewing and Revising Standards

Criticisms of Standard Costs

Budgetary Performance Evaluation

Budget Performance Report

Manufacturing Cost Variances

excel *success*

Direct Materials and Direct Labor Variances

Direct Materials Variances excel *success*

EE **23-1** (page 1040) excel *success*

Direct Labor Variances

EE **23-2** (page 1043)

Factory Overhead Variances

The Factory Overhead Flexible Budget

Variable Factory Overhead Controllable Variance

EE **23-3** (page 1045)

Fixed Factory Overhead Volume Variance

EE **23-4** (page 1047)

Reporting Factory Overhead Variances

Factory Overhead Variances and the Factory Overhead Account

Recording and Reporting Variances from Standards

EE **23-5** (page 1051)

EE **23-6** (page 1053)

Nonfinancial Performance Measures

EE **23-7** (page 1054)

At a Glance   Menu   Turn to pg 1055

South-Western

---

1 Describe the types of standards and how they are established.

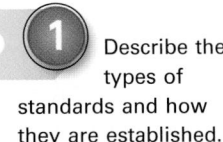

Drivers for United Parcel Service (UPS) are expected to drive a standard distance per day. Salespersons for The Limited are expected to meet sales standards.

Standards

Standards are performance goals. Manufacturing companies normally use **standard cost** for each of the three following product costs:

1. Direct materials
2. Direct labor
3. Factory overhead

Accounting systems that use standards for product costs are called **standard cost systems**. Standard cost systems enable management to determine the following:

1. How much a product *should* cost (standard cost)
2. How much it does cost (actual cost)

Standards may be integrated into computerized manufacturing operations so that variances are automatically detected and reported and operations are adjusted during manufacturing.

When actual costs are compared with standard costs, the exceptions or cost variances are reported. This reporting by the *principle of exceptions* allows management to focus on correcting the cost variances.

Setting Standards

The standard-setting process normally requires the joint efforts of accountants, engineers, and other management personnel. The accountant converts the results of judgments and process studies into dollars and cents. Engineers with the aid of operation managers identify the materials, labor, and machine requirements needed to produce the product. For example, engineers estimate direct materials by studying the product specifications and estimating normal spoilage. Time and motion studies may be used to determine the direct labor required for each manufacturing operation. Engineering studies may also be used to determine standards for factory overhead, such as the amount of power needed to operate machinery.

Setting standards often begins with analyzing past operations. However, caution must be used when relying on past cost data. For example, inefficiencies may be contained within past costs. In addition, changes in technology, machinery, or production methods may make past costs irrelevant for future operations.

Types of Standards

Standards imply an acceptable level of production efficiency. One of the major objectives in setting standards is to motivate employees to achieve efficient operations.

Tight, unrealistic standards may have a negative impact on performance. This is because employees may become frustrated with an inability to meet the standards and may give up trying to do their best. Standards that can be achieved only under perfect operating conditions, such as no idle time, no machine breakdowns, and no materials spoilage, are called **ideal standards** or *theoretical standards*.

Standards that are too loose might not motivate employees to perform at their best. This is because the standard level of performance can be reached too easily. As a result, operating performance may be lower than what could be achieved.

Currently attainable standards, sometimes called *normal standards*, are standards that can be attained with reasonable effort. Such standards, which are used by most companies, allow for normal production difficulties and mistakes. For example, currently attainable standards allow for normal materials spoilage and machine breakdowns. When reasonable standards are used, employees focus more on cost and are more likely to put forth their best efforts.

An example from the game of golf illustrates the distinction between ideal and normal standards. In golf, "par" is an ideal standard for most players. Each player's USGA (United States Golf Association) handicap is the player's normal standard. The motivation of average players is to beat their handicaps because beating par is unrealistic for most players.

The difference between currently attainable and ideal standards is illustrated below.

Currently attainable (personal best)　　　Ideal (world record)

Aluminum beverage cans were redesigned to taper slightly at the top of the can, which reduces the amount of aluminum required per can. As a result, beverage can manufacturers reduced the standard amount of aluminum per can.

Reviewing and Revising Standards

Standard costs should be periodically reviewed to ensure that they reflect current operating conditions. Standards should not be revised, however, just because they differ from actual costs. For example, the direct labor standard would not be revised just because employees are unable to meet properly set standards. On the other hand, standards should be revised when prices, product designs, labor rates, or manufacturing methods change.

Criticisms of Standard Costs

Some criticisms of using standard costs for performance evaluation include the following:

1. Standards limit operating improvements by discouraging improvement beyond the standard.
2. Standards are too difficult to maintain in a dynamic manufacturing environment, resulting in "stale standards."
3. Standards can cause employees to lose sight of the larger objectives of the organization by focusing only on efficiency improvement.
4. Standards can cause employees to unduly focus on their own operations to the possible harm of other operations that rely on them.

Regardless of these criticisms, standards are widely used. In addition, standard costs are only one part of the performance evaluation system used by most companies. As discussed in this chapter, other nonfinancial performance measures are often used to supplement standard costs, with the result that many of the preceding criticisms are overcome.

Integrity, Objectivity, and Ethics in Business

COMPANY REPUTATION: THE BEST OF THE BEST

Harris Interactive annually ranks American corporations in terms of reputation. The ranking is based on how respondents rate corporations on 20 attributes in six major areas. The six areas are emotional appeal, products and services, financial performance, workplace environment, social responsibility, and vision and leadership. What are the five highest-ranked companies in its 2006 survey? The five highest (best) ranked companies were Microsoft, Johnson & Johnson, 3M, Google, and the Coca-Cola Company.

Source: Harris Interactive, February 1, 2007.

---

2 Describe and illustrate how standards are used in budgeting.

Budgetary Performance Evaluation

As discussed in Chapter 22, the master budget assists a company in planning, directing, and controlling performance. The control function, or budgetary performance evaluation, compares the actual performance against the budget.

To illustrate, Western Rider Inc., a manufacturer of blue jeans, uses standard costs in its budgets. The standards for direct materials, direct labor, and factory overhead are separated into the following two components.

1. Standard price
2. Standard quantity

The standard cost per unit for direct materials, direct labor, and factory overhead is computed as follows:

$$\text{Standard Cost per Unit} = \text{Standard Price} \times \text{Standard Quantity}$$

Western Rider's standard costs per unit for its XL jeans are shown in Exhibit 1.

Exhibit 1

Standard Cost for XL Jeans

Manufacturing Costs	Standard Price	×	Standard Quantity per Pair	=	Standard Cost per Pair of XL Jeans
Direct materials	$5.00 per sq. yd.		1.5 sq. yds.		$ 7.50
Direct labor	$9.00 per hr.		0.80 hr. per pair		7.20
Factory overhead	$6.00 per hr.		0.80 hr. per pair		4.80
Total standard cost per pair					$19.50

As shown in Exhibit 1, the standard cost per pair of XL jeans is $19.50, which consists of $7.50 for direct materials, $7.20 for direct labor, and $4.80 for factory overhead.

The standard price and standard quantity are separated for each product cost. For example, Exhibit 1 indicates that for each pair of XL jeans, the standard price for direct materials is $5.00 per square yard and the standard quantity is 1.5 square yards. The standard price and quantity are separated because the department responsible for their control is normally different. For example, the direct materials price per square yard is controlled by the Purchasing Department, and the direct materials quantity per pair is controlled by the Production Department.

As illustrated in Chapter 22, the master budget is prepared based on planned sales and production. The budgeted costs for materials purchases, direct labor, and factory overhead are determined by multiplying their standard costs per unit by the planned level of production. Budgeted (standard) costs are then compared to actual costs during the year for control purposes.

Budget Performance Report

The report that summarizes actual costs, standard costs, and the differences for the units produced is called a **budget performance report**. To illustrate, assume that Western Rider produced the following pairs of jeans during June:

XL jeans produced and sold	5,000 pairs
Actual costs incurred in June:	
Direct materials	$ 40,150
Direct labor	38,500
Factory overhead	22,400
Total costs incurred	$101,050

Exhibit 2 illustrates the budget performance report for June for Western Rider Inc. The report summarizes the actual costs, standard costs, and the differences for each product cost. The differences between actual and standard costs are called **cost variances**. A **favorable cost variance** occurs when the actual cost is less than the standard cost. An **unfavorable cost variance** occurs when the actual cost exceeds the standard cost.

The budget performance report shown in Exhibit 2 is based on the actual units produced in June of 5,000 XL jeans. Even though 6,000 XL jeans might have been *planned* for production, the budget performance report is based on *actual* production.

Exhibit 2

Budget Performance Report

Western Rider Inc.
Budget Performance Report
For the Month Ended June 30, 2010

Manufacturing Costs	Actual Costs	Standard Cost at Actual Volume (5,000 pairs of XL Jeans)*	Cost Variance— (Favorable) Unfavorable
Direct materials	$ 40,150	$37,500	$2,650
Direct labor	38,500	36,000	2,500
Factory overhead	22,400	24,000	(1,600)
Total manufacturing costs	$101,050	$97,500	$3,550

*5,000 pairs × $7.50 per pair = $37,500
5,000 pairs × $7.20 per pair = $36,000
5,000 pairs × $4.80 per pair = $24,000

Manufacturing Cost Variances

The **total manufacturing cost variance** is the difference between total standard costs and total actual cost for the units produced. As shown in Exhibit 2, the total manufacturing cost unfavorable variance and the variance for each product cost is as follows:

	Cost Variance (Favorable) Unfavorable
Direct materials	$ 2,650
Direct labor	2,500
Factory overhead	(1,600)
Total manufacturing variance	$ 3,550

For control purposes, each product cost variance is separated into two additional variances as shown in Exhibit 3.

The total direct materials variance is separated into a *price* and *quantity* variance. This is because standard and actual direct materials costs are computed as follows:

Actual Direct Materials Cost = Actual Price × Actual Quantity
−Standard Direct Materials Cost = −Standard Price × −Standard Quantity
Direct Materials Cost Variance = Price Difference × Quantity Difference

Thus, the actual and standard direct materials costs may differ because of either a price difference (variance) or a quantity difference (variance).

Likewise, the total direct labor variance is separated into a *rate* and a *time* variance. This is because standard and actual direct labor costs are computed as follows:

Actual Direct Labor Cost = Actual Rate × Actual Time
−Standard Direct Labor Cost = −Standard Rate × −Standard Time
Direct Labor Cost Variance = Rate Difference × Time Difference

Therefore, the actual and standard direct labor costs may differ because of either a rate difference (variance) or a time difference (variance).

Exhibit 3

Manufacturing Cost Variances

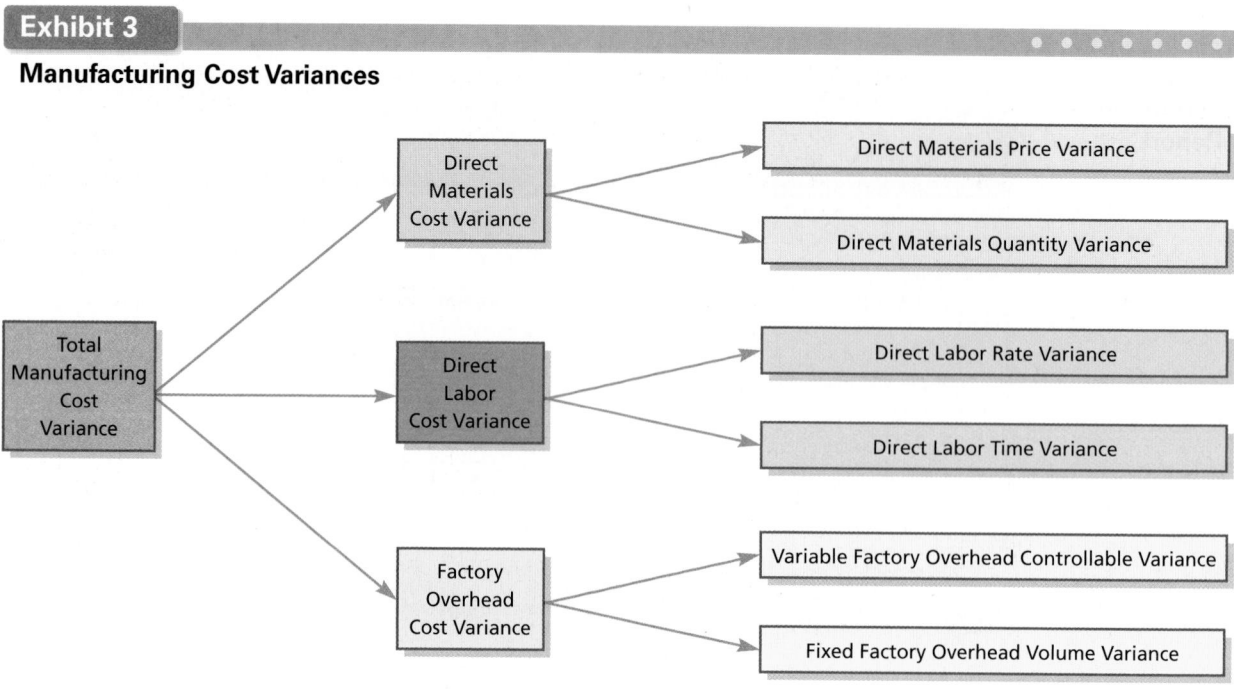

The total factory overhead variance is separated into a *controllable* and *volume* variance. Because factory overhead has fixed and variable cost elements, it is more complex to analyze than direct materials and direct labor, which are variable costs. The controllable variance is similar to a price or rate variance, and the volume variance is similar to the quantity or time variance.

In the next sections, the price and quantity variances for direct materials, the rate and time variances for direct labor, and the controllable and volume variances for factory overhead are further described and illustrated.

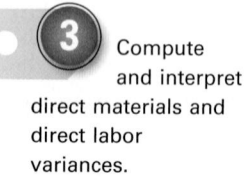

3 Compute and interpret direct materials and direct labor variances.

Direct Materials and Direct Labor Variances

As indicated in the prior section, the total direct materials and direct labor variances are separated into the following variances for analysis and control purposes:

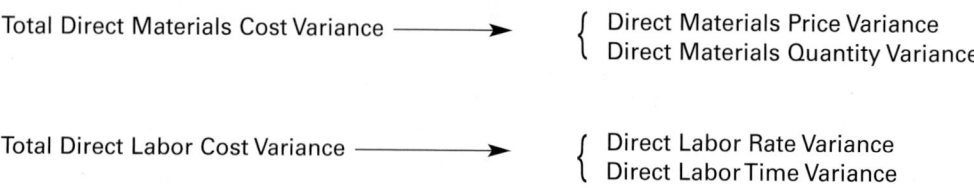

Total Direct Materials Cost Variance ⟶ { Direct Materials Price Variance
Direct Materials Quantity Variance

Total Direct Labor Cost Variance ⟶ { Direct Labor Rate Variance
Direct Labor Time Variance

As a basis for illustration, the variances for Western Rider Inc.'s June operations shown in Exhibit 2 are used.

Direct Materials Variances

During June, Western Rider reported an unfavorable total direct materials cost variance of $2,650 for the production of 5,000 XL style jeans, as shown in Exhibit 2. This variance was based on the following actual and standard costs:

Actual costs	$40,150
Standard costs	37,500
Total direct materials cost variance	$ 2,650

The actual costs incurred of $40,150 consist of the following:

Actual Direct Materials Cost = Actual Price × Actual Quantity
Actual Direct Materials Cost = ($5.50 per sq. yd.) × (7,300 sq. yds.)
Actual Direct Materials Cost = $40,150

The standard costs of $37,500 consist of the following:

Standard Direct Materials Cost = Standard Price × Standard Quantity
Standard Direct Materials Cost = ($5.00 per sq. yd.) × (7,500 sq. yds.)
Standard Direct Materials Cost = $37,500

The standard price of $5.00 per square yard is taken from Exhibit 1. In addition, Exhibit 1 indicates that 1.5 square yards is the standard for producing one pair of XL jeans. Thus, 7,500 (5,000 × 1.5) square yards is the standard for producing 5,000 pairs of XL jeans.

Comparing the actual and standard cost computations shown above indicates that the total direct materials unfavorable cost variance of $2,650 is caused by the following:

1. A price per square yard of $0.50 ($5.50 − $5.00) more than standard
2. A quantity usage of 200 square yards (7,300 sq. yds. − 7,500 sq. yds.) less than standard

The impact of these differences from standard is reported and analyzed as a direct materials *price* variance and direct materials *quantity* variance.

Direct Materials Price Variance
The **direct materials price variance** is computed as follows:

Direct Materials Price Variance = (Actual Price − Standard Price) × Actual Quantity

If the actual price per unit exceeds the standard price per unit, the variance is unfavorable. This positive amount (unfavorable variance) can be thought of as increasing costs (a debit). If the actual price per unit is less than the standard price per unit, the variance is favorable. This negative amount (favorable variance) can be thought of as decreasing costs (a credit).

To illustrate, the direct materials price variance for Western Rider Inc. is computed as follows:[1]

Direct Materials Price Variance = (Actual Price − Standard Price) × Actual Quantity
Direct Materials Price Variance = ($5.50 − $5.00) × 7,300 sq. yds.
Direct Materials Price Variance = $3,650 Unfavorable Variance

As shown above, Western Rider has an unfavorable direct materials price variance of $3,650 for June.

Direct Materials Quantity Variance
The **direct materials quantity variance** is computed as follows:

Direct Materials Quantity Variance = (Actual Quantity − Standard Quantity) × Standard Price

If the actual quantity for the units produced exceeds the standard quantity, the variance is unfavorable. This positive amount (unfavorable variance) can be thought of as

Most restaurants use standards to control the amount of food served to customers. For example, Darden Restaurants, Inc., the operator of the Red Lobster chain, establishes standards for the number of shrimp, scallops, or clams on a seafood plate.

---

1 To simplify, it is assumed that there is no change in the beginning and ending materials inventories. Thus, the amount of materials budgeted for production equals the amount purchased.

increasing costs (a debit). If the actual quantity for the units produced is less than the standard quantity, the variance is favorable. This negative amount (favorable variance) can be thought of as decreasing costs (a credit).

To illustrate, the direct materials quantity variance for Western Rider Inc. is computed as follows:

Direct Materials Quantity Variance = (Actual Quantity − Standard Quantity) × Standard Price
Direct Materials Quantity Variance = (7,300 sq. yds. − 7,500 sq. yds.) × \$5.00
Direct Materials Quantity Variance = −\$1,000 Favorable Variance

As shown above, Western Rider has a favorable direct materials quantity variance of \$1,000 for June.

Direct Materials Variance Relationships The relationship among the *total* direct materials cost variance, the direct materials *price* variance, and the direct materials *quantity* variance is shown in Exhibit 4.

Reporting Direct Materials Variances The direct materials quantity variances should be reported to the manager responsible for the variance. For example, an unfavorable quantity variance might be caused by either of the following:

1. Equipment that has not been properly maintained
2. Low-quality (inferior) direct materials

In the first case, the operating department responsible for maintaining the equipment should be held responsible for the variance. In the second case, the Purchasing Department should be held responsible.

Not all variances are controllable. For example, an unfavorable materials price variance might be due to market-wide price increases. In this case, there is nothing the Purchasing Department might have done to avoid the unfavorable variance. On the other hand, if materials of the same quality could have been purchased from another supplier at the standard price, the variance was controllable.

The price of a pound of copper has doubled since 2005.

Exhibit 4

Direct Materials Variance Relationships

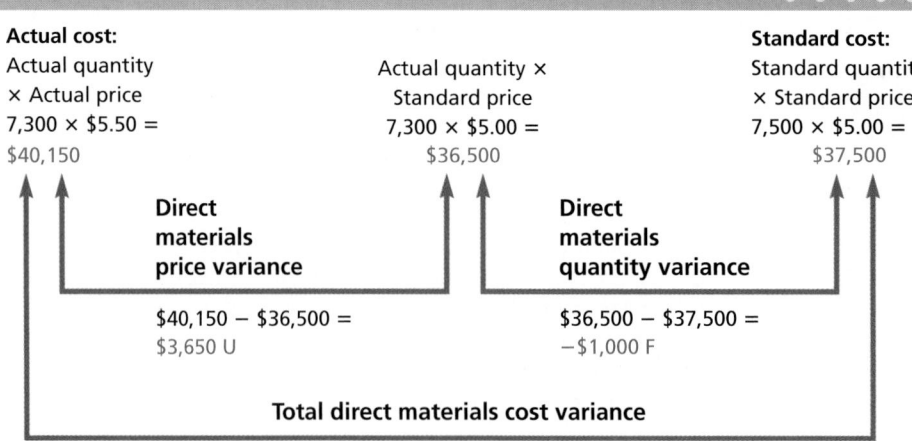

| **Example Exercise 23-1** | **Direct Materials Variances** | | 3 |

Tip Top Corp. produces a product that requires six standard pounds per unit. The standard price is \$4.50 per pound. If 3,000 units required 18,500 pounds, which were purchased at \$4.35 per pound, what is the direct materials (a) price variance, (b) quantity variance, and (c) cost variance?

(continued)

Follow My Example 23-1

a. Direct materials price variance (favorable)   −$2,775 [($4.35 − $4.50) × 18,500 pounds]
b. Direct materials quantity variance (unfavorable) $2,250 [(18,500 pounds − 18,000 pounds*) × $4.50]
c. Direct materials cost variance (favorable)   −$525 [($2,775) + $2,250] or [($4.35 × 18,500 pounds
                                                          −($4.50 × 18,000 pounds)] = $80,475 − $81,000

*3,000 units × 6 pounds

For Practice: PE 23-1A, PE 23-1B

The Internal Revenue Service publishes a time standard for completing a tax return. The average 1040EZ return is expected to require 8.3 hours to prepare.

Direct Labor Variances

During June, Western Rider reported an unfavorable total direct labor cost variance of $2,500 for the production of 5,000 XL style jeans, as shown in Exhibit 2. This variance was based on the following actual and standard costs:

Actual costs	$38,500
Standard costs	36,000
Total direct labor cost variance	$ 2,500

The actual costs incurred of $38,500 consist of the following:

Actual Direct Labor Cost = Actual Rate per Hour × Actual Time
Actual Direct Labor Cost = ($10.00 per hr.) × (3,850 hrs.)
Actual Direct Labor Cost = $38,500

The standard costs of $36,000 consist of the following:

Standard Direct Labor Cost = Standard Rate per Hour × Standard Time
Standard Direct Labor Cost = ($9.00 per hr.) × (4,000 hrs.)
Standard Direct Labor Cost = $36,000

The standard rate of $9.00 per direct labor hour is taken from Exhibit 1. In addition, Exhibit 1 indicates that 0.80 hour is the standard time required for producing one pair of XL jeans. Thus, 4,000 (5,000 × 0.80) direct labor hours is the standard for producing 5,000 pairs of XL jeans.

Comparing the actual and standard cost computations shown above indicates that the total direct labor unfavorable cost variance of $2,500 is caused by the following:

1. A rate of $1.00 per hour ($10.00 − $9.00) more than standard
2. A quantity of 150 hours (4,000 hrs. − 3,850 hrs.) less than standard

The impact of these differences from standard is reported and analyzed as a direct labor *rate* variance and a direct labor *time* variance.

Direct Labor Rate Variance The **direct labor rate variance** is computed as follows:

Direct Labor Rate Variance = (Actual Rate per Hour − Standard Rate per Hour) × Actual Hours

If the actual rate per hour exceeds the standard rate per hour, the variance is unfavorable. This positive amount (unfavorable variance) can be thought of as increasing costs (a debit). If the actual rate per hour is less than the standard rate per hour, the variance is favorable. This negative amount (favorable variance) can be thought of as decreasing costs (a credit).

To illustrate, the direct labor rate variance for Western Rider Inc. is computed as follows:

Direct Labor Rate Variance = (Actual Rate per Hour − Standard Rate per Hour)
                                           × Actual Hours
Direct Labor Rate Variance = ($10.00 − $9.00) × 3,850 hours
Direct Labor Rate Variance = $3,850 Unfavorable Variance

As shown above, Western Rider has an unfavorable direct labor rate variance of $3,850 for June.

Direct Labor Time Variance The **direct labor time variance** is computed as follows:

Direct Labor Time Variance = (Actual Direct Labor Hours − Standard Direct Labor Hours)
× Standard Rate per Hour

If the actual direct labor hours for the units produced exceeds the standard direct labor hours, the variance is unfavorable. This positive amount (unfavorable variance) can be thought of as increasing costs (a debit). If the actual direct labor hours for the units produced is less than the standard direct labor hours, the variance is favorable. This negative amount (favorable variance) can be thought of as decreasing costs (a credit).

To illustrate, the direct labor time variance for Western Rider Inc. is computed as follows:

Direct Labor Time Variance = (Actual Direct Labor Hours − Standard Direct Labor Hours)
× Standard Rate per Hour
Direct Labor Time Variance = (3,850 hours − 4,000 direct labor hours) × $9.00
Direct Labor Time Variance = − $1,350 Favorable Variance

As shown above, Western Rider has a favorable direct labor time variance of $1,350 for June.

Direct Labor Variance Relationships The relationship among the *total* direct labor cost variance, the direct labor *rate* variance, and the direct labor *time* variance is shown in Exhibit 5.

Exhibit 5

Direct Labor Variance Relationships

| Actual cost: Actual hours × Actual rate 3,850 × $10 = $38,500 | Actual hours × Standard rate 3,850 × $9 = $34,650 | Standard cost: Standard hours × Standard rate 4,000 × $9 = $36,000 |

Direct labor rate variance

Direct labor time variance

$38,500 − $34,650 = $3,850 U

$34,650 − $36,000 = −$1,350 F

Total direct labor cost variance

$38,500 − $36,000 = $2,500 U

Reporting Direct Labor Variances Production supervisors are normally responsible for controlling direct labor cost. For example, an investigation could reveal the following causes for unfavorable rate and time variances:

1. An unfavorable rate variance may be caused by the improper scheduling and use of employees. In such cases, skilled, highly paid employees may be used in jobs that are normally performed by unskilled, lower-paid employees. In this case, the unfavorable rate variance should be reported to the managers who schedule work assignments.
2. An unfavorable time variance may be caused by a shortage of skilled employees. In such cases, there may be an abnormally high turnover rate among skilled employees. In this case, production supervisors with high turnover rates should be questioned as to why their employees are quitting.

Direct Labor Standards for Nonmanufacturing Activities Direct labor time standards can also be developed for use in administrative, selling, and service activities. This is most appropriate when the activity involves a repetitive task that produces a

common output. In these cases, the use of standards is similar to that for a manufactured product.

To illustrate, standards could be developed for customer service personnel who process sales orders. A standard time for processing a sales order (the output) could be developed. The variance between the actual and the standard time could then be used to control sales order processing costs. Similar standards could be developed for computer help desk operators, nurses, and insurance application processors.

When labor-related activities are not repetitive, direct labor time standards are less commonly used. This often occurs when the time spent to perform the activity is not directly related to a unit of output. For example, the time spent by a senior executive or the work of a research and development scientist is not easily related to a measurable output. In these cases, the costs and expenses are normally controlled using static budgets.

Example Exercise 23-2   Direct Labor Variances   ●●●●●●●●> ③

TipTop Corp. produces a product that requires 2.5 standard hours per unit at a standard hourly rate of $12 per hour. If 3,000 units required 7,420 hours at an hourly rate of $12.30 per hour, what is the direct labor (a) rate variance, (b) time variance, and (c) cost variance?

Follow My Example 23-2

a. Direct labor rate variance (unfavorable) $2,226 [($12.30 − $12.00) × 7,420 hours]
b. Direct labor time variance (favorable)   −$960 [(7,420 hours − 7,500 hours*) × $12.00]
c. Direct labor cost variance (unfavorable) $1,266 [$2,226 + ($960)] or [($12.30 × 7,420 hours) −
                                               ($12.00 × 7,500 hours)] = $91,266 − $90,000

*3,000 units × 2.5 hours

For Practice: PE 23-2A, PE 23-2B

Factory Overhead Variances

④ Compute and interpret factory overhead controllable and volume variances.

Factory overhead costs are analyzed differently from direct labor and direct materials costs. This is because factory overhead costs have fixed and variable cost elements. For example, indirect materials and factory supplies normally behave as a variable cost as units produced changes. In contrast, straight-line plant depreciation on factory machinery is a fixed cost.

Factory overhead costs are budgeted and controlled by separating factory overhead into fixed and variable costs. Doing so allows the preparation of flexible budgets and analysis of factory overhead controllable and volume variances.

The Factory Overhead Flexible Budget

The preparation of a flexible budget was described and illustrated in Chapter 22. Exhibit 6 illustrates a flexible factory overhead budget for Western Rider Inc. for June 2010.

Exhibit 6 indicates that the budgeted factory overhead rate for Western Rider is $6.00, as computed below.

$$\text{Factory Overhead Rate} = \frac{\text{Budgeted Factory Overhead at Normal Capacity}}{\text{Normal Productive Capacity}}$$

$$\text{Factory Overhead Rate} = \frac{\$30,000}{5,000 \text{ direct labor hrs.}} = \$6.00 \text{ per direct labor hr.}$$

The normal productive capacity is expressed in terms of an activity base such as direct labor hours, direct labor cost, or machine hours. For Western Rider, 100% of normal capacity is 5,000 direct labor hours. The budgeted factory overhead cost at 100% of normal capacity is $30,000, which consists of variable overhead of $18,000 and fixed overhead of $12,000.

Exhibit 6

Factory Overhead Cost Budget Indicating Standard Factory Overhead Rate

	A	B	C	D	E
1	Western Rider Inc.				
2	Factory Overhead Cost Budget				
3	For the Month Ending June 30, 2010				
4	Percent of normal capacity	80%	90%	100%	110%
5	Units produced	5,000	5,625	6,250	6,875
6	Direct labor hours (0.80 hr. per unit)	4,000	4,500	5,000	5,500
7	Budgeted factory overhead:				
8	Variable costs:				
9	Indirect factory wages	$ 8,000	$ 9,000	$10,000	$11,000
10	Power and light	4,000	4,500	5,000	5,500
11	Indirect materials	2,400	2,700	3,000	3,300
12	Total variable cost	$14,400	$16,200	$18,000	$19,800
13	Fixed costs:				
14	Supervisory salaries	$ 5,500	$ 5,500	$ 5,500	$ 5,500
15	Depreciation of plant				
16	and equipment	4,500	4,500	4,500	4,500
17	Insurance and property taxes	2,000	2,000	2,000	2,000
18	Total fixed cost	$12,000	$12,000	$12,000	$12,000
19	Total factory overhead cost	$26,400	$28,200	$30,000	$31,800
20					
21	Factory overhead rate per direct labor hour, $30,000/5,000 hours = $6.00				
22					

For analysis purposes, the budgeted factory overhead rate is subdivided into a variable factory overhead rate and a fixed factory overhead rate. For Western Rider, the variable overhead rate is $3.60 per direct labor hour, and the fixed overhead rate is $2.40 per direct labor hour, as computed below.

$$\text{Variable Factory Overhead Rate} = \frac{\text{Budgeted Fixed Overhead at Normal Capacity}}{\text{Normal Productive Capacity}}$$

$$\text{Variable Factory Overhead Rate} = \frac{\$18,000}{5,000 \text{ direct labor hrs.}} = \$3.60 \text{ per direct labor hr.}$$

$$\text{Fixed Factory Overhead Rate} = \frac{\text{Budgeted Variable Overhead at Normal Capacity}}{\text{Normal Productive Capacity}}$$

$$\text{Fixed Factory Overhead Rate} = \frac{\$12,000}{5,000 \text{ direct labor hrs.}} = \$2.40 \text{ per direct labor hr.}$$

To summarize, the budgeted factory overhead rates for Western Rider Inc. are as follows:

Variable factory overhead rate	$3.60
Fixed factory overhead rate	2.40
Total factory overhead rate	$6.00

As mentioned earlier, factory overhead variances can be separated into a controllable variance and a volume variance as discussed in the next sections.

Variable Factory Overhead Controllable Variance

The variable factory overhead **controllable variance** is the difference between the actual variable overhead costs and the budgeted variable overhead for actual production. It is computed as shown below.

Variable Factory Overhead		Actual		Budgeted
Controllable Variance	=	Variable Factory Overhead	−	Variable Factory Overhead

If the actual variable overhead is less than the budgeted variable overhead, the variance is favorable. If the actual variable overhead exceeds the budgeted variable overhead, the variance is unfavorable.

The **budgeted variable factory overhead** is the standard variable overhead for the *actual* units produced. It is computed as follows:

Budgeted Variable Factory Overhead = Standard Hours for Actual Units Produced
× Variable Factory Overhead Rate

To illustrate, the budgeted variable overhead for Western Rider for June is $14,400, as computed below.

Budgeted Variable Factory Overhead = Standard Hours for Actual Units Produced
× Variable Factory Overhead Rate
Budgeted Variable Factory Overhead = 4,000 direct labor hrs. × $3.60
Budgeted Variable Factory Overhead = $14,400

The preceding computation is based on the fact that Western Rider produced 5,000 XL jeans, which requires a standard of 4,000 (5,000 × 0.8 hr.) direct labor hours. The variable factory overhead rate of $3.60 was computed earlier. Thus, the budgeted variable factory overhead is $14,400 (4,000 direct labor hrs. × $3.60).

During June, assume that Western Rider incurred the following actual factory overhead costs:

	Actual Costs in June
Variable factory overhead	$10,400
Fixed factory overhead	12,000
Total actual factory overhead	$22,400

Based on the actual variable factory overhead incurred in June, the variable factory overhead controllable variance is a $4,000 favorable variance, as computed below.

Variable Factory Overhead   Actual   Budgeted
 Controllable Variance   = Variable Factory Overhead − Variable Factory Overhead

Variable Factory Overhead
 Controllable Variance   = $10,400 − $14,400

Variable Factory Overhead
 Controllable Variance   = −$4,000 Favorable Variance

The variable factory overhead controllable variance indicates the ability to keep the factory overhead costs within the budget limits. Since variable factory overhead costs are normally controllable at the department level, responsibility for controlling this variance usually rests with department supervisors.

Example Exercise 23-3   Factory Overhead Controllable Variance   •••••••• 4

Tip Top Corp. produced 3,000 units of product that required 2.5 standard hours per unit. The standard variable overhead cost per unit is $2.20 per hour. The actual variable factory overhead was $16,850. Determine the variable factory overhead controllable variance.

Follow My Example 23-3

Variable Factory Overhead Controllable Variance = Actual Variable Factory   Budgeted Variable Factory
                                                          Overhead   −   Overhead
Variable Factory Overhead Controllable Variance = $16,850 − [(3,000 units × 2.5 hrs.) × $2.20]
Variable Factory Overhead Controllable Variance = $16,850 − $16,500
Variable Factory Overhead Controllable Variance = $350 Unfavorable Variance

For Practice: PE 23-3A, PE 23-3B

Fixed Factory Overhead Volume Variance

Western Rider's budgeted factory overhead is based on a 100% normal capacity of 5,000 direct labor hours, as shown in Exhibit 6. This is the expected capacity that management believes will be used under normal business conditions. Exhibit 6 indicates that the 5,000 direct labor hours is less than the total available capacity of 110%, which is 5,500 direct labor hours.

The fixed factory overhead **volume variance** is the difference between the budgeted fixed overhead at 100% of normal capacity and the standard fixed overhead for the actual units produced. It is computed as follows:

$$\begin{array}{c}\text{Fixed Factory}\\\text{Overhead}\\\text{Volume Variance}\end{array} = \left(\begin{array}{c}\text{Standard Hours}\\\text{for 100\% of}\\\text{Normal Capacity}\end{array} - \begin{array}{c}\text{Standard Hours for}\\\text{Actual Units}\\\text{Produced}\end{array}\right) \times \begin{array}{c}\text{Fixed Factory}\\\text{Overhead Rate}\end{array}$$

The volume variance measures the use of fixed overhead resources (plant and equipment). The interpretation of an unfavorable and a favorable fixed factory overhead volume variance is as follows:

1. *Unfavorable* fixed factory overhead variance. The actual units produced is *less than* 100% of normal capacity; thus, the company used its fixed overhead resources (plant and equipment) less than would be expected under normal operating conditions.
2. *Favorable* fixed factory overhead variance. The actual units produced is *more than* 100% of normal capacity; thus, the company used its fixed overhead resources (plant and equipment) more than would be expected under normal operating conditions.

To illustrate, the volume variance for Western Rider is a $2,400 unfavorable variance, as computed below.

$$\begin{array}{c}\text{Fixed Factory}\\\text{Overhead}\\\text{Volume Variance}\end{array} = \left(\begin{array}{c}\text{Standard Hours}\\\text{for 100\% of}\\\text{Normal Capacity}\end{array} - \begin{array}{c}\text{Standard Hours for}\\\text{Actual Units}\\\text{Produced}\end{array}\right) \times \begin{array}{c}\text{Fixed Factory}\\\text{Overhead Rate}\end{array}$$

$$\begin{array}{c}\text{Fixed Factory}\\\text{Overhead}\\\text{Volume Variance}\end{array} = \left(\begin{array}{c}\text{5,000 direct}\\\text{labor hrs.}\end{array} - \begin{array}{c}\text{4,000 direct}\\\text{labor hrs.}\end{array}\right) \times \$2.40$$

$$\begin{array}{c}\text{Fixed Factory}\\\text{Overhead}\\\text{Volume Variance}\end{array} = \$2,400 \text{ Unfavorable Variance}$$

Since Western Rider produced 5,000 XL jeans during June, the standard for the actual units produced is 4,000 (5,000 × 0.80) direct labor hours. This is 1,000 hours less then the 5,000 standard hours of normal capacity. The fixed overhead rate of $2.40 was computed earlier. Thus, the unfavorable fixed factory overhead volume variance is $2,400 (1,000 direct labor hrs. × $2.40).

Exhibit 7 illustrates graphically the fixed factory overhead volume variance for Western Rider Inc. The budgeted fixed overhead does not change and is $12,000 at all levels of production. At 100% of normal capacity (5,000 direct labor hours), the standard fixed overhead line intersects the budgeted fixed costs line. For production levels *more than* 100% of normal capacity (5,000 direct labor hours), the volume variance is *favorable*. For production levels *less than* 100% of normal capacity (5,000 direct labor hours), the volume variance is *unfavorable*.

Exhibit 7 indicates that Western Rider's volume variance is unfavorable in June because the actual production is 4,000 direct labor hours, or 80% of normal volume. The unfavorable volume variance of $2,400 can be viewed as the cost of the unused capacity (1,000 direct labor hours).

An unfavorable volume variance may be due to factors such as the following:

1. Failure to maintain an even flow of work
2. Machine breakdowns
3. Work stoppages caused by lack of materials or skilled labor
4. Lack of enough sales orders to keep the factory operating at normal capacity

Exhibit 7

Exhibit 7

Graph of Fixed Overhead Volume Variance

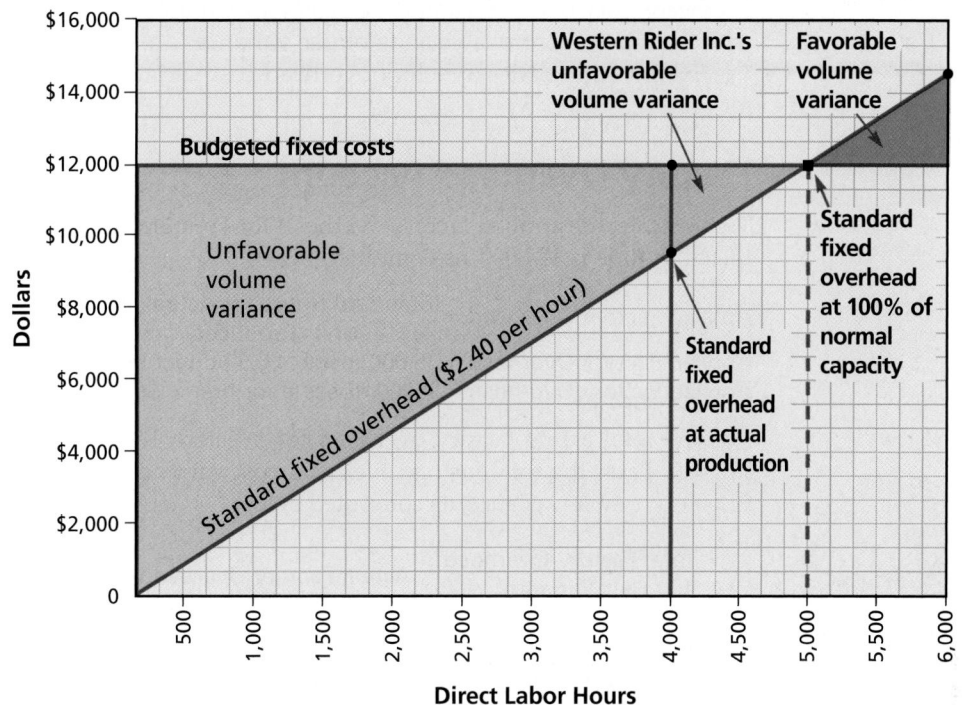

A paper company ran paper machines above normal volume in order to create favorable volume variances. This created a six-months' supply of excess paper inventory that had to be stored in public warehouses, thus, incurring significant storage costs.

Management should determine the causes of the unfavorable variance and consider taking corrective action. For example, a volume variance caused by an uneven flow of work could be remedied by changing operating procedures. Lack of sales orders may be corrected through increased advertising.

Favorable volume variances may not always be desirable. For example, in an attempt to create a favorable volume variance, manufacturing managers might run the factory above the normal capacity. This is favorable when the additional production can be sold. However, if the additional production cannot be sold, it must be stored as inventory, which would incur storage costs. In this case, a favorable volume variance may actually reduce company profits.

Example Exercise 23-4   Factory Overhead Volume Variance ••••••••▸ **4**

Tip Top Corp. produced 3,000 units of product that required 2.5 standard hours per unit. The standard fixed overhead cost per unit is $0.90 per hour at 8,000 hours, which is 100% of normal capacity. Determine the fixed factory overhead volume variance.

Follow My Example 23-4

Fixed Factory Overhead Volume Variance = (Standard Hours for 100% of Normal Capacity − Standard Hours
for Actual Units Produced) × Fixed Factory Overhead Rate
Fixed Factory Overhead Volume Variance = [8,000 hrs. − (3,000 units × 2.5 hrs.)] × $0.90
Fixed Factory Overhead Volume Variance = [8,000 hrs. − 7,500 hrs.] × $0.90
Fixed Factory Overhead Volume Variance = $450 Unfavorable Variance

For Practice: PE 23-4A, PE 23-4B

Reporting Factory Overhead Variances

The total factory overhead cost variance can also be determined as the sum of the factory overhead controllable and volume variances, as shown below for Western Rider Inc.

Variable factory overhead controllable variance	−$4,000 Favorable Variance
Fixed factory overhead volume variance	2,400 Unfavorable Variance
Total factory overhead cost variance	−$1,600 Favorable Variance

A **factory overhead cost variance report** is useful to management in controlling factory overhead costs. Budgeted and actual costs for variable and fixed factory overhead along with the related controllable and volume variances are reported by each cost element.

Exhibit 8 illustrates a factory overhead cost variance report for Western Rider Inc. for June.

Factory Overhead Account

To illustrate, the applied factory overhead for Western Rider for the 5,000 XL jeans produced in June is $24,000, as computed below.

Applied Factory Overhead = $\dfrac{\text{Standard Hours for Actual}}{\text{Units Produced}} \times \dfrac{\text{Total Factory}}{\text{Overhead Rate}}$

Applied Factory Overhead = (5,000 jeans × 0.80 direct labor hr. per pair of jeans) × $6.00
Applied Factory Overhead = 4,000 direct labor hrs. × $6.00 = $24,000

The total actual factory overhead for Western Rider, as shown in Exhibit 8, was $22,400. Thus, the total factory overhead cost variance for Western Rider for June is a $1,600 favorable variance, as computed below.

$\dfrac{\text{Total Factory Overhead}}{\text{Cost Variance}}$ = Actual Factory Overhead − Applied Factory Overhead

$\dfrac{\text{Total Factory Overhead}}{\text{Cost Variance}}$ = $22,400 − $24,000 = −$1,600 Favorable Variance

At the end of the period, the factory overhead account normally has a balance. A debit balance in Factory Overhead represents underapplied overhead. Underapplied

Exhibit 8

Factory Overhead Cost Variance Report

	A	B	C	D	E
1		Western Rider Inc.			
2		Factory Overhead Cost Variance Report			
3		For the Month Ending June 30, 2010			
4	Productive capacity for the month (100% of normal)	5,000 hours			
5	Actual production for the month	4,000 hours			
6					
7		Budget			
8		(at Actual		Variances	
9		Production)	Actual	Favorable	Unfavorable
10	Variable factory overhead costs:				
11	Indirect factory wages	$ 8,000	$ 5,100	$2,900	
12	Power and light	4,000	4,200		$ 200
13	Indirect materials	2,400	1,100	1,300	
14	Total variable factory				
15	overhead cost	$14,400	$10,400		
16	Fixed factory overhead costs:				
17	Supervisory salaries	$ 5,500	$ 5,500		
18	Depreciation of plant and				
19	equipment	4,500	4,500		
20	Insurance and property taxes	2,000	2,000		
21	Total fixed factory				
22	overhead cost	$12,000	$12,000		
23	Total factory overhead cost	$26,400	$22,400		
24	Total controllable variances			$4,200	$ 200
25					
26					
27	Net controllable variance—favorable				$4,000
28	Volume variance—unfavorable:				
29	Capacity not used at the standard rate for fixed				
30	factory overhead—1,000 × $2.40				2,400
31	Total factory overhead cost variance—favorable				$1,600
32					

overhead occurs when actual factory overhead costs exceed the applied factory overhead. A credit balance in Factory Overhead represents overapplied overhead. Overapplied overhead occurs when actual factory overhead costs are less than the applied factory overhead.

The difference between the actual factory overhead and the applied factory overhead is the total factory overhead cost variance. Thus, underapplied and overapplied factory overhead account balances represent the following total factory overhead cost variances:

1.   *Underapplied* Factory Overhead = *Unfavorable* Total Factory Overhead Cost Variance
2.   *Overapplied* Factory Overhead = *Favorable* Total Factory Overhead Cost Variance

The factory overhead account for Western Rider Inc. for the month ending June 30, 2010, is shown below.

Factory Overhead

Actual factory overhead	22,400	24,000	Applied factory overhead
($10,400 + $12,000)			(4,000 hrs. × $6.00 per hr.)
		Bal., June 30 1,600	Overapplied factory overhead

The $1,600 overapplied factory overhead account balance shown above and the total factory cost variance shown in Exhibit 8 are the same.

The variable factory overhead controllable variance and the volume variance can be computed by comparing the factory overhead account with the budgeted total overhead for the actual level produced, as shown below.

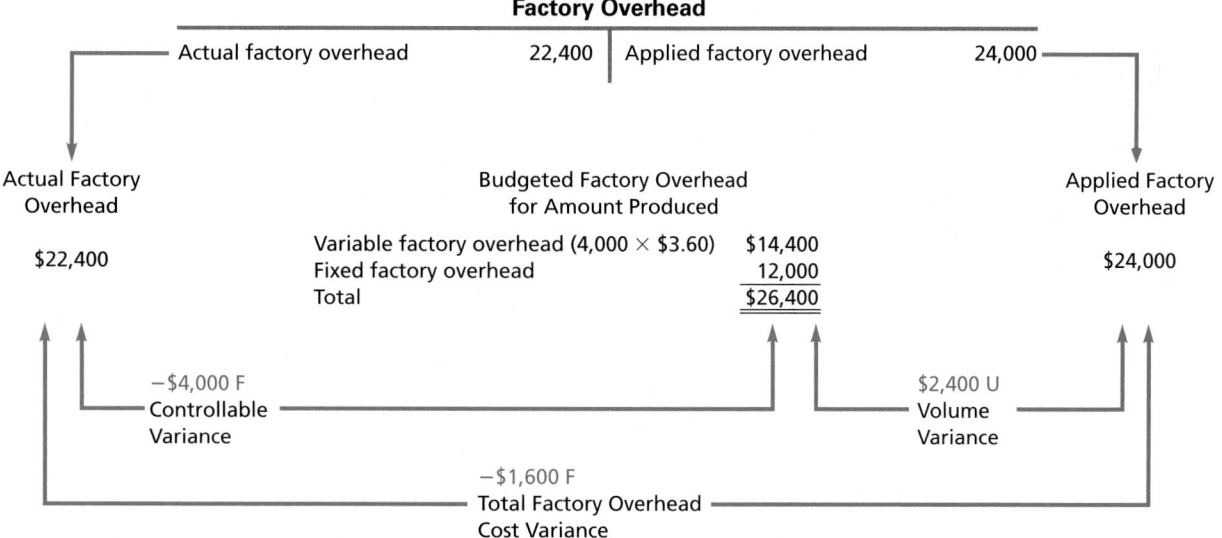

The controllable and volume variances are determined as follows:

1.   The difference between the actual overhead incurred and the budgeted overhead is the *controllable* variance.
2.   The difference between the applied overhead and the budgeted overhead is the *volume* variance.

If the actual factory overhead exceeds (is less than) the budgeted factory overhead, the controllable variance is unfavorable (favorable). In contrast, if the applied factory overhead is less than (exceeds) the budgeted factory overhead, the volume variance is unfavorable (favorable).

For many of the individual factory overhead costs, quantity and price variances can be computed similar to that for direct materials and direct labor. For example, the indirect factory labor cost variance may include both time and rate variances. Likewise, the indirect materials cost variance may include both a quantity variance and a price variance. Such variances are illustrated in advanced textbooks.

A spreadsheet can be used to compute the cost variances as follows:

	A	B	C	D	E	F
1	Inputs:					
2		**Standard**	**Actual**			
3	Direct Materials					
4	Square yards	7,500	7,300			
5	Price per square yard	$ 5.00	$ 5.50			
6						
7	Direct Labor					
8	Hours	4,000	3,850			
9	Rate per hour	$ 9.00	$ 10.00			
10						
11	Factory Overhead					
12	Variable cost		$ 10,400			
13	Fixed cost		12,000			
14	Variable factory overhead rate	$ 3.60				
15	Fixed factory overhead rate	$ 2.40				
16	Normal productive capacity (hrs.)	5,000				
17						
18	Outputs:					
19						
20	Direct Materials Variances					
21	Price variance	=(C5-B5)*C4	(Actual Price - Standard Price) x Actual Quantity				← **a.**
22	Quantity variance	=(C4-B4)*B5	(Actual Quantity - Standard Quantity) x Standard Price			
23	Direct materials cost variance	=SUM(B21:B22)	Sum			
24						
25	Direct Labor Variances					
26	Rate variance	=(C9-B9)*C8	(Actual Rate per Hour - Standard Rate per Hour) x Actual Hours			
27	Time variance	=(C8-B8)*B9	(Actual Hours - Standard Hours) x Standard Rate per Hour			
28	Direct labor cost variance	=SUM(B26:B27)	Sum			
29						
30	Factory Overhead Variance					
31	Variable factory overhead controllable variance	=(C12-(B14*B8)	Actual Variable Factory Overhead - Budgeted Variable Factory Overhead			
32	Fixed factory overhead volume	=(B16-B8)*B15	(Normal Capacity in Hours - Standard Hours for Actual Units) x Fixed Factory Overhead Rate			
33	Factory overhead cost variance	=SUM(B31:B32)	Sum			

The spreadsheet is divided into inputs and outputs. The inputs provide the information needed to develop the cost variance formulas. The formulas for each variance are explained by the adjacent text explanation. Thus, for example, the direct materials price variance is determined as:

a.   (Actual Price - Standard Price) x Actual Quantity

The formula referencing cells from the input area is:

=(C5-B5)*C4

The remaining formulas reference the input cells in a similar manner.

    Go to the hands-on **Excel Tutor** for this example!

5 Journalize the entries for recording standards in the accounts and prepare an income statement that includes variances from standard.

Recording and Reporting Variances from Standards

Standard costs may be used as a management tool to control costs separately from the accounts in the general ledger. However, many companies include standard costs in their accounts. One method for doing so records standard costs and variances at the same time the actual product costs are recorded.

To illustrate, assume that Western Rider Inc. purchased, on account, the 7,300 square yards of blue denim used at $5.50 per square yard. The standard price for direct materials is $5.00 per square yard. The entry to record the purchase and the unfavorable direct materials price variance is as follows:

Materials (7,300 sq. yds. × $5.00)	36,500	
Direct Materials Price Variance	3,650	
Accounts Payable (7,300 sq. yds. × $5.50)		40,150

The materials account is debited for the *actual quantity* purchased at the *standard price*, $36,500 (7,300 square yards × $5.00). Accounts Payable is credited for the $40,150 actual cost and the amount due the supplier. The difference of $3,650 is the unfavorable direct materials price variance [($5.50 − $5.00) × 7,300 sq. yds.]. It is recorded by debiting *Direct Materials Price Variance*. If the variance had been favorable, Direct Materials Price Variance would have been credited for the variance.

A debit balance in the direct materials price variance account represents an unfavorable variance. Likewise, a credit balance in the direct materials price variance account represents a favorable variance.

The direct materials quantity variance is recorded in a similar manner. For example, Western Rider Inc. used 7,300 square yards of blue denim to produce 5,000 pairs of XL jeans. The standard quantity of denim for the 5,000 jeans produced is 7,500 square yards. The entry to record the materials used is as follows:

Work in Process (7,500 sq. yds. × $5.00)	37,500	
Direct Materials Quantity Variance		1,000
Materials (7,300 sq. yds. × $5.00)		36,500

Work in Process is debited for $37,500, which is the standard cost of the direct materials required to produce 5,000 XL jeans (7,500 sq. yds. × $5.00). Materials is credited for $36,500, which is the actual quantity of materials used at the standard price (7,300 sq. yds. × $5.00). The difference of $1,000 is the favorable direct materials quantity variance [(7,300 sq. yds. − 7,500 sq. yds.) × $5.00]. It is recorded by crediting *Direct Materials Quantity Variance*. If the variance had been unfavorable, Direct Materials Quantity Variance would have been debited for the variance.

A debit balance in the direct materials quantity variance account represents an unfavorable variance. Likewise, a credit balance in the direct materials quantity variance account represents a favorable variance.

Example Exercise 23-5 Standard Cost Journal Entries •••••••> 5

Tip Top Corp. produced 3,000 units that require six standard pounds per unit at the $4.50 standard price per pound. The company actually used 18,500 pounds in production. Journalize the entry to record the standard direct materials used in production.

Follow My Example 23-5

Work in Process (18,000* pounds × $4.50) 81,000
Direct Materials Quantity Variance [(18,500 pounds − 18,000 pounds) × $4.50] 2,250
   Materials (18,500 pounds × $4.50) 83,250
*3,000 units × 6 pounds per unit = 18,000 standard pounds for units produced

For Practice: PE 23-5A, PE 23-5B

The journal entries to record the standard costs and variances for *direct labor* are similar to those for direct materials. These entries are summarized below.

1. Work in Process is debited for the standard cost of direct labor.
2. Wages Payable is credited for the actual direct labor cost incurred.
3. Direct Labor Rate Variance is debited for an unfavorable variance and credited for a favorable variance.
4. Direct Labor Time Variance is debited for an unfavorable variance and credited for a favorable variance.

As illustrated in the prior section, the factory overhead account already incorporates standard costs and variances into its journal entries. That is, Factory Overhead is debited for actual factory overhead and credited for applied (standard) factory overhead. The ending balance of factory overhead (overapplied or underapplied) is the total factory overhead cost variance. By comparing the actual factory overhead with the budgeted factory overhead, the controllable variance can be determined. By comparing the budgeted factory overhead with the applied factory overhead, the volume variance can be determined.

When goods are completed, Finished Goods is debited and Work in Process is credited for the standard cost of the product transferred.

At the end of the period, the balances of each of the variance accounts indicate the net favorable or unfavorable variance for the period. These variances may be reported in an income statement prepared for management's use.

Exhibit 9 is an example of an income statement for Western Rider Inc. that includes variances. In Exhibit 9, a sales price of $28 per pair of jeans, selling expenses of $14,500, and administrative expenses of $11,225 are assumed.

Exhibit 9

Variances from Standards in Income Statement

Western Rider Inc.
Income Statement
For the Month Ended June 30, 2010

	Favorable	Unfavorable	
Sales			$140,000[1]
Cost of goods sold—at standard			97,500[2]
Gross profit—at standard			$ 42,500
Less variances from standard cost:			
Direct materials price		$ 3,650	
Direct materials quantity	$1,000		
Direct labor rate		3,850	
Direct labor time	1,350		
Factory overhead controllable	4,000		
Factory overhead volume	_____	2,400	3,550
Gross profit			$ 38,950
Operating expenses:			
Selling expenses		$14,500	
Administrative expenses		11,225	25,725
Income before income tax			$ 13,225

[1]5,000 × $28
[2]$37,500 + $36,000 + $24,000 (from Exhibit 2),
 or 5,000 × $19.50 (from Exhibit 1)

The income statement shown in Exhibit 9 is for internal use by management. That is, variances are not reported to external users. Thus, the variances shown in Exhibit 9 must be transferred to other accounts in preparing an income statement for external users.

In preparing an income statement for external users, the balances of the variance accounts are normally transferred to the Cost of Goods Sold. However, if the variances are significant or if many of the products manufactured are still in inventory, the variances should be allocated to Work in Process, Finished Goods, and Cost of Goods Sold. Such an allocation, in effect, converts these account balances from standard cost to actual cost.

Example Exercise 23-6   Income Statement with Variances   •••••••••❯ 5

Prepare an income statement for the year ended December 31, 2010, through gross profit for Tip Top Corp. using the variance data in Example Exercises 23-1 through 23-4. Assume Tip Top sold 3,000 units at $100 per unit.

Follow My Example 23-6

TIP TOP CORP.
INCOME STATEMENT THROUGH GROSS PROFIT
For the Year Ended December 31, 2010

	Favorable	Unfavorable	
Sales (3,000 units × $100)			$300,000
Cost of goods sold—at standard			194,250*
Gross profit—at standard			$105,750
Less variances from standard cost:			
Direct materials price (EE23-1)	$2,775		
Direct materials quantity (EE23-1)		$2,250	
Direct labor rate (EE23-2)		2,226	
Direct labor time (EE23-2)	960		
Factory overhead controllable (EE23-3)		350	
Factory overhead volume (EE23-4)	_____	450	1,541
Gross profit—actual			$104,209

*Direct materials (3,000 units × 6 lbs. × $4.50)	$ 81,000
Direct labor (3,000 units × 2.5 hrs. × $12.00)	90,000
Factory overhead [3,000 units × 2.5 hrs. × ($2.20 + $0.90)]	23,250
Cost of goods sold at standard	$194,250

For Practice: PE 23-6A, PE 23-6B

6   Describe and provide examples of nonfinancial performance measures.

Nonfinancial Performance Measures

Many companies supplement standard costs and variances from standards with nonfinancial performance measures. A **nonfinancial performance measure** expresses performance in a measure other than dollars. For example, airlines use on-time performance, percent of bags lost, and number of customer complaints as nonfinancial performance measures. Such measures are often used to evaluate the time, quality, or quantity of a business activity.

Using financial and nonfinancial performance measures aids managers and employees in considering multiple performance objectives. Such measures often bring additional perspectives, such as quality of work, to evaluating performance. Some examples of nonfinancial performance measures include the following:

In one company, machine operators were evaluated by a labor time standard (how fast they worked). This resulted in poor-quality products, which led the company to supplement its labor time standard with a product quality standard.

Nonfinancial Performance Measures

Inventory turnover
Percent on-time delivery
Elapsed time between a customer order and product delivery
Customer preference rankings compared to competitors
Response time to a service call
Time to develop new products
Employee satisfaction
Number of customer complaints

Nonfinancial measures are often linked to either the inputs or outputs of an activity or process. A **process** is a sequence of activities for performing a task. The relationship between an activity or a process and its inputs and outputs is shown below.

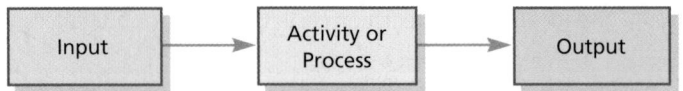

To illustrate, the counter service activity of a fast-food restaurant is used. The following input/outputs could be identified for providing customer service:

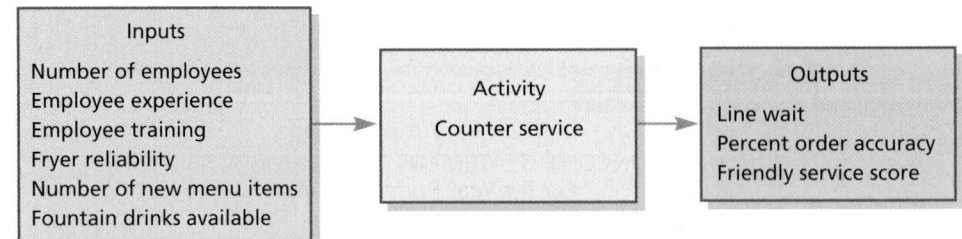

The customer service outputs of the counter service activity include the following:

1. Line wait for the customer
2. Percent order accuracy in serving the customer
3. Friendly service experience for the customer

Some of the inputs that impact the customer service outputs include the following:

1. Number of employees
2. Employee experience
3. Employee training
4. Fryer (and other cooking equipment) reliability
5. Number of new menu items
6. Fountain drink availability

A fast-food restaurant can develop a set of linked nonfinancial performance measures across inputs and outputs. The output measures tell management how the activity is performing, such as keeping the line wait to a minimum. The input measures are used to improve the output measures. For example, if the customer line wait is too long, then improving employee training or hiring more employees could improve the output (decrease customer line wait).

Example Exercise 23-7 Activity Inputs and Outputs   •••••••> 6

The following are inputs and outputs to the baggage claim process of an airline:

Baggage handler training
Time customers wait for returned baggage
Maintenance of baggage handling equipment
Number of baggage handlers
Number of damaged bags
On-time flight performance

Identify whether each is an input or output to the baggage claim process.

Follow My Example 23-7

Baggage handler training	Input
Time customers wait for returned baggage	Output
Maintenance of baggage handling equipment	Input
Number of baggage handlers	Input
Number of damaged bags	Output
On-time flight performance	Input

For Practice: PE 23-7A, PE 23-7B

① Describe the types of standards and how they are established.

		Example Exercises	Practice Exercises
Key Points	**Key Learning Outcomes**		
Standards represent performance benchmarks that can be compared to actual results in evaluating performance. Standards are established so that they are neither too high nor too low, but are attainable.	• Define *ideal* and *normal* *standards* and explain how they are used in setting standards. • Describe some of the criticisms of the use of standards.		

② Describe and illustrate how standards are used in budgeting.

		Example Exercises	Practice Exercises
Key Points	**Key Learning Outcomes**		
Budgets are prepared by multiplying the standard cost per unit by the planned production. To measure performance, the standard cost per unit is multiplied by the actual number of units produced, and the actual results are compared with the standard cost at actual volumes (cost variance).	• Compute the standard cost per unit of production for materials, labor, and factory overhead. • Compute the direct materials, direct labor, and factory overhead cost variances. • Prepare a budget performance report.		

③ Compute and interpret direct materials and direct labor variances.

		Example Exercises	Practice Exercises
Key Points	**Key Learning Outcomes**		
The direct materials cost variance can be separated into direct materials price and quantity variances. The direct labor cost variance can be separated into direct labor rate and time variances.	• Compute and interpret direct materials price and quantity variances.	23-1	23-1A, 23-1B
	• Compute and interpret direct labor rate and time variances.	23-2	23-2A, 23-2B
	• Describe and illustrate how time standards are used in non-manufacturing settings.		

④ Compute and interpret factory overhead controllable and volume variances.

		Example Exercises	Practice Exercises
Key Points	**Key Learning Outcomes**		
The factory overhead cost variance can be separated into a variable factory overhead controllable variance and a fixed factory overhead volume variance.	• Prepare a factory overhead flexible budget.		
	• Compute and interpret the variable factory overhead controllable variance.	23-3	23-3A, 23-3B
	• Compute and interpret the fixed factory overhead volume variance.	23-4	23-4A, 23-4B
	• Prepare a factory overhead cost variance report.		
	• Evaluate factory overhead variances using a T account.		

(continued)

Key Points	Key Learning Outcomes	Example Exercises	Practice Exercises
Standard costs and variances can be recorded in the accounts at the same time the manufacturing costs are recorded in the accounts. Work in Process is debited at standard. Under a standard cost system, the cost of goods sold will be reported at standard cost. Manufacturing variances can be disclosed on the income statement to adjust the gross profit at standard to the actual gross profit.	• Journalize the entries to record the purchase and use of direct materials at standard, recording favorable or unfavorable variances.	**23-5**	23-5A, 23-5B
	• Prepare an income statement, disclosing favorable and unfavorable direct materials, direct labor, and factory overhead variances.	**23-6**	23-6A, 23-6B

Key Points	Key Learning Outcomes	Example Exercises	Practice Exercises
Many companies use a combination of financial and nonfinancial measures in order for multiple perspectives to be incorporated in evaluating performance. Nonfinancial measures are often used in conjunction with the inputs or outputs of a process or an activity.	• Define, provide the rationale for, and provide examples of nonfinancial performance measures.		
	• Identify nonfinancial inputs and outputs of an activity.	**23-7**	23-7A, 23-7B

Key Terms

budget performance report (1036)
budgeted variable factory overhead (1045)
controllable variance (1044)
cost variance (1036)
currently attainable standards (1034)
direct labor rate variance (1041)
direct labor time variance (1042)

direct materials price variance (1039)
direct materials quantity variance (1039)
factory overhead cost variance report (1048)
favorable cost variance (1036)
ideal standards (1034)
nonfinancial performance measure (1053)

process (1054)
standard cost (1033)
standard cost systems (1033)
standards (1033)
total manufacturing cost variance (1037)
unfavorable cost variance (1036)
volume variance (1046)

Illustrative Problem

Hawley Inc. manufactures woven baskets for national distribution. The standard costs for the manufacture of Folk Art style baskets were as follows:

	Standard Costs	Actual Costs
Direct materials	1,500 lbs. at $35	1,600 lbs. at $32
Direct labor	4,800 hrs. at $11	4,500 hrs. at $11.80
Factory overhead	Rates per labor hour, based on 100% of normal capacity of 5,500 labor hrs.:	
	Variable cost, $2.40	$12,300 variable cost
	Fixed cost, $3.50	$19,250 fixed cost

Instructions

1. Determine the quantity variance, price variance, and total direct materials cost variance for the Folk Art style baskets.
2. Determine the time variance, rate variance, and total direct labor cost variance for the Folk Art style baskets.
3. Determine the controllable variance, volume variance, and total factory overhead cost variance for the Folk Art style baskets.

Solution

1.   **Direct Materials Cost Variance**

Quantity variance:

Direct Materials Quantity Variance = (Actual Quantity − Standard Quantity) × Standard Price
Direct Materials Quantity Variance = (1,600 lbs. − 1,500 lbs.) × $35 per lb.
Direct Materials Quantity Variance = $3,500 Unfavorable Variance

Price variance:

Direct Materials Price Variance = (Actual Price − Standard Price) × Actual Quantity
Direct Materials Price Variance = ($32 per lb. − $35 per lb.) × 1,600 lbs.
Direct Materials Price Variance = −$4,800 Favorable Variance

Total direct materials cost variance:

Direct Materials Cost Variance = Direct Materials Quantity Variance + Direct Materials Price Variance
Direct Materials Cost Variance = $3,500 + $(4,800)
Direct Materials Cost Variance = −$1,300 Favorable Variance

2.   **Direct Labor Cost Variance**

Time variance:

Direct Labor Time Variance = (Actual Direct Labor Hours − Standard Direct Labor Hours) × Standard Rate per Hour
Direct Labor Time Variance = (4,500 hrs. − 4,800 hrs.) × $11 per hour
Direct Labor Time Variance = −$3,300 Favorable Variance

Rate variance:

Direct Labor Rate Variance = (Actual Rate per Hour − Standard Rate per Hour) × Actual Hours
Direct Labor Rate Variance = ($11.80 − $11.00) × 4,500 hrs.
Direct Labor Rate Variance = $3,600 Unfavorable Variance

Total direct labor cost variance:

Direct Labor Cost Variance = Direct Labor Time Variance + Direct Labor Rate Variance
Direct Labor Cost Variance = ($3,300) + $3,600
Direct Labor Cost Variance = $300 Unfavorable Variance

3.   **Factory Overhead Cost Variance**

Variable factory overhead—controllable variance:

$$\text{Variable Factory Overhead Controllable Variance} = \text{Actual Variable Factory Overhead} - \text{Budgeted Variable Factory Overhead}$$

$$\text{Variable Factory Overhead Controllable Variance} = \$12,300 - \$11,520^*$$

$$\text{Variable Factory Overhead Controllable Variance} = \$780 \text{ Unfavorable Variance}$$

*4,800 hrs. × $2.40 per hour

Fixed factory overhead volume variance:

$$\text{Fixed Factory Overhead Volume Variance} = \left(\begin{array}{c}\text{Standard Hours for 100\%} \\ \text{of Normal Capacity}\end{array} - \begin{array}{c}\text{Standard Hours for} \\ \text{Actual Units Produced}\end{array}\right) \times \begin{array}{c}\text{Fixed Factory} \\ \text{Overhead Rate}\end{array}$$

$$\text{Fixed Factory Overhead Volume Variance} = (5,500 \text{ hrs.} - 4,800 \text{ hrs.}) \times \$3.50 \text{ per hr.}$$

$$\text{Fixed Factory Overhead Volume Variance} = \$2,450 \text{ Unfavorable Variance}$$

Total factory overhead cost variance:

$$\text{Factory Overhead Cost Variance} = \text{Variable Factory Overhead Controllable Variance} + \text{Fixed Factory Overhead Volume Variance}$$

$$\text{Factory Overhead Cost Variance} = \$780 + \$2,450$$

$$\text{Factory Overhead Cost Variance} = \$3,230 \text{ Unfavorable Variance}$$

Self-Examination Questions (Answers at End of Chapter)

1. The actual and standard direct materials costs for producing a specified quantity of product are as follows:

Actual:	51,000 lbs. at $5.05	$257,550
Standard:	50,000 lbs. at $5.00	$250,000

   The direct materials price variance is:
   A. $50 unfavorable.
   B. $2,500 unfavorable.
   C. $2,550 unfavorable.
   D. $7,550 unfavorable.

2. Bower Company produced 4,000 units of product. Each unit requires 0.5 standard hour. The standard labor rate is $12 per hour. Actual direct labor for the period was $22,000 (2,200 hrs. × $10 per hr.). The direct labor time variance is:
   A. 200 hours unfavorable.
   B. $2,000 unfavorable.
   C. $4,000 favorable.
   D. $2,400 unfavorable.

3. The actual and standard factory overhead costs for producing a specified quantity of product are as follows:

Actual:	Variable factory overhead	$72,500
	Fixed factory overhead	40,000	$112,500
Standard:	19,000 hrs. at $6	
	($4 variable and $2 fixed)	114,000

   If 1,000 hours were unused, the fixed factory overhead volume variance would be:
   A. $1,500 favorable.
   B. $2,000 unfavorable.
   C. $4,000 unfavorable.
   D. $6,000 unfavorable.

4. Ramathan Company produced 6,000 units of Product Y, which is 80% of capacity. Each unit required 0.25 standard machine hour for production. The standard variable factory overhead rate is $5.00 per machine hour. The actual variable factory overhead incurred during the period was $8,000. The variable factory overhead controllable variance is:
   A. $500 favorable.
   B. $500 unfavorable.
   C. $1,875 favorable.
   D. $1,875 unfavorable.

5. Applegate Company has a normal budgeted capacity of 200 machine hours. Applegate produced 600 units. Each unit requires a standard 0.2 machine hour to complete. The standard fixed factory overhead is $12.00 per hour, determined at normal capacity. The fixed factory overhead volume variance is:
   A. $4,800 unfavorable.
   B. $4,800 favorable.
   C. $960 favorable.
   D. $960 unfavorable.

Eye Openers

1. What are the basic objectives in the use of standard costs?
2. How can standards be used by management to help control costs?
3. What is meant by reporting by the "principle of exceptions," as the term is used in reference to cost control?
4. How often should standards be revised?
5. How are standards used in budgetary performance evaluation?
6. a. What are the two variances between the actual cost and the standard cost for direct materials?
   b. Discuss some possible causes of these variances.
7. The materials cost variance report for Nickols Inc. indicates a large favorable materials price variance and a significant unfavorable materials quantity variance. What might have caused these offsetting variances?
8. a. What are the two variances between the actual cost and the standard cost for direct labor?
   b. Who generally has control over the direct labor cost?
9. A new assistant controller recently was heard to remark: "All the assembly workers in this plant are covered by union contracts, so there should be no labor variances." Was the controller's remark correct? Discuss.
10. Would the use of standards be appropriate in a nonmanufacturing setting, such as a fast-food restaurant?
11. a. Describe the two variances between the actual costs and the standard costs for factory overhead.
    b. What is a factory overhead cost variance report?
12. What are budgeted fixed costs at normal volume?
13. If variances are recorded in the accounts at the time the manufacturing costs are incurred, what does a debit balance in Direct Materials Price Variance represent?
14. If variances are recorded in the accounts at the time the manufacturing costs are incurred, what does a credit balance in Direct Materials Quantity Variance represent?
15. Briefly explain why firms might use nonfinancial performance measures.

Practice Exercises

PE 23-1A
Direct materials
variances
obj. 3
EE 23-1   p. 1040

Norris Company produces a product that requires six standard pounds per unit. The standard price is $1.25 per pound. If 500 units required 2,900 pounds, which were purchased at $1.30 per pound, what is the direct materials (a) price variance, (b) quantity variance, and (c) cost variance?

PE 23-1B
Direct materials
variances
obj. 3
EE 23-1   p. 1040

McLean Company produces a product that requires three standard gallons per unit. The standard price is $18.50 per gallon. If 2,500 units required 8,000 gallons, which were purchased at $18.00 per gallon, what is the direct materials (a) price variance, (b) quantity variance, and (c) cost variance?

PE 23-2A
Direct labor variances
obj. 3
EE 23-2   p. 1043

Norris Company produces a product that requires 3.5 standard hours per unit at a standard hourly rate of $12 per hour. If 500 units required 1,500 hours at an hourly rate of $11.50 per hour, what is the direct labor (a) rate variance, (b) time variance, and (c) cost variance?

PE 23-2B
Direct labor variances
obj. 3
EE 23-2   p. 1043

McLean Company produces a product that requires two standard hours per unit at a standard hourly rate of $18 per hour. If 2,500 units required 5,500 hours at an hourly rate of $19 per hour, what is the direct labor (a) rate variance, (b) time variance, and (c) cost variance?

PE 23-3A
Factory overhead
controllable variance
obj. 4
EE 23-3   p. 1045

Norris Company produced 500 units of product that required 3.5 standard hours per unit. The standard variable overhead cost per unit is $0.70 per hour. The actual variable factory overhead was $1,200. Determine the variable factory overhead controllable variance.

PE 23-3B
Factory overhead
controllable variance
obj. 4
EE 23-3   p. 1045

McLean Company produced 2,500 units of product that required two standard hours per unit. The standard variable overhead cost per unit is $2.50 per hour. The actual variable factory overhead was $12,900. Determine the variable factory overhead controllable variance.

PE 23-4A
Factory overhead
volume variance
obj. 4
EE 23-4   p. 1047

Norris Company produced 500 units of product that required 3.5 standard hours per unit. The standard fixed overhead cost per unit is $0.30 per hour at 1,800 hours, which is 100% of normal capacity. Determine the fixed factory overhead volume variance.

PE 23-4B
Factory overhead
volume variance
obj. 4
EE 23-4   p. 1047

McLean Company produced 2,500 units of product that required two standard hours per unit. The standard fixed overhead cost per unit is $1.30 per hour at 4,600 hours, which is 100% of normal capacity. Determine the fixed factory overhead volume variance.

PE 23-5A
Standard cost journal entries
obj. 5

EE 23-5   p. 1051

Norris Company produced 500 units that require six standard pounds per unit at $1.25 standard price per pound. The company actually used 2,900 pounds in production. Journalize the entry to record the standard direct materials used in production.

PE 23-5B
Standard cost journal entries
obj. 5

EE 23-5   p. 1051

McLean Company produced 2,500 units that require three standard gallons per unit at $18.50 standard price per gallon. The company actually used 8,000 gallons in production. Journalize the entry to record the standard direct materials used in production.

PE 23-6A
Income statement with variances
obj. 5

EE 23-6   p. 1053

Prepare an income statement through gross profit for Norris Company using the variance data in Practice Exercises 23-1A, 23-2A, 23-3A, and 23-4A. Assume Norris sold 500 units at $105 per unit.

PE 23-6B
Income statement with variances
obj. 5

EE 23-6   p. 1053

Prepare an income statement through gross profit for McLean Company using the variance data in Practice Exercises 23-1B, 23-2B, 23-3B, and 23-4B. Assume McLean sold 2,500 units at $214 per unit.

PE 23-7A
Activity inputs and outputs
obj. 6

EE 23-7   p. 1054

The following are inputs and outputs to the cooking process of a restaurant:

Percent of meals prepared on time
Number of unexpected cook absences
Number of times ingredients are missing
Number of server order mistakes
Number of hours kitchen equipment is down for repairs
Number of customer complaints

Identify whether each is an input or output to the cooking process.

PE 23-7B
Activity inputs and outputs
obj. 6

EE 23-7   p. 1054

The following are inputs and outputs to the copying process of a copy shop:

Percent jobs done on time
Number of times paper supply runs out
Number of pages copied per hour
Number of employee errors
Number of customer complaints
Copy machine downtime (broken)

Identify whether each is an input or output to the copying process.

Exercises

EX 23-1
Standard direct materials cost per unit
obj. 2

Bavarian Chocolate Company produces chocolate bars. The primary materials used in producing chocolate bars are cocoa, sugar, and milk. The standard costs for a batch of chocolate (5,000 bars) are as follows:

Ingredient	Quantity	Price
Cocoa	510 lbs.	$0.40 per lb.
Sugar	150 lbs.	$0.64 per lb.
Milk	120 gal.	$1.25 per gal.

Determine the standard direct materials cost per bar of chocolate.

EX 23-2
Standard product cost

obj. 2

Hickory Furniture Company manufactures unfinished oak furniture. Hickory uses a standard cost system. The direct labor, direct materials, and factory overhead standards for an unfinished dining room table are as follows:

Direct labor:	standard rate	$18.00 per hr.
	standard time per unit	2.5 hrs.
Direct materials (oak):	standard price	$9.50 per bd. ft.
	standard quantity	18 bd. ft.
Variable factory overhead:	standard rate	$2.80 per direct labor hr.
Fixed factory overhead:	standard rate	$1.20 per direct labor hr.

Determine the standard cost per dining room table.

EX 23-3
Budget performance report

obj. 2

✔ b. Direct labor cost variance, $160 U

Warwick Bottle Company (WBC) manufactures plastic two-liter bottles for the beverage industry. The cost standards per 100 two-liter bottles are as follows:

Cost Category	Standard Cost per 100 Two-Liter Bottles
Direct labor	$1.32
Direct materials	5.34
Factory overhead	0.34
Total	$7.00

At the beginning of July, WBC management planned to produce 650,000 bottles. The actual number of bottles produced for July was 700,000 bottles. The actual costs for July of the current year were as follows:

Cost Category	Actual Cost for the Month Ended July 31, 2010
Direct labor	$ 9,400
Direct materials	36,500
Factory overhead	2,400
Total	$48,300

a. Prepare the July manufacturing standard cost budget (direct labor, direct materials, and factory overhead) for WBC, assuming planned production.
b. Prepare a budget performance report for manufacturing costs, showing the total cost variances for direct materials, direct labor, and factory overhead for July.
c. ━━━▶ Interpret the budget performance report.

EX 23-4
Direct materials variances

obj. 3

✔ a. Price variance, $2,730 F

The following data relate to the direct materials cost for the production of 2,000 automobile tires:

Actual:	54,600 lbs. at $1.80	$98,280
Standard:	53,400 lbs. at $1.85	$98,790

a. Determine the price variance, quantity variance, and total direct materials cost variance.
b. ━━━▶ To whom should the variances be reported for analysis and control?

EX 23-5
Direct materials variances

obj. 3

✔ Quantity variance, $184 U

I-Time, Inc., produces electronic timepieces. The company uses mini-LCD displays for its products. Each timepiece uses one display. The company produced 550 timepieces during March. However, due to LCD defects, the company actually used 570 LCD displays during March. Each display has a standard cost of $9.20. Six hundred LCD displays were purchased for March production at a cost of $6,000.

Determine the price variance, quantity variance, and total direct materials cost variance for March.

EX 23-6
Standard direct materials cost per unit from variance data

objs. 2, 3

The following data relating to direct materials cost for March of the current year are taken from the records of Play Tyme Inc., a manufacturer of plastic toys:

Quantity of direct materials used	5,000 lbs.
Actual unit price of direct materials	$2.40 per lb.
Units of finished product manufactured	1,200 units
Standard direct materials per unit of finished product	4 lbs.
Direct materials quantity variance—unfavorable	$500
Direct materials price variance—favorable	$500

Determine the standard direct materials cost per unit of finished product, assuming that there was no inventory of work in process at either the beginning or the end of the month.

EX 23-7
Standard product cost, direct materials variance

objs. 2, 3

H.J. Heinz Company uses standards to control its materials costs. Assume that a batch of ketchup (1,500 pounds) has the following standards:

	Standard Quantity	Standard Price
Whole tomatoes	2,500 lbs.	$ 0.45 per lb.
Vinegar	140 gal.	2.75 per gal.
Corn syrup	12 gal.	10.00 per gal.
Salt	56 lbs.	2.50 per lb.

The actual materials in a batch may vary from the standard due to tomato characteristics. Assume that the actual quantities of materials for batch K103 were as follows:

2,600 lbs. of tomatoes
135 gal. of vinegar
13 gal. of corn syrup
55 lbs. of salt

a. Determine the standard unit materials cost per pound for a standard batch.
b. Determine the direct materials quantity variance for batch K103.

EX 23-8
Direct labor variances

obj. 3

✔ a. Rate variance, $730 U

The following data relate to labor cost for production of 5,500 cellular telephones:

Actual:	3,650 hrs. at $15.20	$55,480
Standard:	3,710 hrs. at $15.00	$55,650

a. Determine the rate variance, time variance, and total direct labor cost variance.
b. ➔ Discuss what might have caused these variances.

EX 23-9
Direct labor variances

objs. 3, 5

✔ a. Time variance, $510 U

Alpine Bicycle Company manufactures mountain bikes. The following data for May of the current year are available:

Quantity of direct labor used	600 hrs.
Actual rate for direct labor	$12.50 per hr.
Bicycles completed in May	280
Standard direct labor per bicycle	2 hrs.
Standard rate for direct labor	$12.75 per hr.
Planned bicycles for May	310

a. Determine the direct labor rate and time variances.
b. How much direct labor should be debited to Work in Process?

EX 23-10
Direct labor variances

obj. 3

✔ a. Cutting Department rate variance, $350 unfavorable

The Freedom Clothes Company produced 18,000 units during June of the current year. The Cutting Department used 3,500 direct labor hours at an actual rate of $12.10 per hour. The Sewing Department used 5,800 direct labor hours at an actual rate of $11.80 per hour. Assume there were no work in process inventories in either department at the beginning or end of the month. The standard labor rate is $12.00. The standard labor time for the Cutting and Sewing departments is 0.20 hour and 0.30 hour per unit, respectively.

a. Determine the direct labor rate and time variance for the (1) Cutting Department and (2) Sewing Department.
b. ➤ Interpret your results.

EX 23-11
Direct labor
standards for
nonmanufacturing
expenses

obj. 3

✔ a. $1,440

St. Luke Hospital began using standards to evaluate its Admissions Department. The standard was broken into two types of admissions as follows:

Type of Admission	Standard Time to Complete Admission Record
Unscheduled admission	40 min.
Scheduled admission	10 min.

The unscheduled admission took longer, since name, address, and insurance information needed to be determined at the time of admission. Information was collected on scheduled admissions prior to the admissions, which was less time consuming.

The Admissions Department employs two full-time people (40 productive hours per week, with no overtime) at $18 per hour. For the most recent week, the department handled 66 unscheduled and 240 scheduled admissions.

a. How much was actually spent on labor for the week?
b. What are the standard hours for the actual volume for the week?
c. Calculate a time variance, and report how well the department performed for the week.

EX 23-12
Direct labor
standards for
nonmanufacturing
operations

objs. 2, 3

One of the operations in the U.S. Post Office is a mechanical mail sorting operation. In this operation, letter mail is sorted at a rate of one letter per second. The letter is mechanically sorted from a three-digit code input by an operator sitting at a keyboard. The manager of the mechanical sorting operation wishes to determine the number of temporary employees to hire for December. The manager estimates that there will be an additional 34,560,000 pieces of mail in December, due to the upcoming holiday season.

Assume that the sorting operators are temporary employees. The union contract requires that temporary employees be hired for one month at a time. Each temporary employee is hired to work 150 hours in the month.

a. How many temporary employees should the manager hire for December?
b. If each employee earns a standard $18 per hour, what would be the labor time variance if the actual number of letters sorted in December was 33,840,000?

EX 23-13
Direct materials and
direct labor variances

objs. 2, 3

✔ Direct materials
quantity variance,
$600 U

At the beginning of October, Cornerstone Printers Company budgeted 16,000 books to be printed in October at standard direct materials and direct labor costs as follows:

Direct materials	$24,000
Direct labor	8,000
Total	$32,000

The standard materials price is $0.60 per pound. The standard direct labor rate is $10 per hour. At the end of October, the actual direct materials and direct labor costs were as follows:

Actual direct materials	$21,600
Actual direct labor	7,200
Total	$28,800

There were no direct materials price or direct labor rate variances for October. In addition, assume no changes in the direct materials inventory balances in October. Cornerstone Printers Company actually produced 14,000 units during October.

Determine the direct materials quantity and direct labor time variances.

EX 23-14
Flexible overhead budget
obj. 4

✔ Total factory overhead, 12,000 hrs. $158,920

Western Wood Products Company prepared the following factory overhead cost budget for the Press Department for February 2010, during which it expected to require 10,000 hours of productive capacity in the department:

Variable overhead cost:		
Indirect factory labor	$27,500	
Power and light	3,600	
Indirect materials	23,000	
Total variable cost		$ 54,100
Fixed overhead cost:		
Supervisory salaries	$42,000	
Depreciation of plant and equipment	40,000	
Insurance and property taxes	12,000	
Total fixed cost		94,000
Total factory overhead cost		$148,100

Assuming that the estimated costs for March are the same as for February, prepare a flexible factory overhead cost budget for the Press Department for March for 8,000, 10,000, and 12,000 hours of production.

EX 23-15
Flexible overhead budget
obj. 4

Colliers Company has determined that the variable overhead rate is $2.90 per direct labor hour in the Fabrication Department. The normal production capacity for the Fabrication Department is 14,000 hours for the month. Fixed costs are budgeted at $65,800 for the month.

a. Prepare a monthly factory overhead flexible budget for 13,000, 14,000, and 15,000 hours of production.
b. How much overhead would be applied to production if 15,000 hours were used in the department during the month?

EX 23-16
Factory overhead cost variances
obj. 4

✔ Volume variance, $12,750 U

The following data relate to factory overhead cost for the production of 5,000 computers:

Actual:	Variable factory overhead	$125,000
	Fixed factory overhead	34,000
Standard:	5,000 hrs. at $30	150,000

If productive capacity of 100% was 8,000 hours and the factory overhead cost budgeted at the level of 5,000 standard hours was $162,750, determine the variable factory overhead controllable variance, fixed factory overhead volume variance, and total factory overhead cost variance. The fixed factory overhead rate was $4.25 per hour.

EX 23-17
Factory overhead cost variances
obj. 4

✔ a. $1,000 F

Perma Weave Textiles Corporation began January with a budget for 30,000 hours of production in the Weaving Department. The department has a full capacity of 40,000 hours under normal business conditions. The budgeted overhead at the planned volumes at the beginning of January was as follows:

Variable overhead	$ 75,000
Fixed overhead	52,000
Total	$127,000

The actual factory overhead was $128,500 for January. The actual fixed factory overhead was as budgeted. During January, the Weaving Department had standard hours at actual production volume of 31,000 hours.

a. Determine the variable factory overhead controllable variance.
b. Determine the fixed factory overhead volume variance.

EX 23-18
Factory overhead variance corrections
obj. 4

The data related to Acclaim Sporting Goods Company's factory overhead cost for the production of 50,000 units of product are as follows:

Actual:	Variable factory overhead	$269,000
	Fixed factory overhead	180,000
Standard:	76,000 hrs. at $6.00 ($3.60 for variable factory overhead)	456,000

Productive capacity at 100% of normal was 75,000 hours, and the factory overhead cost budgeted at the level of 76,000 standard hours was $456,000. Based on these data, the chief cost accountant prepared the following variance analysis:

Variable factory overhead controllable variance:		
Actual variable factory overhead cost incurred	$269,000	
Budgeted variable factory overhead for 76,000 hours	273,600	
Variance—favorable		−$4,600
Fixed factory overhead volume variance:		
Normal productive capacity at 100%	75,000 hrs.	
Standard for amount produced	76,000	
Productive capacity not used	1,000 hrs.	
Standard variable factory overhead rate	× $6.00	
Variance—unfavorable		6,000
Total factory overhead cost variance—unfavorable		$1,400

Identify the errors in the factory overhead cost variance analysis.

EX 23-19
Factory overhead cost variance report

obj. 4

✔ Net controllable variance, $500 U

Scientific Molded Products Inc. prepared the following factory overhead cost budget for the Trim Department for August 2010, during which it expected to use 10,000 hours for production:

Variable overhead cost:		
Indirect factory labor	$24,000	
Power and light	4,000	
Indirect materials	12,000	
Total variable cost		$ 40,000
Fixed overhead cost:		
Supervisory salaries	$30,000	
Depreciation of plant and equipment	23,400	
Insurance and property taxes	21,600	
Total fixed cost		75,000
Total factory overhead cost		$115,000

Scientific Molded Products has available 15,000 hours of monthly productive capacity in the Trim Department under normal business conditions. During August, the Trim Department actually used 11,000 hours for production. The actual fixed costs were as budgeted. The actual variable overhead for August was as follows:

Actual variable factory overhead cost:	
Indirect factory labor	$27,000
Power and light	4,000
Indirect materials	13,500
Total variable cost	$44,500

Construct a factory overhead cost variance report for the Trim Department for August.

EX 23-20
Recording standards in accounts

obj. 5

Orion Manufacturing Company incorporates standards in its accounts and identifies variances at the time the manufacturing costs are incurred. Journalize the entries to record the following transactions:

a. Purchased 1,700 units of copper tubing on account at $54.50 per unit. The standard price is $56.00 per unit.
b. Used 1,000 units of copper tubing in the process of manufacturing 120 air conditioners. Eight units of copper tubing are required, at standard, to produce one air conditioner.

EX 23-21
Recording standards in accounts

obj. 5

The Assembly Department produced 2,000 units of product during June. Each unit required 1.5 standard direct labor hours. There were 3,200 actual hours used in the Assembly Department during June at an actual rate of $14.00 per hour. The standard direct labor rate is $15 per hour. Assuming direct labor for a month is paid on the fifth day of the following month, journalize the direct labor in the Assembly Department on June 30.

EX 23-22
Income statement indicating standard cost variances

obj. 5

✔ Income before income tax, $74,050

The following data were taken from the records of Parrott Company for December 2010:

Administrative expenses	$ 72,000
Cost of goods sold (at standard)	345,000
Direct materials price variance—favorable	900
Direct materials quantity variance—favorable	1,200
Direct labor rate variance—unfavorable	500
Direct labor time variance—favorable	450
Variable factory overhead controllable variance—favorable	250
Fixed factory overhead volume variance—unfavorable	3,200
Interest expense	2,250
Sales	580,000
Selling expenses	85,800

Prepare an income statement for presentation to management.

EX 23-23
Nonfinancial performance measures

obj. 6

Under Par, Inc., is an Internet retailer of golf equipment. Customers order golf equipment from the company, using an online catalog. The company processes these orders and delivers the requested product from its warehouse. The company wants to provide customers with an excellent purchase experience in order to expand the business through favorable word-of-mouth advertising and to drive repeat business. To help monitor performance, the company developed a set of performance measures for its order placement and delivery process.

> Average computer response time to customer "clicks"
> Dollar amount of returned goods
> Elapsed time between customer order and product delivery
> Maintenance dollars divided by hardware investment
> Number of customer complaints divided by the number of orders
> Number of misfilled orders divided by the number of orders
> Number of orders per warehouse employee
> Number of page faults or errors due to software programming errors
> Number of software fixes per week
> Server (computer) downtime
> Training dollars per programmer

a. For each performance measure, identify it as either an input or output measure related to the "order placement and delivery" process.
b. Provide an explanation for each performance measure.

EX 23-24
Nonfinancial performance measures

obj. 6

Tri-County College wishes to monitor the efficiency and quality of its course registration process.

a. Identify three input and three output measures for this process.
b. Why would Tri-County College use nonfinancial measures for monitoring this process?

Problems Series A

PR 23-1A
Direct materials and direct labor variance analysis

objs. 2, 3

✔ c. Direct labor time variance, $1,095 F

Best Bathware Company manufactures faucets in a small manufacturing facility. The faucets are made from zinc. Manufacturing has 50 employees. Each employee presently provides 36 hours of labor per week. Information about a production week is as follows:

Standard wage per hr.	$14.60
Standard labor time per faucet	15 min.
Standard number of lbs. of zinc	1.6 lbs.
Standard price per lb. of zinc	$11.50
Actual price per lb. of zinc	$11.75
Actual lbs. of zinc used during the week	12,400 lbs.
Number of faucets produced during the week	7,500
Actual wage per hr.	$15.00
Actual hrs. per week	1,800 hrs.

Instructions

Determine (a) the standard cost per unit for direct materials and direct labor; (b) the price variance, quantity variance, and total direct materials cost variance; and (c) the rate variance, time variance, and total direct labor cost variance.

PR 23-2A
Flexible budgeting and variance analysis
objs. 2, 3

✔ 1. a. Direct materials price variance, $18,420 U

Scandia Coat Company makes women's and men's coats. Both products require filler and lining material. The following planning information has been made available:

	Standard Quantity		
	Women's Coats	Men's Coats	Standard Price per Unit
Filler	2.5 lbs.	4.0 lbs.	$1.25
Liner	6.0 yds.	8.5 yds.	6.50
Standard labor time	0.30 hr.	0.45 hr.	
Planned production	4,500 units	5,000 units	
Standard labor rate	$13.40 per hr.	$14.80 per hr.	

Scandia Coat does not expect there to be any beginning or ending inventories of filler and lining material. At the end of the budget year, Scandia Coat experienced the following actual results:

	Women's Coats	Men's Coats
Actual production	4,300	5,500

	Actual Price per Unit	Actual Quantity Purchased and Used
Filler	$1.15 per lb.	31,950
Liner	6.80 per yd.	72,050

	Actual Labor Rate	Actual Labor Hours Used
Woman's Coat	$13.25 per hr.	1,300
Man's Coat	15.00 per hr.	2,425

The expected beginning inventory and desired ending inventory were realized.

Instructions

1. Prepare the following variance analyses, based on the actual results and production levels at the end of the budget year:
   a. Direct materials price, quantity, and total variance.
   b. Direct labor rate, time, and total variance.
2. ➤ Why are the standard amounts in part (1) based on the actual production at the end of the year instead of the planned production at the beginning of the year?

PR 23-3A
Direct materials, direct labor, and factory overhead cost variance analysis
objs. 3, 4

✔ a. Direct materials price variance, $7,060 F

Road Ready Tire Co. manufactures automobile tires. Standard costs and actual costs for direct materials, direct labor, and factory overhead incurred for the manufacture of 5,200 tires were as follows:

	Standard Costs	Actual Costs
Direct materials	71,000 lbs. at $5.10	70,600 lbs. at $5.00
Direct labor	1,300 hrs. at $17.50	1,330 hrs. at $17.80
Factory overhead	Rates per direct labor hr., based on 100% of normal capacity of 1,350 direct labor hrs.:	
	Variable cost, $3.10	$4,000 variable cost
	Fixed cost, $4.90	$6,615 fixed cost

Each tire requires 0.25 hour of direct labor.

Instructions

Determine (a) the price variance, quantity variance, and total direct materials cost variance; (b) the rate variance, time variance, and total direct labor cost variance; and (c) variable factory overhead controllable variance, the fixed factory overhead volume variance, and total factory overhead cost variance.

PR 23-4A
Standard factory overhead variance report

obj. 4

✔ Controllable variance, $640 F

Bio-Care, Inc., a manufacturer of disposable medical supplies, prepared the following factory overhead cost budget for the Assembly Department for March 2010. The company expected to operate the department at 100% of normal capacity of 18,000 hours.

Variable costs:		
Indirect factory wages	$135,000	
Power and light	93,600	
Indirect materials	25,200	
Total variable cost		$253,800
Fixed costs:		
Supervisory salaries	$ 72,000	
Depreciation of plant and equipment	51,500	
Insurance and property taxes	24,100	
Total fixed cost		147,600
Total factory overhead cost		$401,400

During March, the department operated at 16,900 hours, and the factory overhead costs incurred were indirect factory wages, $126,320; power and light, $88,110; indirect materials, $23,220; supervisory salaries, $72,000; depreciation of plant and equipment, $51,500; and insurance and property taxes, $24,100.

Instructions

Prepare a factory overhead cost variance report for March. To be useful for cost control, the budgeted amounts should be based on 16,900 hours.

PR 23-5A
Standards for nonmanufacturing expenses

objs. 3, 6

✔ 2. $256 F

The Radiology Department provides imaging services for Parkside Medical Center. One important activity in the Radiology Department is transcribing digitally recorded analyses of images into a written report. The manager of the Radiology Department determined that the average transcriptionist could type 750 lines of a report in an hour. The plan for the first week in May called for 60,000 typed lines to be written. The Radiology Department has two transcriptionists. Each transcriptionist is hired from an employment firm that requires temporary employees to be hired for a minimum of a 40-hour week. Transcriptionists are paid $16.00 per hour. The manager offered a bonus if the department could type more than 65,000 lines for the week, without overtime. Due to high service demands, the transcriptionists typed more lines in the first week of May than planned. The actual amount of lines typed in the first week of May was 72,000 lines, without overtime. As a result, the bonus caused the average transcriptionist hourly rate to increase to $19.00 per hour during the first week in May.

Instructions

1. If the department typed 60,000 lines according to the original plan, what would have been the labor time variance?
2. What was the labor time variance as a result of typing 72,000 lines?
3. What was the labor rate variance as a result of the bonus?
4. The manager is trying to determine if a better decision would have been to hire a temporary transcriptionist to meet the higher typing demands in the first week of May, rather than paying out the bonus. If another employee was hired from the employment firm, what would have been the labor time variance in the first week?
5. ➡ Which decision is better, paying the bonus or hiring another transcriptionist?
6. ➡ Are there any performance-related issues that the labor time and rate variances fail to consider? Explain.

Problems Series B ● ● ● ● ▶

PR 23-1B
Direct materials and direct labor variance analysis

Vintage Dresses Inc. manufactures dresses in a small manufacturing facility. Manufacturing has 20 employees. Each employee presently provides 35 hours of productive labor per week. Information about a production week is as follows:

objs. 2, 3

✔ c. Rate variance,
$140 U

Standard wage per hr.	$10.80
Standard labor time per dress	12 min.
Standard number of yds. of fabric per dress	3.8 yds.
Standard price per yd. of fabric	$2.90
Actual price per yd. of fabric	$2.75
Actual yds. of fabric used during the week	12,100 yds.
Number of dresses produced during the week	3,250
Actual wage per hr.	$11.00
Actual hrs. per week	700 hrs.

Instructions

Determine (a) the standard cost per dress for direct materials and direct labor; (b) the price variance, quantity variance, and total direct materials cost variance; and (c) the rate variance, time variance, and total direct labor cost variance.

PR 23-2B
Flexible budgeting and variance analysis
objs. 2, 3

✔ 1. a. Direct materials quantity variance, $2,630 F

Cocoa Delights Chocolate Company makes dark chocolate and light chocolate. Both products require cocoa and sugar. The following planning information has been made available:

	Standard Quantity		Standard Price per Pound
	Dark Chocolate	Light Chocolate	
Cocoa	12 lbs.	8 lbs.	$4.50
Sugar	9 lbs.	13 lbs.	0.65
Standard labor time	0.35 hr.	0.50 hr.	
Planned production	3,000 cases	5,000 cases	
Standard labor rate	$14.40 per hr.	$14.00 per hr.	

Cocoa Delights Chocolate does not expect there to be any beginning or ending inventories of cocoa or sugar. At the end of the budget year, Cocoa Delights Chocolate had the following actual results:

	Dark Chocolate	Light Chocolate
Actual production (cases)	2,800	5,500
	Actual Price per Pound	**Actual Pounds Purchased and Used**
Cocoa	$4.65	76,900
Sugar	0.55	97,500
	Actual Labor Rate	**Actual Labor Hours Used**
Dark chocolate	$14.25 per hr.	960
Light chocolate	14.25 per hr.	2,780

Instructions

1. Prepare the following variance analyses, based on the actual results and production levels at the end of the budget year:
   a. Direct materials price, quantity, and total variance.
   b. Direct labor rate, time, and total variance.
2. ➤ Why are the standard amounts in part (1) based on the actual production for the year instead of the planned production for the year?

PR 23-3B
Direct materials, direct labor, and factory overhead cost variance analysis
objs. 3, 4

✔ c. Controllable variance, $150 F

Eastern Polymers, Inc., processes a base chemical into plastic. Standard costs and actual costs for direct materials, direct labor, and factory overhead incurred for the manufacture of 23,500 units of product were as follows:

	Standard Costs	Actual Costs
Direct materials	4,280 lbs. at $8.10	4,250 lbs. at $8.32
Direct labor	2,350 hrs. at $17.50	2,400 hrs. at $17.00
Factory overhead	Rates per direct labor hr., based on 100% of normal capacity of 2,000 direct labor hrs.:	
	Variable cost, $2.20	$5,020 variable cost
	Fixed cost, $3.50	$7,000 fixed cost

Each unit requires 0.1 hour of direct labor.

Instructions

Determine (a) the price variance, quantity variance, and total direct materials cost variance; (b) the rate variance, time variance, and total direct labor cost variance; and (c) variable factory overhead controllable variance, the fixed factory overhead volume variance, and total factory overhead cost variance.

PR 23-4B
Standard factory overhead variance report

obj. **4**

✔ Controllable variance, $130 U

KAT Equipment Inc., a manufacturer of construction equipment, prepared the following factory overhead cost budget for the Welding Department for December 2010. The company expected to operate the department at 100% of normal capacity of 5,600 hours.

Variable costs:		
Indirect factory wages	$17,640	
Power and light	10,080	
Indirect materials	8,400	
Total variable cost		$36,120
Fixed costs:		
Supervisory salaries	$12,000	
Depreciation of plant and equipment	31,450	
Insurance and property taxes	9,750	
Total fixed cost		53,200
Total factory overhead cost		$89,320

During December, the department operated at 6,000 standard hours, and the factory overhead costs incurred were indirect factory wages, $18,760; power and light, $10,620; indirect materials, $9,450; supervisory salaries, $12,000; depreciation of plant and equipment, $31,450; and insurance and property taxes, $9,750.

Instructions

Prepare a factory overhead cost variance report for December. To be useful for cost control, the budgeted amounts should be based on 6,000 hours.

PR 23-5B
Standards for nonmanufacturing expenses

objs. **3, 6**
✔ 3. $960 U

Office Pro, Inc., does software development. One important activity in software development is writing software code. The manager of the WordPro Development Team determined that the average software programmer could write 40 lines of code in an hour. The plan for the first week in May called for 6,000 lines of code to be written on the WordPro product. The WordPro Team has four programmers. Each programmer is hired from an employment firm that requires temporary employees to be hired for a minimum of a 40-hour week. Programmers are paid $28.00 per hour. The manager offered a bonus if the team could generate more than 6,500 lines for the week, without overtime. Due to a project emergency, the programmers wrote more code in the first week of May than planned. The actual amount of code written in the first week of May was 7,000 lines, without overtime. As a result, the bonus caused the average programmer's hourly rate to increase to $34.00 per hour during the first week in May.

Instructions

1. If the team generated 6,000 lines of code according to the original plan, what would have been the labor time variance?
2. What was the actual labor time variance as a result of generating 7,000 lines of code?
3. What was the labor rate variance as a result of the bonus?
4. The manager is trying to determine if a better decision would have been to hire a temporary programmer to meet the higher programming demand in the first week of May, rather than paying out the bonus. If another employee was hired from the employment firm, what would have been the labor time variance in the first week?
5. ⬛➤ Which decision is better, paying the bonus or hiring another programmer?
6. ⬛➤ Are there any performance-related issues that the labor time and rate variances fail to consider? Explain.

Comprehensive Problem 5   ● ● ● ● ●>>

Essence of Persia, Inc., began operations on January 1, 2010. The company produces a hand and body lotion in an eight-ounce bottle called *Eternal Beauty*. The lotion is sold wholesale in 12-bottle cases for $80 per case. There is a selling commission of $16 per case. The January direct materials, direct labor, and factory overhead costs are as follows:

DIRECT MATERIALS

	Cost Behavior	Units per Case	Cost per Unit	Direct Materials Cost per Case
Cream base	Variable	72 ozs.	$0.015	$ 1.08
Natural oils	Variable	24 ozs.	0.250	6.00
Bottle (8-oz.)	Variable	12 bottles	0.400	4.80
				$11.88

DIRECT LABOR

Department	Cost Behavior	Time per Case	Labor Rate per Hour	Direct Labor Cost per Case
Mixing	Variable	16.80 min.	$15.00	$4.20
Filling	Variable	4.20	12.00	0.84
		21.00 min.		$5.04

FACTORY OVERHEAD

	Cost Behavior	Total Cost
Utilities	Mixed	$ 230
Facility lease	Fixed	14,392
Equipment depreciation	Fixed	3,600
Supplies	Fixed	600
		$18,822

Part A—Break-Even Analysis

The management of Essence of Persia, Inc., wishes to determine the number of cases required to break even per month. The utilities cost, which is part of factory overhead, is a mixed cost. The following information was gathered from the first six months of operation regarding this cost:

2010	Case Production	Utility Total Cost
January	300	$230
February	600	263
March	1,000	300
April	900	292
May	750	280
June	825	285

Instructions

1. Determine the fixed and variable portion of the utility cost using the high-low method.
2. Determine the contribution margin per case.
3. Determine the fixed costs per month, including the utility fixed cost from part (1).
4. Determine the break-even number of cases per month.

Part B—August Budgets

During July of the current year, the management of Essence of Persia, Inc., asked the controller to prepare August manufacturing and income statement budgets. Demand was expected to be 1,400 cases at $80 per case for August. Inventory planning information is provided as follows:

Finished Goods Inventory:

	Cases	Cost
Estimated finished goods inventory, August 1, 2010	200	$6,000
Desired finished goods inventory, August 31, 2010	100	3,000

Materials Inventory:

	Cream Base (ozs.)	Oils (ozs.)	Bottles (bottles)
Estimated materials inventory, August 1, 2010	400	240	500
Desired materials inventory, August 31, 2010	600	300	400

There was negligible work in process inventory assumed for either the beginning or end of the month; thus, none was assumed. In addition, there was no change in the cost per unit or estimated units per case operating data from January.

Instructions

5. Prepare the August production budget.
6. Prepare the August direct materials purchases budget.
7. Prepare the August direct labor budget.
8. Prepare the August factory overhead budget.
9. Prepare the August budgeted income statement, including selling expenses.

Part C—August Variance Analysis

During September of the current year, the controller was asked to perform variance analyses for August. The January operating data provided the standard prices, rates, times, and quantities per case. There were 1,500 actual cases produced during August, which was 200 more cases than planned at the beginning of the month. Actual data for August were as follows:

	Actual Direct Materials Price per Case	Actual Direct Materials Quantity per Case
Cream base	$1.05 (for 72 ozs.)	76 ozs.
Natural oils	6.25 (for 24 ozs.)	25 ozs.
Bottle (8-oz.)	4.65 (for 12 bottles)	12.4 bottles

	Actual Direct Labor Rate	Actual Direct Labor Time per Case
Mixing	$15.40	16.00 min.
Filling	11.80	4.60 min.
Actual variable overhead	$158.00	
Normal volume	1,450 cases	

The prices of the materials were different than standard due to fluctuations in market prices. The standard quantity of materials used per case was an ideal standard. The Mixing Department used a higher grade labor classification during the month, thus causing the actual labor rate to exceed standard. The Filling Department used a lower grade labor classification during the month, thus causing the actual labor rate to be less than standard.

Instructions

10. Determine and interpret the direct materials price and quantity variances for the three materials.
11. Determine and interpret the direct labor rate and time variances for the two departments.
12. Determine and interpret the factory overhead controllable variance.
13. Determine and interpret the factory overhead volume variance.
14. Why are the standard direct labor and direct materials costs in the calculations for parts (10) and (11) based on the actual 1,500-case production volume rather than the planned 1,300 cases of production used in the budgets for parts (6) and (7)?

Special Activities

You can access the special activities online at **www.cengage.com/accounting/reeve**.

Excel Success Special Activities

SA 23-1
Direct materials variances

The May Company manufactures plastic toy cars. Each toy car requires 16 standard pounds of resin (plastic). Each pound of resin has a standard cost of $3.25 per pound. Actual production information is as follows:

Volume: 800 toy cars
Actual material price per pound: $3.15
Actual pounds of resin used to produce each car: 16.2
Actual total pounds of used: 12,960 (800 cars × 16.2 pounds)

a. Open the Excel file *SA23-1*.
b. Determine the direct materials price variance, direct materials quantity variance, and the direct materials cost variance.
c. When you have completed the variances, perform a "save as," replacing the entire file name with the following:

SA23-1_[your first name initial]_[your last name]

SA 23-2
Direct labor variances

Each toy car produced by the May Company requires 0.35 standard direct labor hour. Each labor hour has a standard rate of $16 per hour. Actual production information is as follows:

Volume: 800 toy cars
Actual labor rate: $16.50 per hour
Actual direct labor hours per car: 0.32 hours
Actual total direct labor hours: 256 hours (800 cars × 0.32 hours)

a. Open the Excel file *SA23-2*.
b. Determine the direct labor rate variance, direct labor time variance, and the direct labor cost variance.
c. When you have completed the variances, perform a "save as," replacing the entire file name with the following:

SA23-2_[your first name initial]_[your last name]

SA 23-3
Factory overhead variances

The May Company produced 800 toy cars that required 0.32 standard hour per unit to manufacture. The standard variable factory overhead rate per unit is $15.00 per hour. The actual variable factory overhead was $3,775. The normal productive capacity is 300 direct labor hours, and the standard fixed factory overhead rate is $17.00 per direct labor hour. Thus, the budgeted amount of fixed factory overhead is $5,100 (300 direct labor hours × $17.00 per hour).

a. Open the Excel file *SA23-3*.
b. Determine the variable factory overhead controllable variance and the fixed factory overhead volume variance.
c. When you have completed the variances, perform a "save as," replacing the entire file name with the following:

SA23-3_[your first name initial]_[your last name]

SA 23-4
**Direct materials,
direct labor, and
factory overhead
variances**

The Morgan Company produces bed sheets by cutting and sewing fabric. The following production information relates to a recent period:

Inputs	Standard	Actual
Direct Materials		
Square yrds.	34,500	35,200
Price per sq. yrd.	$ 6.50	$ 6.45
Direct Labor		
Hours	6,300	6,450
Rate per hour	$11.50	$ 11.62
Factory Overhead		
Variable cost		$47,900
Fixed cost		42,000
Variable factory overhead rate, per hour	$ 8.20	
Fixed factory overhead rate, per hour	$ 6.00	
Normal productive capacity (hours)	7,000	

a. Open the Excel file *SA23-4*.
b. Prepare a spreadsheet to calculate the direct materials, direct labor, and factory overhead variances.
c. When you have completed the variances, perform a "save as," replacing the entire files name with the following:

   SA23-4_[your first name initial]_[your last name]

Answers to Self-Examination Questions

1. **C** The unfavorable direct materials price variance of $2,550 is determined as follows:

Actual price	$5.05 per lb.
Standard price	5.00
Price variance—unfavorable	$0.05 per lb.

   $0.05 × 51,000 actual lbs. = $2,550

2. **D** The unfavorable direct labor time variance of $2,400 is determined as follows:

Actual direct labor time	2,200
Standard direct labor time	2,000*
Direct labor time variance—unfavorable 200 × $12 standard rate =	$2,400

   *4,000 units × 0.5 hr.

3. **B** The unfavorable factory overhead volume variance of $2,000 is determined as follows:

Productive capacity not used	1,000 hrs.
Standard fixed factory overhead cost rate	× $2
Factory overhead volume variance—unfavorable	$2,000

4. **B** The controllable variable factory overhead variance is determined as follows:

   6,000 units × 0.25 hr. = 1,500 hours
   1,500 hrs. × $5.00 per hr. = $7,500

Actual variable overhead	$8,000
Less budgeted variable overhead at actual volume	7,500
Unfavorable controllable variance	$ 500

5. **D** The fixed factory overhead volume variance can be determined as follows:

   Actual production in standard hours:
   600 units × 0.2 machine hr. = 120 machine hrs.

Practical capacity	200 machine hrs.
Standard hours at actual production	120
Idle capacity	80 machine hrs.

   80 hrs. × $12.00 = $960 unfavorable volume variance

Performance Evaluation for Decentralized Operations

© INDIANHEAD MOUNTAIN SKI RESORT/PRNEWSFOTO [AP TOPIC GALLERY]

K 2   S P O R T S

Have you ever wondered why large retail stores like Wal-Mart, The Home Depot, and Sports Authority are divided into departments? Dividing into departments allows retailers to provide products and expertise in specialized areas, while offering a broad line of products. Departments also allow companies to assign responsibility for financial performance. This information can be used to make product decisions, evaluate operations, and guide company strategy. Strong performance in a department might be attributed to a good department manager, who might be rewarded with a promotion. Poor departmental performance might lead to a change in the mix of products that the department sells.

Like retailers, most businesses organize into operational units, such as divisions and departments. For example, K2 Sports, a leading maker of athletic and outdoor equipment, manages its business across four primary business segments: Marine and Outdoor, Action Sports, Team Sports, and Footwear and Apparel. These segments are further divided into product lines, such as K2 skis, Rawlings athletic equipment, Marmot outdoor products, and WGP Paintball.

Managers are responsible for running the operations of their segment of the business. Each segment is evaluated based on operating profit, and this information is used to plan and control K2's operations.

In this chapter, the role of accounting in assisting managers in planning and controlling organizational units, such as departments, divisions, and stores, is described and illustrated.

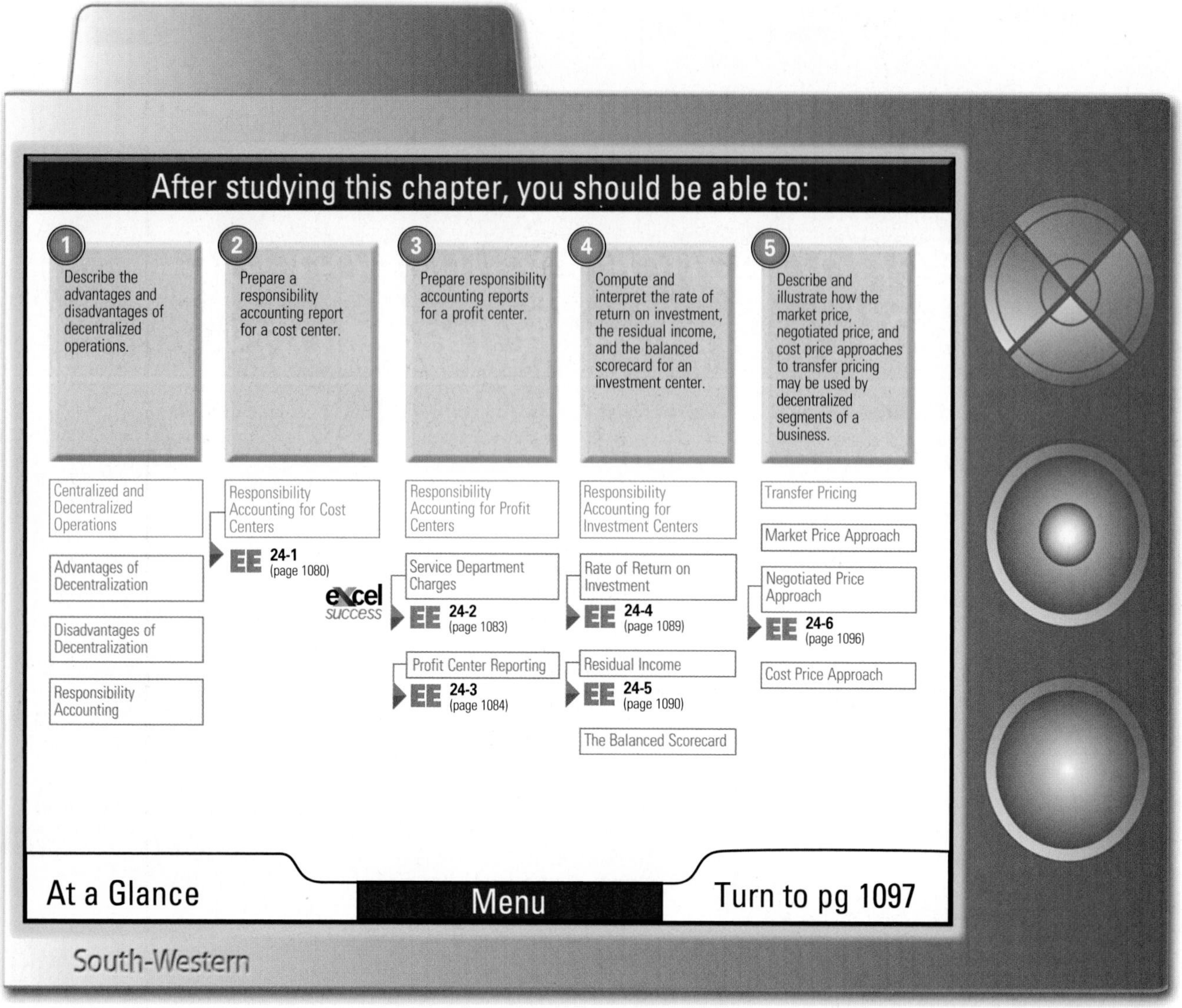

After studying this chapter, you should be able to:

1 Describe the advantages and disadvantages of decentralized operations.

2 Prepare a responsibility accounting report for a cost center.

3 Prepare responsibility accounting reports for a profit center.

4 Compute and interpret the rate of return on investment, the residual income, and the balanced scorecard for an investment center.

5 Describe and illustrate how the market price, negotiated price, and cost price approaches to transfer pricing may be used by decentralized segments of a business.

Centralized and Decentralized Operations	Responsibility Accounting for Cost Centers	Responsibility Accounting for Profit Centers	Responsibility Accounting for Investment Centers	Transfer Pricing
Advantages of Decentralization	**EE** 24-1 (page 1080)	Service Department Charges	Market Price Approach	
Disadvantages of Decentralization	*excel success*	**EE** 24-2 (page 1083)	Rate of Return on Investment	Negotiated Price Approach
Responsibility Accounting		Profit Center Reporting	**EE** 24-4 (page 1089)	**EE** 24-6 (page 1096)
		EE 24-3 (page 1084)	Residual Income	Cost Price Approach
			EE 24-5 (page 1090)	
			The Balanced Scorecard	

At a Glance | Menu | Turn to pg 1097

South-Western

---

1 Describe the advantages and disadvantages of decentralized operations.

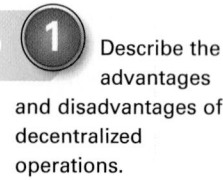

Procter & Gamble is organized around products such as Tide (laundry soap), Braun (home appliance), Charmin (bath tissue), CoverGirl (skin care), and Crest (tooth paste).

Centralized and Decentralized Operations

In a *centralized* company, all major planning and operating decisions are made by top management. For example, a one-person, owner-manager-operated company is centralized because all plans and decisions are made by one person. In a small owner-manager-operated business, centralization may be desirable. This is because the owner-manager's close supervision ensures that the business will be operated in the way the owner-manager wishes.

In a *decentralized* company, managers of separate divisions or units are delegated operating responsibility. The division (unit) managers are responsible for planning and controlling the operations of their divisions. Divisions are often structured around products, customers, or regions.

The proper amount of decentralization for a company depends on the company's unique circumstances. For example, in some companies, division managers have authority over all operations, including fixed asset purchases. In other companies, division managers have authority over profits but not fixed asset purchases.

Advantages of Decentralization

For large companies, it is difficult for top management to do the following:

1. Maintain daily contact with all operations
2. Maintain operating expertise in all product lines and services

Wachovia Corporation, a national bank, decentralized decisions about how the bank does business over the Internet. Each business unit independently decides how it will conduct business over the Internet. For example, the Mortgage Loan Division allows customers to check current mortgage rates and apply for mortgages online.

In such cases, delegating authority to managers closest to the operations usually results in better decisions. These managers often anticipate and react to operating data more quickly than could top management. These managers also can focus their attention on becoming "experts" in their area of operation.

Decentralized operations provide excellent training for managers. Delegating responsibility allows managers to develop managerial experience early in their careers. This helps a company retain managers, some of whom may be later promoted to top management positions.

Managers of decentralized operations often work closely with customers. As a result, they tend to identify with customers and, thus, are often more creative in suggesting operating and product improvements. This helps create good customer relations.

Disadvantages of Decentralization

A primary disadvantage of decentralized operations is that decisions made by one manager may negatively affect the profits of the company. For example, managers of divisions whose products compete with each other might start a price war that decreases the profits of both divisions and, thus, the overall company.

When the Pizza Hut chain added chicken to its menu, Kentucky Fried Chicken (KFC) retaliated with an advertising campaign against Pizza Hut. However, Pizza Hut and KFC are owned by the same company, Yum! Brands, Inc.

Another disadvantage of decentralized operations is that they may result in duplicate assets and expenses. For example, each manager of a product line might have a separate sales force and office support staff.

The advantages and disadvantages of decentralization are summarized in Exhibit 1.

Exhibit 1

Advantages and Disadvantages of Decentralized Operations

Advantages of Decentralization
Allows managers closest to the operations to make decisions
Provides excellent training for managers
Allows managers to become experts in their area of operation
Helps retain managers
Improves creativity and customer relations

Disadvantages of Decentralization
Decisions made by managers may negatively affect the profits of the company
Duplicates assets and expenses

Responsibility Accounting

In a decentralized business, accounting assists managers in evaluating and controlling their areas of responsibility, called *responsibility centers*. **Responsibility accounting** is the process of measuring and reporting operating data by responsibility center.

Three types of responsibility centers are:

1. Cost centers, which have responsibility over costs
2. Profit centers, which have responsibility over revenues and costs
3. Investment centers, which have responsibility over revenue, costs, and investment in assets

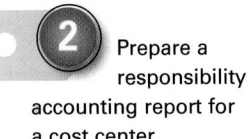

Responsibility Accounting for Cost Centers

A **cost center** manager has responsibility for controlling costs. For example, the supervisor of the Power Department has responsibility for the costs of providing power. A cost center manager does not make decisions concerning sales or the amount of fixed assets invested in the center.

Cost centers may vary in size from a small department to an entire manufacturing plant. In addition, cost centers may exist within other cost centers. For example, an entire university or college could be viewed as a cost center, and each college and department within the university could also be a cost center, as shown in Exhibit 2.

Exhibit 2

Cost Centers in a University

University	College	Department
College of Engineering	Department of Marketing	Department of Accounting
College of Business	Department of Accounting	
College of Arts and Sciences	Department of Management	

Responsibility accounting for cost centers focuses on controlling and reporting of costs. Budget performance reports that report budgeted and actual costs are normally prepared for each cost center.

Exhibit 3 illustrates budget performance reports for the following cost centers:

1. Vice President, Production
2. Manager, Plant A
3. Supervisor, Department 1—Plant A

Exhibit 3 shows how cost centers are often linked together within a company. For example, the budget performance report for Department 1—Plant A supports the report for Plant A, which supports the report for the vice president of production.

The reports in Exhibit 3 show the budgeted costs and actual costs along with the differences. Each difference is classified as either *over* budget or *under* budget. Such reports allow cost center managers to focus on areas of significant differences.

For example, the supervisor for Department 1 of Plant A can focus on why the materials cost was over budget. The supervisor might discover that excess materials were scrapped. This could be due to such factors as machine malfunctions, improperly trained employees, or low quality materials.

Exhibit 3

Responsibility Accounting Reports for Cost Centers

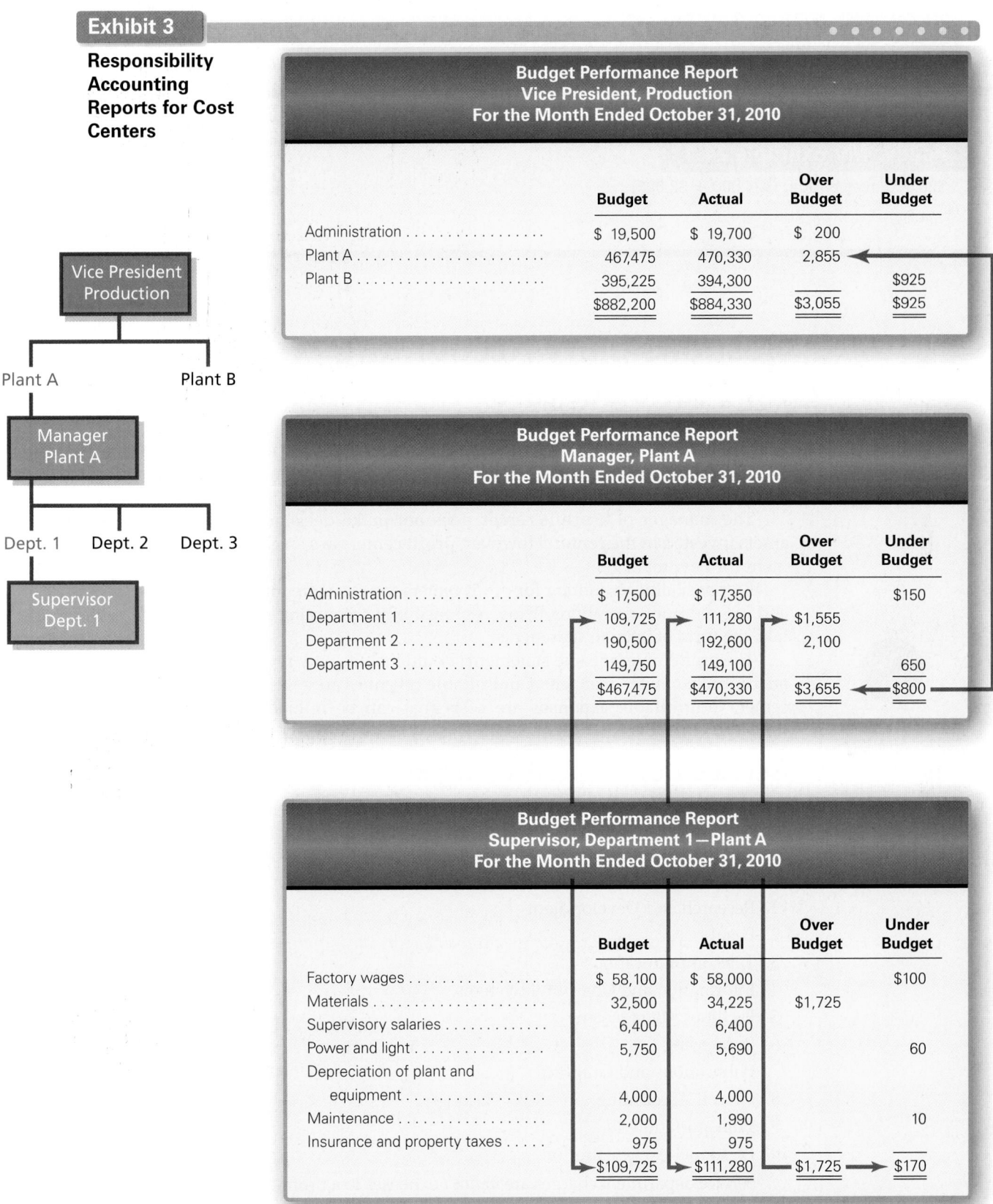

Budget Performance Report
Vice President, Production
For the Month Ended October 31, 2010

	Budget	Actual	Over Budget	Under Budget
Administration	$ 19,500	$ 19,700	$ 200	
Plant A	467,475	470,330	2,855	
Plant B	395,225	394,300		$925
	$882,200	$884,330	$3,055	$925

Budget Performance Report
Manager, Plant A
For the Month Ended October 31, 2010

	Budget	Actual	Over Budget	Under Budget
Administration	$ 17,500	$ 17,350		$150
Department 1	109,725	111,280	$1,555	
Department 2	190,500	192,600	2,100	
Department 3	149,750	149,100		650
	$467,475	$470,330	$3,655	$800

Budget Performance Report
Supervisor, Department 1—Plant A
For the Month Ended October 31, 2010

	Budget	Actual	Over Budget	Under Budget
Factory wages	$ 58,100	$ 58,000		$100
Materials	32,500	34,225	$1,725	
Supervisory salaries	6,400	6,400		
Power and light	5,750	5,690		60
Depreciation of plant and equipment	4,000	4,000		
Maintenance	2,000	1,990		10
Insurance and property taxes	975	975		
	$109,725	$111,280	$1,725	$170

Organization chart (left side):

- Vice President Production
  - Plant A
    - Manager Plant A
      - Dept. 1
        - Supervisor Dept. 1
      - Dept. 2
      - Dept. 3
  - Plant B

As shown in Exhibit 3, responsibility accounting reports are usually more summarized for higher levels of management. For example, the budget performance report for the manager of Plant A shows only administration and departmental data. This report enables the plant manager to identify the departments responsible for major differences. Likewise, the report for the vice president of production summarizes the cost data for each plant.

Example Exercise 24-1   Budgetary Performance for Cost Center ••••••••> **2**

Nuclear Power Company's costs were over budget by $24,000. The company is divided into North and South regions. The North Region's costs were under budget by $2,000. Determine the amount that the South Region's costs were over or under budget.

Follow My Example 24-1

$26,000 over budget ($24,000 + $2,000)

For Practice: PE 24-1A, PE 24-1B

---

3 Prepare responsibility accounting reports for a profit center.

Responsibility Accounting for Profit Centers

A **profit center** manager has the responsibility and authority for making decisions that affect revenues and costs and, thus, profits. Profit centers may be divisions, departments, or products.

The manager of a profit center does not make decisions concerning the fixed assets invested in the center. However, profit centers are an excellent training assignment for new managers.

Responsibility accounting for profit centers focuses on reporting revenues, expenses, and income from operations. Thus, responsibility accounting reports for profit centers take the form of income statements.

The profit center income statement should include only revenues and expenses that are controlled by the manager. **Controllable revenues** are revenues earned by the profit center. **Controllable expenses** are costs that can be influenced (controlled) by the decisions of profit center managers.

Lester B. Korn of Korn/ Ferry International offered the following strategy for young executives en route to top management positions: "Get profit-center responsibility."

Service Department Charges

The controllable expenses of profit centers include *direct operating expenses* such as sales salaries and utility expenses. In addition, a profit center may incur expenses provided by internal centralized *service departments*. Examples of such service departments include the following:

1. Research and Development
2. Legal
3. Telecommunications
4. Information and Computer Systems
5. Facilities Management
6. Purchasing
7. Publications and Graphics
8. Payroll Accounting
9. Transportation
10. Personnel Administration

Service department charges are *indirect* expenses to a profit center. They are similar to the expenses that would be incurred if the profit center purchased the services from outside the company. A profit center manager has control over service department expenses if the manager is free to choose how much service is used. In such cases, **service department charges** are allocated to profit centers based on the usage of the service by each profit center. For example, Exhibit 4 shows the allocation of payroll accounting costs to NEG's Theme Park and Movie Production divisions based on the number of payroll checks processed.

Exhibit 4

Payroll Accounting Department Charges to NEG's Theme Park and Movie Production Divisions

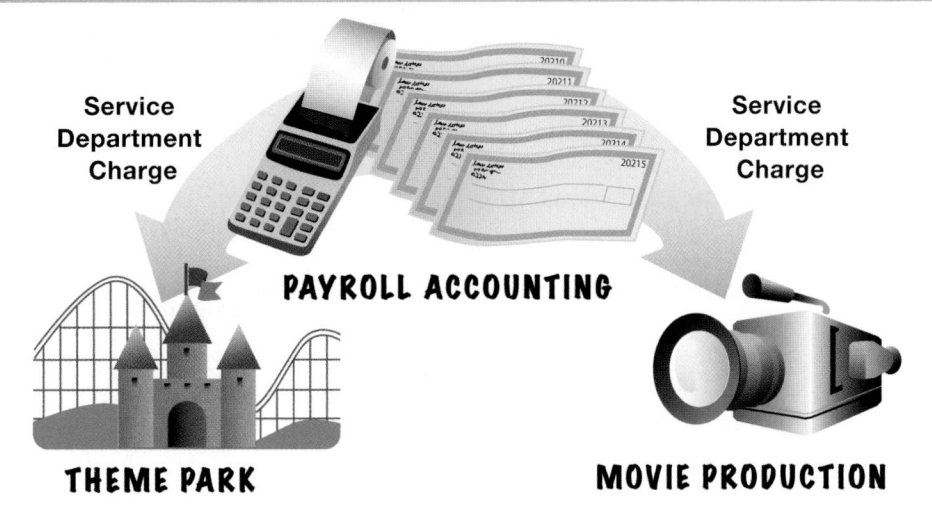

Service Department Charge

Service Department Charge

PAYROLL ACCOUNTING

THEME PARK

MOVIE PRODUCTION

Employees of IBM speak of "green money" and "blue money." Green money comes from customers. Blue money comes from providing services to other IBM departments via service department charges. IBM employees note that blue money is easier to earn than green money; yet from the stockholders' perspective, green money is the only money that counts.

To illustrate, Nova Entertainment Group (NEG), a diversified entertainment company, is used. NEG has the following two operating divisions organized as profit centers:

1. Theme Park Division
2. Movie Production Division

The revenues and direct operating expenses for the two divisions are shown below. The operating expenses consist of direct expenses, such as the wages and salaries of a division's employees.

	Theme Park Division	Movie Production Division
Revenues	$6,000,000	$2,500,000
Operating expenses	2,495,000	405,000

NEG's service departments and the expenses they incurred for the year ended December 31, 2010, are as follows:

Purchasing	$400,000
Payroll Accounting	255,000
Legal	250,000
Total	$905,000

An activity base for each service department is used to charge service department expenses to the Theme Park and Movie Production divisions. The activity base for each service department is a measure of the services performed. For NEG, the service department activity bases are as follows:

Department	Activity Base
Purchasing	Number of purchase requisitions
Payroll Accounting	Number of payroll checks
Legal	Number of billed hours

The use of services by the Theme Park and Movie Production divisions is as follows:

	Service Usage		
Division	Purchasing	Payroll Accounting	Legal
Theme Park	25,000 purchase requisitions	12,000 payroll checks	100 billed hrs.
Movie Production	15,000	3,000	900
Total	40,000 purchase requisitions	15,000 payroll checks	1,000 billed hrs.

The rates at which services are charged to each division are called *service department charge rates*. These rates are computed as follows:

$$\text{Service Department Charge Rate} = \frac{\text{Service Department Expense}}{\text{Total Service Department Usage}}$$

NEG's service department charge rates are computed as follows:

$$\text{Purchasing Charge Rate} = \frac{\$400,000}{40,000 \text{ purchase requisitions}} = \$10 \text{ per purchase requisition}$$

$$\text{Payroll Charge Rate} = \frac{\$255,000}{15,000 \text{ payroll checks}} = \$17 \text{ per payroll check}$$

$$\text{Legal Charge Rate} = \frac{\$250,000}{1,000 \text{ billed hrs.}} = \$250 \text{ per hr.}$$

The services used by each division are multiplied by the service department charge rates to determine the service charges for each division, as shown below.

$$\text{Service Department Charge} = \text{Service Usage} \times \text{Service Department Charge Rate}$$

Exhibit 5 illustrates the service department charges and related computations for NEG's Theme Park and Movie Production divisions.

Exhibit 5

Service Department Charges to NEG Divisions

Nova Entertainment Group
Service Department Charges to NEG Divisions
For the Year Ended December 31, 2010

Service Department	Theme Park Division	Movie Production Division
Purchasing (Note A)	$250,000	$150,000
Payroll Accounting (Note B)	204,000	51,000
Legal (Note C)	25,000	225,000
Total service department charges	$479,000	$426,000

Note A:

25,000 purchase requisitions × $10 per purchase requisition = $250,000

15,000 purchase requisitions × $10 per purchase requisition = $150,000

Note B:

12,000 payroll checks × $17 per check = $204,000

3,000 payroll checks × $17 per check = $51,000

Note C:

100 hours × $250 per hour = $25,000

900 hours × $250 per hour = $225,000

The differences in the service department charges between the two divisions can be explained by the nature of their operations and, thus, usage of services. For example, the Theme Park Division employs many part-time employees who are paid weekly. As a result, the Theme Park Division requires 12,000 payroll checks and incurs a $204,000 payroll service department charge (12,000 × $17). In contrast, the Movie Production Division has more permanent employees who are paid monthly. Thus, the Movie Production Division requires only 3,000 payroll checks and incurs a payroll service department charge of $51,000 (3,000 × $17).

The service department charges can be determined using a spreadsheet as follows:

	A	B	C	D	E
1	*Inputs*				
2					
3	Purchasing	$ 400,000			
4	Payroll Accounting	255,000			
5	Legal	250,000			
6	Total	$ 905,000			
7					
8		**Theme Park Division**	**Movie Production Division**	**Total**	
9	Purchasing	25,000	15,000	40,000	purch. reqs.
10	Payroll Accounting	12,000	3,000	15,000	payroll chks.
11	Legal	100	900	1,000	billed hrs.
12					
13					
14					
15	*Output*				
16		**Nova Entertainment Group**			
17		**Service Department Charges to NEG Division**			
18		**For the Year Ended December 31, 2010**			
19					
20	**Service Department**	**Theme Park Division**	**Movie Production Division**		
21	Purchasing a.	=$B3*(B9/$D9)	=$B3*(C9/$D9)		
22	Payroll Accounting b.	=$B4*(B10/$D10)	=$B4*(C10/$D10)	← c.	
23	Legal	=$B5*(B11/$D11)	=$B5*(C11/$D11)		
24	Total service department charges	=SUM(B21:B23)	=SUM(C21:C23)		

d.

The spreadsheet is divided into input and output sections. The inputs include the expense and activity base data for the service departments. The activity base information is transposed from the table shown in the text. A table is transposed when the columns and rows are reversed. This presentation facilitates copying formulas in the output table.

a.   Enter in cell B21 the formula for the purchasing department charge to the Theme Park Division:

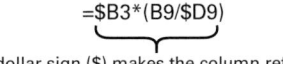

=$B3*(B9/$D9)

The dollar sign ($) makes the column references
absolute (doesn't change when copied).

b.   Copy the formula from B21 to cells B22:B23.

c.   Then copy the cells B21:B23 to C21:C23. If you place the dollar signs as shown in the formula, you will see that the formula copied correctly to all the cells.

d.   Enter in B24:C24 the =SUM function to total the columns.

 Go to the hands-on *Excel Tutor* for this example!

 This Excel Success example uses an Excel function referred to as cell referencing. Go to the *Excel Tutor* titled **Absolute & Relative Cell References** for additional help on this useful Excel function!

Example Exercise 24-2   Service Department Charges   ••••••••▶ 3

The centralized legal department of Johnson Company has expenses of $60,000. The department has provided a total of 2,000 hours of service for the period. The East Division has used 500 hours of legal service during the period, and the West Division has used 1,500 hours. How much should each division be charged for legal services?

(continued)

Follow My Example 24-2

East Division Service Charge for Legal Department:
$15,000 = 500 billed hours × ($60,000/2,000 hours)

West Division Service Charge for Legal Department:
$45,000 = 1,500 billed hours × ($60,000/2,000 hours)

For Practice: PE 24-2A, PE 24-2B

Profit Center Reporting

The divisional income statements for NEG are shown in Exhibit 6.

Exhibit 6

Divisional Income Statements— NEG

Nova Entertainment Group
Divisional Income Statements
For the Year Ended December 31, 2010

	Theme Park Division	Movie Production Division
Revenues*	$6,000,000	$2,500,000
Operating expenses	2,495,000	405,000
Income from operations before service department charges	$3,505,000	$2,095,000
Less service department charges:		
Purchasing	$ 250,000	$ 150,000
Payroll Accounting	204,000	51,000
Legal	25,000	225,000
Total service department charges	$ 479,000	$ 426,000
Income from operations	$3,026,000	$1,669,000

*For a profit center that sells products, the income statement would show: Net sales − Cost of goods sold = Gross profit. The operating expenses would be deducted from the gross profit to get the income from operations before service department charges.

In evaluating the profit center manager, the income from operations should be compared over time to a budget. However, it should not be compared across profit centers, since the profit centers are usually different in terms of size, products, and customers.

Example Exercise 24-3 Income from Operations for Profit Center

Using the data for Johnson Company from Example Exercise 24-2 along with the following data, determine the divisional income from operations for the East and West divisions.

	East Division	West Division
Sales	$300,000	$800,000
Cost of goods sold	165,000	420,000
Selling expenses	85,000	185,000

Follow My Example 24-3

	East Division	West Division
Net sales	$300,000	$800,000
Cost of goods sold	165,000	420,000
Gross profit	$135,000	$380,000
Selling expenses	85,000	185,000
Income from operations before		
service department charges	$ 50,000	$195,000
Service department charges	15,000	45,000
Income from operations	$ 35,000	$150,000

For Practice: PE 24-3A, PE 24-3B

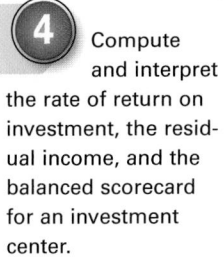

4 Compute and interpret the rate of return on investment, the residual income, and the balanced scorecard for an investment center.

Responsibility Accounting for Investment Centers

An **investment center** manager has the responsibility and the authority to make decisions that affect not only costs and revenues but also the assets invested in the center. Investment centers are often used in diversified companies organized by divisions. In such cases, the divisional manager has authority similar to that of a chief operating officer or president of a company.

Since investment center managers have responsibility for revenues and expenses, *income from operations* is part of investment center reporting. In addition, because the manager has responsibility for the assets invested in the center, the following two additional measures of performance are used:

1. Rate of return on investment
2. Residual income

To illustrate, DataLink Inc., a cellular phone company with three regional divisions, is used. Condensed divisional income statements for the Northern, Central, and Southern divisions of DataLink are shown in Exhibit 7.

Exhibit 7

Divisional Income Statements— DataLink Inc.

DataLink Inc.
Divisional Income Statements
For the Year Ended December 31, 2010

	Northern Division	Central Division	Southern Division
Revenues	$560,000	$672,000	$750,000
Operating expenses	336,000	470,400	562,500
Income from operations before service department charges	$224,000	$201,600	$187,500
Service department charges	154,000	117,600	112,500
Income from operations	$ 70,000	$ 84,000	$ 75,000

Using only income from operations, the Central Division is the most profitable division. However, income from operations does not reflect the amount of assets invested in each center. For example, the Central Division could have twice as many assets as the Northern Division. For this reason, performance measures that consider the amount of invested assets, such as the rate of return on investment and residual income, are used.

Rate of Return on Investment

The interest you earn on a savings account is *your* "rate of return on investment."

Since investment center managers control the amount of assets invested in their centers, they should be evaluated based on the use of these assets. One measure that considers the amount of assets invested is the **rate of return on investment (ROI),** or *rate of return on assets*. It is computed as follows:

$$\text{Rate of Return on Investment (ROI)} = \frac{\text{Income from Operations}}{\text{Invested Assets}}$$

The rate of return on investment is useful because the three factors subject to control by divisional managers (revenues, expenses, and invested assets) are considered. The higher the rate of return on investment, the better the division is using its assets to generate income. In effect, the rate of return on investment measures the income (return) on each dollar invested. As a result, the rate of return on investment can be used as a common basis for comparing divisions with each other.

To illustrate, the invested assets of DataLink's three divisions are as follows:

	Invested Assets
Northern Division	$350,000
Central Division	700,000
Southern Division	500,000

Using the income from operations for each division shown in Exhibit 7, the rate of return on investment for each division is computed below.

Northern Division:

$$\text{Rate of Return on Investment} = \frac{\text{Income from Operations}}{\text{Invested Assets}} = \frac{\$70,000}{\$350,000} = 20\%$$

Central Division:

$$\text{Rate of Return on Investment} = \frac{\text{Income from Operations}}{\text{Invested Assets}} = \frac{\$84,000}{\$700,000} = 12\%$$

Southern Division:

$$\text{Rate of Return on Investment} = \frac{\text{Income from Operations}}{\text{Invested Assets}} = \frac{\$75,000}{\$500,000} = 15\%$$

Although the Central Division generated the largest income from operations, its rate of return on investment (12%) is the lowest. Hence, relative to the assets invested, the Central Division is the least profitable division. In comparison, the rate of return on investment of the Northern Division is 20%, and the Southern Division is 15%.

To analyze differences in the rate of return on investment across divisions, the **DuPont formula** for the rate of return on investment is often used.[1] The DuPont formula views the rate of return on investment as the product of the following two factors:

1. **Profit margin,** which is the ratio of income from operations to sales.
2. **Investment turnover,** which is the ratio of sales to invested assets.

---

1 The DuPont formula was created by a financial executive of E. I. du Pont de Nemours and Company in 1919.

Using the DuPont formula, the rate of return on investment is expressed as follows:

$$\text{Rate of Return on Investment} = \text{Profit Margin} \times \text{Investment Turnover}$$

$$\text{Rate of Return on Investment} = \frac{\text{Income from Operations}}{\text{Sales}} \times \frac{\text{Sales}}{\text{Invested Assets}}$$

The DuPont formula is useful in evaluating divisions. This is because the profit margin and the investment turnover reflect the following underlying operating relationships of each division:

1. Profit margin indicates *operating profitability* by computing the rate of profit earned on each sales dollar.
2. Investment turnover indicates *operating efficiency* by computing the number of sales dollars generated by each dollar of invested assets.

If a division's profit margin increases, and all other factors remain the same, the division's rate of return on investment will increase. For example, a division might add more profitable products to its sales mix and, thus, increase its operating profit, profit margin, and rate of return on investment.

If a division's investment turnover increases, and all other factors remain the same, the division's rate of return on investment will increase. For example, a division might attempt to increase sales through special sales promotions and thus increase operating efficiency, investment turnover, and rate of return on investment.

The graphic at the left illustrates the relationship of the rate of return on investment, the profit margin, and investment turnover. Specifically, more income can be earned by either increasing the investment turnover (turning the crank faster), by increasing the profit margin (increasing the size of the opening), or both.

Using the DuPont formula yields the same rate of return on investment for each of DataLink's divisions, as shown below.

$$\text{Rate of Return on Investment} = \frac{\text{Income from Operations}}{\text{Sales}} \times \frac{\text{Sales}}{\text{Invested Assets}}$$

Northern Division:

$$\text{Rate of Return on Investment} = \frac{\$70,000}{\$560,000} \times \frac{\$560,000}{\$350,000} = 12.5\% \times 1.6 = 20\%$$

Central Division:

$$\text{Rate of Return on Investment} = \frac{\$84,000}{\$672,000} \times \frac{\$672,000}{\$700,000} = 12.5\% \times 0.96 = 12\%$$

Southern Division:

$$\text{Rate of Return on Investment} = \frac{\$75,000}{\$750,000} \times \frac{\$750,000}{\$500,000} = 10\% \times 1.5 = 15\%$$

The Northern and Central divisions have the same profit margins of 12.5%. However, the Northern Division's investment turnover of 1.6 is larger than that of the Central Division's turnover of 0.96. By using its invested assets more efficiently, the Northern Division's rate of return on investment of 20% is 8 percentage points higher than the Central Division's rate of return of 12%.

The Southern Division's profit margin of 10% and investment turnover of 1.5 are lower than those of the Northern Division. The product of these factors results in a return on investment of 15% for the Southern Division, compared to 20% for the Northern Division.

Even though the Southern Division's profit margin is lower than the Central Division's, its higher turnover of 1.5 results in a rate of return of 15%, which is greater than the Central Division's rate of return of 12%.

To increase the rate of return on investment, the profit margin and investment turnover for a division may be analyzed. For example, assume that the Northern Division is in a highly competitive industry in which the profit margin cannot be easily increased. As a result, the division manager might focus on increasing the investment turnover.

To illustrate, assume that the revenues of the Northern Division could be increased by $56,000 through increasing operating expenses, such as advertising, to $385,000. The Northern Division's income from operations will increase from $70,000 to $77,000, as shown below.

Revenues ($560,000 + $56,000)	$616,000
Operating expenses	385,000
Income from operations before service department charges	$231,000
Service department charges	154,000
Income from operations	$ 77,000

The rate of return on investment for the Northern Division, using the DuPont formula, is recomputed as follows:

$$\text{Rate of Return on Investment} = \frac{\text{Income from Operations}}{\text{Sales}} \times \frac{\text{Sales}}{\text{Invested Assets}}$$

$$\text{Rate of Return on Investment} = \frac{\$77,000}{\$616,000} \times \frac{\$616,000}{\$350,000} = 12.5\% \times 1.76 = 22\%$$

Although the Northern Division's profit margin remains the same (12.5%), the investment turnover has increased from 1.6 to 1.76, an increase of 10% (0.16 ÷ 1.6). The 10% increase in investment turnover increases the rate of return on investment by 10% (from 20% to 22%).

The rate of return on investment is also useful in deciding where to invest additional assets or expand operations. For example, DataLink should give priority to expanding operatons in the Northern Division because it earns the highest rate of return on investment. In other words, an investment in the Northern Division will return 20 cents (20%) on each dollar invested. In contrast, investments in the Central and Southern divisions will earn only 12 cents and 15 cents per dollar invested.

A disadvantage of the rate of return on investment as a performance measure is that it may lead divisional managers to reject new investments that could be profitable for the company as a whole. To illustrate, assume the following rates of return for the Northern Division of DataLink:

The CFO of Millennium Chemicals stated: "We had too many divisional executives who failed to spend money on capital projects with more than satisfactory returns because those projects would have lowered the average return on assets of their particular business."

Current rate of return on investment	20%
Minimum acceptable rate of return on investment set by top management	10%
Expected rate of return on investment for new project	14%

If the manager of the Northern Division invests in the new project, the Northern Division's overall rate of return will decrease from 20% due to averaging. Thus, the division manager might decide to reject the project, even though the new project's expected rate of return of 14% exceeds DataLink's minimum acceptable rate of return of 10%.

Example Exercise 24-4   Profit Margin, Investment Turnover, and ROI •••••••➤

Campbell Company has income from operations of $35,000, invested assets of $140,000, and sales of $437,500. Use the DuPont formula to compute the rate of return on investment and show (a) the profit margin, (b) the investment turnover, and (c) the rate of return on investment.

Follow My Example 24-4

a. Profit Margin = $35,000/$437,500 = 8%
b. Investment Turnover = $437,500/$140,000 = 3.125
c. Rate of Return on Investment = 8% × 3.125 = 25%

For Practice: PE 24-4A, PE 24-4B

Residual Income

Residual income is useful in overcoming some of the disadvantages of the rate of return on investment. **Residual income** is the excess of income from operations over a minimum acceptable income from operations, as shown below.[2]

Income from operations	$XXX
Less minimum acceptable income from operations as a percent of invested assets	XXX
Residual income	$XXX

Income from Operations	Minimum Acceptable Rate of Return on Assets	Residual Income

Minus ── Equals

The minimum acceptable income from operations is computed by multiplying the company minimum rate of return by the invested assets. The minimum rate is set by top management, based on such factors as the cost of financing.

To illustrate, assume that DataLink Inc. has established 10% as the minimum acceptable rate of return on divisional assets. The residual incomes for the three divisions are as follows:

	Northern Division	Central Division	Southern Division
Income from operations	$70,000	$84,000	$75,000
Less minimum acceptable income from operations as a percent of invested assets:			
$350,000 × 10%	35,000		
$700,000 × 10%		70,000	
$500,000 × 10%			50,000
Residual income	$35,000	$14,000	$25,000

[2] Another popular term for residual income is economic value added (EVA), which has been trademarked by the consulting firm Stern Stewart & Co.

The Northern Division has more residual income ($35,000) than the other divisions, even though it has the least amount of income from operations ($70,000). This is because the invested assets are less for the Northern Division than for the other divisions.

The major advantage of residual income as a performance measure is that it considers both the minimum acceptable rate of return, invested assets, and the income from operations for each division. In doing so, residual income encourages division managers to maximize income from operations in excess of the minimum. This provides an incentive to accept any project that is expected to have a rate of return in excess of the minimum.

To illustrate, assume the following rates of return for the Northern Division of DataLink:

Current rate of return on investment	20%
Minimum acceptable rate of return on investment set by top management	10%
Expected rate of return on investment for new project	14%

If the manager of Northern Division is evaluated using only return on investment, the division manager might decide to reject the new project. This is because investing in the new project will decrease Northern's current rate of return of 20%. Thus, the manager might reject the new project even though its expected rate of return of 14% exceeds DataLink's minimum acceptable rate of return of 10%.

In contrast, if the manager of the Northern Division is evaluated using residual income, the new project would probably be accepted because it will increase the Northern Division's residual income. In this way, residual income supports both divisional and overall company objectives.

Example Exercise 24-5   Residual Income •••••••• 4

The Wholesale Division of PeanutCo has income from operations of $87,000 and assets of $240,000. The minimum acceptable rate of return on assets is 12%. What is the residual income for the division?

Follow My Example 24-5

Income from operations	$87,000
Minimum acceptable income from operations as a percent of assets ($240,000 × 12%)	28,800
Residual income	$58,200

For Practice: PE 24-5A, PE 24-5B

Merck & Co., Inc. measures the number of drugs in its FDA (Food and Drug Administration) approval pipeline and the length of time it takes to turn ideas into marketable products.

The Balanced Scorecard[3]

The **balanced scorecard** is a set of multiple performance measures for a company. In addition to financial performance, a balanced scorecard normally includes performance measures for customer service, innovation and learning, and internal processes, as shown in Exhibit 8.

Performance measures for learning and innovation often revolve around a company's research and development efforts. For example, the number of new products developed during a year and the time it takes to bring new products to the market are performance

---

3 The balanced scorecard was developed by R. S. Kaplan and D. P. Norton and explained in *The Balanced Scorecard: Translating Strategy into Action* (Cambridge: Harvard Business School Press, 1996).

The Balanced Scorecard

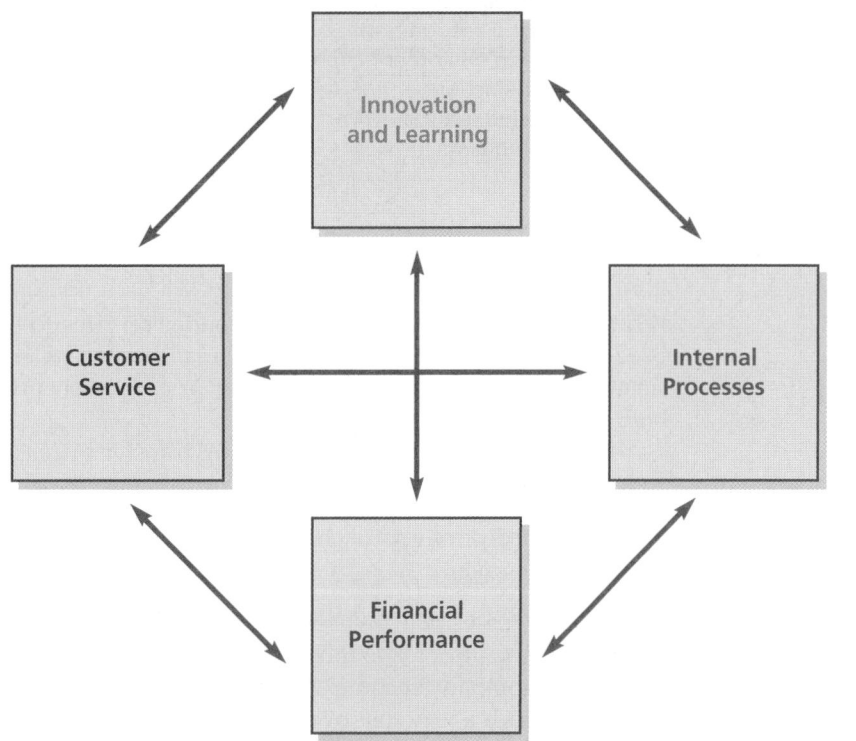

measures for innovation. Performance measures for learning could include the number of employee training sessions and the number of employees who are cross-trained in several skills.

Performance measures for customer service include the number of customer complaints and the number of repeat customers. Customer surveys can also be used to gather measures of customer satisfaction with the company as compared to competitors.

Performance measures for internal processes include the length of time it takes to manufacture a product. The amount of scrap and waste is a measure of the efficiency of a company's manufacturing processes. The number of customer returns is a performance measure of both the manufacturing and sales ordering processes.

All companies will use financial performance measures. Some financial performance measures have been discussed earlier in this chapter and include income from operations, rate of return on investment, and residual income.

The balanced scorecard attempts to identify the underlying nonfinancial drivers, or causes, of financial performance related to innovation and learning, customer service, and internal processes. In this way, the financial performance may be improved. For example, customer satisfaction is often measured by the number of repeat customers. By increasing the number of repeat customers, sales and income from operations can be increased.

Some common performance measures used in the balanced scorecard approach are shown below.

A survey by Bain & Co., a consulting firm, indicated that 57% of large companies use the balanced scorecard.

Hilton Hotels Corporation uses a balanced scorecard to measure employee satisfaction, customer loyalty, and financial performance.

Innovation and Learning	Internal Processes
Number of new products	Waste and scrap
Number of new patents	Time to manufacture products
Number of cross-trained employees	Number of defects
Number of training hours	Number of rejected sales orders
Number of ethics violations	Number of stockouts
Employee turnover	Labor utilization

5 Describe and illustrate how the market price, negotiated price, and cost price approaches to transfer pricing may be used by decentralized segments of a business.

Customer Service	Financial
Number of repeat customers	Sales
Customer brand recognition	Income from operations
Delivery time to customer	Return on investment
Customer satisfaction	Profit margin and investment turnover
Number of sales returns	Residual income
Customer complaints	Actual versus budgeted (standard) costs

Transfer Pricing

When divisions transfer products or render services to each other, a **transfer price** is used to charge for the products or services.[4] Since transfer prices will affect a division's financial performance, setting a transfer price is a sensitive matter for the managers of both the selling and buying divisions.

Three common approaches to setting transfer prices are as follows:

1. Market price approach
2. Negotiated price approach
3. Cost approach

Transfer prices may be used for cost, profit, or investment centers. The objective of setting a transfer price is to motivate managers to behave in a manner that will increase the overall company income. As will be illustrated, however, transfer prices may be misused in such a way that overall company income suffers.

Transfer prices can be set as low as the variable cost per unit or as high as the market price. Often, transfer prices are negotiated at some point between variable cost per unit and market price. Exhibit 9 shows the possible range of transfer prices.

Exhibit 9

Commonly Used Transfer Prices

To illustrate, Wilson Company, a packaged snack food company with no service departments, is used. Wilson Company has two operating divisions (Eastern and Western) that are organized as investment centers. Condensed income statements for Wilson Company, assuming no transfers between divisions, are shown in Exhibit 10.

---

4 The discussion in this chapter highlights the essential concepts of transfer pricing. In-depth discussion of transfer pricing can be found in advanced texts.

Exhibit 10

**Income
Statements—
No Transfers
Between
Divisions**

Wilson Company
Income Statements
For the Year Ended December 31, 2010

	Eastern Division	Western Division	Total Company
Sales:			
50,000 units × $20 per unit	$1,000,000		$1,000,000
20,000 units × $40 per unit		$800,000	800,000
			$1,800,000
Expenses:			
Variable:			
50,000 units × $10 per unit	$ 500,000		$ 500,000
20,000 units × $30* per unit . . .		$600,000	600,000
Fixed	300,000	100,000	400,000
Total expenses	$ 800,000	$700,000	$1,500,000
Income from operations	$ 200,000	$100,000	$ 300,000

*$20 of the $30 per unit represents materials costs, and the remaining $10 per unit represents other variable conversion expenses incurred within the Western Division.

Market Price Approach

Using the **market price approach**, the transfer price is the price at which the product or service transferred could be sold to outside buyers. If an outside market exists for the product or service transferred, the current market price may be a proper transfer price.

$$\text{Transfer Price} = \text{Market Price}$$

To illustrate, assume that materials used by Wilson Company in producing snack food in the Western Division are currently purchased from an outside supplier at $20 per unit. The same materials are produced by the Eastern Division. The Eastern Division is operating at full capacity of 50,000 units and can sell all it produces to either the Western Division or to outside buyers.

A transfer price of $20 per unit (the market price) has no effect on the Eastern Division's income or total company income. The Eastern Division will earn revenues of $20 per unit on all its production and sales, regardless of who buys its product.

Likewise, the Western Division will pay $20 per unit for materials (the market price). Thus, the use of the market price as the transfer price has no effect on the Eastern Division's income or total company income.

In this situation, the use of the market price as the transfer price is proper. The condensed divisional income statements for Wilson Company would be the same as shown in Exhibit 10.

Negotiated Price Approach

If unused or excess capacity exists in the supplying division (the Eastern Division), and the transfer price is equal to the market price, total company profit may not be maximized. This is because the manager of the Western Division will be indifferent toward purchasing materials from the Eastern Division or from outside suppliers. That is, in both cases the Western Division manager pays $20 per unit (the market price). As a result, the Western Division may purchase the materials from outside suppliers.

If, however, the Western Division purchases the materials from the Eastern Division, the difference between the market price of $20 and the variable costs of the Eastern Division of $10 per unit (from Exhibit 10) can cover fixed costs and contribute to overall company profits. Thus, the Western Division manager should be encouraged to purchase the materials from the Eastern Division.

The **negotiated price approach** allows the managers to agree (negotiate) among themselves on a transfer price. The only constraint is that the transfer price be less than the market price, but greater than the supplying division's variable costs per unit, as shown below.

$$\text{Variable Costs per Unit} < \text{Transfer Price} < \text{Market Price}$$

To illustrate, assume that instead of a capacity of 50,000 units, the Eastern Division's capacity is 70,000 units. In addition, assume that the Eastern Division can continue to sell only 50,000 units to outside buyers.

A transfer price less than $20 would encourage the manager of the Western Division to purchase from the Eastern Division. This is because the Western Division is currently purchasing its materials from outside suppliers at a cost of $20 per unit. Thus, its materials cost would decrease, and its income from operations would increase.

At the same time, a transfer price above the Eastern Division's variable costs per unit of $10 (from Exhibit 10) would encourage the manager of the Eastern Division to supply materials to the Western Division. In doing so, the Eastern Division's income from operations would also increase.

Exhibit 11 illustrates the divisional and company income statements, assuming that the Eastern and Western division managers agree to a transfer price of $15.

The Eastern Division increases its sales by $300,000 (20,000 units × $15 per unit) to $1,300,000. As a result, the Eastern Division's income from operations increases by $100,000 ($300,000 sales − $200,000 variable costs) to $300,000, as shown in Exhibit 11.

The increase of $100,000 in the Eastern Division's income can also be computed as follows:

$$\text{Increase in Eastern (Supplying) Division's Income from Operations} = (\text{Transfer Price} - \text{Variable Cost per Unit}) \times \text{Units Transferred}$$

$$\text{Increase in Eastern (Supplying) Division's Income from Operations} = (\$15 - \$10) \times 20{,}000 \text{ units} = \$100{,}000$$

Western Division's materials cost decreases by $5 per unit ($20 − $15) for a total of $100,000 (20,000 units × $5 per unit). Thus, Western Division's income from operations increases by $100,000 to $200,000, as shown in Exhibit 11.

The increase of $100,000 in the Western Division's income can also be computed as follows:

$$\text{Increase in Western (Purchasing) Division's Income from Operations} = (\text{Market Price} - \text{Transfer Price}) \times \text{Units Transferred}$$

$$\text{Increase in Western (Purchasing) Division's Income from Operations} = (\$20 - \$15) \times 20{,}000 \text{ units} = \$100{,}000$$

Comparing Exhibits 10 and 11 shows that Wilson Company's income from operations increased by $200,000, as shown below.

	Income from Operations		
	No Units Transferred (Exhibit 10)	20,000 Units Transferred at $15 per Unit (Exhibit 11)	Increase (Decrease)
Eastern Division	$200,000	$300,000	$100,000
Western Division	100,000	200,000	100,000
Wilson Company	$300,000	$500,000	$200,000

Exhibit 11

Income Statements— Negotiated Transfer Price

Wilson Company
Income Statements
For the Year Ended December 31, 2010

	Eastern Division	Western Division	Total Company
Sales:			
50,000 units × $20 per unit	$1,000,000		$1,000,000
20,000 units × $15 per unit	300,000		300,000
20,000 units × $40 per unit		$800,000	800,000
	$1,300,000	$800,000	$2,100,000
Expenses:			
Variable:			
70,000 units × $10 per unit . . .	$ 700,000		$ 700,000
20,000 units × $25* per unit . .		$500,000	500,000
Fixed	300,000	100,000	400,000
Total expenses	$1,000,000	$600,000	$1,600,000
Income from operations	$ 300,000	$200,000	$ 500,000

*$10 of the $25 represents variable conversion expenses incurred solely within the Western Division, and $15 per unit represents the transfer price per unit from the Eastern Division.

In the preceding illustration, any negotiated transfer price between $10 and $20 is acceptable, as shown below.

$$\text{Variable Costs per Unit} < \text{Transfer Price} < \text{Market Price}$$
$$\$10 < \text{Transfer Price} < \$20$$

Any transfer price within this range will increase the overall income from operations for Wilson Company by $200,000. However, the increases in the Eastern and Western divisions' income from operations will vary depending on the transfer price.

To illustrate, a transfer price of $16 would increase the Eastern Division's income from operations by $120,000, as shown below.

$$\frac{\text{Increase in Eastern (Supplying)}}{\text{Division's Income from Operations}} = (\text{Transfer Price} - \text{Variable Cost per Unit}) \times \text{Units Transferred}$$

$$\frac{\text{Increase in Eastern (Supplying)}}{\text{Division's Income from Operations}} = (\$16 - \$10) \times 20,000 \text{ units} = \$120,000$$

A transfer price of $16 would increase the Western Division's income from operations by $80,000, as shown below.

$$\frac{\text{Increase in Western (Purchasing)}}{\text{Division's Income from Operations}} = (\text{Market Price} - \text{Transfer Price}) \times \text{Units Transferred}$$

$$\frac{\text{Increase in Western (Purchasing)}}{\text{Division's Income from Operations}} = (\$20 - \$16) \times 20,000 \text{ units} = \$80,000$$

With a transfer price of $16, Wilson Company's income from operations still increases by $200,000, which consists of the Eastern Division's increase of $120,000 plus the Western Division's increase of $80,000.

As shown on the previous page, negotiated price provides each division manager with an incentive to negotiate the transfer of materials. At the same time, the overall company's income from operations will also increase. However, the negotiated approach only applies when the supplying division has excess capacity. In other words, the supplying division cannot sell all its production to outside buyers at the market price.

Example Exercise 24-6 Transfer Pricing

•••••••• 5

The materials used by the Winston-Salem Division of Fox Company are currently purchased from outside suppliers at $30 per unit. These same materials are produced by Fox's Flagstaff Division. The Flagstaff Division can produce the materials needed by the Winston-Salem Division at a variable cost of $15 per unit. The division is currently producing 70,000 units and has capacity of 100,000 units. The two divisions have recently negotiated a transfer price of $22 per unit for 30,000 units. By how much will each division's income increase as a result of this transfer?

Follow My Example 24-6

Increase in Flagstaff (Supplying) Division's Income from Operations	= (Transfer Price − Variable Cost per Unit) × Units Transferred
Increase in Flagstaff (Supplying) Division's Income from Operations	= ($22 − $15) × 30,000 units = $210,000
Increase in Winston-Salem (Purchasing) Division's Income from Operations	= (Market Price − Transfer Price) × Units Transferred
Increase in Winston-Salem (Purchasing) Division's Income from Operations	= ($30 − $22) × 30,000 units = $240,000

For Practice: PE 24-6A, PE 24-6B

Cost Price Approach

Under the **cost price approach**, cost is used to set transfer prices. A variety of costs may be used in this approach, including the following:

1. Total product cost per unit
2. Variable product per unit

If total product cost per unit is used, direct materials, direct labor, and factory overhead are included in the transfer price. If variable product cost per unit is used, the fixed factory overhead cost is excluded from the transfer price.

Actual costs or standard (budgeted) costs may be used in applying the cost price approach. If actual costs are used, inefficiencies of the producing (supplying) division are transferred to the purchasing division. Thus, there is little incentive for the producing (supplying) division to control costs. For this reason, most companies use standard costs in the cost price approach. In this way, differences between actual and standard costs remain with the producing (supplying) division for cost control purposes.

The cost price approach is most often used when the responsibility centers are organized as cost centers. When the responsibility centers are organized as profit or investment centers, the cost price approach is normally not used.

For example, using the cost price approach when the supplying division is organized as a profit center ignores the supplying division manager's responsibility for earning profits. In this case, using the cost price approach prevents the supplying division from reporting any profit (revenues − costs) on the units transferred. As a result, the division manager has little incentive to transfer units to another division, even though it may be in the best interests of the company.

Integrity, Objectivity, and Ethics in Business

SHIFTING INCOME THROUGH TRANSFER PRICES

Transfer prices allow companies to minimize taxes by shifting taxable income from countries with high tax rates to countries with low taxes. For example, GlaxoSmithKline, a British company, and the second biggest drug maker in the world, had been in a dispute with the U.S. Internal Revenue Service (IRS) over international transfer prices since the early 1990s. The company pays U.S. taxes on income from its U.S. Division and British taxes on income from the British Division. The IRS, however, claimed that the transfer prices on sales from the British Division to the U.S. Division were too high, which reduced profits and taxes in the U.S. Division. The company received a new tax bill from the IRS in 2005 for almost $1.9 billion related to the transfer pricing issue, raising the total bill to almost $5 billion. In January 2006, the company agreed to settle this dispute with the IRS for $3.4 billion, the largest tax settlement in history.

Source: J. Whalen, "Glaxo Gets New IRS Bill Seeking Another $1.9 Billion in BackTax," *The Wall Street Journal*, January 27, 2005.

At a Glance 24

---

1 Describe the advantages and disadvantages of decentralized operations.

Key Points	**Key Learning Outcomes**	**Example Exercises**	**Practice Exercises**
In a centralized business, all major planning and operating decisions are made by top management. In a decentralized business, these responsibilities are delegated to unit managers. Decentralization may allow a company to be more effective because operational decisions are made by the managers closest to the operations, allowing top management to focus on strategic issues.	• Describe the advantages of decentralization. • Describe the disadvantages of decentralization. • Describe the common types of responsibility centers and the role of responsibility accounting.		

---

2 Prepare a responsibility accounting report for a cost center.

Key Points	**Key Learning Outcomes**	**Example Exercises**	**Practice Exercises**
Cost centers limit the responsibility and authority of managers to decisions related to the costs of their unit. The primary accounting tools for planning and controlling costs for a cost center are budgets and budget performance reports.	• Describe cost centers. • Describe the responsibility reporting for a cost center. • Compute the over (under) budgeted costs for a cost center.	24-1	24-1A, 24-1B

3 Prepare responsibility accounting reports for a profit center.

Key Points	Key Learning Outcomes	Example Exercises	Practice Exercises
In a profit center, managers have the responsibility and authority to make decisions that affect both revenues and costs. Responsibility reports for a profit center usually show income from operations for the unit.	• Describe profit centers.		
	• Determine how service department charges are allocated to profit centers.	**24-2**	24-2A, 24-2B
	• Describe the responsibility reporting for a profit center.		
	• Compute income from operations for a profit center.	**24-3**	24-3A, 24-3B

4 Compute and interpret the rate of return on investment, the residual income, and the balanced scorecard for an investment center.

Key Points	Key Learning Outcomes	Example Exercises	Practice Exercises
In an investment center, the unit manager has the responsibility and authority to make decisions that affect the unit's revenues, expenses, and assets invested in the center. Three measures are commonly used to assess investment center performance: return on investment (ROI), residual income, and the balanced scorecard. These measures are often used to compare and assess investment center performance.	• Describe investment centers.		
	• Describe the responsibility reporting for an investment center.		
	• Compute the rate of return on investment (ROI).	**24-4**	24-4A, 24-4B
	• Compute residual income.	**24-5**	24-5A, 24-5B
	• Describe the balanced scorecard approach.		

5 Describe and illustrate how the market price, negotiated price, and cost price approaches to transfer pricing may be used by decentralized segments of a business.

Key Points	Key Learning Outcomes	Example Exercises	Practice Exercises
When divisions within a company transfer products or provide services to each other, a transfer price is used to charge for the products or services. Transfer prices should be set so that the overall company income is increased when goods are transferred between divisions. One of three common approaches is typically used to establish transfer prices: market price, negotiated price, or cost price.	• Describe how companies determine the price used to transfer products or services between divisions.		
	• Determine transfer prices using the market price approach.		
	• Determine transfer prices using the negotiated price approach.	**24-6**	24-6A, 24-6B
	• Describe the cost price approach to determining transfer price.		

Key Terms

balanced scorecard (1090)
controllable expenses (1080)
controllable revenues (1080)
cost center (1078)
cost price approach (1096)
DuPont formula (1086)

investment center (1085)
investment turnover (1086)
market price approach (1093)
negotiated price approach (1094)
profit center (1080)
profit margin (1086)

rate of return on investment
  (ROI) (1086)
residual income (1089)
responsibility accounting (1077)
service department charges (1080)
transfer price (1092)

Illustrative Problem

Quinn Company has two divisions, Domestic and International. Invested assets and condensed income statement data for each division for the past year ended December 31 are as follows:

	Domestic Division	International Division
Revenues	$675,000	$480,000
Operating expenses	450,000	372,400
Service department charges	90,000	50,000
Invested assets	600,000	384,000

Instructions

1. Prepare condensed income statements for the past year for each division.
2. Using the DuPont formula, determine the profit margin, investment turnover, and rate of return on investment for each division.
3. If management's minimum acceptable rate of return is 10%, determine the residual income for each division.

Solution

1.

Quinn Company
Divisional Income Statements
For the Year Ended December 31, 2010

	Domestic Division	International Division
Revenues	$675,000	$480,000
Operating expenses	450,000	372,400
Income from operations before service department charges	$225,000	$107,600
Service department charges	90,000	50,000
Income from operations	$135,000	$ 57,600

2. Rate of Return on Investment = Profit Margin × Investment Turnover

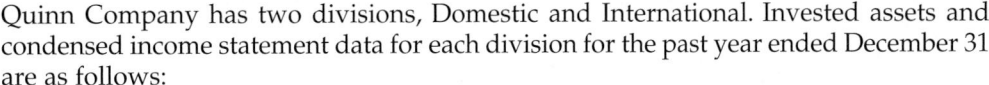

$$\text{Rate of Return on Investment} = \frac{\text{Income from Operations}}{\text{Sales}} \times \frac{\text{Sales}}{\text{Invested Assets}}$$

$$\text{Domestic Division: ROI} = \frac{\$135,000}{\$675,000} \times \frac{\$675,000}{\$600,000}$$

$$\text{ROI} = 20\% \times 1.125$$

$$\text{ROI} = 22.5\%$$

$$\text{International Division: ROI} = \frac{\$57,600}{\$480,000} \times \frac{\$480,000}{\$384,000}$$

$$\text{ROI} = 12\% \times 1.25$$

$$\text{ROI} = 15\%$$

3. Domestic Division: $75,000 [$135,000 − (10% × $600,000)]
    International Division: $19,200 [$57,600 − (10% × $384,000)]

Self-Examination Questions (Answers at End of Chapter)

1. When the manager has the responsibility and authority to make decisions that affect costs and revenues but no responsibility for or authority over assets invested in the department, the department is called a(n):
   A. cost center.
   B. profit center.
   C. investment center.
   D. service department.

2. The Accounts Payable Department has expenses of $600,000 and makes 150,000 payments to the various vendors who provide products and services to the divisions. Division A has income from operations of $900,000, before service department charges, and requires 60,000 payments to vendors. If the Accounts Payable Department is treated as a service department, what is Division A's income from operations?
   A. $300,000
   B. $900,000
   C. $660,000
   D. $540,000

3. Division A of Kern Co. has sales of $350,000, cost of goods sold of $200,000, operating expenses of $30,000, and invested assets of $600,000. What is the rate of return on investment for Division A?
   A. 20%
   B. 25%
   C. 33%
   D. 40%

4. Division L of Liddy Co. has a rate of return on investment of 24% and an investment turnover of 1.6. What is the profit margin?
   A. 6%
   B. 15%
   C. 24%
   D. 38%

5. Which approach to transfer pricing uses the price at which the product or service transferred could be sold to outside buyers?
   A. Cost price approach
   B. Negotiated price approach
   C. Market price approach
   D. Standard cost approach

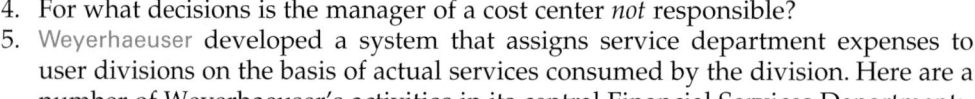

Eye Openers

1. Differentiate between a cost center and a profit center.
2. Differentiate between a profit center and an investment center.
3. In what major respect would budget performance reports prepared for the use of plant managers of a manufacturing business with cost centers differ from those prepared for the use of the various department supervisors who report to the plant managers?
4. For what decisions is the manager of a cost center *not* responsible?
5. Weyerhaeuser developed a system that assigns service department expenses to user divisions on the basis of actual services consumed by the division. Here are a number of Weyerhaeuser's activities in its central Financial Services Department:
   - Payroll
   - Accounts payable
   - Accounts receivable
   - Database administration—report preparation

   For each activity, identify an activity base that could be used to charge user divisions for service.
6. What is the major shortcoming of using income from operations as a performance measure for investment centers?
7. Why should the factors under the control of the investment center manager (revenues, expenses, and invested assets) be considered in computing the rate of return on investment?
8. In a decentralized company in which the divisions are organized as investment centers, how could a division be considered the least profitable even though it earned the largest amount of income from operations?
9. How does using the rate of return on investment facilitate comparability between divisions of decentralized companies?
10. The rates of return on investment for Fosina Co.'s three divisions, East, Central, and West, are 26%, 20%, and 15%, respectively. In expanding operations, which of Fosina Co.'s divisions should be given priority? Explain.
11. Why would a firm use a balanced scorecard in evaluating divisional performance?
12. What is the objective of transfer pricing?

13. When is the negotiated price approach preferred over the market price approach in setting transfer prices?
14. Why would standard cost be a more appropriate transfer cost between cost centers than actual cost?
15. When using the negotiated price approach to transfer pricing, within what range should the transfer price be established?

Practice Exercises

PE 24-1A
Budgetary performance for cost center
obj. 2
EE 24-1   p. 1080

Harding Company's costs were under budget by $200,000. The company is divided into North and South regions. The North Region's costs were over budget by $40,000. Determine the amount that the South Region's costs were over or under budget.

PE 24-1B
Budgetary performance for cost center
obj. 2
EE 24-1   p. 1080

Magic Motion Company's costs were over budget by $63,000. The company is divided into Southwest and Northeast regions. The Southwest Region's costs were under budget by $17,000. Determine the amount that the Northeast Region's costs were over or under budget.

PE 24-2A
Service department charges
obj. 3
EE 24-2   p. 1083

The centralized employee Travel Department of Teapot Dome Company has expenses of $180,000. The department has serviced a total of 2,000 travel reservations for the period. The Norsk Division has made 750 reservations during the period, and the West Division has made 1,250 reservations. How much should each division be charged for travel services?

PE 24-2B
Service department charges
obj. 3
EE 24-2   p. 1083

The centralized Help Desk of Hayman Company has expenses of $140,000. The department has provided a total of 5,000 hours of service for the period. Computer Division has used 2,000 hours of Help Desk service during the period, and Peripheral Division has used 3,000 hours of Help Desk service. How much should each division be charged for Help Desk services?

PE 24-3A
Income from operations for profit center
obj. 3
EE 24-3   p. 1084

Using the data for Teapot Dome Company from Practice Exercise 24-2A, along with the data provided below, determine the divisional income from operations for the Norsk and West divisions.

	Norsk Division	West Division
Sales	$700,000	$770,000
Cost of goods sold	365,000	462,000
Selling expenses	142,500	173,000

PE 24-3B
Income from operations for profit center
obj. 3
EE 24-3   p. 1084

Using the data for the Hayman Company from Practice Exercise 24-2B, along with the data provided below, determine the divisional income from operations for the Computer Division and the Peripheral Division.

	Computer Division	Peripheral Division
Sales	$1,200,000	$1,305,000
Cost of goods sold	610,000	764,000
Selling expenses	264,000	245,000

PE 24-4A
Profit margin,
investment turnover,
and ROI
obj. 4

EE 24-4 p. 1089

Mathews Company has income from operations of $50,000, invested assets of $200,000, and sales of $500,000. Use the DuPont formula to compute the rate of return on investment and show (a) the profit margin, (b) the investment turnover, and (c) the rate of return on investment.

PE 24-4B
Profit margin,
investment turnover,
and ROI
obj. 4

EE 24-4 p. 1089

Wakelin Company has income from operations of $20,125 invested assets of $87,500 and sales of $175,000. Use the DuPont formula to compute the rate of return on investment and show (a) the profit margin, (b) the investment turnover, and (c) the rate of return on investment.

PE 24-5A
Residual income
obj. 4

EE 24-5 p. 1090

The Consumer Division of Woods Company has income from operations of $60,000 and assets of $440,000. The minimum acceptable rate of return on assets is 12%. What is the residual income for the division?

PE 24-5B
Residual income
obj. 4

EE 24-5 p. 1090

The Commercial Division of LaSalle Company has income from operations of $135,000 and assets of $650,000. The minimum acceptable rate of return on assets is 10%. What is the residual income for the division?

PE 24-6A
Transfer pricing
obj. 5

EE 24-6 p. 1096

The materials used by the Laramie Division of Barron Company are currently purchased from outside suppliers at $40 per unit. These same materials are produced by Barron's Astoria Division. The Astoria Division can produce the materials needed by the Laramie Division at a variable cost of $28 per unit. The division is currently producing 80,000 units and has capacity of 100,000 units. The two divisions have recently negotiated a transfer price of $35 per unit for 20,000 units. By how much will each division's income increase as a result of this transfer?

PE 24-6B
Transfer pricing
obj. 5

EE 24-6 p. 1096

The materials used by the Kenosha Division of Ehrlich Company are currently purchased from outside suppliers at $75 per unit. These same materials are produced by the High Point Division. The High Point Division can produce the materials needed by the Kenosha Division at a variable cost of $55 per unit. The division is currently producing 140,000 units and has capacity of 175,000 units. The two divisions have recently negotiated a transfer price of $65 per unit for 30,000 units. By how much will each division's income increase as a result of this transfer?

Exercises

EX 24-1
Budget performance
reports for cost
centers
obj. 2

✔ a. (c) $2,640

Partially completed budget performance reports for Iliad Company, a manufacturer of air conditioners, are provided below.

Iliad Company
Budget Performance Report—Vice President, Production
For the Month Ended April 30, 2010

Plant	Budget	Actual	Over Budget	Under Budget
Mid-Atlantic Region	$ 416,000	$416,000		$ 0
West Region	297,600	296,000		1,600
South Region	(g)	(h)	(i)	
	$ (j)	$ (k)	$ (l)	$1,600

Iliad Company
Budget Peformance Report—Manager, South Region Plant
For the Month Ended April 30, 2010

Department	Budget	Actual	Over Budget	Under Budget
Chip Fabrication	$ (a)	$ (b)	$ (c)	
Electronic Assembly	85,120	86,240	1,120	
Final Assembly	137,120	136,640		$480
	$ (d)	$ (e)	$ (f)	$480

Iliad Company
Budget Performance Report—Supervisor, Chip Fabrication
For the Month Ended April 30, 2010

Department	Budget	Actual	Over Budget	Under Budget
Factory wages	$ 24,640	$ 26,400	$1,760	
Materials	69,600	69,120		$480
Power and light	3,840	4,560	720	
Maintenance	6,720	7,360	640	
	$104,800	$107,440	$3,120	$480

a. Complete the budget performance reports by determining the correct amounts for the lettered spaces.

b. ▅▅▅▅▶ Compose a memo to Dana Johnson, vice president of production for Iliad Company, explaining the performance of the production division for April.

EX 24-2
Divisional income statements
obj. 3
✔ Residential Division income from operations, $78,900

The following data were summarized from the accounting records for DeSalvo Construction Company for the year ended June 30, 2010:

Cost of goods sold:		Service department charges:	
Residential Division	$415,200	Residential Division	$ 56,400
Industrial Division	206,350	Industrial Division	35,480
Administrative expenses:		Net sales:	
Residential Division	$ 74,500	Residential Division	$625,000
Industrial Division	72,400	Industrial Division	367,500

Prepare divisional income statements for DeSalvo Construction Company.

EX 24-3
Service department charges and activity bases
obj. 3

For each of the following service departments, identify an activity base that could be used for charging the expense to the profit center.

a. Central purchasing
b. Legal
c. Accounts receivable
d. Duplication services
e. Electronic data processing
f. Telecommunications

EX 24-4
Activity bases for service department charges
obj. 3

For each of the following service departments, select the activity base listed that is most appropriate for charging service expenses to responsible units.

Service Department	Activity Base
a. Central Purchasing	1. Number of travel claims
b. Training	2. Number of payroll checks
c. Conferences	3. Number of sales invoices
d. Telecommunications	4. Number of purchase requisitions
e. Accounts Receivable	5. Number of telephone lines
f. Employee Travel	6. Number of employees trained
g. Payroll Accounting	7. Number of computers
h. Computer Support	8. Number of conference attendees

EX 24-5
Service department charges
obj. 3
✔ b. Commercial payroll, $12,468

In divisional income statements prepared for Mills Construction Company, the Payroll Department costs are charged back to user divisions on the basis of the number of payroll checks, and the Purchasing Department costs are charged back on the basis of the number of purchase requisitions. The Payroll Department had expenses of $45,900, and the Purchasing Department had expenses of $22,000 for the year. The following annual data for Residential, Commercial, and Government Contract Divisions were obtained from corporate records:

	Residential	Commercial	Government Contract
Sales	$460,000	$610,000	$1,400,000
Number of employees:			
Weekly payroll (52 weeks per year)	125	70	75
Monthly payroll	32	43	30
Number of purchase requisitions per year	2,100	1,500	1,400

a. Determine the total amount of payroll checks and purchase requisitions processed per year by each division.
b. Using the activity base information in (a), determine the annual amount of payroll and purchasing costs charged back to the Residential, Commercial, and Government Contract divisions from payroll and purchasing services.
c. ➤ Why does the Residential Division have a larger service department charge than the other two divisions, even though its sales are lower?

EX 24-6
Service department charges and activity bases
obj. 3

✔ b. Help desk, $30,600

Harris Corporation, a manufacturer of electronics and communications systems, uses a service department charge system to charge profit centers with Computing and Communications Services (CCS) service department costs. The following table identifies an abbreviated list of service categories and activity bases used by the CCS department. The table also includes some assumed cost and activity base quantity information for each service for April.

CCS Service Category	Activity Base	Assumed Cost	Assumed Activity Base Quantity
Help desk	Number of calls	$ 88,400	2,600
Network center	Number of devices monitored	609,375	9,750
Electronic mail	Number of user accounts	67,080	6,450
Local voice support	Number of phone extensions	152,720	9,200

One of the profit centers for Harris Corporation is the Communication Systems (COMM) sector. Assume the following information for the COMM sector:

• The sector has 3,000 employees, of whom 40% are office employees.
• All the office employees have a phone, and 75% of them have a computer on the network.
• Ninety-five percent of the employees with a computer also have an e-mail account.
• The average number of help desk calls for April was 1.0 call per individual with a computer.
• There are 250 additional printers, servers, and peripherals on the network beyond the personal computers.

a. Determine the service charge rate for the four CCS service categories for April.
b. Determine the charges to the COMM sector for the four CCS service categories for April.

EX 24-7
Divisional income statements with service department charges
obj. 3

✔ Retail income from operations, $1,386,134

Encounter Sporting Goods Company has two divisions, Wholesale and Retail, and two corporate service departments, Tech Support and Accounts Payable. The corporate expenses for the year ended December 31, 2010, are as follows:

Tech Support Department	$ 705,000
Accounts Payable Department	278,000
Other corporate administrative expenses	415,000
Total corporate expense	$1,398,000

The other corporate administrative expenses include officers' salaries and other expenses required by the corporation. The Tech Support Department charges the divisions for services rendered, based on the number of computers in the department, and the Accounts Payable Department charges divisions for services, based on the number of checks issued. The usage of service by the two divisions is as follows:

	Tech Support	Accounts Payable
Wholesale Division	300 computers	7,060 checks
Retail Division	200	12,940
Total	500 computers	20,000 checks

The service department charges of the Tech Support Department and the Accounts Payable Department are considered controllable by the divisions. Corporate administrative expenses are not considered controllable by the divisions. The revenues, cost of goods sold, and operating expenses for the two divisions are as follows:

	Wholesale	Retail
Revenues	$6,720,000	$5,712,000
Cost of goods sold	3,528,000	2,688,000
Operating expenses	1,260,000	1,176,000

Prepare the divisional income statements for the two divisions.

EX 24-8
Corrections to service department charges

obj. 3

✔ b. Income from operations, Cargo Division, $80,500

Trans-Continental Airlines, Inc., has two divisions organized as profit centers, the Passenger Division and the Cargo Division. The following divisional income statements were prepared:

Trans-Continental Airlines, Inc.
Divisional Income Statements
For the Year Ended June 30, 2010

	Passenger Division		Cargo Division	
Revenues		$1,400,000		$1,400,000
Operating expenses		950,000		1,200,000
Income from operations before service department charges		$ 450,000		$ 200,000
Less service department charges:				
Training	$ 80,000		$ 80,000	
Flight scheduling	75,000		75,000	
Reservations	105,000	260,000	105,000	260,000
Income from operations		$ 190,000		$ (60,000)

The service department charge rate for the service department costs was based on revenues. Since the revenues of the two divisions were the same, the service department charges to each division were also the same.

The following additional information is available:

	Passenger Division	Cargo Division	Total
Number of personnel trained	200	50	250
Number of flights	250	350	600
Number of reservations requested	14,000	0	14,000

a. Does the income from operations for the two divisions accurately measure performance?
b. Correct the divisional income statements, using the activity bases provided above in revising the service department charges.

EX 24-9
Profit center responsibility reporting

objs. 3, 5

✔ Income from operations, Action Sports Division, $571,400

X-Out Sporting Goods Co. operates two divisions—the Action Sports Division and the Team Sports Division. The following income and expense accounts were provided from the trial balance as of June 30, 2010, the end of the current fiscal year, after all adjustments, including those for inventories, were recorded and posted:

Sales—Action Sports (AS) Division	$14,500,000
Sales—Team Sports (TS) Division	17,600,000
Cost of Goods Sold—Action Sports (AS) Division	8,700,000
Cost of Goods Sold—Team Sports (TS) Division	10,208,000
Sales Expense—Action Sports (AS) Division	2,320,000
Sales Expense—Team Sports (TS) Division	2,464,000
Administrative Expense—Action Sports (AS) Division	1,450,000
Administrative Expense—Team Sports (TS) Division	1,566,400

(continued)

Advertising Expense	$ 642,000
Transportation Expense	314,960
Accounts Receivable Collection Expense	201,750
Warehouse Expense	1,600,000

The bases to be used in allocating expenses, together with other essential information, are as follows:

a. Advertising expense—incurred at headquarters, charged back to divisions on the basis of usage: Action Sports Division, $256,800; Team Sports Division, $385,200.
b. Transportation expense—charged back to divisions at a charge rate of $12.40 per bill of lading: Action Sports Division, 12,000 bills of lading; Team Sports Division, 13,400 bills of lading.
c. Accounts receivable collection expense—incurred at headquarters, charged back to divisions at a charge rate of $7.50 per invoice: Action Sports Division, 12,400 sales invoices; Team Sports Division, 14,500 sales invoices.
d. Warehouse expense—charged back to divisions on the basis of floor space used in storing division products: Action Sports Division, 120,000 square feet; Team Sports Division, 80,000 square feet.

Prepare a divisional income statement with two column headings: Action Sports Division and Team Sports Division. Provide supporting schedules for determining service department charges.

EX 24-10
Rate of return on investment
obj. **4**
✔ a. Health Care Division, 16%

The income from operations and the amount of invested assets in each division of Devon Industries are as follows:

	Income from Operations	Invested Assets
Sporting Goods Division	$80,000	$400,000
Health Care Division	41,600	260,000
Commercial Division	70,400	320,000

a. Compute the rate of return on investment for each division.
b. Which division is the most profitable per dollar invested?

EX 24-11
Residual income
obj. **4**
✔ a. Sporting Goods Division, $40,000

Based on the data in Exercise 24-10, assume that management has established a 10% minimum acceptable rate of return for invested assets.
a. Determine the residual income for each division.
b. Which division has the most residual income?

EX 24-12
Determining missing items in rate of return computation
obj. **4**
✔ d. 0.70

One item is omitted from each of the following computations of the rate of return on investment:

Rate of Return on Investment	=	Profit Margin	×	Investment Turnover
22%	=	10%	×	(a)
(b)	=	16%	×	0.75
18%	=	(c)	×	1.50
14%	=	20%	×	(d)
(e)	=	15%	×	1.60

Determine the missing items, identifying each by the appropriate letter.

EX 24-13
Profit margin, investment turnover, and rate of return on investment
obj. **4**
✔ a. ROI, 15%

The condensed income statement for the International Division of King Industries Inc. is as follows (assuming no service department charges):

Sales	$1,200,000
Cost of goods sold	600,000
Gross profit	$ 600,000
Administrative expenses	300,000
Income from operations	$ 300,000

The manager of the International Division is considering ways to increase the rate of return on investment.

a. Using the DuPont formula for rate of return on investment, determine the profit margin, investment turnover, and rate of return on investment of the International Division, assuming that $2,000,000 of assets have been invested in the International Division.

b. If expenses could be reduced by $60,000 without decreasing sales, what would be the impact on the profit margin, investment turnover, and rate of return on investment for the International Division?

EX 24-14
Rate of return on investment

obj. 4

✔ a. Media Networks ROI, 15.4%

The Walt Disney Company has four major sectors, described as follows:

- **Media Networks:** The ABC television and radio network, Disney channel, ESPN, A&E, E!, and Disney.com.
- **Parks and Resorts:** Walt Disney World Resort, Disneyland, Disney Cruise Line, and other resort properties.
- **Studio Entertainment:** Walt Disney Pictures, Touchstone Pictures, Hollywood Pictures, Miramax Films, and Buena Vista Theatrical Productions.
- **Consumer Products:** Character merchandising, Disney stores, books, and magazines.

Disney recently reported sector income from operations, revenue, and invested assets (in millions) as follows:

	Income from Operations	Revenue	Invested Assets
Media Networks	$4,285	$15,046	$27,692
Parks and Resorts	1,710	10,626	16,311
Studio Entertainment	1,201	7,491	10,812
Consumer Products	631	2,347	1,553

a. Use the DuPont formula to determine the rate of return on investment for the four Disney sectors. Round whole percents to one decimal place and investment turnover to two decimal places.

b. ➡ How do the four sectors differ in their profit margin, investment turnover, and return on investment?

EX 24-15
Determining missing items in rate of return and residual income computations

obj. 4

✔ c. $92,400

Data for Schmidt Company is presented in the following table of rates of return on investment and residual incomes:

Invested Assets	Income from Operations	Rate of Return on Investment	Minimum Rate of Return	Minimum Acceptable Income from Operations	Residual Income
$840,000	$210,000	(a)	14%	(b)	(c)
$500,000	(d)	(e)	(f)	$64,000	$27,500
$320,000	(g)	16%	(h)	$40,000	(i)
$240,000	$48,000	(j)	12%	(k)	(l)

Determine the missing items, identifying each item by the appropriate letter.

EX 24-16
Determining missing items from computations

obj. 4

✔ a. (e) $520,000

Data for the North, South, East and West divisions of McGonigel Company are as follows:

	Sales	Income from Operations	Invested Assets	Rate of Return on Investment	Profit Margin	Investment Turnover
North	$525,000	(a)	(b)	18%	12%	(c)
South	(d)	$65,000	(e)	(f)	10%	1.25
East	$700,000	(g)	$350,000	15%	(h)	(i)
West	$800,000	$140,000	$1,000,000	(j)	(k)	(l)

a. Determine the missing items, identifying each by the letters (a) through (l). Round whole percents to one decimal place and investment turnover to two decimal places.

b. Determine the residual income for each division, assuming that the minimum acceptable rate of return established by management is 10%.

c. Which division is the most profitable in terms of (1) return on investment and (2) residual income?

EX 24-17
Rate of return on investment, residual income

obj. 4

Hilton Hotels Corporation provides lodging services around the world. The company is separated into three major divisions.

- **Hotel Ownership:** Hotels owned and operated by Hilton.
- **Managing and Franchising:** Hotels franchised to others or managed for others.
- **Timeshare:** Resort properties managed for timeshare vacation owners.

Financial information for each division, from a recent annual report, is as follows (in millions):

	Hotel Ownership	Managing and Franchising	Timeshare
Revenues	$4,985	$2,527	$ 650
Income from operations	904	600	152
Total assets	9,681	5,191	1,078

a. Use the DuPont formula to determine the return on investment for each of the Hilton business divisions. Round whole percents to one decimal place and investment turnover to one decimal place.
b. Determine the residual income for each division, assuming a minimum acceptable income of 10% of total assets. Round minimal acceptable return to the nearest million dollars.
c. ➡️ Interpret your results.

EX 24-18
Balanced scorecard

obj. 4

American Express Company is a major financial services company, noted for its American Express® card. Below are some of the performance measures used by the company in its balanced scorecard.

Average cardmember spending
Cards in force
Earnings growth
Hours of credit consultant training
Investment in information technology
Number of Internet features

Number of merchant signings
Number of card choices
Number of new card launches
Return on equity
Revenue growth

For each measure, identify whether the measure best fits the innovation, customer, internal process, or financial dimension of the balanced scorecard.

EX 24-19
Balanced scorecard

obj. 4

Several years ago, United Parcel Service (UPS) believed that the Internet was going to change the parcel delivery market and would require UPS to become a more nimble and customer-focused organization. As a result, UPS replaced its old measurement system, which was 90% oriented toward financial performance, with a balanced scorecard. The scorecard emphasized four "point of arrival" measures, which were:

1. Customer satisfaction index—a measure of customer satisfaction.
2. Employee relations index—a measure of employee sentiment and morale.
3. Competitive position—delivery performance relative to competition.
4. Time in transit—the time from order entry to delivery.

a. ➡️ Why did UPS introduce a balanced scorecard and nonfinancial measures in its new performance measurement system?
b. ➡️ Why do you think UPS included a factor measuring employee sentiment?

EX 24-20
Decision on transfer pricing

obj. 5

✔ a. $1,225,000

Electronic components used by the Engine Division of Armstrong Manufacturing are currently purchased from outside suppliers at a cost of $200 per unit. However, the same materials are available from the Components Division. The Components Division has unused capacity and can produce the materials needed by the Engine Division at a variable cost of $165 per unit.

a. If a transfer price of $180 per unit is established and 35,000 units of materials are transferred, with no reduction in the Components Division's current sales, how much would Armstrong Manufacturing's total income from operations increase?
b. How much would the Engine Division's income from operations increase?
c. How much would the Components Division's income from operations increase?

EX 24-21
Decision on transfer pricing

obj. 5

✔ b. $350,000

Based on Armstrong Manufacturing's data in Exercise 24–20, assume that a transfer price of $190 has been established and that 35,000 units of materials are transferred, with no reduction in the Components Division's current sales.

a. How much would Armstrong Manufacturing's total income from operations increase?
b. How much would the Engine Division's income from operations increase?
c. How much would the Components Division's income from operations increase?
d. ━━━▶ If the negotiated price approach is used, what would be the range of acceptable transfer prices and why?

Problems Series A

PR 24-1A
Budget performance report for a cost center

obj. 2

Amoruso Parts Company sells vehicle parts to automotive companies. The Truck Division is organized as a cost center. The budget for the Truck Division for the month ended October 31, 2010, is as follows (in thousands):

Customer service salaries	$ 260,450
Insurance and property taxes	54,600
Distribution salaries	415,400
Marketing salaries	489,700
Engineer salaries	398,500
Warehouse wages	279,100
Equipment depreciation	87,500
Total	$1,985,250

During October, the costs incurred in the Truck Division were as follows:

Customer service salaries	$ 333,370
Insurance and property taxes	52,960
Distribution salaries	411,250
Marketing salaries	548,460
Engineer salaries	390,530
Warehouse wages	267,930
Equipment depreciation	87,500
Total	$2,092,000

Instructions
1. Prepare a budget performance report for the director of the Truck Division for the month of October.
2. For which costs might the director be expected to request supplemental reports?

PR 24-2A
Profit center responsibility reporting

obj. 3

✔ 1. Income from operations, Metro Division, $274,400

Browning Transportation Co. has three regional divisions organized as profit centers. The chief executive officer (CEO) evaluates divisional performance, using income from operations as a percent of revenues. The following quarterly income and expense accounts were provided from the trial balance as of December 31, 2010:

Revenues—East Division	$600,000
Revenues—West Division	710,000
Revenues—Metro Division	980,000
Operating Expenses—East Division	362,400
Operating Expenses—West Division	393,540
Operating Expenses—Metro Division	527,760
Corporate Expenses—Shareholder Relations	87,500
Corporate Expenses—Customer Support	300,000
Corporate Expenses—Legal	122,400
General Corporate Officers' Salaries	204,000

The company operates three service departments: Shareholder Relations, Customer Support, and Legal. The Shareholder Relations Department conducts a variety of services for shareholders of the company. The Customer Support Department is the company's point of contact for new service, complaints, and requests for repair. The department believes that the number of customer contacts is an activity base for this work. The Legal Department provides legal services for division management. The department believes that the number of hours billed is an activity base for this work. The following additional information has been gathered:

	East	West	Metro
Number of customer contacts	3,750	4,500	6,750
Number of hours billed	850	1,360	1,190

Instructions

1. Prepare quarterly income statements showing income from operations for the three divisions. Use three column headings: East, West, and Metro.
2. Identify the most successful division according to the profit margin. Round to two decimal places.
3. ⟶ Provide a recommendation to the CEO for a better method for evaluating the performance of the divisions. In your recommendation, identify the major weakness of the present method.

PR 24-3A
Divisional income statements and rate of return on investment analysis

obj. 4

✔ 2. Bread Division, ROI, 13.5%

Sunshine Baking Company is a diversified food products company with three operating divisions organized as investment centers. Condensed data taken from the records of the three divisions for the year ended June 30, 2010, are as follows:

	Bread Division	Snack Cake Division	Retail Bakeries Division
Sales	$ 8,100,000	$ 8,700,000	$7,800,000
Cost of goods sold	4,980,000	5,400,000	4,600,000
Operating expenses	1,662,000	1,995,000	1,484,000
Invested assets	10,800,000	10,875,000	6,000,000

The management of Sunshine Baking Company is evaluating each division as a basis for planning a future expansion of operations.

Instructions

1. Prepare condensed divisional income statements for the three divisions, assuming that there were no service department charges.
2. Using the DuPont formula for rate of return on investment, compute the profit margin, investment turnover, and rate of return on investment for each division.
3. ⟶ If available funds permit the expansion of operations of only one division, which of the divisions would you recommend for expansion, based on parts (1) and (2)? Explain.

PR 24-4A
Effect of proposals on divisional performance

obj. 4

✔ 1. ROI, 14.4%

A condensed income statement for the Snowboard Division of New Wave Rides Inc. for the year ended December 31, 2010, is as follows:

Sales	$1,200,000
Cost of goods sold	826,000
Gross profit	$ 374,000
Operating expenses	230,000
Income from operations	$ 144,000
Invested assets	$1,000,000

Assume that the Snowboard Division received no charges from service departments. The president of New Wave Rides has indicated that the division's rate of return on a $1,000,000 investment must be increased to at least 18% by the end of the next year if operations are to continue. The division manager is considering the following three proposals:

Proposal 1: Transfer equipment with a book value of $40,000 to other divisions at no gain or loss and lease similar equipment. The annual lease payments would exceed the amount of depreciation expense on the old equipment by $24,000. This increase in expense would be included as part of the cost of goods sold. Sales would remain unchanged.

Proposal 2: Purchase new and more efficient machining equipment and thereby reduce the cost of goods sold by $120,000. Sales would remain unchanged, and the old equipment, which has no remaining book value, would be scrapped at no gain or loss. The new equipment would increase invested assets by an additional $600,000 for the year.

Proposal 3: Reduce invested assets by discontinuing an engine line. This action would eliminate sales of $330,000, cost of goods sold of $286,300, and operating expenses of $65,000. Assets of $420,000 would be transferred to other divisions at no gain or loss.

Instructions

1. Using the DuPont formula for rate of return on investment, determine the profit margin, investment turnover, and rate of return on investment for the Snowboard Division for the past year.
2. Prepare condensed estimated income statements and compute the invested assets for each proposal.
3. Using the DuPont formula for rate of return on investment, determine the profit margin, investment turnover, and rate of return on investment for each proposal.
4. Which of the three proposals would meet the required 18% rate of return on investment?
5. If the Snowboard Division were in an industry where the profit margin could not be increased, how much would the investment turnover have to increase to meet the president's required 18% rate of return on investment?

PR 24-5A
Divisional performance analysis and evaluation

obj. 4

✔ 2. Touring Bike Division ROI, 24.5%

The vice president of operations of Rucker-Putnam Bike Company is evaluating the performance of two divisions organized as investment centers. Invested assets and condensed income statement data for the past year for each division are as follows:

	Touring Bike Division	Off-Road Bike Division
Sales	$2,800,000	$2,950,000
Cost of goods sold	1,240,000	1,375,000
Operating expenses	1,168,000	1,073,500
Invested assets	1,600,000	2,950,000

Instructions

1. Prepare condensed divisional income statements for the year ended December 31, 2010, assuming that there were no service department charges.
2. Using the DuPont formula for rate of return on investment, determine the profit margin, investment turnover, and rate of return on investment for each division.
3. If management desires a minimum acceptable rate of return of 18%, determine the residual income for each division.
4. ➤ Discuss the evaluation of the two divisions, using the performance measures determined in parts (1), (2), and (3).

PR 24-6A
Transfer pricing

obj. 5

✔ 3. Total income from operations, $253,000

Bay Area Scientific, Inc. manufactures electronic products, with two operating divisions, the Performance Materials and Communication Technologies divisions. Condensed divisional income statements, which involve no intracompany transfers and which include a breakdown of expenses into variable and fixed components, are as follows:

Bay Area Scientific, Inc.
Divisional Income Statements
For the Year Ended December 31, 2010

			Performance Materials Division	Communication Technologies Division	Total
Sales:					
8,000 units	@	$ 78 per unit	$624,000		$ 624,000
12,000 units	@	$152 per unit		$1,824,000	1,824,000
			$624,000	$1,824,000	$2,448,000
Expenses:					
Variable:					
8,000 units	@	$ 58 per unit	$464,000		$ 464,000
12,000 units	@	$108* per unit		$1,296,000	1,296,000
Fixed			124,000	288,000	412,000
Total expenses			$588,000	$1,584,000	$2,172,000
Income from operations			$ 36,000	$ 240,000	$ 276,000

*$78 of the $108 per unit represents materials costs, and the remaining $30 per unit represents other variable conversion expenses incurred within the Communication Technologies Division.

The Performance Materials Division is presently producing 8,000 units out of a total capacity of 9,600 units. Materials used in producing the Communication Technologies Division's product are currently purchased from outside suppliers at a price of $78 per unit. The Performance Materials Division is able to produce the materials used by the Communication Technologies Division. Except for the possible transfer of materials between divisions, no changes are expected in sales and expenses.

Instructions

1. ➤ Would the market price of $78 per unit be an appropriate transfer price for Bay Area Scientific, Inc.? Explain.
2. ➤ If the Communication Technologies Division purchases 1,600 units from the Performance Materials Division, rather than externally, at a negotiated transfer price of $64 per unit, how much would the income from operations of each division and the total company income from operations increase?
3. Prepare condensed divisional income statements for Bay Area Scientific, Inc., based on the data in part (2).
4. ➤ If a transfer price of $70 per unit is negotiated, how much would the income from operations of each division and the total company income from operations increase?
5. a. ➤ What is the range of possible negotiated transfer prices that would be acceptable for Bay Area Scientific, Inc.?
   b. Assuming that the managers of the two divisions cannot agree on a transfer price, what price would you suggest as the transfer price?

Problems Series B

PR 24-1B
Budget performance report for a cost center

obj. 2

The Northeast District of Vidovich Beverages, Inc., is organized as a cost center. The budget for the Northeast District of Vidovich Beverages, Inc., for the month ended May 31, 2010, is as follows:

Sales salaries	$ 569,400
System administration salaries	311,220
Customer service salaries	106,000
Billing salaries	68,560
Maintenance	188,480
Depreciation of plant and equipment	64,050
Insurance and property taxes	28,670
Total	$1,336,380

During May, the costs incurred in the Northeast District were as follows:

Sales salaries	$ 568,680
System administration salaries	310,900
Customer service salaries	125,080
Billing salaries	68,145
Maintenance	189,530
Depreciation of plant and equipment	64,050
Insurance and property taxes	28,770
Total	$1,355,155

Instructions

1. Prepare a budget performance report for the manager of the Northeast District of Vidovich Beverages for the month of May.
2. ➤ For which costs might the supervisor be expected to request supplemental reports?

PR 24-2B
Profit center responsibility reporting

obj. 3

✔ 1. Income from operations, South Region, $399,000

Tri-State Railroad Company organizes its three divisions, the Southeast (SE), East (E), and South (S) regions, as profit centers. The chief executive officer (CEO) evaluates divisional performance, using income from operations as a percent of revenues. The following quarterly income and expense accounts were provided from the trial balance as of December 31, 2010:

Revenues—SE Region	$2,100,000
Revenues—E Region	3,150,000
Revenues—S Region	2,850,000
Operating Expenses—SE Region	1,367,350
Operating Expenses—E Region	2,321,870
Operating Expenses—S Region	1,963,180
Corporate Expenses—Dispatching	165,600
Corporate Expenses—Equipment Management	1,085,000
Corporate Expenses—Treasurer's	425,000
General Corporate Officers' Salaries	860,000

The company operates three service departments: the Dispatching Department, the Equipment Management Department, and the Treasurer's Department. The Dispatching Department manages the scheduling and releasing of completed trains. The Equipment Management Department manages the railroad cars inventories. It makes sure the right freight cars are at the right place at the right time. The Treasurer's Department conducts a variety of services for the company as a whole. The following additional information has been gathered:

	Southeast	East	South
Number of scheduled trains	450	765	585
Number of railroad cars in inventory	4,375	6,125	7,000

Instructions
1. Prepare quarterly income statements showing income from operations for the three regions. Use three column headings: Southeast, East, and South.
2. Identify the most successful region according to the profit margin. Round to two decimal places.
3. ➡ Provide a recommendation to the CEO for a better method for evaluating the performance of the regions. In your recommendation, identify the major weakness of the present method.

PR 24-3B
Divisional income statements and rate of return on investment analysis

obj. 4

✔ 2. Retail Division ROI, 18%

Performance Financial Services Inc. is a diversified investment company with three operating divisions organized as investment centers. Condensed data taken from the records of the three divisions for the year ended June 30, 2010, are as follows:

	Retail Division	Electronic Brokerage Division	Investment Banking Division
Fee revenue	$2,500,000	$1,400,000	$3,250,000
Operating expenses	1,600,000	1,302,000	2,600,000
Invested assets	5,000,000	350,000	4,062,500

The management of Performance Financial Services Inc. is evaluating each division as a basis for planning a future expansion of operations.

Instructions
1. Prepare condensed divisional income statements for the three divisions, assuming that there were no service department charges.
2. Using the DuPont formula for rate of return on investment, compute the profit margin, investment turnover, and rate of return on investment for each division.
3. ➡ If available funds permit the expansion of operations of only one division, which of the divisions would you recommend for expansion, based on parts (1) and (2)? Explain.

PR 24-4B
Effect of proposals on divisional performance

obj. **4**

✔ 3. Proposal 3
ROI, 16%

A condensed income statement for the Water Sports Division of South Mountain Sports Inc. for the year ended January 31, 2010, is as follows:

Sales	$600,000
Cost of goods sold	236,000
Gross profit	$364,000
Operating expenses	274,000
Income from operations	$ 90,000
Invested assets	$500,000

Assume that the Water Sports Division received no charges from service departments.

The president of South Mountain Sports Inc. has indicated that the division's rate of return on a $500,000 investment must be increased to at least 22% by the end of the next year if operations are to continue. The division manager is considering the following three proposals:

Proposal 1: Transfer equipment with a book value of $100,000 to other divisions at no gain or loss and lease similar equipment. The annual lease payments would be less than the amount of depreciation expense on the old equipment by $18,000. This decrease in expense would be included as part of the cost of goods sold. Sales would remain unchanged.

Proposal 2: Reduce invested assets by discontinuing a product line. This action would eliminate sales of $75,000, cost of goods sold of $26,600, and operating expenses of $21,400. Assets of $150,000 would be transferred to other divisions at no gain or loss.

Proposal 3: Purchase new and more efficient machinery and thereby reduce the cost of goods sold by $30,000. Sales would remain unchanged, and the old machinery, which has no remaining book value, would be scrapped at no gain or loss. The new machinery would increase invested assets by $250,000 for the year.

Instructions

1. Using the DuPont formula for rate of return on investment, determine the profit margin, investment turnover, and rate of return on investment for the Water Sports Division for the past year.
2. Prepare condensed estimated income statements and compute the invested assets for each proposal.
3. Using the DuPont formula for rate of return on investment, determine the profit margin, investment turnover, and rate of return on investment for each proposal.
4. Which of the three proposals would meet the required 22% rate of return on investment?
5. If the Water Sports Division were in an industry where the profit margin could not be increased, how much would the investment turnover have to increase to meet the president's required 22% rate of return on investment? Round to two decimal places.

PR 24-5B
Divisional performance analysis and evaluation

obj. **4**

✔ 2. Network
Equipment Division
ROI, 21%

The vice president of operations of Six Layer Computers Inc. is evaluating the performance of two divisions organized as investment centers. Invested assets and condensed income statement data for the past year for each division are as follows:

	Network Equipment Division	**Personal Computing Division**
Sales	$1,400,000	$1,120,000
Cost of goods sold	845,000	690,000
Operating expenses	345,000	206,000
Invested assets	1,000,000	1,400,000

Instructions

1. Prepare condensed divisional income statements for the year ended December 31, 2010, assuming that there were no service department charges.
2. Using the DuPont formula for rate of return on investment, determine the profit margin, investment turnover, and rate of return on investment for each division.
3. If management's minimum acceptable rate of return is 14%, determine the residual income for each division.
4. ━━━ Discuss the evaluation of the two divisions, using the performance measures determined in parts (1), (2), and (3).

PR 24-6B

Transfer pricing

obj. 5

✔ 3. Navigational
Systems Division,
$106,500

Knopfler Industries, Inc. is a diversified aerospace company, including two operating divisions, Specialized Semiconductors and Navigational Systems divisions. Condensed divisional income statements, which involve no intracompany transfers and which include a breakdown of expenses into variable and fixed components, are as follows:

Knopfler Industries, Inc.
Divisional Income Statements
For the Year Ended December 31, 2010

			Specialized Semi-conductors Division	Navigational Systems Division	Total
Sales:					
1,600 units	@	$ 825 per unit	$1,320,000		$1,320,000
2,500 units	@	$1,240 per unit		$3,100,000	3,100,000
			$1,320,000	$3,100,000	$4,420,000
Expenses:					
Variable:					
1,600 units	@	$485 per unit	$ 776,000		$ 776,000
2,500 units	@	$975* per unit		$2,437,500	2,437,500
Fixed			488,000	636,000	1,124,000
Total expenses			$1,264,000	$3,073,500	$4,337,500
Income from operations			$ 56,000	$ 26,500	$ 82,500

*$825 of the $975 per unit represents materials costs, and the remaining $150 per unit represents other variable conversion expenses incurred within the Navigational Systems Division.

The Specialized Semiconductors Division is presently producing 1,600 units out of a total capacity of 2,000 units. Materials used in producing the Navigational Systems Division's product are currently purchased from outside suppliers at a price of $825 per unit. The Specialized Semiconductors Division is able to produce the components used by the Navigational Systems Division. Except for the possible transfer of materials between divisions, no changes are expected in sales and expenses.

Instructions
1. ▬▬▶ Would the market price of $825 per unit be an appropriate transfer price for Knopfler Industries, Inc.? Explain.
2. ▬▬▶ If the Navigational Systems Division purchases 400 units from the Specialized Semiconductors Division, rather than externally, at a negotiated transfer price of $625 per unit, how much would the income from operations of each division and total company income from operations increase?
3. Prepare condensed divisional income statements for Knopfler Industries, Inc., based on the data in part (2).
4. ▬▬▶ If a transfer price of $700 per unit is negotiated, how much would the income from operations of each division and total company income from operations increase?
5. a. ▬▬▶ What is the range of possible negotiated transfer prices that would be acceptable for Knopfler Industries, Inc.?
   b. Assuming that the managers of the two divisions cannot agree on a transfer price, what price would you suggest as the transfer price?

Special Activities   ● ● ● ● ▶

You can access the special activities online at **www.cengage.com/accounting/reeve**.

Excel Success Special Activities

SA 24-1
Service department charges

The Kirkland Company has three central service departments: sales administration, credit, and human resources. The expenses for the three departments are as follows for the year ended December 31, 2011:

Sales administration	$120,000
Credit	84,000
Human resources	185,000
Total	$389,000

Service department expenses are allocated to divisions based on an appropriate activity base. The activity bases associated with each service department to each division for 2011 is as follows:

Service Departments	Northern Division	Southern Division	Total	
Sales administration	1,650	3,850	5,500	sales orders
Credit	4,900	9,100	14,000	customers
Human resources	400	600	1,000	employees

a. Open the Excel file *SA24-1*.
b. Prepare a report showing the service department charges allocated to each division.
c. When you have completed the report, perform a "save as," replacing the entire file name with the following:

 SA24-1_[your first name initial]_[your last name]

SA 24-2
Service department charges

Bass Company allocates central service department expenses from the accounting, travel, and purchasing departments to the Retail, Commercial, and Municipal Divisions. The expenses for the three service departments for the year ended December 31, 2011, are:

Accounting	$264,000
Travel	94,000
Purchasing	192,000
Total	$550,000

The activity base used by each service department in allocating service department expenses to the divisions was determined as follows:

Department	Activity Base
Accounting	Number of transactions
Travel	Number of travel requests
Purchasing	Number of purchase orders

The use of services by the three divisions is as follows:

	Service Usage		
Division	Accounting	Travel	Purchasing
Retail	22,400 trans.	250 trav. req.	1,500 purch. ord.
Commercial	12,500	190	900
Municipal	5,100	60	600
Total	40,000 trans.	500 trav. req.	3,000 purch. ord.

a. Open the Excel file *SA24-2*.
b. Prepare a report showing the service department charges allocated to each division.
c. When you have completed the report, perform a "save as," replacing the entire file name with the following:

 SA24-2_[your first name initial]_[your last name]

SA 24-3
Divisional income statement

The revenues and direct operating expenses for the two divisions of the UniCast Cable Company for the year ended December 31, 2011, are as follows:

	Eastern Division	Western Division
Revenues	$4,100,000	$3,500,000
Operating expenses	2,450,000	2,200,000

There are three central service departments: billing, payroll, and service and repairs. The expenses associated with these central service departments for December 31, 2011, are as follows:

Billing	$ 310,000
Payroll	265,000
Service and repairs	684,000
Total	$1,259,000

The central service department expenses are allocated to the two divisions based on relevant activity bases. The billing, payroll, and service and repairs departments are allocated to the divisions on the basis of bills, payroll checks, and repair requests, respectively. The consumption of activity by the two divisions from the three service departments for 2011 is as follows:

	Eastern Division	Western Division	Total	
Billing	18,500	21,500	40,000	bills
Payroll	1,530	1,870	3,400	payroll chks.
Service and repairs	408	442	850	serv. requests

a. Open the Excel file *SA24-3*.
b. Prepare a divisional income statement for UniCast Cable Company for the year ended December 31, 2011.
c. When you have completed the statement, perform a "save as," replacing the entire file name with the following:

SA24-3_[your first name initial]_[your last name]

Answers to Self-Examination Questions

1. **B** The manager of a profit center (answer B) has responsibility for and authority over costs and revenues. If the manager has responsibility for only costs, the department is called a cost center (answer A). If the responsibility and authority extend to the investment in assets as well as costs and revenues, it is called an investment center (answer C). A service department (answer D) provides services to other departments. A service department could be a cost center, a profit center, or an investment center.

2. **C** $600,000/150,000 = $4 per payment. Division A anticipates 60,000 payments or $240,000 (60,000 × $4) in service department charges from the Accounts Payable Department. Income from operations is thus $900,000 − $240,000, or $660,000. Answer A assumes that all of the service department overhead is assigned to Division A, which would be incorrect, since Division A does not use all of the accounts payable service. Answer B incorrectly assumes that there are no service department charges from Accounts Payable. Answer D incorrectly determines the accounts payable transfer rate from Division A's income from operations.

3. **A** The rate of return on investment for Division A is 20% (answer A), computed as follows:

$$\text{Rate of Return on} = \frac{\text{Income from Operations}}{\text{Invested Assets}}$$

$$\text{ROI} = \frac{\$350,000 - \$200,000 - \$30,000}{\$600,000} = 20\%$$

4. **B** The profit margin for Division L of Liddy Co. is 15% (answer B), computed as follows:

$$\text{Rate of Return on} = \text{Profit Margin} \times \text{Investment Turnover}$$

$$24\% = \text{Profit Margin} \times 1.6$$
$$15\% = \text{Profit Margin}$$

5. **C** The market price approach (answer C) to transfer pricing uses the price at which the product or service transferred could be sold to outside buyers. The cost price approach (answer A) uses cost as the basis for setting transfer prices. The negotiated price approach (answer B) allows managers of decentralized units to agree (negotiate) among themselves as to the proper transfer price. The standard cost approach (answer D) is a version of the cost price approach that uses standard costs in setting transfer prices.

Differential Analysis and Product Pricing

© KEVIN P. CASEY/ASSOCIATED PRESS

R E A L N E T W O R K S ,   I N C .

Many of the decisions that you make depend on comparing the estimated costs of alternatives. The payoff from such comparisons is described in the following report from a University of Michigan study.

Richard Nisbett and two colleagues quizzed Michigan faculty members and university seniors on such questions as how often they walk out on a bad movie, refuse to finish a bad meal, start over on a weak term paper, or abandon a research project that no longer looks promising. They believe that people who cut their losses this way are following sound economic rules: calculating the net benefits of alternative courses of action, writing off past costs that can't be recovered, and weighing the opportunity to use future time and effort more profitably elsewhere.

Among students, those who have learned to use cost-benefit analysis frequently are apt to have far better grades than their Scholastic Aptitude Test scores would have predicted. Again, the more economics courses the students have, the more likely they are to apply cost-benefit analysis outside the classroom.

Dr. Nisbett concedes that for many Americans, cost-benefit rules often appear to conflict with such traditional principles as "never give up" and "waste not, want not."

Managers must also apply cost-benefit rules in making decisions affecting their business. RealNetworks, Inc., the Internet-based music and game company, like most companies must choose between alternatives. Examples of decisions faced by RealNetworks include whether it should expand or discontinue services, such as its recent decision to Mac-enable its digital music service, Rhapsody,® and whether to accept business at special prices, such as special pricing on its Helix Media Delivery System®. Other decisions include whether to replace network equipment, develop its own software, or buy software from others.

In this chapter, differential analysis, which reports the effects of decisions on total revenues and costs, is discussed. Practical approaches to setting product prices are also described and illustrated. Finally, how production bottlenecks influence product mix and pricing decisions is discussed.

Source: Alan L. Otten, "Economic Perspective Produces Steady Yields," from People Patterns, *The Wall Street Journal,* March 31, 1992, p. B1.

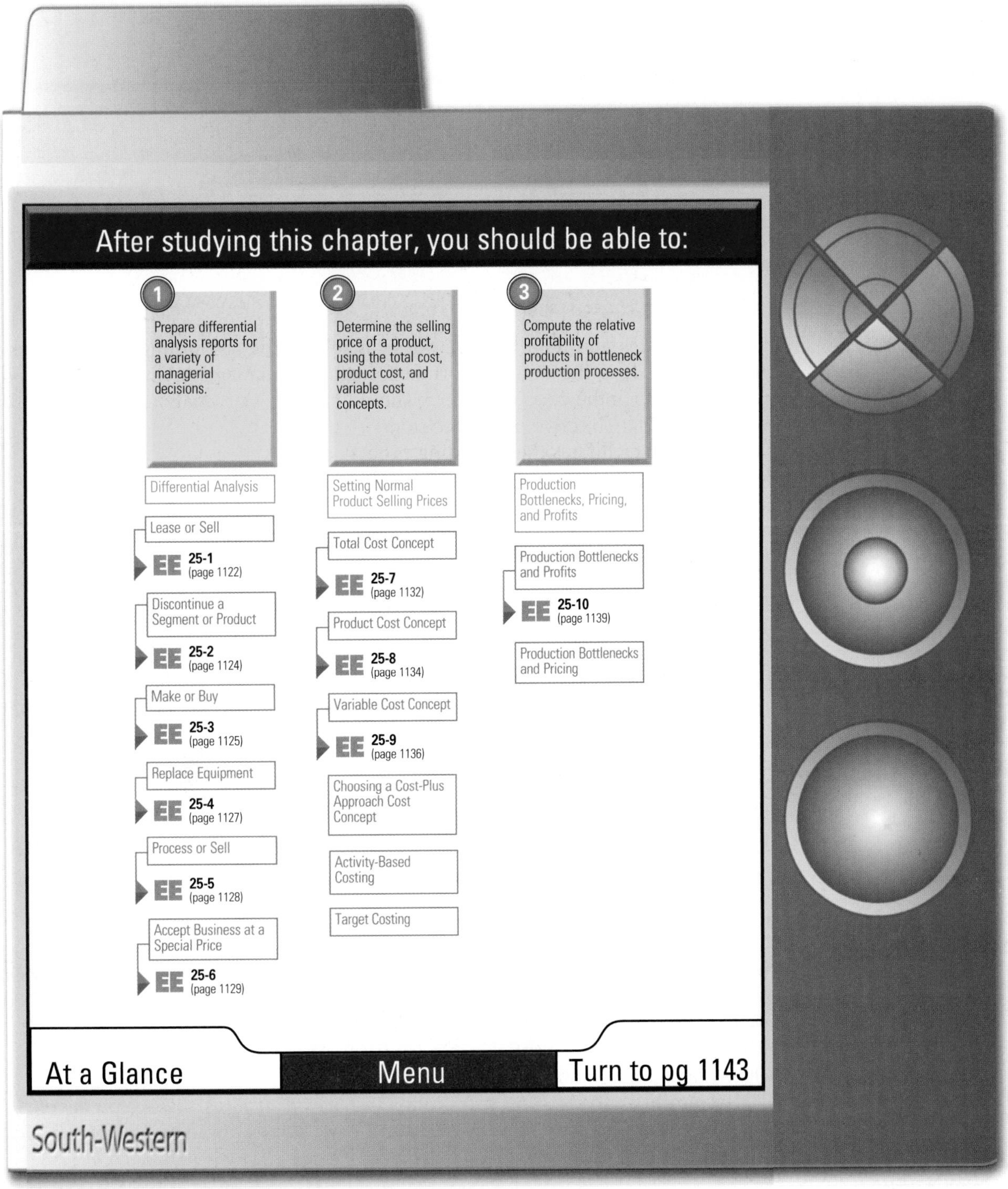

After studying this chapter, you should be able to:

1 Prepare differential analysis reports for a variety of managerial decisions.

2 Determine the selling price of a product, using the total cost, product cost, and variable cost concepts.

3 Compute the relative profitability of products in bottleneck production processes.

Differential Analysis

Lease or Sell
EE 25-1 (page 1122)

Discontinue a Segment or Product
EE 25-2 (page 1124)

Make or Buy
EE 25-3 (page 1125)

Replace Equipment
EE 25-4 (page 1127)

Process or Sell
EE 25-5 (page 1128)

Accept Business at a Special Price
EE 25-6 (page 1129)

Setting Normal Product Selling Prices

Total Cost Concept
EE 25-7 (page 1132)

Product Cost Concept
EE 25-8 (page 1134)

Variable Cost Concept
EE 25-9 (page 1136)

Choosing a Cost-Plus Approach Cost Concept

Activity-Based Costing

Target Costing

Production Bottlenecks, Pricing, and Profits

Production Bottlenecks and Profits
EE 25-10 (page 1139)

Production Bottlenecks and Pricing

At a Glance   Menu   Turn to pg 1143

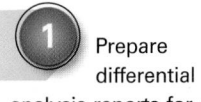
South-Western

Differential Analysis

1 Prepare differential analysis reports for a variety of managerial decisions.

Managerial decision making involves choosing between alternative courses of action. Although the managerial decision-making process varies by the type of decision, it normally involves the following steps:

The objective (Step 1) for most decisions is to maximize the company's profits. The alternative courses of action (Step 2) could include actions such as discontinuing an unprofitable segment, replacing equipment, or offering a product at a special price to an exporter. The relevant information (Step 3) varies by decision, but oftentimes

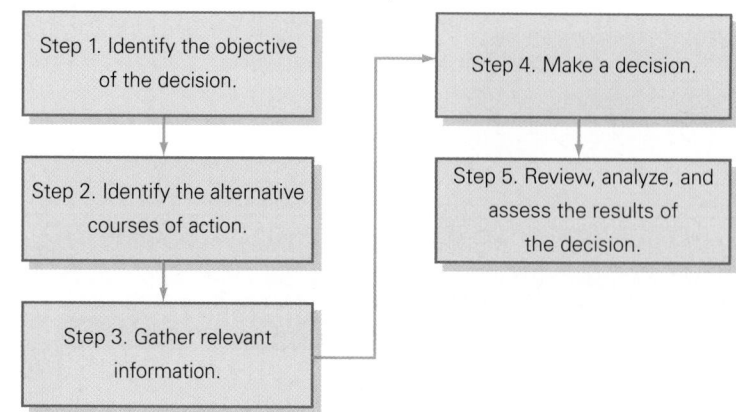

The management of Delta Air Lines decided to discontinue its low-fare Song Airline subsidiary after assessing its profitability.

Have you ever walked out on a bad movie? The cost of the ticket is a sunk cost and, thus, irrelevant to the decision to walk out early.

includes estimates and data that are not available in the accounting records. Making decisions (Step 4) is the most important function of managers. Once the decision is made, the results of the decision (Step 5) should be reviewed, analyzed, and assessed in terms of the initial objective of the decision.

Accounting facilitates the preceding process by:

1. Gathering relevant information for managerial decisions
2. Reporting this information to management
3. Providing management feedback on the results of the decisions

For managerial decisions, estimated future revenues and costs are relevant. Costs that have been incurred in the past are not relevant to the decision. These costs are called **sunk costs**.

Differential revenue is the amount of increase or decrease in revenue that is expected from a course of action as compared to an alternative. To illustrate, assume that equipment can be used to manufacture digital clocks or calculators. The estimated revenue from each product is as follows:

Product	Estimated Revenue
Digital clocks	$175,000
Calculators	150,000
Differential revenue	$ 25,000

The differential revenue from making and selling digital clocks is $25,000.

Differential cost is the amount of increase or decrease in cost that is expected from a course of action as compared to an alternative. For example, if increasing advertising expenses from $100,000 to $150,000 is being considered, the differential cost is $50,000.

Differential income (or **loss**) is the difference between the differential revenue and the differential costs. Differential income indicates that a decision is expected to be profitable, while a differential loss indicates the opposite.

Differential analysis, sometimes called *incremental analysis*, focuses on the effect of alternative courses of action on revenues and costs. An example of a reporting format for differential analysis is shown in Exhibit 1.

Exhibit 1

Differential Analysis

Differential revenue from alternatives:
Revenue from alternative A .... $XXX
Revenue from alternative B XXX
    Differential revenue .... $XXX
Differential cost of alternatives:
Cost of alternative A .... $XXX
Cost of alternative B XXX
    Differential cost XXX
Net differential income or loss from alternatives .... **$XXX**

In this chapter, differential analysis is illustrated for the following decisions:

1. Leasing or selling equipment
2. Discontinuing an unprofitable segment
3. Manufacturing or purchasing a needed part
4. Replacing fixed assets
5. Processing further or selling a product
6. Accepting additional business at a special price

Lease or Sell

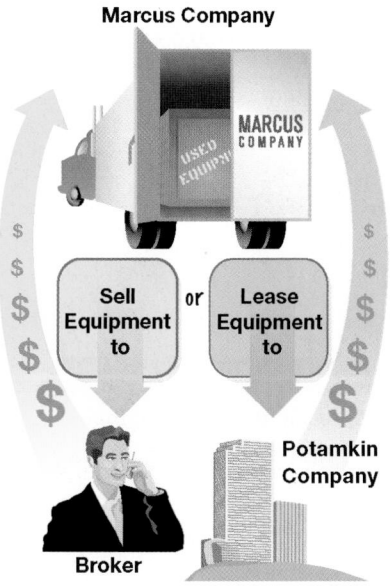

Marcus Company

Management may lease or sell a piece of equipment that is no longer needed. This may occur when a company changes its manufacturing process and can no longer use the equipment in the manufacturing process. In making a decision, differential analysis can be used.

To illustrate, assume that Marcus Company is considering leasing or disposing of the following equipment:

Cost of equipment	$200,000
Less accumulated depreciation	120,000
Book value	$ 80,000
Lease Option:	
Total revenue for five-year lease	$160,000
Total estimated repair, insurance, and property tax expenses during life of lease	35,000
Residual value at end of fifth year of lease	0
Sell Option:	
Sales price	$100,000
Commission on sales	6%

Exhibit 2 shows the differential analysis of whether to lease or sell the equipment.

Exhibit 2

Differential Analysis Report—Lease or Sell

Proposal to Lease or Sell Equipment
June 22, 2010

Differential revenue from alternatives:		
Revenue from lease	$160,000	
Revenue from sale	100,000	
Differential revenue from lease		$60,000
Differential cost of alternatives:		
Repair, insurance, and property tax expenses from lease	$ 35,000	
Commission expense on sale ($100,000 × 6%)	6,000	
Differential cost of lease		29,000
Net differential income from the lease alternative		**$31,000**

Many companies that manufacture expensive equipment give customers the choice of leasing the equipment. For example, construction equipment from Caterpillar can either be purchased outright or leased through Caterpillar's financial services subsidiary.

Exhibit 2 includes only the differential revenues and differential costs associated with the lease or sell decision. The $80,000 book value ($200,000 − $120,000) of the equipment is a *sunk* cost and is not considered in the differential analysis shown in Exhibit 2. In other words, the $80,000 does not affect the decision to lease or sell the equipment. This analysis is verified by the more traditional analysis shown in Exhibit 3.

To simplify, the following factors were not considered in Exhibits 2 and 3:

1. Differential revenue from investing funds
2. Differential income tax

Differential revenue (interest) could arise from investing the cash created by the two alternatives. Differential income tax could arise from differences in the timing of the income from the two alternatives and differences in the amount that is taxed. These factors are discussed in Chapter 26.

Exhibit 3

Traditional Analysis

Lease or Sell

Lease alternative:
Revenue from lease		$160,000
Depreciation expense for remaining five years ...	$80,000	
Repair, insurance, and property tax expenses	35,000	115,000
Net gain			$45,000

Sell alternative:
Sales price		$100,000
Book value of equipment	$80,000	
Commission expense	6,000	86,000
Net gain			14,000
Net differential income from the lease alternative ..			**$31,000**

Example Exercise 25-1 Lease or Sell

Casper Company owns office space with a cost of $100,000 and accumulated depreciation of $30,000 that can be sold for $150,000, less a 6% broker commission. Alternatively, the office space can be leased by Casper Company for 10 years for a total of $170,000, at the end of which there is no residual value. In addition, repair, insurance, and property tax that would be incurred by Casper Company on the rented office space would total $24,000 over the 10 years. Determine the differential income or loss from the lease alternative for Casper Company.

Follow My Example 25-1

Differential revenue from alternatives:
Revenue from lease	$170,000	
Revenue from sale	150,000	
Differential revenue from lease		$20,000

Differential cost of alternatives:
Repair, insurance, and property tax expenses from lease	$ 24,000	
Commission expense on sale	9,000	
Differential cost of lease		15,000
Net differential income from the lease alternative		$ 5,000

For Practice: PE 25-1A, PE 25-1B

Discontinue a Segment or Product

A product, department, branch, territory, or other segment of a business may be generating losses. As a result, management may consider discontinuing (eliminating) the product or segment. In such cases, it may be erroneously assumed that the total company income will increase by eliminating the operating loss.

Discontinuing the product or segment usually eliminates all of the product's or segment's variable costs. Such costs include direct materials, direct labor, variable factory overhead, and sales commissions. However, fixed costs such as depreciation, insurance, and property taxes may not be eliminated. Thus, it is possible for total company income to decrease rather than increase if the unprofitable product or segment is discontinued.

To illustrate, the income statement for Battle Creek Cereal Co. is shown in Exhibit 4. As shown in Exhibit 4, Bran Flakes incurred an operating loss of $11,000. Because Bran Flakes has incurred annual losses for several years, management is considering discontinuing it.

Income (Loss) by Product

Battle Creek Cereal Co. Condensed Income Statement For the Year Ended August 31, 2010				
	Corn Flakes	Toasted Oats	Bran Flakes	Total Company
Sales	$500,000	$400,000	$100,000	$1,000,000
Cost of goods sold:				
Variable costs	$220,000	$200,000	$ 60,000	$ 480,000
Fixed costs	120,000	80,000	20,000	220,000
Total cost of goods sold	$340,000	$280,000	$ 80,000	$ 700,000
Gross profit	$160,000	$120,000	$ 20,000	$ 300,000
Operating expenses:				
Variable expenses	$ 95,000	$ 60,000	$ 25,000	$ 180,000
Fixed expenses	25,000	20,000	6,000	51,000
Total operating expenses	$120,000	$ 80,000	$ 31,000	$ 231,000
Income (loss) from operations	$ 40,000	$ 40,000	$ (11,000)	$ 69,000

If Bran Flakes is discontinued, what would be the total annual operating income of Battle Creek Cereal? The first impression is that total annual operating income would be $80,000, as shown below.

	Corn Flakes	Toasted Oats	Total Company
Income from operations	$40,000	$40,000	$80,000

However, the differential analysis report in Exhibit 5 indicates that discontinuing Bran Flakes actually decreases operating income by $15,000. This is because discontinuing Bran Flakes has no effect on fixed costs and expenses. This is supported by the traditional analysis in Exhibit 6, which indicates that income from operations would decrease from $69,000 to $54,000.

Exhibits 5 and 6 consider only the short-term (one-year) effects of discontinuing Bran Flakes. When discontinuing a product or segment, long-term effects should also be considered. For example, discontinuing Bran Flakes could decrease sales of other products. This might be the case if customers upset with the discontinuance of Bran Flakes quit buying other products from the company. Finally, employee morale and productivity might suffer if employees have to be laid off or relocated.

Differential Analysis Report— Discontinue an Unprofitable Segment

Proposal to Discontinue Bran Flakes September 29, 2010		
Differential revenue from annual sales of Bran Flakes:		
Revenue from sales		$100,000
Differential cost of annual sales of Bran Flakes:		
Variable cost of goods sold	$60,000	
Variable operating expenses	25,000	85,000
Annual differential income from sales of Bran Flakes ...		**$ 15,000**

Exhibit 6

Traditional Analysis

	Bran Flakes, Toasted Oats, and Corn Flakes	Discontinue Bran Flakes*	Toasted Oats and Corn Flakes
Proposal to Discontinue Bran Flakes			
September 29, 2010			
Sales	$1,000,000	$100,000	$900,000
Cost of goods sold:			
Variable costs	$ 480,000	$ 60,000	$420,000
Fixed costs	220,000	—	220,000
Total cost of goods sold	$ 700,000	$ 60,000	$640,000
Gross profit	$ 300,000	$ 40,000	$260,000
Operating expenses:			
Variable expenses	$ 180,000	$ 25,000	$155,000
Fixed expenses	51,000	—	51,000
Total operating expenses	$ 231,000	$ 25,000	$206,000
Income (loss) from operations	$ 69,000	$ 15,000	$ 54,000

*Fixed costs are assumed to remain unchanged with the discontinuance of Bran Flakes.

Example Exercise 25-2   Discontinue a Segment 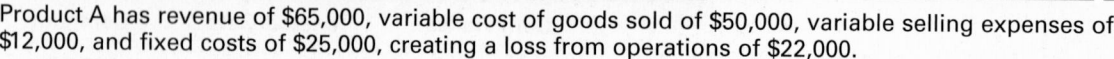 **1**

Product A has revenue of $65,000, variable cost of goods sold of $50,000, variable selling expenses of $12,000, and fixed costs of $25,000, creating a loss from operations of $22,000.

a.   Determine the differential income or loss from sales of Product A.
b.   Should Product A be discontinued?

Follow My Example 25-2

a.   Differential revenue from annual sales of Product A:
  Revenue from sales $65,000
 Differential cost of annual sales of Product A:
  Variable cost of goods sold $50,000
  Variable selling expenses 12,000   62,000
  Annual differential income from sales of Product A .... $ 3,000

b.   Product A should not be discontinued.

For Practice: PE 25-2A, PE 25-2B

Ford Motor Co. purchases spark plugs, GPS units, nuts, and bolts from suppliers.

Make or Buy

Companies often manufacture products made up of components that are assembled into a final product. For example, an automobile manufacturer assembles tires, radios, motors, interior seats, transmissions, and other parts into a finished automobile. In such cases, the manufacturer must decide whether to make a part or purchase it from a supplier.

Differential analysis can be used to decide whether to make or buy a part. The analysis is similar whether management is considering making a part that is currently being purchased or purchasing a part that is currently being made.

To illustrate, assume that an automobile manufacturer has been purchasing instrument panels for $240 a unit. The factory is currently operating at 80% of capacity, and no major increase in production is expected in the near future. The cost per unit of manufacturing an instrument panel internally is estimated as follows:

Direct materials	$ 80
Direct labor	80
Variable factory overhead	52
Fixed factory overhead	68
Total cost per unit	$280

If the make price of $280 is simply compared with the buy price of $240, the decision is to buy the instrument panel. However, if unused capacity could be used in manufacturing the part, there would be no increase in the total fixed factory overhead costs. Thus, only the variable factory overhead costs would be incurred.

The differential report for this make or buy decision is shown in Exhibit 7. As shown in Exhibit 7, there is a cost savings from manufacturing the instrument panel of $28 per panel. However, other factors should also be considered. For example, productive capacity used to make the instrument panel would not be available for other production. The decision may also affect the future business relationship with the instrument panel supplier. For example, if the supplier provides other parts, the company's decision to make instrument panels might jeopardize the timely delivery of other parts.

Exhibit 7

Differential Analysis Report—Make or Buy

Proposal to Manufacture Instrument Panels
February 15, 2010

Purchase price of an instrument panel		$240
Differential cost to manufacture:		
Direct materials	$80	
Direct labor	80	
Variable factory overhead	52	212
Cost savings from manufacturing an instrument panel		**$ 28**

Example Exercise 25-3   Make or Buy

1

A company manufactures a subcomponent of an assembly for $80 per unit, including fixed costs of $25 per unit. A proposal is offered to purchase the subcomponent from an outside source for $60 per unit, plus $5 per unit freight. Provide a differential analysis of the outside purchase proposal.

Follow My Example 25-3

Differential cost to purchase:		
Purchase price of the subcomponent	$60	
Freight for subcomponent	5	$65
Differential cost to manufacture:		
Variable manufacturing costs ($80 − $25 fixed costs)		55
Cost savings from manufacturing subcomponent		$10

For Practice: PE 25-3A, PE 25-3B

Replace Equipment

The usefulness of a fixed asset may decrease before it is worn out. For example, old equipment may no longer be as efficient as new equipment.

Differential analysis can be used for decisions to replace fixed assets such as equipment and machinery. The analysis normally focuses on the costs of continuing to use the old equipment versus replacing the equipment. The book value of the old equipment is a sunk cost and, thus, is irrelevant.

To illustrate, assume that a business is considering replacing the following machine:

Old Machine	
Book value	$100,000
Estimated annual variable manufacturing costs	225,000
Estimated selling price	25,000
Estimated remaining useful life	5 years
New Machine	
Cost of new machine	$250,000
Estimated annual variable manufacturing costs	150,000
Estimated residual value	0
Estimated useful life	5 years

The differential report for the decision to replace the old machine is shown in Exhibit 8.

Exhibit 8

Differential Analysis Report— Replace Machine

Proposal to Replace Machine
November 28, 2010

Annual variable costs—present machine	$225,000	
Annual variable costs—new machine	150,000	
Annual differential decrease in cost	$ 75,000	
Number of years applicable	× 5	
Total differential decrease in cost	$375,000	
Proceeds from sale of present machine	25,000	$400,000
Cost of new machine		250,000
Net differential decrease in cost, five-year total		$150,000
Annual net differential decrease in cost—new machine		**$ 30,000**

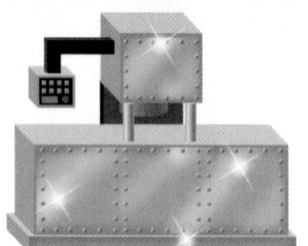

Estimated annual reduction
of costs of $75,000

As shown in Exhibit 8, there is an annual decrease in cost of $30,000 ($150,000 ÷ 5 years) from replacing the old machine. Thus, the decision should be to purchase the new machine and sell the old machine.

Other factors are often important in equipment replacement decisions. For example, differences between the remaining useful life of the old equipment and the estimated life of the new equipment could exist. In addition, the new equipment might improve the overall quality of the product and, thus, increase sales.

The time value of money and other uses for the cash needed to purchase the new equipment could also affect the decision to replace equipment.[1] The revenue that is forgone from an alternative use of an asset, such as cash, is called an **opportunity cost**. Although the opportunity cost is not recorded in the accounting records, it is useful in analyzing alternative courses of action.

To illustrate, assume that in the preceding illustration the cash outlay of $250,000 for the new machine, less the $25,000 proceeds from the sale of the old machine, could be invested to yield a 15% return. Thus, the annual opportunity cost related to the purchase of the new machine is $33,750 (15% × $225,000). Since the opportunity cost of $33,750 exceeds the annual cost savings of $30,000, the old machine should not be replaced.

1 The time value of money in purchasing equipment (capital assets) is discussed in Chapter 26.

Example Exercise 25-4   Replace Equipment

A machine with a book value of $32,000 has an estimated four-year life. A proposal is offered to sell the old machine for $10,000 and replace it with a new machine at a cost of $45,000. The new machine has a four-year life with no residual value. The new machine would reduce annual direct labor costs by $11,000. Provide a differential analysis on the proposal to replace the machine.

Follow My Example 25-4

Annual direct labor cost reduction	$11,000	
Number of years applicable	× 4	
Total differential decrease in cost	$44,000	
Proceeds from sale of old equipment	10,000	$54,000
Cost of new equipment		45,000
Net differential decrease in cost from replacing equipment, four-year total		$ 9,000
Annual net differential decrease in cost—new equipment		$ 2,250

For Practice: PE 25-4A, PE 25-4B

Sell as Kerosene   Sell as Gasoline

Process or Sell

During manufacturing, a product normally progresses through various stages or processes. In some cases, a product can be sold at an intermediate stage of production, or it can be processed further and then sold.

Differential analysis can be used to decide whether to sell a product at an intermediate stage or to process it further. In doing so, the differential revenues and costs from further processing are compared. The costs of producing the intermediate product do not change, regardless of whether the intermediate product is sold or processed further. These costs are sunk costs and are irrelevant to the decision.

To illustrate, assume that a business produces kerosene as follows:

Kerosene:

Batch size	4,000 gallons
Cost of producing kerosene	$2,400 per batch
Selling price	$2.50 per gallon

The kerosene can be processed further to yield gasoline as follows:

Gasoline:

Input batch size	4,000 gallons
Less evaporation (20%)	800 (4,000 × 20%)
Output batch size	3,200 gallons
Additional processing costs	$650 per batch
Selling price	$3.50 per gallon

The differential report for the decision to process the kerosene further is shown in Exhibit 9.

Exhibit 9

Differential Analysis Report— Process or Sell

Proposal to Process Kerosene Further
October 1, 2010

Differential revenue from further processing per batch:		
Revenue from sale of gasoline [(4,000 gallons − 800 gallons evaporation) × $3.50]	$11,200	
Revenue from sale of kerosene (4,000 gallons × $2.50)	10,000	
Differential revenue		$1,200
Differential cost per batch:		
Additional cost of producing gasoline		650
Differential income from further processing gasoline per batch		**$550**

The initial cost of producing the kerosene of $2,400 is not considered in deciding whether to process kerosene further. This initial cost will be incurred, regardless of whether gasoline is produced and, thus, is a sunk cost.

As shown in Exhibit 9, there is additional income from further processing the kerosene into gasoline of $550 per batch. Therefore, the decision should be to process the kerosene further.

Example Exercise 25-5   Process or Sell

Product T is produced for $2.50 per gallon including a $1.00 per gallon fixed cost. Product T can be sold without additional processing for $3.50 per gallon, or processed further into Product V at an additional cost of $1.60 per gallon, including a $0.90 per gallon fixed cost. Product V can be sold for $4.00 per gallon. Provide a differential analysis for further processing into Product V.

Follow My Example 25-5

Differential revenue from further processing per gallon:		
Revenue per gallon from sale of Product V	$4.00	
Revenue per gallon from sale of Product T	3.50	
Differential revenue		$0.50
Differential cost per gallon:		
Additional cost for producing Product V ($1.60 − $0.90)		0.70
Differential loss from further processing into Product V		$0.20

For Practice: PE 25-5A, PE 25-5B

Accept Business at a Special Price

A company may be offered the opportunity to sell its products at prices other than normal prices. For example, an exporter may offer to sell a company's products overseas at special discount prices.

Differential analysis can be used to decide whether to accept additional business at a special price. The differential revenue from accepting the additional business is compared to the differential costs of producing and delivering the product to the customer.

The differential costs of accepting additional business depend on whether the company is operating at full capacity.

The Internet is forcing many companies to respond to "dynamic" pricing. For example, in Priceline.com Inc.'s "name your price" format, customers tell the company what they are willing to pay and then the company must decide if it is willing to sell at that price.

1. If the company is *operating at full capacity*, any additional production increases fixed and variable manufacturing costs. Selling and administrative expenses may also increase because of the additional business.

2. If the company is *operating below full capacity*, any additional production does not increase fixed manufacturing costs. In this case, the differential costs of the additional production are the variable manufacturing costs. Selling and administrative expenses may also increase because of the additional business.

To illustrate, assume that B-Ball Inc. manufactures basketballs as follows:

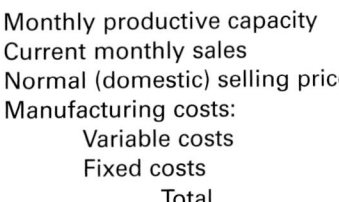

Monthly productive capacity	12,500 basketballs
Current monthly sales	10,000 basketballs
Normal (domestic) selling price	$30.00 per basketball
Manufacturing costs:	
Variable costs	$12.50 per basketball
Fixed costs	7.50
Total	$20.00 per basketball

Order for 5,000
basketballs at $18 each

B-Ball Inc. has received an offer from an exporter for 5,000 basketballs at $18 each. Production can be spread over three months without interfering with normal production or incurring overtime costs. Pricing policies in the domestic market will not be affected.

Comparing the special offer sales price of $18 with the manufacturing cost of $20 per basketball indicates that the offer should be rejected. However, as shown in Exhibit 10, differential analysis indicates that the offer should be accepted.

Exhibit 10

Differential Analysis Report—Sell at Special Price

Proposal to Sell Basketballs to Exporter
March 10, 2010

Differential revenue from accepting offer:	
Revenue from sale of 5,000 additional units at $18	$90,000
Differential cost of accepting offer:	
Variable costs of 5,000 additional units at $12.50	62,500
Differential income from accepting offer	**$27,500**

Proposals to sell products at special prices often require additional considerations. For example, special prices in one geographic area may result in price reductions in other areas with the result that total company sales decrease. Manufacturers must also conform to the Robinson-Patman Act, which prohibits price discrimination within the United States unless price differences can be justified by different costs.

Example Exercise 25-6   Accept Business at Special Price

Product D is normally sold for $4.40 per unit. A special price of $3.60 is offered for the export market. The variable production cost is $3.00 per unit. An additional export tariff of 10% of revenue must be paid for all export products. Determine the differential income or loss per unit from selling Product D for export.

Follow My Example 25-6

Differential revenue from export:		
Revenue per unit from export sale		$3.60
Differential cost from export:		
Variable manufacturing costs	$3.00	
Export tariff (10% × $3.60)	0.36	3.36
Differential income from accepting export sale		$0.24

For Practice: PE 25-6A, PE 25-6B

Setting Normal Product Selling Prices

Determine the selling price of a product, using the total cost, product cost, and variable cost concepts.

The *normal* selling price is the target selling price to be achieved in the long term. The normal selling price must be set high enough to cover all costs and expenses (fixed and variable) and provide a reasonable profit. Otherwise, the business will not survive.

In contrast, in deciding whether to accept additional business at a special price, only differential costs are considered. Any price above the differential costs will increase profits in the short term. However, in the long term, products are sold at normal prices rather than special prices.

Managers can use one of two market methods to determine selling price:

1. Demand-based concept
2. Competition-based concept

Hotels and motels use the demand-based concept in setting room rates. Room rates are set low during off-season travel periods (low demand) and high for peak-season travel periods (high demand) such as holidays.

The demand-based concept sets the price according to the demand for the product. If there is high demand for the product, then the price is set high. Likewise, if there is a low demand for the product, then the price is set low.

The competition-based concept sets the price according to the price offered by competitors. For example, if a competitor reduces the price, then management adjusts the price to meet the competition. The market-based pricing approaches are discussed in greater detail in marketing courses.

Managers can also use one of three cost-plus methods to determine the selling price:

Electronic stores such as Best Buy use the competition-based concept. If a buyer demonstrates that a lower price is available from Circuit City or another competitor, Best Buy will often match the price.

1. Total cost concept
2. Product cost concept
3. Variable cost concept

Cost-plus methods determine the normal selling price by estimating a cost amount per unit and adding a markup, as shown below.

Normal Selling Price = Cost Amount per Unit + Markup

The cost amount per unit depends on the cost concept used. Management determines the **markup** based on the desired profit for the product. The markup should be sufficient to earn the desired profit plus cover any cost and expenses that are not included in the cost amount.

Total Cost Concept

Under the **total cost concept**, manufacturing cost plus the selling and administrative expenses are included in the total cost per unit. The markup per unit is then computed and added to total cost per unit to determine the normal selling price.

The total cost concept is applied using the following steps:

Step 1. Estimate the total manufacturing cost as shown below.

Manufacturing costs:	
Direct materials	$XXX
Direct labor	XXX
Factory overhead	XXX
Total manufacturing cost	$XXX

Step 2. Estimate the total selling and administrative expenses.
Step 3. Estimate the total cost as shown below.

Total manufacturing costs	$XXX
Selling and administrative expenses	XXX
Total cost	$XXX

Step 4. Divide the total cost by the number of units expected to be produced and sold to determine the total cost per unit, as shown below.

TOTAL COST CONCEPT

$$\text{Total Cost per Unit} = \frac{\text{Total Cost}}{\text{Estimated Units Produced and Sold}}$$

MARKUP:
Desired Profit

Step 5. Compute the markup percentage as follows:

$$\text{Markup Percentage} = \frac{\text{Desired Profit}}{\text{Total Cost}}$$

The desired profit is normally computed based on a rate of return on assets as follows:

$$\text{Desired Profit} = \text{Desired Rate of Return} \times \text{Total Assets}$$

TOTAL COST:
Manufacturing Cost
+
Administrative Expense
+
Selling Expense

Step 6. Determine the markup per unit by multiplying the markup percentage times the total cost per unit as follows:

$$\text{Markup per Unit} = \text{Markup Percentage} \times \text{Total Cost per Unit}$$

Step 7. Determine the normal selling price by adding the markup per unit to the total cost per unit as follows:

Total cost per unit	$XXX
Markup per unit	XXX
Normal selling price per unit	$XXX

To illustrate, assume the following data for 100,000 calculators that Digital Solutions Inc. expects to produce and sell during the current year:

Manufacturing costs:		
Direct materials ($3.00 × 100,000)		$ 300,000
Direct labor ($10.00 × 100,000)		1,000,000
Factory overhead:		
Variable costs ($1.50 × 100,000)	$150,000	
Fixed costs	50,000	200,000
Total manufacturing cost		$1,500,000
Selling and administrative expenses:		
Variable expenses ($1.50 × 100,000)	$150,000	
Fixed costs	20,000	
Total selling and administrative expenses		170,000
Total cost		$1,670,000
Desired rate of return		20%
Total assets		$800,000

Using the total cost concept, the normal selling price of $18.30 is determined as follows:

Step 1. Total manufacturing cost: $1,500,000
Step 2. Total selling and administrative expenses: $170,000
Step 3. Total cost: $1,670,000
Step 4. Total cost per unit: $16.70

$$\text{Total Cost per Unit} = \frac{\text{Total Cost}}{\text{Estimated Units Produced and Sold}} = \frac{\$1,670,000}{100,000 \text{ units}} = \$16.70 \text{ per unit}$$

Step 5. Markup percentage: 9.6% (rounded)

$$\text{Desired Profit} = \text{Desired Rate of Return} \times \text{Total Assets} = 20\% \times \$800,000 = \$160,000$$

$$\text{Markup Percentage} = \frac{\text{Desired Profit}}{\text{Total Cost}} = \frac{\$160,000}{\$1,670,000} = 9.6\% \text{ (rounded)}$$

Step 6. Markup per unit: $1.60

> Markup per Unit = Markup Percentage × Total Cost per Unit
> Markup per Unit = 9.6% × $16.70 = $1.60 per unit

Step 7. Normal selling price: $18.30

Total cost per unit	$16.70
Markup per unit	1.60
Normal selling price per unit	$18.30

The ability of the selling price of $18.30 to generate the desired profit of $160,000 is illustrated by the income statement shown below.

Digital Solutions Inc.
Income Statement
For the Year Ended December 31, 2010

Sales (100,000 units × $18.30)		$1,830,000
Expenses:		
Variable (100,000 units × $16.00)	$1,600,000	
Fixed ($50,000 + $20,000)	70,000	1,670,000
Income from operations		$ 160,000

The total cost concept is often used by contractors who sell products to government agencies. This is because in many cases government contractors are required by law to be reimbursed for their products on a total-cost-plus-profit basis.

Example Exercise 25-7   Total Cost Markup Percentage ▸ 2

Apex Corporation produces and sells Product Z at a total cost of $30 per unit, of which $20 is product cost and $10 is selling and administrative expenses. In addition, the total cost of $30 is made up of $18 variable cost and $12 fixed cost. The desired profit is $3 per unit. Determine the markup percentage on total cost.

Follow My Example 25-7

Markup percentage on total cost: $\dfrac{\$3}{\$30} = 10.0\%$

For Practice: PE 25-7A, PE 25-7B

Integrity, Objectivity, and Ethics in Business

PRICE FIXING

Federal law prevents companies competing in similar markets from sharing cost and price information, or what is commonly termed "price fixing." For example, the Federal Trade Commission brought a suit against the major record labels and music retailers for conspiring to set CD prices at a minimum level, or MAP (minimum advertised price). In settling the suit, the major labels ceased their MAP policies and provided $143 million in cash and CDs for consumers.

Product Cost Concept

Under the **product cost concept**, only the costs of manufacturing the product, termed the *product costs*, are included in the cost amount per unit to which the markup is added. Estimated selling expenses, administrative expenses, and desired profit are included in the markup. The markup per unit is then computed and added to the product cost per unit to determine the normal selling price.

The product cost concept is applied using the following steps:

Step 1.   Estimate the total product costs as follows:

Product costs:	
Direct materials	$XXX
Direct labor	XXX
Factory overhead	XXX
Total product cost	$XXX

Step 2.   Estimate the total selling and administrative expenses.

Step 3.   Divide the total product cost by the number of units expected to be produced and sold to determine the total product cost per unit, as shown below.

$$\text{Product Cost per Unit} = \frac{\text{Total Product Cost}}{\text{Estimated Units Produced and Sold}}$$

Step 4.   Compute the markup percentage as follows:

$$\text{Markup Percentage} = \frac{\text{Desired Profit} + \text{Total Selling and Administrative Expenses}}{\text{Total Product Cost}}$$

The numerator of the markup percentage is the desired profit plus the total selling and administrative expenses. These expenses must be included in the markup percentage, since they are not included in the cost amount to which the markup is added.

As illustrated for the total cost concept, the desired profit is normally computed based on a rate of return on assets as follows:

$$\text{Desired Profit} = \text{Desired Rate of Return} \times \text{Total Assets}$$

Step 5.   Determine the markup per unit by multiplying the markup percentage times the product cost per unit as follows:

$$\text{Markup per Unit} = \text{Markup Percentage} \times \text{Product Cost per Unit}$$

Step 6.   Determine the normal selling price by adding the markup per unit to the product cost per unit as follows:

Product cost per unit	$XXX
Markup per unit	XXX
Normal selling price per unit	$XXX

To illustrate, assume the same data for the production and sale of 100,000 calculators by Digital Solutions Inc. as in the preceding example. The normal selling price of $18.30 is determined under the product cost concept as follows:

Step 1.   Total product cost: $1,500,000
Step 2.   Total selling and administrative expenses: $170,000
Step 3.   Total product cost per unit: $15.00

$$\text{Total Cost per Unit} = \frac{\text{Total Product Cost}}{\text{Estimated Units Produced and Sold}} = \frac{\$1,500,000}{100,000 \text{ units}} = \$15.00 \text{ per unit}$$

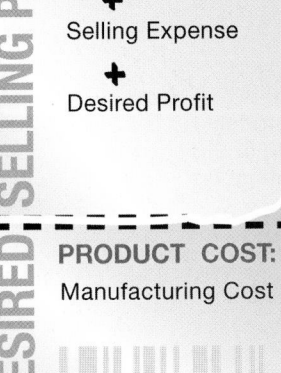
PRODUCT COST CONCEPT

MARKUP:
Administrative Expense
+
Selling Expense
+
Desired Profit

PRODUCT COST:
Manufacturing Cost

DESIRED SELLING PRICE

Step 4. Markup percentage: 22%

Desired Profit = Desired Rate of Return × Total Assets = 20% × $800,000 = $160,000

$$\text{Markup Percentage} = \frac{\text{Desired Profit} + \text{Total Selling and Administrative Expenses}}{\text{Total Product Cost}}$$

$$\text{Markup Percentage} = \frac{\$160,000 + \$170,000}{\$1,500,000} = \frac{\$330,000}{\$1,500,000} = 22\%$$

Step 5. Markup per unit: $3.30

Markup per unit = Markup Percentage × Product Cost per Unit
Markup per unit = 22% × $15.00 = $3.30 per unit

Step 6. Normal selling price: $18.30

Total product cost per unit	$15.00
Markup per unit	3.30
Normal selling price per unit	$18.30

Example Exercise 25-8   Product Cost Markup Percentage ••••••••⟩ ②

Apex Corporation produces and sells Product Z at a total cost of $30 per unit, of which $20 is product cost and $10 is selling and administrative expenses. In addition, the total cost of $30 is made up of $18 variable cost and $12 fixed cost. The desired profit is $3 per unit. Determine the markup percentage on product cost.

Follow My Example 25-8

Markup percentage on product cost: $\dfrac{\$3 + \$10}{\$20} = 65.0\%$

For Practice: PE 25-8A, PE 25-8B

Variable Cost Concept

Under the **variable cost concept**, only variable costs are included in the cost amount per unit to which the markup is added. All variable manufacturing costs, as well as variable selling and administrative expenses, are included in the cost amount. Fixed manufacturing costs, fixed selling and administrative expenses, and desired profit are included in the markup. The markup per unit is then added to the variable cost per unit to determine the normal selling price.

The variable cost concept is applied using the following steps:

Step 1. Estimate the total variable product cost as follows:

Variable product costs:	
Direct materials	$XXX
Direct labor	XXX
Variable factory overhead	XXX
Total variable product cost	$XXX

Step 2. Estimate the total variable selling and administrative expenses.
Step 3. Determine the total variable cost as follows:

Total variable product cost	$XXX
Total variable selling and administrative expenses	XXX
Total variable cost	$XXX

Step 4. Compute the variable cost per unit as follows:

$$\text{Variable Cost per Unit} = \frac{\text{Total Variable Cost}}{\text{Estimated Units Produced and Sold}}$$

Step 5.   Compute the markup percentage as follows:

$$\text{Markup Percentage} = \frac{\text{Desired Profit} + \text{Total Fixed Costs and Expenses}}{\text{Total Variable Cost}}$$

The numerator of the markup percentage is the desired profit plus the total fixed costs (fixed factory overhead) and expenses (selling and administrative). These fixed costs and expenses must be included in the markup percentage, since they are not included in the cost amount to which the markup is added.

As illustrated for the total and product cost concepts, the desired profit is normally computed based on a rate of return on assets as follows:

$$\text{Desired Profit} = \text{Desired Rate of Return} \times \text{Total Assets}$$

Step 6.   Determine the markup per unit by multiplying the markup percentage times the variable cost per unit as follows:

$$\text{Markup per Unit} = \text{Markup Percentage} \times \text{Variable Cost per Unit}$$

Step 7.   Determine the normal selling price by adding the markup per unit to the variable cost per unit as follows:

Variable cost per unit	$XXX
Markup per unit	XXX
Normal selling price per unit	$XXX

To illustrate, assume the same data for the production and sale of 100,000 calculators by Digital Solutions Inc. as in the preceding example. The normal selling price of $18.30 is determined under the variable cost concept as follows:

Step 1.   Total variable product cost: $1,450,000

Variable product costs:	
Direct materials ($3 × 100,000)	$ 300,000
Direct labor ($10 × 100,000)	1,000,000
Variable factory overhead ($1.50 × 100,000)	150,000
Total variable product cost	$1,450,000

Step 2.   Total variable selling and administrative expenses: $150,000 ($1.50 × 100,000)
Step 3.   Total variable cost: $1,600,000 ($1,450,000 + $150,000)
Step 4.   Variable cost per unit: $16.00

$$\frac{\text{Variable Cost}}{\text{per Unit}} = \frac{\text{Total Variable Cost}}{\text{Estimated Units Produced and Sold}} = \frac{\$1,600,000}{100,000 \text{ units}} = \$16 \text{ per unit}$$

Step 5.   Markup percentage: 14.4% (rounded)

Desired Profit = Desired Rate of Return × Total Assets = 20% × $800,000 = $160,000

$$\text{Markup Percentage} = \frac{\text{Desired Profit} + \text{Total Fixed Costs and Expenses}}{\text{Total Variable Cost}}$$

$$\text{Markup Percentage} = \frac{\$160,000 + \$50,000 + \$20,000}{\$1,600,000} = \frac{\$230,000}{\$1,600,000}$$

Markup Percentage = 14.4% (rounded)

Step 6.   Markup per unit: $2..30

Markup per Unit = Markup Percentage × Variable Cost per Unit
Markup per Unit = 14.4% × $16.00 = $2.30 per unit

Step 7.   Normal selling price: $18.30

Total variable cost per unit	$16.00
Markup per unit	2.30
Normal selling price per unit	$18.30

ARIABLE COST CONCEPT

DESIRED SELLING PRICE

MARKUP:
Total Fixed Costs

Desired Profit

VARIABLE COST:
Variable Manufacturing Cost

Variable Administrative and Selling Expenses

Example Exercise 25-9 Variable Cost Markup Percentage ········▶ 2

Apex Corporation produces and sells Product Z at a total cost of $30 per unit, of which $20 is product cost and $10 is selling and administrative expenses. In addition, the total cost of $30 is made up of $18 variable cost and $12 fixed cost. The desired profit is $3 per unit. Determine the markup percentage on variable cost, rounding to one decimal place.

Follow My Example 25-9

Markup percentage on variable cost: $\dfrac{\$3 + \$12}{\$18}$ = 83.3%, rounded to one decimal place

For Practice: PE 25-9A, PE 25-9B

Choosing a Cost-Plus Approach Cost Concept

All three cost-plus concepts produced the same selling price ($18.30) for Digital Solutions Inc. The three cost-plus concepts are summarized in Exhibit 11.

Exhibit 11

Cost-Plus Approach to Setting Normal Selling Prices

Normal Selling Price = Cost Amount per Unit + Markup

$$\text{Cost Amount per Unit} = \frac{\text{Cost Amount}}{\text{Estimated Units Produced and Sold}}$$

Markup = Cost Amount per Unit × Markup Percentage

Cost-Plus Concept	Cost Amount	Markup Percentage

Total cost	Manufacturing (product) costs:
	  Direct materials
	  Direct labor
	  Factory overhead
	Selling and administrative expenses
		$\dfrac{\text{Desired Profit}}{\text{Total Cost}}$

Product cost	Manufacturing (product) costs:
	  Direct materials
	  Direct labor
	  Factory overhead
		$\dfrac{\text{Desired Profit} + \text{Total Selling and Administrative Expenses}}{\text{Total Product Cost}}$

Variable cost	Variable manufacturing (product) costs:
	  Direct materials
	  Direct labor
	  Variable factory overhead
	Variable selling and administrative expenses
		$\dfrac{\text{Desired Profit} + \text{Total Fixed Costs and Expenses}}{\text{Total Variable Cost}}$

Estimated, rather than actual costs and expenses, may be used with any of the three cost-plus concepts. Management should be careful, however, when using estimated or standard costs in applying the cost-plus approach. Specifically, estimates should be based on normal (attainable) operating levels and not theoretical (ideal) levels of performance. In product pricing, the use of estimates based on ideal- or maximum-capacity operating levels could lead to setting product prices too low. In such cases, the costs of such factors as normal spoilage or normal periods of idle time might not be considered.

The decision-making needs of management are also an important factor in selecting a cost concept for product pricing. For example, managers who often make special pricing decisions are more likely to use the variable cost concept. In contrast, a government defense contractor would be more likely to use the total cost concept.

Activity-Based Costing

As illustrated, costs are important in setting product prices and decision making. Inaccurate costs may lead to incorrect decisions and prices. To more accurately measure the costs and expenses, some companies use activity-based costing. **Activity-based costing (ABC)** identifies and traces costs and expenses to activities and then to specific products.

Activity-based costing is particularly useful when manufacturing operations involve large amounts of factory overhead. In such cases, traditional overhead allocation bases such as units produced, direct labor hours, direct labor costs, or machine hours may yield inaccurate cost allocations. This, in turn, may result in distorted product costs and product prices.[2]

Target Costing

Target costing is a method of setting prices that combines market-based pricing with a cost-reduction emphasis. Under target costing, a future selling price is anticipated, using the demand-based or the competition-based concepts. The target cost is then determined by subtracting a desired profit from the expected selling price, as shown below.

Target Cost = Expected Selling Price − Desired Profit

Target costing tries to reduce costs as shown in Exhibit 12. The bar at the left in Exhibit 12 shows the actual cost and profit that can be earned during the current period.

Exhibit 12

Target Cost Concept

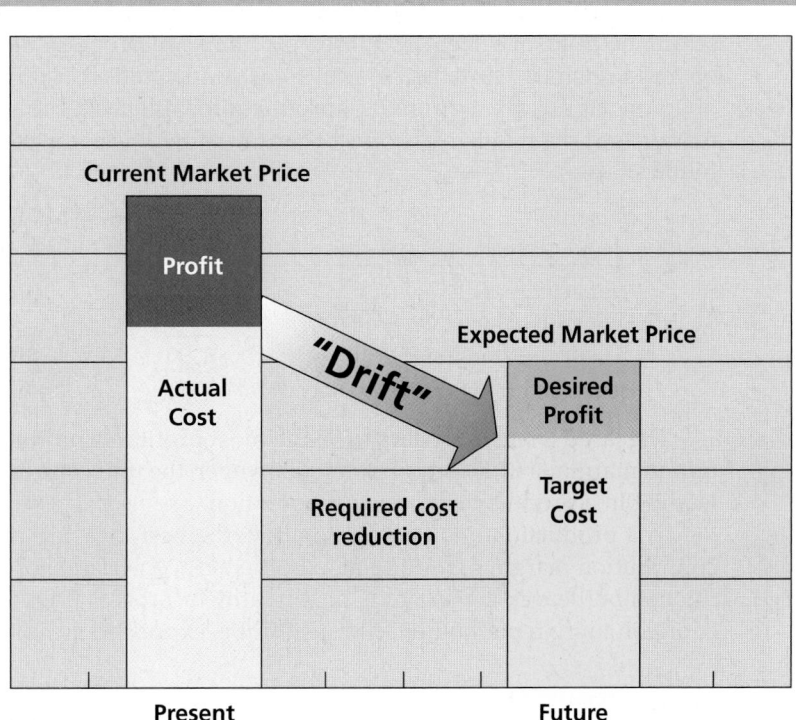

2 Activity-based costing is further discussed and illustrated in the appendix at the end of this chapter.

The bar at the right shows that the market price is expected to decline in the future. The target cost is estimated as the difference between the expected market price and the desired profit.

The target cost is normally less than the current cost. Thus, managers must try to reduce costs from the design and manufacture of the product. The planned cost reduction is sometimes referred to as the cost "drift." Costs can be reduced in a variety of ways such as the following:

1. Simplifying the design
2. Reducing the cost of direct materials
3. Reducing the direct labor costs
4. Eliminating waste

Target costing is especially useful in highly competitive markets such as the market for personal computers. Such markets require continual product cost reductions to remain competitive.

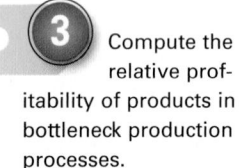

Compute the relative profitability of products in bottleneck production processes.

Production Bottlenecks, Pricing, and Profits

A **production bottleneck** (or *constraint*) is a point in the manufacturing process where the demand for the company's product exceeds the ability to produce the product. The **theory of constraints (TOC)** is a manufacturing strategy that focuses on reducing the influence of bottlenecks on production processes.

Production Bottlenecks and Profits

When a company has a production bottleneck in its production process, it should attempt to maximize its profits, subject to the production bottleneck. In doing so, the unit contribution margin of each product per production bottleneck constraint is used.

To illustrate, assume that PrideCraft Tool Company makes three types of wrenches: small, medium, and large. All three products are processed through a heat treatment operation, which hardens the steel tools. PrideCraft Tool's heat treatment process is operating at full capacity and is a production bottleneck. The product unit contribution margin and the number of hours of heat treatment used by each type of wrench are as follows:

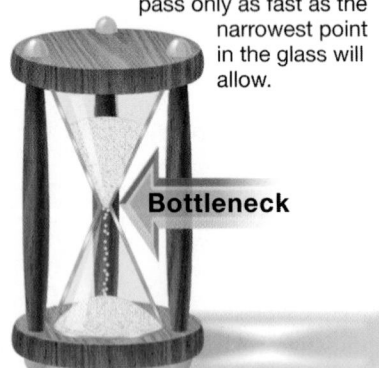

The sand in the hourglass can pass only as fast as the narrowest point in the glass will allow.

Bottleneck

	Small Wrench	Medium Wrench	Large Wrench
Unit selling price	$130	$140	$160
Unit variable cost	40	40	40
Unit contribution margin	$ 90	$100	$120
Heat treatment hours per unit	1 hr.	4 hrs.	8 hrs.

The large wrench appears to be the most profitable product because its unit contribution margin of $120 is the greatest. However, the unit contribution margin can be misleading in a production bottleneck operation.

In a production bottleneck operation, the best measure of profitability is the unit contribution margin per production bottleneck constraint. For PrideCraft Tool, the production bottleneck constraint is heat treatment process hours. Therefore, the unit contribution margin per bottleneck constraint is expressed as follows:

$$\text{Unit Contribution Margin per Production Bottleneck Hour} = \frac{\text{Unit Contribution Margin}}{\text{Heat Treatment Hours per Unit}}$$

The unit contribution per production bottleneck hour for each of the wrenches produced by PrideCraft Tool is computed below.

Small Wrenches

$$\text{Unit Contribution Margin per Production Bottleneck Hour} = \frac{\$90}{1 \text{ hr.}} = \$90 \text{ per hr.}$$

Medium Wrenches

$$\text{Unit Contribution Margin per Production Bottleneck Hour} = \frac{\$100}{4 \text{ hrs.}} = \$25 \text{ per hr.}$$

Large Wrenches

$$\text{Unit Contribution Margin per Production Bottleneck Hour} = \frac{\$120}{8 \text{ hrs.}} = \$15 \text{ per hr.}$$

The small wrench produces the highest unit contribution margin per production bottleneck hour (heat treatment) of $90 per hour. In contrast, the large wrench has the largest contribution margin per unit of $120, but has the smallest unit contribution margin per production bottleneck hour of $15 per hour. Thus, the small wrench is the most profitable product per production bottleneck hour.

Production Bottlenecks and Pricing

When a company has a production bottleneck, the unit contribution margin per bottleneck hour is a measure of each product's profitability. This measure can be used to adjust product prices to reflect the product's use of the bottleneck.

To illustrate, the large wrench produced by PrideCraft Tool Company uses eight bottleneck hours, but produces a contribution margin per unit of only $120. As a result, the large wrench is the least profitable of the wrenches per bottleneck hour ($15 per hour).

PrideCraft Tool Company can improve the profitability of producing large wrenches by any combination of the following:

1. Increase the selling price of the large wrenches.
2. Decrease the variable cost per unit of the large wrenches.
3. Decrease the heat treatment hours required for the large wrenches.

Example Exercise 25-10   Bottleneck Profit   3

Product A has a unit contribution margin of $15. Product B has a unit contribution margin of $20. Product A requires three furnace hours, while Product B requires five furnace hours. Determine the most profitable product, assuming the furnace is a constraint.

Follow My Example 25-10

	Product A	Product B
Unit contribution margin	$15	$20
Furnace hours per unit	÷ 3	÷ 5
Unit contribution margin per production bottleneck hour	$ 5	$ 4
Product A is the most profitable in using bottleneck resources.		

For Practice: PE 25-10A, PE 25-10B

Assume that the variable cost per unit and the heat treatment hours for the large wrench cannot be decreased. In this case, PrideCraft Tool might be able to increase the selling price of the large wrenches.

The price of the large wrench that would make it as profitable as the small wrench is determined as follows:[3]

$$\text{Unit Contribution Margin per Bottleneck Hour for Small Wrench} = \frac{\text{Revised Price of Large Wrench} - \text{Unit Variable Cost for Large Wrench}}{\text{Bottleneck Hours per Unit for Large Wrench}}$$

$$\$90 = \frac{\text{Revised Price of Large Wrench} - \$40}{8}$$

$$\$720 = \text{Revised Price of Large Wrench} - \$40$$

$$\$760 = \text{Revised Price of Large Wrench}$$

If the large wrench's price is increased to $760, it would provide the same unit contribution margin per bottleneck hour as the small wrench, as shown below.

$$\text{Unit Contribution Margin per Bottleneck Hour} = \frac{\text{Unit Contribution Margin}}{\text{Heat Treatment Hours per Unit}}$$

$$\text{Unit Contribution Margin per Bottleneck Hour} = \frac{\$760 - \$40}{8 \text{ hrs.}} = \$90 \text{ per hr.}$$

At a price of $760, PrideCraft Tool Company would be indifferent between producing and selling the small wrench or the large wrench. This assumes that there is unlimited demand for the products. If the market were unwilling to purchase the large wrench at a price of $760, then the company should produce and sell the small wrenches.

3 Assuming that the selling price of the large wrench cannot be increased, the same approach (equation) could be used to determine the decrease in variable cost per unit or decrease in bottleneck hours that is required to make the large wrench as profitable as the small wrench.

A P P E N D I X

Activity-Based Costing

In this chapter, it was indicated that activity-based costing may more accurately identify and trace factory overhead costs to activities and products. This appendix describes and illustrates how activity-based costing provides more accurate and useful factory overhead cost allocations.

Exhibit 13 illustrates an activity-based costing framework for Ruiz Company, which produces snowmobiles and lawnmowers. The activities used in producing snowmobiles and lawnmowers are as follows:

1. Fabrication, which consists of cutting metal to shape the product. This activity is machine intensive.
2. Assembly, which consists of manually assembling machined pieces into a final product. This activity is labor intensive.
3. Setup, which consists of changing tooling in machines in preparing to make a new product. Each production run requires a setup.
4. Quality control inspection, which consists of inspecting the product for conformance to specifications. Inspection requires product teardown and reassembly.
5. Engineering changes, which consist of processing changes in design or process specifications for a product. The document that initiates changing a product or process is called an *engineering change order (ECO)*.

Exhibit 13

Activity-Based Costing—Ruiz Company

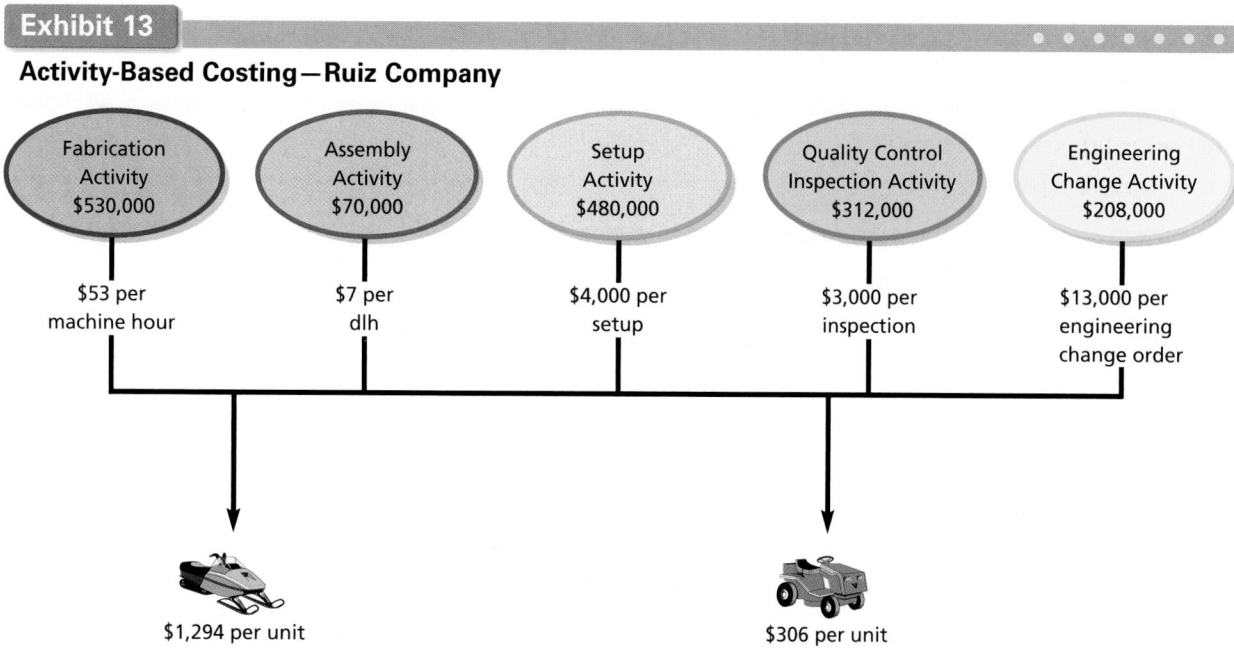

Snowmobiles are a new product for Ruiz Company, and engineers are still making minor design changes. Lawnmowers have been produced by Ruiz Company for many years. Additional information about the two products for Ruiz Company includes the following:

	Snowmobiles	Lawnmowers
Estimated units of total production	1,000 units	1,000 units
Estimated engineering change orders	12 change orders	4 change orders
Estimated setups	100 setups	20 setups
Units per production run	10 units (1,000/100 setups)	50 units (1,000/20 setups)
Quality control inspections	100 inspections (10%)	4 inspections (0.4%)

Each product also uses different amounts of machine and direct labor hours in the fabrication and assembly activities. The estimated activity-base usage, including machine and direct labor hours, is shown in Exhibit 14.

Exhibit 14

Estimated Activity-Base Usage—Ruiz Company

	Activities				
Products	Fabrication (machine hours)	Assembly (direct labor hours)	Setup	Quality Control Inspection	Engineering Change (orders)
Snowmobile	8,000 mh	2,000 dlh	100 setups	100 inspections	12 ECOs
Lawnmower	2,000	8,000	20	4	4
Total activity base	10,000 mh	10,000 dlh	120 setups	104 inspections	16 ECOs

The activity rates for each activity are determined as follows:

$$\text{Activity Rate} = \frac{\text{Budgeted Activity Cost}}{\text{Activity Base Usage}}$$

The activity rates for Ruiz Company are shown in Exhibit 15.

Exhibit 15

Activity Rates—Ruiz Company

Activity	Budgeted Activity Cost ÷	Activity Base Usage	=	Activity Rate
Fabrication	$530,000	10,000 mh		$ 53 per mh
Assembly	70,000	10,000 dlh		7 per dlh
Setup	480,000	120 setups		4,000 per setup
Quality control inspection	312,000	104 inspections		3,000 per inspection
Engineering change	208,000	16 engineering changes		13,000 per ECO

ArvinMeritor, Inc., discovered that incorrect factory overhead cost allocations had "overcosted" its products by roughly 20%. As a result, its product was overpriced and began losing market share.

The factory overhead costs for the snowmobile and lawnmower are computed by multiplying the activity-base usage by the activity rate. The sum of these costs for each product is the total factory overhead cost for the product. This amount is divided by the total number of units of estimated production to determine the factory overhead cost per unit. These computations are shown in Exhibit 16.

As shown in Exhibit 16, snowmobiles and lawnmowers consume factory overhead in different proportions. For example, snowmobiles consume a large proportion of the fabrication, setup, quality control inspections, and engineering change costs. Only under the activity-based approach are these differences reflected in the factory overhead cost allocations and, thus, in the product costs.

Exhibit 16

Activity-Base Product Cost Calculations

Activity	Snowmobile Activity-Base Usage	× Activity Rate	= Activity Cost	Lawnmower Activity-Base Usage	× Activity Rate	= Activity Cost
Fabrication	8,000 mh	$ 53	$ 424,000	2,000 mh	$ 53	$106,000
Assembly	2,000 dlh	7	14,000	8,000 dlh	7	56,000
Setup	100 setups	4,000	400,000	20 setups	4,000	80,000
Quality control inspection	100 inspections	3,000	300,000	4 inspections	3,000	12,000
Engineering change	12 ECOs	13,000	156,000	4 ECOs	13,000	52,000
Total factory overhead cost			$1,294,000			$306,000
Estimated units of production			÷ 1,000			÷ 1,000
Factory overhead cost per unit			$ 1,294			$ 306

1 Prepare differential analysis reports for a variety of managerial decisions.

Key Points	Key Learning Outcomes	Example Exercises	Practice Exercises
Differential analysis reports for leasing or selling, discontinuing a segment or product, making or buying, replacing equipment, processing or selling, and accepting business at a special price are illustrated in the text. Each analysis focuses on the differential revenues and/or costs of the alternative courses of action.	• Prepare a lease or sell differential analysis.	**25-1**	25-1A, 25-1B
	• Prepare a discontinued segment differential analysis.	**25-2**	25-2A, 25-2B
	• Prepare a make-or-buy differential analysis.	**25-3**	25-3A, 25-3B
	• Prepare an equipment replacement differential analysis.	**25-4**	25-4A, 25-4B
	• Prepare a process or sell differential analysis.	**25-5**	25-5A, 25-5B
	• Prepare an accept business at a special price differential analysis.	**25-6**	25-6A, 25-6B

2 Determine the selling price of a product, using the total cost, product cost, and variable cost concepts.

Key Points	Key Learning Outcomes	Example Exercises	Practice Exercises
The three cost concepts commonly used in applying the cost-plus approach to product pricing are the total cost, product cost, and variable cost concepts.	• Compute the markup percentage using the total cost concept.	**25-7**	25-7A, 25-7B
	• Compute the markup percentage using the product cost concept.	**25-8**	25-8A, 25-8B
	• Compute the markup percentage using the variable cost concept.	**25-9**	25-9A, 25-9B
Activity-based costing can be used to provide more accurate cost information in applying cost-plus concepts when indirect costs are significant. Target costing combines market-based methods with a cost-reduction emphasis.	• Describe activity-based costing.		
	• Define and describe target costing.		

3 Compute the relative profitability of products in bottleneck production processes.

Key Points	Key Learning Outcomes	Example Exercises	Practice Exercises
The profitability of a product in a bottleneck production environment is determined by dividing the unit contribution margin by the bottleneck hours per unit. The resulting measure indicates the product's profitability per hour of bottleneck use. This information can be used to support product pricing decisions.	• Compute the unit contribution margin per bottleneck hour.	**25-10**	25-10A, 25-10B
	• Compute the indifference price between products using the unit contribution margin per bottleneck hour.		

Key Terms

activity-based costing (ABC) (1137)
differential analysis (1120)
differential cost (1120)
differential income (or loss) (1120)

differential revenue (1120)
markup (1130)
opportunity cost (1126)
product cost concept (1133)
production bottleneck (1138)

sunk cost (1120)
target costing (1137)
theory of constraints (TOC) (1138)
total cost concept (1130)
variable cost concept (1134)

Illustrative Problem

Inez Company recently began production of a new product, M, which required the investment of $1,600,000 in assets. The costs of producing and selling 80,000 units of Product M are estimated as follows:

Variable costs:	
Direct materials	$ 10.00 per unit
Direct labor	6.00
Factory overhead	4.00
Selling and administrative expenses	5.00
Total	$ 25.00 per unit

Fixed costs:	
Factory overhead	$800,000
Selling and administrative expenses	400,000

Inez Company is currently considering establishing a selling price for Product M. The president of Inez Company has decided to use the cost-plus approach to product pricing and has indicated that Product M must earn a 10% rate of return on invested assets.

Instructions

1. Determine the amount of desired profit from the production and sale of Product M.
2. Assuming that the total cost concept is used, determine (a) the cost amount per unit, (b) the markup percentage, and (c) the selling price of Product M.
3. Assuming that the product cost concept is used, determine (a) the cost amount per unit, (b) the markup percentage, and (c) the selling price of Product M.
4. Assuming that the variable cost concept is used, determine (a) the cost amount per unit, (b) the markup percentage, and (c) the selling price of Product M.
5. Assume that for the current year, the selling price of Product M was $42 per unit. To date, 60,000 units have been produced and sold, and analysis of the domestic market indicates that 15,000 additional units are expected to be sold during the remainder of the year. Recently, Inez Company received an offer from Wong Inc. for 4,000 units of Product M at $28 each. Wong Inc. will market the units in Korea under its own brand name, and no selling and administrative expenses associated with the sale will be incurred by Inez Company. The additional business is not expected to affect the domestic sales of Product M, and the additional units could be produced during the current year, using existing capacity. (a) Prepare a differential analysis report of the proposed sale to Wong Inc. (b) Based on the differential analysis report in part (a), should the proposal be accepted?

Solution

1. $160,000 ($1,600,000 × 10%)
2. a. Total costs:

Variable ($25 × 80,000 units)	$2,000,000
Fixed ($800,000 + $400,000)	1,200,000
Total	$3,200,000

Cost amount per unit: $3,200,000/80,000 units = $40.00

b. Markup Percentage $= \dfrac{\text{Desired Profit}}{\text{Total Costs}}$

Markup Percentage $= \dfrac{\$160,000}{\$3,200,000} = 5\%$

c.
Cost amount per unit	$40.00
Markup ($40 × 5%)	2.00
Selling price	$42.00

3. a. Total manufacturing costs:

Variable ($20 × 80,000 units)	$1,600,000
Fixed factory overhead	800,000
Total	$2,400,000

Cost amount per unit: $2,400,000/80,000 units = $30.00

b. Markup Percentage $= \dfrac{\text{Desired Profit} + \text{Total Selling and Administrative Expenses}}{\text{Total Product Cost}}$

Markup Percentage $= \dfrac{\$160,000 + \$400,000 + (\$5 \times 80,000 \text{ units})}{\$2,400,000}$

Markup Percentage $= \dfrac{\$160,000 + \$400,000 + \$400,000}{\$2,400,000}$

Markup Percentage $= \dfrac{\$960,000}{\$2,400,000} = 40\%$

c.
Cost amount per unit	$30.00
Markup ($30 × 40%)	12.00
Selling price	$42.00

4. a. Variable cost amount per unit: $25.

Total variable costs: $25 × 80,000 units = $2,000,000

b. Markup Percentage $= \dfrac{\text{Desired Profit} + \text{Total Fixed Costs}}{\text{Total Variable Cost}}$

Markup Percentage $= \dfrac{\$160,000 + \$800,000 + \$400,000}{\$2,000,000}$

Markup Percentage $= \dfrac{\$1,360,000}{\$2,000,000} = 68\%$

c.
Cost amount per unit	$25.00
Markup ($25 × 68%)	17.00
Selling price	$42.00

5. a.

Proposal to Sell to Wong Inc.

Differential revenue from accepting offer:	
Revenue from sale of 4,000 additional units at $28	$112,000
Differential cost from accepting offer:	
Variable production costs of 4,000 additional units at $20	80,000
Differential income from accepting offer	$ 32,000

b. The proposal should be accepted.

Self-Examination Questions (Answers at End of Chapter)

1. Marlo Company is considering discontinuing a product. The costs of the product consist of $20,000 fixed costs and $15,000 variable costs. The variable operating expenses related to the product total $4,000. What is the differential cost?
A. $19,000
B. $15,000
C. $35,000
D. $39,000

2. Victor Company is considering disposing of equipment that was originally purchased for $200,000 and has $150,000 of accumulated depreciation to date. The same equipment would cost $310,000 to replace. What is the sunk cost?
A. $50,000
B. $150,000
C. $200,000
D. $310,000

3. Henry Company is considering spending $100,000 for a new grinding machine. This amount could be invested to yield a 12% return. What is the opportunity cost?
   A. $112,000
   B. $88,000
   C. $12,000
   D. $100,000

4. For which cost concept used in applying the cost-plus approach to product pricing are fixed manufacturing costs, fixed selling and administrative expenses, and desired profit allowed for in determining the markup?
   A. Total cost
   B. Product cost
   C. Variable cost
   D. Standard cost

5. Mendosa Company produces three products. All the products use a furnace operation, which is a production bottleneck. The following information is available:

	Product 1	Product 2	Product 3
Unit volume—March	1,000	1,500	1,000
Per-unit information:			
Sales price	$35	$33	$29
Variable cost	15	15	15
Unit contribution margin	$20	$18	$14
Furnace hours	4	3	2

From a profitability perspective, which product should be emphasized in April's advertising campaign?
A. Product 1
B. Product 2
C. Product 3
D. All three

Eye Openers

1. Explain the meaning of (a) differential revenue, (b) differential cost, and (c) differential income.
2. It was reported that Exabyte Corporation, a fast growing Colorado marketer of back-up tape drives, has decided to purchase key components of its product from others. For example, Sony Corporation of America provides Exabyte with mechanical decks, and Solectron Corporation provides circuit boards. A former chief executive officer of Exabyte stated, "If we'd tried to build our own plants, we could never have grown that fast or maybe survived." The decision to purchase key product components is an example of what type of decision illustrated in this chapter?
3. A company could sell a building for $250,000 or lease it for $2,500 per month. What would need to be considered in determining if the lease option would be preferred?
4. A chemical company has a commodity-grade and premium-grade product. Why might the company elect to process the commodity-grade product further to the premium-grade product?
5. A company accepts incremental business at a special price that exceeds the variable cost. What other issues must the company consider in deciding whether to accept the business?
6. A company fabricates a component at a cost of $6.00. A supplier offers to supply the same component for $5.50. Under what circumstances is it reasonable to purchase from the supplier?
7. Many fast-food restaurant chains, such as McDonald's, will occasionally discontinue restaurants in their system. What are some financial considerations in deciding to eliminate a store?
8. In the long run, the normal selling price must be set high enough to cover what factors?

9. Why might the use of ideal standards in applying the cost-plus approach to product pricing lead to setting product prices that are too low?
10. Although the cost-plus approach to product pricing may be used by management as a general guideline, what are some examples of other factors that managers should also consider in setting product prices?
11. What method of determining product cost may be appropriate in settings where the manufacturing process is complex?
12. How does the target cost concept differ from cost-plus approaches?
13. Under what circumstances is it appropriate to use the target cost concept?
14. What is a production bottleneck?
15. What is the appropriate measure of a product's value when a firm is operating under production bottlenecks?

Practice Exercises

PE 25-1A
Lease or sell
obj. 1
EE 25-1   p. 1122

Jefferson Company owns equipment with a cost of $95,000 and accumulated depreciation of $60,000 that can be sold for $40,000, less a 6% sales commission. Alternatively, the equipment can be leased by Jefferson Company for five years for a total of $42,000, at the end of which there is no residual value. In addition, repair, insurance, and property tax that would be incurred by Jefferson Company on the equipment would total $7,000 over the five years. Determine the differential income or loss from the lease alternative for Jefferson Company.

PE 25-1B
Lease or sell
obj. 1
EE 25-1   p. 1122

Grey Company owns a machine with a cost of $320,000 and accumulated depreciation of $60,000 that can be sold for $250,000, less a 5% sales commission. Alternatively, the machine can be leased by Grey Company for three years for a total of $268,000, at the end of which there is no residual value. In addition, repair, insurance, and property tax that would be incurred by Grey Company on the machine would total $24,000 over the three years. Determine the differential income or loss from the lease alternative for Grey Company.

PE 25-2A
Discontinue a segment
obj. 1
EE 25-2   p. 1124

Product L has revenue of $56,000, variable cost of goods sold of $29,000, variable selling expenses of $12,000, and fixed costs of $18,000, creating a loss from operations of $3,000.
a. Determine the differential income or loss from sales of Product L.
b. Should Product L be discontinued?

PE 25-2B
Discontinue a segment
obj. 1
EE 25-2   p. 1124

Product V has revenue of $204,000, variable cost of goods sold of $134,000, variable selling expenses of $74,000, and fixed costs of $14,000, creating a loss from operations of $18,000.
a. Determine the differential income or loss from sales of Product V.
b. Should Product V be discontinued?

PE 25-3A
Make or buy
obj. 1
EE 25-3   p. 1125

A company manufactures various sized plastic bottles for its medicinal product. The manufacturing cost for small bottles is $52 per unit (1,000 bottles), including fixed costs of $15 per unit. A proposal is offered to purchase small bottles from an outside source for $32 per unit, plus $7 per unit for freight. Provide a differential analysis of the outside purchase proposal.

PE 25-3B
Make or buy
obj. 1
EE 25-3   p. 1125

A restaurant bakes its own bread for $160 per unit (100 loaves), including fixed costs of $38 per unit. A proposal is offered to purchase bread from an outside source for $109 per unit, plus $8 per unit for delivery. Provide a differential analysis of the outside purchase proposal.

PE 25-4A
Replace equipment
obj. 1
EE 25-4   p. 1127

A machine with a book value of $48,000 has an estimated five-year life. A proposal is offered to sell the old machine for $50,000 and replace it with a new machine at a cost of $62,000. The new machine has a five-year life with no residual value. The new machine would reduce annual direct labor costs by $2,800. Provide a differential analysis on the proposal to replace the machine.

PE 25-4B
Replace equipment
obj. 1
EE 25-4   p. 1127

A machine with a book value of $250,000 has an estimated six-year life. A proposal is offered to sell the old machine for $243,000 and replace it with a new machine at a cost of $320,000. The new machine has a six-year life with no residual value. The new machine would reduce annual direct labor costs by $12,000. Provide a differential analysis on the proposal to replace the machine.

PE 25-5A
Process or sell
obj. 1
EE 25-5   p. 1128

Product D is produced for $60 per gallon, including a $5 per gallon fixed cost. Product D can be sold without additional processing for $85 per gallon, or processed further into Product E at an additional cost of $19 per gallon, including a $3 per gallon fixed cost. Product E can be sold for $105 per gallon. Provide a differential analysis for further processing into Product E.

PE 25-5B
Process or sell
obj. 1
EE 25-5 p. 1128

Product T is produced for $3.20 per pound, including a $0.20 per pound fixed cost. Product T can be sold without additional processing for $4.10 per pound, or processed further into Product U at an additional cost of $0.50 per pound, including a $0.12 per pound fixed cost. Product U can be sold for $4.45 per pound. Provide a differential analysis for further processing into Product U.

PE 25-6A
Accept business at special price
obj. 1
EE 25-6 p. 1129

Product A is normally sold for $6.50 per unit. A special price of $5.60 is offered for the export market. The variable production cost is $4.50 per unit. An additional export tariff of 25% of revenue must be paid for all export products. Determine the differential income or loss per unit from selling Product A for export.

PE 25-6B
Accept business at special price
obj. 1
EE 25-6 p. 1129

Product R is normally sold for $55 per unit. A special price of $46 is offered for the export market. The variable production cost is $32 per unit. An additional export tariff of 15% of revenue must be paid for all export products. Determine the differential income or loss per unit from selling Product R for export.

PE 25-7A
Total cost markup percentage
obj. 2
EE 25-7 p. 1132

Eden Garden Tools Inc. produces and sells home and garden tools and equipment. A lawnmower has a total cost of $150 per unit, of which $100 is product cost and $50 is selling and administrative expenses. In addition, the total cost of $150 is made up of $125 variable cost and $25 fixed cost. The desired profit is $30 per unit. Determine the markup percentage on total cost.

PE 25-7B
Total cost markup percentage
obj. 2
EE 25-7 p. 1132

Crescent Lighting Inc. produces and sells lighting fixtures. An entry light has a total cost of $80 per unit, of which $36 is product cost and $44 is selling and administrative expenses. In addition, the total cost of $80 is made up of $30 variable cost and $50 fixed cost. The desired profit is $10 per unit. Determine the markup percentage on total cost. Round to one decimal place.

PE 25-8A
Product cost markup percentage
obj. 2
EE 25-8 p. 1134

Eden Garden Tools Inc. produces and sells home and garden tools and equipment. A lawnmower has a total cost of $150 per unit, of which $100 is product cost and $50 is selling and administrative expenses. In addition, the total cost of $150 is made up of $125 variable cost and $25 fixed cost. The desired profit is $30 per unit. Determine the markup percentage on product cost.

PE 25-8B
Product cost markup percentage
obj. 2
EE 25-8 p. 1134

Crescent Lighting Inc. produces and sells lighting fixtures. An entry light has a total cost of $80 per unit, of which $36 is product cost and $44 is selling and administrative expenses. In addition, the total cost of $80 is made up of $30 variable cost and $50 fixed cost. The desired profit is $10 per unit. Determine the markup percentage on product cost.

PE 25-9A
Variable cost markup percentage
obj. 2
EE 25-9 p. 1136

Eden Garden Tools Inc. produces and sells home and garden tools and equipment. A lawnmower has a total cost of $150 per unit, of which $100 is product cost and $50 is selling and administrative expenses. In addition, the total cost of $150 is made up of $125 variable cost and $25 fixed cost. The desired profit is $30 per unit. Determine the markup percentage on variable cost.

PE 25-9B
Variable cost markup percentage
obj. 2
EE 25-9 p. 1136

Crescent Lighting Inc. produces and sells lighting fixtures. An entry light has a total cost of $80 per unit, of which $36 is product cost and $44 is selling and administrative expenses. In addition, the total cost of $80 is made up of $30 variable cost and $50 fixed cost. The desired profit is $10 per unit. Determine the markup percentage on variable cost.

PE 25-10A
Bottleneck profit

obj. 3

EE 25-10 p. 1139

Product K has a unit contribution margin of $240. Product L has a unit contribution margin of $200. Product K requires eight furnace hours, while Product L requires five furnace hours. Determine the most profitable product, assuming the furnace is a constraint.

PE 25-10B
Bottleneck profit

obj. 3

EE 25-10 p. 1139

Product A has a unit contribution margin of $45. Product B has a unit contribution margin of $60. Product A requires three testing hours, while Product B requires five testing hours. Determine the most profitable product, assuming the testing is a constraint.

Exercises

EX 25-1
Lease or sell decision

obj. 1

✔ a. Differential
revenue from lease,
$20,000

Inman Construction Company is considering selling excess machinery with a book value of $280,000 (original cost of $400,000 less accumulated depreciation of $120,000) for $292,000, less a 5% brokerage commission. Alternatively, the machinery can be leased for a total of $312,000 for five years, after which it is expected to have no residual value. During the period of the lease, Inman Construction Company's costs of repairs, insurance, and property tax expenses are expected to be $36,000.

a. Prepare a differential analysis report, dated January 3, 2010, for the lease or sell decision.
b. ━━━━▶ On the basis of the data presented, would it be advisable to lease or sell the machinery? Explain.

EX 25-2
Differential analysis report for a discontinued product

obj. 1

✔ a. Differential
variable costs,
$227,280

A condensed income statement by product line for British Beverage Inc. indicated the following for Royal Cola for the past year:

Sales	$254,000
Cost of goods sold	122,000
Gross profit	$132,000
Operating expenses	156,000
Loss from operations	$ (24,000)

It is estimated that 16% of the cost of goods sold represents fixed factory overhead costs and that 20% of the operating expenses are fixed. Since Royal Cola is only one of many products, the fixed costs will not be materially affected if the product is discontinued.

a. Prepare a differential analysis report, dated March 3, 2010, for the proposed discontinuance of Royal Cola.
b. ━━━━▶ Should Royal Cola be retained? Explain.

EX 25-3
Differential analysis report for a discontinued product

obj. 1

✔ a. Differential
income: bowls,
$17,980

The condensed product-line income statement for Suffolk China Ware Company for the month of December is as follows:

Suffolk China Ware Company
Product-Line Income Statement
For the Month Ended December 31, 2010

	Bowls	Plates	Cups
Sales	$54,000	$68,500	$24,500
Cost of goods sold	22,400	31,700	11,900
Gross profit	$31,600	$36,800	$12,600
Selling and administrative expenses	28,300	25,300	20,400
Income from operations	$ 3,300	$11,500	$ (7,800)

Fixed costs are 15% of the cost of goods sold and 40% of the selling and administrative expenses. Suffolk China Ware assumes that fixed costs would not be materially affected if the Cups line were discontinued.

a. Prepare a differential analysis report for all three products for December 2010.
b. ———► Should the Cups line be retained? Explain.

EX 25-4
Segment analysis,
Charles Schwab
Corporation

obj. 1

The Charles Schwab Corporation is one of the more innovative brokerage and financial service companies in the United States. The company recently provided information about its major business segments as follows (in millions):

	Individual Investor	Institutional Investor	Corporate and Retirement Services
Revenues	$3,352	$1,121	$506
Income from operations	1,237	482	139
Depreciation	98	25	15

a. ———► How do you believe Schwab defines the difference between the "Individual Investor" and "Institutional Investor" segments?
b. Provide a specific example of a variable and fixed cost in the "Individual Investor" segment.
c. Estimate the contribution margin for each segment.
d. If Schwab decided to sell its "Institutional Investor" accounts to another company, estimate how much operating income would decline.

EX 25-5
Decision to
discontinue a
product

obj. 1

On the basis of the following data, the general manager of Sole Mates Inc. decided to discontinue Children's Shoes because it reduced income from operations by $28,000. What is the flaw in this decision?

Sole Mates Inc.
Product-Line Income Statement
For the Year Ended August 31, 2010

	Children's Shoes	Men's Shoes	Women's Shoes	Total
Sales	$170,000	$300,000	$500,000	$970,000
Costs of goods sold:				
Variable costs	$100,000	$150,000	$220,000	$470,000
Fixed costs	50,000	60,000	120,000	230,000
Total cost of goods sold	$150,000	$210,000	$340,000	$700,000
Gross profit	$ 20,000	$ 90,000	$160,000	$270,000
Selling and adminstrative expenses:				
Variable selling and admin. expenses	$ 30,000	$ 45,000	$ 95,000	$170,000
Fixed selling and admin. expenses	18,000	20,000	25,000	63,000
Total selling and admin. expenses	$ 48,000	$ 65,000	$120,000	$233,000
Income (loss) from operations	$(28,000)	$ 25,000	$ 40,000	$ 37,000

EX 25-6
Make-or-buy decision

obj. 1

✔ a. Cost savings
from making, $6.20
per case

Companion Computer Company has been purchasing carrying cases for its portable computers at a delivered cost of $68 per unit. The company, which is currently operating below full capacity, charges factory overhead to production at the rate of 40% of direct labor cost. The fully absorbed unit costs to produce comparable carrying cases are expected to be as follows:

Direct materials	$25.00
Direct labor	32.00
Factory overhead (40% of direct labor)	12.80
Total cost per unit	$69.80

If Companion Computer Company manufactures the carrying cases, fixed factory overhead costs will not increase and variable factory overhead costs associated with the cases are expected to be 15% of the direct labor costs.

a. Prepare a differential analysis report, dated October 11, 2010, for the make-or-buy decision.
b. ———► On the basis of the data presented, would it be advisable to make the carrying cases or to continue buying them? Explain.

EX 25-7
Make-or-buy decision

obj. 1

The Theater Arts Guild of Chicago (TAG-C) employs five people in its Publication Department. These people lay out pages for pamphlets, brochures, and other publications for the TAG-C productions. The pages are delivered to an outside company for printing. The company is considering an outside publication service for the layout work. The outside service is quoting a price of $15 per layout page. The budget for the Publication Department for 2010 is as follows:

Salaries	$220,000
Benefits	35,000
Supplies	30,000
Office expenses	25,000
Office depreciation	30,000
Computer depreciation	22,000
Total	$362,000

The department expects to lay out 20,000 pages for 2010. The computers used by the department have an estimated residual value of $7,000. The Publication Department office space would be used for future administrative needs, if the department's function were purchased from the outside.

a. Prepare a differential analysis report, dated December 15, 2009, for the make-or-buy decision, considering the 2010 differential revenues and costs.
b. ▬▬▶ On the basis of your analysis in part (a), should the page layout work be purchased from an outside company?
c. ▬▬▶ What additional considerations might factor into the decision making?

EX 25-8
Machine replacement decision

obj. 1

A company is considering replacing an old piece of machinery, which cost $600,000 and has $350,000 of accumulated depreciation to date, with a new machine that costs $450,000. The old equipment could be sold for $72,000. The annual variable production costs associated with the old machine are estimated to be $165,000 for eight years. The annual variable production costs for the new machine are estimated to be $112,750 for eight years.

a. Determine the total and annualized differential income or loss anticipated from replacing the old machine.
b. What is the sunk cost in this situation?

EX 25-9
Differential analysis report for machine replacement

obj. 1

✔ a. Annual
differential increase
in costs, $7,200

Singapore Digital Components Company assembles circuit boards by using a manually operated machine to insert electronic components. The original cost of the machine is $60,000, the accumulated depreciation is $24,000, its remaining useful life is five years, and its residual value is negligible. On February 20, 2010, a proposal was made to replace the present manufacturing procedure with a fully automatic machine that will cost $111,000. The automatic machine has an estimated useful life of five years and no significant residual value. For use in evaluating the proposal, the accountant accumulated the following annual data on present and proposed operations:

	Present Operations	Proposed Operations
Sales	$290,000	$290,000
Direct materials	$ 86,000	$ 86,000
Direct labor	40,000	—
Power and maintenance	8,000	30,000
Taxes, insurance, etc.	4,000	7,000
Selling and administrative expenses	65,000	65,000
Total expenses	$203,000	$188,000

a. Prepare a differential analysis report for the proposal to replace the machine. Include in the analysis both the net differential change in costs anticipated over the five years and the net annual differential change in costs anticipated.
b. Based only on the data presented, should the proposal be accepted?
c. ▬▬▶ What are some of the other factors that should be considered before a final decision is made?

EX 25-10

Sell or process further

obj. 1

✔ a. $205

Bunyon Lumber Company incurs a cost of $490 per hundred board feet in processing certain "rough-cut" lumber, which it sells for $635 per hundred board feet. An alternative is to produce a "finished cut" at a total processing cost of $565 per hundred board feet, which can be sold for $840 per hundred board feet. What is the amount of (a) the differential revenue, (b) differential cost, and (c) differential income for processing rough-cut lumber into finished cut?

EX 25-11

Sell or process further

obj. 1

Seattle Roast Coffee Company produces Columbian coffee in batches of 8,000 pounds. The standard quantity of materials required in the process is 8,000 pounds, which cost $5.00 per pound. Columbian coffee can be sold without further processing for $10.80 per pound. Columbian coffee can also be processed further to yield Decaf Columbian, which can be sold for $12.50 per pound. The processing into Decaf Columbian requires additional processing costs of $10,500 per batch. The additional processing will also cause a 5% loss of product due to evaporation.

a. Prepare a differential analysis report for the decision to sell or process further.
b. ➡ Should Seattle Roast sell Columbian coffee or process further and sell Decaf Columbian?
c. Determine the price of Decaf Columbian that would cause neither an advantage or disadvantage for processing further and selling Decaf Columbian.

EX 25-12

Decision on accepting additional business

obj. 1

✔ a. Differential income, $126,000

Down Home Jeans Co. has an annual plant capacity of 65,000 units, and current production is 45,000 units. Monthly fixed costs are $40,000, and variable costs are $22 per unit. The present selling price is $35 per unit. On March 18, 2010, the company received an offer from Fields Company for 18,000 units of the product at $29 each. Fields Company will market the units in a foreign country under its own brand name. The additional business is not expected to affect the domestic selling price or quantity of sales of Down Home Jeans Co.

a. Prepare a differential analysis report for the proposed sale to Fields Company.
b. ➡ Briefly explain the reason why accepting this additional business will increase operating income.
c. What is the minimum price per unit that would produce a contribution margin?

EX 25-13

Accepting business at a special price

obj. 1

Power Serve Company expects to operate at 85% of productive capacity during April. The total manufacturing costs for April for the production of 30,000 batteries are budgeted as follows:

Direct materials	$285,000
Direct labor	104,000
Variable factory overhead	31,000
Fixed factory overhead	58,000
Total manufacturing costs	$478,000

The company has an opportunity to submit a bid for 2,000 batteries to be delivered by April 30 to a government agency. If the contract is obtained, it is anticipated that the additional activity will not interfere with normal production during April or increase the selling or administrative expenses. What is the unit cost below which Power Serve Company should not go in bidding on the government contract?

EX 25-14

Decision on accepting additional business

obj. 1

✔ a. Differential revenue, $1,875,000

Roadworthy Tire and Rubber Company has capacity to produce 170,000 tires. Roadworthy presently produces and sells 130,000 tires for the North American market at a price of $90 per tire. Roadworthy is evaluating a special order from a European automobile company, Euro Motors. Euro is offering to buy 25,000 tires for $75 per tire. Roadworthy's accounting system indicates that the total cost per tire is as follows:

Direct materials	$32
Direct labor	8
Factory overhead (60% variable)	25
Selling and administrative expenses (35% variable)	20
Total	$85

Roadworthy pays a selling commission equal to 5% of the selling price on North American orders, which is included in the variable portion of the selling and administrative expenses. However, this special order would not have a sales commission. If the order was accepted, the tires would be shipped overseas for an additional shipping cost of $6.00 per tire. In addition, Euro has made the order conditional on receiving European safety certification. Roadworthy estimates that this certification would cost $125,000.

a. Prepare a differential analysis report dated May 4, 2010, for the proposed sale to Euro Motors.
b. What is the minimum price per unit that would be financially acceptable to Roadworthy?

EX 25-15
Total cost concept of product costing

obj. 2

✔ d. $318

MyPhone Inc. uses the total cost concept of applying the cost-plus approach to product pricing. The costs of producing and selling 5,000 units of cellular phones are as follows:

Variable costs:		Fixed costs:	
Direct materials	$125 per unit	Factory overhead	$215,000
Direct labor	45	Selling and adm. exp.	75,000
Factory overhead	40		
Selling and adm. exp.	30		
Total	$240 per unit		

MyPhone desires a profit equal to a 25% rate of return on invested assets of $400,000.

a. Determine the amount of desired profit from the production and sale of cellular phones.
b. Determine the total costs and the cost amount per unit for the production and sale of 5,000 units of cellular phones.
c. Determine the total cost markup percentage (rounded to two decimal places) for cellular phones.
d. Determine the selling price of cellular phones. Round to the nearest dollar.

EX 25-16
Product cost concept of product pricing

obj. 2

✔ b. 25.69%

Based on the data presented in Exercise 25-15, assume that MyPhone Inc. uses the product cost concept of applying the cost-plus approach to product pricing.

a. Determine the total manufacturing costs and the cost amount per unit for the production and sale of 5,000 units of cellular phones.
b. Determine the product cost markup percentage (rounded to two decimal places) for cellular phones.
c. Determine the selling price of cellular phones. Round to the nearest dollar.

EX 25-17
Variable cost concept of product pricing

obj. 2

✔ b. 32.5%

Based on the data presented in Exercise 25-15, assume that MyPhone Inc. uses the variable cost concept of applying the cost-plus approach to product pricing.

a. Determine the variable costs and the cost amount per unit for the production and sale of 5,000 units of cellular phones.
b. Determine the variable cost markup percentage (rounded to two decimal places) for cellular phones.
c. Determine the selling price of cellular phones. Round to the nearest dollar.

EX 25-18
Target costing

obj. 2

Toyota Motor Corporation uses target costing. Assume that Toyota marketing personnel estimate that the competitive selling price for the Camry in the upcoming model year will need to be $22,000. Assume further that the Camry's total unit cost for the upcoming model year is estimated to be $18,100 and that Toyota requires a 20% profit margin on selling price (which is equivalent to a 25% markup on total cost).

a. What price will Toyota establish for the Camry for the upcoming model year?
b. ➡ What impact will target costing have on Toyota, given the assumed information?

EX 25-19
Target costing
obj. 2
✔ b. $16

Laser Cast, Inc., manufactures color laser printers. Model A200 presently sells for $400 and has a total product cost of $320, as follows:

Direct materials	$230
Direct labor	60
Factory overhead	30
Total	$320

It is estimated that the competitive selling price for color laser printers of this type will drop to $380 next year. Laser Cast has established a target cost to maintain its historical markup percentage on product cost. Engineers have provided the following cost reduction ideas:

1. Purchase a plastic printer cover with snap-on assembly. This will reduce the amount of direct labor by nine minutes per unit.
2. Add an inspection step that will add six minutes per unit of direct labor but reduce the materials cost by $8 per unit.
3. Decrease the cycle time of the injection molding machine from four minutes to three minutes per part. Thirty percent of the direct labor and 42% of the factory overhead is related to running injection molding machines.

The direct labor rate is $25 per hour.

a. Determine the target cost for Model A200 assuming that the historical markup on product cost is maintained.
b. Determine the required cost reduction.
c. Evaluate the three engineering improvements to determine if the required cost reduction (drift) can be achieved.

EX 25-20
Product decisions under bottlenecked operations
obj. 3

Armstrong Alloys Inc. has three grades of metal product, Type 5, Type 10, and Type 20. Financial data for the three grades are as follows:

	Type 5	Type 10	Type 20
Revenues	$36,000	$40,000	$22,000
Variable cost	$22,500	$20,000	$15,000
Fixed cost	6,000	6,000	6,000
Total cost	$28,500	$26,000	$21,000
Income from operations	$ 7,500	$14,000	$ 1,000
Number of units	÷ 5,000	÷ 5,000	÷ 5,000
Income from operations per unit	$ 1.50	$ 2.80	$ 0.20

Armstrong's operations require all three grades to be melted in a furnace before being formed. The furnace runs 24 hours a day, 7 days a week, and is a production bottleneck. The furnace hours required per unit of each product are as follows:

Type 5:	5 hours
Type 10:	10 hours
Type 20:	5 hours

The Marketing Department is considering a new marketing and sales campaign.
Which product should be emphasized in the marketing and sales campaign in order to maximize profitability?

EX 25-21
Product decisions under bottlenecked operations
obj. 3
✔ a. Total income from operations, $88,000

Ohio Glass Company manufactures three types of safety plate glass: large, medium, and small. All three products have high demand. Thus, Ohio Glass is able to sell all the safety glass that it can make. The production process includes an autoclave operation, which is a pressurized heat treatment. The autoclave is a production bottleneck. Total fixed costs are $74,000. In addition, the following information is available about the three products:

	Large	**Medium**	**Small**
Unit selling price	$120	$100	$90
Unit variable cost	96	85	75
Unit contribution margin	$ 24	$ 15	$15
Autoclave hours per unit	4	2	1
Total process hours per unit	8	6	3
Budgeted units of production	3,000	3,000	3,000

a. Determine the contribution margin by glass type and the total company income from operations for the budgeted units of production.
b. Prepare an analysis showing which product is the most profitable per bottleneck hour.

EX 25-22
Product pricing under bottlenecked operations

obj. 3

✔ Medium, $115

Based on the data presented in Exercise 25-21, assume that Ohio Glass wanted to price all products so that they produced the same profit potential as the highest profit product. Thus, determine the prices for each of the products so that they would produce a profit equal to the highest profit product.

Appendix
EX 25-23
Activity-based costing

✔ Activity cost per stationary bicycle, $71.85

Cardio Care Inc. manufactures stationary bicycles and rowing machines. The products are produced in the Fabrication and Assembly production departments. In addition to production activities, several other activities are required to produce the two products. These activities and their associated activity rates are as follows:

Activity	Activity Rate
Fabrication	$24 per machine hour (mh)
Assembly	$12 per direct labor hour (dlh)
Setup	$40 per setup
Inspecting	$22 per inspection
Production scheduling	$14 per production order
Purchasing	$ 6 per purchase order

The activity-base usage quantities and units produced for each product were as follows:

	Stationary Bicycle	**Rowing Machine**
Machine hours	1,950	975
Direct labor hours	436	162
Setups	48	15
Inspections	725	375
Production orders	68	20
Purchase orders	166	126
Units produced	1,000	1,000

Use the activity rate and usage information to compute the total activity costs and the activity costs per unit for each product.

Appendix
EX 25-24
Activity-based costing

✔ b. Custom, $126.10 per unit

Titan Industries manufactures two types of electrical power units, custom and standard, which involve four overhead activities—production setup, procurement, quality control, and materials management. An activity analysis of the overhead revealed the following estimated costs and activity bases for these activities:

Activity	Cost	Activity Base
Production setup	$ 54,000	Number of setups
Procurement	122,000	Number of purchase orders (PO)
Quality control	170,000	Number of inspections
Materials management	125,000	Number of components
Total	$471,000	

The activity-base usage quantities for each product are as follows:

	Setups	Purchase Orders	Inspections	Components	Unit Volume
Custom	375	900	1,800	300	3,000
Standard	125	100	200	200	3,000
Total	500	1,000	2,000	500	6,000

a. Determine an activity rate for each activity.
b. Assign activity costs to each product, and determine the unit activity cost using the activity rates from part (a).
c. Assume that each product required one direct labor hour per unit. Determine the per-unit cost if factory overhead is allocated on the basis of direct labor hours.
d. ➤ Explain why the answers in parts (b) and (c) are different.

Problems Series A

PR 25-1A
Differential analysis report involving opportunity costs
obj. 1

On March 1, Midway Distribution Company is considering leasing a building and buying the necessary equipment to operate a public warehouse. Alternatively, the company could use the funds to invest in $750,000 of 7% U.S. Treasury bonds that mature in 14 years. The bonds could be purchased at face value. The following data have been assembled:

Cost of equipment	$750,000
Life of equipment	14 years
Estimated residual value of equipment	$76,000
Yearly costs to operate the warehouse, excluding depreciation of equipment	$195,000
Yearly expected revenues—years 1–7	$330,000
Yearly expected revenues—years 8–14	$280,000

Instructions
1. Prepare a report as of March 1, 2010, presenting a differential analysis of the proposed operation of the warehouse for the 14 years as compared with present conditions.
2. Based on the results disclosed by the differential analysis, should the proposal be accepted?
3. If the proposal is accepted, what is the total estimated income from operations of the warehouse for the 14 years?

PR 25-2A
Differential analysis report for machine replacement proposal
obj. 1

Flint Tooling Company is considering replacing a machine that has been used in its factory for two years. Relevant data associated with the operations of the old machine and the new machine, neither of which has any estimated residual value, are as follows:

Old Machine

Cost of machine, eight-year life	$48,000
Annual depreciation (straight-line)	6,000
Annual manufacturing costs, excluding depreciation	14,500
Annual nonmanufacturing operating expenses	2,900
Annual revenue	29,600
Current estimated selling price of the machine	18,000

New Machine

Cost of machine, six-year life	$58,500
Annual depreciation (straight-line)	9,750
Estimated annual manufacturing costs, exclusive of depreciation	5,200

Annual nonmanufacturing operating expenses and revenue are not expected to be affected by purchase of the new machine.

Instructions
1. Prepare a differential analysis report as of May 22, 2010, comparing operations utilizing the new machine with operations using the present equipment. The analysis should indicate the differential income that would result over the six-year period if the new machine is acquired.
2. ▬▬▬► List other factors that should be considered before a final decision is reached.

PR 25-3A
Differential analysis report for sales promotion proposal

obj. 1

✔ 1. Differential income, tennis shoe, $225,000

Glide Shoe Company is planning a one-month campaign for May to promote sales of one of its two shoe products. A total of $125,000 has been budgeted for advertising, contests, redeemable coupons, and other promotional activities. The following data have been assembled for their possible usefulness in deciding which of the products to select for the campaign.

	Tennis Shoe	Walking Shoe
Unit selling price	$110	$100
Unit production costs:		
Direct materials	$ 20	$ 22
Direct labor	8	9
Variable factory overhead	5	6
Fixed factory overhead	12	10
Total unit production costs	$ 45	$ 47
Unit variable selling expenses	7	5
Unit fixed selling expenses	16	12
Total unit costs	$ 68	$ 64
Operating income per unit	$ 42	$ 36

No increase in facilities would be necessary to produce and sell the increased output. It is anticipated that 5,000 additional units of tennis shoes or 6,000 additional units of walking shoes could be sold without changing the unit selling price of either product.

Instructions
1. Prepare a differential analysis report as of May 13, 2010, presenting the additional revenue and additional costs anticipated from the promotion of tennis shoes and walking shoes.
2. ▬▬▬► The sales manager had tentatively decided to promote walking shoes, estimating that operating income would be increased by $91,000 ($36 operating income per unit for 6,000 units, less promotion expenses of $125,000). The manager also believed that the selection of tennis shoes would increase operating income by $85,000 ($42 operating income per unit for 5,000 units, less promotion expenses of $125,000). State briefly your reasons for supporting or opposing the tentative decision.

PR 25-4A
Differential analysis report for further processing

obj. 1

✔ 1. Differential revenue, $25,300

The management of Allegheny Valley Aluminum Co. is considering whether to process aluminum ingot further into rolled aluminum. Rolled aluminum can be sold for $1,600 per ton, and ingot can be sold without further processing for $950 per ton. Ingot is produced in batches of 66 tons by smelting 400 tons of bauxite, which costs $450 per ton. Rolled aluminum will require additional processing costs of $425 per ton of ingot, and 1.2 tons of ingot will produce 1 ton of rolled aluminum (due to trim losses).

Instructions
1. Prepare a report as of December 20, 2010, presenting a differential analysis associated with the further processing of aluminum ingot to produce rolled aluminum.
2. ▬▬▬► Briefly report your recommendations.

PR 25-5A
Product pricing using the cost-plus approach concepts; differential analysis report for accepting additional business

Night Watch Company recently began production of a new product, the halogen light, which required the investment of $500,000 in assets. The costs of producing and selling 12,000 halogen lights are estimated as follows:

objs. 1, 2

✔ 3. b. Markup
percentage, 28%

Variable costs per unit:		Fixed costs:	
Direct materials	$22	Factory overhead	$120,000
Direct labor	12	Selling and administrative expenses	60,000
Factory overhead	6		
Selling and administrative expenses	4		
Total	$44		

Night Watch Company is currently considering establishing a selling price for the halogen light. The president of Night Watch Company has decided to use the cost-plus approach to product pricing and has indicated that the halogen light must earn a 12% rate of return on invested assets.

Instructions

1. Determine the amount of desired profit from the production and sale of the halogen light.
2. Assuming that the total cost concept is used, determine (a) the cost amount per unit, (b) the markup percentage (rounded to two decimal places), and (c) the selling price of the halogen light (rounded to nearest whole dollar).
3. Assuming that the product cost concept is used, determine (a) the cost amount per unit, (b) the markup percentage, and (c) the selling price of the halogen light.
4. Assuming that the variable cost concept is used, determine (a) the cost amount per unit, (b) the markup percentage (rounded to two decimal places), and (c) the selling price of the halogen light (rounded to nearest whole dollar).
5. ━━━▶ Comment on any additional considerations that could influence establishing the selling price for the halogen light.
6. Assume that as of September 1, 2010, 7,000 units of halogen light have been produced and sold during the current year. Analysis of the domestic market indicates that 3,000 additional units of the halogen light are expected to be sold during the remainder of the year at the normal product price determined under the total cost concept. On September 5, Night Watch Company received an offer from Forever Glow Inc. for 2,000 units of the halogen light at $45 each. Forever Glow Inc. will market the units in Japan under its own brand name, and no selling and administrative expenses associated with the sale will be incurred by Night Watch Company. The additional business is not expected to affect the domestic sales of the halogen light, and the additional units could be produced using existing capacity.
   a. Prepare a differential analysis report of the proposed sale to Forever Glow Inc.
   b. Based on the differential analysis report in part (a), should the proposal be accepted?

PR 25-6A
Product pricing and
profit analysis with
bottleneck operations

objs. 1, 3

✔ 1. Ethylene, $34

Delaware Bay Chemical Company produces three products: ethylene, butane, and ester. Each of these products has high demand in the market, and Delaware Bay Chemical is able to sell as much as it can produce of all three. The reaction operation is a bottleneck in the process and is running at 100% of capacity. Delaware Bay wants to improve chemical operation profitability. The variable conversion cost is $7 per process hour. The fixed cost is $550,000. In addition, the cost analyst was able to determine the following information about the three products:

	Ethylene	Butane	Ester
Budgeted units produced	9,000	9,000	9,000
Total process hours per unit	3	3	2
Reactor hours per unit	1.0	0.8	0.5
Unit selling price	$165	$128	$115
Direct materials cost per unit	$110	$75	$85

The reaction operation is part of the total process for each of these three products. Thus, for example, 1.0 of the 3 hours required to process ethylene are associated with the reactor.

Instructions

1. Determine the unit contribution margin for each product.
2. Provide an analysis to determine the relative product profitabilities, assuming that the reactor is a bottleneck.

3. Assume that management wishes to improve profitability by increasing prices on selected products. At what price would ethylene and ester need to be offered in order to produce the same relative profitability as butane?

Problems Series B

PR 25-1B
Differential analysis report involving opportunity costs

obj. 1

On November 1, Essence Stores Inc. is considering leasing a building and purchasing the necessary equipment to operate a retail store. Alternatively, the company could use the funds to invest in $140,000 of 5% U.S. Treasury bonds that mature in 16 years. The bonds could be purchased at face value. The following data have been assembled:

Cost of store equipment	$140,000
Life of store equipment	16 years
Estimated residual value of store equipment	$15,000
Yearly costs to operate the store, excluding depreciation of store equipment	$62,000
Yearly expected revenues—years 1–8	$78,000
Yearly expected revenues—years 9–16	$72,000

Instructions
1. Prepare a report as of November 1, 2010, presenting a differential analysis of the proposed operation of the store for the 16 years as compared with present conditions.
2. Based on the results disclosed by the differential analysis, should the proposal be accepted?
3. If the proposal is accepted, what would be the total estimated income from operations of the store for the 16 years?

PR 25-2B
Differential analysis report for machine replacement proposal

obj. 1

Golden Printing Company is considering replacing a machine that has been used in its factory for four years. Relevant data associated with the operations of the old machine and the new machine, neither of which has any estimated residual value, are as follows:

Old Machine	
Cost of machine, 10-year life	$126,000
Annual depreciation (straight-line)	12,600
Annual manufacturing costs, excluding depreciation	42,500
Annual nonmanufacturing operating expenses	12,300
Annual revenue	95,000
Current estimated selling price of machine	32,400

New Machine	
Cost of machine, six-year life	$144,000
Annual depreciation (straight-line)	24,000
Estimated annual manufacturing costs, exclusive of depreciation	18,900

Annual nonmanufacturing operating expenses and revenue are not expected to be affected by purchase of the new machine.

Instructions
1. Prepare a differential analysis report as of August 13, 2010, comparing operations utilizing the new machine with operations using the present equipment. The analysis should indicate the total differential income that would result over the six-year period if the new machine is acquired.
2. ➤ List other factors that should be considered before a final decision is reached.

PR 25-3B
**Differential analysis
report for sales
promotion proposal**

obj. 1

✔ 1. Moisturizer
differential income,
$177,000

Belle Cosmetics Company is planning a one-month campaign for June to promote sales of one of its two cosmetics products. A total of $120,000 has been budgeted for advertising, contests, redeemable coupons, and other promotional activities. The following data have been assembled for their possible usefulness in deciding which of the products to select for the campaign:

	Moisturizer	Perfume
Unit selling price	$52	$68
Unit production costs:		
Direct materials	$ 9	$11
Direct labor	2	3
Variable factory overhead	3	4
Fixed factory overhead	5	6
Total unit production costs	$19	$24
Unit variable selling expenses	11	15
Unit fixed selling expenses	4	8
Total unit costs	$34	$47
Operating income per unit	$18	$21

No increase in facilities would be necessary to produce and sell the increased output. It is anticipated that 11,000 additional units of moisturizer or 9,000 additional units of perfume could be sold without changing the unit selling price of either product.

Instructions
1. Prepare a differential analysis report as of June 15, 2010, presenting the additional revenue and additional costs anticipated from the promotion of moisturizer and perfume.
2. ▬▬▬▬ The sales manager had tentatively decided to promote moisturizer, estimating that operating income would be increased by $78,000 ($18 operating income per unit for 11,000 units, less promotion expenses of $120,000). The manager also believed that the selection of perfume would have less of an impact on operating income, $69,000 ($21 operating income per unit for 9,000 units, less promotion expenses of $120,000). State briefly your reasons for supporting or opposing the tentative decision.

PR 25-4B
**Differential analysis
report for further
processing**

obj. 1

✔ 1. Differential
revenue, $13,050

The management of Caribbean Sugar Company is considering whether to process further raw sugar into refined sugar. Refined sugar can be sold for $1.90 per pound, and raw sugar can be sold without further processing for $1.10 per pound. Raw sugar is produced in batches of 27,000 pounds by processing 90,000 pounds of sugar cane, which costs $0.25 per pound. Refined sugar will require additional processing costs of $0.35 per pound of raw sugar, and 1.2 pounds of raw sugar will produce 1 pound of refined sugar.

Instructions
1. Prepare a report as of January 30, 2010, presenting a differential analysis of the further processing of raw sugar to produce refined sugar.
2. ▬▬▬▬ Briefly report your recommendations.

PR 25-5B
**Product pricing using
the cost-plus
approach concepts;
differential analysis
report for accepting
additional business**

objs. 1, 2

✔ 3. b. Markup
percentage, 30%

HD Labs Inc. recently began production of a new product, flat panel displays, which required the investment of $1,500,000 in assets. The costs of producing and selling 12,000 units of flat panel displays are estimated as follows:

Variable costs per unit:		Fixed costs:	
Direct materials	$140	Factory overhead	$960,000
Direct labor	30	Selling and administrative expenses	480,000
Factory overhead	50		
Selling and administrative expenses	25		
Total	$245		

HD Labs Inc. is currently considering establishing a selling price for flat panel displays. The president of HD Labs has decided to use the cost-plus approach to product pricing and has indicated that the displays must earn a 20% rate of return on invested assets.

Instructions
1. Determine the amount of desired profit from the production and sale of flat panel displays.
2. Assuming that the total cost concept is used, determine (a) the cost amount per unit, (b) the markup percentage (rounded to two decimal places), and (c) the selling price of flat panel displays (rounded to nearest whole dollar).
3. Assuming that the product cost concept is used, determine (a) the cost amount per unit, (b) the markup percentage, and (c) the selling price of flat panel displays.
4. Assuming that the variable cost concept is used, determine (a) the cost amount per unit, (b) the markup percentage, and (c) the selling price of flat panel displays.
5. ➤ Comment on any additional considerations that could influence establishing the selling price for flat panel displays.
6. Assume that as of August 1, 2010, 5,000 units of flat panel displays have been produced and sold during the current year. Analysis of the domestic market indicates that 4,000 additional units are expected to be sold during the remainder of the year at the normal product price determined under the total cost concept. On August 3, HD Labs Inc. received an offer from Vision Systems Inc. for 1,500 units of flat panel displays at $235 each. Vision Systems Inc. will market the units in Canada under its own brand name, and no selling and administrative expenses associated with the sale will be incurred by HD Labs Inc. The additional business is not expected to affect the domestic sales of flat panel displays, and the additional units could be produced using existing capacity.
   a. Prepare a differential analysis report of the proposed sale to Vision Systems Inc.
   b. Based on the differential analysis report in part (a), should the proposal be accepted?

PR 25-6B
Product pricing and profit analysis with bottleneck operations

objs. 1, 3

✔ 1. High Grade, $30

Gemini Steel Company produces three grades of steel: high, good, and regular grade. Each of these products (grades) has high demand in the market, and Gemini is able to sell as much as it can produce of all three. The furnace operation is a bottleneck in the process and is running at 100% of capacity. Gemini wants to improve steel operation profitability. The variable conversion cost is $8 per process hour. The fixed cost is $410,000. In addition, the cost analyst was able to determine the following information about the three products:

	High Grade	Good Grade	Regular Grade
Budgeted units produced	5,000	5,000	5,000
Total process hours per unit	15	15	12
Furnace hours per unit	5	4	3
Unit selling price	$270	$250	$210
Direct materials cost per unit	$120	$100	$78

The furnace operation is part of the total process for each of these three products. Thus, for example, 5 of the 15 hours required to process High Grade steel are associated with the furnace.

Instructions
1. Determine the unit contribution margin for each product.
2. Provide an analysis to determine the relative product profitabilities, assuming that the furnace is a bottleneck.
3. Assume that management wishes to improve profitability by increasing prices on selected products. At what price would High and Good grades need to be offered in order to produce the same relative profitability as Regular Grade steel?

Special Activities

You can access the special activities online at **www.cengage.com/accounting/reeve**.

Answers to Self-Examination Questions

1. **A** Differential cost is the amount of increase or decrease in cost that is expected from a particular course of action compared with an alternative. For Marlo Company, the differential cost is $19,000 (answer A). This is the total of the variable product costs ($15,000) and the variable operating expenses ($4,000), which would not be incurred if the product is discontinued.

2. **A** A sunk cost is not affected by later decisions. For Victor Company, the sunk cost is the $50,000 (answer A) book value of the equipment, which is equal to the original cost of $200,000 (answer C) less the accumulated depreciation of $150,000 (answer B).

3. **C** The amount of income that could have been earned from the best available alternative to a proposed use of cash is the opportunity cost. For Henry Company, the opportunity cost is 12% of $100,000, or $12,000 (answer C).

4. **C** Under the variable cost concept of product pricing (answer C), fixed manufacturing costs, fixed administrative and selling expenses, and desired profit are allowed for in determining the markup. Only desired profit is allowed for in the markup under the total cost concept (answer A). Under the product cost concept (answer B), total selling and administrative expenses and desired profit are allowed for in determining the markup. Standard cost (answer D) can be used under any of the cost-plus approaches to product pricing.

5. **C** Product 3 has the highest unit contribution margin per bottleneck hour ($14/2 = $7). Product 1 (answer A) has the largest unit contribution margin, but the lowest unit contribution per bottleneck hour ($20/4 = $5), so it is the least profitable product in the constrained environment. Product 2 (answer B) has the highest total profitability in March (1,500 units × $18), but this does not suggest that it has the highest profit potential. Product 2's unit contribution per bottleneck hour ($18/3 = $6) is between Products 1 and 3. Answer D is not true, since the products all have different profit potential in terms of unit contribution margin per bottleneck hour.

Capital Investment Analysis

C A R N I V A L   C O R P O R A T I O N

Why are you paying tuition, studying this text, and spending time and money on a higher education? Most people believe that the money and time spent now will return them more earnings in the future. In other words, the cost of higher education is an investment in your future earning ability. How would you know if this investment is worth it?

One method would be for you to compare the cost of a higher education against the estimated increase in your future earning power. The bigger the difference between your expected future earnings and the cost of your education, the better the investment. The same is true for the investments businesses make in fixed assets. Business organizations use a variety of methods to compare the cost of an investment to its future earnings and cash flows.

For example, Carnival Corporation is the largest vacation cruise company in the world, with over 85 cruise ships that sail to locations around the world. Carnival's fleet required an investment of nearly $29 billion, with each new ship costing approximately $600 million. Carnival used capital investment analysis to compare this investment with the future earnings ability of the ships over their 30-year expected lives. Carnival must be satisfied with their investments, because they have signed agreements with shipyards to add an additional 22 cruise ships to its fleet from 2008–2012.

In this chapter, the methods used to make investment decisions, which may involve thousands, millions, or even billions of dollars, are described and illustrated. The similarities and differences among the most commonly used methods of evaluating investment proposals, as well as the benefits of each method are emphasized. Qualitative considerations affecting investment analyses, considerations complicating investment analyses, and the process of allocating available investment funds among competing proposals are also discussed.

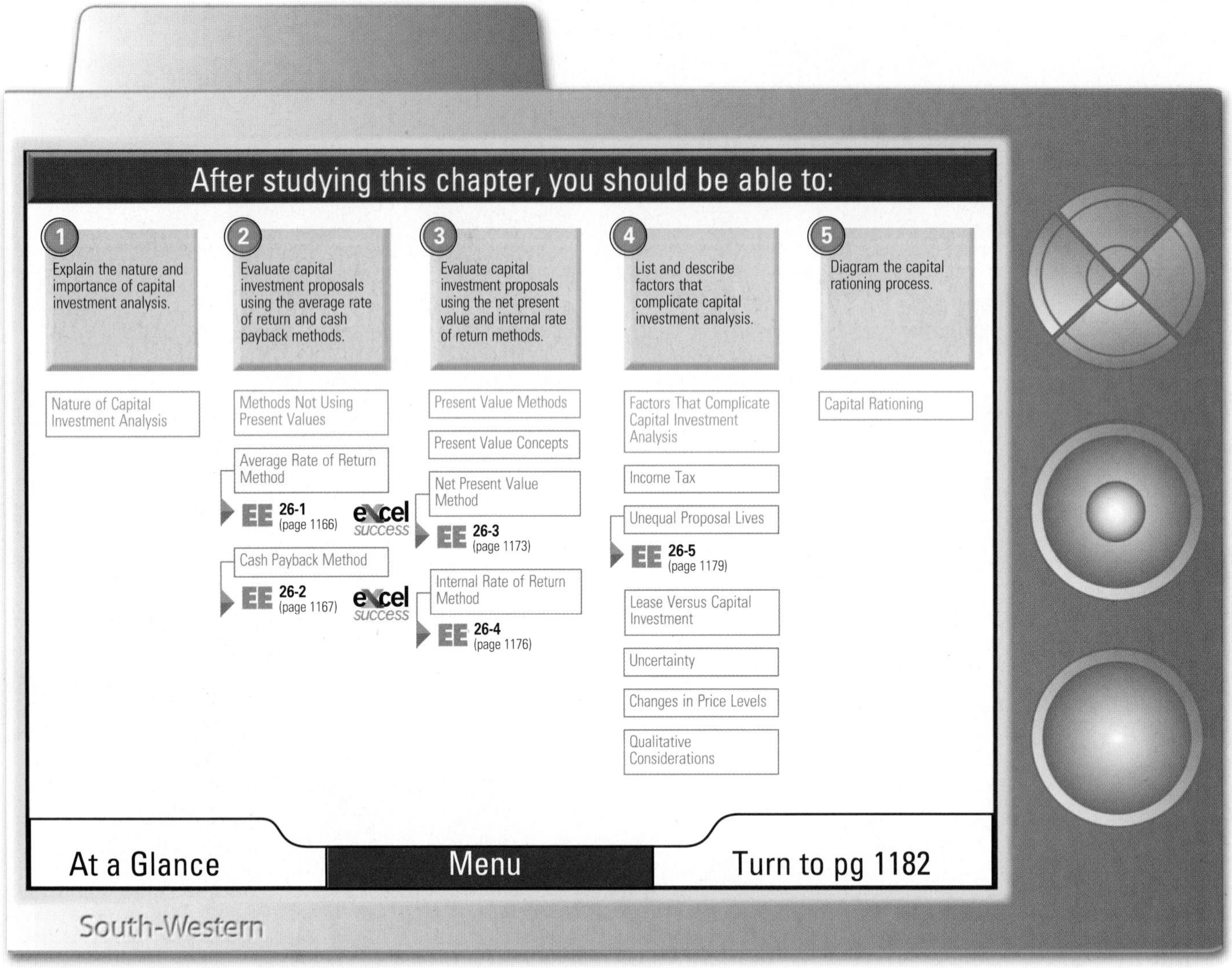

After studying this chapter, you should be able to:

1 Explain the nature and importance of capital investment analysis.

2 Evaluate capital investment proposals using the average rate of return and cash payback methods.

3 Evaluate capital investment proposals using the net present value and internal rate of return methods.

4 List and describe factors that complicate capital investment analysis.

5 Diagram the capital rationing process.

Nature of Capital Investment Analysis

Methods Not Using Present Values

Average Rate of Return Method

EE 26-1 (page 1166) e×cel *success*

Cash Payback Method

EE 26-2 (page 1167) e×cel *success*

Present Value Methods

Present Value Concepts

Net Present Value Method

EE 26-3 (page 1173)

Internal Rate of Return Method

EE 26-4 (page 1176)

Factors That Complicate Capital Investment Analysis

Income Tax

Unequal Proposal Lives

EE 26-5 (page 1179)

Lease Versus Capital Investment

Uncertainty

Changes in Price Levels

Qualitative Considerations

Capital Rationing

| At a Glance | Menu | Turn to pg 1182 |

South-Western

Nature of Capital Investment Analysis

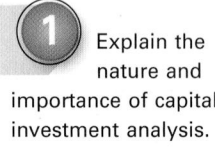

1 Explain the nature and importance of capital investment analysis.

During 2007, Delta Air Lines invested $1.0 billion in capital expenditures, which focused primarily on customer service initiatives, such as new flight equipment and improvements at Delta's Atlanta and New York–JFK hubs.

Companies use capital investment analysis to evaluate long-term investments. **Capital investment analysis** (or *capital budgeting*) is the process by which management plans, evaluates, and controls investments in fixed assets. Capital investments use funds and affect operations for many years and must earn a reasonable rate of return. Thus, capital investment decisions are some of the most important decisions that management makes.

Capital investment evaluation methods can be grouped into the following categories:

Methods That Do Not Use Present Values
1. Average rate of return method
2. Cash payback method

Methods That Use Present Values
1. Net present value method
2. Internal rate of return method

The two methods that use present values consider the time value of money. The **time value of money concept** recognizes that an amount of cash invested today will earn income and thus has value over time.

Evaluate capital investment proposals using the average rate of return and cash payback methods.

Methods Not Using Present Values

The methods not using present values are often useful in evaluating capital investment proposals that have relatively short useful lives. In such cases, the timing of the cash flows (the time value of money) is less important.

Since the methods not using present values are easy to use, they are often used to screen proposals. Minimum standards for accepting proposals are set, and proposals not meeting these standards are dropped. If a proposal meets the minimum standards, it may be subject to further analysis using the present value methods.

A CFO survey of capital investment analysis methods used by large U.S. companies reported the following:

Percentage of Respondents Reporting the Use of the Method as "Always" or "Often"

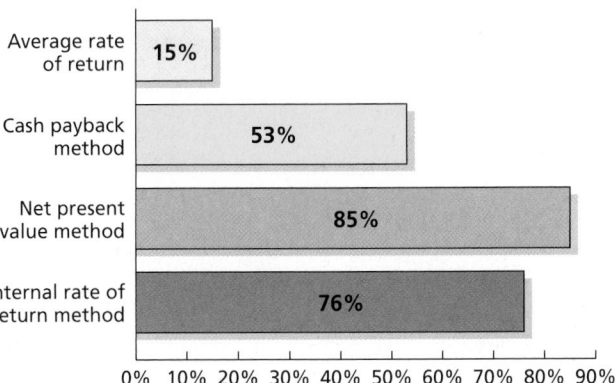

Average rate of return 15%
Cash payback method 53%
Net present value method 85%
Internal rate of return method 76%

0% 10% 20% 30% 40% 50% 60% 70% 80% 90%

Source: Patricia A. Ryan and Glenn P. Ryan, "Capital Budgeting Practice of the Fortune 1000: How Have Things Changed?" *Journal of Business and Management* (Winter 2002).

Average Rate of Return Method

The **average rate of return**, sometimes called the *accounting rate of return*, measures the average income as a percent of the average investment. The average rate of return is computed as follows:

$$\text{Average Rate of Return} = \frac{\text{Estimated Average Annual Income}}{\text{Average Investment}}$$

In the preceding equation, the numerator is the average of the annual income expected to be earned from the investment over its life, after deducting depreciation. The denominator is the average investment (book value) over the life of the investment. Assuming straight-line depreciation, the average investment is computed as follows:

$$\text{Average Investment} = \frac{\text{Initial Cost} + \text{Residual Value}}{2}$$

To illustrate, assume that management is evaluating the purchase of a new machine as follows:

Cost of new machine	$500,000
Residual value	0
Estimated total income from machine	200,000
Expected useful life	4 years

The average estimated annual income from the machine is $50,000 ($200,000/4 years). The average investment is $250,000, as computed below.

$$\text{Average Investment} = \frac{\text{Initial Cost} + \text{Residual Value}}{2} = \frac{\$500,000 + \$0}{2} = \$250,000$$

The average rate of return on the average investment is 20%, as computed below.

$$\text{Average Rate of Return} = \frac{\text{Estimated Average Annual Income}}{\text{Average Investment}} = \frac{\$50,000}{\$250,000} = 20\%$$

The average rate of return of 20% should be compared to the minimum rate of return required by management. If the average rate of return equals or exceeds the minimum rate, the machine should be purchased or considered for further analysis.

Several capital investment proposals can be ranked by their average rates of return. The higher the average rate of return, the more desirable the proposal. For example, assume that management is considering two capital investment proposals with the following average rates of return:

	Proposal A	**Proposal B**
Average Rate of Return	20%	25%

If only the average rate of return is considered, Proposal B, with an average rate of return of 25%, is preferred over Proposal A.

The average rate of return has the following three advantages:

1. It is easy to compute.
2. It includes the entire amount of income earned over the life of the proposal.
3. It emphasizes accounting income, which is often used by investors and creditors in evaluating management performance.

The average rate of return has the following two disadvantages:

1. It does not directly consider the expected cash flows from the proposal.
2. It does not directly consider the timing of the expected cash flows.

Example Exercise 26-1 Average Rate of Return
•••••••> 2

Determine the average rate of return for a project that is estimated to yield total income of $273,600 over three years, has a cost of $690,000, and has a $70,000 residual value.

Follow My Example 26-1

Estimated average annual income	$91,200 ($273,600/3 years)
Average investment	$380,000 ($690,000 + $70,000)/2
Average rate of return	24% ($91,200/$380,000)

For Practice: PE 26-1A, PE 26-1B

Cash Payback Method

A capital investment uses cash and must return cash in the future to be successful. The expected period of time between the date of an investment and the recovery in cash of the amount invested is the **cash payback period**.

When annual net cash inflows are equal, the cash payback period is computed as follows:

$$\text{Cash Payback Period} = \frac{\text{Initial Cost}}{\text{Annual Net Cash Inflow}}$$

To illustrate, assume that management is evaluating the purchase of the following new machine:

Cost of new machine	$200,000
Cash revenues from machine per year	50,000
Expenses of machine per year	30,000
Depreciation per year	20,000

To simplify, the revenues and expenses other than depreciation are assumed to be in cash. Hence, the net cash inflow per year from use of the machine is as follows:

Net cash inflow per year:		
Cash revenues from machine		$50,000
Less cash expenses of machine		
Expenses of machine	$30,000	
Less depreciation	20,000	10,000
Net cash inflow per year		$40,000

The time required for the net cash flow to equal the cost of the new machine is the payback period. Thus, the estimated cash payback period for the investment is five years, as computed below.

$$\text{Cash Payback Period} = \frac{\text{Initial Cost}}{\text{Annual Net Cash Inflow}} = \frac{\$200,000}{\$40,000} = 5 \text{ years}$$

In the preceding illustration, the annual net cash inflows are equal ($40,000 per year). When the annual net cash inflows are not equal, the cash payback period is determined by adding the annual net cash inflows until the cumulative total equals the initial cost of the proposed investment.

To illustrate, assume that a proposed investment has an initial cost of $400,000. The annual and cumulative net cash inflows over the proposal's six-year life are as follows:

Year	Net Cash Flow	Cumulative Net Cash Flow
1	$ 60,000	$ 60,000
2	80,000	140,000
3	105,000	245,000
4	155,000	400,000
5	100,000	500,000
6	90,000	590,000

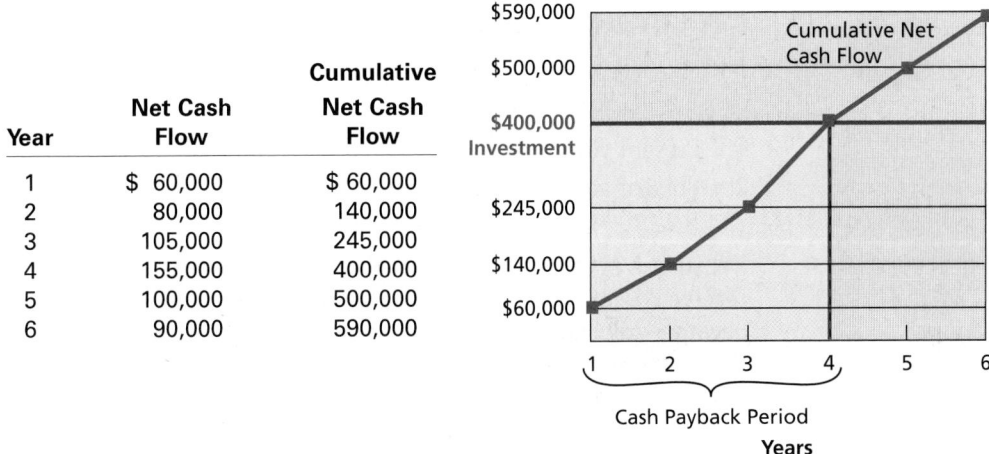

The cumulative net cash flow at the end of Year 4 equals the initial cost of the investment, $400,000. Thus, the payback period is four years.

If the initial cost of the proposed investment had been $450,000, the cash payback period would occur during Year 5. Since $100,000 of net cash flow is expected during Year 5, the additional $50,000 to increase the cumulative total to $450,000 occurs halfway through the year ($50,000/$100,000). Thus, the cash payback period would be $4\frac{1}{2}$ years.[1]

A short cash payback period is desirable. This is because the sooner cash is recovered, the sooner it can be reinvested in other projects. In addition, there is less chance of losses from changing economic conditions or other risks such as a decreasing customer demand when the payback period is short.

A short cash payback period is also desirable for repaying debt used to purchase the investment. The sooner the cash is recovered, the sooner the debt can be paid.

A disadvantage of the cash payback method is that it ignores cash flows occurring after the payback period. In addition, the cash payback method does not use present value concepts in valuing cash flows occurring in different periods.

Example Exercise 26-2   Cash Payback Period ·········▶ 2

A project has estimated annual net cash flows of $30,000. It is estimated to cost $105,000. Determine the cash payback period.

Follow My Example 26-2

3.5 years ($105,000/$30,000)

For Practice: PE 26-2A, PE 26-2B

1 Unless otherwise stated, net cash inflows are received uniformly throughout the year.

3 Evaluate capital investment proposals using the net present value and internal rate of return methods.

Methods Using Present Values

An investment in fixed assets may be viewed as purchasing a series of net cash flows over a period of time. The timing of when the net cash flows will be received is important in determining the value of a proposed investment.

Present value methods use the amount and timing of the net cash flows in evaluating an investment. The two methods of evaluating capital investments using present values are as follows:

1. Net present value method
2. Internal rate of return method

Present value concepts can also be used to evaluate personal finances. For example, you can determine house or car payments under various interest rate and term assumptions using present value concepts.

Present Value Concepts

Both the net present value and the internal rate of return methods use the following two **present value concepts:**[2]

1. Present value of an amount
2. Present value of an annuity

Present Value of an Amount If you were given the choice, would you prefer to receive $1 now or $1 three years from now? You should prefer to receive $1 now, because you could invest the $1 and earn interest for three years. As a result, the amount you would have after three years would be greater than $1.

To illustrate, assume that you have $1 to invest, as follows:

Amount to be invested	$1
Period to be invested	3 years
Interest rate	12%

After one year, the $1 earns interest of $0.12 ($1 × 12%) and, thus, will grow to $1.12 ($1 × 1.12). In the second year, the $1.12 earns 12% interest of $0.134 ($1.12 × 12%) and, thus, will grow to $1.254 ($1.12 × 1.12) by the end of the second year. This process of interest earning interest is called *compounding*. By the end of the third year, your $1 investment will grow to $1.404, as shown below.

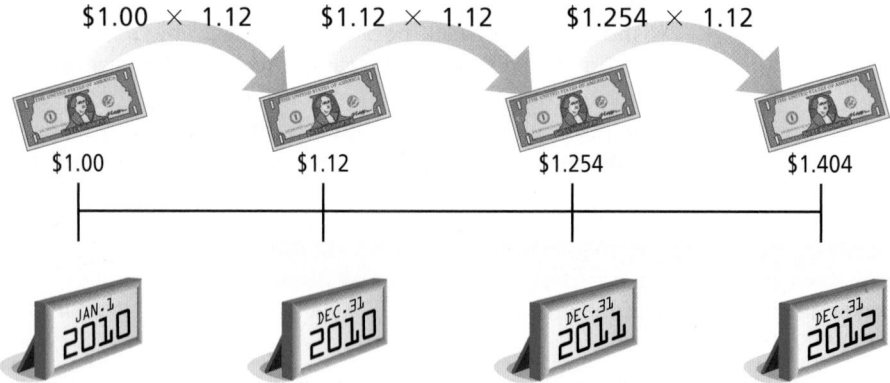

---

2 Present value concepts are also described and illustrated in the appendix to Chapter 14, "Long-Term Liabilities: Bonds and Notes."

On January 1, 2010, what is the present value of $1.404 to be received on December 31, 2012? This is a present value question. The answer can be determined with the aid of a present value of $1 table. For example, the partial table in Exhibit 1 indicates that the present value of $1 to be received in three years with earnings compounded at the rate of 12% a year is 0.712. Multiplying 0.712 by $1.404 yields $1 as follows:

Present Value		Amount to Be Received in 3 Years		Present Value of $1 to Be Received in 3 Years (from Exhibit 1)
$1	=	$1.404	×	0.712

Exhibit 1

Partial Present Value of $1 Table

Present Value of $1 at Compound Interest

Year	6%	10%	12%	15%	20%
1	0.943	0.909	0.893	0.870	0.833
2	0.890	0.826	0.797	0.756	0.694
3	0.840	0.751	0.712	0.658	0.579
4	0.792	0.683	0.636	0.572	0.482
5	0.747	0.621	0.567	0.497	0.402
6	0.705	0.564	0.507	0.432	0.335
7	0.665	0.513	0.452	0.376	0.279
8	0.627	0.467	0.404	0.327	0.233
9	0.592	0.424	0.361	0.284	0.194
10	0.558	0.386	0.322	0.247	0.162

In other words, the present value of $1.404 to be received in three years using a compound interest rate of 12% is $1, as shown below.[3]

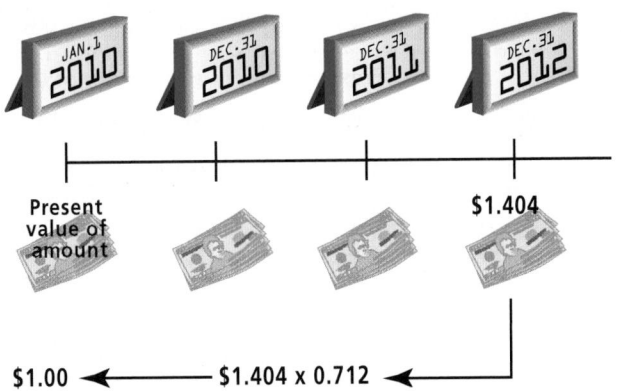

Present Value of an Annuity An **annuity** is a series of equal net cash flows at fixed time intervals. Cash payments for monthly rent, salaries, and bond interest are all examples of annuities.

The present value of an annuity is the sum of the present values of each cash flow. That is, the **present value of an annuity** is the amount of cash needed today to yield a series of equal net cash flows at fixed time intervals in the future.

---

3 The present value factors in the table are rounded to three decimal places. More complete tables of present values are in Appendix A.

To illustrate, the present value of a $100 annuity for five periods at 12% could be determined by using the present value factors in Exhibit 1. Each $100 net cash flow could be multiplied by the present value of $1 at a 12% factor for the appropriate period and summed to determine a present value of $360.50, as shown below.

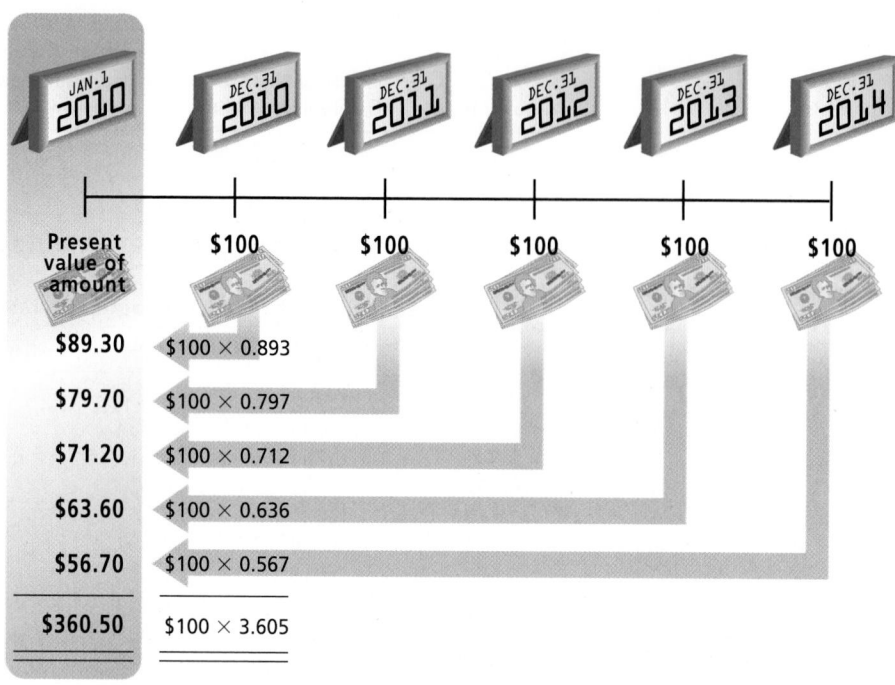

Using a present value of an annuity table is a simpler approach. Exhibit 2 is a partial table of present value of annuity factors.[4]

Exhibit 2

Partial Present Value of an Annuity Table

	Present Value of an Annuity of $1 at Compound Interest				
Year	6%	10%	12%	15%	20%
1	0.943	0.909	0.893	0.870	0.833
2	1.833	1.736	1.690	1.626	1.528
3	2.673	2.487	2.402	2.283	2.106
4	3.465	3.170	3.037	2.855	2.589
5	4.212	3.791	3.605	3.353	2.991
6	4.917	4.355	4.111	3.785	3.326
7	5.582	4.868	4.564	4.160	3.605
8	6.210	5.335	4.968	4.487	3.837
9	6.802	5.759	5.328	4.772	4.031
10	7.360	6.145	5.650	5.019	4.192

The present value factors in the table shown in Exhibit 2 are the sum of the present value of $1 factors in Exhibit 1 for the number of annuity periods. Thus, 3.605 in the annuity table (Exhibit 2) is the sum of the five present value of $1 factors at 12%, as shown on the following page.

---

4 The present value factors in the table are rounded to three decimal places. More complete tables of present values are in Appendix A.

	Present Value of $1 (Exhibit 1)
Present value of $1 for 1 year @12%	0.893
Present value of $1 for 2 years @12%	0.797
Present value of $1 for 3 years @12%	0.712
Present value of $1 for 4 years @12%	0.636
Present value of $1 for 5 years @12%	0.567
Present value of an annuity of $1 for 5 years (from Exhibit 2)	3.605

Multiplying $100 by 3.605 yields the same amount ($360.50) as follows:

Present Value		Amount to Be Received Annually for 5 Years		Present Value of an Annuity of $1 to Be Received for 5 Years (Exhibit 2)
$360.50	=	$100	×	3.605

This amount ($360.50) is the same as what was determined in the preceding illustration by five successive multiplications.

Net Present Value Method

A 55-year-old janitor won a $5 million lottery jackpot, payable in 21 annual installments of $240,245. Unfortunately, the janitor died after collecting only one payment. What happens to the remaining unclaimed payments? In this case, the lottery winnings were auctioned off for the benefit of the janitor's estate. The winning bid approximated the present value of the remaining cash flows, or about $2.1 million.

The **net present value method** compares the amount to be invested with the present value of the net cash inflows. It is sometimes called the *discounted cash flow method*.

The interest rate (return) used in net present value analysis is the company's minimum desired rate of return. This rate, sometimes termed the *hurdle rate*, is based on such factors as the purpose of the investment and the cost of obtaining funds for the investment. If the present value of the cash inflows equals or exceeds the amount to be invested, the proposal is desirable.

To illustrate, assume the following data for a proposed investment in new equipment:

The net present value method compares an investment's initial cash outflow with the present value of its cash inflows.

Cost of new equipment	$ 200,000
Expected useful life	5 years
Minimum desired rate of return	10%
Expected cash flows to be received each year:	
Year 1	$ 70,000
Year 2	60,000
Year 3	50,000
Year 4	40,000
Year 5	40,000
Total expected cash flows	$ 260,000

The present value of the net cash flow for each year is computed by multiplying the net cash flow for the year by the present value factor of $1 for that year, as shown below.

Year	Present Value of $1 at 10%	Net Cash Flow	Present Value of Net Cash Flow
1	0.909	$ 70,000	$ 63,630
2	0.826	60,000	49,560
3	0.751	50,000	37,550
4	0.683	40,000	27,320
5	0.621	40,000	24,840
Total		$260,000	$202,900
Amount to be invested			200,000
Net present value			$ 2,900

The preceding computations are also graphically illustrated on the following page.

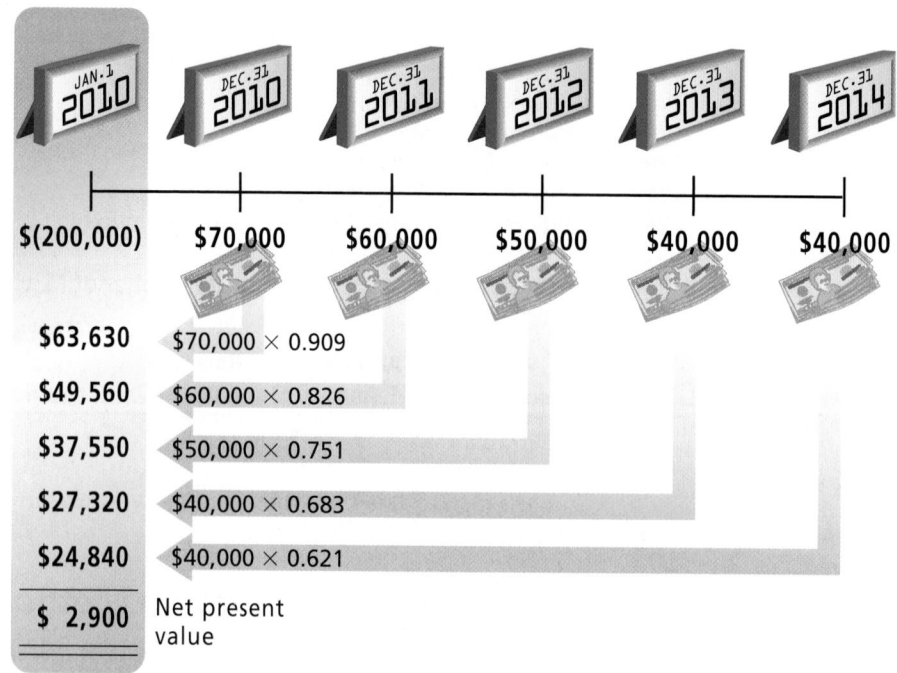

Spreadsheet software can be used to determine the net present value of a project using a specialized function, illustrated as follows:

	A	B
1	Inputs:	
2		
3	Minimum desired rate of return	10%
4		
5		
6	Cost of new equipment	$ 200,000
7		
8		Net Cash Flows
9	Year 1	$70,000
10	Year 2	60,000
11	Year 3	50,000
12	Year 4	40,000
13	Year 5	40,000
14		
15	Output:	
16		
17	Present value of cash flows	=NPV(B4,B9:B13) ← a.
18	Less: amount to be invested	=B6 ← b.
19	Net present value	=B17-B18 ← c.

The inputs include the minimum desired rate of return, cost of the new equipment (amount to be invested), and the end of each year net cash flows expected from the project.

The outputs consist of the following three steps:

a. Enter in B17 the formula for calculating the present value of the net cash flows of the project using the =NPV function as follows,

=NPV(B3,B9:B13)

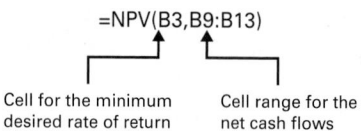

Cell for the minimum desired rate of return   Cell range for the net cash flows

b. Enter in cell B18 the cell reference for the cost of the equipment (amount to be invested), B6.

c.   Enter in cell B19 the difference between the net present value of cash flows and amount to be invested, =B17-B18. In your spreadsheet the net present value will calculate to $2,946. The amount shown in the text, $2,900, is rounded.

 Go to the hands-on **Excel Tutor** for this example!

The net present value of $2,900 indicates that the purchase of the new equipment is expected to recover the investment and provide more than the minimum rate of return of 10%. Thus, the purchase of the new equipment is desirable.

When capital investment funds are limited and the proposals involve different investments, a ranking of the proposals can be prepared by using a present value index. The **present value index** is computed as follows:

$$\text{Present Value Index} = \frac{\text{Total Present Value of Net Cash Flow}}{\text{Amount to Be Invested}}$$

The present value index for the investment in the preceding illustration is 1.0145, as computed below.

$$\text{Present Value Index} = \frac{\text{Total Present Value of Net Cash Flow}}{\text{Amount to Be Invested}}$$

$$\text{Present Value Index} = \frac{\$202,900}{\$200,000} = 1.0145$$

To illustrate, assume that a company is considering three proposals. The net present value and the present value index for each proposal are as follows:

	Proposal A	Proposal B	Proposal C
Total present value of net cash flow	$107,000	$86,400	$86,400
Amount to be invested	100,000	80,000	90,000
Net present value	$ 7,000	$ 6,400	$ (3,600)
Present value index:			
Proposal A ($107,000/$100,000)	1.07		
Proposal B ($86,400/$80,000)		1.08	
Proposal C ($86,400/$90,000)			0.96

A project will have a present value index greater than 1 when the net present value is positive. This is the case for Proposals A and B. When the net present value is negative, the present value index will be less than 1, as is the case for Proposal C.

Although Proposal A has the largest net present value, the present value indices indicate that it is not as desirable as Proposal B. That is, Proposal B returns $1.08 present value per dollar invested, whereas Proposal A returns only $1.07. Proposal B requires an investment of $80,000, compared to an investment of $100,000 for Proposal A. The possible use of the $20,000 difference between Proposals A and B investments should also be considered before making a final decision.

An advantage of the net present value method is that it considers the time value of money. A disadvantage is that the computations are more complex than the average rate of return and cash payback methods. In addition, the net present value method assumes that the cash received from the proposal can be reinvested at the minimum desired rate of return. This assumption may not always be reasonable.

The use of spreadsheet software such as Microsoft Excel can simplify present value computations.

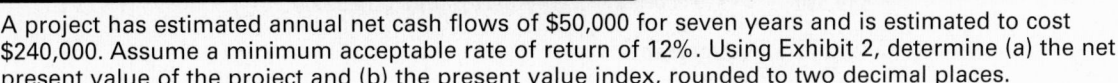

Example Exercise 26-3   Net Present Value   3

A project has estimated annual net cash flows of $50,000 for seven years and is estimated to cost $240,000. Assume a minimum acceptable rate of return of 12%. Using Exhibit 2, determine (a) the net present value of the project and (b) the present value index, rounded to two decimal places.

(continued)

Follow My Example 26-3

a. ($11,800) [($50,000 × 4.564) − $240,000]
b. 0.95   ($228,200/$240,000)

For Practice: PE 26-3A, PE 26-3B

Internal Rate of Return Method

The **internal rate of return (IRR) method** uses present value concepts to compute the rate of return from a capital investment proposal based on its expected net cash flows. This method, sometimes called the *time-adjusted rate of return method*, starts with the proposal's net cash flows and works backward to estimate the proposal's expected rate of return.

To illustrate, assume that management is evaluating the following proposal to purchase new equipment:

Cost of new equipment	$33,530
Yearly expected cash flows to be received	10,000
Expected life	5 years
Minimum desired rate of return	12%

The present value of the net cash flows, using the present value of an annuity table in Exhibit 2, is $2,520, as shown in Exhibit 3.

Exhibit 3

Net Present Value Analysis at 12%

Annual net cash flow (at the end of each of five years)	$ 10,000
Present value of an annuity of $1 at 12% for five years (Exhibit 2)	× 3.605
Present value of annual net cash flows	$36,050
Less amount to be invested	33,530
Net present value	$ 2,520

In Exhibit 3, the $36,050 present value of the cash inflows, based on a 12% rate of return, is greater than the $33,530 to be invested. Thus, the internal rate of return must be greater than 12%. Through trial and error, the rate of return equating the $33,530 cost of the investment with the present value of the net cash flows can be determined to be 15%, as shown below.

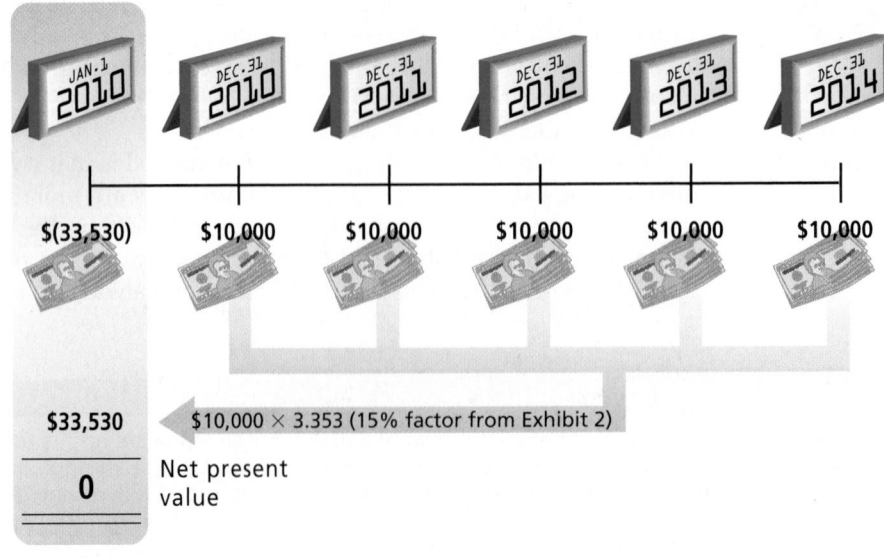

When equal annual net cash flows are expected from a proposal, as in the preceding example, the internal rate of return can be determined as follows:[5]

Step 1. Determine a present value factor for an annuity of $1 as follows:

$$\text{Present Value Factor for an Annuity of \$1} = \frac{\text{Amount to Be Invested}}{\text{Equal Annual Net Cash Flows}}$$

Step 2. Locate the present value factor determined in Step 1 in the present value of an annuity of $1 table (Exhibit 2) as follows:
a. Locate the number of years of expected useful life of the investment in the Year column.
b. Proceed horizontally across the table until you find the present value factor computed in Step 1.

Step 3. Identify the internal rate of return by the heading of the column in which the present value factor in Step 2 is located.

To illustrate, assume that management is evaluating the following proposal to purchase new equipment:

Cost of new equipment	$97,360
Yearly expected cash flows to be received	20,000
Expected useful life	7 years

The present value factor for an annuity of $1 is 4.868, as shown below.

$$\text{Present Value Factor for an Annuity of \$1} = \frac{\text{Amount to Be Invested}}{\text{Equal Annual Net Cash Flows}}$$

$$\text{Present Value Factor for an Annuity of \$1} = \frac{\$97,360}{\$20,000} = 4.868$$

Using the partial present value of an annuity of $1 table shown at the top of the next page and a period of seven years, the factor 4.868 is related to 10%. Thus, the internal rate of return for this proposal is 10%.

Present Value of an Annuity of $1 at Compound Interest

	Year	6%		Step 3 10%	12%
	1	0.943		0.909	0.893
	2	1.833		1.736	1.690
	3	2.673		2.487	2.402
	4	3.465		3.170	3.037
	5	4.212		3.791	3.605
	6	4.917	**Step 2(b)**	4.355	4.111
Step 2(a)	7	5.582		4.868	4.564
	8	6.210		5.335	4.968
	9	6.802		5.759	5.328
	10	7.360		6.145	5.650

Step 1: Determine present value factor for an annuity of $1 $= \frac{\$97,360}{\$20,000} = 4.868$

5 To simplify, equal annual net cash flows are assumed. If the net cash flows are not equal, spreadsheet software can be used to determine the rate of return.

The minimum acceptable rate of return for Owens Corning is 18%; for General Electric Company, it is 20%. The CFO of Owens Corning states, "I'm here to challenge anyone—even the CEO—who gets emotionally attached to a project that doesn't reach our benchmark."

If the minimum acceptable rate of return is 10%, then the proposal is considered acceptable. Several proposals can be ranked by their internal rates of return. The proposal with the highest rate is the most desirable.

A primary advantage of the internal rate of return method is that the present values of the net cash flows over the entire useful life of the proposal are considered. In addition, all proposals can be compared based on their internal rates of return.

The primary disadvantage of the internal rate of return method is that the computations are more complex. Also, like the net present value method, it assumes that the cash received from a proposal can be reinvested at the internal rate of return. This assumption may not always be reasonable.

The internal rate of return can be determined using a spreadsheet formula, as follows:

	A	B
1	Inputs:	
2		
3		
4		Net Cash Flows
5	Cost of new equipment	$(97,360)
6	Year 1	20,000
7	Year 2	20,000
8	Year 3	20,000
9	Year 4	20,000
10	Year 5	20,000
11	Year 6	20,000
12	Year 7	20,000
13		
14	Output:	
15		
16	Internal rate of return	=IRR(B5:B12) ← **a.**

The inputs are the cash flows of the project, beginning with the initial investment entered as a negative number. In this case, the cost of the equipment is $97,360, which is entered in cell B5 as a negative number.

The remaining cash flows are entered individually for each of the years of the project life. The equipment will generate cash flows of $20,000 at the end of each year of the expected seven years of equipment life. These cash flows are entered in B6:B12.

a. The output is the internal rate of return. Enter in cell B16 the Excel =IRR function, as follows:

=IRR(B5:B12)

The range B5:B12 covers the cash flows of the project, including as the first cash flow the initial investment, entered as a negative number. The internal rate of return calculated is 10%, the same rate using the table method.

One advantage of the spreadsheet approach is that the =IRR function can estimate the internal rate of return for a series of unequal cash flows, which is not possible to determine under the table method.

 Go to the hands-on **Excel Tutor** for this example!

Example Exercise 26-4   Internal Rate of Return •••••••• 3

A project is estimated to cost $208,175 and provide annual net cash flows of $55,000 for six years. Determine the internal rate of return for this project, using Exhibit 2.

(continued)

15%   [($208,175/$55,000) = 3.785, the present value of an annuity factor for six periods at 15%, from Exhibit 2]

For Practice: PE 26-4A, PE 26-4B

4 List and describe factors that complicate capital investment analysis.

Factors that Complicate Capital Investment Analysis

Four widely used methods of evaluating capital investment proposals have been described and illustrated in this chapter. In practice, additional factors such as the following may impact capital investment decisions:

1. Income tax
2. Proposals with unequal lives
3. Leasing versus purchasing
4. Uncertainty
5. Changes in price levels
6. Qualitative factors

Income Tax

The impact of income taxes on capital investment decisions can be material. For example, in determining depreciation for federal income tax purposes, useful lives that are much shorter than the actual useful lives are often used. Also, depreciation for tax purposes often differs from depreciation for financial statement purposes. As a result, the timing of the cash flows for income taxes can have a significant impact on capital investment analysis.[6]

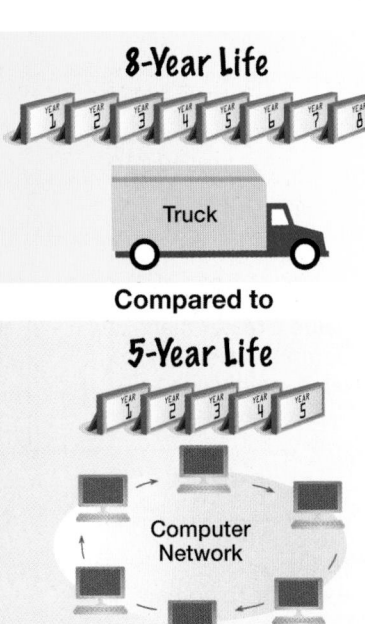

8-Year Life

Truck

Compared to

5-Year Life

Computer Network

for $100,000

Unequal Proposal Lives

The prior capital investment illustrations assumed that the alternative proposals had the same useful lives. In practice, however, proposals often have different lives.

To illustrate, assume that a company is considering purchasing a new truck or a new computer network. The data for each proposal are shown below.

	Truck	Computer Network
Cost	$100,000	$100,000
Minimum desired rate of return	10%	10%
Expected useful life	8 years	5 years
Yearly expected cash flows to be received:		
Year 1	$ 30,000	$ 30,000
Year 2	30,000	30,000
Year 3	25,000	30,000
Year 4	20,000	30,000
Year 5	15,000	35,000
Year 6	15,000	0
Year 7	10,000	0
Year 8	10,000	0
Total	$155,000	$155,000

The expected cash flows and net present value for each proposal are shown in Exhibit 4. Because of the unequal useful lives, however, the net present values in Exhibit 4 are not comparable.

To make the proposals comparable, the useful lives are adjusted to end at the same time. In this illustration, this is done by assuming that the truck will be sold at the end

6 The impact of taxes on capital investment analysis is covered in advanced accounting textbooks.

Exhibit 4

Net Present Value Analysis—Unequal Lives of Proposals

	A	B	C	D
1			Truck	
2	Year	Present	Net	Present
3		Value of	Cash	Value of
4		$1 at 10%	Flow	Net Cash Flow
5	1	0.909	$ 30,000	$ 27,270
6	2	0.826	30,000	24,780
7	3	0.751	25,000	18,775
8	4	0.683	20,000	13,660
9	5	0.621	15,000	9,315
10	6	0.564	15,000	8,460
11	7	0.513	10,000	5,130
12	8	0.467	10,000	4,670
13	Total		$155,000	$112,060
14				
15	Amount to be invested			100,000
16	Net present value			$ 12,060

	A	B	C	D
1			Computer Network	
2	Year	Present	Net	Present
3		Value of	Cash	Value of
4		$1 at 10%	Flow	Net Cash Flow
5	1	0.909	$ 30,000	$ 27,270
6	2	0.826	30,000	24,780
7	3	0.751	30,000	22,530
8	4	0.683	30,000	20,490
9	5	0.621	35,000	21,735
10	Total		$155,000	$116,805
11				
12	Amount to be invested			100,000
13	Net present value			$ 16,805

Exhibit 5

Net Present Value Analysis— Equalized Lives of Proposals

	A	B	C	D
1		Truck—Revised to 5-Year Life		
2	Year	Present	Net	Present
3		Value of	Cash	Value of
4		$1 at 10%	Flow	Net Cash Flow
5	1	0.909	$ 30,000	$ 27,270
6	2	0.826	30,000	24,780
7	3	0.751	25,000	18,775
8	4	0.683	20,000	13,660
9	5	0.621	15,000	9,315
10	5 (Residual			
11	value)	0.621	40,000	24,840
12	Total		$160,000	$118,640
13				
14	Amount to be invested			100,000
15	Net present value			$ 18,640

Truck Net Present Value Greater than Computer Network Net Present Value by $1,835

of five years. The selling price (residual value) of the truck at the end of five years is estimated and included in the cash inflows. Both proposals will then cover five years; thus, the net present value analyses will be comparable.

To illustrate, assume that the truck's estimated selling price (residual value) at the end of Year 5 is $40,000. Exhibit 5 shows the truck's revised present value analysis assuming a five-year life.

As shown in Exhibit 5, the net present value for the truck exceeds the net present value for the computer network by $1,835 ($18,640 − $16,805). Thus, the truck is the more attractive of the two proposals.

Example Exercise 26-5   Net Present Value—Unequal Lives   •••••••> 4

Project 1 requires an original investment of $50,000. The project will yield cash flows of $12,000 per year for seven years. Project 2 has a calculated net present value of $8,900 over a five-year life. Project 1 could be sold at the end of five years for a price of $30,000.. (a) Determine the net present value of Project 1 over a five-year life with residual value, assuming a minimum rate of return of 12%. (b) Which project provides the greatest net present value?

Follow My Example 26-5

Project 1

a. Present value of $12,000 per year at 12% for 5 years $43,260 [$12,000 × 3.605 (Exhibit 2, 12%, 5 years)]
   Present value of $30,000 at 12% at the end of 5 years _17,010_ [$30,000 × 0.567 (Exhibit 1, 12%, 5 years)]
   Total present value of Project 1 $60,270
   Total cost of Project 1   50,000
   Net present value of Project 1 $10,270

b. Project 1—$10,270 is greater than the net present value of Project 2, $8,900.

For Practice: PE 26-5A, PE 26-5B

Lease versus Capital Investment

Leasing fixed assets is common in many industries. For example, hospitals often lease medical equipment. Some advantages of leasing a fixed asset include the following:

1. The company has use of the fixed asset without spending large amounts of cash to purchase the asset.
2. The company eliminates the risk of owning an obsolete asset.
3. The company may deduct the annual lease payments for income tax purposes.

A disadvantage of leasing a fixed asset is that it is normally more costly than purchasing the asset. This is because the lessor (owner of the asset) includes in the rental price not only the costs of owning the asset, but also a profit.

The methods of evaluating capital investment proposals illustrated in this chapter can also be used to decide whether to lease or purchase a fixed asset.

Uncertainty

All capital investment analyses rely on factors that are uncertain. For example, estimates of revenues, expenses, and cash flows are uncertain. This is especially true for long-term capital investments. Errors in one or more of the estimates could lead to incorrect decisions. Methods that consider the impact of uncertainty on capital investment analysis are discussed in advanced accounting and finance textbooks.

Changes in Price Levels

Price levels normally change as the economy improves or deteriorates. General price levels often increase in a rapidly growing economy, which is called **inflation**. During such periods, the rate of return on an investment should exceed the rising price level. If this is not the case, the cash returned on the investment will be less than expected.

Price levels may also change for foreign investments. This occurs as currency exchange rates change. **Currency exchange rates** are the rates at which currency in another country can be exchanged for U.S. dollars.

If the amount of local dollars that can be exchanged for one U.S. dollar increases, then the local currency is said to be weakening to the dollar. When a company has an investment in another country where the local currency is weakening, the return on the investment, as expressed in U.S. dollars, is adversely impacted. This is because the expected amount of local currency returned on the investment would purchase fewer U.S. dollars.[7]

Qualitative Considerations

Some benefits of capital investments are qualitative in nature and cannot be estimated in dollar terms. However, if a company does not consider qualitative considerations, an acceptable investment proposal could be rejected.

Some examples of qualitative considerations that may influence capital investment analysis include the impact of the investment proposal on the following:

1. Product quality
2. Manufacturing flexibility
3. Employee morale
4. Manufacturing productivity
5. Market (strategic) opportunities

Many qualitative factors, such as those listed above, may be as important, if not more important, than quantitative factors.

IBM decided to develop molecular and atomic-level nanotechnology based more on its strategic market potential than on an economic analysis of cash flows.

Integrity, Objectivity, and Ethics in Business

ASSUMPTION FUDGING

The results of any capital budgeting analysis depend on many subjective estimates, such as the cash flows, discount rate, time period, and total investment amount. The results of the analysis should be used to either support or reject a project. Capital budgeting should not be used to justify an assumed net present value. That is, the analyst should not work backwards, filling in assumed numbers that will produce the desired net present value. Such a reverse approach reduces the credibility of the entire process.

5 Diagram the capital rationing process.

Capital Rationing

Capital rationing is the process by which management allocates funds among competing capital investment proposals. In this process, management often uses a combination of the methods described in this chapter.

Exhibit 6 illustrates the capital rationing decision process. Alternative proposals are initially screened by establishing minimum standards using the cash payback and the average rate of return methods. The proposals that survive this screening are further analyzed, using the net present value and internal rate of return methods.

Qualitative factors related to each proposal should also be considered throughout the capital rationing process. For example, new equipment might improve the quality of the product and, thus, increase consumer satisfaction and sales.

At the end of the capital rationing process, accepted proposals are ranked and compared with the funds available. Proposals that are selected for funding are included in the capital expenditures budget. Unfunded proposals may be reconsidered if funds later become available.

---

7 Further discussion on accounting for foreign currency transactions is available on the companion Web site at academic.cengage.com/accounting/warren.

Exhibit 6

Capital Rationing Decision Process

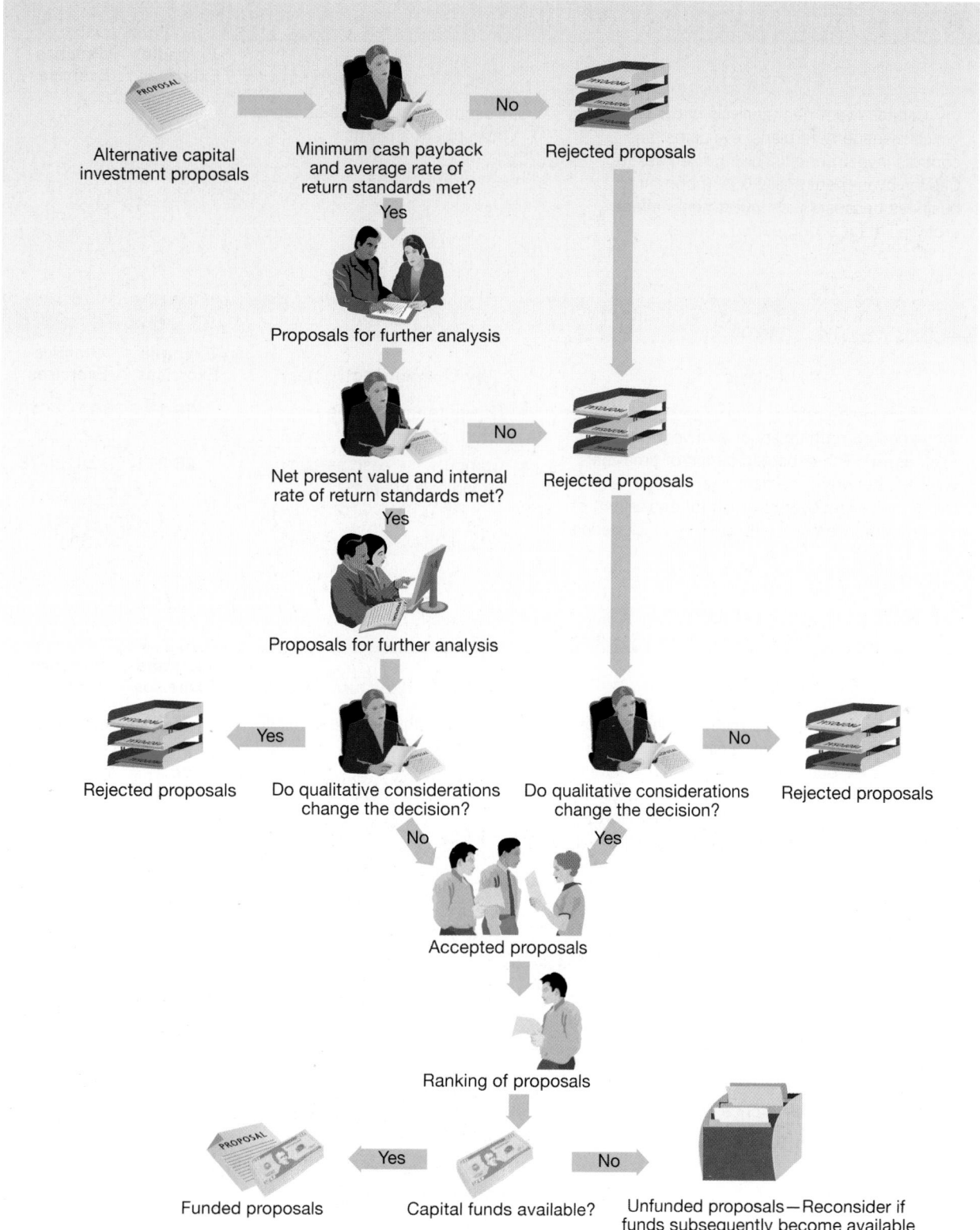

1 Explain the nature and importance of capital investment analysis.

Key Points	Key Learning Outcomes	Example Exercises	Practice Exercises
Capital investment analysis is the process by which management plans, evaluates, and controls investments involving fixed assets. Capital investment analysis is important to a business because such investments affect profitability for a long period of time.	• Describe the purpose of capital investment analysis.		

2 Evaluate capital investment proposals using the average rate of return and cash payback methods.

Key Points	Key Learning Outcomes	Example Exercises	Practice Exercises
The average rate of return method measures the expected profitability of an investment in fixed assets. The expected period of time that will pass between the date of an investment and the complete recovery in cash (or equivalent) of the amount invested is the cash payback period.	• Compute the average rate of return of a project.	26-1	26-1A, 26-1B
	• Compute the cash payback period of a project.	26-2	26-2A, 26-2B

3 Evaluate capital investment proposals using the net present value and internal rate of return methods.

Key Points	Key Learning Outcomes	Example Exercises	Practice Exercises
The net present value method uses present values to compute the net present value of the cash flows expected from a proposal. The internal rate of return method uses present values to compute the rate of return from the net cash flows expected from capital investment proposals.	• Compute the net present value of a project.	26-3	26-3A, 26-3B
	• Compute the internal rate of return of a project.	26-4	26-4A, 26-4B

4 List and describe factors that complicate capital investment analysis.

Key Points	Key Learning Outcomes	Example Exercises	Practice Exercises
Factors that may complicate capital investment analysis include the impact of income tax, unequal lives of alternative proposals, leasing, uncertainty, changes in price levels, and qualitative considerations.	• Describe the impact of income taxes in capital investment analysis.		
	• Evaluate projects with unequal lives.	26-5	26-5A, 26-5B
	• Describe leasing versus capital investment.		
	• Describe uncertainty, changes in price levels, and qualitative considerations in capital investment analysis.		

Key Points	Key Learning Outcomes	Example Exercises	Practice Exercises
Capital rationing refers to the process by which management allocates available investment funds among competing capital investment proposals. A diagram of the capital rationing process appears in Exhibit 6.	• Define *capital rationing*. • Diagram the capital rationing process.		

Key Terms

annuity (1169)
average rate of return (1165)
capital investment analysis (1164)
capital rationing (1180)
cash payback period (1166)

currency exchange rate (1179)
inflation (1179)
internal rate of return (IRR) method (1174)
net present value method (1171)

present value concept (1168)
present value index (1173)
present value of an annuity (1169)
time value of money concept (1165)

Illustrative Problem

The capital investment committee of Hopewell Company is currently considering two investments. The estimated income from operations and net cash flows expected from each investment are as follows:

	Truck		Equipment	
Year	Income from Operations	Net Cash Flow	Income from Operations	Net Cash Flow
1	$ 6,000	$ 22,000	$13,000	$ 29,000
2	9,000	25,000	10,000	26,000
3	10,000	26,000	8,000	24,000
4	8,000	24,000	8,000	24,000
5	11,000	27,000	3,000	19,000
	$44,000	$124,000	$42,000	$122,000

Each investment requires $80,000. Straight-line depreciation will be used, and no residual value is expected. The committee has selected a rate of 15% for purposes of the net present value analysis.

Instructions

1. Compute the following:
   a. The average rate of return for each investment.
   b. The net present value for each investment. Use the present value of $1 table appearing in this chapter.
2. Why is the net present value of the equipment greater than the truck, even though its average rate of return is less?
3. Prepare a summary for the capital investment committee, advising it on the relative merits of the two investments.

1184 Chapter 26 Capital Investment Analysis

Solution

1. a. Average rate of return for the truck:

$$\frac{\$44,000 \div 5}{(\$80,000 + \$0) \div 2} = 22\%$$

Average rate of return for the equipment:

$$\frac{\$42,000 \div 5}{(\$80,000 + \$0) \div 2} = 21\%$$

b. Net present value analysis:

Year	Present Value of $1 at 15%	Net Cash Flow Truck	Net Cash Flow Equipment	Present Value of Net Cash Flow Truck	Present Value of Net Cash Flow Equipment
1	0.870	$ 22,000	$ 29,000	$19,140	$25,230
2	0.756	25,000	26,000	18,900	19,656
3	0.658	26,000	24,000	17,108	15,792
4	0.572	24,000	24,000	13,728	13,728
5	0.497	27,000	19,000	13,419	9,443
Total		$124,000	$122,000	$82,295	$83,849
Amount to be invested				80,000	80,000
Net present value				$ 2,295	$ 3,849

2. The equipment has a lower average rate of return than the truck because the equipment's total income from operations for the five years is $42,000, which is $2,000 less than the truck's. Even so, the net present value of the equipment is greater than that of the truck, because the equipment has higher cash flows in the early years.

3. Both investments exceed the selected rate established for the net present value analysis. The truck has a higher average rate of return, but the equipment offers a larger net present value. Thus, if only one of the two investments can be accepted, the equipment would be the more attractive.

Self-Examination Questions (Answers at End of Chapter)

1. Methods of evaluating capital investment proposals that ignore present value include:
   A. average rate of return.
   B. cash payback.
   C. both A and B.
   D. neither A nor B.

2. Management is considering a $100,000 investment in a project with a five-year life and no residual value. If the total income from the project is expected to be $60,000 and straight-line depreciation is used, the average rate of return is:
   A. 12%.   C. 60%.
   B. 24%.   D. 75%.

3. The expected period of time that will elapse between the date of a capital investment and the complete recovery of the amount of cash invested is called the:

   A. average rate of return period.
   B. cash payback period.
   C. net present value period.
   D. internal rate of return period.

4. A project that will cost $120,000 is estimated to generate cash flows of $25,000 per year for eight years. What is the net present value of the project, assuming an 11% required rate of return? (Use the present value tables in Appendix A.)
   A. ($38,214)   C. $55,180
   B. $8,653   D. $75,000

5. A project is estimated to generate cash flows of $40,000 per year for 10 years. The cost of the project is $226,009. What is the internal rate of return for this project?
   A. 8%   C. 12%
   B. 10%   D. 14%

Eye Openers
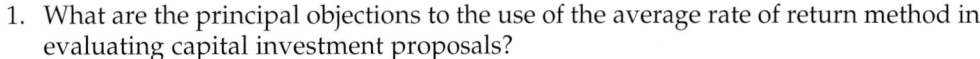

1. What are the principal objections to the use of the average rate of return method in evaluating capital investment proposals?
2. Discuss the principal limitations of the cash payback method for evaluating capital investment proposals.
3. Why would the average rate of return differ from the internal rate of return on the same project?
4. What information does the cash payback period ignore that is included by the net present value method?
5. Your boss has suggested that a one-year payback period is the same as a 100% average rate of return. Do you agree?
6. Why would the cash payback method understate the attractiveness of a project with a large residual value?
7. Why would the use of the cash payback period for analyzing the financial performance of theatrical releases from a motion picture production studio be supported over the net present value method?
8. A net present value analysis used to evaluate a proposed equipment acquisition indicated a $7,900 net present value. What is the meaning of the $7,900 as it relates to the desirability of the proposal?
9. Two projects have an identical net present value of $9,000. Are both projects equal in desirability?
10. What are the major disadvantages of the use of the net present value method of analyzing capital investment proposals?
11. What are the major disadvantages of the use of the internal rate of return method of analyzing capital investment proposals?
12. What provision of the Internal Revenue Code is especially important to consider in analyzing capital investment proposals?
13. What method can be used to place two capital investment proposals with unequal useful lives on a comparable basis?
14. What are the major advantages of leasing a fixed asset rather than purchasing it?
15. Give an example of a qualitative factor that should be considered in a capital investment analysis related to acquiring automated factory equipment.
16. Monsanto Company, a large chemical and fibers company, invested $37 million in state-of-the-art systems to improve process control, laboratory automation, and local area network (LAN) communications. The investment was not justified merely on cost savings but was also justified on the basis of qualitative considerations. Monsanto management viewed the investment as a critical element toward achieving its vision of the future. What qualitative and quantitative considerations do you believe Monsanto would have considered in its strategic evaluation of these investments?

Practice Exercises

PE 26-1A
Average rate of return
obj. 2
EE 26-1   p. 1166

Determine the average rate of return for a project that is estimated to yield total income of $36,000 over three years, has a cost of $65,000, and has a $15,000 residual value. Round to one decimal place.

PE 26-1B
Average rate of return
obj. 2
EE 26-1   p. 1166

Determine the average rate of return for a project that is estimated to yield total income of $136,000 over five years, has a cost of $380,000, and has a $20,000 residual value. Round to one decimal place.

PE 26-2A
Cash payback period
obj. 2
EE 26-2   p. 1167

A project has estimated annual net cash flows of $8,400. It is estimated to cost $37,800. Determine the cash payback period. Round to one decimal place.

PE 26-2B
Cash payback period
obj. 2
EE 26-2   p. 1167

A project has estimated annual net cash flows of $114,000. It is estimated to cost $706,800. Determine the cash payback period. Round to one decimal place.

PE 26-3A
Net present value
obj. 3
EE 26-3   p. 1173

A project has estimated annual net cash flows of $9,000 for four years and is estimated to cost $30,050. Assume a minimum acceptable rate of return of 10%. Using Exhibit 2, determine (1) the net present value of the project and (2) the present value index, rounded to two decimal places.

PE 26-3B
Net present value
obj. 3
EE 26-3   p. 1173

A project has estimated annual net cash flows of $82,000 for five years and is estimated to cost $259,000. Assume a minimum acceptable rate of return of 12%. Using Exhibit 2, determine (1) the net present value of the project and (2) the present value index, rounded to two decimal places.

PE 26-4A
Internal rate of return
obj. 3
EE 26-4   p. 1176

A project is estimated to cost $427,779 and provide annual net cash flows of $87,000 for six years. Determine the internal rate of return for this project, using Exhibit 2.

PE 26-4B
Internal rate of return
obj. 3
EE 26-4   p. 1176

A project is estimated to cost $56,434 and provide annual net cash flows of $14,000 for nine years. Determine the internal rate of return for this project, using Exhibit 2.

PE 26-5A
Net present value—
unequal lives
obj. 4
EE 26-5   p. 1179

Project 1 requires an original investment of $10,000. The project will yield cash flows of $3,000 per year for seven years. Project 2 has a calculated net present value of $2,500 over a four-year life. Project 1 could be sold at the end of four years for a price of $9,000. (a) Determine the net present value of Project 1 over a four-year life with residual value, assuming a minimum rate of return of 20%. (b) Which project provides the greatest net present value?

PE 26-5B
Net present value—
unequal lives
obj. 4
EE 26-5   p. 1179

Project A requires an original investment of $125,000. The project will yield cash flows of $24,000 per year for nine years. Project B has a calculated net present value of $2,400 over a six-year life. Project A could be sold at the end of six years for a price of $60,000. (a) Determine the net present value of Project A over a six-year life with residual value, assuming a minimum rate of return of 12%. (b) Which project provides the greatest net present value?

Exercises

EX 26-1
Average rate of return
obj. 2

✔ Testing
equipment, 5.5%

The following data are accumulated by Eco-Labs, Inc. in evaluating two competing capital investment proposals:

	Testing Equipment	Vehicle
Amount of investment	$80,000	$28,000
Useful life	6 years	8 years
Estimated residual value	0	0
Estimated total income over the useful life	$13,200	$14,000

Determine the expected average rate of return for each proposal. Round to one decimal place.

EX 26-2
Average rate of return—cost savings
obj. 2

Master Fab Inc. is considering an investment in equipment that will replace direct labor. The equipment has a cost of $115,000 with a $10,000 residual value and a 10-year life. The equipment will replace one employee who has an average wage of $26,000 per year. In addition, the equipment will have operating and energy costs of $5,500 per year.

Determine the average rate of return on the equipment, giving effect to straight-line depreciation on the investment.

EX 26-3
Average rate of return—new product
obj. 2

✔ Average annual
income, $138,000

Pocket Pilot Inc. is considering an investment in new equipment that will be used to manufacture a mobile communications device. The device is expected to generate additional annual sales of 6,000 units at $280 per unit. The equipment has a cost of $640,000, residual value of $50,000, and an 8-year life. The equipment can only be used to manufacture the device. The cost to manufacture the device is shown below.

Cost per unit:	
Direct labor	$ 45.00
Direct materials	180.00
Factory overhead (including depreciation)	32.00
Total cost per unit	$257.00

Determine the average rate of return on the equipment.

EX 26-4
Calculate cash flows
obj. 2

Year 1: ($102,900)

Out of Eden, Inc. is planning to invest in new manufacturing equipment to make a new garden tool. The new garden tool is expected to generate additional annual sales of 9,000 units at $42 each. The new manufacturing equipment will cost $156,000 and is expected to have a 10-year life and $12,000 residual value. Selling expenses related to the new product are expected to be 5% of sales revenue. The cost to manufacture the product includes the following on a per-unit basis:

Direct labor	$ 7.00
Direct materials	23.40
Fixed factory overhead—depreciation	1.60
Variable factory overhead	3.60
Total	$35.60

Determine the net cash flows for the first year of the project, Years 2–9, and for the last year of the project.

EX 26-5
Cash payback period
obj. 2

✔ Location 1:
6 years

Primera Banco is evaluating two capital investment proposals for a drive-up ATM kiosk, each requiring an investment of $360,000 and each with an 8-year life and expected total net cash flows of $480,000. Location 1 is expected to provide equal annual net cash flows of $60,000, and Location 2 is expected to have the following unequal annual net cash flows:

Year 1	$120,000	Year 5	$30,000
Year 2	90,000	Year 6	30,000
Year 3	75,000	Year 7	30,000
Year 4	75,000	Year 8	30,000

Determine the cash payback period for both location proposals.

EX 26-6
Cash payback method

obj. **2**

✔ a. Liquid Soap: 3 years

Gentle Care Products Company is considering an investment in one of two new product lines. The investment required for either product line is $500,000. The net cash flows associated with each product are as follows:

Year	Liquid Soap	Body Lotion
1	$190,000	$100,000
2	180,000	100,000
3	130,000	100,000
4	110,000	100,000
5	80,000	100,000
6	50,000	100,000
7	30,000	100,000
8	30,000	100,000
Total	$800,000	$800,000

a. Recommend a product offering to Gentle Care Products Company, based on the cash payback period for each product line.
b. ➤ Why is one product line preferred over the other, even though they both have the same total net cash flows through eight periods?

EX 26-7
Net present value method

obj. **3**

✔ a. NPV ($27,370)

The following data are accumulated by Reynolds Company in evaluating the purchase of $104,000 of equipment, having a four-year useful life:

	Net Income	Net Cash Flow
Year 1	$38,000	$64,000
Year 2	23,000	49,000
Year 3	11,000	37,000
Year 4	(1,000)	25,000

a. Assuming that the desired rate of return is 15%, determine the net present value for the proposal. Use the table of the present value of $1 appearing in Exhibit 1 of this chapter.
b. ➤ Would management be likely to look with favor on the proposal? Explain.

EX 26-8
Net present value method

obj. **3**

✔ a. 2011, $11,000

Rapid Delivery, Inc. is considering the purchase of an additional delivery vehicle for $38,000 on January 1, 2010. The truck is expected to have a five-year life with an expected residual value of $5,000 at the end of five years. The expected additional revenues from the added delivery capacity are anticipated to be $60,000 per year for each of the next five years. A driver will cost $43,000 in 2010, with an expected annual salary increase of $2,000 for each year thereafter. The insurance for the truck is estimated to cost $4,000 per year.

a. Determine the expected annual net cash flows from the delivery truck investment for 2010–2014.
b. Calculate the net present value of the investment, assuming that the minimum desired rate of return is 12%. Use the present value of $1 table appearing in Exhibit 1 of this chapter.
c. Is the additional truck a good investment based on your analysis?

EX 26-9
Net present value method—annuity

obj. **3**

a. $24 million

Hideaway Hotels is considering the construction of a new hotel for $150 million. The expected life of the hotel is 30 years with no residual value. The hotel is expected to earn revenues of $44 million per year. Total expenses, including depreciation, are expected to be $25 million per year. Hideaway management has set a minimum acceptable rate of return of 14%.

a. Determine the equal annual net cash flows from operating the hotel.
b. Calculate the net present value of the new hotel using the present value of an annuity of $1 table found in Appendix A. Round to the nearest million dollars.
c. Does your analysis support construction of the new hotel?

EX 26-10

Net present value method—annuity

obj. 3

✔ a. $69,000

E & T Excavation Company is planning an investment of $245,000 for a bulldozer. The bulldozer is expected to operate for 1,500 hours per year for five years. Customers will be charged $130 per hour for bulldozer work. The bulldozer operator costs $32 per hour in wages and benefits. The bulldozer is expected to require annual maintenance costing $15,000. The bulldozer uses fuel that is expected to cost $42 per hour of bulldozer operation.

a. Determine the equal annual net cash flows from operating the bulldozer.
b. Determine the net present value of the investment, assuming that the desired rate of return is 10%. Use the table of present values of an annuity of $1 in the chapter. Round to the nearest dollar.
c. ━━━━▶ Should E & T invest in the bulldozer, based on this analysis?

EX 26-11

Net present value method

obj. 3

✔ a. $288,800,000

Carnival Corporation has recently placed into service some of the largest cruise ships in the world. One of these ships, the *Carnival Dream*, can hold up to 3,600 passengers and cost $750 million to build. Assume the following additional information:

• There will be 300 cruise days per year operated at a full capacity of 3,600 passengers.
• The variable expenses per passenger are estimated to be $90 per cruise day.
• The revenue per passenger is expected to be $450 per cruise day.
• The fixed expenses for running the ship, other than depreciation, are estimated to be $100,000,000 per year.
• The ship has a service life of 10 years, with a residual value of $120,000,000 at the end of 10 years.

a. Determine the annual net cash flow from operating the cruise ship.
b. Determine the net present value of this investment, assuming a 12% minimum rate of return. Use the present value tables provided in the chapter in determining your answer.

EX 26-12

Present value index

obj. 3

✔ Location A, 1.07

Hot on the Spot Doughnuts has computed the net present value for capital expenditure locations A and B, using the net present value method. Relevant data related to the computation are as follows:

	Location A	Location B
Total present value of net cash flow	$371,290	$396,096
Amount to be invested	347,000	412,600
Net present value	$ (24,290)	$ (16,504)

Determine the present value index for each proposal.

EX 26-13

Net present value method and present value index

obj. 3

✔ b. Packing Machine, 1.18

MVP Sports Equipment Company is considering an investment in one of two machines. The sewing machine will increase productivity from sewing 150 baseballs per hour to sewing 270 per hour. The contribution margin is $0.48 per baseball. Assume that any increased production of baseballs can be sold. The second machine is an automatic packing machine for the golf ball line. The packing machine will reduce packing labor cost. The labor cost saved is equivalent to $26 per hour. The sewing machine will cost $384,600, have an eight-year life, and will operate for 1,700 hours per year. The packing machine will cost $157,900, have an eight-year life, and will operate for 1,600 hours per year. MVP seeks a minimum rate of return of 15% on its investments.

a. Determine the net present value for the two machines. Use the table of present values of an annuity of $1 in the chapter. Round to the nearest dollar.
b. Determine the present value index for the two machines. Round to two decimal places.
c. ━━━━▶ If MVP has sufficient funds for only one of the machines and qualitative factors are equal between the two machines, in which machine should it invest?

EX 26-14
Average rate of return, cash payback period, net present value method

objs. 2, 3

✔ b. 4 years

Great Plains Transportation Inc. is considering acquiring equipment at a cost of $246,000. The equipment has an estimated life of 10 years and no residual value. It is expected to provide yearly net cash flows of $61,500. The company's minimum desired rate of return for net present value analysis is 10%.

Compute the following:

a. The average rate of return, giving effect to straight-line depreciation on the investment.
b. The cash payback period.
c. The net present value. Use the table of the present value of an annuity of $1 appearing in this chapter. Round to the nearest dollar.

EX 26-15
Payback period, net present value analysis, and qualitative considerations

objs. 2, 3, 4

✔ a. 4 years

The plant manager of Shannon Electronics Company is considering the purchase of new automated assembly equipment. The new equipment will cost $2,400,000. The manager believes that the new investment will result in direct labor savings of $600,000 per year for 10 years.

a. What is the payback period on this project?
b. What is the net present value, assuming a 10% rate of return?
c. ▬▬▬▶ What else should the manager consider in the analysis?

EX 26-16
Internal rate of return method

obj. 3

✔ a. 3.326

The internal rate of return method is used by Carlisle Construction Co. in analyzing a capital expenditure proposal that involves an investment of $49,890 and annual net cash flows of $15,000 for each of the six years of its useful life.

a. Determine a present value factor for an annuity of $1 which can be used in determining the internal rate of return.
b. Using the factor determined in part (a) and the present value of an annuity of $1 table appearing in this chapter, determine the internal rate of return for the proposal.

EX 26-17
Internal rate of return method

obj. 3

The Canyons Resort, a Utah ski resort, recently announced a $400 million expansion to lodging properties, lifts, and terrain. Assume that this investment is estimated to produce $95.42 million in equal annual cash flows for each of the first 10 years of the project life.

Determine the expected internal rate of return of this project for 10 years, using the present value of an annuity of $1 table found in Exhibit 2.

EX 26-18
Internal rate of return method—two projects

obj. 3

✔ a. Delivery truck, 15%

Cousin's Salted Snack Company is considering two possible investments: a delivery truck or a bagging machine. The delivery truck would cost $39,287 and could be used to deliver an additional 48,200 bags of taquitos chips per year. Each bag of chips can be sold for a contribution margin of $0.42. The delivery truck operating expenses, excluding depreciation, are $0.60 per mile for 18,000 miles per year. The bagging machine would replace an old bagging machine, and its net investment cost would be $65,718. The new machine would require three fewer hours of direct labor per day. Direct labor is $18 per hour. There are 250 operating days in the year. Both the truck and the bagging machine are estimated to have seven-year lives. The minimum rate of return is 13%. However, Cousin's has funds to invest in only one of the projects.

a. Compute the internal rate of return for each investment. Use the table of present values of an annuity of $1 in the chapter.
b. ▬▬▬▶ Provide a memo to management with a recommendation.

EX 26-19
Net present value method and internal rate of return method

obj. 3

✔ a. ($10,582)

Buckeye Healthcare Corp. is proposing to spend $109,296 on an eight-year project that has estimated net cash flows of $22,000 for each of the eight years.

a. Compute the net present value, using a rate of return of 15%. Use the table of present values of an annuity of $1 in the chapter.
b. ▬▬▬▶ Based on the analysis prepared in part (a), is the rate of return (1) more than 15%, (2) 15%, or (3) less than 15%? Explain.
c. Determine the internal rate of return by computing a present value factor for an annuity of $1 and using the table of the present value of an annuity of $1 presented in the text.

EX 26-20
Identify error in capital investment analysis calculations
obj. 3

Horizon Solutions Inc. is considering the purchase of automated machinery that is expected to have a useful life of five years and no residual value. The average rate of return on the average investment has been computed to be 20%, and the cash payback period was computed to be 5.5 years.

➤ Do you see any reason to question the validity of the data presented? Explain.

EX 26-21
Net present value— unequal lives
objs. 3, 4

✔ Net present value, Apartment Complex, $24,530

Lordsland Development Company has two competing projects: an apartment complex and an office building. Both projects have an initial investment of $720,000. The net cash flows estimated for the two projects are as follows:

	Net Cash Flow	
Year	Apartment Complex	Office Building
1	$225,000	$290,000
2	200,000	290,000
3	200,000	230,000
4	140,000	220,000
5	140,000	
6	105,000	
7	80,000	
8	50,000	

The estimated residual value of the apartment complex at the end of Year 4 is $325,000.

Determine which project should be favored, comparing the net present values of the two projects and assuming a minimum rate of return of 15%. Use the table of present values in the chapter.

EX 26-22
Net present value— unequal lives
objs. 3, 4

Al a Mode, Inc. is considering one of two investment options. Option 1 is a $40,000 investment in new blending equipment that is expected to produce equal annual cash flows of $12,000 for each of seven years. Option 2 is a $45,000 investment in a new computer system that is expected to produce equal annual cash flows of $15,500 for each of five years. The residual value of the blending equipment at the end of the fifth year is estimated to be $8,000. The computer system has no expected residual value at the end of the fifth year.

Assume there is sufficient capital to fund only one of the projects. Determine which project should be selected, comparing the (a) net present values and (b) present value indices of the two projects, assuming a minimum rate of return of 10%. Round the present value index to two decimal places. Use the table of present values in the chapter.

Problems Series A

PR 26-1A
Average rate of return method, net present value method, and analysis
objs. 2, 3

✔ 1.a. 17.5%

The capital investment committee of Cross Continent Trucking Inc. is considering two investment projects. The estimated income from operations and net cash flows from each investment are as follows:

	Warehouse		Tracking Technology	
Year	Income from Operations	Net Cash Flow	Income from Operations	Net Cash Flow
1	$ 42,000	$138,000	$ 89,000	$185,000
2	42,000	138,000	69,000	165,000
3	42,000	138,000	34,000	130,000
4	42,000	138,000	14,000	110,000
5	42,000	138,000	4,000	100,000
Total	$210,000	$690,000	$210,000	$690,000

Each project requires an investment of $480,000. Straight-line depreciation will be used, and no residual value is expected. The committee has selected a rate of 15% for purposes of the net present value analysis.

Instructions

1. Compute the following:
   a. The average rate of return for each investment. Round to one decimal place.
   b. The net present value for each investment. Use the present value of $1 table appearing in this chapter.
2. ➡ Prepare a brief report for the capital investment committee, advising it on the relative merits of the two projects.

PR 26-2A
Cash payback period, net present value method, and analysis

objs. **2, 3**

✔ 1. b. Home & Garden, $127,158

At Home Publications Inc. is considering two new magazine products. The estimated net cash flows from each product are as follows:

Year	Home & Garden	Music Beat
1	$150,000	$125,000
2	120,000	145,000
3	105,000	100,000
4	84,000	70,000
5	41,000	60,000
Total	$500,000	$500,000

Each product requires an investment of $270,000. A rate of 10% has been selected for the net present value analysis.

Instructions

1. Compute the following for each product:
   a. Cash payback period.
   b. The net present value. Use the present value of $1 table appearing in this chapter.
2. ➡ Prepare a brief report advising management on the relative merits of each of the two products.

PR 26-3A
Net present value method, present value index, and analysis

obj. **3**

✔ 2. Branch office expansion, 1.07

United Bankshores, Inc. wishes to evaluate three capital investment projects by using the net present value method. Relevant data related to the projects are summarized as follows:

	Branch Office Expansion	Computer System Upgrade	Install Internet Bill-Pay
Amount to be invested	$700,000	$475,000	$280,000
Annual net cash flows:			
Year 1	350,000	250,000	160,000
Year 2	325,000	225,000	110,000
Year 3	300,000	200,000	80,000

Instructions

1. Assuming that the desired rate of return is 15%, prepare a net present value analysis for each project. Use the present value of $1 table appearing in this chapter.
2. Determine a present value index for each project. Round to two decimal places.
3. ➡ Which project offers the largest amount of present value per dollar of investment? Explain.

PR 26-4A
Net present value method, internal rate of return method, and analysis

obj. **3**

✔ 1. a. Radio station, $110,250

The management of Quest Media Inc. is considering two capital investment projects. The estimated net cash flows from each project are as follows:

Year	Radio Station	TV Station
1	$350,000	$700,000
2	350,000	700,000
3	350,000	700,000
4	350,000	700,000

The radio station requires an investment of $999,250, while the TV station requires an investment of $2,125,900. No residual value is expected from either project.

Instructions
1. Compute the following for each project:
    a. The net present value. Use a rate of 10% and the present value of an annuity of $1 table appearing in this chapter.
    b. A present value index. Round to two decimal places.
2. Determine the internal rate of return for each project by (a) computing a present value factor for an annuity of $1 and (b) using the present value of an annuity of $1 table appearing in this chapter.
3. ➤ What advantage does the internal rate of return method have over the net present value method in comparing projects?

PR 26-5A
Evaluate alternative capital investment decisions

objs. 3, 4

✔ 1. Site B, $159,920

The investment committee of Grid Iron Restaurants Inc. is evaluating two restaurant sites. The sites have different useful lives, but each requires an investment of $565,000. The estimated net cash flows from each site are as follows:

	Net Cash Flows	
Year	Site A	Site B
1	$225,000	$280,000
2	225,000	280,000
3	225,000	280,000
4	225,000	280,000
5	225,000	
6	225,000	

The committee has selected a rate of 20% for purposes of net present value analysis. It also estimates that the residual value at the end of each restaurant's useful life is $0, but at the end of the fourth year, Site A's residual value would be $290,000.

Instructions
1. For each site, compute the net present value. Use the present value of an annuity of $1 table appearing in this chapter. (Ignore the unequal lives of the projects.)
2. For each site, compute the net present value, assuming that Site A is adjusted to a four-year life for purposes of analysis. Use the present value of $1 table appearing in this chapter.
3. ➤ Prepare a report to the investment committee, providing your advice on the relative merits of the two sites.

PR 26-6A
Capital rationing decision involving four proposals

objs. 2, 3, 5

✔ 5. Proposal B, 1.26

Grant Communications Inc. is considering allocating a limited amount of capital investment funds among four proposals. The amount of proposed investment, estimated income from operations, and net cash flow for each proposal are as follows:

	Investment	Year	Income from Operations	Net Cash Flow
Proposal A:	$425,000	1	$ 40,000	$ 125,000
		2	40,000	125,000
		3	40,000	125,000
		4	15,000	100,000
		5	(35,000)	50,000
			$100,000	$ 525,000
Proposal B:	$610,000	1	$158,000	$ 280,000
		2	158,000	280,000
		3	78,000	200,000
		4	28,000	150,000
		5	(22,000)	100,000
			$400,000	$1,010,000
Proposal C:	$275,000	1	$ 45,000	$ 100,000
		2	45,000	100,000
		3	45,000	100,000
		4	45,000	100,000
		5	35,000	90,000
			$215,000	$ 490,000

(continued)

	Investment	Year	Income from Operations	Net Cash Flow
Proposal D:	$190,000	1	$ 22,000	$ 60,000
		2	22,000	60,000
		3	22,000	60,000
		4	2,000	40,000
		5	2,000	40,000
			$ 70,000	$ 260,000

The company's capital rationing policy requires a maximum cash payback period of three years. In addition, a minimum average rate of return of 12% is required on all projects. If the preceding standards are met, the net present value method and present value indexes are used to rank the remaining proposals.

Instructions
1. Compute the cash payback period for each of the four proposals.
2. Giving effect to straight-line depreciation on the investments and assuming no estimated residual value, compute the average rate of return for each of the four proposals. Round to one decimal place.
3. Using the following format, summarize the results of your computations in parts (1) and (2). By placing the calculated amounts in the first two columns on the left and by placing a check mark in the appropriate column to the right, indicate which proposals should be accepted for further analysis and which should be rejected.

Proposal	Cash Payback Period	Average Rate of Return	Accept for Further Analysis	Reject
A				
B				
C				
D				

4. For the proposals accepted for further analysis in part (3), compute the net present value. Use a rate of 12% and the present value of $1 table appearing in this chapter. Round to the nearest dollar.
5. Compute the present value index for each of the proposals in part (4). Round to two decimal places.
6. Rank the proposals from most attractive to least attractive, based on the present values of net cash flows computed in part (4).
7. Rank the proposals from most attractive to least attractive, based on the present value indexes computed in part (5). Round to two decimal places.
8. Based on the analyses, comment on the relative attractiveness of the proposals ranked in parts (6) and (7).

Problems Series B

PR 26-1B
Average rate of return method, net present value method, and analysis

objs. 2, 3

✔ 1. a. 60%

The capital investment committee of Windsor Landscaping Company is considering two capital investments. The estimated income from operations and net cash flows from each investment are as follows:

	Greenhouse		Skid Loader	
Year	Income from Operations	Net Cash Flow	Income from Operations	Net Cash Flow
1	$ 27,000	$ 45,000	$ 47,000	$ 65,000
2	27,000	45,000	32,000	50,000
3	27,000	45,000	24,000	42,000
4	27,000	45,000	17,000	35,000
5	27,000	45,000	15,000	33,000
	$135,000	$225,000	$135,000	$225,000

Each project requires an investment of $90,000. Straight-line depreciation will be used, and no residual value is expected. The committee has selected a rate of 12% for purposes of the net present value analysis.

Instructions
1. Compute the following:
   a. The average rate of return for each investment.
   b. The net present value for each investment. Use the present value of $1 table appearing in this chapter.
2. ➤ Prepare a brief report for the capital investment committee, advising it on the relative merits of the two investments.

PR 26-2B

Cash payback period, net present value method, and analysis

objs. 2, 3

✔ 1. b. Plant
Expansion, $11,100

Be You Apparel Inc. is considering two investment projects. The estimated net cash flows from each project are as follows:

Year	Plant Expansion	Retail Store Expansion
1	$170,000	$200,000
2	170,000	160,000
3	140,000	120,000
4	110,000	120,000
5	120,000	110,000
Total	$710,000	$710,000

Each project requires an investment of $480,000. A rate of 15% has been selected for the net present value analysis.

Instructions
1. Compute the following for each product:
   a. Cash payback period.
   b. The net present value. Use the present value of $1 table appearing in this chapter.
2. ➤ Prepare a brief report advising management on the relative merits of each project.

PR 26-3B

Net present value method, present value index, and analysis

obj. 3

✔ 2. Railcars, 1.17

Atlantic Coast Railroad Company wishes to evaluate three capital investment proposals by using the net present value method. Relevant data related to the proposals are summarized as follows:

	New Maintenance Yard	Acquire Railcars	Route Expansion
Amount to be invested	$14,000,000	$45,000,000	$25,000,000
Annual net cash flows:			
Year 1	7,400,000	32,000,000	18,500,000
Year 2	6,000,000	24,500,000	14,500,000
Year 3	5,500,000	15,800,000	10,800,000

Instructions
1. Assuming that the desired rate of return is 20%, prepare a net present value analysis for each proposal. Use the present value of $1 table appearing in this chapter.
2. Determine a present value index for each proposal. Round to two decimal places.
3. ➤ Which proposal offers the largest amount of present value per dollar of investment? Explain.

PR 26-4B

Net present value method, internal rate of return method, and analysis

obj. 3

✔ 1. a. Generating
unit, $248,240

The management of Mid South Utilities Inc. is considering two capital investment projects. The estimated net cash flows from each project are as follows:

Year	Generating Unit	Distribution Network Expansion
1	$580,000	$210,000
2	580,000	210,000
3	580,000	210,000
4	580,000	210,000

The generating unit requires an investment of $1,761,460, while the distribution network expansion requires an investment of $665,700. No residual value is expected from either project.

Instructions

1. Compute the following for each project:
   a. The net present value. Use a rate of 6% and the present value of an annuity of $1 table appearing in this chapter.
   b. A present value index. Round to two decimal places.
2. Determine the internal rate of return for each project by (a) computing a present value factor for an annuity of $1 and (b) using the present value of an annuity of $1 table appearing in this chapter.
3. ━━━━▶ What advantage does the internal rate of return method have over the net present value method in comparing projects?

PR 26-5B

Evaluate alternative capital investment decisions

objs. **3, 4**

✔ 1. Project II, $79,625

The investment committee of Reliant Insurance Co. is evaluating two projects. The projects have different useful lives, but each requires an investment of $300,000. The estimated net cash flows from each project are as follows:

	Net Cash Flows	
Year	Project I	Project II
1	$90,000	$125,000
2	90,000	125,000
3	90,000	125,000
4	90,000	125,000
5	90,000	
6	90,000	

The committee has selected a rate of 12% for purposes of net present value analysis. It also estimates that the residual value at the end of each project's useful life is $0, but at the end of the fourth year, Project I's residual value would be $175,000.

Instructions

1. For each project, compute the net present value. Use the present value of an annuity of $1 table appearing in this chapter. (Ignore the unequal lives of the projects.)
2. For each project, compute the net present value, assuming that Project I is adjusted to a four-year life for purposes of analysis. Use the present value of $1 table appearing in this chapter.
3. ━━━━▶ Prepare a report to the investment committee, providing your advice on the relative merits of the two projects.

PR 26-6B

Capital rationing decision involving four proposals

objs. **2, 3, 5**

✔ 5. Proposal B, 1.15

Empire Capital Group is considering allocating a limited amount of capital investment funds among four proposals. The amount of proposed investment, estimated income from operations, and net cash flow for each proposal are as follows:

	Investment	Year	Income from Operations	Net Cash Flow
Proposal A:	$420,000	1	$ 86,000	$ 170,000
		2	46,000	130,000
		3	16,000	100,000
		4	(4,000)	80,000
		5	(4,000)	80,000
			$140,000	$ 560,000
Proposal B:	$850,000	1	$130,000	$ 300,000
		2	130,000	300,000
		3	130,000	300,000
		4	130,000	300,000
		5	80,000	250,000
			$600,000	$1,450,000
Proposal C:	$250,000	1	$20,000	$ 70,000
		2	20,000	70,000
		3	20,000	70,000
		4	(10,000)	40,000
		5	(10,000)	40,000
			$ 40,000	$ 290,000

(continued)

	Investment	Year	Income from Operations	Net Cash Flow
Proposal D:	$180,000	1	$ 54,000	$ 90,000
		2	24,000	60,000
		3	24,000	60,000
		4	14,000	50,000
		5	14,000	50,000
			$130,000	$310,000

The company's capital rationing policy requires a maximum cash payback period of three years. In addition, a minimum average rate of return of 12% is required on all projects. If the preceding standards are met, the net present value method and present value indexes are used to rank the remaining proposals.

Instructions

1. Compute the cash payback period for each of the four proposals.
2. Giving effect to straight-line depreciation on the investments and assuming no estimated residual value, compute the average rate of return for each of the four proposals. Round to one decimal place.
3. Using the following format, summarize the results of your computations in parts (1) and (2). By placing the calculated amounts in the first two columns on the left and by placing a check mark in the appropriate column to the right, indicate which proposals should be accepted for further analysis and which should be rejected.

Proposal	Cash Payback Period	Average Rate of Return	Accept for Further Analysis	Reject
A				
B				
C				
D				

4. For the proposals accepted for further analysis in part (3), compute the net present value. Use a rate of 15% and the present value of $1 table appearing in this chapter. Round to the nearest dollar.
5. Compute the present value index for each of the proposals in part (4). Round to two decimal places.
6. Rank the proposals from most attractive to least attractive, based on the present values of net cash flows computed in part (4).
7. Rank the proposals from most attractive to least attractive, based on the present value indexes computed in part (5).
8. ➤ Based on the analyses, comment on the relative attractiveness of the proposals ranked in parts (6) and (7).

Special Activities ● ● ● ● ➤

You can access the special activities online at **www.cengage.com/accounting/reeve**.

Excel Success Special Activities ● ● ● ● ➤

SA 26-1
Net present value

The Cambridge Company is considering expansion into the South. The expansion effort is expected to cost $215,000. The net cash flows expected from this investment are $25,000 per year for the first two years, and $40,000 per year for the remaining eight years of the project life.

a. Open the Excel file *SA26-1*.
b. Determine the net present value of the expansion project assuming a minimum desired rate of return of 12% is desired.

c. When you have completed the analysis, perform a "save as," replacing the entire file name with the following:

SA26-1_[your first name initial]_[your last name]

SA 26-2
Net present value

Gold Software, Inc., is considering an investment in a new game product titled *EagleGolf*. The project will require an investment of $3,800,000. The five-year revenues and cash expenses over the product's life are estimated as follows:

	Revenues	Cash Expenditures
Year 1	$ 500,000	$ 750,000
Year 2	2,600,000	1,500,000
Year 3	3,400,000	1,700,000
Year 4	3,000,000	1,000,000
Year 5	2,100,000	800,000

a. Open the Excel file *SA26-2*.
b. Assuming a minimum desired rate of return of 8%, determine the net present value of the project.
c. When you have completed the analysis, perform a "save as," replacing the entire file name with the following:

SA26-2_[your first name initial]_[your last name]

SA 26-3
Internal rate of return

Celtic Pride Productions, Inc., produces movies. It is estimated that a new movie, *Kelly's Revenge*, will cost $70 million to produce. The movie is estimated to generate net cash flows from ticket, DVD, and cable sales over the next four years as follows:

Year 1	$80,000,000
Year 2	45,000,000
Year 3	15,000,000
Year 4	10,000,000

a. Open the Excel file *SA26-3*.
b. Determine the internal rate of return for this movie.
c. When you have completed the analysis, perform a "save as," replacing the entire file name with the following:

SA26-3_[your first name initial]_[your last name]

SA 26-4
Internal rate of return

Ryder Company is planning one of two alternative investments. The first investment requires a $60,000 investment and will generate net cash flows of $24,000 per year for five years. The second investment requires an investment of $90,000 and will generate net cash flows as follows:

	Net Cash Flows
Year 1	15,000
Year 2	35,000
Year 3	60,000
Year 4	80,000
Year 5	20,000

a. Open the Excel file *SA26-4*.
b. Determine the internal rate of return for each alternative.
c. Indicate in the spreadsheet which alternative should be selected.
d. When you have completed the analysis, perform a "save as," replacing the entire file name with the following:

SA26-4_[your first name initial]_[your last name]

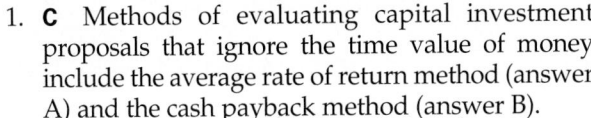

Answers to Self-Examination Questions

1. **C** Methods of evaluating capital investment proposals that ignore the time value of money include the average rate of return method (answer A) and the cash payback method (answer B).

2. **B** The average rate of return is 24% (answer B), determined by dividing the expected average annual earnings by the average investment, as follows:

$$\frac{\$60,000/5}{[(\$100,000) + 0]/2} = 24\%$$

3. **B** Of the four methods of analyzing proposals for capital investments, the cash payback period (answer B) refers to the expected period of time required to recover the amount of cash to be invested. The average rate of return (answer A) is a measure of the anticipated profitability of a proposal. The net present value method (answer C) reduces the expected future net cash

flows originating from a proposal to their present values. The internal rate of return method (answer D) uses present value concepts to compute the rate of return from the net cash flows expected from the investment.

4. **B** The net present value is determined as follows:

Present value of $25,000 for 8 years at 11%	
($25,000 × 5.14612)	$128,653
Less project cost	120,000
Net present value	$ 8,653

5. **C** The internal rate of return for this project is determined by solving for the present value of an annuity factor that when multiplied by $40,000 will equal $226,009. By division, the factor is:

$$\frac{\$226,009}{\$40,000} = 5.65022$$

In Appendix A on pp. A-4 and A-5, scan along the $n = 10$ years row until finding the 5.65022 factor. The column for this factor is 12%.

Appendix A

Interest Tables

Present Value of $1 at Compound Interest Due in _n_ Periods

Periods	5%	5.5%	6%	6.5%	7%	8%
1	0.95238	0.94787	0.94334	0.93897	0.93458	0.92593
2	0.90703	0.89845	0.89000	0.88166	0.87344	0.85734
3	0.86384	0.85161	0.83962	0.82785	0.81630	0.79383
4	0.82270	0.80722	0.79209	0.77732	0.76290	0.73503
5	0.78353	0.76513	0.74726	0.72988	0.71290	0.68058
6	0.74622	0.72525	0.70496	0.68533	0.66634	0.63017
7	0.71068	0.68744	0.66506	0.64351	0.62275	0.58349
8	0.67684	0.65160	0.62741	0.60423	0.58201	0.54027
9	0.64461	0.61763	0.59190	0.56735	0.54393	0.50025
10	0.61391	0.58543	0.55840	0.53273	0.50835	0.46319
11	0.58468	0.55491	0.52679	0.50021	0.47509	0.42888
12	0.55684	0.52598	0.49697	0.46968	0.44401	0.39711
13	0.53032	0.49856	0.46884	0.44102	0.41496	0.36770
14	0.50507	0.47257	0.44230	0.41410	0.38782	0.34046
15	0.48102	0.44793	0.41726	0.38883	0.36245	0.31524
16	0.45811	0.42458	0.39365	0.36510	0.33874	0.29189
17	0.43630	0.40245	0.37136	0.34281	0.31657	0.27027
18	0.41552	0.38147	0.35034	0.32189	0.29586	0.25025
19	0.39573	0.36158	0.33051	0.30224	0.27651	0.23171
20	0.37689	0.34273	0.31180	0.28380	0.25842	0.21455
21	0.35894	0.32486	0.29416	0.26648	0.24151	0.19866
22	0.34185	0.30793	0.27750	0.25021	0.22571	0.18394
23	0.32557	0.29187	0.26180	0.23494	0.21095	0.17032
24	0.31007	0.27666	0.24698	0.22060	0.19715	0.15770
25	0.29530	0.26223	0.23300	0.20714	0.18425	0.14602
26	0.28124	0.24856	0.21981	0.19450	0.17211	0.13520
27	0.26785	0.23560	0.20737	0.18263	0.16093	0.12519
28	0.25509	0.22332	0.19563	0.17148	0.15040	0.11591
29	0.24295	0.21168	0.18456	0.16101	0.14056	0.10733
30	0.23138	0.20064	0.17411	0.15119	0.13137	0.09938
31	0.22036	0.19018	0.16426	0.14196	0.12277	0.09202
32	0.20987	0.18027	0.15496	0.13329	0.11474	0.08520
33	0.19987	0.17087	0.14619	0.12516	0.10724	0.07889
34	0.19036	0.16196	0.13791	0.11752	0.10022	0.07304
35	0.18129	0.15352	0.13010	0.11035	0.09366	0.06764
40	0.14205	0.11746	0.09722	0.08054	0.06678	0.04603
45	0.11130	0.08988	0.07265	0.05879	0.04761	0.03133
50	0.08720	0.06877	0.05429	0.04291	0.03395	0.02132

Present Value of $1 at Compound Interest Due in *n* Periods

Periods	9%	10%	11%	12%	13%	14%
1	0.91743	0.90909	0.90090	0.89286	0.88496	0.87719
2	0.84168	0.82645	0.81162	0.79719	0.78315	0.76947
3	0.77218	0.75132	0.73119	0.71178	0.69305	0.67497
4	0.70842	0.68301	0.65873	0.63552	0.61332	0.59208
5	0.64993	0.62092	0.59345	0.56743	0.54276	0.51937
6	0.59627	0.56447	0.53464	0.50663	0.48032	0.45559
7	0.54703	0.51316	0.48166	0.45235	0.42506	0.39964
8	0.50187	0.46651	0.43393	0.40388	0.37616	0.35056
9	0.46043	0.42410	0.39092	0.36061	0.33288	0.30751
10	0.42241	0.38554	0.35218	0.32197	0.29459	0.26974
11	0.38753	0.35049	0.31728	0.28748	0.26070	0.23662
12	0.35554	0.31863	0.28584	0.25668	0.23071	0.20756
13	0.32618	0.28966	0.25751	0.22917	0.20416	0.18207
14	0.29925	0.26333	0.23199	0.20462	0.18068	0.15971
15	0.27454	0.23939	0.20900	0.18270	0.15989	0.14010
16	0.25187	0.21763	0.18829	0.16312	0.14150	0.12289
17	0.23107	0.19784	0.16963	0.14564	0.12522	0.10780
18	0.21199	0.17986	0.15282	0.13004	0.11081	0.09456
19	0.19449	0.16351	0.13768	0.11611	0.09806	0.08295
20	0.17843	0.14864	0.12403	0.10367	0.08678	0.07276
21	0.16370	0.13513	0.11174	0.09256	0.07680	0.06383
22	0.15018	0.12285	0.10067	0.08264	0.06796	0.05599
23	0.13778	0.11168	0.09069	0.07379	0.06014	0.04911
24	0.12640	0.10153	0.08170	0.06588	0.05323	0.04308
25	0.11597	0.09230	0.07361	0.05882	0.04710	0.03779
26	0.10639	0.08390	0.06631	0.05252	0.04168	0.03315
27	0.09761	0.07628	0.05974	0.04689	0.03689	0.02908
28	0.08955	0.06934	0.05382	0.04187	0.03264	0.02551
29	0.08216	0.06304	0.04849	0.03738	0.02889	0.02237
30	0.07537	0.05731	0.04368	0.03338	0.02557	0.01963
31	0.06915	0.05210	0.03935	0.02980	0.02262	0.01722
32	0.06344	0.04736	0.03545	0.02661	0.02002	0.01510
33	0.05820	0.04306	0.03194	0.02376	0.01772	0.01325
34	0.05331	0.03914	0.02878	0.02121	0.01568	0.01162
35	0.04899	0.03558	0.02592	0.01894	0.01388	0.01019
40	0.03184	0.02210	0.01538	0.01075	0.00753	0.00529
45	0.02069	0.01372	0.00913	0.00610	0.00409	0.00275
50	0.01345	0.00852	0.00542	0.00346	0.00222	0.00143

Present Value of Ordinary Annuity of $1 per Period

Periods	5%	5.5%	6%	6.5%	7%	8%
1	0.95238	0.94787	0.94340	0.93897	0.93458	0.92593
2	1.85941	1.84632	1.83339	1.82063	1.80802	1.78326
3	2.72325	2.69793	2.67301	2.64848	2.62432	2.57710
4	3.54595	3.50515	3.46511	3.42580	3.38721	3.31213
5	4.32948	4.27028	4.21236	4.15568	4.10020	3.99271
6	5.07569	4.99553	4.91732	4.84101	4.76654	4.62288
7	5.78637	5.68297	5.58238	5.48452	5.38923	5.20637
8	6.46321	6.33457	6.20979	6.08875	5.97130	5.74664
9	7.10782	6.95220	6.80169	6.65610	6.51523	6.24689
10	7.72174	7.53763	7.36009	7.18883	7.02358	6.71008
11	8.30641	8.09254	7.88688	7.68904	7.49867	7.13896
12	8.86325	8.61852	8.38384	8.15873	7.94269	7.53608
13	9.39357	9.11708	8.85268	8.59974	8.35765	7.90378
14	9.89864	9.58965	9.29498	9.01384	8.74547	8.22424
15	10.37966	10.03758	9.71225	9.40267	9.10791	8.55948
16	10.83777	10.46216	10.10590	9.76776	9.44665	8.85137
17	11.27407	10.86461	10.47726	10.11058	9.76322	9.12164
18	11.68959	11.24607	10.82760	10.43247	10.05909	9.37189
19	12.08532	11.60765	11.15812	10.73471	10.33560	9.60360
20	12.46221	11.95038	11.46992	11.01851	10.59401	9.81815
21	12.82115	12.27524	11.76408	11.28498	10.83553	10.01680
22	13.16300	12.58317	12.04158	11.53520	11.06124	10.20074
23	13.48857	12.87504	12.30338	11.77014	11.27219	10.37106
24	13.79864	13.15170	12.55036	11.99074	11.46933	10.52876
25	14.09394	13.41393	12.78336	12.19788	11.65358	10.67478
26	14.37518	13.66250	13.00317	12.39237	11.82578	10.80998
27	14.64303	13.89810	13.21053	12.57500	11.98671	10.93516
28	14.89813	14.12142	13.40616	12.74648	12.13711	11.05108
29	15.14107	14.33310	13.59072	12.90749	12.27767	11.15841
30	15.37245	14.53375	13.76483	13.05868	12.40904	11.25778
31	15.59281	14.72393	13.92909	13.20063	12.53181	11.34980
32	15.80268	14.90420	14.08404	13.33393	12.64656	11.43500
33	16.00255	15.07507	14.23023	13.45909	12.75379	11.51389
34	16.19290	15.23703	14.36814	13.57661	12.85401	11.58693
35	16.37420	15.39055	14.49825	13.68696	12.94767	11.65457
40	17.15909	16.04612	15.04630	14.14553	13.33171	11.92461
45	17.77407	16.54773	15.45583	14.48023	13.60552	12.10840
50	18.25592	16.93152	15.76186	14.72452	13.80075	12.23348

Present Value of Ordinary Annuity of $1 per Period

Periods	9%	10%	11%	12%	13%	14%
1	0.91743	0.90909	0.90090	0.89286	0.88496	0.87719
2	1.75911	1.73554	1.71252	1.69005	1.66810	1.64666
3	2.53130	2.48685	2.44371	2.40183	2.36115	2.32163
4	3.23972	3.16986	3.10245	3.03735	2.97447	2.91371
5	3.88965	3.79079	3.69590	3.60478	3.51723	3.43308
6	4.48592	4.35526	4.23054	4.11141	3.99755	3.88867
7	5.03295	4.86842	4.71220	4.56376	4.42261	4.28830
8	5.53482	5.33493	5.14612	4.96764	4.79677	4.63886
9	5.99525	5.75902	5.53705	5.32825	5.13166	4.94637
10	6.41766	6.14457	5.88923	5.65022	5.42624	5.21612
11	6.80519	6.49506	6.20652	5.93770	5.68694	5.45273
12	7.16072	6.81369	6.49236	6.19437	5.91765	5.66029
13	7.48690	7.10336	6.74987	6.42355	6.12181	5.84236
14	7.78615	7.36669	6.96187	6.62817	6.30249	6.00207
15	8.06069	7.60608	7.19087	6.81086	6.46238	6.14217
16	8.31256	7.82371	7.37916	6.97399	6.60388	6.26506
17	8.54363	8.02155	7.54879	7.11963	6.72909	6.37286
18	8.75562	8.20141	7.70162	7.24967	6.83991	6.46742
19	8.95012	8.36492	7.83929	7.36578	6.93797	6.55037
20	9.12855	8.51356	7.96333	7.46944	7.02475	6.62313
21	9.29224	8.64869	8.07507	7.56200	7.10155	6.68696
22	9.44242	8.77154	8.17574	7.64465	7.16951	6.74294
23	9.58021	8.88322	8.26643	7.71843	7.22966	6.79206
24	9.70661	8.98474	8.34814	7.78432	7.28288	6.83514
25	9.82258	9.07704	8.42174	7.84314	7.32998	6.87293
26	9.92897	9.16094	8.48806	7.89566	7.37167	6.90608
27	10.02658	9.23722	8.54780	7.94255	7.40856	6.93515
28	10.11613	9.30657	8.60162	7.98442	7.44120	6.96066
29	10.19828	9.36961	8.65011	8.02181	7.47009	6.98304
30	10.27365	9.42691	8.69379	8.05518	7.49565	7.00266
31	10.34280	9.47901	8.73315	8.08499	7.51828	7.01988
32	10.40624	9.52638	8.76860	8.11159	7.53830	7.03498
33	10.46444	9.56943	8.80054	8.13535	7.55602	7.04823
34	10.51784	9.60858	8.82932	8.15656	7.57170	7.05985
35	10.56682	9.64416	8.85524	8.17550	7.58557	7.07005
40	10.75736	9.77905	8.95105	8.24378	7.63438	7.10504
45	10.88118	9.86281	9.00791	8.28252	7.66086	7.12322
50	10.96168	9.91481	9.04165	8.30450	7.67524	7.13266

Reversing Entries

Some of the adjusting entries recorded at the end of the accounting period affect transactions that occur in the next period. In such cases, a reversing entry may be used to simplify the recording of the next period's transactions.

To illustrate, an adjusting entry for accrued wages expense affects the first payment of wages in the next period. Without using a reversing entry, Wages Payable must be debited for the accrued wages at the end of the preceding period. In addition, Wages Expense must also be debited for only that portion of the payroll that is an expense of the current period.

Using a reversing entry, however, simplifies the analysis and recording of the first wages payment in the next period. As the term implies, a *reversing entry* is the exact opposite of the related adjusting entry. The amounts and accounts are the same as the adjusting entry, but the debits and credits are reversed.

@netsolutions   Reversing entries are illustrated by using the accrued wages for NetSolutions presented in Chapter 3. These data are summarized in Exhibit 1.

Exhibit 1

Accrued Wages

1. Wages are paid on the second and fourth Fridays for the two-week periods ending on those Fridays. The payments were $950 on December 13 and $1,200 on December 27.

2. The wages accrued for Monday and Tuesday, December 30 and 31, are $250.

3. Wages paid on Friday, January 10, total $1,275.

4. Wages expense, January 1–10, $10,025.

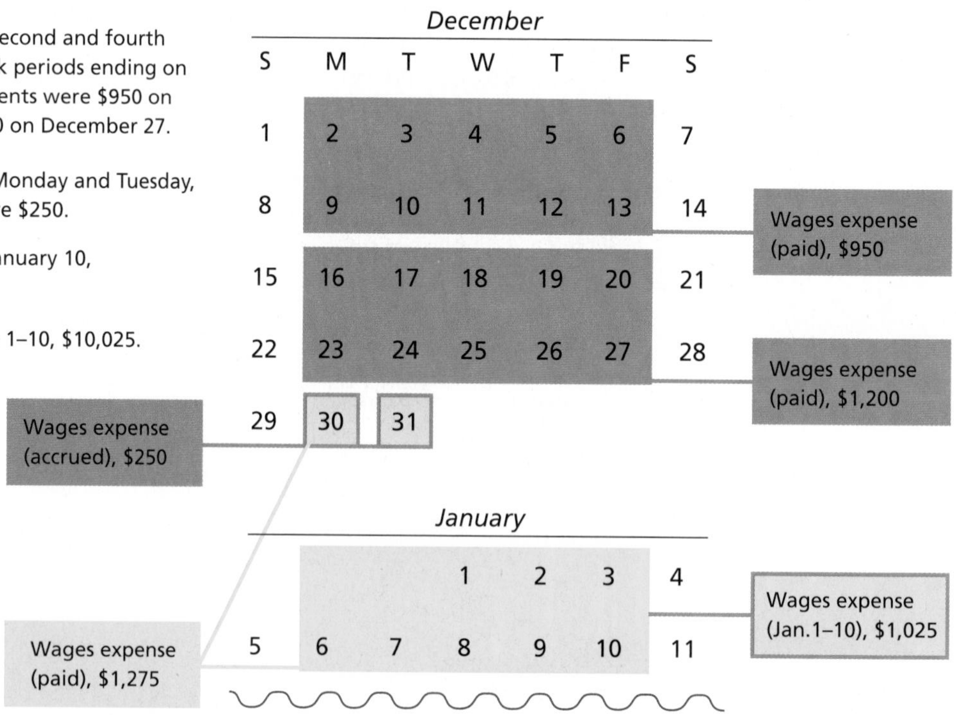

The adjusting entry for the accrued wages of December 30 and 31 is as follows:

2009					
Dec.	31	Wages Expense	51	250	
		Wages Payable	22		250
		Accrued wages.			

After the adjusting entry is recorded, Wages Expense will have a debit balance of $4,525 ($4,275 + $250), as shown on the top of page B-3. Wages Payable will have a credit balance of $250, as shown on page B-3.

After the closing entries are recorded, Wages Expense will have a zero balance. However, since Wages Payable is a liability account, it is not closed. Thus, Wages Payable will have a credit balance of $250 as of January 1, 2010.

Without recording a reversing entry, the payment of the $1,275 payroll on January 10 would be recorded as follows:

2010					
Jan.	10	Wages Payable	22	250	
		Wages Expense	51	1,025	
		Cash	11		1,275

As shown above, to record the January 10 payroll correctly Wages Payable must be debited for $250. This means that the employee who records the January 10 payroll must refer to the December 31, 2009, adjusting entry or to the ledger to determine the amount to debit Wages Payable.

Because the January 10 payroll is not recorded in the normal manner, there is a greater chance that an error may occur. This chance of error is reduced by recording a reversing entry as of the first day of the next period. For example, the reversing entry for the accrued wages expense would be recorded on January 1, 2010, as follows:

2010					
Jan.	1	Wages Payable	22	250	
		Wages Expense	51		250
		Reversing entry.			

The preceding reversing entry transfers the $250 liability from Wages Payable to the credit side of Wages Expense. The nature of the $250 is unchanged—it is still a liability. However, because of its unusual nature, an explanation is written under the reversing entry.

When the payroll is paid on January 10, the following entry is recorded:

Jan.	10	Wages Expense	51	1,275	
		Cash	11		1,275

After the January 10 payroll is recorded, Wages Expense has a debit balance of $1,025. This is the wages expense for the period January 1–10, 2010.

Wages Payable and Wages Expense after posting the adjusting, closing, and reversing entries are shown on the next page.

Account Wages Payable   Account No. 22

Date		Item	Post. Ref.	Debit	Credit	Balance Debit	Balance Credit
2009 Dec.	31	Adjusting	5		250		250
2010 Jan.	1	Reversing	7	250		—	—

Account Wages Expense   Account No. 51

Date		Item	Post. Ref.	Debit	Credit	Balance Debit	Balance Credit
2009 Nov.	30		1	2,125		2,125	
Dec.	13		3	950		3,075	
	27		3	1,200		4,275	
	31	Adjusting	5	250		4,525	
	31	Closing	6		4,525	—	
2010 Jan.	1	Reversing	7		250		250
	10		7	1,275		1,025	

In addition to accrued expenses (accrued liabilities), reversing entries are also used for accrued revenues (accrued assets). To illustrate, the reversing entry for NetSolutions' accrued fees earned as of December 31, 2009, is as follows:

Jan.	1	Fees Earned	41	500	
		Accounts Receivable	12		500
		Reversing entry.			

The use of reversing entries is optional. However, in computerized accounting systems, data entry employees often input routine accounting entries. In such cases, reversing entries may be useful in avoiding errors.

EX B-1
Adjusting and reversing entries

On the basis of the following data, (a) journalize the adjusting entries at December 31, the end of the current fiscal year, and (b) journalize the reversing entries on January 1, the first day of the following year.

1. Sales salaries are uniformly $17,375 for a five-day workweek, ending on Friday. The last payday of the year was Friday, December 26.
2. Accrued fees earned but not recorded at December 31, $19,850.

EX B-2
Adjusting and reversing entries

On the basis of the following data, (a) journalize the adjusting entries at June 30, the end of the current fiscal year, and (b) journalize the reversing entries on July 1, the first day of the following year.

1. Wages are uniformly $25,900 for a five-day workweek, ending on Friday. The last payday of the year was Friday, June 27.
2. Accrued fees earned but not recorded at June 30, $36,100.

EX B-3

Entries posted to the wages expense account

Portions of the wages expense account of a business are shown below.

a. Indicate the nature of the entry (payment, adjusting, closing, reversing) from which each numbered posting was made.

b. Journalize the complete entry from which each numbered posting was made.

Account	Wages Expense						Account No. 53
						Balance	
Date	Item	Post. Ref.	Dr.	Cr.		Dr.	Cr.
2009							
Dec. 26	(1)	49	27,000			1,400,000	
31	(2)	50	16,200			1,416,200	
31	(3)	51		1,416,200		—	—
2010							
Jan. 1	(4)	52		16,200			16,200
2	(5)	53	27,000			10,800	

EX B-4

Entries posted to the salaries expense account

Portions of the salaries expense account of a business are shown below.

Account	Salaries Expense						Account No. 53
						Balance	
Date	Item	Post. Ref.	Dr.	Cr.		Dr.	Cr.
2009							
Dec. 27	(1)	29	17,500			910,000	
31	(2)	30	7,000			917,000	
31	(3)	31		917,000		—	—
2010							
Jan. 1	(4)	32		7,000			7,000
2	(5)	33	17,500			10,500	

a. Indicate the nature of the entry (payment, adjusting, closing, reversing) from which each numbered posting was made.

b. Journalize the complete entry from which each numbered posting was made.

End-of-Period Spreadsheet (Work Sheet) for a Merchandising Business

A merchandising business may use an end-of-period spreadsheet (work sheet) for preparing financial statements and adjusting and closing entries. This appendix illustrates such a spreadsheet for the perpetual inventory system.

@netsolutions

The end-of-period spreadsheet in Exhibit 1 is for NetSolutions on December 31, 2011. Exhibit 1 was prepared using the following steps that are described and illustrated in the appendix to Chapter 4.

Step 1.   Enter the Title.
Step 2.   Enter the Unadjusted Trial Balance.
Step 3.   Enter the Adjustments.
Step 4.   Enter the Adjusted Trial Balance.
Step 5.   Extend the Accounts to the Income Statement and Balance Sheet columns.
Step 6.   Total the Income Statement and Balance Sheet columns, compute the Net Income or Net Loss, and complete the spreadsheet.

The data needed for adjusting the accounts of NetSolutions are as follows:

Physical merchandise inventory on December 31, 2011		$62,150
Office supplies on hand on December 31, 2011		480
Insurance expired during 2011		1,910
Depreciation during 2011 on: Store equipment		3,100
Office equipment		2,490
Salaries accrued on December 31, 2011: Sales salaries	$780	
Office salaries	360	1,140
Rent earned during 2011		600

There is no required order for analyzing the adjustment data and the accounts in the spreadsheet. However, the accounts are normally analyzed in the order in which they appear in the spreadsheet. Using this approach, the adjustment for merchandise inventory shrinkage is listed first as entry (a), followed by the adjustment for office supplies used as entry (b), and so on.

After all the adjustments have been entered, the Adjustments columns are totaled to prove the equality of debits and credits. The adjusted trial balance is entered by combining the adjustments with the unadjusted balances for each account.[1] The Adjusted Trial Balance columns are then totaled to prove the equality of debits and credits. The adjusted balances are then extended to the statement columns. The four statement columns are totaled, and the net income or net loss is determined.

For NetSolutions, the difference between the Credit and Debit columns of the Income Statement section is $75,400, the amount of the net income. The difference between the Debit and Credit columns of the Balance Sheet section is also $75,400, which is the increase in owner's equity as a result of the net income.

---

1 Some accountants prefer to eliminate the Adjusted Trial Balance columns and to extend the adjusted balances directly to the statement columns. Such a spreadsheet (work sheet) is often used if there are only a few adjustment items.

Exhibit 1

End-of-Period Spreadsheet (Work Sheet) for a Merchandising Business Using Perpetual Inventory System

	A	B	C	D	E	F	G	H	I	J	K
1					NetSolutions						
2					End-of-Period Spreadsheet (Work Sheet)						
3					For the Year Ended December 31, 2011						
4	Account Title	Unadjusted Trial Balance		Adjustments		Adjusted Trial Balance		Income Statement		Balance Sheet	
5											
6		Dr.	Cr.	Dr.	Cr.	Dr.	Cr.	Dr.	Cr.	Dr.	Cr.
7	Cash	52,950				52,950				52,950	
8	Accounts Receivable	91,080				91,080				91,080	
9	Merchandise Inventory	63,950			(a)1,800	62,150				62,150	
10	Office Supplies	1,090			(b) 610	480				480	
11	Prepaid Insurance	4,560			(c)1,910	2,650				2,650	
12	Land	20,000				20,000				20,000	
13	Store Equipment	27,100				27,100				27,100	
14	Accum. Depr.—Store Equipment		2,600		(d)3,100		5,700				5,700
15	Office Equipment	15,570				15,570				15,570	
16	Accum. Depr.—Office Equipment		2,230		(e)2,490		4,720				4,720
17	Accounts Payable		22,420				22,420				22,420
18	Salaries Payable				(f)1,140		1,140				1,140
19	Unearned Rent		2,400	(g) 600			1,800				1,800
20	Notes Payable										
21	(final payment due 2019)		25,000				25,000				25,000
22	Chris Clark, Capital		153,800				153,800				153,800
23	Chris Clark, Drawing	18,000				18,000				18,000	
24	Sales		720,185				720,185		720,185		
25	Sales Returns and Allowances	6,140				6,140		6,140			
26	Sales Discounts	5,790				5,790		5,790			
27	Cost of Merchandise Sold	523,505		(a)1,800		525,305		525,305			
28	Sales Salaries Expense	52,650		(f) 780		53,430		53,430			
29	Advertising Expense	10,860				10,860		10,860			
30	Depr. Exp.—Store Equipment			(d)3,100		3,100		3,100			
31	Delivery Expense	2,800				2,800		2,800			
32	Miscellaneous Selling Expense	630				630		630			
33	Office Salaries Expense	20,660		(f) 360		21,020		21,020			
34	Rent Expense	8,100				8,100		8,100			
35	Depr. Exp.—Office Equipment			(e)2,490		2,490		2,490			
36	Insurance Expense			(c)1,910		1,910		1,910			
37	Office Supplies Expense			(b) 610		610		610			
38	Misc. Administrative Expense	760				760		760			
39	Rent Revenue				(g) 600		600		600		
40	Interest Expense	2,440				2,440		2,440			
41		928,635	928,635	11,650	11,650	935,365	935,365	645,385	720,785	289,980	214,580
42	Net income							75,400			75,400
43								720,785	720,785	289,980	289,980
44											

(a) Merchandise inventory shrinkage for period, $1,800 ($63,950 − $62,150).
(b) Office supplies used, $610 ($1,090 − $480).
(c) Insurance expired, $1,910.
(d) Depreciation of store equipment, $3,100.

(e) Depreciation of office equipment, $2,490.
(f) Salaries accrued but not paid (sales salaries, $780; office salaries, $360), $1,140.
(g) Rent earned from amount received in advance, $600.

The income statement, statement of owner's equity, and balance sheet can be prepared from the spreadsheet (work sheet). These financial statements are shown in Exhibits 1, 4, and 5 in Chapter 6. The Adjustments columns in the spreadsheet (work sheet) may be used as the basis for journalizing the adjusting entries. NetSolutions' adjusting entries at the end of 2011 are shown at the top of the following page.

		Journal			Page *28*
Date		**Description**	**Post. Ref.**	**Debit**	**Credit**
		Adjusting Entries			
2011 Dec.	31	Cost of Merchandise Sold	510	1,800	
		Merchandise Inventory	115		1,800
		Inventory shrinkage.			
	31	Office Supplies Expense	534	610	
		Office Supplies	116		610
		Supplies used.			
	31	Insurance Expense	533	1,910	
		Prepaid Insurance	117		1,910
		Insurance expired.			
	31	Depr. Expense—Store Equipment	522	3,100	
		Accumulated Depr.—Store Equipment	124		3,100
		Store equipment depreciation.			
	31	Depr. Expense—Office Equipment	532	2,490	
		Accumulated Depr.—Office Equipment	126		2,490
		Office equipment depreciation.			
	31	Sales Salaries Expense	520	780	
		Office Salaries Expense	530	360	
		Salaries Payable	211		1,140
		Accrued salaries.			
	31	Unearned Rent	212	600	
		Rent Revenue	610		600
		Rent earned.			

The Income Statement columns of the work sheet may be used as the basis for preparing the closing entries. The closing entries for NetSolutions at the end of 2011 are shown on page 276 of Chapter 6.

After the closing entries have been prepared and posted to the accounts, a post-closing trial balance may be prepared to verify the debit-credit equality. The only accounts that should appear on the post-closing trial balance are the asset, contra asset, liability, and owner's capital accounts with balances. These are the same accounts that appear on the end-of-period balance sheet.

PR C-1
End-of-period spreadsheet (work sheet), financial statements, and adjusting and closing entries for perpetual inventory system

✔ 2. Net income: $38,800

The accounts and their balances in the ledger of Rack Saver Co. on December 31, 2010, are as follows:

Cash	$ 12,000	Sales	$800,000
Accounts Receivable	72,500	Sales Returns and Allowances	11,900
Merchandise Inventory	170,000	Sales Discounts	7,100
Prepaid Insurance	9,700	Cost of Merchandise Sold	500,000
Store Supplies	4,200	Sales Salaries Expense	96,400
Office Supplies	2,100	Advertising Expense	25,000
Store Equipment	360,000	Depreciation Expense—	
Accumulated Depreciation—		Store Equipment	—
Store Equipment	60,300	Store Supplies Expense	—
Office Equipment	70,000	Miscellaneous Selling Expense	1,600
Accumulated Depreciation—		Office Salaries Expense	64,000
Office Equipment	17,200	Rent Expense	16,000
Accounts Payable	46,700	Insurance Expense	—
Salaries Payable	—	Depreciation Expense—	
Unearned Rent	3,000	Office Equipment	—
Note Payable		Office Supplies Expense	—
(final payment due 2018)	180,000	Miscellaneous Administrative	
Evan Hoffman, Capital	352,750	Expense	1,650
Evan Hoffman, Drawing	25,000	Rent Revenue	—
Income Summary	—	Interest Expense	10,800

The data needed for year-end adjustments on December 31 are as follows:

Physical merchandise inventory on December 31		$162,500
Insurance expired during the year		3,600
Supplies on hand on December 31:		
Store supplies		1,050
Office supplies		600
Depreciation for the year:		
Store equipment		6,000
Office equipment		3,000
Salaries payable on December 31:		
Sales salaries	$1,800	
Office salaries	1,200	3,000
Unearned rent on December 31		2,000

Instructions
1. Prepare an end-of-period spreadsheet (work sheet) for the fiscal year ended December 31, 2010. List all accounts in the order given.
2. Prepare a multiple-step income statement.
3. Prepare a statement of owner's equity.
4. Prepare a report form of balance sheet, assuming that the current portion of the note payable is $36,000.
5. Journalize the adjusting entries.
6. Journalize the closing entries.

PR C-2
End-of-period spreadsheet (work sheet), financial statements, and adjusting and closing entries for perpetual inventory system

✔ 1. Net income: $38,450

The accounts and their balances in the ledger of Quality Sports Co. on December 31, 2010, are as follows:

Cash	$ 18,000		Sales Discounts	$ 7,100
Accounts Receivable	42,500		Cost of Merchandise Sold	557,000
Merchandise Inventory	218,000		Sales Salaries Expense	101,400
Prepaid Insurance	8,000		Advertising Expense	45,000
Store Supplies	4,200		Depr. Expense—Store Equip.	—
Office Supplies	2,100		Delivery Expense	6,000
Store Equipment	282,000		Store Supplies Expense	—
Accumulated Depr.—Store Equip.	70,300		Miscellaneous. Selling Expense	1,600
Office Equipment	60,000		Office Salaries Expense	64,000
Accumulated Depr.—Office Equip.	17,200		Rent Expense	25,200
Accounts Payable	26,700		Insurance Expense	—
Salaries Payable	—		Depr. Expense—Office Equip.	—
Unearned Rent	2,500		Office Supplies Expense	—
Note Payable (final payment, 2018)	175,000		Misc. Administrative Expense	1,650
Rosario Noe, Capital	286,450		Rent Revenue	—
Rosario Noe, Drawing	10,000		Interest Expense	10,500
Sales	900,000			
Sales Returns and Allowances	13,900			

The data needed for year-end adjustments on December 31 are as follows:

Merchandise inventory on December 31		$211,000
Insurance expired during the year		5,000
Supplies on hand on December 31:		
Store supplies		1,150
Office supplies		750
Depreciation for the year:		
Store equipment		7,500
Office equipment		3,800
Salaries payable on December 31:		
Sales salaries	$1,500	
Office salaries	1,000	2,500
Unearned rent on December 31		500

Instructions

1. Prepare an end-of-period spreadsheet (work sheet) for the fiscal year ended December 31, listing all accounts in the order given.
2. Prepare a multiple-step income statement.
3. Prepare a statement of owner's equity.
4. Prepare a report form of balance sheet, assuming that the current portion of the note payable is $25,000.
5. Journalize the adjusting entries.
6. Journalize the closing entries.

Accounting for Deferred Income Taxes[1]

A corporation determines its taxable income according to the tax laws and files a corporate tax return. In contrast, a corporation prepares its financial statements using generally accepted accounting principles (GAAP). As a result, *taxable income* normally differs from *income before taxes* reported on the income statement.

Temporary Differences

Some differences between *taxable income* and *income before income taxes* are created because items are recognized in one period for tax purposes and in another period for income statement purposes. Such differences, called *temporary differences*, reverse or turn around in later years. Examples of items that create temporary differences include:

1. Revenues or gains that are taxed *after* they are reported in the income statement.

    Example: In some cases, companies make sales under an installment plan in which customers make periodic payments over future time periods. In such cases, the company recognizes revenue for financial reporting purposes when a sale is made but recognizes revenue for tax purposes when the cash is collected.

2. Expenses or losses that are deducted in determining taxable income *after* they are reported in the income statement.

    Example: Product warranty liability expense is estimated and reported in the year of the sale for financial statement reporting but is deducted for tax reporting when paid.

3. Revenues or gains that are taxed *before* they are reported in the income statement.

    Example: Cash received in advance for magazine subscriptions is included in taxable income when received but included in the income statement only when earned in a future period.

4. Expenses or losses that are deducted in determining taxable income *before* they are reported in the income statement.

    Example: MACRS depreciation is used for tax purposes, and the straight-line method is used for financial reporting purposes.

Since temporary differences reverse in later years, they do not change or reduce the total amount of taxable income over the life of a business. Exhibit 1 illustrates the reversing nature of temporary differences.

In Exhibit 1, a corporation uses MACRS depreciation for tax purposes and straight-line depreciation for financial statement purposes. MACRS recognizes more depreciation in the early years and less depreciation in the later years. However, the total depreciation expense is the same for both methods over the life of the asset.

As Exhibit 1 illustrates, temporary differences affect only the timing of when revenues and expenses are reported for tax purposes. The total amount of taxes paid does not change. In other words, only the timing of the payment of taxes is affected.

---

1 Accounting for deferred income taxes is a complex topic that is treated in greater detail in advanced accounting texts. The treatment here provides a general overview and conceptual understanding of the topic.

Exhibit 1

**Temporary
Differences**

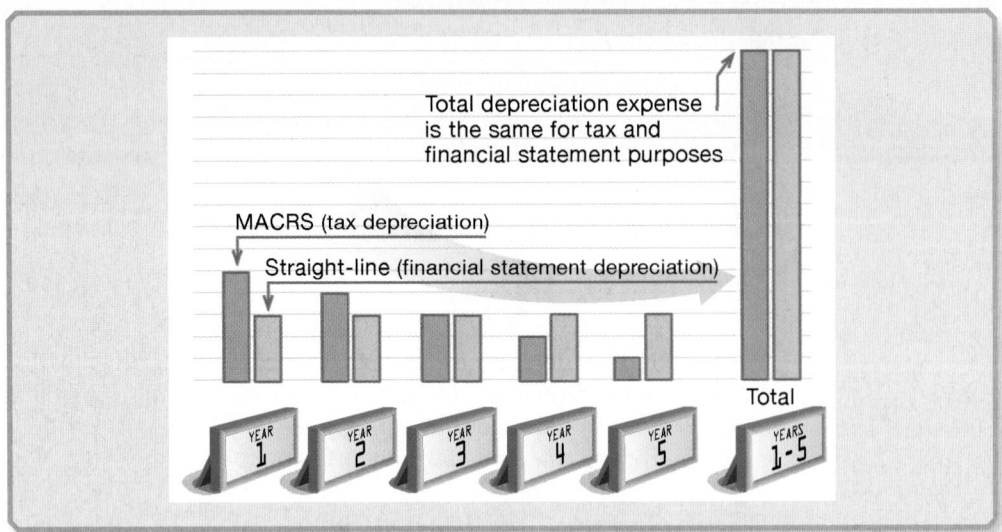

Most corporations use tax-planning methods that delay or defer the payment of taxes to later years. As a result, at the end of each year, most corporations will have two tax liabilities as follows:

1. Current income tax liability, which is due on the current year's taxable income.
2. Postponed or deferred tax liability, which is due in the future when the temporary differences reverse.

To illustrate, assume the following data for the first year of a corporation's operations:

Income before income taxes (income statement)	$ 300,000
Temporary differences	(200,000)
Taxable income (tax return)	$ 100,000
Income tax rate	40%

Based on the preceding data, the income tax expense reported on the income statement is $120,000 ($300,000 × 40%).[2] However, the current income tax liability (income tax due for the year) and reported on the corporate tax return is only $40,000 ($100,000 × 40%). The $80,000 ($120,000 − $40,000) difference is the deferred tax liability that will be paid in future years as shown below.

Income tax expense based on $300,000 reported income at 40%	$120,000
Income tax payable based on $100,000 taxable income at 40%	40,000
Income tax deferred to future years	$ 80,000

On the income statement, income tax expense of $120,000 ($300,000 × 40%) must be reported. This is done so that the current year's expenses (including income tax) are properly matched against the current year's revenue. The entry to record the income tax expense of $120,000 is as shown below.

Income Tax Expense	120,000	
Income Tax Payable		40,000
Deferred Income Tax Payable		80,000
Record income tax expense for the year.		

2 For purposes of illustration, the 40% rate is assumed to include all federal, state, and local income taxes.

The income tax expense reported on the income statement is the total tax, $120,000. Of this amount, $40,000 is currently due and $80,000 will be due in (deferred to) future years.

As the temporary differences reverse and the taxes become due in future years, the $80,000 in *Deferred Income Tax Payable* will be transferred to *Income Tax Payable*. To illustrate, assume that $48,000 of the deferred tax reverses and becomes due in the second year. The journal entry in the second year would be as follows:

Deferred Income Tax Payable	48,000	
Income Tax Payable		48,000
Record income tax payable.		

Reporting Deferred Taxes

The balance of *Deferred Income Tax Payable* at the end of a year is reported as a liability.[3] The amount due within one year is classified as a current liability. The remainder is classified as a long-term liability or reported in a Deferred Credits section following the Long-Term Liabilities section.[4]

Permanent Differences

Differences between taxable income and income (before taxes) reported on the income statement may also arise because of the following:

1. Some revenues are exempt from tax.
2. Some expenses are not deductible in determining taxable income.

Interest from investments in municipal bonds is also tax exempt for individual taxpayers.

The preceding differences, which will not reverse with the passage of time, are called *permanent differences*. For example, interest income on municipal bonds is exempt from federal taxation.

Permanent differences create no special financial reporting problems. This is because the amount of income tax determined according to the tax laws is the *same* amount reported on the income statement.

3 In some cases, a deferred tax asset may arise for tax benefits to be received in the future. Such deferred tax assets are reported as either current or long-term assets, depending on when the benefits are expected to be realized.

4 Additional note disclosures for deferred income taxes are also required. These are discussed in advanced accounting texts.

EX D-1
Deferred tax entries

Ramsey Inc. has $600,000 of income before income taxes, a 35% tax rate, and $320,000 of taxable income. Provide the journal entry for the current year's taxes.

EX D-2
Deferred tax entries

Downstairs Corp. has $180,000 of income before income taxes, a 40% tax rate, and $90,000 of taxable income. Provide the journal entry for the current year's taxes.

EX D-3
Deferred income taxes

Mattress Systems Inc. recognized service revenue of $500,000 on its financial statements in 2009. Assume, however, that the Tax Code requires this amount to be recognized for tax purposes in 2010. The taxable income for 2009 and 2010 is $1,800,000 and $2,400,000, respectively. Assume a tax rate of 40%.

Prepare the journal entries to record the tax expense, deferred taxes, and taxes payable for 2009 and 2010, respectively.

PR D-1
Deferred taxes

✔ 1. Year-end balance, 3rd year, $30,000

Differences between the accounting methods applied to accounts and financial reports and those used in determining taxable income yielded the following amounts for the first four years of a corporation's operations:

	First Year	Second Year	Third Year	Fourth Year
Income before income taxes	$625,000	$750,000	$1,250,000	$1,000,000
Taxable income	500,000	700,000	1,350,000	1,075,000

The income tax rate for each of the four years was 40% of taxable income, and each year's taxes were promptly paid.

Instructions
1. Determine for each year the amounts described by the following captions, presenting the information in the form indicated:

Year	Income Tax Deducted on Income Statement	Income Tax Payments for the Year	Deferred Income Tax Payable	
			Year's Addition (Deduction)	Year-End Balance

2. Total the first three amount columns.

PR D-2
Deferred taxes

✔ 1. Year-end balance, 3rd year, $12,600

Differences between the accounting methods applied to accounts and financial reports and those used in determining taxable income yielded the following amounts for the first four years of a corporation's operations:

	First Year	Second Year	Third Year	Fourth Year
Income before income taxes	$150,000	$195,000	$270,000	$300,000
Taxable income	105,000	180,000	294,000	336,000

The income tax rate for each of the four years was 35% of taxable income, and each year's taxes were promptly paid.

Instructions
1. Determine for each year the amounts described by the following captions, presenting the information in the form indicated:

Year	Income Tax Deducted on Income Statement	Income Tax Payments for the Year	Deferred Income Tax Payable	
			Year's Addition (Deduction)	Year-End Balance

2. Total the first three amount columns.

FORM 10-K

NIKE INC - NKE

Filed: July 27, 2007 (period: May 31, 2007)

Annual report which provides a comprehensive overview of the company for the past year

Nike Inc. Form 10-K – Annual report [Section 13 or 15(d)] of The Securities Exchange Act of 1934 for the fiscal year ended May 31, 2007.

REPORT OF INDEPENDENT REGISTERED PUBLIC ACCOUNTING FIRM

To the Board of Directors and
Shareholders of NIKE, Inc.:

We have completed integrated audits of NIKE, Inc.'s consolidated financial statements and of its internal control over financial reporting as of May 31, 2007, in accordance with the standards of the Public Company Accounting Oversight Board (United States). Our opinions, based on our audits, are presented below.

Consolidated financial statements and financial statement schedule

In our opinion, the consolidated financial statements listed in the index appearing under Item 15(a)(1) present fairly, in all material respects, the financial position of NIKE, Inc. and its subsidiaries at May 31, 2007 and 2006, and the results of their operations and their cash flows for each of the three years in the period ended May 31, 2007 in conformity with accounting principles generally accepted in the United States of America. In addition, in our opinion, the financial statement schedule listed in the index appearing under Item 15(a)(2) presents fairly, in all material respects, the information set forth therein when read in conjunction with the related consolidated financial statements. These financial statements and financial statement schedule are the responsibility of the Company's management. Our responsibility is to express an opinion on these financial statements and financial statement schedule based on our audits. We conducted our audits of these statements in accordance with the standards of the Public Company Accounting Oversight Board (United States). Those standards require that we plan and perform the audit to obtain reasonable assurance about whether the financial statements are free of material misstatement. An audit of financial statements includes examining, on a test basis, evidence supporting the amounts and disclosures in the financial statements, assessing the accounting principles used and significant estimates made by management, and evaluating the overall financial statement presentation. We believe that our audits provide a reasonable basis for our opinion.

As discussed in Note 1 to the consolidated financial statements, effective June 1, 2006, the Company changed the manner in which it accounts for stock-based compensation in accordance with the Statement of Financial Accounting Standards No. 123R "Share-Based Payment."

Internal control over financial reporting

Also, in our opinion, management's assessment, included in "Management's Annual Report on Internal Control Over Financial Reporting" appearing under Item 8, that the Company maintained effective internal control over financial reporting as of May 31, 2007 based on criteria established in *Internal Control — Integrated Framework* issued by the Committee of Sponsoring Organizations of the Treadway Commission ("COSO"), is fairly stated, in all material respects, based on those criteria. Furthermore, in our opinion, the Company maintained, in all material respects, effective internal control over financial reporting as of May 31, 2007, based on criteria established in *Internal Control — Integrated Framework* issued by the COSO. The Company's management is responsible for maintaining effective internal control over financial reporting and for its assessment of the effectiveness of internal control over financial reporting. Our responsibility is to express opinions on management's assessment and on the effectiveness of the Company's internal control over financial reporting based on our audit. We conducted our audit of internal control over financial reporting in accordance with the standards of the Public Company Accounting Oversight Board (United States). Those standards require that we plan and perform the audit to obtain reasonable assurance about whether effective internal control over financial reporting was maintained in all material respects. An audit of internal control over financial reporting includes obtaining an understanding of internal control over financial reporting, evaluating management's assessment, testing and evaluating the design and operating effectiveness of internal control, and performing such other procedures as we consider necessary in the circumstances. We believe that our audit provides a reasonable basis for our opinions.

A company's internal control over financial reporting is a process designed to provide reasonable assurance regarding the reliability of financial reporting and the preparation of financial statements for external purposes in

48

accordance with generally accepted accounting principles. A company's internal control over financial reporting includes those policies and procedures that (i) pertain to the maintenance of records that, in reasonable detail, accurately and fairly reflect the transactions and dispositions of the assets of the company; (ii) provide reasonable assurance that transactions are recorded as necessary to permit preparation of financial statements in accordance with generally accepted accounting principles, and that receipts and expenditures of the company are being made only in accordance with authorizations of management and directors of the company; and (iii) provide reasonable assurance regarding prevention or timely detection of unauthorized acquisition, use, or disposition of the company's assets that could have a material effect on the financial statements.

Because of its inherent limitations, internal control over financial reporting may not prevent or detect misstatements. Also, projections of any evaluation of effectiveness to future periods are subject to the risk that controls may become inadequate because of changes in conditions, or that the degree of compliance with the policies or procedures may deteriorate.

/s/   PRICEWATERHOUSECOOPERS LLP

Portland, Oregon
July 26, 2007

49

NIKE, INC.

CONSOLIDATED STATEMENTS OF INCOME

	Year Ended May 31,		
	2007	**2006**	**2005**
	(In millions, except per share data)		
Revenues	$ 16,325.9	$ 14,954.9	$ 13,739.7
Cost of sales	9,165.4	8,367.9	7,624.3
Gross margin	7,160.5	6,587.0	6,115.4
Selling and administrative expense	5,028.7	4,477.8	4,221.7
Interest (income) expense, net (Notes 1, 6 and 7)	(67.2)	(36.8)	4.8
Other (income) expense, net (Notes 5 and 16)	(0.9)	4.4	29.1
Income before income taxes	2,199.9	2,141.6	1,859.8
Income taxes (Note 8)	708.4	749.6	648.2
Net income	$ 1,491.5	$ 1,392.0	$ 1,211.6
Basic earnings per common share (Notes 1 and 11)	$ 2.96	$ 2.69	$ 2.31
Diluted earnings per common share (Notes 1 and 11)	$ 2.93	$ 2.64	$ 2.24
Dividends declared per common share	$ 0.71	$ 0.59	$ 0.475

The accompanying notes to consolidated financial statements are an integral part of this statement.

50

NIKE, INC.
CONSOLIDATED BALANCE SHEETS

	May 31,	
	2007	**2006**
	(In millions)	
ASSETS		
Current assets:		
Cash and equivalents	$ 1,856.7	$ 954.2
Short-term investments	990.3	1,348.8
Accounts receivable, net	2,494.7	2,382.9
Inventories (Note 2)	2,121.9	2,076.7
Deferred income taxes (Note 8)	219.7	203.3
Prepaid expenses and other current assets	393.2	380.1
Total current assets	8,076.5	7,346.0
Property, plant and equipment, net (Note 3)	1,678.3	1,657.7
Identifiable intangible assets, net (Note 4)	409.9	405.5
Goodwill (Note 4)	130.8	130.8
Deferred income taxes and other assets (Note 8)	392.8	329.6
Total assets	$ 10,688.3	$ 9,869.6
LIABILITIES AND SHAREHOLDERS' EQUITY		
Current liabilities:		
Current portion of long-term debt (Note 7)	$ 30.5	$ 255.3
Notes payable (Note 6)	100.8	43.4
Accounts payable (Note 6)	1,040.3	952.2
Accrued liabilities (Notes 5 and 16)	1,303.4	1,276.0
Income taxes payable	109.0	85.5
Total current liabilities	2,584.0	2,612.4
Long-term debt (Note 7)	409.9	410.7
Deferred income taxes and other liabilities (Note 8)	668.7	561.0
Commitments and contingencies (Notes 14 and 16)	—	—
Redeemable Preferred Stock (Note 9)	0.3	0.3
Shareholders' equity:		
Common stock at stated value (Note 10):		
Class A convertible — 117.6 and 127.8 shares outstanding	0.1	0.1
Class B — 384.1 and 384.2 shares outstanding	2.7	2.7
Capital in excess of stated value	1,960.0	1,447.3
Accumulated other comprehensive income (Note 13)	177.4	121.7
Retained earnings	4,885.2	4,713.4
Total shareholders' equity	7,025.4	6,285.2
Total liabilities and shareholders' equity	$ 10,688.3	$ 9,869.6

The accompanying notes to consolidated financial statements are an integral part of this statement.

51

NIKE, INC.

CONSOLIDATED STATEMENTS OF CASH FLOWS

	Year Ended May 31,		
	2007	2006 (In millions)	2005
Cash provided (used) by operations:			
Net income	$ 1,491.5	$ 1,392.0	$ 1,211.6
Income charges not affecting cash:			
Depreciation	269.7	282.0	257.2
Deferred income taxes	34.1	(26.0)	21.3
Stock-based compensation (Notes 1 and 10)	147.7	11.8	4.9
Amortization and other	0.5	(2.9)	25.6
Income tax benefit from exercise of stock options	—	54.2	63.1
Changes in certain working capital components and other assets and liabilities:			
Increase in accounts receivable	(39.6)	(85.1)	(93.5)
Increase in inventories	(49.5)	(200.3)	(103.3)
(Increase) decrease in prepaid expenses and other current assets	(60.8)	(37.2)	71.4
Increase in accounts payable, accrued liabilities and income taxes payable	85.1	279.4	112.4
Cash provided by operations	1,878.7	1,667.9	1,570.7
Cash provided (used) by investing activities:			
Purchases of short-term investments	(2,133.8)	(2,619.7)	(1,527.2)
Maturities of short-term investments	2,516.2	1,709.8	1,491.9
Additions to property, plant and equipment	(313.5)	(333.7)	(257.1)
Disposals of property, plant and equipment	28.3	1.6	7.2
Increase in other assets, net of other liabilities	(4.3)	(34.6)	(28.0)
Acquisition of subsidiary, net of cash acquired	—	—	(47.2)
Cash provided (used) by investing activities	92.9	(1,276.6)	(360.4)
Cash provided (used) by financing activities:			
Proceeds from issuance of long-term debt	41.8	—	—
Reductions in long-term debt, including current portion	(255.7)	(6.0)	(9.2)
Increase (decrease) in notes payable	52.6	(18.2)	(81.7)
Proceeds from exercise of stock options and other stock issuances	322.9	225.3	226.8
Excess tax benefits from share-based payment arrangements	55.8	—	—
Repurchase of common stock	(985.2)	(761.1)	(556.2)
Dividends — common and preferred	(343.7)	(290.9)	(236.7)
Cash used by financing activities	(1,111.5)	(850.9)	(657.0)
Effect of exchange rate changes	42.4	25.7	6.8
Net increase (decrease) in cash and equivalents	902.5	(433.9)	560.1
Cash and equivalents, beginning of year	954.2	1,388.1	828.0
Cash and equivalents, end of year	$ 1,856.7	$ 954.2	$ 1,388.1
Supplemental disclosure of cash flow information:			
Cash paid during the year for:			
Interest, net of capitalized interest	$ 60.0	$ 54.2	$ 33.9
Income taxes	601.1	752.6	585.3
Dividends declared and not paid	92.9	79.4	65.3

The accompanying notes to consolidated financial statements are an integral part of this statement.

52

NIKE, INC.

CONSOLIDATED STATEMENTS OF SHAREHOLDERS' EQUITY

| | Common Stock | | | | Capital in Excess of Stated Value | Accumulated Other Comprehensive Income (Loss) | Retained Earnings | Total |
| | Class A | | Class B | | | | | |
	Shares	Amount	Shares	Amount				
				(In millions, except per share data)				
Balance at May 31, 2004	155.2	$ 0.1	371.0	$ 2.7	$ 882.3	$ (86.3)	$ 3,982.9	$ 4,781.7
Stock options exercised			8.8		272.2			272.2
Conversion to Class B Common Stock	(11.4)		11.4					—
Repurchase of Class B Common Stock			(13.8)		(8.3)		(547.9)	(556.2)
Dividends on Common stock ($0.475 per share)							(249.4)	(249.4)
Issuance of shares to employees			1.0		21.9			21.9
Stock-based compensation (Note 10):					4.9			4.9
Forfeiture of shares from employees					(1.5)		(0.7)	(2.2)
Comprehensive income (Note 13):								
Net income							1,211.6	1,211.6
Other comprehensive income (net of tax expense of $40.2):								
Foreign currency translation						70.1		70.1
Adjustment for fair value of hedge derivatives						89.6		89.6
Comprehensive income						159.7	1,211.6	1,371.3
Balance at May 31, 2005	143.8	$ 0.1	378.4	$ 2.7	$ 1,171.5	$ 73.4	$ 4,396.5	$ 5,644.2
Stock options exercised			8.0		253.7			253.7
Conversion to Class B Common Stock	(16.0)		16.0					—
Repurchase of Class B Common Stock			(19.0)		(11.3)		(769.9)	(781.2)
Dividends on Common stock ($0.59 per share)							(304.9)	(304.9)
Issuance of shares to employees			1.0		26.9			26.9
Stock-based compensation (Note 10):					11.8			11.8
Forfeiture of shares from employees			(0.2)		(5.3)		(0.3)	(5.6)
Comprehensive income (Note 13):								
Net income							1,392.0	1,392.0
Other comprehensive income (net of tax benefit of $37.8):								
Foreign currency translation						87.1		87.1
Adjustment for fair value of hedge derivatives						(38.8)		(38.8)
Comprehensive income						48.3	1,392.0	1,440.3
Balance at May 31, 2006	127.8	$ 0.1	384.2	$ 2.7	$ 1,447.3	$ 121.7	$ 4,713.4	$ 6,285.2
Stock options exercised			10.7		349.7			349.7
Conversion to Class B Common Stock	(10.2)		10.2					—
Repurchase of Class B Common Stock			(22.1)		(13.2)		(962.0)	(975.2)
Dividends on Common stock ($0.71 per share)							(357.2)	(357.2)
Issuance of shares to employees			1.2		30.1			30.1
Stock-based compensation (Note 10):					147.7			147.7
Forfeiture of shares from employees			(0.1)		(1.6)		(0.5)	(2.1)
Comprehensive income (Note 13):								
Net income							1,491.5	1,491.5
Other comprehensive income (net of tax benefit of $0.5):								
Foreign currency translation						84.6		84.6
Adjustment for fair value of hedge derivatives						(16.7)		(16.7)
Comprehensive income						67.9	1,491.5	1,559.4
Adoption of FAS 158 (net of tax benefit of $5.4) (Note 12):						(12.2)		(12.2)
Balance at May 31, 2007	117.6	$ 0.1	384.1	$ 2.7	$ 1,960.0	$ 177.4	$ 4,885.2	$ 7,025.4

The accompanying notes to consolidated financial statements are an integral part of this statement.

53

NIKE, INC.
NOTES TO CONSOLIDATED FINANCIAL STATEMENTS

Note 1 — Summary of Significant Accounting Policies

Basis of Consolidation

The consolidated financial statements include the accounts of NIKE, Inc. and its subsidiaries (the "Company"). All significant intercompany transactions and balances have been eliminated.

Stock Split

On February 15, 2007 the Board of Directors declared a two-for-one stock split of the Company's Class A and Class B common shares, which was effected in the form of a 100% common stock dividend distributed on April 2, 2007. All references to share and per share amounts in the consolidated financial statements and accompanying notes to the consolidated financial statements have been retroactively restated to reflect the two-for-one stock split.

Recognition of Revenues

Wholesale revenues are recognized when the risks and rewards of ownership have passed to the customer, based on the terms of sale. This occurs upon shipment or upon receipt by the customer depending on the country of the sale and the agreement with the customer. Retail store revenues are recorded at the time of sale. Provisions for sales discounts, returns and miscellaneous claims from customers are made at the time of sale.

Shipping and Handling Costs

Shipping and handling costs are expensed as incurred and included in cost of sales.

Advertising and Promotion

Advertising production costs are expensed the first time the advertisement is run. Media (TV and print) placement costs are expensed in the month the advertising appears.

A significant amount of the Company's promotional expenses result from payments under endorsement contracts. Accounting for endorsement payments is based upon specific contract provisions. Generally, endorsement payments are expensed on a straight-line basis over the term of the contract after giving recognition to periodic performance compliance provisions of the contracts. Prepayments made under contracts are included in prepaid expenses or other assets depending on the period to which the prepayment applies.

Through cooperative advertising programs, the Company reimburses its retail customers for certain of their costs of advertising the Company's products. The Company records these costs in selling and administrative expense at the point in time when it is obligated to its customers for the costs, which is when the related revenues are recognized. This obligation may arise prior to the related advertisement being run.

Total advertising and promotion expenses were $1,912.4 million, $1,740.2 million, and $1,600.7 million for the years ended May 31, 2007, 2006 and 2005, respectively. Prepaid advertising and promotion expenses recorded in prepaid expenses and other assets totaled $253.0 million and $177.1 million at May 31, 2007 and 2006, respectively.

Cash and Equivalents

Cash and equivalents represent cash and short-term, highly liquid investments with maturities of three months or less at date of purchase. The carrying amounts reflected in the consolidated balance sheet for cash and equivalents approximate fair value.

54

NIKE, INC.

NOTES TO CONSOLIDATED FINANCIAL STATEMENTS — (Continued)

Short-term Investments

Short-term investments consist of highly liquid investments, primarily U.S. Treasury debt securities, with maturities over three months from the date of purchase. Debt securities which the Company has the ability and positive intent to hold to maturity are carried at amortized cost. Available-for-sale debt securities are recorded at fair value with any net unrealized gains and losses reported, net of tax, in other comprehensive income. Realized gains or losses are determined based on the specific identification method. The Company holds no investments considered to be trading securities. Amortized cost of both available-for-sale and held-to-maturity debt securities approximates fair market value due to their short maturities. Substantially all short-term investments held at May 31, 2007 have remaining maturities of 180 days or less. Included in interest (income) expense, net for the years ended May 31, 2007, 2006, and 2005, was interest income of $116.9 million, $87.3 million and $34.9 million, respectively, related to short-term investments and cash and equivalents.

Allowance for Uncollectible Accounts Receivable

Accounts receivable consists principally of amounts receivable from customers. We make ongoing estimates relating to the collectibility of our accounts receivable and maintain an allowance for estimated losses resulting from the inability of our customers to make required payments. In determining the amount of the allowance, we consider our historical level of credit losses and make judgments about the creditworthiness of significant customers based on ongoing credit evaluations. Accounts receivable with anticipated collection dates greater than twelve months from the balance sheet date and related allowances are considered non-current and recorded in other assets. The allowance for uncollectible accounts receivable was $71.5 million and $67.6 million at May 31, 2007 and 2006, respectively, of which $33.3 million and $29.2 million was recorded in other assets.

Inventory Valuation

Inventories related to our wholesale operations are stated at lower of cost or market and valued on a first-in, first-out ("FIFO") or moving average cost basis. Inventories related to our retail operations are stated at the lower of average cost or market using the retail inventory method. Under the retail inventory method, the valuation of inventories at cost is calculated by applying a cost-to-retail ratio to the retail value inventories. Permanent and point of sale markdowns, when recorded, reduce both the retail and cost components of inventory on hand so as to maintain the already established cost-to-retail relationship.

Property, Plant and Equipment and Depreciation

Property, plant and equipment are recorded at cost. Depreciation for financial reporting purposes is determined on a straight-line basis for buildings and leasehold improvements over 2 to 40 years and for machinery and equipment over 2 to 15 years. Computer software (including, in some cases, the cost of internal labor) is depreciated on a straight-line basis over 3 to 10 years.

Impairment of Long-Lived Assets

The Company estimates the future undiscounted cash flows to be derived from an asset to assess whether or not a potential impairment exists when events or circumstances indicate the carrying value of a long-lived asset may be impaired. If the carrying value exceeds the Company's estimate of future undiscounted cash flows, the Company then calculates the impairment as the excess of the carrying value of the asset over the Company's estimate of its fair market value.

55

NIKE, INC.

NOTES TO CONSOLIDATED FINANCIAL STATEMENTS — (Continued)

Identifiable Intangible Assets and Goodwill

Goodwill and intangible assets with indefinite lives are not amortized but instead are measured for impairment at least annually in the fourth quarter, or when events indicate that an impairment exists. As required by Statement of Financial Accounting Standards ("SFAS") No. 142, "Goodwill and other Intangible Assets" ("FAS 142"), in the Company's impairment test of goodwill, the Company compares the fair value of the applicable reporting unit to its carrying value. The Company estimates the fair value of its reporting units by using a combination of discounted cash flow analysis and comparisons with the market values of similar publicly traded companies. If the carrying value of the reporting unit exceeds the estimate of fair value, the Company calculates the impairment as the excess of the carrying value of goodwill over its implied fair value. In the impairment tests for indefinite-lived intangible assets, the Company compares the estimated fair value of the indefinite-lived intangible assets to the carrying value. The Company estimates the fair value of indefinite-lived intangible assets and trademarks using the relief from royalty approach, which is a standard form of discounted cash flow analysis used for the valuation of trademarks. If the carrying value exceeds the estimate of fair value, the Company calculates impairment as the excess of the carrying value over the estimate of fair value.

Intangible assets that are determined to have definite lives are amortized over their useful lives and are measured for impairment only when events or circumstances indicate the carrying value may be impaired.

Foreign Currency Translation and Foreign Currency Transactions

Adjustments resulting from translating foreign functional currency financial statements into U.S. dollars are included in the foreign currency translation adjustment, a component of accumulated other comprehensive income in shareholders' equity.

Transaction gains and losses generated by the effect of foreign exchange rates on recorded assets and liabilities denominated in a currency different from the functional currency of the applicable Company entity are recorded in other (income) expense, net, in the period in which they occur.

Accounting for Derivatives and Hedging Activities

The Company uses derivative financial instruments to limit exposure to changes in foreign currency exchange rates and interest rates. The Company accounts for derivatives pursuant to SFAS No. 133, "Accounting for Derivative Instruments and Hedging Activities," as amended and interpreted ("FAS 133"). FAS 133 establishes accounting and reporting standards for derivative instruments and requires that all derivatives be recorded at fair value on the balance sheet. Changes in the fair value of derivative financial instruments are either recognized in other comprehensive income (a component of shareholders' equity) or net income depending on whether the derivative is being used to hedge changes in cash flows or fair value.

See Note 16 for more information on the Company's Risk Management program and derivatives.

Stock-Based Compensation

On June 1, 2006, the Company adopted SFAS No. 123R "Share-Based Payment" ("FAS 123R") which requires the Company to record expense for stock-based compensation to employees using a fair value method. Under FAS 123R, the Company estimates the fair value of options granted under the NIKE, Inc. 1990 Stock Incentive Plan (the "1990 Plan") (see Note 10) and employees' purchase rights under the Employee Stock Purchase Plans ("ESPPs") using the Black-Scholes option pricing model. The Company recognizes this fair value, net of estimated forfeitures, as selling and administrative expense in the Consolidated Statements of Income over the vesting period using the straight-line method.

56

NIKE, INC.

NOTES TO CONSOLIDATED FINANCIAL STATEMENTS — (Continued)

The Company has adopted the modified prospective transition method prescribed by FAS 123R, which does not require the restatement of financial results for previous periods. In accordance with this transition method, the Company's Consolidated Statement of Income for the year ended May 31, 2007 includes (1) amortization of outstanding stock-based compensation granted prior to, but not vested, as of June 1, 2006, based on the fair value estimated in accordance with the original provisions of SFAS No. 123, "Accounting for Stock-Based Compensation" ("FAS 123") and (2) amortization of all stock-based awards granted subsequent to June 1, 2006, based on the fair value estimated in accordance with the provisions of FAS 123R.

The following table summarizes the effects of applying FAS 123R during the year ended May 31, 2007. The resulting stock-based compensation expense primarily relates to stock options.

(in millions, except per share data)	
Addition to selling and administrative expense	$141.9
Reduction to income tax expense	(45.2)
Reduction to net income[1]	$ 96.7
Reduction to earnings per share:	
Basic	$ 0.19
Diluted	$ 0.18

---

[1] In accordance with FAS 123R, stock-based compensation expense reported during the year ended May 31, 2007, includes $24.2 million, net of tax, or $0.04 per diluted share, of accelerated stock-based compensation expense recorded for employees eligible for accelerated stock option vesting upon retirement.

Prior to the adoption of FAS 123R, the Company used the intrinsic value method to account for stock options and ESPP shares in accordance with Accounting Principles Board Opinion No. 25, "Accounting for Stock Issued to Employees" as permitted by FAS 123. If the Company had instead accounted for stock options and ESPP shares issued to employees using the fair value method prescribed by FAS 123 during the years ended May 31, 2006 and 2005 the Company's pro forma net income and pro forma earnings per share would have been reported as follows:

	Year Ended May 31,	
	2006	**2005**
	(In millions, except per share data)	
Net income as reported	$ 1,392.0	$ 1,211.6
Add: Stock option expense included in reported net income, net of tax	0.2	0.6
Deduct: Total stock option and ESPP expense under fair value based method for all awards, net of tax[1]	(76.8)	(64.1)
Pro forma net income	$ 1,315.4	$ 1,148.1
Earnings per share:		
Basic — as reported	$ 2.69	$ 2.31
Basic — pro forma	2.54	2.19
Diluted — as reported	2.64	2.24
Diluted — pro forma	2.50	2.14

---

[1] Accelerated stock-based compensation expense for options subject to accelerated vesting due to employee retirement is not included in the pro forma figures shown above for the years ended May 31, 2006 and 2005. This disclosure reflects the expense of such options ratably over the stated vesting period or upon actual employee retirement. Had the Company recognized the fair value for such stock options on an accelerated

57

NIKE, INC.

NOTES TO CONSOLIDATED FINANCIAL STATEMENTS — (Continued)

basis in this pro forma disclosure, the Company would have recognized additional stock-based compensation expense of $17.5 million, net of tax, or $0.03 per diluted share for the year ended May 31, 2006 and $21.8 million, net of tax, or $0.04 per diluted share for the year ended May 31, 2005.

To calculate the excess tax benefits available for use in offsetting future tax shortfalls as of the date of implementation, the Company is following the alternative transition method discussed in FASB Staff Position No. 123R-3, "Transition Election Relating to Accounting for the Tax Effects of Share-Based Payment Awards."

See Note 10 for more information on the Company's stock programs.

Income Taxes

The Company accounts for income taxes using the asset and liability method. This approach requires the recognition of deferred tax assets and liabilities for the expected future tax consequences of temporary differences between the carrying amounts and the tax basis of assets and liabilities. United States income taxes are provided currently on financial statement earnings of non-U.S. subsidiaries that are expected to be repatriated. The Company determines annually the amount of undistributed non-U.S. earnings to invest indefinitely in its non-U.S. operations. See Note 8 for further discussion.

Earnings Per Share

Basic earnings per common share is calculated by dividing net income by the weighted average number of common shares outstanding during the year. Diluted earnings per common share is calculated by adjusting weighted average outstanding shares, assuming conversion of all potentially dilutive stock options and awards. See Note 11 for further discussion.

Management Estimates

The preparation of financial statements in conformity with generally accepted accounting principles requires management to make estimates, including estimates relating to assumptions that affect the reported amounts of assets and liabilities and disclosure of contingent assets and liabilities at the date of financial statements and the reported amounts of revenues and expenses during the reporting period. Actual results could differ from these estimates.

Reclassifications

Certain prior year amounts have been reclassified to conform to fiscal year 2007 presentation. These changes had no impact on previously reported results of operations or shareholders' equity.

Recently Issued Accounting Standards

In June 2006, the Financial Accounting Standards Board ("FASB") ratified the consensus reached on Emerging Issues Task Force ("EITF") Issue No. 06-3, "How Taxes Collected from Customers and Remitted to Governmental Authorities Should Be Presented in the Income Statement (That Is, Gross versus Net Presentation)" ("EITF 06-3"). EITF 06-3 requires disclosure of the method of accounting for the applicable assessed taxes and the amount of assessed taxes that are included in revenues if they are accounted for under the gross method. EITF 06-3 was adopted in the fourth quarter ended May 31, 2007; however, since the Company presents revenues net of any taxes collected from customers, no additional disclosures were required.

NIKE, INC.

NOTES TO CONSOLIDATED FINANCIAL STATEMENTS — (Continued)

In September 2006, the FASB issued SFAS No. 158, "Employers' Accounting for Defined Benefit Pension and Other Postretirement Plans" ("FAS 158"). FAS 158 requires employers to fully recognize the obligations associated with single-employer defined benefit pension, retiree healthcare and other postretirement plans in their financial statements. The Company adopted the provisions of FAS 158 in the fourth quarter ended May 31, 2007. See Note 12 for additional details.

In September 2006, the SEC staff issued Staff Accounting Bulletin No. 108, "Considering the Effects of Prior Year Misstatements when Quantifying Misstatements in Current Year Financial Statements" ("SAB 108"). SAB 108 requires public companies to quantify errors using both a balance sheet and income statement approach and evaluate whether either approach results in quantifying a misstatement as material, when all relevant quantitative and qualitative factors are considered. The adoption of SAB 108 at May 31, 2007 did not have a material impact on the Company's consolidated financial position or results of operations.

In June 2006, the FASB issued FASB Interpretation No. 48, "Accounting for Uncertainty in Income Taxes" ("FIN 48"). FIN 48 clarifies the accounting for uncertainty in income taxes recognized in the Company's financial statements in accordance with FASB Statement No. 109, "Accounting for Income Taxes". The provisions of FIN 48 are effective for the fiscal year beginning June 1, 2007. The Company has evaluated the impact of the provisions of FIN 48 and does not expect that the adoption will have a material impact on the Company's consolidated financial position or results of operations.

In June 2006, the FASB ratified the consensus reached on EITF Issue No. 06-2, "Accounting for Sabbatical Leave and Other Similar Benefits Pursuant to FASB Statement No. 43" ("EITF 06-2"). EITF 06-2 clarifies recognition guidance on the accrual of employees' rights to compensated absences under a sabbatical or other similar benefit arrangement. The provisions of EITF 06-2 are effective for the fiscal year beginning June 1, 2007 and will be applied through a cumulative effect adjustment to retained earnings. The Company has evaluated the provisions of EITF 06-2 and does not expect that the adoption will have a material impact on the Company's consolidated financial position or results of operations.

In September 2006, the FASB issued SFAS No. 157, "Fair Value Measurements" ("FAS 157"). FAS 157 defines fair value, establishes a framework for measuring fair value in accordance with generally accepted accounting principles, and expands disclosures about fair value measurements. The provisions of FAS 157 are effective for the fiscal year beginning June 1, 2008. The Company is currently evaluating the impact of the provisions of FAS 157.

In February 2007, the FASB issued SFAS No. 159, "The Fair Value Option for Financial Assets and Financial Liabilities — Including an Amendment of FASB Statement No. 115" ("FAS 159"). FAS 159 permits entities to choose to measure many financial instruments and certain other items at fair value. Unrealized gains and losses on items for which the fair value option has been elected will be recognized in earnings at each subsequent reporting date. The provisions of FAS 159 are effective for the fiscal year beginning June 1, 2008. The Company is currently evaluating the impact of the provisions of FAS 159.

Note 2 — Inventories

Inventory balances of $2,121.9 million and $2,076.7 million at May 31, 2007 and 2006, respectively, were substantially all finished goods.

59

NIKE, INC.

NOTES TO CONSOLIDATED FINANCIAL STATEMENTS — (Continued)

Note 3 — Property, Plant and Equipment

Property, plant and equipment includes the following:

	May 31, 2007	May 31, 2006
	(In millions)	
Land	$ 193.8	$ 195.9
Buildings	840.9	842.6
Machinery and equipment	1,817.2	1,661.7
Leasehold improvements	672.8	626.7
Construction in process	94.4	81.4
	3,619.1	3,408.3
Less accumulated depreciation	1,940.8	1,750.6
	$ 1,678.3	$ 1,657.7

Capitalized interest was not material for the years ended May 31, 2007, 2006 and 2005.

Note 4 — Identifiable Intangible Assets and Goodwill:

The following table summarizes the Company's identifiable intangible assets and goodwill balances as of May 31, 2007 and May 31, 2006:

	May 31, 2007			May 31, 2006		
	Gross Carrying Amount	Accumulated Amortization	Net Carrying Amount	Gross Carrying Amount	Accumulated Amortization	Net Carrying Amount
	(In millions)					
Amortized intangible assets:						
Patents	$ 44.1	$ (12.3)	$ 31.8	$ 34.1	$ (10.5)	$ 23.6
Trademarks	49.8	(17.5)	32.3	46.4	(11.8)	34.6
Other	21.6	(17.3)	4.3	21.5	(15.7)	5.8
Total	$115.5	$ (47.1)	$ 68.4	$102.0	$ (38.0)	$ 64.0
Unamortized intangible assets — Trademarks			$ 341.5			$ 341.5
Total			$ 409.9			$ 405.5
Goodwill			$ 130.8			$ 130.8

Amortization expense of identifiable assets with definite lives, which is included in selling and administrative expense, was $9.9 million, $9.8 million and $9.3 million for the years ended May 31, 2007, 2006, and 2005, respectively. The estimated amortization expense for intangible assets subject to amortization for each of the years ending May 31, 2008 through May 31, 2012 is as follows: 2008: $9.7 million; 2009: $8.7 million; 2010: $8.2 million; 2011: $7.7 million; 2012: $6.9 million.

60

NIKE, INC.

NOTES TO CONSOLIDATED FINANCIAL STATEMENTS — (Continued)

Note 5 — Accrued Liabilities

Accrued liabilities include the following:

	May 31,	
	2007	2006
	(In millions)	
Compensation and benefits, excluding taxes	$ 451.6	$ 427.2
Endorser compensation	139.9	124.7
Taxes other than income taxes	133.4	115.1
Dividends payable	92.9	79.5
Fair value of derivatives	90.5	111.2
Import and logistics costs	81.4	63.3
Advertising and marketing	70.6	75.4
Converse arbitration [1]	—	51.9
Other [2]	243.1	227.7
	$ 1,303.4	$ 1,276.0

[1] The Converse arbitration relates to a charge taken during the fourth quarter ended May 31, 2006 as a result of a contract dispute between Converse and a former South American licensee. The dispute was settled during the first quarter ended August 31, 2006.

[2] Other consists of various accrued expenses and no individual item accounted for more than $50 million of the balance at May 31, 2007 or 2006.

Note 6 — Short-Term Borrowings and Credit Lines

Notes payable to banks and interest-bearing accounts payable to Sojitz Corporation of America ("Sojitz America") as of May 31, 2007 and 2006, are summarized below:

	May 31,				
	2007			2006	
	Borrowings	Interest Rate		Borrowings	Interest Rate
		(In millions)			
Notes payable:					
U.S. operations	$ 14.6	0.00%[1]		$ 21.0	0.00%[1]
Non-U.S. operations	86.2	9.85%		22.4	7.72%
	$ 100.8			$ 43.4	
Sojitz America	$ 44.6	6.09%		$ 69.7	5.83%

[1] Weighted average interest rate includes non-interest bearing overdrafts.

The carrying amounts reflected in the consolidated balance sheet for notes payable approximate fair value.

The Company purchases through Sojitz America certain athletic footwear, apparel and equipment it acquires from non-U.S. suppliers. These purchases are for the Company's operations outside of the United States, the Europe, Middle East, and Africa Region and Japan. Accounts payable to Sojitz America are generally due up to 60 days after shipment of goods from the foreign port. The interest rate on such accounts payable is the 60-day London Interbank Offered Rate ("LIBOR") as of the beginning of the month of the invoice date, plus 0.75%.

61

NIKE, INC.

NOTES TO CONSOLIDATED FINANCIAL STATEMENTS — (Continued)

The Company had no borrowings outstanding under its commercial paper program at May 31, 2007 and 2006.

In December 2006, the Company entered into a $1 billion multi-year credit facility that replaced the Company's previous $750 million facility. The facility matures in December 2011, and can be extended for one additional year on both the first and second anniversary date for a total extension of two years. Based on the Company's current long-term senior unsecured debt ratings, the interest rate charged on any outstanding borrowings would be the prevailing LIBOR plus 0.15%. The facility fee is 0.05% of the total commitment. Under this agreement, the Company must maintain, among other things, certain minimum specified financial ratios with which the Company was in compliance at May 31, 2007. No amounts were outstanding under these facilities as of May 31, 2007 or 2006.

In January 2007, one of the Company's Japanese subsidiaries entered into a 3.0 billion yen (approximately $24.7 million as of May 31, 2007) loan facility that replaced certain intercompany borrowings. The interest rate on the facility is based on the six-month Japanese Yen LIBOR plus a spread, resulting in an all-in rate of 0.805% at May 31, 2007. The facility expires December 31, 2007 unless both parties agree to an extension.

Note 7 — Long-Term Debt

Long-term debt includes the following:

	May 31,	
	2007	2006
	(In millions)	
5.5% Corporate Bond, payable August 15, 2006	$ —	$249.3
4.8% Corporate Bond, payable July 9, 2007	25.0	24.7
5.375% Corporate Bond, payable July 8, 2009	24.8	24.6
5.66% Corporate Bond, payable July 23, 2012	24.8	24.6
5.4% Corporate Bond, payable August 7, 2012	14.6	14.4
4.7% Corporate Bond, payable October 1, 2013	50.0	50.0
5.15% Corporate Bonds, payable October 15, 2015	99.6	98.2
4.3% Japanese yen note, payable June 26, 2011	86.4	93.8
1.5% Japanese yen note, payable February 14, 2012	41.1	—
2.6% Japanese yen note, maturing August 20, 2001 through November 20, 2020	51.2	59.7
2.0% Japanese yen note, maturing August 20, 2001 through November 20, 2020	22.9	26.6
Other	—	0.1
Total	440.4	666.0
Less current maturities	30.5	255.3
	$ 409.9	$410.7

The fair value of long-term debt is estimated using discounted cash flow analyses, based on the Company's incremental borrowing rates for similar types of borrowing arrangements. The fair value of the Company's long-term debt, including current portion, is approximately $443.2 million at May 31, 2007 and $674.0 million at May 31, 2006.

The Company had interest rate swap agreements with the same notional amount and maturity dates as the $250.0 million corporate bond that matured on August 15, 2006, whereby the Company received fixed interest payments at the same rate as the bond and paid variable interest payments based on the three-month LIBOR plus a spread. The interest rate payable on these swap agreements was approximately 6.6% at May 31, 2006.

62

NIKE, INC.

NOTES TO CONSOLIDATED FINANCIAL STATEMENTS — (Continued)

The Company has an effective shelf registration statement with the Securities and Exchange Commission for $1 billion of debt securities. The Company has a medium-term note program under the shelf registration ("medium-term note program") that allows the Company to issue up to $500 million in medium-term notes. The Company has issued $240 million in medium-term notes under this program. During the years ended May 31, 2007 and 2006, no notes were issued under the medium-term note program. The issued notes have coupon rates that range from 4.70% to 5.66%. The maturities range from July 9, 2007 to October 15, 2015. For each of these notes, except for the swap for the $50 million note maturing October 1, 2013, the Company has entered into interest rate swap agreements whereby the Company receives fixed interest payments at the same rate as the notes and pays variable interest payments based on the three-month or six-month LIBOR plus a spread. Each swap has the same notional amount and maturity date as the corresponding note. The swap for the $50 million note maturing October 1, 2013, expired October 2, 2006. At May 31, 2007, the interest rates payable on these swap agreements range from approximately 5.2% to 5.9%.

In June 1996, one of the Company's Japanese subsidiaries, NIKE Logistics YK, borrowed 10.5 billion Japanese yen in a private placement with a maturity of June 26, 2011. Interest is paid semi-annually. The agreement provides for early retirement after year ten.

In July 1999, NIKE Logistics YK assumed 13.0 billion in Japanese yen loans as part of its agreement to purchase a distribution center in Japan, which serves as collateral for the loans. These loans mature in equal quarterly installments during the period August 20, 2001 through November 20, 2020. Interest is also paid quarterly.

In February 2007, NIKE Logistics YK entered into a 5.0 billion yen (approximately $41.1 million at May 31, 2007) term loan maturing February 14, 2012 that replaces certain intercompany borrowings. The interest rate on the loan is approximately 1.5% and interest is paid semi-annually.

Amounts of long-term debt maturities in each of the years ending May 31, 2008 through 2012 are $30.5 million, $5.5 million, $30.5 million, $5.5 million and $133.0 million, respectively.

Note 8 — Income Taxes

Income before income taxes is as follows:

	Year Ended May 31,		
	2007	2006	2005
		(In millions)	
Income before income taxes:			
United States	$ 805.1	$ 838.6	$ 755.5
Foreign	1,394.8	1,303.0	1,104.3
	$ 2,199.9	$ 2,141.6	$ 1,859.8

63

NIKE, INC.

NOTES TO CONSOLIDATED FINANCIAL STATEMENTS — (Continued)

The provision for income taxes is as follows:

	Year Ended May 31,		
	2007	2006	2005
		(In millions)	
Current:			
United States			
Federal	$352.6	$359.0	$279.6
State	59.6	60.6	50.7
Foreign	261.9	356.0	292.5
	674.1	775.6	622.8
Deferred:			
United States			
Federal	38.7	(4.2)	21.9
State	(4.8)	(6.8)	(5.3)
Foreign	0.4	(15.0)	8.8
	34.3	(26.0)	25.4
	$708.4	$749.6	$648.2

Deferred tax (assets) and liabilities are comprised of the following:

	May 31,	
	2007	2006
	(In millions)	
Deferred tax assets:		
Allowance for doubtful accounts	$ (12.4)	$ (10.9)
Inventories	(45.8)	(43.9)
Sales return reserves	(42.1)	(39.4)
Deferred compensation	(132.5)	(110.6)
Stock-based compensation	(30.3)	—
Reserves and accrued liabilities	(46.2)	(50.6)
Property, plant, and equipment	(16.3)	(28.6)
Foreign loss carryforwards	(37.5)	(29.2)
Foreign tax credit carryforwards	(3.4)	(9.5)
Hedges	(26.2)	(25.5)
Other	(33.0)	(29.1)
Total deferred tax assets	(425.7)	(377.3)
Valuation allowance	42.3	36.6
Total deferred tax assets after valuation allowance	(383.4)	(340.7)
Deferred tax liabilities:		
Undistributed earnings of foreign subsidiaries	232.6	135.3
Property, plant and equipment	66.1	91.4
Intangibles	97.2	96.8
Hedges	2.5	7.8
Other	17.8	12.5
Total deferred tax liabilities	416.2	343.8
Net deferred tax liability	$ 32.8	$ 3.1

64

NIKE, INC.

NOTES TO CONSOLIDATED FINANCIAL STATEMENTS — (Continued)

A reconciliation from the U.S. statutory federal income tax rate to the effective income tax rate follows:

	Year Ended May 31,		
	2007	2006	2005
Federal income tax rate	35.0%	35.0%	35.0%
State taxes, net of federal benefit	1.6	1.5	1.8
Foreign earnings	(4.1)	(1.5)	(2.8)
Other, net	(0.3)	—	0.9
Effective income tax rate	32.2%	35.0%	34.9%

The effective tax rate for the year ended May 31, 2007 of 32.2% has decreased from the fiscal 2006 effective tax rate of 35%. The decrease is primarily due to a European tax agreement entered into during the three months ended November 30, 2006. The Company recorded a retroactive benefit for the European tax agreement during the year ended May 31, 2007.

During the quarter ended November 30, 2005, the Company's CEO and Board of Directors approved a domestic reinvestment plan as required by the American Jobs Creation Act of 2004 (the "Act") to repatriate $500 million of foreign earnings in fiscal 2006. The Act created a temporary incentive for U.S. multinational corporations to repatriate accumulated income earned outside the U.S. by providing an 85% dividend received deduction for certain dividends from controlled foreign corporations. A $500 million repatriation was made during the quarter ended May 31, 2006 comprised of both foreign earnings for which U.S. taxes have previously been provided and foreign earnings that had been designated as permanently reinvested. Accordingly, the provisions made did not have a material impact on the Company's income tax expense or effective tax rate for the years ended May 31, 2007, 2006 and 2005.

The Company has indefinitely reinvested approximately $1,185.0 million of the cumulative undistributed earnings of certain foreign subsidiaries. Such earnings would be subject to U.S. taxation if repatriated to the U.S. The amount of unrecognized deferred tax liability associated with the permanently reinvested cumulative undistributed earnings was approximately $248.3 million as of May 31, 2007.

Deferred tax assets at May 31, 2007 and 2006 were reduced by a valuation allowance relating to tax benefits of certain foreign subsidiaries with operating losses where it is more likely than not that the deferred tax assets will not be realized.

During the years ended May 31, 2007, 2006, and 2005, income tax benefits attributable to employee stock-based compensation transactions of $56.6 million, $54.2 million, and $63.1 million, respectively, were allocated to shareholders' equity.

Note 9 — Redeemable Preferred Stock

Sojitz America is the sole owner of the Company's authorized Redeemable Preferred Stock, $1 par value, which is redeemable at the option of Sojitz America or the Company at par value aggregating $0.3 million. A cumulative dividend of $0.10 per share is payable annually on May 31 and no dividends may be declared or paid on the common stock of the Company unless dividends on the Redeemable Preferred Stock have been declared and paid in full. There have been no changes in the Redeemable Preferred Stock in the three years ended May 31, 2007, 2006 and 2005. As the holder of the Redeemable Preferred Stock, Sojitz America does not have general voting rights but does have the right to vote as a separate class on the sale of all or substantially all of the assets of the Company and its subsidiaries, on merger, consolidation, liquidation or dissolution of the Company or on the sale or assignment of the NIKE trademark for athletic footwear sold in the United States.

65

NIKE, INC.

NOTES TO CONSOLIDATED FINANCIAL STATEMENTS — (Continued)

Note 10 — Common Stock

The authorized number of shares of Class A Common Stock, no par value, and Class B Common Stock, no par value, are 350 million and 1.5 billion, respectively. Each share of Class A Common Stock is convertible into one share of Class B Common Stock. Voting rights of Class B Common Stock are limited in certain circumstances with respect to the election of directors.

In 1990, the Board of Directors adopted, and the shareholders approved, the NIKE, Inc. 1990 Stock Incentive Plan (the "1990 Plan"). The 1990 Plan provides for the issuance of up to 132 million previously unissued shares of Class B Common Stock in connection with stock options and other awards granted under the plan. The 1990 Plan authorizes the grant of non-statutory stock options, incentive stock options, stock appreciation rights, stock bonuses and the issuance and sale of restricted stock. The exercise price for non-statutory stock options, stock appreciation rights and the grant price of restricted stock may not be less than 75% of the fair market value of the underlying shares on the date of grant. The exercise price for incentive stock options may not be less than the fair market value of the underlying shares on the date of grant. A committee of the Board of Directors administers the 1990 Plan. The committee has the authority to determine the employees to whom awards will be made, the amount of the awards, and the other terms and conditions of the awards. The committee has granted substantially all stock options and restricted stock at 100% of the market price on the date of grant. Substantially all stock option grants outstanding under the 1990 plan were granted in the first quarter of each fiscal year, vest ratably over four years, and expire 10 years from the date of grant.

The weighted average fair value per share of the options granted during the years ended May 31, 2007, 2006 and 2005, as computed using the Black-Scholes pricing model, was $8.80, $9.68 and $13.95, respectively. The weighted average assumptions used to estimate these fair values are as follows:

	Year Ended May 31,		
	2007	2006	2005
Dividend yield	1.6%	1%	1%
Expected volatility	19%	21%	42%
Weighted average expected life (in years)	5.0	4.5	5.0
Risk-free interest rate	5.0%	4.0%	3.7%

For the years ended May 31, 2007 and 2006, the Company estimated the expected volatility based on the implied volatility in market traded options on the Company's common stock with a term greater than one year, along with other factors. For the year ended May 31, 2005, the Company estimated the expected volatility based on the historical volatility of the Company's common stock. The weighted average expected life of options is based on an analysis of historical and expected future exercise patterns. The interest rate is based on the U.S. Treasury (constant maturity) risk-free rate in effect at the date of grant for periods corresponding with the expected term of the options.

66

NIKE, INC.

NOTES TO CONSOLIDATED FINANCIAL STATEMENTS — (Continued)

The following summarizes the stock option transactions under the plan discussed above:

	Shares (In millions)	Weighted Average Option Price
Options outstanding May 31, 2004	37.6	$ 23.71
Exercised	(8.8)	23.17
Forfeited	(0.9)	26.33
Granted	10.8	36.96
Options outstanding May 31, 2005	38.7	27.49
Exercised	(8.0)	24.68
Forfeited	(1.8)	35.75
Granted	11.5	43.68
Options outstanding May 31, 2006	40.4	32.31
Exercised	(10.7)	27.55
Forfeited	(1.6)	37.17
Granted	11.6	39.54
Options outstanding May 31, 2007	39.7	$ 35.50
Options exercisable at May 31,		
2005	14.7	$ 23.01
2006	16.6	25.68
2007	15.3	29.52

The weighted average contractual life remaining for options outstanding and options exercisable at May 31, 2007 was 7.2 years and 5.4 years, respectively. The aggregate intrinsic value for options outstanding and exercisable at May 31, 2007 was $843.7 million and $417.0 million, respectively. The aggregate intrinsic value was the amount by which the market value of the underlying stock exceeded the exercise price of the options. The total intrinsic value of the options exercised during the years ended May 31, 2007, 2006 and 2005 was $204.9 million, $144.0 million and $145.7 million, respectively.

As of May 31, 2007, the Company had $132.4 million of unrecognized compensation costs from stock options, net of estimated forfeitures, to be recognized as selling and administrative expense over a weighted average period of 2.1 years.

In addition to the 1990 Plan, the Company gives employees the right to purchase shares at a discount to the market price under employee stock purchase plans ("ESPPs"). Employees are eligible to participate through payroll deductions up to 10% of their compensation. At the end of each six-month offering period, shares are purchased by the participants at 85% of the lower of the fair market value at the beginning or the ending of the offering period. During the years ended May 31, 2007, 2006 and 2005, employees purchased 0.8 million, 0.8 million and 0.6 million shares, respectively.

From time to time, the Company grants restricted stock and unrestricted stock to key employees under the 1990 Plan. The number of shares granted to employees during the years ended May 31, 2007, 2006 and 2005 were 345,000, 141,000 and 229,000 with weighted average prices of $39.38, $43.38 and $44.65, respectively. Recipients of restricted shares are entitled to cash dividends and to vote their respective shares throughout the period of restriction. The value of all of the granted shares was established by the market price on the date of grant.

67

NIKE, INC.

NOTES TO CONSOLIDATED FINANCIAL STATEMENTS — (Continued)

The following table summarizes the Company's total stock-based compensation expense recognized in selling and administrative expense:

	Year Ended May 31,		
	2007	**2006**	**2005**
		(in millions)	
Stock options	$134.9	$ 0.3	$1.0
ESPPs	7.0	—	—
Restricted stock[(1)]	5.8	11.5	3.9
Total stock-based compensation expense	$147.7	$11.8	$4.9

[(1)] The expense related to restricted stock awards was included in selling and administrative expense in prior years and was not affected by the adoption of FAS 123R.

During the years ended May 31, 2007, 2006 and 2005, the Company also granted shares of stock under the Long-Term Incentive Plan ("LTIP"), adopted by the Board of Directors and approved by shareholders in September 1997. The LTIP provides for the issuance of up to 2.0 million shares of Class B Common Stock. Under the LTIP, awards are made to certain executives in their choice of either cash or stock, based on performance targets established over three-year time periods. Once performance targets are achieved, cash or shares of stock are issued. The shares are immediately vested upon grant. The value of the shares is established by the market price on the date of issuance. Under the LTIP, 3,000, 6,000 and 8,000 shares with a price of $38.84, $40.79 and $34.85, respectively, were issued during the years ended May 31, 2007, 2006 and 2005 for the plan years ended May 31, 2006, 2005 and 2004, respectively. The Company recognized nominal expense related to the shares issued during the years ended May 31, 2007 and 2006, and $0.1 million during the year ended May 31, 2005. The Company recognized $30.0 million, $21.7 million and $22.1 million of selling and administrative expense related to the cash awards during the years ended May 31, 2007, 2006 and 2005, respectively. During the year ended May 31, 2007, LTIP participants agreed to amend their grant agreements to eliminate the ability to receive payments in shares of stock, so shares of stock are no longer awarded. Beginning with the plan year ended May 31, 2007, cash will be awarded if performance targets are achieved.

Note 11 — Earnings Per Share

The following represents a reconciliation from basic earnings per share to diluted earnings per share. Options to purchase an additional 9.5 million, 11.3 million and 0.5 million shares of common stock were outstanding at May 31, 2007, 2006 and 2005, respectively, but were not included in the computation of diluted earnings per share because the options were antidilutive.

	Year Ended May 31,		
	2007	**2006**	**2005**
	(In millions, except per share data)		
Determination of shares:			
Weighted average common shares outstanding	503.8	518.0	525.2
Assumed conversion of dilutive stock options and awards	6.1	9.6	15.4
Diluted weighted average common shares outstanding	509.9	527.6	540.6
Basic earnings per common share	$ 2.96	$ 2.69	$ 2.31
Diluted earnings per common share	$ 2.93	$ 2.64	$ 2.24

68

NIKE, INC.

NOTES TO CONSOLIDATED FINANCIAL STATEMENTS — (Continued)

Note 12 — Benefit Plans

The Company has a profit sharing plan available to most U.S.-based employees. The terms of the plan call for annual contributions by the Company as determined by the Board of Directors. A subsidiary of the Company also has a profit sharing plan available to its U.S.-based employees. The terms of the plan call for annual contributions as determined by the subsidiary's executive management. Contributions of $31.8 million, $33.2 million, and $29.1 million were made to the plans and are included in selling and administrative expenses in the consolidated financial statements for the years ended May 31, 2007, 2006 and 2005, respectively. The Company has various 401(k) employee savings plans available to U.S.-based employees. The Company matches a portion of employee contributions with common stock or cash. Company contributions to the savings plans were $24.9 million, $22.5 million, and $20.3 million for the years ended May 31, 2007, 2006 and 2005, respectively, and are included in selling and administrative expenses.

The Company has pension plans in various countries worldwide. The pension plans are only available to local employees and are generally government mandated. Upon adoption of FAS 158, "Employers' Accounting for Defined Benefit Pension and Other Postretirement Plans" on May 31, 2007, the Company recorded a liability of $17.6 million related to the unfunded pension liabilities of the plans.

Note 13 — Comprehensive Income

Comprehensive income is as follows:

	Year Ended May 31,		
	2007	2006	2005
		(In millions)	
Net income	$1,491.5	$1,392.0	$1,211.6
Other comprehensive income:			
Change in cumulative translation adjustment and other (net of tax (expense) benefit of ($5.4) in 2007, $19.7 in 2006, and $3.9 in 2005)	84.6	87.1	70.1
Changes due to cash flow hedging instruments (Note 16):			
Net loss on hedge derivatives (net of tax benefit of $9.5 in 2007, $2.8 in 2006 and $28.7 in 2005)	(38.1)	(5.6)	(54.0)
Reclassification to net income of previously deferred losses and (gains) related to hedge derivatives (net of tax expense (benefit) of ($3.6) in 2007, $15.3 in 2006 and ($72.8) in 2005)	21.4	(33.2)	143.6
Other comprehensive income	67.9	48.3	159.7
Total comprehensive income	$1,559.4	$1,440.3	$1,371.3

The components of accumulated other comprehensive income are as follows:

	May 31,	
	2007	2006
	(In millions)	
Cumulative translation adjustment and other[1]	$234.3	$161.9
Net deferred loss on hedge derivatives	(56.9)	(40.2)
	$177.4	$121.7

---

[1] Cumulative translation adjustment and other for the year ended May 31, 2007 includes a $12.2 million net-of-tax adjustment relating to the adoption of FAS 158. See Note 12 for additional details.

NIKE, INC.

NOTES TO CONSOLIDATED FINANCIAL STATEMENTS — (Continued)

Note 14 — Commitments and Contingencies

The Company leases space for certain of its offices, warehouses and retail stores under leases expiring from one to twenty-seven years after May 31, 2007. Rent expense was $285.2 million, $252.0 million and $232.6 million for the years ended May 31, 2007, 2006 and 2005, respectively. Amounts of minimum future annual rental commitments under non-cancelable operating leases in each of the five years ending May 31, 2008 through 2012 are $260.9 million, $219.9 million, $183.3 million, $156.7 million, $128.4 million, respectively, and $587.0 million in later years.

As of May 31, 2007 and 2006, the Company had letters of credit outstanding totaling $165.9 million and $347.6 million, respectively. These letters of credit were generally issued for the purchase of inventory.

In connection with various contracts and agreements, the Company provides routine indemnifications relating to the enforceability of intellectual property rights, coverage for legal issues that arise and other items that fall under the scope of FASB Interpretation No. 45, "Guarantor's Accounting and Disclosure Requirements for Guarantees, Including Indirect Guarantees of Indebtedness of Others." Currently, the Company has several such agreements in place. However, based on the Company's historical experience and the estimated probability of future loss, the Company has determined that the fair value of such indemnifications is not material to the Company's financial position or results of operations.

In the ordinary course of its business, the Company is involved in various legal proceedings involving contractual and employment relationships, product liability claims, trademark rights, and a variety of other matters. The Company does not believe there are any pending legal proceedings that will have a material impact on the Company's financial position or results of operations.

Note 15 — Acquisitions

In August 2004, the Company acquired 100% of the equity interests in Official Starter LLC and Official Starter Properties LLC (collectively "Official Starter"). The Exeter Brands Group LLC, a wholly-owned subsidiary of the Company, was formed soon thereafter to develop the Company's business in retail channels serving value-conscious consumers and to operate the Official Starter business. The acquisition was accounted for under the purchase method of accounting. The cash purchase price, including acquisition costs net of cash acquired, was $47.2 million. All assets and liabilities of Exeter Brands Group were initially recorded in the Company's Consolidated Balance Sheet based on their estimated fair values at the date of acquisition. The results of Exeter Brands Group's operations have been included in the consolidated financial statements since the date of acquisition as part of the Company's Other operating segment. The pro forma effect of the acquisition on the combined results of operations was not significant.

Note 16 — Risk Management and Derivatives

The Company is exposed to global market risks, including the effect of changes in foreign currency exchange rates and interest rates. The Company uses derivatives to manage financial exposures that occur in the normal course of business. The Company does not hold or issue derivatives for trading purposes.

The Company formally documents all relationships between hedging instruments and hedged items, as well as its risk-management objective and strategy for undertaking hedge transactions. This process includes linking all derivatives to either specific assets and liabilities on the balance sheet or specific firm commitments or forecasted transactions.

70

NIKE, INC.
NOTES TO CONSOLIDATED FINANCIAL STATEMENTS — (Continued)

Substantially all derivatives outstanding as of May 31, 2007 and 2006 are designated as either cash flow or fair value hedges. All derivatives are recognized on the balance sheet at their fair value. Unrealized gain positions are recorded as other current assets or other non-current assets, depending on the instrument's maturity date. Unrealized loss positions are recorded as accrued liabilities or other non-current liabilities. All changes in fair values of outstanding cash flow hedge derivatives, except the ineffective portion, are recorded in other comprehensive income, until net income is affected by the variability of cash flows of the hedged transaction. Fair value hedges are recorded in net income and are offset by the change in fair value of the underlying asset or liability being hedged.

Cash Flow Hedges

The purpose of the Company's foreign currency hedging activities is to protect the Company from the risk that the eventual cash flows resulting from transactions in foreign currencies, including revenues, product costs, selling and administrative expenses, investments in U.S. dollar-denominated available-for-sale debt securities and intercompany transactions, including intercompany borrowings, will be adversely affected by changes in exchange rates. It is the Company's policy to utilize derivatives to reduce foreign exchange risks where internal netting strategies cannot be effectively employed.

Derivatives used by the Company to hedge foreign currency exchange risks are forward exchange contracts and options. Hedged transactions are denominated primarily in euros, British pounds, Japanese yen, Korean won, Canadian dollars and Mexican pesos. The Company hedges up to 100% of anticipated exposures typically twelve months in advance, but has hedged as much as 32 months in advance. When intercompany loans are hedged, it is typically for their expected duration.

Substantially all foreign currency derivatives outstanding as of May 31, 2007 and 2006 qualify for and are designated as foreign-currency cash flow hedges, including those hedging foreign currency denominated firm commitments.

Changes in fair values of outstanding cash flow hedge derivatives, except the ineffective portion, are recorded in other comprehensive income, until net income is affected by the variability of cash flows of the hedged transaction. In most cases amounts recorded in other comprehensive income will be released to net income some time after the maturity of the related derivative. The consolidated statement of income classification of effective hedge results is the same as that of the underlying exposure. Results of hedges of revenue and product costs are recorded in revenue and cost of sales, respectively, when the underlying hedged transaction affects net income. Results of hedges of selling and administrative expense are recorded together with those costs when the related expense is recorded. Results of hedges of anticipated purchases and sales of U.S. dollar-denominated available-for-sale securities are recorded in other (income) expense, net when the securities are sold.

Results of hedges of anticipated intercompany transactions are recorded in other (income) expense, net when the transaction occurs. Hedges of recorded balance sheet positions are recorded in other (income) expense, net currently together with the transaction gain or loss from the hedged balance sheet position. Net foreign currency transaction gains and losses, which includes hedge results captured in revenues, cost of sales, selling and administrative expense and other (income) expense, net, were a $27.9 million loss, a $49.9 million gain, and a $217.8 million loss for the years ended May 31, 2007, 2006, and 2005, respectively.

Premiums paid on options are initially recorded as deferred charges. The Company assesses effectiveness on options based on the total cash flows method and records total changes in the options' fair value to other comprehensive income to the degree they are effective.

71

NIKE, INC.

NOTES TO CONSOLIDATED FINANCIAL STATEMENTS — (Continued)

As of May 31, 2007, $52.8 million of deferred net losses (net of tax) on both outstanding and matured derivatives accumulated in other comprehensive income are expected to be reclassified to net income during the next twelve months as a result of underlying hedged transactions also being recorded in net income. Actual amounts ultimately reclassified to net income are dependent on the exchange rates in effect when derivative contracts that are currently outstanding mature. As of May 31, 2007, the maximum term over which the Company is hedging exposures to the variability of cash flows for all forecasted and recorded transactions is 18 months.

The Company formally assesses, both at a hedge's inception and on an ongoing basis, whether the derivatives that are used in the hedging transaction have been highly effective in offsetting changes in the cash flows of hedged items and whether those derivatives may be expected to remain highly effective in future periods. When it is determined that a derivative is not, or has ceased to be, highly effective as a hedge, the Company discontinues hedge accounting prospectively.

The Company discontinues hedge accounting prospectively when (1) it determines that the derivative is no longer highly effective in offsetting changes in the cash flows of a hedged item (including hedged items such as firm commitments or forecasted transactions); (2) the derivative expires or is sold, terminated, or exercised; (3) it is no longer probable that the forecasted transaction will occur; or (4) management determines that designating the derivative as a hedging instrument is no longer appropriate.

When the Company discontinues hedge accounting because it is no longer probable that the forecasted transaction will occur in the originally expected period, the gain or loss on the derivative remains in accumulated other comprehensive income and is reclassified to net income when the forecasted transaction affects net income. However, if it is probable that a forecasted transaction will not occur by the end of the originally specified time period or within an additional two-month period of time thereafter, the gains and losses that were accumulated in other comprehensive income will be recognized immediately in net income. In all situations in which hedge accounting is discontinued and the derivative remains outstanding, the Company will carry the derivative at its fair value on the balance sheet, recognizing future changes in the fair value in other (income) expense, net. Any hedge ineffectiveness is recorded in other (income) expense, net. Effectiveness for cash flow hedges is assessed based on forward rates.

For each of the years ended May 31, 2007, 2006 and 2005, the Company recorded in other (income) expense, net an insignificant loss representing the total ineffectiveness of all derivatives. Net income for each of the years ended May 31, 2007, 2006 and 2005 was not materially affected due to discontinued hedge accounting.

Fair Value Hedges

The Company is also exposed to the risk of changes in the fair value of certain fixed-rate debt attributable to changes in interest rates. Derivatives currently used by the Company to hedge this risk are receive-fixed, pay-variable interest rate swaps.

Substantially all interest rate swap agreements are designated as fair value hedges of the related long-term debt and meet the shortcut method requirements under FAS 133. Accordingly, changes in the fair values of the interest rate swap agreements are exactly offset by changes in the fair value of the underlying long-term debt. No ineffectiveness has been recorded to net income related to interest rate swaps designated as fair value hedges for the years ended May 31, 2007, 2006 and 2005.

As discussed in Note 7, during the year ended May 31, 2004, the Company issued a $50 million medium-term note maturing October 1, 2013 and simultaneously entered into a receive-fixed, pay-variable interest rate swap with the same notional amount and fixed interest rate as the note. However, the swap expired

72

NIKE, INC.

NOTES TO CONSOLIDATED FINANCIAL STATEMENTS — (Continued)

October 2, 2006. This interest rate swap was not accounted for as a fair value hedge. Accordingly, changes in the fair value of the swap were recorded to net income each period as a component of other (income) expense, net. The change in the fair value of the swap was not material for the years ended May 31, 2007, 2006 and 2005.

In fiscal 2003, the Company entered into an interest rate swap agreement related to a Japanese yen denominated intercompany loan with one of the Company's Japanese subsidiaries. The Japanese subsidiary pays variable interest on the intercompany loan based on 3-month LIBOR plus a spread. Under the interest rate swap agreement, the subsidiary pays fixed interest payments at 0.8% and receives variable interest payments based on 3-month LIBOR plus a spread based on a notional amount of 8 billion Japanese yen. This interest rate swap is not accounted for as a fair value hedge. Accordingly, changes in the fair value of the swap are recorded to net income each period as a component of other (income) expense, net. The change in the fair value of the swap was not material for the years ended May 31, 2007, 2006 and 2005.

The fair values of all derivatives recorded on the consolidated balance sheet are as follows:

	May 31,	
	2007	2006
	(In millions)	
Unrealized Gains:		
Foreign currency exchange contracts and options	$ 43.5	$ 75.7
Interest rate swaps	0.5	0.9
Unrealized (Losses):		
Foreign currency exchange contracts and options	(90.6)	(122.2)
Interest rate swaps	(2.6)	(6.0)

Concentration of Credit Risk

The Company is exposed to credit-related losses in the event of non-performance by counterparties to hedging instruments. The counterparties to all derivative transactions are major financial institutions with investment grade credit ratings. However, this does not eliminate the Company's exposure to credit risk with these institutions. This credit risk is generally limited to the unrealized gains in such contracts should any of these counterparties fail to perform as contracted. To manage this risk, the Company has established strict counterparty credit guidelines that are continually monitored and reported to senior management according to prescribed guidelines. The Company utilizes a portfolio of financial institutions either headquartered or operating in the same countries the Company conducts its business. As a result of the above considerations, the Company considers the risk of counterparty default to be minimal.

In addition to hedging instruments, the Company is subject to concentrations of credit risk associated with cash and equivalents and accounts receivable. The Company places cash and equivalents with financial institutions with investment grade credit ratings and, by policy, limits the amount of credit exposure to any one financial institution. The Company considers its concentration risk related to accounts receivable to be mitigated by the Company's credit policy, the significance of outstanding balances owed by each individual customer at any point in time and the geographic dispersion of these customers.

Note 17 — Operating Segments and Related Information

Operating Segments.   The Company's operating segments are evidence of the structure of the Company's internal organization. The major segments are defined by geographic regions for operations participating in NIKE brand sales activity excluding NIKE Golf and NIKE Bauer Hockey. Each NIKE brand geographic segment operates predominantly in one industry: the design, production, marketing and selling of sports and fitness

73

NIKE, INC.

NOTES TO CONSOLIDATED FINANCIAL STATEMENTS — (Continued)

footwear, apparel, and equipment. The "Other" category shown below represents activities of Cole Haan, Converse, Exeter Brands Group (beginning August 11, 2004), Hurley, NIKE Bauer Hockey, and NIKE Golf, which are considered immaterial for individual disclosure based on the aggregation criteria in SFAS No. 131 "Disclosures about Segments of an Enterprise and Related Information".

Where applicable, "Corporate" represents items necessary to reconcile to the consolidated financial statements, which generally include corporate activity and corporate eliminations.

Net revenues as shown below represent sales to external customers for each segment. Intercompany revenues have been eliminated and are immaterial for separate disclosure. The Company evaluates performance of individual operating segments based on pre-tax income. On a consolidated basis, this amount represents income before income taxes as shown in the Consolidated Statements of Income. Reconciling items for pre-tax income represent corporate costs that are not allocated to the operating segments for management reporting including corporate activity, certain currency exchange rate gains and losses on transactions and intercompany eliminations for specific income statement items in the Consolidated Statements of Income.

Additions to long-lived assets as presented in the following table represent capital expenditures.

74

NIKE, INC.

NOTES TO CONSOLIDATED FINANCIAL STATEMENTS — (Continued)

Accounts receivable, inventories and property, plant and equipment for operating segments are regularly reviewed by management and are therefore provided below.

Certain prior year amounts have been reclassed to conform to fiscal 2007 presentation.

	Year Ended May 31,		
	2007	2006 (In millions)	2005
Net Revenue			
United States	$ 6,107.1	$ 5,722.5	$ 5,129.3
Europe, Middle East and Africa	4,723.3	4,326.6	4,281.6
Asia Pacific	2,283.4	2,053.8	1,897.3
Americas	952.5	904.9	695.8
Other	2,259.6	1,947.1	1,735.7
	$16,325.9	$14,954.9	$13,739.7
Pre-tax Income			
United States	$ 1,300.3	$ 1,244.5	$ 1,127.9
Europe, Middle East and Africa	1,000.7	960.7	917.5
Asia Pacific	483.7	412.5	399.8
Americas	187.4	172.6	116.5
Other	303.7	153.6	154.8
Corporate	(1,075.9)	(802.3)	(856.7)
	$ 2,199.9	$ 2,141.6	$ 1,859.8
Additions to Long-lived Assets			
United States	$ 67.3	$ 59.8	$ 54.8
Europe, Middle East and Africa	94.9	73.6	38.8
Asia Pacific	20.7	16.8	22.0
Americas	5.3	6.9	6.8
Other	36.0	33.2	31.3
Corporate	89.3	143.4	103.4
	$ 313.5	$ 333.7	$ 257.1
Depreciation			
United States	$ 45.4	$ 54.2	$ 49.0
Europe, Middle East and Africa	47.4	46.9	45.2
Asia Pacific	25.2	28.4	28.3
Americas	6.1	6.4	4.0
Other	28.2	29.0	28.5
Corporate	117.4	117.1	102.2
	$ 269.7	$ 282.0	$ 257.2

75

NIKE, INC.

NOTES TO CONSOLIDATED FINANCIAL STATEMENTS — (Continued)

	Year Ended May 31,		
	2007	2006	2005
		(In millions)	
Accounts Receivable, net			
United States	$ 806.8	$ 717.2	$ 627.0
Europe, Middle East and Africa	739.1	703.3	711.4
Asia Pacific	296.6	319.7	309.8
Americas	184.1	174.5	168.7
Other	404.9	410.0	394.0
Corporate	63.2	58.2	39.0
	$ 2,494.7	$ 2,382.9	$ 2,249.9
Inventories			
United States	$ 796.0	$ 725.9	$ 639.9
Europe, Middle East and Africa	554.5	590.1	496.5
Asia Pacific	214.1	238.3	228.9
Americas	132.0	147.6	96.8
Other	378.7	330.5	316.2
Corporate	46.6	44.3	32.8
	$ 2,121.9	$ 2,076.7	$ 1,811.1
Property, Plant and Equipment, net			
United States	$ 232.7	$ 219.3	$ 216.0
Europe, Middle East and Africa	325.4	266.6	230.0
Asia Pacific	326.1	354.8	380.4
Americas	16.9	17.0	15.7
Other	103.6	98.2	93.4
Corporate	673.6	701.8	670.3
	$ 1,678.3	$ 1,657.7	$ 1,605.8

Revenues by Major Product Lines.   Revenues to external customers for NIKE brand products are attributable to sales of footwear, apparel and equipment. Other revenues to external customers primarily include external sales by Cole Haan Holdings Incorporated, Converse Inc., Exeter Brands Group LLC (beginning August 11, 2004), Hurley International LLC, NIKE Bauer Hockey Corp., and NIKE Golf.

	Year Ended May 31,		
	2007	2006	2005
		(In millions)	
Footwear	$ 8,514.0	$ 7,965.9	$ 7,299.7
Apparel	4,576.5	4,168.0	3,879.4
Equipment	975.8	873.9	824.9
Other	2,259.6	1,947.1	1,735.7
	$ 16,325.9	$ 14,954.9	$ 13,739.7

Revenues and Long-Lived Assets by Geographic Area.   Geographical area information is similar to that shown previously under operating segments with the exception of the Other activity, which has been allocated to the geographical areas based on the location where the sales originated. Revenues derived in the United States were $7,593.7 million, $7,019.0 million, and $6,284.5 million, for the years ended May 31, 2007, 2006, and

76

NIKE, INC.

NOTES TO CONSOLIDATED FINANCIAL STATEMENTS — (Continued)

2005, respectively. The Company's largest concentrations of long-lived assets are in the United States and Japan. Long-lived assets attributable to operations in the United States, which are comprised of net property, plant & equipment were $991.3 million, $998.2 million, and $956.6 million at May 31, 2007, 2006, and 2005, respectively. Long-lived assets attributable to operations in Japan were $260.6 million, $296.3 million, and $321.0 million at May 31, 2007, 2006, and 2005, respectively.

Major Customers. During the years ended May 31, 2007, 2006 and 2005, revenues derived from Foot Locker, Inc. represented 10 percent, 10 percent and 11 percent of the Company's consolidated revenues, respectively. Sales to this customer are included in all segments of the Company.

Item 9. *Changes In and Disagreements with Accountants on Accounting and Financial Disclosure*

There has been no change of accountants nor any disagreements with accountants on any matter of accounting principles or practices or financial statement disclosure required to be reported under this Item.

Item 9A. *Controls and Procedures*

We maintain disclosure controls and procedures that are designed to ensure that information required to be disclosed in our Exchange Act reports is recorded, processed, summarized and reported within the time periods specified in the Securities and Exchange Commission's rules and forms and that such information is accumulated and communicated to our management, including our Chief Executive Officer and Chief Financial Officer, as appropriate, to allow for timely decisions regarding required disclosure. In designing and evaluating the disclosure controls and procedures, management recognizes that any controls and procedures, no matter how well designed and operated, can provide only reasonable assurance of achieving the desired control objectives, and management is required to apply its judgment in evaluating the cost-benefit relationship of possible controls and procedures.

We carry out a variety of on-going procedures, under the supervision and with the participation of our management, including our Chief Executive Officer and Chief Financial Officer, to evaluate the effectiveness of the design and operation of our disclosure controls and procedures. Based on the foregoing, our Chief Executive Officer and Chief Financial Officer concluded that our disclosure controls and procedures were effective at the reasonable assurance level as of May 31, 2007.

"Management's Annual Report on Internal Control Over Financial Reporting" and the related attestation report of PricewaterhouseCoopers LLP are included in Item 8 on pages 46-49 of this Report.

There has been no change in our internal control over financial reporting during our most recent fiscal quarter that has materially affected, or is reasonable likely to materially affect, our internal control over financial reporting.

Item 9B. *Other Information*

No disclosure is required under this Item.

77

A

absorption costing The reporting of the costs of manufactured products, normally direct materials, direct labor, and factory overhead, as product costs. (961)

accelerated depreciation method A depreciation method that provides for a higher depreciation amount in the first year of the asset's use, followed by a gradually declining amount of depreciation. (448)

account An accounting form that is used to record the increases and decreases in each financial statement item. (46)

account form The form of balance sheet that resembles the basic format of the accounting equation, with assets on the left side and Liabilities and Owner's Equity sections on the right side. (16, 259)

account payable The liability created by a purchase on account. (11)

account receivable A claim against the customer created by selling merchandise or services on credit. (12, 59, 394)

accounting An information system that provides reports to stakeholders about the economic activities and condition of a business. (3)

accounting cycle The process that begins with analyzing and journalizing transactions and ends with the post-closing trial balance. (153)

accounting equation Assets = Liabilities + Owner's Equity. (9)

accounting period concept The accounting concept that assumes that the economic life of the business can be divided into time periods. (98)

accounting system The methods and procedures used by a business to collect, classify, summarize, and report financial data for use by management and external users. (205)

accounts payable subsidiary ledger The subsidiary ledger containing the individual accounts with suppliers (creditors). (206)

accounts receivable analysis A company's ability to collect its accounts receivable. (768)

accounts receivable subsidiary ledger The subsidiary ledger containing the individual accounts with customers. (206)

accounts receivable turnover The relationship between net sales and accounts receivable, computed by dividing the net sales by the average net accounts receivable; measures how frequently during the year the accounts receivable are being converted to cash. (411, 768)

accrual basis of accounting Under this basis of accounting, revenues and expenses are reported in the income statement in the period in which they are earned or incurred. (98)

accrued expenses Expenses that have been incurred but not recorded in the accounts. (101)

accrued revenues Revenues that have been earned but not recorded in the accounts. (101)

accumulated depreciation The contra asset account credited when recording the depreciation of a fixed asset. (109)

accumulated other comprehensive income The cumulative effects of other comprehensive income items reported separately in the Stockholders' Equity section of the balance sheet. (681)

activity base (driver) A measure of activity that is related to changes in cost. Used in analyzing and classifying cost behavior. Activity bases are also used in the denominator in calculating the predetermined factory overhead rate to assign overhead costs to cost objects. (854, 937)

activity-based costing (ABC) A cost allocation method that identifies activities causing the incurrence of costs and allocates these costs to products (or other cost objects), based on activity drivers (bases). (854, 1137)

adjusted trial balance The trial balance prepared after all the adjusting entries have been posted. (117)

adjusting entries The journal entries that bring the accounts up to date at the end of the accounting period. (99)

adjusting process An analysis and updating of the accounts when financial statements are prepared. (99)

administrative expenses (general expenses) Expenses incurred in the administration or general operations of the business. (257)

aging the receivables The process of analyzing the accounts receivable and classifying them according to various age groupings, with the due date being the base point for determining age. (401)

Allowance for Doubtful Accounts The contra asset account for accounts receivable. (397)

allowance method The method of accounting for uncollectible accounts that provides an expense for uncollectible receivables in advance of their write-off. (395)

amortization The periodic transfer of the cost of an intangible asset to expense. (455)

annuity A series of equal cash flows at fixed intervals. (635, 1169)

assets The resources owned by a business. (9, 48)

available-for-sale securities Securities that management expects to sell in the future but which are not actively traded for profit. (665)

average inventory cost flow method The method of inventory costing that is based on the assumption that costs should be charged against revenue by using the weighted average unit cost of the items sold. (314)

average rate of return A method of evaluating capital investment proposals that focuses on the expected profitability of the investment. (1165)

B

Bad Debt Expense The operating expense incurred because of the failure to collect receivables. (395)

balance of the account The amount of the difference between the debits and the credits that have been entered into an account. (47)

balance sheet A list of the assets, liabilities, and owner's equity as of a specific date, usually at the close of the last day of a month or a year. (15)

balanced scorecard A performance evaluation approach that incorporates multiple performance dimensions by combining financial and nonfinancial measures. (1090)

bank reconciliation The analysis that details the items responsible for the difference between the cash balance reported in the bank statement and the balance of the cash account in the ledger. (366)

bank statement A summary of all transactions mailed to the depositor or made available online by the bank each month. (363)

bond A form of an interest-bearing note used by corporations to borrow on a long-term basis. (613)

bond indenture The contract between a corporation issuing bonds and the bondholders. (616)

book value The cost of a fixed asset minus accumulated depreciation on the asset. (448)

book value of the asset (or net book value) The difference between the cost of a fixed asset and its accumulated depreciation. (110)

boot The amount a buyer owes a seller when a fixed asset is traded in on a similar asset. (460)

break-even point The level of business operations at which revenues and expired costs are equal. (947)

budget An accounting device used to plan and control resources of operational departments and divisions. (987)

budget performance report A report comparing actual results with budget figures. (1036)

budgetary slack Excess resources set within a budget to provide for uncertain events. (989)

budgeted variable factory overhead The standard variable overhead for the actual units produced. (1045)

business An organization in which basic resources (inputs), such as materials and labor, are assembled and processed to provide goods or services (outputs) to customers. (2)

business combination A business making an investment in another business by acquiring a controlling share, often greater than 50%, of the outstanding voting stock of another corporation by paying cash or exchanging stock. (660)

business entity concept A concept of accounting that limits the economic data in the accounting system to data related directly to the activities of the business. (7)

business transaction An economic event or condition that directly changes an entity's financial condition or directly affects its results of operations. (10)

C

capital account An account used for a proprietorship that represents the owner's equity. (48)

capital expenditures The costs of acquiring fixed assets, adding to a fixed asset, improving a fixed asset, or extending a fixed asset's useful life. (441)

capital expenditures budget The budget summarizing future plans for acquiring plant facilities and equipment. (1006)

capital investment analysis The process by which management plans, evaluates, and controls long-term capital investments involving property, plant, and equipment. (1164)

capital leases Leases that include one or more provisions that result in treating the leased assets as purchased assets in the accounts. (443)

capital rationing The process by which management plans, evaluates, and controls long-term capital investments involving fixed assets. (1180)

carrying amount The balance of the bonds payable account (face amount of the bonds) less any unamortized discount or plus any unamortized premium. (620)

cash Coins, currency (paper money), checks, money orders, and money on deposit that is available for unrestricted withdrawal from banks and other financial institutions. (359)

cash basis of accounting Under this basis of accounting, revenues and expenses are reported in the income statement in the period in which cash is received or paid. (98)

cash budget A budget of estimated cash receipts and payments. (1003)

cash dividend A cash distribution of earnings by a corporation to its shareholders. (583)

cash equivalents Highly liquid investments that are usually reported with cash on the balance sheet. (372)

cash flow per share Normally computed as cash flow from operations per share. (708)

cash flows from financing activities The section of the statement of cash flows that reports cash flows from transactions affecting the equity and debt of the business. (706)

cash flows from investing activities The section of the statement of cash flows that reports cash flows from transactions affecting investments in noncurrent assets. (706)

cash flows from operating activities The section of the statement of cash flows that reports the cash transactions affecting the determination of net income. (705)

cash payback period The expected period of time that will elapse between the date of a capital expenditure and the complete recovery in cash (or equivalent) of the amount invested. (1166)

cash payments journal The special journal in which all cash payments are recorded. (217)

cash receipts journal The special journal in which all cash receipts are recorded. (211)

cash short and over account An account which has recorded errors in cash sales or errors in making change causing the amount of actual cash on hand to differ from the beginning amount of cash plus the cash sales for the day. (361)

Certified Public Accountant (CPA) Public accountants who have met a state's education, experience, and examination requirements. (7)

chart of accounts A list of the accounts in the ledger. (48)

clearing account Another name for the income summary account because it has the effect of clearing the revenue and expense accounts of their balances. (150)

closing entries The entries that transfer the balances of the revenue, expense, and drawing accounts to the owner's capital account. (150)

closing process The transfer process of converting temporary account balances to zero by transferring the revenue and expense account balances to Income Summary, transferring the income summary account balance to the owner's capital account, and transferring the owner's drawing account to the owner's capital account. (150)

closing the books The process of transferring temporary accounts balances to permanent accounts at the end of the accounting period. (150)

common stock The stock outstanding when a corporation has issued only one class of stock. (578)

common-sized statement A financial statement in which all items are expressed only in relative terms. (762)

compensating balance A requirement by some banks requiring depositors to maintain minimum cash balances in their bank accounts. (372)

comprehensive income All changes in stockholders' equity during a period, except those resulting from dividends and stockholders' investments. (681)

consigned inventory Merchandise that is shipped by manufacturers to retailers who act as the manufacturer's selling agent. (328)

consignee The name for the retailer in a consigned inventory arrangement. (328)

consignor The name for the manufacturer in a consigned inventory arrangement. (328)

consolidated financial statements Financial statements resulting from combining parent and subsidiary statements. (660)

contingent liabilities Liabilities that may arise from past transactions if certain events occur in the future. (504)

continuous budgeting A method of budgeting that provides for maintaining a 12-month projection into the future. (990)

continuous process improvement A management approach that is part of the overall total quality management philosophy. The approach requires all employees to constantly improve processes of which they are a part or for which they have managerial responsibility. (817)

contra account (or contra asset account) An account offset against another account. (109)

contract rate The periodic interest to be paid on the bonds that is identified in the bond indenture; expressed as a percentage of the face amount of the bond. (616)

contribution margin Sales less variable costs and variable selling and administrative expenses. (944)

contribution margin ratio The percentage of each sales dollar that is available to cover the fixed costs and provide an operating income. (944)

control environment The overall attitude of management and employees about the importance of controls. (355)

controllable expenses Costs that can be influenced by the decisions of a manager. (1080)

controllable revenues Revenues earned by the profit center. (1080)

controllable variance The difference between the actual amount of variable factory overhead cost incurred and the amount of variable factory overhead budgeted for the standard product. (1044)

controller The chief management accountant of a division or other segment of a business. (816)

controlling A phase in the management process that consists of monitoring the operating results of implemented plans and comparing the actual results with the expected results. (817)

controlling account The account in the general ledger that summarizes the balances of the accounts in a subsidiary ledger. (206)

conversion costs The combination of direct labor and factory overhead costs. (822)

copyright An exclusive right to publish and sell a literary, artistic, or musical composition. (456)

corporation A business organized under state or federal statutes as a separate legal entity. (8)

correcting journal entry An entry that is prepared when an error has already been journalized and posted. (68)

cost A payment of cash (or a commitment to pay cash in the future) for the purpose of generating revenues. (819)

cost accounting system A branch of managerial accounting concerned with accumulating manufacturing costs for financial reporting and decision-making purposes. (847)

cost allocation The process of assigning indirect cost to a cost object, such as a job. (854)

cost behavior The manner in which a cost changes in relation to its activity base (driver). (937)

cost center A decentralized unit in which the department or division manager has responsibility for the control of costs incurred and the authority to make decisions that affect these costs. (1078)

cost concept A concept of accounting that determines the amount initially entered into the accounting records for purchases. (8)

cost method A method of accounting for equity investments representing less than 20% of the outstanding shares of the investee. The purchase is at original cost, and any gains or losses upon sale are recognized by the difference between the sale proceeds and the original cost. (656)

cost object The object or segment of operations to which costs are related for management's use, such as a product or department. (819)

cost of finished goods available The beginning finished goods inventory added to the cost of goods manufactured during the period. (826)

cost of goods manufactured The total cost of making and finishing a product. (826)

cost of goods sold The cost of finished goods available for sale minus the ending finished goods inventory. (826)

cost of goods sold budget A budget of the estimated direct materials, direct labor, and factory overhead consumed by sold products. (1000)

cost of merchandise purchased The cost of net purchases plus transportation costs. (256)

cost of merchandise sold The cost that is reported as an expense when merchandise is sold. (254, 825)

cost of production report A report prepared periodically by a processing department, summarizing (1) the units for which the department is accountable and the disposition of those units and (2) the costs incurred by the department and the allocation of those costs between completed and incomplete production. (893)

cost per equivalent unit The rate used to allocate costs between completed and partially completed production. (898)

cost price approach An approach to transfer pricing that uses cost as the basis for setting the transfer price. (1096)

cost variance The difference between actual cost and the flexible budget at actual volumes. (1036)

cost-volume-profit analysis The systematic examination of the relationships among selling prices, volume of sales and production, costs, expenses, and profits. (943)

cost-volume-profit chart A chart used to assist management in understanding the relationships among costs, expenses, sales, and operating profit or loss. (952)

credit memorandum (credit memo) A form used by a seller to inform the buyer of the amount the seller proposes to credit to the account receivable due from the buyer. (264)

credit period The amount of time the buyer is allowed in which to pay the seller. (263)

credit terms Terms for payment on account by the buyer to the seller. (263)

credits Amounts entered on the right side of an account. (47)

cumulative preferred stock Stock that has a right to receive regular dividends that were not declared (paid) in prior years. (578)

currency exchange rate The rate at which currency in another country can be exchanged for local currency. (1179)

current assets Cash and other assets that are expected to be converted to cash or sold or used up, usually within one year or less, through the normal operations of the business. (149)

current liabilities Liabilities that will be due within a short time (usually one year or less) and that are to be paid out of current assets. (149)

current position analysis A company's ability to pay its current liabilities. (765)

current ratio A financial ratio that is computed by dividing current assets by current liabilities. (766)

currently attainable standards Standards that represent levels of operation that can be attained with reasonable effort. (1034)

D

debit memorandum (debit memo) A form used by a buyer to inform the seller of the amount the buyer proposes to debit to the account payable due the seller. (267)

debits Amounts entered on the left side of an account. (47)

debt securities Notes and bond investments that provide interest revenue over a fixed maturity. (653)

decision making A component inherent in the other management processes of planning, directing, controlling, and improving. (817)

deficiency The debit balance in the owner's equity account of a partner. (549)

deficit A debit balance in the retained earnings account. (577)

defined benefit plan A pension plan that promises employees a fixed annual pension benefit at retirement, based on years of service and compensation levels. (502)

defined contribution plan A pension plan that requires a fixed amount of money to be invested for the employee's behalf during the employee's working years. (502)

depletion The process of transferring the cost of natural resources to an expense account. (454)

depreciate To lose usefulness as all fixed assets except land do. (109)

depreciation The systematic periodic transfer of the cost of a fixed asset to an expense account during its expected useful life. (109, 443)

depreciation expense The portion of the cost of a fixed asset that is recorded as an expense each year of its useful life. (109)

differential analysis The area of accounting concerned with the effect of alternative courses of action on revenues and costs. (1120)

differential cost The amount of increase or decrease in cost expected from a particular course of action compared with an alternative. (1120)

differential income (or loss) The difference between the differential revenue and the differential costs. (1120)

differential revenue The amount of increase or decrease in revenue expected from a particular course of action as compared with an alternative. (1120)

direct costs Costs that can be traced directly to a cost object. (819)

direct labor cost The wages of factory workers who are directly involved in converting materials into a finished product. (821)

direct labor cost budget Budget that estimates direct labor hours and related costs needed to support budgeted production. (998)

direct labor rate variance The cost associated with the difference between the standard rate and the actual rate paid for direct labor used in producing a commodity. (1041)

direct labor time variance The cost associated with the difference between the standard hours and the actual hours of direct labor spent producing a commodity. (1042)

direct materials cost The cost of materials that are an integral part of the finished product. (820)

direct materials price variance The cost associated with the difference between the standard price and the actual price of direct materials used in producing a commodity. (1039)

direct materials purchases budget A budget that uses the production budget as a starting point to budget materials purchases. (997)

direct materials quantity variance The cost associated with the difference between the standard quantity and the actual quantity of direct materials used in producing a commodity. (1039)

direct method A method of reporting the cash flows from operating activities as the difference between the operating cash receipts and the operating cash payments. (706)

direct write-off method The method of accounting for uncollectible accounts that recognizes the expense only when accounts are judged to be worthless. (395)

directing The process by which managers, given their assigned level of responsibilities, run day-to-day operations. (817)

discount The interest deducted from the maturity value of a note or the excess of the face amount of bonds over their issue price. (581, 616)

dishonored note receivable A note that the maker fails to pay on the due date. (409)

dividend yield A ratio, computed by dividing the annual dividends paid per share of common stock by the market price per share at a specific date, that indicates the rate of return to stockholders in terms of cash dividend distributions. (779)

dividends Distribution of a corporation's earning to stockholders. (577)

dividends per share Measures the extent to which earnings are being distributed to common shareholders. (779)

double-declining-balance method A method of depreciation that provides periodic depreciation expense based on the declining book value of a fixed asset over its estimated life. (447)

double-entry accounting system A system of accounting for recording transactions, based on recording increases and decreases in accounts so that debits equal credits. (49)

drawing The account used to record amounts withdrawn by an owner of a proprietorship. (48)

DuPont formula An expanded expression of return on investment determined by multiplying the profit margin by the investment turnover. (1086)

E

earnings per common share (EPS) Net income per share of common stock outstanding during a period. (593, 619)

earnings per share (EPS) on common stock The profitability ratio of net income available to common shareholders to the number of common shares outstanding. (614, 777)

e-commerce The use of the Internet for performing business transactions. (224)

effective interest rate method The method of amortizing discounts and premiums that provides for a constant rate of interest on the carrying amount of the bonds at the beginning of each period; often called simply the "interest method." (619)

effective rate of interest The market rate of interest at the time bonds are issued. (616)

electronic funds transfer (EFT) A system in which computers rather than paper (money, checks, etc.) are used to effect cash transactions. (362)

elements of internal control The control environment, risk assessment, control activities, information and communication, and monitoring. (354)

employee fraud The intentional act of deceiving an employer for personal gain. (354)

employee's earnings record A detailed record of each employee's earnings. (497)

equity method A method of accounting for an investment in common stock by which the investment account is adjusted for the investor's share of periodic net income and cash dividends of the investee. (658)

equity securities The common and preferred stock of a firm. (653)

equivalent units of production The number of production units that could have been completed within a given accounting period, given the resources consumed. (895)

ethics Moral principles that guide the conduct of individuals. (4)

expenses Assets used up or services consumed in the process of generating revenues. (12, 48)

extraordinary item Event or transaction that (1) is significantly different (unusual) from the typical or the normal operating activities of a business and (2) occurs infrequently. (787)

F

factory burden Another term for manufacturing overhead or factory overhead. (821)

factory overhead cost All of the costs of producing a product except for direct materials and direct labor. (821)

factory overhead cost budget Budget that estimates the cost for each item of factory overhead needed to support budgeted production. (999)

factory overhead cost variance report Reports budgeted and actual costs for variable and fixed factory overhead along with the related controllable and volume variances. (1048)

fair value The price that would be received for selling an asset or paying off a liability, often the market price for an equity or debt security. (661)

favorable cost variance A variance that occurs when the actual cost is less than standard cost. (1036)

feedback Measures provided to operational employees or managers on the performance of subunits of the organization. These measures are used by employees to adjust a process

or a behavior to achieve goals. See management by exception. (817)

fees earned Revenue from providing services. (11)

FICA tax Federal Insurance Contributions Act tax used to finance federal programs for old-age and disability benefits (social security) and health insurance for the aged (Medicare). (489)

financial accounting The branch of accounting that is concerned with recording transactions using generally accepted accounting principles (GAAP) for a business or other economic unit and with a periodic preparation of various statements from such records. (4, 814)

Financial Accounting Standards Board (FASB) The authoritative body that has the primary responsibility for developing accounting principles. (7)

financial statements Financial reports that summarize the effects of events on a business. (14)

finished goods inventory The direct materials costs, direct labor costs, and factory overhead costs of finished products that have not been sold. (824)

finished goods ledger The subsidiary ledger that contains the individual accounts for each kind of commodity or product produced. (859)

first-in, first-out (FIFO) inventory cost flow method The method of inventory costing based on the assumption that the costs of merchandise sold should be charged against revenue in the order in which the costs were incurred. (314, 893)

fiscal year The annual accounting period adopted by a business. (165)

fixed asset turnover ratio The number of dollars of sales that are generated from each dollar of average fixed assets during the year, computed by dividing the net sales by the average net fixed assets. (459)

fixed assets (or plant assets) Long-term or relatively permanent tangible assets such as equipment, machinery, and buildings that are used in the normal business operations and that depreciate over time. (109, 149, 438)

fixed costs Costs that tend to remain the same in amount, regardless of variations in the level of activity. (939)

flexible budget A budget that adjusts for varying rates of activity. (991)

FOB (free on board) destination Freight terms in which the seller pays the transportation costs from the shipping point to the final destination. (269)

FOB (free on board) shipping point Freight terms in which the buyer pays the transportation costs from the shipping point to the final destination. (269)

free cash flow The amount of operating cash flow remaining after replacing current productive capacity and maintaining current dividends. (725)

freight in Costs of transportation. (256)

fringe benefits Benefits provided to employees in addition to wages and salaries. (501)

future value The estimated worth in the future of an amount of cash on hand today invested at a fixed rate of interest. (633)

G

general journal The two-column form used for entries that do not "fit" in any of the special journals. (208)

general ledger The primary ledger, when used in conjunction with subsidiary ledgers, that contains all of the balance sheet and income statement accounts. (206)

general-purpose financial statements A type of financial accounting report that is distributed to external users. The term "general purpose" refers to the wide range of decision-making needs that the reports are designed to serve. (4)

generally accepted accounting principles (GAAP) Generally accepted guidelines for the preparation of financial statements. (7)

goal conflict A condition that occurs when individual objectives conflict with organizational objectives. (989)

goodwill An intangible asset that is created from such favorable factors as location, product quality, reputation, and managerial skill. (456)

gross pay The total earnings of an employee for a payroll period. (487)

gross profit Sales minus the cost of merchandise sold. (254)

gross profit method A method of estimating inventory cost that is based on the relationship of gross profit to sales. (332)

H

held-to-maturity securities Investments in bonds or other debt securities that management intends to hold to their maturity. (664)

high-low method A technique that uses the highest and lowest total costs as a basis for estimating the variable cost per unit and the fixed cost component of a mixed cost. (941)

horizontal analysis Financial analysis that compares an item in a current statement with the same item in prior statements. (69, 759)

I

ideal standards Standards that can be achieved only under perfect operating conditions, such as no idle time, no machine breakdowns, and no materials spoilage; also called theoretical standards. (1034)

in arrears Cumulative preferred stock dividends that have not been paid in prior years are said to be in arrears. (579)

income from operations (operating income) Revenues less operating expenses and service department charges for a profit or an investment center. (257)

income statement A summary of the revenue and expenses for a specific period of time, such as a month or a year. (15)

Income Summary An account to which the revenue and expense account balances are transferred at the end of a period. (150)

indirect costs Costs that cannot be traced directly to a cost object. (819)

indirect method A method of reporting the cash flows from operating activities as the net income from operations adjusted for all deferrals of past cash receipts and payments and all accruals of expected future cash receipts and payments. (707)

inflation A period when prices in general are rising and the purchasing power of money is declining. (1179)

installment note A debt that requires the borrower to make equal periodic payments to the lender for the term of the note. (623)

intangible assets Long-term assets that are useful in the operations of a business, are not held for sale, and are without physical qualities. (455)

interest revenue Money received for interest. (11)

internal controls The policies and procedures used to safeguard assets, ensure accurate business information, and ensure compliance with laws and regulations. (206, 352)

internal rate of return (IRR) method A method of analysis of proposed capital investments that uses present value concepts to compute the rate of return from the net cash flows expected from the investment. (1174)

International Accounting Standards Board (IASB) An organization that issues International Financial Reporting Standards for many countries outside the United States. (7)

inventory analysis A company's ability to manage its inventory effectively. (769)

inventory shrinkage (inventory shortage) The amount by which the merchandise for sale, as indicated by the balance of the merchandise inventory account, is larger than the total amount of merchandise counted during the physical inventory. (274)

inventory turnover The relationship between the volume of goods sold and inventory, computed by dividing the cost of goods sold by the average inventory. (330, 770)

investee The company whose stock is purchased by the investor. (656)

investment center A decentralized unit in which the manager has the responsibility and authority to make decisions that affect not only costs and revenues but also the fixed assets available to the center. (1085)

investment turnover A component of the rate of return on investment, computed as the ratio of sales to invested assets. (1086)

investments The balance sheet caption used to report long-term investments in stocks not intended as a source of cash in the normal operations of the business. (653)

investor The company investing in another company's stock. (656)

invoice The bill that the seller sends to the buyer. (209, 262)

J

job cost sheet An account in the work in process subsidiary ledger in which the costs charged to a particular job order are recorded. (860)

job order cost system A type of cost accounting system that provides for a separate record of the cost of each particular quantity of product that passes through the factory. (847)

journal The initial record in which the effects of a transaction are recorded. (50)

journal entry The form of recording a transaction in a journal. (51)

journalizing The process of recording a transaction in the journal. (51)

just-in-time (JIT) processing A processing approach that focuses on eliminating time, cost, and poor quality within manufacturing and nonmanufacturing processes. (909)

L

last-in, first-out (LIFO) inventory cost flow method A method of inventory costing based on the assumption that the most recent merchandise inventory costs should be charged against revenue. (314)

ledger A group of accounts for a business. (48)

liabilities The rights of creditors that represent debts of the business. (9, 48)

limited liability company (LLC) A business form consisting of one or more persons or entities filing an operating agreement with a state to conduct business with limited liability to the owners, yet treated as a partnership for tax purposes. (8, 534)

line department A unit that is directly involved in the basic objectives of an organization. (815)

liquidation The winding-up process when a partnership goes out of business. (545)

long-term liabilities Liabilities that usually will not be due for more than one year. (149)

lower-of-cost-or-market (LCM) method A method of valuing inventory that reports the inventory at the lower of its cost or current market value (replacement cost). (325)

M

management (or managerial) accounting The branch of accounting that uses both historical and estimated data in providing information that management uses in conducting daily operations, in planning future operations, and in developing overall business strategies. (4, 814)

management by exception The philosophy of managing which involves monitoring the operating results of implemented plans and comparing the expected results with the actual results. This feedback allows management to isolate significant variations for further investigation and possible remedial action. (817)

management process The five basic management functions of (1) planning, (2) directing, (3) controlling, (4) improving, and (5) decision making. (816)

Management's Discussion and Analysis (MD&A) An annual report disclosure that provides management's analysis of the results of operations and financial condition. (780)

manufacturing business A type of business that changes basic inputs into products that are sold to individual customers. (3)

manufacturing cells A grouping of processes where employees are cross-trained to perform more than one function. (909)

manufacturing overhead Costs, other than direct materials and direct labor costs, that are incurred in the manufacturing process. (821)

margin of safety Indicates the possible decrease in sales that may occur before an operating loss results. (960)

market price approach An approach to transfer pricing that uses the price at which the product or service transferred could be sold to outside buyers as the transfer price. (1093)

market rate of interest The rate determined from sales and purchases of similar bonds. (616)

markup An amount that is added to a "cost" amount to determine product price. (1130)

master budget The comprehensive budget plan linking all the individual budgets related to sales, cost of goods sold, operating expenses, projects, capital expenditures, and cash. (993)

matching concept (or matching principle) A concept of accounting in which expenses are matched with the revenue generated during a period by those expenses. (15, 98)

materials inventory The cost of materials that have not yet entered into the manufacturing process. (824)

materials ledger The subsidiary ledger containing the individual accounts for each type of material. (849)

materials requisition The form or electronic transmission used by a manufacturing department to authorize materials issuances from the storeroom. (850)

maturity value The amount that is due at the maturity or due date of a note. (408)

merchandise available for sale The cost of merchandise available for sale to customers calculated by adding the beginning merchandise inventory to net purchases. (256, 825)

merchandise inventory Merchandise on hand (not sold) at the end of an accounting period. (254)

merchandising business A type of business that purchases products from other businesses and sells them to customers. (3)

mixed cost A cost with both variable and fixed characteristics, sometimes called a semivariable or semifixed cost. (939)

mortgage notes An installment note that may be secured by a pledge of the borrower's assets. (623)

multiple-step income statement A form of income statement that contains several sections, subsections, and subtotals. (254)

N

natural business year A fiscal year that ends when business activities have reached the lowest point in an annual operating cycle. (166)

negotiated price approach An approach to transfer pricing that allows managers of decentralized units to agree (negotiate) among themselves as to the transfer price. (1094)

net income or net profit The amount by which revenues exceed expenses. (15)

net loss The amount by which expenses exceed revenues. (15)

net pay Gross pay less payroll deductions; the amount the employer is obligated to pay the employee. (487)

net present value method A method of analysis of proposed capital investments that focuses on the present value of the cash flows expected from the investments. (1171)

net purchases Determined when purchases returns and allowances and the purchases discounts are deducted from the total purchases. (256)

net realizable value The estimated selling price of an item of inventory less any direct costs of disposal, such as sales commissions. (326, 397)

net sales Revenue received for merchandise sold to customers less any sales returns and allowances and sales discounts. (255)

nonfinancial performance measure A performance measure expressed in units rather than dollars. (1053)

normal balance of an account The normal balance of an account can be either a debit or a credit depending on whether increases in the account are recorded as debits or credits. (50)

notes receivable A customer's written promise to pay an amount and possibly interest at an agreed-upon rate. (149, 394)

number of days' sales in inventory The relationship between the volume of sales and inventory, computed by dividing the inventory at the end of the year by the average daily cost of goods sold. (330, 770)

number of days' sales in receivables The relationship between sales and accounts receivable, computed by dividing the net accounts receivable at the end of the year by the average daily sales. (411, 769)

number of times interest charges are earned A ratio that measures creditor margin of safety for interest payments, calculated as income before interest and taxes divided by interest expense. (627, 772)

O

objectives (goals) Developed in the planning stage, these reflect the direction and desired outcomes of certain courses of action. (817)

objectivity concept A concept of accounting that requires accounting records and the data reported in financial statements to be based on objective evidence. (8)

operating leases Leases that do not meet the criteria for capital leases and thus are accounted for as operating expenses. (443)

operating leverage A measure of the relative mix of a business's variable costs and fixed costs, computed as contribution margin divided by operating income. (958)

operational planning The development of short-term plans to achieve goals identified in a business's strategic plan. Sometimes called tactical planning. (817)

opportunity cost The amount of income forgone from an alternative to a proposed use of cash or its equivalent. (1126)

other comprehensive income Specified items that are reported separately from net income, including foreign currency items, pension liability adjustments, and unrealized gains and losses on investments. (681)

other expense Expenses that cannot be traced directly to operations. (258)

other income Revenue from sources other than the primary operating activity of a business. (258)

outstanding stock The stock in the hands of stockholders. (578)

overapplied factory overhead The amount of factory overhead applied in excess of the actual factory overhead costs incurred for production during a period. (856)

owner's equity The owner's right to the assets of the business. (9, 48)

P

paid-in capital Capital contributed to a corporation by the stockholders and others. (577)

par The monetary amount printed on a stock certificate. (578)

parent company The corporation owning all or a majority of the voting stock of the other corporation. (660)

partnership An unincorporated business form consisting of two or more persons conducting business as co-owners for profit. (8, 533)

partnership agreement The formal written contract creating a partnership. (533)

patents Exclusive rights to produce and sell goods with one or more unique features. (455)

payroll The total amount paid to employees for a certain period. (487)

payroll register A multicolumn report used to assemble and summarize payroll data at the end of each payroll period. (494)

pension A cash payment to retired employees. (502)

period costs Those costs that are used up in generating revenue during the current period and that are not involved in manufacturing a product, such as selling, general, and administratvie expenses. (822, 860)

periodic inventory system The inventory system in which the inventory records do not show the amount available for sale or sold during the period. (256)

perpetual inventory system The inventory system in which each purchase and sale of merchandise is recorded in an inventory account. (257)

petty cash fund A special cash fund to pay relatively small amounts. (370)

physical inventory A detailed listing of merchandise on hand. (313)

planning A phase of the management process whereby objectives are outlined and courses of action determined. (817)

posting The process of transferring the debits and credits from the journal entries to the accounts. (55)

predetermined factory overhead rate The rate used to apply factory overhead costs to the goods manufactured. The rate is determined by dividing the budgeted overhead cost by the estimated activity usage at the beginning of the fiscal period. (854)

preferred stock A class of stock with preferential rights over common stock. (578)

premium The excess of the issue price of a stock over its par value or the excess of the issue price of bonds over their face amount. (581, 616)

prepaid expenses Items such as supplies that will be used in the business in the future. (11, 100)

present value The estimated worth today of an amount of cash to be received (or paid) in the future. (633)

present value concept Cash to be received (or paid) in the future is not the equivalent of the same amount of money received at an earlier date. (1168)

present value index An index computed by dividing the total present value of the net cash flow to be received from a proposed capital investment by the amount to be invested. (1173)

present value of an annuity The sum of the present values of a series of equal cash flows to be received at fixed intervals. (635, 1169)

price-earnings (P/E) ratio The ratio of the market price per share of common stock, at a specific date, to the annual earnings per share. (778)

prime costs The combination of direct materials and direct labor costs. (822)

prior period adjustments Corrections of material errors related to a prior period or periods, excluded from the determination of net income. (590)

private accounting The field of accounting whereby accountants are employed by a business firm or a not-for-profit organization. (4)

process A sequence of activities linked together for performing a particular task. (1054)

process cost system A type of cost system that accumulates costs for each of the various departments within a manufacturing facility. (848, 887)

process manufacturers Manufacturers that use large machines to process a continuous flow of raw materials through various stages of completion into a finished state. (887)

product cost concept A concept used in applying the cost-plus approach to product pricing in which only the costs of manufacturing the product, termed the product cost, are included in the cost amount to which the markup is added. (1133)

product costs The three components of manufacturing cost: direct materials, direct labor, and factory overhead costs. (822)

production bottleneck A condition that occurs when product demand exceeds production capacity. (1138)

production budget A budget of estimated unit production. (995)

profit The difference between the amounts received from customers for goods or services provided and the amounts paid for the inputs used to provide the goods or services. (2)

profit center A decentralized unit in which the manager has the responsibility and the authority to make decisions that affect both costs and revenues (and thus profits). (1080)

profit margin A component of the rate of return on investment, computed as the ratio of income from operations to sales. (1086)

profit-volume chart A chart used to assist management in understanding the relationship between profit and volume. (954)

profitability The ability of a firm to earn income. (765)

proprietorship A business owned by one individual. (8)

public accounting The field of accounting where accountants and their staff provide services on a fee basis. (7)

purchase order The purchase order authorizes the purchase of the inventory from an approved vendor. (313)

purchase return or allowance From the buyer's perspective, returned merchandise or an adjustment for defective merchandise. (256)

purchases discounts Discounts taken by the buyer for early payment of an invoice. (256)

purchases journal The journal in which all items purchased on account are recorded. (214)

Q

quick assets Cash and other current assets that can be quickly converted to cash, such as marketable securities and receivables. (507, 767)

quick ratio A financial ratio that measures the ability to pay current liabilities with quick assets (cash, marketable securities, accounts receivable). (507, 767)

R

rate earned on common stockholders' equity A measure of profitability computed by dividing net income, reduced by preferred dividend requirements, by common stockholders' equity. (776)

rate earned on stockholders' equity A measure of profitability computed by dividing net income by total stockholders' equity. (775)

rate earned on total assets A measure of the profitability of assets, without regard to the equity of creditors and stockholders in the assets. (774)

rate of return on investment (ROI) A measure of managerial efficiency in the use of investments in assets, computed as income from operations divided by invested assets. (1086)

ratio of fixed assets to long-term liabilities A leverage ratio that measures the margin of safety of long-term creditors, calculated as the net fixed assets divided by the long-term liabilities. (771)

ratio of liabilities to stockholders' equity A comprehensive leverage ratio that measures the relationship of the claims of creditors to stockholders' equity. (771)

ratio of net sales to assets Ratio that measures how effectively a company uses its assets, computed as net sales divided by average total assets. (773)

real (permanent) accounts Term for balance sheet accounts because they are relatively permanent and carried forward from year to year. (150)

realization The sale of assets when a partnership is being liquidated. (545)

receivables All money claims against other entities, including people, business firms, and other organizations. (394)

receiving report The form or electronic transmission used by the receiving personnel to indicate that materials have been received and inspected. (313, 849)

relevant range The range of activity over which changes in cost are of interest to management. (937)

rent revenue Money received for rent. (11)

report form The form of balance sheet with the Liabilities and Owner's Equity sections presented below the Assets section. (259)

residual income The excess of divisional income from operations over a "minimum" acceptable income from operations. (1089)

residual value The estimated value of a fixed asset at the end of its useful life. (444)

responsibility accounting The process of measuring and reporting operating data by areas of responsibility. (1077)

responsibility center An organizational unit for which a manager is assigned responsibility over costs, revenues, or assets. (988)

restrictions Amounts of retained earnings that have been limited for use as dividends. (589)

retail inventory method A method of estimating inventory cost that is based on the relationship of gross profit to sales. (331)

retained earnings Net income retained in a corporation. (577)

retained earnings statement A summary of the changes in the retained earnings in a corporation for a specific period of time, such as a month or a year. (589)

revenue expenditures Costs that benefit only the current period or costs incurred for normal maintenance and repairs of fixed assets. (441)

revenue journal The journal in which all sales and services on account are recorded. (208)

revenue recognition concept The accounting concept that supports reporting revenues when the services are provided to customers. (98)

revenues Increases in owner's equity as a result of selling services or products to customers. (11, 48)

rules of debit and credit In the double-entry accounting system, specific rules for recording debits and credits based on the type of account. (49)

S

sales The total amount charged customers for merchandise sold, including cash sales and sales on account. (11, 254)

sales budget One of the major elements of the income statement budget that indicates the quantity of estimated sales and the expected unit selling price. (995)

sales discounts From the seller's perspective, discounts that a seller may offer the buyer for early payment. (255)

sales mix The relative distribution of sales among the various products available for sale. (957)

sales returns and allowances From the seller's perspective, returned merchandise or an adjustment for defective merchandise. (255)

Sarbanes-Oxley Act of 2002 An act passed by Congress to restore public confidence and trust in the financial statements of companies. (352)

Securities and Exchange Commission (SEC) An agency of the U.S. government that has authority over the accounting and financial disclosures for companies whose shares of ownership (stock) are traded and sold to the public. (7)

selling expenses Expenses that are incurred directly in the selling of merchandise. (257)

service business A business providing services rather than products to customers. (3)

service department charges The costs of services provided by an internal service department and transferred to a responsibility center. (1080)

single-step income statement A form of income statement in which the total of all expenses is deducted from the total of all revenues. (258)

slide An error in which the entire number is moved one or more spaces to the right or the left, such as writing $542.00 as $54.20 or $5,420.00. (67)

solvency The ability of a firm to pay its debts as they come due. (765)

special journals Journals designed to be used for recording a single type of transaction. (207)

special-purpose fund A cash fund used for a special business need. (371)

specific identification inventory cost flow method Inventory method in which the unit sold is identified with a specific purchase. (314)

staff department A unit that provides services, assistance, and advice to the departments with line or other staff responsibilities. (816)

standard cost A detailed estimate of what a product should cost. (1033)

standard cost systems Accounting systems that use standards for each element of manufacturing cost entering into the finished product. (1033)

standards Peformance goals, often relating to how much a product should cost. (1033)

statement of cash flows A summary of the cash receipts and cash payments for a specific period of time, such as a month or a year. (15, 705)

statement of cost of goods manufactured The income statement of manufacturing companies. (826)

statement of members' equity A summary of the changes in each member's equity in a limited liability corporation that have occurred during a specific period of time. (552)

statement of owner's equity A summary of the changes in owner's equity that have occurred during a specific period of time, such as a month or a year. (15)

statement of partnership equity A summary of the changes in each partner's capital in a partnership that have occurred during a specific period of time. (552)

statement of partnership liquidation A summary of the liquidation process whereby cash is distributed to the partners based on the balances in their capital accounts. (546)

statement of stockholders' equity A summary of the changes in the stockholders' equity in a corporation that have occurred during a specific period of time. (591)

static budget A budget that does not adjust to changes in activity levels. (991)

stock Shares of ownership of a corporation. (574)

stock dividend A distribution of shares of stock to its stockholders. (585)

stock split A reduction in the par or stated value of a common stock and the issuance of a proportionate number of additional shares. (592)

stockholders The owners of a corporation. (574)

stockholders' equity The owners' equity in a corporation. (577)

straight-line method A method of depreciation that provides for equal periodic depreciation expense over the estimated life of a fixed asset. (445)

strategic planning The development of a long-range course of action to achieve business goals. (817)

strategies The means by which business goals and objectives will be achieved. (817)

subsidiary company The corporation that is controlled by a parent company. (660)

subsidiary inventory ledger The subsidiary ledger containing individual accounts for items of inventory. (313)

subsidiary ledger A ledger containing individual accounts with a common characteristic. (206)

sunk cost A cost that is not affected by subsequent decisions. (1120)

T

T account The simplest form of an account. (46)

target costing The target cost is determined by subtracting a desired profit from a market method determined price. The resulting target cost is used to motivate cost improvements in design and manufacture. (1137)

temporary (nominal) accounts Accounts that report amounts for only one period. (150)

theory of constraints (TOC) A manufacturing strategy that attempts to remove the influence of bottlenecks (constraints) on a process. (1138)

time tickets The form on which the amount of time spent by each employee and the labor cost incurred for each individual job, or for factory overhead, are recorded. (851)

time value of money concept The concept that an amount of money invested today will earn income. (1165)

total cost concept A concept used in applying the cost-plus approach to product pricing in which all the costs of manufacturing the product plus the selling and administrative expenses are included in the cost amount to which the markup is added. (1130)

total manufacturing cost variance The difference between total standard costs and total actual costs for units produced. (1037)

trade discounts Discounts from the list prices in published catalogs or special discounts offered to certain classes of buyers. (272)

trade-in allowance The amount a seller allows a buyer for a fixed asset that is traded in for a similar asset. (460)

trademark A name, term, or symbol used to identify a business and its products. (456)

trading securities Securities that management intends to actively trade for profit. (661)

transfer price The price charged one decentralized unit by another for the goods or services provided. (1092)

transposition An error in which the order of the digits is changed, such as writing $542 as $452 or $524. (67)

treasury stock Stock that a corporation has once issued and then reacquires. (586)

trial balance A summary listing of the titles and balances of accounts in the ledger. (63)

U

unadjusted trial balance A summary listing of the titles and balances of accounts in the ledger prior to the posting of adjusting entries. (65)

underapplied factory overhead The amount of actual factory overhead in excess of the factory overhead applied to production during a period. (856)

unearned revenue The liability created by receiving revenue in advance. (57, 100)

unfavorable cost variance A variance that occurs when the acutal cost exceeds the standard cost. (1036)

unit contribution margin The dollars available from each unit of sales to cover fixed costs and provide operating profits. (945)

unit of measure concept A concept of accounting requiring that economic data be recorded in dollars. (8)

units-of-production method A method of depreciation that provides for depreciation expense based on the expected productive capacity of a fixed asset. (446)

unrealized gain or loss Changes in the fair value of equity or debt securities for a period. (661)

V

variable cost concept A concept used in applying the cost-plus approach to product pricing in which only the variable costs are included in the cost amount to which the markup is added. (1134)

variable costing The concept that considers the cost of products manufactured to be composed only of those manufacturing costs that increase or decrease as the volume of production rises or falls (direct materials, direct labor, and variable factory overhead). (943)

variable costs Costs that vary in total dollar amount as the level of activity changes. (938)

vertical analysis An analysis that compares each item in a current statement with a total amount within the same statement. (761)

volume variance The difference between the budgeted fixed overhead at 100% of normal capacity and the standard fixed overhead for the actual production achieved during the period. (1046)

voucher A special form for recording relevant data about a liability and the details of its payment. (362)

voucher system A set of procedures for authorizing and recording liabilities and cash payments. (362)

W

whole units The number of units in production during a period, whether completed or not. (895)

work in process inventory The direct materials costs, the direct labor costs, and the applied factory overhead costs that have entered into the manufacturing process but are associated with products that have not been finished. (824)

working capital The excess of the current assets of a business over its current liabilities. (765)

Y

yield A measure of materials usage efficiency. (908)

Z

zero-based budgeting A concept of budgeting that requires all levels of management to start from zero and estimate budget data as if there had been no previous activities in their units. (990)

zero coupon bonds Bonds that provide for only the payment of the face amount at maturity. (636)

A

Absences, compensated, 501
Absorption costing income statement, *illus.*, 962
Absorption costing, *def.*, 961
Accelerated depreciation method, *def.*, 448
Account(s)
  analyzing, 726
  balance of the, 47
  balance sheet, 49
  bank, 363
  cash short and over, 361
  chart of, 48, *illus.*, 49
  clearing, 150
  contra, 109, 264
  contra asset, 109
  controlling, 206
  def., 46
  income statement, 49
  factory overhead, 1048
  nominal, 150
  normal balance of, *illus.*, 50
  offsetting, 264
  other, 728
  permanent, 150
  posting journal entries to, 55
  real, 150
  sales on, 262
  temporary, 150
  types of requiring adjustment, 100
  using to record transactions, 46
Account form, *def.*, 16, 259
Account payable
  def., 11
  See also Accounts payable
Account receivable
  def., 12, 59
  See also Accounts receivable
Accountants
  Certified Public Accountants (CPAs), 7
  management, 815
  opportunities for, 6
Accounting, 357
  accrual basis of, 98
  and business fraud in the 2000s, *illus.*, 5
  career paths and salaries, *illus.*, 6
  cash basis of, 98
  def., 3
  differences between managerial and financial, 814
  environmental, 818
  ethics, 780
  financial, 4, 814
  financial and managerial, *illus.*, 814
  for depreciation, 443
  for dividends, 583
  for notes receivable, 408
  management, 4

managerial, 4, 813, 814
nature of, 2
payroll, 486
private, 4, *illus.*, 6
public, 7, *illus.*, 6
responsibility, 1077
role of ethics in, 4
role of in business, 3
treatment of contingent liabilities, *illus.*, 506
uses of managerial, 827
Accounting cycle
  def., 153
  illustration of, 156, *illus.*, 157
Accounting equation, 9
  business transactions and, 10
  def., 9
Accounting information
  flow of, 144
  users of, *illus.*, 3
Accounting period concept, *def.*, 98
Accounting principles, generally accepted, 7, 354
Accounting rate of return, 1165
Accounting system(s)
  basic, 205
  computerized, 221, 279
  def., 205
  double-entry, 49
  for merchandisers, 277
  for payroll and payroll taxes, 493
  manual, 206
Accounting Trends & Techniques, 459, 586, 589
Accounts payable, 483
  as a percent of total current liabilities, *illus.*, 484
  control account and subsidiary ledger, 219
  subsidiary ledger, *def.*, 206
  See also Account payable
Accounts receivable
  aging of, *illus.*, 402
  control account and subsidiary ledger, 213
  def., 394
  See also Account receivable
Accounts receivable analysis, *def.*, 768
Accounts receivable, subsidiary ledger, *def.*, 206
Accounts receivable turnover, *def.*, 411, 768
Accrual basis of accounting, *def.*, 98
Accruals, 102
Accrued expenses, 107
  def., 101
Accrued revenues, 106
  def., 101
Accrued wages, *illus.*, 108
Accumulated depreciation, *def.*, 109

Accumulated other comprehensive income, 671
  def., 675
ACH (Automated Clearing House), 365
Acid-test ratio, 507, 767
Activity base(s), *def.*, 854, 937
Activity driver, 854, 937
Activity rates, *illus.*, 1142
Activity-base
  product cost calculations, *illus.*, 1142
  usage, estimated, *illus.*, 1141
Activity-based costing (ABC), 1140
  def., 854, 1137,
  illus., 1141
Adjusted trial balance
  def., 117
  enter on the spreadsheet, 172C
  illus., 117, 163
  preparing, 162
  spreadsheet with unadjusted trial balance, adjustments and, *illus.*, 172B3
Adjusting entries
  def., 99
  for inventory shrinkage, 274
  illus., 114, 162
  journalizing and posting, 162
  ledger with, *illus.*, 115–116
  recording, 102
Adjusting process
  and closing process, 274
  def., 99
  nature of, 98
  under periodic inventory system, 282
Adjustment data, assembling and analyzing, 160
Adjustment process, summary of, 111
Adjustments
  accrued revenues and expenses, *illus.*, 101
  and adjusted trial balance, spreadsheet with unadjusted trial balance, *illus.*, 172B3
  enter on the spreadsheet, 172A
  prepaid expenses and unearned revenues, *illus.*, 100
  prior period, 591
  spreadsheet with unadjusted trial balance and, *illus.*, 172B2
  summary of, *illus.*, 112–113
  types of accounts requiring, 100
Administrative expenses, 822
  def., 257
Aging of accounts receivable, *illus.*, 402
Aging the receivables, *def.*, 401
Agreement
  operating, 534
  partnership, 533

Allocation base, 854
Allocation method, 110
Allowance account, write-offs to, 397
Allowance for doubtful accounts,
    def., 397
Allowance method
    and direct write-off methods,
        comparing, 405, *illus.*, 406
    def., 395
    for uncollectible accounts, 397
Allowance, trade-in, 460
Alternative financing plans, effect of,
    $440,000 earnings, *illus.*, 615
    $800,000 earnings, *illus.*, 614
Amortization
    def., 455
    effective interest rate method of,
        632
Amortization of discount
    by interest method, 632
    on bonds payable, *illus.*, 633
Amortization of installment notes,
    illus., 624
Amortization of premium
    by interest method, 633
    on bonds payable, *illus.*, 634
    or discount, 673
Amount, present value of, 1168
Analysis
    accounts receivable, 768
    assumptions of cost-volume-
        profit, 955
    cost-volume-profit, 943
    current position, 765
    differential, 1119, *illus.*, 1120
    horizontal, 759
    incremental, 1120
    inventory, 769
    of receivables method, 401
    profitability, 773
    solvency, 765
    traditional, *illus.*, 1122, 1124
    vertical, 761
    "what if" or sensitivity, 955
Analytical measures
    other, 765
    summary of, 780, *illus.*, 781
Analytical methods, basic, 758
Annual payments, 624
Annual reports, corporate, 780
Annual Statement Studies, 765
Annuity
    def., 630, 1169
    of $1 at compound interest,
        present value of, *illus.*, 630
    of $1, present value of, 630
    present value of, 630, 1169
    table, partial present value of,
        illus., 1170
Application of incorporation, 576
Application service provider (ASP)
    software solutions, 225
Appropriations, 590

Articles of incorporation, 576
Articles of organization, 534
Articles of partnership, 533
Asset disclosures, frequency of
    intangible, *illus.*, 457
Asset improvements, 441
Asset with change in estimate, book
    value of, *illus.*, 451
Assets, 149
    book value of, 110
    comparison of intangible, *illus.*,
        457
    contributing to a partnership, 541
    cost of acquiring fixed, *illus.*, 440
    cost of fixed, 440
    current, 149
    custody of, 357
    def., 9, 48
    discarding fixed, 452
    disposal of fixed, 452
    exchanging similar fixed, 460
    financial, 661
    financial reporting for fixed and
        intangible, 458
    fixed, 109, 149, 438, 439
    fixed, as a percent of total, *illus.*,
        439
    intangible, 455
    leasing fixed, 442
    nature of fixed, 438
    plant, 109, 149, 438
    quick, 507, 767
    rate earned on total, 774
    rate of return on, 1086
    ratio of fixed to long-term
        liabilities, 771
    ratio of net sales to, 773
    revaluation of in partnership, 542
    selling fixed, 453
    tangible, 438
Association of Certified Fraud
    Examiners, 354
Assumption fudging, 1180
Available-for-sale securities, *def.*, 665
Average cost method, 319, 322, 912
    determining costs under, 912
Average inventory cost flow method,
    def., 314
Average rate of return
    def., 1165
    method, 1165

B

Bad debt expense, *def.*, 395
Balance of the account
    def., 47
    normal, 50, *illus.*, 50
Balance sheet, 16, 149, 259, 671
    budgeted, 1007
    budgets, 1002
    classified, 149
    comparative, horizontal analysis,
        illus., 759

comparative, vertical analysis,
    illus., 762
current liabilities on, 504
def., 15
effect of inventory errors on
    current period's, *illus.*, 329
for manufacturing business, 824
income statement and
    comparative, *illus.*, 710
merchandise inventory on, 327
presentation of inventory in
    manufacturing and
    merchandising companies,
    illus., 825
report form of, *illus.*, 260
reporting receivables on, 410
stockholders' equity in, 588
stockholders' equity section of,
    illus., 588
Balance sheet accounts, 49
Balance sheet columns
    extend the accounts to, 172C
    spreadsheet with amounts
        extended to, *illus.*, 172B4
    total, 172C
Balance sheet effects, 328
Balanced scorecard, *def.*, 1090, *illus.*,
    1091
Bank accounts, 363
Bank error in your favor, 370
Bank reconciliation
    def., 366
    illus., 369
Bank statement
    and records, *illus.*, 366
    as control over cash, 365
    def., 363
    illus., 364
Bankers' ratio, 766
Basic analytical methods, 758
Basic earnings per share, 593
Benefits other than pensions,
    postretirement, 503
Bills form, *illus.*, 279
Board of directors, 575
Bond characteristics and
    terminology, 616
Bond discount, amortizing, 619
Bond indenture, *def.*, 616
Bond issued at a discount, 618
Bond premium, amortizing, 621
Bond redemption, 622
Bonds
    callable, 616, 622
    convertible, 616
    debenture, 616
    def., 613
    issued at a premium, 620
    issued at face amount, 617
    pricing of, 630
    proceeds from issuing, 616
    purchase of, 654, 672
    receipt of maturity value of, 674

Bonds (*continued*)
  sale of, 655
  serial, 616
  term, 616
  zero-coupon, 631*fn*
Bonds payable, 718
  accounting for, 617
  amortization of discount on, *illus.*, 633
  amortization of premium on, *illus.*, 634
  nature of, 616
  pricing, 627
Bonuses, 324
  partner, 542, *illus.*, 543
Book value, 458, 659
  def., 448
Book value of the asset
  def., 110
  with change in estimate, *illus.*, 451
Boot, *def.*, 460
Borrowers, 483
Break-even chart, 952
Break-even point
  def., 947
  summary of effects of changes on, 950
Budget(s)
  balance sheet, 1002
  capital expenditures, 1006, *illus.*, 1006
  cash, 1003, *illus.*, 1005
  completing the cash, 1005
  cost of goods sold, 1000, *illus.*, 1001
  def., 987
  direct labor cost, 998, *illus.*, 999
  direct materials purchases, 997, *illus.*, 998
  factory overhead cost, 999, *illus.*, 1000
  factory overhead flexible, 1043
  flexible, *illus.*, 991
  games, 990
  income statement, *illus.*, 994, 995
  master, 993
  performance report, *def.*, 1036, *illus.*, 1037
  production, 995, *illus.*, 996
  sales, 995, *illus.*, 995
  selling and administrative expenses, *illus.*, 1002
  setting conflicting goals, 989
  setting goals too loosely, 989
  setting goals too tightly, 989
  static, *illus.*, 991
  static and flexible, *illus.*, 992
Budgetary performance evaluation, 1035
Budgetary slack, *def.*, 989
Budgeted balance sheet, 1007
Budgeted income statement, 1002, *illus.*, 1003
Budgeted variable factory overhead, *def.*, 1045

Budgeting systems, 990
  computerized, 993
Budgeting
  continuous, *illus.*, 990
  human behavior and, 988
  human behavior problems in, *illus.*, 989
  nature and objectives of, 987, 988
  zero-based, 990
Building, 718
Business
  accept at a special price, 1128
  and accounting fraud in the 2000s, *illus.*, 5
  def., 2
  financial statements for merchandising, 254
  nature of, 2
  nature of merchandising, 253
  network, 958
  role of accounting in, 3
  role of ethics in, 4
  types of, 2
  See also Manufacturing businesses; Merchandising businesses; Service businesses
Business combination, *def.*, 660
Business connection
  Microsoft Corporation, 373
Business entity concept, *def.*, 7
Business transaction
  def., 10
  accounting equation and, 10
Buy or make, 1124
  differential analysis report, *illus.*, 1125
Bylaws, 576

C

Calendar year, 489, 494
Callable bonds, 616, 622
Capital, 577
  account, 48
  budgeting, 1164
  contributed, 577
  legal, 578
  paid-in, 577
  working, 765
Capital crime, 442
Capital deficiency, loss on realization, 549
Capital expenditures, *def.*, 441
Capital expenditures budget
  def., 1006
  illus., 1006
Capital investment analysis
  def., 1164
  factors that complicate, 1177
  nature of, 1164
Capital investment vs. lease, 1179
Capital lease, *def.*, 443

Capital rationing
  decision process, *illus.*, 1181
  def., 1180
Carrying amount, *def.*, 622
Cash, 499
  bank statement as control over, 365
  def., 359
  financial statement reporting of, 371
  investing in current operations, 652
  investing in long-term investments, 653
  investing in temporary investments, 653
  received by EFT, 362
  received from cash sales, 360
  received from customers, 721
  received in the mail, 361
  sales, 260
Cash basis of accounting, *def.*, 98
Cash budget
  completing, 1005
  def., 1003
  illus., 1005
Cash controls over receipts and payments, 359
Cash dividend, *def.*, 583
Cash equivalents, *def.*, 372
Cash flow from operations: direct and indirect methods, *illus.*, 707
Cash flow per share, *def.*, 708
Cash flows
  credit policy and, 716
  free, 725
  illus., 706
  preparing statement of, 719, 728
  reporting, 705
  spreadsheet for statement of, indirect method, 726, *illus.*, 727
  statement of, 15, 18, 705, 709, *illus.*, 720, *illus.*, 724–725
Cash flows from financing activities, 18, 708
  def., 706
Cash flows from investing activities, 18, 708
  def., 706
Cash flows from operating activities, 18, 706
  def., 705
  direct method, 724
  indirect method, *illus.*, 712
Cash funds, special-purpose, 370
Cash inflow, 706
Cash outflow, 706
Cash paid by EFT, 363
Cash payback method, 1166
Cash payback period, *def.*, 1166
Cash payments
  control of, 362
  estimated, 1004
  for income taxes, 724

Cash payments (*continued*)
  for merchandise, 722
  for operating expenses, 723
Cash payments journal
  and postings, *illus.*, 218
  def., 217
  for merchandising business, *illus.*,
    279
Cash receipts
  and revenue in QuickBooks, *illus.*,
    223
  control of, 360
  estimated, 1003
Cash receipts journal
  and postings, *illus.*, 212
  def., 211
  for merchandising business, *illus.*,
    278
Cash short and over account, *def.*, 361
Centralized operations, 1076
Certified Public Accountants
  (CPAs), 782
  def., 7
CFO, 780
Change fund, 360
Character, failure of individual, 4
Chart of accounts, 48
  def., 48
  expanded, *illus.*, 103
  for a merchandising business, 259,
    illus., 261
  illus., 49
  under periodic inventory system,
    281, *illus.*, 281
Charter, 576
Check fraud, 366
Check, payroll, *illus.*, 500
Classified balance sheet, 149
Clean opinion, 782
Clearing account, *def.*, 150
Clock cards, 851
Closing entries, 150, 275
  def., 150
  flowchart of, *illus.*, 152
  illus., 152, 165
  journalizing and posting, 151, 163
  under periodic inventory system, 283
Closing process
  and adjusting process, 274
  def., 150
  illus., 151
Closing the books, *def.*, 150
Collections from sales, schedule of,
  1003, *illus.*, 1004
Commercial substance, 460
Committee of Sponsoring
  Organizations (COSO) of the
  Treadway Commission, 354
Common stock, 717
  def., 578
  dividends and earnings per share
    of, *illus.*, 779
  earnings per share on, 777

Common-sized income statement,
  illus., 763
Common-sized statement, *def.*, 762
Communication and information, 359
Companies, why they invest, 652
Company reputation: best and worst,
  1035
Comparative balance sheet
  horizontal analysis, *illus.*, 759
  income statement and, *illus.*, 710
  vertical analysis, *illus.*, 762
Comparative income statement
  horizontal analysis, *illus.*, 760
  vertical analysis, *illus.*, 763
Comparative retained earnings
  statement, horizontal analysis,
  illus., 761
Comparative schedule of current
  assets, horizontal analysis, *illus.*, 760
Compensated absences, 501
Compensating balance, *def.*, 372
Compounding, 1168
Comprehensive income, 671
  def., 675
Computer system controls, 501
Computerized accounting systems,
  221, 279
Computerized budgeting systems,
  993
Computerized perpetual inventory
  systems, 319
Computers, use of in cost-volume-
  profit analysis, 955
Concept
  accounting period, 98
  business entity, 7
  cost, 8
  matching, 15, 98
  objectivity, 8
  revenue recognition, 98
  unit of measure, 8
Consignee, *def.*, 328
Consignor, *def.*, 328
Consolidated financial statements,
  def., 660
Constraint, 1138
Contingent liabilities, 412
  accounting treatment of, *illus.*, 506
  def., 504
Continuous budgeting
  def., 990
  illus., 990
Continuous process improvement,
  def., 817
Contra account, 264
  def., 109
Contra asset accounts, *def.*, 109
Contract rate, *def.*, 616
Contributed capital, 577
Contribution margin, 961
  def., 944
  income statement, *illus.*, 944
  ratio, *def.*, 944

Control
  environment, *def.*, 355
  human element of, 359
  internal, 352, 354
  of cash payments, 362
  of cash receipts, 360
  of inventory, 312
  over cash, bank statement as, 365
  procedures, 356
Controllable expenses, *def.*, 1080
Controllable revenues, *def.*, 1080
Controllable variance, *def.*, 1044
Controller, *def.*, 816
Controlling
  account, *def.*, 206
  def., 817
  function of management, 988
Conversion costs
  and prime costs, *illus.*, 822
  def., 822
Conversion equivalent units, 897,
  illus., 898
Convertible bonds, 616
Copyright, *def.*, 456
Corporate annual reports, 780
Corporate form, advantages and
  disadvantages of, *illus.*, 575
Corporations, 574
  and their states of incorporation,
    illus., 576
  characteristics of, 574
  def., 8
  financing, 613
  forming, 576
  nature of, 574
  nonpublic, 575
  organizational structure, *illus.*, 575
  private, 575
  public, 575
Correcting journal entry, *def.*, 68
Cosigned inventory, *def.*, 328
Cost accounting system
  def., 847
  overview, 847
Cost allocation, *def.*, 854
Cost behavior concepts, summary of,
  943
Cost behavior, *def.*, 937
Cost center
  def., 1078
  illus., 1078
  responsibility accounting for, 1078
  responsibility accounting reports
    for, *illus.*, 1079
Cost concept
  choosing a cost-plus approach, 1136
  def., 8
  product, 1133
  target, *illus.*, 1137
  variable, 1134
Cost flows
  for a process manufacturer, 890,
    illus., 892

Cost flows (*continued*)
  illus., 905
  labor information and, *illus.*, 852
  materials information and, *illus.*, 850
  summary of, 860
Cost graphs
  fixed, *illus.*, 940
  variable, *illus.*, 938
Cost Management Group of the IMA, 854
Cost method, 586
  def., 656
Cost object, *def.*, 819
Cost of finished goods available, *def.*, 826
Cost of fixed assets, 440
Cost of goods manufactured
  def., 826
  statement of, 826
Cost of goods sold, 760*fn*
  def., 826
  sales and, 860
Cost of goods sold budget
  def., 1000
  illus., 1001
Cost of merchandise purchased, *def.*, 256
Cost of merchandise sold, 760*fn*
  def., 254, 255, 825
  illus., 257
  using periodic inventory system, 280, *illus.*, 281
Cost of production report, 914
  def., 893
  illus., 903, 915
  preparing, 902
  using for decision making, 906
Cost per equivalent unit
  def., 898
  determine, 898, 914
Cost price approach, *def.*, 1096
Cost variances
  def., 1036
  favorable, 1036
  manufacturing, 1037, *illus.*, 1038
  total manufacturing, 1037
  unfavorable, 1036
Cost-benefit considerations, 359
Cost-plus approach
  cost concept, 1136
  to setting, *illus.*, 1136
Costing
  absorption, 961
  variable or direct, 943, 961
Costs
  benefit dollars as a percent of payroll, *illus.*, 501
  classifying, 439, *illus.*, 439
  classifying direct and indirect, *illus.*, 820
  conversion, 822
  criticisms of standard, 1035

def., 819
depreciable, 444
determine units to be assigned, 893, 913
determining under average cost method, 912
differential, 1120
direct and indirect, 819
direct labor, 821
direct materials, 820
effect of changes in fixed, 948
effect of changes in unit variable, 948
estimating inventory, 331
examples of product and period, *illus.*, 823
factory overhead, 821
financial statements and product and period, *illus.*, 823
fixed, 939
flow of manufacturing, *illus.*, 829, 849, 861
flow of through service business, *illus.*, 864
historical, 670
manufacturing operations, 818, 820
mixed, 939, *illus.*, 940
of acquiring fixed assets, *illus.*, 440
opportunity, 1126
period, 860
prime and conversion, *illus.*, 822
product and period, 822
research and development, 456
semivariable or semifixed, 939
standard, 1033, *illus.*, 1036
sunk, 1120
to transferred and partially completed units, allocate, 914
to units transferred out and partially completed units, allocate, 900
variable, 938
Cost-volume-profit analysis
  assumptions of, 955
  def., 943
  graphic approach to, 952
  mathematical approach to, 947
  use of computers in, 955
Cost-volume-profit chart
  def., 952
  illus., 953
  revised, *illus.*, 953
Cost-volume-profit
  relationships, 943
  special relationships, 956
Coupon rate, 616
Credit, 46*fn*, 483
  def., 47
  diagram of the recording and posting of, *illus.*, 55
  line of, 372
  rules of, 49, *illus.*, 50
Credit memo, *def.*, *illus.*, 264

Credit memorandum, *def.*, 264
Credit period, *def.*, 263
Credit policy and cash flow, 716
Credit quality, 617
Credit sales, 768*fn*
Credit terms, *def.*, *illus.*, 263
Creditor, 483
Creditors ledger, 206
Crime, capital, 442
Cumulative preferred stock
  def., 578
  dividends to, *illus.*, 579
Currency exchange rates, *def.*, 1179
Current assets
  comparative schedule of, horizontal analysis, *illus.*, 760
  def., 149
Current liabilities, 483
  accounts payable as a percent of total, *illus.*, 484
  def., 149
  on the balance sheet, 504
Current operations, investing cash in, 652
Current portion of long-term debt, 484
Current position analysis, *def.*, 765
Current ratio, 172
  def., 766
Currently attainable standards, *def.*, 1034
Customer relationship management (CRM), 225
Customers ledger, 206
Customers, cash received from, 721
Cybercash, 360

D

Data
  assembling and analyzing adjustment, 160
  flow in payroll system, *illus.*, 500
Date of declaration, 583
Date of payment, 584
Date of record, 583
Debenture bonds, 616
Debit, 46fn
  def., 47
  diagram of the recording and posting of, *illus.*, 55
  rules of, 49, *illus.*, 50
Debit memo, *def.*, 267, *illus.*, 267
Debit memorandum, *def.*, 267
Debt, current portion of long-term, 484
Debt investments, accounting for, 654
Debt securities, *def.*, 653
Debtors, 483
Decentralization
  advantages of, 1077
  disadvantages of, 1077
Decentralized operations, 1076
  advantages and disadvantages of, *illus.*, 1077

Decision making
  def., 817
  job order costing for, 862
  using cost of production report
    for, 906
Deductions from employee earnings,
  487
Deductions, 487
  other, 489
Deferrals, 102
Deficiency, def., 549
Deficit, def., 577
Defined benefit plan, def., 502
Defined contribution plan, def., 502
Depletion, def., 454
Depreciable cost, 444
Depreciate, def., 109
Depreciation
  accounting for, 443
  accumulated, 109
  def., 109, 443
  for federal income tax, 450
  functional, 443
  physical, 443
  revising estimates, 450
  sum-of-the-years-digits, 459
Depreciation expense, 109
  def., 109
  factors in computing, illus., 444
Depreciation methods
  comparing, 448, illus., 449
  summary of, illus., 449
  use of, illus., 445
Differential analysis, 1119
  def., 11203
  illus., 1120
Differential analysis report
  discontinue an unprofitable
    segment, illus., 1123
  lease or sell, illus., 1121
  make or buy, illus., 1125
  process or sell, illus., 1128
  replace machine, illus., 1126
  sell at special price, illus., 1129
Differential cost, def., 120
Differential income or loss, def., 1120
Differential revenue, def., 1120
Diluted earnings per share, 778
Direct and indirect costs, classifying,
  illus., 820
Direct costing, 943, 961
Direct costs, def., 819
Direct labor
  cost, def., 821, 889
  cost budget, def., 998, illus., 999
  standards for nonmanufacturing
    activities, 1042
Direct labor variances, 1041
  and direct materials, 1038
  rate, def., 1041
  relationships, illus., 1042
  reporting, 1042
  time, def., 1042

Direct materials
  and direct labor variances, 1038
  equivalent units, illus., 896
  purchases budget, def., 997, illus.,
    998
Direct materials cost, 889
  def., 820
Direct materials variances, 1038
  price, def., 1039
  quantity variance, def., 1039
  relationships, 1040, illus., 1040
  reporting, 1040
Direct method, 19fn
  cash flow from operations, illus.,
    707
  cash flows from operating
    activities, 724
  def., 706
  statement of cash flows, 720, illus.,
    724–725
Direct operating expenses, 1080
Direct write-off method
  and allowance methods,
    comparing, 405, illus., 406
  def., 395
  for uncollectible accounts, 396
Directing, def., 817
Directing function of management,
  988
Directors, board of, 575
Discontinue a segment or product,
  1122
Discontinue an unprofitable segment,
  differential analysis report, illus.,
  1123
Discontinued operations, 785
Discount, 412, 486
  amortization of, 673
  amortization of by interest
    method, 632
  bonds issued at, 618
  def., 581, 616
  on bonds payable, amortization
    of, illus., 633
  period, 412
  purchases, 256, 266
  rate, 412, 486
  sales, 255, 262
  trade, 269, 272
Discounted cash flow method, 1171
Discounted note, 486
Discounting notes receivable, 412
Dishonored note receivable, def., 408
Disposal of fixed assets, 452
Dividend revenue, 657
Dividend yield, def., 779
Dividends, 575, 658, 716
  and earnings per share of
    common stock, illus., 779
  accounting for, 583
  cash, 583
  def., 577
  extra, 583

liquidating, 583fn
  receipt of, 657
  recording investee, 659
  special, 583
  stock, 585
  to cumulative preferred stock,
    illus., 579
Dividends per share, def., 779
Dividing income, 536
Divisional income statements, illus.,
  1084, 1085
Double taxation, 575
Double-declining-balance method,
  def., 447
Double-entry accounting system, def.,
  49
Doubtful accounts
  allowance for, 397
  expense, 395
Drawing, def., 48
Due date, 407
DuPont formula, def., 1086
Duties, rotating, 357

E
Earnings
  deductions from employee, 487
  recording employees', 494
  retained, 577
Earnings per common share (EPS),
  def., 593
  assuming dilution, 778
Earnings per share (EPS)
  def., 614
  income statement with, illus., 786
  on common stock, def., 777
  reporting, 786
Earnings record, employee's, 497
  illus., 498–499
E-commerce, def., 224
Economic value added (EVA), 1089
Effective interest rate method
  def., 619
  of amortization, 632
Effective rate of interest, def., 616
Electronic badges, 851
Electronic funds transfers (EFT)
  cash paid by, 363
  cash received by, 362
  def., 362
Elements of internal control
  def., 354
  illus., 355
Employee earnings
  deductions from, 487
  liability for, 487
Employee fraud
  def., 354
  tips on preventing, 357
Employee net pay, computing, 490
Employee's earnings record
  def., 497
  illus., 498–499

Employee's Withholding Allowance Certificate (W-4), 487
illus., 488
Employees, ghost, 853
Employees'
earnings, recording, 494
fringe benefits, 501
Employer's payroll taxes, liability for, 492
End-of-period spreadsheet, 172
illus., 145, 161
preparing, 160
Engineering change order (ECO), 1140
Environmental accounting, 818
Environmentally sustainable resources (being green), 888
Equity
owner's, 48, 149
rate earned on common stockholders', 776
rate earned on stockholders', 775
ratio of liabilities to stockholders', 771
reporting stockholders', 587
shareholders, 577
statement of members', 552
statement of owner's, 258
statement of partnership, 552, *illus.*, 552
statement of stockholders', 591, *illus.*, 590
stockholders', 577
Equity investments, accounting for, 656
Equity method, *def.*, 658
Equity securities, *def.*, 653
Equivalent units
conversion, 897, *illus.*, 898
cost per, 898
determine the cost per, 898, 914
direct materials, *illus.*, 896
materials, 895
Equivalent units of production
compute, 895, 914
def., 895
Errors
affecting the trial balance, 66
in liquidation, 552
inventory, 327
not affecting the trial balance, 67
Estimating uncollectibles, 399
Estimation methods
comparing, 404
differences between, *illus.*, 404
Ethical conduct, guideline for, *illus.*, 5
Ethical indifference, 4
Ethics
accounting, 780
def., 4
role of in accounting, 4
role of in business, 4

European Economic Union (EU), 670
Exchange
gain on, 461
loss on, 461
Ex-dividends, 584
Expected useful life, 444
Expenditures, revenue and capital, 441
Expense(s), 439
accrued, 101, 107
administrative, 257, 822
bad debt, 395
cash payments for operating, 723
controllable, 1080
def., 12, 48
depreciation, 109
direct operating, 1080
doubtful accounts, 395
factors in computing depreciation, 444
general, 257
interest, 723
other, 258
prepaid, 11, 100, 103
selling, 257, selling, 822
uncollectible accounts, 395
Extra dividends, 583
Extraordinary item, *def.*, 785
Extraordinary repairs, 441

F

Face amount, 407
bonds issued at, 617
Factor, 395
in computing depreciation expense, 444
that complicate capital investment analysis, 1177
Factoring, 395
Factory
burden, *def.*, 821
depreciation, 853
labor, 851
overhead account, 1048
overhead balance, disposal of, 857
power, 853
Factory overhead
allocating, 854
applying to jobs, *illus.*, 855
applying to work in process, 855
flexible budget, 1043
overapplied or overabsorbed, 856
underapplied or underabsorbed, 856
Factory overhead cost, 853, 889
def., 821
Factory overhead cost budget
def., 999
illus., 1000
indicating standard factory overhead rate, *illus.*, 1044

Factory overhead cost variance report
def., 1048
illus., 1048
Factory overhead variances, 1043
reporting, 1047
Fair Labor Standards Act, 487
Fair value, *def.*, 661
Fair value accounting, 670
effect of on financial statements, 671
future of, 671
trend to, 670
Favorable cost variance, *def.*, 1036
Favorable fixed factory overhead variance, 1046
Federal income tax, depreciation for, 450
Federal Insurance Contributions Act. *See* FICA
Federal Trade Commission, 1132
Federal unemployment compensation tax, *See* FUTA tax
Federal Wage and Hour Law, 487
Feedback, 206
def., 817
Fees earned, 253
def., 11
FICA tax, 492
def., 489
FIFO and LIFO cost methods, effect of changing costs, *illus.*, 324
Financial accounting, *def.*, 4, 814
Financial Accounting Standards Board (FASB), 359
def., 7
Financial analysis and interpretation, 20, 69, 120, 172, 226, 276, 330, 372, 411, 459, 507, 553, 593, 627, 672, 725
Financial and managerial accounting differences between, 814
illus., 814
Financial assets, 661
Financial statement reporting of cash, 371
Financial statements, 146
consolidated, 660
def., 14
effect of fair value accounting on, 671
effect of inventory errors on, 327
for a merchandising business, 254
for a manufacturing business, 824
for Mornin' Joe, 700
general-purpose, 4
illus., 17, 164
interrelationships among, 20
prepared from work sheet, *illus.*, 147
preparing, 163
product costs, period costs, and, *illus.*, 823

Financial statements (*continued*)
report on fairness of, 782
reporting merchandise inventory
in, 324
under periodic inventory system,
283
Financing activities
cash flows from, 18, 706, 708
noncash, 708
Finished goods, 859
inventory, *def.*, 824
ledger account, *illus.*, 859
Finished goods ledger, 862
def., 859
First-in, first-out (FIFO) inventory
cost flow method, *def.*, 314
method, 316, 320, *def.*, 893
First-in, first-out flow of costs, *illus.*,
321
Fiscal year, *def.*, 166
Fixed asset turnover ratio, *def.*, 459
Fixed assets, 439
as a percent of total assets, *illus.*,
439
cost of, 440
costs of acquiring, *illus.*, 440
def., 109, 149, 438
discarding, 452
disposal of, 452
exchanging similar, 460
financial reporting for, 458
leasing, 442
nature of, 438
selling, 453
to long-term liabilities, ratio of, 771
Fixed charge coverage ratio, 772
Fixed cost graphs, *illus.*, 940
Fixed costs
def., 939
effect of changes in, 948
Fixed factory overhead variance
favorable, 1046
unfavorable, 1046
Fixed overhead volume variance,
1046
graph of, *illus.*, 1047
Flexible and static budgets, *illus.*, 992
Flexible budgets
def., 991
illus., 991
Flowchart of closing entries, *illus.*,
152
FOB (free on board)
destination, *def.*, 269, 327
shipping point, *def.*, 269, 327
Forming and dividing income of a
partnership, 534
Fraud
accounting and business in the
2000s, *illus.*, 5
case of fraudulent price tags, 265
check, 366
employee, 354

journalizing and, 54
online, 224
receivables, 406
round tripping, 148
tips on preventing employee, 357
Free cash flow, *def.*, 725
Free issue basis, office supplies, 104
Freight, 269
Freight in, 282
def., 256
Freight terms, *illus.*, 270
Fringe benefits
def., 501
employees', 501
Frozen Delight, 906
Functional depreciation, 443
Fund
petty cash, 370
sinking, 622*fn*
special-purpose, 371
FUTA tax, 492
Future value, *def.*, 628

G

GAAP. *See* Generally accepted
accounting principles
Gain
on exchange, 461
on realization, 546
on sale of land, 723
unrealized, 661
General expenses, *def.*, 257
General journal, *def.*, 208
General ledger, *def.*, 206
and subsidiary ledgers, *illus.*,
207
General partner, 534
Generally accepted accounting
principles (GAAP), 98, 354, 661,
814
def., 7
General-purpose financial
statements, *def.*, 4
Ghost employees, 853
Goal conflict, *def.*, 989
Goods manufactured
cost of, 826
statement of cost of, 826
Goods sold, cost of, 760*fn*
Goodwill, *def.*, 456
Graph of fixed overhead volume
variance, *illus.*, 1047
Graphic approach to cost-volume-
profit analysis, 952
Greed, culture of, 4
Gross pay, *def.*, 487
Gross profit, *def.*, 254, 257, 962
Gross profit method
def., 332
estimating inventory by, *illus.*,
332
of inventory costing, 332
Guideline for ethical conduct, *illus.*, 5

H

Held-to-maturity investments,
accounting for, 672
Held-to-maturity securities, *def.*, 664
High-low method, *def.*, 941
Historical cost, 670
Holland Beverage Company, 907
Horizontal analysis
comparative balance sheet, *illus.*,
759
comparative income statement,
illus., 760
comparative schedule of current
assets, *illus.*, 760
def., 69, 759
Human behavior
and budgeting, 988
problems in budgeting, *illus.*, 989
Human element of controls, 359
Hurdle rate, 1171

I

Ideal standards, *def.*, 1034
Illusory profits, 324
In arrears, *def.* 579
In-and-out cards, 851
Income
accumulated other
comprehensive, 671
adjustments to net using indirect
method, *illus.*, 711
comprehensive, 671, 675
differential, 1120
(loss) by product, *illus.*, 1123
net, 15
operating, 257
other, 258
shifting through transfer prices,
1097
Income from operations, *def.*, 257,
961, 962, 1085
Income of partnership, dividing, 536
Income statement, 15, 146, 671
absorption costing, *illus.*, 962
accounts, 49
and comparative balance sheet,
illus., 710
budgeted, 1002, *illus.*, 1003
budgets, *illus.*, 994, 995
common-sized, *illus.*, 763
comparative, horizontal analysis,
illus., 760
comparative, vertical analysis,
illus., 763
contribution margin, *illus.*, 944
def., 15
effect of inventory errors on
current period's, *illus.*, 328
effect of inventory errors on two
year's, *illus.*, 329
effects, 328
for a manufacturing company, 825

Income statement (*continued*)
  illus., 862
  multiple-step, 254, *illus.*, 255
  negotiated transfer price, *illus.*, 1095
  no transfers between divisions,
    illus., 1093
  single-step, 258, *illus.*, 259
  unusual items affecting the
    current period's, 785
  unusual items affecting the prior
    period's, 786
  unusual items in, 784, *illus.*, 785
  variable costing, *illus.*, 962
  variances from standards in, *illus.*,
    1052
  with earnings per share, *illus.*, 786
  with statement of costs of goods
    manufactured, (manufacturing
    company), *illus.*, 828
Income statement columns
  extend the accounts to, 172C
  spreadsheet with amounts
    extended to, *illus.*, 172B4
  total, 172C
Income Summary, *def.*, 150
Income taxes, 487, 1177
  cash payments for, 724
  depreciation for federal, 450
Incorporation, application of, 576
Incremental analysis, 1120
Indenture
  bond, 616
  trust, 616
Indirect and direct costs, classifying,
  illus., 820
Indirect costs, *def.*, 819
Indirect labor, 853
Indirect materials, 853
Indirect method, 20*fn*
  adjustments to net income, *illus.*,
    711
  cash flow from operations, *illus.*,
    707, 712
  def., 707
  spreadsheet for statement of cash
    flows, 726, *illus.*, 727
  statement of cash flows, 709, *illus.*,
    720
Inflation, *def.*, 1179
Information
  and communication, 359
  flow of accounting, 144
Installment note
  amortization of, *illus.*, 624
  def., 623
  issuing, 623
Installments, 484
Intangible assets
  comparison of, *illus.*, 457
  def., 455
  disclosures, frequency of, *illus.*,
    457
  financial reporting for, 458

Interest charges, number of times
  earned, 627, 772
Interest expense, 723
Interest in a partnership, purchasing,
  540
Interest method, 619, 632
  amortization of discount by,
    632
  amortization of premium by, 633
Interest rate, 407
Interest revenue, 654
  def., 11
Interest, market or effective rate of,
  616
Internal control, 354, 499
  def., 352
  elements of, 354, *illus.*, 355
  limitations of, 359
  objectives of, 354
  report on, 782
Internal control problems, warning
  signs of, *illus.*, 358
Internal control procedures, *illus.*,
  356
*Internal Control—Integrated
  Framework*, 353, 354
Internal controls, *def.*, 206
  for payroll systems, 499
Internal rate of return (IRR) method,
  def., 1174
International Accounting Standards
  Board (IASB), 670
  def., 7
*International Financial Reporting
  Standards (IFRSs)*, 7, 670
Inventory
  control of, 312
  cosigned, 328
  determining by retail method,
    illus., 331
  estimating by gross profit method,
    illus., 332
  finished goods, 824
  materials, 824
  merchandise, 254
  number of days' sales in, 330, 770
  physical, 313
  reporting of, 313
  safeguarding of, 312
  work in process, 824
Inventory analysis, *def.*, 769
Inventory at lower of cost or market,
  determining, *illus.*, 325
Inventory cost, estimating, 331
Inventory cost flow assumptions, 313
Inventory costing
  gross profit method of, 332
  retail method of, 331
Inventory costing methods
  comparing, 323
  illus., 315
  under periodic inventory system,
    320

  under perpetual inventory system,
    316
  use of, *illus.*, 315
Inventory errors
  on financial statements, effect of,
    327
  effect of on current period's
    balance sheet, *illus.*, 329
  effect of on current period's
    income statement, *illus.*, 328
  effect of on two year's income
    statements, *illus.*, 329
Inventory in manufacturing and
  merchandising companies,
  balance sheet presentation of,
  illus., 825
Inventory in process, 901
Inventory ledger, subsidiary, 313
Inventory profits, 324
Inventory shortage, *def.*, 274
Inventory shrinkage
  adjusting entry for, 274
  def., 274
Inventory turnover, *def.*, 330, 770
Investee
  def., 656
  dividends, recording, 659
  net income, recording, 659
Investing activities
  cash flows from, 18, 706, 708
  noncash, 708
Investment centers
  def., 1085
  responsibility accounting for, 1085
Investment turnover, *def.*, 1086
Investments, 439
  accounting for debt, 654
  accounting for equity, 656
  accounting for held-to-maturity, 672
  def., 653
  dividing of partnership income,
    537
  investing cash in long-term, 653
  rate of return on, 1086
  shareholders', 577
  stock, *illus.*, 656
  summary of valuing and
    reporting of, *illus.*, 668
  valuing and reporting of, 661
Investor, *def.*, 656
Invoice
  def., 209, 262
  form, *illus.*, 280
  illus., 263
Issuance date, 407

J

JIT. *See* just-in-time.
Job cost sheets, 862
  and work in process controlling
    account, *illus.*, 858
  comparing data from, *illus.*, 863
  def., 850

Job order and process cost systems
 compared, *illus.*, 889
 comparing, 888
Job order cost systems, 888
 def., 847
 for manufacturing businesses, 848
 for professional service
 businesses, 863
Job order costing for decision
 making, 862
Job shops, 848
Jobs, 847
 applying factory overhead to,
 illus., 855
Journal
 analyzing and recording
 transactions in, 158
 cash payments, 217
 def., 50
 general, 208
 purchases, 214
 revenue, 208, *illus.*, 209
Journal entries
 for process cost system, 904
 illus., 159–160
 posting to accounts, 55
Journal entry, *def.*, 51
Journalizing, 50
 adjusting entries, 162
 and fraud, 54
 closing entries, 151, 163
 def., 51
Journals
 modified special, 220
 special, 207
Just-in-time processing (JIT), *def.*, 909
Just-in-time production line, *illus.*,
 910

L

Labor information and cost flows,
 illus., 852
Land, 719
 gain on sale of, 723
Last-in, first-out flow of costs, *illus.*,
 322
Last-in, first-out (LIFO) inventory
 cost flow method, *def.*, 314
Last-in, first-out method, 318, 321
Lease, 442
 capital, 443
 operating, 443
Lease or sell, 1121
 differential analysis report, *illus.*,
 1121
Lease vs. capital investment, 1179
Leasing fixed assets, 442
Ledger
 accounts payable subsidiary, 206
 accounts receivable subsidiary,
 206
 additional subsidiary, 220
 creditors, 206

customers, 206
 def., 48
 finished goods, 862
 general and subsidiary, 206, *illus.*,
 207
 illus., 64–65, 154–155, 167–168
 materials, 862
 posting transactions to, 158
 subsidiary, 206
 subsidiary inventory, 313
 with adjusting entries, *illus.*,
 115–116
Legal capital, 578
Lender, 483
Lessee, 443
Lessor, 443
Leverage, 614*fn*, 776
 effect of, *illus.*, 776
Liabilities, 149
 accounts payable as a percent of
 total current, *illus.*, 484
 contingent, 412, 504
 current, 149, 483
 def., 9, 48
 limited, 534, 575
 long-term, 149, 483
 ratio of fixed assets to long-term,
 771
 reporting long-term, 626
 to stockholders' equity, ratio of,
 771
 unlimited, 533
Liability for employee earnings, 487
Liability for employer's payroll taxes,
 492
LIFE, 456
LIFO. *See* Last in first out.
LIFO and FIFO cost methods, effect
 of changing costs, *illus.*, 324
Limitations of internal control, 359
Limited liability, 534, 575
Limited liability company (LLC), 532,
 534
 characteristics of, *illus.*, 535
 def., 8, 534
 proprietorships, and partnerships,
 comparing, 534
Limited life, 533
Limited partners, 534
Limited partnership, 534
Line department, *def.*, 815
Line of credit, 372
Line, 816
Liquidating dividend, 583*fn*
Liquidating partnerships, 545
 steps in, *illus.*, 545
Liquidation
 def., 545
 errors in, 552
Liquidation, statement of
 partnership, 546
 gain on realization, *illus.*, 547
 loss on realization, *illus.*, 548

 loss on realization—capital
 deficiency, *illus.*, 550
LLC. *See* Limited liability company
Long-term debt, current portion of,
 484
Long-term investments, investing
 cash in, 653
Long-term liabilities, 483
 def., 149
 ratio of fixed assets to, 771
 reporting, 626
Loss on exchange, 461
Loss on realization, 547
 capital deficiency, 549
Loss
 differential, 1120
 net, 15
 unrealized, 661
Lower of cost or market (LCM)
 method
 def., 325
 determining inventory at, *illus.*,
 325
 valuation at, 325

M

Maintenance, ordinary, 441
Make or buy, 1124
 differential analysis report, *illus.*,
 1125
Maker, 407
Management accountant in the
 organization, 815
Management accounting, *def.*, 4
Management by exception, *def.*, 817
Management process
 def., 816
 illus., 816
 managerial accounting in, 816
Management
 controlling function of, 988
 directing function of, 988
 planning function of, 988
Management's Discussion and
 Analysis (MD&A), *def.*, 780
Management's philosophy and
 operating style, 355
Managerial accounting, 813
 def., 4, 814
 in management process, 816
 uses of, 827
Managerial and financial accounting
 differences between, 814
 illus., 814
Manager-managed company, 534
Mandatory vacations, 357
Manual accounting systems, 206, 277
 adapting, 220
Manufacturing businesses
 balance sheet for, 824
 def., 3
 financial statements for, 824
 job order cost systems for, 848

Manufacturing cells, *def.*, 909
Manufacturing companies
  balance sheet presentation of
    inventory of, *illus.*, 825
  income statement for, 825
  income statement with statement
    of costs of goods
    manufactured, *illus.*, 828
Manufacturing cost variances, 1037
  illus., 1038
Manufacturing costs, 820
  flow of, *illus.*, 829, 849, 861
  schedule of payments for, 1004,
    illus., 1005
Manufacturing margin, 961
Manufacturing operations, 818
  illus., 818
  summary of, *illus.*, 848
Manufacturing overhead, *def.*, 821
MAP (minimum advertised price),
  1132
Margin of safety, *def.*, 960
Market price approach, *def.*, 1093
Market rate of interest
  def., 616
  of 11%, 631
  of 12%, 631
  of 13%, 631
Markup, *def.*, 1130
Master budget, *def.*, 993
Matching concept, *def.*, 15, 98
Matching principle, *def.*, 98
Materials, 849
  equivalent units, 895
  information and cost flows, *illus.*,
    850
  inventory, *def.*, 824
  ledger, *def.*, 849, 862
  requisitions, *def.*, 850
Mathematical approach to cost-
  volume-profit analysis, 947
Maturity date, 407
Maturity value, *def.*, 408
  of bond, receipt of, 674
Medicare, 489
Member-managed company, 534
Members' equity, statement of, 552
Merchandise
  available for sale, *def.*, 256, 825
  cash payments for, 722
Merchandise inventory
  def., 254
  in financial statements, reporting
    of, 324
  on balance sheet, 327
Merchandise purchased, cost of, 256
Merchandise sold, cost of, 254, 255,
  760*fn*, 825
  illus., 257
Merchandise transactions
  dual nature of, 272
  recording under periodic
    inventory system, 282

Merchandisers, accounting systems
  for, 277
Merchandising business
  cash payments journal for, *illus.*,
    279
  cash receipts journal for, *illus.*, 278
  chart of accounts for, 259, *illus.*,
    261
  def., 3
  financial statements for, 254
  nature of, 253
  purchases journal for, *illus.*, 278
  sales journal for, *illus.*, 277
  statement of owner's equity for,
    illus., 259
Merchandising companies, balance
  sheet presentation of inventory of,
  illus., 825
Merchandising transactions, 259
Mixed costs
  def., 939
  illus., 940
Modified Accelerated Cost Recovery
  System, (MACRS), 450
Monitoring, 358
Mortgage note payable, 149
Mortgage notes, *def.*, 623
Mortgage payable, 149
Moving average, 319
Multiple-step income statement
  def., 254
  illus., 255
Mutual agency, 533

N

Natural business year, *def.*, 166
Natural resources, 454
Negotiated price approach, *def.*, 1094
Net amount, 458
Net book value, *def.*, 110
Net income, 253, 658
  adjustments to using indirect
    method, *illus.*, 711
  completed spreadsheet with, *illus.*,
    172B5
  compute, 172C
  def., 15
  dividing of partnership income
    when allowances exceed, 538
  recording investee, 659
Net loss
  compute, 172C
  def., 15
Net pay, 490
  computing employee, 490
  def., 487
Net present value analysis
  at 12%, *illus.*, 1174
  equalized lives of proposals, *illus.*,
    1178
  unequal lives of proposals, *illus.*,
    1178
Net present value method, *def.*, 1171

Net profit, *def.*, 15
Net purchases, *def.*, 256
Net realizable value
  def., 326, 397
  valuation at, 326
Net sales
  def., 255
  to assets, ratio of, 773
Network business, 958
New York Stock Exchange, 575
Nominal accounts, *def.*, 150
Non taxable entity, 534
Noncash investing and financing
  activities, 708
Nonfinancial performance measure,
  def., 1053
Nonmanufacturing activities, direct
  labor standards for, 1042
Nonpublic corporations, 575
Nontaxable entity, 533
No-par stock, 578, 582
Normal balance of an account, *def.*,
  50
Normal standards, 1034
Note receivable, dishonored, 408
Notes
  amortization of installment, *illus.*,
    624
  installment, 623
  issuing an installment, 623
  mortgage, 623
Notes payable, short-term, 484
Notes receivable, 406
  accounting for, 408
  characteristics of, 406
  def., 149, 394
  discounting, 412
Not-for-profit, 576
NSF (not sufficient funds) checks,
  364
Number of days' sales in inventory,
  def., 330, 770
Number of days' sales in receivables,
  def., 411, 769
Number of times interest charges are
  earned, *def.*, 627, 772
Number of times preferred
  dividends are earned, 772

O

OASDI. *See* Social security
Objective measures, 814
Objectives (goals), *def.*, 817
Objectivity concept, *def.*, 8
Office supplies, free issue basis of,
  104
Offsetting account, 264
Online fraud, 224
Operating activities, cash flows from,
  18, 705, 706
  direct method, 724
  indirect method, *illus.*, 712
Operating agreement, 534

Operating efficiency, 1087
Operating expenses, cash payments for, 723
Operating income, *def.*, 257
Operating lease, *def.*, 443
Operating leverage, *def.*, 958
Operating loss area, 952, 955
Operating profit area, 952, 955
Operating profitability, 1087
Operational planning, *def.*, 817
Operations
    cash flow from, direct and indirect methods, *illus.*, 707
    centralized and decentralized, 1076
    income from, 257
    separating responsibilities for related, 357
Opportunity cost, *def.*, 1126
Ordinary maintenance and repairs, 441
Organization
    article of, 534
    management accountant in, 815
Organization chart, 815
    for Callaway Golf Company, *illus.*, 815
Organizational structure, 355
    of corporation, *illus.*, 575
Orphan Drug Act, 951
Orphan drugs, 951
Other comprehensive income, *def.*, 675
Other expense, *def.*, 258
Other income, *def.*, 258
Other receivables, 395
Outstanding stock, *def.*, 578
Overabsorbed factory overhead, 856
Overapplied factory overhead, *def.*, 856
Owner withdrawals, 50
Owner's equity, 149
    def., 9, 48
    effects of transactions on, *illus.*, 14
    statement of, 15, 16, 148, 258
Ownership
    between 20%–50%, 658
    less than 20%, 656
    more than 50%, 660

P

Paid-in capital
    def., 577
    from issuing stock, 577
Par, *def.*, 578
Par value method, 586*fn*
Parent company, *def.*, 660
Participating preferred stock, 578*fn*
Participation in income, 533
Partner
    general, 534
    limited, 534
Partnership agreement, *def.*, 533

Partnership equity, statement of, *illus.*, 552
Partnership income, dividing of, 536
    by services and investments of partners, 537
    by services of partners, 536
    when allowances exceed net income, 538
Partnership liquidation, statement of, 546
    gain on realization, *illus.*, 547
    loss on realization, *illus.*, 548
    loss on realization—capital deficiency, *illus.*, 550
Partnership property, co-ownership of, 533
Partnerships, 532
    admitting a partner, 540
    characteristics of, *illus.*, 535
    contributing assets to, 541
    death of a partner, 545
    def., 8, 533
    forming and dividing income of, 534
    forming of, 535
    limited, 534
    liquidating, 545
    partner bonuses, 542, *illus.*, 543
    partners admission and withdrawal, 540
    proprietorships, and limited liability companies, comparing, 534
    purchasing an interest in, 540
    revaluation of assets, 542
    steps in liquidating, *illus.*, 545
    two methods of admitting a partner, *illus.*, 540
    tyranny of the majority, 538
    withdrawal of a partner, 544
Patents, *def.*, 455
Pay
    computing employee net, 490
    gross, 487
    net, 487, 490
    take-home, 490
    vacation, 501
Payee, 407
Payments and receipts, cash controls over, 359
Payments for manufacturing costs, schedule of, 1004, *illus.*, 1005
Payroll
    and payroll taxes, accounting systems for, 493
    checks, 497, *illus.*, 500
    costs, benefit dollars as a percent of, *illus.*, 501
    def., 487
    distribution, 494
Payroll accounting, 486
    department charges, *illus.*, 1081

Payroll register
    def., 494
    illus., 494–495
Payroll system diagram, 498
Payroll systems
    flow of data in, *illus.*, 500
    internal controls for, 499
Payroll taxes, 487
    recording and paying, 494
Pension, *def.*, 502
Percent of sales method, 400
Period costs
    and product costs, examples of, *illus.*, 823
    def., 822, 860
    product costs, and financial statements, *illus.*, 823
Periodic inventory system, 280
    adjusting process under, 282
    chart of accounts under, *illus.*, 281
    closing entries under, 283
    cost of merchandise sold using, 280
    def., 256
    financial statements under, 283
    inventory costing methods under, 320
    transactions using, *illus.*, 283
Periodic system, determining cost of merchandise sold using, *illus.*, 281
Permanent accounts, *def.*, 150
Perpetual inventory account (FIFO), entries and, *illus.*, 317–318
Perpetual inventory system
    computerized, 319
    def., 257
    inventory costing methods under, 316
    transactions using, *illus.*, 283
Personnel, competent, 357
Personnel policies, 355
Petty cash custodian, 370
Petty cash fund, *def.*, 370
Physical depreciation, 443
Physical flows for a process manufacturers, *illus.*, 891
Physical inventory, *def.*, 313
Planning
    def., 817
    directing, and controlling, *illus.*, 988
    operational, 817
    strategic, 817
Planning function of management, 988
Plant assets, 438
    def., 109, 149
Post-closing trial balance, 153
    illus., 156, 166
    preparing, 165
Posting
    adjusting entries, 162
    cash payments journal and, *illus.*, 218

Posting (*continued*)
cash receipts journal, *illus.*, 212
closing entries, 151, 163
def., 55
journal entries to accounts, 55
purchases journal and, *illus.*, 215
revenue journal and, *illus.*, 210
transactions to ledger, 158
Postretirement benefits other than
pensions, 503
Predetermined factory overhead rate,
def., 854
Preferred dividends, number of
times earned, 772
Preferred stock
cumulative, 578
def., 578
participating, 578*fn*
Premium
amortization of, 673
amortization of by interest
method, 633
bonds issued at, 620
def., 581, 616
Premium on bonds payable,
amortization of, *illus.*, 634
Premium on stock, 581
Prepaid expenses, 103
def., 11, 100
Present value
def., 628
methods not using, 1165
of $1 at compound interest, *illus.*,
629
of $1 table, 629
of $1 table, partial, *illus.*, 1169
of an amount, 628, 1168
of the periodic receipts, 630
Present value concepts, 627–628
def., 1168
Present value index, *def.*, 1173
Present value methods, 1168
Present value of an annuity
def., 630, 1169
of $1, *def.*, 630
of $1 at compound interest, *illus.*,
630
table, partial, *illus.*, 1170
Price fixing, 1132
Price levels, changes in, 1179
Price-earnings (P/E) ratio, *def.*, 778
Pricing, production bottlenecks and,
1139
Prime costs
and conversion costs, *illus.*, 822
def., 822
Principal, 616, 623
Principle of exceptions, 1034
Prior period adjustments, *def.*, 591
Private accounting
def., 4
illus., 6
Private corporations, 575

Probable and estimable, contingent
liabilities, 504
Probable and not estimable,
contingent liabilities, 505
Proceeds, 412, 486
from issuing bonds, 616
Process, *def.*, 1054
Process and job order cost systems
comparing, 888
illus., 889
Process cost systems, 887
def., 848, 887
journal entries for, 904
Process manufacturers
cost flows for, 890, *illus.*, 892
def., 887
physical flows for, *illus.*, 891
Process or sell, 1127
differential analysis report, *illus.*,
1128
Processing methods, 206
Product, discontinue a, 1122
Product cost concept, *def.*, 1133
Product costs, 1133
and period costs, examples of,
illus., 823
def., 822
period costs, and financial
statements, *illus.*, 823
Product life-cycle management
(PLM), 225
Product selling prices, setting
normal, 1130
Production, compute equivalent
units of, 914
Production bottlenecks
and pricing, 1139
and profits, 1138
def., 1138
Production budget
def., 995
illus., 996
Production line
just-in-time, *illus.*, 910
traditional, *illus.*, 909
Production report
cost of, *illus.*, 903, 914, *illus.*,
915
for decision making, using cost of,
906
preparing cost of, 902
Profit
def., 2
gross, 254, 257
net, 15
target, 950
Profit center
def., 1080
responsibility accounting for, 1080
reporting, 1084
Profit margin, *def.*, 1086
Profitability, *def.*, 765
Profitability analysis, 773

Profits
illusory, 324
inventory, 324
production bottlenecks and, 1138
Profit-volume chart
def., 954
illus., 954
original and revised, *illus.*, 956
Profit-volume ratio, 944
Promissory note, *illus.*, 407
Proofs and security measures, 357
Property, co-ownership of
partnership, 533
Property, plant, and equipment, 149,
438
Proprietorships
characteristics of, *illus.*, 535
def., 8, 532
partnerships, and limited liability
companies, comparing, 534
Protest fee, 412
Public accounting
def., 7
illus., 6
Public Company Accounting
Oversight Board (PCAOB), 6
Public corporations, 572
Publicly held companies, 352
Purchase order, *def.*, 313
Purchase transactions, 266
Purchases, 282
net, 256
Purchases discounts, 266, 282
def., 256
Purchases journal
and postings, *illus.*, 215
def., 214
for merchandising business, *illus.*,
278
Purchases returns and allowances,
267, 282
def., 256

Q

Qualitative considerations, 1180
Quick assets, *def.*, 507, 767
Quick ratio, 767
def., 507, 767

R

Rate earned on common
stockholders' equity, *def.*, 776
Rate earned on operating assets, 774
Rate earned on stockholders' equity,
def., 775
Rate earned on total assets, *def.*, 774
Rate of return
on assets, 1086
on investment (ROI), *def.*, 1086
Ratio
acid-test, 507, 767
bankers', 766
contribution margin, 944

Ratio (*continued*)
current, 766
fixed asset turnover, 459
fixed charge coverage, 772
price-earnings, 778
profit-volume, 944
quick, 507, 767
working capital, 766
Ratio of fixed assets to long-term liabilities, *def.*, 771
Ratio of liabilities to stockholders' equity, *def.*, 771
Ratio of net sales to assets, *def.*, 773
Real accounts, *def.*, 150
Realization
capital deficiency—loss on, 549
def., 545
gain on, 546
loss on, 547
Reasonably possible, contingent liabilities, 505
Receipts and payments, cash controls over, 359
Receivable(s)
accounts, 394
aging the, 401
characteristics of notes, 406
classification of, 394
def., 394
notes, 394, 406
number of days' sales in, 411, 769
other, 395
reporting on the balance sheet, 410
trade, 395
uncollectible, 395
Receivables fraud, 406
Receivables method, analysis of, 401
Receiving report, *def.*, 313, 849
Records and bank statement, *illus.*, 366
Registrar, 581
Related operations, separating responsibilities for, 357
Relative value units, 992
Relevant range, *def.*, 937
Remittance advice, 361
Remote, contingent liabilities, 505
Rent revenue, *def.*, 11
Repairs
extraordinary, 441
ordinary, 441
Replace equipment, 1126
Replace machine, differential analysis report, *illus.*, 1126
Report form
def., 16*fn*, 259
of balance sheet, *illus.*, 260
Report of Independent Registered Public Accounting Firm, 782
Research and development costs, 456
Residual income, *def.*, 1089
Residual value, *def.*, 444

Responsibility accounting
def., 1077
for cost centers, 1078
for investment centers, 1085
for profit centers, 1080
reports for cost centers, *illus.*, 1079
Responsibility centers, 1077
def., 988
Restrictions, *def.*, 590
Résumé padding, 493
Retail inventory method, *def.*, 331
Retail method
determining inventory by, *illus.*, 331
of inventory costing, 331
Retained earnings, 709, 726
def., 577
reporting, 589
Retained earnings statement
comparative, horizontal analysis, *illus.*, 761
def., 589
illus., 589
Revenue
accrued, 101, 106
controllable, 1080
def., 11, 48
differential, 1120
interest, 11
rent, 11
unearned, 57, 100, 105
Revenue and cash receipts in QuickBooks, *illus.*, 223
Revenue expenditures, *def.*, 441
Revenue from sales, 254
Revenue journal
and postings, *illus.*, 210
def., 208
illus., 209
Revenue per employee, 553
Revenue recognition concept, *def.*, 98
Reversing entries, 108*fn*, 155*fn*
Risk assessment, 356
Round tripping, fraud, 148
Rules of debit and credit
def., 49
illus., 50

S

Safety, margin of, 960
Salary, 487
Sale of bonds, 655
Sale of land, gain on, 723
Sale of stock, 657, 659
Sales
and cost of goods sold, 860
cash, 260
def., 11, 254
net, 255
revenue from, 254
schedule of collections from, 1003, *illus.*, 1004

Sales budget
def., 995
illus., 995
Sales discounts, 262
def., 255
Sales journal for merchandising business, *illus.*, 277
Sales method, percent of, 400
Sales mix
considerations, 957
def., 957
Sales on account, 262
Sales returns and allowances, 264
def., 255
Sales taxes, 269, 271
Sales transactions, 260
Salvage value, 444
Sarbanes-Oxley Act (SOX), 6, 352, 499, 575, 576, 782
def., 352
of Nike, *illus.*, 353
Schedule of collections from sales, 1003, *illus.*, 1004
Schedule of payments for manufacturing costs, 1004, *illus.*, 1005
Scrap value, 444
Securities
available-for-sale, 665
debt, 653
equity, 653
held-to-maturity, 664
trading, 661
Securities and Exchange Commission (SEC), *def.*, 7
Security measures and proofs, 357
Segment, discontinue a, 1122
Sell at special price, differential analysis report, *illus.*, 1129
Sell or lease, 1121
differential analysis report, *illus.*, 1121
Sell or process, 1127
differential analysis report, *illus.*, 1139
Selling and administrative expenses budget, *illus.*, 1002
Selling expenses, 822
def., 257
Selling with-dividends, 584
Semifixed costs, 939
Semivariable costs, 939
Sensitivity analysis, 955
Serial bonds, 616
Service activities, 910
Service businesses
def., 3
flow of costs through, *illus.*, 864
job order cost systems for professional, 863
Service department charge rates, 1082

Service department charges
  def., 1080
  illus., 1082
Service departments, 1080
Services of partners, dividing
  income, 536
Shareholders, 574
Shareholders'
  equity, 577
  investment, 577
Short-term notes payable, 484
Single-step income statement
  def., 258
  illus., 259
Sinking fund, 622*fn*
Slide, *def.*, 67
Social security (OASDI), 489
Solvency, 172
  analysis, 765
  def., 765
Special dividends, 583
Special journals, 207
  def., 207
  modified, 220
Special-purpose cash funds, 370
Special-purpose funds, *def.*, 371
Specific identification inventory cost
  flow method, *def.*, 314
Spreadsheet
  complete, 172C
  completed with net income, *illus.*,
    172B5
  end-of-period, *illus.*, 145, *illus.*,
    161, 172
  enter the adjusted trial balance,
    172C
  enter the adjustments, 172A
  enter the title, 172A
  enter the unadjusted trial balance,
    172A
  extend the account to the income
    statement columns, 172C
  extend the accounts to the balance
    sheet columns, 172C
  preparing end-of-period, 160
  with amounts extended to income
    statement and balance sheet
    columns, *illus.*, 172B4
  with unadjusted trial balance and
    adjustments, *illus.*, 172B2
  with unadjusted trial balance,
    adjustments and adjusted trial
    balance, *illus.*, 172B3
  with unadjusted trial balance,
    illus., 172B
  (work sheet), for statement of cash
    flows, indirect method, 726,
    illus., 727
Staff, 816
Staff Accounting Bulletins, 7
Staff department, *def.*, 816
Standard cost
  def., 1033

illus., 1036
  criticisms of, 1035
Standard cost systems, *def.*, 1033
Standard factory overhead rate,
  factory overhead cost budget
  indicating, *illus.*, 1044
Standard treatment protocols,
  1043
Standards
  currently attainable, 1034
  def., 1033
  ideal, 1034
  normal, 1034
  recording and reporting variances
    from, 1050
  reviewing and revising, 1035
  setting of, 1034
  theoretical, 1034
  types of, 1034
Standards for nonmanufacturing
  activities, direct labor, 1042
Standards in income statement,
  variances from, *illus.*, 1052
State unemployment compensation
  tax, *See* SUTA tax
Stated value, 578
Stated value per share, 582
Statement of cash flows, 18
  def., 15, 705
  direct method, 720, *illus.*,
    724–725
  indirect method, 709, *illus.*, 720
  preparing, 719, 728
  spreadsheet for, indirect method,
    726, *illus.*, 727
Statement of cost of goods
  manufactured
  def., 826
  income statement with,
    (manufacturing company),
    illus., 828
Statement of members' equity, *def.*,
  552
Statement of owner's equity, 16, 148,
  258
  def., 15
  for merchandising business, *illus.*,
    259
Statement of partnership equity
  def., 552
  illus., 552
Statement of partnership liquidation
  def., 546
  gain on realization, *illus.*, 547
  loss on realization, *illus.*, 548
  loss on realization—capital
    deficiency, *illus.*, 550
Statement of stockholders' equity
  def., 591
  illus., 590
*Statements of Financial Accounting
  Standards*, 7
Static and flexible budgets, *illus.*, 992

Static budget
  def., 991
  illus., 991
Stock, 575
  characteristics of, 578
  classes of, 578
  common, 578, 717
  cumulative preferred, 578
  def., 574
  dividends to cumulative
    preferred, *illus.*, 579
  issuing, 579
  no-par, 578, 582
  outstanding, 578
  paid-in capital from issuing, 577
  participating preferred, 578*fn*
  preferred, 578
  premium on, 581
  purchase of, 657, 658
  sale of, 657, 659
  treasury, 586
Stock dividend, *def.*, 585
Stock investments, *illus.*, 656
Stock ledger, 859
Stock split, *def.*, 592
Stockholders ledger, 581*fn*
Stockholders, *def.*, 574
Stockholders' equity
  def., 577
  for Mornin' Joe, reporting of, 591
  in balance sheet, 588
  section of balance sheet, *illus.*, 588
  rate earned on, 775
  rate earned on common, 776
  ratio of liabilities to, 771
  reporting, 587
  statement of, 591
  statement of, *illus.*, 590
Straight-line method, 619
  def., 445
Strategic planning, *def.*, 817
Strategies, *def.*, 817
Subjective estimates, 814
Sub-prime woes, 664
Subsidiary company, *def.*, 660
Subsidiary inventory ledger, *def.*, 313
Subsidiary ledger
  accounts payable, 206
  accounts payable control account
    and, 219
  accounts receivable, 206
  accounts receivable control
    account and, 213
  additional, 220
  and general ledger, *illus.*, 207
  def., 206
Sum-of-the-years digits method, 444*fn*
Sum-of-the-years-digits depreciation,
  459
Sunk costs, *def.*, 1120
Supply chain management (SCM),
  225
SUTA tax, 493

T

T account, *def.,* 46
Take-home pay, 490
Tangible assets, 438
Target cost concept, *illus.,* 1137
Target costing, *def.,* 1137
Target profit, 950
Tax payments, responsibility for, *illus.,* 493
Taxation, double, 575
Taxes
  accounting systems for payroll, 493
  cash payments for income, 724
  FICA, 489, 492
  FUTA, 492
  income, 487
  liability for employer's payroll, 492
  payroll, 487
  recording and paying payroll, 494
  sales, 269, 271
  SUTA, 493
Temporary accounts, *def.,* 150
Temporary investments, 653
  investing cash in, 653
Term, 407
Term bonds, 616
Terminology, manufacturing operations, 818
Terms, freight, *illus.,* 270
Theoretical standards, 1034
Theory of constraints (TOC), *def.,* 1138
Time tickets, *def.,* 851
Time value of money concept, 628
  def., 1165
Time-adjusted rate of return method, 1174
Title, enter on the spreadsheet, 172A
Total assets, rate earned on, 774
Total cost concept, *def.,* 1130
Total manufacturing cost variance, *def.,* 1037
Trade discounts, 269
  def., 272
Trade receivables, 395
Trade-in allowance, *def.,* 460
Trade-in value, 444
Trademark, *def.,* 456
Trading securities, *def.,* 661
Traditional analysis, *illus.,* 1122, 1124
Traditional production line, *illus.,* 909
Transactions
  analyzing and recording in the journal, 158
  dual nature of merchandise, 272
  effects of on owner's equity, *illus.,* 14
  illus., 47
  merchandising, 259
  posting to ledger, 158

purchase, 266
recording merchandise under the periodic inventory system, 282
sales, 260
treasury stock, 586
using accounts to record, 46
using periodic and perpetual inventory systems, *illus.,* 283
Transfer agent, 581
Transfer price
  def., 1092
  illus., 1092
  shifting income through, 1097
Transposition, *def.,* 67
Treasury stock
  def., 586
  transactions, 586
Trial balance
  adjusted, *illus.,* 117, *illus.,* 163
  adjustments and adjusted trial balance, spreadsheet with unadjusted, *illus.,* 172B3
  and adjustments, spreadsheet with unadjusted, *illus.,* 172B2
  def., 63
  errors effecting, 66
  errors not affecting, 67
  illus., 65
  post-closing, 153, *illus.,* 156, *illus.,* 166
  preparing a post-closing, 165
  preparing an adjusted, 162
  preparing an unadjusted, 160
  spreadsheet with unadjusted, *illus.,* 172B
  unadjusted, 65, *illus.,* 161
Trust indenture, 616
Turnover
  accounts receivable, 411, 768
  inventory, 330, 770
Tyranny of the majority in partnerships, 538

U

U.S. Chamber of Commerce, 501
U.S. Treasury, 486
Unadjusted trial balance
  adjustments and adjusted trial balance, spreadsheet with, *illus.,* 172B3
  and adjustments, spreadsheet with, *illus.,* 172B2
  def., 65
  enter on the spreadsheet, 172A
  illus., 102, *illus.,* 161
  preparing, 160
  spreadsheet with, *illus.,* 172B
Uncertainty, 1179
Uncollectible accounts
  allowance method for, 397
  direct write-off method for, 396
Uncollectible accounts expense, 395
Uncollectible receivables, 395

Uncollectibles, estimating, 399
Underabsorbed factory overhead, 856
Underapplied factory overhead, *def.,* 856
Unearned revenue(s), 48, 105
  def., 57, 100
Unequal proposal lives, 1177
Unfavorable cost variance, *def.,* 1036
Unfavorable fixed factory overhead variance, 1046
Unit contribution margin, *def.,* 945
Unit of measure concept, *def.,* 8
Unit selling price, effect of changes in, 949
Unit variable costs, effect of changes in, 948
Units
  allocate costs to transferred and partially completed, 914
  allocate costs to units transferred out and partially completed, 900
  started and completed, 901
  whole, 895
Units manufactured exceed units sold, *illus.,* 963
Units to be assigned costs, determine, 893, 913
Units to be costed—mixing department, *illus.,* 894
Units-of-production method, *def.,* 446
Unlimited liability, 533
Unlimited life, 534
Unqualified opinion, 782
Unrealized gain or loss, *def.,* 661
Unusual items
  affecting the current period's income statement, 785
  affecting the prior period's income statement, 786
  in the income statement, *illus.,* 785
  on income statement, 784

V

Vacation pay, 501
Vacations, mandatory, 357
Valuation at lower of cost or market, 325
Valuation at net realizable value, 326
Valuation method, 110
Value
  book, 448, 659
  fair, 661
  future, 628
  maturity, 408
  net book, 110
  net realizable, 326, 397
  present, 628
  residual, scrap, salvage, or trade-in, 444
  stated, 578
Variable cost concept, *def.,* 1134

Variable cost graphs, *illus.*, 938
Variable cost of goods sold, 961
Variable costing, 961
  def., 943
Variable costing income statement, *illus.*, 962
Variable costs, *def.*, 938
Variable factory overhead controllable variance, 1044
Variance relationships
  direct labor, *illus.*, 1042
  direct materials, *illus.*, 1040
Variance(s)
  controllable, 1044
  cost, 1036
  direct labor, 1041
  direct labor and direct materials, 1038
  direct labor rate, 1041
  direct labor time, 1042
  direct materials, 1038
  direct materials price, 1039
  direct materials quantity, 1039
  factory overhead, 1043
  favorable cost, 1036
  favorable fixed factory overhead, 1046
  fixed factory overhead volume, 1046
  graph of fixed overhead volume, *illus.*, 1047

manufacturing cost, 1037, *illus.*, 1038
  reporting direct labor, 1042
  reporting direct materials, 1040
  reporting factory overhead, 1047
  total manufacturing cost, 1037
  unfavorable cost, 1036
  unfavorable fixed factory overhead, 1046
  variable factory overhead controllable, 1044
  volume, 1046
Variances from standards
  in income statement, *illus.*, 1052
  recording and reporting, 1050
Vertical analysis, 120
  comparative balance sheet, *illus.*, 762
  comparative income statement, *illus.*, 763
  def., 761
Volume variance, *def.*, 1046
Voucher system, *def.*, 362
Voucher, *def.*, 362

W

W-4 (Employee's Withholding Allowance Certificate), 487, *illus.*, 488
Wage bracket withholding table, *illus.*, 488

Wages, 487
  accrued, *illus.*, 108
Wall Street Journal, The, 779
Warning signs of internal control problems, *illus.*, 358
Weighted average method, 322
"What if" analysis, 955
Whole units, *def.*, 895
Wholesalers, 272
With-dividends, selling, 584
Withdrawals, owner, 50
Work in process, 858
  accounts, 889
  applying factory overhead to, 855
  controlling account and job cost sheets, *illus.*, 858
  inventory, *def.*, 824
Work sheet, financial statements prepared from, *illus.*, 147
Working capital, 172
  def., 765
  ratio, 766
Write-offs to the allowance account, 397

Y

Yield, *def.*, 908

Z

Zero-based budgeting, *def.*, 990
Zero-coupon bonds, 631*fn*

Company Index

A

Acusphere, Inc., 385
Adams, Stevens & Bradley, Ltd., 395
Adelphia Communications, 5
AgentBlaze, LLC, 531
Airbus, 948
Albertson's, 653
Alcoa Inc., 439, 484, 888, 921
Amazon.com, 3, 225, 242, 316, 360
America Online, Inc., 5
American Airlines, 98, 958
American Express Company, 262, 1108
American Greetings Corporation, 344
American International Group, Inc., (AIG), 5
Amgen Inc., 1213
Anheuser-Busch Companies, Inc., 974
Ann Taylor Retail, Inc., 799, 836
Apple Computer Inc., 45, 344, 455, 472 519, 672, 888
ArvinMeritor, Inc., 1142
AT&T, 484

B

Bain & Co., 1091
Bank of America Corporation, 672, 691, 800
Barnes & Noble, 704
Bear Stearns & Co., 617
Best Buy, 105, 254, 257, 292, 311, 313, 474, 1130
Blockbuster Inc., 593
BMW Group, 1032
Boeing, 420
Briggs & Stratton Corporation, 627
Bristol-Myers Squibb Company (BMS), 225

C

C.H. Robinson Worldwide Inc., 798
Callaway Golf Company, 108, 815–816
Campbell Soup Company, The, 131, 584
Canyons Resort, 1190
Carnival Corporation, 1163, 1189
Caterpillar, 576, 835, 910, 1121
CBS Corp., 534
Charles Schwab Corporation, 1150
Chevron Texaco, 484
Circuit City Stores, Inc., 131, 474, 771, 1130
Cisco Systems, Inc., 225
Citigroup, 664
Coated Sales, Inc., 406
Coca-Cola Company, The, 30, 575, 581, 672, 725, 800, 1016, 1035
Coca-Cola Enterprises, 1016
Colgate-Palmolive Company, 835
Comcast Corporation, 459
Commercial Law League of America, 403

Computer Associates International, Inc., 5
Consolidated Edison Inc., 862
Continental Airlines, Inc., 79, 737, 771
CyberSource, 262

D

DaimlerChrysler, 324
Darden Restaurants, Inc., 1039
DDB Advertising Agency, 888
Deere & Company, 401
Dell Computer Corporation, 3, 133, 225, 242, 325, 519, 797
Deloitte & Touche, 565
Delta Air Lines, 3, 226, 385, 420, 443, 576, 957, 990, 1120, 1164
Digital Theater Systems Inc., 326
Dollar Tree Stores, Inc., 253
Domino Foods, Inc., 921
Donnkenny, Inc., 381
Dow Chemical Company, The, 576
Dreyer's Grand Ice Cream, Inc., 886

E

E. I. du Pont de Nemours and Company (DuPont), 888, 1086fn
eBay Inc., 30, 351, 456, 691, 734, 800
Electronic Arts Inc., 143
Enron, 4, 5
ESPN, 975
eToys Direct, Inc., 316
Exabyte Corporation, 1146
ExxonMobil Corporation, 439, 725

F

Fannie Mae, 5
Fatburger Corporation, 437
FBI, 4
Federated Department Stores, Inc., 178
FedEx Corporation, 182–183, 395, 411
Financial Executives International, **576**
First Chicago Trust Company of New York, 581
Ford Motor Company, 8, 323, 439, 504, 518, 713, 910, 990, 1124
Fox Sports, 975
Fujitsu, 993
Furniture.com, Inc., 316

G

Gap Inc., 484
Gateway, Inc., 133
General Electric Company, 395, 576, 725
General Motors Corporation, 3, 512, 672
GlaxoSmithKline, 1097
Golf Channel, The, 949
Google Inc., 1, 30, 459, 506, 660, 708, 958, 1035
Grant Thornton LLP, 561

H

H.J. Heinz Company, 427, 428, 798, 1062
Harris Corporation, 1104
Hasbro, 573, 797–798
HCA Inc., 401
HealthSouth, 5
Heritage Log Homes, 888
Hershey Foods Company, The, 798, 888, 921
Hewlett-Packard Company (HP), 672, 797, 868
Hilton Hotels Corporation, 946, 1091, 1108
Home Depot, Inc., 8, 35, 256, 299, 576, 672, 1075
Howard Schultz & Associates (HS&A), 362

I

IBM, 484, 1081, 1180
Indian Airlines Limited, 948
Intel Corporation, 395, 441, 888
Internal Revenue Service (IRS), 487, 534, 1041
Intuit Inc., 204, 242, 725, 973

J

Jacobus Pharmaceuticals Company, Inc., 951
JCPenney, 178, 256, 276, 395, 401, 444
JHT Holdings, Inc., 381
Johnson & Johnson, 421, 1035
Jones Soda Co., 704, 741

K

K2 Sports, 1075
Kellogg Company, 576, 922
Kentucky Fried Chicken (KFC), 1077
Kmart Corporation, 84, 178
Kohl's Corporation, 742
Korn/Ferry International, 1080
KPMG LLP, 561
Kroger, 257, 299, 344, 439

L

L.L. Bean, Inc., 242
La-Z-Boy Incorporated, 394
Levi Strauss & Co., 848, 1017
Limited, Inc., The, 178, 427, 428, 1033
Los Angeles Lakers, 955
Lowe's Companies, Inc., 35, 109

M

Macy's, 395
Manpower Inc., 459
Marriott International, Inc., 439, 459
Mars, Incorporated, 575
Marvel Entertainment, Inc., 97
MasterCard, 262, 396
Mattel, Inc., 384, 672, 797–798
McDonald's, 360, 974, 1146

Merck & Co., Inc., 1090, 1214
Merrill Lynch & Co., 664
Metro-Goldwyn-Mayer Studios Inc. (MGM), 1214
MGM Mirage, 420
Microsoft Corporation, 130, 144, 172, 373, 665, 672, 691, 725, 767, 993, 1035, 1173
Millennium Chemicals, 1088
Monster.com, 487
MySpace, 650

N

National Audubon Society, 576
National Check Fraud Center, 366
Nature's Sunshine Products, Inc., 592
Netflix, Inc., 593, 936
NetSuite Inc., 204
New York Bond Exchange, 672
New York Stock Exchange (NYSE), 651
News Corporation, 242, 651
Nike, Inc., 353–354, 641, 744, 757, 782, 808, 888
Nissan Motor Co. Ltd., 484
Norfolk Southern Corporation, 446, 459
North Face, The, 986
Northwest Airlines Corporation, 372
Nova Entertainment Group (NEG), 1081
Novartis AG, 951

O

Oakley, Inc., 393
Office Depot, Inc., 254
OfficeMax, 605
Oracle, 204
Overhill Flowers, Inc., 716
Owens Corning, 1176

P

P.F. Chang's China Bistro, Inc., 515
Pacific Bell, 622
Pacific Gas and Electric Company, 862
Panera Bread, 482, 704
PayPal, 360, 691
PepsiCo, Inc., 30, 395, 796, 888
Pixar Animation Studios, 653
Pizza Hut, 1077
Polo Ralph Lauren Corporation, 427
Priceline.com Inc., 225, 1128
PricewaterhouseCoopers LLP, 353

Procter & Gamble (P&G), 48, 518, 605, 641, 771, 789, 1076
PurchasePro, 5

Q

Qwest Communications International, Inc., 5

R

R.J. Reynolds Tobacco Company, 576
RadioShack Corporation, 106
RealNetworks, Inc., 1118
Red Lobster, 1039
Rite Aid Corp., 484
Ruby Tuesday, Inc., 459

S

Safeway Inc., 344
Sage Software, Inc., 204
SAP, 204
Sears Holding Corporation, 257, 276
Shell Group, 852
Sierra Club, 576
Smurfit-Stone Container Corporation, 242
Societe Generale, 381
Solectron Corporation, 1146
Sony Corporation of America, 456, 1146
Southwest Airlines Co., 205, 459
Speedway Motorsports, Inc., 794
Sports Authority, 1075
Sprint Nextel, 975
St. Paul Companies, 450
Staples, 605
Starbucks Coffee Japan, Ltd., 658
Starbucks Corporation, 2, 188, 242, 484, 576, 658, 704
Steelcase Inc., 1014
Stern Stewart & Co., 1089*fn*
Sun Microsystems, Inc., 576
SunTrust Banks Inc., 661
SUPERVALU Inc., 330
SuperValu, 653

T

Tandy Corporation, 444
Target Corp., 178, 320
Tennessee Valley Authority, 862
3M, 576, 1035
Tiffany & Co., 299
Tiger Woods Design, 888

Time Warner, Inc., 616
Toyota Motor Corporation, 269, 1153
Toys "R" Us., Inc., 178
Tyco International, Ltd., 5

U

U.S. Post Office, 1063
UBS, 664
Under Armour®, Inc., 188, 612
Union Pacific, 798, 949
United Airlines, 420
United Parcel Service, Inc. (UPS), 439, 1033, 1108
Universal Studios, 957

V

Veritas Software, 493
Verizon Communications Inc., 439, 474, 725, 958
VISA, 262, 396

W

W.W. Grainger, Inc., 242
Wachovia Corporation, 1077
Walgreen Co., 439
Wal-Mart, 3, 8, 257, 320, 439, 789, 1075
Walt Disney Company, The, 3, 653, 708, 888, 1107
Warner Bros., 848
Washburn Guitars, 812, 846
Washington Post Company, The, 576
Weyerhaeuser, 1100
Whirlpool Corporation, 225, 576
Williams-Sonoma, 84, 133
Winn-Dixie Stores Inc., 257, 344
WorldCom, 4, 5, 352, 442
Worthington Industries, 1213

X

Xerox Corporation, 5

Y

Yahoo!, 779, 958
YouTube, 660
YRC Worldwide, 798
Yum! Brands, Inc. 1077

Z

Zacks Investment Research, 765
Zale Corporation, 330

Abbreviations and Acronyms Commonly Used in Business and Accounting

AAA	American Accounting Association
ABC	Activity-based costing
AICPA	American Institute of Certified Public Accountants
CIA	Certified Internal Auditor
CIM	Computer-integrated manufacturing
CMA	Certified Management Accountant
CPA	Certified Public Accountant
Cr.	Credit
Dr.	Debit
EFT	Electronic funds transfer
EPS	Earnings per share
FAF	Financial Accounting Foundation
FASB	Financial Accounting Standards Board
FEI	Financial Executives International
FICA tax	Federal Insurance Contributions Act tax
FIFO	First-in, first-out
FOB	Free on board
GAAP	Generally accepted accounting principles
GASB	Governmental Accounting Standards Board
GNP	Gross National Product
IMA	Institute of Management Accountants
IRC	Internal Revenue Code
IRS	Internal Revenue Service
JIT	Just-in-time
LIFO	Last-in, first-out
Lower of C or M	Lower of cost or market
MACRS	Modified Accelerated Cost Recovery System
n/30	Net 30
n/eom	Net, end-of-month
P/E Ratio	Price-earnings ratio
POS	Point of sale
ROI	Return on investment
SEC	Securities and Exchange Commission
TQC	Total quality control

Classification of Accounts

Account Title	Account Classification	Normal Balance	Financial Statement
Accounts Payable	Current liability	Credit	Balance sheet
Accounts Receivable	Current asset	Debit	Balance sheet
Accumulated Depreciation	Contra fixed asset	Credit	Balance sheet
Accumulated Depletion	Contra fixed asset	Credit	Balance sheet
Advertising Expense	Operating expense	Debit	Income statement
Allowance for Doubtful Accounts	Contra current asset	Credit	Balance sheet
Amortization Expense	Operating expense	Debit	Income statement
Bonds Payable	ZLong-term liability	Credit	Balance sheet
Building	Fixed asset	Debit	Balance sheet
_____ Capital	Owner's equity	Credit	Statement of owner's equity/ Balance sheet
Capital Stock	Stockholders' equity	Credit	Balance sheet
Cash	Current asset	Debit	Balance sheet
Cash Dividends	Stockholders' equity	Debit	Retained earnings statement
Cash Dividends Payable	Current liability	Credit	Balance sheet
Common Stock	Stockholders' equity	Credit	Balance sheet
Cost of Merchandise (Goods) Sold	Cost of merchandise (goods sold)	Debit	Income statement
Deferred Income Tax Payable	Current liability/Long-term liability	Credit	Balance sheet
Delivery Expense	Operating expense	Debit	Income Statement
Depletion Expense	Operating expense	Debit	Income statement
Discount on Bonds Payable	Long-term liability	Debit	Balance sheet
Dividend Revenue	Other income	Credit	Income statement
Dividends	Stockholders' equity	Debit	Retained earnings statement
_____ Drawing	Owner's equity	Debit	Statement of owner's equity
Employees Federal Income Tax Payable	Current liability	Credit	Balance sheet
Equipment	Fixed asset	Debit	Balance sheet
Exchange Gain	Other income	Credit	Income statement
Exchange Loss	Other expense	Debit	Income statement
Factory Overhead (Overapplied)	Deferred credit	Credit	Balance sheet (interim)
Factory Overhead (Underapplied)	Deferred debit	Debit	Balance sheet (interim)
Federal Income Tax Payable	Current liability	Credit	Balance sheet
Federal Unemployment Tax Payable	Current liability	Credit	Balance sheet
Finished Goods	Current asset	Debit	Balance sheet
Freight In	Cost of merchandise sold	Debit	Income statement
Freight Out	Operating expense	Debit	Income statement
Gain on Disposal of Fixed Assets	Other income	Credit	Income statement
Gain on Redemption of Bonds	Other income	Credit	Income statement
Gain on Sale of Investments	Other income	Credit	Income statement
Goodwill	Intangible asset	Debit	Balance sheet
Income Tax Expense	Income tax	Debit	Income statement
Income Tax Payable	Current liability	Credit	Balance sheet
Insurance Expense	Operating expense	Debit	Income statement
Interest Expense	Other expense	Debit	Income statement
Interest Receivable	Current asset	Debit	Balance sheet
Interest Revenue	Other income	Credit	Income statement
Investment in Bonds	Investment	Debit	Balance sheet
Investment in Stocks	Investment	Debit	Balance sheet
Investment in Subsidiary	Investment	Debit	Balance sheet
Land	Fixed asset	Debit	Balance sheet
Loss on Disposal of Fixed Assets	Other expense	Debit	Income statement
Loss on Redemption of Bonds	Other expense	Debit	Income statement